AMERICAN DRAMA
COLONIAL TO CONTEMPORARY

STEPHEN WATT

Indiana University

GARY A. RICHARDSON

Mercer University

HARCOURT BRACE COLLEGE PUBLISHERS

Fort Worth   Philadelphia   San Diego   New York   Orlando   Austin   San Antonio
Toronto   Montreal   London   Sydney   Tokyo

Publisher	TED BUCHHOLZ
Senior Acquisitions Editor	STEPHEN T. JORDAN
Senior Developmental Editor	KARL YAMBERT
Project Editor	LAURA J. HANNA
Production Manager	CYNTHIA YOUNG
Art Director	NICK WELCH
Photo/Permissions Editor	LILI WEINER
Cover illustration	LAMBERTO ALVAREZ

ADDRESS FOR EDITORIAL CORRESPONDENCE
HARCOURT BRACE COLLEGE PUBLISHERS, 301 COMMERCE STREET, SUITE 3700, FORT WORTH, TEXAS 76102

ADDRESS FOR ORDERS
HARCOURT BRACE & COMPANY, 6277 SEA HARBOR DRIVE, ORLANDO, FL 32887
1-800-782-4479, OR 1-800-433-0001 (IN FLORIDA)

LIBRARY OF CONGRESS CATALOG CARD NUMBER 93-81045

ISBN: 0-15-500003-9

PRINTED IN THE UNITED STATES OF AMERICA

4 5 6 7 8 9 0 1 2 3   039   9 8 7 6 5 4 3 2 1

To our Children—
Brendan, Caitlin, Kathleen, and Matthew

PREFACE

American Drama: Colonial to Contemporary is intended for students of American drama in English, Theatre, and American Studies courses. Its primary aim is to provide students with a broad historical sense of the transformations of American drama from its beginnings to the present, making certain that this historical sense is as diverse as possible.

As the most comprehensive anthology of American drama available for classroom use, *American Drama* offers a number of distinctive features that underscore its usefulness in a range of courses:

- Its 32 plays and performance pieces represent more than 200 years of American drama, from the early Republic to the 1990s.

- The social, historical, and cultural contexts of the development of American drama are sketched in four historical essays, complemented in turn by uniquely detailed introductions to each play and playwright.

- While providing canonical plays from some of America's best-known dramatists, *American Drama* also includes substantial works by writers too often ignored by, or excluded from, such texts.

- Women playwrights are strongly represented (by 10 selections).

- Two selections (by Karen Finley and Cherríe Moraga) appear in newly revised versions never before anthologized.

- A Glossary defines key dramatic, historical, and critical terms boldfaced in the text.

- A Select Bibliography of books on American drama and theatre and a Select Filmography of American plays widely available on film or videotape provide points of departure for further study of given periods, plays, and playwrights.

- With 9 plays before the rise of modern drama and 13 after 1960, *American Drama* can be used alone or with minimal supplementation in special-topics courses on early or contemporary American theatres.

It is our sincere hope that *American Drama: Colonial to Contemporary* will foster in the reader, as it has rekindled in its authors, an appreciation of the diversity and vitality of the American experience as expressed through drama.

Acknowledgments

We would like to thank all of those readers who thoughtfully shared their knowledge of drama and theatre with us when this was conceived as a decidedly different volume: Thayer W. Beach (Austin Peay State University), Elin Diamond (Rutgers University-New Brunswick), John Glavin (Georgetown University), John Harper (University of Iowa), David Holloway (Portland State University), Keith Hull (University of Wyoming), James Hurt (University of Illinois), William Hutchings (University of Alabama), Katherine Kelly (Texas A & M University), Daniel Kline (Jefferson Community College), Paul Lim (University of Kansas), Tice L. Miller (University of Nebraska), Don Moore (Louisiana State University), Brenda Murphy (University of Connecticut), Lois More Overbeck (Emory University), Vivian Patraka (Bowling Green University), Steven Putzell (Pennsylvania State University-Wilkes Barre), Thelma J. Shinn (Arizona State University), James Stottlar (University of Illinois), and Helen M. Whall (College of the Holy Cross). We also thank Arthur Geffen of the University of Minnesota for his help.

We would also like to express our appreciation to our numerous friends, acquaintances, and colleagues who generously shared their expertise in the field of American drama and theatre and provided invaluable suggestions that have made this a much better book than it otherwise might have been—even when we sometimes chose to disagree with them: Thomas Adler (Purdue University), Katherine Burkman (Ohio State University), J. Ellen Gainor (Cornell University), Norma Jenckes (University of Cincinnati), Keith Newlin (University of North Carolina-Wilmington), Janelle Reinelt (California State University-Sacramento), Judith Roof (Indiana University), Don B. Wilmeth (Brown University), and Toby Zinman (University of the Arts).

Any defects that remain in this volume are ours and can be attributed only to our failure to profit from the excellent advice these scholars provided.

Preparation of a volume of this type can only be completed with the aid of people whose contributions to the project generally remain screened from the reader's view. We therefore gratefully acknowledge our debts to Susan Boome, Virginia Cairns, Valerie Edmonds, Kerri Flaherty, Brian Goldberg, and Laura Walls for their bibliographical and research assistance. Special thanks are also due to Ann Fox for her research and editorial contributions.

We would also like to register our debt to those at Harcourt Brace who have so expertly aided in the structuring and production of this work. To Senior Acquisitions Editor Stephen T. Jordan, we owe thanks for seeing the need for a volume dedicated to American drama and for his continued support throughout the project. To Laura Hanna, our project editor, we express our gratitude for carefully tending to the accuracy of both our commentary and the texts that we present herein. Thanks also to Cynthia Young, production manager, and Nick Welch, art director, for their contributions to this project. To Eleanor Garner, who tracked copyrights and gained permissions, we extend our appreciation. Finally, we convey our profound thanks to the gods of publishing who sent two novice textbook writers Karl Yambert as our senior developmental editor. Karl's graciousness, good humor, keen eyes and ears, and ability to keep track of the thousand details of this project have made our job as authors much easier and more enjoyable.

Finally, to our wives—Nonie Watt and Mary Alice Morgan—who have shared most closely this project's trials, tribulations, and satisfactions, we give public thanks for their many contributions. As always, they have unstintingly sustained our efforts, often deferring their own important work to assist us with ours. For their support, friendship, and inspiration, we thank them.

Stephen Watt
Gary A. Richardson

CONTENTS

INTRODUCTION

A NOTE TO READERS; OR, WHY WE WROTE THIS BOOK

MERICAN DRAMA: COLONIAL TO CONTEMPORARY IS INTENDED TO PROVIDE students of American drama with an introduction to its history. Much as Barnard Hewitt described his objective in writing *Theatre U.S.A.: 1665–1957* (1959), we aim through this collection "to tell the story of our theatre," albeit a somewhat different story than Hewitt's distinguished study relates. Foremost among the several reasons for selecting the 32 individual works that this book comprises is the formation of a new, or at least different, historical narrative from the invariably brief treatment drama receives in thicker volumes of American literature. Parts of this narrative will seem familiar, for any book attempting an overview of American drama must consider those writers and texts that have enjoyed long life on the American stage and in critical accounts of its evolution. At the same time, however, *American Drama: Colonial to Contemporary* endeavors to expand and complicate this history, in part by including plays and writers that have not always been represented—or not always been considered as having played parts—in this story.

Like Hewitt, we cannot mention all the persons involved in the over 300-year chronicle of American drama from the time of *Ye Bare and Ye Cubb,* a play written in colonial Virginia in 1665 that landed its author in court, to such works from the 1990s as Larry Kramer's *The Destiny of Me,* David Mamet's *Oleanna,* and Cherríe Moraga's revised 1994 version of *Giving Up the Ghost.* If we had tried, the result would have been a book too heavy to carry and too expensive for many to buy. And certainly any number of writers *not* included here might have been, perhaps *should* have been, part of this text. Yet factors other than our own predilections or the premises underlying this project had a role in the content of our book as well. In some cases, we were unable to obtain certain plays or performance pieces because of their copyright status, the refusal of an author or an author's estate to grant permission to use the material, or the steep permission fees some agents or publishing houses demanded for reprinting it. Thus, right from the earliest planning stages of this volume, several material, legal, or economic factors emerged to shape it *and* the kind of story it could tell. We hope nonetheless through the works that follow to present the many distinct varieties of plays and performances that together constitute American drama. In addition, through short essays and historical introductions, we attempt to place the writers and works represented here in an historical context (not just a theatrical or literary one), and to suggest the kinds of cultural work these plays accomplish. Given the necessary brevity of our introductory essays, we can only sketch some of these aesthetic and cultural dimensions, leaving it up to both the teacher and industrious student of American drama to complete the picture in more detail.

American Drama: Colonial to Contemporary is, most obviously, an *anthology,* a word coming from a Greek term meaning both a collection of short poems and a garland or gathering of flowers. And we thought it desirable to outline here the criteria by which we selected works to include in this, our garland of American plays, criteria other than the economic and legal factors mentioned above. Even to entitle a book *American Drama: Colonial to Contemporary* is to suggest qualities of scope and diversity, to intimate the contours of a history that is, finally, communicated to a great extent through the inclusion of some dramatic works and the exclusion of others. By what rationale might such decisions be defended? In sum, what principles underlie the construction of a book like this one that intends to relate both a familiar and a more expansive historical narrative?

The answers to these questions lead inevitably to notions of a **canon**[1], by which we mean a body or list of works considered to exemplify, in one or another respect, American drama. And adding the suffix "ize" to "canon," in asserting a writer's or a work's place in a formation, is not a neutral act. On the contrary, because the term "canonize" inevitably connotes both resemblance and elevation or esteem—persons are declared or "canonized" saints by the Catholic Church, for example, in recognition of their virtuous, even exemplary, lives—the noun "canon" conveys a sense of exclusivity, artistic preeminence, value, or "goodness." Decisions about inclusion in a canon, therefore, would seem a matter primarily of aesthetic judgment or assessment: "masterpieces" or great works are part of the canon and lesser ones are not. A number of anthologies in general and collections of drama in particular have been organized on this principle: their editors assumed they knew what made plays great and placed them in their tables of contents. For a number of reasons, however, we have *not* followed such an agenda in editing *American Drama: Colonial to Contemporary,* although persuasive arguments about the "greatness" of many of the plays we *have* selected have been or could be made.

One reason for our reluctance to make claims about dramatic "masterpieces" and structure this book around them is our conviction that such decisions are far more complicated than the seemingly objective assessment of aesthetic value. Among other scholars, John Guillory has considered both the process of canon formation and has identified two fundamentally opposing principles at work. One, the "conservative defense of the canon" to which we have just alluded, rests upon "a belief in the *intrinsic worth* of canonical works" (that is, in their presumed artistry or intellectual merit). Many critiques of this process, conversely, are actually strategic moves toward "opening the canon" and are premised upon the grounds of *representative democracy* (the need to canonize a more diverse body of cultural productions). Such critiques rightly complain, we think, that claims for the intrinsic value of a cultural artifact have everything to do with the authority or privileged position of the person(s) making them. Asseverations of *intrinsic* literary or artistic worth, therefore, are hardly objective; rather, they are inseparable from particular *extrinsic* realities: for example, the positions of institutional authority held by a relatively small group of academicians or theatrical producer-directors. Even the opposition Guillory uses to explain canon formation—intrinsic greatness/democratic representation—might be questioned, for surely some "great" works are also representative of one or another group typically relegated to the margins of conventional histories of American drama and theatre. Proceeding by the logic of Guillory's opposition, any effort to expand or revise the canon in a more "democratic" fashion could be achieved only at the cost of diluting a canon of masterworks with texts of lesser quality. Such is hardly the case.

[1] *Boldfaced terms are defined in the Glossary near the end of the book.*

Canon formation ought to be a more thoughtful process than the opposition between "conservative" defenders of a status quo and their "liberal" or "radical" antagonists. As Guillory asks in reformulating the terms of this debate, "In what social context or institution, then, does the process of canon formation occur?" The answer for most literary genres is quite clearly the academy, although the particular case of drama and performance art is also complicated by matters of theatrical production and the contemporary repertory. Still, canons are formed, for the most part, in college and university classrooms and curricula. What qualifies as American literature is to a considerable extent determined by what works teachers actually place on their course syllabi and by what topics they write about in the journals that other teacher-scholars read. Consequently, editors of anthologies typically endeavor to include those works most often taught in college classrooms, while avoiding those less avidly sought in the intellectual marketplace. (One might also assume that some reciprocity in this relationship exists, that many teachers will teach what gets anthologized or canonized.) Because canons and anthologies are formed, for the most part, within the academy, drama that has been too successful in finding a large popular audience has often been deemed not "literary" enough, thus lacking in substantial value and routinely excluded from consideration. Hence, yet another opposition has frequently inflected canon formation: "high" versus "low" art, a distinction usually defined by the presumed level of sophistication of the consumers of each cultural product. Logically connected to the notion of anthologies as collections of "masterpieces," such an opposition, we feel, also needs to be rejected, for there is no understanding an individual text apart from the larger context of dramatic conventions and theatrical practices in which it was produced. Some of these have emerged in television, film, rock videos, and other mass cultural forms that need to be considered right along with the history of the American drama.

Several anthologies of American drama have preceded this one and, in a sense, we have endeavored to enlarge their respective agendas: Lee Jacobus's *Longman Anthology of American Drama* and the Laurel Drama Series, a group of paperbacks organized by decade and inaugurated with *Famous American Plays of the 1920s* (1959), edited by Kenneth Macgowan, come immediately to mind. Jacobus's text contains 22 plays, five before World War I and several from the 1960s and early 1970s. The *Famous American Plays* series has continued with volumes all the way through the 1980s. Much as Jacobus described his book, we regard our text, in part, as a "monument to talent and greatness." Two of the more obvious and commonly agreed upon "monuments" included here, Eugene O'Neill's *The Iceman Cometh* (1947) and Tennessee Williams's *Cat on a Hot Tin Roof* (1955), were enormously important in their day and continue to exert considerable influence on both the contemporary American drama and on scholarship dedicated to a better understanding of its continuing evolution. Several contributors to the volume *Eugene O'Neill and the Emergence of American Drama* (1989) make this exact point, outlining O'Neill's influence on such later writers as Sam Shepard, whose futuristic rock and roll saga *The Tooth of Crime* (1972) is included here. And, like Macgowan, who viewed the plays he selected as more than "famous" but also "representative" of "the burgeoning theatre of the twenties," we view the 32 works included here as perhaps the most broadly representative of American theatre as have ever been assembled in a single textbook. Many selections, like those in Macgowan's *Famous Plays*, indeed illustrate a particular historical moment or dramatic **form**. No account of drama in nineteenth-century theatre, for example, would be complete without several different examples of **melodrama**; Dion

Boucicault's spectacular melodrama *The Octoroon* (1859) and Augustin Daly's *Under the Gaslight* (1867) have been included for this reason. Anna Cora Mowatt's social comedy *Fashion* (1845) and Bronson Howard's Civil War melodrama *Shenandoah* (1888) represent distinctive types of plays popular on the nineteenth-century stage. More recent selections exemplify other forms of a more modern drama and performance style: Clifford Odets's *Waiting for Lefty* (1935), illustrative of **agit-prop** or activist drama of the 1930s; Arthur Miller's *All My Sons* (1947), an enduring example both of dramatic **realism** and Miller's efforts to write a **tragedy** of the common man; Edward Albee's *The Zoo Story* (1958), exemplary of American **absurdism** in the late 1950s and 1960s; LeRoi Jones' (Amiri Baraka) *Dutchman* (1964), a **guerrilla drama** of the 1960s black liberation movement; and Karen Finley's *We Keep Our Victims Ready* (1989 version), one example of contemporary **performance art**. But just as the dramas in this volume (however monumental some might be) were not selected for reasons of their greatness, these works listed together are far more than a catalogue of dramatic forms. All are inextricably tied to American history, to the progress and inevitable tensions that attend an ever-changing American culture, to the formation of an increasingly diverse national identity.

The matter of the critical neglect of works written by historically marginalized writers—"marginalized" partially definable in terms of gender and ethnicity—reflects this added sense of cultural representativeness. As fine a book as it is, Hewitt's *Theatre U.S.A.* describes an American stage from which Rachel Crothers, Susan Glaspell, Sophie Treadwell, and Langston Hughes, among others, are conspicuously absent. This chronicle is being rewritten by theatre historians, by feminist and other scholars interested in issues of gender and sexuality, and by major repertory theatres as well. For instance, due in large measure to successful revivals of *Machinal* (1928) by the San Francisco Repertory Company in 1983, the Public Theatre in New York in 1990, and Britain's National Theatre in 1993, Sophie Treadwell's work is reaching a new generation of audiences, and we have been fortunate to be able to include it. To take an example of a drama not included here, Zora Neale Hurston's *Spunk*, adapted from her fiction by George C. Wolfe, was revived by several companies for the 1993–1994 season, opening the way for reassessment of the historical importance of such plays of the same period as Hughes' *Mulatto* (1935), which is reprinted here. However, in addition to expanding the scope of historical narration, retelling the story of American drama also means rereading and recontextualizing plays that have traditionally occupied places of preeminence in it. In his *Cowboys, Communists, and Queers* (1992) David Savran attempts precisely this in his rereading of Arthur Miller and Tennessee Williams in the historical light of Cold War America in the early 1950s and the "anti-communism fervor that gripped the national psyche," a fervor or mania that also extended to homosexuals. This kind of reconsideration has influenced our selection of plays for this anthology and, at times, the commentary we have written to accompany them.

In a sense, then, history itself—the history of America and Americans from the pre–Civil War South through World War I, the Great Depression, World War II, the Cold War era, the free speech and civil rights movements, and the post–Vietnam War era—and the role of drama in representing this history have strongly affected our choice of text. Like Shepard's *The Tooth of Crime*, both Adrienne Kennedy's *A Movie Star Has to Star in Black and White* (1976) and Luis Valdez' *I Don't Have to Show You No Stinking Badges!* (1986) concern the influence of mass culture—popular music, film, television—on contemporary American drama. More important, they underscore the influence, even determining power, of mass culture on the consumer, the viewing or listening subject. Related to this issue, two of the more important thematic issues developed in contemporary American drama—feminine subjectivity and the issue of ethnic or racial **Otherness**—are represented here not only by Kennedy's play, but by Ntozake Shange's *Spell #7* (1978), Marsha Norman's *Getting Out* (1978), David Henry Hwang's *M. Butterfly* (1988), and others. Several other works from the contemporary theatre were selected because of their treatment of an issue of importance to life in what some have called **postmodern** America: the war in Vietnam (David Rabe's *Streamers*), gay or lesbian identity (Moraga's *Giving Up the Ghost*), the AIDS crisis (Kramer's *The Destiny of Me*), and sexual harassment in the wake of the televised Senate confirmation of Clarence Thomas for the Supreme Court (Mamet's *Oleanna*).

In sum, all the works in this anthology, this gathering of theatrical flowers, have been chosen for reasons both of their intrinsic value *and* their representativeness, for reasons having to do with our sense of what teachers teach, what scholars write about, and what theatrical companies are producing—and, of course, for reasons of their arrangement as a whole, for the kind of historical story they tell. We have tried throughout to keep editorial intrusions to a minimum, offering the best available text of each work with concise accompanying commentary. Short essays introduce each writer and work, always following a simple formula: a summary of each writer's biography and career, a delineation of the play or performance piece's narrative, and a synopsis of some of the formal, historical, or cultural issues it raises. The volume concludes with three appendices: (1) a *Glossary* of theatrical, dramatic, and historical terms (set in **boldface** in the book's introductory essays); (2) a *Selected Bibliography* of critical works on each writer represented so as to provide a starting point for further inquiry; and (3) a *Selected Filmography* of American plays on film or videocassette or, in some cases, of the screenplays written by dramatists included in this text.

We sincerely hope that you will enjoy *American Drama: Colonial to Contemporary* and that it will spark in you, as it has in us, a reaffirmation of the diversity and cultural importance of the American theatre. Despite allegations to the contrary, there *is* a tradition of drama and theatre in America well worth your attention. We have attempted to sketch the contours of this tradition through the readings that follow.

WORKS CONSULTED

Guillory, John. "Canon." In *Critical Terms for Literary Study*, eds. Frank Lentricchia and Thomas McLaughlin. Chicago: University of Chicago Press, 1990. Pp. 233–249.

Hewitt, Barnard. *Theatre U.S.A.: 1665–1957*. New York: McGraw-Hill, 1959.

Jacobus, Lee A. *The Longman Anthology of American Drama*. New York: Longman, 1982.

Macgowan, Kenneth. *Famous American Plays of the 1920s*. New York: Dell, 1959.

Maufort, Marc, ed. *Eugene O'Neill and the Emergence of American Drama*. Amsterdam/Atlanta: Rodopi, 1989.

Miller, Jordan Y., and Winifred L. Frazer. *American Drama Between the Wars: A Critical History*. Boston: Twayne Publishers, 1991.

Savran, David. *Communists, Cowboys, and Queers: The Politics of Masculinity in the Work of Arthur Miller and Tennessee Williams*. Minneapolis: University of Minnesota Press, 1992.

UNIT I

BEGINNINGS

✦

COLONIAL TO THE CIVIL WAR

ROYALL TYLER, *The Contrast* (1787)

JOHN AUGUSTUS STONE, *Metamora* (1828)

ANNA CORA MOWATT, *Fashion* (1845)

DION BOUCICAULT, *The Octoroon* (1859)

THE OCTOROON

UNDER THE GASLIGHT

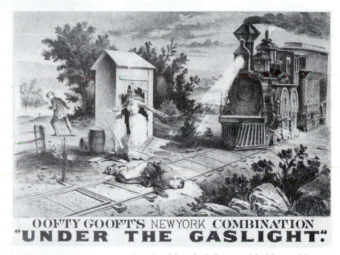

SHENANDOAH

BEGINNINGS

COLONIAL TO THE CIVIL WAR

Think of American drama as an unwanted bastard child; for decades scholars and critics of American literature have thought about it this way, when they have bothered to think about it at all. Historically the most overlooked area in American literary studies, it has also been the most maligned and now, it seems, the most unjustly neglected.

IF AMERICAN DRAMA HAS BEEN THOUGHT OF AS THE UNWELCOMED BASTARD child of American literature, as Susan Harris Smith asserts above, then early American drama has usually been cited as the primary source of its illegitimacy and corruption. No one would deny the greatness of such giants of modernism as O'Neill, Williams, and Miller. But the previous two hundred years of English language dramatic production on this continent were another story. These were best ignored, "more fun than intelligent," as Eric Mordden dismissively phrased it in *The American Theatre* (1981).

But if Mordden's comment is indicative of the customary attitude toward early American drama, is this assessment grounded in an unchallengeable aesthetic evaluation or is it the legacy of an unacknowledged bias? Could it be, as some have asserted, that Americans are simply incapable of writing drama? And, ultimately, even if such an anti-theatrical attitude exists, what import does it have for the contemporary study of American drama? While we can hardly answer these questions in the limited space of this introduction, we *can* make two observations: Drama has occupied a marginal cultural position as a literary form in America, and the continuing critical neglect of early American drama has skewed our understanding of both American drama as an art form and its function within American culture.

In an era without regional playhouses, publicly subsidized theatres, or many managers willing to ignore the box office for very long, early commercial drama faced limited alternatives. Although American playwrights became adept at manipulating popular forms to address new social, political, and economic formations, they broached controversial issues at their peril. Understandably, "safe" subjects in conventional structures are the general rule in the drama before O'Neill. American drama has also suffered in the byplay between nationalistic politics and aesthetics. The early prejudice for European plays retarded the emergence of American playwrights, and those writers who did get their plays mounted often found their work decried as imitative. Ironically, American plays became popular in the nineteenth century by embracing **melodrama**, a form subsequently deprecated by those championing **modernist** aesthetics. Whipsawed by these circumstances, our nation's early dramatic efforts remained on the literary periphery.

Early American Drama: Anti-Theatrical Prejudice and Critical Reception

In the population centers of the colonial Northeast, initial attacks against drama and the-atre stemmed from religious bias. According to Puritan commentators, drama's mimetic replication of a corrupt world tended to confuse the faithful, put before them false values, and ultimately, as the English Puritan cleric Philip Stubbes phrased it, encourage "ydolitarie, heathenrie, and sinne" (quoted in Solberg). This position was hardly new even in seventeenth-century New England, for without the religious patina, this argument stretched back to Plato. But whereas in England the Puritans had been a distinct minority even at the height of the Commonwealth, in New England they exercised significant influ-ence over state affairs.

While drama itself was dangerous, theatre was abomination. The persistent reports of pickpockets, cutpurses, and prostitutes in sixteenth- and seventeenth-century English the-atres had earlier allowed Puritan clergy to extend their moral condemnation of drama from the text to the stage; now it allowed them to cloak economic interests as principled objec-tions. Impoverished, politically alienated, and cut off from the lines of cultural power, English Puritan clergymen had perennially seen themselves as competing with actors' con-gregations for their congregation's limited money, whom the clerics saw as their intellectual, social, and moral inferiors.

Early attitudes in the ostensibly more liberal colonies of the Mid-Atlantic and South were hardly more favorable for would-be founders of a national drama. Though often lack-ing their New England neighbors' epistemological objections and moral outrage, these colonists tended to see drama and theatre as frivolous entertainments at best and as dis-turbances of the civil order at worst. For example, the first evidence of a dramatic per-formance in the English colonies is a 1665 Virginia court record of an anonymous group of actors brought before a justice of the peace who generously acquitted them of having disturbed the peace by performing the now lost *Ye Bare and Ye Cubb.* Similarly, the osten-sibly more reasonable Quakers of Pennsylvania lumped drama together with prizefights and masquerades in a 1682 statute imposing a sentence of hard labor on anyone indulging in these lapses from rectitude.

Whether grounded in moral qualms, economic interest, or concern for the secular com-monweal, this anti-theatrical sentiment survived the colonial period. During the Revolution-ary era, the 1774 Continental Congress passed a resolution to "discourage every species of extravagance and dissipation, especially all horse-racing, . . . cock-fighting, . . . [and] plays" (quoted in Silverman).

Even long after revolutionary sacrifice was no longer needed, drama remained sus-pect. By the beginning of the twentieth century, Ibsenian **realism** and Shavian comedy as well as plays by such American realists as James A. Herne and Clyde Fitch precipitated new calls for censorship. Incidents of repression became increasingly widespread and draconian. One of the most infamous incidents arose from a 1900 production of Fitch's *Sapho* in which a courtesan's pleas for seduction, followed by an exit into her bedroom in her lover's arms, proved too much for New York authorities who arrested the star, Olga

Nethersole, her leading man, and the theatre manager. Although they were later acquitted, continuing moralistic outcries led to laws such as New York's 1927 Wales statute, which allowed authorities not only to arrest actors, producers, and managers, but also to padlock any theatre and deprive it of an operating license for a year. Clearly, one of the first things that we might learn from a more thorough knowledge of a history of early American drama and its biased reception is that shrill debates about the immorality of public art were not conceived in America in the late twentieth century by demagogic politicians or dogmatic religious leaders.

While moral objections periodically generated these spasms of public indignation, pre-Civil War American drama faced a more insidious barrier—audiences' and managers' prejudice for foreign plays. American playwrights (and those who wished to support them) were caught in a double bind. On the one hand, American plays rarely received an unprejudiced hearing. For example, in 1812 William Wood, manager of Philadelphia's Chestnut Street Theatre, convinced his actors and the public that James Nelson Barker's *Marmion* was the work of an English author. After an enthusiastic run of six or seven nights, Wood revealed the ruse—at which point the audiences immediately began to dwindle. On the other hand, if American playwrights somehow succeeded in obtaining the stage, they were often denounced by contemporary and later critics as imitative of European models, of not fulfilling their obligations to produce distinctly "American" plays. Effectively, then, American dramatists were faced with the dilemma of either writing original plays, which almost no one would produce, or suffering critical opprobrium for their lack of originality.

The Founding of a Nation's Drama, 1665–1783

Despite indifference or, occasionally, overt hostility, drama began to appear in America almost from the beginning of European colonization. Initially, the dramatic impulse found expression in collegiate dialogues and rhetorical exercises, which provided oratorical training as well as diversion for aspiring clerics, lawyers, and gentlemen farmers whose future leadership would inevitably necessitate public performances.

Beyond the campuses, the concerns of colonial drama tended to divide along generic lines. Early colonial **comedies,** for example, reveal the political tensions of the period and the increasing dissatisfaction with the administration of British colonial affairs. Ironically, the earliest voice raised on this topic was a Loyalist one, for the first play written and printed in America was New York Royal Governor Robert Hunter's *Androboros: A Biographical Farce in Three Acts* (1715), a Swiftian skewering of New York's colonial Assembly as an insane asylum over which Keeper (Hunter) tries to ride herd. But *Androboros* was soon answered by three works: an untitled, invective-laced work printed in 1732 that lambastes Jonathan Belcher, the last royal governor of Massachusetts; *The Paxton Boys* (1764), a farce about an uprising of Pennsylvanian frontiersmen;

and *The Trial of Atticus* (1771), a loosely structured satire on the corruption of the colonial justice system. While these plays are interesting, the period's most ambitious and artistically satisfying comic play is Robert Munford's *The Candidates; or, the Humours of a Virginia Election*, probably composed in 1770–1771. A roistering farce peopled with Americanized characters, *The Candidates* is an indictment of contemporary electioneering practices. But it is more, too, for it provides an intriguing revelation of the gentry's anxieties concerning democratic rule, specifically the widespread eighteenth-century fear that "the mob" would reduce the world to chaos if the elite were ever to lose their economic, political, and social privileges. Though Munford, who may well have circulated the manuscript among his planter peers, ultimately endorses the system of limited representative democracy embodied in Virginia's House of Burgesses, he does so with trepidation.

Colonial **tragedy** is at once less formally diverse and more varied in subject matter than the comedy of the era. Constrained by the formal dictates of **Augustan tragedy**, both Thomas Godfrey's *The Prince of Parthia* (1759; produced 1767) and Robert Rogers' *Ponteach* (1766) share widely held beliefs that history is instructive and that the proper subject matters of tragedy are honor, the nature of warrior manhood, and free men's natural resistance to despotism. Godfrey's play, the first actually written by an American to be produced in the colonies, is a pseudo-Shakespearean blank verse drama of political machination and romantic dalliance in a modish Oriental setting. *Ponteach*, conversely provides an elevated treatment of Pontiac's rebellion (1763–1766), making it the first full-length representation of a Native American on the American stage.

With the advent of the Revolutionary War, American drama became an effective weapon in the hands of both sides. While the few playhouses that did exist were closed for most of the war, drama found outlets in the press. With both Patriots and Tories utilizing the form, dialogues continued to be popular, conveniently tailored as they were to the broadsheet press of the day. Slightly longer Patriot satiric pieces, such as Mercy Otis Warren's *The Group* (1776) and *The Blockheads* (1776), which excoriated British colonial officials and military officers, respectively, were especially popular in the Boston press. Counterpointing these Patriot attacks in the Loyalist stronghold of New York City was *The Battle of Brooklyn* (1776), an anonymous Tory effort that lacerates Washington and his staff for their Long Island defeat.

In Virginia, Robert Munford sought to restrain what he saw as extremism in *The Patriots* (1777). Running counter to the revolutionary impulse to simplify the political universe into an "us–them" binary, Munford's second play melds farcical, sentimental, and sententious plots to provide "a discourse on the nature of political and personal loyalty and the necessity of tolerance in a period of crisis" (Richardson). Meanwhile in Maryland, in *The Battle of Bunkers-Hill* (1776) and *The Death of General Montgomery* (1777), Hugh Henry Brackenridge sought to provide a new definition of American manhood by showing the heroic efforts and sacrifices of early martyrs to the American cause. John Leacock, a retired Philadelphia goldsmith, tried another tactic in *The Fall of British Tyranny* (1776). An ambitious linking of both satiric and heroic modes, Leacock's play sprawls across the era's political, military, and social topography, encompassing action on both sides of the Atlantic and in both the Northern and Southern colonies. While its structural looseness reveals its amateur origins, Leacock's play is admirable in revealing the emotional core of general Patriot reaction in the early days of the war.

With the end of the war came a moment of self-reflection. No longer British, but not yet certain of what it meant to be "American," the citizens of the new nation sought to discover who, collectively, they were. In this enterprise, the nation's fledgling drama took a willing hand.

Federal Experiments, 1787–1828

The early national period was paradoxically a time of political experimentation in the midst of general cultural conservatism. For many of the social, political, and economic elite, primarily male mercantile capitalists, the transition from British to American seems to have been made somewhat easier by retaining the hierarchical cultural trappings of the previous order while publicly embracing the new political reality. Given the enormous power of these elites, such a disposition had immediate impact upon the theatre world and the drama. This influential group not only owned the physical theatres and were shareholders in the acting companies, but they also exercised control through **benefit performances** for managers and actors and through their purchases of theatre boxes. As Bruce McConachie has argued, these playgoers were most comfortable when the hierarchy of which they were a part found reassuring, conventionally structured expression on the stage. But others, including reviewers, critics, and even some playwrights, argued for a new, distinctly "American" drama, a radical reconfiguration of the dramatic culture to complement the transformations of the polity. The attempts to accommodate these divergent impulses established an enduring tension between aesthetics and ideology in the early national drama. This conflict finds expression in the works of the three major dramatists of the Federal period: Royall Tyler, William Dunlap, and James Nelson Barker.

We shall discuss Tyler's *The Contrast* (1787) in more detail in the introduction to the play, but it is important to note here that the play has been criticized as merely a pale reflection of its English **comedy of manners** forerunners (Tanselle). Certainly, in terms of its structure and its overall aesthetic, Tyler's play seems only superficially American. Nevertheless, the introduction of the Yankee character to the American stage, an implicit concern with the national idiom, and the nationalizing of a heretofore conventionally English conflict between foppish decadence and austere virtue to reflect contemporary political feelings are major accomplishments that counterbalance aesthetic shortcomings in the first noteworthy American comedy to see the stage.

William Dunlap is particularly illustrative of the difficulties encountered by early national dramatists, since as the manager and house playwright for New York's Old American Company from 1796 until 1805, he wrote not in an artistic vacuum but as one intimately involved in the day-to-day workings of a theatrical company. Beset almost continually by financial worries made worse by personal antagonisms among his actors and outbreaks of yellow fever that closed the theatres, Dunlap was forced to turn to adaptations of popular French and German playwrights (notably August von Kotzebue) to keep his company afloat. Dunlap is probably best remembered now in American theatre history for establishing the American taste for melodramas (Grimsted), but his importance to our discussion resides in his major original work, *André* (1798). Another attempt to utilize English forms in the service of a broadly American ideology, *André* represents a first for the American stage—an eighteenth-century tragedy in the classical vein of Addison's *Cato*, in which an American playwright examines the national history critically and produces a play that goes beyond propaganda.

James Nelson Barker's efforts for the Philadelphia theatres produced the most marked insistence upon ideological content as the primary standard of drama's value. In a series of articles published for the *Democratic Press* [Philadelphia] (1816–1817), Barker examined American drama and asserted that the ultimate goal of drama, an end attainable only in a democracy, is "to keep alive the spirit of freedom; and to unite conflicting parties in a common love of liberty and devotedness to country." In his major plays, *Marmion* (1812) and *Superstition* (1824), he provided markedly different strategies to accomplish that end.

In *Marmion*, Barker works by indirection, arguing that heroic literature—with its emphasis on class, validation of aristocratic privilege, and slavish faith in the social and political status quo—has generated aesthetic principles (aristocratic subject matter, stateliness of expression, and formal conservatism) inappropriate to a democracy. Educating the population to the true nature of such an evil system and, thereby, reinforcing American ideals are, according to Barker, much more important for the new nation's drama than replicating superficialities of American characters or locale. In *Superstition*, Barker is more direct. Taking a cue from Dunlap, he chooses an episode from American history and deftly uses it to compose a serious analysis of colonial Puritan intolerance to suggest that, although Americans have escaped the physical confines of the Old World, many remain yoked to outmoded ways of thinking that can easily give way to new tyrannies. Thus, Barker's play not only reinforces conventional messages of the early republic—knowledge of the fragility of liberty and the need for constant vigilance against those within the community who might compromise it—but also exemplifies at least one method of accomplishing those ends—a democratically oriented drama which educates its audience to the lessons of liberty.

"Art" versus "Entertainment" in Drama, 1828–1860

As time passed and national circumstances altered, the influence of the dominantly ideological criteria advanced by the early Federal playwrights diminished somewhat, giving way to two alternative (though in practice not absolutely distinct) approaches to writing American drama. On the one hand, certain dramatists chose to work within the confines of

European-inspired aesthetics, believing that American dramatists were equal in quality to any in the world and that writing in the European vein was the most efficacious way of achieving recognition for American dramatic "art." This posture was made somewhat easier by the concomitant popularity of **romantic tragedy** whose emphasis on the tragic situation of its central characters—usually at odds with some oppressive institution or social order—coincided nicely with America's championing of rugged individualism. Through a series of temporal and geographic displacements, the ideology of the autonomous subject—cornerstone of American bourgeois individualism—became the defining issue of plays set in ancient Rome, South America, and medieval Italy. On the other hand, implicitly conceding that their writings were not "art" (a term too rarefied for their rough-and-tumble audiences) but good, solid "entertainment," aptly conceived and performed for the average working-class American, another group of writers fixed their attention on the people and topics of daily American life. Their plays were designed to appeal to a mass audience who lacked the inclination, and, occasionally, sophistication to appreciate verse tragedy.

Both approaches to the drama sought to deal imaginatively with the issues confronting America during the period. The new states emerging from the old Northwest Territory led to a steady erosion of the older political power bases in New England and Virginia. The election of Jackson in 1828 cast traditional hierarchies into question, putting a new public sanction on individualism, as opposed to the communtarianism popularly associated with the older republicanism of Jefferson and Madison. Economically, an aggressive preindustrial market capitalism tended to reorganize the nation's entire economic structure, heavily emphasizing entrepreneurship. Despite this increased interest in individuality, more traditional liberalism, with its emphasis on collective betterment, found new expression in the period's intensifying focus on temperance and slavery.

These broad social forces had immediate and significant impact upon both elite and popular drama as well as general theatrical operations. The shifting strategies and ideological contours of elite drama can be seen in the central characters of such plays as John Howard Payne's *Brutus* (1819), Robert Montgomery Bird's *The Gladiator* (1831) and *The Broker of Bogota* (1834), and in George Henry Boker's *Francesca da Rimini* (1853). The increasing emphasis on the heroic individual and the individual's emotional life in these plays suggests the ways in which the subject matters and artistic forms of nineteenth-century high culture were adapted to the needs of new audience configurations and to the changing American stage.

Typical of elite drama's paradigm of citizenship at the beginning of the period is Payne's *Brutus*, a retelling of the familiar story of the expulsion of the Tarquin tyrants and the founding of the Roman republic under the leadership of Lucius Junius Brutus. Noble both by birth and character, a powerful military leader, the founder of a predominant republic, and a man so dedicated to justice that he would sacrifice his own son to preserve the state, Brutus was for the elite patriarchs who controlled the theatres of America in the early nineteenth century their fantasy of themselves. By the 1830s, older hierarchies were being supplanted by the new merchant class who found representation as Baptista Febro in Bird's *The Broker of Bogota*. While voicing some of patriarchy's perennial anxieties about the possible loss of authority, Bird's play is most revealing in its shifting of the action out of the public arena into the private, middle-class world of family relations. With *Francesca da Rimini*, elite drama's movement toward an elevation of the interior emotional life is completed. The reappropriation of a Renaissance Italian love triangle from Canto V of Dante's *Inferno* for a mid-nineteenth-century American audience is, on the one hand, a perfectly appropriate gesture for a dramatist who insisted that since art was timeless, it would appeal to any refined audience in any period. On the other hand, Dante's story of tragic love amid political conflict is historically fitting to a class whose control over large sectors of the nation was increasingly removed from public view but who publicly insisted on the importance of manners, social customs, intellectual refinement, and emotional restraint as a way of unobtrusively shaping and indirectly manipulating newly emerging social and economic formations.

If poetic drama articulated the upper class's sense of their nation's adherence to Western cultural values and traditions, the popular drama provided its heterogeneous audiences another attempt to define the nation and its citizenry. Full of spectacle, stereotypical characters, straightforward moral choices, melodramatic plots, and unashamed nationalism, these plays propounded their own ideologies to ensure the continued public and private growth of the United States.

One of the popular plays' enduring subjects of interest was the frontier and its inhabitants. The migrations from the original colonies to the Northwest Territory and then to the lands beyond the Mississippi River had immediate effects not only on those who travelled west, but also on writers. The older versions of heroism detailing the exploits of classical figures, perfectly appropriate to staid bulwarks of high culture such as Boston, New York, and Philadelphia, were being supplanted in the contemporary mind by heroic tales of adventure on the frontier. Thus, the Native American and the frontiersman became part of the popular imagination, growing over the period into heroes of legendary proportion.

Since the **Indian plays** will be discussed later in the context of Stone's *Metamora* (1829), we shall restrict our observations here to the frontiersmen who historically and theatrically supplanted Native Americans. Although the frontiersman could be the straightforward action hero that he was to become in popular culture, the drama of this era provided him with quite varied roles. In plays such as Louisa Medina's *Nick of the Woods* (1838) and W. R. Derr's *Kit Carson, the Hero of the Prairie* (1850), he was the hero who boldly tamed land and savage. But the plays of the period could also utilize the frontiersman as comic social commentator. The most energetic and culturally penetrating example of this latter group is James Kirke Paulding's *The Lion of the West* (1830).

Composed for the actor James H. Hackett's 1830 contest for the best comedy with an American as the central character, *The Lion of the West* became one of Hackett's most popular vehicles, prompting him to have it revised twice—once by John Augustus Stone and once by William Bayle Bernard, who retitled it *The Kentuckian; or, a Trip to New York* for its English premiere. The play's appeal to an 1830s audience was rather direct, for within its farce structure it employs two of the period's favorite comic formulas—crossed courtship and a gauche country eccentric who reveals the foibles of his city "betters." While the vast majority of the play relies upon conventional contrasts between American liberality and British class consciousness and social rigidity, Paulding also manages to suggest the country's growing sectional discord. As we have already noted, the emergence of frontier-inspired Jacksonian democracy with its assertive egalitarianism caused great anxiety among the cultural and political elites whose power was situated in the original colonies' cities. In Nimrod Wildfire, his title character, Paulding presents the audience with the breathing embodiment of this new order but moderated so as to placate all segments of his audience. Paulding at once confirms elitist fears while giving his lower-class viewers one of their own—a bumpkin who has no time for social pretense but is a man who can make sure the heroine ends up in the arms of the deserving hero. He is, in the end, the now traditional, lovable American iconoclast. Like Stone's Metamora and the other Native-American heroes, these frontiersmen did much to give flesh to the emerging myth of the lone individual fighting against mindless social conformity and political injustice.

The popularity of Native Americans and frontiersmen did not banish more established segments of the populace from the stage. While true social comedy had its shining moment in Anna Cora Mowatt's *Fashion* (1845), a play discussed later, the majority of the plays that sought to delineate the American social scene followed the frontier play's lead by focusing on character types. Certain segments of the population were seemingly exhausted in a single play (the New York Dutch as represented in *Rip Van Winkle* for example). But members of other groups appeared as central or supporting figures again and again. One of the most popular of these characters was the Yankee. These descendants of *The Contrast*'s Jonathan were initially content to stay at home in such plays as Lazarus Beach's *Jonathan Postfree* (1807) and A. B. Lindsley's *Love and Friendship* (1809), but eventually they crossed the seas. Charles Mathews' *Jonathan in England* (1824) and James Hackett's *John Bull at Home; or, Jonathan in England*, which placed the irreverent New Englander in Britain, were merely the first step, for Yankees travelled to France, Cuba, Poland, Spain, Algiers, and China, always outraging the local population with their own brand of eccentric chauvinism. So popular was the character type that a succession of notable plays—including Samuel Woodworth's *The Forest Rose* (1825), Joseph S. Jones' *The People's Lawyer; or, Solon Shingle* (1839), and Denman Thompson's *The Old Homestead* (1886)—kept the Yankee on the boards until the early twentieth century.

If the Yankee plays reminded their audiences of both the privilege of eccentricity that freedom guaranteed and the sacrifices necessary to secure that freedom, the slavery plays pointedly insisted to many of the audiences that Southern planters had built their livelihoods on denying freedom to others. And although we shall engage this topic more fully when turning to Dion Boucicault's *The Octoroon* (1859), we cannot leave this period without a few comments about the most popular play in theatrical history—*Uncle Tom's Cabin.*

Harriet Beecher Stowe's sprawling novel seems at first glance rather a poor choice for a dramatic adaptation. An episodic narrative, diffuse focus, and huge cast of characters suggest only a few of the difficulties it presents. However, the novel's enormous popularity upon publication in 1852 led to several adaptations both in the United States and abroad. The most famous, George L. Aiken's six-act distillation, was incredibly popular in its own right, running for over 200 performances in its initial New York City engagement. As Harry Birdoff has noted, in one form or another, the play was before the public continuously until about 1930. In 1879, there were almost 50 troupes crisscrossing the country playing only *Uncle Tom's Cabin;* in 1927, audiences could still sustain a dozen companies. While *Uncle Tom's Cabin* may no longer have aesthetic appeal to contemporary critics, the play's formal qualities were never terribly relevant to understanding its importance to the country and to the country's drama. As Arthur Hobson Quinn noted, "in the catalogue of social forces it remains probably the most potent weapon developed by the literary crusade against slavery." The power of the popular drama to engage contemporary issues and to move people was nowhere better exemplified than in *Uncle Tom's Cabin.*

Before turning to the latter decades of the nineteenth century and to the growth of melodrama, a further brief word on the audiences, players, and theatrical practices is in order. During most of this period, theatres continued the early Federal pattern of relying upon a mixed audience to stay afloat financially. But the foundations of theatrical economics were shifting. Over the course of the 1830s and 1840s, the elite males who had controlled the early Federal theatre found the markedly more egalitarian atmosphere of Jacksonian American theatre increasingly unappealing and shifted away from the theatres to a new and less accessible artistic form—opera. At the same time, a newly emerging elite—the businessman—became the dominant class within the theatrical audience. Women also began to appear in the theatre in greater numbers, a fact that eventually precipitated a division of theatres along class lines and "shattered for good the phenomenon of theatre as a social microcosm of the entire society" (Levine).

The change in the audience was reflected on the boards with the emergence of entrepreneurial "stars" such as Edwin Forrest, James William Wallack, and James H. Hackett. Their rise to prominence spelled the end for **repertoire companies** and hastened the emergence of the **stock company,** which, effectively, became a group of hirelings in support of the stars. The only minor exceptions to this pattern were to be found in the emergence of the **African Theatre,** founded in New York City in 1821 by William Henry Brown, and in the parodic inversion of African-American theatre, the **minstrel show**. In the former instance, the company's relatively small audiences inhibited the development of financially independent actors. In the latter case, the "disguising" of the individual actors and the racial inhibitions to white audience identification with the characters tended to diminish individual stars while lionizing the groups.

As early as the first decades of the nineteenth century, the alternative options of plays as art or as entertainment pulled drama into a broad cultural debate on the role of the arts in a democracy and into a still broader unspoken debate concerning the social organization of American society. The cultural position and roles of drama, acting, and the theatre itself were earnestly debated even by those who despaired of the quality of American plays. And while it is hyperbolic to suggest that the era's theatre was generally a cultural battleground, riots such as the one that took place outside New York City's Astor Place Opera House in 1849 vividly suggest the complex ways in which Americans of the period understood theatrical activity and the preternatural importance which they occasionally attached to it. On that occasion partisans of the American actor Edwin Forrest, intent upon disrupting a performance by the English tragedian William Charles Macready, congregated outside the Astor Place Opera House. Spurred on by a combination of class antagonism, Know-Nothing anti-foreigner feeling, specific anti-English sentiment among recent Irish immigrants in the crowd, and antipathy for "effete" (read English) acting, the pro-Forrest partisans engaged the police and militia who had been brought in to control potential difficulties. The result was a melee that left at least 22 (perhaps as many as 31) dead and 150 injured, and many commentators wondering about the state of the theatre and the nation (Moody).

Political, economic, and social tensions, some of which found expression in the Astor Place riot, mounted steadily during the first half of the nineteenth century. The accommodations hammered out loudly in the halls of Congress and more quietly on the country's stages allowed the nation to grow and prosper throughout most of the period without consciously examining its citizens' underlying and often disparate definitions of the state. Inevitably, those compromises wore thin. Sectional antipathies, conflicting economic models, contradictory urban and rural social structures, and, always, the question of slavery, propelled the nation beyond the possibility of accommodation. The nation descended into civil war. As the forces of chaos began their dance of destruction in Charleston, South Carolina's harbor in April of 1861, no American could have foreseen the changes that the war would precipitate. But as a reflector of American life and as a primary means by which the country defined itself, American drama was inevitably transformed.

WORKS CONSULTED

Barker, James Nelson. "The Drama." Democratic Press [Philadelphia] 18 December 1816–19, February 1817.

Birdoff, Harry. *The World's Greatest Hit: Uncle Tom's Cabin.* New York: Vanni, 1947.

Dunlap, William. *History of the American Theatre.* 2 vols. 1832; Rpt. New York: Burt Franklin, 1963.

Grimsted, David. *Melodrama Unveiled: American Theater and Culture, 1800–1850.* Chicago: University of Chicago Press, 1968.

Levine, Lawrence W. *Highbrow / Lowbrow The Emergence of Cultural Hierarchy in America.* Cambridge, MA: Harvard University Press, 1988.

McConachie, Bruce A. *Melodramatic Formations: American Theatre and Society 1820–1870.* Iowa City: The University of Iowa Press, 1992.

Moody, Richard. *The Astor Place Riot.* Bloomington: Indiana University Press, 1958.

Mordden, Eric. *The American Theatre.* New York: Oxford University Press, 1981.

Quinn, Arthur Hobson. *A History of the American Drama.* 2nd ed. 2 vols. New York: Crofts, 1951.

Richardson, Gary A. *American Drama from the Colonial Period through World War I.* New York: Twayne, 1993.

Silverman, Kenneth. *A Cultural History of the American Revolution.* New York: Crowell, 1976.

Smith, Susan Harris. "Generic Hegemony: American Drama and the Canon." *American Quarterly, 41* (1989): 112–122.

Solberg, Winton U. *Redeem the Time: The Puritan Sabbath in Early America.* Cambridge: Harvard University Press, 1977.

Tanselle, G. Thomas. *Royall Tyler.* Cambridge: Harvard University Press, 1967.

Wood, William. *Personal Recollections of the Stage.* Philadelphia: Henry C. Baird, 1855.

THE CONTRAST (1787)

On the evening of April 16, 1787, the curtain first rose on a professionally produced American comedy with the initial performance of Royall Tyler's *The Contrast* at New York City's John Street Theatre. Five additional performances in April and May at the John Street Theatre and subsequent productions quickly mounted in Baltimore, Philadelphia, Boston, and Charleston indicate that managers immediately recognized the play's appeals. So did the critics. Reviewing the first night's performance for New York's *The Daily Advertiser*, the pseudonymous commentator "Candour" was typical of contemporary audiences, praising the play as "the production of a man of genius" and adding that "nothing can be more praise-worthy than the sentiments of the play throughout. They are the effusions of an honest patriot heart expressed with energy and eloquence." Such enthusiastic praise is remarkable given the play's rapid composition (Tyler finished the play approximately a month after seeing his first theatrical production—a John Street Theatre performance of Sheridan's *The School for Scandal*) and even more noteworthy in light of the fact that Tyler was not a professional writer.

Born in Boston in 1757 to a staunchly patriotic family, Tyler graduated as valedictorian of the Harvard class of 1776 and was simultaneously granted a B.A. by Yale. He read law in Cambridge, Massachusetts, but interrupted his studies to serve with the Independent Company of Boston during the American Revolution. He was admitted to the bar in Maine and afterwards practiced in Braintree, Massachusetts, where he was engaged for a short time to Abigail, the daughter of John Adams. After Abigail broke their engagement, Tyler briefly retired to his mother's home, but by the end of 1785 he was again actively practicing law, this time in Boston, where he met and eventually married Mary Palmer. As aide-de-camp to General Benjamin Lincoln during Shays' Rebellion (1787), Tyler assisted in the suppression of the insurgents and unsuccessfully pursued Shays himself into Vermont. Afterwards sent to New York by Massachusetts Governor Bowdoin, Tyler arrived on March 12, 1787, using the opportunity of official business to see several American Company productions at the John Street Theatre and making the acquaintance of Thomas Wignell, the company's low comedian. Returning to his professional life, Tyler pursued a legal career until 1791 in Boston and afterwards in Vermont, where he eventually served as state's attorney for Windham County (1794–1801), assistant judge (1801–1807) and, ultimately, Chief Justice of the Vermont Supreme Court (1807–1813). Tyler was also professor of jurisprudence at the University of Vermont (1811–1814) as well as a trustee of that institution (1802–1813). He retired from public life in 1821 and died of cancer in Brattleboro, Vermont, on August 16, 1826.

Although he is primarily remembered now as the author of *The Contrast*, Tyler also wrote other plays, essays, poetry, and a novel. After the success of *The Contrast*, Tyler composed a now-lost two-act comic opera, *May Day in Town; or, New York in an Uproar* which was performed at the John Street Theatre on May 19, 1787. The press of his legal career, however, and the demands of beginning a family interrupted his dramatic output for almost a decade. During this period his literary output took the form of occasional prose and poetic collaborations with his friend, Joseph Dennie. Publishing in various New England newspapers and Federalist journals under the names Colon and Spondee, Dennie and Tyler provided satiric essays and poems on various contemporary topics. And, when in 1795 his brother, John, was appointed manager of the Federal Street Theatre in Boston, Tyler once again ventured to write for the stage. Although no copy has survived, *The Farm House; or, The Female Duellists,* an apparent reworking of Charles Kemble's piece of the same name, was performed in May 1796 and is usually attributed to Tyler. There is no doubt, however, that Tyler authored *The Georgia Spec; or, The Land in the Moon,* an afterpiece presented at the Boston's Federal Theatre on October 30, 1797, and at New York's John Street Theatre in December 1797 and again in February 1798. There is no evidence that his later plays were produced, but Tyler continued to write drama, adapting Molière in *The Doctor in Spite of Himself,* dramatizing an episode from Cervantes' *Don Quixote* as *The Island of Barrataria,* and composing three sacred dramas based on Old Testament materials. In addition to his dramatic output, Tyler achieved some note as a novelist with the publication of *The Algerine Captive; or, The Life and Adventures of Dr. Updike Underhill,* the first American novel to be republished in England.

For our purposes, of course, it is Tyler's contributions to American drama in the form of *The Contrast* that demand our attention. It is occasionally difficult to perceive the abiding influence of a play written in the latter decades of the eighteenth century. But *The Contrast*'s impact was immediate and its legacy remains vital. Most immediately, the play provided tentative answers to two questions that bedeviled American writers and dramatists for almost the entire nation's history: is there or can there be an indigenous American literary culture, and, if such a culture exists or is possible, what dramatic expression should it take?

As Donald Seibert and others have noted, Tyler's formal debt to English comedy is heavy (and occasionally heavy-handed), but his play emphatically answers the first question in the af-

firmative. By reworking the **comedy of manners**, Tyler simultaneously staked claim to the English dramatic heritage while, in some senses, turning that heritage against itself. Certainly the accoutrements of manners comedy remain, for the world of *The Contrast* is obsessed with social forms, witty conversation, fashion, and romantic affiliation. But the social assumptions that had made such comedy an upper-class bastion against the witless assaults of the nouveaux riches are turned on their heads. In Tyler's world the audience is not asked to emulate the polished, witty, and ruthless characters whose actions and language reflect social forms unavailable to the uninitiated, but to embrace the doughty and blunt Captain Manly and his sentimental counterpart Maria. While both Thomas Tanselle and Roger Stein have noted that the elevated and slightly pompous speech of Manly and Maria leaves them open to some slight satire, there can be no doubt that Tyler firmly upholds American sincerity against English affectation. Chauvinism aside, Tyler's play provides the American stage with the first incarnation of one of its most enduring stock characters—the Yankee. Jonathan, whose provincial ignorance leads him to mistake a production of *"The School for Scandalization"* for a voyeuristic look into a neighboring house, provides a lower-class counterpart to Manly and suggests that what Daniel Havens has called "the spirit of native worth" is indigenous to even the most remote and uncouth areas of the new country.

But if *The Contrast* spoke to the immediate cultural and dramatic needs of the early republic, its legacy extended beyond its historical moment. On the one hand, for the first time on the American stage, a native-born playwright had chosen to explore the comic possibilities of his fellow citizens' attitudes and actions. In doing so, Tyler carved out a cultural locus where questions of national identity could be examined with good humor and where the foibles and follies of a new nation might be exposed to the healing astringent of an audience's laughter. In this regard, Tyler anticipated American playwrights

from Anna Cora Mowatt and Langdon Mitchell to
Philip Barry and Neil Simon. On the other hand, his
use of regional characters and his keen ear for the
differences among American speech patterns alerted
his audience to the variety of Americas that were being forged. Thus, in ironic ways, Tyler at the beginning of the country's drama struck a note that still
resonates in the work of contemporary dramatists
such as August Wilson, Cherríe Moraga, Luis Valdez,
and Henry David Hwang.

WORKS CONSULTED

Candour. *The Daily Advertiser.* April 18, 1787.
Havens, Daniel F. *The Columbian Muse of Comedy.* Carbondale:
    Southern Illinois University Press, 1973.
Seibert, Donald T., Jr. "Royall Tyler's 'Bold Example': *The Con-
    trast* and the English Comedy of Manners." *Early Ameri-
    can Literature* 13 (1978): 3–11.
Stein, Roger. "Royall Tyler and the Question of Our Speech."
    New England Quarterly 38 (1965): 454–74.
Tanselle, G. Thomas. *Royall Tyler.* Cambridge: Harvard Univer-
    sity Press, 1967.

Prologue

*Written by a Young Gentleman of New-York, and
Spoken by Mr. Wignell*

Exult each patriot heart!—this night is shewn
A piece, which we may fairly call our own;
Where the proud titles of "My Lord! Your Grace!"
To humble Mr. and plain Sir give place.
Our Author pictures not from foreign climes
The fashions, or the follies of the times;
But has confin'd the subject of his work
To the gay scenes—the circles of New-York.
On native themes his Muse displays her pow'rs;
If ours the faults, the virtues too are ours.

Why should our thoughts to distant countries
    roam,
When each refinement may be found at home?
Who travels now to ape the rich or great,
To deck an equipage and roll in state;
To court the graces, or to dance with ease,
Or by hypocrisy to strive to please?
Our free-born ancestors such arts despis'd;
Genuine sincerity alone they priz'd;
Their minds, with honest emulation fir'd,
To solid good—not ornament—aspir'd;
Or, if ambition rous'd a bolder flame,
Stern virtue throve, where indolence was shame.

  But modern youths, with imitative sense,
Deem taste in dress the proof of excellence;
And spurn the meanness of your homespun arts,
Since homespun habits would obscure their parts;
Whilst all, which aims at splendour and parade,
Must come from Europe, and be ready made.
Strange! we should thus our native worth
    disclaim,
And check the progress of our rising fame.
Yet one, whilst imitation bears the sway,
Aspires to nobler heights, and points the way,
Be rous'd, my friends! his bold example view;
Let your own Bards be proud to copy you!
Should rigid critics reprobate our play,
At least the patriotic heart will say,
"Glorious our fall, since in a noble cause.
"The bold attempt alone demands applause."
Still may the wisdom of the Comic Muse
Exalt your merits, or your faults accuse.
But think not, 't is her aim to be severe;—
We all are mortals, and as mortals err.
If candour pleases, we are truly blest;
Vice trembles, when compell'd to stand confess'd.
Let not light Censure on your faults, offend,
Which aims not to expose them, but amend.
Thus does our Author to your candour trust;
Conscious, the free are generous, as just.

CHARACTERS

COL. MANLY	CHARLOTTE
DIMPLE	MARIA
VAN ROUGH	LETITIA
JESSAMY	JENNY
JONATHAN	SERVANTS

SCENE, NEW YORK

N. B. The lines marked with inverted commas, "thus," are omitted in the representation.
(The portions omitted in representation are enclosed in brackets [ ].)

ACT FIRST

SCENE 1: *An Apartment at* CHARLOTTE'S.

CHARLOTTE *and* LETITIA *discovered.*

LETITIA: And so, Charlotte, you really think the pocket-hoop unbecoming.

CHARLOTTE: No, I don't say so: It may be very becoming to saunter round the house of a rainy day; to visit my grand-mamma, or go to Quakers' meeting: but to swim in a minuet, with the eyes of fifty well-dressed beaux upon me, to trip it in the Mall, or walk on the battery, give me the luxurious, jaunty, flowing, bell-hoop. It would have delighted you to have seen me the last evening, my charming girl! I was dangling o'er the battery with Billy Dimple; a knot of young fellows were upon the platform; as I passed them I faultered with one of the most bewitching false steps you ever saw, and then recovered myself with such a pretty confusion, flirting my hoop to discover a jet black shoe and brilliant buckle. Gad! how my little heart thrilled to hear the confused raptures of— *"Demme, Jack, what a delicate foot!" "Ha! General, what a well-turn'd—"*

LETITIA: Fie! fie! Charlotte *(stopping her mouth)*, I protest you are quite a libertine.

CHARLOTTE: Why, my dear little prude, are we not all such libertines? Do you think, when I sat tortured two hours under the hands of my friseur, and an hour more at my toilet, that I had any thoughts of my aunt Susan, or my cousin Betsey? though they are both allowed to be critical judges of dress.

LETITIA: Why, who should we dress to please, but those who are judges of its merit?

CHARLOTTE: Why a creature who does not know *Buffon* from *Souflee*—Man!—my Letitia—Man! for whom we dress, walk, dance, talk, lisp, languish, and smile. Does not the grave Spectator assure us, that even our much bepraised diffidence, modesty, and blushes, are all directed to make ourselves good wives and mothers as fast as we can. Why, I'll undertake with one flirt of this hoop to bring more beaux to my feet in one week, than the grave Maria, and her sentimental circle, can do, by sighing sentiment till their hairs are grey.

LETITIA: Well, I won't argue with you; you always out talk me; let us change the subject. I hear that Mr Dimple and Maria are soon to be married.

CHARLOTTE: You hear true. I was consulted in the choice of the wedding clothes. She is to be married in a delicate white sattin, and has a monstrous pretty brocaded lutestring for the second day. It would have done you good to have seen with what an affected indifference the dear sentimentalist [turned over a thousand pretty things, just as if her heart did not palpitate with her approaching happiness, and at last made her choice, and] arranged her dress with such apathy, as if she did not know that plain white sattin, and a simple blond lace, would shew her clear skin, and dark hair, to the greatest advantage.

LETITIA: But they say her indifference to dress, and even to the gentleman himself, is not entirely affected.

CHARLOTTE: How?

LETITIA: It is whispered, that if Maria gives her hand to Mr Dimple, it will be without her heart.

CHARLOTTE: Though the giving of the heart is one of the last of all laughable considerations in the marriage of a girl of spirit, yet I should like to hear what antiquated notions the dear little piece of old fashioned prudery has got in her head.

LETITIA: Why you know that old Mr John-Richard-Robert - Jacob - Isaac - Abraham - Cornelius Van Dumpling, Billy Dimple's father, (for he has thought fit to soften his name, as well as manners, during his English tour) was the most intimate friend of Maria's father. The old folks, about a year before Mr Van Dumpling's death, proposed this match: the young folks were accordingly introduced, and told they must love one another. Billy was then a good natured, decent, dressing young fellow, with a little dash of the coxcomb, such as our young fellows of fortune usually have. At this time, I really believe she thought she loved him; and had they then been married, I doubt not, they might have jogged on, to the end of the chapter, a good kind of a sing-song lack-a-daysaical life, as other honest married folks do.

CHARLOTTE: Why did they not then marry?

LETITIA: Upon the death of his father, Billy went to England to see the world, and rub off a little of the patroon rust. During his absence, Maria like a good girl, to keep herself constant to her *nown true-love*, avoided company, and betook herself, for her amusement, to her books, and her dear Billy's letters. But, alas! how many ways has the mischievous demon of inconstancy of stealing into a woman's heart! Her love was destroyed by the very means she took to support it.

CHARLOTTE: How?—Oh! I have it—some likely young beau found the way to her study.

LETITIA: Be patient, Charlotte—your head so runs upon beaux.— Why she read *Sir Charles Grandison*, *Clarissa Harlow*, *Shenstone*, and the *Sentimental Journey;* and between whiles, as I said, Billy's letters. But as her taste improved, her love declined. The contrast was so striking betwixt the good sense of her books, and the flimsiness of her love-letters, that she discovered she had unthinkingly engaged her hand without her heart; and then the whole transaction managed by the old folks, now appeared so unsentimental, and looked so like bargaining for a bale of goods, that she found she ought to have rejected, according to every rule of romance, even the man of her choice, if imposed upon her in that manner—Clary Harlow would have scorned such a match.

CHARLOTTE: Well, how was it on Mr Dimple's return? Did he meet a more favourable reception than his letters?

LETITIA: Much the same. She spoke of him with respect abroad, and with contempt in her closet. She watched his conduct and conversation, and found that he had by travelling acquired the wickedness of Lovelace without his wit, and the politeness of Sir Charles Grandison without his generosity. The ruddy youth who washed his face at the cistern every morning, and swore and looked eternal love and constancy, was now metamorphosed into a flippant, palid, polite beau who devotes the morning to his toilet, reads a few pages of Chesterfield's letters, and then minces out, to put the infamous principles in practice upon every woman he meets.

CHARLOTTE: But, if she is so apt at conjuring up these sentimental bugbears, why does she not discard him at once?

LETITIA: Why, she thinks her word too sacred to be trifled with. Besides, her father, who has a great respect for the memory of his deceased friend, is even telling her how he shall renew his years in their union, and repeating the dying injunctions of old Van Dumpling.

CHARLOTTE: A mighty pretty story! And so you would make me believe, that the sensible Maria would give up Dumpling manor, and the all-accomplished Dimple as a husband, for the absurd, ridiculous reason, forsooth, because she despises and abhors him. Just as if a lady could not be privileged to spend a man's fortune, ride in his carriage, be called after his name, and call him her *nown dear love* when she wants money, without loving and respecting the great he-creature. Oh! my dear girl, you are a monstrous prude.

LETITIA: I don't say what I would do; I only intimate how I suppose she wishes to act.

CHARLOTTE: No, no, no! A fig for sentiment. If she breaks, or wishes to break with Mr Dimple, depend upon it, she has some other man in her eye. A woman rarely discards one lover, until she is sure of another.— Letitia little thinks what a clue I have to Dimple's conduct. The generous man submits to render himself disgusting to Maria, in order that she may leave him at liberty to address me. I must change the subject. *(Aside, and rings a bell)*

(Enter SERVANT*)*

Frank, order the horses to.—Talking of marriage—did you hear that Sally Bloomsbury is going to be married next week to Mr Indigo, the rich Carolinian?

LETITIA: Sally Bloomsbury married! Why, she is not yet in her teens.

CHARLOTTE: I do not know how that is but, you may depend upon it, 't is a done affair. I have it from the best authority. There is my aunt Wyerley's Hannah (you know Hannah—though a black, she is a wench that was never caught in a lie in her life); now Hannah has a brother who courts Sarah, Mrs Catgut the milliner's girl, and she told Hannah's brother, and Hannah, who, as I said before, is a girl of

undoubted veracity, told it directly to me, that Mrs Catgut was making a new cap for Miss Bloomsbury, which, as it was very dressy, it is very probable is designed for a wedding cap: now, as she is to be married, who can it be to, but to Mr Indigo? Why, there is no other gentleman that visits at her papa's.

LETITIA: Say not a word more, Charlotte. Your intelligence is so direct and well grounded, it is almost a pity that it is not a piece of scandal.

CHARLOTTE: Oh! I am the pink of prudence. Though I cannot charge myself with ever having discredited a tea-party by my silence, yet I take care never to report any thing of my acquaintance, especially if it is to their credit,— *discredit*, I mean—until I have searched to the bottom of it. It is true, there is infinite pleasure in this charitable pursuit. Oh! how delicious to go and condole with the friends of some backsliding sister, or to retire with some old dowager or maiden aunt of the family, who love scandal so well, that they cannot forbear gratifying their appetite at the expence of the reputation of their nearest relations! And then to return full fraught with a rich collection of circumstances, to retail to the next circle of our acquaintance under the strongest injunctions of secrecy,—ha, ha, ha!— interlarding the melancholy tale with so many doleful shakes of the head, and more doleful, "Ah! who would have thought it! so amiable, so prudent a young lady, as we all thought her, what a monstrous pity! well, I have nothing to charge myself with; I acted the part of a friend, I warned her of the principles of that rake, I told her what would be the consequence; I told her so, I told her so."—Ha, ha, ha!

LETITIA: Ha, ha, ha! Well, but Charlotte, you don't tell me what you think of Miss Bloomsbury's match.

CHARLOTTE: Think! why I think it is probable she cried for a plaything, and they have given her a husband. Well, well, well, the puling chit shall not be deprived of her plaything: 't is only exchanging London dolls for American babies—

Apropos, of babies, have you heard what Mrs Affable's high-flying notions of delicacy have come to?

LETITIA: Who, she that was Miss Lovely?

CHARLOTTE: The same; she married Bob Affable of Schenectady. Don't you remember?
(Enter SERVANT)

SERVANT: Madam, the carriage is ready.

LETITIA: Shall we go to the stores first, or visiting?

CHARLOTTE: I should think it rather too early to visit; especially Mrs Prim: you know she is so particular.

LETITIA: Well, but what of Mrs Affable?

CHARLOTTE: Oh, I'll tell you as we go; come, come, let us hasten. I hear Mrs Catgut has some of the prettiest caps arrived, you ever saw. I shall die if I have not the first sight of them.   *(Exeunt)*

SCENE 2: *A Room in* VAN ROUGH'S *House.* MARIA *sitting disconsolate at a Table, with Books, etc.*

Song

I

The sun sets in night, and the stars shun
     the day;
But glory remains when their lights fade
     away!
Begin, ye tormentors! your threats are in
     vain,
For the son of Alknomook shall never
     complain.

II

Remember the arrows he shot from his
     bow;
Remember your chiefs by his hatchet laid
     low:
Why so slow?—do you wait till I shrink
     from the pain?
No—the son of Alknomook will never
     complain.

III

Remember the wood where in ambush we
     lay;
And the scalps which we bore from your
     nation away:
Now the flame rises fast, you exult in my
     pain;
But the son of Alknomook can never
     complain.

IV

I go to the land where my father is gone;
His ghost shall rejoice in the fame of his
     son:
Death comes like a friend, he relieves
     me from pain;
And thy son, Oh Alknomook! has scorn'd
     to complain.

There is something in this song which ever calls forth my affections. The manly virtue of courage, that fortitude which steels the heart against the keenest misfortunes, which interweaves the laurel of glory amidst the instruments of torture and death, displays something so noble, so exalted, that in despite of the prejudices of education, I cannot but admire it, even in a savage. The prepossession which our sex is supposed to entertain for the character of a soldier, is, I know, a standing piece of raillery among the wits. A cockade, a lapell'd coat, and a feather, they will tell you, are irresistible by a female heart. Let it be so.— Who is it that considers the helpless situation of our sex, that does not see we each moment stand in need of a protector, and that a brave one too. [Formed of the more delicate materials of nature, endowed only with the softer passions, incapable, from our ignorance of the world, to guard against the wiles of mankind, our security for happiness often depends upon their generosity and courage:— Alas! how little of the former do we find.] How inconsistent! that man should be leagued to destroy that honour, upon which, solely rests his respect and esteem. Ten thousand temptations allure us, ten thousand passions betray us; yet the smallest deviation from the path of rectitude is followed by the contempt and insult of man, and the more remorseless pity of woman: years of penitence and tears cannot wash away the stain, nor a life of virtue obliterate its remembrance. [Reputation is the life of woman; yet courage to protect it, is masculine and disgusting; and the only safe asylum a woman of delicacy can find, is in the arms of a man of honour. How naturally then, should we love the brave, and the generous; how gratefully should we bless the arm raised for our protection, when nerv'd by virtue, and directed by honour!] Heaven grant that the man with whom I may be connected—may be connected!—Whither has my imagination transported me—whither does it now lead me?—Am I not indissolubly engaged [by every obligation of honour, which my own consent, and my father's approbation can give,] to a man who can never share my affections, and whom a few days hence, it will be criminal for me to disapprove—to disapprove! would to heaven that were all—to despise. For, can the most frivolous manners, actuated by the most depraved heart, meet, or merit, anything but contempt from every woman of delicacy and sentiment?

(VAN ROUGH, *without*) Mary!

Ha, my father's voice— Sir!—

(*Enter* VAN ROUGH)

VAN ROUGH: What, Mary, always singing doleful ditties, and moping over these plaguy books.

MARIA: I hope, Sir, that it is not criminal to improve my mind with books; or to divert my melancholy with singing at my leisure hours.

VAN ROUGH: Why, I don't know that, child; I don't know that. They us'd to say when I was a young man, that if a woman knew how to make a pudding, and to keep herself out of fire and water, she knew enough for a wife. Now, what good have these books done you? have they not made you melancholy? as you call it. Pray, what right has a girl of your age to be in the dumps? hav n't

you every thing your heart can wish; an't you going to be married to a young man of great fortune; an't you going to have the quit-rent of twenty miles square?

MARIA: One hundredth part of the land, and a lease for life of the heart of a man I could love, would satisfy me.

VAN ROUGH: Pho, pho, pho! child; nonsense, downright nonsense, child. This comes of your reading your story-books; your *Charles Grandisons,* your *Sentimental Journals,* and your *Robinson Crusoes,* and such other trumpery. No, no, no! child, it is money makes the mare go; keep your eye upon the main chance, Mary.

MARIA: Marriage, Sir, is, indeed, a very serious affair.

VAN ROUGH: You are right, child; you are right. I am sure I found it so to my cost.

MARIA: I mean, Sir, that as marriage is a portion for life, and so intimately involves our happiness, we cannot be too considerate in the choice of our companion.

VAN ROUGH: Right, child; very right. A young woman should be very sober when she is making her choice, but when she has once made it, as you have done, I don't see why she should not be as merry as a grig; I am sure she has reason enough to be so— Solomon says, that "there is a time to laugh, and a time to weep"; now a time for a young woman to laugh is when she has made sure of a good rich husband. Now a time to cry, according to you, Mary, is when she is making choice of him: but, I should think, that a young woman's time to cry was, when she despaired of *getting* one.—Why, there was your mother now; to be sure when I popp'd the question to her, she did look a little silly; but when she had once looked down on her apronstrings, as all modest young women us'd to do, and drawled out ye-s, she was as brisk and as merry as a bee.

MARIA: My honoured mother, Sir, had no motive to melancholy; she married the man of her choice.

VAN ROUGH: The man of her choice! And pray, Mary, an't you going to marry the man of your choice—what trumpery notion is this?— It is these vile books *(throwing them away)*. I'd have you to know, Mary, if you won't make young Van Dumpling the man of *your* choice, you shall marry him as the man of *my* choice.

MARIA: You terrify me, Sir. Indeed, Sir, I am all submission. My will is yours.

VAN ROUGH: Why, that is the way your mother us'd to talk. "My will is yours, my dear Mr Van Rough, my will is yours": but she took special care to have her own way though for all that.

MARIA: Do not reflect upon my mother's memory, Sir—

VAN ROUGH: Why not, Mary, why not? She kept me from speaking my mind all her *life*, and do you think she shall henpeck me now she is *dead* too? Come, come; don't go to sniveling: be a good girl, and mind the main chance. I'll see you well settled in the world.

MARIA: I do not doubt your love, Sir; and it is my duty to obey you.— I will endeavor to make my duty and inclination go hand in hand.

VAN ROUGH: Well, well, Mary; do you be a good girl, mind the main chance, and never mind inclination.— Why, do you know that I have been down in the cellar this very morning to examine a pipe of Madeira which I purchased the week you were born, and mean to tap on your wedding day.— That pipe cost me fifty pounds sterling. It was well worth sixty pounds; but I over-reached Ben Bulkhead, the supercargo: I'll tell you the whole story. You must know that—

(Enter SERVANT*)*

SERVANT: Sir, Mr Transfer, the broker, is below.   *(Exit)*

VAN ROUGH: Well, Mary, I must go.—Remember, and be a good girl, and mind the main chance. *(Exit)*

MARIA: *(Alone)* How deplorable is my situation! How distressing for a daughter to find her heart militating with her filial duty! I know my father loves me tenderly, why then do I reluctantly obey him? [Heaven knows! with what reluctance I should oppose the will of a parent, or set an example of filial disobedience]; at a parent's command I could wed aukwardness and deformity. [Were the heart of my husband good, I would so magnify his good qualities with the eye of conjugal affection, that the defects of his person and manners should be lost in the emanation of his virtues.] At a father's command, I could embrace poverty. Were the poor man my husband, I would learn resignation to my lot; I would enliven our frugal meal with good humour, and chase away misfortune from our cottage with a smile. At a father's command, I could almost submit, to what every female heart knows to be the most mortifying, to marry a weak man, and blush at my husband's folly in every company I visited.— But to marry a depraved wretch, whose only virtue is a polished exterior; [who is actuated by the unmanly ambition of conquering the defenceless; whose heart, insensible to the emotions of patriotism, dilates at the plaudits of every unthinking girl]: whose laurels are the sighs and tears of the miserable victims of his specious behaviour.— Can he, who has no regard for the peace and happiness of other families, ever have a due regard for the peace and happiness of his own? Would to heaven that my father were not so hasty in his temper! Surely, if I were to state my reasons for declining this match, he would not compel me to marry a man—whom, though my lips may solemnly promise to honour, I find my heart must ever despise.   *(Exit)*

END   OF   THE   FIRST   ACT

ACT   SECOND

SCENE 1

(Enter CHARLOTTE *and* LETITIA*)*

CHARLOTTE: *(at entering)* Betty, take those things out of the carriage and carry them to my chamber; see that you don't tumble them.— My dear, I protest, I think it was the homeliest of the whole. I declare I was almost tempted to return and change it.

LETITIA: Why would you take it?

CHARLOTTE: [Did n't Mrs Catgut say it was the most fashionable?

LETITIA: But, my dear, it will never sit becomingly on you.

CHARLOTTE: I know that; but did not you hear Mrs Catgut say it was fashionable?

LETITIA: Did you see that sweet airy cap with the white sprig?

CHARLOTTE: Yes, and I longed to take it; but,] my dear, what could I do?— Did not Mrs Catgut say it was the most fashionable; and if I had not taken it, was not that aukward gawky, Sally Slender, ready to purchase it immediately?

[LETITIA: Did you observe how she tumbled over the things at the next shop, and then went off without purchasing any thing, nor even thanking the poor man for his trouble?— But of all the aukward creatures, did you see Miss Blouze, endeavouring to thrust her unmerciful arm into those small kid gloves?

CHARLOTTE: Ha, ha, ha, ha!]

LETITIA: Then did you take notice, with what an affected warmth of friendship she and Miss Wasp met? when all their acquaintances know how much pleasure they take in abusing each other in every company?

CHARLOTTE: Lud! Letitia, is that so extraordinary? Why, my dear, I hope you are not going to turn sentimentalist.—Scandal, you know, is but amusing ourselves with the faults, foibles, follies and reputations of our friends;—indeed, I don't know why we should have friends, if we are not at liberty to make use of them. But no person is so ignorant of the world as to suppose, because I amuse myself with a lady's faults, that I am obliged to quarrel with her person, every time we meet; believe me, my dear, we should have very few acquaintances at that rate.

(SERVANT enters and delivers a letter to CHARLOTTE, and Exits)

CHARLOTTE: You'll excuse me, my dear. (Opens and reads to herself)

LETITIA: Oh, quite excusable.

CHARLOTTE: As I hope to be married, my brother Henry is in the city.

LETITIA: What, your brother, Colonel Manly?

CHARLOTTE: Yes, my dear; the only brother I have in the world.

LETITIA: Was he never in this city?

CHARLOTTE: Never nearer than Harlem Heights, where he lay with his regiment.

LETITIA: What sort of a being is this brother of yours? If he is as chatty, as pretty, as sprightly as you, half the belles in the city will be pulling caps for him.

CHARLOTTE: My brother is the very counterpart and reverse of me: I am gay, he is grave; I am airy, he is solid; I am ever selecting the most pleasing objects for my laughter, he has a tear for every pitiful one. And thus, whilst he is plucking the briars and thorns from the path of the unfortunate, I am strewing my own path with roses.

LETITIA: My sweet friend, not quite so poetical, and little more particular.

CHARLOTTE: Hands off, Letitia. I feel the rage of simile upon me; I can't talk to you in any other way. My brother has a heart replete with the noblest sentiments, but then, it is like—it is like— Oh! you provoking girl, you have deranged all my ideas—it is like—Oh! I have it—his heart is like an old maiden lady's band-box; it contains many costly things, arranged with the most scrupulous nicety, yet the misfortune is, that they are too delicate, costly, and antiquated for common use.

LETITIA: By what I can pick out of your flowery description, your brother is no beau.

CHARLOTTE: No, indeed; he makes no pretension to the character. He'd ride, or rather fly, an hundred miles to relieve a distressed object, or to do a gallant act in the service of his country: but, should you drop your fan or bouquet in his presence, it is ten to one that some beau at the farther end of the room would have the honour of presenting it to you, before he had observed that it fell. I'll tell you one of his antiquated, anti-gallant notions.— He said once in my presence, in a room full of company—would you believe it—in a large circle of ladies, that the best evidence a gentleman could give a young lady of his respect and affection, was, to endeavour in a friendly manner to rectify her foibles. I protest I was crimson to the eyes, upon reflecting that I was known as his sister.

LETITIA: Insupportable creature! tell a lady of her faults! If he is so grave, I fear I have no chance of captivating him.

CHARLOTTE: [His conversation is like a rich old fashioned brocade, it will stand alone; every sentence is a sentiment. Now you may judge what a time I had with him, in my twelve months' visit to my father. He read me such lectures, out of pure brotherly affection, against the extremes of fashion, dress, flirting, and coquetry, and all the other dear things which he knows I doat upon, that, I protest, his conversation made me as melancholy as if I had been at church; and heaven knows, though I never prayed to go there but on one occasion, yet I would have exchanged his conversation for a psalm and a sermon. Church is rather melancholy, to be sure; but then I can ogle the beaux, and be regaled with "here endeth the first lesson"; but his brotherly *here*, you would think had no end.] You captivate him! Why, my dear, he would as soon fall in love with a box of Italian flowers. There is Maria now, if she were not engaged, she might do something.— Oh! how I should like to see that pair of pensorosos together, looking as grave as two sailors' wives of a stormy night, with a flow of sentiment meandering through their conversation like purling streams in modern poetry.

LETITIA: Oh! my dear fanciful—

CHARLOTTE: Hush! I hear some person coming through the entry.

(*Enter* SERVANT)

SERVANT: Madam, there's a gentleman below who calls himself Colonel Manly; do you chuse to be at home?

CHARLOTTE: Shew him in. (*Exit* SERVANT) Now for a sober face.

(*Enter* COLONEL MANLY)

MANLY: My dear Charlotte, I am happy that I once more enfold you within the arms of fraternal affection. I know you are going to ask (amiable impatience!) how our parents do,—the venerable pair transmit you their blessing by me—they totter on the verge of a well-spent life, and wish only to see their children settled in the world, to depart in peace.

CHARLOTTE: I am very happy to hear that they are well. (*Coolly*) Brother, will you give me leave to introduce you to our uncle's ward, one of my most intimate friends.

MANLY: (*Saluting* LETITIA) I ought to regard your friends as my own.

CHARLOTTE: Come, Letitia, do give us a little dash of your vivacity; my brother is so sentimental, and so grave, that I protest he'll give us the vapours.

MANLY: Though sentiment and gravity, I know, are banished the polite world, yet, I hoped, they might find some countenance in the meeting of such near connections as brother and sister.

CHARLOTTE: Positively, brother, if you go one step further in this strain, you will set me crying, and that, you know, would spoil my eyes; and then I should never get the husband which our good papa and mamma have so kindly wished me—never be established in the world.

MANLY: Forgive me, my sister—I am no enemy to mirth; I love your sprightliness; and I hope it will one day enliven the hours of some worthy man; but when I mention the respectable authors of my existence,—the cherishers and protectors of my helpless infancy, whose hearts glow with such fondness and attachment, that they would willingly lay down their lives for my welfare, you will excuse me, if I am so unfashionable as to speak of them with some degree of respect and reverence.

CHARLOTTE: Well, well, brother; if you won't be gay, we'll not differ; I will be as grave as you wish. *(Affects gravity)* And so, brother, you have come to the city to exchange some of your commutation notes for a little pleasure.

MANLY: Indeed, you are mistaken; my errand is not of amusement, but business; and as I neither drink nor game, my expences will be so trivial, I shall have no occasion to sell my notes.

CHARLOTTE: Then you won't have occasion to do a very good thing. Why, there was the Vermont General—he came down some time since, sold all his musty notes at one stroke, and then laid the cash out in trinkets for his dear Fanny. I want a dozen pretty things myself; have you got the notes with you?

MANLY: I shall be ever willing to contribute as far as it is in my power, to adorn, or in any way to please my sister; yet, I hope, I shall never be obliged for this, to sell my notes. I may be romantic, but I preserve them as a sacred deposit. Their full amount is justly due to me, but as embarrassments, the natural consequences of a long war, disable my country from supporting its credit, I shall wait with patience until it is rich enough to discharge them. If that is not in my day, they shall be transmitted as an honourable certificate to posterity, that I have humbly imitated our illustrious WASHINGTON, in having exposed my health and life in the service of my country, without reaping any other reward than the glory of conquering in so arduous a contest.

CHARLOTTE: Well said heroics. Why, my dear Henry, you have such a lofty way of saying things, that I protest I almost tremble at the thought of introducing you to the polite circles in the city. The belles would think you were a player run mad, with your head filled with old scraps of tragedy: and, as to the beaux, they might admire, because they would not understand you.— But, however, I must, I believe, venture to introduce you to two or three ladies of my acquaintance.

LETITIA: And that will make him acquainted with thirty or forty beaux.

CHARLOTTE: Oh! brother, you don't know what a fund of happiness you have in store.

MANLY: I fear, sister, I have not refinement sufficient to enjoy it.

CHARLOTTE: Oh! you cannot fail being pleased.

LETITIA: Our ladies are so delicate and dressy.

CHARLOTTE: And our beaux so dressy and delicate.

LETITIA: Our ladies chat and flirt so agreeably.

CHARLOTTE: And our beaux simper and bow so gracefully.

LETITIA: With their hair so trim and neat.

CHARLOTTE: And their faces so soft and sleek.

LETITIA: Their buckles so tonish and bright.

CHARLOTTE: And their hands so slender and white.

LETITIA: I vow, Charlotte, we are quite poetical.

CHARLOTTE: And then, brother, the faces of the beaux are of such a lily white hue! None of that horrid robustness of constitution, that vulgar corn-fed glow of health, which can only serve to alarm an unmarried lady with apprehensions, and prove a melancholy memento to a married one, that she can never hope for the happiness of being a widow. I will say this to the credit of our city beaux, that such is the delicacy of their complexion, dress, and address, that, even had I no reliance upon the honour of the dear Adonises, I would trust myself in any possible situation with them, without the least apprehensions of rudeness.

MANLY: Sister Charlotte!

CHARLOTTE: Now, now, now brother *(interrupting him)*, now don't go to spoil my mirth with a dash of your gravity; I am so glad to see you, I am in tip-top spirits. Oh! that you could be with us at a little snug party. There is Billy Simper, Jack Chassé, and Colonel Van Titter, Miss Promonade, and the two Miss Tambours, sometimes make a party, with some other ladies, in a side-box at the play. Everything is conducted with such decorum,—first we bow round to the company in general, then to each one in particular, then we have so many inquiries after each other's health, and we are so happy to meet each other, and it is so many ages since we last had that pleasure, [and, if a married lady is in company, we have such a sweet dissertation upon her son Bobby's chin-cough] then the curtain rises, then our sensibility is all awake, and then by the mere force of apprehension, we torture some harmless expression into a double meaning, which the poor author never dreamt of, and then we have recourse to our fans, and then we blush, and then the gentlemen jog one another, peep under the fan and make the prettiest remarks; and then we giggle and they simper, and they giggle and we simper, and then the curtain drops, and then for nuts and oranges, and then we bow, and it's pray Ma'am take it, and pray Sir keep it, and oh! not for the world, Sir: and then the curtain rises again, and then we blush and giggle, and simper, and bow, all over again. Oh! the sentimental charms of side-box conversation!   *(All laugh)*

MANLY: Well, sister, I join heartily with you in the laugh; for, in my opinion, it is as justifiable to laugh at folly, as it is reprehensible to ridicule misfortune.

CHARLOTTE: Well, but brother, positively, I can't introduce you in these clothes: why, your coat looks as if it were calculated for the vulgar purpose of keeping yourself comfortable.

MANLY: This coat was my regimental coat in the late war. The public tumults of our state have induced me to buckle on the sword in support of that government which I once fought to establish. I can only say, sister, that there was a time when this coat was respectable, and some people even thought that those men who had endured so many winter campaigns in the service of their country, without bread, clothing, or pay, at least deserved that the poverty of their appearance should not be ridiculed.

CHARLOTTE: We agree in opinion entirely, brother, though it would not have done for me to have said it: it is the coat makes the man respectable. In the time of the war, when we were almost frightened to death, why, your coat was respectable, that is, fashionable; now another

kind of coat is fashionable, that is, respectable. And pray direct the taylor to make yours the height of the fashion.

MANLY: Though it is of little consequence to me of what shape my coat is, yet, as to the height of the fashion, there you will please to excuse me, sister. You know my sentiments on that subject. I have often lamented the advantage which the French have over us in that particular. In Paris, the fashions have their dawnings, their routine and declensions, and depend as much upon the caprice of the day as in other countries; but there every lady assumes a right to deviate from the general *ton*, as far as will be of advantage to her own appearance. In America, the cry is, what is the fashion? and we follow it, indiscriminately, because it is so.

CHARLOTTE: Therefore it is, that when large hoops are in fashion, we often see many a plump girl lost in the immensity of a hoop petticoat, whose want of height and *em-bon-point* would never have been remarked in any other dress. When the high head-dress is the mode, how then do we see a lofty cushion, with a profusion of gauze, feathers, and ribband, supported by a face no bigger than an apple; whilst a broad full-faced lady, who really would have appeared tolerably handsome in a large head-dress, looks with her smart chapeau as masculine as a soldier.

MANLY: But remember, my dear sister, and I wish all my fair country-women would recollect, that the only excuse a young lady can have for going extravagantly into a fashion, is, because it makes her look extravagantly handsome.— Ladies, I must wish you a good morning.

CHARLOTTE: But, brother, you are going to make home with us.

MANLY: Indeed, I cannot. I have seen my uncle, and explained that matter.

CHARLOTTE: Come and dine with us, then. We have a family dinner about half past four o'clock.

MANLY: I am engaged to dine with the Spanish ambassador. I was introduced to him by an old brother officer; and instead of freezing me with a cold card of compliment to dine with him ten days hence, he, with the true old Castilian frankness, in a friendly manner, asked me to dine with him to-day—an honour I could not refuse. Sister, adieu—Madam, your most obedient— *(Exit)*

CHARLOTTE: I will wait upon you to the door, brother; I have something particular to say to you. *(Exit)*

LETITIA: *(alone)* What a pair!— She the pink of flirtation, he the essence of everything that is *outré* and gloomy.— I think I have completely deceived Charlotte by my manner of speaking of Mr Dimple; she's too much the friend of Maria to be confided in. He is certainly rendering himself disagreeable to Maria, in order to break with her and proffer his hand to me. This is what the delicate fellow hinted in our last conversation. *(Exit)*

SCENE 2: *The Mall*

(Enter JESSAMY)

JESSAMY: Positively this Mall is a very pretty place. I hope the city won't ruin it by repairs. To be sure, it won't do to speak of in the same day with Ranelagh or Vauxhall; however, it's a fine place for a young fellow to display his person to advantage. Indeed, nothing is lost here; the girls have taste, and I am very happy to find they have adopted the elegant London fashion of looking back, after a genteel fellow like me has passed them. Ah! who comes here? This, by his aukwardness, must be the Yankee colonel's servant. I'll accost him.

(Enter JONATHAN)

Votre très—humble serviteur, Monsieur. I understand Colonel Manly, the Yankee officer, has the honour of your services.

JONATHAN: Sir!—

JESSAMY: I say, Sir, I understand that Colonel Manly has the honour of having you for a servant.

JONATHAN: Servant! Sir, do you take me for a neger,—I am Colonel Manly's waiter.

JESSAMY: A true Yankee distinction, egad, without a difference. Why, Sir, do you not perform all the offices of a servant? Do you not even blacken his boots?

JONATHAN: Yes; I do grease them a bit sometimes; but I am a true blue son of liberty, for all that. Father said I should come as Colonel Manly's waiter to see the world, and all that; but no man shall master me: my father has as good a farm as the colonel.

JESSAMY: Well, Sir, we will not quarrel about terms upon the eve of an acquaintance, from which I promise myself so much satisfaction,—therefore sans ceremonie—

JONATHAN: What?—

JESSAMY: I say, I am extremely happy to see Colonel Manly's waiter.

JONATHAN: Well, and I vow, too, I am pretty considerably glad to see you—but what the dogs need of all this outlandish lingo? Who may you be, Sir, if I may be so bold?

JESSAMY: I have the honour to be Mr Dimple's servant, or, if you please, waiter. We lodge under the same roof, and should be glad of the honour of your acquaintance.

JONATHAN: You a waiter! By the living jingo, you look so topping, I took you for one of the agents to Congress.

JESSAMY: The brute has discernment notwithstanding his appearance.— Give me leave to say I wonder then at your familiarity.

JONATHAN: Why, as to the matter of that, Mr— pray, what's your name?

JESSAMY: Jessamy, at your service.

JONATHAN: Why, I swear we don't make any great matter of distinction in our state, between quality and other folks.

JESSAMY: This is, indeed, a levelling principle. I hope, Mr Jonathan, you have not taken part with the insurgents.

JONATHAN: Why, since General Shays has sneaked off, and given us the bag to hold, I don't care to give my opinion; but you'll promise not to tell— put your ear this way—you won't tell?— I vow, I did think the sturgeons were right.

JESSAMY: I thought, Mr Jonathan, you Massachusetts men always argued with a gun in your hand.— Why did n't you join them?

JONATHAN: Why, the colonel is one of those folks called the Shin—shin—dang it all, I can't speak them lignum vitae words—you know what I mean—there is a company of them—they wear a China goose at their button-hole—a kind of gilt thing.— Now the colonel told father and brother,—you must know there are, let me see—there is Elnathan, Silas, and Barnabas, Tabitha—no, no, she's a she—tarnation, now I have it—there's Elnathan, Silas, Barnabas, Jonathan, that's I—seven of us, six went into the wars, and I staid at home to take care of mother. Colonel said that it was a burning shame for the true blue Bunker-hill sons of liberty, who had fought Governor Hutchinson, Lord North, and the Devil, to have any hand in kicking up a cursed dust against a government, which we had every mother's son of us a hand in making.

JESSAMY: Bravo!— Well, have you been abroad in the city since your arrival? What have you seen that is curious and entertaining?

JONATHAN: Oh! I have seen a power of fine sights. I went to see two marble-stone men and a leaden horse, that stands out in doors in all weathers; and when I came where they was, one had got no head, and t' other wer'nt there. They said as how the leaden man was a damn'd tory, and that he took wit in his anger and rode off in the time of the troubles.

JESSAMY: But this was not the end of your excursion.

JONATHAN: Oh, no; I went to a place they call Holy Ground. Now I counted this was a place where folks go to meeting; so I put my hymn-book in my pocket, and walked softly and grave as a minister; and when I came there, the dogs a bit of a meeting-house could I see. At last I spied a young gentlewoman standing by one of the seats, which they have here at the doors—I took her to be the deacon's daughter, and she looked so kind, and so obliging, that I thought I would go and ask her the way to lecture, and

would you think it—she called me dear, and sweeting, and honey, just as if we were married; by the living jingo, I had a month's mind to buss her.

JESSAMY: Well, but how did it end?

JONATHAN: Why, as I was standing talking with her, a parcel of sailor men and boys got round me, the snarl headed curs fell a-kicking and cursing of me at such a tarnal rate, that, I vow, I was glad to take to my heels and split home, right off, tail on end like a stream of chalk.

JESSAMY: Why, my dear friend, you are not acquainted with the city; that girl you saw was a— *(Whispers)*

JONATHAN: Mercy on my soul! was that young woman a harlot!— Well, if this is New York Holy Ground, what must the Holy-day Ground be!

JESSAMY: Well, you should not judge of the city too rashly. We have a number of elegant fine girls here, that make a man's leisure hours pass very agreeably. I would esteem it an honour to announce you to some of them.— Gad! that announce is a select word; I wonder where I picked it up.

JONATHAN: I don't want to know them.

JESSAMY: Come, come, my dear friend, I see that I must assume the honour of being the director of your amusements. Nature has given us passions, and youth and opportunity stimulate to gratify them. It is no shame, my dear Blue-skin, for a man to amuse himself with a little gallantry.

JONATHAN: Girl huntry! I don't altogether understand. I never played at that game. I know how to play hunt the squirrel, but I can't play anything with the girls; I am as good as married.

JESSAMY: Vulgar, horrid brute! Married, and above a hundred miles from his wife, and think that an objection to his making love to every woman he meets! He never can have read, no, he never can have been in a room with a volume of the divine Chesterfield.— So you are married?

JONATHAN: No, I don't say so; I said I was as good as married, a kind of promise.

JESSAMY: As good as married!—

JONATHAN: Why, yes; there's Tabitha Wymen, the deacon's daughter, at home, she and I have been courting a great while, and folks say as how we are to be married; and so I broke a piece of money with her when we parted, and she promised not to spark it with Solomon Dyer while I am gone. You would n't have me false to my true love, would you?

JESSAMY: May be you have another reason for constancy; possibly the young lady has a fortune? Ha! Mr Jonathan, the solid charms; the chains of love are never so binding as when the links are made of gold.

JONATHAN: Why, as to fortune, I must needs say her father is pretty dumb rich; he went representative for our town last year. He will give her—let me see—four times seven is—seven times four—nought and carry one;—he will give her twenty acres of land—somewhat rocky though—a bible, and a cow.

JESSAMY: Twenty acres of rock, a bible, and a cow! Why, my dear Mr Jonathan, we have servant maids, or, as you would more elegantly express it, waitresses, in this city, who collect more in one year from their mistresses' cast clothes.

JONATHAN: You don't say so!—

JESSAMY: Yes, and I'll introduce you to one of them. There is a little lump of flesh and delicacy that lives at next door, wait'ress to Miss Maria; we often see her on the stoop.

JONATHAN: But are you sure she would be courted by me?

JESSAMY: Never doubt it; remember a faint heart never—blisters on my tongue—I was going to be guilty of a vile proverb; flat against the authority of Chesterfield.— I say there can be no doubt, that the brilliancy of your merit will secure you a favourable reception.

JONATHAN: Well, but what must I say to her?

JESSAMY: Say to her! why, my dear friend, though I admire your profound knowledge on every other subject, yet, you will pardon my saying, that your want of opportunity has made the female heart escape the poignancy of your penetration.

Say to her!— Why, when a man goes a-courting, and hopes for success, he must begin with doing, and not saying.

JONATHAN: Well, what must I do?

JESSAMY: Why, when you are introduced you must make five or six elegant bows.

JONATHAN: Six elegant bows! I understand that; six, you say? Well—

JESSAMY: Then you must press and kiss her hand; then press and kiss, and so on to her lips and cheeks; then talk as much as you can about hearts, darts, flames, nectar and ambrosia— the more incoherent the better.

JONATHAN: Well, but suppose she should be angry with I?

JESSAMY: Why, if she should pretend—please to observe, Mr Jonathan—if she should pretend to be offended, you must—But I'll tell you how my master acted in such a case: He was seated by a young lady of eighteen upon a sopha, plucking with a wanton hand the blooming sweets of youth and beauty. When the lady thought it necessary to check his ardour, she called up a frown upon her lovely face, so irresistably alluring, that it would have warmed the frozen bosom of age: remember, said she, putting her delicate arm upon his, remember your character and my honour. My master instantly dropped upon his knees, with eyes swimming with love, cheeks glowing with desire, and in the gentlest modulation of voice, he said— My dear Caroline, in a few months our hands will be indissolubly united at the altar; our hearts I feel are already so—the favours you now grant as evidence of your affection, are favours indeed; yet when the ceremony is once past, what will now be received with rapture, will then be attributed to duty.

JONATHAN: Well, and what was the consequence?

JESSAMY: The consequence!— Ah! forgive me, my dear friend, but you New England gentlemen have such a laudable curiosity of seeing the bottom of every thing;—why, to be honest, I confess I saw the blooming cherub of a consequence smiling in its angelic mother's arms, about ten months afterwards.

JONATHAN: Well, if I follow all your plans, make them six bows, and all that; shall I have such little cherubim consequences?

JESSAMY: Undoubtedly.— What are you musing upon?

JONATHAN: You say you'll certainly make me acquainted?— Why, I was thinking then how I should contrive to pass this broken piece of silver—won't it buy a sugar-dram?

JESSAMY: What is that, the love-token from the deacon's daughter?— You come on bravely. But I must hasten to my master. Adieu, my dear friend.

JONATHAN: Stay, Mr Jessamy—must I buss her when I am introduced to her?

JESSAMY: I told you, you must kiss her.

JONATHAN: Well, but must I buss her?

JESSAMY: Why, kiss and buss, and buss and kiss, is all one.

JONATHAN: Oh! my dear friend, though you have a profound knowledge of all, a pugnancy of tribulation, you don't know everything.   *(Exit)*

JESSAMY: *(alone)* Well, certainly I improve; my master could not have insinuated himself with more address into the heart of a man he despised.— Now will this blundering dog sicken Jenny with his nauseous pawings, until she flies into my arms for very ease. How sweet will the contrast be, between the blundering Jonathan, and the courtly and accomplished Jessamy!

END OF THE SECOND ACT

ACT THIRD

SCENE 1: DIMPLE'S *Room*

DIMPLE: *(discovered at a Toilet, Reading)*
    "Women have in general but one object, which is their beauty." Very true, my lord; positively very true. "Nature has hardly formed a woman ugly enough to be insensible to flattery upon her person." Extremely just, my lord; every day's delightful experience confirms this. "If her face is so shocking that she must, in some degree, be conscious of it, her figure and air, she thinks, make ample amends for it." The sallow Miss Wan is a proof of this.— Upon my telling the distasteful wretch, the other day, that her countenance spoke the pensive language of sentiment, and that Lady Wortley Montague declared, that if the ladies were arrayed in the garb of innocence, the face would be the last part which would be admired as Monsieur Milton expresses it, she grin'd horribly a ghastly smile. "If her figure is deformed, she thinks her face counterbalances it."

(Enter JESSAMY *with letters)*

DIMPLE: Where got you these, Jessamy?

JESSAMY: Sir, the English packet is arrived. [Exit JESSAMY]

*(*DIMPLE *opens and reads a letter enclosing notes)*

DIMPLE: "Sir,
    "I have drawn bills on you in favour of Messrs. Van Cash and Co. as per margin. I have taken up your note to Col. Piquet, and discharged your debts to my Lord Lurcher and Sir Harry Rook. I herewith enclose you copies of the bills, which I have no doubt will be immediately honoured. On failure, I shall empower some lawyer in your country to recover the amounts.
    "I am, Sir,
        "Your most humble servant,
            "JOHN HAZARD."

    Now, did not my lord expressly say, that it was unbecoming a well-bred man to be in a passion, I confess I should be ruffled. *(Reads)* "There is no accident so unfortunate, which a wise man may not turn to his advantage; nor any accident so fortunate, which a fool will not turn to his disadvantage." True, my lord: but how advantage can be derived from this, I can't see. Chesterfield himself, who made, however, the worst practice of the most excellent precepts, was never in so embarrassing a situation. I love the person of Charlotte, and it is necessary I should command the fortune of Letitia. As to Maria!—I doubt not by my *sang-froid* behavior I shall compel her to decline the match; but the blame must not fall upon me. A prudent man, as my lord says, should take all the credit of a good action to himself, and throw the discredit of a bad one upon others. I must break with Maria, marry Letitia, and as for Charlotte—why, Charlotte must be a companion to my wife.—Here, Jessamy!

(Enter JESSAMY)

(DIMPLE folds and seals two letters)

DIMPLE: Here, Jessamy, take this letter to my love. *(Gives one)*

JESSAMY: To which of your honour's loves?— Oh! *(reading)* to Miss Letitia, your honour's rich love.

DIMPLE: And this *(delivers another)* to Miss Charlotte Manly. See that you deliver them privately.

JESSAMY: Yes, your honour. *(Going)*

DIMPLE: Jessamy, who are these strange lodgers that came to the house last night?

JESSAMY: Why, the master is a Yankee colonel; I have not seen much of him; but the man is the most unpolished animal your honour ever disgraced your eyes by looking upon. I have had one of the most *outré* conversations with him!—He really has a most prodigious effect upon my risibility.

DIMPLE: I ought, according to every rule of Chesterfield, to wait on him and insinuate myself into his good graces.—Jessamy, wait on the colonel with my compliments, and if he is disengaged, I will do myself the honour of paying him my respects.— Some ignorant unpolished boor— *(JESSAMY goes off and returns)*

JESSAMY: Sir, the colonel is gone out, and Jonathan, his servant, says that he is gone to stretch his legs upon the Mall—Stretch his legs! what an indelicacy of diction!

DIMPLE: Very well. Reach me my hat and sword. I'll accost him there, in my way to Letitia's, as by accident; pretend to be struck with his person and address, and endeavour to steal into his confidence. Jessamy, I have no business for you at present. *(Exit)*

JESSAMY: *(Taking up the book)*: My master and I obtain our knowledge from the same source;— though, gad! I think myself much the prettier fellow of the two. *(Surveying himself in the glass)* That was a brilliant thought, to insinuate that I folded my master's letters for him; the folding is so neat, that it does honour to the operator. I once intended to have insinuated that I wrote his letters too; but that was before I saw them; it won't do now; no honour there, positively.— "Nothing looks more vulgar *(reading affectedly)*, ordinary, and illiberal, than ugly, uneven, and ragged nails; the ends of which should be kept even and clean, not tipped with black, and cut in small segments of circles"— Segments of circles! surely my lord did not consider that he wrote for the beaux. Segments of circles! what a crabbed term! Now I dare answer, that my master, with all his learning, does not know that this means, according to the present mode, to let the nails grow long, and then cut them off even at top. *(Laughing without)* Ha! that's Jenny's titter. I protest I despair of ever teaching that girl to laugh; she has something so execrably natural in her laugh, that I declare it absolutely discomposes my nerves. How came she into our house!—*(Calls)* Jenny!

(Enter JENNY)

JESSAMY: Prythee, Jenny, don't spoil your fine face with laughing.

JENNY: Why, must n't I laugh, Mr Jessamy?

JESSAMY: You may smile; but, as my lord says, nothing can authorise a laugh.

JENNY: Well, but I can't help laughing—Have you seen him. Mr Jessamy? Ha, ha, ha!

JESSAMY: Seen whom?—

JENNY: Why, Jonathan, the New-England colonel's servant. Do you know he was at the play last night, and the stupid creature don't know where he has been. He would not go to a play for the world; he thinks it was a show, as he calls it.

JESSAMY: As ignorant and unpolished as he is, do you know, Miss Jenny, that I propose to introduce him to the honour of your acquaintance.

JENNY: Introduce him to me! for what?

JESSAMY: Why, my lovely girl, that you may take him under your protection, as Madam Ramboulliet did young Stanhope; that you may, by your plastic hand, mould this uncouth cub into a gentleman. He is to make love to you.

JENNY: Make love to me!—

JESSAMY: Yes, Mistress Jenny, make love to you; and, I doubt not, when he shall become domesticated in your kitchen, that this boor, under your auspices, will soon become *un aimable petit Jonathan*.

JENNY: I must say, Mr Jessamy, if he copies after me, he will be vastly monstrously polite.

JESSAMY: Stay here one moment, and I will call him.—Jonathan!—Mr Jonathan!—   *(Calls)*

JONATHAN: *(Within)* Holla! there.—*(Enters)* You promise to stand by me—six bows you say. *(Bows)*

JESSAMY: Mrs Jenny, I have the honour of presenting Mr Jonathan, Colonel Manly's waiter, to you. I am extremely happy that I have it in my power to make two worthy people acquainted with each other's merit.

JENNY: So, Mr Jonathan, I hear you were at the play last night.

JONATHAN: At the play! why, did you think I went to the devil's drawing-room!

JENNY: The devil's drawing-room!

JONATHAN: Yes; why an't cards and dice the devil's device; and the play-house the shop where the devil hangs out the vanities of the world, upon the tenterhooks of temptation. I believe you have not heard how they were acting the old boy one night, and the wicked one came among them sure enough; and went right off in a storm, and carried one quarter of the play-house with him. Oh! no, no, no! you won't catch me at a play-house, I warrant you.

JENNY: Well, Mr Jonathan, though I don't scruple your veracity, I have some reasons for believing you were there; pray, where were you about six o'clock?

JONATHAN: Why, I went to see one Mr Morrison, the *hocus pocus* man; they said as how he could eat a case knife.

JENNY: Well, and how did you find the place?

JONATHAN: As I was going about here and there, to and again, to find it, I saw a great croud of folks going into a long entry, that had lantherns over the door; so I asked a man, whether that was not the place where they played *hocus pocus?* He was a very civil kind man, though he did speak like the Hessians; he lifted up his eyes and said—"they play *hocus pocus* tricks enough there, Got knows, mine friend."

JENNY: Well—

JONATHAN: So I went right in, and they shewed me away clean up to the garret, just like a meeting-house gallery. And so I saw a power of topping folks, all sitting round in little cabbins, [just like father's corn-cribs;]—and then there was such a squeaking with the fiddles, and such a tarnal blaze with the lights, my head was near turned. At last the people that sat near me set up such a hissing—hiss—like so many mad cats; and then they went thump, thump, thump, just like our Peleg threshing wheat, and stampt away, just like the nation; and called out for one Mr Langolee,—I suppose he helps act[s] the tricks.

JENNY: Well, and what did you do all this time?

JONATHAN: Gor, I—I liked the fun, and so I thumpt away, and hiss'd as lustily as the best of 'em. One sailor-looking man that sat by me, seeing me stamp, and knowing I was a cute fellow, because I could make a roaring noise, clapt me on the shoulder and said, you are a d——d hearty cock, smite my timbers! I told him so I was, but I thought he need not swear so, and make use of such naughty words.

JESSAMY: The savage!—Well, and did you see the man with his tricks?

JONATHAN: Why, I vow, as I was looking out for him, they lifted up a great green cloth, and let us look right into the next neighbour's house. Have you a good many houses in New York made so in that 'ere way?

JENNY: Not many: but did you see the family?

JONATHAN: Yes, swamp it; I see'd the family.

JENNY: Well, and how did you like them?

JONATHAN: Why, I vow they were pretty much like other families;—there was a poor, good natured, curse of a husband, and a sad rantipole of a wife.

JENNY: But did you see no other folks?

JONATHAN: Yes. There was one youngster, they called him Mr Joseph; he talked as sober and as pious as a minister; but like some ministers that I know, he was a sly tike in his heart for all that: He was going to ask a young woman to spark it with him, and—the Lord have mercy on my soul!—she was another man's wife.

JESSAMY: The Wabash!

JENNY: And did you see any more folks?

JONATHAN: Why they came on as thick as mustard. For my part, I thought the house was haunted. There was a soldier fellow, who talked about his row de dow dow, and courted a young woman: but of all the cute folk I saw, I liked one little fellow—

JENNY: Aye! who was he?

JONATHAN: Why, he had red hair, and a little round plump face like mine, only not altogether so handsome. His name was Darby:—that was his baptizing name, his other name I forgot. Oh! it was, Wig—Wag—Wag-all, Darby Wag-all;—pray, do you know him?—I should like to take a sling with him, or a drap of cyder with a pepper-pod in it, to make it warm and comfortable.

JENNY: I can't say I have that pleasure.

JONATHAN: I wish you did, he is a cute fellow. But there was one thing I did n't like in that Mr Darby; and that was, he was afraid of some of them 'ere shooting irons, such as your troopers wear on training days. Now, I'm a true born Yankee American son of liberty, and I never was afraid of a gun yet in all my life.

JENNY: Well, Mr Jonathan, you were certainly at the play-house.

JONATHAN: I at the play-house!—Why did n't I see the play then?

JENNY: Why, the people you saw were players.

JONATHAN: Mercy on my soul! did I see the wicked players?—Mayhap that 'ere Darby that I liked so, was the old serpent himself, and had his cloven foot in his pocket. Why, I vow, now I come to think on 't, the candles seemed to burn blue, and I am sure where I sat it smelt tarnally of brimstone.

JESSAMY: Well, Mr Jonathan, from your account, which I confess is very accurate, you must have been at the play-house.

JONATHAN: Why, I vow I began to smell a rat. When I came away, I went to the man for my money again: you want your money, says he; yes, says I; for what, says he; why, says I, no man shall jocky me out of my money; I paid my money to see sights, and the dogs a bit of a sight have I seen, unless you call listening to people's private business a sight. Why, says he, it is the School for Scandalization.—The School for Scandalization!—Oh, ho! no wonder you New York folks are so cute at it, when you go to school to learn it: and so I jogged off.

JESSAMY: My dear Jenny, my master's business drags me from you; would to heaven I knew no other servitude than to your charms.

JONATHAN: Well, but don't go; you won't leave me so.—

JESSAMY: Excuse me.—Remember the cash. *(Aside to him, and—Exit)*

JENNY: Mr Jonathan, won't you please to sit down. Mr Jessamy tells me you wanted to have some conversation with me. *(Having brought forward two chairs, they sit)*

JONATHAN: Ma'am!—

JENNY: Sir!—

JONATHAN: Ma'am!—

JENNY: Pray, how do you like the city, Sir?

JONATHAN: Ma'am!—

JENNY: I say, Sir, how do you like New York?

JONATHAN: Ma'am!—

JENNY: The stupid creature! but I must pass some little time with him, if it is only to endeavour to learn, whether it was his master that made such an abrupt entrance into our house, and my young mistress's heart, this morning. *(Aside)* As you don't seem to like to talk, Mr Jonathan—do you sing?

JONATHAN: Gor, I—I am glad she asked that, for I forgot what Mr Jessamy bid me say, and I dare as well be hanged as act what he bid me do, I'm so ashamed. *(Aside)* Yes, Ma'am, I can sing—I can sing Mear, Old Hundred, and Bangor.

JENNY: Oh! I don't mean psalm tunes. Have you no little song to please the ladies; such as Roslin Castle, or the Maid of the Mill?

JONATHAN: Why, all my tunes go to meeting tunes, save one, and I count you won't altogether like that 'ere.

JENNY: What is it called?

JONATHAN: I am sure you have heard folks talk about it, it is called Yankee Doodle.

JENNY: Oh! it is the tune I am fond of; and, if I know anything of my mistress, she would be glad to dance to it. Pray, sing?

JONATHAN: *(Sings)*

> Father and I went up to camp,
> Along with Captain Goodwin;
> And there we saw the men and boys,
> As thick as hasty pudding.
>   Yankee Doodle do, etc.

> And there we saw a swamping gun,
> Big as log of maple,
> On a little deuced cart,
> A load for father's cattle.
>   Yankee Doodle do, etc.

> And every time they fired it off,
> It took a horn of powder,
> It made a noise—like father's gun,
> Only a nation louder.
>   Yankee Doodle do, etc.

> There was a man in our town,
> His name was—

No, no, that won't do. Now, if I was with Tabitha Wymen and Jemima Cawley, down at father Chase's, I should n't mind singing this all out before them—you would be affronted if I was to sing that, though that's a lucky thought; if you should be affronted, I have something dang'd cute, which Jessamy told me to say to you.

JENNY: Is that all! I assure you I like it of all things.

JONATHAN: No, no; I can sing more, some other time, when you and I are better acquainted, I'll sing the whole of it—no, no—that's a fib—I can't sing but a hundred and ninety verses: our Tabitha at home can sing it all.—   *(Sings)*

> Marblehead's a rocky place,
> And Cape-Cod is sandy;
> Charleston is burnt down,
> Boston is the dandy.
>   Yankee Doodle do, etc.

I vow, my own town song has put me into such topping spirits, that I believe I'll begin to do a little, as Jessamy says we must when we go a courting—*(Runs and kisses her)* Burning rivers! cooling flames! red hot roses! pig-nuts! hasty-pudding and ambrosia!

JENNY: What means this freedom! you insulting wretch.   *(Strikes him)*

JONATHAN: Are you affronted?

JENNY: Affronted! with what looks shall I express my anger?

JONATHAN: Looks! why, as to the matter of looks, you look as cross as a witch.

JENNY: Have you no feeling for the delicacy of my sex?

JONATHAN: Feeling! Gor, I—I feel the delicacy of your sex pretty smartly *(rubbing his cheek),* though, I vow, I thought when you city ladies courted and married, and all that, you put feeling out of the question. But I want to know whether you are really affronted, or only pretend to be so? 'Cause, if you are certainly right down affronted, I am at the end of my tether;— Jessamy did n't tell me what to say to you.

JENNY: Pretend to be affronted!

JONATHAN: Aye, aye, if you only pretend, you shall hear how I'll go to work to make cherubim consequences. *(Runs up to her)*

JENNY: Begone, you brute!

JONATHAN: That looks like mad; but I won't lose my speech. My dearest Jenny—your name is Jenny, I think? My dearest Jenny, though I have the highest esteem for the sweet favours you have just now granted me—Gor, that's a fib though, but Jessamy says it is not wicked to tell lies to the women. *(Aside)* I say, though I have the highest esteem for the favours you have just now granted me, yet, you will consider, that as soon as the dissolvable knot is tied, they will no longer be favours, but only matters of duty, and matters of course.

JENNY: Marry you! you audacious monster! get out of my sight, or rather let me fly from you. *(Exit hastily)*

JONATHAN: Gor! she's gone off in a swinging passion, before I had time to think of consequences. If this is the way with your city ladies, give me the twenty acres of rock, the bible, the cow, and Tabitha, and a little peaceable bundling.

SCENE 2: *The Mall*

(Enter MANLY*)*

MANLY: It must be so, Montague! and it is not all the tribe of Mandevilles shall convince me, that a nation, to become great, must first become dissipated. Luxury is surely the bane of a nation: Luxury! which enervates both soul and body, by opening a thousand new sources of enjoyment, opens, also, a thousand new sources of contention and want: Luxury! which renders a people weak at home, and accessible to bribery, corruption, and force from abroad. When the Grecian states knew no other tools than the axe and the saw, the Grecians were a great, a free, and a happy people. The kings of Greece devoted their lives to the service of their country, and her senators knew no other superiority over their fellow-citizens than a glorious preeminence in danger and virtue. They exhibited to the world a noble spectacle,—a number of independent states united by a similarity of language, sentiment, manners, common interest, and common consent, in one grand mutual league of protection.—And, thus united, long might they have continued the cherishers of arts and sciences, the protectors of the oppressed, the scourge of tyrants, and the safe asylum of liberty: But when foreign gold, and still more pernicious, foreign luxury, had crept among them, they sapped the vitals of their virtue. The virtues of their ancestors were only found in their writings. Envy and suspicion, the vices of little minds, possessed them. The various states engendered jealousies of each other; and, more unfortunately, growing jealous of their great federal council, the Amphictyons, they forgot that their common safety had existed, and would exist, in giving them an honourable extensive prerogative. The common good was lost in the pursuit of private interest; and that people, who, by uniting, might have stood against the world in arms, by dividing, crumbled into ruin;—their name is now only known in the page of the historian, and what they once were, is all we have left to admire. Oh! that America! Oh! that my country, would in this her day, learn the things which belong to her peace!

(Enter DIMPLE*)*

DIMPLE: You are Colonel Manly, I presume?

MANLY: At your service, Sir.

DIMPLE: My name is Dimple, Sir. I have the honour to be a lodger in the same house with you, and hearing you were in the Mall, came hither to take the liberty of joining you.

MANLY: You are very obliging, Sir.

DIMPLE: As I understand you are a stranger here, Sir, I have taken the liberty to introduce myself to your acquaintance, as possibly I may have it in my power to point out some things in this city worthy your notice.

MANLY: An attention to strangers is worthy a liberal mind, and must ever be gratefully received.
But to a soldier, who has no fixed abode, such
attentions are particularly pleasing.

DIMPLE: Sir, there is no character so respectable
as that of a soldier. And, indeed, when we reflect how much we owe to those brave men who
have suffered so much in the service of their
country, and secured to us those inestimable
blessings that we now enjoy, our liberty and independence, they demand every attention
which gratitude can pay. For my own part, I
never meet an officer, but I embrace him as my
friend, nor a private in distress, but I insensi-
bly extend my charity to him.—I have hit the
Bum[p]kin off very tolerably.   *(Aside)*

MANLY: Give me your hand, Sir! I do not proffer
this hand to everybody; but you steal into my
heart. I hope I am as insensible to flattery as
most men; but I declare (it may be my weak
side), that I never hear the name of soldier
mentioned with respect, but I experience a
thrill of pleasure, which I never feel on any
other occasion.

DIMPLE: Will you give me leave, my dear colonel,
to confer an obligation on myself, by shewing
you some civilities during your stay here, and
giving a similar opportunity to some of my
friends?

MANLY: Sir, I thank you; but I believe my stay in
this city will be very short.

DIMPLE: I can introduce you to some men of excellent sense, in whose company you will esteem
yourself happy; and, by way of amusement, to
some fine girls, who will listen to your soft
things with pleasure.

MANLY: Sir, I should be proud of the honour of
being acquainted with those gentlemen;—but,
as for the ladies, I don't understand you.

DIMPLE: Why, Sir, I need not tell you, that when
a young gentleman is alone with a young lady,
he must say some soft things to her fair
cheek—indeed the lady will expect it. To be
sure, there is not much pleasure, when a man
of the world and a finished coquet[te] meet,

who perfectly know each other; but how delicious is it to excite the emotions of joy, hope,
expectation, and delight, in the bosom of a
lovely girl, who believes every tittle of what
you say to be serious.

MANLY: Serious, Sir! In my opinion, the man,
who, under pretensions of marriage, can plant
thorns in the bosom of an innocent, unsuspect-
ing girl, is more detestable than a common robber, in the same proportion, as private violence
is more despicable than open force, and money
of less value than happiness.

DIMPLE: How he awes me by the superiority of his
sentiments. *(Aside)* As you say, Sir, a gentleman
should be cautious how he mentions marriage.

MANLY: Cautious, Sir! [No person more approves
of an intercourse between the sexes than I do.
Female conversation softens our manners,
whilst our discourse, from the superiority of
our literary advantages, improves their minds.
But, in our young country, where there is no
such thing as gallantry, when a gentleman
speaks of love to a lady, whether he mentions
marriage, or not, she ought to conclude, either
that he meant to insult her, or, that his intentions are the most serious and honourable.]
How mean, how cruel, is it, by a thousand
tender assiduities, to win the affections of an
amiable girl, and though you leave her virtue
unspotted, to betray her into the appearance of
so many tender partialities, that every man of
delicacy would suppress his inclination towards her, by supposing her heart engaged!
Can any man, for the trivial gratification of his
leisure hours, affect the happiness of a whole
life! His not having spoken of marriage, may
add to his perfidy, but can be no excuse for his
conduct.

DIMPLE: Sir, I admire your sentiments;—they are
mine. The light observations that fell from me,
were only a principle of the tongue; they came
not from the heart—my practice has ever disapproved these principles.

MANLY: I believe you, Sir. I should with reluctance suppose that those pernicious sentiment

could find admittance into the heart of a gentleman.

DIMPLE: I am now, Sir, going to visit a family, where, if you please, I will have the honour of introducing you. Mr Manly's ward, Miss Letitia, is a young lady of immense fortune; and his niece, Miss Charlotte Manly, is a young lady of great sprightliness and beauty.

MANLY: That gentleman, Sir, is my uncle, and Miss Manly my sister.

DIMPLE: The devil she is! *(Aside)* Miss Manly your sister, Sir? I rejoice to hear it, and feel a double pleasure in being known to you.— Plague on him! I wish he was at Boston again with all my soul. *(Aside)*

MANLY: Come, Sir, will you go?

DIMPLE: I will follow you in a moment, Sir. *(Exit MANLY)* Plague on it! this is unlucky. A fighting brother is a cursed appendage to a fine girl. Egad! I just stopped in time; had he not discovered himself, in two minutes more I should have told him how well I was with his sister.—Indeed, I cannot see the satisfaction of an intrigue, if one can't have the pleasure of communicating it to our friends. *(Exit)*

E N D   O F   T H E   T H I R D   A C T

A C T   F O U R T H

SCENE 1: CHARLOTTE'S *Apartment*

(CHARLOTTE leading in MARIA)

CHARLOTTE: This is so kind, my sweet friend, to come to see me at this moment. I declare, if I were going to be married in a few days, as you are, I should scarce have found time to visit my friends.

MARIA: Do you think then that there is an impropriety in it?—How should you dispose of your time?

CHARLOTTE: Why, I should be shut up in my chamber; and my head would so run upon—

upon—upon the solemn ceremony that I was to pass through—I declare it would take me above two hours merely to learn that little monosyllable—*Yes.* Ah! my dear, your sentimental imagination does not conceive what that little tiny word implies.

MARIA: Spare me your raillery, my sweet friend; I should love your agreeable vivacity at any other time.

CHARLOTTE: Why this is the very time to amuse you. You grieve me to see you look so unhappy.

MARIA: Have I not reason to look so?

CHARLOTTE: What new grief distresses you?

MARIA: Oh! how sweet it is, when the heart is borne down with misfortune, to recline and repose on the bosom of friendship! Heaven knows, that, although it is improper for a young lady to praise a gentleman, yet I have ever concealed Mr Dimple's foibles, and spoke of him as of one whose reputation I expected would be linked with mine: but his late conduct towards me, has turned my coolness into contempt. He behaves as if he meant to insult and disgust me; whilst my father, in the last conversation on the subject of our marriage, spoke of it as a matter which laid near his heart, and in which he would not bear contradiction.

CHARLOTTE: This works well: oh! the generous Dimple. I'll endeavour to excite her to discharge him. *(Aside)* But, my dear friend, your happiness depends on yourself:—Why don't you discard him? Though the match has been of long standing, I would not be forced to make myself miserable: no parent in the world should oblige me to marry the man I did not like.

MARIA: Oh! my dear, you never lived with your parents, and do not know what influence a father's frowns have upon a daughter's heart. Besides, what have I to allege against Mr Dimple, to justify myself to the world? He carries himself so smoothly, that every one would impute the blame to me, and call me capricious.

CHARLOTTE: And call her capricious! Did ever such an objection start into the heart of woman? For my part, I wish I had fifty lovers to discard, for no other reason, than because I did not fancy them. My dear Maria, you will forgive me; I know your candour and confidence in me; but I have at times, I confess, been led to suppose, that some other gentleman was the cause of your aversion to Mr Dimple.

MARIA: No, my sweet friend, you may be assured, that though I have seen many gentlemen I could prefer to Mr Dimple, yet I never saw one that I thought I could give my hand to, until this morning.

CHARLOTTE: This morning!

MARIA: Yes;—one of the strangest accidents in the world. The odious Dimple, after disgusting me with his conversation, had just left me, when a gentleman, who, it seems, boards in the same house with him, saw him coming out of our door, and the houses looking very much alike, he came into our house instead of his lodgings; nor did he discover his mistake until he got into the parlour, where I was: he then bowed so gracefully; made such a genteel apology, and looked so manly and noble!—

CHARLOTTE: I see some folks, though it is so great an impropriety, can praise a gentleman, when he happens to be the man of their fancy. *(Aside)*

MARIA: I don't know how it was,—I hope he did not think me indelicate—but I asked him, I believe, to sit down, or pointed to a chair. He sat down, and instead of having recourse to observations upon the weather, or hackneyed criticisms upon the theatre, he entered readily into a conversation worthy a man of sense to speak, and a lady of delicacy and sentiment to hear. He was not strictly handsome, but he spoke the language of sentiment, and his eyes looked tenderness and honour.

CHARLOTTE: Oh! *(eagerly)* you sentimental grave girls, when your hearts are once touched, beat us rattles a bar's length. And so, you are quite in love with this he-angel?

MARIA: In love with him! How can you rattle so, Charlotte? am I not going to be miserable? *(Sighs)* In love with a gentleman I never saw but one hour in my life, and don't know

his name!—No: I only wished that the man I shall marry, may look, and talk, and act, just like him. Besides, my dear, he is a married man.

CHARLOTTE: Why, that was good natured.—He told you so, I suppose, in mere charity, to prevent your falling in love with him?

MARIA: He did n't tell me so *(peevishly)*; he looked as if he was married.

CHARLOTTE: How, my dear, did he look sheepish?

MARIA: I am sure he has a susceptible heart, and the ladies of his acquaintance must be very stupid not to—

CHARLOTTE: Hush! I hear some person coming.
    [*(Enter* LETITIA*)*

LETITIA: My dear Maria, I am happy to see you. Lud! what a pity it is that you have purchased your wedding clothes.

MARIA: I think so.   *(Sighing)*

LETITIA: Why, my dear, there is the sweetest parcel of silks come over you ever saw. Nancy Brilliant has a full suit come; she sent over her measure, and it fits her to a hair; it is immensely dressy, and made for a court-hoop. I thought they said the large hoops were going out of fashion.

CHARLOTTE: Did you see the hat?—Is it a fact, that the deep laces round the border is still the fashion?]

DIMPLE: *(within)* Upon my honour, Sir!

MARIA: Ha! Dimple's voice! My dear, I must take leave of you. There are some things necessary to be done at our house.—Can't I go through the other room?
    (Enter DIMPLE *and* MANLY*)*

DIMPLE: Ladies, your most obedient.

CHARLOTTE: Miss Van Rough, shall I present my brother Henry to you? Colonel Manly, Maria,—Miss Van Rough, brother.

MARIA: Her brother! *(Turns and sees* MANLY*)* Oh! my heart! The very gentleman I have been praising.

MANLY: The same amiable girl I saw this morning!

CHARLOTTE: Why, you look as if you were acquainted.

MANLY: I unintentionally intruded into this lady's presence this morning, for which she was so good as to promise me her forgiveness.

CHARLOTTE: Oh! ho! is that the case! Have these two penserosos been together? Were they Henry's eyes that looked so tenderly? *(Aside)* And so you promised to pardon him? and could you be so good natured?—have you really forgiven him? I beg you would do it for my sake. *(Whispering loud to* MARIA*)* But, my dear, as you are in such haste, it would be cruel to detain you: I can show you the way through the other room.

MARIA: Spare me, my sprightly friend.

MANLY: The lady does not, I hope, intend to deprive us of the pleasure of her company so soon.

CHARLOTTE: She has only a mantua-maker who waits for her at home. But, as I am to give my opinion of the dress, I think she cannot go yet. We were talking of the fashions when you came in; but I suppose the subject must be changed to something of more importance now.—Mr Dimple, will you favour us with an account of the public entertainments?

DIMPLE: Why, really, Miss Manly, you could not have asked me a question more *mal-apropos.* For my part, I must confess, that to a man who has travelled, there is nothing that is worthy the name of amusement to be found in this city.

CHARLOTTE: Except visiting the ladies.

DIMPLE: Pardon me, Madam; that is the avocation of a man of taste. But, for amusement, I positively know of nothing that can be called so, unless you dignify with that title the hopping once a fortnight to the sound of two or three squeaking fiddles, and the clattering of the old tavern windows, or sitting to see the miserable mummers, whom you call actors, murder comedy, and make a farce of tragedy.

MANLY: Do you never attend the theatre, Sir?

DIMPLE: I was tortured there once.

CHARLOTTE: Pray, Mr Dimple, was it a tragedy or a comedy?

DIMPLE: Faith, Madam, I cannot tell; for I sat with my back to the stage all the time, admiring a much better actress than any there;—a lady who played the fine woman to perfection;—though, by the laugh of the horrid creatures around me, I suppose it was comedy. Yet, on second thoughts, it might be some hero in a tragedy, dying so comically as to set the whole house in an uproar.—Colonel, I presume you have been in Europe?

MANLY: Indeed, Sir, I was never ten leagues from the continent.

DIMPLE: Believe me, Colonel, you have an immense pleasure to come; and when you shall have seen the brilliant exhibitions of Europe, you will learn to despise the amusements of this country as much as I do.

MANLY: Therefore I do not wish to see them; for I can never esteem that knowledge valuable, which tends to give me a distaste for my native country.

DIMPLE: Well, Colonel, though you have not travelled, you have read.

MANLY: I have, a little: and by it have discovered that there is a laudable partiality, which ignorant, untravelled men entertain for everything that belongs to their native country. I call it laudable;—it injures no one; adds to their own happiness; and, when extended, becomes the noble principle of patriotism. Travelled gentlemen rise superior, in their own opinion, to this: but, if the contempt which they contract for their country is the most valuable acquisition of their travels, I am far from thinking that their time and money are well spent.

MARIA: What noble sentiments!

CHARLOTTE: Let my brother set out from where he will in the fields of conversation, he is sure to end his tour in the temple of gravity.

MANLY: Forgive me, my sister. I love my country; it has its foibles undoubtedly;—some foreigners will with pleasure remark them—but such remarks fall very ungracefully from the lips of her citizens.

DIMPLE: You are perfectly in the right, Colonel—America has her faults.

MANLY: Yes, Sir; and we, her children, should blush for them in private, and endeavour, as individuals, to reform them. But, if our country has its errors in common with other countries, I am proud to say America, I mean the United States, have displayed virtues and achievements which modern nations may admire, but of which they have seldom set us the example.

CHARLOTTE: But, brother, we must introduce you to some of our gay folks, and let you see the city, such as it is. Mr Dimple is known to almost every family in town;—he will doubtless take a pleasure in introducing you.

DIMPLE: I shall esteem every service I can render your brother an honour.

MANLY: I fear the business I am upon will take up all my time, and my family will be anxious to hear from me.

MARIA: His family! But what is it to me that he is married! *(Aside)* Pray, how did you leave your lady, Sir?

CHARLOTTE: My brother is not married *(observing her anxiety)*; it is only an odd way he has of expressing himself.—Pray, brother, is this business, which you make your continual excuse, a secret?

MANLY: No, sister: I came hither to solicit the honourable Congress that a number of my brave old soldiers may be put upon the pension-list, who were, at first, not judged to be so materially wounded as to need the public assistance.—My sister says true: *(To MARIA)* I call my late soldiers my family.—Those who were not in the field in the late glorious contest, and those who were, have their respective merits; but, I confess, my old brother-soldiers are dearer to me than the former description. Friendships made in adversity are lasting; our countrymen may forget us; but that is no reason why we should forget one another. But I must leave you; my time of engagement approaches.

CHARLOTTE: Well, but brother, if you will go, will you please to conduct my fair friend home? You live in the same street;—I was to have gone with her myself— *(Aside)* A lucky thought.

MARIA: I am obliged to your sister, Sir, and was just intending to go.   *(Going)*

MANLY: I shall attend her with pleasure.   *(Exit with MARIA, followed by DIMPLE and CHARLOTTE)*

MARIA: Now, pray don't betray me to your brother.

[CHARLOTTE: *(just as she sees him make a motion to take his leave)* One word with you, brother, if you please.   *(Follows them out)* *(Manent DIMPLE and LETITIA)*

DIMPLE: You received the billet I sent you, I presume?

LETITIA: Hush!—Yes.

DIMPLE: When shall I pay my respects to you?

LETITIA: At eight I shall be unengaged.
    (Re-enter CHARLOTTE)

DIMPLE: Did my lovely angel receive my billet? *(To CHARLOTTE)*

CHARLOTTE: Yes.

DIMPLE: What hour shall I expect with impatience?

CHARLOTTE: At eight I shall be at home, unengaged.

DIMPLE: Unfortunate! I have a horrid engagement of business at that hour.—Can't you finish your visit earlier, and let six be the happy hour?

CHARLOTTE: You know your influence over me.]   *(Exeunt severally)*

SCENE 2: VAN ROUGH'S *House*

(VAN ROUGH, alone)

VAN ROUGH: It cannot possibly be true! The son of my old friend can't have acted so unadvisedly. Seventeen thousand pounds! in bills!—Mr Transfer must have been mistaken. He always appeared so prudent, and talked so well upon money-matters, and even assured me that he intended to change his dress for a suit of clothes which would not cost so much, and look more substantial, as soon as he married.

No, no, no! it can't be; it cannot be.—But, how-ever, I must look out sharp. I did not care what his principles or his actions were, so long as he minded the main chance. Seventeen thousand pounds!—If he had lost it in trade, why the best men may have ill-luck; but to game it away, as Transfer says—why, at this rate, his whole estate may go in one night, and, what is ten times worse, mine into the bargain. No, no; Mary is right. Leave women to look out in these matters; for all they look as if they didn't know a journal from a ledger, when their interest is concerned, they know what's what; they mind the main chance as well as the best of us.—I wonder Mary did not tell me she knew of his spending his money so foolishly. Seventeen thousand pounds! Why, if my daughter was standing up to be married, I would forbid the banns, if I found it was to a man who did not mind the main chance.—Hush! I hear some-body coming. 'T is Mary's voice: a man with her too! I should n't be surprized if this should be the other string to her bow.—Aye, aye, let them alone; women understand the main chance.—Though, i' faith, I'll listen a little. *(Retires into a closet)*

*(*MANLY *leading in* MARIA*)*

MANLY: I hope you will excuse my speaking upon so important a subject, so abruptly; but the moment I entered your room, you struck me as the lady whom I had long loved in imagination, and never hoped to see.

MARIA: Indeed, Sir, I have been led to hear more upon this subject than I ought.

MANLY: Do you then disapprove my suit, Madam, or the abruptness of my introducing it? If the latter, my peculiar situation, being obliged to leave the city in a few days, will, I hope, be my excuse; if the former, I will retire: for I am sure I would not give a moment's inquietude to her, whom I could devote my life to please. I am not so indelicate as to seek your immediate appro-bation; permit me only to be near you, and by a thousand tender assiduities to endeavour to ex-cite a grateful return.

MARIA: I have a father, whom I would die to make happy—he will disapprove—

MANLY: Do you think me so ungenerous as to seek a place in your esteem without his consent? You must—you ever ought to consider that man as unworthy of you, who seeks an interest in your heart, contrary to a father's approbation. A young lady should reflect, that the loss of a lover may be supplied, but nothing can compensate for the loss of a parent's affection. Yet, why do you suppose your father would disapprove? In our country, the affections are not sacrificed to riches, or family aggrandizement:—should you approve, my family is decent, and my rank honourable.

MARIA: You distress me, Sir.

MANLY: Then I will sincerely beg your excuse for obtruding so disagreeable a subject and retire. *(Going)*

MARIA: Stay, Sir! your generosity and good opin-ion of me deserve a return; but why must I de-clare what, for these few hours, I have scarce suffered myself to think?—I am—

MANLY: What?—

MARIA: Engaged, Sir;—and, in a few days, to be married to the gentleman you saw at your sister's.

MANLY: Engaged to be married! And have I been basely invading the rights of another? Why have you permitted this?—Is this the return for the partiality I declared for you?

MARIA: You distress me, Sir. What would you have me say? You are too generous to wish the truth: ought I to say that I dared not suffer my-self to think of my engagement, and that I am going to give my hand without my heart?— Would you have me confess a partiality for you? If so, your triumph is complete; and can be only more so, when days of misery, with the man I cannot love, will make me think of him whom I could prefer.

MANLY: *(after a pause)* We are both unhappy; but it is your duty to obey your parent,—mine to obey my honour. Let us, therefore, both follow the path of rectitude; and of this we may be assured, that if we are not happy, we shall, at least, deserve to be so. Adieu! I dare not trust myself longer with you.   *(Exeunt severally)*

END OF THE FOURTH ACT

ACT FIFTH

SCENE 1: DIMPLE'S *Lodgings*

(JESSAMY meeting JONATHAN)

JESSAMY: Well, Mr Jonathan, what success with the fair?

JONATHAN: Why, such a tarnal cross tike you never saw!—You would have counted she had lived upon crab-apples and vinegar for a fort-night. But what the rattle makes you look so tarnation glum?

JESSAMY: I was thinking, Mr Jonathan, what could be the reason of her carrying herself so coolly to you.

JONATHAN: Coolly, do you call it? Why, I vow, she was fire-hot angry: may be it was because I buss'd her.

JESSAMY: No, no, Mr Jonathan; there must be some other cause: I never yet knew a lady angry at being kissed.

JONATHAN: Well, if it is not the young woman's bashfulness, I vow I can't conceive why she shou'd n't like me.

JESSAMY: May be it is because you have not the Graces, Mr Jonathan.

JONATHAN: Grace! Why, does the young woman expect I must be converted before I court her?

JESSAMY: I mean graces of person; for instance, my lord tells us that we must cut off our nails even at top, in small segments of circles;—though you won't understand that—In the next place, you must regulate your laugh.

JONATHAN: Maple-log seize it! don't I laugh natural?

JESSAMY: That's the very fault, Mr Jonathan. Be-sides, you absolutely misplace it. I was told by a friend of mine that you laughed outright at the play the other night, when you ought only to have tittered.

JONATHAN: Gor! I—what does one go to see fun for if they can't laugh?

JESSAMY: You may laugh;—but you must laugh by rule.

JONATHAN: Swamp it—laugh by rule! Well, I should like that tarnally.

JESSAMY: Why you know, Mr Jonathan, that to dance, a lady to play with her fan, or a gentle-man with his cane, and all other natural motions, are regulated by art. My master has composed an immensely pretty gamut, by which any lady, or gentleman, with a few years' close applica-tion, may learn to laugh as gracefully as if they were born and bred to it.

JONATHAN: Mercy on my soul! A gamut for laugh-ing—just like fa, la, sol?

JESSAMY: Yes. It comprises every possible display of jocularity, from an *affettuoso* smile to a *piano* titter, or full chorus *fortissimo* ha, ha, ha! My master employs his leisure-hours in marking out the plays, like a cathedral chanting-book, that the ignorant may know where to laugh; and that pit, box, and gallery may keep time to-gether, and not have a snigger in one part of the house, a broad grin in the other, and a d——d grum look in the third. How delightful to see the audience all smile together, then look on their books, then twist their mouths into an agreeable simper, then altogether shake the house with a general ha, ha, ha! loud as a full chorus of Handel's, at an Abbey-commemoration.

JONATHAN: Ha, ha, ha! that's dang'd cute, I swear.

JESSAMY: The gentlemen, you see, will laugh the tenor; the ladies will play the counter-tenor; the beaux will squeak the treble; and our jolly friends in the gallery a thorough bass, ho, ho, ho!

JONATHAN: Well, can't you let me see that gamut?

JESSAMY: Oh! yes, Mr Jonathan; here it is. *(Takes out a book)* Oh! no, this is only a titter with its variations. Ah, here it is. *(Takes out another)* Now you must know, Mr Jonathan, this is a piece written by Ben Jonson, which I have set to my master's gamut. The places where you must smile, look grave, or laugh outright, are marked below the line. Now look over me.—"There was a certain man"—now you must smile.

JONATHAN: Well, read it again; I warrant I'll mind my eye.

JESSAMY: "There was a certain man, who had a sad scolding wife,"—now you must laugh.

JONATHAN: Tarnation! That's no laughing matter, though.

JESSAMY: "And she lay sick a-dying;"—now you must titter.

JONATHAN: What, snigger when the good woman's a-dying! Gor, I—

JESSAMY: Yes; the notes say you must—"And she asked her husband leave to make a will,"—now you must begin to look grave;—"and her husband said"—

JONATHAN: Ay, what did her husband say?—Something dang'd cute, I reckon.

JESSAMY: "And her husband said, you have had your will all your life time, and would you have it after you are dead too?"

JONATHAN: Ho, ho, ho! There the old man was even with her; he was up to the notch—ha, ha, ha!

JESSAMY: But, Mr Jonathan, you must not laugh so. Why, you ought to have tittered *piano,* and you have laughed *fortissimo.* Look here; you see these marks, A. B. C. and so on; these are the references to the other part of the book. Let us turn to it, and you will see the directions how to manage the muscles. This *(turns over)* was note D you blundered at.—"You must purse the mouth into a smile, then titter, discovering the lower part of the three front upper teeth."

JONATHAN: How! read it again.

JESSAMY: "There was a certain man"—very well!—"who had a sad scolding wife,"—why don't you laugh?

JONATHAN: Now, that scolding wife sticks in my gizzard so pluckily, that I can't laugh for the blood and nowns of me. Let me look grave here, and I'll laugh your belly full where the old creature's a-dying.—

JESSAMY: "And she asked her husband"—*(Bell rings)* My master's bell! he's returned, I fear—Here, Mr Jonathan, take this gamut; and, I make no doubt but with a few years' close application you may be able to smile gracefully. *(Exeunt severally)*

SCENE 2: CHARLOTTE'S *Apartment*

(Enter MANLY*)*

MANLY: What, no one at home? How unfortunate to meet the only lady my heart was ever moved by, to find her engaged to another, and confessing her partiality for me! Yet engaged to a man, who, by her intimation, and his libertine conversation with me, I fear, does not merit her. Aye! there's the sting; for, were I assured that Maria was happy, my heart is not so selfish, but that it would dilate in knowing it, even though it were with another.—But to know she is unhappy!—I must drive these thoughts from me. Charlotte has some books; and this is what I believe she calls her little library. *(Enters a closet)*

(Enter DIMPLE *leading* LETITIA*)*

LETITIA: And will you pretend to say, now, Mr Dimple, that you propose to break with Maria? Are not the banns published? Are not the clothes purchased? Are not the friends invited? In short, is it not a done affair?

DIMPLE: Believe me, my dear Letitia, I would not marry her.

LETITIA: Why have you not broke with her before this, as you all along deluded me by saying you would?

DIMPLE: Because I was in hopes she would ere this have broke with me.

LETITIA: You could not expect it.

DIMPLE: Nay, but be calm a moment; 't was from my regard to you that I did not discard her.

LETITIA: Regard to me!

DIMPLE: Yes; I have done everything in my power to break with her, but the foolish girl is so fond of me, that nothing can accomplish it. Besides, how can I offer her my hand, when my heart is indissolubly engaged to you?—

LETITIA: There may be reason in this; but why so attentive to Miss Manly?

DIMPLE: Attentive to Miss Manly! For heaven's sake, if you have no better opinion of my constancy, pay not so ill a compliment to my taste.

LETITIA: Did I not see you whisper her to-day?

DIMPLE: Possibly I might—but something of so very trifling a nature, that I have already forgot what it was.

LETITIA: I believe, she has not forgot it.

DIMPLE: My dear creature, how can you for a moment suppose I should have any serious thoughts of that trifling, gay, flighty coquette, that disagreeable—
(Enter CHARLOTTE*)*

DIMPLE: My dear Miss Manly, I rejoice to see you; there is a charm in your conversation that always marks your entrance into company as fortunate.

LETITIA: Where have you been, my dear?

CHARLOTTE: Why, I have been about to twenty shops, turning over pretty things, and so have left twenty visits unpaid. I wish you would step into the carriage and whisk round, make my apology, and leave my cards where our friends are not at home; that you know will serve as a visit. Come, do go.

LETITIA: So anxious to get me out! but I'll watch you. *(Aside)* Oh! yes, I'll go; I want a little exercise.—Positively *(*DIMPLE *offering to accompany her)*, Mr Dimple, you shall not go, why, half my visits are cake and caudle visits; it won't do, you know, for you to go.— *(Exit, but returns to the door in the back scene and listens)*

DIMPLE: This attachment of your brother to Maria is fortunate.

CHARLOTTE: How did you come to the knowledge of it?

DIMPLE: I read it in their eyes.

CHARLOTTE: And I had it from her mouth. It would have amused you to have seen her! She that thought it so great an impropriety to praise a gentleman, that she could not bring out one word in your favour, found a redundancy to praise him.

DIMPLE: I have done everything in my power to assist his passion there: your delicacy, my dearest girl, would be shocked at half the instances of neglect and misbehaviour.

CHARLOTTE: I don't know how I should bear neglect; but Mr Dimple must misbehave himself, indeed, to forfeit my good opinion.

DIMPLE: Your good opinion, my angel, is the pride and pleasure of my heart; and if the most respectful tenderness for you and an utter indifference for all your sex besides, can make me worthy of your esteem, I shall richly merit it.

CHARLOTTE: All my sex besides, Mr Dimple— you forgot your tête-à-tête with Letitia.

DIMPLE: How can you, my lovely angel, cast a thought on that insipid, wry-mouthed, ugly creature!

CHARLOTTE: But her fortune may have charms?

DIMPLE: Not to a heart like mine. The man who has been blessed with the good opinion of my Charlotte, must despise the allurements of fortune.

CHARLOTTE: I am satisfied.

DIMPLE: Let us think no more on the odious subject, but devote the present hour to happiness.

CHARLOTTE: Can I be happy, when I see the man I prefer going to be married to another?

DIMPLE: Have I not already satisfied my charming angel that I can never think of marrying the puling Maria. But, even if it were so, could that be any bar to our happiness; for, as the poet sings—

"Love, free as air, at sight of human ties,
"Spreads his light wings, and in a moment
    flies."

Come then, my charming angel! why delay our bliss! The present moment is ours; the next is in the hand of fate.   *(Kissing her)*

CHARLOTTE: Begone, Sir! By your delusions you had almost lulled my honour asleep.

DIMPLE: Let me lull the demon to sleep again with kisses.   *(He struggles with her; she screams)*
(Enter MANLY*)*

MANLY: Turn, villain! and defend yourself.— *(Draws.* VAN ROUGH *enters and beats down their swords)*

VAN ROUGH: Is the devil in you? are you going to murder one another? *(Holding* DIMPLE*)*

DIMPLE: Hold him, hold him,—I can command my passion.

(Enter JONATHAN*)*

JONATHAN: What the rattle ails you? Is the old one in you? Let the colonel alone, can't you? I feel chock full of fight,—do you want to kill the colonel?—

MANLY: Be still, Jonathan; the gentleman does not want to hurt me.

JONATHAN: Gor! I—I wish he did; I'd shew him Yankee boys play, pretty quick—Don't you see you have frightened the young woman into the *hystrikes?*

VAN ROUGH: Pray, some of you explain this; what has been the occasion of all this racket?

MANLY: That gentleman can explain it to you; it will be a very diverting story for an intended father-in-law to hear.

VAN ROUGH: How was this matter, Mr Van Dumpling?

DIMPLE: Sir,—upon my honour—all I know is, that I was talking to this young lady, and this gentleman broke in on us, in a very extraordinary manner.

VAN ROUGH: Why, all this is nothing to the purpose: can you explain it, Miss? *(To* CHARLOTTE*)*

(Enter LETITIA *through the back scene)*

LETITIA: I can explain it to that gentleman's confusion. Though long betrothed to your daughter *(to* VAN ROUGH*)*, yet allured by my fortune, it seems (with shame do I speak it), he has privately paid his addresses to me. I was drawn in to listen to him by his assuring me that the match was made by his father without his consent, and that he proposed to break with Maria, whether he married me or not. But whatever were his intentions respecting your daughter, Sir, even to me he was false; for he has repeated the same story, with some cruel reflections upon my person, to Miss Manly.

JONATHAN: What a tarnal curse!

LETITIA: Nor is this all, Miss Manly. When he was with me this very morning, he made the same ungenerous reflections upon the weakness of your mind as he has so recently done upon the defects of my person.

JONATHAN: What a tarnal curse and damn too!

DIMPLE: Ha! since I have lost Letitia, I believe I had as good make it up with Maria—Mr Van Rough, at present I cannot enter into particulars; but, I believe I can explain everything to your satisfaction in private.

VAN ROUGH: There is another matter, Mr Van Dumpling, which I would have you explain:— pray, Sir, have Messrs Van Cash and Co. presented you those bills for acceptance?

DIMPLE: The deuce! Has he heard of those bills! Nay, then, all's up with Maria, too; but an affair of this sort can never prejudice me among the ladies; they will rather long to know what the dear creature possesses to make him so agreeable. *(Aside)* Sir, you'll hear from me. *(To* MANLY*)*

MANLY: And you from me, Sir.—

DIMPLE: Sir, you wear a sword.—

MANLY: Yes, Sir:—This sword was presented to me by that brave Gallic hero, the Marquis De La Fayette. I have drawn it in the service of my country, and in private life, on the only occasion where a man is justified in drawing his sword, in defence of a lady's honour. I have fought too many battles in the service of my country to dread the imputation of cowardice.—Death from a man of honour would be a glory you do not merit; you shall live to bear the insult of man, and the contempt of that sex, whose general smiles afforded you all your happiness.

DIMPLE: You won't meet me, Sir?—Then I'll post you for a coward.

MANLY: I'll venture that, Sir.—The reputation of my life does not depend upon the breath of a Mr Dimple. I would have you to know, however, Sir, that I have a cane to chastise the insolence of a scoundrel, and a sword and the good laws of my country, to protect me from the attempts of an assassin.—

DIMPLE: Mighty well! Very fine, indeed!—ladies and gentlemen, I take my leave, and you will please to observe, in the case of my deportment, the contrast between a gentleman, who has read Chesterfield and received the polish of Europe, and an unpolished, untravelled American.   *(Exit)*

(Enter MARIA*)*

MARIA: Is he indeed gone?—

LETITIA: I hope never to return.

VAN ROUGH: I am glad I heard of those bills; though it's plaguy unlucky: I hoped to see Mary married before I died.

MANLY: Will you permit a gentleman, Sir, to offer himself as a suitor to your daughter? Though a stranger to you, he is not altogether so to her, or unknown in this city. You may find a son-in-law of more fortune, but you can never meet with one who is richer in love for her, or respect for you.

VAN ROUGH: Why, Mary, you have not let this gentleman make love to you without my leave?

MANLY: I did not say, Sir—

MARIA: Say, Sir!—I—the gentleman, to be sure, met me accidentally.

VAN ROUGH: Ha, ha, ha! Mark me, Mary; young folks think old folks to be fools; but old fools know young folks to be fools.—Why, I knew all about this affair:—This was only a cunning way I had to bring it about—Hark ye! I was in the closet when you and he were at our house. *(Turns to the company)* I heard that little baggage say she loved her old father, and would die to make him happy! Oh! how I loved the little baggage!—And you talked very prudently, young man. I have inquired into your character, and find you to be a man of punctuality and mind the main chance. And so, as you love Mary, and Mary loves you, you shall have my consent immediately to be married. I'll settle

my fortune on you, and go and live with you the remainder of my life.

MANLY: Sir, I hope—

VAN ROUGH: Come, come, no fine speeches; mind the main chance, young man, and you and I shall always agree.

LETITIA: I sincerely wish you joy *(advancing to* MARIA*)*; and hope your pardon for my conduct.

MARIA: I thank you for your congratulations, and hope we shall at once forget the wretch who has given us so much disquiet, and the trouble that he has occasioned.

CHARLOTTE: And I, my dear Maria,—how shall I look up to you for forgiveness? I, who, in the practice of the meanest arts, have violated the most sacred rights of friendship? I can never forgive myself, or hope charity from the world, but I confess I have much to hope from such a brother; and I am happy that I may soon say, such a sister.—

MARIA: My dear, you distress me; you have all my love.

MANLY: And mine.

CHARLOTTE: If repentance can entitle me to forgiveness, I have already much merit; for I despise the littleness of my past conduct. I now find, that the heart of any worthy man cannot be gained by invidious attacks upon the rights and characters of others;—by countenancing the addresses of a thousand;—or that the finest assemblage of features, the greatest taste in dress, the genteelest address, or the most brilliant wit, cannot eventually secure a coquette from contempt and ridicule.

MANLY: And I have learned that probity, virtue, honour, though they should not have received the polish of Europe, will secure to an honest American the good graces of his fair countrywoman, and, I hope, the applause of THE PUBLIC.

THE END

M E T A M O R A ;   O R ,   T H E   L A S T
O F   T H E   W A M P A N O A G S   (1 8 2 9)

*Philanthropy could not wish to see this con-
tinent restored to the condition in which it
was found by our forefathers. What good
man would prefer a country covered with
forests and ranged by a few thousand savages to our extensive Republic, studded with
cities, towns, and prosperous farms, embel-
lished with all improvements which art can
devise or industry execute, occupied by more
than 12,000,000 happy people, and filled
with all the blessings of liberty, civilization,
and religion?*

So spoke President Andrew Jackson in his Annual
Address to Congress in 1830. Jackson's remarks represent a recurrent theme of his administration and
provide rhetorical traces of the cultural clash between native and colonial peoples that dated from
the beginnings of European, especially English, settlement of North America. Jackson's justifications for
the removal of indigenous peoples from their homelands (land reconstituted by white settlers' plows and
rifles as the United States) constitute more than a
mere backdrop to John Augustus Stone's *Metamora.*
As Stone's play filled theatres throughout America,
Jackson and other federal and state officials were using language, representations, and ideologies similar
to those found in Stone's play in a cultural and political drama on the national stage. As the actor Edwin
Forrest thrilled audiences as the heroic seventeenth-
century Wampanoag chieftain Metamora, the remnants of the Native American population east of the
Mississippi River were being forced to the lands
beyond white settlement west of the river. As in
his dreams Metamora foresaw the supplanting of

indigenous cultures by the new intruders, Native
Americans were being transformed into the "Indians" of the American imagination. Simultaneously
a facilitator and reflector of these national phenomena, *Metamora* is one of the earliest examples of
American drama's treatment of racial diversity and
racial conflict's importance to the ongoing process of
national self-definition.

At the same time, the history of the play's genesis is indicative of some of the forces that shaped the
drama of the Jacksonian period, an era dominated by
the emergence of a few "star" actors and entrepreneurial managers. The author, John Augustus Stone,
was born in Concord, Massachusetts, December 15,
1800, and took to the stage at 20, debuting in Boston
as Old Norval in John Home's *Douglas.* This initial
effort set the pattern for his acting career, which
consisted in the main of character roles, primarily
gruff older men and comic eccentrics. He moved to
New York in 1822, becoming an audience favorite
from his first appearance. After working for several
years in New York, during which time he married
the actress Amelia Greene Legge and began a family, he removed himself and his family to Philadelphia in 1831, working until the end of his life at the
Walnut Street and Chestnut Street theatres. He suffered from ill health during his brief tenure in
Philadelphia and, after sinking into despondency,
committed suicide by throwing himself into the
Schuylkill River on May 29, 1834.

While chiefly an actor, Stone occasionally
wrote plays and recrafted the work of others. *Tan-
cred* (1837), the only play published during his life,
was never mounted. But Stone's craftsmanship was
such that *Restoration* (1824), *The Lion of the West*

(1831, a revision of James Kirke Paulding's play of the same title), *The Demoniac* (1831), and *The Ancient Briton* (1833) all saw productions. Stone also provided George H. Hill with one of his most popular Yankee roles in *The Golden Fleece, or The Yankee of Spain* (1834). Without doubt, however, Stone's reputation as a playwright rests upon *Metamora.*

Stone wrote the play as an entry for the first of the actor Edwin Forrest's nine playwrighting contests. Over the years, this device was to pay Forrest handsome dividends by providing him three of his most popular parts—Metamora, Jack Cade, and Spartacus. In the first contest, Forrest's personal background, his public persona as an arch-patriot, and his business acumen came together to establish the parameters of the contest. Having early in his career been personally impressed by a Choctaw chief, Push-ma-ta-ha, desiring to be perceived as a supporter of American arts, and seeking a role uniquely suited to his acting strengths and physical attributes, Forrest offered 500 dollars and a half-share of a **benefit performance** "for the best tragedy, in five acts, of which the hero, or principal character, shall be an aboriginal of this country." A panel of prominent literary and theatrical men, which included William Cullen Bryant, James Lawson, and Prosper M. Wetmore, selected Stone's effort from the 14 plays submitted.

Given Forrest's sponsorship, Stone's background as an actor, and the fact that Stone had seen Forrest in the supporting role of the Indian chief in a production of M. M. Noah's *She Would Be a Soldier*, it is not surprising that Stone's offering played to Forrest's particular strengths. From its opportunities to dominate the stage in a costume that showed muscular arms and legs to advantage, to the physically demanding action of the play, to the speeches that called for an emotionally powerful voice, *Metamora* testifies to Stone's knowledge of what worked on stage and specifically what would work for Edwin Forrest. It is hardly a surprise, then, that the play became Forrest's premier non-Shakespearean vehicle. As Richard Moody has documented, *Metamora* was in Forrest's hands a veritable money-making machine, again and again rescuing both Forrest and

the managers who hired him from otherwise disappointing seasons (*Dramas*). Along with Custis' *The Indian Prophecy, Metamora* formed the vanguard of a host of plays about North and South American natives that held the stage for several years. Though the popularity of the **Indian plays** would eventually fade, in the hands of Forrest *Metamora* remained popular until the actor's death in 1872.

This success could hardly have been forecast before Stone and Forrest's collaboration, for previous Indian plays such as Robert Rogers' *Ponteach* (1766) and James Nelson Barker's *The Indian Princess* (1808) had either never been produced or been indifferently received. Only George Washington Parke Custis' *The Indian Prophecy* (1827) had succeeded, running for 12 nights at the Chestnut Street Theater in 1827. However, even the influence of this particular antecedent on either Stone or Forrest is problematic. In the adulatory age following George Washington's death in 1799, Washington's central role in his grandson's drama may well have been the guarantor of the play's popularity. Certainly the period advertisements reproduced by Murray Nelligan suggest that Washington, rather than the Native American, was the focal point of the attention.

Even in the case of Stone and Forrest's effort, the Native American subject seems more an attempt to domesticate romantic tragedy than anything else. Certainly, Forrest's admiration for Push-ma-ta-ha and his ability to recognize the potentials of the right "Indian" play should not be confused with any political agenda. There is no evidence that either Stone or Forrest was deeply concerned for Native Americans. As Montrose Moses has commented, the actor's "fervor for the Indians seems to have died out when his sentiments were embodied in 'Metamora'."

While Stone's and Forrest's motives appear to have been purely monetary, the "sentiments" to which Moses refers linked the figure of Metamora so closely to the American public that the play itself provides a telling insight into the ideological conflicts that were part of the "Indian Question" that beset the United States in the early decades of the nineteenth century. Basic to this issue were two operations of mind that have significance for an understanding of *Metamora*. The first was the European propensity to efface the differences among various Native American groups. As Roy Harvey Pearce has commented, "white understanding of the Indian was in crucial part derived from a conflation of all Indians, tribes and subtribes into one: *the* Indian." For the audience, viewing a performance of *Metamora* through this distorting lens, the Wampanoags of the seventeenth century became the Creeks, Cherokees, and Choctaws of the nineteenth century, and the Puritan settlers of Massachusetts became contemporary Americans. History dissolved into myth, and the play rehearsed not only the events of a historical moment but, more important, a timeless narrative in which "Americans" were always fated to displace "Indians."

The second turn of mind, that which gave moral sanction to the violation of the native population's prior claim to the land, recast native and colonial conflicts as a struggle between evil savages and civilized saints. Originated, as Slotkin and Folsom have argued, by Puritan historians seeking to explain the wars of the late seventeenth century, this conception effectively elevated the conflict beyond the mundane concerns over control of New England and friction created by colonists' desires for additional native lands. Instead, as Jeffrey Mason contends, these conflicts were transformed into a cosmic battle in which savage natives acting as the agents of Satan were pitted against the colonists, the forces of light representing the true God.

There can be little doubt that not only the audience but also Stone and Forrest actively saw the play in these terms. Although Metamora himself may be called "the grandest model of a mighty man," may love wife and child, may be motivated only by an appropriate desire to preserve his nation, and may save the white heroine's life and virtue, he is ultimately "only" a savage. More appealing as a model of manhood than the run-of-the-mill colonists who oppose him, Metamora's stature as an individual is undermined by his lack of civilization and his implicit unwillingness to embrace the "true" faith. As Priscilla Sears has noted, such virtues and vices "render him a worthy opponent and an estimable trophy for the Anglo-Europeans." When in the play's first act Walter catalogues Metamora's virtues, the young hero concludes by suggesting that "Heaven alone must judge" Metamora's faith. In the course of the play, Heaven seemingly passes its judgment. Although the audience is invited vicariously to savor the satisfactions of heroic martyrdom as Metamora dies cursing the English, its members imaginatively stand with their European forefathers as the curtain lowers. The message is clear. The course of empire is inevitable, justified by the very civilization whose instruments strike down the last "noble savage."

WORKS CONSULTED

Mason, Jeffrey D. *Melodrama and the Myth of America.* Bloomington: Indiana University Press, 1993.

Moody, Richard. *Dramas from the American Theatre, 1762–1909.* Cleveland: World Publishing, 1966.

Moses, Montrose J. *The Fabulous Forrest: The Record of an American Actor.* [1929]. New York: Blom, 1969.

Nelligan, Murray H. "American Nationalism on the Stage: The Plays of George Washington Parke Custis (1781–1857)." *The Virginia Magazine of History and Biography,* 58 (1950): 299–324.

Pearce, Roy Harvey. *Savagism and Civilization: A Study of the Indian and the American Mind.* Rev. ed. of *The Savages of America.* 1953. Berkeley: University of California Press, 1988.

Richardson, James D., ed. *A Compilation of the Messages and Papers of the Presidents,* Vol. III. New York: Bureau of National Literature, 1897.

Sears, Priscilla. *A Pillar of Fire to Follow: American Indian Dramas: 1808–1859.* Bowling Green, OH: Bowling Green University Popular Press, 1982.

Slotkin, Richard and James K. Folsom, eds. *"So Dreadful a Judgment": Puritan Response to King Philip's War, 1676–1677.* Middletown, CT: Wesleyan University Press, 1978.

CHARACTERS

INDIANS

METAMORA . . . . chief of the Wampanoags

KANESHINE . . . . an Indian prophet

ANNAWANDAH . . . . the traitor

OTAH . . . . an Indian boy

INDIAN BOY . . . . child of Metamora

NAHMEOKEE . . . . wife of Metamora

INDIANS, WARRIORS, ETC.

ENGLISH

LORD FITZARNOLD

SIR ARTHUR VAUGHAN

MORDAUNT

ERRINGTON . . . . chief of the council

WALTER . . . . an orphan

CAPTAIN CHURCH

WOLFE

GOODENOUGH

TRAMP

OCEANA . . . . Mordaunt's daughter

SOLDIERS, SAILORS, PEASANTS, ETC.*

* The text reproduced here was painstakingly reconstructed by Professor Richard Moody, emeritus professor at Indiana University, from partial versions found at the Edwin Forrest Home in Philadelphia and the University of Utah Library augmented by a copy found by Professor Moody among the Lord Chamberlain's plays in the British Library.

Prologue

Written by Mr Prosper M. Wetmore.
Spoken by Mrs Barrett, New Park Theater,
New York, December 15, 1829.

Not from the records of Imperial Rome,
Or classic Greece—the muses' chosen home—
From no rich legends of the olden day
Our bard hath drawn the story of his play;
Led by the guiding hand of genius on,
He here hath painted Nature on her throne;
His eye hath pierced the forest's shadowy gloom,
And read strange lessons from a nation's tomb:
Brief are the annals of that blighted race—
These halls usurp a monarch's resting-place—
Traditions's mist-enshrouded page alone
Tells that an empire was—we know 'tis gone!
From foreign climes full oft the muse has brought
Her glorious treasures of gigantic thought;
And here, beneath the witchery of her power,
The eye hath poured its tributary shower:
When modern pens have sought th' historic page,
To picture forth the deeds of former age—
O'er soft Virginia's sorrows ye have sighed,
And dropt a tear when spotless beauty died;
When Brutus "cast his cloud aside"; to stand

The guardian of the tyrant-trampled land—
When patriot Tell his clime from thraldom freed,
And bade th' avenging arrow do its deed.
Your bosoms answered with responsive swell,
For freedom triumphed when th' oppressors fell!
These were the melodies of humbler lyres,
The lights of Genius, yet without his fires;
But when the master-spirit struck the chords,
And inspiration breathed her burning words—
When passion's self stalked living o'er the stage,
To plead with love, or rouse the soul to rage—
When Shakespeare led his bright creations forth,
And conjured up the mighty dead from earth—
Breathless—entranced—ye've listened to the line,
And felt the minstrel's power, all but divine!
While thus your plaudits cheer the stranger lay,
Shall native pens in vain the field essay?
To-night we test the strength of native powers,
Subject, and bard, and actor, all our ours—
'Tis yours to judge, if worthy of a name,
And bid them live within the halls of fame!

ACT I

SCENE 1: *Sunset. A wild, picturesque scene; high, craggy rocks in distance; dark pine trees, etc. Rocks cross stage, with platform cross behind. Steps, etc., at back. A rude tomb, flowers growing around it. Half dark.* MORDAUNT *discovered leaning on tomb. Slow music.*

MORDAUNT: The sun has sunk behind yon craggy rocks; and day's last beams are fading from the clouds that fleet in hurrying masses through the sky, like tattered banners of a flying host! England, my home! When will thy parent arms again enfold me? Oh! When for me will dawn a day of hope? Will not sincere repentance from my scathed brow efface the brand of regicide?

TRAMP: *(outside)* What ho! Good Master Mordaunt! *(Cannon)*

MORDAUNT: Ha! What mean those sounds? Now, your news? *(Enter* TRAMP*)*

TRAMP: A gallant bark, urged by the favoring breeze, makes for the crowded shore.

MORDAUNT: From England! Ha!

TRAMP: St. George's banner floats from her high mast, and her long signal pennon gleams with green and gold.

MORDAUNT: 'Tis he—he comes and with him hope arrives. Go, hasten, fellow; seek my daughter; say the Lord Fitzarnold comes to greet her. *(*TRAMP *crosses to R. behind)* Marshal my followers in their best array—away to the beach and let loud music welcome him ashore. *(Exit* TRAMP*)* What mingled feelings crowd about my heart, blended so strange and wild? Sunned by his sovereign's smile, Fitzarnold comes to woo and wed my daughter. Born on the heaving deep, the child of storms, and reared in savage wilds, her worth and beauty well may grace the courtly halls of England. And yet, to force her gentle will, whose every thought has been to soothe my sorrows and relieve my cares! Yet must she wed Fitzarnold. His alliance can with oblivion shroud the past, clear from my scutcheon every rebel stain, and give my franchised spirit liberty.

Exit. Slow music, four bars. Enter OCEANA, *looking around as if in search*

OCEANA: Sure, 'twas my father's voice, and loud in converse. Father! Dear father! Not here? And yet I thought—*(Flute heard, distant)* Ha! whence that strain? So soft yet strange. Methinks some pious minstrel seeks the moonlight hour to breathe devotion forth in melody. *(Music changes)* Hark! It changes place and measure, too. Now deeper in the woods it warbles, now it seems aloft floating in plaintive tones through the air. This place—the hour—the day—heavens! 'tis my mother's birthday, and her grave undecked with flowers! O my mother, my dear mother! Perhaps her angel spirit hovers here o'er her lone daughter's steps, a guardian still. *(Kneels to tomb)* Ah, what flower is this?

"Forgetmenot!" *(Music ceases)* My mother, look from thy seraph home upon thy child, and when for those thou lovest on earth thou breathest a prayer, oh, then forget me not. *(Places flower in bosom. Enter* WALTER*)*

WALTER: Oceana!

OCEANA: Walter, was thine the strain but now I heard?

WALTER: 'Twas but an humble tribute to thy beauty, but could not match the sweetness of thy voice, whose every tone, attuned to dulcet sounds, can melt the soul to nature's harmony.

OCEANA: Walter, this from thee.

WALTER: Nay, blame me not; although dependent on Sir Arthur Vaughan, nameless and poor, yet do I not despair, for in my heart a sacred treasure lies I would not barter for my patron's gold.

OCEANA: What means't thou, Walter?

WALTER: Thine own sweet image, which naught on earth can banish or efface—a whispered hope I dare not speak aloud—a light thine own bright eyes have kindled up.

OCEANA: Nay, Walter, you ask not of the danger I escaped!

WALTER: Danger! What danger? When?

OCEANA: 'Twas yestere'en, when I was lingering on the eastern beach, all heedless of the coming night, a panther growling from the thicket rushed and marked me for his prey. Powerless I stood—my blood stood still—I shrieked as I strove to fly, when at the instant, from a ready hand, swift as the lightning's flash, an arrow came and felled the monster as he crouched to spring.

WALTER: Didst mark who sent it?

OCEANA: Full well I did. High on a craggy rock an Indian stood, with sinewy arm and eye that pierced the glen. His bowstring drawn to wing a second death, a robe of fur was o'er his shoulder thrown, and o'er his long, dark hair an eagle's plume waved in the breeze, a feathery diadem. Firmly he stood upon the jutting height, as if a sculptor's hand had carved him there. With awe I gazed as on the cliff he turned—the grandest model of a mighty man.

WALTER: 'Twas Haups great chieftain, Metamora called; our people love him not, nor is it strange; he stands between them and extended sway, ready alike with words of power to urge, or gleaming weapon force his princely dues.

METAMORA: *(outside)* Hah! Ha!

OCEANA: *(going up)* Behold his dread encounter with a wolf. His vanquished foe with mighty arm he hurls down the steep height where mortal never trod.

METAMORA: Hah! Hah! *(Enters on rock, passes across and off)*

WALTER: *(at* METAMORA'S *exit)* 'Tis Metamora, the noble sachem of a valiant race—the white man's dread, the Wampanoag's hope. *(Enter* META-MORA *down R.)*

METAMORA: Ha, ha, ha! Turned on me—brave beast; he died like a red man.

OCEANA: Chief, you are hurt; this scarf will staunch the wound. *(Offers it)*

METAMORA: No! *(Rejects it)*

WALTER: 'Tis Oceana—she whose life you saved.

METAMORA: Metamora will take the white maiden's gift. *(*OCEANA *ties his arm with scarf)*

OCEANA: But yestere'en thou savedst my life, great chief; how can I pay thee for the generous deed?

METAMORA: Hearken, daughter of the pale face; Metamora forgives not a wrong and forgets not a kindness. In the days of his age, Massasoit, my father, was in the white man's dwelling; while there, the spirit of the grave touched him and he laid down to die. A soft hand was stretched out to save him; it was the hand of thy mother. She that healed him sleeps in yonder tomb; but why should Metamora let his arrows sleep in the quiver when her daughter's life was in danger and her limbs shook with fear? Metamora loves the mild-eyed and the kind, for such is Nahmeokee.

WALTER: Such words, and more than all, such deeds, should win you, chief, the love of all our people. Would you were more among us. Why never seek our homes? Sir Arthur Vaughan's doors will open to the Indian chief.

OCEANA: My sire will thank thee for his daughter's life.

METAMORA: The red man's heart is on the hills where his father's shafts have flown in the chase. Ha! I have been upon the high mountain top where the grey mists were beneath my feet, and the Great Spirit passed by me in his wrath. He spake in anger and the old rocks crumbled beneath the flash of his spear. Then I was proud and smiled, for I had slain the great bird whose wing never tires, and whose eye never shrinks; and his feathers would adorn the long black hair of Nahmeokee, daughter of Miantonemo, the great hunter. The war and the chase are the red man's brother and sister. The storm cloud in its fury frights him not. Wrapt in the spoils he has won, he lays him down and no one comes near to steal. The Great Spirit hears his evening prayer, and he sleeps amidst the roar of a mighty cataract.

WALTER: Were all thy nation mild and good like thee, how soon the fire of discord might be quenched.

METAMORA: Metamora has been the friend of the white man; yet if the flint be smitten too hard it will show that in its heart is fire. The Wampanoag will not wrong his white brother who comes from the land that is first touched by the rising sun; but he owns no master, save that One who holds the sun in his right hand, who rides on a dark storm, and who cannot die. *(Crosses to L.)*

WALTER: That lofty bearing—that majestic mien— the regal impress sits upon his brow, and earth seems conscious of her proudest son. *(Conch shell heard sounding, R.)*

METAMORA: Ha! My young men return from their evening toil, and their hands are filled with the sweet fish of the lake. Come to my wigwam; ye shall eat of fish that the Great Spirit of the waters sends, and your hearts shall be made glad. *(Going R. but returns and takes from his head an eagle plume)* Maiden, take this; it means speed and safety; when the startling whoop is heard and the war hatchet gleams in the red blaze, let it be found in thy braided hair. Despise not the red man's gift; it will bring more good to you than the yellow earth the white man worships as his god. Take it—no Wampanoag's hand will e'er be raised against the head or hand that bears the eagle plume. *(Crosses to* WALTER*)* Young man, be thou like the oak in its spreading power and let thy tough branches shelter the tender flower that springs up under them. Look to the maiden of the eagle plume, and—come to my wigwam. *(Exit)*

OCEANA: Teach him, Walter; make him like to us.

WALTER: 'Twould cost him half his native virtues. Is justice goodly? Metamora's just. Is bravery virtue? Metamora's brave. If love of country, child and wife and home, be to deserve them all—he merits them.

OCEANA: Yet he is a heathen.

WALTER: True, Oceana, but his worship though untaught and rude flows from his heart, and Heaven alone must judge of it. *(Enter* TRAMP*)*

TRAMP: Your father, lady, requires your presence.

OCEANA: Say I come. *(A distant drum)*

WALTER: What is that?

TRAMP: The drum that summons Lord Fitzarnold's escort. He comes a suitor for my lady's hand. *(Exit* TRAMP*)*

WALTER: Deny it, Oceana—say 'tis false!

OCEANA: It is—

WALTER: Untrue?

OCEANA: Oh, most unwelcome.

WALTER: Heavens! You tremble—and your cheek is pale—my Lord Fitzarnold, that most courtly gentleman, and must my hopes—

OCEANA: Walter, dost thou mean—

WALTER: Obey thy sire. I cannot say farewell. But, oh, when highborn revelers carouse, and proud Fitzarnold lords it at the board, give one brief thought to me! That blessed thought shall soothe the fond complainings of my heart and hush them to repose. *(Exit* WALTER *L.* OCEANA *exit R.)*

SCENE 2: *Lights up. A room in* SIR ARTHUR'S *house. Enter* SIR ARTHUR *and* WALTER.

WALTER: Yet hear me, sir.

SIR ARTHUR: Forebear; thou art too hot.

WALTER: 'Tis not the meanness of our state that galls us, but men's opinions. Poverty and toil and consciousness of lowly destiny sit lightly where no scorn is heaped upon them. But yesterday I was indeed content, for none despised, none had learned to scoff the son of charity, the wretched ship boy who could trace existence no further than the wreck from which you plucked him; but now 'tis changed, all suddenly begin to find me base.

SIR ARTHUR: Marry, go to! You wrong yourself and me. Have I not fostered you—like a father tutored you? In early life bereft of wife and child, wearied of discord and fierce civil strife, I left the haunts of wild and factious men, to woo contentment in this wilderness. My heart was vacant and received thee in. Do not by any rash, unworthy act forsake that heart. Who is it finds thee base?

WALTER: All, since Fitzarnold is expected here.

SIR ARTHUR: Fitzarnold! What a plague! There is naught talked of or thought of but Lord Fitzarnold! And yet this noble viscount, but for his coat and title were a man to look with scorn upon—a profligate and spendthrift as fame already has too truly shown him.

WALTER: And 'tis for such a man that Master Mordaunt sets me aside—for such a man his daughter must cast me off.

SIR ARTHUR: Tut! Master Mordaunt is too wise a man to give his daughter to this Lord Fitzarnold. Patience awhile, and watch the progress of this meteor. Patience, and trust to fortune. *(Exit)*

WALTER: This lordly suitor comes to wake me from my cherished dreams, and crush the hopes which lately looked so fair. And shall I yield the glorious prize I deemed was wholly mine? Yield, and without a struggle? No, by heaven! Look to thyself, Fitzarnold. Let Oceana be but true. I heed not all thy power, thy wealth, thy titles, backed though they be by Mordaunt's selfish views. *(Exit)*

SCENE 3: *The harbor. Ships anchored in the distance. Military music,* MORDAUNT, ERRINGTON, GOODENOUGH, CHURCH, SOLDIERS, CITIZENS *(male and female) discovered. A boat comes on from L., with* FITZARNOLD, WOLFE, *and* SAILORS, *who land. Shout.*

MORDAUNT: Long live the king! Welcome Fitzarnold! Rest to the sea-worn! Joy to each and all!

FITZARNOLD: I thank thee, Mordaunt! But I did not think to see such faces in the wilderness! Thy woody shores are bright with sparkling eyes, like Argonaut's adventurous sailors. But where's the golden boon we look for, sir? Fair Oceana—Mordaunt, where is she? *(*WALTER *enters, L., and stands against wing)*

MORDAUNT: So please you, my lord, at home, eager to pay your lordship's kindness back, and prove she can discern thy courtesy.

WALTER: *(aside)* Indeed! Dost say so, worldling?

MORDAUNT: Pray thee, regard these gentlemen, my lord—our council's father, Errington—and this our army's leader; elders of the State. *Introducing them severally;* FITZARNOLD *salutes them, and at last approaching* WALTER, *extends his hand;* WALTER *bows coldly but does not take it. Music eight bars*

FITZARNOLD: How now, young sir? Mordaunt, who is this?

MORDAUNT: My noble lord, I pray thee, heed him not! A wayward youth, somewhat o'er worn with study. *(Crosses to* WALTER*)* Rash boy! Be wise and tempt me not; I can destroy—

WALTER: Thy daughter's peace and wed her there. *(*MORDAUNT *gives* WALTER *a look of hate and turns from him)*

MORDAUNT: Forth to the hall—a strain of music there. *(Crosses to R.)*

FITZARNOLD: Young sir, I shall desire some further converse with you.

WALTER: At injury's prompting, deeds, not words, were best. My lord, you shall find me. *(Touches his sword)*

FITZARNOLD: Now for thy fair daughter, Mordaunt, come.

Music. Exeunt all but WALTER *and* WOLFE. PEASANTS *and* SOLDIERS *exeunt, R.*

WOLFE: Thou goest not with them?

WALTER: No, nor before, nor follow after. But why dost thou ask?

WOLFE: Because I know thee.

WALTER: Then thou knowest one who will not take a lordling by the hand, because his fingers shine with hoops of gold—nor shun the beggar's grasp if it be honest. Thou knowest me?

WOLFE: Yes!

WALTER: To know oneself was thought task enough in olden time. What dost thou know?

WOLFE: That thou wert wrecked and saved.

WALTER: Aye, more's the pity! *(Aside)* Had I been drowned I had not lived to love and have no hope.

WOLFE: Thou art a good man's son.

WALTER: A pity then, again. Were I a rascal's offspring, I might thrive. What more?

WOLFE: Thou shalt possess thy mistress.

WALTER: Didst mark that lord?

WOLFE: He is my master.

WALTER: Then I am dumb. Be faithful to him, and now farewell. *(Crosses to L.)*

WOLFE: Yet in good time I will say that you will bestow a blessing for.

WALTER: Indeed! What mean you?

Enter TRAMP, *L., with packet*

TRAMP: News from the Indians. *(Shows packet)* 'Tis for the council by a horseman left, who bade me see it with all haste delivered. The Indian tribes conspire from east to west and faithful Sasamond has found his grave! This packet must be borne to Mordaunt.

WALTER: Trust it with me.

TRAMP: That I will readily, so thou wilt bear it safely.

WALTER: Aye, and quickly, too. *(Takes packet, crosses to R.)* Let me remember Metamora's

words—"Look to the maiden of the eagle plume."

Exit hastily, followed by WOLFE, *and* TRAMP. *Quick curtain*

ACT II

SCENE 1: *Music. Interior of a wigwam; a skin rolled. Stage covered with skins, etc. Child on skin near R. entrance.* NAHMEOKEE *near it.* METAMORA *at L., preparing for the chase.*

NAHMEOKEE: Thou wilt soon be back from the chase.

METAMORA: Yes, before the otter has tasted his midday food on the bank of the stream, his skin shall make a garment for Nahmeokee when the snow whitens the hunting grounds and the cold wind whistles through the trees. Nahmeokee, take our little one from his rest; he sleeps too much.

NAHMEOKEE: Oh, no! But thou, Metamora, sleepst too little. In the still hour of midnight when Wekolis has sung his song, and the great light has gone down behind the hills, when Nahmeokee's arms like the growing vine were round thee—as if some danger lay waiting in the thick wood—thou didst bid me bring thy tomahawk and the spear that Massasoit had borne when the war cry of the Wampanoags was loudest in the place of blood! Why is thy rest like the green lake when the sudden blast passes across its bosom?

METAMORA: Nahmeokee, the power of dreams has been on me, and the shadows of things that are to be have passed before me. My heart is big with a great thought. When I sleep I think the knife is red in my hand, and the scalp of the white man is streaming.

NAHMEOKEE: Metamora, is not the white man our brother? And does not the Great Spirit look on him as he does on us? Do not go towards his home today because thy wrath is kindled and it spreads like the flames which the white man makes in the dark bosom of the forest. Let Nahmeokee clasp her arms around thee; rest thy head upon her bosom, for it is hot and thy eye is red with the thoughts that burn! Our old men counsel peace, and the aim of the white man will spare.

METAMORA: Yes, when our fires are no longer red, on the high places of our fathers; when the bones of our kindred make fruitful the fields of the stranger, which he has planted amidst the ashes of our wigwams; when we are hunted back like the wounded elk far toward the going down of the sun, our hatchets broken, our bows unstrung and war whoop hushed; then will the stranger spare, for we will be too small for his eye to see.
       Trumpet. Enter OTAH

OTAH: O son of Massasoit, the power of the white man approaches, and he looks not like one who seeks the Wampanoag's friendship! Look where the bright weapons flash through the clouds of his track.

METAMORA: Ha! Let the paleface come with the calumet or with the knife, Metamora does not fear their power. Where is Annawandah, skilled in talk? Let him approach me.
       Exit OTAH

NAHMEOKEE: Our child would not rest in the mid-hour of night for the hidden snake had bitten him as he lay stretched in the rays of the sun. I rose from my seat to get the dried leaves the Good Spirit has filled with power to heal; the moon was bright and a shadow passed me. It was Annawandah passed our wigwam; his step was like the course of the serpent and he paused and listened. My eye followed him to the seaside, and his light canoe shot like an arrow across the slumbering waters.

METAMORA: Humph! Was he alone?

NAHMEOKEE: Alone.

METAMORA: And he went with fear?

NAHMEOKEE: Like one who goes to steal.
       Trumpet. Enter OTAH

OTAH: Look! The white warrior comes.

Enter CHURCH, SIR ARTHUR VAUGHAN, *and* GOODENOUGH, *with musqueteers [sic]*

CHURCH: Although we come unbidden, chieftain, yet is our purpose friendly.

METAMORA: Why do you bring your fire weapons if you come to hold a talk of peace?

CHURCH: It is our custom.

METAMORA: Well, speak; my ears are open to hear.

SIR ARTHUR: Philip, our mission is—

METAMORA: Philip! I am the Wampanoag chief, Metamora.

SIR ARTHUR: We are directed by our council's head, for the times are filled with doubt, and to make *sure* our bond of peace and love to urge your presence at the council.

NAHMEOKEE: *(aside)* Do not go.

METAMORA: Daughter of Miantonemo, peace! *(To them)* I will go.

CHURCH: Our troops shall form thy escort there.

METAMORA: I know the path.

SIR ARTHUR: We must not go without thee, chief.

METAMORA: I have breasted the cold winds of forty winters and to those that spoke kindly to me in the words of love I have been pliant—aye, very yielding like the willow that droops over the stream, but till with a single arm you can move the mighty rock that mocks the lightning and the storm seek not to stir Metamora when his heart says no. I will come! *(Crosses to R.)*

CHURCH: We shall expect thee, chief.

METAMORA: Metamora cannot lie.

CHURCH: Stand to your arms.
       Trumpet. Exit CHURCH, GOODENOUGH, OTAH *and* SOLDIERS

SIR ARTHUR: Be thou not rash, but with thy tongue of manly truth dispel all charge that wrongs thy noble nature. Throw not the brand that kindles bloody war lest thou thyself should be the victim. *(*SIR ARTHUR *going L.)*

METAMORA: My father's deeds shall be my counsellors, and the Great Spirit will hear the words of my mouth. *(Exit* SIR ARTHUR*)* Now, Nahmeokee, I will talk to thee. Dost thou not love this little one, Nahmeokee?

NAHMEOKEE: Oh, yes!

METAMORA: When first his little eyes unclosed, thou saidst they were like mine; and my people rejoiced with a mighty joy, that the grandson of Massasoit, the white man's friend, should rule in the high places of his kindred; and hoped that his days would be long and full of glory. Nahmeokee, by the blood of his warlike race, he shall not be the white man's slave.

NAHMEOKEE: Thy talk is strange, and fear creeps over me. Thy heart is beating at thy side, as if thy bosom could not hold it.

METAMORA: Because 'tis full of thee—and thee, my little one. Humph! Bring me the knife thy brother wore in battle—my hatchet—the spear that was thy father's when Uncas slew him for the white man's favor. Humph! These things thou gavest me with thyself; thinkest thou this arm can wield them in the fight?

NAHMEOKEE: Ah! Thy bravery will lose thee to me.

METAMORA: Let not thy heart be troubled. If I require assistance from my people, I will lift up a flame on the lofty hill that shall gleam afar through the thick darkness.

NAHMEOKEE: I shall remember thy words.

METAMORA: Take in thy babe; I am going. (Crosses to L.)

NAHMEOKEE: Metamora, dost thou go alone?

METAMORA: No; Manito is with me.

Exit. NAHMEOKEE *exit*

SCENE 2: *A room in the house of* MORDAUNT. *Enter* OCEANA.

OCEANA: Free from Fitzarnold's gaze, I feel myself again. Why came he here? His looks appalled [me] yet my father smiled—ah! he comes.
Enter MORDAUNT

MORDAUNT: How now, my daughter; how is this? Why have you left his lordship thus?

OCEANA: I thought 'twas time.

MORDAUNT: It is not time to play the prude, when noble men confess thy charms and come fair suitors to thee. Fitzarnold loves thee and his alliance is so dear to me, I'll have no scruples of a timid girl to weigh against it. For long years

I've nursed this fondness and I now command obedience.

OCEANA: That union must remain unblessed wherein the helpless hand is giving no heart to bear it company. O my father, how at the altar can I take that vow my heart now whispers never can be kept.

MORDAUNT: Hear me, rash girl, now that none o'erhear our converse. Learn thy father's destiny—the name I bear is not my own!

OCEANA: My father!

MORDAUNT: Thou didst not know my former life and deeds. Hardy adventure and the shock of arms, civil contention and a monarch's death make up the past, and poison all who come! 'Tis thou alone can clothe my future days with peace and shed one cheering ray o'er a dark scene of terror.

OCEANA: Art thou distraught?

MORDAUNT: Do not deny me, girl, and make me so! I am an outcast and a man forbid. Fitzarnold knows me and he asks my child—has power, and gaining thee preserves thy sire. Speak, Oceana! Thy resolve: what is it?

OCEANA: Thou canst not mean it, father! No, it cannot be!

MORDAUNT: Girl, it is as certain as our earthly doom. Decide, then, now between my honor and my instant death! For by thy mother's memory and by my soul, if my despair do find thee pitiless, my own right hand shall end a wretched life and leave thee nothing for a bridal dower but my curses and a blighted name. (Crosses to R.)

OCEANA: My throat is parched! I pray a moment's peace, a moment's pause.
Business. MORDAUNT *paces the stage in great agitation, at last falls on his knee to* OCEANA. WALTER *enters, starts at seeing them and remains at back*

MORDAUNT: Look at thy father, lowly begging life of thee. I will not swear, I will not rave, my child, but I'll implore thee! If thou hast ever loved me and dost so still, show that affection now! Let not thy father's name forever stand a mark for men to heap their curses on—relent, my child.

OCEANA: I can endure no more—rise, my father.

MORDAUNT: Dost thou promise?

OCEANA: All, all!

MORDAUNT: Swear, by truth! by honor! By the dead—

OCEANA: To wed Fitzarnold—

WALTER: *(comes up)* Hold! Hold, rash girl, forebear! Thou art ensnared and wouldst pronounce thy doom.

MORDAUNT: Lightning consume thee, meddling fool! What bringst thou here?

WALTER: No pleasant duty, sir; a message which the council sends thee here. *(Gives packet to* MORDAUNT*)* I am no spy, nor do I care to know secrets too dread for thine own heart to hold.

MORDAUNT: Beggar, begone!
Strikes him with packet and crosses to L. WALTER *draws sword.* OCEANA *interposes*

OCEANA: It is my father, Walter, mine.

WALTER: A blow.

OCEANA: Oh, thou wilt forgive him!

WALTER: Never! I will forth, and ere he shall enforce thee where thou hast no joy, will rend the mask he cheats us with. *(Crosses to L.)*

OCEANA: And if thou dost, by heaven I'll ne'er be thine.

WALTER: *(sheathes sword)* Old man, an angel's bosom shelters thine. Instruct Fitzarnold in our quarrel's cause. No daughter bars my way to him.
Exit. Enter FITZARNOLD

FITZARNOLD: How now, you tremble; what has chanced?

MORDAUNT: A moody beggar who abused my love and I chastised him for it—that's all.

OCEANA: My father—

MORDAUNT: Go to thy chamber.

OCEANA: Would it were my grave. *(Exit)*

MORDAUNT: My noble lord, that moody stripling whom you saw last night—whether set on by Vaughan, his patron, or by the vainness of his own conceits, resolves to break my daughter's marriage.

FITZARNOLD: And wilt thou suffer this? What is the villain's state?

MORDAUNT: Dependence on Sir Arthur Vaughan; his wealth a goodly person and the [law?] love of schools. [*sic*] *(Bell tolls)* Hark! I am summoned to the council. Wilt thou along?
FITZARNOLD *crosses to L.*

FITZARNOLD: I trust he finds no favor with your daughter.

MORDAUNT: She shall be thine, my lord; thine with free will and full contentment. Now for the council.
Exeunt

SCENE 3:   *Flourish. The council chamber.* ERRINGTON, SIR ARTHUR *and* CHURCH *on raised platform.* MORDAUNT *and* FITZARNOLD *seated at table, L.* ELDERS, *etc.* GOODENOUGH *and* SOLDIERS, *R.* VILLAGERS, *etc.* WALTER *and* TRAMP.

ERRINGTON: 'Tis news that asks from us most speedy action. Heaven has in sounds most audible and strange, in sights, too, that amazed the lookers-on, forewarned our people of their peril. 'Tis time to lift the arm so long supine, and with one blow cut off this heathen race, who spite of reason and the word revealed, continue hardened in their devious ways, and make the chosen tremble. Colleagues, your voices—speak—are you for peace or war?

SIR ARTHUR: What is your proof your Indian neighbors mean not as fairly towards our settlements as did King Philip's father, Massasoit?

ERRINGTON: Sir, we have full proof that Philip is our foe. Sasamond, the faithful servant of our cause, has been dispatched by Philip's men, set on to murder him. One of his tribe confessed the horrid truth—and will, when time shall call, give horrid proof on't. I say this chieftain is a man of blood, and Heaven will bless the valiant arm that slays him.
METAMORA *enters suddenly and remains at C. When* METAMORA *enters, all start and grasp their swords. The soldiers prepare to fire. All are silent and confused*

METAMORA: You sent for me and I am come. Humph! If you have nothing to say I will go back—if you fear to question, Metamora does not fear to answer.

ERRINGTON: Philip, 'tis thought you love us not, and all unmindful of our league of peace, plot with the Narragansetts, and contrive fatal disorder to our colony.

METAMORA: Do your fears counsel you? What is it makes your old men grave? And your young men grasp their fire weapons as if they awaited the onset of the foe? Brothers, what has Metamora done that doubt is in all your faces and your spirits seem troubled? The good man's heart is a stranger to fear, and his tongue is ready to speak the words of truth.

ERRINGTON: We are informed that thou gavest shelter to a banished man, whose deeds unchristian met our just reproof—one by our holy synod doomed—whom it is said you housed, and thereby hast incurred our church's censure—and given just cause to doubt thy honesty.

METAMORA: Why was that man sent away from the home of his joy? Because the Great Spirit did not speak to him as he had spoken to you? Did you not come across the great waters and leave the smoke of your fathers' hearth because the iron hand was held out against you, and your hearts were sorrowful in the high places of prayer. Why do you that have just plucked the red knife from your own wounded sides, strive to stab your brother?

ERRINGTON: Indian, this is no reply for us. Didst thou not know the sentence of the court on him whom thou didst shelter?

METAMORA: If my rarest enemy had crept unarmed into my wigwam and his heart was sore, I would not have driven him from my fire nor forbidden him to lie down upon my mat. Why then should the Wampanoag shut out the man of peace when he came with tears in his eyes and his limbs torn by the sharp thorns of the thicket? Your great book, you say, tells you to give good gifts to the stranger and deal kindly with him whose heart is sad; the Wampanoag needs no such counselor, for the Great Spirit has with his own fingers written it upon his heart.

MORDAUNT: Why dost thou put arms into thy people's hands, thereby engendering mischief towards us?

METAMORA: If my people do wrong, I am quick to punish. Do you not set a snare for them that they may fall, and make them mad with the fire water the Great Spirit gave you in his wrath? The red man sickens in the house of the palefaces, and the leaping stream of the mountains is made impure by the foul brooks that mingle with it.

SIR ARTHUR: Chieftain, since these things are so, sell us thy lands and seek another biding place.

METAMORA: And if I did, would you not stretch out your hand to seize that also? No! White man, no! Never will Metamora forsake the home of his fathers, and let the plough of the strangers disturb the bones of his kindred.

CHURCH: These are bold words, chief.

METAMORA: They are true ones.

ERRINGTON: They give no token of thy love of peace. We would deal fairly with thee—nay, be generous.

METAMORA: Then would you pay back that which fifty snows ago you received from the hands of my father, Massasoit. Ye had been tossed about like small things upon the face of the great waters, and there was no earth for your feet to rest on; your backs were turned upon the land of your fathers. The red man took you as a little child *and opened the door of his wigwam. The keen blast of the north howled in the leafless wood, but the Indian covered you with his broad right hand and put it back. Your little ones smiled when they heard the loud voice of the storm, for our fires were warm and the Indian was the white man's friend.*

ERRINGTON: Such words are needless now.

METAMORA: I will speak no more; I am going.

Lines between asterisks are reprinted from the Forrest Home manuscript, because they are illegible in the University of Utah manuscript.

MORDAUNT: Hold! A moment, Philip; we have yet to tell of the death of Sasamond, who fell in secret and by treachery.

METAMORA: So should the treacherous man fall, by the keen knife in the darkness and not ascend from the strife of battle to the bright haven where the dead warrior dwells in glory.

ERRINGTON: Didst thou contrive his murder?

METAMORA: I will not answer.

ERRINGTON: We have those can prove thou didst.

METAMORA: I have spoken.

ERRINGTON: Bring in the witness. *(Exit* GOODENOUGH*)* We, too, long have stayed the arm of power from execution. Come, we parley with a serpent and his wiles are deep.

METAMORA: Injurious white man! Do not tread too hard upon the serpent's folds. His fangs are not taken out, nor has its venom lost the power to kill.

ERRINGTON: Approach!

GOODENOUGH *returns with* ANNAWANDAH

METAMORA: Annawandah!

ERRINGTON: Behold, deceitful man, thy deeds are known.

METAMORA: Let me see his eye. Art thou he whom I snatched from the war club of the Mohigan [*sic*], when thou hadst sung thy death song, and the lips of the foe were thirsty for thy blood? Has Metamora cherished thee in his wigwam and hast thou put a knife into the white man's hand to slay him! The foul spirit hath entered thee, and the pure blood of the Wampanoag has left thy veins. Thy heart is a lie, and thine eye cannot rest upon the face of truth, when like the great light it shines on thee in unclouded glory. Elders, can he speak to you the words of truth, when he is false to his brother, his country and his god?

ERRINGTON: He was thy trusty agent, Philip, and conscience-smote revealed thy wickedness.

METAMORA: You believe his words?

ERRINGTON: We do, and will reward his honesty.

METAMORA: Wampanoag! No, I will not call thee so. Red man, say unto these people they have bought thy tongue, and thou hast uttered a lie!

ERRINGTON: He does not answer.

METAMORA: I am Metamora, thy father and thy king.

ERRINGTON: Philip o'erawes him—send the witness home.

METAMORA: I will do that! Slave of the white man, go follow Sasamond.
Stabs ANNAWANDAH, *who staggers off, R. All stand up, general movement*

ERRINGTON: Seize and bind him.
SOLDIERS *make a forward movement*

METAMORA: Come! My knife has drunk the blood of the false one, yet it is not satisfied! White man, beware! The mighty spirits of the Wampanoag race are hovering o'er your heads; they stretch out their shadowy arms to me and ask for vengeance; they shall have it. The wrath of the wronged Indian shall fall upon you like a cataract that dashes the uprooted oak down the mighty chasms. The war whoop shall start you from your dreams at night, and the red hatchet gleam in the blaze of your burning dwellings! From the east to the west, in the north and in the south shall cry of vengeance burst, till the lands you have stolen groan under your feet no more!

ERRINGTON: Secure him!

METAMORA: Thus do I smite your nation and defy your power.

ERRINGTON: Fire on him.
Business. METAMORA *hurls hatchet into stage, and rushes out, C. Soldiers fire after him.* MORDAUNT, *who has moved forward, receives a shot and falls in chair. Tableau. Drums, trumpets, and general confusion. Quick curtain*

A C T   I I I

SCENE 1: *A chamber in* MORDAUNT'S *house. Enter* FITZARNOLD.

FITZARNOLD: Mordaunt wounded, and perhaps to death, struck by a shot that was leveled at the chief; and the fierce storm of war at distance heard, which soon may burst tremendous o'er our heads! This is no place for me. She must be mine tonight! Aye, this night, for fear his death may snatch his gold and daughter from me. Within there, Wolfe! *(Enter WOLFE)* Go get a surgeon for this Mordaunt's wounds, a scribe and priest for me—wilt be silent?

WOLFE: I will observe! Does my lord wed tomorrow?

FITZARNOLD: No, this night; and with tomorrow's sun I spread my sail for England.

WOLFE: Ha!

FITZARNOLD: How now! What meanest thou? Wouldst thou to rival me?

WOLFE: My lord!

FITZARNOLD: Well, well; go see thy duty done. *(Exit)*

WOLFE: My lord, be sure on't. Now for young Walter. I will fulfill my duty but not to thee, my Lord Fitzarnold! Thou wilt not thank me for the priest I'll bring. *(Exit)*

SCENE 2: *An Indian village, deep wood, set wigwam, R. Lights half down. Conch shell heard.* NAHMEOKEE *enters from wigwam.*

NAHMEOKEE: Sure 'twas the shell of Metamora, and spoke the strain it was wont when the old men were called to council, or when the scout returns from his long travel.

METAMORA: *(outside)* Nahmeokee!

NAHMEOKEE: It is—it is Metamora.
Enter METAMORA

METAMORA: Is our little one well, Nahmeokee?

NAHMEOKEE: He is. How didst thou leave the white man with whom thou hast been to hold a talk?

METAMORA: Like the great stream of the mountain when the spirit of the storm passes furiously over its bosom. Where are my people?

NAHMEOKEE: Here in the deep woods where Kaweshine,* the aged priest, tells them the

From this point on, the manuscript reads Kaweshine *instead of the original reading,* Kaneshine.

mighty deeds of their people, and interprets to them the will of the Great Spirit.

METAMORA: Otah! *(OTAH enters)* Summon my warriors; bid them with speed to council. *(Exit OTAH)* I have escaped the swift flight of the white man's bullets but like the bounding elk when the hunters who follow close upon his heels. *(Reenter OTAH with KAWESHINE and all the INDIANS. Indian march, eight bars. Indians form at L.)* Warriors, I took a prisoner from the uplifted weapon of the Mohigan, when the victor's limbs were bloody and the scalps at his belt had no number. He lived in my wigwam; I made him my brother. When the spirit of sleep was upon me, he crept like a guilty thing away, and put into the white man's hand a brand of fire to consume me, and drive my people far away where there are no hunting grounds and where the Wampanoag has no protecting Spirit.

KAWESHINE: Annawandah?

METAMORA: Annawandah!

KAWESHINE: Where is he, chief of thy people, and where is the dog whose head the Great Spirit will smite with fire?

METAMORA: Where the ravenous bird of night may eat the flesh of his body. Here is the blood of the traitor's heart! *(Shows knife)* My people, shall I tell you the thoughts that fill me?

KAWESHINE: Speak, Metamora, speak!

METAMORA: When the strangers came from afar off, they were like a little tree; but now they are grown up and their spreading branches threaten to keep the light from you. They ate of your corn and drank of your cup, and now they lift up their arms against you. Oh my people, the race of the red man has fallen away like the trees of the forest before the axes of the palefaces. The fair places of his father's triumphs hear no more the sound of his footsteps. He moves in the region his proud fathers bequeathed him, not like a lord of the soil, but like a wretch who comes for plunder and for prey.
Distant thunder and lightning

KAWESHINE: The chief has spoken truly and the stranger is worthy to die! But the fire of our warriors is burnt out and their hatchets have no edge. O son of Massasoit, thy words are to me like the warm blood of the foe, and I will drink till I am full! Speak again!

METAMORA: "Chief of the people," said a voice from the deep as I lay by the seaside in the eyes of the moon—"Chief of the people, wake from thy dream of peace, and make sharp the point of thy spear, for the destroyer's arm is made bare to smite. O son of my old age, arise like the tiger in great wrath and snatch thy people from the devourer's jaws!" My father spoke no more; a mist passed before me, and from the mist the Spirit bent his eyes imploringly on me. I started to my feet and shouted the shrill battle cry of the Wampanoags. The high hills sent back the echo, and rock, hill and ocean, earth and air opened their giant throats and cried with me, "Red man, arouse! Freedom! Revenge or death!" *(Thunder and lightning. All quail but* METAMORA*)* Hark, warriors! The Great Spirit hears me and pours forth his mighty voice with mine. Let your voice in battle be like his, and the flash from your fire weapons as quick to kill. Nahmeokee, take this knife, carry it to the Narragansett, to thy brother; tell him the hatchet is dug from the grave where the grass is grown old above it; thy tongue will move him more than the voice of all our tribe in the loud talk of war.

NAHMEOKEE: Nahmeokee will not fail in her path; and her eyes will be quick to see where the stranger has set his snare.

METAMORA: Warriors! Your old and infirm must you send into the country of the Narragansett, that your hearts may not be made soft in the hour of battle.

NAHMEOKEE: Go you tonight, Metamora?

METAMORA: Tonight! I will not lay down in my wigwam till the foe has drawn himself together and comes in his height to destroy. Nahmeokee, I still will be the red man's father and his king, or the sacred rock whereon my father spoke so long the words of wisdom shall be made red with the blood of his race.

Hurried music. METAMORA *and* INDIANS *exeunt.* NAHMEOKEE *goes in wigwam*

SCENE 3: *A chamber in* MORDAUNT'S *house. Clock strikes twelve as scene opens. Thunder distant. Enter* OCEANA *in plain attire.*

OCEANA: I know not how it is but every thunder peal seems to bear words portentous. The moaning blast has meaning in its sound and tells of distant horror—it is the hour when I bade Walter come! Can he have braved the tempest? Hark, I hear a step! *(Knock)* How my heart beats. *(Enter* FITZARNOLD*)* It is—it is Fitzarnold!

FITZARNOLD: Fitzarnold, lady! Why this wonder? Is it fear? Can she whom thunder frights not shrink from me?

OCEANA: My lord, the hour is late; I feign would know who sent thee hither.

FITZARNOLD: Thy honored father.

OCEANA: Thy purpose?

FITZARNOLD: Read it there. *(Gives letter)*

OCEANA: Ha! Tonight! Be thine tonight?

FITZARNOLD: Aye, tonight. I have thy father's secret.

OCEANA: I know thou hast, and in that mean advantage wouldst mar his daughter's happiness forever—away! I blush that thus I parley words with thee—get thee gone. *(Crosses to L.)*

FITZARNOLD: Yes, when thou goest with me; not till then, lady. I will not waste the time that grows more precious every moment to me. *(Thunder)* What though the lightning flash and thunder roll—what though the tempest pours its fury down, Fitzarnold's soul does swell above the din! Nay more, dares brave the storm within thy breast, and shrinks not from the lightning of thine eye.

OCEANA: Would it could kill thee!

FITZARNOLD: It can do more—can conquer like the fiery serpent. It pierces, and as it pierces charms—Oceana!

OCEANA: Stand back! I will alarm my sire.

FITZARNOLD: And if thou dost, he will not aid thee. My treasures are embarked, aye, all but thee; thy father gives consent, the priest waits and ere morning, father, daughter, son, shall all be riding on the wave for England.

OCEANA: No, never!

FITZARNOLD: Convince thyself—*(Stamps his foot. WALTER enters disguised as a priest)* Now, scornful lady, thy bridal hour has come; thy tauntings do but fan the flame that rages here.

OCEANA: Is there no refuge?

FITZARNOLD: None, but in these arms.

OCEANA: No hope—no rescue!

FITZARNOLD: None! None!

OCEANA: Walter, on thee I call—Walter, where art thou?

WALTER: *(throws off disguise)* Walter is here.

FITZARNOLD: Villain! Thy life or mine!

FITZARNOLD draws, OCEANA throws herself between them

OCEANA: Forebear! No blood! *(To WALTER)* Thou must come stainless to these arms.

WALTER: Sayest thou? Wilt thou take me to them?

OCEANA: I will—I do.

They embrace

FITZARNOLD: Thy father's blood be on thee; he is Fitzarnold's victim.

Exit, R. Bell rings. Enter TRAMP, L.

TRAMP: The savages approach! The Wampanoag chieftain and his crew, at distance, peal their startling yell of war! Haste, sir, to meet them.

WALTER: Retire thee for a while, my Oceana—thou, sir, on the instant follow me—your sword! your sword!

Exit, R. with OCEANA, TRAMP follows

SCENE 4: *A view of MORDAUNT'S house on the beach, R. Sea in distance, ship on fire. Garden and staircase leading down to the water. Lights down at opening of scene. Distant yells heard. Enter FITZARNOLD hastily.*

FITZARNOLD: Almighty powers! Hemmed in on every side! No hope. *(War whoop)* Hark to their savage yells! No means are left for flight, for on the waves my precious vessel burns—by the fell savage mastered! No retreat!

War whoops. Exit FITZARNOLD hastily. METAMORA and all the INDIANS enter up staircase entrances. Music hurried, forte till all are on

METAMORA: *(pointing to FITZARNOLD)* Follow him! *(To others)* Go into the white man's dwelling and drag him to me that my eye can look upon his torture and his scalp may tell Metamora's triumph to his tribe—go.

OTAH and KAWESHINE are about to enter the house when OCEANA appears

OCEANA: Forebear, ye shall not enter.

METAMORA: Warriors, have I not spoken.

Throws her around to L., INDIANS go in

OCEANA: Great Chieftain! Dost thou not know me?

METAMORA: I am a Wampanoag in the home of mine enemy; I ride on my wrongs, and vengeance cries out for blood.

OCEANA: Wilt thou not hear me?

METAMORA: Talk to the rattling storm or melt the high rocks with tears; thou canst not move me. My foe! my foe! my foe!

OCEANA: Have mercy, Heaven!

The INDIANS return dragging in MORDAUNT and down R.

METAMORA: Hah!

MORDAUNT: Mercy! Mercy!

OCEANA: My father! Spare my father! *(Rushes to MORDAUNT)*

METAMORA: He must die! Drag him away to the fire of the sacrifice that my ear may drink the music of his dying groans.

OCEANA: Fiends and murderers!

METAMORA: The white man has made us such. Prepare.

Business

OCEANA: Then smite his heart through mine; our mangled breasts shall meet in death—one grave shall hold us. Metamora, dost thou remember this? *(Shows eagle plume)*

METAMORA: Yes.

OCEANA: It was thy father's. Chieftain, thou gavest it to me.

METAMORA: Say on.

OCEANA: Thou saidst it would prove a guardian to me when the conflict raged. Were thy words true when with thy father's tongue thou saidst, whatever being wore the gift, no Indian of thy tribe should do that being harm.

METAMORA: The Wampanoag cannot lie.

OCEANA: Then do I place it here. *(Places it on* MORDAUNT'S *bosom)*

METAMORA: Hah!

OCEANA: The Wampanoag cannot lie, and I can die for him who gave existence to me.

MORDAUNT: My child! My child!

Red fire in house

METAMORA: Take them apart! (INDIANS *separate them)* Old man, I cannot let the tomahawk descend upon thy head, or bear thee to the place of sacrifice; but here is that shall appease the red man's wrath. *(Seizes* OCEANA; *flames seen in house)* The fire is kindled in thy dwelling, and I will plunge her in the hot fury of the flames.

MORDAUNT: No, no, thou wilt not harm her.

OCEANA: Father, farewell! Thy nation, savage, will repent this act of thine.

METAMORA: If thou art just, it will not. Old man, take thy child. *(Throws her to him)* Metamora cannot forth with the maiden of the eagle plume; and he disdains a victim who has no color in his face nor fire in his eye.

Bugle sounds

MORDAUNT: Gracious heavens!

METAMORA: Hark! The power of the white man comes! Launch your canoes! We have drunk blood enough. Spirit of my father, be at rest! Thou art obeyed, thy people are avenged.

Exit hastily followed by the INDIANS. *Drums and trumpet till curtain. Enter* WALTER, GOODENOUGH, CHURCH, SOLDIERS, PEASANTS, *male and female, all from behind house.* SOLDIERS *are about to fire, when* WALTER *throws himself before them and exclaims*

WALTER: Forebear! Forebear!

WALTER and OCEANA embrace. Tableau. Curtain

ACT IV

SCENE 1: *Enter* ERRINGTON—LORD FITZARNOLD—WALTER *and* CHURCH *L. H. A room in* SIR ARTHUR'S *house.*

SIR ARTHUR: Welcome my brother.

ERRINGTON: The strife is over: but the wail of those who mourn some captive friend still wounds the ear and fills our hearts with sadness.

FITZARNOLD: The follower of mine, surprised or else too venturous in the fight, was dragged away in bondage.

SIR ARTHUR: Old Wolfe.

FITZARNOLD: The same—a moody but a faithful man doomed no doubt to torture or to death.

WALTER: Faithful indeed. But not to him thou think'st. *(Aside)*

ERRINGTON: He will avenge the captives fall.

WALTER: But must they fall—is there no way to save them?

ERRINGTON: None young sir unless thy wisdom find it.

WALTER: They might be ransomed.

SIR ARTHUR: True they might. And from my wealth I'll pay whatever price the Indians' power will yield them for.

ERRINGTON: But who so rash to bear such offer unto Philip in his present mood?

FITZARNOLD: *(aside)* Could I but tempt this stripling to his death.

ERRINGTON: Say is there one so reckless and so brave will dare the peril to preserve his fellows?

FITZARNOLD: Grave sirs, I know of none more truly fit than young Walter to achieve the deed. How proud the name required by such an act. How vast the joy his daring heart must feel. Whose arm against such terror shall prevail. And rescue numbers from a lingering death.

WALTER: If my Lord so dearly holds the prize, Why not himself adventure to attain it? But I will go—for I have reasons for it Would move me, felt I not my Lord's great pity for the captives woe.

SIR ARTHUR: Bravely said thou deserve'st our thanks,
And if thou canst persuade the hostile chief
To draw his arm'd bands away and save the blood, that else must flow so terribly.

ERRINGTON: Take swiftest horse young man and Heaven protect thee.

WALTER: No tongue so blest as that which heralds peace—
No heart so mailed as that which beats, warm for his fellow man.

Fare you well. *(Exit* WALTER*)*

ERRINGTON: Now to our labours—those new levies made—
We may exterminate, with one full blow
This savage race, hated of man—unblessed of Heaven—
Surely a land so fair was ne'er designed to feed the heartless infidel.
Cry L. H. "Indians! Indians!"

ERRINGTON: Hah! More massacre! Mercy Heaven!
Enter OCEANA *L. H.*

OCEANA: Oh Sirs shew pity to a captive wretch whom heartless men abuse with taunts and blows. If ye are men oh let the helpless find in you kind pity—mercy and protection.

ERRINGTON: Maiden,
Whom dost thou speak of?

OCEANA: An Indian woman
And her infant child, by these made prisoners.
Look there, they have ta'en her child from her.
Enter NAHMEOKEE *with* OFFICER, *two* GUARDS, *as prisoner.* GOODENOUGH *with the child. L. H.*

ERRINGTON: How now, who hast thou there?

GOODENOUGH: An Indian woman, we captured in the glen.
A spy, 'tis thought sent by the cursed foe.

ERRINGTON: Came she alone?

GOODENOUGH: No, a young and nimble man
Was with her, but he 'scap'd pursuit.
I am sure he is wounded, for I saw him fall.

ERRINGTON: Woman what art thou?

NAHMEOKEE: Give poor woman her child?

ERRINGTON: Dost thou hear my question?

NAHMEOKEE: Give poor Indian woman her child?

OCEANA: Do so.

GOODENOUGH: Why 'twas I that caught the creature—and—

OCEANA: Man didst thou hear me? *(Takes child from him)*

GOODENOUGH: Hard times indeed to lose so good a prize. [The brat is saleable]* Tis mine.

OCEANA: Measureless brute.

GOODENOUGH: For what? Tis only an Indian boy.
OCEANA *gives* NAHMEOKEE *her child, who touch'd with her kindness, takes her scarf to wipe* OCEANA'S *eyes. The latter recognises it to be the one bound round* METAMORA'S *arm in first scene*

OCEANA: Nahmeokee!

NAHMEOKEE: Hush!

ERRINGTON: Who art thou woman?

NAHMEOKEE: I am the servant of the Great Spirit.

ERRINGTON: Who is thy husband?

NAHMEOKEE: One thou dost not love.

ERRINGTON: His name?

NAHMEOKEE: I will not tell thee.

ERRINGTON: We can enforce an answer.

NAHMEOKEE: Poor Indian woman cannot keep her limbs from pain; but she can keep silence.

ERRINGTON: Woman what is thy nation & thy race?

NAHMEOKEE: White man the Sun is my father and the Earth my mother—I will speak no more.

ERRINGTON: Captain take charge of this same stubborn wretch
Who neither will her name nor purpose tell.
If she do prove as alleg'd a spy,
Nothing shall save her from a public death;
We must o'erawe our treacherous foe.
[And this obdurate & blasphemous witch
May in her death, keep death from many more.]*
Summon our Elders—my Lord Fitzarnold
Your counsel now may aid us.

FITZARNOLD: 'Tis thine,—& my poor service.

ERRINGTON: Take her away. *(Cross R.)* Justice is sometimes slow,
Yet is she sure.

*Lined out in the original.

NAHMEOKEE: Thy nation white man, yet may find it so.
   Exeunt ERRINGTON *R. H.* GOODENOUGH, CHURCH, NAHMEOKEE *and* SOLDIERS *L. H.*
OCEANA: Fitzarnold of the Council—could I move His sympathy? *(Approaching him tremblingly)* My lord.
FITZARNOLD: Well lady?
OCEANA: I have offended thee.
FITZARNOLD: I have forgotten it.
OCEANA: I have a boon to ask.
FITZARNOLD: Sayst thou—of me?
OCEANA: It will not cost thee much.
FITZARNOLD: No price too great to purchase thy sweet smiles of thee.
OCEANA: Then be this female's advocate my lord. Thou canst be eloquent and the heart of good, But much misguided men may by thy speech Be moved to pity and to pardon her.
FITZARNOLD: How so—a wandering wretch unknown?
OCEANA: Metamora has helpless prisoners.
FITZARNOLD: 'Tis true—and thou dost deeply feel for them.
   Young Walter now seeks their enfranchisement.
OCEANA: I know it sir. *(Aside)* Be still my throbbing heart.
   My lord what vengeance will her husband take. Think you will aught appease dread Philip's wrath—
   When he is told—chieftain thy wife's a slave?
FITZARNOLD: His wife—the Queen! Indeed! Dost say so?
OCEANA: Give not the secret unto mortal ear— It might destroy all hopes of unity.
   Preserve this captive from impending doom And countless prayers shall pay thee for it.
FITZARNOLD: Thy kind approval is reward enough.
OCEANA: Shall she be saved?
FITZARNOLD: She shall be free—a word of mine can do it.
OCEANA: Thanks! Thanks! My Lord deceive me not.
FITZARNOLD: Fear not fair Lady. I have pledged my word.

Exit OCEANA *L. H.*
FITZARNOLD: Thou thinks't me kind—ha! ha! I will be so. Philip has
   Captives—& young Walter's there.
   The Council dare not take this woman's life for that would doom their captive countrymen. Imprisoned she is free from danger for the law protects her. But turn her loose to the wild fury of the senseless crowd *she dies* ere justice or the Elder's arms can reach her. Ah! This way conducts me straight to the goal. I am resolved to reach and seal at once my hated rival's doom.
   [Oh! I will plead as Angels do in Heaven For mortals when they err and mourn for it.]*
   Her freedom is her death—the zealot crowd Will rush upon her like the loosen'd winds And prove as merciless—while the lion husband,
   Madden'd with his loss, sheds blood to surfeiting.
   Oh yes, dear pleader for the captive one Thy boon is granted. She shall be free! *(Exit R. H.)*

SCENE 2: *One-half dark. An Indian Retreat.* WOLFE *bound to the Stake R. H.* METAMORA *at a distance leaning on his rifle.* KANESHINE† *& WARRIORS. Lights one-half down.*

KANESHINE: Warriors, our enemies have been met, and the blood of the Stranger has sunk deep into the sand—yet the spirit of those who have fallen by the power of the foe are not yet appeas'd—prepare the captives for their hour of death. Come round the tree of sacrifice and lift up the flame, till it devour in its fiery rage, the abhor'd usurpers *(Gun L. H.)* of the red man's soil! Come my lips are dry for the captive's blood.
   As they are about to fire the pile, a shot is heard. Enter WALTER

*Lined out in the original.
†The Lord Chamberlain's copy uses the original spelling.

METAMORA: Hold! Let the young man say why he comes into our country unbidden. Why does he tempt the ire of our warriors, when their weapons are red with the blood of the battle?

WALTER: That I come friendly let this emblem speak.
To check the dire advance of bloody war,
To urge the Wampanoags to disarm his band
And once again renew with us the bond
That made the white and red man brothers.

METAMORA: No, young man, the blood my warriors have tasted, has made their hearts glad and their hands are thrust out for more. Let the white man fear. The arrow he has shot into the mountain has turned back and pierced his own side. What are the Elder's words?

WALTER: Let Philip take our wampum and our coin
Restore his captives and remove his dead
And rest from causeless and destructive war,
Until such terms of lasting peace are made
As shall forever quell our angry feuds
And sink the hatchet to be raised no more.

METAMORA: *Humph!* And meanwhile he sharpens his long weapons in secret, and each day grows more numerous. When the great stream of the mountains first springs from the earth it is very weak, and I can stand up against its waters, but when the great rain descends, it is swift and swollen, death dwells in its white bosom and it will not spare.

WALTER: By Him who moves the stars and lights the Sun,
If thou dost shed the trembling captive's blood,
A thousand warlike men will rush to arms
And terribly avenge their countryman.

METAMORA: Well, let them come! Our arms are as strong as the white man's. And the use of the fire-weapon he has taught us. My ears are shut against thee.

WALTER: *(TO WOLFE):* Oh, my friend! I will achieve thy rescue if gold or prayers can move them.

WOLFE: I was prepared to die, and only mourned
For I am childless and a lonely man.
I had not told the secret of thy birth.
And shewn thy father to thee.

WALTER: My Father! Sayst thou?

WOLFE: Walter, listen to me.

OTAH: *(speaks without)* Metamora!

METAMORA: Ha! *(Enter OTAH)*

OTAH: Nahmeokee!

METAMORA: Dead!

OTAH: Our feet grew weary in the path, and we sate down to rest in the dark wood—the fire-weapons blazed in the thicket, and my arm was wounded, with the other I grasped the keen knife you gave Nahmeokee, but I sank down powerless and the white men bore off the queen a captive.

METAMORA: *Humph*—Nahmeokee is the white man's prisoner. Where is thy horse?

WALTER: Beneath yonder tree.

METAMORA: Unbind the captive! Young man! You must abide with the Wampanoag till Nahmeokee returns to her home. Woe unto you if the hard hand has been laid upon her. Take the white man to my wigwam.

WALTER: I thank thee Chieftain, this is kindness to me. Come good Wolfe tell me my father's name.

METAMORA: If one drop fall from Nahmeokee's eye, one hair from her head, the axe shall hew your quivering limbs asunder and the ashes of your bones be carried away on the rushing winds. Come old man.
Exeunt

SCENE 3: *Enter FITZARNOLD.*

FITZARNOLD: Nahmeokee now is free, and the fanatic herd all cry aloud, "Oh mad rulers! Mercy to her"—she comes—and witch, hag and Indian din her ears. They come this way—I must avoid their clamor. *(Enter NAHMEOKEE)*

NAHMEOKEE: Let them not kill the poor Indian women.

FITZARNOLD: Woman away.

NAHMEOKEE: They will murder my child.

FITZARNOLD: Hold off—I cannot help thee. *(Exit FITZARNOLD)*

NAHMEOKEE: They come upon me from every side of the path. My limbs can bear me no farther. Mercy! Hah! They have missed my track and seek in the wood, and in the caves for my blood. Who is he that rides a swift horse there, through the narrow path way of the glen! The shade of the coming night is over him and he dimly appears a red man riding the swift cloud. *(Shouts)* Ha, they have traced me by the white garment, the brambles tore from me in my flight. They come. Cling to me my child. Cling to thy mother's bosom. *(Enter* GOODENOUGH *and 4* PEASANTS*)*

GOODENOUGH: Foul Indian witch thy race is run. Drag her to the lake. Take her child from her. *(Enter* METAMORA*)*

METAMORA: Stand back! or the swift death shall take wing. Which of you has lived too long? Let him lift up his arm against her.

OFFICER: How is this? King Philip ventures here? What comest thou for?

METAMORA: Boy! Thou art a child, there is no mark of the war upon thee. Send me thy Elder, or thy Chief. I'll make my talk to him.

GOODENOUGH: Here comes Master Errington. *(Enter* ERRINGTON *&* SOLDIERS*)*

ERRINGTON: Philip a Prisoner!

METAMORA: No! He has arms in his hand and courage in his heart, he comes near you of his own will, and when he has done his work, he'll go back to his wigwam.

ERRINGTON: Indian, you answer boldly.

METAMORA: What is there I should fear?

ERRINGTON: Savage! The wrath of him who hates the Heathen and the man of blood.

METAMORA: Does he love mercy; and is he the white man's friend?

ERRINGTON: Yes.

METAMORA: How did Nahmeokee and her infant wrong you, that you hunted her through the thorny pathway of the glen, and scented her blood like the fierce red wolf in his hunger?

CHURCH: Why hold parley with him! Call our musqueteers and bear them both to trial and to doom. Heaven smiles on us—Philip in our power. His cursed followers would sue for peace.

METAMORA: Not till the blood of twenty English captives be poured out as a sacrifice. Elders beware, the knife is sharpened—the stake is fixed—and the captive's limbs tremble under the burning gaze of the prophet of wrath. Woe come to them when my people shall hear their chief has been slain by the pale faces or is bound in the dark place of doom.

NAHMEOKEE: Do not tempt them Metamora, they are many like the leaves of the forest and we are but as two lone trees standing in their midst.

METAMORA: Which can easier escape the hunter's spear? The tiger that turns on it in his wrath, or the lamb that sinks down and trembles? Thou has seen me look unmoved at a torturing death—shall mine eye be turned downward when the white man frowns?

ERRINGTON: Philip, the peace our young man offered thee. Didst thou regard his words?

METAMORA: Yes.

ERRINGTON: And wilt thou yield compliance?

METAMORA: I will. Nahmeokee shall bear the tidings to my people that the prisoners may return to their homes, and the war-whoop shall not go forth on the evening gale.

ERRINGTON: Let her set forth. Friends let me advise you,

    Keep the Chieftain prisoner, let's muster men.

    And in unlook'd for hour with one blow we will overwhelm

    This accursed race. And furthermore— *(Converses apart)*

NAHMEOKEE: *(to* METAMORA*)* I will remember thy words.

METAMORA: Grieve not that I linger in the dark place of the condemned, for the eye of the Great Spirit will be on me there.

ERRINGTON: We greet thee Philip and accept thy love. Nahmeokee may return.

METAMORA: 'Tis very good. The horse stands neath the brow of the hill—speak not—I read thy thought in thy eye. Go—go. Nahmeokee. I am ready to follow you.

ERRINGTON: Conduct him forth to prison. *(*SOLDIERS *attempt to take his gun)*

METAMORA: No! This shall be to me as my child and I will talk to it, until I go back to my people.

GOODENOUGH: Right well conceived, could it but talk.

METAMORA: It can—when the land of my great fore-fathers is trampled on by the foot of the foe—or when treachery lurks round the Wampanoag, while he bides in the white man's home.

ACT V

SCENE 1: *Same as Act I, Scene 1. Lights down.* OCEANA *discovered leaning against tomb. Slow music, four bars.*

OCEANA: Tomb of the silent dead, thou seemest my only refuge! O Walter, where art thou? Alas! the kindly promptings of thy noble heart have led thee to captivity, perhaps to death! Welcome the hour when these dark portals shall unfold again, and reunite parent and child in the long sleep of death. *(Enter* FITZARNOLD*)* Ah! Fitzarnold here!

FITZARNOLD: I come with words of comfort to thee and feign would soothe thy sorrow.

OCEANA: I do not ask your sympathy, my lord.

FITZARNOLD: A sea of danger is around thee, lady, and I would be the skillful pilot to guide thy struggling bark to safety.

OCEANA: Nay, but let me rather perish in the waves than reach a haven to be shared with thee.

FITZARNOLD: Thou hast no choice; thy father willed thee mine, and with his latest breath bequeathed thee to me. Walter, my stripling rival in thy love, has left thee here defenseless and alone. I deem as nothing thy unnatural hate, and only see thy fair and lovely form; and though thy flashing eyes were armed with lightning, thus would my arms enfold thee.

OCEANA: *(clings to tomb)* Now, if thou darest, approach me—now whilst with my mother's spirit hovering o'er me—whilst thus with tearful eyes and breaking heart I call on Heaven to blast the bold audacious wretch, who seeks a daughter's ruin o'er her parent's grave.

FITZARNOLD: Aye, despite of all.

METAMORA: *(in tomb)* Hold! Touch her not!

OCEANA: Hark to that voice! Kind Heaven has heard my prayers.

The door of the tomb opens, and METAMORA *appears.* OCEANA *faints and falls*

FITZARNOLD: Philip here!

METAMORA: He is the Great Spirit [who?] has sent me;* the ghosts are waiting for thee in the dark place of doom! Now thou must go. Tremble, for the loud cry is terrible and the blaze of their eyes, like the red fire of war, gleams awfully in the night.

FITZARNOLD: I have not wronged thee.

METAMORA: Not? Didst thou not contrive the death of Nahmeokee, when the treacherous white man thirsted for her blood? Did she not with bended knees, her eyes streaming with woes of the heart, catch hold of thy shining broad garment thinking it covered man? Was not thy hand upraised against her, and thy heart, like thy hand, flint that wounds the weary one who rests upon it?

FITZARNOLD: No! no!

METAMORA: I saw thee when my quick step was on the hills, and the joy of Metamora's eyes felt thy blows. I feel them now! "Revenge!" cried the shadow of my father as he looked on with me. I, too, cried revenge and now I have it! The blood of my heart grows hotter as I look on him who smote the red cheek of Nahmeokee.

FITZARNOLD: As reparation I will give thee gold.

METAMORA: No! Give me back the happy days, the fair hunting ground, and the dominion my great forefathers bequeathed me.

FITZARNOLD: I have not robbed thee of them.

METAMORA: Thou art a white man, and thy veins hold the blood of a robber! Hark! The spirits of the air howl for thee! Prepare—*(Throws him around to R.)*

This is the actual reading of the manuscript. A more plausible reading would probably be: "He is. The Great Spirit has sent me."

FITZARNOLD: Thou shalt not conquer ere thou killest me. This sword a royal hand bestowed! This arm can wield it still.
Draws; METAMORA *disarms and kills him*
METAMORA: Metamora's arm has saved thee from a common death; who dies by me dies nobly! *(Turns to* OCEANA*)* For thee, Metamora's home shall screen thee from the spreading fury of his nation's wrath.
Hurry till change. Exit bearing OCEANA

SCENE 2: *A chamber. Enter* SIR ARTHUR, *meeting* ERRINGTON *and* CHURCH.

SIR ARTHUR: I have news will startle you.
ERRINGTON: Is't of the chief?
SIR ARTHUR: It is; he has escaped our power!
ERRINGTON: Escaped! Confusion! How?
SIR ARTHUR: But now we sought his prison and found it tenantless.
ERRINGTON: But how escaped he? There was no egress thence, unless some treacherous hand unlocked the door.
SIR ARTHUR: And so we thought, at first; but on minute search we found some stones displaced, which showed a narrow opening into a subterranean passage, dark and deep, through which we crept until, to our surprise, we reached the tomb of Mordaunt.
ERRINGTON: The tomb of Mordaunt?
SIR ARTHUR: The ruined pile which now serves as our prison was, years since, when first he sought these shores, the residence of Mordaunt, and this secret passage, doubtless, was formed by him for concealment or escape in time of danger.
ERRINGTON: Indeed!
SIR ARTHUR: Yes, and he had cause to be so guarded, for once, unseen by him, I heard that wretched man commune with Heaven, and sue for pardon for the heinous sin of Hammond of Harrington!
ERRINGTON: Hammond! The outlawed regicide?
SIR ARTHUR: Even so; it was himself he prayed for, the guilty man who gave to death the king, his lord, the royal martyr Charles. As Mordaunt, he here sought refuge from the wrath of the rightful heir now seated on the throne.
ERRINGTON: Think you the chieftain knew this secret way?
SIR ARTHUR: 'Tis likely that he did, or else by chance discovered it and thus has won his freedom and his life.
CHURCH: We must summon our men. Double the guard and have their range extended.
Exeunt CHURCH *and* ERRINGTON
WOLFE: *(without)* Where is Sir Arthur Vaughan?
SIR ARTHUR: Who calls? *(Enter* WOLFE*)* Now, who art thou?
WOLFE: A supplicant for pardon.
SIR ARTHUR: Pardon—for what?
WOLFE: A grievous sin, I now would feign confess.
SIR ARTHUR: Indeed! Go on! Declare it then; I will forgive thee!
WOLFE: Long years have passed since then, but you must still remember when at Naples with your wife and child.
SIR ARTHUR: Ha! Dost thou mean—
WOLFE: The flames consumed thy dwelling and thou together with thy wife and boy, escaped almost by miracle.
SIR ARTHUR: Ha!
WOLFE: I there looked on midst the assembled throng, a stranger mariner. Urged by the fiend, and aided by the wild confusion of the scene, I snatched your boy and through the noisy throng I bore him to my anchored bark, thinking his waiting parents soon would claim with gold their darling. Next day came on a tempest and the furious winds far from the city drove us and thy child.
SIR ARTHUR: Heavens! Can this be true?
WOLFE: He grew up the sharer of my sea-born perils. One awful night our vessel stuck upon the rocks near these shores and the greedy ocean swelled over her shattered frame—thy son—
SIR ARTHUR: Go on—go on—
WOLFE: Was by mysterious power preserved and guided to his unconscious father. Walter is thy son.

SIR ARTHUR: Man! Why didst thou not tell me?

WOLFE: I feared thy just anger and the force of law. I became Fitzarnold's follower but to this hour has memory tortured me.

SIR ARTHUR: And Walter is a hostage to the savage foe; perchance they have murdered him!

WOLFE: No! Oceana's kindness to the Indian queen has purchased his freedom and my own.

SIR ARTHUR: Where is he?

WOLFE: Looking for her he loves, fair Oceana! Whom 'tis said, a party of the foe carried off.

SIR ARTHUR: Quick, let us arm and follow him. For thee, this act of justice pardons thee.
Exeunt

SCENE 3: *Indian village.* GROUPS OF INDIANS. KAWESHINE *and* OTAH *discovered.* KAWESHINE *has been addressing them. His looks are gloomy and bewildered.*

METAMORA: *(outside, at change of scene)* Where are my people?

KAWESHINE: Ha! 'Tis our chief—I know the sound of his voice, and some quick danger follows him.
METAMORA *enters, bearing* OCEANA. NAHMEOKEE *enters from wigwam*

METAMORA: Nahmeokee, take the white maiden in; I would speak to my people; go in and follow not the track of the warrior's band.

NAHMEOKEE: Come in, my mat is soft, and the juice of the sweet berry shall give joy to thy lips. Come in, thou art pale and yielding, like the lily, when it is borne down by the running waters.
She leads OCEANA *into wigwam*

METAMORA: Warriors, I have escaped from the hands of the white man, when the fire was kindled to devour me. Prepare for the approaching hour if ye love the high places your fathers trod in majesty and strength. Snatch your keen weapons and follow me! If ye love the silent spots where the bones of your kindred repose, sing the dread song of war and follow me! If you love the bright lakes which the Great Spirit gave you when the sun first blazed with the fires of his touch, shout the war song of the Wampanoag race, and on to the battle follow me! Look at the bright glory that is wrapped like a mantle around the slain in battle! Call on the happy spirits of the warriors dead, and cry, "Our lands! Our nation's freedom! Or the grave!"

KAWESHINE: O chieftain, take my counsel and hold out to the palefaces the pipe of peace. Ayantic and the great Mohigan join with our foes against us, and the power of our brother, the Narragansett is no more! List, o chieftain, to the words that I tell of the time to come.

METAMORA: Ha! Dost thou prophesy?

KAWESHINE: In the deep wood, when the moon shone bright, my spirit was sad and I sought the ear of Manito in the sacred places; I heard the sound as of one in pain, and I beheld gasping under a hemlock, the lightning had sometime torn, a panther wounded and dying in his thick red gore. I thought of the tales of our forefathers who told us that such was an omen of coming evil. I spoke loudly the name of Metamora, and the monster's eyes closed instantly and he writhed no more. I turned and mourned, for I said, Manito loves no more the Wampanoag and our foes will prevail.

METAMORA: Didst thou tell my people this?

KAWESHINE: Chieftain, yes; my spirit was troubled.

METAMORA: Shame of the tribe, thou art no Wampanoag, thy blood is tainted—thou art half Mohigan, thy breath has sapped the courage of my warriors' hearts. Begone, old man, thy life is in danger.

KAWESHINE: I have spoken the words of truth, and the Great Manito has heard them.

METAMORA: Liar and coward! Let him preserve thee now!
About to stab him when NAHMEOKEE *enters from wigwam and interposes*

NAHMEOKEE: He is a poor old man—he healed the deep wound of our little one. (*Gets to L. of* METAMORA)

METAMORA: Any breast but Nahmeokee's had felt the keen edge of my knife! Go, corrupted one, thy presence makes the air unwholesome round hope's high places. Begone!

KAWESHINE: Metamora drives me from the wigwam before the lightning descends to set it on fire. Chieftain, beware the omen. (*Exit*)

NAHMEOKEE: (*aside*) Will he not become the white man's friend and show him the secret path of our warriors? Manito guard the Wampanoag!

METAMORA: Men of Po-hon-e-ket, the palefaces come towards your dwellings and no warrior's hatchet is raised for vengeance. The war whoop is hushed in the camp and we hear no more the triumph of battle. Manito hates you, for you have fallen from the high path of your fathers and Metamora must alone avenge the Wampanoag's wrongs.

OMNES: Battle! Battle!

METAMORA: Ha! The flame springs up afresh in your bosoms; a woman's breath has brought back the lost treasure of your souls. (*Distant march, drums and trumpet heard*) Ha! they come! Go, warriors, and meet them, and remember the eye of a thousand ages looks upon you. (WARRIORS *exeunt silently*) Nahmeokee, should the palefaces o'ercome our strength, go thou with our infant to the sacred place of safety. My followers slain, there will the last of the Wampanoags pour out his heart's blood on the giant rock, his father's throne.

NAHMEOKEE: O Metamora!

METAMORA: Come not near me or thou wilt make my heart soft, when I would have it hard like the iron and gifted with many lives. Go in, Nahmeokee. (*Distant trumpets.* NAHMEOKEE *goes in wigwam.* METAMORA *kneels*) The knee that never bent to man I bend to thee, Manito. As the arm was broken that was put out against Nahmeokee, so break thou the strength of the oppressor's nation, and hurl them down from the high hill of their pride and power, with the loud thunder of thy voice. Confound them—smite them with the lightning of thine eye—while thus I bare my red war arm—while thus I wait the onset of the foe—(*Loud alarm*) They come! Death! Death, or my nation's freedom! *Rushes off. Loud shouts. Drums and trumpets till change*

SCENE 4: *Rocky pass. Trumpet sounds retreat. Enter* ERRINGTON *and* CHURCH.

ERRINGTON: They fly! They fly—the field is ours! This blow destroys them. Victory cheaply bought at twice our loss; the red man's power is broken now forever. (*Enter* WALTER) Is Oceana slain?

WALTER: No; the chieftain Metamora rescued her from the base passions of the Lord Fitzarnold whom Metamora slew to avenge the wrongs he offered to his wife, and Oceana by the chief was borne in safety to his lodge.

ERRINGTON: In safety?

WALTER: Yes; from the hands of Nahmeokee I received her, just as some Indians maddened by defeat, prepared to offer her a sacrifice.

ERRINGTON: Away then, Walter. (WALTER *crosses to R.*) Sir Arthur now seeks thee out to claim thee as his own son. [*sic.*]

WALTER: My father! I fly to seek him. (*Exit*)

ERRINGTON: The victory is ours; yet while Philip lives we are in peril! Come, let us find this Indian prophet whom Metamora banished from his tribe. He may be bribed to show us the chieftain's place of safety. *Exeunt. Change*

SCENE 5: METAMORA'S *stronghold. Rocks, bridge and waterfall.* NAHMEOKEE *discovered listening. The child lays under a tree, R., covered with furs. Slow music, four bars.*

NAHMEOKEE: He comes not, yet the sound of the battle has died away like the last breath of a storm! Can he be slain? O cruel white man, this day will stain your name forever.

Slow music, sixteen bars. METAMORA *enters on bridge. Crosses and enters L.*

METAMORA: Nahmeokee, I am weary of the strife of blood. Where is our little one? Let me take him to my burning heart and he may quell its mighty torrent.

NAHMEOKEE: *(With broken utterance)* He is here!

(Lifts the furs and shows the child dead)

METAMORA: Ha! Dead! Dead! Cold!

NAHMEOKEE: Nahmeokee could not cover him with her body, for the white men were around her and over her. I plunged into the stream and the unseen shafts of the fire weapons flew with a great noise over my head. One smote my babe and he sunk into the deep water; the foe shouted with a mighty shout, for he thought Nahmeokee and her babe had sunk to rise no more.

METAMORA: His little arms will never clasp thee more; his little lips will never press the pure bosom which nourished him so long! Well, is he not happy? Better to die by the stranger's hand than live his slave.

NAHMEOKEE: O Metamora! *(Falls on his neck)*

METAMORA: Nay, do not bow down thy head; let me kiss off the hot drops that are running down thy red cheeks. Thou wilt see him again in the peaceful land of spirits, and he will look smilingly as—as—as I do now, Nahmeokee.

NAHMEOKEE: Metamora, is our nation dead? Are we alone in the land of our fathers?

METAMORA: The palefaces are all around us, and they tread in blood. The blaze of our burning wigwams flashes awfully in the darkness of their path. We are destroyed—not vanquished; we are no more, yet we are forever—Nahmeokee.

NAHMEOKEE: What wouldst thou?

METAMORA: Dost thou not fear the power of the white man?

NAHMEOKEE: No.

METAMORA: He may come hither in his might and slay thee.

NAHMEOKEE: Thou art with me.

METAMORA: He may seize thee, and bear thee off to the far country, bind these arms that have so often clasped me in the dear embrace of love, scourge thy soft flesh in the hour of his wrath, and force thee to carry burdens like the beasts of the fields.

NAHMEOKEE: Thou wilt not let them.

METAMORA: We cannot fly, for the foe is all about us; we cannot fight, for this is the only weapon I have saved from the strife of blood.

NAHMEOKEE: It was my brother's—Coanchett's.

METAMORA: It has tasted the white man's blood, and reached the cold heart of the traitor; it has been our truest friend: it is our only treasure.

NAHMEOKEE: Thine eye tells me the thought of thy heart, and I rejoice at it. *(Sinks on his bosom)*

METAMORA: Nahmeokee, I look up through the long path of thin air, and I think I see our infant borne onward to the land of the happy, where the fair hunting grounds know no storms or snows, and where the immortal brave feast in the eyes of the giver of good. Look upwards, Nahmeokee, the spirit of thy murdered father beckons thee.

NAHMEOKEE: I will go to him.

METAMORA: Embrace me, Nahmeokee—'twas like the first you gave me in the days of our strength and joy—they are gone. *(Places his ear to the ground)* Hark! In the distant wood I faintly hear the cautious tread of men! They are upon us. Nahmeokee—the home of the happy is made ready for thee. *(Stabs her, she dies)* She felt no white man's bondage—free as the air she lived—pure as the snow she died! In smiles she died! Let me taste it, ere her lips are cold as the ice.

Loud shouts. Roll of drums. KAWESHINE *leads* CHURCH *and* SOLDIERS *on bridge, R.*

CHURCH: He is found! Philip is our prisoner.

METAMORA: No! He lives—last of his race—but still your enemy—lives to defy you still. Though numbers overpower me and treachery surround

me, though friends desert me, I defy you still!
Come to me—come singly to me! And this true
knife that has tasted the foul blood of your nation and now is red with the purest of mine, will
feel a grasp as strong as when it flashed in the
blaze of your burning dwellings, or was lifted
terribly over the fallen in battle.

CHURCH: Fire upon him!

METAMORA: Do so, I am weary of the world for ye
are dwellers in it; I would not turn upon my
heel to save my life.

CHURCH: Your duty, soldiers.

They fire. METAMORA *falls. Enter* WALTER,
OCEANA, WOLFE, SIR ARTHUR, ERRINGTON,
GOODENOUGH, TRAMP, *and* PEASANTS. *Roll of
drums and trumpet till all on*

METAMORA: My curses on you, white men! May
the Great Spirit curse you when he speaks in
his war voice from the clouds! Murderers! The
last of the Wampanoags' curse be on you! May
your graves and the graves of your children be
in the path the red man shall trace! And may
the wolf and panther howl o'er your fleshless
bones, fit banquet for the destroyers! Spirits of
the grave, I come! But the curse of Metamora
stays with the white man! I die! My wife! My
Queen! My Nahmeokee!

*Falls and dies; a tableau is formed. Drums and
trumpet sound a retreat till curtain. Slow curtain*

EPILOGUE

Written by Mr James Lawson.
Spoken by Mrs Hilson, New Park Theater.
New York, December 15, 1829.

Before this bar of beauty, taste, and wit,
This host of critics, too, who throng the pit,
A trembling bard has been this night
    arraigned;
And I am counsel in the cause retained.
Here come I, then, to plead with nature's art,
And speak, less to the law, than to the heart.
    A native bard—a native actor too,

Have drawn a native picture to your view;
In fancy, this bade Indian wrongs arise,
While that embodied all before your eyes;
Inspired by genius, and by judgment led,
Again the Wampanoag fought and bled;
Rich plants are both of our own fruitful land,
Your smiles the sun that made their leaves
    expand;
Yet, not that they are native do I plead,
'Tis for their worth alone I ask your meed.
How shall I ask ye? Singly? Then I will—
But should I fail? Fail! I must try my skill.
    Sir, I know you—I've often seen your face;
And always seated in that selfsame place;
Now, in my ear—what think you of our play?
That it has merit truly, he did say;
And that the hero, prop'd on genius' wing,
The Indian forest scoured, like Indian king!
    See that fair maid, the tear still in her eye,
And hark! hear not you now that gentle sigh?
Ah! these speak more than language could
    relate,
The woe-fraught heart o'er Nahmeokee's fate;
She scans us not by rigid rules of art,
Her test is feeling, and her judge the heart.
    What dost thou say, thou bushy-whiskered
    beau?
He nods approval—whiskers are the go.
    Who is he sits the fourth bench from the
    stage?
There; in the pit!—why he looks wondrous
    sage!
He seems displeased, his lip denotes a
    sneer—
O! he's a critic that looks so severe!
Why, in his face I see the attic salt—
A critic's merit is to find a fault.
What fault find you, sir? eh! or you, sir?
    None!
Then, if the critic's mute, my cause is won.
Yea, by that burst of loud heartfelt applause,
I feel that I have gained my client's cause.
Thanks, that our strong demerits you forgive,
And bid our bard and Metamora live.

FASHION; OR, LIFE IN NEW YORK (1845)

It is that rare thing, a social satire based on real knowledge of the life it depicts, but painting it without bitterness, without nastiness, and without affectation.

Arthur Hobson Quinn's assessment of *Fashion; or, Life in New York* is typical of critical response to the play since its premier at New York's Park Theatre on March 24, 1845. Generally witty dialogue, well-conceived characters, and a brisk comic action have consistently enthralled audiences and made the play one of the most often revived of nineteenth-century American comedies. Even those with distinctly different aesthetic orientations have recognized the play's charms. For example, one of the most successful ventures in the 1924–1925 season of the reconstituted Provincetown Players, led by the triumvirate of Robert Edmond Jones, Kenneth Macgowan, and Eugene O'Neill, was the 235-performance run of *Fashion*. But, while the play's comedic appeals are clear, it is perhaps unwise to restrict too readily the play's significance to its status as the best American **comedy of manners** of the nineteenth century. *Fashion* is certainly a comedy of manners, but it is much more than that. As an artifact of a particular woman writer's career, the play's history provides an entrée to the world of women playwrights on the early American stage. And, understood within its original cultural context, *Fashion* also reveals the class tensions that resided just below the surface of antebellum America as well as one of the mechanisms of control being deployed by the remnants of patriciate in the face of a growing emphasis on acquisition within American society during this period.

Given the social conventions of the day, Anna Cora Ogden seems at first blush one of the women least likely to enter upon a theatrical career. Born into a wealthy and genteel American family in Bordeaux, France in 1819, she spent her earliest years happily among her 16 siblings. Her father, a successful merchant, and her mother, the granddaughter of a signer of the Declaration of Independence, encouraged their children in amateur theatrical activities, and *Fashion*'s author recounts in her *Autobiography of an Actress* (1854) that one of her earliest memories is of debuting (at four years old) as a judge in a French-language version of *Othello* produced for her father's birthday. The family returned to New York in 1825 and she entered boarding school. At 13, she found herself the object of the affections of James Mowatt, a lawyer and family friend. Mowatt proposed marriage when she turned 14, and although her family was not averse to Mowatt's suit, they insisted that Anna Cora delay her marriage until she was 17. In 1834, unable to resist Mowatt's continuing entreaties, she secretly married him. She was 15.

Soon reconciled with her family, Anna Cora Mowatt enjoyed a life of ease as the wife of a successful lawyer, highlighted by elaborate parties, concerts, and private theatricals in the family home. But her life was not without its challenges, especially frequent sickness. Her writing career began, almost by chance, as a diversion during a bout of tuberculosis when she composed a long romantic poem, *Pelayo, or The Cavern of Covadonga* (later published under the pseudonym "Isabel"). When her health declined again in 1837, she went abroad, traveling in England, Germany, and France for three years. After a year in Europe, she was joined by her husband, whose vision had deteriorated to such an extent that he could no longer follow his profession. Soon after their return in 1840, James Mowatt informed his wife that his speculations had bankrupted the family. Determined to aid in the situation, she embarked upon a series of dramatic readings. In an era in which the Lyceum circuit made household names of the scientist Louis Agassiz and the early fighter for women's rights Frances Wright and amplified the influence of the philosopher–poet Ralph Waldo Emerson and the orator Daniel Webster, Anna Cora Mowatt found fame and a small fortune giving readings of such works as Scott's *The Lay of the Last Minstrel*. She augmented this income by writing stories and sketches under various names for popular magazines of the day, including *Ladies' Companion*, *Goodey's*, and *Graham's*. Eventually, she was prevailed upon to write a play for public presentation (she had already composed at least two for private theatricals), and *Fashion* was born.

Having survived the falling away of friends who considered her venture into public life an unpardonable breach of upper-class decorum, having become more intimately acquainted with the actual theatrical operations through her work with the cast of *Fashion*, and having recognized what she later asserted in her autobiography as Providence's plan for her life, Anna Cora Mowatt entered upon a career as an actress, debuting on June 13, 1845, at New York's Park Theatre as Pauline in Edward Bulwer-Lytton's *The Lady of Lyons*. For the next nine years, except for episodes of illness and a brief period after James Mowatt's death in 1851, she pursued her career to general applause. In June 1854, shortly after her triumphal farewell tour, she married William F. Ritchie, the editor of the Richmond *Enquirer*. The marriage was apparently not a happy one and after 1860 she lived alone abroad, dying in England on July 28, 1870.

On one level, *Fashion* is a descendent of Tyler's *The Contrast* and another in a long line of comedies of manners. As a manners comedy, *Fashion*'s primary subjects are the social mores of New York's upper class and the absurdity that arises when the Tiffany family tries to utilize social forms they do not understand to become part of what Mrs Tiffany tellingly calls the "ee-light." Combining the outlandish fashion consciousness of such Restoration fops as Sir George Etherege's Sir Fopling Flutter with the language-mangling ability of Richard Brinsley Sheridan's Mrs Malaprop, Mrs Tiffany is a masterful reworking of manners comedy character conventions. But as a former upstate New York milliner, she is sufficiently American to serve as the perfect lightning rod for Mowatt's localized satire. Beyond the rich comedy that flows from Mrs Tiffany's atrocious attempts to be one of the beau monde, Mowatt seems to be using her play to broach a social and economic question of some import for members of her class, a question which is particularly adeptly addressed by manners comedy.

The action of a traditional manners comedy distinguishes between those who ape the social mores of fashionable society in an inevitably vain attempt to obtain admission to that group and those for whom their manners are signs simultaneously of their position and of the ideology which undergirds that status. Though writers of sentimental comedy had to a degree shifted the ideological foundation of the privileged class from an older witty, hereditary aristocracy to a new elite of feeling, manners comedy's assumption remained that society was ordered hierarchically. For Americans, one of whose most cherished myths was the equality of all men, such a hierarchy was potentially troubling. Even if classes existed in society, any stage representation of society had to justify carefully the existence of classes and the bases of their distinctions. Mowatt's play does just that, for it is a particularly complex response to an ideological contest between an older social formation, represented by Trueman, and an emerging one embodied in Mrs Tiffany, Snobson, and the ersatz Count Jolimaitre.

But, ultimately, this is a play about not only the possible supplanting of one economic group by another, but also the potential substitution of one set of values by another. In the vicious production-consumption cycle that has turned Mr Tiffany's "flesh into dollars and mortgaged . . . [his] soul in the bargain" in order that Mrs Tiffany can foolishly indulge her search for the "jenny-says-quoi" in all her material possessions, the new acquisitive economic model finds expression. In the Tiffanys' willingness to sell their daughter either to silence the blackmailing Snobson or gain a title, Mowatt suggests a newly sanctioned variety of economic prostitution. As Daniel Havens has noted, the world of *Fashion* is "the ugly image of the American-dream-gone-sour. It is a decadent extreme of the Jacksonian promise."

The choices presented by the play could hardly have escaped the first night audience's notice. Eric Wollencott Barnes, Anna Cora Mowatt's biographer, observes that unlike the middle-class and business-class crowds which regularly frequented the Park Theatre on a typical night, *Fashion*'s opening night crowd was "composed almost exclusively of people of education and taste" and of "the litterati." Although Edgar Allan Poe, in his review for *The Broadway Journal,* could entertain the idea that Mowatt had moved beyond the typical subject of the comedy of manners to satirize fashion *as* fashion, the fact remains that her most obvious targets are those whose economic, social, political, and moral shortcomings seem, in Mowatt's view, to preclude them from assuming leadership of the country. This is not a play that attacks social stratification, but one that seeks widespread endorsement of the proposition that the demarcations as currently constituted between classes must and should exist. Strategically, this is not a play that seeks positively to justify the bases of Adam Trueman comic heroism. Rather, *Fashion* anatomizes the alternative presented in the Tiffany crowd and leaves the audience to draw its own conclusion. By ridiculing the ineptitudes of the Tiffanys and by eventually securing the removal of the Tiffany women to the countryside, Mowatt's play metaphorically reestablishes the clear boundaries between the worlds of high society and business, allowing them to mingle in the commercial sphere while preserving the deferential social order valued by an older social formation.

Given the continuing social flux that permeated American society in the 1840s and 1850s, it is easy to understand the theatrical impact of the play. As Walter Meserve has noted, the success of *Fashion* and Mowatt's own popularity as an actress initiated a series of comedies taking New York City life of one class or another as their subjects. In a sense all the comedies that followed *Fashion* tried to attain the same goal—to present the tensions underlying American society and to seek a new accommodation between the older order and new alternatives. To the extent that they have succeeded, we have been able to see both ourselves and our fellow citizens more clearly.

WORKS CONSULTED

Barnes, Eric Wollencott. *The Lady of Fashion: The Life and Theatre of Anna Cora Mowatt.* New York: Charles Scribner's Sons, 1954.

Havens, Daniel F. *The Columbian Muse of Comedy: The Development of a Native Tradition in Early American Comedy, 1787–1845.* Carbondale: Southern Illinois University Press, 1973.

Meserve, Walter J. "Social Awareness of Stage: 1850–1859." *The American Stage: Social and Economic Issues from the Colonial Period to the Present.* Eds. Ron Engle and Tice L. Miller. Cambridge: Cambridge University Press, 1993, 81–100.

Mowatt, Anna Cora. *Autobiography of an Actress: or, Eight Years on the Stage.* Boston: Ticknor and Fields, 1854.

Poe, Edgar Allan. "Mrs. Mowatt's Comedy Reconsidered." *The American Theatre as Seen by Its Critics, 1752–1934.* Eds. Montrose J. Moses and John Mason Brown. New York: Norton, 1934. 63–66.

Quinn, Arthur Hobson. *A History of the American Drama: From the Beginning to the Civil War.* 2nd ed. New York: Crofts, 1944.

CHARACTERS

ACT FIRST

SCENE 1: *A splendid Drawing Room in the House of* MRS TIFFANY. *Open folding doors, discovering a Conservatory. On either side glass windows down to the ground. Doors on right and left. Mirror, couches, ottomans, a table with albums, beside it an arm chair.* MILLINETTE *dusting furniture.* ZEKE *in a dashing livery, scarlet coat.*

ZEKE: Dere's a coat to take de eyes ob all Broadway! Ah! Missy, it am de fixin's dat make de natural *born* gemman. A libery for ever! Dere's a pair ob insuppressibles to 'stonish de colored population.

MILLINETTE: Oh, *oui*, Monsieur Zeke. *(Very politely)* I not *comprend* one word he say! *(Aside)*

ZEKE: I tell 'ee what, Missy, I'm 'stordinary glad to find dis a bery 'spectabul like situation! Now, as you've made de acquaintance ob dis here family, and dere you've had a supernumerary advantage ob me—seeing dat I only receibed my appointment dis morning.

What I wants to know is your publicated opinion, privately expressed, ob de domestic circle.

MILLINETTE: You mean vat *espèce*, vat kind of personnes are Monsieur and Madame Tiffany? Ah! Monsieur is not de same ting as Madame,—not at all.

ZEKE: Well, I s'pose he ain't altogether.

MILLINETTE: Monsieur is man of business,—Madame is lady of fashion. Monsieur make de money,—Madame spend it. Monsieur nobody at all,—Madame everybody altogether. Ah! Monsieur Zeke, de money is all dat is *necessaire* in dis country to make one lady of fashion. Oh! it is quite anoder ting in *la belle France!*

ZEKE: A bery lucifer explanation. Well, now we've disposed ob de heads ob de family, who come next?

MILLINETTE: First, dere is Mademoiselle Seraphina Tiffany. Mademoiselle is not at all one proper *personne*. Mademoiselle Seraphina is one coquette. Dat is not de mode in *la belle France*; de ladies, dere, never learn *la coquetrie* until dey do get one husband.

ZEKE: I tell 'ee what, Missy, I disreprobate dat proceeding altogeder!

MILLINETTE: Vait! I have not tell you all *la famille* yet. Dere is Ma'mselle Prudence—Madame's sister, one very *bizarre* personne. Den dere is Ma'mselle Gertrude, but she not anybody at all; she only teach Mademoiselle Seraphina *la musique*.

ZEKE: Well now, Missy, what 's your own special defunctions?

MILLINETTE: I not understand, Monsieur Zeke.

ZEKE: Den I'll amplify. What 's de nature ob your exclusive services?

MILLINETTE: *Ah, oui! je comprend.* I am Madame's *femme de chambre*—her lady's maid, Monsieur Zeke. I teach Madame *les modes de Paris*, and Madame set de fashion for all New York. You see, Monsieur Zeke, dat it is me, *moi-même,* dat do lead de fashion for all de American *beau monde!*

ZEKE: Yah! yah! yah! I hab de idea by de heel. Well now, p'raps you can 'lustrify my officials?

MILLINETTE: Vat you will have to do? Oh! much tings, much tings. You vait on de table,—you tend de door,—you clean de boots,—you run de errands,—you drive de carriage,—you rub de horses,—you take care of de flowers,—you carry de water,—you help cook de dinner,—you wash de dishes,—and den you always remember to do everything I tell you to!

ZEKE: Wheugh, am dat *all?*

MILLINETTE: All I can tink of now. To-day is Madame's day of reception, and all her grand friends do make her one *petite* visit. You mind run fast ven de bell do ring.

ZEKE: Run? If it was n't for dese superfluminous trimmings, I tell 'ee what, Missy, I'd run—

MRS TIFFANY: *(outside)* Millinette!

MILLINETTE: Here comes Madame! You better go, Monsieur Zeke.

ZEKE: Look ahea, Massa Zeke, does n't dis open rich! *(Aside)*   *(Exit* ZEKE)
(Enter MRS TIFFANY, *dressed in the most extravagant height of fashion)*

MRS TIFFANY: Is everything in order, Millinette? Ah! very elegant, very elegant, indeed! There is a *jenny-says-quoi* look about this furniture,—an air of fashion and gentility perfectly bewitching. Is there not, Millinette?

MILLINETTE: Oh, *oui* , Madame!

MRS TIFFANY: But where is Miss Seraphina? It is twelve o'clock; our visitors will be pouring in, and she has not made her appearance. But I hear that nothing is more fashionable than to keep people waiting.—None but vulgar persons pay any attention to punctuality. Is it not so, Millinette?

MILLINETTE: Quite *comme il faut.*—Great personnes always do make little personnes wait, Madame.

MRS TIFFANY: This mode of receiving visitors only upon one specified day of the week is a most convenient custom! It saves the trouble of keeping the house continually in order and of being always dressed. I flatter myself that *I* was the first to introduce it amongst the New York *ee-light.* You are quite sure that it is strictly a Parisian mode, Millinette?

MILLINETTE: Oh, *oui*, Madame; entirely *mode de Paris.*

MRS TIFFANY: This girl is worth her weight in gold. *(Aside)* Millinette, how do you say *arm-chair* in French?

MILLINETTE: *Fauteuil,* Madame.

MRS TIFFANY: *Fo-tool!* That has a foreign—an out-of-the-wayish sound that is perfectly charming—and so genteel! There is something about our American words decidedly vulgar. *Fowtool!* how refined. *Fowtool! Arm-chair!* what a difference!

MILLINETTE: Madame have one charmante pronunciation. *Fowtool (mimicking aside)* charmante, Madame!

MRS TIFFANY: Do you think so, Millinette? Well, I believe I have. But a woman of refinement and of fashion can always accommodate herself to everything foreign! And a week's study of that invaluable work—"*French without a Master,*" has made me quite at home in the court language of Europe! But where is the new valet?

I'm rather sorry that he is black, but to obtain a white American for a domestic is almost impossible; and they call this a free country! What did you say was the name of this new servant, Millinette?

MILLINETTE: He do say his name is Monsieur Zeke.

MRS TIFFANY: Ezekiel, I suppose. Zeke! Dear me, such a vulgar name will compromise the dignity of the whole family. Can you not suggest something more aristocratic, Millinette? Something *French!*

MILLINETTE: *Oh, oui,* Madame; *Adolph* is one very fine name.

MRS TIFFANY: A-dolph! Charming! Ring the bell, Millinette! (MILLINETTE *rings the bell*) I will change his name immediately, besides giving him a few directions.
(*Enter* ZEKE. MRS TIFFANY *addresses him with great dignity*)
Your name, I hear, is *Ezekiel.*—I consider it too plebeian an appellation to be uttered in my presence. In future you are called A-dolph. Don't reply,—never interrupt me when I am speaking. A-dolph, as my guests arrive, I desire that you will inquire the name of every person, and then announce it in a loud, clear tone. That is the fashion in Paris. (MILLINETTE *retires up the stage*)

ZEKE: Consider de office discharged, Missus. (*Speaking very loudly*)

MRS TIFFANY: Silence! Your business is to obey and not to talk.

ZEKE: I 'm dumb, Missus!

MRS TIFFANY: (*pointing up stage*) A-dolph, place that *fowtool* behind me.

ZEKE: (*looking about him*) I hab n't got dat far in de dictionary yet. No matter, a genus gets his learning by nature. (*Takes up the table and places it behind* MRS TIFFANY, *then expresses in dumb show great satisfaction.* MRS TIFFANY, *as she goes to sit, discovers the mistake*)

MRS TIFFANY: You dolt! Where have you lived not to know that *fow-tool* is the French for *armchair?* What ignorance! Leave the room this instant. (MRS TIFFANY *draws forward an armchair and sits.* MILLINETTE *comes forward suppressing her merriment at* ZEKE'S *mistake and removes the table*)

ZEKE: Dem 's de defects ob not having a libery education.   (*Exit*)
(PRUDENCE *peeps in*)

PRUDENCE: I wonder if any of the fine folks have come yet. Not a soul,—I knew they had n't. There 's Betsy all alone. (*Walks in*) Sister Betsy!

MRS TIFFANY: Prudence! how many times have I desired you to call me *Elizabeth? Betsy* is the height of vulgarity.

PRUDENCE: Oh! I forgot. Dear me, how spruce we do look here, to be sure,—everything in first rate style now, Betsy. (MRS TIFFANY *looks at her angrily*) *Elizabeth,* I mean. Who would have thought, when you and I were sitting behind that little mahogany-colored counter, in Canal Street, making up flashy hats and caps—

MRS TIFFANY: Prudence, *what do* you mean? Millinette, leave the room.

MILLINETTE: *Oui,* Madame. (MILLINETTE *pretends to arrange the books upon a side table, but lingers to listen*)

PRUDENCE: But I always predicted it,—I always told you so, Betsy,—I always said you were destined to rise above your station!

MRS TIFFANY: Prudence! Prudence! have I not told you that—

PRUDENCE: No, Betsy, it was *I* that told *you,* when we used to buy our silks and ribbons of Mr Antony Tiffany—"*talking Tony,*" you know we used to call him, and when you always put on the finest bonnet in our shop to go to his,—and when you staid so long smiling and chattering with him, I always told you that *something* would grow out of it—and didn't it?

MRS TIFFANY: Millinette, send Seraphina here instantly. Leave the room.

MILLINETTE: *Oui,* Madame. So dis Americaine ladi of fashion vas one *milliner?* Oh, vat a fine country for *les marchandes des modes!* I shall send for all my relation by de next packet! (*Aside*) (*Exit* MILLINETTE)

MRS TIFFANY: Prudence! never let me hear you mention this subject again. Forget what we *have* been, it is enough to remember that we *are* of the *upper ten thousand!* (PRUDENCE *goes up and sits down*)

(*Enter* SERAPHINA, *very extravagantly dressed*)

MRS TIFFANY: How bewitchingly you look, my dear! Does Millinette say that that head dress is strictly Parisian?

SERAPHINA: Oh, yes, Mamma, all the rage! They call it a *lady's tarpaulin,* and it is the exact pattern of one worn by the Princess Clementina at the last court ball.

MRS TIFFANY: Now, Seraphina, my dear, don't be too particular in your attentions to gentlemen not eligible. There is Count Jolimaitre, decidedly the most fashionable foreigner in town,—and so refined,—so much accustomed to associate with the first nobility in his own country that he can hardly tolerate the vulgarity of Americans in general. You may devote yourself to him. Mrs Proudacre is dying to become acquainted with him. By the by, if she or her daughters should happen to drop in, be sure you don't introduce them to the Count. It is not the fashion in Paris to introduce—Millinette told me so.

(*Enter* ZEKE)

ZEKE: (*in a very loud voice*) Mister T. Tennyson Twinkle!

MRS TIFFANY: Show him up.   (*Exit* ZEKE)

PRUDENCE: I must be running away!   (*Going*)

MRS TIFFANY: Mr T. Tennyson Twinkle—a very literary young man and a sweet poet! It is all the rage to patronize poets! Quick, Seraphina, hand me that magazine.—Mr Twinkle writes for it. (SERAPHINA *hands the magazine,* MRS TIFFANY *seats herself in an arm-chair and opens the book*)

PRUDENCE: (*returning*) There 's Betsy trying to make out that reading without her spectacles. (*Takes a pair of spectacles out of her pocket and hands them to* MRS TIFFANY) There, Betsy, I knew you were going to ask for them. Ah! they're a blessing when one is growing old!

MRS TIFFANY: What do you mean, Prudence? A woman of fashion *never* grows old! Age is always out of fashion.

PRUDENCE: Oh, dear! what a delightful thing it is to be fashionable. (*Exit* PRUDENCE. MRS TIFFANY *resumes her seat*)

(*Enter* TWINKLE. *He salutes* SERAPHINA)

TWINKLE: Fair Seraphina! the sun itself grows dim,

Unless you aid his light and shine on him!

SERAPHINA: Ah! Mr Twinkle, there is no such thing as answering you.

TWINKLE: (*looks around and perceives* MRS TIFFANY) The "New Monthly Vernal Galaxy." Reading my verses by all that's charming! Sensible woman! I won't interrupt her. (*Aside*)

MRS TIFFANY: (*rising and coming forward*) Ah! Mr Twinkle, is that you? I was perfectly *abimé* at the perusal of your very *distingué* verses.

TWINKLE: I am overwhelmed, Madam. Permit me. (*Taking the magazine*) Yes, they do read tolerably. And you must take into consideration, ladies, the rapidity with which they were written. Four minutes and a half by the stop watch! The true test of a poet is the *velocity* with which he composes. Really they do look very prettily, and they read tolerably,—*quite* tolerably—*very* tolerably,—especially the first verse. (*Reads*) "To Seraphina T——."

SERAPHINA: Oh! Mr Twinkle!

TWINKLE: (*reads*) "Around my heart"—

MRS TIFFANY: How touching! Really, Mr Twinkle, quite tender!

TWINKLE: (*recommencing*) "Around my heart"—

MRS TIFFANY: Oh, I must tell you, Mr Twinkle! I heard the other day that poets were the aristocrats of literature. That's one reason I like them, for I do dote on all aristocracy!

TWINKLE: Oh, Madam, how flattering! Now pray lend me your ears!   (*Reads*) "Around my heart thou weavest"—

SERAPHINA: That is such a *sweet* commencement, Mr Twinkle!

TWINKLE: (*aside*) I wish she would n't interrupt me! (*Reads*) "Around my heart thou weavest a spell"—

MRS TIFFANY: Beautiful! But excuse me one moment, while I say a word to Seraphina! Don't

be too affable, my dear! Poets are very ornamental appendages to the drawing room, but
they are always as poor as their own verses.
They don't make eligible husbands! *(Aside to*
Seraphina*)*

TWINKLE: Confound their interruptions! *(Aside)*
My dear Madam, unless you pay the utmost at-
tention you cannot catch the ideas. Are you
ready? Well, now you shall hear it to the end!
(Reads)
"Around my heart thou weavest a spell
"Whose"—
(Enter ZEKE*)*

ZEKE: Mister Augustus Fogg! A bery misty lookin
young gemman? *(Aside)*

MRS TIFFANY: Show him up, Adolph!! *(Exit* ZEKE*)*

TWINKLE: This is too much!

SERAPHINA: Exquisite verses, Mr Twinkle,—
exquisite!

TWINKLE: Ah, lovely Seraphina! your smile of approval transports me to the summit of Olympus.

SERAPHINA: Then I must frown, for I would not
send you so far away.

TWINKLE: Enchantress! It's all over with her.
(Aside)   *(Retire up and converse)*

MRS TIFFANY: Mr Fogg belongs to one of our oldest families,—to be sure he is the most difficult person in the world to entertain, for he
never takes the trouble to talk, and never notices anything or anybody,—but then I hear
that nothing is considered so vulgar as to betray any emotion, or to attempt to render oneself agreeable!
(Enter MR FOGG, *fashionably attired but in*
very dark clothes)

FOGG: *(bowing stiffly)* Mrs Tiffany, your most
obedient. Miss Seraphina, yours. How d' ye do,
Twinkle?

MRS TIFFANY: Mr Fogg, how do you do? Fine
weather,—delightful, is n't it?

FOGG: I am indifferent to weather, Madam.

MRS TIFFANY: Been to the opera, Mr Fogg? I hear
that the *bow monde* make their *debutt* there every evening.

FOGG: I consider operas a bore, Madam.

SERAPHINA: *(advancing)* You must hear Mr Twinkle's verses, Mr Fogg!

FOGG: I am indifferent to verses, Miss Seraphina.

SERAPHINA: But Mr Twinkle's verses are addressed to me!

TWINKLE: Now pay attention, Fogg! *(Reads)*—
"Around my heart thou weavest a spell
"Whose magic I"—
(Enter ZEKE*)*

ZEKE: Mister—No, he say he ain't no Mister—

TWINKLE: "Around my heart thou weavest a spell
"Whose magic I can never tell!"

MRS TIFFANY: Speak in a loud, clear tone, A-dolph!

TWINKLE: This is terrible!

ZEKE: Mister Count Jolly-made-her!

MRS TIFFANY: Count Jolimaitre! Good gracious!
Zeke, Zeke—A-dolph I mean,—Dear me, what
a mistake! *(Aside)* Set that chair out of the
way,—put that table back. Seraphina, my dear,
are you all in order? Dear me! dear me! Your
dress is so tumbled! *(Arranges her dress)* What
are you grinning at? *(To* ZEKE*)* Beg the Count to
honor us by walking up!   *(Exit* ZEKE*)*
     Seraphina, my dear *(aside to her)*, remem-
ber now what I told you about the Count. He is
a man of the highest,—good gracious! I am so
flurried; and nothing is so ungenteel as agitation! what will the Count think! Mr Twinkle,
pray stand out of the way! Seraphina, my dear,
place yourself on my right! Mr Fogg, the conservatory—beautiful flowers,—pray amuse
yourself in the conservatory.

FOGG: I am indifferent to flowers, Madam.

MRS TIFFANY: Dear me! the man stands right in
the way,—just where the Count must make his
entray! *(Aside)* Mr Fogg,—pray—
(Enter COUNT JOLIMAITRE, *very dashingly*
dressed, wears a moustache)

MRS TIFFANY: Oh, Count, this unexpected honor—

SERAPHINA: Count, this inexpressible pleasure—

COUNT: Beg you won't mention it, Madam! Miss
Seraphina, your most devoted!   *(Crosses)*

MRS TIFFANY: What condescension! *(Aside)* Count,
may I take the liberty to introduce—Good gracious! I forgot. *(Aside)* Count, I was about to

remark that we never introduce in America. All our fashions are foreign, Count. (TWINKLE, *who has stepped forward to be introduced, shows great indignation*)

COUNT: Excuse me, Madam, our fashions have grown antediluvian before you Americans discover their existence. You are lamentably behind the age—lamentably! 'Pon my honor, a foreigner of refinement finds great difficulty in existing in this provincial atmosphere.

MRS TIFFANY: How dreadful, Count! I am very much concerned. If there is anything which I can do, Count—

SERAPHINA: Or I, Count, to render your situation less deplorable—

COUNT: Ah! I find but one redeeming charm in America—the superlative loveliness of the feminine portion of creation,—and the wealth of their obliging papas. *(Aside)*

MRS TIFFANY: How flattering! Ah! Count, I am afraid you will turn the head of my simple girl here. She is a perfect child of nature, Count.

COUNT: Very possibly, for though you American women are quite charming, yet, demme, there's a deal of native rust to rub off!

MRS TIFFANY: *Rust?* Good gracious, Count! where do you find any rust? *(Looking about the room)*

COUNT: How very unsophisticated!

MRS TIFFANY: Count, I am so much ashamed,—pray excuse me! Although a lady of large fortune, and one, Count, who can boast of the highest connections, I blush to confess that I have never travelled,—while you, Count, I presume are at home in all the courts of Europe.

COUNT: *Courts?* Eh? Oh, yes, Madam, very true. I believe I am pretty well known in some of the courts of Europe—*police courts. (Aside, crossing)* In a word, Madam, I had seen enough of civilized life—wanted to refresh myself by a sight of barbarous countries and customs—had my choice between the Sandwich Islands and New York—chose New York!

MRS TIFFANY: How complimentary to our country! And, Count, I have no doubt you speak every conceivable language? You talk English like a native.

COUNT: Eh, what? Like a native? Oh, ah, demme, yes, I am something of an Englishman. Passed one year and eight months with the Duke of Wellington, six months with Lord Brougham, two and a half with Count d'Orsay—knew them all more intimately than their best friends—no heroes to me—had n't a secret from me, I assure,—*especially of the toilet. (Aside)*

MRS TIFFANY: Think of that, my dear! Lord Wellington and Duke Broom! *(Aside to* SERAPHINA*)*

SERAPHINA: And only think of Count d'Orsay, Mamma! *(Aside to* MRS TIFFANY*)* I am so wild to see Count d'Orsay!

COUNT: Oh! a mere man milliner. Very little refinement out of Paris! Why, at the very last dinner given at Lord—Lord Knowswho, would you believe it, Madam, there was an individual present who wore a *black* cravat and took *soup twice!*

MRS TIFFANY: How shocking! the sight of him would have spoilt my appetite! Think what a great man he must be, my dear, to despise lords and counts in that way. *(Aside to* SERAPHINA*)* I must leave them together. *(Aside)* Mr Twinkle, your arm. I have some really very *foreign exotics* to show you.

TWINKLE: I fly at your command. I wish all her exotics were blooming in their native soil! *(Aside, and glancing at the* COUNT*)*

MRS TIFFANY: Mr Fogg, will you accompany us? My conservatory is well worthy a visit. It cost an immense sum of money.

FOGG: I am indifferent to conservatories, Madam; flowers are such a bore!

MRS TIFFANY: I shall take no refusal. Conservatories are all the rage,—I could not exist without mine! Let me show you,—let me show you. *(Places her arm through* MR FOGG'S, *without his consent. Exeunt* MRS TIFFANY, FOGG, *and* TWINKLE *into the conservatory, where they are seen walking about)*

SERAPHINA: America, then, has no charms for you, Count?

COUNT: Excuse me,—some exceptions. I find you, for instance, particularly charming! Can't say

I admire your country. Ah! if you had ever breathed the exhilarating air of Paris, ate creams at Tortoni's, dined at the Café Royale, or if you had lived in London—felt at home at St. James's, and every afternoon driven a couple of Lords and a Duchess through Hyde Park, you would find America—where you have no kings, queens, lords, nor ladies—insupportable!

SERAPHINA: Not while there was a Count in it? *(Enter* ZEKE, *very indignant)*

ZEKE: Where's de Missus? *(Enter* MRS TIFFANY, FOGG, *and* TWINKLE, *from the conservatory)*

MRS TIFFANY: Whom do you come to announce, A-dolph?

ZEKE: He said he would n't trust me—no, not eben wid so much as his name; so I would n't trust him up stairs, den he ups wid *his stick* and I *cuts mine.*

MRS TIFFANY: Some of Mr Tiffany's vulgar acquaintances. I shall die with shame. *(Aside)* A-dolph, inform him that I am *not at home. (Exit* ZEKE*)*

My nerves are so shattered, I am ready to sink. Mr Twinkle, that *fow tool*, if you please!

TWINKLE: What? What do you wish, Madam?

MRS TIFFANY: The ignorance of these Americans! *(Aside)* Count, may I trouble you? That *fow tool*, if you please!

COUNT: She's not talking English, nor French, but I suppose it's American. *(Aside)*

TRUEMAN: *(outside)* Not at home!

ZEKE: No, Sar—Missus say she's not at home.

TRUEMAN: Out of the way, you grinning nigger! *(Enter* ADAM TRUEMAN, *dressed as a farmer, a stout cane in his hand, his boots covered with dust.* ZEKE *jumps out of his way as he enters)*   *(Exit* ZEKE*)*

TRUEMAN: Where 's this woman that's not *at home* in her own house? May I be shot! if I wonder at it! I should n't think she'd ever feel *at home* in such a showbox as this! *(Looking round)*

MRS TIFFANY: What a plebeian looking old farmer! I wonder who he is? *(Aside)* Sir—*(advancing very agitatedly)* what do you mean, Sir, by this *ow*dacious conduct? How dare you intrude yourself into my parlor? Do you know who I am,

Sir? *(With great dignity)* You are in the presence of Mrs Tiffany, Sir!

TRUEMAN: Antony's wife, eh? Well now, I might have guessed that—ha! ha! ha! for I see you make it a point to carry half your husband's shop upon your back! No matter; that's being a good helpmate—for he carried the whole of it once in a pack on his own shoulders—now you bear a share!

MRS TIFFANY: How dare you, you impertinent, *ow*dacious, ignorant old man! It's all an invention. You're talking of somebody else. What will the Count think! *(Aside)*

TRUEMAN: Why, I thought folks had better manners in the city! This is a civil welcome for your husband's old friend, and after my coming all the way from Catteraugus to see you and yours! First a grinning nigger tricked out in scarlet regimentals—

MRS TIFFANY: Let me tell you, Sir, that liveries are all the fashion!

TRUEMAN: The fashion, are they? To make men wear the *badge of servitude* in a free land,—that's the fashion, is it? Hurrah, for republican simplicity! I will venture to say now, that you have your coat of arms too!

MRS TIFFANY: Certainly, Sir; you can see it on the panels of my *voyture.*

TRUEMAN: Oh! no need of that. I know what your escutcheon must be! A bandbox *rampant* with a bonnet *couchant*, and a peddler's pack *passant!* Ha, ha, ha! that shows both houses united!

MRS TIFFANY: Sir! you are most profoundly ignorant,—what do you mean by this insolence, Sir? How shall I get rid of him? *(Aside)*

TRUEMAN: *(looking at* SERAPHINA*)* I hope that is not Gertrude! *(Aside)*

MRS TIFFANY: Sir, I'd have you know that—Seraphina, my child, walk with the gentlemen into the conservatory. *(Exeunt* SERAPHINA, TWINKLE, FOGG *into conservatory)* Count Jolimaitre, pray make due allowances for the errors of this rustic! I do assure you, Count—*(Whispers to him)*

TRUEMAN: Count! She calls that critter with a shoe brush over his mouth, Count! To look at him, I should have thought he was a tailor's walking advertisement! *(Aside)*

COUNT: *(addressing* TRUEMAN, *whom he has been inspecting through his eyeglass)* Where did you say you belonged, my friend? Dug out of the ruins of Pompeii, eh?

TRUEMAN: I belong to a land in which I rejoice to find that you are a foreigner.

COUNT: What a barbarian! He doesn 't see the honor I'm doing his country! Pray, Madam, is it one of the aboriginal inhabitants of the soil? To what tribe of Indians does he belong—the Pawnee or Choctaw? Does he carry a tomahawk?

TRUEMAN: Something quite as useful,—do you see that? *(Shaking his stick)* (COUNT *runs behind* MRS TIFFANY)

MRS TIFFANY: Oh, dear! I shall faint! Millinette! *(Approaching)* Millinette!
(Enter MILLINETTE *without advancing into the room)*

MILLINETTE: *Oui,* Madame.

MRS TIFFANY: A glass of water! *(Exit* MILLINETTE*)* Sir, *(crossing to* TRUEMAN*)* I am shocked at your plebeian conduct! 'Tis a gentleman of the highest standing, Sir! He is a *Count,* Sir!
(Enter MILLINETTE, *bearing a salver with a glass of water. In advancing towards* MRS TIFFANY, *she passes in front of the* COUNT, *starts and screams. The* COUNT, *after a start of surprise, regains his composure, plays with his eyeglass, and looks perfectly unconcerned)*

MRS TIFFANY: What is the matter? What *is* the matter?

MILLINETTE: Noting, noting,—only— *(Looks at* COUNT *and turns away her eyes again)* only— noting at all!

TRUEMAN: Don't be afraid, girl! Why, did you never see a live Count before? He's tame;—I dare say your mistress there leads him about by the ears.

MRS TIFFANY: This is too much! Millinette, send for Mr Tiffany instantly! *(Crosses to* MILLINETTE, *who is going)*

MILLINETTE: He just come in, Madame!

TRUEMAN: My old friend! Where is he? Take me to him,—I long to have one more hearty shake of the hand!

MRS TIFFANY: *(crosses to him)* Count, honor me by joining my daughter in the conservatory, I will return immediately. (COUNT *bows and walks towards conservatory,* MRS TIFFANY *following part of the way and then returning to* TRUEMAN*)*

TRUEMAN: What a Jezebel! These women always play the very devil with a man, and yet I don't believe such a damaged bale of goods as *that (looking at* MRS TIFFANY*)* has smothered the heart of little Antony!

MRS TIFFANY: This way, Sir, sal vous plait. *(Exit with great dignity)*

TRUEMAN: *Sal vous plait.* Ha, ha, ha! We'll see what Fashion has done for him. *(Exit)*

END OF ACT FIRST

ACT SECOND

SCENE 1: *Inner apartment of* MR TIFFANY'S *Counting House.* MR TIFFANY, *seated at a desk looking over papers.* MR SNOBSON, *on a high stool at another desk, with a pen behind his ear.*

SNOBSON: *(rising, advances to the front of the stage, regards* TIFFANY *and shrugs his shoulders)* How the old boy frets and fumes over those papers, to be sure! He's working himself into a perfect fever—exactly,—therefore *bleeding's* the prescription! So here goes! *(Aside)* Mr Tiffany, a word with you, if you please, Sir?

MR TIFFANY: *(sitting still)* Speak on, Mr Snobson, I attend.

SNOBSON: What I have to say, Sir, is a matter of the first importance to the credit of the concern—the *credit* of the concern, Mr Tiffany!

MR TIFFANY: Proceed, Mr Snobson.

SNOBSON: Sir, you've a handsome house—fine carriage—nigger in livery—feed on the fat of the land—everything first rate—

MR TIFFANY: Well, Sir?

SNOBSON: My salary, Mr Tiffany!

MR TIFFANY: It has been raised three times within the last year.

SNOBSON: Still it is insufficient for the necessities of an honest man,—mark me, an *honest* man, Mr Tiffany.

MR TIFFANY: *(crossing)* What a weapon he has made of that word! *(Aside)* Enough—another hundred shall be added. Does that content you?

SNOBSON: There is one other subject, which I have before mentioned, Mr Tiffany,—your daughter,—what's the reason you can't let the folks at home know at once that I'm to be *the man?*

MR TIFFANY: Villain! And must the only seal upon this scoundrel's lips be placed there by the hand of my daughter? *(Aside)* Well, Sir, it shall be as you desire.

SNOBSON: And Mrs Tiffany shall be informed of your resolution?

MR TIFFANY: Yes.

SNOBSON: Enough said! That's the ticket! The CREDIT *of the concern's safe*, Sir!   *(Returns to his seat)*

MR TIFFANY: How low have I bowed to this insolent rascal! To rise himself he mounts upon my shoulders, and unless I can shake him off he must crush me! *(Aside)*
(Enter TRUEMAN*)*

TRUEMAN: Here I am, Antony, man! I told you I'd pay you a visit in your money-making quarters. *(Looks around)* But it looks as dismal here as a cell in the States' prison!

MR TIFFANY: *(forcing a laugh)* Ha, ha, ha! States' prison! You are so facetious! Ha, ha, ha!

TRUEMAN: Well, for the life of me I can't see anything so amusing in that! I should think the States' prison plaguy uncomfortable lodgings. And you laugh, man, as though you fancied yourself there already.

MR TIFFANY: Ha, ha, ha!

TRUEMAN: *(imitating him)* Ha, ha, ha! What on earth do you mean by that ill-sounding laugh, that has nothing of a laugh about it! This

fashion-worship has made heathens and hypocrites of you all! *Deception* is your household God! A man laughs as if he were crying, and cries as if he were laughing in his sleeve. Everything is something else from what it seems to be. I have lived in your house only three days, and I've heard more lies than were ever invented during a Presidential election! First your fine lady of a wife sends me word that she's not at home—I walk up stairs, and she takes good care that *I* shall not be *at home*—wants to turn me out of doors. Then *you* come in—take your old friend by the hand—whisper, the deuce knows what, in your wife's ear, and the tables are turned in a tangent! Madam curtsies—says she's enchanted to see me—and orders her grinning nigger to show me a room.

MR TIFFANY: We were exceedingly happy to welcome you as our guest!

TRUEMAN: Happy? *You* happy? Ah, Antony! Antony! that hatchet face of yours, and those criss-cross furrows tell quite another story! It's many a long day since you were *happy* at anything! You look as if you'd melted down your flesh into dollars, and mortgaged your soul in the bargain! Your warm heart has grown cold over your ledger—your light spirits heavy with calculation! You have traded away your youth—your hopes—your tastes, for wealth! and now you *have* the wealth you coveted, what does it profit you? Pleasure it cannot buy; for you have lost your *capacity* for enjoyment—Ease it will not bring; for the love of gain is never satisfied! It has made your counting house a penitentiary, and your home a fashionable *museum* where there is no niche for you! You have spent so much time *ciphering* in the one, that you find yourself at last a very *cipher* in the other! See me, man! seventy-two last August!—strong as a hickory and every whit as sound!

MR TIFFANY: I take the greatest pleasure in remarking your superiority, Sir.

TRUEMAN: Bah! no man takes pleasure in remarking the superiority of another! Why the deuce, can't you speak the truth, man? But it's not the *fashion* I suppose! I have not seen one frank, open face since—no, no, I can't say that either, though lying *is* catching! There's that girl, Gertrude, who is trying to teach your daughter music—but Gertrude was bred in the country!

MR TIFFANY: A good girl; my wife and daughter find her very useful.

TRUEMAN: Useful? Well, I must say you have queer notions of *use!*—But come, cheer up, man! I'd rather see one of your old smiles, than know you'd realized another thousand! I hear you are making money on the true, American, high pressure system—better go slow and sure—the more steam, the greater danger of the boiler's bursting! All sound, I hope? Nothing rotten at the core?

MR TIFFANY: Oh, sound—quite sound!

TRUEMAN: Well, that's pleasant—though I must say you don't look very pleasant about it!

MR TIFFANY: My good friend, although I am solvent, I may say, perfectly solvent—yet you—the fact is, you can be of some assistance to me!

TRUEMAN: That's the *fact* is it? I'm glad we've hit upon one *fact* at last! Well— *(SNOBSON, who during this conversation has been employed in writing, but stops occasionally to listen, now gives vent to a dry chuckling laugh)*

TRUEMAN: Hey? What's that? Another of those deuced ill-sounding, city laughs! *(Sees SNOBSON)* Who's that perched up on the stool of repentance—eh, Antony?

SNOBSON: The old boy has missed his text there— *that's* the stool of repentance! *(Aside and looking at TIFFANY'S seat)*

MR TIFFANY: One of my clerks—my confidential clerk!

TRUEMAN: Confidential? Why he looks for all the world like a spy—the most inquisitorial, hang-dog face—ugh! the sight of it makes my blood run cold! Come, *(crosses)* let us talk over matters where this critter can't give us the benefit of his opinion! Antony, the next time you choose a confidential clerk, take one that carries his credentials in his face—those in his pocket are not worth much without! *(Exeunt TRUEMAN and TIFFANY)*

SNOBSON: *(jumping from his stool and advancing)* The old prig has got the tin, or Tiff would never be so civil! All right—Tiff will work every shiner into the concern—all the better for me! Now I'll go and make love to Seraphina. The old woman need n't try to knock me down with any of her French lingo! Six months from to-day if I ain't driving my two footmen tandem, down Broadway—and as fashionable as Mrs Tiffany herself, then I ain't the trump I thought I was! that's all. *(Looks at his watch)* Bless me! eleven o'clock and I have n't had my julep yet! Snobson, I'm ashamed of you! *(Exit)*

SCENE 2: *The interior of a beautiful conservatory; walk through the centre; stands of flower pots in bloom; a couple of rustic seats.* GERTRUDE, *attired in white, with a white rose in her hair; watering the flowers.* COLONEL HOWARD *regarding her.*

HOWARD: I am afraid you lead a sad life here, Miss Gertrude?

GERTRUDE: *(turning round gaily)* What! amongst the flowers? *(Continues her occupation)*

HOWARD: No, amongst the thistles, with which Mrs Tiffany surrounds you; the tempests, which her temper raises!

GERTRUDE: They never harm me. Flowers and herbs are excellent tutors. I learn prudence from the reed, and bend until the storm has swept over me!

HOWARD: Admirable philosophy! But still this frigid atmosphere of fashion must be uncongenial to you? Accustomed to the pleasant companionship of your kind friends in Geneva, surely you must regret this cold exchange?

GERTRUDE: Do you think so? Can you suppose that I could possibly prefer a ramble in the woods to a promenade in Broadway? A wreath of scented wild flowers to a bouquet of these sickly exotics? The odour of new-mown hay to the heated air of this crowded conservatory?

Or can you imagine that I could enjoy the quiet conversation of my Geneva friends, more than the edifying chit-chat of a fashionable drawing room? But I see you think me totally destitute of taste?

HOWARD: You have a merry spirit to jest thus at your grievances!

GERTRUDE: I have my *mania*,—as some wise person declares that all mankind have,—and mine is a love of independence! In Geneva, my wants were supplied by two kind old maiden ladies, upon whom I know not that I have any claim. I had abilities, and desired to use them. I came here at my own request; for here I am no longer *dependent! Voilà tout*, as Mrs Tiffany would say.

HOWARD: Believe me, I appreciate the confidence you repose in me!

GERTRUDE: Confidence! Truly, Colonel Howard, the *confidence* is entirely on your part, in supposing that I confide that which I have no reason to conceal! I think I informed you that Mrs Tiffany only received visitors on her reception day—she is therefore not prepared to see you. Zeke—Oh! I beg his pardon—Adolph, made some mistake in admitting you.

HOWARD: Nay, Gertrude, it was not Mrs Tiffany, nor Miss Tiffany, whom I came to see; it—it was—

GERTRUDE: The conservatory perhaps? I will leave you to examine the flowers at leisure! *(Crosses)*

HOWARD: Gertrude—listen to me. If I only dared to give utterance to what is hovering upon my lips! *(Aside)* Gertrude!

GERTRUDE: Colonel Howard!

HOWARD: Gertrude, I must—must—

GERTRUDE: Yes, indeed you *must*, must leave me! I think I hear somebody coming—Mrs Tiffany would not be well pleased to find you here—pray, pray leave me—that door will lead you into the street. *(Hurries him out through door; takes up her watering pot, and commences watering flowers, tying up branches, &c)* What a strange being is man! Why should he hesitate to say—nay, why should I prevent his saying,

what I would most delight to hear? Truly man *is* strange—but woman is quite as incomprehensible! *(Walks about gathering flowers)*
(Enter COUNT JOLIMAITRE*)*

COUNT: There she is—the bewitching little creature! Mrs Tiffany and her daughter are out of ear-shot. I caught a glimpse of their feathers floating down Broadway, not ten minutes ago. Just the opportunity I have been looking for! Now for an engagement with this captivating little piece of prudery! 'Pon honor, I am almost afraid she will not resist a *Count* long enough to give value to the conquest. *(Approaching her) Ma belle petite*, were you gathering roses for me?

GERTRUDE: *(starts on first perceiving him, but instantly regains her self-possession)* The roses here, Sir, are carefully guarded with thorns—if you have the right to gather, pluck for yourself!

COUNT: Sharp as ever, little Gertrude! But now that we are alone, throw off this frigidity, and be at your ease.

GERTRUDE: Permit me to *be alone*, Sir, that I *may* be at my ease!

COUNT: Very good, *ma belle*, well said! *(Applauding her with his hands)* Never yield too soon, even to a *title!* But as the old girl may find her way back before long, we may as well come to particulars at once. I love you; but that you know already. *(Rubbing his eyeglass unconcernedly with his handkerchief)* Before long I shall make Mademoiselle Seraphina my wife, and, of course, you shall remain in the family!

GERTRUDE: *(indignantly)* Sir—

COUNT: 'Pon my honor you shall! In France we arrange these little matters without difficulty!

GERTRUDE: But I am an *American!* Your conduct proves that you are not one!   *(Going, crosses)*

COUNT: *(preventing her)* Don't run away, my immaculate *petite Americaine!* Demme, you've quite overlooked my condescension—the difference of our stations—you a species of upper servant—an orphan—no friends.

(Enter TRUEMAN *unperceived)*

GERTRUDE: And therefore more entitled to the respect and protection of every *true gentleman!* Had you been one, you would not have insulted me!

COUNT: My charming little orator, patriotism and declamation become you particularly! *(Approaches her)* I feel quite tempted to taste—

TRUEMAN: *(thrusting him aside)* An American hickory-switch! *(Strikes him)* Well, how do you like it?

COUNT: Old matter-of-fact! *(Aside)* Sir, how dare you?

TRUEMAN: My stick has answered that question!

GERTRUDE: Oh! now I am quite safe!

TRUEMAN: Safe! not a bit safer than before! All women would be safe, if they knew how virtue became them! As for you, Mr Count, what have you to say for yourself? Come, speak out!

COUNT: Sir,—aw—aw—you don't understand these matters!

TRUEMAN: That's a fact! Not having had *your* experience, I don't believe I *do* understand them!

COUNT: A piece of pleasantry—a mere joke—

TRUEMAN: A joke was it? I'll show you a joke worth two of that! I'll teach you the way we natives joke with a puppy who don't respect an honest woman! *(Seizing him)*

COUNT: Oh! oh! demme—you old ruffian! let me go. What do you mean?

TRUEMAN: Oh! a piece of pleasantry—a mere joke—very pleasant is n't it?
(Attempts to strike him again; COUNT *struggles with him. Enter* MRS TIFFANY *hastily, in her bonnet and shawl)*

MRS TIFFANY: What is the matter? I am perfectly *abimé* with terror. Mr Trueman, what has happened?

TRUEMAN: Oh! we have been *joking!*

MRS TIFFANY: *(to* COUNT, *who is re-arranging his dress)* My dear Count, I did not expect to find you here—how kind of you!

TRUEMAN: Your *dear* Count has been showing his *kindness* in a very *foreign* manner. Too *foreign* I think, he found it to be relished by an *unfashionable native!* What do you think of a puppy, who insults an innocent girl all in the way of *kindness?* This Count of yours—this importation of—

COUNT: My dear Madam, demme, permit me to explain. It would be unbecoming—demme—particular unbecoming of you—aw—aw—to pay any attention to this ignorant person. *(Crosses to* TRUEMAN) Anything that he says concerning a man of my standing—aw—the truth is, Madam—

TRUEMAN: Let us have the truth by all means,—if it is only for the novelty's sake!

COUNT: *(turning his back to* TRUEMAN) You see, Madam, hoping to obtain a few moments' private conversation with Miss Seraphina—with *Miss Seraphina* I say and—aw—and knowing her passion for flowers, I found my way to your very tasteful and *recherché* conservatory. *(Looks about him approvingly)* Very beautifully arranged—does you great credit, madam! Here I encountered this young person. She was inclined to be talkative; and I indulged her with—with a—aw—demme—a few *common places!* What passed between us was mere *harmless badinage*—on *my* part. You, madam, you—so conversant with our European manners—you are aware that when a man of fashion—that is, when a woman—a man is bound—amongst noblemen, you know—

MRS TIFFANY: I comprehend you perfectly—*parfittement,* my dear Count.

COUNT: 'Pon my honor, that's very obliging of her. *(Aside)*

MRS TIFFANY: I am shocked at the plebeian forwardness of this conceited girl!

TRUEMAN: *(walking up to* COUNT) Did you ever keep a reckoning of the lies you tell in an hour?

MRS TIFFANY: Mr Trueman, I blush for you! *(Crosses to* TRUEMAN)

TRUEMAN: Don't do that—you have no blushes to spare!

MRS TIFFANY: It is a man of rank whom you are addressing, Sir!

TRUEMAN: A rank villain, Mrs Antony Tiffany! A *rich one* he would be, had he as much *gold* as *brass!*

MRS TIFFANY: Pray pardon him, Count; he knows nothing of *bon ton!*

COUNT: Demme, he's beneath my notice. I tell you what, old fellow—(TRUEMAN *raises his stick as* COUNT *approaches, the latter starts back*) the sight of him discomposes me—aw—I feel quite uncomfortable—aw—let us join your charming daughter? I can't do you the honor to shoot you, Sir—*(to* TRUEMAN*)* you are beneath me—a nobleman can't fight a commoner! Good bye, old Truepenny! I—aw—I'm insensible to your insolence!   *(Exeunt* COUNT *and* MRS TIFFANY*)*

TRUEMAN: You won't be insensible to a cow hide in spite of your nobility! The next time he practises any of his foreign fashions on you, Gertrude, you'll see how I'll wake up his sensibilities!

GERTRUDE: I do not know what I should have done without you, sir.

TRUEMAN: Yes, you do—you know that you would have done well enough! Never tell a lie, girl! not even for the sake of pleasing an old man! When you open your lips let your heart speak. Never tell a lie! Let your face be the looking-glass of your soul—your heart its clock—while your tongue rings the hours! But the glass must be clear, the clock true, and then there's no fear but the tongue will do its duty in a woman's head!

GERTRUDE: You are very good, Sir!

TRUEMAN: That's as it may be!—How my heart warms towards her! *(Aside)* Gertrude, I hear that you have no mother?

GERTRUDE: Ah! no, Sir; I wish I had.

TRUEMAN: So do I! Heaven knows, so do I! *(Aside, and with emotion)* And you have no father, Gertrude?

GERTRUDE: No, Sir—I often wish I had!

TRUEMAN: *(hurriedly)* Don't do that, girl! don't do that! Wish you had a mother—but never wish that you had a father again! Perhaps the one you had did not deserve such a child!
(Enter PRUDENCE*)*

PRUDENCE: Seraphina is looking for you, Gertrude.

GERTRUDE: I will go to her. *(Crosses)* Mr Trueman, you will not permit me to thank you, but you cannot prevent my gratitude!   *(Exit)*

TRUEMAN: *(looking after her)* If falsehood harbours there, I'll give up searching after truth!
(Crosses, retires up the stage musingly, and commences examining the flowers)

PRUDENCE: What a nice old man he is to be sure! I wish he would say something! *(Aside)*
(Crosses, walks after him, turning when he turns—after a pause)
Don't mind *me*, Mr Trueman!

TRUEMAN: Mind you? Oh! no, don't be afraid *(crosses)*—I was n't minding you. Nobody seems to mind you much!
*(Continues walking and examining the flowers—*PRUDENCE *follows)*

PRUDENCE: Very pretty flowers, ain't they? Gertrude takes care of them.

TRUEMAN: Gertrude? So I hear—*(advancing)* I suppose you can tell me now who this Gertrude—

PRUDENCE: Who she's in love with? I *knew* you were going to say that! I'll tell you all about it! Gertrude, she's in love with—Mr Twinkle! and he's in love with her. And Seraphina she's in love with Count Jolly—what-d' ye-call-it: but Count Jolly don't take to her at all—but Colonel Howard—he's the man—he's desperate about her!

TRUEMAN: Why you feminine newspaper! Howard in love with that quintessence of affectation! Howard—the only, frank, straightforward fellow that I've met since—I'll tell him my mind on the subject! And Gertrude hunting for happiness in a rhyming dictionary! The girl's a greater fool than I took her for!   *(Crosses)*

PRUDENCE: So she is—you see I know all about them!

TRUEMAN: I see you do! You've a wonderful knowledge—wonderful—of *other people's concerns!* It may do here, but take my word for it, in the county of Catteraugus you'd get the name of a great *busy-body.* But perhaps you know that too?

PRUDENCE: Oh! I always know what's coming. I feel it beforehand all over me. I knew something was going to happen the day you came here—and what's more I can always tell a married man from a single—I felt right off that you were a bachelor!

TRUEMAN: Felt right off I was a bachelor did you? you were sure of it—sure?—quite sure? (PRUDENCE *assents delightedly*) Then you felt wrong!—a bachelor and a widower are not the same thing!

PRUDENCE: Oh! but it all comes to the same thing—a widower's as good as a bachelor any day! And besides I knew that you were a farmer *right off.*

TRUEMAN: On the spot, eh? I suppose you saw cabbages and green peas growing out of my hat?

PRUDENCE: No, I did n't—but I knew all about you. And I knew—(*looking down and fidgeting with her apron*) I knew you were for getting married soon! For last night I dream't I saw your funeral going along the streets, and the mourners all dressed in white. And a funeral is a sure sign of a wedding, you know! (*Nudging him with her elbow*)

TRUEMAN: (*imitating her voice*) Well I can't say that I *know* any such thing! you know! (*Nudging her back*)

PRUDENCE: Oh! it does, and there's no getting over it! For my part, I like farmers—and I know all about setting hens and turkeys, and feeding chickens, and laying eggs, and all that sort of thing!

TRUEMAN: May I be shot! if mistress newspaper is not putting in an advertisement for herself! This is your city mode of courting I suppose, ha, ha, ha! (*Aside*)

PRUDENCE: I've been west, a little; but I never was in the county of Catteraugus, myself.

TRUEMAN: Oh! you were not? And you have taken a particular fancy to go there, eh?

PRUDENCE: Perhaps I should n't object—

TRUEMAN: Oh!—ah!—so I suppose. Now pay attention to what I am going to say, for it is a matter of great importance to yourself.

PRUDENCE: Now it's coming—I know what he's going to say! (*Aside*)

TRUEMAN: The next time you want to tie a man for life to your apron-strings, pick out one that don't come from the county of Catteraugus—for greenhorns are scarce in those parts, and modest women plenty! (*Exit*)

PRUDENCE: Now who'd have thought he was going to say that! But I won't give him up yet—I won't give him up. (*Exit*)

END OF ACT SECOND

ACT THIRD

SCENE 1: MRS TIFFANY'S *Parlor. Enter* MRS TIFFANY, *followed by* MR TIFFANY.

MR TIFFANY: Your extravagance will ruin me, Mrs Tiffany!

MRS TIFFANY: And your stinginess will ruin me, Mr Tiffany! It is totally and *toot a fate* impossible to convince you of the necessity of *keeping up appearances.* There is a certain display which every woman of fashion is forced to make!

MR TIFFANY: And pray who made *you* a woman of fashion?

MRS TIFFANY: What a vulgar question! All women of fashion, Mr Tiffany—

MR TIFFANY: In this land are *self-constituted,* like you, Madam—and *fashion* is the cloak for more sins than charity ever covered! It was for *fashion's* sake that you insisted upon my purchasing this expensive house—it was for *fashion's* sake that you ran me in debt at every exorbitant upholsterer's and extravagant furniture warehouse in the city—it was for *fashion's* sake that you built that ruinous conservatory—hired more servants than they have persons to wait upon—and dressed your footman like a harlequin!

MRS TIFFANY: Mr Tiffany, you are thoroughly plebeian, and insufferably *American*, in your grovelling ideas! And, pray, what was the occasion of these very *mal-ap-pro-pos* remarks? Merely because I requested a paltry fifty dollars to purchase a new style of head-dress—a *bijou* of an article just introduced in France.

MR TIFFANY: Time was, Mrs Tiffany, when you manufactured your own French head-dresses—took off their first gloss at the public balls, and then sold them to your shortest-sighted customers. And all you knew about France, or French either, was what you spelt out at the bottom of your fashion plates—but now you have grown so fashionable, forsooth, that you have forgotten how to speak your mother tongue!

MRS TIFFANY: Mr Tiffany, Mr Tiffany! Nothing is more positively vulgarian—more *unaristocratic* than any allusion to the past!

MR TIFFANY: Why I thought, my dear, that *aristocrats* lived principally upon the past—and traded in the market of fashion with the bones of their ancestors for capital?

MRS TIFFANY: Mr Tiffany, such vulgar remarks are only suitable to the counting house, in my drawing room you should—

MR TIFFANY: Vary my sentiments with my locality, as you change your *manners* with your *dress!*

MRS TIFFANY: Mr Tiffany, I desire that you will purchase Count d'Orsay's "Science of Etiquette," and learn how to conduct yourself—especially before you appear at the grand ball, which I shall give on Friday!

MR TIFFANY: Confound your balls, Madam; they make *footballs* of my money, while you dance away all that I am worth! A pretty time to give a ball when you know that I am on the very brink of bankruptcy!

MRS TIFFANY: So much the greater reason that nobody should suspect your circumstances, or you would lose your credit at once. Just at this crisis a ball is absolutely *necessary* to save your reputation! There is Mrs Adolphus Dashaway—she gave the most splendid fête of the season—and I hear on very good authority that her husband has not paid his baker's bill in three months. Then there was Mrs Honeywood—

MR TIFFANY: Gave a ball the night before her husband shot himself—perhaps you wish to drive me to follow his example? *(Crosses)*

MRS TIFFANY: Good gracious! Mr Tiffany, how you talk! I beg you won't mention anything of the kind. I consider black the most unbecoming color. I'm sure I've done all that I could to gratify you. There is that vulgar old torment, Trueman, who gives one the lie fifty times a day—have n't I been very civil to him?

MR TIFFANY: Civil to his *wealth*, Mrs Tiffany! I told you that he was a rich, old farmer—the early friend of my father—my own benefactor—and that I had reason to think he might assist me in my present embarrassments. Your civility was *bought*—and like most of your *own* purchases has yet to be *paid* for. *(Crosses)*

MRS TIFFANY: And will be, no doubt! The condescension of a woman of fashion should command any price. Mr Trueman is insupportably indecorous—he has insulted Count Jolimaitre in the most outrageous manner. If the Count was not so deeply interested—so *abimé* with Seraphina, I am sure he would never honor us by his visits again!

MR TIFFANY: So much the better—he shall never marry my daughter!—I am resolved on that. Why, Madam, I am told there is in Paris a regular matrimonial stock company, who fit out indigent dandies for this market. How do I know but this fellow is one of its creatures, and that he has come here to increase its dividends by marrying a fortune?

MRS TIFFANY: Nonsense, Mr Tiffany. The Count, the most fashionable young man in all New York—the intimate friend of all the dukes and lords in Europe—not marry my daughter? Not permit Seraphina to become a Countess? Mr Tiffany, you are out of your senses!

MR TIFFANY: That would not be very wonderful, considering how many years I have been united to you, my dear. Modern physicians pronounce lunacy infectious!

MRS TIFFANY: Mr Tiffany, he is a man of fashion—

MR TIFFANY: Fashion makes fools, but cannot *feed* them. By the bye, I have a request,—since you are bent upon ruining me by this ball, and there is no help for it,—I desire that you will send an invitation to my confidential clerk, Mr Snobson.

MRS TIFFANY: Mr Snobson! Was there ever such an *you-nick* demand! Mr Snobson would cut a pretty figure amongst my fashionable friends! I shall do no such thing, Mr Tiffany.

MR TIFFANY: Then, Madam, the ball shall not take place. Have I not told you that I am in the power of this man? That there are circumstances which it is happy for you that you do not know—which you cannot comprehend,—but which render it essential that you should be civil to Mr Snobson? Not you merely, but Seraphina also. He is a more appropriate match for her than your foreign favorite.

MRS TIFFANY: A match for Seraphina, indeed! *(Crosses)* Mr Tiffany, you are determined to make a *fow pas*.

MR TIFFANY: Mr Snobson intends calling this morning. *(Crosses)*

MRS TIFFANY: But, Mr Tiffany, this is not reception day—my drawing-rooms are in the most terrible disorder—

MR TIFFANY: Mr Snobson is not particular—he must be admitted.

(Enter ZEKE)

ZEKE: Mr Snobson.

(Enter SNOBSON, exit ZEKE)

SNOBSON: How dye do, Marm? *(Crosses)* How are you? Mr Tiffany, your most!—

MRS TIFFANY: *(formally)* Bung jure. Comment vow portè vow, Monsur Snobson?

SNOBSON: Oh, to be sure—very good of you—fine day.

MRS TIFFANY: *(pointing to a chair with great dignity)* Sassoyez vow, Monsur Snobson.

SNOBSON: I wonder what she's driving at? I ain't up to the fashionable lingo yet! *(Aside)* Eh? what? Speak a little louder, Marm?

MRS TIFFANY: What ignorance! *(Aside)*

MR TIFFANY: I presume Mrs Tiffany means that you are to take a seat.

SNOBSON: Ex-actly—very obliging of her—so I will. *(Sits)* No ceremony amongst friends, you know—and likely to be nearer—you understand? *O. K.*, all correct. How *is* Seraphina?

MRS TIFFANY: Miss Tiffany is not visible this morning.   *(Retires up)*

SNOBSON: Not visible? *(Jumping up)* suppose that's the English for can't see her? Mr Tiffany, Sir—*(walking up to him)* what am I to understand by this *de-fal-ca-tion*, Sir? I expected your word to be as good as your bond—beg pardon, Sir—I mean *better*—considerably better—no humbug about it, Sir.

MR TIFFANY: Have patience, Mr Snobson. *(Rings bell)*

(Enter ZEKE)

Zeke, desire my daughter to come here.

MRS TIFFANY: *(coming down)* Adolph—I say, Adolph—

(ZEKE straightens himself and assumes foppish airs, as he turns to MRS TIFFANY)

MR TIFFANY: Zeke.

ZEKE: Don't know any such nigga, Boss.

MR TIFFANY: Do as I bid you instantly, or off with your livery and quit the house!

ZEKE: Wheugh! I'se all dismission!   *(Exit)*

MRS TIFFANY: A-dolph, A-dolph!   *(Calling after him)*

SNOBSON: I brought the old boy to his bearings, did n't I though! Pull that string, and he is sure to work right. *(Aside)* Don't make any stranger of me, Marm—I'm quite at home. If you've got any odd jobs about the house to do up, I sha'n't miss you. I'll amuse myself with Seraphina when she comes—we'll get along very cosily by ourselves.

MRS TIFFANY: Permit me to inform you, Mr Snobson, that a French mother never leaves her daughter alone with a young man—she knows your sex too well for that!

SNOBSON: Very *dis*-obliging of her—but as we're none French—

MRS TIFFANY: You have yet to learn, Mr Snobson, that the American *ee-light*—the aristocracy—the *bon-ton*—as a matter of conscience, scrupulously follow the foreign fashions.

SNOBSON: Not when they are foreign to their interests, Marm—for instance—*(enter* SERAPHINA*)* There you are at last, eh, Miss? How d' ye do? Ma said you were n't visible. Managed to get a peep at her, eh, Mr Tiffany?

SERAPHINA: I heard you were here, Mr Snobson, and came without even arranging my toilette; you will excuse my negligence?

SNOBSON: Of everything but *me*, Miss.

SERAPHINA: I shall never have to ask your pardon for *that*, Mr Snobson.

MRS TIFFANY: Seraphina—child—really—
(As she is approaching SERAPHINA, MR TIFFANY *plants himself in front of his wife)*

MR TIFFANY: Walk this way, Madam, if you please. To see that she fancies the surly fellow takes a weight from my heart. *(Aside)*

MRS TIFFANY: Mr Tiffany, it is highly improper and not at all *distingué* to leave a young girl—
(Enter ZEKE*)*

ZEKE: Mr Count Jolly-made-her!

MRS TIFFANY: Good gracious! The Count—Oh, dear!—Seraphina, run and change your dress,—no there's not time! A-dolph, admit him. *(Exit* ZEKE*)* Mr Snobson, get out of the way, will you? Mr Tiffany, what are you doing at home at this hour?
(Enter COUNT JOLIMAITRE, *ushered by* ZEKE*)*

ZEKE: Dat's de genuine article ob a gemman. *(Aside)*   *(Exit)*

MRS TIFFANY: My dear Count, I am overjoyed at the very sight of you.

COUNT: Flattered myself you'd be glad to see me, Madam—knew it was not your *jour de reception.*

MRS TIFFANY: But for you, Count, all days—

COUNT: I thought so. Ah, Miss Tiffany, on my honor, you're looking beautiful.   *(Crosses)*

SERAPHINA: Count, flattery from you—

SNOBSON: What? Eh? What's that you say?

SERAPHINA: Nothing but what etiquette requires. *(Aside to him)*

COUNT: *(regarding* MR TIFFANY *through his eyeglass)* Your worthy Papa, I believe? Sir, your most obedient.
(MR TIFFANY bows coldly; COUNT *regards* SNOBSON *through his glass, shrugs his shoulders and turns away)*

SNOBSON: *(to* MRS TIFFANY*)* Introduce me, will you? I never knew a Count in all my life—what a strange-looking animal!

MRS TIFFANY: Mr Snobson, it is not the fashion to introduce in France!

SNOBSON: But, Marm, we're in America. *(*MRS TIFFANY *crosses to* COUNT*)* The woman thinks she's somewhere else than where she is—she wants to make an *alibi?*   *(Aside)*

MRS TIFFANY: I hope that we shall have the pleasure of seeing you on Friday evening, Count?

COUNT: Really, madam, my invitations—my engagements—so numerous—I can hardly answer for myself: and you Americans take offence so easily—

MRS TIFFANY: But, Count, everybody expects you at our ball—you are the principal attraction—

SERAPHINA: Count, you *must* come!

COUNT: Since you insist—aw—aw—there's no resisting you, Miss Tiffany.

MRS TIFFANY: I am so thankful. How can I repay your condescension! *(*COUNT *and* SERAPHINA *converse)* Mr Snobson, will you walk this way?—I have *such* a cactus in full bloom—remarkable flower! Mr Tiffany, pray come here—I have something particular to say.

MR TIFFANY: Then speak out, my dear—I thought it was highly improper just now to leave a girl with a young man?   *(Aside to her)*

MRS TIFFANY: Oh, but the Count—that is different!

MR TIFFANY: I suppose you mean to say there's nothing of *the man* about him?
(Enter MILLINETTE *with a scarf in her hand)*

MILLINETTE: Adolph tell me he vas here. *(Aside)* Pardon, Madame, I bring dis scarf for Mademoiselle.

MRS TIFFANY: Very well, Millinette; you know best what is proper for her to wear.
(MR and MRS TIFFANY and SNOBSON retire up; she engages the attention of both gentlemen)
(MILLINETTE crosses towards SERAPHINA, gives the COUNT a threatening look, and commences arranging the scarf over SERAPHINA'S shoulders)

MILLINETTE: Mademoiselle, *permettez-moi. Perfide! (Aside to* COUNT) If Mademoiselle vil stand *tranquille* one *petit moment. (Turns* SERAPHINA'S *back to the* COUNT, *and pretends to arrange the scarf)* I must speak vid you to-day, or I tell all— you find me at de foot of de stair ven you go. *Prends garde! (Aside to* COUNT)

SERAPHINA: What is that you say, Millinette?

MILLINETTE: Dis scarf make you so very beautiful, Mademoiselle—*Je vous salue, mes dames.* *(Curtsies)* *(Exit)*

COUNT: Not a moment to lose! *(Aside)* Miss Tiffany, I have an unpleasant—a particularly unpleasant piece of intelligence—you see, I have just received a letter from my friend— the—aw—the Earl of Airshire; the truth is, the Earl's daughter—beg you won't mention it—has distinguished me by a tender *penchant.*

SERAPHINA: I understand—and they wish you to return and marry the young lady; but surely you will not leave us, Count?

COUNT: If *you* bid me stay—I should n't have the conscience—I could n't *afford* to tear myself away. I'm sure that's honest. *(Aside)*

SERAPHINA: Oh, Count!

COUNT: Say but one word—say that you should n't mind being made a Countess—and I'll break with the Earl to-morrow.

SERAPHINA: Count, this surprise—but don't think of leaving the country, Count—we could not pass the time without you! I—yes—yes, Count—I do consent!

COUNT: I thought she would! *(Aside, while he embraces her)* Enchanted, rapture, bliss, ecstasy, and all that sort of thing—words can't express it, but you understand. But it must be kept a secret—positively it *must!* If the rumour of our engagement were whispered abroad—the Earl's daughter—the delicacy of my situation, aw—you comprehend? It is even possible that our nuptials, my charming Miss Tiffany, *our nuptials* must take place in private!

SERAPHINA: Oh, that is quite impossible!

COUNT: It's the latest fashion abroad—the very latest. Ah, I knew that would determine you. Can I depend on your secrecy?

SERAPHINA: Oh, yes! Believe me.

SNOBSON: *(coming forward in spite of* MRS TIFFANY'S *efforts to detain him)* Why, Seraphina, hav[e] n't you a word to throw to a dog?

MR TIFFANY: I should n't think she had after wasting so many upon a puppy. *(Aside)*
(Enter ZEKE, *wearing a three-cornered hat)*

ZEKE: Missus, de bran new carriage am below.

MRS TIFFANY: Show it up,—I mean, Very well, A-dolph. *(Exit* ZEKE)
Count, my daughter and I are about to take an airing in our new *voyture,* —will you honor us with your company?

COUNT: Madam, I—I have a most *pressing* engagement. A letter to write to the *Earl of Airshire* —who is at present residing in the *Isle of Skye.* I must bid you good morning.

MRS TIFFANY: Good morning, Count. *(Exit* COUNT)

SNOBSON: *I'm* quite at leisure, *(crosses to* MRS TIFFANY) Marm. Books balanced—ledger closed—nothing to do all the afternoon,—I'm for you.

MRS TIFFANY: *(without noticing him)* Come, Seraphina, come!
(As they are going SNOBSON *follows them)*

SNOBSON: But, Marm—I was saying, Marm, I am quite at leisure—not a thing to do; have I, Mr Tiffany?

MRS TIFFANY: Seraphina, child—your red shawl— remember—Mr Snobson, *bon swear!*
(Exit, leading SERAPHINA)

SNOBSON: Swear! Mr Tiffany, Sir, am I to be fobbed off with a *bon swear?* D—n it, I will swear!

MR TIFFANY: Have patience, Mr Snobson, if you will accompany me to the counting house—

SNOBSON: Don't count too much on me, Sir. I'll make up no more accounts until these are settled! I'll run down and jump into the carriage in spite of her *bon swear.*   *(Exit)*

MR TIFFANY: You'll jump into a hornet's nest, if you do! Mr Snobson, Mr Snobson! *(Exit after him)*

SCENE 2: *Housekeeper's room.*

(Enter MILLINETTE*)*

MILLINETTE: I have set dat bête, Adolph, to vatch for him. He say he would come back so soon as Madame's voiture drive from de door. If he not come—but he vill—he vill—he *bien étourdi,* but he have *bon coeur.*
(Enter COUNT*)*

COUNT: Ah! Millinette, my dear, you see what a good-natured dog I am to fly at your bidding—

MILLINETTE: Fly? Ah! *trompeur!* Vat for you fly from Paris? Vat for you leave me—and I love you so much? Ven you sick—you almost die—did I not stay by you—take care of you—and you have no else friend? Vat for you leave Paris?

COUNT: Never allude to disagreeable subjects, *mon enfant!* I was forced by uncontrollable circumstances to fly to the land of liberty—

MILLINETTE: Vat you do vid all de money I give you? The last sou I had—did I not give you?

COUNT: I dare say you did, ma petite—wish you'd been better supplied! *(Aside)* Don't ask any questions here—can't explain now—the next time we meet—

MILLINETTE: But, ah! ven shall ve meet—ven? You not deceive me, not any more.

COUNT: Deceive you! I'd rather deceive myself—I wish I could! I'd persuade myself you were once more washing linen in the Seine! *(Aside)*

MILLINETTE: I vil tell you ven ve shall meet—On Friday night Madame give one grand ball—you come *sans doute*—den ven de supper is served—de Americans tink of noting else ven de supper come—den you steal out of de room, and you find me here—and you give me one grand *explanation!*
(Enter GERTRUDE*, unperceived)*

COUNT: Friday night—while supper is serving—*parole d'honneur* I will be here—I will explain every thing—my sudden departure from Paris—my—demme, my countship—every thing! Now let me go—if any of the family should discover us—

GERTRUDE: *(who during the last speech has gradually advanced)* They might discover more than you think it advisable for them to know!

COUNT: The devil!

MILLINETTE: *Mon Dieu!* Mademoiselle Gertrude!

COUNT: *(Recovering himself)* My dear Miss Gertrude, let me explain—aw—aw—nothing is more natural than the situation in which you find me—

GERTRUDE: I am inclined to believe that, Sir.

COUNT: Now—'pon my honor, that's not fair. Here is Millinette will bear witness to what I am about to say—

GERTRUDE: Oh, I have not the slightest doubt of that, Sir.

COUNT: You see, Millinette happened to be lady's-maid in the family of—of—the Duchess Chateau D'Espagne—and I chanced to be a particular friend of the Duchess—*very particular* I assure you! Of course I saw Millinette, and she, demme, she saw me! Did n't you, Millinette?

MILLINETTE: Oh! *oui*—Mademoiselle, I knew him ver vell.

COUNT: Well, it is a remarkable fact that—being in correspondence with this very Duchess—at this very time—

GERTRUDE: That is sufficient, Sir—I am already so well acquainted with your extraordinary talents for improvisation, that I will not further tax your invention—

MILLINETTE: Ah! Mademoiselle Gertrude do not betray us—have pity!

COUNT: *(assuming an air of dignity)* Silence, Millinette! My word has been doubted—the word of a nobleman! I will inform my friend, Mrs Tiffany, of this young person's audacity.   *(Going)*

GERTRUDE: His own weapons alone can foil this villain! *(Aside)* Sir—Sir—Count! *(At the last word the* COUNT *turns)* Perhaps, Sir, the least said about this matter the better!

COUNT: *(delightedly)* The least said? We won't say anything at all. She's coming round—could n't resist me. *(Aside)* Charming Gertrude—

MILLINETTE: *Quoi?* Vat that you say?

COUNT: My sweet, adorable Millinette, hold your tongue, will you? *(Aside to her)*

MILLINETTE: *(Aloud)* No, I vill not! If you do look so from out your eyes at her again, I vill tell all!

COUNT: Oh, I never could manage two women at once,—jealousy makes the dear creatures so spiteful. The only valor is in flight! *(Aside)* Miss Gertrude, I wish you good morning. Millinette, *mon enfant,* adieu. *(Exit)*

MILLINETTE: But I have one word more to say. Stop, Stop! *(Exit after him)*

GERTRUDE: *(musingly)* Friday night, while supper is serving, he is to meet Millinette here and explain—what? This man is an impostor! His insulting me—his familiarity with Millinette—his whole conduct—prove it. If I tell Mrs Tiffany this she will disbelieve me, and one word may place this so-called Count on his guard. To convince Seraphina would be equally difficult, and her rashness and infatuation may render her miserable for life. No—she shall be saved! I must devise some plan for opening their eyes. Truly, if I *cannot* invent one, I shall be the first woman who was ever at a loss for a stratagem—especially to punish a villain or to shield a friend. *(Exit)*

END OF ACT THIRD

ACT FOURTH

SCENE 1: *Ball room splendidly illuminated. A curtain hung at the further end.* MR *and* MRS TIFFANY, SERAPHINA, GERTRUDE, FOGG, TWINKLE, COUNT, SNOBSON, COLONEL HOWARD, *a number of guests— some seated, some standing. As the curtain rises, a cotillion is danced;* GERTRUDE *dancing with* HOWARD, SERAPHINA *with* COUNT.

COUNT: *(advancing with* SERAPHINA *to the front of the stage)* To-morrow then—to-morrow—I may salute you as my bride—demme, my Countess!
(Enter ZEKE, *with refreshments)*

SERAPHINA: Yes, to-morrow.
(As the COUNT *is about to reply,* SNOBSON *thrusts himself in front of* SERAPHINA)

SNOBSON: You said you'd dance with me, Miss—now take my fin, and we'll walk about and see what's going on.
*(*COUNT *raises his eyeglass, regards* SNOBSON, *and leads* SERAPHINA *away;* SNOBSON *follows, endeavoring to attract her attention, but encountering* ZEKE, *bearing a waiter of refreshments; stops him, helps himself, and puts some in his pockets)*
Here's the treat! get my to-morrow's luncheon out of Tiff.
(Enter TRUEMAN, *yawning and rubbing his eyes)*

TRUEMAN: What a nap I've had, to be sure! *(Looks at his watch)* Eleven o'clock, as I'm alive! Just the time when country folks are comfortably *turned in,* and here your grand *turn-out* has hardly begun yet. *(To* TIFFANY, *who approaches)*

GERTRUDE: *(advancing)* I was just coming to look for you, Mr Trueman. I began to fancy that you were paying a visit to dream-land.

TRUEMAN: So I was, child—so I was—and I saw a face—like yours—but brighter!—even brighter. *(To* TIFFANY) There's a smile for you, man! It makes one feel that the world has something worth living for in it yet! Do you remember a smile like that, Antony? Ah! I see you don't—but I do—I do! *(Much moved)*

HOWARD: *(advancing)* Good evening, Mr Trueman. *(Offers his hand)*

TRUEMAN: That's right, man; give me your whole hand! When a man offers me the tips of his fingers, I know at once there's nothing in him worth seeking beyond his fingers' ends.

(TRUEMAN *and* HOWARD, GERTRUDE *and* TIFFANY *converse*)

MRS TIFFANY: *(advancing)* I'm in such a fidget lest that vulgar old fellow should disgrace us by some of his plebeian remarks! What it is to give a ball, when one is forced to invite vulgar people!

(MRS TIFFANY *advances towards* TRUEMAN; SERAPHINA *stands conversing flippantly with the gentlemen who surround her; amongst them is* TWINKLE, *who having taken a magazine from his pocket, is reading to her, much to the undisguised annoyance of* SNOBSON)

Dear me, Mr Trueman, you are very late—quite in the fashion, I declare!

TRUEMAN: Fashion! And pray what is *fashion,* madam? An agreement between certain persons to live without using their souls! to substitute etiquette for virtue—decorum for purity—manners for morals! to affect a shame for the works of their Creator! and expend all their rapture upon the works of their tailors and dressmakers!

MRS TIFFANY: You have the most *ow-tray* ideas, Mr Trueman—quite rustic, and deplorably *American!* But pray walk this way.

(MRS TIFFANY *and* TRUEMAN *go up*)

COUNT: *(advancing to* GERTRUDE, HOWARD *a short distance behind her)* Miss Gertrude—no opportunity of speaking to you before—in demand you know!

GERTRUDE: I have no choice, I must be civil to him. *(Aside)* What were you remarking, Sir?

COUNT: Miss Gertrude—charming Ger—aw—aw—I never found it so difficult to speak to a woman before. *(Aside)*

GERTRUDE: Yes, a very charming ball—many beautiful faces here.

COUNT: Only one!—aw—aw—one—the fact is—
(Talks to her in dumb show)

HOWARD: What could old Trueman have meant by saying she fancied that puppy of a Count—that paste jewel thrust upon the little finger of society.

COUNT: Miss Gertrude—aw—'pon my honor—you don't understand—really—aw—aw—will you dance the polka with me?

(GERTRUDE *bows and gives him her hand; he leads her to the set forming;* HOWARD *remains looking after them*)

HOWARD: Going to dance with him too! A few days ago she would hardly bow to him civilly—could old Trueman have had reasons for what he said? *(Retires up)*

(Dance, the polka; SERAPHINA, *after having distributed her bouquet, vinaigrette and fan amongst the gentlemen, dances with* SNOBSON)

PRUDENCE: *(peeping in as dance concludes)* I don't like dancing on Friday; something strange is always sure to happen! I'll be on the look out. *(Remains peeping and concealing herself when any of the company approach)*

GERTRUDE: *(advancing hastily)* They are preparing the supper—now if I can only dispose of Millinette while I unmask this insolent pretender!   *(Exit)*

PRUDENCE: *(peeping)* What's that she said? It's coming!

(Re-enter GERTRUDE, *bearing a small basket filled with bouquets; approaches* MRS TIFFANY; *they walk to the front of the stage*)

GERTRUDE: Excuse me, Madam—I believe this is just the hour at which you ordered supper?

MRS TIFFANY: Well, what's that to you! So you've been dancing with the Count—how dare you dance with a nobleman—*you?*

GERTRUDE: I will answer that question half an hour hence. At present I have something to propose, which I think will gratify you and please your guests. I have heard that at the most elegant balls in Paris, it is customary—

MRS TIFFANY: What? what?

GERTRUDE: To station a servant at the door with a basket of flowers. A bouquet is then presented to every lady as she passes in—I prepared this basket a short time ago. As the company walk in to supper, might not the flowers be distributed to advantage?

MRS TIFFANY: How *distingué!* You are a good creature, Gertrude—there, run and hand the *bokettes* to them yourself! You shall have the whole credit of the thing.

GERTRUDE: Caught in my own net! *(Aside)* But, Madam, *I* know so little of fashions—Millinette, being French herself, will do it with so much more grace. I am sure Millinette—

MRS TIFFANY: So am I. She will do it a thousand times better than you—there go call her.

GERTRUDE: *(giving basket)* But, Madam, pray order Millinette not to leave her station till supper is ended—as the company pass out of the supper room she may find that some of the ladies have been overlooked.

MRS TIFFANY: That is true—very thoughtful of you, Gertrude. *(Exit GERTRUDE)* What a *recherché* idea! *(Enter MILLINETTE)* Here, Millinette, take this basket. Place yourself there, and distribute these *bokettes* as the company pass in to supper; but remember not to stir from the spot until supper is over. It is a French fashion you know, Millinette. I am so delighted to be the first to introduce it—it will be all the rage in the *bow-monde!*

MILLINETTE: Mon Dieu! dis vill ruin all! *(Aside)* Madame, Madame, let me tell you, Madame, dat in France, in Paris, it is de custom to present *les* bouquets ven every body first come—long before de supper. Dis vould be *outré! barbare!* not at all la mode! Ven dey do come in—dat is de fashion in Paris!

MRS TIFFANY: Dear me! Millinette, what is the difference? besides I'd have you to know that Americans always improve upon French fashions! here, take the basket, and let me see that you do it in the most *you-nick* and genteel manner.

(MILLINETTE poutingly takes the basket and retires up stage. A MARCH. Curtain hung at the further end of the room is drawn back, and discloses a room, in the centre of which stands a supper table, beautifully decorated and illuminated; the company promenade two by two into the supper room; MILLINETTE presents bouquets as they pass; COUNT leads MRS TIFFANY)

TRUEMAN: *(Encountering FOGG, who is hurrying alone to the supper room)* Mr Fogg, never mind the supper, man! Ha, ha, ha! Of course you are indifferent to suppers!

FOGG: Indifferent! suppers—oh, ah—no, Sir—suppers? no—no—I'm not indifferent to suppers! *(Hurries away towards table)*

TRUEMAN: Ha, ha, ha! Here's a new discovery I've made in the fashionable world! Fashion don't permit the critters to have *heads* or *hearts,* but it allows them stomachs! *(To TIFFANY, who advances)* So it's not fashionable to *feel,* but it's fashionable to *feed,* eh, Antony? ha, ha, ha!

(TRUEMAN and TIFFANY retire towards supper room. Enter GERTRUDE, followed by ZEKE)

GERTRUDE: Zeke, go to the supper room instantly,—whisper to Count Jolimaitre that all is ready, and that he must keep his appointment without delay,—then watch him, and as he passes out of the room, place yourself in front of Millinette in such a manner, that the Count cannot see her nor she him. Be sure that they do not see each other—every thing depends upon that. *(Crosses)*

ZEKE: Missey, consider dat business brought to a scientific conclusion.

(Exit into supper room. Exit GERTRUDE)

PRUDENCE: *(who has been listening)* What can she want of the Count? I always suspected that Gertrude, because she is so merry and busy! Mr Trueman thinks so much of her too—I'll tell him this! There's something wrong—but it all comes of giving a ball on a Friday! How astonished the dear old man will be when he finds out how much I know!

(Advances timidly towards the supper room)

SCENE 2: *Housekeeper's room; dark stage; table, two chairs.*

(Enter GERTRUDE, with a lighted candle in her hand)

GERTRUDE: So far the scheme prospers! and yet this imprudence—if I fail? Fail! to lack courage in a difficulty, or ingenuity in a dilemma, are not woman's failings!

(Enter ZEKE, with a napkin over his arm, and a bottle of champagne in his hand)

Well, Zeke—Adolph!

ZEKE: Dat's right, Missey; I feels just now as if dat was my legitimate title; dis here's de stuff to make a nigger feel like a gemman!

GERTRUDE: But he is coming?

ZEKE: He's coming! *(Sound of a champagne cork heard)* Do you hear dat, Missey? Don't it put you all in a froth, and make you feel as light as a cork? Dere's nothing like the *union brand,* to wake up de harmonies ob de heart. *(Drinks from bottle)*

GERTRUDE: Remember to keep watch upon the outside—do not stir from the spot; when I call you, come in quickly with a light—now, will you be gone!

ZEKE: I'm off, Missey, like a champagne cork wid de strings cut.   *(Exit)*

GERTRUDE: I think I hear the Count's step. *(Crosses, stage dark; she blows out candle)* Now if I can but disguise my voice, and make the best of my French.

(Enter COUNT)

COUNT: Millinette, where are you? How am I to see you in the dark?

GERTRUDE: *(imitating MILLINETTE'S voice in a whisper)* Hush! *parle bas.*

COUNT: Come here and give me a kiss.

GERTRUDE: Non—non—*(retreating alarmed, COUNT follows)* make haste, I must know all.

COUNT: You did not use to be so deuced particular.

ZEKE: *(without)* No admission, gemman! Box office closed, tickets stopped!

TRUEMAN: *(without)* Out of my way; do you want me to try if your head is as hard as my stick?

GERTRUDE: What shall I do? Ruined, ruined!

(She stands with her hands clasped in speechless despair)

COUNT: Halloa! they are coming here, Millinette! Millinette, why don't you speak?

Where can I hide myself? *(Running about stage, feeling for a door)* Where are all your closets? If I could only get out—or get in somewhere; may I be smothered in a clothes' basket, if you ever catch me in such a scrape again! *(His hand accidentally touches the knob of a door opening into a closet)* Fortune's favorite yet! I'm safe!

(Gets into closet and closes door. Enter PRUDENCE, TRUEMAN, MRS TIFFANY, and COLONEL HOWARD, followed by ZEKE, bearing a light; lights up)

PRUDENCE: Here they are, the Count and Gertrude! I told you so!

(Stops in surprise on seeing only GERTRUDE)

TRUEMAN: And you see what a lie you told!

MRS TIFFANY: Prudence, how dare you create this disturbance in my house? To suspect the Count too—a nobleman!

HOWARD: My sweet Gertrude, this foolish old woman would—

PRUDENCE: Oh! you need n't talk—I heard her make the appointment—I know he's here—or he's been here. I wonder if she has n't hid him away!

(Runs peeping about the room)

TRUEMAN: *(following her angrily)* You're what I call a confounded—troublesome—meddling—old—prying—*(as he says the last word, PRUDENCE opens closet where the COUNT is concealed)* Thunder and lightning!

PRUDENCE: I told you so!

(They all stand aghast; MRS TIFFANY, with her hands lifted in surprise and anger; TRUEMAN, clutching his stick; HOWARD, looking with an expression of bewildered horror from the COUNT to GERTRUDE)

MRS TIFFANY: *(Shaking her fist at GERTRUDE)* You depraved little minx! this is the meaning of your dancing with the Count!

COUNT: *(Stepping from the closet and advancing)* I don't know what to make of it! Millinette not here! Miss Gertrude—oh! I see—a disguise—the girl's desperate about me—the way with them all. *(Aside)*

TRUEMAN: I'm choking—I can't speak—Gertrude—no—no—it is some horrid mistake! *(Partly aside, changes his tone suddenly)* The villain! I'll hunt the truth out of him, if there's any in—*(crosses, approaches* COUNT *threateningly)* do you see this stick? You made its first acquaintance a few days ago; it is time you were better known to each other.

(As TRUEMAN *attempts to seize him,* COUNT *escapes, and shields himself behind* MRS TIFFANY, TRUEMAN *following)*

COUNT: You ruffian! would you strike a woman?—Madam—my dear Madam—keep off that barbarous old man, and I will explain! Madam, with—aw—your natural *bon gout*—aw—your fashionable refinement—aw—your—aw—your knowledge of *foreign customs*—

MRS TIFFANY: Oh! Count, I hope it ain't a *foreign custom* for the nobility to shut themselves up in the dark with young women? We think such things *dreadful* in *America*.

COUNT: Demme—aw—hear what I have to say, Madam—I'll satisfy all sides—I am perfectly innocent in this affair—'pon my honor I am! That young lady shall inform you that I am so herself!—can't help it, sorry for her. Old matter-of-fact won't be convinced any other way,—that club of his is so particularly unpleasant! *(Aside)* Madam, I was summoned here *malgré moi,* and not knowing whom I was to meet—Miss Gertrude, favor the company by saying whether or not you directed—that—aw—aw—that colored individual to conduct me here?

GERTRUDE: Sir, you well know—

COUNT: A simple yes or no will suffice.

MRS TIFFANY: Answer the Count's question instantly, Miss.

GERTRUDE: I did—but—

COUNT: You hear, Madam—

TRUEMAN: I won't believe it—I can't! Here, you nigger, stop rolling up your eyes, and let us know whether she told you to bring that critter here?

ZEKE: I'se refuse to gib ebidence; dat's de device ob de skilfullest counsels ob de day! Can't answer, Boss—neber git a word out ob dis child—Yah! yah! *(Exit)*

GERTRUDE: Mrs Tiffany,—Mr Trueman, if you will but have patience—

TRUEMAN: Patience! Oh, Gertrude, you've taken from an old man something better and dearer than his patience—the one bright hope of nineteen years of self-denial—of nineteen years of—

(Throws himself upon a chair, his head leaning on table)

MRS TIFFANY: Get out of my house, you *ow*dacious—you ruined—you *abimé* young woman! You will corrupt all my family. Good gracious! don't touch me,—don't come near me. Never let me see your face after to-morrow. Pack. *(Goes up)*

HOWARD: Gertrude, I have striven to find some excuse for you—to doubt—to disbelieve—but this is beyond all endurance! *(Exit)*

(Enter MILLINETTE *in haste)*

MILLINETTE: I could not come before—*(Stops in surprise at seeing the persons assembled)* Mon Dieu! vat does dis mean?

COUNT: Hold your tongue, fool! You will ruin everything, I will explain to-morrow. *(Aside to her)* Mrs Tiffany—Madam—my dear Madam, let me conduct you back to the ballroom. *(She takes his arm)* You see I am quite innocent in this matter; a man of my standing, you know,—aw, aw—you comprehend the whole affair.

(Exit COUNT *leading* MRS TIFFANY)*

MILLINETTE: I will say to him von vord, I will! *(Exit)*

GERTRUDE: Mr Trueman, I beseech you—I insist upon being heard,—I claim it as a right!

TRUEMAN: Right? How dare you have the face, girl, to talk of rights? *(Comes down)* You had more rights than you thought for, but you have forfeited them all! All right to love, respect, protection, and to not a little else that you don't dream of. Go, go! I'll start for Catteraugus to-morrow,—I've seen enough of what fashion can do!   *(Exit)*

PRUDENCE: *(wiping her eyes)* Dear old man, how he takes on! I'll go and console him!   *(Exit)*

GERTRUDE: This is too much! How heavy a penalty has my imprudence cost me!—his esteem, and that of one dearer—my home—my— *(Burst of lively music from ballroom)* They are dancing, and I—I should be weeping, if pride had not sealed up my tears.
(She sinks into a chair. Band plays the polka behind till Curtain falls)

END OF ACT FOURTH

ACT FIFTH

SCENE 1: MRS TIFFANY'S *Drawing Room—same Scene as Act First.* GERTRUDE *seated at a table, with her head leaning on her hand; in the other hand she holds a pen. A sheet of paper and an ink-stand before her.*

GERTRUDE: How shall I write to them? What shall I say? Prevaricate I cannot—*(rises and comes forward)* and yet if I write the truth—simple souls! how can they comprehend the motives for my conduct? Nay—the truly pure see no imaginary evil in others! It is only vice, that reflecting its own image, suspects even the innocent. I have no time to lose—I must prepare them for my return. *(Resumes her seat and writes)* What a true pleasure there is in daring to be frank! *(After writing a few lines more pauses)* Not so frank either,—there is one name that I cannot mention. Ah! that he should suspect—should despise me.   *(Writes)*
(Enter TRUEMAN*)*

TRUEMAN: There she is! If this girl's soul had only been as fair as her face,—yet she dared to speak the truth,—I'll not forget that! A woman who refuses to tell a lie has one spark of heaven in her still. *(Approaches her)* Gertrude, *(*GERTRUDE *starts and looks up)* what are you writing there? Plotting more mischief, eh, girl?

GERTRUDE: I was writing a few lines to some friends in Geneva.

TRUEMAN: The Wilsons, eh?

GERTRUDE: *(surprised, rising)* Are you acquainted with them, Sir?

TRUEMAN: I should n't wonder if I was. I suppose you have taken good care not to mention the dark room—that foreign puppy in the closet—the pleasant surprise—and all that sort of thing, eh?

GERTRUDE: I have no reason for concealment, Sir! for I have done nothing of which I am ashamed!

TRUEMAN: Then I can't say much for your modesty.

GERTRUDE: I should not wish you to say more than I deserve.

TRUEMAN: There's a bold minx! *(Aside)*

GERTRUDE: Since my affairs seem to have excited your interest—I will not say *curiosity,* perhaps you even feel a desire to inspect my correspondence? There, *(handing the letter)* I pride myself upon my good nature,—you may like to take advantage of it?

TRUEMAN: With what an air she carries it off! *(Aside)* Take advantage of it? So I will. *(Reads)* What's this? "French chambermaid — Count — impostor — infatuation—Seraphina—Millinette—disguised myself—expose him." Thunder and lightning! I see it all! Come and kiss me, girl! *(*GERTRUDE *evinces surprise)* No, no—I forgot—it won't do to come to that yet! She's a rare girl! I'm out of my senses with joy! I don't know what to do with myself! Tol, de rol, de rol, de ra. *(Capers and sings)*

GERTRUDE: What a remarkable old man! *(Aside)* Then you do me justice, Mr Trueman?

TRUEMAN: I say I don't! Justice? You're above all dependence upon justice! Hurrah! I've found one true woman at last? *True? (Pauses thoughtfully)* Humph! I did n't think of that flaw!

Plotting and manœuvering—not much truth in that? An honest girl should be above stratagems!

GERTRUDE: But my *motive*, Sir, was good.

TRUEMAN: That's not enough—your *actions* must be *good* as well as your *motives!* Why could you not tell the silly girl that man was an impostor?

GERTRUDE: I did inform her of my suspicions—she ridiculed them; the plan I chose was an imprudent one, but I could not devise—

TRUEMAN: I hate devising! Give me a woman with the *firmness* to be *frank!* But no matter—I had no right to look for an angel out of Paradise; and I am as happy—as happy as a Lord! that is, ten times happier than any Lord ever was! Tol, de rol, de rol! Oh! you—you—I'll thrash every fellow that says a word against you!

GERTRUDE: You will have plenty of employment then, Sir, for I do not know of one just now who would speak in my favor!

TRUEMAN: Not *one*, eh? Why, where's your dear Mr Twinkle? I know all about it—can't say that I admire your choice of a husband! But there's no accounting for a girl's taste.

GERTRUDE: Mr Twinkle! Indeed you are quite mistaken!

TRUEMAN: No—really? Then you're not taken with him, eh?

GERTRUDE: Not even with his rhymes.

TRUEMAN: Hang that old mother meddle-much! What a fool she has made of me. And so you're quite free, and I may choose a husband for you myself? Heart-whole, eh?

GERTRUDE: I—I—I trust there is nothing *unsound* about my heart.

TRUEMAN: There it is again. Don't prevaricate, girl! I tell you an *evasion* is a *lie in contemplation*, and I hate lying! Out with the truth! Is your heart *free* or not?

GERTRUDE: Nay, Sir, since you *demand* an answer, permit *me* to demand by what right you ask the question?
(Enter HOWARD*)*
Colonel Howard here!

TRUEMAN: I'm out again! What's the Colonel to her? *(Retires up)*

HOWARD: *(crosses to her)* I have come, Gertrude, to bid you farewell. To-morrow I resign my commission and leave this city, perhaps for ever. You, Gertrude, it is you who have exiled me! After last evening—

TRUEMAN: *(coming forward to* HOWARD*)* What the plague have you got to say about last evening?

HOWARD: Mr Trueman!

TRUEMAN: What have you got to say about last evening? and what have you to say to that little girl at all? It's Tiffany's precious daughter you're in love with.

HOWARD: Miss Tiffany? Never! I never had the slightest pretension—

TRUEMAN: That lying old woman! But I'm glad of it! Oh! Ah! Um! *(Looking significantly at* GERTRUDE *and then at* HOWARD*)* I see how it is. So you don't choose to marry Seraphina, eh? Well now, whom do you choose to marry?
(Glancing at GERTRUDE*)*

HOWARD: I shall not marry at all!

TRUEMAN: You won't? *(Looking at them both again)* Why you don't mean to say that you don't like—
(Points with his thumb to GERTRUDE*)*

GERTRUDE: Mr Trueman, I may have been wrong to boast of my good nature, but do not presume too far upon it.

HOWARD: You like frankness, Mr Trueman, therefore I will speak plainly. I have long cherished a dream from which I was last night rudely awakened.

TRUEMAN: And that's what you call speaking plainly? Well, I differ with you! But I can guess what you mean. Last night you suspected Gertrude there of—*(angrily)* of what no man shall ever suspect her again while I'm above ground! You did her injustice,—it was a mistake! There, now that matter's settled. Go, and ask her to forgive you,—she's woman enough to do it! Go, go!

HOWARD: Mr Trueman, you have forgotten to whom you dictate.

TRUEMAN: Then you won't do it? you won't ask her pardon?

HOWARD: Most undoubtedly I will not—not at any man's bidding. I must first know—

TRUEMAN: You won't do it? Then if I don't give you a lesson in politeness—

HOWARD: It will be because you find me your *tutor* in the same science. I am not a man to brook an insult, Mr Trueman! but we'll not quarrel in presence of the lady.

TRUEMAN: Won't we? I don't know that—

GERTRUDE: Pray, Mr Trueman—Colonel Howard, pray desist, Mr Trueman, for my sake! *(Taking hold of his arm to hold him back)* Colonel Howard, if you will read this letter it will explain everything.   *(Hands letter to HOWARD, who reads)*

TRUEMAN: He don't deserve an explanation! Didn't I tell him that it was a mistake? Refuse to beg your pardon! I'll teach him, I'll teach him!

HOWARD: *(After reading)* Gertrude, how have I wronged you!

TRUEMAN: Oh, you'll beg her pardon now? *(Between them)*

HOWARD: Hers, Sir, and yours! Gertrude, I fear—

TRUEMAN: You need n't,—she'll forgive you. You don't know these women as well as I do,—they're always ready to pardon; it's their nature, and they can't help it. Come along, I left Antony and his wife in the dining room; we'll go and find them. I've a story of my own to tell! As for you, Colonel, you may follow. Come along. Come along! *(Leads out GERTRUDE, followed by HOWARD)*

(Enter MR *and* MRS TIFFANY, MR TIFFANY *with a bundle of bills in his hand)*

MRS TIFFANY: I beg you won't mention the subject again, Mr Tiffany. Nothing is more plebeian than a discussion upon economy—nothing more *ungenteel* than looking over and fretting over one's bills!

MR TIFFANY: Then I suppose, my dear, it is quite as ungenteel to *pay* one's bills?

MRS TIFFANY: Certainly! I hear the *ee-light* never condescend to do anything of the kind. The honor of their invaluable patronage is sufficient for the persons they employ!

MR TIFFANY: *Patronage* then is a newly invented food upon which the working classes fatten? What convenient appetites poor people must have! Now listen to what I am going to say. As soon as my daughter marries Mr Snobson— *(Enter* PRUDENCE, *a three-cornered note in her hand)*

PRUDENCE: Oh, dear! oh, dear! what shall we do! Such a misfortune! Such a disaster! Oh, dear! oh, dear!

MRS TIFFANY: Prudence, you are the most tiresome creature! What *is* the matter?

PRUDENCE: *(pacing up and down the stage)* Such a disgrace to the whole family! But I always expected it. Oh, dear! oh, dear!

MRS TIFFANY: *(following her up and down the stage)* What are you talking about, Prudence? Will you tell me what has happened?

PRUDENCE: *(still pacing,* MRS TIFFANY *following)* Oh! I can't, I can't! You'll feel so dreadfully! How could she do such a thing! But I expected nothing else! I never did, I never did!

MRS TIFFANY: *(still following)* Good gracious! what do you mean, Prudence? Tell me, will you tell me? I shall get into such a passion! What *is* the matter?

PRUDENCE: *(still pacing)* Oh, Betsy, Betsy! That your daughter should have come to that! Dear me, dear me!

MR TIFFANY: Seraphina? Did you say Seraphina? What has happened to her? what has she done? *(Following* PRUDENCE *up and down the stage on the opposite side from* MRS TIFFANY*)*

MRS TIFFANY: *(still following)* What *has* she done? what *has* she done?

PRUDENCE: Oh! something dreadful—dreadful—shocking!

MR TIFFANY: *(still following)* Speak quickly and plainly—you torture me by this delay,—Prudence, be calm, and speak! What is it?

PRUDENCE: *(stopping)* Zeke just told me—he carried her travelling trunk himself—she gave him a whole dollar! Oh, my!

MR TIFFANY: Her trunk? where? where?

PRUDENCE: Round the corner!

MRS TIFFANY: What did she want with her trunk? You are the most vexatious creature, Prudence! There is no bearing your ridiculous conduct!

PRUDENCE: Oh, you will have worse to bear—worse! Seraphina's gone!

MR TIFFANY: Gone! where?

PRUDENCE: Off!—eloped—eloped with the Count! Dear me, dear me! I always told you she would!

MR TIFFANY: Then I am ruined! (Stands with his face buried in his hands)

MRS TIFFANY: Oh, what a ridiculous girl! And she might have had such a splendid wedding! What could have possessed her?

MR TIFFANY: The devil himself possessed her, for she has ruined me past all redemption! Gone, Prudence, did you say gone? Are you sure they are gone?

PRUDENCE: Did n't I tell you so! Just look at this note—one might know by the very fold of it—

MR TIFFANY: (snatching the note) Let me see it! (Opens the note and reads) "My dear Ma,—When you receive this I shall be a countess! Is n't it a sweet title? The Count and I were forced to be married privately, for reasons which I will explain in my next. You must pacify Pa, and put him in a good humour before I come back, though now I'm to be a countess I suppose I should n't care!" Undutiful huzzy! "We are going to make a little excursion and will be back in a week

"Your dutiful daughter—Seraphina." A man's curse is sure to spring up at his own hearth,—here is mine! The sole curb upon that villain gone, I am wholly in his power! Oh! the first downward step from honor—he who takes it cannot pause in his mad descent and is sure to be hurried on to ruin!

MRS TIFFANY: Why, Mr Tiffany, how you do take on! And I dare say to elope was the most fashionable way after all!

(Enter TRUEMAN, leading GERTRUDE, and followed by HOWARD)

TRUEMAN: Where are all the folks? Here, Antony, you are the man I want. We've been hunting for you all over the house. Why—what's the matter? There's a face for a thriving city merchant! Ah! Antony, you never wore such a hang-dog look as that when you trotted about the country with your pack upon your back! Your shoulders are no broader now—but they've a heavier load to carry—that's plain!

MRS TIFFANY: Mr Trueman, such allusions are highly improper! What would my daughter, the Countess, say!

GERTRUDE: The Countess? Oh! Madam!

MRS TIFFANY: Yes, the Countess! My daughter Seraphina, the Countess dee Jolimaitre! What have you to say to that? No wonder you are surprised after your recherché, abimé conduct! I have told you already, Miss Gertrude, that you were not a proper person to enjoy the inestimable advantages of my patronage. You are dismissed—do you understand? Discharged!

TRUEMAN: Have you done? Very well, it's my turn now. Antony, perhaps what I have to say don't concern you as much as some others—but I want you to listen to me. You remember, Antony, (his tone becomes serious), a blue-eyed, smiling girl—

MR TIFFANY: Your daughter, Sir? I remember her well.

TRUEMAN: None ever saw her to forget her! Give me your hand, man. There—that will do! Now let me go on. I never coveted wealth—yet twenty years ago I found myself the richest farmer in Catteraugus. This cursed money made my girl an object of speculation. Every idle fellow that wanted to feather his nest was sure to come courting Ruth. There was one—my heart misgave me the instant I laid eyes on him—for he was a city chap, and not over fond of the truth. But Ruth—ah! she was too pure herself to look for guile! His fine words and his fair looks—the old story—she was taken with him—I said, "no"—but the girl liked her own way better than her old father's—girls always do! and one morning—the rascal robbed me—not of my money, he would have been welcome to that—but of the only treasure I cherished—my daughter!

MR TIFFANY: But you forgave her!

TRUEMAN: I did! I knew she would never forgive herself—that was punishment enough! The scoundrel thought he was marrying my gold with my daughter—he was mistaken! I took care that they should never want; but that was all. She loved him—what will not woman love? The villain broke her heart—mine was tougher, or it would n't have stood what it did. A year after they were married, he forsook her! She came back to her old home—her old father! It could n't last long—she pined—and pined—and—then—she died! Don't think me an old fool—though I am one—for grieving won't bring her back.   *(Bursts into tears)*

MR TIFFANY: It was a heavy loss!

TRUEMAN: So heavy, that I should not have cared how soon I followed her, but for the child she left! As I pressed that child in my arms, I swore that my unlucky wealth should never curse it, as it had cursed its mother! It was all I had to love—but I sent it away—and the neighbors thought it was dead. The girl was brought up tenderly but humbly by my wife's relatives in Geneva. I had her taught true independence—she had hands—capacities—and should use them! Money should never buy her a husband! for I resolved not to claim her until she had made her choice, and found the man who was willing to take her for herself alone. She turned out a rare girl! and it's time her old grandfather claimed her. Here he is to do it! And there stands Ruth's child! Old Adam's heiress! Gertrude, Gertrude!—my child!

(GERTRUDE rushes into his arms)

PRUDENCE: *(After a pause)* Do tell; I want to know! But I knew it! I always said Gertrude would turn out somebody, after all!

MRS TIFFANY: Dear me! Gertrude an heiress! My dear Gertrude, I always thought you a very charming girl—quite YOU-NICK—an heiress! I must give her a ball! I'll introduce her into society myself—of course an heiress must make a sensation! *(Aside)*

HOWARD: I am too bewildered even to wish her joy. Ah! there will be plenty to do that now—but the gulf between us is wider than ever.

(Aside)

TRUEMAN: Step forward, young man, and let us know what you are muttering about. I said I would never claim her until she had found the man who loved her for herself. I *have* claimed her—yet I never break my word—I think I *have* found that man! and here he is. *(Strikes HOWARD on the shoulder)* Gertrude's yours! There—never say a word, man—don't bore me with your thanks—you can cancel all obligations by making that child happy! There—take her!—Well, girl, and what do you say?

GERTRUDE: That I rejoice too much at having found a parent for my first act to be one of disobedience!   *(Gives her hand to HOWARD)*

TRUEMAN: How very dutiful! and how disinterested!

(TIFFANY retires up—and paces the stage, exhibiting great agitation)

PRUDENCE: *(To TRUEMAN)* All the *single folks* are getting married!

TRUEMAN: No they are not. You and I are single folks, and we're not likely to get married.

MRS TIFFANY: My dear Mr Trueman—my sweet Gertrude, when my daughter, the Countess, returns, she will be delighted to hear of this *deenooment!* I assure you that the Countess will be quite charmed!

GERTRUDE: The Countess? Pray, Madam, where *is* Seraphina?

MRS TIFFANY: The Countess *dee* Jolimaitre, my dear, is at this moment on her way to—to Washington! Where after visiting all the fashionable curiosities of the day—including the President—she will return to grace her native city!

GERTRUDE: I hope you are only jesting, Madam? Seraphina is not married?

MRS TIFFANY: Excuse me, my dear, my daughter had this morning the honor of being united to the Count *dee* Jolimaitre!

GERTRUDE: Madam! He is an impostor!

MRS TIFFANY: Good gracious! Gertrude, how can you talk in that disrespectful way of a man of rank? An heiress, my dear, should have better manners! The Count—

(Enter MILLINETTE, *crying)*

MILLINETTE: Oh! Madame! I will tell everyting—oh! dat monstre! He break my heart!

MRS TIFFANY: Millinette, what is the matter?

MILLINETTE: Oh! he promise to marry me—I love him much—and now Zeke say he run away vid Mademoiselle Seraphina!

MRS TIFFANY: What insolence! The girl is mad! Count Jolimaitre marry my *femmy de chamber!*

MILLINETTE: Oh! Madame, he is not one Count, not at all! Dat is only de title he go by in dis country. De foreigners always take de large title ven dey do come here. His name *à Paris* vas Gustave Treadmill. But he not one Frenchman at all, but he do live one long time *à Paris.* First he live vid Monsieur Vermicelle—dere he vas de head cook! Den he live vid Monsieur Tire-nez, de barber! After dat he live wid Monsieur le Comte Frippon-fin—and dere he vas le Comte's valet! Dere, now I tell everyting I feel one great deal better!

MRS TIFFANY: Oh! good gracious! I shall faint! Not a Count! What will everybody say? It's no such thing! I say he *is* a Count! One can see the foreign *jenny says quoi* in his face! Don't you think I can tell a Count when I see one? I say he *is* a Count!

(Enter SNOBSON, *his hat on—his hands thrust in his pocket—evidently a little intoxicated)*

SNOBSON: I won't stand it! I say I won't!

MR TIFFANY: *(rushing up to him)* Mr Snobson, for heaven's sake— *(Aside)*

SNOBSON: Keep off! I'm a hard customer to get the better of! You'll see if I don't come out strong!

TRUEMAN: *(quietly knocking off* SNOBSON's *hat with his stick)* Where are your manners, man?

SNOBSON: My business ain't with you, Catteraugus; you 've waked up the wrong passenger!—Now the way I'll put it into Tif will be a caution. I'll make him wince! That extra mint julep has put the true pluck in me. Now for it! *(Aside)* Mr Tiffany, Sir—you need n't think to come over me, Sir—you'll have to get up a little earlier in the morning before you do *that,* Sir! I'd like to know, Sir, how you came to assist your daughter in running away with that foreign loafer? It was a downright swindle, Sir. After the conversation I and you had on that subject she was n't your property, Sir.

TRUEMAN: What, Antony, is that the way your city clerk bullies his boss?

SNOBSON: You're drunk, Catteraugus—don't expose yourself—you're drunk! Taken a little too much toddy, my old boy! Be quiet! I'll look after you, and they won't find it out. If you want to be busy, you may take care of my *hat*—I feel so deuced weak in the chest, I don't think I *could* pick it up myself.—Now to put the screws to Tiff. *(Aside)* Mr Tiffany, Sir—you have broken your word, as no virtuous individual—no honorable member—of—the—com—mu—ni—ty—

MR TIFFANY: Have some pity, Mr Snobson, I beseech you! I had nothing to do with my daughter's elopement! I will agree to anything you desire—your salary shall be doubled—trebled— *(Aside to him)*

SNOBSON: *(aloud)* No you don't. No bribery and corruption.

MR TIFFANY: I implore you to be silent. You shall become partner of the concern, if you please—only do not speak. You are not yourself at this moment. *(Aside to him)*

SNOBSON: Ain't I, though? I feel *twice* myself. I feel like two Snobsons rolled into one, and I'm chock full of the spunk of a dozen! Now Mr Tiffany, Sir—

MR TIFFANY: I shall go distracted! Mr Snobson, if you have one spark of manly feeling— *(Aside to him)*

TRUEMAN: Antony, why do you stand disputing with that drunken jackass? Where's your nigger? Let him kick the critter out, and be of use for once in his life.

SNOBSON: Better be quiet, Catteraugus. This ain't your hash, so keep your spoon out of the dish. Don't expose yourself, old boy.

TRUEMAN: Turn him out, Antony!

SNOBSON: He dare n't do it! Ain't I up to him? Ain't he in my power? Can't I knock him into a cocked hat with a word? And now he's got my steam up—I *will* do it!

MR TIFFANY: *(beseechingly)* Mr Snobson—my friend—

SNOBSON: It's no go—steam's up—and I don't stand at anything!

TRUEMAN: You won't *stand* here long unless you mend your manners—you're not the first man I've *upset* because he did n't know his place.

SNOBSON: I know where Tiff's place is, and that's in the *States' Prison!* It's bespoke already. He would have it! He would n't take pattern of me, and behave like a gentleman! He's a *forger*, Sir! *(TIFFANY throws himself into a chair in an attitude of despair; the others stand transfixed with astonishment)* He's been forging Dick Anderson's endorsements of his notes these ten months. He's got a couple in the bank that will send him to the wall anyhow—if he can't make a raise. I took them there myself! Now you know what he's worth. I said I'd expose him, and I have done it!

MRS TIFFANY: Get out of the house! You ugly, little, drunken brute, get out! It's not true. Mr Trueman, put him out; you have got a stick—put him out!

(Enter SERAPHINA, in her bonnet and shawl—a parasol in her hand)

SERAPHINA: I hope Zeke has n't delivered my note.

(Stops in surprise at seeing the persons assembled)

MRS TIFFANY: Oh, here is the Countess! *(Advances to embrace her)*

MR TIFFANY: *(starting from his seat, and seizing SERAPHINA violently by the arm)* Are—you—married?

SERAPHINA: Goodness, Pa, how you frighten me! No, I'm not married, *quite*.

MR TIFFANY: Thank heaven.

MRS TIFFANY: *(drawing SERAPHINA aside)* What's the matter? Why did you come back?

SERAPHINA: The clergyman was n't at home—I came back for my jewels—the Count said nobility could n't get on without them.

MR TIFFANY: I may be saved yet! Seraphina, my child, you will not see me disgraced—ruined! I have been a kind father to you—at least I have tried to be one—although your mother's extravagance made a *madman* of me! The Count is an impostor—you seemed to like him—*(pointing to SNOBSON)*. Heaven forgive me! *(Aside)* Marry *him* and save *me*. You, Mr Trueman, you will be my friend in this hour of extreme need—you will advance the sum which I require—I pledge myself to return it. My wife—my child—who will support them were I—the thought makes me frantic! You will aid me? You had a child yourself.

TRUEMAN: But I did not *sell* her—it was her own doings. Shame on you, Antony! Put a price on your own flesh and blood! Shame on such foul traffic!

MR TIFFANY: Save me—I conjure you—for my father's sake.

TRUEMAN: For your *father's* SON's sake I will *not* aid you in becoming a greater villain than you are!

GERTRUDE: Mr Trueman—Father, I should say—save him—do not embitter our happiness by permitting this calamity to fall upon another—

TRUEMAN: Enough—I did not need your voice, child. I am going to settle this matter my own way.

(Goes up to SNOBSON—who has seated himself and fallen asleep—tilts him out of the chair)

SNOBSON: *(waking up)* Eh? Where's the fire? Oh! it's you, Catteraugus.

TRUEMAN: If I comprehend aright, you have been for some time aware of your principal's forgeries?

(As he says this, he beckons to HOWARD, who advances as witness)

SNOBSON: You've hit the nail, Catteraugus! Old chap saw that I was up to him six months ago; left off throwing dust into my eyes—

TRUEMAN: Oh, he did!

SNOBSON: Made no bones of forging Anderson's name at my elbow.

TRUEMAN: Forged at your elbow? You saw him do it?

SNOBSON: I did.

TRUEMAN: Repeatedly.

SNOBSON: Re—pea—ted—ly.

TRUEMAN: Then you, Rattlesnake, if he goes to the States' Prison, you'll take up your quarters there too. You are an accomplice, an *accessory!* (TRUEMAN *walks away and seats himself,* HOWARD *rejoins* GERTRUDE. SNOBSON *stands for some time bewildered*)

SNOBSON: The deuce, so I am! I never thought of that! I must make myself scarce. I'll be off! Tif, I say, Tif! (*Going up to him and speaking confidentially*) that drunken old rip has got us in his power. Let's give him the slip and be off. They want men of genius at the West,—we're sure to get on! You—you can set up for a writing master, and teach copying *signatures;* and I—I'll give lectures on *temperance!* You won't come, eh? Then I'm off without you. Good bye, Catteraugus! Which is the way to California? (*Steals off*)

TRUEMAN: There's one debt your city owes me. And now let us see what other nuisances we can abate. Antony, I'm not given to preaching, therefore I shall not say much about what you have done. Your face speaks for itself,— the crime has brought its punishment along with it.

MR TIFFANY: Indeed it has, Sir! In *one year* I have lived a *century* of misery.

TRUEMAN: I believe you, and upon one condition I will assist you—

MR TIFFANY: My friend—my first, ever kind friend,—only name it!

TRUEMAN: You must sell your house and all these gew gaws, and bundle your wife and daughter off to the country. There let them learn economy, true independence, and home virtues, instead of foreign follies. As for yourself, continue your business—but let moderation, in future, be your counsellor, and let *honesty* be your confidential clerk.

MR TIFFANY: Mr Trueman, you have made existence once more precious to me! My wife and daughter shall quit the city to-morrow, and—

PRUDENCE: It's all coming right! It's all coming right! We'll go to the county of Catteraugus. (*Walking up to* TRUEMAN)

TRUEMAN: No, you won't,—I make that a stipulation, Antony; keep clear of Catteraugus. None of your fashionable examples there! (JOLIMAITRE *appears in the Conservatory and peeps into the room unperceived*)

COUNT: What can detain Seraphina? We ought to be off!

MILLINETTE: (*turns round, perceives him, runs and forces him into the room*) Here he is! Ah, Gustave, mon cher Gustave! I have you now and we never part no more. Don't frown, Gustave, don't frown—

TRUEMAN: Come forward, Mr Count! and for the edification of fashionable society confess that you 're an impostor.

COUNT: An impostor? Why, you abominable old—

TRUEMAN: Oh, your feminine friend has told us all about it, the cook—the valet—barber and all that sort of thing. Come, confess, and something may be done for you.

COUNT: Well, then, I do confess I am no count; but really, ladies and gentlemen, I may recommend myself as the most capital cook.

MRS TIFFANY: Oh, Seraphina!

SERAPHINA: Oh, Ma!

(*They embrace and retire up*)

TRUEMAN: Promise me to call upon the whole circle of your fashionable acquaintances with your own advertisements and in your cook's attire, and I will set you up in business to-morrow. Better turn stomachs than turn heads!

MILLINETTE: But you will marry me?

COUNT: Give us your hand, Millinette! Sir, command me for the most delicate *paté* —the daintiest *croquette à la royale* —the most transcendent *omelette soufflée* that ever issued from a French pastry-cook's oven. I hope you will pardon my conduct, but I heard that in America, where you pay homage to titles while you profess to scorn them—where *Fashion* makes the basest coin current—where you have no kings, no princes, no *nobility* —

TRUEMAN: Stop there! I object to your use of that word. When justice is found only among lawyers—health among physicians—and patriotism among politicians, *then* may you say that there is no *nobility* where there are no titles! But we *have* kings, princes, and nobles in abundance—of *Nature's stamp*, if not of *Fashion's*,—we have honest men, warm hearted and brave, and we have women—gentle, fair, and true, to whom no *title* could add *nobility*.

EPILOGUE

PRUDENCE: I told you so! And now you hear and see.
  I told you *Fashion* would the fashion be!
TRUEMAN: Then both its point and moral I distrust.
COUNT: Sir, is that liberal?
HOWARD: Or is it just?
TRUEMAN: The guilty have escaped!

MR TIFFANY: Is, therefore, sin
  Made charming? Ah! there's punishment within!
  Guilt ever carries his own scourge along.
GERTRUDE: Virtue her own reward!
TRUEMAN: You're right, I'm wrong.
MRS TIFFANY: How we have been deceived!
PRUDENCE: I told you so.
SERAPHINA: To lose at once a title and a beau!
COUNT: A count no more. I'm no more of *account*.
TRUEMAN: But to a nobler title you may mount,
  And be in time—who knows?—an honest man!
COUNT: Eh, Millinette?
MILLINETTE: Oh, *oui*—I know you can!
GERTRUDE: *(to audience)* But ere we close the scene, a word with you,—
We charge you answer,—Is this picture true?
Some little mercy to our efforts show,
Then let the world your honest verdict know.
Here let it see portrayed its ruling passion,
And learn to prize at its just value—*Fashion*.

CURTAIN

THE OCTOROON (1859)

There were various opinions as to which way the play leaned—whether it was Northern or Southern in its sympathy. The truth of the matter was it was noncommittal. The dialogue and characters of the play made one feel for the South, but the action proclaimed against slavery, and called loudly for its abolition.

Joseph Jefferson III's assessment of the political and theatrical tightrope that Dion Boucicault managed to walk in *The Octoroon* helps to explain the success of this play in a New York City deeply divided by the question of slavery—especially four days after the execution of John Brown. It also provides a clue to the financial, artistic, and political problems facing the authors writing for mid-nineteenth-century American theatre. Though all American writers of the era risked contentious receptions when they broached slavery, playwrights were particularly vulnerable to the force of public opinion—often delivered from the gallery in the form of rotten vegetables. While today such reactions would be considered beyond the pale of acceptable behavior for theatre audiences, the relationship between producer and consumer of theatrical entertainments was much less deferential in the 1850s. A recognition of this distinction in audience norms is imperative as we examine Boucicault's play and seek to understand its emotive power for its original audiences, for the reception of this era's plays has often been clouded by viewing these plays with modern expectations. These were not, as has often been claimed by advocates of other dramatic styles, entertainments to match the "less demanding" tastes of the day. These were plays crafted to make their authors' points *through* their audience's expectations.

Confirming in some senses Hans Robert Jauss' observation that entertainment, as distinct from art, tends to fulfill its original audience's expectations, Boucicault and the other writers of popular entertainment sought to evoke their viewers' sympathy rather than to portray ideological or aesthetic conflict. Nevertheless, like today's occasionally more confrontational popular entertainment, these plays reflected the America their authors saw, while simultaneously entering the debate about the country's future direction. In analyzing the political impact of popular entertainment, we might do well to see plays such as Boucicault's *The Octoroon* as the antecedents of movies such as *Boyz 'N the Hood* or *Schindler's List*. Although the style has changed, the goal of transforming society remains vital.

Even though Dionysius Lardner Boucicault himself asserted that he was born in 1822, Richard Fawkes, his most recent biographer, maintains that Boucicault was born in Dublin, Ireland, on 27 December 1820 to Anne and Samuel Boursiquot. His ostensible father was a Dublin wine merchant of Huguenot extraction. But it is much more likely that Dion's actual father was his mother's lover, Dionysius Lardner, Trinity College lecturer and author of the 134-volume *The Cabinet Cyclopedia*. An indifferent student and lonely young man, Boucicault threw over Lardner's intentions that he should become a civil engineer and entered upon a theatrical career in 1838, acting in English provincial theatres under the name Lee Morton. After moving to London in 1840, Boucicault continued to act and made the rounds trying to sell plays. His break came in 1841. A dismal early season induced Madame Vestris and Charles Mathews, her husband, the lessees of Covent Garden (one of London's two **patent theatres** sanctioned by the government to provide serious drama for the English capital) to stage Boucicault's *London Assurance.* When it became a rousing success, Boucicault's playwrighting career was firmly launched. For the next 12 years, he continued to act while perfecting his playwrighting skills, updating older forms such as **Restoration comedy** and adapting contemporary French **farces** and **melodramas** for Mathews and, later, Charles Kean. In 1852, he became involved with Kean's ward, the actress Agnes Robertson. When her guardian objected to their relationship, Agnes moved in with Boucicault and he turned impresario, booking Agnes into New York City's Burton's Theatre. By 1853, they were together in New York, probably married, and Boucicault began the first American phase of his career.

Boucicault's initial years in America were devoted to furthering his wife's career, touring, and trying his hand briefly at theatre managing. His first American success came by adapting a French original into *The Poor of New York* (1857), a play that used the financial panics of 1837 and 1857 as background for a typical melodramatic action in which a villain impoverishes a family until his crime is revealed in the fifth act. (The formula was so popular that Boucicault later refashioned the play as *The Streets of Philadelphia, The Poor of the London Streets, The Poor of Liverpool,* and so on, allowing his audiences to watch a "local" tenement burn on stage.) He followed this with *Jessie Brown,* a story taken from the contemporary newspaper reports about the 1857 Sepoy revolt in India. Two years later he turned his hand to a distinctly American topic with *The Octoroon; or Life in Louisiana,* an enormously popular play that opened December 6, 1859, at the Winter Garden in New York City. After a rift with the management of the Winter Garden, Boucicault and Agnes Robertson left and joined Laura Keene at the theatre that bore her name. There, on March 29, 1860, Boucicault brought out the first of his successful Irish plays, *The Colleen Bawn,* which played to capacity houses until it was withdrawn in May.

Flush with his American triumph, Boucicault and Agnes Robertson returned to England in July 1860 and took up residence there, remaining until 1872. In that period, Boucicault's fortunes rose and fell, from a low point of personal bankruptcy after a failed managerial effort in 1863 to personal triumph with the 1864 premier in Dublin of his second major Irish play, *Arrah-na-Pogue.* While this was not a particularly productive writing period for Boucicault, he did manage to craft the actor Joseph Jefferson III's most famous role in *Rip Van Winkle* (1865) and such pieces as *Flying Scud* (1866) and the contemporaneously scandalous *Formosa* (1869). By 1872, Boucicault had once again tired of England and returned to the United States and to American citizenship.

The last phase of Boucicault's career brought both his greatest artistic achievements and his most resounding personal failures. In 1874, *The Shaughraun* opened at Wallack's in New York and made Boucicault his final fortune, an astonishing $500,000 in its American runs alone. For the rest of his life he vainly tried to repeat *The Shaughraun*'s success. Meanwhile his personal life became increasingly troubling. His shameless liaisons with various actresses finally proved too much for Agnes Robertson, who sued him for divorce in 1880. For eight years Agnes's action dragged through the English courts. After he returned from an 1885 Australian tour with a new wife and the public assertion that he had never actually been married to Agnes Robertson at all, Agnes branded him a bigamist. After she was finally granted the divorce in 1888, Boucicault went through another ceremony with his last wife, Louise Thorndyke. By this time, Boucicault's fortunes were exhausted and, at 68, his phenomenal energy was ebbing. Nevertheless, he stayed active, managing a drama school, trying to write and adapt plays, and writing for magazines such as *The North American Review.* After a heart attack, he succumbed to a bout of pneumonia September 18, 1890.

The Octoroon was, of course, not the first play to broach the slavery question. A host of adapters had reworked Harriet Beecher Stowe's *Uncle Tom's Cabin* for the stage. But the adaptations, which tried to build upon the novel's popularity by transferring as many characters and plot lines as possible from Stowe's original, had only limited success as adaptations. As Jeffrey D. Mason has pointed out, while the novel and its reworkings share certain characters and central concerns, the adaptations tended to contort many of Stowe's original arguments. Boucicault based the plot of his play on the much lesser-known novel *The Quadroon* by Mayne Reid and, as a result, was able to construct a play, which, while not carrying the emotional power of *Uncle Tom's Cabin*, was a much tighter, more finished piece of drama. At the same time he was able to tailor his play to the audiences he expected to encounter at the Winter Garden.

While it is certainly unwarranted to say that Boucicault was himself an abolitionist in sympathy, Fawkes is probably correct in his assessment that Boucicault's status as Irishman made him sympathetic to the fate of any people subjugated by another. To convince his audience of slavery's evils, he carefully balanced indictment with endorsement, terror-inspiring action with humorous banter. Like most of the slavery plays of this era, *The Octoroon* sentimentalizes the central issue by examining the effects of slavery upon a family, the ideological and psychological bastion of the middle and lower classes who comprised most of its audience. In the process, Boucicault develops a discourse on legality that casts into grave doubt the operation of the law as a guarantor of widely held sentimental and moral beliefs. While Boucicault manipulates the play's ending ultimately to avoid the implications of the play's earlier action, he implicitly leads his audience to question either political "remedies" such as the Fugitive Slave Law of 1850 or the judicial challenges that arose in the face of the 1857 Dred Scott decision.

Boucicault's strategy is evident from the play's beginning. There, among Pete, Paul, Grace, and a host of other "happy darkies" derived from the **minstrel show** tradition, George Peyton encounters the pernicious evil of slavery when he falls in love with Zoe, the octoroon of the title. The European-educated George is willing to ignore local miscegenation statutes, but Zoe herself resists, citing the "ineffaceable curse of Cain" that stems from her mixed racial heritage. While Boucicault's English audiences would later demand that the hero and heroine marry, the original American audiences, sharing the prevailing racial theories of the day, accepted Boucicault's resolution of the couple's dilemma in Zoe's suicide. Thus, in *The Octoroon* Boucicault was able to accomplish two antithetical ends simultaneously. On the one hand, he was able to secure overwhelming sympathy for his central character. His play provided Agnes and the other actors the opportunity to achieve what he considered their highest aspirations as actors—to deprive the audience "of their separate individualities, and fuse all listening minds into one—to make all hearts beat as one; and, as [they lead] them to beat, to bring them irresistibly into one current of sympathy." Such sympathy might have provided the basis for a call to radical political action. On the other hand, by accepting the racial theories of the day, he reinscribed blacks as the inherently tainted beings his contemporaries believed them to be. As Joseph Roach has observed, *The Octoroon*, like most white popular representations of blacks in the period, restricted itself to eroticizing and exoticizing the fate of an imperiled mixed-race heroine. Rather than calling for a radical political solution, Boucicault vitiated the sympathy he had produced and muted the moral force of the play's argument. The final tableau of Wahnotee at Paul's grave standing over the corpse of M'Closky starkly reduces the audience's political and moral choices either to personal sympathy for the heroine or political action, which might potentially return humanity to the rule of the savage. Thus, *The Octoroon* is ambivalent at a level more fundamental than Jefferson's reference to America's mid-century sectional dispute reflects.

WORKS CONSULTED

Boucicault, Dion. "Theatres, Halls, and Audiences." *The North American Review,* 149 *(October, 1889): 425–456.*

Fawkes, Richard. *Dion Boucicault*. London: Quartet Books, 1979.

Jauss, Hans Robert. *Toward an Aesthetic of Reception*. Trans. Timothy Bahti. Minneapolis: University of Minnesota Press, 1982.

Jefferson, Joseph, III. *Rip Van Winkle: An Autobiography*. New York: 1890.

Mason, Jeffrey D. *Melodrama and the Myth of America*. Bloomington: Indiana University Press, 1993.

Richardson, Gary A. "Boucicault's *The Octoroon* and American Law." *Theatre Journal*, 34 (1982): 155–164.

Roach, Joseph R. "Slave Spectacles and Tragic Octoroons: A Cultural Genealogy of Antebellum Performance." *Theatre Survey*, 33 (1992): 167–187.

CHARACTERS

GEORGE PEYTON	JACKSON
SALEM SCUDDER	OLD PETE
MR SUNNYSIDE	PAUL (a boy slave)
JACOB M'CLOSKY	SOLON
WAHNOTEE	MRS PEYTON
LAFOUCHE	ZOE
CAPTAIN RATTS	DORA SUNNYSIDE
COLONEL POINTDEXTER	GRACE
JULES THIBODEAUX	MINNIE
JUDGE CAILLOU	DIDO

ACT FIRST

The scene opens on a view of the Plantation Terrebonne, in Louisiana. A branch of the Mississippi is seen winding through the Estate. A low built, but extensive Planter's Dwelling, surrounded with a veranda, and raised a few feet from the ground, occupies the left side. On the right stand a table and chairs. GRACE *is discovered sitting at breakfast-table with the negro children.*

(SOLON *enters, from the house*)

SOLON: Yah! you bomn'ble fry—git out—a gen'leman can't pass for you.

GRACE: *(seizing a fly whisk)* Hee!—ha git out! *(She drives the children away; in escaping they tumble against* SOLON, *who falls with the tray; the children steal the bananas and rolls that fall about)*

(*Enter* PETE, *who is lame; he carries a mop and pail*)

PETE: Hey! laws a massey! why, clar out! drop dat banana! I'll murder this yer crowd. *(He chases children about; they leap over railing at back)*

(*Exit* SOLON)

Dem little niggers is a judgment upon dis generation.

(*Enter* GEORGE, *from the house*)

GEORGE: What's the matter, Pete?

PETE: It's dem black trash, Mas'r George; dis ere property wants claring; dem's getting too numerous round: when I gets time I'll kill some on 'em, sure!

GEORGE: They don't seem to be scared by the threat.

PETE: Stop, you varmin! stop till I get enough of you in one place!

GEORGE: Were they all born on this estate?

PETE: Guess they nebber was born—dem tings! what, dem?—get away! Born here—dem darkies? What, on Terrebonne! Don't b'lieve it, Mas'r George; dem black tings never was born at all; dey swarmed one mornin' on a sassafras tree in the swamp; I cotched 'em; dey ain't no 'count. Don't believe dey'll turn out niggers when dey're growed; dey'll come out sunthin' else.

GRACE: Yes, Mas'r George, dey was born here; and old Pete is fonder on 'em dan he is of his fiddle on a Sunday.

PETE: What? dem tings—dem?—get away. *(Makes blow at the children)* Born here! dem darkies! What, on Terrebonne? Don't b'lieve it, Mas'r George,—no. One morning dey swarmed on a sassafras tree in de swamp, and I cotched 'em all in a sieve,—dat's how dey come on top of dis yearth—git out, you,—ya, ya! *(Laughs)* *(Exit* GRACE*)*

(Enter MRS PEYTON, *from the house)*

MRS PEYTON: So, Pete, you are spoiling those children as usual!

PETE: Dat's right, missus! gib it to ole Pete! he's allers in for it. Git away dere! Ya! if dey ain't all lighted, like coons, on dat snake fence, just out of shot. Look dar! Ya, ya! Dem debils. Ya!

MRS PEYTON: Pete, do you hear?

PETE: Git down dar! I'm arter you! *(Hobbles off)*

MRS PEYTON: You are out early this morning, George.

GEORGE: I was up before daylight. We got the horses saddled, and galloped down the shell road over the Piney Patch; then coasting the Bayou Lake, we crossed the long swamps, by Paul's Path, and so came home again.

MRS PEYTON: *(laughing)* You seem already familiar with the names of every spot on the estate.

(Enter PETE, *who arranges breakfast)*

GEORGE: Just one month ago I quitted Paris. I left that siren city as I would have left a beloved woman.

MRS PEYTON: No wonder! I dare say you left at least a dozen beloved women there, at the same time.

GEORGE: I feel that I departed amid universal and sincere regret. I left my loves and my creditors equally inconsolable.

MRS PEYTON: George, you are incorrigible. Ah! you remind me so much of your uncle, the judge.

GEORGE: Bless his dear old handwriting, it's all I ever saw of him. For ten years his letters came every quarter-day, with a remittance and a word of advice in his formal cavalier style; and then a joke in the postscript, that upset the dignity of the foregoing. Aunt, when he died, two years ago, I read over those letters of his, and if I did n't cry like a baby—

MRS PEYTON: No, George; say you wept like a man. And so you really kept those foolish letters?

GEORGE: Yes; I kept the letters, and squandered the money.

MRS PEYTON: *(embracing him)* Ah! why were you not my son—you are so like my dear husband. *(Enter* SALEM SCUDDER*)*

SCUDDER: Ain't he! Yes—when I saw him and Miss Zoe galloping through the green sugar crop, and doing ten dollars' worth of damage at every stride, says I, how like his old uncle he do make the dirt fly.

GEORGE: O, aunt! what a bright, gay creature she is!

SCUDDER: What, Zoe! Guess that you did n't leave anything female in Europe that can lift an eyelash beside that gal. When she goes along, she just leaves a streak of love behind her. It's a good drink to see her come into the cotton fields—the niggers get fresh on the sight of her. If she ain't worth her weight in sunshine you may take one of my fingers off, and choose which you like.

MRS PEYTON: She need not keep us waiting breakfast, though. Pete, tell Miss Zoe that we are waiting.

PETE: Yes, missus. Why, Minnie, why don't you run when you hear, you lazy crittur? *(*MINNIE *runs off)* Dat's de laziest nigger on dis yere property. *(Sitting down)* Don't do nuffin.

MRS PEYTON: My dear George, you are left in your uncle's will heir to this estate.

GEORGE: Subject to your life interest and an annuity to Zoe, is it not so?

MRS PEYTON: I fear that the property is so involved that the strictest economy will scarcely recover it. My dear husband never kept any accounts, and we scarcely know in what condition the estate really is.

SCUDDER: Yes, we do, ma'am; it's in a darned bad condition. Ten years ago the judge took as overseer a bit of Connecticut hardware called M'Closky. The judge did n't understand accounts—the overseer did. For a year or two all went fine. The judge drew money like Bourbon whisky from a barrel, and never turned off the tap. But out it flew, free for everybody or anybody to beg, borrow, or steal. So it went, till one day the judge found the tap would n't run. He looked in to see what stopped it, and pulled out a big mortgage. "Sign that," says the overseer; "it's only a formality." "All right," says the judge, and away went a thousand acres; so at the end of eight years, Jacob M'Closky, Esquire, finds himself proprietor of the richest half of Terrebonne—

GEORGE: But the other half is free.

SCUDDER: No, it ain't; because, just then, what does the judge do, but hire another overseer—a Yankee—a Yankee named Salem Scudder.

MRS PEYTON: O, no, it was—

SCUDDER: Hold on, now! I'm going to straighten this account clear out. What was this here Scudder? Well, he lived in New York by sittin' with his heels up in front of French's Hotel, and inventin'—

GEORGE: Inventing what?

SCUDDER: Improvements—anything, from a stay-lace to a fire-engine. Well, he cut that for the photographing line. He and his apparatus arrived here, took the judge's likeness and his fancy, who made him overseer right off. Well, sir, what does this Scudder do but introduces his inventions and improvements on this estate. His new cotton gins broke down, the steam sugar-mills burst up, until he finished off with his folly what Mr M'Closky with his knavery began.

MRS PEYTON: O, Salem! how can you say so? Have n't you worked like a horse?

SCUDDER: No, ma'am, I worked like an ass—an honest one, and that's all. Now, Mr George, between the two overseers, you and that good old lady have come to the ground; that is the state of things, just as near as I can fix it.   (ZOE *sings without*)

GEORGE: 'T is Zoe.

SCUDDER: O, I have not spoiled that anyhow. I can't introduce any darned improvement there. Ain't that a cure for old age; it kinder lifts the heart up, don't it?

MRS PEYTON: Poor child! what will become of her when I am gone? If you have n't spoiled her, I fear I have. She has had the education of a lady.

GEORGE: I have remarked that she is treated by the neighbors with a kind of familiar condescension that annoyed me.

SCUDDER: Don't you know that she is the natural daughter of the judge, your uncle, and that old lady thar just adored anything her husband cared for; and this girl, that another woman would 'a' hated, she loves as if she'd been her own child.

GEORGE: Aunt, I am prouder and happier to be your nephew and heir to the ruins of Terrebonne, than I would have been to have had half Louisiana without you.

(Enter ZOE, *from the house*)

ZOE: Am I late? Ah! Mr Scudder, good morning.

SCUDDER: Thank 'ye. I'm from fair to middlin', like a bamboo cane, much the same all the year round.

ZOE: No; like a sugar cane; so dry outside, one would never think there was so much sweetness within.

SCUDDER: Look here: I can't stand that gal! if I stop here, I shall hug her right off. (*He sees* PETE, *who has set his pail down up stage, and goes to sleep on it)* If that old nigger ain't asleep, I'm blamed. Hillo!

(He kicks pail from under PETE, *and lets him down. Exit)*

PETE: Hi! Debbel's in de pail! Whar's breakfass?

(Enter SOLON *and* DIDO *with coffee-pot and dishes)*

DIDO: Bless'ee, Missey Zoe, here it be. Dere's a dish of penpans—jess taste, Mas'r George—and here's fried bananas; smell 'em do, sa glosh.

PETE: Hole yer tongue, Dido. Whar's de coffee? *(He pours it out)* If it don't stain de cup, your wicked ole life's in danger, sure! dat right! black as nigger; clar as ice. You may drink dat, Mas'r George. *(Looks off)* Yah! here's Mas'r Sunnyside, and Missey Dora, jist drove up. Some of you niggers run and hole de hosses; and take dis, Dido.

(He gives her coffee-pot to hold, and hobbles off, followed by SOLON *and* DIDO*)*

(Enter SUNNYSIDE *and* DORA*)*

SUNNYSIDE: Good day, ma'am. *(He shakes hands with* GEORGE*)* I see we are just in time for breakfast. *(He sits)*

DORA: O, none for me; I never eat. *(She sits)*

GEORGE: *(aside)* They do not notice Zoe.— *(Aloud)* You don't see Zoe, Mr Sunnyside.

SUNNYSIDE: Ah! Zoe, girl; are you there?

DORA: Take my shawl, Zoe. *(ZOE helps her)* What a good creature she is.

SUNNYSIDE: I dare say, now, that in Europe you have never met any lady more beautiful in person, or more polished in manners, than that girl.

GEORGE: You are right, sir; though I shrank from expressing that opinion in her presence, so bluntly.

SUNNYSIDE: Why so?

GEORGE: It may be considered offensive.

SUNNYSIDE: *(astonished)* What? I say, Zoe, do you hear that?

DORA: Mr Peyton is joking.

MRS PEYTON: My nephew is not acquainted with our customs in Louisiana, but he will soon understand.

GEORGE: Never, aunt! I shall never understand how to wound the feelings of any lady; and, if that is the custom here, I shall never acquire it.

DORA: Zoe, my dear, what does he mean?

ZOE: I don't know.

GEORGE: Excuse me, I'll light a cigar. *(He goes up)*

DORA: *(aside to* ZOE*)* Is n't he sweet! O, dear, Zoe, is he in love with anybody?

ZOE: How can I tell?

DORA: Ask him, I want to know; don't say I told you to inquire, but find out. Minnie, fan me, it is so nice—and his clothes are French, ain't they?

ZOE: I think so; shall I ask him that too?

DORA: No, dear. I wish he would make love to me. When he speaks to one he does it so easy, so gentle; it is n't bar-room style; love lined with drinks, sighs tinged with tobacco—and they say all the women in Paris were in love with him, which I feel *I* shall be. Stop fanning me; what nice boots he wears.

SUNNYSIDE: *(to* MRS PEYTON*)* Yes, ma'am, I hold a mortgage over Terrebonne; mine's a ninth, and pretty near covers all the property, except the slaves. I believe Mr M'Closky has a bill of sale on them. O, here he is.

(Enter M'CLOSKY*)*

SUNNYSIDE: Good morning, Mr M'Closky.

M'CLOSKY: Good morning, Mr Sunnyside; Miss Dora, your servant.

DORA: *(seated)* Fan me, Minnie.— *(Aside)* I don't like that man.

M'CLOSKY: *(aside)* Insolent as usual. —*(Aloud)* You begged me to call this morning. I hope I'm not intruding.

MRS PEYTON: My nephew, Mr Peyton.

M'CLOSKY: O, how d' ye do, sir? *(He offers his hand,* GEORGE *bows coldly) (Aside)* A puppy—if he brings any of his European airs here we'll fix him.— *(Aloud)* Zoe, tell Pete to give my mare a feed, will ye?

GEORGE: *(angrily)* Sir!

M'CLOSKY: Hillo! did I tread on ye?

MRS PEYTON: What is the matter with George?

ZOE: *(she takes fan from* MINNIE*)* Go, Minnie, tell Pete; run! *(Exit* MINNIE*)*

MRS PEYTON: Grace, attend to Mr M'Closky.

M'CLOSKY: A julep, gal, that's my breakfast, and a bit of cheese.

GEORGE: *(aside to* MRS PEYTON*)* How can you ask that vulgar ruffian to your table!

MRS PEYTON: Hospitality in Europe is a courtesy; here, it is an obligation. We tender food to a stranger, not because he is a gentleman, but because he is hungry.

GEORGE: Aunt, I will take my rifle down to the Atchafalaya. Paul has promised me a bear and a deer or two. I see my little Nimrod yonder, with his Indian companion. Excuse me, ladies. Ho! Paul!   *(He enters house)*

PAUL: *(outside)* I'ss, Mas'r George.
(Enter PAUL *with the Indian)*

SUNNYSIDE: It's a shame to allow that young cub to run over the swamps and woods, hunting and fishing his life away instead of hoeing cane.

MRS PEYTON: The child was a favorite of the judge, who encouraged his gambols. I could n't bear to see him put to work.

GEORGE: *(returning with rifle)* Come, Paul, are you ready?

PAUL: I'ss, Mas'r George. O, golly! ain't that a pooty gun.

M'CLOSKY: See here, you imp; if I catch you, and your redskin yonder, gunning in my swamps, I'll give you rats, mind. Them vagabonds, when the game's about, shoot my pigs. *(Exit* GEORGE *into house)*

PAUL: You gib me rattan, Mas'r Clostry, but I guess you take a berry long stick to Wahnotee. Ugh, he make bacon of you.

M'CLOSKY: Make bacon of me, you young whelp! Do you mean that I'm a pig? Hold on a bit.
(He seizes whip, and holds PAUL*)*

ZOE: O, sir! don't, pray, don't.

M'CLOSKY: *(slowly lowering his whip)* Darn you, redskin, I'll pay you off some day, both of ye.
(He returns to table and drinks)

SUNNYSIDE: That Indian is a nuisance. Why don't he return to his nation out West?

M'CLOSKY: He's too fond of thieving and whiskey.

ZOE: No; Wahnotee is a gentle, honest creature, and remains here because he loves that boy with the tenderness of a woman. When Paul was taken down with the swamp fever the Indian sat outside the hut, and neither ate, slept, nor spoke for five days, till the child could recognize and call him to his bedside. He who can love so well is honest—don't speak ill of poor Wahnotee.

MRS PEYTON: Wahnotee, will you go back to your people?

WAHNOTEE: Sleugh.

PAUL: He don't understand; he speaks a mash-up of Indian and Mexican. Wahnotee Patira na sepau assa wigiran?

WAHNOTEE: Weal Omenee.

PAUL: Says he'll go if I'll go with him. He calls me Omenee, the Pigeon, and Miss Zoe is Ninemoosha, the Sweetheart.

WAHNOTEE: *(pointing to* ZOE*)* Ninemoosha.

ZOE: No, Wahnotee, we can't spare Paul.

PAUL: If Omenee remain, Wahnotee will die in Terrebonne.
(During the dialogue, WAHNOTEE *has taken* GEORGE'S *gun)*
(Enter GEORGE*)*

GEORGE: Now I'm ready.
*(GEORGE *tries to regain his gun;* WAHNOTEE *refuses to give it up;* PAUL *quietly takes it from him and remonstrates with him)*

DORA: Zoe, he's going; I want him to stay and make love to me; that's what I came for to-day.

MRS PEYTON: George, I can't spare Paul for an hour or two; he must run over to the landing; the steamer from New Orleans passed up the river last night, and if there's a mail they have thrown it ashore.

SUNNYSIDE: I saw the mail-bags lying in the shed this morning.

MRS PEYTON: I expect an important letter from Liverpool; away with you, Paul; bring the mail-bags here.

PAUL: I'm 'most afraid to take Wahnotee to the shed, there's rum there.

WAHNOTEE: Rum!

PAUL: Come, then, but if I catch you drinkin', O, laws a mussey, you'll get snakes! I'll gib it you! now mind. *(Exit with Indian)*

GEORGE: Come, Miss Dora, let me offer you my arm.

DORA: Mr George, I am afraid, if all we hear is true, you have led a dreadful life in Europe.

GEORGE: That's a challenge to begin a description of my feminine adventures.

DORA: You have been in love, then?

GEORGE: Two hundred and forty-nine times! Let me relate you the worst cases.

DORA: No! no!

GEORGE: I'll put the naughty parts in French.

DORA: I won't hear a word! O, you horrible man! go on.

(Exit GEORGE and DORA to the house)

M'CLOSKY: Now, ma'am, I'd like a little business, if agreeable. I bring you news; your banker, old Lafouche, of New Orleans, is dead; the executors are winding up his affairs, and have foreclosed on all overdue mortgages, so Terrebonne is for sale. Here's the *Picayune (Producing paper)* with the advertisement.

ZOE: Terrebonne for sale!

MRS PEYTON: Terrebonne for sale, and you, sir, will doubtless become its purchaser.

M'CLOSKY: Well, ma'am, I s'pose there's no law agin my bidding for it. The more bidders, the better for you. You'll take care, I guess, it don't go too cheap.

MRS PEYTON: O, sir, I don't value the place for its price, but for the many happy days I've spent here; that landscape, flat and uninteresting though it may be, is full of charm for me; those poor people, born around me, growing up about my heart, have bounded my view of life; and now to lose that homely scene, lose their black, ungainly faces! O, sir, perhaps you should be as old as I am, to feel as I do, when my past life is torn away from me.

M'CLOSKY: I'd be darned glad if somebody would tear my past life away from *me*. Sorry I can't help you, but the fact is, you're in such an all-fired mess that you could n't be pulled out without a derrick.

MRS PEYTON: Yes, there is a hope left yet, and I cling to it. The house of Mason Brothers, of Liverpool, failed some twenty years ago in my husband's debt.

M'CLOSKY: They owed him over fifty thousand dollars.

MRS PEYTON: I cannot find the entry in my husband's accounts; but you, Mr M'Closky, can doubtless detect it. Zoe, bring here the judge's old desk; it is in the library. *(Exit ZOE to the house)*

M'CLOSKY: You don't expect to recover any of this old debt, do you?

MRS PEYTON: Yes; the firm has recovered itself, and I received a notice two months ago that some settlement might be anticipated.

SUNNYSIDE: Why, with principal and interest this debt has been more than doubled in twenty years.

MRS PEYTON: But it may be years yet before it will be paid off, if ever.

SUNNYSIDE: If there's a chance of it, there's not a planter round here who would n't lend you the whole cash, to keep your name and blood amongst us. Come, cheer up, old friend.

MRS PEYTON: Ah! Sunnyside, how good you are; so like my poor Peyton.

(Exit MRS PEYTON and SUNNYSIDE to the house)

M'CLOSKY: Curse their old families—they cut me—a bilious, conceited, thin lot of dried up aristocracy. I hate 'em. Just because my grandfather was n't some broken-down Virginia transplant, or a stingy old Creole, I ain't fit to sit down to the same meat with them. It makes my blood so hot I feel my heart hiss. I'll sweep these Peytons from this section of the country. Their presence keeps alive the reproach against me that I ruined them. Yet, if this money should come! Bah! There's no chance of it. Then, if they go, they'll take Zoe—she'll follow them. Darn that girl; she makes me quiver when I think of her; she's took me for all I'm worth. *(Enter* ZOE *from house, with the desk)* O, here, do you know what the annuity the old judge left you is worth to-day? Not a picayune.

ZOE: It's surely worth the love that dictated it; here are the papers and accounts. *(Putting the desk on the table)*

M'CLOSKY: Stop, Zoe; come here! How would you like to rule the house of the richest planter on Atchafalaya—eh? or say the word, and I'll buy this old barrack, and you shall be mistress of Terrebonne.

ZOE: O, sir, do not speak so to me!

M'CLOSKY: Why not! look here, these Peytons are bust; cut 'em; I am rich, jine me; I'll set you up grand, and we'll give these first families here our dust, until you'll see their white skins shrivel up with hate and rage; what d' ye say?

ZOE: Let me pass! O, pray, let me go!

M'CLOSKY: What, you won't, won't ye? If young George Peyton was to make you the same offer, you'd jump at it pretty darned quick, I guess. Come, Zoe, don't be a fool; I'd marry you if I could, but you know I can't; so just say what you want. Here, then, I'll put back these Peytons in Terrebonne, and they shall know you done it; yes, they'll have you to thank for saving them from ruin.

ZOE: Do you think they would live here on such terms?

M'CLOSKY: Why not? We'll hire out our slaves, and live on their wages.

ZOE: But I'm not a slave.

M'CLOSKY: No; if you were I'd buy you, if you cost all I'm worth.

ZOE: Let me pass!

M'CLOSKY: Stop.

(Enter SCUDDER*)*

SCUDDER: Let her pass.

M'CLOSKY: Eh?

SCUDDER: Let her pass!

(He takes out his knife. Exit ZOE *to house)*

M'CLOSKY: Is that you, Mr Overseer? *(He examines paper)*

SCUDDER: Yes, I'm here, somewhere, interferin'.

M'CLOSKY: *(sitting)* A pretty mess you've got this estate in—

SCUDDER: Yes—me and Co.—we done it; but, as you were senior partner in the concern, I reckon you got the big lick.

M'CLOSKY: What d' ye mean?

SCUDDER: Let me proceed by illustration. *(Sits)* Look thar! *(Points with his knife off)* D' ye see that tree?—it's called a live oak, and is a native here; beside it grows a creeper; year after year that creeper twines its long arms round and round the tree—sucking the earth dry all about its roots—living on its life—overrunning its branches, until at last the live oak withers and dies out. Do you know what the niggers round here call that sight? they call it the Yankee hugging the Creole.

M'CLOSKY: Mr Scudder, I've listened to a great many of your insinuations, and now I'd like to come to an understanding what they mean. If you want a quarrel—

SCUDDER: No, I'm the skurriest crittur at a fight you ever see; my legs have been too well brought up to stand and see my body abused; I take good care of myself, I can tell you.

M'CLOSKY: Because I heard that you had traduced my character.

SCUDDER: Traduced! Whoever said so lied. I always said you were the darndest thief that ever escaped a white jail to misrepresent the North to the South.

M'CLOSKY: *(he raises hand to back of his neck)* What!

SCUDDER: Take your hand down—take it down. *(*M'CLOSKY *lowers his hand)* Whenever I gets into company like yours, I always start with the advantage on my side.

M'CLOSKY: What d 'ye mean?

SCUDDER: I mean that before you could draw that bowie-knife, you wear down your back, I'd cut you into shingles. Keep quiet, and let's talk sense. You wanted to come to an understanding, and I'm coming thar as quick as I can. Now, Jacob M'Closky, you despise me because you think I'm a fool; I despise you because I know you to be a knave. Between us we've ruined these Peytons; you fired the judge, and I finished off the widow. Now, I feel bad about my share in the business. I'd give half the balance of my life to wipe out my part of the work. Many a night I've laid awake and thought how to pull them through, till I've cried like a child over the sum I could n't do; and you know how darned hard 't is to make a Yankee cry.

M'CLOSKY: Well, what's that to me?

SCUDDER: Hold on, Jacob, I'm coming to that—I tell ye, I 'm such a fool—I can't bear the feeling, it keeps at me like a skin complaint, and if this family is sold up—

M'CLOSKY: What then?

SCUDDER: *(rising)* I 'd cut my throat—or yours—yours I 'd prefer.

M'CLOSKY: Would you now? why don't you do it?

SCUDDER: 'Cos I's skeered to try! I never killed a man in my life—and civilization is so strong in me I guess I could n't do it—I 'd like to, though!

M'CLOSKY: And all for the sake of that old woman and that young puppy—eh? No other cause to hate—to envy me—to be jealous of me—eh?

SCUDDER: Jealous? what for?

M'CLOSKY: Ask the color in your face: d' ye think I can't read you, like a book? With your New England hypocrisy, you would persuade yourself that it was this family alone you cared for; it ain't—you know it ain't—'t is the "Octoroon"; and you love her as I do; and you hate me because I 'm your rival—that 's where the tears come from, Salem Scudder, if you ever shed any—that 's where the shoe pinches.

SCUDDER: Wal, I do like the gal; she 's a—

M'CLOSKY: She 's in love with young Peyton; it made me curse whar it made you cry, as it does now; I see the tears on your cheeks now.

SCUDDER: Look at 'em, Jacob, for they are honest water from the well of truth. I ain't ashamed of it—I do love the gal; but I ain't jealous of you, because I believe the only sincere feeling about you is your love for Zoe, and it does your heart good to have her image thar; but I believe you put it thar to spile. By fair means I don't think you can get her, and don't you try foul with her,

'cause if you do, Jacob, civilization be darned, I'm on you like a painter, and when I'm drawed out I'm pizin. *(Exit SCUDDER to house)*

M'CLOSKY: Fair or foul, I 'll have her—take that home with you! *(He opens desk)* What 's here—judgments? yes, plenty of 'em; bill of costs; account with Citizens' Bank—what's this? "Judgment, $40,000, 'Thibodeaux against Peyton,'"—surely, that is the judgment under which this estate is now advertised for sale— *(He takes up paper and examines it)* yes, "Thibodeaux against Peyton, 1838." Hold on! whew! this is worth taking to—in this desk the judge used to keep one paper I want—this should be it. *(Reads)* "The free papers of my daughter Zoe, registered February 4th, 1841." Why, judge, was n't you lawyer enough to know that while a judgment stood against you it was a lien on your slaves? Zoe is your child by a quadroon slave, and you did n't free her; blood! if this is so, she 's mine! this old Liverpool debt—that may cross me—if it only arrive too late—if it don't come by this mail—Hold on! this letter the old lady expects—that 's it; let me only head off that letter, and Terrebonne will be sold before they can recover it. That boy and the Indian have gone down to the landing for the post-bags; they'll idle on the way as usual; my mare will take me across the swamp, and before they can reach the shed, I'll have purified them bags—ne'er a letter shall show this mail. Ha, ha!—*(Calls)* Pete, you old turkey-buzzard, saddle my mare. Then, if I sink every dollar I'm worth in her purchase, I'll own that Octoroon.

ACT SECOND

The Wharf with goods, boxes, and bales scattered about—a camera on a stand; DORA *being photographed by* SCUDDER, *who is arranging photographic apparatus,* GEORGE *and* PAUL *looking on at back.*

SCUDDER: Just turn your face a leetle this way—fix your—let's see—look here.

DORA: So?

SCUDDER: That's right. *(Putting his head under the darkening apron)* It's such a long time since I did this sort of thing, and this old machine has got so dirty and stiff, I 'm afraid it won't operate. That's about right. Now don't stir.

PAUL: Ugh! she looks as though she war gwine to have a tooth drawed!

SCUDDER: I 've got four plates ready, in case we miss the first shot. One of them is prepared with a self-developing liquid that I 've invented. I hope it will turn out better than most of my notions. Now fix yourself. Are you ready?

DORA: Ready!

SCUDDER: Fire!—one, two, three. *(SCUDDER takes out watch)*

PAUL: Now it 's cooking; laws mussey! I feel it all inside, as if I was at a lottery.

SCUDDER: So! *(Throws down apron)* That's enough. *(Withdrawing slide, turns and sees PAUL)* What! what are you doing there, you young varmint! Ain't you took them bags to the house yet?

PAUL: Now, it ain't no use trying to get mad, Mas'r Scudder. I'm gwine! I only come back to find Wahnotee; whar is dat ign'ant Injiun?

SCUDDER: You'll find him scenting round the rum store, hitched up by the nose. *(Exit into the room)*

PAUL: *(calling at the door)* Say, Mas'r Scudder, take me in dat telescope?

SCUDDER: *(inside the room)* Get out, you cub! clar out!

PAUL: You got four of dem dishes ready. Gosh, would n't I like to hab myself took! What 's de charge, Mas'r Scudder? *(He runs off)* *(Enter SCUDDER, from the room)*

SCUDDER: Job had none of them critters on his plantation, else he'd never ha' stood through so many chapters. Well, that has come out clear, ain't it? *(Showing the plate)*

DORA: O, beautiful! Look, Mr Peyton.

GEORGE: *(looking)* Yes, very fine!

SCUDDER: The apparatus can't mistake. When I travelled round with this machine, the homely folks used to sing out, "Hillo, mister, this ain't like me!" "Ma'am," says I, "the apparatus can't mistake." "But, mister, that ain't my nose." "Ma'am, your nose drawed it. The machine can't err—you may mistake your phiz but the apparatus don't." "But, sir, it ain't agreeable." "No, ma'am, the truth seldom is." *(Enter PETE, puffing)*

PETE: Mas'r Scudder! Mas'r Scudder!

SCUDDER: Hillo! what are you blowing about like a steamboat with one wheel for?

PETE: *You* blow, Mas'r Scudder, when I tole you: dere's a man from Noo Aleens just arriv'd at de house, and he's stuck up two papers on de gates: "For sale—dis yer property," and a heap of oder tings—an he seen missus, and arter he shown some papers she burst out crying—I yelled; den de corious of little niggers dey set up, den de hull plantation children—de live stock reared up and created a purpiration of lamentation as did de ole heart good to har.

DORA: What's the matter?

SCUDDER: He's come.

PETE: Dass it—I saw 'm!

SCUDDER: The sheriff from New Orleans has taken possession—Terrebonne is in the hands of the law. *(Enter ZOE)*

ZOE: O, Mr Scudder! Dora! Mr Peyton! come home—there are strangers in the house.

DORA: Stay, Mr Peyton: Zoe, a word! *(She leads her forward—aside)* Zoe, the more I see of George Peyton the better I like him; but he is too modest—that is a very impertinent virtue in a man.

ZOE: I'm no judge, dear.

DORA: Of course not, you little fool; no one ever made love to you, and you can't understand; I mean, that George knows I am an heiress; my fortune would release this estate from debt.

ZOE: O, I see!

DORA: If he would only propose to marry me I would accept him, but he don't know that, and he will go on fooling, in his slow European way, until it is too late.

ZOE: What's to be done?

DORA: You tell him.

ZOE: What? that he is n't to go on fooling in his slow—

DORA: No, you goose! twit him on his silence and abstraction—I'm sure it 's plain enough, for he has not spoken two words to me all the day; then joke round the subject, and at last speak out.

SCUDDER: Pete, as you came here, did you pass Paul and the Indian with the letter-bags?

PETE: No, sar; but dem vagabonds neber take the 'specable straight road, dey goes by de swamp. *(Exit up the path)*

SCUDDER: Come, sir!

DORA: *(to* ZOE*)* Now's your time.—*(Aloud)* Mr Scudder, take us with you—Mr Peyton is so slow, there's no getting him on.
(Exit DORA *and* SCUDDER*)*

ZOE: They are gone!—*(Glancing at* GEORGE*)* Poor fellow, he has lost all.

GEORGE: Poor child! how sad she looks now she has no resource.

ZOE: How shall I ask him to stay?

GEORGE: Zoe, will you remain here? I wish to speak to you.

ZOE: *(aside)* Well, that saves trouble.

GEORGE: By our ruin you lose all.

ZOE: O, I'm nothing; think of yourself.

GEORGE: I can think of nothing but the image that remains face to face with me; so beautiful, so simple, so confiding, that I dare not express the feelings that have grown up so rapidly in my heart.

ZOE: *(aside)* He means Dora.

GEORGE: If I dared to speak!

ZOE: That's just what you must do, and do it at once, or it will be too late.

GEORGE: Has my love been divined?

ZOE: It has been more than suspected.

GEORGE: Zoe, listen to me, then. I shall see this estate pass from me without a sigh, for it possesses no charm for me; the wealth I covet is the love of those around me—eyes that are rich in fond looks, lips that breathe endearing words; the only estate I value is the heart of one true woman, and the slaves I'd have are her thoughts.

ZOE: George, George, your words take away my breath!

GEORGE: The world, Zoe, the free struggle of minds and hands is before me; the education bestowed on me by my dear uncle is a noble heritage which no sheriff can seize; with that I can build up a fortune, spread a roof over the heads I love, and place before them the food I have earned; I will work—

ZOE: Work! I thought none but colored people worked.

GEORGE: Work, Zoe, is the salt that gives savor to life.

ZOE: Dora said you were slow; if she could hear you now—

GEORGE: Zoe, you are young; your mirror must have told you that you are beautiful. Is your heart free?

ZOE: Free? of course it is!

GEORGE: We have known each other but a few days, but to me those days have been worth all the rest of my life. Zoe, you have suspected the feeling that now commands an utterance—you have seen that I love you.

ZOE: Me! you love *me?*

GEORGE: As my wife,—the sharer of my hopes, my ambitions, and my sorrows; under the shelter of your love I could watch the storms of fortune pass unheeded by.

ZOE: *My* love! *My* love? George, you know not what you say! *I* the sharer of your sorrows—your wife! Do you know what I am?

GEORGE: Your birth—I know it. Has not my dear aunt forgotten it—she who had the most right to remember it? You are illegitimate, but love knows no prejudice.

ZOE: *(aside)* Alas! he does not know, he does not know! and will despise me, spurn me, loathe me, when he learns who, what, he has so loved.—*(aloud)* George, O, forgive me! Yes, I love you—I did not know it until your words showed me what has been in my heart; each of them awoke a new sense, and now I know how unhappy—how very unhappy I am.

GEORGE: Zoe, what have I said to wound you?

ZOE: Nothing; but you must learn what I thought you already knew. George, you cannot marry me; the laws forbid it!

GEORGE: Forbid it?

ZOE: There is a gulf between us, as wide as your love, as deep as my despair; but, O, tell me, say you will pity me! that you will not throw me from you like a poisoned thing!

GEORGE: Zoe, explain yourself—your language fills me with shapeless fears.

ZOE: And what shall I say? I—my mother was—no, no—not her! Why should I refer the blame to her? George, do you see that hand you hold? look at these fingers; do you see the nails are of a bluish tinge?

GEORGE: Yes, near the quick there is a faint blue mark.

ZOE: Look in my eyes; is not the same color in the white?

GEORGE: It is their beauty.

ZOE: Could you see the roots of my hair you would see the same dark, fatal mark. Do you know what that is?

GEORGE: No.

ZOE: That is the ineffaceable curse of Cain. Of the blood that feeds my heart, one drop in eight is black—bright red as the rest may be, that one drop poisons all the flood; those seven bright drops give me love like yours—hope like yours—ambition like yours—life hung with passions like dew-drops on the morning flowers; but the one black drop gives me despair, for I'm an unclean thing—forbidden by the laws—I'm an Octoroon!

GEORGE: Zoe, I love you none the less; this knowledge brings no revolt to my heart, and I can overcome the obstacle.

ZOE: But *I* cannot.

GEORGE: We can leave this country, and go far away where none can know.

ZOE: And your mother, she who from infancy treated me with such fondness, she who, as you said, has most reason to spurn me, can she forget what I am? Will she gladly see you wedded to the child of her husband's slave?

No! she would revolt from it, as all but you would; and if I consented to hear the cries of my heart, if I did not crush out my infant love, what would she say to the poor girl on whom she had bestowed so much? No, no!

GEORGE: Zoe, must we immolate our lives on her prejudice?

ZOE: Yes, for I'd rather be black than ungrateful! Ah, George, our race has at least one virtue—it knows how to suffer!

GEORGE: Each word you utter makes my love sink deeper into my heart.

ZOE: And I remained here to induce you to offer that heart to Dora!

GEORGE: If you bid me do so I will obey you—

ZOE: No, no! if you cannot be mine, O, let me not blush when I think of you.

GEORGE: Dearest Zoe! *(Exit* GEORGE *and* ZOE) *(As they exit,* M'CLOSKY *rises from behind a rock and looks after them)*

M'CLOSKY: She loves him! I felt it—and how she can love! *(Advances)* That one black drop of blood burns in her veins and lights up her heart like a foggy sun. O, how I lapped up her words, like a thirsty bloodhound! I'll have her, if it costs me my life! Yonder the boy still lurks with those mail-bags; the devil still keeps him here to tempt me, darn his yellow skin! I arrived just too late, he had grabbed the prize as I came up. Hillo! he's coming this way, fighting with his Injiun.   *(Conceals himself)* *(Enter* PAUL, *wrestling with* WAHNOTEE)

PAUL: It ain't no use now: you got to gib it up!

WAHNOTEE: Ugh!

PAUL: It won't do! You got dat bottle of rum hid under your blanket—gib it up now, you—. Yar! *(Wrenching it from him)* You nasty, lying Injiun! It's no use you putting on airs; I ain't gwine to sit up wid you all night and you drunk. Hillo! war's de crowd gone? And dar's de 'paratus—O, gosh, if I could take a likeness ob dis child! Uh—uh, let's have a peep. *(Looking through camera)* O, golly! yar, you Wahnotee! you stan' dar, I see you. Ta demine usti.

(He looks at WAHNOTEE *through the camera;* WAHNOTEE *springs back with an expression of alarm)*

WAHNOTEE: No tue Wahnotee.

PAUL: Ha, ha! he tinks it's a gun. You ign'ant Injiun, it can't hurt you! Stop, here's dem dishes—plates—dat's what he call 'em, all fix: I see Mas'r Scudder do it often—tink I can take likeness—stay dere, Wahnotee.

WAHNOTEE: No, carabine tue.

PAUL: I must operate and take my own likeness too—how debbel I do dat? Can't be ober dar an' here too—I ain't twins. Ugh! ach! 'Top; you look, you Wahnotee; you see dis rag, eh? Well when I say go, den lift dis rag like dis, see! den run to dat pine tree up dar *(points)* and back ag'in, and den pull down de rag so, d' ye see?

WAHNOTEE: Hugh!

PAUL: Den you hab glass ob rum.

WAHNOTEE: Rum!

PAUL: Dat wakes him up. Coute, Wahnotee in omenee dit go Wahnotee, poina la fa, comb a pine tree, la revieut sala, la fa.

WAHNOTEE: Fire-water!

PAUL: Yes, den a glass ob fire-water; now den. *(Throwing mail-bags down and sitting on them)* Pret, now den go.

*(*WAHNOTEE *raises the apron and runs off.* PAUL *sits for his picture*—M'CLOSKY *appears)*

M'CLOSKY: Where are they? Ah, yonder goes the Indian!

PAUL: De time he gone just 'bout enough to cook dat dish plate.

M'CLOSKY: Yonder is the boy—now is my time! What's he doing; is he asleep? *(Advancing)* He is sitting on my prize! darn his carcass! I'll clear him off there—he'll never know what stunned him. *(He takes Indian's tomahawk and steals to* PAUL*)*

PAUL: Dam dat Injiun! is dat him creeping dar? I dare n't move fear to spile myself. *(*M'CLOSKY *strikes him on the head—he falls dead)*

M'CLOSKY: Hooraw; the bags are mine—now for it!—*(Opening the mail-bags)* What's here? Sunnyside, Pointdexter, Jackson, Peyton; here it is—the Liverpool postmark, sure enough!—

(Opening letter—reads) "Madam, we are instructed by the firm of Mason and Co., to inform you that a dividend of forty per cent. is payable on the 1st proximo, this amount in consideration of position, they send herewith, and you will find enclosed by draft to your order, on the Bank of Louisiana, which please acknowledge—the balance will be paid in full, with interest, in three, six, and nine months—your drafts on Mason Brothers at those dates will be accepted by La Palisse and Compagnie, N. O., so that you may command immediate use of the whole amount at once, if required. Yours, etc., James Brown." What a find! this infernal letter would have saved all. *(During the reading of letter he remains nearly motionless under the focus of the camera)* But now I guess it will arrive too late—these darned U. S. mails are to blame. The Injiun! he must not see me. *(Exit rapidly)*

*(*WAHNOTEE *runs on, and pulls down the apron. He sees* PAUL, *lying on the ground and speaks to him, thinking that he is shamming sleep. He gesticulates and jabbers to him and moves him with his feet, then kneels down to rouse him. To his horror he finds him dead. Expressing great grief he raises his eyes and they fall upon the camera. Rising with a savage growl, he seizes the tomahawk and smashes the camera to pieces. Going to* PAUL *he expresses in pantomime grief, sorrow, and fondness, and takes him in his arms to carry him away)*

ACT THIRD

(A Room in MRS PEYTON'S *house showing the entrance on which an auction bill is posted.* SOLON *and* GRACE *are there)*

PETE: *(outside)* Dis way—dis way.
   (Enter PETE, POINTDEXTER, JACKSON, LAFOUCHE *and* CAILLOU*)*

PETE: Dis way, gen'l'men; now, Solon—Grace—dey's hot and tirsty—sangaree, brandy, rum.

JACKSON: Well, what d 'ye say, Lafouche—d 'ye smile?
(Enter THIBODEAUX *and* SUNNYSIDE*)*
THIBODEAUX: I hope we don't intrude on the family.
PETE: You see dat hole in dar, sar? I was raised on dis yar plantation—nebber see no door in it—always open, sar, for stranger to walk in.
SUNNYSIDE: And for substance to walk out.
(Enter RATTS*)*
RATTS: Fine southern style that, eh!
LAFOUCHE: *(reading the bill)* "A fine, well-built old family mansion, replete with every comfort."
RATTS: There's one name on the list of slaves scratched, I see.
LAFOUCHE: Yes; No. 49, Paul, a quadroon boy, aged thirteen.
SUNNYSIDE: He's missing.
POINTDEXTER: Run away, I suppose.
PETE: *(indignantly)* No, sar; nigger nebber cut stick on Terrebonne; dat boy's dead, sure.
RATTS: What, Picayune Paul, as we called him, that used to come aboard my boat?—poor little darkey, I hope not; many a picayune he picked up for his dance and nigger songs, and he supplied our table with fish and game from the Bayous.
PETE: Nebber supply no more, sar—nebber dance again. Mas'r Ratts, you hard him sing about de place where de good niggers go, de last time.
RATTS: Well!
PETE: Well, he gone dar hisself; why I tink so—'cause we missed Paul for some days, but nebber tout nothin' till one night dat Injiun Wahnotee suddenly stood right dar 'mongst us—was in his war paint, and mighty cold and grave—he sit down by de fire. "Whar's Paul?" I say—he smoke and smoke, but nebber look out ob de fire; well knowing dem critters, I wait a long time—den he say, "Wahnotee great chief"; den I say nothing—smoke anoder time—last, rising to go, he turn round at door, and say berry low—O, like a woman's voice he say, "Omenee Pangeuk,"—dat is, Paul is dead—nebber see him since.

RATTS: That red-skin killed him.
SUNNYSIDE: So we believe; and so mad are the folks around, if they catch the red-skin they'll lynch him sure.
RATTS: Lynch him! Darn his copper carcass, I've got a set of Irish deck-hands aboard that just loved that child; and after I tell them this, let them get a sight of the red-skin, I believe they would eat him, tomahawk and all. Poor little Paul!
THIBODEAUX: What was he worth?
RATTS: Well, near on five hundred dollars.
PETE: *(scandalized)* What, sar! You p'tend to be sorry for Paul, and prize him like dat! Five hundred dollars! *(To* THIBODEAUX*)* Tousand dollars, Massa Thibodeau.
(Enter SCUDDER*)*
SCUDDER: Gentlemen, the sale takes place at three. Good morning, Colonel. It's near that now, and there's still the sugar-houses to be inspected. Good day, Mr Thibodeaux—shall we drive down that way? Mr Lafouche, why, how do you do, sir? you're looking well.
LAFOUCHE: Sorry I can't return the compliment.
RATTS: Salem's looking a kinder hollowed out.
SCUDDER: What, Mr Ratts, are you going to invest in swamps?
RATTS: No; I want a nigger.
SCUDDER: Hush.
PETE: Eh! wass dat?
SCUDDER: Mr Sunnyside, I can't do this job of showin' round the folks; my stomach goes agin it. I want Pete here a minute.
SUNNYSIDE: I'll accompany them certainly.
SCUDDER: *(eagerly)* Will ye? Thank ye; thank ye.
SUNNYSIDE: We must excuse Scudder, friends. I'll see you round the estate.
(Enter GEORGE *and* MRS PEYTON*)*
LAFOUCHE: Good morning, Mrs Peyton.
(All salute)
SUNNYSIDE: This way, gentlemen.
RATTS: *(aside to* SUNNYSIDE*)* I say, I'd like to say summit soft to the old woman; perhaps it would n't go well, would it?
THIBODEAUX: No; leave it alone.

RATTS: Darn it, when I see a woman in trouble, I feel like selling the skin off my back.
(*Exit* THIBODEAUX, SUNNYSIDE, RATTS, POINTDEXTER, GRACE, JACKSON, LAFOUCHE, CAILLOU, SOLON)

SCUDDER: (*aside to* PETE) Go outside there; listen to what you hear, then go down to the quarters and tell the boys, for I can't do it. O, get out.

PETE: He said "I want a nigger." Laws, mussey! What am goin' to cum ob us! (*Exit slowly, as if trying to conceal himself*)

GEORGE: My dear aunt, why do you not move from this painful scene? Go with Dora to Sunnyside.

MRS PEYTON: No, George; your uncle said to me with his dying breath, "Nellie, never leave Terrebonne," and I never *will* leave it, till the law compels me.

SCUDDER: Mr George, I'm going to say somethin' that has been chokin' me for some time. I know you'll excuse it. Thar's Miss Dora—that girl's in love with you; yes, sir, her eyes are startin' out of her head with it: now her fortune would redeem a good part of this estate.

MRS PEYTON: Why, George, I never suspected this!

GEORGE: I did, aunt, I confess, but—

MRS PEYTON: And you hesitated from motives of delicacy?

SCUDDER: No, ma'am; here's the plan of it. Mr George is in love with Zoe.

GEORGE: Scudder!

MRS PEYTON: George!

SCUDDER: Hold on, now! things have got so jammed in on top of us, we ain't got time to put kid gloves on to handle them. He loves Zoe, and has found out that she loves him. (*Sighing*) Well, that's all right; but as he can't marry her, and as Miss Dora would jump at him—

MRS PEYTON: Why did n't you mention this before?

SCUDDER: Why, because *I* love Zoe, too, and I could n't take that young feller from her; and she's jist living on the sight of him, as I saw her do; and they so happy in spite of this yer misery around them, and they reproachin' themselves with not feeling as they ought. I've seen it, I tell you; and darn it, ma'am, can't you see

that 's what 's been a hollowing me out so—I beg your pardon.

MRS PEYTON: O, George,—my son, let me call you,—I do not speak for my own sake, nor for the loss of the estate, but for the poor people here: they will be sold, divided, and taken away—they have been born here. Heaven has denied me children; so all the strings of my heart have grown around and amongst them, like the fibres and roots of an old tree in its native earth. O, let all go, but save them! With them around us, if we have not wealth, we shall at least have the home that they alone can make—

GEORGE: My dear mother—Mr Scudder—you teach me what I ought to do; if Miss Sunnyside will accept me as I am, Terrebonne shall be saved: I will sell myself, but the slaves shall be protected.

MRS PEYTON: *Sell* yourself, George! Is not Dora worth any man's—

SCUDDER: Don't say that, ma'am; don't say that to a man that loves another gal. He's going to do an heroic act; don't spile it.

MRS PEYTON: But Zoe is only an Octoroon.

SCUDDER: She's won this race agin the white, anyhow; it's too late now to start her pedigree. (*As* DORA *enters*) Come, Mrs Peyton, take my arm. Hush! here's the other one: she's a little too thoroughbred—too much of the greyhound; but the heart's there, I believe.
(*Exeunt* SCUDDER *and* MRS PEYTON)

DORA: Poor Mrs Peyton.

GEORGE: Miss Sunnyside, permit me a word: a feeling of delicacy has suspended upon my lips an avowal, which—

DORA: (*aside*) O, dear, has he suddenly come to his senses?
(*Enter* ZOE, *stopping at back*)

GEORGE: In a word, I have seen and admired you!

DORA: (*aside*) He has a strange way of showing it. European, I suppose.

GEORGE: If you would pardon the abruptness of the question, I would ask you, Do you think the sincere devotion of my life to make yours happy would succeed?

DORA: *(aside)* Well, he has the oddest way of making love.

GEORGE: You are silent?

DORA: Mr Peyton, I presume you have hesitated to make this avowal because you feared, in the present condition of affairs here, your object might be misconstrued, and that your attention was rather to my fortune than myself. *(A pause)* Why don't he speak?—I mean, you feared I might not give you credit for sincere and pure feelings. Well, you wrong me. I don't think you capable of anything else but—

GEORGE: No, I hesitated because an attachment I had formed before I had the pleasure of seeing you had not altogether died out.

DORA: *(smiling)* Some of those sirens of Paris, I presume. *(Pausing)* I shall endeavor not to be jealous of the past; perhaps I have no right to be. *(Pausing)* But now that vagrant love is— eh, faded—is it not? Why don't you speak, sir?

GEORGE: Because, Miss Sunnyside, I have not learned to lie.

DORA: Good gracious—who wants you to?

GEORGE: I do, but I can't do it. No, the love I speak of is not such as you suppose,—it is a passion that has grown up here since I arrived; but it is a hopeless, mad, wild feeling, that must perish.

DORA: Here! since you arrived! Impossible: you have seen no one; whom can you mean?

ZOE: *(advancing)* Me.

GEORGE: Zoe!

DORA: You!

ZOE: Forgive him, Dora; for he knew no better until I told him. Dora, you are right. He is incapable of any but sincere and pure feelings—so are you. He loves me—what of that? You know you can't be jealous of a poor creature like me. If he caught the fever, were stung by a snake, or possessed of any other poisonous or unclean thing, you could pity, tend, love him through it, and for your gentle care he would love you in return. Well, is he not thus afflicted now? I am his love—he loves an Octoroon.

GEORGE: O, Zoe, you break my heart!

DORA: At college they said I was a fool—I must be. At New Orleans, they said, "She's pretty, very pretty, but no brains." I'm afraid they must be right; I can't understand a word of all this.

ZOE: Dear Dora, try to understand it with your heart. You love George; you love him dearly; I know it; and you deserve to be loved by him. He will love you—he must. His love for me will pass away—it shall. You heard him say it was hopeless. O, forgive him and me!

DORA: *(weeping)* O, why did he speak to me at all then? You've made me cry, then, and I hate you both! *(Exit through room)*

(Enter MRS PEYTON *and* SCUDDER, M'CLOSKY *and* POINTDEXTER*)*

M'CLOSKY: I'm sorry to intrude, but the business I came upon will excuse me.

MRS PEYTON: Here is my nephew, sir.

ZOE: Perhaps I had better go.

M'CLOSKY: Wal, as it consarns you, perhaps you better had.

SCUDDER: Consarns Zoe?

M'CLOSKY: I don't know; she may as well hear the hull of it. Go on, Colonel—Colonel Pointdexter, ma'am—the mortgagee, auctioneer, and general agent.

POINTDEXTER: Pardon me, madam, but do you know these papers? *(He hands the papers to* MRS PEYTON*)*

MRS PEYTON: *(taking them)* Yes, sir; they were the free papers of the girl Zoe; they were in my husband's secretary. How came they in your possession?

M'CLOSKY: I—I found them.

GEORGE: And you purloined them?

M'CLOSKY: Hold on, you'll see. Go on, Colonel.

POINTDEXTER: The list of your slaves is incomplete—it wants one.

SCUDDER: The boy Paul—we know it.

POINTDEXTER: No, sir, you have omitted the Octoroon girl, Zoe.

MRS PEYTON: ⎫ Zoe
ZOE: ⎭ Me!

POINTDEXTER: At the time the judge executed those free papers to his infant slave, a judgment stood recorded against him; while that was on record he had no right to make away with his property. That judgment still exists: under it and others this estate is sold to-day. Those free papers ain't worth the sand that's on 'em.

MRS PEYTON: Zoe a slave! It is impossible!

POINTDEXTER: It is certain, madam: the judge was negligent, and doubtless forgot this small formality.

SCUDDER: But the creditors will not claim the gal?

M'CLOSKY: Excuse me; one of the principal mortgagees has made the demand.

(Exeunt M'CLOSKY *and* POINTDEXTER*)*

SCUDDER: Hold on yere, George Peyton; you sit down there. You're trembling so, you'll fall down directly. This blow has staggered me some.

MRS PEYTON: O, Zoe, my child! don't think too hard of your poor father.

ZOE: I shall do so if you weep. See, I'm calm.

SCUDDER: Calm as a tombstone, and with about as much life. I see it in your face.

GEORGE: It cannot be! It shall not be!

SCUDDER: Hold your tongue—it must. Be calm— darn the things; the proceeds of this sale won't cover the debts of the estate. Consarn those Liverpool English fellers, why could n't they send something by the last mail? Even a letter, promising something—such is the feeling round amongst the planters. Darn me, if I could n't raise thirty thousand on the envelope alone, and ten thousand more on the postmark.

GEORGE: Zoe, they shall not take you from us while I live.

SCUDDER: Don't be a fool; they'd kill you and then take her, just as soon as—stop: old Sunnyside, he'll buy her; that'll save her.

ZOE: No, it won't; we have confessed to Dora that we love each other. How can she then ask her father to free me?

SCUDDER: What in thunder made you do that?

ZOE: Because it was the truth, and I had rather be a slave with a free soul, than remain free with a slavish, deceitful heart. My father gives me

freedom—at least he thought so. May Heaven bless him for the thought, bless him for the happiness he spread around my life. You say the proceeds of the sale will not cover his debts. Let me be sold then, that I may free his name. I give him back the liberty he bestowed upon me; for I can never repay him the love he bore his poor Octoroon child, on whose breast his last sigh was drawn, into whose eyes he looked with the last gaze of affection.

MRS PEYTON: O, my husband! I thank Heaven you have not lived to see this day.

ZOE: George, leave me! I would be alone a little while.

GEORGE: Zoe!

(Turning away overpowered)

ZOE: Do not weep, George. Dear George, you now see what a miserable thing I am.

GEORGE: Zoe!

SCUDDER: I wish they could sell *me!* I brought half this ruin on this family, with my all-fired improvements. I deserve to be a nigger this day—I feel like one, inside. *(Exit* SCUDDER*)*

ZOE: Go now, George—leave me—take her with you. *(Exit* MRS PEYTON *and* GEORGE*)* A slave! a slave! Is this a dream—for my brain reels with the blow? He said so. What! then I shall be sold!—sold! and my master—O! *(She falls on her knees, with her face in her hands)* No— no master but one. George—George—hush— they come! save me! No, *(Looks off)* 't is Pete and the servants—they come this way. *(Enters the inner room)*

(Enter PETE, GRACE, MINNIE, SOLON, DIDO, *and all Niggers)*

PETE: Cum yer now—stand round, 'cause I've got to talk to you darkies—keep dem chil'n quiet— don't make no noise, de missus up dar har us.

SOLON: Go on, Pete.

PETE: Gen'l'men, my colored frens and ladies, dar's mighty bad news gone round. Dis yer prop'ty to be sold—old Terrebonne—whar we all been raised, is gwine—dey's gwine to tak it away—can't stop here nohow.

OMNES: O-o!—O-o!

PETE: Hold quiet, you trash o' niggers! tink anybody wants you to cry? Who's you to set up screeching?—be quiet! But dis ain't all. Now, my cullud brethren, gird up your lines, and listen—hold on yer bref—it's a comin'. We tought dat de niggers would belong to de ole missus, and if she lost Terrebonne, we must live dere allers, and we would hire out, and bring our wages to ole Missus Peyton.

OMNES: Ya! ya! Well—

PETE: Hush! I tell ye, 't ain't so—we can't do it—we've got to be sold—

OMNES: Sold!

PETE: Will you hush? she will har you. Yes! I listen dar jess now—dar was ole lady cryin'—Mas'r George—ah! you seen dem big tears in his eyes. O, Mas'r Scudder, he did n't cry zackly; both ob his eyes and cheek look like de bad Bayou in low season—so dry dat I cry for him. *(Raising his voice)* Den say de missus, "'T ain't for de land I keer, but for dem poor niggers—dey'll be sold—dat wot stagger me." "No," say Mas'r George, "I'd rather sell myself fuss; but dey shan't suffer, nohow,—I see 'em dam fuss."

OMNES: O, bless 'um! Bless Mas'r George.

PETE: Hole yer tongues. Yes, for you, for me, for dem little ones, dem folks cried. Now, den, if Grace dere wid her chil'n were all sold, she'll begin screechin' like a cat. She did n't mind how kind old judge was to her; and Solon, too, he'll holler, and break de ole lady's heart.

GRACE: No, Pete; no, I won't. I'll bear it.

PETE: I don't tink you will any more, but dis here will; 'cause de family spile Dido, dey has. She nebber was worth much a' dat nigger.

DIDO: How dar you say dat, you black nigger, you? I fetch as much as any odder cook in Louisiana.

PETE: What's the use of your takin' it kind, and comfortin' de missus' heart, if Minnie dere, and Louise, and Marie, and Julie is to spile it?

MINNIE: We won't, Pete; we won't.

PETE: *(to the men)* Dar, do you hear dat, ye mis'able darkies; dem gals is worth a boat load of kinder men dem is. Cum, for de pride of de family, let every darky look his best for the judge's sake—dat ole man so good to us and dat ole woman—so dem strangers from New Orleans shall say, Dem's happy darkies, dem's a fine set of niggers; every one say when he's sold, "Lor' bless dis yer family I'm gwine out of, and send me as good a home."

OMNES: We'll do it, Pete; we'll do it.

PETE: Hush! hark! I tell ye dar's somebody in dar. Who is it?

GRACE: It's Missy Zoe. See! see!

PETE: Come along; she har what we say, and she's cryin' for us. None o' ye ign'rant niggers could cry for yerselves like dat. Come here quiet: now quiet. *(Exeunt* PETE *and all the Negroes, slowly)*

(Enter ZOE *who is supposed to have overheard the last scene)*

ZOE: O! must I learn from these poor wretches how much I owe, and how I ought to pay the debt? Have I slept upon the benefits I received, and never saw, never felt, never knew that I was forgetful and ungrateful? O, my father! my dear, dear father! forgive your poor child. You made her life too happy, and now these tears will flow. Let me hide them till I teach my heart. O, my—my heart! *(Exit, with a low, wailing, suffocating cry)*

(Enter M'CLOSKY, LAFOUCHE, JACKSON, SUNNYSIDE *and* POINTDEXTER*)*

POINTDEXTER: *(looking at his watch)* Come, the hour is past. I think we may begin business. Where is Mr Scudder?

JACKSON: I want to get to Ophelensis tonight.

(Enter DORA*)*

DORA: Father, come here.

SUNNYSIDE: Why, Dora, what's the matter? Your eyes are red.

DORA: Are they? thank you. I don't care, they were blue this morning, but it don't signify now.

SUNNYSIDE: My darling! who has been teasing you?

DORA: Never mind. I want you to buy Terrebonne.

SUNNYSIDE: Buy Terrebonne! What for?

DORA: No matter—buy it!

SUNNYSIDE: It will cost me all I'm worth. This is folly, Dora.

DORA: Is my plantation at Comptableau worth this?

SUNNYSIDE: Nearly—perhaps.

DORA: Sell it, then, and buy this.

SUNNYSIDE: Are you mad, my love?

DORA: Do you want *me* to stop here and *bid* for it?

SUNNYSIDE: Good gracious, no!

DORA: Then I'll do it if you don't.

SUNNYSIDE: I will! I will! But for Heaven's sake go—here comes the crowd. *(Exit* DORA*)* What on earth does that child mean or want?
(Enter SCUDDER, GEORGE, RATTS, CAILLOU, PETE, GRACE, MINNIE, *and all the Negroes. A large table is in the center of the background.* POINTDEXTER *mounts the table with his hammer, his clerk sitting at his feet. The Negro mounts the table from behind. The rest sit down)*

POINTDEXTER: Now, gentlemen, we shall proceed to business. It ain't necessary for me to dilate, describe or enumerate; Terrebonne is known to you as one of the richest bits of sile in Louisiana, and its condition reflects credit on them as had to keep it. I'll trouble you for that piece of baccy, Judge—thank you—so, gentlemen, as life is short, we'll start right off. The first lot on here is the estate in block, with its sugar-houses, stock, machines, implements, good dwelling-houses and furniture. If there is no bid for the estate and stuff, we'll sell it in smaller lots. Come, Mr Thibodeaux, a man has a chance once in his life—here's yours.

THIBODEAUX: Go on. What's the reserve bid?

POINTDEXTER: The first mortgagee bids forty thousand dollars.

THIBODEAUX: Forty-five thousand.

SUNNYSIDE: Fifty thousand.

POINTDEXTER: When you have done joking, gentlemen, you'll say one hundred and twenty thousand. It carried that easy on mortgage.

LAFOUCHE: Then why don't you buy it yourself, Colonel?

POINTDEXTER: I'm waiting on your fifty thousand bid.

CAILLOU: Eighty thousand.

POINTDEXTER: Don't be afraid: it ain't going for that, Judge.

SUNNYSIDE: Ninety thousand.

POINTDEXTER: We're getting on.

THIBODEAUX: One hundred—

POINTDEXTER: One hundred thousand bid for this mag—

CAILLOU: One hundred and ten thousand—

POINTDEXTER: Good again—one hundred and—

SUNNYSIDE: Twenty.

POINTDEXTER: And twenty thousand bid. Squire Sunnyside is going to sell this at fifty thousand advance to-morrow. *(Looking round)* Where's that man from Mobile that wanted to give one hundred and eighty thousand?

THIBODEAUX: I guess he ain't left home yet, Colonel.

POINTDEXTER: I shall knock it down to the Squire—going—gone—for one hundred and twenty thousand dollars. *(Raising hammer)* Judge, you can raise the hull on mortgage—going for half its value. *(Knocking on the table)* Squire Sunnyside, you've got a pretty bit o' land, Squire. Hillo, darkey, hand me a smash dar.

SUNNYSIDE: I got more than I can work now.

POINTDEXTER: Then buy the hands along with the property. Now, gentlemen, I'm proud to submit to you the finest lot of field hands and house servants that was ever offered for competition: they speak for themselves, and do credit to their owners. *(Reading)* "No. 1, Solon, a guest boy, and a good waiter."

PETE: That's my son—buy him, Mas'r Ratts; he's sure to sarve you well.

POINTDEXTER: Hold your tongue!

RATTS: Let the old darkey alone—eight hundred for that boy.

CAILLOU: Nine.

RATTS: A thousand.

SOLON: Thank you, Mas'r Ratts: I die for you, sar; hold up for me, sar.

RATTS: Look here, the boy knows and likes me, Judge; let him come my way!

CAILLOU: Go on—I'm dumb.

POINTDEXTER: One thousand bid. He's yours. Captain Ratts, Magnolia steamer. (SOLON *goes and stands behind* RATTS) "No. 2, the yellow girl, Grace, with two children—Saul, aged four, and Victoria five." *(They get on table)*

SCUDDER: That's Solon's wife and children, Judge.

GRACE: *(to* RATTS*)* Buy me, Mas'r Ratts, do buy me, sar?

RATTS: What in thunder should I do with you and those devils on board my boat?

GRACE: Wash, sar—cook, sar—anyting.

RATTS: Eight hundred agin, then—I'll go it.

JACKSON: Nine.

RATTS: I'm broke, Solon—I can't stop the Judge.

THIBODEAUX: What's the matter, Ratts? I'll lend you all you want. Go it, if you're a mind to.

RATTS: Eleven.

JACKSON: Twelve.

SUNNYSIDE: O, O!

SCUDDER: *(to* JACKSON*)* Judge, my friend. The Judge is a little deaf. Hello! *(Speaking in his ear-trumpet)* This gal and them children belong to that boy Solon there. You're bidding to separate them, Judge.

JACKSON: The devil I am! *(Rising)* I'll take back my bid, Colonel.

POINTDEXTER: All right, Judge; I thought there was a mistake. I must keep you, Captain, to the eleven hundred.

RATTS: Go it.

POINTDEXTER: Eleven hundred—going—going—sold! "No. 3, Pete, a house servant."

PETE: Dat's me—yer, I'm comin'—stand around dar. *(Tumbles upon the table)*

POINTDEXTER: Aged seventy-two.

PETE: What's dat? A mistake, sar—forty-six.

POINTDEXTER: Lame.

PETE: But don't mount to nuffin—kin work cannel. Come, Judge, pick up. Now's your time, sar.

JACKSON: One hundred dollars.

PETE: What, sar? me! for me—look ye here! *(He dances)*

GEORGE: Five hundred.

PETE: Mas'r George—ah, no, sar—don't buy me—keep your money for some udder dat is to be sold. I ain't no 'count, sar.

POINTDEXTER: Five hundred bid—it's a good price. He's yours, Mr George Peyton. (PETE *goes down)* "No. 4, the Octoroon girl, Zoe." *(Enter* ZOE, *very pale, and stands on table.* M'CLOSKY *who hitherto has taken no interest in the sale, now turns his chair)*

SUNNYSIDE: *(rising)* Gentlemen, we are all acquainted with the circumstances of this girl's position, and I feel sure that no one here will oppose the family who desires to redeem the child of our esteemed and noble friend, the late Judge Peyton.

OMNES: Hear! bravo! hear!

POINTDEXTER: While the proceeds of this sale promises to realize less than the debts upon it, it is my duty to prevent any collusion for the depreciation of the property.

RATTS: Darn ye! You're a man as well as an auctioneer, ain't ye?

POINTDEXTER: What is offered for this slave?

SUNNYSIDE: One thousand dollars.

M'CLOSKY: Two thousand.

SUNNYSIDE: Three thousand.

M'CLOSKY: Five thousand.

GEORGE: Demon!

SUNNYSIDE: I bid seven thousand, which is the last dollar this family possesses.

M'CLOSKY: Eight.

THIBODEAUX: Nine.

OMNES: Bravo!

M'CLOSKY: Ten. It's no use, Squire.

SCUDDER: Jacob M'Closky, you shan't have that girl. Now, take care what you do. Twelve thousand.

M'CLOSKY: Shan't I! Fifteen thousand. Beat that any of ye.

POINTDEXTER: Fifteen thousand bid for the Octoroon.
(Enter DORA)

DORA: Twenty thousand.

OMNES: Bravo!

M'CLOSKY: Twenty-five thousand.

OMNES: *(groan)* O! O!

GEORGE: Yelping hound—take that.

(He rushes on M'CLOSKY. M'CLOSKY *draws his knife)*

SCUDDER: *(darting between them)* Hold on, George Peyton—stand back. This is your own house; we are under your uncle's roof; recollect yourself. And, strangers, ain't we forgetting there's a lady present? *(The knives disappear)* If we can't behave like Christians, let's try and act like gentlemen. Go on, Colonel.

LAFOUCHE: He did n't ought to bid against a lady.

M'CLOSKY: O, that's it, is it? Then I'd like to hire a lady to go to auction and buy my hands.

POINTDEXTER: Gentlemen, I believe none of us have two feelings about the conduct of that man; but he has the law on his side—we may regret, but we must respect it. Mr M'Closky has bid twenty-five thousand dollars for the Octoroon. Is there any other bid? For the first time, twenty-five thousand—last time! *(Brings hammer down)* To Jacob M'Closky, the Octoroon girl, Zoe, twenty-five thousand dollars.

ACT FOURTH

SCENE: *The Wharf. The Steamer "Magnolia," alongside, a bluff rock.* RATTS *discovered, superintending the loading of ship.*

(Enter LAFOUCHE *and* JACKSON)

JACKSON: How long before we start, captain?

RATTS: Just as soon as we put this cotton on board.

(Enter PETE, *with a lantern, and* SCUDDER, *with note book)*

SCUDDER: One hundred and forty-nine bales. Can you take any more?

RATTS: Not a bale. I 've got engaged eight hundred bales at the next landing, and one hundred hogsheads of sugar at Patten's Slide—that'll take my guards under—hurry up thar.

VOICE: *(outside)* Wood's aboard.

RATTS: All aboard then.

(Enter M'CLOSKY)

SCUDDER: Sign that receipt, captain, and save me going up to the clerk.

M'CLOSKY: See here—there's a small freight of turpentine in the fore hold there, and one of the barrels leaks; a spark from your engines might set the ship on fire, and you'll go with it.

RATTS: You be darned! Go and try it, if you've a mind to.

LAFOUCHE: Captain, you've loaded up here until the boat is sunk so deep in the mud she won't float.

RATTS: *(calling off)* Wood up thar, you Pollo—hang on to the safety valve—guess she'll crawl off on her paddles.   *(Shouts heard)*

JACKSON: What's the matter?

(Enter SOLON)

SOLON: We got him!

SCUDDER: Who?

SOLON: The Injiun!

SCUDDER: Wahnotee? Where is he? D'ye call running away from a fellow catching him?

RATTS: Here he comes.

OMNES: Where? Where?

(Enter WAHNOTEE. *They are all about to rush on him)*

SCUDDER: Hold on! stan' round thar! no violence—the critter don't know what we mean.

JACKSON: Let him answer for the boy then.

M'CLOSKY: Down with him—lynch him.

OMNES: Lynch him!   *(Exit* LAFOUCHE)

SCUDDER: Stan' back, I say! I'll nip the first that lays a finger on him. Pete, speak to the red-skin.

PETE: Whar's Paul, Wahnotee? What's come ob de child?

WAHNOTEE: Paul wunce—Paul pangeuk.

PETE: Pangeuk—dead!

WAHNOTEE: Mort!

M'CLOSKY: And you killed him? *(They approach him)*

SCUDDER: Hold on!

PETE: Um, Paul reste?

WAHNOTEE: Hugh vieu. *(Goes)* Paul reste ci!

SCUDDER: Here, stay! (*Examining the ground*) The earth has been stirred here lately.

WAHNOTEE: Weenee Paul.

(*He points down, and shows by pantomime how he buried* PAUL)

SCUDDER: The Injun means that he buried him there! Stop! here's a bit of leather (*Drawing out the mail-bags*) The mail-bags that were lost! (*Sees the tomahawk in* WAHNOTEE'S *belt—draws it out and examines it*) Look! here are marks of blood—look thar, red-skin, what's that?

WAHNOTEE: Paul! (*Makes a sign that* PAUL *was killed by a blow on the head*)

M'CLOSKY: He confesses it; the Indian got drunk, quarrelled with him, and killed him.

(*Re-enter* LAFOUCHE, *with smashed apparatus*)

LAFOUCHE: Here are evidences of the crime; this rum-bottle half emptied—this photographic apparatus smashed—and there are marks of blood and footsteps around the shed.

M'CLOSKY: What more d'ye want—ain't that proof enough? Lynch him!

OMNES: Lynch him! Lynch him!

SCUDDER: Stan' back boys! He's an Injiun—fair play.

JACKSON: Try him, then—try him on the spot of his crime.

OMNES: Try him! Try him!

LAFOUCHE: Don't let him escape!

RATTS: I'll see to that. (*Drawing revolver*) If he stirs, I'll put a bullet through his skull, mighty quick.

M'CLOSKY: Come, form a court then, choose a jury—we'll fix this varmin.

(*Enter* THIBODEAUX *and* CAILLOU)

THIBODEAUX: What's the matter?

LAFOUCHE: We've caught this murdering Injiun, and are going to try him.

(WAHNOTEE *sits, rolled in blanket*)

PETE: Poor little Paul—poor little nigger!

SCUDDER: This business goes agin me, Ratts—'t ain't right.

LAFOUCHE: We're ready; the jury's impanelled—go ahead—who'll be accuser?

RATTS: M'Closky.

M'CLOSKY: Me?

RATTS: Yes; you was the first to hail Judge Lynch.

M'CLOSKY: Well, what's the use of argument whar guilt sticks out so plain; the boy and Injiun were alone when last seen.

SCUDDER: Who says that?

M'CLOSKY: Everybody—that is, I heard so.

SCUDDER: Say what you know—not what you heard.

M'CLOSKY: I know then that the boy was killed with that tomahawk—the red-skin owns it—the signs of violence are all round the shed—this apparatus smashed—ain't it plain that in a drunken fit he slew the boy, and when sober concealed the body yonder?

OMNES: That's it—that's it.

RATTS: Who defends the Injiun?

SCUDDER: I will; for it is agin my natur' to b'lieve him guilty; and if he be, this ain't the place, nor you the authority to try him. How are we sure the boy is dead at all? There are no witnesses but a rum bottle and an old machine. Is it on such evidence you'd hang a human being?

RATTS: His own confession.

SCUDDER: I appeal against your usurped authority. This lynch law is a wild and lawless proceeding. Here's a pictur' for a civilized community to afford; yonder, a poor, ignorant savage, and round him a circle of hearts, white with revenge and hate, thirsting for his blood: you call yourselves judges—you ain't—you're a jury of executioners. It is such scenes as these that bring disgrace upon our Western life.

M'CLOSKY: Evidence! Evidence! Give us evidence. We've had talk enough; now for proof.

OMNES: Yes, yes! Proof, proof!

SCUDDER: Where am I to get it? The proof is here, in my heart.

PETE: (*who has been looking about the camera*) 'Top, sar! 'Top a bit! O, laws-a-mussey, see dis! here's a pictur' I found stickin' in that yar telescope machine, sar! look, sar!

SCUDDER: A photographic plate. (PETE *holds his lantern up*) What's this, eh? two forms! The child—'t is he! dead—and above him—Ah! ah! Jacob M'Closky, 't was you murdered that boy!

M'CLOSKY: Me?

SCUDDER: You! You slew him with that tomahawk; and as you stood over his body with the letter in your hand, you thought that no witness saw the deed, that no eye was on you—but there was, Jacob M'Closky, there was. The eye of the Eternal was on you—the blessed sun in heaven, that, looking down, struck upon this plate the image of the deed. Here you are, in the very attitude of your crime!

M'CLOSKY: 'T is false!

SCUDDER: 'T is true! the apparatus can't lie. Look there, jurymen. (Showing plate to jury) Look there. O, you wanted evidence—you called for proof—Heaven has answered and convicted you.

M'CLOSKY: What court of law would receive such evidence? (Going)

RATTS: Stop! this would! You called it yourself; you wanted to make us murder that Injiun; and since we've got our hands in for justice, we'll try it on you. What say ye? shall we have one law for the red-skin and another for the white?

OMNES: Try him! Try him!

RATTS: Who'll be accuser?

SCUDDER: I will! Fellow-citizens, you are convened and assembled here under a higher power than the law. What's the law? When the ship's abroad on the ocean, when the army is before the enemy, where in thunder's the law? It is in the hearts of brave men, who can tell right from wrong, and from whom justice can't be bought. So it is here, in the wilds of the West, where our hatred of crime is measured by the speed of our executions—where necessity is law! I say, then, air you honest men? air you true? Put your hands on your naked breasts, and let every man as don't feel a real American heart there, bustin' up with freedom, truth, and right, let that man step out—that's the oath I put to ye—and then say, Darn ye, go it!

OMNES: Go on! Go on!

SCUDDER: No! I won't go on; that man's down. I won't strike him, even with words. Jacob, your accuser is that picture of the crime—let that speak—defend yourself.

M'CLOSKY: (drawing knife) I will, quicker than lightning.

RATTS: Seize him, then! (They rush on M'CLOSKY, and disarm him) He can fight though he's a painter: claws all over.

SCUDDER: Stop! Search him, we may find more evidence.

M'CLOSKY: Would you rob me first, and murder me afterwards?

RATTS: (searching him) That's his programme—here's a pocket-book.

SCUDDER: (opening it) What's here? Letters! Hello! To "Mrs Peyton. Terrebonne, Louisiana, United States." Liverpool postmark. Ho! I've got hold of the tail of a rat—come out. (Reading) What's this? A draft for eighty-five thousand dollars, and credit on Palisse and Co., of New Orleans, for the balance. Hi! the rat's out. You killed the boy to steal this letter from the mail-bags—you stole this letter, that the money should not arrive in time to save the Octoroon; had it done so, the lien on the estate would have ceased, and Zoe be free.

OMNES: Lynch him! Lynch him! Down with him!

SCUDDER: Silence in the court: stand back, let the gentlemen of the jury retire, consult, and return their verdict.

RATTS: I'm responsible for the crittur—go on.

PETE: (to WAHNOTEE) See, Injiun; look dar, (Showing him the plate) see dat innocent; look, dar's de murderer of poor Paul.

WAHNOTEE: Ugh! (Examining the plate)

PETE: Ya! as he? Closky tue Paul—kill de child with your tomahawk dar: 't was n't you, no—ole Pete allus say so. Poor Injiun lub our little Paul. (WAHNOTEE rises and looks at M'CLOSKY—he is in his war paint and fully armed)

SCUDDER: What say ye, gentlemen? Is the prisoner guilty, or is he not guilty?

OMNES: Guilty!

SCUDDER: And what is to be his punishment?

OMNES: Death! (All advance)

WAHNOTEE: (crosses to M'CLOSKY) Ugh!

SCUDDER: No, Injiun; we deal out justice here, not revenge. 'T ain't you he has injured, 't is the white man, whose laws he has offended.

RATTS: Away with him—put him down the aft hatch, till we rig his funeral.

M'CLOSKY: Fifty against one! O! if I had you one by one alone in the swamp, I'd rip ye all. *(He is borne off in boat struggling)*

SCUDDER: Now, then, to business.

PETE: *(re-enters from boat)* O, law, sir, dat debil Closky, he tore hisself from de gen'lam, knock me down, take my light, and trows it on de turpentine barrels, and de shed's all afire! *(Fire seen)*

JACKSON: *(re-entering)* We are catching fire forward: quick, cut free from the shore.

RATTS: All hands aboard there—cut the starn ropes—give her headway!

OMNES: Ay, ay!

(Cry of "Fire" heard—Engine bells heard—steam whistle noise)

RATTS: Cut all away, for'ard—overboard with every bale afire. *(The steamer moves off with the fire still blazing)*

(M'CLOSKY re-enters, swimming)

M'CLOSKY: Ha! have I fixed ye? Burn! burn! that's right. You thought you had cornered me, did ye? As I swam down, I thought I heard something in the water, as if pursuing me—one of them darned alligators, I suppose—they swarm hereabout—may they crunch every limb of ye.   *(Exit)*

(WAHNOTEE is seen swimming. He finds trail and follows M'CLOSKY. The steamer floats on at back, burning)

ACT FIFTH

SCENE 1: *Negroes' Quarters.*

(Enter ZOE)

ZOE: It wants an hour yet to daylight—here is Pete's hut—*(Knocks)* He sleeps—no: I see a light.

DIDO: *(enters from hut)* Who dat?

ZOE: Hush, aunty! 'T is I—Zoe.

DIDO: Missey Zoe? Why you out in de swamp dis time ob night; you catch de fever sure—you is all wet.

ZOE: Where's Pete?

DIDO: He gone down to de landing last night wid Mas'r Scudder; not come back since—kint make it out.

ZOE: Aunty, there is sickness up at the house; I have been up all night beside one who suffers, and I remembered that when I had the fever you gave me a drink, a bitter drink, that made me sleep—do you remember it?

DIDO: Did n't I? Dem doctors ain't no 'count; dey don't know nuffin.

ZOE: No; but you, aunty, you are wise—you know every plant, don't you, and what it is good for?

DIDO: Dat you drink is fust rate for red fever. Is de folks' head bad?

ZOE: Very bad, aunty; and the heart aches worse, so they can get no rest.

DIDO: Hold on a bit, I get you de bottle.   *(Exit)*

ZOE: In a few hours that man, my master, will come for me: he has paid my price, and he only consented to let me remain here this one night, because Mrs Peyton promised to give me up to him to-day.

DIDO: *(re-enters with phial)* Here 't is—now you give one timble-full—dat's nuff.

ZOE: All there is there would kill one, would n't it?

DIDO: Guess it kill a dozen—nebber try.

ZOE: It's not a painful death, aunty, is it? You told me it produced a long, long sleep.

DIDO: Why you tremble so? Why you speak so wild? What you's gwine to do, missey?

ZOE: Give me the drink.

DIDO: No. Who dat sick at de house?

ZOE: Give it to me.

DIDO: No. You want to hurt yourself. O, Miss Zoe, why you ask old Dido for dis pizen?

ZOE: Listen to me. I love one who is here, and he loves me—George. I sat outside his door all night—I heard his sighs—his agony—torn from him by my coming fate; and he said, "I'd rather see her dead than this!"

DIDO: Dead!

ZOE: He said so—then I rose up, and stole from the house, and ran down to the bayou: but its cold, black, silent stream terrified me—drowning must be so horrible a death. I could not do it. Then as I knelt there, weeping for courage a snake rattled beside me. I shrunk from it and fled. Death was there beside me, and I dared not take it. O I'm afraid to die; yet I am more afraid to live.

DIDO: Die!

ZOE: So I came here to you; to you, my own dear nurse; to you, who so often hushed me to sleep when I was a child; who dried my eyes and put your little Zoe to rest. Ah! give me the rest that no master but One can disturb—the sleep from which I shall awake free! You can protect me from that man—do let me die without pain.

DIDO: No, no—life is good for young ting like you.

ZOE: O! good, good nurse: you will, you will.

DIDO: No—g' way.

ZOE: Then I shall never leave Terrebonne—the drink, nurse; the drink; that I may never leave my home—my dear, dear home. You will not give me to that man? Your own Zoe, that loves you, aunty, so much, so much. *(She gets the phial)* Ah! I have it.

DIDO: No, missey. O! no—don't.

ZOE: Hush!   *(Runs off)*

DIDO: Here, Solon, Minnie, Grace.
       (They enter)

ALL: Was de matter?

DIDO: Miss Zoe got de pizen.   *(Exit)*

ALL: O! O!   *(Exeunt)*

SCENE 2: *In a Cane-brake Bayou, on a bank, with a canoe near by,* M'CLOSKY *is seen asleep.*

M'CLOSKY: Burn, burn! blaze away. How the flames crack. I'm not guilty; would ye murder me? Cut, cut the rope—I choke—choke!—Ah! *(Waking)* Hello! where am I? Why, I was dreaming—curse it! I can never sleep now without dreaming. Hush! I thought I heard the sound of a paddle in the water. All night, as I fled through the cane-brake, I heard footsteps behind me. I lost them in the cedar swamp—again they haunted my path down the bayou, moving as I moved, resting when I rested—hush! there again!—no; it was only the wind over the canes. The sun is rising. I must launch my dug-out, and put for the bay, and in a few hours I shall be safe from pursuit on board of one of the coasting schooners that run from Galveston to Matagorda. In a little time this darned business will blow over, and I can show again. Hark! there's that noise again! If it was the ghost of that murdered boy haunting me! Well—I did n't mean to kill him, did I? Well, then, what has my all-cowardly heart got to skeer me so for?
(He gets in canoe and rows off. WAHNOTEE *appears in another canoe. He gets out and finds trail and paddles off after* M'CLOSKY)

SCENE 3: *A cedar Swamp*

(Enter SCUDDER *and* PETE)

SCUDDER: Come on, Pete, we shan't reach the house before midday.

PETE: Nebber mind, sa, we bring good news—it won't spile for de keeping.

SCUDDER: Ten miles we've had to walk, because some blamed varmin onhitched our dug-out. I left it last night all safe.

PETE: P'r'aps it floated away itself.

SCUDDER: No; the hitching line was cut with a knife.

PETE: Say, Mas'r Scudder, s'pose we go in round by de quarters and raise de darkies, den dey cum long wid us, and we 'proach dat ole house like Gin'ral Jackson when he took London out dar.

SCUDDER: Hello, Pete, I never heard of that affair.

PETE: I tell you, sa—hush!

SCUDDER: What?

PETE: Was dat?—a cry out dar in the swamp—dar again!

SCUDDER: So it is. Something forcing its way through the undergrowth—it comes this way—it's either a bear or a run-away nigger.

(He draws a pistol. M'CLOSKY *rushes on, and falls at* SCUDDER'S *feet)*

SCUDDER: Stand off—what are ye?

PETE: Mas'r Clusky.

M'CLOSKY: Save me—save me! I can go no farther. I heard voices.

SCUDDER: Who's after you?

M'CLOSKY: I don't know, but I feel it's death! In some form, human, or wild beast, or ghost, it has tracked me through the night. I fled; it followed. Hark! there it comes—it comes—don't you hear a footstep on the dry leaves!

SCUDDER: Your crime has driven you mad.

M'CLOSKY: D 'ye hear it—nearer—nearer—ah!

*(*WAHNOTEE *rushes on, and attacks* M'CLOSKY*)*

SCUDDER: The Injiun! by thunder.

PETE: You'se a dead man, Mas'r Closky—you got to b'lieve dat.

M'CLOSKY: No—no. If I must die, give me up to the law; but save me from the tomahawk. You are a white man; you'll not leave one of your own blood to be butchered by the red-skin?

SCUDDER: Hold on now, Jacob; we've got to figure on that—let us look straight at the thing. Here we are on the selvage of civilization. It ain't our side, I believe, rightly; but Nature has said that where the white man sets his foot, the red man and the black man shall up sticks and stand around. But what do we pay for that possession? In cash? No—in kind—that is, in protection, forbearance, gentleness, in all them goods that show the critters the difference between the Christian and the savage. Now, what have you done to show them the distinction? for, darn me, if I can find out.

M'CLOSKY: For what I have done, let me be tried.

SCUDDER: You have been tried—honestly tried and convicted. Providence has chosen your executioner. I shan't interfere.

PETE: O, no; Mas'r Scudder, don't leave Mas'r Closky like dat—don't, sa—'t ain't what good Christian should do.

SCUDDER: D' ye hear that, Jacob? This old nigger, the grandfather of the boy you murdered, speaks for you—don't that go through you? D' ye feel it?

Go on, Pete, you've waked up the Christian here, and the old hoss responds. *(He throws bowie-knife to* M'CLOSKY*)* Take that, and defend yourself.

(Exeunt SCUDDER *and* PETE. WAHNOTEE *faces him. They fight.* M'CLOSKY *runs off,* WAHNOTEE *follows him.—Screams outside)*

SCENE 4: *Parlor at Terrebonne*

(Enter ZOE*)*

ZOE: My home, my home! I must see you no more. Those little flowers can live, but I cannot. To-morrow they'll bloom the same—all will be here as now, and I shall be cold. O! my life, my happy life; why has it been so bright?

(Enter MRS PEYTON *and* DORA*)*

DORA: Zoe, where have you been?

MRS PEYTON: We felt quite uneasy about you.

ZOE: I've been to the negro quarters. I suppose I shall go before long, and I wished to visit all the places, once again, to see the poor people.

MRS PEYTON: Zoe, dear, I'm glad to see you more calm this morning.

DORA: But how pale she looks, and she trembles so.

ZOE: Do I? *(Enter* GEORGE*)* Ah! he is here.

DORA: George, here she is.

ZOE: I have come to say good-by, sir; two hard words—so hard, they might break many a heart; might n't they?

GEORGE: O, Zoe! can you smile at this moment?

ZOE: You see how easily I have become reconciled to my fate—so it will be with you. You will not forget poor Zoe! but her image will pass away like a little cloud that obscured your happiness a while—you will love each other; you are both too good not to join your hearts. Brightness will return amongst you. Dora, I once made you weep; those were the only tears I caused anybody. Will you forgive me?

DORA: Forgive you—*(Kisses her)*

ZOE: I feel you do, George.

GEORGE: Zoe, you are pale. Zoe!—she faints!

ZOE: No; a weakness, that's all—a little water. *(*DORA *gets some water)* I have a restorative here—will you pour it in the glass? (DORA *attempts to take it*) No; not you—George. (GEORGE *pours the contents of the phial into glass*) Now, give it to me. George, dear George, do you love me?

GEORGE: Do you doubt it, Zoe?

ZOE: No! (*She drinks*)

DORA: Zoe, if all I possess would buy your freedom, I would gladly give it.

ZOE: I am free! I had but one Master on earth, and he has given me my freedom!

DORA: Alas! but the deed that freed you was not lawful.

ZOE: Not lawful—no—but I am going to where there is no law—where there is only justice.

GEORGE: Zoe, you are suffering—your lips are white—your cheeks are flushed.

ZOE: I must be going—it is late. Farewell, Dora. (*Retiring*)

PETE: (*outside*) Whar's Missus—whar's Mas'r George?

GEORGE: They come.
(*Enter* SCUDDER)

SCUDDER: Stand around and let me pass—room thar! I feel so big with joy, creation ain't wide enough to hold me. Mrs Peyton, George Peyton, Terrebonne is yours. It was that rascal M'Closky—but he got rats, I swow—he killed the boy, Paul, to rob this letter from the mailbags—the letter from Liverpool you know—he sot fire to the shed—that was how the steamboat got burned up.

MRS PEYTON: What d' ye mean?

SCUDDER: Read—read that.
(*He gives letter to them*)

GEORGE: Explain yourself.
(*Enter* SUNNYSIDE)

SUNNYSIDE: Is it true?

SCUDDER: Every word of it, Squire. Here, you tell it, since you know it. If I was to try, I'd bust.

MRS PEYTON: Read, George. Terrebonne is yours.
(*Enter* PETE, DIDO, SOLON, MINNIE, *and* GRACE)

PETE: Whar is she—whar is Miss Zoe?

SCUDDER: What's the matter?

PETE: Don't ax me. Whar's de gal? I say.

SCUDDER: Here she is—Zoe!—water—she faints.

PETE: No—no. 'T ain't no faint—she's a dying, sa: she got pizon from old Dido here, this mornin'.

GEORGE: Zoe!

SCUDDER: Zoe! is this true?—no, it ain't—darn it, say it ain't. Look here, you're free, you know; nary a master to hurt you now: you will stop here as long as you're a mind to, only don't look so.

DORA: Her eyes have changed color.

PETE: Dat's what her soul's gwine to do. It's going up, dar, whar dere's no line atween folks.

GEORGE: She revives.

ZOE: (*on the sofa*) George—where—where—

GEORGE: O, Zoe! what have you done?

ZOE: Last night I overheard you weeping in your room, and you said, "I'd rather see her dead than so!"

GEORGE: Have I then prompted you to this?

ZOE: No; but I loved you so, I could not bear my fate; and then I stood between your heart and hers. When I am dead she will not be jealous of your love for me, no laws will stand between us. Lift me; so—(GEORGE *raises her head*)—let me look at you, that your face may be the last I see of this world. O! George, you may, without a blush, confess your love for the Octoroon.
(*She dies.* GEORGE *lowers her head gently and kneels beside her*)

CURTAIN

BEGINNINGS

CIVIL WAR TO WORLD WAR I

AUGUSTIN DALY, *Under the Gaslight* (1867)

BRONSON HOWARD, *Shenandoah* (1888)

JAMES A. HERNE, *Margaret Fleming* (1890)

WILLIAM VAUGHN MOODY, *The Great Divide* (1903)

RACHEL CROTHERS, *He and She* (1911)

CIVIL WAR TO WORLD WAR I

The Worlds of Melodrama, 1860–1910

A S NEW MIDDLE-, BUSINESS-, AND WORKING-CLASS AUDIENCES CAME TO dominate the theatres, as some theatres (old and new) began to hone their appeal to particular segments of the theatre-going population, and as theatres continued to try to satisfy these audiences' desires for an entertaining education in the shifting reality of America, an already well-established dramatic form and style were consolidating their positions on the American stage. That form was **melodrama**. The pervasiveness of melodrama in all of its permutations is hard to overestimate. In fact, melodrama came to dominate the stage on both sides of the Atlantic so thoroughly that the partisans for the next formal paradigm to sweep Western culture—realism—were forced to wage an aesthetic campaign for over 40 years before realist drama could even approach the popularity of melodrama. Since we will have the opportunity to address some of the specific varieties and uses of melodrama when we discuss Augustin Daly's *Under the Gaslight* (1867) and Bronson Howard's *Shenandoah* (1888), we will restrict ourselves at this juncture to a few observations on melodrama's basic structural paradigm and how it served the audiences who flocked to it.

In the last 100 years, the stereotypical distillation of stage melodrama—a mustache-twirling villain; a beautiful, chaste, and inevitably imperiled heroine; and a stalwart hero to save her (Snidely Whiplash, Nell Fenwick, and Dudley Doright, if you are a fan of "Rocky and Bullwinkle")—have passed from unconscious to almost self-parodic elements of American popular culture. Realist, modernist, and formalist condemnations of melodrama as artistic dross have so colored subsequent critical discussions that, until recently, we have failed to recognize melodrama's "durability, its cross-cultural popularity, its service as an agent of socialization, or its later function as a forum in which conflicting ideologies could confront each other and, to a certain extent, resolve the social and political tensions of the emerging western industrial-capitalist states of the nineteenth-century" (Richardson). However, as recent critics such as David Grimsted, Bruce McConachie, and Jeffrey Mason have insisted, to understand how American melodrama functioned during its late nineteenth-century heyday, one must understand not only the general appeals of the form but also the particular context in which these plays met their original audiences.

Melodrama's fundamental characteristics are readily apparent to the first-time viewer or reader. As Michael Booth notes, "essentially, melodrama is a simplification and idealization of human experience dramatically presented." Melodrama uses all of the theatre's devices (including atmospheric music, from which the form draws its name) to present life as a relatively straightforward contest between "good" and "evil." But this simplification, ironically enough, may explain melodrama's enduring audience appeal, for as James Smith has observed, such elementary division "expresses the reality of the human condition as we all experience it most of the time." The result is a drama that facilitates audience identification with the heroes and heroines and allows, within the context of the dramatic production, the emergence of collective identities embodied in the hero and heroine. In a plot usually characterized by extravagant coincidences, a hero faces physical danger, the indifference or hostility of society, or a villain's inexplicable antipathy (or some combination of the three) in order to save a typically passive heroine who symbolically serves as the repository of the cultural values necessary to perpetuate civilized society. Formally, then, right will always triumph; order will always reassert itself.

On the other hand, although the formal pattern is one of a return to stability, the psychological paradigm is one which emphasizes anxiety, threat, even terror. While the play may begin and end happily, the great body of the plot is consumed by plunges over a series of emotional cataracts whose cumulative effect upon the audience is to tap a deep-seated fear that one of these times the moral, social, and domestic order may actually change. For members of older social formations in the audience, the operation of melodrama confirmed the world as they had always known it. For the members of emerging formations whose very presence in the theatre testified to their increasing, but as yet tenuous, economic standing, melodrama provided a means of facing and putting to rest their economic and social nightmares. As Jeffrey Mason has commented, "If society can change, if it can evolve or transform into something new rather than experiencing a restoration to its former condition, then it is possible for such a change to leave the subject behind, rendering him marginal, rejected, and out of place. This is the fear of erasure or displacement, of being cast aside and left alone." Such fears were hardly groundless in America in the midst of this period's unprecedented change.

During the golden age of American melodrama, roughly between 1865 and 1900, America was drastically transfigured. In spite of the Civil War, the nation's population doubled in the second half of the century. Much of that growth was concentrated in about a dozen cities where immigrants joined recent arrivals from the country to seek employment in the new commercial hubs of America. Economically, Currier and Ives' America of family farms and small businesses was being supplanted by industry as the prime employer of the American work force. A new, more intense class consciousness was emerging in the country as tension and suspicion between the new capitalists and a fragmented and various labor force became a fact of life. Displacements from earlier economic and social patterns generated a nostalgia for an earlier, more comprehensible, and stable form of life and led to efforts to use the theatre and imaginative literature, in general, to understand the new realities of American society. For both immigrant and native-born, the theatre became a primary means of seeing the world, of learning how to deal with that world, of being reassured that the promise of America remained an achievable goal.

One of the most obvious groups to use the theatre as the site of both education and entertainment was immigrants. Though ethnic theatres catering specifically to particular communities began to emerge during the nineteenth century (their activity peaked from 1900 to 1930), immigrants also found themselves portrayed and inscribed in the mainstream commercial houses (Seller). Italians, Germans, Bohemians, Chinese, and, above all, the Irish found representation on the melodramatic stage. Besides offering the immigrant a glimpse of home and the native born a peek at their newest countrymen's ostensibly exotic backgrounds, these melodramas asserted the essential humanity beneath the surface variety of national characters and, thus, more often than not, served to decrease ethnic tensions. Occasionally, as in the case of Dion Boucicault's Irish nationalist melodramas, the plays served several functions at once. But to recognize the way in which Boucicault intervened culturally in the social formation of the day, it is necessary to understand the outlines of Irish-American history in this period.

The Irish had long been the targets of nativist bias, reviled by such groups as the Know-Nothing party which asserted that the Irish affiliation with Roman Catholicism meant that most could not be absolutely loyal to the United States. Even after the Civil War, the social position of the Irish remained problematic. Although they had made great political strides (capturing New York City government, for instance), they were still usually presented on stage and in the newspapers as rowdy drunkards and wastrels. To lessen anti-Irish prejudice in the United States, to aid his native countrymen in their nationalist struggle, to provide himself a series of marvelous parts, and, to a large degree, to attract a ready audience (after all, there were more Irishmen attending the theatre in New York for most of the nineteenth century than there were in Dublin), Boucicault produced a series of enormously successful Irish plays in the 1860s and 1870s. While all of these plays are set in Ireland, they are obviously designed to speak primarily to American playgoers (only *Arrah-na-Pogue* [1865] premiered in Dublin) for they subvert Anglo-American stereotypes about the Irish in order to insinuate that, despite their differences, Anglo-Americans and Irish-Americans share two important traits—a deep love of personal freedom and a healthy distrust of the English.

If Boucicault looked to the "old country" to explain the new America and its latest inhabitants, any number of playwrights used melodrama to examine America's ongoing westward expansion. In the wake of the Civil War, older frontier play conventions were reworked for a new audience, an audience less optimistic than its pre-1861 counterpart, one seeking the reassuring, less complicated world that the melodramatic vision provided. The proven formulas of previous eras resurfaced, particularly in portraits of stock characters and in romantic attitudes toward nature. Thus, the heroic frontiersman endured in such plays as Frank Murdock's *Davy Crockett* (1872), and the rude frontiersman continued to provide comic fodder in Charles H. Hoyt's *A Texas Steer* (1890). And, just as *Metamora* had partaken of the romantic idea of nature's inherently spiritual essence, so too Joaquin Miller's *The Danites in the Sierras* (1877) and David Belasco's *The Girl of the Golden West* (1905) appealed through their intricate scenic designs and dialogue to the nation's enduring faith that God was to be discovered most directly in unmediated nature.

But if these plays' use of earlier frontier dramas' conventions provided a measure of reassurance to their audiences, the plays' actions also forced them to reflect more consciously on new, potentially troubling realities. Primary among these was a pervasive insistence upon representing economic production as a part of Western life. Goldfield plays such as Miller's *The Danites in the Sierras*, Belasco's *The Girl of the Golden West*, and Bartley Campbell's *My Partner* (1879) acknowledge what the audience knew unconsciously—almost all westward expansion was rooted in an initial rush for gold or silver. While these plays often ignored the reality of heavily capitalized, large-scale mining operations run by syndicates in favor of the more picturesque placer miner panning his life toward economic empowerment and independence, they could not help but acknowledge that it was the West as a locale that seemed to provide this remote chance of economic freedom. But in the majority of these plays the hope of achieving that independence proved illusory. As the plays made clear, those who travelled west often brought with them many of the evils they sought to escape—moral decay, violence, ethnic and racial bias, and a nagging tendency to replicate vapid social orders. Thus, though their intention could hardly be seen as polemic, many of these melodramas provided telling social commentary in the guise of reassuring entertainment.

The Emergence of Realism and the End of the Early Drama, 1870–1917

Although there is no doubt that melodrama was the dominant dramatic mode between 1860 and 1910, there is also no doubt that over that same period an alternative dramatic orientation was insinuating itself into some of the best critical and theatrical minds of the period. Encompassing now one aspect of characterization, now another of performance, now still another of production, what has come to be called **realism** emerged in fits and starts. Nor did realism, a multivalent critical term now fraught with extensive interpretive and theoretical baggage, mean the same thing to all people at all times in the period. It emerged from a particular historical moment and responded to the same political, social, economic, and cultural forces to which melodrama reacted. Certainly, then, it is better to understand "realism" in this period as part of a dialectic whose other member was "idealism" than to imagine that it was in itself a wholly positive, self-contained critical concept. This is particularly important when considering the statements of the period's major critics, people such as William Dean Howells and Henry James, who, as writers of narrative fiction as well as drama, nearly always speak of "realism" as a goal rather than a set of established convention or settled practice.

The realists' essential objection to late nineteenth-century melodrama was what they perceived as its insistence upon simplifying and idealizing. While the concept of an objective, verifiable reality is far more problematic than theoreticians such as Émile Zola (whose set of 1870s essays on "naturalism in the theatre" is usually credited with beginning the realist critical debate) acknowledged, these writers insisted that drama could and should deal with issues of vital interest in a natural and honest manner. For the realists, the "objective" reality was to be represented in a structure that replicated the flow of the events themselves rather than in a form superimposed to fit some preconceived aesthetic dictum. Added to these essentials was a dramatic language that, as much as possible, should foster the illusion that the audience was listening to real people speaking. While this approach to diction and dialogue did not preclude figurative language, it rendered rhetorical flourishes and pervasive lyricism, as well as soliloquies and asides, beyond the pale. Hence, even if it meant the incorporation of vulgarities, colloquialisms, and dialects, the drama on the stage was to sound as much like what the audience heard outside the theatre as possible. While the playwrights were to give them a new language to speak, the actors presenting the play were to learn a new, quieter style of acting—more understated, more nuanced, and more evocative. Gone were the days of "chewing the scenery," of engaging in the type of histrionics in a domestic tragedy that might (according to the more conservative realist theorists of the day, such as James) remain appropriate for a historically and aesthetically distanced forerunner such as a Shakespearean tragedy. If the actors were to restrain themselves, so too the theatre technicians—the carpenters, musicians, costumers, and lighting specialists—were to redirect their efforts away from the "sensation scenes," which, according to realist critics, served to disguise the essential falsity of melodramatic action toward a physical verisimilitude that would enhance the realism of the play.

Ultimately, these new plays would allow the playwrights, actors, and audiences to examine the same vital issues and moral choices that the melodramatists were considering but presented through ordinary characters engaged in normal daily lives rather than through extraordinary characters caught up in an idealized world. While it is impossible to deal with the entire scope of American dramatic realism's emergence or the varieties of resistance the process encountered, a brief glance at plays by William Dean Howells, Steele MacKaye, Bronson Howard, and William Gillette will enhance our ability to appreciate the works after the turn of the century, which build upon or implicitly respond to the issues raised by the realists.

None of the individuals writing before the turn of the century, with the exception of James A. Herne, whose *Margaret Fleming* is introduced later in this anthology, consistently wrote what could be called fully realistic plays. Each of the playwrights we will discuss, however, contributed to the eventual ascendancy of realism as American drama's dominant mode in the first half of the twentieth century. Beyond a dogged critical campaign to gain acceptance for realism waged from his editorial chairs at the *Atlantic Monthly* and *Harper's Magazine,* and minimally successful commercial pieces such as *The Counterfeit Presentiment* (1877), Howells' greatest contributions to the writing of realist drama were a series of short realistic comedies which regularly appeared in the *Atlantic Monthly* and *Harper's Magazine* and provided models for his contemporaries and the aspiring writers who followed him. The key realist elements of Howells' popular comedies were restrained dialogue, situations, and characters typical of Howells' middle-class audience, and a social comedy that emerged, more often than not, from character rather than situation.

This increased interest in the realistic representation of character is also the primary contribution of both Steele MacKaye and Bronson Howard. While in such early efforts as *Marriage* (1872) MacKaye sought to pare his plots and focus on serious social issues, his greatest successes were more modest in their accomplishments in the cause of realism. In both *Hazel Kirke* (1880; first acted as *An Iron Will* in 1879) and *Paul Kauver; or Anarchy* (1887), MacKaye takes pains to provide carefully delineated characters who seem, in many senses, ill-fitted to the plays' traditionally melodramatic plots. To a degree, Bronson Howard is more successful in matching realist characters and a realist plot in *The Henrietta* (1887), his exploration of the private and business lives of New York financiers. Convinced that the primary concern of the American stage ought to be the portrayal of American business, Howard replaced the traditional slavering businessman of melodrama with the much more complex characters of Nicholas Vanalstyne and his son. ("Old Nick" and his son may seem somewhat overdrawn until one remembers that the original audience's daily newspapers treated them to the similar exploits of men such as Jay Gould,

John D. Rockefeller, and Andrew Carnegie. Given that historical circumstance, it is quite possible to read this play's central characters as falling well within the bounds created by turning daily reality into satiric comedy.)

The most difficult major figure to describe effectively in this context is William Gillette, for his contributions were of a more ephemeral nature, situated as they were within performance practice. Gillette, who scored enormous successes in plays such as *Secret Service* (1895) and *Sherlock Holmes* (1899) (an adaptation of three of Doyle's stories), was not actually much concerned with the philosophical debates concerning realism. However, his own inclination toward restrained acting and his meticulous attention to the visual components of his performances led him inadvertently to aid its growth. While the plots of Gillette's works rarely evidenced any commitment to realism, their performances immersed the audience in a world of such physical verisimilitude that the melodramatic premises of the plays were often forgotten.

By the turn of the century, the advocates of realism within literature generally and drama particularly seemed to have carried the aesthetic debate if not the publishing houses and theatres. Although the forces of melodrama had hardly been beaten from the field, they were fighting a rearguard action and the nation's drama increasingly seemed to embrace realism's premises. Nevertheless, the American theatre had not yet entered the period of realist ascendancy associated with the 1920s and 1930s. Plays tended still to combine both realistic and melodramatic—and on occasion, fantastic—elements. Additionally, two circumstances—one emerging from the operation of the theatrical business, and the other from the realist/melodrama debate—tended to retard the full-blown development of a dominantly realistic American drama.

At a secret meeting in 1895, the owners of the vast majority of American theatres secretly entered into an agreement to control competition and prices. Known as the Theatrical Syndicate, this group of producers and theatre owners effectively stifled dramatic experimentation for many years by treating the theatre as a "bottom line business." After the advent of the Shubert brothers in the first decade of the century some competition was reintroduced to the theatrical scene, but things did not improve much for the commercial houses or the audiences who attended them. The Shuberts' "Independent Movement," which sought to offset the Syndicate by providing audiences alternate theatres and attractions, intensified competition between the groups with the ironic effect of minimizing still further the freedom of playwrights to grapple with new subject matter in a more realistic form. For the Syndicate and the Shuberts, the rich vein of melodrama, which had sustained their theatres for years, had not yet played out. Not surprisingly, groups such as the Provincetown Players who wished to go beyond the conventional formulas of commercial success began to spring up and provide American audiences more regular access to innovative dramatists such as Shaw, Ibsen, Chekhov, O'Neill, and Glaspell. In a very real sense, such groups as New York's Washington Square Players, and its successors, The Theatre Guild, and The Group Theatre, collectively dedicated to providing new spaces for noncommercial drama, are the direct heirs of this period of theatrical monopoly.

Also proving something of a restriction to the further expansion of its influence was the belief that realism—at least as understood by its early formulators—had encouraged character analysis at the expense of the broader dramatic canvas that had been the forte of romantic drama and melodrama. Many playwrights at the beginning of the century, therefore, tended to focus on the private rather than the social world, sublimating or displacing their social critiques in ways similar to the techniques employed by post–Civil War melodramas. While many of American drama's traditional subjects—sectional identity, racial and ethnic strife, differences between country and city, relationships between men and women, life among the social elite, the pressures for social conformity, and the desire for individuality—are represented in the era, they are almost always rendered within a domestic form. With the major exception of plays dealing with women's issues under the rubric of the "Woman's Question," the variety of broad social critique that one often associates with the muckraking journalists or the novels of Dreiser, Lewis, and Wharton is absent from the plays of this era.

The growth of the city has been a perennial topic since *The Contrast*, but by the turn of the century it had come to dominate the literary imagination of a host of American poets and novelists. It is not surprising that in a period of enormous urban physical and demographic growth, dramatists, too, would find the city a vital subject for their examination. Indeed, the period produced two of the most interesting American dramas to treat the city, Langdon Mitchell's *The New York Idea* (1906) and Clyde Fitch's *The City* (1909). Mitchell's play is probably the best comedy of manners written in America between Anna Cora Mowatt's *Fashion* (1845) and Philip Barry's *Holiday* (1928). Sparkling with the kind of wit and verbal play that one associates with Congreve and Sheridan, Mitchell's play skewers the frivolity of his upper-class targets. While finally more social satire than social criticism, *The New York Idea* uses its counterpointing of the unconventional freedoms of American youth with the stuffy formalities of the older generation to give the play a charmingly American flavor. While Mitchell does make some interesting observations about the symbiotic relationship between the city and the upper class, ultimately the city serves more as backdrop for the "fast life" of the upper class than a key factor in understanding the characters.

In *The City*, Fitch is careful to construct his play so as to take advantage of the contrast between the American myth of the small town with its closely knit families, good friends, and upright lives and the bustling city with its disintegrating families, promiscuous life style, and cutthroat competition. Despite appeals to condemn the city as the genesis of his characters' final act failings, Fitch's play refuses to indulge the popular myth that the city is responsible. Through the use of melodramatic elements, Fitch's play clearly establishes the moral contrasts he wishes his audience to recognize. But in its refusal to end the action happily and its care to utilize contemporary concerns about greed and political corruption in New York, the play suggests that realism has complicated its conception.

If Mitchell and Fitch used contemporary events and mores to give their plays a veneer of realism, Edward Sheldon carefully rendered his character studies in such a way as to allow for the serious investigation of social ills while maintaining an audience whose tastes had been formed by melodrama's reliance on sensational action. In a series of notable successes—including *Salvation Nell* (1908), *The Nigger* (1909), and *The Boss* (1911)—Sheldon turned a cold eye on abiding problems within American society, examining, in turn, the effects of urban poverty, racism, and machine politics. While Sheldon's plays are hardly the social dramas of a Kingsley or an Odets, they do provide a kind of dramatic refraction of the Progressive movement. For all of their engagement with the social forces of the day, Sheldon's plays finally pull back from suggesting organized or governmental intervention. Sheldon ultimately restricts his interest to complex characters rather than social programs, and his solution to the problems he sees is ultimately a very traditional one—personal moral transformation. Paradoxically, the plays of the period best able to delineate the fates of the abused and neglected and, thus, lay the groundwork for social action do not seem grounded in a vision that can grasp the possibility of a social or political solution to these problems. There can be little doubt that Sheldon's willingness to address social issues places him in the mainstream of the American social play tradition and that the coincidence of his plays' productions during the era's social flux give them a historical importance that rivals the antislavery plays of the 1850s. Nevertheless, his equivocal attitude suggests both the enduring conservatism of the commercial theatre and the necessity of circumventing that theatre to speak to those issues.

While Sheldon and, to a lesser extent, Fitch and Mitchell were analyzing the nation's shortcomings, another group of dramatists was repudiating the assumptions that grounded those investigations and embracing a new vision. Turning from broad social concerns that seemed to consume their contemporaries, these playwrights sought to reexamine the status of the individual in America. In such works as Augustus Thomas' *The Witching Hour* (1907), Percy MacKaye's *The Scarecrow* (1908), and William Vaughn Moody's *The Great Divide* (1906) and *The Faith Healer* (1909), these writers sought to raise questions about the nature of human existence, the individual's relationship to society, and the existence and nature of transcendent realities. As we shall see in our later discussion of Moody's *The Great Divide*, through their belief in and focus on the power within the individual, these writers sought to explore forces that the ostensible rationality of modernity denied or repressed. Collectively they suggest a counterpolitics to the emphasis on collective social problems and a reassertion of the primacy of the individual on the American stage. Dramatically, the plays reveal a fascination with sources of characterization beyond those recognized by the era's dramatic realism and raise questions that will not arise again on the American stage until raised by O'Neill. Although Moody's early death and MacKaye's redirection of his efforts to noncommercial theatre greatly reduced the lasting impact of these plays on the direction of American drama, their presence in our dramatic history is a telling reminder that, despite a continuing interest in its social context, American drama also encompasses those visions that insist upon resisting the pull of particular historical and social circumstances.

In the first two decades of the twentieth century, as in most centuries, it would be difficult to find plays that did not deal with issues of gender. But the seemingly changing circumstances of women in this period gave a new urgency to dramatic representations of women's issues. In addition to the continuing treatment by men, women's issues received a new perspective in another group of plays, plays written by women themselves. This heightened dramatic interest in women was in some senses the result of several converging forces. The growth of women's educational opportunities after the Civil War meant, among other things, that a new and larger group of extremely literate women was available as both literary artists and literary consumers. Additionally, women's visibility outside the home increased as they assumed positions of leadership in social and moral movements—as varied as Carrie Nation's temperance campaign and Jane Addams' social work at Hull House—and in the professions and business. Finally, within the political and legal fields, the long legal ascendancy of men was beginning to be challenged ever so slightly. New divorce laws gave women greater legal freedom (although most lacked the economic independence to take advantage of their legal options), and in 1920 the culmination of a long struggle was reached when women gained the franchise. For many in the period, it seemed that the assumptions that had underpinned the social, legal, economic, emotional, not to mention dramatic relationships between women and men in America had been thrown into relief and were available for reexamination. Little surprise then that, given these circumstances, playwrights, especially women such as Rachel Crothers and Susan Glaspell, would choose to devote much of their creative energies to examining such a vital topic.

Despite the semblance of change, however, the new representations of women often replicated at basic levels those assumptions, which had grounded earlier, yet in more overtly oppressive social and dramatic formations. As Judith Stephens has cogently argued, the Progressive era tended to couch social reform within a context that inevitably restricted the power and opportunities of women. By attempting to use the widely held belief that women were more "moral" than men as the basis for greater participation in the world, female reformers employed a conventional sentiment that would ultimately restrict them. When linked with the dramatic convention that all plays must present a moral view, this reliance upon superior morality inevitably couched women as the moral spokesperson and, thereby, reinforced the dominant gender ideology. As we shall see in our discussions of Herne's *Margaret Fleming,* Moody's *The Great Divide,* Crothers' *He and She,* and Glaspell's *Trifles,* all of these plays lodge critiques of the dominant gender ideology only, paradoxically, to reinforce it.

Ironically, the advent of independent theatre companies (such as the Provincetown Players, of which Glaspell was a founding member) seems to have had little effect on the representations of women in the early decades of the century. The continuing control of the major commercial houses by the Theatrical Syndicate and the Shuberts meant that radical critiques of the social order which these organizations reflected were not going to be tolerated by men fixated on the bottom line. And even alternative theatre companies tended to be ruled just as firmly by men. Typical is the fact that women are conspicuously absent from administrative leadership roles in the Provincetown Players, the Washington Square Players, and The Theatre Guild.

As the world spun toward the cataclysm of World War I, the American drama was dragged like most American institutions toward a new reality. Events and experimental companies like the Provincetown Players pulled American drama from its provincial early history into a new artistic phase. The social, political, artistic, and cultural assumptions which, in the main, had sustained the nation's drama for over 200 years were obliterated. Gone was the innocent belief that American experience or the drama that reflected that experience was or could any longer remain apart from the events, political and artistic, of those beyond its shores. Some older writers would continue to produce after the war, but, old or new, the writers who sought to people the stage after 1917 were forever changed by the experience of that war.

WORKS CONSULTED

Booth, Michael. *Hiss the Villain: Six English and American Melodramas.* New York: Benjamin Blom, 1964.

Grimsted, David. *Melodrama Unveiled: American Theater and Culture, 1800–1850.* Chicago: University of Chicago Press, 1968.

Mason, Jeffrey D. *Melodrama and the Myth of America.* Bloomington: Indiana University Press, 1993.

McConachie, Bruce A. *Melodramatic Formations.* Iowa City: University of Iowa Press, 1992.

Murphy, Brenda. *American Realism and American Drama, 1880–1940.* Cambridge: Cambridge University Press, 1987.

Seller, Maxine Schwartz, ed. *Ethnic Theatre in the United States.* Westport, CT: Greenwood Press, 1983.

Smith, James L. *Melodrama.* London: Methuen, 1973.

Stephens, Judith. "Gender Ideology and Dramatic Convention in Progressive Era Plays, 1890–1920." *Theatre Journal,* 41 (1989): 45–55.

UNDER THE GASLIGHT (1867)

The piece is, in fact, nothing more than a stage carpenter's drama. The play has been fitted to the scenes as the poetry in the old annuals used to be to the plates, or just as Nicholas Nickleby's drama was adapted to bring in the pump and two water tubs that Mr. Vincent Crummles had bought at a bargain. Everything the management could do to make the piece a success has been done. It was admirably put upon the stage, and the full house showed that the excellence of the scenery was appreciated. Of the drama itself, however, nothing good can be said.

Such, Odell reminds us, was *The Herald* reviewer's estimate of *Under the Gaslight,* the **sensation melodrama** that secured Augustin Daly's reputation as a playwright and launched his career as a major figure in the American theatre in the last half of the nineteenth century. If *The Herald* reviewer could find nothing to satisfy his taste, the audiences who thrilled to the sensation scene in which the heroine chopped her way out of a railroad switching shed, loosened her loyal companion's ropes, and rescued him from an oncoming train in more than 100 performances during that first season did not seem to share his indifference. The *New York Times'* review provides a hint to explain the play's success when it notes that on opening night "a crowded and brilliant audience . . . testified their approbation of the several scenes by hearty applause." Just as *The Octoroon* focused its audiences' attentions on the primary social, moral, and political issues of the antebellum period, *Under the Gaslight* addressed similar issues arising from the increasing urbanization of American society after the war. *The Octoroon's* focus on slavery had unavoidably raised race and ethnicity as defining elements of an individual's identity.

Similarly, *Under the Gaslight's* conflict between the rich and poor of New York City drew attention to post–Civil War economic flux and the way class increasingly determined social identity. But, while both plays examined issues central to individual as well as national self-definition, the psychic trajectory of each play was distinctly different. *The Octoroon* had managed to evoke sympathy from its white audiences for Zoe's tragic plight while simultaneously distancing viewers' potential anxieties by rendering Zoe ultimately "other" by dint of her race. In *Under the Gaslight,* the audience was required not merely to sympathize but to empathize with Laura Courtland, whose fall from middle-class security to lower-class subsistence represented the collective economic nightmare of Daly's middle- and business-class audience.

As his younger brother and biographer, Joseph Francis Daly, tells us, John Augustin Daly was born on July 20, 1838, in Plymouth, North Carolina, to Captain Denis Daly, a shipowner, and Elizabeth Duffey Daly. Daly's mother was widowed in 1841, and the same year she moved the family to Norfolk, Virginia. Finally, at the insistence of her sister, Elizabeth Daly moved her family to New York City. Augustin Daly briefly attended public school but soon began working for a firm of house furnishers. Daly frequently spent his free time attending the theatre, and by the later 1850s was unsuccessfully peddling plays to established stars such as W. E. Burton, Laura Keene, and Joseph Jefferson III. In December 1859, Daly began covering theatrical affairs, among other things, in a weekly column for the *Sunday Courier.* Over the course of the next few years, he expanded his readership by becoming the drama critic for the *Evening Express* (1864), the *Sun* (1866), the *New York Times,* and the *Citizen* (1867). For a brief time in 1867, Daly was writing for all five papers at once. After increasing successes as a playwright, beginning with *Leah, the Forsaken* (1862), and extending through *Under the Gaslight* and *Norwood* (both 1867), Daly resigned from all of the newspapers but the *New York Times*. By 1869, he had given up that position also, choosing to devote his time to his bride, Mary Duff, and his first, full-time managerial position.

With his move into theatre management, Daly was able to put into practice the principles that he earlier espoused in his dramatic criticism. As William Winter later recalled, Daly asserted that his theatre would produce "whatever is novel, original, entertaining, and unobjectionable" and revive "whatever is rare and worthy in legitimate drama." Daly's purpose was clear. He was intent upon securing the theatre as an institution against all future "moral attacks," of accomplishing what William Dunlap had tried to do nearly 100 years before, of providing an environment in which his middle-class clientele could be uplifted as well as entertained. For the next 30 years, through success and failure, he would steadfastly hold to and accomplish his major goals.

Daly's contributions to American theatre are arguably much greater than his contribution to the national drama. While Daly was to have such notable original successes as *Horizon* (1871) later in his career, his duties as a manager-director consumed great amounts of his time and energy, and he became widely known for his localized adaptations and his elaborate productions of pieces from the classical repertoire, especially Shakespearean comedy in collaboration with the celebrated actress, Ada Rehan. Daly's contributions include being the first American manager to tour Europe with an American company (a tour his companies completed nine times) and being the first American manager to establish a permanent London playhouse for his own company. In 1899, he left New York City for England to settle legal questions arising from his London theatre. After a severe bout of pneumonia in transit Daly collapsed of a heart attack while on a shopping excursion to Paris and died June 7, 1899.

Under the Gaslight, coming as it does early in Daly's career, reveals the influence of a host of plays that had earlier addressed New York City life. Rahill reminds us that such pieces as Benjamin Baker's *A Glance at New York* (1848) with Mose the ruffian and volunteer fireman Cornelius Matthews' *Broadway and the Bowery* (1856), *The Rich of New York* (1857), and *Gotham, or Daylight and Gaslight* (1857) had long established the farcical appeals of the lower-class denizens of the city to lower-class audiences. Boucicault's *The Poor of New York* (1857) elevated the subgenre by adding a distinctly middle-class caste to the action. Daly combined the rough-hewn charms of the character farces with the serious action of Boucicault's success of the previous decade to produce a piece cannily suited to address the middle-class audience that often found New York City a disquieting environment.

As Seymour Mandelbaum notes, New York City in the 1860s and 1870s experienced enormous flux. Forty-four percent of the nearly one million residents had been born abroad. The streets were often dirty, inadequately drained, and often the final resting places of dead animals. The mid-1860s' death rate of 40/1000 was the highest in the Western world among large cities. The power which drove the commercial and banking worlds was widely distributed, but as a whole the distribution of income in the city was radically skewed to either the rich or the very poor. Those of moderate means were rare. It is little wonder that given this social and economic reality, *Under the Gaslight* spoke forcefully to the local realities of those who entered Daly's theatre.

The story of Laura Courtland, as Bruce McConachie has argued, evidences a dawning awareness among the emergent business-class audiences (and the playwrights who sought to speak to and through them) of the flaws in previous melodrama's insistence upon a strict causal correlation between social success and individual respectability. But while McConachie is correct in asserting that "sensation melodrama decoupled this linkage by acknowledging that chance often interferes with the best-laid plans of business-class heroes and heroines to maintain their social positions," he is less convincing in suggesting that such plays as *Under the Gaslight* "shift the definition of respectability from inner qualities of character and morality to 'natural' attributes resulting from birth and upbringing." Laura (whose very name seems to imply her heritage in romantic literature) is effectively the new middle-class romance heroine, a fact that the original reviewer for the *New York Times* recognized when he remarked that the play reminded him of nothing so much as the tale of Sir Gawain and the loathly lady. Like the already popular Horatio Alger tales, *Under the Gaslight* acknowledges "luck" or "chance" or "fate," but it reinscribes the importance of individual character at the same time that it suggests that integrity is not an absolute stay against the vicissitudes of circumstance. As an answer to the popularized theories of nature *vs.* nurture in the wake of the evolutionist writings of Charles Darwin and Herbert Spencer, *Under the Gaslight* implies both that environment does not wholly determine character (as distinct from class) and that respectability remains a function of character rather than of class. As the spectators applaud Laura's return to the economic well-being that nobility of character seems to warrant, the audience simultaneously embraces a reassuring projection of itself which allays its fears of its own tenuous social construction. *Under the Gaslight* is, finally, a play that speaks less to the aspirations of those separated by class, education, and birth from the goal of respectability than to those who fear losing their status as respectable members of the bourgeoisie. As Laura's story suggests, though society can foolishly dismiss from its ranks individuals who confront economic hard times, fate cannot remove that which is part of a person's identity.

WORKS CONSULTED

Daly, Joseph Francis. *The Life of Augustin Daly.* New York: Macmillan, 1917.

Felheim, Marvin. *The Theatre of Augustin Daly.* Cambridge: Harvard University Press, 1956.

Jefferson, Joseph, III. *Rip van Winkle: An Autobiography.* New York: 1890.

Mandelbaum, Seymour J. *Boss Tweed's New York.* (1965). Chicago: Elephant Paperback, 1990.

McConachie, Bruce A. *Melodramatic Formations: American Theatre and Society, 1820–1870.* Iowa City: University of Iowa Press, 1992.

New York Times. Review of *Under the Gaslight.* New York Theatre. New York City. 13 August 1867: 5.

Odell, George Clinton Densmore. *Annals of the New York Stage.* 15 vols. 1927–1949. New York: AMS Press, 1970.

Rahill, Frank. *The World of Melodrama.* University Park: Pennsylvania State University, 1967.

Shattuck, Charles H. "Augustin Daly and the Shakespeare Comedies." In *Shakespeare on the American Stage.* Vol. 2. Washington: Folger Books, 1987. 54–92.

Winter, William. *Vagrant Memories.* New York: George H. Doran, 1915.

CHARACTERS

RAY TRAFFORD	a rich young man
LAURA COURTLAND	his sweetheart
PEARL COURTLAND	her cousin
EDWARD DEMILT	
WINDEL	
MRS VAN DAM	fashionable members of society
MISS EARLIE	
SNORKEY	a messenger
MARTIN	a servant
BYKE	a villain
JUDAS	his associate
PEACHBLOSSOM	a servant

BERMUDAS ⎫
PEANUTS ⎰ .... street sellers

JUSTICE BOWLING

SPLINTER .... an attorney

PETER RICH .... a vagrant boy

POLICEMAN 999

RAFFERDI .... an organ-grinder

SAM .... a negro

POLICE SERGEANT

SIGNALMAN

     Negro servant, Officers of the police court, Dock boys, Policemen, Ladies and Gentlemen

ACT I

SCENE I: *Parlour at the* COURTLANDS, *deep window at back showing snowy exterior—street lamp lighted—time, night—the place elegantly furnished, chandelier, &c.*

RAY TRAFFORD *is discovered lounging on tête-à-tête,* PEARL *is taking leave of* DEMILT, WINDEL, MRS VAN DAM, *and* SUE EARLIE, *who are all dressed and muffled to go out.*

MRS VAN DAM: Goodnight! Of course we'll see you on Tuesday.

PEARL: To be sure you will.

DEMILT: Never spent a jollier hour. Goodnight, Ray.

RAY: *(on sofa)* Goodnight.

MRS VAN DAM: You won't forget the sociable on Tuesday, Ray?

RAY: Oh, I won't forget.

ALL: *(at door)* Goodnight—goodnight.

    (Exeunt DEMILT, WINDEL, MRS VAN DAM, *and* MISS EARLIE*)*

PEARL: Goodnight. Oh, dear, now they're gone and the holiday's gone with them. *(Goes to window)* There they go. *(Laughter without)* Ray, do

come and look at the Van Dams' new sleigh. How they have come out.

RAY: Yes, it's the gayest thing in the park.

PEARL: I wonder where they got the money! I thought you said Van Dam had failed.

RAY: Well, yes. He failed to pay, but he continues to spend.

PEARL: *(as if to those outside)* Goodnight! *(Response from without as sleigh bells jingle 'goodnight')* I wish I was in there with you. It's delightful for a sleigh ride, if it wasn't New Year's. Oh! there's Demilt over. *(Laughter outside, cracking of whips,* RAY *saunters up to window, sleigh bells jingle, sleigh music heard to die away,* RAY *and* PEARL *wave their handkerchiefs)*

PEARL: *(closing lace curtains)* Isn't it a frightful thing to be shut up here on such a beautiful night, and New Year's of all others? Pshaw, we've had nothing but mopes all day. Oh, dear, I hate mourning, though it does become me, and I hate everything but fun, larks, and dancing.

RAY: Where in the world is Laura?

PEARL: Oh, do forget her for a second, can't you? She'll be here presently. You're not in the house a minute but it's 'Where's Laura?' 'Why don't Laura come?'

RAY: *(taking her hand)* Well, if anybody in the world could make me forget her it would be you. But if you had a lover, wouldn't you like him to be as constant as that?

PEARL: That's quite another thing.

RAY: But this doesn't answer my question. Where is she?

PEARL: I sent for her as soon as I saw you coming. She has hardly been down here a moment all this evening. Oh, dear! Now don't you think I'm a victim, to be cooped up in this way instead of receiving calls as we used to?

RAY: You forget that your mother died only last summer.

PEARL: No, I don't forget. Pshaw, you're just like Laura. She's only my cousin, and yet she keeps always saying 'Poor aunt Mary. Let us not forget how she would have sorrowed for us.'

RAY: Well, don't you know she would, too?

PEARL: I don't know anything about it. I was always at boarding school, and she only saw me once a year. Laura was always at home, and it's very different. But don't let's talk about it. To die—ugh! I don't want to die till I don't want to live—and that'll not be for a million years. Come, tell me, where have you been today? How many calls did you make?

RAY: About sixty.

PEARL: That's all? You're lazy. Demilt and Windel made a hundred and thirty, and they say that's nothing. Won't you have a cup of coffee?

RAY: No.

PEARL: Ain't you hungry?

RAY: No—you torment.

PEARL: Oh, dear! I suppose it's because you're going to be married shortly to Laura. If there's one time that a man's stupid to his friends, it's when he's going to be married shortly. Tell me whom you saw. (RAY *has sauntered off and is looking over cards on table*) Where are you? Oh, you needn't be so impatient to see her. Do be agreeable. Sit here and tell me something funny, or I shall drop down and fall asleep.

RAY: You witch! Why didn't I fall in love with you?

PEARL: *(laughing)* I don't know—why didn't you?

RAY: You never keep me waiting. *(Listening)* Ah! that's her step. No.

PEARL: Do sit down.

RAY: *(sitting)* This calling's a great bore, but as you and Laura insisted I should go through it I did. First I—*(jumping up)* I knew it was she. *(Goes to door, meets* LAURA, *who enters)* How you did keep me waiting! *(Kisses both her hands)*

LAURA: And you, sir, we have been looking for you since eight o'clock.

RAY: Oh, I was fulfilling your orders. I've been engaged in the business of calling from ten o'clock in the morning till now, ten at night.

LAURA: Well, you can make this your last one, for you have leave to spend a nice long hour chatting here before you go. Won't you have some supper?

RAY: I don't care if I do, I'm rather famished.

PEARL: Well, I declare! Did Laura bring your appetite with her? (LAURA *rings*)

RAY: I don't know how it is, but she brings me a relish for everything in life, I believe. Laura, I think if I were to lose you I'd mope to death and starve to death.

LAURA: Well, that's as much to say I'm a sort of life pill.

(Enter MARTIN)

Martin, supper. *(Exit)*

RAY: You may joke about it, but it's so. You take the lounge.

*(*LAURA *and* PEARL *sit on tête-à-tête)*

PEARL: You don't want me to go away, do you? *(Putting her head on* LAURA'S *shoulder)*

LAURA: Certainly not. What an idea!

PEARL: I'm sure you'll have time enough to be alone when you are married. And I do so want to talk and be talked to.

LAURA: Well, Ray shall talk to you.

PEARL: He was just going to tell me about his calls today.

LAURA: That's exactly what we want to hear about. Did you call on everyone we told you to?

RAY: Everyone. There was Miss—

PEARL: Did you go to Henrietta Liston's first?

RAY: Yes, and wasn't she dressed! Speaking of dress, are you going to have your new pink for the sociable Tuesday?

LAURA: Yes, Pearl, and I will do credit to the occasion, as it is our first for a year.

RAY: (taking LAURA's hand) And our last.

PEARL: Our last!

RAY: Laura's and mine. For when we are married, you know, we shall be tabooed—where maids and bachelors only are permitted.

PEARL: Oh, bless me! (Rising) How do you do, Mrs Trafford?

LAURA: (rising, sadly) I wish you hadn't said that, Pearl. You know the old proverb, 'Call a maid by a married name.'

RAY: Nonsense! (Putting his arm about LAURA's waist) It's only a few days to wait, and we'll live long enough, you know. For nothing but death shall separate us.

(MARTIN appears at door)

PEARL: Oh, here's supper.

MARTIN: Beg pardon, Miss.

LAURA: What's the matter?

MARTIN: There's a person below, miss, who says he's been sent with a bouquet for you, miss, and must deliver it in person.

LAURA: For me? Whose servant is it?

MARTIN: I don't know, miss, he looks like one of those soldier messengers, red cap and all that.

LAURA: Show him up here. (Exit MARTIN)

PEARL: How romantic. So late at night. It's a rival in disguise, Ray.

(Re-enter MARTIN showing in SNORKEY with an air of disdain. SNORKEY has a large bouquet in his left hand, and his hat is under the stump of his right arm, which is cut off)

LAURA: You wished to see me.

SNORKEY: Are you Miss Laura Courtland?

LAURA: Yes.

SNORKEY: Then I was told to give you this.

LAURA: By whom?

SNORKEY: Now, that's what I don't know myself. You see I was down by the steps of the Fifth Avenue Hotel taking a light supper off a small toothpick, when a big chap dressed in black came by, and says he, 'Hallo, come with me if you want to earn a quarter.' That (confidentially to all) being my very frame of mind, I went up one street and down another till we came here. 'Just you take this up there,' says he, 'and ask for Miss Laura Courtland, and give it to her and no one else.'

LAURA: It is some folly of our late visitors.

SNORKEY: I'm one of the soldier messengers, miss. A South Carolina gentleman took such a fancy to me at Fredericksburg! Wouldn't have no denial—cut off my arm to remember me by; he was very fond of me. I wasn't any use to Uncle Sam then, so I came home, put a red band round my blue cap, and with my empty sleeve, as a character from my last place, set up for light porter and general messenger. All orders executed with neatness and dispatch.

LAURA: Poor fellow! Martin, be sure and give him a glass of wine before he goes.

SNORKEY: I'm much obliged, miss, but I don't think it would be good for me on an empty stomach after fasting all day.

LAURA: Well, Martin shall find you some supper, too.

SNORKEY: Is this Martin? What a nice young man! Mayn't he have a drop of something, too? He must have caught cold letting me in, he has got such a dreadful stiffness in the back of his neck. (Exit MARTIN)

RAY: (giving pencilled address) Call on me at this place tomorrow, and you shan't regret it.

SNORKEY: All right, cap'n. I haven't forgot the army regulations about punctuality and promotion. Ladies, if ever either of you should want a light porter think of Joe Snorkey—wages no objection. (Exit)

PEARL: (who has been examining the bouquet) Oh, Laura, only look, here's a billet-doux.

RAY: Nonsense, crazy-head, who would dare? (Takes bouquet) A letter! (Takes a paper from bouquet)

LAURA: A letter?

PEARL: I am crazy—am I?

RAY: 'For Miss Laura Courtland. Confidential.'

LAURA: *(laughs)* Ha, ha! From some goose who has made one call too many today. Read it, Ray.

RAY: 'Dear Laura . . .' *(Refusing the letter and going to* PEARL*)*

LAURA: *(looks at it a moment, when the whole expression of face changes, then reads slowly and deliberately)* 'I respectfully beg you to grant me the favour of an interview tonight. I have waited until your company retired. I am waiting across the street now.'

PEARL: *(runs to window)* A tall man in black is just walking away.

LAURA: 'If you will have the door opened as soon as you get this I will step over; if you don't, I will ring; under all circumstances I will get in. There is no need to sign my name; you will remember me as the strange man whom you once saw talking with your mother in the parlour, and who frightened you so much.' What can be the meaning of this? Pearl—no. *(Goes to bell on table and rings)*

RAY: Laura, you—

LAURA: Ask me nothing. I will tell you by and by. *(Enter* MARTIN*)*

MARTIN: Miss—

LAURA: Admit no one till you bring me the name.

MARTIN: I was about to tell you, miss, that a strange man has forced himself in at the door and asks to see you, but will give no name.

RAY: Kick the rascal out.

PEARL: Oh, don't let him come here.

MARTIN: He's a very strange-looking person, miss.

RAY: I'll find out what this means. *(Is going to door when* BYKE *appears at it smiling and bowing)*

BYKE: I'll spare you the trouble if you'll hear me a minute.

RAY: *(violently)* Who are you, fellow?

BYKE: Don't, I beg you. Don't speak so crossly; I might answer back; then you'd kick me out, and you'd never forgive yourself for it as long as I lived.

RAY: Your business? Come, speak quickly and begone.

BYKE: Business, on this happy day! I came for pleasure—to see Miss Courtland, my little pupil—grown so—only think, sir, I knew her when she was only a little child; I taught her music—she was so musical—and so beautiful—I adored her, and her mother told me I needn't come again. But I did, and her mother was glad to see me, wasn't she, little pupil? *(to* LAURA, *who is pale with terror, leaning on* PEARL*)* and begged me to stay—but I said no—I'd call occasionally—to see my dear little pupil and to receive any trifling contribution her mother might give me. Won't you shake hands, little pupil? *(Advances suddenly, when* RAY *grasps him by the collar.* BYKE *glares at him a moment, then quickly, as before)* Don't, please, don't; the stuff is old and I've no other.

RAY: The fellow's drunk. Leave the house.

BYKE: What, after sending that touching bouquet?

LAURA: It was you, then? I knew it.

BYKE: You see she knows me. Ah, memory, how it blooms again where the plough of time has passed.

LAURA: Leave this house at once.

BYKE: Not until I have spoken to you.

RAY: *(seizing him)* You miserable rascal.

BYKE: Don't, pray don't. I weigh a hundred and ninety-eight pounds, and if you attempt to throw me about you'll strain yourself.

LAURA: Go; tomorrow in the morning I will see you.

BYKE: Thanks. I thank you, miss, for your forbearance. I am also obliged to you, sir, for not throwing me out at the window. I am indeed. I wish you goodnight and many happy returns of the day. *(Bows and turns to go, then familiarly to servant)* Many calls today, John? *(Exit)*

*(*RAY *runs to* LAURA, *who is pale and agitated)*

LAURA: *(pointing after* BYKE*)* See that he goes. *(Exit* RAY, LAURA, *taking both of* PEARL'S *hands in her own)* Pearl, he must know everything.

PEARL: Oh, dear, this is dreadful. I do hate scenes.

LAURA: He must know everything, I tell you; and you must relate all. He will question, he will ponder—leave him nothing to ask.

PEARL: If you wish it, but—

LAURA: I desire it; speak of me as you will, but tell him the truth.

(Enter RAY, hastily)

Stay with her, don't follow me. (Exit LAURA)

RAY: Pearl, what does this mean?

PEARL: Oh, it's only a little cloud that I want to clear up for you.

RAY: Cloud? How? Where?

PEARL: Don't I tell you I am going to tell you? Sit down here by me.

RAY: He said he knew her. And she gave him an interview for tomorrow. That drunken wretch—

PEARL: Do sit down. I can never speak while you are walking about so. Sit by me, won't you, for I've got something strange to tell you.

RAY: You serious? I'd as soon expect to see the lightning tamed. Well, I listen.

PEARL: I have something to say to you, Ray, which you must settle with your own heart. You love Laura, do you not?

RAY: Pearl, I do more; I adore her. I adore the very air that she breathes. I will never be happy without her, I can swear that.

PEARL: Laura is twenty now. How do you think she looked when I first saw her?

RAY: Were you at home when she first came into this earthly sphere?

PEARL: Yes.

RAY: Well then, I suppose she looked very small and very pink.

PEARL: She was covered with rags, barefooted, unkempt, crying, and six years old.

RAY: (shocked) Explain.

PEARL: One night father and mother were going to the opera. When they were crossing Broadway, the usual crowd of children accosted them for alms. As mother felt in her pocket for some change, her fingers touched a cold and trembling hand which had clutched her purse.

RAY: A pickpocket! Well?

PEARL: This hand my mother grasped in her own, and so tightly that a small, feeble voice uttered an exclamation of pain. Mother looked down, and there beside her was a little ragged girl.

RAY: The thief.

PEARL: Yes, but a thief hardly six years old, with a face like an angel's. 'Stop!' said my mother, 'what are you doing?' 'Trying to steal,' said the child. 'Don't you know that it's wicked to do so?' asked my father. 'No,' said the girl, 'but it's dreadful to be hungry.' 'Who told you to steal?' asked my mother. 'She—there!' said the child, pointing to a squalid woman in a doorway opposite, who fled suddenly down the street. 'That is Old Judas,' said the girl.

RAY: Old Judas! What a name. But how does this story interest us?

PEARL: This child was Laura. My father was about to let her go unharmed, but my mother said, 'No, it is not enough. We have a duty to perform, even to her,' and acting on a sudden impulse, took her to our home. On being questioned there, the child seemed to have no recollection save of misery and blows. My mother persuaded father, and the girl was sent to a country clergyman's for instruction, and there she remained for several years.

RAY: Pearl, you are joking with me.

PEARL: In beauty, and accomplishments, and dignity, Laura, as mother named her, exceeded every girl of her age. In gratitude she was all that father could have wished. She was introduced, as you know, into society as my cousin, and no one dreams of her origin.

RAY: (starting up) Laura an outcast—a thief!

PEARL: (rising) No, that is what she might have been.

RAY: And this man—tonight?

PEARL: All I know about him is that four years ago this man came with a cruel-looking woman, to see mother. There was a fearful scene between them, for Laura and I sat trembling on the stairs and overheard some awful words. At last they went away, the man putting money into his pocket as he left.

RAY: But who were they?

PEARL: Laura never told me, and mother would not. But, of course, they must have been Laura's father and mother. (RAY sinks on chair as if overcome)

PEARL: Mother made me promise never to tell anybody this, and you would have known nothing had not Laura made me speak. You see, she would not conceal anything from you. Ray, why don't you speak—shall I go after Laura? Shall I tell her to come to you? Why don't you answer? I'll go and tell her you want to see her. I'm going to send her to you, Ray. (*Goes off still looking back at him*)

RAY: (*starting up*) What a frightful story. Laura Courtland a thief. A drunken wretch who knows her history and a squalid beggar woman can claim her at any moment as their own child. And I was about to marry her. Yes, and I love her. But what would my mother think? My friends? Society? No—no—no—I cannot think of it. I will write her—I will tell her—pshaw! she knows, of course, that I cannot wed her now. (*Goes to the table*) Here is paper. (*Sits*) What am I about to do? What will be said of me? But I owe a duty to myself—to society—I must perform it. (*Writes*) 'Laura, I have heard all from your sister.' What have I said? (*crosses out last words*)—'from Pearl. You know that I love you, but my mother will demand of me a wife who will not blush to own her kindred, and who is not the daughter of obscurity and crime.' It is just—it is I who have been deceived. (*Folds letter and addresses it*) I will leave it for her. (*Puts on light overcoat which hangs on chair at back*) I must go before she returns. Her step—too late! (*Crams the letter into pocket of overcoat*) (LAURA *enters*)

LAURA: (*gently*) Ray.

RAY: Miss—Miss Courtland. (LAURA *looks at him a moment, smiles, and then crosses without further noticing him, and sits down on tête-à-tête*) What have I said? What ought I to have said? (*He takes a step towards her—she rises, without looking at him, goes to window, looks out, then looks over books on table*) Laura—I—

LAURA: Pshaw, where is my book?

RAY: What book do you want, Laura?

LAURA: Sir!

RAY: (*repulsed*) Oh, (*pause*) I've been a fool. How lovely she looks. (*He follows her mechanically to table*) Can I find it for you?

LAURA: (*picking up book and re-seating herself*) Don't trouble yourself, I beg.

RAY: (*coming forward and leaning over her seat*) Laura.

LAURA: (*without lifting her head*) Well.

RAY: (*toying with her hair*) Look at me. (LAURA *turns round and looks full at him*)

RAY: No, no, not that way—as you used to. You act as if I were a stranger.

LAURA: They are only strangers who call me Miss Courtland. (*Resumes reading*)

RAY: Forgive me, I beg you to forgive me. I was mad—it was so sudden—this miserable story—but I don't care what they say. Oh, do listen to me. I thought you hated reading.

LAURA: I often wish that I were ugly, wretched, and repulsive, like the heroine in this story.

RAY: Why?

LAURA: Because then I could tell who really loved me.

RAY: And don't you know?

LAURA: No, I do not.

RAY: Well, I know.

LAURA: Do tell me then, please.

RAY: He has told you so himself a hundred times.

LAURA: You?

RAY: I!

LAURA: (*laughing heartily at him, then seriously*) How happy must those women be who are poor, and friendless, and plain, when some true heart comes and says 'I wish to marry you!'

RAY: Laura, you act very strangely tonight.

LAURA: Will you put this book away?

RAY: (*throws it on table*) There, Laura. (*Seats himself beside her*)

LAURA: (*rising*) There's Pearl calling me.

RAY: (*rising and taking her hand*) Laura, why don't you let me speak to you?

LAURA: About what?

RAY: About my love.

LAURA: For whom? Not me. This is only marriage and giving in marriage. I hate the very word.

RAY: You did not think so once.

LAURA: I wish I had. I am frightened now; I begin to understand myself better.

RAY: And I am frightened because I understand you less.

LAURA: Do not try to; goodnight. (*Stops by door as she is going out*) Goodnight Mr Trafford. (*Exit* LAURA, *laughing*)

RAY: I've been an ass. No, I wrong that noble animal. The ass recognized the angel, and I, like Balaam, was blind. But I see now. After all, what have I to fear? (*Takes letter from pocket*) No one knows of this. (*Puts it in his pocket again*) Let things go on; we'll be married, go straight to Europe, and live there ten years. That's the way we'll fix it. (*Exit* RAY—*scene closes in*)

SCENE II: (*1st grooves*)—*the gentlemen's coat-room at Delmonico's—opening* C., *for hats and coats. Chairs* L. *Pier-glass on flat.*

(*Enter* WINDEL *and* DEMILT *muffled, and with umbrellas; they proceed to disrobe*)

DEMILT: Phew! wet as the deuce, and cold too. There'll be nobody here.

WINDEL: It's an awful night. The rooms are almost empty.

DEMILT: Sam! Where the dickens is that darkey? (*Enter* SAM, *fetching in a chair, and boot-black box and brush*)

SAM: Here, sah.

DEMILT: (*sitting in chair*) Hurry up with my boots. Who's here?

SAM: Berry few gemman, sah; only lebben overcoats and ten overshoes. Dem overshoes is spilin the polishin' business.

DEMILT: Look out and don't give me any knocks.

WINDEL: (*handing in his coat at window and getting check for it*) I wonder if the Courtland girls have come yet.

DEMILT: What did Laura Courtland ever see in Trafford to fall in love with? The Van Dam party is my fancy.

WINDEL: (*brushing his hair at glass*) She's ten years older than you, and has a husband.

DEMILT: Yes, a fine old banker, on whom she can draw for everything but attention and affection. She has to get that by her own business tact. (*Other parties enter, exchange goodnights, and deposit their coats; some go out at once, some arrange themselves at glass*)

DEMILT: That'll do, Sam, take my coat. (*Enter* RAY TRAFFORD)

WINDEL: Hallo, Trafford, this is a night, ain't it? Have the Courtlands come?

RAY: Not with me. Here, Sam, take my coat. (*His coat is pulled off by* SAM, *and four letters drop out*) Stupid!

DEMILT: Save the pieces. Mind the love letters.

RAY: (*picking them up*) Look out well next time. There's that cursed letter I was going to send to Laura. Confound it, I must destroy it when I go home. (*Puts letter back in overcoat pocket—gets his boots touched up*)

DEMILT: I say, Trafford, what'll you take and let a fellow read those? Windel, I guess if the girls could get into the cloakroom, it would be better than the dead-letter office. What a time they'd have! Are you ready?

WINDEL: What's the use of hurrying? There is no life in the party till Laura Courtland comes. By Jove, Trafford! you're in luck. She's the prettiest girl in New York.

RAY: And the best. (*March music heard*)

DEMILT: There's the march music; let's go. (*Gets a final brush as they all go off*)

RAY: Come along. (*Exeunt*)

SAM: (*picking up a letter dropped from* RAY'S *pocket*) Dere's anoder of dem billy dooses; wonder if it am Mist' Trafford's. Eh, golly! mustn't mix dem gentlemen's letter,—mustn't mix 'em nohow—or nobody or nuffing wouldn't be able to stop fighting in dis city for de nex' month. (*Exit, carrying a chair, &c.*)

SCENE III: *The blue room at Delmonico's. Waltz music as the scene opens. Waltzers in motion —*PEARL *is dancing with* MRS VAN DAM.

(Enter RAY TRAFFORD, DEMILT *and* WINDEL*)*

PEARL:　There's Ray. I've had enough; I want to speak with him. *(Bursts away from* MRS VAN DAM, *runs up to* TRAFFORD. DEMILT *goes up to* MRS VAN DAM*)*

PEARL:　*(to* RAY*)* You lazy fellow, where have you been?

DEMILT:　You're not tired, are you?

MRS VAN DAM:　I feel as fresh as a daisy.

DEMILT:　Have a waltz with me. *(Waltz music, piano, as they dance,* WINDEL *goes to* MISS EARLIE*)*

RAY:　Where's Laura?

PEARL:　She wasn't ready, and I was dying to come. Been fixed since eight o'clock; so I came with Miss Earlie. So you made it up with Laura?

RAY:　Yes. Don't say anything more about the horrid subject. We've made it all up. But what on earth keeps her tonight? It's eleven already. Confound it, I tremble every moment she's out of my sight. I fear that terrible man and his secret.

MRS VAN DAM:　*(coming up with* DEMILT*)* Trafford, you look very uneasy; what's the matter?

RAY:　Oh, nothing. I think I ought to go for Laura. I will, too. *(SERVANT passes at back)* Here! go upstairs for my overcoat. *(Gives the man a card, and he goes out)*

MRS VAN DAM:　Nonsense! She'll be here in good time. You shan't leave us. Hold him, Pearl. We want a nine-pin quadrille; we haven't half enough gentlemen. Come, be jolly about it. You lovers are always afraid someone will carry your girls away.

RAY:　*(uneasy)* I? I'm not afraid.

PEARL:　Come, come! I never saw such a restless fellow.

(Enter SERVANT *with coat)*

SERVANT:　Here's your coat, sir.

MRS VAN DAM:　Give it to me. I'm determined you shan't go. *(Takes coat carelessly)* I'll make you a promise—if Laura isn't here in fifteen minutes, you shall have your coat, and may go for her.

RAY:　Well, I suppose I'll have to wait.

MRS VAN DAM:　There, take him off, Pearl. *(RAY goes off with* PEARL—*to* SERVANT*)* Here, take this back. *(Flings coat to* SERVANT, *as she does so letters drop from it)* Well, there! *(MISS EARLIE and another lady run forward and pick up letters)* Love letters, of course! *(Smelling them)* Perfumed to suffocation.

MISS EARLIE:　Here's one for Laura, it's unsealed and not delivered.

MRS VAN DAM *(tremolo waltz music)* A fair prize, let's see it. *(Music—takes and opens it, puts on eyeglasses and reads)* 'Laura,' well, come, that's cool for a lover, 'I have heard all from'—something scratched out—ah! 'your sister, Pearl—your obscure origin—terrible family connexions—the secret of the tie which binds you to a drunken wretch—my mother, society—will demand of me a wife who will not blush to own her kindred—or start at the name of outcast and thief.—Signed, RAY TRAFFORD.' *(All stand speechless and look at each other—all this time the rest have been dancing)*

MISS EARLIE:　What can it mean?

MRS VAN DAM:　It means that the rumours of ten years ago are proven. It was then suspected that the girl whom Mrs Courtland brought every year from some unnamed place in the country, and introduced to everybody as her niece, was an imposter, which that foolish woman, in a freak of generosity, was thrusting upon society. The rumours died out for want of proof, and before Laura's beauty and dignity, but now they are confirmed; she is some beggar's child.

MISS EARLIE:　What do you think we ought to do? *(TRAFFORD surrenders* PEARL *to* DEMILT *and comes down)*

MRS VAN DAM:　Tell it—tell it everywhere, of course. The best blood of New York is insulted by the girl's presence.

RAY:　What have you three girls got your heads together for? Some conspiracy, I know.

MRS VAN DAM:　*(to ladies)* Go, girls, tell it everywhere.

RAY:　*(as the ladies distribute themselves about the groups)* What is it all about? Your face is like a portrait of mystery.

MRS VAN DAM: *(showing letter)* Look at this, and tell me what it means.

RAY: *(quickly)* Where did you get this?

MRS VAN DAM: It is you who must answer, and society that will question. So Laura is not a Courtland?

RAY: *(overcome)* You know, then—

MRS VAN DAM: Everything! And will you marry this creature? You cannot, society will not permit your sacrifice.

RAY: This is not your business. Give me that letter.

MRS VAN DAM: Certainly, take it. But let me say one word—its contents are known. In an hour every tongue will question you about this secret, every eye will inquire.

RAY: I implore you! Do not breathe a word for her sake. *(She turns scornfully away)*

MRS VAN DAM: The secret's not mine.

RAY: Who knows it?

MRS VAN DAM: Look! *(points to others who are grouped about whispering and motioning towards RAY)*
(Enter PEARL and speaks to lady and gentlemen)

RAY: *(wildly)* What will they do?

MRS VAN DAM: Expose her! Expel her from society in which she is an intruder!

RAY: You dare not!

PEARL: Oh Ray, what is the meaning of this?

RAY: *(bitterly)* It means that society is a terrible avenger of insult. Have you ever heard of the Siberian wolves? When one of the pack falls through weakness the others devour him. It is not an elegant comparison, but there is something wolfish in society. Laura has mocked it with a pretence, and society, which is made up of pretences, will bitterly resent the mockery.

MRS VAN DAM: Very good! This handsome thief has stolen your breeding as well as your brains, I see.

RAY: If you speak a word against her I will say that what you utter is a lie!

MRS VAN DAM: As you please, we will be silent. But you will find that the world speaks most forcibly when it utters no sound.

PEARL: Oh, go and prevent her coming here.

RAY: That I can do. *(Going up hastily sees LAURA entering)* Too late. *(He retreats)*

MRS VAN DAM: Come, girls! Let us look after our things. They are no longer safe when an accomplished thief enters. *(Music low, continues while all except PEARL and RAY pass out, eyeing LAURA superciliously)*

PEARL: Ray, Ray! why do you not come to her?

MRS VAN DAM: *(surrounded by others)* Are you not coming with us, Trafford?

PEARL: *(to LAURA)* Let us go home.

LAURA: No, stay with *him!* *(Pointing to RAY, who has held off)* He shall not suffer the disgrace long. *(About to faint; RAY runs forward, she proudly waves him away)* It is Heaven's own blow!

ACT II

SCENE I: *Interior of a basement. Street and railings seen through window at back. Entrance door L., stove with long pipe in fire-place, R. Table between two windows at back, with flowers, &c.—humble furniture. Table C., three chairs. Closet, L. (2nd grooves.)*

PEACHBLOSSOM *is discovered polishing stove— (a slip-shod girl).*

SONG—PEACHBLOSSOM
A lordly knight and a lovely dame were
    walking in the meadow.
But a jealous rival creeping came,
    a-watching in the shadow.
They heeded not, but he whet his knife
    and dogged them in the shadow;
The knight was brave, and the dame was
    true, the rival fared but badly;
For the knight he drew and ran him
    through, and left him groaning sadly.
The knight and dame soon wedded were,
    with bells a-chiming gladly.

PEACHBLOSSOM: The stove won't shine. It's the fault of the polish, I know. That boy that comes here just fills the bottles with mud, and calls it stove polish. Only let me catch him. Ah! Ah! *(threatening gesture with brush)* I declare I'd give it up if I didn't want to make everything look smart, before Miss Nina comes in. Miss Nina is the only friend I ever had since I ran away from mother Judas. I wonder where old Judas is now? I know she's drunk, she always was; perhaps that's why she never tried to find out what became of me. If she did she could not take me away. Miss Nina begged me off a policeman. I belong to her. I wonder why she ain't got any other friends? She's awful mysterious. Tells me never to let any strangers see her. She's afraid of somebody, I know. It looks just as if she was hiding. I thought only bad girls, such as I, had to hide. If I was good and pretty like her, I wouldn't hide from the President. *(Still polishing—*JUDAS *appears at window with basket of ornaments, &c.)*

JUDAS: Hum! Is your ma in, my dear?

PEACHBLOSSOM: *(starting)* Oh! *(Aside)* Old Judas! She's found me out at last. No she ain't, or she'd have got me by the hair before she spoke, that's *her* way.

JUDAS: *(coming in at door—*PEACHBLOSSOM *keeps her back towards her)* Any old clothes to change for chany, my dear? Where's your ma's old skirts and shawls, my pet? Get 'em quick, before mother comes in, and I'll give you a beautiful chany mug or a tea-pot for them. Come here, my ducky—see the pretty—*(recognises* PEACHBLOSSOM*).* Eh! why you jail-bird, what are you doing here? Are you sneakin' it? Answer me, or I'll knock your head agin the wall. *(Catches her by the hair)*

PEACHBLOSSOM: You just leave me be. I'm honest, I am. I'm good!

JUDAS: You're good? Where's my shoe? I'll take the goodness out of you.

PEACHBLOSSOM: Oh, oh! please don't beat me. I ain't good. I'm only trying to be.

JUDAS: You're only trying to be, eh? Trying to be good, and here's me as was a-weeping every night, thinking as you was sent up for six months. Who're you living with—you ain't a-keeping house, are you?

PEACHBLOSSOM: I'm living with Miss Nina.

JUDAS: Nina, what's she, concert saloon girl?

PEACHBLOSSOM: No, she's a lady.

JUDAS: A lady—and have such baggage as you about? Where's my shoe? I'll make you speak the truth.

PEACHBLOSSOM: I don't know what she is. She met me when the police were taking me up for loafin' down Hudson Street, and she begged me off.

JUDAS: Has she any money?

PEACHBLOSSOM: No, she's poor.

JUDAS: Any nice clothes?

PEACHBLOSSOM: Oh, she's got good clothes.

JUDAS: Where are they?

PEACHBLOSSOM: Locked up, and she's got the key.

JUDAS: You're lying; I see it in your eye. You're always shamefaced when you are telling the truth, and now you're as bold as brass. Where's my shoe? *(Making a dash at her)*

PEACHBLOSSOM: *(shouting)* There's Miss Nina. *(As if curtseying to someone behind* JUDAS.*)* Good morning, miss.

JUDAS: *(changing her tone)* Ah, my pretty dear! What a good lady to take you in and give you a home. *(Turns and discovers the deception—in a rage)* You hussy. *(*PEACHBLOSSOM *retreats)* Wait till I get you in my clutches again, and it won't be long. Miss Nina takes care of you, does she? Who will take care of her? Let her look to it. *(*LAURA *enters, plainly dressed, at back.)* Beg pardon, Miss, I just called to see if you had any old clothes you'd like to exchange.

LAURA: No, I don't want anything, my good woman.

JUDAS: *(eyeing her sharply and going to door)* That's her—I'd know her anywhere! *(Malicious glance, and exit)*

LAURA: You've been very good this morning, Blossom. The room is as nice as I could wish.

PEACHBLOSSOM: Please 'm, I tried because you are so good to me. Shall I sweep out the airy? I guess I'd better—then she'll be alone, as she loves to be. *(Takes broom and exit)*

LAURA: *(opening a package and taking out photographs)* No pay yet for colouring 'till I have practised a week longer. Then I shall have all the work I can do. They say at the photographer's I colour well, and the best pictures will be given me. The best! Already I have had beneath my brush so many faces that I know—friends of the old days. The silent eyes seem to wonder at me for bringing them to this strange and lowly home. *(Picking up letters from table)* Letters, ah! answers to my advertisement for employment. No, only a circular 'To the lady of this house.' What's that! *(Starting)* Only Blossom sweeping. Every time there is a noise I dread the entrance of someone that knows me. But they could never find me in New York. I left them all so secretly and suddenly. None of them can expect I would have descended to this. But it is natural, everything will find its level. I sprang from poverty, and I return to it. Poor Pearl. How she must have wondered the next morning—Laura gone! But three months have passed, and they have forgotten me. Ray will cheer her.

(Wrangling outside; PEACHBLOSSOM *bursts in, dragging* BERMUDAS, *with his professional tape, pins, blacking, and baskets)*

PEACHBLOSSOM: Here he is 'm.

BERMUDAS: Leave go, I tell yer, or I'll make yer.

LAURA: What is the matter?

PEACHBLOSSOM: He's the boy that sold me that stove polish what isn't stove polish.

BERMUDAS: What is it then—s-a-a-y?

PEACHBLOSSOM: It's mud! it's mud at tenpence a bottle.

BERMUDAS: Ah, where could I get mud? Ain't the streets clean? Mud's dearer than stove polish now.

PEACHBLOSSOM: And your matches is wet, and your pins won't stick, and your shoe-strings is rotten, there now!

BERMUDAS: Well, how am I to live? it ain't my fault, it's the taxes. Ain't I got to pay my income tax, and how am I to pay it if I gives you your money's worth? Sa-a-y?

LAURA: Do let the boy alone, Blossom. Send him away.

(Enter PEANUTS*)*

PEANUTS: Extra! Hollo, Bermudas! how's your sister? Papers, Miss. Extra! Revolution in Mexico!

LAURA: Dear, dear, this is the way I'm worried from morning till night.

BERMUDAS: Here, just you get out! This is my beat.

PEANUTS: Vell, I ain't blacking or hairpins now, I'm papers. How'm I hurting you?

BERMUDAS: Vell, I'm papers at four o'clock, and this is my beat. Take care of me, I'm training for a fight. I'm a bruiser, I am.

PEANUTS: Hold yer jaw. *(They fight)*

PEACHBLOSSOM: *(beats them with broom)* Get out with you, both of you! *(Grand escapade, and exit of boys)*

LAURA: Don't let's be troubled in this way again. Have you got the things for dinner?

PEACHBLOSSOM: Lor, no, miss. It's twelve o'clock, and I forgot.

*(*PEACHBLOSSOM *gets shawl, big bonnet from hooks on the wall, basket from closet, while* LAURA *opens her pocket-book for money)*

LAURA: What did we have for dinner yesterday, Blossom?

PEACHBLOSSOM: Beefsteak 'm. Let's have some leg o' mutton today. We've never had that.

LAURA: But I don't know how to cook it. Do you?

PEACHBLOSSOM: No, but I'd just slap it on, and it's sure to come out right.

LAURA: Slap it on what?

PEACHBLOSSOM: The gridiron!

LAURA: *(giving money)* No, we'd better not try a leg of mutton today. Get some lamb chops; we know how to manage them.

PEACHBLOSSOM: *(as she is going)* Taters, as usual, 'mum?

LAURA: Yes; and stop, Blossom—while you're buying the chops, just ask the butcher—off hand, you know—how he would cook a leg of mutton, if he were going to eat it himself—as if you wanted to know for yourself.

PEACHBLOSSOM: Yes 'm, but I'm sure it's just as good broiled as fried. *(Exit)*

LAURA: Now to be cook. *(Laughing)* The Tuesday Sociable ought to see me now. Artist in the morning, cook at noon, artist in the afternoon. *(SNORKEY raps at the door and enters)*

SNORKEY: *(with letter)* Beg pardon, is there anybody here as answers to the name of A. B. C.?

LAURA: *(aside)* My advertisement for work—Yes, give it to me.

SNORKEY: *(seeing her face)* If I'd been taking something this morning, I'd say that I'd seen that face in a different sort of place from this.

LAURA: Is there anything to pay? Why do you wait?

SNORKEY: Nothing, Miss. It's all right. *(Going— and aside)* But it ain't all right, Snorkey, old boy. *(Goes out after looking at her, stops at window, and gazes in)*

LAURA: Yes, an answer to my advertisement. *(Reads)* 'To A. B. C.—Your advertisement promises that you are a good linguist, and can teach children of any age. I have two daughters for whom I wish to engage your services while on a tour of Europe. Call at seven o'clock this evening, at No. 207, West 34th Street, Annersley.' Hope at last, a home, and in another land soon. I was sure the clouds would not always be black above me. *(Kisses letter, SNORKEY re-entering)*

SNORKEY: Miss, I say Miss? *(LAURA starts)* Sh—

LAURA: What do you want?

SNORKEY: Only one word, and perhaps it may be of service to you. I'd do anything to serve you.

LAURA: And why me?

SNORKEY: I'm a blunt fellow, Miss, but I hope my way don't offend. Ain't you the lady that I brought a bouquet to on New Year's night—not here, but in a big house, all bright and rich, and who was so kind to a poor soldier?

LAURA: *(faint and leaning against chair)* Whoever you may be, promise to tell no one you saw me here.

SNORKEY: No fear, Miss. I promise.

LAURA: Sacredly?

SNORKEY: No need to do more than promise, Miss—I keeps my word. I promised Uncle Sam I'd stick to the flag—though they tore my arm off, and by darnation I stuck! I don't want to tell on you, Miss, I want to tell on someone else.

LAURA: What do you mean?

SNORKEY: They're looking for you.

LAURA: Who?

SNORKEY: Byke. *(LAURA utters a loud cry, and sinks on chair)* He's on it day and night. I've got his money in my pocket now, and you've got his letter in your hand this minute. *(LAURA drops the letter in dismay)*

LAURA: This?

SNORKEY: Yes, it's his writin'—looks like a woman's, don't it? Lord! the snuff that man's up to would make Barnum sneeze his head off. He's kept me in hand, 'cause he thinks I know you, having seen you that once. Every day he reads the advertisements, and picks out a dozen or so, and says to me—'Snorkey, that's like my little pet,' and then he sits down and answers them, and gets the advertisers to make appointments with him, which he keeps regularly, and regularly comes back cussing at his ill luck. See here, Miss, I've a bundle of answers to deliver as usual, to advertisers. I calls 'em Byke's Target Practice, and this time, you see, he's accidentally hit the mark.

LAURA: For heaven's sake do not betray me to him! I've got very little money; I earn it hardly, but take it, take it—and save me. *(Offers money)*

SNORKEY: No, miss, not a cent of it. Though Byke is a devil, and would kick me hard if he thought I would betray him.

LAURA: I don't want you to suffer for my sake; take the money.

SNORKEY: No, I stood up to be shot at for thirteen dollars a month, and I can take my chances of a kickin' for nothing. But Byke ain't the only one, miss; there's another's looking for you.

LAURA: *(her look of joy changing to fear)* Another! Who?

SNORKEY: *(approaching smilingly and confidential)* Mr Trafford. *(LAURA turns aside despairingly)* He's been at me every day for more than six weeks. 'Snorkey,' says he, 'do you remember that beautiful young lady you brought the bouquet to on New Year's night?' 'Well,' says I, 'Cap'n, the young lady I slightly disremember, but the cakes and wine I got there that night I shall never forget.' 'Search for that young lady,' says he, 'and when you find her'—

LAURA: No, no, no; not even he must know. Do you hear—not he—not anyone. You have served them well; serve me and be silent.

SNORKEY: Just as you please, miss, but I hate to serve you by putting your friends off the track—it don't seem natural—Byke I don't mind, but the cap'n wouldn't do you any harm. Just let me give him a bit of a hint. *(LAURA makes an entreating gesture)* Well I'm mum, but as I've only got one hand, it's hard work to hold my tongue. Not the least bit of a hint? *(LAURA appeals to him and then turns away)* They say when a woman says no she means yes. I wonder if I dare tell her that he's not far off. Perhaps I'd better not. But I can tell him. *(Exit)*

LAURA: How shall I ever escape that dreadful man? And Ray searching for me too. Our friends, then, remember us, as well as our enemies.

(Enter PEACHBLOSSOM, quickly, shutting the door behind her, with basket, which she places on table)

PEACHBLOSSOM: Oh, Miss Nina, whatever is into the people? There's a strange man coming down the entry; I heard him asking that red cap fellow about you.

LAURA: Byke! Fasten the door, quick. *(PEACHBLOSSOM runs to door, it is slightly opened, she pushes it against someone on the other side)*

PEACHBLOSSOM: Oh, dear, he's powerful strong; I can't keep it shut. Go away, you willin: Oh! *(The door is forced and RAY TRAFFORD enters)*

RAY: Laura, it is I!

LAURA: Ray! *(Shrinks from him)*

RAY: Dear Laura—*(he stops as he becomes conscious that PEACHBLOSSOM with her basket on her arm and her bonnet hanging on her back is staring at him)* I say, my girl, haven't you some particular business somewhere else to attend to?

PEACHBLOSSOM: *(seriously)* No, sir, I've swept the sidewalk and gone a-marketing, and now I'm indoors and I mean to stay.

RAY: And wouldn't you oblige me by going for a sheet of paper and an envelope? Here's a dollar—try and see how slow you can be.

PEACHBLOSSOM: *(firmly)* You can't sheet of paper me, mister, I'm protecting Miss Nina, and I'm not to be enveloped.

LAURA: Go as the gentleman asks you, Blossom.

PEACHBLOSSOM: Oh! *(Takes money, fixes her bonnet)* First it's 'Keep the man out,' now it's 'Let him stay in alone with me.' But I suppose she's like all of us—it makes a great difference which man it is. *(Exit)*

RAY: *(after watching PEACHBLOSSOM out)* Laura, when I approached you you shrank from me. Why did you do so?

LAURA: Look around you and find your answer.

RAY: *(shuddering)* Pardon me, I did not come here to insult your misery. When I saw you I forgot everything else.

LAURA: And now it's time for us to remember everything. I told you to look around that you might understand that in such a place I am no longer Laura Courtland, nor anything I used to be. But I did not ask your pity. There is no misery here.

RAY: Alone, without means, exposed to every rudeness, unprotected, is this not misery for you?

LAURA: *(laughing)* Oh, it's not so bad as that.

RAY: Laura, don't trifle with me. You cannot have exchanged everything that made you happy for this squalid poverty, and not feel it deeply.

LAURA: I have not time to feel anything deeply. *(Takes basket up, goes to table, busies herself about preparing dinner)* I work from sunrise till night, and I sleep so soundly that I have not even dreams to recall the past. Just as you came in I was about to cook our dinner. Only think—lamb chops.

RAY: Lamb chops! It makes me shudder to hear you speak.

LAURA: Does it? Then wait till I get the gridiron on the fire and you'll shiver. And if you want to be transfixed with horror stop and take dinner.

RAY: I will not hear you mock yourself thus, Laura. I tell you in this self-banishment you have acted thoughtlessly—you have done wrong.

LAURA: Why?

RAY: Because, let the miserable creatures who slandered you say what they might, you had still a home and friends.

LAURA: A home! Where the very servants would whisper and point, friends who would be ashamed to acknowledge me. You are mistaken. That is neither home nor friendship.

RAY: And you are resolved to surrender the past for ever?

LAURA: The past has forgotten me in spite of myself.

RAY: Look at me.

LAURA: Well, then, there's one who has not forgotten me, but I desire that he may. You speak to me of bitterness. Your presence, your words, cause me the first pang I have felt since the night I fled unnoticed from my chamber, and began my life anew. Therefore I entreat you to leave me, to forget me.

RAY: Laura, by the tie that once bound us!

LAURA: Yes, *once*. It *is* a long time ago.

RAY: What have I said? The tie which still—

LAURA: *(sharply turning)* Mr Trafford, must I remind you of that night when all arrayed themselves so pitilessly against me, when a gesture from you might have saved me, and you saw me without stretching a finger to the woman who had felt the beating of your heart. No, you made your choice then—the world without me. I make my choice now—the wide, wide, world without you.

RAY: I have been bitterly punished, for we are never so humiliated as when we despise ourselves. But, by the heaven above us both, I love you, Laura—I have never ceased to love you.

LAURA: I thank you. I know how to construe the love which you deny in the face of society to offer me behind its back.

RAY: Will you drive me mad? I tell you, Laura, your misery, your solitude is as nothing to the anguish I have suffered. The maniac who in his mental darkness stabs to the heart the friend he loved never felt in returning reason the remorse my error has earned me. Everyday it says to me 'You have been false to the heart that loved you, and you shall account for it to your conscience all your life. You shall find that the bitterest drops in the cup of sorrow are the tears of the woman you have forsaken.' And it is true. Oh, forgive me—have pity on me.

LAURA: *(moved)* I forgive you. Yes, and I pity you—and so good-bye for ever.

RAY: Of course I am nothing to you now; that is some comfort to me. I have only to be sorry on my own account, but I come to you on behalf of others.

LAURA: Whom?

RAY: My mother and Pearl, they ask for you. For them I have sought you, to urge you to return to them.

LAURA: Dear little Pearl.

RAY: Yes, she has been quite ill.

LAURA: She has been ill?

RAY: Think of those two hearts which you have caused to suffer and do not drive me from you. It is not only wealth, luxury, and refinement which you have surrendered—you have also cast away those greater riches, loving and devoted friends. But they shall persuade you themselves—yes, I'll go and bring them to you; you cannot resist their entreaties.

LAURA: No, no, they must not come here, they must never know where *I* hide my shame, and you must never reveal it.

RAY: I promise it if you will go to them with me. Think, they will insist on coming unless you do.

LAURA: Poor Pearl. If I go with you, you promise not to detain me—to permit me to come back and to trouble me and my poor life no more?

RAY: I promise, but I know you will release me from it when you see them. I will get a carriage, so that no one will meet you. Wait for me, I shall not be long. It is agreed?

LAURA: *(smiling)* Yes, it is agreed.
(Enter PEACHBLOSSOM, *with a sheet of paper foolscap and some enormous envelopes)*

PEACHBLOSSOM: Here they are.

RAY: That's a good girl, keep them till I come back. In half an hour, Laura, be ready. *(Exit)*

PEACHBLOSSOM: *(with an air)* What's he going to do in half an hour?

LAURA: He's going to take me away with him for a little while, Peachblossom, and while I'm gone I wish you to be a good girl, and watch the house and take care of it till I return.

PEACHBLOSSOM: I don't believe it, you won't return. *(Crying)* That's what our Sal said when she went off with her young man, and she never came back at all. You shan't go; I hate him. He shan't take you away.

LAURA: *(who is getting ready, putting her hat on, &c.)* Blossom!

PEACHBLOSSOM: I don't care, if you go away I'll go away; I'll bite and scratch him if he comes back. *(Fiercely tearing up the paper and envelopes)* Let him come back—let him dare come back.

LAURA: Blossom, you're very wicked. Go into the corner this minute and put your apron over your head.

PEACHBLOSSOM: *(crying at* LAURA'S *feet)* Oh, please, Miss Nina, let me go with you and I'll be so good and not say a word to anyone. Do let me go with you. Let me ask him to let me go with you. *(Figure passes the window)* Here he is; I see him coming.

LAURA: Run, run, open the door. *(*PEACHBLOSSOM *runs to door, throws it open, disclosing* BYKE— *exclamation of horror from* LAURA*)*

BYKE: Ah, my dear little runaway, found you at last, and just going out. How lucky! I wanted you to take a walk with me.

LAURA: Instantly leave this place!

BYKE: How singular! You are always ordering me out and I am always coming in. We want a change. I will go out, and I request you to come with me.

LAURA: Blossom, go find an officer, tell him this wretch is insulting me.

BYKE: Blossom? Ah—exactly! Here, you Judas.
*(*JUDAS *enters)*

PEACHBLOSSOM: Oh, miss, save me.

BYKE: *(throws* PEACHBLOSSOM *over to* JUDAS, *who drags her out)* Take care of that brat, and as for you, daughter, come with me.

LAURA: Daughter!

BYKE: Yes, it is time to declare myself. Paternal feeling has been too long smothered in my breast. Come to my arms, my child—my long-estranged child. *(Takes out dirty handkerchief and presses his eyes with pretended feeling)*

LAURA: Heavens! is there no help? *(She attempts to escape,* BYKE *seizes her)*

BYKE: What an unfilial girl; you take advantage of a father's weakness and try to bolt. *(Clutching her by the arm)* Come, go with me and cheer my old age. Ain't I good to take you back after all these years? *(Drags her out, she calling 'help! help!')*

SCENE II: *The Tombs Police Court. Long high desk with three seats across back, from R. to L., on platform. Railing in front, railing around L., with opening L. C. In front of railing, a bench R. and L.—gate in C. of railing. Judge* BOWLING *and another* JUSTICE *seated behind high desk C., with clerk on his L.* JUSTICE *is reading paper, with his feet upon desk R.* POLICEMEN *at R. and L.* POLICEMAN *999 at gate. Hard-looking set of men and women on benches R. and L.—Lawyer* SPLINTER *is talking to* RAFFERDI, *an organ-man, who is in crowd. As the curtain rises, noisy buzz is heard.*

BOWLING: Smithers, keep those people quiet. (POLICEMAN *handling people roughly*) Here, easy—officer, treat those poor people decently. Well, whom have you got there?

POLICEMAN: (*dragging urchin within railing*) Pickpocket, your honour. Caught in the act.

BOWLING: What's he got to say for himself? Nothing, eh? What's his name?

POLICEMAN: (*stooping down to boy as if asking him*) Says his name is Peter Rich.

BOWLING: You stand a poor chance, Rich. Take him away. (BOWLING *consults with another Justice, as the boy is taken off*)

SPLINTER: (*to* RAFFERDI, *who has his monkey and organ*) So you want to get out, eh? How much money have you got?

RAFFERDI: Be jabers! half a dollar in cents is all the money I'm worth in the world.

SPLINTER: Give it to me. I thought you organ fellows were Italians.

RAFFERDI: Divil doubt it! Ain't I got a monkey?

POLICEMAN: Here, you—come up here. (*Takes* RAFFERDI *inside the railing*)

BOWLING: Now then, what's this, officer?

POLICEMAN: (RAFFERDI *takes stand*) Complaint of disturbing the neighbourhood.

BOWLING: What have you got to say for yourself?

SPLINTER: If your honour please, I appear for this man.

BOWLING: Well, what have you got to say for him?

SPLINTER: Here is an unfortunate man, your honour—a native of sunny Italy. He came to our free and happy country, and being a votary of music, he bought an organ and a monkey, and tried to earn his bread. But the myrmidons of the law were upon him, and the Eagle of Liberty drooped his pinions as Rafferdi was hurried to his dungeon.

BOWLING: Rafferdi, you're an Irishman, ain't you? What do you mean by deceiving us?

RAFFERDI: Sure I didn't. It's the lawyer chap there. I paid him fifty cents and he's lying out the worth of it.

BOWLING: You fellows are regular nuisances. I've a great mind to commit you.

SPLINTER: Commit him? If the court please, reflect—commit him to prison? What will become of his monkey?

BOWLING: Well, I'll commit him too.

SPLINTER: You cannot. I defy the Court to find anything in the Statutes authorising the committal of the monkey.

BOWLING: Well, we'll leave out the monkey.

SPLINTER: And if the Court please, what is the monkey to do in the wide world, with his natural protector in prison? I appeal to those kindlier feelings in your honour's breast, which must ever temper justice with mercy. This monkey is perhaps an orphan!

BOWLING: (*laughing*) Take them both away, and don't let me catch you here again, Mr Rafferdi, or you'll go to jail. (SPLINTER *goes down*— RAFFERDI *exits*)

POLICEMAN: (*pulling* SAM, *a nigger, who is drunk, out of a crowd*) Get up here.

SAM: (*noisily*) Look yah—don't pull me around.

BOWLING: Silence there! what's all this noise about?

SAM: Whar's de court? I want to see de Judge.

SPLINTER: My coloured friend, can I assist you?

SAM: Am you a Counseller-at-law?

SPLINTER: Yes, retain me. How much money have you got?

SAM: I ain't got no money, but I've got a policy ticket. It's bound to draw a prize.

SPLINTER: Got any pawn tickets?

SAM: Ob course. (*Giving him a handful*)

BOWLING: Well, what's the charge?

POLICEMAN: Drunk and disorderly.

BOWLING: Well, my man, what have you to say?

SAM: Dis here gemman represents me.

SPLINTER: We admit, if the Court please, that we were slightly intoxicated, but we claim the privilege, as the equal of the white man.

BOWLING: (*to clerk*) Very good. Commit him for ten days.

SPLINTER: But this is an outrage, your honour.

BOWLING: *(to officer)* Take him off. *(Motioning to* SAM—SPLINTER *sits down discomfited*—SAM *very wroth)*

SAM: What?

BOWLING: Take him away.

SAM: Look here, judge, hab you read the Civil Right Bill? You can't send dis nigger to prison, while dat bill am de law ob de land.

BOWLING: That'll do, remove him.

SAM: I ain't no gipsy. I'm one of de Bureau niggers, I am. Where am de law? Don't touch me, white man! Dis am corruption—dis am 'ficial delinquency! *(POLICEMAN collars him and carries him off)*

BOWLING: Any more prisoners? *(Noise)* What noise is that?

(OFFICER goes out. BYKE enters, followed by the OFFICER, who escorts LAURA)

BYKE: Where is the judge? Oh, where is the good, kind judge?

BOWLING: Well, my dear sir, what is the matter?

BYKE: Oh, sir, forgive my tears. I'm a broken-hearted man!

BOWLING: Be calm, my dear sir. Officer, bring this gentleman a chair. *(OFFICER hands chair)*

BYKE: Ah, sir, you are very good to a poor distressed father, whose existence has been made a desert on account of his child.

BOWLING: Repress your emotion, and tell me what you want.

BYKE: I want my child.

BOWLING: Where is she?

BYKE: She is here, sir—here—my darling, my beautiful child, and so unfilial—so unnatural.

BOWLING: How is this, young lady?

LAURA: *(standing inside railing)* It is all a lie. He is not my father.

BYKE: Not your father? Oh, dear, oh, dear, you will break my heart!

BOWLING: This needs some explanation. If not his child, who are you?

LAURA: I am—I dare not say it. I know not who I am, but I feel that he cannot be my father.

BYKE: Oh, dear—Oh!—

BOWLING: *(sharply)* Silence! *(To* LAURA, *sternly)* You say you don't know who you are. Do you know this man?

LAURA: Yes.

BOWLING: Where and with whom do you live?

LAURA: I have lived alone for four months.

BOWLING: And with whom did you live before that!

LAURA: Oh, forgive me, if I seem disobedient— but I cannot tell.

BOWLING: Then I must look to this gentleman for information.

BYKE: And I will gladly give it. Yes, sir, I will gladly tell. She was taken from me years ago, when she was but a little child, by rich people who wanted to adopt her. I refused—they paid me—I was poor—I was starving—I forebore to claim her—she was happy, but they turned her forth four months ago into the street. I could not see her suffer—my child—the prop of my declining days. I begged her to come—she refused. My enemies had poisoned my daughter's mind against *me,* her father. I am still poor. I taught school, but I have saved a little money, only for her,

BOWLING: How old is she?

BYKE: Nineteen.

BOWLING: Your father is your legal guardian during your minority, and is entitled to your custody. Why are you so undutiful? Try to correct this.

BYKE: Oh, bless you, dear good judge for these words.

LAURA: Oh, have I no friends, must I go with him?

BOWLING: Certainly.

LAURA: Anything then. Exposure! Disgrace, rather than that! *(JUDGES consult)*
(Enter SNORKEY)

BYKE: *(aside)* Snorkey! the devil!

SNORKEY: Can I help you, miss? Only tell me what to do, and if it takes my other arm off, I'll save you.

LAURA: Yes, yes, you can help me! *(To JUDGES)* Will you let me send a message.

BOWLING: You may do that.

LAURA: Run to that house—not my house—but the one in which you saw me first. Do you remember it?

SNORKEY: Don't I, and the wine and cakes.

LAURA: Ask for Miss Pearl. Tell her where I am. Tell her to come instantly. (SNORKEY *going*) Stay—tell her to bring the ebony box in mother's cabinet. Can you recollect?

SNORKEY: Can I what? Gaze at this giant intellect and don't ask me! The ebony box—all right— I'm off. *(Exit)*

BOWLING: It would have been as well, young lady, to have answered frankly at first.

BYKE: Oh, sir! Don't be harsh with her! Don't be harsh with my poor child.

BOWLING: Your father has a most Christian disposition.

LAURA: Sir, I have told you, and I now solemnly repeat it, that this man is no relation of mine. I desire to remain unknown, for I am most unfortunate; but the injustice you are about to commit forces me to reveal myself, though in doing so I shall increase a sorrow already hard to bear.

BOWLING: We sit here to do right, according to the facts before us. And let me tell you, young lady, that your father's statement is correct. Further, unless the witnesses you have sent for can directly contradict him, we shall not alter our decision.

LAURA: Let it be so. He says he gave me into the care of certain wealthy people when I was a little child.

BYKE: I am willing to swear to it.

LAURA: Then he will be able to describe the clothes in which I was dressed at the time. They were safely kept, I have sent for them.

BYKE: Let them be produced—and I will recognise every little precious garment. *(Aside)* This is getting ferociously hot for me! Ha!
(Re-enter SNORKEY with RAY hastily)

SNORKEY: *(excitedly)* Here's a witness! Here's evidence. (POLICEMAN *admonishes him*)

LAURA: (RAY *takes her hand through the rail*) Ray!

BOWLING: Who is this?

RAY: I am a friend, sir, of this lady.

BYKE: He is a dreadful character—a villain who wants to lead my child astray! Don't—please don't let him contaminate her!

BOWLING: Silence! *(To RAY)* Can you disprove that this young lady is his daughter?

RAY: His daughter?

LAURA: He knows nothing.

BOWLING: Let him answer. Come—have you any knowledge of this matter?

RAY: I had been told, sir, that—(LAURA *looks at him*) No—I know nothing.

LAURA: Have you brought the ebony box? It contained the clothes which I wore when—

RAY: I understand; but in my haste, and not knowing your peril I brought nothing. But can you not remember them yourself?

LAURA: Perfectly.

RAY: Write, then! *(Handing her a memorandum book—to BOWLING)* Sir, this lady will hand you a description of those articles which she wore when she was found thirteen years ago. Then let this scoundrel be questioned—and if he fails to answer, I will accuse him of an attempted abduction.

BOWLING: That's the way.

BYKE: *(aside)* It will not be a great effort for me to remember.

BOWLING: *(taking the book from RAY)* Now, sir, I will listen to you. (RAY *and* LAURA *are eager and expectant*)

BYKE: *(deliberately)* A soiled gingham frock, patched and torn. (LAURA *gives a shudder and turns aside*)

BOWLING: What kind of shoes and stockings?

BYKE: Her feet were bare.

BOWLING: And the colour of her hood?

BYKE: Her dear little head was uncovered.

BOWLING: *(handing book back)* He has answered correctly.

LAURA: It is useless to struggle more! Heaven alone can help me!

RAY: You can see, sir, that this lady cannot be his daughter. Look at her and at him.

BOWLING: I only see that he has pretty well proven his case. She must go with him, and let her learn to love him as a daughter should.

RAY: She shall not! I shall follow him wherever he goes.

BYKE: (taking LAURA'S hand) I appeal to the Court.

BOWLING: Officer, take charge of that person, until this gentleman is gone.

BYKE: (coming forward with LAURA, who is dumb and despairing) My child, try and remember the words of the good judge. 'You must learn to love me as a daughter should.'

SNORKEY: (to RAY) Stay here, sir, I'll track him. No one suspects me. (Music—tableau—closed in by next scene)

SCENE III: Exterior of the Tombs, with ballads on strings upon the railings.

(Enter JUDAS, followed by PEACHBLOSSOM)

PEACHBLOSSOM: Only tell me where he has taken her, and I'll go with you—indeed I will.

JUDAS: We don't want you, we wouldn't be bothered with you; she's our game.

PEACHBLOSSOM: What are you going to do with her?

JUDAS: Do! why we'll coin her. Turn her into dollars. We've had it on foot for a long time.

PEACHBLOSSOM: What! Is she the rich young lady I heard you and Byke speak of so often before I got away from you?

JUDAS: (savagely) Heard me speak of! What did you hear?

PEACHBLOSSOM: (dancing off) Oh, I know! I know more than you suppose. When you used to lock me up in the back cellar for running away, you forgot that doors had key-holes.

JUDAS: (aside) This girl must be silenced.

PEACHBLOSSOM: What are you muttering about— don't you know how Byke used to throw you down and trample on you for muttering?

JUDAS: I'll have you yet, my beauty.

PEACHBLOSSOM: I think you are a great fool, Judas.

JUDAS: Likely, likely.

PEACHBLOSSOM: Why don't you give up Miss Nina to that handsome young gentleman? He'd pay you well for the secret. He'd give his whole fortune for her, I know, I saw it in his face. And he'd treat you better than Byke does.

JUDAS: Not yet my chicken; besides, what does he care for her now? Isn't he going to marry the other girl—she's the one will pay when the time comes—but we intend to hold the goods 'till the price is high.

PEACHBLOSSOM: Then if you won't, I'll—I'll tell him all I used to overhear about babies and cradles, and he'll understand it, perhaps, if I don't.

JUDAS: (aside) Hang her—she'll make mischief. (Aloud) Well, come along with me, my beauty, and I'll talk it over with you.

PEACHBLOSSOM: Don't touch me; I won't trust you with your hands on me. (JUDAS makes a dart at her) I knew that was your game. But I'll be even with you yet. (Dancing off tantalisingly before JUDAS—Both exit)

(Enter SNORKEY)

SNORKEY: (desponding) I'm no more use than a gun without a trigger. I tried to follow Byke, but he smoked in a minute. Then I tried to make up with him, but he swore that I went against him in Court, and so he wouldn't have me at no price. Then I ran after the carriage that he got into with the lady, till a darn'd old woman caught me for upsetting her apple stand and bursting up her business. What am I to do now? I'm afraid to go back to the cap'n, he won't have me at any price either, I suppose. (Gazing at ballads, hands in his pockets—going from one to the other)

(Enter BERMUDAS, with ballads in his hands, and preparing to take others off the line, as if to shut up shop)

BERMUDAS: (after gazing at SNORKEY) What are you a-doing of—sa-a-y? (SNORKEY takes no notice) This here's one of the fellows as steals the bread of the poor man. Reading all the songs for nothin', and got bags of gold at home. Sa-a-y!

SNORKEY: Well, youngster, what are you groaning about? Have you got the cholera?

BERMUDAS: Ah! what are you doing? Taking the bloom off my songs? You've read them 'ere ballads till they're in rags.

SNORKEY: I was looking for the 'Prairie Bird'.

BERMUDAS: Perary Bird, eh? There ain't no perary bird. There's a 'Perary Flower'.

SNORKEY: Now don't go into convulsions. I'll find it. *(Turns to songs)*

BERMUDAS: Sa-ay—you needn't look no further for that bird! I've found him and no mistake. He's a big Shanghae with a red comb and no feathers.

SNORKEY: He's dropped on me.

BERMUDAS: Ain't you a mean cuss, sa-ay? Why don't you come down with your two cents, and support trade?

SNORKEY: But I ain't got two cents. What's a fellow to do if he hasn't got a red?

BERMUDAS: *(toning down)* Hain't you? Where's your messages?

SNORKEY: Haven't had one go today.

BERMUDAS: Where do you hang out?

SNORKEY: Nowheres.

BERMUDAS: My eye—no roost?

SNORKEY: No.

BERMUDAS: I tell you what, come along with us— we've got a bully place—no rent—no taxes— no nothin'.

SNORKEY: Where is it?

BERMUDAS: Down under the pier! I discovered it. I was in swimmin' and seed a hole and went in. Lots of room, just the place for a quiet roost. We has jolly times every night, I tell you, on the dock; and when it is time to turn in we goes below, and has it as snug as a hotel; come down with us.

SNORKEY: I will! These young rascals will help me to track that scoundrel yet.

BERMUDAS: Now, help me to take in my shop windows; it's time to shut up shop.
(Enter RAY TRAFFORD)

RAY: If what that crazy girl has told me can be true, Laura may yet be restored to her friends, if not to me, for I have dispelled that dream for ever. But that villain must be traced immediately, or he will convey his victim far beyond our reach or rescue. *(*SNORKEY, *helping to take down songs, sees* TRAFFORD*)*

SNORKEY: Hollo! Cap'n!

RAY: The man of all I wanted. You tracked him?

SNORKEY: They was too much for me, sir— two horses was, but I saw them turn into Greenwich-street, near Jay.

RAY: This may give us a clue. I have learned from a girl who knows this fellow that he has some hiding-place over the river, and owns a boat which is always fastened near the pier where the Boston steamers are.

SNORKEY: Well, cap'n, if anything's to be done, you'll find me at Pier—what's the number of our pier, Shorty?

BERMUDAS: Pier 30! Downstairs!

SNORKEY: Pier 30. That's my new home, and if you want me, say the word.

RAY: You will help me?

SNORKEY: You bet, cap'n. I was on Columbia's side for four years, and I'll fight for her daughters for the rest of my life, if you say so. If there's any fightin' count me in, cap'n.

RAY: Thank you, brave fellow. Here take this—no nonsense—take it. Pier 30, is it?

SNORKEY: Pier 30. *(Exit* TRAFFORD*)*

BERMUDAS: *(eyeing money)* How much, Perary?

SNORKEY: One—two—three—four—four dollars.

BERMUDAS: Four dollars! Sa-ay—don't you want to buy a share in a paying business? I'm looking out for a partner with a cash capital for the ballad business. Or I tell you what to do. Lay your money on me in a mill. I'm going to be a prize-fighter, and get reported in the respectable dailies. 'Rattling Mill, *99*th round, Bermudas the victor, having knocked his antagonist into nowheres.'

SNORKEY: Come along, you young imp. I could floor you with my own arm, and then the report would be: '25th round—Snorkey came up first, while his antagonist showed great signs of distress.'

BERMUDAS: Say, Perary, what are you going to do with all that money?

SNORKEY: I won't bet it on you, sure.

BERMUDAS: I'll tell you what to do; let's go and board at the Metropolitan Hotel for an hour.

SNORKEY: What will we do for toothpicks?

BERMUDAS: Oh, go along. You can't get anything to eat for four dollars. (*Exeunt* SNORKEY *and* BERMUDAS *squaring off*)

SCENE IV: *Foot of Pier 30, North River—Transparent set water pieces—a pier projecting into the river. A large cavity in front. Bow of a vessel at back, and other steamers, vessels and piers in perspective on either side. The flat gives view of Jersey City and the river shipping by starlight. Music of distant serenade heard.*

(Enter BYKE, *sculling a boat, which he fastens to the pier.* JUDAS *is on the pier, smoking pipe, looking down*)

JUDAS: Have you fixed everything across the river?

BYKE: Yes, I have a horse and waggon waiting near the shore to carry her to the farm. Has anyone been around here?

JUDAS: Not a soul. I've been waiting here for an hour. What made you so long?

BYKE: I pulled down the river for a spell to throw any spies off the track. It was necessary after what you told me of that girl's threat to blab about the Boston pier.

JUDAS: Pshaw! she'd never dare.

BYKE: Never mind, it's best to be certain. Is the prize safe?

JUDAS: Yes, she was worn out, and slept when I came away. How her blood tells—she wouldn't shed a tear.

BYKE: Bah! if she'd been more of a woman and set up a screaming, we shouldn't have been able to get her at all. Success to all girls of spirit, say I.

JUDAS: Don't you think it might be worth while to treat with this young spark, Trafford, and hear what he has to offer?

BYKE: Satan take him, no! That'll spoil your game about the other girl, Pearl. He was making up to her all right, and if he gets this one back he'll upset the whole game by marrying her. I tell you he's got the old feeling for her, spite of her running away. Now you can judge for yourself, and do as you please.

JUDAS: Then I do as you do—get her out of the city. When Pearl is married to him we can treat for Laura's ransom by threatening them with the real secret.

BYKE: Then that's settled. (*Taking out flask*) Here's the precious infant's health. Do you think she'll go easy, or shall we drug her?

JUDAS: Just tell her it's to meet her beau and get her ransom, or give her a reason and she'll be as mild as a lamb.

BYKE: Ha! let me get hold of her, and I'll answer she goes across, reason or no reason. (BERMUDAS *calls outside*) There's a noise.

JUDAS: It's only the market boys coming down for a swim.

BYKE: Softly then, come along. (*Music—exeunt*) (Enter BERMUDAS, PEANUTS, *and two other boys*)

BERMUDAS: Say, Peanuts, go down and see if any of the fellows is come yet. (PEANUTS *scrambles down to hole in front on side of dock—comes out again*)

PEANUTS: There's nobody there.

SNORKEY: (*without*) Hollo!

BERMUDAS: Hollo! that's our new chum. Hollo! follow your front teeth, and you'll get here afore you knows it.

(Enter SNORKEY, *with more boys*)

SNORKEY: What a very airy location.

BERMUDAS: It's a very convenient hotel. Hot and cold saltwater baths at the very door of your bedrooms, and sometimes when the tide rises we has the bath brought to us in bed, doesn't we, Peanuts?

PEANUTS: That's so.

SNORKEY: Come, what do you do before you go to bed?

BERMUDAS: We'll have a swarry. Say, one of you fellows, go down and bring up the piany forty.

(PEANUTS *goes into hole and gets banjo)* What'll I give you?

SNORKEY: Something lively. *(Music, nigger songs, and various entertainments—trained dogs, street acrobats, &c., ending with dance by boys, given according to capacity and talent. At the end of it a general shout of jubilee)*

SERGEANT: *(aside)* Here, boys! less noise.

BERMUDAS: It's Acton and the police. Let's go to bed. *(BERMUDAS and boys get down into hole)*

SERGEANT: *(entering in patrol boat)* If you boys don't make less noise, I'll have to clear you out.

BERMUDAS: *(on the pier)* It's an extra occasion, Mr Acton; we've got a distinguished military guest, and we're entertaining him. *(Boat passes out)* Come along, Perary, let's go to bed. *(SNORKEY is about to descend)*

(Enter RAY TRAFFORD on pier)

RAY: Is that you, Snorkey?

SNORKEY: *(quickly whispering)* Here, sir. Anything turned up?

RAY: Byke was overheard to say he intended crossing the river tonight. He will doubtless use that boat which he keeps by the Boston pier. The river patrol are on the watch for him, but I will meet him before he can embark.

SNORKEY: Which Boston pier is it, cap'n? There are three on this river.

RAY: Three?

SNORKEY: Yes, one of them is two slips below. I tell you what, cap'n; you get the officers, go by the shore way, search all the ships; I'll find a boat here, and will drop down the river, and keep an eye around generally.

VOICE: *(without)* This way, sir.

RAY: That's the patrol calling me. Your idea is a good one. Keep a sharp eye down the stream. *(Exit)*

SNORKEY: *(alone)* Now for my lay.

BERMUDAS: *(popping his head up)* Say, can't I do nothin? I'm the Fifth-Ward Chicken, and if there's any muss, let me have a shy.

SNORKEY: No; get in and keep quiet. *(BERMUDAS disappears)* I wonder where I can find a boat.

There ought to be plenty tied up about here. My eye! *(Discovering BYKE'S)* Here's one for the wishin'—sculls too. I'm in luck. Say, Bermudas, whose boat is this?

BERMUDAS: Yours, if you like. Turn it loose. *(SNORKEY jumps down, enters boat, pushes off)*

BERMUDAS: *(inside)* Keep your toe out of my ear. *(Pause—Enter BYKE, LAURA, and JUDAS, on pier)*

LAURA: Is this the place? There is no one here; you have deceived me.

BYKE: Well, we have, but we won't do so any longer.

LAURA: What do you mean?

BYKE: *(drawing pistol)* Do you see this? It is my dog Trusty. It has a very loud voice, and a sharp bite; and if you scream out, I'll try if it can't outscream you. Judas, unfasten the boat.

LAURA: What are you about to do? You will not murder me?

BYKE: No, we only mean to take you to the other shore, where your friends won't think of finding you. Quick, Judas!

JUDAS: The boat's gone.

BYKE: Damn you, what do you mean? Where is it? Here, hold her. Where the devil is that boat?

SNORKEY: *(re-appearing in boat)* Here!

BYKE: Snorkey! We're betrayed. Come. *(Drags LAURA away)*

SNORKEY: The police are there. Turn, you coward, don't run away from a one-armed man!

BYKE: Judas, take her. *(SNORKEY strikes at him with oar, BYKE takes oar from him and strikes him—he falls in boat)*

SNORKEY: Help! Bermudas! *(The boys hear the noise, and scramble up at back. The patrol boat appears with lights)*

BERMUDAS: Hi! Ninety-ninth round! First blood for Bermudas! *(Jumps at BYKE)*

BYKE: *(flinging BERMUDAS off)* Judas, toss her over. *(JUDAS throws LAURA over back of pier. RAY enters. Boys all get on pier and surround BYKE, fighting him. Officers enter—RAY leaps into water after LAURA—Curtain—Moonlight on during scene)*

ACT III

SCENE I: *Long Branch. Ground floor of an elegant residence—open windows from floor to ceiling at back opening upon a balcony or promenade. Perspective of the shore and sea in distance. Doors R. and L. Sunset. The curtain rises to lively music.*

(Enter PEARL, MRS VAN DAM, MISS EARLIE, and other ladies in summer costume, DEMILT and WINDEL with them.)

PEARL: And so the distinguished foreigner is in love with me? I thought he looked excessively solemn last night. Do you know, I can't imagine a more serious spectacle than a Frenchman or an Italian in love. One always imagines them to be unwell. *(To MRS VAN DAM)* Do fasten my glove—there's a dear.

MRS VAN DAM: Where's Ray?

PEARL: Oh, he's somewhere. I never saw such another. Isn't he cheerful? He never smiles, and seldom talks.

MRS VAN DAM: But the foreigner does. What an ecstasy he was in over your singing; sing us a verse, won't you, while we're waiting for Ray?

ALL: It will be delightful—do.

PEARL: Well!

AIR, *'When the War Is Over, Mary'*
Now the summer days are fading,
   Autumn sends its dreary blast
Moaning through the silent forest
   Where the leaves are falling fast.
Soon dread winter will enfold us—
   Chilling in its arms of snow,
Flowers that the summer cherished,
   Birds that sing, and streams that flow.
Say, shall all things droop and wither,
   That are born this summer day?
Shall the happy love it brought us—
   Like the flowers fade away?
Go; be still thou flutt'ring bosom—
   Seasons change and years glide by,
They may not harm what is immortal—
   Darling—love shall never die!

Now, I've sung that to Ray a dozen times, and he never even said it was nice. He hasn't any soul for music; oh, dear, what a creature!

MRS VAN DAM: Yes, and what a victim you will be, with a husband who has 600,000 dollars per annum income!

PEARL: That's some comfort, isn't it?

(Enter RAY TRAFFORD bowing to others)

RAY: Going out, Pearl?

PEARL: Yes, we're off to Shrewsbury. Quite a party's going—four carriages—and we mean to stay and ride home by moonlight.

RAY: Couldn't you return a little earlier?

MRS VAN DAM: Earlier! Pshaw! What's in you, Trafford? *(The ladies and gentlemen go up)*

RAY: You know that Laura will be quite alone, and she is still suffering.

PEARL: Well, she'll read and read, as she always did, and never miss me.

RAY: But at least she ought to have some little attention.

PEARL: Dear, dear, what an unreasonable fellow you are. Isn't she happy now—didn't you save her from drowning, and haven't I been as good to her as I can be—what more do you want?

RAY: I don't like to hear you talk so, Pearl, and remember what she and you were once. And you know that she was something else once—something that you are now to me. And yet how cheerful, how gentle she is. She has lost everything, and does not complain.

PEARL: Well, what a sermon! There, I know you're hurt and I'm a fool. But I can't help it. People say 'she's good-looking, but she's got no heart!' I'd give anything for one, but they ain't to be bought.

RAY: Well, don't moan about it, I didn't mean to reprove you.

PEARL: But you *do* reprove me. I'm sure I haven't been the cause of Laura's troubles. I didn't tell the big ugly man to come and take her away, although I was once glad he did.

RAY: Pearl!

PEARL: Because I thought I had gained you by it. *(RAY turns away)* But now I've got you, I don't seem to make you happy. But I might as well complain that you don't make me happy—but I don't complain, I'm satisfied, and I want you to be satisfied. There, *are* you satisfied?

MRS VAN DAM: *(who, with others, has been promenading up and down the balcony)* Here are the carriages.

PEARL: I'm coming. Can't you get me my shawl, Ray? *(RAY gets it from chair)*

MRS VAN DAM: And here's your foreign admirer on horseback.

(Exeunt MISS EARLIE, DEMILT and WINDEL)

PEARL: Bye, bye, Ray. *(Exit PEARL)*

MRS VAN DAM: Are you not coming, Trafford?

RAY: I? No!

MRS VAN DAM: Do come on horseback, here's a horse ready for you.

PEARL: *(without)* Ray! Ray!

MRS VAN DAM: Pearl's calling you. Be quick or Count Carom will be before you, and hand her in the carriage.

RAY: *(taking his hat slowly)* Oh, by all means, let the Count have some amusement.

MRS VAN DAM: *(taking RAY'S arm)* You're a perfect icicle. *(They exeunt. Noise of whips and laughter. Plaintive music as LAURA enters, and gazes out at them)*

LAURA: Poor Pearl. It is a sad thing to want for happiness, but it is a terrible thing to see another groping about blindly for it when it is almost within the grasp. And yet she can be very happy with him. Her sunny temper and her joyous face will brighten any home. *(Sits on table, on which are books)* How happy I feel to be alone with these friends, who are ever ready to talk to me—with no longings for what I may not have—my existence hidden from all save two in the wide world, and making my joy out of the joy of that innocent child who will soon be his wife. (PEACHBLOSSOM *appears at back, looking in cautiously, grotesquely attired)*

PEACHBLOSSOM: If you please.

LAURA: *(aloud)* Who's there?

PEACHBLOSSOM: *(running in)* Oh, it's Miss Nina! Oh, I'm so glad; I've had such a hunt for you.

Don't ask me nothing yet. I'm so happy. I've been looking for you so long, and I've had such hard luck. Lord what a tramp—miles on miles.

LAURA: Did anyone see you come here? How did you find me?

PEACHBLOSSOM: I asked 'em at the hotel where Mr Trafford was, and they said at Courtlands, and I asked 'em where Courtlands was, and they said down the shore, and I walked down lookin' at every place till I came here.

LAURA: Speak low, Blossom. My existence is a secret, and no one must hear you.

PEACHBLOSSOM: Well, miss, I says to Snorkey—says I—

LAURA: Is he with you?

PEACHBLOSSOM: No, miss, but we are great friends. He wants me to keep house for him some day. I said to him—'I want to find out where Miss Nina's gone,' and so he went to Mr Trafford's and found he was come to Long Branch, but never a word could we hear of you.

LAURA: And the others—those dreadful people?

PEACHBLOSSOM: Byke and old Judas? Clean gone! They hasn't been seen since they was took up for throwing you into the water, and let off because no one came to Court agin 'em. Bermudas says he's seen 'em in Barnum's wax-work show, but Bermudas is *such* a liar. He brought me up here.

LAURA: Brought you up here?

PEACHBLOSSOM: Yes, he sells papers at Stetson's; he's got the exclusive trade here, and he has a little waggon and a horse, and goes down to the junction every night to catch the extras from the express train what don't come here. He says he'll give me lots of nice rides if I'll stay here.

LAURA: But you must not stay here. You must go back to New York this evening.

PEACHBLOSSOM: Back! No, I won't.

LAURA: Blossom!

PEACHBLOSSOM: I won't, I won't, I won't! I'll never let you away again. I did it once and you was took away and chucked overboard and almost drowned. I won't be any trouble, indeed, I won't. I'll hire out at the hotel, and run over when my work is done at night, when nobody can see me, to look up at your window. Don't send me away. You're the only one as ever was good to me.

LAURA: *(aside)* It's too dangerous. She certainly would reveal me sooner or later. I must send her back.

PEACHBLOSSOM: Besides, I've got something to tell you. Dreadful! dreadful! about old Judas and Byke—a secret.

LAURA: A secret! what in the world are you saying?

PEACHBLOSSOM: Is it wicked to listen at doors when people talk?

LAURA: It is very wicked.

PEACHBLOSSOM: Well, I suppose that's why I did it. I used to listen to Byke and Judas when they used to talk about a rich lady whom they called Mrs Courtland.

LAURA: Ah!

PEACHBLOSSOM: Judas used to be a nurse at Mrs Courtland's, and was turned off for stealing. And wasn't she and Byke going to make money off her! and Byke was to pretend to be some beautiful lady's father. Then when they took you, Judas says to me: 'Did you ever hear of children being changed in their cradles?'—and that you wasn't her child, but she was going to make money off the real one at the proper time.

LAURA: What do you tell me?

PEACHBLOSSOM: Oh! I'm not crazy. I know a heap, don't I? And I want you [to] think I'm somebody, and not send me away.

LAURA: *(to herself)* She must speak the truth. And yet if I were to repeat her strange words here, I should be suspected of forging the tale. No! better let it rest as it is. She must go—and I must go too.

PEACHBLOSSOM: You ain't mad with me?

LAURA: No, no; but you must go away from here. Go back to the hotel, to your friend—anywhere, and wait for me; I will come to you.

PEACHBLOSSOM: It is a promise?

LAURA: *(nervously)* Yes, go.

PEACHBLOSSOM: Then I'll go; for I know you always keep your word—you ain't angry 'cause I came after you? I did it because I loved you—

because I wanted to see you put in the right place. Honour bright, you ain't sending me away now? Well, I'll go; goodbye! *(Exit)*

LAURA: *(animated)* I must return to the city, no matter what dangers may lurk there. It is dangerous enough to be concealed here, with a hundred Argus-eyed women about me every day, but with this girl, detection would be certain. I must go—secretly if I can—openly if I must.

RAY: *(outside)* No, I shall not ride again. Put him up. *(Entering)* Laura, I knew I should find you here.

LAURA: *(sitting and pretending composure)* I thought you had gone with Pearl.

RAY: I did go part of the way, but I left the party a mile down the road.

LAURA: You and Pearl had no disagreement?

RAY: No—yes; that is, we always have. Our social barometers always stand at 'cloudy' and 'overcast.'

LAURA: And whose fault is that?

RAY: *(pettishly)* Not mine. I know I do all I can—I say all I can—but she—

LAURA: But she is to be your wife. Ray, my friend, courtship is the text from which the whole solemn sermon of married life takes its theme. Do not let yours be discontented and unhappy.

RAY: To be my wife; yes. In a moment of foolishness, dazzled by her airs, and teased by her coquettishness, I asked her to be my wife.

LAURA: And you repent already?

RAY: *(taking her hand)* I lost you, and I was at the mercy of any flirt that chose to give me an inviting look. It was your fault—you know it was! Why did you leave me?

LAURA: *(after conflict with her feelings)* Ray, the greatest happiness I have ever felt has been the thought that all your affections were for ever bestowed upon a virtuous lady, your equal in family, fortune and accomplishments. What a revelation do you make to me now! What is it makes you continually at war with your happiness?

RAY: I don't know what it is. I was wrong to accuse you. Forgive me! I have only my own cowardice to blame for my misery. But Pearl—

LAURA: You must not accuse her.

RAY: When you were gone, she seemed to have no thought—no wish—but for my happiness. She constantly invited me to her house, and when I tried to avoid her, met me at every turn. Was she altogether blameless?

LAURA: Yes, it was her happiness she sought, and she had a right to seek it.

RAY: Oh! men are the veriest fools on earth; a little attention, a little sympathy, and they are caught—caught by a thing without soul or brains, while some noble woman is forsaken and forgotten.

LAURA: Ray, will you hear me?

RAY: *(looking at her hopefully)* Yes, speak to me as you used to speak. Be to me as you used to be.

LAURA: *(smiling sadly)* I cannot be that to you; but I can speak as the spirit of the Laura who is dead to you for ever.

RAY: Be it as you will.

LAURA: Let the woman you look upon be wise or vain, beautiful or homely, rich or poor, she has but one thing she can really give or refuse—her heart! Her beauty, her wit, her accomplishments, she may sell to you—but her love is the treasure without money and without price.

RAY: How well I have learned that.

LAURA: She only asks in return, that when you look upon her, your eyes shall speak a mute devotion; that when you address her, your voice shall be gentle, loving and kind. That you shall not despise her because she cannot understand, all at once, your vigorous thoughts and ambitious designs; for when misfortune and evil have defeated your greatest purposes—her love remains to console you. You look to the trees for strength and grandeur—do not despise the flowers, because their fragrance is all they have to give. Remember, love is all a woman has to give; but it is the only earthly thing which God permits us to carry beyond the grave.

RAY: You are right. You are always right. I asked Pearl to be my wife, knowing what she was, and I will be just to her. I will do my duty though it break my heart.

LAURA: Spoken like a hero.

RAY: But it is to you I owe the new light that guides me; and I will tell her—

LAURA: Tell her nothing—never speak of me. And when you see her, say to her it is she, and she alone, whom you consult and to whom you listen.

RAY: And you?

LAURA: You will see me no more.

RAY: You will leave me?

LAURA: Something of me will always be with you—my parting words—my prayers for your happiness. *(Distant music heard)*

RAY: *(falling on his knees)* Oh, Laura, you leave me to despair.

LAURA: No; to the happiness which follows duty well performed. Such happiness as I feel in doing mine. *(Picture. During last of this scene the sun has set, and night comes on. Close in. Stage dark)*

SCENE II: *Woods near Shrewsbury Station.*

(Enter BYKE, *shabbily dressed)*

BYKE: It's getting darker and darker, and I'm like to lose my way. Where the devil is Judas? It must be nine o'clock, and she was to be at the bend with the waggon half an hour ago. *(Rumble of wheels heard)* Humph—at last.

(Enter JUDAS*)*

JUDAS: Is that you, Byke?

BYKE: Who did you suppose it was? I've been tramping about the wet grass for an hour.

JUDAS: It was a hard job to get the horse and waggon.

BYKE: Give me a match. *(Lights pipe and leans against a tree)* Did you get the bearings of the crib?

JUDAS: Yes, it is on the shore, well away from the other cottages and hotels.

BYKE: That's good. Nothing like peace and quietness. Who's in the house?

JUDAS: Only the two girls and the servants.

BYKE: How many of them?

JUDAS: Four.

BYKE: It'll be mere child's play to go through that house. Have you spied about the swag?

JUDAS: They have all their diamonds and jewels there. Pearl wears them constantly; they're the talk of the whole place.

BYKE: We'll live in luxury off that girl all our lives. She'll settle a handsome thing on us, won't she? when she knows what we know, and pays us to keep dark—if t'other one don't spoil the game.

JUDAS: Curse her! I could cut her throat.

BYKE: Oh, I'll take care of that!

JUDAS: You always do things for the best, dear old Byke!

BYKE: Of course I do. What time is it?

JUDAS: Not ten yet.

BYKE: An hour to wait.

JUDAS: But, Byke, you won't peach on me before my little pet is married, will you?

BYKE: What's the fool about now?

JUDAS: I can't help trembling; nothing is safe while Laura is there.

BYKE: I've provided for that. I've had the same idea as you—while she's in the way, and Trafford unmarried, our plans are all smoke, and we might as well be sitting on the hob with a keg of powder in the coals.

JUDAS: That we might. But what have you thought to do?

BYKE: Why, I've thought what an unfortunate creature Laura is—robbed of her mother, her home, and her lover; nothing to live for; it would be a mercy to put her out of the way.

JUDAS: That's it; but how—how—how—

BYKE: It's plain she wasn't born to be drowned, or the materials are very handy down here. What made you talk about cutting her throat? It was very wrong! When a thing gets into my head, it sticks there.

JUDAS: You oughtn't to mind me.

BYKE: Make your mind easy on that score.

JUDAS: *(alarmed)* Byke, I heard someone in the bushes just there. *(Points off)*

BYKE: *(nervously and quickly)* Who? Where?

JUDAS: Where the hedge is broken. I could swear I saw the shadow of a man.

BYKE: Stop here. I'll see. *(Goes off)*

JUDAS: I begin to shiver. But it must be done or we starve. Why should I tremble? It's the safest job we ever planned. If they discover us, our secret will save us—we know too much to be sent to jail.
(Re-enter BYKE, slowly)

BYKE: There are traces, but I can see no one. *(Looking off)*

JUDAS: Suppose we should have been overheard!

BYKE: *(glaring at her)* Overheard? Bah! no one could understand.

JUDAS: Come, let us go to the waggon and be off.

BYKE: *(always looking off)* Go you, I will follow. Bring it round by the station, and wait for me in the shadows of the trees. I will follow. *(JUDAS goes off. BYKE, after a moment, still looking, buttons up his coat and hides behind wood)* Heigho! I must be off.
(Enter SNORKEY, slowly)

SNORKEY: Tracked 'em again! We're the latest fashionable arrivals at Long Branch. 'Mr Byke and Lady, and Brigadier-General Snorkey, of New York'; there's an item for the papers! With a horse and waggon, they'll be at the seaside in two hours; but in the train I think I'll beat 'em. Then to find Cap'n Trafford, and give him the wink, and be ready to receive the distinguished visitors with all the honours. Robbery; burglary; murder; that's Byke's catechism. 'What's to be done when you're hard up?—Steal! What's to be done if you're caught at it?—Kill!' It's short and easy, and he lives up to it like a good many Christians don't live up to their laws. *(Looking off)* They're out of sight. Phew! it's midsummer, but I'm chilled to the bone; something like a piece of ice has been stuck between my shoulders all day, and something like a black mist is always before me. (BYKE *is behind tree*) Just like old Nettly told me he felt, the night before Fredericksburg—and next day he was past all feeling—hit with a shell, and knocked into so many pieces, I didn't know which to call my old friend. Well *(slapping his chest)*, we've all got to go; and if I can save *them*, I'll have some little capital to start the next world on. The next world! perhaps I shan't be the maimed beggar *there* that I am in this. *(Takes out pistol, examines cap; goes off,* BYKE *gliding after him)*

SCENE III: *Railroad Station at Shrewsbury Bend, R. Platform around it, and door at side, window in front. At L. clump of shrubs and trees. The railroad track runs from L. to R. View of Shrewsbury River in perspective. Night —moonlight. The switch, with a red lantern and a signalman's coat hanging on it L. C. The signal lamp and post beside it. As the scene opens, several packages are lying about the stage, among them a bundle of axes. The* SIGNALMAN *is wheeling in a small barrel, whistling at his work.*

(Enter LAURA, *in walking dress, feebly)*

LAURA: It is impossible for me to go further. A second time I've fled from home and friends, but now they will never find me. The trains must all have passed, and there are no conveyances till tomorrow.

SIGNALMAN: Beg pardon, ma'am, looking for anybody?

LAURA: Thank you, no. Are you the man in charge of this station?

SIGNALMAN: Yes, ma'am.

LAURA: When is there another train for New York?

SIGNALMAN: New York? Not till morning. We've only one more train tonight; that's the down one; it'll be here in about twenty minutes—express train.

LAURA: What place is that?

SIGNALMAN: That? That's the signal station shed. It serves for store-room, depot, baggage-room, and everything.

LAURA: Can I stay there tonight?

SIGNALMAN: There? Well it's an odd place, and I should think you would hardly like it. Why don't you go to the hotel?

LAURA: I have my reasons—urgent ones. It is not because I want money. You shall have this *(producing porte-monnaie)* if you let me remain here.

SIGNALMAN: Well, I've locked up a good many things in there over-night, but I never had a young lady for freight before. Besides, ma'am, I don't know anything about you. You know it's odd that you won't go to a decent hotel, and plenty of money in your pocket.

LAURA: You refuse me—well—I shall only have to sit here all night.

SIGNALMAN: Here, in the open air? Why, it would kill you.

LAURA: So much the better.

SIGNALMAN: Excuse me for questions, miss, but you're a-running away from someone, ain't you?

LAURA: Yes.

SIGNALMAN: Well, I'd like to help you. I'm a plain man you know, and I'd like to help you, but there's one thing would go agin me to assist in. *(*LAURA *interested)* I'm on to fifty years of age, and I've many children, some on 'em daughters grown. There's many temptations for young gals, and sometimes the old man has to put on the brakes a bit, for some young men are wicked enough to persuade the gals to steal out of their father's house in the dead of the night, and go to shame and misery. So tell me this—it ain't the old man, and the old man's home you've left, young lady?

LAURA: No, you good, honest fellow—no, I have no father.

SIGNALMAN: Then, by Jerusalem, I'll do for you what I can. Anything but run away from them that have not their interest but yours at heart. Come, you may stay there, but I'll have to lock you in.

LAURA: I desire that you should.

SIGNALMAN: It's for your safety as much as mine. I've got a patent lock on that door that would give a skeleton the rheumatism to fool with it. You don't mind the baggage; I'll have to put it in with you, hoes, shovels, mowing machines, and what is this? axes—yes, a bundle of axes. If the superintendent finds me out I'll ask him if he was afraid you'd run off with these. *(Laughs)* So, if you please, I'll first tumble 'em in. *(Puts goods in house,* LAURA *sitting on platform looking at him. When all in he comes towards her, taking up cheese-box to put it in station)* I say, miss, I ain't curious, but, of course, it's a *young man* you're a-going to?

LAURA: So far from that, it's a young man I'm running away from.

SIGNALMAN: *(dropping a box)* Running away from a young man; let me shake hands with you. *(Shakes her hand)* Lord, it does my heart good. At your age, too. *(Seriously)* I wish you'd come and live down in my neighbourhood awhile; among my gals *(shaking his head)* you'd do a power of good. *(Putting box in station)*

LAURA: I've met an excellent friend—and here at least I can be concealed until tomorrow—then for New York. My heart feels lighter already—it's a good omen.

SIGNALMAN: Now, miss, bless your heart, here's your hotel ready. *(Goes to switch and takes off coat, putting it on)*

LAURA: Thanks, my good friend, but not a word to anyone till tomorrow, not even—not even to your girls.

SIGNALMAN: Not a word, I promise you. If I told my girls it would be over the whole village before morning. *(She goes in, he locks door. LAURA appears at window facing audience)*

LAURA: Lock me in safely.

SIGNALMAN: Ah, be sure I will. There! *(Tries door)* Safe as a jail. *(Pulls out watch and then looking at track with lantern)* Ten minutes and down she comes. It's all safe this way, my noisy beauty, and you may come as soon as you like. Goodnight, miss.

LAURA: *(at window)* Goodnight.

SIGNALMAN: Running away from a young man, ha! ha! ha! *(He goes to track, then looks down it, lights his pipe and is trudging off)* *(Enter SNORKEY)*

SNORKEY: Ten minutes before the train comes, I'll wait here for it. *(To SIGNALMAN, who re-enters)* Hallo, I say, the train won't stop here too long, will it?

SIGNALMAN: Too long? it won't stop here at all.

SNORKEY: I must reach the shore tonight, there'll be murder done unless I can prevent it.

SIGNALMAN: Murder or no murder, the train can't be stopped.

SNORKEY: It's a lie. By waving the red signal for danger the engineer must stop, I tell you.

SIGNALMAN: Do you think I'm a fool? What, disobey orders and lose my place; then what's to become of my family? *(Exit)*

SNORKEY: I won't be foiled; I will confiscate some farmer's horse about here and get there before them somehow.
(Enter BYKE at back with loose coil of rope in his hand)
Then when Byke arrives in his donkey cart he'll be ready to sit for a picture of surprise.

BYKE: *(suddenly throwing the coil over SNORKEY)* Will he?

SNORKEY: Byke!

BYKE: Yes, Byke. Where's that pistol of yours? *(Tightening rope round his arm)*

SNORKEY: In my breast pocket.

BYKE: *(taking it)* Just what I wanted.

SNORKEY: You ain't a-going to shoot me?

BYKE: No!

SNORKEY: Well, I'm obliged to you for that.

BYKE: *(leading him to platform)* Just sit down a minute, will you.

SNORKEY: What for? *(LAURA appears horror-struck at window)*

BYKE: You'll see.

SNORKEY: Well, I don't mind if I do take a seat. *(Sits down, BYKE coils the rope round his legs)* Hollo, what's this?

BYKE: You'll see. *(Picks the helpless SNORKEY up)*

SNORKEY: Byke, what are you going to do?

BYKE: Put you to bed. *(Lays him across the railroad track)*

SNORKEY: Byke, you don't mean to—My God, you are a villain!

BYKE: *(fastening him to rails)* I'm going to put you to bed. You won't toss much. In less than ten minutes you'll be sound asleep. There, how do you like it? You'll get down to the Branch before me, will you? You'll dog me and play the eavesdropper, eh! Now do it if you can. When you hear the thunder under your head and see the lights dancing in your eyes, and feel the iron wheels a foot from your neck, remember Byke. *(Exit)*

LAURA: Oh, Heavens, he will be murdered before my eyes! How can I aid him?

SNORKEY: Who's that?

LAURA: It is I, do you not know my voice?

SNORKEY: That I do, but I almost thought I was dead and it was an angel's. Where are you?

LAURA: In the station.

SNORKEY: I can't see you, but I can hear you. Listen to me, miss, for I've got only a few minutes to live.

LAURA: *(shaking door)* And I cannot aid you.

SNORKEY: Never mind me, miss, I might as well die now and here, as at any other time. I'm not afraid. I've seen death in almost every shape, and none of them scare me; but for the sake of those you love, I would live. Do you hear me?

LAURA: Yes! yes!

SNORKEY: They are on the way to your cottage— Byke and Judas—to rob and murder.

LAURA: *(in agony)* Oh, I must get out! *(Shakes window bars)* What shall I do?

SNORKEY: Can't you burst the door?

LAURA: It is locked fast.

SNORKEY: Is there nothing in there? no hammer? no crowbar?

LAURA: Nothing. *(Faint steam whistle heard in the distance)* Oh, Heavens! The train! *(Paralysed for an instant)* The axe!!!

SNORKEY: Cut the woodwork! Don't mind the lock, cut round it. How my neck tingles! *(A blow at door is heard)* Courage! *(Another)* Courage! *(The steam whistle heard again—nearer, and rumble of train on track—another blow)* That's a true woman. Courage! *(Noise of locomotive heard, with whistle. A last blow—the door swings open, mutilated, the lock hanging—and* LAURA *appears, axe in hand)*

SNORKEY: Here—quick! *(She runs and unfastens him. The locomotive lights glare on scene)* Victory! Saved! Hooray! *(*LAURA *leans exhausted against switch)* And these are the women who ain't to have a vote! *(As* LAURA *takes his head*

from the track, the train of cars rushes past with roar and whistle)

ACT IV

SCENE I: *An elegant boudoir at Courtland Cottage, Long Branch. Open window and balcony at back— moonlight exterior—tree overhanging balcony. Bed is at* L., *toilette table* R., *arm chair* C., *door* L., *lighted lamp on toilette table—dresses on chair by bed, and by window on* R. *Music.*

PEARL: *(discovered, en negligée, brushing her hair out at table before mirror)* I don't feel a bit sleepy. What a splendid drive we had. I like that foreigner. What an elegant fellow he is! Ray is nothing to him. I wonder if I'm in love with him. Pshaw—what an idea! I don't believe I could love anybody much. How sweetly he writes! *(Picks up letter)* 'You were more lovely than ever tonight—with one thing more, you'd be an angel!' Now that's perfectly splendid—'with one thing more, you'd be an angel—that one thing is love. They tell me Mr Trafford is your professed admirer. I'm sure he could never be called your lover, for he seems incapable of any passion but melancholy.' It's quite true, Ray does not comprehend me. *(Takes up another letter)* 'Pearl, forgive me if I have been cross and cold. For the future, I will do my duty, as your affianced husband, better.' Now, did ever anyone hear such talk as that from a lover? Lover! Oh, dear! I begin to feel that he can love—but not me. Well, I'd just as soon break, if he'd be the first to speak. How sweet and fresh the air is. *(She turns down lamp)* It's much nicer here, than going to bed. *(Settles herself in tête-à-tête for a nap. Pause. Moonbeams fall on* BYKE, *who appears above the balcony. He gets over the rail and enters)*

BYKE: Safely down. I've made no mistake—no, this is her room. What a figure I am for a lady's chamber. (*Goes to table, picks up delicate lace handkerchief, and wipes his face*) Phew! hot! (*Puts handkerchief in his pocket*) Now for my bearings. (*Taking huge clasp-knife from his pocket*) There's the bed where she's sleeping like a precious infant, and here—(*Sees* PEARL *in chair, and steals round at back, looking down at her*) It's so dark—I can't recognise the face. It's a wonder she don't feel me in the air and dream of me. If she does she'll wake sure—but it's easy to settle that. (*Takes phial of chloroform, from his pocket, saturates the handkerchief he picked up, and applies it*) So—now my charmer, we'll have the earrings. (*Takes them out*) What's here? (*Going to table*) Bracelets—diamonds! (*Going to dresses, and feeling in the pockets*) Money! That's handy. (*He puts all in a bag, and hands them over balcony*) Now for the drawers; there's where the treasure must be. Locked? (*Tries them with bunch of keys*) Patent lock of course. It amuses me to see people buying patent locks when there's one key will fit 'em all. (*Produces small crowbar, and just as he is about to force the drawer, a shout is heard, and noise of waggon*) What's that? (*Jumps, catching at a chair, which falls over*) Damnation!

PEARL: (*starting up*) Who's there? What's that?

BYKE: Silence, or I'll kill you.

PEARL: Help! Help!

BYKE: (*running to bureau for knife*) You will have it, my pretty one.

PEARL: (*runs to door*) Save me! save me! (BYKE *pursues her, she dodges him round the table, &c. Just as* BYKE *overtakes her, the door bursts open and* RAY *and* LAURA *enter.* BYKE *turns and runs to balcony, and confronts* SNORKEY *and* BERMUDAS, *who have clambered over*)

LAURA: Just in time.

RAY: (*seizing* BYKE) Scoundrel!

SNORKEY: Hold him, governor. Hold him! (*Assists* RAY *to bind* BYKE *in chair*)

BERMUDAS: Sixty-sixth and last round. The big 'un floored, and Bermudas as fresh as a daisy.

PEARL: Dear, dear Laura, you have saved me.

RAY: Yes, Pearl, from more than you can tell.

LAURA: No, no; her preservers are there. (*Pointing to* BERMUDAS *and* SNORKEY) Had it not been for the one, I should never have learned your danger, and but for the other, we could never have reached you in time.

SNORKEY: Bermudas and his fourth editions did it. Business enterprise and Bermudas' pony express worked the oracle this time.

BERMUDAS: The way we galloped! Sa-ay, my pony must have thought the extras was full of lively intelligence.

PEARL: Darling Laura, you shall never leave us again.

RAY: No, never!

SNORKEY: Beg pardon, cap'n, what are we to do with this here game we've brought down?

RAY: The magistrates will settle with him.

SNORKEY: Come, old fellow.

BYKE: One word, I beg. My conduct, I know, has been highly reprehensible. I have acted injudiciously, and have been the occasion of more or less inconvenience to everyone here. But I wish to make amends, and therefore I tender you all, in this public manner, my sincere apologies. I trust this will be entirely satisfactory.

RAY: Villain!

BYKE: I have a word to say to you, sir.

SNORKEY: Come, that's enough.

BYKE: My good fellow, don't interrupt gentlemen who are conversing together. (*To* RAY) I address you, sir—you design to commit me to the care of the officers of the law?

RAY: Most certainly.

BYKE: And you will do your best towards having me incarcerated in the correctional establishments of this country? (RAY *bows*)

SNORKEY: How very genteel.

BYKE: Then I have to say, if you will, I shall make a public exposure of certain matters connected with a certain young lady.

LAURA: Do not think that will deter us from your punishment. I can bear even more than I have—for the sake of justice.

BYKE: Excuse me, I did not even remotely refer to you.

LAURA: To whom, then?

BYKE: *(pointing to* PEARL*)* To her.

RAY: Miss Courtland?

BYKE: Oh dear—no sir. The daughter of old Judas—the spurious child placed in *your* cradle, Miss Laura Courtland, when you were abducted from it by your nurse.

PEARL: What does he say?

BYKE: That you're a beggar's child—we have the proofs! Deliver me to prison, and I produce them.

RAY: Wretch!

PEARL: Then it's you, dear Laura, have been wronged—while I—

LAURA: You are my sister still—whatever befalls!

PEARL: Oh, I'm so glad it's so! Ray won't want to marry me, now—at least, I hope so; for I know he loves you—he always loved you—and you will be happy together.

RAY: Pearl, what are you saying?

PEARL: Don't interrupt me! I mean every word of it. Laura, I've been very foolish, I know. I ought to have tried to reunite you—but there is time.

RAY: Dear Laura! Is there, indeed, still time? *(She gives her hand)*

BYKE: Allow me to suggest that a certain proposition I had the honour to submit has not yet been answered.

RAY: Release him. *(*SNORKEY *undoes his cords)*

BYKE: Thank you—not so rough! Thank you.

RAY: Now, go—but remember, if you ever return to these parts you shall be tried, not only for this burglary, but for the attempt to kill that poor fellow.

BYKE: Thank you. Good-bye. *(To* SNORKEY*)* Good-bye, my dear friend; overlook our little dispute, and write to me. *(Aside)* They haven't caught Judas, and she shall make them pay handsomely for her silence yet.

(Enter PEACHBLOSSOM*)*

PEACHBLOSSOM: Oh, Miss! Oh, such an accident—old Judas!

LAURA: ⎱
BYKE: ⎰Well?

PEACHBLOSSOM: She was driving along the road away from here just now, when her horse dashed close to the cliff and tumbled her down all of a heap. They've picked her up, and they tell me she is stone dead.

BYKE: *(aside)* Dead! And carried her secret with her! All's up. I'll have to emigrate. *(Aloud)* My friends, pardon my emotion—this melancholy event has made me a widower. I solicit your sympathies in my bereavement. *(Exit* BYKE*)*

BERMUDAS: Go to Hoboken and climb a tree! I guess I'll follow him and see he don't pick up anything on his way out. *(Exit* BERMUDAS*)*

SNORKEY: Well, there goes a pretty monument of grief. Ain't he a cool 'un? If I ever sets up an ice-cream saloon, I'll have him for head freezer.

PEACHBLOSSOM: Oh, Miss Laura, mayn't I live with you now, and never leave no more?

LAURA: Yes, you shall live with me as long as you please.

SNORKEY: That won't be long if I can help it. *(*PEACHBLOSSOM *blushes)* Beg pardon. I suppose we'd better be going! The ladies must be tired, cap'n, at this time of night.

RAY: Yes, it is night! It is night always for me. *(Moving towards door)*

LAURA: *(placing one hand on his shoulder, taking his hand)* But there is a tomorrow. You see, it cannot be dark for ever.

PEARL: Hope for tomorrow, Ray.

LAURA: We shall have cause to bless it, for it will bring the long sought sunlight of our lives.

CURTAIN

BRONSON HOWARD

SHENANDOAH (1888)

A Klee painting named "Angelus Novus" shows an angel looking as though he is about to move away from something he is fixedly contemplating. His eyes are staring, his mouth is open, his wings are spread. This is how one pictures the angel of history. Where we perceive a chain of events, he sees one single catastrophe which keeps piling wreckage upon wreckage and hurls it in front of his feet. The angel would like to stay, awaken the dead, and make whole what has been smashed. But a storm is blowing from Paradise; it has got caught in his wings with such violence that the angel can no longer close them. This storm irresistibly propels him into the future to which his back is turned, while the pile of debris before him grows skyward. This storm is what we call progress.

Walter Benjamin's ninth thesis on the philosophy of history raises the interrelated questions of past, future, and the perspectives from which communities see both. This particular constellation of questions is very much at the heart of Bronson Howard's *Shenandoah*, a preeminent example of American **melodrama's** use of the past for subject matter and an equally cogent instance of America's tendency to melodramatize its history into a hegemonic narrative. The strategies utilized and conclusions drawn by Howard's play are typical of an abiding strand of the national discourse, particularly strong in late nineteenth-century America, which suggests that what Lincoln called "the last, best hope of the earth" has found embodiment in an America always progressing into an ever brighter future. George Santayana reiterated the point when he observed that for

late nineteenth-century Americans, "The world . . . was a safe place, watched over by a kindly God, who exacted nothing but cheerfulness and good-will from his children; and the American flag was a sort of rainbow in the sky, promising that all storms were over. Or if storms came, such as the Civil War, they would not be harder than was necessary to test the national spirit and raise it to a new efficiency." It is that movement—from storm to rainbow—that is the essence of Howard's play.

Born to Charles and Margaret Howard in Detroit on October 7, 1842, Bronson Crocker Howard grew up the son of a commission merchant who became the mayor of Detroit in 1849. He was educated in Detroit until at 16 he was sent to Russell's Institute in New Haven, Connecticut, to prepare for entrance to Yale. In 1861 he entered Yale, but an eye infection caused him to withdraw. He returned home, accepting a job as the drama critic for the Detroit *Free Press*. His interest in writing drama manifested itself in 1864 when his first play, *Fantine*, a dramatization of some episodes from Hugo's *Les Misérables*, was mounted by the Detroit Theatre. Encouraged by the play's reception, he went to New York the next year, working as a journalist at first for the *Tribune* and later the *Post*. In 1870, *Saratoga*, his first New York theatrical endeavor, premiered at Augustin Daly's Fifth Avenue Theatre, where it enjoyed a first run of 101 nights. Perhaps taking a hint from his contemporary, Augustin Daly, Howard retained his newspaper job while writing a series of relatively insignificant pieces. Included in this group was *Lillian's Last Love* (1873), a play that Howard later revised with great success as *The Banker's Daughter* (1878) and made the subject of his *Autobiography of a Play* (1914), originally an 1886 lecture to the Shakespeare Club at Harvard in which he laid out many of his principles of dramatic construction.

Howard continued to write and adapt plays, devoting himself exclusively to his playwrighting after 1876 when he ended his journalism career. (The decision to live by his dramatic work—and its successful implementation—gives Bronson Howard the distinction of being the first truly professional playwright in America who was not also an actor or a theatre manager.) British productions of Howard's plays occasioned regular trips to England, and on one such trip he met Alice Wyndham, the sister of Charles Wyndham, the manager of London's Court Theatre, where *Saratoga* was being produced under its British title, *Brighton*. A romance developed and in 1880 they were married. Howard's next major dramatic achievement was *Young Mrs. Winthrop* (1882), a study of a marriage's near dissolution in the face of the husband's obsession with business and the wife's preoccupation with high society. Howard addressed the "international theme" popularized in the fiction of Henry James and William Dean Howells in *One of Our Girls* (1885). He returned to the theme of business and family life in *The Henrietta* (1887), a play whose combination of ticker-tape machines, high finance maneuverings, and romantic intrigues grossed a half million dollars in its initial run. *Shenandoah*, Howard's last major play, premiered in Boston in 1888 to unenthusiastic response. However, Charles Frohman, just beginning his managerial career, convinced Howard to make certain revisions, and, with the help of Al Hayman, his future Theatrical Syndicate partner, Frohman produced the play at New York's Star Theatre in 1889. With General William Tecumseh Sherman in the audience, the play began a 250-performance initial run. Howard was never to recapture the success of *Shenandoah*, though he would continue to write and have plays produced until 1899. In 1891, he founded the American Dramatists Club to agitate for playwrights having their property rights secure against piracy. He died on August 4, 1906.

In *Autobiography of a Play*, Howard enunciated an insistently businesslike approach to the writing of plays for an American audience. As a playwright who eschewed literary pretensions, his audience was the final authority on a play's form, and their desires were to be satisfied if at all possible. While this approach may sound artistically craven and mercenary, it actually sprang from Howard's beliefs as to the ways that plays appeal to their audiences and it made him one of the preeminent melodramatists of his day. At the core of his belief was the idea that "laws of dramatic construction exist in the passions and sympathies of the human race." Given his egalitarian turn of mind, Howard found that essential to any playwright's success was an appeal not to the grand sweep of history but to the hearts which contained those passions and sympathies. The most straightforward method of doing this was to focus his plays upon love. As he rationalized it, "the dramatist appeals to a thousand hearts at the same moment; he has no choice in the matter, he must do this; and it is only when he deals with the love of the sexes that his work is most interesting to that aggregate of human hearts we call 'the audience.'" Not surprisingly, *Shenandoah* carefully reflects these premises. But in following these assumptions, *Shenandoah* becomes a telling example of the ways in which Howard's audiences saw *their* history and how that history was fashioned to serve *them*.

Shenandoah was not the first play to deal with the Civil War or the issues surrounding it. As noted in the earlier discussion of Dion Boucicault's *The Octoroon*, plays examining slavery were popular before the war broke out. During the war, flag-waving patriotic spectacles were common on both sides of the Mason-Dixon line. After the war, with the exception of amateur productions for veterans groups, the subject was rarely addressed by the major playwrights of the day. After Daly produced *Norwood* (1867), which included a scene at the Battle of Gettysburg, and Boucicault then refined the soon-to-be-ubiquitous Southern belle heroine in *Belle Lamar* (1874), the topic was mainly ignored until William Gillette's blockbuster *Held by the Enemy* (1886). Nevertheless, as Jeffrey Mason has argued, a pattern for discussing the war had clearly emerged by the time that Howard began writing *Shenandoah*. The most salient features of this design were a suppression of discussions of slavery as a generative cause of the war; a rhetorical distribution of claims to be fighting for freedom, liberty, and independence to both sides; and a reframing of the war as a type of tumultuous sectional love affair in which (usually) a Northern hero wins back his Southern love.

Howard utilizes this general formula in *Shenandoah* but complicates and amplifies its possibilities. He first attempts to remove from view and earshot as many of the widely acknowledged causes and lingering consequences of the war as he can: he excludes blacks from the cast and thereby relieves himself and his audience of encountering even a reminder of the question of slavery; he also eliminates anything more than a brief first-act acknowledgment of the regional differences which underpinned the conflict; and, finally, he downplays the war's harsher military realities by focusing the audience's attention upon his central characters' interlocked loves. All of these dramatic choices evidence Howard's sense of a widespread desire for sectional rapprochement. While such strategies ameliorate the causes and the pain caused by the war's actual prosecution, Howard also undertakes to suggest abiding affinities that provide the ground for an emotional reunion to match the political one forged on battlefields such as Cedar Creek. By emphasizing the similarities of the combatants; by circumscribing the conflict within a romantic melodrama framework which metaphorically renders reunion of the nation an inevitable consequence to the formal imperative of uniting the lovers; by naturalizing the Union ideological belief in the indivisibility of the nation; by doubling Northern and Southern heroes and heroines; by soliciting sympathy for the losses of both sides of the conflict; and by incorporating as many age groups and classes into his play as he can manage (with the obvious exception of blacks), Howard actively asserts that the nation was always and already indivisible even in the midst of the war that to his audience had settled that question forever.

That Howard was successful in his appropriation of history is evident not only from the play's long run, but in the reviewers' comments as well. In his "Editor's Study" segment for *Harper's Monthly*, William Dean Howells remarked upon the conciliatory note to which Howard's play aspired: "The swiftly moving history is expressed from the patriotic point of view in such terms and characters as do justice to the high motives and unselfish heroism on both sides." The *New York Times'* Edward A. Dithmar, reviewing the play's opening night, pointed out that "the author has spared no effort to emphasize the sentimental idea of the brotherhood of the contesting parties in our terrible war, and the recognition by individuals on either side of the natural ties which bound them to their foes." Dithmar repeated his observation the following Sunday in his summation of the week's theatrical events, noting that Howard "handled the war with delicate care, almost gingerly," a circumstance which Dithmar attributed in some measure to Howard's recognition that the war "is still too near for the great body of Americans to view its incidents calmly and dispassionately."

Shenandoah marked a significant moment in the nation's movement beyond the particular passions of the Civil War, but it was only a small part of a more complex configuration of circumstances that made such a reconciliation "inevitable." On the cultural front, Northern and Southern writers such as John William De Forest, George Washington Cable, and Joel Chandler Harris were busily constructing the "Old South" myth. Meanwhile in the economic and business world, the Panic of 1873 brought Northern prosperity to an abrupt halt and made revitalized Southern markets a necessity for Northern industries. In the political arena, the accommodations in early 1877 which allowed the Republicans to retain the presidency in the person of Rutherford B. Hayes also ended Reconstruction and restored the South as a political force. If *Shenandoah* did not accomplish the tasks of the angel—if it could not raise the dead and make whole what had been smashed—it did manage to suggest that a new day replete with rainbows was predestined. The hegemonic narrative of the forward march of "the last, best hope of earth" could have no other conclusion.

WORKS CONSULTED

Benjamin, Walter. *Illuminations*. ed. Hannah Arendt. New York: Schocken Books, 1968.

Dithmar, Edward A. Review of *Shenandoah* by Bronson Howard. *New York Times*, Sept. 10, 1889: 4.

————. Review of *Shenandoah* by Bronson Howard. *New York Times*, Sept. 15, 1889: 3.

Howard, Bronson. *Autobiography of a Play*. New York: Dramatic Museum of Columbia University, 1914.

Howells, William Dean. "Editor's Study." *Harper's Monthly*, June 1890: 155.

Mason, Jeffrey D. *Melodrama and the Myth of America*. Bloomington: Indiana University Press, 1993.

Richardson, Gary A. *American Drama from the Colonial Period through World War I*. New York: Twayne, 1993.

Santayana, George. *Character and Opinion in the United States*. New York: Norton, 1920.

CHARACTERS

GENERAL HAVERHILL*

COLONEL KERCHIVAL WEST

CAPTAIN HEARTSEASE . . . . Officers of Sheridan's Cavalry

LIEUTENANT FRANK BEDLOE

MAJOR-GENERAL FRANCIS BUCKTHORN . . . . Commander of the 19th Army Corps

SERGEANT BARKET

COLONEL ROBERT ELLINGHAM . . . . 10th Virginia

CAPTAIN THORNTON . . . . Secret Service, C. S. A.

MRS CONSTANCE HAVERHILL

GERTRUDE ELLINGHAM

MADELINE WEST

JENNY BUCKTHORN

MRS EDITH HAVERHILL

HARDWICK . . . . Surgeon

CAPTAIN LOCKWOOD . . . . U. S. Signal Corps

LIEUTENANT OF SIGNAL CORPS

LIEUTENANT OF INFANTRY

CORPORAL DUNN

BENSON

OLD MARGERY

JANNETTE

WILKINS

*After the character list, the family name is consistently called "Haverill." Howard also promotes Haverill from colonel to general without comment between acts one and two.

ACT FIRST

CHARLESTON HARBOR IN 1861. "AFTER THE BALL."

SCENE: *The Interior of a Southern Residence on the shore of Charleston Harbor. Large double doors at the rear of the stage are open. A large, wide window, with low sill, extends down the right side of the stage. A veranda is seen through the doors and the window. There is a wide opening on the left with a corridor beyond. The furniture and appointments are quaint and old-fashioned, but the general tone of the walls and upholstery is that of the old Colonial period in its more ornamental and decorative phase, as shown in the early days of Charleston. Old candlesticks and candelabra, with lighted candles nearly burned down, light the room, and in addition the moon-light streams in. Beyond the central doors and the window there is a lawn, with Southern foliage, extending down to the shores of the harbor; a part of the bay lies in the distance, with low-lying land beyond. The lights of Charleston are seen over the water along the shore. The gray twilight of early morning gradually steals over the scene as the Act progresses. As the curtain rises,* KERCHIVAL WEST *is sitting in a chair, his feet extended and his head thrown back, a handkerchief over his face.* ROBERT ELLINGHAM *strolls in on the veranda, beyond the window, smoking. He looks to the right, starts and moves to the window; leans against the upper side of the window and looks across.*

ELLINGHAM: Kerchival!

KERCHIVAL: *(under the handkerchief)* Eh? H'm!

ELLINGHAM: Can you sleep at a time like this? My own nerves are on fire.

KERCHIVAL: Fire? Oh—yes—I remember. Any more fire-works, Bob?

ELLINGHAM: A signal rocket from one of the batteries, now and then. *(He goes up beyond the window.* KERCHIVAL *arouses himself, taking the handkerchief from his eyes)*

KERCHIVAL: What a preposterous hour to be up. The ball was over an hour ago, all the guests are gone, and it's nearly four o'clock. *(Looking at his watch)* Exactly ten minutes of four. *(He takes out a cigar)* Our Southern friends assure us that General Beauregard is to open fire on Fort Sumter this morning. I don't believe it. *(Lighting the cigar and rising, he looks out through the window)* There lies the old fort—solemn and grim as ever, and the flag-staff stands above it, like a warning finger. If they do fire upon it *(shutting his teeth for a moment and looking down at the cigar in his hand)* the echo of that first shot will be heard above their graves, and Heaven knows how many of our own, also; but the flag will still float!—over the graves of both sides.

*(*ELLINGHAM *enters from the central door and approaches him)*

Are you Southerners all mad, Robert?

ELLINGHAM: Are you Northerners all blind? *(*KERCHIVAL *sits down)* We Virginians would prevent a war if we could. But your people in the North do not believe that one is coming. You do not understand the determined frenzy of my fellow Southerners. Look! *(Pointing toward the rear of the stage)* Do you see the lights of the city, over the water? The inhabitants of Charleston are gathering, even now, in the gray, morning twilight, to witness the long-promised bombardment of Fort Sumter. It is to be a gala day for them. They have talked and dreamed of nothing else for weeks. The preparations have become a part of their social life—of their amusement—their gayeties. This very night at the ball—here—in the house of my own relatives—what was their talk? What were the jests they laughed at? Sumter! War! Ladies were betting bonbons that the United States would not dare to fire a shot in return, and pinning ribbons on the breasts of their "heroes." There was a signal rocket from one of the forts, and the young men who were dancing here left their partners standing on the floor to return to the batteries—as if it were the night before another Waterloo. The ladies themselves hurried away to watch the "spectacle" from their own verandas. You won't see the truth! I tell you, Kerchival, a war between the North and South is inevitable!

KERCHIVAL: And if it does come, you Virginians will join the rest.

ELLINGHAM: Our State will be the battle ground, I fear. But every loyal son of Virginia will follow her flag. It is our religion!

KERCHIVAL: My State is New York. If New York should go against the old flag, New York might go to the devil. That is my religion.

ELLINGHAM: So differently have we been taught what the word "patriotism" means!

KERCHIVAL: You and I are officers of the same regiment of the United States Regular Army, Robert; we were classmates at West Point, and we have fought side by side on the plains. You saved my scalp once; I'd have to wear a wig, now, if you had n't. I say, old boy, are we to be enemies?

ELLINGHAM: *(laying his hand over his shoulder)* My dear old comrade, whatever else comes, our friendship shall be unbroken!

KERCHIVAL: Bob! *(looking up at him)* I only hope that we shall never meet in battle!

ELLINGHAM: In battle? The idea is horrible!

KERCHIVAL: *(rising and crossing to him)* My dear old comrade, one of us will be wrong in this great fight, but we shall both be honest in it. *(He gives his hand; ELLINGHAM grasps it warmly, then turns away)*

ELLINGHAM: Colonel Haverill is watching the forts, also; he has been as sad to-night as we have. Next to leaving you, my greatest regret is that I must resign from his regiment.

KERCHIVAL: You are his favorite officer.

ELLINGHAM: Naturally, perhaps; he was my guardian.
(Enter HAVERILL from the rear. He walks down, stopping in the center of the stage)

HAVERILL: Kerchival! I secured the necessary passports to the North yesterday afternoon; this one is yours; I brought it down for you early in the evening. (KERCHIVAL *takes the paper and goes to the window)* I am ordered direct to Washington at once, and shall start with Mrs Haverill this forenoon. You will report to Captain Lyon, of the 2d Regiment, in St. Louis.

Robert! I have hoped for peace to the last, but it is hoping against hope. I feel certain, now, that the fatal blow will be struck this morning. Our old regiment is already broken up, and you, also, will now resign, I suppose, like nearly all your fellow Southerners in the Service.

ELLINGHAM: You know how sorry I am to leave your command, Colonel!

HAVERILL: I served under your father in Mexico; he left me, at his death, the guardian of you and your sister, Gertrude. Even since you became of age, I have felt that I stood in his place. But you must be your sister's only guardian now. Your father fell in battle, fighting for our common country, but you—

ELLINGHAM: He would have done as I shall do, had he lived. He was a Virginian!

HAVERILL: I am glad, Robert, that he was never called upon to decide between two flags. He never knew but one, and we fought under it together. *(Exit)*

ELLINGHAM: Kerchival! Something occurred in this house to-night which—which I should n't mention under ordinary circumstances, but I— I feel that it may require my further attention, and you, perhaps, can be of service to me. Mrs Haverill, the wife of the Colonel—

KERCHIVAL: Fainted away in her room.

ELLINGHAM: You know?

KERCHIVAL: I was one of the actors in the little drama.

ELLINGHAM: Indeed!

KERCHIVAL: About half-past nine this evening, while the ladies were dressing for the ball, I was going upstairs; I heard a quick, sharp cry, sprang forward, found myself at an open door. Mrs Haverill lay on the floor inside, as if she had just reached the door to cry for help, when she fell. After doing all the unnecessary and useless things I could think of, I rushed out of the room to tell your sister, Gertrude, and my own sister, Madeline, to go and take care of the lady. Within less than twenty minutes afterwards, I saw Mrs Haverill sail into the drawing-room, a thing of beauty, and with the glow of perfect health on her cheek. It was an immense relief to me when I saw her. Up to that time I had a vague idea that I had committed a murder.

ELLINGHAM: Murder!

KERCHIVAL: M—m. A guilty conscience. Every man, of course, does exactly the wrong thing when a woman faints. When I rushed out of Mrs Haverill's room, I left my handkerchief soaked with water upon her face. I must ask her for it, it's a silk one. Luckily, the girls got there in time to take it off; she would n't have come to if they had n't. It never occurred to me that she'd need to breathe in my absence. That's all I know about the matter. What troubles you? I suppose every woman has a right to faint whenever she chooses. The scream that I heard was so sharp, quick and intense that—

ELLINGHAM: That the cause must have been a serious one.

KERCHIVAL: Yes! So I thought. It must have been a mouse.

ELLINGHAM: Mr Edward Thornton has occupied the next room to that of Mrs Haverill to-night.

KERCHIVAL: (quickly) What do you mean?

ELLINGHAM: During the past month or more he has been pressing, not to say insolent, in his attentions to Mrs Haverill.

KERCHIVAL: I've noticed that myself.

ELLINGHAM: And he is an utterly unscrupulous man; it is no fault of mine that he was asked to be a guest at this house to-night. He came to Charleston, some years ago, from the North, but if there are any vices and passions peculiarly strong in the South, he has carried them all to the extreme. In one of the many scandals connected with Edward Thornton's name, it was more than whispered that he entered a lady's room unexpectedly at night. But, as he killed the lady's husband in a duel a few days afterwards, the scandal dropped.

KERCHIVAL: Of course; the gentleman received ample satisfaction as an outraged husband, and Mr Thornton apologized, I suppose, to his widow.

ELLINGHAM: He has repeated the adventure.

KERCHIVAL: Do—you—think—that?

ELLINGHAM: I was smoking on the lawn, and glanced up at the window; my eyes may have deceived me, and I must move cautiously in the matter; but it could n't have been imagination; the shadow of Edward Thornton's face and head appeared upon the curtain.

KERCHIVAL: Whew! The devil!

ELLINGHAM: Just at that moment I, too, heard the stifled scream.

(Enter EDWARD THORNTON)

THORNTON: Gentlemen!

ELLINGHAM: Your name was just on my tongue, Mr Thornton.

THORNTON: I thought I heard it, but you are welcome to it. Miss Gertrude has asked me to ride over to Mrs Pinckney's with her, to learn if there is any further news from the batteries. I am very glad the time to attack Fort Sumter has come at last!

ELLINGHAM: I do not share your pleasure.

THORNTON: You are a Southern gentleman.

ELLINGHAM: And you are a Northern "gentleman."

THORNTON: A Southerner by choice; I shall join the cause.

ELLINGHAM: We native Southerners will defend our own rights, sir; you may leave them in our keeping. It is my wish, Mr Thornton, that you do not accompany my sister.

THORNTON: Indeed!

ELLINGHAM: Her groom, alone, will be sufficient.

THORNTON: As you please, sir. Kindly offer my excuses to Miss Gertrude. You and I can chat over the subject later in the day, when we are alone. (Moving up the stage)

ELLINGHAM: By all means, and another subject, also, perhaps.

THORNTON: I shall be entirely at your service. (Exit to the veranda)

ELLINGHAM: Kerchival, I shall learn the whole truth, if possible, to-day. If it is what I suspect—what I almost know—I will settle with him myself. He has insulted our Colonel's wife and outraged the hospitality of my friends. (Walking to the right)

KERCHIVAL: *(walking to the left)* I think it ought to be my quarrel. I'm sure I'm mixed up in it enough.

MADELINE: *(without, calling)* Kerchival!

ELLINGHAM: Madeline. *(Aside, starting,* KERCHIVAL *looks across at him sharply)*

KERCHIVAL: *(aside)* I distinctly saw Bob give a start when he heard Madeline. Now what can there be about my sister's voice to make a man jump like that?

GERTRUDE: *(without)* Brother Robert!

KERCHIVAL: Gertrude! *(Aside, starting,* ELLINGHAM *looks at him sharply)* How the tones of a woman's voice thrill through a man's soul! *(Enter* MADELINE*)*

MADELINE: Oh, Kerchival—here you are. *(Enter* GERTRUDE, *from the apartment, in a riding habit, with a whip)*

GERTRUDE: Robert, dear! *(Coming down to* ROBERT; *they converse in dumb show)*

MADELINE: Where are your field glasses? I've been rummaging all through your clothes, and swords, and sashes, and things. I've turned everything in your room upside down.

KERCHIVAL: Have you?

MADELINE: I can't find your glasses anywhere. I want to look at the forts. Another rocket went up just now. *(Runs up the stage and stands on the piazza looking off)*

KERCHIVAL: A sister has all the privileges of a wife to upset a man's things, without her legal obligation to put them straight again. *(Glances at* GERTRUDE*)* I wish Bob's sister had the same privileges in my room that my own has.

GERTRUDE: Mr Thornton is n't going with me, you say?

ELLINGHAM: He requested me to offer you his apologies.

KERCHIVAL: May *I* accompany you? *(*ELLINGHAM *turns to the window on the right)*

GERTRUDE: My groom, old Pete, will be with me, of course; there's no particular need of anyone else. But you may go along, if you like. I've got my hands full of sugar plums for Jack. Dear old Jack—he always has his share when we have

company. I'm going over to Mrs Pinckney's to see if she's had any more news from General Beauregard; her son is on the General's staff.

MADELINE: *(looking off to the right)* There's another rocket from Fort Johnson; and it is answered from Fort Moultrie. Ah! *(Angrily)* General Beauregard is a bad, wicked man! *(Coming down)*

GERTRUDE: Oh! Madeline! You are a bad, wicked Northern girl to say such a thing.

MADELINE: I *am* a Northern girl.

GERTRUDE: And I am a Southern girl. *(They face each other)*

KERCHIVAL: *(dropping into a chair)* The war has begun. *(*ELLINGHAM *has turned from the window; he strolls across the stage, watching the girls)*

GERTRUDE: General Beauregard is a patriot.

MADELINE: He is a Rebel.

GERTRUDE: So am I.

MADELINE: Gertrude!—You—you—

GERTRUDE: Madeline!—You—

MADELINE: I—I—

GERTRUDE: I—

BOTH: O—O-h! *(Bursting into tears and rushing into each other's arms, sobbing, then suddenly kissing each other vigorously)*

KERCHIVAL: I say, Bob, if the North and South do fight, that will be the end of it.

GERTRUDE: I've got something to say to you, Madeline, dear. *(Confidentially and turning with her arms about her waist. The girls sit down talking earnestly)*

ELLINGHAM: Kerchival, old boy! There's—there's something I'd like to say to you before we part to-day.

KERCHIVAL: I'd like a word with you, also!

MADELINE: You don't really mean that, Gertrude—with me?

ELLINGHAM: I'm in love with your sister, Madeline.

KERCHIVAL: The devil you are!

ELLINGHAM: I never suspected such a thing until last night.

GERTRUDE: Robert was in love with you six weeks ago. *(*MADELINE *kisses her)*

KERCHIVAL: *I've* made a discovery, too, Bob.

MADELINE: *I've* got something to say to *you,* Gertrude.

KERCHIVAL: I'm in love with *your* sister.

ELLINGHAM: *(astonished)* You are?

MADELINE: Kerchival has been in love with you for the last three months. (GERTRUDE *offers her lips—they kiss)*

KERCHIVAL: I fell in love with her the day before yesterday. *(The two gentlemen grasp each other's hands warmly)*

ELLINGHAM: We understand each other, Kerchival. *(He turns up the stage and stops at the door)* Miss Madeline, you said just now that you wished to watch the forts. Would you like to walk down to the shore?

MADELINE: Yes! *(Rising and going up to him. He takes one of her hands in his own and looks at her earnestly)*

ELLINGHAM: This will be the last day that we shall be together, for the present. But we shall meet again—sometime—if we both live.

MADELINE: If we both live! You mean—if *you* live. You must go into this dreadful war, if it comes.

ELLINGHAM: Yes, Madeline, I must. Come let us watch for our fate.   *(Exeunt to the veranda)*

KERCHIVAL: *(aside)* I must leave Charleston to-day. *(He sighs)* Does she love me?

GERTRUDE: I am ready to start, Mr West, when you are.

KERCHIVAL: Oh! Of course, I forgot. *(Rising)* I shall be delighted to ride at your side.

GERTRUDE: At my side! *(Rising)* There is n't a horse in America that can keep by the side of my Jack, when I give him his head, and I'm sure to do it. You may follow us. But you can hardly ride in that costume; while you are changing it, I'll give Jack his bonbons. *(Turning to the window)* There he is, bless him! Pawing the ground, and impatient for me to be on his back. Let him come, Pete. *(Holding up bonbons at window)* I love you.

KERCHIVAL: Eh? *(Turning suddenly)*

GERTRUDE: *(looking at him)* What?

KERCHIVAL: You were saying—

GERTRUDE: Jack! *(Looking out. The head of a large black horse appears through the window)* You dear old fellow. *(She feeds him with bonbons)* Jack has been my boy ever since he was a little colt. I brought you up, did n't I, Jack? He's the truest, and kindest, and best of friends; I would n't be parted from him for the world, and I'm the only woman he'll allow to be near him.

KERCHIVAL: *(earnestly)* You are the only woman, Miss Gertrude, that I—

GERTRUDE: Dear Jack!

KERCHIVAL: *(aside)* Jack embarrasses me. He's a third party.

GERTRUDE: There! That will do for the present, Jack. Now go along with Pete! If you are a very good boy, and don't let Lieutenant Kerchival West come within a quarter of a mile of me, after the first three minutes, you shall have some more sugar plums when we get to Mrs Pinckney's. *(An old negro leads the horse away.* GERTRUDE *looks around at* KERCHIVAL*)* You have n't gone to dress, yet; we shall be late. Mrs Pinckney asked a party of friends to witness the bombardment this morning, and breakfast together on the piazza while they are looking at it. We can remain and join them, if you like.

KERCHIVAL: I hope they won't wait for breakfast until the bombardment begins.

GERTRUDE: I'll bet you an embroidered cigar-case, Lieutenant, against a box of gloves that it will begin in less than an hour.

KERCHIVAL: Done! You will lose the bet. But you shall have the gloves; and one of the hands that go inside them shall be—*(Taking one of her hands; she withdraws it)*

GERTRUDE: My own—until some one wins it. You don't believe that General Beauregard will open fire on Fort Sumter this morning?

KERCHIVAL: No; I don't.

GERTRUDE: Everything is ready.

KERCHIVAL: It's so much easier to get everything ready to do a thing than it is to do it. I have been ready a dozen times, this very night, to say to you, Miss Gertrude, that I—that I— *(Pauses)*

GERTRUDE: *(looking down and tapping her skirt with her whip)* Well?

KERCHIVAL: But I did n't.

GERTRUDE: *(glancing up at him suddenly)* I dare say, General Beauregard has more nerve than you have.

KERCHIVAL: It is easy enough to set the batteries around Charleston Harbor, but the man who fires the first shot at a woman—

GERTRUDE: Woman!

KERCHIVAL: At the American flag—must have nerves of steel.

GERTRUDE: You Northern men are so slow, to—

KERCHIVAL: I have been slow; but I assure you, Miss Gertrude, that my heart—

GERTRUDE: What subject are we on now?

KERCHIVAL: You were complaining because I was too slow.

GERTRUDE: I was doing nothing of the kind, sir!— let me finish, please. You Northern men are so slow, to believe that our Southern heroes— Northern *men* and Southern *heroes*—you recognize the distinction I make—you won't believe that they will keep their promises. They have sworn to attack Fort Sumter this morning, and—they—will do it. This "American Flag" you talk of is no longer our flag: it is foreign to us!—It is the flag of an enemy!

KERCHIVAL: *(tenderly and earnestly)* Am I your enemy?

GERTRUDE: You have told me that you will return to the North, and take the field.

KERCHIVAL: Yes, I will. *(Decisively)*

GERTRUDE: You will be fighting against my friends, against my own brother, against me. We *shall* be enemies.

KERCHIVAL: *(firmly)* Even that, Gertrude—*(She looks around at him, he looks squarely into her eyes as he proceeds)*—if you will have it so. If my country needs my services, I shall not refuse them, though it makes us enemies! *(She wavers a*

moment, under strong emotion, and turns away; sinks upon the seat, her elbow on the back of it, and her tightly-clenched fist against her cheek, looking away from him)*

GERTRUDE: I will have it so! I am a Southern woman!

KERCHIVAL: We have more at stake between us, this morning, than a cigar-case and a box of gloves. *(Turning up the stage)*
(Enter MRS HAVERILL from apartment)

MRS HAVERILL: Mr West! I've been looking for you. I have a favor to ask.

KERCHIVAL: Of me?—with pleasure.

MRS HAVERILL: But I am sorry to have interrupted you and Gertrude. *(As she passes down KERCHIVAL moves up the stage. GERTRUDE rises) (Apart)* There are tears in your eyes, Gertrude, dear!

GERTRUDE: *(apart)* They have no right there.

MRS HAVERILL: *(apart)* I'm afraid I know what has happened. A quarrel! and you are to part with each other so soon. Do not let a girl's coquetry trifle with her heart until it is too late. You remember the confession you made to me last night?

GERTRUDE: *(apart)* Constance! *(Starting)* That is my secret; more a secret now than ever.

MRS HAVERILL: *(apart)* Yes, dear; but you do love him. *(GERTRUDE moves up the stage)*

GERTRUDE: You need not ride over with me, Mr West.

KERCHIVAL: I can be ready in one moment.

GERTRUDE: I choose to go alone! Old Pete will be with me; and Jack, himself, is a charming companion.

KERCHIVAL: If you prefer Jack's company to mine—

GERTRUDE: I do.   *(Exit on the veranda)*

KERCHIVAL: Damn Jack! But you will let me assist you to mount.   *(Exit after her)*

MRS HAVERILL: We leave for the North before noon, but every hour seems a month. If my husband should learn what happened in my room to-night, he would kill that man. What encouragement could I have given him? Innocence is never on its guard—but, *(drawing up)* the last I remember before I fell unconscious, he was crouching before me like a whipped cur! *(She starts as she looks out of the window)* There is Mr Thornton, now—Ah! *(Angrily)* No—I must control my own indignation. I must keep him and Colonel Haverill from meeting before we leave Charleston. Edward Thornton would shoot my husband down without remorse. But poor Frank! I must not forget him, in my own trouble. I have but little time left to care for his welfare.

(Re-enter KERCHIVAL*)*

KERCHIVAL: You said I could do you a favor, Mrs Haverill?

MRS HAVERILL: Yes, I wanted to speak with you about General Haverill's son, Frank. I should like you to carry a message to Charleston for me as soon as it is light. It is a sad errand. You know too well the great misfortune that has fallen upon my husband in New York.

KERCHIVAL: His only son has brought disgrace upon his family name, and tarnished the reputation of a proud soldier. Colonel Haverill's fellow officers sympathize with him most deeply.

MRS HAVERILL: And poor young Frank! I could hardly have loved the boy more if he had been my own son. If he had not himself confessed the crime against the bank, I could not have believed him guilty. He has escaped from arrest. He is in the City of Charleston. I am the only one in all the world he could turn to. He was only a lad of fourteen when his father and I were married, six years ago; and the boy has loved me from the first. His father is stern and bitter now in his humiliation. This note from Frank was handed to me while the company were here last evening. I want you to find him and arrange for me to meet him, if you can do it with safety. I shall give you a letter for him.

KERCHIVAL: I'll get ready at once; and I will do all I can for the boy.

MRS HAVERILL: And—Mr West! Gertrude and Madeline have told me that—that—I was under obligations to you last evening.

KERCHIVAL: Don't mention it. I merely ran for them, and I—I'm very glad you did n't choke—before they reached you. I trust you are quite well now?

MRS HAVERILL: I am entirely recovered, thank you. And I will ask another favor of you, for we are old friends. I desire very much that General Haverill should not know that—that any accident occurred to me to-night—or that my health has not been perfect.

KERCHIVAL: Certainly, madam!

MRS HAVERILL: It would render him anxious without cause.

KERCHIVAL: *(aside)* It looks as if Robert was right; she does n't want the two men to meet. *(Enter* HAVERILL, *a white silk handkerchief in his hand)*

HAVERILL: Constance, my dear, I've been all over the place looking for you. I thought you were in your room. But—by the way, Kerchival, this is your handkerchief; your initials are on it.

*(*KERCHIVAL *turns and stares at him a second.* MRS HAVERILL *starts slightly and turns front.* HAVERILL *glances quickly from one to the other, then extends his hands toward* KERCHIVAL, *with the handkerchief.* KERCHIVAL *moves to him and takes it.* MRS HAVERILL *drops into the chair)*

KERCHIVAL: Thank you. *(He walks up and exits with a quick glance back.* HAVERILL *looks at* MRS HAVERILL, *who sits nervously, looking away. He then glances up after* KERCHIVAL. *A cloud comes over his face and he stands a second in thought. Then, with a movement as if brushing away a passing suspicion, he smiles pleasantly and approaches* MRS HAVERILL; *leaning over her)*

HAVERILL: My fair Desdemona! *(Smiling)* I found Cassio's handkerchief in your room. Have you a kiss for me? *(She looks up, he raises her chin with a finger and kisses her)* That's the way I shall smother you.

MRS HAVERILL: *(rising and dropping her head upon his breast)* Husband!

HAVERILL: But what is this they have been telling me?

MRS HAVERILL: What have they said to you?

HAVERILL: There was something wrong with you in the early part of the evening; you are trembling and excited, my girl!

MRS HAVERILL: It was nothing, John; I—I—was ill, for a few moments, but I am well now.

HAVERILL: You said nothing about it to me.

MRS HAVERILL: Do not give it another thought.

HAVERILL: Was there anything besides your health involved in the affair? There was. *(Aside)* How came this handkerchief in her room?

MRS HAVERILL: My husband! I do not want to say anything more—at—at present—about what happened to-night. There has never been a shadow between us—will you not trust me?

HAVERILL: Shadow! You stand in a bright light of your own, my wife; it shines upon my whole life—there can be no shadow there. Tell me as much or as little as you like, and in your own time. I am sure you will conceal nothing from me that I ought to know. I trust my honor and my happiness to you, absolutely.

MRS HAVERILL: They will both be safe, John, in my keeping. But there is something else that I wish to speak with you about; something very near to your heart—your son!

HAVERILL: My son!

MRS HAVERILL: He is in Charleston.

HAVERILL: And not—in prison? To me he is nowhere. I am childless.

MRS HAVERILL: I hope to see him to-day; may I not take him some kind word from you?

HAVERILL: My lawyers in New York had instructions to provide him with whatever he needed.

MRS HAVERILL: They have done so, and he wants for nothing; he asks for nothing, except that I will seek out the poor young wife—only a girl herself—whom he is obliged to desert, in New York.

HAVERILL: His marriage was a piece of reckless folly, but I forgave him that.

MRS HAVERILL: I am sure that it was only after another was dependent on him that the debts of a mere spendthrift were changed to fraud—and crime.

HAVERILL: You may tell him that I will provide for her.

MRS HAVERILL: And may I take him no warmer message from his father?

HAVERILL: I am an officer of the United States Army. The name which my son bears came to me from men who had borne it with honor, and I transmitted it to him without a blot. He has disgraced it, by his own confession.

MRS HAVERILL: *I* cannot forget the poor mother who died when he was born; her whose place I have tried to fill, to both Frank and to you. I never saw her, and she is sleeping in the old graveyard at home. But I am doing what she would do to-day, if she were living. No pride—no disgrace—could have turned her face from him. The care and the love of her son has been to me the most sacred duty which one woman can assume for another.

HAVERILL: You have fulfilled that duty, Constance. Go to my son! I would go with you, but he is a man now; he could not look into my eyes, and I could not trust myself. But I will send him something which a man will understand. Frank loves you as if you were his own mother; and I—I would like him to—to think tenderly of me, also. He will do it when he looks at this picture. *(Taking a miniature from his pocket)*

MRS HAVERILL: Of me!

HAVERILL: I have never been without it one hour, before, since we were married. He will recognize it as the one that I have carried through every campaign, in every scene of danger on the Plains; the one that has always been with me. He is a fugitive from justice. At times, when despair might overcome him, this may give him nerve to meet his future life manfully. It has often nerved me, when I might have failed without it. Give it to him, and tell him that I send it. *(Giving her the miniature)* I could not send a kinder message, and he will understand it. *(Turning, he stands a moment in thought.* THORNTON *appears at the window looking at them quietly, over his shoulder, a cigar in his hand.* MRS HAVERILL *sees him, and starts with a suppressed breath, then looks at* HAVERILL, *who moves away. He speaks aside)* My son! My son! We shall never meet again! *(Exit)* (MRS HAVERILL *looks after him earnestly, then turns and looks at* THORNTON, *drawing up to her full height.* THORNTON *moves up the stage, beyond the window)*

MRS HAVERILL: Will he dare to speak to me again? *(Enter* THORNTON; *he comes down the stage quietly. He has thrown away the cigar)*

THORNTON: Mrs Haverill! I wish to offer you an apology.

MRS HAVERILL: I have not asked for one, sir!

THORNTON: Do you mean by that, that you will not accept one?

MRS HAVERILL: *(aside)* What can I say? *(Aloud)* Oh, Mr Thornton!—for my husband's sake, I—

THORNTON: Ah! You are afraid that your husband may become involved in an unpleasant affair. Your solicitude for his safety, madame, makes me feel that my offense to-night was indeed unpardonable. No gentleman can excuse himself for making such a mistake as I have made. I had supposed that it was Lieutenant Kerchival West, who—

MRS HAVERILL: What do you mean, sir?

THORNTON: But if it is your husband that stands between us—

MRS HAVERILL: Let me say this, sir: whatever I may fear for my husband, he fears nothing for himself.

THORNTON: He knows? *(Looking at her, keenly)* *(Enter* KERCHIVAL WEST, *now in riding suit)* *(He stops, looking at them)* You are silent. Your husband does know what occurred to-night; that relieves my conscience. *(Lightly)* Colonel Haverill and I can now settle it between us.

MRS HAVERILL: No, Mr Thornton! My husband knows nothing, and, I beg of you, do not let this horrible affair go further. *(Sees* KERCHIVAL)

KERCHIVAL: Pardon me. *(Stepping forward)* I hope I am not interrupting you. *(Aside)* It *was*

Thornton. *(Aloud)* You said you would have a letter for me to carry, Mrs Haverill.

MRS HAVERILL: Yes, I—I will go up and write it at once. *(As she leaves she stops and looks back. Aside)* I wonder how much he overheard.

KERCHIVAL: *(quietly)* I suppose eight o'clock will be time enough for me to go?

MRS HAVERILL: Oh, yes! *(glancing at him a moment)* —quite.   *(Exit)*

KERCHIVAL: *(quietly)* Mr Thornton! you are a scoundrel! Do I make myself plain?

THORNTON: You make the fact that you desire to pick a quarrel with me quite plain, sir; but I choose my own quarrels and my own enemies.

KERCHIVAL: Colonel Haverill is my commander, and he is beloved by every officer in the regiment.

THORNTON: On what authority, may I ask, do you—

KERCHIVAL: The honor of Colonel Haverill's wife is under our protection.

THORNTON: Under your protection? You have a better claim than that, perhaps, to act as her champion. Lieutenant Kerchival West is Mrs Haverill's favorite officer in the regiment.

KERCHIVAL: *(approaching him)* You dare to suggest that I—

THORNTON: If I accept your challenge, I shall do so not because you are her protector, but my rival.

KERCHIVAL: Bah! *(Striking him sharply on the cheek with his glove. The two men stand facing each other a moment)* Is it my quarrel now?

THORNTON: I think you are entitled to my attention, sir.

KERCHIVAL: My time here is limited.

THORNTON: We need not delay. The Bayou La Forge is convenient to this place.

KERCHIVAL: I'll meet you there, with a friend, at once.

THORNTON: It will be light enough to see the sights of our weapons in about one hour. *(They bow to each other, and* THORNTON *goes out)*

KERCHIVAL: I've got ahead of Bob.

GERTRUDE: *(without)* Whoa! Jack! Old boy! Steady, now—that's a good fellow.

KERCHIVAL: She has returned. I *must* know whether Gertrude Ellingham loves me—before Thornton and I meet. He is a good shot.

GERTRUDE: *(without, calling)* O—h! Pete! You may take Jack to the stable. Ha—ha—ha! *(She appears at window; to* KERCHIVAL*)* Old Pete, on the bay horse, has been doing his best to keep up with us; but Jack and I have led him such a race! Ha—ha—ha—ha! *(Disappearing beyond the window)*

KERCHIVAL: Does she love me?

GERTRUDE: *(entering at the rear and coming down)* I have the very latest news from the headquarters of the Confederate Army in South Carolina. At twenty minutes after three this morning General Beauregard sent this message to Major Anderson in Fort Sumter: "I shall open fire in one hour!" The time is up!—and he will keep his word! *(Turning and looking out of the window.* KERCHIVAL *moves across to her)*

KERCHIVAL: Gertrude! I must speak to you; we may never meet again; but I must know the truth. I love you. *(Seizing her hand)* Do you love me? *(She looks around at him as if about to speak; hesitates)* Answer me! *(She looks down with a coquettish smile, tapping her skirt with her riding whip)* Well? *(A distant report of a cannon, and low rumbling reverberations over the harbor.* GERTRUDE *turns suddenly, looking out.* KERCHIVAL *draws up, also looking off)*

GERTRUDE: A low—bright—line of fire—in the sky! It is a shell. *(A second's pause; she starts slightly)* It has burst upon the fort. *(Looks over her shoulder at* KERCHIVAL, *drawing up to her full height)* Now!—do you believe that we Southerners are in deadly earnest?

KERCHIVAL: We Northerners are in deadly earnest, too. I have received my answer. *(He crosses quickly and then turns)* We are—enemies! *(They look at each other for a moment)* *(Exit* KERCHIVAL*)*

GERTRUDE: Kerchival! *(Moving quickly half across stage, looking after him eagerly, then stops)* Enemies! *(She drops into the chair sobbing bitterly. Another distant report, and low, long reverberation as the curtain descends)*

ACT SECOND

The scene is the exterior of the Ellingham Homestead in the Shenandoah Valley. Three Top Mountain is seen in the distance. A corner of the house, with the projecting end of the veranda, is seen on the left. A low wall extends from the veranda across the stage to the center, then with a turn to the right it is continued off the stage. There is a wide opening in the wall at the center, with a low, heavy stone post, with flat top, on each side. Beyond the wall and the opening, a road runs across the stage. At the back of this road there is an elevation of rock and turf. This slopes up the rear, is level on the top about twelve feet, then slopes down to the road, and also out behind the wood, which is seen at the right. The level part in the center rises to about four feet above the stage. Beyond this elevation in the distance is a broad valley, with Three Top Mountain rising on the right. The foliage is appropriate to Northern Virginia. Rustic seats and table are on the right. There is a low rock near the stone post. When curtain rises it is sunset. As the act proceeds this fades into twilight and then brightens into moonlight. At the rise of the curtain a trumpet signal is heard, very distant. GERTRUDE *and* MADELINE *are standing on the elevation.* GERTRUDE *shading her eyes with her hand and looking off to the left.* MADELINE *stands a little below her, on the incline, resting her arm about* GERTRUDE'S *waist, also looking off.*

GERTRUDE: It is a regiment of Union Cavalry. The Federal troops have their line three miles beyond us, and only a month ago the Confederate Army was north of Winchester. One army or the other has been marching up and down the Shenandoah Valley for three years. I wonder what the next change will be. We in Virginia have had more than our share of the war. *(Looking off)*

MADELINE: You have, indeed, Gertrude. *(Walking down to a seat)* And we at home in Washington have pitied you so much. But everybody says that there will be peace in the valley after this. *(Dropping into the seat)*

GERTRUDE: Peace! *(Coming down)* That word means something very different to us poor Southerners from what it means to you.

MADELINE: I know, dear; and we in the North know how you have suffered, too. We were very glad when General Buckthorn was appointed to the command of the Nineteenth Army Corps, so that Jenny could get permission for herself and me to come and visit you.

GERTRUDE: The old General will do anything for Jenny, I suppose.

MADELINE: Yes. *(Laughing)* We say in Washington that Jenny is in command of the Nineteenth Army Corps herself.

GERTRUDE: I was never more astonished or delighted in my life than when you and Jenny Buckthorn rode up, this morning, with a guard from Winchester; and Madeline, dear, I—I only wish that my brother Robert could be here, too. Do you remember in Charleston, darling—that morning—when I told you that—that Robert loved you?

MADELINE: He—*(looking down)*—he told me so himself only a little while afterwards, and while we were standing there, on the shore of the bay—the—the shot was fired which compelled him to enter this awful war—and me to return to my home in the North.

GERTRUDE: I was watching for that shot, too. *(Turning)*

MADELINE: Yes—*(rising)*—you and brother Kerchival—

GERTRUDE: We won't talk about that, my dear. We were speaking of Robert. As I told you this morning, I have not heard from him since the battle of Winchester, a month ago. Oh, Madeline! the many, many long weeks, like these, we have suffered, after some terrible battle in which he has been engaged. I do not know, now, whether he is living or dead.

MADELINE: The whole war has been one long suspense to me. *(Dropping her face into her hands)*

GERTRUDE: My dear sister! *(Placing her arm about her waist and moving to the left)* You are a Northern girl, and I am a Rebel—but we are sisters. *(They mount the veranda and pass out. An old countryman comes in. He stops and glances back, raises a broken portion of the capstone of the post, and places a letter under it. GERTRUDE has stepped back on the veranda and is watching him. He raises his head sharply, looking at her and bringing his finger to his lips. He drops his head again, as with age, and goes out. GERTRUDE moves down to the stage and up to the road, looks to the right and left, raises the broken stone, glancing back as she does so, then takes the letter and moves down)* Robert is alive! It is his handwriting! *(She tears open the wrapper)* Only a line from him! and this—a dispatch—and also a letter to me! Why, it is from Mrs Haverill—from Washington—with a United States postmark. *(She reads from a scrap of paper)* "The enclosed dispatch must be in the hands of Captain Edward Thornton before eight o'clock to-night. We have signaled to him from Three Top Mountain, and he is waiting for it at the bend in Oak Run. Our trusty scout at the Old Forge will carry it if you will put it in his hands." The scout is not there, now; I will carry it to Captain Thornton myself. I—I have n't my own dear horse to depend on now; Jack knew every foot of the way through the woods about here; he could have carried a dispatch himself. I can't bear to think of Jack; it's two years since he was captured by the enemy—and if he is still living—I—I suppose he is carrying one of their officers. No! Jack would n't fight on that side. He was a Rebel—as I am. He was one of the Black Horse Cavalry—his eyes always flashed towards the North. Poor Jack! my pet. *(Brushing her eyes)* But this is no time for tears. I must do the best I can with the gray horse. Captain Thornton shall have the dispatch. *(She reads from note)* "I also enclose a letter for you. I found it in a United States mail-bag which we captured from the enemy." Oh—that's the way Mrs Haverill's letter came—Ha—ha—ha—by way of the Rebel army! *(Opens it; reads)* "My Darling Gertrude: When Colonel Kerchival West was in Washington last week, on his way from Chattanooga, to serve under Sheridan in the Shenandoah Valley, he called upon me. It was the first time I had seen him since the opening of the war. I am certain that he still loves you, dear." *(She kisses the letter eagerly, then draws up)* It is quite immaterial to me whether Kerchival West still loves me or not. *(Reads)* "I have kept your secret, my darling."—Ah! My secret!— "but I was sorely tempted to betray the confidence you reposed in me at Charleston. If Kerchival West had heard you say, as I did, when your face was hidden in my bosom, that night, that you loved him with your whole heart—"—Oh! I could bite my tongue out now for making that confession— *(She looks down at letter with a smile)* "I am certain that he still loves you." *(A Trumpet Signal. She kisses the letter repeatedly. The Signal is repeated louder than at first. She starts, listening)*

*(*JENNY BUCKTHORN *runs in, on the veranda)*

JENNY: Do you hear, Gertrude, they are going to pass this very house. *(A Military band is playing "John Brown" in the distance. A chorus of soldiers is heard)* I've been watching them through my glass; it is Colonel Kerchival West's regiment.

GERTRUDE: *(eagerly, then coldly)* Colonel West's! It is perfectly indifferent to me whose regiment it is.

JENNY: Oh! Of course. *(Coming down)* It is equally indifferent to me; Captain Heartsease is in command of the first troop. *(Trumpet Signal sounds)* Column right! *(She runs up to the road. Looking off to the left)* They are coming up the hill.

GERTRUDE: At my very door! And Kerchival West in command! I will not stand here and see them pass. The dispatch for Captain Thornton! I will carry it to him as soon as they are gone. *(Exit up the veranda, the band and chorus increasing in volume)*

JENNY: Cavalry! That's the branch of the service I was born in; I was in a fort at the time—on the Plains. Sergeant Barket always said that my first baby squall was a command to the garrison; if any officer or soldier, from my father down, failed to obey my orders, I court-martialed him on the spot. I'll make 'em pass in review. *(Jumping up on the rustic seat)* Yes! *(Looking off to the left)* There's Captain Heartsease himself, at the head of the first troop. Draw sabre! *(With parasol)* Present! *(Imitating the action. The band and chorus are now full and loud; she swings the parasol in time. A Trumpet Signal. Band and chorus suddenly cease)* Halt! Why, they are stopping here. *(Trumpet Signal sounds)* Dismount! I—I wonder if they are going to—I do believe—(Looking eagerly. Trumpet Signal)* Assembly of Guard Details! As sure as fate, they are going into camp here. We girls will have a jolly time. *(Jumping down)* Ha—ha— ha—ha! Let me see. How shall I receive Captain Heartsease? He deserves a court-martial, for he stole my lace handkerchief—at Mrs Grayson's reception—in Washington. He was called away by orders to the West that very night, and we have n't met since. *(Sighs)* He's been in lots of battles since then; I suppose he's forgotten all about the handkerchief. We girls, at home, don't forget such things. We are n't in battles. All we do is to—to scrape lint and flirt with other officers.

(Enter CAPTAIN HEARTSEASE, *followed by* COLONEL ROBERT ELLINGHAM, *then stops at the gate)*

HEARTSEASE: This way, Colonel Ellingham. *(They enter. As they come down* HEARTSEASE *stops suddenly, looking at* JENNY, *and puts up his glasses)* Miss Buckthorn!

JENNY: Captain Heartsease!

HEARTSEASE: *(very quietly and with perfect composure)* I am thunderstruck. The unexpected sight of you has thrown me into a fever of excitement.

JENNY: Has it? *(Aside)* If he gets so excited as that in battle it must be awful. *(Aloud)* Colonel Ellingham!

ELLINGHAM: Miss Buckthorn! You are visiting my sister? I am what may be called a visitor—by force—myself.

JENNY: Oh! You're a prisoner!

ELLINGHAM: I ventured too far within the Union lines to-night, and they have picked me up. But Major Wilson has kindly accepted my parole, and I shall make the best of it.

JENNY: Is Major Wilson in command of the regiment?

HEARTSEASE: Yes. Colonel West is to join us at this point, during the evening.

ELLINGHAM: I am very glad you are here, Miss Buckthorn, with Gertrude.

JENNY: Somebody here will be delighted to see you, Colonel.

ELLINGHAM: My sister can hardly be pleased to see me as a prisoner.

JENNY: Not your sister. *(Passing him and crossing to the veranda. She turns and beckons to him. She motions with her thumb, over her shoulder. He goes up the steps of the veranda and turns)*

ELLINGHAM: What do you mean?

JENNY: I mean this—*(Reaching up her face, he leans down, placing his ear near her lips)*— somebody else's sister! When she first sees you, be near enough to catch her.

ELLINGHAM: I understand you! Madeline! *(Exit on veranda.* JENNY *runs up steps after him, then stops and looks back at* HEARTSEASE *over the railing.* HEARTSEASE *takes a lace handkerchief from his pocket)*

JENNY: I do believe that's my handkerchief. *(A guard of Sentries marches in and across the stage in the road. The Corporal in command orders halt and a sentry to post, then marches the guard out. The sentry stands with his back to the* audience, *afterwards moving out and in, appearing and disappearing during the Act)*

HEARTSEASE: Miss Buckthorn! I owe you an apology. After I left your side, the last time we met, I found your handkerchief in my possession. I assure you, it was an accident.

JENNY: *(aside, pouting)* I thought he *intended* to steal it. *(Aloud)* That was more than a year ago. *(Then brightly)* Do you always carry it with you?

HEARTSEASE: Always; there. *(Indicating his left breast pocket)*

JENNY: Next to his heart!

HEARTSEASE: Shall I return it to you?

JENNY: Oh, if a lace handkerchief can be of any use to you, Captain, during the hardships of a campaign—you—you may keep that one. You soldiers have so few comforts—and it's real lace.

HEARTSEASE: Thank you. *(Returning the handkerchief to his pocket)* Miss Buckthorn, your father is in command of the Nineteenth Army Corps. He does n't like me.

JENNY: I know it.

HEARTSEASE: But you are in command of him.

JENNY: Yes; I always have been.

HEARTSEASE: If ever you decide to assume command of any other man, I—I trust you will give *me* your orders.

JENNY: *(aside, starting back)* If that was intended for a proposal, it 's the queerest-shaped one I ever heard of. *(Aloud)* Do you mean, Captain, that—that you—I must command myself now. *(Shouldering her parasol)* 'Bout—face! March! *(Turning squarely around, marching up and out, on the veranda)*

HEARTSEASE: I have been placed on waiting orders. *(Stepping up the stage and looking after her; then very quietly and without emotion)* I am in an agony of suspense. The sight of that girl always arouses the strongest emotions of my nature. *(Enter* COLONEL KERCHIVAL WEST, *looking at the paper in his hand. The sentinel, in the road, comes to a salute)* Colonel West!

KERCHIVAL: Captain!

HEARTSEASE: You have rejoined the regiment sooner than we expected.

KERCHIVAL: *(looking at the paper)* Yes; General Haverill is to meet me here at seven o'clock. Major Wilson tells me that some of your company captured Colonel Robert Ellingham, of the Tenth Virginia.

HEARTSEASE: He is here under parole.

KERCHIVAL: And this is the old Ellingham homestead. *(Aside)* Gertrude herself is here, I suppose; almost a prisoner to me, like her brother; and my troops surround their home. She must, indeed, feel that I am her enemy now. Ah, well, war is war. *(Aloud)* By the bye, Heartsease, a young Lieutenant, Frank Bedloe, has joined our troop?

HEARTSEASE: Yes; an excellent young officer.

KERCHIVAL: I sent for him as I came through the camp. Lieutenant Frank "Bedloe" is the son of General Haverill.

HEARTSEASE: Indeed! Under an assumed name!

KERCHIVAL: He was supposed to have been killed in New Orleans more than a year ago; but he was taken prisoner instead.

HEARTSEASE: He is here.

KERCHIVAL: I should never have known him; with his full beard and bronzed face. His face was as smooth as a boy's when I last met him in Charleston.

(Enter LIEUTENANT FRANK BEDLOE; he stops, saluting)

FRANK: You wished me to report to you, Colonel?

KERCHIVAL: You have been assigned to the regiment during my absence.

FRANK: Yes, sir.

(KERCHIVAL moves to him and grasps his hand; looks into his eyes a moment before speaking)

KERCHIVAL: Frank Haverill.

FRANK: You—you know me, sir?

KERCHIVAL: I saw Mrs Haverill while I was passing through Washington on Saturday. She told me that you had escaped from prison in Richmond, and had re-entered the service. She did not know then that you had been assigned to my regiment. I received a letter from her, in Winchester, this morning, informing me of the fact, and asking for my good offices in your behalf. But here is the letter. *(Taking a letter from wallet and giving it to him)* It is for you rather than for me. I shall do everything I can for you, my dear fellow.

FRANK: Thank you, sir. *(He opens the letter, dropping the envelope upon the table)* Kind, thoughtful and gentle to my faults, as ever—*(Looking at the letter)*—and always thinking of my welfare. My poor little wife, too, is under her protection. Gentlemen, I beg of you not to reveal my secret to my father.

KERCHIVAL: General Haverill shall know nothing from us, my boy, you have my word for that.

HEARTSEASE: Nothing.

KERCHIVAL: And he cannot possibly recognize you. What with your full beard, and thinking as he does, that you are—

FRANK: That I am dead. I am dead to him. It would have been better if I had died. Nothing but my death—not even that—can wipe out the disgrace which I brought upon his name.

HEARTSEASE: General Haverill has arrived.

(Enter GENERAL HAVERILL, with a Staff Officer)

FRANK: *(moving down)* My father!

HAVERILL: *(after exchanging salutes with the three officers, he turns to the Staff Officer, giving him a paper and brief instructions in dumb show. The Officer goes out over the incline. Another Staff Officer enters, salutes and hands him a paper, then stands up)* Ah! The men are ready. *(Looking at the paper, then to KERCHIVAL)* Colonel! I have a very important matter to arrange with you; there is not a moment to be lost. I will ask Captain Heartsease to remain. *(FRANK salutes and starts up the stage; HAVERILL looks at him, starting slightly; raises his hand to detain him)* One moment; your name!

HEARTSEASE: Lieutenant Bedloe, General, of my own troop, and one of our best officers. *(HAVERILL steps to FRANK, looking into his face a moment)*

HAVERILL: Pardon me! *(He steps down the stage. FRANK moves away from him, then stops and *looks back at him.* HAVERILL *stands up a moment in thought, covers his face with one hand, then draws up)* Colonel West! We have a most dangerous piece of work for a young officer— *(FRANK starts joyfully)*—to lead a party of men, whom I have already selected. I cannot *order* an officer to undertake anything so nearly hopeless; he must be a volunteer.

FRANK: Oh, sir, General! Let me be their leader.

HAVERILL: I thought you had passed on.

FRANK: Do not refuse me, sir. *(HAVERILL looks at him a moment.* HEARTSEASE *and* KERCHIVAL *exchange glances)*

HAVERILL: You are the man we need, my young friend. You shall go. Listen! We wish to secure a key to the cipher dispatches, which the enemy are now sending from their signal station on Three Top Mountain. There is another Confederate Signal Station in the valley, just beyond Buckton's Ford. *(Pointing to the left)* Your duty will be this: First, to get inside the enemy's line; then to follow a path through the woods, with one of our scouts as your guide; attack the Station suddenly, and secure their code, if possible. I have this moment received word that the scout and the men are at the fort, now, awaiting their leader. Major McCandless, of my staff, will take you to the place. *(Indicating the Staff Officer.* FRANK *exchanges salutes with him)* My young friend! I do not conceal from you the dangerous nature of the work on which I am sending you. If—if you do not return, I—I will write, myself, to your friends. *(Taking out a note book)* Have you a father living?

FRANK: My—father—is—is—he is—

HAVERILL: I understand you. A mother? Or—

KERCHIVAL: I have the address of Lieutenant Bedloe's friends, General.

HAVERILL: I will ask you to give it to me, if necessary. *(He extends his hand)* Good-bye, my lad. *(FRANK moves to him.* HAVERILL *grasps his hand, warmly)* Keep a brave heart and come back to us.

(FRANK moves up the stage. Exit Staff Officer)

FRANK: He is my father still.   *(Exit)*

HAVERILL: My dead boy's face! *(Dropping his face into both hands)*

HEARTSEASE: *(apart to* KERCHIVAL*)* He shall not go alone. *(Aloud)* General! Will you kindly give me leave of absence from the command?

HAVERILL: Leave of absence! To an officer in active service—and in the presence of the enemy?

KERCHIVAL: *(taking his hand. Apart)* God bless you, old fellow! Look after the boy.

HAVERILL: A—h— *(With a sudden thought, turns)* I think I understand you, Captain Heartsease. Yes; you may have leave of absence.

HEARTSEASE: Thank you. *(He salutes.* HAVERILL *and* KERCHIVAL *salute. Exit* HEARTSEASE*)*

KERCHIVAL: Have you any further orders for me, General?

HAVERILL: I wish you to understand the great importance of the duty to which I have just assigned this young officer. General Sheridan started for Washington this noon, by way of Front Royal. Since his departure, we have had reason to believe that the enemy are about to move, and we must be able to read their signal dispatches, if possible. *(Sitting down)* I have ordered Captain Lockwood, of our own Signal Corps, to report to you here, with officers and men. *(He takes up the empty envelope on table, unconsciously, as he speaks, tapping it on the table)* If Lieutenant Bedloe succeeds in getting the key to the enemy's cipher, we can signal from this point—*(pointing to the elevation)*—to our station at Front Royal. Men and horses are waiting there now, to carry forward a message, if necessary, to General Sheridan himself. *(He starts suddenly, looking at the envelope in his hand; reads address. Aside)* "Colonel Kerchival West"—in my wife's handwriting!

KERCHIVAL: I'll attend to your orders.

HAVERILL: Postmarked at Washington, yesterday. *(Reads)* "Private and confidential." *(Aloud)* Colonel West! I found a paragraph, to-day, in a paper published in Richmond, taken from a prisoner. I will read it to you. *(He takes a newspaper slip from his wallet and reads)* "From the *Charleston Mercury.* Captain Edward Thornton, of the Confederate Secret Service, has been assigned to duty in the Shenandoah Valley. Our gallant Captain still bears upon his face the mark of his meeting, in 1861, with Lieutenant, now Colonel Kerchival West, who is also to serve in the valley, with Sheridan's Army. Another meeting between these two men would be one of the strange coincidences of the war, as they were at one time, if not indeed at present, interested in the same beautiful woman." *(Rises)* I will ask you to read the last few lines, yourself. *(Crossing, he hands* KERCHIVAL *the slip)*

KERCHIVAL: *(reading)* "The scandal connected with the lovely wife of a Northern officer, at the opening of the war, was overshadowed, of course, by the attack on Fort Sumter; but many Charlestonians will remember it. The lady in defense of whose good name Captain Thornton fought the duel"—he defended her good name!—"is the wife of General Haverill, who will be Colonel West's immediate commander." *(He pauses a moment, then hands back the slip)* General! I struck Mr Thornton, after a personal quarrel.

HAVERILL: And the cause of the blow? There is much more in this than I have ever known of. I need hardly say that I do not accept the statement of this scandalous paragraph as correct. I will ask you to tell me the whole story, frankly, as man to man.

KERCHIVAL: *(after a moment's thought)* I will tell you—all—frankly, General.

(Enter SERGEANT BARKET*)*

BARKET: Colonel Wist? Adjutant Rollins wishes to report—a prisoner—just captured.

HAVERILL: We will meet again later, to-night when the camp is at rest. We are both soldiers, and have duties before us, at once. For the present, Colonel, be on the alert; we must watch the enemy. *(He moves up the stage.* BARKET *salutes.* HAVERILL *stops and looks at envelope in his hands, reading)* "Private and confidential."   *(Exit)*

KERCHIVAL: Sergeant Barket! Lieutenant Bedloe has crossed the enemy's line, at Buckton's Ford, with a party of men. I wish you to ride to the ford yourself, and remain there, with your horse in readiness and fresh. As soon as any survivor of the party returns, ride back with the first news at full speed.

BARKET: Yes, sir. *(Starting)*

KERCHIVAL: You say a prisoner has been captured? Is it a spy?

BARKET: Worse—a petticoat.

KERCHIVAL: A female prisoner! *(Dropping into the seat)*

BARKET: I towld the byes your honor would n't thank us fer the catchin' of her. The worst of it is she's a lady; and what's worse still, it's a purty one.

KERCHIVAL: Tell Major Wilson, for me, to let her take the oath, and everything else she wants. The Government of the United States will send her an apology and a new bonnet.

BARKET: The young lady is to take the oath, is it? She says she'll see us damned first.

KERCHIVAL: A lady, Barket?

BARKET: Well! she did n't use thim exact words. That's the way I understand her emphasis. Ivery time she looks at me, I feel like getting under a boom-proof. She was dashing through the woods on a gray horse, sur; and we had the divil's own chase. But we came up wid her, at last, down by the bend in Oak Run. Just at that moment we saw the figure of a Confederate officer, disappearing among the trays on the ither side.

KERCHIVAL: A—h!

BARKET: Two of us rayturned wid the girl; and the rist wint after the officer. Nothing has been heard of thim yet.

KERCHIVAL: Have you found any dispatches on the prisoner?

BARKET: Well!—yer honor, I'm a bachelor, meself; and I'm not familiar with the taypography of the sex. We byes are in mortal terror for fear somebody might order us to go on an exploring expedition.

KERCHIVAL: Tell them to send the prisoner here, Barket, and hurry to Buckton's Ford yourself, at once.

BARKET: As fast as me horse can carry me, sir, and it's a good one.   *(Exit)*

KERCHIVAL: I'd rather deal with half the Confederate army than with one woman, but I must question her. They captured her down by the Bend in Oak Run. *(Taking out the map, and looking at it)* I see. She had just met, or was about to meet, a Confederate officer at that point. It is evident that she was either taking him a dispatch or was there to receive one. Oak Run. *(CORPORAL DUNN and two soldiers enter, with GERTRUDE as a prisoner. They stop, KERCHIVAL sits, studying the map. GERTRUDE glances at him and marches down with her head erect; she stops, with her back to him)*

DUNN: The prisoner, Colonel West!

KERCHIVAL: Ah! Very well, Corporal; you can go. *(Rising; he motions the guard to retire. DUNN gives the necessary orders and exit with guard)* Be seated, madam. *(GERTRUDE draws up, folding her arms and planting her foot, spitefully. KERCHIVAL shrugs his shoulders. Aside)* I wish they'd capture a tigress for me, or some other female animal that I know how to manage better than I do a woman. *(Aloud)* I am very sorry, madam; but, of course, my duty as a military officer is paramount to all other considerations. You have been captured within the lines of this army, and under circumstances which lead me to think that you have important dispatches upon your person. I trust that you will give me whatever you have, at once. I shall be exceedingly sorry if you compel me to adopt the extreme—and the very disagreeable course—for both of us—of having—you—I—I hesitate even to use the word, madame—but military law is absolute—having you—

GERTRUDE: Searched! If you dare, Colonel West! *(Turning to him suddenly and drawing up to her full height)*

KERCHIVAL: Gertrude Ellingham! *(Springs across to her, with his arms extended)* My dear Gertrude!

GERTRUDE: *(turning her back upon him)* Not "dear Gertrude" to you, sir!

KERCHIVAL: Not?—Oh! I forgot.

GERTRUDE: *(coldly)* I am your prisoner.

KERCHIVAL: Yes. *(Drawing up firmly, with a change of manner)* We will return to the painful realities of war. I am very sorry that you have placed yourself in a position like this, and, believe me, Gertrude—*(With growing tenderness)*—I am still more sorry to be in such a position myself. *(Resting one hand on her arm, and his other arm about her waist)*

GERTRUDE: *(after looking down at his hands)* You don't like the position? *(He starts back, drawing up with dignity)* Is that the paramount duty of a military officer?

KERCHIVAL: You will please hand me whatever dispatches or other papers may be in your possession.

GERTRUDE: *(looking away)* You will *force* me, I suppose. I am a woman; you have the power. Order in the guard! A Corporal and two men—you'd better make it a dozen—I am dangerous! Call the whole regiment to arms! Beat the long roll! I won't give up, if all the armies of the United States surround me.

(Enter GENERAL BUCKTHORN)

KERCHIVAL: General Buckthorn! *(Saluting)*

BUCKTHORN: Colonel West.

GERTRUDE: *(aside)* Jenny's father! *(BUCKTHORN glances at GERTRUDE, who still stands looking away. He moves down to KERCHIVAL)*

BUCKTHORN: *(apart, gruffly)* I was passing with my staff, and I was informed that you had captured a woman bearing dispatches to the enemy. Is this the one?

KERCHIVAL: Yes, General.

BUCKTHORN: Ah! *(Turning, he looks at her)*

GERTRUDE: I wonder if he will recognize me. He has n't seen me since I was a little girl. *(She turns toward him)*

BUCKTHORN: *(turning to KERCHIVAL and punching him in the ribs)* Fine young woman!—*(He turns and bows to her very gallantly, removing his hat. She bows deeply in return)* A-h-e-m! *(Suddenly pulling himself up to a stern, military air; then gruffly to KERCHIVAL, extending his hand)* Let me see the dispatches.

KERCHIVAL: She declines positively to give them up.

BUCKTHORN: Oh! Does she? *(Walks up the stage thoughtfully, and turns)* My dear young lady! I trust you will give us no further trouble. Kindly let us have those dispatches.

GERTRUDE: *(looking away)* I have no dispatches, and I would not give them to you if I had.

BUCKTHORN: What! You defy my authority? Colonel West, I command you! Search the prisoner!
(GERTRUDE turns suddenly towards KERCHIVAL, facing him defiantly. He looks across at her, aghast. A moment's pause)

KERCHIVAL: General Buckthorn—I decline to obey that order.

BUCKTHORN: You—you decline to obey my order! *(Moves down to him fiercely)*

KERCHIVAL: *(apart)* General! It is the woman I love.

BUCKTHORN: *(apart)* Is it? Damn you, sir! I would n't have an officer in my army corps who *would* obey me, under such circumstances. I'll have to look for those dispatches myself.

KERCHIVAL: *(facing him, angrily)* If you dare, General Buckthorn!

BUCKTHORN: *(apart)* Blast your eyes! I'd kick you out of the army if you'd *let* me search her; but it's my military duty to swear at you. *(To GERTRUDE)* Colonel West has sacrificed his life to protect you.

GERTRUDE: His life!

BUCKTHORN: I shall have him shot for insubordination to his commander, immediately. *(Gives KERCHIVAL a huge wink, and turns up stage)*

GERTRUDE: Oh, sir! General! I have told you the truth. I have no dispatches. Believe me, sir, I have n't so much as a piece of paper about me, except—

BUCKTHORN: Except? *(Turning sharply)*

GERTRUDE: Only a letter. Here it is. *(Taking letter from the bosom of her dress)* Upon my soul, it is all I have. Truly, it is.

BUCKTHORN: *(taking the letter)* Colonel West, you're reprieved. *(Winks at KERCHIVAL, who turns away, laughing. BUCKTHORN reads letter)* "Washington"—Ho—ho! From within our own lines—"Colonel Kerchival West"—

KERCHIVAL: Eh?

GERTRUDE: Please, General!—Don't read it aloud.

BUCKTHORN: Very well! I won't.

KERCHIVAL: *(aside)* I wonder what it has to do with me.

BUCKTHORN: *(Reading. Aside)* "If Kerchival West had heard you say, as I did—m—m—that you loved him with your whole heart—" *(He glances up at GERTRUDE, who drops her head, coyly)* This is a very important military document. *(Turns to the last page)* "Signed, Constance Haverill." *(Turns to front page)* "My dear Gertrude!" Is this Miss Gertrude Ellingham?

GERTRUDE: Yes, General.

BUCKTHORN: I sent my daughter, Jenny, to your house, with an escort, this morning.

GERTRUDE: She is here.

BUCKTHORN: *(tapping her under the chin)* You're an arrant little Rebel, my dear; but I like you immensely. *(Draws up suddenly, with an Ahem!, then turns to KERCHIVAL)* Colonel West, I leave this dangerous young woman in your charge. *(KERCHIVAL approaches)* If she disobeys you in any way, or attempts to escape— read that letter! *(Giving him the letter)*

GERTRUDE: Oh! General!

BUCKTHORN: But not till then.

KERCHIVAL: *(tenderly, taking her hand)* My— prisoner!

GERTRUDE: *(aside)* I could scratch my own eyes out—or his, either—rather than have him read that letter.
(Enter CORPORAL DUNN, with a guard of four soldiers and CAPTAIN EDWARD THORNTON as a prisoner)

KERCHIVAL: Edward Thornton!

GERTRUDE: They have taken him, also! He has the dispatch!

DUNN: The Confederate Officer, Colonel, who was pursued by our troops at Oak Run, after they captured the young lady.

BUCKTHORN: The little witch has been communicating with the enemy!

KERCHIVAL: *(to GERTRUDE)* You will give me your parole of honor until we next meet?

GERTRUDE: Yes. *(Aside)* That letter! I *am* his prisoner. *(She walks up the steps, looking back at Captain Thornton, and then leaves the stage)*

KERCHIVAL: We will probably find the dispatches we have been looking for now, General.

BUCKTHORN: Prisoner! You will hand us what papers you may have.

THORNTON: I will hand you nothing.

BUCKTHORN: Colonel! (KERCHIVAL *motions to* THORNTON, *who looks at him sullenly)*

KERCHIVAL: Corporal Dunn!—search the prisoner. *(*DUNN *steps to* THORNTON, *taking him by the shoulder and turning him rather roughly so that* THORNTON'S *back is to the audience.* DUNN *throws open his coat, takes the paper from his breast, hands it to* KERCHIVAL, *who gives it to* BUCKTHORN*)* Proceed with the search. *(*DUNN *continues the search.* BUCKTHORN *drops upon the seat, lights a match and looks at the paper)*

BUCKTHORN: *(reading)* "General Rosser will rejoin General Early with all the cavalry in his command, at—" This is important.
(Continues to read with matches. The CORPORAL *hands a packet to* KERCHIVAL. *He removes the covering)*

KERCHIVAL: *(starting)* A portrait of Mrs Haverill! *(He touches* CORPORAL DUNN *on the shoulder quickly and motions him to retire.* DUNN *falls back to the guard.* KERCHIVAL *speaks apart to* THORNTON, *who has turned front)* How did this portrait come into your possession?

THORNTON: That is my affair, not yours!

BUCKTHORN: Anything else, Colonel?

KERCHIVAL: *(placing the miniature in his pocket)* Nothing!

THORNTON: *(apart, over* KERCHIVAL'S *shoulder)* A time will come, perhaps, when I can avenge the insult of this search, and also this scar. *(Pointing to a scar on his face)* Your aim was better than mine in Charleston, but we shall meet again; give me back that picture.

KERCHIVAL: Corporal! Take your prisoner!

THORNTON: Ah!
(He springs viciously at KERCHIVAL; CORPORAL DUNN *springs forward, seizes* THORNTON *and*

throws him back to the Guard. KERCHIVAL *walks to the right,* DUNN *stands with his carbine levelled at* THORNTON, *looks at* KERCHIVAL, *who quietly motions him out.* CORPORAL DUNN *gives the orders to the men and marches out, with* THORNTON*)*

BUCKTHORN: Ah! *(Still reading with matches)* Colonel! *(Rising)* The enemy has a new movement on foot, and General Sheridan has left the army! Listen! *(Reads from dispatches with matches)* "Watch for a signal from Three Top Mountain to-night."

KERCHIVAL: We hope to be able to read that signal ourselves.

BUCKTHORN: Yes, I know. Be on your guard. I will speak with General Haverill, and then ride over to General Wright's headquarters. Keep us informed.

KERCHIVAL: I will, General.
(Saluting. BUCKTHORN *salutes and exit)*

KERCHIVAL: "Watch for a signal from Three Top Mountain to-night." *(Looking up at Mountain)* We shall be helpless to read it unless Lieutenant Bedloe is successful. I only hope the poor boy is not lying dead, already, in those dark woods beyond the ford. *(He turns down, taking the miniature from his pocket)* How came Edward Thornton to have this portrait of Mrs Haverill in his possession? *(*GERTRUDE *runs in on the veranda)*

GERTRUDE: Oh, Colonel West! He's here! *(Looks back)* They are coming this way with him.

KERCHIVAL: Him! Who?

GERTRUDE: Jack.

KERCHIVAL: Jack!

GERTRUDE: My own horse!

KERCHIVAL: Ah, I remember! He and I were acquainted in Charleston.

GERTRUDE: Two troopers are passing through the camp with him.

KERCHIVAL: He is not in your possession?

GERTRUDE: He was captured at the battle of Fair Oaks, but I recognized him the moment I saw him; and I am sure he knew me, too, when I went up to him. He whinnied and looked so happy. You are in command here— *(Running down)*—you will compel them to give him up to me?

KERCHIVAL: If he is in my command, your pet shall be returned to you. I'll give one of my own horses to the Government as a substitute, if necessary.

GERTRUDE: Oh, thank you, my dear Kerchival! *(Going to him; he takes her hand, looking into her eyes)* I—I could almost—

KERCHIVAL: Can you almost confess, at last, Gertrude, that you—love me? *(Tenderly; she draws back, hanging her head, but leaving her hand in his)* Have I been wrong? I felt that that confession was hovering on your tongue when we were separated in Charleston. Have I seen that confession in your eyes since we met again to-day—even among the angry flashes which they have shot out at me? During all this terrible war—in the camp and the trench—in the battle—I have dreamed of a meeting like this. You are still silent?

(Her hand is still in his. She is looking down. A smile steals over her face, and she raises her eyes to his, taking his hand in both her own)

GERTRUDE: Kerchival! I— *(Enter BENSON. She looks around over her shoulder. KERCHIVAL looks up. A trooper leading a large black horse, now caparisoned in military saddle, bridle, follows BENSON across; another trooper follows)* Jack!

(She runs up the stage, meeting the horse. KERCHIVAL turns)

KERCHIVAL: Confound Jack! That infernal horse was always in my way!

GERTRUDE: *(with her arm about her horse's neck)* My darling old fellow! Is he not beautiful, Kerchival? They have taken good care of him. How soft his coat is!

KERCHIVAL: Benson, explain this!

BENSON: I was instructed to show this horse and his leader through the lines, sir.

KERCHIVAL: What are your orders, my man? *(Moving up, the trooper hands him a paper. He moves down a few steps, reading it)*

GERTRUDE: You are to be mine again, Jack, mine! *(Resting her cheek against the horse's head and patting it)* The Colonel has promised it to me.

KERCHIVAL: Ah! *(With a start, as he reads the paper. GERTRUDE raises her head and looks at him)* This is General Sheridan's horse, on his way to Winchester, for the use of the General when he returns from Washington.

GERTRUDE: General Sheridan's horse? He is mine!

KERCHIVAL: I have no authority to detain him. He must go on.

GERTRUDE: I have hold of Jack's bridle, and you may order your men to take out their sabres and cut my hand off.

KERCHIVAL: *(he approaches her and gently takes her hand as it holds the bridle)* I would rather have my own hand cut off, Gertrude, than bring tears to your eyes, but there is no alternative! *(GERTRUDE releases the bridle and turns front, brushing her eyes, her hand still held in his, his back to the audience. He returns the order and motions troopers out; they move out, with the horse. KERCHIVAL turns to move. GERTRUDE starts after the horse; he turns quickly to check her)* You forget—that—you are my prisoner.

GERTRUDE: I *will* go!

KERCHIVAL: General Buckthorn left me special instructions—*(taking out the wallet and letter)*—in case you declined to obey my orders—

GERTRUDE: Oh, Colonel! Please don't read that letter. *(She stands near him, dropping her head. He glances up at her from the letter. She glances up at him and drops her eyes again)* I will obey you.

KERCHIVAL: *(aside)* What the deuce can there be in that letter?

GERTRUDE: Colonel West! Your men made me a prisoner this afternoon; to-night you have robbed me, by your own orders, of—of—Jack is only a pet, but I love him; and my brother is also a captive in your hands. When we separated in Charleston you said that we were enemies. What is there lacking to make those words true to-day? You *are* my enemy! A few moments ago you asked me to make a confession to you. You can judge for yourself whether it is likely to be a confession of—love—or of hatred!

KERCHIVAL: Hatred!

GERTRUDE: *(facing him)* Listen to my confession, sir! From the bottom of my heart—

KERCHIVAL: Stop!

GERTRUDE: I will not stop!

KERCHIVAL: I command you.

GERTRUDE: Indeed! *(He throws open the wallet in his hand and raises the letter)* Ah! *(She turns away; turns again, as if to speak. He half opens the letter. She stamps her foot and walks up steps of the veranda. Here she turns again)* I tell you, I— *(He opens the letter. She turns, and exits with a spiteful step)*

KERCHIVAL: I wonder if that document orders me to cut her head off! *(Returning it to wallet and pocket)* Was ever lover in such a position? I am obliged to cross the woman I love at every step.

(Enter CORPORAL DUNN, *very hurriedly)*

DUNN: A message from Adjutant Rollins, sir! The prisoner, Capt. Thornton, dashed away from the special guard which was placed over him, and he has escaped. He had a knife concealed, and two of the Guard are badly wounded. Adjutant Rollins thinks the prisoner is still within the lines of the camp—in one of the houses or the stables.

KERCHIVAL: Tell Major Wilson to place the remainder of the Guard under arrest, and to take every possible means to recapture the prisoner. *(DUNN salutes, and exit)* So! Thornton has jumped his guard, and he is armed. I wonder if he is trying to get away, or to find me. From what I know of the man, he does n't much care which he succeeds in doing. That scar which I gave him in Charleston is deeper in his heart than it is in his face. *(A signal light suddenly appears on Three Top Mountain. The "Call.")* Ah!—the enemy's signal!

(Enter CAPTAIN LOCKWOOD, *followed by the* LIEUTENANT OF SIGNAL CORPS)*

Captain Lockwood! You are here! Are your signalmen with you?

LOCKWOOD: Yes, Colonel; and one of my Lieutenants.

(The LIEUTENANT *is looking up at the signal with his glass.* CAPTAIN LOCKWOOD *does the same)*

*(*HAVERILL *enters, followed by two staff officers)*

HAVERILL: *(as he enters)* Can you make anything of it, Captain?

LOCKWOOD: Nothing, General! Our services are quite useless unless Lieutenant Bedloe returns with the key to their signals.

HAVERILL: A—h! We shall fail. It is time he had returned, if successful.

SENTINEL: *(without)* Halt! Who goes there? *(*KERCHIVAL *runs up the stage and half way up the incline, looking off)* Halt! *(A shot is heard without)*

BARKET: *(without)* Och!—Ye murtherin spalpeen!

KERCHIVAL: Sentinel! Let him pass; it is Sergeant Barket.

SENTINEL: *(without)* Pass on.

KERCHIVAL: He did n't give the countersign. News from Lieutenant Bedloe, General!

BARKET: *(hurrying in, up the slope)* Colonel Wist, our brave byes wiped out the enemy, and here's the papers.

KERCHIVAL: Ah! *(Taking the papers.—Then to* LOCKWOOD) Is that the key?

LOCKWOOD: Yes. Lieutenant!

*(*LIEUTENANT *hurries up to the elevation, looking through his glass.* LOCKWOOD *opens the book)*

HAVERILL: What of Lieutenant Bedloe, Sergeant?

BARKET: Sayreously wounded, and in the hands of the inimy!

HAVERILL: *(sighing)* A—h.

BARKET: *(coming down the stone steps)* It is reported that Captain Heartsease was shot dead at his side.

KERCHIVAL: Heartsease dead!

LIEUTENANT OF SIGNAL CORPS: *(reading Signals)* Twelve—Twenty-two—Eleven.

BARKET: Begorra! I forgot the Sintinil entirely, but he did n't forget me. *(Holding his left arm)*

HAVERILL: Colonel West! We must make every possible sacrifice for the immediate exchange of Lieutenant Bedloe, if he is still living. It is due to him. Colonel Robert Ellingham is a prisoner in this camp; offer him his own exchange for young Bedloe.

KERCHIVAL: He will accept, of course. I will ride to the front with him myself, General, and show him through the lines.

HAVERILL: At once! (KERCHIVAL *crosses front and exit on the veranda*) Can you follow the dispatch, Captain?

LOCKWOOD: Perfectly; everything is here.

HAVERILL: Well!

LIEUTENANT OF SIGNAL CORPS: Eleven—Twenty-two—One—Twelve.

LOCKWOOD: (*from the book*) "General Longstreet is coming with—"

HAVERILL: Longstreet!

LIEUTENANT OF SIGNAL CORPS: One—Twenty-one.

LOCKWOOD: "With eighteen thousand men."

HAVERILL: Longstreet and his corps!

LIEUTENANT OF SIGNAL CORPS: Two—Eleven—Twenty-two.

LOCKWOOD: "Sheridan is away!"

HAVERILL: They have discovered his absence!

LIEUTENANT OF SIGNAL CORPS: Two—Twenty-two—Eleven—One—Twelve—One.

LOCKWOOD: "We will crush the Union Army before he can return."

HAVERILL: Signal that dispatch from here to our Station at Front Royal. Tell them to send it after General Sheridan—and ride for their lives. (LOCKWOOD *hurries out*) Major Burton! We will ride to General Wright's headquarters at once—our horses!

(*The noise of a struggle is heard without*)

BARKET: What the devil is the row out there? (*Exit, also one of the Staff Officers*)

HAVERILL: (*looking off to the left*) What is this! Colonel West wounded!

(*Enter* KERCHIVAL WEST, *his coat thrown open, with* ELLINGHAM, BARKET *assisting*)

ELLINGHAM: Steady, Kerchival, old boy! You should have let us carry you.

KERCHIVAL: Nonsense, old fellow! It's a mere touch with the point of the knife. I—I'm faint—with the loss of a little blood—that's all. Bob!—I—

(*He reels suddenly and is caught by* ELLINGHAM *as he sinks to the ground, insensible*)

ELLINGHAM: Kerchival. (*Kneeling at his side*)

HAVERILL: Go for the Surgeon! (*To the Staff Officer, who goes out quickly on veranda*) How did this happen?

(*Enter* CORPORAL DUNN *and Guard, with* THORNTON. *He is in his shirt sleeves and disheveled, his arms folded. They march down*) Captain Thornton!

ELLINGHAM: We were leaving the house together; a hunted animal sprang suddenly across our path, like a panther. (*Looking over his shoulder*) There it stands. Kerchival!—my brother!

DUNN: We had just brought this prisoner to bay, but I'm afraid we were too late.

HAVERILL: This is assassination, sir, not war. If you have killed him—

THORNTON: Do what you like with me; we need waste no words. I had an old account to settle, and I have paid my debt.

ELLINGHAM: General Haverill! I took these from his breast when he first fell.

(*Handing up wallet and miniature to* HAVERILL. HAVERILL *starts as he looks at the miniature.* THORNTON *watches him*)

HAVERILL: (*aside*) My wife's portrait!

THORNTON: If I have killed him—your honor will be buried in the same grave.

HAVERILL: Her picture on his breast! She gave it to him—not to my son!

(*Dropping into the seat.* CAPTAIN LOCKWOOD *enters with a Signalman, who has a burning torch on a long pole; he hurries up the elevation.* CAPTAIN LOCKWOOD *stands below, facing him. Almost simultaneously with the entrance of the Signalman,* GERTRUDE *runs in on veranda*)

GERTRUDE: They are calling for a surgeon! Who is it? Brother!—you are safe. Ah! (*Uttering a scream, as she sees* KERCHIVAL, *and falling on her knees at his side*) Kerchival! Forget those last bitter words I said to you. Can't you hear my confession? I do love you. Can't you hear me? I love you!

(The Signalman is swinging the torch as the curtain descends, LOCKWOOD *looking out to the right)*

ACT THIRD

The scene is the same as in the Second Act. It is now bright daylight, with sunshine flecking the foreground and bathing the distant valley and mountains. As the curtain rises JENNY BUCKTHORN *is sitting on the low stone post, in the center of the stage, looking toward the left. She imitates a Trumpet Signal on her closed fists.*

JENNY: What a magnificent line! Guides-posts! Every man and every horse is eager for the next command. There comes the flag! *(As the scene progresses Trumpet Signals are heard without and she follows their various meanings in her speech)* To the standard! The regiment is going to the front. Oh! I do wish I could go with it. I always do, the moment I hear the trumpets. Boots and Saddles! Mount! I wish I was in command of the regiment. It was born in me. Fours right! There they go! Look at those horses' ears! Forward. *(A military band is heard without, playing "The Battle Cry of Freedom."* JENNY *takes the attitude of holding a bridle and trotting)* Rappity—plap—plap—plap, etc. *(She imitates the motions of a soldier on horseback, stepping down to the rock at side of post; thence to the ground and about the stage, with the various curvettings of a spirited horse. A chorus of soldiers is heard without, with the band. The music becomes more and more distant.* JENNY *gradually stops as the music is dying away, and stands, listening. As it dies entirely away, she suddenly starts to an enthusiastic attitude)* Ah! If I were only a man! The enemy! On Third Battalion, left, front, into line, march! Draw sabres! Charge! *(Imitates a Trumpet Signal. As she finishes, she rises to her full height, with both arms raised, and trembling with enthusiasm)* Ah! *(She suddenly drops her arms and changes to an attitude and expression of disappointment—pouting)* And the first time Old Margery took me to Father, in her arms, she had to tell him I was a girl. Father was as much disgusted as I was. But he 'd never admit it; he says I 'm as good a soldier as any of 'em—just as I am.

(Enter BARKET, *on the veranda, his arm in a sling)*

BARKET: Miss Jenny!

JENNY: Barket! The regiment has marched away to the front, and we girls are left here, with just you and a corporal's guard to look after us.

BARKET: I 've been watching the byes mesilf. *(Coming down)* If a little military sugar-plum like you, Miss Jenny, objects to not goin' wid 'em, what do you think of an ould piece of hard tack like me? I can't join the regiment till I 've taken you and Miss Madeline back to Winchester, by your father's orders. But it is n't the first time I 've escorted you, Miss Jenny. Many a time, when you was a baby, on the Plains, I commanded a special guard to accompany ye's from one fort to anither, and we gave the command in a whisper, so as not to wake ye's up.

JENNY: I told you to tell Father that I 'd let him know when Madeline and I were ready to go.

BARKET: I tould him that I 'd as soon move a train of army mules.

JENNY: I suppose we must start for home again to-day?

BARKET: Yes, Miss Jenny, in charge of an ould Sargeant wid his arm in a sling and a couple of convalescent throopers. This department of the United States Army will move to the rear in half an hour.

JENNY: Madeline and I only came yesterday morning.

BARKET: Whin your father got ye's a pass to the front, we all thought the fightin' in the Shenandoey Valley was over. It looks now as if it was just beginning. This is no place for women, now. Miss Gertrude Ellingham ought to go wid us, but she won't.

JENNY: Barket! Captain Heartsease left the regiment yesterday, and he has n't rejoined it; he is n't with them, now, at the head of his company. Where is he?

BARKET: I can't say where he is, Miss Jenny. *(Aside)* Lyin' unburied in the woods, where he was shot, I 'm afraid.

JENNY: When Captain Heartsease does rejoin the regiment, Barket, please say to him for me, that—that I—I may have some orders for him, when we next meet. *(Exit, on veranda)*

BARKET: Whin they nixt mate. They tell us there is no such thing as marriage in Hiven. If Miss Jenny and Captain Heartsease mate there, they 'll invint somethin' that 's mighty like it. While I was lyin' wounded in General Buckthorn's house at Washington, last summer, and ould Margery was taking care of me, Margery told me, confidentially, that they was in love wid aitch ither; and I think she was about right. I 've often seen Captain Heartsease take a sly look at a little lace handkerchief, just before we wint into battle. *(Looking off the stage)* Here 's General Buckthorn himself. He and I must make it as aisy as we can for Miss Jenny's poor heart.

(Enter GENERAL BUCKTHORN*)*

BUCKTHORN: Sergeant Barket! You have n't started with those girls yet?

BARKET: They 're to go in half an hour, sir.

BUCKTHORN: Be sure they do go. Is General Haverill here?

BARKET: Yes, sur; in the house with some of his staff, and the Surgeon.

BUCKTHORN: Ah! The Surgeon. How is Colonel West, this morning, after the wound he received last night?

BARKET: He says, himself, that he 's as well as iver he was; but the Colonel and Surgeon don't agray on that subject. The dochter says he must n't lave his room for a month. The knife wint dape; and there 's somethin' wrong inside of him. But the Colonel, bein' on the outside himsilf, can't see it. He 's as cross as a bear, baycause they would n't let him go to the front this morning, at the head of his regiment.

I happened to raymark that the Chaplain was prayin' for his raycovery. The Colonel said he 'd court-martial him if he did n't stop that— quick; there 's more important things for the Chaplain to pray for in his official capacity. Just at that moment the trumpets sounded, "Boots and Saddles." I had to dodge one of his boots, and the Surgeon had a narrow escape from the ither one. It was lucky for us both his saddle was n't in the room.

BUCKTHORN: That looks encouraging. I think Kerchival will get on.

BARKET: Might I say a word to you, sur, about Miss Jenny?

BUCKTHORN: Certainly, Barket. You and old Margery and myself have been a sort of triangular mother, so to speak, to the little girl since her own poor mother left her to our care, when she was only a baby, in the old fort on the Plains. *(He unconsciously rests his arm over* BARKET'S *shoulder, familiarly, and then suddenly draws up)* Ahem! *(Gruffly)* What is it? Proceed.

BARKET: Her mother's bosom would have been the softest place for her poor little head to rest upon, now, sur.

BUCKTHORN: *(touching his eyes)* Well!

BARKET: Ould Margery told me in Washington that Miss Jenny and Captain Heartsease were in love wid aitch ither.

BUCKTHORN: *(starting)* In love!

BARKET: I approved of the match.

BUCKTHORN: What the devil!

*(*BARKET *salutes quickly and starts up stage and out.* BUCKTHORN *moves up after him, and stops at the post.* BARKET *stops in the road)*

BARKET: So did ould Margery.

BUCKTHORN: *(angrily)* March! *(*BARKET *salutes suddenly and marches off)* Heartsease! That young jackanapes! A mere fop; he 'll never make a soldier. My girl in love with—bah! I don't believe it; she 's too good a soldier, herself. *(Enter* HAVERILL, *on the veranda)* Ah, Haverill!

HAVERILL: General Buckthorn! Have you heard anything of General Sheridan since I sent that dispatch to him last evening?

BUCKTHORN: He received it at midnight and sent back word that he considers it a ruse of the enemy. General Wright agrees with him. The reconnaissance yesterday showed no hostile force, on our right, and Crook reports that Early is retreating up the valley. But General Sheridan may, perhaps, give up his journey to Washington, and he has ordered some changes in our line, to be executed this afternoon at four o'clock. I rode over to give you your instructions in person. You may order General McCuen to go into camp on the right of Meadow Brook, with the second division.
(HAVERILL *is writing in his note-book*)
(*Enter* JENNY, *on the veranda*)

JENNY: Oh, Father! I 'm so glad you 've come. I 've got something to say to you. (*Running down and jumping into his arms, kissing him. He turns with her, and sets her down, squarely on her feet and straight before him*)

BUCKTHORN: And I 've got something to say to you—about Captain Heartsease.

JENNY: Oh! That 's just what I wanted to talk about.

BUCKTHORN: Fall in! Front face! (*She jumps into military position, turning towards him*) What 's this I hear from Sergeant Barket? He says you 've been falling in love.

JENNY: I have. (*Saluting*)

BUCKTHORN: Young woman! Listen to my orders. Fall out! (*Turns sharply and marches to* HAVERILL) Order the Third Brigade of Cavalry, under Colonel Lowell, to occupy the left of the pike.

JENNY: Father! (*Running to him and seizing the tail of his coat*) Father, dear!

BUCKTHORN: Close in Colonel Powell on the extreme left—(*slapping his coat-tails out of* JENNY'S *hands, without looking around*)—and hold Custer on the second line, at Old Forge Road. That is all at present. (*Turning to* JENNY) Good-bye, my darling! (*Kisses her*) Remember your orders! You little pet! (*Chuckling, as he taps her chin; draws up suddenly and turns to* HAVERILL) General! I bid you good-day.

HAVERILL: Good-day, General Buckthorn.
(*They salute with great dignity.* BUCKTHORN *starts up stage;* JENNY *springs after him, seizing his coat-tails*)

JENNY: But I want to talk with you, Father; I can't fall out. I—I—have n't finished yet.
(*Clinging to his coat, as* BUCKTHORN *marches out rapidly, in the road, holding back with all her might*)

HAVERILL: It may have been a ruse of the enemy, but I hope that General Sheridan has turned back from Washington. (*Looking at his note-book*) We are to make changes in our line at four o'clock this afternoon. (*Returning the book to his pocket, he stands in thought*) The Surgeon tells me that Kerchival West will get on well enough if he remains quiet; otherwise not. He shall not die by the hand of a common assassin; he has no right to die like that. My wife gave my own picture of herself to him—not to my son—and she looked so like an angel when she took it from my hand! They were both false to me, and they have been true to each other. I will save his life for myself.
(*Enter* GERTRUDE, *on the veranda*)

GERTRUDE: General Haverill! (*Anxiously, coming down*) Colonel West persists in disobeying the injunctions of the Surgeon. He is preparing to join his regiment at the front. Give him your orders to remain here. Compel him to be prudent!

HAVERILL: (*quickly*) The honor of death at the front is not in reserve for him.

GERTRUDE: Eh? What did you say, General?

HAVERILL: Gertrude! I wish to speak to you, as your father's old friend; and I was once your guardian. Your father was my senior officer in the Mexican War. Without his care I should have been left dead in a foreign land. He, himself, afterwards fell fighting for the old flag.

GERTRUDE: The old flag. (*Aside*) My father died for it, and he—(*looking toward the left*)—is suffering for it—the old flag!

HAVERILL: I can now return the kindness your father did to me, by protecting his daughter from something that may be worse than death.

GERTRUDE: What do you mean?

HAVERILL: Last night I saw you kneeling at the side of Kerchival West; you spoke to him with all the tender passion of a Southern woman. You said you loved him. But you spoke into ears that could not hear you. Has he ever heard those words from your lips? Have you ever confessed your love to him before?

GERTRUDE: Never. Why do you ask?

HAVERILL: Do not repeat those words. Keep your heart to yourself, my girl.

GERTRUDE: General! Why do you say this to me? And at such a moment—when his life—

HAVERILL: His life! *(Turning sharply)* It belongs to me!

GERTRUDE: Oh!

KERCHIVAL: Sergeant! *(Without. He steps into the road, looking back.* HAVERILL *comes down)* See that my horse is ready at once. General! *(Saluting)* Are there any orders for my regiment beyond those given to Major Wilson, in my absence, this morning? I am about to ride on after the troops and reassume my command.

HAVERILL: *(quietly)* It is my wish, Colonel, that you remain here under the care of the Surgeon.

KERCHIVAL: My wound is a mere trifle. This may be a critical moment in the campaign, and I cannot rest here. I must be with my own men.

HAVERILL: *(quietly)* I beg to repeat the wish I have already expressed.

(KERCHIVAL walks to him, and speaks apart, almost under his breath, but very earnest in tone)

KERCHIVAL: I have had no opportunity, yet, to explain certain matters, as you requested me to do yesterday; but whatever there may be between us, you are now interfering with my duty and my privilege as a soldier; and it is my right to be at the head of my regiment.

HAVERILL: *(quietly)* It is my positive order that you do not reassume your command.

KERCHIVAL: General Haverill, I protest against this—

HAVERILL: *(quietly)* You are under arrest, sir.

KERCHIVAL: Arrest!

GERTRUDE: Ah!

(KERCHIVAL unclasps his belt and offers his sword to HAVERILL)

HAVERILL: *(quietly)* Keep your sword; I have no desire to humiliate you; but hold yourself subject to further orders from me.

KERCHIVAL: My regiment at the front!—and I under arrest! *(Exit)*

HAVERILL: Gertrude! If your heart refuses to be silent—if you feel that you must confess your love to that man—first tell him what I have said to you, and refer him to me for an explanation. *(Exit)*

GERTRUDE: What can he mean? He would save me from something worse than death, he said. "His life—It belongs to me!" What can he mean? Kerchival told me that he loved me—it seems many years since that morning in Charleston—and when we met again, yesterday, he said that he had never ceased to love me. I will not believe that he told me a falsehood. I have given him my love, my whole soul and my faith. *(Drawing up to her full height)* My perfect faith!

(JENNY runs in, to the road, and up the slope. She looks down the hill, then toward the left and enters)

JENNY: A flag of truce, Gertrude. And a party of Confederate soldiers, with an escort, coming up the hill. They are carrying someone; he is wounded.

(Enter, up the slope, a Lieutenant of Infantry with an escort of Union Soldiers, their arms at right shoulder, and a party of Confederate Soldiers bearing a rustic stretcher. LIEUTENANT FRANK BEDLOE *lies on the stretcher.* MAJOR HARDWICK, *a Confederate Surgeon, walks at his side.* MADELINE *appears at the veranda, watching them.* GERTRUDE *stands with her back to the audience. The Lieutenant gives orders in a low tone, and the front escort moves toward the right, in the road. The Confederate bearers and the Surgeon pass through the gate. The rear escort moves on in the road, under the Lieutenant's orders. The bearers halt in the front of the stage; on a sign from the Surgeon, they leave the stretcher on the ground, stepping back)*

HARDWICK: Is General Haverill here?

GERTRUDE: Yes; what can we do, sir?

MADELINE: The General is just about mounting with his staff, to ride away. Shall I go for him, sir?

HARDWICK: Say to him, please, that Colonel Robert Ellingham, of the Tenth Virginia, sends his respects and sympathy. He instructed me to bring this young officer to this point, in exchange for himself, as agreed upon between them last evening. *(Exit* MADELINE*)*

JENNY: Is he unconscious or sleeping, sir?

HARDWICK: Hovering between life and death. I thought he would bear the removal better. He is waking. Here, my lad! *(Placing his canteen to the lips of* FRANK, *who moves, reviving)* We have reached the end of our journey.

FRANK: My father!

HARDWICK: He is thinking of his home.

*(*FRANK *rises on one arm, assisted by the Surgeon)*

FRANK: I have obeyed General Haverill's orders, and I have a report to make.

GERTRUDE: We have already sent for him. *(Stepping to him)* He will be here in a moment.

FRANK: *(looking into her face, brightly)* Is not this—Miss—Gertrude Ellingham?

GERTRUDE: You know me? You have seen me before?

FRANK: Long ago! Long ago! You know the wife of General Haverill?

GERTRUDE: I have no dearer friend in the world.

FRANK: She will give a message for me to the dearest friend *I* have in the world. My little wife! I must not waste even the moment we are waiting. Doctor! My note-book! *(Trying to get it from his coat. The Surgeon takes it out. A torn and blood-stained lace handkerchief also falls out.* GERTRUDE *kneels at his side)* Ah! I—I—have a message from another—*(holding up the handkerchief)*—from Captain Heartsease. *(*JENNY *makes a quick start towards him)* He lay at my side in the hospital, when they brought me away; he had only strength enough to put this in my hand, and he spoke a woman's name; but I—I—forget what it is. The red spots upon it are the only message he sent.

*(*GERTRUDE *takes the handkerchief and looks back at* JENNY, *extending her hand.* JENNY *moves to her, takes the handkerchief and turns back, looking down on it. She drops her face into her hands and goes out sobbing, on the veranda)*

(Enter MADELINE *on the veranda)*

MADELINE: General Haverill is coming. I was just in time. He was already on his horse.

FRANK: Ah! He is coming. *(Then suddenly)* Write! Write! *(*GERTRUDE *writes in the note-book as he dictates)* "To—my wife—Edith:—Tell our little son, when he is old enough to know—how his father died; not how he lived. And tell her who filled my own mother's place so lovingly—she is your mother, too—that my father's portrait of her, which she gave to me in Charleston, helped me to be a better man!" And—Oh! I must not forget this—"It was taken away from me while I was a prisoner in Richmond, and it is in the possession of Captain Edward Thornton, of the Confederate Secret Service. But her face is still beside your own in my heart. My best—warmest, last—love—to you, darling." I will sign it.

*(*GERTRUDE *holds the book, and he signs it, then sinks back very quietly, supported by the Surgeon.* GERTRUDE *rises and walks away)*

MADELINE: General Haverill is here.

(The Surgeon lays the fold of the blanket over FRANK'S *face and rises)*

GERTRUDE: Doctor!

HARDWICK: He is dead.

*(*MADELINE, *on the veranda, turns and looks away. The Lieutenant orders the guard, "Present Arms.")*

(Enter HAVERILL, *on the veranda. He salutes the guard as he passes. The Lieutenant orders, "Carry Arms."* HAVERILL *comes down)*

HAVERILL: I am too late?

HARDWICK: I 'm sorry, General. His one eager thought as we came was to reach here in time to see you.

*(*HAVERILL *moves to the bier, looks down at it, then folds back the blanket from the face. He starts slightly as he first sees it)*

HAVERILL: Brave boy! I hoped once to have a son like you. I shall be in your father's place to-day, at your grave. *(He replaces the blanket and steps back)* We will carry him to his comrades in the front. He shall have a soldier's burial, in sight of the mountain-top beneath which he sacrificed his young life; that shall be his monument.

HARDWICK: Pardon me, General. We Virginians are your enemies, but you cannot honor this young soldier more than we do. Will you allow my men the privilege of carrying him to his grave? *(HAVERILL inclines his head. The Surgeon motions to the Confederate Soldiers, who step to the bier and raise it gently)*

HAVERILL: Lieutenant!

(The Lieutenant orders the guard "Left Face." The Confederate bearers move through the gate, preceded by LIEUTENANT HARDWICK. HAVERILL draws his sword, reverses it, and moves up behind the bier with bowed head. The Lieutenant orders "Forward March," and the cortège disappears. While the girls are still watching it, the heavy sound of distant artillery is heard, with booming reverberations among the hills and in the valley)

MADELINE: What is that sound, Gertrude?

GERTRUDE: Listen!

(Another and more prolonged distant sound, with long reverberations)

MADELINE: Again! Gertrude!

(GERTRUDE raises her hand to command silence; listens. Distant cannon again)

GERTRUDE: It is the opening of a battle.

MADELINE: Ah! *(Running down stage. The sounds are heard again, prolonged)*

GERTRUDE: How often have I heard that sound! *(Coming down)* This is war, Madeline! You are face to face with it now.

MADELINE: And Robert is there! He may be in the thickest of the danger—at this very moment.

GERTRUDE: Yes. Let our prayers go up for him; mine do, with all a sister's heart.

(KERCHIVAL enters on veranda, without coat or vest, his sash about his waist, looking back as he comes in)

Kerchival!

KERCHIVAL: Go on! Go on! Keep the battle to yourselves. I 'm out of it. *(The distant cannon and reverberations are rising in volume)*

MADELINE: I pray for Robert Ellingham—and for the *cause* in which he risks his life! *(KERCHIVAL looks at her, suddenly; also GERTRUDE)* Heaven forgive me if I am wrong, but I am praying for the enemies of my country. His people are my people, his enemies are my enemies. Heaven defend him and his, in this awful hour.

KERCHIVAL: Madeline! My sister!

MADELINE: Oh, Kerchival! *(Turning and dropping her face on his breast)* I cannot help it—I cannot help it!

KERCHIVAL: My poor girl! Every woman's heart, the world over, belongs not to any country or any flag, but to her husband—and her lover. Pray for the man you love, sister—it would be treason not to. *(Passes her before him to the left of the stage. Looks across to GERTRUDE)* Am I right? *(GERTRUDE drops her head. MADELINE moves up veranda and out)* Is what I have said to Madeline true?

GERTRUDE: Yes! *(Looks up)* Kerchival!

KERCHIVAL: Gertrude! *(Hurries across to her, clasps her in his arms. He suddenly staggers and brings his hand to his breast)*

GERTRUDE: Your wound!

(Supporting him as he reels and sinks into seat)

KERCHIVAL: Wound! I have no wound! You do love me! *(Seizing her hand)*

GERTRUDE: Let me call the Surgeon, Kerchival.

KERCHIVAL: You can be of more service to me than he can. *(Detaining her. Very heavy sounds of the battle; she starts, listening)* Never mind that! It 's only a battle. You love me!

GERTRUDE: Be quiet, Kerchival, dear. I do love you. I told you so, when you lay bleeding here, last night. But you could not hear me. *(At his side, resting her arm about him, stroking his head)* I said that same thing to—to—another, more than three years ago. It is in that letter that General Buckthorn gave you. *(KERCHIVAL starts)* No— no—you must be very quiet, or I will not say another word. If you obey me, I will repeat that part of the letter, every word; I know it by heart, for I read it a dozen times. The letter is from Mrs Haverill.

KERCHIVAL: *(quietly)* Go on.

GERTRUDE: "I have kept your secret, my darling, but I was sorely tempted to betray the confidence you reposed in me at Charleston. If Kerchival West—*(she retires backward from him as she proceeds)*—had heard you say, as I did, when your face was hidden in my bosom, that night, that you loved him with your whole heart—"

KERCHIVAL: Ah!

(Starting to his feet. He sinks back. She springs to support him)

GERTRUDE: I will go for help.

KERCHIVAL: Do not leave me at such a moment as this. You have brought me a new life. *(Bringing her to her knees before him and looking down at her)* Heaven is just opening before me. *(His hands drop suddenly and his head falls back)*

GERTRUDE: Ah! Kerchival! You are dying! *(Musketry. A sudden sharp burst of musketry, mingled with the roar of artillery near by. KERCHIVAL starts, seizing GERTRUDE's arm and holding her away, still on her knees. He looks eagerly toward the left)*

KERCHIVAL: The enemy is close upon us!

(BARKET runs in, up the slope)

BARKET: Colonel Wist! The devils have sprung out of the ground. They 're pouring over our lift flank like Noah's own flood. The Union Army has started back for Winchester, on its way to the North Pole; our own regiment, Colonel, is coming over the hill in full retrate.

KERCHIVAL: My own regiment! *(Starting up)* Get my horse, Barket. *(Turns)* Gertrude, my life! *(Embraces GERTRUDE)*

BARKET: Your horse is it? I 'm wid ye! There 's a row at Finnegan's ball, and we 're in it. *(Springs to the road, and runs out)*

KERCHIVAL: *(turns away. Stops)* I am under arrest. *(The retreat begins. Fugitives begin to straggle across the stage from the left)*

GERTRUDE: You must not go, Kerchival; it will kill you.

KERCHIVAL: Arrest be damned! *(Starts up toward the center, raising his arms above his head with clenched fist, and rising to full height)* Stand out of my way, you cowards!

(They cower away from him as he rushes out among them. The stream of fugitives passing across the stage swells in volume. GERTRUDE runs through them and up to the elevation, turning)

GERTRUDE: Men! Are you soldiers? Turn back! There is a leader for you! Turn back! Fight for your flag—and mine!—the flag my father died for! Turn back! *(She looks out toward the left and then turns toward the front)* He has been marked for death already, and I—I can only pray. *(Dropping to her knees)*

(The stream of fugitives continues, now over the elevation also. Rough and torn uniforms, bandaged arms and legs; some limping and supported by others, some dragging their muskets after them, others without muskets, others using them as crutches. There is a variety of uniforms, both cavalry and infantry; flags are draggled on the ground, the rattle of near musketry and roar of cannon continue; two or three wounded fugitives drop down beside the hedge. BENSON staggers in and drops upon a rock near the post. Artillerists, rough, torn and wounded, drag and force a field-piece across. CORPORAL DUNN, wounded, staggers to the top of elevation. There is a lull in the sounds of the battle. Distant cheers are heard without)

DUNN: Listen, fellows! Stop! Listen! Sheridan! General Sheridan is coming!

(Cheers from those on stage. GERTRUDE rises quickly. The wounded soldiers rise, looking over the hedge. All on stage stop, looking eagerly toward the left. The cheers without come nearer, with shouts of "Sheridan! Sheridan!") The horse is down; he is worn out.

GERTRUDE: No! He is up again! He is on my Jack! Now, for your life, Jack, and for me! You 've never failed me yet. *(The cheers without now*

swell to full volume and are taken up by those on the stage. The horse sweeps by with General Sheridan) Jack! Jack!! Jack!!!
(Waving her arms as he passes. She throws up her arms and falls backward, caught by DUNN. *The stream of men is reversed and surges across the stage to the left, in the road and on the elevation, with shouts, and throwing up of hats. The field-piece is forced up the slope with a few bold, rough movements; the artillerists are loading it, and the stream of returning fugitives is still surging by in the road as the curtain falls)*

ACT FOURTH

A living room in the residence of GENERAL BUCK-THORN *in Washington. There is a fireplace slanting upward from the left toward the center of the stage. On the right toward the center there is a small alcove. On the left there is an opening to the hall with a stair-case beyond. There is a door on the right and a wide opening with portières leads on the left toward another room. There is an upright piano toward the front of the stage on the right and an armchair and low stool stand before the fireplace. A small table is set for tea. It is afternoon;* MRS HAVERILL, *in an arm-chair, is resting her face upon her hand, and looking into the fire.* EDITH *is on a low stool at her side, sewing a child's garment.*

EDITH: It seems hardly possible that the war is over, and that General Lee has really surrendered. There is music in the streets nearly all the time, now, and everybody looks so cheerful and bright. *(Distant fife and drums are heard playing "Johnnie Comes Marching Home."* EDITH *springs up and runs up to window, looking out)* More troops returning! The old tattered battle-flag is waving in the wind, and people are running after them so merrily. Every day, now, seems like a holiday. The war is over. All the women ought to feel very happy, whose—whose husbands are—coming back to them.

MRS HAVERILL: Yes, Edith; those women whose—husbands are coming back to them. *(Still looking into the fire)*

EDITH: Oh! *(Dropping upon the stool, her head upon the arm of the chair)*

MRS HAVERILL: *(resting her arm over her)* My poor, little darling! *Your* husband will not come back.

EDITH: Frank's last message has never reached me.

MRS HAVERILL: No; but you have one sweet thought always with you. Madeline West heard part of it, as Gertrude wrote it down. His last thought was a loving one, of you.

EDITH: Madeline says that he was thinking of you, too. He knew that you were taking such loving care of his little one, and of me. You have always done that, since you first came back from Charleston, and found me alone in New York.

MRS HAVERILL: I found a dear, sweet little daughter. *(Stroking her head)* Heaven sent you, darling! You have been a blessing to me. I hardly know how I should have got through the past few months at all without you at my side.

EDITH: What is your own trouble, dear? I have found you in tears so often; and since last October, after the battle of Cedar Creek, you—you have never shown me a letter from—from my—Frank's father. General Haverill arrived in Washington yesterday, but has not been here yet. Is it because I am here? He has never seen me, and I fear that he has never forgiven Frank for marrying me.

MRS HAVERILL: Nonsense, my child; he did think the marriage was imprudent, but he told me to do everything I could for you. If General Haverill has not been to see either of us, since his arrival in Washington, it is nothing that you need to worry your dear little head about. How are you getting on with your son's wardrobe?

EDITH: Oh! Splendidly! Frankie is n't a baby any longer; he 's a man, now, and he has to wear a man's clothes. *(Holding up a little pair of trousers, with maternal pride)* He 's rather young to be dressed like a man, but I want Frank to grow up as soon as possible. I long to have him old enough to understand me when I repeat to him the words in which General Haverill told the whole world how his father died! *(Rising)* And yet, even in his official report to the Government, he only honored him as Lieutenant Bedloe. He has never forgiven his son for the disgrace he brought upon his name.

MRS HAVERILL: I know him so well—*(rising)*—the unyielding pride, that conquers even the deep tenderness of his nature. He can be silent, though his own heart is breaking. *(Aside)* He can be silent, too, though *my* heart is breaking. *(Dropping her face in her hand)*

EDITH: *Mother! (Putting her arm about her)*
(Enter JANNETTE*)*

JANNETTE: A letter for you, Madam.

MRS HAVERILL: *(taking note. Aside)* He has answered me. *(She opens and reads the letter, and inclines her head to* JANNETTE, *who goes out to the hall. Aloud)* General Haverill will be here this afternoon, Edith.   *(Exit)*

EDITH: There is something that she cannot confide to me, or to anyone. General Haverill returned to Washington yesterday, and he has not been here yet. He will be here to-day. I always tremble when I think of meeting him.
*(*GENERAL BUCKTHORN *appears in the hall)*

BUCKTHORN: Come right in; this way, Barket. Ah, Edith!

BARKET: *(entering)* As I was saying, sur—just after the battle of Sayder Creek began—

BUCKTHORN: *(to* EDITH*)* More good news! The war is, indeed, over now!

BARKET: Whin Colonel Wist rode to the front to mate his raytrating rigiment—

BUCKTHORN: General Johnston has surrendered his army, also; and that, of course, does end the war.

EDITH: I 'm very glad that all the fighting is over.

BUCKTHORN: So am I; but my occupation, and old Barket's, too, is gone. Always at work on new clothes for our little soldier?

EDITH: He 's growing so, I can hardly make them fast enough for him. But this is the time for his afternoon nap. I must go now, to see if he is sleeping soundly.

BUCKTHORN: Our dear little mother! *(Tapping her chin)* I always claim the privilege of my white hair, you know. *(She puts up her lips; he kisses her. She goes out)* The sweetest young widow I ever saw! *(*BARKET *coughs.* BUCKTHORN *turns sharply;* BARKET *salutes)* Well! What the devil are you thinking about now?

BARKET: The ould time, sur. Yer honor used to claim the same privilege for brown hair.

BUCKTHORN: You old rascal! What a memory you have! You were telling me for the hundredth time about the battle of Cedar Creek; go on. I can never hear it often enough. Kerchival West was a favorite of mine, poor fellow!

BARKET: Just afther the battle of Sayder Creek began, when the Colonel rode to the front to mate his raytrating rigiment—

BUCKTHORN: I 'll tell Old Margery to bring in tea for both of us, Barket.

BARKET: For both of us, sur?

BUCKTHORN: Yes; and later in the evening we 'll have something else, together. This is a great day for all of us. I 'm not your commander to-day, but your old comrade in arms—*(Laying his arm over* BARKET'S *shoulder)*—and I 'm glad I don't have to pull myself up now every time I forget my dignity. Ah! you and I will be laid away before long, but we 'll be together again in the next world, won't we, Barket?

BARKET: Wid yer honor's permission. *(Saluting)*

BUCKTHORN: Ha—ha—ha! *(Laughing)* If we do meet there, I 'm certain you 'll salute me as your superior officer. There 's Old Margery, now. *(Looking toward the door and calling)* Margery! Tea for two!

MARGERY: *(without)* The tay be waiting for ye, sur; and it be boilin' over wid impatience.

BUCKTHORN: Bring up a chair, Barket. *(Sitting down in the arm-chair)*

BARKET: *(having placed table and drawing up a chair)* Do you know, Gineral, I don't fale quite aisy in my moind. I 'm not quite sure that Margery will let us take our tay together. *(Sits down, doubtfully)*

BUCKTHORN: I had n't thought of that. I—*(Glancing to the right)*—I hope she will, Barket. But, of course, if she won't—she 's been commander-in-chief of my household ever since Jenny was a baby.

BARKET: At Fort Duncan, in Texas.

BUCKTHORN: You and Old Margery never got along very well in those days; but I thought you had made it all up; she nursed you through your wound, last summer, and after the battle of Cedar Creek, also.

BARKET: Yis, sur, bliss her kind heart, she 's been like a wife to me; and that 's the trouble. A man's wife is such an angel when he 's ill that he dreads to get well; good health is a misfortune to him. Auld Margery and I have had anither misunderstanding.

BUCKTHORN: I 'll do the best I can for both of us, Barket. You were telling me about the battle of—

BARKET: Just afther the battle of Sayder Creek began, whin Colonel Wist rode to the front to mate his raytrating rigiment—
(Enter OLD MARGERY, with a tea-tray. She stops abruptly, looking at BARKET. He squirms in his chair. BUCKTHORN rises and stands with his back to the mantel. OLD MARGERY moves to the table, arranges things on it, glances at BARKET, then at BUCKTHORN, who looks up at the ceiling, rubbing his chin. OLD MARGERY takes up one of the cups, with saucer)

MARGERY: I misunderstood yer order, sur. I see there 's no one here but yerself.   *(Going)*

BUCKTHORN: Ah, Margery! *(She stops)* Barket tells me that there has been a slight misunderstanding between you and him.

MARGERY: Day before yisterday, the ould Hibernian dhrone had the kitchen upside down, to show anither old milithary vagabone loike himself how the battle of Sayder Creek was fought. He knocked the crame pitcher into the basket of clane clothes, and overturned some raspberry jam and the flat-irons into a pan of fresh eggs. There *has* been a misunderstanding betwane us.

BUCKTHORN: I see there has. I suppose Barket was showing his friend how Colonel Kerchival West rode forward to meet his regiment, when he was already wounded dangerously.

MARGERY: Bliss the poor, dear young man! He and I was always good frinds, though he was something of a devil in the kitchen himself, whin he got there. *(Wiping her eye with one corner of her apron)* And bliss the young Southern lady that was in love wid him, too. *(Changing the cup and wiping the other eye with the corner of her apron)* Nothing was iver heard of ayther of thim after that battle was over, to this very day.

BUCKTHORN: Barket was at Kerchival's side when he rode to the front. *(OLD MARGERY hesitates a moment, then moves to the table, sets down the cup and marches out. BUCKTHORN sits in the arm-chair again, pouring tea)* I could always find some way to get Old Margery to do what I wanted her to do.

BARKET: You 're a great man, Gineral; we 'd niver have conquered the South widout such men.

BUCKTHORN: Now go on, Barket; you were interrupted.

BARKET: Just afther the battle of Sayder Creek began, whin—
(Enter JANNETTE, with a card, which she hands to BUCKTHORN)

BUCKTHORN: *(reading card)* Robert Ellingham! *(Rises)* I will go to him. *(To JANNETTE)* Go upstairs and tell Miss Madeline to come down.

JANNETTE: Yes, sir.   *(Going)*

BUCKTHORN: And, Jannette, simply say there is a caller; don't tell her who is here. *(Exit JANNETTE. BUCKTHORN follows her out to the hall)* Ellingham! My dear fellow!
(Extending his hand and disappearing)

BARKET: Colonel Ellingham and Miss Madeline—lovers! That 's the kind o' volunteers the country nades now!
(Enter BUCKTHORN and ELLINGHAM)

BUCKTHORN: *(as he enters)* We 've been fighting four years to keep you out of Washington, Colonel, but we are delighted to see you within the lines, now.

ELLINGHAM: I am glad, indeed, General, to have so warm a welcome. But can you tell me anything about my sister, Gertrude?

BUCKTHORN: About your sister? Why, can't you tell us? And have you heard nothing of Kerchival West on your side of the line?

ELLINGHAM: All I can tell you is this: As soon as possible after our surrender at Appomattox, I made my way to the Shenandoah Valley. Our home there is utterly deserted. I have hurried down to Washington in the hopes that I might learn something of you. There is no human being about the old homestead; it is like a haunted house—empty, and dark, and solitary. You do not even know where Gertrude is?

BUCKTHORN: We only know that Kerchival was not found among the dead of his own regiment at Cedar Creek, though he fell among them during the fight. The three girls searched the field for him, but he was not there. As darkness came on, and they were returning to the house, Gertrude suddenly seized the bridle of a stray horse, sprang upon its back and rode away to the South, into the woods at the foot of Three Top Mountain. The other two girls watched for her in vain. She did not return, and we have heard nothing from her since.

ELLINGHAM: Poor girl! I understand what was in her thoughts, and she was right. We captured fourteen hundred prisoners that day, although we were defeated, and Kerchival must have been among them. Gertrude rode away, alone, in the darkness, to find him. I shall return to the South at once and learn where she now is.

(JANNETTE has re-entered, down the stairs)

JANNETTE: Miss Madeline will be down in a moment. *(Exit in hall)*

BARKET: *(aside)* That name wint through his chist like a rifle ball.

BUCKTHORN: Will you step into the drawing-room, Colonel? I will see Madeline myself, first. She does not even know that you are living.

ELLINGHAM: I hardly dared ask for her. Is she well?

BUCKTHORN: Yes; and happy—or soon will be.

ELLINGHAM: Peace, at last!

(Exit to the apartment. BUCKTHORN closes the portières)

BUCKTHORN: I ought to prepare Madeline a little, Barket; you must help me.

BARKET: Yis, sur, I will.

(Enter MADELINE, down the stairs)

MADELINE: Uncle! Jannette said you wished to see me; there is a visitor here. Who is it?

BARKET: Colonel Robert Ellingham.

MADELINE: Ah! *(Staggering)*

BUCKTHORN: *(supporting her)* You infernal idiot! I 'll put you in the guard-house!

BARKET: You wanted me to help ye, Gineral.

MADELINE: Robert is alive—and here?

(Rising from his arms, she moves to the portières, holds them aside, peeping in; gives a joyful start, tosses aside the portières and runs through)

BUCKTHORN: Barket! There 's nothing but that curtain between us and Heaven.

BARKET: I don't like stayin' out o' Hiven, myself, sur. Gineral! I 'll kiss Ould Margery—if I die for it! *(Exit)*

BUCKTHORN: Kiss Old Margery! I 'll give him a soldier's funeral.

(Enter JENNY from hall, demurely)

Ah! Jenny, my dear! I have news for you. Colonel Robert Ellingham is in the drawing-room.

JENNY: Oh! I am delighted. *(Starting)*

BUCKTHORN: A-h-e-m!

JENNY: Oh!—exactly. I see. I have some news for *you*, papa. Captain Heartsease has arrived in Washington.

BUCKTHORN: Oh! My dear! I have often confessed to you how utterly mistaken I was about that young man. He is a soldier—as good a soldier as you are. I 'll ask him to the house.

JENNY: *(demurely)* He is here now.

BUCKTHORN: Now?

JENNY: He's been here an hour; in the library.

BUCKTHORN: Why! Barket and I were in the library fifteen minutes ago.

JENNY: Yes, sir. We were in the bay-window; the curtains were closed.

BUCKTHORN: Oh! exactly; I see. You may tell him he has my full consent.

JENNY: He has n't asked for it.

BUCKTHORN: Has n't he? And you 've been in the bay-window an hour? Well, my darling—I was considered one of the best Indian fighters in the old army, but it took me four years to propose to your mother. I 'll go and see the Captain.   *(Exit)*

JENNY: I wonder if it will take Captain Heartsease four years to propose to me. Before he left Washington, nearly two years ago, he told everybody in the circle of my acquaintance, except me, that he was in love with me. I 'll be an old lady in caps before our engagement commences. Poor, dear mother! The idea of a girl's waiting four years for a chance to say, "Yes." It 's been on the tip of my tongue so often, I 'm afraid it 'll pop out, at last, before he pops the question.

(Enter BUCKTHORN *and* HEARTSEASE *from the hall)*

BUCKTHORN: Walk right in, Captain; this is the family room. You must make yourself quite at home here.

HEARTSEASE: Thank you. *(Walking down toward the right)*

BUCKTHORN: My dear! *(Apart to* JENNY*)* The very first thing he said to me, after our greeting, was that he loved my daughter.

JENNY: Now he 's told my father!

BUCKTHORN: He 's on fire!

JENNY: Is he? *(Looking at* HEARTSEASE, *who stands quietly stroking his mustache)* Why does n't he tell *me?*

BUCKTHORN: You may have to help him a little; your mother assisted me. When you and Jenny finish your chat, Captain—*(Lighting a cigar at the mantel)*—you must join me in the smoking room.

HEARTSEASE: I shall be delighted. By the way, General—I have been in such a fever of excitement since I arrived at this house—

JENNY: *(aside)* Fever? Chills!

HEARTSEASE: That I forgot it entirely. I have omitted a very important and a very sad commission. I have brought with me the note-book of Lieutenant Frank Bedloe—otherwise Haverill—in which Miss Gertrude Ellingham wrote down his last message to his young wife.

JENNY: Have you seen Gertrude?

BUCKTHORN: *(taking the book)* How did this note-book come into your possession?

HEARTSEASE: Miss Ellingham visited the prison in North Carolina where I was detained. She was going from hospital to hospital, from prison to prison, and from burial-place to burial-place, to find Colonel Kerchival West, if living—or some record of his death.

BUCKTHORN: Another Evangeline! Searching for her lover through the wilderness of this great war!

HEARTSEASE: I was about to be exchanged at the time, and she requested me to bring this to her friends in Washington. She had not intended to carry it away with her. I was not exchanged, as we then expected, but I afterwards escaped from prison to General Sherman's Army.

BUCKTHORN: I will carry this long-delayed message to the widowed young mother.   *(Exit)*

JENNY: I remember so well, when poor Lieutenant Haverill took out the note-book and asked Gertrude to write for him. He—he brought me a message at the same time.

(Their eyes meet. He puts up his glasses. She turns away, touching her eyes)

HEARTSEASE: I—I remember the circumstances you probably allude to; that is—when he left my side—I—I gave him my—I mean your— lace handkerchief.

JENNY: It is sacred to me!

HEARTSEASE: Y-e-s—I would say—is it?

JENNY: *(wiping her eyes)* It was stained with the life-blood of a hero!

HEARTSEASE: I must apologize to you for its condition. I had n't any chance to have it washed and ironed.

JENNY: *(looking around at him, suddenly; then, aside)* What could any girl do with a lover like that? *(Turning up the stage)*

HEARTSEASE: *(aside)* She seems to remember that incident so tenderly! My blood boils!

JENNY: Did n't you long to see your—your friends at home—when you were in prison, Captain?

HEARTSEASE: Yes—especially—I longed especially, Miss Buckthorn, to see—

JENNY: Yes!—to see—

HEARTSEASE: But there were lots of jolly fellows in the prison.

(JENNY turns away)

HEARTSEASE: We had a dramatic society, and a glee club, and an orchestra. I was one of the orchestra. I had a banjo, with one string; I played one tune on it, that I used to play on the piano, with one finger. But, Miss Buckthorn, I am a prisoner again, to-night—your prisoner.

JENNY: *(aside)* At last!

HEARTSEASE: I 'll show you how that tune went. *(Turns to the piano and sits)*

JENNY: *(aside)* Father said I 'd have to help him, but I don't see an opening.

(HEARTSEASE plays part of an air with one finger and strikes two or three wrong notes)

HEARTSEASE: There are two notes down there, somewhere, that I never could get right. The fellows in prison used to dance while I played—*(playing)*—that is, the lame ones did; those that were n't lame could n't keep the time.

JENNY: You must have been in great danger, Captain, when you escaped from prison.

HEARTSEASE: Y-e-s. I was badly frightened several times. One night I came face to face, on the road, with a Confederate Officer. It was Captain Thornton.

JENNY: Oh! What did you do?

HEARTSEASE: I killed him. *(Very quietly, and trying the tune again at once. Enter JANNETTE, from the hall; she glances into the room and goes up the stairs)* I used to skip those two notes on the banjo. It 's very nice for a soldier to come home from the war, and meet those—I mean the one particular person—that he—you see, when a soldier loves a woman, as—as—

JENNY: *(aside)* As he loves me. *(Approaches him)*

HEARTSEASE: As soldiers often do—*(Plays; she turns away, petulantly; he plays the tune through correctly)* That 's it!

JENNY: *(aside)* I 'm not going to be made love to by piece-meal, like this, any longer. *(Aloud)* Captain Heartsease! Have you anything in particular to say to me? *(He looks up)*

HEARTSEASE: Y-e-s. *(Rising)*

JENNY: Say it! You told my father, and all my friends, that you were in love with me. Whom are you going to tell next?

HEARTSEASE: I *am* in love with you.

JENNY: It was my turn.

HEARTSEASE: *(going near to her)* Do you love me?

JENNY: *(laying her head quietly on his breast)* I must take time to consider.

HEARTSEASE: *(quietly)* I assume that this means "Yes."

JENNY: It is n't the way a girl says "No."

HEARTSEASE: My darling!

JENNY: Why! His heart is beating as fast as mine is!

HEARTSEASE: *(quietly)* I am frantic with joy. *(He kisses her. She hides her face on his breast. Enter MRS HAVERILL, down-stairs, followed by JANNETTE. MRS HAVERILL stops suddenly. JANNETTE stands in the doorway. HEARTSEASE inclines his head to her, quietly looking at her over JENNY)* I am delighted to see you, after so long an absence; I trust that we shall meet more frequently hereafter.

JENNY: *(looking at him)* Eh?

HEARTSEASE: *(looking down at her)* I think, perhaps, it might be as well for us to repair to another apartment, and continue our interview, there!

JENNY: *(dropping her head on his breast again)* This room is very comfortable.

MRS HAVERILL: Jenny, dear!

*(*JENNY *starts up; looks from* MRS HAVERILL *to* HEARTSEASE*)*

JENNY: Constance! I—'Bout face! March! *(She turns and goes out)*

MRS HAVERILL: I am glad to see you again, Captain, and happy as well as safe.

HEARTSEASE: Thank you, Madam. I am happy. If you will excuse me, I will join—my father—in the smoking room. *(*MRS HAVERILL *inclines her head, and* HEARTSEASE *walks out)*

MRS HAVERILL: Jannette! You may ask General Haverill to come into this room. *(Exit* JAN-NETTE. MRS HAVERILL *walks down the stage, reading a note)* "I have hesitated to come to you personally, as I have hesitated to write to you. If I have been silent, it is because I could not bring my hand to write what was in my mind and in my heart. I do not know that I can trust my tongue to speak it, but I will come." *(Enter* HAVERILL, *from the hall; he stops)*

HAVERILL: Constance!

MRS HAVERILL: My husband! May I call you husband? After all these months of separation, with your life in almost daily peril, and my life— what? Only a weary longing for one loving word—and you are silent.

HAVERILL: May I call you wife? I do not wish to speak that word except with reverence. You have asked me to come to you. I am here. I will be plain, direct and brief. Where is the portrait of yourself, which I gave you, in Charleston, for my son?

MRS HAVERILL: Your son is dead, sir; and my portrait lies upon his breast, in the grave. *(*HAVERILL *takes the miniature from his pocket and holds it towards her in his extended hand. She starts back)* He gave it to you? And you ask me where it is?

HAVERILL: It might have lain in the grave of Kerchival West!

MRS HAVERILL: Ah!

HAVERILL: Not in my son's. I found it upon *his* breast. *(She turns front, dazed)* Well! I am listening! It was not I that sought this interview,

madam; and if you prefer to remain silent, I will go. You know, now, why I have been silent so long.

MRS HAVERILL: My only witnesses to the truth are both dead. I shall remain silent. *(Turning towards him)* We stand before each other, living, but not so happy as they. We are parted, forever. Even if you should accept my unsupported word—if I could so far forget my pride as to give it to you—suspicion would still hang between us. I remain silent.

*(*HAVERILL *looks at her, earnestly, for a moment, then approaches her)*

HAVERILL: I cannot look into your eyes and not see truth and loyalty there. Constance!

MRS HAVERILL: No, John! *(Checking him)* I will not accept your blind faith! *(Moving)*

HAVERILL: *(looking down at the picture in his hand)* My faith is blind; blind as my love! I do not wish to see!

(Enter EDITH. *She stops and looks at* HAVERILL. *He raises his head and looks at her)*

EDITH: This is General Haverill? *(Dropping her eyes)* I am Edith, sir.

HAVERILL: *(gently)* My son's wife. *(Kisses her forehead)* You shall take the place he once filled in my heart. His crime and his disgrace are buried in a distant grave.

EDITH: And you have not forgiven him, even yet?

MRS HAVERILL: Is there no atonement for poor Frank's sin—not even his death? Can you only bury the wrong and forget the good?

HAVERILL: The good?

MRS HAVERILL: Your own words to the Government, as his commander!

HAVERILL: What do you mean?

MRS HAVERILL: "The victory of Cedar Creek would have been impossible without the sacrifice of this young officer."

HAVERILL: My own words, yes—but—

EDITH: "His name must take its place forever, in the roll of names which his countrymen honor."

HAVERILL: Lieutenant Bedloe!

MRS HAVERILL: Haverill! You did not know?

HAVERILL: My—son.

EDITH: You did not receive mother's letter?—after his death?

HAVERILL: My son! *(Sinking upon a chair)* I left him alone in his grave, unknown; but my tears fell for him, then, as they do now. He died before I reached him.

EDITH: Father! *(Laying her hand gently on his shoulder)* You shall see Frank's face again. His little son is lying asleep upstairs; and when he wakes up, Frank's own eyes will look into yours. I have just received his last message. I will read it to you. *(She opens the note-book and reads)* "Tell our little son how his father died, not how he lived. And tell her who filled my own mother's place so lovingly." *(She looks at* MRS HAVERILL, *moves to her and hides her face in her bosom)* My mother!

MRS HAVERILL: Edith—my child! Frank loved us both.

EDITH: *(reading)* "Father's portrait of her, which she gave to me in Charleston—(HAVERILL *starts)*—helped me to be a better man."

HAVERILL: *(rising to his feet)* Constance!

EDITH: *(reading)* "It was taken from me in Richmond, and it is in the possession of Captain Edward Thornton."

HAVERILL: One moment! Stop! Let me think! *(*EDITH *looks at him)* Thornton was a prisoner—and to Kerchival West. A dispatch had been found upon him—he was searched! *(He moves to her and takes both her hands in his own, bowing his head over them)* My head is bowed in shame.

MRS HAVERILL: Speak to me, John, as you used to speak! Tell me you still love me!

HAVERILL: The—the words will come—but they are—choking me—now. *(He presses her hand to his lips)*

MRS HAVERILL: We will think no more of the past except of what was bright in it. Frank's memory, and our own love, will be with us always. *(Enter* BUCKTHORN, *followed by* HEARTSEASE*)*

BUCKTHORN: Haverill! You are back from the war, too. It begins to look like peace in earnest.

HAVERILL: Yes. Peace and home. *(Shaking hands with him.* MRS HAVERILL *joins* EDITH*)* *(Enter* BARKET*)*

BARKET: Gineral! (BUCKTHORN *moves to him.* HAVERILL *joins* MRS HAVERILL *and* EDITH. BARKET *speaks apart, twisting one side of his face)* I kissed her!

BUCKTHORN: Have you sent for a surgeon?

BARKET: I felt as if the inimy had surprised us agin, and Sheridan was sixty miles away.

HAVERILL: This is old Sergeant Barket. *(*BARKET *salutes)* You were the last man of us all that saw Colonel West.

BARKET: Just afther the battle of Sayder Creek began—whin Colonel Wist rode to the front to mate his raytrating rigiment—the byes formed in line, at sight of him, to raysist the victorious inimy. It was just at the brow of a hill—about there, sur—*(pointing with his cane)* and—here! *(He takes the tray from the table and sets it on the carpet, then lays the slices of bread in a row)* That be the rigiment. *(All are interested.* MADELINE *and* ELLINGHAM *enter, and look on.* BARKET *arranges the two cups and saucers in a row)* That be the inimy's batthery, sur. *(Enter* MARGERY. *She goes to the table, then looks around, sharply at* BARKET*)*

MARGERY: Ye ould Hibernian dhrone! What are yez doin' wid the china on the floor? You 'll break it all!

BUCKTHORN: Ah—Margery! Barket is telling us where he last saw Colonel Kerchival West.

MARGERY: The young Colonel! The taycups and saucers be's the inimy's batthery? Yez may smash 'em, if ye loike!

BUCKTHORN: Go on, Barket. *(*JENNY *and* HEARTSEASE *have entered, as* BARKET *proceeds, the whole party lean forward, intensely interested.* GERTRUDE *enters in the hall, looks in, beckons as if to some one without, and* KERCHIVAL *follows. They move to the center of the stage, back of the rest and listen unseen)*

BARKET: Just as the rigiment was rayformed in line, and Colonel Wist was out in front—widout any coat or hat, and wid only a shtick in his hand—we heard cheers in the rear. Gineral Sheridan was coming! One word to the men—and we swept over the batthery like a whirlwind! *(Slashing his cane through the cups and saucers)*

MARGERY: Hoo-roo!

BARKET: The attack on the lift flank was checked. But when we shtopped to take breath, Colonel Wist was n't wid us. *(*GERTRUDE *turns lovingly to* KERCHIVAL. *He places his arm about her)* Heaven knows where he is now. After the battle was over, poor Miss Gertrude wint off by hersilf into the wilderness to find him.

KERCHIVAL: My wife! You saved my life, at last. *(Embracing her)*

BARKET: They 'll niver come together in this world. I saw Miss Gertrude, myself, ride away into the woods and disappear behind a schoolhouse on the battle-field, over there.

GERTRUDE: No, Barket—*(All start and look)*—it was the little church; we were married there this morning!

M A R G A R E T   F L E M I N G   (1 8 9 0)

The power of this story, as presented in Mr. Herne's every-day phrase, and in the naked simplicity of Mrs. Herne's acting of the wife's part, was terrific. It clutched the heart. It was common; it was pitilessly plain; it was ugly; but it was true, and it was irresistible.

* * *

Margaret Fleming is, indeed, the quintessence of the commonplace. Its language is the colloquial English of the shops and the streets and the kitchen fire-place. Its personages are the every-day nonentities that some folks like to forget when they go to the theatre. . . . The life it portrays is sordid and mean, and its effect upon a sensitive mind is depressing.

The status of *Margaret Fleming* among its contemporaries is starkly epitomized by these two contrasting evaluations of the play. The first is taken from William Dean Howells' review for *Harper's Monthly* of the original Boston production of the play; the latter is from the *New York Times'* Edward Dithmar after the play's New York premier. This contrast of attitudes about the play that most legitimately lays claim to having brought the realistic aesthetic of Gustave Flaubert and Henrik Ibsen to the American stage reveals the friction between two cultural tectonic plates—the Victorian and the modern. As both literary work and cultural intervention, *Margaret Fleming*'s existence suggests the aesthetic and cultural changes that were overtaking the country in the last decade of the nineteenth century. While it is tempting to contend that *Margaret Fleming* was as revolutionary as Howells, Hamlin Garland, and

others of the play's supporters asserted that it was, the reality is that the play was a theatrical failure while Herne was alive. Economic and aesthetic forces combined to keep the play from the public, and, when it did receive a hearing, the general audience, educated by **melodrama** to expect a different style of play, stayed away in droves. While its immediate theatrical influence was not great, *Margaret Fleming* set a standard against which later American **realist** dramatists were to measure themselves. As an episode in the career of James A. Herne, it marked a failed experiment that propelled his endeavors in other, equally realistic and much more profitable directions.

James Ahern was born February 1, 1838, in Cohoes, New York, to Ann Temple and Patrick Ahern. John Perry, Herne's biographer, depicts Patrick Ahern as a narrow-minded, devout, and poor Irish immigrant who had converted from Catholicism to the Calvinist Dutch Reformed Church and whose intolerance instilled in his son a lifelong repugnance of organized religion. His mother was the one family member who could understand James' desires to move beyond working in a brush factory and, when he left home in 1859 with his $165 savings to become an actor, he apparently left with his mother's blessing. Over the next few years, he changed his name to James A. Herne and steadily progressed from unpaid "apprentice" actor on a rural New York circuit, through supporting player in Albany, to a working actor in some of the major houses in Baltimore, Philadelphia, and Montreal. Along the way, he married (1866) and divorced (1868) Helen Western, and toured California as the leading man of her sister, Lucille. In 1869, James Fisk hired Herne as manager of New York's Grand Opera House at a princely salary of $10,000, but that position lasted only one year.

After spending four years playing principally in New York and Montreal, Herne returned to California, where he managed theatres in San Francisco, was encouraged to write by David Belasco, and met and married (1878) Katherine Corcoran, the Irish-born actress whose support for her husband's writing and subtle characterizations of many of his female leads (including that of Margaret Fleming) did much to secure the family's fortune and her husband's reputation. In a very real sense, the close working relationship between James and Katherine Herne represented a partnership of such completeness that there is a significant argument to be made that Katherine Corcoran Herne is entitled to share in authorship of several of Herne's plays, especially *Margaret Fleming.*

Herne's writing career had its first major success with *Hearts of Oak* (1879), written in conjunction with David Belasco. Though initially unsuccessful in San Francisco, Belasco and the Hernes moved the play across the country, eventually finding a receptive audience in Chicago, where in the face of the unwillingness of the principal Chicago managers to produce the play, they rented a dilapidated variety theatre and put the play on themselves. After some legal complications arising from Belasco's borrowing the plot from an earlier English melodrama, *The Mariner's Compass,* the play moved on to Philadelphia and New York, where its reception was lukewarm. Having quarreled with Belasco in Philadelphia and subsequently bought up his rights to the play, Herne moved on to Boston, where he and Katherine settled, began their family, and from which he launched his seasonal tours throughout the country. His summers he spent at home writing new plays and preparing the next year's tour. Herne's next effort, *The Minute Men of 1774–5* (1886), with its reliance upon historical material and complex plotting, indicated a direction that he would not pursue again. After touring with *Hearts of Oak* in 1887, Herne brought out *Drifting Apart* (1888), a sober picture of a man destroyed by alcoholism. Again, as in the case of *Hearts of Oak,* theatre managers of major houses refused to book a play

on such a serious subject and Herne exhausted his personal fortune trying to keep *Drifting Apart* before the public.

This was followed by *Margaret Fleming* (1890), which Herne premiered in Lynn, Massachusetts, in an attempt to secure the backing of Boston's managers. The strategy failed. Any play that wanted to broach the subject of adultery openly and had stage action that included the title character unbuttoning her dress to nurse her husband's illegitimate child was beyond the pale. Herne was forced to delay opening the play, accepting a stage managership with Abraham Erlanger to support his family. In May of 1891, accepting the advice of William Dean Howells, the Hernes rented a concert hall above a piano dealership, borrowed furnishings, made their own stage curtains, secured other professional and amateur performers, and staged the play. While the intelligentsia and literary community were, in the main, lavishly enthusiastic, the underwriters withdrew their support after three weeks and the play closed. While Herne would eventually return to the sober discussion of social issues in *Griffith Davenport* (1899), his Civil War play exploring slavery and regional conflict, the audience's rebuff of his *Margaret Fleming* sent him for a while in another direction. In 1892, Herne produced *Shore Acres* at McVicker's Theatre in Chicago with minor success. In February 1893 it opened in Boston and the response was overwhelming. The kind and decent Uncle Nat and the tribulations of his New England family captivated audiences and the play remained an audience favorite well into the next century. Herne had at last hit upon a way of presenting what he would have deemed "truth" as "art." Herne put forth his aesthetic principles most clearly in "Art for Truth's Sake in the Drama," an article which expresses what audiences perceived in *Shore Acres* and Herne's last play, *Sag Harbor* (1899). In that article, he contended that the nature of the realist aesthetic might not generate "beautiful" art, but in its truthful portrait of representative reality, it found an alternative which earlier art had overlooked. If its objects were not beautiful in a conventionally aesthetic sense, they did "[perpetuate] the everyday life of its time," present "the latent beauty of the so-called common-places of life, . . . [dignify] labor and [reveal] the divinity of the common man." This aesthetic sensibility, which in his later plays could be read as affectionate local color portraits of common Americans, finally won him a popular audience. But his fame and success came rather too late; after a steady decline over six months, Herne died on June 2, 1901.

To accommodate various managers' demands, Herne rewrote *Margaret Fleming* several times. The play reprinted here represents the play's final version as reconstructed by Katherine Corcoran Herne after the original manuscript was lost in a house fire. In the original version, the last act takes place four years after the third-act curtain. Philip meets Joe on Boston Common and tells him that Margaret has disappeared, his business has failed, and he has lived a life of misery and regret. Joe becomes convinced that the child who, Maria has maintained, was her sister's is actually Lucy Fleming and takes Philip off to show him the child. Meantime, the still-blind Margaret has accidentally discovered Maria and Lucy. Maria at first denies that Lucy is Margaret's daughter but then confesses. Margaret takes away the child. When Philip arrives, Maria maintains that she has sold the child. The final scene takes place in a police station where Maria, Joe, Lucky, Philip, and Margaret meet. When the police inspector leaves them alone to reconcile, Margaret tells Philip that "the wife-heart has gone out of me" and they agree to part. The play ends as the police go back to the usual routine. As this summary of the earlier version suggests, in the final version Herne moved steadily away from melodrama, excluding melodramatic elements such as the kidnapping of Margaret's daughter from the version here.

The power of *Margaret Fleming* emerges from Herne's ability to weld various elements of realistic dramaturgy into what Arthur Hobson Quinn accurately assessed as a whole "unequalled in realism by any other known American drama of its century." Herne produces an action whose unfolding brings greater understanding of the play's very real characters and their situation. His dialogue is plain and straightforward and avoids the rhetorical flourishes or use of asides still common to much contemporary melodrama. His characters' inner lives can be represented through understated acting. His simple sets use the technical resources of the theatre to facilitate understanding of the characters and the situation, and not as mere spectacle or ornamentation. Finally, Herne consciously tackles important issues. For the first time on the American stage, a playwright chooses to attack the sexual double standard and, in the process, to question seriously the assumptions of the dominant patriarchal social and moral codes. Though we may agree with Judith Stephens that ultimately the play reinscribes women within roles reserved for them by traditional patriarchy, the fact remains that Herne raises the issue. In addition, as Frank Galassi argues, Herne provides one of the most telling portraits in the nineteenth-century American theatre of the "Economic/Industrial Man," a personification of the economic and social forces that were driving America into the acquisitive mode which would come to dominate it during the rise of industrial capitalism.

Nearly 30 years after *Margaret Fleming*'s premier, William Winter asserted in his *The Life of David Belasco* that "*Margaret Fleming* . . . is one of those crude and completely ineffectual pieces of hysterical didacticism which are from time to time produced on the stage with a view to the dismay of libertines by an exhibition of some of the evil consequences of licentious conduct." Like the plates whose movements precipitate earthquakes, the movement from one literary epoch to the next is rarely as rapid, complete, and uniform as traditional literary periodization implicitly suggests. Winter, a surviving member of those Victorians who longed for the idealized world that had long since receded into memory by 1918, could never quite forgive writers such as Herne for propelling American drama into modernity. Perhaps it is wise that we not forget.

WORKS CONSULTED

Dithmar, Edward A. *Review of Margaret Fleming* by James A. Herne. *New York Times.* Dec. 10, 1891. 4: 7.

Edwards, Herbert J., and Julie A. Herne. *James A. Herne: The Rise of Realism in the American Drama*. Orono: University of Maine Press, 1964.

Galassi, Frank. "The Acquisitive Sense in American Drama." *Praxis*, 2, ii (Winter 1976): 149–155.

Herne, James A. "Art for Truth's Sake in the Drama." *Arena, 17* (1897): 361–70. In *American Drama and Its Critics*, ed. Alan S. Downer. Chicago: University of Chicago Press, 1965. 1–9.

Howells, William Dean. "Editor's Study." *Harper's Monthly*. August 1891: 478.

Perry, John. *James A. Herne: The American Ibsen*. Chicago: Nelson-Hall, 1978.

Quinn, Arthur Hobson. *The Literature of the American People*. New York: Appleton-Century-Crofts, 1951.

Stephens, Judith. "Gender Ideology and Dramatic Convention in Progressive Era Plays, 1890–1920." *Theatre Journal*, 41 (1989): 45–55.

Winter, William. *The Life of David Belasco*. New York: Moffat Yard & Company, 1918.

C H A R A C T E R S*

PHILIP FLEMING . . . . mill owner

DOCTOR LARKIN

JOE FLETCHER

MR FOSTER . . . . manager of the mill

WILLIAMS . . . . foreman

BOBBY . . . . office boy

CHARLEY BURTON

MARGARET FLEMING . . . . wife of Philip Fleming

MARIA BINDLEY . . . . a nurse

MRS BURTON

HANNAH . . . . the cook

JANE . . . . a maid

ACT I

SCENE 1—Philip Fleming's private office at the mill.
SCENE 2—The living-room in Margaret's home.

ACT II

The living-room in Margaret's home.

ACT III

A room in Mrs Burton's cottage.

ACT IV

The living-room in Margaret's home.

The action takes place in Canton, Mass., in 1890.

The play in its earliest form contained several characters not in the revised version, which in its turn includes two not in the first version. To give all the actors in the various versions would therefore lead to confusion. Mrs. Herne acted Margaret in all the productions of 1890, 1891, 1892 and 1894. Mr. Herne acted in 1890, in May, 1891, and in 1892, but not in the Boston production in October, 1891, or in the New York production of 1894.

ACT FIRST

SCENE 1:   *It is a morning in Spring in* PHILIP FLEM-ING'S *private office at the mill. Bright sunlight floods the room at first. Later it becomes cloudy until at the end of the act, rain is falling fitfully. The*

*room is handsomely furnished. There is a table in
the center at the back between two windows. Above
the table and attached to the wall is a cabinet with
a mirror in the door. In the right corner is an
umbrella-stand and hat-rack beside a door leading
to the street. There are two windows below the door. A
little to the right of the center of the room is an arm-
chair, and in the same position on the left is a flat-
top office desk, with a chair on either side. Behind it
on the left is a door leading to the mill. There is a
bunch of flowers on the desk, and two silver frames
holding pictures of* MARGARET *and* LUCY. *There are
also pictures on the wall, including one of the mill
and one of* PHILIP'S *father as a young man.*

As the curtain rises, BOBBY *enters from the left with
a desk-basket of mail, which he places on the desk.
He rearranges the chairs slightly. As he is about to
go out a key is heard in the door on the right.* BOBBY
pauses expectantly. PHILIP FLEMING, *carrying an
umbrella and a rain-coat, enters from the street door
on the right. He is a well dressed, prosperous, happy-
looking man about thirty-five. He hangs up his hat
and coat, and places his umbrella in the stand. Then
he glances carelessly into the hat-rack mirror and
runs his hand lightly over his hair.*

PHILIP: *(in a friendly manner)* Good morning,
    Bobby.

BOBBY: *(grinning appreciatively)* Good morning,
    sir.
    *(*PHILIP *goes to his desk and, shifting one or
    two articles out of his way, begins the duties of
    the day)*

PHILIP: Did you get wet this morning in that big
    shower?

BOBBY: Yes, sir, a little, but I'm all right now.
    *(*PHILIP *glances rapidly through the letters and
    with an eager manner selects two large en-
    velopes, opens one, glances through a document
    it contains and places it in his inside coat-
    pocket with a satisfied smile)*

PHILIP: *(chatting, as he continues his work)* Still
    doing the four mile sprint?

BOBBY: Yes, sir. Oh, I like it, sir—when it don't
    rain.

*(*PHILIP *opens other letters rapidly, glancing
with a quick, comprehensive eye through each
before placing it in the growing heap on the
desk)*

PHILIP: How about the bicycle?

BOBBY: Well, sir, Mr Foster says he thinks he'll
    be able to recommend me for a raise pretty
    soon, if I keep up my record.

PHILIP: *(looking at him quizzically)* A raise,
    Bobby?

BOBBY: Yes, Mr Fleming, and my mother says I
    can save all I get and I guess I'll have a bicycle
    pretty soon then.

PHILIP: How long have you been here?

BOBBY: Six months the day after tomorrow.

PHILIP: *(smiling kindly)* I guess I'll have to talk to
    Foster, myself.

BOBBY: Oh, thank you, Mr Fleming.
    *(*PHILIP *opens a letter which appears to disturb
    him. He pauses over it with a worried frown)*

PHILIP: Ask Mr Foster to come here at once, please.
    (As BOBBY *starts to go)* And tell Williams I want
    to see him.

BOBBY: Yes, sir. *(He goes out the door on the left.
    There is a moment's pause, and then* FOSTER *en-
    ters from the same door. He is a bright, active
    young man about twenty-eight or thirty)*

PHILIP: Good morning, Foster.

FOSTER: Good morning, Mr Fleming.

PHILIP: Here's a letter from the receiver for Reed
    and Vorst. He wants to know if we'll accept an
    immediate settlement of forty percent.

FOSTER: *(becoming serious)* Gee, Mr Fleming, I
    don't see how we can. I was depending on at
    least fifty percent to carry us through the sum-
    mer. It's always a dull season, you know, and—

PHILIP: Why, we have more orders now than we
    had this time last year.

FOSTER: Yes, I know, sir. But, I was going to speak
    to you. The Cotton Exchange Bank doesn't want
    to renew those notes.

PHILIP: Doesn't, eh? Well, then, we'll have to ac-
    cept Reed and Vorst's offer.

FOSTER: I think it would be a mistake just now,
    sir. If we hold out they've got big assets.

PHILIP: Can't be helped. I'm hard-pressed. We're short of ready money.

FOSTER: I don't understand it. We've had a better winter than we've had for years.

PHILIP: *(smiling)* That last little flier I took wasn't as successful as the former ones.

FOSTER: You've been too lenient with the retailers.

PHILIP: "Live and let live" 's my motto.

FOSTER: I'd hate to see anything happen to the mill.

PHILIP: Nothing's going to happen. Let me do the worrying. Our credit's good. I'll raise the money tomorrow.

FOSTER: I hope so, sir. Anything else?

PHILIP: *(giving him the letters)* Wire the answers to these right away. That's all.

FOSTER: All right, sir. *(He goes out)*

(PHILIP takes up a large sheet of paper which contains a report from one of the departments of the mill. He scans it closely and makes some calculations upon a sheet of paper. WILLIAMS enters)

PHILIP: *(looking up)* Good morning, Williams.

(WILLIAMS is quite an old man, but has the attitude of one who knows his business and can do things. He stands with bent shoulders and arms hanging limp. He is chewing tobacco, and speaks with a quick, sharp, New England accent)

WILLIAMS: Good morning, Mr Fleming.

PHILIP: *(holding the report in his hand)* Williams, a short time ago you told me that the main supply belt in the finishing room was only repaired a few times during the last six months. I find here from your report that it has broken down about twice a week since last January. How long does it take to make a repair?

WILLIAMS: Oh, sometimes about ten minutes—other times again, twenty minutes. We have done it in five minutes.

PHILIP: There are about one hundred and ten operators in that room?

WILLIAMS: One hundred and seven.

PHILIP: Why, you should have reported this condition the first week it arose. Poor economy, Williams. *(He makes a few, rapid calculations upon the back of a report)* Twelve hundred dollars lost time. *(He shakes his head)* We could have bought a new belt a year ago and saved money in the bargain.

WILLIAMS: I told Mr Baker several times, sir, in the beginning and he didn't seem to think anything of it.

PHILIP: Well, report all such details to me in the future. *(He writes a few lines rapidly and rings the bell. BOBBY enters briskly)* Tell Mr Foster to get those firms over long distance, and whichever one can make the quickest delivery to place orders there—see?

BOBBY: Yes, sir. *(He has a soiled card in his hand, which he offers to PHILIP with a grin)* A man outside told me to hand you his visiting card.

WILLIAMS: Is that all, sir?

PHILIP: Yes. *(He smiles as he reads the card)* Joe Fletcher! Tell him to come in. *(He resumes work at his desk. WILLIAMS goes out)*

BOBBY: Yes, sir. *(He follows WILLIAMS)*

(After a moment JOE FLETCHER enters. He is a man of middle age, well made but heavy and slouching in manner. He has a keen, shrewd eye in a weak and dissipated face, which is made attractive, nevertheless, by a genial and ingratiating smile. He is wearing a shabby linen coat called a "duster," which hangs, crushed and limp, from his neck to his ankles. Strung from his left shoulder is a cord hung with sponges of various sizes. Several lengths of chamois are dangling with the sponges across his breast and back, draping his right hip and leg. In one hand he has a weather beaten satchel. He carries by a leather thong a heavy stone hanging from a cracked plate. There are two holes in the rim of the plate through one of which runs the thong by which it is carried. The other, the big stone, is fastened to it with a piece of chain. He carries it unconscious of its weight. There is a pervading sense of intimacy between the man and his equipment, and from his battered hat to his spreading shoes the stains of the road, like a varnish, bind them together in a mellow fellowship)

PHILIP: Hello, Joe. (*He looks at him with humorous curiosity*)

JOE: (*light-heartedly*) How d'do, Mr Fleming. (*His voice is broken and husky. He gives a little, dry cough now and then in an ineffectual attempt to clear it. He crosses to the corner of the table, and shows by his step that his feet are sore and swollen*)

PHILIP: What are you doing now, Joe?

JOE: (*indicating his effects. While he talks he places the stone against a corner of the table on the floor, and puts the valise on the edge of the table*) Traveling merchant; agent for Brummell's Giant Cement; professional corn doctor—soft and hard corns—calluses—bunions removed instantly, ingrowing nails treated 'thout pain or loss of blood—*or* money *re*funded. Didn't ye read m'card? (*He coughs*)

PHILIP: (*laughing*) Well, not all of it, Joe.

JOE: (*reminiscently*) Inventor of Dr. Fletcher's famous cough mixture, warranted to cure coughs—colds, hoarseness and loss o' voice. An infallible remedy fur all chronic conditions of the *pull-mon*-ary organs. (*He coughs again*) When not too fur gone. (*He takes a labelled bottle, containing a brown mixture from his inside pocket, shakes it and holds it up proudly before* PHILIP) Kin I sell ye a bottle? (*He smiles ingratiatingly*)

PHILIP: (*smiling but shaking his head*) No, Joe, I guess not today.

JOE: (*opening the satchel insinuatingly*) Mebbe a few boxes o' corn salve? It's great. (PHILIP *shakes his head*) Would ye like to consider a box o' cement?

PHILIP: (*still smiling*) No, but I'll take one of those big sponges.

JOE: I thought I could sell ye something. (*He unhooks a large sponge and lays it upon the desk.* PHILIP *hands him a bill. He takes it carelessly, looks at it, shakes his head regretfully and puts it into his pocket. Then he feels in his other pocket and taps his vest pockets*) Gosh, I'm sorry, but I ain't got a bit of change.

PHILIP: Oh, never mind the change, Joe. (*He laughs indulgently*)

JOE: (*regretfully*) Well, I'd feel better if I *hed* the change. (JOE *has been standing to the left of the desk*) Kin I set down fur a minnit, Mr Fleming? M'feet gets so tired.

PHILIP: Yes, Joe, sit down.

JOE: I got pretty wet a while ago in that shower. My, but it did come down.

PHILIP: (*warmly*) Perhaps you'd like a hot drink? (*He indicates with a nod of the head, the cabinet back of* JOE, *as the latter is about to sit down.* JOE *shows a lively interest*)

JOE: (*glancing at* PHILIP *with a shy twinkle in his eye*) Oh, kin I, Mr Fleming? Thank ye. (*He shuffles over to the cabinet, opens the door and gloats over the vision of joy which greets him. He selects a bottle*)

PHILIP: Hold on, Joe. Wait for some hot water.

JOE: (*hastily*) No, thank ye. I'm afraid I'd be like the Irishman in the dream.

PHILIP: What was that, Joe?

JOE: (*as he pours out a generous portion*) Well, the Irishman was dreaming that he went to see the priest, and the priest asked him to have a drink. "I will, thank ye kindly," says Pat. "Is it hot or cold ye'll have it?" says the priest? "Hot, if ye plaze, yer Riverence," says Pat, and while they were waiting fur the hot water, Pat wakes up. "Bad luck to me," says he, "why didn't I take it cold?" (*He drains the glass, smacks his lips and chuckles*) My, but that's good stuff! Mr Fleming, are ye as fond of it yourself as ye used to be?

PHILIP: (*smiling and shaking his head*) No, Joe. I've got through with all that foolishness. I've sowed my wild oats.

JOE: (*chuckling as he sits in the chair*) You must have got a pretty slick crop out o' yourn.

PHILIP: Every man gets a pretty full crop of those, Joe, before he gets through.

JOE: Ye've turned over a new leaf, eh?

PHILIP: Yes—married.

JOE: Married?

PHILIP: Yes, and got a baby.

JOE: Thet so! Did ye marry out'n the mill?

PHILIP: Oh, no. She was a Miss Thorp, of Niagara. *(He hands the picture of the child to* JOE*)*

JOE: *(showing interest immediately, and gazing at the picture, while gradually a gentle responsive smile plays over his features. He says, admiringly)* By George! that's a great baby! *(He gives a chuckling laugh at it)* Boy?

PHILIP: *(proudly)* No. Girl!

JOE: Thet so! Should a thought you'd a wanted a boy. *(With sly significance, and chuckling at his own joke)* Ye've hed so many girls.

PHILIP: *(he laughs lightly)* Tut, tut, Joe, no more of that for me. *(He hands him the frame containing* MARGARET'S *picture)* My wife.

JOE: *(his expression becoming grave as the sweetness and dignity of the face touches him. He takes a long breath)* My, but that's a fine face. Gee, if she's as good as that, you're a lucky man, Mr Fleming.

PHILIP: Yes, Joe, I've got more than I deserve, I guess. *(He becomes serious for the first time and a shadow flits over his face. He sighs)*

JOE: *(sympathetically)* Oh, I understand just how you feel. I'm married m'self. *(He sits down facing the audience, his hands clasped, his thumbs gently rolling over each other. A far-away tender look comes into his eyes)*

PHILIP: *(surprised)* Married? *(*JOE *nods his head)* Where's your wife?

JOE: Left me. *(He gives a sigh of self pity)*

PHILIP: *(touched)* Left you! *(he shakes his head compassionately, then the thought comes to him)* If my wife left me I'd kill myself.

JOE: *(philosophically)* Oh, no, no, ye wouldn't. You'd get over it, just as I did. *(He sighs)*

PHILIP: How did it happen? What did you do?

JOE: *(innocently)* Not a durn thing! She was a nice, German woman, too. She kept a gent's furnishing store down in South Boston, and I married her.

PHILIP: *(recovering himself and speaking gaily)* Oh, Joe. *(He shakes his head in mock reproval)*

You married her for her money, eh? *(He laughs at him)*

JOE: *(ingenuously)* No, I didn't, honest. I thought I might get a whack at the till once in a while, but I didn't.

PHILIP: *(quizzing him)* Why not, Joe?

JOE: She fixed me up a pack and sent me out on the road to sell goods, and when I got back, she was gone. There was a new sign on the store, "Isaac Litchenstein, Ladies and Gents' Drygoods." *(He draws a big sigh)*

PHILIP: And you've never seen her since?

JOE: *(shaking his head sadly)* No, siree, never!

PHILIP: *(serious again, impressed by* JOE*)* That's pretty tough, Joe.

*(*BOBBY *enters)*

BOBBY: Doctor Larkin would like to see you, sir.

JOE: *(gathering himself and his merchandise together)* Well, I guess I'll get out and drum up a few sales. Much obliged to you, Mr Fleming.

PHILIP: Oh, stop at the house, Joe. Mrs Fleming might want something. It's the old place on Linden Street.

JOE: Got a dog?

PHILIP: Yes.

JOE: That settles it.

PHILIP: Only a pug, Joe.

JOE: Oh, a snorer. I'll sell him a bottle of cough mixture. *(As* DR LARKIN *enters)* Hello, Doc! How are you? Raining?

*(*JOE *goes to the door on the right, crossing the* DOCTOR *who is walking toward* PHILIP *on the left)*

DOCTOR: *(looking at him, mystified)* Good morning, sir. No, it's not raining. (*JOE *goes out.* DR LARKIN *is a tall, gaunt man who looks older than he is, with quite a stoop in his shoulders. He has dark brown hair and a beard, streaked with grey, and soft, kind blue eyes. He carries the medicine satchel of a homeopathic physician. His manner is usually distant and cold but extremely quiet and gentle. In the opening of this scene he is perturbed and irritated, later he becomes stern and authoritative)*

PHILIP: Good morning, Doctor Larkin.

DOCTOR: *(turning to* PHILIP*)* Who is that fellow? *(He looks after* JOE *as he goes out)*

PHILIP: Don't you remember him? That's Joe Fletcher. (PHILIP *is standing to the right of the desk, and* DOCTOR LARKIN *at the left center of the stage)*

DOCTOR: Is that Joe Fletcher? Why he used to be quite a decent sort of fellow. Wasn't he a foreman here in your father's time?

PHILIP: Yes, he was one of the best men in the mill.

DOCTOR: *(shaking his head)* He is a sad example of what liquor and immorality will bring a man to. He has indulged his appetites until he has no real moral nature left.

PHILIP: *(lightly)* Oh, I don't think Joe ever had much "moral nature."
(The sunlight leaves the room. It is growing cloudy outside)

DOCTOR: Every man has a moral nature. In this case it is love of drink that has destroyed it. There are some men who are moral lepers, even lacking the weakness of the tippler as an excuse.

PHILIP: Have you been to the house, doctor? About midnight Margaret thought little Lucy had a fever. She was going to call you up— but—

DOCTOR: *(abruptly)* She would not have found me in at midnight.

PHILIP: Ah, is that so? Someone very ill? *(The telephone rings)* Excuse me, doctor. Hello. Oh, is that you, Margaret? How is Lucy now? Good! I knew she'd be all right. Yes, of course. Do— bring her. *(To the* DOCTOR*)* She's bringing baby to the 'phone. Hello, Lucy. Many happy returns of the day. Good-bye. Yes, I'll be home at twelve sharp. Apple pie? Yes, of course, I like it. That is, *your* apple pie. *(He leaves the phone with a joyous air)* This is baby's birthday, you know, doctor.

DOCTOR: I've just left a baby *(He speaks bitterly, looking at* PHILIP *significantly)* that should never have had a birthday.

PHILIP: *(without noticing the* DOCTOR'S *manner, he goes to the cabinet and, taking a box of cigars, offers the box to the* DOCTOR*)* Why, Doctor, you're morbid today. Take a cigar, it will quiet your nerves.
(The rain begins to fall, beating heavily against the windows)

DOCTOR: No, thank you. *(With a subtle shade of repugnance in his tone)* I'll smoke one of my own. (PHILIP *smiles indulgently, goes to the desk, sits in the chair to the left of it, lights a cigar, leans back luxuriously, with his hands in his pockets, and one leg over the other, and tips back the legs of the chair)*

PHILIP: *(carelessly)* What's the matter, doctor? You used to respect my cigars.

DOCTOR: *(hotly)* I used to respect you.

PHILIP: *(rather surprised but laughing good-naturedly)* Well, doctor, and don't you now? *(He is bantering him)*

DOCTOR: *(quietly but sternly)* No, I don't.

PHILIP: *(smoking placidly)* Good Lord—why?

DOCTOR: *(his satchel resting upon his knees, his hands clasping the metal top, he leans over a trifle and, looking impressively into* PHILIP'S *face, says, in a low, calm voice)* At two o'clock last night Lena Schmidt gave birth to a child.

PHILIP: *(becoming livid with amazement and fear, and staring blankly before him, the cigar dropping from his parted lips)* In God's name, how did they come to send for you?

DOCTOR: Doctor Taylor—he called me in consultation. He was frightened after the girl had been in labor thirty-six hours.

PHILIP: *(murmuring to himself)* Thirty-six hours! Good God! *(There is a pause, then he partly recovers himself)* I suppose she told you?

DOCTOR: She told me nothing. It was a lucky thing for you that I was there. The girl was delirious.

PHILIP: Delirious! Well, I've done all I could for her, doctor.

DOCTOR: Have you? *(His tone is full of scorn)*

PHILIP: She's had all the money she wanted.

DOCTOR: Has she? *(He speaks in the same tone)*

PHILIP: I tried to get her away months ago, but she wouldn't do it. She was as stubborn as a mule.

DOCTOR: Strange she should want to remain near the father of her child, isn't it?

PHILIP: If she'd done as I told her to, this thing would never have happened.

DOCTOR: You'd have forced some poor devil to run the risk of state's prison. By God, you're worse than I thought you were.

PHILIP: Why, doctor, you must think I'm—

DOCTOR: I don't think anything about it. I know just what brutes such men as you are.

PHILIP: Well, I'm not wholly to blame. You don't know the whole story, doctor.

DOCTOR: I don't want to know it. The *girl's* not to blame. She's a product of her environment. Under present social conditions, she'd probably have gone wrong anyhow. But you! God Almighty! If we can't look for decency in men like you—representative men,—where in God's name are we to look for it, I'd like to know?

PHILIP: If my wife hears of this, my home will be ruined.

DOCTOR: *(scornfully)* Your home! Your home! It is just such damn scoundrels as you that make and destroy homes.

PHILIP: Oh, come now, doctor, aren't you a little severe?

DOCTOR: Severe! Severe! Why, do you realize, if this thing should become known, it will stir up a stench that will offend the moral sense of every man, woman and child in this community?

PHILIP: Well, after all, I'm no worse than other men. Why, I haven't seen the girl for months.

DOCTOR: Haven't you? Well, then suppose you go and see her now.

PHILIP: *(he springs to his feet)* I'll do nothing of the sort.

DOCTOR: Yes, you will. She shan't lie there and die like a dog.

PHILIP: *(he walks around the room greatly perturbed)* I tell you I'll not go!

DOCTOR: Yes, you will.

PHILIP: *(he comes over to the* DOCTOR *and looks down upon him)* What'll you do if I don't?

DOCTOR: I don't know, but you'd best go and see that girl.

PHILIP: *(he turns away)* Well, what do you want me to say to her?

DOCTOR: Lie to her as you have before. Tell her you love her.

PHILIP: I never lied to her. I never told her I loved her.

DOCTOR: Faugh!

PHILIP: I tell you I never did!

DOCTOR: *(rising from his chair)* You'd better get Mrs Fleming away from here until this thing blows over. When I think of a high-minded, splendid little woman like her married to a man like you—ugh! *(The* DOCTOR *goes out quickly)* *(*PHILIP, *left alone, walks about like an old man, seems dazed for a moment, then goes mechanically to the telephone)*

PHILIP: Lindon, 3721. Margaret. *(He speaks in a broken, hushed voice)* Margaret! Yes, it's I, Philip. Yes! Well, I'm tired. No, I can't come home now. I will not be home to luncheon. I have a business engagement. No, I cannot break it off. It's too important. Eh? Why, with a man from Boston. Yes, certainly, I will, just as soon as I can get away. Yes, dear—I will—good-bye. *(Just before he finishes,* FOSTER *enters)* Hello, Foster.

FOSTER: *(consulting a memorandum)* I couldn't get the Harry Smith Company, New York, until noon, sir. They say that the belting can be shipped by fast express at once. The Boston people want ten cents a square foot more than they ask, but we can save that in time and express rates.

PHILIP: When would the New York shipment get here?

FOSTER: At the earliest, tomorrow afternoon.

PHILIP: White and Cross can ship at once, you say?

FOSTER: Yes, sir.

PHILIP: Well, give them the order. Their stuff is better, anyhow. Have a covered wagon at the station for the four-ten train. Keep enough men over time tonight to put it up.

FOSTER: Yes, sir, the sooner it's done, the better.

PHILIP: Yes, Williams is getting old. He's not the best man for that finishing room. Put him where you can keep an eye on him. He's all right. I have an appointment and will not be in the office again today. Get the interest on those notes off.

FOSTER: Yes, I've attended to that already. Anything else?

PHILIP: No.

FOSTER: All right, sir. Good morning.

(PHILIP *who has braced himself for this, relaxes again. The rain continues. He goes about the room, lights a cigar, puts on a rain-coat, looks at his watch, buttons his coat, all the while sunk in deep thought. He takes his umbrella and hat and goes out quietly, shutting the door so that the click of the latch is heard, as the curtain falls*)

SCENE 2: *The scene is the living-room in* MARGARET'S *home. At the back large glass doors open on to a spacious porch with a garden beyond. There is a fire-place with logs burning, in the corner on the left, and beside it a French window opening on the garden. Below it is a door leading to another room. There is another door on the right going to the main part of the house. There is a table in the center, a baby grand piano on the lower right, and a baby carriage close by the doors at the back. The room is furnished in exquisite taste showing in its distinct character the grace and individuality of a well-bred woman.*

MARGARET *is seated in a low rocking-chair near the fire with the baby in her lap. A large bath towel is spread across her knees. She is exquisitely dressed in an evening gown.*

MARIA BINDLEY, *the nurse-maid, is dressed in a black dress, cap and apron. She is a middle-aged German woman, dark in complexion, and of medium build and height. She speaks with a not too pronounced German accent. She is gathering up the baby's garments which are scattered about* MARGARET'S *feet. She is furtively weeping and makes an occasional effort to overcome her emotion.* MARGARET *is putting the last touches to the baby's night toilet. She is laughing and murmuring mother talk to her. A shaded lamp is burning on the table to the right. The effect of the light is subdued. The glare of the fire is the high note, making a soft radiance about* MARGARET *and the child.* MARIA *is in the shadow, except as she flits into the light whenever she moves near* MARGARET. *The sound of the rain beating against the windows, is heard now and then.*

MARGARET: *(in a low, laughing tone)* No—no—no! You little beggar. You've had your supper! *(She fastens the last two or three buttons of her dress)* No more! Time to go to sleep now! No use staying awake any longer for naughty father. Two, whole, hours—late! No, he doesn't care a bit about you; not a bit! *(She shakes her head)* No, nor me either. Never mind, darling, we'll punish him well for this. Yes, we will. Perhaps we'll leave *him* some day, and then we'll see how he likes being left alone. Naughty, bad father—isn't he? *Yes he is!* Staying away all day! Never mind, ladybird—hush, go to sleep now—Mother loves her! Go to sleep—close your eyes. *(This is all said in a cooing, soothing voice. She begins to sing a lullaby)* Go—to—sleep—blossom—go to sl—

(MARIA *comes close to* MARGARET *and picks up two little socks. As she rises, she sniffs in an effort to suppress her tears. This attracts* MARGARET'S *attention, and immediately she is all commiseration*)

MARGARET: Don't cry, Maria—please don't—it distresses me to see you cry.

MARIA: *(smiling a little at* MARGARET'S *sympathy. As she talks, she smooths the socks and folds them)* I cannot help it, Mrs Fleming—I am an unhappy woman. I try not to cry, but I cannot keep back de tears. *(She puts the socks in the basket on the table)* I have had an unhappy life—my fadder vas a brute. *(She picks up the dress and shakes it)* My first husband, Ralph Bindley, vas a goot, honest man. *(She puts the dress in the basket)* Und my second husband vas dot tramp vot vas here dis morning. Vat I have told you aboudt already. *(She gathers together the other garments)* Und now my sister—my little Lena—is dying.

MARGARET: *(in dismay)* Dying! Why, you didn't tell me *that*, Maria!

MARIA: Vell, she is not dying yust this very moment, but the doctor says she vill never leave dot bed alive. My sweet little Lena! My lovely little sister. I have nursed her, Mrs Fleming, yust like you nurse your baby now.

MARGARET: *(holding the child to her breast)* What did you say her name was?

MARIA: *(working mechanically and putting the things neatly away)* Lena,—Lena Schmidt. She does not go by my name—she goes by my fadder's name.

MARGARET: And, you say, she ran away from you?

MARIA: Ya—I tried to find her every place. I hunted high und low, but she does not come, und von day I meet an olt friend on Vashington Street, Chris Anderson, und Chris, he tell me that two or three weeks before he see her by the public gartens. Und she vas valking by the arm of a fine, handsome gentleman—und she look smiling and happy, und Chris, he says dot he knows *dot* gentleman—*dot* he vas a rich man vot lives down in Canton where Chris vonce worked when he comes to dis country first.

MARGARET: And didn't you ask the man's name?

MARIA: Ach, I forget. Und Chris go back to de olt country, und I never find out. Und den I tink maybe she is married to dot man—und she is ashamed of me and dot miserable husband of mine. I say to myself, "I vill go and see—und find oudt if she is happy." Den I vill go far away, where she vill never see me again. Und I come here to Canton, und at last I find her—und Ach Gott! She is going to be a mutter—und she is no man's vife! *(She has been weeping silently but*

has continued to work, only pausing at some point in her story that moved her)

MARGARET: *(deeply touched)* Did she tell you the man's name?

MARIA: Ach! No! You could not drag dot oudt of her mit red-hot irons. She says she loves dis man, und she vill make him no trouble. But, by Gott, I vill find dot man oudt, und I vill choke it from his troat. *(She is beside herself with vindictive passion)*

MARGARET: *(terrified at her ferocity and crushing her child to her breast)* Oh, Maria—don't— please don't! You frighten me!

MARIA: *(at once all humility)* Excuse me, Mrs Fleming. I did not mean to do dot.

MARGARET: *(kindly)* You need not remain any longer. I can manage baby myself. You had best go to your sister at once. If I can be of any help to you, please tell me, won't you?

MARIA: Ya, Mrs Fleming, I tank you. Und if she is vorse maybe I stay all night.

MARGARET: Yes, certainly. You need not come back tonight.

MARIA: *(very softly and humbly)* I am much obliged to you, Mrs Fleming.

MARGARET: *(as MARIA is going)* Oh! You had best take my rain-coat.

MARIA: Ah, you are very goot, Mrs Fleming. *(She has finished her work and is going but hesitates a moment and turns back)* If you please, don't tell Mr Fleming about me und my poor sister!

MARGARET: *(slightly annoyed)* Decidedly not! Why should I tell such things to him?

MARIA: Vell—men don't have sympathy mit peoples like us. He is a fine gentleman, und if he knowed about *her*—he might not like to have *me* by his vife und child. He might tink *I* vas as badt as she was. Good night, Mrs Fleming.

MARGARET: Good night, Maria. No need to hurry back in the morning. *(There is a wistful sympathy in her face. As her eyes rest upon the door through which MARIA has passed, she is lost in thought. Presently a door slams, then she is all alert with expectation. There is a moment's pause, she listens then quickly puts the child in the baby carriage and runs to the door)* Is that you, Philip?

JANE: *(outside)* No, ma'am, it is not Mr Fleming. It was only the post man.

(MARGARET turns away with a sigh of disappointment, goes to the French window and peers out at the rain. The MAID enters with several letters, leaves them on the table and goes out. MARGARET turns from the window, brushes the tears away impatiently, and drifts purposelessly across the room toward the right, her hands clasped behind her back. Finding herself at the piano she listlessly sits before it and plays a plaintive air, softly. Then suddenly she dashes into a prelude to a gay love song. As she sings half through a stanza, the song gradually loses spirit. Her hands grow heavy over the keys, her voice breaks, and the words come slow and faltering. She ends by breaking into tears, with her head lowered and her fingers resting idly upon the keys. The child attracts her and she goes quickly to her. She laughs through her tears into the wide-open eyes, and begins scolding her for not going to sleep. Soft endearing notes come and go in her voice. A tender joy takes possession of her spirit. She takes the child in her arms)

MARGARET: Well, my lady, wide awake! Come, come, no more nonsense, now! No. Go to sleep! Late hours—will—certainly spoil—your beauty. Yes! Close up your eyes—quick! Come! There, that's nice. She's a sweet, good child! *(She hums)* Go—to—sleep! *(She sways slowly from right to left, then swinging with a rhythmic step with the lullaby, she lilts softly)* Blow, blow, Blossom go—into the world below—I am the west wind wild and strong—blossoms must go when they hear my song. *(She puts out the lamp, leaving the room in the warm glare of the firelight)* Go, little blossom, go—into the world below. Rain, rain, rain is here. Blossoms must learn to weep. *(She reaches the French window. As she turns PHILIP is seen through the filmy curtains. He enters unnoticed)* I am the east wind, bleak and cold, poor little blossoms their petals must fold.

Weep, little blossoms, weep, into your cradles creep. *(She is unconscious of PHILIP'S presence. His rain-coat and hat are dripping wet. He is pale and weary, his manner is listless and abstracted and he looks as though he had been wandering about in the rain for hours. He drifts into the room. MARGARET turns around and takes a step, her eyes upon the child, then her lullaby grows indistinct as she notices that the baby is asleep. Another step takes her into PHILIP'S arms. She gives a cry of alarm)*

MARGARET: . . . Oh, Philip! You frightened me! Why did you do that?

PHILIP: Why are you in the dark, Margaret? *(He goes toward her as if to take her in his arms)* Dearest!

MARGARET: *(drawing back from him with a shade of petulance)* You're all wet. Don't come near baby. She was wakeful. I've put her to sleep. Where have you been all day?

PHILIP: Didn't I tell you over the 'phone I had an engagement?

MARGARET: *(as she flits swiftly into the room on the left)* Did it take you all day to keep it? *(She remains in the room long enough to put the child in the crib and then returns)*

PHILIP: Yes. A lot of things came up—that I didn't expect. I've been detained. *(He is still standing where she left him)*

MARGARET: *(turning up the lamp)* Why, dear, look! Your umbrella is dripping all over the floor.

PHILIP: *(noticing the little puddle of water)* Oh, how stupid of me! *(He hurries out the door on the right, removes his hat and rain-coat, leaves the umbrella, and returns quickly)*

(MARGARET, meanwhile has mopped up the water. Then she turns on the lamp on the table to the right)

MARGARET: *(reproachfully)* We've been awfully lonesome here all day, baby and I!

PHILIP: *(by the fire)* Forgive me, sweetheart. I've had a very hard day.

MARGARET: Did you forget it was Lucy's birthday?

PHILIP: *(smiling gravely)* No, I didn't forget. You have both been in my mind the whole day.

MARGARET: *(glowing with love and a welcome that she refused to give until now)* Oh, Philip! *(She throws herself in his arms)* It's good to get you back. So good! *(After a moment she rings the bell. The* MAID *answers)* Jane, I wish you would serve dinner in here.

JANE: Yes, Mrs Fleming.

PHILIP: *(drawing her close to him again)* Dear little wife! *(As though a long time had passed since he parted from her)*

JANE: *(coming in with a tray containing food and silver, and going to the center table)* Shall I lay the table here, Mrs Fleming?

MARGARET: No—here—cosy—by the fire. *(JANE dresses the table deftly and without bustle. She goes away and returns with the dinner)* You need not return, Jane. I'll ring if we need you.

JANE: Very well, Mrs Fleming. *(She goes off)*

PHILIP: *(sitting to the right of the table, and taking a large envelope from his pocket, he withdraws a bank book and hands it to* MARGARET, *who is about to sit down on the left)* Here, Margaret—I want you to look over that.

MARGARET: *(taking the book and reading the cover)* Margaret Fleming in account with Boston Providence Savings Bank. *(She opens the book and reads)* "By deposit, May 3, 1890, $5,000." Five thousand dollars! Oh, Philip!

PHILIP: *(smiling complacently)* There's something else.

MARGARET: Yes? *(*PHILIP *nods his head, and hands her a large envelope which he has taken from his pocket. She looks at it and reads)* "Margaret Fleming, guardian for Lucy Fleming." *(She takes a document from the envelope)* A certificate for $20,000 worth of United States bonds, maturing 1930. Why, Philip! How wonderful. But, can you afford it? *(He smiles and nods his head, and then begins to serve the dinner.* MARGARET, *in childish joy, rushes to the door of the room where the child is)* Oh, baby! Lucy! You are rich, rich! *(She stops and peeps in)* Oh, my, I must not wake her. The little heiress! *(She sits at the table and begins to serve)*

PHILIP: *(handing her another envelope. Tenderly)* For you Margaret!

MARGARET: *(taking it and becoming breathless as she reads it)* It's a deed for this house and all the land! Ah, Philip, how generous you are, and this is what has kept you away all day! And I was cross with you. *(Tears come to her eyes)* Forgive me, dear, please do. *(She goes to him and kneels by his side)* But, why do you do all this? What need? What necessity for me to have a deed of property from you?

PHILIP: Well, things have not been going just our way at the mill. The new tariff laws may help some, but I doubt it. At all events, before anything serious—

MARGARET: *(a little awed)* Serious?

PHILIP: Well, you never can be sure. At any rate, in times of stress a business man should protect his family.

MARGARET: Is there danger—of—trouble?

PHILIP: No! I hope not. I think I'll be able to tide it over.

MARGARET: But, dear—you—this property, is worth a lot of money. Why not sell it? Wouldn't that be a great help? A resource in case—

PHILIP: Sell the home?

MARGARET: No, sell the house. The home is where we are. *(She rises and stands partly back of his chair with her arms about his neck)* Where *love* is—no matter *where*, just so long as we three are there together. A big house—a little house—of course, I do love this place, where you were born, and baby— *(Taking a long breath)* It's very precious—but— *(She has moved back to the head of the table and now lays down the deed)* I cannot take it, dear. It frightens me. It's too valuable—all this—land—no—let us guard it together and if bad times come, it will be—a fine thing to have—

PHILIP: *(protesting)* Now, my dear!

MARGARET: I don't want the responsibility. Suppose something happened to me. *(She sits at the table, on the left)*

PHILIP: Ah—Margaret—

MARGARET: *(laughing)* Well—I just said "suppose."

PHILIP: *(laughing)* Well—*don't say it.* We'll think of nothing "suppose." *Nothing*, but bright—*beautiful* things.

MARGARET: Come, dear, eat. I should think you were famished. You've touched nothing yet.

PHILIP: I don't feel hungry. I'm tired—awfully tired.

MARGARET: No wonder, after all you've been through today. I'll make up a cup of tea. *(She rings the bell.* JANE *enters)* Boiling water, Jane, please, and bring the tea things. *(While she is busy over the tea things she stops and looks at him quizzically)* Who was that tramp you sent here this morning?

PHILIP: *(innocently)* What tramp?

MARGARET: Why, the one with the plate and the big stone—the cough medicine,—the sponges and *the voice. (She imitates* JOE*)*

PHILIP: *(laughing)* Ah, he's not a tramp—that's Joe Fletcher.

MARGARET: Did you know that he was Maria's husband?

PHILIP: *(amazed)* What! Maria's husband? What did he say to her?

MARGARET: *(smiling reminiscently)* He didn't say much—*She* did all the talking.

PHILIP: What did *she* say?

MARGARET: I don't know. She spoke in German. I think, she was swearing at him. When I came she had him by the ears and was trying to pull his head off. Then she got him to the floor and threw him down the front steps. It was the funniest thing I ever saw. I couldn't help laughing, yet my heart ached for her.

PHILIP: Poor Joe! That's the second time she's thrown him out.

MARGARET: She never did that before?

PHILIP: He says she did.

MARGARET: Well, she didn't. He robbed her and left her.

PHILIP: What?

MARGARET: She went out on the road to sell goods and left him in charge of the shop. When she came back he was gone and he had sold out the place to a secondhand dealer.

PHILIP: *(in wonderment)* What a liar that fellow is!

MARGARET: Well, if he told you any other story—he certainly is. *(She notices a change in his face)* Why, Philip! You look awfully white! Are you ill? Are you keeping anything from me? Oh, please tell me—do. Let me share your trouble. *(She goes to him, and puts her arms about his shoulders, with her face against his as she finishes the last line)*

PHILIP: No—no—dear heart—nothing! There's nothing more to tell. I'm very tired.

MARGARET: Oh, how selfish of me. You should have gone to bed the moment you came.

PHILIP: I'll be all right in the morning. I must have caught a chill. *(He shudders)* My blood seems to be congealed.

MARGARET: *(alarmed)* Oh, my dear—my poor boy! It was a dreadful thing you did. *(He starts guiltily)* Going about in the rain all day. *(She goes swiftly into the room on the left and returns with a handsome dressing gown and slippers.* PHILIP *has gone over to the fire)* I must give you some aconite. A hot drink—and a mustard foot bath. *(She fusses over him, helps him to get into his dressing gown, and warms his slippers by the fire)*

PHILIP: I don't think I need anything, dear, but a hot drink, perhaps, and a night's rest. I'll be all right in the morning. I think I'll take a little brandy.

MARGARET: *(quickly)* I'll get it for you, dear. Keep by the fire. *(She rushes out the door on the right, and returns quickly with a silver tray holding a cut-glass decanter of brandy and a glass. She pours out some and holds up the glass)* Is that enough?

PHILIP: Plenty—thank you! *(He drinks it, while* MARGARET *replaces the tray on the small table at the back)*

MARGARET: Now, dear, I'll look after that mustard bath.

PHILIP: *(protesting)* Oh, Margaret, please don't bother. I really don't need it.

MARGARET: *(laughing at him)* Yes, you do. *(She shakes her finger threateningly at him)* You might just as well make up your mind that you've got to have it.

PHILIP: *(smiling resignedly)* All right—"*boss.*"

MARGARET: *(laughing at him as she starts to go)* You know, Philip, dear, you gave me the strangest feeling when you stood there—the rain dripping from you—you didn't look a bit like yourself. *(She gives an apologetic laugh)* You gave me a dreadful fright. Just like a spirit! A lost spirit. *(She laughs again)* Now, wasn't that silly of me? *(She runs off to the right, still laughing)*

(PHILIP sits in the fire light looking sadly after her, as the curtain falls)

ACT SECOND

The scene is the same as the Second Scene of the First Act. The large doors at the back are open showing a luxuriant garden in brilliant sunshine. The baby is in her carriage by the garden door. MARGARET, *in a dainty house dress, is seated in a low chair in the center of the room, mending one of the baby's dresses.* DR LARKIN, *sitting at the table on the left with his back turned to her, is folding little packages of medicine.* MARGARET *looks happy and contented as she chats with him.*

DOCTOR: You say you have no pain in the eyes?

MARGARET: No pain at all . . . only, once in awhile there is . . . a . . . sort of a dimness.

DOCTOR: Yes, a dimness.

MARGARET: As if my eyes were tired.

DOCTOR: Yes!

MARGARET: When I read too long, or . . .

DOCTOR: *(turning about and looking at her)* Do you know what would be a good thing for you to do?

MARGARET: What, doctor?

DOCTOR: Wear glasses.

MARGARET: Why, doctor, aren't you dreadful! *(She laughs at him)* Why, I'd look a sight.

DOCTOR: Well, it would be a good idea, all the same. You should wear glasses when you are reading or sewing, at least.

MARGARET: *(laughing gaily at him)* Well, I'll do nothing of the sort. Time enough for me to wear glasses, years and years from now.

DOCTOR: *(smiling indulgently)* It would be a good thing to do now. How is "Topsy" this morning?

MARGARET: *(glancing proudly in the direction of the baby)* Oh, she's blooming.

DOCTOR: Mrs Fleming, any time you want to sell that baby, Mrs Larkin and I will give you ten thousand dollars for her.

MARGARET: *(laughing and beaming with pride)* Yes . . . doctor . . . *when* we *want* to sell her. How is Mrs Larkin?

DOCTOR: She's doing very nicely. I'm going to try to get her up to the mountains this summer. *(He finishes the packages)* There . . . take one of these powders three times a day. Rest your eyes as much as possible. Don't let anything fret or worry you, and keep out-doors all you can. *(He closes the bag after putting a couple of bottles and a small medicine case in it)*

MARGARET: Oh, doctor, aren't you going to leave something for Philip?

DOCTOR: *(giving a dry, little grunt)* Hum! I forgot about him. *(Standing by the table, he takes a small case from his satchel, removes two large bottles of pellets from it, fills two phials from them and makes a number upon the cork of each with a fountain pen)* You say he was pretty wet when he came home last night?

MARGARET: Yes, and tired out. He had a very hard day, I think. I never saw him so completely fagged. It seemed to me he had been tramping in the rain for hours. I gave him a good scolding too, I tell you. I doctored him up as well as I could and put him to bed. *(Smiling contentedly)* He's as bright as a lark this morning, but all the same, I insisted upon his remaining home for a rest.

DOCTOR: You take good care of him, don't you? *(He beams upon her kindly)*

MARGARET: *(playfully)* I've got to . . . he's all I have, and men like Philip are not picked up every day, now, I tell you.

DOCTOR: *(drily)* No, men like Philip Fleming are certainly not to be found easily.

MARGARET: I hope there's nothing wrong with him. I was worried last night. You know, he has been working awfully hard lately.

DOCTOR: *(kindly)* Now, don't fret about imaginary ills. He's probably a little over-worked. It might be a good idea to have him go away for a week or two.

MARGARET: *(entering into the suggestion)* Yes . . . a little trip somewhere would help him a lot, I'm sure.

DOCTOR: *(holding up his finger)* But, you must go with him, though.

(MARGARET, by this time, is standing up, with the baby's dress tucked under her arm. She takes stitches as she talks)

MARGARET: *(eagerly)* Of course! I wouldn't let him go alone. Somebody might steal him from me. *(She smiles)*

DOCTOR: *(snapping the clasp of his satchel, vehemently murmurs under his breath)* Hum! They'd bring him back mighty quick, I guess. *(He turns to her)* Give him these. Tell him to take two alternately every hour.

MARGARET: *(taking the phials, and nodding her head as if to remember)* Two every hour—thank you.

(PHILIP enters from the garden, gaily humming an air. He has a freshly plucked rose in his hand)

PHILIP: Good morning, doctor.

DOCTOR: *(coldly)* Good morning.

MARGARET: *(noticing the rose, regretfully)* Oh, Philip, you plucked that rose.

PHILIP: Yes, isn't it lovely? It's the first of the season. *(He smells it)*

MARGARET: Yes, and I've been watching it. I wanted it to open yesterday for baby's birthday.

PHILIP: *(playfully)* It saved itself for today for baby's mother. *(He puts it on her breast)*

MARGARET: *(pleased)* Well, I'd rather it had bloomed yesterday for her. Excuse me, doctor, I must run into the kitchen. We have a new cook and she needs watching.

PHILIP: *(gaily)* And she's a dandy. *(He breaks into a chant)* Oh, I'm glad we've got a new cookie. I'm glad we've got a new cook. She's . . .

MARGARET: *(laughing at him)* Hush! Hush! Philip, stop—be quiet! *(She puts her hand over his mouth. He tries to sing through her fingers)* She'll hear you. Oh, doctor, isn't he terrible? He's poking fun at her all the time, but she is funny, though. *(She runs off joyously to the right)*

PHILIP: What a glorious morning, after yesterday.

DOCTOR: *(eyeing him coldly)* Yes—it is—you're in high feather this morning, eh?

PHILIP: *(cheerily)* Of course I am. What's the good in worrying over things you can't help?

DOCTOR: Have you seen . . . ?

PHILIP: *(quickly)* Yes. *(In a low voice)* I've made arrangements for her to go away as soon as she is well enough.

DOCTOR: *Humph!*

PHILIP: It's a terrible mess. I'll admit I never realized what I was doing, but, I shall make things all right for this girl, and her child. *(He sits on the edge of the table to the left. The DOCTOR is standing to the right of him)* Doctor I'm going to tell my wife this whole miserable story.

DOCTOR: *(aghast)* What?

PHILIP: *(hastily interrupting)* Ah, not now—in the future. When we both have grown closer together. When I have shown her by an honest and decent life that I ought to be forgiven—when I feel sure of her faith and confidence—then I shall confess and ask her to forgive me.

DOCTOR: *(shaking his head)* That would be a mighty hazardous experiment. You would draw a woman's heart strings closer and closer about you—and then deliberately tear them asunder. Best keep silent forever.

PHILIP: There would be no hazard. I know Margaret—of course if she found me out now—I admit it—it would be a terrible thing, but—

DOCTOR: *(abruptly)* You'd better get Mrs Fleming away from here for a few weeks.

PHILIP: *(surprised)* Away? *(He smiles confidently)* What need?

DOCTOR: She is threatened with a serious affection of the eyes.

PHILIP: *(his smile fading away, then recovering quickly and laughing lightly)* Aren't you trying to frighten me, doctor?

DOCTOR: *(annoyed by his levity)* I don't care anything about you, but, I tell you, your wife has a tendency to an affection of the eyes called glaucoma.

PHILIP: *(interested)* Glaucoma? Affection of the eyes? Why, Margaret has magnificent eyes.

DOCTOR: Yes, she has magnificent eyes, but, her child is the indirect cause of the development of an inherent weakness in them.

PHILIP: In what way?

DOCTOR: Conditions incident to motherhood. Shock. She is showing slight symptoms now that if aggravated would cause very serious consequences.

PHILIP: *(puzzled)* I do not understand.

DOCTOR: The eye—like other organs, has its own special secretion, which keeps it nourished and in a healthy state. The inflow and outflow of this secretion is equal. The physician sometimes comes across a patient of apparently sound physique, in whom he will find an abnormal condition of the eye where this natural function is through some inherent weakness, easily disturbed. When the patient is subject to illness, great physical or mental suffering—the too great emotion of a sudden joy or sorrow,—the stimulus of any one of these causes may produce in the eyes a super-abundant influx of this perfectly healthy fluid and the fine outflowing ducts cannot carry it off.

PHILIP: Yes. What then?

DOCTOR: The impact continues—until the result—is—

PHILIP: Yes? What is the result?

DOCTOR: Blindness.

PHILIP: *(awed)* Why—that is horrible—is there no remedy?

DOCTOR: Yes. A very delicate operation.

PHILIP: Always successful?

DOCTOR: If performed under proper conditions— yes.

PHILIP: And my wife is in danger of this? *(He walks up and down the room)*

DOCTOR: There is no danger whatever to Mrs Fleming, if the serenity of her life is not disturbed. There are slight, but nevertheless serious symptoms that must be remedied at once, with ordinary care. She will outgrow this weakness. Perhaps you will understand now, how necessary it is that she leave Canton for a few weeks.

PHILIP: *(deeply impressed by the* DOCTOR'S *recital)* Yes, I do. I will set about getting her away at once. I can leave the mill for a while in Foster's hands.

DOCTOR: Yes, he is an honest, capable fellow. Above all things, do not let Mrs Fleming suspect that there is anything serious the matter. Keep her cheerful.

PHILIP: Ah, Margaret is the sunniest, happiest disposition—nothing troubles her.

DOCTOR: Well, you keep her so. *(*PHILIP *takes out his cigar case and offers it to the* DOCTOR. *The latter refuses laconically)* Thank you, I have my own. *(He has taken a cigar from his vest pocket.* PHILIP *strikes a match and offers it to the doctor. At the same time, the* DOCTOR *is lighting his cigar with his own match, ignoring* PHILIP'S *attention.* PHILIP *shrugs his shoulders indulgently, lights his cigar and good-naturedly watches the* DOCTOR, *who takes up his satchel and leaves the room hastily with a curt)* Good morning.

PHILIP: *(genially)* Good morning, Dr Larkin. *(He sits in the armchair to the right and comfortably contemplates the convolutions of the cigar smoke) (The closing of the front door is heard.* JOE

FLETCHER *appears at the French window, stealthily peering into the room. He sees* PHILIP *and coughs)*

JOE: Hello, Mr Fleming!

PHILIP: *(looking up)* Hello, Joe—come in.

JOE: *(in a whisper)* Is it safe?

PHILIP: *(laughing)* Yes, I guess so.

JOE: *(slouching inside)* Where's Maria?

PHILIP: Gone out.

JOE: *(relieved)* Say, that was a damn mean trick you played on me yesterday.

PHILIP: What trick?

JOE: Sending me up here—you knew durn well she'd go fer me.

PHILIP: *(laughing)* I didn't know Maria was your wife, honest I didn't.

JOE: Oh, tell that to the marines. I want my sign. *(As* PHILIP *looks puzzled)* The sample of Giant's Cement with the plate.

PHILIP: *(remembering)* Oh, yes. *(He chuckles to himself, goes to the door at the right and brings back the cracked plate with the big stone hung to it.* JOE *takes it and turns to go)* Why did you lie to me yesterday?

JOE: I didn't lie to you.

PHILIP: You told me your wife ran away from you.

JOE: So she did.

PHILIP: *She* says you robbed her and left her.

JOE: She's a liar, and I'll tell it to her face.

PHILIP: *(laughing)* Come, Joe, you wouldn't dare.

JOE: She's a liar. I'm not afraid of her.

PHILIP: She made you run yesterday.

JOE: *(holding up the sign)* Didn't she have this? What chance has a fellow got when a woman has a *weapon* like this?

PHILIP: *(laughing at him)* And you were in the war.

JOE: Yes, and I was in the war! The Johnnies didn't fight with things like this.

PHILIP: *(enjoying the situation)* Come, Joe, I believe she'd make you run without that.

JOE: She's a liar. I can lick her. *(With conviction)* I have licked her. *(He grows bolder)* An' I'll lick her again.

PHILIP: *(laughing heartily)* Come, Joe, that'll do. The best way for you to lick 'er is there. *(He points to the decanter upon the side table.* JOE *gazes upon it tenderly and chuckles with unctuous satisfaction)*

JOE: That's a great joke, Mr Fleming. *Kin* I? *(He shuffles over to the decanter)*

PHILIP: Yes, go ahead.

(JOE *pours the liquor into a glass.* MARIA *walks hastily in through the window and sees* PHILIP*)*

MARIA: *(diffidently)* Excuse me, Mr Fleming, I did not know you vas here. I always come in dot way mit de baby. *(* JOE *is in the act of carrying the glass to his lips. He hears* MARIA'S *voice and stands terrified.* MARIA *sees him and becomes inflamed with indignation. She puts her hands on her hips and glares at him)* Vell, you dom scoundrel!

JOE: *(soothingly extending a hand to her)* There now, Maria, keep cool. Don't lose your temper.

MARIA: *(mocking him)* Yah, don't lose my temper. Didn't I tell you never to darken dis house again? Du Teufel aus Hölle! *(She makes a lunge at him. He dodges and hops on tip-toe from side to side in a zig-zag)*

JOE: Just a minute, Maria! *(He gulps)* I can—I can explain—the whole—thing. *(He makes a desperate bolt, but* MARIA *is on his heels. He stumbles and falls sprawling upon his hands and face, with his head to the front, in the center of the room. She swoops upon him, digs her hands into the loose folds of his coat between the shoulders and drags him to his feet. He limps with fright, puffing and spluttering, awkwardly helping himself and dropping the sign)* Maria, for God's sake, don't! I ain't ever done anything to you.

MARIA: *(dragging him toward the window)* Ach, Gott! No, you have never done nutting to me.

JOE: I'll make it all right with you. Let me go. I want my sign! Ugh! *(She throws him through the French window. He stumbles and staggers out of sight.* MARIA *picks up the sign and flings it after him. All the time she is scolding and weeping with anger)*

MARIA: Don't you dare come here no more to a decent house, you loafer. You can't explain nutting to me, you tief—you loafer— *(She sinks into the chair at the right of the table, leans her arms across the table, buries her face in them and sobs bitterly. All her fury has vanished and she is crushed and broken)*

PHILIP: *(laughing and calling after* JOE*)* Joe, come back! Joe! *(He goes out through the window)* Joe!

MARGARET: *(rushing in and up to the garden door, afraid some harm has come to the child)* What on earth is the matter? An earthquake?

MARIA: *(sobbing)* No. Mrs Fleming. It vas dot miserable husband of me.

MARGARET: What?

MARIA: Yah, I yust came in now, und I find him dere drinking of Mr Fleming's brandy.

MARGARET: Good gracious—what did you do, Maria?

MARIA: I skipped dot gutter mit him, I bet my life. *(She is still weeping)*

MARGARET: *(a smile flickering about her lips)* There, Maria, don't cry. Don't let him trouble you so. How is your sister?

MARIA: Vorse, Mrs Fleming.

MARGARET: Worse. Oh, I'm so sorry.

MARIA: Yah. I don't tink she vill ever leave dot bed alive. My poor little Lena. Mrs Fleming, I ask you—mebbe you vill come to see her. She talks about you all de time now.

MARGARET: *(surprised)* Talks about me? Why, how does she know me?

MARIA: Vell, she ask about you—a lot—und I tell her of you and your beautiful home and your little baby, und how she says she'd like yust once to look into your face.

MARGARET: *(hesitating a moment)* Well, I'll go. If I only could do anything for her, poor girl.

MARIA: Yah, she is a poor girl, Mrs Fleming. Mebbe she vill tell you the name of dis man vot—

MARGARET: *(with repugnance)* Oh, no, no! I don't want to know the brute, or his name.

MARIA: *(vindictively)* Oh, Gott! If I vould know it—

MARGARET: *(breaking in upon her, kindly)* But, I'll go to see her.

MARIA: Tank you, Mrs Fleming. You are a goodt lady.

MARGARET: Where did you say she lives?

MARIA: *(still quietly weeping)* Forty-two Millbrook St. By Mrs Burton's cottage.

MARGARET: Very well. *(*PHILIP'S *voice is heard outside, laughing)* Oh, there's Mr Fleming. Come, Maria, don't let him see you crying. Come, go to the kitchen and tell Hannah— *(She has urged* MARIA *to her feet and is pressing her toward the door)*

MARIA: Is dot new girl come?

MARGARET: Yes.

MARIA: Hannah is her name?

MARGARET: *(pressing her)* Yes, tell her to make you a nice cup of tea, and then you'd best go back to your sister.

MARIA: Tank you, Mrs Fleming. I don't want no tea. Mebbe she needs me. I go right back to her. You'll come sure, Mrs Fleming?

MARGARET: *(putting her through the door on the right as* PHILIP *comes in through the window on the left)* Yes, I'll come in a little while.

PHILIP: Oh, Margaret, I wish you'd been here. *(He begins to laugh)* Such a circus. The funniest thing I ever saw.

MARGARET: Yes, Maria told me. Poor thing. I'm sorry for her. *(*PHILIP *laughs. She goes to her work basket which is on the center table, and takes out the two phials.* PHILIP *crosses to the right and* MARGARET *goes to him)* Here, dear— some medicine Dr Larkin left for you.

PHILIP: *(pushing her hand away gently)* Oh, I don't want any medicine. There's nothing the matter with me. *(He begins to chuckle again)* If you could—

MARGARET: *(shaking him by the lapels of his jacket)* Yes, there is a great deal the matter with you. *(She looks at him seriously and he becomes serious)* Doctor says you're all run down. You've got to have a rest. Here, now, take two of these pellets, alternating every hour. *(He takes the phials and puts them in his vest pocket)* Take some now!

PHILIP: Oh! Now? Must I?

MARGARET: *(shaking him)* Yes, this minute. *(He takes two pellets and pretends to choke. She shakes him again)* Look at your watch. Note the time.

PHILIP: Yes'm.

MARGARET: Well, in an hour, take two from the other phial.

PHILIP: Yes'm. *(He lights a fresh cigar, and MARGARET gives a cry of reproval)*

MARGARET: Philip! What are you doing? *(She rushes at him and takes the cigar from him)* Don't you know you mustn't smoke when you are taking medicine.

PHILIP: Why not?

MARGARET: It'll kill the effect of it. You may smoke in an hour.

PHILIP: I've got to take more medicine in an hour?

MARGARET: Well, I guess you'll have to give up smoking.

PHILIP: What!

MARGARET: Until you're well.

PHILIP: But, I'm well now.

MARGARET: *(going through the door on the left) Until you have stopped taking those pellets!*

PHILIP: All right. I'll forget them.

MARGARET: Philip!

PHILIP: *(going to the baby in the garden doorway)* The cigars! What are you doing?

MARGARET: Changing my gown. I'm going out.

PHILIP: Where are you going?

MARGARET: Oh, just a little errand.

PHILIP: Well, hurry back.

MARGARET: Yes, I won't be long. *(She gives a little scream)* Oh!

PHILIP: What's the matter?

MARGARET: Nothing. Stuck a pin into my finger, that's all.

PHILIP: My! You gave me a shock. *(He puts his hand to his heart playfully)*

MARGARET: *(laughing)* Sorry. Did you see my gloves?

PHILIP: Yes.

MARGARET: Where?

PHILIP: On your hands, of course.

MARGARET: Now, don't be silly!

PHILIP: *(playing with the baby)* Margaret, you know baby's eyes are changing.

MARGARET: No.

PHILIP: Yes. They're growing like yours.

MARGARET: Nonsense. She has your eyes.

PHILIP: *(eyeing the baby critically)* No, they're exactly like yours. She's got my nose though.

MARGARET: *(giving a little cry of protest)* Oh, Philip—don't say that.

PHILIP: Why?

MARGARET: It would be terrible if she had your nose. Just imagine my dainty Lucy with a great big nose like yours.

PHILIP: *(feeling his nose)* Why, I think I have a very nice nose.

MARGARET: *(coming in, laughing)* Oh, yes, it's a good enough nose—as noses go—but— *(She touches the bell)*

PHILIP: *(noticing her gown)* Your new suit?

MARGARET: *(gaily)* Yes. Like it?

PHILIP: It's a dandy. Turn around. *(She dances over to him and twirls about playfully)* Wait, there's a thread. *(He picks it off her skirt)* *(JANE enters)*

MARGARET: Jane, please tell Hannah to come here.

JANE: Yes, ma'am. *(She goes)* *(PHILIP begins to chuckle)*

MARGARET: Now, Philip, I implore you to keep still. Please don't get me laughing while I'm talking to her.

PHILIP: *(indignantly)* I'm not going to say anything. *(HANNAH appears. She is very large, stout and dignified)*

MARGARET: *(hurriedly, in haste to be off)* Hannah! I'm going out and I shall not be able to look after the baking of the bread. When the loaves have raised almost to the top of the pans put them in the oven.

HANNAH: *(who has been studying admiringly* MARGARET'S *costume)* Yes, Ma'am. I does always put the bread in when it's almost up to the top in the pans.

MARGARET: And bake them just one hour.

HANNAH: Ah! Yes, ma'am. I always bakes 'em an hour.

(PHILIP smothers a laugh in a cough. MARGARET *stares at him)*

MARGARET: And, have luncheon on at half past twelve, please.

HANNAH: Yes, I always has the lunch on at half past twelve, sharp.

MARGARET: *(who has been putting on her gloves)* Thank you, Hannah, that's all. Well, I'm off. *(To* PHILIP*)* Good-bye, dear. *(She starts off hastily)*

HANNAH: Good-bye, ma'am. *(She goes out)*

MARGARET: *(pausing to look at* PHILIP *as he plays with the baby in the carriage)* Oh, how dear you both look there together.

PHILIP: *(looking at his watch)* You'd best hurry if you want to get back at *half past twelve sharp.* *(He imitates* HANNAH*)*

MARGARET: *(rapturously gazing at them)* Oh, if I could paint, what a picture I would make of you two!

PHILIP: Are you going?

MARGARET: Yes, I'm going. *(She notices* PHILIP *giving the baby his watch, and giving a little scream of alarm, she rushes at him)* Philip, what are you doing?

PHILIP: That's all right. She won't hurt it.

MARGARET: Suppose she'd swallow it.

PHILIP: Well!

MARGARET: *(mocking him)* Well! There, put it in your pocket. And have some sense. *(She picks up the rattle and the big rubber ball and puts them in his hands)* There, you can play with these. *(They both laugh with the fun of it all)*

PHILIP: Oh! Go on Margaret, and hurry home.

MARGARET: *(kissing him and the baby)* All right. Won't be long. Don't forget your medicine, and

please don't smoke when my back is turned. *(She dances out through the French window, overflowing with fun and animation. This scene must be played rapidly, with a gay, light touch)*

ACT THIRD

The scene is a neat, plainly furnished sitting-room in MRS BURTON'S *cottage. The walls are covered with old-fashioned wall paper of a faded green color. Sunlight streams in through two windows at the back. In one there is a small table holding a few pots of geraniums, and in the second, a hanging basket of ivy. A few straggling vines creep about the window-frame. There are doors at the left center, down left and on the right. In the center of the room stands a table with a chair to the right of it, and a few hair-cloth chairs are here and there. A sofa stands against the left wall below the door, and there is a low rocking-chair on the left.*

The room is empty and after a moment the stillness is broken by the wail of an infant. The hushed notes of a woman's voice are heard from the open door on the left, soothing the child. A low knock is heard at the door to the right. The door opens slowly and DOCTOR LARKIN *enters.* MRS BURTON *emerges from the room on the left with a tiny baby wrapped in a soft white shawl in her arms. She is a motherly woman, large and placid, with a benign immobility of countenance. She speaks with a New England drawl.*

MRS BURTON: Good morning, doctor. I didn't hear ye knock.

DOCTOR: How is your patient this morning?

MRS BURTON: Why, ain't yer seen Dr Taylor? Didn't he tell ye?

DOCTOR: No. She's—?

MRS BURTON: *(nodding her head)* Yes.

DOCTOR: When did it happen?

MRS BURTON: About an hour ago. She seemed brighter this morning. After her sister went out she slept for a while. When I came in the room she opened her eyes and asked me for a pencil and paper. I brought 'em to her and she writ for quite a spell. Then she lay back on the pillow. I asked her if she wouldn't take a little nourishment. She smiled and shook her head. Then she gave a long sigh—an'—an'—that was all there was to it.

DOCTOR: How's the child?

MRS BURTON: Poor little critter— *(She looks down at it)* I can't do nothing for it. I've tried everything. It ought to have mother's milk—that's all there is to it. Be quiet, you poor little motherless critter.

DOCTOR: It would be better for it if it had gone with her.

MRS BURTON: Why, doctor, ain't ye awful?

DOCTOR: Why, what chance has that child got in this world? I'll send you something for it. *(He turns to go)*

MRS BURTON: Don't ye want to see her?

DOCTOR: No! What good can I be to her now, poor devil?

(CHARLEY BURTON, a sturdy lad of ten, breaks boisterously into the room from the door on the right, carrying a baseball and bat)

CHARLEY: Ma! Ma! Here's a woman wants to see Mrs Bindley.

MRS BURTON: *(reprimanding him)* Lady! And take your hat off.

(DR LARKIN and MRS BURTON look expectantly toward the door. MARGARET enters slowly, her eyes bent upon her glove which she is unfastening. DR LARKIN is dumbfounded at the sight of her. She takes a few steps toward him and looks up)

MARGARET: *(pleasantly surprised at seeing him)* Why, doctor! I didn't know that you were on this case.

DOCTOR: *(confused)* I'm not. Dr Taylor—he—called me in consultation. But, what in the name of all that's wonderful brings you here?

MARGARET: Maria!

DOCTOR: What Maria? Not—

MARGARET: Yes, our Maria—this sick girl is her sister. *(She removes her hat and places it with her gloves on the table)*

DOCTOR: *(in consternation)* Her sister! Then you know?

MARGARET: I know that there is a poor sick girl here who wants—

DOCTOR: *(going to her, brusquely)* Mrs Fleming, you'd best not remain here—the girl is dead. Go home.

MARGARET: *(pityingly)* Dead? Poor thing!

DOCTOR: Yes. Does your husband know you are here?

MARGARET: *(shaking her head)* Oh, no!

DOCTOR: Come, you must go home! *(He almost pushes her out of the room in his urgency)*

MARGARET: *(resisting him gently)* Ah, no, doctor. Now that I am here, let me stay. I can be of some help, I know.

DOCTOR: No, you can be of no use. Everything has been done.

MARGARET: Well, I'll just say a word to Maria. Where is she?

DOCTOR: I don't know—I don't know anything about Maria.

MRS BURTON: She's in there. *(She nods toward the door on the left)*

(The DOCTOR has crowded MARGARET almost through the door in his eagerness to have her out of the house. She is reluctantly yielding to him, when MRS BURTON's voice arrests her. She turns quickly and, looking over the DOCTOR's shoulder, notices the child in MRS BURTON's arms. She impulsively brushes the DOCTOR aside and goes toward her, her face beaming with tender sympathy)

MARGARET: Oh, is this the baby?

MRS BURTON: Yes'm.

MARGARET: *(going close to her on tip-toes and gazing with maternal solicitude down upon the child)* Poor little baby! What a dear mite of a thing it is.

MRS BURTON: Yes'm.

MARGARET: *(impulsively)* Doctor, we must take care of this baby.

DOCTOR: *(impatiently)* You've got a baby of your *own*, Mrs Fleming.

MARGARET: Yes, and that's why I pity this one. I suppose, I always did love babies, anyhow. They are such wonderful, mysterious little things, aren't they?

MRS BURTON: Yes'm.

DOCTOR: *(spurred by a growing sense of catastrophe)* Mrs Fleming, there is danger to your child in your remaining here.

MARGARET: *(alarmed)* Oh, doctor!

DOCTOR: I hated to tell you this before—but—there is contagion in this atmosphere.

MARGARET: *(hastily taking her hat from the table)* Doctor, why didn't you— *(She is hurrying away when she is checked by a poignant moan. She turns a frightened face and sees MARIA coming from the room on the left with a letter in her hand. MARIA'S face is distorted by grief)*

MARIA: Ah, Mrs Burton, I have found out who dot man is. He is— *(She sees MARGARET and smiles bitterly upon her)* So,—you have come, Mrs Fleming?

MARGARET: *(making a movement of sympathy)* Maria!

MARIA: Vell, you may go back again. You can do nutting for her now. She is dead. *(Perversely)* But, ven you do go, you vill take dot baby back mit you. He shall now have two babies instead of one.

MARGARET: *(smiling)* What do you mean, Maria? Who shall have two babies?

MARIA: *(fiercely)* Philip Fleming—dot's who. *(MARGARET stares at her, only comprehending half what MARIA means. DR LARKIN goes quickly to her)*

DOCTOR: Come away, Mrs Fleming—the woman is crazy. *(He tries to draw her away)*

MARIA: *(contemptuously)* No, I ain't crazy! *(She shakes the letter at MARGARET)* You read dot letter and see if I vas crazy! *(MARGARET, in a dazed way, reaches for the letter, and tries to read it, turning it different ways)*

MARGARET: I cannot make it out. *(She hands it to the doctor, and says helplessly)* Read it—to me—doctor—please.

DOCTOR: *(beside himself and snatching the letter)* No, nor shall you. *(He makes a motion to tear the letter)*

MARIA: *(threateningly)* Don't you tear dot letter, doctor.

MARGARET: *(putting her hand out gently)* You must not destroy that letter, doctor. Give it back to me. *(DR LARKIN returns the letter reluctantly. MARGARET attempts to read it, fails, becomes impatient, and hands it to MARIA, helplessly)* You read it to me, Maria.
(MARIA, whose passion has subsided, takes the letter in an awed manner and begins to read it. The DOCTOR is in a daze. MARGARET sinks into the chair to the right of the table. She has recovered her calm poise, but does not seem to be at all the same MARGARET)

MARIA: *(reading in a simple, unaffected manner)*

Canton, June 10,

DEAR MR FLEMING:

You was good to come to see me, and I thank you. I will not trouble you no more. I am sorry for what has happened. I know you never loved me and I never asked you to, but I loved you. It was all my fault. I will never trouble you no more. You can do what you like with the baby. I do not care. Do not be afraid, I shall never tell. They tried to get me to but I never shall. Nobody will ever know. No more at present, from your obedient servant,

LENA SCHMIDT

MARGARET: *(turning to the DOCTOR, who is standing close to her chair)* Did you know—anything of this—doctor?

DOCTOR: *(evasively)* Well—I knew—something of it—but, this girl may be lying. Such as she is—will say anything sometimes.

MARIA: *(fiercely)* Don't you say dot, doctor. She would not tell nutting to hurt him, not to save her soul.

DOCTOR: *(with finality)* Well, now that you know the worst, come away from here—come home.

MARIA: *(bitterly)* Oh! Ya! She can go home. She have alvays got a home und a husband und fine clothes, because she is his vife, but my poor sister don't have any of dese tings, because she is only de poor mistress. But, by

Gott, she shall not go home unless she takes dot baby back mit her.

DOCTOR: She shall do nothing of the sort.

MARIA: Vell, den, I vill take it, und fling it in his face.

MARGARET: (calmly, and rising from the chair) You shall not go near him. You shall not say— one word to him!

MARIA: Von't I? Who is going to stop me? I vould yust like to know dot?

MARGARET: (quite calmly) I am!

MARIA: (mockingly) You—you vill take his part, because you are his vife! (Fiercely) Vell! (She draws a pistol from her dress pocket) Do you see dot gun? Vell, I buy dot gun, und I swore dot ven I find out dot man I vill have his life. Und, if you try to stop me, I vill lay you stiff und cold beside her.

MARGARET: (calmly, pityingly, holding out her hand as though to quiet her) Maria! Stop! How dare you talk like that to me? Give me that pistol. (MARIA, awed by MARGARET's spirit, meekly hands her the weapon) You think—I— am happy—because I am his wife? Why, you poor fool, that girl (She points to the door on the left) never in all her life suffered one thousandth part what I have suffered in these past five minutes. Do you dare to compare her to me? I have not uttered one word of reproach, even against her, and yet she has done me a wrong, that not all the death-bed letters that were ever written can undo. I wonder what I have ever done to deserve this! (She loses control of herself and sinks sobbing, into the chair, her arms upon the table, and her head dropping upon them)

DOCTOR: (overcome by the situation, throws his arms about her and tries to draw her to her feet) For God's sake, Mrs Fleming, let me take you out of this hell.

MARGARET: (gently resisting him) Ah, doctor, you cannot take this hell out of my breast. (Suddenly her manner changes. She says with quick decision) Maria, get me a sheet of writing paper. Doctor, give me a pencil.

(DR LARKIN puts his hand into his vest pocket. MARIA, who seems dazed, looks helplessly about as though the paper might be within reach. Then suddenly thinking of the letter in her hand, she tears off the blank half of it and quickly lays it on the table before MARGARET)

DOCTOR: (giving her the pencil) What are you going to do?

MARGARET: Send—for him!

DOCTOR: No—not here!

MARGARET: Yes—here— (She writes nervously, mumbling what she writes) "Philip: I am waiting for you, here. That girl is dead." (She folds the letter) Where's that boy?

(MARIA and MRS BURTON both make a movement in search of CHARLEY)

MARIA: Charley! (She goes to the door at the back and calls again in a hushed voice) Charley! (CHARLEY enters. She whispers to him that the lady wants him) You, go quick! (CHARLEY goes to MARGARET)

MARGARET: (in tense nervousness) Charley, do you know Mr Fleming?

CHARLEY: Yes'm.

MARGARET: Do you know where he lives?

CHARLEY: Yes'm—on Canton Street.

MARGARET: Yes—go there—don't ring the bell— go through the garden—you will find him there, playing with the baby. Give him this.

CHARLEY: Any answer?

MARGARET: (at nervous tension) No! Go quick! Quick! (She springs to her feet) Now, doctor—I want you to leave me!

DOCTOR: Mrs Fleming, for God's sake don't see him here.

MARGARET: Yes, here—and—alone! Please go. (The DOCTOR does not respond) I don't want you or any other living being to hear what passes between him and me, and (She points to the room) that dead girl. Please go!

DOCTOR: Mrs Fleming, as your physician, I order you to leave this place at once.

MARGARET: No, doctor—I must see him, here.

DOCTOR: (with gentle persuasion) Mrs Fleming, you have no right to do this. Think of your child.

MARGARET: (remembering) My baby! My poor, little innocent baby! Oh, I wish to God that she were dead. *(She is beside herself and not realizing what she says. She crosses to the left)*

DOCTOR: *(following her)* Mrs Fleming, in God's name, calm yourself! I have tried to keep it from you, but, I am forced to tell you— *(He is so deeply moved that he is almost incoherent)* If you continue in this way, dear lady, you are exposing yourself to a terrible affliction—this—trouble—with your eyes. You are threatened with—if you keep up this strain—a sudden blindness may fall upon you.

MARGARET: *(appalled)* Blind! Blind! *(She speaks in a low terrified voice)* Oh, no doctor, not *that*—not *now*—not until after I've seen him.

DOCTOR: Not only that, but if you keep up this strain much longer, it may cost you your life.

MARGARET: I don't care—what happens to me, only, let me *see* him, and then, the sooner it all comes the better. *(She crosses to the left with the* DOCTOR *following her)*

DOCTOR: *(Growing desperate, and throwing his arms about her)* Mrs Fleming, you must leave this place! Come home.

MARGARET: No. Doctor, please leave me alone. *(She draws herself from him)* I tell you I've got to see him here. *(Then with a sweet intimacy, she goes to him)* A woman has a strange feeling for the physician who brings her child into the world—I love you—I have always obeyed your orders, haven't I? *(She speaks brokenly)*

DOCTOR: *(quietly)* Always.

MARGARET: Then, let me be the doctor now, and I order you to leave this house at once.

DOCTOR: *(hopelessly)* You are determined to do this thing?

MARGARET: *(with finality)* Yes.

DOCTOR: Very well then—good-bye. *(He holds out his hand, which she takes mechanically. He holds her hand warmly for a moment. She clings to him as though afraid to let him go, then slowly draws away)*

MARGARET: Good-bye!

(The DOCTOR *leaves the room quickly.* MARGARET *takes a step after him until she touches the left side of the table in the center. She stands there gazing into space, the calmness of death upon her face. The sunlight streaming through the window falls upon her.* MRS BURTON *is sitting in a rocking-chair in the corner of the room.* MARIA *is sitting on the sofa at the left, weeping silently, with clasped hands, her arms lying in her lap, her body bent. She makes a plaintive moan before she speaks)*

MARIA: Ah—Mrs Fleming, you must not do dis ting. Vat vas I—vot was she, I'd like to know—dot ve should make dis trouble for you? You come here, like an angel to help us, und I have stung you like a snake in dot grass. *(She goes to* MARGARET *and falls upon her knees beside her)* Oh, Mrs Fleming, on my knees I ask you to forgive me.

*(*MARGARET *stands immobile at the table, her right hand resting upon its edge—her left hand partly against her cheek. She is lost in spiritual contemplation of the torment she is suffering. She shows impatience at the sound of* MARIA'S *voice as though loath to be disturbed. She replies wearily)*

MARGARET: I have nothing to forgive. Get up, Maria. You have done nothing to me—go away!

MARIA: *(in a paroxysm of contrition)* Oh, I beg, Mrs Fleming, dot you vill take dot gun and blow my brains out.

MARGARET: Don't go on like that, Maria! *(*MARIA'S *weeping irritates her)* Get up! Please go away. Go away! I say.

*(*MARIA *slinks away quietly into the back room.* MARGARET *takes a long, sobbing breath, which ends in a sigh. She stares into space and a blank look comes into her face as though she were gazing at things beyond her comprehension. Presently the silence is broken by a low wail from the infant. It half arouses her)*

MARGARET: What is the matter with that child? *(Her voice seems remote. Her expression remains fixed)* Why don't you keep it quiet?

MRS BURTON: *(in a hushed voice)* It's hungry.

MARGARET: *(in the same mood, but her voice is a little querulous)* Well, then, why don't you feed it?

MRS BURTON: I can't get nothing fit for it. I've tried everything I could think of, but it's no use. *(She gets up and places the child upon the *sofa to the left)* There, be still, you poor little critter, an' I'll see what I ken get fer ye. *(As she goes to the door at the back,* MARGARET *speaks wearily)*

MARGARET: Bring a lamp—it's getting dark here. *(She is still in the same attitude by the table. There is a silence, then the child's wail arouses her. She half turns her head in its direction— and tries to quiet it)* Hush—child—hush— *(Then she reaches out her hand as if to pat it)* There—there—poor little thing. Don't fret—it's no use to fret, child—be quiet now—there— there, now. (She turns and slowly gropes her way to the sofa, sits on the edge of it, and feels for the child and gently pats it. She murmurs softly)* Hush—baby—go to sleep.

(There is a silence while a soft flood of sunshine plays about her. A pitying half smile flits across her face. She utters a faint sigh and again drifts away into that inner consciousness where she evidently finds peace. Again the child is restless—it arouses her and, hopeless of comforting it, she takes it in her arms. After a moment, she rises to her feet and stumbles toward the table. She knocks against the low chair. At the same moment, PHILIP FLEMING *dashes breathlessly into the room through the door on the right. He pauses in horror as* MARGARET *raises her head, her eyes wide open, staring into his—her face calm and remote. She hushes the child softly, and sits in the low chair.* PHILIP *stands in dumb amazement watching her. The child begins to fret her again. She seems hopeless of comforting it. Then scarcely conscious of what she is doing, suddenly with an impatient, swift movement she unbuttons her dress to give nourishment to the child, when the picture fades away into darkness)*

ACT FOURTH

The scene is the same as the Second Act. The doors and window leading into the garden are open.

MARIA *is seated close to the open door, sewing. She occasionally looks into the garden as if guarding something. She is neatly dressed, fresh and orderly looking. Her manner is subdued. A bell rings and a closing door is heard. Then* DR LARKIN *enters.* MARIA *goes to meet him and scans his face anxiously.*

MARIA: Goot morning, doctor.

DOCTOR: Good morning. Well! Any news?

MARIA: *(losing interest and shaking her head sadly)* No, doctor. No vord from him yet. It is seven days now—I hoped—mebbe you might have some.

DOCTOR: No—nothing. How is Mrs Fleming? *(*MARIA *sits down to the left of the center of the room and the doctor to the right)*

MARIA: Yust the same as yesterday, und the day before, und all the udder days. Ach, so bright, und so cheerful, but I tink all the same she is breaking her heart. Ach, ven I look into her sad eyes—vot cannot see me—I am ashamed to hold my head up. *(She brushes away the tears)*

DOCTOR: Does she talk about him at all?

MARIA: No, she never speaks his name.

DOCTOR: How is the child?

MARIA: *(brightening)* She is fine. Dot little tooth came trough dis morning und she don't fret no more now.

DOCTOR: And, the *other* one?

MARIA: *(indifferently)* Oh, he's all right. I put him beside Lucy in her crib dis morning und she laughs and pulls at him und plays mit him yust like he vas a little kitten. Dis is no place for him, doctor. Ven Mr Fleming comes home he vill fix tings, und I vill take him away by myself—vere she no more can be troubled mit him.

DOCTOR: Things will come out all right. You'd best keep quiet. Have nothing whatever to say in this matter.

MARIA: Ya. I make enough trouble already mit my tongue. You bet I keep it shut in my head now. Shall I call Mrs Fleming? She is in the garden.

DOCTOR: She's there a great deal now, isn't she?

MARIA: Ya, she is always dere by the blossoms, und the babies. *(She goes to the door and says in slow, deferential voice)* Mrs Fleming, Doctor Larkin is here.

MARGARET: *(outside)* Yes, I'll come. *(She slowly emerges from the garden into the doorway, her arms filled with flowers. She is daintily dressed and there is a subtle dignity and reserve about her. She smiles cheerily)* Good morning, doctor. Maria, there are some daffodils out by the yellow bed. Bring them, please. *(She slowly enters the room)*

(The DOCTOR goes to her and gently leads her to the table on the right where she puts the flowers, after carefully locating a place to lay them)

DOCTOR: Well, well, where did you get such a lot of roses? I couldn't gather so many in a month from my scrubby bushes. The bugs eat 'em all up.

MARGARET: Why don't you spray them? *(MARIA brings a large loose bunch of daffodils)* Bring some jars, Maria.

DOCTOR: I did spray them.

MARGARET: When?

DOCTOR: When I saw the rose bugs.

MARGARET: *(smiling)* That's a fine time to spray bushes. Don't you know that the time to prevent trouble is to look ahead? From potatoes to roses, spray before anything happens—*then* nothing *will* happen.

DOCTOR: *(laughing)* Yes, of course, I know, but I forgot to do it until I saw two big, yellow bugs in the heart of every rose and all the foliage chewed up.

MARGARET: There's no use in it now. You are just wasting time. Start early next year before the leaves open.

DOCTOR: *(admiringly)* What a brave, cheery little woman you are.

MARGARET: What's the use in being anything else? I don't see any good in living in this world, unless you can live right.

DOCTOR: And this world needs just such women as you.

MARGARET: What does the world know or care about me?

(The bell rings and the door opens and shuts)

DOCTOR: Very little, but it's got to feel your influence. *(He pats her hand)*

(The MAID enters)

MAID: Mr Foster wishes to see you for a moment, Mrs Fleming.

MARGARET: Tell him to come in. *(The MAID goes out. In a moment FOSTER enters, flurried and embarrassed)* Good morning, Mr Foster. *(She holds out her hands to him)* Anything wrong at the mill?

FOSTER: Good morning, Mrs Fleming. Oh, no—not at all, not at all. How do you do, doctor? *(He shakes hands with the DOCTOR with unusual warmth)*

DOCTOR: *(somewhat surprised and looking at him quizzically)* Hello, Foster.

MARGARET: Will you sit down, Mr Foster?

FOSTER: Thank you—yes, I will. What beautiful flowers. Mother says you have the loveliest garden in Canton.

MARGARET: *(pleased)* That's awfully nice of her. I had a delightful visit with her yesterday.

FOSTER: *(nervously)* Yes, she told me so.

MARGARET: We sat in the garden. What a sweet, happy soul she is.

FOSTER: *(fussing with his hat and getting up and moving his chair close to the DOCTOR'S)* Yes. Mother always sees the bright side of the worst things.

MARGARET: She's very proud of you.

FOSTER: *(laughing foolishly)* Oh, yes, she is happy over anything I do. *(He looks at MARGARET furtively, then at the doctor. He evidently has something to say. Suddenly in a tense whisper he speaks to the doctor)* Mr Fleming has come back.

DOCTOR: Hush! Where is he? At the mill?

FOSTER: No. Here—outside.

DOCTOR: How does he look?

FOSTER: He's a wreck. He wants to see her.

DOCTOR: Well, tell her—I'll go— *(He rises)*

FOSTER: No! *(He grabs him by the coat)* For God's sake, don't go. You tell her—you're her doctor. *(MARGARET, who has been busy with the flowers, becomes suddenly interested)*

MARGARET: What are you two whispering about?

FOSTER: *(laughing nervously)* Oh, just a little advice, that's all. *(He goes to* MARGARET*)* I'll say good morning, Mrs Fleming. Glad to see you—er—looking—ah—so well. *(He shakes hands and rushes out)*

*(*MARGARET *stands a little mystified. The* DOCTOR *approaches her gently)*

DOCTOR: *(very tenderly)* Mrs Fleming—I have something to say to you.

MARGARET: *(standing tense and with ominous conviction)* Philip is dead!

DOCTOR: No. He is not dead.

MARGARET: Where is he?

DOCTOR: *Outside.*

MARGARET: Why doesn't he come in?

DOCTOR: He's ashamed—afraid.

MARGARET: This is his home. Why should he be afraid to enter it? I will go to him.

(She starts toward the door, and then staggers. The DOCTOR *puts an arm around her)*

DOCTOR: There now. Keep up your courage. Don't forget, everything depends upon you.

MARGARET: *(brokenly)* I'm brave, doctor. I—perhaps it's best for you to tell him to come here.

DOCTOR: *(patting her on the shoulder)* Remember, you are very precious to us all. We cannot afford to lose *you.*

*(*MARGARET *stands by the table, calm and tense.* PHILIP *comes in from the right, carrying his cap in his hands. He looks weary and broken. He crosses behind* MARGARET *to the center of the stage and, standing humbly before her, murmurs her name softly)*

PHILIP: Margaret!

MARGARET: Well, Philip. *(After a slight pause)* You have come back.

PHILIP: *(humbly)* Yes.

MARGARET: *(gently)* Why did you go away?

PHILIP: *(overwhelmed with shame)* I couldn't face you. I wanted to get away somewhere, and hide forever. *(He looks sharply at her)* Can't you see me, Margaret?

MARGARET: *(shaking her head)* No!

PHILIP: *(awed)* You are blind! Oh!

*(*MARGARET *sits down in a chair by the table.* PHILIP *remains standing)*

MARGARET: Don't mind. I shall be cured. Doctor Norton sees me every day. He will operate as soon as he finds me normal.

PHILIP: You have been suffering?

MARGARET: Oh, no. *(After a pause)* Philip, do you think that was right? To run away and hide?

PHILIP: I did not consider whether it was right or wrong. *(He speaks bitterly)* I did not know the meaning of those words. I never have.

MARGARET: Oh, you are a man—people will soon forget.

PHILIP: *(fiercely)* I do not care about others. It is you, Margaret—will you ever forget? Will you ever forgive?

MARGARET: *(shaking her head and smiling sadly)* There is nothing to forgive. And, I want to forget.

PHILIP: *(bewildered by her magnanimity but full of hope)* Then you will let me come back to you? You will help me to be a better—a wiser man?

MARGARET: *(smiling gently)* Yes, Philip.

(A quick joy takes hold of PHILIP*. He makes a warm movement to go to her, then checks himself, and approaches her slowly while speaking, overcome by the wonder and beauty of her kindness)*

PHILIP: All my life, Margaret, I will make amends for what I have done. I will atone for my ignorance— Oh, my wife—my dear, dear wife. *(He hangs over her tenderly, not daring to touch her)* *(At the word "wife"* MARGARET *rises, shrinking from him as though some dead thing was near her. A look of agony flits across her face)*

MARGARET: No! Philip, not that! No! *(She puts out her hands to ward him off)*

PHILIP: *(beseechingly)* Margaret!

MARGARET: *(her face poignant with suppressed emotion, she confesses, brokenly)* The wife-heart has gone out of me.

PHILIP: Don't—don't say that, Margaret.

MARGARET: I must. Ah, Philip, how I worshipped you. You were my idol. Is it my fault that you lie broken at my feet?

PHILIP: *(with urgency)* You say you want to forget—that you forgive! Will you—?

MARGARET: Can't you understand? It is not a
question of forgetting, or of forgiving— *(For
an instant she is at a loss how to convince him)*
Can't you understand? Philip! *(Then suddenly)* Suppose—I—had been unfaithful to
you?

PHILIP: *(with a cry of repugnance)* Oh, Margaret!

MARGARET: *(brokenly)* There! You see! You are
a man, and you have your ideals of—the—
sanctity—of—the thing you love. Well, I am a
woman—and perhaps—I, too, have the same
ideals. I don't know. But, I, too, cry "pollution." *(She is deeply moved)*

PHILIP: *(abashed)* I did not know. I never realized
before, the iniquity—of my—behavior. Oh, if I
only had my life to live over again. Men, as a
rule, do not consider others when urged on by
their desires. How you must hate me.

MARGARET: No, I don't—I love you—I pity you.

PHILIP: Dear, not now—but in the future—some
time—away in the future—perhaps, the old
Margaret—

MARGARET: Ah, Philip, the old Margaret is dead.
The truth killed her.

PHILIP: Then—there is no hope for me?
*(There is a dignity and a growing manliness in
his demeanor as the scene progresses)*

MARGARET: *(warmly)* Yes. Every hope.

PHILIP: Well, what do you want me to do? Shall I
go away?

MARGARET: No. Your place is here. You cannot
shirk your responsibilities now.

PHILIP: I do not want to shirk my responsibilities,
Margaret. I want to do whatever you think is
best.

MARGARET: Very well. It is best for us both to remain here, and take up the old life together.
It will be a little hard for you, but you are a
man—you will soon live it down.

PHILIP: Yes—I *will* live it down.

MARGARET: Go to the mill tomorrow morning and
take up your work again, as though this thing
had never happened.

PHILIP: Yes. All right. I'll do that.

MARGARET: Mr Foster, you know, you have an unusually capable man there?

PHILIP: Yes, I appreciate Foster. He's a nice chap,
too.

MARGARET: He has carried through a very critical week at the mill.

PHILIP: Don't worry, Margaret, everything will be
all right there now. I will put my whole heart
and soul into the work.

MARGARET: Then, you must do something for your
child.

PHILIP: Yes, our dear child.

MARGARET: No, not our child—not Lucy. Your son.

PHILIP: My son?

MARGARET: Yes.

PHILIP: Where is he?

MARGARET: Here.

PHILIP: *(resentfully)* Who brought him here?

MARGARET: I did.

PHILIP: *(amazed)* You brought that child here?

MARGARET: Yes, where else should he go?

PHILIP: You have done that?

MARGARET: What other thing was there for me to
do? Surely if he was good enough to bring into
the world, he is good enough to find a shelter
under your roof.

PHILIP: *(moved by her magnanimity)* I never
dreamed that you would do that, Margaret.

MARGARET: Well, he is here. Now, what are you
going to do with him?

PHILIP: *(helplessly)* What can I do?

MARGARET: Give him a name, educate him. Try to
make atonement for the wrong you did his
mother. You must teach him never to be ashamed
of her, to love her memory—motherhood is a divine thing—remember that, Philip, no matter
when, or how. You can do fine things for this unfortunate child.

PHILIP: *(contemptuously)* Fine things for him! I
am not fit to guide a young life. A fine thing
I have made of my own.

MARGARET: There is no use now lamenting what
was done yesterday. That's finished. Tomorrow?
What are you going to do with that?

PHILIP: There does not seem any "tomorrow" worth while for me. The past—

MARGARET: The past is dead. We must face the living future. Now, Philip, there are big things ahead for you, if you will only look for them. They certainly will not *come* to *you*. I will help you—we will fight this together.

PHILIP: Forgive me, please. I'll not talk like that any more.

MARGARET: Of course, there will be a lot of talk— mean talk—but they will get tired of that in the end. Where have you been all this time?

PHILIP: In Boston.

MARGARET: What have you been doing?

PHILIP: Nothing—I've been—in the hospital.

MARGARET: *(stretching out her arms to him with an infinite tenderness)* Ah, Philip, you have been ill?

PHILIP: No!

MARGARET: What was it. *(He is silent)* Please tell me.

PHILIP: *(rather reluctantly reciting his story)* I was walking across the bridge over the Charles River one night—I was sick of myself—the whole world—I believed I should never see your face again. The water looked so quiet, it fascinated me. I just dropped into it and went down. It seemed like going to sleep. Then I woke up and I was in a narrow bed in a big room.

MARGARET: *(breathless)* The hospital?

PHILIP: Yes.

MARGARET: Oh, that was a cruel thing to do. Were they kind to you there?

PHILIP: Yes. There was an old nurse there—she was sharp. She told me not to be a fool, but to go back to my wife. She said—"If she's any good, she will forgive you." *(He smiles whimsically)* Margaret, some day I am going to earn your respect, and then—I know, I shall be able to win you back to me all over again.

MARGARET: *(smiling sadly)* I don't know. That would be a wonderful thing. *(She weeps silently)* A very wonderful thing. *(Then suddenly she springs to her feet)* Ah, dreams! Philip! Dreams! And we must get to work.

(PHILIP is inspired by her manner, and there is a quickening of his spirit, a response to her in the new vibration in his voice)

PHILIP: Work! Yes—I'll not wait until tomorrow. I'll go to the mill now.

MARGARET: That's fine. Do it.

PHILIP: Yes, I'll take a bath and get into some fresh clothing first.

MARGARET: Do. You must look pretty shabby knocking about for a week without a home.

PHILIP: Oh, I'll be all right. I'd like to see Lucy. *(He looks about)* Where is she?

(MARGARET is at the table occupied with the flowers)

MARGARET: They are both out there. *(She indicates with a turn of her head)* In the garden.

(PHILIP goes quickly to the door opening upon the garden and gazes out eagerly. MARGARET, at the table, pauses in her work, gives a long sigh of relief and contentment. Her eyes look into the darkness and a serene joy illuminates her face. The picture slowly fades out as PHILIP steps buoyantly into the garden)

THE END OF THE PLAY

THE GREAT DIVIDE (1906)

I am heart and soul dedicated to the conviction that modern life can be presented on the stage in the poetic mediums and adequately presented only in that way.

* * *

The fact is that Mr. Moody, who has already placed himself at the head of modern American poets, has not ceased to be a poet in assaying the stage—though his play is written in the simplest and most unaffected prose.

It is one of the ironies of American dramatic history that the play which many critics have called the first modern American drama was written by a poet/playwright who felt, as stated in the first epigraph above, taken from his letter to contemporary dramatist Percy MacKaye, that the best expressions of the contemporary condition were to be contained within his verse plays. But as the *New York Sun*'s reviewer John Corbin noted in his critique of the New York opening, also quoted above, William Vaughn Moody's play employs its prose in a most poetic fashion, utilizing a host of **imagistic** devices to sustain its contrast between the binary opposites that form the core of the play's meaning. At its heart, *The Great Divide* addresses what Moody considered two abiding, interconnected problems at the core of American culture in particular and of "modern" culture in general, which prevented people from achieving happiness and fulfillment in life. The first of these is humanity's increasingly sterile spiritual existence, a state made evident, to Moody, by people's seemingly innate longing after a reunion with the divine. The second challenge is the legacy of Puritan religious repression, which couches humanity's collective life in terms of sin, mortification, atonement, and sacrifice. In dramatizing the internal struggles of Ruth Jordan and Stephen Ghent in the face of these dilemmas, Moody furthered the **modernist** move from plot-driven to character-based drama.

William Vaughn Moody was born in Spencer, Indiana, to Burdette and Henriette Moody on July 8, 1869. His father had been a steamboat captain on the Ohio and Mississippi rivers until his boat was confiscated at Memphis during the Civil War. Shortly after his son's birth, the elder Moody moved his family to New Albany, Indiana, right across the Ohio River from Louisville, Kentucky, so that he might take a job in his brother-in-law's iron works. William Vaughn Moody grew up in New Albany nurtured by his father's tales of freedom on the river and by his mother's love of music, art, and literature. Moody early indicated a contemplative disposition and was encouraged to attend college in the East. After his mother died in 1884 and his father succumbed in 1886, Moody taught high school for a year and then secured a job as a tutor to a student studying for admission to Yale. This position allowed Moody to study at the Riverview Academy in Poughkeepsie, New York, an Ivy League preparatory school from which he graduated in 1889. He entered Harvard on scholarship, supplemented by a loan from an uncle and his own efforts as a proctor, tutor, typist, and editor. He quickly established himself among the literary-minded students, writing poems for Harvard's literary magazines. After graduating in a remarkable three years, he toured Europe as a tutor, returning to Harvard to secure a master's degree in 1894. He joined Harvard's faculty as an instructor of English the same year, but moved on to become assistant professor of English at the University of Chicago in 1895. Though conscientious, Moody much preferred his own writing to correcting papers and worked steadily to minimize his teaching responsibilities.

The financial rewards of textbooks on English literature that he coauthored with Robert M. Lovett eventually allowed him to leave his teaching position, and after 1902 he did not return to full-time teaching for the remainder of his life.

Moody's first verse play of a projected three-part cycle, *The Masque of Judgment*, was published in 1900, followed by a book of poetry, *Poems* (1901), which secured his reputation as a major American poet. A second verse play, *The Fire-Bringer*, followed in 1904. His stature was given another boost by his election to the National Institute of Arts and Letters. His first prose effort for the stage, *The Great Divide*, originally entitled *The Sabine Woman*, was produced in 1906, although not published until 1909. His achievements were again recognized when Yale conferred upon him the honorary Doctor of Letters. *The Faith Healer*, which Moody had begun before *The Great Divide*, was not performed until 1909. Throughout this period of intense productivity (which generated not only his plays and poems but numerous essays, reviews, and textbooks), Moody became increasingly romantically involved with his longtime friend, Harriet Brainerd. Their letters reveal an energetic and affectionate couple, whose brief marriage was plagued by Moody's deteriorating health. After Harriet nursed him through a severe typhoid fever attack, the two finally married May 7, 1909, spending the summer travelling in Europe in a vain hope that the relaxation would restore Moody's failing eyesight. Two subsequent operations at Johns Hopkins for a brain tumor proved unsuccessful. After a brief sojourn in California during which time he wrote an act of *The Death of Eve* (intended as the third play of his trilogy), Moody died in Colorado Springs, Colorado, October 17, 1910. He was 41 years old.

While at first glance *The Great Divide* may seem a bit of a departure for a poet whose previous dramatic work had been in verse, Maurice Brown makes the excellent point that "the theme of salvation through masculine strength and the power of passion is central to Moody's earlier work," including *The Fire-Bringer*. Moody constantly wrestles with spiritual issues throughout his poetry as well as his verse and prose plays. For Moody, as for Henry Adams and many others at the turn of the century, the march of modernity encompassed a displacement of older spiritual formulations in favor of newer, technological ones—the replacement of the Virgin by the Dynamo, as Adams expressed it in *The Education of Henry Adams* (1907). For both Moody and Adams, the modern age in general, and modern America in particular, seemed intent upon ignoring or repressing spiritual life in its rush into the industrial, technological future. Against the modern world's materialist rigidity, Moody posited a mystical union between the individual and the Life-Force, a concept seemingly derived from Moody's own reading of Greek literature and philosophy. This position had significant consequences, for, as Gary Richardson has noted elsewhere, embracing "Almighty Nature" as the path to spiritual enlightenment struck a telling blow "both at the conventional, emotionally stultifying, religious foundations of the country as well as at the assumptions associated with economic, biological and social determinism."

Another major contribution to American drama was Moody's reconfiguration of the frontier myth. Unlike the simple binary opposition between civilization and wilderness that had been a permanent fixture in the American theatre since at least Stone's *Metamora*, Moody insists that the sublimity of the West offers modern Americans their last opportunity to apprehend Almighty Nature without the constrictions imposed by the rigid moralism of traditional religion, especially Calvinist Christianity. In a strategy that startlingly anticipates such plays as Sam Shepard's *True West*, Moody begins the play by seemingly embracing the romanticized version of the frontier popularized by a host of Western **melodramas**. Slowly, however, he deconstructs this naturalized frontier to reveal a less tidy, more disturbing primal force embodied in Stephen Ghent, the savage of male fantasy, and of female fantasy—at least as male writers create and project those fantasies. Ghent is little more than a sexual caveman who can say without apology that most "good women" are taken "by main strength and fraud," and that wives, specifically, are all "paid for in some good coin or other." The commercialization of the female body, which turns Ruth into property to be purchased by the person with the largest cache of gold nuggets and the quickest pistol, gives neither the playwright nor his protagonist pause. Whatever the shortcomings of his gender ideology, however, Ghent offers an energy, which can, Moody suggests, reinvigorate the staid, passionless Eastern world personified by Ruth.

If Ghent represents the Western Life-Force in all its vitality *and* violence, Ruth embodies the legacy of dessicated Puritan self-loathing and abnegation. Like many a Civil War melodrama heroine, Ruth clings to an ideology whose essential falsity she herself reveals in the moment in which she intuitively chooses life over death by deciding not to kill either Ghent or herself when she has the chance. But she represses the "truth," choosing instead to indulge the soul-numbing mortification rituals of her Puritan ancestors in an attempt to regain the spiritual purity she feels Ghent has stripped from her. The result, however, is not the romantic transfiguration of *The Scarlet Letter*'s Hester Prynne, but the tormented spiral toward self-dissolution of Arthur Dimmesdale. Ruth's final acceptance of her husband suggests the reconciliation of the Eastern intellect and the Western body, the rebirth of the classical ideal of a sound mind in a sound body. But from the woman's perspective this reintegration of body and mind comes at a high price.

Despite Moody's pointed questioning of the double standard, his play's gender assumptions are ultimately less radical than they seemed to the play's contemporary audiences. The feeling of liberation that permeates the play's conclusion tends to deflect the audience's attention from the subtle reconstitution of male and female roles that, while strikingly at odds with contemporary practice, nevertheless reinscribes long-standing, foundational arguments about gender difference. While the force of Ghent's—and Moody's—argument hinges upon the tacit admission of women's sexuality (a position quite daring given the period's representation of women as either angelic wife/mother or demonic seductress), the configuration that Ghent establishes once again posits women as humanity's moral transformative agent. Moody certainly does not reassert the sexual double standard as his generation knew it. But, as Lois Gottlieb asserts, while Moody transforms the terms of the debate, he does not fundamentally challenge the premises of the double standard itself. While new Romans may seize new Sabine women, the consequences remain the same—the growth of a spiritually vital civilization whose highest ideals embrace the male "spiritual necessity" of occasionally violating the rules of civilization itself in order to remain true to the "Almighty Spirit" that prompts them.

The Great Divide does indicate a new direction in American drama. Though Moody's personal influence was limited by his untimely death, the reception of his best-known play indicated that the American theatrical public might be ready for a **realism** that transcended the representational verisimilitude for which Moody's contemporary David Belasco was noted. Through subtle characterization, poetic expression, a telling use of landscape, and piercing psychological insight into the way America constructed gender roles and, thus, the way American men and women interacted with one another, Moody's *The Great Divide* paved the way for the next generation of playwrights and that generation's greatest practitioner, Eugene O'Neill.

WORKS CONSULTED

Brown, Maurice. *Estranging Dawn: The Life and Works of William Vaughn Moody.* Carbondale: Southern Illinois University Press, 1973.

Corbin, John. Review of *The Great Divide. New York Sun,* Oct. 4, 1906. Rpt. in *The American Theatre as Seen by Its Critics, 1752–1934.* Eds. Montrose J. Moses and John Mason Brown. New York: Norton, 1934. 176–178.

Gottlieb, Lois C. "The Double Standard Debate in Early 20th–Century American Drama." *Michigan Academician,* 7 (1975): 441–452.

Halpern, Martin. *William Vaughn Moody.* New York: Twayne, 1964.

Moody, William Vaughn. *Some Letters of William Vaughn Moody.* Ed. Daniel Gregory Mason. Boston and New York: Houghton Mifflin, 1913.

———. *Letters to Harriet.* Ed. Percy MacKaye. Boston: Houghton Mifflin, 1935.

———. *Some Letters of William Vaughn Moody.* Ed. Daniel Gregory Mason. Boston and New York: Houghton Mifflin, 1913.

———. *The Plays and Poems of William Vaughn Moody.* 2 Vols. Ed. John M. Manly. Boston and New York: Houghton Mifflin, 1912.

Richardson, Gary A. *American Drama from the Colonial Period through World War I: A Critical History.* New York: Twayne, 1993.

Stephens, Judith L. "Subverting the Demon-Angel Dichotomy: Innovation and Feminist Intervention in Twentieth-Century Drama." *Text and Performance Quarterly,* 1 (1989): 53–64.

C H A R A C T E R S

PHILIP JORDAN

POLLY JORDAN . . . . Philip's wife

MRS JORDAN . . . . his mother

RUTH JORDAN . . . . his sister

WINTHROP NEWBURY

DR NEWBURY . . . . Winthrop's father

STEPHEN GHENT

LON ANDERSON

BURT WILLIAMS

DUTCH

A MEXICAN

A CONTRACTOR

AN ARCHITECT

A BOY

ACT I

Interior of PHILIP JORDAN'S *cabin in southern Arizona, on a late afternoon in spring. A large room rudely built, adorned with blankets, pottery, weapons, and sacred images of the local Indian tribes, and hung with trophies of the chase, together with hunting-knives, saddles, bridles, nose-bags for horses, lariats, and other paraphernalia of frontier life. Through a long low window at the back the desert is seen, intensely colored, and covered with the uncouth shapes of giant cacti, dotted with bunches of gorgeous bloom. The entrance door is on the left (from the spectator's standpoint), in a projecting elbow of the room; farther to the left is a door leading to the sleeping-quarters. On the right is a cook-stove, a cupboard for dishes and household utensils, and a chimney-piece, over which hangs a bleached cow's-skull supporting a rifle.*

At a rude table in the centre sits PHILIP JORDAN, *a man of thirty-four, mending a bridle.* POLLY, *his wife, kneels before an open trunk, assisted in her packing by* WINTHROP NEWBURY, *a recent graduate of an Eastern medical college.* RUTH JORDAN, PHILIP'S *sister, a girl of nineteen, stands at the window looking out.*

WINTHROP: *(as he hands the last articles to* POLLY) What on earth possessed you to bring such a load of duds to Arizona?

POLLY: They promised me a good time, meaning one small shindig—one—in the three months I've spent in this unholy place.
   (PHILIP *makes an impatient movement with the bridle; speaks gruffly*)

PHILIP: You'd better hurry. It's getting late.

RUTH: (*from the window*) It's getting cooler, which is more to the point. We can make the railroad easily by sunrise, with this delicious breeze blowing.

POLLY: (*gives the finishing touches to the trunk and locks the lid*) There, at last! Heaven help the contents.

PHILIP: (*gruffly, as he rises*) Give me a lift with the trunk, Win.
   (*They carry the trunk outside.* POLLY, *with the aid of a cracked mirror, puts on her travelling hat and cloak*)

RUTH: My, Pollikins! You'll be the talk of all the jack rabbits and sage hens between here and the railroad.

POLLY: Phil is furious at me for going, and it *is* rather mean to sneak off for a visit in a grand house in San Francisco, when you poor dears have to slave on here. But really, I can't endure this life a day longer.

RUTH: It isn't in nature that you should. Fancy *that* (*she indicates* POLLY *with a grandiose gesture*) nourishing itself on salt-pork, chickory beans, and airtight!

POLLY: Do you really mean to say that apart from your pride in helping your brother, making the project go, and saving the family fortunes, you really *enjoy* yourself here?

RUTH: Since Phil and I came out, one day has been more radiantly exciting than the other. I don't know what's the matter with me. I think I shall be punished for being so happy.

POLLY: Punished for being happy! There's your simon-pure New-Englander.

RUTH: True! I was discovered at the age of seven in the garret, perusing "The Twelve Pillars and Four Cornerstones of a Godly Life."

POLLY: (*pointing at* RUTH's *heart, speaks with mock solemnity*) If Massachusetts and Arizona ever get in a mix-up in there, woe be!—Are you ever going to have that coffee done?

RUTH: I hope soon, before you get me analyzed out of existence.

POLLY: (*as* RUTH *busies herself at the stove*) The main point is this, my dear, and you'd better listen to what the old lady is a-tellin' of ye. Happiness is its own justification, and it's the sacreder the more unreasonable it is. It comes or it doesn't, that's all you can say about it. And when it comes, one has the sense to grasp it or one hasn't. There you have the Law and the Prophets.
   (WINTHROP *and* PHILIP *enter from outside.* RUTH, *who has set out the coffee and sandwiches on the table, bows elaborately, with napkin over arm*)

RUTH: *Messieurs et Mesdames!*

WINTHROP: Coffee! Well, rather, with an all-night ride in the desert ahead of us. (*They drink their coffee,* PHILIP *standing sullenly apart*) Where do we get our next feed?

RUTH: With luck, at Cottonwood Wash.

WINTHROP: And how far may Cottonwood Wash be?

RUTH: Thirty miles.

WINTHROP: (*sarcastically*) Local measurement?

POLLY: (*poking* PHILIP) Phil, for Heaven's sake say something. You diffuse the gloom of the Pit.

PHILIP: I've had my say out, and it makes absolutely no impression on you.

POLLY: It's the impression on the public I'm anxious about.

PHILIP: The public will have to excuse me.

POLLY: I *am* horribly sorry for you two poor dears, left alone in this dreadful place. When Dr Newbury goes, I don't see how you'll support life. I should like to know how long this sojourn in the wilderness is going to last, anyhow.
   (*During the following,* RUTH *takes a candle from the shelf, lights it, and brings it to the table. The sunset glow has begun to fade*)

RUTH: Till Cactus Fibre makes our eternal fortune.

WINTHROP: And how long will that be?

RUTH: (*counts on her fingers*) Two years to pay back the money we raised on mother's estate, two years of invested profits, two years of hard luck and marking time, two years of booming prosperity. Say eight years!

POLLY: Shades of the tomb! How long do you expect to live.

RUTH: Forever!

(The sound of a galloping horse is heard, muffled by the sand)

WINTHROP: Listen. What's that?

(A boy of fifteen, panting from his rapid ride, appears at the open door)

PHILIP: *(rising and going toward the door)* What's the matter?

BOY: I've come for the doctor.

PHILIP: Who wants a doctor?

BOY: Your man Sawyer, over to Lone Tree.—He's broke his leg.

RUTH: Broken his leg! Sawyer? Our foreman?

PHILIP: There's a nice piece of luck!—How did it happen?

BOY: They was doin' some Navajo stunts on horseback, pullin' chickens out of the sand at a gallop and takin' a hurdle on the upswing. Sawyer's horse renigged, and lunged off agin a 'dobe wall. Smashed his leg all to thunder.

(WINTHROP looks vaguely about for his kit and travelling necessaries, while POLLY gives the boy food, which he accepts shyly as he goes outside with PHILIP. RUTH has snatched saddle and bridle from their peg)

RUTH: I'll have Buckskin saddled for you in a jiffy. How long will it take you to set the leg?

WINTHROP: Perhaps an hour, perhaps three.

RUTH: It's a big detour, but you can catch us at Cottonwood Wash by sunrise, allowing three hours for Sawyer. Buckskin has done it before. *(She goes out)*

POLLY: *(pouting)* This will spoil all our fun! Why can't the creature wait till you get back?

WINTHROP: Did you ever have a broken leg?

POLLY: Well, no, not exactly a leg. But I've had a broken heart! In fact, I've got one now, if you're not going with us.

WINTHROP: To tell you the truth, mine is broken too. *(Pause)* Did you ever dream of climbing a long hill, and having to turn back before you saw what was on the other side? *(POLLY nods enthusiastically)* I feel as if I'd had my chance to-night to see what was over there, and lost it.

POLLY: You'll excuse me if it sounds personal, Dr Newbury, but did you expect to discern a—sort of central figure in the outrolled landscape?

WINTHROP: *(embarrassed, repenting of his sentimental outburst)* No. That is—

POLLY: *(with a sweep of her arm)* O, I see. Just scenery!

(She laughs and goes into the inner room, L. RUTH reenters. The sky has partly faded and a great full moon begins to rise)

RUTH: Buckskin is ready, and so is the moon. The boy knows the trails like an Indian. He will bring you through to Cottonwood by daylight.

WINTHROP: *(taking heart)* We shall have the ride back together, at any rate.

RUTH: Yes.—I would go with you, and try to do something to make poor Sawyer comfortable, but we haven't another horse that can do the distance. *(She holds out her hand)* Good-bye.

WINTHROP: *(detaining her hand)* Won't you make it up to me? *(He draws her toward him)*

RUTH: *(gently but firmly)* No, Win. Please not.

WINTHROP: Never?

RUTH: Life is so good just as it is! Let us not change it.

(He drops her hand, and goes out, without looking back. POLLY reenters. The women wave WINTHROP good-bye)

POLLY: *(takes RUTH by the shoulders and looks at her severely)* Conscience clear?

RUTH: *(humoring her)* Crystal!

POLLY: *(counts on her fingers)* Promising young physician, charming girl, lonely ranch, horseback excursions, spring of the year!

RUTH: Not guilty.

POLLY: Gracious! Then it's not play, it's earnest.

RUTH: Neither the one nor the other. It's just your little blonde romantic noddle. *(She takes POLLY'S head between her hands and shakes it as if to show its emptiness)* Do you think if

I wanted to flirt, I would select a youth I've played hookey with, and seen his mother spank? *(Suddenly sobered)* Poor dear Win! He's so good, so gentle and chivalrous. But— *(With a movement of lifted arms, as if for air)* ah me, he's—finished! I want one that isn't finished!

POLLY: Are you out of your head, you poor thing?

RUTH: You know what I mean well enough. Winthrop is all rounded off, a completed product. But the man I sometimes see in my dreams is—*(Pausing for a simile)*—well, like this country out here, don't you know—? *(She breaks off, searching for words, and makes a vague outline in the air, to indicate bigness and incompletion)*

POLLY: *(drily)* Yes, thank you. I do know! Heaven send you joy of him!

RUTH: Heaven won't, because, alas, he doesn't exist! I am talking of a sublime abstraction—of the glorious unfulfilled—of the West—the Desert.

POLLY: *(lifts* RUTH'S *chin, severely)* We haven't by chance, some spring morning, riding over to the trading-station or elsewhere—just by the merest chance *beheld* a sublime abstraction—say in blue overalls and jumper? *(*RUTH *shakes her head)* Honest? *(More emphatic head-shaking.* POLLY *drops* RUTH'S *chin with a shrug of the shoulders.* PHILIP *enters)*

RUTH: *(putting on her riding-hat)* Is Pinto saddled?

PHILIP: Pinto is gone.

RUTH: *(astonished)* Gone where?

PHILIP: To that Mexican blow-out over at Lone Tree. Every man-jack on the ranch has disappeared, without leave asked or notice given, except this paper which I just found nailed to the factory door. *(*RUTH *takes the note and reads it anxiously. Then she slowly removes her hat and lays it away)* What are you up to now? We've no time to lose!

RUTH: *(with quiet determination)* I am not going.

POLLY: *(as* PHILIP *turns in surprise)* Not going?

RUTH: I must stay and look after the ranch.

PHILIP: O, come, that's out of the question!

RUTH: We have put all mother's money into this venture. We can't take any risks.

PHILIP: The men will be back to-morrow. It's not to be thought of—your staying here all alone.

POLLY: *(seats herself with decision)* One thing is certain: either Ruth goes or I stay.

PHILIP: *(takes off his hat and sets down the provision basket)* That suits me perfectly!

POLLY: *(hysterical)* But I can't stay! I won't stay! I shall go mad if I spend another night in this place.

RUTH: No, you mustn't stay. You would never get us worked up to the point of letting you go, another time. *(She lifts* POLLY, *and with arm around her waist leads her to the door)*

PHILIP: I refuse to leave you here alone, just to satisfy a whim of Polly's. That's flat!

RUTH: But, Phil, you forget the stores you're to fetch back. They will be dumped out there on the naked sand, and by to-morrow night— *(She blows across her palm, as if scattering thistledown)*

PHILIP: Well, what of it? A few hundred dollars' worth of stuff!

RUTH: A few hundred dollars means sink or swim with us just now.—Besides, there's poor Sawyer. He'll be brought back here to-morrow, and nobody to nurse him. Then inflammation, fever, and good-bye Sawyer. *(*PHILIP, *with a gesture of accepting the inevitable, picks up the grain-sacks and basket)*

POLLY: *(at the door, embracing* RUTH*)* Good-bye, dear. Aren't you really afraid to stay?

RUTH: I'm awfully sorry to miss the fun, but as for danger, the great Arizona Desert is safer than Beacon Hill.

POLLY: You're sure?

RUTH: If marauders prowl, I'll just fire the blunderbuss out the window, and they won't stop running this side of the Great Divide.

POLLY: *(kissing her)* Good-bye, dear.

RUTH: Good-bye. *(*POLLY *goes out)*

PHILIP: *(pausing beside* RUTH, *at the door)* Mind you put out the light early. It can be seen from the Goodwater Trail. There's no telling what riff-raff will be straggling back that way after the dance.

RUTH: Riff-raff! They're my sworn knights and brothers.

PHILIP: In that case, what makes you uneasy about the property?

RUTH: O, property! That's different.

PHILIP: Well, you mind what I say and put out the light.

RUTH: Yours for prudence! *(She puts her arm around his waist and draws him to her, kissing him tenderly)* Good-bye, Phil. *(He kisses her and starts to go. She still detains him. When she speaks again, her voice is softened and awed)* What a lovely night! Who would ever think to call this a desert, this moonlit ocean of flowers? What millions of cactus blooms have opened since yesterday!

PHILIP: *(looking at her dubiously)* What's the matter with you to-night?

RUTH: Nothing. Everything. Life!—I don't know what's got into me of late. I'm just drunk with happiness the whole time.

PHILIP: Well, you're a queer one.—Good-bye. I shall get back as soon as horseflesh will do it. *(He goes out)*

RUTH: *(as the rumble of the wagon is heard)* Good-bye! Good-bye, Pollikins! Good-bye! *(She takes the candle from the table and stands in the door for a time, then raises the light in one hand and waves her handkerchief with the other. She sets the candle again on the table, goes to the mantel-shelf, and takes down a photograph)* Dear Win! I forgot how disappointed *you* were going to be. *(Pause, during which she still gazes at the picture)* Clear, kind heart! *(After a moment she replaces it brusquely on the mantel-shelf, and raises her arms above her head with a deep breath. She stands thus, with arms crossed behind her head, looking at the photograph. Her gaze becomes amused and mischievous; she*

points her finger at the picture and whispers mockingly)* Finished! Finished!
(She begins to prepare for bed, taking down her hair, and re-coiling it loosely during the following. She hums a tune vaguely and in snatches, then with a stronger rhythm; at last she sings)

Heart, wild heart,
Brooding apart,
Why dost thou doubt, and why art thou
  sullen?
Flower and bird
Wait but thy word—

(She breaks off, picks up a photograph from the table, and looks at it for a moment in silence) Poor little mother! You look out at me with such patient, anxious eyes. There are better days coming for you, and it's troublesome me that's bringing them. Only you trust me!
(A man's face appears at the edge of the window, gazing stealthily in. As RUTH *turns, he disappears. She lays down the picture and sings again)*

This is the hour,
And thine is the power.
Heart, high heart, be brave to begin it.
Dare you refuse?
Think what we lose!
Think what we gain—

(The words grow indistinct as she takes up the candle and passes into the other room, from which her voice sounds from time to time in interrupted song. The man again appears, shading his face with a peaked Mexican hat so as to see into the darkened room. He turns and waves his hand as if signalling distant persons to approach, then enters through the open door. He looks cautiously about the room, tip-toes to the inner door and listens, then steals softly out, and is seen again at the window, beckoning. RUTH *reenters, carrying the candle. She is shod in moccasins, and clad in a loose, dark sleeping-dress, belted at the waist, with wide,*

hanging sleeves and open throat. As she crosses to the table she sings)

Heart which the cold
Long did enfold—
Hark, from the dark eaves the night thaw
    drummeth!
Now as a god,
Speak to the sod,
Cry to the sky that the miracle cometh!

(*She passes her hand over a great bunch of wild flowers on the table*)

Be still, you beauties! You'll drive me to distraction with your color and your odor. I'll take a hostage for your good behavior.
(*She selects a red flower, puts it in the dark mass of her hair, and looks out at the open door*)
What a scandal the moon is making, out there in that great crazy world! Who but me could think of sleeping on such a night?
(*She sits down, folds the flowers in her arms, and buries her face in them. After a moment she starts up, listens, goes hurriedly to the door, and peers out. She then shuts and bolts the door, draws the curtains before the window, comes swiftly to the table, and blows out the light. The room is left in total darkness. There are muttering voices outside, the latch is tried, then a heavy lunge breaks the bolt. A man pushes in, but is hurled back by a taller man, with a snarling oath. A third figure advances to the table, and strikes a match. As soon as the match is lighted* RUTH *levels the gun, which she has taken from its rack above the mantel. There is heard the click of the hammer, as the gun misses fire. It is instantly struck from her hand by the first man [*DUTCH*] who attempts to seize her. She evades him, and tries to wrest a pistol from a holster on the wall. She is met by the second man [*SHORTY*] who frustrates the attempt, pocketing the weapon. While this has been going on the third man [*GHENT*] has been fumbling with the lamp, which he has at last succeeded in*

lighting. All three are dressed in rude frontier fashion; the one called SHORTY *is a* MEXICAN *half-breed, the others are Americans.* GHENT *is younger than* DUTCH, *and taller, but less powerfully built. All are intoxicated, but not sufficiently so to incapacitate them from rapid action. The* MEXICAN *has seized* RUTH *and attempts to drag her toward the inner room. She breaks loose, and flies back again to the chimney-piece, where she stands at bay.* GHENT *remains motionless and silent by the table, gazing at her*)

DUTCH: (*uncorking a whiskey flask*) Plucky little catamount. I drink its health. (*Drinks*)

RUTH: What do you want here?

DUTCH: (*laughs, with sinister relish*) Did you hear that, Steve? (*He drinks again, and reaches out the flask to* RUTH) Take one, and pull in its purty little claws, eh? Jolly time. No more fuss and fury. (RUTH *reaches for a knife, hidden behind the elbow of the chimney.* DUTCH *wrests the knife from her and seizes her in his arms*) Peppery little devil!
(*With desperate strength she breaks from his clutch and reels from him in sickness of horror.* GHENT *remains gazing at her in a fascinated semi-stupor. Meanwhile, after closing the door, the* MEXICAN *has taken dice from his pocket, and, throwing them into a small vase on the table, shakes them and holds out the vase to* DUTCH. *He takes it and turns to* GHENT; *the latter has moved a step or two toward* RUTH, *who in her retreat has reached the chimney-piece and stands at bay*)

DUTCH: Come, get into the game, curse you, Steve! This is going to be a free-for-all, by God!
(*As he rattles the dice,* RUTH *makes a supplicating gesture to* GHENT)

RUTH: Save me! save me! (*Her gesture is frozen by his advancing towards her. She looks wildly about, shrinking from him, then with sudden desperate resolution speaks*) Save me, and I will make it up to you! (GHENT *again advances; she goes on pantingly, as she stands at bay*) Don't touch me! Listen! Save me from these others, and from yourself, and I will pay you—with my life.

GHENT: *(with dull wonder)* With—your life?

RUTH: With all that I am or can be.

GHENT: What do you mean?—*(Pause)* You mean you'll go along with me out of this? Stick to me—on the square?

RUTH: *(in a tragic whisper)* Yes.

GHENT: On the dead square?

RUTH: Yes.

GHENT: You won't peach, and spoil it?

RUTH: No.

(Pause, during which he looks at her fixedly)

GHENT: Give me your hand on it!

(She gives him her hand. The other men, at the table, have drawn their weapons, and hold them carelessly, but alert to the slightest suspicious movement on the part of GHENT)

DUTCH: *(as GHENT turns to them)* Shorty and me's sittin' in this game, and interested, eh, Shorty? *(The MEXICAN nods. GHENT comes slowly to the table, eyeing the two. DUTCH holds out the vase containing the dice)* Shake for her!

GHENT: Shake how?

DUTCH: Any damn way! Sole and exclusive rights. License to love and cherish on the premises! *(GHENT takes the vase, shakes the dice meditatively, is about to throw, then sets the vase down. He searches through his pockets and produces a few bills and a handful of silver, which he lays on the table)*

GHENT: There's all I've got in my clothes. Take it, and give me a free field, will you?

DUTCH: *(leaning over the table to GHENT, in plaintive remonstrance)* You don't mean me, Steve!

GHENT: *(to the MEXICAN)* Well, you, then! *(The MEXICAN spreads the money carelessly with his left hand to ascertain its amount, then thrusts it away with a disgusted grunt of refusal)*

DUTCH: Don't blame you, Shorty! A ornery buck of a dirt-eatin' Mojave'd pay more'n that for his squaw. *(RUTH covers her face shudderingly. GHENT stands pondering, watching the two men under* his brows, and slowly gathering up the money. As if on a sudden thought, he opens his shirt, and unwinds from his neck a string of gold nuggets in the rough, strung on a leather thread)*

GHENT: Well, it ain't much, that's sure. But there's a string of gold nuggets I guess is worth some money. *(He throws it on the table, speaking to both men)* Take that, and clear out.

DUTCH: *(draws up angrily)* I've give you fair warning!

GHENT: We'll keep everything friendly between me and you. A square stand-up shoot, and the best man takes her.

DUTCH: *(mollified)* Now you're comin' to!

GHENT: *(to the MEXICAN)* Then it's up to you, and you'd better answer quick!

THE MEXICAN: *(eyeing GHENT and RUTH, points to the gun lying on the floor)* I take him, too.

GHENT: No, you don't. You leave everything here the way you found it.

THE MEXICAN: Alla right.

(He pockets the chain and starts for the door)

GHENT: Hold on a minute. You've got to promise to tie the man who falls, on his horse, and take him to Mesa Grande. Bargain? *(The MEXICAN nods)* And mouth shut, mind you, or—*(He makes a sign across his throat)*

THE MEXICAN: *(nods)* Alla right. *(He goes out)*

GHENT: *(motioning toward the door)* Outside.

DUTCH: *(surprised)* What for?

GHENT: *(sternly)* Outside!

(They move toward the door. DUTCH stops and waves his hand to RUTH)

DUTCH: Don't worry, my girl. Back soon.

GHENT: *(threateningly)* Cut that out!

DUTCH: What's eatin' you? She ain't yours yet, and I guess she won't be, not till hell freezes over.

(He taps his pistol and goes out. GHENT picks up the rifle which has previously missed fire; he unloads it, throws it on the window-seat, and follows DUTCH. RUTH stands beside the table, listening. Four shots are heard. After a short time GHENT appears and watches from the door

the vanishing horses. He comes to the table opposite RUTH)

RUTH: *(in a low voice)* Is he dead?

GHENT: No; but he'll stay in the coop for a while. *(She sinks down in a chair.* GHENT *seats himself at the other side of the table, draws a whiskey flask from his pocket, and uncorks it awkwardly, using only his right hand)*

RUTH: *(as he is about to drink)* Don't!

GHENT: *(lowers the bottle and looks at her in a dazed way)* Is this on the square?

RUTH: I gave you my promise.

(Gazing at her, he lets the bottle sink slowly by his side; the liquor runs out, while he sits as if in a stupor. RUTH *glances toward the door, and half starts from her seat, sinking back as he looks up)*

GHENT: Give me a drink of water.

(She brings the water from a bucket in the corner. He sets the empty bottle on the table, drinks deeply of the water, takes a handkerchief from his neck, wets it, and mops his face)

GHENT: Where are your folks?

RUTH: My brother has gone out to the railroad.

GHENT: Him and you ranching it here by yourselves?

RUTH: Yes.

GHENT: Write him a note. *(He shoves paper, pen, and ink before her)* Fix it up anyway you like.

RUTH: Tell me first what you mean to do with me.

GHENT: *(ponders awhile in silence)* Have you got a horse to ride?

RUTH: Yes.

GHENT: We can reach San Jacinto before sun-up. Then we're off for the Cordilleras. I've got a claim tucked away in them hills that'll buy you the city of Frisco some day, if you have a mind to it! *(She shrinks and shudders)* What you shivering at? *(*RUTH *does not answer, but begins to write.* GHENT, *still using only one hand, takes a pistol from his pocket, examines it, and lays it carelessly on the table, within* RUTH'S *reach. He rises and goes to the fireplace, takes a cigarette from his pocket and lights it, and examines the objects on the mantel-shelf.* RUTH *stops writing, takes up the pistol, then lays it down, as he*

speaks without turning around) Read what you've written. *(*RUTH, *about to read, snatches up the pistol again, rises, and stands trembling and irresolute)* Why don't you shoot? *(He turns around deliberately)* You promised on the square, but there's nothing square about this deal. You ought to shoot me like a rattlesnake!

RUTH: I know that.

GHENT: Then why don't you?

RUTH: *(slowly)* I don't know.

GHENT: I guess you've got nerve enough, for that or anything.—Answer me; why not?

RUTH: I don't—know.—You laid it there for me.— And—you have no right to die.

GHENT: How's that?

RUTH: You must live—to pay for having spoiled your life.

GHENT: Do you think it is spoiled?

RUTH: Yes.

GHENT: And how about your life?

RUTH: I tried to do it.

GHENT: To do what?

RUTH: To take my life. I ought to die. I have a right to die. But I cannot, I cannot! I love my life, I must live. In torment, in darkness—it doesn't matter. I want my life. I will have it! *(She drops the weapon on the table, pushes it toward him, and covers her eyes)* Take it away! Don't let me see it. If you want me on these terms, take me, and may God forgive you for it; but if there is a soul in you to be judged, don't let me do myself violence. *(She sinks down by the table, hiding her face in her hands)* O, God have pity on me!

*(*GHENT *puts the pistol back into his belt, goes slowly to the outer door, opens it, and stands for some moments gazing out. He then closes the door, and takes a step or two toward the table. As he speaks,* RUTH'S *sobs cease, she raises her head and looks strangely at him)*

GHENT: I've lived hard and careless, and lately I've been going down hill pretty fast. But I haven't got so low yet but what I can tell one woman from another. If that was all of it, I'd be miles away from here by now, riding like hell for liquor to wash the taste of shame out of my mouth. But that ain't all. I've seen what I've been looking the world over for, and never knew it.—Say your promise holds, and I'll go away now.

RUTH: O, yes, go, go! You will be merciful. You will not hold me to my cruel oath.

GHENT: And when I come back? (RUTH *does not answer. He takes a step nearer*) And when I come back?

RUTH: You never—could—come back.

GHENT: No, I guess I never could.

RUTH: (*eager, pleading*) You *will* go?

GHENT: For good?

RUTH: Yes.

GHENT: Do you mean that?

RUTH: (*wildly*) Yes, yes, ten thousand times!

GHENT: Is that your last word?

RUTH: Yes. (*Pause. She watches him with strained anxiety*) O, why did you come here to-night?

GHENT: I come because I was blind-drunk and sun-crazy, and looking for damnation the nearest way. That's why I come. But that's not why I'm staying. I'm talking to you in my right mind now. I want you to try and see this thing the way it is.

RUTH: O, that is what I want you to do! You did yourself and me a hideous wrong by coming here. Don't do us both a more hideous wrong still! I was in panic fear. I snatched at the first thing I could. Think what our life would be, beginning as we have begun! O, for God's pity go away now, and never come back! Don't you see there can never be anything between us but hatred, and misery, and horror?

GHENT: (*hardening*) We'll see about that!—Are you ready to start? (RUTH, *conscious for the first time of her undress condition, shrinks, and folds her gown closer about her neck*) Go, and be quick about it. (*She starts toward her room; he detains her*) Where's your saddle?

(*She points at it and goes out.* GHENT *picks up the note she has written, reads it, and stands for a moment in reflection before laying it down. He*

gets more water from the bucket, drinks deeply, mops his face, and rolls up the sleeve of his left arm, which is soaked with blood. He tries awkwardly to stanch a wound in his forearm, gives it up in disgust, and rolls down his sleeve again. He reads the note once more, then takes RUTH's saddle and bridle from the wall and goes out. RUTH comes in; her face is white and haggard, but her manner determined and collected. She comes to the table, and sees the bloody handkerchief and basin of water. As GHENT enters, she turns to him anxiously)*

RUTH: You are hurt.

GHENT: It's no matter.

RUTH: Where? (*He indicates his left arm. She throws off her hooded riding-cloak, and impulsively gathers together water, towels, liniment, and bandages; she approaches him, quite lost in her task, flushed and eager*) Sit down.—Roll up your sleeve. (*He obeys mechanically. She rapidly and deftly washes and binds the wound, speaking half to herself, between long pauses*) Can you lift your arm?—The bone is not touched.—It will be all right in a few days.—This balsam is a wonderful thing to heal.

GHENT: (*watching her dreamily, as she works*) What's your name?

RUTH: Ruth—Ruth—Jordan. (*Long pause*) There, gently.—It must be very painful.
(*He shakes his head slowly, with half-humorous protest*)

GHENT: It's not fair!

RUTH: What isn't fair?

GHENT: To treat me like this. It's not in the rules of the game.

RUTH: (*as the sense of the situation again sweeps over her*) Binding your wound? I would do the same service for a dog.

GHENT: Yes, I dare say. But the point is, I ain't a dog; I'm a human—the worst way! (*She rises and puts away the liniment and bandages. He starts up, with an impulsive gesture*) Make this bad business over into something good for both of us! You'll never regret it! I'm a strong man!

(He holds out his right arm, rigid) I used to feel sometimes, before I went to the bad, that I could take the world like that and tilt her over. And I can do it, too, if you say the word! I'll put you where you can look down on the proudest. I'll give you the kingdoms of the world and all the glory of 'em. *(She covers her face with her hands. He comes nearer)* Give me a chance, and I'll make good. By God, girl, I'll make good!— I'll make a queen of you. I'll put the world under your feet! *(RUTH makes a passionate gesture, as if to stop her ears)* What makes you put your hands over your ears like that? Don't you like what I'm saying to you?

RUTH: *(taking the words with difficulty)* Do you remember what that man said just now?

GHENT: What about?

RUTH: About the Indian—and—his squaw.

GHENT: Yes. There was something in it, too. I was a fool to offer him that mean little wad.

RUTH: For—me!

GHENT: Well, yes, for you, if you want to put it that way.

RUTH: But—a chain of nuggets—that comes nearer being a fair price?

GHENT: O, to buy off a greaser!

RUTH: But to buy the soul of a woman—one must go higher. A mining-claim! The kingdoms of the world and all the glory of them! *(Breaking down in sudden sobs)* O, be careful how you treat me! Be careful! I say it as much for your sake as mine. Be careful!

GHENT: *(turns from her, his bewilderment and discomfiture translating itself into gruffness)* Well, I guess we'll blunder through.—Come along! We've no time to lose.—Where are your things? *(At her gesture, he picks up the saddle-pack which she has brought out of the bedroom with her, and starts toward the door)*

RUTH: *(taking a hammer from the window-ledge and handing it to GHENT)* Fix the bolt. My brother must not know.

(He drives in the staple of the bolt, while she throws the blood-stained water and handkerchief into the fire. He aids her in replacing the weapons on the walls, then takes the saddle-pack and stands at the door, waiting. She picks up her mother's picture, and thrusts it in her bosom. After standing a moment in hesitation, she takes the picture out, kisses it, lays it on the mantel, face down. She extinguishes the lamp, and goes out hastily. He follows, closing the door)

THE CURTAIN FALLS IN DARKNESS

ACT II

STEPHEN GHENT'S *home, in the Cordilleras. At the right, crowning a rude terrace, is an adobe cabin, stained of pale buff, mellowed to ivory by sun and dust. Over it clamber vines loaded with purple bloom. The front of the cabin is turned at an angle toward the spectator, the farther side running parallel with the brink of the cañon, of which the distant wall and upper reaches are crimsoned by the afternoon light. In the level space before the rocky terrace is a stone table and seats, made of natural rocks roughly worked with the chisel. The rude materials have manifestly been touched by a refined and artistic hand, bent on making the most of the glorious natural background. Against the rocks on the left stands a large hand-loom of the Navajo type, with weaving-stool, and a blanket half woven. On the table lies a half-finished Indian basket, and strips of colored weaving-materials lie in a heap on the ground. Cactus plants in blossom fill the niches of the rocks and lift their fantastic forms above the stones which wall the cañon brink. At one point this wall is broken, where a path descends into the cañon.*

LON ANDERSON, *a venerable-looking miner, with gray hair and beard, sits smoking before the cabin.* BURT WILLIAMS, *a younger man, peeps up over the edge of the cañon, from the path.*

BURT: Hello, Lon. Is the Missus inside? *(LON smokes on, without looking at the questioner)* Look here, I put a nickel in you, you blame rusty old slot-machine. Push out something!

LON: *(removes his pipe deliberately)* What you wantin' off'n her now? A music lesson or a headache powder?

BURT: Boss's waitin' down at the mine, with a couple o' human wonders he's brought back with him from wherever he's been this time. Something doin' on the quiet.

LON: You can tell him his wife ain't nowheres about.

(BURT produces an enormous bandana from his pocket, mounts the wall, and waves it. He sits on the wall and smokes for a moment in silence, looking down into the cañon, as if watching the approaching party. He points with his pipe at the cabin)

BURT: Funny hitch-up—this here one—I think.

LON: *(after a pause)* How much you gittin' a day now?

BURT: Same little smilin' helpless three and six-bits.

LON: Anything extry for thinkin'?

BURT: Nope! Throwed in. *(They smoke again. BURT glances down to reassure himself, then points at the loom and basket)* Queer business—this rug-weavin' and basket-makin', ain't it?—What d'ye s'pose she wants to sit, day in and day out, like a half-starved Navajo, slavin' over them fool things fur?—Boss ain't near, is he? Don't keep her short of ice-cream sodas and trolley-rides, does 'e? *(LON rises and approaches BURT, regarding him grimly)* Saw 'er totin' a lot o' that stuff burro-back over to the hotel week 'fore last.—An' Dod Ranger—you know what a disgustin' liar Dod is—he tells how he was makin' tests over in the cross-cañon, an' all of a sudden plump he comes on her talkin' to a sawed-off Mexican hobo, and when she sees Dod, she turns white's a sheet.

LON: *(with suppressed ferocity)* You tell Dod Ranger to keep his mouth shet, and you keep yourn shet too—or by Jeehosophat, I'll make the two of ye eat yer Adam's apples and swaller the core!

BURT: O, git down off'n yer hind legs, Lon! Nobody's intendin' any disrespect.

LON: You boys keep yer blatherin' tongues off'n her! Or you'll get mixed up with Alonzo P. Anderson—*(He taps his breast)*—so's it'll take a coroner to untangle ye!

BURT: *(deprecatingly)* I guess I'd stick up fur 'er 's quick as you would, come to that.

LON: Well, we don't need no stickin' up fur 'er. What we need is less tongue. *(He leans down and speaks lower)* Especially when the boss is round. You tell the boys so.

(BURT looks at him in surprise and is about to speak; LON makes a warning signal, indicating the approach of the party below. BURT descends, saluting GHENT respectfully)

GHENT: *(peeping up over the edge of the cañon)* Coast clear, eh, Lon?

LON: Yes, sir.

GHENT: Where is she?

LON: *(points along the brink of the cañon)* Kind o' think she went out to Look-off Ledge.—Guess she didn't expect you back to-day.

GHENT: *(speaking below)* Come up, gentlemen. *(GHENT emerges from the cañon, followed by an ARCHITECT, a dapper young Easterner, and a CONTRACTOR, a bluff Western type. GHENT is neatly dressed in khaki, with riding-boots and broad felt hat. He has a prosperous and busy air, and is manifestly absorbed in the national game of making money)* Take a seat.

CONTRACTOR: *(seats himself by the table)* Don't care if I do. That new stage of yours just jumped stiff-legged from the go-off. And the trail up here from the mine is a good deal of a proposition for the see-dentary.

ARCHITECT: *(as he takes in the stupendous view)* What a wonderful place! Even better than you described it.

GHENT: Yes. My wife picked it out.—Let's see your plans.

(He removes basket from the table, where the ARCHITECT unrolls several sheets of blue paper)

ARCHITECT: I have followed your instructions to the letter. I understand that nothing is to be touched except the house.

GHENT: Not a stone, sir; not a head of cactus. Even the vines you've got to keep, exactly as they are.

ARCHITECT: *(smiling)* That will be a little difficult.

GHENT: You can put 'em on a temporary trellis.— A little pains will do it.

CONTRACTOR: Maybe, with a man to shoo the masons off with a shot-gun.

GHENT: *(over the plans)* Provide a dozen men, if necessary, with machine guns.

CONTRACTOR: As you please, Mr Ghent. The owner of the Verde mine has a right to his whims, I reckon.

ARCHITECT: I have designed the whole house in the Spanish style, very broad and simple. This open space where we stand—*(Points to the plans)*—I have treated as a semi-enclosed *patio*, with arcaded porches.

GHENT: *(dubiously)* Good.

ARCHITECT: This large room fronting the main arcade is the living-room.

GHENT: I guess we'll have 'em all living-rooms. This place is to be lived in, from the word go.

ARCHITECT: *(humoring him)* To be sure, everything cheerful and open.—Here on the left of the inner court is the library and music-room.

GHENT: I'm afraid we won't have much use for that. My wife don't go in much for frills. I used to play the concertina once, but it was a long while ago.

ARCHITECT: It can be used for other purposes. For instance, as a nursery, though I had put that on the other side.

GHENT: *(embarrassed and delighted)* Um, yes, nursery.—Stamping-ground for the—? *(The* ARCHITECT *nods; the* CONTRACTOR *follows suit, with emphasis.* LON *nods solemnly over his pipe)* Good. *(The* ARCHITECT *bends over to make a note with his pencil.* GHENT *restrains him and says somewhat sheepishly in his ear)* You can leave it music-room on the map.

ARCHITECT: *(continuing his explanation)* This wing—
*(*GHENT, *interrupting him, holds the plan at arm's length, with head on one side and eyes squinted, as he looks from the drawings to the cabin and surroundings)*

GHENT: Looks a little—*sprawly* on paper. I had sort of imagined something more—more up in the air, like them swell tepees on the Hill in Frisco.
(He makes a grandiose outline of high roofs and turrets in the air)

ARCHITECT: I think this is more harmonious with the surroundings.

CONTRACTOR: *(in answer to* GHENT'S *inquiring look)* Won't look so showy from the new hotel across yonder. *(He points to the left, down the curve of the cañon wall)*

GHENT: What's your estimate on this plan, now you've seen the location?

CONTRACTOR: It's a long way to haul the stuff.—Say somewheres between twenty and twenty-five thousand. Twenty-five will be safe.

GHENT: *(slightly staggered)* That's a big lot of money, my friend!

CONTRACTOR: *(with cold scorn)* I thought we was talkin' about a *house!* I can build you a good sheep-corral for a right smart less.

GHENT: Well, I guess we don't want any sheep-corrals.

CONTRACTOR: I should think not, with the Verde pumping money at you the way they tell she does.

GHENT: *(holds up the plans again and looks at them in perplexed silence)* I'll tell you, gentlemen, I'll have to consult my wife about this before I decide. The fact is, I've been working the thing out on the sly, up to now.

CONTRACTOR: Expect to build it of an afternoon, while the lady was takin' her see-ester?

GHENT: I thought I'd smuggle her off somewhere for a while. *(He is silent a moment, pondering)* No! It's her house and she must O. K. the plans before ground is broke. *(He looks along the cañon rim)* Would you mind waiting a few minutes till I see if I can find her? *(He starts irresolutely, then turns back)* Or better still, leave the plans, and I'll see you at the hotel to-morrow morning. I haven't been over there since it was opened. I'd like to know what they're making of it.

CONTRACTOR: *(astonished)* Hain't been over to the Buny Visty yet?

GHENT: Too busy.

CONTRACTOR: Well, you'll find it an up-to-date joint, and chock full of tourist swells and lungers.

GHENT: Good-afternoon, gentlemen. You'll excuse me. You can find your way back all right? Take the left-hand path. It's better going.
(The ARCHITECT bows ceremoniously, the CONTRACTOR nods. GHENT disappears along the cañon brink behind the cabin)

ARCHITECT: *(has been examining the work on the loom, and has then picked up the unfinished basket, admiringly)* What a beautiful pattern! I say, this is like those we saw at the hotel. *(To LON)* May I ask who is making this? *(Lon smokes in silence; the ARCHITECT raises his voice, slightly sharp)* May I ask who is making this?

LON: *(benignly)* You kin, my friend, you kin!

ARCHITECT: Well, then, the question is put.

LON: And very clear-put, too. You'd ought to be in the law business, young man. *(He gets up deliberately)* Or some other business that'd take up all yer time.

ARCHITECT: *(between wrath and amusement)* Well, I'll be hanged! *(He follows his companion down the cañon path, stopping a moment at the brink to look round with a professional air at the house and surroundings, then at LON)* Tart old party! *(He descends. LON crosses to the table, looks over the plans, makes outlines in the air in imitation of GHENT, then shakes his head dubiously, as he rolls up the plans. RUTH appears, emerging from the cañon path. She wears the same dress as at the close of Act I, with a dark scarf-like handkerchief thrown over her head. She is pale and exhausted. She sinks on the rocks at the edge of the cañon)*

LON: *(approaching her, anxiously)* It's too much fer you, ma'am. You'd oughter let me go.
(He brings her a glass of water from an Indian water-jar before the cabin)

RUTH: *(tasting the water)* O, I thought I should never get back! *(She leans against a rock, with closed eyes, then rouses herself again)* Lon, take the glass, and see if you can make out any one down yonder, on the nearer trail. I—I thought some one was following me.

LON: *(speaks low)* Excuse me askin', Mis' Ghent, but is that dod-blamed Mexican a-botherin' you again?

RUTH: No. He has gone away, for good. It's some one I saw at the hotel—some one I used to know.—Look if you can make out a man's figure, coming up.

LON: *(takes the glass from the niche in the rocks, and scans the cañon path)* Can't see nothin' but a stray burro, an' he ain't got no figger to speak of.—Might be t'other side o' Table Rock, down in the pinyon scrub. *(RUTH gets up with an effort, takes the glass and looks through it, then lays it on the ledge)* Excuse me, ma'am, but—Mister Ghent come home this afternoon.

RUTH: *(startled)* Where is he?

LON: Huntin' for you down Look-off Ledge way. I 'lowed you was there, not knowin' what else to say.

RUTH: Thank you, Lon.—You can go now.
(He goes down the cañon path. RUTH looks once more through the glass, then crosses to the table, where she sits down and begins to finger the roll of plans. GHENT reenters. He approaches with soft tread and bends over RUTH. She starts up with a little cry, avoiding his embrace)

RUTH: You frightened me.—When did you come back?

GHENT: An hour ago.

RUTH: Was your journey successful?

GHENT: Yes. But my home-coming—that looks rather like a failure. *(Pause)* I expected to find you out on the bluff.

RUTH: Lon was mistaken. I had gone the other way. *(As she stands at the table, she begins to unroll the plans)* What are these papers?

GHENT: Haven't you one word of welcome for me, after five days? (RUTH *remains silent, with averted head, absently unrolling the packet*) Not a look even? (*He waits a moment, then sighs and seats himself moodily by the table*) I never can remember! After I've been away from you for twelve hours, I forget completely.

RUTH: Forget what?

GHENT: How it stands between us. It's childish, but for the life of me I can't help it.—After I've been away a few hours, this place gets all lit up with bright colors in my mind, like—(*Searching for a simile*)—well, like a Christmas tree! I dare say a Christmas tree don't amount to much in real life, but I saw one once, in a play,—I was a little mining-camp roust-about, so high,—and ever since it has sort of stood to me for the gates o' glory.

RUTH: (*with a hysterical laugh*) A Christmas tree! (*She bows her head in her hands, and repeats the words, as if to herself, in a tone in which bitterness has given place to tragic melancholy*) A Christmas tree!
(GHENT, *watching her moodily, crumples up the plans and throws them upon the ground. He goes toward the cabin, hesitates, turns, and comes back to the table, where* RUTH *still sits with buried head. He draws from his pocket a jewel-case, which he opens and lays before her*)

GHENT: There is a little present I brought home for you. And here are some more trinkets. (*He takes out several pieces of jewelry and tumbles them together on the table*) I know you don't care much for these things, but I had to buy something, the way I was feeling. And these papers—(*Picks them up and spreads them out on the table*)—these mean that you're not to live much longer in a mud shanty, with pine boxes for furniture. These are the drawings for a new house that I want to talk over with you. (*He points at the map and speaks glibly, trying to master his discomfiture at her lack of interest*) Spanish style, everything broad and simple! Large living-room opening on inner court. Library and music-room, bless your

heart. Bedrooms; kitchen and thereunto pertaining. Wing where the proprietor retires to express his inmost feelings. General effect sprawly, but harmonious with the surroundings. Twenty thousand estimated, twenty-five limit. Is she ours?

RUTH: (*in a dead, flat tone*) How much did you say the house is to cost?

GHENT: Twenty-five thousand dollars at the outside.

RUTH: And these—trinkets?

GHENT: O, I don't know.—A few hundred.

RUTH: (*draws the plans toward her and pours the jewels in a heap upon them from her lifted hands*) Twenty-five thousand dollars and the odd hundreds! (*She laughs suddenly and jarringly*) My price has risen! My price has risen! (*She laughs again, as she rises from the table and looks down the cañon path*) Keep those displayed to show to our visitors! My honor is at stake. (*She points down the path*) There is one coming now!

GHENT: Visitors? What visitors?

RUTH: Only an old school-friend of mine; a Mr Winthrop Newbury.

GHENT: What are you talking about? Are you crazy? (*He joins her, where she stands looking down into the cañon*) This fellow, is he really what you say? (RUTH *nods, with unnaturally bright eyes and mocking smile*) What does this mean?

RUTH: It means that he caught sight of me, an hour ago, in the hotel.

GHENT: In the hotel? What were you doing there?

RUTH: (*with biting calm*) Nothing wicked—as yet. They don't pay twenty-five thousand dollars over there—at least not yet! (GHENT *turns sharply, as if stung by a physical blow. She raises her hands to him, in a swift revulsion of feeling*) O, don't judge me! Don't listen to me! I am not in my right mind.

GHENT: (*sweeps the jewels together, and throws them over the cliff*) Do you want me to be here, while you see him? (*She does not answer*) Won't you answer me?

RUTH: (*again cold*) Act as you think best.

GHENT: It's a question of what will be easiest for you.

RUTH: O, it's all easy for me!
(GHENT *stands irresolute, then raises his hand in a gesture of perplexity and despair, and goes into the house, closing the door.* WINTHROP NEWBURY *appears at the top of the cañon path, looks curiously about, catches sight of* RUTH'S *averted figure, and rushes toward her*)

WINTHROP: Ruth! Is it really you?
(RUTH *starts involuntarily toward him, stretching out her arms. As he advances, she masters herself, and speaks in a natural voice, with an attempt at gayety, as she takes his hand*)

RUTH: Well, of all things! Winthrop Newbury! How did you find your way to this eagle's nest?

WINTHROP: I—we saw you—we caught a glimpse of you at the hotel, but we weren't sure. We followed you, but lost you in the cañon.

RUTH: We? Who is we?

WINTHROP: Your brother and his wife.

RUTH: (*turning the shock, which she has been unable to conceal, into conventional surprise*) Philip and Polly here!

WINTHROP: They took the other turn, down there where the path forks. We didn't know which way you had gone.

RUTH: Yes, but why on earth are they here at all?

WINTHROP: They are on their way East. They stopped over to see me.

RUTH: To see you? Are you—living here?

WINTHROP: I have been here only a week. (*He starts impulsively, trying to break through the conventional wall which she has raised between them*) Ruth—for God's sake—!

RUTH: (*interrupting him, with exaggerated animation*) But tell me! I am all curiosity. How do you happen to be here—of all places?

WINTHROP: What does it matter? I am here. We have found you, after all these miserable months of anxiety and searching. O Ruth—why—

RUTH: I have acted badly, I know. But I wish not to talk of that. Not now. I will explain everything later. Tell me about yourself—about Philip and Polly—and mother. I am thirsty for news. What have you been doing all these months, since—our queer parting?

WINTHROP: (*solemnly*) Looking for you. (*Pause*) O Ruth—how could you do it? How could you do it?

RUTH: (*touches him on the arm, and looks at him with dumb entreaty, speaking low*) Winthrop!

WINTHROP: (*in answer to her unspoken words*) As you will.

RUTH: (*resumes her hard, bright tone*) You haven't told me about mother. How is she?

WINTHROP: Well. Or she will be, now. Ruth, you ought at least to have written to her. She has suffered cruelly.

RUTH: (*quickly, with a nervous uplift of her arms*) Yes, yes, I know that!—And you are—settled here? You mean to remain?

WINTHROP: I am physician at the End-of-the-Rainbow mines, three miles below. At least I— I am making a trial of it. (*Pause*) How pale and worn you are.—Don't turn away. Look at me. (*She flinches, then summons her courage and looks him steadily in the face*) You are—you are ill—I fear you are desperately ill!

RUTH: (*moving away nervously*) Nonsense. I was never better in my life. (*She goes toward the cañon brink*) You haven't praised our view. We are very proud of it.

WINTHROP: (*following her*) Yes, very fine. Magnificent.

RUTH: But you're not looking at it at all! Do you see that bit of smoke far down yonder? That is the stamp mill of the Rio Verde mine.

WINTHROP: (*compelling himself to follow her lead*) Yes—the Rio Verde. One of the big strikes of the region. Dispute about the ownership, I believe.

RUTH: None that I ever heard of, and I ought to know. For—(*she makes a sweeping bow*)—we are the Rio Verde, at your service.

WINTHROP: You—your—husband is the owner of the Verde mine?

RUTH: No less!

WINTHROP: (*embarrassed*) We found the record of your marriage at San Jacinto. The name was Ghent—Stephen Ghent.

RUTH: Yes. He will be so glad to see some of my people. (WINTHROP'S *eyes have fallen on the basket at the foot of the table. He picks it up, examines it curiously, and looks meaningly at* RUTH, *who snatches it from his hand and throws it over the cliff*) A toy I play with! You know I always have to keep my hands busy pottering at some rubbishy craft or other.

WINTHROP: (*is about to speak, but checks himself. He points at the loom*) And the blanket, too?

RUTH: Yes, another fad of mine. It is really fascinating work. The Indian women who taught me think I am a wonder of cleverness.

WINTHROP: So do—the women—over there. (*He points across the cañon*)

RUTH: (*flushing*) Ah, yes, you saw some of my stuff at the hotel. You know how vain I am. I had to show it.

WINTHROP: Perhaps. But why should the wife of the man who owns the Verde mine *sell* her handiwork, and under such—such vulgar conditions?

RUTH: (*brilliantly explanatory*) To see if it *will* sell, of course! That is the test of its merit.
(*He looks at her in mute protest, then with a shake of the head, rises and puts on his hat*)

WINTHROP: Do you want to see the others?

RUTH: Why, yes, to be sure I do. How should I not?

WINTHROP: You haven't seemed very anxious—these last eight months.

RUTH: True. I have been at fault. I so dread explanations. And Phil's tempests of rage! Poor boy, he must feel sadly ill-used.

WINTHROP: He does. (*Hesitates*) If there is any reason why you would rather he didn't see you, just now,—

RUTH: There is no reason. At least, none valid.

WINTHROP: Then I will bring them up.

RUTH: By all means. (*She holds out her hand, smiling*) Auf wiedersehen!
(WINTHROP *releases her hand and goes toward the cañon path. He waves, and turns to* RUTH)

WINTHROP: They are just below. (*As* RUTH *advances he takes her hand and looks searchingly into her eyes*) For old friendship's sake, won't you give me one human word before they come? At least answer me honestly one human question?

RUTH: (*keeping up her hard, bright gayety*) In the great lottery of a woman's answers there is always one such prize!

WINTHROP: (*dejectedly, as he drops her hand*) It's no use, if that is your mood.

RUTH: My mood! You old bugbear! I am as sober-serious as my stars ever let me be.

WINTHROP: Did you, that night you bade me good-bye, know that—this was going to happen?

RUTH: (*cordially explanatory*) No. It was half accident, half wild impulse. Phil left me at the ranch alone. My lover came, impatient, importunate, and I—went with him.

WINTHROP: And your—this man—to whom you are married—pardon me, you don't need to answer unless you wish—for how long had you known him?

RUTH: (*solemnly, as she looks him straight in the eyes*) All my life! And for aeons before.
(*He looks at her for a moment, then goes toward the cañon path.* POLLY'S *voice is heard calling*)

POLLY: (*not yet visible*) Win! Win!

WINTHROP: (*calls down the cañon*) Come up! Come up!
(RUTH *goes past him down the cañon path. In a moment she reappears, with* POLLY. *They are laughing and talking as they come*)

POLLY: Ruth!

RUTH: Dear old Polly!

POLLY: You *naughty* girl!

RUTH: If our sins must find us out, you are the kind of Nemesis I choose.

POLLY: My! But you're a shady character. And sly!
(PHILIP *appears.* RUTH *hurries to embrace him, while* POLLY, *fanning herself with her handkerchief, examines the house and surroundings with curiosity*)

RUTH: O Phil!—Dear old man! (*She covers his face lightly with her hands*) No scolding, no frowns. This is the finding of the prodigal, and she expects a robe and a ring.

POLLY: (*seating herself on a rock*) Heavens, what a climb!—I'm a rag.

RUTH: *(motions to the men to be seated)* The cabin wouldn't hold us all, but there's one good thing about this place; there's plenty of outdoors.

WINTHROP: *(looking about)* I should say there was!

POLLY: To think of our practical Ruth doing the one really theatrical thing known in the annals of Milford Corners, Mass.!—And what a setting! My dear, your stage arrangements are perfect.

RUTH: In this case Providence deserves the credit. We may have come here to have our pictures taken, but we stayed to make a living. *(PHILIP has drawn apart, gloomy and threatening. POLLY keeps up her heroic efforts to give the situation a casual and humorous air)*

POLLY: *(with jaunty challenge)* Well, where is he?

RUTH: Who?

POLLY: He! *(RUTH points at the cabin, smiling)* Well, produce him!

RUTH: *(following, with gratitude in her eyes, the key of lightness and raillery which POLLY has struck)* You insist?

POLLY: Absolutely.

RUTH: O, very well!

(She goes up the rocky incline, and enters the cabin, calling: "Steve! Steve!" POLLY goes to PHILIP and shakes him)

POLLY: Now you behave! *(Indicates WINTHROP)* He's behaving.

(RUTH reappears in the doorway, followed by GHENT)

RUTH: *(with elaborate gayety, as they descend the rocks)* Well, Stephen, since they've run us to earth, I suppose we must put a good face on it, and acknowledge them.—This is Polly, of whom I've talked so much. Polly the irresistible. Beware of her! *(POLLY shakes his hand cordially)* And this is—my brother Philip. *(GHENT extends his hand, which PHILIP pointedly ignores. RUTH goes on hastily, to cover the insult)* And this is my old school-friend, Winthrop Newbury. *(They shake hands)*

WINTHROP: *(to PHILIP, formally explanatory)* Mr Ghent is the owner of the famous Verde mine.

GHENT: Part owner, sir. I hadn't the capital to develop with, so I had to dispose of a half-interest.

WINTHROP: Isn't there some litigation under way?

RUTH: *(looking at GHENT, surprised)* Litigation?

GHENT: Yes—a whole rigmarole.

POLLY: *(catching at a straw to make talk)* Heaven help you if you have got entangled in the law! I can conceive of nothing more horrible or ghostly than a court of law; unless *(She glances at PHILIP)* it is that other court of high justice, which people hold in private to judge their fellows, from hearsay and half-knowledge!

RUTH: *(keeping up the play desperately, as she blesses POLLY with a look)* But there must be law, just the same, and penalties and rewards and all that. Else what's the use of being good?

POLLY: Like you—for instance!

RUTH: Well, yes, like me!

POLLY: You are not good, you are merely magnificent. I want to be magnificent! I want to live on the roof of the world and own a gold mine! *(To GHENT)* Show me where the sweet thing is.

GHENT: We can get a better view of the plant from the ledge below. Will you go down?

(GHENT, POLLY, and WINTHROP go down the cañon path. RUTH takes PHILIP by the arm, to lead him after)

PHILIP: No. We must have a word together, before the gabble begins again. Winthrop has given me your explanation, which explains nothing.

RUTH: *(trying to keep up the light tone)* Hasn't that usually been the verdict on explanations of my conduct?

PHILIP: Don't try to put me off! Tell me in two words how you came to run away with this fellow.

RUTH: *(hardening)* Remember to whom you are speaking and about whom.

PHILIP: I got your note, with its curt announcement of your resolve. Later, by mere accident, we found the record of your marriage at San Jacinto—if you call it a marriage, made hugger-mugger at midnight by a tipsy justice of the peace. I don't want to question its validity. I only pray that no one will. But I want to know how it came to be made, in such hurry and secrecy—how it came to be made at all, for that matter. How did you ever come to disgrace yourself and your family by clandestine meetings and a hedgerow marriage with a person of this class? And why, after the crazy leap was taken, did you see fit to hide yourself away without a word to me or your distracted mother? Though that perhaps is easier to understand!

RUTH: The manner of your questions absolves me from the obligation to answer them.

PHILIP: I refuse to be put off with any such patent subterfuge.

RUTH: Subterfuge or not, it will have to suffice, until you remember that my right to choose my course in life is unimpeachable, and that the man whose destiny I elect to share cannot be insulted in my presence.

PHILIP: Very well, I can wait. The truth will come out some day. Meanwhile, you can take comfort from the fact that your desertion at the critical moment of our enterprise has spelled ruin for me.

RUTH: *(overwhelmed)* Philip, you don't mean—!

PHILIP: Absolute and irretrievable ruin.

RUTH: Then you are going back East—for good?

PHILIP: Yes.

RUTH: But—mother's money! What will she do? *(PHILIP shrugs his shoulders)* Is everything gone—everything?

PHILIP: I shall get something from the sale. Perhaps enough to make a fresh start, somewhere, in some small way.

RUTH: *(comes to him, and lays her arms on his shoulders)* Phil, I am sorry, sorry!
(He caresses her; she bursts into suppressed convulsive weeping and clings to him, hiding her face in his breast)

PHILIP: Ruth, you are not happy! You have made a hideous mistake. Come home with me. *(RUTH shakes her head)* At least for a time. You are not well. You look really ill. Come home with us, if only for a month.

RUTH: No, no, dear Phil, dear brother! *(She draws down his face and kisses him; then lifts her head, with an attempt at lightness)* There! I have had my cry, and feel better. The excitement of seeing you all again is a little too much for me.

PHILIP: If there is anything that you want to tell me about all this, tell me now.

RUTH: O, there will be plenty of time for explanations and all that! Let us just be happy now in our reunion.

PHILIP: There will not be plenty of time. We leave to-morrow morning.

RUTH: Then you will take me on trust—like a dear good brother. Perhaps I shall never explain! I like my air of mystery.

PHILIP: Remember that if you ever have anything to complain of—in your life—it is my right to know it. The offender shall answer to me, and dearly, too.

RUTH: *(takes his head between her hands, and shakes it, as with recovered gayety)* Of course they will, you old fire-eater!

PHILIP: *(pointing to the blanket on the loom)* Ruth, at least tell me why—.
(RUTH does not see his gesture, as she is looking at the others, who come up from below. The men linger in the background, GHENT pointing out objects in the landscape)

RUTH: *(to POLLY, who advances)* Well, what do you think of us, in a bird's-eye view?

POLLY: In a bird's-eye view you are superb! *(She draws RUTH to her, and speaks in a lower tone)* And looked at near, you are an enthralling puzzle.

RUTH: *(half to herself)* If you only knew how much!

POLLY: *(taking RUTH by the chin as in Act I)* So you *had*—just by chance—riding over to the trading-station or so—met the glorious unfulfilled—in blue overalls and a jumper! I thought so! *(RUTH bows her head in a spasm of pain. POLLY, who does not see her face, goes on teasingly)* I see now what you meant about wanting one that wasn't finished. This one certainly isn't finished. But when he is, he'll be grand! *(RUTH moves away with averted head. POLLY follows her, peeping round to view her face)* Don't sulk! I meant nothing disrespectful. On the contrary, I'm crazy about him. *(In a louder tone)* And now that I've seen the outside of you, I *must* peep into that fascinating little house!

RUTH: *(to* GHENT, *who has drawn nearer)* Polly wants to go inside the cabin. I can't let her until we have shown her what it's going to be. *(With* GHENT'S *aid she spreads out the plans, which* POLLY *examines with curiosity)* These are the plans for our new house. You call us magnificent. We will show you that we are not. We are overwhelming!

WINTHROP: *(looking at his watch)* I am afraid we must be getting back. It grows dark very suddenly in the cañon.

RUTH: *(to* POLLY*)* Well, then you may come in, if you will promise to view the simple present in the light of the ornate future.

*(*POLLY *goes in.* RUTH, *lingering at the door for an instant, looks back anxiously at the men)*

PHILIP: *(curtly, to* GHENT*)* If you will permit me, I should like a word with you.

GHENT: Certainly.

*(*WINTHROP *effaces himself, making and lighting a cigarette, as he looks out over the cañon)*

PHILIP: In deference to my sister's wishes, I refrain from asking you for the explanation which is due me. *(*GHENT *bows in silence)* But there is one thing which I think I am at liberty to question.

GHENT: Do so.

PHILIP: I hear of your interest in a valuable mine. I hear of plans for an elaborate house. Why, then, is my sister compelled to peddle her own handiwork in a public caravansery?

GHENT: What do you mean? I don't understand you.

PHILIP: *(points at the loom)* Her rugs and baskets are on sale in the corridor of the hotel, fingered and discussed by the tourist mob.

GHENT: *(astonished)* This can't be true!

PHILIP: It is, however.

GHENT: I know nothing of it. I've had to be away a great deal. I knew she worked too hard over these things, but I took it for a mere pastime. Perhaps—No, I can't understand it at all!

PHILIP: I advise you to make inquiries. She has taken pains to conceal her identity, but it is known nevertheless, and the subject of public curiosity.

*(*POLLY *and* RUTH *come out from the cabin)*

POLLY: *(to* PHILIP*)* Take me away quickly, or I shall never enjoy upholstery again! *(To* RUTH*)* Please change your mind, dear, and come with us for the night.

RUTH: No. I will see you in the morning.

WINTHROP: We leave by the early stage.

RUTH: *(looking at him quickly)* You too?

WINTHROP: Yes, I have decided so.

RUTH: I will be there in good time, trust me. *(She kisses* POLLY *and* PHILIP*)* Good-bye, till morning. *(Gives her hand to* WINTHROP*)* Good-bye. *(*PHILIP *ignores* GHENT *pointedly in the leave-takings.* POLLY *bids him farewell with corresponding cordiality)*

POLLY: Good-bye, Mr Ghent. *(As they descend the cañon path, she is heard chatting enthusiastically)* O Phil, you ought to have seen the inside of that delightful little house! *(Her voice is heard for some time, indistinctly.* RUTH, *at the top of the path, waves to them as they descend)*

GHENT: *(looks long at her, with deep gratitude)* God bless you! *(She sits down on the rocks of the cabin terrace. He walks up and down in anxious thought. Once or twice he makes as if to speak. At length he stops before her)* You must go in and lie down. You are worn out.

RUTH: *(rousing herself)* No, there is something I must tell you first.

GHENT: *(points at the rug)* It's about this—work you have been doing?

RUTH: *(slightly startled)* You know of that?

GHENT: Your brother told me. I should have found it out to-morrow anyhow. *(Pause)* Have you wanted money?

RUTH: Yes.

GHENT: I thought I—I thought you had enough. I have often begged you to take more.

RUTH: I haven't spent what you gave me. It is in there. *(She points toward the house)*

GHENT: *(astonished)* You haven't spent—any of it?

RUTH: A little. Nothing for myself.

GHENT: But there has been no need to save, not after the first month or two. You surely knew that!

RUTH: Yes, I knew it. It was not economy.

GHENT: *(slowly)* You haven't been willing to take money from me?

RUTH: No. I know it was small of me, but I couldn't help it. I have paid for everything.—I have kept account of it—O, to the last dreadful penny! These clothes are the ones I wore from my brother's house that night. This shelter—you know I helped to raise that with my own hands. And—and some things I paid for secretly, from the little hoard I brought away with me. You were careless; you did not notice.

GHENT: *(sits down, dizzy from the shock of her words)* I must try to grasp this! *(There is a silence, during which he sits perfectly motionless. At last he turns to her)* Why—why did you stand up so plucky, so splendid, just now? Put a good face on everything about our life? Call me by my first name and all that—before your own people?

RUTH: We are man and wife. Beside that, my own people are as strangers.

GHENT: *(eagerly)* You say that? You can still say that?

RUTH: *(looks up, startled)* Can't you? *(She awaits his answer tensely)*

GHENT: *(desperately)* O, I don't know. I can't say or think anything, after what you have just told me!

RUTH: *(wails)* You can't say it! And it isn't true! It is we who are strangers.—Worse, a thousand times worse!

GHENT: *(rises and stands over her)* Don't let us dash ourselves to hell in one crazy minute! *(He pauses and hesitates. When he speaks again it is with wistful tenderness)* Ruth, do you remember our journey here? *(She lifts her head, looking at him with white, thirsty face)* I thought—it seemed to me you had—begun to care for me.

RUTH: That night, when we rode away from the justice's office at San Jacinto, and the sky began to brighten over the desert—the ice that had gathered here—*(She touches her heart)*—began to melt in spite of me. And when the next night and

the next day passed, and the next, and still you spared me and treated me with beautiful rough chivalry, I said to myself, "He has heard my prayer to him. He knows what a girl's heart is." As you rode before me down the arroyos, and up over the mesas, through the dazzling sunlight and the majestic silence, it seemed as if you were leading me out of a world of little codes and customs into a great new world.—So it was for those first days.—And then—and then—I woke, and saw you standing in my tent-door in the starlight! I knew before you spoke that we were lost. You hadn't the strength to save us!

GHENT: *(huskily)* Surely it hasn't all been—hateful to you? There have been times, since that.—The afternoon we climbed up here. The day we made the table; the day we planted the vines.

RUTH: *(in a half whisper)* Yes!—Beautiful days! *(She puts her hands suddenly before her face and sobs)* O, it was not my fault! I have struggled against it. You don't know how I have struggled!

GHENT: Against what? Struggled against what?

RUTH: Against the hateful image you had raised up beside your own image.

GHENT: What do you mean?

RUTH: I mean that sometimes—often—when you stand there before my eyes, you fade away, and in your place I see—the Other One!

GHENT: Speak plainly, for God's sake! I don't understand this talk.

RUTH: *(looking steadfastly, as at an invisible shape, speaks in a horrified whisper)* There he stands behind you now!—The human beast, that goes to its horrible pleasure as not even a wild animal will go—*in pack, in pack!* (GHENT, *stung beyond endurance, rises and paces up and down.* RUTH *continues in a broken tone, spent by the violence of her own words)* I have tried—O, you don't know how I have tried to save myself from these thoughts.—While we were poor and struggling I thought I could do it.—Then—*(She points toward the cañon)*—then that hole down there began belching its stream of gold. You began to load me with gifts—to force easy ways upon me—

GHENT: Well, what else did I care to make money for?

(RUTH *does not answer for a moment, then speaks slowly, taking the words with loathing upon her tongue*)

RUTH: Every time you give me anything, or talk about the mine and what it is going to do, there rings in my ears that dreadful sneer: "A dirt-eating Mojave would pay more than that for his squaw!" (*She rises, lifting her arms*) I held myself so dear! And you bought me for a handful of gold, like a woman of the street! You drove me before you like an animal from the market! (GHENT *has seated himself again, elbows on knees and face in his hands.* RUTH *takes slowly from her bosom the nugget chain and holds it crumpled up in her palm. Her tone is quiet, almost matter-of-fact*)

I have got back the chain again.

GHENT: (*looks up*) Chain?—What chain?

RUTH: (*in the same tone, as she holds it up, letting it unwind*) The one you bought me with.

GHENT: (*dumfounded*) Where the devil—? Has that fellow been around here?

RUTH: It would have had no meaning for me except from his hand.

GHENT: So that's what you've been doing with this rug-weaving and basket-making tomfoolery? (RUTH *does not answer, but continues looking at the chain, running it through her fingers and weighing it in her hand*) How long has this been going on?

RUTH: How long?—How long can one live without breathing? Two minutes? A few life-times? How long!

GHENT: It was about a month after we came here that you began to potter with this work.

RUTH: (*draws her hand about her neck as if loosening something there; convulsively*) Since then this has been round my neck, around my limbs, a chain of eating fire. Link by link I have unwound it. You will never know what it has cost me, but I have paid it all. Take it and let me go free. (*She tries to force it upon him, with wailing entreaty*) Take it, take it, I beseech you!

GHENT: (*holding himself under stern control*) You are killing yourself. You mustn't go on this way. Go and rest. We will talk of this to-morrow.

RUTH: Rest! To-morrow! O, how little you have understood of all I have said! I know it is only a symbol—a make-believe. I know I am childish to ask it. Still, take it and tell me I am free. (GHENT *takes the chain reluctantly, stands for a moment looking at it, then speaks with iron firmness*)

GHENT: As you say, your price has risen. This is not enough. (*He throws the chain about her neck and draws her to him by it*) You are mine, mine, do you hear? Now and forever! (*He starts toward the house. She holds out her hand blindly to detain him*)

RUTH: (*in a stifled voice*) Wait! There is—something else. (*He returns to her, anxiously, and stands waiting. She goes on, touching the chain*) It isn't only for my sake I ask you to take this off me, nor only for your sake. There is—another life—to think of.

GHENT: (*leaning to look into her averted face*) Ruth!—Is it true?—Thank God!

RUTH: Now will you take this off me?

GHENT: (*starts to do so, then draws back*) No. Now less than ever. For now, more than ever, you are mine.

RUTH: But—*how* yours? O, remember, have pity! *How* yours?

(PHILIP *appears at the head of the cañon path. Hearing their voices, he waits, half concealed*)

GHENT: No matter how! Bought if you like, but mine! Mine by blind chance and the hell in a man's veins, if you like! Mine by almighty Nature whether you like it or not!

RUTH: Nature! Almighty Nature! (*She takes the chain slowly from her neck*) Not yours! By everything my people have held sacred! (*She drops the chain*) Not yours! Not yours!

(*She turns slowly.* PHILIP *has come forward, and supports her as she sinks half fainting upon his neck*)

PHILIP: (*to* GHENT) I came back to get my sister for the night.—I don't know by what ugly spell you have held her, but I know, from her own

lips, that it is broken. *(To* RUTH*)* Come! I have
horses below.

GHENT: No!

PHILIP: *(measuring him)* Yes. *(Pause)*

GHENT: Let her say!

RUTH: *(looks long at* GHENT, *then at the house and
surroundings. At last she turns to her brother)*
Take me—with you. Take me—home!

*(*PHILIP, *supporting her, leads her down the
cañon path.* GHENT *stands gazing after them as
they disappear below the rim. He picks up the
chain and goes back, looking down after the descending figures. The sunset light has faded,
and darkness has begun to settle over the mountain world)*

CURTAIN

ACT III

Sitting-room of MRS JORDAN'S *house at Milford Corners, Massachusetts. An old-fashioned New England
interior, faded but showing signs of former distinction. The walls are hung with family portraits, several in clerical attire of the eighteenth century, one in
the uniform of the Revolutionary War. Doors open
right and left. At the back is a fireplace, flanked by
windows, the curtains of which are drawn. On the left
is a small table, with a lamp, books, and magazines;
on the right, near the fireplace, a sewing-table, with
lamp and sewing-basket. A bookcase and a writing-
desk occupy opposite corners of the room, forward.*

WINTHROP *and* PHILIP *stand near the desk, chatting.*
POLLY *is reading a newspaper at the table, left.* RUTH
*sits before the grate, sewing; her face is turned away
toward the fire.*

PHILIP: *(offers* WINTHROP *his cigar-case)* Have
another cigar.

WINTHROP: Well, as a celebration. *(Takes one and
lights it)*

PHILIP: Rather small business for the Jordan family, to be celebrating a bare escape from the
poor-house.

WINTHROP: Where did you scare up the benevo-
lent uncle? I never heard of him before.

PHILIP: Nor I, scarcely. He's always lived abroad.
*(*WINTHROP, *strolling about, peeps over* POLLY'S
shoulder)

WINTHROP: *(to* PHILIP, *with a scandalized gesture)*
Stock reports!

PHILIP: Her latest craze.

WINTHROP: Last week it was Japanese Samurai.

POLLY: *(crushingly)* And next week it will be—
Smart Alecks.

(The door on the left opens, and MRS JORDAN *enters, with* DR NEWBURY. *During the preceding
conversation* RUTH *has sat sewing, paying no
heed to the chatter.* MRS JORDAN *and the* DOCTOR
*look at her as they come in, but she does not look
up)*

MRS JORDAN: Sit down, Doctor, at least for a
moment.

DR NEWBURY: *(seats himself,* MRS JORDAN *near
him)* I can never resist such an invitation, in
this house.

MRS JORDAN: Dear Doctor, you've been a wonderful friend to me and mine all these years, since
poor Josiah was taken.

DR NEWBURY: But just when you needed help
most—

MRS JORDAN: I know how gladly you would have
offered it, if you could.

DR NEWBURY: Your brother-in-law in England
was able to redeem the property?

MRS JORDAN: *(hastily)* Yes, yes.—But what we are
to do for the future, with my little capital
gone—*(She speaks lower)* O, that dreadful West!
If my children had only stayed where they were
born and bred.

(She glances at RUTH, *who has let her sewing fall into her lap and sits staring into the
fire)*

DR NEWBURY: *(sotto voce)* Poor child!

*(*POLLY *looks up from the newspaper excitedly,
holding her finger at a place on the sheet)*

POLLY: I say, Phil! Win! Look here.

*(*PHILIP *and* WINTHROP, *who have been chatting and smoking apart, come to the table)*

PHILIP: What is it now?

POLLY: *(tapping on the paper)* Something about your Arizona scheme.

PHILIP: *(bending over her, reads)* "Allegheny pig-iron, 93¾, National Brick—"

POLLY: *(pointing)* No, there!

PHILIP: Arizona Cactus Fibre, 84. *(He picks up the paper, astounded)* Cactus Fibre listed! Selling at 84! *(He tosses the paper to* WINTHROP*)* This is the last straw!

MRS JORDAN: *(who has been listening anxiously)* What does it mean, Phil?

PHILIP: Only that the people who bought our plant and patents for a song, have made a fortune out of them.

*(*RUTH *has resumed her needle-work.* WINTHROP *offers her the paper, with his finger at the line. She takes it, looks at it vaguely, and lays it on the table)*

POLLY: *(leaning across)* Doesn't that interest you?

RUTH: *(tonelessly)* O, yes.

(She rises, lays her work aside, and goes toward the door, left)

DR NEWBURY: *(as she passes him)* Won't you bid me good-night, my child?

RUTH: *(giving him her hand)* Good-night, Doctor.

DR NEWBURY: *(shaking his finger)* Remember, no more moping! And from to-morrow, outdoors with you.

*(*RUTH *looks at him vacantly, attempting to smile. She moves toward the door, which* WINTHROP *opens for her)*

WINTHROP: *(holding out his hand)* You must bid me good-night, too, and good-bye.

RUTH: *(with a faint kindling of interest)* Are you going away?

WINTHROP: Only back to Boston. Some time, when you are stronger, you will come down and see our new sailor's hospital.

RUTH: Yes.—Good-bye.

(She goes out, WINTHROP *closing the door)*

WINTHROP: *(to* DR NEWBURY*)* I must be going along, father. Good-night, everybody! *(Patting* PHILIP'S *shoulder)* Hard luck, old man!

(He goes out by the hall door on the right, PHILIP *accompanying him)*

DR NEWBURY: *(looking after his son)* Brave boy! Brave boy! He keeps up a good show.

MRS JORDAN: You think he still grieves over her?

DR NEWBURY: Ah, poor chap! He's made of the right stuff, if he is mine.

MRS JORDAN: Let us not talk of it. It is too sad, too dreadful.

*(*PHILIP *reenters)*

DR NEWBURY: About part of it we must talk. *(He speaks so as to include* PHILIP *and* POLLY *in the conversation)* Mrs Jordan, I don't want to alarm you, but your daughter—I may as well put it bluntly—is in a dangerous state.

MRS JORDAN: *(frightened)* Doctor! I thought she seemed so much stronger.

DR NEWBURY: She is, so far as her body is concerned.

*(*MRS JORDAN *sits in an attitude of nervous attention, gazing at the doctor as if trying to formulate one of many questions pressing upon her.* PHILIP *comes forward and sits by the table, near them)*

PHILIP: Don't you think that the routine of life which she has taken up will soon restore her to a normal state of mind?

DR NEWBURY: Perhaps.—I hope so.—I would have good hope of it, if it were not for her attitude toward her child.

MRS JORDAN: *(overwhelmed)* You have noticed that, too! I haven't spoken to you of it, because—I haven't been willing to see it myself.

PHILIP: I can't see that there is anything particularly strange in her attitude. She takes care of the brat scrupulously enough.

POLLY: Brat!

MRS JORDAN: Brat! *(To* DR NEWBURY, *after a reproachful gaze at* PHILIP*)* With the most watchful, the minutest care, but—*(She speaks in a constrained voice, with a nervous glance at the door)*—exactly as if it were a piece of machinery!—Phil, do please lay down that paper-knife before you break it! Your father brought that to me from India. *(He obeys, but picks it up again absentmindedly, after a few seconds)* Pardon me, Doctor. She goes about her daily business, and answers when she is spoken to, but as for her really being here—*(She breaks out)* Doctor, what *shall* we do?

DR NEWBURY: She must be roused from this state, but how to do it, I don't know.

POLLY: *(rising, with heightened color and nervous emphasis)* Well, I do!

MRS JORDAN: *(looking at her with frightened interrogation)* Polly—?

POLLY: What she needs is her husband, and I have sent for him!

PHILIP: *(inarticulate with surprise and anger)* You—!

POLLY: Yes, I. He's been here a week. And he's an angel, isn't he, mother?

(PHILIP *snaps the paper-knife in two, flings the pieces to the floor, and rises, pale with rage)*

MRS JORDAN: *(gathering up the pieces with a wail)* O Phil! How could you! One of my most precious relics!

PHILIP: *(to* MRS JORDAN*)* Is this true, or is it another of her tedious jokes?

POLLY: *(protesting)* O, my dear, tedious!

MRS JORDAN: *(wipes her eyes, after ruefully fitting the broken pieces of the knife together and laying them tenderly on the table)* You don't deserve to have me answer you, but it is true.

PHILIP: Was this action taken with your knowledge?

MRS JORDAN: I do not expect to be spoken to in that tone. Polly telegraphed merely the facts. He came at his own instance.

PHILIP: But you have consented to enter into relations with him?

MRS JORDAN: I have seen him several times.

POLLY: *(triumphantly)* And yesterday we showed him the baby! Such fun, wasn't it, mother?

MRS JORDAN: *(wiping her eyes, sheepishly)* Yes, it was rather—enjoyable.

PHILIP: He can't be in this town. I should have heard of it.

POLLY: We've hid him safe.

PHILIP: Where?

POLLY: Never mind. He's on tap, and the sooner we turn on the spigot the better, is what I think. Doctor, what do you think?

DR NEWBURY: Let me ask you again to state your view of Ruth's case. I don't think I quite grasp your view.

POLLY: *(pluming herself, doctrinaire)* Well! Here on the one hand is the primitive, the barbaric woman, falling in love with a romantic stranger, who, like some old Viking on a harry, cuts her with his two-handed sword from the circle of her kinsmen, and bears her away on his dragon ship toward the midnight sun. Here on the other hand is the derived, the civilized woman, with a civilized nervous system, observing that the creature eats bacon with his bowie knife, knows not the manicure, has the conversation of a preoccupied walrus, the instincts of a jealous caribou, and the endearments of a dancing crab in the mating season.

MRS JORDAN: Polly! What ideas! What language!

DR NEWBURY: Don't be alarmed, Mrs Jordan. The vocabulary has changed since our day, and—the point of view has shifted a little. *(To* POLLY*)* Well?

POLLY: Well, Ruth is one of those people who can't live in a state of divided feeling. She sits staring at this cleavage in her life, like—like that man in Dante, don't you know, who is pierced by the serpent, and who stands there in hell staring at his wound, yawning like a sleepy man.

MRS JORDAN: O, Polly, do please try not to get our heads muddled up with literature!

POLLY: All I mean is that when she married her man she married him for keeps. And he did the same by her.

(PHILIP *rises, with uncontrollable impatience, and goes back to the mantelpiece, against which he leans, nervously tearing a bit of paper to pieces)*

DR NEWBURY: Don't you think that a mere difference of cultivation, polish—or—or something of that sort—is rather small to have led to a rupture, and so painful a one too?

POLLY: *(a little nonplussed)* Well, yes, perhaps it does *look* small. But we don't know the particulars; and men *are* such *colossal* brutes, you know, dear Doctor!

DR NEWBURY: *(judicially)* Yes, so they are, so they are!

POLLY: And then her pride! You know when it comes to pride, Ruth would make Lucifer look like a charity-boy asking for more soup.

DR NEWBURY: I think perhaps the plan should be tried. *(After a pause)* Yes, I think so decidedly.

PHILIP: I call this a plot against her dignity and peace of mind!

DR NEWBURY: *(rising)* Well, this conspirator must be going. *(He shakes hands with POLLY and MRS JORDAN, takes his hat and stick. PHILIP remains plunged in angry reflection. DR NEWBURY taps PHILIP jestingly on the shoulder with the tip of his cane)* When you have lived as long as I have, my boy, you'll—you'll be just as old as I am!

(He goes out, POLLY accompanying him to the door. PHILIP, disregarding his mother's conciliatory look and gesture as he passes her, goes out left. POLLY stretches her arms and draws a deep breath as the door closes after him)

MRS JORDAN: *(looking at her severely)* Pray what does that mean?

POLLY: O, Phil is such a walking thunder-cloud, these days. It's a relief to get rid of him.

MRS JORDAN: Have you done what you could to make his life brighter?

POLLY: I never had a chance. He has always been too much wrapped up in Ruth to think of me.

MRS JORDAN: How can you say such a thing? What do you suppose he married you for?

POLLY: Heaven knows! What do they ever do it for? It is a most curious and savage propensity. But immensely interesting to watch.

MRS JORDAN: *(with a despairing gesture)* If you hold such heathenish views, why are you so bent on bringing those two together?

POLLY: *(soberly)* Because they represent—what Philip and I have missed.

MRS JORDAN: And pray what have "Philip and I" missed?

POLLY: O, we're all right. But we're not like those two.

MRS JORDAN: I should hope not!

POLLY: Even I believe that now and then a marriage is made in Heaven. This one was. They are predestined lovers!

MRS JORDAN: *(mournfully, hypnotized by the evangelical note)* I pray it may be so. *(She looks suspiciously at POLLY)* You wretched girl! Predestined lovers and marriage made in Heaven, after all you've just been saying about how impossible he is.

POLLY: He is quite impossible, but he's the kind we can't resist, any of us. He'd only have to crook his little finger at me.

MRS JORDAN: *(lifting her hands in despair)* What are you young women coming to! *(Pause)* He seems to me a good man.

POLLY: *(delighted)* O, he's *good!* so is a volcano between eruptions. And commonplace, too, until you happen to get a glimpse down one of the old volcanic rifts in his surface, and see—far below—underneath the cold lava-beds—fire, fire, the molten heart of a continent!

MRS JORDAN: I only hope you have some vague general notion of what you are talking about.

POLLY: Amen.—And now let's consider when, where, and how we are to hale this dubious pair together.

MRS JORDAN: One thing is sure, it mustn't be here.

POLLY: Why not?

MRS JORDAN: On Philip's account.

POLLY: O, bother Philip! Wasn't that the doorbell?

MRS JORDAN: Yes. You had better go.

(POLLY goes out. After a moment she reenters, excitedly)

POLLY: It's Mr Ghent!

MRS JORDAN: *(amazed)* Mr Ghent? *(POLLY nods enthusiastically. GHENT enters. He is conventionally dressed, a black string tie and the broad-brimmed hat which he carries being the only suggestions of Western costume remaining. MRS JORDAN receives him in a flutter of excitement and alarm)* Mr Ghent—! Surely at this hour—!

GHENT: I beg your pardon. There was no other way. I am going West to-night.—Can I see you alone?

MRS JORDAN: *(looks at Polly, who goes out, pouting)* Going West to-night?

GHENT: Yes. Trouble at the mine.

MRS JORDAN: Isn't your business partner competent to attend to it?

GHENT: He's competent to steal the whole outfit. In fact, is doing it, or has done it already.

MRS JORDAN: *(vaguely alarmed)* And—my property here? Is that involved in the danger?

GHENT: Certainly not.

MRS JORDAN: *(relieved)* I have gone through such months of misery at the thought of losing the dear old place!—If Ruth only knew that we owe the very roof over our heads to you—

GHENT: Well, she isn't to know, that's understood, isn't it? Besides, it's nothing to speak of. Glad if you think it a service. She wouldn't.

MRS JORDAN: You mean—?

GHENT: I mean that if she knew about it, she wouldn't stay here overnight.

MRS JORDAN: Sit down. *(She motions him to a seat at the table; she sits near him, speaking with nervous impulsiveness)* Tell me what is the trouble between you! It has all been a dreadful mystery from the beginning!

GHENT: Is it a mystery that a woman like your daughter—?

(He stops and sinks into gloomy thought)

MRS JORDAN: Should have chosen you?—Pardon me, I don't mean anything unkind—*(He makes a gesture of brusque exoneration)* But having chosen—and broken faith with her brother to do it—

GHENT: *(nervously)* Let's drop that! *(Pause)* Mrs Jordan, you come of the old stock. Do you believe in the devil?

MRS JORDAN: Perhaps not in the sense you mean.

GHENT: *(tapping his breast)* I mean the devil inside of a man—the devil in the heart!

MRS JORDAN: O, yes. We are all forced by our lives to believe in that.

GHENT: Our lives! *(He looks slowly round the room)* How long have you lived here?

MRS JORDAN: For thirty years, in this house. Before I was married I lived in the old house down the road yonder, opposite the church.

GHENT: *(to himself)* Think of it!

MRS JORDAN: What did you say?

GHENT: *(gathers himself together)* Mrs Jordan, I want you to promise that what I put in your hands from time to time comes to your daughter as if from another source.

MRS JORDAN: You are going away for good?

GHENT: Yes.

MRS JORDAN: You give her up?

GHENT: A man can't give up what isn't his.

MRS JORDAN: What isn't his? She is your wife.

GHENT: No. Never has been.

MRS JORDAN: *(terrified)* O, pitiful heavens!

GHENT: I beg your pardon.—I was only trying to say—I used to think that when a couple was married, there they were, man and wife, and that was the end of it. I used to think that when they had a child, well, sure enough it was their child, and all said.—And there's something in that, too. *(He stares before him, smiting the table, and speaking with low intensity)* Damn me if there ain't something eternal in it! *(He sits for a moment more in gloomy thought)* Do you think she'll make up to the young one, after a bit?

MRS JORDAN: O, surely! To think otherwise would be too dreadful!

GHENT: I'd give a good deal to know.—It's kind of lonesome for the little rooster, sitting out there all by himself on the world's doorstep!—I must see her for a minute before I go.—Do your best for me.

MRS JORDAN: I will do what I can.

GHENT: You can put it as a matter of business. There is a matter of business I want to talk over with her, if I can get up the gumption.

MRS JORDAN: Hadn't you better tell me what it is?

GHENT: Well, it's about your son Philip. That little scheme he started out in my country—the Cactus Fibre industry.

MRS JORDAN: Yes?

GHENT: I believe he thinks his sister's going away when she did queered his game.

MRS JORDAN: It was a severe blow to him in every way. She was the life and soul of his enterprise.

GHENT: I want her to give him back the Cactus Fibre outfit, worth something more than when he dropped it.

MRS JORDAN: Give it back to him? She?

GHENT: *(takes papers from his pocket)* Yes. I happened to hear it was knocking around for nothing in the market, and I bought it—for the house, really. Hated to see that go to the dogs. Then I looked over the plant, and got a hustler to boom it. I thought as a matter of transfer, to cancel her debt, or what she thinks her debt— *(Pause)*

MRS JORDAN: *(fingering the paper with hesitation)* Mr Ghent, we really can't accept such a thing. Your offer is quixotic.

GHENT: Quix—what?

MRS JORDAN: Quixotic, it really is.

GHENT: *(doubtfully)* I guess you're right. It depends on the way you look at it. One way it looks like a pure business proposition—so much lost, so much made good. The other way it looks, as you say, quix—um—. Anyway, there are the papers! Do what you think best with them.

(He lays the papers on the table, and picks up his hat)

MRS JORDAN: Wait in the parlor. *(He opens the hall door)* The second door on the left.

(With an awkward bow to MRS JORDAN, he partly closes the door after him, when the inner door opens and RUTH appears. She goes to the sewing-table and picks up her sewing. Her mother, with a frightened glance at the half-open hall door, draws her back and kisses her. GHENT, unseen by RUTH, remains standing, with his hand on the doorknob)

MRS JORDAN: Ruth, you are a brave girl, and I will treat you like one.—Your husband is here.

RUTH: Here?—Where?

(GHENT pushes the door open, and closes it behind him. RUTH, sinking back against the opposite wall, stares at him blankly)

MRS JORDAN: He is leaving for the West again tonight. He has asked to see you before he goes. *(RUTH covers her face with her hands, then fumbles blindly for the latch of the door. Her mother restrains her)* It is your duty to hear what he has to say. You owe that to the love you once bore him.

RUTH: He killed my love before it was born!

MRS JORDAN: It is your duty to hear him, and part with him in a Christian spirit, for our sakes, if not for your own.

RUTH: For whose sake?

MRS JORDAN: For mine, and your brother's.—We owe it to him, as a family.

GHENT: *(raises his hand restrainingly)* Mrs Jordan—!

RUTH: Owe?

MRS JORDAN: We owe it to him, for what he has done and wishes to do.

RUTH: What he has done?—Wishes to do?

MRS JORDAN: Yes, don't echo me like a parrot! He has done a great deal for us, and is anxious to do more, if you will only let him.

RUTH: What is this? Explain it to me quickly.

MRS JORDAN: *(with growing impatience)* Don't think to judge your mother!

RUTH: I demand to hear what all this is! Tell me.

MRS JORDAN: *(losing control of herself)* He has kept us from being turned into the street! *(GHENT, who has tried dumbly to restrain her, turns away in stoic resignation to his fate)* He has given us the very roof over our heads!

RUTH: You said that uncle—

MRS JORDAN: Well, it was not your uncle! I said so to shield you in your stubborn and cold-hearted pride.

RUTH: Is there more of this?

MRS JORDAN: Yes, there *is* more. You wronged your brother to follow your own path of wilful love, and now you wrong him again by following your own path of wilful aversion. Here comes your husband, offering to make restitution—

RUTH: What restitution?

MRS JORDAN: He has bought Philip's property out there, and wants you to give it back to him. *(RUTH stands motionless for a moment, then looks vacantly about, speaking in a dull voice, as at first)*

RUTH: I must go away from this house.

MRS JORDAN: You don't understand. He claims nothing. He is going away himself immediately. Whatever this dreadful trouble is between you,

you are his wife, and he has a right to help you and yours.

RUTH: I am not his wife.

MRS JORDAN: Ruth, don't frighten me. He said those same words—

RUTH: He said—what?

MRS JORDAN: That you were not his wife.

RUTH: He said—that?

MRS JORDAN: Yes, but afterward he explained—

RUTH: *(flaming into white wrath)* Explained! Did he explain that when I was left alone that night at the ranch he came—with two others—and when gun and knife had failed me, and nothing stood between me and their drunken fury, I sold myself to the strongest of them, hiding my head behind the name of marriage? Did he explain that between him and the others money clinked—*(She raps on the table)*—my price in hard money on the table? And now that I have run away to the only refuge I have on earth, he comes to buy the very house where I have hidden, and every miserable being within it!

(Long pause. She looks about blankly and sinks down by the table)

MRS JORDAN: *(cold and rigid)* And you—married him—after that? *(She turns away in horror-stricken judgment)* You ought to have—died—first! *(PHILIP opens the door and enters, staring at GHENT with dislike and menace)* O Philip, she has told me!—You can't imagine what horrors!

(RUTH rises, with fright in her face, and approaches her brother to restrain him)

PHILIP: Horrors? What horrors?

MRS JORDAN: It was your fault! You ought never to have left her alone in that dreadful place! She—she married him—to save herself—from—O horrible!

(PHILIP waits an instant, the truth penetrating his mind slowly. Then, with mortal rage in his face, he starts toward GHENT)

PHILIP: You—dog!

(RUTH throws herself in PHILIP'S path)

RUTH: No, no, no!

PHILIP: Get out of my way. This is my business now.

RUTH: No, it is mine. I tell you it is mine.

PHILIP: We'll see whose it is. I said that if the truth ever came out, this man should answer to me, and now, by God, he shall answer!

(With another access of rage he tries to thrust RUTH from his path. MRS JORDAN, terrified at the storm she has raised, clings desperately to her son's arm)

RUTH: I told him long ago it should be between us. Now it shall be between us.

MRS JORDAN: Philip! For my sake, for your father's sake! Don't, don't! You will only make it worse. In pity's name, leave them alone together. Leave them alone—together!

(They force PHILIP back to the door, where he stands glaring at GHENT)

PHILIP: *(to GHENT)* My time will come. Meanwhile, hide behind the skirts of the woman whose life you have ruined and whose heart you have broken. Hide behind her. It is the coward's privilege. Take it.

(PHILIP, with MRS JORDAN still clinging to his arm, goes out, RUTH closing the door after them. She and GHENT confront each other in silence for a moment, across the width of the room)

RUTH: God forgive me! You never can.

GHENT: It was a pity—but—you were in a corner. I drove you to it, by coming here.

RUTH: It was base of me—base!

GHENT: The way your mother took it showed me one thing.—I've never understood you, because—I don't understand your people.

RUTH: You mean—her saying I ought to have died rather than accept life as I did?

GHENT: Yes.

RUTH: She spoke the truth. I have always seen it.

GHENT: Ruth, it's a queer thing for me to be saying, but—it seems to me, you've never seen the truth between us.

RUTH: What is the truth—between us?

GHENT: The truth is—*(He pauses, then continues with a disconsolate gesture)* Well, there's no use going into that. *(He fumbles in his pocket, and takes from it the nugget chain, which he looks at in silence for a time, then speaks in quiet resignation)* I've got here the chain, that's come, one way and another, to have a meaning for us. For you it's a bitter meaning, but, all the same, I want you to keep it. Show it some day to the boy, and tell him—about me. *(He lays it on the desk and goes toward the door)*

RUTH: What is the truth—between us?

GHENT: I guess it was only of myself I was thinking.

RUTH: What is it—about yourself?

GHENT: *(after a pause)* I drifted into one of your meeting-houses last Sunday, not knowing where else to go, and I heard a young fellow preaching about what he called "The Second Birth." A year and a half ago I should have thought it was all hocus-pocus, but you can believe me or not, the way he went on he might have been behind the door that night in that little justice den at San Jacinto, saying to the Recording Angel: "Do you see that rascal? Take notice! There ain't an ounce of bone or a drop of blood in him but what's new man!"

RUTH: You think it has been all my fault—the failure we've made of our life?

GHENT: It's been no failure. However it is, it's been our life, and in my heart I think it's been—all—right!

RUTH: All right! O, how can you say that? *(She repeats the words with a touch of awe and wonder)* All right!

GHENT: Some of it has been wrong, but as a whole it has been right—right! I know that doesn't happen often, but it has happened to us, because— *(He stops, unable to find words for his idea)* because—because the first time our eyes met, they burned away all that was bad in our meeting, and left only the fact that we *had* met—pure good—pure joy—a fortune of it—for both of us. Yes, for both of us! You'll see it yourself some day.

RUTH: If you had only heard me cry to you, to wait, to cleanse yourself and me—by suffering and sacrifice—before we dared begin to live! But you wouldn't see the need!—O, if you could

have felt for yourself what I felt for you! If you could have said, "The wages of sin is death!" and suffered the anguish of death, and risen again purified! But instead of that, what you had done fell off from you like any daily trifle.

GHENT: *(steps impulsively nearer her, sweeping his hand to indicate the portraits on the walls)* Ruth, it's these fellows are fooling you! It's they who keep your head set on the wages of sin, and all that rubbish. What have we got to do with suffering and sacrifice? That may be the law for some, and I've tried hard to see it as our law, and thought I had succeeded. But I haven't! Our law is joy, and selfishness; the curve of your shoulder and the light on your hair as you sit there says that as plain as preaching.—Does it gall you the way we came together? You asked me that night what brought me, and I told you whiskey, and sun, and the devil. Well, I tell you now I'm thankful on my knees for all three! Does it rankle in your mind that I took you when I could get you, by main strength and fraud? I guess most good women are taken that way, if they only knew it. Don't you want to be paid for? I guess every wife is paid for in some good coin or other. And as for you, I've paid for you not only with a trumpery chain, but with the heart in my breast, do you hear? That's one thing you can't throw back at me—the man you've made of me, the life and the meaning of life you've showed me the way to! *(RUTH's face is hidden in her hands, her elbows on the table. He stands over her, flushed and waiting. Gradually the light fades from his face. When he speaks again, the ring of exultation which has been in his voice is replaced by a sober intensity)* If you can't see it my way, give me another chance to live it out in yours. *(He waits, but she does not speak or look up. He takes a package of letters and papers from his pocket, and runs them over, in deep reflection)* During the six months I've been East—

RUTH: *(looking up)* Six months? Mother said a week!

GHENT: Your sister-in-law's telegram was forwarded to me here. I let her think it brought me, but as a matter of fact, I came East in the next train after yours. It was a rather low-lived thing to do, I suppose, hanging about and bribing your servant for news—(RUTH *lets her head sink in her hands. He pauses and continues ruefully*) I might have known how that would strike you! Well, it would have come out sooner or later.—That's not what I started to talk about.—You ask me to suffer for my wrong. Since you left me I *have* suffered—God knows! You ask me to make some sacrifice. Well—how would the mine do? Since I've been away they've as good as stolen it from me. I could get it back easy enough by fighting; but supposing I don't fight. Then we'll start all over again, just as we stand in our shoes, and make another fortune—for our boy. (RUTH *utters a faint moan as her head sinks in her arms on the table. With trembling hands,* GHENT *caresses her hair lightly, and speaks between a laugh and a sob*) Little mother! Little mother! What does the past matter, when we've got the future—and him? (RUTH *does not move. He remains bending over her for some moments, then straightens up, with a gesture of stoic despair*) I know what you're saying there to yourself, and I guess you're right. Wrong is wrong, from the moment it happens till the crack of doom, and all the angels in Heaven, working overtime, can't make it less or different by a hair. That seems to be the law. I've learned it hard, but I guess I've learned it. I've seen it written in mountain letters across the continent of this life.—Done is done, and lost is lost, and smashed to hell is smashed to hell. We fuss and potter and patch up. You might as well try to batter down the Rocky Mountains with a rabbit's heart-beat! (*He goes to the door, where he turns*) You've fought hard for me, God bless you for it.—But it's been a losing game with you from the first!—You belong here, and I belong out yonder—beyond the Rockies, beyond—the Great Divide!

(*He opens the door and is about to pass out.* RUTH *looks up with streaming eyes*)

RUTH: Wait! (*He closes the door and stands waiting for her to speak.* RUTH *masters herself and goes on, her eyes shining, her face exalted*) Tell me you know that if I could have followed you, and been your wife, without struggle and without bitterness, I would have done it.

GHENT: (*solemnly*) I believe you would.

RUTH: Tell me you know that when I tore down with bleeding fingers the life you were trying to build for us, I did it only—because—I loved you!

GHENT: (*comes slowly to the table, looking at her with bewilderment*) How was that?

RUTH: O, I don't wonder you ask! Another woman would have gone straight to her goal. You might have found such a one. But instead you found me, a woman in whose ears rang night and day the cry of an angry Heaven to us both— "Cleanse yourselves!" And I went about doing it in the only way I knew—(*She points at the portraits on the wall*)—the only way my fathers knew—by wretchedness, by self-torture, by trying blindly to pierce your careless heart with pain. And all the while you—O, as I lay there and listened to you, I realized it for the first time—you had risen, in one hour, to a wholly new existence, which flooded the present and the future with brightness, yes, and reached back into our past, and made of it—made of all of it—something to cherish! (*She takes the chain, and comes closer*) You have taken the good of our life and grown strong. I have taken the evil and grown weak, weak unto death. Teach me to live as you do!

(*She puts the chain around her neck*)

GHENT: (*puzzled, not yet realizing the full force of her words*) Teach you—to live—as I do?

RUTH: And teach—*him!*

GHENT: (*unable to realize his fortune*) You'll let me help make a kind of a happy life for—the little rooster?

RUTH: (*holds out her arms, her face flooded with happiness*) And for us! For us!

CURTAIN

HE AND SHE (1911)

To study the life and career of Rachel Crothers (1878–1958) is to encounter key questions facing those interested in women playwrights of the early decades of the twentieth century. How responsible were these women for the ongoing "Woman Question," and how could they advance women's causes in a way that did not further exclude them from the already male-dominated, highly commercial world of the theatre? At one point, Crothers seemed to attribute her extensive treatment of women's issues to the topicality of the subject rather than to a feminist agenda: "I [do not] go out stalking the footsteps of women's progress. It is something that comes to me subconsciously. I may say I even sense the trend before I have hearsay or direct knowledge of it." Yet Crothers returned to the subject of women trying to negotiate a new place in society time and time again across her 23 full-length plays, in a manner that very often reworked conventional **realist** stage depictions of women. Hers is a career marked by her own balancing act, as she tried to exercise her own vision fully while reaching as large an audience as possible. *He and She* is a prime example of this negotiation, for while it offers the timely figure of a New Woman torn between career and family, it poses no easy answers to the dilemma. The same might be said of much of Crothers' work.

Like Susan Glaspell, Crothers was a product of the Midwest; she was born to Dr. Eli Kirk Crothers and Dr. Marie Depew Crothers in December 1878 in Bloomington, Illinois. Her mother, who had left for Philadelphia and Chicago to complete her medical degree after Crothers was born, served as an early example to her daughter of what heights women could reach. Crothers exhibited her own penchant for theatre as a child and young adult; she loved theatricals, and wrote and produced childhood melodramas. The new drama whose concern with social issues of the day she would later emulate appealed to her early on; she even suggested at one point to the Bloomington Dramatic Society that they launch a production of Henrik Ibsen's *A Doll House*. Upon her graduation from Illinois State Normal University High School in 1891, she attended the New England School of Dramatic Instruction in Boston; after one term, certified in teaching elocution, she returned to her hometown. Her family disapproved of her burgeoning theatrical aspirations, so she contented herself with giving lessons and performing locally. She finally moved to New York City in 1896 or 1897 to gain a foothold in theatre, and between 1897 and 1902 became connected with the Stanhope-Wheatcroft school of acting, first as a student, then as a teacher. In the meantime, she made her acting debut in 1897 with E. H. Sothern's company; she appeared with his Lyceum stock company in New York, and in a touring company of *The Christian*.

Throughout her tenure at the school, Crothers composed one-act plays as vehicles for her drama students; between 1899 and 1903, her works began to attract notice. She gained several skills while overseeing these plays, talents upon which she would rely on for the rest of her career; she took charge of producing, coaching the actors, and designing the sets and costumes. Crothers agreed with Bernard Shaw, who believed that the playwright trained in stagecraft was the best director of his or her own play, for that ensured a consistency of vision when different parties were responsible for assembling the production. Of the 35 professional productions of her work mounted, she would later direct and design sets for two-thirds of them. It should be emphasized that not only was this a rare step for a playwright to take at this time, it was practically unheard of for a woman.

The Three of Us (1906), her first successful foray onto Broadway, marked the start of a long and formidable career upon the American stage, one that would largely center itself around the depiction of what Crothers called a "*Comédie Humaine de la Femme* or a Dramatic History of Woman." Such early plays as *The Three of Us* (1906), *Myself Bettina* (1908), *A Man's World* (1910), and *He and She* (1911) largely centered around the figure of a New Woman opposing society's conventions in the hope of erasing the double standard that existed for men and women. The heroines in these works are far from typical; Rhy MacChesney in *The Three of Us*, for example, tries both to raise her two brothers and run a failing mine in the West. Pitted against the resentment of a brother at being bossed by a woman and the attempts of a rival to compromise her honor, Mac-Chesney attempts to break free of the stereotypical roles that would force her to submit to either one of them. Her success in the end, however, is questionable; she marries her suitor Stephen Townley in the hopes that his influence as a male role model can help reform her brother. The heroine of *A Man's World*, Frank Ware, is arguably more successful. A social activist and writer, Frank rejects the love of her life, Malcolm Gaskell, when she discovers he is the father of the illegitimate child she has adopted, Kiddie. Angry at his refusal to accept responsibility for his actions, as well as his inability to see beyond a sexual double standard, she breaks with him.

He and She emerges in the context of these works, portraying the struggle of a woman to achieve her full potential in the face of society's expectations of her. Artist Ann Herford enjoys a free and equal relationship with her husband and fellow artist Tom, until she wins a commission for a frieze that he had hoped to sculpt as well. Ann's work on the commission takes her away from her family to the point of crisis; her daughter runs away, determined to be married, and Ann is forced to choose between her child and her work. Ann gives up the commission to her husband in order to take her daughter away, but not without a sense of bitterness at what this will cost her as an artist and as a woman seeking to realize her potential.

The play suffered a somewhat problematic production history. First produced in 1912 under the name *The Herfords* at the Plymouth Theatre, it failed to survive two years of provincial tryouts. It was not brought to New York until 1920 when it had a short run at the Little Theatre, in a production in which Crothers herself starred as Ann. We can speculate as to what extent the mixed reception was caused by the complicated nature of the play's message; that is, Ann felt equally the importance of her responsibilities as a mother and her duty to be true to herself as an artist, and refused to make quietly the choice society demanded between children and career. Audiences, however, tended to take one side or the other, even though Crothers' ultimate point seems to be that one choice is no more "right" than the other, and that a society that allows a woman a chance to explore only one part of her potential is essentially unjust.

Viewing Crothers' artistry as a depiction of the evolution of the modern woman, one can identify three further periods of change in her drama. Following the production of the "social problem" plays such as *He and She*, she wrote six commercial comedies that dealt in no significant way with women's concerns. With the 1920s, Crothers reintensified her focus on multidimensional female characters; her typical heroine now, however, was no longer the noble, solitary figure struggling for social change, but a woman struggling to negotiate as best she could the uncertainty of male-female relationships in postwar society. An early play of the decade, *Nice People* (1921), centered around the extreme of the flapper, while plays such as *Mary the Third* (1923) and *A Lady's Virtue* (1925) featured heroines struggling with developing notions of domesticity. In the last period of her writing stretching through the 1930s, Crothers' fully evolved New Woman has to confront the real dimensions of her "advancement" and the dissatisfaction and loneliness still present in her life, despite her freedom. *Let Us Be Gay* (1929), for example, explores the extent to which sexual freedom alone cannot add meaning to a woman's life.

When Ladies Meet (1933) concerns the relationship of two women, a wife and a mistress, competing for the same man. They meet without knowing each other's identity and, when it is discovered, they decide their loyalties to each other as women must outweigh all else. The play was a critical success and was awarded the Megrue Prize in Comedy in 1933. Crothers' final play to be produced, *Susan and God* (1937), was a critical triumph and concluded her ongoing look at the developing New Woman. In it, Susan Trexel, a religious convert who attempts to convert others, is revealed as a figure more interested in doing so for her own glory than theirs. Crothers was able in this way to sound a "warning to the modern woman concerning the ever-present potential for selfishness present in the pursuit of self-fulfillment and independence." Crothers' playwrighting was cut short by World War II; as she had during World War I, she founded a war relief effort composed of theatre artists. She returned to playwrighting after the war, but withdrew both *Bill Comes Back* (1945) and *My South Window* (1950) before production; because the latter was comic, she feared it would be inappropriate to stage during the Korean War.

The plays of Rachel Crothers do not embody the **expressionist** impulse seen in the works of such contemporaries as Sophie Treadwell and Susan Glaspell; rather, she wrote largely in the realist vein that was becoming commercially popular. Partly as a result, Crothers is a somewhat vexed figure for those trying to assess the feminism of her plays, since it is sometimes unclear how extensively she actually challenged the prevailing social order. Yet the fact that she took over the design of most of her productions is too often neglected; thus, her contribution to making design more symbolically meaningful is still undervalued. She advocated women helping each other (indeed, a woman gave Crothers her start), and considered women a prime dramatic subject; at the same time, she eschewed the label "*woman* playwright" and typed many such artists as ineffectual and inexperienced. One must remember that at the time Crothers was writing, "lady playwrights" were largely stereotyped as dealing with light, trivial subjects. Crothers' distancing herself from a label should not be mistaken for a lack of concern with women's development, nor should the fact that her portraits of women vary and are not always flattering. Instead, these facts should be seen as constituting a feminist vision that takes into account the experiences of women old and young, rich and poor, from several different walks of life. The issues—the double standard, where a "liberated" woman's true place in the world lies—cut across such boundaries and, indeed, are still timely today, as the 1973 and 1980 revivals of *He and She* in Washington and New York, respectively, point out. Crothers was able to document the change of her day in a way that was commercially viable, adopting popular realist tenets of the times and thus reaching a great number of people; likewise, she was able to make her plays universal enough in theme that they still speak to women's concerns. This duality tells us much about our dramatic heritage and is certainly justification for further study of Crothers.

WORKS CONSULTED

Abramson, Doris. "Rachel Crothers: Broadway Feminist." In *Modern American Drama: The Female Canon*, ed. June Schleuter. London and Toronto: Associated University Presses, 1990. 55–65.

Friedman, Sharon. "Feminism as Theme in Twentieth-Century American Women's Drama." *American Studies*, 25 (1984): 69–89.

Gottlieb, Lois C. "The Double Standard Debate in Early Twentieth-Century American Drama." *Michigan Academician*, 7 (1975): 441–52.

———. *Rachel Crothers*. Boston: Twayne Publishers, 1979.

Sutherland, Cynthia. "American Women Playwrights as Mediators of the 'Woman Problem.'" *Modern Drama*, 21 (1978): 219–236.

CHARACTERS

ACT I

SCENE: *The Herford Studio.*

The room is in the basement floor of a large old fashioned house in lower New York—and shows that it has been made over and adapted to the needs of a sculptor.

At right center back are double doors opening into the workroom. At right of these doors is a recess showing it has been cut in. The ceiling of the half of the room which is towards the audience is much higher than the other part—showing that the room which is on the floor above has been used to give height to this part of the studio.

The break made in the ceiling is supported by an interesting old carved column—very evidently brought from Italy—and in the overhanging part of the wall is set a very beautiful old Italian frieze in bas relief—a few faded colors showing.

At lower left is a large studio window.

At lower right side a single door leading into hall. At upper left corner, a cupboard is built in, in harmony with the construction of the room, and showing, when opened, drawers and compartments for holding sculptors' tools, etc.

Before the window, at right center, is a scaffold built to hold a section of a frieze. At its base is a revolving table, holding modeling clay, tools, etc. In front of the scaffold is a short pair of steps. At centre is a long table holding rolls of sketches, a desk set—a book or two, pencils, compasses, several pieces of modeling.

There are a number of chairs about and a piece of rich brocade in vivid coloring thrown over the back of one.

The room is simple, dignified, beautiful, full of taste and strength. Soft afternoon sunshine streams in from the wide window. KEITH MCKENZIE *and* TOM HERFORD *are lifting one section of a bas relief frieze about 3 by 5—and placing it on the scaffolding.*

MCKENZIE *is about 35, tall, good-looking, in a pleasing, common-place way; also wearing a sculptor's working clothes—but of a practical and not artistic sort.*

TOM HERFORD *is 40, a fine specimen of the vigorous American-artist type. Virile, fresh, alive and generous in nature and viewpoint. He wears the stamp of confidence and success.*

TOM: *(as they lift the frieze)* Come on! There she is! Put her over—no, this way, about half a foot. That's right. There! Let's have a look. *(*TOM *goes down to hanging switch and turns on the light. As he does so, he says:)* Wait! *(The lights are turned up) (Turning to* KEITH*)* What do you think?

KEITH: It's a great thing, Governor! Going to be a walk-away for you. You'll win it as sure as guns. I *know* it. I bet you land the $100,000.00 as sure as you're standing there, governor.

TOM: Oh, I don't know. The biggest fellows in the country are going in for this competition.

KEITH: Well—you're *one* of the biggest. *I* think you're *the* biggest—and you've turned out the best thing you've ever done in your life. *(Going to stand above table)*

TOM: That's damned nice of you, McKenzie. It *does* look pretty good out here. Doesn't it? *(He goes up on the steps—to touch the frieze)*

KEITH: *(after a pause)* Governor.

TOM: *(working at his frieze)* Um?

KEITH: I want to ask you something. Not from curiosity—but because—I'd like to know for my own sake. You needn't answer of course—if you don't want to.

TOM: Go on. Fire away.

KEITH: Have you ever been sorry that Mrs Herford is a sculptor—instead of just your wife?

TOM: Not for a minute.

KEITH: I've been thinking a lot about it all lately.

TOM: About you and Ruth, you mean?

KEITH: Yes. She'll marry me in the fall if I let her keep on working.

TOM: And?

KEITH: Well—I—Hang it all! I don't *want* her to. I can take care of her now. At first it was different—when I was grubbing along—but since I've been with you, you've put me on my feet. I'll never be *great*—I know that all right—but I can take care of her.

TOM: *(working at frieze)* But she *wants* to keep on, doesn't she?

KEITH: Yes, but—

TOM: Good Heavens, boy—you're not bitten with that bug I hope. "I want my girl by my own fireside to live for me alone."

KEITH: Oh—

TOM: Why Ruth Creel's a howling success—the way she's climbed up in that magazine—why in the name of Christopher, do you want her to stop?

KEITH: *(at right end of table, figuring mechanically on some papers on table)* How can she keep on at that and keep house too?

TOM: Well they *do*, you know—somehow.

KEITH: Oh, Mrs Herford's different. She's working right here with you—and her time is her own. But Ruth's tied down to office hours and it's slavery—that's what it is.

TOM: *She* doesn't think so. Does she?

KEITH: I want a home. I want children.

TOM: Of course. But that doesn't mean she'll have to give up her profession forever.

KEITH: Oh, I'm strong for women doing anything they want to do—in *general*—But when it's the girl you love and want to marry, it's different.

TOM: It ought not to be.

KEITH: When you come down to brass tacks—

ANN: *(coming quickly in from the workroom, and stopping as she sees the frieze)* Oh Tom!
(ANN HERFORD is 38. Intensely feminine and a strong vibrating personality which radiates warmth and vitality. She wears a long linen working smock—a soft rich red in color. Her sleeves are rolled up and her general appearance shows that she is at work and has stopped only to look at TOM'S frieze)

KEITH: Looks great out here—doesn't it, Mrs Herford?

ANN: Um.

KEITH: Aren't you—more sure now than ever it will win?

ANN: Um. — *(Starting to speak and checking herself)*

TOM: What?

ANN: Nothing. Your horses *are* marvelous, Tom. I wish we could see it all together—now. Don't you? The rest of the twenty sections—so we could see how much we—how much we—*feel* the running.

TOM: Don't you feel it in this piece?

ANN: Of course.

KEITH: I do—tremendously. I think it's wonderful. *(He goes into workroom)*

TOM: Ann—what were you going to say a minute ago about the frieze?

ANN: A—I don't know.

TOM: Don't hedge. Several times lately you've started to say something and haven't got it out. What is it? Any suggestions?

ANN: How do you feel about it yourself, boy? Are you satisfied?

TOM: Does that mean you aren't?

ANN: I asked you.

TOM: Well—it's the best that's in me. Why? What's the matter? You don't like it after all.

ANN: Like it? It's a strong—noble—beautiful thing.

TOM: *But*—

ANN: Dearest—is it—just exactly what your first conception of it was? Has it turned out just as you first felt it?

TOM: Why yes—not absolutely in detail of course. It's improved a lot I think—in the working—but in the main, yes—it's *just* the same. Why do you say that?

ANN: You know of course, but—

TOM: Say it—Say it. What have you got in your mind?

ANN: I don't know that I can—but in the beginning it had a feeling of swiftness, of rushing—swirling—as if your soul were let loose in it, Tom—too big, too free to be held in and confined. But, somehow, now that it's finished—

TOM: Go on.

ANN: That wild thing has gone out of it. It's crystalized into something magnificent but a little conventional.

TOM: Good heavens, Ann, you can't call that *conventional?*

ANN: Well—orthodox then. It's noble of course—but that inexplainable thing which made it great—is *gone*—for me. Perhaps it's just me—my imagination—because I care so much.

TOM: It is imagination. It's much stronger than when I began.

ANN: Is it?

TOM: Of course. You're trying to put something fantastic into it which never was there at all. That's not *me*. What I've done I've got through a certain strong solid boldness. That's why I think this stands a good chance. It's the very best thing I've ever done, Ann, by all—

KEITH: *(opening the workroom door)* Governor—will you show Guido and me about something please—Just a minute? *(There is a slight pause)* *(*TOM *looks at the frieze)*

TOM: I don't see what you mean at all, dear girl. Thanks a lot—but I think you're wrong this time. *(He goes into workroom.* ANN *looks again at the frieze as* RUTH CREEL *comes in from hall)*

ANN: *(going quickly to* RUTH*)* Oh, Ruth—bless you! *(She kisses her warmly)*

RUTH: I came straight from the office and I'm dirty as a pig. *(*ANN *points to* TOM'S *frieze)* Is that it? *(*ANN *nods)* Well?

ANN: Oh, Ruth—I'm sick in the bottom of my soul. I hope—I hope—I'm wrong. I *must* be wrong. Tom knows better than I do; but—I can't help it. I tell myself I'm a fool—and the more I try to persuade myself the more it comes back. Ruth, it isn't the same. It isn't. What ever it was that lifted it above good work and made it a thing of inspiration—is gone. It's gone—*gone*.

RUTH: Have you—told Tom how you feel?

ANN: Just this minute. He says I'm wrong absolutely—that it's the best thing he's ever done.

RUTH: I hope to God you are wrong—but I bet you're not. You *know*. Did you—have you told him the other thing?

ANN: Not yet. But I've finished it.

RUTH: Absolutely?

ANN: I worked down here last night till three o'clock this morning.

RUTH: Well—how is it?

ANN: Oh, I don't dare think. It can't be as good as it seems to me.

RUTH: *Of course* it can. Why shouldn't it be? Aren't you going to offer it to him right away—before it's too late?

ANN: How *can* I? It frightens me to pieces to even think of it—but, oh,—my dear, my dear—it's alive and fresh and *new*. It is. It is. If he only would take it—my idea—and put his wonderful work—his wonderful execution into it.

RUTH: Perhaps he'll be *fired* with it—jump at it.

ANN: I'm afraid, he won't—and I'm afraid of *this* for him. It would nearly kill him to lose. He's counting on winning. Keith and everybody are so dead sure of him.

RUTH: Show him yours for goodness—

ANN: Be careful. He'll be back in a minute.

RUTH: I'll skip upstairs and make myself presentable.

ANN: Go in my room, dear. *(RUTH goes out through hall. TOM and KEITH come back from workroom. ANN goes to TOM—they stand a moment—looking at the frieze. ANN slaps TOM on the back, without speaking, and goes on into workroom)*

KEITH: *(after a pause)* I agree with you in general, governor. But when it comes down to the girl you love and want to marry, it's different.

TOM: Why is it?

KEITH: The world has got to have homes to live in and who's going to make 'em if the women don't do it?

TOM: *(smiling at KEITH tolerantly)* Oh, come—come.

KEITH: Do you mean to say you wouldn't rather your sister Daisy was married and keeping her own house instead of working here as your secretary?

TOM: But she *isn't* married— and she won't live with Ann and me unless it's a business proposition. I respect her *tremendously* for it—tremendously.

KEITH: Well, Daisy's a big, plucky, independent thing anyway—but Ruth's a little delicate fragile—

TOM: With a mind bigger than most of the *men* you know.

KEITH: Oh, mind be damned. I want a wife.

DAISY: *(coming in from the hall)* Oh—Tom—it's out here. How corking!

(DAISY HERFORD is twenty-eight—strong, wholesome, handsome, with the charm of health and freshness. She wears a severe serge gown and carries a pencil and stenographer's pad)

TOM: Well—sis, how do you like it?

DAISY: I adore it. I hope you haven't any doubts now about winning.

TOM: I've plenty of 'em—but somehow today it looks as if it stood a pretty good chance.

DAISY: Chance! I never was so sure of anything in my life.

KEITH: Daisy—maybe you know just *what* ought to be *where* with *this stuff.*

DAISY: I've been itching to get at it. Let's put all the tools on that side.

KEITH: I *have* started.

DAISY: And throw the trash in here. *(Pushing the box with her foot)*

KEITH: Can you help me now?

DAISY: Yes. Tom, do you want me to write to the Ward people about that marble again?

TOM: Yes I do. Shake them up. Tell 'em if it isn't here by the first of the month I won't take it.

DAISY: *(making a note in her note-book)* Um—um. *(MILLICENT HERFORD rushes in from hall at left. MILLICENT is 16—pretty—eager—full of vitality and will—half child, half woman. She is charmingly dressed in an afternoon frock and picture hat and is at the moment happy and exhilarated)*

MILLICENT: Father, where's mother?

TOM: In the work room. But you can't go in. *(As MILLICENT starts to workroom)*

MILLICENT: Why not?

TOM: She's finishing something and said not to let *any* one stop her.

MILLICENT: Oh *dear!* I think I *might.* It's awfully important. Couldn't I just poke my head in the door a minute?

TOM: Not for a second.

MILLICENT: Sakes, I wish Mother wouldn't work in my Christmas vacation. It's an awful bore. Don't you think she might stop the little while I'm at home, Aunt Daisy?

DAISY: None of my business. Don't ask me.

KEITH: If you ask *me*—yes I think she might.

TOM: That's nonsense. Your mother's doing about everything that *can* be done to make your vacation a success, isn't she?

MILLICENT: Yes, of course.

TOM: Then I don't see that there's any reason why she shouldn't be allowed a little time for herself.

MILLICENT: But I want her *now*. Aren't my new pumps stemmy, Aunt Daisy?

DAISY: Aren't they what?

MILLICENT: Stemmy. Wake up, Aunt Daisy. Oh, the luncheon was gorgeous. All the girls were there and the matinee was heavenly.

KEITH: What play?

MILLICENT: "The Flame of Love." You needn't laugh, father. It's the best play in town. The leading man is a peach. Honestly, he's the best looking thing I ever saw in my life. We were all crazy about him. Belle Stevens took off her violets and threw them right *at* him. She makes me tired, though. I don't think seventeen is so terribly much older than sixteen, do you, Aunt Daisy?

DAISY: *(still at the cupboard)* It depends on whether you're sixteen or seventeen—how much older it is.

MILLICENT: I don't care—I wouldn't wear a ring as big as hers if I had one. Oh, Aunt Daisy, may I borrow your earrings? *(Going to DAISY)*

DAISY: Help yourself.

MILLICENT: Thanks, you're a duck. I could combostulate you for that. How much longer do you think mother will be, daddie?

TOM: Couldn't say.

MILLICENT: Well, tell her I *have* to see her the minute she comes out. Don't forget. *(She hurries off through hall)*

TOM: She's grown up over night somehow. I can't get used to it.

KEITH: And she went away to school a few months ago just a girl. Amazing, isn't it?

DAISY: Not a bit. What do you expect? She's free now—cut loose. Boarding school does that pretty quickly.

TOM: I suppose so—and I suppose it's good for her. *(Looking at the frieze he goes into the workroom)*

KEITH: The Governor's darned cheerful about the frieze to-day.

DAISY: I should think he *would* be. It's great. *(KEITH and DAISY go on clearing out cupboard)*

KEITH: I'd give a good deal to know what Mrs Herford actually thinks of it.

DAISY: Why she *loves* it.

KEITH: She looks at it with such a sort of a—I don't know. I can't help wondering if she *is* so dead certain of it as the rest of us are.

DAISY: I hope she doesn't discourage Tom. After all *he* likes it and he knows more about it than anybody else. Ann's criticism is wonderful, of course, but still Tom *is the artist*.

KEITH: You're just as jealous for your brother as you can be, aren't you, Daisy? All right for the missus to be clever, but you want Tom to be supreme in everything, don't you?

DAISY: He *is*. *(Leaning over the box)*

KEITH: You're a brick. Daisy, have you ever been in love in your life?

DAISY: What do you mean? *(Lifting her head—startled and embarrassed)*

KEITH: I've been thinking an awful lot lately about this business of married women working. What do *you* think of it—now honestly?

DAISY: What difference does it make—what I think?

KEITH: Of course, there's no reason on earth why you shouldn't be in it. You don't care a hang for men—and—

DAISY: You mean men don't care a hang for me.

KEITH: No I don't. I don't mean that at all. But you're so independent men are sort of afraid of you.

DAISY: Oh, don't apologize. You mean I'm a plain, practical girl meant to take care of myself.

KEITH: Well—that's what you *want* to be, isn't it?

DAISY: Never mind about me. Let's change the subject.

KEITH: You needn't be so touchy. I talk awfully frankly about my affairs and you never say a word about yourself.

DAISY: Why should I? I'm not interesting and you're not interested.

KEITH: I am too. You're the best pal a fellow ever had. I don't know any other girl I could have worked with all this time—day in and day out and not either been dead sick of or sort of—you know sweet on, in a way.

DAISY: You needn't rub it in.

KEITH: Why, Daisy, old girl, what *is* the matter? What in the dickens are you so huffy about?

DAISY: Just let me and my idiosyncrasies alone, please.

KEITH: Heavens! Can't I say what I think?

DAISY: No, you can't. I don't want to hear it. I know just what I seem like to other people—so there's no use explaining me to myself.

KEITH: All I meant was if you *were* in love would you give up your job and—

DAISY: But I'm *not* in love, so stop thinking about it.

KEITH: Gosh! I thought *you* had common sense, but you're just as queer as the rest of them. What I want to know is—if a girl loves a man well enough to marry him why in hell she can't stay at home and—

DAISY: What's the matter? (As KEITH *cuts his finger on the tool he is holding*) Did you cut your finger?

KEITH: Not much.

DAISY: (*with a sudden tenderness*) Let me see.

KEITH: It's nothing.

DAISY: It is too. Hold still. I'll tie it up for you. (*She ties his finger with her own handkerchief*) Anything the—hold still. Anything the matter with one of your fingers would put you out of commission.

KEITH: Might be a good idea. I don't think Ruth believes in me much. Doesn't think I'll get much farther.

DAISY: (*warmly*) I don't know why. I think you've got plenty for her to believe in. Well—speaking of angels. How are you, Ruth? (As RUTH *comes in from the hall*)

KEITH: Oh—hello, dear.

RUTH: Hello. What's the matter?

KEITH: Nothing.

DAISY: Keith was waxing emphatic about *you* and over emphasized a finger. (*She turns back to cupboard*)

RUTH: I'm sorry. (*Touching* KEITH'S *hand as he comes down to her*)

KEITH: How are you?

RUTH: Dead. This day's been twenty-four hours long. (*Sitting at left end of table*)

KEITH: (*coming down to* RUTH) *Has* anything gone wrong?

RUTH: No—but a young author from the eloquent West has been fighting me since nine o'clock this morning.

KEITH: What about?

RUTH: He's got a perfectly magnificent story—or idea for one, rather—but it's so crudely written that it's impossible to publish it.

DAISY: I suppose you can re-write it for him.

RUTH: No, he won't let me. Wants to do it all himself. Oh, he's so stubborn and so funny and so splendid. So outlandishly conceited and so adorably boyish I wanted to slap him one minute and kiss him the next.

KEITH: Why didn't you do both and you'd have got what you wanted.

RUTH: I was afraid to risk it.

KEITH: (*nodding towards* TOM'S *frieze*) Doesn't that hit you in the eye?

RUTH: Awfully like Tom, isn't it? Strong and splendid.

KEITH: What are you thinking—

RUTH: Oh, nothing—only I wish Ann had—I wish Ann had gone in for this competition too.

KEITH: What?

DAISY: Why on earth should she?

RUTH: Why shouldn't she?

DAISY: Ruth, you're daffy about Ann. Always have been.

KEITH: She does beautiful work for a woman—but ye gods—she's not in *this* class.

RUTH: And she never *will* be if she's held back and told she's limited. I think she has genius and the sooner she makes a bold dash and tries for something big the better.

DAISY: Nonsense! Tom's pushed her and believed in her always. You can't say *he's* held her back.

RUTH: (*to* KEITH) I've heard *you* say she has genius—lots of times.

KEITH: So she has—in a way. She has more imagination than the governor, but, great Peter, when it comes to execution and the real thing she isn't *in* it with him. How could she be? She's a woman.

RUTH: Don't be any more antedeluvian or prehistoric than you can help, Keith. Don't *you* think Ann's more original and really innately gifted than Tom is, Daisy?

DAISY: *I do not.* She's terribly good. Of course—no doubt about that—but good Lord, Tom's *great* — a really *great* artist. (DAISY *starts to hall door*)

RUTH: Why do you go, Daisy?

DAISY: Must. I have bushels of letters to get off.

RUTH: You look as fresh and rosy as if you were just beginning the day. How do you do it?

DAISY: Oh, I'm not expressing my soul in my job— merely earning my bread and butter. I suppose that's why I look so husky at twilight. (DAISY *goes out through hall*)

RUTH: (*looking after* DAISY) Do you know—I don't believe Daisy likes me any more.

KEITH: (*sitting on left end of table near* RUTH) Kiss me. (RUTH *leans her head towards* KEITH. *He kisses her cheek*)

RUTH: She's so marvelously good-natured—queer she's getting snappy at me lately.

KEITH: I'm awfully glad you came.

RUTH: Does it hurt? (*Touching his finger*)

KEITH: Not much.

RUTH: I wonder why she doesn't like me?

KEITH: What are you talking about? I'm asked to stay to dinner, too.

RUTH: That's nice.

KEITH: I can't bear to see you so tired, dear.

RUTH: I'll be all right when I have some tea.

KEITH: This time next year you could be in your own home—away from those damnable office hours and the drudgery—if you only would. If you only *would.*

RUTH: It never seems to occur to you that I might be a little less tired but bored to death without my job.

KEITH: If you really cared for me the way you used to—you wouldn't be bored.

RUTH: Oh let's not begin that.

KEITH: But do you love me, dear. *Do* you?

RUTH: I've been telling you so for a pretty long time, haven't I?

KEITH: Are you tired of it?

RUTH: There isn't any reason on earth why you should *think* I am.

KEITH: Well, I do think it. I worry about it all the time. I know you're brilliant and successful— but you—after all you say you love me—and I don't see— (*He stops with a sigh*) You're awful pretty today. Your face is like a flower.

RUTH: Oh—

KEITH: Yes, it is. I love you so.

RUTH: Dear old boy! I love you.

KEITH: Do you, Ruth? *Do* you?

RUTH: I've never loved anyone else. You've filled all that side of my life and you've made it beautiful. We must hang together dear— (*Putting both her hands over one of his*) And understand and give things up for each other. But it must be fifty-fifty, dearest. I can make you happy, Keith—Oh I can. And I'll be so happy and contented with you if you'll only— (KEITH *turns away impatiently*) I've never had a home for a minute—in my whole life—nor a relative since I was three—of any sort or description—not a soul who belonged to me but you.

KEITH: I want you to have the sweetest little home in the world.

RUTH: Think of having our own little dinners and all the nice people we know at our table—*ours.*

KEITH: Yes—but—*how can you do it if you're away all day?*

RUTH: Oh Keith, dear boy, you—the whole trouble is you think housekeeping is making a home—and the two things aren't the same at all—at all, at all.

KEITH: Well, they can't be separated.

RUTH: Oh, yes, they can. Love—love makes a home—not tables and chairs. We can *afford* more if I work, too. We can *pay* some one to do the stuff you think I ought to do. And you'll go on climbing up in your work and I'll go on in mine and we'll both grow to something and *be* somebody and have something to give each other. It will be fair—we'll be pulling together—pals and lovers like Tom and Ann. That's why they're so ideally happy.

KEITH: Yes, but we're different. We couldn't—

RUTH: You're not fair, Keith.

KEITH: Great guns, Ruth—neither are you.

RUTH: I am. I am perfectly. *(Their voices rise together)*

TOM: *(coming back from the workroom)* What's the row? Hello, Ruthie Creel.

RUTH: *(giving her hand to* TOM*)* Hello, you nice Tommie Herford. I always lose my heart to you in your working clothes.

TOM: You have my heart in any kind of clothes.

RUTH: Keith's cross with me, Tom. You're much nicer to me than he is.

KEITH: You never spring any of your revolutionary speeches on Herford. You save all your really soothing remarks for me.

RUTH: Tom, am I revolutionary? Aren't I just a little cooing dove?

TOM: Absolutely.

DAISY: *(coming in from hall)* Dr Remington's here. Millicent's bringing him down. But he says he wants to sit upstairs on the parlor sofa, not down in the cellar. Tom, will you sign these letters now? *(Daisy puts the letters on the table—*TOM *goes towards the table as* MILLICENT *comes in from the hall bringing* DR REMINGTON *by the hand)*

(DR REMINGTON is 65. He is inclined to portliness and his keen humor and kindliness are combined with an understanding and wisdom which make him a very strong and a very lovable man. His manner and speech are a little deliberate. He has a twinkling readiness to tease but the weight and dignity of a successful and important physician)

TOM: Hello—hello—hello.

REMINGTON: How are you?

KEITH: *(taking* REMINGTON'S *overcoat)* How are you, Dr Remington? *(*RUTH *comes to the doctor to take his hat and stick)*

REMINGTON: Hello, McKenzie. And here's that pretty little Ruth thing—knowing so much it makes my head ache.

RUTH: So long as it's your head and not mine I don't mind.

MILLICENT: Oh, thank you for the chocolates, grandfather. They're just the kind I adore. I could absolutely combostulate you— *(Giving him a violent hug)* Five pounds, daddie.

TOM: You're a fine doctor!

REMINGTON: Chocolate's about the best medicine I know of if you want a girl to love you. Where's your mother?

MILLICENT: In the cave. *(Pointing to workroom)*

REMINGTON: Can't she be excavated? Go and dig her out.

MILLICENT: They won't let me. You do it.

REMINGTON: Hasn't anybody got the courage to do it? *(*KEITH *starts towards the door with box)*

DAISY: Not me.

REMINGTON: Well, McKenzie, go and tell her to let the work go to thunder and come and see her dad. *(*KEITH *goes into workroom)* Is that the thing that's going to get the hundred thousand for you?

TOM: If—yes.

REMINGTON: Well, go to it—boy. I hope you hit it. *(Sitting in the large chair at left)*

TOM: Thanks. I'm doing my durndest. Daisy, you've got some of these dimensions wrong. Keith will have to give them to you again.

DAISY: Oh, I'm sorry.

REMINGTON: It's a good thing you're working for your own brother, Daisy—nobody else would have you.

DAISY: You're the only person in the whole world who isn't impressed with my business ability.

REMINGTON: Stuff! I wager you say in your prayers every night—Oh, Lord, deliver me from this job and get me a good husband.

DAISY: *(laughing with the others and going to* REMINGTON*)* That's a very stemmy tie you're wearing. Do you get me?

REMINGTON: Not exactly. All I know is I'd rather be stemmy than seedy.

KEITH: *(opening the workroom door)* Don't you want me to carry that in for you, Mrs Herford?

ANN: *(from within)* No, no—I'd rather do it myself.

KEITH: It's too heavy for you.

ANN: No it isn't. *(*ANN *comes in carrying the figure of a woman in the nude—about a foot high. The figure is in wet clay and stands on a modeling board)*

TOM: Steady there! Steady! Let me take it.

ANN: Don't touch it!

REMINGTON: Hello there!

ANN: Hello, daddy! I couldn't come out until I finished my lady. Isn't she nice? She's ready to be cast now. Come and look at her, Tom. She isn't so bad?

TOM: She looks pretty good to me.

REMINGTON: She looks a little chilly to me. Why don't you put a full suit of clothes on one of 'em—just for a change, Ann?

ANN: You nice, horrid, sweet, adorable, cross old thing! Why didn't you come yesterday? I don't see why I love you so when you never do anything I want you to.

REMINGTON: If I did I wouldn't be half as irresistible. Aren't you going to stop for the day now and pay a little attention to me?

ANN: I *am.*

MILLICENT: Mother, when can I see you? Alone I mean.

ANN: After awhile. Have you had a nice day, dear?

MILLICENT: Gorgeous! But I have to see you about something.

ANN: You do? (*Holding* MILLICENT) Look at her—dad. Hasn't she grown?

MILLICENT: Mother, may I stay home from school one more day?

ANN: Gracious! Is that what you want to see me about?

MILLICENT: That's just one thing. Can't I, mother? All the girls are staying over. Mayn't I? Please—please.

ANN: I have to think a little. Let's wait and talk it over. Daisy, aren't we going to have some tea?

DAISY: It will be ready in a minute.

REMINGTON: Thank God! Then we'll go upstairs.

ANN: No, down here—it's much nicer. You'll have to get used to it, dad.

MILLICENT: Well—you be thinking—but you be thinking—*yes*—for I've just *got* to stay over. I've just got to. It would be perfectly ridiculous if I didn't. (*She goes out through hall*)

REMINGTON: (*nodding after* MILLICENT) Getting more like you every day, Ann.

ANN: She's *your* grandchild, you know.

REMINGTON: I like 'em that way. I'd rather she was stubborn as a mule than have a wabbly spine.

ANN: (*taking off her smock*) But a little wabbling once in a while is rather a pleasant thing to live with. For instance, it would make me very happy indeed if you wabbled enough to admit that this is a beautiful studio and that having it in the house where we live is the most sensible thing in the world.

REMINGTON: It would be all right if you'd stay upstairs and mind your own business. Tom, if you don't look out you'll be so mixed up you'll be upstairs keeping house and Ann will be downstairs keeping shop.

TOM: I don't know how I'd keep house—but Ann could keep shop all right.

REMINGTON: Is that the way you feel about it, McKenzie? When you're married are you going to stay at home and polish up while Ruth goes on running the magazine?

KEITH: It looks as if that's about the way it'll have to be.

RUTH: (*bringing the cake down to table*) That's a splendid suggestion, Dr Remington. Keith thinks somebody's got to do it for a successful marriage—and *I* won't—so why not you, dear? (*Pointing at* KEITH) (KEITH *looks at* RUTH *and turns away in hopeless disgust*)

REMINGTON: (*winking at* RUTH *and lowering his voice to her*) Keep at it. He'll come to it. (ANN *laughs as she cuts the cake*)

KEITH: I don't see that it's so funny.

REMINGTON: (*going to table to get a piece of cake*) You bet it's not funny. Daisy, would you like your husband to wash the dishes if you happened to be too much occupied to do it yourself?

DAISY: I'd kill him if he did. (*Bringing the cream and sugar to large table*)

REMINGTON: Oh—well—with one perfectly normal woman in the room I'm much more comfortable. (*He settles himself elaborately in his chair at left*)

KEITH: I'm serious. I'd like to know if there's anything queer or preposterous in a fellow wanting a girl to give up hard, slavish work and let him take care of her when she marries him.

RUTH: When she wants to do the work. Don't leave that out.

TOM: I don't see that you, Keith, or any other fellow has got any kick coming so long as the girl makes you happy.

KEITH: I'd like to hear your angle on it if you don't mind, doctor.

RUTH: Yes. Keith loves to hear his mid-Victorian ideas well supported.

REMINGTON: Oh, I'm not so moth-eaten as I may look. In fact, I'm a damned sight more advanced than you women are. You're still yelling about your right to do anything on land or sea you want to do. We gave you that long ago.

ANN: So nice of you!

RUTH: *(sitting below the table at right)* Why talk about it all then? What else is there to it?

REMINGTON: Put this in your pipe. The more women make good—the more they come into the vital machinery of running the world, the more they complicate their own lives and the more tragedies they lay up for themselves.

RUTH: The more they escape—you mean.

ANN: *(as she pours the tea)* There isn't a single hard thing that can happen to a woman that isn't made easier by being able to make her own living. And you know it.

REMINGTON: Oh. It's a hopeless subject for conversation. What everybody says is true. There's the rub.

DAISY: Two?

REMINGTON: Three. (KEITH *gives a cup of tea to* REMINGTON)

TOM: Go on. What were you going to say?

ANN: Yes, go on, dad.

REMINGTON: *(to* ANN) You hang on to yourself then till I get through. The development of women hasn't changed the laws of creation.

ANN: Oh yes it has. (REMINGTON *looks at her*) Sorry. Go on.

REMINGTON: Sex is still the strongest force in the world. *(He looks at* ANN *again)*

ANN: *(smiling)* Go on.

REMINGTON: And no matter how far she goes she doesn't change the fundamental laws of her own—

TOM: Individuality?

RUTH: Type?

DAISY: Character?

KEITH: Ego.

RUTH: Psychology.

ANN: Species.

TOM: Breed.

DAISY: Spots.

REMINGTON: *No!*—Mechanism—mechanism. And when the sensitive—involved—complex elements of a woman's nature become entangled in the responsibility of a man's work—and the two things fight for first place in her—she's got a hell of a mess on hand.

ANN: But her psychological mechanism *has* changed.

REMINGTON: No.

ANN: Yes.

TOM: Yes, I think it has.

KEITH: It couldn't.

RUTH: But it *has.* Women who are really doing things nowadays are an absolutely different breed from the one-sided domestic animals they used to be.

ANN: But men don't realize how deeply and fiercely creative women love their work.

REMINGTON: That's just it—Just what I'm getting at. A woman of genius puts in her work the same fierce love she puts into her child or her man. That's where her fight is—for one or the other of 'em has got to be the stronger in her. It isn't a question of her *right* to do things—nor her ability—God knows—plenty of 'em are beating men at their own jobs now. Why, I sometimes think she'll go so far that the great battle of the future will be between the sexes for supremacy. But I tell you—she has tragedies ahead of her—the tragedy of choice between the two sides of her own nature.

RUTH: Well, thank you—I'll take any and all of the hard things that go *with* my job—but none of the ones that come from being a dub and giving it up.

REMINGTON: How about you, Daisy? Could any man on earth make you stop typewriting and live for him alone?

DAISY: Oh, I'm not in this class. Ann and Ruth both have men to depend on if they want them. I'm taking care of myself because I've *got* to—and I must say this soul tragedy of choice stuff makes me a little tired. *(She starts toward hall)*

REMINGTON: *(stopping* DAISY *by taking her hand)* If I were twenty or thirty years younger, I'd go in for you strong.

DAISY: Yes, I know—I'm just the kind that *older* men appreciate very deeply. *(She goes out)*

REMINGTON: Poor Daisy.

ANN: Poor Daisy. She's the happiest, most independent thing in the world. *(Straightening the things on the table*—KEITH *having taken the tea tray away)*

RUTH: Much to be envied. No strings to *her* independence.

KEITH: And so cocky and spunky—nobody can even ask her if she's ever been in love.

REMINGTON: Sure sign she has been then.

TOM: But she never has.

REMINGTON: How do you know?

TOM: I've been pretty close to her all my life. No blighted bud about Daisy.

REMINGTON: She's putting up a darned good bluff, I must say.

RUTH: Bluff? What do you mean?

ANN: Father thinks there isn't a girl alive who wouldn't rather have a beau than a job.

REMINGTON: I do. And Daisy *looks* so self-reliant she *has* to be cocky to keep up appearances. Under her skin, she's not half the man that little lady-like looking thing Ruth is.

RUTH: Now, Dr Remington, you may go upstairs.

REMINGTON: I haven't time now. I've wasted it all down here.

RUTH: Oh, come and look at the living room just a minute. It's too beautiful.

REMINGTON: Has it got a carpet on it yet?

ANN: Yes, absolutely finished.

REMINGTON: Because I don't mind saying my feet are like ice from this confounded brick floor.

RUTH: Oh, the beautiful tiles!

REMINGTON: I'll take a little less Italian beauty and a little more American comfort in mine.

(RUTH, REMINGTON and KEITH go out through hall)

TOM: *(stopping* ANN *as she starts with the others)* Ann—about this thing. Why in the name of heaven didn't you say you were disappointed in it long ago?

ANN: I kept hoping each day I was mistaken; that what I missed would come back. But when I saw it out here—I'm afraid of it, Tom.

TOM: Afraid of what? That I'll fail? Lose it? *(*ANN *nods)* Nonsense! You're tired of it. There can't be such a change in it as all that. The idea's absolutely the same and I've *worked* as I never—

ANN: I know. I know! And oh, the beauty—the beauty of the work! That's the pity.

TOM: Pity?

ANN: I mean somebody without *half* your skill as an artist may have an idea—an *idea* that's *new*.

TOM: Oh bosh! Nothing can be done, anyhow. It's too late. Besides, I don't agree with you. I honestly do not, Ann. I know you're saying this because you're trying to boost me and get the best out of me; but the thing's done, you know. Don't confuse me. I must go on now. What's the use of talking about it? It's too late.

ANN: No, it isn't.

TOM: It is. Of course it is. You can't expect me to begin all over again and put into it a subtle intangible something I don't even feel. Damn it! It will have to fail then.

ANN: *(taking hold of* TOM *quickly)* It can't. You've got to win, Tom. You've *got* to. It's the most important thing you've ever done. Think of where it will put you. Think of the money.

TOM: I *have* thought. I've done the best that's *in* me, I tell you. It *is* the best, the very best I've ever—

ANN: But it isn't. It isn't. It isn't as great as your last two things—

TOM: Oh—

ANN: Tom—listen—you don't know how hard it is to say it. I'd rather you won this than anything that could possibly happen. You know that. Don't you?

TOM: Of course. But this isn't getting anywhere. It will have to go in as it stands.

ANN: Wait—I—I've wanted to talk to you about something for a long time—but I wasn't sure—and now I *am.*

TOM: Well—

MILLICENT: *(coming back through hall)* Thank goodness, mother. I can't wait any longer.

ANN: *(to* MILLICENT*)* Oh, just a minute, dear.

TOM: No, that's all right. There's nothing more to be said.

ANN: I appreciate what you mean—yes I do. But it doesn't get me. And all I can do is to go after it as I see it. *(He goes into workroom.* ANN *stands looking at the frieze)*

MILLICENT: *(pulling* ANN *toward table)* Mother—come here. Mother, *please.* Why—what I wanted to—sit down. *(Putting* ANN *into a chair above the long table)* Every *one* of the girls are staying over tomorrow. It looks as if you were having such a slow time that you didn't have anything to do *but* go back to school if you don't stay. And I want—Why Fanny's going to have a party tomorrow night—just a little one, and I want to have eight of them to dinner first. *(Sitting at right end of table)*

ANN: Oh—

MILLICENT: Only eight. You see, Fanny's brother's home, too, and—you see it's—Everybody has dinners and things you know before they go to the dance, you know, and—will you, Mother? Can't I?

ANN: But dearest you've done so much since you've been home. You can't get back to school too soon. New York is dreadful. It really is! The sensible mothers can't compete with the idiotic ones who let girls do all these silly things.

MILLICENT: Don't be foolish, Mother.

ANN: And school does begin tomorrow. And they expect—

MILLICENT: They don't expect us to be back. All the really smart girls stay over. It's only the deadly slow ones who are there on time. Please, mother—*please.* There'll only be eight of us; and Fanny's done so much for me I think it's as little as I could do to have her brother to dinner. Don't you?

ANN: Is he nice?

MILLICENT: Yes he is. He's older, you know and more fun. He got full dress clothes this Christmas—long tails, you know, and he looks perfectly—Mother, you're not listening. *(*ANN'S *eyes have gone back to the frieze again)*

ANN: Yes, I am dear—Yes I am. Full dress clothes.

MILLICENT: Well—May I?

ANN: Dearest—I may be frightfully busy tomorrow. I may have to do the most important thing I've ever done in my life and if I do it would be awfully hard to have—

MILLICENT: Oh, now mother! Fanny's mother's had a party or something for her *every* single night. She took her to the Plaza to dance after the matinee today and I've never been to a hotel or any exciting place in my life. You try to keep me so young mother and, jiminy cricket, I'm sixteen.

ANN: Positively ancient.

MILLICENT: Well—sixteen's old enough for *any* thing. Will you mother—please—*please. (Kissing her mother's throat)*

ANN: But what would I do if I had to do this other thing?

MILLICENT: What other thing? Can't it wait?

ANN: No it can't. That's just it. Your father may—I may be working with him all day tomorrow.

MILLICENT: You needn't have such a terribly *elaborate* dinner,—you know, but I'm crazy to do it. In fact I just have to. I've already asked most of them and they're dying to come.

ANN: You didn't, Kitten—how could you?

MILLICENT: But Mother, it's so *important*—and I don't see how I can get out of it now. You wouldn't want me to be compromised or anything, would you?

ANN: *(laughing and kissing* MILLICENT*)* You blessed baby—you ought to be spanked.

MILLICENT: You're an angel, Mummie. You will—won't you? *(Putting her cheek against* ANN'S*)*

ANN: What have you got in your ears?

MILLICENT: Earrings of course.

ANN: Heavens! Take them off.

MILLICENT: Oh, *mother!* All the girls wear them.

ANN: Take them off!

MILLICENT: But they have so much style.

ANN: Style your granny! Take them off or I'll bite 'em off. (MILLICENT *squirms and giggles as* ANN *bites her ears*)

MILLICENT: Wait—wait. I will. I think you're mean to make me. You have such terribly strict ideas.

ANN: Your ears are much prettier than those things. Can't you understand that nothing is so attractive as just being natural? Why cover up with stuff like that?

MILLICENT: You *are* funny! You'll stay at home and meet everybody tomorrow night, won't you? I want them to see you. You are sweet, mummy.

ANN: Do you love me a lot?

MILLICENT: Of course. (*Kissing* ANN)

ANN: (*rising suddenly and going to look at the frieze*) Oh, I'm so unhappy.

MILLICENT: Why? What's the matter? I should think you'd be tickled to death if father's going to get all that money.

TOM: (*coming in from the workroom quickly*) You say— (*He stops, seeing* MILLICENT)

MILLICENT: Aren't you coming up, now to plan it all?

ANN: In a few—

TOM: Go on Millicent. (MILLICENT *skips out*) Why didn't you speak the minute you saw it go wrong—or thought you did?

ANN: I was never *sure*, until today, dear.

TOM: I don't agree with you at all but still it isn't exactly inspiring—knowing you think I'm going to fail.

ANN: Tom—I'm sorry.

TOM: It's all right—but you know I care more what you think than anybody in the world and—I—it's sort of a knockout.

ANN: I had to tell you the truth—when I *was* sure. I *had* to. Tom—listen—since you've been working at this an idea has come to me. At first I thought the idea was too big for me—that I never could carry it out—and then I said I won't *let* myself be afraid—and it's grown and grown

night and day. Last night I finished it—down here—

TOM: The—

ANN: The drawings—I want you to look at them—and if—if you like it—if you think the idea is better than yours I want you to take it—use it, instead of yours.

TOM: Why Ann, you're not serious. (*She nods*) Good heavens, child, you know—you know how tremendous this thing is as well as I do.

ANN: Yes I do! But I tell you my idea is big. Oh, I knew you'd look like that when I told you. You can't believe it of course—but Tom—It's there—something vital and *alive*—with a strange charm in it. And I offer it to you dear—if you want it.

TOM: (*taking her in his arms strongly and kissing her passionately*) You generous darling! It's like you to do this. You dear—I love you for it.

ANN: (*responding warmly to his love*) I want you to have it. It's more than I ever dared dream I could do.

TOM: But darling—you couldn't possibly do anything for a scheme as big as this.

ANN: Why do you take that for granted? Why do you say that—before you've even seen my sketches?

TOM: (*after a pause*) Well—where are they?

ANN: (*taking a key out of her pocket*) In the lower drawer in my cupboard.

TOM: (*taking the key*) No, don't come with me.

ANN: But I—

TOM: I don't want you to explain anything. I want it to strike me fresh. But I'm going to hit hard—right from the shoulder. If it's good—all right. If it's bad—all right. And I expect you to take it like a man. (ANN *nods.* TOM *hurries into workroom as* RUTH *comes in from hall*)

RUTH: Have you told him?

ANN: Yes—he's gone to look at my sketches now.

RUTH: Ann—I've been thinking. You're a fool to give away your ideas. Make your models and send them in yourself.

ANN: What?

RUTH: Certainly. Why not?

ANN: Oh, Ruth—I couldn't. Some day I will. Some day.

RUTH: Some day! You've got the biggest idea you've ever had. Do it—send it in—yourself—on your *own feet*.

ANN: Tom would think I was out of my—

RUTH: *You* know it's good—don't you!

ANN: *Yes, I do.*

RUTH: It belongs to *you*—and if you don't take care of it and give it its chance, you kill something which is more important than you are. Don't forget *that*. You're not just the talented woman, you've got *downright genius* and you ought to make everything give way to that. *Everything*. If you don't you're weak.

ANN: Wait and see what Tom says. He'll know. He's so dead right about my stuff—always.

RUTH: Oh, you lucky people! Pulling together. If Keith only had a little of it towards me. Ann, what *shall* I do?

ANN: *(with quick sympathy)* What, dear?

RUTH: He's never, never, never going to know what a sacrifice it will be for me to stop just as I'm getting what I've slaved and struggled for all these years. And I can't bear to hurt him.

ANN: Dear old Keith. He just *can't see*. And he loves you so.

KEITH: *(coming in from hall)* Why did you come back down here?

RUTH: Just to run away from—you. No, I didn't. *(Going to him sweetly)* You know I didn't.

ANN: *(as* DAISY *comes in from hall)* Daisy, tell me the minute Tom comes out.

KEITH: *(to* RUTH*)* I'll be up in a minute. I've got to cover some stuff in there. *(exit* ANN *and* RUTH*)*

KEITH: You're a wonder, Daisy. You don't mind sitting up late to get your letters off, do you?

DAISY: Oh, no—I'm healthy.

KEITH: You're a peach. I'm sorry I made you huffy. All I meant was that no man would ever think he could ask you to marry him unless he had an awfully big bank-roll to offer.

*(*REMINGTON *comes in from hall to get his hat and stick—just in time to hear* KEITH'S *last*

remark. DAISY *rises—consciously.* KEITH *goes into workroom.* REMINGTON *goes to end of table)*

DAISY: I suppose that speech sounded rather queer. He was talking about Ruth, of course.

REMINGTON: Don't apologize or you'll make me suspicious.

DAISY: Now—

REMINGTON: It sounded very much as if he were making love to *you*.

DAISY: Oh—

REMINGTON: I wish to God he would. You'd—be a much better wife for him than the other one.

DAISY: You—

REMINGTON: You know you would. Why don't you go in and get him? Cut the other one out.

DAISY: How *dare* you say such a thing to me?

REMINGTON: Why shouldn't I say it?

DAISY: Because you have no *right* to. I haven't the slightest interest in Keith McKenzie—not the slightest.

REMINGTON: No. I can see that.

DAISY: What do you mean?

REMINGTON: *(suddenly understanding)* Why my dear girl, I didn't mean anything. I'm sorry.

DAISY: I don't know why in the world you said such a thing to me.

REMINGTON: Well—well—forget it.

DAISY: You don't think from anything I've ever done or said—

REMINGTON: I don't think anything—I don't know anything . . .

DAISY: I don't see *why* you said it.

ANN: *(coming from hall)* What's the matter?
(As DAISY *breaks away from* REMINGTON *who is holding her by the wrists)*

DAISY: Let me go, please. I'm in a hurry. *(*DAISY *rushes out through hall)*

ANN: What on earth are you doing to Daisy?

REMINGTON: She's doing things to me.

ANN: What?

REMINGTON: Convincing me of some of my old-fashioned ideas. *(*TOM *rushes in from the workroom with a large roll of drawings)*

TOM: Ann—they're wonderful.

ANN: Oh—Tom!

TOM: *(spreading the roll of sketches on the table—* ANN *helping him)* Beautiful! Astoundingly beautiful! Well as I know you, I didn't think you had it in you.

ANN: I can't believe it. Are you going to use it?

TOM: Oh, my dear girl. That's different. Now don't be hurt. Why Ann—it isn't possible. You—you're mistaken—way off. I don't know what's got into you. This is imaginative and charming and graceful—full of abandon and fantasy and even vitality—but ye gods, child, it isn't in *this* class.

ANN: But you could strengthen it. It will grow. You'll see more in it. Really you will. Don't make up your mind yet.

REMINGTON: What are you talking about? What has she done?

TOM: Drawings for a frieze—like this. And they're amazing, doctor. Positively amazing.

REMINGTON: You don't say.

TOM: Wait—let's see what McKenzie says. McKenzie—

ANN: *(pounding on the workroom door)* Keith— Keith—come here—quickly.

REMINGTON: Looks beautiful to me, daughter. When did you do all this? Do you mean to say you didn't know anything about it, Tom?

TOM: Not a thing. She's been— *(*KEITH *comes in)* Here McKenzie. Look at this. Here's a scheme Mrs Herford's worked out. Begins here—See— see? Get it? What do you think?

KEITH: Mrs Herford?

TOM: Yes. Do you get it?

McKENZIE: Of course.

TOM: Well? What do you say?

KEITH: I say it's as beautiful as anything I ever saw.

TOM: Great! And what do you think of it for a big place like mine?

KEITH: For *that?*

TOM: Yes.

KEITH: Oh—I—too fanciful, isn't it? Would the crowd understand it? Needs a big clear striking thing like that. Don't you think?

TOM: Then you don't think it's as good as mine for this competition.

KEITH: As yours? Heavens no!

ANN: *(standing at right—facing the three men)* Then do you know what I'm going to do?

KEITH AND TOM: What?

ANN: Make my models and send them in myself.

TOM, KEITH AND REMINGTON: What?

ANN: Why not?

REMINGTON: You don't mean it, daughter.

ANN: I do. I mean it with my whole soul.

REMINGTON: Why do you want to do anything so foolish?

ANN: Because I *made* it. Because it's my work. You all say it's good. Why shouldn't I send it? I don't mind failure. I only want it to stand its little chance with the rest. I love it. It means more to me than I can possibly—why shouldn't I? I *want* to.

TOM: Then do it. Why not? It's your own affair. Go ahead. *(Putting out the hand of a good pal-ship to her)*

ANN: Oh, Tom—thank you. You're splendid. *(The curtain falls)*

ACT II

TIME: *Four months later—about nine in the evening. The living room in the Herford house.*

The room is long and wide, dignified and restful in proportions. At center back a large fireplace with a severe mantel in cream marble. A wide window covers the entire left wall, and wide doors at right lead into the library. A single door at back, left of fireplace, leads into hall. The walls are hung in a soft dull silk which throws out the strong simple lines of the woodwork. A bright wood fire is burning and soft lights throw a warm glow over the gray carpet and the furniture which is distinguished and artistic but distinctly comfortable, giving the room the air of being much lived in and used.

AT CURTAIN: *The room is empty a moment.* DAISY *is singing in the library at right.* ELLEN, *a maid, middle-aged and kindly, comes from hall carrying a silver coffee service.*

DAISY: *(as she comes in from library)* Here's your coffee, girls. Come in here. Put the flowers over there, Ellen.

(ELLEN moves the vase of flowers and makes room for the coffee service on table right center. RUTH comes in from the library with a book. ELLEN goes to fire and pokes it, then straightens the writing things on the desk)

DAISY: Ann, here's your coffee.

ANN: *(calling from library)* I don't want any, thank you. What time is it, Daisy?

DAISY: About nine. Why?

ANN: Oh, the postman. I'm waiting for the last mail.

DAISY: Well, don't. A watched pot you know. *(To RUTH)* She's watched every mail for a week. I almost think Ann will be more disappointed than Tom himself if he doesn't get the commission. *(They take their coffee to the fire)*

RUTH: I hope to goodness he does. Everybody's so dead sure of him.

DAISY: Almost too sure. I'm beginning to be frightened myself. The time is about up.

ANN: *(hurrying in from the library)* That's the postman—isn't it?

ELLEN: No ma'am. Beggin' your pardon. It ain't— I'm listenin' too.

ANN: Are you, Ellen? Keep on and bring it up the minute it comes.

ELLEN: Faith I will. I've got the habit meself lately of watchin' for the mail.

ANN: Have you?

ELLEN: Every time I hear the whistle I drop whatever I'm doin' like it was hot—and run.

ANN: Do you?

ELLEN: And just before I open the door I say— The Holy Saints be praised, I hope it's come this time—whatever it is they're lookin' for. *(She goes out through the hall)*

ANN: Oh, dear! It gets worse as the time grows shorter.

DAISY: Ann, working yourself up like this won't make Tom get the commission. Stop thinking about it.

ANN: But I can't, Daisy Dimple. He ought to hear tonight if he's ever going to.

DAISY: Well, I'll be glad when it's all over and we know one way or the other—and can settle down to ordinary life again. It's almost given me nervous indigestion.

ANN: Listen! There's the postman.

RUTH: *(jumping so that her cup and saucer almost fall)* Oh, Ann, you're getting me so excited, I'll listen for the postman all the rest of my life.

ANN: I know I shall. Oh, Tom must get it. He *must*. If he does, I'll wire Millicent. *(Taking up a picture of Millicent which stands in a frame on the table)* I think I'll run up to school Sunday just to give her a good hug. I get so hungry for her!

RUTH: Isn't it splendid the school is so really what it ought to be?

ANN: Yes. So much that's sweet and right that one can't get in New York for a girl.

DAISY: *(sewing on a frock which is nearly finished)* She seems pretty keen about it herself.

ANN: Yes—rather. Easter vacation when I was working day and night to get my models off, she was perfectly contented to stay at school.

RUTH: She's an adorable kiddie but I don't envy you your job.

ANN: Why?

RUTH: I think being a mother is the most gigantic, difficult, important and thankless thing in the world.

DAISY: That's the most sensible remark I ever heard you give vent to, Ruth.

ANN: There's something much more glorious in it than being thanked. You'll miss the most wonderful thing in the world, Ruth, if you don't have children.

RUTH: I know. I know. But work has taken that all out of me. It does, you know. It would bore me stiff to take care of a baby.

DAISY: That's a pleasant prospect for Keith. Do you expect *him* to do it?

RUTH: *(making herself comfortable on the couch)* I'm not going to *have* children.

ANN: *(going to sit at the fire)* That's perfectly fair if he knows it. No reason why you should if you don't want 'em.

DAISY: Well, I think it's a *rotten* way to live.

RUTH: Wait till you decide to marry somebody yourself, young lady, and see how *you* like giving up everything that interests you most.

DAISY: Well, by Jove, if I ever *do* marry, I'll *marry* and do all the things that belong to my side of the game. No halfway business for me. You might as well be a man's mistress and be done with it.

RUTH: *(half serious—half joking)* That's the ideal relationship for a man and woman. Each to keep his independence in absolutely every way—and live together merely because they charm each other. But somehow we don't seem to be able to make it respectable.

DAISY: I suppose that's very clever and modern.

RUTH: Oh, no—it's as old as the everlasting hills. The trouble is children are apt to set in and mess things up. It's hard on *them*.

DAISY: So far as I can see most everything that's modern is hard on children.

ANN: *(laughing)* How's the gown getting on, Daisy?

DAISY: Most finished.

RUTH: That's awfully pretty.

ANN: Slip it on so we can see.

DAISY: Oh, I can't.

ANN: *(rising and walking to* DAISY*)* Yes, you can—over that one—just to give us an idea.

DAISY: I'll look a tub and it really makes me quite respectably straight up and down.

ANN: You're a perfectly scrumptious size and shape. Isn't she, Ruth?

RUTH: Magnificent!

DAISY: Yes, Ruth, skinny women always enthuse over their fat friends.

RUTH: *(rising and goes to* DAISY*)* Oh, you aren't fat, Daisy. That is, not too fat. How does this go. It's terribly complicated, isn't it?

DAISY: No—perfectly simple. Wait—this goes over here.

ANN: No, it doesn't, does it?

DAISY: Yes, it does. Right there. Don't you see? The style of the whole gown depends on that.

RUTH: You must have it on wrong side before.

DAISY: Nonsense! Can't you see, Ann? It's as simple as can be.

ANN: Yes, I know dear—but does this go on the shoulder—or down on your hip? *(They all talk at once for a moment on the subject of where the end of the girdle fastens)* Oh, here! I see, of course! There!

DAISY: Now, does it make me look big?

RUTH: You want to look big, don't you?

DAISY: Well, I want to look life size. Don't you see how much better I am through here than I was last year, Ann? *(Touching her hip)*

ANN: Much. The female form divine is improving all the time anyway—gradually getting back to what it was in the beginning.

DAISY: I don't expect to look like you in it, Ruth.

RUTH: Oh, don't you, dear? Then why don't you have it stick out this way as much as possible so everybody will know you *mean* to look broad? There's everything in that, you know.

DAISY: I think it would be awfully good on you—to fill out what you haven't got. Then everybody would know you didn't *mean* to look so narrow—even if you *are*.

ANN: You're both delightful. Perfect specimens of your types. When I look at Ruth I think the most alluring charm a woman can have is beautiful bones without a superfluous ounce of flesh on them. And when I look at you, Daisy, I think after all, there's nothing so stunning as a big strong girl with perfectly natural lines—so natural that we know she'd be even better looking with no clothes on at all.

DAISY: Heavens, Ann! Your sculptor's eye is a little embarrassing.

RUTH: Evidently you think my clothes help me out a good deal. But at least I'm free and comfortable, too. Can you touch the floor, Daisy?

DAISY: Of course. *(The two women bend—touching the floor with the tips of their fingers)*

(TOM, REMINGTON *and* KEITH *come in from the hall*)

TOM: What's going on?

REMINGTON: What are you trying to do, Ruth—swim or fly?

ANN: We're just saying that the waist measure expands as we *broaden* in our ideas.

KEITH: Is that the fashion now?

RUTH: Yes—broad and free.

REMINGTON: That's *one* thing you women have to acknowledge men have more sense about than you have.

ANN, RUTH, DAISY: What?

REMINGTON: Our figures. We've had the same shape since the Garden of Eden and you've had hundreds of absolutely different kinds.

ANN: Turn around, Daisy, I want to try something. *(She accidentally sticks a pin into DAISY's shoulder)*

DAISY: Ouch!

ANN: Oh, I'm sorry! You seem to be so close to your clothes.

REMINGTON: What are you doing to her?

DAISY: She's sticking pins into me.

ANN: For her own good. Isn't that pretty?

TOM: What?

ANN: The frock.

TOM: Is that new?

KEITH: Which?

DAISY: Do you mean to say you don't realize I have on something different from what I wore at dinner?

RUTH: No use dressing for Keith. He never sees anything.

DAISY: I'm going to undress now. Perhaps that will interest you more. *(ANN begins to unfasten the gown)*

REMINGTON: Much more.

ANN: Was *that* the postman?

DAISY: No, it was *not*.

REMINGTON: The postman habit is getting on my nerves. You're all jumping and listening till you'll have St. Vitus dance if you don't stop.

ANN: How can we help it?

REMINGTON: After all, a few other competitions have been lost and won—and people have lived through it. It's not the only thing in life.

TOM: You'd think it was if you had $100,000 at stake. *(ELLEN comes in from hall and takes out the coffee tray)*

ANN: Aren't we going to have some bridge? Who wants to play? I know you do, daddy.

REMINGTON: I have to get even with you for that last rubber, Tom.

TOM: You can't do it.

DAISY: I want to play, with you, doctor.

REMINGTON: Come on.

RUTH: I'm afraid to play *against* you.

REMINGTON: *(turning at the library door)* What's that?

OTHERS: What?

REMINGTON: The postman!

OTHERS: Oh! *(RUTH and DAISY go into library, R. with REMINGTON)*

ANN: *(to TOM and KEITH)* Coming?

TOM: You go, Keith. I want to look at the paper a minute.

KEITH: Oh, my game's no good. You go.

ANN: Now don't stay out here and listen and wait. If there is any mail Ellen will bring it straight up.

TOM: I won't. I'll be with you—in two minutes.

ANN: Anyway—tonight doesn't necessarily decide it. There may be still two or three more days. Isn't that so, Keith?

KEITH: Yes, I think so.

REMINGTON, RUTH, DAISY: *(calling from the library)* Come on. Come on.

ANN: Coming. *(She goes in)*

KEITH: That's straight. I do think so—*(A pause. TOM reads)* Don't you?

TOM: I'm trying to—but these last few days of waiting have been—

KEITH: Don't lose your nerve, Herford. I'm just as sure as I was the first day. If by any wild chance you *don't* get it—it will be a fluke.

TOM: Oh, no. Oh, no, not by any means. The men judging this *know*. I'd trust them with anything.

The fellows who lose will have no kick coming on that score.

KEITH: Well—I don't see how you *can* lose.

TOM: A man's a fool to let himself count on an uncertainty. I don't mean that I've lost sight of the fact that I might lose—not for a second—but I confess—as the time has grown shorter I've realized I *want* it even more than I thought I did.

KEITH: Of course you want it. Aside from the glory—it's an *awful lot of money*—governor, an awful lot of money.

TOM: *It is.* It would put us straight—clear up the house entirely and make it possible to do only the things a fellow wants to do. That's what I'm after. Then—No more competitions for me, thank you. Is that the 'phone? I'm as bad as Ann—jumping and listening. Damn it! I want to *know*—one way or the other.

KEITH: Of course you do. The cursed waiting is enough to make you cut your throat.

ELLEN: *(opening the hall door)* The telephone for Mr Herford.

TOM: Who is it?

ELLEN: I couldn't just get the name, sir.

KEITH: Want me to go?

TOM: If you don't mind, old man. *(ELLEN goes out)*

KEITH: *(starting to the door and turning)* It couldn't be—you wouldn't get word that way—would you?

TOM: Uh?—Oh—nonsense! No—no—nonsense! I'll go—No, I—you go—old man. That's not it— of course. *(TOM listens a moment—showing a tense anxiety)*

RUTH: *(coming in from the library)* They're waiting for you, Tom. The cards are dealt. Where's Keith?

TOM: He'll be back in a minute.

RUTH: Aren't you going in?

TOM: Why don't you take my place? I don't feel a bit—

RUTH: I did offer to but Dr Remington said he would like to *play* bridge this evening, not *teach* it. Wouldn't it be seventh heaven to

speak the truth on all occasions as unconcernedly as Dr Remington does? Imagine the sheer bliss of letting go and spitting it all out. Have you ever counted the lies you told in just one day, Tom?

TOM: No—I've never had time. *(TOM starts to go into the library and turns to see if RUTH is coming)*

RUTH: No—I'm going to wait for Keith. *(TOM goes in—RUTH reads for a moment)*

KEITH: *(coming back from the hall)* That was—

RUTH: What?

KEITH: Millicent or her school or something. Such a bad connection; they're going to call again in a few minutes. Is that dress new, dear?

RUTH: I've had it three years.

KEITH: It's awfully pretty. I wish you'd wear it all the time.

RUTH: I do.

KEITH: Aren't we going in to play?

RUTH: No, I don't feel like it. Come and sit down, dear. Oh, are you going to sit way over there?

KEITH: Not 'specially. *(Drawing chair near the couch—KEITH sits facing RUTH)*

RUTH: Comfortable?

KEITH: Not very.

RUTH: Have you read this?

KEITH: No. Any good?

RUTH: Yes—Good enough. *(She rises, going to the fireplace)*

KEITH: What's the matter? I thought you wanted to talk. Where are you going?

RUTH: No place.

KEITH: You got the fidgets too?

RUTH: Sort of.

KEITH: Well, stop it. Herford's going to be all right. There'll be news in a day or so now.

RUTH: I wasn't thinking of that. I have something to tell you.

KEITH: Then why don't you come and tell it?

RUTH: And if you aren't fine about it—it will be the greatest disappointment in my whole life. *(Going to KEITH and putting a hand on his shoulder)*

KEITH: You mean if I don't think just what you want me to about it. Go on. I s'pose I know, anyway.

RUTH: Then if you do—but you don't. It's so wonderful you couldn't guess. And you'll just *have* to see it the right way, because if you don't it would mean you're what I know you're *not*. Down in your real soul, Keith, you're generous and fair and right.

KEITH: Suppose you communicate it to me first and discuss my soul afterwards.

RUTH: *(sitting on couch facing* KEITH*)* Well—Oh you *will* be sweet won't you, Keithie?

KEITH: I can see it's going to be something *very* pleasant for *me*.

RUTH: It is if you . . .

KEITH: It's wonderful if I'm not a fool and a pig. Yes, I know. Go on. Go on.

RUTH: Now don't begin that way—please dear. Don't shut up your mind before I even tell you.

KEITH: Suppose you *do* tell me.

RUTH: Well—last week there was a row in the office over a matter concerning the policy of the magazine and I differed with all the men in my department. At last I was sent for by the Editor in Chief. He was terribly severe at first, and I was frightened to pieces—but I stuck to my guns—and bless your soul he sent for me again today and said they had had a meeting of the directors and that they decided—oh, it's too—

KEITH: What? What?

RUTH: They had decided to make me Editor of the Woman's Magazine. *(Fighting back her tears)* Isn't it funny?

KEITH: And I suppose all this introduction means you accepted—without even asking me?

RUTH: Why, of course. Oh, Keith, don't you understand what this means to me?

KEITH: I understand that unless it means more to you than I do—you wouldn't hesitate a minute to chuck it.

RUTH: It's hopeless—we'll never—never see it the same way.

KEITH: You've never made the slightest effort to see it *my* way.

RUTH: What you ask of me is to cut off one half of my life and throw it away. What I ask of you is only an experiment—to let me try and see if I can't make things comfortable and smooth and happy for us—and still take this big thing that has come as a result of all my years of hard work and fighting for it.

KEITH: You'll never stop if you don't now. Once you get deeper in it you'll be swamped—eaten up by it.

RUTH: Don't, Keith. I can't bear it. It's too unutterably selfish.

KEITH: *(rising and pushing his chair away)* All right—I'm selfish—but I'm human—and I'll bet my hat I'm just like every nine men out of ten. What in the name of heaven does loving a girl amount to if you don't want to take care of her from start to finish? A man's no good if he doesn't feel that way, I tell you. He's a pup—and ought to be shot.

RUTH: *(rising)* But what about *me*—and what I want and have to have—in order to be happy?

KEITH: That's it. That is the point. You won't be happy without it. You want the excitement of it—that hustle and bustle outside.

RUTH: I want it just as you want your work—and you haven't any more right to ask me to give up mine than I have to ask you to stop *yours*.

KEITH: You simply don't *love* me.

RUTH: What rot! What nonsense!

KEITH: You don't love me.

RUTH: It's hopeless. You've decided then. You won't compromise—so we'll end it.

KEITH: What do you mean?

RUTH: *(going to the hall door)* You've made your own choice. We'll end it now.

KEITH: *(following her)* No—Ruth—I won't give you up.

RUTH: You have. You have given me up.

KEITH: Ruth—wait.

RUTH: It's best, Keith. Don't hate me. You'll see it's best in a little while. We'll learn to be friends. I want you to be happy, dear boy—I do. And I couldn't make you so. We'll end it now. It's the best for us both.

KEITH: Ruth—

(*She goes out quickly, closing the door.* KEITH *turns to the fire*)

DAISY: (*knocking and opening the library door*) Excuse me. May I come in to get my sewing? Where's Ruth?

KEITH: (*with his back to* DAISY) Don't know.

DAISY: Well, don't bite my head off. I can always tell when you and Ruth have been discussing the *emancipation* of women.

(*Sitting below table and taking her dress to sew*)

KEITH: You *all* think you're superior beings.

DAISY: Of course.

KEITH: (*beginning to walk about*) Yes, you do. You're just as bad as the rest of them—worse. The minute a woman makes enough to buy the clothes on her back, she thinks she and God Almighty are running the earth and men are just little insects crawling around. (DAISY *laughs*) Oh, you can laugh. It's so—and you *know* it. Every one of you that have got the bee in your bonnet of doing something—*doing* something, are through with the men. Look at *you*. You've cut men out entirely and you think you're too smart to marry one. Now, don't you? Isn't that the reason?

DAISY: (*threading her needle*) Don't bully-rag me. Say it all to Ruth.

KEITH: I tell you it's all rot—business for women. It spoils every one of you. Why aren't *you* in a home of your own instead of hustling for your bread and butter? It's because you're too damned conceited. You think you know more than any man you ever saw and you think you don't need one. You wait—You'll see—some day.

(*Going back to the fire*)

DAISY: You amuse me.

KEITH: There you *are*—that's about what I'm for.

DAISY: There's a button off your coat. Looks horrid.

KEITH: I know. I've got it.

(*Putting his finger in waistcoat pocket*)

DAISY: Have you got it there? (KEITH *shows her the button*) Come here, I'll do it.

KEITH: Never mind. I'll *nail* it on.

DAISY: Come here. (KEITH *goes slowly to her*) You'll have to take your coat off. It's bad luck to sew anything *on* you.

KEITH: Oh—

DAISY: Go on—take it off. (KEITH *takes off his coat reluctantly and watches* DAISY *as she examines the coat*) Good Gracious, the lining's ripped, too.

KEITH: Yes.

DAISY: Poor old fellow! Are these some of your stitches?

KEITH: (*drawing the chair from C. and sitting L. before* DAISY) What's the matter with 'em?

DAISY: Looks like carpet thread. (*Snipping some threads*) See, I'll just draw this together and that'll be all right.

(*She begins to sing an old ditty—* KEITH *gradually hums with her, keeping time with his hands and feet and relaxing into a good humor*)

KEITH: (*soothed for a moment*) How does it happen you're so handy with a needle? I thought you were all for business.

DAISY: Well, I can sew a button on if *you* can.

KEITH: I tell you it changes all women—business. They make a little money themselves and want luxury and won't live without it.

DAISY: Sometimes—yes. But there are lots and lots and lots of women taking care of themselves—putting up the bluff of being independent and happy who would be so glad to live in a little flat and do their own work—just to be the nicest thing in the world to some man.

KEITH: Wouldn't you think that Ruth would like that better than the office?

DAISY: No—not the lamp light and the needle for Ruth. Keith, don't ask her to give up her work—don't you see, she's more clever, in her way than you are in yours. She'll go further, and if you make her stop, she'll hate you some day because she'll think you've kept her back. That's a hard thing to say—but it's the truth.

KEITH: You mean I'm a failure.

DAISY: (*genuinely*) No—no—I don't mean that, Keith.

KEITH: I work—Gosh, how I work, but I'll never *do* anything. Why haven't I got what Mrs Herford's got? She sent models off for this frieze that any *man* would be proud to send. Why couldn't I?

DAISY: Seems kind of mixed up and unfair—doesn't it?

KEITH: You bet it's unfair. I work like a dog and never get anywhere. If Ruth throws me over, I'll never have the home I'm working for. That's what I want—a home. I'll never have it now.

DAISY: Oh, yes you will.

KEITH: I'm done for.

DAISY: No, you're not. There are too many women in the world—who—could—love you.

KEITH: I'm no good.

DAISY: Some woman might think that you—your—the way you work—and your honesty and *loyalty* are the greatest things a man can have.

KEITH: Um!

DAISY: *Some* woman might use all her cleverness and ingenuity to make the little flat beautiful—to show you what your own home—could be—to give you a better dinner than you thought you could afford.

KEITH: *(sitting with his head in his hands)* That kind of a woman is a thing of the past.

DAISY: Oh no, they're not. They're lying around *thick*. The trouble is—a *woman* can't *ask*. Even if a man is—just at her hand—and she knows she could make him happy—she can't *tell* him—she can't open his eyes—she has to hide what might make things right for both of them. Because she's a woman.

KEITH: Oh—love doesn't cut much ice with a woman. Women are all *brain* nowadays.

DAISY: *(with sudden warmth)* That's enough to use all the brains a woman's got—to make a home—to bring up children—and to keep a man's love.

KEITH: *(raising his head slowly and looking at Daisy)* I never expected to hear *you* say a thing like that. There's some excuse for *you* being in business.

DAISY: Yes, of course. *(Rising and holding the coat)* I'm not the marrying kind.

KEITH: *(getting into the coat)* Much obliged. Would *you* be willing to give up work and marry a man on a small salary—if you loved him?

DAISY: You make me laugh.

KEITH: What's the matter, Daisy?

DAISY: Nothing.

KEITH: I never saw tears in your eyes before. Women are funny things.

DAISY: Yes, we're funny. There's only one thing on earth funnier.

KEITH: What?

DAISY: Men.

REMINGTON: *(coming in from the library)* Did I leave my other glasses in here?

DAISY: *(beginning to look for them)* I haven't seen them.

REMINGTON: I've lost one game because I didn't have 'em and I don't propose to give 'em another.

DAISY: What a shame! Help look for them, Keith.

REMINGTON: I'm pretty blind—but thank God not quite as bad as you, Keith.

KEITH: What? There's nothing the matter with my eyes.

REMINGTON: *(looking insinuatingly at Daisy)* Don't you think there is, Daisy?

DAISY: *(trying to look unconscious)* Are you *sure* you left those glasses in here?

REMINGTON: It's as bad a case of short sightedness as I ever saw.

DAISY: Oh—

(The doctor holds her and turns her, pushing her toward KEITH)

REMINGTON: Daisy, don't you see that queer blind look in his eyes?

DAISY: No—I don't.

KEITH: What do you mean? *(REMINGTON laughs)* Do you see the joke, Daisy?

REMINGTON: It's no joke—is it Daisy?

DAISY: I don't know what on earth you're talking about. I'm going to get those glasses. *(Going to hall door)* You probably left them in your hoat in the call. I mean your hall in the coat—I mean—

REMINGTON: That's all right, Daisy—we know what you mean. At least I do.

DAISY: Oh you— (ELLEN *comes in from hall*)
   What is it, Ellen?
ELLEN: The telephone, Miss Herford.
DAISY: For me?
ELLEN: They said any one of the family.
DAISY: I'll go.
   (She goes out followed by ELLEN*)*
REMINGTON: *There's* a woman who knows how to
   take care of a man.
KEITH: I'm afraid that's not her object in life.
   They all have something else to do.
REMINGTON: What's the matter with you?
KEITH: I'm done for.
REMINGTON: Ruth, you mean?
KEITH: She won't marry me unless she goes on
   working.
REMINGTON: She's right, too.
KEITH: What?
REMINGTON: Of course. You haven't any more
   right to ask that clever little woman to throw
   away half her life and to be the tail to your kite
   than you have to ask her to cut her throat. Open
   your eyes and look around. There are always
   other women.
KEITH: *Never.* Never in the world for me.
REMINGTON: I give you about three months.
KEITH: Do you think I could ever—
REMINGTON: Certainly I do. Look at Daisy, for instance. A fine, sweet wholesome girl with no
   kinks and no abnormal ambitions.
KEITH: Daisy?
REMINGTON: Don't blow your brains out for a couple of days. Talk it over with her. She thinks
   you're about the finest thing going.
KEITH: *What?*
REMINGTON: Fact! Don't try to hold on to the
   woman who's getting away from you, but take
   the one who is coming your way.
KEITH: You're crazy. Mad as a hatter. What are
   you giving me?
REMINGTON: Just a little professional advice—
   free. She's head over heels in love with you, I
   tell you.
DAISY: *(coming in from hall in great excitement. She has a case for glasses in her hand)*

Dr Remington, that was long distance. They
   telephoned from school that Millicent has
   gone.
KEITH: Gone?
REMINGTON: Gone where?
DAISY: Left school suddenly tonight without say-
   ing a word to anyone.
REMINGTON AND KEITH: What?
DAISY: As soon as they knew—they 'phoned the
   station, and found she had taken the train for
   New York.
REMINGTON: What train?
DAISY: The one that gets here at nine o'clock.
KEITH: *(looking at his watch)* It's 9:15 now.
DAISY: Shall I tell Ann?
REMINGTON: No—no—wait. We'll give her fifteen
   minutes more to get to the house. No use fright-
   ening Ann.
KEITH: Do you think she *is* coming home?
DAISY: Why do you say that, Keith? What put
   such an idea into your head?
KEITH: Why wouldn't she say so—wire or write or
   something?
DAISY: Oh, it's too horrible. Doctor, oughtn't we to
   tell them now?
REMINGTON: No—no—
DAISY: But we're wasting time. What if she
   shouldn't come?
KEITH: I think I'll dash down to the station any-
   way. The train might be late.
REMINGTON: No—no. They'd ask where you'd
   gone. Wait fifteen minutes—I think she'll be
   here. I don't want to frighten—
   (ANN comes in from the library)
ANN: Well, I never saw people so wildly keen
   about playing as you are. What's the matter
   with you?
REMINGTON: I've been waiting all this time—for
   my glasses. Come on Daisy.
   (Taking the glasses from DAISY, *he goes into
   library)*
ANN: You look worried, Daisy.
DAISY: No—I'm only—
ELLEN: *(coming in from hall with eight letters on
   a small tray)* The mail, Mrs Herford.

ANN: Oh! *(She snatches the letters, taking off the three top ones)* It's come! Tom's letter.

KEITH AND DAISY: What?

(ELLEN goes out through hall L. C.)

ANN: It is! It is—as true as I live.

KEITH: Great Scott!

DAISY: Then he's got it. He's got it.

ANN: Sh! Ask him to come here.

DAISY: It's too good to be true. It's too good!

(DAISY goes into the library)

KEITH: I can't tell you how glad I am, Mrs Herford. I can't tell you.

ANN: *(scarcely able to speak)* Ask him to come here.

KEITH: *(going into library)* Mrs Herford wants you, Governor.

TOM: *(within)* Come and play, Ann.

ANN: *(throwing the other letters on the table)* Come here just a minute, Tom, please.

TOM: *(coming to door)* What is it?

ANN: Shut the door. It's come. *(Showing the letter. TOM opens and reads it. A look of sickening disappointment comes into his face)* No? Oh, Tom!

TOM: I was their *second* choice!

ANN: Oh, Tom, don't take it like that. What difference does it make after all? You know you did a big thing. It's all luck—anyway.

TOM: I'll pull up in a minute. Well, it means taking hold of something else pretty quick. Going at it again.

ANN: Yes, keeping at it—that's it. What a TERRIBLE lot chance has to do with it.

TOM: Oh no, that isn't it.

ANN: Yes, it is, too.

TOM: No—I failed. I didn't get it, that's all.

ANN: You'll do something greater—next time—because of this.

TOM: *(taking her hand)* You're a brick! Now, see here, don't you be cut up about this. It's not the end of everything, you know. Stop that! You're not crying, I hope?

ANN: No, I'm not. Of course, I'm not! *(With passionate tenderness)* Oh, my boy. I never loved you so much—never believed in you as I do now. This is only a little hard place that will make you all the stronger.

TOM: Dear old girl! What would I do without you? I'll tell the others and get it over. *(Rising, he stops, staring at one of the letters on the table)* Ann!

ANN: Um?

TOM: *(taking up a letter)* Ann—here's one for you, too.

ANN: What? *(She tears open the letter)* Tom! They've given the commission to me! Look! Read it! Is that what it says? Is it? Now aren't you glad you let me do it? You haven't lost! We've got it. Say you're glad. Say you're proud of me, dear. That's the best part of it all.

TOM: Of course, I am, dear, of course I am.

ANN: Oh, Tom, I wanted you to get it more than I ever wanted anything in my life, but this is SOMETHING to be thankful for. Doesn't this almost make it right?

TOM: Yes, dear, yes. Don't think of me. That's over—that part of it. Tell the others now.

ANN: Wait!

TOM: Aren't you going to?

ANN: I only want to be sure that you're just as happy that *I* won, as I would have been if YOU had.

TOM: Of course, I am. You know that.
(Kissing her)

ANN: Tell the others, then, Tom—I can't.

TOM: *(opening the library doors)* What do you think has happened?

DAISY: *(rushing in)* Tom got it. Didn't you, Tom? You did. You did! Oh, I'm so glad. *(She kisses him)*

KEITH: *(following DAISY in)* Well—governor— what did I tell you?

REMINGTON: *(in doorway)* Pretty fine—isn't it?

ANN: You tell them, Tom.

TOM: Ann got it!

DAISY: What?

TOM: Isn't it great?

ANN: You won't believe it. But you can see the letter. Now, father, don't you think getting that is better than being nursemaid and housekeeper! Now, don't you, honestly?

REMINGTON: I do not.

ANN: What?

REMINGTON: I do not.

ANN: Oh, I can laugh at your theories now. You haven't a leg to stand on. Has he, Tom? Be a dear father and say you're glad.

REMINGTON: I'm not. I'd rather you'd failed a thousand times over—for your own good. What are you going to do with Millicent while you're making this thing?

ANN: How can you be so hard and narrow, Father?

REMINGTON: What if you did win? You've got something far greater than making statues to do.

TOM: Doctor, you're excited.

REMINGTON: Not a bit. I'm only telling the truth. This is your *business* you know—and it would have been far better for *both* of you if *you'd won the thing.*

TOM: I don't see the argument. Ann got it because she sent in a better model than I did. I don't see that anything else has anything to do with the case.

(TOM *goes out through hall*)

ANN: (*turning to sit on the couch*) At least *Tom's* glad I got it.

REMINGTON: He's stung to the quick. You've humiliated him in his own eyes. (*He goes to the fireplace*)

ANN: I *can't* understand why you feel this way about it, father.

DAISY: Oh, it's *natural* enough.

ANN: (*turning to* DAISY *in amazement*) Aren't *you* glad for me—Daisy?

DAISY: Yes, but—I—I'm awfully sorry for Tom. (*She goes out through hall*)

ANN: What's the matter with them all, Keith?

KEITH: Oh—as Daisy says—it's natural, Mrs Herford.

(*He goes out after* DAISY)

REMINGTON: (*coming down to* ANN) Daughter, I'm afraid I was a little too stiff just now. I didn't mean to be unkind.

ANN: (*rising and starting to hall door*) Oh, it doesn't matter.

REMINGTON: (*stopping her*) Yes, it does matter. I wouldn't hurt you for the world.

ANN: But you've *always* fought me, Father. You've *never* thought I had any right to work—never believed in my ability, now that I've proved I have some— Why can't you acknowledge it?

REMINGTON: Ann, this is a dangerous moment in your life. Tom's beaten—humiliated—knocked out. You did it—he can't stand it.

ANN: What have I done? Tom has a big nature. He's not little and petty enough to be hurt because I won.

REMINGTON: You're *blind.* He's had a blow tonight that no man on earth could stand.

ANN: Not Tom. I won't believe it.

REMINGTON: Yes, I say. I know what I'm talking about. Ann, be careful how you move now. Use your woman's tact, your love. Make Tom know that he is the greatest thing in the world to you— that you'd even give up all this work idea—if— he wanted—you to.

ANN: *What?* Tom wouldn't let me.

REMINGTON: Ask him. Ask him. See what he'd say.

ANN: Why, I wouldn't insult him. He'd think I thought he was—

(TOM *comes in from the hall*—ANN *checks herself and turns away quickly to fire*)

TOM: (*after a pause*) What's the matter?

REMINGTON: Nothing—nothing. Ann and I were just having a little argument as usual. I'll be back in a few minutes.

(*Looking at his watch he goes into hall*)

TOM: (*going slowly to* ANN) I hope you're not still fighting about the—your frieze?

ANN: They're all so funny, Tom—the way they act about it. It hurts. But so long as you're glad, it doesn't matter what anyone else thinks. Say you're glad, dear. I want you to be as happy as I would be if you had won.

TOM: You know I am, dear. You know that.

ANN: (*with a sigh of relief* ANN *sits at left of fire*) Think how I'll have to work. I can't even go to the country in the summer.

TOM: (*sitting opposite* ANN *at the fire*) And what will you do with Millicent this summer?

ANN: Oh, there are lots of nice things for her to do. The money! Think what it will mean to you!

TOM: Let me tell you one thing, Ann, in the beginning. I'll never touch a penny of the money.

ANN: What?

TOM: Not a cent of it.

ANN: What are you talking about?

TOM: That's your money. Put it away for yourself.

ANN: I never heard you say anything so absolutely unreasonable before in my life.

TOM: If you think I'm unreasonable, all right. But that's understood about the money. We won't discuss it.

ANN: Well, we *will* discuss it. Why shouldn't you use my money as well as I yours?

TOM: That's about as different as day and night.

ANN: Why is it?

TOM: Because I'm taking care of *you*. It's all right if you never do another day's work in your life. You're doing it because you want to, I'm doing it because I've got to. If you were alone it would be a different thing. But I'm here, and so long as I am I'll make what keeps us going.

ANN: But I'll help you.

TOM: No, you won't.

ANN: I *will*. I'm going on just as far as I have ability to go, and if you refuse to take any money I may make—if you refuse to use it for our mutual good, you're unjust and taking an unfair advan——Oh, Tom! what are we saying? We're out of our senses—both of us. You didn't mean what you said. Did you? It would——I simply couldn't bear it if you did. You didn't—did you?

TOM: I did—of course.

ANN: Tom—after all these years of pulling together, now that I've *done* something, why do you suddenly balk?

TOM: *(rising)* Good Heavens! Do you think I'm going to use your money? Don't try to run my end of it. It's the same old story—when you come down to it, a woman can't mix up in a man's business. *(He moves away)*

ANN: Mix up in it? Isn't it a good thing for you that I got this commission?

TOM: No. I don't know that it's a good thing from any standpoint to have it known that I failed, but my wife succeeded.

ANN: I thought you said you were glad—proud of me.

TOM: It's too—distracting—too—takes you away from more important things.

ANN: What things?

TOM: Millicent and me.

ANN: Oh, Tom——don't. You know that you and Millicent come before everything on earth to me.

TOM: No.

ANN: You do.

TOM: We don't—now. Your ambition comes first.

ANN: *(she rises, going to him)* Tom, I worship you. You know that, don't you?

TOM: I'm beginning to hate this work and everything in connection with it.

ANN: But you taught me—helped me—pushed me on. What's changed you?

TOM: I let you do it in the first place because I thought it was right. I wanted you to do the thing you wanted to do.

ANN: Well?

TOM: I was a fool. I didn't see what it would lead to. It's taking you away from everything else—and there'll be no end to it. Your ambition will carry you away till the home and Millicent and I are nothing to you!

ANN: Tom—look at me. Be honest. Are you sorry——*sorry* I got this commission?

TOM: I'm sorry it's the most important thing in the world to you.

ANN: Oh! Why do you say that to me? How can you?

TOM: Haven't I just seen it? You're getting rid of Millicent now because you don't want her to interfere with your work.

ANN: No!

TOM: You're pushing her out of your life.

ANN: No!

TOM: You said just now you were going to send her away alone in the summer. I don't like that. She's got to be with you—I want you to keep her with you.

ANN: But that's impossible. You know that. If I stop work now I might as well give up the frieze entirely.

TOM: Then give it up.

ANN: What?

TOM: Give up the whole thing—forever. Why shouldn't you?

ANN: Do you mean that?

TOM: Yes.

ANN: Tom—I love you. Don't ask this sacrifice of me to prove my love.

TOM: Could you make it? Could you?

ANN: Don't ask it! Don't ask it for your own sake. I want to keep on loving you. I want to believe you're what I thought you were. Don't make me think you're just like every other man.

TOM: I am a man—and you're my wife and Millicent's our daughter. Unless you come back to the things a woman's always had to do—and always will—we can't go on. We can't go on.

ANN: *(following him around the table)* Tom—if you're just a little hurt—just a little jealous because I won——

TOM: Oh——

ANN: That's natural—I can understand that.

TOM: Oh—don't——

ANN: But, oh, Tom, the other——to ask me to give it all up. I could never forgive that. Take it back, Tom—take it back.

TOM: Good God, Ann, can't you see? You're a woman and I'm a man. You're not free in the same way. If you won't stop because I ask it—I say you *must*.

ANN: You can't say that to me. You can't.

TOM: I do say it.

ANN: No!

TOM: I say it because I know it's *right*.

ANN: It isn't.

TOM: I can't make you see it.

ANN: It isn't.

TOM: I don't know how—but everything in me tells me it's right.

ANN: Tom—listen to me.

TOM: If you won't do it because I ask you—I demand it. I say you've *got* to.

ANN: Tom—you can kill our love by just what you do now.

TOM: Then this work *is* the biggest thing in the world to you?

ANN: What is more important to us both—to our happiness than just that?

MILLICENT: *(calling outside door L. C.)* Mother! *(A startled pause as* ANN *and* TOM *turn towards hall door)* Mother! I'm home, where are you? *(*MILLICENT *opens the hall door and rushes into the room)*

ANN: Millicent! What are you doing here?

MILLICENT: I came home, mother.

ANN: Why?

MILLICENT: Because I had to.

ANN: Are you ill, dear?

MILLICENT: No. No.

TOM: Is anything wrong at school?

MILLICENT: No, but I won't go back.

TOM: But why won't you? What's the trouble?

MILLICENT: I won't go back.

TOM: But you can't do a thing like this. I won't allow it.

MILLICENT: You wouldn't let me come home when I wanted to and now I can't go back. I won't——everything's different now. I won't go back and you can't make me.

(She turns and rushes out of the room and TOM *and* ANN *stare at each other as the curtain falls)*

ACT III

TIME: *Half an hour later.*

SCENE: *Same as Act II.* RUTH *is writing at the desk.* DAISY *opens the hall door and stops, listening back into the hall.*

RUTH: *(quickly)* What's the matter?

DAISY: Nothing. I was looking to see who went up the stairs. It's Dr Remington.

RUTH: How's Millicent now?

DAISY: Ann's with her—getting her to bed.

RUTH: Do you know yet why she came home?

DAISY: I don't know whether Ann's got it out of her yet or not.

RUTH: What do you think? Why on earth didn't she tell them at school?

DAISY: I haven't the dimmest—but she didn't do it without some good reason. I'll bet anything on that. Millicent's a pretty level-headed youngster.

RUTH: She's a pretty self-willed one. Ann will send her right back of course.

DAISY: I don't know whether she will or not. Millicent's got some rather decided ideas of her own on that.

RUTH: But she'll *have* to go. Why shouldn't she? Ann will make her.

DAISY: Tom will have something to say about it.

RUTH: It's for Ann to decide surely.

DAISY: Not at all. I don't see why. She is Tom's child, too, you know, and this is his house and he pays the bills at school and if he doesn't want her to go back you can bet she jolly well won't go. I only hope Millicent tells the whole business whatever it is. Ann is so excited over the frieze I don't know whether she'll have the patience to handle Millicent right or not. She's not easy.

RUTH: It's awful for Ann to be upset now—of all times—when she has to begin this gigantic work.

DAISY: Oh—I wish the damned frieze were in Guinea and that Ann had nothing to do but take care of Tom and Millicent—like any other woman. I'd give *anything* if she hadn't won the competition.

RUTH: Daisy!

DAISY: Oh, I would. I have a ghastly feeling that something horrible is going to come of it—if it hasn't already come.

RUTH: What do you mean?

DAISY: I tell you it is not possible for a man and woman to love each other and live together and be happy—unless the man is—*it*.

RUTH: Speaking of the dark ages! You ought to live in a harem. How any girl who makes her own bread and butter can be so old fashioned as you are—I can't see.

DAISY: You've got so used to your own ideas you forget that I am the average normal woman the world is full of.

RUTH: Nonsense! You're almost extinct. I'm the average normal woman the world is full of— and it's going to be fuller and fuller.

DAISY: I'll bet on plenty of us—left—*(Indicating herself)* on Judgment day.

RUTH: I want to laugh when I think how mistaken we've been calling you a bachelor girl. Why you'd make the best wife of anybody I know.

DAISY: I s'pose you mean that as an insult.

RUTH: But you *seem* so self reliant men are sort of afraid of you—

REMINGTON: *(coming in from hall and feeling a certain restraint in the two girls)* Am I in the wrong camp?

RUTH AND DAISY: No, no. Come in.

REMINGTON: I have to stay some place. I'm going to hang around till Millicent quiets down—and then I'll clear out.

DAISY: Is she ill?

REMINGTON: Oh, no. Just a little worked up and excited.

RUTH: Why do you think she came home, Dr Remington?

REMINGTON: I don't know what to think—unless she has *"boy"* in the head.

DAISY: Goodness no! Not yet!

REMINGTON: She's sixteen. You can't choke it off to save your life.

RUTH: Oh, she's a baby!

REMINGTON: Don't fool yourself. She won't wait as long as you two have to sit by her own fireside with children on her knee.

RUTH: Oh—

REMINGTON: That's the only thing in the game that's worth a cent—anyway. *(As* KEITH *comes in from the hall)* Isn't that so, Keith?

KEITH: What's that?

REMINGTON: I've just been telling these two that love and children are the greatest things on earth. Ruth doesn't agree with me—but Daisy—

RUTH: I must go.

DAISY: I must go up to Ann. *(*RUTH *goes out)*

REMINGTON: Let *me* go. They both seem terribly anxious to get out when you come in, Keith. Or maybe I'm in the way. I'll go.

DAISY: Don't be silly. I really must see if I can do anything for Ann.

REMINGTON: No, you mustn't. She's waiting for me to see Millicent. By the way, Keith—tomorrow's Sunday. I always take a run into the country in the motor on Sunday. Come along and bring either Ruth or Daisy. Take your choice. I know which one I'd take. *(He goes into the hall)*

DAISY: Isn't he a goose.

KEITH: Would it bore you to go, Daisy?

DAISY: Nonsense! Ruth will.

KEITH: It would be awfully good of you. Tomorrow's going to be a hard day for me to get through. Ruth told me tonight that she—I'm afraid it's all over.

DAISY: Why don't you compromise?

KEITH: There's nothing to compromise about. She's all wrong. Don't you think so?

DAISY: Oh, don't ask me. I don't know anything about it.

KEITH: Wait a minute. I—won't you go tomorrow, Daisy?

DAISY: Ask Ruth. It will be a good chance to make up.

KEITH: You're so *practical* and like such *different* things—maybe you'd think flying along through the country and lunching at some nice little out-of-the-way place was too frivolous—

DAISY: Oh yes, I don't like anything but being shut up in the house all day, pounding at my typewriter and splitting my head to get the bills straight. To actually go off with a man—for a whole day—and have a little fun—like any other woman—would be too unheard of. Of course, I couldn't do anything as silly as that.

KEITH: Oh—

DAISY: I wouldn't be amusing anyway. Dr Remington—well, he's sixty, and you'd be thinking of Ruth and I'd sit there like a stick—the sensible, practical woman who couldn't possibly be interesting and fascinating because no man would take the trouble to find out how devilish and alluring and altogether exciting I could be if I had the chance.

(She throws open the door and goes out. KEITH stares after her)

TOM: *(coming in from library after a moment)* I thought you'd gone, McKenzie.

KEITH: No, but I'm going.

REMINGTON: *(coming back from hall)* Good night, McKenzie. I'll dig you up in the morning, ten o'clock. Sharp, mind. And I'll call for Daisy first.

KEITH: *(at hall door)* All right. Much obliged, Doctor. *(Turning back)* How'd you know it was Daisy?

REMINGTON: I didn't—but I do now.

KEITH: Good night. *(He goes out)*

TOM: Well—how is she? How is Millicent?

REMINGTON: Oh, she's not ill—but the child's nervous as a witch—all strung up. She's worried about something—got something on her mind and naturally her head aches and she has a little fever—but that won't hurt her.

TOM: Got something on her mind? What?

REMINGTON: She didn't confide in me.

TOM: What *could* she have on her mind?

REMINGTON: I don't think she's committed murder—but she's *got* a mind, you know—There's no reason why she shouldn't have something *on* it.

TOM: Well, *I* don't know what to do with her.

REMINGTON: If you think she ought *not* to go back to school, say so. Tell Ann those are your orders.

TOM: I don't give orders to Ann.

REMINGTON: The devil you don't. She'd like it. A woman—a dog and a walnut tree—the more you beat 'em, the better they be.

TOM: The walnut tree business doesn't work with Ann. I made a fool of myself tonight by telling her I wouldn't touch the money she gets out of this thing. She doesn't understand. I've made her think I'm jealous because she won.

REMINGTON: Well, aren't you?

TOM: *No!* I tell you it's something else. Something sort of gave way under my feet when I opened her letter.

REMINGTON: I know. I know.

TOM: Doctor, for the Lord's sake, don't think I'm mean. I don't want to drag her back—but she seems gone somehow—she doesn't *need* me any more. *That's* what hurts.

REMINGTON: Of course, it hurts.

TOM: Much as I've loved to have her with me—working away at my elbow—wonderful as it all was—sometimes I've wished I hadn't seen her all day—that I had her to go home to—fresh and rested—waiting for *me* and that I was running the machine alone for her. She'll never understand. I've acted like a skunk.

REMINGTON: Y-e-s—I guess you have—so have I—unjust—pig-headed. No more right to say the things I've said to her than I have to spank her—except that she's—the most precious thing in the world to me—and I'd rather see her happy—as a woman—than *the greatest artist in the world.*

TOM: That's it. I want her here—*mine.* But I s'pose that's rotten and wrong.

REMINGTON: Yes—I s'pose it is. But you're despising yourself for something that's been in your bones—boy—since the beginning of time. Men and women will go through hell over this before it shakes down into shape. *You're* right and *she's* right and you're tearing each other like mad dogs over it because you love each other.

TOM: That's it. If another *man* had got it I'd take my licking without whining. What's the matter with me? Why can't I be that way to *her?*

REMINGTON: *(shaking his head with a wistful smile)* Male and female created He them. I don't take back any of the stuff I said to her before she went into this. She's fighting you now for her rights—but she laid her genius at your feet once and she'd do it again if—

ANN: *(coming in from the hall and speaking after a pause)* Well, father—what do you say about Millicent?

REMINGTON: My advice is that you let her stay at home for a while.

ANN: This is only a caprice—and it would be the worst thing in the world to give in to her. Unless you say as a physician—that she's too ill to—

REMINGTON: I don't say she's too ill—physically. You must decide for yourself. I'll go up and see her again and if she isn't asleep then I'll give her a mild sleeping powder. Ann, I put her in your arms first—and the look that came into your eyes then was as near divinity as we ever get. Oh, my daughter—don't let the new restlessness and strife of the world about you blind you to the old things—the real things. *(He goes out)*

ANN: *(after a pause)* You agree with me, don't you, that it's better for her to go back.

TOM: Do whatever you think best.

ANN: But what do *you* think?

TOM: It doesn't matter what I think, does it?

MILLICENT: *(opening the door)* Mother, aren't you coming back? (MILLICENT *wears a soft robe over her night gown. Her hair is down her back)*

ANN: Millicent—why did you get out of bed?

MILLICENT: I couldn't sleep. *(Running and jumping into the middle of the couch)*

ANN: Run back—quickly.

MILLICENT: In a minute. It's so quiet upstairs I couldn't sleep. I'm used to the girls.

ANN: You'll catch cold.

MILLICENT: Goodness, mother, I'm roasting.

ANN: *Millicent*—what *shall* I do with you?

MILLICENT: Is that what you and dad were talking about? What did Grandfather say? I don't care what he says. I'm not going back to school. You're on my side—aren't you, Dad?

TOM: Whatever your mother thinks is right, of course.

MILLICENT: Is it true—what Daisy told me—that you got the contract for a big frieze and not father? Is it? Is it, father? *(Looking from one to the other)*

TOM: Yes. It's quite true.

ANN: Millicent, go to bed.

MILLICENT: I think that's perfectly horrid, mother. Why should they give it to you? I think father ought to have it—he's the man. Don't you think people will think it's funny that you didn't get it? I should think it would make them lose confidence in you. *(A pause.* TOM *stalks out—closing the door)* Is father hurt because you got it? I should think he would be.

ANN: Millicent, I've had quite enough of this. Go up to bed at once.

MILLICENT: Will you come up and sleep with me?

ANN: Of course not. *(Walking about restlessly)*

MILLICENT: Why not?

ANN: Neither one of us would sleep a wink.

MILLICENT: That wouldn't matter. I don't want to be alone.

ANN: Come now—I won't speak to you again.

MILLICENT: What have you decided about school?

ANN: I'll tell you in the morning.

MILLICENT: I won't go up till you tell me.

ANN: Millicent—you will go at once, I say.

MILLICENT: Oh, Mother, don't be cross. Sit down and talk a minute.

ANN: It's late, dear. You must—

MILLICENT: That's nothing. We girls often talk till twelve.

ANN: Till twelve? Do the teachers know it?

MILLICENT: Oh, Mother, you're lovely! Don't you suppose they *know* that they don't know everything that's going on? Come and sit down, Mummie.

ANN: No! You must go to bed.

MILLICENT: But I won't go back to school.

ANN: *(going to* MILLICENT, *who is still on the couch)* You make it terribly hard for me, Millicent. You don't know what's good for you, of course. I don't expect you to—but I *do* expect you to be obedient.

MILLICENT: But, Mother, I tell you I—

ANN: Don't be so rebellious. Now come upstairs, please dear, and—

MILLICENT: But I won't go back to school, Mother, dear. I won't.

ANN: You say I treat you like a child. You *force* me to. If you don't want me to punish you—go upstairs at once and don't say another word.

MILLICENT: I won't go back.

ANN: Stop, I say!

MILLICENT: I know what I want to do. I'm sixteen.

ANN: *(their voices rising together)* You're my child. You will obey me.

MILLICENT: But I won't. You don't understand. I can't mother, I can't—I can't.

ANN: Why? Why can't you?

MILLICENT: Because I—I'm going to be married.

ANN: You silly child!

MILLICENT: It's the truth, Mother. I am.

ANN: Don't say a thing like that, even in fun.

MILLICENT: It's the truth, I tell you. I'm going to be married.

ANN: Some time you are, of course—you mean.

MILLICENT: No—now—soon. That's why I left. That's why I'm not going back.

ANN: *(after drawing a chair to the couch and sitting before* MILLICENT*)* What do you mean?

MILLICENT: I—he—we—we're engaged.

ANN: He—who?

MILLICENT: You—You don't know him.

ANN: Who?

MILLICENT: He's—he's perfectly wonderful.

ANN: *Who is he?*

MILLICENT: Now, Mother, wait. He—he isn't rich—

ANN: Well—

MILLICENT: He's poor—but he's perfectly wonderful—he works and he's so noble about it.

ANN: What does he do?

MILLICENT: He—he—Oh, mother, it's hard to explain, because he's so different.

ANN: *What does he do?*

MILLICENT: Well—just now he—he drives the motor at school—because you see he's so proud he—

ANN: Drives the motor—a chauffeur, you mean?

MILLICENT: People call him that, of course—but he isn't—*(*ANN *rises)* Mother—*(*ANN *goes to the door and locks it—going back to* MILLICENT, *who had risen)* Now, Mother, don't look like that.

ANN: Sit down.

MILLICENT: *Don't* look like that. Let me tell you about it.

ANN: *(sitting again)* Yes, tell me about it.

MILLICENT: Oh, I—hardly know how to begin.

ANN: He drives the motor—the school motor, you say?

MILLICENT: Yes—to the trains, you know—and into town and to church.

ANN: Who is his father?

MILLICENT: Why—I—I don't know who he is. I've never met his father.

ANN: What is his name?

MILLICENT: His father's name? I don't know.

ANN: The *boy's* name.

MILLICENT: Willie Kern.

ANN: How does he happen to drive a motor?

MILLICENT: Well, I don't know just *how* it happened—he's so clever you know, and of course he isn't really a chauffeur at all.

ANN: What is he then?

MILLICENT: Oh, Mother! He just happens to run the school motor.

ANN: And what did he do before that?

MILLICENT: Why he—he ran *another* motor. Oh, now, Mother, you don't understand at all. *(She breaks into sobs and throws herself full length on the couch.* ANN *sits rigidly)* Just because he's poor and clever and drives a motor is no reason why you should act this way. *(Sitting up)* He's going to do something else. He's going to come to New York to get a different position. And we'll be married as soon as he gets it, and that's why I came home—to tell you. So there—you see I can't go back to school. *(She rises and starts to the door)*

ANN: Millicent! Come here.

MILLICENT: That's all there is to tell. I'm going to bed now.

ANN: *(rising)* You know this is the most wild and impossible thing in the world.

MILLICENT: I don't. It *isn't* impossible. I'm going to marry him. I love him better than you or father or anybody in the world and I'm going to marry him.

ANN: Stop! Do you want to disgrace us? How any child of mine could speak—even speak to such a— Oh, the disappointment! Where's your pride? How *could* you? How could you? Millicent, if you'll promise me to give this up I won't say a word to your father.

MILLICENT: No—no—I'm going.

ANN: Don't unlock that door.

MILLICENT: I want to go now.

ANN: You'll never see this boy again. Never speak to him—never write to him—never hear of him. I shall send you away where he'll never know—

MILLICENT: *(coming back to couch)* You won't! He loves me and I love him. He understands me. All that vacation when you wouldn't let me come home and all the other girls had gone he was just as good to me as he could be. He knew how lonely I was and he—we got engaged that vacation. You wouldn't let me come home.

ANN: Millicent—you don't know what you're saying. You don't know what you're doing.

MILLICENT: Oh, yes, I do, Mother. It's you that don't know. You don't understand.

ANN: *(kneeling before* MILLICENT*)* My darling—why—didn't you tell me this when you said you wanted to come home? Why didn't you tell me then? *(Sobbing,* ANN *buries her face in* MILLICENT'S *lap)*

MILLICENT: I would have told you—if you'd let me come home—but you wouldn't—and I was so lonely there without the girls and—we—we got engaged. You don't understand, Mother.

ANN: *(lifting her face to* MILLICENT*)* Oh, yes, I do, dear. Yes, I do. Tell me—all about it. When did you first know him? How did you—happen to speak to him—I mean to—to love him.

MILLICENT: Oh, Mother, why I—he—I just did—he's so handsome and so nice. You haven't any idea how nice he is, Mother.

ANN: Haven't I, dear? What is he like? Tell me *everything*—how did it begin?

MILLICENT: He—the first time I really knew he was so different you know—

ANN: Yes, dear.

MILLICENT: Was one Sunday morning I was ready for church before anybody else and I went out to get in the motor and ran down the steps and fell, and he jumped out and picked me up and put me in the motor, and of course I thanked him and we had to wait quite a while for the others, and I found out how different and really wonderful he was. All the girls were crazy about him. Here's his picture. *(Drawing out a locket which is on a chain around her neck)* It's just a little snapshot which I took myself one morning—and you can't really tell from this how awfully good looking he is. *(*ANN *seizes the locket and looks closely at the picture)* His eyes are the most wonderful—and his lashes are the longest I ever saw. You can't see his teeth and they are—well, you'd just love his teeth, Mother.

ANN: Would I, dear? Have you seen very much of him? Have you see him any place besides in the motor, I mean? *(*MILLICENT *hesitates)* Tell me, dear—everything. I shall understand.

MILLICENT: Well, of course, Mother—I *had* to see him some place else after school began again and the girls were all back and I wasn't going for the mail any more.

ANN: Of course; and where *did* you see him?

MILLICENT: Why, you see, it—it was awfully hard, Mummie, because I couldn't tell anybody. Nobody would have *understood*—except Fanny. She's such a dear. She's been so sympathetic through the whole thing, and she has helped me a lot. There is a fire escape out of our room and Mondays and Thursdays at nine o'clock at night—

ANN: Oh—

MILLICENT: What, Mother?

ANN: Nothing—go on, dear.

MILLICENT: At exactly nine I'd put on Fanny's long black coat and go down, and he was always there and we always went down in the arbor just a little while.

ANN: The arbor? Where was the arbor?

MILLICENT: Down the path of the other side of the drive—not far from the house; but of course nobody went near it at that time of night—in cold weather and—and we'd talk a while and then I'd run back. You don't mind, do you, Mother. What else could I do?

ANN: And—he's kissed you—of course?

MILLICENT: Of course.

ANN: And you've kissed him?

MILLICENT: *(lowering her eyes)* Why yes—Mother—we're engaged.

ANN: And what did he say to you there in the arbor?

MILLICENT: I can't tell you *everything* he said, Mother.

ANN: Why not, Millicent? I'm your mother. No one on earth is so close to you—or loves you so much—or cares so much for your happiness—and understands so well. I remember when I was engaged to your father—I wasn't much older than you—I know, dear. Tell me what he said.

MILLICENT: He thinks I'm pretty, Mother.

ANN: Yes, dear.

MILLICENT: And he thinks I'm wonderful to understand him and to know what he really is in spite of what he happens to be doing.

ANN: Yes—and how long did you usually stay there in the arbor?

MILLICENT: Oh, not very long, only last time it was longer. He teased so and I couldn't help it. He—he—I—

ANN: How long was it that time?

MILLICENT: Oh—it—it was almost two hours last time.

ANN: And what did you do all that time? Wasn't it cold?

MILLICENT: He made me put on his overcoat—He *just made* me.

ANN: *(holding* MILLICENT *close in her arms)* And he held you close—and kissed you—and told you how much he loved you?

MILLICENT: Yes, I love him so—Mother—but—I—tonight, was the last night to go again—but I—

ANN: *(holding* MILLICENT *off as she searches her face)* Yes, dear?

MILLICENT: I—I was—afraid to go.

ANN: *(shrieking)* Why?

MILLICENT: Oh, Mother—Was it wicked to be afraid? I ran away—I wanted to be with you. *(*ANN *snatches* MILLICENT *in her arms. Her head falls against* MILLICENT *and* MILLICENT'S *arms hold her close as she sobs. Someone tries the door and knocks)*

TOM: *(in the hall)* Ann!—Ann!

ANN: Yes?

TOM: Why is the door locked?

ANN: Millicent and I are talking. Wait just a few minutes. And Tom—tell her grandfather not to wait to see Millicent again tonight. She's all right.

TOM: Sure?

ANN: I'm sure.

MILLICENT: *(in a whisper—after listening a moment)* What are you going to tell father?

ANN: *(sitting on the floor)* Well—you see, dear—you're too young to be married now—much too young—and—

MILLICENT: Oh, now, Mother, if you're going to talk *that* way. Wait till you see him.

ANN: That's just what I want to do. I've got such a lovely plan for us—for the summer.

MILLICENT: But I want to be married as soon as he gets his—

ANN: I know, his position—and while he's looking and getting settled you and I will go abroad.

MILLICENT: You're awfully good, Mother, but if you really want to do something for me—I'd rather you'd give me that money to be married.

ANN: But Millicent, my dear child—I *have* to go. I'm so tired. I've been working awfully hard this winter. You're the only one in the world who could really be with me and take care of me. I *need* you.

MILLICENT: Poor Mother! I don't want to be *selfish* and if you *need* me—I'll go.

ANN: *(catching MILLICENT in her arms)* Thank you, dear.

MILLICENT: *If* you'll promise me that I can be married when I get back.

ANN: *(getting to her feet)* If—you—*still*—want to—marry him when you come—back with me—you may. I promise.

MILLICENT: Mother! I didn't know you loved me so much.

ANN: Didn't you, dear? Now go to bed. *(They start to the door together. ANN catches MILLICENT again, kissing her tenderly as though she were something new and precious)*

MILLICENT: What's the matter, Mother?

ANN: Nothing, dear— Good night.

MILLICENT: Good night.

TOM: *(coming into doorway as MILLICENT unlocks and opens the door)* Not in bed yet?

MILLICENT: *(throwing her arms about her father's neck)* Oh, Dad. I'm so happy. *(She goes out)*

ANN: *(sitting at the fire)* Come, in, Tom. I want to talk to you about Millicent.

TOM: *(closing the door and going to ANN)* What's the matter?

ANN: She thinks she's in love.

TOM: What?

ANN: Our baby. She wants to be married.

TOM: What do you mean?

ANN: That's why she came home.

TOM: Good Heavens, Ann! Married? What has she got mixed up in? How did such a thing happen? How *could* it?

ANN: Because I didn't let her come home when she wanted to. Don't say anything, Tom. I can't bear it now.

TOM: *(putting a hand on her head tenderly)* Don't dear! Don't! It—might have—happened—anyway.

ANN: Oh, the things that *can* happen!

TOM: Has she told you everything?

ANN: Everything.

TOM: What have you said to her? What are you going to do?

ANN: I'm going to take her away—and win her—till she gives up of her own free will—I shall have to have the wisdom of all the ages. I shall have to be more fascinating than the boy. That's a pretty big undertaking, Tom. I wonder if I'll be equal to it.

TOM: You mean you're going to give up your frieze and go away with her? *(ANN nods her head)* You can't do it, Ann.

ANN: *(rising and moving away)* Oh, yes, I can.

TOM: You cannot. Don't lose your head. You're pledged to finish it and deliver it at a certain time. You can't play fast and loose with a big piece of work like that.

ANN: *You'll* have to make my frieze, Tom.

TOM: I will not! I utterly and absolutely refuse to. You make Millicent behave and break this thing up and you go on with your—

ANN: I can't. I can't. She's been in danger—absolute danger.

TOM: How?

ANN: Oh, I'll tell you. I'll tell you. She ran away to me—to me—and I was pushing her off. My little girl! She's got to be held tight in my arms and carried through.

TOM: Ann, I'm not going to allow this to wipe out what you've done. I'll settle her—

ANN: Tom, you can't speak of it to her—not breathe it—

TOM: Of course I will.

ANN: No you won't. If we cross her she'll get at him some way—somehow.

TOM: I'm not going to let you sacrifice yourself for a wayward—

ANN: It's my job. She is what I've given to life. If I fail her now—my whole life's a failure. Will you make my frieze, dear, will you?

TOM: No. It's *yours*. You've got to have the glory of it. Ann, I haven't been fair—but you're going to have this and all that's coming to you. I'm not going to let anything take it away from you. It's too important. My God, you've not only beaten me—you've won over the biggest men in the field—with your own brain and your own hands—in a fair, fine, hard fight. You're cut up now—but if you should give this thing up—there'll be times when you'd eat your heart out to be at work on it—when the artist in you will *yell* to be let out.

ANN: I know. I know. And I'll hate you because you're doing it—and I'll hate myself because I gave it up—and I'll almost—hate—her. I know. I know. You needn't tell me. Why I've seen my men and women up there—their strong limbs stretched—their hair blown back. I've seen the crowd looking up—I've heard people say—"A woman did that" and my heart has almost burst with pride—not so much that *I* had done it—but for *all* women. And then the door opened—and Millicent came in. There isn't any choice, Tom—she's part of my body—part of my soul. Will you make my frieze, dear, will you? (*Falling against him*)

TOM: (*taking her in his arms*) My darling! I'll do whatever makes it easiest for you. Don't think I don't know *all—all*—it means to you. My God, it's hard.

ANN: (*releasing herself and going to the hall door*) Put out the light. I hope she's asleep. (*They go out into the lighted hall. After a moment*

THE CURTAIN FALLS

MODERN

Susan Glaspell, *Trifles* (1916)

Sophie Treadwell, *Machinal* (1928)

Philip Barry, *Holiday* (1928)

Lillian Hellman, *The Children's Hour* (1934)

Clifford Odets, *Waiting for Lefty* (1935)

Langston Hughes, *Mulatto* (1935)

Eugene O'Neill, *The Iceman Cometh* (1946)

Arthur Miller, *All My Sons* (1947)

Tennessee Williams, *Cat on a Hot Tin Roof* (1955)

©1993 Martha Swope

THE CHILDREN'S HOUR

MACHINAL

VanDamm Collection/The New York Public Library for the

©1993 Martha Swope

THE ICEMAN COMETH

CAT ON A HOT TIN ROOF

©1993 Martha Swope

THE MODERN AMERICAN STAGE

From 1900 to World War I, [Broadway] was provincial and parochial; it bore no serious relation to art or life. Between the two world wars, it was bursting with energy and enterprise; the new dramatists . . . and the people of the theatre were full of hope and fresh ideas.

LTHOUGH SOME MIGHT OBJECT TO BROOKS ATKINSON'S DIAGNOSIS OF Broadway's artistic malaise before World War I—and while Broadway should not to be equated with the larger American theatre—few would question his enthusiasm for the progress of American drama around the time of World War I. For while America was drawing closer to involvement in the war in Europe, an explosion of theatrical activity was occurring at home. As Broadway theatres began to be invigorated by a new generation of dramatists, actors, and artisans, important new theatres were being founded across the country, a phenomenon repeated later in the 1950s, and again in the 1960s, when the **Off-Broadway** and **Off-Off Broadway** movements were paralleled by the establishment of important regional theatres. The careers of such European *grandes dames* of an earlier theatrical moment as Sarah Bernhardt and the much-acclaimed Italian actress Eleonora Duse, performers who brought respectability with them on their visits to America, were near their respective conclusions by the end of World War I. At the same time, numerous intellectual and artistic discourses were emerging to influence the trajectory American drama would take: socialism and the Bolshevik Revolution of 1917; Freudian psychoanalysis, disseminated by such journals as *The Psychoanalytic Review,* first published by the American Psychological Association in 1914; German expressionism, as conveyed by imported dramas and films; the New Stagecraft employed by European companies that toured the United States during the second and third decades of this century; the theory of acting developed by Konstantin Stanislavski at the Moscow Art Theatre, which appeared in New York in 1923; and others. This is not to say that as American doughboys returned from Europe such residual genres as **melodrama** and the **musical comedies** Atkinson deprecates as "parochial" could not find appreciative audiences. But around the time of World War I, new dramatic forms were emerging and important "revolts" were taking place in the American theatre—and in international modern drama as well.

This section of *American Drama: Colonial to Contemporary* attempts to recapture some of this revolutionary energy and, through the nine selections of drama from this period, to delineate the various intellectual and artistic shapes this revolt assumed. What follows is a brief account of these advances in stage design, actor training, and, most important, the writing of American drama.

AMERICA REVOLTS:
THE TWENTIES AND THIRTIES

I can't live without the theatre, but I can't live with it. The theatre gives itself lofty graces, claims a noble lineage, but has no more dimension than a bordello.

Like Atkinson's depiction of early twentieth-century Broadway, Harold Clurman's derogation of the New York theatre in the early 1920s as a "bordello" portrays an institution corrupted by commercialism and in need of artistic revitalization. Viewing the 1920s as a decade distinguished mainly by the incessant party-throwing in theatrical and intellectual circles, Clurman epitomizes a youthful critique of commercial theatres and conventional drama that would endeavor to transform Broadway from a provincial outpost dominated by European stars and imported plays into an authentic American theatre. This revisionist project took numerous forms, involving a rich *mélange* of homegrown talent and European influences and occurring at a number of sites in and outside New York. Clurman himself would play a central part in this project in the 1930s as a cofounder of **The Group Theatre** and later with his direction of some of America's most important plays.

As World War I was beginning, a Little Theatre Movement was part of a heretofore unprecedented expansion of American theatre. Assessing this growth, Maurice Browne, British impresario and founder of the Chicago Little Theatre, asserts that at "the end of 1912 there were two Little Theatres in the country; five years later there were said to be more than thirty within a radius of fifty miles from Times Square, more than three hundred beyond it; by 1920 there were thousands." Among these new venues were The Players in Providence, Rhode Island (founded in 1909); the Wisconsin Dramatic Society in Madison and Milwaukee (1911), and Mrs. Lyman Gale's Boston Toy Theatre (1912). Browne's Chicago Little Theatre was one of the more important of these for several reasons. First, as the term "little" implies, it was dedicated to staging plays that would not draw a popular audience, but rather attract a smaller, more sophisticated following. As Charles Lock observes, the Chicago Little Theatre was supported by such playgoers as social activist Emma Goldman, novelist Theodore Dreiser, labor leader and prominent socialist Eugene Debs, and others to see, "often for the first time in America," dramas by Henrik Ibsen, August Strindberg, Bernard Shaw, Maurice Maeterlinck, and William Butler Yeats. Herein resides one definition of the culture of modernism: its implicit "plea for the marginal, the suppressed" that too easily became transposed into the register of a cultural "elite." Second, and more important for our purposes, Browne's Chicago theatre influenced George Cram "Jig" Cook and Floyd Dell, who helped found the Provincetown Players in 1915. The process of influence was also reciprocal, as Cook and Dell encouraged Browne to produce more contemporary, previously unperformed, plays and in particular more works by American writers. Among the results of this collision of energetic young Americans with European drama and innovative theatrical techniques—both in the Chicago Little Theatre's experimentation with mime, puppetry, and dance, and in theatres across the country, including New York—were new conceptions of stage design, lighting, and acting, and some of the most enduring drama this country has ever produced, several examples of which are included in this anthology.

The movement in American theatre toward a modern drama was facilitated not only by such theatres as Browne's in Chicago, but also by a number of tours by prominent European companies before and shortly after World War I. In 1911, for example, performances by the Irish Players from Dublin's Abbey Theatre of J. M. Synge's *The Playboy of the Western World* not only sparked rioting ("ructions," as the Irish call it) in cities like New York and Boston with large Irish-American populations, but also motivated a number of Americans to write peasant plays similar to those Synge and Lady Gregory wrote for the Abbey. Black dramatists in particular like Randolph Edmonds and Gloria Douglas Johnson followed Alain Locke's suggestion in *The New Negro* (1925) and James Weldon Johnson's similar observation that Harlem should play a role in America analogous to that which Dublin played in Ireland; this role included the creation of a "native and poetic" drama from the "living language of the people" that would banish invidious stereotypes of African Americans from the stage. What cultural historians term the **Harlem Renaissance** of the 1920s was thus inflected, in part, by the Irish peasant play as black artists created "folk plays" inspired by the example of the Abbey Theatre.

Other European companies touring America early in this century contributed much to an ongoing revision of predominant notions of scenic decoration, acting, and dramatic writing. In 1915, for instance, the New Stage Society of New York asked British actor-playwright Harley Granville-Barker to present a series of plays at Wallack's Theatre; following Barker's stint, both French and German companies appeared in New York and presented variations of what became known as the **New Stagecraft**. Associated with British artist Edward Gordon Craig, the New Stagecraft marked a reaction against the representational sets used in both melodrama and **realistic** drama. Craig's designs made little concession to either historical accuracy (the reigning concept of scenic decoration at the time being the so-called "archaeological approach") or realistic portrayal; rather, they privileged the interplay of three or four dominant colors, relying on lighting effects that highlighted or altered these colors, movement, and geometric shapes instead of on heavy furnishings. Yeats, who lectured on the modern theatre using a model Craig constructed for him, declared "naturalistic scene painting" ably refuted by the "more delicate art" of Craig's "decorative scene-painting," one as "inseparable from the movements as from the robes of the players and from the falling of the light." Craig's stagecraft was clearly more compatible with Yeats's poetic drama than with the acting theories of Stanislavsky, with whom Craig collaborated, albeit with difficulty, at the Moscow Art Theatre on a production of *Hamlet* in 1912. Because Craig also worked with Max Reinhardt in Germany and with various companies and artists in France, England, and Italy, when Granville-Barker, Reinhardt, and the Moscow Art Theatre appeared in New York, American audiences and theatrical artisans alike were exposed to Craig's highly influential principles of scenic decoration. Robert Edmond Jones also observed Reinhardt's Deutsches Theater for a year, and Lee Simonson, designer and founding member of the **Theatre Guild**, studied in Paris for three years. The result? A greatly expanded repertory of decorative and lighting practices, and a modern American drama molded from a myriad of intellectual, historical, and theatrical materials.

And where was this drama performed? For British drama critic and translator William Archer, *not* on Broadway: "In the region of Washington Square or Greenwich Village, or . . . among the sand dunes of Cape Cod—we must look for the real birthplace

of the American drama." What is more, in what in retrospect seems a remarkable historical coincidence, at about the same time in 1915 groundbreaking theatrical experimentation and innovative dramatic writing were taking place at all three of the locations
Archer mentions. These revisions of a dramatic orthodoxy would blossom into major
achievements in the 1920s when the Neighborhood Playhouse, the Theatre Guild, and
the Provincetown Players began to produce new American plays staged in fresh and exciting ways.

The **Provincetown Players** exemplify both the theatrical and intellectual radicalism well under way in America during the second decade of this century. Founded in
Provincetown, Massachusetts, as a playwright's theatre in the summer of 1915, a group of
young intellectuals and theatrical amateurs congregated at the home of journalist John
Reed, later the author of *Ten Days That Shook the World* on the Russian revolution. Members of the Provincetown Players at this time, included, as mentioned above, "Jig" Cook
and his wife Susan Glaspell, and designer Robert Edmond Jones. Reed, who died in Russia and is buried in the Kremlin, maintained an active interest in international socialism,
as did his wife Louise Bryant and later member Max Eastman, an editor of, and contributor to, the socialist publication *Masses*. And several of the group's earliest productions,
Cook and Glaspell's *Suppressed Desires* for instance, staged in Provincetown at the Wharf
Theatre during the summer of 1915, reveal the extent to which Freudian psychoanalysis
informed (perhaps too heavily) intellectual debate at the time. It would remain equally
prominent in much of the mature work of the Provincetown Players' most important writer,
Eugene O'Neill.

Moving to New York in 1916 to a brownstone in Greenwich Village, the Provincetown
Players established themselves with productions of plays by Cook, Glaspell, and O'Neill,
and later produced the early work of writers destined for fame in other media: Edna St.
Vincent Millay, for example, who also acted with the Players and won a Pulitzer Prize for
her poetry in 1923; and Djuna Barnes, an active voice in the suffrage movement and an
important novelist in her own right. Among other plays in the repertory during the company's early years were Glaspell's *Trifles* (reprinted here), Cook's *The Athenian Women*,
and several of O'Neill's one-act plays of the sea. But it was the production of his expressionistic play *The Emperor Jones* in January 1920 that secured the company's—and
O'Neill's—reputations. Critics like Heywood Broun of the *New York Tribune* proclaimed
him "the most promising playwright in America," and a month later the Provincetown
Players staged O'Neill's Pulitzer Prize–winning drama, *Beyond the Horizon*.

After winning a second Pulitzer in 1922 for *Anna Christie* and travelling in Europe
with Glaspell and Cook, O'Neill, with Jones and critic Kenneth Macgowan, left the
Provincetown Players to form The Experimental Theatre, Incorporated. During the winters of 1923–1924 and 1924–1925, they staged 16 plays, among them two of O'Neill's
destined for both controversy and critical acclaim: *All God's Chillun Got Wings*, with Paul
Robeson, and *Desire under the Elms*, designed by Jones and starring Walter Huston. The
former work, which concerns an interracial marriage, led to O'Neill's receipt of numerous
death threats; the successful run of the latter, which centers around a son's desire for his
older stepmother and her desire for him, was halted by the district attorney amid charges
of immorality. The frank representation of sexuality in the theatre sparked similar controversy earlier in the century—actress Olga Nethersole's highly publicized trial in 1900

over her lascivious "osculations" in Clyde Fitch's *Sapho,* as we mentioned earlier—but in the 1920s not everyone was ready for playwrights like O'Neill. Blacks playing major roles was still a new idea for the American stage, and as long as they embodied a racial **Other** in plays like *The Emperor Jones*—which presents a superstitious, fatuous stereotype of an African American against whom white audiences could define themselves and find ample rationalization for their cultural hegemony—popular acceptance seemed to follow. Representations of miscegenation or Oedipal desire, however, were another matter. Nevertheless, O'Neill continued over the next quarter-century to write what are arguably two of the greatest plays of the American stage, *Long Day's Journey Into Night,* first produced in 1956 after his death, and *The Iceman Cometh* (1946), which is reprinted here. The Provincetown Players disbanded in 1929.

O'Neill's plays were produced by other theatres as well, one of which was the Theatre Guild, founded in 1915 as the Washington Square Players and organized around the single principle that, as its directors later described it when introducing a volume of plays it produced, "the theatre itself is bigger than any of the workers in it . . . and should be employed for the creation of the finest drama of the time." As the Washington Square Players, the Guild presented some 68 plays before changing its name in 1918, assuming control of the Garrick Theatre in the spring of 1919, and establishing itself with a production of Irish playwright St. John Ervine's *John Ferguson.* Throughout the 1920s and 1930s it not only mounted plays by such European dramatists as Bernard Shaw and Ferenc Molnar, but also staged a number of enormously influential works by a new generation of American playwrights: Elmer Rice's expressionistic *The Adding Machine* (1923), with its sharp criticism of American capitalism culminating in the protagonist's crawling upon a giant business machine; Sidney Howard's Freudian drama *The Silver Cord* (1926), which probed a complicated mother-son relationship; and O'Neill's epic-length "psychological novel" *Strange Interlude* (1928), composed of nine acts and over five hours of performance. Later, in the 1940s, some of America's most popular musicals—Richard Rodgers and Oscar Hammerstein II's *Oklahoma!* (1943) and *Carousel* (1945), for instance—were produced by the Theatre Guild.

In addition to the Theatre Guild's production of *Strange Interlude,* the decade of the 1920s—one central to the evolution of the drama in America—brought with it other advances and, at the end of the decade, setbacks for American theatre. For Langston Hughes, the stock market crash of 1929 signaled the decline of what is now known as the Harlem Renaissance. Throughout the 1920s African-American writers like Hughes, Nella Larsen, Claude McKay, and Zora Neale Hurston produced important novels, poems, plays, and political commentary that interrogated the very possibility of a black art in America. A return to black folklore and music, as in the folk plays mentioned above, and to jazz and the blues, formed a complement to novels like Larsen's *Quicksand* (1928) and *Passing* (1929), which for the most part represented the lives of African Americans in cities like New York and Chicago. Throughout the 1920s, of course, stereotypical black protagonists and supporting players (often in roles as domestic servants or chauffeurs) appeared on Broadway, but the decade also brought with it distinguished efforts by many African-American writers and intellectuals to identify and then rebut the insidious cultural work such stock characterizations accomplished. These included the founding in 1921 of *Crisis,* published by the NAACP and edited by W. E. B. DuBois, and the publication of *Fire,* edited by Wallace Thurman, to which, among others, Hughes and Hurston contributed.

The decade of the 1920s, one in which, according to Macgowan, the American drama "came of age," ended with the 1929 production of *Street Scene* at the Playhouse, which eventually earned Rice a Pulitzer Prize, and the lively interchanges on theatrical matters between Harold Clurman, a script reader for the Theatre Guild, and Lee Strasberg, an actor-director there, who envisioned a different kind of repertory company and were preparing to make their own mark on the American theatre. Sophie Treadwell's *Machinal* (1928) and Rice's *Street Scene* together paint a bleak picture of the pressures and dehumanizing effects of life in a modern city, a picture in the latter case greatly enhanced by the stage designs of Jo Mielziner who, perhaps even more so than Jones or Lee Simonson, was the most celebrated theatre artist in America from the mid-1920s until his death in 1976. Robert Littell, in *Theatre Arts Monthly*, called Mielziner's work for *Street Scene* a "breath-taking piece of American scene design" complete with sophisticated and highly realistic sound effects—"the gigantic ebbing and flowing buzz" of a great city, the "roaring loneliness" of New York—created by a combination of phonographs and amplifiers. Plays like Rice's, Littell opined, recalled the artistry of the Moscow Art Theatre during its tour of America in the 1920s and compared favorably with it.

But great plays required skilled actors, and for Clurman and Strasberg the Theatre Guild operated too much like a business, hiring players as parts became available with the effect, as Clurman lamented, that the actor's self-development as "a growing craftsman was neglected." Clurman and Strasberg, joined by Theatre Guild manager Cheryl Crawford and such experienced actors as Sanford Meisner, Morris Carnovsky, and Franchot Tone, met in late 1930 to contemplate the founding of a company dedicated, as Clurman observed, to bringing the actor "much closer to the content of the play, to link the actor as an individual with the creative purpose of the playwright." The disappointment all of these young iconoclasts felt with the Theatre Guild, coupled with the influence of the Moscow Art Theatre's visit and the work of such Russian acting teachers as Richard Boleslavski and Maria Ouspenskaya at the American Laboratory Theatre (1923–1933), led to Clurman, Crawford, and Strasberg's founding of the **Group Theatre** in 1931. In the ten years the Group was together, designer Mordecai Gorelik and director Elia Kazan refined their talents; Strasberg, Meisner, Robert Lewis, and Stella Adler developed their theories of acting and practice of training actors; and all four went on, in their different ways, to define the so-called Method System and teach many of America's greatest actors: Marlon Brando, Paul Newman, Joanne Woodward, and many more.

In the summer of 1931, 28 actors followed Crawford, Clurman, and Strasberg to Brookfield Center, Connecticut, eventually to rehearse the Group's first play, Paul Green's *The House of Connelly*, and to receive training from Strasberg in, among other skills, relaxation techniques and the development of **affective (or emotional) memory**. Later, as head of the **Actors Studio**, Strasberg described affective memory as that recollection of "emotional experiences" from the actor's past that can be rendered "serviceable" and "fused" with the character and event being portrayed. Bolstered by such attentiveness to the actor's art and by Maxwell Anderson's commentary on rehearsals, Green's play opened in New York at the Martin Beck Theatre on September 23, 1931, to enthusiastic reviews. The Group had its share of failures in the next few seasons—1932 was a particularly discouraging year—but realized critical acclaim again in 1933 with Sidney Kingsley's hospital drama, *Men in White*. The pinnacle of the Group's ten-year history was reached on January 14, 1935, when it produced *Waiting for Lefty* (reprinted here), a play written by one of its members, Clifford

Odets, based on a strike among taxi drivers the previous year. At a celebration of the Group Theatre held in 1987, actress Shelley Winters, an audience member for an early production of *Lefty*, recalled the play's closing tableau with cast and audience rising as one to yell "Strike!" Odets's **agitprop** play struck a responsive chord in a Depression-weary audience grown increasingly sensitive to the exploitation of workers and the plight of the nation's poor. And many members of the Group, particularly those who had joined the Communist Party of America or felt ideological affinity with it, believed that Odets's play represented precisely what they had been working toward: an ensemble acting company and a theatre of socio-political commitment. Clurman describes the play and the extraordinary opening night: "'Strike!' was *Lefty*'s lyric message . . . strike for greater dignity, strike for a bolder humanity, strike for the full stature of man." Odets's "delirious" audience "stormed" the stage "dazed and happy: a new awareness and confidence had entered their lives." At the same time, such productions offered a counter to the witty, generally successful comedies of S. N. Behrman, Philip Barry, and others—Behrman's *The Second Man* and *End of Summer* (1936), Barry's *Paris Bound* (1927), *Holiday* (1928), and *The Philadelphia Story* (1939), for instance—which presented audiences in the later 1920s, 1930s, and 1940s with the predicaments of an affluent class that spent more money hosting parties than Odets's cabbies made in an entire year.

Waiting for Lefty is just one example of memorable American drama originating both in Depression-era hardship and in what for many became an increasingly attractive socialist critique of the causes of such conditions. As American and international economies declined, the American theatre, in numerous respects, reflected this broader economic crisis and, somewhat paradoxically, flourished in spite of it. Broadway was sent reeling by the nearly 40 percent drop in total national income between 1929 and 1932. The same conditions that sparked demonstrations by unemployed workers in 38 cities in 1930 and, by 1931, necessitated the feeding of 82,000 indigents daily by 82 breadlines in New York alone, wreaked havoc with the professional theatre. In the first two years of the decade, 26 of 78 Broadway theatres closed, with the remainder in operation only some 20 weeks a year on average. According to Mordecai Gorelik, who not only designed for the Group Theatre but also cofounded the Theatre Collective, one of numerous leftist theatre groups that organized in the 1930s, by 1934 more than 80 percent of all stage workers in New York were unemployed. Among other results, these desperate conditions led to the founding of The League of Workers Theatres in 1932, and a broadly felt commitment to produce plays that foregrounded economic problems and addressed them to a working-class audience. The League included the Workers Laboratory Theatre, the Negro People's Theatre, the Theatre of Action, and Solidarity Players in Boston, the Blue Blouses of Chicago, and Rebel Players of Los Angeles. And, as these troupes formed, the American drama evolved in a direction scarcely imaginable just a few years earlier.

Ideologically compatible with agitprop dramas like *Waiting for Lefty* and Langston Hughes' *Don't You Want to Be Free?* (1938), which ends with black and white workers uniting to struggle together for improved conditions, were **Living Newspapers** like *Triple-A Plowed Under* (1936) and *Power* (1937), produced by the **Federal Theatre Project** under Hallie Flanagan's directorship from 1935 to 1939. These documentary dramas treated contemporary economic and social problems in what Flanagan terms a "rapid, cinematic form" that did not require star-actors, and brought together unemployed newspaper reporters and theatre workers not only in New York, but in Chicago, Cleveland, and Norwalk, Connecticut, as well. Romanian emigré John Houseman directed the Negro Theatre Project in New York for the W.P.A. (Works Progress Administration), devoting himself to "the performance of classical works . . . without concession or reference to color." One such production was the "voodoo" *Macbeth* in 1936, set in Haiti and redacted as a kind of suspense thriller, staged by Houseman and the young actor-director Orson Welles, with whom Houseman would cofound the Mercury Theatre in 1937 (and which in 1941 Welles would employ for his film masterpiece, *Citizen Kane*). In the early 1930s, Eva Le Gallienne continued her successful management of the Civic Repertory Theatre (which began in 1926), staging works by, among others, Chekhov, Ibsen, and Glaspell. Hughes' *Mulatto* ran successfully on Broadway in 1935, and Hughes went on in the 1930s to establish the Harlem Suitcase Theatre in New York and the New Negro Theatre in Los Angeles. As the decade of the 1930s drew to a close, Thornton Wilder won the Pulitzer Prize for *Our Town* (1938), a formally inventive, **metatheatrical** examination of "small-town" U.S.A. and American idealism that evokes comparison with the images Norman Rockwell created for covers of *The Saturday Evening Post*.

But by the end of the decade, America was on the brink of involvement in another war; not surprisingly, Wilder's *Our Town* and leftist plays of social protest were joined by what Thomas Adler views as a recurring meditation in American drama on the war in Europe. That is, as American drama evolved throughout the 1930s, it responded not only to opposing explanations of the causes of the Depression and putative solutions, but also in two of Robert E. Sherwood's three Pulitzer Prize-winning plays—*Idiot's Delight* (1936) and *There Shall Be No Night* (1941)—to a changing national perspective of American intervention in World War II. As Adler points out, the former play, like Jean Renoir's antiwar film *Grand Illusion* (1937) and a host of other filmic and theatrical examples, diagnoses the "virus" of a "chauvinistic nationalism" as the cause of conflict in Europe and advocates both "pacifism and isolationism." By 1941, Sherwood's *There Shall Be No Night*, much like Philip Barry's allegorical *Liberty Jones* and Lillian Hellman's *Watch on the Rhine* (both produced the same year), seemed to assert just the opposite: that fighting fascism and Germany's aggression toward its European neighbors could redeem an America which, in many respects, had sunk into what Sherwood's play terms "ruthless materialism" and "intellectual impotence." Such redemption, unfortunately, is seldom attained without cost—as Sherwood's Oscar-winning screenplay about disabled soldiers *The Best Years of Our Lives* (1946) shows so poignantly—or outside the context of the business of waging war, one theme of Arthur Miller's *All My Sons* (1947). These later reflections aside, however, as the 1930s closed and America prepared for war, one further fact seems clear: another generation of playwrights was preparing yet again to reshape the American drama and re-examine the national identity.

THE FORTIES AND FIFTIES

"Prosperity—Strictly Limited" is how Barnard Hewitt describes the fiscal condition of the American theatre from 1940 to 1957. An improved economy, lifted out of the Depression by wartime industrial production, was infusing the Broadway theatres that survived the hard times with capital generated by longer runs and a greater demand for entertainment. But, like the costs in human misery of waging a war, the price of success for American theatre in the 1940s, especially that Broadway was compelled to pay, was high: Production expenses grew steeper and the necessity of staging "hit" shows seemed greater than ever. It is, then, hardly coincidental that, among other popular genres, the musical seemed to come into its own during the 1940s. In 1941, while some audiences were considering the politics of Hellman's *Watch on the Rhine*, others were enjoying *Lady in the Dark*, a musical by Moss Hart, Ira Gershwin, and Kurt Weill. For a number of reviewers, *Lady in the Dark*, built around psychoanalytic issues, marked a point when the musical comedy reached for greater levels of complexity in plot and theme. While audiences in late 1942 experienced the theatrical iconoclasm of Wilder's *The Skin of Our Teeth*—its simultaneous representation of past and present, its dissolution of the barrier or **"fourth wall"** between actor and audience—the next spring they were enjoying Rodgers and Hammerstein's *Oklahoma!*, in the early stages of its 2,248-performance run in New York. Richard Rodgers, a popular composer with Lorenz Hart in the 1920s and 1930s of *On Your Toes* (1936), *The Boys from Syracuse* (1938), and *Pal Joey* (1940), teamed with Oscar Hammerstein II in 1943 to write some of America's most popular musicals, including *Carousel, South Pacific* (1949), *The King and I* (1951), and *The Sound of Music* (1959). In 1943, Alan Jay Lerner and Frederick Loewe also initiated their long partnership, leading to such musicals as *Brigadoon* (1947), *Paint Your Wagon* (1951), *My Fair Lady* (1956), and *Camelot* (1960). It is arguable, however, that the enormous success of *Oklahoma!* was due not only to its music and Hammerstein's libretto, which, like that of *Lady in the Dark* seemed to some critics more dramatically complex than that of conventional musicals, but also to its ideological implications that a wartime audience found consoling: America is a great country; the future will be better than the past; keep an optimistic faith.

As C. W. E. Bigsby observes in *Modern American Drama, 1945–1990*, as America entered the war Arthur Miller was writing protest plays, and Tennessee Williams began working with a radical theatre company. For Bigsby, the assumptions of both playwrights were "formed" by the "pre-history" of the Depression, and many of their most enduring plays "seem to bear the impress of the thirties." So, while for some critics—Brooks Atkinson, for example—the progress achieved by the American theatre in the 1920s was stalled by the end of the 1930s, Bigsby points to the importance of the thirties in shaping the work of two of America's best dramatists (not to mention several fine plays by Wilder, Hellman, William Saroyan, and Maxwell Anderson, to name just a few). Williams's *A Streetcar Named Desire* (1947), *Cat on a Hot Tin Roof* (1955), and *Sweet Bird of Youth* (1959) and Miller's *All My Sons* and *Death of a Salesman* (1949) also owed another debt to the 1930s that had little to do with dramatic craftsmanship: their direction by Elia Kazan, former member of the Group Theatre. Said Miller of the rehearsals of *All My Sons*, Kazan was "driving it to ever more intensified climaxes, working it like a piece of music that had to be sustained here and hushed there. . . . He had the devil's energy and knew how to pay attention to what the writer or his actors were trying to tell him." Kazan went on to Hollywood and directed, among other films, *A Streetcar Named Desire* (1951), *On the Waterfront* (1954), and *East of Eden* (1955); Williams and Miller, of course, went on to become giants of the American theatre.

The collaboration between Williams and Kazan provides a telling model of changed relationships in the workings of theatrical production, and reveals an American drama striving to transcend the boundaries of photographic realism. Agreeing with playwright Robert Ardrey, Brenda Murphy contends that the Williams-Kazan collaboration that began with *A Streetcar Named Desire* reflects a basic change in the conventional working relationships of dramatist, director, and producer. One of several reformations attributable to the Group Theatre, this revised arrangement brought the playwright into more immediate contact with the rehearsal and subsequent revision of his or her script. No longer the solitary author who simply delivered a completed text to the director and disappeared from the production process, Williams, especially in the case of *Cat on a Hot Tin Roof*, worked closely with Kazan during rehearsals (which is one reason why two versions of the play are printed in this anthology). Yet, perhaps more important is what Murphy characterizes as Williams's adamant stand "against the theatrical realism that was the dominant mode in American drama before World War II" (Wilder's *The Skin of Our Teeth* and Miller's *Death of a Salesman* are the products of similar "stands"). From his earliest full-length works—his self-described "lyrical play about memories and the loneliness of them," *Battle of Angels* (1940), and his "memory play" *The Glass Menagerie* (1944)—Williams resisted the formal constraints imposed by realism. The representation of memories on stage required formal and technical experimentation, and Murphy points to Williams's manifesto-like notes to *The Glass Menagerie* as one indication of his determination to find a poetic means of expressing subjective experience on stage.

In his notes to *The Glass Menagerie*, Williams remarks that "expressionism and all other conventional techniques in drama have only one valid aim, and that is a closer approach to truth." For Williams, dramatic realism, with its "genuine Frigidaire and authentic ice-cubes" (and equally prosaic language), was incapable of capturing "truth, life, or reality . . . which the poetic imagination can represent or suggest, in essence, only through transformation, through changing into other forms than those which were merely present in appearance." For *The Glass Menagerie*, Williams used slides and legends printed on screens; and for both this play and *A Streetcar Named Desire*, Jo Mielziner supported Williams's aim by making scrims of gauze upon which the outsides of buildings were painted. By dimming lights shining on the buildings and turning up light inside, the walls were rendered transparent, allowing the audience an instantaneous view of the interior. Mielziner employed similar devices in designing Miller's *Death of a Salesman* and Williams's *Cat on a Hot Tin Roof*, the latter which Eric Bentley discussed in the *New Republic:* "The general scheme is that . . . a view of *man's* exterior is also a view of his interior, the habitat of his body and the country of his memories and dreams. A theatre historian would probably call this world a combination of naturalism and expressionism." Bentley was right, for theatre historians have regarded such work as suggesting this precise combination. Williams continued to transgress the boundaries of realism in his "dream play" *Camino Real* (1953) and, while revising *The Night of the Iguana* during a pre-Broadway run in Chicago in 1961, explained that the play owed much to Samuel Beckett, Harold Pinter, Edward Albee, and the **theatre of the absurd**, which was just beginning to take drama even further away from conventional realism.

The 1940s brought not only the war plays alluded to above, but also plays gauging the changed structure of feeling in postwar America. Hellman's *The Searching Wind* (1944), for example, anticipates Arthur Laurents' *Home of the Brave* (1945) and, more obviously, Miller's *All My Sons* (reprinted here), which juxtaposes the idealism of a returning soldier with the dark secrets—or harsh realities—of the father he loves and thought he knew. But insofar as the father, Joe Keller, and his family form the hub around which an entire neighborhood revolves, Miller's tragic thesis might be extended more broadly to the decaying values and glossily deceptive surface of the entire country. In *Death of a Salesman* Miller more pointedly interrogates the so-called American Dream, one unattainable for society's weaker and older citizens like Willy Loman. Mourning at his graveside in the play's epilogue, Linda Loman demands that attention be paid to such men as her late husband but, much as the family home is surrounded in Miller's initial stage directions by taller and newer buildings, Willy has been similarly overwhelmed by forces over which he can exert no control. In his autobiography *Timebends,* Miller regards New York theatre in the late 1940s as similarly impossible for playwrights to control. In 1949, *Death of a Salesman,* at least by Miller's own account, appealed to an audience that "was basically the same for musicals and light entertainments as for the ambitious stuff . . . an audience representing, more or less, all of America." He rejects any tendency to romanticize the late 1940s and early 1950s as "some type of renaissance in the New York theatre," a theatre he perceived as a "temple being rotted out with commercialized junk." A "good piece of work" like *Death of a Salesman,* he observed, makes it to Broadway "mostly by accident." The story of Willy's misfortune, as it happens, has proven a happy "accident" for Miller and American drama, continuing to find appreciative audiences in the United States, Europe, and China.

Miller's view of Broadway in the early postwar years was shared by many, and such a view is in part responsible for a rejuvenated Off-Broadway movement that continued the Little Theatre Movement and the ambitions of groups like the Provincetown Players earlier in the century. Smaller houses opened in the late 1940s and early 1950s outside the Broadway area surrounding Times Square, many of which were dedicated to producing experimental plays on small budgets and hiring young, unknown actors to replace the star system that dominated Broadway and accelerated the vertiginous spiral of costs associated with Broadway productions. An off-Broadway revival in 1952 of Williams's *Summer and Smoke,* first produced with unspectacular results on Broadway in 1948, verified for many the possibility of emancipating serious drama from a system so ill-suited to it and moving it to a more thoughtful theatrical context. This revival by the Circle in the Square Theatre won widespread critical acclaim, an acclaim typically accompanied by a sharp indictment of Broadway like John Gassner's in the *Educational Theatre Journal*: "As if to upbraid Broadway for the ignoble season of 1951–1952, an intrepid Greenwich Village group calling itself Circle in the Square revived *Summer and Smoke* shortly after the season was officially closed. . . . As staged by talented new director José Quintero, *Summer and Smoke* represented a triumph of atmosphere and theatrical poetry over all the mediocre realism that gluts the market place of tired Broadway showmanship." A few years later, reviewing what he termed Quintero's "flawless" Circle in the Square production of *Long Day's Journey into Night* (November 1956), Gassner was even more exasperated with Broadway drama. He opined that "little space is needed for the assessment of [Broadway] productions which ranged, with few exceptions, from the commonplace of failure to the commonplaces of success." Quintero and Circle in the Square have become renowned for their productions of O'Neill's later plays; other Off-Broadway houses have staged new plays by Beckett, Albee, Joe Orton, Jean Genet, Jack Gelber, and numerous other contemporary writers; Joseph Papp founded the New York Shakespeare Festival off-Broadway in 1954. Not long after this, however, as Gerald Weales complains, "the words *off-Broadway theatre,*" which once "called up a picture of a dedicated group, held together by aesthetic or ideational concerns, determined to change the state of the theatre or the state of the world," were starting to lose their radical force. So by the early 1960s, Weales suggests, "Broadway and off-Broadway appear to operate through the same economic (and artistic) motivations." (Thus arose the necessity of moving *off-off* Broadway in the early 1960s, a matter to be taken up later in this text.)

The 1950s, as Kazan would later recall, were also a time in which his "world of friends"—artists and intellectuals working in New York and particularly those in Hollywood—"was in political as well as personal turmoil." Some dozen years after the Group disbanded, some twenty years after the audience at the premiere of *Waiting for Lefty* had felt what Harold Clurman called a "new awareness and confidence," the "swelling power of the [political] right" was preparing to impose its "particular type of terror" on any communists or intellectuals sympathetic to socialism that the **House Un-American Activities Committee** (HUAC) and Senator Joseph McCarthy could find. And they found many of them in the film industry and in the circle of artists involved in political theatre in the 1930s and early 1940s. John Howard Lawson, Clifford Odets, Elia Kazan, Lillian Hellman, Arthur Miller—all were subpoenaed, all were asked to name the names of communists they knew. Film stars like John Garfield were threatened with blacklisting, as was Kazan, who finally named many names and suffered the inevitable ostracism that resulted. Kazan found the occasion of his testimony an opportunity to review his outrage at being bullied in the past by communist "comrades" to make productions more "right thinking" and thus, although strongly pressured to inform, cooperated with a certain intellectual principle. Hellman and others refused. This infamous inquisition of the politics—and, not infrequently, the sexuality—of a long line of American theatre and film artists, among other American citizens, was felt throughout the decade. Lives and careers were ruined; intellectual freedom was, quite obviously, seriously threatened.

Nevertheless, as the history of American drama throughout the twentieth century shows, the stirrings of a radically different emergent drama were soon to be felt, and by the early 1960s, American theatre was to undergo a change as extraordinary as those initiated in Provincetown and Greenwich Village nearly a half-century earlier. Taken together, the nine plays in this section of *American Drama* form a distinguished roster of theatre for the period in which American drama truly was "bursting with energy and enterprise."

WORKS CONSULTED

Adler, Thomas P. *Mirror on the Stage: The Pulitzer Plays as an Approach to American Drama.* West Lafayette, IN: Purdue University Press, 1987.

Atkinson, Brooks. *Broadway.* New York: Macmillan, 1970.

Bablet, Denis. *The Theatre of Gordon Craig.* London: Eyre Methuen, 1981.

Bentley, Eric. "Review." *New Republic,* April 4, 1955, 22.

Bigsby, C.W.E. *Modern American Drama, 1945–1990.* Cambridge: Cambridge University Press, 1992.

Browne, Maurice. *Too Late to Lament: An Autobiography.* Bloomington: Indiana University Press, 1956.

Brustein, Robert. *The Theatre of Revolt: An Approach to the Modern Drama.* Boston: Little, Brown and Company, 1962.

Clurman, Harold. *The Fervent Years.* New York: Harcourt Brace Jovanovich, 1975.

Deutsch, Helen, and Stella Hanau. *The Provincetown Players: A Story of the Theatre.* New York: Farrar & Rinehart, 1931.

Flanagan, Hallie. *Arena: The History of the Federal Theatre.* New York: Duell, Sloan & Pearce, 1940.

France, Richard. *The Theatre of Orson Welles.* Lewisburg, PA: Bucknell University Press, 1977.

Gassner, John. "Broadway in Review." *Educational Theatre Journal* 4 (1952): 323–334.

———. "Broadway in Review." *Educational Theatre Journal* 9 (1957): 38–45.

Gorelik, Mordecai. "Theatre Is a Weapon." *Theatre Arts Monthly, 18* (June 1934): 420–433.

Hatch, James V., ed. *Black Theater, U.S.A.: Forty-Five Plays by Black Americans, 1847–1974.* New York: Free Press, 1974.

Hethmon, Robert H., ed. *Strasberg at the Actors Studio: Tape-Recorded Sessions.* New York: Viking, 1968.

Hewitt, Barnard. *Theatre U.S.A.—1665 to 1957.* New York: McGraw-Hill, 1959.

Kazan, Elia. *Elia Kazan: A Life.* New York: Alfred A. Knopf, 1988.

Littell, Robert. "Brighter Lights—Broadway in Review." *Theatre Arts Monthly, 13* (March 1929): 164–176.

Lock, Charles. "Maurice Browne and the Chicago Little Theatre." *Modern Drama, 31* (1988): 106–116.

Locke, Alain, ed. *The New Negro: Voices of the Harlem Renaissance* (1925). Rpt. New York: Atheneum, 1992.

Miller, Arthur. *Timebends: A Life.* New York: Grove Press, 1987.

Murphy, Brenda. *Tennessee Williams and Elia Kazan: A Collaboration in the Theatre.* Cambridge: Cambridge University Press, 1992.

Sarlos, Robert. *Jig Cook and the Provincetown Players: Theatre in Ferment.* Amherst: University of Massachusetts Press, 1982.

Smiley, Sam. *The Drama of Attack: Didactic Plays of the American Depression.* Columbia: University of Missouri Press, 1972.

Smith, Wendy. *Real-life Drama: The Group Theatre, 1931–1940.* New York: Knopf, 1990.

Theatre Guild Board of Directors. "Introduction." *The Theatre Guild Anthology.* New York: Random House, 1936.

Weales, Gerald. *American Drama Since World War II.* New York: Harcourt, Brace & World, 1962.

Williams, Tennessee. *The Theatre of Tennessee Williams.* 8 vols. New York: New Directions, 1971.

Wilmeth, Don B., and Tice Miller, eds. *The Cambridge Guide to American Theatre.* Cambridge: Cambridge University Press, 1993.

TRIFLES (1916)

She is one of America's great playwrights and one of its most neglected: Davenport ingénue and Greenwich Village bohemian, devoted wife and New Woman. The contradictions represented in the character of Susan Glaspell (1876–1948), contradictions that have made her not **modernist** enough in the eyes of some theatre scholars, actually constitute a playwright very American in character. The study of Glaspell's life and works, fortunately, has enjoyed something of a rebirth in recent years. Feminist scholars have sought to reclaim an artistic vision previously rejected as "too woman-centered," and show the greater complexities behind it. For it is a very real fact that, as a founding member of the **Provincetown Players**, Glaspell was a major contributor to a company that set a new direction for the American theatre, one that reached towards **expressionist** and **symbolist** devices. Glaspell's play *Trifles* (1916) is a key part of the evolutionary process that began there; a traditional one-acter, with its action in a familiar setting, it nevertheless asks the audience to develop very different ways of reading and considering human relations.

Glaspell's pioneering artistic spirit was seemingly preordained by her birthdate (1 July 1876) and definitely fostered by her upbringing. The proximity of her birthdate to the American centennial was a coincidence that seemed fated for a playwright who, born and bred in America's heartland, would come to identify with those who settled it. She was born Susan Keating Glaspell to Alice Keating and Elmer S. Glaspell in Davenport, Iowa, where her family had settled as early as 1839. Middle-class, she was educated in the Davenport schools; her upbringing appears to have been as "typically American" as her later life would be unconventional. Upon graduation from high school, she exchanged her diploma for a byline—"Susie K. Glaspell"—and worked first as reporter for the *Davenport Morning Republican*, then as society editor for the *Weekly Outlook*, a Davenport society magazine.

"Susie" did not last long as a creation; in a radical departure from what was considered "adequate" education for a woman of her time, Glaspell left her reporting job and Davenport for Des Moines to enroll in Drake University, from which she graduated in 1899. She remained in Des Moines to work for the *Des Moines Daily News* as a statehouse and legislative reporter, a job that provided ample material for her writing. During this time she covered the famous Hassock murder case, in which Margaret Hassock was accused of striking her husband, farmer John Hassock, with an axe as he slept. That story would later become the basis for *Trifles* and its short story version, "Jury of Her Peers" (1917). Glaspell returned to Davenport in 1901, determined to make a living as a writer, and seemed destined to become a local colorist along the lines of another well-known Davenport author, Alice French. Between 1903 and 1912, she published several stories about Iowa politics, later collected (and recently reissued) in a volume entitled *Lifted Masks*. She moved to Chicago in 1902 to enroll in graduate school in English; upon her return home in 1904 she enjoyed a successful career as a writer and popular figure in Davenport social circles. There she became involved with the intelligentsia of the Monist Society, and met her future husband, George Cram "Jig" Cook, a prominent scholarly figure. They were married in 1913, and divided their time between the intellectual circles of New York's Greenwich Village and Provincetown, Massachusetts.

It was involvement with this community that led to the founding of a major force in the development of American drama as part of the ongoing **Little Theatre Movement**. Glaspell and Cook, capitalizing on the craze for psychoanalysis, coauthored a satire called *Suppressed Desires* in 1914. Unable to get it staged, and disheartened by what they saw as the stagnant state of contemporary American theatre, Glaspell and Cook helped found an alternative theatre in Provincetown. They sought to model the more imaginative productions being staged in Europe, and indeed, the inspiration for the endeavor came from seeing a 1911 visit to the United States by the **Abbey Theatre's** Irish Players. During the summer of 1915, Cook procured the use of a seaside fish house, to be renamed the Wharf Theatre, and the Provincetown Players were born. Glaspell would go on to contribute seven plays to the company in as many years, second only to Eugene O'Neill, who had also entered into his famous affiliation with the group. She also acted in, produced, and directed several of her plays. Cook eventually moved the group to its permanent home in New York City, but due to conflicts within the company, he and Glaspell took a year's sabbatical in 1919. They eventually made a final split with the Provincetown Players (whom they accused of emphasizing the spectacle of production over the art of playwriting), traveling to Greece in 1922 as part of a lifelong dream of Cook's.

It was during her association with the Provincetown Players that Glaspell was her most prolific and innovative as a playwright. While her earlier prose had drawn heavily on her experiences—from the short stories based on time spent in the Iowa statehouse and Drake University to the novels set in the Midwest—critics like Veronica Makowsky generally agree that "what reputation Glaspell has today can be credited to her plays, which are more radical and experimental." The complicated nature of Glaspell's personal life—raised squarely in the heartland, but subscribing to the free, modern life-style of the city—is strongly echoed in her playwriting. Although her work could appear fairly traditional (after all, *Trifles* is set in the most untheatrical and ordinary of settings, a farm kitchen), it served as a place for Glaspell both to test predominant innovations in playwriting of the time and create her own. In this regard, Christine Dymkowski has suggested

that as a playwright, Glaspell was always "on the edge," trying to make her work serve as a theatrical "front line" for ways of seeing and performing.

Trifles is regarded today as the play in which Glaspell first exercised this intellectual and artistic pioneer spirit. As with many of her later plays, the struggle of women as a disenfranchised group is at the heart of the action. Two women, Mrs Peters and Mrs Hale, accompany a group of law officials to an isolated farmhouse where the officials seek evidence with which to convict Minnie Wright of the murder of her husband. The women quickly discover that all was not right at the Wrights, and that Minnie (the characteristically absent central character in Glaspell's plays) may have indeed been justified in murdering a cruel, subjugating husband. The codes by which they discover her oppression also signal their own **otherness**; the clues exist in the "trifles" that the men in the play are so quick to dismiss: crooked sewing, unbaked bread, and an unkempt house. The women continually leave the meanings of what they find only half said; but as Linda Ben-Zvi writes, "Glaspell's women are what they seem to be: tentative and often halting, trying to find themselves and their voices." In the case of *Trifles*, these women are trying to reassign significance to the activities of one woman the world has left behind, and in so doing, give a voice to all women. The class differences between the men in the play suggest there are kinds of subjugation other than gender-based ones; but in this case, all the men unite inflexibly against what they perceive as an unimportant "woman's sphere." Ultimately, the women decide to band together and ignore the moral code of the male world, concealing the evidence they have discerned of Minnie's crime.

In several of the plays that followed *Trifles*— *The Outside* (1917), *Woman's Honor* (1918), and *The Verge* (1921)—Glaspell further attempted to explore what it meant for women to seek self-actualization in a man's world. The means by which this revolutionary idea was explored varied, but continually involved Glaspell pushing the boundaries of her artistic sense. In *Woman's Honor*, for example, the gender types society found so comforting became self-evident and self-mocking; the narrowly defined women in this play are not named formally, but characterized as "The Shielded One," "The Mercenary One," and "The Motherly One," while the inept men in the life of the dynamic heroine in *The Verge* are simply like every other "Tom, Dick and Harry," who are their namesakes. But while the characters in these plays are exaggerated for satirical purposes, Glaspell also designed characters who moved towards more hopeful ends, as in the case of Mrs Patrick and Allie Mayo of *The Outside*, two women living in self-imposed exile by the sea. In this play, the influence of symbolist techniques is evident. The futile attempt to resuscitate a drowned man leads to a discussion that eventually allows them to revive their own sense of place in the life going on around them, thus feeling less marginalized. Less successful in achieving a goal so symbolically expressed is Claire Archer, *The Verge*'s central character, whose attempts to cultivate new plant species bespeak her own wish to re-create her own life. Like Yank in O'Neill's *The Hairy Ape*, she seeks a place to belong outside the conventional roles society has defined for her as wife, mother, and even mistress. Unable to fulfill her ultimate goals as a scientist and as a New Woman, Claire goes insane; to represent this, *The Verge* also uses compressed, distorted spaces, suggestive lighting, and the nonrealistic supporting characters typically associated with symbolist drama.

Glaspell was never to match the dynamism of her years spent with the Provincetown Players, although she continued her theatrical involvement. Following Cook's death in 1924, she returned to the United States, settled in Davenport, and wrote a biography of him, *The Road to the Temple*. She collaborated with her lover Norman Matson to write a play, *The Comic Artist;* their relationship dissolved in 1931 after his lack of success and infidelity. That same year, Glaspell won the Pulitzer Prize for *Alison's House*, a play based on the life of Emily Dickinson. Although her absence from the theatre as a

playwright was to extend for 14 years after receiving the Pulitzer, Glaspell agreed to become Midwest director for the **Federal Theatre Project** in 1934. Her tenure was brief; nevertheless, she spent her time actively seeking out new kinds of drama, especially as it expressed the spirit of the Midwest. Returning to Provincetown, she spent the rest of her life writing novels and living quietly, due to poor health. An attempt to return to writing drama in 1945 was not successful.

Something of an outsider to conventional society, Glaspell resembled the characters who dominate her plays. Still, she contributed significantly to the social change of her day; the Provincetown Players, for example, for whom such women as Djuna Barnes, Edna Ferber, and Edna St. Vincent Millay wrote, offered women a forum for their plays that had never been available before. Glaspell has not been fully acknowledged for experimenting with the new theatrical forms that contemporaries such as O'Neill tried, and though writers such as Sophie Treadwell would "make it new" in their works to an even greater extent, Glaspell's initial forays into these areas on the behalf of women playwrights should not be discounted.

WORKS CONSULTED

Ben-Zvi, Linda. "Susan Glaspell's Contributions to Contemporary Women Playwrights." *Feminine Focus: The New Women Playwrights*, Ed. Enoch Brater. Oxford: Oxford University Press, 1989. 147–166.

Dymkowski, Christine. "On the Edge: The Plays of Susan Glaspell." *Modern Drama*, 31 (1988): 91–105.

Friedman, Sharon. "Feminism as Theme in Twentieth-Century American Women's Drama." *American Studies*, 25 (1984): 69–89.

Makowsky, Veronica. *Susan Glaspell's Century of American Women: A Critical Interpretation of Her Work*. New York: Oxford University Press, 1993.

Noe, Marcia. *Susan Glaspell: Voice from the Heartland*. Macomb, IL: Western Illinois University Press, 1983.

Oziebolo, Barbara. "Rebellion and Rejection: The Plays of Susan Glaspell." *Modern American Drama: The Female Canon*, Ed. June Schleuter. Rutherford, NJ: Fairleigh Dickinson University Press, 1990. 66–76.

CHARACTERS

GEORGE HENDERSON . . . . County Attorney

HENRY PETERS . . . . Sheriff

LEWIS HALE . . . . A Neighboring Farmer

MRS PETERS

MRS HALE

THE SETTING: *The kitchen in the now abandoned farmhouse of* JOHN WRIGHT

SCENE: *The kitchen in the now abandoned farmhouse of* JOHN WRIGHT, *a gloomy kitchen, and left without having been put in order—unwashed pans under the sink, a loaf of bread outside the breadbox, a dish towel on the table—other signs of incompleted work. At the rear the outer door opens and the* SHERIFF *comes in followed by the* COUNTY ATTORNEY *and* HALE. *The* SHERIFF *and* HALE *are men in middle life, the* COUNTY ATTORNEY *is a young man; all are much bundled up and go at once to the stove. They are followed by the two women—the* SHERIFF'S *wife first; she is a slight wiry woman, a thin nervous face.* MRS HALE *is larger and would ordinarily be called more comfortable looking, but she is disturbed now and looks fearfully about as she enters. The women have come in slowly, and stand close together near the door.*

COUNTY ATTORNEY: *(rubbing his hands)* This feels good. Come up to the fire, ladies.

MRS PETERS: *(after taking a step forward)* I'm not—cold.

SHERIFF: *(unbuttoning his overcoat and stepping away from the stove as if to mark the beginning of official business)* Now, Mr Hale, before we move things about, you explain to Mr Henderson just what you saw when you came here yesterday morning.

COUNTY ATTORNEY: By the way, has anything been moved? Are things just as you left them yesterday?

SHERIFF: *(looking about)* It's just the same. When it dropped below zero last night I thought I'd better send Frank out this morning to make a fire for us—no use getting pneumonia with a big case on, but I told him not to touch anything except the stove—and you know Frank.

COUNTY ATTORNEY: Somebody should have been left here yesterday.

SHERIFF: Oh—yesterday. When I had to send Frank to Morris Center for that man who went crazy—I want you to know I had my hands full yesterday, I knew you could get back from Omaha by today and as long as I went over everything here myself—

COUNTY ATTORNEY: Well, Mr Hale, tell just what happened when you came here yesterday morning.

HALE: Harry and I had started to town with a load of potatoes. We came along the road from my place and as I got here I said, "I'm going to see if I can't get John Wright to go in with me on a party telephone." I spoke to Wright about it once before and he put me off, saying folks talked too much anyway, and all he asked was peace and quiet—I guess you know about how much he talked himself; but I thought maybe if I went to the house and talked about it before his wife, though I said to Harry that I didn't know as what his wife wanted made much difference to John—

COUNTY ATTORNEY: Let's talk about that later, Mr Hale. I do want to talk about that, but tell now just what happened when you got to the house.

HALE: I didn't hear or see anything; I knocked at the door, and still it was all quiet inside. I knew they must be up, it was past eight o'clock. So I knocked again, and I thought I heard somebody say, "Come in." I wasn't sure, I'm not sure yet, but I opened the door—this door *(indicating the door by which the two women are still standing)* and there in that rocker—*(pointing to it)* sat Mrs Wright.
  (They all look at the rocker.)

COUNTY ATTORNEY: What—was she doing?

HALE: She was rockin' back and forth. She had her apron in her hand and was kind of—pleating it.

COUNTY ATTORNEY: And how did she—look?

HALE: Well, she looked queer.

COUNTY ATTORNEY: How do you mean—queer?

HALE: Well, as if she didn't know what she was going to do next. And kind of done up.

COUNTY ATTORNEY: How did she seem to feel about your coming?

HALE: Why, I don't think she minded—one way or other. She didn't pay much attention. I said, "How do, Mrs Wright, it's cold, ain't it?" And she said, "Is it?"—and went on kind of pleating at her apron. Well, I was surprised; she didn't ask me to come up to the stove, or to set down, but just sat there, not even looking at me, so I said, "I want to see John." And then she—laughed. I guess you would call it a laugh. I thought of Harry and the team outside, so I said a little sharp: "Can't I see John?" "No," she says, kind o' dull like. "Ain't he home?" says I. "Yes," says she, "he's home." "Then why can't I see him?" I asked her, out of patience. "'Cause he's dead," says she. *"Dead?"* says I. She just nodded her head, not getting a bit excited, but rockin' back and forth. "Why—where is he?" says I, not knowing what to say. She just pointed upstairs—like that *(Himself pointing to the room above)*. I got up, with the idea of going up there. I walked from there to here—then I says, "Why, what did he die of?" "He died of a rope round his neck," says she, and just went on pleatin' at her apron. Well, I went out and called Harry. I thought I might—need help. We went upstairs and there he was lyin'—

COUNTY ATTORNEY: I think I'd rather have you go into that upstairs, where you can point it all out. Just go on now with the rest of the story.

HALE: Well, my first thought was to get that rope off. It looked . . . *(Stops, his face twitches)* . . . but Harry, he went up to him, and he said, "No, he's dead all right, and we'd better not touch anything." So we went back down stairs. She was still sitting that same way. "Has anybody been notified?" I asked. "No," says she, unconcerned. "Who did this, Mrs Wright?" said Harry. He said it businesslike—and she stopped pleatin' of her apron. "I don't know," she says. "You don't *know?*" says Harry. "No," says she. "Weren't you sleepin' in the bed with him?" says Harry. "Yes," says she, "but I was on the inside." "Somebody slipped a rope round his neck and strangled him and you didn't wake up?" says Harry. "I didn't wake up," she said after him. We must 'a looked as if we didn't see how that could be, for after a minute she said, "I sleep sound." Harry was going to ask her more questions but I said maybe we ought to let her tell her story first to the coroner, or the sheriff, so Harry went fast as he could to Rivers' place, where there's a telephone.

COUNTY ATTORNEY: And what did Mrs Wright do when she knew that you had gone for the coroner?

HALE: She moved from that chair to this one over here *(Pointing to a small chair in the corner)* and just sat there with her hands held together and looking down. I got a feeling that I ought to make some conversation, so I said I had come in to see if John wanted to put in a telephone, and at that she started to laugh, and then she stopped and looked at me—scared. *(The* COUNTY ATTORNEY, *who has had his notebook out, makes a note)* I dunno, maybe it wasn't scared. I wouldn't like to say it was. Soon Harry got back, and then Dr Lloyd came, and you, Mr Peters, and so I guess that's all I know that you don't.

COUNTY ATTORNEY: *(looking around)* I guess we'll go upstairs first—and then out to the barn and around there. *(To the* SHERIFF*)* You're convinced that there was nothing important here—nothing that would point to any motive.

SHERIFF: Nothing here but kitchen things.

(The COUNTY ATTORNEY, *after again looking around the kitchen, opens the door of a cupboard closet. He gets up on a chair and looks on a shelf. Pulls his hand away, sticky.)*

COUNTY ATTORNEY: Here's a nice mess.

(The women draw nearer.)

MRS PETERS: *(to the other woman)* Oh, her fruit; it did freeze. *(To the* COUNTY ATTORNEY*)* She worried about that when it turned so cold. She said the fire'd go out and her jars would break.

SHERIFF: Well, can you beat the women! Held for murder and worryin' about her preserves.

COUNTY ATTORNEY: I guess before we're through she may have something more serious than preserves to worry about.

HALE: Well, women are used to worrying over trifles.

(The two women move a little closer together.)

COUNTY ATTORNEY: *(with the gallantry of a young politician)* And yet, for all their worries, what would we do without the ladies? *(The women do not unbend. He goes to the sink, takes a dipperful of water from the pail and, pouring it into a basin, washes his hands. Starts to wipe them on the roller towel, turns it for a cleaner place)* Dirty towels! *(Kicks his foot against the pans under the sink)* Not much of a housekeeper, would you say, ladies?

MRS HALE: *(stiffly)* There's a great deal of work to be done on a farm.

COUNTY ATTORNEY: To be sure. And yet *(With a little bow to her)* I know there are some Dickson county farmhouses which do not have such roller towels.

(He gives it a pull to expose its full length again.)

MRS HALE: Those towels get dirty awful quick. Men's hands aren't always as clean as they might be.

COUNTY ATTORNEY: Ah, loyal to your sex, I see. But you and Mrs Wright were neighbors. I suppose you were friends, too.

MRS HALE: *(shaking her head)* I've not seen much of her of late years. I've not been in this house—it's more than a year.

COUNTY ATTORNEY: And why was that? You didn't like her?

MRS HALE: I liked her all well enough. Farmers' wives have their hands full, Mr Henderson. And then—

COUNTY ATTORNEY: Yes—?

MRS HALE: *(looking about)* It never seemed a very cheerful place.

COUNTY ATTORNEY: No—it's not cheerful. I shouldn't say she had the homemaking instinct.

MRS HALE: Well, I don't know as Wright had, either.

COUNTY ATTORNEY: You mean that they didn't get on very well?

MRS HALE: No, I don't mean anything. But I don't think a place'd be any cheerfuller for John Wright's being in it.

COUNTY ATTORNEY: I'd like to talk more of that a little later. I want to get the lay of things upstairs now.

(He goes to the left, where three steps lead to a stair door.)

SHERIFF: I suppose anything Mrs Peters does'll be all right. She was to take in some clothes for her, you know, and a few little things. We left in such a hurry yesterday.

COUNTY ATTORNEY: Yes, but I would like to see what you take, Mrs Peters, and keep an eye out for anything that might be of use to us.

MRS PETERS: Yes, Mr Henderson.

(The women listen to the men's steps on the stairs, then look about the kitchen.)

MRS HALE: I'd hate to have men coming into my kitchen, snooping around and criticising.

(She arranges the pans under sink which the COUNTY ATTORNEY *had shoved out of place.)*

MRS PETERS: Of course it's no more than their duty.

MRS HALE: Duty's all right, but I guess that deputy sheriff that came out to make the fire might have got a little of this on. *(Gives the roller towel a pull)* Wish I'd thought of that sooner. Seems mean to talk about her for not having things slicked up when she had to come away in such a hurry.

MRS PETERS: *(who has gone to a small table in the left rear corner of the room, and lifted one end of a towel that covers a pan)* She had bread set. *(Stands still)*

MRS HALE: *(eyes fixed on a loaf of bread beside the breadbox, which is on a low shelf at the other side of the room. Moves slowly toward it)* She was going to put this in there. *(Picks up loaf, then abruptly drops it. In a manner of returning to familiar things)* It's a shame about her fruit. I wonder if it's all gone. *(Gets up on the chair and looks)* I think there's some here that's all right, Mrs Peters. Yes—here; *(Holding it toward the window)* this is cherries, too. *(Looking again)* I declare I believe that's the only one. *(Gets down, bottle in her hand. Goes to the sink and wipes it off on the outside)* She'll feel awful bad after all her hard work in the hot weather. I remember the afternoon I put up my cherries last summer. *(She puts the bottle on the big kitchen table, center of the room. With a sigh, is about to sit down in the rocking-chair. Before she is seated realizes what chair it is; with a slow look at it, steps back. The chair which she has touched rocks back and forth.)*

MRS PETERS: Well, I must get those things from the front room closet. *(She goes to the door at the right, but after looking into the other room, steps back)* You coming with me, Mrs Hale? You could help me carry them.

(They go in the other room; reappear, MRS PETERS carrying a dress and skirt, MRS HALE following with a pair of shoes.)

MRS PETERS: My, it's cold in there.

(She puts the clothes on the big table, and hurries to the stove.)

MRS HALE: *(examining the skirt)* Wright was close. I think maybe that's why she kept so much to herself. She didn't even belong to the Ladies Aid. I suppose she felt she couldn't do her part, and then you don't enjoy things when you feel shabby. She used to wear pretty clothes and be lively, when she was Minnie Foster, one of the town girls singing in the choir. But that—oh, that was thirty years ago. This all you was to take in?

MRS PETERS: She said she wanted an apron. Funny thing to want, for there isn't much to get you dirty in jail, goodness knows. But I suppose just to make her feel more natural. She said they was in the top drawer in this cupboard. Yes, here. And then her little shawl that always hung behind the door. *(Opens stair door and looks)* Yes, here it is.

(Quickly shuts door leading upstairs)

MRS HALE: *(abruptly moving toward her)* Mrs Peters?

MRS PETERS: Yes, Mrs Hale?

MRS HALE: Do you think she did it?

MRS PETERS: *(in a frightened voice)* Oh, I don't know.

MRS HALE: Well, I don't think she did. Asking for an apron and her little shawl. Worrying about her fruit.

MRS PETERS: *(starts to speak, glances up, where footsteps are heard in the room above. In a low voice)* Mr Peters says it looks bad for her. Mr Henderson is awful sarcastic in a speech and he'll make fun of her sayin' she didn't wake up.

MRS HALE: Well, I guess John Wright didn't wake when they was slipping that rope under his neck.

MRS PETERS: No, it's strange. It must have been done awful crafty and still. They say it was such a —funny way to kill a man, rigging it all up like that.

MRS HALE: That's just what Mr Hale said. There was a gun in the house. He says that's what he can't understand.

MRS PETERS: Mr Henderson said coming out that what was needed for the case was a motive; something to show anger, or—sudden feeling.

MRS HALE: *(who is standing by the table)* Well, I don't see any signs of anger around here. *(She puts her hand on the dish towel which lies on the table, stands looking down at table, one half of which is clean, the other half messy)* It's wiped to here. *(Makes a move as if to finish work, then turns and looks at loaf of bread outside the breadbox. Drops towel. In that voice of coming back to familiar things)* Wonder how they are finding things upstairs. I hope she had it a little more red-up up there. You know, it seems kind of *sneaking.* Locking her up in town and then coming out here and trying to get her own house to turn against her!

MRS PETERS: But Mrs Hale, the law is the law.

MRS HALE: I s'pose 'tis. *(Unbuttoning her coat)* Better loosen up your things, Mrs Peters. You won't feel them when you go out.

(MRS PETERS takes off her fur tippet, goes to hang it on hook at back of room, stands looking at the under part of the small corner table.)

MRS PETERS: She was piecing a quilt.

(She brings the large sewing basket and they look at the bright pieces.)

MRS HALE: It's log cabin pattern. Pretty, isn't it? I wonder if she was goin' to quilt it or just knot it?

(Footsteps have been heard coming down the stairs. The SHERIFF enters followed by HALE and the COUNTY ATTORNEY.)

SHERIFF: They wonder if she was going to quilt it or just knot it!

(The men laugh; the women look abashed.)

COUNTY ATTORNEY: *(rubbing his hands over the stove)* Frank's fire didn't do much up there, did it? Well, let's go out to the barn and get that cleared up.

(The men go outside.)

MRS HALE: *(resentfully)* I don't know as there's anything so strange, our takin' up our time with little things while we're waiting for them to get the evidence. *(She sits down at the big table smoothing out a block with decision)* I don't see as it's anything to laugh about.

MRS PETERS: *(apologetically)* Of course they've got awful important things on their minds.

(Pulls up a chair and joins MRS HALE at the table)

MRS HALE: *(examining another block)* Mrs Peters, look at this one. Here, this is the one she was working on, and look at that sewing! All the rest of it has been so nice and even. And look at this! It's all over the place! Why, it looks as if she didn't know what she was about!

(After she has said this they look at each other, then start to glance back at the door. After an instant MRS HALE has pulled at a knot and ripped the sewing.)

MRS PETERS: Oh, what are you doing, Mrs Hale?

MRS HALE: *(mildly)* Just pulling out a stitch or two that's not sewed very good. *(Threading a needle)* Bad sewing always made me fidgety.

MRS PETERS: *(nervously)* I don't think we ought to touch things.

MRS HALE: I'll just finish up this end. *(Suddenly stopping and leaning forward)* Mrs Peters?

MRS PETERS: Yes, Mrs Hale?

MRS HALE: What do you suppose she was so nervous about?

MRS PETERS: Oh—I don't know. I don't know as she was nervous. I sometimes sew awful queer when I'm just tired. *(MRS HALE starts to say something, looks at MRS PETERS, then goes on sewing)* Well, I must get these things wrapped up. They may be through sooner than we think. *(Putting apron and other things together)* I wonder where I can find a piece of paper, and string.

MRS HALE: In that cupboard, maybe.

MRS PETERS: *(looking in cupboard)* Why, here's a birdcage. *(Holds it up)* Did she have a bird, Mrs Hale?

MRS HALE: Why, I don't know whether she did or not—I've not been here for so long. There was a man around last year selling canaries cheap, but I don't know as she took one; maybe she did. She used to sing real pretty herself.

MRS PETERS: *(glancing around)* Seems funny to think of a bird here. But she must have had one, or why would she have a cage? I wonder what happened to it.

MRS HALE: I s'pose maybe the cat got it.

MRS PETERS: No, she didn't have a cat. She's got that feeling some people have about cats—being afraid of them. My cat got in her room and she was real upset and asked me to take it out.

MRS HALE: My sister Bessie was like that. Queer, ain't it?

MRS PETERS: *(examining the cage)* Why, look at this door. It's broke. One hinge is pulled apart.

MRS HALE: *(looking too)* Looks as if someone must have been rough with it.

MRS PETERS: Why, yes.
(She brings the cage forward and puts it on the table.)

MRS HALE: I wish if they're going to find any evidence they'd be about it. I don't like this place.

MRS PETERS: But I'm awful glad you came with me, Mrs Hale. It would be lonesome for me sitting here alone.

MRS HALE: It would, wouldn't it? *(Dropping her sewing)* But I tell you what I do wish, Mrs Peters. I wish I had come over sometimes when *she* was here. I—*(Looking around the room)*—wish I had.

MRS PETERS: But of course you were awful busy, Mrs Hale—your house and your children.

MRS HALE: I could've come. I stayed away because it weren't cheerful—and that's why I ought to have come. I—I've never liked this place. Maybe because it's down in a hollow and you don't see the road. I dunno what it is, but it's a lonesome place and always was. I wish I had come over to see Minnie Foster sometimes. I can see now—
(Shakes her head)

MRS PETERS: Well you mustn't reproach yourself, Mrs Hale. Somehow we just don't see how it is with other folks until—something comes up.

MRS HALE: Not having children makes less work—but it makes a quiet house, and Wright out to work all day, and no company when he did come in. Did you know John Wright, Mrs Peters?

MRS PETERS: Not to know him; I've seen him in town. They say he was a good man.

MRS HALE: Yes—good; he didn't drink, and kept his word as well as most, I guess, and paid his debts. But he was a hard man, Mrs Peters. Just to pass the time of day with him—*(Shivers)* Like a raw wind that gets to the bone. *(Pauses, her eye falling on the cage)* I should think she would 'a wanted a bird. But what do you suppose went with it?

MRS PETERS: I don't know, unless it got sick and died.
(She reaches over and swings the broken door, swings it again. Both women watch it.)

MRS HALE: You weren't raised round here, were you? *(*MRS PETERS *shakes her head)* You didn't know—her?

MRS PETERS: Not till they brought her yesterday.

MRS HALE: She—come to think of it, she was kind of like a bird herself—real sweet and pretty, but kind of timid and—fluttery. How—she—did—change. *(Silence; then as if struck by a happy thought and relieved to get back to everyday things)* Tell you what, Mrs Peters, why don't you take the quilt in with you? It might take up her mind.

MRS PETERS: Why, I think that's a real nice idea, Mrs Hale. There couldn't possibly be any objection to it, could there? Now, just what would I take? I wonder if her patches are in here—and her things.
(They look in the sewing basket.)

MRS HALE: Here's some red. I expect this has got sewing things in it. *(Brings out a fancy box)* What a pretty box. Looks like something somebody would give you. Maybe her scissors are in here. *(Opens box. Suddenly puts her hand to her nose)* Why—(*MRS PETERS *bends nearer, then turns her face away)* There's something wrapped up in this piece of silk.

MRS PETERS: Why, this isn't her scissors.

MRS HALE: *(lifting the silk)* Oh, Mrs Peters—it's—
*(*MRS PETERS *bends closer.)*

MRS PETERS: It's the bird.

MRS HALE: *(jumping up)* But, Mrs Peters—look at it! Its neck! Look at its neck! It's all—other side *too.*

MRS PETERS: Somebody—wrung—its—neck. *(Their eyes meet. A look of growing comprehension, of horror. Steps are heard outside.* MRS HALE *slips box under quilt pieces, and sinks into her chair. Enter* SHERIFF *and* COUNTY ATTORNEY. MRS PETERS *rises.)*

COUNTY ATTORNEY: *(as one turning from serious things to little pleasantries)* Well, ladies, have you decided whether she was going to quilt it or knot it?

MRS PETERS: We think she was going to—knot it.

COUNTY ATTORNEY: Well, that's interesting, I'm sure. *(Seeing the birdcage)* Has the bird flown?

MRS HALE: *(putting more quilt pieces over the box)* We think the—cat got it.

COUNTY ATTORNEY: *(preoccupied)* Is there a cat? *(*MRS HALE *glances in a quick covert way at* MRS PETERS.*)*

MRS PETERS: Well, not *now.* They're superstitious, you know. They leave.

COUNTY ATTORNEY: *(to* SHERIFF PETERS *continuing an interrupted conversation)* No sign at all of anyone having come from the outside. Their own rope. Now let's go up again and go over it piece by piece. *(They start upstairs)* It would have to have been someone who knew just the— *(*MRS PETERS *sits down. The two women sit there not looking at one another, but as if peering into something and at the same time holding back. When they talk now it is in the manner of feeling their way over strange ground, as if afraid of what they are saying, but as if they cannot help saying it.)*

MRS HALE: She liked the bird. She was going to bury it in that pretty box.

MRS PETERS: *(in a whisper)* When I was a girl—my kitten—there was a boy took a hatchet, and before my eyes—and before I could get there— *(Covers her face an instant)* If they hadn't held me back I would have—*(Catches herself, looks upstairs where steps are heard, falters weakly)*— hurt him.

MRS HALE: *(with a slow look around her)* I wonder how it would seem never to have had any children around. *(Pause)* No, Wright wouldn't like the bird—a thing that sang. She used to sing. He killed that, too.

MRS PETERS: *(moving uneasily)* We don't know who killed the bird.

MRS HALE: I knew John Wright.

MRS PETERS: It was an awful thing was done in this house that night, Mrs Hale. Killing a man while he slept, slipping a rope around his neck that choked the life out of him.

MRS HALE: His neck. Choked the life out of him. *(Her hand goes out and rests on the birdcage.)*

MRS PETERS: *(with rising voice)* We don't know who killed him. We don't know.

MRS HALE: *(her own feeling not interrupted)* If there'd been years and years of nothing, then a bird to sing to you, it would be awful—still, after the bird was still.

MRS PETERS: *(something within her speaking)* I know what stillness is. When we homesteaded in Dakota, and my first baby died—after he was two years old, and me with no other then—

MRS HALE: *(moving)* How soon do you suppose they'll be through, looking for the evidence?

MRS PETERS: I know what stillness is. *(Pulling herself back)* The law has got to punish crime, Mrs Hale.

MRS HALE: *(not as if answering that)* I wish you'd seen Minnie Foster when she wore a white dress with blue ribbons and stood up there in the choir and sang. *(A look around the room)* Oh, I *wish* I'd come over here once in a while! That was a crime! That was a crime! Who's going to punish that?

MRS PETERS: *(looking upstairs)* We mustn't—take on.

MRS HALE: I might have known she needed help! I know how things can be—for women. I tell you, it's queer, Mrs Peters. We live close together and we live far apart. We all go through the same things—it's all just a different kind of the same thing. *(Brushes her eyes; noticing the bottle of fruit, reaches out for it)* If I was you I wouldn't tell her her fruit was gone. Tell her it *ain't.* Tell her it's all right. Take this in to prove it to her.

She—she may never know whether it was broke or not.

MRS PETERS: *(takes the bottle, looks about for something to wrap it in, takes petticoat from the clothes brought from the other room, very nervously begins winding this around the bottle. In a false voice)* My, it's a good thing the men couldn't hear us. Wouldn't they just laugh! Getting all stirred up over a little thing like a—dead canary. As if that could have anything to do with—with—wouldn't they *laugh!)* *(The men are heard coming down stairs.)*

MRS HALE: *(under her breath)* Maybe they would—maybe they wouldn't.

COUNTY ATTORNEY: No, Peters, it's all perfectly clear except a reason for doing it. But you know juries when it comes to women. If there was some definite thing. Something to show—something to make a story about—a thing that would connect up with this strange way of doing it—

(The women's eyes meet for an instant. Enter HALE from outer door.)

HALE: Well, I've got the team around. Pretty cold out there.

COUNTY ATTORNEY: I'm going to stay here a while by myself. *(To the SHERIFF)* You can send Frank out for me, can't you? I want to go over everything. I'm not satisfied that we can't do better.

SHERIFF: Do you want to see what Mrs Peters is going to take in?

(The COUNTY ATTORNEY goes to the table, picks up the apron, laughs.)

COUNTY ATTORNEY: Oh, I guess they're not very dangerous things the ladies have picked out.

(Moves a few things about, disturbing the quilt pieces which cover the box. Steps back) No, Mrs Peters doesn't need supervising. For that matter, a sheriff's wife is married to the law. Ever think of it that way, Mrs Peters?

MRS PETERS: Not—just that way.

SHERIFF: *(chuckling)* Married to the law. *(Moves toward the other room)* I just want you to come in here a minute, George. We ought to take a look at these windows.

COUNTY ATTORNEY: *(scoffingly)* Oh, windows!

SHERIFF: We'll be right out, Mr Hale.

(HALE goes outside. The SHERIFF follows the COUNTY ATTORNEY into the other room. Then MRS HALE rises, hands tight together, looking intensely at MRS PETERS, whose eyes make a slow turn, finally meeting MRS HALE'S. A moment MRS HALE holds her, then her own eyes point the way to where the box is concealed. Suddenly MRS PETERS throws back quilt pieces and tries to put the box in the bag she is wearing. It is too big. She opens box, starts to take bird out, cannot touch it, goes to pieces, stands there helpless. Sound of a knob turning in the other room. MRS HALE snatches the box and puts it in the pocket of her big coat. Enter COUNTY ATTORNEY and SHERIFF.)

COUNTY ATTORNEY: *(facetiously)* Well, Henry, at least we found out that she was not going to quilt it. She was going to—what is it you call it, ladies?

MRS HALE: *(her hand against her pocket)* We call it—knot it, Mr Henderson.

MACHINAL (1928)

In her notes on Sophie Treadwell (1885–1970) in an edition of *Machinal* published to coincide with a 1993 production by Great Britain's National Theatre, Judith E. Barlow observes that in recent years feminist scholars have attempted to "write women back into the theatrical history from which they have been erased." One such woman is Treadwell, who "rarely rates more than a line or two if she is acknowledged at all" in standard histories of American drama and theatre. Both Treadwell and *Machinal* (pronounced mock-en-AHL), her best-known play, will receive more than a line or two here. But more than securing her position in theatre history is at stake, for there is no understanding a broadly construed American drama if writers like Treadwell are overlooked. Moreover, revivals of *Machinal* in the 1980s and 1990s have both garnered generally positive critical reviews and attracted enthusiastic audiences in London, New York, and San Francisco.

Treadwell was born in California and graduated from the University of California in 1906. She worked for a number of years as a journalist—specifically, as a war correspondent from 1916 through 1918 and as a special correspondent in Mexico for a time during World War II—and authored some 30 plays, four novels, and several film scenarios and scripts. Seven of her plays were produced in New York, including *Gringo* (1922), *Plumes in the Dust* (1936), and *Hope for a Harvest* (1941), although Barlow suggests that unflattering critical response to this last, autobiographical play caused Treadwell to retire as a writer for the New York stage. Retaining her maiden name after marrying journalist William O. McGeehan, she also took an active role in the suffrage movement and wrote frequently on issues of concern to women.

One point of interest seldom mentioned in recent commentary is that her concern for society's less fortunate manifests itself not only in her writing, but in the disposition of her estate with the Roman Catholic Church of the Diocese of Tucson, Arizona, to which royalties for her work are paid to help support local orphanages.

Treadwell, as Louise Heck-Rabi explains, was never content to identify one type of play she wrote best and then "refine that form" until "commercial success" was assured. Rather, she experimented with a variety of dramatic forms and generic conventions, one of them the ill-fated *For Saxaphone* [sic] (1934), a cinematic and musical drama centering around what Heck-Rabi describes as "one core character and her three satellite selves." In this respect, *For Saxaphone* anticipates the representation not merely of psychically divided or "doubled" characters so prominent in Eugene O'Neill's work, but also the creation of multiple selves and subject positions for a single character in such feminist dramas as Marsha Norman's *Getting Out* and Cherríe Moraga's *Giving Up the Ghost,* both of which are reprinted in this volume. In addition, the unique form of the play, as Treadwell discussed in a letter to Robert Edmond Jones, who was interested in producing it, was derived from various mass cultural genres such as music, radio, and the cinema. In this way, her aesthetic innovations foreshadow, among others, Adrienne Kennedy's in *A Movie Star Has to Star in Black and White* that appropriate structures and scenes from well-known films. *Machinal,* however, as virtually every commentator remarks, is attributable to two other sources: a notorious 1927 trial Treadwell covered as a reporter in which a wife was convicted of murdering her husband, and the influence of **expressionism** on American drama, one clearly visible in such other American plays of the 1920s as O'Neill's *The Emperor Jones* (1920) and Elmer Rice's *The Adding Machine* (1923).

The Ruth Snyder murder trial was a highly sensational media event, consistently making headlines for much of 1927 and the first two weeks of 1928. Like the Young Woman in *Machinal*, whose name we eventually learn is Helen, Snyder died in the electric chair, the first woman so executed in the state of New York. And, like the court reporters in Episode Eight of the play who renarrate Helen's testimony in the disparate stories that best suit their own and their editors' needs, reporters tended to cast Snyder into what Ginger Strand identifies as one of two predictable roles: either guilty temptress or innocent victim, whore or virgin, "evil subject or helpless object." *Machinal*, however, complicates this conceptually inadequate opposition, showing Helen as entrapped within various apparatuses as employee, daughter, wife, mother, lover, defendant, and finally criminal. She becomes, as Treadwell describes her, typical or emblematic of an "ordinary young woman, any woman," performing the various roles afforded her by an "essentially hard, mechanized" society. Commenting on the New York Public Theater production of *Machinal* in 1990, Jill Dolan sees all of these professional and domestic roles as reiterating the same gendered reality, as the play's episodes are located within "interlocking social and political discourses . . . unified to discipline and punish the very material body of the Young Woman." The unrelenting quality of such discipline is underscored in Episode Nine when the priest's ministrations are juxtaposed to the strains of a Negro spiritual outside; the priest offers Helen little spiritual freedom or consolation, and she asks him with no success for a prayer she can finally understand.

Treadwell's critique of the gendered nature of modern cruelties for all but the privileged members of a dominant class (like Helen's employer-husband) parallels depictions of a dehumanizing industrial capitalism in much expressionist film and drama, which by the 1920s had influenced writers as diverse as O'Neill, Rice, Glaspell, and the Irish dramatist Sean O'Casey. The works of German playwright Ernst Toller and such film directors as Fritz Lang and F. W. Murnau are generally credited as introducing expressionist techniques to British and American artists; certainly Treadwell's text and Arthur Hopkins' 1928 production designed by Robert Edmond Jones reveal some of this influence. For Brooks Atkinson, who reviewed *Machinal* for the *New York Times* in 1928 (and later, in 1960, reviewed an off-Broadway revival of the play), this influence was evident in several ways: in the play's episodic structure and the "tatters" of office conversation in the opening scene; Jones's evocative but "skeletonized" settings (nonrepresentational ones, that is); the "clatter" of machinery, music, or airplanes throughout; and Jones's well-chosen lighting effects. Atkinson was particularly struck by the end of the production when, after the lights have been completely dimmed, the Young Woman's last cries of "Somebody! Somebod—!" are accompanied suddenly by a "pulsating flood of terrifying crimson light." In Hopkins's 1928 production and more recent ones, the coldness of a mechanized world that has subjugated Helen is represented by drab metallic office cabinets, hospital beds, and prison bars; and, along with these elements of the set and the constant mechanical clatter Atkinson describes, the play of light and shadow reinforces themes of entrapment, mechanization, and alienation that Treadwell's script develops.

Some critics have complained that *Machinal* as produced on the contemporary stage is merely a museum piece or relic, a once-obscure expressionist drama recovered by scholars and producers primarily for its feminist critique, but not an especially "great" play. For some, Treadwell's "essentially soft, tender" Young Woman is an inadequate protagonist; for others, the play is too humorless, predictable, and condescending to the working class. Perhaps, but in his review in the *New York Times* of the 1990 Public Theater production, Frank Rich took another stance, calling *Machinal* both "an authentic artifact of a distant civilization and a piece of living art that seems timeless," and a "startling collision of past and present." In what precise ways these characterizations may or may not be true is a matter for each reader to decide for him- or herself.

WORKS CONSULTED

Atkinson, Brooks. "A Tragedy of Submission." *New York Times,* 8 September 1928: 10:3.

Barlow, Judith E. "Introduction to *Machinal.*" London: Royal National Theatre/Nick Hern Books, 1993.

Dolan, Jill. "Machinal." *Theatre Journal,* 44 (1992): 96–97.

Heck-Rabi, Louise. "Sophie Treadwell: Agent for Change." *Women in American Theater: Careers, Images, Movements.*

Eds. Helen Krich Chinoy and Linda Walsh Jenkins. New York: Crown, 1981. 157–162.

Parent, Jennifer. "Arthur Hopkins' Production of Sophie Treadwell's *Machinal.*" *The Drama Review, 26* (1982): 87–100.

Rich, Frank. "A Nightmarish Vision of Urban America As Assembly Line." *New York Times* 16 October 1990: C13–14.

Strand, Ginger. "Treadwell's Neologism: *Machinal.*" *Theatre Journal, 44* (1992): 163–175.

CHARACTERS

YOUNG WOMAN	MAN
TELEPHONE GIRL	ANOTHER MAN
STENOGRAPHER	WAITER
FILING CLERK	JUDGE
ADDING CLERK	LAWYER FOR DEFENSE
MOTHER	LAWYER FOR PROSECUTION
HUSBAND	COURT REPORTER
BELLBOY	BAILIFF
NURSE	REPORTER
DOCTOR	SECOND REPORTER
YOUNG MAN	THIRD REPORTER
GIRL	JAILER
MAN	MATRON
BOY	PRIEST

Episode I: To Business
Episode II: At Home
Episode III: Honeymoon
Episode IV: Maternal
Episode V: Prohibited
Episode VI: Intimate
Episode VII: Domestic
Episode VIII: The Law
Episode IX: A Machine

THE PLOT *is the story of a woman who murders her husband—an ordinary young woman, any woman.*

THE PLAN *is to tell this story by showing the different phases of life that the woman comes in contact with, and in none of which she finds any place, any*

peace. The woman is essentially soft, tender, and the life around her is essentially hard, mechanized. Business, home, marriage, having a child, seeking pleasure—all are difficult for her—mechanical, nerve nagging. Only in an illicit love does she find anything with life in it for her, and when she loses this, the desperate effort to win free to it again is her undoing.

The story is told in nine scenes. In the dialogue of these scenes there is the attempt to catch the rhythm of our common city speech, its brassy sound, its trick of repetition, etc.

Then there is, also, the use of many different sounds chosen primarily for their inherent emotional effect (steel riveting, a priest chanting, a Negro singing, jazz band, etc.), but contributing also to the creation of a background, an atmosphere.

THE HOPE *is to create a stage production that will have "style," and at the same time, by the story's own innate drama, by the directness of its telling, by the variety and quick changingness of its scenes, and the excitement of its sounds, to create an interesting play.*

SCENICALLY *this play is planned to be handled in two basic sets (or in one set with two backs).*

The first division—(The first Four Episodes)—needs an entrance at one side, and a back having a door and a large window. The door gives, in

Episode 1—*to Vice President's office*
    "   2—*to hall*
    "   3—*to bathroom*
    "   4—*to corridor*
          And the window shows, in
    "   1—*an opposite office*
    "   2—*an inner apartment court*
    "   3—*window of a dance casino opposite*
    "   4—*steel girders*

(Of these, only the casino window is important. Sky could be used for the others.)

The second division—(the last Five Episodes)—has the same side entrance, but the back has only one opening—for a small window (barred).

Episode 5—*window is masked by electric piano*
    "   6—*window is disclosed (sidewalk outside)*
    "   7—*window is curtained*
    "   8—*window is masked by Judge's bench*
    "   9—*window is disclosed (sky outside)*

There is a change of furniture, and props for each episode—(only essential things, full of character).

For Episode 9, the room is closed in from the sides, and there is a place with bars and a door in it, put straight across stage down front (back far enough to leave a clear passageway in front of it).

LIGHTING *concentrated and intense: Light and shadow—bright light and darkness. This darkness,* already in the scene, grows and blacks out the light for dark stage when the scene changes are made.*

OFFSTAGE VOICES

*Characters in the Background
Heard, but Unseen*

*A Janitor
A Baby
A Boy and a Girl
A Husband and Wife
A Husband and Wife
A Radio Announcer
A Negro Singer*

MECHANICAL
OFFSTAGE SOUNDS

*A small jazz band
A hand organ
Steel riveting
Telegraph instruments
Aeroplane engine*

MECHANICAL
OFFSTAGE SOUNDS

*Office Machines (Typewriters, telephones, etc.)
Electric piano.*

CHARACTERS

*In the Background
Seen, Not Heard*

(See, off the main set; i.e., through a window or door)

*Couples of men and women dancing
A Woman in a bathrobe
A Woman in a wheel chair
A Nurse with a covered basin
A Nurse with a tray
The feet of men and women passing in the street.*

EPISODE ONE: TO BUSINESS

SCENE: *An Office*
          A Switchboard
          Filing Cabinet
          Adding Machine
          Typewriter and Table
          Manifold Machine

SOUNDS: *Office Machines*
          Typewriters
          Adding Machine
          Manifold
          Telephone Bells
          Buzzers

CHARACTERS AND THEIR MACHINES:
A YOUNG WOMAN *(Typewriter)*
A STENOGRAPHER *(Typewriter)*
A FILING CLERK *(Filing cabinet and manifold)*
AN ADDING CLERK *(Adding Machine)*
TELEPHONE OPERATOR *(Switchboard)*

(BEFORE THE CURTAIN—*Sounds of Machines going. They continue throughout the scene, and accompany the* YOUNG WOMAN'S *thoughts after the scene is blacked out.*)

(AT THE RISE OF THE CURTAIN: *All the Machines are disclosed, and all the characters with the exception of* THE YOUNG WOMAN.)

Of these characters, THE YOUNG WOMAN, *going any day to any business. Ordinary. The confusion of her own inner thoughts, emotions, desires, dreams cuts her off from any actual adjustment to the routine of work. She gets through this routine with a very small surface of her consciousness. She is not homely and she is not pretty. She is preoccupied with herself— with her person. She has well kept hands, and a trick of constantly arranging her hair over her ears.*

The STENOGRAPHER *is the faded, efficient woman office worker. Drying, dried.*

The ADDING CLERK *is her male counterpart.*

The FILING CLERK *is a boy not grown, callow adolescence.*

The TELEPHONE GIRL, *young, cheap and amorous.*

Lights come up on office scene. Two desks R. *and* L. *Telephone booth back* R.C. *Filing cabinet back of* C. *Adding machine back* L.C.

ADDING CLERK: *(in the monotonous voice of his monotonous thoughts; at his adding machine)* 2490, 28, 76, 123, 36842, 1, ¼, 37, 804, 23½, 982.

FILING CLERK: *(in the same way—at his filing desk)* Accounts—A. Bonds—B. Contracts— C. Data—D. Earnings—E.

STENOGRAPHER: *(in the same way—Left)* Dear Sir—in re—your letter—recent date—will state—

TELEPHONE GIRL: Hello—Hello—George H. Jones Company good morning—hello hello— George H. Jones Company good morning— hello.

FILING CLERK: Market—M. Notes—N. Output— O. Profits—P.—! *(Suddenly)* What's the matter with Q?

TELEPHONE GIRL: Matter with it—Mr J.—Mr K. wants you— What you mean matter? Matter with what?

FILING CLERK: Matter with Q.

TELEPHONE GIRL: Well—what is? Spring 1726?

FILING CLERK: I'm asking yuh——

TELEPHONE GIRL: WELL?

FILING CLERK: Nothing filed with it——

TELEPHONE GIRL: Well?

FILING CLERK: Look at A. Look at B. What's the matter with Q?

TELEPHONE GIRL: Ain't popular. Hello—Hello— George H. Jones Company.

FILING CLERK: Hot dog! Why ain't it?

ADDING CLERK: Has it personality?

STENOGRAPHER: Has it Halitosis?

TELEPHONE GIRL: Has it got it?

FILING CLERK: Hot dog!

TELEPHONE GIRL: What number do you want? *(Recognizing but not pleased)* Oh—hello—sure I know who it is—tonight? Uh, uh— *(Negative, but each with a different inflection)*—you heard me—No!

FILING CLERK: Don't you like him?

STENOGRAPHER: She likes 'em all.

TELEPHONE GIRL: I do not!

STENOGRAPHER: Well—pretty near all!

TELEPHONE GIRL: What number do you want? Wrong number. Hello—hello—George H. Jones Company. Hello, hello—

STENOGRAPHER: Memorandum—attention Mr Smith—at a conference of——

ADDING CLERK: 125—83¾—22—908—34—¼—28593——

FILING CLERK: Report—R, Sales—S, Trade—T.

TELEPHONE GIRL: Shh—! Yes, Mr J.—? No—Miss A. ain't in yet—I'll tell her, Mr J.—just the minute she gets in.

STENOGRAPHER: She's late again, huh?

TELEPHONE GIRL: Out with her sweetie last night, huh?

FILING CLERK: Hot dog.

ADDING CLERK: She ain't got a sweetie.

STENOGRAPHER: How do you know?

ADDING CLERK: I know.

FILING CLERK: Hot dog.

ADDING CLERK: She lives alone with her mother.

TELEPHONE GIRL: Spring 1876? Hello—Spring 1876. Spring! Hello, Spring 1876? 1876! Wrong number! Hello! Hello!

STENOGRAPHER: Director's meeting semi-annual report card.

FILING CLERK: Shipments—Sales—Schedules—S.

ADDING CLERK: She doesn't belong in an office.

TELEPHONE GIRL: Who does?

STENOGRAPHER: I do!

ADDING CLERK: You said it!

FILING CLERK: Hot dog!

TELEPHONE GIRL: Hello—hello—George H. Jones Company—hello—hello—

STENOGRAPHER: I'm efficient. She's inefficient.

FILING CLERK: She's inefficient.

TELEPHONE GIRL: She's got J. going.

STENOGRAPHER: Going?

TELEPHONE GIRL: Going and coming.

FILING CLERK: Hot dog.

   (*Enter* JONES.)

JONES: Good morning, everybody.

TELEPHONE GIRL: Good morning.

FILING CLERK: Good morning.

ADDING CLERK: Good morning.

STENOGRAPHER: Good morning, Mr J.

JONES: Miss A. isn't in yet?

TELEPHONE GIRL: Not yet, Mr J.

FILING CLERK: Not yet.

ADDING CLERK: Not yet.

STENOGRAPHER: She's late.

JONES: I just wanted her to take a letter.

STENOGRAPHER: I'll take the letter.

JONES: One thing at a time and that done well.

ADDING CLERK: (*yessing*) Done well.

STENOGRAPHER: I'll finish it later.

JONES: Hew to the line.

ADDING CLERK: Hew to the line.

STENOGRAPHER: Then I'll hurry.

JONES: Haste makes waste.

ADDING CLERK: Waste.

STENOGRAPHER: But if you're in a hurry.

JONES: I'm never in a hurry— That's how I get ahead! (*Laughs. They all laugh*) First know you're right—then go ahead.

ADDING CLERK: Ahead.

JONES: (*to* TELEPHONE GIRL) When Miss A. comes in tell her I want her to take a letter. (*Turns to go in—then*) It's important.

TELEPHONE GIRL: (*making a note*) Miss A.—important.

JONES: (*starts up—then*) And I don't want to be disturbed.

TELEPHONE GIRL: You're in conference?

JONES: I'm in conference. (*turns—then*) Unless it's A.B.—of course.

TELEPHONE GIRL: Of course—A.B.

JONES: (*starts—turns again; attempts to be facetious*) Tell Miss A. the early bird catches the worm.

   (*Exit* JONES.)

TELEPHONE GIRL: The early worm gets caught.

ADDING CLERK: He's caught.

TELEPHONE GIRL: Hooked.

ADDING CLERK: In the pan.

FILING CLERK: Hot dog.

STENOGRAPHER: We beg leave to announce——

(Enter YOUNG WOMAN. *Goes behind telephone booth to desk* R.)

STENOGRAPHER: You're late!

FILING CLERK: You're late.

ADDING CLERK: You're late.

STENOGRAPHER: And yesterday!

FILING CLERK: The day before.

ADDING CLERK: And the day before.

STENOGRAPHER: You'll lose your job.

YOUNG WOMAN: No!

STENOGRAPHER: No?

*(*WORKERS *exchange glances.)*

YOUNG WOMAN: I can't!

STENOGRAPHER: Can't?

(Same business.)

FILING CLERK: Rent—bills—installments—miscellaneous.

ADDING CLERK: A dollar ten—ninety-five—3.40—35—12.60.

STENOGRAPHER: Then why are you late?

YOUNG WOMAN: Why?

STENOGRAPHER: Excuse!

ADDING CLERK: Excuse!

FILING CLERK: Excuse.

TELEPHONE GIRL: Excuse it, please.

STENOGRAPHER: Why?

YOUNG WOMAN: The subway?

TELEPHONE GIRL: Long distance?

FILING CLERK: Old stuff!

ADDING CLERK: That stall!

STENOGRAPHER: Stalled?

YOUNG WOMAN: No——

STENOGRAPHER: What?

YOUNG WOMAN: I had to get out!

ADDING CLERK: Out!

FILING CLERK: Out?

STENOGRAPHER: Out where?

YOUNG WOMAN: In the air!

STENOGRAPHER: Air?

YOUNG WOMAN: All those bodies pressing.

FILING CLERK: Hot dog!

YOUNG WOMAN: I thought I would faint! I had to get out in the air!

FILING CLERK: Give her the air.

ADDING CLERK: Free air—

STENOGRAPHER: Hot air.

YOUNG WOMAN: Like I'm dying.

STENOGRAPHER: Same thing yesterday. *(Pause)* And the day before.

YOUNG WOMAN: Yes—what am I going to do?

ADDING CLERK: Take a taxi!

*(*THEY *laugh.)*

FILING CLERK: Call a cop!

TELEPHONE GIRL: Mr J. wants you.

YOUNG WOMAN: Me?

TELEPHONE GIRL: You!

YOUNG WOMAN: *(rises)* Mr J.!

STENOGRAPHER: Mr J.

TELEPHONE GIRL: He's bellowing for you!

*(*YOUNG WOMAN *gives last pat to her hair—goes off into door—back.)*

STENOGRAPHER: *(after her)* Get it just right.

FILING CLERK: She's always doing that to her hair.

TELEPHONE GIRL: It gives a line—it gives a line—

FILING CLERK: Hot dog.

ADDING CLERK: She's artistic.

STENOGRAPHER: She's inefficient.

FILING CLERK: She's inefficient.

STENOGRAPHER: Mr J. knows she's inefficient.

ADDING CLERK: 46-23-84-2-2-2-1,492—678.

TELEPHONE GIRL: Hello—hello—George H. Jones Company—hello—Mr Jones? He's in conference.

STENOGRAPHER: *(sarcastic)* Conference!

ADDING CLERK: Conference.

FILING CLERK: Hot dog!

TELEPHONE GIRL: Do you think he'll marry her?

ADDING CLERK: If she'll have him.

STENOGRAPHER: If she'll have him!

FILING CLERK: Do you think she'll have him?

TELEPHONE GIRL: How much does he get?

ADDING CLERK: Plenty—5,000—10,000—15,000—20,000—25,000.

STENOGRAPHER: And plenty put away.

ADDING CLERK: Gas Preferred—4's—steel—5's—oil—6's.

FILING CLERK: Hot dog.

STENOGRAPHER: Will she have him? Will she have him? This agreement entered into—party of the first part—party of the second part—will he have her?

TELEPHONE GIRL: Well, I'd hate to get into bed with him. *(Familiar melting voice)* Hello—humhum—hum—hum—hold the line a minute—will you—hum hum. *(Professional voice)* Hell, hello—A.B., just a minute, Mr A.B.—Mr J.? Mr A.B.—go ahead, Mr A.B. *(Melting voice)* We were interrupted—huh—huh—huh-huhuh—hum—hum.
(Enter YOUNG WOMAN—*she goes to her chair, sits with folded hands.)*

FILING CLERK: That's all you ever say to a guy—

STENOGRAPHER: Hum—hum—or uh huh— *(Negative)*

TELEPHONE GIRL: That's all you have to. *(To phone)* Hum—hum—hum hum—hum hum—

STENOGRAPHER: Mostly hum hum.

ADDING CLERK: You've said it!

FILING CLERK: Hot dog.

TELEPHONE GIRL: Hum hum huh hum humhumhum—tonight? She's got a date—she told me last night—humhumhuh—hum—all right. *(Disconnects)* Too bad—my boy friend's got a friend—but my girl friend's got a date.

YOUNG WOMAN: You have a good time.

TELEPHONE GIRL: Big time.

STENOGRAPHER: Small time.

ADDING CLERK: A big time on the small time.

TELEPHONE GIRL: I'd ask you, kid, but you'd be up to your neck!

STENOGRAPHER: Neckers!

ADDING CLERK: Petters!

FILING CLERK: Sweet papas.

TELEPHONE GIRL: Want to come?

YOUNG WOMAN: Can't.

TELEPHONE GIRL: Date?

YOUNG WOMAN: My mother.

STENOGRAPHER: Worries?

TELEPHONE GIRL: Nags—hello—George H. Jones Company—Oh hello—
*(*YOUNG WOMAN *sits before her machine—hands in lap, looking at them.)*

STENOGRAPHER: Why don't you get to work?

YOUNG WOMAN: *(dreaming)* What?

ADDING CLERK: Work!

YOUNG WOMAN: Can't.

STENOGRAPHER: Can't?

YOUNG WOMAN: My machine's out of order.

STENOGRAPHER: Well, fix it!

YOUNG WOMAN: I can't—got to get somebody.

STENOGRAPHER: Somebody! Somebody! Always somebody! Here, sort the mail, then!

YOUNG WOMAN: *(rises)* All right.

STENOGRAPHER: And hurry! You're late.

YOUNG WOMAN: *(sorting letters)* George H. Jones & Company—George H. Jones Inc. George H. Jones—

STENOGRAPHER: You're always late.

ADDING CLERK: You'll lose your job.

YOUNG WOMAN: *(hurrying)* George H. Jones—George H. Jones Personal—

TELEPHONE GIRL: Don't let 'em get your goat, kid—tell 'em where to get off.

YOUNG WOMAN: What?

TELEPHONE GIRL: Ain't it all set?

YOUNG WOMAN: What?

TELEPHONE GIRL: You and Mr J.

STENOGRAPHER: You and the boss.

FILING CLERK: You and the big chief.

ADDING CLERK: You and the big cheese.

YOUNG WOMAN: Did he tell you?

TELEPHONE GIRL: I told you!

ADDING CLERK: I told you!

STENOGRAPHER: I don't believe it.

ADDING CLERK: 5,000—10,000—15,000.

FILING CLERK: Hot dog.

YOUNG WOMAN: No—it isn't so.

STENOGRAPHER: Isn't it?

YOUNG WOMAN: No.

TELEPHONE GIRL: Not yet.

ADDING CLERK: But soon.

FILING CLERK: Hot dog.
(Enter JONES.)*

TELEPHONE GIRL: *(busy)* George H. Jones Company—Hello—Hello.

STENOGRAPHER: Awaiting your answer—

ADDING CLERK: 5,000—10,000—15,000—

JONES: *(crossing to* YOUNG WOMAN—*puts hand on her shoulder,* ALL *stop and stare)* That letter done?

YOUNG WOMAN: No. *(She pulls away)*

JONES: What's the matter?

STENOGRAPHER: She hasn't started.

JONES: O.K.—want to make some changes.

YOUNG WOMAN: My machine's out of order.

JONES: O.K.—use the one in my room.

YOUNG WOMAN: I'm sorting the mail.

STENOGRAPHER: *(sarcastic)* One thing at a time!

JONES: *(retreating—goes back* C.*)* O.K. *(To* YOUNG WOMAN*)* When you're finished. *(Starts back to his room)*

STENOGRAPHER: Haste makes waste.

JONES: *(at door)* O.K.—don't hurry. *(Exits)*

STENOGRAPHER: Hew to the line!

TELEPHONE GIRL: He's hewing.

FILING CLERK: Hot dog.

TELEPHONE GIRL: Why did you flinch, kid?

YOUNG WOMAN: Flinch?

TELEPHONE GIRL: Did he pinch?

YOUNG WOMAN: No!

TELEPHONE GIRL: Then what?

YOUNG WOMAN: Nothing!— Just his hand.

TELEPHONE GIRL: Oh—just his hand—*(Shakes her head thoughtfully)* Uhhuh. *(Negative)* Uh-huh. *(Decisively)* No! Tell him no.

STENOGRAPHER: If she does she'll lose her job.

ADDING CLERK: Fired.

FILING CLERK: The sack!

TELEPHONE GIRL: *(on the defensive)* And if she doesn't?

ADDING CLERK: She'll come to work in a taxi!

TELEPHONE GIRL: Work?

FILING CLERK: No work.

STENOGRAPHER: No worry.

ADDING CLERK: Breakfast in bed.

STENOGRAPHER: *(sarcastic)* Did Madame ring?

FILING CLERK: Lunch in bed!

TELEPHONE GIRL: A double bed! *(In phone)* Yes, Mr J. *(To* YOUNG WOMAN*)* J. wants you.

YOUNG WOMAN: *(starts to get to her feet—but doesn't)* I can't—I'm not ready—In a minute. *(Sits staring ahead of her)*

ADDING CLERK: 5,000—10,000—15,000—

FILING CLERK: Profits—plans—purchase—

STENOGRAPHER: Call your attention our prices are fixed.

TELEPHONE GIRL: Hello—hello—George H. Jones Company—hello—hello—

YOUNG WOMAN: *(thinking her thoughts aloud — to the subdued accompaniment of the office sounds and voices)* Marry me — wants to marry me — George H. Jones — George H. Jones and Company — Mrs George H. Jones — Mrs George H. Jones. Dear Madame—marry—do you take this man to be your wedded husband—I do—to love honor and to love — kisses — no — I can't — George H. Jones — How would you like to marry me — What do you say — Why Mr Jones I — let me look at your little hands — you have such pretty little hands—let me hold your pretty little hands — George H. Jones — Fat hands — flabby hands—don't touch me—please—fat hands are never weary — please don't — married — all girls—most girls—married—babies—a baby—curls—little curls all over its head — George H. Jones—straight—thin—bald—don't touch me—please — no — can't — must — somebody — something—no rest—must rest—no rest—must rest—no rest—late today—yesterday—before—late — subway — air — pressing — bodies pressing—bodies—trembling—air—stop—air—late—job—no job—fired—late—alarm clock—alarm clock—alarm clock—hurry—job—ma—nag—nag — nag — ma — hurry — job — no job — no money — installments due — no money — money—George H. Jones—money—Mrs George H. Jones—money—no work—no worry—free!—rest — sleep till nine — sleep till ten — sleep till noon — now you take a good rest this morning—don't get up till you want to — thank you — oh thank you—oh don't!—please don't touch me—I want to rest — no rest — earn — got to earn — married—earn—no—yes—earn—all girls—most girls—ma—pa—ma—all women—most women — I can't — must — maybe — must — somebody — something — ma — pa — ma — can I, ma? Tell me, ma — something — somebody.

BLACK OUT

(The sounds of the office machines continue until the scene lights into Episode 2—and the office sounds become the sound of a radio [offstage].)

EPISODE TWO: AT HOME

SCENE: A KITCHEN
Table—chairs—plates and food—
Garbage can—a pair of rubber gloves.
The door at the back now opens on a hall—
    the window, on an apartment house court.

CHARACTERS:
    YOUNG WOMAN
    MOTHER

OUTSIDE VOICES: *Characters heard, but not seen:*
    A JANITOR
    A BABY
    A MOTHER AND A SMALL BOY
    A YOUNG BOY AND YOUNG GIRL
    A HUSBAND AND A WIFE
    ANOTHER HUSBAND AND A WIFE

SOUNDS:
    Buzzer
    Radio (Voice of Announcer)
        (Music and Singer)

AT RISE:
    YOUNG WOMAN *and* MOTHER *eating—Radio*
    offstage—Radio stops.

YOUNG WOMAN: Ma—I want to talk to you.
MOTHER: Aren't you eating a potato?
YOUNG WOMAN: No.
MOTHER: Why not?
YOUNG WOMAN: I don't want one.
MOTHER: That's no reason. Here! Take one.
YOUNG WOMAN: I don't want it.
MOTHER: Potatoes go with stew—here!
YOUNG WOMAN: Ma, I don't want it!
MOTHER: Want it! Take it!
YOUNG WOMAN: But I—oh, all right. *(Takes it—then)* Ma, I want to ask you something.
MOTHER: Eat your potato.
YOUNG WOMAN: *(takes a bite—then)* Ma, there's something I want to ask you—something important.
MOTHER: Is it mealy?
YOUNG WOMAN: S'all right. Ma—tell me.

MOTHER: Three pounds for a quarter.
YOUNG WOMAN: Ma—tell me—
    (Buzzer.)
MOTHER: *(her dull voice brightening)* There's the garbage. *(Goes to door—or dumbwaiter—opens it)*
    (Stop radio.)
JANITOR'S VOICE: *(offstage)* Garbage.
MOTHER: *(pleased—busy)* All right. *(Gets garbage can—puts it out.* YOUNG WOMAN *walks up and down)* What's the matter now?
YOUNG WOMAN: Nothing.
MOTHER: That jumping up from the table every night the garbage is collected! You act like you're crazy.
YOUNG WOMAN: Ma, do all women—
MOTHER: I suppose you think you're too nice for anything so common! Well, let me tell you, my lady, that it's a very important part of life.
YOUNG WOMAN: I know, but, Ma, if you—
MOTHER: If it weren't for garbage cans where would we be? Where would we all be? Living in filth—that's what! Filth! I should think you'd be glad! I should think you'd be grateful!
YOUNG WOMAN: Oh, Ma!
MOTHER: Well, are you?
YOUNG WOMAN: Am I what?
MOTHER: Glad! Grateful.
YOUNG WOMAN: Yes!
MOTHER: You don't act like it!
YOUNG WOMAN: Oh, Ma, don't talk!
MOTHER: You just said you wanted to talk.
YOUNG WOMAN: Well now—I want to think. I got to think.
MOTHER: Aren't you going to finish your potato?
YOUNG WOMAN: Oh, Ma!
MOTHER: Is there anything the matter with it?
YOUNG WOMAN: No—
MOTHER: Then why don't you finish it?
YOUNG WOMAN: Because I don't want it.
MOTHER: Why don't you?
YOUNG WOMAN: Oh, Ma! Let me alone!
MOTHER: Well, you've got to eat! If you don't eat—
YOUNG WOMAN: Ma! Don't nag!

MOTHER: Nag! Just because I try to look out for you—nag! Just because I try to care for you—nag! Why, you haven't sense enough to eat! What would become of you I'd like to know—if I didn't nag!

(Offstage—a sound of window opening—all these offstage sounds come in through the court window at the back.)

WOMAN'S VOICE: Johnny—Johnny—come in now!

A SMALL BOY'S VOICE: Oh, Ma!

WOMAN'S VOICE: It's getting cold.

A SMALL BOY'S VOICE: Oh, Ma!

WOMAN'S VOICE: You heard me! *(Sound of window slamming)*

YOUNG WOMAN: I'm grown up, Ma.

MOTHER: Grown up! What do you mean by that?

YOUNG WOMAN: Nothing much—I guess. *(Offstage sound of baby crying.* MOTHER *rises, clatters dishes)* Let's not do the dishes right away, Ma. Let's talk—I gotta.

MOTHER: Well, I can't talk with dirty dishes around—you may be able to but—*(Clattering—clattering.)*

YOUNG WOMAN: Ma! Listen! Listen!—There's a man wants to marry me.

MOTHER: *(stops clattering—sits)* What man?

YOUNG WOMAN: He says he fell in love with my hands.

MOTHER: In love! Is that beginning again! I thought you were over that!

(Offstage BOY'S VOICE—*whistles*—GIRL'S VOICE *answers.)*

BOY'S VOICE: Come on out.

GIRL'S VOICE: Can't.

BOY'S VOICE: Nobody'll see you.

GIRL'S VOICE: I can't.

BOY'S VOICE: It's dark now—come on.

GIRL'S VOICE: Well—just for a minute.

BOY'S VOICE: Meet you round the corner.

YOUNG WOMAN: I got to get married, Ma.

MOTHER: What do you mean?

YOUNG WOMAN: I gotta.

MOTHER: You haven't got in trouble, have you?

YOUNG WOMAN: Don't talk like that!

MOTHER: Well, you say you got to get married—what do you mean?

YOUNG WOMAN: Nothing.

MOTHER: Answer me!

YOUNG WOMAN: All women get married, don't they?

MOTHER: Nonsense!

YOUNG WOMAN: You got married, didn't you?

MOTHER: Yes, I did!

(Offstage voices.)

WOMAN'S VOICE: Where you going?

MAN'S VOICE: Out.

WOMAN'S VOICE: You were out last night.

MAN'S VOICE: Was I?

WOMAN'S VOICE: You're always going out.

MAN'S VOICE: Am I?

WOMAN'S VOICE: Where you going?

MAN'S VOICE: Out.

(End of offstage voices.)

MOTHER: Who is he? Where did you come to know him?

YOUNG WOMAN: In the office.

MOTHER: In the office!

YOUNG WOMAN: It's Mr J.

MOTHER: Mr J.?

YOUNG WOMAN: The Vice-President.

MOTHER: Vice-President! His income must be—Does he know you've got a mother to support?

YOUNG WOMAN: Yes.

MOTHER: What does he say?

YOUNG WOMAN: All right.

MOTHER: How soon you going to marry him?

YOUNG WOMAN: I'm not going to.

MOTHER: Not going to!

YOUNG WOMAN: No! I'm not going to.

MOTHER: But you just said—

YOUNG WOMAN: I'm not going to.

MOTHER: Are you crazy?

YOUNG WOMAN: I can't, Ma! I can't!

MOTHER: Why can't you?

YOUNG WOMAN: I don't love him.

MOTHER: Love!—what does that amount to! Will it clothe you? Will it feed you? Will it pay the bills?

YOUNG WOMAN: No! But it's real just the same!

MOTHER: Real!

YOUNG WOMAN: If it isn't—what can you count on in life?

MOTHER: I'll tell you what you can count on! You can count that you've got to eat and sleep and get up and put clothes on your back and take 'em off again—that you got to get old—and that you got to die, That's what you can count on! All the rest is in your head!

YOUNG WOMAN: But Ma—didn't you love Pa?

MOTHER: I suppose I did—I don't know—I've forgotten—what difference does it make—now?

YOUNG WOMAN: But then!—oh Ma, tell me!

MOTHER: Tell you what?

YOUNG WOMAN: About all that—love!
    (Offstage voices.)

WIFE'S VOICE: Don't.

HUSBAND'S VOICE: What's the matter—don't you want me to kiss you?

WIFE'S VOICE: Not like that.

HUSBAND'S VOICE: Like what?

WIFE'S VOICE: That silly kiss!

HUSBAND'S VOICE: Silly kiss?

WIFE'S VOICE: You look so silly—oh I know what's coming when you look like that—and kiss me like that—don't—go away—
    (End of offstage voices.)

MOTHER: He's a decent man, isn't he?

YOUNG WOMAN: I don't know. How should I know—yet.

MOTHER: He's a Vice-President—of course he's decent.

YOUNG WOMAN: I don't care whether he's decent or not. I won't marry him.

MOTHER: But you just said you wanted to marry—

YOUNG WOMAN: Not him.

MOTHER: Who?

YOUNG WOMAN: I don't know—I don't know—I haven't found him yet!

MOTHER: You talk like you're crazy!

YOUNG WOMAN: Oh, Ma—tell me!

MOTHER: Tell you what?

YOUNG WOMAN: Tell me— *(Words suddenly pouring out)* Your skin oughtn't to curl—ought it—when he just comes near you—ought it? That's wrong, ain't it? You don't get over that, do you—ever, do you or do you? How is it, Ma—do you?

MOTHER: Do you what?

YOUNG WOMAN: Do you get used to it—so after a while it doesn't matter? Or don't you? Does it always matter? You ought to be in love, oughtn't you, Ma? You must be in love, mustn't you, Ma? That changes everything, doesn't it—or does it? Maybe if you just like a person it's all right—is it? When he puts a hand on me, my blood turns cold. But your blood oughtn't to run cold, ought it? His hands are—his hands are—fat, Ma—don't you see—his hands are fat—and they sort of press—and they're fat—don't you see?—Don't you see?

MOTHER: *(stares at her bewildered)* See what?

YOUNG WOMAN: *(rushing on)* I've always thought I'd find somebody—somebody young—and—and attractive—with wavy hair—wavy hair—I always think of children with curls—little curls all over their head—somebody young—and attractive—that I'd like—that I'd love—But I haven't found anybody like that yet—I haven't found anybody— I've hardly known anybody—you'd never let me go with anybody and—

MOTHER: Are you throwing it up to me that—

YOUNG WOMAN: No—let me finish, Ma! No—let me finish! I just mean I've never found anybody—anybody—nobody's ever asked me—till now—he's the only man that's ever asked me—And I suppose I got to marry somebody—all girls do—

MOTHER: Nonsense.

YOUNG WOMAN: But, I can't go on like this, Ma—I don't know why—but I can't—it's like I'm all tight inside—sometimes I feel like I'm stifling!— You don't know—stifling. *(Walks up and down)* I can't go on like this much longer—going to work—coming home—going to work—coming home—I can't— Sometimes in the subway I think I'm going to die—sometimes even in the office if something don't happen—I got to do something—I don't know—it's like I'm all tight inside.

MOTHER: You're crazy.

YOUNG WOMAN: Oh, Ma!

MOTHER: You're crazy!

YOUNG WOMAN: Ma—if you tell me that again I'll kill you! I'll kill you!

MOTHER: If that isn't crazy!

YOUNG WOMAN: I'll kill you— Maybe I am crazy— I don't know. Sometimes I think I am—the thoughts that go on in my mind—sometimes I think I am—I can't help it if I am— I do the best I can—I do the best I can and I'm nearly crazy! *(MOTHER rises and sits)* Go away! Go away! You don't know anything about anything! And you haven't got any pity—no pity—you just take it for granted that I go to work every day—and come home every night and bring my money every week—you just take it for granted—you'd let me go on forever—and never feel any pity— *(Offstage RADIO—a voice singing a sentimental Mother song or popular home song.)* *(MOTHER begins to cry—crosses to chair L.— sits.)*

YOUNG WOMAN: Oh Ma—forgive me! Forgive me!

MOTHER: My own child! To be spoken to like that by my own child!

YOUNG WOMAN: I didn't mean it, Ma—I didn't mean it! *(She goes to her mother—crosses to L.)*

MOTHER: *(clinging to her hand)* You're all I've got in the world—and you don't want me—you want to kill me.

YOUNG WOMAN: No—no, I don't, Ma! I just said that!

MOTHER: I've worked for you and slaved for you!

YOUNG WOMAN: I know, Ma.

MOTHER: I brought you into the world.

YOUNG WOMAN: I know, Ma.

MOTHER: You're flesh of my flesh and—

YOUNG WOMAN: I know, Ma, I know.

MOTHER: And—

YOUNG WOMAN: You rest, now, Ma—you rest—

MOTHER: *(struggling)* I got to do the dishes.

YOUNG WOMAN: I'll do the dishes— You listen to the music, Ma—I'll do the dishes. *(MOTHER sits.)* *(YOUNG WOMAN crosses to behind screen.)* *(Takes a pair of rubber gloves and begins to put them on.)*

(The MOTHER sees them—they irritate her— there is a return of her characteristic mood.)

MOTHER: Those gloves! I've been washing dishes for forty years and I never wore gloves! But my lady's hands! My lady's hands!

YOUNG WOMAN: Sometimes you talk to me like you're jealous, Ma.

MOTHER: Jealous?

YOUNG WOMAN: It's my hands got me a husband.

MOTHER: A husband? So you're going to marry him now!

YOUNG WOMAN: I suppose so.

MOTHER: If you ain't the craziest— *(The scene blacks out.)* *(In the darkness, the Mother song goes into jazz—very faint—as the scene lights into)*

EPISODE THREE: HONEYMOON

SCENE: HOTEL BEDROOM
Bed, chair, mirror
The door at the back now opens on a bathroom; the window, on a dance casino opposite.

CHARACTERS:
YOUNG WOMAN
HUSBAND
BELLBOY

OFFSTAGE:
Seen but not heard—MEN *and* WOMEN *dancing in couples.*

SOUNDS:
A small jazz band (violin, piano, saxophone—very dim, at first, then louder).

AT RISE:
Set dark.

BELLBOY, HUSBAND, *and* YOUNG WOMAN *enter.* BELLBOY *carries luggage. He switches on light by door.*
Stop music.

HUSBAND: Well, here we are. *(Throws hat on bed.)*

(BELLBOY *puts luggage down, crosses to window, raises shade three inches, opens window three inches.*)

(*Sounds of jazz music louder. Offstage.*)

BELLBOY: (*comes to man for tip*) Anything else, Sir? (*Receives tip. Exits.*)

HUSBAND: Well, here we are.

YOUNG WOMAN: Yes, here we are.

HUSBAND: Aren't you going to take your hat off—stay a while? (YOUNG WOMAN *looks around as though looking for a way out, then takes off her hat, pulls the hair automatically around her ears*) This is all right, isn't it? Huh? Huh?

YOUNG WOMAN: It's very nice.

HUSBAND: Twelve bucks a day! They know how to soak you in these pleasure resorts. Twelve bucks! (*Music*) Well—we'll get our money's worth out of it all right. (*Goes toward bathroom*) I'm going to wash up. (*Stops at door*) Don't you want to wash up? (YOUNG WOMAN *shakes head "No"*) I do! It was a long trip! I want to wash up! (*Goes off—closes door. Sings in bathroom.* YOUNG WOMAN *goes to window—raises shade—sees the dancers going round and round in couples. Music is louder. Re-enter* HUSBAND) Say, pull that blind down! They can see in!

YOUNG WOMAN: I thought you said there'd be a view of the ocean!

HUSBAND: Sure there is.

YOUNG WOMAN: I just see people—dancing.

HUSBAND: The ocean's beyond.

YOUNG WOMAN: (*desperately*) I was counting on seeing it!

HUSBAND: You'll see it tomorrow—what's eating you? We'll take in the boardwalk— Don't you want to wash up?

YOUNG WOMAN: No!

HUSBAND: It was a long trip. Sure you don't? (YOUNG WOMAN *shakes her head "No."* HUSBAND *takes off his coat—puts it over chair*) Better make yourself at home. I'm going to. (*She stares at him—moves away from the window*) Say, pull down that blind! (*Crosses to chair down* L.—*sits.*)

YOUNG WOMAN: It's close—don't you think it's close?

HUSBAND: Well—you don't want people looking in, do you? (*Laughs*) Huh—huh?

YOUNG WOMAN: No.

HUSBAND: (*laughs*) I guess not. Huh? (*Takes off shoes.* YOUNG WOMAN *leaves the window, and crosses down to the bed.*) Say—you look a little white around the gills! What's the matter?

YOUNG WOMAN: Nothing.

HUSBAND: You look like you're scared.

YOUNG WOMAN: No.

HUSBAND: Nothing to be scared of. You're with your husband, you know. (*Takes her to chair, left.*)

YOUNG WOMAN: I know.

HUSBAND: Happy?

YOUNG WOMAN: Yes.

HUSBAND: (*sitting*) Then come here and give us a kiss. (*He puts her on his knee*) That's the girlie. (*He bends her head down, and kisses her along the back of her neck*) Like that? (*She tries to get to her feet*) Say—stay there! What you moving for? —You know—you got to learn to relax, little girl— (*Dancers go off. Dim lights. Pinches her above knee*) Say, what you got under there?

YOUNG WOMAN: Nothing.

HUSBAND: Nothing! (*Laughs*) That's a good one! Nothing, huh? Huh? That reminds of the story of the Pullman porter and the—what's the matter—did I tell you that one?

(*Music dims off and out.*)

YOUNG WOMAN: I don't know.

HUSBAND: The Pullman porter and the tart?

YOUNG WOMAN: No.

HUSBAND: It's a good one—well—the train was just pulling out and the tart—

YOUNG WOMAN: You did tell that one!

HUSBAND: About the—

YOUNG WOMAN: Yes! Yes! I remember now!

HUSBAND: About the—

YOUNG WOMAN: Yes!

HUSBAND: All right—if I did. You're sure it was the one about the—

YOUNG WOMAN: I'm sure.

HUSBAND: When he asked her what she had underneath her seat and she said—

YOUNG WOMAN: Yes! Yes! That one!

HUSBAND: All right— But I don't believe I did. (SHE *tries to get up again, as* HE *holds her*) You know you have got something under there— what is it?

YOUNG WOMAN: Nothing—just—just my garter.

HUSBAND: Your garter! Your garter! Say did I tell you the one about—

YOUNG WOMAN: Yes! Yes!

HUSBAND: (*with dignity*) How do you know which one I meant?

YOUNG WOMAN: You told me them all!

HUSBAND: (*pulling her back to his knee*) No, I didn't! Not by a jugful! I got a lot of 'em up my sleeve yet—that's part of what I owe my success to—my ability to spring a good story— You know—you got to learn to relax, little girl—haven't you?

YOUNG WOMAN: Yes.

HUSBAND: That's one of the biggest things to learn in life. That's part of what I owe my success to. Now you go and get those heavy things off— and relax.

YOUNG WOMAN: They're not heavy.

HUSBAND: You haven't got much on—have you? But you'll feel better with 'em off. (*Gets up*) Want me to help you?

YOUNG WOMAN: No.

HUSBAND: I'm your husband, you know.

YOUNG WOMAN: I know.

HUSBAND: You aren't afraid of your husband, are you?

YOUNG WOMAN: No—of course not—but I thought maybe—can't we go out for a little while?

HUSBAND: Out? What for?

YOUNG WOMAN: Fresh air—walk—talk.

HUSBAND: We can talk here—I'll tell you all about myself. Go along now. (YOUNG WOMAN *goes toward bathroom door—gets bag.*) Where are you going?

YOUNG WOMAN: In here.

HUSBAND: I thought you'd want to wash up.

YOUNG WOMAN: I just want to—get ready.

HUSBAND: You don't have to go in there to take your clothes off!

YOUNG WOMAN: I want to.

HUSBAND: What for?

YOUNG WOMAN: I always do.

HUSBAND: What?

YOUNG WOMAN: Undress by myself.

HUSBAND: You've never been married till now— have you? (*Laughs*) Or have you been putting something over on me?

YOUNG WOMAN: No.

HUSBAND: I understand—kind of modest—huh? Huh?

YOUNG WOMAN: Yes.

HUSBAND: I understand women— (*Indulgently*) Go along. (*She goes off—starts to close door.* YOUNG WOMAN *exits.*) Don't close the door— thought you wanted to talk. (*He looks around the room with satisfaction—after a pause— Rises— takes off his collar.*) You're awful quiet—what are you doing in there?

YOUNG WOMAN: Just—getting ready—

HUSBAND: (*still in his mood of satisfaction*) I'm going to enjoy life from now on— I haven't had such an easy time of it. I got where I am by hard work and self denial—now I'm going to enjoy life—I'm going to make up for all I missed— aren't you about ready?

YOUNG WOMAN: Not yet.

HUSBAND: Next year maybe we'll go to Paris. You can buy a lot of that French underwear—and Switzerland—all my life I've wanted a Swiss watch—that I bought right there— I coulda' got a Swiss watch here, but I always wanted one that I bought right there— Isn't that funny—huh? Isn't it? Huh? Huh?

YOUNG WOMAN: Yes.

HUSBAND: All my life I've wanted a Swiss watch that I bought right there. All my life I've counted on having that some day—more than anything— except one thing—you know what?

YOUNG WOMAN: No.

HUSBAND: Guess.

YOUNG WOMAN: I can't.

HUSBAND: Then I'm coming in and tell you.

YOUNG WOMAN: No! Please! Please don't.

HUSBAND: Well hurry up then! I thought you women didn't wear much of anything these days—huh? Huh? I'm coming in!

YOUNG WOMAN: No—no! Just a minute!

HUSBAND: All right. Just a minute!

(YOUNG WOMAN *is silent.*)

HUSBAND: *(laughs and takes out watch)* 13— 14— I'm counting the seconds on you—that's what you said, didn't you—just a minute! — 49—50—51—52—53—

(Enter YOUNG WOMAN.)

YOUNG WOMAN: *(at the door)* Here I am.

(*She wears a little white gown that hangs very straight. She is very still, but her eyes are wide with a curious, helpless, animal terror.*)

HUSBAND: *(starts toward her—stops. The room is in shadow except for one dim light by the bed. Sound of* YOUNG WOMAN *weeping)* You crying? *(Sound of weeping)* What you crying for? *(Crosses to her)*

YOUNG WOMAN: *(crying out)* Ma! Ma! I want my mother!

HUSBAND: I thought you were glad to get away from her.

YOUNG WOMAN: I want her now—I want somebody.

HUSBAND: You got me, haven't you?

YOUNG WOMAN: Somebody—somebody—

HUSBAND: There's nothing to cry about. There's nothing to cry about.

BLACK OUT

(*The music continues until the lights go up for* EPISODE FOUR.)

(*Rhythm of the music is gradually replaced by the sound of steel riveting for* EPISODE FOUR.)

EPISODE FOUR: MATERNAL

SCENE: *A room in a hospital. The door in the back now opens on a corridor; the window, on a tall building going up.*

Bed. Chair.

CHARACTERS IN THE SCENE:
  YOUNG WOMAN
  DOCTORS
  NURSES
  HUSBAND

OUTSIDE—CORRIDOR LIFE:

CHARACTERS SEEN BUT NOT HEARD:
  WOMAN IN WHEEL CHAIR
  WOMAN IN BATHROBE
  STRETCHER WAGON
  NURSE WITH TRAY
  NURSE WITH COVERED BASIN

SOUNDS:
(*outside window*) *Riveting.*

AT RISE:
YOUNG WOMAN *lies still in bed.*

The door is open.

In the corridor, a stretcher wagon goes by.

Enter NURSE.

NURSE: How are you feeling today? *(No response from* YOUNG WOMAN) Better? *(No response)* No pain? *(No response.* NURSE *takes her watch in one hand,* YOUNG WOMAN'S *wrist in the other— stands, then goes to chart at foot of bed—writes)* You're getting along fine. *(No response)* Such a sweet baby you have, too. *(No response)* Aren't you glad it's a girl? *(*YOUNG WOMAN *makes sign with her head, "No")* You're not! Oh, my! That's no way to talk! Men want boys—women ought to want girls. *(No response)* Maybe you didn't want either, eh? *(*YOUNG WOMAN *signs "No." Riveting machine)* You'll feel different when it begins to nurse. You'll just love it then. Your milk hasn't come yet—has it? *(Sign—"No")* It will! *(Sign— "No")* Oh, you don't know Doctor! *(Goes to door—turns)* Anything else you want? *(*YOUNG WOMAN *points to window)* Draft? *(Sign—"No")* The noise? *(*YOUNG WOMAN *signs "Yes")* Oh, that can't be helped. Hospital's got to have a new wing. We're the biggest Maternity Hospital in the world. I'll close the window, though. *(*YOUNG WOMAN *signs "No")* No?

YOUNG WOMAN: *(whispers)* I smell everything then.

NURSE: *(starting out the door—Riveting machine)* Here's your man!

(Enter HUSBAND with large bouquet. Crosses to bed.)

HUSBAND: Well, how are we today?

(YOUNG WOMAN—no response)

NURSE: She's getting stronger!

HUSBAND: Of course she is!

NURSE: *(taking flowers)* See what your husband brought you.

HUSBAND: Better put 'em in water right away. *(Exit NURSE)* Everything O.K.? *(YOUNG WOMAN signs "No")* Now see here, my dear, you've got to brace up, you know! And—and face things! Everybody's got to brace up and face things! That's what makes the world go round. I know all you've been through but— *(YOUNG WOMAN signs "No")* Oh, yes I do! I know all about it! I was right outside all the time! *(YOUNG WOMAN makes violent gesture of "No." Ignoring)* Oh yes! But you've got to brace up now! Make an effort! Pull yourself together! Start the uphill climb! Oh I've been down—but I haven't stayed down. I've been licked but I haven't stayed licked! I've pulled myself up by my own bootstraps, and that's what you've got to do! Will power! That's what conquers! Look at me! Now you've got to brace up! Face the music! Stand the gaff! Take life by the horns! Look it in the face! —Having a baby's natural! Perfectly natural thing—why should—

(YOUNG WOMAN chokes—points wildly to door. Enter NURSE with flowers in a vase.)

NURSE: What's the matter?

HUSBAND: She's got that gagging again—like she had the last time I was here.

(YOUNG WOMAN gestures him out.)

NURSE: Better go, sir.

HUSBAND: *(at door)* I'll be back.

(YOUNG WOMAN gasping and gesturing.)

NURSE: She needs rest.

HUSBAND: Tomorrow then. I'll be back tomorrow—tomorrow and every day—goodbye.

(Exits.)

NURSE: You got a mighty nice husband, I guess you know that? *(Writes on chart)* Gagging.

(Corridor life—WOMAN IN BATHROBE passes door. Enter DOCTOR, YOUNG DOCTOR, NURSE wheeling surgeon's wagon with bottles, instruments, etc.)

DOCTOR: How's the little lady today? *(Crosses to bed.)*

NURSE: She's better, Doctor.

DOCTOR: Of course she's better! She's all right—aren't you? *(YOUNG WOMAN does not respond)* What's the matter? Can't you talk?

(Drops her hand—takes chart.)

NURSE: She's a little weak yet, Doctor.

DOCTOR: *(at chart)* Milk hasn't come yet?

NURSE: No, Doctor.

DOCTOR: Put the child to breast. *(YOUNG WOMAN—"No—no!"—Riveting machine)* No? Don't you want to nurse your baby? *(YOUNG WOMAN signs "No")* Why not? *(No response)* These modern neurotic women, eh, Doctor? What are we going to do with 'em? *(YOUNG DOCTOR laughs. NURSE smiles)* Bring the baby!

YOUNG WOMAN: No!

DOCTOR: Well—that's strong enough. I thought you were too weak to talk—that's better. You don't want your baby?

YOUNG WOMAN: No.

DOCTOR: What do you want?

YOUNG WOMAN: Let alone—let alone.

DOCTOR: Bring the baby.

NURSE: Yes, Doctor—she's behaved very badly every time, Doctor—very upset—maybe we better not.

DOCTOR: I decide what we better and better not here, Nurse!

NURSE: Yes, Doctor.

DOCTOR: Bring the baby.

NURSE: Yes, Doctor.

DOCTOR: *(with chart)* Gagging—you mean nausea.

NURSE: Yes, Doctor, but—

DOCTOR: No buts, nurse.

NURSE: Yes, Doctor.

DOCTOR: Nausea!— Change her diet!—What is her diet?

NURSE: Liquids.

DOCTOR: Give her solids.

NURSE: Yes, Doctor. She says she can't swallow solids.

DOCTOR: Give her solids.

NURSE: Yes, Doctor. *(Starts to go)*

(Riveting machine.)

DOCTOR: Wait—I'll change her medicine. *(Takes pad and writes prescription in Latin. Hands it to* NURSE*)* After meals. *(To door)* Bring her baby. *(Exit* DOCTOR, *followed by* YOUNG DOCTOR *and* NURSE *with surgeon's wagon.)*

NURSE: Yes, Doctor.

(Exits.)

YOUNG WOMAN: *(alone)* Let me alone — let me alone — let me alone — I've submitted to enough — I won't submit to any more — crawl off — crawl off in the dark — Vixen crawled under the bed — way back in the corner under the bed — they were all drowned — puppies don't go to heaven — heaven — golden stairs — long stairs — long — too long — long golden stairs — climb those golden stairs — stairs — stairs — climb — tired — too tired — dead — no matter — nothing matters — dead — stairs — long stairs — all the dead going up — going up to be in heaven — heaven — golden stairs — all the children coming down — coming down to be born — dead going up — children coming down — going up — coming down — going up — coming down — going up — coming down — going up — stop — stop — no — no traffic cop — no — no traffic cop in heaven — traffic cop — traffic cop — can't you give us a smile — tired — too tired — no matter — it doesn't matter — St. Peter — St. Peter at the gate — you can't come in — no matter — it doesn't matter — I'll rest — I'll lie down — down — all written down — down in a big book — no matter — it doesn't matter — I'll lie down — it weighs me — it's over me — it weighs — weighs — it's heavy — it's a heavy book — no matter — lie still — don't move — can't move — rest — forget — they say you forget — a girl — aren't you glad it's a girl — a little girl — with no hair — none — little curls all over his head — a little bald girl — curls — curls all over his head — what kind of hair has God? no matter — it doesn't matter — everybody loves God — they've got to — got to — got to love God — God is love — even if he's bad they got to love him — even if he's got fat hands — fat hands — no no — he wouldn't be God — His hands make you well — He lays on his hands — well — and happy — no matter — doesn't matter — far — too far — tired — too tired Vixen crawled off under bed — eight — there were eight — a woman crawled off under the bed — a woman has one — two three four — one two three four — one two three four — two plus two is four — two times two is four — two times four is eight Vixen had eight — one two three four five six seven eight — eight — Puffie had eight — all drowned — drowned — drowned in blood — blood — oh God! God — God never had one — Mary had one — in a manger — the lowly manger — God's on a high throne — far — too far — no matter — it doesn't matter — God Mary Mary God Mary — Virgin Mary — Mary had one — the Holy Ghost — the Holy Ghost — George H. Jones — oh don't — please don't! Let me rest — now I can rest — the weight is gone — inside the weight is gone — it's only outside — outside — all around — weight — I'm under it — Vixen crawled under the bed — there were eight — I'll not submit any more — I'll not submit — I'll not submit —

(The scene BLACKS OUT. *The sound of riveting continues until it goes into the sound of an electric piano and the scene lights up for* EPISODE FIVE.*)*

EPISODE FIVE: PROHIBITED

SCENE: *Bar—Bottles—Tables—Chairs—Electric piano.*

SOUND: *Electric piano.*

CHARACTERS:

MAN *behind the bar*
POLICEMAN *at bar*

WAITER

At Table 1. A MAN *and a* WOMAN

At Table 2. A MAN *and a* BOY

At Table 3. TWO MEN *waiting for* TWO GIRLS, *who are*

TELEPHONE GIRL *of Episode One and* YOUNG WOMAN.

AT RISE: *Everyone except the* GIRLS *on. Of the characters, the* MAN *and* WOMAN *at Table 1 are an ordinary man and woman.* THE MAN *at Table 2 is a middle-aged fairy; the* BOY *is young, untouched. At Table 3,* 1ST MAN *is pleasing, common, vigorous. He has coarse, wavy hair.* 2ND MAN *is an ordinary salesman type.*

1ST MAN: *(at Table 3)* I'm going to beat it.

2ND MAN: Oh, for the love of Mike.

1ST MAN: They ain't going to show.

2ND MAN: Sure they'll show.

1ST MAN: How do you know they'll show?

2ND MAN: I tell you you can't keep that baby away from me—just got to—*(Snaps fingers)*—She comes running.

1ST MAN: Looks like it.

2ND MAN: *(to* WAITER—*makes sign "2," with his fingers)* The same.

(WAITER *goes to the bar.*)

MAN: *(at Table 2)* Oh, I'm sorry I brought you here.

BOY: Why?

MAN: This Purgatory of noise! I brought you here to give you pleasure—let you taste pleasure. This sherry they have here is bottled—heaven. Wait till you taste it.

BOY: But I don't drink.

MAN: Drink! This isn't drink! Real amontillado is sunshine and orange groves—it's the Mediterranean and blue moonlight and—love? Have you ever been in love?

BOY: No.

MAN: Never in love with—a woman?

BOY: No—not really.

MAN: What do you mean—really?

BOY: Just—that.

MAN: Ah! *(Makes sign to* WAITER*)* Two—you know what I want—Two.

(WAITER *goes to the bar.*)

MAN: *(at Table 1)* Well, are you going through with it, or ain't you?

WOMAN: That's what I want to do—go through with it.

MAN: But you can't.

WOMAN: Why can't I?

MAN: How can yuh? *(Silence)* It's nothing—most women don't think anything about it—they just—Bert told me a doctor to go to—gave me the address—

WOMAN: Don't talk about it!

MAN: Got to talk about it—you got to get out of this. *(Silence—*MAN *makes sign to* WAITER*)* What you having?

WOMAN: Nothing—I don't want anything. I had enough.

MAN: Do you good. The same?

WOMAN: I suppose so.

MAN: *(makes sign "2" to* WAITER*)* The same.

(WAITER *goes to the bar.*)

(*At Table 3.*)

1ST MAN: I'm going to beat it.

2ND MAN: Oh say, listen! I'm counting on you to take the other one off my hands.

1ST MAN: I'm going to beat it.

2ND MAN: For the love of Mike have a heart! Listen—as a favor to me—I got to be home by six—I promised my wife—sure. That don't leave me no time at all if we got to hang around—entertain some dame. You got to take her off my hands.

1ST MAN: Maybe she won't fall for me.

2ND MAN: Sure she'll fall for you! They all fall for you—even my wife likes you—tries to kid herself it's your brave exploits, but I know what it is—sure she'll fall for you.

(*Enter two girls*—TELEPHONE GIRL *and* YOUNG WOMAN.*)

GIRL: *(coming to table)* Hello—

2ND MAN: *(grouch)* Good night.

GIRL: Good night? What's eatin' yuh?

2ND MAN: *(same)* Nothin's eatin' me—thought somethin' musta swallowed you.

GIRL: Why?

2ND MAN: You're late!

GIRL: *(unimpressed)* Oh—(*Brushing it aside*)—Mrs Jones—Mr Smith.

2ND MAN: Meet my friend, Mr Roe. *(They all sit. To the* WAITER*)* The same, and two more. *(*WAITER *goes.)*

GIRL: So we kept you waiting, did we?

2ND MAN: Only about an hour.

YOUNG WOMAN: Was it that long?

2ND MAN: We been here that long—ain't we, Dick?

1ST MAN: Just about, Harry.

2ND MAN: For the love of God what delayed yuh?

GIRL: Tell Helen that one.

2ND MAN: *(to* YOUNG WOMAN*)* The old Irish woman that went to her first race? Bet on the skate that came in last—she went up to the jockey and asked him, "For the love of God, what delayed yuh?" *(All laugh)*

YOUNG WOMAN: Why, that's kinda funny!

2ND MAN: Kinda!—What do you mean kinda?

YOUNG WOMAN: I just mean there are not many of 'em that are funny at all.

2ND MAN: Not if you haven't heard the funny ones.

YOUNG WOMAN: Oh I've heard 'em all.

1ST MAN: Not a laugh in a carload, eh?

GIRL: Got a cigarette?

2ND MAN: *(with package)* One of these?

GIRL: *(taking one)* Uhhuh.

(He offers the package to YOUNG WOMAN.*)*

YOUNG WOMAN: *(taking one)* Uhhuh.

2ND MAN: *(to* 1ST MAN*)* One of these?

1ST MAN: *(showing his own package)* Thanks—I like these. *(He lights* YOUNG WOMAN's *cigarette)*

2ND MAN: *(lighting* GIRL's *cigarette)* Well—baby—how they comin', huh?

GIRL: Couldn't be better.

2ND MAN: How's every little thing?

GIRL: Just great.

2ND MAN: Miss me?

GIRL: I'll say so—when did you get in?

2ND MAN: Just a coupla hours ago.

GIRL: Miss me?

2ND MAN: Did I? You don't know the half of it.

YOUNG WOMAN: *(interrupting restlessly)* Can we dance here?

2ND MAN: Not here.

YOUNG WOMAN: Where do we go from here?

2ND MAN: Where do we go from here! You just got here!

1ST MAN: What's the hurry?

2ND MAN: What's the rush?

YOUNG WOMAN: I don't know.

GIRL: Helen wants to dance.

YOUNG WOMAN: I just want to keep moving.

1ST MAN: *(smiling)* You want to keep moving, huh?

2ND MAN: You must be one of those restless babies! Where do we go from here!

YOUNG WOMAN: It's only some days—I want to keep moving.

1ST MAN: You want to keep moving, huh? *(He is staring at her smilingly)*

YOUNG WOMAN: *(nods)* Uhhuh.

1ST MAN: *(quietly)* Stick around a while.

2ND MAN: Where do we go from here! Say, what kind of a crowd do you run with, anyway?

GIRL: Helen don't run with any crowd—do you, Helen?

YOUNG WOMAN: *(embarrassed)* No.

1ST MAN: Well, I'm not a crowd—run with me.

2ND MAN: *(gratified)* All set, huh?—Dick was about ready to beat it.

1ST MAN: That's before I met the little lady. *(*WAITER *serves drinks.)*

1ST MAN: Here's how.

2ND MAN: Here's to you.

GIRL: Here's looking at you.

YOUNG WOMAN: Here's—happy days. *(They all drink.)*

1ST MAN: That's good stuff!

2ND MAN: Off a boat.

1ST MAN: Off a boat?

2ND MAN: They get all their stuff here—off a boat.

GIRL: That's what *they* say.

2ND MAN: No! Sure! Sure they do! Sure!

GIRL: It's all right with me.

2ND MAN: But they do! Sure!

GIRL: I believe you, darling!

2ND MAN: Did you miss me?

GIRL: Uhhuh. (*Affirmative*)

2ND MAN: Any other daddies?

GIRL: Uhhuh. (*Negative*)

2ND MAN: Love any daddy but daddy?

GIRL: Uhhuh. (*Negative*)

2ND MAN: Let's beat it!

GIRL: (*a little self-conscious before* YOUNG WOMAN) We just got here.

2ND MAN: Don't I know it—Come on!

GIRL: But—(*Indicates* YOUNG WOMAN)

2ND MAN: (*not understanding*) They're all set—aren't you?

1ST MAN: (*to* YOUNG WOMAN) Are we?
(*She doesn't answer*)

2ND MAN: I got to be out to the house by six—come on—(*Rising—to* GIRL) Come on, kid—let's us beat it! (GIRL *indicates* YOUNG WOMAN) (*Now understanding—very elaborate.*) Business is business, you know! I got a lot to do yet this afternoon—thought you might go along with me—help me out—how about it?

GIRL: (*rising, her dignity preserved*) Sure—I'll go along with you—help you out.
(*Both rise.*)

2ND MAN: All right with you folks?

1ST MAN: All right with me.

2ND MAN: All right with you? (*To* YOUNG WOMAN)

YOUNG WOMAN: All right with me.

2ND MAN: Come on, kid. (*They rise*) Where's the damage?

1ST MAN: Go on!

2ND MAN: No!

1ST MAN: Go on!

2ND MAN: I'll match you.

YOUNG WOMAN: Heads win!

GIRL: Heads I win—tails you lose.

2ND MAN: (*impatiently*) He's matching me.

1ST MAN: Am I matching you or you matching me?

2ND MAN: I'm matching you. (*They match*) You're stung!

1ST MAN: (*contentedly*) Not so you can notice it.
(*Smiles at* YOUNG WOMAN)

GIRL: That's for you, Helen.

2ND MAN: She ain't dumb! Come on.

GIRL: (*to* 1ST MAN) You be nice to her now. She's very fastidious. —Goodbye.
(*Exit* 2ND MAN *and* GIRL.)

YOUNG WOMAN: I know what business is like.

1ST MAN: You do—do yuh?

YOUNG WOMAN: I used to be a business girl myself before—

1ST MAN: Before what?

YOUNG WOMAN: Before I quit.

1ST MAN: What did you quit for?

YOUNG WOMAN: I just quit.

1ST MAN: You're married, huh?

YOUNG WOMAN: Yes—I am.

1ST MAN: All right with me.

YOUNG WOMAN: Some men don't seem to like a woman after she's married—
(WAITER *comes to the table.*)

1ST MAN: What's the difference?

YOUNG WOMAN: Depends on the man, I guess.

1ST MAN: Depends on the woman, I guess. (*To* WAITER, *makes sign of "2"*) The same.
(WAITER *goes to the bar.*)

(*At Table 1.*)

MAN: It don't amount to nothing. God! Most women just—

WOMAN: I know—I know—I know.

MAN: They don't think nothing of it. They just—

WOMAN: I know—I know—I know.
(*Re-enter* 2ND MAN *and* GIRL. *They go to Table 3.*)

2ND MAN: Say, I forgot—I want you to do something for me, will yuh?

1ST MAN: Sure—what is it?

2ND MAN: I want you to telephone me out home tomorrow—and ask me to come into town—will yuh?

1ST MAN: Sure—why not?

2ND MAN: You know—business—get me?

1ST MAN: I get you.

2ND MAN: I've worked the telegraph gag to death—and my wife likes you.

1ST MAN: What's your number?

2ND MAN: I'll write it down for you. (*Writes*)

1ST MAN: How is your wife?

2ND MAN: She's fine.

1ST MAN: And the kid?

2ND MAN: Great. *(Hands him the card)* Come on, kid. *(To* GIRL. *Turns back to* YOUNG WOMAN*)* Get this bird to tell you about himself.

GIRL: Keep him from it.

2ND MAN: Get him to tell you how he killed a couple a spig down in Mexico.

GIRL: You been in Mexico?

2ND MAN: He just came up from there.

GIRL: Can you teach us the tango?

YOUNG WOMAN: You killed a man?

2ND MAN: Two of 'em! With a bottle! Get him to tell you—with a bottle. Come on, kid. Goodbye. *(Exit* 2ND MAN *and* GIRL.*)*

YOUNG WOMAN: Why did you?

1ST MAN: What?

YOUNG WOMAN: Kill 'em?

1ST MAN: To get free.

YOUNG WOMAN: Oh.

(At Table 2.)

MAN: You really must taste this—just taste it. It's a real amontillado, you know.

BOY: Where do they get it here?

MAN: It's always down the side streets one finds the real pleasures, don't you think?

BOY: I don't know.

MAN: Learn. Come, taste this! Amontillado! Or don't you like amontillado?

BOY: I don't know. I never had any before.

MAN: Your first taste! How I envy you! Come, taste it! Taste it! And die. *(BOY tastes wine—finds it disappointing.)*

MAN: *(gilding it)* Poe was a lover of amontillado. He returns to it continually, you remember—or are you a lover of Poe?

BOY: I've read a lot of him.

MAN: But are you a lover?

(At Table 3.)

1ST MAN: There were a bunch of bandidos—bandits, you know, took me into the hills—holding me there—what was I to do? I got the two birds that guarded me drunk one night, and then I filled the empty bottle with small stones—and let 'em have it!

YOUNG WOMAN: Oh!

1ST MAN: I had to get free, didn't I? I let 'em have it—

YOUNG WOMAN: Oh—then what did you do?

1ST MAN: Then I beat it.

YOUNG WOMAN: Where to—?

1ST MAN: Right here. *(Pause)* Glad?

YOUNG WOMAN: *(nods)* Yes.

1ST MAN: *(makes sign to* WAITER *of "2")* The same. *(WAITER goes to bar.)*

(At Table 1.)

MAN: You're just scared because this is the first time and—

WOMAN: I'm not scared.

MAN: Then what are you for Christ's sake?

WOMAN: I'm not scared. I want it—I want to have it—that ain't being scared, is it?

MAN: It's being goofy.

WOMAN: I don't care.

MAN: What about your folks?

WOMAN: I don't care.

MAN: What about your job? *(Silence)* You got to keep your job, haven't you? *(Silence)* Haven't you?

WOMAN: I suppose so.

MAN: Well—there you are!

WOMAN: *(silence—then)* All right—let's go now— You got the address?

MAN: Now you're coming to. *(They get up and go off.)* *(Exit* MAN *and* WOMAN.*)*

(At Table 3.)

YOUNG WOMAN: A bottle like that? *(She picks it up)*

1ST MAN: Yeah—filled with pebbles.

YOUNG WOMAN: What kind of pebbles?

1ST MAN: Pebbles! Off the ground.

YOUNG WOMAN: Oh.

1ST MAN: Necessity, you know, mother of invention. *(As* YOUNG WOMAN *handles the bottle)* Ain't a bad weapon—first you got a sledge hammer—then you got a knife.

YOUNG WOMAN: Oh. *(Puts bottle down)*

1ST MAN: Women don't like knives, do they? *(Pours drink)*

YOUNG WOMAN: No.

1ST MAN: Don't mind a hammer so much, though, do they?

YOUNG WOMAN: No—

1ST MAN: I didn't like it myself—any of it—but I had to get free, didn't I? Sure I had to get free, didn't I? *(Drinks)* Now I'm damn glad I did.

YOUNG WOMAN: Why?

1ST MAN: You know why. *(He puts his hand over hers)*

(At Table 2.)

MAN: Let's go to my rooms—and I'll show them to you—I have a first edition of Verlaine that will simply make your mouth water. *(They stand up)* Here—there's just a sip at the bottom of my glass— (BOY *takes it)* That last sip that's sweetest— Wasn't it?

BOY: *(laughs)* And I always thought that was dregs.

(Exit MAN followed by BOY.)

(At Table 3.)

(The MAN is holding her hand across the table.)

YOUNG WOMAN: When you put your hand over mine! When you just touch me!

1ST MAN: Yeah? *(Pause)* Come on, kid, let's go!

YOUNG WOMAN: Where?

1ST MAN: You haven't been around much, have you, kid?

YOUNG WOMAN: No.

1ST MAN: I could tell that just to look at you.

YOUNG WOMAN: You could?

1ST MAN: Sure I could. What are you running around with a girl like that other one for?

YOUNG WOMAN: I don't know. She seems to have a good time.

1ST MAN: So that's it?

YOUNG WOMAN: Don't she?

1ST MAN: Don't you?

YOUNG WOMAN: No.

1ST MAN: Never?

YOUNG WOMAN: Never.

1ST MAN: What's the matter?

YOUNG WOMAN: Nothing—just me, I guess.

1ST MAN: You're all right.

YOUNG WOMAN: Am I?

1ST MAN: Sure. You just haven't met the right guy—that's all—a girl like you—you got to meet the right guy.

YOUNG WOMAN: I know.

1ST MAN: You're different from girls like that other one—any guy'll do her. You're different.

YOUNG WOMAN: I guess I am.

1ST MAN: You didn't fall for that business gag—did you—when they went off?

YOUNG WOMAN: Well, I thought they wanted to be alone probably, but—

1ST MAN: And how!

YOUNG WOMAN: Oh—so that's it.

1ST MAN: That's it. Come along—let's go—

YOUNG WOMAN: Oh, I couldn't! Like this?

1ST MAN: Don't you like me?

YOUNG WOMAN: Yes.

1ST MAN: Then what's the matter?

YOUNG WOMAN: Do—you—like me?

1ST MAN: Like yuh? You don't know the half of it—listen—you know what you seem like to me?

YOUNG WOMAN: What?

1ST MAN: An angel. Just like an angel.

YOUNG WOMAN: I do?

1ST MAN: That's what I said! Let's go!

YOUNG WOMAN: Where?

1ST MAN: Where do you live?

YOUNG WOMAN: Oh, we can't go to my place.

1ST MAN: Then come to my place.

YOUNG WOMAN: Oh I couldn't—is it far?

1ST MAN: Just a step—come on—

YOUNG WOMAN: Oh I couldn't—what is it—a room?

1ST MAN: No—an apartment—a one-room apartment.

YOUNG WOMAN: That's different.

1ST MAN: On the ground floor—no one will see you—coming or going.

YOUNG WOMAN: *(getting up)* I couldn't.

1ST MAN: *(rises)* Wait a minute—I got to pay the damage—and I'll get a bottle of something to take along.

YOUNG WOMAN: No—don't.

1ST MAN: Why not?

YOUNG WOMAN: Well—don't bring any pebbles.

1ST MAN: Say—forget that! Will you?

YOUNG WOMAN: I just meant I don't think I'll need anything to drink.

1ST MAN: *(leaning to her eagerly)* You like me— don't you, kid?

YOUNG WOMAN: Do you me?

1ST MAN: Wait!

(He goes to the bar. She remains, her hands outstretched on the table staring ahead.)

(Enter a MAN and a GIRL. They go to one of the empty tables. The WAITER goes to them.)

MAN: *(to GIRL)* What do you want?

GIRL: Same old thing.

MAN: *(to the WAITER)* The usual. *(Makes a sign "2.")*

(The 1ST MAN crosses to YOUNG WOMAN with a wrapped bottle under his arm. She rises and starts out with him. As they pass the piano, he stops and puts in a nickel—the music starts as they exit.)

BLACK OUT

(The music of the electric piano continues until the lights go up for EPISODE SIX, and the music has become the music of a hand organ, very very faint.)

EPISODE SIX: INTIMATE

SCENE: *A dark room.*

SOUNDS: *A hand organ. Footbeats, of passing feet.*

CHARACTERS:
  MAN
  YOUNG WOMAN

AT RISE:

  DARKNESS. *Nothing can be discerned. From the outside comes the sound of a hand organ, very faint, and the irregular rhythm of passing feet. The hand organ is playing "Cielito Lindo," that Spanish song that has been on every hand organ lately.*

MAN: You're awful still, honey. What you thinking about?

WOMAN: About sea shells. *(The sound of her voice is beautiful)*

MAN: Sheshells? Gee! I can't say it!

WOMAN: When I was little my grandmother used to have a big pink sea shell on the mantle behind the stove. When we'd go to visit her they'd let me hold it, and listen. That's what I was thinking about now.

MAN: Yeah?

WOMAN: You can hear the sea in 'em, you know.

MAN: Yeah, I know.

WOMAN: I wonder why that is?

MAN: Search me. *(Pause)*

WOMAN: You going?
  (He has moved.)

MAN: No. I just want a cigarette.

WOMAN: *(glad, relieved)* Oh.

MAN: Want one?

WOMAN: No. *(Taking the match)* Let me light it for you.

MAN: You got mighty pretty hands, honey. *(The match is out)* This little pig went to market. This little pig stayed home. This little pig went—

WOMAN: *(laughs)* Diddle diddle dee. *(Laughs again)*

MAN: You got awful pretty hands.

WOMAN: I used to have. But I haven't taken much care of them lately. I will now— *(Pause. The music gets clearer)* What's that?

MAN: What?

WOMAN: That music?

MAN: A dago hand organ. I gave him two bits the first day I got here—so he comes every day.

WOMAN: I mean—what's that he's playing?

MAN: "Cielito Lindo."

WOMAN: What does that mean?

MAN: Little Heaven.

WOMAN: Little Heaven?

MAN: That's what lovers call each other in Spain.

WOMAN: Spain's where all the castles are, ain't it?

MAN: Yeah.

WOMAN: Little Heaven—sing it!

MAN: *(singing to the music of the hand organ)* De la sierra morena viene, bajando viene, bajando; un par de ojitos negros—cielito lindo—da contrabando.

WOMAN: What does it mean?

MAN: From the high dark mountains.

WOMAN: From the high dark mountains—?

MAN: Oh it doesn't mean anything. It doesn't make sense. It's love. *(Taking up the song)* Ay-ay-ay-ay.

WOMAN: I know what that means.

MAN: What?

WOMAN: Ay-ay-ay-ay.

(They laugh.)

MAN: *(taking up the song)* Canta no llores— Sing don't cry—

WOMAN: *(taking up song)* La-la-la-la-la-la-la-la-la-la—Little Heaven!

MAN: You got a nice voice, honey.

WOMAN: Have I?

(Laughs—tickles him.)

MAN: You bet you have—hey!

WOMAN: *(laughing)* You ticklish?

MAN: Sure I am! Hey! *(They laugh)* Go on, honey, sing something.

WOMAN: I couldn't.

MAN: Go on—you got a fine voice.

WOMAN: *(laughs and sings)*

Hey, diddle, diddle, the cat and the
   fiddle,
The cow jumped over the moon
The little dog laughed to see the sport
And the dish ran away with the spoon—

(Both laugh) I never thought that had any sense before—now I get it.

MAN: You got me beat.

WOMAN: It's you and me.—La—lalalalalala—lalalalalalala—Little Heaven. You're the dish and I'm the spoon.

MAN: You're a little spoon all right.

WOMAN: And I guess I'm the little cow that jumped over the moon. *(A pause)* Do you believe in sorta guardian angels?

MAN: What?

WOMAN: Guardian angels?

MAN: I don't know. Maybe.

WOMAN: I do. *(Taking up the song again)* Lalalalala-lalalalala-lalalala—Little Heaven. *(Talking)* There must be something that looks out for you and brings you your happiness, at last—look at us! How did we both happen to go to that place today if there wasn't something!

MAN: Maybe you're right.

WOMAN: Look at us!

MAN: Everything's us to you, kid—ain't it?

WOMAN: Ain't it?

MAN: All right with me.

WOMAN: We belong together! We belong together! And we're going to stick together, ain't we?

MAN: Sing something else.

WOMAN: I tell you I can't sing!

MAN: Sure you can!

WOMAN: I tell you I hadn't thought of singing since I was a little bit of a girl.

MAN: Well sing anyway.

WOMAN: *(singing)* And every little wavelet had its night cap on—its night cap on—its night cap on—and every little wave had its night cap on—so very early in the morning. *(Talking)* Did you used to sing that when you were a little kid?

MAN: Nope.

WOMAN: Didn't you? We used to—in the first grade—little kids—we used to go round and round in a ring—and flop our hands up and down—supposed to be the waves. I remember it used to confuse me—because we did just the same thing to be little angels.

MAN: Yeah?

WOMAN: You know why I came here?

MAN: I can make a good guess.

WOMAN: Because you told me I looked like an angel to you! That's why I came.

MAN: Jeez, honey, all women look like angels to me—all white women. I ain't been seeing nothing but Indians, you know, for the last couple of years. Gee, when I got off the boat here the other day—and saw all the women—gee I pretty near went crazy—talk about looking like angels—why—

WOMAN: You've had a lot of women, haven't you?

MAN: Not so many—real ones.

WOMAN: Did you—like any of 'em—better than me?

MAN: Nope—there wasn't one of 'em any sweeter than you, honey—not as sweet—no—not as sweet.

WOMAN: I like to hear you say it. Say it again—

MAN: *(protesting good humoredly)* Oh—

WOMAN: Go on—tell me again!

MAN: Here! *(Kisses her)* Does that tell you?

WOMAN: Yes. *(Pause)* We're going to stick together—always—aren't we?

MAN: *(honestly)* I'll have to be moving on, kid—some day, you know.

WOMAN: When?

MAN: Quien sabe?

WOMAN: What does that mean?

MAN: Quien sabe? You got to learn that, kid, if you're figuring on coming with me. It's the answer to everything—below the Rio Grande.

WOMAN: What does it mean?

MAN: It means—who knows?

WOMAN: Keen sabe?

MAN: Yep—don't forget it—now.

WOMAN: I'll never forget it!

MAN: Quien sabe?

WOMAN: And I'll never get to use it.

MAN: Quien sabe.

WOMAN: I'll never get—below the Rio Grande—I'll never get out of here.

MAN: Quien sabe.

WOMAN: *(change of mood)* That's right! Keen sabe? Who knows?

MAN: That's the stuff.

WOMAN: You must like it down there.

MAN: I can't live anywhere else—for long.

WOMAN: Why not?

MAN: Oh—you're free down there! You're free! *(A Street Light is lit outside. The outlines of a window take form against this light. There are bars across it, and from outside it, the sidewalk cuts across almost at the top. [It is a basement room.] The constant going and coming of passing feet, [mostly feet of couples] can be dimly seen. Inside, on the ledge, there is a lily blooming in a bowl of rocks and water.)*

WOMAN: What's that?

MAN: Just the street light going on.

WOMAN: Is it as late as that?

MAN: Late as what?

WOMAN: Dark.

MAN: It's been dark for hours—didn't you know that?

WOMAN: No!—I must go! *(Rises)*

MAN: Wait—the moon will be up in a little while—full moon.

WOMAN: It isn't that! I'm late! I must go! *(She comes into the light. She wears a white chemise that might be the tunic of a dancer, and as she comes into the light she fastens about her waist a little skirt. She really wears almost exactly the clothes that women wear now, but the finesse of their cut, and the grace and ease with which she puts them on, must turn this episode of her dressing into a personification, an idealization of a woman clothing herself. All her gestures must be unconscious, innocent, relaxed, sure and full of natural grace. As she sits facing the window pulling on a stocking.)* What's that?

MAN: What?

WOMAN: On the window ledge.

MAN: A flower.

WOMAN: Who gave it to you?

MAN: Nobody gave it to me. I bought it.

WOMAN: For yourself?

MAN: Yeah—why not?

WOMAN: I don't know.

MAN: In Chinatown—made me think of Frisco where I was a kid—so I bought it.

WOMAN: Is that where you were born—Frisco?

MAN: Yep. Twin Peaks.

WOMAN: What's that?

MAN: A couple hills—together.

WOMAN: One for you and one for me.

MAN: I bet you'd like Frisco.

WOMAN: I know a woman went out there once!

MAN: The bay and the hills! Jeez, that's the life! Every Saturday we used to cross the Bay—get a couple nags and just ride—over the hills. One would have a blanket on the saddle—the other, the grub. At night, we'd make a little fire and eat—and then roll up in the old blanket and—

WOMAN: Who? Who was with you?

MAN: (indifferently) Anybody. (Enthusiastically) Jeez, that dry old grass out there smells good at night—full of tar weed—you know—

WOMAN: Is that a good smell?

MAN: Tar weed? Didn't you ever smell it? (She shakes her head, "No") Sure it's a good smell! The bay and the hills. (She goes to the mirror of the dresser, to finish dressing. She has only a dress to put on that is in one piece—with one fastening on the side. Before slipping it on, she stands before the mirror and stretches. Appreciatively but indifferently) You look in good shape, kid. A couple of months riding over the mountains with me, you'd be great.

WOMAN: Can I?

MAN: What?

WOMAN: Some day—ride mountains with you?

MAN: Ride mountains? Ride donkeys!

WOMAN: It's the same thing!—with you!—Can I—some day? The high dark mountains?

MAN: Who knows?

WOMAN: It must be great!

MAN: You ever been off like that, kid?—high up? On top of the world?

WOMAN: Yes.

MAN: When?

WOMAN: Today.

MAN: You're pretty sweet.

WOMAN: I never knew anything like this way! I never knew that I could feel like this! So,—so purified! Don't laugh at me!

MAN: I ain't laughing, honey.

WOMAN: Purified.

MAN: It's a hell of a word—but I know what you mean. That's the way it is—sometimes.

WOMAN: (she puts on a little hat, then turns to him) Well—goodbye.

MAN: Aren't you forgetting something? (Rises)

WOMAN: (she looks toward him, then throws her head slowly back, lifts her right arm—this gesture that is in so many statues of women [Volupté]—He comes out of the shadow, puts his arm around her, kisses her. Her head and arm go further back,—then she brings her arm around with a wide encircling gesture, her hand closes over his head, her fingers spread. Her fingers are protective, clutching. When he releases her, her eyes are shining with tears. She turns away. She looks back at him—and the room—and her eyes fasten on the lily) Can I have that?

MAN: Sure—why not?

(She takes it—goes. As she opens the door, the music is louder. The scene blacks out.)

WOMAN: Goodbye. And— (Hesitates) And— thank you.

M U S I C — C U R T A I N — B L A C K   O U T

(The music continues until the Curtain goes up for EPISODE SEVEN— It goes up on silence.)

E P I S O D E   S E V E N :   D O M E S T I C

SCENE: A Sitting Room (A divan—a telephone—a window.)

CHARACTERS:
HUSBAND
YOUNG WOMAN

They are seated on opposite ends of the divan. They are both reading papers—to themselves.

HUSBAND: Record production.

YOUNG WOMAN: Girl turns on gas.

HUSBAND: Sale hits a million—

YOUNG WOMAN: Woman leaves all for love—

HUSBAND: Market trend steady—

YOUNG WOMAN: Young wife disappears—

HUSBAND: Owns a life interest— *(Phone rings. YOUNG WOMAN looks toward it)* That's for me. *(In phone)* Hello—oh hello, A.B. It's all settled?—Everything signed? Good. Good! Tell R.A. to call me up. *(Closes phone—to YOUNG WOMAN)* Well, it's all settled. They signed!—aren't you interested? Aren't you going to ask me?

YOUNG WOMAN: *(by rote)* Did you put it over?

HUSBAND: Sure I put it over.

YOUNG WOMAN: Did you swing it?

HUSBAND: Sure I swung it.

YOUNG WOMAN: Did they come through?

HUSBAND: Sure they came through.

YOUNG WOMAN: Did they sign?

HUSBAND: I'll say they signed.

YOUNG WOMAN: On the dotted line?

HUSBAND: On the dotted line.

YOUNG WOMAN: The property's yours?

HUSBAND: The property's mine. I'll put a first mortgage. I'll put a second mortgage and the property's mine. Happy?

YOUNG WOMAN: *(by rote)* Happy.

HUSBAND: *(going to her)* The property's mine! It's not all that's mine! *(Pinching her cheek—happy and playful)* I got a first mortgage on her—I got a second mortgage on her—and she's mine! *(YOUNG WOMAN pulls away swiftly)* What's the matter?

YOUNG WOMAN: Nothing—what?

HUSBAND: You flinched when I touched you.

YOUNG WOMAN: No.

HUSBAND: You haven't done that in a long time.

YOUNG WOMAN: Haven't I?

HUSBAND: You used to do it every time I touched you.

YOUNG WOMAN: Did I?

HUSBAND: Didn't know that, did you?

YOUNG WOMAN: *(unexpectedly)* Yes. Yes, I know it.

HUSBAND: Just purity.

YOUNG WOMAN: No.

HUSBAND: Oh, I liked it. Purity.

YOUNG WOMAN: No.

HUSBAND: You're one of the purest women that ever lived.

YOUNG WOMAN: I'm just like anybody else only— *(Stops)*

HUSBAND: Only what?

YOUNG WOMAN: *(a pause)* Nothing.

HUSBAND: It must be something.
(Phone rings.)
(She gets up and goes to window.)

HUSBAND: *(in phone)* Hello—hello, R.A.—well, I put it over—yeah, I swung it—sure they came through—did they sign? On the dotted line! The property's mine. I made the proposition. I sold them the idea. Now watch me. Tell D.D. to call me up. *(Hangs up)* That was R.A. What are you looking at?

YOUNG WOMAN: Nothing.

HUSBAND: You must be looking at something.

YOUNG WOMAN: Nothing—the moon.

HUSBAND: The moon's something, isn't it?

YOUNG WOMAN: Yes.

HUSBAND: What's it doing?

YOUNG WOMAN: Nothing.

HUSBAND: It must be doing something.

YOUNG WOMAN: It's moving—moving—
(She comes down restlessly)

HUSBAND: Pull down the shade, my dear.

YOUNG WOMAN: Why?

HUSBAND: People can look in. *(Phone rings)* Hello—hello D.D.—Yes—I put it over—they came across—I put it over on them—yep—yep—yep—I'll say I am—yep—on the dotted line—Now you watch me—yep. Yep yep. Tell B.M. to phone me. *(Hangs up)* That was D.D. *(To YOUNG WOMAN, who has come down to davenport and picked up a paper)* Aren't you listening?

YOUNG WOMAN: I'm reading.

HUSBAND: What you reading?

YOUNG WOMAN: Nothing.

HUSBAND: Must be something. *(He sits and picks up his paper)*

YOUNG WOMAN: *(reading)* Prisoner escapes— lifer breaks jail—shoots way to freedom—

HUSBAND: Don't read that stuff—listen—here's a first rate editorial. I agree with this. I agree absolutely. Are you listening?

YOUNG WOMAN: I'm listening.

HUSBAND: *(importantly)* All men are born free and entitled to the pursuit of happiness. *(YOUNG WOMAN gets up)* My, you're nervous tonight.

YOUNG WOMAN: I try not to be.

HUSBAND: You inherit that from your mother. She was in the office today.

YOUNG WOMAN: Was she?

HUSBAND: To get her allowance.

YOUNG WOMAN: Oh—

HUSBAND: Don't you know it's the *first*.

YOUNG WOMAN: Poor Ma.

HUSBAND: What would she do without me?

YOUNG WOMAN: I know. You're very good.

HUSBAND: One thing—she's grateful.

YOUNG WOMAN: Poor Ma—poor Ma.

HUSBAND: She's got to have care.

YOUNG WOMAN: Yes. She's got to have care.

HUSBAND: A mother's a very precious thing—a good mother.

YOUNG WOMAN: *(excitedly)* I try to be a good mother.

HUSBAND: Of course you're a good mother.

YOUNG WOMAN: I try! I try!

HUSBAND: A mother's a very precious thing— *(Resuming his paper)* And a child's a very precious thing. Precious jewels.

YOUNG WOMAN: *(reading)* Sale of jewels and precious stones. *(YOUNG WOMAN puts her hand to throat)*

HUSBAND: What's the matter?

YOUNG WOMAN: I feel as though I were drowning.

HUSBAND: Drowning?

YOUNG WOMAN: With stones around my neck.

HUSBAND: You just imagine that.

YOUNG WOMAN: Stifling.

HUSBAND: You don't breathe deep enough— breathe now—look at me. *(He breathes)* Breath is life. Life is breath.

YOUNG WOMAN: *(suddenly)* And what is death?

HUSBAND: *(smartly)* Just—no breath!

YOUNG WOMAN: *(to herself)* Just no breath. *(Takes up paper)*

HUSBAND: All right?

YOUNG WOMAN: All right.

HUSBAND: *(reads as she stares at her paper. Looks up after a pause)* I feel cold air, my dear.

YOUNG WOMAN: Cold air?

HUSBAND: Close the window, will you?

YOUNG WOMAN: It isn't open.

HUSBAND: Don't you feel cold air?

YOUNG WOMAN: No—you just imagine it.

HUSBAND: I never imagine anything. *(YOUNG WOMAN is staring at the paper.)* What are you reading?

YOUNG WOMAN: Nothing.

HUSBAND: You must be reading something.

YOUNG WOMAN: Woman finds husband dead.

HUSBAND: *(uninterested)* Oh. *(Interested)* Here's a man says "I owe my success to a yeast cake a day—my digestion is good—I sleep very well— and—*(His wife gets up, goes toward door)* Where you going?

YOUNG WOMAN: No place.

HUSBAND: You must be going some place.

YOUNG WOMAN: Just—to bed.

HUSBAND: It isn't eleven yet. Wait.

YOUNG WOMAN: Wait?

HUSBAND: It's only ten-forty-six—wait! *(Holds out his arms to her.)* Come here!

YOUNG WOMAN: *(takes a step toward him—recoils)* Oh—I want to go away!

HUSBAND: Away? Where?

YOUNG WOMAN: Anywhere—away.

HUSBAND: Why, what's the matter?

YOUNG WOMAN: I'm scared.

HUSBAND: What of?

YOUNG WOMAN: I can't sleep—I haven't slept.

HUSBAND: That's nothing.

YOUNG WOMAN: And the moon—when it's full moon.

HUSBAND: That's nothing.

YOUNG WOMAN: I can't sleep.

HUSBAND: Of course not. It's the light.

YOUNG WOMAN: I don't see it! I feel it! I'm afraid.

HUSBAND: *(kindly)* Nonsense—come here.

YOUNG WOMAN: I want to go away.

HUSBAND: But I can't get away now.

YOUNG WOMAN: Alone!

HUSBAND: You've never been away alone.

YOUNG WOMAN: I know.

HUSBAND: What would you do?

YOUNG WOMAN: Maybe I'd sleep.

HUSBAND: Now you wait.

YOUNG WOMAN: *(desperately)* Wait?

HUSBAND: We'll take a trip—we'll go to Europe—I'll get my watch—I'll get my Swiss watch—I've always wanted a Swiss watch that I bought right there—isn't that funny? Wait—wait. *(*YOUNG WOMAN *comes down to davenport—sits.* HUSBAND *resumes his paper)* Another revolution below the Rio Grande.

YOUNG WOMAN: Below the Rio Grande?

HUSBAND: Yes—another—

YOUNG WOMAN: Anyone—hurt?

HUSBAND: No.

YOUNG WOMAN: Any prisoners?

HUSBAND: No.

YOUNG WOMAN: All free?

HUSBAND: All free.

(He resumes his paper.)

*(*YOUNG WOMAN *sits, staring ahead of her—The music of the hand organ sounds off very dimly, playing "Cielito Lindo." Voices begin to sing it—'Ay-ay-ay-ay'—and then the words—the music and voices get louder.)*

THE VOICE OF HER LOVER: They were a bunch of bandidos—bandits you know—holding me there—what was I to do—I had to get free—didn't I? I had to get free—

VOICES: Free—free—free—

LOVER: I filled an empty bottle with small stones—

VOICES: Stones—stones—precious stones—millstones—stones—stones—millstones—

LOVER: Just a bottle with small stones.

VOICES: Stones—stones—small stones—

LOVER: You only need a bottle with small stones.

VOICES: Stones—stones—small stones—

VOICE OF A HUCKSTER: Stones for sale—stones—stones—small stones—precious stones—

VOICES: Stones — stones — precious stones—

LOVER: Had to get free, didn't I? Free?

VOICES: Free? Free?

LOVER: Quien sabe? Who knows? Who knows?

VOICES: Who'd know? Who'd know? Who'd know?

HUCKSTER: Stones—stones—small stones—big stones—millstones—cold stones—head stones—

VOICES: Head stones—head stones—head stones. *(The music,—the voices—mingle—increase—the* YOUNG WOMAN *flies from her chair and cries out in terror.)*

YOUNG WOMAN: Oh! Oh!

(The scene BLACKS OUT—*the music and the dim voices, "Stones—stones—stones," continue until the scene lights for* EPISODE EIGHT.*)*

EPISODE EIGHT: THE LAW

SCENE: *Courtroom*

SOUNDS: *Clicking of telegraph instruments offstage*

CHARACTERS:

> JUDGE
> JURY
> LAWYERS
> SPECTATORS
> REPORTERS
> MESSENGER BOYS
> LAW CLERKS
> BAILIFF
> COURT REPORTER
> YOUNG WOMAN

The words and movements of all these people except the YOUNG WOMAN *are routine—mechanical— Each is going through the motions of his own game.*

AT RISE: ALL *assembled, except* JUDGE.

(Enter JUDGE.*)*

BAILIFF: *(mumbling)* Hear ye—hear ye—hear ye!

*(*ALL *rise.* JUDGE *sits.* ALL *sit.)*

*(*LAWYER FOR DEFENSE *gets to his feet—He is the verbose, 'eloquent'—typical criminal defense lawyer.)*

*(*JUDGE *signs to him to wait—turns to* LAW CLERKS, *grouped at foot of the bench.)*

1ST CLERK: *(handing up a paper—routine voice)* State versus Kling—stay of execution.

JUDGE: Denied.

(1ST CLERK goes.)

2ND CLERK: Bing vs. Ding—demurrer.

(JUDGE signs.)

(2ND CLERK goes.)

3RD CLERK: Case of John King—habeas corpus.

(JUDGE signs.)

(3RD CLERK goes.)

(JUDGE signs to BAILIFF.)

BAILIFF: *(mumbling)* People of the State of _____ versus Helen Jones.

JUDGE: *(to LAWYER FOR THE DEFENSE)* Defense ready to proceed?

LAWYER FOR DEFENSE: We're ready, your Honor.

JUDGE: Proceed.

LAWYER FOR DEFENSE: Helen Jones.

BAILIFF: HELEN JONES!

(YOUNG WOMAN rises.)

LAWYER FOR DEFENSE: Mrs Jones, will you take the stand?

(YOUNG WOMAN goes to witness stand.)

1ST REPORTER: *(writing rapidly)* The defense sprang a surprise at the opening of court this morning by putting the accused woman on the stand. The prosecution was swept off its feet by this daring defense strategy and—

(Instruments get louder.)

2ND REPORTER: Trembling and scarcely able to stand, Helen Jones, accused murderess, had to be almost carried to the witness stand this morning when her lawyer—

BAILIFF: *(mumbling—with Bible)* Do you swear to tell the truth, the whole truth and nothing but the truth—so help you God?

YOUNG WOMAN: I do.

JUDGE: You may sit.

(She sits in witness chair.)

COURT REPORTER: What is your name?

YOUNG WOMAN: Helen Jones.

COURT REPORTER: Your age?

YOUNG WOMAN: *(hesitates—then)* Twenty-nine.

COURT REPORTER: Where do you live?

YOUNG WOMAN: In prison.

LAWYER FOR DEFENSE: This is my client's legal address. *(Hands a scrap of paper.)*

LAWYER FOR PROSECUTION: *(jumping to his feet)* I object to this insinuation on the part of counsel on any illegality in the holding of this defendant in jail when the law—

LAWYER FOR DEFENSE: I made no such insinuation.

LAWYER FOR PROSECUTION: You implied it—

LAWYER FOR DEFENSE: I did not!

LAWYER FOR PROSECUTION: You're a—

JUDGE: Order!

BAILIFF: Order!

LAWYER FOR DEFENSE: Your Honor, I object to counsel's constant attempt to—

LAWYER FOR PROSECUTION: I protest—I—

JUDGE: Order!

BAILIFF: Order!

JUDGE: Proceed with the witness.

LAWYER FOR DEFENSE: Mrs Jones, you are the widow of the late George H. Jones, are you not?

YOUNG WOMAN: Yes.

LAWYER FOR DEFENSE: How long were you married to the late George H. Jones before his demise?

YOUNG WOMAN: Six years.

LAWYER FOR DEFENSE: Six years! And it was a happy marriage, was it not? *(YOUNG WOMAN hesitates)* Did you quarrel?

YOUNG WOMAN: No, sir.

LAWYER FOR DEFENSE: Then it was a happy marriage, wasn't it?

YOUNG WOMAN: Yes, sir.

LAWYER FOR DEFENSE: In those six years of married life with your late husband, the late George H. Jones, did you EVER have a quarrel?

YOUNG WOMAN: No, sir.

LAWYER FOR DEFENSE: Never one quarrel?

LAWYER FOR PROSECUTION: The witness has said—

LAWYER FOR DEFENSE: Six years without one quarrel! Six years! Gentlemen of the jury, I ask you to consider this fact! Six years of married life without a quarrel! *(The JURY grins)* I ask you to consider it seriously! Very seriously! Who of us—and this is not intended as any reflection on the sacred institution of marriage—no—but!

JUDGE: Proceed with your witness.

LAWYER FOR DEFENSE: You have one child—have you not, Mrs Jones?

YOUNG WOMAN: Yes, sir.

LAWYER FOR DEFENSE: A little girl, is it not?

YOUNG WOMAN: Yes, sir.

LAWYER FOR DEFENSE: How old is she?

YOUNG WOMAN: She's five—past five.

LAWYER FOR DEFENSE: A little girl of past five. Since the demise of the late Mr Jones you are the only parent she has living, are you not?

YOUNG WOMAN: Yes, sir.

LAWYER FOR DEFENSE: Before your marriage to the late Mr Jones, you worked and supported your mother, did you not?

LAWYER FOR PROSECUTION: I object, your honor! Irrelevant—immaterial—and—

JUDGE: Objection sustained!

LAWYER FOR DEFENSE: In order to support your mother and yourself as a girl, you worked, did you not?

YOUNG WOMAN: Yes, sir.

LAWYER FOR DEFENSE: What did you do?

YOUNG WOMAN: I was a stenographer.

LAWYER FOR DEFENSE: And since your marriage you have continued as her sole support, have you not?

YOUNG WOMAN: Yes, sir.

LAWYER FOR DEFENSE: A devoted daughter, gentlemen of the jury! As well as a devoted wife and a devoted mother!

LAWYER FOR PROSECUTION: Your Honor!

LAWYER FOR DEFENSE: *(quickly)* And now, Mrs Jones, I will ask you—the law expects me to ask you—it demands that I ask you—did you—or did you not—on the night of June 2nd last or the morning of June 3rd last—kill your husband, the late George H. Jones—did you, or did you not?

YOUNG WOMAN: I did not.

LAWYER FOR DEFENSE: You did not?

YOUNG WOMAN: I did not.

LAWYER FOR DEFENSE: Now, Mrs Jones, you have heard the witnesses for the State—They were not many—and they did not have much to say—

LAWYER FOR PROSECUTION: I object.

JUDGE: Sustained.

LAWYER FOR DEFENSE: You have heard some police and you have heard some doctors. None of whom was present! The prosecution could not furnish any witness to the crime—not one witness!

LAWYER FOR PROSECUTION: Your Honor!

LAWYER FOR DEFENSE: Nor one motive.

LAWYER FOR PROSECUTION: Your Honor—I protest! I—

JUDGE: Sustained.

LAWYER FOR DEFENSE: But such as these witnesses were, you have heard them try to accuse you of deliberately murdering your own husband, this husband with whom, by your own statement, you had never had a quarrel—not one quarrel in six years of married life, murdering him, I say, or rather they say, while he slept, by brutally hitting him over the head with a bottle—a bottle filled with small stones—Did you, I repeat this, or did you not?

YOUNG WOMAN: I did not.

LAWYER FOR DEFENSE: You did not! Of course you did not! *(Quickly)* Now, Mrs Jones, will you tell the jury in your own words exactly what happened on the night of June 2nd or the morning of June 3rd last, at the time your husband was killed.

YOUNG WOMAN: I was awakened by hearing somebody—something—in the room, and I saw two men standing by my husband's bed.

LAWYER FOR DEFENSE: Your husband's bed—that was also your bed, was it not, Mrs Jones?

YOUNG WOMAN: Yes.

LAWYER FOR DEFENSE: You hadn't the modern idea of separate beds, had you, Mrs Jones?

YOUNG WOMAN: Mr Jones objected.

LAWYER FOR DEFENSE: I mean you slept in the same bed, did you not?

YOUNG WOMAN: Yes.

LAWYER FOR DEFENSE: Then explain just what you meant by saying 'my husband's bed.'

YOUNG WOMAN: Well—I—

LAWYER FOR DEFENSE: You meant his side of the bed, didn't you?

YOUNG WOMAN: Yes. His side.

LAWYER FOR DEFENSE: That is what I thought, but I wanted the jury to be clear on that point. *(To the* JURY*)* Mr and Mrs Jones slept in the same bed. *(To her)* Go on, Mrs Jones. *(As she is silent)* You heard a noise and—

YOUNG WOMAN: I heard a noise and I awoke and saw two men standing beside my husband's side of the bed.

LAWYER FOR DEFENSE: Two men?

YOUNG WOMAN: Yes.

LAWYER FOR DEFENSE: Can you describe them?

YOUNG WOMAN: Not very well—I couldn't see them very well.

LAWYER FOR DEFENSE: Could you say whether they were big or small—light or dark, thin or—

YOUNG WOMAN: They were big dark looking men.

LAWYER FOR DEFENSE: Big dark looking men?

YOUNG WOMAN: Yes.

LAWYER FOR DEFENSE: And what did you do, Mrs Jones, when you suddenly awoke and saw two big dark looking men standing beside your bed?

YOUNG WOMAN: I didn't do anything!

LAWYER FOR DEFENSE: You didn't have time to do anything—did you?

YOUNG WOMAN: No. Before I could do anything—one of them raised—something in his hand and struck Mr Jones over the head with it.

LAWYER FOR DEFENSE: And what did Mr Jones do?

*(*SPECTATORS *laugh.)*

JUDGE: Silence.

BAILIFF: Silence.

LAWYER FOR DEFENSE: What did Mr Jones do, Mrs Jones?

YOUNG WOMAN: He gave a sort of groan and tried to raise up.

LAWYER FOR DEFENSE: Tried to raise up!

YOUNG WOMAN: Yes!

LAWYER FOR DEFENSE: And then what happened?

YOUNG WOMAN: The man struck him again and he fell back.

LAWYER FOR DEFENSE: I see. What did the men do then? The big dark looking men.

YOUNG WOMAN: They turned and ran out of the room.

LAWYER FOR DEFENSE: I see. What did you do then, Mrs Jones?

YOUNG WOMAN: I saw Mr Jones was bleeding from the temple. I got towels and tried to stop it, and then I realized he had—passed away—

LAWYER FOR DEFENSE: I see. What did you do then?

YOUNG WOMAN: I didn't know what to do. But I thought I'd better call the police. So I went to the telephone and called the police.

LAWYER FOR DEFENSE: What happened then?

YOUNG WOMAN: Nothing. Nothing happened.

LAWYER FOR DEFENSE: The police came, didn't they?

YOUNG WOMAN: Yes—they came.

LAWYER FOR DEFENSE: *(quickly)* And that is all you know concerning the death of your husband in the late hours of June 2nd or the early hours of June 3rd last, isn't it?

YOUNG WOMAN: Yes sir.

LAWYER FOR DEFENSE: All?

YOUNG WOMAN: Yes sir.

LAWYER FOR DEFENSE: *(to* LAWYER FOR PROSECUTION*)* Take the witness.

1ST REPORTER: *(writing)* The accused woman told a straightforward story of—

2ND REPORTER: The accused woman told a rambling, disconnected story of—

LAWYER FOR PROSECUTION: You made no effort to cry out, Mrs Jones, did you, when you saw those two big dark men standing over your helpless husband, did you?

YOUNG WOMAN: No sir. I didn't. I—

LAWYER FOR PROSECUTION: And when they turned and ran out of the room, you made no effort to follow them or cry out after them, did you?

YOUNG WOMAN: No sir.

LAWYER FOR PROSECUTION: Why didn't you?

YOUNG WOMAN: I saw Mr Jones was hurt.

LAWYER FOR PROSECUTION: Ah! You saw Mr Jones was hurt! You saw this—how did you see it?

YOUNG WOMAN: I just saw it.

LAWYER FOR PROSECUTION: Then there was a light in the room?

YOUNG WOMAN: A sort of light.

LAWYER FOR PROSECUTION: What do you mean—a sort of light? A bed light?

YOUNG WOMAN: No. No, there was no light on.

LAWYER FOR PROSECUTION: Then where did it come from—this sort of light?

YOUNG WOMAN: I don't know.

LAWYER FOR PROSECUTION: Perhaps—from the window.

YOUNG WOMAN: Yes—from the window.

LAWYER FOR PROSECUTION: Oh, the shade was up!

YOUNG WOMAN: No—no, the shade was down.

LAWYER FOR PROSECUTION: You're sure of that?

YOUNG WOMAN: Yes. Mr Jones always wanted the shade down.

LAWYER FOR PROSECUTION: The shade was down—there was no light in the room—but the room was light—how do you explain this?

YOUNG WOMAN: I don't know.

LAWYER FOR PROSECUTION: You don't know!

YOUNG WOMAN: I think where the window was open—under the shade—light came in—

LAWYER FOR PROSECUTION: There is a street light there?

YOUNG WOMAN: No—there's no street light.

LAWYER FOR PROSECUTION: Then where did this light come from—that came in under the shade?

YOUNG WOMAN: *(desperately)* From the moon!

LAWYER FOR PROSECUTION: The moon!

YOUNG WOMAN: Yes! It was bright moon!

LAWYER FOR PROSECUTION: It was bright moon—you are sure of that!

YOUNG WOMAN: Yes.

LAWYER FOR PROSECUTION: How are you sure?

YOUNG WOMAN: I couldn't sleep—I never can sleep in the bright moon. I never can.

LAWYER FOR PROSECUTION: It was bright moon. Yet you could not see two big dark looking men—but you could see your husband bleeding from the temple.

YOUNG WOMAN: Yes sir.

LAWYER FOR PROSECUTION: And did you call a doctor?

YOUNG WOMAN: No.

LAWYER FOR PROSECUTION: Why didn't you?

YOUNG WOMAN: The police did.

LAWYER FOR PROSECUTION: But you didn't?

YOUNG WOMAN: No.

LAWYER FOR PROSECUTION: Why didn't you? *(No answer)* Why didn't you?

YOUNG WOMAN: *(whispers)* I saw it was—useless.

LAWYER FOR PROSECUTION: Ah! You saw that! You saw that—very clearly.

YOUNG WOMAN: Yes.

LAWYER FOR PROSECUTION: And you didn't call a doctor.

YOUNG WOMAN: It was—useless.

LAWYER FOR PROSECUTION: What did you do?

YOUNG WOMAN: It was useless—there was no use of anything.

LAWYER FOR PROSECUTION: I asked you what you did.

YOUNG WOMAN: Nothing.

LAWYER FOR PROSECUTION: Nothing!

YOUNG WOMAN: I just sat there.

LAWYER FOR PROSECUTION: You sat there! A long while, didn't you?

YOUNG WOMAN: I don't know.

LAWYER FOR PROSECUTION: You don't know? *(Showing her the neck of a broken bottle)* Mrs Jones, did you ever see this before?

YOUNG WOMAN: I think so.

LAWYER FOR PROSECUTION: You think so.

YOUNG WOMAN: Yes.

LAWYER FOR PROSECUTION: What do you think it is?

YOUNG WOMAN: I think it's the bottle that was used against Mr Jones.

LAWYER FOR PROSECUTION: Used against him—yes—that's right. You've guessed right. This neck and these broken pieces and these pebbles were found on the floor and scattered over the bed. There were no fingerprints, Mrs Jones, on this bottle. None at all. Doesn't that seem strange to you?

YOUNG WOMAN: No.

LAWYER FOR PROSECUTION: It doesn't seem strange to you that this bottle held in the big dark hand of one of those big dark men left no mark! No print! That doesn't seem strange to you?

YOUNG WOMAN: No.

LAWYER FOR PROSECUTION: You are in the habit of wearing rubber gloves at night, Mrs Jones—are you not? To protect—to soften your hands—are you not?

YOUNG WOMAN: I used to.

LAWYER FOR PROSECUTION: Used to—when was that?

YOUNG WOMAN: Before I was married.

LAWYER FOR PROSECUTION: And after your marriage you gave it up?

YOUNG WOMAN: Yes.

LAWYER FOR PROSECUTION: Why?

YOUNG WOMAN: Mr Jones did not like the feeling of them.

LAWYER FOR PROSECUTION: You always did everything Mr Jones wanted?

YOUNG WOMAN: I tried to—Anyway I didn't care any more—so much—about my hands.

LAWYER FOR PROSECUTION: I see—so after your marriage you never wore gloves at night any more?

YOUNG WOMAN: No.

LAWYER FOR PROSECUTION: Mrs Jones, isn't it true that you began wearing your rubber gloves again—in spite of your husband's expressed dislike—about a year ago—a year ago this spring?

YOUNG WOMAN: No.

LAWYER FOR PROSECUTION: You did not suddenly begin to care particularly for your hands again—about a year ago this spring?

YOUNG WOMAN: No.

LAWYER FOR PROSECUTION: You're quite sure of that?

YOUNG WOMAN: Yes.

LAWYER FOR PROSECUTION: Quite sure?

YOUNG WOMAN: Yes.

LAWYER FOR PROSECUTION: Then you did not have in your possession, on the night of June 2nd last, a pair of rubber gloves?

YOUNG WOMAN: *(shakes her head)* No.

LAWYER FOR PROSECUTION: *(to JUDGE)* I'd like to introduce these gloves as evidence at this time, your Honor.

JUDGE: Exhibit 24.

LAWYER FOR PROSECUTION: I'll return to them later—now, Mrs Jones—this nightgown—you recognize it, don't you?

YOUNG WOMAN: Yes.

LAWYER FOR PROSECUTION: Yours, is it not?

YOUNG WOMAN: Yes.

LAWYER FOR PROSECUTION: The one you were wearing the night your husband was murdered, isn't it?

YOUNG WOMAN: The night he died,—yes.

LAWYER FOR PROSECUTION: Not the one you wore under your peignoir—I believe that is what you call it, isn't it? A peignoir? When you received the police—but the one you wore before that—isn't it?

YOUNG WOMAN: Yes.

LAWYER FOR PROSECUTION: This was found—not where the gloves were found—no—but at the bottom of the soiled clothes hamper in the bathroom—rolled up and wet—why was it wet, Mrs Jones?

YOUNG WOMAN: I had tried to wash it.

LAWYER FOR PROSECUTION: Wash it? I thought you had just sat?

YOUNG WOMAN: First—I tried to make things clean.

LAWYER FOR PROSECUTION: Why did you want to make this—clean—as you say?

YOUNG WOMAN: There was blood on it.

LAWYER FOR PROSECUTION: Spattered on it?

YOUNG WOMAN: Yes.

LAWYER FOR PROSECUTION: How did that happen?

YOUNG WOMAN: The bottle broke—and the sharp edge cut.

LAWYER FOR PROSECUTION: Oh, the bottle broke and the sharp edge cut!

YOUNG WOMAN: Yes. That's what they told me afterwards.

LAWYER FOR PROSECUTION: Who told you?

YOUNG WOMAN: The police—that's what they say happened.

LAWYER FOR PROSECUTION: Mrs Jones, why did you try so desperately to wash that blood away—before you called the police?

LAWYER FOR DEFENSE: I object!

JUDGE: Objection overruled.

LAWYER FOR PROSECUTION: Why, Mrs Jones?

YOUNG WOMAN: I don't know. It's what anyone would have done, wouldn't they?

LAWYER FOR PROSECUTION: That depends, doesn't it? (*Suddenly taking up bottle*) Mrs Jones—when did you first see this?

YOUNG WOMAN: The night my husband was—done away with.

LAWYER FOR PROSECUTION: Done away with! You mean killed?

YOUNG WOMAN: Yes.

LAWYER FOR PROSECUTION: Why don't you say killed?

YOUNG WOMAN: It sounds so brutal.

LAWYER FOR PROSECUTION: And you never saw this before then?

YOUNG WOMAN: No sir.

LAWYER FOR PROSECUTION: You're quite sure of that?

YOUNG WOMAN: Yes.

LAWYER FOR PROSECUTION: And these stones—when did you first see them?

YOUNG WOMAN: The night my husband was done away with.

LAWYER FOR PROSECUTION: Before that night your husband was murdered—you never saw them? Never before then?

YOUNG WOMAN: No sir.

LAWYER FOR PROSECUTION: You are quite sure of that?

YOUNG WOMAN: Yes.

LAWYER FOR PROSECUTION: Mrs Jones, do you remember about a year ago, a year ago this spring, bringing home to your house—a lily, a Chinese water lily?

YOUNG WOMAN: No—I don't think I do.

LAWYER FOR PROSECUTION: You don't think you remember bringing home a water lily growing in a bowl filled with small stones?

YOUNG WOMAN: No—No I don't.

LAWYER FOR PROSECUTION: I'll show you this bowl, Mrs Jones. Does that refresh your memory?

YOUNG WOMAN: I remember the bowl—but I don't remember—the lily.

LAWYER FOR PROSECUTION: You recognize the bowl then?

YOUNG WOMAN: Yes.

LAWYER FOR PROSECUTION: It is yours, isn't it?

YOUNG WOMAN: It was in my house—yes.

LAWYER FOR PROSECUTION: How did it come there?

YOUNG WOMAN: How did it come there?

LAWYER FOR PROSECUTION: Yes—where did you get it?

YOUNG WOMAN: I don't remember.

LAWYER FOR PROSECUTION: You don't remember?

YOUNG WOMAN: No.

LAWYER FOR PROSECUTION: You don't remember about a year ago bringing this bowl into your bedroom filled with small stones and some water and a lily? You don't remember tending very carefully that lily till it died? And when it died you don't remember hiding the bowl full of little stones away on the top shelf of your closet—and keeping it there until—you don't remember?

YOUNG WOMAN: No, I don't remember.

LAWYER FOR PROSECUTION: You may have done so?

YOUNG WOMAN: No—no—I didn't! I didn't! I don't know anything about all that.

LAWYER FOR PROSECUTION: But you do remember the bowl?

YOUNG WOMAN: Yes. It was in my house—you found it in my house.

LAWYER FOR PROSECUTION: But you don't remember the lily or the stones?

YOUNG WOMAN: No—No I don't!

(LAWYER FOR PROSECUTION *turns to look among his papers in a brief case.*)

1ST REPORTER: (*writing*) Under the heavy artillery fire of the State's attorney's brilliant cross-questioning, the accused woman's defense was badly riddled. Pale and trembling she—

2ND REPORTER: (*writing*) Undaunted by the Prosecution's machine-gun attack, the defendant was able to maintain her position of innocence in the face of rapid-fire questioning that threatened, but never seriously menaced her defense. Flushed but calm she—

LAWYER FOR PROSECUTION: *(producing paper)* Your Honor, I'd like to introduce this paper in evidence at this time.

JUDGE: What is it?

LAWYER FOR PROSECUTION: It is an affidavit taken in the State of Guanajuato, Mexico.

LAWYER FOR DEFENSE: Mexico? Your Honor, I protest. A Mexican affidavit! Is this the United States of America or isn't it?

LAWYER FOR PROSECUTION: It's properly executed—sworn to before a notary—and certified to by an American Consul.

LAWYER FOR DEFENSE: Your Honor! I protest! In the name of this great United States of America—I protest—are we to permit our sacred institutions to be thus—

JUDGE: What is the purpose of this document—who signed it?

LAWYER FOR PROSECUTION: It is signed by one Richard Roe, and its purpose is to refresh the memory of the witness on the point at issue—and incidentally supply a motive for this murder—this brutal and cold-blooded murder of a sleeping man by—

LAWYER FOR DEFENSE: I protest, your Honor! I object!

JUDGE: Objection sustained. Let me see the document. *(Takes paper which is handed up to him—looks at it)* Perfectly regular. Do you offer this affidavit as evidence at this time for the purpose of refreshing the memory of the witness at this time?

LAWYER FOR PROSECUTION: Yes, your Honor.

JUDGE: You may introduce the evidence.

LAWYER FOR DEFENSE: I object! I object to the introduction of this evidence at this time as irrelevant, immaterial, illegal, biased, prejudicial, and—

JUDGE: Objection overruled.

LAWYER FOR DEFENSE: Exception.

JUDGE: Exception noted. Proceed.

LAWYER FOR PROSECUTION: I wish to read the evidence to the jury at this time.

JUDGE: Proceed.

LAWYER FOR DEFENSE: I object.

JUDGE: Objection overruled.

LAWYER FOR DEFENSE: Exception.

JUDGE: Noted.

LAWYER FOR DEFENSE: Why is this witness himself not brought into court—so he can be cross-questioned?

LAWYER FOR PROSECUTION: The witness is a resident of the Republic of Mexico and as such not subject to subpoena as a witness to this court.

LAWYER FOR DEFENSE: If he was out of the jurisdiction of this court how did you get this affidavit out of him?

LAWYER FOR PROSECUTION: This affidavit was made voluntarily by the deponent in the furtherance of justice.

LAWYER FOR DEFENSE: I suppose you didn't threaten him with extradition on some other trumped-up charge so that—

JUDGE: Order!

BAILIFF: Order!

JUDGE: Proceed with the evidence.

LAWYER FOR PROSECUTION: *(reading)* In the matter of the State of _____ vs. Helen Jones, I Richard Roe, being of sound mind, do herein depose and state that I know the accused, Helen Jones, and have known her for a period of over one year immediately preceding the date of the signature on this affidavit. That I first met the said Helen Jones in a so-called speakeasy somewhere in the West 40s in New York City. That on the day I met her, she went with me to my room, also somewhere in the West 40s in New York City, where we had intimate relations—

YOUNG WOMAN: *(moans)* Oh!

LAWYER FOR PROSECUTION: *(continues reading)* —and where I gave her a blue bowl filled with pebbles, also containing a flowering lily. That from the first day we met until I departed for Mexico in the Fall, the said Helen Jones was an almost daily visitor to my room where we continued to—

YOUNG WOMAN: No! No!

(Moans.)

LAWYER FOR PROSECUTION: What is it, Mrs Jones—what is it?

YOUNG WOMAN: Don't read any more! No more!

LAWYER FOR PROSECUTION: Why not?

YOUNG WOMAN: I did it! I did it! I did it!

LAWYER FOR PROSECUTION: You confess?

YOUNG WOMAN: Yes—I did it!

LAWYER FOR DEFENSE: I object, your Honor.

JUDGE: You confess you killed your husband?

YOUNG WOMAN: I put him out of the way—yes.

JUDGE: Why?

YOUNG WOMAN: To be free.

JUDGE: To be free? Is that the only reason?

YOUNG WOMAN: Yes.

JUDGE: If you just wanted to be free—why didn't you divorce him?

YOUNG WOMAN: Oh I couldn't do that! I couldn't hurt him like that!

(Burst of laughter from ALL *in the court. The* YOUNG WOMAN *stares out at them, and then seems to go rigid.)*

JUDGE: Silence!

BAILIFF: Silence!

(There is a gradual silence.)

JUDGE: Mrs Jones, why— (YOUNG WOMAN *begins to moan—suddenly—as though the realization of her enormity and her isolation had just come upon her. It is a sound of desolation, of agony, of human woe. It continues until the end of the scene)* Why—?

*(*YOUNG WOMAN *cannot speak.)*

LAWYER FOR DEFENSE: Your Honor, I ask a recess to—

JUDGE: Court's adjourned.

*(*SPECTATORS *begin to file out. The* YOUNG WOMAN *continues in the witness box, unseeing, unheeding.)*

1ST REPORTER: Murderess confesses.

2ND REPORTER: Paramour brings confession.

3RD REPORTER: I did it! Woman cries!

(There is a great burst of speed from the telegraphic instruments. They keep up a constant accompaniment to the WOMAN'S *moans. The scene* BLACKS OUT *as the courtroom empties and* TWO POLICEMEN *go to stand by the woman.)*

BLACK OUT

(The sound of the telegraph instruments continues until the scene lights into EPISODE NINE— *and the prayers of the* PRIEST.*)*

EPISODE NINE: A MACHINE

SCENE: *A Prison Room. The front bars face the audience. (They are set back far enough to permit a clear passageway across the stage.)*

SOUNDS: *The voice of a Negro singing. The whir of an aeroplane flying.*

CHARACTERS:
YOUNG WOMAN
A PRIEST
A JAILER
TWO BARBERS
A MATRON
MOTHER
TWO GUARDS

AT RISE:
In front of the bars, at one side, sits a MAN; *at the opposite side, a* WOMAN.

(The JAILER *and the* MATRON*).*
Inside the bars, a MAN *and a* WOMAN.

(The YOUNG WOMAN *and a* PRIEST*).*
The YOUNG WOMAN *sits still with folded hands. The* PRIEST *is praying.*

PRIEST: Hear, oh Lord, my prayer; and let my cry come to Thee. Turn not away Thy face from me; in the day when I am in trouble, incline Thy ear to me. In what day soever I shall call upon Thee, hear me speedily. For my days are vanished like smoke; and my bones are grown dry, like fuel for the fire. I am smitten as grass, and my heart is withered; because I forgot to eat my bread. Through the voice of my groaning, my bone hath cleaved to my flesh. I am become like to a pelican of the wilderness. I am like a night raven in the house. I have watched and become as a sparrow all alone on the housetop. All the day long my enemies reproach me; and they that praised me did swear against me. My days have declined like a shadow, and I am withered like grass. But Thou, oh Lord, end rest forever. Thou shalt arise and have mercy, for it is time to have mercy. The time is come. *(Voice of* NEGRO *offstage—Begins to sing a Negro spiritual.)*

PRIEST: The Lord hath looked upon the earth, that He might hear the groans of them that are in fetters, that He might release the children of—

*(*VOICE OF NEGRO *grown louder.)*

JAILER: Stop that nigger yelling.

YOUNG WOMAN: No, let him sing. He helps me.

MATRON: You can't hear the Father.

YOUNG WOMAN: He helps me.

PRIEST: Don't I help you, daughter?

YOUNG WOMAN: I understand him. He is condemned. I understand him.

*(*THE VOICE OF THE NEGRO SINGER *goes on louder, drowning out the voice of the* PRIEST.*)*

PRIEST: *(chanting in Latin)* Gratiam tuum, quaesumus, Domine, metibus nostris infunde, ut qui, angelo nuntiante, Christifilii tui incarnationem cognovimus, per passionem eius et crucem ad ressurectionis gloriam perducamus. Per eumdem Christum Dominum nostrum.

(Enter TWO BARBERS. *There is a rattling of keys.)*

1ST BARBER: How is she?

MATRON: Calm.

JAILER: Quiet.

YOUNG WOMAN: *(rising)* I am ready.

1ST BARBER: Then sit down.

YOUNG WOMAN: *(in a steady voice)* Aren't you the death guard come to take me?

1ST BARBER: No, we ain't the death guard. We're the barbers.

YOUNG WOMAN: The barbers.

MATRON: Your hair must be cut.

JAILER: Must be shaved.

BARBER: Just a patch. *(The* BARBERS *draw near her.)*

YOUNG WOMAN: No!

PRIEST: Daughter, you're ready. You know you are ready.

YOUNG WOMAN: *(crying out)* Not for this! Not for this!

MATRON: The rule.

JAILER: Regulations.

BARBER: Routine. *(The* BARBERS *take her by the arms.)*

YOUNG WOMAN: No! No! Don't touch me—touch me! *(*THEY *take her and put her down in the chair, cut a patch from her hair)* I will not be submitted—this indignity! No! I will not be submitted!—Leave me alone! Oh my God am I never to be let alone! Always to have to submit—to submit! No more—not now—I'm going to die—I won't submit! Not now!

BARBER: *(finishing cutting a patch from her hair)* You'll submit, my lady. Right to the end, you'll submit! There, and a neat job too.

JAILER: Very neat.

MATRON: Very neat.

(Exit BARBERS.*)*

YOUNG WOMAN: *(her calm shattered)* Father, Father! Why was I born?

PRIEST: I came forth from the Father and have come into the world—I leave the world and go into the Father.

YOUNG WOMAN: *(weeping)* Submit! Submit! Is nothing mine? The hair on my head! The very hair on my head—

PRIEST: Praise God.

YOUNG WOMAN: Am I never to be let alone! Never to have peace! When I'm dead, won't I have peace?

PRIEST: Ye shall indeed drink of my cup.

YOUNG WOMAN: Won't I have peace tomorrow?

PRIEST: I shall raise Him up at the last day.

YOUNG WOMAN: Tomorrow! Father! Where shall I be tomorrow?

PRIEST: Behold the hour cometh. Yea, is now come. Ye shall be scattered every man to his own.

YOUNG WOMAN: In Hell! Father! Will I be in Hell?

PRIEST: I am the Resurrection and the Life.

YOUNG WOMAN: Life has been hell to me, Father!

PRIEST: Life has been hell to you, daughter, because you never knew God! Gloria in excelsis Deo.

YOUNG WOMAN: How could I know Him, Father? He never was around me.

PRIEST: You didn't seek Him, daughter. Seek and ye shall find.

YOUNG WOMAN: I sought something—I was always seeking something.

PRIEST: What? What were you seeking?

YOUNG WOMAN: Peace. Rest and peace. Will I find it tonight, Father? Will I find it?

PRIEST: Trust in God.

(*A shadow falls across the passage in the front of the stage—and there is a shirring sound.*)

YOUNG WOMAN: What is that? Father! Jailer! What is that?

JAILER: An aeroplane.

MATRON: Aeroplane.

PRIEST: God in His Heaven.

YOUNG WOMAN: Look, Father! A man flying! He has wings! But he is not an angel!

JAILER: Hear his engine.

MATRON: Hear the engine.

YOUNG WOMAN: He has wings—but he isn't free! I've been free, Father! For one moment—down here on earth—I have been free! When I did what I did I was free! Free and not afraid! How is that, Father? How can that be? A great sin— a mortal sin—for which I must die and go to hell—but it made me free! One moment I was free! How is that, Father? Tell me that?

PRIEST: Your sins are forgiven.

YOUNG WOMAN: And that other sin—that other sin—that sin of love— That's all I ever knew of Heaven—heaven on earth! How is that, Father? How can that be—a sin—a mortal sin—all I know of heaven?

PRIEST: Confess to Almighty God.

YOUNG WOMAN: Oh, Father, pray for me—a prayer—that I can understand!

PRIEST: I will pray for you, daughter, the prayer of desire. Behind the King of Heaven, behold Thy Redeemer and God, Who is even now coming; prepare thyself to receive Him with love, invite him with the ardor of thy desire; come, oh my Jesus, come to thy soul which desires Thee! Before Thou givest Thyself to me, I desire to give Thee my miserable heart. Do Thou accept it, and come quickly to take possession of it! Come my God, hasten! Delay no longer! My only and Infinite Good, my Treasure, my Life, my Paradise, my Love, my all, my wish is to receive Thee with the love with which—

(*Enter the* MOTHER. *She comes along the passageway and stops before the bars.*)

YOUNG WOMAN: (*recoiling*) Who's that woman?

JAILER: Your mother.

MATRON: Your mother.

YOUNG WOMAN: She's a stranger—take her away—she's a stranger.

JAILER: She's come to say goodbye to you—

MATRON: To say goodbye.

YOUNG WOMAN: But she's never known me—never known me—ever— (*To the* MOTHER) Go away! You're a stranger! Stranger! Stranger! (MOTHER *turns and starts away. Reaching out her hands to her*) Oh Mother! Mother!

(*They embrace through the bars.*)

(*Enter* TWO GUARDS.)

PRIEST: Come, daughter.

1ST GUARD: It's time.

2ND GUARD: Time.

YOUNG WOMAN: Wait! Mother, my child; my little strange child! I never knew her! She'll never know me! Let her live, Mother. Let her live! Live! Tell her—

PRIEST: Come, daughter.

YOUNG WOMAN: Wait! wait! Tell her—

(*The* JAILER *takes the* MOTHER *away.*)

GUARD: It's time.

YOUNG WOMAN: Wait! Wait! Tell her! Wait! Just a minute more! There's so much I want to tell her—Wait—

(*The* JAILER *takes the* MOTHER *off.*)

(*The* TWO GUARDS *take the* YOUNG WOMAN *by the arms, and start through the door in the bars and down the passage, across stage and off.*)

(The PRIEST *follows; the* MATRON *follows the* PRIEST; *the* PRIEST *is praying.)*
(The scene BLACKS OUT.*)*
(The voice of the PRIEST *gets dimmer and dimmer.)*

PRIEST: Lord have mercy—Christ have mercy—Lord have mercy—Christ hear us! God the Father of Heaven! God the Son, Redeemer of the World, God the Holy Ghost—Holy Trinity one God—Holy Mary—Holy Mother of God—Holy Virgin of Virgins—St. Michael—St. Gabriel—St. Raphael—
(His voice dies out.)
(Out of the darkness come the voices of REPORTERS.*)*

1ST REPORTER: What time is it now?
2ND REPORTER: Time now.
3RD REPORTER: Hush.
1ST REPORTER: Here they come.
3RD REPORTER: Hush.
PRIEST: *(his voice sounds dimly—gets louder—continues until the end)* St. Peter pray for us—St. Paul pray for us—St. James pray for us—St. John pray for us—all ye holy Angels and Archangels—all ye blessed orders of holy spirits—St. Joseph—St. John the Baptist—St. Thomas—
1ST REPORTER: Here they are!
2ND REPORTER: How little she looks! She's gotten smaller.
3RD REPORTER: Hush.
PRIEST: St. Philip pray for us. All ye Holy Patriarchs and prophets—St. Philip—St.

Matthew—St. Simon—St. Thaddeus—All ye holy apostles—all ye holy disciples—all ye holy innocents—Pray for us—Pray for us—Pray for us.—
1ST REPORTER: Suppose the machine shouldn't work!
2ND REPORTER: It'll work!—It always works!
3RD REPORTER: Hush!
PRIEST: Saints of God make intercession for us—Be merciful—Spare us, oh Lord—be merciful—
1ST REPORTER: Her lips are moving—what is she saying?
2ND REPORTER: Nothing.
3RD REPORTER: Hush!
PRIEST: Oh Lord deliver us from all evil—from all sin—from Thy wrath—from the snares of the devil—from anger and hatred and every evil will—from—
1ST REPORTER: Did you see that? She fixed her hair under the cap—pulled her hair out under the cap.
3RD REPORTER: Hush!
PRIEST: —Beseech Thee—hear us—that Thou would'st spare us—that Thou would'st pardon us—Holy Mary—pray for us—
2ND REPORTER: There—
YOUNG WOMAN: *(calling out)* Somebody! Somebod—
(Her voice is cut off.)
PRIEST: Christ have mercy—Lord have mercy—Christ have mercy—

CURTAIN

HOLIDAY (1928)

With his marvelous gift for spinning, spiraling humors, Philip Barry keeps life gay through most of his new spindrift comedy, Holiday.

The *New York Times* review of Philip Barry's *Holiday* is typical of those that his most successful plays received in the late 1920s and 1930s. Barry, along with S. N. Behrman, Robert E. Sherwood, Elmer Rice, Sidney Howard, Maxwell Anderson, and, of course, Eugene O'Neill, epitomize a period when, to use Kenneth Macgowan's phrasing, Broadway was "burgeoning" and American drama was "coming of age." This success, however, was neither consistent nor universally conceded, as Carl Carmer's criticism of Barry published in a 1929 issue of *Theatre Arts Monthly* indicates. Barry, whose plays were produced more frequently outside of New York than those of any of his contemporaries save for O'Neill, was for Carmer a "widely acclaimed dramatist who has yet to write a play both popular and important." Put differently, Carmer and to a lesser extent Brooks Atkinson of the *New York Times* saw in Barry's work an unfortunate paradox: While his "serious" drama could not win support at the box office, his several **comedies** like *Holiday* proved enormously popular. Such commentators as Joseph Wood Krutch have generally followed the theatregoing public in this assessment, commending Barry and Behrman in particular for their writing of sparkling, consistently witty dialogue in "cosmopolitan" **high comedies** occupied to a great extent by sophisticated characters of "ease and gaiety and grace."

Philip Barry (1896–1949) was raised in a Roman Catholic family in Rochester, New York, and enrolled at Yale University in 1913. His college career was interrupted by World War I when he was assigned to the American Embassy in London. Once home from Europe, he returned to Yale, from which he graduated in 1919, and later enrolled in what at the time was America's most distinguished workshop for young dramatists, George Pierce Baker's Workshop 47 at Harvard, which other writers such as O'Neill, Behrman, and Howard attended as well at various times. Barry, who around this time fell in love with and eventually married the daughter of a wealthy New Yorker, left writing for a time to take a job as an advertising clerk, but returned to Harvard to write his first full-length play produced by the Workshop during the 1921–1922 season. Retitled *You and I*, the play opened at the Belmont Theatre in early 1923 and ran for 170 performances. Not yet 27, the young playwright whom Carmer described as "most representative of America's academically schooled dramatists" saw his first professional production become a considerable Broadway success.

Barry went on to write such comedies as *Paris Bound* (1927), *Holiday* (1928), *The Animal Kingdom* (1932), and his most enduringly popular play, *The Philadelphia Story* (1939), starring Katharine Hepburn. Occasionally, he turned to more serious material—in *John* (1927), for example, a play about John the Baptist, which closed after only 11 performances and which partially explains Carmer's thesis that by 1929 Barry had failed to write a play that was both "popular and important." *Tomorrow and Tomorrow* (1931) might qualify as achieving both, yet even this question betrays a familiar and questionable bias against comedy that, among other weaknesses, tends to ignore the important cultural work it can perform in questioning stereotypes, challenging accepted values or mores, and working toward redefined senses of social community. Given the booming business in video rentals and the accessibility of films from Hollywood's big-studio era, Barry is also remembered today through film versions of his plays

Holiday and *The Philadelphia Story*, which came to epitomize a sophisticated variety of comedy in the 1930s and '40s. The film version of *Holiday* (1938), starring Hepburn and Cary Grant, was followed by such comedies as Howard Hawks' *Bringing Up Baby* (1938), again starring Hepburn and Grant, *His Girl Friday* (1939), starring Grant and Rosalind Russell, and George Cukor's version of *The Philadelphia Story* (1940), starring Grant, Hepburn, and James Stewart. For their performances Hepburn won a New York Film Critics Award and was nominated for her third Academy Award, and Stewart received an Oscar as Best Actor.

Holiday and *The Philadelphia Story*, while by no means identical in plot and characterization, are nonetheless similar in several respects: the affluence of their central characters, for instance. As Stanley Cavell maintains, the narratives of Hollywood "Comedies of Remarriage" in the 1930s and 1940s like *The Philadelphia Story* emphasize questions of the "heroine's identity"; hence, the "subject of the genre is well described as the creation of the woman, or of the new woman, or the new creation of the human." Cavell points to other features that distinguish such works from, among others, Shakespearean **romantic comedies** (*A Midsummer Night's Dream, As You Like It*) concerned with the relationships of young lovers and paternal objections to their marriage. In *The Philadelphia Story*, in contrast to Shakespeare's plays, the central character Tracy Lord is 24, exceptionally mature and independent, and has already been married to and divorced from Dexter Haven, a wealthy man of 28. Tracy's relationship to her father is crucial to the play's action and to her evolving sense of self, as is her growing uncertainty about her impending marriage to George Kittredge. But her father, unlike those in romantic comedy and more like Linda Seton's in *Holiday*, can scarcely prevent Tracy from doing as she pleases. As Haven says near the end of the play after Kittredge believes Tracy has had an affair with Mike Connor, a journalist assigned to cover the wedding, it is not so much that a man expects his wife to "behave herself. Naturally"; rather, a husband should want his wife to "behave

herself naturally." Through this rephrasing, Barry's audience could easily formulate a crucial distinction between Tracy's two suitors: While Kittredge believes a wife owes a "natural" debt of obedience to her husband, Dexter represents a level of freedom impossible for Tracy to attain under Kittredge's patriarchal rule. The difference between the two articulations marks the distance between constraint and liberty, suppression of one's desire and the freedom to express it—in short, self-realization on one's own terms.

For Johnny Case and Linda Seton in *Holiday*, such self-fulfillment does not reside in the values of Linda's father and sister Julia, to whom Johnny is engaged. Both Julia and her father are driven by notions of social class, wealth, and success from which Case—and, soon afterward, Linda—must escape if they are to find freedom and inner peace. This conflict or opposition of values is registered in several different ways in the play. Most obviously, Linda's "playroom," to which she and a select few friends retreat for a private party in Act Two, constitutes an oppositional site to the ballroom below where Julia and her three hundred guests are gathered, awaiting the announcement of her engagement. Even the stage directions with which *Holiday* opens reflect the weightiness and confinement of the Seton house: The panelling and curtains are "heavy," the appointments are "rich, very rich," and a portrait of Linda's grandfather (and the tradition of business and wealth it represents) is prominently displayed over a fireplace. Against such solidity and tradition, Johnny's desire to retire from business while he is still young so as to "find out who I am and what I am" can only be seen as a rationalization for self-indulgence or a symptom, in Julia's last act assessment, of being an "idler." Loving the feeling of "being free" more than he loves Julia, Johnny opts to escape what, from his perspective, can only be imprisonment. Thus, it is not so much Edward Seton's opposition to Julia's marriage to Johnny that prevents it, but Julia's own subscription to her father's sense of values. For Linda, in love with Johnny, his decision to escape signals her one chance for happiness, and as the curtain falls she begins her pursuit of the man worth more to her than all her material possessions.

Linda's conflict between love for her sister and growing affection for her sister's fiancé may seem insignificant compared to the poverty of Elmer Rice's tenement dwellers in *Street Scene* (1929) or the entrapment of Helen Jones in Sophie Tread-well's *Machinal*. And, in some senses, it may be. But it is both an interesting and instructive histori-cal fact that in 1928 both *Machinal* and *Holiday* were designed and produced at the same theatre and by the same men—Robert Edmond Jones and Arthur Hopkins, respectively—*Machinal* in Sep-tember and *Holiday* two months later. Both plays, along with *Street Scene*, were anthologized in Burns Mantle's *The Best Plays of 1928–29;* both plays at-tracted their share of audience support. Both plays, however different, help define American drama in the 1920s and, at the same time, perhaps tell us something about the theatregoing public. In his book on Hollywood comedy, Cavell rejects the no-tion that, by the later 1930s, such texts were merely "fairy tales for the depression." Yet implicit in his argument that such works amount to something more than vehicles of escape for their audiences, Cavell opens up questions as to precisely what viewers took away from films like *The Philadelphia Story* or, in this case, plays like *Holiday*. And how might a theatre audience of *Holiday* in 1928, be-fore the great Stock Market Crash of 1929, have re-sponded differently from the film audience that saw the Hepburn-Grant version a decade later (or what is today the lesser-known 1930 film adapta-tion starring Mary Astor)? The answers to these questions might lead to a revaluation of the notion that Barry was incapable of writing a play that is both "popular" and "important."

WORKS CONSULTED

Atkinson, Brooks. "Review." *New York Times*, November 27, 1928: 36:1.

Carmer, Carl. "Philip Barry." *Theatre Arts Monthly* (November 1929): 819–826.

Cavell, Stanley. *Pursuits of Happiness: The Hollywood Comedy of Remarriage.* Cambridge, MA: Harvard University Press, 1981.

Krutch, Joseph Wood. *The American Drama Since 1918: An In-formal History.* New York: George Braziller, 1957.

Macgowan, Kenneth. "Introduction." *Famous American Plays of the 1920s.* New York: Laurel Books, 1959.

CHARACTERS

LINDA SETON . . . . She is twenty-seven, and looks about twenty-two. She is slim, rather boyish, exceedingly fresh. She is smart, she is pretty, but beside JULIA'S grace, JULIA'S beauty, she seems a trifle gauche, and almost plain.

JOHNNY CASE . . . . Is thirty, medium-tall, slight, attractive-looking, luck-ily not quite handsome.

JULIA SETON . . . . Is twenty-eight, and quite beautiful.

NED SETON . . . . He is twenty-six. He is as handsome in his way as JULIA is in hers. His features are fine, a little too fine. He dis-places very little, but no one minds: he is a nice boy.

SUSAN . . . . Is thirty, smart and attractive.

NICK POTTER . . . . He is about thirty-four, with an attractive, amusing face.

EDWARD SETON . . . . He is fifty-eight, large, nervous, distinguished.

LAURA . . . . SETON'S wife, is thirty-two, a shade taller than SETON, with a rather handsome, rather disagreeable face. She is as smartly dressed as a poor figure will allow.

SETON CRAM . . . . He is thirty-six, somewhat bald, inclined to a waist-line, but well turned out.

HENRY . . . . He is fifty, of pleasant appearance, of pleasant manner.

CHARLES . . . . A younger man-servant.

DELIA . . . . A housemaid of about thirty-five.

ACT I. *Room on the Third Floor of* EDWARD SETON'S *House in New York.*
ACT II. *Room on the Top Floor.*
ACT III. *Room on the Third Floor.*

ACT ONE

SCENE: *A room on the third floor of* EDWARD SETON'S *house in New York. The only entrance is at Left. It is a very large rectangular room of the Stanford White period. The panelling is heavy, the mouldings are heavy, the three long windows looking out over the park at Back are hung with heavy curtains. The portrait of* SETON'S *father, by a contemporary English master, hangs over the fireplace, at the right. It is a handsome room, and quite a comfortable room, but rich, very rich. At Right and Left are two comfortable sofas, a table behind each. On one table are two telephones, one for the house, the second for outside. On the other table, magazines and newspaper, and a cigarette-box. This side of the sofa, near Center, are two upholstered benches, and at Right and Left of each a large chair. In the corners of the room, at Back, stand two more chairs, a table and lamp beside each.*

TIME: *It is about twelve o'clock on a bright, cold Sunday morning in mid-December, this year.*

AT RISE: *A fire is burning in the fireplace. Sunday papers are strewn upon a low table and beside a chair near it.*

JULIA SETON *is seated at a desk, Right, writing a note. She is twenty-eight, and quite beautiful. She writes in silence for a few minutes, then calls, in response to a knock at the door:*

JULIA: Yes? (HENRY *enters from Left.* HENRY *is the butler. He is fifty, of pleasant appearance, of pleasant manner*) Oh, hello, Henry. How have you been? *(She seals the note.)*
HENRY: Well, thank you, Miss. We're very glad to have you back again.
JULIA: It was a lovely trip.
HENRY: A Mr Case to see you, Miss. He said you expected him, so Charles is bringing him up.
JULIA: That's right. How many are we for lunch?
HENRY: Six, I believe. Only Mr and Mrs Cram are expected.
JULIA: Hasn't Miss Linda friends, too?
HENRY: Not as we've been told, Miss.
JULIA: Have an extra place set, will you?
HENRY: Yes, Miss. (HENRY *collects the newspapers from the floor and chairs, and piles them in a neat pile upon a table. After a moment* CHARLES, *a younger man-servant, appears in the doorway.)*
CHARLES: Mr Case, Miss.

JULIA: *(rises from the desk and calls in the direction of the hall)* Come in, Johnny! Quick!—Of all slow people. (CHARLES *stands aside to admit* JOHNNY CASE, *and enters after him.* JOHNNY *is thirty, medium-tall, slight, attractive-looking, luckily not quite handsome. He goes at once to* JULIA.)

JOHNNY: There was a traffic-jam. Men were dying like flies.—Did you really go to church?

JULIA: Yes, but I ducked the sermon. I was sure you'd get here before me. You're staying for lunch, you know.

JOHNNY: Thanks, I'd love to. (BOTH *look warily at the* TWO MEN *tidying up the room)* I'm actually hungry again. Those same old shooting-pains.

JULIA: Isn't it extraordinary the appetite that place gives you? You should have seen the breakfast I ate on the train.

JOHNNY: Why wouldn't you join me? You were invited.

JULIA: Miss Talcott would have swooned away. She's the world's worriedest chaperon as it is. (HENRY *goes out.* CHARLES *has begun to gather ashtrays upon a larger tray)* —You can leave the trays till later, Charles.

CHARLES: Very well, Miss. *(He moves toward the door.* JULIA *talks against his exit.)*

JULIA: *(to* JOHNNY*)* Have you ever known such cold?

JOHNNY: Never.

JULIA: It's hard to believe it was twenty degrees lower at Placid.

JOHNNY: You don't feel it, there.

JULIA: That's what they say.—And you can close the door, Charles. It makes a draught.

CHARLES: Yes, Miss.

JULIA: When Mr Seton comes in, would you ring this room from the door? Two short ones.

CHARLES: Very good, Miss. *(He goes out, closing the door after him. For a moment* JULIA *and* JOHNNY *stand transfixed, looking at each other. Then* JULIA *smiles slightly and says)*

JULIA: Hello, Sweet— *(In an instant* JOHNNY *is beside her and she is in his arms, being kissed.*

At length she stands off from him, murmuring) Johnny—Johnny—mind your manners.

JOHNNY: But dear, where are we?

JULIA: We're here, all right. (JOHNNY *moves away from her and looks about him.)*

JOHNNY: But where's "here"?

JULIA: Where I live. Don't you like it?

JOHNNY: But Julia, seriously, what *is* all this?

JULIA: All what?

JOHNNY: All this house—and armies of men underfoot picking up newspapers, and—

JULIA: Aren't you silly, Johnny. I told you where I lived. *(She seats herself upon a sofa)* —I wrote it on the back of an envelope for you.

JOHNNY: But it's enormous. I'm overcome. It's the Grand Central. How can you stand it?

JULIA: I seem to manage.

JOHNNY: Don't you find you rattle around a good deal in it?

JULIA: I hadn't noticed that I did.

JOHNNY: *(cups his hands and calls through them)* Hoo! *(Then)* There's a bad echo.

JULIA: You stop criticizing this house, or I'll call the bouncer.

JOHNNY: But you must all be so *rich*, Julia!

JULIA: Well, we aren't poor.

JOHNNY: You should have told me, you really should.

JULIA: Would it have made any difference?

JOHNNY: *(laughs)* Lord, yes! I'd have asked you to marry me in two days, instead of ten.

JULIA: *(a pause. Then)* How do you mean?

JOHNNY: I went through an awful struggle. You've no idea. I had very definite plans for the next few years, and at first a wife looked like quite a complication.

JULIA: What were the plans?

JOHNNY: For one thing, I was worried about having enough for both of us. If I'd known, I'd have spared myself. It's simply swell now. Good Julia.

JULIA: Aren't you funny, Johnny.

JOHNNY: Why?

JULIA: To talk about it.

JOHNNY: It? Money? Why? Is it so sacred?

JULIA: Of course not. But—

JOHNNY: I'm simply delighted, that's all.

JULIA: —That I have—uh—money?

JOHNNY: Yes. Sure. *(She laughs.)*

JULIA: You're amazing.

JOHNNY: But why not?—If I'd suddenly discovered you could play the piano I'd be delighted, wouldn't I?

JULIA: Is it like knowing how to play the piano?

JOHNNY: Well, they're both very pleasant accomplishments in a girl.

JULIA: But, my dear, you're going to make millions, yourself!

JOHNNY: Oh, no, I'm not.

JULIA: You are too!

JOHNNY: —Am not.

JULIA: Are too. *(A brief pause.)*

JOHNNY: How did you happen to decide I'd do, Julia?

JULIA: I fell in love with you, silly.

JOHNNY: You might have done that, and still not have wanted to marry me.

JULIA: I do, though.

JOHNNY: You know awfully little about me.

JULIA: *I* know enough.—You aren't trying to get out of anything, are you, Johnny?

JOHNNY: Watch me.

JULIA: Because you haven't a chance, you know. *(She rises and goes to the window at Back.)*

JOHNNY: But what's there different about me? What did it?

JULIA: You're utterly, utterly different.

JOHNNY: —I am a man of the pee-pul—

JULIA: That might be one reason.

JOHNNY: I began life with these two bare hands.

JULIA: —So did the gentleman over the fireplace. *(*JOHNNY *looks at the portrait above the mantel)* —Take heart from Grandfather.

JOHNNY: You wouldn't tell me you're *those* Setons!

JULIA: Forgive us, Johnny, but we are.

JOHNNY: *(overwhelmed, lowers his head)* It's too much.

JULIA: *(lightly)* —What man has done, man can do—or words to that effect. *(She is looking out the window, down into the street.)*

JOHNNY: See here, child—if you think I'm a budding young Captain of Industry, or—

JULIA: Sh— wait a minute.

JOHNNY: What's the matter?

JULIA: It's the motor. At least I think—yes, it is.

JOHNNY: Him?

JULIA: Wait a minute— No—it's only Linda. Father must have decided to walk home with Ned.

JOHNNY: Did you tell him, as you planned to?

JULIA: *(again moves toward the sofa)* Father? Just exactly as I planned to.

JOHNNY: I'm still not sure that church was a good place.

JULIA: I wanted to give him a chance to think, before he started talking. He never talks in church.

JOHNNY: What did you say?

JULIA: I said, "Look here, Father: I'm going to marry Johnny Case." And he said, "What's that?" And I said, "I said, I'm going to marry Johnny Case."

JOHNNY: And he never even peeped?

JULIA: Oh, yes.—"And who may Johnny Chase be?" "Case," I said. "Not Chase." "Well, Case, then?"—I told him I'd met you at Placid, that he'd meet you at luncheon and that you were with Sloan, Hobson, Hunt and Sloan.—That was right, wasn't it?

JOHNNY: Sloan, Hobson, *Hunter* and Sloan.

JULIA: It was near enough. He said, "I know Sam Hobson," and began to pray rapidly—and that was all there was to it.

JOHNNY: But probably there'll be more.

JULIA: Yes, probably a lot more—I hope you're feeling strong. *(They seat themselves together upon the sofa at Right.)*

JOHNNY: Seriously, how do you think he'll take it?

JULIA: *(laughs)* —Seriously! *(Then)* You'll have one big thing in your favor, Johnny.

JOHNNY: What?

JULIA: You'll see.

JOHNNY: I know: It's this necktie.

JULIA: Johnny—

JOHNNY: Julia—

JULIA: Don't jest, boy.

JOHNNY: Oh, darling, let's not let the fun go out of it!

JULIA: Is it likely to?

JOHNNY: No, but—

JULIA: Say it.

JOHNNY: What was the point of spilling it so quickly?

JULIA: I had to tell Father. It would have been different if Mother were alive. I could have broken it gently through her, I suppose. But as it is—

JOHNNY: —Eventually, I know. But why the rush?

JULIA: I had to tell him. He'd never have forgiven me.

JOHNNY: It could have been such a swell guilty secret for awhile.

JULIA: I can't see what particular fun a secret would have been.

JOHNNY: Can't you, dear?

JULIA: No.

JOHNNY: All right.

JULIA: Oh, don't say "all right" that way! You don't mean "all right."

JOHNNY: *(smiles)* All right.

JULIA: You're the most outspoken, direct man I've ever known, and you sit there, sobbing over—

JOHNNY: It's all right, dear. Really it is.

JULIA: I thought you wanted us to be married as soon as possible.

JOHNNY: I do.

JULIA: Well, then.

JOHNNY: When shall we?

JULIA: There's another place Father comes in.

JOHNNY: I should think it would be pretty much up to you.

JULIA: You don't know Father.

JOHNNY: But let's not have an elaborate one— wedding, I mean.

JULIA: I doubt if we can avoid it. We've got to think of Father.

JOHNNY: It's getting pretty complicated.

JULIA: You didn't think it would be simple, did you?

JOHNNY: I suppose I just didn't think.

JULIA: You couldn't have. *(In sudden exasperation)* Oh, Johnny, *Johnny*—what's the matter with you?

JOHNNY: I just hate the thought of sitting down with a man and being practical about you—so soon, I mean. *(*JULIA *softens.)*

JULIA: —Angel. *(She kisses him, lightly)* It's got to be done, though.

JOHNNY: All right. I'll gird up my loins.—You know, I'll bet he'll hate this necktie. It doesn't look substantial.

JULIA: You might sit like this—covering it with your hand.

JOHNNY: I love you, Julia.

JULIA: I love you, Johnny.

JOHNNY: That's the main thing, isn't it?

JULIA: Darling, that's everything—

JOHNNY: Kiss?

JULIA: With pleasure— *(They kiss.)*

JOHNNY: —Don't go.

JULIA: I wouldn't think of it.

JOHNNY: It'd be swell to have this whole day free with no ordeals to face.

JULIA: It'll be over soon.—I think we'll have Ned and Linda on our side.

JOHNNY: Lord, do they have to mix in, too?

JULIA: Well, they're my brother and sister.

JOHNNY: Are they good guys?

JULIA: —Dears. Ned's a little inclined to drink too much, but I think he'll outgrow it. You ought to be able to help him, I think. Linda's a curious girl. She's developed the queerest—I don't know—attitude toward life. I can't make her out. She doesn't think as we do at all, any more.

JOHNNY: We?

JULIA: —The family. Father's worried sick about her. I think *we* can help her a lot, though—I hope we can.

JOHNNY: *(rises and goes to the fireplace)* She might prefer to work it out for herself. So might Ned.

JULIA: You *are* strange this morning, Johnny.

JOHNNY: How?

JULIA: You seem—not to like things quite as much as you might.

JOHNNY: Oh, yes, I do!

JULIA: We can't just wander forever up snowy mountains through pine woods with never a care, you know.

JOHNNY: Come here, darling. *(He goes to her, she to him. They meet)* —We can do better than that.

JULIA: Do you suppose?

JOHNNY: I know. *(JULIA'S head drops.)*

JULIA: Oh, I feel so awfully sad all at once.

JOHNNY: Don't—*don't*. Don't ever— *(His grasp tightens upon her shoulders)* Look up here—! *(With an effort, she looks up)* —Now please kiss me several times. *(She kisses him, once, twice, lightly.)*

JULIA: Is that all right?

JOHNNY: All right, hell. It's perfect. *(He bends to kiss her again, when the door suddenly opens and LINDA SETON enters, in hat and fur coat. LINDA is twenty-seven, and looks about twenty-two. She is slim, rather boyish, exceedingly fresh. She is smart, she is pretty, but beside JULIA'S grace, JULIA'S beauty, she seems a trifle gauche, and almost plain. She is pulling off her hat.)*

LINDA: I must say, that of all the boring— *(She stops at the sight of JULIA and JOHNNY)* Why, Julia. For shame, Julia. *(JULIA and JOHNNY part. LINDA throws her hat and gloves upon a chair)* Is this a way to spend Sunday morning? Who's your partner? Anyone I know?

JULIA: It's— *(She recovers her composure)* —This is Mr Case—my sister, Linda.

JOHNNY: How do you do?

LINDA: Well, thanks.—And you?

JOHNNY: I couldn't be better.

LINDA: Good.

JULIA: *(with dignity)* —*Johnny* Case, his name is. I'm going to marry him.

LINDA: That makes it all right, then. *(She takes off her coat)* Who's coming to lunch? Susan and Nick didn't telephone, did they?

JULIA: —In just about one month I'm going to marry him.

LINDA: Stand over here in the light, will you, Case? *(JOHNNY turns to her scrutiny)* —But I've never even seen you before.

JULIA: Neither had I, until ten days ago at Placid.

LINDA: *(to JOHNNY, with hope)* You aren't a guide, are you?

JOHNNY: No. I'm a lawyer.

LINDA: Wouldn't you know it.

JULIA: *(seats herself upon a chair at Right)* I want you to be maid-of-honor, Linda.

LINDA: I accept. What'll we wear? *(She sits upon the bench at Left, and JOHNNY upon the sofa facing her)* Listen: is this what came over Father in church?

JULIA: I imagine so.

LINDA: Then you've told him already.

JULIA: Yes.

LINDA: Tsch-tsch, this modern generation. *(To JOHNNY)* Well, young man, I hope you realize what you're getting in for.

(DELIA, a housemaid of about thirty-five, comes in, takes LINDA'S coat, hat and gloves, and goes out with them.)

JULIA: That's pleasant.

LINDA: I don't mean you. You're divine. I mean Father—and Cousin Seton Cram and Laura and the rest of the outlying Setons—and the general atmosphere of plenty, with the top riveted down on the cornucopia—

JULIA: Johnny will try to bear up, won't you, Johnny?

JOHNNY: I'll do my best.

LINDA: *(goes to JULIA and seats herself upon the bench facing her)* But how *did* you happen to get together? Tell Linda everything.

JULIA: Well, I was walking along the road with Miss Talcott one morning on the way to the rink and who should I see but—

LINDA: —*Whom* should I see but—

JULIA: —And who should I see but this man coming along, carrying skis.

LINDA: Fancy that. A downright romance. Go on, dear—

JULIA: Do you really want to know?

LINDA: I'm hungry for romance, Sister. If you knew the way my little heart is beating against its bars right this minute.

JULIA: He had a queer look on his face.

LINDA: I can believe that. His eyes must have been burning.

JULIA: As a matter of fact, the trouble was with his nose. So I stopped him and said: "I suppose you don't realize it, but your nose is frozen." And he said: "Thanks, I hadn't realized it." And I said: "Well, it is." And he said: "I don't suppose there's anything you personally could do about it."

LINDA: Fresh.

JULIA: I thought so too.

JOHNNY: She was fresh to mention it. It looked to me like an out-and-out pick-up.

LINDA: Obviously.

JULIA: I know a good thing when I see it.

LINDA: *(to JOHNNY)* —So you swept her off her snowshoes?

JOHNNY: It was touch-and-go with us.

LINDA: *(to JULIA)* I think I like this man.

JULIA: I was sure you would.

LINDA: Well, my dears, take your happiness while you may.

JOHNNY: Watch us.

JULIA: *(laughs)* No—*don't* watch us! Hello, Ned—

(NED SETON enters from the hall. He is twenty-six. He is as handsome in his way as JULIA is in hers. His features are fine, a little too fine. He displaces very little, but no one minds: he is a nice boy. JOHNNY rises. NED goes to JULIA.)

NED: Oh, *you're* back.—Then it was you who took that shaker out of my room.

JULIA: This is Mr Case—my brother Ned. *(JOHNNY moves to NED. They shake hands briefly.)*

NED: How do you do?—It was you who took it, Julia, and I'm getting sick of your meddling in my affairs.

JULIA: I'm going to marry him. *(NED turns slowly, as JULIA's words penetrate, and regards JOHNNY.)*

NED: You've got a familiar look about you.

JOHNNY: That's good.

NED: Is your name Johnny Case?

JOHNNY: Johnny Case.

NED: —One Saturday, quite a while ago, I went down to New Haven for a game. Afterwards, you took me all the way home from the Field, and put me to bed somewhere.

LINDA: How sweet.

JOHNNY: Call me Nana. *(He goes to the sofa at Right.)*

NED: I never got a chance to thank you. Thanks.

JOHNNY: It's all right.—Any time.

NED: *(settles down with a newspaper on the sofa at Left)* He's a good man, this Case fellow.

LINDA: The point is, there's no moss apparent, nor yet the slightest touch of decay.

NED: I expect Father'll be a job. When do they come to grips?

JULIA: Before luncheon, I suppose.

LINDA: *(rises)* That soon? See here, Case, *I* think you need some coaching.

JOHNNY: I'd be grateful for anything in this trouble.

LINDA: Have you anything at all but your winning way to your credit?

JOHNNY: Not a thing.

JULIA: Oh, hasn't he, though!

LINDA: The first thing Father will want to know is, how are you fixed?

JOHNNY: Fixed?

LINDA: *(firmly)* —Fixed.—Are you a man of means, and if so, how much?

JULIA: Linda!

LINDA: Be still, Beauty. *(To JOHNNY)* I know you wouldn't expect that of a man in Father's position, but the fact is, money is our god here.

JULIA: Linda, I'll—! —Johnny, it isn't true at all.

NED: *(looks up from his paper)* No?—What is, then?

LINDA: Well, young man?

JOHNNY: *(goes to her)* I have in my pocket now, thirty-four dollars, and a package of Lucky Strikes. Will you have one?

LINDA: Thanks. *(She takes a cigarette from him)* —But no gilt-edged securities? No rolling woodlands?

JOHNNY: I've got a few shares of common stock tucked away in a warm place.

LINDA: —Common? Don't say the word. *(She accepts a light from him)* I'm afraid it won't do, Julia.—He's a comely boy, but probably just another of the vast army of clock-watchers. *(She moves toward the window. JOHNNY laughs and seats himself on the sofa at Right.)*

NED: *(from behind his newspaper)* How are you socially?

JOHNNY: Nothing there, either.

LINDA: *(turning)* You mean to say your mother wasn't even a Whoozis?

JOHNNY: Not even that.

JULIA: Linda, I do wish you'd shut up.

NED: Maybe he's got a judge somewhere in the family.

LINDA: Yes, that might help. Old Judge Case's boy. White pillars. Guitars a-strummin'. Evenin', Massa.

NED: You must know some prominent people. Drop a few names.

LINDA: —Just casually, you know: "When I was to Mrs Onderdonk's cock-fight last Tuesday, whom should I see but Mrs Marble. Well, sir, I thought we'd die laughing—"

JULIA: *(to JOHNNY)* This is a lot of rot, you know.

JOHNNY: I'm having a grand time.

LINDA: "'Johnny,' she says to me—she calls me 'Johnny'—"

JULIA: Oh, will you be *quiet!* What on earth has set you off this time?

LINDA: But it's dreadful, Sister. *(To JOHNNY)* —Just what do you think you're going to prove with Edward Seton, financier and cotillion-leader?

JOHNNY: Well, I'll tell you: when I find myself in a position like this, I ask myself: What would General Motors do? Then I do the opposite.

LINDA: *(laughs and reseats herself. To JULIA)* It'll be a pity, if it doesn't come off. It'll be a real pity.

JULIA: It will come off. *(To JOHNNY)* Father isn't at all as they say he is.

JOHNNY: No?

JULIA: Not in the least.—Ned, where is he? Didn't he come in with you?

JOHNNY: Don't hurry him. There's no hurry.

NED: He said he had to stop to see Sam Hobson about something.

JULIA: *(to JOHNNY)* You.

JOHNNY: That's nice. I hope I get a good character.

LINDA: If it does go through all right, are you really going to make it quick?

JULIA: The second week in January. The tenth.

LINDA: —Announcing when?

JULIA: Right away—next Saturday, say.

LINDA: *(eagerly)* Oh, darling, let me give a party for it!

JULIA: *(puzzled)* Do you want to? I thought you hated the thought of—

LINDA: *I* want to! Not Father. *I* want to.

JULIA: Why, of course, dear. We'd love it.

NED: Who'd like a drink? *(No one bothers with him.)*

LINDA: —Father's to have nothing to do with it. And we *won't* send out cards. I'll telephone people.—Saturday's New Year's Eve, do you know it? Oh, Lord, Lord—let's have some fun in this house before you leave it!

JULIA: Why, Linda—

LINDA: I mean it! Let me, won't you?

JULIA: If Father doesn't mind.

LINDA: No ifs at all!—And just a few people—very few. Not a single bank of pink roses and no String Quartet during supper. All I want by way of entertainment is just one good tap-dancer. Let me plan it. Let me give it. Julia, let *me* do something for you once—*me*, Julia.

JULIA: I'd love it, dear. I really would.

LINDA: It won't be a ball, it'll be a simple sit-down supper—and you know where?—The old playroom.

JULIA: Why, not the—

LINDA: —Because the playroom's the one room in this house anyone's ever had fun in!

NED: I haven't been up there for ten years.

LINDA: That's your loss, Neddy. I've installed a newfangled gramophone, and I sit and play to myself by the hour. Come up some time. It's worth the trip. *(She turns suddenly to JOHNNY)* —Do you know any living people, Case? That's a cry from the heart.

JOHNNY: One or two.

LINDA: Give me a list. *(To JULIA)* —Seton and Laura can't have a look-in—is that understood? *(To JOHNNY)* —A terrible cousin and his wife—the Seton Crams. They're coming for lunch today. I hope your digestion's good. *(To JULIA)* —Not a look-in, remember.

JULIA: I don't know how you'll keep them out.

LINDA: *(rises abruptly)* Oh, Julia—this is important to me!—No one must touch my party but me, do you hear?

JULIA: All right, darling.

LINDA: If anyone does, I won't come to it.

NED: —At that, you might have a better time. *(He rises)* Look here, Case—

JOHNNY: Yes?

NED: Cocktails aren't allowed at mid-day, so just before luncheon's announced I'll ask you if you care to brush up.

JOHNNY: And guess what I'll say.

JULIA: There'll be wine with lunch, Ned.

NED: You have to give it something to build on, don't you? *(A BUZZER sounds twice. JULIA and JOHNNY rise.)*

JULIA: —It's Father! He's home.

LINDA: He'll go up to his sitting-room first.

JULIA: *(moves toward the door)* I know. Come on with me, Ned.

NED: I don't want to see him.

JULIA: Please come with me. *(NED goes out. She turns to JOHNNY)* You wait here with Linda a moment. I'll either come down again or send word. Just talk a while. *(She follows NED out. A brief pause. Then LINDA goes to the bench at Left, and JOHNNY to the one at Right.)*

LINDA: However do you do, Mr Case?

JOHNNY: —And you, Miss—uh—?

LINDA: Seton is the name.

JOHNNY: Not one of the bank Setons!

LINDA: The same.

JOHNNY: Fancy!—I hear a shipment of ear-marked gold is due in on Monday. *(Now they are seated)*

LINDA: *(in her most social manner)* Have you been to the Opera much lately?

JOHNNY: Only in fits and starts, I'm afraid.

LINDA: But, my dear, we must do *something* for them! They entertained us in Rome.

JOHNNY: —And you *really* saw Mount Everest?

LINDA: Chit.

JOHNNY: Chat.

LINDA: Chit-chat.

JOHNNY: Chit-chat.

LINDA: Will that go for the preliminaries?

JOHNNY: It's all right with me.

LINDA: I love my sister Julia more than anything else in this world.

JOHNNY: I don't blame you. So do I.

LINDA: She's so sweet, you don't know.

JOHNNY: Yes, I do.

LINDA: She's beautiful.

JOHNNY: She's all of that.

LINDA: —And exciting, too—don't you think?

JOHNNY: —Don't. I'll start gittering.

LINDA: It's terribly important that she should marry the right person.

JOHNNY: That's important for everyone.

LINDA: It's particularly so for Julia.—I suppose you realize you're a rather strange bird in these parts.

JOHNNY: How's that?

LINDA: You don't know the kind of men we see as a rule.—Where have you been?

JOHNNY: Oh—working hard.

LINDA: Nights?

JOHNNY: Nights too.

LINDA: What about these little jaunts to Placid? Come clean, Case.

JOHNNY: That's the first holiday I've ever had.

LINDA: *(unconvinced)* Yes.

JOHNNY: You heard what I said.

LINDA: Then you can't have been working long.

JOHNNY: Just since I was ten. *(She frowns, puzzled.)*

LINDA: —Ten. At what?

JOHNNY: —Anything I could get. Law, the last few years.

LINDA: —Must be ambitious.

JOHNNY: *(expels his breath in a long, tired jet)* I am. Not for that, though.

LINDA: For what, then?

JOHNNY: Oh—to live. Do you mind? *(There is a pause.)*

LINDA: What is it you've been doing?

JOHNNY: I don't call what I've been doing, living.

LINDA: No? *(He shakes his head.)*

JOHNNY: —A while ago you asked me if I knew any living people. I know damn few.

LINDA: There aren't but damn few.

JOHNNY: Well, I mean to be one of them some day. Johnny's dream.

LINDA: So do I. Linda's longing.

JOHNNY: There's a pair called Nick and Susan Potter—

LINDA: So you know Nick and Susan?

JOHNNY: I should say I do.

LINDA: So that's where I've heard your name. Aren't they grand?

JOHNNY: It seems to me they know just about everything. Maybe I'm wrong.

LINDA: You're not, though.

JOHNNY: Life must be swell when you have some idea of what goes on, the way they do.

LINDA: They get more fun out of nothing than anyone I know.

JOHNNY: You don't have such a bad time yourself, do you?

LINDA: (leaning forward) Case, are you drawing me out? (JOHNNY laughs.)

JOHNNY: Sure! Come on!

LINDA: Well, compared to the time I have, the last man in a chain-gang thoroughly enjoys himself.

JOHNNY: But how does that happen?

LINDA: You tell me, and I'll give you a rosy red apple.

JOHNNY: It seems to me you've got everything.

LINDA: Oh, it does, does it?

JOHNNY: What's the matter? Are you fed up?

LINDA: —To the neck.—Now tell me about your operation.

JOHNNY: I had been ailing for years—I don't know—life seemed to have lost its savor—

LINDA: Couldn't you do your housework?

JOHNNY: Every time I ran upstairs I got all rundown. (LINDA laughs. JOHNNY leans forward) You'd better come on a party with Julia and me.

LINDA: Any time you need an extra girl, give me a ring.—When?

JOHNNY: How's Tuesday?

LINDA: Splendid, thanks.—And how's Thursday?

JOHNNY: Blooming.

LINDA: (reflectively) —Looked badly the last time we met.

JOHNNY: —Just nerves, nothing but nerves.

LINDA: (a moment's pause. Then) —Do I seem to you to complain a good deal?

JOHNNY: I hadn't noticed it.

LINDA: Then I can let myself go a little: this is a hell of a life, Case.

JOHNNY: (looks about him) What do you mean? All this luxe? All this—?

LINDA: You took the words right out of my mouth.

JOHNNY: Well, for that matter, so's mine.

LINDA: What's the answer?

JOHNNY: Maybe you need some time off, too—I mean from what you're doing, day in, day out—

LINDA: Days out, please—years out—

JOHNNY: All right: take it. Take the time—

LINDA: —And of course that's so easy.

JOHNNY: —It can be done. I intend to do it. I intend to take quite a lot of it—when I'm not so busy just making the wherewithal.

LINDA: Case, you astonish me. I thought you were a Willing Worker.

JOHNNY: I am, if I can get what I'm working for.

LINDA: And what would that be?

JOHNNY: Mine is a simple story: I just want to save part of my life for myself. There's a catch to it, though. It's got to be part of the young part.

LINDA: You'll never get on and up that way.

JOHNNY: All right, but I want my time while I'm young. And let me tell you, the minute I get hold of just about twenty nice round thousands, I'm going to knock off for as long as they last, and—

LINDA: Quit?

JOHNNY: Quit. Retire young, and work old. That's what I want to do.

LINDA: —Grand. Does Julia know about it?

JOHNNY: No—there's no use getting her hopes up until it happens.—Don't tell her, will you?

LINDA: She has enough of her own for two right now—or ten, for that matter. Mother and Grandfather did us pretty pretty.

JOHNNY: *(shakes his head)* Thanks, but I've got to do myself—only just pretty enough.

LINDA: I see. That's foolish—but you're all right, Case. You haven't been bitten with it yet—you haven't been caught by it.

JOHNNY: By what?

LINDA: *(so reverently)* The reverence for riches.

JOHNNY: *(laughs)* You *are* a funny girl.

LINDA: —Funny, am I? And what about you, you big stiff?

JOHNNY: *(laughs, and rises)* —Just take Johnny's hand, and come into the Light, sister. *(JULIA enters. JOHNNY turns to her)* Did you see him?

JULIA: I saw him.

LINDA: Julia! How was he?

JULIA: I don't know yet.—Johnny, you go up to Ned's room. You haven't arrived yet. Take the elevator—Father's coming down the stairs. Quick, will you?

JOHNNY: When do I arrive?

JULIA: One o'clock. It's quarter to.

JOHNNY: This is getting a little complicated, if you ask me.

JULIA: Nobody asked you. Go on! Do as you're told.

JOHNNY: *(turns)* See here, you saucy—

LINDA: *(goes to the fireplace)* Go on, Case. Don't expect simplicity here—just think of our Fifth Avenue frontage. *(JOHNNY laughs and goes out. LINDA turns to JULIA)* Tell me: was Father awful?

JULIA: —The same old story, of course: I'm being married for my money.

LINDA: That's always flattering.—But Case didn't know our foul secret, did he?

JULIA: No.

LINDA: Even if he had, what of it?—And what good's all this jack we've got, anyway—unless to get us a superior type of husband?

JULIA: I hate you to talk like that! I hate it!

LINDA: Listen to me, Julia: I'm sore all the way through. I've been sore for a long time now, ever since I really saw how it—oh, never mind.

Anyway, I don't doubt that if Case *had* known he'd still be running. You're in luck there.

JULIA: You do like him, don't you?

LINDA: She asks me if I like him!—My dear girl, do you realize that *life* walked into this house this morning? Marry him quick. Don't let him get away. And if Father starts the usual—where *is* Big Business, anyhow?

JULIA: He said he'd be right down.

LINDA: Stand your ground, Julia. If you don't know your own mind by now, you haven't got a mind. Name your date and stick to it. I'm telling you.

JULIA: *(slowly)* I want Father to see that Johnny has the selfsame qualities Grandfather had,—and that there's no reason why he shouldn't arrive just where he did.

LINDA: —If he wants to.

JULIA: —Wants to! You don't know Johnny. You don't know how far he's come already—and from what—

LINDA: —Or where he's going.

JULIA: *I* do! *I* know! I can see it clear as day! *(A moment. Then)* Linda—

LINDA: What?

JULIA: It'll be awful to leave you.

LINDA: I don't know exactly what I'll do, when you go. I've got to do something—get out—quit on it—change somehow, or I'll go mad. I could curl up and die right now.

JULIA: *(touched)* Why, darling—

LINDA: Why, my foot. I don't look sick, do I? *(She moves to the fireplace)* Oh, Lord, if I could only get *warm* in this barn! *(She crouches before the fire and holds her hands to it)* —Never mind about me. I'll be all right. Look out for yourself. When Big Business comes down, just watch you don't let him— *(The door opens. She looks over her shoulder and sees her Father)* —But by a strange coincidence, here he is now.

JULIA: Did you see Mr Hobson, Father?

(EDWARD SETON enters. He is fifty-eight, large, nervous, distinguished. He wears a black morning coat, a white carnation in the buttonhole, and gray striped trousers. He takes nose glasses

from his nose and folds them away in a silver case.)

EDWARD: Yes.—Of course, my dear, there is another thing to be considered: What is the young man's background? Is he the sort of person that—? Ah, good morning, Linda.

LINDA: You saw me in church, Father. What's on your mind? You look worried.

EDWARD: I presume Julia has told you her story?

LINDA: Story? She's told me the facts.

EDWARD: But we mustn't rush into things, must we? *(A glance passes between* JULIA *and* LINDA.*)*

JULIA: *(goes to him)* I want to be married on January tenth, Father. That's—that's just two weeks from Tuesday.

EDWARD: *(moves to the table behind the sofa at Right, and begins to search through the newspapers)* Quite impossible.

LINDA: Why?

JULIA: Yes, why? I—I'm sure I couldn't stand a long engagement.

EDWARD: As yet, there is no engagement to stand.

LINDA: The boy has loads of charm, Father.

EDWARD: *(quickly)* You know him?

LINDA: I've heard tell of him.

EDWARD: *(tastes the word)* Charm.

LINDA: —I suppose it's solid merit you're after. Well, the rumor is he's got that, too. Sterling chap, on the whole. A catch, in fact. *(* NED *wanders in and seats himself upon the sofa at Left, with a newspaper.)*

JULIA: What did Mr Hobson say, Father?

EDWARD: We must find out about the young man's background.

JULIA: What did he say?

EDWARD: Have you the financial section of the *Times*, Ned?

NED: No, I try to take Sundays off, when I can.

EDWARD: —Which reminds me: I should like you to make a practice of remaining in the office until six o'clock.

NED: Six!—What for?

EDWARD: As an example to the other men.

NED: But there's nothing for me to do after three.

EDWARD: You will find something.

NED: Look here, Father—if you think I'm going to fake a lot of—

EDWARD: Did you understand me, Ned? *(A moment:* NED *loses)*

NED: —Oh, all right.

JULIA: What did Mr Hobson say about Johnny, Father?

EDWARD: *(settles himself upon the sofa with the financial section, now happily found)* His report was not at all unfavorable.

LINDA: That must have been a blow.

JULIA: —But what did he *say?*

EDWARD: We must find out more about the young man, Julia. He seems to have some business ability—he has put through what looks like a successful reorganization of Seaboard Utilities. He holds some of the stock.

NED: Seaboard! Poor fellow—

EDWARD: —Shrewd fellow, perhaps. Hobson says signs are not unfavorable for Seaboard.—We'll buy some in the morning, Ned.

LINDA: Just another ill wind blowing money to Da-Da.

EDWARD: But we *must* know more about Mr Chase's background.

JULIA: Case, Father, Case.

LINDA: Let it go. Chase has such a sweet banking sound.

JULIA: He's from Baltimore.

LINDA: Fine old pre-war stock, I imagine.

NED: Wasn't there a Judge Case somewhere?

EDWARD: We shall see. We shall take steps to—

LINDA: Father, if you reach for a Social Register, I'll cry out with pain.

EDWARD: *(with decision)* Well, I most certainly intend to know more about the young man than his name and his birthplace.—He does not, of course, realize that you have spoken to me, as yet?

NED: Of course not.

LINDA: Julia works fast, but not *that* fast, do you, Julia? *(* JULIA *does not answer.)*

EDWARD: I propose not to allow the subject of an engagement to come up in my first talk with him. I believe I am competent to direct the conversation.—You and Ned, Julia, may excuse yourselves on one pretext or another. I should like you to stay, Linda.

LINDA: I *knew* I should have learned shorthand. (EDWARD *smiles.* HENRY *enters.*)

EDWARD: I shall trust your memory.—Yes, Henry?

HENRY: Mr Case wishes to be announced, sir.

EDWARD: Yes. (HENRY *goes out, closing the door after him.* EDWARD *arranges his cuffs, and takes a firmer seat in his chair.*)

LINDA: —So does Mr Case's engagement. I want to give a party for it New Year's Eve, Father.

JULIA: Wait a minute, dear—

EDWARD: *(watching the doorway)* You may give a party if you like, Linda, but whether to announce an engagement, we shall see—

LINDA: —Another point about my party is that it's *my* party—mine.

EDWARD: Yes?

LINDA: Yes—and as such, I'd like to run it. I can do quite well without your secretary this time, darling—and without Seton's and Laura's helpful hints, I can do brilliantly.—There's someone at the door.

NED: Keep a stiff upper lip, Father. No doubt the fellow is an impostor.

EDWARD: *(laughs)* Oh, we shall learn many things this morning! He is not the first young man to be interviewed by me.

JULIA: Father—

EDWARD: Yes, Daughter?

JULIA: Remember: I know what I want. (JOHNNY *enters*) Oh, here you are!

JOHNNY: Here I am.

JULIA: Father, this is—Mr Case. (JOHNNY *goes to* EDWARD. *They shake hands.* NED *rises.*)

EDWARD: How do you do, Mr Case?

JOHNNY: How do you do, sir?

EDWARD: —My daughter, Linda.

LINDA: How do you do?

JOHNNY: How do you do?

EDWARD: And my son, Ned.

JOHNNY: How do you do?

NED: I recall your face, but your figure puzzles me.

EDWARD: Julia, if you and Ned will do the telephoning I spoke of, Linda and I will try to entertain Mr Case until the others come—won't we, Linda?

LINDA: Sure. I'm game.

JULIA: *(moves toward the door)* —Coming, Ned?

NED: *(following her)* I wonder what we'd do without the telephone. *(They go out.)*

EDWARD: Sit down, Mr Case.

JOHNNY: Thank you. *(He seats himself upon the bench, Left, and* LINDA *upon a small stool at the fireplace.)*

EDWARD: I presume, like all young people, you have the bad habit of smoking before luncheon?

JOHNNY: I'm afraid I have.

EDWARD: —A cigar?

JOHNNY: Not right now, thank you.

EDWARD: *(lets himself down into a sofa)* We've been quite at the mercy of the snow these days, haven't we?

JOHNNY: It doesn't seem much after Placid.

EDWARD: Placid—ah, yes! My daughter Julia has just come from there.

JOHNNY: I know.

EDWARD: *(a brief pause. Then)* —You are in business in New York, Mr Case?

JOHNNY: Yes, I'm in the Law. I'm with Sloan, Hobson.

EDWARD: An excellent firm.—And a born New Yorker?

JOHNNY: No. I was born in Baltimore.—In eighteen ninety-seven. July sixth. I'm thirty.

EDWARD: Baltimore—I used to have many friends in Baltimore.—The Whites—the Clarence Whites—Possibly you knew them.

JOHNNY: No, I don't believe I ever did.

EDWARD: —And then there was Archie Fuller's family—

JOHNNY: I'm afraid not.

EDWARD: —And let me see now—Colonel Evans—old Philip Evans—

JOHNNY: Nope. *(There is a silence. Then)* I haven't been there in some years. And I shouldn't be likely to know them, anyway. My mother and father died when I was quite young. My father had a small grocery store in Baltimore, which he was never able to make a go of. He left a number of debts which my mother worked very hard to clear up. I was the only child, and I wasn't in a position to help very much. She died the May before my sixteenth birthday. (LINDA *is listening with growing interest*)

EDWARD: But how sad.

JOHNNY: It *was* pretty sad.—I hadn't any connections, except for an uncle who's in the roofing business in Wilmington. He wasn't much good, though—he was inclined to get drunk—still is—

LINDA: We have an uncle like that, but he keeps off roofs.

JOHNNY: (*smiles at her, and continues*) —But I was what's called a bright boy, and I managed to wangle a couple of scholarships. They helped a good deal in school and college, and there were always plenty of ways to make up the difference. In term-time I usually ran eating-joints and typed lecture notes. In summers I sold aluminum pots and pans—

EDWARD: (*weakly*) Linda! Are you there, Linda?

LINDA: Yes, Father.

JOHNNY: —Or worked in a factory or on a newspaper. Once I got myself engaged as a tutor. That was pretty unpleasant. Then there were department stores at Christmas and florists at Easter. During law school I slept all night on a couch in a doctor's office, and got fifteen a week for it. That was soft.

EDWARD: (*it is all he can say*) Admirable!

JOHNNY: No—it simply happened to be the only way to get through. (*A brief pause. Then*) Anything else, sir?

EDWARD: I beg your pardon?

LINDA: (*rises*) I should think you would.

JOHNNY: —Is there anything more I can tell you about myself?

EDWARD: Why, uh—that is to say, uh— (*He flounders and stops. A moment, then* JOHNNY *moves toward him.*)

JOHNNY: Well, Mr Seton, how about it?

EDWARD: About it? About what?

JOHNNY: Julia and me.

EDWARD: You and Julia? I'm afraid I—

JOHNNY: —About our getting married.

EDWARD: (*there is a silence. Then*) This is a complete surprise, Mr Case. I don't know quite what to say to you.

JOHNNY: (*smiles*) "Yes" would be pleasant.

EDWARD: I am sure it would. However, we must go into it rather more carefully, I am afraid.

JOHNNY: The only difficulty is the time. Julia's idea is January tenth. It's mine, too.

EDWARD: We shall see about that.

JOHNNY: May I ask *how* we shall see, sir?

EDWARD: Mr Case, I do not know you at all.

JOHNNY: I'll give you every opportunity you permit me. How's lunch tomorrow?

EDWARD: Tomorrow I have several—

JOHNNY: —Tuesday?

EDWARD: (*hesitates*) Will you meet me at the Bankers' Club at one on Friday?

JOHNNY: I'm terribly sorry, but Friday's out. I've got to go to Boston on business.—Better make it tomorrow. (*A moment.* NED *and* JULIA *re-enter. Then* EDWARD *speaks, hastily*)

EDWARD: —Very well. I shall arrange my appointments.—Ah, Ned, Julia—and what do you suppose can be keeping the Crams? (*But* JOHNNY *cuts in before they can reply.*)

JOHNNY: —Thank you. In the meantime, I think Mr Hobson or Mr Sloan might say a good word for me. I'm nobody at all, as things go. But I'm quite decent and fairly civilized, and I love your daughter very much—which isn't a bit hard. She seems to like me quite a lot too, and that's about all that can be said for me—except that I think we've a simply grand chance to be awfully happy.—What do *you* say, Julia?

JULIA: Oh, so do I!

LINDA: Come on, Father, be an angel. *I* think he's a very good number.

EDWARD: I am afraid it is too important a matter to be decided off-hand.

JULIA: But I want to be married on the—

EDWARD: *(with sudden sharpness)* You will be married, Julia, when I have reached a favorable decision—and upon a day which I will name.

JULIA: I—our plan was—the tenth, and sail that night on—

EDWARD: The tenth is out of the question.

JULIA: Oh, but Father—! I—

EDWARD: —And we shall let it rest at that, for the moment.

LINDA: But you'll come round, Father! I have a swell hunch you'll come round. Oh, Lordy, Lordy, what fun! Let's all join hands and— *(VOICES are heard from the hall)*

EDWARD: Seton?—Laura?—Is that you I hear?

LINDA: You bet it is.—Let's *not* join hands. *(SETON CRAM and his wife, LAURA, enter. SETON is thirty-six, somewhat bald, inclined to a waistline, but well turned out in a morning coat, striped trousers and spats. LAURA is thirty-two, a shade taller than SETON, with a rather handsome, rather disagreeable face. She is as smartly dressed as a poor figure will allow.)*

SETON: Hello, hello!

EDWARD: —How are you, young man?

SETON: Blooming, thanks. We walked all the way up. *(They shake hands with EDWARD)*

LAURA: I do hope we're not late, Uncle Ned.

EDWARD: No, indeed!

LINDA: You're early.

LAURA: Julia, my dear, you're back. *(She kisses her and then bears down upon LINDA)* —And Linda! How simply stunning!

LINDA: *(wards off the impending kiss)* Careful, Laura—I've got the most terrible cold.

LAURA: *(returning)* But I never saw you looking better!—Hello, Ned.

NED: Hello.   *(Warn CURTAIN)*

EDWARD: This is—uh—Mr Case—my nephew, Mr Cram, and Mrs Cram. *(LAURA inclines her head.)*

SETON: How do you do?

JOHNNY: How do you do? *(NED edges away from LAURA. EDWARD, still stunned, stares in front of himself)*

LAURA: —Isn't it horrid how chapped one's hands get in this weather? I don't know *what* to do. How was Placid, Julia?—You must have had *such* a divine time. Were there loads of amusing people there?—And lots of beaux, too— Oh, you needn't deny it!—We know Julia, don't we, Seton?—And you, Linda—we haven't seen *you* for ages— *(She seats herself upon the bench at Right)* —Now sit right down and tell us *everything* you've been doing—

LINDA: Well, take the average day: I get up about eight-thirty, bathe, dress, and have my coffee. —Aren't you going to brush up before lunch, Ned?

NED: —Would you care to brush up before lunch, Case?

JOHNNY: I think I shall, if I may. *(He follows NED to the door)*

LINDA: —Julia?

JULIA: I'm all right, thanks.

LINDA: But look at *me*, will you! *(She moves quickly across the room after NED and JOHNNY, flicking imaginary dust from her dress as she goes)* — Simply *covered* with dust!—Wait, boys!

CURTAIN

ACT   TWO

SCENE: *The Playroom on the top floor is a long and spacious low-ceilinged room with white woodwork and pale blue walls upon which are lightly traced story-book designs in silver, white and green.*

At Right and Left there are two windows with window seats below them, curtained in a white-starred cretonne of a deeper blue than the walls.

The only entrance is from the hall at Back.

At Right there is a low platform for horizontal bars and a punching-bag, above which a pair of trapezes swing from the ceiling. At present they are tied up. Against the back wall behind them is a glass cabinet containing a collection of old toys, arranged on shelves in orderly rows.

Also at Right is a table, with tablecloth spread, and four small chairs. Against the back wall at Left is an old-fashioned music-box, and in the corner near it a small electric gramophone. Also at Left is a low couch and a table, a miniature easy-chair and a folding cushion.

TIME: *New Year's Eve, this year.*

AT RISE: *The Playroom is empty, and lit only by a pale NIGHT GLOW from the windows. A moment, then* JULIA *opens the door, and calls:*

JULIA: Linda! *(There is no answer. Dance MUSIC is heard from downstairs)* She isn't here.

NED: *(reaches past her to an electric button and lights the room)* I didn't say she was. All I said was it's where she comes, as a rule, when she finds herself in a jam. *(They come into the room.* BOTH *are in evening clothes. In one hand* NED *carries two whisky and sodas. He puts one glass on the table and retains the other)*

JULIA: I don't believe she's in the house.

NED: *(takes a swallow of his drink)* Maybe not.

JULIA: I told them all at dinner that she had a blinding headache, but expected to come down later.

NED: That's as good as anything— *(And another swallow)* Let's get out of here. This room gives me a funny feeling.

JULIA: Wait a minute.—You know how furious Father was when she wasn't there for dinner— *(She goes and shuts the door, closing out the MUSIC)* What can we do, Ned?

NED: Search me.

JULIA: *(she moves to a chair and seats herself)* But it's her party!

NED: Don't make me laugh, Julia. It was, maybe, until you and Father took it over.

JULIA: *I* did?

NED: You stood by and saw it done. Then the Crams got hold of it. Among you, you asked the whole list—which was just what Linda didn't want. You threw out the team of dancers she'd

engaged for supper, and got in that troupe of Scotch Songbirds. You let Farley, with his Flower Fancies, turn it into a house of mourning. Among you, you made Linda's funny little bust into a first-class funeral. I can't say I blame her, no. However—*(He raises his glass)* —drink to Linda.

JULIA: Well, I do! She should have realized that Father couldn't announce my engagement without *some* fuss.

NED: She should have, yes. But unlike me, Linda always hopes. *(Again his glass is raised)* Bottoms up to Linda.

JULIA: Don't, Ned.

NED: Don't what?

JULIA: You've been drinking steadily since eight o'clock.

NED: Yes?—Funny old Ned. On New Year's Eve, too. *(He drains his glass and takes up the other)*

JULIA: Will you kindly stop it?

NED: Darling sister, I shall drink as much as I like at any party I agree to attend. *(She turns from him with an exclamation)* —And as much as I like is as much as I can hold. It's my protection against your tiresome friends. Linda's out of luck, she hasn't one.

JOHNNY: *(comes in. MUSIC and VOICES are heard from downstairs)* —Believe it or not, I've been talking politics with an Admiral. *(He looks about him)* —What a nice room!

NED: It's too full of ghosts for me. It gives me the creeps.

JULIA: She isn't here, Johnny.

JOHNNY: Linda?

JULIA: Yes, of course.

JOHNNY: Did you expect she would be?

JULIA: Ned thought so.

NED: Ned was wrong.

*(*HENRY *and* CHARLES *enter.* HENRY *carries table linen and silver and a tray of plates and glasses;* CHARLES, *a pail of ice containing two bottles of champagne and a plate of sandwiches. They go to the table.)*

JULIA: Isn't there room for everyone downstairs, Henry?

HENRY: Miss Linda telephoned to serve supper here for six at half-past eleven, Miss.

NED: Ned was right.

JULIA: From where did she telephone, do you know?

HENRY: She didn't say, Miss. (*There is a pause.* HENRY *and* CHARLES *proceed to set the table*)

JOHNNY: (*to* JULIA) I think I know where she is, if that's any help.

JULIA: You? Where—?

JOHNNY: With Nick and Susan Potter.

JULIA: What's she doing with them?

JOHNNY: Dining, I imagine.

NED: It's eleven-twenty now.

JULIA: Where did you get your information, Johnny?

JOHNNY: I met her coming in this afternoon. She said she wouldn't stay in the house tonight. Apparently it meant more to her than anyone thought.

NED: Not than I thought. I warned Father.

JOHNNY: It was no use talking to her. She was going out to dine somewhere by herself. I knew that Nick and Susan were having Pete Jessup and Mary Hedges, so I telephoned Susan and asked her to ask Linda, too.

JULIA: I wish you had spoken to me first.

JOHNNY: Why?

JULIA: People like that aren't good for Linda.

JOHNNY: (*looks at her for a moment, puzzled, and then laughs*) What are you talking about, Julia?

JULIA: They make her even more discontented than she is. Heavens knows why, but they do.

NED: Apparently she's bringing them back with her. (HENRY *and* CHARLES *go out, closing the door after them*)

JULIA: Well, they certainly can't expect to have supper up here by themselves.

NED: No? Why not?

JULIA: They simply can't, that's all.

NED: What is this conspiracy against Linda, anyway? Are you all afraid she might cause a good time here, for once—and if she did, the walls might fall down? Is that it? (JULIA *does not reply.* JOHNNY *seats himself near her*)

JOHNNY: I do love this room, don't you, Julia?

JULIA: (*briefly*) Yes.—It was Mother's idea for us.

JOHNNY: She must have been sweet.

JULIA: She was.

NED: —Father wanted a big family, you know. So she had Julia straight off, to oblige him. But Julia was a girl, so she promptly had Linda. But Linda was a girl—it looked hopeless. (*His voice rises*) —So the next year she had me, and there was much joy in the land.—It was a boy, and the fair name of Seton would flourish. (JULIA *looks at him in alarm*) —It must have been a great consolation to Father. Drink to Mother, Johnny—she tried to be a Seton for a while, then gave up and died.—Drink to Mother—

JOHNNY: (*laughs uneasily*) You're talking through your hat, Ned.

NED: But I'm not.

JULIA: (*to* JOHNNY) Can't you possibly persuade him that he's had enough?

NED: It's all right, Julia: you heard what I said. —There's a bar in my room, if you want anything, Johnny. Tell as many of the men as you think need it. It's all very pleasant and hole-in-the-wall like everything else that's any relief in this house.—Drink to Father. (*He drains his glass, sets it down upon a table, turns on his heel and goes out, closing the door after him*)

JULIA: We must do something about them—we *must*, Johnny!

JOHNNY: —Him and Linda.

JULIA: Yes, yes!

JOHNNY: I don't see what.—It seems a lot more goes on inside them than we've any idea of. Linda must be at the end of some rope or other. As for Ned—

JULIA: He always does this—always—

JOHNNY: (*rises*) He began some time.—I'll keep an eye on him, though, and if he stops making sense I'll get him to bed somehow.

JULIA: —And Linda's got to bring her friends downstairs.—People know there's something wrong, now—they must know.—She's simply *got* to!

JOHNNY: All right, darling. Only—

JULIA: Only what—

JOHNNY: —Do try to enjoy tonight, won't you?

JULIA: But I am, Johnny. I think it's a lovely party!

JOHNNY: Then how about getting that frown from between your eyes and not feeling personally responsible for three hundred guests, and a brother and sister?

JULIA: —Someone's got to be.

JOHNNY: —Let your Father, then.

JULIA: Poor man. Reporters have been after him all day long.

JOHNNY: Me, too. I've never felt so important.

JULIA: I hope you didn't talk.

JOHNNY: I just asked for offers for the story of how I wooed and won you. Farm Boy Weds Heiress as Blizzard Grips City.

JULIA: *(laughs)* What *did* you say?

JOHNNY: I didn't see them.

JULIA: That's right. Father was awfully anxious that nothing be added to what he sent in—except, of course, what they're bound to add themselves.

JOHNNY: Evidently it's a good deal.

JULIA: Well, that we can't help.

JOHNNY: The French Line wrote me. They want to give us a suite, in place of the cabin.

JULIA: I doubt if we ought to accept it.

JOHNNY: No? Why not?

JULIA: I think it might not look so well. I'll ask Father.

JOHNNY: *(a brief pause. Then)* Perhaps we oughtn't to go abroad at all. Perhaps *that's* too great an evidence of wealth.

JULIA: Now, Johnny—

JOHNNY: —But we're going, my dear, and in the most comfortable quarters they choose to provide.

JULIA: What a curious tone for you to take. *(He looks at her in amazement, then laughs genuinely)*

JOHNNY: Julia, don't be ridiculous! "Tone to take." *(She turns from him)* —We may be suddenly and unexpectedly important to the world, but I don't see that we're quite important enough to bend over backwards.

JULIA: *(a silence. Then)* Of course, I'll do whatever you like about it.

JOHNNY: It would be nice if you'd like it too.

JULIA: *(she returns to him)* And I'll like it too, Johnny. *(He bends and kisses her lightly)*

JOHNNY: —Sweet. *(He takes her by the hand and draws her toward the door)* —Come on, let's go below and break into a gavotte.

JULIA: *(stops)* —Do something for me, will you?

JOHNNY: Sure.

JULIA: —Stay here till Linda arrives, then make her come down. I can't wait. *Some* female member of the household's got to be around, if it's only the cook.

JOHNNY: —I'll *ask* her to come down.

JULIA: Insist on it!

JOHNNY: Well, I'll do whatever a gent can in the circumstances.

JULIA: You're *so* irritating! Honestly, I hate the sight of you.

JOHNNY: Julia—

JULIA: What?

JOHNNY: Like hell you do.

JULIA: I know. It's hopeless. *(She goes to the door, opens it, then turns to him again. LAUGHTER is heard from downstairs)* Do as you like—I love you very much.

JOHNNY: —You get through that door quick and close it after you, or you won't get out at all.

JULIA: —Just to look at you makes my spine feel like—feel like— *(He moves swiftly toward her, but finds the door closed. He stands for a moment staring at it, transfixed, then pulls it open, calling "Darling!"—But instead of* JULIA, *he finds* NICK POTTER.)

NICK: Hey! What is this?

JOHNNY: Nick! *(*NICK *moves away from him, scowling, and straightening his coat. He is about thirty-four, with an attractive, amusing face)*

NICK: —Get fresh with me, and I'll knock your block off. *(He sees the champagne and goes to it)* What have we here—some kind of a grape beverage?

JOHNNY: Mum's the word.—Where's Susan?

NICK: Coming.—I hear you're engaged. Many happy returns. Is it announced yet?

JOHNNY: Thanks.—No, it's to come with a roll of drums at midnight—"A lady has lost a diamond and platinum wrist watch."

NICK: —With that gifted entertainer, Mr Edward Seton, at the microphone—

JOHNNY: That's the plan.

NICK: I heard about his work with this party.—He has the true ashman's touch, that man.

JOHNNY: He's been all right to me.

NICK: Oh, sure—he believes you're a comer. That's what won him over so quickly—the same stuff as Grandpa Seton himself—up-from-nothing—hew to the line—eat yeast. Me—of course I'm God's great social menace because I never got out and did Big Things.

JOHNNY: I really like him. I like him a lot.

NICK: Keep your men on him, though. Don't relax your vigilance. *(He is opening the bottles and filling the glasses. MUSIC and VOICES are heard through the open door)*

JOHNNY: —You think, for instance, that if *I* should quit business—

NICK: Just try it once. Why, he'd come down on you like Grant took Bourbon.

JOHNNY: You've got him all wrong, Nick.

NICK: Maybe.—Anyhow, you're not really thinking of it, are you?

JOHNNY: *(goes to the couch)* I am, you know!

NICK: On what, may I ask?

JOHNNY: Well, I've got a nice little mess of common stock that's begun to move about two years before I thought it would. And if it goes where I think it will—

NICK: —Haven't you and Julia a pretty good life ahead as it is, Johnny?

JOHNNY: You and Susan have a better one.

NICK: Listen, baby—I don't think I'd try any enlightened living stuff on this family. They wouldn't know what you were talking about.

JOHNNY: Julia would.

NICK: —Might. But the old man's a terror, Johnny. Honestly—you don't *know*.

JOHNNY: Enough of your jibes, Potter. You answer to me for your slurs on a Seton.

NICK: *(moves toward him)* —Seats on a Slurton—I want to get three seats on a Slurton for Tuesday

night. *(—And confronts him with an empty bottle)* Go on, hit me, why don't you? Just hit me. Take off your glasses—*(And returns to the table)*—I was dragged against my will to this function. And somehow I don't seem to so well.

JOHNNY: What?

NICK: —Function.

(LINDA and SUSAN enter. SUSAN is thirty, smart and attractive. She goes straight to JOHNNY and kisses him.)

SUSAN: Cheers from me, Johnny.

JOHNNY: Thanks, Susan.

SUSAN *and* NICK: *(together)* We only hope that you will be happy as we have been. *(LINDA closes the door. VOICES and MUSIC cease to be heard. NICK continues to fill the glasses)*

JOHNNY: *(to LINDA)* What did you do with Pete and Mary?

LINDA: They're coming in a heated barouche.

JOHNNY: Linda, I'm to inform you that there's another party going on in the house.

LINDA: You mean that low-class dance hall downstairs? *(She moves toward NICK)* Don't speak of it. *(NICK gives her a glass of wine, and then one to SUSAN)*

NICK: Here, Pearl, wet your pretty whistle with this. *(NICK and JOHNNY take glasses. SUSAN raises hers)*

SUSAN: —To Johnny and his Julia.

JOHNNY: Julia— *(They drink. LINDA seats herself in a chair near the table)*

SUSAN: —Merry Christmas, from Dan to Beersheba.

NICK: *(examining the table)* —Only sandwiches? What a house!

LINDA: There's solid food on the way.

NICK: I'll trade twenty marbles and a jack-knife for the carcass of one chicken, in good repair.

LINDA: You should have been with us, Johnny. Not one word of sense was spoken from eight to eleven.

SUSAN: —When Linda got homesick.

LINDA: I'm a die-hard about this evening and this room. I only hope nobody else wanders in. *(JOHNNY seats himself near LINDA.)*

NICK: I tell you who'd be fun.

LINDA: Who?

NICK: Seton and Laura.

LINDA: They wouldn't stay long.—You see those trapezes?

NICK: Yes?

LINDA: Time was when Seton and I used to swing from them by our knees, and spit at each other.

NICK: Great!

LINDA: I'm happy to say now, I rarely missed.

JOHNNY: But aren't we going downstairs?

LINDA: No, Angel, we're not.

NICK: It's grand here. It takes sixty years off these old shoulders. *(He looks at his watch)* Eleven-forty.—Doctor Stork's on the way, dears, with Little Baby New Year. *(He goes and seats himself with* JOHNNY *and* LINDA*)*

LINDA: I wish someone would tell me what *I'm* to do next year—and the year after—and the year after that—

SUSAN: What you need is a husband, Linda. *(She joins the group)*

LINDA: Have you got any addresses?

SUSAN: He'll arrive. I only hope you'll know how to act when he does.

LINDA: Well, I won't take No for an answer.

NICK: Don't you do it.

LINDA: And in the meanwhile what? Hot-foot it around the world with a maid and a dog? Lie on one beach after another, getting brown?

NICK: Oo, I *love* to play in the sand.

SUSAN: *(to* LINDA*)* —You just won't stay put, will you, child?

LINDA: And grow up to be a committee-woman and sit on Boards? Excuse me, Susan, but from now on any charity work *I* do will be for the rich. They need it more. *(*NICK, SUSAN *and* JOHNNY *are eating sandwiches and sipping their wine)*

NICK: Now look, Linda—let me tell you about yourself, will you?

LINDA: Go ahead.

NICK: There's more of your grandfather in you than you think.

LINDA: Boo.

NICK: There is, though. He wasn't satisfied with the life he was born into, so he made one for

himself. Now, you don't like *his* five-story log cabin so you're out in the woods again with your own little hatchet.

SUSAN: The Little Pioneer, with Linda Seton.

JOHNNY: —Linda's off on the wrong foot, though. She's headed up the fun-alley. She thinks having fun is the whole answer to life.

LINDA: *I* do?

JOHNNY: You do.—Me—it's not just entertainment *I'm* after—oh, no—I want all of it—inside, outside—smooth and rough—let 'er come!

NICK: You're right, too.—Life's a grand little ride, if you take it yourself.

JOHNNY: —And no good at all if someone else takes you on it. Damn it, there's *no* life any good but the one you make for yourself.

SUSAN: *(a protest)* Hey, hey—

JOHNNY: —Except yours and Nick's, maybe.

LINDA: But they *have* made theirs!—Haven't you, Susan?

SUSAN: About half-and-half, I should say. I don't know quite what we'd do if we had to earn our own living.

NICK: Earn it.—Is it settled about the wedding, Johnny?

JOHNNY: The twelfth—a week from Friday.

LINDA: Why not the tenth?

JOHNNY: Your father had a corporation meeting.—Ushers' dinner on Monday, Nick.

NICK: *(to* SUSAN*)* Don't wait lunch for me Tuesday.

SUSAN: Just come as you are.—Oh, I gave a scream.

LINDA: What's the matter?

SUSAN: *(to* JOHNNY*)* —Then you've put off your sailing, too?

JOHNNY: We had to.

SUSAN: Don't tell me it's the *Paris* now?

JOHNNY: Yes. Why?

SUSAN: But we changed ours from the tenth to the *Paris* so as not to bump into your wedding trip!

NICK: Well, we'll change back again.

JOHNNY: Don't think of it. It'll be great fun.

LINDA: Guess what *I* did in a wild moment this morning—

NICK: What?

LINDA: —Had my passport renewed—and Ned's. I want to get him away.

SUSAN: You're sailing then too?—It's a field day!

LINDA: No—not till a week or so after.

JOHNNY: Come along with us, Linda. It'd be grand. We'd own the boat.

LINDA: You'll have had plenty of family by then, little man. We'll join up later.

JOHNNY: How long do you plan to stay over, Nick?

NICK: Oh—June—August—September—like the dirty loafers we are.

LINDA: Loafers nothing!

JOHNNY: You've got the life, you two.

LINDA: Haven't they? *(To* SUSAN*)* You know, you've always seemed to me the rightest, wisest, happiest people ever I've known.

SUSAN: Why, Linda, thanks!

LINDA: You're my one real hope in the world.

JOHNNY: Mine, too.

SUSAN: Well, when we're with a pair like you— shall I say it, Nick?

NICK: Just let them look at us: Beam, darling—

SUSAN: *(beams)* —The Beaming Potters.

NICK: —In ten minutes of clean fun—

NICK *and* SUSAN: *(together)* We hope you'll like us! *(Then)*

NICK: —And what about you, Johnny? How long will you and Julia be there? *(A moment.* JOHNNY *smiles. Then)*

JOHNNY: Well—maybe indefinitely.

LINDA: How do you mean? Julia said March.

JOHNNY: Julia doesn't know yet.

LINDA: Johnny, what *is* this?!

JOHNNY: Well, some stock that I got at about eight was kind enough to touch fifteen today. And if a deal I think's going through does go through, it'll do twice that.

SUSAN: *(puzzled)* I must be dumb, but—

JOHNNY: Friends, there's a very fair chance I'll quit business next Saturday.

LINDA: Johnny!

NICK: For good?

JOHNNY: —For as long as it lasts.

SUSAN: As what lasts? Have you made some money?

JOHNNY: I think I shall have, by Saturday.

SUSAN: Good boy!

LINDA: Oh, very good boy!

NICK: —And Julia doesn't know your little plan?

JOHNNY: I haven't breathed a word of it to her. I wanted to be sure first. It all depends on what a Boston crowd called Bay State Power does about it. I'll know that Monday.

LINDA: They'll do it! I don't know what it is, but I know they'll do it! Oh, Lord, am I happy! *(A moment. Then)* But, Johnny—

JOHNNY: What?

LINDA: I'm scared.

JOHNNY: Of what?

LINDA: Listen to me a moment: Father and Julia— *(She stops, as* SETON *and* LAURA *appear in the doorway, and exclaims in disgust)* My God, it's Winnie-the-Pooh! *(*JOHNNY *and* NICK *rise.* LAURA *gazes about her)*

LAURA: But isn't this lovely!

SETON: Well, well, so here you are! *(He comes into the room.* LAURA *follows.)*

NICK: So we are.

SETON: Hello, Nick.—Hello, Susan!

NICK: How are you?

LAURA: *(to* SUSAN*)* My dear, what fun! We simply never meet any more.

SUSAN: —Just a pair of parallel lines, I expect.

LAURA: I must say you're a picture, Susan.

SUSAN: *(rises and goes to the couch)* —Madame is in a satin bed-jacket, by Hammacher-Schlemmer.

LAURA: May we sit down a minute? *(She seats herself in* NICK'S *chair.)*

LINDA: Why not?

LAURA: I've never been up here. It's awfully pleasant.

LINDA: We like it.

NICK: Of course, it's rather far from the carline—

SUSAN: And the water isn't all it might be—

NICK *and* SUSAN: *(together)* —But *we* like it!

JOHNNY: Don't change it, friends. It's the poor man's club.

LAURA: What on earth are you all talking about?

LINDA: *(rises and goes to the table)* Oh, just banter—airy nothings—give and take—

NICK: It's our defense against the ashman's touch.

LAURA: I *love* the decorations.

LINDA: They *love* to be loved.

LAURA: I'm afraid I don't follow you. You're not all tight, are you?

LINDA: On the continent, dear, on the continent.

NICK: We have a very high boiling-point.

SETON: *(leans over and plucks* JOHNNY'S *sleeve)* You old fox, you.

JOHNNY: Yes? How's that?

SETON: Sam Hobson's downstairs. He's just been telling me about your little haul in Seaboard. You might have let your friends in on it.

JOHNNY: There's still time. Climb aboard if you like.

SETON: I have already.—Do you know there's an order in our office to buy sixty thousand shares for Ross, of Bay State Power, all the way up to thirty?

JOHNNY: *(quickly)* Are you sure of that?

SETON: I took the order myself.

JOHNNY: Then that cinches it.

SUSAN: Is it a real killing, Johnny?

JOHNNY: For me it is!

SETON: *(impressively)* —Just thirty or forty thousand, that's all.

SUSAN: —No odd cents?

LINDA: Johnny—Johnny—

NICK: Let this be a lesson to you, young man.

SETON: —Anyone mind if I talk a little business? —The impression in our part of town is, it's you who put Seaboard on the map.

JOHNNY: I wouldn't go so far as that.

SETON: Ross said so himself.—Look here: we'd damn well like to have you with us, in Pritchard, Ames.

JOHNNY: Thanks, I've heard about that.

SETON: The Chief's told you already?

JOHNNY: I saw him this afternoon.

SETON: *(to* NICK*)* —To begin at twice what he gets now—and probably a directorship in Seaboard, to boot.

NICK: Well, well—to boot, eh?

SETON: *(to* JOHNNY*)* I hope you said yes.

JOHNNY: I told him I'd let him know.

SETON: Believe me when I tell you the first fifty thousand is the hardest.—It's plain sailing after that.

LINDA: *(suddenly)* Look out, Johnny!

SETON: —In two years we'll make your forty thousand, eighty—in five, two hundred.

NICK: *(edges over to* JOHNNY*)* —Lend a fellow a dime for a cup of coffee, mister? *(*JOHNNY *laughs)*

SETON: Well, how about it?

JOHNNY: I'll let him know.

SETON: You couldn't do better than to come with us—not possibly.

JOHNNY: *(rises and puts his glass on the table)* It's awfully nice of you, it really is.

LINDA: Look out, look *out!*

JOHNNY: Don't worry, Linda.

SETON: —Just let me give you a brief outline of the possibilities—

LINDA: That will do for business tonight, Seton.

SETON: I just want to tell Johnny—

LINDA: It's enough, really.

SETON: *(laughs and rises)* You're the hostess! — Then let's all go downstairs and celebrate, shall we?

LAURA: *(rises)* Yes, let's.—Its such a wonderful party.

LINDA: I'm not going downstairs.

SETON: Oh, come along, Linda—don't be foolish.

LAURA: Do come, dear. Your father said to tell you he—

LINDA: Yes—I thought so.—But I'm not going downstairs.

NICK: *(moves away from them to the other side of the room)* Where's the old music-box we used to play, Linda?

LINDA: Over there—but I've got something better— *(She goes to the gramophone in the corner)* Listen—it's electric—it'll melt your heart with its—

NICK: Take it away. *(*SUSAN *rises.* SETON *and* LAURA *move toward the door)*

SUSAN: Nick—you wouldn't go whimsical on us!

NICK: Oh, God, for the old scenes—the old times—

SETON: It's a quarter to twelve now, you know—

NICK: *(is examining the music-box)* Welcome, little New Year—

LAURA: Linda, I really think that—

LINDA: I know, Laura.

NICK: *(reads the music-box's repertory from a card)* "Sweet Marie"—"Fatal Wedding"—"Southern Roses"—

SUSAN: —And *this* is the way they used to dance when Grandmamma was a girl.

NICK: *(covers his eyes, and gulps)* Don't. My old eyes can scarcely see for the tears.

LAURA: You're all absolutely mad.
(HENRY *and* CHARLES *enter, with a chafing-dish and a platter of cold meats. A CHORUS of male voices is heard from downstairs.)*

SUSAN: Heavens, what would that be?

LINDA: It's the Scottish Singers, the little dears—
(She is watching JOHNNY)

NICK: I wouldn't have come if I'd known the Campbells were coming—(CHARLES *closes the door.* LINDA *starts a loud new dance-record on the gramophone)*

SETON: *(angrily)* What do you think this gets you, anyway?

LINDA: Peace and quiet!

NICK: *(huddles himself in his arms)* What a night! What a night!

SUSAN: What Nick really wants is some nice beer to cry into.

LINDA: Will everybody please stop sobbing! Stop it!—Take some wine, will you, Case?

JOHNNY: Thanks.

LINDA: *(intensely)* If you weaken now—!

JOHNNY: I never felt stronger.

LINDA: *(turns to* SUSAN*)* Peter and Mary—they couldn't have ditched us, could they?

SUSAN: Oh, no, they'll be along—

NICK: Eleven forty-seven—what *can* be keeping old Doctor Stork? *(*HENRY *and* CHARLES, *having placed the platter and chafing-dish upon the table, go out)*

LAURA: *(at the door)* Linda—really—people are beginning to wonder a little—

LINDA: I am *not going downstairs.*

LAURA: *(laughs unpleasantly)* Well, of course, if—

LINDA: But I wouldn't dream of keeping anyone who wants to—

LAURA: *(stares a moment, then turns to* SETON*)* Apparently we aren't welcome here.

SETON: I gathered that some time ago.—Linda, I think your conduct toward your guests tonight is outrageous.

LAURA: And so do I.

LINDA: I imagined that was what brought you up, you sweet things.

SETON: If you ask me, it's one of the worst cases of downright rudeness I've ever seen.

LINDA: And has someone asked you?

LAURA: —When a girl invites three hundred people to her house, and then proceeds to—

LINDA: I invited six people—three of whom you see before you. The others came on someone else's say-so—yours and Father's, I believe.

LAURA: Perhaps we'd better go home, Seton.

LINDA: Oh, you're here now. Stay, if you like. I'd prefer it, however, if you'd do your commenting on my behavior not to my face, but behind my back as usual—

LAURA: *(opens the door)* Come, Seton—*(She goes out, with all the hauteur she can command)*

SETON: *(to* LINDA*)* When I think of the—

LINDA: —Before you go, you wouldn't care to swing on the old trapeze a while, would you—? *(He stares. She turns away)* I suppose not. *(*SETON *goes out, closing the door after him.* LINDA *moves toward the table)* Oh, the cheek, the cheek!

NICK: Some day they'll draw themselves up like that and won't be able to get down again. *(He goes to* JOHNNY*)* Well, Johnny—!

JOHNNY: *(at the table)* Lord, it's the grandest feeling—Oh, wait till Julia hears! On tonight of all nights, too! What a break that is!

LINDA: I've never been so happy for anyone in my life.

NICK: Go to it, boy!

JOHNNY: Oh, won't I? Watch me! *(Then)* — Where'll we spend the Spring?—Let's all spend the Spring together!

NICK: What do you say, Susan? Do you think we could stand them?

SUSAN: There'll always be a curse and a blow for you with us, Johnny.

LINDA: Can I come? Please, can I come, too—? *(She trots in among them)*

NICK: Don't leave us, darling. We want you. We need you. *(SUSAN joins them. She sits at the end of the table, opposite NICK, and JOHNNY and LINDA behind it, facing the front. JOHNNY refills the glasses and SUSAN and LINDA serve the food)*

SUSAN: How about the south of France?

JOHNNY: Why not?

LINDA: No, no—the air reeks of roses and the nightingales make the nights hideous.

JOHNNY: *(overcome)* Don't—don't—*(He gives each of them a glass of wine)*

NICK: *(a suggestion)* If we went to Norway, we could all paint a house at midnight.

JOHNNY: —Norway's out. It's got to be some place you can swim all day long.—You know, it's just dawned on me that I've never swum enough. That's one of the things I want to do: *swim.*

NICK: *(rises and leans upon the table)* Young man, in the bright lexicon of youth there is no such word. Swimming is for idlers.

SUSAN: —And Hawaiians.

LINDA: —And fish.

NICK: Are you a fish? Answer me that.—Can you look yourself squarely in the eye and say "I am a fish"? No. You cannot.

JOHNNY: You are a hard man, sir.

NICK: It is life that has made me hard, son.

JOHNNY: —But I want only to be like you, Daddy—how can I be like you?

NICK: You ask me for the story of my success? —Well, I'll tell you—

LINDA: Come—gather close, children. *(They turn their chairs and face him)*

NICK: —I arrived in this country at the age of three months, with nothing in my pockets but five cents and an old hat-check. I had no friends, little or no education, and sex to me was still the Great Mystery. But when I came down the gang-plank of that little sailing-vessel—steam was then unknown, except to the very rich—Friends, can you picture that manly little figure without a tug at your heart strings, and a faint wave of nausea? But I just pulled my belt a little tighter, and told myself, "Don't forget you're a Potter, Nick"—I called myself "Nick"—and so I found myself at my first job, in the glass works. Glass was in its infancy then—we had barely scratched the surface—but I have never shirked work—and if there was an errand to be run, I ran five errands. If someone wanted to get off at the third floor, I took him to the tenth floor.—Then one day came my big chance. I was in the glass-blowing department then—now Miss Murphy's department—and a very capable little woman she is—

LINDA: Why, Mr. Potter, I'm no such thing.

NICK: Oh, yes, you are, Miss Murphy! Well, sir, I was blowing glass like a two-year-old, whistling as I blew. Suddenly I looked down and found in my hand—*a bottle*—or what we now know as a bottle. I rushed to my employer, a Mr Grandgent, and said, "Look, Mr Grandgent—I think I've got something here." Mr Grandgent looked—and laughed—*laughed,* do you understand?—I went from city to city like some hunted thing, that laugh still in my ears. But with me went my bottle. They called it Potter's Folly. They said it would never work. Well, time has shown how right they were. Now the bottle is in every home. I have made the bottle a National Institution!—And that, my dears, is how I met your grandmother. *(He bows)*

LINDA: *(rises, champagne-glass in hand)* —To one who, in the face of every difficulty, has proved himself a Christian gentleman.—Music, music! *(She goes to the gramophone and starts a record)*

SUSAN: *(rises)* —To one who has been friend to rich and poor alike—

JOHNNY: *(rises)* —To one who, as soldier—

LINDA: —As statesman—

SUSAN: —As navigator—

JOHNNY: —As man about town—

LINDA: —As scout-leader—

NICK: —As Third Vice-President of the second largest spat factory in East St. Louis—

JOHNNY: On behalf of the hook-and-ladder company of the First Reformed Church, I want to say a few words about our brave Fire Laddies. Has it occurred to you—*(The door opens and* JULIA *and* EDWARD *enter)*

EDWARD: Linda!

LINDA: Yes?

EDWARD: Please turn that machine off. *(*SUSAN *goes to* NICK*)*

LINDA: You know Mr and Mrs Potter, Father—

EDWARD: *(curtly)* How do you do? *(Then to* LINDA*)* Turn it off, Linda—*(*LINDA *stops the record)*

NICK: *(to* SUSAN*)* —Fell, or was pushed.

JOHNNY: *(moves eagerly toward* JULIA*)* Julia! Listen, darling! I've got a grand surprise for you—

EDWARD: Just a moment!—You must all come down, now. It's nearly twelve, and we want the entire party together to see the New Year in.

LINDA: But there are two parties, Father—the one down there and mine—*here.*

EDWARD: Please do as I say, Linda.

LINDA: I asked for permission to have a few of my friends here tonight. You said I might. I've got some of them, now, and—

EDWARD: —I noticed you had.

LINDA: —And more are coming.

JULIA: They've come, haven't they?

LINDA: How do you mean?

JULIA: Peter Jessup and what's-her-name—Mary Hedges—

LINDA: What about them?

JULIA: They're downstairs.

LINDA: They—?—How long have they been there?

JULIA: Twenty minutes or so. I said you'd be down.

LINDA: Oh, you did, did you?

JULIA: —They're being very amusing. I said we expected them to be. Jessup has done his trained-seal act to perfection, and now I think Mary Hedges is about to give her imitations. *(There is a silence.* LINDA *stares at her, speechless)* They're a great success, really.

LINDA: *(without turning)* Nick—will you and Susan bring them up to my sitting-room? I'll be there in a minute.

SUSAN: All right, Linda. *(She moves toward the door.* NICK *follows, gazing anxiously at the ceiling as he goes)*

NICK: —The New Year ought to be just about passing over Stamford. *(They go out, closing the door after them)*

JOHNNY: *(goes to* JULIA*)* Julia! Big news, dear— guess what's happened?

LINDA: *(to* EDWARD *and* JULIA, *before* JULIA *can reply)* Oh, this is so humiliating.—Peter and Mary are my guests, do you understand? Not paid entertainers—*(She moves away from them)*

JULIA: I'm sorry. I simply couldn't imagine mixing in people like that to no purpose.

LINDA: Couldn't you?

JULIA: No.—But of course I can't follow your reasoning these days, Linda. I can't follow it at all.

EDWARD: *(to* LINDA*)* There's no cause for temper, child. Just run along now, and we'll follow. Julia and I want to talk to Johnny for a moment.

JULIA: *(turns again to* JOHNNY*)* What is it, Johnny? Quick, tell me!

LINDA: —Listen to me, Father: tonight means a good deal to me—I don't know what, precisely—and I don't know how. Something is trying to take it away from me, and I can't let it go. I'll put in an appearance downstairs, if you like. Then I want to bring a few people up here—the few people in the world I can talk to, and feel something for. And I want to sit with them and have supper with them, and we won't disturb anyone. That's all right with you, isn't it?

EDWARD: Your place is downstairs.

LINDA: Once more, Father: this is important to me. Don't ask me why. I don't know. It has something to do with—when I was a child here—and this room—and good times in it—and—

EDWARD: What special virtue this room has, I'm sure I don't see.

LINDA: You don't, do you—no—you can't. Well, I'll tell you this room's my home. It's the only home I've got. There's something here that I understand, and that understands me. Maybe it's Mother.

EDWARD: Please do as I have told you, Linda.

LINDA: I suppose you know it's the end of us, then.

EDWARD: Don't talk nonsense. Do as I say.

LINDA: It *is* the end. But all the same, I'm going to have supper here tonight in my home with my friends.

EDWARD: I have told you—

LINDA: —You thought I'd come around, didn't you? You always think people will come around. Not me: not tonight. And I shan't be bothered here, either. Because if there's one thing you can't stand it's a scene. I can promise you one, if you interfere. I can promise you a beauty. *(EDWARD turns from her. LINDA looks about her, at the room)*

EDWARD: —Well, Johnny, so there's good news, is there?

LINDA: *(suddenly)* Was Mother a sweet soul, Father? Was she exciting?

EDWARD: *(to* JOHNNY*)* —A happy day all around, eh? An engagement to be announced, New Year's to celebrate—and now—

LINDA: Was Mother a sweet soul, Father? Was she exciting?

EDWARD: Your mother was a very beautiful and distinguished woman. *(to* JOHNNY*)* Naturally, I am delighted that—

LINDA: Was she a sweet soul, Father? Was she exciting? *(For an instant* EDWARD *loses control of himself)*

EDWARD: Linda, if you are not happy here, why don't you go away? I should be glad if next month you would take your maid and Miss Talcott and go on a trip somewhere. You distress me. You cause nothing but trouble and upsets. You—

LINDA: All right, Father. That's just what I'm going to do, after the wedding. No maid and no Miss Talcott, though. Just me—Linda—the kid herself—

EDWARD: As you wish.

LINDA: I've wanted to get out for years. I've never known it so well as tonight. I can't bear it here any longer. It's doing terrible things to me.

EDWARD: —And will you leave this room now, please?

LINDA: This room—this room—I don't think you'll be able to stand it long. I'll come back when you've left it—*(She goes out. There is a silence. Then)*

JULIA: She's dreadful tonight. She's made one situation after another.

EDWARD: Never mind, my dear. Things will settle themselves. *(He seats himself in a chair at Right)* Well, Johnny—I don't think I need worry about the way *you'll* take care of Julia, need I?

JOHNNY: *(laughs, uncertainly)* We'll try to manage!

EDWARD: I consider what you've done a fine piece of work. I congratulate you.

JULIA: Oh, and so do I—so do *I*, dear! *(She sits near her father)*

JOHNNY: —But you don't know yet, do you?

EDWARD: The fact is, Seton has just now told us.

JULIA: Isn't it marvelous?—Oh, what a New Year!

EDWARD: —Your stock is going up with a rush, it seems. It's time to make hay, I think.

JOHNNY: Hay?

EDWARD: *(with relish)* Money! Money!

JULIA: *Now* all those years you worked so hard—they'll pay interest now, Johnny! *(The frown grows between* JOHNNY'S *eyes)*

EDWARD: Of course, I could put you into the Bank tomorrow—but I am not sure that that would be advisable at present.

JULIA: —That will come, won't it, Johnny? *(To* EDWARD*)* You'd better not wait *too* long, though—he may cost you too much!

EDWARD: *(smiles)* We'll have to risk that. People always do. *(Then seriously)* Pritchard, Ames is an excellent house. In my opinion, you could not do better than to go with them. Then, in five or six years, you come to us on your own merit. After that, as the children put it, "the sky's the limit." You're in a fair way to be a man of means at forty-five. I'm proud of you.

JOHNNY: *(there is a pause. Finally)* But—I'd made up my mind not to take the Pritchard, Ames offer.

EDWARD: What? And why not?

JOHNNY: I don't want to get tied up for life quite so soon. You see, I'm a kind of a queer duck, in a way. I'm afraid I'm not as anxious as I might be for the things most people work toward. I don't *want* too much money.

EDWARD: Too *much* money?

JOHNNY: Well, more than I need to live by. *(He seats himself facing them and begins eagerly, hopefully, to tell him his plan)* —You see, it's always been my plan to make a few thousands early in the game, if I could, and then quit for as long as they last, and try to find out who I am and what I am and what goes on and what about it—now, while I'm young, and feel good all the time.—I'm sure Julia understands what I'm getting at—don't you, Julia?

JULIA: *(laughs, uncertainly)* I'm not sure I do, Johnny!

EDWARD: You wish to occupy yourself otherwise, is that it?—with some—er—art or other, say—

JOHNNY: Oh, no, I've got no abilities that way. I'm not one of the frail ones with a longing to get away from it all and indulge a few tastes, either. I haven't any tastes. Old china and first editions and gate-legged tables don't do a thing to me. I don't want to live any way or in any time but my own—now—in New York—and Detroit—and Chicago—and Phoenix—any place but here—but I do want to live!

EDWARD: —As a gentleman of leisure.

JOHNNY: —As a man whose time, for a while at least, is his own. That's what I've been plugging for ever since I was ten. Please don't make me feel guilty about it, sir. Whether I'm right or wrong, it's more important to me than anything in the world but Julia. Even if it turns out to be just one of those fool ideas that people dream about and then go flat on—even if I find I've had enough of it in three months, still I want it. I've got a feeling that if I let this chance go by, there'll never be another for me. So I don't think anyone will mind if I—just have a go at it—will they, Julia? *(JULIA is silent)* —Will they, dear? (JULIA *rises*. JOHNNY *rises with her)*

JULIA: *(after a moment)* Father—will you let Johnny and me talk a while?

EDWARD: Just a moment—*(He rises and turns to* JOHNNY) —As I understand it, you have some objection, perhaps, to our manner of living—

JOHNNY: Not for you, sir. I haven't the slightest doubt it's all right for you—or that it's the answer for a lot of people. But for me—well, you see I don't *want* to live in what they call "a certain way." In the first place I'd be no good at it and besides that I don't want to be identified with any one class of people. I want to live every which way, among all kinds—and know them—and understand them—and love them—*that's* what I want!—Don't you, Julia?

JULIA: Why, I—It sounds—

EDWARD: In all my experiences, I have never heard such a—

JOHNNY: I want these years now, sir.

JULIA: Father—please—*(He turns to her. Their eyes meet)* —It will be all right, I promise you.

EDWARD: *(moves toward the door, where he turns once more to* JOHNNY) Case, it strikes me that you chose a strange time to tell us this, a very strange time.

JOHNNY: *(puzzled)* I don't quite—

EDWARD: —In fact, if I had not already sent the announcement to the newspapers—asked a number of our friends here tonight to—

JULIA: Father!

JOHNNY: *(very quietly)* Oh, I see.

JULIA: Father—please go down. We'll come in a minute. (EDWARD *hesitates an instant, then goes out)*

JOHNNY: *(still hopeful, turns to* JULIA) —Darling, he didn't get what I'm driving at, at all! My plan is—

JULIA: Oh, Johnny, Johnny, why did you do it?

JOHNNY: Do what?

JULIA: You knew how all that talk would antagonize him.

JOHNNY: *(a moment)* You think talk is all it was?

JULIA: I think it was less than that! I'm furious with you.

JOHNNY: It wasn't just talk, Julia.

JULIA: Well, if you think you can persuade me that a man of your energy and your ability possibly *could* quit at thirty for *any* length of time, you're mistaken.

JOHNNY: I'd like a try at it.

JULIA: It's ridiculous—and why you chose tonight of all nights to go on that way to Father—

JOHNNY: Wait a minute, dear: we'd better get clear on this—

JULIA: I'm clear on it now! If you're tired, and need a holiday, we'll have it. We'll take two months instead of one, if you like. We'll—

JOHNNY: That wouldn't settle anything.

JULIA: Johnny, I've known quite a few men who don't work—and of all the footling, unhappy existences—it's inconceivable that you could stand it—it's unthinkable you could!

JOHNNY: —I might do it differently.

JULIA: Differently!

JOHNNY: *(a moment. Then)* Julia, do you love me? *(She looks at him swiftly, then looks away)*

JULIA: *(lowly)* You—you have a great time standing me against a wall and throwing knives around me, don't you? *(In an instant he has taken her in his arms)*

JOHNNY: Oh, sweet—

JULIA: *(against his shoulder)* What do you do things like that for? What's the matter with you, anyway?

JOHNNY: *(he stands off and looks at her)* Haven't you the remotest idea of what I'm after? *(She looks at him, startled)* I'm after—all that's in me, all I am. I want to get it out—where I can look at it, know it. That takes time.—Can't you understand that?

JULIA: But you haven't an idea yet of how exciting *business* can be—you're just beginning! Oh, Johnny, see it through! You'll love it. I know you will. There's no such thrill in the world as making money. It's the most—what are you staring at?

JOHNNY: Your face.

JULIA: *(she turns away)* Oh—you won't listen to me—you won't hear me—

JOHNNY: Yes, I will.

JULIA: *(a pause. Then JULIA speaks in another voice)* And you'd expect me to live on—this money you've made, too, would you?

JOHNNY: Why, of course not. You have all you'll ever need for anything you'd want, haven't you?

JULIA: *(another pause, then)* —I suppose it doesn't occur to you how badly it would *look* for you to stop now, does it—?

JOHNNY: Look? How? *(She does not answer)* —Oh—you mean there'd be those who'd think I'd married money and called it a day—

JULIA: There would be. There'd be plenty of them.

JOHNNY: —And you'd mind that, would you?

JULIA: Well, I'm not precisely anxious to have it thought of you.

JOHNNY: —Because *I* shouldn't mind it—and I think that lookout's mine. Oh, darling, you don't see what I'm aiming at, either—but try a little blind faith for a while, won't you? Come along with me—

JULIA: Johnny—*(She reaches for his hand)*

JOHNNY: —The whole way, dear.

JULIA: —Wait till next year—or two years, and we'll think about it again. If it's right, it can be done, then as well as now.—You can do that for me—for us—can't you? *(A moment. Then he slowly brings her around and looks into her eyes)*

JOHNNY: You think by then I'd have "come around." That's what you think, isn't it?—I'd have "come around"—

JULIA: But surely you can at least see that if—! *(She stops, as LINDA re-enters)*

LINDA: It lacks six minutes of the New Year, if anyone's interested. *(A moment, then JULIA moves toward the door)*

JULIA: Come on, Johnny.

JOHNNY: *(to LINDA)* Where are the others?

LINDA: My pretty new friends? Well, it seems they've ditched me. *(She starts a tune on the music-box)* —This won't make too much noise, do you think?

JOHNNY: How do you mean, Linda?

LINDA: I imagine Peter and Mary got tired of being put through their tricks, and slid out when they could. Nick and Susan left a message upstairs with Delia saying that they had to go after them. I'm supposed to follow, but I don't think I will, somehow.

JULIA: Oh, I *am* sorry.

LINDA: Are you, Julia? That's a help, *(She goes to the supper-table)* —Anyone care for a few cold cuts before the fun starts?

JOHNNY: You're not going to stay up here all alone—

LINDA: Why not? I'm just full of resources. I crack all kinds of jokes with myself—and they say the food's good. *(She takes a bit of a sandwich and puts it down again)* Ugh! Kiki—

JULIA: Linda, this is plain stubbornness, and you know it.

LINDA: *(wheels about sharply)* Listen, Julia—! *(She stops, and turns away)* No—that gets you nowhere, does it?

JULIA: *(to* JOHNNY*)* Are you coming?

JOHNNY: I think I'll wait a moment with Linda, if you don't mind.

JULIA: But I do mind!—Will you come, please?

JOHNNY: —In a moment, Julia. *(*JULIA *looks at him. He meets her gaze steadily. She turns and goes out. There is a pause. Then)*

LINDA: You'd better run on down, don't you think?

JOHNNY: Not right away. *(another pause)*

LINDA: I'm afraid I don't know how to entertain you. I've done all my stuff.

JOHNNY: I don't need entertaining.

LINDA: *(another pause, a very long one.* LINDA *looks uncertainly toward the music-box. Finally)* — You wouldn't care to step into a waltz, Mr Case?

JOHNNY: I'd love it. *(She extends her arms. He takes her in his. They begin to waltz slowly to the music-box)* —There's a conspiracy against you and me, child.

LINDA: What's that?

JOHNNY: The Vested Interests—

LINDA: I know.

JOHNNY: —They won't let you have any fun, and they won't give me time to think.

LINDA: I suppose, like the great fathead you are, you told them all your little hopes and dreams.

JOHNNY: Um.

LINDA: —Pretty disappointing?

JOHNNY: Bad enough.

LINDA: Poor boy.

JOHNNY: How about your own evening?

LINDA: Not so good, either.

JOHNNY: Poor girl.

LINDA: But we won't mind, will we?

JOHNNY: Hell, no, we won't mind.

LINDA: We'll get there—

JOHNNY: We'll get there! *(She stops in the dance and looks up at him for a moment, curiously. Then he smiles at her and she smiles back)*

JOHNNY: —Place head, A, against cheek, B, and proceed as before—*(They begin to dance again)* —Of course they may be right.

LINDA: Don't you believe it!

JOHNNY: They seem—awfully sure.

LINDA: It's your ride still, isn't it? You know where you want to go, don't you?

JOHNNY: Well, I thought I did.

LINDA: So did I.—Pathetic, wasn't it—all my fuss and fury over anything so unimportant as this party.

JOHNNY: Maybe it was important.

LINDA: Well, if it was, I'm not. And I guess that's the answer.

JOHNNY: Not quite.

LINDA: —Me and my little what-do-you-call-it— defense mechanism—so pathetic. Yes, I'm just chock-full of pathos, I am.

JOHNNY: You're a brick, Linda.

LINDA: Oh, shut your silly face—*(Then)* You're right, you know—there *is* nothing up the fun-alley.

JOHNNY: Fun-alley?

LINDA: I had a nice little seven-word motto for my life, but I guess she don't work—

JOHNNY: What was it?

LINDA: "Not very important—but pretty good entertainment."

JOHNNY: H'm—

LINDA: For "pretty good" read "rotten." *(They dance for a few moments, silently. Then* LINDA *stops)* There. That's enough. I'm getting excited.

JOHNNY: —What?

LINDA: —It was grand. Thanks. You can go now. *(She has not yet left his arms. Suddenly from outside comes the sound of BELLS tolling. Her grasp tightens upon his arm)* Listen! *(She*

*looks over her shoulder toward the window.
HORNS begin to be heard from the distance,
long-drawn-out, insistent)*

JOHNNY: It's it, all right.

LINDA: *(again she turns her face to his)* Happy
New Year, Johnny.

JOHNNY: *(he bends and kisses her)* Happy New
Year, dear. *(For an instant she clings to him,
then averts her face)*

LINDA: *(in a breath)* Oh, Johnny, you're so attractive—

JOHNNY: *(with difficulty)* You're —you're all right
yourself—*(There is a dead silence. Then she
leaves his arms, turns and smiles to him)*

LINDA: —You can count on Sister Linda.—Run
on down now—quick! They'll be waiting.

JOHNNY: *(hesitates)* Linda—

LINDA: What?

JOHNNY: They've—your father—I've been put in
a position that—

LINDA: Do you love Julia, Johnny? *(He turns
away)*

JOHNNY: Of course I do.
*(NED enters silently, another glass in hand. He
stands in the shadow at Left, watching them,
swaying almost imperceptibly.)*

LINDA: —Well, if ever she needed you, she needs
you now. Once it's announced she'll go through
with it. Then you can help her. I can't do anything any more. I've tried for twenty years.
You're all that's left. Go on, Johnny—*(He goes to
the door. From downstairs a swelling CHORUS of
male voices begins "Auld Lang Syne")*—And tell
those choir-boys for me that I'll be in Scotland
before them.
*(JOHNNY goes out, closing the door after him.
LINDA stops the music-box, then moves slowly to
the window, Right, where she stands silently for
a moment, looking out. NED is still watching
her, immobile. At length she turns to him)*

LINDA: —Just take any place, Ned. *(He goes to
the couch and sits there)*

NED: —Rum party down there, isn't it?

LINDA: A hundred million dollars knocking together never made many sparks that I could

see. *(She takes a glass of wine from the table)*
What's it like to get drunk, Ned?

NED: It's—How drunk?

LINDA: Good and drunk.

NED: Grand.

LINDA: *(she seats herself near the table, facing
him)* How is it?

NED: Well, to begin with, it brings you to life.

LINDA: Does it?

NED: Yes.—And after a little while you begin to
know all about it. You feel—I don't know—
important—

LINDA: That must be good.

NED: It is.—Then pretty soon the game starts.

LINDA: What game?

NED: —That you play with yourself. It's a swell
game—there's not a sweller game on this earth,
really—

LINDA: *(sips her wine)* How does it go?

NED: Well, you think clear as crystal, but every
move, every sentence is a problem. That—gets
pretty interesting.

LINDA: I see.

NED: Swell game. Most terribly exciting game.

LINDA: You—get beaten, though, don't you?

NED: Sure. But that's good, too. Then you don't
mind anything—not anything at all. Then you
sleep.

LINDA: *(she is watching him, fascinated)* How—
long can you keep it up?

NED: A long while. As long as you last.

LINDA: Oh, Ned—that's awful!

NED: Think so?—Other things are worse.

LINDA: But—but where do you end up?

NED: Where does everybody end up? You die.—
And that's all right, too.

LINDA: *(a pause. Then)* Ned, can you do it on
champagne?

NED: Why—*(He stops and looks at her, intently)*
—What's the matter, Linda?

LINDA: *(she finishes her glass and sets it down)*
Nothing.

NED: I know.

LINDA: Yes?

NED: Johnny.

LINDA: Give me some more wine, Ned.

NED: *(rises and goes over to her)* He's a funny guy, isn't he?

LINDA: Give me some, Ned—

NED: *(he goes to the table, refills her glass, returns, and give it to her)* —You can tell me about it, dear.

LINDA: *(looks up at him. A moment, then)* I love the boy, Neddy.

NED: I thought so.—Hell, isn't it?

LINDA: I guess it will be. *(Warn CURTAIN.)*

NED: *(raises his glass)* Here's luck to you—

LINDA: *(stares at her glass)* I don't want any luck. *(NED moves away from her to the table near the couch. He finishes his drink, leaves it there and sinks down upon the couch. LINDA carefully sets her glass of wine, untouched, upon the supper table, and rises)* I think what I'd better do is— *(She moves slowly to the door, and opens it. The SONG is just finishing. It is APPLAUDED. LINDA hesitates at the door)* Ned—*(He does not answer. Suddenly, from downstairs, comes a long roll of DRUMS. LINDA stiffens. She starts to close the door, but is held there, her hand upon the knob. EDWARD'S VOICE begins to be heard)*

EDWARD: Ladies and gentlemen—my very good friends: I have the honor to announce to you the engagement of my daughter, Julia, to Mr John Case—an event which doubles the pleasure I take in wishing you—and them—a most happy and prosperous New Year. *(There is a prolonged APPLAUSE and through it CONGRATULATIONS and LAUGHTER. Slowly she closes the door, but still stands with her hand upon it. Finally she speaks, without turning)*

LINDA: Ned—*(He does not answer)* Ned—maybe I ought to go down and—I'm not sure I *will* stay up here—do you mind? *(He is silent. She turns and sees him)* Ned! *(He is asleep. She goes to him swiftly, speaking again, in a low voice)* Ned—*(A moment. Then)* Poor lamb. *(She bends and kisses him. She goes to the doorway, turns off the LIGHTS in the Playroom, and opens the door. A confusion of excited VOICES is heard from downstairs. In the lighted hallway LINDA turns to the stairs, raises her head and goes out, calling above the voices)* Hello!—Hello, everyone!

CURTAIN

ACT THREE

SCENE: *The same as Act I.*

TIME: *Twelve days later. Ten o'clock at night. The curtains are drawn and the lamps lighted. Coffee service is on a small table near the fireplace.* NICK *and* SUSAN *are taking their coffee.* LINDA'S *cup is on the table. She stands near the sofa at Left Center, frowning at* NICK.

LINDA: No?

NICK: *(shakes his head)* Not possibly. *(He is behind the sofa at Right, upon which* SUSAN *is seated.)*

SUSAN: Why should Johnny pick a place like that?

LINDA: Why should he go away at all?

NICK: I'd have done the same thing—I'd have just giv' 'er a look, I would, and flounced out.

SUSAN: Hush, Nick. This is no time for fooling.

LINDA: *(thinks a minute, then head down, eyes on the floor, she paces across the room and back, and cross again. She stops opposite them and turns)*—Atlantic City.

SUSAN: You don't go to Atlantic City for six days to think.

NICK: Old Chinese proverb.

LINDA: But where can he be, then?—*Where?*

SUSAN: Don't worry, Linda. I'm sure he's all right.

NICK: Susan and I parted forever at least forty times. *(To* SUSAN*)* —Or was it forty-seven?

SUSAN: Of course.—And they haven't even done that. They've just put off the wedding a while.

LINDA: I know, but—*(She looks away, anxiously)* Oh, Lordy, Lordy—

NICK: Johnny will come around, Linda. He's up against the old fight between spirit and matter—anyone want to take a hundred on spirit?

LINDA: I will! I'll take two hundred!

NICK: It's a bet, Madam. *(He looks at his watch)*

SUSAN: Don't forget we have to go back to the house for our bags, Nick.

NICK: There's lots of time. She doesn't sail until midnight. "She"—a boat that size, "she"—the big nance. *(To* LINDA*)* —You don't really want to see us off, do you?

LINDA: Oh, yes! But can you stop back for me on your way down?

SUSAN: If you like.

LINDA: I don't want to leave here till the last minute. I keep feeling that something may happen.

SUSAN: Where's Julia now?

LINDA: She went to dine some place with Father. He won't let her out of his sight—or into mine.

NICK: No wonder Johnny took to the woods.

LINDA: *(quickly)*—The woods?

NICK: —Or wherever he did take to.

LINDA: Now I know!

SUSAN: Yes?

LINDA: It was at Placid they met. It was at Placid they—of course! *(She goes to the telephone behind the sofa, at Left)*

NICK: *(to* SUSAN*)* It may be. They say they always return to the scene of the crime.

LINDA: Long distance, please.

SUSAN: —In which case, I suppose Julia wins.

NICK: I don't know. It's pretty cold at Placid. There's nothing for a rapid pulse like a little wet snow up the sleeve.

LINDA: Long distance, please—

SUSAN: *(to* NICK*)* Would you mind telling me how a man like Johnny is attracted to a girl like that, in the first place?

NICK: *(to* SUSAN*)* You're too young to know, Susan.

LINDA: *(at the telephone)*—Long distance?

SUSAN: I can think of several people who'd be better for Johnny than Julia.

LINDA: I want to speak with Lake Placid, New York—

NICK: I can think of one, anyway.

LINDA: —Placid—the Lake Placid Club.

SUSAN: Do you suppose she's in love with him?

NICK: Suppose? I know. Look at her.

LINDA: "P-l-a-c-i-d"—

NICK: Tiger, Tiger, Tiger.

LINDA: Quiet a minute, will you? *(To the telephone)*—Placid—calm—peaceful. Yes. And I'd like to speak with Mr John Case.

SUSAN: If I could grab you the way I did, she can—

NICK: But there's more in this than meets the ear, darling—Julia.

LINDA: Quiet! *(Then, to the telephone)*—Miss Seton. *Linda* Seton. *(To* SUSAN*)*—I don't want to give him heart-failure, thinking it's—*(To the telephone)*—John Case—Lake Placid Club—Linda Seton. Thanks. *(She replaces the receiver and returns to* NICK *and* SUSAN*)* I'm sure he's there. I feel it in my bones.

NICK: *(a pause. Then)* Linda, Johnny asked me not to tell anyone, but I think you ought to know something: the fact is, he's got a single cabin on the *Paris* for himself tonight.

LINDA: He—? How do you know?

NICK: Because I got it for him.

LINDA: You don't seriously think he'd do it?

NICK: No—I can't say I do.

LINDA: Well, *I* do! Oh, Lord—then he's in New York now!

NICK: Maybe so.

LINDA: He can't be, or he'd be here.—Where did he go to, Nick?

NICK: —Of that, I wasn't informed.

LINDA: You know, this is ageing me.

SUSAN: We know something else you don't know, Linda.

LINDA: Oh! What is it?

NICK: —Look out, Susan. Steady, girl.

LINDA: *(glances at them, quickly, then lights a cigarette)* What is it?

SUSAN: How did you happen to decide not to come abroad, as you planned?

LINDA: Why, I—well, I thought probably Johnny and Julia—they'd rather not have any family tagging along, and besides that, I want to get Ned off on a trip with me—out West, if I can.

SUSAN: I know. But—

NICK: *(again* NICK *cuts across her)*—I saw Ned in Jimmy's last night. He was—well, if I may use the word—

SUSAN: Look here, Linda—

LINDA: *(to* NICK*)*—I think he's all right tonight. He went to a show with the Wheelers.

NICK: *(reflects)* I wonder if they're really in love with each other.

LINDA: They're terribly in love.

SUSAN: What makes you think so?

LINDA: I know it. Johnny couldn't help but be, and Julia—

SUSAN: *(glances at* NICK*)* You meant the Wheelers, didn't you?

NICK: Why, I—yes, I did.

LINDA: I don't know about them. *(She moves away from them, then back again)*

SUSAN: Can't *you* do anything with her, Linda?

LINDA: Who—Julia?

SUSAN: Yes.

LINDA: I've talked myself blue in the face. It's no good. She won't listen. I've had the cold-shoulder and the deaf-ear so long now I'm all hoarse and half frozen.

SUSAN: I thought she's always depended on you.

LINDA: Well, she doesn't any more.

SUSAN: You love her a great deal, don't you?

LINDA: *(laughs shortly)* I expect I do!

SUSAN: —But my dear child, don't you see that if she thinks just as your father does—

LINDA: Johnny'll fix that. Johnny'll fix everything.

SUSAN: He'll never change *them*, Linda.

LINDA: Susan, you don't know that man.

NICK: —It'd be a pity to deprive your father of the pleasure he'd take in putting him over on the town.

LINDA: Don't speak of it. That's one thing Johnny's been spared so far. I don't think he's had an inkling of *it* yet.

NICK: It will come: Mr and Mrs John Sebastian Case have closed their Sixty-fourth Street house and gone to Coney Island for the hunting. Mrs

Case will be remembered as Julia Seton, of Seton Pretty.

SUSAN: I'd like a picture of him, when it happens.

NICK: I wouldn't.

LINDA: —If they'd only listen to me—I've got to make them listen!—And he's so sweet, he's so attractive. What's the matter with the girl, anyway? She ought to know by now that men like Johnny don't grow on every bush.

SUSAN: —But you see, the things you like in him are just what she can't stand, Linda. And the fate you say he'll save her from is the one fate in this whole world she wants.

LINDA: I don't believe it.—Even so, she loves him—and there's been a break—and wouldn't you think she'd at least be woman enough to hang on—*hang on!*

SUSAN: I don't know. There's another who isn't woman enough to grab.

LINDA: *(there is a silence. Finally* LINDA *speaks)*—I don't quite get you, Susan.

SUSAN: Well, to make it plain, no man's lost this side of the altar.

NICK: She's talking a lot of—*(Then, to* SUSAN*)* Come on, Pearl—ups-a-daisy.

LINDA: Susan—

SUSAN: Yes, dear?

LINDA: Julia has never in her life loved anyone but Johnny.

SUSAN: —And you.

LINDA: —And me.

NICK: *(in spite of himself)*—And herself.

LINDA: *(turns on him sharply)* That's not true!—Even in this it's of him she's thinking—she may be mistaken, but it *is* of him!

SUSAN: I've no doubt she believes that.

LINDA: Well, I believe it too!

NICK: —Come on, will you, Susan?

LINDA: I think it's rotten of you to suspect things of Julia that aren't Julia at all, and I think it's worse of you to—

NICK: We're sorry, Linda, really we are.

LINDA: You aren't sorry! You're—*(Suddenly she covers her face with her hands)* Oh, what's the matter with me?

SUSAN: Linda, I could shake you.

LINDA: I wish you would.—I wish someone would, till there was nothing left to shake.

SUSAN: —And there's not a thing to do about it?

LINDA: What there is to do, I'm doing. *(She goes to the window at Back. A silence. Then)*

SUSAN: —And if you did anything else, I expect you wouldn't be Linda.

NICK: Linda, I think you're just about the—*(But that is as close as he can get to a declaration of faith)*—Oh, hell—*(He turns to* SUSAN*)* Will you come, dear? It's ten-thirty.

SUSAN: *(rises and moves toward* LINDA. NICK *follows)* But if Johnny should—*(*LINDA *faces her)*—Promise us one thing, Linda.

LINDA: What?

SUSAN: *(after a moment)* Nothing.

LINDA: I love you two.

SUSAN: —And so do we love you.

LINDA: —Call back for me when?

SUSAN: In half an hour.

NICK: Less.

LINDA: —Then could your car possibly take me out to Mary Hedges'?

SUSAN: But of course! What a good idea—

LINDA: Mary asked if—I'll have a bag packed. *(*JULIA *comes in.)* Oh, hello, dear.—Are you back already?

JULIA: Isn't it late? Hello, Susan. Hello, Nick. I thought you were sailing. *(She leaves her evening wrap on the sofa, Left, and moves toward the writing table at Right.)*

SUSAN: We are.

NICK: At the crack of twelve. On the way now, in fact.

JULIA: I hope you have a grand trip.

SUSAN: Thanks. *(*DELIA *enters and takes* JULIA'S *wrap from the sofa)*

LINDA: —Delia, will you pack a bag for me, please? I'm going to Mrs Hedges until Tuesday.

DELIA: Yes, Miss. *(She goes out.* NICK *and* SUSAN *stand at Center, facing* JULIA*)*

SUSAN: I'm sorry we won't be here for the wedding, Julia.

JULIA: I'm sorry too, Susan.

NICK: When's it to be?

JULIA: We haven't quite—set a date, yet.

SUSAN: —In the Spring, some time?

JULIA: Possibly before.

NICK: Let us know, won't you?

JULIA: Of course.

NICK: *(a brief pause. Then)*—Then you're not coming down to the boat tonight?

JULIA: I'm afraid I can't. Bon voyage, though.

NICK: *(thinks rapidly)* Thanks. Can we take any word to Johnny for you?

JULIA: To Johnny?

NICK: Yes.—Or a basket of fruit, maybe?

JULIA: He'll be there, will he?

NICK: *(this, at any rate,* NICK *can do)* I should imagine so, if he's sailing.

JULIA: Sailing!

NICK: Isn't he?

JULIA: I wasn't aware of it.

NICK: Well, all I know is that the morning he left for wherever he went to, he telephoned me to get him a single cabin through Andrews, of the French Line. I don't believe it's been given up, or I'd have heard from them. I thought of course you knew, or I—

JULIA: I think I should—if he were going.

NICK: Yes, I suppose so. *(To* SUSAN*)* We won't expect him, then.

SUSAN: No.—Goodbye, Julia. *(They move together toward the door)*

NICK: Look us up, when you arrive. Immigrant's Bank.—We'll see you later, Linda.

LINDA: I'll be ready.

SUSAN: Thanks. Lovely evening—

NICK *and* SUSAN: *(together)*—And you must come and see *us* some time! *(They go out. There is a silence.* JULIA *looks for a cigarette)*

LINDA: It may be true, Julia. I think the chances are it is.

JULIA: What?

LINDA: —That Johnny's going with them.

JULIA: *(laughs)* Not possibly, darling!—Why don't they keep these cigarette-boxes filled—

LINDA: Stop it, Julia!

JULIA: Stop it?

LINDA: —Pretending you don't give a damn.

JULIA: *(finds and lights a cigarette)* You seem to be taking my little difficulty more seriously than I am. *(She moves toward the sofa at Left)*

LINDA: If you don't want Johnny to go off tonight and make a hash of both your lives, you'd better send him some word to the boat.

JULIA: *(smiles)* Somehow, I don't think that's necessary.

LINDA: Why not?

JULIA: Well, for one reason, because he won't be there. He's no more sailing tonight than I am.

LINDA: You don't know that he's not!

JULIA: I don't know that he is, so I think I'm safe in assuming it.—Do you want to go to the Todds' dinner on Wednesday? They telephoned—

LINDA: —Julia, why do you want to shut me out in the cold like this?

JULIA: I wasn't aware that I was.

LINDA: —But won't you just *talk* to me! Oh, please, Julia—

JULIA: I don't know what there is to say.

LINDA: Never so long as I remember has there been anything we couldn't—

JULIA: If there's been any shutting out done, it's you who've done it, Linda.

LINDA: Me?!

JULIA: Johnny and I have had a difference of opinion, and you're siding with him, aren't you?

LINDA: But he's right! He's right for you as well as for himself—

JULIA: I think that's for me to decide.

LINDA: Not Father?

JULIA: Father has nothing to do with it—

LINDA: Oh, no!

JULIA: He happens to agree with me where you don't, that's all.

LINDA: We've always agreed before—always.

JULIA: No—I think quite often I've given in, in order to avoid scenes and upsets and—oh, well—

LINDA: *(a silence. Then)*—Is that true, Julia?

JULIA: You've always been the "stronger character," haven't you? At least people have always thought so. You've made all the decisions, you've always had the ideas—

LINDA: —And you've been resenting me right from the very—*(She moves away from her, toward the fireplace)* Oh—I can't believe it—

JULIA: It's nothing to get in a state about—and I didn't say I resented you. You've been an immense help, often. But when it comes to determining my future, and the future of the man I'm going to marry—

LINDA: *(turns on her sharply)*—Your future! What do you want, Julia—just security? Sit back in your feather-boa among the Worthies of the World?

JULIA: Well, I'm certain that one thing I *don't* want is to start this endless, aimless discussion all over again.

LINDA: But I tell you you can't *stand* this sort of life forever—not if you're the person I think you are. And when it starts going thin on you, what'll you have to hold on to?—Lois Evans shot herself—why? Franny Grant's up the Hudson in a sanitarium—why?

JULIA: I'm sure I don't know.

LINDA: —Nothing left to do or have or want—that's why—and no insides! There's not a poor girl in town who isn't happier than we are—at least they still *want* what we've got—*they* think it's good. *(She turns away)*—If they knew!

JULIA: —And *I* think it's good.

LINDA: Lord, Julia, don't tell me that you *want* it!

JULIA: I want it, and it's all I want.

LINDA: *(there is a silence. Then)*—Then it's goodbye, Julia.

JULIA: Oh, Linda, for Heaven's sake don't be so ridiculous! If you're so damn set on being violent, get a few Russians in and talk life with a great big L to them.

EDWARD: *(comes in, an admonishing finger raised)* Ah—ah—ah!

LINDA: *(turns to him)*—Father, I think you're both giving Johnny the rottenest kind of a deal.

EDWARD: In what way?

LINDA: Every way! Why do you do it? It can't be that you think he's out to marry for money. You must realize how simple it would have been for him—to conform to specifications now, and then just not get up some fine morning.

EDWARD: *(moves to the table behind the sofa at Right)* I don't regard the young man as a fortune-hunter, Linda.

LINDA: Well, what is it, then?

EDWARD: *(finds a cigarette and comes forward with it)*—I think his outlook has merely become—somewhat confused, shall we say, and—

LINDA: —And you'll straighten it out for him.

EDWARD: *(to JULIA)* We shall try, shan't we, Daughter?

LINDA: Why hasn't he a right to spend some part of his life as he wants to? He can afford it. What's he got to do? Pile up so much that he can be comfortable on the income of his income?

EDWARD: *(seats himself in a chair near the sofa)*—That would be an excellent aim, but I think we shall hardly require it of him.

LINDA: I'd like to hear the requirements.

EDWARD: Any self-respecting young man wishes to earn enough to support his wife and his family.

LINDA: Even when his wife already has—? Even when there's no possible need of it?

EDWARD: Even then.

LINDA: Oh, Father, what a fake idea that is!

EDWARD: I don't think so. Nor does Julia.—In addition, he has somehow developed a very curious attitude toward work—

LINDA: It seems to me saner than most. He wants his leisure at this end—good sense, I call it.—Which is harder to do, anyway—? Go to an office and rustle papers about or sit under a tree and look at your own soul?

JULIA: *(contemptuously)* Heavens!—The office, I should say.

LINDA: Then you've never looked, Julia.

JULIA: You can't talk to her, Father.

EDWARD: I should like to understand what he—and you—are aiming at, Linda, but I must confess I cannot. *(NED comes in)*—I consider his whole attitude deliberately un-American.

LINDA: *(stares at EDWARD)* Are you serious?

EDWARD: Entirely.

LINDA: *(she stares for a moment more)*—You're right. I believe it is.

NED: *(seats himself on the sofa, at Left)* I've always said the Americans were a great little people.

LINDA: —Then he's a bad one, and will go to hell when he dies. Because apparently he can't quite believe that a life devoted to piling up money is all it's cracked up to be.—That's strange, isn't it—when he has us, right before his eyes, for such a shining example?

JULIA: I thought *you* were the one who found leisure so empty.

LINDA: —You think I call this, leisure? A life-sentence to *this?*—Or that he does?

JULIA: I think any variety of it he'd find quite as empty.

LINDA: —Even if it should be, he's got a right to discover it for himself! Can't you see that?

JULIA: I can see the discovery would come, quick enough.

LINDA: —And you don't want to be with him to lend a hand, if it should? *(JULIA is silent.)*

EDWARD: Linda, I listened most attentively to our young dreamer the other day. I have listened quite as attentively to you this evening. I am not entirely without intelligence, but I must still confess that most of your talk seems to me to be of the seventeen-year-old variety.

LINDA: I'm glad if it is! We're all grand at seventeen. It's after that that the—sickness sets in.

EDWARD: *(chuckles, shakes his head and rises)*—I feel very well, myself—and you look in perfect health, my dear. *(He moves toward the door)*

LINDA: —You both think he'll come around, Father—compromise, anyway. You'll get fooled. He won't give way one little inch.

EDWARD: *(at the door EDWARD turns, smiling)* Stubborn—?

LINDA: Right! And sure he's right!

EDWARD: We shall see—*(He goes out, victor)*

JULIA: —Is that all, Linda?

LINDA: Where are you going?

JULIA: To bed.

LINDA: Now?

JULIA: Yes. Have you any objections?

LINDA: You actually won't lift a finger to keep him off that boat tonight?

JULIA: He has no idea of taking it.

LINDA: You don't know him!

JULIA: Well, I think I know him a little better than you. I happen to be engaged to him.
(HENRY *has entered with a tray containing a decanter of whisky, ice, a bottle of soda, and one glass.*)

NED: Thanks, Henry. (HENRY *bows and goes out*)

JULIA: Ned, I thought you went to the theatre with the Wheelers—

NED: I did, but it was so bad I left. (*He rises, goes behind the table and makes himself a drink*)

JULIA: Wasn't that just a trifle rude?

NED: I don't know, Julia. Look it up under R in the book of etiquette, will you?

JULIA: I can't imagine what you're thinking of these days.—Drinking alone—that's pretty too, isn't it?

NED: I never thought of the aesthetic side, but I see what you mean. (*He takes a long swallow of his drink*)

JULIA: (*regards him contemptuously, then, to* LINDA) If there's any message of any sort, I wish you'd ring my room.

LINDA: All right. (JULIA *goes out.* LINDA *seats herself and stares moodily in front of her.*)

NED: —Like a drink?

LINDA: No, thanks.

NED: (*again settles down upon the sofa*) —You know, most people, including Johnny and yourself, make a big mistake about Julia.

LINDA: What's that?

NED: They're taken in by her looks. At bottom she's a very dull girl, and the life she pictures for herself is the life she belongs in. (*The* TELEPHONE *rings.* LINDA *goes to it*)

LINDA: —You've never hit it off, that's all. (*At the telephone*) Hello.—Yes.—Yes.—What? When, do you know?—Well, ask, will you? (*To* NED) He *was* there.

NED: Who and where?

LINDA: Johnny—Placid. (*To the telephone*) Yes? This—? I see. No. No. That's right. Thanks. (*She puts down the telephone and turns again to* NED) —And left this noon.

NED: Then he'll be around tonight.

LINDA: You think so? This late?

NED: He'll be around.

LINDA: (*a moment. Then*) Ned—

NED: What?

LINDA: Do you remember what we talked about New Year's Eve?

NED: (*a brief pause. Then*) Sure—I remember.

LINDA: Tell me something—

NED: Sure.

LINDA: Does it stand out all over me?

NED: Why?

LINDA: Nick and Susan—I think they got it.

NED: Anyone who loves you would, Linda.

LINDA: Oh, that's awful. I'm so ashamed— (*Then she raises her head*) I'm not, though!

NED: Why should you be?

LINDA: (*suddenly*) Look here, Ned—you're in a jam too, aren't you?

NED: Me?

LINDA: You.

NED: Sure, I suppose so.

LINDA: Is it that you hate this— (*Her gesture includes the house and all it represents*) —Or that you love that— (*She indicates his drink*)

NED: H'm— (*He looks about him*) Well, God knows I hate all this— (*And lifts the glass before his eyes*) —and God knows I'm crazy mad over this— (*He takes a deep swallow and sets the glass down*) I guess it's both.

LINDA: What are we going to do?

NED: Nothing, that I know of.

LINDA: But we must!

NED: (*hunches down into the sofa*) I'm all right.

LINDA: You're not—but you'll pull out of it—and *I'll* pull out of it.

NED: I'm all right. I don't mind any more.

LINDA: You've got to mind. We can't just let go, can we?

NED: *I* can. I have.

LINDA: No. No!

NED: Listen, Linda: I've had the whole thing out with myself, see? All of it. A lot of times. And I've developed my what-do-you-call-it—technique. I'm all right. There's no reason for stewing over me. I'm—*(He squints at his glass)* —very happy.

LINDA: There must be some sort of life for you—

NED: —But there *is!* Haven't I got the swell Seton name to uphold? *(He laughs shortly)* —Only that's where I'll fox it. I'll make *it* uphold me.

LINDA: Neddy—listen: After the wedding we'll go out to Boulder, both of us.—We'll live on horseback and in trout streams all day long every day until we're in hand again. We'll get so damn tired that we won't be able to want anything or think of anything but sleep.

NED: You make it too hard. Come on—have a drink.

LINDA: Oh, you're dying, Neddy!

NED: *(very patiently)* All right, Linda.

LINDA: Won't you do that with me?

NED: Thanks, but uh-uh. Nope.

LINDA: *(moves away from him to the other side of the room)* Oh, won't anyone ever again do what I *know* they should do?

NED: That's what's the matter with you, Linda. You worry so much over other people's troubles you don't get anywhere with your own. *(HENRY enters. LINDA is staring at NED)*

HENRY: —Mr Case, Miss.

LINDA: *(a silence, then LINDA recovers herself)* Yes?—Have him come up, will you? *(HENRY bows and goes out. A moment. NED watches her. Then)*

NED: —Are you sure you *want* to get over him?

LINDA: No. I'm not. And that's what scares me most. I feel alive, and I love it. I feel at last something's happening to me. But it can't get anywhere, so it's like living on—*your* stuff. I've *got* to get over it.

NED: —Because it seems so hopeless, is that it?

LINDA: Seems! What do you mean?

NED: Don't you know? *(LINDA can only look at him. He goes to her)* —Then let me tell you something: you're twice as attractive as Julia ever thought of being. You've got twice the looks, and

twice the mind, and ten times the guts. You've lived in her shade for years now, and there's nothing to it. You could charm a bird off a tree, if you would. And why not? If you were in her way, she'd ride you down like a rabbit.

LINDA: *(softly)* Oh, you stinker—knowing the way she loves him—you stinker, Ned.

NED: *(shrugs)* All right. *(He wanders in the direction of the door)* —Tell him Hello for me, will you?

LINDA: *(LINDA's voice rises)* —If there's one thing I'll do in my life, it'll be to let the fresh air back into you again, hear me?—I'll do it if I have to shoot you.

NED: *(turns and smiles back at her)* —All right. *(He goes out. With an exclamation LINDA goes to the window and looks out, huddling herself in her arms)*

JOHNNY: *(enters. A moment, then)* Hello, Linda.

LINDA: Hello, Johnny.

JOHNNY: Is—? *(LINDA moves to the telephone)*

LINDA: I'll send for her.

JOHNNY: Wait a minute. *(A silence. He looks about him)* I feel as if I'd—been away quite a while.

LINDA: Yes.

JOHNNY: I went to Placid.

LINDA: I see.

JOHNNY: It was horrible there.

LINDA: I can imagine it.

JOHNNY: Oh, Linda, I love her so—

LINDA: Of course you do, Johnny.

JOHNNY: It—makes anything else—any plans—ideas—anything—

LINDA: —Seem so unimportant, of course.

JOHNNY: But I know they are important! I know that!

LINDA: *(smiles)* Still—

JOHNNY: *(turns away)* That's it—*still*—

LINDA: *(a moment)* I think it'll come out all right, Johnny.

JOHNNY: Maybe, in the long run.

LINDA: Have you—I suppose you've decided something or other—

JOHNNY: I'm going to stay at my job, if that's what you mean.

LINDA: *(after a moment, very quietly)* I see.

JOHNNY: But only for a while! Only a couple of years, say—just until I can get through to her that—well, it's what she asked, and after all, a couple of years isn't a lifetime.

LINDA: No, of course not.

JOHNNY: I can see the way they look at it—I could hardly expect them suddenly to do a complete about-face, and—but hang it, they ought at least to see what I'm getting at!

LINDA: Perhaps eventually they will.

JOHNNY: That's what I'm counting on.

LINDA: *(another silence. Then)* The fun's gone out of you, Johnny. That's too bad.

JOHNNY: *(stares at the floor)* It'll be back.

LINDA: I hope.

JOHNNY: *(looks up suddenly)* Linda—you agree that there's only the one thing for me to do now—

LINDA: *(smiles again)* Compromise—

JOHNNY: Yes, damn it! But *you* think that's right, don't you?

LINDA: I don't think it matters a bit what I think—

JOHNNY: *(goes to her suddenly and seizes her wrists)* It does, though! You think it's right, don't you? Say you think it's right!

LINDA: Shall I send for Julia?

JOHNNY: Say it first!

LINDA: *(with difficulty)* Johnny—when two people love each other as much as you, anything that keeps them apart must be wrong.—Will that do? *(JOHNNY drops her hand and moves away from her.)* —And shall I send for her now?

JOHNNY: Go ahead.

LINDA: *(goes to the telephone and presses a button in the box beside it)* With luck, we'll manage not to include Father this time.

JOHNNY: Oh, Lord, yes! (LINDA *again presses the button, and again several times)* Asleep, probably—

LINDA: Of course not. *(She presses it again. Then)* Julia—yes—would you come down a minute? No—but there's no telegram *to* send up. Will you come, Julia? *(Her voice changes)* Julia, it's terribly important that you come down here at once. *(She replaces the telephone and turns to* JOHNNY*)* She'll be right down.

JOHNNY: If she doesn't fall asleep again.

LINDA: Johnny—don't talk like that. I can't stand to hear your voice do that.

JOHNNY: You care more what happens to me than she does.

LINDA: *(startled)* What? Don't be silly. *(Then, with difficulty)* Maybe I feel things about you that she doesn't because—well, maybe just because *I'm* not in love with you.

JOHNNY: You know what I think of you, don't you?

LINDA: *(smiles)* I'd be glad to hear.

JOHNNY: I like you better than anyone else in the world.

LINDA: That's very nice, Johnny—because I like you a good deal, too. *(For a long moment their eyes hold them together. Then* EDWARD *comes in and, with a start,* LINDA *sees him)* Oh, for the love of Pete—

EDWARD: *(advances to* JOHNNY, *hand outstretched)* Well, well—good evening!

JOHNNY: Good evening, sir. *(They shake hands)*

LINDA: *(turns away)* —Both members of this club.

EDWARD: They tell me you've been away. Very pleasant, having you back.

JOHNNY: It's pleasant to be back.

EDWARD: —Quite at the mercy of the snow these days, aren't we?

JOHNNY: Quite.

EDWARD: *(moves toward the fireplace)* Still, they say Americans need four seasons, so I suppose we oughtn't to complain, eh?

JOHNNY: I suppose not.

LINDA: Father—Johnny came tonight to see Julia—

EDWARD: —That doesn't surprise me a great deal, Daughter—not a great deal!

LINDA: —Julia—not you and me.—Come on—let's go byebye.

JULIA: *(enters)* Linda, what's the idea of—? *(She sees* JOHNNY*)* Oh—

JOHNNY: *(goes to her swiftly)* Get a wrap, will you? We're going out—

JULIA: *(hesitates)* Father—you won't mind if Johnny and I—

EDWARD: Please close the door. I wish to speak with both of you. *(*JULIA *gestures helplessly to* JOHNNY *and closes the door)* —You insist upon putting me in a position that I don't in the least relish—

(JULIA *seats herself upon the bench at Left. The door is opened again, tentatively*) Who's that?— Oh, come in, Ned, come in.

NED: (*enters and moves toward his drink*) Sorry.— I just wanted—

EDWARD: Sit down, Son— (NED *seats himself upon the sofa Left.* EDWARD *continues to* JULIA *and* JOHNNY) —Coming between two young people in love is furthest from my wish and intention.— Love, true love, is a very rare and beautiful thing, and— (NED *rises and moves silently toward the door*) Where are you going? Please sit down! (*He waits until* NED *had returned to his place, then continues*) —And I believe its path— that is to say, the path of true love, contrary to the adage, *should* run smooth. But in order that it may—I am a man of fifty-eight years, and speak from a long experience and observation— it is of paramount importance that—

JOHNNY: I beg your pardon, sir.

EDWARD: Yes?

JOHNNY: If Pritchard, Ames still want me, I'll go with them when we get back from our wedding-trip—about March first, say. (LINDA *turns away. There is a silence. Then*)

JULIA: (*softly*) Oh, Johnny— (*She goes to him*)

JOHNNY: I'm still not convinced—I still don't believe in it, but it's what Julia wishes and—and I'm—glad to defer to her wish.

LINDA: And now, in Heaven's name, may they be left alone—or shall we all move over to Madison Square Garden?

EDWARD: (*disregarding her*) You are not convinced, you say— (LINDA *exclaims impatiently*)

JOHNNY: Would you like me to lie to you, sir?

JULIA: It's enough for me, Father.

JOHNNY: Julia said a year or two. I'll stay with them three years. I'll work harder than ever I've worked before. I'll do everything I can to make a success of it. I only ask that if at the end of the three years I still feel that it's wise to quit for a while, there won't be any more objections.

EDWARD: I doubt if by that time there'll be reason for any.

JOHNNY: We'll have to see about that, sir.

JULIA: Well, Father?

EDWARD: (*a pause. Then*) When is it you wish to be married?

JULIA: As soon as possible.

JOHNNY: Sooner.

EDWARD: The invitations must be out for ten days at least.—How would two weeks from Wednesday suit you?

JULIA: That would be perfect.

EDWARD: No doubt there will be a sailing later that week.—Well, now, the sun's shining once more, isn't it?—And we're all friends again, eh?

LINDA: Just one big family.

EDWARD: —And what are your plans for your wedding-trip, may I ask?

JOHNNY: We haven't any very definite ones. Mostly France, I expect.

EDWARD: It's well to arrange even honeymoons a bit in advance.—Now let me suggest a little itinerary: You'll land at Plymouth or Southampton, and proceed straight to London. I'll cable my sister tomorrow. She and her husband will be delighted to have you stay with them.

LINDA: Good Lord, Father—

EDWARD: (*to* JOHNNY) He is Sir Horace Porter— one of the most important men in British banking circles.

JULIA: Father, I'm not sure—

EDWARD: You can scarcely go abroad and not stop with your Aunt Helen, Julia. In addition, it will save hotel expense and Johnny will be able to learn something of British methods.—Then I shall cable the Bouviers in Paris.—He was expert adviser to the Minister of Finance in the late war—a very good man for you to know. If they aren't already in Cannes, they will be very glad to have you visit them. And if they are, you could not do better than go straight to the South yourselves and—

JOHNNY: I had thought of this as more of a lark than a business trip, sir.

EDWARD: —But there's no harm in combining a little business with pleasure, is there? I've never found there was.

JULIA: *(to* JOHNNY*)* They have a lovely place in Cannes.

EDWARD: A week in London—a week in Paris—

LINDA: An hour in the Louvre—

EDWARD: —Ten days in Cannes—ideal! Then you might sail from Genoa and return by the Southern route. *(To* JULIA*)* I'll arrange to have your house ready for you to go into March first.

JULIA: —Thanks, dear.

JOHNNY: What house is that, Julia?

JULIA: Father's lending us the sweetest little place on Sixty-fourth Street.

NED: *(to* LINDA*)* Would you call the Sixty-fourth Street house little?

LINDA: *(watching* JOHNNY*)* —By comparison.

EDWARD: *(to* JULIA*)* And I have also decided to turn the cottage at The Poplars over to you for the summers.

JULIA: Father, you shouldn't—you really should not! *(She goes to him and takes his hand)*

NED: Now there *is* a small place—hasn't even got a ballroom.

JULIA: Oh, Johnny—wait till you see it!

EDWARD: *(is beaming)* This is not a deed of gift, you know—not yet. Perhaps when you have occupied them for—er—five years or so, my hard old heart may soften.

JULIA: —Listen to him—*his* hard old heart! *(To* JOHNNY*)* —Have you ever known of anyone so sweet?

JOHNNY: *(after a moment)* Julia—I'm sorry—but I can't stand it.

JULIA: *(a silence. Then)* Would you—mind telling me what you mean?

JOHNNY: If we begin loaded down with possessions, obligations, responsibilities, how would we ever get out from under them? We never would.

EDWARD: Ah?

JOHNNY: —No. You're extremely generous—and kind—but it's not for me.

EDWARD: And may I ask what *is* for you?

JOHNNY: I don't know yet, but I do know it's not this.

EDWARD: *(very quietly)* We are to understand, then, that you are *not* returning to work.

JOHNNY: That work? For this? *(He shakes his head)* —No.

JULIA: But you said—!

JOHNNY: —I'm back where I was, now. I can see now that it's got to be a clean break, it's simply got to.

EDWARD: But the other day, if I remember correctly, you intimated that you might follow some occupation—

JOHNNY: Eventually, yes. I think I may still be fairly active at thirty-five or forty.

EDWARD: —And in the meantime you expect just to lie fallow, is that it?

JOHNNY: Not lie—be! I expect to dig and plow and water for all I'm worth.

EDWARD: Toward the—er—eventual occupation which is to overtake you—

JOHNNY: Exactly.

EDWARD: I see.—Julia, if you marry this young man now, I doubt if he will ever again earn one penny. *(He moves to the table behind the sofa, at Right)*

JOHNNY: *(advances)* Julia, if it's important to you, I'll promise you I shall always earn my own living. And what's more, if there's need of it, I'll always earn yours.

JULIA: Thanks.

JOHNNY: Oh, my dear, we've got to make our own life—there's nothing to it if we don't—there's no other way to live it!—Let's forget wedding invitations and two weeks from Wednesday. Let's go now. Let's be married tonight. *(*EDWARD *turns, in amazement)*

JULIA: I must decide now, must I?

JOHNNY: Please—

JULIA: —And if I say No—not unless you—?

JOHNNY: —Then I'm going tonight, by myself.

JULIA: *(a moment. Then)* Very well—you can go. Because I don't quite see myself with an idler for a husband.

JOHNNY: *(a silence. Then* JOHNNY *speaks slowly)* I suppose the fact is, I love feeling free inside even better than I love you, Julia.

JULIA: Apparently—or what you call feeling free.

JOHNNY: *(turns to* EDWARD*)* Goodbye, sir. I'm sorry we couldn't make a go of it. Thanks for trying, anyhow. *(He goes to* LINDA *and takes both her hands)* —Goodbye to you, Linda. You've been sweet.

LINDA: Goodbye, Johnny. So have you.—I hope you find what you're looking for.

JOHNNY: I hope *you* do.

LINDA: You did want someone along with you on the big search, didn't you?

JOHNNY: I did, you know.

LINDA: Poor boy.

JOHNNY: —But we won't mind, will we?

LINDA: Hell, no—*we* won't mind.

JOHNNY: We'll get there—

LINDA: Sure! *We'll* get there!

JOHNNY: Linda—

LINDA: *(she leans toward him)* Oh, please do—

JOHNNY: *(bends, kisses her briefly, and moves toward the door)* Goodbye, Ned. *(*NED *attempts a goodbye, but cannot say it.* JOHNNY *goes out. There is a complete silence for a moment. Then* LINDA *murmurs)*

LINDA: I'll miss that man. *(Another silence, which* JULIA *finally breaks)*

JULIA: *(half to herself)* —He's really gone, then.

EDWARD: Yes.—And in my opinion—

LINDA: *(turns sharply)* —Good riddance, eh? *(*EDWARD *nods sagely)*

JULIA: —Really gone—

LINDA: *(goes to her)* —Oh, never mind, dear, never mind. If he loves you, he'll be back!

JULIA: *(turns upon her)* —Be back? Be *back*, did you say? What do you think I am? Do you think all I've got to do with my time is to persuade a—a lightweight like him that there's something to life but having fun and more fun? *(*LINDA *stares, unable to speak)*

EDWARD: I hope, Julia, that this experience, hard as it may have been, will teach you that—

JULIA: Oh, don't worry about me! I'm all right. *(She laughs briefly)* —Even a little more than all right, I should say.

NED: *(rises)* —Um.—Narrow squeak, wasn't it? *(Suddenly* LINDA *grasps* JULIA'S *arm)*

JULIA: What's the matter with you?

LINDA: You don't love him.

JULIA: Will you kindly let go my arm?

LINDA: You don't love him!

JULIA: Will you *please*—

LINDA: Answer me! Do you or do you not?

JULIA: And what's that to you, may I ask?

EDWARD: Now, children—

LINDA: What's it to me! Oh, what's it to me! *(Her grasp tightens on* JULIA'S *arm)* Answer me!

JULIA: Father—what's the matter with her?

LINDA: You don't, do you? I can *see* you don't. It's written all over you. You're relieved he's gone—*relieved!*

JULIA: And suppose I am?

LINDA: —She asks me suppose she is! *(Again she confronts* JULIA*)* Are you? Say it!

JULIA: *(wrenches herself free)* —I'm so relieved I could sing with it.—Is that what you want?

LINDA: Yes!—Thanks! *(She throws back her head and laughs with joy, and moves quickly to the table behind the sofa at Left)* Oh, Lordy, Lordy—have I got a job now! *(From her handbag on the table she takes two brown envelopes, goes to* NED *and gives him one of them)*

NED: What is it? *(He sees)* Passport—

LINDA: What do you say?

NED: When?

LINDA: Now. Tonight.

NED: Oh, I couldn't tonight.

LINDA: Of course you could! If I can, you can.

EDWARD: *(advances)* Linda, where are you off to?

LINDA: *(to* NED*)* Will you come?

NED: Well, you know I'd like to, but—

LINDA: Then come!

EDWARD: Linda, where are you going? Tell me instantly.

LINDA: —On a trip. On a big ride. Oh, what a ride! Do you mind?

NED: Listen, Father, I'd—

EDWARD: A trip now is out of the question. Please remember you have a position to fill. You are not an idler. *(To* LINDA*)* —A trip where?

LINDA: *(to* NED*)* You won't?

NED: I can't.

LINDA: —Caught.

NED: Maybe.

LINDA: —I'll be back for you, Ned.

NED: *(almost inaudibly)* I'll—be here—

DELIA: *(enters)* Excuse me, Miss Linda—Mr and Mrs Potter are waiting in the car. Your bag has gone down.

LINDA: Bring my fur coat, will you, Delia?—And throw a couple of hats in the hatbox and take it down, too.

DELIA: Very well, Miss. *(*DELIA *goes out)*

LINDA: *(turns to* JULIA*)* —You've got no faith in Johnny, have you, Julia? His little dream may fall flat, you think—yes! So it may! What about it? What if it should? There'll be another—the point is, he *does* dream! Oh, I've got all the faith in the world in Johnny. Whatever he does is all right with me. If he wants to sit on his tail, he can sit on his tail. If he wants to come back and sell peanuts, Lord how I'll believe in those peanuts!—Goodbye, Julia.—Goodbye, Father. *(She leaves them and goes to* NED*)* Goodbye, Neddy—
(Warn CURTAIN*.)*

NED: Goodbye, kid—good luck— *(For a moment they cling together. Then)*

LINDA: Oh, never you fear, I'll be back for you, my fine bucko!

NED: All right, kid. *(She moves toward the door.* NED *is drawn after her.* DELIA *enters with the fur coat.* LINDA *takes it from her.* DELIA *goes out)*

EDWARD: As yet you have not said where it is you are—

JULIA: *(exclaims suddenly)* I know!

LINDA: *(going out)* —And try to stop me, some-one! Oh, please—someone try to stop me! *(She is gone)*

NED: *(stands looking after her, murmuring softly)* Oh, God, oh, God—

EDWARD: I shall not permit it! I shall—

NED: —Permit it!—Permit Linda?—Don't make me laugh, Father.

JULIA: *(advancing)* She's going *with* them, isn't she? *Isn't* she?

NED: *(smiles and picks up his glass again)* —Going to get her Johnny.

JULIA: *(laughs shortly)* A fine chance she's got!

NED: —Any bets? *(Then savagely)* —Any bets, Julia? *(He raises his glass)* —To Linda— *(The portrait above the fireplace catches his eye)* —And while we're at it—Grandfather! *(He drinks.)*

CURTAIN

THE CHILDREN'S HOUR (1934)

The hardest lesson in the theatre is to take nobody too seriously.

In this epigraph taken from a chapter entitled simply "Theatre" in *Pentimento* (1973), her widely acclaimed book of prose "portraits," Lillian Hellman recalls a disgruntled actress's anti-Semitic slur of Harold Clurman, who at that time was directing Hellman's play, *The Autumn Garden* (1951). By 1951, she had eight screenplays and several well-known stage plays to her credit, including *The Little Foxes* (1939), *Watch on the Rhine* (1941, for which she won a New York Drama Critics Circle Award), *The Searching Wind* (1944), and *Another Part of the Forest* (1946). There was, inevitably, the occasional failure, such as with *Days to Come* (1936), which closed after only seven performances. And, even though *The Children's Hour* was a tremendous success, running for 691 performances on Broadway, it and Hellman received their shares of criticism: the play was little more than melodrama, the last act was structurally flawed, and so on. Fortunately, the Hellman of 1934 followed advice the older Hellman offered nearly 40 years later; just as she had with the misguided attack on Clurman, she did not take those responses critical of her ability "too seriously" and went on to become one of the most important women who has ever written for the American stage. In the later years of her career, she wrote such plays as *Toys in the Attic* (New York Drama Critics Circle Award Winner for 1960) and several autobiographical volumes, including *An Unfinished Woman* (1969), *Pentimento*, and *Scoundrel Time* (1976).

If Hellman chose not to take drama reviewers overly seriously, the same cannot be said of her political convictions—or of the weight of her political opinions with her contemporaries. Arthur Miller, for example, recalls her inviting him to a dinner party in the late 1940s to hear two Yugoslav diplomats enumerate Josef Stalin's many crimes against their country. Like Clifford Odets, John Howard Lawson, Langston Hughes, and other writers during the Depression-weary 1930s, Hellman was attracted to socialism for both ideological reasons and more personal ones as well. In particular, as she discovered during a brief stay in Europe in 1929, an anti-Semitic variety of fascism was growing in Nazi Germany. Also, Hellman's longtime friend, a medical student living in Vienna pseudonymously named Julia in *Pentimento* and a 1977 film of the same title, advised Hellman as early as 1933 to learn about "the holocaust that is on its way" and later in 1937 asked her to sneak $50,000 into Germany to aid an anti-Hitler group. (Julia was killed the following year.) On that evening a decade later, Miller sensed that Hellman could hardly bring herself to believe that Russia, which fought the Nazis so vigorously during the war, could "so exploit a sister socialist state" by "bleeding Yugoslavia white." Although Miller could not ignore the Yugoslavs' account, Hellman, who by this time "ran kind of a salon through which what could be called the significant world passed" and to whom the young diplomats looked for approval, could not resist the "deep pull of loyalty to the past and the antifascist, pro-Soviet sentiments of years gone by." In 1952, the **House Un-American Activities Committee (HUAC)** would ask her to delineate these sentiments—which she did—and to name Communist sympathizers of her acquaintance— which she refused to do. Her refusal led to her being blacklisted in Hollywood and audited by the Internal Revenue Service, and to her writing a controversial account of the hearings, *Scoundrel Time*.

Hellman's background scarcely seemed to foreshadow her political activism, although it clearly influenced several of the dramas she wrote, particularly her representation of the New South in *The Little Foxes* and *Another Part of the Forest*. Lillian Hellman (1905–1984) was born in New Orleans as the only child of Max Hellman, whose family had emigrated in the 1840s from Germany, and Julia Newhouse Hellman, originally from Alabama. There is some uncertainty about the year of Hellman's birth, as most sources place it either in 1905 or 1906 (or, occasionally, 1907). In her study of Hellman, Doris Falk outlines this inconsistency (which continues into the 1990s) and decides upon 1905 on the grounds that Hellman herself identified this as the year of her birth when testifying before HUAC; further, in *An Unfinished Woman* Hellman describes her husband Arthur Kober's accepting a position as a screenwriter at Paramount Studio in 1930 and her having turned 25 the June before. Shortly after arriving in Hollywood, Hellman took a position herself at $50 a week as a script reader at Metro-Goldwyn-Mayer.

Like much of her adult life, Hellman's childhood involved a considerable amount of travel. She recalls moving to New York when she was about six and returning frequently for six-month stays to New Orleans and her father's two sisters. As a result, Hellman describes her formal education as "a kind of frantic tennis game" between the two very different worlds of New York and New Orleans, a possible reason for her mediocre performance as a student. She attended New York University and Columbia University, where she first became aware of philosophy and such writers as Karl Marx and Friedrich Engels, but left before graduation to become a reader for what was then one of New York's preeminent publishers, Horace Liveright. There she met influential writers, attended lavish parties, and met Kober, to whom she was married from 1927 to 1932. She travelled with him to Paris, wrote short stories and later screenplays in Hollywood, and there became acquainted with successful detective writer, Dashiell Hammett, with whom she developed an intimate, albeit occasionally stormy, relationship that lasted until his death in 1961. She travelled to Russia, served as correspondent during the Spanish Civil War, dined with Ernest Hemingway and numerous writers of the so-called **lost generation**, and became an important figure in her own right.

It was Hammett, author of such detective novels (and later films) as *The Maltese Falcon* (1930) and *The Thin Man* (1932), who first introduced Hellman to William Roughead's *Bad Companions* (1931), which included an account of an early nineteenth-century Scottish school for young women that was ruined by the accusations of a manipulative and malicious student. Mary Tilford's allegation of lesbianism against her teachers Karen Wright and Martha Dobie in *The Children's Hour* is believed by Mary's grandmother, Mrs Amelia Tilford, and as the curtain lowers on Act Two, scene one, Mrs Tilford phones the parents of other students at the Wright-Dobie School for girls, effectively destroying it and the reputation of the two teachers. By the end of the act, a young girl whom Mary has blackmailed corroborates her lie, even though the inconsistencies of Mary's story are obvious. Unfortunately for Karen and Martha, both the parents of their students and a jury that heard the libel case they brought against Mrs Tilford believed they indeed possessed what the judge termed "sinful sexual knowledge of one another." As the third act of the play begins, Karen and Martha appear ruined, angry, and despondent. Martha, however, in a moment of self-recognition, or Aristotelian **anagnorisis**, reveals that the entire ordeal has clarified at least one thing: namely, that she really *does* love Karen in "the way they said." Karen, engaged to Joseph Cardin and "horrified" by this admission, pleads with Martha to put such thoughts out of her mind. Moments later, Martha is dead by her own hand.

Several plays in *American Drama: Colonial to Contemporary* end with the suicide of a central character. *The Children's Hour*, however, is not one of them, a structural fact that prompted sharp criticism of Hellman as a dramatist. A chastened Mrs Tilford, aware of the great wrong she has perpetrated against the two women, appears to plead for forgiveness after Martha's body is discovered. She is too late— and, for some critics, her desire to find expiation of her guilt is too distracting and anticlimactic.

Bernard Dick, taking Hellman's part against such complaints, argues for the play's resemblance to an Aristotelian tragedy: its **unity of action**, movement from ignorance to knowledge, tragic climax, and so on. Hellman herself responded to criticism by explaining that she could not resist a kind of moral "summing-up" in the conclusion. Some commentators found the play more melodramatic than tragic, with the powerful forces of evil represented by Mary and her affluent family triumphing over Karen and Martha. When Hellman directed the play herself in late 1952 within the Cold War context of the HUAC hearings and the destruction of people's lives and careers, *The Children's Hour* took on an entirely different political resonance. It stands today as the first dramatic success of a playwright whose politics led to an injustice analogous to that suffered by her characters—and as a play that can be successfully revived so long as a dominant and powerful class can find ways to subjugate those who attempt to survive at society's margins. This issue of social injustice Hellman *did* take seriously.

WORKS CONSULTED

Dick, Bernard F. *Hellman in Hollywood*. Rutherford, NJ: Fairleigh Dickinson University Press, 1982.

Falk, Doris. *Lillian Hellman*. New York: Frederick Ungar, 1978.

Hellman, Lillian. *Pentimento: A Book of Portraits*. Boston: Little, Brown, 1973.

———. *An Unfinished Woman—A Memoir*. Boston: Little, Brown, 1969.

Krutch, Joseph Wood. *The American Drama Since 1918: An Informal History*. New York: George Braziller, 1957.

Miller, Arthur. *Timebends: A Life*. New York: Grove Press, 1987.

CHARACTERS

PEGGY ROGERS	MARY TILFORD
MRS LILY MORTAR	KAREN WRIGHT
EVELYN MUNN	MARTHA DOBIE
HELEN BURTON	DOCTOR JOSEPH CARDIN
LOIS FISHER	AGATHA
CATHERINE	MRS AMELIA TILFORD
ROSALIE WELLS	A GROCERY BOY

ACT ONE

Living room of the Wright-Dobie School
Late afternoon in April.

ACT TWO

Scene 1. Living room at Mrs Tilford's.
        A few hours later.
Scene 2. The same. Later that evening.

ACT THREE

The same as Act One. November.

ACT ONE

SCENE: *A room in the Wright-Dobie School for girls, a converted farmhouse about ten miles from the town of Lancet, Massachusetts. It is a comfortable, unpretentious room used as an afternoon study-room and at all other times as the living room.*

A large door left center faces the audience. There is a single door right. Against both back walls are bookcases. A large desk is at right; a table, two sofas, and eight or ten chairs.

It is early in an afternoon in April.

AT RISE: MRS LILY MORTAR *is sitting in a large chair right center, with her head back and her eyes closed. She is a plump, florid woman of forty-five with dyed reddish hair. Her dress is too fancy for a classroom.*

Seven girls, from twelve to fourteen years old, are informally grouped on chairs and sofa. Six of them are sewing with no great amount of industry on pieces of white material. One of the others, EVELYN MUNN, *is using her scissors to trim the hair of* ROSALIE, *who sits, nervously, in front of her: she has* ROSALIE'S *head bent back at an awkward angle and is enjoying herself.*

The eighth girl, PEGGY ROGERS, *is sitting in a higher chair than the others. She is reading aloud from a book. She is bored and she reads in a singsong, tired voice.*

PEGGY: "It is twice blest; it blesseth him that gives and him that takes: 'tis mightiest in the mightiest; it becomes the throned monarch better than his crown; his sceptre shows the force of temporal power, the attribute to awe and majesty, wherein . . ." *(*MRS MORTAR *suddenly opens her eyes and stares at the hair-cutting. The children make efforts to warn* EVELYN. PEGGY *raises her voice until she is shouting)* "doth sit the dread and fear of kings; but mercy is above . . ."

MRS MORTAR: Evelyn! What are you doing?

EVELYN: *(she lisps)* Uh—nothing, Mrs Mortar.

MRS MORTAR: You are certainly doing something. You are ruining the scissors for one thing.

PEGGY: *(loudly)* "But mercy is above. It . . ."

MRS MORTAR: Just a moment, Peggy. It is very unfortunate that you girls cannot sit quietly with your sewing and drink in the immortal words of the immortal bard. *(She sighs)* Evelyn, go back to your sewing.

EVELYN: I can't get the hem thtraight. Honeth, I've been trying for three weekth, but I jutht can't do it.

MRS MORTAR: Helen, please help Evelyn with the hem.

HELEN: *(rises, holding up the garment* EVELYN *has been working on. It is soiled and shapeless and* so much has been cut off that it is now hardly large enough for a child of five. Giggling*)* She can't ever wear *that*, Mrs Mortar.

MRS MORTAR: *(vaguely)* Well, try to do something with it. Make some handkerchiefs or something. Be clever about it. Women must learn these tricks. *(To* PEGGY*)* Continue. "Mightiest in the mightiest."

PEGGY: "'Tis mightiest in the mightiest; it becomes the throned monarch better than his crown; his sceptre—his sceptre shows the force of temporal power, the attribute to awe and majesty, wherein —"

LOIS: *(from the back of the room chants softly and monotonously through the previous speech)* Ferebam, ferebas, ferebat, ferebamus, ferebatis, fere—fere—

CATHERINE: *(two seats away, the book propped in front of her)* Ferebant.

LOIS: Ferebamus, ferebatis, fere*bant*.

MRS MORTAR: Who's doing that?

PEGGY: *(the noise ceases. She hurries on)* "Wherein doth sit the dread and fear of kings; but mercy is above this sceptred sway, it is enthroned in the hearts of kings, it is an attribute to God himself—"

MRS MORTAR: *(sadly)* Peggy, can't you imagine yourself as Portia? Can't you read the lines with some feeling, some pity? *(Dreamily)* Pity. Ah! As Sir Henry said to me many's the time, pity makes the actress. Now, why can't *you* feel pity?

PEGGY: I guess I feel pity.

LOIS: Ferebamus, ferebatis, fere—fere—fere—

CATHERINE: Fere*bant*, stupid.

MRS MORTAR: How many people in this room are talking? Peggy, read the line again. I'll give you the cue.

PEGGY: What's a cue?

MRS MORTAR: A cue is a line or word given the actor or actress to remind them of their next speech.

HELEN: *(softly)* To remind *him* or *her*.

ROSALIE: *(a fattish girl with glasses)* Weren't you ever in the movies, Mrs Mortar?

MRS MORTAR: I had many offers, my dear. But the cinema is a shallow art. It has no—no—*(Vaguely)* no fourth dimension. Now, Peggy, if you would only try to submerge yourself in this problem. You are pleading for the life of a man. *(She rises and there are faint sighs from the girls, who stare at her with blank, bored faces. She recites with gestures)* "But mercy is above this sceptred sway; it is enthroned in the hearts of kings, it is an attribute to God himself; and earthly power doth then show likest God's when mercy seasons justice."

LOIS: *(almost singing it)* Utor, fruor, fungor, potior, and vescor take the dative.

CATHERINE: Take the *ablative.*

LOIS: Oh, dear. Utor, fruor, fung—

MRS MORTAR: *(to* LOIS, *with sarcasm)* You have something to tell the class?

LOIS: *(apologetically)* We've got a Latin exam this afternoon.

MRS MORTAR: And you intend to occupy the sewing and elocution hour learning what should have been learnt yesterday?

CATHERINE: *(wearily)* It takes her more than yesterday to learn it.

MRS MORTAR: Well, I cannot allow you to interrupt us like this.

CATHERINE: But we're finished sewing.

LOIS: *(admiringly)* I bet you were good at Latin, Mrs Mortar.

MRS MORTAR: Long ago, my dear, long ago. Now, take your book over by the window and don't disturb our enjoyment of Shakespeare. *(*CATHERINE *and* LOIS *rise, go to window, stand mumbling and gesturing)* Let us go back again. "It is an attribute to—" *(At this point the door opens far enough to let* MARY TILFORD, *clutching a slightly faded bunch of wild flowers, squeeze cautiously in. She is fourteen, neither pretty nor ugly. She is an undistinguished-looking girl)* "And earthly power doth then show likest God's when mercy seasons justice. We do pray for mercy, and that same prayer doth teach—"

PEGGY: *(happily)* You've skipped three lines.

MRS MORTAR: In my entire career I've never missed a line.

PEGGY: But you did skip three lines. *(Goes to* MRS MORTAR *with book)* See?

MRS MORTAR: *(seeing* MARY *sidling along wall toward other end of the room, turns to her to avoid* PEGGY *and the book)* Mary!

MARY: Yes, Mrs Mortar?

MRS MORTAR: This is a pretty time to be coming to your sewing class, I must say. Even if you have no interest in your work you might at least remember that you owe me a little courtesy. Courtesy is breeding. Breeding is an excellent thing. *(Turns to class)* Always remember that.

ROSALIE: Please, Mrs Mortar, can I write that down?

MRS MORTAR: Certainly. Suppose you all write it down.

PEGGY: But we wrote it down last week.
  *(*MARY *giggles)*

MRS MORTAR: Mary, I am still awaiting your explanation. Where have you been?

MARY: I took a walk.

MRS MORTAR: So you took a walk. And may I ask, young lady, are we in the habit of taking walks when we should be at our classes?

MARY: I am sorry, Mrs Mortar, I went to get you these flowers. I thought you would like them and I didn't know it would take so long to pick them.

MRS MORTAR: *(flattered)* Well, well.

MARY: You were telling us last week how much you liked flowers, and I thought that I would bring you some and—

MRS MORTAR: That was very sweet of you, Mary; I always like thoughtfulness. But you must not allow anything to interfere with your classes. Now run along, dear, and get a vase and some water to put my flowers in. *(*MARY *turns, sticks out her tongue at* HELEN, *says* "A-a-a," *and exits left)* You may put that book away, Peggy. I am sure your family need never worry about your going on the stage.

PEGGY: I don't want to go on the stage. I want to be a lighthouse keeper's wife.

MRS MORTAR: Well, I certainly hope you won't read to him.

(The laughter of the class pleases her. PEGGY *sits down among the other girls, who are making a great show of doing nothing.* MRS MORTAR *returns to her chair, puts her head back, closes her eyes)*

CATHERINE: How much longer, O Cataline, are you going to abuse our patience? *(To* LOIS*)* Now translate it, and for goodness' sakes try to get it right this time.

MRS MORTAR: *(for no reason)* "One master passion in the breast, like Aaron's serpent, swallows all the rest."

(She and LOIS *are murmuring during* KAREN WRIGHT'S *entrance.* KAREN *is an attractive woman of twenty-eight, casually pleasant in manner, without sacrifice of warmth or dignity. She smiles at the girls, goes to the desk. With her entrance there is an immediate change in the manner of the girls: they are fond of her and they respect her. She gives* MORTAR, *whose quotation has reached her, an annoyed look.)*

LOIS: "Quo usque tandem a*but*ere . . ."

KAREN: *(automatically)* "A*butere.*" *(Opens drawer in desk)* What's happened to your hair, Rosalie?

ROSALIE: It got cut, Miss Wright.

KAREN: *(smiling)* I can see that. A new style? Looks as though it has holes in it.

EVELYN: *(giggling)* I didn't mean to do it that bad, Mith Wright, but Rothalie'th got funny hair. I thaw a picture in the paper, and I wath trying to do it that way.

ROSALIE: *(feels her hair, looks pathetically at* KAREN*)* Oh, what shall I do, Miss Wright? *(Gesturing)* It's long here, and it's long here, and it's short here and—

KAREN: Come up to my room later and I'll see if I can fix it for you.

MRS MORTAR: And hereafter we'll have no more haircutting.

KAREN: Helen, have you found your bracelet?

HELEN: No, I haven't, and I've looked everywhere.

KAREN: Have another look. It must be in your room somewhere.

*(*MARY *comes in right, with her flowers in a vase.* KAREN *looks at the flowers in surprise)*

MARY: Good afternoon, Miss Wright. *(Sits down, looks at* KAREN, *who is staring hard at the flowers)*

KAREN: Hello, Mary.

MRS MORTAR: *(fluttering around)* Peggy has been reading Portia for us.
*(*PEGGY *sighs.)*

KAREN: Peggy doesn't like Portia?

MRS MORTAR: I don't think she quite appreciates it, but—

KAREN: *(patting* PEGGY *on the head)* I don't think I do either. Where'd you get those flowers, Mary?

MRS MORTAR: She picked them for me. *(Hurriedly)* It made her a little late to class, but she heard me say I loved flowers, and she went to get them for me. *(With a sigh)* The first wild flowers of the season.

KAREN: But not the very first, are they, Mary?

MARY: I don't know.

KAREN: Where did you get them?

MARY: Near Conway's cornfield, I think.

KAREN: It wasn't necessary to go so far. There was a bunch exactly like this in the garbage can this morning.

MRS MORTAR: *(after a second)* Oh, I can't believe it! What a nasty thing to do! *(To* MARY*)* And I suppose you have just as fine an excuse for being an hour late to breakfast this morning, and last week—*(To* KAREN*)* I haven't wanted to tell you these things before, but—

KAREN: *(hurriedly, as a bell rings off stage)* There's the bell.

LOIS: *(walking toward door)* Ad, ab, ante, in, de, inter, con, post, præ—*(Looks up at* KAREN*)* I *can't* seem to remember the rest.

KAREN: Præ, pro, sub, super. Don't worry, Lois. You'll come out all right. *(*LOIS *smiles, exits.* MARY *attempts to make a quick exit)* Wait a minute, Mary. *(Reluctantly* MARY *turns back as the girls file out.* KAREN *moves the small chairs, clearing the room as she talks)* Mary, I've had the feeling—and I don't think I'm wrong—that the girls here are happy; that they like Miss

Dobie and me, that they like the school. Do you think that's true?

MARY: Miss Wright, I have to get my Latin book.

KAREN: I thought it was true until you came here a year ago. I don't think you're very happy here, and I'd like to find out why. *(Looks at* MARY, *waits for an answer, gets none, shakes her head)* Why, for example, do you find it necessary to lie to us so often?

MARY: *(without looking up)* I'm not lying. I went out walking and I saw the flowers and they looked pretty and I didn't know it was so late.

KAREN: *(impatiently)* Stop it, Mary! I'm not interested in hearing that foolish story again. I *know* you got the flowers out of the garbage can. What I do want to know is why you feel you have to lie out of it.

MARY: I *did* pick the flowers near Conway's. You never believe me. You believe everybody but me. It's always like that. Everything I say you fuss at me about. Everything I do is wrong.

KAREN: You know that isn't true. *(Goes to* MARY, *puts her arm around her, waits until the sobbing has stopped)* Look, Mary, look at me. *(Raises* MARY'S *face with her hand)* Let's try to understand each other. If you feel that you *have* to take a walk, or that you just *can't* come to class, or that you'd like to go into the village by yourself, come and tell me—I'll try to understand. I don't say that I'll always agree that you should do exactly what you want to do, but I've had feelings like that, too—everybody has—and I won't be unreasonable about yours. But this way, this kind of lying you do, makes everything wrong.

MARY: *(looking steadily at* KAREN*)* I got the flowers near Conway's cornfield.

KAREN: *(looks at* MARY, *sighs, moves back toward desk and stands there for a moment)* Well, there doesn't seem to be any other way with you; you'll have to be punished. Take your recreation periods alone for the next two weeks. No horseback riding and no hockey. Don't leave the school grounds for any reason whatsoever. Is that clear?

MARY: *(carefully)* Saturday, too?

KAREN: Yes.

MARY: But you said I could go to the boat races.

KAREN: I'm sorry, but you can't go.

MARY: I'll tell my grandmother. I'll tell her how everybody treats me here and the way I get punished for every little thing I do. I'll tell her, I'll—

MRS MORTAR: Why, I'd slap her hands!

KAREN: *(turning back from door, ignoring* MRS MORTAR'S *speech. To* MARY*)* Go upstairs, Mary.

MARY: I don't feel well.

KAREN: *(wearily)* Go upstairs now.

MARY: I've got a pain. I've had it all morning. It hurts right here. *(Pointing vaguely in the direction of her heart)* Really it does.

KAREN: Ask Miss Dobie to give you some hot water and bicarbonate of soda.

MARY: It's a bad pain. I've never had it before. My heart! It's my heart! It's stopping or something. I can't breathe. *(She takes a long breath and falls awkwardly to the floor.)*

KAREN: *(sighs, shakes her head, kneels beside* MARY. *To* MRS MORTAR*)* Ask Martha to phone Joe.

MRS MORTAR: *(going out)* Do you think—? Heart trouble is very serious in a child.

*(*KAREN *picks* MARY *up from the floor and carries her off right. After a moment* MARTHA DOBIE *enters center. She is about the same age as* KAREN. *She is a nervous, high-strung woman.)*

KAREN: *(enters right)* Did you get Joe?

MARTHA: *(nodding)* What happened to her? She was perfectly well a few hours ago.

KAREN: She probably still is. I told her she couldn't go to the boat races and she had a heart attack. *(Sits down at desk and begins to mark papers)* She's a problem, that kid. Her latest trick was kidding your aunt out of a sewing lesson with those faded flowers we threw out. Then she threatened to go to her grandmother with some tale about being mistreated.

MARTHA: And, please God, Grandma would believe her and take her away.

KAREN: Which would give the school a swell black eye. But we ought to do something.

MARTHA: How about having a talk with Mrs
   Tilford?

KAREN: *(smiling)* You want to do it? (MARTHA
   shakes her head) I hate to do it. She's been so
   nice to us. Anyway, it wouldn't do any good.
   She's too crazy about Mary to see her faults
   very clearly—and the kid knows it.

MARTHA: How about asking Joe to say something
   to her? She'd listen to him.

KAREN: That would be admitting that we can't do
   the job ourselves.

MARTHA: Well, we can't, and we might as well admit it. We've tried everything we can think of.
   She's had more attention than any other three
   kids put together. And we still haven't the
   faintest idea what goes on inside her head.

KAREN: She's a strange girl.

MARTHA: That's putting it mildly.

KAREN: *(laughs)* We always talk about her as if
   she were a grown woman.

MARTHA: It's not so funny. There's something the
   matter with the kid. That's been true ever since
   the first day she came. She causes trouble
   here; she's bad for the other girls. I don't know
   what it is—it's a feeling I've got that it's wrong
   somewhere—

KAREN: All right, all right, we'll talk it over with
   Joe. Now what about our other pet nuisance?

MARTHA: *(laughs)* My aunt the actress? What's
   she been up to now?

KAREN: Nothing unusual. Last night at dinner she
   was telling the girls about the time she lost
   her trunks in Butte, Montana, and how she
   gave her best performance of Rosalind during
   a hurricane. Today in the kitchen you could
   hear her on what Sir Henry said to her.

MARTHA: Wait until she does Hedda Gabler standing on one foot. Sir Henry taught her to do it that
   way. He said it was a test of great acting.

KAREN: You must have had a gay childhood.

MARTHA: *(bitterly)* Oh, I did. I did, indeed. God,
   how I used to hate all that—

KAREN: Couldn't we get rid of her soon, Martha? I
   hate to make it hard on you, but she really
   ought not to be here.

MARTHA: *(after a moment)* I know.

KAREN: We can scrape up enough money to send
   her away. Let's do it.

MARTHA: *(goes to her, affectionately pats her
   head)* You've been very patient about it. I'm
   sorry and I'll talk to her today. It'll probably be
   a week or two before she can be ready to leave.
   Is that all right?

KAREN: Of course. *(Looks at her watch)* Did you
   get Joe himself on the phone?

MARTHA: He was already on his way. Isn't he always on his way over here?

KAREN: *(laughs)* Well, I'm going to marry him,
   you know.

MARTHA: *(looking at her)* You haven't talked of
   marriage for a long time.

KAREN: I've talked of it with Joe.

MARTHA: Then you *are* thinking about it—soon?

KAREN: Perhaps when the term is over. By that
   time we ought to be out of debt, and the school
   should be paying for itself.

MARTHA: *(nervously playing with a book on the
   table)* Then we won't be taking our vacation together?

KAREN: Of course we will. The three of us.

MARTHA: I had been looking forward to someplace by the lake—just you and me—the way
   we used to at college.

KAREN: *(cheerfully)* Well, now there will be three
   of us. That'll be fun, too.

MARTHA: *(after a pause)* Why haven't you told me
   this before?

KAREN: I'm not telling you anything we haven't
   talked about often.

MARTHA: But you're talking about it as *soon* now.

KAREN: I'm glad to be able to. I've been in love
   with Joe a long time. (MARTHA *crosses to window and stands looking out, her back to* KAREN.
   KAREN *finishes marking papers and rises)* It's a
   big day for the school. Rosalie's finally put an
   "l" in could.

MARTHA: *(not turning from window)* You really
   are going to leave, aren't you?

KAREN: I'm not going to leave, and you know it.
   Why do you say things like that? We agreed a

long time ago that my marriage wasn't going to make any difference to the school.

MARTHA: But it will. You know it will. It can't help it.

KAREN: That's nonsense. Joe doesn't want me to give up here.

MARTHA: (turning from window) It's been so damned hard building this thing up, slaving and going without things to make ends meet— think of having a winter coat without holes in the lining again!—and now when we're getting on our feet, you're all ready to let it go to hell.

KAREN: This is a silly argument, Martha. Let's quit it. You haven't listened to a word I've said. I'm not getting married tomorrow, and when I do, it's not going to interfere with my work here. You're making something out of nothing.

MARTHA: It's going to be hard going on alone afterward.

KAREN: For God's sake, do you expect me to give up my marriage?

MARTHA: I don't mean that, but it's so— (Door, center, opens and DOCTOR JOSEPH CARDIN comes in. He is a large, pleasant-looking, carelessly dressed man of about thirty-five.)

CARDIN: Hello, darling. Hi, Martha. What's the best news?

MARTHA: Hello, Joe.

KAREN: We tried to get you on the phone. Come in and look at your little cousin.

CARDIN: What's the matter with her now?

KAREN: You'd better come and see her. She says she has a pain in her heart. (Goes out, right.)

CARDIN: (stopping to light a cigarette) Our little Mary pops up in every day's dispatches.

MARTHA: (impatiently) Go and see her. Heart attacks are nothing to play with.

CARDIN: (looks at her) Never played with one in my life. (Exits right.)
(MARTHA walks around room and finally goes to stare out window. MRS MORTAR enters right.)

MRS MORTAR: I was asked to leave the room. (MARTHA pays no attention) It seems that I'm not wanted in the room during the examination.

MARTHA: (over her shoulder) What difference does it make?

MRS MORTAR: What difference does it make? Why, it was a deliberate snub.

MARTHA: There's very little pleasure in watching a man use a stethoscope.

MRS MORTAR: Isn't it natural that the child should have me with her? Isn't it natural that an older woman should be present? (No answer) Very well, if you are so thick-skinned that you don't resent these things—

MARTHA: What are you talking about? Why, in the name of heaven, should you be with her?

MRS MORTAR: It—it's customary for an older woman to be present during an examination.

MARTHA: (laughs) Tell that to Joe. Maybe he'll give you a job as duenna for his office.

MRS MORTAR: It was I who saved Delia Lampert's life the time she had that heart attack in Buffalo. We almost lost her that time. Poor Delia! We went over to London together. She married Robert Laffonne. Not seven months later he left her and ran away with Eve Cloun, who was playing the Infant Phenomenon in Birmingham—

MARTHA: Console yourself. If you've seen one heart attack, you've seen them all.

MRS MORTAR: So you don't resent your aunt being snubbed and humiliated?

MARTHA: Oh, Aunt Lily!

MRS MORTAR: Karen is consistently rude to me, and you know it.

MARTHA: I know that she is very polite to you, and—what's more important—very patient.

MRS MORTAR: Patient with me? I, who have worked my fingers to the bone!

MARTHA: Don't tell yourself that too often, Aunt Lily; you'll come to believe it.

MRS MORTAR: I know it's true. Where could you have gotten a woman of my reputation to give these children voice lessons, elocution lessons? Patient with me! Here I've donated my services—

MARTHA: You are being paid.

MRS MORTAR: That small thing! I used to earn twice that for one performance.

MARTHA: The gilded days. It was very extravagant of them to pay you so much. *(Suddenly tired of the whole thing)* You're not very happy here, are you, Aunt Lily?

MRS MORTAR: Satisfied enough, I guess, for a poor relation.

MARTHA: *(makes a motion of distaste)* But you don't like the school or the farm or—

MRS MORTAR: I told you at the beginning you shouldn't have bought a place like this. Burying yourself on a farm! You'll regret it.

MARTHA: We like it here. *(After a moment)* Aunt Lily, you've talked about London for a long time. Would you like to go over?

MRS MORTAR: *(with a sigh)* It's been twenty years, and I shall never live to see it again.

MARTHA: Well, you can go any time you like. We can spare the money now, and it will do you a lot of good. You pick out the boat you want and I'll get the passage. *(She has been talking rapidly, anxious to end the whole thing)* Now that's all fixed. You'll have a grand time seeing all your old friends, and if you live sensibly I ought to be able to let you have enough to get along on. *(She begins to gather books, notebooks, and pencils.)*

MRS MORTAR: *(slowly)* So you want me to leave?

MARTHA: That's not the way to put it. You've wanted to go ever since I can remember.

MRS MORTAR: You're trying to get rid of me.

MARTHA: That's it. We don't want you around when we dig up the buried treasure.

MRS MORTAR: So? You're turning me out? At my age! Nice, grateful girl you are.

MARTHA: Oh, my God, how can anybody deal with you? You're going where you want to go, and we'll be better off alone. That suits everybody. You complain about the farm, you complain about the school, you complain about Karen, and now you have what you want and you're still looking for something to complain about.

MRS MORTAR: *(with dignity)* Please do not raise your voice.

MARTHA: You ought to be glad I don't do worse.

MRS MORTAR: I absolutely refuse to be shipped off three thousand miles away. I'm not going to England. I shall go back to the stage. I'll write to my agents tomorrow, and as soon as they have something good for me—

MARTHA: The truth is I'd like you to leave soon. The three of us can't live together, and it doesn't make any difference whose fault it is.

MRS MORTAR: You wish me to go tonight?

MARTHA: Don't act, Aunt Lily. Go as soon as you've found a place you like. I'll put the money in the bank for you tomorrow.

MRS MORTAR: You think I'd take your money? I'd rather scrub floors first.

MARTHA: You'll change your mind.

MRS MORTAR: I should have known by this time that the wise thing is to stay out of your way when *he's* in the house.

MARTHA: What are you talking about now?

MRS MORTAR: Never mind. I should have known better. You always take your spite out on me.

MARTHA: Spite? *(Impatiently)* Oh, don't let's have any more of this today. I'm tired. I've been working since six o'clock this morning.

MRS MORTAR: Any day that he's in the house is a bad day.

MARTHA: When *who* is in the house?

MRS MORTAR: Don't think you're fooling me, young lady. I wasn't born yesterday.

MARTHA: Aunt Lily, the amount of disconnected unpleasantness that goes on in your head could keep a psychologist busy for years. Now go take your nap.

MRS MORTAR: I know what I know. Every time that man comes into this house, you have a fit. It seems like you just can't stand the idea of them being together. God knows what you'll do when they get married. You're jealous of him, that's what it is.

MARTHA: *(her voice is tense and the previous attitude of good-natured irritation is gone)* I'm very fond of Joe, and you know it.

MRS MORTAR: You're fonder of Karen, and I know that. And it's unnatural, just as unnatural as it can be. You don't like their being together. You were always like that even as a child. If you had a little girl friend, you always got mad when she liked anybody else. Well, you'd better get a beau of your own now—a woman of your age.

MARTHA: The sooner you get out of here the better. You are making me sick and I won't stand for it any longer. I want you to leave—
(At this point there is a sound outside the large doors center. MARTHA breaks off. After a moment she crosses to the door and opens it. EVELYN and PEGGY are to be seen on the staircase. For a second she stands still as they stop and look at her. Then, afraid that her anger with her aunt will color anything she might say to the children, she crosses the room again and stands with her back to them.)

MARTHA: What were you doing outside the door?

EVELYN: *(hurriedly)* We were going upththairth, Mith Dobie.

PEGGY: We came down to see how Mary was.

MARTHA: And you stopped long enough to see how we were. Did you deliberately listen?

PEGGY: We didn't mean to. We heard voices and we couldn't help—

MRS MORTAR: *(a social tone)* Eavesdropping is something nice young ladies just don't do.

MARTHA: *(turning to face the children)* Go upstairs now. We'll talk about this later. *(Slowly shuts door as they begin to climb the stairs.)*

MRS MORTAR: You mean to say you're not going to do anything about that? *(No answer. She laughs nastily)* That's the trouble with these new-fangled notions of discipline and—

MARTHA: *(thoughtfully)* You know, it's really bad having you around children.

MRS MORTAR: What exactly does that mean?

MARTHA: It means that I don't like them hearing the things you say. Oh, I'll "do something about it," but the truth is that this is their home, and things shouldn't be said in it that they can't hear. When you're at your best, you're not for tender ears.

MRS MORTAR: So now it's my fault, is it? Just as I said, whenever he's in the house you think you can take it out on me. You've got to have some way to let out steam and—
(Door opens, right, and CARDIN comes in.)

MARTHA: How is Mary?
(MRS MORTAR, head in air, gives MARTHA a malicious half-smile and exits center.)

MRS MORTAR: Good day, Joseph.

CARDIN: What's the matter with the Duchess?

MARTHA: Just keeping her hand in, in case Sir Henry's watching her from above. What about Mary?

CARDIN: Nothing. Absolutely nothing.

MARTHA: *(sighs)* I thought so.

CARDIN: I could have managed a better faint than that when I was six years old.

MARTHA: Nothing the matter with her at all?

CARDIN: *(laughs)* No, ma'am, not a thing. Just a little something she thought up.

MARTHA: But it's such a silly thing to do. She knew we'd have you in. *(Sighs)* Maybe she's not so bright. Any idiots in your family, Joe? Any inbreeding?

CARDIN: Don't blame her on me. It's another side of the family. *(Laughs)* You can look at Aunt Amelia and tell: old New England stock, never married out of Boston, still thinks honor is honor and dinner's at eight. Yes, ma'am, we're a proud old breed.

MARTHA: The Jukes were an old family, too. Look, Joe, have you any idea what is the matter with Mary? I mean, has she always been like this?

CARDIN: She's always been a honey. Aunt Amelia's spoiling hasn't helped any, either.

MARTHA: We're reaching the end of our rope with her. This kind of thing—

CARDIN: *(looking at her)* Aren't you taking it too seriously?

MARTHA: *(after a second)* I guess I am. But you stay around kids long enough and you won't know what to take seriously, either. But I do think somebody ought to talk to Mrs Tilford about her.

CARDIN: You wouldn't be meaning me now, would you, Miss Dobie?

MARTHA: Well, Karen and I were talking about it this afternoon and—

CARDIN: Listen, friend, I'm marrying Karen, but I'm not writing Mary Tilford in the contract. *(MARTHA moves slightly. CARDIN takes her by the shoulders and turns her around to face him again. His face is grave, his voice gentle)* Forget Mary for a minute. You and I have got something to fight about. Every time anything's said about marrying—about Karen marrying me—you— I'm fond of you. I always thought you liked me. What is it? I know how fond you are of Karen, but our marriage oughtn't to make a great deal of difference—

MARTHA: *(pushing his hands from her shoulders)* God damn you. I wish—*(She puts her face in her hands.* CARDIN *watches her in silence, mechanically lighting a cigarette. When she takes her hands from her face, she holds them out to him. Contritely)* Joe, please, I'm sorry. I'm a fool, a nasty, bitter—

CARDIN: *(takes her hands in one of his, patting them with his other hand)* Aw, shut up. *(He puts an arm around her, and she leans her head against his lapel. They are standing like that when* KAREN *comes in, right.)*

MARTHA: *(to* KAREN, *as she wipes her eyes)* Your friend's got a nice shoulder to weep on.

KAREN: He's an admirable man in every way. Well, the angel child is now putting her clothes back on.

MARTHA: The angel child's influence is abroad even while she's unconscious. Her roommates were busy listening at the door while Aunt Lily and I were yelling at each other.

KAREN: We'll have to move those girls away from one another.

(A bell rings from the rear of the house.)

MARTHA: That's my class. I'll send Peggy and Evelyn down. You talk to them.

KAREN: All right. *(As* MARTHA *exits center,* KAREN *goes toward door, right. As she passes* CARDIN *she kisses him)* Mary!

*(*MARY *opens door, comes in, stands buttoning the neck of her dress.)*

CARDIN: *(to* MARY) How's it feel to be back from the grave?

MARY: My heart hurts.

CARDIN: *(laughing. To* KAREN) Science has failed. Try a hairbrush.

MARY: It's *my* heart, and it hurts.

KAREN: Sit down.

MARY: I want to see my grandmother. I want to—
*(*EVELYN *and* PEGGY *timidly enter center.)*

KAREN: Sit down, girls, I want to talk to you.

PEGGY: We're awfully sorry, really. We just didn't think and—

KAREN: I'm sorry too, Peggy. *(Thoughtfully)* You and Evelyn never used to do things like this. We'll have to separate you three.

EVELYN: Ah, Mith Wright, we've been together almotht a year.

KAREN: Peggy, you will move into Lois's room, and Lois will move in with Evelyn. Mary will go in with Rosalie.

MARY: Rosalie hates me.

KAREN: I can't imagine Rosalie hating anyone.

MARY: *(starting to cry)* And it's all because I had a pain. If anybody else was sick they'd be put to bed and petted. You're always mean to me. I get blamed and punished for everything. *(To* CARDIN) I do, Cousin Joe. All the time for everything.
*(*MARY *by now is crying violently and as* KAREN *half moves toward her,* CARDIN, *who has been frowning, picks* MARY *up and puts her down on the couch.)*

CARDIN: You've been unpleasant enough to Miss Wright. Lie here until you've stopped working yourself into a fit. *(Picks up his hat and bag, smiles at* KAREN) I've got to go now. She's not going to hurt herself crying. The next time she faints, I'd wait until she got tired lying on the floor. *(Passing* MARY, *he pats her head. She jerks away from him.)*

KAREN: Wait a minute. I'll walk to the car with you. *(To* GIRLS) Go up now and move your things. Tell Lois to get her stuff ready.
*(*SHE *and* CARDIN *exit center. A second after the door is closed,* MARY *springs up and throws a cushion at the door.)*

EVELYN: Don't do that. She'll hear you.

MARY: Who cares if she does? *(Kicks table)* And she can hear that, too.
(Small ornament falls off table and breaks on floor. EVELYN *and* PEGGY *gasp.)*

EVELYN: *(frightened)* Now what are you going to do?

PEGGY: *(stooping down in a vain effort to pick up the pieces)* You'll get the devil now. Dr Cardin gave it to Miss Wright. I guess it was kind of a lover's gift. People get awfully angry about a lover's gift.

MARY: Oh, leave it alone. She'll never know we did it.

PEGGY: *We* didn't do it. You did it yourself.

MARY: And what will you do if I say *we* did do it? *(Laughs)* Never mind, I'll think of something else. The wind could've knocked it over.

EVELYN: Yeh. She'th going to believe that one.

MARY: Oh, stop worrying about it. I'll get out of it.

EVELYN: Did you really have a pain?

MARY: I fainted, didn't I?

PEGGY: I wish I could faint sometimes. I've never even worn glasses, like Rosalie.

MARY: A lot it'll get you to faint.

EVELYN: What did Mith Wright do to you when the clath left?

MARY: Told me I couldn't go to the boat races.

EVELYN: Whew!

PEGGY: But we'll remember everything that happens and we'll give you all the souvenirs and things.

MARY: I won't let you go if I can't go. But I'll find some way to go. What were *you* doing?

PEGGY: We came down to see what was happening to you, but the doors were closed and we could hear Miss Dobie and Mortar having an awful row. Then Miss Dobie opens the door and there we were.

MARY: And a lot of crawling and crying you both did too, I bet.

EVELYN: We were thort of thorry about lithening. I gueth it wathn't—

MARY: Ah, you're always sorry about everything. What were they saying?

PEGGY: What was who saying?

MARY: Dobie and Mortar, silly.

PEGGY: *(evasively)* Just talking, I guess.

EVELYN: Fighting, you mean.

MARY: About what?

EVELYN: Well, they were talking about Mortar going away to England and—

PEGGY: You know, it really wasn't very nice to've listened, and I think it's worse to tell.

MARY: You do, do you? You just don't tell me and see what happens.
(PEGGY sighs.)

EVELYN: Mortar got awful thore at that and thaid they juth wanted to get rid of her, and then they thtarted talking about Dr Cardin.

MARY: What about him?

PEGGY: We'd better get started moving; Miss Wright will be back first thing we know.

MARY: *(fiercely)* Shut up! Go on, Evelyn.

EVELYN: They're going to be married.

MARY: Everybody knows that.

PEGGY: But everybody doesn't know that Miss Dobie doesn't want them to get married. How do you like that?
(The door opens and ROSALIE WELLS *sticks her head in.)*

ROSALIE: I have a class soon. If you're going to move your things—

MARY: Close that door, you idiot. *(ROSALIE closes door, stands near it)* What do you want?

ROSALIE: I'm trying to tell you. If you're going to move your things—not that I want you in with me—you'd better start right now. Miss Wright's coming in a minute.

MARY: Who cares if she is?

ROSALIE: *(starts for door)* I'm just telling you for your own good.

PEGGY: *(getting up)* We're coming.

MARY: No. Let Rosalie move our things.

ROSALIE: You crazy?

PEGGY: *(nervously)* It's all right. Evelyn and I'll get your things. Come on, Evelyn.

MARY: Trying to get out of telling me, huh? Well, you won't get out of it that way. Sit down and stop being such a sissy. Rosalie, you go on up and move my things and don't say a word about our being down here.

ROSALIE: And who was your French maid yesterday, Mary Tilford?

MARY: *(laughing)* You'll do for today. Now go on, Rosalie, and fix our things.

ROSALIE: You crazy?

MARY: And the next time we go into town, I'll let you wear my gold locket and buckle. You'll like that, won't you, Rosalie?

ROSALIE: *(draws back, moves her hands nervously)* I don't know what you're talking about.

MARY: Oh, I'm not talking about anything in particular. You just run along now and remind me the next time to get my buckle and locket for you.

ROSALIE: *(stares at her a moment)* All right, I'll do it this time, but just 'cause I got a good disposition. But don't think you're going to boss me around, Mary Tilford.

MARY: *(smiling)* No, indeed. (ROSALIE *starts for door*) And get the things done neatly, Rosalie. Don't muss my white linen bloomers—
(The door slams as MARY *laughs.)*

EVELYN: Now what do you think of that? What made her tho agreeable?

MARY: Oh, a little secret we got. Go on, now, what else did they say?

PEGGY: Well, Mortar said that Dobie was jealous of them, and that she was like that when she was a little girl, and that she'd better get herself a beau of her own because it was unnatural, and that she never wanted anybody to like Miss Wright, and that was unnatural. Boy! Did Miss Dobie get sore at that!

EVELYN: Then we didn't hear any more. Peggy dropped a book.

MARY: What'd she mean Dobie was jealous?

PEGGY: What's unnatural?

EVELYN: Un for not. Not natural.

PEGGY: It's funny, because everybody gets married.

MARY: A lot of people don't—they're too ugly.

PEGGY: *(jumps up, claps her hand to her mouth)* Oh, my God! Rosalie'll find that copy of *Mademoiselle de Maupin.* She'll blab like the dickens.

MARY: Ah, she won't say a word.

EVELYN: Who getth the book when we move?

MARY: You can have it. That's what I was doing this morning—finishing it. There's one part in it—

PEGGY: What part?
*(*MARY *laughs.)*

EVELYN: Well, what wath it?

MARY: Wait until you read it.

PEGGY: It's a shame about being moved. I've got to go in with Helen, and she blows her nose all night. Lois told me.

MARY: It was a dirty trick making us move. She just wants to see how much fun she can take away from me. She hates me.

PEGGY: No, she doesn't, Mary. She treats you just like the rest of us—almost better.

MARY: That's right, stick up for your crush. Take her side against mine.

PEGGY: I didn't mean it that way.

EVELYN: *(looks at her watch)* We'd better get upthtairth.

MARY: I'm not going.

PEGGY: Rosalie isn't so bad.

EVELYN: What you going to do about the vathe?

MARY: I don't care about Rosalie and I don't care about the vase. I'm not going to be here.

EVELYN *and* PEGGY: *(together)* Not going to be here! What do you mean?

MARY: *(calmly)* I'm going home.

PEGGY: Oh, Mary—

EVELYN: You can't do that.

MARY: Can't I? You just watch. *(Begins to walk around the room)* I'm not staying here. I'm going home and tell Grandma I'm not staying anymore. *(Smiles to herself)* I'll tell her I'm not happy. They're scared of Grandma—she helped 'em when they first started, you know—and when she tells 'em something, believe me, they'll sit up and listen. They can't get away with treating me like this, and they don't have to think they can.

PEGGY: *(appalled)* You just going to walk out like that?

EVELYN: What you going to tell your grandmother?

MARY: Oh, who cares? I'll think of something to tell her. I can always do it better on the spur of the moment.

PEGGY: She'll send you right back.

MARY: You let me worry about that. Grandma's very fond of me, on account my father was her favorite son. I can manage *her* all right.

PEGGY: I don't think you ought to go, really, Mary. It's just going to make an awful lot of trouble.

EVELYN: What'th going to happen about the vathe?

MARY: Say I did it—it doesn't make a bit of difference anymore to me. Now listen, you two got to help. They won't miss me before dinner if you make Rosalie shut the door and keep it shut. Now, I'll go through the field to French's, and then I can get the bus to Homestead.

EVELYN: How you going to get to the thtreetcar?

MARY: Taxi, idiot.

PEGGY: How are you going to get out of here in the first place?

MARY: I'm going to walk out. You know where the front door is? Well, I'm going right out that front door.

EVELYN: Gee, I wouldn't have the nerve.

MARY: Of course you wouldn't. You'd let 'em do anything to you they want. Well, they can't do it to me. Who's got any money?

EVELYN: Not me. Not a thent.

MARY: I've got to have at least a dollar for the taxi and a dime for the bus.

EVELYN: And where you going to find it?

PEGGY: See? Why don't you just wait until your allowance comes Monday, and then you can go anyplace you want. Maybe by that time—

MARY: I'm going today. *Now.*

EVELYN: You can't *walk* to Lanthet.

MARY: (goes to PEGGY) You've got money. You've got two dollars and twenty-five cents.

PEGGY: I—I—

MARY: Go get it for me.

PEGGY: No! No! I won't get it for you.

EVELYN: You can't have *that* money, Mary—

MARY: Get it for me.

PEGGY: (her voice is scared) I won't. I won't. Mamma doesn't send me much allowance—not half as much as the rest of you get—I saved this so long—you took it from me last time—

EVELYN: Ah, she wantth that bithycle tho bad.

PEGGY: I haven't gone to the movies, I haven't had any candy, I haven't had anything the rest of you get all the time. It took me so long to save that and I—

MARY: Go upstairs and get me the money.

PEGGY: (hysterically, backing away from her) I won't. I won't. I won't.
(MARY makes a sudden move for her, grabs her left arm, and jerks it back, hard and expertly. PEGGY screams softly. EVELYN tries to take MARY's arm away. Without releasing her hold on PEGGY, MARY slaps EVELYN's face. EVELYN begins to cry.)

MARY: Just say when you've had enough.

PEGGY: (softly, stiflingly) All—all right—I'll get it.
(MARY nods her head as the curtain falls.)

CURTAIN

ACT TWO

SCENE 1: *Living room at* MRS TILFORD'S. *It is a formal room, without being cold or elegant. The furniture is old, but excellent. The exit to the hall is left; glass doors, right, lead to a dining room that cannot be seen.*

AT RISE: *Stage is empty. Voices are heard in the hall.*

AGATHA: (offstage) What are *you* doing here? Well, come on in—don't stand there gaping at me. Have they given you a holiday or did you just decide you'd get a better dinner here? (AGATHA *enters left, followed by* MARY. AGATHA *is a sharp-faced maid, not young, with a querulous voice*) Can't you even say hello?

MARY: Hello, Agatha. You didn't give me a chance. Where's Grandma?

AGATHA: Why aren't you in school? Look at your face and clothes. Where have you been?

MARY: I got a little dirty coming home. I walked part of the way through the woods.

AGATHA: Why didn't you put on your middy blouse and your old brown coat?

MARY: Oh, stop asking me questions. Where's Grandma?

AGATHA: Where ought any clean person be at this time of day? She's taking a bath.

MARY: Is anybody coming for dinner?

AGATHA: She didn't say anything about you coming.

MARY: How could she, stupid? She didn't know.

AGATHA: Then what are you doing here?

MARY: Leave me alone. I don't feel well.

AGATHA: Why don't you feel well? Who ever heard of a person going for a walk in the woods when they didn't feel well?

MARY: Oh, leave me alone. I came home because I was sick.

AGATHA: You look all right.

MARY: But I don't feel all right. I can't even come home without everybody nagging at me.

AGATHA: Don't think you're fooling me, young lady. You might pull the wool over some people's eyes, but—I bet you've been up to something again. *(Stares suspiciously at* MARY*)* Well, you wait right here till I tell your grandmother. And if you feel so sick, you certainly won't want any dinner. A good dose of rhubarb and soda will fix you up. *(Exits left.)*

*(*MARY *makes a face in the direction* AGATHA *has gone and stops sniffling. She looks nervously around the room, then goes to a low mirror and tries several experiments with her face in an attempt to make it look sick and haggard.* MRS TILFORD, *followed by* AGATHA, *enters left.* MRS TILFORD *is a large, dignified woman in her sixties, with a pleasant, strong face.)*

AGATHA: *(to* MRS TILFORD, *as she follows her into the room)* Why didn't you put some cold water on your chest? Do you want to catch your death of cold at your age? Did you have to hurry so?

MRS TILFORD: Mary, what are you doing home?

*(*MARY *rushes to her and buries her head in* MRS TILFORD'S *dress, crying.* MRS TILFORD *pats her head, then puts an arm around her and leads her to a sofa.)*

MRS TILFORD: Never mind, dear; now stop crying and tell me what is the matter.

MARY: *(gradually stops crying, fondling* MRS TILFORD'S *hand)* It's so good to see you, Grandma. You didn't come to visit me all last week.

MRS TILFORD: I was coming tomorrow.

MARY: I missed you so. *(Smiling up at* MRS TILFORD*)* I was awful homesick.

MRS TILFORD: I'm glad that's all it was. I was frightened when Agatha said you were not well.

AGATHA: Did I say that? I said she needed a good dose of rhubarb and soda. Most likely she only came home for Wednesday night fudge cake.

MRS TILFORD: We all get homesick. But how did you get here? Did Miss Karen drive you over?

MARY: I—I walked most of the way, and then a lady gave me a ride and—*(Looks timidly at* MRS TILFORD.*)*

AGATHA: Did she have to walk through the woods in her very best coat?

MRS TILFORD: Mary! Do you mean you left without permission?

MARY: *(nervously)* I ran away, Grandma. They didn't know—

MRS TILFORD: That was a very bad thing to do, and they'll be worried. Agatha, phone Miss Wright and tell her Mary is here. John will drive her back before dinner.

MARY: *(as* AGATHA *starts toward telephone)* No, Grandma, don't do that. Please don't do that. Please let me stay.

MRS TILFORD: But, darling, you can't leave school anytime you please.

MARY: Oh, please, Grandma, don't send me back right away. You don't know how they'll punish me.

MRS TILFORD: I don't think they'll be that angry. Come, you're acting like a foolish little girl.

MARY: *(hysterically, as she sees* AGATHA *about to pick up the telephone)* Grandma! Please! I can't go back! I can't! They'll kill me! They will, Grandma! They'll kill me!

*(*MRS TILFORD *and* AGATHA *stare at* MARY *in amazement. She puts her head in* MRS TILFORD'S *lap and sobs.)*

MRS TILFORD: *(motioning with a hand for* AGATHA *to leave the room)* Never mind phoning now, Agatha.

AGATHA: If you're going to let her—

*(*MRS TILFORD *repeats the gesture.* AGATHA *exits, right.)*

MRS TILFORD: Stop crying, Mary.

MARY: It's so nice here, Grandma.

MRS TILFORD: I'm glad you like being home with me, but at your age you can hardly—What made you say such a terrible thing about Miss Wright and Miss Dobie? You know they wouldn't hurt you.

MARY: Oh, but they would. They—I— *(Breaks off, looks around as if hunting for a clue)* I fainted today!

MRS TILFORD: Fainted?

MARY: Yes, I did. My heart—I had a pain in my heart. I couldn't help having a pain in my heart, and when I fainted right in class, they called Cousin Joe and he said I didn't. He said it was maybe only that I ate my breakfast too fast and Miss Wright blamed me for it.

MRS TILFORD: *(relieved)* I'm sure if Joseph said it wasn't serious, it wasn't.

MARY: But I did have a pain in my heart—honest.

MRS TILFORD: Have you still got it?

MARY: I guess I haven't got it much anymore, but I feel a little weak, and I was so scared of Miss Wright being so mean to me just because I was sick.

MRS TILFORD: Scared of Karen? Nonsense. It's perfectly possible that you had a pain, but if you had really been sick your Cousin Joseph would certainly have known it. It's not nice to frighten people by pretending to be sick when you aren't.

MARY: I didn't *want* to be sick, but I'm always getting punished for everything.

MRS TILFORD: *(gently)* You mustn't imagine things like that, child, or you'll grow up to be a very unhappy woman. I'm not going to scold you anymore for coming home this time, though I suppose I should. Run along upstairs and wash your face and change your dress, and after dinner John will drive you back. Run along.

MARY: *(happily)* I can stay for dinner?

MRS TILFORD: Yes.

MARY: Maybe I could stay till the first of the week. Saturday's your birthday and I could be here with you.

MRS TILFORD: We don't celebrate my birthday, dear. You'll have to go back to school after dinner.

MARY: But—*(She hesitates, then goes up to* MRS TILFORD *and puts her arms around the older woman's neck. Softly)* How much do you love me?

MRS TILFORD: *(smiling)* As much as all the words in all the books in all the world.

MARY: Remember when I was little and you used to tell me that right before I went to sleep? And it was a rule nobody could say another single word after you finished? You used to say "Wor-rr-ld," and then I had to shut my eyes tight. I miss you an awful lot, Grandma.

MRS TILFORD: And I miss you, but I'm afraid my Latin is too rusty—you'll learn it better in school.

MARY: But couldn't I stay out the rest of this term? After the summer maybe I won't mind it so much. I'll study hard, honest, and—

MRS TILFORD: You're an earnest little coaxer, but it's out of the question. Back you go tonight. *(Gives* MARY *a playful slap)* Let's not have any more talk about it now, and let's have no more running away from school ever.

MARY: *(slowly)* Then I really have to go back there tonight?

MRS TILFORD: Of course.

MARY: You don't love me. You don't care whether they kill me or not.

MRS TILFORD: Mary.

MARY: You don't! You don't! You don't care what happens to me.

MRS TILFORD: *(sternly)* But I *do* care that you're talking this way.

MARY: I'm sorry I said that, Grandma. I didn't mean to hurt your feelings. *(Puts her arms around* MRS TILFORD'S *neck)* Forgive me?

MRS TILFORD: What made you talk like that?

MARY: *(in a whisper)* I'm scared, Grandma, I'm scared. They'll do dreadful things to me.

MRS TILFORD: Dreadful? Nonsense. They'll punish you for running away. You deserve to be punished.

MARY: It's not that. It's not anything I do. It never is. They—they just punish me anyhow, just like they got something against me. I'm afraid of them, Grandma.

MRS TILFORD: That's ridiculous. What have they ever done to you that is so terrible?

MARY: A lot of things—all the time. Miss Wright says I can't go to the boat races and—*(Realizing the inadequacy of this reply, she breaks off, hesitates, and finally stammers)* It's—it's after what happened today.

MRS TILFORD: You mean something else besides your naughtiness in pretending to faint and then running away?

MARY: I *did* faint. I didn't pretend. They just said that to make me feel bad. Anyway, it wasn't anything that I did.

MRS TILFORD: What was it, then?

MARY: I can't tell you.

MRS TILFORD: Why?

MARY: *(sulkily)* Because you're just going to take their part.

MRS TILFORD: *(a little annoyed)* Very well. Now run upstairs and get ready for dinner.

MARY: It was—it was all about Miss Dobie and Mrs Mortar. They were talking awful things and Peggy and Evelyn heard them and Miss Dobie found out, and then they made us move our rooms.

MRS TILFORD: What has that to do with you? I don't understand a word you're saying.

MARY: They made us move our rooms. They said we couldn't be together anymore. They're afraid to have us near them, that's what it is, and they're taking it out on me. They're scared of you.

MRS TILFORD: For a little girl you're imagining a lot of big things. Why should they be scared of me?

MARY: They're afraid you'll find out.

MRS TILFORD: Find out what?

MARY: *(vaguely)* Things.

MRS TILFORD: Run along, Mary.

MARY: *(slowly starting for door)* All right. But there're a lot of things. They have secrets or something, and they're afraid I'll find out and tell you.

MRS TILFORD: There's not necessarily anything wrong with people having secrets.

MARY: But they've got funny ones. Peggy and Evelyn heard Mrs Mortar telling Miss Dobie that she was jealous of Miss Wright marrying Cousin Joe.

MRS TILFORD: You shouldn't repeat things like that.

MARY: But that's what she said, Grandma. She said it was unnatural for a girl to feel that way.

MRS TILFORD: What?

MARY: I'm just telling you what she said. She said there was something funny about it, and that Miss Dobie had always been like that, even when she was a little girl, and that it was unnatural—

MRS TILFORD: Stop using that silly word, Mary.

MARY: *(vaguely realizing that she is on the right track, hurries on)* But that was the word *she* kept using, Grandma, and then they got mad and told Mrs Mortar she'd have to get out.

MRS TILFORD: That was probably not the reason at all.

MARY: *(nodding vigorously)* I bet it was, because honestly, Miss Dobie does get cranky and mean every time Cousin Joe comes, and today I heard her say to him: "God damn you," and then she said she was just a jealous fool and—

MRS TILFORD: You have picked up some fine words, haven't you, Mary?

MARY: That's just what she said, Grandma, and one time Miss Dobie was crying in Miss Wright's room, and Miss Wright was trying to stop her, and she said that all right, maybe she wouldn't get married right away if—

MRS TILFORD: How do you know all this?

MARY: We couldn't help hearing because they—I mean Miss Dobie—was talking awful loud, and their room is right next to ours.

MRS TILFORD: Whose room?

MARY: Miss Wright's room, I mean, and you can just ask Peggy and Evelyn whether we didn't hear. Almost always Miss Dobie comes in after we go to bed and stays a long time. I guess that's why they want to get rid of us—of me—because we hear things. That's why they're making us move our room, and they punish me all the time for—

MRS TILFORD: For eavesdropping, I should think. *(She has said this mechanically. With nothing definite in her mind, she is making an effort to conceal the fact that* MARY'S *description of the life at school has worried her)* Well, now I think we've had enough gossip, don't you? Dinner's almost ready, and I can't eat with a girl who has such a dirty face.

MARY: *(softly)* I've heard other things, too. I've heard other things. Plenty of other things, Grandma.

MRS TILFORD: What things?

MARY: Bad things.

MRS TILFORD: Well, what were they?

MARY: I can't tell you.

MRS TILFORD: Mary, you're annoying me very much. If you have anything to say, then say it and stop acting silly.

MARY: I mean I can't say it out loud.

MRS TILFORD: There couldn't possibly be anything so terrible that you couldn't say it out loud. Now either tell the truth or be still.

MARY: Well, a lot of things I don't understand. But it's awful, and sometimes they fight and then they make up, and Miss Dobie cries and Miss Wright gets mad, and then they make up again, and there are funny noises and we get scared.

MRS TILFORD: Noises? I suppose you girls have a happy time imagining a murder.

MARY: And we've seen things, too. Funny things. *(Sees the impatience of her grandmother)* I'd tell you, but I got to whisper it.

MRS TILFORD: Why must you whisper it?

MARY: I don't know. I just got to. *(Climbs on the sofa next to* MRS TILFORD *and begins whispering. At first the whisper is slow and hesitant, but it gradually works up to fast, excited talking. In the middle of it* MRS TILFORD *stops her.)*

MRS TILFORD: *(trembling)* Do you know what you're saying? *(Without answering,* MARY *goes back to the whispering until the older woman takes her by the shoulders and turns her around to stare in her face)* Mary! *Are you telling me the truth?*

MARY: Honest, honest. You just ask Peggy and Evelyn and—*(After a moment* MRS TILFORD *gets up and begins to pace about the room. She is no longer listening to* MARY, *who keeps up a running fire of conversation)* They know too. And maybe there're other kids who know, but we've always been frightened and so we didn't ask, and one night I was going to go and find out, but I got scared and we went to bed early so we wouldn't hear, but sometimes I couldn't help it, but we never talked about it much, because we thought they'd find out and—Oh, Grandma, don't make me go back to that awful place.

MRS TILFORD: *(abstractedly)* What? *(Starts to move about again.)*

MARY: Don't make me go back to that place. I just couldn't stand it anymore. Really, Grandma, I'm so unhappy there, and if only I could stay out the rest of the term, why, then—

MRS TILFORD: *(makes irritated gesture)* Be still a minute. *(After a moment)* You can stay here tonight.

MARY: *(hugging* MRS TILFORD*)* You're the nicest, loveliest grandma in all the world. You—you're not mad at me?

MRS TILFORD: I'm not mad at you. Now get ready for dinner. *(MARY kisses her and runs happily out left.* MRS TILFORD *stands staring after her for a long moment. Then, very slowly, she puts on her eyeglasses and crosses to the phone. She dials a number)* Is Miss Wright—is Miss Wright in? *(Waits a second, hurriedly puts down the receiver)* Never mind, never mind. *(Dials another number)* Dr Cardin, please. Mrs Tilford. *(She remains absolutely motionless while she waits. When she does speak, her voice is low and tense)* Joseph? Joseph? Can you come to see me right away? Yes, I'm perfectly well. No, but it's important, Joseph, very important. I must see you right away. I—I can't tell you over the phone. Can't you come sooner? It's not about Mary's fainting—I said it's not about Mary, Joseph; in one way it's about Mary—*(Suddenly quiet)* But will the hospital take so long? Very well, Joseph, make it as soon as you can. *(Hangs up the receiver, sits for a moment undecided. Then, taking a breath, she dials another number)* Mrs Munn, please. This is Mrs Tilford. Miriam?

This is Amelia Tilford. Could you come over right away? I want some advice—I want to tell you—Thank you.

CURTAIN

SCENE 2: *The same as Scene 1. The curtain has been lowered to mark the passing of a few hours.*

AT RISE: MARY *is lying on the floor playing with a puzzle.* AGATHA *appears lugging blankets and pillows across the room. Almost at the door, she stops and gives* MARY *an annoyed look.*

AGATHA: And see to it that she doesn't get my good quilt all dirty, and let her wear your green pajamas.

MARY: Who?

AGATHA: Who? Rosalie Wells is coming over to spend the night with you.

MARY: You mean she's going to sleep *here?*

AGATHA: You heard me.

MARY: What for?

AGATHA: Do I know all the crazy things that are happening around here? Mrs Munn comes over and then they phone Mrs Wells all the way to New York, three dollars and eighty-five cents and families starving, and Mrs Wells wanted to know if Rosalie could stay here until tomorrow.

MARY: *(relieved)* Oh. Couldn't Evelyn Munn come instead?

AGATHA: Sure. We'll have the whole town over to entertain you.

MARY: I won't let Rosalie Wells wear my new pajamas.

AGATHA: *(exits as the front doorbell rings)* Don't tell me what you won't do. You'll act like a lady for once in your life. *(Offstage)* Come on in, Rosalie. Just go on in there and make yourself at home. Have you had your dinner?

ROSALIE: *(offstage)* Good evening. Yes'm.

AGATHA: *(offstage)* Hang up your pretty coat. Have you had your bath?

ROSALIE: *(offstage)* Yes, ma'am. This morning.

AGATHA: *(offstage)* Well, you better have another one. *(She is climbing the stairs as* ROSALIE *comes into the room.* MARY, *lying in front of the couch, is hidden from her. Gingerly* ROSALIE *sits down on a chair.)*

MARY: *(softly)* Whooooooo. *(*ROSALIE *jumps)* Whooooooo. *(*ROSALIE, *frightened, starts hurriedly for the door.* MARY *sits up, laughs)* You're a goose.

ROSALIE: *(belligerently)* Oh, so it's you. Well, who likes to hear funny noises at night? You could have been a werewolf.

MARY: A werewolf sure wouldn't want you.

ROSALIE: You know everything, don't you? *(*MARY *laughs.* ROSALIE *comes over, stands staring at puzzle)* Isn't it funny about school?

MARY: What's funny about it?

ROSALIE: Don't act like you can come home every night.

MARY: Maybe I can from now on. *(Rolls over on her back luxuriously)* Maybe I'm never going back.

ROSALIE: Am I going back? I don't want to stay home.

MARY: What'll you give to know?

ROSALIE: Nothing. I'll ask Mamma.

MARY: Will you give me a free T.L. if I tell you?

ROSALIE: *(thinks for a moment)* All right. Lois Fisher told Helen that you were very smart.

MARY: That's an old one. I won't take it.

ROSALIE: You got to take it.

MARY: Nope.

ROSALIE: *(laughs)* You don't know, anyway.

MARY: I know what I heard, and I know Grandma phoned your mother in New York. You're just going to spend the night here.

ROSALIE: But what's happened? Peggy and Helen and Evelyn and Lois went home tonight, too. Do you think somebody's got scarlet fever or something?

MARY: No.

ROSALIE: Do *you* know what it is? How'd you find out? *(No answer)* You're always pretending you know everything. You're just faking. *(Flounces away)* Never mind, don't bother telling me. I think curiosity is very unladylike, anyhow. I have no concern with your silly secrets.

MARY: Suppose I told you that I just may have said that you were in on it?

ROSALIE: In on what?

MARY: The secret. Suppose I told you that I *may have* said that you told me about it?

ROSALIE: Why, Mary Tilford! You can't do a thing like that. I didn't tell you about anything. (MARY *laughs*) Did you tell your grandmother such a thing?

MARY: Maybe.

ROSALIE: Did you?

MARY: Maybe.

ROSALIE: Well, I'm going right up to your grandmother and tell her I didn't tell you anything—whatever it is. You're just trying to get me into trouble and I'm not going to let you. (*Starts for door.*)

MARY: Wait a minute, I'll come with you. I want to tell her about Helen Burton's bracelet.

ROSALIE: (*sits down suddenly*) What about it?

MARY: Just that you stole it.

ROSALIE: Shut up. I didn't do any such thing.

MARY: Yes, you did.

ROSALIE: (*tearfully*) You made it up. You're always making things up.

MARY: You can't call me a fibber, Rosalie Wells. That's a kind of a dare and I won't take a dare. I guess I'll go tell Grandma, anyway. Then she can call the police and they'll come for you and you'll spend the rest of your life in one of those solitary prisons and you'll get older and older, and when you're very old and can't see anymore, they'll let you out maybe and your mother and father will be dead and you won't have anyplace to go and you'll beg on the streets—

ROSALIE: I didn't steal anything. I borrowed the bracelet and I was going to put it back as soon as I'd worn it to the movies. I never meant to keep it.

MARY: Nobody'll believe that, least of all the police. You're just a common, ordinary thief. Stop that bawling. You'll have the whole house down here in a minute.

ROSALIE: You won't tell? Say you won't tell.

MARY: Am I a fibber?

ROSALIE: No.

MARY: Then say: "I apologize on my hands and knees."

ROSALIE: I apologize on my hands and knees. Let's play with the puzzle.

MARY: Wait a minute. Say: "From now on, I, Rosalie Wells, am the vassal of Mary Tilford and will do and say whatever she tells me under the solemn oath of a knight."

ROSALIE: I won't say that. That's the worst oath there is. (MARY *starts for the door*) Mary! Please don't—

MARY: Will you swear it?

ROSALIE: (*sniffling*) But then you could tell me to do anything.

MARY: And you'd have to do it. Say it quick or I'll—

ROSALIE: (*hurriedly*) From now on, I, Rosalie Wells, am the vassal of Mary Tilford and will do and say whatever she tells me under the solemn oath of a knight. (*She gasps, and sits up straight as* MRS TILFORD *enters.*)

MARY: Don't forget that.

MRS TILFORD: Good evening, Rosalie, you're looking very well.

ROSALIE: Good evening, Mrs Tilford.

MARY: She's getting fatter every day.

MRS TILFORD: (*abstractedly*) Then it's very becoming. (*Doorbell rings*) That must be Joseph. Mary, take Rosalie into the library. Be sure you're both fast asleep by half past ten. (ROSALIE *starts to exit right, sees* MARY, *stops and hesitates.*)

MARY: Go on, Rosalie. (*Waits until* ROSALIE *reluctantly exits*) Grandma.

MRS TILFORD: Yes?

MARY: Grandma, Cousin Joe'll say I've got to go back. He'll say I really wasn't—
(CARDIN *enters and she runs from the room.*)

CARDIN: Hello, Amelia. (*Looks curiously at the fleeing* MARY) Mary home, eh?

MRS TILFORD: (*watching* MARY *as she leaves*) Hello, Joseph. Sit down. (*He sits down, looks at her curiously, waits for her to speak*) Whisky?

CARDIN: Please. How are you feeling? Headaches again?

MRS TILFORD: *(puts drink on table)* No.

CARDIN: Those are good powders. Bicarbonate of soda and water. Never hurt anybody yet.

MRS TILFORD: Yes. How have you been, Joseph? *(Vaguely, sparring for time)* I haven't seen you the last few weeks. Agatha misses you for Sunday dinners.

CARDIN: I've been busy. We're getting the results from the mating season right about now.

MRS TILFORD: Did I take you away from a patient?

CARDIN: No. I was at the hospital.

MRS TILFORD: How's it getting on?

CARDIN: Just the same. No money, badly equipped, a lousy laboratory, everybody growling at everybody else—Amelia, you didn't bring me here to talk about the hospital. What's the matter with you?

MRS TILFORD: I—I have something to tell you.

CARDIN: Well, out with it.

MRS TILFORD: It's a very hard thing to say, Joseph.

CARDIN: Hard for you to say to *me?* *(No answer)* Don't be worried about Mary. I guessed that she ran home to tell you about her faint. It was caused by nothing but bad temper and was very clumsily managed, at that. Amelia, she's a terribly spoilt—

MRS TILFORD: I heard about the faint. That's not what is worrying me.

CARDIN: *(gently)* Are you in some trouble?

MRS TILFORD: We all are in trouble. Bad trouble.

CARDIN: We? Me, you mean? Nothing's the matter with me.

MRS TILFORD: When did you last see Karen?

CARDIN: Today. This afternoon.

MRS TILFORD: Oh. Not since seven o'clock?

CARDIN: What's happened since seven o'clock?

MRS TILFORD: Joseph, you've been engaged to Karen for a long time. Are your plans any more definite than they were a year ago?

CARDIN: You can get ready to buy the wedding present. We'll have the wedding here, if you don't mind. The smell of clean little girls and boiled linen would worry me.

MRS TILFORD: Why has Karen decided so suddenly to make it definite?

CARDIN: She has not suddenly decided anything. The school is pretty well on its feet, and now that Mrs Mortar is leaving—

MRS TILFORD: I've heard about their putting Mrs Mortar out.

CARDIN: Putting her out? Well, maybe. But a nice sum for a trip and a promise that a good niece will support you the rest of your life is an enviable way of being put out.

MRS TILFORD: *(slowly)* Don't you find it odd, Joseph, that they want so much to get rid of that silly, harmless woman?

CARDIN: I don't know what you're talking about, but it isn't odd at all. Lily Mortar is not a harmless woman, although God knows she's silly enough. She's a tiresome, spoilt old bitch. If you're forming a Mortar Welfare Society, you're wasting your time. *(Gets up, puts down his glass)* It's not like you to waste your time. Now, what's it that's really on your mind?

MRS TILFORD: You must not marry Karen.

CARDIN: *(shocked, he grins)* You're a very impertinent lady. Why must I—*(imitates her)* not marry Karen?

MRS TILFORD: Because there's something wrong with Karen—something horrible.

(The doorbell is heard to ring loud and long.)

CARDIN: I cannot allow you to say things like that, Amelia.

MRS TILFORD: I have good reason for saying it. *(Breaks off as she hears voices offstage)* Who is that?

KAREN: *(offstage)* Mrs Tilford, Agatha. Is she in?

AGATHA: *(offstage)* Yes'm. Come on in.

MRS TILFORD: I won't have her here.

CARDIN: *(angrily)* What are you talking about?

MRS TILFORD: I won't have her here.

CARDIN: Then you don't want me here either. *(Turns to face KAREN and MARTHA)* Darling, what?—

KAREN: *(stops when she sees him, puts her hand over her eyes)* Is it a joke, Joe?

MARTHA: *(with great force to MRS TILFORD)* We've come to find out what you are doing.

CARDIN: *(kissing* KAREN*)* What is it?

KAREN: It's crazy! It's crazy! What did she do it for?

CARDIN: What are you talking about? What do you mean?

MRS TILFORD: You shouldn't have come here.

CARDIN: What is all this? What's happened?

KAREN: I tried to reach you. Hasn't she told you?

CARDIN: Nobody's told me anything. I haven't heard anything but wild talk. What is it, Karen? *(She starts to speak, then dumbly shakes her head)* What's happened, Martha?

MARTHA: *(violently)* An insane asylum has been let loose. How do we know what's happened?

CARDIN: What was it?

KAREN: We didn't know what it was. Nobody would talk to us, nobody would tell us anything.

MARTHA: I'll tell you, I'll tell you. You see if you can make any sense out of it. At dinnertime, Mrs Munn's chauffeur said that Evelyn must be sent home right away. At half past seven Mrs Burton arrived to tell us that she wanted Helen's things packed and that she'd wait outside because she didn't want to enter a place like ours. Five minutes later the Wells's butler came for Rosalie.

CARDIN: What was it?

MARTHA: It was a madhouse. People rushing in and out, the children being pushed into cars—

KAREN: Mrs Rogers finally told us.

CARDIN: What? What?

KAREN: That—that Martha and I are—in love with each other. In love with each other. Mrs Tilford told them.

CARDIN: *(for a moment stands staring at her incredulously. Then he walks across the room, stares out of the window, and finally turns to* MRS TILFORD*)* Did you tell them that?

MRS TILFORD: Yes.

CARDIN: Are you sick?

MRS TILFORD: You know I'm not sick.

CARDIN: *(snapping the words out)* Then what did you do it for?

MRS TILFORD: *(slowly)* Because it's true.

KAREN: *(incredulously)* You think it's true, then?

MARTHA: You fool! You damned, vicious—

KAREN: Do you realize what you're saying?

MRS TILFORD: I realize it very well. And—

MARTHA: You realize nothing, nothing, nothing.

MRS TILFORD: And that's why I don't think you should have come here. *(Quietly)* I shall not call you names, and I will not allow you to call me names. I can't trust myself to talk about it with you now or ever.

KAREN: What's she talking about, Joe? What's she mean? What is she trying to do to us? What is everybody doing to us?

MARTHA: *(softly, as though to herself)* Pushed around. We're being pushed around by crazy people. *(Shakes herself slightly)* That's an awful thing. And we're standing here—*(*CARDIN *puts his arm around* KAREN, *walks with her to the window. They stand there together)* We're standing here taking it. *(Suddenly with violence)* Didn't you know we'd come here? Were we supposed to lie down and grin while you kicked us around with these lies?

MRS TILFORD: This can't do any of us any good, Miss Dobie.

MARTHA: *(scornfully imitating her)* "This can't do any of us any good." Listen, listen. Try to understand this: you're not playing with paper dolls. We're human beings, see? It's our lives you're fooling with. *Our* lives. That's serious business for us. Can you understand that?

MRS TILFORD: I can understand that, and I regret it. But you've been playing with children's lives, and that's why I stopped you. *(More calmly)* I know how serious this is for you, how serious it is for all of us.

CARDIN: *(bitterly)* I don't think you do know.

MRS TILFORD: I wanted to avoid this meeting because it can't do any good. You came here to find out if I had made the charge. You've found out. Let's end it there. I'm sorry this had to be done to you, Joseph.

CARDIN: I don't like your sympathy.

MRS TILFORD: Very well. There's nothing I mean to do, nothing I want to do. There's nothing anybody can do.

CARDIN: *(carefully)* You have already done a terrible thing.

MRS TILFORD: I have done what I had to do. What they are may be their own business. It becomes a great deal more than that when children are involved.

KAREN: *(wildly)* It's not true. Not a word of it is true; can't you understand that?

MRS TILFORD: There won't be any punishment for either of you. This—this thing is your own. Go away with it. I don't understand it and I don't want any part of it.

MARTHA: *(slowly)* So you thought we would go away?

MRS TILFORD: I think that's best for you.

MARTHA: There must be something we can do to you, and, whatever it is, we'll find it.

MRS TILFORD: That will be very unwise.

KAREN: You are right to be afraid.

MRS TILFORD: I am not afraid, Karen.

CARDIN: You *are* old—and you *are* irresponsible.

KAREN: *(goes to* MRS TILFORD*)* I don't want to have anything to do with your mess, do you hear me? It makes me feel dirty and sick to be forced to say this, but here it is; there isn't a single word of truth in anything you've said. We're standing here defending ourselves—and against what? Against a lie. A great, awful lie.

MRS TILFORD: I'm sorry that I can't believe that.

KAREN: Damn you!

CARDIN: But you can believe this: they've worked eight long years to save enough money to buy that farm, to start that school. They did without everything that young people ought to have. You wouldn't know about that. That school meant things to them: self-respect, and bread and butter, and honest work. Do you know what it is to try so hard for anything? Well, now it's gone. *(Suddenly hits the side of the table with his hand)* What the hell did you do it for?

MRS TILFORD: *(softly)* It had to be done.

CARDIN: Righteousness is a great thing.

MRS TILFORD: *(gently)* I know how you must feel.

CARDIN: You don't know anything about how I feel. And you don't know how they feel, either.

MRS TILFORD: I've loved you as much as I loved my own boys. I wouldn't have spared them; I couldn't spare you.

CARDIN: *(fiercely)* I believe you.

MARTHA: What is there to do to you? What can we do to you? There must be something—something that makes you feel the way we do tonight. You don't want any part of this, you said. But you'll get a part. More than you bargained for. *(Suddenly)* Listen: are you willing to stand by everything you've said tonight?

MRS TILFORD: Yes.

MARTHA: All right. That's fine. But don't get the idea we'll let you whisper this lie: you made it and you'll come out with it. Shriek it to your town of Lancet. We'll *make* you shriek it—and we'll make you do it in a courtroom. *(Quietly)* Tomorrow, Mrs Tilford, you will have a libel suit on your hands.

MRS TILFORD: That will be very unwise.

KAREN: Very unwise—for you.

MRS TILFORD: It is you I am thinking of. I am frightened for you. It was wrong of you to brazen it out here tonight; it would be criminally foolish of you to brazen it out in public. That can bring you nothing but pain. You must not be punished any further.

MARTHA: You feel that you are too old to be punished. You believe we should spare you.

MRS TILFORD: You know that is not what I meant.

CARDIN: *(turns from the window)* So you took a child's word for it?

MARTHA: *(looks at him)* I knew it, too.

KAREN: That is really where you got it? I can't believe—it couldn't be. Why, she's a child.

MARTHA: She's not a child any longer.

KAREN: Oh, my God, it all fits so well now. That girl has hated us for a long time. We never knew why, we never could find out. There didn't seem to be any reason—

MARTHA: There wasn't any reason. She hates everybody and everything.

KAREN: Your Mary's a strange girl, a bad girl. There's something very awful the matter with her.

MRS TILFORD: I was waiting for you to say that, Miss Wright.

KAREN: I'm telling you the truth. We should have told it to you long ago. *(Stops, sighs)* It's no use.

MARTHA: Where is she? Bring her out here and let us hear what she has to say.

MRS TILFORD: You cannot see her.

CARDIN: Where is she?

MRS TILFORD: I won't have that, Joseph.

CARDIN: I'm going to talk to her.

MRS TILFORD: *(to* KAREN *and* MARTHA*)* You came here demanding explanations. It was I who should have asked them from you. You attack me, you attack Mary. I've told you I didn't mean you any harm. I still don't. You claim that it isn't true; it may be natural that you should say that, but I *know* that it is true. No matter what you say, you know very well I wouldn't have acted until I was absolutely sure. All I wanted was to get those children away. That has been done. There won't be any talk about it or about you—I'll see to that. You have been in my house long enough. Get out.

KAREN: *(gets up)* The wicked very young, and the wicked very old. Let's go home.

CARDIN: Sit down. *(To* MRS TILFORD*)* When two people come here with their lives spread on the table for you to cut to pieces, then the only honest thing to do is to give them a chance to come out whole. Are you honest?

MRS TILFORD: I've always thought so.

CARDIN: Then where is Mary? *(After a moment she moves her head to door, right. Quickly* CARDIN *goes to the door and opens it)* Mary! Come here. *(After a moment* MARY *appears, stands nervously near door. Her manner is shy and afraid.)*

MRS TILFORD: *(gently)* Sit down, dear, and don't be afraid.

MARTHA: *(her lips barely moving)* Make her tell the truth.

CARDIN: *(walking about in front of* MARY*)* Look, everybody lies all the time. Sometimes they have to, sometimes they don't. I've lied for a lot of different reasons, but there was seldom a time when, if I'd been given a second chance, I wouldn't have taken back the lie and told the truth. You're lucky if you ever get that chance. I'm telling you this because I'm about to ask you a question. Before you answer the question, I want to tell you that if you've l—, if you made a mistake, you must take this chance and say so. You won't be punished for it. Do you get all that?

MARY: *(timidly)* Yes, Cousin Joe.

CARDIN: *(grimly)* All right, let's get started. Were you telling your grandmother the truth this afternoon? The exact truth about Miss Wright and Miss Dobie?

MARY: *(without hesitation)* Oh, yes.

*(*KAREN *sighs deeply.* MARTHA, *her fists closed tight, turns her back to the child.* CARDIN *smiles as he looks at* MARY.*)*

CARDIN: All right, Mary, that was your chance; you passed it up. *(Pulls up a chair, sits down in front of her)* Now let's find out things.

MRS TILFORD: She's told you. Aren't you through?

CARDIN: Not by a long shot. You've started something and we'll finish it for you. Will you answer some more questions, Mary?

MARY: Yes, Cousin Joe.

MARTHA: Stop that sick, sweet tone.

*(*MRS TILFORD *half rises;* CARDIN *motions her back.)*

CARDIN: Why don't you like Miss Dobie and Miss Wright?

MARY: Oh, I do like them. They just don't like me. They never have liked me.

CARDIN: How do you know?

MARY: They're always picking on me. They're always punishing me for everything that happens. No matter what happens, it's always me.

CARDIN: Why do you think they do that?

MARY: Because—because they're—because they— *(Stops, turns)* Grandma, I—

CARDIN: All right, we'll skip that one. Did you get punished today?

MARY: Yes, and it was just because Peggy and Evelyn heard them and so they took it out on me.

KAREN: That's a lie.

CARDIN: Ssh. Heard what, Mary?

MARY: Mrs Mortar told Miss Dobie that there was something funny about her. She said that she had a funny feeling about Miss Wright, and Mrs Mortar said that was unnatural. That was why we got punished, just because—

KAREN: That was not the reason they got punished.

MRS TILFORD: *(to* MARTHA*)* Miss Dobie?

MARTHA: My aunt is a stupid woman. What she said was unpleasant; it was said to annoy me. It meant nothing more than that.

MARY: And, Cousin Joe, she said every time you came to the school Miss Dobie got jealous, and that she didn't want you to get married.

MARTHA: *(to* CARDIN*)* She said that, too. This— this child is taking little things, little family things, and making them have meanings that— *(Stops, suddenly regards* MARY *with a combination of disgust and interest)* Where did you learn so much in so little time?

CARDIN: What do you think Mrs Mortar meant by all that, Mary?

MRS TILFORD: Stop it, Joseph!

MARY: I don't know, but it was always kind of funny and she always said things like that and all the girls would talk about it when Miss Dobie went and visited Miss Wright late at night—

KAREN: *(angrily)* And we go to the movies at night and sometimes we read at night and sometimes we drink tea at night. Those are guilty things, too, Mrs Tilford.

MARY: And there are always funny sounds and we'd stay awake and listen because we couldn't help hearing and I'd get frightened because the sounds were like—

MARTHA: Be still!

KAREN: *(with violence)* No, no. You don't want her still now. What else did you hear?

MARY: Grandma, I—

MRS TILFORD: *(bitterly to* CARDIN*)* You are trying to make her name it.

CARDIN: *(ignoring her, speaks to* MARY*)* Go on.

MARY: I don't know; there were just sounds.

CARDIN: But what did you think they were? Why did they frighten you?

MARY: *(weakly)* I don't know.

CARDIN: *(smiles at* MRS TILFORD*)* She doesn't know.

MARY: *(hastily)* I saw things, too. One night there was so much noise I thought somebody was sick or something and I looked through the keyhole and they were kissing and saying things and then I got scared because it was different sort of and I—

MARTHA: *(her face distorted, turns to* MRS TILFORD*)* That child—that child is sick.

KAREN: Ask her again how she could see us.

CARDIN: How could you see Miss Dobie and Miss Wright?

MARY: I—I—

MRS TILFORD: Tell him what you whispered to me.

MARY: It was at night and I was leaning down by the keyhole.

KAREN: *There's no keyhole on my door.*

MRS TILFORD: What?

KAREN: There—is—no—keyhole—on—my— door.

MARY: *(quickly)* It wasn't her room, Grandma, it was the other room, I guess. It was *Miss Dobie's* room. I saw them through the keyhole in Miss Dobie's room.

CARDIN: How did you know anybody was in Miss Dobie's room?

MARY: I told you, I told you. Because we heard them. Everybody heard them—

MARTHA: I share a room with my aunt. It is on the first floor at the other end of the house. It is impossible to hear anything from there. *(To* CARDIN*)* Tell her to come and see for herself.

MRS TILFORD: *(her voice shaken)* What is this, Mary? Why did you say you saw through a keyhole? *Can* you hear from your room?—

MARY: *(starts to cry)* Everybody is yelling at me. I don't know what I'm saying with everybody mixing me all up. I did see it! I did see it!

MRS TILFORD: *What* did you see? *Where* did you see it? I want the truth, now. The truth, whatever it is.

CARDIN: *(gets up, moves his chair back)* We can go home. We are finished here. *(Looks around)* It's not a pleasant place to be.

MRS TILFORD: *(angrily)* Stop that crying, Mary. Stand up.

(MARY gets up, crying hysterically. MRS TILFORD stands directly in front of her.)

MRS TILFORD: *I want the truth.*

MARY: All—all right.

MRS TILFORD: What is the truth?

MARY: It was Rosalie who saw them. I just said it was me so I wouldn't have to tattle on Rosalie.

CARDIN: *(wearily)* Oh, my God!

MARY: It *was* Rosalie, Grandma, she told us all about it. She said she had read about it in a book and she knew. *(Desperately)*. You ask Rosalie. You just ask Rosalie. She'll tell you. We used to talk about it all the time. That's the truth, that's the honest truth. She said it was when the door was open once and she told us all about it. I was just trying to save Rosalie, and everybody jumps on me.

MRS TILFORD: *(to CARDIN)* Please wait a minute. *(Goes to library door)* Rosalie!

CARDIN: You're giving yourself an awful beating, Amelia, and you deserve whatever you get.

MRS TILFORD: *(stands waiting for ROSALIE, passes her hand over her face)* I don't know. I don't know, anymore. Maybe it's what I do deserve. *(As ROSALIE, frightened, appears at the door, making bows to everybody, she takes the child gently by the hand, brings her down center, talking nervously)* I'm sorry to keep you up so late, Rosalie. You must be tired. *(Speaks rapidly)* Mary says there's been a lot of talk in the school

lately about Miss Wright and Miss Dobie. Is that true?

ROSALIE: I—I don't know what you mean.

MRS TILFORD: That things have been said among you girls.

ROSALIE: *(wide-eyed, frightened)* What things? I never—I—I—

KAREN: *(gently)* Don't be frightened.

MRS TILFORD: What was the talk about, Rosalie?

ROSALIE: *(utterly bewildered)* I don't know what she means, Miss Wright.

KAREN: Rosalie, Mary has told her grandmother that certain things at school have been—er—puzzling you girls. You, particularly.

ROSALIE: History puzzles me. I guess I'm not very good at history, and Helen helps me sometimes, if that—

KAREN: No, that's not what she meant. She says that you told her that you saw certain—certain acts between Miss Dobie and myself. She says that once, when the door was open, you saw us kissing each other in a way that—*(Unable to bear the child's look, she turns her back)* women don't kiss one another.

ROSALIE: Oh, Miss Wright, I didn't, didn't, I didn't. I *never* said such a thing.

MRS TILFORD: *(grimly)* That's true, my dear?

ROSALIE: I never saw any such thing. Mary always makes things up about me and everybody else. *(Starts to weep in excitement)* I never said any such thing ever. Why I never even could have thought of—

MARY: *(staring at her, speaks very slowly)* Yes, you did, Rosalie. You're just trying to get out of it. I remember just when you said it. I remember it, because it was the day Helen Burton's bracelet was—

ROSALIE: *(stands fascinated and fearful, looking at MARY)* I never did. I—I—you're just—

MARY: It was the day Helen's bracelet was stolen, and nobody knew who did it, and Helen said that if her mother found out, she'd have the thief put in jail.

KAREN: *(puzzled, as are the others, by the sudden change in ROSALIE'S manner)* There's nothing to cry about. You must help us by telling the truth. Why, what's the matter, Rosalie?

MARY: Grandma, there's something I've got to tell you that—

ROSALIE: *(with a shrill cry)* Yes. Yes. I did see it. I told Mary. What Mary said was right. I said it. I said it—

(Throws herself on the couch, weeping hysterically; MARTHA *stands leaning against the door;* KAREN, CARDIN, *and* MRS TILFORD *are staring at* ROSALIE; MARY *slowly sits down as the curtain falls.)*

CURTAIN

ACT THREE

SCENE: *The same as Act One. Living room of the school.*

AT RISE: *The room has changed. It is not dirty, but it is dull and dark and uncared for. The windows are tightly shut, the curtains tightly drawn.* KAREN *is sitting in a large chair, right center, feet flat on floor.* MARTHA *is lying on the couch, her face buried against the pillows, her back to* KAREN. *It is a minute or two after the rise of the curtain before either speaks.*

MARTHA: It's cold in here.
KAREN: Yes.
MARTHA: What time is it?
KAREN: I don't know.
MARTHA: I was hoping it was time for my bath.
KAREN: Take it early today.
MARTHA: *(laughs)* Oh, I couldn't do that. I look forward all day to that bath. It's my last touch with the full life. It makes me feel important to know that there's one thing ahead of me, one thing I've *got* to do. You ought to get yourself something like that. I tell you, at five o'clock every day you comb your hair. How's that? It's better for you, take my word. You wake up in the morning and you say to yourself, the day's

not entirely empty, life is rich and full: at five o'clock I'll comb my hair.

(They fall back into silence. A moment later the phone rings. Neither of them pays the slightest attention to it. But the ringing becomes too insistent. KAREN *rises, takes the receiver off, goes back to her chair and sits down.)*

KAREN: It's raining.
MARTHA: Hungry?
KAREN: No. You?
MARTHA: No, but I'd like to be hungry. Remember how much we used to eat at college?
KAREN: That was ten years ago.
MARTHA: Well, maybe we'll be hungry in another ten years. It's cheaper this way.
KAREN: What's the old thing about time being more nourishing than bread?
MARTHA: Maybe.
KAREN: Joe's late today. What time is it?
MARTHA: *(turns again to lie on her side)* We've been sitting here for eight days asking each other the time. Haven't you heard? There isn't any time anymore.
KAREN: It's been days since we've been out of this house.
MARTHA: Well, we'll have to get off these chairs sooner or later. In a couple of months they'll need dusting.
KAREN: What'll we do when we get off?
MARTHA: God knows.
KAREN: *(almost in a whisper)* It's awful.
MARTHA: Let's not talk about it. *(After a moment)* What about eggs for dinner?
KAREN: All right.
MARTHA: I'll make some potatoes with onions, the way you used to like them.
KAREN: It's a week ago Thursday. It never seemed real until the last day. It seems real enough now, all right. Let's go out.
MARTHA: *(turns over, stares at her)* Where to?
KAREN: We'll take a walk.
MARTHA: Where'll we walk?
KAREN: Why shouldn't we take a walk? We won't see anybody, and suppose we do, what of it? We'll just—

MARTHA: *(slowly gets up)* Come on. We'll go through the park.

KAREN: They might see us. *(They stand looking at each other)* Let's not go. (MARTHA *goes back, lies down again)* We'll go tomorrow.

MARTHA: *(laughs)* Stop kidding yourself.

KAREN: But Joe says we've got to go out. He says that all the people who don't think it's true will begin to wonder if we keep hiding this way.

MARTHA: If it makes you feel better to think there *are* such people, go ahead.

KAREN: He says we ought to go into town and go shopping and act as though—

MARTHA: Shopping? That's a sound idea. There aren't three stores in Lancet that would sell us anything. Hasn't he heard about the ladies' clubs and their meetings and their circulars and their visits and their—

KAREN: *(softly)* Don't tell him.

MARTHA: *(gently)* I won't. *(There are footsteps in the hall, and the sound of something being dragged)* There's our friend.

(A GROCERY BOY *appears lugging a box. He brings it into the room, stands staring at them, giggles a little. Walks toward* KAREN, *stops, examines her. She sits tense, looking away from him. Without taking his eyes from* KAREN, *he speaks.)*

GROCERY BOY: I knocked on the kitchen door but nobody answered.

MARTHA: You said that yesterday. All right. Thanks. Good-bye.

KAREN: *(unable any longer to stand the stare)* Make him stop it.

GROCERY BOY: Here are the things. *(Giggles, moves toward* MARTHA, *stands looking at her. Suddenly* MARTHA *thrusts her hand in the air.)*

MARTHA: I've got eight fingers, see? I'm a freak.

GROCERY BOY: *(giggling)* There's a car comin' here. *(Starts backing out of door, still looking.)* Good-bye. *(Exits.)*

MARTHA: You still think we should go into town?

KAREN: I don't know. I don't know anything anymore. *(After a moment)* Martha, Martha, Martha—

MARTHA: *(gently)* What is it, Karen?

KAREN: What are we going to do? It's like that dark hour of the night when half awake you struggle through the black mess you've been dreaming. Then, suddenly, you wake up and you see your own bed or your own nightgown and you know you're back again in a solid world. But now it's all the nightmare; there is no solid world. Oh, Martha, *why* did it happen. *What* happened? What are we doing here like this?

MARTHA: Waiting.

KAREN: For what?

MARTHA: I don't know.

KAREN: We've got to get out of this place. I can't stand it anymore.

MARTHA: You'll be getting married soon. Everything will be all right then.

KAREN: *(vaguely)* Yes.

MARTHA: *(looks up at the tone)* What is it?

KAREN: Nothing.

MARTHA: There mustn't be anything wrong between you and Joe. Never.

KAREN: *(without conviction)* Nothing's wrong. *(As footsteps are heard in the hall, her face lights up)* There's Joe now.

*(*MRS MORTAR, *small suitcase in hand, stands in the doorway, her face pushed coyly forward.)*

MRS MORTAR: And here I am. Hello, hello.

MARTHA: *(she has turned over on her back and is staring at her aunt. She speaks to* KAREN*)* The Duchess, isn't it? Returned at long last. *(Too jovially)* Come on in. We're delighted to see you. Are you tired from your journey? Is there something I can get you?

MRS MORTAR: *(surprised)* I'm very glad to see you both, and *(looks around)* I'm very glad to see the old place again. How is everything?

MARTHA: Everything's fine. We're splendid, thank you. You're just in time for tea.

MRS MORTAR: You know, I should like some tea, if it isn't too much trouble.

MARTHA: No trouble at all. Some small sandwiches and a little brandy?

MRS MORTAR: *(puzzled).* Why, Martha.

MARTHA: Where the hell have you been?

MRS MORTAR: Around, around. I had a most interesting time. Things—

MARTHA: Why didn't you answer my telegrams?

MRS MORTAR: Things have changed in the theater—drastically changed, I might say.

MARTHA: *Why didn't you answer my telegrams?*

MRS MORTAR: Oh, Martha, there's your temper again.

MARTHA: Answer me and don't bother about my temper.

MRS MORTAR: *(nervously)* I was moving around a great deal. *(Conversationally)* You know, I think it will throw a very revealing light on the state of the new theater when I tell you that the Lyceum in Rochester now has a toilet backstage.

MARTHA: To hell with the toilet in Rochester. Where were you?

MRS MORTAR: Moving around, I tell you.

KAREN: What difference does it all make now?

MRS MORTAR: Karen is quite right. Let bygones be bygones. As I was saying, there's an effete something in the theater now, and that accounts for—

MARTHA: Why did you refuse to come back here and testify for us?

MRS MORTAR: Why, Martha, I didn't refuse to come back at all. That's the wrong way to look at it. I was on a tour; that's a moral obligation, you know. Now don't let's talk about unpleasant things anymore. I'll go up and unpack a few things; tomorrow's plenty of time to get my trunk.

KAREN: *(laughs)* Things have changed here, you know.

MARTHA: She doesn't know. She expected to walk right up to a comfortable fire and sit down and she very carefully waited until the whole thing was over. *(Leans forward, speaking to* MRS MORTAR*)* Listen. Karen Wright and Martha Dobie brought a libel suit against a woman called Tilford because her grandchild had accused them of having what the judge called "sinful sexual knowledge of one another." *(*MRS MORTAR *holds up her hand in protest, and* MARTHA *laughs)* Don't like that, do you? Well, a great part of the defense's case was based on remarks made by Lily Mortar, actress in the toilets of Rochester, against her niece, Martha. And a greater part of the defense's case rested on the telling fact that Mrs Mortar would not appear in court to deny or explain those remarks. Mrs Mortar had a moral obligation to the theater. As you probably read in the papers, we lost the case.

MRS MORTAR: I didn't think of it that way, Martha. It couldn't have done any good for all of us to get mixed up in that unpleasant notoriety—*(Sees* MARTHA'S *face. Hastily)* But now that you've explained it, why, I do see it your way, and I'm sorry I didn't come back. But now that I am here, I'm going to stand shoulder to shoulder with you. I know what you've gone through, but the body and heart *do* recover, you know. I'll be here working right along with you and we'll—

MARTHA: There's an eight o'clock train. Get on it.

MRS MORTAR: Martha.

MARTHA: You've come back to pick the bones dry. There's nothing here for you.

MRS MORTAR: *(sniffling a little)* How can you talk to me like that?

MARTHA: Because I hate you. I've always hated you.

MRS MORTAR: *(gently)* God will punish you for that.

MARTHA: He's been doing all right.

MRS MORTAR: When you wish to apologize, I will be temporarily in my room. *(Starts to exit, almost bumps into* CARDIN, *steps back with dignity)* How do you do?

CARDIN: *(laughs)* Look who's here. A little late, aren't you?

MRS MORTAR: So it's you. Now, I call *that* loyal. A lot of men wouldn't still be here. They would have felt—

MARTHA: Get out of here.

KAREN: *(opening door)* I'll call you when it's time for your train.

(MRS MORTAR looks at her, exits.)

CARDIN: Now, what do you think brought her back?

KAREN: God knows.

MARTHA: I know. She was broke.

CARDIN: *(pats MARTHA on the shoulder)* Don't let her worry you this time, Martha. We'll give her some money and get rid of her. *(Pulls KAREN to him)* Been out today, darling?

KAREN: We started to go out.

CARDIN: *(shakes his head)* Feel all right?

(KAREN leans over to kiss him. Almost imperceptibly he pulls back.)

KAREN: Why did you do that?

MARTHA: Karen.

CARDIN: Do what?

KAREN: Draw back that way.

CARDIN: *(laughs, kisses her)* If we sit around here much longer, we'll all be bats. I sold my place today to Foster.

KAREN: You did what?

CARDIN: We're getting married this week. Then we're going away—all three of us.

KAREN: You can't leave here. I won't have you do this for me. What about the hospital and—

CARDIN: Shut up, darling, it's all fixed. We're going to Vienna and we're going quick. Fischer wrote that I can have my old place back.

KAREN: No! No! I'm not going to let you.

CARDIN: It's already done. Fischer can't pay me much, but it'll be enough for the three of us. Plenty if we live cheap.

MARTHA: I couldn't go with you, Joe.

CARDIN: Nonsense, Martha, we're all going. We're going to have fun again.

KAREN: *(slowly)* You don't want to go back to Vienna.

CARDIN: No.

KAREN: Then why?

CARDIN: Look: I don't want to go to Vienna; I'd rather have stayed here. But then you don't want to go to Vienna; you'd rather have stayed here. Well, to hell with that. We *can't* stay here, and Vienna offers enough to eat and sleep and drink beer on. Now don't object any more, please, darling. All right?

KAREN: All right.

MARTHA: I can't go. It's better for all of us if I don't.

CARDIN: *(puts his arm around her)* Not now. You stay with us now. Later on, if you want it that way. All right?

MARTHA: *(smiles)* All right.

CARDIN: Swell. I'll buy you good coffee cakes and take you both to Ischl for a honeymoon.

MARTHA: *(picking up grocery box, she starts for door)* A big coffee cake with a lot of raisins. It would be nice to like something again. *(Exits.)*

CARDIN: *(with a slightly forced heartiness)* I'll be going back with a pretty girl who belongs to me. I'll show you off all over the place—to Dr Engelhardt, and the nurse at the desk, and to the fat gal in the cake shop, and to Fischer. *(Laughs)* The last time I saw him was at the railroad station. He took me back of the baggage car. *(With an imitation of an accent)* "Joseph," he said, "you'll be a good doctor; I would trust you to cut up my Minna. But you're not a great doctor, and you never will be. Go back where you were born and take care of your sick. Leave the fancy work to the others." I came home.

KAREN: You'll be coming home again someday.

CARDIN: Let's not talk about it. *(After a moment)* You'll need some clothes?

KAREN: A few. Oh, your Dr Fischer was so right. This is where you belong.

CARDIN: I need an overcoat and a suit. You'll need a lot of things—heavy things. It's cold there now, much colder than you'd expect—

KAREN: I've done this to you. I've taken you away from everything you want.

CARDIN: But it's lovely in the mountains, and that's where we'll go for a month.

KAREN: They—*they've* done it. They've taken away every chance we had. Everything we wanted, everything we were going to be.

CARDIN: And we've got to stop talking like that. *(Takes her by the shoulder)* We've got a chance.

But it's just one chance, and if we miss it we're done for. It means that we've got to start putting the whole business behind us now. *Now,* Karen. What you've done, you've done—and that's that.

KAREN: What *I've* done?

CARDIN: *(impatiently)* What's been done to you.

KAREN: What did you mean? *(When there is no answer)* What did you mean when you said: "What you've done"?

CARDIN: *(shouting)* Nothing. Nothing. *(Then very quietly)* Karen, there are a lot of people in this world who've had bad trouble in their lives. We're three of those people. We could sit around the rest of our lives and exist on that trouble, until in the end we had nothing else and we'd want nothing else. That's something I'm not coming to and I'm not going to let you come to.

KAREN: I know. I'm sorry. *(After a moment)* Joe, can we have a baby right away?

CARDIN: *(vaguely)* Yes, I guess so. Although we won't have much money now.

KAREN: You used to want one right away. You always said that was the way you wanted it. There's some reason for your changing.

CARDIN: My God, we *can't* go on like this. Everything I say to you is made to mean something else. We don't talk like people anymore. Oh, let's get out of here as fast as we can.

KAREN: *(as though she is finishing the sentence for him)* And every word will have a new meaning. You think we'll be able to run away from that? Woman, child, love, lawyer—no words that we can use in safety anymore. *(Laughs)* Sick, high-tragic people. That's what we'll be.

CARDIN: *(gently)* No, we won't, darling. Love is casual—that's the way it should be. We must find that out all over again. We must learn again to live and love like other people.

KAREN: It won't work.

CARDIN: What?

KAREN: The two of us together.

CARDIN: *(sharply)* Stop talking like that.

KAREN: It's true. *(Suddenly).* I want you to say it now.

CARDIN: I don't know what you're talking about.

KAREN: Yes, you do. We've both known for a long time. I knew surely the day we lost the case. I was watching your face in court. It was ashamed—and sad at being ashamed. Say it now, Joe. Ask it now.

CARDIN: I have nothing to ask. Nothing—*(Quickly)* All right. Is it—was it ever—

KAREN: *(puts her hand over his mouth).* No. Martha and I have never touched each other. *(Pulls his head down on her shoulder)* That's all right, darling. I'm glad you asked. I'm not mad a bit, really.

CARDIN: I'm sorry, Karen, I'm sorry. I didn't mean to hurt you, I—

KAREN: I know. You wanted to wait until it was all over, you really never wanted to ask at all. You didn't know for sure; you thought there might be just a little truth in it all. *(With great feeling)* You've been good to me and loyal. You're a fine man. *(Afraid of tears, she pats him, walks away)* Now go and sit down, Joe. I have things to say. They're all mixed up and I must get them clear.

CARDIN: Don't let's talk any more. Let's forget and go ahead.

KAREN: *(puzzled)* Go ahead?

CARDIN: Yes, Karen.

KAREN: You believe me, then?

CARDIN: Of course I believe you. I only had to hear you say it.

KAREN: No, no, no. That isn't the way things work. Maybe you believe me. I'd never know whether you did or not. You'd never know whether you did, either. We couldn't do it that way. Can't you see what would happen? We'd be hounded by it all our lives. I'd be frightened, always, and in the end my own fright would make me—would make me hate you. *(Sees slight movement he makes)* Yes, it would; I know it would. I'd hate you for what I thought I'd done to you. And I'd hate myself, too. It would grow and grow until we'd be ruined by it. *(Sees him about to speak)* Ah, Joe, you've seen all that yourself. You knew it first.

CARDIN: *(softly)* I didn't mean it that way; I don't now.

KAREN: *(smiles)* You're still trying to spare me, still trying to tell yourself that we might be all right again. But we won't be all right. Not ever, ever, ever. I don't know all the reasons why. Look, I'm standing here. I haven't changed. *(Holds out her hands)* My hands look just the same, my face is the same, even my dress is old. We're in a room we've been in so many times before; you're sitting where you always sit; it's nearly time for dinner. I'm like everybody else. I can have all the things that everybody has. I can have you and I can go to market, and we can go to the movies, and people will talk to me and—*(Suddenly notices the pain in his face)* Oh, I'm sorry. I mustn't talk like that. That couldn't be true anymore.

CARDIN: It could be, Karen. We'll make it be like that.

KAREN: No. That's only what we'd like to have had. It's what we can't have now. Go home, darling.

CARDIN: *(with force)* Don't talk like that. No matter what it is, we can't leave each other. I can't leave you—

KAREN: Joe, Joe. Let's do it now and quick; it will be too hard later on.

CARDIN: No, no, no. We love each other. *(His voice breaks)* I'd give anything not to have asked questions, Karen.

KAREN: It had to be asked sooner or later—and answered. You're a good man—the best I'll ever know—and you've been better to me than—But it's no good now, for either of us; you can see that.

CARDIN: It can be. You say I helped you. Help me now; help me to be strong and good enough to—*(Goes toward her with his arms out)* Karen!

KAREN: *(drawing back)* No, Joe! *(Then, as he stops)* Will you do something for me?

CARDIN: No. I won't—

KAREN: Will you—will you go away for two days— a day—and think this all over by yourself— away from me and love and pity? Will you? And then decide.

CARDIN: *(after a long pause)* Yes, if you want, but it won't make any difference. We will—

KAREN: Don't say anything. Please go now. *(She sits down, smiles, closes her eyes. For a moment he stands looking at her, then slowly puts on his hat)* And all my heart goes with you.

CARDIN: *(at door, leaving)* I'll be coming back. *(Exits, slowly, reluctantly, closing door.)*

KAREN: *(a moment after he has gone)* No, you won't. Never, darling. *(Stays as she is until* MARTHA *enters right.)*

MARTHA: *(goes to lamp, lights it)* It gets dark so early now. *(Sits down, stretches, laughs)* Cooking always makes me feel better. Well, I guess we'll have to give the Duchess some dinner. When the hawks descend, you've got to feed 'em. Where's Joe? *(No answer)* Where's Joe?

KAREN: Gone.

MARTHA: A patient? Will he be back in time for dinner?

KAREN: No.

MARTHA: *(watching her)* We'll save dinner for him, then. Karen! What's the matter?

KAREN: He won't be back anymore.

MARTHA: *(slowly and carefully)* You mean he won't be back anymore tonight.

KAREN: He won't be back at all.

MARTHA: *(quickly, walks to* KAREN) What happened? *(*KAREN *shakes her head)* What happened, Karen?

KAREN: He thought that we had been lovers.

MARTHA: *(tensely)* I don't believe you.
(Wearily KAREN *turns her head away.)*

KAREN: All right.

MARTHA: *(automatically)* I don't believe it. He's never said a word all these months, all during the trial—*(Suddenly grabs* KAREN *by the shoulder, shakes her)* Didn't you tell him? For God's sake, didn't you tell him it wasn't true?

KAREN: Yes.

MARTHA: He didn't believe you?

KAREN: I guess he believed me.

MARTHA: *(angrily)* Then what have you done?

KAREN: What had to be done.

MARTHA: It's all wrong. It's silly. He'll be back in a little while and you'll clear it all up—*(Realizes why that can't be, covers her mouth with her hand)* Oh, God, I wanted that for you so much.

KAREN: Don't. I feel sick to my stomach.

MARTHA: *(goes to couch opposite* KAREN, *puts her head in her arms)* What's happened to us? What's really happened to us?

KAREN: I don't know. I want to be sleepy. I want to go to sleep.

MARTHA: Go back to Joe. He's strong; he'll understand. It's too much for you this way.

KAREN: *(irritably)* Stop talking about it. Let's pack and get out of here. Let's take the train in the morning.

MARTHA: The train to where?

KAREN: I don't know. Someplace; anyplace.

MARTHA: A job? Money?

KAREN: In a big place we could get something to do.

MARTHA: They'd know about us. We've been famous.

KAREN: A small town, then.

MARTHA: They'd know more about us.

KAREN: *(as a child would say it)* Isn't there anywhere to go?

MARTHA: No. We're bad people. We'll sit. We'll be sitting the rest of our lives wondering what's happened to us. You think this scene is strange? Well, get used to it; we'll be here for a long time. *(Suddenly pinches* KAREN *on the arm)* Let's pinch each other sometimes. We can tell whether we're still living.

KAREN: *(shivers, listlessly gets up, starts making a fire in the fireplace)* But this isn't a new sin they tell us we've done. Other people aren't destroyed by it.

MARTHA: They are the people who believe in it, who want it, who've chosen it. We aren't like that. We don't love each other. *(Suddenly stops, crosses to fireplace, stands looking abstractedly at* KAREN. *Speaks casually)* I don't love you. We've been very close to each other, of course. I've loved you like a friend, the way thousands of women feel about other women.

KAREN: *(only half listening)* Yes.

MARTHA: Certainly that doesn't mean anything. There's nothing wrong about that. It's

perfectly natural that I should be fond of you, that I should—

KAREN: *(listlessly)* Why are you saying all this to me?

MARTHA: Because I love you.

KAREN: *(vaguely)* Yes, of course.

MARTHA: I love you that way—maybe the way they said I loved you. I don't know. *(Waits, gets no answer, kneels down next to* KAREN) Listen to me!

KAREN: What?

MARTHA: *I have loved you the way they said.*

KAREN: You're crazy.

MARTHA: There's always been something wrong. Always—as long as I can remember. But I never knew it until all this happened.

KAREN: *(for the first time looks up)* Stop it!

MARTHA: You're afraid of hearing it; I'm more afraid than you.

KAREN: *(puts her hands over her ears)* I won't listen to you.

MARTHA: Take your hands down. *(Leans over, pulls* KAREN'S *hands away)* You've got to know it. I can't keep it any longer. I've got to tell you how guilty I am.

KAREN: *(deliberately).* You are guilty of nothing.

MARTHA: I've been telling myself that since the night we heard the child say it; I've been praying I could convince myself of it. I can't, I can't any longer. It's there. I don't know how, I don't know why. But I did love you. I do love you. I resented your marriage; maybe because I wanted you; maybe I wanted you all along; maybe I couldn't call it by a name; maybe it's been there ever since I first knew you—

KAREN: *(tensely)* It's a lie. You're telling yourself a lie. We never thought of each other that way.

MARTHA: *(bitterly)* No, of course *you* didn't. But who says I didn't? I never felt that way about anybody but you. I've never loved a man— *(Stops. Softly)* I never knew why before. Maybe it's that.

KAREN: *(carefully)* You are tired and sick.

MARTHA: *(as though she were talking to herself)* It's funny; it's all mixed up. There's something in you, and you don't know it and you don't do anything about it. Suddenly a child gets bored and lies—and there you are, seeing it for the first time. *(Closes her eyes)* I don't know. It all seems to come back to *me*. In some way I've ruined your life. I've ruined my own. I didn't even *know*. *(Smiles)* There's a big difference between us now, Karen. I feel all dirty and— *(Puts out her hand, touches* KAREN'S *head)* I can't stay with you anymore, darling.

KAREN: *(in a shaken, uncertain tone)* All this isn't true. You've never said it; we'll forget it by tomorrow—

MARTHA: Tomorrow? Karen, we would have had to invent a new language, as children do, without words like tomorrow.

KAREN: *(crying)* Go and lie down, Martha. You'll feel better.

*(*MARTHA *looks around the room, slowly, carefully. She is very quiet. Exits right, stands at door for a second looking at* KAREN, *then slowly shuts the door behind her.* KAREN *sits alone without moving. There is no sound in the house until, a few minutes after* MARTHA'S *exit, a shot is heard. The sound of the shot should not be too loud or too strong. For a few seconds after the noise has died out,* KAREN *does not move. Then, suddenly, she springs from the chair, crosses the room, pulls open door, right. Almost at the same moment footsteps are heard on the staircase.)*

MRS MORTAR: What was that? Where is it? *(Enters door center, frightened, aimlessly moving about)* Karen! Martha! Where are you? I heard a shot. What was—*(Stops as she sees* KAREN *reappear, right. Walks toward her, still talking. Stops when she sees* KAREN'S *face)* What—what is it? *(*KAREN *moves her hands, shakes her head slightly, passes* MRS MORTAR, *and goes toward window.* MRS MORTAR *stares at her for a moment, rushes past her through door right. Left alone,* KAREN *leans against the window.* MRS MORTAR *reenters crying. After a minute)* What shall we do? What shall we do?

KAREN: *(in a toneless voice)* Nothing.

MRS MORTAR: We've got to get a doctor—right away. *(Goes to phone, nervously, fumblingly starts to dial.)*

KAREN: *(without turning)* There isn't any use.

MRS MORTAR: We've got to do something. Oh, it's awful. Poor Martha. I don't know what we can do—*(Puts phone down, collapses in chair, sobs quietly)* You think she's dea—

KAREN: Yes.

MRS MORTAR: Poor, poor Martha. I can't realize it's true. Oh, how could she—she was so—I don't know what—*(Looks up, still crying, surprised)* I'm—I'm frightened.

KAREN: Don't cry.

MRS MORTAR: I can't help it. How can I help it? *(Gradually the sobs cease, and she sits rocking herself)* I'll never forgive myself for the last words I said to her. But I was good to her, Karen, and you know God will excuse me for that once. I always tried to do everything I could. *(Suddenly)* Suicide's a sin. *(No answer. Timidly)* Shouldn't we call somebody to—

KAREN: In a little while.

MRS MORTAR: She shouldn't have done it, she shouldn't have done it. It was because of all this awful business. She would have got a job and started all over again—she was just worried and sick and—

KAREN: That isn't the reason she did it.

MRS MORTAR: What—why—?

KAREN: *(wearily)* What difference does it make now?

MRS MORTAR: *(reproachfully)* You're not crying.

KAREN: No.

MRS MORTAR: What will happen to me? I haven't anything. Poor Martha—

KAREN: She was very good to you; she was good to us all.

MRS MORTAR: Oh, I know she was, Karen, and I was good to her too. I did everything I could. I—I haven't any place to go. *(After a few seconds of silence)* I'm afraid. It seems so queer—in the next room. *(Shivers.)*

KAREN: Don't be afraid.

MRS MORTAR: It's different for you. You're young. *(The doorbell rings.* MRS MORTAR *jumps.* KAREN *doesn't move. It rings again.)*

MRS MORTAR: *(nervously).* Who is it? *(The bell rings again)* Shall I answer it? *(*KAREN *shrugs)* I think we'd better. *(Exits through*

center doors. *Returns in a minute followed by*
AGATHA, *who stands in the door)* It's a woman.
(No answer) It's a woman to see you, Karen.
(Getting no answer, she turns to AGATHA*)* You
can't come in now; we've had a—we've had
trouble here.

AGATHA: Miss Karen, I've *got* to speak to you.

KAREN: *(turns slowly, mechanically)* Agatha.

AGATHA: *(goes to* KAREN*)* Please, Miss Karen.
We've tried so hard to get you. I been phoning
here all the time. Trying to get you. Phoning and
phoning. Please, please let her come in. Just for
a minute, Miss Karen. Please—

MRS MORTAR: Who wants to come in here?

AGATHA: Mrs Tilford. *(Looks at* KAREN*)* Don't you
feel well? *(*KAREN *shakes her head)* You ain't
mad at *me?*

MRS MORTAR: That woman can't come in here.
She caused all—

KAREN: I'm not mad at you, Agatha.

AGATHA: Can I—can I get you something?

KAREN: No.

AGATHA: You poor child. You look like you got a
pain. *(Hesitates, takes* KAREN'S *hands)* I only
came cause she's so bad off. She's got to see
you, Miss Karen, she's just got to. She's been
sittin' outside in the car, hoping you'd come
out. She can't get Dr Joe. He—he won't talk to
her anymore. I wouldn't a come—I always
been on your side—but she's sick. If only you
could see her, you'd let her come for just a
minute.

KAREN: I couldn't do that, Agatha.

AGATHA: I don't blame you. But I had to tell you.
She's old. It's going to kill her.

KAREN: *(bitterly)* Kill her? Where is Mrs Tilford?

AGATHA: Outside.

KAREN: All right.

AGATHA: *(presses* KAREN'S *arm)* You always been
a good girl. *(Hurriedly exits.)*

MRS MORTAR: You going to allow that woman to
come in here? With Martha lying there? How
can you be so feelingless? *(She starts to cry)* I
won't stay and see it. I won't have anything to do
with it. I'll never let that woman—*(Rushes sobbing from the room.)*

(A second after, MRS TILFORD *appears in the doorway. Her face, her walk, her voice have changed.)*

MRS TILFORD: Karen, let me come in.

(Without turning, KAREN *bows her head.* MRS
TILFORD *enters, stands staring at the floor.)*

KAREN: Why have you come here?

MRS TILFORD: I had to come. *(Stretches out her
hand to* KAREN, *who does not turn. She drops her
hand)* I know now; I know it wasn't true.

KAREN: What?

MRS TILFORD: *(carefully)* I know it wasn't true,
Karen.

KAREN: *(stares at her, shudders)* You know it wasn't
true? I don't care what you know. It doesn't matter anymore. If that's what you had to say, you've
said it. Go away.

MRS TILFORD: *(puts her hand to her throat)* I've
got to tell you.

KAREN: I don't want to hear you.

MRS TILFORD: Last Tuesday Mrs Wells found a
bracelet in Rosalie's room. The bracelet had
been hidden for several months. We found out
that Rosalie had taken the bracelet from another girl, and that Mary—*(Closes her eyes)* that
Mary knew that and used it to force Rosalie into
saying that she had seen you and Miss Dobie
together. I—I've talked to Mary. I've found out.
*(*KAREN *suddenly begins to laugh, high and
sharp)* Don't do that, Karen. I have only a little
more to say. I've tried to say it to you for six
days. I've talked to Judge Potter. He will make
all arrangements. There will be a public apology and an explanation. The damage suit will be
paid to you in full and—and any more that you
will be kind enough to take from me. I—I must
see that you won't suffer anymore.

KAREN: We're not going to suffer anymore. Martha
is dead. *(*MRS TILFORD *gasps, shakes her head as
though to shake off the truth, and covers her face.*
KAREN *watches her for a minute)* So you've come
here to relieve your conscience? Well, I won't be
your confessor. It's choking you, is it? *(Violently)*
And you want to stop the choking, don't you?
You've done a wrong and you have to right that
wrong or you can't rest your head again. You
want to be "just," don't you, and you wanted us

to help you be just? You've come to the wrong place for help. You want to be a "good" woman again, don't you? *(Bitterly)* Oh, I know. You told us that night you had to do what you did. Now you "have" to do this. A public apology and money paid, and you can sleep again and eat again. That done and there'll be peace for you. You're old, and the old are callous. Ten, fifteen years left for you. But what of me? It's a whole life for me. A whole God-damned life. *(Suddenly quiet, points to door, right)* And what of her?

MRS TILFORD: *(she is crying)* You are still living.

KAREN: Yes. I guess so.

MRS TILFORD: *(with a tremendous effort to control herself)* I didn't come here to relieve myself. I swear to God I didn't. I came to try—to try anything. I knew there wasn't any relief for me, Karen, and that there never would be again. *(Tensely)* But what I am or why I came doesn't matter. The only thing that matters is you and— You, now.

KAREN: There's nothing for me.

MRS TILFORD: Oh, let's try to make something for you. You're young and I—I can help you.

KAREN: *(smiles)* You can help me?

MRS TILFORD: *(with great feeling)* Take whatever I can give you. Take it for yourself and use it for yourself. It won't bring me peace, if that's what's worrying you. *(Smiles)* Those ten or fifteen years you talk about! They will be bad years.

KAREN: I'm tired, Mrs Tilford. You will have a hard time ahead, won't you?

MRS TILFORD: Yes.

KAREN: Mary?

MRS TILFORD: I don't know.

KAREN: You can send her away.

MRS TILFORD: No. I could never do that. Whatever she does, it must be to me and no one else. She's—she's—

KAREN: Yes. Your very own, to live with the rest of your life. *(For a moment she watches* MRS TILFORD'S *face)* It's over for me now, but it will never end for you. She's harmed us both, but she's harmed you more, I guess. *(Sits down beside* MRS TILFORD*)* I'm sorry.

MRS TILFORD: *(clings to her)* Then you'll try for yourself.

KAREN: All right.

MRS TILFORD: You and Joe.

KAREN: No. We're not together anymore.

MRS TILFORD: *(looks up at her)* Did I do that, too?

KAREN: I don't think anyone did anything, anymore.

MRS TILFORD: *(makes a half-movement to rise)* I'll go to him right away.

KAREN: No, it's better now the way it is.

MRS TILFORD: But he must know what I know, Karen. You must go back to him.

KAREN: *(smiles)* No, not anymore.

MRS TILFORD: You must, you must—*(Sees her face, hesitates)* Perhaps later, Karen?

KAREN: Perhaps.

MRS TILFORD: *(after a moment in which they both sit silent)* Come away from here now, Karen. *(*KAREN *shakes her head)* You can't stay with— *(Moves her hand toward door, right.)*

KAREN: When she is buried, then I will go.

MRS TILFORD: You'll be all right?

KAREN: I'll be all right, I suppose. Good-bye, now. *(They both rise.* MRS TILFORD *speaks, pleadingly.)*

MRS TILFORD: You'll let me help you? You'll let me try?

KAREN: Yes, if it will make you feel better.

MRS TILFORD: *(with great feeling)* Oh, yes, oh, yes, Karen. *(*KAREN *walks toward the window.)*

KAREN: *(suddenly)* Is it nice out?

MRS TILFORD: It's been cold. *(*KAREN *opens the window slightly, sits on the ledge.)*

KAREN: It feels very good.

MRS TILFORD: You'll write me sometime?

KAREN: If I ever have anything to say. Good-bye, now.

MRS TILFORD: Good-bye, my dear. *(*KAREN *smiles as* MRS TILFORD *exits. She does not turn, but a minute later she raises her hand.)*

KAREN: Good-bye.

CURTAIN

WAITING FOR LEFTY (1935)

An Odets play was awaited like news hot off the press, as though through him we would know what to think of ourselves and our prospects.

In this reminiscence from his autobiography *Time-bends,* Arthur Miller recalls Clifford Odets's almost meteoric rise to prominence in the late 1930s, and suggests his impact on theatregoers and young playwrights like Miller himself. An actor in the influential Group Theatre in the early 1930s, Odets (1906–1963) had four plays produced on Broadway in 1935: *Awake and Sing!, Till the Day I Die, Paradise Lost,* and the play initially responsible for his rise to notoriety, *Waiting for Lefty.* First performed in a benefit on January 5, 1935, for the *New Theatre Magazine* published by the New Theatre League— a group of small companies such as the Workers Laboratory and the New Playwrights' Theatre dedicated to addressing a working-class audience— *Waiting for Lefty* quickly became one of the most controversial and influential dramas of the decade. By June of 1935, as reported in *Time* magazine, although *Waiting for Lefty* was being produced all across America, it was also banned in New Haven (even after winning the George Pierce Baker Drama Cup at Yale University in March), Boston, Newark, and four other American cities on "one ambiguous pretext or another"—building code violations, allegations of "profanity and blasphemy," and so on. Its impact in Europe was also appreciable. Ewan Mac-Coll, an important figure in Britain's Workers Theatre Movement of the 1930s, declared Odets's play "ideal" for Manchester's Theatre of Action in the early months of 1935, for it provided not only a successful vehicle with which to articulate social protest, but it is also a catalyst for envisioning a proletarian theatre which toured working-class areas.

Waiting for Lefty, in short, powerfully depicts Depression-era frustrations among the working class, as it also exemplifies one theatrical form developed to express these, the **agitprop** drama.

Given Odets's biography, there is a certain irony and, perhaps, historical inaccuracy in remembering him primarily as a working-class dramatist of political *agitation* or subversive *propaganda,* the root words of the term "agitprop." Born in Philadelphia to a middle-class family, Odets's father moved his family to the Bronx, New York (the setting for *Awake and Sing!*) when young Clifford was six. There his father rose from working in a printing plant to eventually owning it; later, after returning to Philadelphia, he assumed the vice-presidency of a boiler company and bought an advertising agency. Dropping out of high school after two years to become a writer, the younger Odets took minor jobs at various small theatres and in 1929 was an understudy for Spencer Tracy in a Broadway play. He acted for the Theatre Guild and appeared in several roles for the Group Theatre, including one in Sidney Kingsley's Pulitzer Prize–winning hospital drama, *Men in White* (1933). But it is surely attributable to the energy, enthusiasm, and collective intelligence of the Group Theatre—with founders Lee Strasberg, Harold Clurman, and Cheryl Crawford, and such consummate actors as Stella Adler, Luther Adler, Morris Carnovsky, Sanford Meisner, and others—that Odets's career as a playwright blossomed.

In addition to the four dramas produced in 1935, Odets's plays appeared on Broadway throughout the late 1930s and early 1940s: *Golden Boy* (1937), *Rocket to the Moon* (1938), *Night Music* (1940), and *Clash by Night* (1941). And in 1936, after the success of his plays during the previous year, several Hollywood studios made lucrative offers to him to work as a screenwriter. Odets, who in the early years of the Group Theatre earned a minimal salary and lived in cramped quarters with several other members of the company, was reportedly offered as much as $4,000 a week to write screenplays. He finally signed a contract with Paramount for $2,500 per week, writing or co-writing (and occasionally directing) such films as *The General Died* (1936) and *Humoresque* (1947). His popular later play *The Country Girl* (1950) was made into an equally successful movie in 1954, one for which Grace Kelly won an Academy Award for Best Actress. And, in the years immediately preceding his death from cancer in 1963, Odets worked for NBC television as a writer and script editor for *The Richard Boone Show.*

Odets's commitment to social issues and to the Group's project of reinventing the American theatre clearly came into conflict with his work in the film industry, a conflict evident in what is commonly regarded as his partially autobiographical critique of Hollywood, *The Big Knife* (1949). On the one hand, Odets was committed to the Group Theatre and the artistic integrity for which it stood; as a result, he used his screenwriting salary to underwrite Group productions on several occasions until the company's dissolution in 1941. Yet, on the other hand, in the late 1930s he was building both a personal and professional life in California. In 1937, he married Luise Rainer, winner of two consecutive Academy Awards as Best Actress for her performances in *The Great Ziegfeld* (1936) and *The Good Earth* (1937), only to be separated from her two years later. Charlie Castle, star-actor and central character of *The Big Knife*, experiences pressures that were doubtless similar to those afflicting Odets, as his virtual entrapment in the film business destroys his marriage and, eventually, his life. Before committing suicide, Castle accuses the variety of mass culture produced by Hollywood as guilty of "murder [of] the highest dreams and hopes of a whole great people," a position his wife Marion had argued earlier in attempting to persuade him to return to a New York theatre devoid of Hollywood's corrosive "atmosphere of flattery and deceit." Odets never really

effected such a clean break, negotiating much of his life between the New York theatre and Hollywood studios.

The California life-style of the Castles in *The Big Knife*, with its cocktail parties and swimming pools, is about as far removed from the lives of Odets's impoverished cabdrivers in *Waiting for Lefty* as Hollywood is from New York. In *The Big Knife*, Castle is coerced into signing an acting contract for over three and one-half million dollars; in Act One of *Waiting for Lefty*, a desperate housewife tries to persuade her cabdriver-husband to organize a strike in protest of the meager six to seven dollars a week he earns. Yet in some ways, both the cabdriver and the movie star are fighting the respective systems that enslave them. The episodic structure of *Waiting for Lefty*, with its platform oratory and riveting conclusion interrupted by five narrative flashbacks, delineates the variety of oppressions suffered by the working class. The first episode between a cabdriver and his wife, for example, reiterates the harsh material circumstances that partially motivated the 1934 cabdrivers' strike upon which *Waiting for Lefty* is loosely based. (When it was published in *New Theatre*, the play actually had the subtitle "A Play in Six Scenes, Based on the New York Strike of February, 1934.") The abject poverty of which Edna complains to Joe in this episode is followed by the corruption and class biases of an industrialist and doctor in later scenes—and the destruction of young people's dreams in the episode between a young "hack" and his girl. Poverty, the moral corruption of the ruling class and of even such supposedly beneficent institutions as a hospital, the exploitation of workers in a capitalist system which is indifferent to their suffering—these are the ideological appeals of *Waiting for Lefty*. Or, as Arthur Miller put it, Odets seemed "pure, revolutionary, and the bearer of the light" in making his "comradely outcry against the intolerable present."

This outcry is, of course, primarily a socialist or Marxist one. It was almost inevitable, therefore, that when in the early moments of the Cold War in 1947 the **House Un-American Activities Committee** (HUAC) turned to well-known writers and actors in its investigation of the subversive content of Hollywood movies, Odets would be called to testify. He admitted to being a member of the Communist Party for several months in the early 1930s, and was known to associate with several figures who became prime targets of the Committee's work, Charles Chaplin and John Howard Lawson, for instance. Lawson, a leftist writer whose play *Processional* (1925) clearly influenced Odets, and whose *Gentlewoman* (1932) was produced by the Group, co-wrote the film *Blockade* with Odets in 1938 and later became president of the Screen Writers' Guild. One of a group of Hollywood artists known as the Hollywood Ten blacklisted after appearing in front of HUAC, Lawson was imprisoned in 1948. Chaplin, as Charles Maland describes it, spent several evenings near the end of the war with such "political progressives" as Lawson and Odets, and FBI files contained reports of Chaplin's attending parties at Odets's home. For his part, Odets suggested to his HUAC interrogators that he actually took no part in strikes and explained that he borrowed the form of *Waiting for Lefty* from the American **minstrel show** with its on-stage audience, solo performances, and actors sitting in the audience. More recent commentators also point to the 1934 production of *Newsboy* by the Workers Laboratory Theatre as another influence on Odets—and, at the same time, another confirmation of his leftist politics.

Whatever the case or influences, *Waiting for Lefty* electrified audiences. Just as *Newsboy* ends with an expression of racial harmony, a cry for all men to "REVOLT!" against the sources of their subjugation, *Waiting for Lefty* ends with three words—"STRIKE! STRIKE! STRIKE"—uniting audience and actors in a moment of shared social commitment. Unlike much Broadway drama of the 1920s and 1930s—the witty high comedy of Philip Barry or S. N. Behrman, for example, or the psychological realism of Eugene O'Neill—Odets introduced Broadway and the entire country to the worlds of the working and middle classes in plays like *Waiting for Lefty, Awake and Sing!,* and *Rocket to the Moon.* One part of these worlds and part of Odets's contribution to American drama is linguistic; indeed, Arthur Miller credits Odets with "disposing of middle-class gentility" and introducing characters with propensities for "screaming and yelling and cursing like somebody off the Manhattan streets." This linguistic shift would seem only appropriate, for *Waiting for Lefty* represents the everyday predicaments of the Depression-era poor, calling for an end to their suffering. Played on a nearly bare stage, therefore easily transportable to union halls or street corners, *Waiting for Lefty* is not only representative of proletarian drama during the Depression, but also confirms the theatrical fact that even the simplest or most basic formal elements, if combined ingeniously, can create memorable drama. If, as Joseph Wood Krutch observed in reviewing the play for the *Nation*, Odets in *Waiting for Lefty* "invented a form which turns out to be a very effective dramatic equivalent of soap-box oratory," then we might read the most political of contemporary plays for traces of the conventions Odets so skillfully refined over a half-century ago.

WORKS CONSULTED

"Agit-Prop." *Time*, 17 June 1935: 38.

Clurman, Harold. *The Fervent Years: The Group Theatre and the Thirties.* New York: Harcourt Brace Jovanovich, 1975.

Gorney, Howard, and Ewan MacColl, eds. *Agit-Prop to Theatre Workshop.* Manchester: Manchester University Press, 1986.

Krutch, Joseph Wood. *The American Drama Since 1918: An Informal History.* New York: George Braziller, 1957.

Maland, Charles. *Chaplin and American Culture: The Evolution of a Star Image.* Princeton: Princeton University Press, 1989.

Miller, Arthur. *Timebends: A Life.* New York: Grove Press, 1987.

Miller, Gabriel, ed. *Critical Essays on Clifford Odets.* Boston: G. K. Hall, 1991.

Odets, Clifford. *The Big Knife.* New York: Samuel French, 1949.

CHARACTERS

FATT	CLAYTON
JOE	AGATE KELLER
EDNA	HENCHMAN
MILLER	REILLY
FAYETTE	DR BARNES
IRV	DR BENJAMIN
FLORENCE	A MAN
SID	

As the curtain goes up we see a bare stage. On it are sitting six or seven men in a semi-circle. Lolling against the proscenium down left is a young man chewing a toothpick: a gunman. A fat man of porcine appearance is talking directly to the audience. In other words he is the head of a union and the men ranged behind him are a committee of workers. They are now seated in interesting different attitudes and present a wide diversity of type, as we shall soon see. The fat man is hot and heavy under the collar, near the end of a long talk, but not too hot: he is well fed and confident. His name is HARRY FATT.

FATT: You're so wrong I ain't laughing. Any guy with eyes to read knows it. Look at the textile strike—out like lions and in like lambs. Take the San Francisco tie-up—starvation and broken heads. The steel boys wanted to walk out too, but they changed their minds. It's the trend of the times, that's what it is. All we workers got a good man behind us now. He's top man of the country—looking out for our interests—the man in the White House is the one I'm referrin' to. That's why the times ain't ripe for a strike. He's working day and night—

VOICE: *(from the audience)* For who? *(The GUN-MAN stirs himself)*

FATT: For you! The records prove it. If this was the Hoover régime, would I say don't go out, boys? Not on your tintype! But things is different now. You read the papers as well as me. You know it. And that's why I'm against the strike. Because we gotta stand behind the man who's standin' behind us! The whole country—

ANOTHER VOICE: Is on the blink! *(The GUNMAN looks grave)*

FATT: Stand up and show yourself, you damn red! Be a man, let's see what you look like! *(Waits in vain)* Yellow from the word go! Red and yellow makes a dirty color, boys. I got my eyes on four or five of them in the union here. What the hell'll they do for you? Pull you out and run away when trouble starts. Give those birds a chance and they'll have your sisters and wives in the whore houses, like they done in Russia. They'll tear Christ off his bleeding cross. They'll wreck your homes and throw your babies in the river. You think that's bunk? Read the papers! Now listen, we can't stay here all night. I gave you the facts in the case. You boys got hot suppers to go to and—

ANOTHER VOICE: Says you!

GUNMAN: Sit down, Punk!

ANOTHER VOICE: Where's Lefty? *(Now this question is taken up by the others in unison. FATT pounds with gavel.)*

FATT: That's what I wanna know. Where's your pal, Lefty? You elected him chairman—where the hell did he disappear?

VOICES: We want Lefty! Lefty! Lefty!

FATT: *(pounding)* What the hell is this—a circus? You got the committee here. This bunch of cowboys you elected. *(Pointing to man on extreme right end.)*

MAN: Benjamin.

FATT: Yeah, Doc Benjamin. *(Pointing to other men in circle in seated order)* Benjamin, Miller, Stein, Mitchell, Phillips, Keller. It ain't my fault Lefty took a run-out powder. If you guys—

A GOOD VOICE: What's the committee say?

OTHERS: The committee! Let's hear from the committee! *(FATT tries to quiet the crowd, but one of the seated men suddenly comes to the front. The GUNMAN moves over to center stage, but FATT says)*

FATT: Sure, let him talk. Let's hear what the red boys gotta say! *(Various shouts are coming from the audience. FATT insolently goes back to his seat in the middle of the circle. He sits on his raised platform and relights his cigar. The GUNMAN goes back to his post. JOE, the new speaker, raises his hand for quiet. Gets it quickly. He is sore.)*

JOE: You boys know me. I ain't a red boy one bit! Here I'm carryin' a shrapnel that big I picked up in the war. And maybe I don't know it when it rains! Don't tell me red! You know what we are? The black and blue boys! We been kicked around so long we're black and blue from head to toes. But I guess anyone who says straight out he don't like it, he's a red boy to the leaders of the union. What's this crap about goin' home to hot suppers? I'm asking to your faces how many's got hot suppers to go home to? Anyone who's sure of his next meal, raise his hand! A certain gent sitting behind me can raise them both. But not in front here! And that's why we're talking strike—to get a living wage!

VOICE: Where's Lefty?

JOE: I honest to God don't know, but he didn't take no run-out powder. That Wop's got more guts than a slaughter house. Maybe a traffic jam got him, but he'll be here. But don't let this red stuff scare you. Unless fighting for a living scares you. We gotta make up our minds. My wife made up my mind last week, if you want the truth. It's plain as the nose on Sol Feinberg's face we need a strike. There's us comin' home every night—eight, ten hours on the cab. "God," the wife says, "eighty cents ain't money—don't buy beans almost. You're workin' for the company," she says to me, "Joe! you ain't workin' for me or the family no more!" She says to me, "If you don't start . . ."

I. JOE AND EDNA

The lights fade out and a white spot picks out the playing space within the space of seated men. The seated men are very dimly visible in the outer dark, but more prominent is FATT smoking his cigar and often blowing the smoke in the lighted circle.

A tired but attractive woman of thirty comes into the room, drying her hands on an apron. She stands there sullenly as JOE comes in from the other side, home from work. For a moment they stand and look at each other in silence.

JOE: Where's all the furniture, honey?

EDNA: They took it away. No installments paid.

JOE: When?

EDNA: Three o'clock.

JOE: They can't do that.

EDNA: Can't? They did it.

JOE: Why, the palookas, we paid three-quarters.

EDNA: The man said read the contract.

JOE: We must have signed a phoney. . . .

EDNA: It's a regular contract and you signed it.

JOE: Don't be so sour, Edna. . . . *(Tries to embrace her.)*

EDNA: Do it in the movies, Joe—they pay Clark Gable big money for it.

JOE: This is a helluva house to come home to. Take my word!

EDNA: Take MY word! Whose fault is it?

JOE: Must you start that stuff again?

EDNA: Maybe you'd like to talk about books?

JOE: I'd like to slap you in the mouth!

EDNA: No you won't.

JOE: (sheepishly) Jeez, Edna, you get me sore some time. . . .

EDNA: But just look at me—I'm laughing all over!

JOE: Don't insult me. Can I help it if times are bad? What the hell do you want me to do, jump off a bridge or something?

EDNA: Don't yell. I just put the kids to bed so they won't know they missed a meal. If I don't have Emmy's shoes soled tomorrow, she can't go to school. In the meantime let her sleep.

JOE: Honey, I rode the wheels off the chariot today. I cruised around five hours without a call. It's conditions.

EDNA: Tell it to the A & P!

JOE: I booked two-twenty on the clock. A lady with a dog was lit . . . she gave me a quarter tip by mistake. If you'd only listen to me— we're rolling in wealth.

EDNA: Yeah? How much?

JOE: I had "coffee and—" in a beanery. (Hands her silver coins) A buck four.

EDNA: The second month's rent is due tomorrow.

JOE: Don't look at me that way, Edna.

EDNA: I'm looking through you, not at you. . . . Everything was gonna be so ducky! A cottage by the waterfall, roses in Picardy. You're a four-star-bust! If you think I'm standing for it much longer, you're crazy as a bedbug.

JOE: I'd get another job if I could. There's no work—you know it.

EDNA: I only know we're at the bottom of the ocean.

JOE: What can I do?

EDNA: Who's the man in the family, you or me?

JOE: That's no answer. Get down to brass tacks. Christ, gimme a break, too! A coffee and java all day. I'm hungry, too, Babe. I'd work my fingers to the bone if—

EDNA: I'll open a can of salmon.

JOE: Not now. Tell me what to do!

EDNA: I'm not God!

JOE: Jeez, I wish I was a kid again and didn't have to think about the next minute.

EDNA: But you're not a kid and you do have to think about the next minute. You got two blondie kids sleeping in the next room. They need food and clothes. I'm not mentioning anything else—But we're stalled like a flivver in the snow. For five years I laid awake at night listening to my heart pound. For God's sake, do something, Joe, get wise. Maybe get your buddies together, maybe go on strike for better money. Poppa did it during the war and they won out. I'm turning into a sour old nag.

JOE: (defending himself) Strikes don't work!

EDNA: Who told you?

JOE: Besides that means not a nickel a week while we're out. Then when it's over they don't take you back.

EDNA: Suppose they don't! What's to lose?

JOE: Well, we're averaging six-seven dollars a week now.

EDNA: That just pays for the rent.

JOE: That is something, Edna.

EDNA: It isn't. They'll push you down to three and four a week before you know it. Then you'll say, "That's somethin'," too!

JOE: There's too many cabs on the street, that's the whole damn trouble.

EDNA: Let the company worry about that, you big fool! If their cabs didn't make a profit, they'd take them off the streets. Or maybe you think they're in business just to pay Joe Mitchell's rent!

JOE: You don't know a-b-c, Edna.

EDNA: I know this—your boss is making suckers outa you boys every minute. Yes, and suckers out of all the wives and the poor innocent kids who'll grow up with crooked spines and sick bones. Sure, I see it in the papers, how good orange juice is for kids. But damnit our kids get colds one on top of the other. They look like little ghosts. Betty never saw a grapefruit. I took her to the store last week and she pointed to a stack of grapefruits. "What's that!" she said. My God, Joe—the world is supposed to be for all of us.

JOE: You'll wake them up.

EDNA: I don't care, as long as I can maybe wake you up.

JOE: Don't insult me. One man can't make a strike.

EDNA: Who says one? You got hundreds in your rotten union!

JOE: The union ain't rotten.

EDNA: No? Then what are they doing? Collecting dues and patting your back?

JOE: They're making plans.

EDNA: What kind?

JOE: They don't tell us.

EDNA: It's too damn bad about you. They don't tell little Joey what's happening in his bitsie witsie union. What do you think it is—a ping pong game?

JOE: You know they're racketeers. The guys at the top would shoot you for a nickel.

EDNA: Why do you stand for that stuff?

JOE: Don't you wanna see me alive?

EDNA: *(after a deep pause)* No . . . I don't think I do, Joe. Not if you can lift a finger to do something about it, and don't. No, I don't care.

JOE: Honey, you don't understand what—

EDNA: And any other hackie that won't fight . . . let them all be ground to hamburger!

JOE: It's one thing to—

EDNA: Take your hand away! Only they don't grind me to little pieces! I got different plans. *(Starts to take off her apron.)*

JOE: Where are you going?

EDNA: None of your business.

JOE: What's up your sleeve?

EDNA: My arm'd be up my sleeve, darling, if I had a sleeve to wear.
   (Puts neatly folded apron on back of chair.)

JOE: Tell me!

EDNA: Tell you what?

JOE: Where are you going?

EDNA: Don't you remember my old boy friend?

JOE: Who?

EDNA: Bud Haas. He still has my picture in his watch. He earns a living.

JOE: What the hell are you talking about?

EDNA: I heard worse than I'm talking about.

JOE: Have you seen Bud since we got married?

EDNA: Maybe.

JOE: If I thought . . . *(He stands looking at her.)*

EDNA: See much? Listen, boy friend, if you think I won't do this it just means you can't see straight.

JOE: Stop talking bull!

EDNA: This isn't five years ago, Joe.

JOE: You mean you'd leave me and the kids?

EDNA: I'd leave *you* like a shot!

JOE: No. . . .

EDNA: Yes! *(JOE turns away, sitting in a chair with his back to her. Outside the lighted circle of the playing stage we hear the other seated members of the strike committee. "She will . . . she will . . . it happens that way," etc. This group should be used throughout for various comments, political, emotional and as general chorus. Whispering. . . . The fat boss now blows a heavy cloud of smoke into the scene.)*

JOE: *(finally)* Well, I guess I ain't got a leg to stand on.

EDNA: No?

JOE: *(suddenly mad)* No, you lousy tart, no! Get the hell out of here. Go pick up that bull-thrower on the corner and stop at some cushy hotel downtown. He's probably been coming here every morning and laying you while I hacked my guts out!

EDNA: You're crawling like a worm!

JOE: You'll be crawling in a minute.

EDNA: You don't scare me that much! *(Indicates a half inch on her finger.)*

JOE: This is what I slaved for!

EDNA: Tell it to your boss!

JOE: He don't give a damn for you or me!

EDNA: That's what I say.

JOE: Don't change the subject!

EDNA: This is the subject, the *exact subject!* Your boss makes this subject. I never saw him in my life, but he's putting ideas in my head a mile a minute. He's giving your kids that fancy disease called the rickets. He's making a jellyfish outa you and putting wrinkles in my face.

This is the subject every inch of the way! He's throwing me into Bud Haas' lap. When in hell will you get wise—

JOE: I'm not so dumb as you think! But you are talking like a red.

EDNA: I don't know what that means. But when a man knocks you down you get up and kiss his fist! You gutless piece of baloney.

JOE: One man can't—

EDNA: *(with great joy)* I don't say one man! I say a hundred, a thousand, a whole million, I say. But start in your own union. Get those hack boys together! Sweep out those racketeers like a pile of dirt! Stand up like men and fight for the crying kids and wives. God-damnit! I'm tired of slavery and sleepless nights.

JOE: *(with her)* Sure, sure! . . .

EDNA: Yes. Get brass toes on your shoes and know where to kick!

JOE: *(suddenly jumping up and kissing his wife full on the mouth)* Listen, Edna, I'm goin' down to 174th Street to look up Lefty Costello. Lefty was saying the other day . . . *(He suddenly stops)* How about this Haas guy?

EDNA: Get out of here!

JOE: I'll be back! *(Runs out. For a moment* EDNA *stands triumphant. There is a blackout and when the regular lights come up,* JOE MITCHELL *is concluding what he has been saying.)*

JOE: You guys know this stuff better than me. We gotta walk out!

(Abruptly he turns and goes back to his seat.)

BLACK OUT

II. LAB ASSISTANT EPISODE

Discovered: MILLER, *a lab assistant, looking around; and* FAYETTE, *an industrialist.*

FAYETTE: Like it?

MILLER: Very much. I've never seen an office like this outside the movies.

FAYETTE: Yes, I often wonder if interior decorators and bathroom fixture people don't get all their ideas from Hollywood. Our country's extraordinary that way. Soap, cosmetics, electric refrigerators—just let Mrs Consumer know they're used by the Crawfords and Garbos—more volume of sale than one plant can handle!

MILLER: I'm afraid it isn't that easy, Mr Fayette.

FAYETTE: No, you're right—gross exaggeration on my part. Competition is cutthroat today. Market's up flush against a stone wall. The astronomers had better hurry—open Mars to trade expansion.

MILLER: Or it will be just too bad!

FAYETTE: Cigar?

MILLER: Thank you, don't smoke.

FAYETTE: Drink?

MILLER: Ditto, Mr Fayette.

FAYETTE: I like sobriety in my workers . . . the trained ones, I mean. The pollacks and niggers, they're better drunk—keeps them out of mischief. Wondering why I had you come over?

MILLER: If you don't mind my saying—very much.

FAYETTE: *(patting him on the knee)* I like your work.

MILLER: Thanks.

FAYETTE: No reason why a talented young man like yourself shouldn't string along with us—a growing concern. Loyalty is well repaid in our organization. Did you see Siegfried this morning?

MILLER: He hasn't been in the laboratory all day.

FAYETTE: I told him yesterday to raise you twenty dollars a month. Starts this week.

MILLER: You don't know how happy my wife'll be.

FAYETTE: Oh, I can appreciate it. *(He laughs.)*

MILLER: Was that all, Mr Fayette?

FAYETTE: Yes, except that we're switching you to laboratory A tomorrow. Siegfried knows about it. That's why I had you in. The new work is very important. Siegfried recommended you very highly as a man to trust. You'll work directly under Dr Brenner. Make you happy?

MILLER: Very. He's an important chemist!

FAYETTE: *(leaning over seriously)* We think so, Miller. We think so to the extent of asking you to stay within the building throughout the time you work with him.

MILLER: You mean sleep and eat in?

FAYETTE: Yes. . . .

MILLER: It can be arranged.

FAYETTE: Fine. You'll go far, Miller.

MILLER: May I ask the nature of the new work?

FAYETTE: *(looking around first)* Poison gas. . . .

MILLER: Poison!

FAYETTE: Orders from above. I don't have to tell you from where. New type poison gas for modern warfare.

MILLER: I see.

FAYETTE: You didn't know a new war was that close, did you?

MILLER: I guess I didn't.

FAYETTE: I don't have to stress the importance of absolute secrecy.

MILLER: I understand!

FAYETTE: The world is an armed camp today. One match sets the whole world blazing in forty-eight hours. Uncle Sam won't be caught napping!

MILLER: *(addressing his pencil)* They say 12 million men were killed in that last one and 20 million more wounded or missing.

FAYETTE: That's not our worry. If big business went sentimental over human life there wouldn't be big business of any sort!

MILLER: My brother and two cousins went in the last one.

FAYETTE: They died in a good cause.

MILLER: My mother says "no!"

FAYETTE: She won't worry about you this time. You're too valuable behind the front.

MILLER: That's right.

FAYETTE: All right, Miller. See Siegfried for further orders.

MILLER: You should have seen my brother—he could ride a bike without hands. . . .

FAYETTE: You'd better move some clothes and shaving tools in tomorrow. Remember what I said—you're with a growing organization.

MILLER: He could run the hundred yards in 9:8 flat. . . .

FAYETTE: Who?

MILLER: My brother. He's in the Meuse-Argonne Cemetery. Mama went there in 1926. . . .

FAYETTE: Yes, those things stick. How's your handwriting, Miller, fairly legible?

MILLER: Fairly so.

FAYETTE: Once a week I'd like a little report from you.

MILLER: What sort of report?

FAYETTE: Just a few hundred words once a week on Dr Brenner's progress.

MILLER: Don't you think it might be better coming from the Doctor?

FAYETTE: I didn't ask you that.

MILLER: Sorry.

FAYETTE: I want to know what progress he's making, the reports to be purely confidential—between you and me.

MILLER: You mean I'm to watch him?

FAYETTE: Yes!

MILLER: I guess I can't do that. . . .

FAYETTE: Thirty a month raise . . .

MILLER: You said twenty. . . .

FAYETTE: Thirty!

MILLER: Guess I'm not built that way.

FAYETTE: Forty. . . .

MILLER: Spying's not in my line, Mr Fayette!

FAYETTE: You use ugly words, Mr Miller!

MILLER: For ugly activity? Yes!

FAYETTE: Think about it, Miller. Your chances are excellent. . . .

MILLER: No.

FAYETTE: You're doing something for your country. Assuring the United States that when those goddamn Japs start a ruckus we'll have offensive weapons to back us up! Don't you read your newspapers, Miller?

MILLER: Nothing but Andy Gump.

FAYETTE: If you were on the inside you'd know I'm talking cold sober truth! Now, I'm not asking you to make up your mind on the spot. Think about it over your lunch period.

MILLER: No.

FAYETTE: Made up your mind already?

MILLER: Afraid so.

FAYETTE: You understand the consequences?

MILLER: I lose my raise—

Simultaneously:
{
MILLER: And my job!
FAYETTE: And your job!
MILLER: You misunderstand—
}

MILLER: Rather dig ditches first!

FAYETTE: That's a big job for foreigners.

MILLER: But sneaking—and making poison gas— that's for Americans?

FAYETTE: It's up to you.

MILLER: My mind's made up.

FAYETTE: No hard feelings?

MILLER: Sure hard feelings! I'm not the civilized type, Mr Fayette. Nothing suave or sophisticated about me. Plenty of hard feelings! Enough to want to bust you and all your kind square in the mouth! (*Does exactly that.*)

BLACK OUT

III. THE YOUNG HACK AND HIS GIRL

Opens with girl and brother. FLORENCE *waiting for* SID *to take her to a dance.*

FLORENCE: I gotta right to have something out of life. I don't smoke, I don't drink. So if Sid wants to take me to a dance, I'll go. Maybe if you was in love you wouldn't talk so hard.

IRV: I'm saying it for your good.

FLORENCE: Don't be so good to me.

IRV: Mom's sick in bed and you'll be worryin' her to the grave. She don't want that boy hanging around the house and she don't want you meeting him in Crotona Park.

FLORENCE: I'll meet him anytime I like!

IRV: If you do, yours truly'll take care of it in his own way. With just one hand, too!

FLORENCE: Why are you all so set against him?

IRV: Mom told you ten times—it ain't him. It's that he ain't got nothing. Sure, we know he's serious, that he's stuck on you. But that don't cut no ice.

FLORENCE: Taxi drivers used to make good money.

IRV: Today they're makin' five and six dollars a week. Maybe you wanta raise a family on that. Then you'll be back here living with us again and I'll be supporting two families in one. Well . . . over my dead body.

FLORENCE: Irv, I don't care—I love him!

IRV: You're a little kid with half-baked ideas!

FLORENCE: I stand there behind the counter the whole day. I think about him—

IRV: If you thought more about Mom it would be better.

FLORENCE: Don't I take care of her every night when I come home? Don't I cook supper and iron your shirts and . . . you give me a pain in the neck, too. Don't try to shut me up! I bring a few dollars in the house, too. Don't you see I want something else out of life. Sure, I want romance, love, babies. I want everything in life I can get.

IRV: You take care of Mom and watch your step!

FLORENCE: And if I don't?

IRV: Yours truly'll watch it for you!

FLORENCE: You can talk that way to a girl. . . .

IRV: I'll talk that way to your boy friend, too, and it won't be with words! Florrie, if you had a pair of eyes you'd see it's for your own good we're talking. This ain't no time to get married. Maybe later—

FLORENCE: "Maybe Later" never comes for me, though. Why don't we send Mom to a hospital? She can die in peace there instead of looking at the clock on the mantelpiece all day.

IRV: That needs money. Which we don't have!

FLORENCE: Money, Money, Money!

IRV: Don't change the subject.

FLORENCE: This is the subject!

IRV: You gonna stop seeing him? (*She turns away*) Jesus, kiddie, I remember when you were a baby with curls down your back. Now I gotta stand here yellin' at you like this.

FLORENCE: I'll talk to him, Irv.

IRV: When?

FLORENCE: I asked him to come here tonight. We'll talk it over.

IRV: Don't get soft with him. Nowadays is no time to be soft. You gotta be hard as a rock or go under.

FLORENCE: I found that out. There's the bell. Take the egg off the stove I boiled for Mom. Leave us alone Irv. (SID *comes in—the two men look at each other for a second.* IRV *exits.*)

SID: *(enters)* Hello, Florrie.

FLORENCE: Hello, Honey. You're looking tired.

SID: Naw, I just need a shave.

FLORENCE: Well, draw your chair up to the fire and I'll ring for brandy and soda . . . like in the movies.

SID: If this was the movies I'd bring a big bunch of roses.

FLORENCE: How big?

SID: Fifty or sixty dozen—the kind with long, long stems—big as that. . . .

FLORENCE: You dope. . . .

SID: Your Paris gown is beautiful.

FLORENCE: *(acting grandly)* Yes, Percy, velvet panels are coming back again. Madame La Farge told me today that Queen Marie herself designed it.

SID: Gee . . . !

FLORENCE: Every princess in the Balkans is wearing one like this. *(Poses grandly)*

SID: Hold it. *(Does a nose camera—thumbing nose and imitating grinding of camera with other hand. Suddenly she falls out of the posture and swiftly goes to him, to embrace him, to kiss him with love. Finally)*

SID: You look tired, Florrie.

FLORENCE: Naw, I just need a shave. *(She laughs tremulously)*

SID: You worried about your mother?

FLORENCE: No.

SID: What's on your mind?

FLORENCE: The French and Indian War.

SID: What's on your mind?

FLORENCE: I got us on my mind, Sid. Night and day, Sid!

SID: I smacked a beer truck today. Did I get hell! I was driving along thinking of US, too. You don't have to say it—I know what's on your mind. I'm rat poison around here.

FLORENCE: Not to me. . . .

SID: I know to who . . . and I know why. I don't blame them. We're engaged now for three years. . . .

FLORENCE: That's a long time. . . .

SID: My brother Sam joined the navy this morning—get a break that way. They'll send him down to Cuba with the hootchy-kootchy girls. He don't know from nothing, that dumb basket ball player!

FLORENCE: Don't you do that.

SID: Don't you worry, I'm not the kind who runs away. But I'm so tired of being a dog, Baby, I could choke. I don't even have to ask what's going on in your mind. I know from the word go, 'cause I'm thinking the same things, too.

FLORENCE: It's yes or no—nothing in between.

SID: The answer is no—a big electric sign looking down on Broadway!

FLORENCE: We wanted to have kids. . . .

SID: But that sort of life ain't for the dogs which is us. Christ, Baby! I get like thunder in my chest when we're together. If we went off together I could maybe look the world straight in the face, spit in its eye like a man should do. God-damnit, it's trying to be a man on the earth. Two in life together.

FLORENCE: But something wants us to be lonely like that—crawling alone in the dark. Or they want us trapped.

SID: Sure, the big shot money men want us like that.

FLORENCE: Highly insulting us—

SID: Keeping us in the dark about what is wrong with us in the money sense. They got the power and mean to be damn sure they keep it. They know if they give in just an inch, all the dogs like us will be down on them together—an ocean knocking them to hell and back and each singing cuckoo with stars coming from their nose and ears. I'm not raving, Florrie—

FLORENCE: I know you're not, I know.

SID: I don't have the words to tell you what I feel. I never finished school. . . .

FLORENCE: I know. . . .

SID: But it's relative, like the professors say. We worked like hell to send him to college—my kid brother Sam, I mean—and look what he done—joined the navy! The damn fool don't see the cards is stacked for all of us. The money man dealing himself a hot royal flush. Then giving you and me a phony hand like a pair of tens or something. Then keep on losing the pots 'cause the cards is stacked against you. Then he says, what's the matter you can't win—no stuff on the ball, he says to you. And kids like my brother believe it 'cause they don't know better. For all their education, they don't know from nothing. But wait a minute! Don't he come around and say to you—this millionaire with a jazz band—listen Sam or Sid or what's-your-name, you're no good, but here's a chance. The whole world'll know who you are. Yes sir, he says, get up on that ship and fight those bastards who's making the world a lousy place to live in. The Japs, the Turks, the Greeks. Take this gun—kill the slobs like a real hero, he says, a real American. Be a hero! And the guy you're poking at? A real louse, just like you, 'cause they don't let him catch more than a pair of tens, too. On that foreign soil he's a guy like me and Sam, a guy who wants his baby like you and hot sun on his face! They'll teach Sam to point the guns the wrong way, that dumb basket ball player!

FLORENCE: I got a lump in my throat, Honey.

SID: You and me—we never even had a room to sit in somewhere.

FLORENCE: The park was nice . . .

SID: In winter? The hallways . . . I'm glad we never got together. This way we don't know what we missed.

FLORENCE: (in a burst) Sid, I'll go with you—we'll get a room somewhere.

SID: Naw . . . they're right. If we can't climb higher than this together—we better stay apart.

FLORENCE: I swear to God I wouldn't care.

SID: You would, you would—in a year, two years, you'd curse the day. I seen it happen.

FLORENCE: Oh, Sid. . . .

SID: Sure, I know. We got the blues, Babe—the 1935 blues. I'm talkin' this way 'cause I love you. If I didn't, I wouldn't care. . . .

FLORENCE: We'll work together, we'll—

SID: How about the backwash? Your family needs your nine bucks. My family—

FLORENCE: I don't care for them!

SID: You're making it up, Florrie. Little Florrie Canary in a cage.

FLORENCE: Don't make fun of me.

SID: I'm not, Baby.

FLORENCE: Yes, you're laughing at me.

SID: I'm not. (They stand looking at each other, unable to speak. Finally, he turns to a small portable phonograph and plays a cheap, sad, dance tune. He makes a motion with his hand; she comes to him. They begin to dance slowly. They hold each other tightly, almost as though they would merge into each other. The music stops, but the scratching record continues to the end of the scene. They stop dancing. He finally looses her clutch and seats her on the couch, where she sits, tense and expectant)

SID: Hello, Babe.

FLORENCE: Hello. (For a brief time they stand as though in a dream)

SID: (finally) Good-bye, Babe. (He waits for an answer, but she is silent. They look at each other)

SID: Did you ever see my Pat Rooney imitation? (He whistles "Rosy O'Grady" and soft-shoes to it. Stops. He asks)

SID: Don't you like it?

FLORENCE: (finally) No. (Buries her face in her hands. Suddenly he falls on his knees and buries his face in her lap.)

BLACK OUT

IV. LABOR SPY EPISODE

FATT: You don't know how we work for you. Shooting off your mouth won't help. Hell, don't you guys ever look at the records like me? Look in your own industry. See what happened when the hacks walked out in Philly three months ago! Where's Philly? A thousand miles away? An hour's ride on the train.

VOICE: Two hours!!

FATT: Two hours . . . what the hell's the difference. Let's hear from someone who's got the practical experience to back him up. Fellers, there's a man here who's seen the whole parade in Philly, walked out with his pals, got knocked down like the rest—and blacklisted after they went back. That's why he's here. He's got a mighty interestin' word to say. *(Announces)* Tom Clayton! *(As* CLAYTON *starts up from the audience,* FATT *gives him a hand which is sparsely followed in the audience.* CLAYTON *comes forward)* Fellers, this is a man with practical strike experience—Tom Clayton from little ole Philly.

CLAYTON: *(a thin, modest individual)* Fellers, I don't mind your booing. If I thought it would help us hacks get better living conditions, I'd let you walk all over me, cut me up to little pieces. I'm one of you myself. But what I wanna say is that Harry Fatt's right. I only been working here in the big town five weeks, but I know conditions just like the rest of you. You know how it is—don't take long to feel the sore spots, no matter where you park.

CLEAR VOICE: *(from audience)* Sit down!

CLAYTON: But Fatt's right. Our officers is right. The time ain't ripe. Like a fruit don't fall off the tree until it's ripe.

CLEAR VOICE: Sit down, you fruit!

FATT: *(on his feet)* Take care of him, boys.

VOICE: *(in audience, struggling)* No one takes care of me. *(Struggle in house and finally the owner of the voice runs up on stage, says to speaker)*

SAME VOICE: Where the hell did you pick up that name! Clayton! This rat's name is Clancy, from the old Clancys, way back! Fruit! I almost wet myself listening to that one!

FATT: *(gunman with him)* This ain't a barn! What the hell do you think you're doing here!

SAME VOICE: Exposing a rat!

FATT: You can't get away with this. Throw him the hell outa here.

VOICE: *(preparing to stand his ground)* Try it yourself. . . . When this bozo throws that slop around. You know who he is? That's a company spy.

FATT: Who the hell are you to make—

VOICE: I paid dues in this union for four years, that's who's me! I gotta right and this pussy-footed rat ain't coming in here with ideas like that. You know his record. Lemme say it out—

FATT: You'll prove all this or I'll bust you in every hack outfit in town!

VOICE: I gotta right. I gotta right. Looka *him*, he don't say boo!

CLAYTON: You're a liar and I never seen you before in my life!

VOICE: Boys, he spent two years in the coal fields breaking up any organization he touched. Fifty guys he put in jail. He's ranged up and down the east coast—shipping, textiles, steel—he's been in everything you can name. Right now—

CLAYTON: That's a lie!

VOICE: Right now he's working for that Bergman outfit on Columbus Circle who furnishes rats for any outfit in the country, before, during, and after strikes. *(The man who is the hero of the next episode goes down to his side with other committee men)*

CLAYTON: He's trying to break up the meeting, fellers!

VOICE: We won't search you for credentials. . . .

CLAYTON: I got nothing to hide. Your own secretary knows I'm straight.

VOICE: Sure. Boys, you know who this sonovabitch is?

CLAYTON: I never seen you before in my life!!

VOICE: Boys, I slept with him in the same bed sixteen years. HE'S MY OWN LOUSY BROTHER!!

FATT: *(after pause)* Is this true? *(No answer from* CLAYTON*)*

VOICE: *(to* CLAYTON*)* Scram, before I break your neck! *(*CLAYTON *scrams down center aisle,* VOICE *says, watching him)* Remember his map—he can't change that—Clancy! *(Standing in his place says)* Too bad you didn't know about this, Fatt! *(After a pause)* The Clancy family tree is bearing nuts! *(Standing isolated clear on the stage is the hero of the next episode.)*

B L A C K   O U T

V. I N T E R N E   E P I S O D E

Dr Barnes, an elderly distinguished man, is speaking on the telephone. He wears a white coat.

DR BARNES: No, I gave you my opinion twice. You outvoted me. You did this to Dr Benjamin yourself. That is why you can tell him yourself. *(Hangs up phone, angrily. As he is about to pour himself a drink from a bottle on the table, a knock is heard)*

BARNES: Who is it?

BENJAMIN: *(without)* Can I see you a minute, please?

BARNES: *(hiding the bottle)* Come in, Dr Benjamin, come in.

BENJAMIN: It's important—excuse me—they've got Leeds up there in my place—He's operating on Mrs Lewis—the hysterectomy—it's my job. I washed up, prepared . . . they told me at the last minute. I don't mind being replaced, Doctor, but Leeds is a damn fool! He shouldn't be permitted—

BARNES: *(dryly)* Leeds is the nephew of Senator Leeds.

BENJAMIN: He's incompetent as hell.

BARNES: *(obviously changing subject, picks up lab jar)* They're doing splendid work in brain surgery these days. This is a very fine specimen. . . .

BENJAMIN: I'm sorry, I thought you might be interested.

BARNES: *(still examining jar)* Well, I am, young man, I am! Only remember it's a charity case!

BENJAMIN: Of course. They wouldn't allow it for a second, otherwise.

BARNES: Her life is in danger?

BENJAMIN: Of course! You know how serious the case is!

BARNES: Turn your gimlet eyes elsewhere, Doctor. Jigging around like a cricket on a hot grill won't help. Doctors don't run these hospitals. He's the Senator's nephew and there he stays.

BENJAMIN: It's too bad.

BARNES: I'm not calling you down either. *(Plopping down jar suddenly)* Goddamnit, do you think it's my fault?

BENJAMIN: *(about to leave)* I know . . . I'm sorry.

BARNES: Just a minute. Sit down.

BENJAMIN: Sorry, I can't sit.

BARNES: Stand then!

BENJAMIN: *(sits)* Understand, Dr Barnes, I don't mind being replaced at the last minute this way, but . . . well, this flagrant bit of class distinction—because she's poor—

BARNES: Be careful of words like that—"class distinction." Don't belong here. Lots of energy, you brilliant young men, but idiots. Discretion! Ever hear that word?

BENJAMIN: Too radical?

BARNES: Precisely. And some day like in Germany, it might cost you your head.

BENJAMIN: Not to mention my job.

BARNES: So they told you?

BENJAMIN: Told me what?

BARNES: They're closing Ward C next month. I don't have to tell you the hospital isn't self-supporting. Until last year that board of trustees met deficits. . . . You can guess the rest. At a board meeting Tuesday, our fine feathered friends discovered they couldn't meet the last quarter's deficit—a neat little sum well over $100,000. If the hospital is to continue at all, its damn—

BENJAMIN: Necessary to close another charity ward!

BARNES: So they say. . . . *(A wait)*

BENJAMIN: But that's not all?

BARNES: *(ashamed)* Have to cut down on staff too. . . .

BENJAMIN: That's too bad. Does it touch me?

BARNES: Afraid it does.

BENJAMIN: But after all I'm top man here. I don't mean I'm better than others, but I've worked harder.

BARNES: And shown more promise. . . .

BENJAMIN: I always supposed they'd cut from the bottom first.

BARNES: Usually.

BENJAMIN: But in this case?

BARNES: Complications.

BENJAMIN: For instance? (BARNES *hesitant*)

BARNES: I like you, Benjamin. It's one ripping shame.

BENJAMIN: I'm no sensitive plant—what's the answer.

BARNES: An old disease, malignant, tumescent. We need an antitoxin for it.

BENJAMIN: I see.

BARNES: What?

BENJAMIN: I met that disease before—at Harvard first.

BARNES: You have seniority here, Benjamin.

BENJAMIN: But I'm a Jew! (BARNES *nods his head in agreement.* BENJAMIN *stands there a moment and blows his nose*)

BARNES: (*blows his nose*) Microbes!

BENJAMIN: Pressure from above?

BARNES: Don't think Kennedy and I didn't fight for you!

BENJAMIN: Such discrimination, with all those wealthy brother Jews on the board?

BARNES: I've remarked before—doesn't seem to be much difference between wealthy Jews and rich Gentiles. Cut from the same piece!

BENJAMIN: For myself I don't feel sorry. My parents gave up an awful lot to get me this far. They ran a little dry goods shop in the Bronx until their pitiful savings went in the crash last year. Poppa's peddling neckties. . . . Saul Ezra Benjamin—a man who's read Spinoza all his life.

BARNES: Doctors don't run medicine in this country. The men who know their jobs don't run anything here, except the motormen on trolley cars. I've seen medicine change—plenty—anesthesia, sterilization—but not because of

rich men—in *spite* of them! In a rich man's country your true self's buried deep. Microbes! Less. . . . Vermin! See this ankle, this delicate sensitive hand? Four hundred years to breed that. Out of a revolutionary background! Spirit of '76! Ancestors froze at Valley Forge! What's it all mean! Slops! The honest workers were sold out then, in '76. The Constitution's for rich men then and now. Slops! (*The phone rings*)

BARNES: (*angrily*) Dr Barnes. (*Listens a moment, looks at* BENJAMIN) I see. (*Hangs up, turns slowly to the younger Doctor*) They lost your patient. (BENJAMIN *stands solid with the shock of this news but finally hurls his operation gloves to the floor*)

BARNES: That's right . . . that's right. Young, hot, go and do it! I'm very ancient, fossil, but life's ahead of you, Dr Benjamin, and when you fire the first shot say, "This one's for old Doc Barnes!" Too much dignity—bullets. Don't shoot vermin! Step on them! If I didn't have an invalid daughter—

BARNES: (*goes back to his seat, blows his nose in silence*) I have said my piece, Benjamin.

BENJAMIN: Lots of things I wasn't certain of. Many things these radicals say . . . you don't believe theories until they happen to you.

BARNES: You lost a lot today, but you won a great point.

BENJAMIN: Yes, to know I'm right? To really begin believing in something? Not to say, "What a world!", but to say, "Change the world!" I wanted to go to Russia. Last week I was thinking about it—the wonderful opportunity to do good work in their socialized medicine—

BARNES: Beautiful, beautiful!

BENJAMIN: To be able to work—

BARNES: Why don't you go? I might be able—

BENJAMIN: Nothing's nearer what I'd like to do!

BARNES: Do it!

BENJAMIN: No! Our work's here—America! I'm scared. . . . What future's ahead, I don't know. Get some job to keep alive—maybe drive a cab—and study and work and learn my place—

BARNES: And step down hard!

BENJAMIN: Fight! Maybe get killed, but goddamn! We'll go ahead! (BENJAMIN *stands with clenched fist raised high*)

B L A C K   O U T

VI. S T R I K E   E P I S O D E

AGATE: *Ladies and Gentlemen,* and don't let anyone tell you we ain't got some ladies in this sea of upturned faces! Only they're wearin' pants. Well, maybe I don't know a thing; maybe I fell outa the cradle when I was a kid and ain't been right since—you can't tell!

VOICE: Sit down, cockeye!

AGATE: Who's paying you for those remarks, Buddy?—Moscow Gold? Maybe I got a *glass eye,* but it come from working in a factory at the age of eleven. They hooked it out because they didn't have a shield on the works. But I wear it like a medal 'cause it tells the world where I belong—deep down in the working class! We had delegates in the union there—all kinds of secretaries and treasurers . . . walkin' delegates, but not with blisters on their feet! Oh no! On their fat little ass from sitting on cushions and raking in mazuma. (SECRETARY *and* GUNMAN *remonstrate in words and actions here*) Sit down, boys. I'm just sayin' that about unions in general. I know it ain't true here! Why no, our officers is all aces. Why, I seen our own secretary Fatt walk outa his way not to step on a cockroach. No boys, don't think—

FATT: *(breaking in)* You're out of order!

AGATE: *(to audience)* Am I outa order?

ALL: No, no. Speak. Go on, etc.

AGATE: Yes, our officers is all aces. But I'm a member here—and no experience in Philly either! Today I couldn't wear my union button. The damnedest thing happened. When I take the old coat off the wall, I see she's smoking. I'm a sonovagun if the old union button isn't on

fire! Yep, the old celluloid was makin' the most god-awful stink: the landlady come up and give me hell! You know what happened? That old union button just blushed itself to death! Ashamed! Can you beat it?

FATT: Sit down, Keller! Nobody's interested!

AGATE: Yes they are!

GUNMAN: Sit down like he tells you!

AGATE: *(continuing to audience)* And when I finish—*(His speech is broken by* FATT *and* GUNMAN *who physically handle him. He breaks away and gets to other side of stage. The two are about to make for him when some of the committee men come forward and get in between the struggling parties.* AGATE'S *shirt has been torn)*

AGATE: *(to audience)* What's the answer, boys? The answer is, if we're reds because we wanna strike, then we take over their salute too! Know how they do it? *(Makes Communist salute)* What is it? An uppercut! The good old uppercut to the chin! Hell, some of us boys ain't even got a shirt to our backs. What's the boss class tryin' to do—make a nudist colony outa us? *(The audience laughs and suddenly* AGATE *comes to the middle of the stage so that the other cabmen back him up in a strong clump)*

AGATE: Don't laugh! Nothing's funny! This is your life and mine! It's skull and bones every incha the road! Christ, we're dyin' by inches! For what? For the debutant-ees to have their sweet comin' out parties in the Ritz! Poppa's got a daughter she's gotta get her picture in the papers. Christ, they make 'em with our blood. Joe said it. Slow death or fight. It's war! *(Throughout this whole speech* AGATE *is backed up by the other six workers, so that from their activity it is plain that the whole group of them are saying these things. Several of them may take alternate lines out of this long last speech)*

You Edna, God love your mouth! Sid and Florrie, the other boys, old Doc Barnes—fight with us for right! It's war! Working class, unite and fight! Tear down the slaughter house of our old lives! Let freedom really ring.

These slick slobs stand here telling us about bogeymen. That's a new one for the kids—the reds is bogeymen! But the man who got me food in 1932, he called me Comrade! The one who picked me up where I bled—he called me Comrade too! What are we waiting for. . . . Don't wait for Lefty! He might never come. Every minute—*(This is broken into by a man who has dashed up the center aisle from the back of the house. He runs up on stage, says)*

MAN: Boys, they just found Lefty!

OTHERS: What? What? What?

SOME: Shhh. . . . Shhh. . . .

MAN: They found Lefty. . . .

AGATE: Where?

MAN: Behind the car barns with a bullet in his head!

AGATE: *(crying)* Hear it, boys, hear it? Hell, listen to me! Coast to coast! HELLO AMERICA! HELLO. WE'RE STORMBIRDS OF THE WORKING-CLASS. WORKERS OF THE WORLD. . . . OUR BONES AND BLOOD! And when we die they'll know what we did to make a new world! Christ, cut us up to little pieces. We'll die for what is right! put fruit trees where our ashes are!

(To audience) Well, what's the answer?

ALL: STRIKE!

AGATE: LOUDER!

ALL: STRIKE!

AGATE *and* OTHERS *on Stage:* AGAIN!

ALL: STRIKE, STRIKE, STRIKE!!!

CURTAIN

MULATTO (1935)

My old man died in a fine big house.
My ma died in a shack.
I wonder where I'm going to die,
Being neither white nor black?

This last stanza of Langston Hughes's poem "Cross" (1924) foreshadows one of the central tensions of *Mulatto,* which in 1935 earned the distinction of being the longest-running Broadway play ever written by an African American. Yet unlike the vast majority of playwrights in *American Drama: Colonial to Contemporary,* Hughes (1902–1967) was not known primarily as a dramatist, but as a poet, essayist, journalist, novelist, and central figure in the **Harlem Renaissance** of the 1920s. During this period, Harlem became an important site for African-American writers and intellectuals who together contributed substantially to modern American culture in general and to literary **modernism** in particular. Hughes's contributions to both were enormous.

As he recalls in *The Big Sea* (1940), one of Hughes's two volumes of autobiography, the 1920s marked a period in which "every season there was at least one hit play on Broadway acted by a Negro cast. And when books by Negro authors were being published with greater frequency and much more publicity than ever before or since. . . . It was the period when the Negro was in vogue." With this wave of interest in African-American culture came the rise of such performers as Paul Robeson, Bessie Smith, Ethel Waters, Josephine Baker, and Rose McLendon (who played Cora in the original production of *Mulatto*); of such writers as Claude McKay and Alain Locke, poet Countée Cullen, novelists Zora Neale Hurston, Nella Larsen, Jean Toomer, and Jessie Fauset; and of such publications as *The Messenger* and *Fire* (edited by Wallace Thurman and

which Hughes and Hurston, among others, helped cofound). In a moment of exuberance, Helga Crane, the mulatto protagonist of Larsen's *Quicksand* (1928), describes Harlem in the 1920s as a "continuously gorgeous panorama" that "fascinated" and "thrilled" her. Like "thousands of other Harlem dwellers, she patronized its shops, its theatres, its art galleries, and its restaurants, and read its papers. . . . For her this Harlem was enough." Sadly, it was not enough for long, as Larsen's protagonist suffers from psychological conflicts much like those afflicting the mulatto in Hughes's "Cross." Similarly, this moment of cultural ascendancy for African Americans could not survive for long. As Hughes postulates in his autobiography, the Stock Market crash of 1929 formed one of several causes for the eventual decline of the Harlem that Helga Crane found so enthralling. Hughes's distinguished career, however, flourished long after the 1920s, continuing until his death in 1967.

James Mercer Langston Hughes was born in 1902 in Joplin, Missouri, to James and Carrie Langston Hughes, a couple frequently gone while he was a toddler, thus necessitating his movement among relatives. His father, attempting to reconcile with his wife, brought the family to Mexico City where he was working but, after surviving a severe earthquake in 1907, Hughes's mother returned to America bringing her young son with her. Hughes lived with his grandmother in Lawrence, Kansas, while his mother worked in Topeka, and, after his grandmother's death, he moved in for a time with friends of the family. In 1915, remarried and relocated in Lincoln, Illinois, his mother sent for him, and while completing the eighth grade there he was elected class poet. In 1916, both Hughes and his mother followed her second husband to a new job in Cleveland, where at Central High School Hughes's interest in poetry grew. He read Walt Whitman and Carl Sandburg, edited the Central High *Monthly*, and there began to publish his poems and short fiction. Hughes spent the summer of 1919 with his father in Mexico and, upon reentering the United States in September, Hughes confronted what biographer Arnold Rampersad describes as a "nation inflamed by racial strife." Among other factors, inflated postwar expectations and large-scale migration, especially to urban areas, sparked rioting and violence across the country: Thirty-eight blacks died in Chicago during a July riot, 200 in Arkansas; blood was shed in over two dozen American cities. As the young writer prepared for his senior year in high school, a number of factors that would surface in much of his later work began to coalesce: acute loneliness, a sense of homelessness, the experience of racial tension, and a deep-felt concern over the present dilemmas and the future lives of African Americans in this country.

Hughes returned to Mexico in 1920 and placed his first poem in the *Crisis*, published by the NAACP and edited by W. E. B. DuBois, in 1921. After spending a year at Columbia University, Hughes worked several different jobs before going to sea in 1923 and living for brief periods in Africa, France, and Italy. He returned to New York in 1924, moved shortly thereafter to Washington, DC, and later enrolled at Lincoln University on a scholarship, graduating in 1929. But long before his graduation Hughes established himself as a poet with the publication of two books of poems, *The Weary Blues* (1926) and *Fine Clothes to the Jew* (1927). Publishing his first novel, *Not Without Laughter*, in 1930, he was well on his way to a prolific career before reaching his thirtieth birthday. More than this, as Amiri Baraka maintains in his "Foreword" to a reprinting of *The Big Sea*, Hughes's 1926 essay "The Negro Artist and the Racial Mountain" amounts to a "manifesto" of the Harlem Renaissance, "critical to our understanding of the social, aesthetic and class-conscious development of black literature." Published in the *Nation*, "The Negro Artist and the Racial Mountain" identifies for Baraka and the **Black Arts Movement** that followed in the 1960s several formidable obstacles to

the advancement of African-American art: "the urge within the race toward whiteness, the desire to pour racial individuality into the mold of American standardization, and to be as little Negro and as much American as possible." Hughes indicts the black middle class as especially culpable in teaching its children to see beauty through the mediating "pattern" of Caucasian values, an allegation and tension prominent not only in Hughes's work, but in such plays of Baraka's as *Dutchman* (1964), reprinted in this volume, and *The Slave* (1964) as well.

Yet in the same essay, these obstacles notwithstanding, Hughes recognizes the emergence of "an honest American Negro literature" and music, declaring jazz, a strong influence on his poetry, one of the "inherent expressions of Negro life in America." "Now," Hughes says, "I await the rise of the Negro theatre." "Await" here should not suggest that he sat idly by while others created such a theatre, for he also made significant contributions both to the New York theatre and to regional theatres. He founded, for example, three dramatic groups for the production of African-American drama: the Suitcase Theatre in Harlem (1938), the Negro Art Theatre in Los Angeles (1939), and the Skyloft Players in Chicago (1949). The Suitcase Theatre, it should be added, was also dedicated to advancing the cause of workers, as was the case with much Depression-era theatre, and was opened as a branch of the International Workers Order. Hughes's short play *Don't You Want to Be Free?*, a kind of **agitprop** play enlivened with elements of blues and Negro spirituals that was often compared to Clifford Odets's *Waiting for Lefty*, opened there in April 1938. Playing only three times a week, it ran some 135 performances. Of the nine plays Hughes saw through to professional production, however, *Mulatto* and *Simply Heavenly* (1957), a comedy set in Harlem and based on the life of a character about whom Hughes had written in other texts, were clearly the most successful. In addition to these, he also wrote musicals, a movie script, and a radio drama.

Don't You Want to Be Free? provides a sharp contrast to *Mulatto:* While the former moves from the era of slavery to the modern city, the latter is set in a rural Georgia reminiscent of the antebellum South; while the former culminates with blacks and whites, cast and audience members, joining hands to "fight, fight, fight" together to "lead the workers toward the light," the latter underscores racial hatred and division; while the former ends with reconciliation, the latter closes with madness and death. Such a comparison also reveals Hughes's adeptness both at drawing urban scenes and at appropriating from folk customs and regional dialects of the American South. Most important, he clearly intended for *Mulatto,* as its subtitle *A Tragedy of the Deep South* implies, to constitute a serious, even poetic representation of the oppression of blacks in contemporary America. His disappointment, therefore, seems hardly surprising when he learned that the Broadway production in 1935 over which he had no legal control included several key revisions of his text, making the play more melodramatic and sensational (for example, Sallie Lewis, who appears only in the first act of the text, reappears later as a rape victim). In fact, the original text printed here was first published nearly 30 years after the Broadway production in *Five Plays by Langston Hughes* (1963). This is not to suggest, as Webster Smalley contends, that *Mulatto* does not contain elements of melodrama or traces of the kind of exaggerated oppositions that obtain in many political plays of the 1930s. Rather, this version of *Mulatto*—Hughes's original version—is a different play from the one Broadway audiences viewed in 1935.

Robert "Bert" Lewis in *Mulatto* is more complicated, more sympathetic, than the stereotypical villains in melodramas like Dion Boucicault's *The Octoroon;* and, indeed, the figure of the mulatto appears frequently in modern American literature and drama: in Gertrude Stein's "Melanctha" from *Three Lives* (1909), Paul Green's Pulitzer Prize–winning drama *In Abraham's Bosom* (1926), and Nella Larsen's *Quicksand* and *Passing* (1929), for instance. Like Stein's Melanctha, who could be so

"awful blue" that her friend Rose Johnson feared she might kill herself, Bert in *Mulatto* also suffers emotionally. His seething anger and ambitions for the future will not allow him to return to the social and professional "place" reserved for blacks in Georgia, yet the institutionalized racism represented by his white father, Colonel Norwood, will not allow Bert the privileges he feels are owed him. Bert also wants Norwood to recognize him as his son, a wish which Norwood's own prejudice will not allow him to grant. So, as is often the case in tragic drama, father and son come into conflict; death and madness are the seemingly inevitable result.

Although Broadway audiences supported *Mulatto* at the box office, many reviewers were not so generous. And more recent critics, even those generally admiring of Hughes's work, like Darwin Turner, tend to regard *Mulatto* as a kind of flawed dramatic experiment, the result of a young playwright's inexperience (Hughes actually wrote the play in 1930). Such aesthetic considerations, like those in regard to Hughes's representation of the South, his use of the mulatto figure, and the development of Cora Lewis's madness, might constitute a starting point for reflection on the tragic and/or melodramatic dimensions of *Mulatto.*

WORKS CONSULTED

Hughes, Langston. *The Big Sea: An Autobiography* (1940). Rpt. New York: Thunder's Mouth Press, 1986.

———. *Five Plays by Langston Hughes,* Ed. Webster Smalley. Bloomington: Indiana University Press, 1963.

———. "The Negro Artist and the Racial Mountain." *Nation,* 122 (June 23, 1926): 692–694.

Larsen, Nella. *An Intimation of Things Distant: The Collected Fiction of Nella Larsen,* ed. Charles R. Larson. New York: Anchor Books, 1992.

Rampersad, Arnold. *The Life of Langston Hughes.* 2 vols. New York: Oxford University Press, 1986.

Turner, Darwin T. "Langston Hughes as Playwright." *CLA Journal,* 11 (1968): 297–309.

CHARACTERS

COLONEL THOMAS NORWOOD . . . . Plantation owner, a still vigorous man of about sixty, nervous, refined, quick-tempered, and commanding; a widower who is the father of four living mulatto children by his Negro house-keeper

CORA LEWIS . . . . A brown woman in her forties who has kept the house and been the mistress of COLONEL NORWOOD for some thirty years

WILLIAM LEWIS . . . . The oldest son of CORA LEWIS and the COLONEL; a fat, easy-going, soft-looking mulatto of twenty-eight; married

SALLIE LEWIS . . . . The seventeen-year-old daughter, very light with sandy hair and freckles, who could pass for white

ROBERT LEWIS . . . . Eighteen, the youngest boy; strong and well-built; a light mulatto with ivory-yellow skin and proud thin features like his father's; as tall as the COLONEL, with the same gray-blue eyes, but with curly black hair instead of brown; of a fiery, impetuous temper—immature and willful—resenting his blood and the circumstances of his birth

FRED HIGGINS . . . . A close friend of COLONEL NORWOOD; a county politician; fat and elderly, conventionally Southern

SAM . . . . An old Negro retainer, a personal servant of the COLONEL

BILLY . . . . The small son of WILLIAM LEWIS; a chubby brown kid about five

TALBOT . . . . The overseer

MOSE . . . . An elderly Negro, chauffeur for FRED HIGGINS

A STOREKEEPER

AN UNDERTAKER

UNDERTAKER'S HELPER . . . . Voice off-stage only

THE MOB

ACT ONE

TIME: *An afternoon in early fall.*

THE SETTING: *The living room of the Big House on a plantation in Georgia. Rear center of the room, a vestibule with double doors leading to the porch; at* each side of the doors, a large window with lace curtains and green shades; at left a broad flight of stairs leading to the second floor; near the stairs, downstage, a doorway leading to the dining room and kitchen; opposite, at right of stage, a door to the library. The room is furnished in the long out-dated horsehair and walnut style of the nineties; a crystal *chandelier, a large old-fashioned rug, a marble-topped table, upholstered chairs. At the right there is a small cabinet. It is a very clean, but somewhat shabby and rather depressing room, dominated by a large oil painting of* NORWOOD'S *wife of his youth on the center wall. The windows are raised. The afternoon sunlight streams in.*

ACTION: *As the curtain rises, the stage is empty. The door at the right opens and* COLONEL NORWOOD *enters, crossing the stage toward the stairs, his watch in his hand. Looking up, he shouts:*

NORWOOD: Cora! Oh, Cora!

CORA: *(heard above)* Yes, sir, Colonel Tom.

NORWOOD: I want to know if that child of yours means to leave here this afternoon?

CORA: *(at head of steps now)* Yes, sir, she's goin' directly. I's gettin' her ready now, packin' up an' all. 'Course, she wants to tell you goodbye 'fore she leaves.

NORWOOD: Well, send her down here. Who's going to drive her to the railroad? The train leaves at three—and it's after two now. You ought to know you can't drive ten miles in no time.

CORA: *(above)* Her brother's gonna drive her. Bert. He ought to be back here most any time now with the Ford.

NORWOOD: *(stopping on his way back to the library)* Ought to be *back* here? Where's he gone?

CORA: *(coming downstairs nervously)* Why, he driv in town 'fore noon, Colonel Tom. Said he were lookin' for some tubes or somethin' 'nother by de mornin' mail for de radio he's been riggin' up out in de shed.

NORWOOD: Who gave him permission to be driving off in the middle of the morning? I bought that Ford to be used when I gave orders for it to be used, not . . .

CORA: Yes, sir, Colonel Tom, but . . .

NORWOOD: But what? *(Pausing. Then deliberately)* Cora, if you want that hardheaded yellow son of yours to get along around here, he'd better listen to me. He's no more than any other black buck on this plantation—due to work like the

rest of 'em. I don't take such a performance from nobody under me—driving off in the middle of the day to town, after I've told him to bend his back in that cotton. How's Talbot going to keep the rest of those darkies working right if that boy's allowed to set that kind of an example? Just because Bert's your son, and I've been damn fool enough to send him off to school for five or six years, he thinks he has a right to privileges, acting as if he owned this place since he's been back here this summer.

CORA: But, Colonel Tom . . .

NORWOOD: Yes, I know what you're going to say. I don't give a damn about him! There's no nigger-child of mine, yours, ours—no darkie—going to disobey me. I put him in that field to work, and he'll stay on this plantation till I get ready to let him go. I'll tell Talbot to use the whip on him, too, if he needs it. If it hadn't been that he's yours, he'd-a had a taste of it the other day. Talbot's a damn good overseer, and no saucy, lazy Nigras stay on this plantation and get away with it. *(To* CORA*)* Go on back upstairs and see about getting Sallie out of here. Another word from you and I won't send your *(Sarcastically)* pretty little half-white daughter anywhere, either. Schools for darkies! Huh! If you take that boy of yours for an example, they do 'em more harm than good. He's learned nothing in college but impudence, and he'll stay here on this place and work for me awhile before he gets back to any more schools. *(He starts across the room)*

CORA: Yes, sir, Colonel Tom. *(Hesitating)* But he's just young, sir. And he was mighty broke up when you said last week he couldn't go back to de campus. *(*COLONEL NORWOOD *turns and looks at* CORA *commandingly. Understanding, she murmurs)* Yes, sir. *(She starts upstairs, but turns back)* Can't I run and fix you a cool drink, Colonel Tom?

NORWOOD: No, damn you! Sam'll do it.

CORA: *(sweetly)* Go set down in de cool, then, Colonel. 'Taint good for you to be going' on this way in de heat. I'll talk to Robert maself soon's he comes in. He don't mean nothing—just smart and young and kinder careless, Colonel Tom, like ma mother said you used to be when you was eighteen.

NORWOOD: Get on upstairs, Cora. Do I have to speak again? Get on! (*He pulls the cord of the servants' bell*)

CORA: (*on the steps*) Does you still be in the mind to tell Sallie goodbye?

NORWOOD: Send her down here as I told you. (*Impatiently*) Where's Sam? Send him here first. (*Fuming*) Looks like he takes his time to answer that bell. You colored folks are running the house to suit yourself nowadays.

CORA: (*coming downstairs again and going toward door under the steps*) I'll get Sam for you. (CORA *exits left.* NORWOOD *paces nervously across the floor. Goes to the window and looks out down the road. Takes a cigar from his pocket, sits in a chair with it unlighted, scowling. Rises, goes toward servants' bell and rings it again violently as* SAM *enters, out of breath.*)

NORWOOD: What the hell kind of a tortoise race is this? I suppose you were out in the sun somewhere sleeping?

SAM: No, sah, Colonel Norwood. Just tryin' to get Miss Sallie's valises down to de yard so's we can put 'em in de Ford, sah.

NORWOOD: (*out of patience*) Huh! Darkies waiting on darkies! I can't get service in my own house. Very well. (*Loudly*) Bring me some whiskey and soda, and ice in a glass. Is that damn Frigidaire working right? Or is Livonia still too thick-headed to know how to run it? Any ice cubes in the thing?

SAM: Yes, sah, Colonel, yes, sah. (*Backing toward door left*) 'Scuse me, please sah, but (*as* NORWOOD *turns toward library*) Cora say for me to ask you is it all right to bring that big old trunk what you give Sallie down by de front steps. We ain't been able to tote it down them narrer little back steps, sah. Cora say, can we bring it down de front way through here?

NORWOOD: No other way? (SAM *shakes his head*) Then pack it on through to the back, quick. Don't let me catch you carrying any of Sallie's

baggage out of that front door here. You-all'll be wanting to go in and out the front way next. (*Turning away, complaining to himself*) Darkies have been getting mighty fresh in this part of the country since the war. The damn Germans should've . . . (*To* SAM) Don't take that trunk out that front door.

SAM: (*evilly, in a cunning voice*) I's seen Robert usin' de front door—when you ain't here, and he comes up from de cabin to see his mammy. (SALLIE, *the daughter, appears at the top of the stairs, but hesitates about coming down*)

NORWOOD: Oh, you have, have you? Let me catch him and I'll break his young neck for him. (*Yelling at* SAM) Didn't I tell you some whiskey and soda an hour ago?

(SAM *exits left.* SALLIE *comes shyly down the stairs and approaches her father. She is dressed in a little country-style coat-suit ready for traveling. Her features are Negroid, although her skin is very fair.* COLONEL NORWOOD *gazes down at her without saying a word as she comes meekly toward him, half-frightened.*)

SALLIE: I just wanted to tell you goodbye, Colonel Norwood, and thank you for letting me go back to school another year, and for letting me work here in the house all summer where mama is. (NORWOOD *says nothing. The girl continues in a strained voice as if making a speech*) You mighty nice to us colored folks certainly, and mama says you the best white man in Georgia. (*Still* NORWOOD *says nothing. The girl continues*) You been mighty nice to your—I mean to us colored children, letting my sister and me go off to school. The principal says I'm doing pretty well and next year I can go to Normal and learn to be a teacher. (*Raising her eyes*) You reckon I can, Colonel Tom?

NORWOOD: Stand up straight and let me see how you look. (*Backing away*) Hum-m-m! Getting kinder grown, ain't you? Do they teach you in that school to have good manners, and not be afraid of work, *and to respect white folks?*

SALLIE: Yes, sir, I been taking up cooking and sewing, too.

NORWOOD: Well, that's good. As I recall it, that school turned your sister out a right smart cook. Cora tells me she's got a good job in some big hotel in Chicago. I'm thinking about you going on up North there with her in a year or two. You're getting too old to be around here, and too womanish. *(He puts his hands on her arms as if feeling her flesh)*

SALLIE: *(drawing back slightly)* But I want to live down here with mama. I want to teach school in that there empty school house by the Cross Roads what hasn't had a teacher for five years. *(SAM has been standing with the door cracked, overhearing the conversation. He enters with the drink and places it on the table, right. NORWOOD sits down, leaving the girl standing, as SAM pours out a drink.)*

NORWOOD: Don't get that into your head, now. There's been no teacher there for years—and there won't be any teacher there, either. Cotton teaches these pickaninnies enough around here. Some of 'em's too smart as it is. The only reason I did have a teacher there once was to get you young ones o' Cora's educated. I gave you all a chance and I hope you appreciate it. *(He takes a long drink)* Don't know why I did it. No other white man in these parts ever did it, as I know of. *(To SAM)* Get out of here! *(SAM exits left)* Guess I couldn't stand to see Cora's kids working around here dumb as the rest of these no good darkies—need a dozen of 'em to chop one row of cotton, or to keep a house clean. Or maybe I didn't want to see Talbot eyeing you gals. *(Taking another drink)* Anyhow, I'm glad you and Bertha turned out right well. Yes, hum-m-m! *(Straightening up)* You know I tried to do something for those brothers of yours, too, but William's stupid as an ox—good for work, though—and that Robert's just an impudent, hardheaded, yellow young fool. I'm gonna break his damn neck for him if he don't watch out. Or else put Talbot on him.

SALLIE: *(suddenly frightened)* Please, sir, don't put the overseer on Bert, Colonel Tom. He was the smartest boy at school, Bert was. On the football team, too. Please, sir, Colonel Tom. Let brother work here in the house, or somewhere else where Talbot can't mistreat him. He ain't used . . .

NORWOOD: *(rising)* Telling me what to do, heh? *(Staring at her sternly)* I'll use the back of my hand across your face if you don't hush. *(He takes another drink. The noise of a Ford is heard outside)* That's Bert now, I reckon. He's to take you to the railroad line, and while you're riding with him, you better put some sense into his head. And tell him I want to see him as soon as he gets back here. *(CORA enters left with a bundle and an umbrella. SAM and WILLIAM come downstairs with a big square trunk, and exit hurriedly, left)*

SALLIE: Yes, sir, I'll tell him.

CORA: Colonel Tom, Sallie ain't got much time now. *(To the girl)* Come on, chile. Bert's here. Yo' big brother and Sam and Livonia and everybody's all waiting at de back door to say goodbye. And your baggage is being packed in. *(Noise of another car is heard outside)* Who else is that there coming up de drive? *(CORA looks out the window)* Mr Higgins' car, Colonel Tom. Reckon he's coming to see you . . . Hurry up out o' this front room, Sallie. Here, take these things of your'n *(Hands her the bundle and parasol)* while I opens de door for Mr Higgins. *(In a whisper)* Hurry up, chile! Get out! *(NORWOOD turns toward the front door as CORA goes to open it)*

SALLIE: *(shyly to her father)* Goodbye, Colonel Tom.

NORWOOD: *(his eyes on the front door, scarcely noticing the departing SALLIE, he motions)* Yes, yes, goodbye! Get on now! *(CORA opens the front door as her daughter exits left)* Well, well! Howdy do, Fred. Come in, come in! *(CORA holds the outer door of the vestibule wide as FRED HIGGINS enters with rheumatic dignity, supported on the arm of his chauffeur, MOSE, a very black Negro in a slouchy uniform. CORA closes the door and exits left hurriedly, following SALLIE)*

NORWOOD: *(smiling)* How's the rheumatiz today? Women or licker or heat must've made it worse—from the looks of your speed!

HIGGINS: *(testily, sitting down puffing and blowing in a big chair)* I'm in no mood for fooling, Tom, not now. *(To* MOSE*)* All right. *(The* CHAUFFEUR *exits front.* HIGGINS *continues angrily)* Norwood, that damned yellow nigger buck of yours that drives that new Ford tried his best just now to push my car off the road, then got in front of me and blew dust in my face for the last mile coming down to your gate, trying to beat me in here—which he did. Such a deliberate piece of impudence I don't know if I've ever seen out of a nigger before in all the sixty years I've lived in this county. *(The noise of the Ford is heard going out the drive, and the cries of the* NEGROES *shouting farewells to* SALLIE. HIGGINS *listens indignantly)* What kind of crazy coons have you got on your place, anyhow? Sounds like a black Baptist picnic to me. *(Pointing to the window with his cane)* Tom, listen to that.

NORWOOD: *(flushing)* I apologize to you, Fred, for each and every one of my darkies. *(*SAM *enters with more ice and another glass)* Permit me to offer you a drink. I realize I've got to tighten down here.

HIGGINS: Mose tells me that was Cora's boy in that Ford—and that young black fool is what I was coming here to talk to you about today. That boy! He's not gonna be around here long—not the way he's acting. The white folks in town'll see to that. Knowing he's one of your yard niggers, Norwood, I thought I ought to come and tell you. The white folks at the Junction aren't intending to put up with him much longer. And I don't know what good the jail would do him once he got in there.

NORWOOD: *(tensely)* What do you mean, Fred—jail? Don't I always take care of the folks on my plantation without any help from the Junction's police force? Talbot can do more with an unruly black buck than your marshal.

HIGGINS: Warn't lookin' at it that way, Tom. I was thinking how weak the doors to that jail is. They've broke 'em down and lynched four niggers to my memory since it's been built. After what happened this morning, you better keep that yellow young fool out o' town from now on. It might not be safe for him around there—today, nor no other time.

NORWOOD: What the hell? *(Perturbed)* He went in just now to take his sister to the depot. Damn it, I hope no ruffians'll break up my new Ford. What was it, Fred, about this morning?

HIGGINS: You haven't heard? Why, it's all over town already. He sassed out Miss Gray in the post office over a box of radio tubes that come by mail.

NORWOOD: He did, heh?

HIGGINS: Seems like the stuff was sent C. O. D. and got here all smashed up, so he wouldn't take it. Paid his money first before he saw the box was broke. Then wanted the money order back. Seems like the post office can't give money orders back—rule against it. Your nigger started to argue, and the girl at the window—Miss Gray—got scared and yelled for some of the mail clerks. They threw Bert out of the office, that's all. But that's enough. Lucky nothing more didn't happen. *(Indignantly)* That Bert needs a damn good beating—talking back to a white woman—and I'd like to give it to him myself, the way he kicked the dust up in my eyes all the way down the road coming out here. He was mad, I reckon. That's one yellow buck don't know his place, Tom, and it's your fault he don't—sending 'em off to be educated.

NORWOOD: Well, by God, I'll show him. I wish I'd have known it before he left here just now.

HIGGINS: Well, he's sure got mighty aggravating ways for a buck his color to have. Drives down the main street and don't stop for nobody, white or black. Comes in my store and if he ain't waited on as quick as the white folks are, he walks out and tells the clerk his money's as good as a white man's any day. Said last week standing out on my store front that he wasn't *all* nigger no how; said his name was Norwood—not Lewis, like the rest of his family—and part of your plantation here would be his when you passed out—and all that kind of stuff, boasting to the walleyed coons listening to him.

NORWOOD: *(astounded)* Well, I'll be damned!

HIGGINS: Now, Tom, you know that don't go 'round these parts 'o Georgia, nor nowhere else in the South. A darkie's got to keep in his place down here. Ruinous to other niggers hearing that talk, too. All this postwar propaganda on the radio about freedom and democracy—why the niggers think it's meant for them! And that Eleanor Roosevelt, she ought to been muzzled. She's driving our niggers crazy—your boy included! Crazy! Talking about civil rights. Ain't been no race trouble in our country for three years—since the Deekin's lynching—but I'm telling you, Norwood, you better see that that buck of yours goes away from here. I'm speaking on the quiet, but I can see ahead. And what happened this morning about them radio tubes wasn't none too good.

NORWOOD: *(beside himself with rage)* A black ape! I——I . . .

HIGGINS: You been too decent to your darkies, Norwood. That's what's the matter with you. And then the whole county suffers from a lot of impudent bucks who take lessons from your crowd. Folks been kicking about that, too. Guess you know it. Maybe that's the reason you didn't get that nomination for committeeman a few years back.

NORWOOD: Maybe 'tis, Higgins. *(Rising and pacing the room)* God damn niggers! *(Furiously)* Everything turns on niggers, niggers, niggers! No wonder Yankees call this the Black Belt! *(He pours a large drink of whiskey)*

HIGGINS: *(soothingly)* Well, let's change the subject. Hand me my glass, there, too.

NORWOOD: Pardon me, Fred. *(He puts ice in his friend's glass and passes him the bottle)*

HIGGINS: Tom, you get excited too easy for warm weather . . . Don't ever show black folks they got you going, though. I think sometimes that's where you make your mistake. Keep calm, keep calm—and then you command. Best plantation manager I ever had never raised his voice to a nigger—and they were scared to death of him.

NORWOOD: Have a smoke. *(Pushes cigars toward HIGGINS)*

HIGGINS: You ought've married again, Tom—brought a white woman out here on this damn place o' yours. A woman could help you run things. Women have soft ways, but they can keep things humming. Nothing but blacks in the house—a man gets soft like niggers are inside. *(Puffing at cigar)* And living with a colored woman! Of course, I know we all have 'em—I didn't know you could make use of a white girl till I was past twenty. Thought too much o' white women for that—but I've given many a yellow gal a baby in my time. *(Long puff at cigar)* But for a man's own house you need a wife, not a black woman.

NORWOOD: Reckon you're right, Fred, but it's too late to marry again now. *(Shrugging his shoulders)* Let's get off of darkies and women for awhile. How's crops? *(Sitting down)* How's politics going?

HIGGINS: Well, I guess you know the Republicans is trying to stir up trouble for us in Washington. I wish the South had more men like Bilbo and Rankin there. But, say, by the way, Lawyer Hotchkiss wants to see us both about that budget money next week. He's got some real Canadian stuff at his office, in his filing case, too—brought back from his vacation last summer. Taste better'n this old mountain juice we get around here. Not meaning to insult your drinks, Tom, but just remarking. I serve the same as you myself, label and all.

NORWOOD: *(laughing)* I'll have you know, sir, that this is prewar licker, sir!

HIGGINS: Hum-m-m! Well, it's got me feelin' better'n I did when I come in here—whatever it is.

(Puffs at his cigar) Say, how's your cotton this year?

NORWOOD: Doin' right well, specially down in the south field. Why not drive out that road when you leave and take a look at it? I'll ride down with you. I want to see Talbot, anyhow.

HIGGINS: Well, let's be starting. I got to be back at the Junction by four o'clock. Promised to let that boy of mine have the car to drive over to Thomasville for a dance tonight.

NORWOOD: One more shot before we go. *(He pours out drinks)* The young ones must have their fling, I reckon. When you and I grew up down here it used to be a carriage and the best pair of black horses when you took the ladies out—now it's an automobile. That's a good lookin' new car of yours, too.

HIGGINS: Right nice.

NORWOOD: Been thinking about getting a new one myself, but money's been kinder tight this year, and conditions are none too good yet, either. Reckon that's why everybody's so restless. *(He walks toward stairs calling)* Cora! Oh, Cora! . . . If I didn't have a few thousand put away, I'd feel the pinch myself. *(As CORA appears on the stairs)* Bring me my glasses up there by the side of my bed . . . Better whistle for Mose, hadn't I, Higgins? He's probably 'round back with some of his women. *(Winking)* You know I got some nice black women in this yard.

HIGGINS: Oh, no, not Mose. I got my servants trained to stay in their places—right where I want 'em—while they're working for me. Just open the door and tell him to come in here and help me out. *(NORWOOD goes to the door and calls the CHAUFFEUR. MOSE enters and assists his master out to the car. CORA appears with the glasses, goes to the vestibule and gets the COLONEL'S hat and cane which she hands him)*

NORWOOD: *(To CORA)* I want to see that boy o' yours soon as I get back. That won't be long, either. And tell him to put up that Ford of mine and don't touch it again.

CORA: Yes, sir, I'll have him waiting here. *(In a whisper)* It's hot weather, Colonel Tom. Too much of this licker makes your heart upset. It ain't good for you, you know. *(NORWOOD pays her no attention as he exits toward the car. The noise of the departing motor is heard. CORA begins to tidy up the room. She takes a glass from a side table. She picks up a doily that was beneath the glass and looks at it long and lovingly. Suddenly she goes to the door left and calls toward the kitchen)* William, you William! Com'ere, I want to show you something. Make haste, son. *(As CORA goes back toward the table, her eldest son, WILLIAM, enters carrying a five-year-old boy)* Look here at this purty doily yo' sister made this summer while she been here. She done learned all about sewing and making purty things at school. Ain't it nice, son?

WILLIAM: Sho' is. Sallie takes after you, I reckon. She's a smart little crittur, ma. *(Sighs)* De Lawd knows, I was dumb at school. *(To his child)* Get down, Billy, you's too heavy. *(He puts the boy on the floor)* This here sewin's really fine.

BILLY: *(running toward the big upholstered chair and jumping up and down on the spring seat)* Gityap! I's a mule driver. Haw! Gee!

CORA: You Billy, get out of that chir 'fore I skins you alive. Get on into de kitchen, sah.

BILLY: I'm playin' horsie, grandma. *(Jumps up in the chair)* Horsic! Horsie!

CORA: Get! That's de Colonel's favorite chair. If he knows any little darkie's been jumpin' on it, he raise sand. Get on, now.

BILLY: Ole Colonel's ma grandpa, ain't he? Ain' he ma white grandpa?

WILLIAM: *(snatching the child out of the chair)* Boy, I'm gonna fan your hide if you don't hush!

CORA: Shs-ss-s! You Billy, hush yo' mouth! Chile, where you hear that? *(To her son)* Some o' you all been talking too much in front o' this chile. *(To the boy)* Honey, go on in de kitchen till yo' daddy come. Get a cookie from 'Vonia and set down on de back porch. *(Little BILLY exits left)*

WILLIAM: Ma, you know it 'twarn't me told him. Bert's the one been goin' all over de plantation

since he come back from Atlanta remindin'
folks right out we's Colonel Norwood's chilluns.

CORA: *(catching her breath)* Huh!

WILLIAM: He comes down to my shack tellin' Billy
and Marybell they got a white man for grandpa.
He's gonna get my chilluns in trouble sho'—
like he got himself in trouble when Colonel Tom
whipped him.

CORA: Ten or 'leven years ago, warn't it?

WILLIAM: And Bert's *sho'* in trouble now. Can't go
back to that college like he could-a if he'd-a
had any sense. You can't fool with white folks—
and de Colonel ain't never really liked Bert
since that there first time he beat him, either.

CORA: No, he ain't. Leastwise, he ain't understood
him. *(Musing sadly in a low voice)* Time Bert
was 'bout seven, warn't it? Just a little bigger'n
yo' Billy.

WILLIAM: Yes.

CORA: Went runnin' up to Colonel Tom out in de
horse stables when de Colonel was showin' off
his horses—I 'members so well—to fine white
company from town. Lawd, that boy's always
been foolish! He went runnin' up and grabbed
a-holt de Colonel and yelled right in front o' de
white folks' faces, "O, papa, Cora say de dinner's ready, papa!" Ain't never called him papa
before, and I don't know where he got it from.
And Colonel Tom knocked him right backwards under de horse's feet.

WILLIAM: And when de company were gone, he
beat that boy unmerciful.

CORA: I thought sho' he were gonna kill ma chile
that day. And he were mad at me, too, for
months. Said I was teaching you chilluns who
they pappy were. Up till then Bert had been
his favorite little colored child round here.

WILLIAM: Sho' had.

CORA: But he never liked him no more. That's
why he sent him off to school so soon to stay,
winter and summer, all these years. I had to
beg and plead to have him home this summer—but I's sorry now I ever got that boy back
here again.

WILLIAM: He's sho' growed more like de Colonel
all de time, ain't he? Bert thinks he's a real

white man hisself now. Look at de first thing he
did when he come home, he ain't seen de
Colonel in six years—and Bert sticks out his
hand fo' to shake hands with him!

CORA: Lawd! That chile!

WILLIAM: Just like white folks! And de Colonel
turns his back and walks off. Can't blame him.
He ain't used to such doings from colored folks.
God knows what's got into Bert since he come
back. He's acting like a fool—just like he was a
boss man round here. Won't even say "Yes, sir"
and "No, sir" no more to de white folks. Talbot
asked him warn't he gonna work in de field this
mornin'. Bert says "No!" and turn and walk
away. White man so mad, I could see him nearly
foam at de mouth. If he warn't yo' chile, ma,
he'd been knocked in de head fo' now.

CORA: You's right.

WILLIAM: And you can't talk to him. I tried to tell
him something the other day, but he just laughed
at me, and said we's all just scared niggers on
this plantation. Says he ain't no nigger, no how.
He's a Norwood. He's half-white, and he's gonna
act like it. *(In amazement at his brother's daring)*
And this is Georgia, too!

CORA: I's scared to death for de boy, William. I
don't know what to do. De Colonel says he won't
send him off to school no mo'. Says he's mo'
sassy and impudent now than any nigger he ever
seed. Bert never has been like you was, and de
girls, quiet and sensible like you knowed you
had to be. *(She sits down)* De Colonel say he's
gonna make Bert stay here now and work on this
plantation like de rest of his niggers. He's gonna
show him what color he is. Like that time when
he beat him for callin' him "papa." He say he's
gwine to teach him his place and make de boy
know where he belongs. Seems like me or you
can't show him. Colonel Tom has to take him in
hand, or these white folks'll kill him around
here and then—oh, My God!

WILLIAM: A nigger's just got to know his place in
de South, that's all, ain't he, ma?

CORA: Yes, son. That's all, I reckon.

WILLIAM: And ma brother's one damn fool nigger.
Don't seems like he knows nothin'. He's gonna

ruin us all round here. Makin' it bad for everybody.

CORA: Oh, Lawd, have mercy! *(Beginning to cry)* I don't know what to do. De way he's acting up can't go on. Way he's acting to de Colonel can't last. Somethin's gonna happen to ma chile. I had a bad dream last night, too, and I looked out and seed de moon all red with blood. I seed a path o' living blood across this house, I tell you, in my sleep. Oh, Lawd, have mercy! *(Sobbing)* Oh, Lawd, help me in ma troubles. *(The noise of the returning Ford is heard outside.* CORA *looks up, rises, and goes to the window)* There's de chile now, William. Run out to de back door and tell him I wants to see him. Bring him in here where Sam and Livonia and de rest of 'em won't hear ever'thing we's sayin'. I got to talk to ma boy. He's ma baby boy, and he don't know de way.

(Exit WILLIAM *through the door left.* CORA *is wiping her eyes and pulling herself together when the front door is flung open with a bang and* ROBERT *enters.)*

ROBERT: *(running to his mother and hugging her teasingly)* Hello, ma! Your daughter got off, and I've come back to keep you company in the parlor! Bring out the cookies and lemonade. *Mister* Norwood's here!

CORA: *(beginning to sob anew)* Take yo' hands off me, boy! Why don't you mind? Why don't you mind me?

ROBERT: *(suddenly serious, backing away)* Why, mamma, what's the matter? Did I scare you? Your eyes are all wet! Has somebody been telling you 'bout this morning?

CORA: *(not heeding his words)* Why don't you mind me, son? Ain't I told you and told you not to come in that front door, never? *(Suddenly angry)* Will somebody have to beat it into you? What's got wrong with you when you was away at that school? What am I gonna do?

ROBERT: *(carelessly)* Oh, I knew that the Colonel wasn't here. I passed him and old man Higgins on the road down by the south patch. He wouldn't even look at me when I waved at him. *(Half-playfully)* Anyhow, isn't this my old man's

house? Ain't I his son and heir? *(Grandly, strutting around)* Am I not Mr Norwood, Junior?

CORA: *(utterly serious)* I believes you goin' crazy, Bert. I believes you wants to get us all killed or run away or something awful like that. I believes . . . (WILLIAM *enters left*)

WILLIAM: Where's Bert? He ain't come round back——*(Seeing his brother in the room)* How'd you get in here?

ROBERT: *(grinning)* Houses have front doors.

WILLIAM: Oh, usin' de front door like de white folks, heh? You gwine do that once too much.

ROBERT: Yes, like de white folks. What's a front door for, you rabbit-hearted coon?

WILLIAM: Rabbit-hearted coon's better'n a dead coon any day.

ROBERT: I wouldn't say so. Besides, you and me's only half-coons, anyhow, big boy. And I'm gonna act like my white half, not my black half. Get me, kid?

WILLIAM: Well, you ain't gonna act like it long here in de middle o' Georgy. And you ain't gonna act like it when de Colonel's around, either.

ROBERT: Oh, no? My stay down here'll be short and sweet, boy, short and sweet. The old man won't send me away to college no more—so you think I'm gonna stick around and work in the fields? Like fun? I might stay here awhile and teach some o' you darkies to think like men, maybe—till it gets too much for the old Colonel—but no more bowing down to white folks for me—not Robert Norwood.

CORA: Hush, son!

ROBERT: Certainly not right on my own old man's plantation—Georgia or no Georgia.

WILLIAM: *(scornfully)* I hears you.

ROBERT: *You* can do it if you want to, but I'm ashamed of you. I've been away from here six years. *(Boasting)* I've learned something, seen people in Atlanta, and Richmond, and Washington where the football team went—real colored people who don't have to take off their hats to white folks or let 'em go to bed with their sisters—like that young Higgins boy, asking me what night Sallie was comin' to town. A damn cracker! *(To* CORA) 'Scuse me, ma. *(Continuing)*

Back here in these woods maybe Sam and Livonia and you and mama and everybody's got their places fixed for 'em, but not me. *(Seriously)* Nobody's gonna fix a place for me. I'm old man Norwood's son. Nobody fixed a place for him. *(Playfully again)* Look at me. I'm a 'fay boy. *(Pretends to shake his hair back)* See these gray eyes? I got the right to everything everybody else has. *(Punching his brother in the belly)*, Don't talk to me, old slavery-time Uncle Tom.

WILLIAM: *(resentfully)* I ain't playin', boy. *(Pushes younger brother back with some force)* I ain't playin' a-tall.

CORA: All right, chilluns, stop. Stop! And William, you take Billy and go on home. 'Vonia's got to get supper and she don't like no young-uns under her feet in de kitchen. I wants to talk to Bert in here now 'fore Colonel Tom gets back. *(Exit* WILLIAM *left.* CORA *continues to* BERT*)* Sit down, child, right here a minute, and listen.

ROBERT: *(sitting down)* All right, ma.

CORA: Hard as I's worked and begged and humbled maself to get de Colonel to keep you chilluns in school, you comes home wid yo' head full o' stubbornness and yo' mouth full o' sass for me an' de white folks an' everybody. You know can't no colored boy here talk like you's been doin' to no white folks, let alone to de Colonel and that old devil of a Talbot. They ain't gonna stand fo' yo' sass. Not only you, but I 'spects we's all gwine to pay fo' it, every colored soul on this place. I was scared to death today fo' yo' sister, Sallie, scared de Colonel warn't gwine to let her go back to school, neither, 'count o' yo' doins, but he did, thank Gawd—and then you come near makin' her miss de train. Did she have time to get her ticket and all?

ROBERT: Sure! Had to drive like sin to get there with her, though. I didn't mean to be late getting back here for her, ma, but I had a little run-in about them radio tubes in town.

CORA: *(worried)* What's that?

ROBERT: The tubes was smashed when I got 'em, and I had already made out my money order, so the woman in the post office wouldn't give the three dollars back to me. All I did was explain to her that we could send the tubes back—but she got hot because there were two or three white folks waiting behind me to get stamps, I guess. So she yells at me to move on and not give her any of my "educated nigger talk." So I said, "I'm going to finish showing you these tubes before I move on"—and then she screamed and called the mail clerk working in the back, and told him to throw me out. *(Boasting)* He didn't do it by himself, though. Had to call all the white loafers out in the square to get me through that door.

CORA: *(fearfully)* Lawd have mercy!

ROBERT: Guess if I hadn't-a had the Ford then, they'd've beat me half-to-death, but when I saw how many crackers there was, I jumped in the car and beat it on away.

CORA: Thank God for that!

ROBERT: Not even a football man *(Half-boasting)* like me could tackle the whole Junction. 'Bout a dozen colored guys standing around, too, and not one of 'em would help me—the dumb jigaboos! They been telling me ever since I been here, *(Imitating darky talk)* "You can't argue wid whut folks, man. You better stay out o' this Junction. You must ain't got no sense, nigger! You's a fool" . . . Maybe I am a fool, ma—but I didn't want to come back here nohow.

CORA: I's sorry I sent for you.

ROBERT: Besides you, there ain't nobody in this country but a lot of evil white folks and cowardly niggers. *(Earnestly)* I'm no nigger, anyhow, am I, ma? I'm half-white. The Colonel's my father—the richest man in the county—and I'm not going to take a lot of stuff from nobody if I do have to stay here, not from the old man either. He thinks I ought to be out there in the sun working, with Talbot standing over me like I belonged in the chain gang. Well, he's got another thought coming! *(Stubbornly)* I'm a Norwood—not a field-hand nigger.

CORA: You means you ain't workin' no mo'?

ROBERT: *(flaring)* No, I'm not going to work in the fields. What did he send me away to school for—just to come back here and be his servant, or pick his hills of cotton?

CORA: He sent you away to de school because *I* asked him and begged him, and got down on my knees to him, that's why. *(Quietly)* And now I just wants to make you see some sense, if you can. I knows, honey, you reads in de books and de papers, and you knows a lot more'n I do. But, chile, you's in Georgy—and I don't see how it is you don't know where you's at. This ain't up North—and even up yonder where we hears it's so fine, yo' sister has to pass for white to get along good.

ROBERT: *(bitterly)* I know it.

CORA: She ain't workin' in no hotel kitchen like de Colonel thinks. She's in a office typewriting. And Sallie's studyin' de typewriter, too, at de school, but yo' pappy don't know it. I knows we ain't s'posed to study nothin' but cookin' and hard workin' here in Georgy. That's all I ever done, or knowed about. I been workin' on this very place all ma life—even 'fore I come to live in this Big House. When de Colonel's wife died, I come here, and borned you chilluns. And de Colonel's been real good to me in his way. Let you all sleep in this house with me when you was little, and sent you all off to school when you growed up. Ain't no white man in this county done that with his cullud chilluns before, far as I can know. But you—Robert, be awful, awful careful! When de Colonel comes back, in a few minutes, he wants to talk to you. Talk right to him, boy. Talk like you was colored, 'cause you ain't white.

ROBERT: *(angrily)* And I'm not black, either. Look at me, mama. *(Rising and throwing up his arms)* Don't I look like my father? Ain't I as light as he is? Ain't my eyes gray like his eyes are? *(The noise of a car is heard outside)* Ain't this our house?

CORA: That's him now. *(Agitated)* Hurry, chile, and let's we get out of this room. Come on through yonder to the kitchen. *(She starts toward the door left)* And I'll tell him you're here.

ROBERT: I don't want to run into the kitchen. Isn't this our house? *(As CORA crosses hurriedly left, ROBERT goes toward the front door)* The Ford is parked out in front, anyway.

CORA: *(at the door left to the rear of the house)* Robert! Robert! *(As ROBERT nears the front door, COLONEL NORWOOD enters, almost runs into the boy, stops at the threshold and stares unbelievingly at his son. CORA backs up against the door left.)*

NORWOOD: Get out of here! *(He points toward the door to rear of the house where CORA is standing)*

ROBERT: *(half-smiling)* Didn't you want to talk to me?

NORWOOD: Get out of here!

ROBERT: Not that way. *(The COLONEL raises his cane to strike the boy. CORA screams. BERT draws himself up to his full height, taller than the old man and looking very much like him, pale and proud. The man and the boy face each other. NORWOOD does not strike)*

NORWOOD: *(in a hoarse whisper)* Get out of here. *(His hand is trembling as he points)*

CORA: Robert! Come on, son, come on! Oh, my God, come on. *(Opening the door left)*

ROBERT: Not that way, ma. *(ROBERT walks proudly out the front door. NORWOOD, in an impotent rage, crosses the room to a small cabinet right, opens it nervously with a key from his pocket, takes out a pistol, and starts toward the front door. CORA overtakes him, seizes his arm, stops him)*

CORA: He's our son, Tom. *(She sinks slowly to her knees, holding his body)* Remember, he's our son.

CURTAIN

ACT TWO

SCENE ONE

TIME: *After supper. Sunset.*

SETTING: *The same.*

ACTION: *As the curtain rises, the stage is empty. Through the windows the late afternoon sun makes two bright paths toward the footlights.* SAM, *carrying a tray bearing a whiskey bottle and a bowl of ice, enters left and crosses toward the library. He stoops at the door right, listens a moment, knocks, then opens the door and goes in. In a moment* SAM *returns. As he leaves the library, he is heard replying to a request of* NORWOOD'S.

SAM: Yes, sah, Colonel! Sho' will, sah! Right away, sah! Yes, sah, I'll tell him. *(He closes the door and crosses the stage muttering to himself)* Six o'clock. Most nigh that now. Better tell Cora to get that boy right in here. Can't nobody else do nothin' with that fool Bert but Cora. *(He exits left. Can be heard calling)* Cora! You, Cora . . .
(Again the stage is empty. Off stage, outside, the bark of a dog is heard, the sound of Negroes singing down the road, the cry of a child. The breeze moves the shadows of leaves and tree limbs across the sunlit paths from the windows. The door left opens and CORA *enters, followed by* ROBERT.)

CORA: *(softly to* ROBERT *behind her in the dining room)* It's all right, son. He ain't come out yet, but it's nearly six, and that's when he said he wanted you, but I was afraid maybe you was gonna be late. I sent for you to come up here to de house and eat supper with me in de kitchen. Where'd you eat yo' vittuals at, chile?

ROBERT: Down at Willie's house, ma. After the old man tried to hit me you still want me to hang around and eat up here?

CORA: I wanted you to be here on time, honey, that's all. *(She is very nervous)* I kinder likes to have you eat with me sometimes, too, but you ain't et up here more'n once this summer. But this evenin' I just wanted you to be here when de Colonel sent word for you, 'cause we's done had enough trouble today.

ROBERT: He's not here on time, himself, is he?

CORA: He's in de library. Sam couldn't get him to eat no supper tonight, and I ain't seen him a-tall.

ROBERT: Maybe he wants to see me in the library, then.

CORA: You know he don't 'low no colored folks in there 'mongst his books and things 'cept Sam. Some o' his white friends goes in there, but none o' us.

ROBERT: Maybe he wants to see *me* in there, though.

CORA: Can't you never talk sense, Robert? This ain't no time for foolin' and jokin.' Nearly thirty years in this house and I ain't never been in there myself, not once, 'mongst de Colonel's papers. *(The clock strikes six)* Stand over yonder and wait till he comes out. I's gwine on upstairs now, so's he can talk to you. And don't aggravate him no mo' fo' God's sake. Agree to whatever he say. I's scared fo' you, chile, de way you been actin,' and de fool tricks you done today, and de trouble about de post office besides. Don't aggravate him. Fo' yo' sake, honey, 'cause I loves you—and fo' all de po' colored folks on this place what has such a hard time when his humors get on him—agree to whatever he say, will you, Bert?

ROBERT: All right, ma. *(Voice rising)* But he better not start to hit me again.

CORA: Shs-ss-s! He'll hear you. He's right in there.

ROBERT: *(sullenly)* This was the day I ought to have started back to school—like my sister. I stayed my summer out here, didn't I? Why didn't he keep his promise to me? You said if I came home I could go back to college again.

CORA: Shs-ss-s! He'll be here now. Don't say nothin', chile. I's done all I could.

ROBERT: All right, ma.

CORA: *(approaching the stairs)* I'll be in ma room, honey, where I can hear you when you goes out. I'll come down to de back door and see you 'fore you goes back to de shack. Don't aggravate him, chile.
(She ascends the stairs. The boy sits down sullenly, left, and stares at the door opposite from which his father must enter. The clock strikes the quarter after six. The shadows of the window curtains have lengthened on the carpet. The sunshine has deepened to a pale orange, and the light paths grow less distinct across the floor. The boy sits up straight in his chair. He

looks at the library door. It opens. NORWOOD *enters. He is bent and pale. He looks across the room and sees the boy. Suddenly he straightens up. The old commanding look comes into his face. He strides directly across the room toward his son. The boy, half afraid, half defiant, yet sure of himself, rises. Now that* ROBERT *is standing, the white man turns, goes back to a chair near the table, right, and seats himself. He takes out a cigar, cuts off the end and lights it, and in a voice of mixed condescension and contempt, he speaks to his son.* ROBERT *remains standing near the chair.)*

NORWOOD: I don't want to have to beat you another time as I did when you were a child. The next time I might not be able to control myself. I might kill you if I touched you again. I been runnin' this plantation for thirty-five years, and I never had to beat a Nigra as old as you are. I never had to beat one of Cora's children either— but you. The rest of 'em had sense 'nough to keep out of my sight, and to speak to me like they should . . . I don't have any trouble with my colored folks. Never have trouble. They do what I say, or what Mr Talbot says, and that's all there is to it. I give 'em a chance. If they turn in crops they get paid. If they're workin' for wages, they get paid. If they want to spend their money on licker, or buy an old car, or fix up their cabins, they can. Do what they choose long as they know their places and it don't hinder their work. And to Cora's young ones I give all the chances any colored folks ever had in these parts. More'n many a white child's had. I sent you all off to school. Let Bertha go on up North when she got grown and educated. Intend to let Sallie do the same. Gave your brother William that house he's living in when he got married, pay him for his work, help him out if he needs it. None of my darkies suffer. Sent you to college. Would have kept on, would have sent you back today, but I don't intend to pay for no darky, or white boy either if I had one, that acts the way you've been acting. And certainly for no black fool. Now I want to know what's wrong with you? I

don't usually talk about what I'm going to do with anybody on this place. It's my habit to tell people *what to do,* not discuss it with 'em. But I want to know what's the matter with you— whether you're crazy or not. In that case, you'll have to be locked up. And if you aren't, you'll have to change your ways a damn sight or it won't be safe for you here, and you know it—venting your impudence on white women, parking the car in front of my door, driving like mad through the Junction, and going, everywhere, just as you please. Now, I'm going to let you talk to me, but I want you to talk right.

ROBERT: *(still standing)* What do you mean, "talk right"?

NORWOOD: I mean talk like a nigger should to a white man.

ROBERT: Oh! But I'm not a nigger, Colonel Tom. I'm your son.

NORWOOD: *(testily)* You're Cora's boy.

ROBERT: Women don't have children by themselves.

NORWOOD: Nigger women don't know the fathers. You're a bastard.

*(*ROBERT *clenches his fist.* NORWOOD *turns toward the drawer where the pistol is, takes it out, and lays it on the table. The wind blows the lace curtains at the windows, and sweeps the shadows of falling leaves across the paths of sunlight on the floor.)*

ROBERT: I've heard that before. I've heard it from Negroes, and I've heard it from white folks. Now I hear it from you. *(Slowly)* You're talking about my mother.

NORWOOD: I'm talking about Cora, yes. Her children are bastards.

ROBERT: *(quickly)* And you're their father. *(Angrily)* How come I look like you, if you're not my father?

NORWOOD: Don't shout at me, boy. I can hear you. *(Half-smiling)* How come your skin is yellow and your elbows rusty? How come they threw you out of the post office today for talking to a white woman? How come you're the crazy young buck you are?

ROBERT: They had no right to throw me out. I asked for my money back when I saw the broken tubes. Just as you had no right to raise that cane today when I was standing at the door of this house where *you* live, while *I* have to sleep in a shack down the road with the field hands. *(Slowly)* But my mother sleeps with you.

NORWOOD: You don't like it?

ROBERT: No, I don't like it.

NORWOOD: What can you do about it?

ROBERT: *(after a pause)* I'd like to kill all the white men in the world.

NORWOOD: *(starting)* Niggers like you are hung to trees.

ROBERT: I'm not a nigger.

NORWOOD: You don't like your own race? *(ROBERT is silent)* Yet you don't like white folks either?

ROBERT: *(defiantly)* You think I ought to?

NORWOOD: You evidently don't like me.

ROBERT: *(boyishly)* I used to like you, when I first knew you were my father, when I was a little kid, before that time you beat me under the feet of your horses. *(Slowly)* I liked you until then.

NORWOOD: *(a little pleased)* So you did, heh? *(Fingering his pistol)* A pickaninny calling me "papa." I should've broken your young neck for that first time. I should've broken your head for you today, too—since I didn't then.

ROBERT: *(laughing scornfully)* You should've broken my head?

NORWOOD: Should've gotten rid of you before this. But you was Cora's child. I tried to help you. *(Aggrieved)* I treated you decent, schooled you. Paid for it. But tonight you'll get the hell off this place and stay off. Get the hell out of this county. *(Suddenly furious)* Get out of this state. Don't let me lay eyes on you again. Get out of here now. Talbot and the storekeeper are coming up here this evening to talk cotton with me. I'll tell Talbot to *see* that you go. That's all. *(NORWOOD motions toward the door, left)* Tell Sam to come in here when you go out. Tell him to make a light here.

ROBERT: *(impudently) Ring* for Sam—I'm not going through the kitchen. *(He starts toward the front door)* I'm not your servant. You're not going to

tell me what to do. You're not going to have Talbot run me off the place like a field hand you don't want to use any more.

NORWOOD: *(springing between his son and the front door, pistol in hand)* You black bastard! *(ROBERT goes toward him calmly, grasps his father's arm and twists it until the gun falls to the floor. The older man bends backward in startled fury and pain)* Don't you dare put your . . .

ROBERT: *(laughing)* Why don't you shoot, papa? *(Louder)* Why don't you shoot?

NORWOOD: *(gasping as he struggles, fighting back)* . . . black . . . hands . . . on . . . you . . .

ROBERT: *(hysterically, as he takes his father by the throat)* Why don't you shoot, papa? *(NORWOOD's hands claw the air helplessly. ROBERT chokes the struggling white man until his body grows limp)* Why don't you shoot! *(Laughing)* Why don't you shoot? Huh? Why?

(CORA appears at the top of the stairs, hearing the commotion. She screams.)

CORA: Oh, my God! *(She rushes down. ROBERT drops the body of his father at her feet in a path of flame from the setting sun. CORA starts and stares in horror)*

ROBERT: *(wildly)* Why didn't he shoot, mama? He didn't want *me* to live. Why didn't he shoot? *(Laughing)* He was the boss. Telling me what to do. Why didn't he shoot, then? He was the white man.

CORA: *(falling on the body)* Colonel Tom! Colonel Tom! Tom! Tom! *(Gazes across the corpse at her son)* He's yo' father, Bert.

ROBERT: He's dead. The white man's dead. My father's dead. *(Laughing)* I'm living.

CORA: Tom! Tom! Tom!

ROBERT: Niggers are living. He's dead. *(Picks up the pistol)* This is what he wanted to kill me with, but he's dead. I can use it now. Use it on all the white men in the world, because they'll be coming looking for me now. *(Stuffs the pistol into his shirt)* They'll want me now.

CORA: *(rising and running toward her boy)* Quick, chile, out that way, *(pointing toward the front door)* so they won't see you in de kitchen. Make for de swamp, honey. Cross de fields fo' de swamp. Go de crick way. In runnin' water, dogs can't smell no tracks. Hurry, chile!

ROBERT: Yes, mama. I can go out the front way now, easy. But if I see they gonna get me before I can reach the swamp, I'm coming back here, mama, and *(Proudly)* let them take me out of my father's house—if they can. *(Pats the gun under his shirt)* They're not going to string me up to some roadside tree for the crackers to laugh at.

CORA: *(moaning aloud)* Oh, O-o-o! Hurry! Hurry, chile!

ROBERT: I'm going, ma. *(He opens the door. The sunset streams in like a river of blood)*

CORA: Run, chile!

ROBERT: Not out of my father's house. *(He exits slowly, tall and straight against the sun)*

CORA: Fo' God's sake, hurry, chile! *(Glancing down the road)* Lawd have mercy! There's Talbot and de storekeeper in de drive. They sees my boy! *(Moaning)* They sees ma boy. *(Relieved)* But thank God, they's passin' him! *(CORA backs up against the wall in the vestibule. She stands as if petrified as* TALBOT *and the* STOREKEEPER *enter)*

TALBOT: Hello, Cora. What's the matter with you? Where's that damn fool boy o' your'n goin', coming out the front door like he owned the house? What's the matter with you, woman? Can't you talk? Can't you talk? Where's Norwood? Let's have some light in this dark place. *(He reaches behind the door and turns on the lights.* CORA *remains backed up against the wall, looking out into the twilight, watching* ROBERT *as he goes across the field)* Good God, Jim! Look at this! *(The* TWO WHITE MEN *stop in horror before the sight of* NORWOOD's *body on the floor)*

STOREKEEPER: He's blue in the face. *(Bends over the body)* That nigger we saw walking out the door! *(Rising excitedly)* That nigger bastard of Cora's . . . *(Stooping over the body again)* Why the Colonel's dead!

TALBOT: That nigger! *(Rushes toward the door)* He's running toward the swamp now . . . We'll get him . . . Telephone town—there, in the library. Telephone the sheriff. Get men, white men, after that nigger.

(STOREKEEPER rushes into the library. He can be heard talking excitedly on the phone.)

STOREKEEPER: Sheriff! Sheriff! Is this the sheriff? I'm calling from Norwood's plantation. That nigger, Bert, has just killed Norwood—and run, headed for the swamp. Notify the gas station at the crossroads! Tell the boys at the sawmill to head him off at the creek. Warn everybody to be on the lookout. Call your deputies! Yes! Yes! Spread a dragnet. Get out the dogs. Meanwhile we'll start after him. *(He slams the phone down and comes back into the room)* Cora, where's Norwood's car? In the barn? *(CORA does not answer)*

TALBOT: Talk, you black bitch!

(She remains silent. TALBOT *runs, yelling and talking, out into the yard, followed by the* STOREKEEPER. *Sounds of excited shouting outside, and the roar of a motor rushing down the drive. In the sky the twilight deepens into early night.* CORA *stands looking into the darkness.)*

CORA: My boy can't get to de swamp now. They's telephoned the white folks down that way. So he'll come back home now. Maybe he'll turn into de crick and follow de branch home directly. *(Protectively)* But they shan't get him. I'll make a place for to hide him. I'll make a place upstairs down under de floor, under ma bed. In a minute ma boy'll be runnin' from de white folks with their hounds and their ropes and their guns and everything they uses to kill po' colored folks with. *(Distressed)* Ma boy'll be out there runnin'. *(Turning to the body on the floor)* Colonel Tom, you hear me? Our boy, out there runnin'. *(Fiercely)* You said he was ma boy—*ma* bastard boy. I heard you . . . but he's yours too . . . but yonder in de dark runnin'—runnin' from yo' people, from white people. *(Pleadingly)* Why don't you get up and stop 'em? He's *your* boy. His eyes is gray—like your eyes. He's tall like you's tall. He's proud like you's proud. And he's runnin'—runnin' from po' white trash what ain't worth de little finger o' nobody what's got your blood in 'em, Tom. *(Demandingly)* Why don't you get up from there and stop 'em, Colonel Tom? What's that you say? He ain't your chile? He's ma bastard chile? My yellow bastard chile? *(Proudly)* Yes, he's mine. But don't call him that. Don't you touch him. Don't you put your white hands on him. You's beat him enough, and cussed him enough. Don't you touch him now. He *is* ma boy, and no white folks gonna touch him now. That's finished. I'm gonna make a place for him upstairs under ma bed. *(Backs away from the body toward the stairs)* He's ma chile. Don't you come in ma bedroom while he's up there. Don't you come to my bed no mo'. I calls you to help me now, and you just lays there. I calls you for to wake up, and you just lays there. Whenever you called me, in de night, I woke up. When you called for me to love, I always reached out ma arms fo' you. I borned you five chilluns and now one of 'em is out yonder in de dark runnin' from yo' people. Our youngest boy out yonder in de dark runnin'. *(Accusingly)* He's runnin' from you, too. You said he warn't your'n—he's just Cora's po' little yellow bastard. But he *is* your'n, Colonel Tom. *(Sadly)* And he's runnin' from you. You are out yonder in de dark, *(Points toward the door)* runnin' our chile, with de hounds and de gun in yo' hand, and Talbot's followin' 'hind you with a rope to hang Robert with. *(Confidently)* I been sleepin' with you too long, Colonel Tom, not to know that this ain't you layin' down there with yo' eyes shut on de floor. You can't fool me—you ain't never been so still like this before—you's out yonder runnin' ma boy. *(Scornfully)* Colonel Thomas Norwood, runnin' ma boy through de fields in de dark, runnin' ma poor little helpless Bert through de fields in de dark to lynch him . . . Damn you, Colonel Norwood! *(Backing slowly up the stairs, staring at the rigid body below her)* Damn you, Thomas Norwood! God damn you!

CURTAIN

SCENE TWO

TIME: *One hour later. Night.*

SETTING: *The same.*

ACTION: *As the curtain rises, the* UNDERTAKER *is talking to* SAM *at the outer door. All through this scene the approaching cries of the manhunt are heard.*

UNDERTAKER: Reckon there won't be no orders to bring his corpse back out here, Sam. None of us ain't seen Talbot or Mr Higgins, but I'm sure they'll be having the funeral in town. The coroner told us to bring the body into the Junction. Ain't nothin' but niggers left out here now.

SAM: *(very frightened)* Yes, sah! Yes, sah! You's right, sah! Nothin' but us niggers, sah!

UNDERTAKER: The Colonel didn't have no relatives far as you know, did he, Sam?

SAM: No, sah. Ain't had none. No, sah! You's right, sah!

UNDERTAKER: Well, you got everything o' his locked up around here, ain't you? Too bad there ain't no white folks about to look after the Colonel's stuff, but every white man that's able to walk's out with the posse. They'll have that young nigger swingin' before ten.

SAM: *(trembling)* Yes, sah, yes, sah! I 'spects so. Yes, sah!

UNDERTAKER: Say, where's that woman the Colonel's been living with—where's that black housekeeper, Cora, that murderin' bastard's mother?

SAM: She here, sah! She's up in her room.

UNDERTAKER: *(curiously)* I'd like to see how she looks. Get her down here. Say, how about a little drink before we start that ride back to town, for me and my partner out there with the body?

SAM: Cora got de keys to all de licker, sah!

UNDERTAKER: Well, get her down here then, double quick! *(SAM goes up the stairs. The UNDERTAKER leans in the front doorway talking to his partner outside in the wagon)* Bad business, a white man having saucy nigger children on his hands, and his black woman living in his own house.

VOICE OUTSIDE: Damn right, Charlie.

UNDERTAKER: Norwood didn't have a gang o' yellow gals, though, like Higgins and some o' these other big bugs. Just this one bitch far's I know, livin' with him damn near like a wife. Didn't even have much company out here. And they tell me ain't been a white woman stayed here overnight since his wife died when I was a baby. (SAM'S *shuffle is heard on the stairs*) Here comes a drink, I reckon, boy. You needn't get down off the ambulance. I'll have Sam bring it out there to you. (SAM *descends followed by* CORA *who comes down the stairs. She says nothing. The UN-DERTAKER looks up grinning at* CORA) Well, so you're the Cora that's got these educated nigger children? Hum-m! Well, I guess you'll see one of 'em swinging full of bullet holes when you wake up in the morning. They'll probably hang him to that tree down here by the Colonel's gate— 'cause they tell me he strutted right out the front gate past that tree after the murder. Or maybe they'll burn him. How'd you like to see him swinging there roasted in the morning when you wake up, girlie?

CORA: *(calmly)* Is that all you wanted to say to me?

UNDERTAKER: Don't get smart! Maybe you think there's nobody to boss you now. We gonna have a little drink before we go. Get out a bottle of rye.

CORA: I takes ma orders from Colonel Norwood, sir.

UNDERTAKER: Well, you'll take no more orders from him. He's dead out there in my wagon— so get along and get the bottle.

CORA: He's out yonder with de mob, not in your wagon.

UNDERTAKER: I tell you he's in my wagon!

CORA: He's out there with de mob.

UNDERTAKER: God damn! *(To his partner outside)* I believe this black woman's gone crazy in here. *(To* CORA) Get the keys out for that licker, and be quick about it! (CORA *does not move.* SAM *looks from one to the other, frightened*)

VOICE OUTSIDE: Aw, to hell with the licker, Charlie. Come on, let's start back to town. We want to get in on some of that excitement, too. They should've found that nigger by now—and I want to see 'em drag him out here.

UNDERTAKER: All right, Jim. *(To* CORA *and* SAM) Don't you all go to bed until you see that bonfire. You niggers are getting besides yourselves around Polk County. We'll burn a few more of you if you don't be careful. *(He exits, and the noise of the dead-wagon going down the road is heard)*

SAM: Oh, Lawd, hab mercy on me! I prays, Lawd hab mercy! O, ma Lawd, ma Lawd, ma Lawd! Cora, is you a fool? *Is* you a fool? Why didn't you give de mens de licker, riled as these white folks is? In ma old age is I gonna be burnt by de crackers? Lawd, is I sinned? Lawd, what has I done? *(Suddenly stops moaning and becomes schemingly calm)* I don't have to stay here tonight, does I? I done locked up de Colonel's library, and he can't be wantin' nothin'. No, ma Lawd, he won't want nothin' now. He's with Jesus—or with de devil, one. *(To* CORA) I's gwine on away from here. Sam's gwine in town to his chilluns' house, and I ain't gwine by no road either. I gwine through de holler where I don't have to pass no white folks.

CORA: Yes, Samuel, you go on. De Colonel can get his own drinks when he comes back tonight.

SAM: *(bucking his eyes in astonishment at* CORA) Lawd God Jesus!
(He bolts out of the room as fast as his old legs will carry him. CORA *comes down stairs, looks for a long moment out into the darkness, then closes the front door and draws the blinds. She looks down at the spot where the* COLONEL'S *body lay.)*

CORA: All de colored folks are runnin' from you tonight. Po' Colonel Tom, you too old now to be out with de mob. You got no business goin', but you had to go, I reckon. I 'members that time they hung Luke Jordon, you sent yo' dogs out to hunt him. The next day you killed all de dogs. You were kinder softhearted. Said you didn't like that kind of sport. Told me in bed one night you could hear them dogs howlin' in yo' sleep. But de time they burnt de courthouse when that po' little cullud boy was locked up in it cause they said he hugged a white girl, you was with 'em again. Said you had to go help 'em. Now you's out chasin' ma boy. *(As she stands at the window, she sees a passing figure)* There goes yo' other woman, Colonel Tom, Livonia is runnin' from you too, now. She would've wanted you last night. Been wantin' you again ever since she got old and fat and you stopped layin' with her and put her in the kitchen to cook. Don't think I don't know, Colonel Tom. Don't think I don't remember them nights when you used to sleep in that cabin down by de spring. I knew 'Vonia was there with you. I ain't no fool, Colonel Tom. But she ain't bore you no chilluns. I'm de one that bore 'em. *(Musing)* White mens, and colored womens, and little bastard chilluns—that's de old way of de South—but it's ending now. Three of your yellow brothers yo' father had by Aunt Sallie Deal—what had to come and do your laundry to make her livin'—you got colored relatives scattered all over this county. Them de ways o' de South—mixtries, mixtries. *(WILLIAM enters left, silently, as his mother talks. She is sitting in a chair now. Without looking up)* Is that you, William?

WILLIAM: Yes, ma, it's me.

CORA: Is you runnin' from him, too?

WILLIAM: *(hesitatingly)* Well, ma, you see . . . don't you think kinder . . . well, I reckon I ought to take Libby and ma babies on down to de church house with Reverend Martin and them, or else get 'long to town if I can hitch up them mules. They's scared to be out here, my wife and her ma. All de folks done gone from de houses down yonder by de branch, and you can hear de hounds a bayin' off yonder by de swamp, and cars is tearin' up that road, and de white folks is yellin' and hollerin' and carryin' on somethin' terrible over toward de brook. I done told Robert 'bout his foolishness. They's gonna hang him sure. Don't you think you better be comin' with us, ma. That is, do you want to? 'Course we can go by ourselves, and maybe

you wants to stay here and take care o' de big house. I don't want to leave you, ma, but I . . . I . . .

CORA: Yo' brother'll be back, son, then I won't be by myself.

WILLIAM: *(bewildered by his mother's sureness)* I though Bert went . . . I thought he run . . . I thought . . .

CORA: No, honey. He went, but they ain't gonna get him out there. I sees him comin' back here now, to be with me. I's gwine to guard him 'till he can get away.

WILLIAM: Then de white folks'll come here, too.

CORA: Yes, de Colonel'll come back here sure. *(The deep baying of the hounds is heard at a distance through the night)* Colonel Tom will come after his son.

WILLIAM: My God, ma! Come with us to town.

CORA: Go on, William, go on! Don't wait for them to get back. You never was much like neither one o' them—neither de Colonel or Bert—you's mo' like de field hands. Too much o' ma blood in you, I guess. You never liked Bert much, neither, and you always was afraid of de Colonel. Go on, son, and hide yo' wife and her ma and your chilluns. Ain't nothin' gonna hurt you. You never did go against nobody. Neither did I, till tonight. Tried to live right and not hurt a soul, white or colored. *(Addressing space)* I tried to live right, Lord. *(Angrily)* Tried to live right, Lord. *(Throws out her arms resentfully as if to say, "and this is what you give me")* What's de matter, Lawd, you ain't with me? *(The hounds are heard howling again.)*

WILLIAM: I'm gone, ma. *(He exits fearfully as his mother talks)*

CORA: *(bending over the spot on the floor where the COLONEL has lain. She calls)* Colonel Tom! Colonel Tom! Colonel Tom! Look! Bertha and Sallie and William and Bert, all your chilluns, runnin' from you, and you layin' on de floor there, dead! *(Pointing)* Out yonder with the mob, dead. And when you come home, upstairs in my bed on top of my body, dead. *(Goes to the window, returns, sits down, and begins to speak as if remembering a far-off dream)* Colonel Thomas Norwood! I'm just poor Cora Lewis, Colonel Norwood. Little black Cora Lewis, Colonel Norwood. I'm just fifteen years old. Thirty years ago, you put your hands on me to feel my breasts, and you say, "You a pretty little piece of flesh, ain't you? Black and sweet, ain't you?" And I lift up ma face, and you pull me to you, and we laid down under the trees that night, and I wonder if your wife'll know when you go back up the road into the big house. And I wonder if my mama'll know it, when I go back to our cabin. Mama said she nursed you when you was a baby, just like she nursed me. And I loved you in the dark, down there under that tree by de gate, afraid of you and proud of you, feelin' your gray eyes lookin' at me in de dark. Then I cried and cried and told ma mother about it, but she didn't take it hard like I thought she'd take it. She said fine white mens like de young Colonel always took good care o' their colored womens. She said it was better than marryin' some black field hand and workin' all your life in de cotton and cane. Better even than havin' a job like ma had, takin' care o' de white chilluns. Takin' care o' you, Colonel Tom. *(As* CORA *speaks the sounds of the approaching mob gradually grow louder and louder. Auto horns, the howling of dogs, the far-off shouts of men, full of malignant force and power, increase in volume)* And I was happy because I liked you, 'cause you was tall and proud, 'cause you said I was sweet to you and called me purty. And when yo' wife died—de Mrs Norwood *(Scornfully)* that never bore you any chilluns, the pale beautiful Mrs Norwood that was like a slender pine tree in de winter frost . . . I knowed you wanted me. I was full with child by you then—William, it was—our first boy. And ma mammy said, go up there and keep de house for Colonel Tom, sweep de floors and make de beds, and by and by, you won't have to sweep de floors and make no beds. And

what my mammy said was right. It all come true. Sam and Rusus and 'Vonia and Lucy did de waitin' on you and me, and de washin' and de cleanin' and de cookin'. And all I did was a little sewin' now and then, and a little preservin' in de summer and a little makin' of pies and sweet cakes and things you like to eat on Christmas. And de years went by. And I was always ready for you when you come to me in de night. And we had them chilluns, your chilluns and mine, Tom Norwood, all of 'em! William, born dark like me, dumb like me, and then Baby John what died; then Bertha, white and smart like you; and then Bert with your eyes and your ways and your temper, and mighty nigh your color; then Sallie, nearly white, too, and smart, and purty. But Bert was yo' chile! He was always yo' child . . . Good-looking, and kind, and headstrong, and strange, and stubborn, and proud like you, and de one I could love most 'cause he needed de most lovin'. And he wanted to call you "papa," and I tried to teach him no, but he did it anyhow and *(Sternly)* you beat him, Colonel Thomas Norwood. And he growed up with de beatin' in his heart, and your eyes in his head, and your ways, and your pride. And this summer he looked like you that time I first knowed you down by de road under them trees, young and fiery and proud. There was no touchin' Bert, just like there was no touchin' you. I could only love him, like I loved you. I could only love him. But I couldn't talk to him, because he hated you. He had your ways—and you beat him! After you beat that chile, then you died, Colonel Norwood. You died here in this house, and you been living dead a long time. You lived dead. *(Her voice rises above the nearing sounds of the mob)* And when I said this evenin', "Get up! Why don't you help me?" You'd done been dead a long time—a long time before you laid down on this floor, here, with the breath choked out o' you—and Bert standin' over you living, living, living. That's why you hated him. And you want to kill him. Always, you wanted to kill him. Out there with de hounds and de torches and de cars and de guns, you want to kill ma boy. But you won't kill him! He's comin' home first. He's comin' home to me. He's comin' home! *(Outside the noise is tremendous now, the lights of autos flash on the window curtains, there are shouts and cries.* CORA *sits, tense, in the middle of the room)* He's comin' home!

A MAN'S VOICE: *(outside)* He's somewhere on this lot.

ANOTHER VOICE: Don't shoot, men. We want to get him alive.

VOICE: Close in on him. He must be in them bushes by the house.

FIRST VOICE: Porch! Porch! Porch! There he is yonder—running to the door!
(Suddenly shots are heard. The door bursts open and ROBERT *enters, firing back into the darkness. The shots are returned by the mob, breaking the windows. Flares, lights, voices, curses, screams.)*

VOICES: Nigger! Nigger! Nigger! Get the nigger!
*(*CORA *rushes toward the door and bolts it after her son's entrance.)*

CORA: *(leaning against the door)* I was waiting for you, honey. Yo' hiding place is all ready, upstairs, under ma bed, under de floor. I sawed a place there fo' you. They can't find you there. Hurry—before yo' father comes.

ROBERT: *(panting)* No time to hide, ma. They're at the door now. They'll be coming up the back way, too. *(Sounds of knocking and the breaking of glass)* They'll be coming in the windows. They'll be coming in everywhere. And only one bullet left, ma. It's for me.

CORA: Yes, it's fo' you, chile. Save it. Go upstairs in mama's room. Lay on ma bed and rest.

ROBERT: *(going slowly toward the stairs with the pistol in his hand)* Goodnight, ma. I'm awful tired of running, ma. They been chasing me for hours.

CORA: Goodnight, son.
*(*CORA *follows him to the foot of the steps. The door begins to give at the forcing of the mob. As* ROBERT *disappears above, it bursts open. A great crowd of white men pour into the room with guns, ropes, clubs, flashlights, and knives.* CORA *turns on the stairs, facing them quietly.* TALBOT, *the leader of the mob, stops.)*

TALBOT: Be careful, men. He's armed. *(To* CORA*)* Where is that yellow bastard of yours—upstairs?

CORA: Yes, he's going to sleep. Be quiet, you all. Wait. *(She bars the way with outspread arms)*

TALBOT: *(harshly)* Wait, hell! Come on, boys, let's go! *(A single shot is heard upstairs)* What's that?

CORA: *(calmly)* My boy . . . is gone . . . to sleep!
*(*TALBOT *and some of the men rush up the stairway,* CORA *makes a final gesture of love toward the room above. Yelling and shouting, through all the doors and windows, a great crowd pours into the room. The roar of the mob fills the house, the whole night, the whole world. Suddenly* TALBOT *returns at the top of the steps and a hush falls over the crowd.)*

TALBOT: Too late, men. We're just a little too late. *(A sigh of disappointment rises from the mob.* TALBOT *comes down the stairs, walks up to* CORA *and slaps her once across the face. She does not move. It is as though no human hand can touch her again.)*

CURTAIN

THE ICEMAN COMETH (1946)

When Eugene O'Neill (1888–1953) began writing *The Iceman Cometh* in June 1939, he undertook a project for which he had been preparing most of his adult life. By 1939, O'Neill had reached both the apex of artistic success and the nadir of physical and psychological exhaustion caused by bouts with neuritis, rheumatism, and alcoholism. In 1936, he became the first American dramatist to win the Nobel Prize for Literature; to this day, no other American playwright has been so honored. And, while some questioned the Nobel committee's selection of O'Neill, the theatrical world, for the most part, endorsed it with great enthusiasm. Bernard Shaw and William Butler Yeats, themselves Nobel laureates, were but two of the many important writers who expressed their approbation of O'Neill's selection. This influential prize matched the magnitude of both the past accomplishments and future aspirations of America's first great playwright, for only a year earlier in 1935, O'Neill began work on what was to be his greatest achievement: *A Tale of Possessors Self-Dispossessed*, a cycle tracing several generations of a family composed of nine full-length and independent, yet intimately linked, plays. By the time of his death, however, he had completed to his satisfaction only *A Touch of the Poet* (1935–1942; first produced, 1956); a second, unfinished play, *More Stately Mansions*, was revised and produced in 1967.

Despite O'Neill's failure to conclude this cycle, his most distinguished plays are the products of these later years: *The Iceman Cometh, Long Day's Journey Into Night* (1939–1941; first produced, 1956), and *A Moon for the Misbegotten* (1943; first produced, 1957). All three dramas are wrought from events in his life (or, in the case of *A Moon for the Misbegotten*, in the life of his older brother, Jamie).

O'Neill's parents James and Ella Quinlan O'Neill both came from Irish-Catholic families that had immigrated to America, and both his father and Jamie were actors. James O'Neill was in fact a celebrated performer on the nineteenth- and early twentieth-century stages who, in his younger years, enjoyed the status of matinée idol due in large measure to his celebrated and often repeated portrayal of Edmond Dantes in an adaptation of Alexandre Dumas' romantic novel, *The Count of Monte Cristo*. But regardless of James's success, the O'Neill family suffered from serious problems and longstanding internal conflicts. As *Long Day's Journey Into Night* suggests, O'Neill's brother was prone to cynicism and alcoholism, and his mother suffered both from an addiction to morphine first prescribed to ease her pain in childbirth and from unrelenting feelings of guilt over the death of a third son, Edmund, from the measles when he was but 18 months old. James O'Neill was frequently vilified by his sons, particularly by Jamie, for his philandering as a younger man and for his miserliness, or for causing Ella's drug addiction due to the elder O'Neill's failures to provide her with a decent home or a competent doctor. At middle age, Eugene O'Neill looked into his past for the raw materials of these three dramas, and the guilt and internal conflict so prevalent in his earlier work inevitably surfaced in them.

Both *Long Day's Journey Into Night* and *The Iceman Cometh* are set in 1912, a year crucial to O'Neill's life and development as a playwright. Expelled from Princeton in 1907 and secretly married in 1909, O'Neill had yet to find himself professionally, so his father arranged for him to travel to Honduras on a gold-mining expedition. Following six months in Central America, he signed on as an assistant stage manager for a touring melodrama in which his father was starring.

But neither prospecting nor stage management appealed to him. His experience traveling between Honduras and the United States, however, whetted O'Neill's appetite for the life of a seaman; so after his unhappy stint as a stage manager ended, he embarked upon voyages to South America and Europe. These experiences eventually led to O'Neill's writing a number of one-act "plays of the sea," several of which were adapted into a single narrative by filmmaker John Ford in *Long Voyage Home* (1939). It was in between such trips that in 1911 he happened across the rooming-house bar near the dockside area of lower Manhattan that would serve as the setting for *The Iceman Cometh*. For three dollars a month, O'Neill rented a room over the saloon that would become Harry Hope's bar in the play, spending most of his money on cheap whiskey and beer, five cents a glass or schooner. Here, in the company of the dissolute residents of the place, O'Neill nearly drank himself to death. And in 1912, after another unsuccessful foray into the theatre with his father, he attempted suicide, a project at which his fellow boarder, Jimmy Byth, later Jimmy Tomorrow in *The Iceman Cometh*, succeeded. Over a quarter of a century after O'Neill lived there, many of the alcoholic denizens of "Jimmy-the-Priest's" (so-called after its owner, James J. Condon) reappeared as central characters in *The Iceman Cometh*.

In the winter of 1914, after short stints as a sailor and journalist, O'Neill enrolled in George Pierce Baker's Workshop 47, and in 1915 joined the **Provincetown Players** on Cape Cod whose members included Susan Glaspell and her husband "Jig" Cook, Robert Edmond Jones, and social activist John Reed. The Provincetown Players, both in Massachusetts and in Greenwich Village where the company moved in 1916, produced such early O'Neill plays of the sea as *Bound East for Cardiff*, *In the Zone*, *The Moon of the Caribbees*, and *Long Voyage Home*. Its 1920 production of *The Emperor Jones*, O'Neill's **expressionist** representation of a black train porter-turned-dictator, helped establish the company's artistic credentials in New York and sparked controversy when Charles Gilpin, the actor who played

Brutus Jones, accused O'Neill of racism. Nevertheless, Gilpin's portrayal achieved historical importance as one of the first featured roles played by a black actor on the American stage; many more such roles followed in the 1920s and 1930s.

Between 1916 and his receipt of the Nobel Prize in 1936, O'Neill established himself as America's preeminent dramatist, earning Pulitzer Prizes for his first full-length play, *Beyond the Horizon* (1920), and later for *Anna Christie* (1922) and *Strange Interlude* (1927). His other works include *The Hairy Ape* (1921), *Desire Under the Elms* (1924), *The Great God Brown* (1925), the epic-length *Mourning Becomes Electra* (1928), and *Days Without End* (1934), all of which reflect O'Neill's interest in and study of psychoanalysis, an interest shared by many American intellectuals outside of Provincetown and Greenwich Village. As the Provincetown Players were forming, European psychoanalysis was becoming institutionalized in America; and in 1914 the American Psychoanalytic Association (APA) began publication of *The Psychoanalytic Review*, in which the work of Freud and such members of his inner circle as Carl Jung and Otto Rank was regularly featured. European analysts were routinely invited to speak at annual conventions of the APA, and psychoanalytic thought informed conversations in the intellectual and artistic circles in which O'Neill traveled. Cook and Glaspell poke fun at those infatuated with psychoanalytic explanations in their one-act play *Suppressed Desires* (1914), in which Freudian theory is applied in laughable ways by devotees who speak to each other in a dialogue replete with analytic jargon.

If merely an intellectual fad for some, O'Neill took analysis very seriously; indeed, a psychiatrist he saw for six weeks in 1926 advised him that his excessive drinking was caused by unresolved guilt over his unacknowledged Oedipal impulses. And critical readings of such plays as *Desire Under the Elms*, *Strange Interlude*, and *Mourning Becomes Electra* also tend to take their Freudian thematics seriously. In *O'Neill: Son and Artist*, for example, Louis Sheaffer emphasizes the Oedipal nature of hostility between father and son in *Desire Under the Elms*, and Charles Marsden in *Strange Interlude* alludes mockingly to the preeminent position psychoanalytic theory had achieved among American intellectuals: "O Oedipus, O my King! The World is adopting you!" *Strange Interlude* also owes much to Freud's *Beyond the Pleasure Principle* (1920), one of several books by Freud and Jung that O'Neill mentions when discussing works that have influenced him. And O'Neill describes his intention in *Mourning Becomes Electra*, a trilogy of plays formed into one dramatic text and modeled after Aeschylus' *Oresteia*, as an attempt to create a tragedy from a psychological equivalent of the "Greek sense of fate." If he achieves this intention, he does so not only by refashioning devices appropriated from the classical stage—the mask-like faces of the Mannon family, the play's central characters, and his use of townspeople as a kind of chorus—but also by employing split characters or "doubles," mirror-image figures who struggle with Oedipal anxiety, misdirected sexual longing, and overwhelming guilt. These are serious matters, to be sure, with tragic consequences for the central characters of the play.

The Iceman Cometh also contains psychoanalytic resonances, albeit not quite so overt ones as those in some of his earlier works. The dramatic action of the play hovers between tragedy and pathos, especially after Theodore Hickman ("Hickey") enters the scene near the end of Act One. Hickey's arrival is much anticipated by his former drinking cronies, yet he has come to Hope's saloon on this occasion not to preside over a drunken party, but to lead them out of their self-created illusions or "pipe dreams," as he often calls them. Rather like one premise of Freud's analytic practice, Hickey's plan is based on the notion that only after confronting their own inner truths will his friends find any lasting "peace," another of his favorite terms. His friends are not eager to accept his cure, although several do attempt to confront their illusions, and only after Hickey has been led away by the police is there any peace for his friends in Hope's saloon. This return to "normalcy" is ironic and bittersweet at best, for it includes the restoration of several characters' impossible dreams of regaining their former statures before their lives were

destroyed by alcoholism. The title of the play suggests such a formal ambiguity, as the "iceman" is both a central character in a dirty joke told by Hickey and a figure of death; O'Neill apparently intended a parallel between the title of his play and a Biblical passage with the words: "Death cometh." Hickey, as Larry Slade recognizes in Act Three, is the "iceman" of death: "I'm damned sure he's brought death here with him. I feel the cold touch of it on him."

In a reading of the play that recalls Aristotelian theories of tragic drama, Robert Bechtold Heilman refers to O'Neill's vision as inherently "antitragic." Heilman bases his thesis on Hickey's ultimate failure to convince his friends of the importance of dispelling their "pipe dreams." That is to say, in the *Poetics* Aristotle emphasizes the importance to tragic action of what the Greeks referred to as **peripeteia** and **anagnorisis** (reversal of fortune and self-recognition), respectively. After the fortune of the tragic hero begins to reverse, he reaches a new level of self-understanding, as Oedipus does in Sophocles' tragedy *Oedipus the King*. Because O'Neill's characters fail to achieve such self-knowledge—even Hickey, whose claims of attaining "peace" are belied by his desire to be punished for his crime—Heilman regards O'Neill's implicit argument in *The Iceman Cometh* as concerning the "impossibility of tragic experience: man cannot bear self-knowledge [and] must therefore live in illusion." Among other characters, Martha Dobie in Lillian Hellman's *The Children's Hour* and Joe Keller in Arthur Miller's *All My Sons* might be viewed as confirming this thesis, as their own acquisition of self-knowledge precipitates their suicides.

While such a reading relies on perhaps too narrow an understanding of Aristotle's *Poetics*, it also underscores the difficulties of applying traditional conceptions of genre to plays of the modern and contemporary eras. Who *is* the tragic hero in *The Iceman Cometh*? In what ways is his—or their—fall "tragic"? How are audiences or readers to regard the return of peace to the residents of Hope's boardinghouse? *The Iceman Cometh* thus leaves its audience not only with a sense of the desperation of its principal characters, but also with a number of questions about genre, dramatic form, and theme. In addition, the production history of *The Iceman Cometh* would seem to indicate that audiences have responded to these questions—and to the play itself—in quite different ways. First given a problematic production by the Theatre Guild in October 1946, the play received a number of reviews that Louis Sheaffer aptly terms "sharply critical" and "lukewarm" (although three critics endorsed *The Iceman* for the New York Drama Critics Circle Award as Play of the Year, a prize which went to Miller's *All My Sons*). Ten years later in an **Off-Broadway** production at the Circle in the Square theatre starring Jason Robards, director José Quintero succeeded in bringing out the qualities of O'Neill's play that Broadway could not. Quintero and Robards went on to collaborate in, among other productions, *Long Day's Journey into Night* in November 1956, securing their reputations as America's preeminent interpreters of O'Neill's work. Thus, after a long absence in the late 1930s and early 1940s, O'Neill returned to New York and

American theatre, reclaiming his place and challenging new audiences as he plumbed heretofore undiscovered depths of meaning in his plays—and, inevitably, in his life.

WORKS CONSULTED

Bogard, Travis. *Contour in Time: The Plays of Eugene O'Neill.* New York: Oxford University Press, 1972.

Gelb, Arthur, and Barbara Gelb. *O'Neill.* New York: Harper & Row, 1962.

Heilman, Robert Bechtold. *The Iceman, the Arsonist, and the Troubled Agent: Tragedy and Melodrama on the Modern Stage.* Seattle: University of Washington Press, 1973.

Raleigh, John Henry, ed. *Twentieth Century Interpretations of The Iceman Cometh.* Englewood Cliffs, NJ: Prentice-Hall, 1968.

Sheaffer, Louis. *O'Neill: Son and Artist.* Boston: Little, Brown, 1973.

———. *O'Neill: Son and Playwright.* Boston: Little, Brown, 1968.

Watt, Stephen. "O'Neill and Otto Rank: Doubles, 'Death Instincts,' and the Trauma of Birth." *Comparative Drama,* 20 (1986): 211–230.

CHARACTERS

HARRY HOPE . . . . proprietor of a saloon and rooming house*

ED MOSHER . . . . Hope's brother-in-law, one-time circus man*

PAT MCGLOIN . . . . one-time Police Lieutenant*

WILLIE OBAN . . . . a Harvard Law School alumnus*

JOE MOTT . . . . one-time proprietor of a Negro gambling house

PIET WETJOEN ("THE GENERAL") . . . . one-time leader of a Boer commando*

CECIL LEWIS ("THE CAPTAIN") . . . . one-time Captain of British infantry*

JAMES CAMERON ("JIMMY TOMORROW") . . . . one-time Boer War correspondent*

HUGO KALAMAR . . . . one-time editor of Anarchist periodicals

LARRY SLADE . . . . one-time Syndicalist-Anarchist*

ROCKY PIOGGI . . . . night bartender*

DON PARRITT*

*Roomers at Harry Hope's.

PEARL*
MARGIE* } .... street walkers
CORA
CHUCK MORELLO .... day bartender*
THEODORE HICKMAN (HICKEY) .... a hardware salesman
MORAN
LIEB

Synopsis of Scenes

Harry Hope's is a Raines-Law hotel of the period, a cheap gin-mill of the five-cent whiskey, last-resort variety situated on the downtown West Side of New York. The building, owned by Hope, is a narrow five-story structure of the tenement type, the second floor a flat occupied by the proprietor. The renting of rooms on the upper floors, under the Raines-Law loopholes, makes the establishment legally a hotel and gives it the privilege of serving liquor in the back room of the bar after closing hours and on Sundays, provided a meal is served with the booze, thus making a back room legally a hotel restaurant. This food provision was generally circumvented by putting a property sandwich in the middle of each table, an old desiccated ruin of dust-laden bread and mummified ham or cheese which only the drunkest yokel from the sticks ever regarded as anything but a noisome table decoration. But at Harry Hope's, Hope being a former minor Tammanyite and still possessing friends, this food technicality is ignored as irrelevant, except during the fleeting alarms of reform agitation. Even Hope's back room is not a separate room, but simply the rear of the barroom divided from the bar by drawing a dirty black curtain across the room.

ACT ONE

SCENE: *The back room and a section of the bar of* HARRY HOPE'S *saloon on an early morning in summer, 1912. The right wall of the back room is a dirty black curtain which separates it from the bar. At rear, this curtain is drawn back from the wall so the bartender can get in and out. The back room is crammed with round tables and chairs placed so close together that it is a difficult squeeze to pass between them. In the middle of the rear wall is a door opening on a hallway. In the left corner, built out into the room, is the toilet with a sign "This is it" on the door. Against the middle of the left wall is a nickel-in-the-slot phonograph. Two windows, so glazed with grime one cannot see through them, are in the left wall, looking out on a backyard. The walls and ceiling once were white, but it was a long time ago, and they are now so splotched, peeled,* stained and dusty that their color can best be described as dirty. The floor, with iron spittoons placed here and there, is covered with sawdust. Lighting comes from single wall brackets, two at left and two at rear.

There are three rows of tables, from front to back. Three are in the front line. The one at left-front has four chairs; the one at center-front, four; the one at right-front, five. At rear of, and half between, front tables one and two is a table of the second row with five chairs. A table, similarly placed at rear of front tables two and three, also has five chairs. The third row of tables, four chairs to one and six to the other, is against the rear wall on either side of the door.

At right of this dividing curtain is a section of the barroom, with the end of the bar seen at rear, a door to the hall at left of it. At front is a table with four chairs. Light comes from the street windows off right, the gray subdued light of early morning in a narrow street. In the back room, LARRY SLADE and HUGO KALAMAR are at the table at left-front, HUGO in a chair facing right, LARRY at rear of table facing front, with an empty chair between them. A fourth chair is at right of table, facing left. HUGO is a small man in his late fifties. He has a head much too big for his body, a high forehead, crinkly long black hair streaked with gray, a square face with a pug nose, a walrus mustache, black eyes which peer near-sightedly from behind thick-lensed spectacles, tiny hands and feet. He is dressed in threadbare black clothes and his white shirt is frayed at collar and cuffs, but everything about him is fastidiously clean. Even his flowing Windsor tie is neatly tied. There is a foreign atmosphere about him, the stamp of an alien radical, a strong resemblance to the type Anarchist as portrayed, bomb in hand, in newspaper cartoons. He is asleep now, bent forward in his chair, his arms folded on the table, his head resting sideways on his arms.

LARRY SLADE is sixty. He is tall, raw-boned, with coarse straight white hair, worn long and raggedly cut. He has a gaunt Irish face with a big nose, high cheekbones, a lantern jaw with a week's stubble of beard, a mystic's meditative pale-blue eyes with a gleam of sharp sardonic humor in them. As slovenly as HUGO is neat, his clothes are dirty and much slept

in. His gray flannel shirt, open at the neck, has the appearance of having never been washed. From the way he methodically scratches himself with his long-fingered, hairy hands, he is lousy and reconciled to being so. He is the only occupant of the room who is not asleep. He stares in front of him, an expression of tired tolerance giving his face the quality of a pitying but weary old priest's.

All four chairs at the middle table, front, are occupied. JOE MOTT sits at left-front of the table, facing front. Behind him, facing right-front, is PIET WETJOEN ("The General"). At center of the table, rear, JAMES CAMERON ("Jimmy Tomorrow") sits facing front. At right of table, opposite JOE, is CECIL LEWIS ("The Captain").

JOE MOTT is a Negro, about fifty years old, brown-skinned, stocky, wearing a light suit that had once been flashily sporty but is now about to fall apart. His pointed tan buttoned shoes, faded pink shirt and bright tie belong to the same vintage. Still, he manages to preserve an atmosphere of nattiness and there is nothing dirty about his appearance. His face is only mildly negroid in type. The nose is thin and his lips are not noticeably thick. His hair is crinkly and he is beginning to get bald. A scar from a knife slash runs from his left cheekbone to jaw. His face would be hard and tough if it were not for its good nature and lazy humor. He is asleep, his nodding head supported by his left hand.

PIET WETJOEN, the Boer, is in his fifties, a huge man with a bald head and a long grizzled beard. He is slovenly dressed in a dirty shapeless patched suit, spotted by food. A Dutch farmer type, his once great muscular strength has been debauched into flaccid tallow. But despite his blubbery mouth and sodden bloodshot blue eyes, there is still a suggestion of old authority lurking in him like a memory of the drowned. He is hunched forward, both elbows on the table, his hand on each side of his head for support.

JAMES CAMERON ("Jimmy Tomorrow") is about the same size and age as HUGO, a small man. Like HUGO, he wears threadbare black, and everything about him is clean. But the resemblance ceases there. JIMMY has a face like an old well-bred, gentle bloodhound's, with folds of flesh hanging from each side of his mouth, and big brown friendly guileless eyes, more bloodshot than any bloodhound's ever were. He has mouse-colored thinning hair, a little bulbous nose, buck teeth in a small rabbit mouth. But his forehead is fine, his eyes are intelligent and there once was a competent ability in him. His speech is educated, with the ghost of a Scotch rhythm in it. His manners are those of a gentleman. There is a quality about him of a prim, Victorian old maid, and at the same time of a likable, affectionate boy who has never grown up. He sleeps, chin on chest, hands folded in his lap.

CECIL LEWIS ("The Captain") is as obviously English as Yorkshire pudding and just as obviously the former army officer. He is going on sixty. His hair and military mustache are white, his eyes bright blue, his complexion that of a turkey. His lean figure is still erect and square-shouldered. He is stripped to the waist, his coat, shirt, undershirt, collar and tie crushed up into a pillow on the table in front of him, his head sideways on this pillow, facing front, his arms dangling toward the floor. On his lower left shoulder is the big ragged scar of an old wound.

At the table at right-front, HARRY HOPE, the proprietor, sits in the middle, facing front, with PAT MCGLOIN on his right and ED MOSHER on his left, the other two chairs being unoccupied.

Both MCGLOIN and MOSHER are big paunchy men. MCGLOIN has his old occupation of policeman stamped all over him. He is in his fifties, sandy-haired, bullet-headed, jowly, with protruding ears and little round eyes. His face must once have been brutal and greedy, but time and whiskey have melted it down into a good-humored, parasite's characterlessness. He wears old clothes and is slovenly. He is slumped sideways on his chair, his head drooping jerkily toward one shoulder.

ED MOSHER is going on sixty. He has a round kewpie's face—a kewpie who is an unshaven habitual drunkard. He looks like an enlarged, elderly, bald edition of the village fat boy—a sly fat boy, congenitally indolent, a practical joker, a born grafter and con merchant. But amusing and essentially harmless, even in his most enterprising days, because always too lazy to carry crookedness beyond petty swindling.

The influence of his old circus career is apparent in his get-up. His worn clothes are flashy; he wears phony rings and a heavy brass watch-chain (not connected to a watch). Like MCGLOIN, he is slovenly. His head is thrown back, his big mouth open.

HARRY HOPE is sixty, white-haired, so thin the description "bag of bones" was made for him. He has the face of an old family horse, prone to tantrums, with balkiness always smoldering in its wall eyes, waiting for any excuse to shy and pretend to take the bit in its teeth. HOPE is one of those men whom everyone likes on sight, a softhearted slob, without malice, feeling superior to no one, a sinner among sinners, a born easy mark for every appeal. He attempts to hide his defenselessness behind a testy truculent manner, but this has never fooled anyone. He is a little deaf, but not half as deaf as he sometimes pretends. His sight is failing but is not as bad as he complains it is. He wears five-and-ten-cent-store spectacles which are so out of alignment that one eye at times peers half over one glass while the other eye looks half under the other. He has badly fitting store teeth, which click like castanets when he begins to fume. He is dressed in an old coat from one suit and pants from another.

In a chair facing right at the table in the second line, between the first two tables, front, sits WILLIE OBAN, his head on his left arm outstretched along the table edge. He is in his late thirties, of average height, thin. His haggard, dissipated face has a small nose, a pointed chin, blue eyes with colorless lashes and brows. His blond hair, badly in need of a cut, clings in a limp part to his skull. His eyelids flutter continually as if any light were too strong for his eyes. The clothes he wears belong on a scarecrow. They seem constructed of an inferior grade of dirty blotting paper. His shoes are even more disreputable, wrecks of imitation leather, one laced with twine, the other with a bit of wire. He has no socks, and his bare feet show through holes in the soles, with his big toes sticking out of the uppers. He keeps muttering and twitching in his sleep.

As the curtain rises, ROCKY, the night bartender, comes from the bar through the curtain and stands looking over the back room. He is a Neapolitan-American in his late twenties, squat and muscular, *with a flat, swarthy face and beady eyes. The sleeves of his collarless shirt are rolled up on his thick, powerful arms and he wears a soiled apron. A tough guy but sentimental, in his way, and good-natured. He signals to* LARRY *with a cautious "Sstt" and motions him to see if* HOPE *is asleep.* LARRY *rises from his chair to look at* HOPE *and nods to* ROCKY. ROCKY *goes back to the bar but immediately returns with a bottle of bar whiskey and a glass. He squeezes between the tables to* LARRY.

ROCKY: *(in a low voice out of the side of his mouth)* Make it fast. *(* LARRY *pours a drink and gulps it down.* ROCKY *takes the bottle and puts it on the table where* WILLIE OBAN *is)* Don't want de Boss to get wise when he's got one of his tightwad buns on. *(He chuckles with an amused glance at* HOPE*)* Jees, ain't de old bastard a riot when he starts dat bull about turnin' over a new leaf? "Not a damned drink on de house," he tells me, "and all dese bums got to pay up deir room rent. Beginnin' tomorrow," he says. Jees, yuh'd tink he meant it!
(He sits down in the chair at LARRY'S *left.)*

LARRY: *(grinning)* I'll be glad to pay up—tomorrow. And I know my fellow inmates will promise the same. They've all a touching credulity concerning tomorrows. *(A half-drunken mockery in his eyes)* It'll be a great day for them, tomorrow—the Feast of All Fools, with brass bands playing! Their ships will come in, loaded to the gunwales with cancelled regrets and promises fulfilled and clean slates and new leases!

ROCKY: *(cynically)* Yeah, and a ton of hop!

LARRY: *(leans toward him, a comical intensity in his low voice)* Don't mock the faith! Have you no respect for religion, you unregenerate Wop? What's it matter if the truth is that their favoring breeze has the stink of nickel whiskey on its breath, and their sea is a growler of lager and ale, and their ships are long since looted and scuttled and sunk on the bottom? To hell with the truth! As the history of the world proves, the truth has no bearing on anything.

It's irrelevant and immaterial, as the lawyers say. The lie of a pipe dream is what gives life to the whole misbegotten mad lot of us, drunk or sober. And that's enough philosophic wisdom to give you for one drink of rotgut.

ROCKY: *(grins kiddingly)* De old Foolosopher, like Hickey calls yuh, ain't yuh? I s'pose you don't fall for no pipe dream?

LARRY: *(a bit stiffly)* I don't, no. Mine are all dead and buried behind me. What's before me is the comforting fact that death is a fine long sleep, and I'm damned tired, and it can't come too soon for me.

ROCKY: Yeah, just hangin' around hopin' you'll croak, ain't yuh? Well, I'm bettin' you'll have a good long wait. Jees, somebody'll have to take an axe to croak you!

LARRY: *(grins)* Yes, it's my bad luck to be cursed with an iron constitution that even Harry's booze can't corrode.

ROCKY: De old anarchist wise guy dat knows all de answers! Dat's you, huh?

LARRY: *(frowns)* Forget the anarchist part of it. I'm through with the Movement long since. I saw men didn't want to be saved from themselves, for that would mean they'd have to give up greed, and they'll never pay that price for liberty. So I said to the world, God bless all here, and may the best man win and die of gluttony! And I took a seat in the grandstand of philosophical detachment to fall asleep observing the cannibals do their death dance. *(He chuckles at his own fancy—reaches over and shakes* HUGO'S *shoulder)* Ain't I telling him the truth, Comrade Hugo?

ROCKY: Aw, fer Chris' sake, don't get dat bughouse bum started!

HUGO: *(raises his head and peers at* ROCKY *blearily through his thick spectacles—in a guttural declamatory tone)* Capitalist swine! Bourgeois stool pigeons! Have the slaves no right to sleep even? *(Then he grins at* ROCKY *and his manner changes to a giggling, wheedling playfulness, as though he were talking to a child)* Hello, leedle Rocky! Leedle monkey-face! Vere is your leedle slave girls? *(With an abrupt change to a bully-ing tone)* Don't be a fool! Loan me a dollar! Damned bourgeois Wop! The great Malatesta is my good friend! Buy me a trink!

(He seems to run down, and is overcome by drowsiness. His head sinks to the table again and he is at once fast asleep.)

ROCKY: He's out again. *(More exasperated than an-gry)* He's lucky no one don't take his cracks seri-ous or he'd wake up every mornin' in a hospital.

LARRY: *(regarding* HUGO *with pity)* No. No one takes him seriously. That's his epitaph. Not even the comrades any more. If I've been through with the Movement long since, it's been through with him, and, thanks to whiskey, he's the only one doesn't know it.

ROCKY: I've let him get by wid too much. He's goin' to pull dat slavegirl stuff on me once too often. *(His manner changes to defensive argu-ment)* Hell, yuh'd tink I wuz a pimp or some-thin'. Everybody knows me knows I ain't. A pimp don't hold no job. I'm a bartender. Dem tarts, Margie and Poil, dey're just a side line to pick up some extra dough. Strictly business, like dey was fighters and I was deir manager, see? I fix the cops fer dem so's dey can hustle widout gettin' pinched. Hell, dey'd be on de Is-land most of de time if it wasn't fer me. And I don't beat dem up like a pimp would. I treat dem fine. Dey like me. We're pals, see? What if I do take deir dough? Dey'd on'y trow it away. Tarts can't hang on to dough. But I'm a bartender and I work hard for my livin' in dis dump. You know dat, Larry.

LARRY: *(with inner sardonic amusement—flat-teringly)* A shrewd business man, who doesn't miss any opportunity to get on in the world. That's what I'd call you.

ROCKY: *(pleased)* Sure ting. Dat's me. Grab an-other ball, Larry. *(*LARRY *pours a drink from the bottle on* WILLIE'S *table and gulps it down.* ROCKY *glances around the room)* Yuh'd never tink all dese bums had a good bed upstairs to go to. Scared if dey hit the hay dey wouldn't be here when Hickey showed up, and dey'd miss a coupla drinks. Dat's what kept you up too, ain't it?

LARRY: It is. But not so much the hope of booze, if you can believe that. I've got the blues and Hickey's a great one to make a joke of every-thing and cheer you up.

ROCKY: Yeah, some kidder! Remember how he woiks up dat gag about his wife, when he's cock-eyed, cryin' over her picture and den springin' it on yuh all of a sudden dat he left her in de hay wid de iceman? *(He laughs)* I wonder what's happened to him. Yuh could set your watch by his periodicals before dis. Always got here a coupla days before Harry's birthday party, and now he's on'y got till tonight to make it. I hope he shows soon. Dis dump is like de morgue wid all dese bums passed out.

*(*WILLIE OBAN *jerks and twitches in his sleep and begins to mumble. They watch him.)*

WILLIE: *(blurts from his dream)* It's a lie! *(Miser-ably)* Papa! Papa!

LARRY: Poor devil. *(Then angry with himself)* But to hell with pity! It does no good. I'm through with it!

ROCKY: Dreamin' about his old man. From what de old-timers say, de old gent sure made a pile of dough in de bucket-shop game before de cops got him. *(He considers* WILLIE *frowningly)* Jees, I've seen him bad before but never dis bad. Look at dat get-up. Been playin' de old reliever game. Sold his suit and shoes at Solly's two days ago. Solly give him two bucks and a bum outfit. Yesterday he sells de bum one back to Solly for four bits and gets dese rags to put on. Now he's through. Dat's Solly's final edition he wouldn't take back for nuttin'. Willie sure is on de bot-tom. I ain't never seen no one so bad, except Hickey on de end of a coupla his bats.

LARRY: *(sardonically)* It's a great game, the pur-suit of happiness.

ROCKY: Harry don't know what to do about him. He called up his old lady's lawyer like he al-ways does when Willie gets licked. Yuh remem-ber dey used to send down a private dick to give him the rush to a cure, but de lawyer tells Harry nix, de old lady's off of Willie for keeps dis time and he can go to hell.

LARRY: (watches WILLIE, *who is shaking in his sleep like an old dog*) There's the consolation that he hasn't far to go! (*As if replying to this,* WILLIE *comes to a crisis of jerks and moans.* LARRY *adds in a comically intense, crazy whisper*) Be God, he's knocking on the door right now!

WILLIE: (*suddenly yells in his nightmare*) It's a God-damned lie! (*He begins to sob*) Oh, Papa! Jesus!
(*All the occupants of the room stir on their chairs but none of them wakes up except* HOPE.)

ROCKY: (*grabs his shoulder and shakes him*) Hey, you! Nix! Cut out de noise!
(WILLIE *opens his eyes to stare around him with a bewildered horror.*)

HOPE: (*opens one eye to peer over his spectacles—drowsily*) Who's that yelling?

ROCKY: Willie, Boss. De Brooklyn boys is after him.

HOPE: (*querulously*) Well, why don't you give the poor feller a drink and keep him quiet? Bejees, can't I get a wink of sleep in my own back room?

ROCKY: (*indignantly to* LARRY) Listen to that blind-eyed, deef old bastard, will yuh? He give me strict orders not to let Willie hang up no more drinks, no matter—

HOPE: (*mechanically puts a hand to his ear in the gesture of deafness*) What's that? I can't hear you. (*Then drowsily irascible*) You're a cockeyed liar. Never refused a drink to anyone needed it bad in my life! Told you to use your judgment. Ought to know better. You're too busy thinking up ways to cheat me. Oh, I ain't as blind as you think. I can still see a cash register, bejees!

ROCKY: (*grins at him affectionately now—flatteringly*) Sure, Boss. Swell chance of foolin' you!

HOPE: I'm wise to you and your sidekick, Chuck. Bejees, you're burglars, not barkeeps! Blind-eyed, deef old bastard, am I? Oh, I heard you! Heard you often when you didn't think. You and Chuck laughing behind my back, telling

people you throw the money up in the air and whatever sticks to the ceiling is my share! A fine couple of crooks! You'd steal the pennies off your dead mother's eyes!

ROCKY: (*winks at* LARRY) Aw, Harry, me and Chuck was on'y kiddin'.

HOPE: (*more drowsily*) I'll fire both of you. Bejees, if you think you can play me for an easy mark, you've come to the wrong house. No one ever played Harry Hope for a sucker!

ROCKY: (*to* LARRY) No one but everybody.

HOPE: (*His eyes shut again—mutters*) Least you could do—keep things quiet—
(*He falls asleep.*)

WILLIE: (*pleadingly*) Give me a drink, Rocky. Harry said it was all right. God, I need a drink.

ROCKY: Den grab it. It's right under your nose.

WILLIE: (*avidly*) Thanks.
(*He takes the bottle with both twitching hands and tilts it to his lips and gulps down the whiskey in big swallows.*)

ROCKY: (*sharply*) When! When! (*He grabs the bottle*) I didn't say, take a bath! (*Showing the bottle to* LARRY—*indignantly*) Jees, look! He's killed a half pint or more!
(*He turns on* WILLIE *angrily, but* WILLIE *has closed his eyes and is sitting quietly, shuddering, waiting for the effect.*)

LARRY: (*with a pitying glance*) Leave him be, the poor devil. A half pint of that dynamite in one swig will fix him for a while—if it doesn't kill him.

ROCKY: (*shrugs his shoulders and sits down again*) Aw right by me. It ain't my booze.
(*Behind him, in the chair at left of the middle table,* JOE MOTT, *the Negro, has been waking up.*)

JOE: (*his eyes blinking sleepily*) Whose booze? Gimme some. I don't care whose. Where's Hickey? Ain't he come yet? What time's it, Rocky?

ROCKY: Gettin' near time to open up. Time you begun to sweep up in de bar.

JOE: (*lazily*) Never mind de time. If Hickey ain't come, it's time Joe goes to sleep again. I was dreamin' Hickey come in de door, crackin' one of dem drummer's jokes, wavin' a big bankroll and we was all goin' be drunk for two weeks. Wake up and no luck. *(Suddenly his eyes open wide)* Wait a minute, dough. I got idea. Say, Larry, how 'bout dat young guy, Parritt, come to look you up last night and rented a room? Where's he at?

LARRY: Up in his room, asleep. No hope in him, anyway, Joe. He's broke.

JOE: Dat what he told you? Me and Rocky knows different. Had a roll when he paid you his room rent, didn't he, Rocky? I seen it.

ROCKY: Yeah. He flashed it like he forgot and den tried to hide it quick.

LARRY: *(surprised and resentful)* He did, did he?

ROCKY: Yeah, I figgered he don't belong, but he said he was a friend of yours.

LARRY: He's a liar. I wouldn't know him if he hadn't told me who he was. His mother and I were friends years ago on the Coast. *(He hesitates—then lowering his voice)* You've read in the papers about that bombing on the Coast when several people got killed? Well, the one woman they pinched, Rosa Parritt, is his mother. They'll be coming up for trial soon, and there's no chance for them. She'll get life, I think. I'm telling you this so you'll know why if Don acts a bit queer, and not jump on him. He must be hard hit. He's her only kid.

ROCKY: *(nods—then thoughtfully)* Why ain't he out dere stickin' by her?

LARRY: *(frowns)* Don't ask questions. Maybe there's a good reason.

ROCKY: *(stares at him—understandingly)* Sure. I get it. *(Then wonderingly)* But den what kind of a sap is he to hang on to his right name?

LARRY: *(irritably)* I'm telling you I don't know anything and I don't want to know. To hell with the Movement and all connected with it! I'm out of it, and everything else, and damned glad to be.

ROCKY: *(shrugs his shoulders—indifferently)* Well, don't tink I'm interested in dis Parritt guy. He's nuttin' to me.

JOE: Me neider. If dere's one ting more'n anudder I cares nuttin' about, it's de sucker game you and Hugo call de Movement. *(He chuckles—reminiscently)* Reminds me of damn fool argument me and Mose Porter has de udder night. He's drunk and I'm drunker. He says, "Socialist and Anarchist, we ought to shoot dem dead. Dey's all no-good sons of bitches." I says, "Hold on, you talk's if Anarchists and Socialists was de same." "Dey is," he says. "Dey's both no-good bastards." "No, dey ain't," I says. "I'll explain the difference. De Anarchist he never works. He drinks but he never buys, and if he do ever get a nickel, he blows it in on bombs, and he wouldn't give you nothin'. So go ahead and shoot him. But de Socialist, sometimes, he's got a job, and if he gets ten bucks, he's bound by his religion to split fifty-fifty wid you. You say—how about my cut, Comrade? And you gets de five. So you don't shoot no Socialists while I'm around. Dat is, not if dey got anything. Of course, if dey's broke, den dey's no-good bastards, too." *(He laughs, immensely tickled.)*

LARRY: *(grins with sardonic appreciation)* Be God, Joe, you've got all the beauty of human nature and the practical wisdom of the world in that little parable.

ROCKY: *(winks at* JOE*)* Sure, Larry ain't de on'y wise guy in dis dump, hey, Joe? *(At a sound from the hall he turns as* DON PARRITT *appears in the doorway.* ROCKY *speaks to* LARRY *out of the side of his mouth)* Here's your guy.

*(*PARRITT *comes forward. He is eighteen, tall and broad-shouldered but thin, gangling and awkward. His face is good-looking, with blond curly hair and large regular features, but his personality is unpleasant. There is a shifting defiance and ingratiation in his light-blue eyes and an irritating aggressiveness in his manner. His clothes and shoes are new, comparatively expensive, sporty in style. He looks as though he belonged in a pool room patronized by would-be sports. He glances around defensively, sees* LARRY *and comes forward.)*

PARRITT: Hello, Larry. (*He nods to* ROCKY *and* JOE) Hello.

(*They nod and size him up with expressionless eyes.*)

LARRY: (*without cordiality*) What's up? I thought you'd be asleep.

PARRITT: Couldn't make it. I got sick of lying awake. Thought I might as well see if you were around.

LARRY: (*indicates the chair on the right of table*) Sit down and join the bums then. (PARRITT *sits down.* LARRY *adds meaningfully*) The rules of the house are that drinks may be served at all hours.

PARRITT: (*forcing a smile*) I get you. But, hell, I'm just about broke. (*He catches* ROCKY'S *and* JOE'S *contemptuous glances—quickly*) Oh, I know you guys saw— You think I've got a roll. Well, you're all wrong. I'll show you. (*He takes a small wad of dollar bills from his pocket*) It's all ones. And I've got to live on it till I get a job. (*Then with defensive truculence*) You think I fixed up a phony, don't you? Why the hell would I? Where would I get a real roll? You don't get rich doing what I've been doing. Ask Larry. You're lucky in the Movement if you have enough to eat.

(LARRY *regards him puzzledly.*)

ROCKY: (*coldly*) What's de song and dance about? We ain't said nuttin'.

PARRITT: (*lamely—placating them now*) Why, I was just putting you right. But I don't want you to think I'm a tightwad. I'll buy a drink if you want one.

JOE: (*cheering up*) If? Man, when I don't want a drink, you call de morgue, tell dem come take Joe's body away, 'cause he's sure enuf dead. Gimme de bottle quick, Rocky, before he changes his mind!

(ROCKY *passes him the bottle and glass. He pours a brimful drink and tosses it down his throat, and hands the bottle and glass to* LARRY.)

ROCKY: I'll take a cigar when I go in de bar. What're you havin'?

PARRITT: Nothing. I'm on the wagon. What's the damage?

(*He holds out a dollar bill.*)

ROCKY: Fifteen cents.

(*He makes change from his pocket.*)

PARRITT: Must be some booze!

LARRY: It's cyanide cut with carbolic acid to give it a mellow flavor. Here's luck!

(*He drinks.*)

ROCKY: Guess I'll get back in de bar and catch a coupla winks before opening-up time.

(*He squeezes through the tables and disappears, right-rear, behind the curtain. In the section of bar at right, he comes forward and sits at the table and slumps back, closing his eyes and yawning.*)

JOE: (*stares calculatingly at* PARRITT *and then looks away—aloud to himself, philosophically*) One-drink guy. Dat well done run dry. No hope till Harry's birthday party. 'Less Hickey shows up. (*He turns to* LARRY) If Hickey comes, Larry, you wake me up if you has to bat me wid a chair.

(*He settles himself and immediately falls asleep.*)

PARRITT: Who's Hickey?

LARRY: A hardware drummer. An old friend of Harry Hope's and all the gang. He's a grand guy. He comes here twice a year regularly on a periodical drunk and blows in all his money.

PARRITT: (*with a disparaging glance around*) Must be hard up for a place to hang out.

LARRY: It has its points for him. He never runs into anyone he knows in his business here.

PARRITT: (*lowering his voice*) Yes, that's what I want, too. I've got to stay under cover, Larry, like I told you last night.

LARRY: You did a lot of hinting. You didn't tell me anything.

PARRITT: You can guess, can't you? (*He changes the subject abruptly*) I've been in some dumps on the Coast, but this is the limit. What kind of joint is it, anyway?

LARRY: *(with a sardonic grin)* What is it? It's the No Chance Saloon. It's Bedrock Bar, The End of the Line Café, The Bottom of the Sea Rathskeller! Don't you notice the beautiful calm in the atmosphere? That's because it's the last harbor. No one here has to worry about where they're going next, because there is no farther they can go. It's a great comfort to them. Although even here they keep up the appearances of life with a few harmless pipe dreams about their yesterdays and tomorrows, as you'll see for yourself if you're here long.

PARRITT: *(stares at him curiously)* What's your pipe dream, Larry?

LARRY: *(hiding resentment)* Oh, I'm the exception. I haven't any left, thank God. *(Shortly)* Don't complain about this place. You couldn't find a better for lying low.

PARRITT: I'm glad of that, Larry. I don't feel any too damned good. I was knocked off my base by that business on the Coast, and since then it's been no fun dodging around the country, thinking every guy you see might be a dick.

LARRY: *(sympathetically now)* No, it wouldn't be. But you're safe here. The cops ignore this dump. They think it's as harmless as a graveyard. *(He grins sardonically)* And, be God, they're right.

PARRITT: It's been lonely as hell. *(Impulsively)* Christ, Larry, I was glad to find you. I kept saying to myself, "If I can only find Larry. He's the one guy in the world who can understand—" *(He hesitates, staring at* LARRY *with a strange appeal.)*

LARRY: *(watching him puzzledly)* Understand what?

PARRITT: *(hastily)* Why, all I've been through. *(Looking away)* Oh, I know you're thinking, This guy has a hell of a nerve. I haven't seen him since he was a kid. I'd forgotten he was alive. But I've never forgotten you, Larry. You were the only friend of Mother's who ever paid attention to me, or knew I was alive. All the others were too busy with the Movement. Even Mother. And I had no Old Man. You used to take me on your knee and tell me stories and crack jokes and make me laugh. You'd ask me questions and take what I said seriously. I guess I got to feel in the years you lived with us that you'd taken the place of my Old Man. *(Embarrassedly)* But, hell, that sounds like a lot of mush. I suppose you don't remember a damned thing about it.

LARRY: *(moved in spite of himself)* I remember well. You were a serious lonely little shaver. *(Then resenting being moved, changes the subject)* How is it they didn't pick you up when they got your mother and the rest?

PARRITT: *(in a lowered voice but eagerly, as if he wants this chance to tell about it)* I wasn't around, and as soon as I heard the news I went under cover. You've noticed my glad rags. I was staked to them—as a disguise, sort of. I hung around pool rooms and gambling joints and hooker shops, where they'd never look for a Wobblie,° pretending I was a sport. Anyway, they'd grabbed everyone important, so I suppose they didn't think of me until afterward.

LARRY: The papers say the cops got them all dead to rights, that the Burns dicks knew every move before it was made, and someone inside the Movement must have sold out and tipped them off.

PARRITT: *(turns to look* LARRY *in the eyes—slowly)* Yes, I guess that must be true, Larry. It hasn't come out who it was. It may never come out. I suppose whoever it was made a bargain with the Burns men to keep him out of it. They won't need his evidence.

LARRY: *(tensely)* By God, I hate to believe it of any of the crowd, if I am through long since with any connection with them. I know they're damned fools, most of them, as stupidly greedy for power as the worst capitalist they attack, but I'd swear there couldn't be a yellow stool pigeon among them.

Wobblie *(also spelled Wobbly): informal term for a member of the Industrial Workers of the World, a labor union organized in 1905 and disintegrated after 1920.*

PARRITT: Sure. I'd have sworn that, too, Larry.

LARRY: I hope his soul rots in hell, whoever it is!

PARRITT: Yes, so do I.

LARRY: (after a pause—shortly) How did you locate me? I hoped I'd found a place of retirement here where no one in the Movement would ever come to disturb my peace.

PARRITT: I found out through Mother.

LARRY: I asked her not to tell anyone.

PARRITT: She didn't tell me, but she'd kept all your letters and I found where she'd hidden them in the flat. I sneaked up there one night after she was arrested.

LARRY: I'd never have thought she was a woman who'd keep letters.

PARRITT: No, I wouldn't, either. There's nothing soft or sentimental about Mother.

LARRY: I never answered her last letters. I haven't written her in a couple of years— or anyone else. I've gotten beyond the desire to communicate with the world—or, what's more to the point, to let it bother me any more with its greedy madness.

PARRITT: It's funny Mother kept in touch with you so long. When she's finished with anyone, she's finished. She's always been proud of that. And you know how she feels about the Movement. Like a revivalist preacher about religion. Anyone who loses faith in it is more than dead to her; he's a Judas who ought to be boiled in oil. Yet she seemed to forgive you.

LARRY: (sardonically) She didn't, don't worry. She wrote to denounce me and try to bring the sinner to repentance and a belief in the One True Faith again.

PARRITT: What made you leave the Movement, Larry? Was it on account of Mother?

LARRY: (starts) Don't be a damned fool! What the hell put that in your head?

PARRITT: Why, nothing—except I remember what a fight you had with her before you left.

LARRY: (resentfully) Well, if you do, I don't. That was eleven years ago. You were only seven. If we did quarrel, it was because I told her I'd become convinced the Movement was only a beautiful pipe dream.

PARRITT: (with a strange smile) I don't remember it that way.

LARRY: Then you can blame your imagination— and forget it. (He changes the subject abruptly) You asked me why I quit the Movement. I had a lot of good reasons. One was myself, and another was my comrades, and the last was the breed of swine called men in general. For myself, I was forced to admit, at the end of thirty years' devotion to the Cause, that I was never made for it. I was born condemned to be one of those who has to see all sides of a question. When you're damned like that, the questions multiply for you until in the end it's all question and no answer. As history proves, to be a worldly success at anything, especially revolution, you have to wear blinders like a horse and see only straight in front of you. You have to see, too, that this is all black, and that is all white. As for my comrades in the Great Cause, I felt as Horace Walpole° did about England, that he could love it if it weren't for the people in it. The material the ideal free society must be constructed from is men themselves and you can't build a marble temple out of a mixture of mud and manure. When man's soul isn't a sow's ear, it will be time enough to dream of silk purses. (He chuckles sardonically—then irritably as if suddenly provoked at himself for talking so much) Well, that's why I quit the Movement, if it leaves you any wiser. At any rate, you see it had nothing to do with your mother.

PARRITT: (smiles almost mockingly) Oh, sure, I see. But I'll bet Mother has always thought it was on her account. You know her, Larry. To hear her go on sometimes, you'd think she was the Movement.

LARRY: (stares at him, puzzled and repelled— sharply) That's a hell of a way for you to talk, after what happened to her!

Horace Walpole (1717–1797): English novelist and essayist.

PARRITT: *(at once confused and guilty)* Don't get me wrong. I wasn't sneering, Larry. Only kidding. I've said the same thing to her lots of times to kid her. But you're right. I know I shouldn't now. I keep forgetting she's in jail. It doesn't seem real. I can't believe it about her. She's always been so free. I— But I don't want to think of it. *(LARRY is moved to a puzzled pity in spite of himself. PARRITT changes the subject)* What have you been doing all the years since you left—the Coast, Larry?

LARRY: *(sardonically)* Nothing I could help doing. If I don't believe in the Movement, I don't believe in anything else either, especially not the State. I've refused to become a useful member of its society. I've been a philosophical drunken bum, and proud of it. *(Abruptly his tone sharpens with resentful warning)* Listen to me. I hope you've deduced that I've my reason for answering the impertinent questions of a stranger, for that's all you are to me. I have a strong hunch you've come here expecting something of me. I'm warning you, at the start, so there'll be no misunderstanding, that I've nothing left to give, and I want to be left alone, and I'll thank you to keep your life to yourself. I feel you're looking for some answer to something. I have no answer to give anyone, not even myself. Unless you call what Heine° wrote in his poem to morphine an answer.

(He quotes a translation of the closing couplet sardonically.)

"Lo, sleep is good; better is death; in
     sooth,
The best of all were never to be born."

PARRITT: *(shrinks a bit frightenedly)* That's the hell of an answer. *(Then with a forced grin of bravado)* Still, you never know when it might come in handy.

(He looks away. LARRY stares at him puzzledly, interested in spite of himself and at the same time vaguely uneasy.)

LARRY: *(forcing a casual tone)* I don't suppose you've had much chance to hear news of your mother since she's been in jail?

PARRITT: No. No chance. *(He hesitates—then blurts out)* Anyway, I don't think she wants to hear from me. We had a fight just before that business happened. She bawled me out because I was going around with tarts. That got my goat, coming from her. I told her, "You've always acted the free woman, you've never let anything stop you from—" *(He checks himself—goes on hurriedly)* That made her sore. She said she wouldn't give a damn what I did except she'd begun to suspect I was too interested in outside things and losing interest in the Movement.

LARRY: *(stares at him)* And were you?

PARRITT: *(hesitates—then with intensity)* Sure I was! I'm no damned fool! I couldn't go on believing forever that gang was going to change the world by shooting off their loud traps on soapboxes and sneaking around blowing up a lousy building or a bridge! I got wise it was all a crazy pipe dream! *(Appealingly)* The same as you did, Larry. That's why I came to you. I knew you'd understand. What finished me was this last business of someone selling out. How can you believe anything after a thing like that happens? It knocks you cold! You don't know what the hell is what! You're through! *(Appealingly)* You know how I feel, don't you, Larry? *(LARRY stares at him, moved by sympathy and pity in spite of himself, disturbed, and resentful at being disturbed, and puzzled by something he feels about PARRITT that isn't right. But before he can reply, HUGO suddenly raises his head from his arms in a half-awake alcoholic daze and speaks.)*

HUGO: *(quotes aloud to himself in a guttural declamatory style)* "The days grow hot, O Babylon! 'Tis cool beneath thy villow trees!" *(PARRITT turns startledly as HUGO peers*

Heinrich Heine *(1797–1856): German lyric poet and journalist.*

muzzily without recognition at him. HUGO *exclaims automatically in his tone of denunciation)* Gottammed stool pigeon!

PARRITT: *(shrinks away—stammers)* What? Who do you mean? *(Then furiously)* You lousy bum, you can't call me that! *(He draws back his fist.)*

HUGO: *(ignores this—recognizing him now, bursts into his childish teasing giggle)* Hello, leedle Don! Leedle monkey-face. I did not recognize you. You have grown big boy. How is your mother? Where you come from? *(He breaks into his wheedling, bullying tone)* Don't be a fool! Loan me a dollar! Buy me a trink! *(As if this exhausted him, he abruptly forgets it and plumps his head down on his arms again and is asleep.)*

PARRITT: *(with eager relief)* Sure, I'll buy you a drink, Hugo. I'm broke, but I can afford one for you. I'm sorry I got sore. I ought to have remembered when you're soused you call everyone a stool pigeon. But it's no damned joke right at this time. *(He turns to* LARRY, *who is regarding him now fixedly with an uneasy expression as if he suddenly were afraid of his own thoughts—forcing a smile)* Gee, he's passed out again. *(He stiffens defensively)* What are you giving me the hard look for? Oh, I know. You thought I was going to hit him? What do you think I am? I've always had a lot of respect for Hugo. I've always stood up for him when people in the Movement panned him for an old drunken has-been. He had the guts to serve ten years in the can in his own country and get his eyes ruined in solitary. I'd like to see some of them here stick that. Well, they'll get a chance now to show— *(Hastily)* I don't mean— But let's forget that. Tell me some more about this dump. Who are all these tanks? Who's that guy trying to catch pneumonia?

(He indicates LEWIS.*)*

LARRY: *(stares at him almost frightenedly—then looks away and grasps eagerly this chance to change the subject. He begins to describe the sleepers with sardonic relish but at the same time showing his affection for them)* That's Captain Lewis, a one-time hero of the British Army. He

strips to display that scar on his back he got from a native spear whenever he's completely plastered. The bewhiskered bloke opposite him is General Wetjoen, who led a commando in the War. The two of them met when they came here to work in the Boer War° spectacle at the St. Louis Fair and they've been bosom pals ever since. They dream the hours away in happy dispute over the brave days in South Africa when they tried to murder each other. The little guy between them was in it, too, as correspondent for some English paper. His nickname here is Jimmy Tomorrow. He's the leader of our Tomorrow Movement.

PARRITT: What do they do for a living?

LARRY: As little as possible. Once in a while one of them makes a successful touch somewhere, and some of them get a few dollars a month from connections at home who pay it on condition they never come back. For the rest, they live on free lunch and their old friend, Harry Hope, who doesn't give a damn what anyone does or doesn't do, as long as he likes you.

PARRITT: It must be a tough life.

LARRY: It's not. Don't waste your pity. They wouldn't thank you for it. They manage to get drunk, by hook or crook, and keep their pipe dreams, and that's all they ask of life. I've never known more contented men. It isn't often that men attain the true goal of their heart's desire. The same applies to Harry himself and his two cronies at the far table. He's so satisfied with life he's never set foot out of this place since his wife died twenty years ago. He has no need of the outside world at all. This place has a fine trade from the Market people across the street and the waterfront workers, so in spite of Harry's thirst and his generous heart, he comes out even. He never worries in hard times because there's always old friends from the days

---

Boer War: *War in South Africa fought between Great Britain and Dutch colonists (Boers) of the Transvaal and Orange Free State between 1899 and 1902.*

when he was a jitney Tammany° politician, and a friendly brewery to tide him over. Don't ask me what his two pals work at because they don't. Except at being his lifetime guests. The one facing this way is his brother-in-law, Ed Mosher, who once worked for a circus in the ticket wagon. Pat McGloin, the other one, was a police lieutenant back in the flush times of graft when everything went. But he got too greedy and when the usual reform investigation came he was caught red-handed and thrown off the Force. (*He nods at* JOE) Joe here has a yesterday in the same flush period. He ran a colored gambling house then and was a hell of a sport, so they say. Well, that's our whole family circle of inmates, except the two barkeeps and their girls, three ladies of the pavement that room on the third floor.

PARRITT: (*bitterly*) To hell with them! I never want to see a whore again! (*As* LARRY *flashes him a puzzled glance, he adds confusedly*) I mean, they always get you in dutch.

(*While he is speaking* WILLIE OBAN *has opened his eyes. He leans toward them, drunk now from the effect of the huge drink he took, and speaks with a mocking suavity.*)

WILLIE: Why omit me from your Who's Who in Dypsomania, Larry? An unpardonable slight, especially as I am the only inmate of royal blood. (*To* PARRITT—*ramblingly*) Educated at Harvard, too. You must have noticed the atmosphere of culture here. My humble contribution. Yes, Generous Stranger—I trust you're generous—I was born in the purple, the son, but unfortunately not the heir, of the late world-famous Bill

Oban, King of the Bucket Shops.° A revolution deposed him, conducted by the District Attorney. He was sent into exile. In fact, not to mince matters, they locked him in the can and threw away the key. Alas, his was an adventurous spirit that pined in confinement. And so he died. Forgive these reminiscences. Undoubtedly all this is well known to you. Everyone in the world knows.

PARRITT: (*uncomfortably*) Tough luck. No, I never heard of him.

WILLIE: (*blinks at him incredulously*) Never heard? I thought everyone in the world— Why, even at Harvard I discovered my father was well known by reputation, although that was some time before the District Attorney gave him so much unwelcome publicity. Yes, even as a freshman I was notorious. I was accepted socially with all the warm cordiality that Henry Wadsworth Longfellow° would have shown a drunken Negress dancing the cancan at high noon on Brattle Street. Harvard was my father's idea. He was an ambitious man. Dictatorial, too. Always knowing what was best for me. But I did make myself a brilliant student. A dirty trick on my classmates, inspired by revenge, I fear. (*He quotes*) "Dear college days, with pleasure rife! The grandest gladdest days of life!" But, of course, that is a Yale hymn, and they're given to rah-rah exaggeration at New Haven. I was a brilliant student at Law School, too. My father wanted a lawyer in the family. He was a calculating man. A thorough knowledge of the law close at hand in the house to help him find fresh ways to evade it. But I discovered the loophole of whiskey and escaped his jurisdiction. (*Abruptly to* PARRITT) Speaking of whiskey, sir, reminds me—and, I hope, reminds you—that

Tammany: Founded in 1789 as the Society of St. Tammany (a nonexistent personage), a political organization in New York City formed to resist aristocratic tendencies in the growing Republic whose reputation in the latter half of the nineteenth century was marred by allegations of election fraud and corruption. It reached the height of its influence during the administration of Jimmy Walker, mayor of New York, who resigned in 1932 over charges of political corruption.

Bucket Shop: an establishment believed to sell and trade securities or commodities that in reality involved itself in gambling and fraud.
Henry Wadsworth Longfellow (1807–1882): American poet and professor of foreign languages at both Bowdoin College and Harvard.

when meeting a Prince the customary salutation is "What'll you have?"

PARRITT: *(with defensive resentment)* Nix! All you guys seem to think I'm made of dough. Where would I get the coin to blow everyone?

WILLIE: *(sceptically)* Broke? You haven't the thirsty look of the impecunious. I'd judge you to be a plutocrat, your pockets stuffed with ill-gotten gains. Two or three dollars, at least. And don't think we will question how you got it. As Vespasian° remarked, the smell of all whiskey is sweet.

PARRITT: What do you mean, how I got it? *(To* LARRY, *forcing a laugh)* It's a laugh, calling me a plutocrat, isn't it, Larry, when I've been in the Movement all my life.

*(*LARRY *gives him an uneasy suspicious glance, then looks away, as if avoiding something he does not wish to see.)*

WILLIE: *(disgustedly)* Ah, one of those, eh? I believe you now, all right! Go away and blow yourself up, that's a good lad. Hugo is the only licensed preacher of that gospel here. A dangerous terrorist, Hugo! He would as soon blow the collar off a schooner of beer as look at you! *(To* LARRY*)* Let us ignore this useless youth, Larry. Let us join in prayer that Hickey, the Great Salesman, will soon arrive bringing the blessed burgeois long green! Would that Hickey or Death would come! Meanwhile, I will sing a song. A beautiful old New England folk ballad which I picked up at Harvard amid the debris of education.

(He sings in a boisterous baritone, rapping on the table with his knuckles at the indicated spots in the song:)

"Jack, oh Jack, was a sailor lad
And he came to a tavern for gin.
He rapped and he rapped with a *(Rap, rap, rap)*
But never a soul seemed in."

Vespasian (A.D. 9–79): *Titus Flavius Sabinus Vespasianus, Roman emperor from* A.D. *69 until 79.*

(The drunks at the tables stir. ROCKY *gets up from his chair in the bar and starts back for the entrance to the back room.* HOPE *cocks one irritable eye over his specs.* JOE MOTT *opens both of his and grins.* WILLIE *interposes some drunken whimsical exposition to* LARRY*)* The origin of this beautiful ditty is veiled in mystery, Larry. There was a legend bruited about in Cambridge lavatories that Waldo Emerson° composed it during his uninformative period as a minister, while he was trying to write a sermon. But my own opinion is, it goes back much further, and Jonathan Edwards° was the author of both words and music.

(He sings:)

"He rapped and rapped, and tapped and
    tapped
Enough to wake the dead
Till he heard a damsel *(Rap, rap, rap)*
On a window right over his head."

(The drunks are blinking their eyes now, grumbling and cursing. ROCKY *appears from the bar at rear, right, yawning.)*

HOPE: *(with fuming irritation)* Rocky! Bejees, can't you keep that crazy bastard quiet?

*(*ROCKY *starts for* WILLIE.*)*

WILLIE: And now the influence of a good woman enters our mariner's life. Well, perhaps "good" isn't the word. But very, very kind.

(He sings:)

"Oh, come up," she cried, "my sailor
    lad,
And you and I'll agree,
And I'll show you the prettiest *(Rap, rap,
    rap)*
That ever you did see."

Ralph Waldo Emerson (1803–1882): *Graduate of Harvard College and the Harvard Divinity School and American essayist and poet; leader of the so-called "Transcendentalist" movement in American literature.*

Jonathan Edwards (1703–1758): *American theologian and writer of such sermons as "Sinners in the Hands of an Angry God."*

(He speaks) You see, Larry? The lewd Puritan touch, obviously, and it grows more marked as we go on.
(He sings:)

"Oh, he put his arm around her waist,
He gazed in her bright blue eyes
And then he—"

(But here ROCKY *shakes him roughly by the shoulder.)*

ROCKY: Piano! What d'yuh tink dis dump is, a dump?

HOPE: Give him the bum's rush upstairs! Lock him in his room!

ROCKY: *(yanks* WILLIE *by the arm)* Come on, Bum.

WILLIE: *(dissolves into pitiable terror)* No! Please, Rocky! I'll go crazy up in that room alone! It's haunted! I— *(He calls to* HOPE*)* Please, Harry! Let me stay here! I'll be quiet!

HOPE: *(immediately relents—indignantly)* What the hell you doing to him, Rocky? I didn't tell you to beat up the poor guy. Leave him alone, long as he's quiet.

*(*ROCKY *lets go of* WILLIE *disgustedly and goes back to his chair in the bar.)*

WILLIE: *(huskily)* Thanks, Harry. You're a good scout.

(He closes his eyes and sinks back in his chair exhaustedly, twitching and quivering again.)

HOPE: *(addressing* MCGLOIN *and* MOSHER, *who are sleepily awake—accusingly)* Always the way. Can't trust nobody. Leave it to that Dago to keep order and it's like bedlam in a cathouse, singing and everything. And you two big barflies are a hell of a help to me, ain't you? Eat and sleep and get drunk! All you're good for, bejees! Well, you can take that "I'll-have-the-same" look off your maps! There ain't going to be no more drinks on the house till hell freezes over! *(Neither of the two is impressed either by his insults or his threats. They grin hangover grins of tolerant affection at him and wink at each other.* HARRY *fumes)*

Yeah, grin! Wink, bejees! Fine pair of sons of bitches to have glued on me for life!

(But he can't get a rise out of them and he subsides into a fuming mumble. Meanwhile, at the middle table, CAPTAIN LEWIS *and* GENERAL WETJOEN *are as wide awake as heavy hangovers permit.* JIMMY TOMORROW *nods, his eyes blinking.* LEWIS *is gazing across the table at* JOE MOTT, *who is still chuckling to himself over* WILLIE'S *song. The expression on* LEWIS' *face is that of one who can't believe his eyes.)*

LEWIS: *(aloud to himself, with a muzzy wonder)* Good God! Have I been drinking at the same table with a bloody Kaffir?

JOE: *(grinning)* Hello, Captain. You comin' up for air? Kaffir? Who's he?

WETJOEN: *(blurrily)* Kaffir, dot's a nigger, Joe. *(*JOE *stiffens and his eyes narrow.* WETJOEN *goes on with heavy jocosity)* Dot's joke on him, Joe. He don't know you. He's still plind drunk, the ploody Limey chentleman! A great mistake I missed him at the pattle of Modder River.° Vit mine rifle I shoot damn fool Limey officers py the dozen, but him I miss. De pity of it! *(He chuckles and slaps* LEWIS *on his bare shoulder)* Hey, wake up, Cecil, you ploody fool! Don't you know your old friend, Joe? He's no damned Kaffir! He's white, Joe is!

LEWIS: *(light dawning—contritely)* My profound apologies, Joseph, old chum. Eyesight a trifle blurry, I'm afraid. Whitest colored man I ever knew. Proud to call you my friend. No hard feelings, what?

(He holds out his hand.)

JOE: *(at once grins good-naturedly and shakes his hand)* No, Captain, I know it's mistake. Youse regular, if you is a Limey. *(Then his face hardening)* But I don't stand for "nigger" from nobody. Never did. In de old days, people calls me "nigger" wakes up in de hospital. I was de leader ob de Dirty Half-Dozen Gang. All six of

---

Modder River *(misspelling of Moder River): River of Northern Alsace, a tributary of the Rhine.*

us colored boys, we was tough and I was de toughest.

WETJOEN: *(inspired to boastful reminiscence)* Me, in old days in Transvaal, I vas so tough and strong I grab axle of ox wagon mit full load and lift like feather.

LEWIS: *(smiling amiably)* As for you, my balmy Boer that walks like a man, I say again it was a grave error in our foreign policy ever to set you free, once we nabbed you and your commando with Cronje. We should have taken you to the London zoo and incarcerated you in the baboons' cage. With a sign: "Spectators may distinguish the true baboon by his blue behind."

WETJOEN: *(grins)* Gott! to dink ten better Limey officers, at least, I shoot clean in the mittle of forehead at Spion Kopje, and you I miss! I neffer forgive myself!

(JIMMY TOMORROW blinks benignantly from one to the other with a gentle drunken smile.)

JIMMY: *(sentimentally)* Now, come, Cecil, Piet! We must forget the War. Boer and Briton, each fought fairly and played the game till the better man won and then we shook hands. We are all brothers within the Empire united beneath the flag on which the sun never sets. *(Tears come to his eyes. He quotes with great sentiment, if with slight application)* "Ship me somewhere east of Suez—"

LARRY: *(breaks in sardonically)* Be God, you're there already, Jimmy. Worst is best here, and East is West, and tomorrow is yesterday. What more do you want?

JIMMY: *(with bleary benevolence, shaking his head in mild rebuke)* No, Larry, old friend, you can't deceive me. You pretend a bitter, cynic philosophy, but in your heart you are the kindest man among us.

LARRY: *(disconcerted—irritably)* The hell you say!

PARRITT: *(leans toward him—confidentially)* What a bunch of cuckoos!

JIMMY: *(as if reminded of something—with a pathetic attempt at a brisk, no-more-nonsense air)* Tomorrow, yes. It's high time I straightened out and got down to business again. *(He brushes his sleeve fastidiously)* I must have this suit cleaned and pressed. I can't look like a tramp when I—

JOE: *(who has been brooding—interrupts)* Yes, suh, white folks always said I was white. In de days when I was flush, Joe Mott's de only colored man dey allows in de white gamblin' houses. "You're all right, Joe, you're white," dey says. *(He chuckles)* Wouldn't let me play craps, dough. Dey know I could make dem dice behave. "Any odder game and any limit you like, Joe," dey says. Man, de money I lost! *(He chuckles—then with an underlying defensiveness)* Look at de Big Chief in dem days. He knew I was white. I'd saved my dough so I could start my own gamblin' house. Folks in de know tells me, see de man at de top, den you never has trouble. You git Harry Hope give you a letter to de Chief. And Harry does. Don't you, Harry?

HOPE: *(preoccupied with his own thoughts)* Eh? Sure. Big Bill was a good friend of mine. I had plenty of friends high up in those days. Still could have if I wanted to go out and see them. Sure, I gave you a letter. I said you was white. What the hell of it?

JOE: *(to CAPTAIN LEWIS who has relapsed into a sleepy daze and is listening to him with an absurd strained attention without comprehending a word)* Dere. You see, Captain. I went to see de Chief, shakin' in my boots, and dere he is sittin' behind a big desk, lookin' as big as a freight train. He don't look up. He keeps me waitin' and waitin', and after 'bout an hour, seems like to me, he says slow and quiet like dere wasn't no harm in him, "You want to open a gamblin' joint, does you, Joe?" But he don't give me no time to answer. He jumps up, lookin' as big as two freight trains, and he pounds his fist like a ham on de desk, and he shouts, "You black son of a bitch, Harry says you're white and you better be white or dere's a little iron room up de river waitin' for you!" Den he sits down and says quiet again, "All right. You can open. Git de hell outa here!" So I opens, and he finds out I'se white, sure 'nuff, 'cause I run wide open for years and pays my sugar on de dot, and de cops and I is friends. *(He chuckles with pride)* Dem old days! Many's de night I come in here. Dis was a first-class hangout for sports in dem days. Good whiskey, fifteen cents, two for two bits. I t'rows down a fifty-dollar bill like it was trash paper and says, "Drink it up, boys, I don't want no change." Ain't dat right, Harry?

HOPE: *(caustically)* Yes, and bejees, if I ever seen you throw fifty cents on the bar now, I'd know I had delirium tremens! You've told that story ten million times and if I have to hear it again, that'll give me D.T.s anyway!

JOE: *(chuckling)* Gittin' drunk every day for twenty years ain't give you de Brooklyn boys. You needn't be scared of me!

LEWIS: *(suddenly turns and beams on HOPE)* Thank you, Harry, old chum. I will have a drink, now you mention it, seeing it's so near your birthday. *(The others laugh.)*

HOPE: *(puts his hand to his ear—angrily)* What's that? I can't hear you.

LEWIS: *(sadly)* No, I fancied you wouldn't.

HOPE: I don't have to hear, bejees! Booze is the only thing you ever talk about!

LEWIS: *(sadly)* True. Yet there was a time when my conversation was more comprehensive. But as I became burdened with years, it seemed rather pointless to discuss my other subject.

HOPE: You can't joke with me! How much room rent do you owe me, tell me that?

LEWIS: Sorry. Adding has always baffled me. Subtraction is my forte.

HOPE: *(snarling)* Arrh! Think you're funny! Captain, bejees! Showing off your wounds! Put on your clothes, for Christ's sake! This ain't no Turkish bath! Lousy Limey army! Took 'em years to lick a gang of Dutch hayseeds!

WETJOEN: Dot's right, Harry. Gif him hell!

HOPE: No lip out of you, neither, you Dutch spinach! General, hell! Salvation Army, that's what you'd ought t'been General in! Bragging what a shot you were, and, bejees, you missed him! And he missed you, that's just as bad! And now the two of you bum on me! *(Threateningly)*

But you've broke the camel's back this time, bejees! You pay up tomorrow or out you go!

LEWIS: *(earnestly)* My dear fellow, I give you my word of honor as an officer and a gentleman, you shall be paid tomorrow.

WETJOEN: Ve swear it, Harry! Tomorrow vidout fail!

McGLOIN: *(a twinkle in his eye)* There you are, Harry. Sure, what could be fairer?

MOSHER: *(With a wink at McGLOIN)* Yes, you can't ask more than that, Harry. A promise is a promise—as I've often discovered.

HOPE: *(turns on them)* I mean the both of you, too! An old grafting flatfoot and a circus bunco steerer! Fine company for me, bejees! Couple of con men living in my flat since Christ knows when! Getting fat as hogs, too! And you ain't even got the decency to get me upstairs where I got a good bed! Let me sleep on a chair like a bum! Kept me down here waitin' for Hickey to show up, hoping I'd blow you to more drinks!

McGLOIN: Ed and I did our damnedest to get you up, didn't we, Ed?

MOSHER: We did. But you said you couldn't bear the flat because it was one of those nights when memory brought poor old Bessie back to you.

HOPE: *(his face instantly becoming long and sad and sentimental—mournfully)* Yes, that's right, boys. I remember now. I could almost see her in every room just as she used to be—and it's twenty years since she—

(His throat and eyes fill up. A suitable sentimental hush falls on the room.)

LARRY: *(in a sardonic whisper to PARRITT)* Isn't a pipe dream of yesterday a touching thing? By all accounts, Bessie nagged the hell out of him.

JIMMY: *(who has been dreaming, a look of prim resolution on his face, speaks aloud to himself)* No more of this sitting around and loafing. Time I took hold of myself. I must have my shoes soled and heeled and shined first thing tomorrow morning. A general spruce-up. I want to have a well-groomed appearance when I—

(His voice fades out as he stares in front of him. No one pays any attention to him except LARRY *and* PARRITT.*)*

LARRY: *(as before, in a sardonic aside to* PARRITT*)* The tomorrow movement is a sad and beautiful thing, too!

MCGLOIN: *(with a huge sentimental sigh—and a calculating look at* HOPE*)* Poor old Bessie! You don't find her like in these days. A sweeter woman never drew breath.

MOSHER: *(in a similar calculating mood)* Good old Bess. A man couldn't want a better sister than she was to me.

HOPE: *(mournfully)* Twenty years, and I've never set foot out of this house since the day I buried her. Didn't have the heart. Once she'd gone, I didn't give a damn for anything. I lost all my ambition. Without her, nothing seemed worth the trouble. You remember, Ed, you, too, Mac—the boys was going to nominate me for Alderman. It was all fixed. Bessie wanted it and she was so proud. But when she was taken, I told them, "No, boys, I can't do it. I simply haven't the heart. I'm through." I would have won the election easy, too. *(He says this a bit defiantly)* Oh, I know there was jealous wise guys said the boys was giving me the nomination because they knew they couldn't win that year in this ward. But that's a damned lie! I knew every man, woman and child in the ward, almost. Bessie made me make friends with everyone, helped me remember all their names. I'd have been elected easy.

MCGLOIN: You would, Harry. It was a sure thing.

MOSHER: A dead cinch, Harry. Everyone knows that.

HOPE: Sure they do. But after Bessie died, I didn't have the heart. Still, I know while she'd appreciate my grief, she wouldn't want it to keep me cooped up in here all my life. So I've made up my mind I'll go out soon. Take a walk around the ward, see all the friends I used to know, get together with the boys and maybe tell 'em I'll let 'em deal me a hand in their game again. Yes, bejees, I'll do it. My birthday, tomorrow, that'd be the right time to turn over a new leaf. Sixty. That ain't too old.

MCGLOIN: *(flatteringly)* It's the prime of life, Harry.

MOSHER: Wonderful thing about you, Harry, you keep young as you ever was.

JIMMY: *(dreaming aloud again)* Get my things from the laundry. They must still have them. Clean collar and shirt. If I wash the ones I've got on any more, they'll fall apart. Socks, too. I want to make a good appearance. I met Dick Trumbull on the street a year or two ago. He said, "Jimmy, the publicity department's never been the same since you got—resigned. It's dead as hell." I said, "I know. I've heard rumors the management were at their wits' end and would be only too glad to have me run it for them again. I think all I'd have to do would be go and see them and they'd offer me the position. Don't you think so, Dick?" He said, "Sure, they would, Jimmy. Only take my advice and wait a while until business conditions are better. Then you can strike them for a bigger salary than you got before, do you see?" I said, "Yes, I do see, Dick, and many thanks for the tip." Well, conditions must be better by this time. All I have to do is get fixed up with a decent front tomorrow, and it's as good as done.

HOPE: *(glances at* JIMMY *with a condescending affectionate pity—in a hushed voice)* Poor Jimmy's off on his pipe dream again. Bejees, he takes the cake!

(This is too much for LARRY. *He cannot restrain a sardonic guffaw. But no one pays any attention to him.)*

LEWIS: *(opens his eyes, which are drowsing again—dreamily to* WETJOEN*)* I'm sorry we had to postpone our trip again this April, Piet. I hoped the blasted old estate would be settled up by then. The damned lawyers can't hold up the settlement much longer. We'll make it next year, even if we have to work and earn our passage money, eh? You'll stay with me at the old place as long as you like, then you can take the *Union Castle* from Southampton to Cape Town. *(Sentimentally,* *with real yearning)* England in April. I want you to see that, Piet. The old veldt has its points, I'll admit, but it isn't home—especially home in April.

WETJOEN: *(blinks drowsily at him—dreamily)* Ja, Cecil, I know how beautiful it must be, from all you tell me many times. I vill enjoy it. But I shall enjoy more ven I am home, too. The veldt, ja! You could put England on it, and it would look like a farmer's small garden. Py Gott, there is space to be free, the air like vine is, you don't need booze to be drunk! My relations vill so surprised be. They vill not know me, it is so many years. Dey vill be so glad I haf come home at last.

JOE: *(dreamily)* I'll make my stake and get my new gamblin' house open before you boys leave. You got to come to de openin'. I'll treat you white. If you're broke, I'll stake you to buck any game you chooses. If you wins, dat's velvet for you. If you loses, it don't count. Can't treat you no whiter dan dat, can I?

HOPE: *(again with condescending pity)* Bejees, Jimmy's started them off smoking the same hop. *(But the three are finished, their eyes closed again in sleep or a drowse.)*

LARRY: *(aloud to himself—in his comically tense, crazy whisper)* Be God, this bughouse will drive me stark, raving loony yet!

HOPE: *(turns on him with fuming suspicion)* What? What d'you say?

LARRY: *(placatingly)* Nothing, Harry. I had a crazy thought in my head.

HOPE: *(irascibly)* Crazy is right! Yah! The old wise guy! Wise, hell! A damned old fool Anarchist I-Won't-Worker! I'm sick of you and Hugo, too. Bejees, you'll pay up tomorrow, or I'll start a Harry Hope Revolution! I'll tie a dispossess bomb to your tails that'll blow you out in the street! Bejees, I'll make your Movement move! *(The witticism delights him and he bursts into a shrill cackle. At once* MCGLOIN *and* MOSHER *guffaw enthusiastically.)*

MOSHER: *(flatteringly)* Harry, you sure say the funniest things! *(He reaches on the table as if*

he expected a glass to be there—then starts with well-acted surprise)* Hell, where's my drink? That Rocky is too damned fast cleaning tables. Why, I'd only taken one sip of it.

HOPE: *(his smiling face congealing)* No, you don't! *(Acidly)* Any time you only take one sip of a drink, you'll have lockjaw and paralysis! Think you can kid me with those old circus con games?—me, that's known you since you was knee-high, and, bejees, you was a crook even then!

MCGLOIN: *(grinning)* It's not like you to be hardhearted, Harry. Sure, it's hot, parching work laughing at your jokes so early in the morning on an empty stomach!

HOPE: Yah! You, Mac! Another crook! Who asked you to laugh? We was talking about poor old Bessie, and you and her no-good brother start to laugh! A hell of a thing! Talking mush about her, too! "Good old Bess." Bejees, she'd never forgive me if she knew I had you two bums living in her flat, throwing ashes and cigar butts on her carpet. You know you opinion of you, Mac. "That Pat McGloin is the biggest drunken grafter that ever disgraced the police force," she used to say to me. "I hope they send him to Sing Sing for life."

MCGLOIN: *(unperturbed)* She didn't mean it. She was angry at me because you used to get me drunk. But Bess had a heart of gold underneath her sharpness. She knew I was innocent of all the charges.

WILLIE: *(jumps to his feet drunkenly and points a finger at* MCGLOIN—*imitating the manner of a cross-examiner—coldly)* One moment, please. Lieutenant McGloin! Are you aware you are under oath? Do you realize what the penalty for perjury is? *(Purringly)* Come now, Lieutenant, isn't it a fact that you're as guilty as hell? No, don't say, "How about your old man?" I am asking the questions. The fact that he was a crooked old bucket-shop bastard has no bearing on your case. *(With a change to maudlin joviality)* Gentlemen of the Jury, court will now recess while the D.A. sings out a little ditty he

learned at Harvard. It was composed in a wanton moment by the Dean of the Divinity School on a moonlight night in July, 1776, while sobering up in a Turkish bath.
(He sings:)

"Oh, come up," she cried, "my sailor
 lad,
And you and I'll agree.
And I'll show you the prettiest *(Rap, rap,
 rap on table)*
That ever you did see."

(Suddenly he catches HOPE'S *eyes fixed on him condemningly, and sees* ROCKY *appearing from the bar. He collapses back on his chair, pleading miserably)* Please, Harry! I'll be quiet! Don't make Rocky bounce me upstairs! I'll go crazy alone! *(To* McGLOIN) I apologize, Mac. Don't get sore. I was only kidding you.
*(*ROCKY, *at a relenting glance from* HOPE, *returns to the bar)*

McGLOIN: *(good-naturedly)* Sure, kid all you like, Willie. I'm hardened to it. *(He pauses— seriously)* But I'm telling you some day before long I'm going to make them reopen my case. Everyone knows there was no real evidence against me, and I took the fall for the ones higher up. I'll be found innocent this time and reinstated. *(Wistfully)* I'd like to have my old job on the Force back. The boys tell me there's fine pickings these days, and I'm not getting rich here, sitting with a parched throat waiting for Harry Hope to buy a drink.
(He glances reproachfully at HOPE.)

WILLIE: Of course, you'll be reinstated, Mac. All you need is a brilliant young attorney to handle your case. I'll be straightened out and on the wagon in a day or two. I've never practiced but I was one of the most brilliant students in Law School, and your case is just the opportunity I need to start. *(Darkly)* Don't worry about my not forcing the D.A. to reopen your case. I went through my father's papers before the cops destroyed them, and I remember a lot of people,

even if I can't prove— *(Coaxingly)* You will let me take your case, won't you, Mac?

McGLOIN: *(soothingly)* Sure I will and it'll make your reputation, Willie.
*(*MOSHER *winks at* HOPE, *shaking his head, and* HOPE *answers with identical pantomime, as though to say, "Poor dopes, they're off again!")*

LARRY: *(aloud to himself more than to* PARRITT— *with irritable wonder)* Ah, be damned! Haven't I heard their visions a thousand times? Why should they get under my skin now? I've got the blues, I guess. I wish to hell Hickey'd turn up.

MOSHER: *(calculatingly solicitous—whispering to* HOPE) Poor Willie needs a drink bad, Harry— and I think if we all joined him it'd make him feel he was among friends and cheer him up.

HOPE: More circus con tricks! *(Scathingly)* You talking of your dear sister! Bessie had you sized up. She used to tell me, "I don't know what you can see in that worthless, drunken, petty-larceny brother of mine. If I had my way," she'd say, "he'd get booted out in the gutter on his fat behind." Sometimes she didn't say behind, either.

MOSHER: *(grins genially)* Yes, dear old Bess had a quick temper, but there was no real harm in her. *(He chuckles reminiscently)* Remember the time she sent me down to the bar to change a ten-dollar bill for her?

HOPE: *(has to grin himself)* Bejees, do I! She coulda bit a piece out of a stove lid, after she found it out.
(He cackles appreciatively.)

MOSHER: I was sure surprised when she gave me the ten spot. Bess usually had better sense, but she was in a hurry to go to church. I didn't really mean to do it, but you know how habit gets you. Besides, I still worked then, and the circus season was going to begin soon, and I needed a little practice to keep my hand in. Or, you never can tell, the first rube that came to my wagon for a ticket might have left with the right change and I'd be disgraced. *(He chuckles)* I said, "I'm sorry, Bess, but I had to take it all in dimes. Here, hold out your hands and I'll count it out for you, so you won't kick afterwards I short-changed you." *(He begins a count which grows more rapid as he goes on)* Ten, twenty, thirty, forty, fifty, sixty, seventy, eighty, ninety, a dollar. Ten, twenty, thirty, forty, fifty, sixty—You're counting with me, Bess, aren't you?—eighty, ninety, two dollars. Ten, twenty—Those are pretty shoes you got on, Bess—forty, fifty, seventy, eighty, ninety, three dollars. Ten, twenty, thirty—What's on at the church tonight, Bess? —fifty, sixty, seventy, ninety, four dollars. Ten, twenty, thirty, fifty, seventy, eighty, ninety— That's a swell new hat, Bess, looks very becoming—six dollars. *(He chuckles)* And so on. I'm bum at it now for lack of practice, but in those days I could have short-changed the Keeper of the Mint.

HOPE: *(grinning)* Stung her for two dollars and a half, wasn't it, Ed?

MOSHER: Yes. A fine percentage, if I do say so, when you're dealing to someone who's sober and can count. I'm sorry to say she discovered my mistakes in arithmetic just after I beat it around the corner. She counted it over herself. Bess somehow never had the confidence in me a sister should. *(He sighs tenderly)* Dear old Bess.

HOPE: *(indignant now)* You're a fine guy bragging how you short-changed your own sister! Bejees, if there was a war and you was in it, they'd have to padlock the pockets of the dead!

MOSHER: *(a bit hurt at this)* That's going pretty strong, Harry. I always gave a sucker some chance. There wouldn't be no fun robbing the dead. *(He becomes reminiscently melancholy)* Gosh, thinking of the old ticket wagon brings those days back. The greatest life on earth with the greatest show on earth! The grandest crowd of regular guys ever gathered under one tent! I'd sure like to shake their hands again!

HOPE: *(acidly)* They'd have guns in theirs. They'd shoot you on sight. You've touched every damned one of them. Bejees, you've even borrowed fish from the trained seals and peanuts from every elephant that remembered you!

(This fancy tickles him and he gives a cackling laugh.)

MOSHER: *(overlooking this—dreamily)* You know, Harry, I've made up my mind I'll see the boss in a couple of days and ask for my old job. I can get back my magic touch with change easy, and I can throw him a line of bull that'll kid him I won't be so unreasonable about sharing the profits next time. *(With insinuating complaint)* There's no percentage in hanging around this dive, taking care of you and shooing away your snakes, when I don't even get an eye-opener for my trouble.

HOPE: *(implacably)* No! (MOSHER *sighs and gives up and closes his eyes. The others, except* LARRY *and* PARRITT, *are all dozing again now.* HOPE *goes on grumbling)* Go to hell or the circus, for all I care. Good riddance, bejees! I'm sick of you! *(Then worriedly)* Say, Ed, what the hell you think's happened to Hickey? I hope he'll turn up. Always got a million funny stories. You and the other bums have begun to give me the graveyard fantods. I'd like a good laugh with old Hickey. *(He chuckles at a memory)* Remember that gag he always pulls about his wife and the iceman? He'd make a cat laugh!

*(*ROCKY *appears from the bar. He comes front, behind* MOSHER'S *chair, and begins pushing the black curtain along the rod to the rear wall.)*

ROCKY: Openin' time, Boss. *(He presses a button at rear which switches off the lights. The back room becomes drabber and dingier than ever in the gray daylight that comes from the street windows, off right, and what light can penetrate the grime of the two backyard windows at left.* ROCKY *turns back to* HOPE—*grumpily)* Why don't you go up to bed, Boss? Hickey'd never turn up dis time of de mornin'!

HOPE: *(starts and listens)* Someone's coming now.

ROCKY: *(listens)* Aw, dat's on'y my two pigs. It's about time dey showed.

(He goes back toward the door at left of the bar)

HOPE: *(sourly disappointed)* You keep them dumb broads quiet. I don't want to go to bed. I'm going to catch a couple more winks here and I don't want no damn-fool laughing and screeching. *(He settles himself in his chair, grumbling)* Never thought I'd see the day when Harry Hope's would have tarts rooming in it. What'd Bessie think? But I don't let 'em use my rooms for business. And they're good kids. Good as anyone else. They got to make a living. Pay their rent, too, which is more than I can say for— *(He cocks an eye over his specs at* MOSHER *and grins with satisfaction)* Bejees, Ed, I'll bet Bessie is doing somersaults in her grave!

(He chuckles. But MOSHER'S *eyes are closed, his head nodding, and he doesn't reply, so* HOPE *closes his eyes.* ROCKY *has opened the barroom door at rear and is standing in the hall beyond it, facing right. A girl's laugh is heard.)*

ROCKY: *(warningly)* Nix! Piano!

(He comes in, beckoning them to follow. He goes behind the bar and gets a whiskey bottle and glasses and chairs. MARGIE *and* PEARL *follow him, casting a glance around. Everyone except* LARRY *and* PARRITT *is asleep or dozing. Even* PARRITT *has his eyes closed. The two girls, neither much over twenty, are typical dollar street walkers, dressed in the usual tawdry get-up.* PEARL *is obviously Italian with black hair and eyes.* MARGIE *has brown hair and hazel eyes, a slum New Yorker of mixed blood. Both are plump and have a certain prettiness that shows even through their blobby make-up. Each retains a vestige of youthful freshness, although the game is beginning to get them and give them hard, worn expressions. Both are sentimental, feather-brained, giggly, lazy, good-natured and reasonably contented with life. Their attitude toward* ROCKY *is much that of two maternal, affectionate sisters toward a bullying brother whom they like to tease and spoil. His attitude toward them is that of the owner of two performing pets he has trained to do a profitable act under his management. He feels a proud proprietor's affection for them, and is tolerantly lax in his discipline.)*

MARGIE: *(glancing around)* Jees, Poil, it's de Morgue wid all de stiffs on deck. *(She catches* LARRY'S *eye and smiles affectionately)* Hello, Old Wise Guy, ain't you died yet?

LARRY: *(grinning)* Not yet, Margie. But I'm waiting impatiently for the end.

*(*PARRITT *opens his eyes to look at the two girls, but as soon as they glance at him he closes them again and turns his head away.)*

MARGIE: *(as she and* PEARL *come to the table at right, front, followed by* ROCKY*)* Who's de new guy? Friend of yours, Larry? *(Automatically she smiles seductively at* PARRITT *and addresses him in a professional chant)* Wanta have a good time, kid?

PEARL: Aw, he's passed out. Hell wid him!

HOPE: *(cocks an eye over his specs at them—with drowsy irritation)* You dumb broads cut the loud talk.

(He shuts his eye again.)

ROCKY: *(admonishing them good-naturedly)* Sit down before I knock yuh down. *(*MARGIE *and* PEARL *sit at left, and rear, of table,* ROCKY *at right of it. The girls pour drinks.* ROCKY *begins in a brisk, business-like manner but in a lowered voice with an eye on* HOPE*)* Well, how'd you tramps do?

MARGIE: Pretty good. Didn't we, Poil?

PEARL: Sure. We nailed a coupla all-night guys.

MARGIE: On Sixth Avenoo. Boobs from de sticks.

PEARL: Stinko, de bot' of 'em.

MARGIE: We thought we was in luck. We steered dem to a real hotel. We figgered dey was too stinko to bother us much and we could cop a good sleep in beds that ain't got cobble stones in de mattress like de ones in dis dump.

PEARL: But we was outa luck. Dey didn't bother us much dat way, but dey wouldn't go to sleep either, see? Jees, I never hoid such gabby guys.

MARGIE: Dey got onta politics, drinkin' outa de bottle. Dey forgot we was around. "De Bull Moosers° is de on'y reg'lar guys," one guy says.

Bull Moosers: *members of the "Bull Moose" Party, nickname for the Progressive Party, founded by Theodore Roosevelt and supporters in 1912 after the Republican convention nominated William Howard Taft for president.*

And de other guy says, "You're a God-damned liar! And I'm a Republican!" Den dey'd laugh.

PEARL: Den dey'd get mad and make a bluff dey was goin' to scrap, and den dey'd make up and cry and sing "School Days." Jees, imagine tryin' to sleep wid dat on de phonograph!

MARGIE: Maybe you tink we wasn't glad when de house dick come up and told us all to git dressed and take de air!

PEARL: We told de guys we'd wait for dem 'round de corner.

MARGIE: So here we are.

ROCKY: *(sententiously)* Yeah. I see you. But I don't see no dough yet.

PEARL: *(with a wink at* MARGIE—*teasingly)* Right on de job, ain't he, Margie?

MARGIE: Yeah, our little business man! Dat's him!

ROCKY: Come on! Dig!
(They both pull up their skirts to get the money from their stockings. ROCKY *watches this move carefully.)*

PEARL: *(amused)* Pipe him keepin' cases, Margie.

MARGIE: *(amused)* Scared we're holdin' out on him.

PEARL: Way he grabs, yuh'd tink it was him done de woik. *(She holds out a little roll of bills to* ROCKY*)* Here y'are, Grafter!

MARGIE: *(holding hers out)* We hope it chokes yuh. *(*ROCKY *counts the money quickly and shoves it in his pocket)*

ROCKY: *(genially)* You dumb baby dolls gimme a pain. What would you do wid money if I wasn't around? Give it all to some pimp.

PEARL: *(teasingly)* Jees, what's the difference—? *(Hastily)* Aw, I don't mean dat, Rocky.

ROCKY: *(his eyes growing hard—slowly)* A lotta difference, get me?

PEARL: Don't get sore. Jees, can't yuh take a little kiddin'?

MARGIE: Sure, Rocky, Poil was on'y kiddin'. *(Soothingly)* We know yuh got a reg'lar job. Dat's why we like yuh, see? Yuh don't live offa us. Yuh're a bartender.

ROCKY: *(genially again)* Sure, I'm a bartender. Everyone knows me knows dat. And I treat you goils right, don't I? Jees, I'm wise yuh hold out on me, but I know it ain't much, so what the hell, I let yuh get away wid it. I tink yuh're a coupla good kids. Yuh're aces wid me, see?

PEARL: You're aces wid us, too. Ain't he, Margie?

MARGIE: Sure, he's aces. *(*ROCKY *beams complacently and takes the glasses back to the bar.* MARGIE *whispers)* Yuh sap, don't yuh know enough not to kid him on dat? Serve yuh right if he beat yuh up!

PEARL: *(admiringly)* Jees, I'll bet he'd give yuh an awful beatin', too, once he started. Ginnies got awful tempers.

MARGIE: Anyway, we wouldn't keep no pimp, like we was reg'lar old whores. We ain't dat bad.

PEARL: No. We're tarts, but dat's all.

ROCKY: *(rinsing glasses behind the bar)* Cora got back around three o'clock. She woke up Chuck and dragged him outa de hay to go to a chop suey joint. *(Disgustedly)* Imagine him standin' for dat stuff!

MARGIE: *(disgustedly)* I'll bet dey been sittin' around kiddin' demselves wid dat old pipe dream about gettin' married and settlin' down on a farm. Jees, when Chuck's on de wagon, dey never lay off dat dope! Dey give yuh an earful everytime yuh talk to 'em!

PEARL: Yeah. Chuck wid a silly grin on his ugly map, de big boob, and Cora gigglin' like she was in grammar school and some tough guy'd just told her babies wasn't brung down de chimney by a boid!

MARGIE: And her on de turf long before me and you was! And bot' of 'em arguin' all de time, Cora sayin' she's scared to marry him because he'll go on drunks again. Just as dough any drunk could scare Cora!

PEARL: And him swearin', de big liar, he'll never go on no more periodicals! An' den her pretendin'— But it gives me a pain to talk about it. We ought to phone de booby hatch to send round de wagon for 'em.

ROCKY: *(comes back to the table—disgustedly)* Yeah, of all de pipe dreams in dis dump, dey got de nuttiest! And nuttin' stops dem. Dey been dreamin' it for years, every time Chuck goes on de wagon. I never could figger it. What would gettin' married get dem? But de farm stuff is de sappiest part. When bot' of 'em was dragged up in dis ward and ain't never been nearer a farm dan Coney Island! Jees, dey'd tink dey'd gone deef if dey didn't hear de El rattle! Dey'd get D.T.s if dey ever hoid a cricket choip! I hoid crickets once on my cousin's place in Joisey. I couldn't sleep a wink. Dey give me de heebie-jeebies. *(With deeper disgust)* Jees, can yuh picture a good barkeep like Chuck diggin' spuds? And imagine a whore hustlin' de cows home! For Christ sake! Ain't dat a sweet picture!

MARGIE: *(rebukingly)* Yuh oughtn't to call Cora dat, Rocky. She's a good kid. She may be a tart, but—

ROCKY: *(considerately)* Sure, dat's all I meant, a tart.

PEARL: *(giggling)* But he's right about de damned cows, Margie. Jees, I bet Cora don't know which end of de cow has de horns! I'm goin' to ask her. *(There is the noise of a door opening in the hall and the sound of a man's and woman's arguing voices.)*

ROCKY: Here's your chance. Dat's dem two nuts now.
(CORA and CHUCK look in from the hallway and then come in. CORA is a thin peroxide blonde, a few years older than PEARL and MARGIE, dressed in similar style, her round face showing more of the wear and tear of her trade than theirs, but still with traces of a doll-like prettiness. CHUCK is a tough, thick-necked, barrel-chested Italian-American, with a fat, amiable, swarthy face. He has on a straw hat with a vivid band, a loud suit, tie and shirt, and yellow shoes. His eyes are clear and he looks healthy and strong as an ox.)

CORA: *(gaily)* Hello, bums. *(She looks around)* Jees, de Morgue on a rainy Sunday night! *(She waves to LARRY—affectionately)* Hello, Old Wise Guy! Ain't you croaked yet?

LARRY: *(grins)* Not yet, Cora. It's damned tiring, this waiting for the end.

CORA: Aw, gwan, you'll never die! Yuh'll have to hire someone to croak yuh wid an axe.

HOPE: *(cocks one sleepy eye at her—irritably)* You dumb hookers, cut the loud noise! This ain't a cathouse!

CORA: *(teasingly)* My, Harry! Such language!

HOPE: *(closes his eyes—to himself with a gratified chuckle)* Bejees, I'll bet Bessie's turning over in her grave!
(CORA sits down between MARGIE and PEARL. CHUCK takes an empty chair from HOPE's table and puts it by hers and sits down. At LARRY's table, PARRITT is glaring resentfully toward the girls)

PARRITT: If I'd known this dump was a hooker hangout, I'd never have come here.

LARRY: *(watching him)* You seem down on the ladies.

PARRITT: *(vindictively)* I hate every bitch that ever lived! They're all alike! *(Catching himself guiltily)* You can understand how I feel, can't you, when it was getting mixed up with a tart that made me have that fight with Mother? *(Then with a resentful sneer)* But what the hell does it matter to you? You're in the grandstand. You're through with life.

LARRY: *(sharply)* I'm glad you remember it. I don't want to know a damned thing about your business.
(He closes his eyes and settles on his chair as if preparing for sleep. PARRITT stares at him sneeringly. Then he looks away and his expression becomes furtive and frightened.)

CORA: Who's de guy wid Larry?

ROCKY: A tightwad. To hell wid him.

PEARL: Say, Cora, wise me up. Which end of a cow is de horns on?

CORA: *(embarrassed)* Aw, don't bring dat up. I'm sick of hearin' about dat farm.

ROCKY: You got nuttin' on us!

CORA: *(ignoring this)* Me and dis overgrown tramp has been scrappin' about it. He says Joisey's de best place, and I says Long Island because we'll be near Coney. And I tells him,

"How do I know yuh're off of periodicals for life? I don't give a damn how drunk yuh get, the way we are, but I don't wanta be married to no soak."

CHUCK: And I tells her I'm off de stuff for life. Den she beefs we won't be married a month before I'll trow it in her face she was a tart. "Jees, Baby," I tells her. "Why should I? What de hell yuh tink I tink I'm marryin', a voigin? Why should I kick as long as yuh lay off it and don't do no cheatin' wid de iceman or nobody?" *(He gives her a rough hug)* Dat's on de level, Baby. *(He kisses her.)*

CORA: *(kissing him)* Aw, yuh big tramp!

ROCKY: *(shakes his head with profound disgust)* Can yuh tie it? I'll buy a drink. I'll do anything. *(He gets up.)*

CORA: No, dis round's on me. I run into luck. Dat's why I dragged Chuck outa bed to celebrate. It was a sailor. I rolled him. *(She giggles)* Listen, it was a scream. I've run into some nutty souses, but dis guy was de nuttiest. De booze dey dish out around de Brooklyn Navy Yard must be as turrible bug-juice as Harry's. My dogs was givin' out when I seen dis guy holdin' up a lamp-post, so I hurried to get him before a cop did. I says, "Hello, Handsome, wanta have a good time?" Jees, he was paralyzed! One of dem polite jags. He tries to bow to me, imagine, and I had to prop him up or he'd fell on his nose. And what d'yuh tink he said? "Lady," he says, "can yuh kindly tell me de nearest way to de Museum of Natural History?" *(They all laugh)* Can yuh imagine! At two A.M. As if I'd know where de dump was anyway. But I says, "Sure ting, Honey Boy, I'll be only too glad." So I steered him into a side street where it was dark and propped him against a wall and give him a frisk. *(She giggles)* And what d'yuh tink he does? Jees, I ain't lyin', he begins to laugh, de big sap! He says, "Quit ticklin' me." While I was friskin' him for his roll! I near died! Den I toined him 'round and give him a push to start him. "Just keep goin'," I told him. "It's a big white building on your right.

You can't miss it." He must be swimmin' in de North River yet! *(They all laugh.)*

CHUCK: Ain't Uncle Sam de sap to trust guys like dat wid dough!

CORA: *(with a business-like air)* I picked twelve bucks offa him. Come on, Rocky. Set 'em up. *(ROCKY goes back to the bar. CORA looks around the room)* Say, Chuck's kiddin' about de iceman a minute ago reminds me. Where de hell's Hickey?

ROCKY: Dat's what we're all wonderin'.

CORA: He oughta be here. Me and Chuck seen him.

ROCKY: *(excited, comes back from the bar, forgetting the drinks)* You seen Hickey? *(He nudges HOPE)* Hey, Boss, come to! Cora's seen Hickey. *(HOPE is instantly wide awake and everyone in the place, except HUGO and PARRITT, begins to rouse up hopefully, as if a mysterious wireless message had gone round.)*

HOPE: Where'd you see him, Cora?

CORA: Right on de next corner. He was standin' dere. We said, "Welcome to our city. De gang is expectin' yuh wid deir tongues hangin' out a yard long." And I kidded him, "How's de iceman, Hickey? How's he doin' at your house?" He laughs and says, "Fine." And he says, "Tell de gang I'll be along in a minute. I'm just finishin' figurin' out de best way to save dem and bring dem peace."

HOPE: *(chuckles)* Bejees, he's thought up a new gag! It's a wonder he didn't borry a Salvation Army uniform and show up in that! Go out and get him, Rocky. Tell him we're waitin' to be saved! *(ROCKY goes out, grinning)*

CORA: Yeah, Harry, he was only kiddin'. But he was funny, too, somehow. He was different, or somethin'.

CHUCK: Sure, he was sober, Baby. Dat's what made him different. We ain't never seen him when he wasn't on a drunk, or had de willies gettin' over it.

CORA: Sure! Gee, ain't I dumb?

HOPE: *(with conviction)* The dumbest broad I ever seen! *(Then puzzledly)* Sober? That's funny. He's always lapped up a good starter on his way here. Well, bejees, he won't be sober long! He'll be good and ripe for my birthday party tonight at twelve. *(He chuckles with excited anticipation—addressing all of them)* Listen! He's fixed some new gag to pull on us. We'll pretend to let him kid us, see? And we'll kid the pants off him.

(They all say laughingly, "Sure, Harry," "Righto," "That's the stuff," "We'll fix him," etc., etc., their faces excited with the same eager anticipation. ROCKY appears in the doorway at the end of the bar with HICKEY, his arm around HICKEY's shoulders.)

ROCKY: *(with an affectionate grin)* Here's the old son of a bitch!

(They all stand up and greet him with affectionate acclaim, "Hello, Hickey!" etc. Even HUGO comes out of his coma to raise his head and blink through his thick spectacles with a welcoming giggle.)

HICKEY: *(jovially)* Hello, Gang! *(He stands a moment, beaming around at all of them affectionately. He is about fifty, a little under medium height, with a stout, roly-poly figure. His face is round and smooth and big-boyish with bright blue eyes, a button nose, a small, pursed mouth. His head is bald except for a fringe of hair around his temples and the back of his head. His expression is fixed in a salesman's winning smile of self-confident affability and hearty good fellowship. His eyes have the twinkle of a humor which delights in kidding others but can also enjoy equally a joke on himself. He exudes a friendly, generous personality that makes everyone like him on sight. You get the impression, too, that he must have real ability in his line. There is an efficient, business-like approach in his manner, and his eyes can take you in shrewdly at a glance. He has the salesman's mannerisms of speech, an easy flow of glib, persuasive convincingness. His clothes are those of a successful drummer whose territory consists of minor cities and small towns—not flashy but* conspicuously spic and span. He immediately puts on an entrance act, places a hand affectedly on his chest, throws back his head, and sings in a falsetto tenor) "It's always fair weather, when good fellows get together!" *(Changing to a comic bass and another tune)* "And another little drink won't do us any harm!" *(They all roar with laughter at this burlesque which his personality makes really funny. He waves his hand in a lordly manner to* ROCKY*)* Do your duty, Brother Rocky. Bring on the rat poison! *(*ROCKY *grins and goes behind the bar to get drinks amid an approving cheer from the crowd.* HICKEY *comes forward to shake hands with* HOPE*—with affectionate heartiness)* How goes it, Governor?

HOPE: *(enthusiastically)* Bejees, Hickey, you old bastard, it's good to see you! *(*HICKEY *shakes hands with* MOSHER *and* MCGLOIN; *leans right to shake hands with* MARGIE *and* PEARL; *moves to the middle table to shake hands with* LEWIS, JOE MOTT, WETJOEN *and* JIMMY; *waves to* WILLIE, LARRY *and* HUGO. *He greets each by name with the same affectionate heartiness and there is an interchange of "How's the kid?" "How's the old scout?" "How's the boy?" "How's everything?" etc., etc.* ROCKY *begins setting out drinks, whiskey glasses with chasers, and a bottle for each table, starting with* LARRY's *table.* HOPE *says)* Sit down, Hickey. Sit down. *(*HICKEY *takes the chair, facing front, at the front of the table in the second row which is half between* HOPE's *table and the one where* JIMMY TOMORROW *is.* HOPE *goes on with excited pleasure)* Bejees, Hickey, it seems natural to see your ugly, grinning map. *(With a scornful nod to* CORA*)* This dumb broad was tryin' to tell us you'd changed, but you ain't a damned bit. Tell us about yourself. How've you been doin'? Bejees, you look like a million dollars.

ROCKY: *(coming to* HICKEY's *table, puts a bottle of whiskey, a glass and a chaser on it—then hands* HICKEY *a key)* Here's your key, Hickey. Same old room.

HICKEY: *(shoves the key in his pocket)* Thanks, Rocky. I'm going up in a little while and grab a snooze. Haven't been able to sleep lately and I'm tired as hell. A couple of hours good kip will fix me.

HOPE: *(as* ROCKY *puts drinks on his table)* First time I ever heard you worry about sleep. Bejees, you never would go to bed. *(He raises his glass, and all the others except* PARRITT *do likewise)* Get a few slugs under your belt and you'll forget sleeping. Here's mud in your eye, Hickey. *(They all join in with the usual humorous toasts.)*

HICKEY: *(heartily)* Drink hearty, boys and girls! *(They all drink, but* HICKEY *drinks only his chaser)*

HOPE: Bejees, is that a new stunt, drinking your chaser first?

HICKEY: No, I forgot to tell Rocky— You'll have to excuse me, boys and girls, but I'm off the stuff. For keeps. *(They stare at him in amazed incredulity.)*

HOPE: What the hell— *(Then with a wink at the others, kiddingly)* Sure! Joined the Salvation Army, ain't you? Been elected President of the W.C.T.U?° Take that bottle away from him, Rocky. We don't want to tempt him into sin. *(He chuckles and the others laugh.)*

HICKEY: *(earnestly)* No, honest, Harry. I know it's hard to believe but— *(He pauses—then adds simply)* Cora was right, Harry. I have changed. I mean, about booze. I don't need it any more. *(They all stare, hoping it's a gag, but impressed and disappointed and made vaguely uneasy by the change they now sense in him.)*

HOPE: *(his kidding a bit forced)* Yeah, go ahead, kid the pants off us! Bejees, Cora said you was coming to save us! Well, go on. Get this joke off your chest! Start the service! Sing a God-damned hymn if you like. We'll all join in the chorus. "No drunkard can enter this beautiful home." That's a good one. *(He forces a cackle.)*

HICKEY: *(grinning)* Oh, hell, Governor! You don't think I'd come around here peddling some brand of temperance bunk, do you? You know me better than that! Just because I'm through with the stuff don't mean I'm going Prohibition. Hell, I'm not that ungrateful! It's given me too many good times. I feel exactly the same as I always did. If anyone wants to get drunk, if that's the only way they can be happy, and feel at peace with themselves, why the hell shouldn't they? They have my full and entire sympathy. I know all about that game from soup to nuts. I'm the guy that wrote the book. The only reason I've quit is— Well, I finally had the guts to face myself and throw overboard the damned lying pipe dream that'd been making me miserable, and do what I had to do for the happiness of all concerned—and then all at once I found I was at peace with myself and I didn't need booze any more. That's all there was to it. *(He pauses. They are staring at him, uneasy and beginning to feel defensive.* HICKEY *looks round and grins affectionately—apologetically)* But what the hell! Don't let me be a wet blanket, making fool speeches about myself. Set 'em up again, Rocky. Here. *(He pulls a big roll from his pocket and peels off a ten-dollar bill. The faces of all brighten)* Keep the balls coming until this is killed. Then ask for more.

ROCKY: Jees, a roll dat'd choke a hippopotamus! Fill up, youse guys. *(They all pour out drinks.)*

HOPE: That sounds more like you, Hickey. That water-wagon bull—Cut out the act and have a drink, for Christ's sake.

HICKEY: It's no act, Governor. But don't get me wrong. That don't mean I'm a teetotal grouch and can't be in the party. Hell, why d'you suppose I'm here except to have a party, same as I've always done, and help celebrate your birthday tonight? You've all been good pals to me, the best friends I've ever had. I've been thinking about you ever since I left the house—all the time I was walking over here—

HOPE: Walking? Bejees, do you mean to say you walked?

HICKEY: I sure did. All the way from the wilds of darkest Astoria. Didn't mind it a bit, either. I seemed to get here before I knew it. I'm a bit tired and sleepy but otherwise I feel great. *(Kiddingly)* That ought to encourage you, Governor—show you a little walk around the ward is nothing to be so scared about. *(He winks at the others.* HOPE *stiffens resentfully for a second.* HICKEY *goes on)* I didn't make such bad time either for a fat guy, considering it's a hell of a ways, and I sat in the park a while thinking. It was going on twelve when I went in the bedroom to tell Evelyn I was leaving. Six hours, say. No, less than that. I'd been standing on the corner some time before Cora and Chuck came along, thinking about all of you. Of course, I was only kidding Cora with that stuff about saving you. *(Then seriously)* No, I wasn't either. But I didn't mean booze. I meant save you from pipe dreams. I know now, from my experience, they're the things that really poison and ruin a guy's life and keep him from finding any peace. If you knew how free and contented I feel now. I'm like a new man. And the cure for them is so damned simple, once you have the nerve. Just the old dope of honesty is the best policy—honesty with yourself, I mean. Just stop lying about yourself and kidding yourself about tomorrows. *(He is staring ahead of him now as if he were talking aloud to himself as much as to them. Their eyes are fixed on him with uneasy resentment. His manner becomes apologetic again)* Hell, this begins to sound like a damned sermon on the way to lead the good life. Forget that part of it. It's in my blood, I guess. My old man used to whale salvation into my heinie with a birch rod. He was a preacher in the sticks of Indiana, like I've told you. I got my knack of sales gab from him, too. He was the boy who could sell those Hoosier hayseeds building lots along the Golden Street! *(Taking on a salesman's persuasiveness)* Now listen, boys and girls, don't look at me as if I was trying to sell you a gold-brick. Nothing up my sleeve, honest. Let's take an example. Any one of you. Take you, Governor. That walk around the ward you never take—

HOPE: *(defensively sharp)* What about it?

HICKEY: *(grinning affectionately)* Why, you know as well as I do, Harry. Everything about it.

HOPE: *(defiantly)* Bejees, I'm going to take it!

HICKEY: Sure, you're going to—this time. Because I'm going to help you. I know it's the thing you've got to do before you'll ever know what real peace means. *(He looks at* JIMMY TOMORROW*)* Same thing with you, Jimmy. You've got to try and get your old job back. And no tomorrow about it! *(As* JIMMY *stiffens with a pathetic attempt at dignity—placatingly)* No, don't tell me, Jimmy. I know all about tomorrow. I'm the guy that wrote the book.

JIMMY: I don't understand you. I admit I've foolishly delayed, but as it happens, I'd just made up my mind that as soon as I could get straightened out—

HICKEY: Fine! That's the spirit! And I'm going to help you. You've been damned kind to me, Jimmy, and I want to prove how grateful I am. When it's all over and you don't have to nag at yourself any more, you'll be grateful to me, too! *(He looks around at the others)* And all the rest of you, ladies included, are in the same boat, one way or another.

LARRY: *(who has been listening with sardonic appreciation—in his comically intense, crazy whisper)* Be God, you've hit the nail on the head, Hickey! This dump is the Palace of Pipe Dreams!

HICKEY: *(grins at him with affectionate kidding)* Well, well! The Old Grandstand Foolosopher speaks! You think you're the big exception, eh? Life doesn't mean a damn to you any more, does it? You're retired from the circus. You're just waiting impatiently for the end—the good old Long Sleep! *(He chuckles)* Well, I think a lot of you, Larry, you old bastard. I'll try and make an honest man of you, too!

LARRY: *(stung)* What the devil are you hinting at, anyway?

HICKEY: You don't have to ask me, do you, a wise old guy like you? Just ask yourself. I'll bet you know.

PARRITT: *(is watching* LARRY'S *face with a curious sneering satisfaction)* He's got your number all right, Larry! *(He turns to* HICKEY) That's the stuff, Hickey. Show the old faker up! He's got no right to sneak out of everything.

HICKEY: *(regards him with surprise at first, then with a puzzled interest)* Hello. A stranger in our midst. I didn't notice you before, Brother.

PARRITT: *(embarrassed, his eyes shifting away)* My name's Parritt. I'm an old friend of Larry's. *(His eyes come back to* HICKEY *to find him still sizing him up—defensively)* Well? What are you staring at?

HICKEY: *(continuing to stare—puzzledly)* No offense, Brother. I was trying to figure— Haven't we met before some place?

PARRITT: *(reassured)* No. First time I've ever been East.

HICKEY: No, you're right. I know that's not it. In my game, to be a shark at it, you teach yourself never to forget a name or a face. But still I know damned well I recognized something about you. We're members of the same lodge— in some way.

PARRITT: *(uneasy again)* What are you talking about? You're nuts.

HICKEY: *(dryly)* Don't try to kid me, Little Boy. I'm a good salesman—so damned good the firm was glad to take me back after every drunk—and what made me good was I could size up anyone. *(Frowningly puzzled again)* But I don't see— *(Suddenly breezily good-natured)* Never mind. I can tell you're having trouble with yourself and I'll be glad to do anything I can to help a friend of Larry's.

LARRY: Mind your own business, Hickey. He's nothing to you—or to me, either. (HICKEY *gives him a keen inquisitive glance.* LARRY *looks away and goes on sarcastically)* You're keeping us all in suspense. Tell us more about how you're going to save us.

HICKEY: *(good-naturedly but seeming a little hurt)* Hell, don't get sore, Larry. Not at me. We've always been good pals, haven't we? I know I've always liked you a lot.

LARRY: *(a bit shamefaced)* Well, so have I liked you. Forget it, Hickey.

HICKEY: *(beaming)* Fine! That's the spirit! *(Looking around at the others, who have forgotten their drinks)* What's the matter, everybody? What is this, a funeral? Come on and drink up! A little action! *(They all drink)* Have another. Hell, this is a celebration! Forget it, if anything I've said sounds too serious. I don't want to be a pain in the neck. Any time you think I'm talking out of turn, just tell me to go chase myself! *(He yawns with growing drowsiness and his voice grows a bit muffled)* No, boys and girls, I'm not trying to put anything over on you. It's just that I know now from experience what a lying pipe dream can do to you—and how damned relieved and contented with yourself you feel when you're rid of it. *(He yawns again)* God, I'm sleepy all of a sudden. That long walk is beginning to get me. I better go upstairs. Hell of a trick to go dead on you like this. *(He starts to get up but relaxes again. His eyes blink as he tries to keep them open)* No, boys and girls, I've never known what real peace was until now. It's a grand feeling, like when you're sick and suffering like hell and the Doc gives you a shot in the arm, and the pain goes, and you drift off. *(His eyes close)* You can let go of yourself at last. Let yourself sink down to the bottom of the sea. Rest in peace. There's no farther you have to go. Not a single damned hope or dream left to nag you. You'll all know what I mean after you— *(He pauses—mumbles)* Excuse—all in—got to grab forty winks— Drink up, everybody—on me—

(The sleep of complete exhaustion overpowers him. His chin sags to his chest. They stare at him with puzzled uneasy fascination.)

HOPE: *(forcing a tone of irritation)* Bejees, that's a fine stunt, to go to sleep on us! *(Then fumingly to the crowd)* Well, what the hell's the matter with you bums? Why don't you drink up? You're always crying for booze, and now you've got it under your nose, you sit like dummies! *(They start and gulp down their whiskies and pour another.* HOPE *stares at* HICKEY) Bejees, I can't figure Hickey. I still say he's kidding us. Kid his own grandmother, Hickey would. What d'you think, Jimmy?

JIMMY: *(unconvincingly)* It must be another of his jokes, Harry, although— Well, he does appear changed. But he'll probably be his natural self again tomorrow— *(Hastily)* I mean, when he wakes up.

LARRY: *(staring at* HICKEY *frowningly—more aloud to himself than to them)* You'll make a mistake if you think he's only kidding.

PARRITT: *(in a low confidential voice)* I don't like that guy, Larry. He's too damned nosy. I'm going to steer clear of him.

*(*LARRY *gives him a suspicious glance, then looks hastily away.)*

JIMMY: *(with an attempt at open-minded reasonableness)* Still, Harry, I have to admit there was some sense in his nonsense. It is time I got my job back—although I hardly need him to remind me.

HOPE: *(with an air of frankness)* Yes, and I ought to take a walk around the ward. But I don't need no Hickey to tell me, seeing I got it all set for my birthday tomorrow.

LARRY: *(sardonically)* Ha! *(Then in his comically intense, crazy whisper)* Be God, it looks like he's going to make two sales of his peace at least! But you'd better make sure first it's the real McCoy and not poison.

HOPE: *(disturbed—angrily)* You bughouse I-Won't-Work harp, who asked you to shove in an oar? What the hell d'you mean, poison? Just because he has your number— *(He immediately feels ashamed of this taunt and adds apologetically)* Bejees, Larry, you're always croaking about something to do with death. It gets my nanny. Come on, fellers, let's drink up. *(They drink.* HOPE's *eyes are fixed on* HICKEY *again)* Stone cold sober and dead to the world! Spilling that business about pipe dreams! Bejees, I don't get it. *(He bursts out again in angry complaint)* He ain't like the old Hickey! He'll be a fine wet

blanket to have around at my birthday party! I wish to hell he'd never turned up!

MOSHER: *(who has been the least impressed by* HICKEY'S *talk and is the first to recover and feel the effect of the drinks on top of his hangover— genially)* Give him time, Harry, and he'll come out of it. I've watched many cases of almost fatal teetotalism, but they all came out of it completely cured and as drunk as ever. My opinion is the poor sap is temporarily bughouse from overwork. *(Musingly)* You can't be too careful about work. It's the deadliest habit known to science, a great physician once told me. He practiced on street corners under a torchlight. He was positively the only doctor in the world who claimed that rattlesnake oil, rubbed on the prat, would cure heart failure in three days. I remember well his saying to me, "You are naturally delicate, Ed, but if you drink a pint of bad whiskey before breakfast every evening, and never work if you can help it, you may live to a ripe old age. It's staying sober and working that cuts men off in their prime."

(While he is talking, they turn to him with eager grins. They are longing to laugh, and as he finishes they roar. Even PARRITT *laughs.* HICKEY *sleeps on like a dead man, but* HUGO, *who had passed into his customary coma again, head on table, looks up through his thick spectacles and giggles foolishly.)*

HUGO: *(blinking around at them. As the laughter dies he speaks in his giggling, wheedling manner, as if he were playfully teasing children)* Laugh, leedle bourgeois monkey-faces! Laugh like fools, leedle stupid peoples! *(His tone suddenly changes to one of guttural soapbox denunciation and he pounds on the table with a small fist)* I vill laugh, too! But I vill laugh last! I vill laugh at you! *(He declaims his favorite quotation)* "The days grow hot, O Babylon! 'Tis cool beneath thy villow trees!"

(They all hoot him down in a chorus of amused jeering. HUGO *is not offended. This is evidently their customary reaction. He giggles good-naturedly.* HICKEY *sleeps on. They have*

all forgotten their uneasiness about him now and ignore him.)

LEWIS: *(tipsily)* Well, now that our little Robespierre has got the daily bit of guillotining off his chest, tell me more about your doctor friend, Ed. He strikes me as the only bloody sensible medico I ever heard of. I think we should appoint him house physician here without a moment's delay.

(They all laughingly assent.)

MOSHER: *(warming to his subject, shakes his head sadly)* Too late! The old Doc has passed on to his Maker. A victim of overwork, too. He didn't follow his own advice. Kept his nose to the grindstone and sold one bottle of snake oil too many. Only eighty years old when he was taken. The saddest part was that he knew he was doomed. The last time we got paralyzed together he told me: "This game will get me yet, Ed. You see before you a broken man, a martyr to medical science. If I had any nerves I'd have a nervous breakdown. You won't believe me, but this last year there was actually one night I had so many patients, I didn't even have time to get drunk. The shock to my system brought on a stroke which, as a doctor, I recognized was the beginning of the end." Poor old Doc! When he said this he started crying. "I hate to go before my task is completed, Ed," he sobbed. "I'd hoped I'd live to see the day when, thanks to my miraculous cure, there wouldn't be a single vacant cemetery lot left in this glorious country." *(There is a roar of laughter. He waits for it to die and then goes on sadly)* I miss Doc. He was a gentleman of the old school. I'll bet he's standing on a street corner in hell right now, making suckers of the damned, telling them there's nothing like snake oil for a bad burn.

(There is another roar of laughter. This time it penetrates HICKEY'S *exhausted slumber. He stirs on his chair, trying to wake up, managing to raise his head a little and force his eyes half open. He speaks with a drowsy, affectionately encouraging smile. At once the laughter stops abruptly and they turn to him startledly.)*

HICKEY: That's the spirit—don't let me be a wet blanket—all I want is to see you happy—
(He slips back into heavy sleep again. They all stare at him, their faces again puzzled, resentful and uneasy.)

CURTAIN

ACT TWO

SCENE: *The back room only. The black curtain dividing it from the bar is the right wall of the scene. It is getting on toward midnight of the same day.*

The back room has been prepared for a festivity. At center, front, four of the circular tables are pushed together to form one long table with an uneven line of chairs behind it, and chairs at each end. This improvised banquet table is covered with old table cloths, borrowed from a neighboring beanery, and is laid with glasses, plates and cutlery before each of the seventeen chairs. Bottles of bar whiskey are placed at intervals within reach of any sitter. An old upright piano and stool have been moved in and stand against the wall at left, front. At right, front, is a table without chairs. The other tables and chairs that had been in the room have been moved out, leaving a clear floor space at rear for dancing. The floor has been swept clean of sawdust and scrubbed. Even the walls show evidence of having been washed, although the result is only to heighten their splotchy leprous look. The electric light brackets are adorned with festoons of red ribbon. In the middle of the separate table at right, front, is a birthday cake with six candles. Several packages, tied with ribbon, are also on the table. There are two necktie boxes, two cigar boxes, a fifth containing a half dozen handkerchiefs, the sixth is a square jeweler's watch box.

As the curtain rises, CORA, CHUCK, HUGO, LARRY, MARGIE, PEARL *and* ROCKY *are discovered.* CHUCK, ROCKY *and the three girls have dressed up for the occasion.* CORA *is arranging a bouquet of flowers in a vase, the vase being a big schooner glass from the bar, on top of the piano.* CHUCK *sits in a chair at the foot (left) of the banquet table. He has turned it so he can watch her. Near the middle of the row of chairs behind the table,* LARRY *sits, facing front, a drink of whiskey before him. He is staring before him in frowning, disturbed meditation. Next to him, on his left,* HUGO *is in his habitual position, passed out, arms on table, head on arms, a full whiskey glass by his head. By the separate table at right, front,* MARGIE *and* PEARL *are arranging the cake and presents, and* ROCKY *stands by them. All of them, with the exception of* CHUCK *and* ROCKY, *have had plenty to drink and show it, but no one, except* HUGO, *seems to be drunk. They are trying to act up in the spirit of the occasion but there is something forced about their manner, an undercurrent of nervous irritation and preoccupation.*

CORA: *(standing back from the piano to regard the flower effect)* How's dat, Kid?

CHUCK: *(grumpily)* What de hell do I know about flowers?

CORA: Yuh can see dey're pretty, can't yuh, yuh big dummy?

CHUCK: *(mollifying)* Yeah, Baby, sure. If yuh like 'em, dey're aw right wid me.
*(*CORA *goes back to give the schooner of flowers a few more touches.)*

MARGIE: *(admiring the cake)* Some cake, huh, Poil? Lookit! Six candles. Each for ten years.

PEARL: When do we light de candles, Rocky?

ROCKY: *(grumpily)* Ask dat bughouse Hickey. He's elected himself boss of dis boithday racket. Just before Harry comes down, he says. Den Harry blows dem out wid one breath, for luck. Hickey was goin' to have sixty candles, but I says, Jees, if de old guy took dat big a breath, he'd croak himself.

MARGIE: *(challengingly)* Well, anyways, it's some cake, ain't it?

ROCKY: *(without enthusiasm)* Sure, it's aw right by me. But what de hell is Harry goin' to do wid a cake? If he ever et a hunk, it'd croak him.

PEARL: Jees, yuh're a dope! Ain't he, Margie?

MARGIE: A dope is right!

ROCKY: *(stung)* You broads better watch your step or—

PEARL: *(defiantly)* Or what?

MARGIE: Yeah! Or what?
(They glare at him truculently)

ROCKY: Say, what de hell's got into youse? It'll be twelve o'clock and Harry's boithday before long. I ain't lookin' for no trouble.

PEARL: *(ashamed)* Aw, we ain't neider, Rocky.
(For the moment this argument subsides.)

CORA: *(over her shoulder to* CHUCK—*acidly)* A guy what can't see flowers is pretty must be some dumbbell.

CHUCK: Yeah? Well, if I was as dumb as you— *(Then mollifyingly)* Jees, yuh got your scrappin' pants on, ain't yuh? *(Grins good-naturedly)* Hell, Baby, what's eatin' yuh? All I'm tinkin' is, flowers is dat louse Hickey's stunt. We never had no flowers for Harry's boithday before. What de hell can Harry do wid flowers? He don't know a cauliflower from a geranium.

ROCKY: Yeah, Chuck, it's like I'm tellin' dese broads about de cake. Dat's Hickey's wrinkle, too. *(Bitterly)* Jees, ever since he woke up, yuh can't hold him. He's taken on de party like it was his boithday.

MARGIE: Well, he's payin' for everything, ain't he?

ROCKY: Aw, I don't mind de boithday stuff so much. What gets my goat is de way he's tryin' to run de whole dump and everyone in it. He's buttin' in all over de place, tellin' everybody where dey get off. On'y he don't really tell yuh. He just keeps hintin' around.

PEARL: Yeah. He was hintin' to me and Margie.

MARGIE: Yeah, de lousy drummer.

ROCKY: He just gives yuh an earful of dat line of bull about yuh got to be honest wid yourself and not kid yourself, and have de guts to be what yuh are. I got sore. I told him dat's aw right for de bums in dis dump. I hope he makes dem wake up. I'm sick of listenin' to dem hop demselves up. But it don't go wid me, see? I don't kid myself wid no pipe dream. *(*PEARL *and* MARGIE *exchange a derisive look. He catches it and his eyes narrow)* What are yuh grinnin' at?

PEARL: *(her face hard—scornfully)* Nuttin'.

MARGIE: Nuttin'.

ROCKY: It better be nuttin'! Don't let Hickey put no ideas in your nuts if you wanta stay healthy! *(Then angrily)* I wish de louse never showed up! I hope he don't come back from de delicatessen. He's gettin' everyone nuts. He's ridin' someone every minute. He's got Harry and Jimmy Tomorrow run ragged, and de rest is hidin' in deir rooms so dey won't have to listen to him. Dey're all actin' cagey wid de booze, too, like dey was scared if dey get too drunk, dey might spill deir guts, or somethin'. And everybody's gettin' a prize grouch on.

CORA: Yeah, he's been hintin' round to me and Chuck, too. Yuh'd tink he suspected me and Chuck hadn't no real intention of gettin' married. Yuh'd tink he suspected Chuck wasn't goin' to lay off periodicals—or maybe even didn't want to.

CHUCK: He didn't say it right out or I'da socked him one. I told him, "I'm on de wagon for keeps and Cora knows it."

CORA: I told him, "Sure, I know it. And Chuck ain't never goin' to trow it in my face dat I was a tart, neider. And if yuh tink we're just kiddin' ourselves, we'll show yuh!"

CHUCK: We're goin' to show him!

CORA: We got it all fixed. We've decided Joisey is where we want de farm, and we'll get married dere, too, because yuh don't need no license. We're goin' to get married tomorrow. Ain't we, Honey?

CHUCK: You bet, Baby.

ROCKY: *(disgusted)* Christ, Chuck, are yuh lettin' dat bughouse louse Hickey kid yuh into—

CORA: *(turns on him angrily)* Nobody's kiddin' him into it, nor me neider! And Hickey's right. If dis big tramp's goin' to marry me, he ought to do it, and not just shoot off his old bazoo about it.

ROCKY: *(ignoring her)* Yuh can't be dat dumb, Chuck.

CORA: You keep outa dis! And don't start beefin' about crickets on de farm drivin' us nuts. You and your crickets! Yuh'd tink dey was elephants!

MARGIE: *(coming to* ROCKY'S *defense—sneeringly)* Don't notice dat broad, Rocky. Yuh heard her say "tomorrow," didn't yuh? It's de same old crap.

CORA: *(glares at her)* Is dat so?

PEARL: *(lines up with* MARGIE*—sneeringly)* Imagine Cora a bride! Dat's a hot one! Jees, Cora, if all de guys you've stayed wid was side by side, yuh could walk on 'em from here to Texas!

CORA: *(starts moving toward her threateningly)* Yuh can't talk like dat to me, yuh fat Dago hooker! I may be a tart, but I ain't a cheap old whore like you!

PEARL: *(furiously)* I'll show yuh who's a whore! *(They start to fly at each other, but* CHUCK *and* ROCKY *grab them from behind.)*

CHUCK: *(forcing* CORA *onto a chair)* Sit down and cool off, Baby.

ROCKY: *(doing the same to* PEARL*)* Nix on de rough stuff, Poil.

MARGIE: *(glaring at* CORA*)* Why don't you leave Poil alone, Rocky? She'll fix dat blonde's clock! Or if she don't, I will!

ROCKY: Shut up, you! *(Disgustedly)* Jees, what dames! D'yuh wanta gum Harry's party?

PEARL: *(a bit shamefaced—sulkily)* Who wants to? But nobody can't call me a —.

ROCKY: *(exasperatedly)* Aw, bury it! What are you, a voigin? *(*PEARL *stares at him, her face growing hard and bitter. So does* MARGIE*)*

PEARL: Yuh mean you tink I'm a whore, too, huh?

MARGIE: Yeah, and me?

ROCKY: Now don't start nuttin'!

PEARL: I suppose it'd tickle you if me and Margie did what dat louse, Hickey, was hintin' and come right out and admitted we was whores.

ROCKY: Aw right! What of it? It's de truth, ain't it?

CORA: *(lining up with* PEARL *and* MARGIE*—indignantly)* Jees, Rocky, dat's a fine hell of a ting to say to two goils dat's been as good to yuh as Poil and Margie! *(To* PEARL*)* I didn't mean to call yuh dat, Poil. I was on'y mad.

PEARL: *(accepts the apology gratefully)* Sure, I was mad, too, Cora. No hard feelin's.

ROCKY: *(relieved)* Dere. Dat fixes everyting, don't it?

PEARL: *(turns on him—hard and bitter)* Aw right, Rocky. We're whores. You know what dat makes you, don't you?

ROCKY: *(angrily)* Look out, now!

MARGIE: A lousy little pimp, dat's what!

ROCKY: I'll loin yuh!

(He gives her a slap on the side of the face.)

PEARL: A dirty little Ginny pimp, dat's what!

ROCKY: *(gives her a slap, too)* And dat'll loin you!

(But they only stare at him with hard sneering eyes.)

MARGIE: He's provin' it to us, Poil.

PEARL: Yeah! Hickey's convoited him. He's give up his pipe dream!

ROCKY: *(furious and at the same time bewildered by their defiance)* Lay off me or I'll beat de hell—

CHUCK: *(growls)* Aw, lay off dem. Harry's party ain't no time to beat up your stable.

ROCKY: *(turns to him)* Whose stable? Who d'yuh tink yuh're talkin' to? I ain't never beat dem up! What d'yuh tink I am? I just give dem a slap, like any guy would his wife, if she got too gabby. Why don't yuh tell dem to lay off me? I don't want no trouble on Harry's boithday party.

MARGIE: *(a victorious gleam in her eye—tauntingly)* Aw right, den, yuh poor little Ginny. I'll lay off yuh till de party's over if Poil will.

PEARL: *(tauntingly)* Sure, I will. For Harry's sake, not yours, yuh little Wop!

ROCKY: *(stung)* Say, listen, youse! Don't get no wrong idea—*(But an interruption comes from* LARRY *who bursts into a sardonic laugh. They all jump startledly and look at him with unanimous hostility.* ROCKY *transfers his anger to him)* Who de hell yuh laughin' at, yuh half-dead old stew bum?

CORA: *(sneeringly)* At himself, he ought to be! Jees, Hickey's sure got his number!

LARRY: *(ignoring them, turns to* HUGO *and shakes him by the shoulder—in his comically intense, crazy whisper)* Wake up, Comrade! Here's the Revolution starting on all sides of you and you're sleeping through it! Be God, it's not to Bakunin's° ghost you ought to pray in your dreams, but to the great Nihilist,° Hickey! He's started a movement that'll blow up the world!

HUGO: *(blinks at him through his thick spectacles—with guttural denunciation)* You, Larry! Renegade! Traitor! I vill have you shot! *(He giggles)* Don't be a fool! Buy me a trink! *(He sees the drink in front of him, and gulps it down. He begins to sing the "Carmagnole"° in a guttural basso, pounding on the table with his glass)* "Dansons la Carmagnole! Vive le son! Vive le son! Dansons la Carmagnole! Vive le son des canons!"

ROCKY: Can dat noise!

HUGO: *(ignores this—to* LARRY, *in a low tone of hatred)* That bourgeois svine, Hickey! He laughs like good fellow, he makes jokes, he dares make hints to me so I see what he dares to think. He thinks I am finish, it is too late, and so I do not vish the Day come because it vill not be my Day. Oh, I see what he thinks! He thinks lies even vorse, dat I— *(He stops abruptly with a guilty look, as if afraid he was letting something slip—then revengefully)* I vill have him hanged the first one of all on de first lamppost! *(He changes his mood abruptly and peers around at* ROCKY *and the others—giggling again)* Vhy you so serious, leedle monkey-faces? It's all great joke, no? So ve get drunk, and ve laugh like hell, and den ve die, and de pipe dream vanish! *(A bitter mocking contempt creeps into his tone)* But be of good cheer, leedle stupid peoples! "The days grow hot, O Babylon!" Soon, leedle proletarians, ve vill have free picnic in the cool shade, ve vill eat hot dogs and trink free beer beneath the villow trees! Like hogs, yes! Like beautiful

Bakunin, *Mikhail Aleksandrovich (1814–1876): Russian anarchist.*

Nihilist: *a believer in nihilism; here an allusion to a movement in Russia (c. 1860–1917) which advocated revolutionary reform and used both terrorism and assassination to achieve it.*

"Carmagnole": *a lively song and dance popular during the French Revolution.*

leedle hogs! *(He stops startledly, as if confused and amazed at what he has heard himself say. He mutters with hatred)* Dot Gottamned liar, Hickey. It is he who makes me sneer. I want to sleep. *(He lets his head fall forward on his folded arms again and closes his eyes.* LARRY *gives him a pitying look, then quickly drinks his drink.)*

CORA: *(uneasily)* Hickey ain't overlookin' no bets, is he? He's even give Hugo de woiks.

LARRY: I warned you this morning he wasn't kidding.

MARGIE: *(sneering)* De old wise guy!

PEARL: Yeah, still pretendin' he's de one exception, like Hickey told him. He don't do no pipe dreamin'! Oh, no!

LARRY: *(sharply resentful)* I—! *(Then abruptly he is drunkenly good-natured, and you feel this drunken manner is an evasive exaggeration)* All right, take it out on me, if it makes you more content. Sure, I love every hair of your heads, my great big beautiful baby dolls, and there's nothing I wouldn't do for you!

PEARL: *(stiffly)* De old Irish bunk, huh? We ain't big. And we ain't your baby dolls! *(Suddenly she is mollified and smiles)* But we admit we're beautiful. Huh, Margie?

MARGIE: *(smiling)* Sure ting! But what would he do wid beautiful dolls, even if he had de price, de old goat? *(She laughs teasingly—then pats* LARRY *on the shoulder affectionately)* Aw, yuh're aw right at dat, Larry, if yuh are full of bull!

PEARL: Sure. Yuh're aces wid us. We're noivous, dat's all. Dat lousy drummer—why can't he be like he's always been? I never seen a guy change so. You pretend to be such a fox, Larry. What d'yuh tink's happened to him?

LARRY: I don't know. With all his gab I notice he's kept that to himself so far. Maybe he's saving the great revelation for Harry's party. *(Then irritably)* To hell with him! I don't want to know. Let him mind his own business and I'll mind mine.

CHUCK: Yeah, dat's what I say.

CORA: Say, Larry, where's dat young friend of yours disappeared to?

LARRY: I don't care where he is, except I wish it was a thousand miles away! *(Then, as he sees they are surprised at his vehemence, he adds hastily)* He's a pest.

ROCKY: *(breaks in with his own preoccupation)* I don't give a damn what happened to Hickey, but I know what's gonna happen if he don't watch his step. I told him, "I'll take a lot from you, Hickey, like everyone else in dis dump, because yuh've always been a grand guy. But dere's tings I don't take from you nor nobody, see? Remember dat, or you'll wake up in a hospital—or maybe worse, wid your wife and de iceman walkin' slow behind yuh."

CORA: Aw, yuh shouldn't make dat iceman crack, Rocky. It's aw right for him to kid about it but—I notice Hickey ain't pulled dat old iceman gag dis time. *(Excitedly)* D'yuh suppose dat he did catch his wife cheatin'? I don't mean wid no iceman, but wid some guy.

ROCKY: Aw, dat's de bunk. He ain't pulled dat gag or showed her photo around because he ain't drunk. And if he'd caught her cheatin' he'd be drunk, wouldn't he? He'd have beat her up and den gone on de woist drunk he'd ever staged. Like any other guy'd do. *(The girls nod, convinced by this reasoning.)*

CHUCK: Sure! Rocky's got de right dope, Baby. He'd be paralyzed. *(While he is speaking, the Negro,* JOE, *comes in from the hallway. There is a noticeable change in him. He walks with a tough, truculent swagger and his good-natured face is set in sullen suspicion.)*

JOE: *(to* ROCKY—*defiantly)* I's stood tellin' people dis dump is closed for de night all I's goin' to. Let Harry hire a doorman, pay him wages, if he wants one.

ROCKY: *(scowling)* Yeah? Harry's pretty damned good to you.

JOE: *(shamefaced)* Sure he is. I don't mean dat. Anyways, it's all right. I told Schwartz, de cop, we's closed for de party. He'll keep folks away. *(Aggressively again)* I want a big drink, dat's what!

CHUCK: Who's stoppin' yuh? Yuh can have all yuh want on Hickey.

JOE: *(has taken a glass from the table and has his hand on a bottle when* HICKEY'S *name is mentioned. He draws his hand back as if he were going to refuse—then grabs it defiantly and pours a big drink)* All right, I's earned all de drinks on him I could drink in a year for listenin' to his crazy bull. And here's hopin' he gets de lockjaw! *(He drinks and pours out another)* I drinks on him but I don't drink wid him. No, suh, never no more!

ROCKY: Aw, bull! Hickey's aw right. What's he done to you?

JOE: *(sullenly)* Dat's my business. I ain't buttin' in yours, is I? *(Bitterly)* Sure, you think he's all right. He's a white man, ain't he? *(His tone becomes aggressive)* Listen to me, you white boys! Don't you get it in your heads I's pretendin' to be what I ain't, or dat I ain't proud to be what I is, get me? Or you and me's goin' to have trouble! *(He picks up his drink and walks left as far away from them as he can get and slumps down on the piano stool.)*

MARGIE: *(in a low angry tone)* What a noive! Just because we act nice to him, he gets a swelled nut! If dat ain't a coon all over!

CHUCK: Talkin' fight talk, huh? I'll moider de nigger! *(He takes a threatening step toward* JOE, *who is staring before him guiltily now.)*

JOE: *(speaks up shamefacedly)* Listen, boys, I's sorry. I didn't mean dat. You been good friends to me. I's nuts, I guess. Dat Hickey, he gets my head all mixed up wit' craziness. *(Their faces at once clear of resentment against him.)*

CORA: Aw, dat's aw right, Joe. De boys wasn't takin' yuh serious. *(Then to the others, forcing a laugh)* Jees, what'd I say, Hickey ain't overlookin' no bets. Even Joe. *(She pauses—then adds puzzledly)* De funny ting is, yuh can't stay sore at de bum when he's around. When he forgets de bughouse preachin', and quits tellin' yuh where yuh get off, he's de same old Hickey. Yuh can't help likin' de louse. And yuh got to admit he's got de right dope—*(She adds hastily)* I mean, on some of de bums here.

MARGIE: *(with a sneering look at* ROCKY*)* Yeah, he's coitinly got one guy I know sized up right! Huh, Poil?

PEARL: He coitinly has!

ROCKY: Cut it out, I told yuh!

LARRY: *(is staring before him broodingly. He speaks more aloud to himself than to them)* It's nothing to me what happened to him. But I have a feeling he's dying to tell us, inside him, and yet he's afraid. He's like that damned kid. It's strange the queer way he seemed to recognize him. If he's afraid, it explains why he's off booze. Like that damned kid again. Afraid if he got drunk, he'd tell— *(While he is speaking,* HICKEY *comes in the doorway at rear. He looks the same as in the previous act, except that now his face beams with the excited expectation of a boy going to a party. His arms are piled with packages.)*

HICKEY: *(booms in imitation of a familiar Polo Grounds bleacherite cry—with rising volume)* Well! Well!! Well!!! *(They all jump startledly. He comes forward, grinning)* Here I am in the nick of time. Give me a hand with these bundles, somebody. *(*MARGIE *and* PEARL *start taking them from his arms and putting them on the table. Now that he is present, all their attitudes show the reaction* CORA *has expressed. They can't help liking him and forgiving him.)*

MARGIE: Jees, Hickey, yuh scared me outa a year's growth, sneakin' in like dat.

HICKEY: Sneaking? Why, me and the taxi man made enough noise getting my big surprise in the hall to wake the dead. You were all so busy drinking in words of wisdom from the Old Wise Guy here, you couldn't hear anything else. *(He grins at* LARRY*)* From what I heard, Larry, you're not so good when you start playing Sherlock Holmes. You've got me all wrong. I'm not afraid of anything now—not even myself. You better stick to the part of Old Cemetery, the Barker for

the Big Sleep—that is, if you can still let yourself get away with it!

(He chuckles and gives LARRY *a friendly slap on
the back.* LARRY *gives him a bitter angry look)*

CORA: *(giggles)* Old Cemetery! That's him, Hickey.
We'll have to call him dat.

HICKEY: *(watching* LARRY *quizzically)* Beginning
to do a lot of puzzling about me, aren't you,
Larry? But that won't help you. You've got to
think of yourself. I couldn't give you my peace.
You've got to find your own. All I can do is help
you, and the rest of the gang, by showing you
the way to find it.

*(He has said this with a simple persuasive
earnestness. He pauses, and for a second they
stare at him with fascinated resentful uneasiness.)*

ROCKY: *(breaks the spell)* Aw, hire a church!

HICKEY: *(placatingly)* All right! All right! Don't
get sore, boys and girls. I guess that did sound
too much like a lousy preacher. Let's forget it
and get busy on the party.

(They look relieved.)

CHUCK: Is dose bundles grub, Hickey? You bought
enough already to feed an army.

HICKEY: *(with boyish excitement again)* Can't be
too much! I want this to be the biggest birthday
Harry's ever had. You and Rocky go in the hall
and get the big surprise. My arms are busted
lugging it.

(They catch his excitement. CHUCK *and* ROCKY
*go out, grinning expectantly. The three girls
gather around* HICKEY, *full of thrilled curiosity.)*

PEARL: Jees, yuh got us all het up! What is it,
Hickey?

HICKEY: Wait and see. I got it as a treat for the
three of you more than anyone. I thought to myself, I'll bet this is what will please those whores
more than anything. *(They wince as if he had
slapped them, but before they have a chance to be
angry, he goes on affectionately)* I said to myself,
I don't care how much it costs, they're worth it.
They're the best little scouts in the world, and
they've been damned kind to me when I was
down and out! Nothing is too good for them.

(Earnestly) I mean every word of that, too—and
then some! *(Then, as if he noticed the expression
on their faces for the first time)* What's the matter? You look sore. What—? *(Then he chuckles)*
Oh, I see. But you know how I feel about that.
You know I didn't say it to offend you. So don't be
silly now.

MARGIE: *(lets out a tense breath)* Aw right,
Hickey. Let it slide.

HICKEY: *(jubilantly, as* CHUCK *and* ROCKY *enter
carrying a big wicker basket)* Look! There it
comes! Unveil it, boys.

*(They pull off a covering burlap bag. The bas-
ket is piled with quarts of champagne.)*

PEARL: *(with childish excitement)* It's champagne!
Jees, Hickey, if you ain't a sport!

*(She gives him a hug, forgetting all animosity,
as do the other girls.)*

MARGIE: I never been soused on champagne.
Let's get stinko, Poil.

PEARL: You betcha my life! De bot' of us!

*(A holiday spirit of gay festivity has seized them
all. Even* JOE MOTT *is standing up to look at the
wine with an admiring grin, and* HUGO *raises
his head to blink at it.)*

JOE: You sure is hittin' de high spots, Hickey.
(Boastfully) Man, when I runs my gamblin'
house, I drinks dat old bubbly water in steins!
(He stops guiltily and gives HICKEY *a look of
defiance)* I's goin' to drink it dat way again, too,
soon's I make my stake! And dat ain't no pipe
dream, neider!

*(He sits down where he was, his back turned to
them.)*

ROCKY: What'll we drink it outa, Hickey? Dere
ain't no wine glasses.

HICKEY: *(enthusiastically)* Joe has the right idea!
Schooners! That's the spirit for Harry's birthday!
*(ROCKY *and* CHUCK *carry the basket of wine
into the bar. The three girls go back and stand
around the entrance to the bar, chatting excitedly among themselves and to* CHUCK *and*
ROCKY *in the bar.)*

HUGO: *(with his silly giggle)* Ve vill trink vine beneath the villow trees!

HICKEY: *(grins at him)* That's the spirit, Brother— and let the lousy slaves drink vinegar!

(Hugo blinks at him startledly, then looks away.)

HUGO: *(mutters)* Gottamned liar!

(He puts his head back on his arms and closes his eyes, but this time his habitual pass-out has a quality of hiding.)

LARRY: *(gives Hugo a pitying glance—in a low tone of anger)* Leave Hugo be! He rotted ten years in prison for his faith! He's earned his dream! Have you no decency or pity?

HICKEY: *(quizzically)* Hello, what's this? I thought you were in the grandstand. *(Then with a simple earnestness, taking a chair by LARRY, and putting a hand on his shoulder)* Listen, Larry, you're getting me all wrong. Hell, you ought to know me better. I've always been the best-natured slob in the world. Of course, I have pity. But now I've seen the light, it isn't my old kind of pity—the kind yours is. It isn't the kind that lets itself off easy by encouraging some poor guy to go on kidding himself with a lie—the kind that leaves the poor slob worse off because it makes him feel guiltier than ever—the kind that makes his lying hopes nag at him and reproach him until he's a rotten skunk in his own eyes. I know all about that kind of pity. I've had a bellyful of it in my time, and it's all wrong! *(With a salesman's persuasiveness)* No, sir. The kind of pity I feel now is after final results that will really save the poor guy, and make him contented with what he is, and quit battling himself, and find peace for the rest of his life. Oh, I know how you resent the way I have to show you up to yourself. I don't blame you. I know from my own experience it's bitter medicine, facing yourself in the mirror with the old false whiskers off. But you forget that, once you're cured. You'll be grateful to me when all at once you find you're able to admit, without feeling ashamed, that all the grandstand foolosopher bunk and the waiting for the Big Sleep stuff is a pipe dream. You'll say to yourself, I'm just an old man who is scared of life, but even more scared of dying. So I'm keeping drunk and hanging on to life at any price, and what of it? Then you'll know what real peace means, Larry, because you won't be scared of either life or death any more. You simply won't give a damn! Any more than I do!

LARRY: *(has been staring into his eyes with a fascinated wondering dread)* Be God, if I'm not beginning to think you've gone mad! *(With a rush of anger)* You're a liar!

HICKEY: *(injuredly)* Now, listen, that's no way to talk to an old pal who's trying to help you. Hell, if you really wanted to die, you'd just take a hop off your fire escape, wouldn't you? And if you really were in the grandstand, you wouldn't be pitying everyone. Oh, I know the truth is tough at first. It was for me. All I ask is for you to suspend judgment and give it a chance. I'll absolutely guarantee— Hell, Larry, I'm no fool. Do you suppose I'd deliberately set out to get under everyone's skin and put myself in dutch with all my old pals, if I wasn't certain, from my own experience, that it means contentment in the end for all of you? *(LARRY again is staring at him fascinatedly. HICKEY grins)* As for my being bughouse, you can't crawl out of it that way. Hell, I'm too damned sane. I can size up guys, and turn 'em inside out, better than I ever could. Even where they're strangers like that Parritt kid. He's licked, Larry. I think there is only one possible way out you can help him to take. That is, if you have the right kind of pity for him.

LARRY: *(uneasily)* What do you mean? *(Attempting indifference)* I'm not advising him, except to leave me out of his troubles. He's nothing to me.

HICKEY: *(shakes his head)* You'll find he won't agree to that. He'll keep after you until he makes you help him. Because he has to be punished, so he can forgive himself. He's lost all his guts. He can't manage it alone, and you're the only one he can turn to.

LARRY: For the love of God, mind your own business! *(With forced scorn)* A lot you know about him! He's hardly spoken to you!

HICKEY: No, that's right. But I do know a lot about him just the same. I've had hell inside me. I can spot it in others. *(Frowning)* Maybe that's what gives me the feeling there's something familiar about him, something between us. *(He shakes his head)* No, it's more than that. I can't figure it. Tell me about him. For instance, I don't imagine he's married, is he?

LARRY: No.

HICKEY: Hasn't he been mixed up with some woman? I don't mean trollops. I mean the old real love stuff that crucifies you.

LARRY: *(with a calculating relieved look at him— encouraging him along this line)* Maybe you're right. I wouldn't be surprised.

HICKEY: *(grins at him quizzically)* I see. You think I'm on the wrong track and you're glad I am. Because then I won't suspect whatever he did about the Great Cause. That's another lie you tell yourself, Larry, that the good old Cause means nothing to you any more. *(LARRY is about to burst out in denial but HICKEY goes on)* But you're all wrong about Parritt. That isn't what's got him stopped. It's what's behind that. And it's a woman. I recognize the symptoms.

LARRY: *(sneeringly)* And you're the boy who's never wrong! Don't be a damned fool. His trouble is he was brought up a devout believer in the Movement and now he's lost his faith. It's a shock, but he's young and he'll soon find another dream just as good. *(He adds sardonically)* Or as bad.

HICKEY: All right. I'll let it go at that, Larry. He's nothing to me except I'm glad he's here because he'll help me make you wake up to yourself. I don't even like the guy, or the feeling there's anything between us. But you'll find I'm right just the same, when you get to the final showdown with him.

LARRY: There'll be no showdown! I don't give a tinker's damn—

HICKEY: Sticking to the old grandstand, eh? Well, I knew you'd be the toughest to convince of all the gang, Larry. And, along with Harry and Jimmy Tomorrow, you're the one I want most to help. *(He puts an arm around LARRY's shoulder and gives him an affectionate hug)* I've always liked you a lot, you old bastard! *(He gets up and his manner changes to his bustling party excitement—glancing at his watch)* Well, well, not much time before twelve. Let's get busy, boys and girls. *(He looks over the table where the cake is)* Cake all set. Good. And my presents, and yours, girls, and Chuck's, and Rocky's. Fine. Harry'll certainly be touched by your thought of him. *(He goes back to the girls)* You go in the bar, Pearl and Margie, and get the grub ready so it can be brought right in. There'll be some drinking and toasts first, of course. My idea is to use the wine for that, so get it all set. I'll go upstairs now and root everyone out. Harry the last. I'll come back with him. Somebody light the candles on the cake when you hear us coming, and you start playing Harry's favorite tune, Cora. Hustle now, everybody. We want this to come off in style. *(He bustles into the hall. MARGIE and PEARL disappear in the bar. CORA goes to the piano. JOE gets off the stool sullenly to let her sit down.)*

CORA: I got to practice. I ain't laid my mits on a box in Gawd knows when. *(With the soft pedal down, she begins gropingly to pick out "The Sunshine of Paradise Alley")* Is dat right, Joe? I've forgotten dat has-been tune. *(She picks out a few more notes)* Come on, Joe, hum de tune so I can follow.

(JOE begins to hum and sing in a low voice and correct her. He forgets his sullenness and becomes his old self again.)

LARRY: *(suddenly gives a laugh—in his comically intense, crazy tone)* Be God, it's a second feast of Belshazzar,° with Hickey to do the writing on the wall!

CORA: Aw, shut up. Old Cemetery! Always beefin'! *(WILLIE comes in from the hall. He is in a pitiable state, his face pasty, haggard with sleeplessness and nerves, his eyes sick and haunted. He is sober. CORA greets him over her shoulder kiddingly)* If it ain't Prince Willie!

Belshazzar *(6th century B.C.): According to the Book of Daniel (5: 30), the son of Nebuchadnezzar II who died at the capture of Babylon in 539 B.C.*

(Then kindly) Gee, kid, yuh look sick. Git a coupla shots in yuh.

WILLIE: *(tensely)* No, thanks. Not now. I'm tapering off.

(He sits down weakly on LARRY'S *right.)*

CORA: *(astonished)* What d'yuh know? He means it!

WILLIE: *(leaning toward* LARRY *confidentially—in a low shaken voice)* It's been hell up in that damned room, Larry! The things I've imagined! *(He shudders)* I thought I'd go crazy. *(With pathetic boastful pride)* But I've got it beat now. By tomorrow morning I'll be on the wagon. I'll get back my clothes the first thing. Hickey's loaning me the money. I'm going to do what I've always said—go to the D.A.'s office. He was a good friend of my Old Man's. He was only assistant, then. He was in on the graft, but my Old Man never squealed on him. So he certainly owes it to me to give me a chance. And he knows that I really was a brilliant law student. *(Self-reassuringly)* Oh, I know I can make good, now I'm getting off the booze forever. *(Moved)* I owe a lot to Hickey. He's made me wake up to myself—see what a fool— It wasn't nice to face but— *(With bitter resentment)* It isn't what he says. It's what you feel behind—what he hints—Christ, you'd think all I really wanted to do with my life was sit here and stay drunk. *(With hatred)* I'll show him!

LARRY: *(masking pity behind a sardonic tone)* If you want my advice, you'll put the nearest bottle to your mouth until you don't give a damn for Hickey!

WILLIE: *(stares at a bottle greedily, tempted for a moment—then bitterly)* That's fine advice! I thought you were my friend!

(He gets up with a hurt glance at LARRY, *and moves away to take a chair in back of the left end of the table, where he sits in dejected, shaking misery, his chin on his chest.)*

JOE: *(to* CORA) No, like dis. *(He beats time with his finger and sings in a low voice)* "She is the sunshine of Paradise Alley." *(She plays)* Dat's more like it. Try it again.

(She begins to play through the chorus again. DON PARRITT *enters from the hall. There is a frightened look on his face. He slinks in furtively, as if he were escaping from someone. He looks relieved when he sees* LARRY *and comes and slips into the chair on his right.* LARRY *pretends not to notice his coming, but he instinctively shrinks with repulsion.* PARRITT *leans toward him and speaks ingratiatingly in a low secretive tone.)*

PARRITT: Gee, I'm glad you're here, Larry. That damned fool, Hickey, knocked on my door. I opened up because I thought it must be you, and he came bustin' in and made me come downstairs. I don't know what for. I don't belong in this birthday celebration. I don't know this gang and I don't want to be mixed up with them. All I came here for was to find you.

LARRY: *(tensely)* I've warned you—

PARRITT: *(goes on as if he hadn't heard)* Can't you make Hickey mind his own business? I don't like that guy, Larry. The way he acts, you'd think he had something on me. Why, just now he pats me on the shoulder, like he was sympathizing with me, and says, "I know how it is, Son, but you can't hide from yourself, not even here on the bottom of the sea. You've got to face the truth and then do what must be done for your own peace and the happiness of all concerned." What did he mean by that, Larry?

LARRY: How the hell would I know?

PARRITT: Then he grins and says, "Never mind, Larry's getting wise to himself. I think you can rely on his help in the end. He'll have to choose between living and dying, and he'll never choose to die while there is a breath left in the old bastard!" And then he laughs like it was a joke on you. *(He pauses.* LARRY *is rigid on his chair, staring before him.* PARRITT *asks him with a sudden taunt in his voice)* Well, what do you say to that, Larry?

LARRY: I've nothing to say. Except you're a bigger fool than he is to listen to him.

PARRITT: *(with a sneer)* Is that so? He's no fool where you're concerned. He's got your number, all right! (LARRY'S *face tightens but he keeps silent.* PARRITT *changes to a contrite, appealing air)* I don't mean that. But you keep acting as if you were sore at me, and that gets my goat. You know what I want most is to be friends with you, Larry. I haven't a single friend left in the world. I hoped you— *(Bitterly)* And you could be, too, without it hurting you. You ought to, for Mother's sake. She really loved you. You loved her, too, didn't you?

LARRY: *(tensely)* Leave what's dead in its grave.

PARRITT: I suppose, because I was only a kid, you didn't think I was wise about you and her. Well, I was. I've been wise, ever since I can remember, to all the guys she's had, although she'd tried to kid me along it wasn't so. That was a silly stunt for a free Anarchist woman, wasn't it, being ashamed of being free?

LARRY: Shut your damned trap!

PARRITT: *(guiltily but with a strange undertone of satisfaction)* Yes, I know I shouldn't say that now. I keep forgetting she isn't free any more. *(He pauses)* Do you know, Larry, you're the one of them all she cared most about? Anyone else who left the Movement would have been dead to her, but she couldn't forget you. She'd always make excuses for you. I used to try and get her goat about you. I'd say, "Larry's got brains and yet he thinks the Movement is just a crazy pipe dream." She'd blame it on booze getting you. She'd kid herself that you'd give up booze and come back to the Movement— tomorrow! She'd say, "Larry can't kill in himself a faith he's given his life to, not without killing himself." *(He grins sneeringly)* How about it, Larry? Was she right? (LARRY *remains silent. He goes on insistently)* I suppose what she really meant was, come back to her. She was always getting the Movement mixed up with herself. But I'm sure she really must have loved you, Larry. As much as she could love anyone besides herself. But she wasn't faithful to you, even at that, was she? That's why you finally walked out on her, isn't it? I remember that last fight you had with her. I was listening. I was on your side, even if she was my mother, because I liked you so much; you'd been so good to me—like a father. I remember her putting on her high-and-mighty free-woman stuff, saying you were still a slave to bourgeois morality and jealousy and you thought a woman you loved was a piece of private property you owned. I remember that you got mad and you told her, "I don't like living with a whore, if that's what you mean!"

LARRY: *(bursts out)* You lie! I never called her that!

PARRITT: *(goes on as if* LARRY *hadn't spoken)* I think that's why she still respects you, because it was you who left her. You were the only one to beat her to it. She got sick of the others before they did of her. I don't think she ever cared much about them, anyway. She just had to keep on having lovers to prove to herself how free she was *(He pauses—then with a bitter repulsion)* It made home a lousy place. I felt like you did about it. I'd get feeling it was like living in a whorehouse—only worse, because she didn't have to make her living—

LARRY: You bastard! She's your mother! Have you no shame?

PARRITT: *(bitterly)* No! She brought me up to believe that family-respect stuff is all bourgeois, property-owning crap. Why should I be ashamed?

LARRY: *(making a move to get up)* I've had enough!

PARRITT: *(catches his arm—pleadingly)* No! Don't leave me! Please! I promise I won't mention her again! (LARRY *sinks back in his chair)* I only did it to make you understand better. I know this isn't the place to—Why didn't you come up to my room, like I asked you? I kept waiting. We could talk everything over there.

LARRY: There's nothing to talk over!

PARRITT: But I've got to talk to you. Or I'll talk to Hickey. He won't let me alone! I feel he knows, anyway! And I know he'd understand, all right—in his way. But I hate his guts! I don't want anything to do with him! I'm scared of him, honest. There's something not human behind his damned grinning and kidding.

LARRY: *(starts)* Ah! You feel that, too?

PARRITT: *(pleadingly)* But I can't go on like this. I've got to decide what I've got to do. I've got to tell you, Larry!

LARRY: *(again starts up)* I won't listen!

PARRITT: *(again holds him by the arm)* All right! I won't. Don't go! (LARRY *lets himself be pulled down on his chair.* PARRITT *examines his face and becomes insultingly scornful)* Who do you think you're kidding? I know damned well you've guessed—

LARRY: I've guessed nothing!

PARRITT: But I want you to guess now! I'm glad you have! I know now, since Hickey's been after me, that I meant you to guess right from the start. That's why I came to you. *(Hurrying on with an attempt at a plausible frank air that makes what he says seem doubly false)* I want you to understand the reason. You see, I began studying American history. I got to admiring Washington and Jefferson and Jackson and Lincoln. I began to feel patriotic and love this country. I saw it was the best government in the world, where everybody was equal and had a chance. I saw that all the ideas behind the Movement came from a lot of Russians like Bakunin and Kropotkin° and were meant for Europe, but we didn't need them here in a democracy where we were free already. I didn't want this country to be destroyed for a damned foreign pipe dream. After all, I'm from old American pioneer stock. I began to feel I was a traitor for helping a lot of cranks and bums and free women plot to overthrow our government. And then I saw it was my duty to my country—

LARRY: *(nauseated—turns on him)* You stinking rotten liar! Do you think you can fool me with

Kropotkin, *Prince Petr Alekseyevich (1842–1921): Russian anarchist and writer.*

such hypocrite's cant! *(Then turning away)* I don't give a damn what you did! It's on your head—whatever it was! I don't want to know—and I won't know!

PARRITT: *(as if* LARRY *had never spoken—falteringly)* But I never thought Mother would be caught. Please believe that, Larry. You know I never would have—

LARRY: *(his face haggard, drawing a deep breath and closing his eyes—as if he were trying to hammer something into his own brain)* All I know is I'm sick of life! I'm through! I've forgotten myself! I'm drowned and contented on the bottom of a bottle. Honor or dishonor, faith or treachery are nothing to me but the opposites of the same stupidity which is ruler and king of life, and in the end they rot into dust in the same grave. All things are the same meaningless joke to me, for they grin at me from the one skull of death. So go away. You're wasting breath. I've forgotten your mother.

PARRITT: *(jeers angrily)* The old foolosopher, eh? *(He spits out contemptuously)* You lousy old faker!

LARRY: *(so distracted he pleads weakly)* For the love of God, leave me in peace the little time that's left to me!

PARRITT: Aw, don't pull that pitiful old-man junk on me! You old bastard, you'll never die as long as there's a free drink of whiskey left!

LARRY: *(stung—furiously)* Look out how you try to taunt me back into life, I warn you! I might remember the thing they call justice there, and the punishment for— *(He checks himself with an effort—then with a real indifference that comes from exhaustion)* I'm old and tired. To hell with you! You're as mad as Hickey, and as big a liar. I'd never let myself believe a word you told me.

PARRITT: *(threateningly)* The hell you won't! Wait till Hickey gets through with you!
  *(*PEARL *and* MARGIE *come in from the bar. At the sight of them,* PARRITT *instantly subsides and becomes self-conscious and defensive, scowling at them and then quickly looking away.)*

MARGIE: *(eyes him jeeringly)* Why, hello, Tight-wad Kid. Come to join de party? Gee, don't he act bashful, Poil?

PEARL: Yeah. Especially wid his dough. *(PAR-RITT slinks to a chair at the left end of the table, pretending he hasn't heard them. Suddenly there is a noise of angry, cursing voices and a scuffle from the hall. PEARL yells)* Hey, Rocky! Fight in de hall!

(ROCKY and CHUCK run from behind the bar curtain and rush into the hall. ROCKY's voice is heard in irritated astonishment, "What de hell?" and then the scuffle stops and ROCKY appears holding CAPTAIN LEWIS by the arm, followed by CHUCK with a similar hold on GENERAL WETJOEN. Although these two have been drinking they both are sober, for them. Their faces are sullenly angry, their clothes disarranged from the tussle.)

ROCKY: *(leading LEWIS forward—astonished, amused and irritated)* Can yuh beat it? I've heard youse two call each odder every name yuh could think of but I never seen you— *(Indignantly)* A swell time to stage your first bout, on Harry's boithday party! What started de scrap?

LEWIS: *(forcing a casual tone)* Nothing, old chap. Our business, you know. That bloody ass, Hickey, made some insinuation about me, and the boorish Boer had the impertinence to agree with him.

WETJOEN: Dot's a lie! Hickey made joke about me, and this Limey said yes, it was true!

ROCKY: Well, sit down, de bot' of yuh, and cut out de rough stuff.

(He and CHUCK dump them down in adjoining chairs toward the left end of the table, where, like two sulky boys, they turn their backs on each other as far as possible in chairs which both face front.)

MARGIE: *(laughs)* Jees, lookit de two bums! Like a coupla kids! Kiss and make up, for Gawd's sakes!

ROCKY: Yeah. Harry's party begins in a minute and we don't want no soreheads around.

LEWIS: *(stiffly)* Very well. In deference to the occasion, I apologize, General Wetjoen—provided that you do also.

WETJOEN: *(sulkily)* I apologize, Captain Lewis—because Harry is my good friend.

ROCKY: Aw, hell! If yuh can't do better'n dat—! *(MOSHER and McGLOIN enter together from the hall. Both have been drinking but are not drunk.)*

PEARL: Here's de star boarders.

(They advance, their heads together, so interested in a discussion they are oblivious to everyone.)

McGLOIN: I'm telling you, Ed, it's serious this time. That bastard, Hickey, has got Harry on the hip. *(As he talks, MARGIE, PEARL, ROCKY and CHUCK prick up their ears and gather round. CORA, at the piano, keeps running through the tune, with soft pedal, and singing the chorus half under her breath, with JOE still correcting her mistakes. At the table, LARRY, PARRITT, WILLIE, WETJOEN and LEWIS sit motionless, staring in front of them. HUGO seems asleep in his habitual position)* And you know it isn't going to do us no good if he gets him to take that walk tomorrow.

MOSHER: You're damned right. Harry'll mosey around the ward, dropping in on everyone who knew him when. *(Indignantly)* And they'll all give him a phony glad hand and a ton of good advice about what a sucker he is to stand for us.

McGLOIN: He's sure to call on Bessie's relations to do a little cryin' over dear Bessie. And you know what that bitch and all her family thought of me.

MOSHER: *(with a flash of his usual humor—rebukingly)* Remember, Lieutenant, you are speaking of my sister! Dear Bessie wasn't a bitch. She was a God-damned bitch! But if you think my loving relatives will have time to discuss you, you don't know them. They'll be too busy telling Harry what a drunken crook I am and saying he ought to have me put in Sing Sing!

McGLOIN: *(dejectedly)* Yes, once Bessie's relations get their hooks in him, it'll be as tough for us as if she wasn't gone.

MOSHER: *(dejectedly)* Yes, Harry has always been weak and easily influenced, and now he's getting old he'll be an easy mark for those grafters. *(Then with forced reassurance)* Oh, hell, Mac, we're saps to worry. We've heard Harry pull that bluff about taking a walk every birthday he's had for twenty years.

McGLOIN: *(doubtfully)* But Hickey wasn't sicking him on those times. Just the opposite. He was asking Harry what he wanted to go out for when there was plenty of whiskey here.

MOSHER: *(with a change to forced carelessness)* Well, after all, I don't care whether he goes out or not. I'm clearing out tomorrow morning anyway. I'm just sorry for you, Mac.

McGLOIN: *(resentfully)* You needn't be, then. Ain't I going myself? I was only feeling sorry for you.

MOSHER: Yes, my mind is made up. Hickey may be a lousy, interfering pest, now he's gone teetotal on us, but there's a lot of truth in some of his bull. Hanging around here getting plastered with you, Mac, is pleasant, I won't deny, but the old booze gets you in the end, if you keep lapping it up. It's time I quit for a while. *(With forced enthusiasm)* Besides, I feel the call of the old carefree circus life in my blood again. I'll see the boss tomorrow. It's late in the season but he'll be glad to take me on. And won't all the old gang be tickled to death when I show up on the lot!

McGLOIN: Maybe—if they've got a rope handy!

MOSHER: *(turns on him—angrily)* Listen! I'm damned sick of that kidding!

McGLOIN: You are, are you? Well, I'm sicker of your kidding me about getting reinstated on the Force. And whatever you'd like, I can't spend my life sitting here with you, ruining my stomach with rotgut. I'm tapering off, and in the morning I'll be fresh as a daisy. I'll go and have a private chin with the Commissioner. *(With forced enthusiasm)* Man alive, from what the boys tell me, there's sugar galore these days, and I'll soon be ridin' around in a big red automobile—

MOSHER: *(derisively—beckoning an imaginary Chinese)* Here, One Lung Hop! Put fresh peanut oil in the lamp and cook the Lieutenant another dozen pills! It's his gowed-up night!

McGLOIN: *(stung—pulls back a fist threateningly)* One more crack like that and I'll—!

MOSHER: *(putting up his fists)* Yes? Just start—! *(CHUCK and ROCKY jump between them.)*

ROCKY: Hey! Are you guys nuts? Jees, it's Harry's boithday party! *(They both look guilty)* Sit down and behave.

MOSHER: *(grumpily)* All right. Only tell him to lay off me. *(He lets ROCKY push him in a chair, at the right end of the table, rear.)*

McGLOIN: *(grumpily)* Tell him to lay off me. *(He lets CHUCK push him into the chair on MOSHER's left. At this moment HICKEY bursts in from the hall, bustling and excited.)*

HICKEY: Everything all set? Fine! *(He glances at his watch)* Half a minute to go. Harry's starting down with Jimmy. I had a hard time getting them to move! They'd rather stay hiding up there, kidding each other along. *(He chuckles)* Harry don't even want to remember it's his birthday now! *(He hears a noise from the stairs)* Here they come! *(Urgently)* Light the candles! Get ready to play, Cora! Stand up, everybody! Get that wine ready, Chuck and Rocky! *(MARGIE and PEARL light the candles on the cake. CORA gets her hands set over the piano keys, watching over her shoulder. ROCKY and CHUCK go in the bar. Everybody at the table stands up mechanically. HUGO is the last, suddenly coming to and scrambling to his feet. HARRY HOPE and JIMMY TOMORROW appear in the hall outside the door. HICKEY looks up from his watch)* On the dot! It's twelve! *(Like a cheer leader)* Come on now, everybody, with a Happy Birthday, Harry!

(With his voice leading they all shout "Happy Birthday, Harry!" in a spiritless chorus. HICKEY signals to CORA, who starts playing and singing in a whiskey soprano "She's the Sunshine of Paradise Alley." HOPE and JIMMY stand in the doorway. Both have been drinking heavily. In HOPE

the effect is apparent only in a bristling, touchy, pugnacious attitude. It is entirely different from the usual irascible beefing he delights in and which no one takes seriously. Now he really has a chip on his shoulder. JIMMY, *on the other hand, is plainly drunk, but it has not had the desired effect, for beneath a pathetic assumption of gentlemanly poise, he is obviously frightened and shrinking back within himself.* HICKEY *grabs* HOPE'S *hand and pumps it up and down. For a moment* HOPE *appears unconscious of this handshake. Then he jerks his hand away angrily.*)

HOPE: Cut out the glad hand, Hickey. D'you think I'm a sucker? I know you, bejees, you sneaking, lying drummer! (*With rising anger, to the others*) And all you bums! What the hell you trying to do, yelling and raising the roof? Want the cops to close the joint and get my license taken away? (*He yells at* CORA *who has stopped singing but continues to play mechanically with many mistakes*) Hey, you dumb tart, quit banging that box! Bejees, the least you could do is learn the tune!

CORA: (*stops—deeply hurt*) Aw, Harry! Jees, ain't I—
(*Her eyes begin to fill*)

HOPE: (*glaring at the other girls*) And you two hookers, screaming at the top of your lungs! What d'you think this is, a dollar cathouse? Bejees, that's where you belong!

PEARL: (*miserably*) Aw, Harry—
(*She begins to cry*)

MARGIE: Jees, Harry, I never thought you'd say that—like yuh meant it. (*She puts her arm around* PEARL—*on the verge of tears herself*) Aw, don't bawl, Poil. He don't mean it.

HICKEY: (*reproachfully*) Now, Harry! Don't take it out on the gang because you're upset about yourself. Anyway, I've promised you you'll come through all right, haven't I? So quit worrying. (*He slaps* HOPE *on the back encouragingly.* HOPE *flashes him a glance of hate*) Be yourself, Governor. You don't want to bawl out the old gang just when they're congratulating you on your birthday, do you? Hell, that's no way!

HOPE: (*looking guilty and shamefaced now—forcing an unconvincing attempt at his natural tone*) Bejees, they ain't as dumb as you. They know I was only kidding them. They know I appreciate their congratulations. Don't you, fellers? (*There is a listless chorus of "Sure, Harry," "Yes," "Of course we do," etc. He comes forward to the two girls, with* JIMMY *and* HICKEY *following him, and pats them clumsily*) Bejees, I like you broads. You know I was only kidding.
(*Instantly they forgive him and smile affectionately.*)

MARGIE: Sure we know, Harry.

PEARL: Sure.

HICKEY: (*grinning*) Sure. Harry's the greatest kidder in this dump and that's saying something! Look how he's kidded himself for twenty years! (*As* HOPE *gives him a bitter, angry glance, he digs him in the ribs with his elbow playfully*) Unless I'm wrong, Governor, and I'm betting I'm not. We'll soon know, eh? Tomorrow morning. No, by God, it's *this* morning now!

JIMMY: (*with a dazed dread*) *This* morning?

HICKEY: Yes, it's today at last, Jimmy. (*He pats him on the back*) Don't be so scared! I've promised I'll help you.

JIMMY: (*trying to hide his dread behind an offended, drunken dignity*) I don't understand you. Kindly remember I'm fully capable of settling my own affairs!

HICKEY: (*earnestly*) Well, isn't that exactly what I want you to do, settle with yourself once and for all? (*He speaks in his ear in confidential warning*) Only watch out on the booze, Jimmy. You know, not too much from now on. You've had a lot already, and you don't want to let yourself duck out of it by being too drunk to move—not this time!
(JIMMY *gives him a guilty, stricken look and turns away and slumps into the chair on* MOSHER'S *right.*)

HOPE: (*to* MARGIE—*still guiltily*) Bejees, Margie, you know I didn't mean it. It's that lousy drummer riding me that's got my goat.

MARGIE: I know. *(She puts a protecting arm around* HOPE *and turns him to face the table with the cake and presents)* Come on. You ain't noticed your cake yet. Ain't it grand?

HOPE: *(trying to brighten up)* Say, that's pretty. Ain't ever had a cake since Bessie—Six candles. Each for ten years, eh? Bejees, that's thoughtful of you.

PEARL: It was Hickey got it.

HOPE: *(his tone forced)* Well, it was thoughtful of him. He means well, I guess. *(His eyes, fixed on the cake, harden angrily)* To hell with his cake. *(He starts to turn away.* PEARL *grabs his arm.)*

PEARL: Wait, Harry. Yuh ain't seen de presents from Margie and me and Cora and Chuck and Rocky. And dere's a watch all engraved wid your name and de date from Hickey.

HOPE: To hell with it! Bejees, he can keep it! *(This time he does turn away.)*

PEARL: Jees, he ain't even goin' to look at our presents.

MARGIE: *(bitterly)* Dis is all wrong. We gotta put some life in dis party or I'll go nuts! Hey, Cora, what's de matter wid dat box? Can't yuh play for Harry? Yuh don't have to stop just because he kidded yuh!

HOPE: *(rouses himself—with forced heartiness)* Yes, come on, Cora. You was playing it fine. *(*CORA *begins to play half-heartedly.* HOPE *suddenly becomes almost tearfully sentimental)* It was Bessie's favorite tune. She was always singing it. It brings her back. I wish— *(He chokes up.)*

HICKEY: *(grins at him—amusedly)* Yes, we've all heard you tell us you thought the world of her, Governor.

HOPE: *(looks at him with frightened suspicion)* Well, so I did, bejees! Everyone knows I did! *(Threateningly)* Bejees, if you say I didn't—

HICKEY: *(soothingly)* Now, Governor. I didn't say anything. You're the only one knows the truth about that. *(*HOPE *stares at him confusedly.* CORA *continues to play. For a moment there is a pause, broken by* JIMMY TOMORROW *who speaks with muzzy, self-pitying melancholy out of a sentimental dream.)*

JIMMY: Marjorie's favorite song was "Loch Lomond." She was beautiful and she played the piano beautifully and she had a beautiful voice. *(With gentle sorrow)* You were lucky, Harry. Bessie died. But there are more bitter sorrows than losing the woman one loves by the hand of death—

HICKEY: *(with an amused wink at* HOPE*)* Now, listen, Jimmy, you needn't go on. We've all heard that story about how you came back to Cape Town and found her in the hay with a staff officer. We know you like to believe that was what started you on the booze and ruined your life.

JIMMY: *(stammers)* I—I'm talking to Harry. Will you kindly keep out of— *(With a pitiful defiance)* My life is not ruined!

HICKEY: *(ignoring this—with a kidding grin)* But I'll bet when you admit the truth to yourself, you'll confess you were pretty sick of her hating you for getting drunk. I'll bet you were really damned relieved when she gave you such a good excuse. *(*JIMMY *stares at him strickenly.* HICKEY *pats him on the back again—with sincere sympathy)* I know how it is, Jimmy. I— *(He stops abruptly and for a second he seems to lose his self-assurance and become confused.)*

LARRY: *(seizing on this with vindictive relish)* Ha! So that's what happened to you, is it? Your iceman joke finally came home to roost, did it? *(He grins tauntingly)* You should have remembered there's truth in the old superstition that you'd better look out what you call because in the end it comes to you!

HICKEY: *(himself again—grins to* LARRY *kiddingly)* Is that a fact, Larry? Well, well! Then you'd better watch out how you keep calling for that old Big Sleep! *(*LARRY *starts and for a second looks superstitiously frightened. Abruptly* HICKEY *changes to his jovial, bustling, master-of-ceremonies manner)* But what are we waiting for, boys and girls? Let's start the party rolling! *(He shouts to the bar)* Hey, Chuck and Rocky! Bring on the big surprise! Governor, you sit at the head of the table here. *(He makes* HARRY *sit down on the chair at the end of the table, right. To* MARGIE *and* PEARL*)* Come on, girls, sit down. *(They sit side by side on* JIMMY'S *right.* HICKEY *bustles down to the left end of table)* I'll sit here at the foot.

(He sits, with CORA *on his left and* JOE *on her left.* ROCKY *and* CHUCK *appear from the bar, each bearing a big tray laden with schooners of champagne which they start shoving in front of each member of the party.)*

ROCKY: *(with forced cheeriness)* Real champagne, bums! Cheer up! What is dis, a funeral? Jees, mixin' champagne wid Harry's redeye will knock yuh paralyzed! Ain't yuh never satisfied?

(He and CHUCK *finish serving out the schooners, grab the last two themselves and sit down in the two vacant chairs remaining near the middle of the table. As they do so,* HICKEY *rises, a schooner in his hand.)*

HICKEY: *(rapping on the table for order when there is nothing but a dead silence)* Order! Order, Ladies and Gents! *(He catches* LARRY'S *eyes on the glass in his hand)* Yes, Larry, I'm going to drink with you this time. To prove I'm not teetotal because I'm afraid booze would make me spill my secrets, as you think. *(LARRY looks sheepish.* HICKEY *chuckles and goes on)* No, I gave you the simple truth about that. I don't need booze or anything else any more. But I want to be sociable and propose a toast in honor of our old friend, Harry, and drink it with you. *(His eyes fix on* HUGO, *who is out again, his head on his plate — To* CHUCK, *who is on* HUGO'S *left)* Wake up our demon bomb-tosser, Chuck. We don't want corpses at this feast.

CHUCK: *(gives* HUGO *a shake)* Hey, Hugo, come up for air! Don't yuh see de champagne?

(HUGO blinks around and giggles foolishly)

HUGO: Ve vill eat birthday cake and trink champagne beneath the villow tree! *(He grabs his schooner and takes a greedy gulp—then sets it back on the table with a grimace of distaste—in a strange, arrogantly disdainful tone, as if he were rebuking a butler)* Dis vine is unfit to trink. It has not properly been iced.

HICKEY: *(amusedly)* Always a high-toned swell at heart, eh, Hugo? God help us poor bums if you'd ever get to telling us where to get off! You'd have been drinking our blood beneath those willow trees! *(He chuckles.* HUGO *shrinks back in his chair, blinking at him, but* HICKEY *is now looking up the table at* HOPE. *He starts his toast, and as he goes on he becomes more moved and obviously sincere)* Here's the toast, Ladies and Gents! Here's to Harry Hope, who's been a friend in need to every one of us! Here's to the old Governor, the best sport and the kindest, biggest-hearted guy in the world! Here's wishing you all the luck there is, Harry, and long life and happiness! Come on, everybody! To Harry! Bottoms up!

(They have all caught his sincerity with eager relief. They raise their schooners with an enthusiastic chorus of "Here's how, Harry!" "Here's luck, Harry!" etc., and gulp half the wine down, HICKEY *leading them in this.)*

HOPE: *(deeply moved—his voice husky)* Bejees, thanks, all of you. Bejees, Hickey, you old son of a bitch, that's white of you! Bejees, I know you meant it, too.

HICKEY: *(moved)* Of course I meant it, Harry, old friend! And I mean it when I say I hope today will be the biggest day in your life, and in the lives of everyone here, the beginning of a new life of peace and contentment where no pipe dreams can ever nag at you again. Here's to that, Harry!

(He drains the remainder of his drink, but this time he drinks alone. In an instant the attitude of everyone has reverted to uneasy, suspicious defensiveness.)

ROCKY: *(growls)* Aw, forget dat bughouse line of bull for a minute, can't yuh?

HICKEY: *(sitting down—good-naturedly)* You're right, Rocky, I'm talking too much. It's Harry we want to hear from. Come on, Harry! *(He pounds his schooner on the table)* Speech! Speech!

(They try to recapture their momentary enthusiasm, rap their schooners on the table, call "Speech," but there is a hollow ring in it. HOPE *gets to his feet reluctantly, with a forced smile, a smoldering resentment beginning to show in his manner.)*

HOPE: *(lamely)* Bejees, I'm no good at speeches. All I can say is thanks to everybody again for remembering me on my birthday. *(Bitterness coming out)* Only don't think because I'm sixty I'll be a bigger damned fool easy mark than ever! No, bejees! Like Hickey says, it's going to be a new day! This dump has got to be run like other dumps, so I can make some money and not just split even. People has got to pay what they owe me! I'm not running a damned orphan asylum for bums and crooks! Nor a God-damned hooker shanty, either! Nor an Old Men's Home for lousy Anarchist tramps that ought to be in jail! I'm sick of being played for a sucker! *(They stare at him with stunned, bewildered hurt. He goes on in a sort of furious desperation, as if he hated himself for every word he said, and yet couldn't stop)* And don't think you're kidding me right now, either! I know damned well you're giving me the laugh behind my back, thinking to yourselves, The old, lying, pipe-dreaming faker, we've heard his bull about taking a walk around the ward for years, he'll never make it! He's yellow, he ain't got the guts, he's scared he'll find out— *(He glares around at them almost with hatred)* But I'll show you, bejees! *(He glares at HICKEY)* I'll show you, too, you son of a bitch of a frying-pan-peddling bastard!

HICKEY: *(heartily encouraging)* That's the stuff, Harry! Of course you'll try to show me! That's what I want you to do!

(HARRY glances at him with helpless dread—then drops his eyes and looks furtively around the table. All at once he becomes miserably contrite.)

HOPE: *(his voice catching)* Listen, all of you! Bejees, forgive me. I lost my temper! I ain't feeling well! I got a hell of a grouch on! Bejees, you know you're all as welcome here as the flowers in May!

(They look at him with eager forgiveness. ROCKY is the first one who can voice it)

ROCKY: Aw, sure, Boss, you're always aces wid us, see?

HICKEY: *(rises to his feet again. He addresses them now with the simple, convincing sincerity of one making a confession of which he is genuinely ashamed)* Listen, everybody! I know you are sick of my gabbing, but I think this is the spot where I owe it to you to do a little explaining and apologize for some of the rough stuff I've had to pull on you. I know how it must look to you. As if I was a damned busybody who was not only interfering in your private business, but even sicking some of you on to nag at each other. Well, I have to admit that's true, and I'm damned sorry about it. But it simply had to be done! You must believe that! You know old Hickey. I was never one to start trouble. But this time I had to—for your own good! I had to make you help me with each other. I saw I couldn't do what I was after alone. Not in the time at my disposal. I knew when I came here I wouldn't be able to stay with you long. I'm slated to leave on a trip. I saw I'd have to hustle and use every means I could. *(With a joking boastfulness)* Why, if I had enough time, I'd get a lot of sport out of selling my line of salvation to each of you all by my lonesome. Like it was fun in the old days, when I traveled house to house, to convince some dame, who was sicking the dog on me, her house wouldn't be properly furnished unless she bought another wash boiler. And I could do it with you, all right. I know every one of you, inside and out, by heart. I may have been drunk when I've been here before, but old Hickey could never be so drunk he didn't have to see through people. I mean, everyone except himself. And, finally, he had to see through himself, too. *(He pauses. They stare at him, bitter, uneasy and fascinated. His manner changes to deep earnestness)* But here's the point to get. I swear I'd never act like I have if I wasn't absolutely sure it will be worth it to you in the end, after you're rid of the damned guilt that makes you lie to yourselves you're something you're not, and the remorse that nags at you and makes you

hide behind lousy pipe dreams about tomorrow. You'll be in a today where there is no yesterday or tomorrow to worry you. You won't
give a damn what you are any more. I wouldn't
say this unless I knew, Brothers and Sisters.
This peace is real! It's a fact! I know! Because
I've got it! Here! Now! Right in front of you!
You see the difference in me! You remember
how I used to be! Even when I had two quarts
of rotgut under my belt and joked and sang
"Sweet Adeline," I still felt like a guilty
skunk. But you can all see that I don't give a
damn about anything now. And I promise you,
by the time this day is over, I'll have every one
of you feeling the same way! *(He pauses. They
stare at him fascinatedly. He adds with a grin)*
I guess that'll be about all from me, boys and
girls—for the present. So let's get on with the
party.
(He starts to sit down.)

LARRY: *(sharply)* Wait! *(Insistently—with a sneer)*
I think it would help us poor pipe-dreaming sinners along the sawdust trail to salvation if you
told us now what it was happened to you that
converted you to this great peace you've found.
*(More and more with a deliberate, provocative
taunting)* I notice you didn't deny it when I
asked you about the iceman. Did this great revelation of the evil habit of dreaming about tomorrow come to you after you found your wife
was sick of you?
*(While he is speaking the faces of the gang have
lighted up vindictively, as if all at once they saw
a chance to revenge themselves. As he finishes, a
chorus of sneering taunts begins, punctuated by
nasty, jeering laughter.)*

HOPE: Bejees, you've hit it, Larry! I've noticed he
hasn't shown her picture around this time!

MOSHER: He hasn't got it! The iceman took it
away from him!

MARGIE: Jees, look at him! Who could blame her?

PEARL: She must be hard up to fall for an iceman!

CORA: Imagine a sap like him advisin' me and
Chuck to git married!

CHUCK: Yeah! He done so good wid it!

JIMMY: At least I can say Marjorie chose an officer and a gentleman.

LEWIS: Come to look at you, Hickey, old chap,
you've sprouted horns like a bloody antelope!

WETJOEN: Pigger, py Gott! Like a water buffalo's!

WILLIE: *(sings to his "Sailor Lad" tune)*

"Come up," she cried, "my iceman lad,
  And you and I'll agree—"

*(They all join in a jeering chorus, rapping with
knuckles or glasses on the table at the indicated
spot in the lyric.)*

"And I'll show you the prettiest *(Rap,
    rap, rap)*
That ever you did see!"

*(A roar of derisive, dirty laughter. But HICKEY
has remained unmoved by all this taunting. He
grins good-naturedly, as if he enjoyed the joke
at his expense, and joins in the laughter.)*

HICKEY: Well, boys and girls, I'm glad to see you
getting in good spirits for Harry's party, even if
the joke is on me. I admit I asked for it by always pulling that iceman gag in the old days. So
laugh all you like. *(He pauses. They do not laugh
now. They are again staring at him with baffled
uneasiness. He goes on thoughtfully)* Well, this
forces my hand, I guess, your bringing up the
subject of Evelyn. I didn't want to tell you yet.
It's hardly an appropriate time. I meant to wait
until the party was over. But you're getting the
wrong idea about poor Evelyn, and I've got to
stop that. *(He pauses again. There is a tense stillness in the room. He bows his head a little and
says quietly)* I'm sorry to tell you my dearly
beloved wife is dead.
*(A gasp comes from the stunned company. They
look away from him, shocked and miserably
ashamed of themselves, except LARRY who continues to stare at him.)*

LARRY: *(aloud to himself with a superstitious
shrinking)* Be God, I felt he'd brought the
touch of death on him! *(Then suddenly he is*

even more ashamed of himself than the others and stammers) Forgive me, Hickey! I'd like to cut my dirty tongue out!
(This releases a chorus of shamefaced mumbles from the crowd. "Sorry, Hickey." "I'm sorry, Hickey." "We're sorry, Hickey.")

HICKEY: *(looking around at them—in a kindly, reassuring tone)* Now look here, everybody. You mustn't let this be a wet blanket on Harry's party. You're still getting me all wrong. There's no reason—You see, I don't feel any grief. *(They gaze at him startledly. He goes on with convincing sincerity)* I've got to feel glad, for her sake. Because she's at peace. She's rid of me at last. Hell, I don't have to tell you—you all know what I was like. You can imagine what she went through, married to a no-good cheater and drunk like I was. And there was no way out of it for her. Because she loved me. But now she is at peace like she always longed to be. So why should I feel sad? She wouldn't want me to feel sad. Why, all that Evelyn ever wanted out of life was to make me happy.
(He stops, looking around at them with a simple, gentle frankness. They stare at him in bewildered, incredulous confusion.)

CURTAIN

ACT THREE

SCENE: *Barroom of* HARRY HOPE'S, *including a part of what had been the back room in Acts One and Two. In the right wall are two big windows, with the swinging doors to the street between them. The bar itself is at rear. Behind it is a mirror, covered with white mosquito netting to keep off the flies, and a shelf on which are barrels of cheap whiskey with spigots and a small showcase of bottled goods. At left of the bar is the doorway to the hall. There is a table at left, front, of barroom proper, with four chairs. At right, front, is a small free-lunch counter, facing left, with a space between it and the window for the dealer to stand*

when he dishes out soup at the noon hour. Over the mirror behind the bar are framed photographs of Richard Croker° and Big Tim Sullivan,° flanked by framed lithographs of John L. Sullivan° and Gentleman Jim Corbett° in ring costume.

At left, in what had been the back room, with the dividing curtain drawn, the banquet table of Act Two has been broken up, and the tables are again in the crowded arrangement of Act One. Of these, we see one in the front row with five chairs at left of the barroom table, another with five chairs at left-rear of it, a third back by the rear wall with five chairs, and finally, at extreme left-front, one with four chairs, partly on and partly off stage, left.

It is around the middle of the morning of HOPE'S *birthday, a hot summer day. There is sunlight in the street outside, but it does not hit the windows and the light in the back-room section is dim.*

JOE MOTT *is moving around, a box of sawdust under his arm, strewing it over the floor. His manner is sullen, his face set in gloom. He ignores everyone. As the scene progresses, he finishes his sawdusting job, goes behind the lunch counter and cuts loaves of bread.* ROCKY *is behind the bar, wiping it, washing glasses, etc. He wears his working clothes, sleeves rolled up. He looks sleepy, irritable and worried. At the barroom table, front,* LARRY *sits in a chair, facing right-front. He has no drink in front of him. He stares ahead, deep in harried thought. On his right,*

Richard Croker (1841–1922): Native of Ireland who emigrated as a child, Croker became a wealthy politician associated with Tammany Hall and, in later life, an owner of successful race horses.

Big Tim Sullivan (1862–1913): New York saloon owner and politician associated with Tammany Hall; known as the uncrowned king of the lower east side and much beloved for his annual Christmas dinner for thousands of New York derelicts.

John L. Sullivan (1858–1918): American heavyweight prizefighter and London Prize Ring bare knuckle champion, 1882–1892.

Gentleman Jim Corbett (1866–1933): Heavyweight prizefighter and First Marquis of Queensberry champion, 1892–1897; defeated Sullivan in 1892 in first championship fight to use oversized boxing gloves.

in a chair facing right, HUGO *sits sprawled forward, arms and head on the table as usual, a whiskey glass beside his limp hand. At rear of the front table at left of them, in a chair facing left,* PARRITT *is sitting. He is staring in front of him in a tense, strained immobility.*

As the curtain rises, ROCKY *finishes his work behind the bar. He comes forward and drops wearily in the chair at right of* LARRY'S *table, facing left.*

ROCKY: Nuttin' now till de noon rush from de Market. I'm goin' to rest my fanny. *(Irritably)* If I ain't a sap to let Chuck kid me into workin' his time so's he can take de mornin' off. But I got sick of arguin' wid 'im. I says, "Aw right, git married! What's it to me?" Hickey's got de bot' of dem bugs. *(Bitterly)* Some party last night, huh? Jees, what a funeral! It was jinxed from de start, but his tellin' about his wife croakin' put de K.O. on it.

LARRY: Yes, it turned out it wasn't a birthday feast but a wake!

ROCKY: Him promisin' he'd cut out de bughouse bull about peace—and den he went on talkin' and talkin' like he couldn't stop! And all de gang sneakin' upstairs, leavin' free booze and eats like dey was poison! It didn't do dem no good if dey thought dey'd shake him. He's been hoppin' from room to room all night. Yuh can't stop him. He's got his Reform Wave goin' strong dis mornin'! Did yuh notice him drag Jimmy out de foist ting to get his laundry and his clothes pressed so he wouldn't have no excuse? And he give Willie de dough to buy his stuff back from Solly's. And all de rest been brushin' and shavin' demselves wid de shakes—

LARRY: *(defiantly)* He didn't come to my room! He's afraid I might ask him a few questions.

ROCKY: *(scornfully)* Yeah? It don't look to me he's scared of yuh. I'd say you was scared of him.

LARRY: *(stung)* You'd lie, then!

PARRITT: *(jerks round to look at* LARRY—*sneeringly)* Don't let him kid you, Rocky. He had his door locked. I couldn't get in, either.

ROCKY: Yeah, who d'yuh tink yuh're kiddin', Larry? He's showed you up, aw right. Like he says, if yuh was so anxious to croak, why wouldn't yuh hop off your fire escape long ago?

LARRY: *(defiantly)* Because it'd be a coward's quitting, that's why!

PARRITT: He's all quitter, Rocky. He's a yellow old faker!

LARRY: *(turns on him)* You lying punk! Remember what I warned you—!

ROCKY: *(scowls at* PARRITT*)* Yeah, keep outta dis, you! Where d'yuh get a license to butt in? Shall I give him de bum's rush, Larry? If you don't want him around, nobody else don't.

LARRY: *(forcing an indifferent tone)* No. Let him stay. I don't mind him. He's nothing to me.
*(*ROCKY *shrugs his shoulders and yawns sleepily)*

PARRITT: You're right, I have nowhere to go now. You're the only one in the world I can turn to.

ROCKY: *(drowsily)* Yuh're a soft old sap, Larry. He's a no-good louse like Hickey. He don't belong. *(He yawns)* I'm all in. Not a wink of sleep. Can't keep my peepers open.
(His eyes close and his head nods. PARRITT *gives him a glance and then gets up and slinks over to slide into the chair on* LARRY'S *left, between him and* ROCKY. LARRY *shrinks away, but determinedly ignores him.)*

PARRITT *(bending toward him—in a low, ingratiating, apologetic voice)* I'm sorry for riding you, Larry. But you get my goat when you act as if you didn't care a damn what happened to me, and keep your door locked so I can't talk to you. *(Then hopefully)* But that was to keep Hickey out, wasn't it? I don't blame you. I'm getting to hate him. I'm getting more and more scared of him. Especially since he told us his wife was dead. It's that queer feeling he gives me that I'm mixed up with him some way. I don't know why, but it started me thinking about Mother—as if she was dead. *(With a strange undercurrent of something like satisfaction in his pitying tone)* I suppose she might as well be. Inside herself, I mean. It must kill her when she thinks of me—I know she doesn't want to, but she can't help it. After all, I'm her only kid. She used to spoil me and made a pet of me. Once in a great while, I mean. When she remembered me. As if she wanted to make up for something. As if she felt guilty. So she must have loved me a little, even if she never let it interfere with her freedom. *(With a strange pathetic wistfulness)* Do you know, Larry, I once had a sneaking suspicion that maybe, if the truth was known, you were my father.

LARRY: *(violently)* You damned fool! Who put that insane idea in your head? You know it's a lie! Anyone in the Coast crowd could tell you I never laid eyes on your mother till after you were born.

PARRITT: Well, I'd hardly ask them, would I? I know you're right, though, because I asked her. She brought me up to be frank and ask her anything, and she'd always tell me the truth. *(Abruptly)* But I was talking about how she must feel now about me. My getting through with the Movement. She'll never forgive that. The Movement is her life. And it must be the final knockout for her if she knows I was the one who sold—

LARRY: Shut up, damn you!

PARRITT: It'll kill her. And I'm sure she knows it must have been me. *(Suddenly with desperate urgency)* But I never thought the cops would get her! You've got to believe that! You've got to see what my only reason was! I'll admit what I told you last night was a lie—that bunk about getting patriotic and my duty to my country. But here's the true reason, Larry—the only reason! It was just for money! I got stuck on a whore and wanted dough to blow it on her and have a good time! That's all I did it for! Just money! Honest!

(He has the terrible grotesque air, in confessing his sordid baseness, of one who gives an excuse which exonerates him from any real guilt.)

LARRY: *(grabs him by the shoulder and shakes him)* God damn you, shut up! What the hell is it to me?

(ROCKY starts awake)

ROCKY: What's comin' off here?

LARRY: *(controlling himself)* Nothing. This gabby young punk was talking my ear off, that's all. He's a worse pest than Hickey.

ROCKY: *(drowsily)* Yeah, Hickey—Say, listen, what d'yuh mean about him bein' scared you'd ask him questions? What questions?

LARRY: Well, I feel he's hiding something. You notice he didn't say what his wife died of.

ROCKY: *(rebukingly)* Aw, lay off dat. De poor guy— What are yuh gettin' at, anyway? Yuh don't tink it's just a gag of his?

LARRY: I don't. I'm damned sure he's brought death here with him. I feel the cold touch of it on him.

ROCKY: Aw, bunk! You got croakin' on de brain, Old Cemetery. *(Suddenly ROCKY's eyes widen)* Say! D'yuh mean yuh tink she committed suicide, 'count of his cheatin' or something?

LARRY: *(grimly)* It wouldn't surprise me. I'd be the last to blame her.

ROCKY: *(scornfully)* But dat's crazy! Jees, if she'd done dat, he wouldn't tell us he was glad about it, would he? He ain't dat big a bastard.

PARRITT: *(speaks up from his own preoccupation— strangely)* You know better than that, Larry. You know she'd never commit suicide. She's like you. She'll hang on to life even when there's nothing left but—

LARRY: *(stung—turns on him viciously)* And how about you? Be God, if you had any guts or decency—!

(He stops guiltily.)

PARRITT: *(sneeringly)* I'd take that hop off your fire escape you're too yellow to take, I suppose?

LARRY: *(as if to himself)* No! Who am I to judge? I'm done with judging.

PARRITT: *(tauntingly)* Yes, I suppose you'd like that, wouldn't you?

ROCKY: *(irritably mystified)* What de hell's all dis about? *(To PARRITT)* What d'you know about Hickey's wife? How d'you know she didn't—?

LARRY: *(with forced belittling casualness)* He doesn't. Hickey's addled the little brains he's got. Shove him back to his own table, Rocky. I'm sick of him.

ROCKY: *(to* PARRITT, *threateningly)* Yuh heard Larry? I'd like an excuse to give yuh a good punch in de snoot. So move quick!

PARRITT: *(gets up—to* LARRY*)* If you think moving to another table will get rid of me! *(He moves away—then adds with bitter reproach)* Gee, Larry, that's a hell of a way to treat me, when I've trusted you, and I need your help.

(He sits down in his old place and sinks into a wounded, self-pitying brooding.)

ROCKY: *(going back to his train of thought)* Jees, if she committed suicide, yuh got to feel sorry for Hickey, huh? Yuh can understand how he'd go bughouse and not be responsible for all de crazy stunts he's stagin' here. *(Then puzzledly)* But how can yuh be sorry for him when he says he's glad she croaked, and yuh can tell he means it? *(With weary exasperation)* Aw, nuts! I don't get nowhere tryin' to figger his game. *(His face hardening)* But I know dis. He better lay off me and my stable! *(He pauses—then sighs)* Jees, Larry, what a night dem two pigs give me! When de party went dead, dey pinched a coupla bottles and brung dem up deir room and got stinko. I don't get a wink of sleep, see? Just as I'd drop off on a chair here, dey'd come down lookin' for trouble. Or else dey'd raise hell upstairs, laughin' and singin', so I'd get scared dey'd get de joint pinched and go up to tell dem to can de noise. And every time dey'd crawl my frame wid de same old argument. Dey'd say, "So yuh agreed wid Hickey, do yuh, yuh dirty little Ginny? We're whores, are we? Well, we agree wid Hickey about you, see! Yuh're nuttin' but a lousy pimp!" Den I'd slap dem. Not beat 'em up, like a pimp would. Just slap dem. But it don't do no good. Dey'd keep at it over and over. Jees, I get de earache just thinkin' of it! "Listen," dey'd say, "If we're whores we gotta right to have a reg'lar pimp and not stand for no punk imitation! We're sick of wearin' out our dogs poundin' sidewalks for a double-crossin' bartender, when all de thanks we get is he looks down on us. We'll find a guy who really needs us to take care of

him and ain't ashamed of it. Don't expect us to work tonight, 'cause we won't, see? Not if de streets was blocked wid sailors! We're goin' on strike and yuh can like it or lump it!" *(He shakes his head)* Whores goin' on strike! Can yuh tie dat? *(Going on with his story)* Dey says, "We're takin' a holiday. We're goin' to beat it down to Coney Island and shoot the chutes and maybe we'll come back and maybe we won't. And you can go to hell!" So dey put on deir lids and beat it, de bot' of dem stinko.

(He sighs dejectedly. He seems grotesquely like a harried family man, henpecked and browbeaten by a nagging wife. LARRY *is deep in his own bitter preoccupation and hasn't listened to him.* CHUCK *enters from the hall at rear. He has his straw hat with the gaudy band in his hand and wears a Sunday-best blue suit with a high stiff collar. He looks sleepy, hot, uncomfortable and grouchy.)*

CHUCK: *(glumly)* Hey, Rocky. Cora wants a sherry flip. For her noives.

ROCKY: *(turns indignantly)* Sherry flip! Christ, she don't need nuttin' for her noive! What's she tink dis is, de Waldorf?

CHUCK: Yeah, I told her, what would we use for sherry, and dere wasn't no egg unless she laid one. She says, "Is dere a law yuh can't go out and buy de makings, yuh big tramp?" *(Resentfully puts his straw hat on his head at a defiant tilt)* To hell wid her! She'll drink booze or nuttin'!

(He goes behind the bar to draw a glass of whiskey from a barrel.)

ROCKY: *(sarcastically)* Jees, a guy oughta give his bride anything she wants on de weddin' day, I should tink! *(As* CHUCK *comes from behind the bar,* ROCKY *surveys him derisively)* Pipe de bridegroom, Larry! All dolled up for de killin'! *(*LARRY *pays no attention.)*

CHUCK: Aw, shut up!

ROCKY: One week on dat farm in Joisey, dat's what I give yuh! Yuh'll come runnin' in here some night yellin' for a shot of booze 'cause de crickets is after yuh! *(Disgustedly)* Jees, Chuck, dat louse Hickey's coitinly made a prize coupla suckers outa youse.

CHUCK: *(unguardedly)* Yeah. I'd like to give him one sock in de puss—just one! *(Then angrily)* Aw, can dat! What's he got to do wid it? Ain't we always said we was goin' to? So we're goin' to, see? And don't give me no argument! *(He stares at* ROCKY *truculently. But* ROCKY *only shrugs his shoulders with weary disgust and* CHUCK *subsides into complaining gloom)* If on'y Cora'd cut out de beefin'. She don't gimme a minute's rest all night. De same old stuff over and over! Do I really want to marry her? I says, "Sure, Baby, why not?" She says, "Yeah, but after a week yuh'll be tinkin' what a sap you was. Yuh'll make dat an excuse to go off on a periodical, and den I'll be tied for life to a no-good soak, and de foist ting I know yuh'll have me out hustlin' again, your own wife!" Den she'd bust out cryin', and I'd get sore. "Yuh're a liar," I'd say. "I ain't never taken your dough 'cept when I was drunk and not workin'!" "Yeah," she'd say, "and how long will yuh stay sober now? Don't tink yuh can kid me wid dat water-wagon bull! I've heard it too often." Dat'd make me sore and I'd say, "Don't call me a liar. But I wish I was drunk right now, because if I was, yuh wouldn't be keepin' me awake all night beefin'. If yuh opened your yap, I'd knock de stuffin' outa yuh!" Den she'd yell, "Dat's a sweet way to talk to de goil yuh're goin' to marry." *(He sighs explosively)* Jees, she's got me hangin' on de ropes! *(He glances with vengeful yearning at the drink of whiskey in his hand)* Jees, would I like to get a quart of dis redeye under my belt!

ROCKY: Well, why de hell don't yuh?

CHUCK: *(instantly suspicious and angry)* Sure! You'd like dat, wouldn't yuh? I'm wise to you! Yuh don't wanta see me get married and settle down like a reg'lar guy! Yuh'd like me to stay paralyzed all de time, so's I'd be like you, a lousy pimp!

ROCKY: *(springs to his feet, his face hardened viciously)* Listen! I don't take dat even from you, see!

CHUCK: *(puts his drink on the bar and clenches his fists)* Yeah? Wanta make sometin' of it? *(Jeeringly)* Don't make me laugh! I can lick ten of youse wid one mit!

ROCKY: *(reaching for his hip pocket)* Not wid lead in your belly, yuh won't!

JOE: *(has stopped cutting when the quarrel started—expostulating)* Hey, you, Rocky and Chuck! Cut it out! You's ole friends! Don't let dat Hickey make you crazy!

CHUCK: *(turns on him)* Keep outa our business, yuh black bastard!

ROCKY: *(like* CHUCK, *turns on* JOE, *as if their own quarrel was forgotten and they became natural allies against an alien)* Stay where yuh belong, yuh doity nigger!

JOE: *(snarling with rage, springs from behind the lunch counter with the bread knife in his hand)* You white sons of bitches! I'll rip your guts out! *(*CHUCK *snatches a whiskey bottle from the bar and raises it above his head to hurl at* JOE. ROCKY *jerks a short-barreled, nickel-plated revolver from his hip pocket. At this moment* LARRY *pounds on the table with his fist and bursts into a sardonic laugh.)*

LARRY: That's it! Murder each other, you damned loons, with Hickey's blessing! Didn't I tell you he'd brought death with him? *(His interruption startles them. They pause to stare at him, their fighting fury suddenly dies out and they appear deflated and sheepish.)*

ROCKY: *(to* JOE) Aw right, you. Leggo dat shiv and I'll put dis gat away.

*(*JOE *sullenly goes back behind the counter and slaps the knife on top of it.* ROCKY *slips the revolver back in his pocket.* CHUCK *lowers the bottle to the bar.* HUGO, *who has awakened and raised his head when* LARRY *pounded on the table, now giggles foolishly.)*

HUGO: Hello, leddle peoples! Neffer mind! Soon you vill eat hot dogs beneath the villow trees and trink free vine— *(Abruptly in a haughty fastidious tone)* The champagne vas not properly iced. *(With guttural anger)* Gottamned liar, Hickey! Does that prove I vant to be aristocrat? I love only the proletariat! I vill lead them! I vill be like a Gott to them! They vill be my slaves! *(He stops in bewildered self-amazement—to* LARRY *appealingly)* I am very trunk, no, Larry? I talk foolishness. I am so trunk, Larry, old friend, am I not, I don't know vhat I say?

LARRY: *(pityingly)* You're raving drunk, Hugo. I've never seen you so paralyzed. Lay your head down now and sleep it off.

HUGO: *(gratefully)* Yes. I should sleep. I am too crazy trunk.

(He puts his head on his arms and closes his eyes.)

JOE: *(behind the lunch counter—brooding superstitiously)* You's right, Larry. Bad luck come in de door when Hickey come. I's an ole gamblin' man and I knows bad luck when I feels it! *(Then defiantly)* But it's white man's bad luck. He can't jinx me! *(He comes from behind the counter and goes to the bar—addressing* ROCKY *stiffly)* De bread's cut and I's finished my job. Do I get de drink I's earned? *(*ROCKY *gives him a hostile look but shoves a bottle and glass at him.* JOE *pours a brimful drink—sullenly)* I's finished wid dis dump for keeps. *(He takes a key from his pocket and slaps it on the bar)* Here's de key to my room. I ain't comin' back. I's goin' to my own folks where I belong. I don't stay where I's not wanted. I's sick and tired of messin' round wid white men. *(He gulps down his drink—then looking around defiantly he deliberately throws his whiskey glass on the floor and smashes it)*

ROCKY: Hey! What de hell—!

JOE: *(with a sneering dignity)* I's on'y savin' you de trouble, White Boy. Now you don't have to break it, soon's my back's turned, so's no white man kick about drinkin' from de same glass. *(He walks stiffly to the street door—then turns for a parting shot—boastfully)* I's tired of loafin' 'round wid a lot of bums. I's a gamblin' man. I's gonna get in a big crap game and win me a big bankroll. Den I'll get de okay to open up my old gamblin' house for colored men. Den maybe I comes back here sometime to see de bums. Maybe I throw a twenty-dollar bill on de bar and

say, "Drink it up," and listen when dey all pat me on de back and say, "Joe, you sure is white." But I'll say, "No, I'm black and my dough is black man's dough, and you's proud to drink wid me or you don't get no drink!" Or maybe I just says, "You can all go to hell. I don't lower myself drinkin' wid no white trash!" *(He opens the door to go out—then turns again)* And dat ain't no pipe dream! I'll get de money for my stake today, somehow, somewheres! If I has to borrow a gun and stick up some white man, I gets it! You wait and see!

(He swaggers out through the swinging doors.)

CHUCK: *(angrily)* Can yuh beat de noive of dat dinge! Jees, if I wasn't dressed up, I'd go out and mop up de street wid him!

ROCKY: Aw, let him go, de poor old dope! Him and his gamblin' house! He'll be back tonight askin' Harry for his room and bummin' me for a ball. *(Vengefully)* Den I'll be de one to smash de glass. I'll loin him his place!

(The swinging doors are pushed open and WILLIE OBAN *enters from the street. He is shaved and wears an expensive, well-cut suit, good shoes and clean linen. He is absolutely sober, but his face is sick, and his nerves in a shocking state of shakes.)*

CHUCK: Another guy all dolled up! Got your clothes from Solly's, huh, Willie? *(Derisively)* Now yuh can sell dem back to him again tomorrow.

WILLIE: *(stiffly)* No, I—I'm through with that stuff. Never again.

(He comes to the bar.)

ROCKY: *(sympathetically)* Yuh look sick, Willie. Take a ball to pick yuh up.

(He pushes a bottle toward him.)

WILLIE: *(eyes the bottle yearningly but shakes his head—determinedly)* No, thanks. The only way to stop is to stop. I'd have no chance if I went to the D.A.'s office smelling of booze.

CHUCK: Yuh're really goin' dere?

WILLIE: *(stiffly)* I said I was, didn't I? I just came back here to rest a few minutes, not because I needed any booze. I'll show that cheap drummer I don't have to have any Dutch courage—

(Guiltily) But he's been very kind and generous staking me. He can't help his insulting manner, I suppose. *(He turns away from the bar)* My legs are a bit shaky yet. I better sit down a while. *(He goes back and sits at the left of the second table, facing* PARRITT, *who gives him a scowling, suspicious glance and then ignores him.* ROCKY *looks at* CHUCK *and taps his head disgustedly.* CAPTAIN LEWIS *appears in the doorway from the hall)*

CHUCK: *(mutters)* Here's anudder one.

*(*LEWIS *looks spruce and clean-shaven. His ancient tweed suit has been brushed and his frayed linen is clean. His manner is full of a forced, jaunty self-assurance. But he is sick and beset by katzenjammer.)*

LEWIS: Good morning, gentlemen all. *(He passes along the front of bar to look out in the street)* A jolly fine morning, too. *(He turns back to the bar)* An eye-opener? I think not. Not required, Rocky, old chum. Feel extremely fit, as a matter of fact. Though can't say I slept much, thanks to that interfering ass, Hickey, and that stupid bounder of a Boer. *(His face hardens)* I've had about all I can take from that fellow. It's my own fault, of course, for allowing a brute of a Dutch farmer to become familiar. Well, it's come to a parting of the ways now, and good riddance. Which reminds me, here's my key. *(He puts it on the bar)* I shan't be coming back. Sorry to be leaving good old Harry and the rest of you, of course, but I can't continue to live under the same roof with that fellow.

(He stops, stiffening into hostility as WETJOEN *enters from the hall, and pointedly turns his back on him.* WETJOEN *glares at him sneeringly. He, too, has made an effort to spruce up his appearance, and his bearing has a forced swagger of conscious physical strength. Behind this, he is sick and feebly holding his booze-sodden body together.)*

ROCKY: *(to* LEWIS—*disgustedly putting the key on the shelf in back of the bar)* So Hickey's kidded the pants offa you, too? Yuh tink yuh're leavin' here, huh?

WETJOEN: *(jeeringly)* Ja! Dot's vhat he kids himself.

LEWIS: *(ignores him—airily)* Yes, I'm leaving, Rocky. But that ass, Hickey, has nothing to do with it. Been thinking things over. Time I turned over a new leaf, and all that.

WETJOEN: He's going to get a job! Dot's what he says!

ROCKY: What at, for Chris' sake?

LEWIS: *(keeping his airy manner)* Oh, anything. I mean, not manual labor, naturally, but anything that calls for a bit of brains and education. However humble. Beggars can't be choosers. I'll see a pal of mine at the Consulate. He promised any time I felt an energetic fit he'd get me a post with the Cunard—clerk in the office or something of the kind.

WETJOEN: Ja! At Limey Consulate they promise anything to get rid of him vhen he comes there tronk! They're scared to call the police and have him pinched because it vould scandal in the papers make about a Limey officer and chentleman!

LEWIS: As a matter of fact, Rocky, I only wish a post temporarily. Means to an end, you know. Save up enough for a first-class passage home, that's the bright idea.

WETJOEN: He's sailing back to home, sveet home! Dot's biggest pipe dream of all. What leetle brain the poor Limey has left, dot isn't in whiskey pickled, Hickey has made crazy!

*(*LEWIS' *fists clench, but he manages to ignore this.)*

CHUCK: *(feels sorry for* LEWIS *and turns on* WETJOEN—*sarcastically)* Hickey ain't made no sucker outa you, huh? You're too foxy, huh? But I'll bet you tink yuh're goin' out and land a job, too.

WETJOEN: *(bristles)* I am, ja. For me, it is easy. Because I put on no airs of chentleman. I am not ashamed to vork with my hands. I vas a farmer before the war ven ploody Limey thieves steal my country. *(Boastfully)* Anyone I ask for job can see with one look I have the great strength to do work of ten ordinary mens.

LEWIS: *(sneeringly)* Yes, Chuck, you remember he gave a demonstration of his extraordinary muscles last night when he helped to move the piano.

CHUCK: Yuh couldn't even hold up your corner. It was your fault de damned box almost fell down de stairs.

WETJOEN: My hands vas sweaty! Could I help dot my hands slip? I could de whole veight of it lift! In old days in Transvaal, I lift loaded oxcart by the axle! So vhy shouldn't I get job? Dot longshoreman boss, Dan, he tell me any time I like, he take me on. And Benny from de Market he promise me same.

LEWIS: You remember, Rocky, it was one of those rare occasions when the Boer that walks like a man—spelled with a double o, by the way—was buying drinks and Dan and Benny were stony. They'd bloody well have promised him the moon.

ROCKY: Yeah, yuh big boob, dem boids was on'y kiddin' yuh.

WETJOEN: *(angrily)* Dot's lie! You vill see dis morning I get job! I'll show dot bloody Limey chentleman, and dot liar, Hickey! And I need vork only leetle vhile to save money for my passage home. I need not much money because I am not ashamed to travel steerage. I don't put on first-cabin airs! *(Tauntingly)* Und *I* can go home to my country! When I get there, they vill let *me* come in!

LEWIS: *(grows rigid—his voice trembling with repressed anger)* There was a rumor in South Africa, Rocky, that a certain Boer officer—if you call the leaders of a rabble of farmers officers—kept advising Cronje to retreat and not stand and fight—

WETJOEN: And I vas right! I vas right! He got surrounded at Poardeberg! He had to surrender!

LEWIS: *(ignoring him)* Good strategy, no doubt, but a suspicion grew afterwards into a conviction among the Boers that the officer's caution was prompted by a desire to make his personal escape. His countrymen felt extremely savage about it, and his family disowned him. So I imagine there would be no welcoming committee waiting on the dock, nor delighted relatives making the veldt ring with their happy cries—

WETJOEN: *(with guilty rage)* All lies! You Gottamned Limey—*(Trying to control himself and copy* LEWIS' *manner)* I also haf heard rumors of a Limey officer who, after the war, lost all his money gambling vhen he vas tronk. But they found out it was regiment money, too, he lost—

LEWIS: *(loses his control and starts for him)* You bloody Dutch scum!

ROCKY: *(leans over the bar and stops* LEWIS *with a straight-arm swipe on the chest)* Cut it out!
(At the same moment CHUCK *grabs* WETJOEN *and yanks him back.)*

WETJOEN: *(struggling)* Let him come! I saw them come before—at Modder River, Magersfontein, Spion Kopje—waving their silly swords, so afraid they couldn't show off how brave they vas!—and I kill them vith my rifle so easy! *(Vindictively)* Listen to me, you Cecil! Often vhen I am tronk and kidding you I say I am sorry I missed you, but now, py Gott, I am sober, and I don't joke, and I say it!

LARRY: *(gives a sardonic guffaw—with his comically crazy, intense whisper)* Be God, you can't say Hickey hasn't the miraculous touch to raise the dead, when he can start the Boer War raging again!
(This interruption acts like a cold douche on LEWIS *and* WETJOEN. *They subside, and* ROCKY *and* CHUCK *let go of them.* LEWIS *turns his back on the Boer.)*

LEWIS: *(attempting a return of his jaunty manner, as if nothing had happened)* Well, time I was on my merry way to see my chap at the Consulate. The early bird catches the job, what? Good-bye and good luck, Rocky, and everyone.
(He starts for the street door.)

WETJOEN: Py Gott, if dot Limey can go, I can go! *(He hurries after* LEWIS. *But* LEWIS, *his hand about to push the swinging doors open, hesitates, as though struck by a sudden paralysis of the will, and* WETJOEN *has to jerk back to avoid bumping into him. For a second they stand there, one behind the other, staring over the swinging doors into the street.)*

ROCKY: Well, why don't yuh beat it?

LEWIS: *(guiltily casual)* Eh? Oh, just happened to think. Hardly the decent thing to pop off without saying good-bye to old Harry. One of the best, Harry. And good old Jimmy, too. They ought to be down any moment. *(He pretends to notice* WETJOEN *for the first time and steps away from the door—apologizing as to a stranger)* Sorry, I seem to be blocking your way out.

WETJOEN: *(stiffly)* No. I vait to say good-bye to Harry and Jimmy, too.

(He goes to right of door behind the lunch counter and looks through the window, his back to the room. LEWIS *takes up a similar stand at the window on the left of door.)*

CHUCK: Jees, can yuh beat dem simps! *(He picks up* CORA'S *drink at the end of the bar)* Hell, I'd forgot Cora. She'll be trowin' a fit.

(He goes into the hall with the drink.)

ROCKY: *(looks after him disgustedly)* Dat's right, wait on her and spoil her, yuh poor sap!

(He shakes his head and begins to wipe the bar mechanically.)

WILLIE: *(is regarding* PARRITT *across the table from him with an eager, calculating eye. He leans over and speaks in a low confidential tone)* Look here, Parritt. I'd like to have a talk with you.

PARRITT: *(starts—scowling defensively)* What about?

WILLIE: *(his manner becoming his idea of a crafty criminal lawyer's)* About the trouble you're in. Oh, I know. You don't admit it. You're quite right. That's my advice. Deny everything. Keep your mouth shut. Make no statements whatever without first consulting your attorney.

PARRITT: Say! What the hell—?

WILLIE: But you can trust me. I'm a lawyer, and it's just occurred to me you and I ought to co-operate. Of course I'm going to see the D.A. this morning about a job on his staff. But that may take time. There may not be an immediate opening. Meanwhile it would be a good idea for me to take a case or two, on my own, and prove my

brilliant record in Law School was no flash in the pan. So why not retain me as your attorney?

PARRITT: You're crazy! What do I want with a lawyer?

WILLIE: That's right. Don't admit anything. But you can trust me, so let's not beat about the bush. You got in trouble out on the Coast, eh? And now you're hiding out. Any fool can spot that. *(Lowering his voice still more)* You feel safe here, and maybe you are, for a while. But remember, they get you in the end. I know from my father's experience. No one could have felt safer than he did. When anyone mentioned the law to him, he nearly died laughing. But—

PARRITT: You crazy mutt! *(Turning to* LARRY *with a strained laugh)* Did you get that, Larry? This damned fool thinks the cops are after me!

LARRY: *(bursts out with his true reaction before he thinks to ignore him)* I wish to God they were! And so should you, if you had the honor of a louse!

*(*PARRITT *stares into his eyes guiltily for a second. Then he smiles sneeringly)*

PARRITT: And you're the guy who kids himself he's through with the Movement! You old lying faker, you're still in love with it!

*(*LARRY *ignores him again now)*

WILLIE: *(disappointedly)* Then you're not in trouble, Parritt? I was hoping— But never mind. No offense meant. Forget it.

PARRITT: *(condescendingly—his eyes on* LARRY*)* Sure. That's all right, Willie. I'm not sore at you. It's that damned old faker that gets my goat. *(He slips out of his chair and goes quietly over to sit in the chair beside* LARRY *he had occupied before—in a low, insinuating, intimate tone)* I think I understand, Larry. It's really Mother you still love—isn't it?—in spite of the dirty deal she gave you. But hell, what did you expect? She was never true to anyone but herself and the Movement. But I understand how you can't help still feeling—because I still love her, too. *(Pleading in a strained, desperate tone)* You know I do, don't you? You must! So you see I couldn't have expected they'd catch her! You've got to believe me that I sold them out just to get a few lousy dollars to blow in on a whore. No other reason, honest! There couldn't possibly be any other reason!

(Again he has a strange air of exonerating himself from guilt by this shameless confession.)

LARRY: *(trying not to listen, has listened with increasing tension)* For the love of Christ will you leave me in peace! I've told you you can't make me judge you! But if you don't keep still, you'll be saying something soon that will make you vomit your own soul like a drink of nickel rotgut that won't stay down! *(He pushes back his chair and springs to his feet)* To hell with you! *(He goes to the bar)*

PARRITT: *(jumps up and starts to follow him—desperately)* Don't go, Larry! You've got to help me!

(But LARRY *is at the bar, back turned, and* ROCKY *is scowling at him. He stops, shrinking back into himself helplessly, and turns away. He goes to the table where he had been before, and this time he takes the chair at rear facing directly front. He puts his elbows on the table, holding his head in his hands as if he had a splitting headache.)*

LARRY: Set 'em up, Rocky. I swore I'd have no more drinks on Hickey, if I died of drought, but I've changed my mind! Be God, he owes it to me, and I'd get blind to the world now if it was the Iceman of Death himself treating! *(He stops, startledly, a superstitious awe coming into his face)* What made me say that, I wonder. *(With a sardonic laugh)* Well, be God, it fits, for Death was the Iceman Hickey called to his home!

ROCKY: Aw, forget dat iceman gag! De poor dame is dead. *(Pushing a bottle and glass at* LARRY) Gwan and get paralyzed! I'll be glad to see one bum in dis dump act natural.

*(*LARRY *downs a drink and pours another.* ED MOSHER *appears in the doorway from the hall. The same change which is apparent in the manner and appearance of the others shows in him. He is sick, his nerves are shattered, his eyes are* apprehensive, but he, too, puts on an exaggeratedly self-confident bearing. He saunters to the bar between* LARRY *and the street entrance.)*

MOSHER: Morning, Rocky. Hello, Larry. Glad to see Brother Hickey hasn't corrupted you to temperance. I wouldn't mind a shot myself. *(As* ROCKY *shoves a bottle toward him he shakes his head)* But I remember the only breath-killer in this dump is coffee beans. The boss would never fall for that. No man can run a circus successfully who believes guys chew coffee beans because they like them. *(He pushes the bottle away)* No, much as I need one after the hell of a night I've had— *(He scowls)* That drummer son of a drummer! I had to lock him out. But I could hear him through the wall doing his spiel to someone all night long. Still at it with Jimmy and Harry when I came down just now. But the hardest to take was that flannel-mouth, flatfoot Mick trying to tell me where I got off! I had to lock him out, too.

(As he says this, MCGLOIN *comes in the doorway from the hall. The change in his appearance and manner is identical with that of* MOSHER *and the others.)*

MCGLOIN: He's a liar, Rocky! It was me locked him out!

*(*MOSHER *starts to flare up—then ignores him. They turn their backs on each other.* MCGLOIN *starts into the back-room section.)*

WILLIE: Come and sit here, Mac. You're just the man I want to see. If I'm to take your case, we ought to have a talk before we leave.

MCGLOIN: *(contemptuously)* We'll have no talk. You damned fool, do you think I'd have your father's son for my lawyer? They'd take one look at you and bounce us both out on our necks! *(*WILLIE *winces and shrinks down in his chair.* MCGLOIN *goes to the first table beyond him and sits with his back to the bar)* I don't need a lawyer, anyway. To hell with the law! All I've got to do is see the right ones and get them to pass the word. They will, too. They know I was framed. And once they've passed the word, it's as good as done, law or no law.

MOSHER: God, I'm glad I'm leaving this madhouse! *(He pulls his key from his pocket and slaps it on the bar)* Here's my key, Rocky.

McGLOIN: *(pulls his from his pocket)* And here's mine. *(He tosses it to* ROCKY*)* I'd rather sleep in the gutter than pass another night under the same roof with that loon, Hickey, and a lying circus grifter! *(He adds darkly)* And if that hat fits anyone here, let him put it on!

(MOSHER turns toward him furiously but ROCKY leans over the bar and grabs his arm.)

ROCKY: Nix! Take it easy! *(MOSHER subsides. ROCKY tosses the keys on the shelf—disgustedly)* You boids gimme a pain. It'd soive you right if I wouldn't give de keys back to yuh tonight.

(They both turn on him resentfully, but there is an interruption as CORA *appears in the doorway from the hall with* CHUCK *behind her. She is drunk, dressed in her gaudy best, her face plastered with rouge and mascara, her hair a bit disheveled, her hat on anyhow.)*

CORA: *(comes a few steps inside the bar—with a strained bright giggle)* Hello, everybody! Here we go! Hickey just told us, ain't it time we beat it, if we're really goin'. So we're showin' de bastard, ain't we, Honey? He's comin' right down wid Harry and Jimmy. Jees, dem two look like dey was goin' to de electric chair! *(With frightened anger)* If I had to listen to any more of Hickey's bunk, I'd brain him. *(She puts her hand on* CHUCK'S *arm)* Come on, Honey. Let's get started before he comes down.

CHUCK: *(sullenly)* Sure, anyting yuh say, Baby.

CORA: *(turns on him truculently)* Yeah? Well, I say we stop at de foist reg'lar dump and yuh gotta blow me to a sherry flip—or four or five, if I want 'em!—or all bets is off!

CHUCK: Aw, yuh got a fine bun on now!

CORA: Cheap skate! I know what's eatin' you, Tightwad! Well, use my dough, den, if yuh're so stingy. Yuh'll grab it all, anyway, right after de ceremony. I know you! *(She hikes her skirt up and reaches inside the top of her stocking)* Here, yuh big tramp!

CHUCK: *(knocks her hand away—angrily)* Keep your lousy dough! And don't show off your legs to dese bums when yuh're goin' to be married, if yuh don't want a sock in de puss!

CORA: *(pleased—meekly)* Aw right, Honey. *(Looking around with a foolish laugh)* Say, why don't all you barflies come to de weddin'? *(But they are all sunk in their own apprehensions and ignore her. She hesitates, miserably uncertain)* Well, we're goin', guys. *(There is no comment. Her eyes fasten on* ROCKY*—desperately)* Say, Rocky, yuh gone deaf? I said me and Chuck was goin' now.

ROCKY: *(wiping the bar—with elaborate indifference)* Well, good-bye. Give my love to Joisey.

CORA: *(tearfully indignant)* Ain't yuh goin' to wish us happiness, yuh doity little Ginny?

ROCKY: Sure. Here's hopin' yuh don't moider each odder before next week.

CHUCK: *(angrily)* Aw, Baby, what d'we care for dat pimp? *(ROCKY turns on him threateningly, but* CHUCK *hears someone upstairs in the hall and grabs* CORA'S *arm)* Here's Hickey comin'! Let's get outa here!

(They hurry into the hall. The street door is heard slamming behind them.)

ROCKY: *(gloomily pronounces an obituary)* One regular guy and one all-right tart gone to hell. *(Fiercely)* Dat louse Hickey oughta be croaked! *(There is a muttered growl of assent from most of the gathering. Then* HARRY HOPE *enters from the hall, followed by* JIMMY TOMORROW, *with* HICKEY *on his heels.* HOPE *and* JIMMY *are both putting up a front of self-assurance, but* CORA'S *description of them was apt. There is a desperate bluff in their manner as they walk in, which suggests the last march of the condemned.* HOPE *is dressed in an old black Sunday suit, black tie, shoes, socks, which give him the appearance of being in mourning.* JIMMY'S *clothes are pressed, his shoes shined, his white linen immaculate. He has a hangover and his gently appealing dog's eyes have a boiled look.* HICKEY'S *face is a bit drawn from lack of sleep and his voice is hoarse from continual talking, but his bustling energy appears nervously intensified, and his beaming expression is one of triumphant accomplishment.)*

HICKEY: Well, here we are! We've got this far, at least! *(He pats* JIMMY *on the back)* Good work, Jimmy. I told you you weren't half as sick as you pretended. No excuse whatever for postponing—

JIMMY: I'll thank you to keep your hands off me! I merely mentioned I would feel more fit tomorrow. But it might as well be today, I suppose.

HICKEY: Finish it now, so it'll be dead forever, and you can be free! *(He passes him to clap* HOPE *encouragingly on the shoulder)* Cheer up, Harry. You found your rheumatism didn't bother you coming downstairs, didn't you? I told you it wouldn't. *(He winks around at the others. With the exception of* HUGO *and* PARRITT, *all their eyes are fixed on him with bitter animosity. He gives* HOPE *a playful nudge in the ribs)* You're the damnedest one for alibis, Governor! As bad as Jimmy!

HOPE: *(putting on his deaf manner)* Eh? I can't hear—*(Defiantly)* You're a liar! I've had rheumatism on and off for twenty years. Ever since Bessie died. Everybody knows that.

HICKEY: Yes, we know it's the kind of rheumatism you turn on and off! We're on to you, you old faker!

(He claps him on the shoulder again, chuckling.)

HOPE: *(looks humiliated and guilty—by way of escape he glares around at the others)* Bejees, what are all you bums hanging round staring at me for? Think you was watching a circus! Why don't you get the hell out of here and 'tend to your own business, like Hickey's told you? *(They look at him reproachfully, their eyes hurt. They fidget as if trying to move.)*

HICKEY: Yes, Harry, I certainly thought they'd have had the guts to be gone by this time. *(He grins)* Or maybe I did have my doubts. *(Abruptly he becomes sincerely sympathetic and earnest)* Because I know exactly what you're up

against, boys. I know how damned yellow a man can be when it comes to making himself face the truth. I've been through the mill, and I had to face a worse bastard in myself than any of you will have to in yourselves. I know you become such a coward you'll grab at any lousy excuse to get out of killing your pipe dreams. And yet, as I've told you over and over, it's exactly those damned tomorrow dreams which keep you from making peace with yourself. So you've got to kill them like I did mine. *(He pauses. They glare at him with fear and hatred. They seem about to curse him, to spring at him. But they remain silent and motionless. His manner changes and he becomes kindly bullying)* Come on, boys! Get moving! Who'll start the ball rolling? You, Captain, and you, General. You're nearest the door. And besides, you're old war heroes! You ought to lead the forlorn hope! Come on, now, show us a little of that good old battle of Modder River spirit we've heard so much about! You can't hang around all day looking as if you were scared the street outside would bite you!

LEWIS: *(turns with humiliated rage—with an attempt at jaunty casualness)* Right you are, Mister Bloody Nosey Parker! Time I pushed off. Was only waiting to say good-bye to you, Harry, old chum.

HOPE: *(dejectedly)* Good-bye, Captain. Hope you have luck.

LEWIS: Oh, I'm bound to, Old Chap, and the same to you. *(He pushes the swinging doors open and makes a brave exit, turning to his right and marching off outside the window at right of door.)*

WETJOEN: Py Gott, if dot Limey can, I can! *(He pushes the door open and lumbers through it like a bull charging an obstacle. He turns left and disappears off rear, outside the farthest window.)*

HICKEY: *(exhortingly)* Next? Come on, Ed. It's a fine summer's day and the call of the old circus lot must be in your blood!

(MOSHER *glares at him, then goes to the door.* McGLOIN *jumps up from his chair and starts moving toward the door.* HICKEY *claps him on the back as he passes)* That's the stuff, Mac.

MOSHER: Good-bye, Harry.

(He goes out, turning right outside.)

McGLOIN: *(glowering after him)* If that crooked grafter has the guts—

(He goes out, turning left outside. HICKEY *glances at* WILLIE *who, before he can speak, jumps from his chair.)*

WILLIE: Good-bye, Harry, and thanks for all your kindness.

HICKEY: *(claps him on the back)* That's the way, Willie! The D.A.'s a busy man. He can't wait all day for you, you know.

*(*WILLIE *hurries to the door.)*

HOPE: *(dully)* Good luck, Willie.

*(*WILLIE *goes out and turns right outside. While he is doing so,* JIMMY, *in a sick panic, sneaks to the bar and furtively reaches for* LARRY'S *glass of whiskey.)*

HICKEY: And now it's your turn, Jimmy, old pal. *(He sees what* JIMMY *is at and grabs his arm just as he is about to down the drink)* Now, now, Jimmy! You can't do that to yourself. One drink on top of your hangover and an empty stomach and you'll be oreyeyed. Then you'll tell yourself you wouldn't stand a chance if you went up soused to get your old job back.

JIMMY: *(pleads abjectly)* Tomorrow! I will tomorrow! I'll be in good shape tomorrow! *(Abruptly getting control of himself—with shaken firmness)* All right. I'm going. Take your hands off me.

HICKEY: That's the ticket! You'll thank me when it's all over.

JIMMY: *(in a burst of futile fury)* You dirty swine! *(He tries to throw the drink in* HICKEY'S *face, but his aim is poor and it lands on* HICKEY'S *coat.* JIMMY *turns and dashes through the door, disappearing outside the window at right of door.)*

HICKEY: *(brushing the whiskey off his coat— humorously)* All set for an alcohol rub! But

no hard feelings. I know how he feels. I wrote the book. I've seen the day when if anyone forced me to face the truth about my pipe dreams, I'd have shot them dead. *(He turns to* HOPE—*encouragingly)* Well, Governor, Jimmy made the grade. It's up to you. If he's got the guts to go through with the test, then certainly you—

LARRY: *(bursts out)* Leave Harry alone, damn you!

HICKEY: *(grins at him)* I'd make up my mind about myself if I was you, Larry, and not bother over Harry. He'll come through all right. I've promised him that. He doesn't need anyone's bum pity. Do you, Governor?

HOPE: *(with a pathetic attempt at his old fuming assertiveness)* No, bejees! Keep your nose out of this, Larry. What's Hickey got to do with it? I've always been going to take this walk, ain't I? Bejees, you bums want to keep me locked up in here 's if I was in jail! I've stood it long enough! I'm free, white and twenty-one, and I'll do as I damned please, bejees! You keep your nose out, too, Hickey! You'd think you was boss of this dump, not me. Sure, I'm all right! Why shouldn't I be? What the hell's to be scared of, just taking a stroll around my own ward? *(As he talks he has been moving toward the door. Now he reaches it)* What's the weather like outside, Rocky?

ROCKY: Fine day, Boss.

HOPE: What's that? Can't hear you. Don't look fine to me. Looks 's if it'd pour down cats and dogs any minute. My rheumatism— *(He catches himself)* No, must be my eyes. Half blind, bejees. Makes things look black. I see now it's a fine day. Too damned hot for a walk, though, if you ask me. Well, do me good to sweat the booze out of me. But I'll have to watch out for the damned automobiles. Wasn't one of them around the last time, twenty years ago. From what I've seen of 'em through the window, they'd run over you as soon as look at you. Not that I'm scared of 'em. I can take care of myself. *(He puts a reluctant hand on the swinging door)* Well, so long— *(He stops and looks* back—*with frightened irascibility)* Bejees, where are you, Hickey? It's time we got started.

HICKEY: *(grins and shakes his head)* No, Harry. Can't be done. You've got to keep a date with yourself alone.

HOPE: *(with forced fuming)* Hell of a guy, you are! Thought you'd be willing to help me across the street, knowing I'm half blind. Half deaf, too. Can't bear those damned automobiles. Hell with you! Bejees, I've never needed no one's help and I don't now! *(Egging himself on)* I'll take a good long walk now I've started. See all my old friends. Bejees, they must have given me up for dead. Twenty years is a long time. But they know it was grief over Bessie's death that made me— *(He puts his hand on the door)* Well, the sooner I get started— *(Then he drops his hand—with sentimental melancholy)* You know, Hickey, that's what gets me. Can't help thinking the last time I went out was to Bessie's funeral. After she'd gone, I didn't feel life was worth living. Swore I'd never go out again. *(Pathetically)* Somehow, I can't feel it's right for me to go, Hickey, even now. It's like I was doing wrong to her memory.

HICKEY: Now, Governor, you can't let yourself get away with that one any more!

HOPE: *(cupping his hand to his ear)* What's that? Can't hear you. *(Sentimentally again but with desperation)* I remember now clear as day the last time before she—It was a fine Sunday morning. We went out to church together. *(His voice breaks on a sob.)*

HICKEY: *(amused)* It's a great act, Governor. But I know better, and so do you. You never did want to go to church or any place else with her. She was always on your neck, making you have ambition and go out and do things, when all you wanted was to get drunk in peace.

HOPE: *(falteringly)* Can't hear a word you're saying. You're a Goddamned liar, anyway! *(Then in a sudden fury, his voice trembling with hatred)* Bejees, you son of a bitch, if there was a mad dog outside I'd go and shake hands with it rather than stay here with you!

(The momentum of his fit of rage does it. He pushes the door open and strides blindly out into the street and as blindly past the window behind the free-lunch counter.)

ROCKY: *(in amazement)* Jees, he made it! I'd a give yuh fifty to one he'd never— *(He goes to the end of the bar to look through the window—disgustedly)* Aw, he's stopped. I'll bet yuh he's comin' back.

HICKEY: Of course, he's coming back. So are all the others. By tonight they'll all be here again. You dumbell, that's the whole point.

ROCKY: *(excitedly)* No, he ain't neider! He's gone to de coib. He's lookin' up and down. Scared stiff of automobiles. Jees, dey ain't more'n two an hour comes down dis street, de old boob! *(He watches excitedly, as if it were a race he had a bet on, oblivious to what happens in the bar.)*

LARRY: *(turns on HICKEY with bitter defiance)* And now it's my turn, I suppose? What is it I'm to do to achieve this blessed peace of yours?

HICKEY: *(grins at him)* Why, we've discussed all that, Larry. Just stop lying to yourself—

LARRY: You think when I say I'm finished with life, and tired of watching the stupid greed of the human circus, and I'll welcome closing my eyes in the long sleep of death—you think that's a coward's lie?

HICKEY: *(chuckling)* Well, what do you think, Larry?

LARRY: *(with increasing bitter intensity, more as if he were fighting with himself than with HICKEY)* I'm afraid to live, am I?—and even more afraid to die! So I sit here, with my pride drowned on the bottom of a bottle, keeping drunk so I won't see myself shaking in my britches with fright, or hear myself whining and praying: Beloved Christ, let me live a little longer at any price! If it's only for a few days more, or a few hours even, have mercy, Almighty God, and let me still clutch greedily to my yellow heart this sweet treasure, this jewel beyond price, the dirty, stinking bit of withered old flesh which is my beautiful little life! *(He laughs with a sneering, vindictive self-loathing, staring inward at himself with contempt and hatred. Then abruptly he makes* HICKEY *again the antagonist)* You think you'll make me admit that to myself?

HICKEY: *(chuckling)* But you just did admit it, didn't you?

PARRITT: *(lifts his head from his hands to glare at* LARRY—*jeeringly)* That's the stuff, Hickey! Show the old yellow faker up! He can't play dead on me like this! He's got to help me!

HICKEY: Yes, Larry, you've got to settle with him. I'm leaving you entirely in his hands. He'll do as good a job as I could at making you give up that old grandstand bluff.

LARRY: *(angrily)* I'll see the two of you in hell first!

ROCKY: *(calls excitedly from the end of the bar)* Jees, Harry's startin' across de street! He's goin' to fool yuh, Hickey, yuh bastard! *(He pauses, watching—then worriedly)* What de hell's he stoppin' for? Right in de middle of de street! Yuh'd tink he was paralyzed or somethin'! *(Disgustedly)* Aw, he's quittin'! He's turned back! Jees, look at de old bastard travel! Here he comes!

*(*HOPE *passes the window outside the free-lunch counter in a shambling, panic-stricken run. He comes lurching blindly through the swinging doors and stumbles to the bar at* LARRY'S *right.)*

HOPE: Bejees, give me a drink quick! Scared me out of a year's growth! Bejees, that guy ought to be pinched! Bejees, it ain't safe to walk in the streets! Bejees, that ends me! Never again! Give me that bottle! *(He slops a glass full and drains it and pours another— To* ROCKY, *who is regarding him with scorn—appealingly)* You seen it, didn't you, Rocky?

ROCKY: Seen what?

HOPE: That automobile, you dumb Wop! Feller driving it must be drunk or crazy. He'd run right over me if I hadn't jumped. *(Ingratiatingly)* Come on, Larry, have a drink. Everybody have a drink. Have a cigar, Rocky. I know you hardly ever touch it.

ROCKY: *(resentfully)* Well, dis is de time I do touch it! *(Pouring a drink)* I'm goin' to get

stinko, see! And if yuh don't like it, yuh know what yuh can do! I gotta good mind to chuck my job, anyways. *(Disgustedly)* Jees, Harry, I thought yuh had some guts! I was bettin' yuh'd make it and show dat four-flusher up! *(He nods at* HICKEY—*then snorts)* Automobile, hell! Who d'yuh tink yuh're kiddin'? Dey wasn' no automobile! Yuh just quit cold!

HOPE: *(feebly)* Guess I ought to know! Bejees, it almost killed me!

HICKEY: *(comes to the bar between him and* LARRY, *and puts a hand on his shoulder—kindly)* Now, now, Governor. Don't be foolish. You've faced the test and come through. You're rid of all that nagging dream stuff now. You know you can't believe it any more.

HOPE: *(appeals pleadingly to* LARRY) Larry, you saw it, didn't you? Drink up! Have another! Have all you want! Bejees, we'll go on a grand old souse together! You saw that automobile, didn't you?

LARRY: *(compassionately, avoiding his eyes)* Sure, I saw it, Harry. You had a narrow escape. Be God, I thought you were a goner!

HICKEY: *(turns on him with a flash of sincere indignation)* What the hell's the matter with you, Larry? You know what I told you about the wrong kind of pity. Leave Harry alone! You'd think I was trying to harm him, the fool way you act! My oldest friend! What kind of a louse do you think I am? There isn't anything I wouldn't do for Harry, and he knows it! All I've wanted to do is fix it so he'll be finally at peace with himself for the rest of his days! And if you'll only wait until the final returns are in, you'll find that's exactly what I've accomplished! *(He turns to* HOPE *and pats his shoulder—coaxingly)* Come now, Governor, What's the use of being stubborn, now when it's all over and dead? Give up that ghost automobile.

HOPE: *(beginning to collapse within himself— dully)* Yes, what's the use—now? All a lie! No automobile. But, bejees, something ran over me! Must have been myself, I guess. *(He forces a feeble smile—then wearily)* Guess I'll sit down. Feel all in. Like a corpse, bejees. *(He*

picks a bottle and glass from the bar and walks to the first table and slumps down in the chair, facing left-front. His shaking hand misjudges the distance and he sets the bottle on the table with a jar that rouses HUGO, *who lifts his head from his arms and blinks at him through his thick spectacles.* HOPE *speaks to him in a flat, dead voice)* Hello, Hugo. Coming up for air? Stay passed out, that's the right dope. There ain't any cool willow trees—except you grow your own in a bottle.
(He pours a drink and gulps it down.)

HUGO: *(with his silly giggle)* Hello, Harry, stupid proletarian monkey-face! I vill trink champagne beneath the villow— *(With a change to aristocratic fastidiousness)* But the slaves must ice it properly! *(With guttural rage)* Gottamned Hickey! Peddler pimp for nouveau-riche capitalism! Ven I lead the jackass mob to the sack of Babylon, I vill make them hang him to a lamppost the first one!

HOPE: *(spiritlessly)* Good work. I'll help pull on the rope. Have a drink, Hugo.

HUGO: *(frightenedly)* No, thank you. I am too trunk now. I hear myself say crazy things. Do not listen, please. Larry vill tell you I haf never been so crazy trunk. I must sleep it off. *(He starts to put his head on his arms but stops and stares at* HOPE *with growing uneasiness)* Vhat's matter, Harry? You look funny. You look dead. Vhat's happened? I don't know you. Listen, I feel I am dying, too. Because I am so crazy trunk! It is very necessary I sleep. But I can't sleep here vith you. You look dead.
(He scrambles to his feet in a confused panic, turns his back on HOPE *and settles into the chair at the next table which faces left. He thrusts his head down on his arms like an ostrich hiding its head in the sand. He does not notice* PARRITT, *nor* PARRITT *him.)*

LARRY: *(to* HICKEY *with bitter condemnation)* Another one who's begun to enjoy your peace!

HICKEY: Oh, I know it's tough on him right now, the same as it is on Harry. But that's only the first shock. I promise you they'll both come through all right.

LARRY: And you believe that! I see you do! You mad fool!

HICKEY: Of course, I believe it! I tell you I know from my own experience!

HOPE: *(spiritlessly)* Close that big clam of yours, Hickey. Bejees, you're a worse gabber than that nagging bitch, Bessie, was.
(He drinks his drink mechanically and pours another.)

ROCKY: *(in amazement)* Jees, did yuh hear dat?

HOPE: *(dully)* What's wrong with this booze? There's no kick in it.

ROCKY: *(worriedly)* Jees, Larry, Hugo had it right. He does look like he'd croaked.

HICKEY: *(annoyed)* Don't be a damned fool! Give him time. He's coming along all right. *(He calls to* HOPE *with a first trace of underlying uneasiness)* You're all right, aren't you, Harry?

HOPE: *(dully)* I want to pass out like Hugo.

LARRY: *(turns to* HICKEY—*with bitter anger)* It's the peace of death you've brought him.

HICKEY: *(for the first time loses his temper)* That's a lie! *(But he controls this instantly and grins)* Well, well, you did manage to get a rise out of me that time. I think such a hell of a lot of Harry— *(Impatiently)* You know that's damned foolishness. Look at me. I've been through it. Do I look dead? Just leave Harry alone and wait until the shock wears off and you'll see. He'll be a new man. Like I am. *(He calls to* HOPE *coaxingly)* How's it coming, Governor? Beginning to feel free, aren't you? Relieved and not guilty any more?

HOPE: *(grumbles spiritlessly)* Bejees, you must have been monkeying with the booze, too, you interfering bastard! There's no life in it now. I want to get drunk and pass out. Let's all pass out. Who the hell cares?

HICKEY: *(lowering his voice—worriedly to* LARRY) I admit I didn't think he'd be hit so hard. He's always been a happy-go-lucky slob. Like I was. Of course, it hit me hard, too. But only for a minute. Then I felt as if a ton of guilt had been lifted off my mind. I saw what had happened was the only possible way for the peace of all concerned.

LARRY: (sharply) What was it happened? Tell us that! And don't try to get out of it! I want a straight answer! (Vindictively) I think it was something you drove someone else to do!

HICKEY: (puzzled) Someone else?

LARRY: (accusingly) What did your wife die of? You've kept that a deep secret, I notice—for some reason!

HICKEY: (reproachfully) You're not very considerate, Larry. But, if you insist on knowing now, there's no reason you shouldn't. It was a bullet through the head that killed Evelyn.

(There is a second's tense silence.)

HOPE: (dully) Who the hell cares? To hell with her and that nagging old hag, Bessie.

ROCKY: Christ. You had de right dope, Larry.

LARRY: (revengefully) You drove your poor wife to suicide? I knew it! Be God, I don't blame her! I'd almost do as much myself to be rid of you! It's what you'd like to drive us all to— (Abruptly he is ashamed of himself and pitying) I'm sorry, Hickey. I'm a rotten louse to throw that in your face.

HICKEY: (quietly) Oh, that's all right, Larry. But don't jump at conclusions. I didn't say poor Evelyn committed suicide. It's the last thing she'd ever have done, as long as I was alive for her to take care of and forgive. If you'd known her at all, you'd never get such a crazy suspicion. (He pauses—then slowly) No, I'm sorry to have to tell you my poor wife was killed.

(LARRY stares at him with growing horror and shrinks back along the bar away from him. PARRITT jerks his head up from his hands and looks around frightenedly, not at HICKEY, but at LARRY. ROCKY'S round eyes are popping. HOPE stares dully at the table top. HUGO, his head hidden in his arms, gives no sign of life.)

LARRY: (shakenly) Then she—was murdered.

PARRITT: (springs to his feet—stammers defensively) You're a liar, Larry! You must be crazy to say that to me! You know she's still alive! (But no one pays any attention to him.)

ROCKY: (blurts out) Moidered? Who done it?

LARRY: (his eyes fixed with fascinated horror on HICKEY—frightenedly) Don't ask questions, you dumb Wop! It's none of our damned business! Leave Hickey alone!

HICKEY: (smiles at him with affectionate amusement) Still the old grandstand bluff, Larry? Or is it some more bum pity? (He turns to ROCKY—matter-of-factly) The police don't know who killed her yet, Rocky. But I expect they will before very long. (As if that finished the subject, he comes forward to HOPE and sits beside him, with an arm around his shoulder—affectionately coaxing) Coming along fine now, aren't you, Governor? Getting over the first shock? Beginning to feel free from guilt and lying hopes and at peace with yourself?

HOPE: (with a dull callousness) Somebody croaked your Evelyn, eh? Bejees, my bets are on the iceman! But who the hell cares? Let's get drunk and pass out. (He tosses down his drink with a lifeless, automatic movement—complainingly) Bejees, what did you do to the booze, Hickey? There's no damned life left in it.

PARRITT: (stammers, his eyes on LARRY, whose eyes in turn remain fixed on HICKEY) Don't look like that, Larry! You've got to believe what I told you! It had nothing to do with her! It was just to get a few lousy dollars!

HUGO: (suddenly raises his head from his arms and, looking straight in front of him, pounds on the table frightenedly with his small fists) Don't be a fool! Buy me a trink! But no more vine! It is not properly iced! (With guttural rage) Gottamned stupid proletarian slaves! Buy me a trink or I vill have you shot! (He collapses into abject begging) Please, for Gott's sake! I am not trunk enough! I cannot sleep! Life is a crazy monkey-face! Always there is blood beneath the villow trees! I hate it and I am afraid! (He hides his face on his arms, sobbing muffledly) Please, I am crazy trunk! I say crazy things! For Gott's sake, do not listen to me!

(But no one pays any attention to him. LARRY stands shrunk back against the bar. ROCKY is

leaning over it. They stare at HICKEY. PARRITT
stands looking pleadingly at LARRY.)

HICKEY: *(gazes with worried kindliness at* HOPE*)*
You're beginning to worry me, Governor. Something's holding you up somewhere. I don't see
why—You've faced the truth about yourself.
You've done what you had to do to kill your nagging pipe dreams. Oh, I know it knocks you
cold. But only for a minute. Then you see it was
the only possible way to peace. And you feel
happy. Like I did. That's what worries me about
you, Governor. It's time you began to feel
happy—

C U R T A I N

A C T   F O U R

SCENE: *Same as Act One—the back room with the
curtain separating it from the section of the barroom with its single table at right of curtain, front.
It is around half past one in the morning of the following day.*

*The tables in the back room have a new ar-
rangement. The one at left, front, before the window
to the yard, is in the same position. So is the one at
the right, rear, of it in the second row. But this table
now has only one chair. This chair is at right of it,
facing directly front. The two tables on either side of
the door at rear are unchanged. But the table which
was at center, front, has been pushed toward right
so that it and the table at right, rear, of it in the second row, and the last table at right in the front row,
are now jammed so closely together that they form
one group.*

*LARRY, HUGO and PARRITT are at the table at left,
front. LARRY is at left of it, beside the window, facing
front. HUGO sits at rear, facing front, his head on his
arms in his habitual position, but he is not asleep. On
HUGO's left is PARRITT, his chair facing left, front. At
right of table, an empty chair, facing left. LARRY's
chin is on his chest, his eyes fixed on the floor. He will*

not look at PARRITT, *who keeps staring at him with a
sneering, pleading challenge.*

*Two bottles of whiskey are on each table,
whiskey and chaser glasses, a pitcher of water.*

*The one chair by the table at right, rear, of them
is vacant.*

At the first table at right of center, CORA *sits at
left, front, of it, facing front. Around the rear of this
table are four empty chairs. Opposite* CORA, *in a sixth
chair, is* CAPTAIN LEWIS, *also facing front. On his left,*
MCGLOIN *is facing front in a chair before the middle
table of his group. At right, rear, of him, also at this
table,* GENERAL WETJOEN *sits facing front. In back of
this table are three empty chairs.*

At right, rear, of WETJOEN, *but beside the last
table of the group, sits* WILLIE. *On* WILLIE's *left, at
rear of table, is* HOPE. *On* HOPE's *left, at right, rear, of
table, is* MOSHER. *Finally, at right of table is* JIMMY
TOMORROW. *All of the four sit facing front.*

*There is an atmosphere of oppressive stagnation
in the room, and a quality of insensibility about all
the people in this group at right. They are like wax
figures, set stiffly on their chairs, carrying out mechanically the motions of getting drunk but sunk in
a numb stupor which is impervious to stimulation.*

In the bar section, JOE *is sprawled in the chair
at right of table, facing left. His head rolls forward
in a sodden slumber.* ROCKY *is standing behind his
chair, regarding him with dull hostility.* ROCKY's
*face is set in an expression of tired, callous tough-
ness. He looks now like a minor Wop gangster.*

ROCKY: *(shakes* JOE *by the shoulder)* Come on,
yuh damned nigger! Beat it in de back room!
It's after hours. *(But* JOE *remains inert.* ROCKY
gives up) Aw, to hell wid it. Let de dump get
pinched. I'm through wid dis lousy job, anyway! *(He hears someone at rear and calls)*
Who's dat? *(*CHUCK *appears from rear. He has
been drinking heavily, but there is no lift to his
jag; his manner is grouchy and sullen. He has
evidently been brawling. His knuckles are raw
and there is a mouse under one eye. He has lost
his straw hat, his tie is awry, and his blue suit is
dirty.* ROCKY *eyes him indifferently)* Been

scrappin', huh? Started off on your periodical, ain't yuh?

(For a second there is a gleam of satisfaction in his eyes.)

CHUCK: Yeah, ain't yuh glad? *(Truculently)* What's it to yuh?

ROCKY: Not a damn ting. But dis is someting to me. I'm out on my feet holdin' down your job. Yuh said if I'd take your day, yuh'd relieve me at six, and here it's half past one A.M. Well, yuh're takin' over now, get me, no matter how plastered yuh are!

CHUCK: Plastered, hell! I wisht I was. I've lapped up a gallon, but it don't hit me right. And to hell wid de job. I'm goin' to tell Harry I'm quittin'.

ROCKY: Yeah? Well, I'm quittin', too.

CHUCK: I've played sucker for dat crummy blonde long enough, lettin' her kid me into woikin'. From now on I take it easy.

ROCKY: I'm glad yuh're gettin' some sense.

CHUCK: And I hope yuh're gettin' some. What a prize sap you been, tendin' bar when yuh got two good hustlers in your stable!

ROCKY: Yeah, but I ain't no sap now. I'll loin dem, when dey get back from Coney. *(Sneeringly)* Jees, dat Cora sure played you for a dope, feedin' yuh dat marriage-on-de-farm hop!

CHUCK: *(dully)* Yeah. Hickey got it right. A lousy pipe dream. It was her pulling sherry flips on me woke me up. All de way walkin' to de ferry, every ginmill we come to she'd drag me in to blow her. I got tinkin', Christ, what won't she want when she gets de ring on her finger and I'm hooked? So I tells her at de ferry, "Kiddo, yuh can go to Joisey, or to hell, but count me out."

ROCKY: She says it was her told you to go to hell, because yuh'd started hittin' de booze.

CHUCK: *(ignoring this)* I got tinkin', too, Jees, won't I look sweet wid a wife dat if yuh put all de guys she's stayed wid side by side, dey'd reach to Chicago. *(He sighs gloomily)* Dat kind of dame, yuh can't trust 'em. De minute your back is toined, dey're cheatin' wid de iceman or some-one. Hickey done me a favor, makin' me wake up. *(He pauses—then adds pathetically)* On'y it

was fun, kinda, me and Cora kiddin' ourselves— *(Suddenly his face hardens with hatred)* Where is dat son of a bitch, Hickey? I want one good sock at dat guy—just one!—and de next buttin' in he'll do will be in de morgue! I'll take a chance on goin' to de Chair—!

ROCKY: *(starts—in a low warning voice)* Piano! Keep away from him, Chuck! He ain't here now, anyway. He went out to phone, he said. He wouldn't call from here. I got a hunch he's beat it. But if he does come back, yuh don't know him, if anyone asks yuh, get me? *(As CHUCK looks at him with dull surprise he lowers his voice to a whisper)* De Chair, maybe dat's where he's goin'. I don't know nuttin', see, but it looks like he croaked his wife.

CHUCK: *(with a flash of interest)* Yuh mean she really was cheatin' on him? Den I don't blame de guy—

ROCKY: Who's blamin' him? When a dame asks for it— But I don't know nuttin' about it, see?

CHUCK: Is any of de gang wise?

ROCKY: Larry is. And de boss ought to be. I tried to wise de rest of dem up to stay clear of him, but dey're all so licked, I don't know if dey got it. *(He pauses—vindictively)* I don't give a damn what he done to his wife, but if he gets de Hot Seat I won't go into no mournin'!

CHUCK: Me, neider!

ROCKY: Not after his trowin' it in my face I'm a pimp. What if I am? Why de hell not? And what he's done to Harry. Jees, de poor old slob is so licked he can't even get drunk. And all de gang. Dey're all licked. I couldn't help feelin' sorry for de poor bums when dey showed up tonight, one by one, lookin' like pooches wid deir tails between deir legs, dat everyone'd been kickin' till dey was too punch-drunk to feel it no more. Jimmy Tomorrow was de last. Schwartz, de copper, brung him in. Seen him sittin' on de dock on West Street, lookin' at de water and cryin'! Schwartz thought he was drunk and I let him tink it. But he was cold sober. He was tryin' to jump in and didn't have de noive, I figgered it. Noive! Jees, dere ain't enough guts left in de whole gang to battle a mosquito!

CHUCK: Aw, to hell wid 'em! Who cares? Gimme a drink. (ROCKY *pushes the bottle toward him apathetically*) I see you been hittin' de redeye, too.

ROCKY: Yeah. But it don't do no good. I can't get drunk right. (CHUCK *drinks.* JOE *mumbles in his sleep.* CHUCK *regards him resentfully*) Dis doity dinge was able to get his snootful and pass out. Jees, even Hickey can't faze a nigger! Yuh'd tink he was fazed if yuh'd seen him come in. Stinko, and he pulled a gat and said he'd plug Hickey for insultin' him. Den he dropped it and begun to cry and said he wasn't a gamblin' man or a tough guy no more; he was yellow. He'd borrowed de gat to stick up someone, and den didn't have de guts. He got drunk panhandlin' drinks in nigger joints, I s'pose. I guess dey felt sorry for him.

CHUCK: He ain't got no business in de bar after hours. Why don't yuh chuck him out?

ROCKY: (*apathetically*) Aw, to hell wid it. Who cares?

CHUCK: (*lapsing into the same mood*) Yeah. I don't.

JOE: (*suddenly lunges to his feet dazedly—mumbles in humbled apology*) Scuse me, White Boys. Scuse me for livin'. I don't want to be where I's not wanted.

(*He makes his way swayingly to the opening in the curtain at rear and tacks down to the middle table of the three at right, front. He feels his way around it to the table at its left and gets to the chair in back of* CAPTAIN LEWIS.)

CHUCK: (*Gets up—in a callous, brutal tone*) My pig's in de back room, ain't she? I wanna collect de dough I wouldn't take dis mornin', like a sucker, before she blows it.

(*He goes rear.*)

ROCKY: (*getting up*) I'm comin', too. I'm trough woikin'. I ain't no lousy bartender.

(*CHUCK comes through the curtain and looks for* CORA *as* JOE *flops down in the chair in back of* CAPTAIN LEWIS.)

JOE: (*taps* LEWIS *on the shoulder—servilely apologetic*) If you objects to my sittin' here, Captain, just tell me and I pulls my freight.

LEWIS: No apology required, old chap. Anybody could tell you I should feel honored a bloody Kaffir would lower himself to sit beside me. (JOE *stares at him with sodden perplexity—then closes his eyes.* CHUCK *comes forward to take the chair behind* CORA'S, *as* ROCKY *enters the back room and starts over toward* LARRY'S *table.*)

CHUCK: (*his voice hard*) I'm waitin', Baby. Dig!

CORA: (*with apathetic obedience*) Sure. I been expectin' yuh. I got it all ready. Here. (*She passes a small roll of bills she has in her hand over her shoulder, without looking at him. He takes it, glances at it suspiciously, then shoves it in his pocket without a word of acknowledgment.* CORA *speaks with a tired wonder at herself rather than resentment toward him*) Jees, imagine me kiddin' myself I wanted to marry a drunken pimp.

CHUCK: Dat's nuttin', Baby. Imagine de sap I'da been, when I can get your dough just as easy widout it!

ROCKY: (*takes the chair on* PARRITT'S *left, facing* LARRY—*dully*) Hello, Old Cemetery. (LARRY *doesn't seem to hear. To* PARRITT) Hello, Tightwad. You still around?

PARRITT: (*keeps his eyes on* LARRY—*in a jeeringly challenging tone*) Ask Larry! He knows I'm here, all right, although he's pretending not to! He'd like to forget I'm alive! He's trying to kid himself with that grandstand philosopher stuff! But he knows he can't get away with it now! He kept himself locked in his room until a while ago, alone with a bottle of booze, but he couldn't make it work! He couldn't even get drunk! He had to come out! There must have been something there he was even more scared to face than he is Hickey and me! I guess he got looking at the fire escape and thinking how handy it was, if he was really sick of life and only had the nerve to die! (*He pauses sneeringly.* LARRY'S *face has tautened, but he pretends he doesn't hear.* ROCKY *pays no attention. His head has sunk forward, and he stares at the table top, sunk in the same stupor as the other occupants of the room.* PARRITT *goes on, his tone becoming more insistent)* He's been thinking of me, too, Rocky. Trying to figure a way to get out of helping me! He doesn't want to be bothered understanding. But he does understand all right! He used to love her, too. So he thinks I ought to take a hop off the fire escape! *(He pauses,* LARRY'S *hands on the table have clenched into fists, as his nails dig into his palms, but he remains silent.* PARRITT *breaks and starts pleading)* For God's sake, Larry, can't you say something? Hickey's got me all balled up. Thinking of what he must have done has got me so I don't know any more what I did or why. I can't go on like this! I've got to know what I ought to do—

LARRY: *(in a stifled tone)* God damn you! Are you trying to make me your executioner?

PARRITT: *(starts frightenedly)* Execution? Then you do think—?

LARRY: I don't think anything!

PARRITT: *(with forced jeering)* I suppose you think I ought to die because I sold out a lot of loud-mouthed fakers, who were cheating suckers with a phony pipe dream, and put them where they ought to be, in jail? *(He forces a laugh)* Don't make me laugh! I ought to get a medal! What a damned old sap you are! You must still believe in the Movement! *(He nudges* ROCKY *with his elbow)* Hickey's right about him, isn't he, Rocky? An old no-good drunken tramp, as dumb as he is, ought to take a hop off the fire escape!

ROCKY: *(dully)* Sure. Why don't he? Or you? Or me? What de hell's de difference? Who cares? *(There is a faint stir from all the crowd, as if this sentiment struck a responsive chord in their numbed minds. They mumble almost in chorus as one voice, like sleepers talking out of a dully irritating dream, "The hell with it!" "Who cares?" Then the sodden silence descends again on the room.* ROCKY *looks from* PARRITT *to* LARRY *puzzledly. He mutters)* What am I doin' here wid youse two? I remember I had something on my mind to tell yuh. What—? Oh, I got it now.

(He looks from one to the other of their oblivious faces with a strange, sly, calculating look—ingratiatingly) I was tinking how you was bot' reg'lar guys. I tinks, ain't two guys like dem saps to be hangin' round like a coupla stew bums and wastin' demselves. Not dat I blame yuh for not woikin'. On'y suckers woik. But dere's no percentage in bein' broke when yuh can grab good jack for yourself and make someone else woik for yuh, is dere? I mean, like I do. So I tinks, Dey're my pals and I ought to wise up two good guys like dem to play my system, and not be lousy barflies, no good to demselves or nobody else. *(He addresses* PARRITT *now—persuasively)* What yuh tink, Parritt? Ain't I right? Sure, I am. So don't be a sucker, see? Yuh ain't a bad-lookin' guy. Yuh could easy make some gal who's a good hustler, an' start a stable. I'd help yuh and wise yuh up to de inside dope on de game. *(He pauses inquiringly.* PARRITT *gives no sign of having heard him.* ROCKY *asks impatiently)* Well, what about it? What if dey do call yuh a pimp? What de hell do you care—any more'n I do.

PARRITT: *(without looking at him—vindictively)* I'm through with whores. I wish they were all in jail—or dead!

ROCKY: *(ignores this—disappointedly)* So yuh won't touch it, huh? Aw right, stay a bum! *(He turns to* LARRY*)* Jees, Larry, he's sure one dumb boob, ain't he? Dead from de neck up! He don't know a good ting when he sees it. *(Oily, even persuasive again)* But how about you, Larry? You ain't dumb. So why not, huh? Sure, yuh're old, but dat don't matter. All de hustlers tink yuh're aces. Dey fall for yuh like yuh was deir uncle or old man or someting. Dey'd like takin' care of yuh. And de cops 'round here, dey like yuh, too. It'd be a pipe for yuh, 'specially wid me to help yuh and wise yuh up. Yuh wouldn't have to worry where de next drink's comin' from, or wear doity clothes. *(Hopefully)* Well, don't it look good to yuh?

LARRY: *(glances at him—for a moment he is stirred to sardonic pity)* No, it doesn't look good, Rocky. I mean, the peace Hickey's brought you. It isn't contented enough, if you have to make everyone else a pimp, too.

ROCKY: (*stares at him stupidly—then pushes his chair back and gets up, grumbling*) I'm a sap to waste time on yuh. A stew bum is a stew bum and yuh can't change him. (*He turns away—then turns back for an afterthought*) Like I was sayin' to Chuck, yuh better keep away from Hickey. If anyone asks yuh, yuh don't know nuttin', get me? Yuh never even hoid he had a wife. (*His face hardens*) Jees, we all ought to git drunk and stage a celebration when dat bastard goes to de Chair.

LARRY: (*vindictively*) Be God, I'll celebrate with you and drink long life to him in hell! (*Then guiltily and pityingly*) No! The poor mad devil— (*Then with angry self-contempt*) Ah, pity again! The wrong kind! He'll welcome the Chair!

PARRITT: (*contemptuously*) Yes, what are you so damned scared of death for? I don't want your lousy pity.

ROCKY: Christ, I hope he don't come back, Larry. We don't know nuttin' now. We're on'y guessin', see? But if de bastard keeps on talkin'—

LARRY: (*grimly*) He'll come back. He'll keep on talking. He's got to. He's lost his confidence that the peace he's sold us is the real McCoy, and it's made him uneasy about his own. He'll have to prove to us—

(*As he is speaking* HICKEY *appears silently in the doorway at rear. He has lost his beaming salesman's grin. His manner is no longer self-assured. His expression is uneasy, baffled and resentful. It has the stubborn set of an obsessed determination. His eyes are on* LARRY *as he comes in. As he speaks, there is a start from all the crowd, a shrinking away from him.*)

HICKEY: (*angrily*) That's a damned lie, Larry! I haven't lost confidence a damned bit! Why should I? (*Boastfully*) By God, whenever I made up my mind to sell someone something I knew they ought to want, I've sold 'em! (*He suddenly looks confused—haltingly*) I mean— It isn't kind of you, Larry, to make that kind of crack when I've been doing my best to help—

ROCKY: (*moving away from him toward right—sharply*) Keep away from me! I don't know nuttin' about yuh, see?

(*His tone is threatening but his manner as he turns his back and ducks quickly across to the bar entrance is that of one in flight. In the bar he comes forward and slumps in a chair at the table, facing front.*)

HICKEY: (*comes to the table at right, rear, of* LARRY'S *table and sits in the one chair there, facing front. He looks over the crowd at right, hopefully and then disappointedly. He speaks with a strained attempt at his old affectionate jollying manner*) Well, well! How are you coming along, everybody? Sorry I had to leave you for a while, but there was something I had to get finally settled. It's all fixed now.

HOPE: (*in the voice of one reiterating mechanically a hopeless complaint*) When are you going to do something about this booze, Hickey? Bejees, we all know you did something to take the life out of it. It's like drinking dishwater! We can't pass out! And you promised us peace.

(*His group all join in in a dull, complaining chorus, "We can't pass out! You promised us peace!"*)

HICKEY: (*bursts into resentful exasperation*) For God's sake, Harry, are you still harping on that damned nonsense! You've kept it up all afternoon and night! And you've got everybody else singing the same crazy tune! I've had about all I can stand—That's why I phoned—(*He controls himself*) Excuse me, boys and girls. I don't mean that. I'm just worried about you, when you play dead on me like this. I was hoping by the time I got back you'd be like you ought to be! I thought you were deliberately holding back, while I was around, because you didn't want to give me the satisfaction of showing me I'd had the right dope. And I did have! I know from my own experience. (*Exasperatedly*) But I've explained that a million times! And you've all done what you needed to do! By rights you should be contented now, without a single damned hope or lying dream left to torment you! But here you are, acting like a lot of stiffs cheating the undertaker! *(He looks around accusingly)* I can't figure it—unless it's just your damned pigheaded stubbornness! *(He breaks—miserably)* Hell, you oughtn't to act this way with me! You're my old pals, the only friends I've got. You know the one thing I want is to see you all happy before I go— *(Rousing himself to his old brisk, master-of-ceremonies manner)* And there's damned little time left now. I've made a date for two o'clock. We've got to get busy right away and find out what's wrong. *(There is a sodden silence. He goes on exasperatedly)* Can't you appreciate what you've got, for God's sake? Don't you know you're free now to be yourselves, without having to feel remorse or guilt, or lie to yourselves about reforming tomorrow? Can't you see there is no tomorrow now? You're rid of it forever! You've killed it! You don't have to care a damn about anything any more! You've finally got the game of life licked, don't you see that? *(Angrily exhorting)* Then why the hell don't you get pie-eyed and celebrate? Why don't you laugh and sing "Sweet Adeline"? *(With bitterly hurt accusation)* The only reason I can think of is, you're putting on this rotten half-dead act just to get back at me! Because you hate my guts! *(He breaks again)* God, don't do that, gang! It makes me feel like hell to think you hate me. It makes me feel you suspect I must have hated you. But that's a lie! Oh, I know I used to hate everyone in the world who wasn't as rotten a bastard as I was! But that was when I was still living in hell—before I faced the truth and saw the one possible way to free poor Evelyn and give her the peace she'd always dreamed about.

(He pauses. Everyone in the group stirs with awakening dread and they all begin to grow tense on their chairs.)

CHUCK: *(without looking at* HICKEY—*with dull, resentful viciousness)* Aw, put a bag over it! To hell wid Evelyn! What if she was cheatin'? And who cares what yuh did to her? Dat's your funeral. We don't give a damn, see? *(There is a dull, resentful chorus of assent, "We don't give a damn."* CHUCK *adds dully)* All we want outa you is keep de hell away from us and give us a rest. *(A muttered chorus of assent.)*

HICKEY: *(as if he hadn't heard this—an obsessed look on his face)* The one possible way to make up to her for all I'd made her go through, and get her rid of me so I couldn't make her suffer any more, and she wouldn't have to forgive me again! I saw I couldn't do it by killing myself, like I wanted to for a long time. That would have been the last straw for her. She'd have died of a broken heart to think I could do that to her. She'd have blamed herself for it, too. Or I couldn't just run away from her. She'd have died of grief and humiliation if I'd done that to her. She'd have thought I'd stopped loving her. *(He adds with a strange impressive simplicity)* You see, Evelyn loved me. And I loved her. That was the trouble. It would have been easy to find a way out if she hadn't loved me so much. Or if I hadn't loved her. But as it was, there was only one possible way. *(He pauses—then adds simply)* I had to kill her.

(There is a second's dead silence as he finishes—then a tense indrawn breath like a gasp from the crowd, and a general shrinking movement.)

LARRY: *(bursts out)* You mad fool, can't you keep your mouth shut! We may hate you for what you've done here this time, but we remember the old times, too, when you brought kindness and laughter with you instead of death! We don't want to know things that will make us help send you to the Chair!

PARRITT: *(with angry scorn)* Ah, shut up, you yellow faker! Can't you face anything? Wouldn't I deserve the Chair, too, if I'd— It's worse if you kill someone and they have to go on living. I'd be glad of the Chair! It'd wipe it out! It'd square me with myself!

HICKEY: *(disturbed—with a movement of repulsion)* I wish you'd get rid of that bastard, Larry. I can't have him pretending there's something in common between him and me. It's what's in your heart that counts. There was love in my heart, not hate.

PARRITT: *(glares at him in angry terror)* You're a liar! I don't hate her! I couldn't! And it had nothing to do with her, anyway! You ask Larry!

LARRY: *(grabs his shoulder and shakes him furiously)* God damn you, stop shoving your rotten soul in my lap!

(PARRITT subsides, hiding his face in his hands and shuddering.)

HICKEY: *(goes on quietly now)* Don't worry about the Chair, Larry. I know it's still hard for you not to be terrified by death, but when you've made peace with yourself, like I have, you won't give a damn. *(He addresses the group at right again— earnestly)* Listen, everybody. I've made up my mind the only way I can clear things up for you, so you'll realize how contented and carefree you ought to feel, now I've made you get rid of your pipe dreams, is to show you what a pipe dream did to me and Evelyn. I'm certain if I tell you about it from the beginning, you'll appreciate what I've done for you and why I did it, and how damned grateful you ought to be—instead of hating me. *(He begins eagerly in a strange running narrative manner)* You see, even when we were kids, Evelyn and me—

HOPE: *(bursts out, pounding with his glass on the table)* No! Who the hell cares? We don't want to hear it. All we want is to pass out and get drunk and a little peace!

(They are all, except LARRY and PARRITT, seized by the same fit and pound with their glasses, even HUGO, and ROCKY in the bar, and shout in chorus, "Who the hell cares? We want to pass out!")

HICKEY: *(with an expression of wounded hurt)* All right, if that's the way you feel. I don't want to cram it down your throats. I don't need to tell anyone. I don't feel guilty. I'm only worried about you.

HOPE: What did you do to this booze? That's what we'd like to hear. Bejees, you done something. There's no life or kick in it now. *(He appeals mechanically to* JIMMY TOMORROW*)* Ain't that right, Jimmy?

JIMMY: *(more than any of them, his face has a wax-figure blankness that makes it look embalmed. He answers in a precise, completely lifeless voice, but his reply is not to* HARRY'S *question, and he does not look at him or anyone else)* Yes. Quite right. It was all a stupid lie—my nonsense about tomorrow. Naturally, they would never give me my position back. I would never dream of asking them. It would be hopeless. I didn't resign. I was fired for drunkenness. And that was years ago. I'm much worse now. And it was absurd of me to excuse my drunkenness by pretending it was my wife's adultery that ruined my life. As Hickey guessed, I was a drunkard before that. Long before. I discovered early in life that living frightened me when I was sober. I have forgotten why I married Marjorie. I can't even remember now if she was pretty. She was a blonde, I think, but I couldn't swear to it. I had some idea of wanting a home, perhaps. But, of course, I much preferred the nearest pub. Why Marjorie married me, God knows. It's impossible to believe she loved me. She soon found I much preferred drinking all night with my pals to being in bed with her. So, naturally, she was unfaithful. I didn't blame her. I really didn't care. I was glad to be free—even grateful to her, I think, for giving me such a good tragic excuse to drink as much as I damned well pleased.

(He stops like a mechanical doll that has run down. No one gives any sign of having heard him. There is a heavy silence. Then ROCKY, *at the table in the bar, turns grouchily as he hears a noise behind him. Two men come quietly forward. One,* MORAN, *is middle-aged. The other,* LIEB, *is in his twenties. They look ordinary in every way, without anything distinctive to indicate what they do for a living.)*

ROCKY: *(grumpily)* In de back room if yuh wanta drink.

(MORAN makes a peremptory sign to be quiet. All of a sudden ROCKY senses they are detectives and springs up to face them, his expression freezing into a wary blankness. MORAN pulls back his coat to show his badge.)

MORAN: *(in a low voice)* Guy named Hickman in the back room?

ROCKY: Tink I know de names of all de guys—?

MORAN: Listen, you! This is murder. And don't be a sap. It was Hickman himself phoned in and said we'd find him here around two.

ROCKY: *(dully)* So dat's who he phoned to. *(He shrugs his shoulders)* Aw right, if he asked for it. He's de fat guy sittin' alone. *(He slumps down in his chair again)* And if yuh want a confession all yuh got to do is listen. He'll be tellin' all about it soon. Yuh can't stop de bastard talkin'.

(MORAN gives him a curious look, then whispers to LIEB, who disappears rear and a moment later appears in the hall doorway of the back room. He spots HICKEY and slides into a chair at the left of the doorway, cutting off escape by the hall. MORAN goes back and stands in the opening in the curtain leading to the back room. He sees HICKEY and stands watching him and listening.)

HICKEY: *(suddenly bursts out)* I've got to tell you! Your being the way you are now gets my goat! It's all wrong! It puts things in my mind—about myself. It makes me think, if I got balled up about you, how do I know I wasn't balled up about myself? And that's plain damned foolishness. When you know the story of me and Evelyn, you'll see there wasn't any other possible way out of it, for her sake. Only I've got to start way back at the beginning or you won't understand. *(He starts his story, his tone again becoming musingly reminiscent)* You see, even as a kid I was always restless. I had to keep on the go. You've heard the old saying, "Ministers' sons are sons of guns." Well, that was me, and then some. Home was like a jail. I didn't fall for the religious bunk. Listening to my old man whooping up hell fire and scaring those Hoosier suckers into shelling out their dough only handed me a laugh, although I had to hand it to him, the way he sold them nothing for something. I guess I take after him, and that's what made me a good salesman. Well, anyway, as I said, home was like jail, and so was school, and so was that damned hick town. The only place I liked was the pool rooms, where I could smoke Sweet Caporals, and mop up a couple of beers, thinking I was a hell-on-wheels sport. We had one hooker shop in town, and, of course, I liked that, too. Not that I hardly ever had entrance money. My old man was a tight old bastard. But I liked to sit around in the parlor and joke with the girls, and they liked me because I could kid 'em along and make 'em laugh. Well, you know what a small town is. Everyone got wise to me. They all said I was a no-good tramp. I didn't give a damn what they said. I hated everybody in the place. That is, except Evelyn. I loved Evelyn. Even as a kid. And Evelyn loved me.

(He pauses. No one moves or gives any sign except by the dread in their eyes that they have heard him. Except PARRITT, who takes his hands from his face to look at LARRY pleadingly.)

PARRITT: I loved Mother, Larry! No matter what she did! I still do! Even though I know she wishes now I was dead! You believe that, don't you? Christ, why can't you say something?

HICKEY: *(too absorbed in his story now to notice this—goes on in a tone of fond, sentimental reminiscence)* Yes, sir, as far back as I can remember, Evelyn and I loved each other. She always stuck up for me. She wouldn't believe the gossip—or she'd pretend she didn't. No one could convince her I was no good. Evelyn was stubborn as all hell once she'd made up her mind. Even when I'd admit things and ask her forgiveness, she'd make excuses for me and defend me against myself. She'd kiss me and say she knew I didn't mean it and I wouldn't do it again. So I'd promise I wouldn't. I'd have to promise, she was so sweet and good, though I knew darned well—*(A touch of strange bitterness comes into his voice for a moment)* No, sir, you couldn't stop Evelyn. Nothing on earth could shake her faith in me. Even I couldn't. She was a sucker for a pipe dream. *(Then quickly)* Well, naturally, her family forbid her seeing me. They were one of the town's best, rich for that hick burg, owned the trolley line and lumber company. Strict Methodists, too. They hated my guts. But they couldn't stop Evelyn. She'd sneak notes to me and meet me on the sly. I was getting more rest-less. The town was getting more like a jail. I made up my mind to beat it. I knew exactly what I wanted to be by that time. I'd met a lot of drummers around the hotel and liked 'em. They were always telling jokes. They were sports. They kept moving. I liked their life. And I knew I could kid people and sell things. The hitch was how to get the railroad fare to the Big Town. I told Mollie Arlington my trouble. She was the madame of the cathouse. She liked me. She laughed and said, "Hell, I'll stake you, Kid! I'll bet on you. With that grin of yours and that line of bull, you ought to be able to sell skunks for good ratters!" *(He chuckles)* Mollie was all right. She gave me confidence in myself. I paid her back, the first money I earned. Wrote her a kid-ding letter, I remember, saying I was peddling baby carriages and she and the girls had better take advantage of our bargain offer. *(He chuck-les)* But that's ahead of my story. The night be-fore I left town, I had a date with Evelyn. I got all worked up, she was so pretty and sweet and good. I told her straight, "You better forget me, Evelyn, for your own sake. I'm no good and never will be. I'm not worthy to wipe your shoes." I broke down and cried. She just said, looking white and scared, "Why, Teddy? Don't you still love me?" I said, "Love you? God, Eve-lyn, I love you more than anything in the world. And I always will!" She said, "Then nothing else matters, Teddy, because nothing but death could stop my loving you. So I'll wait, and when you're ready you send for me and we'll be mar-ried. I know I can make you happy, Teddy, and once you're happy you won't want to do any of the bad things you've done any more." And I said, "Of course, I won't, Evelyn!" I meant it, too. I believed it. I loved her so much she could make me believe anything.

(He sighs. There is a suspended, waiting silence. Even the two detectives are drawn into it. Then HOPE *breaks into dully exasperated, brutally callous protest.)*

HOPE: Get it over, you long-winded bastard! You married her, and you caught her cheating with the iceman, and you croaked her, and who the hell cares? What's she to us? All we want is to pass out in peace, bejees! *(A chorus of dull, re-sentful protest from all the group. They mumble, like sleepers who curse a person who keeps awak-ening them, "What's it to us? We want to pass out in peace!"* HOPE *drinks and they mechanically follow his example. He pours another and they do the same. He complains with a stupid, nagging insistence)* No life in the booze! No kick! Dish-water. Bejees, I'll never pass out!

HICKEY: *(goes on as if there had been no interrup-tion)* So I beat it to the Big Town. I got a job easy, and it was a cinch for me to make good. I had the knack. It was like a game, sizing people up quick, spotting what their pet pipe dreams were, and then kidding 'em along that line, pre-tending you believed what they wanted to be-lieve about themselves. Then they liked you, they trusted you, they wanted to buy something to show their gratitude. It was fun. But still, all the while I felt guilty, as if I had no right to be having such a good time away from Evelyn. In each letter I'd tell her how I missed her, but I'd keep warning her, too. I'd tell her all my faults, how I liked my booze every once in a while, and so on. But there was no shaking Evelyn's belief in me, or her dreams about the future. After each letter of hers, I'd be as full of faith as she was. So as soon as I got enough saved to start us off, I sent for her and we got married. Christ, wasn't I happy for a while! And wasn't she happy! I don't care what anyone says, I'll bet there never was two people who loved each other more than me and Evelyn. Not only then but always after, in spite of everything I did— *(He pauses—then sadly)* Well, it's all there, at the start, everything that happened afterwards. I never could learn to handle temptation. I'd want to reform and mean it. I'd promise Evelyn, and I'd promise myself, and I'd believe it. I'd tell her, it's the last time. And she'd say, "I know it's the last time, Teddy. You'll never do it again." That's what made it so hard. That's what made me feel such a rotten skunk—her always forgiving me. My playing around with women, for instance. It was only a harmless good time to me. Didn't mean anything. But I'd know what it meant to Evelyn. So I'd say to myself, never again. But you know how it is, traveling around. The damned hotel rooms. I'd get seeing things in the wall paper. I'd get bored as hell. Lonely and homesick. But at the same time sick of home. I'd feel free and I'd want to celebrate a little. I never drank on the job, so it had to be dames. Any tart. What I'd want was some tramp I could be myself with without being ashamed—someone I could tell a dirty joke to and she'd laugh.

CORA: *(with a dull, weary bitterness)* Jees, all de lousy jokes I've had to listen to and pretend was funny!

HICKEY: *(goes on obliviously)* Sometimes I'd try some joke I thought was a corker on Evelyn. She'd always make herself laugh. But I could tell she thought it was dirty, not funny. And Evelyn always knew about the tarts I'd been with when I came home from a trip. She'd kiss me and look in my eyes, and she'd know. I'd see in her eyes how she was trying not to know, and then telling herself even if it was true, he couldn't help it, they tempt him, and he's lonely, he hasn't got me, it's only his body, anyway, he doesn't love them. I'm the only one he loves. She was right, too. I never loved anyone else. Couldn't if I wanted to. *(He pauses)* She forgave me even when it all had to come out in the open. You know how it is when you keep taking chances. You may be lucky for a long time, but you get nicked in the end. I picked up a nail from some tart in Altoona.

CORA: *(dully, without resentment)* Yeah. And she picked it up from some guy. It's all in de game. What de hell of it?

HICKEY: I had to do a lot of lying and stalling when I got home. It didn't do any good. The quack I went to got all my dough and then told me I was cured and I took his word. But I wasn't, and poor Evelyn—But she did her best to make me believe she fell for my lie about how traveling men get things from drinking cups on trains. Anyway, she forgave me. The same way she forgave me every time I'd turn up after a periodical drunk. You all know what I'd be like at the end of one. You've seen me. Like something lying in the gutter that no alley cat would lower itself to drag in—something they threw out of the D.T. ward in Bellevue along with the garbage, something that ought to be dead and isn't! *(His face is convulsed with self-loathing)* Evelyn wouldn't have heard from me in a month or more. She'd have been waiting there alone, with the neighbors shaking their heads and feeling sorry for her out loud. That was before she got me to move to the outskirts, where there weren't any next-door neighbors. And then the door would open and in I'd stumble—looking like what I've said—into her home, where she kept everything so spotless and clean. And I'd sworn it would never happen again, and now I'd have to start swearing again this was the last time. I could see disgust having a battle in her eyes with love. Love always won. She'd make herself kiss me, as if nothing had happened, as if I'd just come home from a business trip. She'd never complain or bawl me out. *(He bursts out in a tone of anguish that has anger and hatred beneath it)* Christ, can you imagine what a guilty skunk she made me feel! If she'd only admitted once she didn't believe any more in her pipe dream that some day I'd behave! But she never would. Evelyn was stubborn as hell. Once she'd set her heart on anything, you couldn't shake her faith that it had to come true— tomorrow! It was the same old story, over and over, for years and years. It kept piling up, inside her and inside me. God, can you picture all I made her suffer, and all the guilt she made me feel, and how I hated myself! If she only hadn't been so damned good—if she'd been the same kind of wife I was a husband. God, I used to pray sometimes she'd—I'd even say to her, "Go on, why don't you, Evelyn? It'd serve me right. I wouldn't mind. I'd forgive you." Of course, I'd pretend I was kidding—the same way I used to joke here about her being in the hay with the iceman. She'd have been so hurt if I'd said it seriously. She'd have thought I'd stopped loving her. *(He pauses—then looking around at them)* I suppose you think I'm a liar, that no woman could have stood all she stood and still loved me so much—that it isn't human for any woman to be so pitying and forgiving. Well, I'm not lying, and if you'd ever seen her, you'd realize I wasn't. It was written all over her face, sweetness and love and pity and forgiveness. *(He reaches mechanically for the inside pocket of his coat)* Wait! I'll show you. I always carry her picture. *(Suddenly he looks startled. He stares before him, his hand falling back—quietly)* No, I'm forgetting I tore it up—afterwards. I didn't need it any more.

(He pauses. The silence is like that in the room of a dying man where people hold their breath, waiting for him to die.)

CORA: *(with a muffled sob)* Jees, Hickey! Jees!
(She shivers and puts her hands over her face.)

PARRITT: *(to* LARRY *in a low insistent tone)* I burnt up Mother's picture, Larry. Her eyes followed me all the time. They seemed to be wishing I was dead!

HICKEY: It kept piling up, like I've said. I got so I thought of it all the time. I hated myself more and more, thinking of all the wrong I'd done to the sweetest woman in the world who loved me so much. I got so I'd curse myself for a lousy bastard every time I saw myself in the mirror. I felt such pity for her it drove me crazy. You wouldn't believe a guy like me, that's knocked around so much, could feel such pity. It got so every night I'd wind up hiding my face in her lap, bawling and begging her forgiveness. And, of course, she'd always comfort me and say, "Never mind, Teddy, I know you won't ever again." Christ, I loved her so, but I began to hate that pipe dream! I began to be afraid I was going bughouse, because sometimes I couldn't forgive her for forgiving me. I even caught myself hating her for making me hate myself so much. There's a limit to the guilt you can feel and the forgiveness and the pity you can take! You have to begin blaming someone else, too. I got so sometimes when she'd kiss me it was like she did it on purpose to humiliate me, as if she'd spit in my face! But all the time I saw how crazy and rotten of me that was, and it made me hate myself all the more. You'd never believe I could hate so much, a good-natured, happy-go-lucky slob like me. And as the time got nearer to when I was due to come here for my drunk around Harry's birthday, I got nearly crazy. I kept swearing to her every night that this time I really wouldn't, until I'd made it a real final test to myself—and to her. And she kept encouraging me and saying, "I can see you really mean it now, Teddy. I know you'll conquer it this time, and we'll be so happy, dear." When she'd say that and kiss me, I'd believe it, too. Then she'd go to bed, and I'd stay up alone because I couldn't sleep and I didn't want to disturb her, tossing and rolling around. I'd get so damned lonely. I'd get thinking how peaceful it was here, sitting around with the old gang, getting drunk and forgetting love, joking and laughing and singing and swapping lies. And finally I knew I'd have to come. And I knew if I came this time, it was the finish. I'd never have the guts to go back and be forgiven again, and that would break Evelyn's heart because to her it would mean I didn't love her any more. *(He pauses)* That last night I'd driven myself crazy trying to figure some way out for her. I went in the bedroom. I was going to tell her it was the end. But I couldn't do that to her. She was sound asleep. I thought, God, if she'd only never wake up, she'd never know! And then it came to me—the only possible way out, for her sake. I remembered I'd given her a gun for protection while I was away and it was in the bureau drawer. She'd never feel any pain, never wake up from her dream. So I—

HOPE: *(tries to ward this off by pounding with his glass on the table—with brutal, callous exasperation)* Give us a rest, for the love of Christ! Who the hell cares? We want to pass out in peace!

(They all, except PARRITT *and* LARRY, *pound with their glasses and grumble in chorus: "Who the hell cares? We want to pass out in peace!"* MORAN, *the detective, moves quietly from the entrance in the curtain across the back of the room to the table where his companion,* LIEB, *is sitting.* ROCKY *notices his leaving and gets up from the table in the rear and goes back to stand and watch in the entrance.* MORAN *exchanges a glance with* LIEB, *motioning him to get up. The latter does so. No one notices them. The clamor of banging glasses dies out as abruptly as it started.* HICKEY *hasn't appeared to hear it.)*

HICKEY: *(simply)* So I killed her.

(There is a moment of dead silence. Even the detectives are caught in it and stand motionless.)

PARRITT: *(suddenly gives up and relaxes limply in his chair—in a low voice in which there is a strange exhausted relief)* I may as well confess, Larry. There's no use lying any more. You know, anyway. I didn't give a damn about the money. It was because I hated her.

HICKEY: *(obliviously)* And then I saw I'd always known that was the only possible way to give her peace and free her from the misery of loving me. I saw it meant peace for me, too, knowing she was at peace. I felt as though a ton of guilt was lifted off my mind. I remember I stood by the bed and suddenly I had to laugh. I couldn't help it, and I knew Evelyn would forgive me. I remember I heard myself speaking to her, as if it was something I'd always wanted to say: "Well, you know what you can do with your pipe dream now, you damned bitch!" *(He stops with a horrified start, as if shocked out of a nightmare, as if he couldn't believe he heard what he had just said. He stammers)* No I never—!

PARRITT: *(to* LARRY—*sneeringly)* Yes, that's it! Her and the damned old Movement pipe dream! Eh, Larry?

HICKEY: *(bursts into frantic denial)* No! That's a lie! I never said—! Good God, I couldn't have said that! If I did, I'd gone insane! Why, I loved Evelyn better than anything in life! *(He appeals brokenly to the crowd)* Boys, you're all

my old pals! You've known old Hickey for years! You know I'd never—(*His eyes fix on* HOPE) You've known me longer than anyone, Harry. You know I must have been insane, don't you, Governor?

HOPE: *(at first with the same defensive callousness—without looking at him)* Who the hell cares? *(Then suddenly he looks at* HICKEY *and there is an extraordinary change in his expression. His face lights up, as if he were grasping at some dawning hope in his mind. He speaks with a groping eagerness)* Insane? You mean—you went really insane?

(At the tone of his voice, all the group at the tables by him start and stare at him as if they caught his thought. Then they all look at HICKEY *eagerly, too.)*

HICKEY: Yes! Or I couldn't have laughed! I couldn't have said that to her!

*(*MORAN *walks up behind him on one side, while the second detective,* LIEB, *closes in on him from the other.)*

MORAN: *(taps* HICKEY *on the shoulder)* That's enough, Hickman. You know who we are. You're under arrest. *(He nods to* LIEB, *who slips a pair of handcuffs on* HICKEY'S *wrists.* HICKEY *stares at them with stupid incomprehension.* MORAN *takes his arm)* Come along and spill your guts where we can get it on paper.

HICKEY: No, wait, Officer! You owe me a break! I phoned and made it easy for you, didn't I? Just a few minutes! *(To* HOPE—*pleadingly)* You know I couldn't say that to Evelyn, don't you, Harry—unless—

HOPE: *(eagerly)* And you've been crazy ever since? Everything you've said and done here—

HICKEY: *(for a moment forgets his own obsession and his face takes on its familiar expression of affectionate amusement and he chuckles)* Now, Governor! Up to your old tricks, eh? I see what you're driving at, but I can't let you get away with—(*Then, as* HOPE'S *expression turns to resentful callousness again and he looks away, he adds hastily with pleading desperation)* Yes, Harry, of course, I've been out of my mind ever since! All the time I've been here! You saw I was insane, didn't you?

MORAN: *(with cynical disgust)* Can it! I've had enough of your act. Save it for the jury. *(Addressing the crowd, sharply)* Listen, you guys. Don't fall for his lies. He's starting to get foxy now and thinks he'll plead insanity. But he can't get away with it.

(The crowd at the grouped tables are grasping at hope now. They glare at him resentfully.)

HOPE: *(begins to bristle in his old-time manner)* Bejees, you dumb dick, you've got a crust trying to tell us about Hickey! We've known him for years, and every one of us noticed he was nutty the minute he showed up here! Bejees, if you'd heard all the crazy bull he was pulling about bringing us peace—like a bughouse preacher escaped from an asylum! If you'd seen all the damned-fool things he made us do! We only did them because—*(He hesitates—then defiantly)* Because we hoped he'd come out of it if we kidded him along and humored him. *(He looks around at the others)* Ain't that right, fellers?

(They burst into a chorus of eager assent: "Yes, Harry!" "That's it, Harry!" "That's why!" "We knew he was crazy!" "Just to humor him!")

MORAN: A fine bunch of rats! Covering up for a dirty, cold-blooded murderer.

HOPE: *(stung into recovering all his old fuming truculence)* Is that so? Bejees, you know the old story, when Saint Patrick drove the snakes out of Ireland they swam to New York and joined the police force! Ha! *(He cackles insultingly)* Bejees, we can believe it now when we look at you, can't we, fellers? *(They all growl assent, glowering defiantly at* MORAN. MORAN *glares at them, looking as if he'd like to forget his prisoner and start cleaning out the place.* HOPE *goes on pugnaciously)* You stand up for your rights, bejees, Hickey! Don't let this smart-aleck dick get funny with you. If he pulls any rubber-hose tricks, you let me know! I've still got friends at the Hall! Bejees, I'll have him back in uniform pounding a beat where the

only graft he'll get will be stealing tin cans from the goats!

MORAN: *(furiously)* Listen, you cockeyed old bum, for a plugged nickel I'd— *(Controlling himself, turns to* HICKEY, *who is oblivious to all this, and yanks his arm)* Come on, you!

HICKEY: *(with a strange mad earnestness)* Oh, I want to go, Officer. I can hardly wait now. I should have phoned you from the house right afterwards. It was a waste of time coming here. I've got to explain to Evelyn. But I know she's forgiven me. She knows I was insane. You've got me all wrong, Officer. I want to go to the Chair.

MORAN: Crap!

HICKEY: *(exasperatedly)* God, you're a dumb dick! Do you suppose I give a damn about life now? Why, you bonehead, I haven't got a single damned lying hope or pipe dream left!

MORAN: *(jerks him around to face the door to the hall)* Get a move on!

HICKEY: *(as they start walking toward rear—insistently)* All I want you to see is I was out of my mind afterwards, when I laughed at her! I was a raving rotten lunatic or I couldn't have said— Why, Evelyn was the only thing on God's earth I ever loved! I'd have killed myself before I'd ever have hurt her!

(They disappear in the hall. HICKEY'S *voice keeps on protesting.)*

HOPE: *(calls after him)* Don't worry, Hickey! They can't give you the Chair! We'll testify you was crazy! Won't we, fellers? *(They all assent. Two or three echo* HOPE'S *"Don't worry, Hickey." Then from the hall comes the slam of the street door.* HOPE'S *face falls—with genuine sorrow)* He's gone. Poor crazy son of a bitch! *(All the group around him are sad and sympathetic, too.* HOPE *reaches for his drink)* Bejees, I need a drink. *(They grab their glasses.* HOPE *says hopefully)* Bejees, maybe it'll have the old kick, now he's gone.

(He drinks and they follow suit.)

ROCKY: *(comes forward from where he has stood in the bar entrance—hopefully)* Yeah, Boss, maybe we can get drunk now.

(He sits in the chair by CHUCK *and pours a drink and tosses it down. Then they all sit still, waiting for the effect, as if this drink were a crucial test, so absorbed in hopeful expectancy that they remain oblivious to what happens at* LARRY'S *table.)*

LARRY: *(his eyes full of pain and pity—in a whisper, aloud to himself)* May the Chair bring him peace at last, the poor tortured bastard!

PARRITT: *(leans toward him—in a strange low insistent voice)* Yes, but he isn't the only one who needs peace, Larry. I can't feel sorry for him. He's lucky. He's through, now. It's all decided for him. I wish it was decided for me. I've never been any good at deciding things. Even about selling out, it was the tart the detective agency got after me who put it in my mind. You remember what Mother's like, Larry. She makes all the decisions. She's always decided what I must do. She doesn't like anyone to be free but herself. *(He pauses, as if waiting for comment, but* LARRY *ignores him)* I suppose you think I ought to have made those dicks take me away with Hickey. But how could I prove it, Larry? They'd think I was nutty. Because she's still alive. You're the only one who can understand how guilty I am. Because you know her and what I've done to her. You know I'm really much guiltier than he is. You know what I did is a much worse murder. Because she is dead and yet she has to live. For a while. But she can't live long in jail. She loves freedom too much. And I can't kid myself like Hickey, that she's at peace. As long as she lives, she'll never be able to forget what I've done to her even in her sleep. She'll never have a second's peace. *(He pauses—then bursts out)* Jesus, Larry, can't you say something? *(*LARRY *is at the breaking point.* PARRITT *goes on)* And I'm not putting up any bluff, either, that I was crazy afterwards when I laughed to myself and thought, "You know what you can do with your freedom pipe dream now, don't you, you damned old bitch!"

LARRY: *(snaps and turns on him, his face convulsed with detestation. His quivering voice has a condemning command in it)* Go! Get the hell out of life, God damn you, before I choke it out of you! Go up—!

PARRITT: *(his manner is at once transformed. He seems suddenly at peace with himself. He speaks simply and gratefully)* Thanks, Larry. I just wanted to be sure. I can see now it's the only possible way I can ever get free from her. I guess I've really known that all my life. *(He pauses—then with a derisive smile)* It ought to comfort Mother a little, too. It'll give her the chance to play the great incorruptible Mother of the Revolution, whose only child is the Proletariat. She'll be able to say: "Justice is done! So may all traitors die!" She'll be able to say: "I am glad he's dead! Long live the Revolution!" *(He adds with a final implacable jeer)* You know her, Larry! Always a ham!

LARRY: *(pleads distractedly)* Go, for the love of Christ, you mad tortured bastard, for your own sake!

*(*HUGO *is roused by this. He lifts his head and peers uncomprehendingly at* LARRY. *Neither* LARRY *nor* PARRITT *notices him.)*

PARRITT: *(stares at* LARRY. *His face begins to crumble as if he were going to break down and sob. He turns his head away, but reaches out fumblingly and pats* LARRY'S *arms and stammers)* Jesus, Larry, thanks. That's kind. I knew you were the only one who could understand my side of it.

(He gets to his feet and turns toward the door.)

HUGO: *(looks at* PARRITT *and bursts into his silly giggle)* Hello, leedle Don, leedle monkey-face! Don't be a fool! Buy me a trink!

PARRITT: *(puts on an act of dramatic bravado—forcing a grin)* Sure, I will, Hugo! Tomorrow! Beneath the willow trees!

(He walks to the door with a careless swagger and disappears in the hall. From now on, LARRY *waits, listening for the sound he knows is coming from the backyard outside the window, but trying not to listen, in an agony of horror and cracking nerve.)*

HUGO: *(stares after* PARRITT *stupidly)* Stupid fool! Hickey make you crazy, too. *(He turns to the oblivious* LARRY—*with a timid eagerness)* I'm glad, Larry, they take that crazy Hickey away to asylum. He makes me have bad dreams. He makes me tell lies about myself. He makes me want to spit on all I have ever dreamed. Yes, I am glad they take him to asylum. I don't feel I am dying now. He vas selling death to me, that crazy salesman. I think I have a trink now, Larry. *(He pours a drink and gulps it down.)*

HOPE: *(jubilantly)* Bejees, fellers, I'm feeling the old kick, or I'm a liar! It's putting life back in me! Bejees, if all I've lapped up begins to hit me, I'll be paralyzed before I know it! It was Hickey kept it from—Bejees, I know that sounds crazy, but he was crazy, and he'd got all of us as bughouse as he was. Bejees, it does queer things to you, having to listen day and night to a lunatic's pipe dreams—pretending you believe them, to kid him along and doing any crazy thing he wants to humor him. It's dangerous, too. Look at me pretending to start for a walk just to keep him quiet. I knew damned well it wasn't the right day for it. The sun was broiling and the streets full of automobiles. Bejees, I could feel myself getting sunstroke, and an automobile damn near ran over me. *(He appeals to* ROCKY, *afraid of the result, but daring it)* Ask Rocky. He was watching. Didn't it, Rocky?

ROCKY: *(a bit tipsily)* What's dat, Boss? Jees, all de booze I've mopped up is beginning to get to me. *(Earnestly)* De automobile, Boss? Sure, I seen it! Just missed yuh! I thought yuh was a goner. *(He pauses—then looks around at the others, and assumes the old kidding tone of the inmates, but hesitantly, as if still a little afraid)* On de woid of a honest bartender!

(He tries a wink at the others. They all respond with smiles that are still a little forced and uneasy.)

HOPE: *(flashes him a suspicious glance. Then he understands—with his natural testy manner)* You're a bartender, all right. No one can say different. (*ROCKY looks grateful*) But, bejees, don't pull that honest junk! You and Chuck ought to have cards in the Burglars' Union! *(This time there is an eager laugh from the group.* HOPE *is*

delighted) Bejees, it's good to hear someone laugh again! All the time that bas— poor old Hickey was here, I didn't have the heart— Bejees, I'm getting drunk and glad of it! *(He cackles and reaches for the bottle)* Come on, fellers. It's on the house. *(They pour drinks. They begin rapidly to get drunk now.* HOPE *becomes sentimental)* Poor old Hickey! We mustn't hold him responsible for anything he's done. We'll forget that and only remember him the way we've always known him before—the kindest, biggest-hearted guy ever wore shoe leather. *(They all chorus hearty sentimental assent: "That's right, Harry!" "That's all!" "Finest fellow!" "Best scout!" etc.* HOPE *goes on)* Good luck to him in Matteawan! Come on, bottoms up! *(They all drink. At the table by the window* LARRY'S *hands grip the edge of the table. Unconsciously his head is inclined toward the window as he listens.)*

LARRY: *(cannot hold back an anguished exclamation)* Christ! Why don't he—!

HUGO: *(beginning to be drunk again—peers at him)* Vhy don't he what? Don't be a fool! Hickey's gone. He vas crazy. Have a trink. *(Then as he receives no reply—with vague uneasiness)* What's matter with you, Larry? You look funny. What you listen to out in backyard, Larry? *(CORA begins to talk in the group at right)*

CORA: *(tipsily)* Well, I thank Gawd now me and Chuck did all we could to humor de poor nut. Jees, imagine us goin' off like we really meant to git married, when we ain't even picked out a farm yet!

CHUCK: *(eagerly)* Sure ting, Baby. We kidded him we was serious.

JIMMY: *(confidently—with a gentle, drunken unction)* I may as well say I detected his condition almost at once. All that talk of his about tomorrow, for example. He had the fixed idea of the insane. It only makes them worse to cross them.

WILLIE: *(eagerly)* Same with me, Jimmy. Only I spent the day in the park. I wasn't such a damned fool as to—

LEWIS: *(getting jauntily drunk)* Picture my predicament if I *had* gone to the Consulate.

The pal of mine there is a humorous blighter. He would have got me a job out of pure spite. So I strolled about and finally came to roost in the park. (*He grins with affectionate kidding at* WETJOEN) And lo and behold, who was on the neighboring bench but my old battlefield companion, the Boer that walks like a man—who, if the British Government had taken my advice, would have been removed from his fetid kraal on the veldt straight to the baboon's cage at the London Zoo, and little children would now be asking their nurses: "Tell me, Nana, is that the Boer General, the one with the blue behind?" (*They all laugh uproariously.* LEWIS *leans over and slaps* WETJOEN *affectionately on the knee*) No offense meant, Piet, old chap.

WETJOEN: (*beaming at him*) No offense taken, you damned Limey! (WETJOEN *goes on—grinningly*) About a job, I felt the same as you, Cecil.

(*At the table by the window* HUGO *speaks to* LARRY *again.*)

HUGO: (*with uneasy insistence*) What's matter, Larry? You look scared. What you listen for out there?

(*But* LARRY *doesn't hear, and* JOE *begins talking in the group at right.*)

JOE: (*with drunken self-assurance*) No, suh, I wasn't fool enough to git in no crap game. Not while Hickey's around. Crazy people puts a jinx on you.

(MCGLOIN *is now heard. He is leaning across in front of* WETJOEN *to talk to* ED MOSHER *on* HOPE'S *left.*)

MCGLOIN: (*with drunken earnestness*) I know you saw how it was, Ed. There was no good trying to explain to a crazy guy, but it ain't the right time. You know how getting reinstated is.

MOSHER: (*decidedly*) Sure, Mac. The same way with the circus. The boys tell me the rubes are wasting all their money buying food and times never was so hard. And I never was one to cheat for chicken feed.

HOPE: (*looks around him in an ecstasy of bleary sentiment content*) Bejees, I'm cockeyed! Bejees, you're all cockeyed! Bejees, we're all all right! Let's have another!

(*They pour out drinks. At the table by the window* LARRY *has unconsciously shut his eyes as he listens.* HUGO *is peering at him frightenedly now.*)

HUGO: (*reiterates stupidly*) What's matter, Larry? Why you keep eyes shut? You look dead. What you listen for in backyard? (*Then, as* LARRY *doesn't open his eyes or answer, he gets up hastily and moves away from the table, mumbling with frightened anger*) Crazy fool! You vas crazy like Hickey! You give me bad dreams, too.

(*He shrinks quickly past the table where* HICKEY *had sat to the rear of the group at right.*)

ROCKY: (*greets him with boisterous affection*) Hello, dere, Hugo! Welcome to de party!

HOPE: Yes, bejees, Hugo! Sit down! Have a drink! Have ten drinks, bejees!

HUGO: (*forgetting* LARRY *and bad dreams, gives his familiar giggle*) Hello, leedle Harry! Hello, nice, leedle, funny monkey-faces! (*Warming up, changes abruptly to his usual declamatory denunciation*) Gottamned stupid bourgeois! Soon comes the Day of Judgment! (*They make derisive noises and tell him to sit down. He changes again, giggling good-naturedly, and sits at rear of the middle table*) Give me ten trinks, Harry. Don't be a fool. (*They laugh.* ROCKY *shoves a glass and bottle at him. The sound of* MARGIE'S *and* PEARL'S *voices is heard from the hall, drunkenly shrill. All of the group turn toward the door as the two appear. They are drunk and look blowsy and disheveled. Their manner as they enter hardens into a brazen defensive truculence.*)

MARGIE: (*stridently*) Gangway for two good whores!

PEARL: Yeah! And we want a drink quick!

MARGIE: (*glaring at* ROCKY) Shake de lead outa your pants, Pimp! A little soivice!

ROCKY: (*his black bullet eyes sentimental, his round Wop face grinning welcome*) Well, look who's here! (*He goes to them unsteadily, opening his arms*) Hello, dere, Sweethearts! Jees, I was beginnin' to worry about yuh, honest!

(*He tries to embrace them. They push his arms away, regarding him with amazed suspicion.*)

PEARL: What kind of a gag is dis?

HOPE: *(calls to them effusively)* Come on and join the party, you broads! Bejees, I'm glad to see you!

(The girls exchange a bewildered glance, taking in the party and the changed atmosphere.)

MARGIE: Jees, what's come off here?

PEARL: Where's dat louse, Hickey?

ROCKY: De cops got him. He'd gone crazy and croaked his wife. *(The girls exclaim, "Jees!" But there is more relief than horror in it.* ROCKY *goes on)* He'll get Matteawan. He ain't responsible. What he's pulled don't mean nuttin'. So forget dat whore stuff. I'll knock de block off anyone calls you whores! I'll fill de bastard full of lead! Yuh're tarts, and what de hell of it? Yuh're as good as anyone! So forget it, see?

(They let him get his arms around them now. He gives them a hug. All the truculence leaves their faces. They smile and exchange maternally amused glances.)

MARGIE: *(with a wink)* Our little bartender, ain't he, Poil?

PEARL: Yeah, and a cute little Ginny at dat!

(They laugh)

MARGIE: And is he stinko!

PEARL: Stinko is right. But he ain't got nuttin' on us. Jees, Rocky, did we have a big time at Coney!

HOPE: Bejees, sit down, you dumb broads! Welcome home! Have a drink! Have ten drinks, bejees! *(They take the empty chairs on* CHUCK'S *left warmly welcomed by all.* ROCKY *stands in back of them, a hand on each of their shoulders, grinning with proud proprietorship.* HOPE *beams over and under his crooked spectacles with the air of a host whose party is a huge success, and rambles on happily)* Bejees, this is all right! We'll make this my birthday party, and forget the other. We'll get paralyzed! But who's missing? Where's the Old Wise Guy? Where's Larry?

ROCKY: Over by de window, Boss. Jees, he's got his eyes shut. De old bastard's asleep *(They turn to look.* ROCKY *dismisses him)* Aw, to hell wid him. Let's have a drink.

(They turn away and forget him.)

LARRY: *(torturedly arguing to himself in a shaken whisper)* It's the only way out for him! For the peace of all concerned, as Hickey said! *(Snapping)* God damn his yellow soul, if he doesn't soon, I'll go up and throw him off!—like a dog with its guts ripped out you'd put out of misery! *(He half rises from his chair just as from outside the window comes the sound of something hurtling down, followed by a muffled, crunching thud.* LARRY *gasps and drops back on his chair, shuddering, hiding his face in his hands. The group at right hear it but are too preoccupied with drinks to pay much attention.)*

HOPE: *(wonderingly)* What the hell was that?

ROCKY: Aw, nuttin'. Someting fell off de fire escape. A mattress, I'll bet. Some of dese bums been sleepin' on de fire escapes.

HOPE: *(his interest diverted by this excuse to beef—testily)* They've got to cut it out! Bejees, this ain't a fresh-air cure. Mattresses cost money.

MOSHER: Now don't start crabbing at the party, Harry. Let's drink up.

(HOPE forgets it and grabs his glass, and they all drink.)

LARRY: *(in a whisper of horrified pity)* Poor devil! *(A long-forgotten faith returns to him for a moment and he mumbles)* God rest his soul in peace. *(He opens his eyes—with a bitter self-derision)* Ah, the damned pity—the wrong kind, as Hickey said! Be God, there's no hope! I'll never be a success in the grandstand—or anywhere else! Life is too much for me! I'll be a weak fool looking with pity at the two sides of everything till the day I die! *(With an intense bitter sincerity)* May that day come soon! *(He pauses startledly, surprised at himself—then with a sardonic grin)* Be God, I'm the only real convert to death Hickey made here. From the bottom of my coward's heart I mean that now!

HOPE: *(calls effusively)* Hey there, Larry! Come over and get paralyzed! What the hell you doing, sitting there? *(Then as* LARRY *doesn't reply he immediately forgets him and turns to the party. They are all very drunk now, just a few drinks ahead of the passing-out stage, and hilariously happy about it)* Bejees, let's sing! Let's celebrate! It's my birthday party! Bejees, I'm oreyeyed! I want to sing!

(He starts the chorus of "She's the Sunshine of Paradise Alley," and instantly they all burst into song. But not the same song. Each starts the chorus of his or her choice. JIMMY TOMORROW'S *is "A Wee Dock and Doris";* ED MOSHER'S, *"Break the News to Mother";* WILLIE OBAN'S *the "Sailor Lad" ditty he sang in Act One;* GENERAL WETJOEN'S, *"Waiting at the Church";* MCGLOIN'S, *"Tammany";* CAPTAIN LEWIS', *"The Old Kent Road";* JOE'S, *"All I Got Was Sympathy";* PEARL'S *and* MARGIE'S, *"Everybody's Doing It";* ROCKY'S, *"You Great Big Beautiful Doll";* CHUCK'S, *"The Curse of an Aching Heart";* CORA'S, *"The Oceana Roll"; while* HUGO *jumps to his feet and, pounding on the table with his fist, bellows in his guttural basso the French Revolutionary "Carmagnole." A weird cacophony results from this mixture and they stop singing to roar with laughter. All but* HUGO, *who keeps on with drunken fervor.)*

HUGO:

Dansons la Carmagnole!
Vive le son! Vive le son!
Dansons la Carmagnole!
Vive le son des canons!

(They all turn on him and howl him down with amused derision. He stops singing to denounce them in his most fiery style) Capitalist svine! Stupid bourgeois monkeys! *(He declaims)* "The days grow hot, O Babylon!" *(They all take it up and shout in enthusiastic jeering chorus)* "'Tis cool beneath thy willow trees!"

(They pound their glasses on the table, roaring with laughter, and HUGO *giggles with them. In his chair by the window,* LARRY *stares in front of him, oblivious to their racket.)*

CURTAIN

ALL MY SONS (1947)

In the opening chapter of *American Drama Since World War II* (1962), Gerald Weales introduces Arthur Miller with a statement suggestive of the often contradictory critical reception Miller has received: "It is generally conceded, even by those who persist in not admiring his work, that Miller is one of the two playwrights of the postwar American theatre who deserve any consideration as major dramatists. Tennessee Williams is the other." The canon of American drama, of course, is considerably different now from what it was in 1962, as a number of arguably "major" dramatists have emerged since then. Yet if it is "generally conceded" that Miller is one of this country's most important playwrights, some critics have persisted in "not admiring" *All My Sons*, his first successful play. In a single dismissive sentence, Robert Bechtold Heilman characterizes *All My Sons* as mostly an "over-plotted play in the well-made tradition." More recently, Harold Bloom maintains that although the play is "admirably constructed," it is neither "adequately expressed" nor so "crucial" in importance as Eugene O'Neill's *The Iceman Cometh*, its principal rival for the New York Drama Critics Circle Award in 1947—which Miller won. Other critical generalizations similar to Heilman's about the play's domestic **realism** or its resemblance to the **well-made play** of the nineteenth century, about Miller's oft-stated project of writing tragic drama for the modern stage, and his self-acknowledged indebtedness to Henrik Ibsen have become commonplace. And, although avoiding the evaluative registers in which such earlier commentary is pitched, recent discussions of Miller's politics and the cultural work his drama performs mirror the mixed reception that greeted *All My Sons* a half-century ago. Whatever their supposed limitations, however, Miller and *All My Sons* continue to be the topics of critical essays, books, and debate; thus, as Weales asserted in the

early 1960s, Miller remains a preeminent figure in the history of modern American drama. Running for 328 performances in its inaugural production at New York's Coronet Theatre in January 1947, *All My Sons* marks the beginning of this preeminence.

Arthur Miller (1915–) was born in Manhattan to a manufacturer father and schoolteacher mother, one origin of the significance of the business ethos and the intense self-reflection in both *All My Sons* and his Pulitzer Prize–winning drama of the decline of the aging Willy Loman, *Death of a Salesman* (1949). Miller's own account of his childhood and adolescence in his autobiography *Timebends* (1987) suggests such a reading of the early plays. Moving to Brooklyn when he was 13 and growing up during the Depression, Miller remembers that by 1932, the year in which he graduated from high school, his family could no longer "disguise" its "fears" of poverty. "Producing even the fifty-dollars-a-month mortgage payment was becoming a strain," Miller observes—so much so that his older brother was forced to drop out of New York University to help his father in a garment business doomed later to fail. Miller also recalls that at about this time, outside a neighborhood pharmacy where teenage boys gathered to play handball, he first heard a college student allude to Marxism and an imminent social revolution that would "transform every country" by demolishing an unfair class system, effecting a more equitable distribution of wealth and restoring a greater sense of social justice. In 1932 the "concept of a classless society had a disarming sweetness," for "the *true* condition of man," it seemed to the young Miller, "was the complete opposite of the competitive system" he knew so well. Socialism's "comradely embrace" signified for him the exact opposite of the mores of his father, the failed businessman: "For deep down in the comradely world of the Marxist promise is parricide." Here social theory meets the Oedipus of classical drama and Sigmund Freud's psychoanalysis; here, some scholars have asserted, resides one source of a dramatic tension between fathers and sons—and, in Willy Loman's case, between his utopian dreams and the harsh reality of life in the modern city—so central to *All My Sons* and *Death of a Salesman*.

After graduating from high school, Miller worked at various jobs for two years before being admitted to and eventually graduating from the University of Michigan in 1938. At the university, he wrote editorials for the campus newspaper and won two successive Avery Hopwood Awards for plays, one of which (*No Villain*) was revised and won the Theatre Guild Award of $1,250 in 1938. At about this time he became engaged to the first of his three wives, Mary Grace Slattery, worked briefly with the Federal Theatre Project in 1940, and wrote scripts for several radio programs. He travelled to army camps during the war, writing a prose account of what he saw and in 1945 published his first novel, *Focus*. But the theatre was his main love, and in 1944 he finally saw one of his plays produced in New York, the ill-fated and ironically entitled *The Man Who Had All the Luck,* which closed after only four performances. But after this, Miller, who claims that the failure was essential to his education as a dramatist, went on to write *All My Sons, Death of a Salesman,* and an adaptation of Ibsen's *An Enemy of the People* (1950). Miller then transposed the **HUAC** interrogation of suspected communists into the Salem witch trials of Puritan America in his Tony Award–winning play, *The Crucible* (1953). Among the dramas that followed are *A View from the Bridge* (1955), *After the Fall* (1964), *The Price* (1968), *The Archbishop's Ceiling* (1977), *The American Clock* (1980), *The Ride Down Mount Morgan* (1991), and *Broken Glass* (1994). Miller has also written three screenplays, most notably *The Misfits* (1961), starring his second wife, Marilyn Monroe, and *Playing for Time* (1980). With his third wife, photographer Ingeborg Morath, he has also authored several travel books, including an account of *Death of a Salesman* in China.

Politics, political causes, and the theatre have been and remain Miller's principal passions, and it is in these arenas that he has both realized his greatest achievements and, occasionally, caused the greatest controversy. He served as president of International PEN, an organization of writers established after World War I to fight against censorship and political pressure exerted on writers; he attended the 1968 national convention of the Democratic Party as a state delegate from Connecticut; and in 1985, on behalf of PEN and the Helsinki Watch Committee, he and British playwright Harold Pinter went to Turkey in an effort to gain the release of writers imprisoned for their political convictions. Most famously, Miller testified in 1956 in front of HUAC, receiving a citation for contempt of Congress for refusing to inform on his friends and associates of leftist political ideology. (The sentence, which was to have included imprisonment, was later reversed.) Willing to admit responsibility for his own involvement in organizations and causes the committee deemed subversive, Miller's commitment to social change parallels the issue of individual responsibility to community and the world at large developed in such plays as *All My Sons*. In his "Introduction to the Collected Plays," Miller delineates the importance of both this idea and Ibsen's influence on his early work.

During World War II, Joe Keller, the protagonist of *All My Sons*, sold defective engine-heads to the Army Air Force, causing the deaths of 21 pilots. An amiable and well-liked man, Keller nonetheless represents, as Miller explains in his introductory essay, a "threat to society" not because he cannot tell right from wrong, but because "his cast of mind cannot admit that he, personally, has any viable connection with his world, his universe, or his society." Such myopia or "cast of mind," left uncorrected, will create what Miller describes as a "jungle existence for all of us no matter how high our buildings soar." In the climax of the play, Keller's son Chris forces his father to recognize his vital relationship to the rest of the world, one he has violated, and the recognition inevitably necessitates his self-punishment. To move the plot to this point, as Miller acknowledges, he must replicate one characteristic of such Ibsen plays as *A Doll's House* (1879) and *Hedda Gabler* (1890): He must spend a great deal of dramatic time "bringing the past into the present." As unfashionable or archaic as such lengthy exposition might be regarded, Miller claims to "take it as a truth that the end of drama is the creation of a higher consciousness." Ibsen's "insistence upon valid causation" preceding such a creation, at least in Miller's view, "cannot be dismissed as a wooden notion." Nor can the possibility of writing tragedy in a modern age. But, as he explains in his essay "Tragedy and the Common Man" (1949), tragedy requires a balancing of the individual or the psychological with the sociological: "Our lack of tragedy may be partially accounted for by the turn which modern literature has taken toward the purely psychiatric, or purely sociological. . . . From neither of these views can tragedy derive." *All My Sons* can be regarded as one of Miller's earliest efforts at constructing such a balance in what Raymond Williams has termed a "liberal tragedy" inspired by Ibsen, in which an individual aspiring against a corrupt society finally becomes aware of his or her own corruption, his or her own guilt.

Miller goes on to refine this concern in such plays as *Death of a Salesman* and *The Crucible*. For C.W.E. Bigsby, one "striking" phenomenon is the artistic "distance" Miller travels between *All My Sons* and *Death of a Salesman*, where the balance between social responsibility and individual psychology is conveyed by a dramatic **form** far more complex than that of *All My Sons*. In the later play Miller melds social **realism** with **expressionism** in representing Willy Loman's dreams and fantasies, struggles and failures; for this reason, Jo Mielziner, one of New York's most inventive designers, created a set that allowed past and present to intermingle almost seamlessly, as characters from Willy's memory "walk" through the walls of his house. Yet, like earlier critical commentary, recent studies of Miller are not always paeans to his talent. In his critique of Miller, David Savran, for example, endeavors not so much to chart his artistic evolution, but rather to situate his drama more precisely within the history of Cold War America. For Savran, Miller's stance before HUAC interrogators notwithstanding, his plays reveal not only their author's liberal politics,

but also his formulation of a problematic "liberal subject" ("who is seen as the repository of free will, moral responsibility, sovereign desires, and the power 'to follow the dictates of his or her own conscience'") and his reinforcement of traditional constructions of gender. That is to say, at the same time that Miller regarded his political ideology as "radical," his own sexual politics and that emerging in his plays were strikingly orthodox: Joe Keller, the "man among men" as described in the stage directions, and, more obviously, Willy and Biff Loman in *Death of a Salesman* aspire to a "rugged and heroic virility" marked by its exclusion of women. Savran, then, interrogates the contradictory quality of Miller's politics, which is both leftist in trajectory and nonetheless informed by all-too-familiar notions of gender.

As these very different critical perspectives are intended to suggest, Arthur Miller remains a vital force in the history of American drama, asking important questions in his plays and provoking varied, and at times negative, responses from his critics. Because *All My Sons* marks the beginning of his role in this history, it seems an appropriate place for new audiences to begin formulating their own reactions to Miller's work.

WORKS CONSULTED

Bigsby, C.W.E. *Modern American Drama, 1945–1990*. Cambridge, MA: Cambridge University Press, 1992.

Bloom, Harold. "Introduction," *Arthur Miller's All My Sons*. Ed. Harold Bloom. New York: Chelsea House, 1988.

Heilman, Robert Bechtold. *The Iceman, the Arsonist, and the Troubled Agent*. Seattle: University of Washington Press, 1973.

Miller, Arthur. "Introduction to the Collected Plays." *Arthur Miller's Collected Plays*. New York: Viking, 1957.

————. *Timebends: A Life*. New York: Grove, 1987.

————. "Tragedy and the Common Man." *New York Times*, 27 February 1949, Sec. 2, pp. 1, 3.

Savran, David. *Cowboys, Communists, and Queers: The Politics of Masculinity in the Work of Arthur Miller and Tennessee Williams*. Minneapolis: University of Minnesota Press, 1992.

Weales, Gerald. *American Drama Since World War II*. New York: Harcourt, Brace & World, 1962.

Williams, Raymond. *Modern Tragedy*. Stanford, CA: Stanford University Press, 1966.

CHARACTERS

JOE KELLER	DR. JIM BAYLISS
KATE KELLER	SUE BAYLISS
CHRIS KELLER	FRANK LUBEY
ANN DEEVER	LYDIA LUBEY
GEORGE DEEVER	BERT

ACT ONE

The back yard of the Keller home in the outskirts of an American town. August of our era.

The stage is hedged on right and left by tall, closely planted poplars which lend the yard a secluded atmosphere. Upstage is filled with the back of the house and its open, unroofed porch which extends into the yard some six feet. The house is two stories high and has seven rooms. It would have cost perhaps fifteen thousand in the early twenties when it was built. Now it is nicely painted, looks tight and comfortable, and the yard is green with sod, here and there plants whose season is gone. At the right, beside the house, the entrance of the driveway can be seen, but the poplars cut off view of its continuation downstage. In the left corner, downstage, stands the four-foot-high stump of a slender apple tree whose upper trunk and branches lie toppled beside it, fruit still clinging to its branches.

Downstage right is a small, trellised arbor, shaped like a sea shell, with a decorative bulb hanging from its forward-curving roof. Garden chairs and a table are scattered about. A garbage pail on the ground next to the porch steps, a wire leaf-burner near it.

On the rise: It is early Sunday morning. JOE KELLER *is sitting in the sun reading the want ads of the Sunday paper, the other sections of which lie neatly on the ground beside him. Behind his back, inside the arbor,* DOCTOR JIM BAYLISS *is reading part of the paper at the table.*

KELLER *is nearing sixty. A heavy man of stolid mind and build, a business man these many years, but with the imprint of the machine-shop worker and boss still upon him. When he reads, when he speaks, when he listens, it is with the terrible concentration of the uneducated man for whom there is still wonder in many commonly known things, a man whose judgments must be dredged out of experience and a peasant-like common sense. A man among men.*

DOCTOR BAYLISS *is nearly forty. A wry self-controlled man, an easy talker, but with a wisp of sadness that clings even to his self-effacing humor.*

At curtain, JIM *is standing at left, staring at the broken tree. He taps a pipe on it, blows through the pipe, feels in his pockets for tobacco, then speaks.*

JIM: Where's your tobacco?

KELLER: I think I left it on the table. (JIM *goes slowly to table on the arbor, finds a pouch, and sits there on the bench, filling his pipe*) Gonna rain tonight.

JIM: Paper says so?

KELLER: Yeah, right here.

JIM: Then it can't rain.

(FRANK LUBEY *enters, through a small space between the poplars.* FRANK *is thirty-two but balding. A pleasant, opinionated man, uncertain of himself, with a tendency toward peevishness when crossed, but always wanting it pleasant and neighborly. He rather saunters in, leisurely, nothing to do. He does not notice* JIM *in the arbor. On his greeting,* JIM *does not bother looking up.*)

FRANK: Hya.

KELLER: Hello, Frank. What's doin'?

FRANK: Nothin'. Walking off my breakfast. *(looks up at the sky)* That beautiful? Not a cloud.

KELLER: *(looking up)* Yeah, nice.

FRANK: Every Sunday ought to be like this.

KELLER: *(indicating the sections beside him)* Want the paper?

FRANK: What's the difference, it's all bad news. What's today's calamity?

KELLER: I don't know, I don't read the news part any more. It's more interesting in the want ads.

FRANK: Why, you trying to buy something?

KELLER: No, I'm just interested. To see what people want, y'know? For instance, here's a guy is lookin' for two Newfoundland dogs. Now what's he want with two Newfoundland dogs?

FRANK: That is funny.

KELLER: Here's another one. Wanted—old dictionaries. High prices paid. Now what's a man going to do with an old dictionary?

FRANK: Why not? Probably a book collector.

KELLER: You mean he'll make a living out of that?

FRANK: Sure, there's a lot of them.

KELLER: *(shaking his head)* All the kind of business goin' on. In my day, either you were a lawyer, or a doctor, or you worked in a shop. Now—

FRANK: Well, I was going to be a forester once.

KELLER: Well, that shows you; in my day, there was no such thing. *(scanning the page, sweeping it with his hand)* You look at a page like this you realize how ignorant you are. *(softly, with wonder, as he scans page)* Psss!

FRANK: *(noticing tree)* Hey, what happened to your tree?

KELLER: Ain't that awful? The wind must've got it last night. You heard the wind, didn't you?

FRANK: Yeah, I got a mess in my yard, too. *(goes to tree)* What a pity. *(turning to* KELLER*)* What'd Kate say?

KELLER: They're all asleep yet. I'm just waiting for her to see it.

FRANK: *(struck)* You know?—it's funny.

KELLER: What?

FRANK: Larry was born in August. He'd been twenty-seven this month. And his tree blows down.

KELLER: *(touched)* I'm surprised you remember his birthday, Frank. That's nice.

FRANK: Well, I'm working on his horoscope.

KELLER: How can you make him a horoscope? That's for the future, ain't it?

FRANK: Well, what I'm doing is this, see. Larry was reported missing on November twenty-fifth, right?

KELLER: Yeah?

FRANK: Well, then, we assume that if he was killed it was on November twenty-fifth. Now, what Kate wants—

KELLER: Oh, Kate asked you to make a horoscope?

FRANK: Yeah, what she wants to find out is whether November twenty-fifth was a favorable day for Larry.

KELLER: What is that, favorable day?

FRANK: Well, a favorable day for a person is a fortunate day, according to his stars. In other words it would be practically impossible for him to have died on his favorable day.

KELLER: Well, was that his favorable day?—November twenty-fifth?

FRANK: That's what I'm working on to find out. It takes time! See, the point is, if November twenty-fifth was his favorable day, then it's completely possible he's alive somewhere, because—I mean it's possible. *(he notices* JIM *now.* JIM *is looking at him as though at an idiot. To* JIM*—with an uncertain laugh)* I didn't even see you.

KELLER: *(to* JIM*)* Is he talkin' sense?

JIM: Him? He's all right. He's just completely out of his mind, that's all.

FRANK: *(peeved)* The trouble with you is, you don't *believe* in anything.

JIM: And your trouble is that you believe in *anything. You* didn't see my kid this morning, did you?

FRANK: No.

KELLER: Imagine? He walked off with his thermometer. Right out of his bag.

JIM: *(getting up)* What a problem. One look at a girl and he takes her temperature. *(goes to driveway, looks upstage toward street)*

FRANK: That boy's going to be a real doctor; he's smart.

JIM: Over my dead body he'll be a doctor. A good beginning, too.

FRANK: Why? It's an honorable profession.

JIM: *(looking at him tiredly)* Frank, will you stop talking like a civics book? *(KELLER laughs)*

FRANK: Why, I saw a movie a couple of weeks ago, reminded me of you. There was a doctor in that picture—

KELLER: Don Ameche!

FRANK: I think it was, yeah. And he worked in his basement discovering things. That's what you ought to do; you could help humanity, instead of—

JIM: I would love to help humanity on a Warner Brothers salary.

KELLER: *(pointing at him, laughing)* That's very good, Jim.

JIM: *(looking toward house)* Well, where's the beautiful girl was supposed to be here?

FRANK: *(excited)* Annie came?

KELLER: Sure, sleepin' upstairs. We picked her up on the one o'clock train last night. Wonderful thing. Girl leaves here, a scrawny kid. Couple of years go by, she's a regular woman. Hardly recognized her, and she was running in and out of this yard all her life. That was a very happy family used to live in your house, Jim.

JIM: Like to meet her. The block can use a pretty girl. In the whole neighborhood there's not a damned thing to look at. *(SUE, JIM's wife, enters. She is rounding forty, an overweight woman who fears it. On seeing her JIM wryly adds)* Except my wife, of course.

SUE: *(in same spirit)* Mrs. Adams is on the phone, you dog.

JIM: *(to KELLER)* Such is the condition which prevails—*(going to his wife)* my love, my light.

SUE: Don't sniff around me. *(pointing to their house)* And give her a nasty answer. I can smell her perfume over the phone.

JIM: What's the matter with her now?

SUE: I don't know, dear. She sounds like she's in terrible pain—unless her mouth is full of candy.

JIM: Why don't you just tell her to lay down?

SUE: She enjoys it more when you tell her to lay down. And when are you going to see Mr. Hubbard?

JIM: My dear; Mr. Hubbard is not sick, and I have better things to do than to sit there and hold his hand.

SUE: It seems to me that for ten dollars you could hold his hand.

JIM: *(to KELLER)* If your son wants to play golf tell him I'm ready. Or if he'd like to take a trip around the world for about thirty years. *(he exits)*

KELLER: Why do you needle him? He's a doctor, women are supposed to call him up.

SUE: All I said was Mrs. Adams is on the phone. Can I have some of your parsley?

KELLER: Yeah, sure. *(she goes to parsley box and pulls some parsley)* You were a nurse too long, Susie. You're too . . . too . . . realistic.

SUE: *(laughing, pointing at him)* Now you said it! *(LYDIA LUBEY enters. She is a robust, laughing girl of twenty-seven.)*

LYDIA: Frank, the toaster—*(sees the others)* Hya.

KELLER: Hello!

LYDIA: *(to FRANK)* The toaster is off again.

FRANK: Well, plug it in, I just fixed it.

LYDIA: *(kindly, but insistently)* Please, dear, fix it back like it was before.

FRANK: I don't know why you can't learn to turn on a simple thing like a toaster! *(he exits)*

SUE: *(laughing)* Thomas Edison.

LYDIA: *(apologetically)* He's really very handy. *(she sees broken tree)* Oh, did the wind get your tree?

KELLER: Yeah, last night.

LYDIA: Oh, what a pity. Annie get in?

KELLER: She'll be down soon. Wait'll you meet her, Sue, she's a knockout.

SUE: I should've been a man. People are always introducing me to beautiful women. *(to* JOE*)* Tell her to come over later: I imagine she'd like to see what we did with her house. And thanks. *(she exits)*

LYDIA: Is she still unhappy, Joe?

KELLER: Annie? I don't suppose she goes around dancing on her toes, but she seems to be over it.

LYDIA: She going to get married? Is there anybody—?

KELLER: I suppose—say, it's a couple years already. She can't mourn a boy forever.

LYDIA: It's so strange—Annie's here and not even married. And I've got three babies. I always thought it'd be the other way around.

KELLER: Well, that's what a war does. I had two sons, now I got one. It changed all the tallies. In my day when you had sons it was an honor. Today a doctor could make a million dollars if he could figure out a way to bring a boy into the world without a trigger finger.

LYDIA: You know, I was just reading—
(Enter CHRIS KELLER *from house, stands in doorway.)*

LYDIA: Hya, Chris.
*(*FRANK *shouts from offstage.)*

FRANK: Lydia, come in here! If you want the toaster to work don't plug in the malted mixer.

LYDIA: *(embarrassed, laughing)* Did I?

FRANK: And the next time I fix something don't tell me I'm crazy! Now come in here!

LYDIA: *(to* KELLER*)* I'll never hear the end of this one.

KELLER: *(calling to* FRANK*)* So what's the difference? Instead of toast have a malted!

LYDIA: Sh! sh! *(she exits, laughing)*
*(*CHRIS *watches her off. He is thirty-two; like his father, solidly built, a listener. A man capable of immense affection and loyalty. He has a cup of coffee in one hand, part of a doughnut in the other.)*

KELLER: You want the paper?

CHRIS: That's all right, just the book section. *(he bends down and pulls out part of paper on porch floor)*

KELLER: You're always reading the book section and you never buy a book.

CHRIS: *(coming down to settee)* I like to keep abreast of my ignorance. *(he sits on settee)*

KELLER: What is that, every week a new book comes out?

CHRIS: Lot of new books.

KELLER: All different.

CHRIS: All different.
*(*KELLER *shakes his head, puts knife down on bench, takes oilstone up to the cabinet.)*

KELLER: Psss! Annie up yet?

CHRIS: Mother's giving her breakfast in the dining room.

KELLER: *(looking at broken tree)* See what happened to the tree?

CHRIS: *(without looking up)* Yeah.

KELLER: What's Mother going to say?
*(*BERT *runs on from driveway. He is about eight. He jumps on stool, then on* KELLER'S *back.)*

BERT: You're finally up.

KELLER: *(swinging him around and putting him down)* Ha! Bert's here! Where's Tommy? He's got his father's thermometer again.

BERT: He's taking a reading.

CHRIS: What!

BERT: But it's only oral.

KELLER: Oh, well, there's no harm in oral. So what's new this morning, Bert?

BERT: Nothin'. *(he goes to broken tree, walks around it)*

KELLER: Then you couldn't've made a complete inspection of the block. In the beginning, when I first made you a policeman you used to come in every morning with something new. Now, nothin's ever new.

BERT: Except some kids from Thirtieth Street. They started kicking a can down the block, and I made them go away because you were sleeping.

KELLER: Now you're talkin', Bert. Now you're on the ball. First thing you know I'm liable to make you a detective.

BERT: *(pulling him down by the lapel and whispering in his ear)* Can I see the jail now?

KELLER: Seein' the jail ain't allowed, Bert. You know that.

BERT: Aw, I betcha there isn't even a jail. I don't see any bars on the cellar windows.

KELLER: Bert, on my word of honor there's a jail in the basement. I showed you my gun, didn't I?

BERT: But that's a hunting gun.

KELLER: That's an arresting gun!

BERT: Then why don't you ever arrest anybody? Tommy said another dirty word to Doris yesterday, and you didn't even demote him. *(KELLER chuckles and winks at CHRIS, who is enjoying all this.)*

KELLER: Yeah, that's a dangerous character, that Tommy. *(beckons him closer)* What word does he say?

BERT: *(backing away quickly in great embarrassment)* Oh, I can't say that.

KELLER: *(grabbing him by the shirt and pulling him back)* Well, gimme an idea.

BERT: I can't. It's not a nice word.

KELLER: Just whisper it in my ear. I'll close my eyes. Maybe I won't even hear it. *(BERT, on tiptoe, puts his lips to KELLER'S ear, then in unbearable embarrassment steps back.)*

BERT: I can't, Mr. Keller.

CHRIS: *(laughing)* Don't make him do that.

KELLER: Okay, Bert. I take your word. Now go out, and keep both eyes peeled.

BERT: *(interested)* For what?

KELLER: For what! Bert, the whole neighborhood is depending on you. A policeman don't ask questions. Now peel them eyes!

BERT: *(mystified, but willing)* Okay. *(he runs off stage back of arbor)*

KELLER: *(calling after him)* And mum's the word, Bert. *(BERT stops and sticks his head through the arbor.)*

BERT: About what?

KELLER: Just in general. Be v-e-r-y careful.

BERT: *(nodding in bewilderment)* Okay. *(he exits)*

KELLER: *(laughing)* I got all the kids crazy!

CHRIS: One of these days, they'll all come in here and beat your brains out.

KELLER: What's she going to say? Maybe we ought to tell her before she sees it.

CHRIS: She saw it.

KELLER: How could she see it? I was the first one up. She was still in bed.

CHRIS: She was out here when it broke.

KELLER: When?

CHRIS: About four this morning. *(indicating window above them)* I heard it cracking and I woke up and looked out. She was standing right here when it cracked.

KELLER: What was she doing out here four in the morning?

CHRIS: I don't know. When it cracked she ran back into the house and cried in the kitchen.

KELLER: Did you talk to her?

CHRIS: No, I—I figured the best thing was to leave her alone. *(pause)*

KELLER: *(deeply touched)* She cried hard?

CHRIS: I could hear her right through the floor of my room.

KELLER: *(after slight pause)* What was she doing out here at that hour? *(CHRIS silent. With an undertone of anger showing)* She's dreaming about him again. She's walking around at night.

CHRIS: I guess she is.

KELLER: She's getting just like after he died. *(slight pause)* What's the meaning of that?

CHRIS: I don't know the meaning of it. *(slight pause)* But I know one thing, Dad. We've made a terrible mistake with Mother.

KELLER: What?

CHRIS: Being dishonest with her. That kind of thing always pays off, and now it's paying off.

KELLER: What do you mean, dishonest?

CHRIS: You know Larry's not coming back and I know it. Why do we allow her to go on thinking that we believe with her?

KELLER: What do you want to do, argue with her?

CHRIS: I don't want to argue with her, but it's time she realized that nobody believes Larry is alive any more. *(KELLER simply moves away, thinking, looking at the ground)* Why shouldn't she dream of him, walk the nights waiting for him?

Do we contradict her? Do we say straight out that we have no hope any more? That we haven't had any hope for years now?

KELLER: *(frightened at the thought)* You can't say that to her.

CHRIS: We've got to say it to her.

KELLER: How're you going to prove it? Can you prove it?

CHRIS: For God's sake, three years! Nobody comes back after three years. It's insane.

KELLER: To you it is, and to me. But not to her. You can talk yourself blue in the face, but there's no body and there's no grave, so where are you?

CHRIS: Sit down, Dad. I want to talk to you.

(KELLER looks at him searchingly a moment.)

KELLER: The trouble is the Goddam newspapers. Every month some boy turns up from nowhere, so the next one is going to be Larry, so—

CHRIS: All right, all right, listen to me. *(slight pause.* KELLER *sits on settee)* You know why I asked Annie here, don't you?

KELLER: *(he knows, but—)* Why?

CHRIS: You know.

KELLER: Well, I got an idea, but— What's the story?

CHRIS: I'm going to ask her to marry me. *(slight pause)*

(KELLER nods.)

KELLER: Well, that's only your business, Chris.

CHRIS: You know it's not only my business.

KELLER: What do you want me to do? You're old enough to know your own mind.

CHRIS: *(asking, annoyed)* Then it's all right, I'll go ahead with it?

KELLER: Well, you want to be sure Mother isn't going to—

CHRIS: Then it isn't just my business.

KELLER: I'm just sayin'—

CHRIS: Sometimes you infuriate me, you know that? Isn't it your business, too, if I tell this to Mother and she throws a fit about it? You have such a talent for ignoring things.

KELLER: I ignore what I gotta ignore. The girl is Larry's girl.

CHRIS: She's not Larry's girl.

KELLER: From Mother's point of view he is not dead and you have no right to take his girl. *(slight pause)* Now you can go on from there if you know where to go, but I'm tellin' you I don't know where to go. See? I don't know. Now what can I do for you?

CHRIS: I don't know why it is, but every time I reach out for something I want, I have to pull back because other people will suffer. My whole bloody life, time after time after time.

KELLER: You're a considerate fella, there's nothing wrong in that.

CHRIS: To hell with that.

KELLER: Did you ask Annie yet?

CHRIS: I wanted to get this settled first.

KELLER: How do you know she'll marry you? Maybe she feels the same way Mother does?

CHRIS: Well, if she does, then that's the end of it. From her letters I think she's forgotten him. I'll find out. And then we'll thrash it out with Mother? Right? Dad, don't avoid me.

KELLER: The trouble is, you don't see enough women. You never did.

CHRIS: So what? I'm not fast with women.

KELLER: I don't see why it has to be Annie.

CHRIS: Because it is.

KELLER: That's a good answer, but it don't answer anything. You haven't seen her since you went to war. It's five years.

CHRIS: I can't help it. I know her best. I was brought up next door to her. These years when I think of someone for my wife, I think of Annie. What do you want, a diagram?

KELLER: I don't want a diagram . . . I—I'm— She thinks he's coming back, Chris. You marry that girl and you're pronouncing him dead. Now what's going to happen to Mother? Do you know? I don't! *(pause)*

CHRIS: All right, then, Dad.

KELLER: *(thinking* CHRIS *has retreated)* Give it some more thought.

CHRIS: I've given it three years of thought. I'd hoped that if I waited, Mother would forget Larry and then we'd have a regular wedding and everything happy. But if that can't happen here, then I'll have to get out.

KELLER: What the hell is *this?*

CHRIS: I'll get out. I'll get married and live some place else. Maybe in New York.

KELLER: Are you crazy?

CHRIS: I've been a good son too long, a good sucker. I'm through with it.

KELLER: You've got a business here, what the hell is this?

CHRIS: The business! The business doesn't inspire me.

KELLER: Must you be inspired?

CHRIS: Yes. I like it an hour a day. If I have to grub for money all day long at least at evening I want it beautiful. I want a family, I want some kids, I want to build something I can give myself to. Annie is in the middle of that. Now . . . where do I find it?

KELLER: You mean— *(goes to him)* Tell me something, you mean you'd leave the business?

CHRIS: Yes. On this I would.

KELLER: *(after a pause)* Well . . . you don't want to think like that.

CHRIS: Then help me stay here.

KELLER: All right, but—but don't think like that. Because what the hell did I work for? That's only for you, Chris, the whole shootin' match is for you!

CHRIS: I know that, Dad. Just you help me stay here.

KELLER: *(putting a fist up to* CHRIS's *jaw)* But don't think that way, you hear me?

CHRIS: I am thinking that way.

KELLER: *(lowering his hand)* I don't understand you, do I?

CHRIS: No, you don't. I'm a pretty tough guy.

KELLER: Yeah. I can see that.

   *(*MOTHER *appears on porch. She is in her early fifties, a woman of uncontrolled inspirations and an overwhelming capacity for love.)*

MOTHER: Joe?

CHRIS: *(going toward porch)* Hello, Mom.

MOTHER: *(indicating house behind her; to* KELLER*)* Did you take a bag from under the sink?

KELLER: Yeah, I put it in the pail.

MOTHER: Well, get it out of the pail. That's my potatoes.

   *(*CHRIS *bursts out laughing—goes up into alley.)*

KELLER: *(laughing)* I thought it was garbage.

MOTHER: Will you do me a favor, Joe? Don't be helpful.

KELLER: I can afford another bag of potatoes.

MOTHER: Minnie scoured that pail in boiling water last night. It's cleaner than your teeth.

KELLER: And I don't understand why, after I worked forty years and I got a maid, why I have to take out the garbage.

MOTHER: If you would make up your mind that every bag in the kitchen isn't full of garbage you wouldn't be throwing out my vegetables. Last time it was the onions.

   *(*CHRIS *comes on, hands her bag.)*

KELLER: I don't like garbage in the house.

MOTHER: Then don't eat. *(she goes into the kitchen with bag)*

CHRIS: That settles you for today.

KELLER: Yeah, I'm in last place again. I don't know, once upon a time I used to think that when I got money again I would have a maid and my wife would take it easy. Now I got money, and I got a maid, and my wife is workin' for the maid. *(he sits in one of the chairs)*

   *(*MOTHER *comes out on last line. She carries a pot of string beans)*

MOTHER: It's her day off, what are you crabbing about?

CHRIS: *(to* MOTHER*)* Isn't Annie finished eating?

MOTHER: *(looking around preoccupiedly at yard)* She'll be right out. *(moves)* That wind did some job on this place. *(of the tree)* So much for that, thank God.

KELLER: *(indicating chair beside him)* Sit down, take it easy.

MOTHER: *(pressing her hand on top of her head)* I've got such a funny pain on the top of my head.

CHRIS: Can I get you an aspirin?

   *(*MOTHER *picks a few petals off ground, stands there smelling them in her hand, then sprinkles them over plants.)*

MOTHER: No more roses. It's so funny . . . everything decides to happen at the same time. This month is his birthday; his tree blows down. Annie comes. Everything that happened seems to be coming back. I was just down the cellar, and what do I stumble over? His baseball glove. I haven't seen it in a century.

CHRIS: Don't you think Annie looks well?

MOTHER: Fine. There's no question about it. She's a beauty . . . I still don't know what brought her here. Not that I'm not glad to see her, but—

CHRIS: I just thought we'd all like to see each other again. (MOTHER *just looks at him, nodding ever so slightly—almost as though admitting something*) And I wanted to see her myself.

MOTHER: (*as her nods halt, to* KELLER) The only thing is I think her nose got longer. But I'll always love that girl. She's one that didn't jump into bed with somebody else as soon as it happened with her fella.

KELLER: (*as though that were impossible for* ANNIE) Oh, what're you—?

MOTHER: Never mind. Most of them didn't wait till the telegrams were opened. I'm just glad she came, so you can see I'm not *completely* out of my mind. (*sits, and rapidly breaks string beans in the pot*)

CHRIS: Just because she isn't married doesn't mean she's been mourning Larry.

MOTHER: (*with an undercurrent of observation*) Why then isn't she?

CHRIS: (*a little flustered*) Well . . . it could've been any number of things.

MOTHER: (*directly at him*) Like what, for instance?

CHRIS: (*embarrassed, but standing his ground*) I don't know. Whatever it is. Can I get you an aspirin?
(MOTHER *puts her hand to her head. She gets up and goes aimlessly toward the trees on rising.*)

MOTHER: It's not like a headache.

KELLER: You don't sleep, that's why. She's wearing out more bedroom slippers than shoes.

MOTHER: I had a terrible night. (*she stops moving*) I never had a night like that.

CHRIS: (*looking at* KELLER) What was it, Mom? Did you dream?

MOTHER: More, more than a dream.

CHRIS: (*hesitantly*) About Larry?

MOTHER: I was fast asleep, and— (*raising her arm over the audience*) Remember the way he used to fly low past the house when he was in training? When we used to see his face in the cockpit going by? That's the way I saw him. Only high up. Way, way up, where the clouds are. He was so real I could reach out and touch him. And suddenly he started to fall. And crying, crying to me . . . Mom, Mom! I could hear him like he was in the room. Mom! . . . it was his voice! If I could touch him I knew I could stop him, if I could only— (*breaks off, allowing her outstretched hand to fall*) I woke up and it was so funny— The wind . . . it was like the roaring of his engine. I came out here . . . I must've still been half asleep. I could hear that roaring like he was going by. The tree snapped right in front of me—and I like—came awake. (*she is looking at tree. She suddenly realizes something, turns with a reprimanding finger shaking slightly at* KELLER) See? We should never have planted that tree. I said so in the first place; it was too soon to plant a tree for him.

CHRIS: (*alarmed*) Too soon!

MOTHER: (*angering*) We rushed into it. Everybody was in such a hurry to bury him. I *said* not to plant it yet. (*to* KELLER) I *told* you to—!

CHRIS: Mother, Mother! (*she looks into his face*) The wind blew it down. What significance has that got? What are you talking about? Mother, please . . . Don't go through it all again, will you? It's no good, it doesn't accomplish anything. I've been thinking, y'know?— maybe we ought to put our minds to forgetting him?

MOTHER: That's the third time you've said that this week.

CHRIS: Because it's not right; we never took up our lives again. We're like at a railroad station waiting for a train that never comes in.

MOTHER: *(pressing top of her head)* Get me an aspirin, heh?

CHRIS: Sure, and let's break out of this, heh, Mom? I thought the four of us might go out to dinner a couple of nights, maybe go dancing out at the shore.

MOTHER: Fine. *(to* KELLER*)* We can do it tonight.

KELLER: Swell with me!

CHRIS: Sure, let's have some fun. *(to* MOTHER*)* You'll start with this aspirin. *(he goes up and into house with new spirit. Her smile vanishes)*

MOTHER: *(with an accusing undertone)* Why did he invite her here?

KELLER: Why does that bother you?

MOTHER: She's been in New York three and a half years, why all of a sudden—?

KELLER: Well, maybe—maybe he just wanted to see her.

MOTHER: Nobody comes seven hundred miles "just to see."

KELLER: What do you mean? He lived next door to the girl all his life, why shouldn't he want to see her again? *(*MOTHER *looks at him critically)* Don't look at me like that, he didn't tell me any more than he told you.

MOTHER: *(—a warning and a question)* He's not going to marry her.

KELLER: How do you know he's even thinking of it?

MOTHER: It's got that about it.

KELLER: *(sharply watching her reaction)* Well? So what?

MOTHER: *(alarmed)* What's going on here, Joe?

KELLER: Now listen, kid—

MOTHER: *(avoiding contact with him)* She's not his girl, Joe; she knows she's not.

KELLER: You can't read her mind.

MOTHER: Then why is she still single? New York is full of men, why isn't she married? *(pause)* Probably a hundred people told her she's foolish, but she's waited.

KELLER: How do you know why she waited?

MOTHER: She knows what I know, that's why. She's faithful as a rock. In my worst moments, I think of her waiting, and I know again that I'm right.

KELLER: Look, it's a nice day. What are we arguing for?

MOTHER: *(warningly)* Nobody in this house dast take her faith away, Joe. Strangers might. But not his father, not his brother.

KELLER: *(exasperated)* What do you want me to do? What do you want?

MOTHER: I want you to act like he's coming back. Both of you. Don't think I haven't noticed you since Chris invited her. I won't stand for any nonsense.

KELLER: But, Kate—

MOTHER: Because if he's not coming back, then I'll kill myself! Laugh. Laugh at me. *(she points to tree)* But why did that happen the very night she came back? Laugh, but there are meanings in such things. She goes to sleep in his room and his memorial breaks in pieces. Look at it; look. *(she sits on bench)* Joe—

KELLER: Calm yourself.

MOTHER: Believe with me, Joe. I can't stand all alone.

KELLER: Calm yourself.

MOTHER: Only last week a man turned up in Detroit, missing longer than Larry. You read it yourself.

KELLER: All right, all right, calm yourself.

MOTHER: You above all have got to believe, you—

KELLER: *(rising)* Why me about all?

MOTHER: Just don't stop believing.

KELLER: What does that mean, me above all?

*(*BERT *comes rushing on.)*

BERT: Mr. Keller! Say, Mr. Keller . . . *(pointing up driveway)* Tommy just said it again!

KELLER: *(not remembering any of it)* Said what? Who?

BERT: The dirty word.

KELLER: Oh. Well—

BERT: Gee, aren't you going to arrest him? I warned him.

MOTHER: *(with suddenness)* Stop that, Bert. Go home. *(*BERT *backs up, as she advances)* There's no jail here.

KELLER: *(as though to say, "Oh-what-the-hell-let-him-believe-there-is")* Kate—

MOTHER: *(turning on* KELLER *furiously)* There's no jail here! I want you to stop that jail business! *(He turns, shamed, but peeved.)*

BERT: *(past her to* KELLER*)* He's right across the street.

MOTHER: Go home, Bert. *(*BERT *turns around and goes up driveway. She is shaken. Her speech is bitten off, extremely urgent)* I want you to stop that, Joe. That whole jail business!

KELLER: *(alarmed, therefore angered)* Look at you, look at you shaking.

MOTHER: *(trying to control herself, moving about clasping her hands)* I can't help it.

KELLER: What have I got to hide? What the hell is the matter with you, Kate?

MOTHER: I didn't say you had anything to hide, I'm just telling you to stop it! Now stop it! *(As* ANN *and* CHRIS *appear on porch.* ANN *is twenty-six, gentle but despite herself capable of holding fast to what she knows.* CHRIS *opens door for her)*

ANN: Hya, Joe! *(She leads off a general laugh that is not self-conscious because they know one another too well)*

CHRIS: *(bringing* ANN *down, with an outstretched, chivalric arm)* Take a breath of that air, kid. You never get air like that in New York.

MOTHER: *(genuinely overcome with it)* Annie, where did you get that dress!

ANN: I couldn't resist. I'm taking it right off before I ruin it. *(swings around)* How's that for three weeks' salary?

MOTHER: *(to* KELLER*)* Isn't she the most—? *(to* ANN*)* It's gorgeous, simply gor—

CHRIS: *(to* MOTHER*)* No kidding, now, isn't she the prettiest gal you ever saw?

MOTHER: *(caught short by his obvious admiration, she finds herself reaching out for a glass of water and aspirin in his hand, and—)* You gained a little weight, didn't you, darling? *(she gulps pill and drinks)*

ANN: It comes and goes.

KELLER: Look how nice her legs turned out!

ANN: *(as she runs to fence)* Boy, the poplars got thick, didn't they?

*(*KELLER *moves to settee and sits.)*

KELLER: Well, it's three years, Annie. We're gettin' old, kid.

MOTHER: How does Mom like New York? *(*ANN *keeps looking through trees)*

ANN: *(a little hurt)* Why'd they take our hammock away?

KELLER: Oh, no, it broke. Couple of years ago.

MOTHER: What broke? He had one of his light lunches and flopped into it.

ANN: *(laughs and turns back toward* JIM'S *yard)* Oh, excuse me!

*(*JIM *has come to fence and is looking over it. He is smoking a cigar. As she cries out, he comes on around on stage.)*

JIM: How do you do. *(To* CHRIS*)* She looks very intelligent!

CHRIS: Ann, this is Jim—Doctor Bayliss.

ANN: *(shaking* JIM'S *hand)* Oh, sure, he writes a lot about you.

JIM: Don't you believe it. He likes everybody. In the battalion he was known as Mother McKeller.

ANN: I can believe it. You know—? *(To* MOTHER*)* It's so strange seeing him come out of that yard. *(To* CHRIS*)* I guess I never grew up. It almost seems that Mom and Pop are in there now. And you and my brother doing algebra, and Larry trying to copy my home-work. Gosh, those dear dead days beyond recall.

JIM: Well, I hope that doesn't mean you want me to move out?

SUE: *(calling from offstage)* Jim, come in here! Mr. Hubbard is on the phone!

JIM: I told you I don't want—

SUE: *(commandingly sweet)* Please, dear! Please!

JIM: *(resigned)* All right, Susie. *(trailing off)* All right, all right . . . *(to* ANN*)* I've only met you, Ann, but if I may offer you a piece of advice—When you marry, never—even in your mind—never count your husband's money.

SUE: *(from offstage)* Jim?

JIM: At once! *(turns and goes off)* At once. *(he exits)*

MOTHER: *(*ANN *is looking at her. She speaks meaningfully)* I told her to take up the guitar. It'd be a common interest for them. *(they laugh)* Well, he loves the guitar!

*(*ANN, *as though to overcome* MOTHER, *becomes suddenly lively, crosses to* KELLER *on settee, sits on his lap.)*

ANN: Let's eat at the shore tonight! Raise some hell around here, like we used to before Larry went!

MOTHER: *(emotionally)* You think of him! You see? *(triumphantly)* She thinks of him!

ANN: *(with an uncomprehending smile)* What do you mean, Kate?

MOTHER: Nothing. Just that you—remember him, he's in your thoughts.

ANN: That's a funny thing to say; how could I help remembering him?

MOTHER: *(—it is drawing to a head the wrong way for her; she starts anew. She rises and comes to* ANN*)* Did you hang up your things?

ANN: Yeah . . . *(to* CHRIS*)* Say, you've sure gone in for clothes. I could hardly find room in the closet.

MOTHER: No, don't you remember? That's Larry's room.

ANN: You mean . . . they're Larry's?

MOTHER: Didn't you recognize them?

ANN: *(slowly rising, a little embarrassed)* Well, it never occurred to me that you'd—I mean the shoes are all shined.

MOTHER: Yes, dear. *(slight pause.* ANN *can't stop staring at her.* MOTHER *breaks it by speaking with the relish of gossip, putting her arm around* ANN *and walking with her)* For so long I've been aching for a nice conversation with you, Annie. Tell me something.

ANN: What?

MOTHER: I don't know. Something nice.

CHRIS: *(wryly)* She means do you go out much?

MOTHER: Oh, shut up.

KELLER: And are any of them serious?

MOTHER: *(laughing, sits in her chair)* Why don't you both choke?

KELLER: Annie, you can't go into a restaurant with that woman any more. In five minutes thirty-nine strange people are sitting at the table telling her their life story.

MOTHER: If I can't ask Annie a personal question—

KELLER: Askin' is all right, but don't beat her over the head. You're beatin' her, you're beatin' her. *(they are laughing)*

*(*ANN *takes pan of beans off stool, puts them on floor under chair and sits.)*

ANN: *(to* MOTHER*)* Don't let them bulldoze you. Ask me anything you like. What do you want to know, Kate? Come on, let's gossip.

MOTHER: *(to* CHRIS *and* KELLER*)* She's the only one is got any sense. *(to* ANN*)* Your mother—she's not getting a divorce, heh?

ANN: No, she's calmed down about it now. I think when he gets out they'll probably live together. In New York, of course.

MOTHER: That's fine. Because your father is still—I mean he's a decent man after all is said and done.

ANN: I don't care. She can take him back if she likes.

MOTHER: And you? You—*(shakes her head negatively)*—go out much? *(slight pause)*

ANN: *(delicately)* You mean am I still waiting for him?

MOTHER: Well, no. I don't expect you to wait for him but—

ANN: *(kindly)* But that's what you mean, isn't it?

MOTHER: Well . . . yes.

ANN: Well, I'm not, Kate.

MOTHER: *(faintly)* You're not?

ANN: Isn't it ridiculous? You don't really imagine he's—?

MOTHER: I know, dear, but don't say it's ridiculous, because the papers were full of it; I don't know about New York, but there was half a page about a man missing even longer than Larry, and he turned up from Burma.

CHRIS: *(coming to* ANN*)* He couldn't have wanted to come home very badly, Mom.

MOTHER: Don't be so smart.

CHRIS: You can have a helluva time in Burma.

ANN: (*rises and swings around in back of* CHRIS) So I've heard.

CHRIS: Mother, I'll bet you money that you're the only woman in the country who after three years is still—

MOTHER: You're sure?

CHRIS: Yes, I am.

MOTHER: Well, if you're sure then you're sure. (*she turns her head away an instant*) They don't say it on the radio but I'm sure that in the dark at night they're still waiting for their sons.

CHRIS: Mother, you're absolutely—

MOTHER: (*waving him off*) Don't be so damned smart! Now stop it! (*slight pause*) There are just a few things you *don't* know. All of you. And I'll tell you one of them, Annie. Deep, deep in your heart you've always been waiting for him.

ANN: (*resolutely*) No, Kate.

MOTHER: (*with increasing demand*) But deep in your heart, Annie!

CHRIS: She ought to know, shouldn't she?

MOTHER: Don't let them tell you what to think. Listen to your heart. Only your heart.

ANN: Why does your heart tell you he's alive?

MOTHER: Because he has to be.

ANN: But why, Kate?

MOTHER: (*going to her*) Because certain things have to be, and certain things can never be. Like the sun has to rise, it has to be. That's why there's God. Otherwise anything could happen. But there's God, so certain things can never happen. I would know, Annie—just like I knew the day he—(*indicates* CHRIS)—went into that terrible battle. Did he write me? Was it in the papers? No, but that morning I couldn't raise my head off the pillow. Ask Joe. Suddenly, I knew. I knew! And he was nearly killed that day. Ann, you *know* I'm right!

(ANN *stands there in silence, then turns trembling, going upstage.*)

ANN: No, Kate.

MOTHER: I have to have some tea.

(FRANK *appears, carrying ladder.*)

FRANK: Annie! (*coming down*) How are you, gee whiz!

ANN: (*taking his hand*) Why, Frank, you're losing your hair.

KELLER: He's got responsibility.

FRANK: Gee whiz!

KELLER: Without Frank the stars wouldn't know when to come out.

FRANK: (*laughs; to* ANN) You look more womanly. You've matured. You—

KELLER: Take it easy, Frank, you're a married man.

ANN: (*as they laugh*) You still haberdashering?

FRANK: Why not? Maybe I too can get to be president. How's your brother? Got his degree, I hear.

ANN: Oh, George has his own office now!

FRANK: Don't say! (*funereally*) And your dad? Is he—?

ANN: (*abruptly*) Fine. I'll be in to see Lydia.

FRANK: (*sympathetically*) How about it, does Dad expect a parole soon?

ANN: (*with growing ill-ease*) I really don't know, I—

FRANK: (*staunchly defending her father for her sake*) I mean because I feel, y'know, that if an intelligent man like your father is put in prison, there ought to be a law that says either you execute him, or let him go after a year.

CHRIS: (*interrupting*) Want a hand with that ladder, Frank?

FRANK: (*taking cue*) That's all right, I'll— (*picks up ladder*) I'll finish the horoscope tonight, Kate. (*embarrassed*) See you later, Ann, you look wonderful. (*he exits. They look at* ANN)

ANN: (*to* CHRIS, *as she sits slowly on stool*) Haven't they stopped talking about Dad?

CHRIS: (*comes down and sits on arm of chair*) Nobody talks about him any more.

KELLER: (*rises and comes to her*) Gone and forgotten, kid.

ANN: Tell me. Because I don't want to meet anybody on the block if they're going to—

CHRIS: I don't want you to worry about it.

ANN: (*to* KELLER) Do they still remember the case, Joe? Do they talk about you?

KELLER: The only one still talks about it is my wife.

MOTHER: That's because you keep on playing policeman with the kids. All their parents hear out of you is jail, jail, jail.

KELLER: Actually what happened was that when I got home from the penitentiary the kids got very interested in me. You know kids. I was—(laughs)—like the expert on the jail situation. And as time passed they got it confused and . . . I ended up a detective. (laughs)

MOTHER: Except that *they* didn't get it confused. (to ANN) He hands out police badges from the Post Toasties boxes. (they laugh)
(ANN *rises and comes to* KELLER, *putting her arm around his shoulder.*)

ANN: (wondrously at them, happy) Gosh, it's wonderful to hear you laughing about it.

CHRIS: Why, what'd you expect?

ANN: The last thing I remember on this block was one word—"Murderers!" Remember that, Kate?—Mrs. Hammond standing in front of our house and yelling that word? She's still around, I suppose?

MOTHER: They're all still around.

KELLER: Don't listen to her. Every Saturday night the whole gang is playin' poker in this arbor. All the ones who yelled murderer takin' my money now.

MOTHER: Don't, Joe; she's a sensitive girl, don't fool her. (to ANN) They still remember about Dad. It's different with him. (indicates JOE) He was exonerated, your father's still there. That's why I wasn't so enthusiastic about your coming. Honestly, I know how sensitive you are, and I told Chris, I said—

KELLER: Listen, you do like I did and you'll be all right. The day I come home, I got out of my car—but not in front of the house . . . on the corner. You should've been here, Annie, and you too, Chris; you'd-a seen something. Everybody knew I was getting out that day; the porches were loaded. Picture it now; none of them believed I was innocent. The story was, I pulled a fast one getting myself exonerated. So I get out of my car, and I walk down the street. But very slow. And with a smile. The beast! I was the beast; the guy who sold cracked cylinder heads to the Army Air Force; the guy who made twenty-one P-40s crash in Australia. Kid, walkin' down the street that day I was guilty as hell. Except I wasn't, and there was a court paper in my pocket to prove I wasn't, and I walked . . . past . . . the porches. Result? Fourteen months later I had one of the best shops in the state again, a respected man again; bigger than ever.

CHRIS: (with admiration) Joe McGuts.

KELLER: (now with great force) That's the only way you lick 'em is guts! (to ANN) The worst thing you did was to move away from here. You made it tough for your father when he gets out. That's why I tell you, I like to see him move back right on this block.

MOTHER: (pained) How could they move back?

KELLER: It ain't gonna end *till* they move back! (to ANN) Till people play cards with him again, and talk with him, and smile with him—you play cards with a man you know he can't be a murderer. And the next time you write him I like you to tell him just what I said. (ANN *simply stares at him*) You hear me?

ANN: (surprised) Don't you hold anything against him?

KELLER: Annie, I never believed in crucifying people.

ANN: (mystified) But he was your partner, he dragged you through the mud.

KELLER: Well, he ain't my sweetheart, but you gotta forgive, don't you?

ANN: You, either, Kate? Don't you feel any—?

KELLER: (to ANN) The next time you write Dad—

ANN: I don't write him.

KELLER: (struck) Well, every now and then you—

ANN: (a little shamed, but determined) No, I've *never* written to him. Neither has my brother. (to CHRIS) Say, do you feel this way, too?

CHRIS: He murdered twenty-one pilots.

KELLER: What the hell kinda talk is that?

MOTHER: That's not a thing to say about a man.

ANN: What else can you say? When they took him away I followed him, went to him every visiting day. I was crying all the time. Until the news came about Larry. Then I realized. It's wrong to pity a man like that. Father or no father, there's only one way to look at him. He knowingly shipped out parts that would crash an airplane. And how do you know Larry wasn't one of them?

MOTHER: I was waiting for that. *(going to her)* As long as you're here, Annie, I want to ask you never to say that again.

ANN: You surprise me. I thought you'd be mad at him.

MOTHER: What your father did had nothing to do with Larry. Nothing.

ANN: But we can't know that.

MOTHER: *(striving for control)* As long as you're here!

ANN: *(perplexed)* But, Kate—

MOTHER: Put that out of your head!

KELLER: Because—

MOTHER: *(quickly to KELLER)* That's all, that's enough. *(places her hand on her head)* Come inside now, and have some tea with me. *(she turns and goes up steps)*

KELLER: *(to ANN)* The one thing you—

MOTHER: *(sharply)* He's not dead, so there's no argument! Now come!

KELLER: *(angrily)* In a minute! *(MOTHER turns and goes into house)* Now look, Annie—

CHRIS: All right, Dad, forget it.

KELLER: No, she doesn't feel that way. Annie—

CHRIS: I'm sick of the whole subject, now cut it out.

KELLER: You want her to go on like this? *(to ANN)* Those cylinder heads went into P-40s only. What's the matter with you? You know Larry never flew a P-40.

CHRIS: So who flew those P-40s, pigs?

KELLER: The man was a fool, but don't make a murderer out of him. You got no sense? Look what it does to her! *(to ANN)* Listen, you gotta appreciate what was doin' in that shop in the war. The both of you! It was a madhouse. Every half hour the Major callin' for cylinder heads, they were whippin' us with the telephone. The trucks were hauling them away hot, damn near. I mean just try to see it human, see it human. All of a sudden a batch comes out with a crack. That happens, that's the business. A fine, hairline crack. All right, so—so he's a little man, your father, always scared of loud voices. What'll the Major say?—Half a day's production shot. . . . What'll I say? You know what I mean? Human. *(he pauses)* So he takes out his tools and he— covers over the cracks. All right—that's bad, it's wrong, but that's what a little man does. If I could have gone in that day I'd a told him—junk 'em, Steve, we can afford it. But alone he was afraid. But I know he meant no harm. He believed they'd hold up a hundred per cent. That's a mistake, but it ain't murder. You mustn't feel that way about him. You understand me? It ain't right.

ANN: *(she regards him a moment)* Joe, let's forget it.

KELLER: Annie, the day the news came about Larry he was in the next cell to mine—Dad. And he cried, Annie—he cried half the night.

ANN: *(touched)* He shoulda cried all night. *(slight pause)*

KELLER: *(almost angered)* Annie, I do not understand why you—!

CHRIS: *(breaking in—with nervous urgency)* Are you going to stop it?

ANN: Don't yell at him. He just wants everybody happy.

KELLER: *(clasps her around waist, smiling)* That's my sentiments. Can you stand steak?

CHRIS: And champagne!

KELLER: Now you're operatin'! I'll call Swanson's for a table! Big time tonight, Annie!

ANN: Can't scare me.

KELLER: *(to CHRIS, pointing at ANN)* I like that girl. Wrap her up. *(they laugh. Goes up porch)* You got nice legs, Annie! . . . I want to see everybody drunk tonight. *(pointing to CHRIS)* Look at him, he's blushin'! *(he exits, laughing, into house)*

CHRIS: *(calling after him)* Drink your tea, Casanova. *(he turns to* ANN*)* Isn't he a great guy?

ANN: You're the only one I know who loves his parents.

CHRIS: I know. It went out of style, didn't it?

ANN: *(with a sudden touch of sadness)* It's all right. It's a good thing. *(she looks about)* You know? It's lovely here. The air is sweet.

CHRIS: *(hopefully)* You're not sorry you came?

ANN: Not sorry, no. But I'm—not going to stay.

CHRIS: Why?

ANN: In the first place, your mother as much as told me to go.

CHRIS: Well—

ANN: You saw that—and then you—you've been kind of—

CHRIS: What?

ANN: Well . . . kind of embarrassed ever since I got here.

CHRIS: The trouble is I planned on kind of sneaking up on you over a period of a week or so. But they take it for granted that we're all set.

ANN: I knew they would. Your mother anyway.

CHRIS: How did you know?

ANN: From *her* point of view, why else would I come?

CHRIS: Well . . . would you want to? *(*ANN *still studies him)* I guess you know this is why I asked you to come.

ANN: I guess this is why I came.

CHRIS: Ann, I love you. I love you a great deal. *(finally)* I love you. *(pause. She waits)* I have no imagination . . . that's all I know to tell you. *(*ANN *is waiting, ready)* I'm embarrassing you. I didn't want to tell it to you here. I wanted some place we'd never been; a place where we'd be brand new to each other. . . . You feel it's wrong here, don't you? This yard, this chair? I want you to be ready for me. I don't want to win you away from anything.

ANN: *(putting her arms around him)* Oh, Chris, I've been ready a long, long time!

CHRIS: Then he's gone forever. You're sure.

ANN: I almost got married two years ago.

CHRIS: Why didn't you?

ANN: You started to write to me—*(slight pause)*

CHRIS: You felt something that far back?

ANN: Every day since!

CHRIS: Ann, why didn't you let me know?

ANN: I was waiting for you, Chris. Till then you never wrote. And when you did, what did you say? You sure can be ambiguous, you know.

CHRIS: *(looks toward house, then at her, trembling)* Give me a kiss, Ann. Give me a—*(they kiss)* God, I kissed you, Annie, I kissed Annie. How long, how long I've been waiting to kiss you!

ANN: I'll never forgive you. Why did you wait all these years? All I've done is sit and wonder if I was crazy for thinking of you.

CHRIS: Annie, we're going to live now! I'm going to make you so happy. *(he kisses her, but without their bodies touching)*

ANN: *(a little embarrassed)* Not like that you're not.

CHRIS: I kissed you . . .

ANN: Like Larry's brother. Do it like you, Chris. *(he breaks away from her abruptly)* What is it, Chris?

CHRIS: Let's drive some place . . . I want to be alone with you.

ANN: No . . . what is it, Chris, your mother?

CHRIS: No—nothing like that.

ANN: Then what's wrong? Even in your letters, there was something ashamed.

CHRIS: Yes. I suppose I have been. But it's going from me.

ANN: You've got to tell me—

CHRIS: I don't know how to start. *(he takes her hand)*

ANN: It wouldn't work this way. *(Slight pause)*

CHRIS: *(speaks quietly, factually at first)* It's all mixed up with so many other things. . . . You remember, overseas, I was in command of a company?

ANN: Yeah, sure.

CHRIS: Well, I lost them.

ANN: How many?

CHRIS: Just about all.

ANN: Oh, gee!

CHRIS: It takes a little time to toss that off. Because they weren't just men. For instance, one time it'd been raining several days and this kid came to me, and gave me his last pair of dry socks. Put them in my pocket. That's only a little thing—but . . . that's the kind of guys I had. They didn't die; they killed themselves for each other. I mean that exactly; a little more selfish and they'd 've been here today. And I got an idea—watching them go down. Everything was being destroyed, see, but it seemed to me that one new thing was made. A kind of—responsibility. Man for man. You understand me?—To show that, to bring that onto the earth again like some kind of a monument and everyone would feel it standing there, behind him, and it would make a difference to him. *(pause)* And then I came home and it was incredible. I—there was no meaning in it here; the whole thing to them was a kind of a—bus accident. I went to work with Dad, and that rat-race again. I felt—what you said—ashamed somehow. Because nobody was changed at all. It seemed to make suckers out of a lot of guys. I felt wrong to be alive, to open the bank-book, to drive the new car, to see the new refrigerator. I mean you can take those things out of a war, but when you drive that car you've got to know that it came out of the love a man can have for a man, you've got to be a little better because of that. Otherwise what you have is really loot, and there's blood on it. I didn't want to take any of it. And I guess that included you.

ANN: And you still feel that way?

CHRIS: I want you now, Annie.

ANN: Because you mustn't feel that way any more. Because you have a right to whatever you have. Everything, Chris, understand that? To me, too . . . And the money, there's nothing wrong in your money. Your father put hundreds of planes in the air, you should be proud. A man should be paid for that . . .

CHRIS: Oh Annie, Annie . . . I'm going to make a fortune for you!

KELLER: *(offstage)* Hello . . . Yes. Sure.

ANN: *(laughing softly)* What'll I do with a fortune? *(They kiss.* KELLER *enters from house.)*

KELLER: *(thumbing toward house)* Hey, Ann, your brother—*(they step apart shyly.* KELLER *comes down, and wryly)* What is this, Labor Day?

CHRIS: *(waving him away, knowing the kidding will be endless)* All right, all right.

ANN: You shouldn't burst out like that.

KELLER: Well, nobody told me it was Labor Day. *(looks around)* Where's the hot dogs?

CHRIS: *(loving it)* All right. You said it once.

KELLER: Well, as long as I know it's Labor Day from now on, I'll wear a bell around my neck.

ANN: *(affectionately)* He's so subtle!

CHRIS: George Bernard Shaw as an elephant.

KELLER: George!—hey, you kissed it out of my head—your brother's on the phone.

ANN: *(surprised)* My brother?

KELLER: Yeah, George. Long distance.

ANN: What's the matter, is anything wrong?

KELLER: I don't know, Kate's talking to him. Hurry up, she'll cost him five dollars.

ANN: *(takes a step upstage, then comes down toward* CHRIS*)* I wonder if we ought to tell your mother yet? I mean I'm not very good in an argument.

CHRIS: We'll wait till tonight. After dinner. Now don't get tense, just leave it to me.

KELLER: What're you telling her?

CHRIS: Go ahead, Ann. *(with misgivings,* ANN *goes up and into house)* We're getting married, Dad. *(*KELLER *nods indecisively)* Well, don't you say anything?

KELLER: *(distracted)* I'm glad, Chris, I'm just— George is calling from Columbus.

CHRIS: Columbus!

KELLER: Did Annie tell you he was going to see his father today?

CHRIS: No, I don't think she knew anything about it.

KELLER: *(asking uncomfortably)* Chris! You—you think you know her pretty good?

CHRIS: *(hurt and apprehensive)* What kind of a question?

KELLER: I'm just wondering. All these years George don't go to see his father. Suddenly he goes . . . and she comes here.

CHRIS: Well, what about it?

KELLER: It's crazy, but it comes to my mind. She don't hold nothin' against me, does she?

CHRIS: *(angry)* I don't know what you're talking about.

KELLER: *(a little more combatively)* I'm just talkin'. To his last day in court the man blamed it all on me; and this is his daughter. I mean if she was sent here to find out something?

CHRIS: *(angered)* Why? What is there to find out?

ANN: *(on phone, offstage)* Why are you so excited, George? What happened there?

KELLER: I mean if they want to open up the case again, for the nuisance value, to hurt us?

CHRIS: Dad . . . how could you think that of her?

ANN: *(still on phone)* But what did he say to you, for God's sake?

> *Together*

KELLER: It couldn't be, heh. You know.

CHRIS: Dad, you amaze me . . .

KELLER: *(breaking in)* All right, forget it, forget it. *(with great force, moving about)* I want a clean start for you, Chris. I want a new sign over the plant—Christopher Keller, Incorporated.

CHRIS: *(a little uneasily)* J. O. Keller is good enough.

KELLER: We'll talk about it. I'm going to build you a house, stone, with a driveway from the road. I want you to spread out, Chris, I want you to use what I made for you. *(he is close to him now)* I mean, with joy, Chris, without shame . . . with joy.

CHRIS: *(touched)* I will, Dad.

KELLER: *(with deep emotion)* Say it to me.

CHRIS: Why?

KELLER: Because sometimes I think you're . . . ashamed of the money.

CHRIS: No, don't feel that.

KELLER: Because it's good money, there's nothing wrong with that money.

CHRIS: *(a little frightened)* Dad, you don't have to tell me this.

KELLER: *(—with overriding affection and self-confidence now. He grips* CHRIS *by the back of the neck, and with laughter between his determined jaws)* Look, Chris, I'll go to work on Mother for you. We'll get her so drunk tonight we'll all get married! *(steps away, with a wide gesture of his arm)* There's gonna be a wedding, kid, like there never was seen! Champagne, tuxedos—!

(He breaks off as ANN'S *voice comes out loud from the house where she is still talking on phone.)*

ANN: Simply because when you get excited you don't control yourself. . . . *(*MOTHER *comes out of house)* Well, what did he tell you for God's sake? *(pause)* All right, come then. *(pause)* Yes, they'll all be here. Nobody's running away from you. And try to get hold of yourself, will you? *(pause)* All right, all right. Good-by.

(there is a brief pause as ANN *hangs up receiver, then comes out of kitchen.)*

CHRIS: Something happen?

KELLER: He's coming here?

ANN: On the seven o'clock. He's in Columbus. *(to* MOTHER*)* I told him it would be all right.

KELLER: Sure, fine! Your father took sick?

ANN: *(mystified)* No, George didn't say he was sick. I—*(shaking it off)* I don't know, I suppose it's something stupid, you know my brother— *(she comes to* CHRIS*)* Let's go for a drive, or something . . .

CHRIS: Sure. Give me the keys, Dad.

MOTHER: Drive through the park. It's beautiful now.

CHRIS: Come on, Ann. *(to them)* Be back right away.

ANN: *(as she and* CHRIS *exit up driveway)* See you. *(*MOTHER *comes down toward* KELLER, *her eyes fixed on him.)*

KELLER: Take your time. *(to* MOTHER*)* What does George want?

MOTHER: He's been in Columbus since this morning with Steve. He's gotta see Annie right away, he says.

KELLER: What for?

MOTHER: I don't know. *(she speaks with warning)* He's a lawyer now, Joe. George is a lawyer. All these years he never even sent a postcard to Steve. Since he got back from the war, not a postcard.

KELLER: So what?

MOTHER: *(her tension breaking out)* Suddenly he takes an airplane from New York to see him. An airplane!

KELLER: Well? So?

MOTHER: *(trembling)* Why?

KELLER: I don't read minds. Do you?

MOTHER: Why, Joe? What has Steve suddenly got to tell him that he takes an airplane to see him?

KELLER: What do I care what Steve's got to tell him?

MOTHER: You're sure, Joe?

KELLER: *(frightened, but angry)* Yes, I'm sure.

MOTHER: *(sits stiffly in a chair)* Be smart now, Joe. The boy is coming. Be smart.

KELLER: *(desperately)* Once and for all, did you hear what I said? I said I'm sure!

MOTHER: *(nods weakly)* All right, Joe. *(he straightens up)* Just . . . be smart.

(KELLER, in hopeless fury, looks at her, turns around, goes up to porch and into house, slamming screen door violently behind him. MOTHER sits in chair downstage, stiffly, staring, seeing.)

C U R T A I N

A C T   T W O

As twilight falls, that evening.

On the rise, CHRIS is discovered sawing the broken-off tree, leaving stump standing alone. He is dressed in good pants, white shoes, but without a shirt. He disappears with tree up the alley when MOTHER appears on porch. She comes down and stands watching him. She has on a dressing gown, carries a tray of grape juice drink in a pitcher, and glasses with sprigs of mint in them.

MOTHER: *(calling up alley)* Did you have to put on good pants to do that? *(she comes downstage and puts tray on table in the arbor. Then looks around uneasily, then feels pitcher for coolness. CHRIS enters from alley brushing off his hands)* You notice there's more light with that thing gone?

CHRIS: Why aren't you dressing?

MOTHER: It's suffocating upstairs. I made a grape drink for Georgie. He always liked grape. Come and have some.

CHRIS: *(impatiently)* Well, come on, get dressed. And what's Dad sleeping so much for? *(he goes to table and pours a glass of juice)*

MOTHER: He's worried. When he's worried he sleeps. *(pauses. Looks into his eyes)* We're dumb, Chris. Dad and I are stupid people. We don't know anything. You've got to protect us.

CHRIS: You're silly; what's there to be afraid of?

MOTHER: To his last day in court Steve never gave up the idea that Dad made him do it. If they're going to open the case again I won't live through it.

CHRIS: George is just a damn fool, Mother. How can you take him seriously?

MOTHER: That family hates us. Maybe even Annie—

CHRIS: Oh, now, Mother . . .

MOTHER: You think just because you like everybody, they like you!

CHRIS: All right, stop working yourself up. Just leave everything to me.

MOTHER: When George goes home tell her to go with him.

CHRIS: *(noncommittally)* Don't worry about Annie.

MOTHER: Steve is her father, too.

CHRIS: Are you going to cut it out? Now, come.

MOTHER: *(going upstage with him)* You don't realize how people can hate, Chris, they can hate so much they'll tear the world to pieces.

(ANN, dressed up, appears on porch.)

CHRIS: Look! She's dressed already. *(as he and MOTHER mount porch)* I've just got to put on a shirt.

ANN: *(in a preoccupied way)* Are you feeling well, Kate?

MOTHER: What's the difference, dear. There are certain people, y'know, the sicker they get the longer they live. *(she goes into house)*

CHRIS: You look nice.

ANN: We're going to tell her tonight.

CHRIS: Absolutely, don't worry about it.

ANN: I wish we could tell her now. I can't stand scheming. My stomach gets hard.

CHRIS: It's not scheming, we'll just get her in a better mood.

MOTHER: *(offstage, in the house)* Joe, are you going to sleep all day!

ANN: *(laughing)* The only one who's relaxed is your father. He's fast asleep.

CHRIS: I'm relaxed.

ANN: Are you?

CHRIS: Look. *(he holds out his hand and makes it shake)* Let me know when George gets here.
(He goes into the house. ANN moves aimlessly, and then is drawn toward tree stump. She goes to it, hesitantly touches broken top in the hush of her thoughts. Offstage LYDIA calls, "Johnny! Come get your supper!" SUE enters, and halts, seeing ANN.)

SUE: Is my husband—?

ANN: *(turns, startled)* Oh!

SUE: I'm terribly sorry.

ANN: It's all right, I—I'm a little silly about the dark.

SUE: *(looks about)* It is getting dark.

ANN: Are you looking for your husband?

SUE: As usual. *(laughs tiredly)* He spends so much time here, they'll be charging him rent.

ANN: Nobody was dressed so he drove over to the depot to pick up my brother.

SUE: Oh, your brother's in?

ANN: Yeah, they ought to be here any minute now. Will you have a cold drink?

SUE: I will, thanks. *(ANN goes to table and pours)* My husband. Too hot to drive me to beach. Men are like little boys; for the neighbors they'll always cut the grass.

ANN: People like to do things for the Kellers. Been that way since I can remember.

SUE: It's amazing. I guess your brother's coming to give you away, heh?

ANN: *(giving her drink)* I don't know. I suppose.

SUE: You must be all nerved up.

ANN: It's always a problem getting yourself married, isn't it?

SUE: That depends on your shape, of course. I don't see why you should have had a problem.

ANN: I've had chances—

SUE: I'll bet. It's romantic . . . it's very unusual to me, marrying the brother of your sweetheart.

ANN: I don't know. I think it's mostly that whenever I need somebody to tell me the truth I've always thought of Chris. When he tells you something you know it's so. He relaxes me.

SUE: And he's got money. That's important, you know.

ANN: It wouldn't matter to me.

SUE: You'd be surprised. It makes all the difference. I married an intern. On my salary. And that was bad, because as soon as a woman supports a man he owes her something. You can never owe somebody without resenting them. *(ANN laughs)* That's true, you know.

ANN: Underneath, I think the doctor is very devoted.

SUE: Oh, certainly. But it's bad when a man always sees the bars in front of him. Jim thinks he's in jail all the time.

ANN: Oh . . .

SUE: That's why I've been intending to ask you a small favor, Ann. It's something very important to me.

ANN: Certainly, if I can do it.

SUE: You can. When you take up housekeeping, try to find a place away from here.

ANN: Are you fooling?

SUE: I'm very serious. My husband is unhappy with Chris around.

ANN: How is that?

SUE: Jim's a successful doctor. But he's got an idea he'd like to do medical research. Discover things. You see?

ANN: Well, isn't that good?

SUE: Research pays twenty-five dollars a week minus laundering the hair shirt. You've got to give up your life to go into it.

ANN: How does Chris—

SUE: *(with growing feeling)* Chris makes people want to be better than it's possible to be. He does that to people.

ANN: Is that bad?

SUE: My husband has a family, dear. Every time he has a session with Chris he feels as though he's compromising by not giving up everything for research. As though Chris or anybody else isn't compromising. It happens with Jim every couple of years. He meets a man and makes a statue out of him.

ANN: Maybe he's right. I don't mean that Chris is a statue, but—

SUE: Now darling, you know he's not right.

ANN: I don't agree with you. Chris—

SUE: Let's face it, dear. Chris is working with his father, isn't he? He's taking money out of that business every week in the year.

ANN: What of it?

SUE: You ask me what of it?

ANN: I certainly do. *(she seems about to burst out)* You oughtn't cast aspersions like that, I'm surprised at you.

SUE: You're surprised at me!

ANN: He'd never take five cents out of that plant if there was anything wrong with it.

SUE: You know that.

ANN: I know it. I resent everything you've said.

SUE: *(moving toward her)* You know what I resent, dear?

ANN: Please, I don't want to argue.

SUE: I resent living next door to the Holy Family. It makes me look like a bum, you understand?

ANN: I can't do anything about that.

SUE: Who is he to ruin a man's life? Everybody knows Joe pulled a fast one to get out of jail.

ANN: That's not true!

SUE: Then why don't you go out and talk to people? Go on, talk to them. There's not a person on the block who doesn't know the truth.

ANN: That's a lie. People come here all the time for cards and—

SUE: So what? They give him credit for being smart. I do, too, I've got nothing against Joe. But if Chris wants people to put on the hair shirt let him take off his broadcloth. He's driving my husband crazy with that phony idealism of his, and I'm at the end of my rope on it! *(CHRIS enters on porch, wearing shirt and tie now. She turns quickly, hearing. With a smile)* Hello, darling. How's Mother?

CHRIS: I thought George came.

SUE: No, it was just us.

CHRIS: *(coming down to them)* Susie, do me a favor, heh? Go up to Mother and see if you can calm her. She's all worked up.

SUE: She still doesn't know about you two?

CHRIS: *(laughs a little)* Well, she senses it, I guess. You know my mother.

SUE: *(going up to porch)* Oh, yeah, she's psychic.

CHRIS: Maybe there's something in the medicine chest.

SUE: I'll give her one of everything. *(on porch)* Don't worry about Kate; couple of drinks, dance her around a little . . . She'll love Ann. *(to ANN)* Because you're the female version of him. *(CHRIS laughs)* Don't be alarmed, I said version. *(She goes into house)*

CHRIS: Interesting woman, isn't she?

ANN: Yeah, she's very interesting.

CHRIS: She's a great nurse, you know, she—

ANN: *(in tension, but trying to control it)* Are you still doing that?

CHRIS: *(sensing something wrong, but still smiling)* Doing what?

ANN: As soon as you get to know somebody you find a distinction for them. How do you know she's a great nurse?

CHRIS: What's the matter, Ann?

ANN: The woman hates you. She despises you!

CHRIS: Hey . . . What's hit you?

ANN: Gee, Chris—

CHRIS: What happened here?

ANN: You never— Why didn't you tell me?

CHRIS: Tell you what?

ANN: She says they think Joe is guilty.

CHRIS: What difference does it make what they think?

ANN: I don't care what they think, I just don't understand why you took the trouble to deny it. You said it was all forgotten.

CHRIS: I didn't want you to feel there was anything wrong in you coming here, that's all. I know a lot of people think my father was guilty, and I assumed there might be some question in your mind.

ANN: But I never once said I suspected him.

CHRIS: Nobody says it.

ANN: Chris, I know how much you love him, but it could never—

CHRIS: Do you think I could forgive him if he'd done that thing?

ANN: I'm not here out of a blue sky, Chris. I turned my back on my father, if there's anything wrong here now—

CHRIS: I know that, Ann.

ANN: George is coming from Dad, and I don't think it's with a blessing.

CHRIS: He's welcome here. You've got nothing to fear from George.

ANN: Tell me that . . . Just tell me that.

CHRIS: The man is innocent, Ann. Remember he was falsely accused once and it put him through hell. How would you behave if you were faced with the same thing again? Annie, believe me, there's nothing wrong for you here, believe me, kid.

ANN: All right, Chris, all right. *(they embrace as* KELLER *appears quietly on porch.* ANN *simply studies him)*

KELLER: Every time I come out here it looks like Playland! *(they break and laugh in embarrassment)*

CHRIS: I thought you were going to shave?

KELLER: *(sitting on bench)* In a minute. I just woke up, I can't see nothin'.

ANN: You look shaved.

KELLER: Oh, no. *(massages his jaw)* Gotta be extra special tonight. Big night, Annie. So how's it feel to be a married woman?

ANN: *(laughs)* I don't know, yet.

KELLER: *(to* CHRIS) What's the matter, you slippin'? *(he takes a little box of apples from under the bench as they talk)*

CHRIS: The great roué!

KELLER: What is that, roué?

CHRIS: It's French.

KELLER: Don't talk dirty. *(they laugh)*

CHRIS: *(to* ANN) You ever meet a bigger ignoramus?

KELLER: Well, somebody's got to make a living.

ANN: *(as they laugh)* That's telling him.

KELLER: I don't know, everybody's gettin' so Goddam educated in this country there'll be nobody to take away the garbage. *(they laugh)* It's gettin' so the only dumb ones left are the bosses.

ANN: You're not so dumb, Joe.

KELLER: I know, but you go into our plant, for instance. I got so many lieutenants, majors and colonels that I'm ashamed to ask somebody to sweep the floor. I gotta be careful I'll insult somebody. No kiddin'. It's a tragedy: you stand on the street today and spit, you're gonna hit a college man.

CHRIS: Well, don't spit.

KELLER: *(breaks apple in half, passing it to* ANN *and* CHRIS) I mean to say, it's comin' to a pass. *(he takes a breath)* I been thinkin', Annie . . . your brother, George. I been thinkin' about your brother George. When he comes I like you to *brooch* something to him.

CHRIS: Broach.

KELLER: What's the matter with brooch?

CHRIS: *(smiling)* It's not English.

KELLER: When I went to night school it was brooch.

ANN: *(laughing)* Well, in day school it's broach.

KELLER: Don't surround me, will you? Seriously, Ann . . . You say he's not well. George, I been thinkin', why should he knock himself out in New York with that cut-throat competition, when I got so many friends here; I'm very friendly with some big lawyers in town. I could set George up here.

ANN: That's awfully nice of you, Joe.

KELLER: No, kid, it ain't nice of me. I want you to understand me. I'm thinking of Chris. *(slight pause)* See . . . this is what I mean. You get older, you want to feel that you—accomplished something. My only accomplishment is my son. I ain't brainy. That's all I accomplished. Now, a year, eighteen months, your father'll be a free man. Who is he going to come to, Annie? His baby. You. He'll come, old, mad, into your house.

ANN: That can't matter any more, Joe.

KELLER: I don't want that to come between us. *(gestures between* CHRIS *and himself)*

ANN: I can only tell you that that could never happen.

KELLER: You're in love now, Annie, but believe me, I'm older than you and I know—a daughter is a daughter, and a father is a father. And it could happen. *(he pauses)* I like you and George to go to him in prison and tell him . . . "Dad, Joe wants to bring you into the business when you get out."

ANN: *(surprised, even shocked)* You'd have him as a partner?

KELLER: No, no partner. A good job. *(pause. He sees she is shocked, a little mystified. He gets up, speaks more nervously)* I want him to know, Annie . . . while he's sitting there I want him to know that when he gets out he's got a place waitin' for him. It'll take his bitterness away. To know you got a place . . . it sweetens you.

ANN: Joe, you owe him nothing.

KELLER: I owe him a good kick in the teeth, but he's your father.

CHRIS: Then kick him in the teeth! I don't want him in the plant, so that's that! You understand? And besides, don't talk about him like that. People misunderstand you!

KELLER: And I don't understand why she has to crucify the man.

CHRIS: Well, it's her father, if she feels—

KELLER: No, no.

CHRIS: *(almost angrily)* What's it to you? Why—?

KELLER: *(—a commanding outburst in high nervousness)* A father is a father! *(as though the outburst had revealed him, he looks about, wanting to retract it. His hand goes to his cheek)* I better—I better shave. *(he turns and a smile is on his face. To* ANN*)* I didn't mean to yell at you, Annie.

ANN: Let's forget the whole thing, Joe.

KELLER: Right. *(to* CHRIS*)* She's likeable.

CHRIS: *(a little peeved at the man's stupidity)* Shave, will you?

KELLER: Right again.

(As he turns to porch LYDIA *comes hurrying from her house.)*

LYDIA: I forgot all about it. *(seeing* CHRIS *and* ANN*)* Hya. *(to* JOE*)* I promised to fix Kate's hair for tonight. Did she comb it yet?

KELLER: Always a smile, hey, Lydia?

LYDIA: Sure, why not?

KELLER: *(going up on porch)* Come on up and comb my Katie's hair. *(*LYDIA *goes up on porch)* She's got a big night, make her beautiful.

LYDIA: I will.

KELLER: *(holds door open for her and she goes into kitchen. To* CHRIS *and* ANN*)* Hey, that could be a song. *(he sings softly)*
"Come on up and comb my Katie's hair . . .
Oh, come on up, 'cause she's my lady fair—"
(to ANN*)* How's that for one year of night school? *(he continues singing as he goes into kitchen)*
"Oh, come on up, come on up, and comb my
           lady's hair—"
*(*JIM BAYLISS *rounds corner of driveway, walking rapidly.* JIM *crosses to* CHRIS, *motions him and pulls him down excitedly.* KELLER *stands just inside kitchen door, watching them.)*

CHRIS: What's the matter? Where is he?

JIM: Where's your mother?

CHRIS: Upstairs, dressing.

ANN: *(crossing to them rapidly)* What happened to George?

JIM: I asked him to wait in the car. Listen to me now. Can you take some advice? *(They wait)* Don't bring him in here.

ANN: Why?

JIM: Kate is in bad shape, you can't explode this in front of her.

ANN: Explode what?

JIM: You know why he's here, don't try to kid it away. There's blood in his eye; drive him somewhere and talk to him alone.

(ANN *turns to go up drive, takes a couple of steps, sees* KELLER, *and stops. He goes quietly on into house.*)

CHRIS: (*shaken, and therefore angered*) Don't be an old lady.

JIM: He's come to take her home. What does that mean? (*to* ANN) You know what that means. Fight it out with him some place else.

ANN: (*comes back down toward* CHRIS) I'll drive . . . him somewhere.

CHRIS: (*goes to her*) No.

JIM: Will you stop being an idiot?

CHRIS: Nobody's afraid of him here. Cut that out!

(*He starts for driveway, but is brought up short by* GEORGE, *who enters there.* GEORGE *is* CHRIS'S *age, but a paler man, now on the edge of his self-restraint. He speaks quietly, as though afraid to find himself screaming. An instant's hesitation and* CHRIS *steps up to him, hand extended, smiling.*)

CHRIS: Helluva way to do; what're you sitting out there for?

GEORGE: Doctor said your mother isn't well, I—

CHRIS: So what? She'd want to see you, wouldn't she? We've been waiting for you all afternoon. (*he puts his hand on* GEORGE'S *arm, but* GEORGE *pulls away, coming across toward* ANN)

ANN: (*touching his collar*) This is filthy, didn't you bring another shirt?

(GEORGE *breaks away from her, and moves down, examining the yard. Door opens, and he turns rapidly, thinking it is* KATE, *but it's* SUE. *She looks at him; he turns away and moves to fence. He looks over it at his former home.* SUE *comes downstage.*)

SUE: (*annoyed*) How about the beach, Jim?

JIM: Oh, it's too hot to drive.

SUE: How'd you get to the station—Zeppelin?

CHRIS: This is Mrs. Bayliss, George. (*calling, as* GEORGE *pays no attention, staring at house*) George! (GEORGE *turns*) Mrs. Bayliss.

SUE: How do you do.

GEORGE: (*removing his hat*) You're the people who bought our house, aren't you?

SUE: That's right. Come and see what we did with it before you leave.

GEORGE: (*walks down and away from her*) I liked it the way it was.

SUE: (*after a brief pause*) He's frank, isn't he?

JIM: (*pulling her off*) See you later. . . . Take it easy, fella. (*they exit*)

CHRIS: (*calling after them*) Thanks for driving him! (*turning to* GEORGE) How about some grape juice? Mother made it especially for you.

GEORGE: (*with forced appreciation*) Good old Kate, remembered my grape juice.

CHRIS: You drank enough of it in this house. How've you been, George?—Sit down.

GEORGE: (*keeps moving*) It takes me a minute. (*looking around*) It seems impossible.

CHRIS: What?

GEORGE: I'm back here.

CHRIS: Say, you've gotten a little nervous, haven't you?

GEORGE: Yeah, toward the end of the day. What're you, big executive now?

CHRIS: Just kind of medium. How's the law?

GEORGE: I don't know. When I was studying in the hospital it seemed sensible, but outside there doesn't seem to be much of a law. The trees got thick, didn't they? (*points to stump*) What's that?

CHRIS: Blew down last night. We had it there for Larry. You know.

GEORGE: Why, afraid you'll forget him?

CHRIS: (*starts for* GEORGE) Kind of a remark is that?

ANN: (*breaking in, putting a restraining hand on* CHRIS) When did you start wearing a hat?

GEORGE: (*discovers hat in his hand*) Today. From now on I decided to look like a lawyer, anyway. (*he holds it up to her*) Don't you recognize it?

ANN: Why? Where—?

GEORGE: Your father's— He asked me to wear it.

ANN: How is he?

GEORGE: He got smaller.

ANN: Smaller?

GEORGE: Yeah, little. *(holds out his hand to measure)* He's a little man. That's what happens to suckers, you know. It's good I went to him in time—another year there'd be nothing left but his smell.

CHRIS: What's the matter, George, what's the trouble?

GEORGE: The trouble? The trouble is when you make suckers out of people once, you shouldn't try to do it twice.

CHRIS: What does that mean?

GEORGE: *(to ANN)* You're not married yet, are you?

ANN: George, will you sit down and stop—?

GEORGE: Are you married yet?

ANN: No. I'm not married yet.

GEORGE: You're not going to marry him.

ANN: Why am I not going to marry him?

GEORGE: Because his father destroyed your family.

CHRIS: Now look, George . . .

GEORGE: Cut it short, Chris. Tell her to come home with me. Let's not argue, you know what I've got to say.

CHRIS: George, you don't want to be the voice of God, do you?

GEORGE: I'm—

CHRIS: That's been your trouble all your life, George, you dive into things. What kind of a statement is that to make? You're a big boy now.

GEORGE: I'm a big boy now.

CHRIS: Don't come bulling in here. If you've got something to say, be civilized about it.

GEORGE: Don't civilize me!

ANN: Shhh!

CHRIS: *(ready to hit him)* Are you going to talk like a grown man or aren't you?

ANN: *(quickly, to forestall an outburst)* Sit down, dear. Don't be angry, what's the matter? *(he allows her to seat him, looking at her)* Now what happened? You kissed me when I left, now you—

GEORGE: *(breathlessly)* My life turned upside down since then. I couldn't go back to work when you left. I wanted to go to Dad and tell him you were going to be married. It seemed impossible not to tell him. He loved you so much. *(he pauses)* Annie—we did a terrible thing. We can never be forgiven. Not even to send him a card at Christmas. I didn't see him once since I got home from the war! Annie, you don't know what was done to that man. You don't know what happened.

ANN: *(afraid)* Of course I know.

GEORGE: You can't know, you wouldn't be here. Dad came to work that day. The night foreman came to him and showed him the cylinder heads . . . they were coming out of the process with defects. There was something wrong with the process. So Dad went directly to the phone and called here and told Joe to come down right away. But the morning passed. No sign of Joe. So Dad called again. By this time he had over a hundred defectives. The Army was screaming for stuff and Dad didn't have anything to ship. So Joe told him . . . on the phone he told him to weld, cover up the cracks in any way he could, and ship them out.

CHRIS: Are you through now?

GEORGE: *(surging up at him)* I'm not through now! *(back to ANN)* Dad was afraid. He wanted Joe there if he was going to do it. But Joe can't come down . . . He's sick. Sick! He suddenly gets the flu! Suddenly! But he promised to take responsibility. Do you understand what I'm saying? On the telephone you can't have responsibility! In a court you can always deny a phone call and that's exactly what he did. They knew he was a liar the first time, but in the appeal they believed that rotten lie and now Joe is a big shot and your father is the patsy. *(he gets up)* Now what're you going to do? Eat his food, sleep in his bed? Answer me; what're you going to do?

CHRIS: What're you going to do, George?

GEORGE: He's too smart for me, I can't prove a phone call.

CHRIS: Then how dare you come in here with that rot?

ANN: George, the court—

GEORGE: The court didn't know your father! But you know him. You know in your heart Joe did it.

CHRIS: *(whirling him around)* Lower your voice or I'll throw you out of here!

GEORGE: She knows. She knows.

CHRIS: *(to* ANN*)* Get him out of here, Ann. Get him out of here.

ANN: George, I know everything you've said. Dad told that whole thing in court, and they—

GEORGE: *(—almost a scream)* The court did not know him, Annie!

ANN: Shhh!—But he'll say anything, George. You know how quick he can lie.

GEORGE: *(turning to* CHRIS, *with deliberation)* I'll ask you something, and look me in the eye when you answer me.

CHRIS: I'll look you in the eye.

GEORGE: You know your father—

CHRIS: I know him well.

GEORGE: And he's the kind of boss to let a hundred and twenty-one cylinder heads be repaired and shipped out of his shop without even knowing about it?

CHRIS: He's that kind of boss.

GEORGE: And that's the same Joe Keller who never left his shop without first going around to see that all the lights were out.

CHRIS: *(with growing anger)* The same Joe Keller.

GEORGE: The same man who knows how many minutes a day his workers spend in the toilet.

CHRIS: The same man.

GEORGE: And my father, that frightened mouse who'd never buy a shirt without somebody along—that man would dare do such a thing on his own?

CHRIS: On his own. And because he's a frightened mouse this is another thing he'd do—throw the blame on somebody else because he's not man enough to take it himself. He tried it in court but it didn't work, but with a fool like you it works!

GEORGE: Oh, Chris, you're a liar to yourself!

ANN: *(deeply shaken)* Don't talk like that!

CHRIS: *(sits facing* GEORGE*)* Tell me, George. What happened? The court record was good enough for you all these years, why isn't it good now? Why did you believe it all these years?

GEORGE: *(after a slight pause)* Because you believed it. . . . That's the truth, Chris. I believed everything, because I thought you did. But today I heard it from his mouth. From his mouth it's altogether different than the record. Anyone who knows him, and knows your father, will believe it from his mouth. Your Dad took everything we have. I can't beat that. But she's one item he's not going to grab. *(he turns to* ANN*)* Get your things. Everything they have is covered with blood. You're not the kind of a girl who can live with that. Get your things.

CHRIS: Ann . . . you're not going to believe that, are you?

ANN: *(goes to him)* You know it's not true, don't you?

GEORGE: How can he tell you? It's his father. *(to* CHRIS*)* None of these things ever even cross your mind?

CHRIS: Yes, they crossed my mind. Anything can cross your mind!

GEORGE: *He knows,* Annie. He knows!

CHRIS: The voice of God!

GEORGE: Then why isn't your name on the business? Explain that to her!

CHRIS: What the hell has that got to do with—?

GEORGE: Annie, why isn't his name on it?

CHRIS: Even when I don't own it!

GEORGE: Who're you kidding? Who gets it when he dies? *(to* ANN*)* Open your eyes, you know the both of them, isn't that the first thing they'd do, the way they love each other?—J. O. Keller and Son? *(pause.* ANN *looks from him to* CHRIS.*)* I'll settle it. Do you want to settle it, or are you afraid to?

CHRIS: What do you mean?

GEORGE: Let me go up and talk to your father. In ten minutes you'll have the answer. Or are you afraid of the answer?

CHRIS: I'm not afraid of the answer. I know the answer. But my mother isn't well and I don't want a fight here now.

GEORGE: Let me go to him.

CHRIS: You're not going to start a fight here now.

GEORGE: *(to* ANN*)* What more do you want! *(there is a sound of footsteps in the house)*

ANN: *(turns her head suddenly toward house)* Someone's coming.

CHRIS: *(to* GEORGE, *quietly)* You won't say anything now.

ANN: You'll go soon. I'll call a cab.

GEORGE: You're coming with me.

ANN: And don't mention marriage, because we haven't told her yet.

GEORGE: You're coming with me.

ANN: You understand? Don't— George, you're not going to start anything now! *(she hears footsteps)* Shsh!

*(*MOTHER *enters on porch. She is dressed almost formally; her hair is fixed. They are all turned toward her. On seeing* GEORGE *she raises both hands, comes down toward him.)*

MOTHER: Georgie, Georgie.

GEORGE: *(—he has always liked her)* Hello, Kate.

MOTHER: *(cups his face in her hands)* They made an old man out of you. *(touches his hair)* Look, you're gray.

GEORGE: *(—her pity, open and unabashed, reaches into him, and he smiles sadly)* I know, I—

MOTHER: I told you when you went away, don't try for medals.

GEORGE: *(laughs, tiredly)* I didn't try, Kate. They made it very easy for me.

MOTHER: *(actually angry)* Go on. You're all alike. *(to* ANN*)* Look at him, why did you say he's fine? He looks like a ghost.

GEORGE: *(relishing her solicitude)* I feel all right.

MOTHER: I'm sick to look at you. What's the matter with your mother, why don't she feed you?

ANN: He just hasn't any appetite.

MOTHER: If he ate in my house he'd have an appetite. *(to* ANN*)* I pity your husband! *(to* GEORGE*)* Sit down. I'll make you a sandwich.

GEORGE: *(—sits with an embarrassed laugh)* I'm really not hungry.

MOTHER: Honest to God, it breaks my heart to see what happened to all the children. How we worked and planned for you, and you end up no better than us.

GEORGE: *(with deep feeling for her)* You . . . you haven't changed at all, you know that, Kate?

MOTHER: None of us changed, Georgie. We all love you. Joe was just talking about the day you were born and the water got shut off. People were carrying basins from a block away—a stranger would have thought the whole neighborhood was on fire! *(they laugh. She sees the juice. To* ANN*)* Why didn't you give him some juice!

ANN: *(defensively)* I offered it to him.

MOTHER: *(scoffingly)* You offered it to him! *(thrusting glass into* GEORGE'S *hand)* Give it to him! *(to* GEORGE, *who is laughing)* And now you're going to sit here and drink some juice . . . and look like something!

GEORGE: *(sitting)* Kate, I feel hungry already.

CHRIS: *(proudly)* She could turn Mahatma Gandhi into a heavyweight!

MOTHER: *(to* CHRIS, *with great energy)* Listen, to hell with the restaurant! I got a ham in the icebox, and frozen strawberries, and avocados, and—

ANN: Swell, I'll help you!

GEORGE: The train leaves at eight-thirty, Ann.

MOTHER: *(to* ANN*)* You're leaving?

CHRIS: No, Mother, she's not—

ANN: *(breaking through it, going to* GEORGE*)* You hardly got here; give yourself a chance to get acquainted again.

CHRIS: Sure, you don't even know us any more.

MOTHER: Well, Chris, if they can't stay, don't—

CHRIS: No, it's just a question of George, Mother, he planned on—

GEORGE: *(gets up politely, nicely, for* KATE'S *sake)* Now wait a minute, Chris . . .

CHRIS: *(smiling and full of command, cutting him off)* If you want to go, I'll drive you to the station now, but if you're staying, no arguments while you're here.

MOTHER: *(at last confessing the tension)* Why should he argue? *(she goes to him. With desperation and compassion, stroking his hair)* Georgie and us have no argument. How could we have an argument, Georgie? We all got hit by the same lightning, how can you—? Did you see what happened to Larry's tree, Georgie? *(she has taken his arm, and unwillingly he moves across stage with her)* Imagine? While I was dreaming of him in the middle of the night, the wind came along and—

(LYDIA enters on porch. As soon as she sees him):

LYDIA: Hey, Georgie! Georgie! Georgie! Georgie! Georgie! *(she comes down to him eagerly. She has a flowered hat in her hand, which KATE takes from her as she goes to GEORGE)*

GEORGE: *(as they shake hands eagerly, warmly)* Hello, Laughy. What'd you do, grow?

LYDIA: I'm a big girl now.

MOTHER: Look what she can do to a hat!

ANN: *(to LYDIA, admiring the hat)* Did you make that?

MOTHER: In ten minutes! *(she puts it on)*

LYDIA: *(fixing it on her head)* I only rearranged it.

GEORGE: You still make your own clothes?

CHRIS: *(of MOTHER)* Ain't she classy! All she needs now is a Russian wolfhound.

MOTHER: *(moving her head)* It feels like somebody is sitting on my head.

ANN: No, it's beautiful, Kate.

MOTHER: *(kisses LYDIA. To GEORGE)* She's a genius! You should've married her. *(they laugh)* This one can feed you!

LYDIA: *(strangely embarrassed)* Oh, stop that, Kate.

GEORGE: *(to LYDIA)* Didn't I hear you had a baby?

MOTHER: You don't hear so good. She's got three babies.

GEORGE: *(a little hurt by it—to LYDIA)* No kidding, three?

LYDIA: Yeah, it was one, two, three— You've been away a long time, Georgie.

GEORGE: I'm beginning to realize.

MOTHER: *(to CHRIS and GEORGE)* The trouble with you kids is you *think* too much.

LYDIA: Well, we think, too.

MOTHER: Yes, but not all the time.

GEORGE: *(with almost obvious envy)* They never took Frank, heh?

LYDIA: *(a little apologetically)* No, he was always one year ahead of the draft.

MOTHER: It's amazing. When they were calling boys twenty-seven Frank was just twenty-eight, when they made it twenty-eight he was just twenty-nine. That's why he took up astrology. It's all in when you were born, it just goes to show.

CHRIS: What does it go to show?

MOTHER: *(to CHRIS)* Don't be so intelligent. Some superstitions are very nice! *(to LYDIA)* Did he finish Larry's horoscope?

LYDIA: I'll ask him now, I'm going in. *(to GEORGE, a little sadly, almost embarrassed)* Would you like to see my babies? Come on.

GEORGE: I don't think so, Lydia.

LYDIA: *(understanding)* All right. Good luck to you, George.

GEORGE: Thanks. And to you . . . And Frank. *(she smiles at him, turns and goes off to her house. GEORGE stands staring after her)*

LYDIA: *(as she runs off)* Oh, Frank!

MOTHER: *(reading his thoughts)* She got pretty, heh?

GEORGE: *(sadly)* Very pretty.

MOTHER: *(as a reprimand)* She's beautiful, you damned fool!

GEORGE: *(looks around longingly; and softly, with a catch in his throat)* She makes it seem so nice around here.

MOTHER: *(shaking her finger at him)* Look what happened to you because you wouldn't listen to me! I told you to marry that girl and stay out of the war!

GEORGE: *(laughs at himself)* She used to laugh too much.

MOTHER: And you didn't laugh enough. While you were getting mad about Fascism Frank was getting into her bed.

GEORGE: *(to CHRIS)* He won the war, Frank.

CHRIS: All the battles.

MOTHER: *(in pursuit of this mood)* The day they started the draft, Georgie, I told you you loved that girl.

CHRIS: *(laughs)* And truer love hath no man!

MOTHER: I'm smarter than any of you.

GEORGE: *(laughing)* She's wonderful!

MOTHER: And now you're going to listen to me, George. You had big principles, Eagle Scouts the three of you; so now I got a tree, and this one—*(indicating* CHRIS*)*—when the weather gets bad he can't stand on his feet; and that big dope—*(pointing to* LYDIA'S *house)*—next door who never reads anything but Andy Gump has three children and his house paid off. Stop being a philosopher, and look after yourself. Like Joe was just saying—you move back here, he'll help you get set, and I'll find you a girl and put a smile on your face.

GEORGE: Joe? Joe wants me here?

ANN: *(eagerly)* He asked me to tell you, and I think it's a good idea.

MOTHER: Certainly. Why must you make believe you hate us? Is that another principle?—that you have to hate us? You don't hate us, George, I know you, you can't fool me, I diapered you. *(suddenly, to* ANN*)* You remember Mr. Marcy's daughter?

ANN: *(laughing, to* GEORGE*)* She's got you hooked already! *(*GEORGE *laughs, is excited)*

MOTHER: You look her over, George; you'll see she's the most beautiful—

CHRIS: She's got warts, George.

MOTHER: *(to* CHRIS*)* She hasn't got warts! *(to* GEORGE*)* So the girl has a little beauty mark on her chin—

CHRIS: And two on her nose.

MOTHER: You remember. Her father's the retired police inspector.

CHRIS: Sergeant, George.

MOTHER: He's a very kind man!

CHRIS: He looks like a gorilla.

MOTHER: *(to* GEORGE*)* He never shot anybody.
(They all burst out laughing, as KELLER *appears in doorway.* GEORGE *rises abruptly and stares at* KELLER, *who comes rapidly down to him.)*

KELLER: *(—the laughter stops. With strained joviality)* Well! Look who's here! *(Extending his hand)* Georgie, good to see ya.

GEORGE: *(shaking hands—somberly)* How're you, Joe?

KELLER: So-so. Gettin' old. You comin' out to dinner with us?

GEORGE: No, got to be back in New York.

ANN: I'll call a cab for you. *(she goes up into the house)*

KELLER: Too bad you can't stay, George. Sit down. *(to* MOTHER*)* He looks fine.

MOTHER: He looks terrible.

KELLER: That's what I said, you look terrible, George. *(they laugh)* I wear the pants and she beats me with the belt.

GEORGE: I saw your factory on the way from the station. It looks like General Motors.

KELLER: I wish it was General Motors, but it ain't. Sit down, George. Sit down. *(takes cigar out of his pocket)* So you finally went to see your father, I hear?

GEORGE: Yes, this morning. What kind of stuff do you make now?

KELLER: Oh, little of everything. Pressure cookers, an assembly for washing machines. Got a nice, flexible plant now. So how'd you find Dad? Feel all right?

GEORGE: *(searching* KELLER, *speaking indecisively)* No, he's not well, Joe.

KELLER: *(lighting his cigar)* Not his heart again, is it?

GEORGE: It's everything, Joe. It's his soul.

KELLER: *(blowing out smoke)* Uh huh—

CHRIS: How about seeing what they did with your house?

KELLER: Leave him be.

GEORGE: *(to* CHRIS, *indicating* KELLER*)* I'd like to talk to him.

KELLER: Sure, he just got here. That's the way they do, George. A little man makes a mistake and they hang him by the thumbs; the big ones become ambassadors. I wish you'd-a told me you were going to see Dad.

GEORGE: *(studying him)* I didn't know you were interested.

KELLER: In a way, I am. I would like him to know, George, that as far as I'm concerned, any time he wants, he's got a place with me. I would like him to know that.

GEORGE: He hates your guts, Joe. Don't you know that?

KELLER: I imagined it. But that can change, too.

MOTHER: Steve was never like that.

GEORGE: He's like that now. He'd like to take every man who made money in the war and put him up against a wall.

CHRIS: He'll need a lot of bullets.

GEORGE: And he'd better not get any.

KELLER: That's a sad thing to hear.

GEORGE: *(with bitterness dominant)* Why? What'd you expect him to think of you?

KELLER: *(—the force of his nature rising, but under control)* I'm sad to see he hasn't changed. As long as I know him, twenty-five years, the man never learned how to take the blame. You know that, George.

GEORGE: *(—he does)* Well, I—

KELLER: But you do know it. Because the way you come in here you don't look like you remember it. I mean like in nineteen thirty-seven when we had the shop on Flood Street. And he damn near blew us all up with that heater he left burning for two days without water. He wouldn't admit that was his fault, either. I had to fire a mechanic to save his face. You remember that.

GEORGE: Yes, but—

KELLER: I'm just mentioning it, George. Because this is just another one of a lot of things. Like when he gave Frank that money to invest in oil stock.

GEORGE: *(distressed)* I know that, I—

KELLER: *(driving in, but restrained)* But it's good to remember those things, kid. The way he cursed Frank because the stock went down. Was that Frank's fault? To listen to him Frank was a swindler. And all the man did was give him a bad tip.

GEORGE: *(gets up, moves away)* I know those things . . .

KELLER: Then remember them, remember them. *(ANN comes out of house)* There are certain men in the world who rather see everybody hung before they'll take blame. You understand me, George?

(They stand facing each other, GEORGE *trying to judge him.)*

ANN: *(coming downstage)* The cab's on its way. Would you like to wash?

MOTHER: *(with the thrust of hope)* Why must he go? Make the midnight, George.

KELLER: Sure, you'll have dinner with us!

ANN: How about it? Why not? We're eating at the lake, we could have a swell time.

(A long pause, as GEORGE *looks at* ANN, CHRIS, KELLER, *then back to her.)*

GEORGE: All right.

MOTHER: Now you're talking.

CHRIS: I've got a shirt that'll go right with that suit.

MOTHER: Size fifteen and a half, right, George?

GEORGE: Is Lydia—? I mean—Frank and Lydia coming?

MOTHER: I'll get you a date that'll make her look like a— *(she starts upstage)*

GEORGE: *(laughing)* No, I don't want a date.

CHRIS: I know somebody just for you! Charlotte Tanner! *(he starts for the house)*

KELLER: Call Charlotte, that's right.

MOTHER: Sure, call her up. *(CHRIS goes into house)*

ANN: You go up and pick out a shirt and tie.

GEORGE: *(stops, looks around at them and the place)* I never felt at home anywhere but here. I feel so— *(he nearly laughs, and turns away from them)* Kate, you look so young, you know? You didn't change at all. It . . . rings an old bell. *(turns to* KELLER*)* You too, Joe, you're amazingly the same. The whole atmosphere is.

KELLER: Say, I ain't got time to get sick.

MOTHER: He hasn't been laid up in fifteen years.

KELLER: Except my flu during the war.

MOTHER: Huhh?

KELLER: My flu, when I was sick during . . . the war.

MOTHER: Well, sure . . . *(to* GEORGE*)* I mean except for that flu. *(GEORGE stands perfectly still)* Well, it slipped my mind, don't look at me that way. He wanted to go to the shop but he couldn't lift himself off the bed. I thought he had pneumonia.

GEORGE: Why did you say he's never—?

KELLER: I know how you feel, kid, I'll never forgive myself. If I could've gone in that day I'd never allow Dad to touch those heads.

GEORGE: She said you've never been sick.

MOTHER: I said he was sick, George.

GEORGE: (*going to* ANN) Ann, didn't you hear her say—?

MOTHER: Do you remember every time you were sick?

GEORGE: I'd remember pneumonia. Especially if I got it just the day my partner was going to patch up cylinder heads . . . What happened that day, Joe?

(FRANK *enters briskly from driveway, holding* LARRY'S *horoscope in his hand. He comes to* KATE.)

FRANK: Kate! Kate!

MOTHER: Frank, did you see George?

FRANK: (*extending his hand*) Lydia told me, I'm glad to . . . you'll have to pardon me. (*pulling* MOTHER *over*) I've got something amazing for you, Kate, I finished Larry's horoscope.

MOTHER: You'd be interested in this, George. It's wonderful the way he can understand the—

CHRIS: (*entering from house*) George, the girl's on the phone—

MOTHER: (*desperately*) He finished Larry's horoscope!

CHRIS: Frank, can't you pick a better time than this?

FRANK: The greatest men who ever lived believed in the stars!

CHRIS: Stop filling her head with that junk!

FRANK: Is it junk to feel that there's a greater power than ourselves? I've studied the stars of his life! I won't argue with you, I'm telling you. Somewhere in this world your brother is alive!

MOTHER: (*instantly to* CHRIS) Why isn't it possible?

CHRIS: Because it's insane.

FRANK: Just a minute now. I'll tell you something and you can do as you please. Just let me say it. He was supposed to have died on November twenty-fifth. But November twenty-fifth was his favorable day.

CHRIS: Mother!

MOTHER: Listen to him!

FRANK: It was a day when everything good was shining on him, the kind of day he should've married on. You can laugh at a lot of it, I can understand you laughing. But the odds are a million to one that a man won't die on his favorable day. That's known, that's known, Chris!

MOTHER: Why isn't it possible, why isn't it possible, Chris!

GEORGE: (*to* ANN) Don't you understand what she's saying? She just told you to go. What are you waiting for now?

CHRIS: Nobody can tell her to go. (*a car horn is heard*)

MOTHER: (*to* FRANK) Thank you, darling, for your trouble. Will you tell him to wait, Frank?

FRANK: (*as he goes*) Sure thing.

MOTHER: (*calling out*) They'll be right out, driver!

CHRIS: She's not leaving, Mother.

GEORGE: You heard her say it, he's never been sick!

MOTHER: He misunderstood me, Chris! (CHRIS *looks at her, struck*)

GEORGE: (*to* ANN) He simply told your father to kill pilots, and covered himself in bed!

CHRIS: You'd better answer him, Annie. Answer him.

MOTHER: I packed your bag, darling.

CHRIS: What?

MOTHER: I packed your bag. All you've got to do is close it.

ANN: I'm not closing anything. He asked me here and I'm staying till he tells me to go. (*to* GEORGE) Till Chris tells me!

CHRIS: That's all! Now get out of here, George!

MOTHER: (*to* CHRIS) But if that's how he feels—

CHRIS: That's all, nothing more till Christ comes, about the case or Larry as long as I'm here! (*to* GEORGE) Now get out of here, George!

GEORGE: (*to* ANN) You tell me. I want to hear you tell me.

ANN: Go, George!

(*They disappear up the driveway,* ANN *saying*) "Don't take it that way, Georgie! Please don't take it that way."

CHRIS: *(turning to his mother)* What do you mean, you packed her bag? How dare you pack her bag?

MOTHER: Chris—

CHRIS: How dare you pack her bag?

MOTHER: She doesn't belong here.

CHRIS: Then I don't belong here.

MOTHER: She's Larry's girl.

CHRIS: And I'm his brother and he's dead, and I'm marrying his girl.

MOTHER: Never, never in this world!

KELLER: You lost your mind?

MOTHER: You have nothing to say!

KELLER: *(cruelly)* I got plenty to say. Three and a half years you been talking like a maniac—
(MOTHER smashes him across the face.)

MOTHER: Nothing. You have nothing to say. Now I say. He's coming back, and everybody has got to wait.

CHRIS: Mother, Mother—

MOTHER: Wait, wait—

CHRIS: How long? How long?

MOTHER: *(rolling out of her)* Till he comes; forever and ever till he comes!

CHRIS: *(as an ultimatum)* Mother, I'm going ahead with it.

MOTHER: Chris, I've never said no to you in my life, now I say no!

CHRIS: You'll never let him go till I do it.

MOTHER: I'll never let him go and you'll never let him go!

CHRIS: I've let him go. I've let him go a long—

MOTHER: *(with no less force, but turning from him)* Then let your father go. *(pause. CHRIS stands transfixed)*

KELLER: She's out of her mind.

MOTHER: Altogether! *(to CHRIS, but not facing them)* Your brother's alive, darling, because if he's dead, your father killed him. Do you understand me now? As long as you live, that boy is alive. God does not let a son be killed by his father. Now you see, don't you? Now you see. *(beyond control, she hurries up and into house)*

KELLER: *(—CHRIS has not moved. He speaks insinuatingly, questioningly)* She's out of her mind.

CHRIS: *(in a broken whisper)* Then . . . you did it?

KELLER: *(with the beginning of plea in his voice)* He never flew a P-40—

CHRIS: *(struck; deadly)* But the others.

KELLER: *(insistently)* She's out of her mind. *(He takes a step toward CHRIS, pleadingly)*

CHRIS: *(unyielding)* Dad . . . you did it?

KELLER: He never flew a P-40, what's the matter with you?

CHRIS: *(still asking, and saying)* Then you did it. To the others.
(Both hold their voices down.)

KELLER: *(afraid of him, his deadly insistence)* What's the matter with you? What the hell is the matter with you?

CHRIS: *(quietly, incredibly)* How could you do that? How?

KELLER: What's the matter with you!

CHRIS: Dad . . . Dad, you killed twenty-one men!

KELLER: What, killed?

CHRIS: You killed them, you murdered them.

KELLER: *(as though throwing his whole nature open before CHRIS)* How could I kill anybody?

CHRIS: Dad! Dad!

KELLER: *(trying to hush him)* I didn't kill anybody!

CHRIS: Then explain it to me. What did you do? Explain it to me or I'll tear you to pieces!

KELLER: *(horrified at his overwhelming fury)* Don't, Chris, don't—

CHRIS: I want to know what you did, now what did you do? You had a hundred and twenty cracked engine-heads, now what did you do?

KELLER: If you're going to hang me then I—

CHRIS: I'm listening. God Almighty, I'm listening!

KELLER: *(—their movements now are those of subtle pursuit and escape. KELLER keeps a step out of CHRIS's range as he talks)* You're a boy, what could I do! I'm in business, a man is in business; a hundred and twenty cracked, you're out of business; you got a process, the process don't work you're out of business; you don't know how to operate, your stuff is no good; they close you up, they tear up your contracts, what the hell's it to them? You lay forty years into a

business and they knock you out in five minutes, what could I do, let them take forty years,
let them take my life away? *(his voice cracking)*
I never thought they'd install them. I swear to
God. I thought they'd stop 'em before anybody
took off.

CHRIS: Then why'd you ship them out?

KELLER: By the time they could spot them I thought
I'd have the process going again, and I could
show them they needed me and they'd let it go
by. But weeks passed and I got no kick-back, so
I was going to tell them.

CHRIS: Then why didn't you tell them?

KELLER: It was too late. The paper, it was all over
the front page, twenty-one went down, it was too
late. They came with handcuffs into the shop,
what could I do? *(he sits on bench)* Chris . . .
Chris, I did it for you, it was a chance and I took
it for you. I'm sixty-one years old, when would I
have another chance to make something for
you? Sixty-one years old you don't get another
chance, do ya?

CHRIS: You even knew they wouldn't hold up in
the air.

KELLER: I didn't say that.

CHRIS: But you were going to warn them not to
use them—

KELLER: But that don't mean—

CHRIS: It means you knew they'd crash.

KELLER: It don't mean that.

CHRIS: Then you *thought* they'd crash.

KELLER: I was afraid maybe—

CHRIS: You were afraid maybe! God in heaven,
what kind of a man are you? Kids were hanging
in the air by those heads. You knew that!

KELLER: For you, a business for you!

CHRIS: *(with burning fury)* For me! Where do you
live, where have you come from? For me!—I
was dying every day and you were killing my
boys and you did it for me? What the hell do
you think I was thinking of, the Goddam business? Is that as far as your mind can see, the
business? What is that, the world—the business? What the hell do you mean, you did it for
me? Don't you have a country? Don't you live

in the world? What the hell are you? You're not
even an animal, no animal kills his own, what
are you? What must I do to you? I ought to tear
the tongue out of your mouth, what must I do?
*(with his fist he pounds down upon his father's
shoulder. He stumbles away, covering his face
as he weeps)* What must I do, Jesus God, what
must I do?

KELLER: Chris . . . My Chris . . .

CURTAIN

ACT THREE

Two o'clock the following morning, MOTHER *is discovered on the rise, rocking ceaselessly in a chair,
staring at her thoughts. It is an intense, slight, sort
of rocking. A light shows from upstairs bedroom,
lower floor windows being dark. The moon is strong
and casts its bluish light.*

Presently JIM, *dressed in jacket and hat, appears, and seeing her, goes up beside her.*

JIM: Any news?

MOTHER: No news.

JIM: *(gently)* You can't sit up all night, dear, why
don't you go to bed?

MOTHER: I'm waiting for Chris. Don't worry about
me, Jim, I'm perfectly all right.

JIM: But it's almost two o'clock.

MOTHER: I can't sleep. *(slight pause)* You had an
emergency?

JIM: *(tiredly)* Somebody had a headache and
thought he was dying. *(slight pause)* Half of
my patients are quite mad. Nobody realizes how
many people are walking around loose, and
they're cracked as coconuts. Money. Money-
money-money-money. You say it long enough it
doesn't mean anything. *(she smiles, makes a silent laugh)* Oh, how I'd love to be around when
that happens!

MOTHER: *(shaking her head)* You're so childish,
Jim! Sometimes you are.

JIM: *(looks at her a moment)* Kate. *(pause)* What happened?

MOTHER: I told you. He had an argument with Joe. Then he got in the car and drove away.

JIM: What kind of an argument?

MOTHER: An argument, Joe . . . He was crying like a child, before.

JIM: They argued about Ann?

MOTHER: *(after slight hesitation)* No, not Ann. Imagine? *(indicates lighted window above)* She hasn't come out of that room since he left. All night in that room.

JIM: *(looks at window, then at her)* What'd Joe do, tell him?

MOTHER: *(stops rocking)* Tell him what?

JIM: Don't be afraid, Kate, I know. I've always known.

MOTHER: How?

JIM: It occurred to me a long time ago.

MOTHER: I always had the feeling that in the back of his head, Chris . . . almost knew. I didn't think it would be such a shock.

JIM: *(gets up)* Chris would never know how to live with a thing like that. It takes a certain talent—for lying. You have it, and I do. But not him.

MOTHER: What do you mean . . . He's not coming back?

JIM: Oh, no, he'll come back. We all come back, Kate. These private little revolutions always die. The compromise is always made. In a peculiar way. Frank is right—every man does have a star. The star of one's honesty. And you spend your life groping for it, but once it's out it never lights again. I don't think he went very far. He probably just wanted to be alone to watch his star go out.

MOTHER: Just as long as he comes back.

JIM: I wish he wouldn't, Kate. One year I simply took off, went to New Orleans; for two months I lived on bananas and milk, and studied a certain disease. It was beautiful. And then she came, and she cried. And I went back home with her. And now I live in the usual darkness; I can't find myself; it's even hard sometimes to remember the kind of man I wanted to be. I'm a good husband; Chris is a good son—he'll come back.

(KELLER comes out on porch in dressing gown and slippers. He goes upstage—to alley. JIM goes to him.)

JIM: I have a feeling he's in the park. I'll look around for him. Put her to bed, Joe; this is no good for what she's got. *(JIM exits up driveway)*

KELLER: *(coming down)* What does he want here?

MOTHER: His friend is not home.

KELLER: *(comes down to her. His voice is husky)* I don't like him mixing in so much.

MOTHER: It's too late, Joe. He knows.

KELLER: *(apprehensively)* How does he know?

MOTHER: He guessed a long time ago.

KELLER: I don't like that.

MOTHER: *(laughs dangerously, quietly into the line)* What you don't like.

KELLER: Yeah, what I don't like.

MOTHER: You can't bull yourself through this one, Joe, you better be smart now. This thing—this thing is not over yet.

KELLER: *(indicating lighted window above)* And what is she doing up there? She don't come out of the room.

MOTHER: I don't know, what is she doing? Sit down, stop being mad. You want to live? You better figure out your life.

KELLER: She don't know, does she?

MOTHER: She saw Chris storming out of here. It's one and one—she knows how to add.

KELLER: Maybe I ought to talk to her?

MOTHER: Don't ask me, Joe.

KELLER: *(—almost an outburst)* Then who do I ask? But I don't think she'll do anything about it.

MOTHER: You're asking me again.

KELLER: I'm askin' you. What am I, a stranger? I thought I had a family here. What happened to my family?

MOTHER: You've got a family. I'm simply telling you that I have no strength to think any more.

KELLER: You have no strength. The minute there's trouble you have no strength.

MOTHER: Joe, you're doing the same thing again; all your life whenever there's trouble you yell at me and you think that settles it.

KELLER: Then what do I do? Tell me, talk to me, what do I do?

MOTHER: Joe . . . I've been thinking this way. If he comes back—

KELLER: What do you mean "if"? He's comin' back!

MOTHER: I think if you sit him down and you— explain yourself. I mean you ought to make it clear to him that you know you did a terrible thing. *(not looking into his eyes)* I mean if he saw that you realize what you did. You see?

KELLER: What ice does that cut?

MOTHER: *(a little fearfully)* I mean if you told him that you want to pay for what you did.

KELLER: *(sensing . . . quietly)* How can I pay?

MOTHER: Tell him—you're willing to go to prison. *(pause)*

KELLER: *(struck, amazed)* I'm willing to—?

MOTHER: *(quickly)* You wouldn't go, he wouldn't ask you to go. But if you told him you wanted to, if he could feel that you wanted to pay, maybe he would forgive you.

KELLER: He would forgive me! For what?

MOTHER: Joe, you know what I mean.

KELLER: I don't know what you mean! You wanted money, so I made money. What must I be forgiven? You wanted money, didn't you?

MOTHER: I didn't want it that way.

KELLER: I didn't want it that way, either! What difference is it what you want? I spoiled the both of you. I should've put him out when he was ten like I was put out, and make him earn his keep. Then he'd know how a buck is made in this world. Forgiven! I could live on a quarter a day myself, but I got a family so I—

MOTHER: Joe, Joe . . . It don't excuse it that you did it for the family.

KELLER: It's got to excuse it!

MOTHER: There's something bigger than the family to him.

KELLER: Nothin' is bigger!

MOTHER: There is to him.

KELLER: There's nothin' he could do that I wouldn't forgive. Because he's my son. Because I'm his father and he's my son.

MOTHER: Joe, I tell you—

KELLER: Nothin's bigger than that. And you're goin' to tell him, you understand? I'm his father and he's my son, and if there's something bigger than that I'll put a bullet in my head!

MOTHER: You stop that!

KELLER: You heard me. Now you know what to tell him. *(pause. He moves from her—halts)* But he wouldn't put me away though . . . He wouldn't do that . . . Would he?

MOTHER: He loved you, Joe, you broke his heart.

KELLER: But to put me away . . .

MOTHER: I don't know. I'm beginning to think we don't really know him. They say in the war he was such a killer. Here he was always afraid of mice. I don't know him. I don't know what he'll do.

KELLER: Goddam, if Larry was alive he wouldn't act like this. He understood the way the world is made. He listened to me. To him the world had a forty-foot front, it ended at the building line. This one, everything bothers him. You make a deal, overcharge two cents, and his hair falls out. He don't understand money. Too easy, it came too easy. Yes, sir. Larry. That was a boy we lost, Larry. Larry. *(he slumps on chair in front of her)* What am I gonna do, Kate?

MOTHER: Joe, Joe, please . . . You'll be all right, nothing is going to happen.

KELLER: *(desperately, lost)* For you, Kate, for both of you, that's all I ever lived for . . .

MOTHER: I know, darling, I know. *(ANN enters from house. They say nothing, waiting for her to speak)*

ANN: Why do you stay up? I'll tell you when he comes.

KELLER: *(rises, goes to her)* You didn't eat supper, did you? *(to MOTHER)* Why don't you make her something?

MOTHER: Sure, I'll—

ANN: Never mind, Kate, I'm all right. *(they are unable to speak to each other)* There's something I want to tell you. *(she starts, then halts)* I'm not going to do anything about it.

MOTHER: She's a good girl! *(to* KELLER*)* You see? She's a—

ANN: I'll do nothing about Joe, but you're going to do something for me. *(directly to* MOTHER*)* You made Chris feel guilty with me. Whether you wanted to or not, you've crippled him in front of me. I'd like you to tell him that Larry is dead and that you know it. You understand me? I'm not going out of here alone. There's no life for me that way. I want you to set him free. And then I promise you, everything will end, and we'll go away, and that's all.

KELLER: You'll do that. You'll tell him.

ANN: I know what I'm asking, Kate. You had two sons. But you've only got one now.

KELLER: You'll tell him.

ANN: And you've got to say it to him so he knows you mean it.

MOTHER: My dear, if the boy was dead, it wouldn't depend on my words to make Chris know it. . . . The night he gets into your bed, his heart will dry up. Because he knows and you know. To his dying day he'll wait for his brother! No, my dear, no such thing. You're going in the morning, and you're going alone. That's your life, that's your lonely life. *(she goes to porch, and starts in)*

ANN: Larry is dead, Kate.

MOTHER: *(—she stops)* Don't speak to me.

ANN: I said he's dead. I know! He crashed off the coast of China November twenty-fifth! His engine didn't fail him. But he died. I know . . .

MOTHER: How did he die? You're lying to me. If you know, how did he die?

ANN: I loved him. You know I loved him. Would I have looked at anyone else if I wasn't sure? That's enough for you.

MOTHER: *(moving on her)* What's enough for me? What're you talking about? *(she grasps* ANN'S *wrists)*

ANN: You're hurting my wrists.

MOTHER: What are you talking about! *(pause. She stares at* ANN *a moment, then turns and goes to* KELLER*)*

ANN: Joe, go in the house.

KELLER: Why should I—

ANN: Please go.

KELLER: Lemme know when he comes. *(*KELLER *goes into house)*

MOTHER: *(as she sees* ANN *taking a letter from her pocket)* What's that?

ANN: Sit down. *(*MOTHER *moves left to chair, but does not sit)* First you've got to understand. When I came, I didn't have any idea that Joe—I had nothing against him or you. I came to get married. I hoped . . . So I didn't bring this to hurt you. I thought I'd show it to you only if there was no other way to settle Larry in your mind.

MOTHER: Larry? *(snatches letter from* ANN'S *hand)*

ANN: He wrote it to me just before he— *(*MOTHER *opens and begins to read letter)* I'm not trying to hurt you, Kate. You're making me do this, now remember you're— Remember. I've been so lonely, Kate . . . I can't leave here alone again. *(a long, low moan comes from* MOTHER'S *throat as she reads)* You made me show it to you. You wouldn't believe me. I told you a hundred times, why wouldn't you believe me!

MOTHER: Oh, my God . . .

ANN: *(with pity and fear)* Kate, please, please . . .

MOTHER: My God, my God . . .

ANN: Kate, dear, I'm so sorry . . . I'm so sorry. *(*CHRIS *enters from driveway. He seems exhausted.)*

CHRIS: What's the matter—?

ANN: Where were you? . . . You're all perspired. *(*MOTHER *doesn't move)* Where were you?

CHRIS: Just drove around a little. I thought you'd be gone.

ANN: Where do I go? I have nowhere to go.

CHRIS: *(to* MOTHER*)* Where's Dad?

ANN: Inside lying down.

CHRIS: Sit down, both of you. I'll say what there is to say.

MOTHER: I didn't hear the car . . .

CHRIS: I left it in the garage.

MOTHER: Jim is out looking for you.

CHRIS: Mother . . . I'm going away. There are a couple of firms in Cleveland, I think I can get a place. I mean, I'm going away for good. *(to* ANN *alone)* I know what you're thinking, Annie. It's true. I'm yellow. I was made yellow in this house because I suspected my father and I did nothing about it, but if I knew that night when I came home what I know now, he'd be in the district attorney's office by this time, and I'd have brought him there. Now if I look at him, all I'm able to do is cry.

MOTHER: What are you talking about? What else can you do?

CHRIS: I could jail him! I could jail him, if I were human any more. But I'm like everybody else now. I'm practical now. You made me practical.

MOTHER: But you have to be.

CHRIS: The cats in that alley are practical, the bums who ran away when we were fighting were practical. Only the dead ones weren't practical. But now I'm practical, and I spit on myself. I'm going away. I'm going now.

ANN: *(going up to him)* I'm coming with you.

CHRIS: No, Ann.

ANN: Chris, I don't ask you to do anything about Joe.

CHRIS: You do, you do.

ANN: I swear I never will.

CHRIS: In your heart you always will.

ANN: Then do what you have to do!

CHRIS: Do what? What is there to do? I've looked all night for a reason to make him suffer.

ANN: There's reason, there's reason!

CHRIS: What? Do I raise the dead when I put him behind bars? Then what'll I do it for? We used to shoot a man who acted like a dog, but honor was real there, you were protecting something. But here? This is the land of the great big dogs, you don't love a man here, you eat him! That's the principle; the only one we live by— it just happened to kill a few people this time, that's all. The world's that way, how can I take it

out on him? What sense does that make? This is a zoo, a zoo!

ANN: *(to* MOTHER*)* You know what he's got to do! Tell him!

MOTHER: Let him go.

ANN: I won't let him go. You'll tell him what he's got to do . . .

MOTHER: Annie!

ANN: Then I will!

(KELLER *enters from house.* CHRIS *sees him, goes down near arbor.)*

KELLER: What's the matter with you? I want to talk to you.

CHRIS: I've got nothing to say to you.

KELLER: *(taking his arm)* I want to talk to you!

CHRIS: *(pulling violently away from him)* Don't do that, Dad. I'm going to hurt you if you do that. There's nothing to say, so say it quick.

KELLER: Exactly what's the matter? What's the matter? You got too much money? Is that what bothers you?

CHRIS: *(with an edge of sarcasm)* It bothers me.

KELLER: If you can't get used to it, then throw it away. You hear me? Take every cent and give it to charity, throw it in the sewer. Does that settle it? In the sewer, that's all. You think I'm kidding? I'm tellin' you what to do, if it's dirty then burn it. It's your money, that's not my money. I'm a dead man, I'm an old dead man, nothing's mine. Well, talk to me! What do you want to do!

CHRIS: It's not what I want to do. It's what you want to do.

KELLER: What should I want to do? (CHRIS *is silent)* Jail? You want me to go to jail? If you want me to go, say so! Is that where I belong? Then tell me so! *(slight pause)* What's the matter, why can't you tell me? *(furiously)* You say everything else to me, say that! *(slight pause)* I'll tell you why you can't say it. Because you know I don't belong there. Because you know! *(with growing emphasis and passion, and a persistent tone of desperation)* Who worked for nothin' in that war? When they work for nothin', I'll work for nothin'. Did they ship a gun or a truck outa Detroit before they got their price? Is that clean? It's dollars and cents, nickels and dimes; war and peace, it's nickels and dimes, what's clean? Half the Goddam country is gotta go if I go! That's why you can't tell me.

CHRIS: That's exactly why.

KELLER: Then . . . why am *I* bad?

CHRIS: *I* know you're no worse than most men but I thought you were better. I never saw you as a man. I saw you as my father. *(almost breaking)* I can't look at you this way, I can't look at myself! *(He turns away, unable to face* KELLER. ANN *goes quickly to* MOTHER, *takes letter from her and starts for* CHRIS. MOTHER *instantly rushes to intercept her.)*

MOTHER: Give me that!

ANN: He's going to read it! *(she thrusts letter into* CHRIS'S *hand)* Larry. He wrote it to me the day he died.

KELLER: Larry!

MOTHER: Chris, it's not for you. *(he starts to read)* Joe . . . go away . . .

KELLER: *(mystified, frightened)* Why'd she say, Larry, what—?

MOTHER: *(desperately pushes him toward alley, glancing at* CHRIS) Go to the street, Joe, go to the street! *(she comes down beside* KELLER) Don't, Chris . . . *(pleading from her whole soul)* Don't tell him.

CHRIS: *(quietly)* Three and one half years . . . talking, talking. Now you tell me what you must do . . . This is how he died, now tell me where you belong.

KELLER: *(pleading)* Chris, a man can't be a Jesus in this world!

CHRIS: I know all about the world. I know the whole crap story. Now listen to this, and tell me what a man's got to be! *(reads)* "My dear Ann: . . ." You listening? He wrote this the day he died. Listen, don't cry. . . . Listen! "My dear Ann: It is impossible to put down the things I feel. But I've got to tell you something. Yesterday they flew in a load of papers from the States and I read about Dad and your father

being convicted. I can't express myself. I can't tell you how I feel—I can't bear to live any more. Last night I circled the base for twenty minutes before I could bring myself in. How could he have done that? Every day three or four men never come back and he sits back there doing business. . . . I don't know how to tell you what I feel. . . . I can't face anybody. . . . I'm going out on a mission in a few minutes. They'll probably report me missing. If they do, I want you to know that you mustn't wait for me. I tell you, Ann, if I had him there now I could kill him—" *(*KELLER *grabs letter from* CHRIS'S *hand and reads it. After a long pause)* Now blame the world. Do you understand that letter?

KELLER: *(speaking almost inaudibly)* I think I do. Get the car. I'll put on my jacket. *(he turns and starts slowly for the house.* MOTHER *rushes to intercept him)*

MOTHER: Why are you going? You'll sleep, why are you going?

KELLER: I can't sleep here. I'll feel better if I go.

MOTHER: You're so foolish. Larry was your son too, wasn't he? You know he'd never tell you to do this.

KELLER: *(looking at letter in his hand)* Then what is this if it isn't telling me? Sure, he was my son. But I think to him they were all my sons. And I guess they were, I guess they were. I'll be right down. *(exits into house)*

MOTHER: *(to* CHRIS, *with determination)* You're not going to take him!

CHRIS: I'm taking him.

MOTHER: It's up to you, if you tell him to stay he'll stay. Go and tell him!

CHRIS: Nobody could stop him now.

MOTHER: You'll stop him! How long will he live in prison? Are you trying to kill him?

CHRIS: *(holding out letter)* I thought you read this!

MOTHER: *(of* LARRY, *the letter)* The war is over! Didn't you hear? It's over!

CHRIS: Then what was Larry to you? A stone that fell into the water? It's not enough for him to be sorry. Larry didn't kill himself to make you and Dad sorry.

MOTHER: What more can we be!

CHRIS: You can be better! Once and for all you can know there's a universe of people outside and you're responsible to it, and unless you know that, you threw away your son because that's why he died.

(A shot is heard in the house. They stand frozen for a brief second. CHRIS *starts for porch, pauses at step, turns to* ANN.)

CHRIS: Find Jim! *(he goes on into the house and* ANN *runs up driveway.* MOTHER *stands alone, transfixed)*

MOTHER: *(softly, almost moaning)* Joe . . . Joe . . . Joe . . . Joe . . . *(*CHRIS *comes out of house, down to* MOTHER's *arms)*

CHRIS: *(almost crying)* Mother, I didn't mean to—

MOTHER: Don't dear. Don't take it on yourself. Forget now. Live. *(*CHRIS *stirs as if to answer)* Shhh . . . *(she puts his arms down gently and moves toward porch)* Shhh . . . *(as she reaches porch steps she begins sobbing).*

C U R T A I N

CAT ON A HOT TIN ROOF (1955)

In an interview published in *Playboy* in 1973, Tennessee Williams confided to C. Robert Jennings that although *The Glass Menagerie* (1944) "may be my best play, *Cat on a Hot Tin Roof* is still my favorite." Williams goes on to say that he "hated" Richard Brooks's 1958 film adaptation of the play which, along with its stars Paul Newman and Elizabeth Taylor, was nominated for an Academy Award (ironically, Brooks and James Poe were also nominated for writing the very screenplay Williams so disliked). In particular, Williams objected to Taylor's casting as Maggie, and in a later interview in *The Partisan Review* voiced his dismay at the film's optimistic ending, one in which Brooks "sweetens up" the material and "makes it all hunky-dory." The film, of course, given the censurious Production Code of the Motion Picture Producers and Distributors of America (M.P.P.D.A.) in effect at the time, did much more than "sweeten up" the conclusion of *Cat on a Hot Tin Roof*. It effected major changes in Williams's play, ranging all the way from the rewording of a phrase (Maggie's reference to Brick as an "ass-aching Puritan" is changed to "back-aching Puritan," for example) to the more serious matter of erasing all references both to the homosexual couple who once owned the plantation Big Daddy Pollitt operates and to the homoerotic in his son Brick's feelings of guilt over his past relationship with Skipper, his dead teammate and friend. As revised for the screen, *Cat on a Hot Tin Roof*, especially in its presentation of the origin of Brick and Maggie's troubled marriage, bears little resemblance to Williams's play, one whose origin dates back to his story "Three Players of a Summer Game," written in 1952 and published in a collection of short fiction, *Hard Candy* (1954).

In addition to the film, several other versions of *Cat on a Hot Tin Roof* exist, a testament to Williams's abiding interest in his favorite play. Two of these are printed here, as they are in the eight-volume *The Theatre of Tennessee Williams* (1971): Williams's original version and the Broadway version with its revised third act. The changes in the latter were suggested to Williams by Elia Kazan, director of such distinguished plays as Williams's *Streetcar Named Desire* (1947) and Arthur Miller's *Death of a Salesman* (1949), and of such films as *On the Waterfront* (1954) and *East of Eden* (1955). As Williams observes in a "Note of Explanation" published along with the Broadway version, Kazan believed that the play's third act required three revisions: Big Daddy, whom Kazan regarded as crucial to the play's action, needed to reappear; Brick needed to be at least somewhat transformed after his emotional encounter with his father; and Maggie needed to be drawn in a more sympathetic light. For the Broadway production of *Cat on a Hot Tin Roof* Williams, who writes in his explanatory note that "no living playwright . . . hasn't something valuable to learn about his own work from a director so keenly perceptive as Elia Kazan," acceded only to the third of Kazan's suggestions and refashioned Maggie's character. In the same *Playboy* interview and elsewhere, Williams expresses his view that no piece of writing is "ever what one wishes it to be," and perhaps this sentiment partially explains his rewriting the play for the American Shakespeare Theatre in 1974, nearly 20 years after its Broadway opening. In this later version, Williams appears to have pointed at least one revision in the direction Kazan had outlined so many years before, for here (as in the film as well) Big Daddy returns in Act Three, bursting with crude humor and a desire to survey his "twenty-eight thousand acres of th' richest land this side of the valley Nile." As in his original 1955 script—and unlike the saccharine ending of the film with Brick kissing Maggie as his desire for her is reborn—the 1974 *Cat on a Hot Tin Roof* ends with Maggie expressing her love for Brick, who echoes the question Big Daddy uttered earlier in the play, "Wouldn't it be funny if that was true?" How significant these changes are to the 1974 *Cat* is a matter of some debate, an issue about which even Williams seemed uncertain: In the prefatory material for this later revision, he claims that the third act is "completely rewritten, along with other substantial revisions," but in the *Partisan Review* interview he states that he "made some changes in the end, [but] not as much as I anticipated." Readers of all of these versions will have to draw their own conclusions about shades of difference between them, starting with the two different versions printed here that readers and audiences alike experienced in 1955.

Thomas Lanier, later Tennessee, Williams (1911–1983) was born to C. C. and Edwina Williams in Columbus, Mississippi, and moved to St. Louis at age seven when his father, a travelling shoe salesman, was named branch sales manager for the International Shoe Company. For the next several years the family moved to eight different apartments in St. Louis, where young Tom endured his parents' increasingly violent quarrels. In 1922, his mother bought him a secondhand typewriter, and by 1927 he was earning small amounts of money and cash prizes for his essays and film reviews. In 1929, he enrolled at the University of Missouri, but two years later, after failing ROTC, his father refused to allow him to continue. Williams later studied at Washington University in St. Louis, and in 1936 local theatre groups produced two of his one-act plays. In 1937, he enrolled at the University of Iowa and completed his degree during the summer of 1938. After graduating, Williams moved to New Orleans, where he worked as a waiter and continued to write stories and plays, submitting several plays to a contest sponsored by the **Group Theatre** in New York. He received $100 from the Group (and, more importantly, introduced himself to such theatre professionals as Kazan), travelled with a friend to California and toured Mexico, and upon returning moved back to St. Louis. He

won a grant from the Rockefeller Foundation and in January, 1940, enrolled in a seminar on playwriting conducted by Theresa Helburn, executive director of the **Theatre Guild**, and John Gassner, essayist and distinguished professor. After two years of writing, revision, and the rejection of plays by various New York producers, Williams began work on *The Gentleman Caller*, later named *The Glass Menagerie*, which opened in Chicago in 1944 and became a huge success when moved to New York the following March. Williams's career, one of the most distinguished in the history of the American theatre—and, in some ways, one of the most poignant—had begun.

Over the next two decades came a string of successful plays and film adaptations: *A Streetcar Named Desire* (1947), which won both the New York Drama Critics Circle Award and the Pulitzer Prize; *Summer and Smoke* (1948); *The Rose Tattoo* (1951), winner of the Tony Award for Best Play; *Cat on a Hot Tin Roof*, which was awarded both the New York Drama Critics Circle Award and the Pulitzer Prize; *Suddenly Last Summer* (1958); *Sweet Bird of Youth* (1959); and *The Night of the Iguana* (1961), winner of the New York Drama Critics Circle Award. There were, along the way, the inevitable failures: the highly experimental "dream play" *Camino Real* (1953) received sharp reviews and closed after just 60 performances (although a 1970 revival of the play achieved considerable success), and *Orpheus Descending* (1956) closed after only 68 performances. By the early 1960s, professional failure and personal distress had taken their toll on him; he had begun psychiatric analysis in 1956, the year his father died, and his longtime companion Frank Merlo died of lung cancer in 1963. "The Sixties were no good for me even from the beginning, from *Night of the Iguana* on," Williams observed in his *Playboy* interview. "My professional decline began after *Iguana*. . . . I was broken as much by repeated failures in the theater as by Frank's death. Everything went wrong. My life—private and professional—and ultimately my mind broke." The abuse of alcohol and prescribed sleeping pills, depression, professional failure—by 1969 Williams's life was in a shambles, and he spent the last three months of the year in a hospital. Williams returned in the 1970s, however, to write such plays as *Out Cry* (1971), *Small Craft Warnings* (1972), and others before his death in 1983.

The success of *Cat on a Hot Tin Roof* is, in some respects, the product of Williams at the height of his artistic powers and of Kazan and designer Jo Mielziner at the height of theirs. Reviewing the play for the *New Republic*, Eric Bentley emphasized the relationship between the set and lighting effects for *Cat* and those of both *A Streetcar Named Desire* and *Death of a Salesman*. In all three productions, and especially in *Cat*, which marked for Bentley an even further departure from naturalism than the earlier two plays, a minimalist "exterior" is deftly made to represent a troubled psychological "interior": a "view of *man's* exterior . . . is also a view of his interior, the habitat of his body and the country of his memories and dreams. A theatre historian would probably call this world a combination of **naturalism** and **expressionism**." C. W. E. Bigsby alludes to the same phenomenon when he locates the "great strength" of the play in "Williams's ability to fuse the psychological, the social, and the metaphysical in a play whose realistic set belies its symbolic force." For Bigsby, then, *Cat on a Hot Tin Roof* concerns more than individual psychology; like much of Williams's work, it depicts a "society on the turn." The southern setting of this and many of his plays is redolent of a past on the wane and no longer recoverable; when Big Daddy dies, part of an older South will die with him.

Reviewers in 1955 and critics now underscore the relationship between sexuality and capitalism in *Cat on a Hot Tin Roof*. As the play begins, the large Pollitt clan awaits the return of Big Daddy, whom Bentley with strong justification terms a "shocking vulgarian," from a battery of medical tests that will indicate he is dying of cancer. The disposition of his immense estate is at issue, as Gooper, the lawyer with five "monstrous" children and a "good breeder" of a wife, intends to secure it for himself rather than see it fall into the hands of his alcoholic brother. Alcoholism, however, is not Brick's only problem, for he finds it impossible to sustain any sexual intimacy

with Maggie because of his past relationship with Skipper—one Brick describes as an "exceptional friendship," something "clean and decent"—and his guilt over hanging up on Skipper immediately before his suicide. This "exceptional friendship" is juxtaposed to Big Daddy's leering after Maggie and his stated desire to "cut loose" with a younger woman and "hump her from hell to breakfast." Thus, Big Daddy, the "Ugly American" who has gone to Europe with his wife and brought back a small fortune in goods, also becomes what David Savran terms the "exemplar of normative masculinity." Citing Arthur Miller's response to the play, Savran calls Big Daddy "the very image of power, of materiality, of authority," and the model of a promiscuous "orthodox heterosexualized masculinity in the 1950s that simultaneously desires and degrades women"; conversely, homosexual desire is "cast not as masculinity's anathema but as that which already inheres inside the male subject (like a cancer)." In *Cat on a Hot Tin Roof*, such complexities of sexuality and gender construction are implicated in a narrative about family, acquisitiveness, and a young man's idealized yearning for an honest, "deep" relationship he unfortunately cannot find with his wife. Williams's favorite play, it remains an important work in its own right and an intriguing artifact of a moment in American history when such matters were just beginning to be discussed with the frankness Williams offers.

WORKS CONSULTED

Bentley, Eric. "Review." *The New Republic*, 4 April 1955, p. 22.

Bigsby, C.W.E. *Modern American Drama, 1945–1990*. Cambridge, MA: Cambridge University Press, 1992.

Brown, Cecil. "Interview with Tennessee Williams." *Conversations with Tennessee Williams*. Ed. Albert J. Devlin. Jackson: University of Mississippi Press, 1986. 251–283.

Jennings, C. Robert. "*Playboy* Interview: Tennessee Williams." In *Conversations with Tennessee Williams*. 224–250.

Londré, Felicia Hardison. *Tennessee Williams*. New York: Ungar, 1979.

Murphy, Brenda. *Tennessee Williams and Elia Kazan: A Collaboration in the Theatre*. Cambridge, MA: Cambridge University Press, 1992.

Savran, David. *Communists, Cowboys, and Queers: The Politics of Masculinity in the Work of Arthur Miller and Tennessee Williams.* Minneapolis: University of Minnesota Press, 1992.

Williams, Tennessee. *Cat on a Hot Tin Roof.* New York: New Directions, 1975.

———. *The Theatre of Tennessee Williams.* 8 vols. New York: New Directions, 1971.

Person to Person

Of course it is a pity that so much of all creative work is so closely related to the personality of the one who does it.

It is sad and embarrassing and unattractive that those emotions that stir him deeply enough to demand expression, and to charge their expression with some measure of light and power, are nearly all rooted, however changed in their surface, in the particular and sometimes peculiar concerns of the artist himself, that special world, the passions and images of it that each of us weaves about him from birth to death, a web of monstrous complexity, spun forth at a speed that is incalculable to a length beyond measure, from the spider mouth of his own singular perceptions.

It is a lonely idea, a lonely condition, so terrifying to think of that we usually don't. And so we talk to each other, write and wire each other, call each other short and long distance across land and sea, clasp hands with each other at meeting and at parting, fight each other and even destroy each other because of this always somewhat thwarted effort to break through walls to each other. As a character in a play once said, "We're all of us sentenced to solitary confinement inside our own skins."

Personal lyricism is the outcry of prisoner to prisoner from the cell in solitary where each is confined for the duration of his life.

I once saw a group of little girls on a Mississippi sidewalk, all dolled up in their mothers' and sisters' castoff finery, old raggedy ball gowns and plumed hats and high-heeled slippers, enacting a meeting of ladies in a parlor with a perfect mimicry of polite Southern gush and simper. But one child

was not satisfied with the attention paid her enraptured performance by the others, they were too involved in their own performances to suit her, so she stretched out her skinny arms and threw back her skinny neck and shrieked to the deaf heavens and her equally oblivious playmates, "Look at me, look at me, look at me!"

And then her mother's high-heeled slippers threw her off balance and she fell to the sidewalk in a great howling tangle of soiled white satin and torn pink net, and still nobody looked at her.

I wonder if she is not, now, a Southern writer.

Of course it is not only Southern writers, of lyrical bent, who engage in such histrionics and shout, "Look at me!" Perhaps it is a parable of all artists. And not always do we topple over and land in a tangle of trappings that don't fit us. However, it is well to be aware of that peril, and not to content yourself with a demand for attention, to know that out of your personal lyricism, your sidewalk histrionics, something has to be created that will not only attract observers but participants in the performance.

I try very hard to do that.

The fact that I want you to observe what I do for your possible pleasure and to give you knowledge of things that I feel I may know better than you, because my world is different from yours, as different as every man's world is from the world of others, is not enough excuse for a personal lyricism that has not yet mastered its necessary trick of rising above the singular to the plural concern, from personal to general import. But for years and years now, which may have passed like a dream because of this obsession, I have been trying to learn how to perform this trick and make it truthful, and sometimes I feel that I am able to do it. Sometimes, when the enraptured streetcorner performer in me cries out "Look at me!," I feel that my hazardous footwear and fantastic regalia may not quite throw me off balance. Then, suddenly, you fellow-performers in the sidewalk show may turn to give me your attention and allow me to hold it, at least for the interval between 8:40 and 11 something P.M.

Eleven years ago this month of March, when I was far closer than I knew, only nine months away from that long-delayed, but always expected, something that I lived for, the time when I would first catch and hold an audience's attention, I wrote my first preface to a long play. The final paragraph went like this:

> There is too much to say and not enough time to say it. Nor is there power enough. I am not a good writer. Sometimes I am a very bad writer indeed. There is hardly a successful writer in the field who cannot write circles around me . . . but I think of writing as something more organic than words, something closer to being and action. I want to work more and more with a more plastic theatre than the one I have (worked with) before. I have never for one moment doubted that there are people—millions!—to say things to. We come to each other, gradually, but with love. It is the short reach of my arms that hinders, not the length and multiplicity of theirs. With love and with honesty, the embrace is inevitable.

This characteristically emotional, if not rhetorical, statement of mine at that time seems to suggest that I thought of myself as having a highly personal, even intimate relationship with people who go to see plays. I did and I still do. A morbid shyness once prevented me from having much direct communication with people, and possibly that is why I began to write to them plays and stories. But even now when that tongue-locking, face-flushing, silent and crouching timidity has worn off with the passage of the troublesome youth that it sprang from, I still find it somehow easier to "level with" crowds of strangers in the hushed twilight of orchestra and balcony sections of theatres than with individuals across a table from me. Their being strangers somehow makes them more familiar and more approachable, easier to talk to.

Of course I know that I have sometimes presumed too much upon corresponding sympathies and interest in those to whom I talk boldly, and this has led to rejections that were painful and costly enough to inspire more prudence. But when I weigh one thing against another, an easy liking against a hard respect, the balance always tips the same way, and whatever the risk of being turned a cold shoulder, I still don't want to talk to people only about the surface aspects of their lives, the sort of things that acquaintances laugh and chatter about on ordinary social occasions.

I feel that they get plenty of that, and heaven knows so do I, before and after the little interval of time in which I have their attention and say what I have to say to them. The discretion of social conversation, even among friends, is exceeded only by the discretion of "the deep six," that grave wherein nothing is mentioned at all. Emily Dickinson, that lyrical spinster of Amherst, Massachusetts, who wore a strict and savage heart on a taffeta sleeve, commented wryly on that kind of posthumous discourse among friends in these lines:

> I died for beauty, but was scarce
> Adjusted in the tomb,
> When one who died for truth was lain
> In an adjoining room.
>
> He questioned softly why I failed?
> "For beauty," I replied.
> "And I for truth,—the two are one;
> We brethren are," he said.
>
> And so, as kinsmen met a night,
> We talked between the rooms,
> Until the moss had reached our lips,
> And covered up our names.

Meanwhile!—I want to go on talking to you as freely and intimately about what we live and die for as if I knew you better than anyone else whom you know.

TENNESSEE WILLIAMS

CHARACTERS

MARGARET

BRICK

MAE .... sometimes called Sister Woman

BIG MAMA

DIXIE .... a little girl

BIG DADDY

REVEREND TOOKER

GOOPER .... sometimes called Brother Man

DOCTOR BAUGH .... pronounced "Baw"

LACEY .... a Negro servant

SOOKEY .... another

Another little girl and two small boys

(The playing script of Act III also includes TRIXIE,
another little girl, also DAISY, BRIGHTIE *and* SMALL,
servants.)

Notes for the Designer

The set is the bed-sitting-room of a plantation home in
the Mississippi Delta. It is along an upstairs gallery
which probably runs around the entire house; it has
two pairs of very wide doors opening onto the gallery;
showing white balustrades against a fair summer sky
that fades into dusk and night during the course of the
play, which occupies precisely the time of its performance, excepting, of course, the fifteen minutes of intermission.

Perhaps the style of the room is not what you
would expect in the home of the Delta's biggest cotton-
planter. It is Victorian with a touch of the Far East. It
hasn't changed much since it was occupied by the
original owners of the place, Jack Straw and Peter
Ochello, a pair of old bachelors who shared this room
all their lives together. In other words, the room must
evoke some ghosts; it is gently and poetically haunted
by a relationship that must have involved a tenderness which was uncommon. This may be irrelevant or
unnecessary, but I once saw a reproduction of a faded
photograph of the verandah of Robert Louis Steven-
son's home on that Samoan Island where he spent
his last years, and there was a quality of tender light
on weathered wood, such as porch furniture made of
bamboo and wicker, exposed to tropical suns and tropical rains, which came to mind when I thought about
the set for this play, bringing also to mind the grace
and comfort of light, the reassurance it gives, on a
late and fair afternoon in summer, the way that no
matter what, even dread of death, is gently touched
and soothed by it. For the set is the background for a
play that deals with human extremities of emotion,
and it needs that softness behind it.

The bathroom door, showing only pale-blue tile
and silver towel racks, is in one side wall; the hall
door in the opposite wall. Two articles of furniture
need mention: a big double bed which staging should

make a functional part of the set as often as suitable, the surface of which should be slightly raked to make figures on it seen more easily; and against the wall space between the two huge double doors upstage: a monumental monstrosity peculiar to our times, a huge console combination of radio-phonograph *(Hi-Fi with three speakers)* TV set *and* liquor cabinet, *bearing and containing many glasses and bottles, all in one piece, which is a composition of muted silver tones, and the opalescent tones of reflecting glass, a chromatic link, this thing, between the sepia (tawny gold) tones of the interior and the cool (white and blue) tones of the gallery and sky. This piece of furniture (?!), this monument, is a very complete and compact little shrine to virtually all the comforts and illusions behind which we hide from such things as the characters in the play are faced with. . . . The set should be far less realistic than I have so far implied in this description of it. I think the walls below the ceiling should dissolve mysteriously into air; the set should be roofed by the sky; stars and moon suggested by traces of milky pallor, as if they were observed through a telescope lens out of focus.*

Anything else I can think of? Oh, yes, fanlights (transoms shaped like an open glass fan) above all the doors in the set, with panes of blue and amber, and above all, the designer should take as many pains to give the actors room to move about freely (to show their restlessness, their passion for breaking out) as if it were a set for a ballet.

An evening in summer. The action is continuous, with two intermissions.

ACT ONE

At the rise of the curtain someone is taking a shower in the bathroom, the door of which is half open. A pretty young woman, with anxious lines in her face, enters the bedroom and crosses to the bathroom door.

MARGARET: *(shouting above roar of water)* One of those no-neck monsters hit me with a hot buttered biscuit so I have t' change!

*(*MARGARET'S *voice is both rapid and drawling. In her long speeches she has the vocal tricks of a priest delivering a liturgical chant, the lines are almost sung, always continuing a little beyond her breath so she has to gasp for another. Sometimes she intersperses the lines with a little wordless singing, such as "Da-da-daaaa!")*
(Water turns off and BRICK *calls out to her, but is still unseen. A tone of politely feigned interest, masking indifference, or worse, is characteristic of his speech with* MARGARET.*)*

BRICK: Wha'd you say, Maggie? Water was on s' loud I couldn't hearya. . . .

MARGARET: Well, I!—just remarked that!—one of th' no-neck monsters messed up m' lovely lace dress so I got t'—cha-a-ange. . . .
(She opens and kicks shut drawers of the dresser.)

BRICK: Why d'ya call Gooper's kiddies no-neck monsters?

MARGARET: Because they've got no necks! Isn't that a good enough reason?

BRICK: Don't they have any necks?

MARGARET: None visible. Their fat little heads are set on their fat little bodies without a bit of connection.

BRICK: That's too bad.

MARGARET: Yes, it's too bad because you can't wring their necks if they've got no necks to wring! Isn't that right, honey?
(She steps out of her dress, stands in a slip of ivory satin and lace.)

Yep, they're no-neck monsters, all no-neck people are monsters . . .
*(*CHILDREN *shriek downstairs.)*

Hear them? Hear them screaming? I don't know where their voice-boxes are located since they don't have necks. I tell you I got so nervous at that table tonight I thought I would throw back my head and utter a scream you could hear across the Arkansas border an' parts of Louisiana an' Tennessee. I said to your charming sister-in-law, Mae, honey, couldn't you feed those precious little things at a separate table with an oilcloth cover? They make such a mess an' the lace cloth looks *so* pretty!

She made enormous eyes at me and said, "Ohhh, noooooo! On Big Daddy's birthday? Why, he would never forgive me!" Well, I want you to know, Big Daddy hadn't been at the table two minutes with those five no-neck monsters slobbering and drooling over their food before he threw down his fork an' shouted, "Fo' God's sake, Gooper, why don't you put them pigs at a trough in th' kitchen?"—Well, I swear, I simply could have di-ieed!

Think of it, Brick, they've got five of them and number six is coming. They've brought the whole bunch down here like animals to display at a county fair. Why, they have those children doin' tricks all the time! "Junior, show Big Daddy how you do this, show Big Daddy how you do that, say your little piece fo' Big Daddy, Sister. Show your dimples, Sugar. Brother, show Big Daddy how you stand on your head!"—It goes on all the time, along with constant little remarks and innuendos about the fact that you and I have not produced any children, are totally childless and therefore totally useless!—Of course it's comical but it's also disgusting since it's so obvious what they're up to!

BRICK: *(without interest)* What are they up to, Maggie?

MARGARET: Why, you know what they're up to!

BRICK: *(appearing)* No, I don't know what they're up to.

(He stands there in the bathroom doorway drying his hair with a towel and hanging onto the towel rack because one ankle is broken, plastered and bound. He is still slim and firm as a boy. His liquor hasn't started tearing him down outside. He has the additional charm of that cool air of detachment that people have who have given up the struggle. But now and then, when disturbed, something flashes behind it, like lightning in a fair sky, which shows that at some deeper level he is far from peaceful. Perhaps in a stronger light he would show some signs of deliquescence, but the fading, still warm, light from the gallery treats him gently.)

MARGARET: I'll tell you what they're up to, boy of mine!—They're up to cutting you out of your father's estate, and—

(She freezes momentarily before her next remark. Her voice drops as if it were somehow a personally embarrassing admission.)

—Now we know that Big Daddy's dyin' of—cancer. . . .

(There are voices on the lawn below: long-drawn calls across distance. MARGARET raises her lovely bare arms and powders her armpits with a light sigh.)

(She adjusts the angle of a magnifying mirror to straighten an eyelash, then rises fretfully saying:)

There's so much light in the room it—

BRICK: *(softly but sharply)* Do we?

MARGARET: Do we what?

BRICK: Know Big Daddy's dyin' of cancer?

MARGARET: Got the report today.

BRICK: Oh . . .

MARGARET: *(letting down bamboo blinds which cast long, gold-fretted shadows over the room)* Yep, got th' report just now . . . it didn't surprise me, Baby. . . .

(Her voice has range, and music; sometimes it drops low as a boy's and you have a sudden image of her playing boys' games as a child.)

I recognized the symptoms soon's we got here last spring and I'm willin' to bet you that Brother Man and his wife were pretty sure of it, too. That more than likely explains why their usual summer migration to the coolness of the Great Smokies was passed up this summer in favor of—hustlin' down here ev'ry whipstitch with their whole screamin' tribe! And why so many allusions have been made to Rainbow Hill lately. You know what Rainbow Hill is? Place that's famous for treatin' alcoholics an' dope fiends in the movies!

BRICK: I'm not in the movies.

MARGARET: No, and you don't take dope. Otherwise you're a perfect candidate for Rainbow Hill, Baby, and that's where they aim to ship you—over my dead body! Yep, over my dead body they'll ship you there, but nothing would please them better. Then Brother Man could get a-hold of the purse strings and dole out remittances to us, maybe get power-of-attorney and sign checks for us and cut off our credit wherever, whenever he wanted! Son-of-a-bitch!—How'd you like that, Baby?—Well, you've been doin' just about ev'rything in your power to bring it about, you've just been doin' ev'rything you can think of to aid and abet them in this scheme of theirs! Quittin' work, devoting yourself to the oc-cupation of drinkin'!—Breakin' your ankle last night on the high school athletic field: doin' what? Jumpin' hurdles? At two or three in the morning? Just fantastic! Got in the paper. *Clarksdale Register* carried a nice little item about it, human interest story about a well-known former athlete stagin' a one-man track meet on the Glorious Hill High School athletic field last night, but was slightly out of condition and didn't clear the first hurdle! Brother Man Gooper claims he exercised his influence t' keep it from goin' out over AP or UP or every goddam "P." But, Brick? You still have one big advantage!

(During the above swift flood of words, BRICK *has reclined with contrapuntal leisure on the snowy surface of the bed and has rolled over care-fully on his side or belly.)*

BRICK: *(wryly)* Did you *say* something, Maggie?

MARGARET: Big Daddy dotes on you, honey. And he can't stand Brother Man and Brother Man's wife, that monster of fertility, Mae; she's down-right odious to him! Know how I know? By little expressions that flicker over his face when that woman is holding fo'th on one of her choice top-ics such as—how she refused twilight sleep!—when the twins were delivered! Because she feels motherhood's an experience that a woman ought to experience fully!—in order to fully ap-preciate the wonder and beauty of it! HAH!

(This loud "HAH!" is accompanied by a violent action such as slamming a drawer shut.)

—and how she made Brother Man come in an' stand beside her in the delivery room so he would not miss out on the "wonder and

beauty" of it either!—producin' those no-neck monsters. . . .

(A speech of this kind would be antipathetic from almost anybody but MARGARET; *she makes it oddly funny, because her eyes constantly twinkle and her voice shakes with laughter which is basi-cally indulgent.)*

—Big Daddy shares my attitude toward those two! As for me, well—I give him a laugh now and then and he tolerates me. In fact!—I some-times suspect that Big Daddy harbors a little unconscious "lech" fo' me. . . .

BRICK: What makes you think that Big Daddy has a lech for you, Maggie?

MARGARET: Way he always drops his eyes down my body when I'm talkin' to him, drops his eyes to my boobs an' licks his old chops! Ha ha!

BRICK: That kind of talk is disgusting.

MARGARET: Did anyone ever tell you that you're an ass-aching Puritan, Brick?

I think it's mighty fine that that ole fellow, on the doorstep of death, still takes in my shape with what I think is deserved appreciation!

And you wanta know something else? Big Daddy didn't know how many little Maes and Goopers had been produced! "How many kids have you got?" he asked at the table, just like Brother Man and his wife were new acquain-tances to him! Big Mama said he was jokin', but that ole boy wasn't jokin', Lord, no!

And when they infawmed him that they had five already and were turning out number six!—the news seemed to come as a sort of un-pleasant surprise . . .

(Children yell below.)

Scream, monsters!

(Turns to Brick with a sudden, gay, charming smile which fades as she notices that he is not looking at her but into fading gold space with a troubled expression.)

(It is constant rejection that makes her humor "bitchy.")

Yes, you should of been at that supper-table, Baby.

(Whenever she calls him "Baby" the word is a soft caress.)

Y'know, Big Daddy, bless his ole sweet soul, he's the dearest ole thing in the world, but he does hunch over his food as if he preferred not to notice anything else. Well, Mae an' Gooper were side by side at the table, direckly across from Big Daddy, watchin' his face like hawks while they jawed an' jabbered about the cuteness an' brilliance of th' no-neck monsters!

(She giggles with a hand fluttering at her throat and her breast and her long throat arched.)

(She comes downstage and re-creates the scene with voice and gesture.)

And the no-neck monsters were ranged around the table, some in high chairs and some on th' *Books of Knowledge,* all in fancy little paper caps in honor of Big Daddy's birthday, and all through dinner, well, I want you to know that Brother Man an' his partner never once, for one moment, stopped exchanging pokes an' pinches an' kicks an' signs an' signals!—Why, they were like a couple of cardsharps fleecing a sucker.— Even Big Mama, bless her ole sweet soul, she isn't th' quickest an' brightest thing in the world, she finally noticed, at last, an' said to Gooper, "Gooper, what are you an' Mae makin' all these signs at each other about?"—I swear t' goodness, I nearly choked on my chicken!

(MARGARET, back at the dressing-table, still doesn't see BRICK. He is watching her with a look that is not quite definable.—Amused? shocked? contemptuous?—part of those and part of something else.)

Y'know—your brother Gooper still cherishes the illusion he took a giant step up on the social ladder when he married Miss Mae Flynn of the Memphis Flynns.

(MARGARET moves about the room as she talks, stops before the mirror, moves on.)

But I have a piece of Spanish news for Gooper. The Flynns never had a thing in this world but money and they lost that, they were nothing at all but fairly successful climbers. Of course, Mae Flynn came out in Memphis eight years before I made my debut in Nashville, but I had friends at Ward-Belmont who came from Memphis and they used to come to see me and I used

to go to see them for Christmas and spring vacations, and so I know who rates an' who doesn't rate in Memphis society. Why, y'know ole Papa Flynn, he barely escaped doing time in the Federal pen for shady manipulations on th' stock market when his chain stores crashed, and as for Mae having been a cotton carnival queen, as they remind us so often, lest we forget, well, that's one honor that I don't envy her for!—Sit on a brass throne on a tacky float an' ride down Main Street, smilin', bowin', and blowin' kisses to all the trash on the street—

(She picks out a pair of jeweled sandals and rushes to the dressing-table.)

Why, year before last, when Susan McPheeters was singled out fo' that honor, y'know what happened to her? Y'know what happened to poor little Susie McPheeters?

BRICK: *(absently)* No. What happened to little Susie McPheeters?

MARGARET: Somebody spit tobacco juice in her face.

BRICK: *(dreamily)* Somebody spit tobacco juice in her face?

MARGARET: That's right, some old drunk leaned out of a window in the Hotel Gayoso and yelled, "Hey, Queen, hey, hey, there, Queenie!" Poor Susie looked up and flashed him a radiant smile and he shot out a squirt of tobacco juice right in poor Susie's face.

BRICK: Well, what d'you know about that.

MARGARET: *(gaily)* What do I know about it? I was there, I saw it!

BRICK: *(absently)* Must have been kind of funny.

MARGARET: Susie didn't think so. Had hysterics. Screamed like a banshee. They had to stop th' parade an' remove her from her throne an' go on with—

(She catches sight of him in the mirror, gasps slightly, wheels about to face him. Count ten.)

—Why are you looking at me like that?

BRICK: *(whistling softly, now)* Like what, Maggie?

MARGARET: *(intensely, fearfully)* The way y' were lookin' at me just now, befo' I caught your eye in the mirror and you started t' whistle! I don't know how t' describe it but it froze my blood!—

I've caught you lookin' at me like that so often lately. What are you thinkin' of when you look at me like that?

BRICK: I wasn't conscious of lookin' at you, Maggie.

MARGARET: Well, I was conscious of it! What were you thinkin'?

BRICK: I don't remember thinking of anything, Maggie.

MARGARET: Don't you think I know that—? Don't you—?—Think I know that—?

BRICK: *(coolly)* Know *what*, Maggie?

MARGARET: *(struggling for expression)* That I've gone through this—*hideous!*—transformation, before—*hard! Frantic!*
(Then she adds, almost tenderly:)
—*cruel!!*
That's what you've been observing in me lately. How could y' help but observe it? That's all right. I'm not—thin-skinned any more, can't afford t' be thin-skinned any more.
(She is now recovering her power.)
—But Brick? Brick?

BRICK: Did you say something?

MARGARET: I was *goin'* t' say something: that I get—lonely. Very!

BRICK: Ev'rybody gets that . . .

MARGARET: Living with someone you love can be lonelier—than living entirely *alone!*—if the one that y' love doesn't love you. . . .
(There is a pause. BRICK hobbles downstage and asks, without looking at her:)

BRICK: Would you like to live alone, Maggie?
(Another pause: then—after she has caught a quick, hurt breath:)

MARGARET: *No!—God!—I wouldn't!*
(Another gasping breath. She forcibly controls what must have been an impulse to cry out. We see her deliberately, very forcibly, going all the way back to the world in which you can talk about ordinary matters.)
Did you have a nice shower?

BRICK: Uh-huh.

MARGARET: Was the water cool?

BRICK: No.

MARGARET: But it made y' feel fresh, huh?

BRICK: Fresher. . . .

MARGARET: I know something would make y' feel *much* fresher!

BRICK: What?

MARGARET: An alcohol rub. Or cologne, a rub with cologne!

BRICK: That's good after a workout but I haven't been workin' out, Maggie.

MARGARET: You've kept in good shape, though.

BRICK: *(indifferently)* You think so, Maggie?

MARGARET: I always thought drinkin' men lost their looks, but I was plainly mistaken.

BRICK: *(wryly)* Why, thanks, Maggie.

MARGARET: You're the only drinkin' man I know that it never seems t' put fat on.

BRICK: I'm gettin' softer, Maggie.

MARGARET: Well, sooner or later it's bound to soften you up. It was just beginning to soften up Skipper when—
(She stops short.)
I'm sorry. I never could keep my fingers off a sore—I wish you *would* lose your looks. If you did it would make the martyrdom of Saint Maggie a little more bearable. But no such goddam luck. I actually believe you've gotten better looking since you've gone on the bottle. Yeah, a person who didn't know you would think you'd never had a tense nerve in your body or a strained muscle.
(There are sounds of croquet on the lawn below: the click of mallets, light voices, near and distant.)
Of course, you always had that detached quality as if you were playing a game without much concern over whether you won or lost, and now that you've lost the game, not lost but just quit playing, you have that rare sort of charm that usually only happens in very old or hopelessly sick people, the charm of the defeated.—You look so cool, so cool, so enviably cool.
(Music is heard.)
They're playing croquet. The moon has appeared and it's white, just beginning to turn a little bit yellow. . . .
You were a wonderful lover. . . .

Such a wonderful person to go to bed with, and I think mostly because you were really indifferent to it. Isn't that right? Never had any anxiety about it, did it naturally, easily, slowly, with absolute confidence and perfect calm, more like opening a door for a lady or seating her at a table than giving expression to any longing for her. Your indifference made you wonderful at lovemaking—*strange?*—but true. . . .

You know, if I thought you would never, never, *never* make love to me again—I would go downstairs to the kitchen and pick out the longest and sharpest knife I could find and stick it straight into my heart, I swear that I would!

But one thing I don't have is the charm of the defeated, my hat is still in the ring, and I am determined to win!

(There is the sound of croquet mallets hitting croquet balls.)

—What is the victory of a cat on a hot tin roof?—I wish I knew. . . .

Just staying on it, I guess, as long as she can. . . .

(More croquet sounds.)

Later tonight I'm going to tell you I love you an' maybe by that time you'll be drunk enough to believe me. Yes, they're playing croquet. . . .

Big Daddy is dying of cancer. . . .

What were you thinking of when I caught you looking at me like that? Were you thinking of Skipper?

(BRICK takes up his crutch, rises.)

Oh, excuse me, forgive me, but laws of silence don't work! No, laws of silence don't work. . . .

(BRICK crosses to the bar, takes a quick drink, and rubs his head with a towel.)

Laws of silence don't work. . . .

When something is festering in your memory or your imagination, laws of silence don't work, it's just like shutting a door and locking it on a house on fire in hope of forgetting that the house is burning. But not facing a fire doesn't put it out. Silence about a thing just

magnifies it. It grows and festers in silence, becomes malignant. . . .

Get dressed, Brick.

(He drops his crutch.)

BRICK: I've dropped my crutch.

(He has stopped rubbing his hair dry but still stands hanging onto the towel rack in a white towel-cloth robe.)

MARGARET: Lean on me.

BRICK: No, just give me my crutch.

MARGARET: Lean on my shoulder.

BRICK: *I don't want to lean on your shoulder, I want my crutch!*

(This is spoken like sudden lightning.)

Are you going to give me my crutch or do I have to get down on my knees on the floor and—

MARGARET: *Here, here, take it, take it!*

(She has thrust the crutch at him.)

BRICK: *(hobbling out)* Thanks . . .

MARGARET: We mustn't scream at each other, the walls in this house have ears. . . .

(He hobbles directly to liquor cabinet to get a new drink.)

—but that's the first time I've heard you raise your voice in a long time, Brick. A crack in the wall?—Of composure?

—I think that's a good sign. . . .

A sign of nerves in a player on the defensive!

(BRICK turns and smiles at her coolly over his fresh drink.)

BRICK: It just hasn't happened yet, Maggie.

MARGARET: What?

BRICK: The click I get in my head when I've had enough of this stuff to make me peaceful. . . . Will you do me a favor?

MARGARET: Maybe I will. What favor?

BRICK: Just, just keep your voice down!

MARGARET: *(in a hoarse whisper)* I'll do you that favor, I'll speak in a whisper, if not shut up completely, if *you* will do *me* a favor and make that drink your last one till after the party.

BRICK: What party?

MARGARET: Big Daddy's birthday party.

BRICK: Is this Big Daddy's birthday?

MARGARET: You know this is Big Daddy's birthday!

BRICK: No, I don't, I forgot it.

MARGARET: Well, I remembered it for you. . . .
(They are both speaking as breathlessly as a pair of kids after a fight, drawing deep exhausted breaths and looking at each other with faraway eyes, shaking and panting together as if they had broken apart from a violent struggle.)

BRICK: Good for you, Maggie.

MARGARET: You just have to scribble a few lines on this card.

BRICK: You scribble something, Maggie.

MARGARET: It's got to be your handwriting; it's your present, I've given him my present; it's got to be your handwriting!
(The tension between them is building again, the voices becoming shrill once more.)

BRICK: I didn't get him a present.

MARGARET: I got one for you.

BRICK: All right. You write the card, then.

MARGARET: And have him know you didn't remember his birthday?

BRICK: I didn't remember his birthday.

MARGARET: You don't have to prove you didn't!

BRICK: I don't want to fool him about it.

MARGARET: Just write "Love, Brick!" for God's—

BRICK: No.

MARGARET: You've *got* to!

BRICK: I don't have to do anything I don't want to do. You keep forgetting the conditions on which I agreed to stay on living with you.

MARGARET: *(out before she knows it)* I'm not living with you. We occupy the same cage.

BRICK: You've got to remember the conditions agreed on.

MARGARET: They're impossible conditions!

BRICK: Then why don't you—?

MARGARET: HUSH! Who is out there? Is somebody at the door?
(There are footsteps in hall.)

MAE: *(outside)* May I enter a moment?

MARGARET: Oh, *you!* Sure. Come in, Mae.
(MAE enters bearing aloft the bow of a young lady's archery set.)

MAE: Brick, is this thing yours?

MARGARET: Why, Sister Woman—that's my Diana Trophy. Won it at the intercollegiate archery contest on the Ole Miss campus.

MAE: It's a mighty dangerous thing to leave exposed round a house full of nawmal rid-blooded children attracted t'weapons.

MARGARET: "Nawmal rid-blooded children attracted t'weapons" ought t'be taught to keep their hands off things that don't belong to them.

MAE: Maggie, honey, if you had children of your own you'd know how funny that is. Will you please lock this up and put the key out of reach?

MARGARET: Sister Woman, nobody is plotting the destruction of your kiddies. —Brick and I still have our special archers' license. We're goin' deer-huntin' on Moon Lake as soon as the season starts. I love to run with dogs through chilly woods, run, run, leap over obstructions—
(She goes into the closet carrying the bow.)

MAE: How's the injured ankle, Brick?

BRICK: Doesn't hurt. Just itches.

MAE: Oh, my! Brick—Brick, you should've been downstairs after supper! Kiddies put on a show. Polly played the piano, Buster an' Sonny drums, an' then they turned out the lights an' Dixie an' Trixie puhfawmed a toe dance in fairy costume with *spahkluhs!* Big Daddy just beamed! He just beamed!

MARGARET: *(from the closet with a sharp laugh)* Oh, I bet. It breaks my heart that we missed it! *(She reenters.)* But Mae? Why did y'give dawgs' names to all your kiddies?

MAE: *Dogs' names?*
(MARGARET has made this observation as she goes to raise the bamboo blinds, since the sunset glare has diminished. In crossing she winks at BRICK.)

MARGARET: *(sweetly)* Dixie, Trixie, Buster, Sonny, Polly!—Sounds like four dogs and a parrot . . . animal act in a circus!

MAE: Maggie?
(MARGARET turns with a smile.)
Why are you so catty?

MARGARET: 'Cause I'm a cat! But why can't *you* take a joke, Sister Woman?

MAE: Nothin' pleases me more than a joke that's funny. You know the real names of our kiddies. Buster's real name is Robert. Sonny's real name is Saunders. Trixie's real name is Marlene and Dixie's—

(Someone downstairs calls for her. "Hey, Mae!"— She rushes to door, saying:)

Intermission is over!

MARGARET: *(As MAE closes door)* I wonder what Dixie's real name is?

BRICK: Maggie, being catty doesn't help things any . . .

MARGARET: I know! *WHY!*—Am I so catty?— 'Cause I'm consumed with envy an' eaten up with longing?—Brick, I've laid out your beautiful Shantung silk suit from Rome and one of your monogrammed silk shirts. I'll put your cuff-links in it, those lovely star sapphires I get you to wear so rarely. . . .

BRICK: I can't get trousers on over this plaster cast.

MARGARET: Yes, you can, I'll help you.

BRICK: I'm not going to get dressed, Maggie.

MARGARET: Will you just put on a pair of white silk pajamas?

BRICK: Yes, I'll do that, Maggie.

MARGARET: *Thank* you, thank you so *much!*

BRICK: Don't mention it.

MARGARET: *Oh, Brick!* How long does it have t' go on? This punishment? Haven't I done time enough, haven't I served my term, can't I apply for a—pardon?

BRICK: Maggie, you're spoiling my liquor. Lately your voice always sounds like you'd been running upstairs to warn somebody that the house was on fire!

MARGARET: Well, no wonder, no wonder. Y'know what I feel like, Brick?

(Children's and grownups' voices are blended, below, in a loud but uncertain rendition of "My Wild Irish Rose.")

I feel all the time like a cat on a hot tin roof!

BRICK: Then jump off the roof, jump off it, cats can jump off roofs and land on their four feet uninjured!

MARGARET: Oh, yes!

BRICK: Do it!—fo' God's sake, do it . . .

MARGARET: Do what?

BRICK: Take a lover!

MARGARET: I can't see a man but you! Even with my eyes closed, I just see you! Why don't you get ugly, Brick, why don't you please get fat or ugly or something so I could stand it?

(She rushes to hall door, opens it, listens.)

The concert is still going on! Bravo, no-necks, bravo!

(She slams and locks door fiercely.)

BRICK: What did you lock the door for?

MARGARET: To give us a little privacy for a while.

BRICK: You know better, Maggie.

MARGARET: No, I don't know better. . . .

(She rushes to gallery doors, draws the rose-silk drapes across them.)

BRICK: Don't make a fool of yourself.

MARGARET: I don't mind makin' a fool of myself over you!

BRICK: I mind, Maggie. I feel embarrassed for you.

MARGARET: Feel embarrassed! But don't continue my torture. I can't live on and on under these circumstances.

BRICK: You agreed to—

MARGARET: I know but—

BRICK: —Accept that condition!

MARGARET: *I CAN'T! CAN'T! CAN'T!*

(She seizes his shoulder.)

BRICK: Let go!

(He breaks away from her and seizes the small boudoir chair and raises it like a lion-tamer facing a big circus cat.)

(Count five. She stares at him with her fist pressed to her mouth, then bursts into shrill, almost hysterical laughter. He remains grave for a moment, then grins and puts the chair down.)

(BIG MAMA calls through closed door.)

BIG MAMA: Son? Son? Son?

BRICK: What is it, Big Mama?

BIG MAMA: *(outside)*

Oh, son! We got the most wonderful news about Big Daddy. I just had t' run up an' tell you right this—

(She rattles the knob.)

—What's this door doin', locked, faw? You all think there's robbers in the house?

MARGARET: Big Mama, Brick is dressin', he's not dressed yet.

BIG MAMA: That's all right, it won't be the first time I've seen Brick not dressed. Come on, open this door!

(MARGARET, with a grimace, goes to unlock and open the hall door, as BRICK hobbles rapidly to the bathroom and kicks the door shut. BIG MAMA has disappeared from the hall.)

MARGARET: Big Mama?

(BIG MAMA appears through the opposite gallery doors behind MARGARET, huffing and puffing like an old bulldog. She is a short, stout woman; her sixty years and 170 pounds have left her somewhat breathless most of the time; she's always tensed like a boxer, or rather, a Japanese wrestler. Her "family" was maybe a little superior to Big Daddy's, but not much. She wears a black or silver lace dress and at least half a million in flashy gems. She is very sincere.)

BIG MAMA: *(loudly, startling MARGARET)* Here— I come through Gooper's and Mae's gall'ry door. Where's Brick? *Brick*—Hurry on out of there, son, I just have a second and want to give you the news about Big Daddy.—I hate locked doors in a house. . . .

MARGARET: *(with affected lightness)* I've noticed you do, Big Mama, but people have got to have *some* moments of privacy, don't they?

BIG MAMA: No, ma'am, not in *my* house. *(Without pause)* Whacha took off you' dress faw? I thought that little lace dress was so sweet on yuh, honey.

MARGARET: I thought it looked sweet on me, too, but one of m' cute little table-partners used it for a napkin so—!

BIG MAMA: *(picking up stockings on floor)* What?

MARGARET: You know, Big Mama, Mae and Gooper's so touchy about those children— thanks, Big Mama . . .

(BIG MAMA has thrust the picked-up stockings in MARGARET's hand with a grunt.)

—that you just don't dare to suggest there's any room for improvement in their—

BIG MAMA: Brick, hurry out!—Shoot, Maggie, you just don't like children.

MARGARET: I do SO like children! Adore them!— well brought up!

BIG MAMA: *(gentle—loving)* Well, why don't you have some and bring them up well, then, instead of all the time pickin' on Gooper's an' Mae's?

GOOPER: *(shouting up the stairs)* Hey, hey, Big Mama, Betsy an' Hugh got to go, waitin' t' tell yuh g'by!

BIG MAMA: Tell 'em to hold their hawses, I'll be right down in a jiffy!

(She turns to the bathroom door and calls out.)

Son? Can you hear me in there?

(There is a muffled answer.)

We just got the full report from the laboratory at the Ochsner Clinic, completely negative, son, ev'rything negative, right on down the line! Nothin' a-tall's wrong with him but some little functional thing called a spastic colon. Can you hear me, son?

MARGARET: He can hear you, Big Mama.

BIG MAMA: Then why don't he say something? God Almighty, a piece of news like that should make him shout. It made *me* shout, I can tell you. I shouted and sobbed and fell right down on my knees—Look!

(She pulls up her skirt.)

See the bruises where I hit my kneecaps? Took both doctors to haul me back on my feet!

(She laughs—she always laughs like hell at herself.)

Big Daddy was furious with me! But ain't that wonderful news?

(Facing bathroom again, she continues:)

After all the anxiety we been through to git a report like that on Big Daddy's birthday? Big Daddy tried to hide how much of a load that

news took off his mind, but didn't fool *me*. He was mighty close to crying about it *himself!*
(Goodbyes are shouted downstairs, and she rushes to door.)
Hold those people down there, don't let them go!—Now, git dressed, we're all comin' up to this room fo' Big Daddy's birthday party because of your ankle.—How's his ankle, Maggie?

MARGARET: Well, he broke it, Big Mama.

BIG MAMA: I know he broke it.
(A phone is ringing in hall. A Negro voice answers: "Mistuh Polly's res'dence.")
I mean does it hurt him much still.

MARGARET: I'm afraid I can't give you that information, Big Mama. You'll have to ask Brick if it hurts much still or not.

SOOKEY: *(in the hall)* It's Memphis, Mizz Polly, it's Miss Sally in Memphis.

BIG MAMA: Awright, Sookey.
(BIG MAMA rushes into the hall and is heard shouting on the phone:)
Hello, Miss Sally. How are you, Miss Sally?—Yes, well, I was just gonna call you about it. *Shoot!*—
(She raises her voice to a bellow.)
Miss Sally? Don't ever call me from the Gayoso Lobby, too much talk goes on in that hotel lobby, no wonder you can't hear me! Now listen, Miss Sally. They's nothin' serious wrong with Big Daddy. We got the report just now, they's nothin' wrong but a thing called a—spastic! *SPASTIC!*—colon . . .
(She appears at the hall door and calls to MARGARET.*)*
—Maggie, come out here and talk to that fool on the phone. I'm shouted breathless!

MARGARET: *(goes out and is heard sweetly at phone)* Miss Sally? This is Brick's wife, Maggie. So nice to hear your voice. Can you hear *mine?* Well, *good!*—Big Mama just wanted you to know that they've got the report from the Ochsner Clinic and what Big Daddy has is a spastic colon. Yes. Spastic colon, Miss Sally. That's right, spastic colon. *G'bye, Miss Sally, hope I'll see you real soon!*

(Hangs up a little before MISS SALLY *was probably ready to terminate the talk. She returns through the hall door.)*
She heard me perfectly. I've discovered with deaf people the thing to do is not shout at them but just enunciate clearly. My rich old Aunt Cornelia was deaf as the dead but I could make her hear me just by sayin' each word slowly, distinctly, close to her ear. I read her the *Commercial Appeal* ev'ry night, read her the classified ads in it, even, she never missed a word of it. But was she a mean ole thing! Know what I got when she died? Her unexpired subscriptions to five magazines and the Book-of-the-Month Club and a LIBRARY full of ev'ry dull book ever written! All else went to her hellcat of a sister . . . meaner than she was, even!
(BIG MAMA has been straightening things up in the room during this speech.)

BIG MAMA: *(closing closet door on discarded clothes)* Miss Sally sure is a case! Big Daddy says she's always got her hand out fo' somethin'. He's not mistaken. That poor ole thing always has her hand out fo' somethin'. I don't think Big Daddy gives her as much as he should.
(Somebody shouts for her downstairs and she shouts:)
I'm comin'!
(She starts out. At the hall door, turns and jerks a forefinger, first toward the bathroom door, then toward the liquor cabinet, meaning: "Has Brick been drinking?" MARGARET *pretends not to understand, cocks her head and raises her brows as if the pantomimic performance was completely mystifying to her.)*
(BIG MAMA rushes back to MARGARET:*)*
Shoot! Stop playin' so dumb!—I mean has he been drinkin' that stuff much yet?

MARGARET: *(with a little laugh)* Oh! I think he had a highball after supper.

BIG MAMA: Don't laugh about it!—Some single men stop drinkin' when they git married and others start! Brick never touched liquor before he—!

MARGARET: (crying out) *THAT'S NOT FAIR!*

BIG MAMA: Fair or not fair I want to ask you a question, one question: D'you make Brick happy in bed?

MARGARET: Why don't you ask if he makes *me* happy in bed?

BIG MAMA: Because I know that—

MARGARET: *It works both ways!*

BIG MAMA: Something's not right! You're childless and my son drinks!

(*Someone has called her downstairs and she has rushed to the door on the line above. She turns at the door and points at the bed.*)

—When a marriage goes on the rocks, the rocks are *there*, right *there*!

MARGARET: *That's*—

(BIG MAMA *has swept out of the room and slammed the door.*)

—not—*fair* . . .

(MARGARET *is alone, completely alone, and she feels it. She draws in, hunches her shoulders, raises her arms with fists clenched, shuts her eyes tight as a child about to be stabbed with a vaccination needle. When she opens her eyes again, what she sees is the long oval mirror and she rushes straight to it, stares into it with a grimace and says: "Who are you?"—Then she crouches a little and answers herself in a different voice which is high, thin, mocking: "I am Maggie the Cat!"—Straightens quickly as bathroom door opens a little and* BRICK *calls out to her.*)

BRICK: Has Big Mama gone?

MARGARET: She's gone.

(*He opens the bathroom door and hobbles out, with his liquor glass now empty, straight to the liquor cabinet. He is whistling softly.* MARGARET'S *head pivots on her long, slender throat to watch him.*)

(*She raises a hand uncertainly to the base of her throat, as if it was difficult for her to swallow, before she speaks:*)

You know, our sex life didn't just peter out in the usual way, it was cut off short, long before the natural time for it to, and it's going to revive again, just as sudden as that. I'm confident of it. That's what I'm keeping myself attractive for. For the time when you'll see me again like other men see me. Yes, like other men see me. They still see me, Brick, and they like what they see. Uh-huh. Some of them would give their—Look, Brick!

(*She stands before the long oval mirror, touches her breast and then her hips with her two hands.*)

How high my body stays on me!—Nothing has fallen on me—not a fraction. . . .

(*Her voice is soft and trembling: a pleading child's. At this moment as he turns to glance at her—a look which is like a player passing a ball to another player, third down and goal to go— she has to capture the audience in a grip so tight that she can hold it till the first intermission without any lapse of attention.*)

Other men still want me. My face looks strained, sometimes, but I've kept my figure as well as you've kept yours, and men admire it. I still turn heads on the street. Why, last week in Memphis everywhere that I went men's eyes burned holes in my clothes, at the country club and in restaurants and department stores, there wasn't a man I met or walked by that didn't just eat me up with his eyes and turn around when I passed him and look back at me. Why, at Alice's party for her New York cousins, the best lookin' man in the crowd—followed me upstairs and tried to force his way in the powder room with me, followed me to the door and tried to force his way in!

BRICK: Why didn't you let him, Maggie?

MARGARET: Because I'm not that common, for one thing. Not that I wasn't almost tempted to. You like to know who it was? It was Sonny Boy Maxwell, that's who!

BRICK: Oh, yeah, Sonny Boy Maxwell, he was a good end-runner but had a little injury to his back and had to quit.

MARGARET: He has no injury now and has no wife and still has a lech for me!

BRICK: I see no reason to lock him out of a powder room in that case.

MARGARET: And have someone catch me at it? I'm not that stupid. Oh, I might sometime cheat on you with someone, since you're so insultingly eager to have me do it!—But if I do, you can be damned sure it will be in a place and a time where no one but me and the man could possibly know. Because I'm not going to give you any excuse to divorce me for being unfaithful or anything else. . . .

BRICK: Maggie, I wouldn't divorce you for being unfaithful or anything else. Don't you know that? Hell. I'd be relieved to know that you'd found yourself a lover.

MARGARET: Well, I'm taking no chances. No, I'd rather stay on this hot tin roof.

BRICK: A hot tin roof's 'n uncomfo'table place t' stay on. . . .

(He starts to whistle softly.)

MARGARET: *(through his whistle)* Yeah, but I can stay on it just as long as I have to.

BRICK: You could leave me, Maggie.

(He resumes whistle. She wheels about to glare at him.)

MARGARET: *Don't want to and will not!* Besides if I did, you don't have a cent to pay for it but what you get from Big Daddy and he's dying of cancer!

(For the first time a realization of BIG DADDY'S *doom seems to penetrate to* BRICK'S *consciousness, visibly, and he looks at* MARGARET.*)*

BRICK: Big Mama just said he *wasn't*, that the report was okay.

MARGARET: That's what she thinks because she got the same story that they gave Big Daddy. And was just as taken in by it as he was, poor ole things. . . .

But tonight they're going to tell her the truth about it. When Big Daddy goes to bed, they're going to tell her that he is dying of cancer.
(She slams the dresser drawer.)
—It's malignant and it's terminal.

BRICK: Does Big Daddy know it?

MARGARET: Hell, do they *ever* know it? Nobody says, "You're dying." You have to fool them. They have to fool *themselves*.

BRICK: Why?

MARGARET: *Why?* Because human beings dream of life everlasting, that's the reason! But most of them want it on earth and not in heaven.

(He gives a short, hard laugh at her touch of humor.)

Well. . . . *(She touches up her mascara.)* That's how it is, anyhow. . . . *(She looks about.)* Where did I put down my cigarette? Don't want to burn up the home-place, at least not with Mae and Gooper and their five monsters in it!

(She has found it and sucks at it greedily. Blows out smoke and continues:)

So this is Big Daddy's last birthday. And Mae and Gooper, they know it, oh, *they* know it, all right. They got the first information from the Ochsner Clinic. That's why they rushed down here with their no-neck monsters. Because. Do you know something? Big Daddy's made no will? Big Daddy's never made out any will in his life, and so this campaign's afoot to impress him, forcibly as possible, with the fact that you drink and I've borne no children!

(He continues to stare at her a moment, then mutters something sharp but not audible and hobbles rather rapidly out onto the long gallery in the fading, much faded, gold light.)

MARGARET: *(continuing her liturgical chant)* Y'know, I'm *fond* of Big Daddy, I am genuinely fond of that old man, I really *am*, you know. . . .

BRICK: *(faintly, vaguely)* Yes, I know you are. . . .

MARGARET: I've always sort of admired him in spite of his coarseness, his four-letter words and so forth. Because Big Daddy *is* what he *is*, and he makes no bones about it. He hasn't turned gentleman farmer, he's still a Mississippi red neck, as much of a red neck as he must have been when he was just overseer here on the old Jack Straw and Peter Ochello place. But he got hold of it an' built it into th' biggest an' finest plantation in the Delta.—I've always *liked* Big Daddy. . . .

(She crosses to the proscenium.)

Well, this is Big Daddy's last birthday. I'm sorry about it. But I'm facing the facts. It takes money to take care of a drinker and that's the office that I've been elected to lately.

BRICK: You don't have to take care of me.

MARGARET: Yes, I do. Two people in the same boat have got to take care of each other. At least you want money to buy more Echo Spring when this supply is exhausted, or will you be satisfied with a ten-cent beer?

Mae an' Gooper are plannin' to freeze us out of Big Daddy's estate because you drink and I'm childless. But we can defeat that plan. We're *going* to defeat that plan!

Brick, y'know, I've been so God damn disgustingly poor all my life!—That's the *truth*, Brick!

BRICK: I'm not sayin' it isn't.

MARGARET: Always had to suck up to people I couldn't stand because they had money and I was poor as Job's turkey. You don't know what that's like. Well, I'll tell you, it's like you would feel a thousand miles away from Echo Spring!—And had to get back to it on that broken ankle . . . without a crutch!

That's how it feels to be as poor as Job's turkey and have to suck up to relatives that you hated because they had money and all you had was a bunch of hand-me-down clothes and a few old moldy three per cent government bonds. My daddy loved his liquor, he fell in love with his liquor the way you've fallen in love with Echo Spring!—And my poor Mama, having to maintain some semblance of social position, to keep appearances up, on an income of one hundred and fifty dollars a month on those old government bonds!

When I came out, the year that I made my debut, I had just two evening dresses! One Mother made me from a pattern in *Vogue*, the other a hand-me-down from a snotty rich cousin I hated!

—The dress that I married you in was my grandmother's weddin' gown. . . .

So that's why I'm like a cat on a hot tin roof!

(BRICK *is still on the gallery. Someone below calls up to him in a warm Negro voice, "Hiya, Mistuh Brick, how yuh feelin'?"* BRICK *raises his liquor glass as if that answered the question.*)

MARGARET: You can be young without money but you can't be old without it. You've got to be old *with* money because to be old without it is just too awful, you've got to be one or the other, either *young* or *with money,* you can't be old and *without* it.—That's the truth, Brick. . . .

(BRICK *whistles softly, vaguely.*)

Well, now I'm dressed, I'm all dressed, there's nothing else for me to do.

(*Forlornly, almost fearfully.*)

I'm dressed, all dressed, nothing else for me to do. . . .

(*She moves about restlessly, aimlessly, and speaks, as if to herself.*)

I know when I made my mistake.—What am I—? Oh!—my bracelets. . . .

(*She starts working a collection of bracelets over her hands onto her wrists, about six on each, as she talks.*)

I've thought a whole lot about it and now I know when I made my mistake. Yes, I made my mistake when I told you the truth about that thing with Skipper. Never should have confessed it, a fatal error, tellin' you about that thing with Skipper.

BRICK: Maggie, shut up about Skipper. I mean it, Maggie; you got to shut up about Skipper.

MARGARET: You ought to understand that Skipper and I—

BRICK: You don't think I'm serious, Maggie? You're fooled by the fact that I am saying this quiet? Look, Maggie. What you're doing is a dangerous thing to do. You're—you're—you're—foolin' with something that—nobody ought to fool with.

MARGARET: This time I'm going to finish what I have to say to you. Skipper and I made love, if love you could call it, because it made both of us feel a little bit closer to you. You see, you son of a bitch, you asked too much of people, of me, of him, of all the unlucky poor damned sons of bitches that happen to love you, and there was a whole pack of them, yes, there was a pack of them besides me and Skipper, you asked too goddam much of people that loved you, you—superior creature!—you godlike being!—And so we made love to each other to dream it was you, both of us! Yes, yes, yes! Truth, truth! What's so awful about it? I like it, I think the truth is—yeah! I shouldn't have told you. . . .

BRICK: *(holding his head unnaturally still and uptilted a bit)* It was Skipper that told me about it. Not you, Maggie.

MARGARET: I told you!

BRICK: After he told me!

MARGARET: What does it matter who—?

(BRICK turns suddenly out upon the gallery and calls:)

BRICK: Little girl! Hey, little girl!

LITTLE GIRL: *(at a distance)* What, Uncle Brick?

BRICK: Tell the folks to come up!—Bring everybody upstairs!

MARGARET: I can't stop myself! I'd go on telling you this in front of them all, if I had to!

BRICK: Little girl! Go on, go on, will you? Do what I told you, call them!

MARGARET: Because it's got to be told and you, you!—you never let me!

(She sobs, then controls herself, and continues almost calmly.)

It was one of those beautiful, ideal things they tell about in the Greek legends, it couldn't be anything else, you being you, and that's what made it so sad, that's what made it so awful, because it was love that never could be carried through to anything satisfying or even talked about plainly. Brick, I tell you, you got to believe me, Brick, I *do* understand all about it! I—I think it was—*noble!* Can't you tell I'm sincere when I say I respect it? My only point, the only point that I'm making, is life has got to be allowed to continue even after the *dream* of life is—all—over. . . .

(BRICK is without his crutch. Leaning on furniture, he crosses to pick it up as she continues as if possessed by a will outside herself:)

Why I remember when we double-dated at college, Gladys Fitzgerald and I and you and Skipper, it was more like a date between you and Skipper. Gladys and I were just sort of tagging along as if it was necessary to chaperone you!—to make a good public impression—

BRICK: *(turns to face her, half lifting his crutch)* Maggie, you want me to hit you with this crutch? Don't you know I could kill you with this crutch?

MARGARET: Good Lord, man, d' you think I'd care if you did?

BRICK: One man has one great good true thing in his life. One great good thing which is true!—I had friendship with Skipper.—You are naming it dirty!

MARGARET: I'm not naming it dirty! I am naming it clean.

BRICK: Not love with you, Maggie, but friendship with Skipper was that one great true thing, and you are naming it dirty!

MARGARET: Then you haven't been listenin', not understood what I'm saying! I'm naming it so damn clean that it killed poor Skipper!—You two had something that had to be kept on ice, yes, incorruptible, yes!—and death was the only icebox where you could keep it. . . .

BRICK: I married you, Maggie. Why would I marry you, Maggie, if I was—?

MARGARET: Brick, don't brain me yet, let me finish!—I know, believe me I know, that it was only Skipper that harbored even any *unconscious* desire for anything not perfectly pure between you two!—Now let me skip a little. You married me early that summer we graduated out of Ole Miss, and we were happy, weren't we, we were blissful, yes, hit heaven together ev'ry time that we loved! But that fall you an' Skipper turned down wonderful offers of jobs in order to keep on bein' football heroes—pro-football heroes. You organized the Dixie Stars that fall, so you could keep on bein' team-mates forever! But somethin' was not right with it!—*Me included!*—between you. Skipper began hittin' the bottle . . . you got a spinal injury—couldn't play the Thanksgivin' game in Chicago, watched it on TV from a traction bed in Toledo. I joined Skipper. The Dixie Stars lost because poor Skipper was drunk. We drank together that night all night in the bar of the Blackstone and when cold day was comin' up over the Lake an' we were comin' out drunk to take a dizzy look at it, I said, "SKIPPER! STOP LOVIN' MY HUSBAND OR TELL HIM HE'S GOT TO LET YOU ADMIT IT TO HIM!"—one way or another!

HE SLAPPED ME HARD ON THE MOUTH!—then turned and ran without stopping once, I am sure, all the way back into his room at the Blackstone. . . .

—When I came to his room that night, with a little scratch like a shy little mouse at his door, he made that pitiful, ineffectual little attempt to prove that what I had said wasn't true. . . .

(BRICK *strikes at her with crutch, a blow that shatters the gemlike lamp on the table.*)

—In this way, I destroyed him, by telling him truth that he and his world which he was born and raised in, yours and his world, had told him could not be told?

—From then on Skipper was nothing at all but a receptacle for liquor and drugs. . . .

—*Who shot cock-robin? I with my*—
(*She throws back her head with tight shut eyes.*)
—*merciful arrow!*
(BRICK *strikes at her; misses.*)

Missed me!—Sorry,—I'm not tryin' to whitewash my behavior, Christ, no! Brick, I'm not good. I don't know why people have to pretend to be good, nobody's good. The rich or the well-to-do can afford to respect moral patterns, conventional moral patterns, but I could never afford to, yeah, but—I'm honest! Give me credit for just that, will you *please?*—Born poor, raised poor, expect to die poor unless I manage to get us something out of what Big Daddy leaves when he dies of cancer! But Brick?!—*Skipper is dead! I'm alive! Maggie the cat is*—
(BRICK *hops awkwardly forward and strikes at her again with his crutch.*)
—*alive! I am alive, alive! I am* . . .
(*He hurls the crutch at her, across the bed she took refuge behind, and pitches forward on the floor as she completes her speech.*)
—*alive!*

(*A little girl,* DIXIE, *bursts into the room, wearing an Indian war bonnet and firing a cap pistol at* MARGARET *and shouting: "Bang, bang, bang!"*)

(*Laughter downstairs floats through the open hall door.* MARGARET *had crouched gasping to bed at child's entrance. She now rises and says with cool fury:*)

Little girl, your mother or someone should teach you—(*Gasping*)—to knock at a door before you come into a room. Otherwise people might think that you—lack—good breeding. . . .

DIXIE: Yanh, yanh, yanh, what is Uncle Brick doin' on th' floor?

BRICK: I tried to kill your Aunt Maggie, but I failed—and I fell. Little girl, give me my crutch so I can get up off th' floor.

MARGARET: Yes, give your uncle his crutch, he's a cripple, honey, he broke his ankle last night jumping hurdles on the high school athletic field!

DIXIE: What were you jumping hurdles for, Uncle Brick?

BRICK: Because I used to jump them, and people like to do what they used to do, even after they've stopped being able to do it. . . .

MARGARET: That's right, that's your answer, now go away, little girl.
(DIXIE *fires cap pistol at* MARGARET *three times.*)
Stop, you stop that, monster! You little no-neck monster!
(*She seizes the cap pistol and hurls it through gallery doors.*)

DIXIE: (*with a precocious instinct for the cruelest thing*) You're *jealous!*—You're just jealous because you can't have babies!
(*She sticks out her tongue at* MARGARET *as she sashays past her with her stomach stuck out, to the gallery.* MARGARET *slams the gallery doors and leans panting against them. There is a pause.* BRICK *has replaced his spilt drink and sits, faraway, on the great four-poster bed.*)

MARGARET: You see?—they gloat over us being childless, even in front of their five little no-neck monsters!
(*Pause. Voices approach on the stairs.*)
Brick?—I've been to a doctor in Memphis, a— a gynecologist. . . .

I've been completely examined, and
there is no reason why we can't have a child
whenever we want one. And this is my time by
the calendar to conceive. Are you listening to
me? Are you? Are you LISTENING TO ME!

BRICK: Yes. I hear you, Maggie.

(His attention returns to her inflamed face.)

—But how in hell on earth do you imagine—
that you're going to have a child by a man that
can't stand you?

MARGARET: That's a problem that I will have to
work out.

(She wheels about to face the hall door.)

Here they come!

(The lights dim.)

CURTAIN

ACT TWO

There is no lapse of time. MARGARET *and* BRICK *are
in the same positions they held at the end of Act I.*

MARGARET: *(at door)*   Here they come!

*(BIG DADDY appears first, a tall man with a
fierce, anxious look, moving carefully not to betray his weakness even, or especially, to himself.)*

BIG DADDY: Well, Brick.

BRICK: Hello, Big Daddy.—Congratulations!

BIG DADDY: —Crap. . . .

*(Some of the people are approaching through the
hall, others along the gallery: voices from both
directions.* GOOPER *and* REVEREND TOOKER *become visible outside gallery doors, and their
voices come in clearly.)*

(They pause outside as GOOPER *lights a cigar.)*

REVEREND TOOKER: *(vivaciously)*   Oh, but St.
Paul's in Grenada has three memorial windows, and the latest one is a Tiffany stained-
glass window that cost twenty-five hundred
dollars, a picture of Christ the Good Shepherd
with a Lamb in His arms.

GOOPER: Who give that window, Preach?

REVEREND TOOKER: Clyde Fletcher's widow. Also
presented St. Paul's with a baptismal font.

GOOPER: Y'know what somebody ought t' give
your church is a *coolin'* system, Preach.

REVEREND TOOKER: Yes, siree, Bob! And y'know
what Gus Hamma's family gave in his memory
to the church at Two Rivers? A complete new
stone parish-house with a basketball court in
the basement and a—

BIG DADDY: *(uttering a loud barking laugh which
is far from truly mirthful)*   Hey, Preach! What's
all this talk about memorials, Preach? Y' think
somebody's about t' kick off around here? 'S
that it?

(Startled by this interjection, REVEREND TOOKER
*decides to laugh at the question almost as loud as
he can.)*

*(How he would answer the question we'll never
know, as he's spared that embarrassment by the
voice of* GOOPER'S *wife,* MAE, *rising high and
clear as she appears with "*DOC*"* BAUGH, *the
family doctor, through the hall door.)*

MAE: *(almost religiously)*   —Let's see now, they've
had their *tyyy-*phoid shots, and their tetanus
shots, their diphtheria shots and their hepatitis
shots and their polio shots, they got *those*
shots every month from May through September, and—Gooper? Hey! Gooper!—What all
have the kiddies been shot faw?

MARGARET: *(overlapping a bit)*   Turn on the Hi-Fi,
Brick! Let's have some music t' start off th'
party with!

*(The talk becomes so general that the room
sounds like a great aviary of chattering birds.
Only* BRICK *remains unengaged, leaning upon
the liquor cabinet with his faraway smile, an
ice cube in a paper napkin with which he now
and then rubs his forehead. He doesn't respond
to* MARGARET'S *command. She bounds forward
and stoops over the instrument panel of the
console.)*

GOOPER: We gave 'em that thing for a third an-
niversary present, got three speakers in it.

*(The room is suddenly blasted by the climax of
a Wagnerian opera or a Beethoven symphony.)*

BIG DADDY: *Turn that dam thing off!*

(Almost instant silence, almost instantly broken by the shouting charge of BIG MAMA, *entering through hall door like a charging rhino.)*

BIG MAMA: *Wha's my Brick, wha's mah precious baby!!*

BIG DADDY: *Sorry! Turn it back on!*

(Everyone laughs very loud. BIG DADDY *is famous for his jokes at* BIG MAMA'S *expense, and nobody laughs louder at these jokes than* BIG MAMA *herself, though sometimes they're pretty cruel and* BIG MAMA *has to pick up or fuss with something to cover the hurt that the loud laugh doesn't quite cover.)*

(On this occasion, a happy occasion because the dread in her heart has also been lifted by the false report on BIG DADDY'S *condition, she giggles, grotesquely, coyly, in* BIG DADDY'S *direction and bears down upon* BRICK, *all very quick and alive.)*

BIG MAMA: Here he is, here's my precious baby! What's that you've got in your hand? You put that liquor down, son, your hand was made fo' holdin' somethin' better than that!

GOOPER: Look at Brick put it down!

*(*BRICK *has obeyed* BIG MAMA *by draining the glass and handing it to her. Again everyone laughs, some high, some low.)*

BIG MAMA: Oh, you bad boy, you, you're my bad little boy. Give Big Mama a kiss, you bad boy, you!—Look at him shy away, will you? Brick never liked bein' kissed or made a fuss over, I guess because he's always had too much of it! Son, you turn that thing off!

*(*BRICK *has switched on the TV set.)*

I can't stand TV, radio was bad enough but TV has gone it one better, I mean—*(Plops wheezing in chair)*—one worse, ha ha! Now what'm I sittin' down here faw? I want t' sit next to my sweetheart on the sofa, hold hands with him and love him up a little!

*(*BIG MAMA *has on a black and white figured chiffon. The large irregular patterns, like the markings of some massive animal, the luster of her great diamonds and many pearls, the brilliants set in the silver frames of her glasses, her*

riotous voice, booming laugh, have dominated the room since she entered.* BIG DADDY *has been regarding her with a steady grimace of chronic annoyance.)*

BIG MAMA: *(still louder)* Preacher, Preacher, hey, Preach! Give me you' hand an' help me up from this chair!

REVEREND TOOKER: None of your tricks, Big Mama!

BIG MAMA: What tricks? You give me you' hand so I can get up an'—

*(*REVEREND TOOKER *extends her his hand. She grabs it and pulls him into her lap with a shrill laugh that spans an octave in two notes.)*

Ever seen a preacher in a fat lady's lap? Hey, hey, folks! Ever seen a preacher in a fat lady's lap?

*(*BIG MAMA *is notorious throughout the Delta for this sort of inelegant horseplay.* MARGARET *looks on with indulgent humor, sipping Dubonnet "on the rocks" and watching* BRICK, *but* MAE *and* GOOPER *exchange signs of humorless anxiety over these antics, the sort of behavior which* MAE *thinks may account for their failure to quite get in with the smartest young married set in Memphis, despite all. One of the Negroes,* LACEY *or* SOOKEY, *peeks in, cackling. They are waiting for a sign to bring in the cake and champagne. But* BIG DADDY'S *not amused. He doesn't understand why, in spite of the infinite mental relief he's received from the doctor's report, he still has these same old fox teeth in his guts. "This spastic thing sure is something," he says to himself, but aloud he roars at* BIG MAMA:)*

BIG DADDY: *BIG MAMA, WILL YOU QUIT HORSIN'?*—You're too old an' too fat fo' that sort of crazy kid stuff an' besides a woman with your blood-pressure—she had two hundred last spring!—is riskin' a stroke when you mess around like that. . . .

BIG MAMA: *Here comes Big Daddy's birthday!*

*(*NEGROES *in white jackets enter with an enormous birthday cake ablaze with candles and carrying buckets of champagne with satin ribbons about the bottle necks.)*

(MAE *and* GOOPER *strike up song, and everybody, including the* NEGROES *and* CHILDREN, *joins in. Only* BRICK *remains aloof.*)

EVERYONE: Happy birthday to you.
Happy birthday to you.
Happy birthday, Big Daddy—
(Some sing: "Dear, Big Daddy!")
Happy birthday to you.
(Some sing: "How old are you?")
*(*MAE *has come down center and is organizing her children like a chorus. She gives them a barely audible: "One, two, three!" and they are off in the new tune.)*

CHILDREN: Skinamarinka—dinka—dink
Skinamarinka—do
We love you.
Skinamarinka—dinka—dink
Skinamarinka—do
(All together, they turn to BIG DADDY.*)*
Big Daddy, you!
(They turn back front, like a musical comedy chorus.)
We love you in the morning;
We love you in the night.
We love you when we're with you,
And we love you out of sight.
Skinamarinka—dinka—dink
Skinamarinka—do.
*(*MAE *turns to* BIG MAMA.*)*
Big Mama, too!
*(*BIG MAMA *bursts into tears. The* NEGROES *leave.)*

BIG DADDY: Now Ida, what the hell is the matter with you?

MAE: She's just so happy.

BIG MAMA: I'm just so happy, Big Daddy, I have to cry or something.
(Sudden and loud in the hush:)
Brick, do you know the wonderful news that Doc Baugh got from the clinic about Big Daddy? Big Daddy's one hundred per cent!

MARGARET: Isn't that wonderful?

BIG MAMA: He's just one hundred per cent. Passed the examination with flying colors. Now that we know there's nothing wrong with Big Daddy but

a spastic colon, I can tell you something. I was worried sick, half out of my mind, for fear that Big Daddy might have a thing like—
*(*MARGARET *cuts through this speech, jumping up and exclaiming shrilly:)*

MARGARET: Brick, honey, aren't you going to give Big Daddy his birthday present?
(Passing by him, she snatches his liquor glass from him.)
(She picks up a fancily wrapped package.)
Here it is, Big Daddy, this is from Brick!

BIG MAMA: This is the biggest birthday Big Daddy's ever had, a hundred presents and bushels of telegrams from—

MAE: *(at same time)* What is it, Brick?

GOOPER: I bet 500 to 50 that Brick don't *know* what it is.

BIG MAMA: The fun of presents is not knowing what they are till you open the package. Open your present, Big Daddy.

BIG DADDY: Open it you'self. I want to ask Brick somethin'! Come here, Brick.

MARGARET: Big Daddy's callin' you, Brick.
(She is opening the package.)

BRICK: Tell Big Daddy I'm crippled.

BIG DADDY: I see you're crippled. I want to know how you got crippled.

MARGARET: *(making diversionary tactics)* Oh, look, oh, look, why, it's a cashmere robe!
(She holds the robe up for all to see.)

MAE: You sound surprised, Maggie.

MARGARET: I never saw one before.

MAE: That's funny.—*Hah!*

MARGARET: *(turning on her fiercely, with a brilliant smile)* Why is it funny? All my family ever had was family—and luxuries such as cashmere robes still surprise me!

BIG DADDY: *(ominously)* Quiet!

MAE: *(heedless in her fury)* I don't see how you could be so surprised when you bought it yourself at Loewenstein's in Memphis last Saturday. You know how I know?

BIG DADDY: I said, Quiet!

MAE: —I know because the salesgirl that sold it to you waited on me and said, Oh, Mrs Pollitt, your sister-in-law just bought a cashmere robe for your husband's father!

MARGARET: Sister Woman! Your talents are wasted as a housewife and mother, you really ought to be with the FBI or—

BIG DADDY: QUIET!

(REVEREND TOOKER'S *reflexes are slower than the others'. He finishes a sentence after the bellow.*)

REVEREND TOOKER: *(to* DOC BAUGH*)* —the Stork and the Reaper are running neck and neck!

(*He starts to laugh gaily when he notices the silence and* BIG DADDY'S *glare. His laugh dies falsely.*)

BIG DADDY: Preacher, I hope I'm not butting in on more talk about memorial stained-glass windows, am I, Preacher?

(REVEREND TOOKER *laughs feebly, then coughs dryly in the embarrassed silence.*)

Preacher?

BIG MAMA: Now, Big Daddy, don't you pick on Preacher!

BIG DADDY: *(raising his voice)* You ever hear that expression all hawk and no spit? You bring that expression to mind with that little dry cough of yours, all hawk an' no spit. . . .

(*The pause is broken only by a short startled laugh from* MARGARET, *the only one there who is conscious of and amused by the grotesque.*)

MAE: *(raising her arms and jangling her bracelets)* I wonder if the mosquitoes are active tonight?

BIG DADDY: What's that, Little Mama? Did you make some remark?

MAE: Yes, I said I wondered if the mosquitoes would eat us alive if we went out on the gallery for a while.

BIG DADDY: Well, if they do, I'll have your bones pulverized for fertilizer!

BIG MAMA: *(quickly)* Last week we had an airplane spraying the place and I think it done some good, at least I haven't had a—

BIG DADDY: *(cutting her speech)* Brick, they tell me, if what they tell me is true, that you done some jumping last night on the high school athletic field?

BIG MAMA: Brick, Big Daddy is talking to you, son.

BRICK: *(smiling vaguely over his drink)* What was that, Big Daddy?

BIG DADDY: They said you done some jumping on the high school track field last night.

BRICK: That's what they told me, too.

BIG DADDY: Was it jumping or humping that you were doing out there? What were you doing out there at three A.M., layin' a woman on that cinder track?

BIG MAMA: Big Daddy, you are off the sick-list, now, and I'm not going to excuse you for talkin' so—

BIG DADDY: Quiet!

BIG MAMA: —*nasty* in front of Preacher and—

BIG DADDY: *QUIET!*—I ast you, Brick, if you was cuttin' you'self a piece o' poon-tang last night on that cinder track? I thought maybe you were chasin' poon-tang on that track an' tripped over something in the heat of the chase—'sthat it?

(GOOPER *laughs, loud and false, others nervously following suit.* BIG MAMA *stamps her foot, and purses her lips, crossing to* MAE *and whispering something to her as* BRICK *meets his father's hard, intent, grinning stare with a slow, vague smile that he offers all situations from behind the screen of his liquor.*)

BRICK: No, sir, I don't think so. . . .

MAE: *(at the same time, sweetly)* Reverend Tooker, let's you and I take a stroll on the widow's walk.

(*She and the preacher go out on the gallery as* BIG DADDY *says:*)

BIG DADDY: Then what the hell were you doing out there at three o'clock in the morning?

BRICK: Jumping the hurdles, Big Daddy, runnin' and jumpin' the hurdles, but those high hurdles have gotten too high for me, now.

BIG DADDY: 'Cause you was drunk?

BRICK: *(his vague smile fading a little)* Sober I wouldn't have tried to jump the *low* ones. . . .

BIG MAMA: *(quickly)* Big Daddy, blow out the candles on your birthday cake!

MARGARET: *(at the same time)* I want to propose a toast to Big Daddy Pollitt on his sixty-fifth birthday, the biggest cotton-planter in—

BIG DADDY: *(bellowing with fury and disgust) I told you to stop it, now stop it, quit this—!*

BIG MAMA: *(coming in front of* BIG DADDY *with the cake)* Big Daddy, I will not allow you to talk that way, not even on your birthday, I—

BIG DADDY: I'll talk like I want to on my birthday, Ida, or any other goddam day of the year and anybody here that don't like it knows what they can do!

BIG MAMA: You don't mean that!

BIG DADDY: What makes you think I don't mean it?

(Meanwhile various discreet signals have been exchanged and GOOPER *has also gone out on the gallery.)*

BIG MAMA: I just know you don't mean it.

BIG DADDY: You don't know a goddam thing and you never did!

BIG MAMA: Big Daddy, you don't mean that.

BIG DADDY: Oh, yes, I do, oh, yes, I do, I mean it! I put up with a whole lot of crap around here because I thought I was dying. And you thought I was dying and you started taking over, well, you can stop taking over now, Ida, because I'm not gonna die, you can just stop now this business of taking over because you're not taking over because I'm not dying, I went through the laboratory and the goddam exploratory operation and there's nothing wrong with me but a spastic colon. And I'm not dying of cancer which you thought I was dying of. Ain't that so? Didn't you think that I was dying of cancer, Ida?

(Almost everybody is out on the gallery but the two old people glaring at each other across the blazing cake.)

*(*BIG MAMA'S *chest heaves and she presses a fat fist to her mouth.)*

*(*BIG DADDY *continues, hoarsely:)*

Ain't that so, Ida? Didn't you have an idea I was dying of cancer and now you could take control of this place and everything on it? I got that impression, I seemed to get that impression. Your loud voice everywhere, your fat old body butting in here and there!

BIG MAMA: Hush! The Preacher!

BIG DADDY: Rut the goddam preacher!

*(*BIG MAMA *gasps loudly and sits down on the sofa which is almost too small for her.)*

Did you hear what I said? I said rut the goddam preacher!

(Somebody closes the gallery doors from outside just as there is a burst of fireworks and excited cries from the children.)

BIG MAMA: I never seen you act like this before and I can't think what's got in you!

BIG DADDY: I went through all that laboratory and operation and all just so I would know if you or me was boss here! Well, now it turns out that I am and you ain't—and that's my birthday present—and my cake and champagne!—because for three years now you been gradually taking over. Bossing. Talking. Sashaying your fat old body around the place I made! I made this place! I was overseer on it! I was the overseer on the old Straw and Ochello plantation. I quit school at ten! I quit school at ten years old and went to work like a nigger in the fields. And I rose to be overseer of the Straw and Ochello plantation. And old Straw died and I was Ochello's partner and the place got bigger and bigger and bigger and bigger and bigger! I did all that myself with no goddam help from you, and now you think you're just about to take over. Well, I am just about to tell you that you are not just about to take over, you are not just about to take over a goddam thing. Is that clear to you, Ida? Is that very plain to you, now? Is that understood completely? I been through the laboratory from A to Z. I've had the goddam exploratory operation, and nothing is wrong with me but a spastic colon—made spastic, I guess, by *disgust!* By all the goddam lies and liars that I have had to put up with, and all the goddam hypocrisy that I lived with all these forty years that we been livin' together! Hey! Ida!! Blow out the candles on the birthday cake! Purse up your lips and draw a deep breath and blow out the goddam candles on the cake!

BIG MAMA: Oh, Big Daddy, oh, oh, oh, Big Daddy!

BIG DADDY: What's the matter with you?

BIG MAMA: *In all these years you never believed that I loved you??*

BIG DADDY: Huh?

BIG MAMA: *And I did, I did so much, I did love you!*—I even loved your hate and your hardness, Big Daddy!

(She sobs and rushes awkwardly out onto the gallery.)

BIG DADDY: *(to himself)* *Wouldn't it be funny if that was true.* . . .

(A pause is followed by a burst of light in the sky from the fireworks.)

BRICK! HEY, BRICK!

(He stands over his blazing birthday cake.)

(After some moments, BRICK hobbles in on his crutch, holding his glass.)

(MARGARET follows him with a bright, anxious smile.)

I didn't call you, Maggie. I called Brick.

MARGARET: I'm just delivering him to you.

(She kisses BRICK on the mouth which he immediately wipes with the back of his hand. She flies girlishly back out. BRICK and his father are alone.)

BIG DADDY: Why did you do that?

BRICK: Do what, Big Daddy?

BIG DADDY: Wipe her kiss off your mouth like she'd spit on you.

BRICK: I don't know. I wasn't conscious of it.

BIG DADDY: That woman of yours has a better shape on her than Gooper's but somehow or other they got the same look about them.

BRICK: What sort of look is that, Big Daddy?

BIG DADDY: I don't know how to describe it but it's the same look.

BRICK: They don't look peaceful, do they?

BIG DADDY: No, they sure in hell don't.

BRICK: They look nervous as cats?

BIG DADDY: That's right, they look nervous as cats.

BRICK: Nervous as a couple of cats on a hot tin roof?

BIG DADDY: That's right, boy, they look like a couple of cats on a hot tin roof. It's funny that you and Gooper being so different would pick out the same type of woman.

BRICK: Both of us married into society, Big Daddy.

BIG DADDY: Crap . . . I wonder what gives them both that look?

BRICK: Well. They're sittin' in the middle of a big piece of land, Big Daddy, twenty-eight thousand acres is a pretty big piece of land and so they're squaring off on it, each determined to knock off a bigger piece of it than the other whenever you let it go.

BIG DADDY: I got a surprise for those women. I'm not gonna let it go for a long time yet if that's what they're waiting for.

BRICK: That's right, Big Daddy. You just sit tight and let them scratch each other's eyes out. . . .

BIG DADDY: You bet your life I'm going to sit tight on it and let those sons of bitches scratch their eyes out, ha ha ha. . . , But Gooper's wife's a good breeder, you got to admit she's fertile. Hell, at supper tonight she had them all at the table and they had to put a couple of extra leafs in the table to make room for them, she's got five head of them, now, and another one's comin'.

BRICK: Yep, number six is comin'. . . .

BIG DADDY: Brick, you know, I swear to God, I don't know the way it happens.

BRICK: The way what happens, Big Daddy?

BIG DADDY: You git you a piece of land, by hook or crook, an' things start growin' on it, things accumulate on it, and the first thing you know it's completely out of hand, completely out of hand!

BRICK: Well, they say nature hates a vacuum, Big Daddy.

BIG DADDY: That's what they say, but sometimes I think that a vacuum is a hell of a lot better than some of the stuff that nature replaces it with.

Is someone out there by that door?

BRICK: Yep.

BIG DADDY: Who?

(He has lowered his voice.)

BRICK: Someone int'rested in what we say to each other.

BIG DADDY: Gooper?——*GOOPER!*

(After a discreet pause, MAE appears in the gallery door.)

MAE: Did you call Gooper, Big Daddy?

BIG DADDY: Aw, it was you.

MAE: Do you want Gooper, Big Daddy?

BIG DADDY: No, and I don't want you. I want some privacy here, while I'm having a confidential talk with my son Brick. Now it's too hot in here to close them doors, but if I have to close those rutten doors in order to have a private talk with my son Brick, just let me know and I'll close 'em. Because I hate eavesdroppers, I don't like any kind of sneakin' an' spyin'.

MAE: Why, Big Daddy—

BIG DADDY: You stood on the wrong side of the moon, it threw your shadow!

MAE: I was just—

BIG DADDY: You was just nothing but *spyin'* an' you *know* it!

MAE: *(begins to sniff and sob)* Oh, Big Daddy, you're so unkind for some reason to those that really love you!

BIG DADDY: Shut up, shut up, shut up! I'm going to move you and Gooper out of that room next to this! It's none of your goddam business what goes on in here at night between Brick an' Maggie. You listen at night like a couple of rutten peek-hole spies and go and give a report on what you hear to Big Mama an' she comes to me and says they say such and such and so and so about what they heard goin' on between Brick an' Maggie, and Jesus, it makes me sick. I'm goin' to move you an' Gooper out of that room, I can't stand sneakin' an' spyin', it makes me sick. . . .

(MAE throws back her head and rolls her eyes heavenward and extends her arms as if invoking God's pity for this unjust martyrdom; then she presses a handkerchief to her nose and flies from the room with a loud swish of skirts.)

BRICK: *(now at the liquor cabinet)* They listen, do they?

BIG DADDY: Yeah. They listen and give reports to Big Mama on what goes on in here between you and Maggie. They say that—
(He stops as if embarrassed.)

—You won't sleep with her, that you sleep on the sofa. Is that true or not true? If you don't like Maggie, get rid of Maggie!—What are you doin' there now?

BRICK: Fresh'nin' up my drink.

BIG DADDY: Son, you know you got a real liquor problem?

BRICK: Yes, sir, yes, I know.

BIG DADDY: Is that why you quit sports-announcing, because of this liquor problem?

BRICK: Yes, sir, yes, sir, I guess so.
(He smiles vaguely and amiably at his father across his replenished drink.)

BIG DADDY: Son, don't guess about it, it's too important.

BRICK: *(vaguely)* Yes, sir.

BIG DADDY: And listen to me, don't look at the damn chandelier. . . .
(Pause. BIG DADDY'S voice is husky.)
—Somethin' else we picked up at th' big fire sale in Europe.
(Another pause.)
Life is important. There's nothing else to hold onto. A man that drinks is throwing his life away. Don't do it, hold onto your life. There's nothing else to hold onto. . . .
Sit down over here so we don't have to raise our voices, the walls have ears in this place.

BRICK: *(hobbling over to sit on the sofa beside him)* All right, Big Daddy.

BIG DADDY: Quit!—how'd that come about? Some disappointment?

BRICK: I don't know. Do you?

BIG DADDY: I'm askin' you, goddam it! How in hell would I know if you don't?

BRICK: I just got out there and found that I had a mouth full of cotton. I was always two or three beats behind what was goin' on on the field and so I—

BIG DADDY: Quit!

BRICK: *(amiably)* Yes, quit.

BIG DADDY: Son?

BRICK: Huh?

BIG DADDY: *(inhales loudly and deeply from his cigar; then bends suddenly a little forward,*

*exhaling loudly and raising a hand to his fore-
head)* —Whew!—ha ha!—I took in too much
smoke, it made me a little light-headed. . . .
(The mantel clock chimes.)
Why is it so damn hard for people to talk?

BRICK: Yeah. . . .

*(The clock goes on sweetly chiming till it has
completed the stroke of ten.)*

—Nice peaceful-soundin' clock, I like to hear
it all night. . . .

(He slides low and comfortable on the sofa; BIG
DADDY *sits up straight and rigid with some unspoken anxiety. All his gestures are tense and
jerky as he talks. He wheezes and pants and sniffs
through his nervous speech, glancing quickly,
shyly, from time to time, at his son.)*

BIG DADDY: We got that clock the summer we wint
to Europe, me an' Big Mama on that damn Cook's
Tour, never had such an awful time in my life,
I'm tellin' you, son, those gooks over there, they
gouge your eyeballs out in their grand hotels.
And Big Mama bought more stuff than you
could haul in a couple of boxcars, that's no crap.
Everywhere she wint on this whirlwind tour, she
bought, bought, bought. Why, half that stuff
she bought is still crated up in the cellar, under
water last spring!

(He laughs.)

That Europe is nothin' on earth but a great big
auction, that's all it is, that bunch of old worn-
out places, it's just a big fire sale, the whole
rutten thing, an' Big Mama wint wild in it, why,
you couldn't hold that woman with a mule's
harness! Bought, bought, bought!—lucky I'm a
rich man, yes siree, Bob, an' half that stuff is
mildewin' in th' basement. It's lucky I'm a rich
man, it sure is lucky, well, I'm a rich man,
Brick, yep, I'm a mighty rich man.

(His eyes light up for a moment.)

Y'know how much I'm worth? Guess, Brick!
Guess how much I'm worth!

*(*BRICK *smiles vaguely over his drink.)*

Close on ten million in cash an' blue chip
stocks, outside, mind you, of twenty-eight

thousand acres of the richest land this side of
the valley Nile!

*(A puff and crackle and the night sky blooms
with an eerie greenish glow.* CHILDREN *shriek
on the gallery.)*

But a man can't buy his life with it, he can't buy
back his life with it when his life has been
spent, that's one thing not offered in the Europe
fire sale or in the American markets or any markets on earth, a man can't buy his life with it, he
can't buy back his life when his life is
finished. . . .

That's a sobering thought, a very sobering
thought, and that's a thought that I was turning
over in my head, over and over and over—until
today. . . .

I'm wiser and sadder, Brick, for this experience which I just gone through. They's one
thing else that I remember in Europe.

BRICK: What is that, Big Daddy?

BIG DADDY: The hills around Barcelona in the
country of Spain and the children running over
those bare hills in their bare skins beggin' like
starvin' dogs with howls and screeches, and how
fat the priests are on the streets of Barcelona, so
many of them and so fat and so pleasant, ha
ha!—Y'know I could feed that country? I got
money enough to feed that goddam country, but
the human animal is a selfish beast and I don't
reckon the money I passed out there to those
howling children in the hills around Barcelona
would more than upholster one of the chairs in
this room, I mean pay to put a new cover on this
chair!

Hell, I threw them money like you'd scatter
feed corn for chickens, I threw money at them
just to get rid of them long enough to climb back
into th' car and—drive away. . . .

And then in Morocco, them Arabs, why,
prostitution begins at four or five, that's no exaggeration, why, I remember one day in Mar-
rakech, that old walled Arab city, I set on a
broken-down wall to have a cigar, it was fearful hot there and this Arab woman stood in the

road and looked at me till I was embarrassed, she stood stock still in the dusty hot road and looked at me till I was embarrassed. But listen to this. She had a naked child with her, a little naked girl with her, barely able to toddle, and after a while she set this child on the ground and give her a push and whispered something to her. This child come toward me, barely able t' walk, come toddling up to me and—

Jesus, it makes you sick t' remember a thing like this!

It stuck out its hand and tried to unbutton my trousers!

That child was not yet five! Can you believe me? Or do you think that I am making this up? I wint back to the hotel and said to Big Mama, Git packed! We're clearing out of this country. . . .

BRICK: Big Daddy, you're on a talkin' jag tonight.

BIG DADDY: *(ignoring this remark)* Yes, sir, that's how it is, the human animal is a beast that dies but the fact that he's dying don't give him pity for others, no, sir, it—

—Did you say something?

BRICK: Yes.

BIG DADDY: What?

BRICK: Hand me over that crutch so I can get up.

BIG DADDY: Where you goin'?

BRICK: I'm takin' a little short trip to Echo Spring.

BIG DADDY: To where?

BRICK: Liquor cabinet. . . .

BIG DADDY: Yes, sir, boy—

(He hands BRICK *the crutch.)*

—the human animal is a beast that dies and if he's got money he buys and buys and buys and I think the reason he buys everything he can buy is that in the back of his mind he has the crazy hope that one of his purchases will be life everlasting!—Which it never can be. . . . The human animal is a beast that—

BRICK: *(at the liquor cabinet)* Big Daddy, you sure are shootin' th' breeze here tonight.

(There is a pause and voices are heard outside.)

BIG DADDY: I been quiet here lately, spoke not a word, just sat and stared into space. I had something heavy weighing on my mind but tonight that load was took off me. That's why I'm talking.—The sky looks diff'rent to me. . . .

BRICK: You know what I like to hear most?

BIG DADDY: What?

BRICK: Solid quiet. Perfect unbroken quiet.

BIG DADDY: Why?

BRICK: Because it's more peaceful.

BIG DADDY: Man, you'll hear a lot of that in the grave.

(He chuckles agreeably.)

BRICK: Are you through talkin' to me?

BIG DADDY: Why are you so anxious to shut me up?

BRICK: Well, sir, ever so often you say to me, Brick, I want to have a talk with you, but when we talk, it never materializes. Nothing is said. You sit in a chair and gas about this and that and I look like I listen. I try to look like I listen, but I don't listen, not much. Communication is—awful hard between people an'—somehow between you and me, it just don't—

BIG DADDY: Have you ever been scared? I mean have you ever felt downright terror of something?

(He gets up.)

Just one moment. I'm going to close these doors. . . .

(He closes doors on gallery as if he were going to tell an important secret.)

BRICK: What?

BIG DADDY: Brick?

BRICK: Huh?

BIG DADDY: Son, I thought I had it!

BRICK: Had what? Had what, Big Daddy?

BIG DADDY: Cancer!

BRICK: Oh . . .

BIG DADDY: I thought the old man made out of bones had laid his cold and heavy hand on my shoulder!

BRICK: Well, Big Daddy, you kept a tight mouth about it.

BIG DADDY: A pig squeals. A man keeps a tight mouth about it, in spite of a man not having a pig's advantage.

BRICK: What advantage is that?

BIG DADDY: Ignorance—of mortality—is a comfort. A man don't have that comfort, he's the only living thing that conceives of death, that knows what it is. The others go without knowing, which is the way that anything living should go, go without knowing, without any knowledge of it, and yet a pig squeals, but a man sometimes, he can keep a tight mouth about it. Sometimes he—

(There is a deep, smoldering ferocity in the old man.)

—can keep a tight mouth about it. I wonder if—

BRICK: What, Big Daddy?

BIG DADDY: A whiskey highball would injure this spastic condition?

BRICK: No, sir, it might do it good.

BIG DADDY: *(grins suddenly, wolfishly)* Jesus, I can't tell you! The sky is open! Christ, it's open again! It's open, boy, it's open!

(BRICK looks down at his drink.)

BRICK: You feel better, Big Daddy?

BIG DADDY: Better? Hell! I can breathe!—All of my life I been like a doubled up fist. . . .

(He pours a drink.)

—Poundin', smashin', drivin'!—now I'm going to loosen these doubled up hands and touch things *easy* with them. . . .

(He spreads his hands as if caressing the air.)

You know what I'm contemplating?

BRICK: *(vaguely)* No, sir. What are you contemplating?

BIG DADDY: Ha ha!—*Pleasure!*—pleasure with *women!*

(BRICK'S smile fades a little but lingers.)

Brick, this stuff burns me!—

—Yes, boy. I'll tell you something that you might not guess. I still have desire for women and this is my sixty-fifth birthday.

BRICK: I think that's mighty remarkable, Big Daddy.

BIG DADDY: Remarkable?

BRICK: *Admirable*, Big Daddy.

BIG DADDY: You're damn right it is, remarkable and admirable both. I realize now that I never had me enough. I let many chances slip by because of scruples about it, scruples, convention—crap. . . . All that stuff is bull, bull, bull!—It took the shadow of death to make me see it. Now that shadow's lifted, I'm going to cut loose and have, what is it they call it, have me a—ball!

BRICK: A ball, huh?

BIG DADDY: That's right, a ball, a ball! Hell!—I slept with Big Mama till, let's see, five years ago, till I was sixty and she was fifty-eight, and never even liked her, never did!

(The phone has been ringing down the hall. BIG MAMA enters, exclaiming:)

BIG MAMA: Don't you men hear that phone ring? I heard it way out on the gall'ry.

BIG DADDY: There's five rooms off this front gall'ry that you could go through. Why do you go through this one?

(BIG MAMA makes a playful face as she bustles out the hall door.)

Hunh!—Why, when Big Mama goes out of a room, I can't remember what that woman looks like, but when Big Mama comes back into the room, boy, then I see what she looks like, and I wish I didn't!

(Bends over laughing at this joke till it hurts his guts and he straightens with a grimace. The laugh subsides to a chuckle as he puts the liquor glass a little distrustfully down on the table.)

(BRICK has risen and hobbled to the gallery doors.)

Hey! Where you goin'?

BRICK: Out for a breather.

BIG DADDY: Not yet you ain't. Stay here till this talk is finished, young fellow.

BRICK: I thought it was finished, Big Daddy.

BIG DADDY: It ain't even begun.

BRICK: My mistake. Excuse me. I just wanted to feel that river breeze.

BIG DADDY: Turn on the ceiling fan and set back down in that chair.

(BIG MAMA'S *voice rises, carrying down the hall.*)

BIG MAMA: Miss Sally, you're a case! You're a caution, Miss Sally. Why didn't you give me a chance to explain it to you?

BIG DADDY: Jesus, she's talking to my old maid sister again.

BIG MAMA: Well, goodbye, now, Miss Sally. You come down real soon, Big Daddy's dying to see you! Yaisss, goodbye, Miss Sally. . . .

(*She hangs up and bellows with mirth.* BIG DADDY *groans and covers his ears as she approaches.*)

(*Bursting in*)

Big Daddy, that was Miss Sally callin' from Memphis again! You know what she done, Big Daddy? She called her doctor in Memphis to git him to tell her what that spastic thing is! Ha-*HAAAA!*— And called back to tell me how relieved she was that—Hey! Let me in!

(BIG DADDY *has been holding the door half closed against her.*)

BIG DADDY: Naw I ain't. I told you not to come and go through this room. You just back out and go through those five other rooms.

BIG MAMA: Big Daddy? Big Daddy? Oh, big Daddy!—You didn't mean those things you said to me, did you?

(*He shuts door firmly against her but she still calls.*)

Sweetheart? Sweetheart? Big Daddy? You didn't mean those awful things you said to me?—I know you didn't. I know you didn't mean those things in your heart. . . .

(*The childlike voice fades with a sob and her heavy footsteps retreat down the hall.* BRICK *has risen once more on his crutches and starts for the gallery again.*)

BIG DADDY: All I ask of that woman is that she leave me alone. But she can't admit to herself that she makes me sick. That comes of having slept with her too many years. Should of quit much sooner but that old woman she never got

enough of it—and I was good in bed . . . I never should of wasted so much of it on her. . . . They say you got just so many and each one is numbered. Well, I got a few left in me, a few, and I'm going to pick me a good one to spend 'em on! I'm going to pick me a choice one, I don't care how much she costs, I'll smother her in—minks! Ha ha! I'll strip her naked and smother her in minks and choke her with diamonds! Ha ha! I'll strip her naked and choke her with diamonds and smother her with minks and hump her from hell to breakfast. *Ha aha ha ha ha!*

MAE: (*gaily at door*) Who's that laughin' in there?

GOOPER: Is Big Daddy laughin' in there?

BIG DADDY: Crap!—them two—*drips*. . . .

(*He goes over and touches* BRICK'S *shoulder.*)

Yes, son. Brick, boy.—I'm—*happy!* I'm happy, son, I'm happy!

(*He chokes a little and bites his under lip, pressing his head quickly, shyly against his son's head and then, coughing with embarrassment, goes uncertainly back to the table where he set down the glass. He drinks and makes a grimace as it burns his guts.* BRICK *sighs and rises with effort.*)

What makes you so restless? Have you got ants in your britches?

BRICK: Yes, sir . . .

BIG DADDY: Why?

BRICK: —Something—hasn't—happened. . . .

BIG DADDY: Yeah? What is that?

BRICK: (*sadly*) —the click. . . .

BIG DADDY: Did you say click?

BRICK: Yes, click.

BIG DADDY: What click?

BRICK: A click that I get in my head that makes me peaceful.

BIG DADDY: I sure in hell don't know what you're talking about, but it disturbs me.

BRICK: It's just a mechanical thing.

BIG DADDY: What is a mechanical thing?

BRICK: This click that I get in my head that makes me peaceful. I got to drink till I get it. It's just a mechanical thing, something like a—like a—like a—

BIG DADDY: Like a—

BRICK: Switch clicking off in my head, turning the hot light off and the cool night on and—
(He looks up, smiling sadly.)
—all of a sudden there's—peace!

BIG DADDY: *(whistles long and soft with astonishment; he goes back to* BRICK *and clasps his son's two shoulders)* Jesus! I didn't know it had gotten that bad with you. Why, boy, you're—*alcoholic!*

BRICK: That's the truth, Big Daddy. I'm alcoholic.

BIG DADDY: This shows how I—let things go!

BRICK: I have to hear that little click in my head that makes me peaceful. Usually I hear it sooner than this, sometimes as early as—noon, but—
—Today it's—dilatory. . . .
—I just haven't got the right level of alcohol in my bloodstream yet!
(This last statement is made with energy as he freshens his drink.)

BIG DADDY: Uh—huh. Expecting death made me blind. I didn't have no idea that a son of mine was turning into a drunkard under my nose.

BRICK: *(gently)* Well, now you do, Big Daddy, the news has penetrated.

BIG DADDY: UH-huh, yes, now I do, the news has—penetrated. . . .

BRICK: And so if you'll excuse me—

BIG DADDY: No, I won't excuse you.

BRICK: —I'd better sit by myself till I hear that click in my head, it's just a mechanical thing but it don't happen except when I'm alone or talking to no one. . . .

BIG DADDY: You got a long, long time to sit still, boy, and talk to no one, but now you're talkin' to me. At least I'm talking to you. And you set there and listen until I tell you the conversation is over!

BRICK: But this talk is like all the others we've ever had together in our lives! It's nowhere, nowhere!—it's—it's *painful*, Big Daddy. . . .

BIG DADDY: All right, then let it be painful, but don't you move from that chair!—I'm going to remove that crutch. . . .
(He seizes the crutch and tosses it across room.)

BRICK: I can hop on one foot, and if I fall, I can crawl!

BIG DADDY: If you ain't careful you're gonna crawl off this plantation and then, by Jesus, you'll have to hustle your drinks along Skid Row!

BRICK: That'll come, Big Daddy.

BIG DADDY: Naw, it won't. You're my son and I'm going to straighten you out; now that *I'm* straightened out, I'm going to straighten out you!

BRICK: Yeah?

BIG DADDY: Today the report come in from Oschner Clinic. Y'know what they told me?
(His face glows with triumph.)
The only thing that they could detect with all the instruments of science in that great hospital is a little spastic condition of the colon! And nerves torn to pieces by all that worry about it.
(A little GIRL *bursts into room with a sparkler clutched in each fist, hops and shrieks like a monkey gone mad and rushes back out again as* BIG DADDY *strikes at her.)*
(Silence. The two men stare at each other. A WOMAN *laughs gaily outside.)*
I want you to know I breathed a sigh of relief almost as powerful as the Vicksburg tornado!

BRICK: You weren't ready to go?

BIG DADDY: GO WHERE?—crap. . . .
—When you are gone from here, boy, you are long gone and no where! The human machine is not no different from the animal machine or the fish machine or the bird machine or the reptile machine or the insect machine! It's just a whole goddam lot more complicated and consequently more trouble to keep together. Yep. I thought I had it. The earth shook under my foot, the sky come down like the black lid of a kettle and I couldn't breathe!—Today!!—that lid was lifted, I drew my first free breath in— how many years?—God!—three. . . .
(There is laughter outside, running footsteps, the soft, plushy sound and light of exploding rockets.)

(BRICK *stares at him soberly for a long moment; then makes a sort of startled sound in his nostrils and springs up on one foot and hops across the room to grab his crutch, swinging on the furniture for support. He gets the crutch and flees as if in horror for the gallery. His father seizes him by the sleeve of his white silk pajamas.*)

Stay here, you son of a bitch!—till I say go!

BRICK: I can't.

BIG DADDY: You sure in hell will, goddam it.

BRICK: No, I can't. We talk, you talk, in—circles! We get nowhere, nowhere! It's always the same, you say you want to talk to me and don't have a ruttin' thing to say to me!

BIG DADDY: Nothin' to say when I'm tellin' you I'm going to live when I thought I was dying?!

BRICK: Oh—*that!*—Is that what you have to say to me?

BIG DADDY: Why, you son of a bitch! Ain't that, ain't that—*important?!*

BRICK: Well, you said that, that's said, and now I—

BIG DADDY: Now you set back down.

BRICK: You're all balled up, you—

BIG DADDY: I ain't balled up!

BRICK: You are, you're all balled up!

BIG DADDY: Don't tell me what I am, you drunken whelp! I'm going to tear this coat sleeve off if you don't set down!

BRICK: Big Daddy—

BIG DADDY: Do what I tell you! I'm the boss here, now! I want you to know I'm back in the driver's seat now!

(BIG MAMA *rushes in, clutching her great heaving bosom.*)

What in hell do you want in here, Big Mama?

BIG MAMA: Oh, Big Daddy! Why are you shouting like that? I just cain't *stainnnnnnnnd*—it. . . .

BIG DADDY: (*raising the back of his hand above his head*) GIT!—outa here.

(*She rushes back out, sobbing.*)

BRICK: (*softly, sadly*) Christ. . . .

BIG DADDY: (*fiercely*) Yeah! Christ!—is right

. . .

(BRICK *breaks loose and hobbles toward the gallery.*)

(BIG DADDY *jerks his crutch from under* BRICK *so he steps with the injured ankle. He utters a hissing cry of anguish, clutches a chair and pulls it over on top of him on the floor.*)

Son of a—tub of—hog fat. . . .

BRICK: Big Daddy! Give me my crutch.

(BIG DADDY *throws the crutch out of reach.*)

Give me that crutch, Big Daddy.

BIG DADDY: Why do you drink?

BRICK: Don't know, give me my crutch!

BIG DADDY: You better think why you drink or give up drinking!

BRICK: Will you please give me my crutch so I can get up off this floor?

BIG DADDY: First you answer my question. Why do you drink? Why are you throwing your life away, boy, like somethin' disgusting you picked up on the street?

BRICK: (*getting onto his knees*) Big Daddy, I'm in pain, I stepped on that foot.

BIG DADDY: Good! I'm glad you're not too numb with the liquor in you to feel some pain!

BRICK: You—spilled my—drink . . .

BIG DADDY: I'll make a bargain with you. You tell me why you drink and I'll hand you one. I'll pour you the liquor myself and hand it to you.

BRICK: Why do I drink?

BIG DADDY: Yeah! Why?

BRICK: Give me a drink and I'll tell you.

BIG DADDY: Tell me first!

BRICK: I'll tell you in one word.

BIG DADDY: What word?

BRICK: DISGUST!

(*The clock chimes softly, sweetly.* BIG DADDY *gives it a short, outraged glance.*)

Now how about that drink?

BIG DADDY: What are you disgusted with? You got to tell me that, first. Otherwise being disgusted don't make no sense!

BRICK: Give me my crutch.

BIG DADDY: You heard me, you got to tell me what I asked you first.

BRICK: I told you, I said to kill my disgust!

BIG DADDY: DISGUST WITH WHAT!

BRICK: You strike a hard bargain.

BIG DADDY: What are you disgusted with?—an' I'll pass you the liquor.

BRICK: I can hop on one foot, and if I fall, I can crawl.

BIG DADDY: You want liquor that bad?

BRICK: *(dragging himself up, clinging to bedstead)* Yeah, I want it that bad.

BIG DADDY: If I give you a drink, will you tell me what it is you're disgusted with, Brick?

BRICK: Yes, sir, I will try to.

(The old man pours him a drink and solemnly passes it to him.)

(There is silence as BRICK drinks.)

Have you ever heard the word "mendacity"?

BIG DADDY: Sure. Mendacity is one of them five dollar words that cheap politicians throw back and forth at each other.

BRICK: You know what it means?

BIG DADDY: Don't it mean lying and liars?

BRICK: Yes, sir, lying and liars.

BIG DADDY: Has someone been lying to you?

CHILDREN: *(chanting in chorus offstage)* We want Big Dad-dee!

We want Big Dad-dee!

(GOOPER appears in the gallery door.)

GOOPER: Big Daddy, the kiddies are shouting for you out there.

BIG DADDY: *(fiercely)* Keep out, Gooper!

GOOPER: 'Scuse *me!*

(BIG DADDY slams the doors after GOOPER.)

BIG DADDY: Who's been lying to you, has Margaret been lying to you, has your wife been lying to you about something, Brick?

BRICK: Not her. That wouldn't matter.

BIG DADDY: Then who's been lying to you, and what about?

BRICK: No one single person and no one lie. . . .

BIG DADDY: Then what, what then, for Christ's sake?

BRICK: —The whole, the whole—thing. . . .

BIG DADDY: Why are you rubbing your head? You got a headache?

BRICK: No, I'm tryin' to—

BIG DADDY: —Concentrate, but you can't because your brain's all soaked with liquor, is that the trouble? Wet brain!

(He snatches the glass from BRICK'S hand.)

What do you know about this mendacity thing? Hell! I could write a book on it! Don't you know that? I could write a book on it and still not cover the subject? Well, I could, I could write a goddam book on it and still not cover the subject anywhere near enough!!—Think of all the lies I got to put up with!—Pretenses! Ain't that mendacity? Having to pretend stuff you don't think or feel or have any idea of? Having for instance to act like I care for Big Mama!—I haven't been able to stand the sight, sound, or smell of that woman for forty years now!—even when I *laid* her!—regular as a piston. . . . Pretend to love that son of a bitch of a Gooper and his wife Mae and those five same screechers out there like parrots in a jungle? Jesus! Can't stand to look at 'em!

Church!—it bores the Bejesus out of me but I go!—I go an' sit there and listen to the fool preacher!

Clubs!—Elks! Masons! Rotary!—*crap!*

(A spasm of pain makes him clutch his belly. He sinks into a chair and his voice is softer and hoarser.)

You I *do* like for some reason, did always have some kind of real feeling for—affection—respect—yes, always. . . .

You and being a success as a planter is all I ever had any devotion to in my whole life!—and that's the truth. . . .

I don't know why, but it is!

I've lived with mendacity!—Why can't *you* live with it? Hell, you *got* to live with it, there's nothing *else* to *live* with except mendacity, is there?

BRICK: Yes, sir. Yes, sir there is something else that you can live with!

BIG DADDY: What?

BRICK: (*lifting his glass*) This!—Liquor. . . .

BIG DADDY: That's not living, that's dodging away from life.

BRICK: I want to dodge away from it.

BIG DADDY: Then why don't you kill yourself, man?

BRICK: I like to drink. . . .

BIG DADDY: Oh, God, I can't talk to you. . . .

BRICK: I'm sorry, Big Daddy.

BIG DADDY: Not as sorry as I am. I'll tell you something. A little while back when I thought my number was up—

(*This speech should have torrential pace and fury.*)

—before I found out it was just this—spastic—colon, I thought about you. Should I or should I not, if the jig was up, give you this place when I go—since I hate Gooper an' Mae an' know that they hate me, and since all five same monkeys are little Maes an' Goopers.—And I thought, No!—Then I thought, Yes!—I couldn't make up my mind. I hate Gooper and his five same monkeys and that bitch Mae! Why should I turn over twenty-eight thousand acres of the richest land this side of the valley Nile to not my kind?—But why in hell, on the other hand, Brick—should I subsidize a goddam fool on the bottle?—Liked or not liked, well, maybe even—*loved!*—Why should I do that?—Subsidize worthless behavior? Rot? Corruption?

BRICK: (*smiling*) I understand.

BIG DADDY: Well, if you do, you're smarter than I am, God damn it, because I don't understand. And this I will tell you frankly. I didn't make up my mind at all on that question and still to this day I ain't made out no will!—Well, now I don't *have* to. The pressure is gone. I can just wait and see if you pull yourself together or if you don't.

BRICK: That's right, Big Daddy.

BIG DADDY: You sound like you thought I was kidding.

BRICK: (*rising*) No, sir, I know you're not kidding.

BIG DADDY: But you don't care—?

BRICK: (*hobbling toward the gallery door*) No, sir, I don't care. . . .

Now how about taking a look at your birthday fireworks and getting some of that cool breeze off the river?

(*He stands in the gallery doorway as the night sky turns pink and green and gold with successive flashes of light.*)

BIG DADDY: *WAIT!*—Brick. . . .

(*His voice drops. Suddenly there is something shy, almost tender, in his restraining gesture.*)

Don't let's—leave it like this, like them other talks we've had, we've always—talked around things, we've—just talked around things for some rutten reason. I don't know what, it's always like something was left not spoken, something avoided because neither of us was honest enough with the—other. . . .

BRICK: I never lied to you, Big Daddy.

BIG DADDY: Did I ever to *you?*

BRICK: No, sir. . . .

BIG DADDY: Then there is at least two people that never lied to each other.

BRICK: But we've never *talked* to each other.

BIG DADDY: We can *now.*

BRICK: Big Daddy, there don't seem to be anything much to say.

BIG DADDY: You say that you drink to kill your disgust with lying.

BRICK: You said to give you a reason.

BIG DADDY: Is liquor the only thing that'll kill this disgust?

BRICK: Now. Yes.

BIG DADDY: But not once, huh?

BRICK: Not when I was still young an' believing. A drinking man's someone who wants to forget he isn't still young an' believing.

BIG DADDY: Believing what?

BRICK: Believing. . . .

BIG DADDY: Believing *what?*

BRICK: (*stubbornly evasive*) Believing. . . .

BIG DADDY: I don't know what the hell you mean by believing and I don't think you know what you mean by believing, but if you still got sports in your blood, go back to sports announcing and—

BRICK: Sit in a glass box watching games I can't play? Describing what I can't do while players do it? Sweating out their disgust and confusion in contests I'm not fit for? Drinkin' a coke, half bourbon, so I can stand it? That's no goddam good any more, no help—time just outran me, Big Daddy—got there first . . .

BIG DADDY: I think you're passing the buck.

BRICK: You know many drinkin' men?

BIG DADDY: (with a slight, charming smile) I have known a fair number of that species.

BRICK: Could any of them tell you why he drank?

BIG DADDY: Yep, you're passin' the buck to things like time and disgust with "mendacity" and—crap!—if you got to use that kind of language about a thing, it's ninety-proof bull, and I'm not buying any.

BRICK: I had to give you a reason to get a drink!

BIG DADDY: You started drinkin' when your friend Skipper died.

(Silence for five beats. Then BRICK makes a startled movement, reaching for his crutch.)

BRICK: What are you suggesting?

BIG DADDY: I'm suggesting nothing.

(The shuffle and clop of BRICK's rapid hobble away from his father's steady, grave attention.)
—But Gooper an' Mae suggested that there was something not right exactly in your—

BRICK: (stopping short downstage as if backed to a wall) "Not right"?

BIG DADDY: Not, well, exactly normal in your friendship with—

BRICK: They suggested that, too? I thought that was Maggie's suggestion.

(BRICK's detachment is at last broken through. His heart is accelerated; his forehead sweat-beaded; his breath becomes more rapid and his voice hoarse. The thing they're discussing, timidly and painfully on the side of BIG DADDY, fiercely, violently on BRICK's side, is the inadmissible thing that Skipper died to disavow between them. The fact that if it existed it had to be disavowed to "keep face" in the world they lived in, may be at the heart of the "mendacity" that BRICK drinks to kill his disgust with. It

may be the root of his collapse. Or maybe it is only a single manifestation of it, not even the most important. The bird that I hope to catch in the net of this play is not the solution of one man's psychological problem. I'm trying to catch the true quality of experience in a group of people, that cloudy, flickering, evanescent—fiercely charged!—interplay of live human beings in the thundercloud of a common crisis. Some mystery should be left in the revelation of character in a play, just as a great deal of mystery is always left in the revelation of character in life, even in one's own character to himself. This does not absolve the playwright of his duty to observe and probe as clearly and deeply as he legitimately can: but it should steer him away from "pat" conclusions, facile definitions which make a play just a play, not a snare for the truth of human experience.)

(The following scene should be played with great concentration, with most of the power leashed but palpable in what is left unspoken.)
Who else's suggestion is it, is it yours? How many others thought that Skipper and I were—

BIG DADDY: (gently) Now, hold on, hold on a minute, son.—I knocked around in my time.

BRICK: What's that got to do with—

BIG DADDY: I said "Hold on!"—I bummed, I bummed this country till I was—

BRICK: Whose suggestion, who else's suggestion is it?

BIG DADDY: Slept in hobo jungles and railroad Y's and flophouses in all cities before I—

BRICK: Oh, you think so, too, you call me your son and a queer. Oh! Maybe that's why you put Maggie and me in this room that was Jack Straw's and Peter Ochello's, in which that pair of old sisters slept in a double bed where both of 'em died!

BIG DADDY: Now just don't go throwing rocks at—
(Suddenly REVEREND TOOKER appears in the gallery doors, his head slightly, playfully, fatuously cocked, with a practised clergyman's smile, sincere as a bird-call blown on a hunter's whistle,

the living embodiment of the pious, conventional lie.)

(BIG DADDY gasps a little at this perfectly timed, but incongruous, apparition.)

—What're you lookin' for, Preacher?

REVEREND TOOKER: The gentleman's lavatory, ha ha!—heh, heh . . .

BIG DADDY: *(with strained courtesy)* —Go back out and walk down to the other end of the gallery, Reverend Tooker, and use the bathroom connected with my bedroom, and if you can't find it, ask them where it is!

REVEREND TOOKER: Ah, thanks.

(He goes out with a deprecatory chuckle.)

BIG DADDY: It's hard to talk in this place . . .

BRICK: Son of a—!

BIG DADDY: *(leaving a lot unspoken)* —I seen all things and understood a lot of them, till 1910. Christ, the year that—I had worn my shoes through, hocked my—I hopped off a yellow dog freight car half a mile down the road, slept in a wagon of cotton outside the gin—Jack Straw an' Peter Ochello took me in. Hired me to manage this place which grew into this one.—When Jack Straw died—why, old Peter Ochello quit eatin' like a dog does when its master's dead, and died, too!

BRICK: Christ!

BIG DADDY: I'm just saying I understand such—

BRICK: *(violently)* Skipper is dead. I have not quit eating!

BIG DADDY: No, but you started drinking.

(BRICK wheels on his crutch and hurls his glass across the room shouting.)

BRICK: YOU THINK SO, TOO?

BIG DADDY: *Shhh!*

(Footsteps run on the gallery. There are women's calls.)

(BIG DADDY goes toward the door.)

Go away!—Just broke a glass. . . .

(BRICK is transformed, as if a quiet mountain blew suddenly up in volcanic flame.)

BRICK: You think so, too? You think so, too? You think me an' Skipper did, did, did!—*sodomy!*—together?

BIG DADDY: Hold—!

BRICK: That what you—

BIG DADDY: —*ON*—a minute!

BRICK: You think we did dirty things between us, Skipper an'—

BIG DADDY: Why are you shouting like that? Why are you—

BRICK: —Me, is that what you think of Skipper, is that—

BIG DADDY: —so excited? I don't think nothing. I don't know nothing. I'm simply telling you what—

BRICK: You think that Skipper and me were a pair of dirty old men!

BIG DADDY: Now that's—

BRICK: Straw? Ochello? A couple of—

BIG DADDY: Now just—

BRICK: —ducking sissies? Queers? Is that what you—

BIG DADDY: Shhh.

BRICK: —think?

(He loses his balance and pitches to his knees without noticing the pain. He grabs the bed and drags himself up.)

BIG DADDY: Jesus!—Whew. . . . Grab my hand!

BRICK: Naw, I don't want your hand. . . .

BIG DADDY: Well, I want yours. Git up!

(He draws him up, keeps an arm about him with concern and affection.)

You broken out in a sweat! You're panting like you'd run race with—

BRICK: *(freeing himself from his father's hold)* Big Daddy, you shock me, Big Daddy, you, you—*shock* me. Talkin' so—

(He turns away from his father.)

—casually!—about a—thing like that . . .

—Don't you know how people *feel* about things like that? How, how *disgusted* they are by things like that? Why, at Ole Miss when it was discovered a pledge to our fraternity, Skipper's and mine, did a, *attempted* to do a, unnatural thing with—

We not only dropped him like a hot rock!—We told him to git off the campus, and he did, he got!—All the way to—

(He halts, breathless.)

BIG DADDY: Where?

BRICK: North Africa, last I heard!

BIG DADDY: Well, I have come back from further away than that. I have just now returned from the other side of the moon, death's country, son, and I'm not easy to shock by anything here.

(He comes downstage and faces out.)

I always, anyhow, lived with too much space around me to be infected by ideas of other people. One thing you can grow on a big place more important than cotton!—is *tolerance!*—I own it.

(He returns toward BRICK.)

BRICK: Why can't exceptional friendship, *real, real, deep, deep friendship!* between two men be respected as something clean and decent without being thought of as—

BIG DADDY: It can, it is, for God's sake.

BRICK: *Fairies.* . . .

(In his utterance of this word, we gauge the wide and profound reach of the conventional mores he got from the world that crowned him with early laurel.)

BIG DADDY: I told Mae an' Gooper—

BRICK: Frig Mae and Gooper, frig all dirty lies and liars!—Skipper and me had a clean, true thing between us!—had a clean friendship, practically all our lives, till Maggie got the idea you're talking about. Normal? No!—It was too rare to be normal, any true thing between two people is too rare to be normal. Oh, once in a while he put his hand on my shoulder or I'd put mine on his, oh, maybe even, when we were touring the country in pro-football an' shared hotel-rooms we'd reach across the space between the two beds and shake hands to say goodnight, yeah, one or two times we—

BIG DADDY: Brick, nobody thinks that that's not normal!

BRICK: Well, they're mistaken, it was! It was a pure an' true thing an' that's not normal.

(They both stare straight at each other for a long moment. The tension breaks and both turn away as if tired.)

BIG DADDY: Yeah, it's—hard t'—talk. . . .

BRICK: All right, then, let's—let it go. . . .

BIG DADDY: Why did Skipper crack up? Why have you?

*(*BRICK *looks back at his father again. He has already decided, without knowing that he has made this decision, that he is going to tell his father that he is dying of cancer. Only this could even the score between them: one inadmissible thing in return for another.)*

BRICK: *(ominously)* All right. You're asking for it, Big Daddy. We're finally going to have that real true talk you wanted. It's too late to stop it, now, we got to carry it through and cover every subject.

(He hobbles back to the liquor cabinet.)

Uh-huh.

(He opens the ice bucket and picks up the silver tongs with slow admiration of their frosty brightness.)

Maggie declares that Skipper and I went into pro-football after we left Ole Miss because we were scared to grow up . . .

(He moves downstage with the shuffle and clop of a cripple on a crutch. As MARGARET *did when her speech became "recitative," he looks out into the house, commanding its attention by his direct, concentrated gaze—a broken, "tragically elegant" figure telling simply as much as he knows of "the Truth":)*

—Wanted to—keep on tossing—those long, long!—high, high!—passes that—couldn't be intercepted except by time, the aerial attack that made us famous! And so we did, we did, we kept it up for one season, that aerial attack, we held it high!—Yeah, but—

—that summer, Maggie, she laid the law down to me, said, Now or never, and so I married Maggie. . . .

BIG DADDY: How was Maggie in bed?

BRICK: *(wryly)* Great! the greatest!

*(*BIG DADDY *nods as if he thought so.)*

She went on the road that fall with the Dixie Stars. Oh, she made a great show of being the world's best sport. She wore a—wore a—tall bearskin cap! A shako, they call it, a dyed moleskin coat, a moleskin coat dyed red!—Cut up crazy! Rented hotel ballrooms for victory celebrations, wouldn't cancel them when it—turned out—defeat. . . .

MAGGIE THE CAT! Ha ha!

(BIG DADDY *nods.*)

—But Skipper, he had some fever which came back on him which doctors couldn't explain and I got that injury—turned out to be just a shadow on the X-ray plate—and a touch of bursitis. . . .

I lay in a hospital bed, watched our games on TV, saw Maggie on the bench next to Skipper when he was hauled out of a game for stumbles, fumbles!—Burned me up the way she hung on his arm!—Y'know, I think that Maggie had always felt sort of left out because she and me never got any closer together than two people just get in bed, which is not much closer than two cats on a—fence humping. . . .

So! She took this time to work on poor dumb Skipper. He was a less than average student at Ole Miss, you know that, don't you?!—Poured in his mind the dirty, false idea that what we were, him and me, was a frustrated case of that ole pair of sisters that lived in this room, Jack Straw and Peter Ochello!—He, poor Skipper, went to bed with Maggie to prove it wasn't true, and when it didn't work out, he thought it *was* true!—Skipper broke in two like a rotten stick—nobody ever turned so fast to a lush—or died of it so quick. . . .

—Now are you satisfied?

(BIG DADDY *has listened to this story, dividing the grain from the chaff. Now he looks at his son.*)

BIG DADDY: Are *you* satisfied?

BRICK: With what?

BIG DADDY: That half-ass story!

BRICK: What's half-ass about it?

BIG DADDY: Something's left out of that story. What did you leave out?

(*The phone has started ringing in the hall. As if it reminded him of something,* BRICK *glances suddenly toward the sound and says:*)

BRICK: Yes!—I left out a long-distance call which I had from Skipper, in which he made a drunken confession to me and on which I hung up!—last time we spoke to each other in our lives. . . .

(*Muted ring stops as someone answers phone in a soft, indistinct voice in hall.*)

BIG DADDY: You hung up?

BRICK: Hung up. Jesus! Well—

BIG DADDY: Anyhow now!—we have tracked down the lie with which you're disgusted and which you are drinking to kill your disgust with, Brick. You been passing the buck. This disgust with mendacity is disgust with yourself.

You!—dug the grave of your friend and kicked him in it!—before you'd face truth with him!

BRICK: *His* truth, not *mine!*

BIG DADDY: His truth, okay! But you wouldn't face it with him!

BRICK: Who *can* face truth? Can *you?*

BIG DADDY: Now don't start passin' the rotten buck again, boy!

BRICK: *How about these birthday congratulations, these many, many happy returns of the day, when ev'rybody but you knows there won't be any!*

(*Whoever has answered the hall phone lets out a high, shrill laugh; the voice becomes audible saying: "no, no, you got it all wrong! Upside down! Are you crazy?"*)

(BRICK *suddenly catches his breath as he realizes that he has made a shocking disclosure. He hobbles a few paces, then freezes, and without looking at his father's shocked face, says:*)

Let's, let's—go out, now, and—

(BIG DADDY *moves suddenly forward and grabs hold of the boy's crutch like it was a weapon for which they were fighting for possession.*)

BIG DADDY: Oh, no, no! No one's going out. What did you start to say?

BRICK: I don't remember.

BIG DADDY: "Many happy returns when they know there won't be any"?

BRICK: Aw, hell, Big Daddy, forget it. Come on out on the gallery and look at the fireworks they're shooting off for your birthday. . . .

BIG DADDY: First you finish that remark you were makin' before you cut off. "Many happy returns when they know there won't be any"?—Ain't that what you just said?

BRICK: Look, now. I can get around without that crutch if I have to but it would be a lot easier on the furniture an' glassware if I didn' have to go swinging along like Tarzan of th'—

BIG DADDY: FINISH! WHAT YOU WAS SAYIN'!

(An eerie green glow shows in sky behind him.)

BRICK: *(sucking the ice in his glass, speech becoming thick)* Leave th' place to Gooper and Mae an' their five little same little monkeys. All I want is—

BIG DADDY: "LEAVE TH' PLACE," did you say?

BRICK: *(vaguely)* All twenty-eight thousand acres of the richest land this side of the valley Nile.

BIG DADDY: Who said I was "leaving the place" to Gooper or anybody? This is my sixty-fifth birthday! I got fifteen years or twenty years left in me! I'll outlive *you!* I'll bury you an' have to pay for your coffin!

BRICK: Sure. Many happy returns. Now let's go watch the fireworks, come on, let's—

BIG DADDY: Lying, have they been lying? About the report from th'—clinic? Did they, did they—find something?—*Cancer.* Maybe?

BRICK: Mendacity is a system that we live in. Liquor is one way out an' death's the other. . . .

(He takes the crutch from BIG DADDY'S loose grip and swings out on the gallery leaving the doors open.)

(A song, "Pick a Bale of Cotton," is heard.)

MAE: *(appearing in door)* Oh, Big Daddy, the field-hands are singin' fo' you!

BIG DADDY: *(shouting hoarsely)* BRICK! BRICK!

MAE: He's outside drinkin', Big Daddy.

BIG DADDY: *BRICK!*

(MAE retreats, awed by the passion of his voice. CHILDREN call BRICK in tones mocking BIG DADDY. His face crumbles like broken yellow plaster about to fall into dust.)

(There is a glow in the sky. BRICK swings back through the doors, slowly, gravely, quite soberly.)

BRICK: I'm sorry, Big Daddy. My head don't work any more and it's hard for me to understand how anybody could care if he lived or died or was dying or cared about anything but whether or not there was liquor left in the bottle and so I said what I said without thinking. In some ways I'm no better than the others, in some ways worse because I'm less alive. Maybe it's being alive that makes them lie, and being almost *not* alive makes me sort of accidentally truthful—I don't know but—anyway—we've been friends . . .

—And being friends is telling each other the truth. . . .

(There is a pause.)

You told *me!* I told *you!*

(A CHILD rushes into the room and grabs a fistful of firecrackers and runs out again.)

CHILD: *(screaming)* Bang, bang, bang, bang bang, bang, bang, bang, bang!

BIG DADDY: *(slowly and passionately)* CHRIST—DAMN—ALL—LYING SONS OF—LYING BITCHES!

(He straightens at last and crosses to the inside door. At the door he turns and looks back as if he had some desperate question he couldn't put into words. Then he nods reflectively and says in a hoarse voice:)

Yes, all liars, all liars, all lying dying liars!

(This is said slowly, slowly, with a fierce revulsion. He goes on out.)

—Lying! Dying! Liars!

(His voice dies out. There is the sound of a child being slapped. It rushes, hideously bawling, through room and out the hall door.)

(BRICK remains motionless as the lights dim out and the curtain falls.)

CURTAIN

ACT THREE

There is no lapse of time.
MAE *enters with* REVEREND TOOKER.

MAE: Where is Big Daddy! Big Daddy?

BIG MAMA: *(entering)* Too much smell of burnt
fireworks makes me feel a little bit sick at my
stomach.—Where is Big Daddy?

MAE: That's what I want to know, where has Big
Daddy gone?

BIG MAMA: He must have turned in, I reckon he
went to baid. . . .
*(*GOOPER *enters.)*

GOOPER: Where is Big Daddy?

MAE: We don't know where he is!

BIG MAMA: I reckon he's gone to baid.

GOOPER: Well, then, now we can talk.

BIG MAMA: What *is* this talk, *what* talk?
*(*MARGARET *appears on gallery, talking to* DR
BAUGH.)*

MARGARET: *(musically)* My family freed their
slaves ten years before abolition, my great-
great-grandfather gave his slaves their freedom
five years before the war between the States
started!

MAE: Oh, for God's sake! Maggie's climbed back
up in her family tree!

MARGARET: *(sweetly)* What, Mae?—Oh, where's
Big Daddy?!
*(The pace must be very quick. Great Southern
animation.)*

BIG MAMA: *(addressing them all)* I think Big
Daddy was just worn out. He loves his family,
he loves to have them around him, but it's a
strain on his nerves. He wasn't himself tonight,
Big Daddy wasn't himself, I could tell he was
all worked up.

REVEREND TOOKER: I think he's remarkable.

BIG MAMA: Yaisss! Just remarkable. Did you all notice the food he ate at that table? Did you all notice the supper he put away? Why, he ate like a
hawss!

GOOPER: I hope he doesn't regret it.

BIG MAMA: Why, that man—ate a huge piece of
cawn-bread with molasses on it! Helped himself twice to hoppin' john.

MARGARET: Big Daddy loves hoppin' john.—We
had a real country dinner.

BIG MAMA: *(overlapping* MARGARET*)* Yais, he
simply adores it! An' candied yams? That man
put away enough food at that table to stuff a
nigger *field*-hand!

GOOPER: *(with grim relish)* I hope he don't have to
pay for it later on. . . .

BIG MAMA: *(fiercely)* What's *that*, Gooper?

MAE: Gooper says he hopes Big Daddy doesn't
suffer tonight.

BIG MAMA: Oh, shoot, Gooper says, Gooper says!
Why should Big Daddy suffer for satisfying a
normal appetite? There's nothin' wrong with
that man but nerves, he's sound as a dollar!
And now he knows he is an' that's why he ate
such a supper. He had a big load off his mind,
knowin' he wasn't doomed t'—what he thought
he was doomed to. . . .

MARGARET: *(sadly and sweetly)* Bless his old
sweet soul. . . .

BIG MAMA: *(vaguely)* Yais, bless his heart, wher's
Brick?

MAE: Outside.

GOOPER: —Drinkin' . . .

BIG MAMA: I know he's drinkin'. You all don't have
to keep tellin' *me* Brick is drinkin'. Cain't I see
he's drinkin' without you continually tellin' me
that boy's drinkin'?

MARGARET: Good for you, Big Mama!
(She applauds.)

BIG MAMA: Other people *drink* and *have* drunk an'
will *drink*, as long as they make that stuff an'
put it in bottles.

MARGARET: That's the truth. I never trusted a
man that didn't drink.

MAE: Gooper never drinks. Don't you trust Gooper?

MARGARET: Why, Gooper don't you drink? If I'd
known you didn't drink, I wouldn't of made that
remark—

BIG MAMA: *Brick?*

MARGARET: —at least not in your presence.
(She laughs sweetly.)

BIG MAMA: *Brick!*

MARGARET: He's still on the gall'ry. I'll go bring him in so we can talk.

BIG MAMA: *(worriedly)* I don't know what this mysterious family conference is about.

(Awkward silence. BIG MAMA looks from face to face, then belches slightly and mutters, "Excuse me. . . ." She opens an ornamental fan suspended about her throat, a black lace fan to go with her black lace gown, and fans her wilting corsage, sniffing nervously and looking from face to face in the uncomfortable silence as MARGARET calls "Brick?" and BRICK sings to the moon on the gallery.)

I don't know what's wrong here, you all have such long faces! Open that door on the hall and let some air circulate through here, will you please, Gooper?

MAE: I think we'd better leave that door closed, Big Mama, till after the talk.

BIG MAMA: Reveren' Tooker, will *you* please open that door?!

REVEREND TOOKER: I sure will, Big Mama.

MAE: I just didn't think we ought t' take any chance of Big Daddy hearin' a word of this discussion.

BIG MAMA: I *swan!* Nothing's going to be said in Big Daddy's house that he cain't hear if he wants to!

GOOPER: Well, Big Mama, it's—

(MAE gives him a quick, hard poke to shut him up. He glares at her fiercely as she circles before him like a burlesque ballerina, raising her skinny bare arms over her head, jangling her bracelets, exclaiming:)

MAE: A breeze! A breeze!

REVEREND TOOKER: I think this house is the coolest house in the Delta.—Did you all know that Halsey Banks' widow put air-conditioning units in the church and rectory at Friar's Point in memory of Halsey?

(General conversation has resumed; everybody is chatting so that the stage sounds like a big bird-cage.)

GOOPER: Too bad nobody cools your church off for you. I bet you sweat in that pulpit these hot Sundays, Reverend Tooker.

REVEREND TOOKER: Yes, my vestments are drenched.

MAE: *(at the same time to DR BAUGH)* You reckon those vitamin B_{12} injections are what they're cracked up t' be, Doc Baugh?

DOCTOR BAUGH: Well, if you want to be stuck with something I guess they're as good to be stuck with as anything else.

BIG MAMA: *(at gallery door)* Maggie, Maggie, aren't you comin' with Brick?

MAE: *(suddenly and loudly, creating a silence)* I have a strange feeling, I have a peculiar feeling!

BIG MAMA: *(turning from gallery)* What feeling?

MAE: That Brick said somethin' he shouldn't of said t' Big Daddy.

BIG MAMA: Now what on earth could Brick of said t' Big Daddy that he shouldn't say?

GOOPER: Big Mama, there's somethin'—

MAE: NOW, WAIT!

(She rushes up to BIG MAMA and gives her a quick hug and kiss. BIG MAMA pushes her impatiently off as the REVEREND TOOKER's voice rises serenely in a little pocket of silence:)

REVEREND TOOKER: Yes, last Sunday the gold in my chasuble faded into th' purple. . . .

GOOPER: Reveren', you must of been preachin' hell's fire last Sunday!

(He guffaws at this witticism but the REVEREND is not sincerely amused. At the same time BIG MAMA has crossed over to DR BAUGH and is saying to him:)

BIG MAMA: *(her breathless voice rising high-pitched above the others)* In my day they had what they call the Keeley cure for heavy drinkers. But now I understand they just take some kind of tablets, they call them "Annie Bust" tablets. But *Brick* don't need to take *nothin'.*

(BRICK appears in gallery doors with MARGARET behind him.)

BIG MAMA: *(unaware of his presence behind her)* That boy is just broken up over Skipper's death. You know how poor Skipper died. They

gave him a big, big dose of that sodium amytal stuff at his home and then they called the ambulance and give him another big, big dose of it at the hospital and that and all of the alcohol in his system fo' months an' months an' months just proved too much for his heart. . . . I'm scared of needles! I'm more scared of a needle than the knife. . . . I think more people have been needled out of this world than—
(She stops short and wheels about.)
OH!—here's Brick! My precious baby—
(She turns upon BRICK *with short, fat arms extended, at the same time uttering a loud, short sob, which is both comic and touching.)*
*(*BRICK *smiles and bows slightly, making a burlesque gesture of gallantry for* MAGGIE *to pass before him into the room. Then he hobbles on his crutch directly to the liquor cabinet and there is absolute silence, with everybody looking at* BRICK *as everybody has always looked at* BRICK *when he spoke or moved or appeared. One by one he drops ice cubes in his glass, then suddenly, but not quickly, looks back over his shoulder with a wry, charming smile, and says:)*

BRICK: I'm sorry! Anyone else?

BIG MAMA: *(sadly)* No, son. I *wish* you wouldn't!

BRICK: I wish I didn't have to, Big Mama, but I'm still waiting for that click in my head which makes it all smooth out!

BIG MAMA: Aw, Brick, you—BREAK MY HEART!

MARGARET: *(at the same time)* Brick, go sit with Big Mama!

BIG MAMA: I just cain't staiiiiiiiii-nnnnnd—it. . . .
(She sobs.)

MAE: Now that we're all assembled—

GOOPER: We kin talk. . . .

BIG MAMA: Breaks my heart. . . .

MARGARET: Sit with Big Mama, Brick, and hold her hand.
*(*BIG MAMA *sniffs very loudly three times, almost like three drum beats in the pocket of silence.)*

BRICK: You do that, Maggie. I'm a restless cripple. I got to stay on my crutch.

*(*BRICK *hobbles to the gallery door; leans there as if waiting.)*
*(*MAE *sits beside* BIG MAMA, *while* GOOPER *moves in front and sits on the end of the couch, facing her.* REVEREND TOOKER *moves nervously into the space between them; on the other side,* DR BAUGH *stands looking at nothing in particular and lights a cigar.* MARGARET *turns away.)*

BIG MAMA: Why're you all *surroundin'* me—like this? Why're you all starin' at me like this an' makin' signs at each other?
*(*REVEREND TOOKER *steps back startled.)*

MAE: Calm yourself, Big Mama.

BIG MAMA: Calm you'self, *you'self*, Sister Woman. How could I calm myself with everyone starin' at me as if big drops of blood had broken out on m'face? What's this all about, Annh! What?
*(*GOOPER *coughs and takes a center position.)*

GOOPER: Now, Doc Baugh.

MAE: Doc Baugh?

BRICK: *(suddenly)* SHHH!—
(Then he grins and chuckles and shakes his head regretfully.)
—Naw!—that wasn't th' click.

GOOPER: Brick, shut up or stay out there on the gallery with your liquor! We got to talk about a serious matter. Big Mama wants to know the complete truth about the report we got today from the Ochsner Clinic.

MAE: *(eagerly)* —on Big Daddy's condition!

GOOPER: Yais, on Big Daddy's condition, we got to face it.

DOCTOR BAUGH: Well. . . .

BIG MAMA: *(terrified, rising)* Is there? Something? Something that I? Don't—Know?
(In these few words, this startled, very soft, question, BIG MAMA *reviews the history of her forty-five years with* BIG DADDY, *her great, almost embarrassingly true-hearted and simple-minded devotion to* BIG DADDY, *who must have had something* BRICK *has, who made himself loved so much by the "simple expedient" of not loving enough to disturb his charming detachment, also once coupled, like* BRICK'S, *with virile beauty.)*

(BIG MAMA *has a dignity at this moment: she almost stops being fat.*)

DOCTOR BAUGH: *(after a pause, uncomfortably)* Yes?—Well—

BIG MAMA: *I!!!—want to—knowwwwwww. . . .* (*Immediately she thrusts her fist to her mouth as if to deny that statement.*)
(*Then, for some curious reason, she snatches the withered corsage from her breast and hurls it on the floor and steps on it with her short, fat feet.*)
—*Somebody must be lyin'!—I want to know!*

MAE: Sit down, Big Mama, sit down on this sofa.

MARGARET: *(quickly)* Brick, go sit with Big Mama.

BIG MAMA: *What is it, what is it?*

DOCTOR BAUGH: I never have seen a more thorough examination than Big Daddy Pollitt was given in all my experience with the Ochsner Clinic.

GOOPER: It's one of the best in the country.

MAE: It's *THE* best in the country—bar *none!*
(*For some reason she gives* GOOPER *a violent poke as she goes past him. He slaps at her hand without removing his eyes from his mother's face.*)

DOCTOR BAUGH: Of course they were ninety-nine and nine-tenths percent sure before they even started.

BIG MAMA: Sure of what, sure of what, sure of—what?—what!
(*She catches her breath in a startled sob.* MAE *kisses her quickly. She thrusts* MAE *fiercely away from her, staring at the doctor.*)

MAE: Mommy, be a brave girl!

BRICK: *(in the doorway, softly)* "By the light, by the light,
Of the sil-ve-ry mo-ooo-n . . ."

GOOPER: Shut up!—Brick.

BRICK: —Sorry. . . .
(*He wanders out on the gallery.*)

DOCTOR BAUGH: But now, you see, Big Mama, they cut a piece off this growth, a specimen of the tissue and—

BIG MAMA: Growth? You told Big Daddy—

DOCTOR BAUGH: Now wait.

BIG MAMA: *(fiercely)* You told me and Big Daddy there wasn't a thing wrong with him but—

MAE: Big Mama, they always—

GOOPER: Let Doc Baugh talk, will yuh?

BIG MAMA: —little spastic condition of—
(*Her breath gives out in a sob.*)

DOCTOR BAUGH: Yes, that's what we told Big Daddy. But we had this bit of tissue run through the laboratory and I'm sorry to say the test was positive on it. It's—well—malignant. . . .
(*Pause.*)

BIG MAMA: —Cancer?! Cancer?!
(DR BAUGH *nods gravely.*)
(BIG MAMA *gives a long gasping cry.*)

MAE and GOOPER: Now, now, now, Big Mama, you had to know. . . .

BIG MAMA: *WHY DIDN'T THEY CUT IT OUT OF HIM? HANH? HANH?*

DOCTOR BAUGH: Involved too much, Big Mama, too many organs affected.

MAE: Big Mama, the liver's affected and so's the kidneys, both! It's gone way past what they call a—

GOOPER: A surgical risk.

MAE: —Uh-huh. . . .
(BIG MAMA *draws a breath like a dying gasp.*)

REVEREND TOOKER: Tch, tch, tch, tch, tch!

DOCTOR BAUGH: Yes, it's gone past the knife.

MAE: *That's why he's turned yellow, Mommy!*

BIG MAMA: *Git away from me, git away from me, Mae!*
(*She rises abruptly.*)
I want Brick! Where's Brick? Where is my only son?

MAE: Mama! Did she say "*only son*"?

GOOPER: What does that make *me?*

MAE: A sober responsible man with five precious children!—*Six!*

BIG MAMA: I want Brick to tell me! Brick! Brick!

MARGARET: *(rising from her reflections in a corner)* Brick was so upset he went back out.

BIG MAMA: *Brick!*

MARGARET: Mama, let *me* tell you!

BIG MAMA: No, no, leave me alone, you're not my blood!

GOOPER: *Mama, I'm your son!* Listen to *me!*

MAE: Gooper's your son, he's your first-born!

BIG MAMA: Gooper never liked Daddy.

MAE: (*as if terribly shocked*) That's not TRUE!
   (*There is a pause. The* MINISTER *coughs and rises.*)

REVEREND TOOKER: (*to* MAE) I think I'd better slip away at this point.

MAE: (*sweetly and sadly*) Yes, Doctor Tooker, you go.

REVEREND TOOKER: (*discreetly*) Goodnight, goodnight, everybody, and God bless you all . . . on this place. . . .
   (*He slips out.*)

DOCTOR BAUGH: That man is a good man but lacking in tact. Talking about people giving memorial windows—if he mentioned one memorial window, he must have spoke of a dozen, and saying how awful it was when somebody died intestate, the legal wrangles, and so forth.
   (MAE *coughs, and points at* BIG MAMA.)

DOCTOR BAUGH: Well, Big Mama. . . .
   (*He sighs.*)

BIG MAMA: It's all a mistake, I know it's just a bad dream.

DOCTOR BAUGH: We're gonna keep Big Daddy as comfortable as we can.

BIG MAMA: Yes, it's just a bad dream, that's all it is, it's just an awful dream.

GOOPER: In my opinion Big Daddy is having some pain but won't admit that he has it.

BIG MAMA: Just a dream, a bad dream.

DOCTOR BAUGH: That's what lots of them do, they think if they don't admit they're having the pain they can sort of escape the fact of it.

GOOPER: (*with relish*) Yes, they get sly about it, they get real sly about it.

MAE: Gooper and I think—

GOOPER: Shut up, Mae!—Big Daddy ought to be started on morphine.

BIG MAMA: Nobody's going to give Big Daddy morphine.

DOCTOR BAUGH: Now, Big Mama, when that pain strikes it's going to strike mighty hard and Big Daddy's going to need the needle to bear it.

BIG MAMA: I tell you, nobody's going to give him morphine.

MAE: Big Mama, you don't want to see Big Daddy suffer, you know you—
   (GOOPER *standing beside her gives her a savage poke.*)

DOCTOR BAUGH: (*placing a package on the table*) I'm leaving this stuff here, so if there's a sudden attack you all won't have to send out for it.

MAE: I know how to give a hypo.

GOOPER: Mae took a course in nursing during the war.

MARGARET: Somehow I don't think Big Daddy would want Mae to give him a hypo.

MAE: You think he'd want *you* to do it?
   (DR BAUGH *rises.*)

GOOPER: Doctor Baugh is goin'.

DOCTOR BAUGH: Yes, I got to be goin'. Well, keep your chin up, Big Mama.

GOOPER: (*with jocularity*) She's gonna keep *both* chins up, aren't you Big Mama?
   (BIG MAMA *sobs.*)
   Now stop that, Big Mama.

MAE: Sit down with me, Big Mama.

GOOPER: (*at door with* DR BAUGH) Well, Doc, we sure do appreciate all you done. I'm telling you, we're surely obligated to you for—
   (DR BAUGH *has gone out without a glance at him.*)

GOOPER: —I guess that doctor has got a lot on his mind but it wouldn't hurt him to act a little more human. . . .
   (BIG MAMA *sobs.*)
   Now be a brave girl, Mommy.

BIG MAMA: It's not true, I know that it's just not true!

GOOPER: Mama, those tests are infallible!

BIG MAMA: Why are you so determined to see your father daid?

MAE: Big Mama!

MARGARET: (*gently*) I know what Big Mama means.

MAE: (*fiercely*) Oh, do you?

MARGARET: (*quietly and very sadly*) Yes, I think I do.

MAE: For a newcomer in the family you sure do show a lot of understanding.

MARGARET: Understanding is needed on this place.

MAE: I guess you must have needed a lot of it in your family, Maggie, with your father's liquor problem and now you've got Brick with his!

MARGARET: Brick does not have a liquor problem at all. Brick is devoted to Big Daddy. This thing is a terrible strain on him.

BIG MAMA: Brick is Big Daddy's boy, but he drinks too much and it worries me and Big Daddy, and, Margaret, you've got to cooperate with us, you've got to cooperate with Big Daddy and me in getting Brick straightened out. Because it will break Big Daddy's heart if Brick don't pull himself together and take hold of things.

MAE: Take hold of *what* things, Big Mama?

BIG MAMA: The place.

(There is a quick violent look between MAE and GOOPER.)

GOOPER: Big Mama, you've had a shock.

MAE: Yais, we've all had a shock, but. . . .

GOOPER: Let's be realistic—

MAE: —Big Daddy would never, would *never*, be foolish enough to—

GOOPER: —put this place in irresponsible hands!

BIG MAMA: Big Daddy ain't going to leave the place in anybody's hands; Big Daddy is *not* going to die. I want you to get that in your heads, all of you!

MAE: Mommy, Mommy, Big Mama, we're just as hopeful an' optimistic as you are about Big Daddy's prospects, we have faith in *prayer*— but nevertheless there are certain matters that have to be discussed an' dealt with, because otherwise—

GOOPER: Eventualities have to be considered and now's the time. . . . Mae, will you please get my briefcase out of our room?

MAE: Yes, honey.

(She rises and goes out through the hall door.)

GOOPER: *(standing over BIG MAMA)* Now Big Mom. What you said just now was not at all true and you know it. I've always loved Big Daddy in my own quiet way. I never made a show of it, and I know that Big Daddy has always been fond of me in a quiet way, too, and he never made a show of it neither.

(MAE returns with GOOPER'S briefcase.)

MAE: Here's your briefcase, Gooper, honey.

GOOPER: *(handing the briefcase back to her)* Thank you. . . . Of cou'se, my relationship with Big Daddy is different from Brick's.

MAE: You're eight years older'n Brick an' always had t'carry a bigger load of th' responsibilities than Brick ever had t'carry. He never carried a thing in his life but a football or a highball.

GOOPER: Mae, will y' let me talk, please?

MAE: Yes, honey.

GOOPER: Now, a twenty-eight thousand acre plantation's a mighty big thing t'run.

MAE: Almost singlehanded.

(MARGARET has gone out onto the gallery, and can be heard calling softly to BRICK.)

BIG MAMA: You never had to run this place! What are you talking about? As if Big Daddy was dead and in his grave, you had to run it? Why, you just helped him out with a few business details and had your law practice at the same time in Memphis!

MAE: Oh, Mommy, Mommy, Big Mommy! Let's be fair! Why, Gooper has given himself body and soul to keeping this place up for the past five years since Big Daddy's health started failing. Gooper won't say it, Gooper never thought of it as a duty, he just did it. And what did Brick do? Brick kept living in his past glory at college! Still a football player at twenty-seven!

MARGARET: *(returning alone)* Who are you talking about, now? Brick? A football player? He isn't a football player and you know it. Brick is a sports announcer on TV and one of the best-known ones in the country!

MAE: I'm talking about what he was.

MARGARET: Well, I wish you would just stop talking about my husband.

GOOPER: I've got a right to discuss my brother with other members of MY OWN family which don't include *you.* Why don't you go out there and drink with Brick?

MARGARET: I've never seen such malice toward a brother.

GOOPER: How about his for me? Why, he can't stand to be in the same room with me!

MARGARET: This is a deliberate campaign of vilification for the most disgusting and sordid reason on earth, and I know what it is! It's *avarice, avarice, greed, greed!*

BIG MAMA: *Oh, I'll scream! I will scream in a moment unless this stops!*

(GOOPER *has stalked up to* MARGARET *with clenched fists at his sides as if he would strike her.* MAE *distorts her face again into a hideous grimace behind* MARGARET'S *back.*)

MARGARET: We only remain on the place because of Big Mom and Big Daddy. If it is true what they say about Big Daddy we are going to leave here just as soon as it's over. Not a moment later.

BIG MAMA: *(sobs)* Margaret. Child. Come here. Sit next to Big Mama.

MARGARET: Precious Mommy. I'm sorry, I'm sorry, I—!

(*She bends her long graceful neck to press her forehead to* BIG MAMA'S *bulging shoulder under its black chiffon.*)

GOOPER: How beautiful, how touching, this display of devotion!

MAE: Do you know why she's childless? She's childless because that big beautiful athlete husband of hers won't go to bed with her!

GOOPER: You jest won't let me do this in a nice way, will yah? Aw right—Mae and I have five kids with another one coming! I don't give a goddam if Big Daddy likes me or don't like me or did or never did or will or will never! I'm just appealing to a sense of common decency and fair play. I'll tell you the truth. I've resented Big Daddy's partiality to Brick ever since Brick was born, and the way I've been treated like I was just barely good enough to spit on and sometimes not even good enough for that. Big Daddy is dying of cancer, and it's

spread all through him and it's attacked all his vital organs including the kidneys and right now he is sinking into uremia, and you all know what uremia is, it's poisoning of the whole system due to the failure of the body to eliminate its poisons.

MARGARET: *(to herself, downstage, hissingly) Poisons, poisons! Venomous thoughts and words! In hearts and minds!—That's poisons!*

GOOPER: *(overlapping her)* I am asking for a square deal, and I expect to get one. But if I don't get one, if there's any peculiar shenanigans going on around here behind my back, or before me, well, I'm not a corporation lawyer for nothing, I know how to protect my own interests.—*OH! A late arrival!*

(BRICK *enters from the gallery with a tranquil, blurred smile, carrying an empty glass with him.*)

MAE: Behold the conquering hero comes!

GOOPER: The fabulous Brick Pollitt! Remember him?—Who could forget him!

MAE: He looks like he's been injured in a game!

GOOPER: Yep, I'm afraid you'll have to warm the bench at the Sugar Bowl this year, Brick!

(MAE *laughs shrilly.*)

Or was it the Rose Bowl that he made that famous run in?

MAE: The punch bowl, honey. It was in the punch bowl, the cut-glass punch bowl!

GOOPER: Oh, that's right, I'm getting the bowls mixed up!

MARGARET: Why don't you stop venting your malice and envy on a sick boy?

BIG MAMA: *Now you two hush, I mean it, hush, all of you, hush!*

GOOPER: All right, Big Mama. A family crisis brings out the best and the worst in every member of it.

MAE: *That's the truth.*

MARGARET: *Amen!*

BIG MAMA: *I said, hush! I won't tolerate any more catty talk in my house.*

(MAE *gives* GOOPER *a sign indicating briefcase.*)

(BRICK'S *smile has grown both brighter and vaguer. As he prepares a drink, he sings softly:*)

BRICK:

Show me the way to go home,
I'm tired and I wanta go to bed,
I had a little drink about an hour ago—

GOOPER: (*at the same time*) Big Mama, you know it's necessary for me t'go back to Memphis in th' mornin' t'represent the Parker estate in a lawsuit.

(MAE *sits on the bed and arranges papers she has taken from the briefcase.*)

BRICK: (*continuing the song*)

Wherever I may roam,
On land or sea or foam.

BIG MAMA: Is it, Gooper?

MAE: Yaiss.

GOOPER: That's why I'm forced to—to bring up a problem that—

MAE: Somethin' that's too important t' be put off!

GOOPER: If Brick was sober, he ought to be in on this.

MARGARET: Brick is present; we're here.

GOOPER: Well, good. I will now give you this outline my partner, Tom Bullitt, an' me have drawn up—a sort of dummy—trusteeship.

MARGARET: Oh, that's it! You'll be in charge an' dole out remittances, will you?

GOOPER: This we did as soon as we got the report on Big Daddy from th' Ochsner Laboratories. We did this thing, I mean we drew up this dummy outline with the advice and assistance of the Chairman of the Boa'd of Directors of th' Southern Plantahs Bank and Trust Company in Memphis, C. C. Bellowes, a man who handles estates for all th' prominent fam'lies in West Tennessee and th' Delta.

BIG MAMA: Gooper?

GOOPER: (*crouching in front of* BIG MAMA) Now this is not—not final, or anything like it. This is just a preliminary outline. But it does provide a basis—a design—a—possible, feasible—*plan!*

MARGARET: Yes, I'll bet.

MAE: It's a plan to protect the biggest estate in the Delta from irresponsibility an'—

BIG MAMA: Now you listen to me, all of you, you listen here! They's not goin' to be any more catty talk in my house! And Gooper, you put that away before I grab it out of your hand and tear it right up! I don't know what the hell's in it, and I don't want to know what the hell's in it. I'm talkin' in Big Daddy's language now; I'm his *wife*, not his *widow*, I'm still his *wife!* And I'm talkin' to you in his language an'—

GOOPER: Big Mama, what I have here is—

MAE: Gooper explained that it's just a plan. . . .

BIG MAMA: I don't care what you got there. Just put it back where it came from, an' don't let me see it again, not even the outside of the envelope of it! Is that understood? Basis! Plan! Preliminary! Design! I say—what is it Big Daddy always says when he's disgusted?

BRICK: (*from the bar*) Big Daddy says "crap" when he's disgusted.

BIG MAMA: (*rising*) That's right—*CRAP!* I say *CRAP* too, like Big Daddy!

MAE: Coarse language doesn't seem called for in this—

GOOPER: Somethin' in me is *deeply outraged* by hearin' you talk like this.

BIG MAMA: *Nobody's goin' to take nothin'!*—till Big Daddy lets go of it, and maybe, just possibly, not—not even then! No, not even then!

BRICK:

You can always hear me singin' this song,
Show me the way to go home.

BIG MAMA: Tonight Brick looks like he used to look when he was a little boy, just like he did when he played wild games and used to come home all sweaty and pink-cheeked and sleepy, with his—red curls shining. . . .

(*She comes over to him and runs her fat shaky hand through his hair. He draws aside as he does from all physical contact and continues the song in a whisper, opening the ice bucket and dropping in the ice cubes one by one as if he were mixing some important chemical formula.*)

BIG MAMA: (*continuing*) Time goes by so fast. Nothin' can outrun it. Death commences too early—almost before you're half-acquainted with life—you meet with the other. . . .

Oh, you know we just got to love each other an' stay together, all of us, just as close as we can, especially now that such a *black* thing has come and moved into this place without invitation.

(Awkwardly embracing BRICK, *she presses her head to his shoulder.)*

*(*GOOPER *has been returning papers to* MAE, *who has restored them to briefcase with an air of severely tried patience.)*

GOOPER: Big Mama? Big Mama?

(He stands behind her, tense with sibling envy.)

BIG MAMA: *(oblivious of* GOOPER*)* Brick, you hear me, don't you?

MARGARET: Brick hears you, Big Mama, he understands what you're saying.

BIG MAMA: Oh, Brick, son of Big Daddy! Big Daddy does so love you! Y'know what would be his fondest dream come true? If before he passed on, if Big Daddy has to pass on, you gave him a child of yours, a grandson as much like his son as his son is like Big Daddy!

MAE: *(zipping briefcase shut: an incongruous sound)* Such a pity that Maggie an' Brick can't oblige!

MARGARET: *(suddenly and quietly but forcefully)* Everybody listen.

(She crosses to the center of the room, holding her hands rigidly together.)

MAE: Listen to what, Maggie?

MARGARET: I have an announcement to make.

GOOPER: A sports announcement, Maggie?

MARGARET: Brick and I are going to—*have a child!*

*(*BIG MAMA *catches her breath in a loud gasp.)*

(Pause. BIG MAMA *rises.)*

BIG MAMA: Maggie! Brick! This is too good to believe!

MAE: That's right, too good to believe.

BIG MAMA: Oh, my, my! This is Big Daddy's dream, his dream come true! I'm going to tell him right now before he—

MARGARET: We'll tell him in the morning. Don't disturb him now.

BIG MAMA: I want to tell him before he goes to sleep, I'm going to tell him his dream's come true this minute! And Brick! A child will make you pull yourself together and quit this drinking! *(She seizes the glass from his hand.)* The responsibilities of a father will—

(Her face contorts and she makes an excited gesture; bursting into sobs, she rushes out, crying.)

I'm going to tell Big Daddy right this minute!

(Her voice fades out down the hall.)

*(*BRICK *shrugs slightly and drops an ice cube into another glass.* MARGARET *crosses quickly to his side, saying something under her breath, and she pours the liquor for him, staring up almost fiercely into his face.)*

BRICK: *(coolly)* Thank you, Maggie, that's a nice big shot.

*(*MAE *has joined* GOOPER *and she gives him a fierce poke, making a low hissing sound and a grimace of fury.)*

GOOPER: *(pushing her aside)* Brick, could you possibly spare me one small shot of that liquor?

BRICK: Why, help yourself, Gooper boy.

GOOPER: I will.

MAE: *(shrilly)* Of course we know that this is—

GOOPER: *Be still, Mae!*

MAE: I won't be still! I know she's made this up!

GOOPER: God damn it, I said to shut up!

MARGARET: Gracious! I didn't know that my little announcement was going to provoke such a storm!

MAE: *That* woman isn't *pregnant!*

GOOPER: Who said she was?

MAE: *She* did.

GOOPER: The doctor didn't. Doc Baugh didn't.

MARGARET: I haven't gone to Doc Baugh.

GOOPER: Then who'd you go to, Maggie?

MARGARET: One of the best gynecologists in the South.

GOOPER: Uh huh, uh huh!—I see. . . .

(He takes out pencil and notebook.)

—May we have his name, please?

MARGARET: No, you may not, Mister Prosecuting Attorney!

MAE: He doesn't have any name, he doesn't exist!

MARGARET: Oh, he exists all right, and so does my child, Brick's baby!

MAE: You can't conceive a child by a man that won't sleep with you unless you think you're— (BRICK *has turned on the phonograph. A scat song cuts* MAE'S *speech.*)

GOOPER: *Turn that off!*

MAE: We know it's a lie because we hear you in here; he won't sleep with you, we hear you! So don't imagine you're going to put a trick over on us, to fool a dying man with a— (*A long drawn cry of agony and rage fills the house.* MARGARET *turns phonograph down to a whisper.*) (*The cry is repeated.*)

MAE: (*awed*) Did you hear that, Gooper, did you hear that?

GOOPER: Sounds like the pain has struck.

MAE: Go see, Gooper!

GOOPER: Come along and leave these love birds together in their nest! (*He goes out first.* MAE *follows but turns at the door, contorting her face and hissing at* MARGARET.)

MAE: *Liar!* (*She slams the door.*) (MARGARET *exhales with relief and moves a little unsteadily to catch hold of* BRICK'S *arm.*)

MARGARET: Thank you for—keeping still . . .

BRICK: OK, Maggie.

MARGARET: It was gallant of you to save my face!

BRICK: —It hasn't happened yet.

MARGARET: What?

BRICK: The click. . . .

MARGARET: —the click in your head that makes you peaceful, honey?

BRICK: Uh-huh. It hasn't happened. . . . I've got to make it happen before I can sleep. . . .

MARGARET: —I—know what you—mean. . . .

BRICK: Give me that pillow in the big chair, Maggie.

MARGARET: I'll put it on the bed for you.

BRICK: No, put it on the sofa, where I sleep.

MARGARET: Not tonight, Brick.

BRICK: I want it on the sofa. That's where I sleep. (*He has hobbled to the liquor cabinet. He now pours down three shots in quick succession and stands waiting, silent. All at once he turns with a smile and says:*) There!

MARGARET: What?

BRICK: The *click.* . . . (*His gratitude seems almost infinite as he hobbles out on the gallery with a drink. We hear his crutch as he swings out of sight. Then, at some distance, he begins singing to himself a peaceful song.*) (MARGARET *holds the big pillow forlornly as if it were her only companion, for a few moments, then throws it on the bed. She rushes to the liquor cabinet, gathers all the bottles in her arms, turns about undecidedly, then runs out of the room with them, leaving the door ajar on the dim yellow hall.* BRICK *is heard hobbling back along the gallery, singing his peaceful song. He comes back in, sees the pillow on the bed, laughs lightly, sadly, picks it up. He has it under his arm as* MARGARET *returns to the room.* MARGARET *softly shuts the door and leans against it, smiling softly at* BRICK.)

MARGARET: Brick, I used to think that you were stronger than me and I didn't want to be overpowered by you. But now, since you've taken to liquor—you know what?—I guess it's bad, but now I'm stronger than you and I can love you more truly!

Don't move that pillow. I'll move it right back if you do!—Brick? (*She turns out all the lamps but a single rose-silk-shaded one by the bed.*) I really have been to a doctor and I know what to do and—Brick?—this is my time by the calendar to conceive!

BRICK: Yes, I understand, Maggie. But how are you going to conceive a child by a man in love with his liquor?

MARGARET: By locking his liquor up and making him satisfy my desire before I unlock it!

BRICK: Is that what you've done, Maggie?

MARGARET: Look and see. That cabinet's mighty empty compared to before!

BRICK: Well, I'll be a son of a—

(He reaches for his crutch but she beats him to it and rushes out on the gallery, hurls the crutch over the rail and comes back in, panting.)

(There are running footsteps. BIG MAMA *bursts into the room, her face all awry, gasping, stammering.)*

BIG MAMA: Oh, my God, oh, my God, oh, my God, where is it?

MARGARET: Is this what you want, Big Mama?

*(*MARGARET *hands her the package left by the doctor.)*

BIG MAMA: I can't bear it, oh, God! Oh, Brick! Brick, baby!

(She rushes at him. He averts his face from her sobbing kisses. MARGARET *watches with a tight smile.)*

My son, Big Daddy's boy! Little Father!

(The groaning cry is heard again. She runs out, sobbing.)

MARGARET: And so tonight we're going to make the lie true, and when that's done, I'll bring the liquor back here and we'll get drunk together, here, tonight, in this place that death has come into. . . .

        —What do you say?

BRICK: I don't say anything. I guess there's nothing to say.

MARGARET: Oh, you weak people, you weak, beautiful people!—who give up.—What you want is someone to—

(She turns out the rose-silk lamp.)

—take hold of you.—Gently, gently, with love! And—

(The curtain begins to fall slowly.)

I *do* love you, Brick, I *do*!

BRICK: *(smiling with charming sadness)* Wouldn't it be funny if that was true?

THE CURTAIN COMES DOWN

Note of Explanation

Some day when time permits I would like to write a piece about the influence, its dangers and its values, of a powerful and highly imaginative director upon the development of a play, before and during production. It does have dangers, but it has them only if the playwright is excessively malleable or submissive, or the director is excessively insistent on ideas or interpretations of his own. Elia Kazan and I have enjoyed the advantages and avoided the dangers of this highly explosive relationship because of the deepest mutual respect for each other's creative function: we have worked together three times with a phenomenal absence of friction between us and each occasion has increased the trust. If you don't want a director's influence on your play, there are two ways to avoid it, and neither is good. One way is to arrive at an absolutely final draft of your play before you let your director see it, then hand it to him saying, Here it is, take it or leave it! The other way is to select a director who is content to put your play on the stage precisely as you conceived it with no ideas of his own. I said neither is a good way, and I meant it. No living playwright, that I can think of, hasn't something valuable to learn about his own work from a director so keenly perceptive as Elia Kazan. It so happened that in the case of Streetcar, Kazan was given a script that was completely finished. In the case of Cat, he was shown the first typed version of the play, and he was excited by it, but he had definite reservations about it which were concentrated in the third act. The gist of his reservations can be listed as three points: one, he felt that Big Daddy was too vivid and important a character to disappear from the play except as an offstage cry after the second act curtain; two, he felt that the character of Brick should undergo some apparent mutation as a result of the virtual vivisection that he undergoes in his interview with his father in Act Two. Three, he felt that the character of Margaret, while he understood that I sympathized with her and liked her myself, should be, if possible, more clearly sympathetic to an audience.

It was only the third of these suggestions that I embraced wholeheartedly from the outset, because it so happened that Maggie the Cat had become steadily more charming to me as I worked on her characterization. I didn't want Big Daddy to reappear in Act Three and I felt that the moral paralysis of Brick was a root thing in his tragedy, and to show a dramatic progression would obscure the meaning of that tragedy in him and because I don't believe that a conversation, however revelatory, ever effects so immediate a change in the heart or even conduct of a person in Brick's state of spiritual disrepair.

However, I wanted Kazan to direct the play, and though these suggestions were not made in the form of an ultimatum, I was fearful that I would lose his interest if I didn't re-examine the script from his point of view. I did. And you will find included in this published script the new third act that resulted from his creative influence on the play. The reception of the playing-script has more than justified, in my opinion, the adjustments made to that influence. A failure reaches fewer people, and touches fewer, than does a play that succeeds.

It may be that Cat number one would have done just as well, or nearly, as Cat number two; it's an interesting question. At any rate, with the publication of both third acts in this volume, the reader can, if he wishes, make up his own mind about it.

TENNESSEE WILLIAMS

ACT THREE

AS PLAYED IN NEW YORK PRODUCTION

BIG DADDY *is seen leaving as at the end of Act II.*

BIG DADDY: *(shouts, as he goes out* D.R. *on gallery)* ALL — LYIN' — DYIN' — LIARS! LIARS! LIARS!

(After BIG DADDY *has gone,* MARGARET *enters from* D.R. *on gallery, into room through* D.S. *door. She X to* BRICK *at* L.C.*)*

MARGARET: Brick, what in the name of God was goin' on in this room?
*(*DIXIE *and* TRIXIE *rush through the room from the hall,* L. *to gallery* R., *brandishing cap pistols, which they fire repeatedly, as they shout:* "Bang! Bang! Bang!")
*(*MAE *appears from* D.R. *gallery entrance, and turns the children back* U.L., *along gallery. At the same moment,* GOOPER, REVEREND TOOKER *and* DR BAUGH *enter from* L. *in the hall.)*

MAE: Dixie! You quit that! Gooper, will y'please git these kiddies t'baid? Right now?
*(*GOOPER *and* REVEREND TOOKER *X along upper gallery.* DR BAUGH *holds,* U.C., *near hall door.* REVEREND TOOKER *X to* MAE *near section of gallery just outside doors,* R.*)*

GOOPER: *(urging the children along)* Mae—you seen Big Mama?

MAE: Not yet.
*(*DIXIE *and* TRIXIE *vanish through hall,* L.*)*

REVEREND TOOKER: *(to* MAE*)* Those kiddies are so full of vitality. I think I'll have to be startin' back to town.
*(*MARGARET *turns to watch and listen.)*

MAE: Not yet, Preacher. You know we regard you as a member of this fam'ly, one of our closest an' dearest, so you just got t'be with us when Doc Baugh gives Big Mama th' actual truth about th' report from th' clinic.
(Calls through door:)
Has Big Daddy gone to bed, Brick?
*(*GOOPER *has gone out* D.R. *at the beginning of the exchange between* MAE *and* REVEREND TOOKER.*)*

MARGARET: *(replying to* MAE*)* Yes, he's gone to bed.
(To BRICK:*)* Why'd Big Daddy shout "liars"?

GOOPER: *(off* D.R.*)* Mae!
*(*MAE *exits* D.R. REVEREND TOOKER *drifts along upper gallery.)*

BRICK: I didn't lie to Big Daddy. I've lied to nobody, nobody but myself, just lied to myself.

The time has come to put me in Rainbow Hill, put me in Rainbow Hill, Maggie, I ought to go there.

MARGARET: Over my dead body!

(BRICK *starts* R. *She holds him.*)

Where do you think you're goin'?

(MAE *enters from* D.R. *on gallery, X to* REVEREND TOOKER, *who comes to meet her.*)

BRICK: (X *below to* C.) Out for some air, I want air—

GOOPER: (*entering from* D.R. *to* MAE, *on gallery*) Now, where is that old lady?

MAE: Cantcha find her, Gooper?

(REVEREND TOOKER *goes out* D.R.)

GOOPER: (X *to* DOC *above hall door*) She's avoidin' this talk.

MAE: I think she senses somethin'.

GOOPER: (*calls off* L.) Sookey! Go find Big Mama an' tell her Doc Baugh an' the Preacher've got to go soon.

MAE: Don't let Big Daddy hear yuh!

(*Brings* DR BAUGH *to* R. *on gallery.*)

REVEREND TOOKER: (*off* D.R., *calls*) Big Mama.

SOOKEY *and* DAISY: (*running from* L. *to* R. *on lawn, calling*) Miss Ida! Miss Ida!

(*They go out* U.R.)

GOOPER: (*calling off upper gallery*) Lacey, you look downstairs for Big Mama!

MARGARET: Brick, they're going to tell Big Mama the truth now, an' she needs you!

(REVEREND TOOKER *appears in lawn area,* U.R., X C.)

DOCTOR BAUGH: (*to* MAE, *on* R. *gallery*) This is going to be painful.

MAE: Painful things can't always be avoided.

DOCTOR BAUGH: That's what I've noticed about 'em, Sister Woman.

REVEREND TOOKER: (*on lawn, points off* R.) I see Big Mama!

(*Hurries off* L. *and reappears shortly in hall.*)

GOOPER: (*hurrying into hall*) She's gone round the gall'ry to Big Daddy's room. Hey, Mama!

(*Off:*)

Hey, Big Mama! Come here!

MAE: (*calls*) Hush, Gooper! Don't holler, go to her!

(GOOPER *and* REVEREND TOOKER *now appear together in hall.* BIG MAMA *runs in from* D.R., *carrying a glass of milk. She X past* DR BAUGH *to* MAE, *on* R. *gallery.* DR BAUGH *turns away.*)

BIG MAMA: Here I am! What d'you all want with me?

GOOPER: (*steps toward* BIG MAMA) Big Mama, I told you we got to have this talk.

BIG MAMA: What talk you talkin' about? I saw the light go on in Big Daddy's bedroom an' took him his glass of milk, an' he just shut the shutters right in my face.

(*Steps into room through* R. *door.*)

When old couples have been together as long as me an' Big Daddy, they, they get irritable with each other just from too much—devotion! Isn't that so?

(X *below wicker seat to* R.C. *area.*)

MARGARET: (X *to* BIG MAMA, *embracing her*) Yes, of course it's so.

(BRICK *starts out* U.C. *through hall, but sees* GOOPER *and* REVEREND TOOKER *entering, so he hobbles through* C. *out* D.S. *door and onto gallery.*)

BIG MAMA: I think Big Daddy was just worn out. He loves his fam'ly. He loves to have 'em around him, but it's a strain on his nerves. He wasn't himself tonight, Brick—

(X C. *toward* BRICK. BRICK *passes her on his way out,* D.S.)

Big Daddy wasn't himself, I could tell he was all worked up.

REVEREND TOOKER: (U.S.C.) I think he's remarkable.

BIG MAMA: Yaiss! Just remarkable.

(*Faces* U.S., *turns, X to bar, puts down glass of milk.*)

Did you notice all the food he ate at that table?

(X R. *a bit.*)

Why he ate like a hawss!

GOOPER: (U.S.C.) I hope he don't regret it.

BIG MAMA: (*turns* U.S. *toward* GOOPER) What! Why that man ate a huge piece of cawn bread with molasses on it! Helped himself twice to hoppin' john!

MARGARET: *(X to* BIG MAMA*)* Big Daddy loves hoppin' john. We had a real country dinner.

BIG MAMA: Yais, he simply adores it! An' candied yams. Son—
(X to D.S. *door, looking out at* BRICK. MARGARET *X above* BIG MAMA *to her* L.*)*
That man put away enough food at that table to stuff a fieldhand.

GOOPER: I hope he don't have to pay for it later on.

BIG MAMA: *(turns* U.S.*)* What's that, Gooper?

MAE: Gooper says he hopes Big Daddy doesn't suffer tonight.

BIG MAMA: *(turns to* MARGARET, D.C.*)* Oh, shoot, Gooper says, Gooper says! Why should Big Daddy suffer for satisfyin' a nawmal appetite? There's nothin' wrong with that man but nerves; he's sound as a dollar! An' now he knows he is, an' that's why he ate such a supper. He had a big load off his mind, knowin' he wasn't doomed to—what—he thought he was—doomed t'—
(She wavers.)
*(*MARGARET *puts her arms around* BIG MAMA.*)*

GOOPER: *(urging* MAE *forward)* MAE!
*(*MAE *runs forward below wicker seat. She stands below* BIG MAMA, MARGARET *above* BIG MAMA. *They help her to the wicker seat.* BIG MAMA *sits.* MARGARET *sits above her.* MAE *stands behind her.)*

MARGARET: Bless his ole sweet soul.

BIG MAMA: Yes—bless his heart.

BRICK: *(*D.S. *on gallery, looking out front)* Hello, moon, I envy you, you cool son of a bitch.

BIG MAMA: I want Brick!

MARGARET: He just stepped out for some fresh air.

BIG MAMA: Honey! I want Brick!

MAE: Bring li'l Brother in here so we kin talk.
*(*MARGARET *rises, X through* D.S. *door to* BRICK *on gallery.)*

BRICK: *(to the moon)* I envy you—you cool son of a bitch.

MARGARET: Brick, what're you doin' out here on the gall'ry, Baby?

BRICK: Admirin' an' complimentin' th' man in the moon.

*(*MAE *X to* DR BAUGH *on* R. *gallery.* REVEREND TOOKER *and* GOOPER *move* R.U.C., *looking at* BIG MAMA.*)*

MARGARET: *(to* BRICK*)* Come in, Baby. They're gettin' ready to tell Big Mama the truth.

BRICK: I can't witness that thing in there.

MAE: Doc Baugh, d'you think those vitamin B$_{12}$ injections are all they're cracked up t'be?
(Enters room to upper side, behind wicker seat.)

DOCTOR BAUGH: *(X to below wicker seat)* Well, I guess they're as good t'be stuck with as anything else.
(Looks at watch; X through to L.C.*)*

MARGARET: *(to* BRICK*)* Big Mama needs you!

BRICK: I can't witness that thing in there!

BIG MAMA: What's wrong here? You all have such long faces, you sit here waitin' for somethin' like a bomb—to go off.

GOOPER: We're waitin' for Brick an' Maggie to come in for this talk.

MARGARET: *(X above* BRICK, *to his* R.*)* Brother Man an' Mae have got a trick up their sleeves, an' if you don't go in there t'help Big Mama, y'know what I'm goin' to do—?

BIG MAMA: Talk. Whispers! Whispers!
(Looks out D.R.*)*
Brick! . . .

MARGARET: *(answering* BIG MAMA'S *call)* Comin', Big Mama!
(to BRICK.*)*
I'm goin' to take every dam' bottle on this place an' pitch it off th' levee into th' river!

BIG MAMA: Never had this sort of atmosphere here before.

MAE: *(sits above* BIG MAMA *on wicker seat)* Before what, Big Mama?

BIG MAMA: This occasion. What's Brick an' Maggie doin' out there now?

GOOPER: *(X* D.C., *looks out)* They seem to be havin' some little altercation.
*(*BRICK *X toward* D.S. *step.* MAGGIE *moves* R. *above him to portal* D.R. REVEREND TOOKER *joins* DR BAUGH, L.C.*)*

BIG MAMA: *(taking a pill from pill box on chain at her wrist)* Give me a little somethin' to wash this tablet down with. Smell of burnt fireworks always makes me sick.

(MAE *X to bar to pour glass of water.* DR BAUGH *joins her.* GOOPER *X to* REVEREND TOOKER, L.C.)

BRICK: (*to* MAGGIE*)* You're a live cat, aren't you?

MARGARET: You're dam' right I am!

BIG MAMA: Gooper, will y'please open that hall door—an' let some air circulate in this stiflin' room?

(GOOPER *starts* U.S., *but is restrained by* MAE, *who X through* C. *with glass of water.* GOOPER *turns to men* D.L.C.)

MAE: (*X to* BIG MAMA *with water, sits above her*) Big Mama, I think we ought to keep that door closed till after we talk.

BIG MAMA: I swan!

(*Drinks water. Washes down pill.*)

MAE: I just don't think we ought to take any chance of Big Daddy hearin' a word of this discussion.

BIG MAMA: (*hands glass to* MAE*)* What discussion of what? Maggie! Brick! Nothin' is goin' to be said in th' house of Big Daddy Pollitt that he can't hear if he wants to!

(MAE *rises, X to bar, puts down glass, joins* GOOPER *and the two men,* L.C.)

BRICK: How long are you goin' to stand behind me, Maggie?

MARGARET: Forever, if necessary.

(BRICK *X* U.S. *to* R. *gallery door.*)

BIG MAMA: Brick!

(MAE *rises, looks out* D.S., *sits.*)

GOOPER: That boy's gone t'pieces—he's just gone t'pieces.

DOCTOR BAUGH: Y'know, in my day they used to have somethin' they called the Keeley cure for drinkers.

BIG MAMA: Shoot!

DOCTOR BAUGH: But nowadays, I understand they take some kind of tablets that kill their taste for the stuff.

GOOPER: (*turns to* DR BAUGH*)* Call 'em anti-bust tablets.

BIG MAMA: Brick don't need to take nothin'. That boy is just broken up over Skipper's death. You

know how poor Skipper died. They gave him a big, big dose of that sodium amytal stuff at his home an' then they called the ambulance an' give him another big, big dose of it at th' hospital an' that an' all the alcohol in his system fo' months an' months just proved too much for his heart an' his heart quit beatin'. I'm scared of needles! I'm more scared of a needle than th' knife—

(BRICK *has entered the room to behind the wicker seat. He rests his hand on* BIG MAMA'S *head.* GOOPER *has moved a bit* U.R.C., *facing* BIG MAMA.)

BIG MAMA: Oh! Here's Brick! My precious baby!

(DR BAUGH *X to bar, puts down drink.* BRICK *X below* BIG MAMA *through* C. *to bar.*)

BRICK: Take it, Gooper!

MAE: (*rising*) What?

BRICK: Gooper knows what. Take it, Gooper!

(MAE *turns to* GOOPER U.R.C. DR BAUGH *X to* REVEREND TOOKER. MARGARET, *who has followed* BRICK U.S. *on* R. *gallery before he entered the room, now enters room, to behind wicker seat.*)

BIG MAMA: (*to* BRICK*)* You just break my heart.

BRICK: (*at bar*) Sorry—anyone else?

MARGARET: Brick, sit with Big Mama an' hold her hand while we talk.

BRICK: You do that, Maggie. I'm a restless cripple. I got to stay on my crutch.

(MAE *sits above* BIG MAMA. GOOPER *moves in front, below, and sits on couch, facing* BIG MAMA. REVEREND TOOKER *closes in to* R.C. DR BAUGH *X* D.C., *faces upstage, smoking cigar.* MARGARET *turns away to* R. *doors.*)

BIG MAMA: Why're you all *surroundin'* me?—like this? Why're you all starin' at me like this an' makin' signs at each other?

(BRICK *hobbles out hall door and X along* R. *gallery.*)

I don't need nobody to hold my hand. Are you all crazy? Since when did Big Daddy or me need anybody—?

(REVEREND TOOKER *moves behind wicker seat.*)

MAE: Calm yourself, Big Mama.

BIG MAMA: Calm you'self *you'self*, Sister Woman! How could I calm myself with everyone starin' at me as if big drops of blood had broken out on m'face? What's this all about, Annh! What?

GOOPER: Doc Baugh—

(MAE *rises.*)

Sit down, Mae—

(MAE *sits.*)

—Big Mama wants to know the complete truth about th' report we got today from the Ochsner Clinic!

(DR BAUGH *buttons his coat, faces group at* R.C.)

BIG MAMA: Is there somethin'—somethin' that I don't know?

DOCTOR BAUGH: Yes—well . . .

BIG MAMA: (*rises*) I—want to—*knowwwww!*

(*X to* DR BAUGH.)

Somebody must be lyin'! *I want to know!*

(MAE, GOOPER, REVEREND TOOKER *surround* BIG MAMA.)

MAE: Sit down, Big Mama, sit down on this sofa!

(BRICK *has passed* MARGARET *Xing* D.R. *on gallery.*)

MARGARET: Brick! Brick!

BIG MAMA: *What is it, what is it?*

(BIG MAMA *drives* DR BAUGH *a bit* D.L.C. *Others follow, surrounding* BIG MAMA.)

DOCTOR BAUGH: I never have seen a more thorough examination than Big Daddy Pollitt was given in all my experience at the Ochsner Clinic.

GOOPER: It's one of th' best in th' country.

MAE: It's *THE* best in th' country—bar none!

DOCTOR BAUGH: Of course they were ninety-nine and nine-tenths per cent certain before they even started.

BIG MAMA: Sure of what, sure of what, sure of what—*what!?*

MAE: Now, Mommy, be a brave girl!

BRICK: (*on* D.R. *gallery, covers his ears, sings*) "By the light, by the light, of the silvery moon!"

GOOPER: (*breaks* D.R. *Calls out to* BRICK) Shut up, Brick!

(*Returns to group* L.C.)

BRICK: Sorry . . .

(*Continues singing.*)

DOCTOR BAUGH: But now, you see, Big Mama, they cut a piece off this growth, a specimen of the tissue, an'—

BIG MAMA: Growth? You told Big Daddy—

DOCTOR BAUGH: Now, wait—

BIG MAMA: You told me an' Big Daddy there wasn't a thing wrong with him but—

MAE: Big Mama, they always—

GOOPER: Let Doc Baugh talk, will yuh?

BIG MAMA: —little spastic condition of—

REVEREND TOOKER: (*throughout all this*) Shh! Shh! Shh!

(BIG MAMA *breaks* U.C., *they all follow.*)

DOCTOR BAUGH: Yes, that's what we told Big Daddy. But we had this bit of tissue run through the laboratory an' I'm sorry t'say the test was positive on it. It's malignant.

(*Pause.*)

BIG MAMA: *Cancer! Cancer!*

MAE: Now now, Mommy—

GOOPER: (*at the same time*) You had to know, Big Mama.

BIG MAMA: *Why didn't they cut it out of him? Hanh? Hannh?*

DOCTOR BAUGH: Involved too much, Big Mama, too many organs affected.

MAE: Big Mama, the liver's affected, an' so's the kidneys, both. It's gone way past what they call a—

GOOPER: —a surgical risk.

(BIG MAMA *gasps.*)

REVEREND TOOKER: Tch, tch, tch.

DOCTOR BAUGH: Yes, it's gone past the knife.

MAE: That's why he's turned yellow!

(BRICK *stops singing, turns away* U.R. *on gallery.*)

BIG MAMA: (*pushes* MAE D.S.) Git away from me, git away from me, Mae!

(*X* D.S.R.)

I want Brick! Where's Brick! *Where's my only son?*

MAE: *(a step after* BIG MAMA*)* Mama! Did she say "only" son?

GOOPER: *(following* BIG MAMA*)* What does that make me?

MAE: *(above* GOOPER*)* A sober responsible man with five precious children—*six!*

BIG MAMA: I want Brick! Brick! Brick!

MARGARET: *(a step to* BIG MAMA *above couch)* Mama, let *me* tell you.

BIG MAMA: *(pushing her aside)* No, no, leave me alone, you're not my blood!
(She rushes onto the D.S. *gallery.)*

GOOPER: *(X to* BIG MAMA *on gallery)* Mama! I'm your son! Listen to me!

MAE: Gooper's your son, Mama, he's your first-born!

BIG MAMA: Gooper never liked Daddy!

MAE: That's not true!

REVEREND TOOKER: *(*U.C.*)* I think I'd better slip away at this point. Goodnight, goodnight everybody, and God bless you all—on this place. *(Goes out through hall.)*

DOCTOR BAUGH: *(X* D.R. *to above* D.S. *door)* Well, Big Mama—

BIG MAMA: *(leaning against* GOOPER, *on lower gallery)* It's all a mistake, I know it's just a bad dream.

DOCTOR BAUGH: We're gonna keep Big Daddy as comfortable as we can.

BIG MAMA: Yes, it's just a bad dream, that's all it is, it's just an awful dream.

GOOPER: In my opinion Big Daddy is havin' some pain but won't admit that he has it.

BIG MAMA: Just a dream, a bad dream.

DOCTOR BAUGH: That's what lots of 'em do, they think if they don't admit they're havin' the pain they can sort of escape th' fact of it.
*(*BRICK *X* U.S. *on* R. *gallery.* MARGARET *watches him from* R. *door.)*

GOOPER: Yes, they get sly about it, get real sly about it.

MAE: *(X to* R. *of* DR BAUGH*)* Gooper an' I think—

GOOPER: Shut up, Mae!—Big Mama, I really do think Big Daddy should be started on morphine.

BIG MAMA: *(pulling away from* GOOPER*)* Nobody's goin' to give Big Daddy morphine!

DOCTOR BAUGH: Now, Big Mama, when that pain strikes it's goin' to strike mighty hard an' Big Daddy's goin' t'need the needle to bear it.

BIG MAMA: *(X to* DR BAUGH*)* I tell you, nobody's goin' to give him morphine!

MAE: Big Mama, you don't want to see Big Daddy suffer, y'know y'—

DOCTOR BAUGH: *(X to bar)* Well, I'm leavin' this stuff here
(Puts packet of morphine, etc., on bar.)
so if there's a sudden attack you won't have to send out for it.
*(*BIG MAMA *hurries to* L. *side bar.)*

MAE: *(X* C., *below* DR BAUGH*)* I know how to give a hypo.

BIG MAMA: Nobody's goin' to give Big Daddy morphine!

GOOPER: *(X* C.*)* Mae took a course in nursin' durin' th' war.

MARGARET: Somehow I don't think Big Daddy would want Mae t'give him a hypo.

MAE: *(to* MARGARET*)* You think he'd want *you* to do it?

DOCTOR BAUGH: Well—

GOOPER: Well, Doc Baugh is goin'—

DOCTOR BAUGH: Yes, I got to be goin'. Well, keep your chin up, Big Mama.
(X to hall.)

GOOPER: *(as he and* MAE *follow* DR BAUGH *into the hall)* She's goin' to keep her ole chin up, aren't you, Big Mama?
(They go out L.*)*
Well, Doc, we sure do appreciate all you've done. I'm telling you, we're obligated—

BIG MAMA: Margaret!
(X R.C.*)*

MARGARET: *(meeting* BIG MAMA *in front of wicker seat)* I'm right here, Big Mama.

BIG MAMA: Margaret, you've got to cooperate with me an' Big Daddy to straighten Brick out now—

GOOPER: *(off L., returning with MAE)* I guess that Doctor has got a lot on his mind, but it wouldn't hurt him to act a little more human—

BIG MAMA: —because it'll break Big Daddy's heart if Brick don't pull himself together an' take hold of things here. *(BRICK X D.S.R. on gallery.)*

MAE: *(U.C., overhearing)* Take hold of what things, Big Mama?

BIG MAMA: *(sits in wicker chair, MARGARET standing behind chair)* The place.

GOOPER: *(U.C.)* Big Mama, you've had a shock.

MAE: *(X with GOOPER to BIG MAMA)* Yais, we've all had a shock, but—

GOOPER: Let's be realistic—

MAE: Big Daddy would not, would *never*, be foolish enough to—

GOOPER: —put this place in irresponsible hands!

BIG MAMA: Big Daddy ain't goin' t'put th' place in anybody's hands, Big Daddy is *not* goin' t'die! I want you to git that into your haids, all of you! *(MAE sits above BIG MAMA, MARGARET turns R. to door, GOOPER X L.C. a bit.)*

MAE: Mommy, Mommy, Big Mama, we're just as hopeful an' optimistic as you are about Big Daddy's prospects, we have faith in prayer— but nevertheless there are certain matters that have to be discussed an' dealt with, because otherwise—

GOOPER: Mae, will y'please get my briefcase out of our room?

MAE: Yes, honey. *(Rises, goes out through hall L.)*

MARGARET: *(X to BRICK on D.S. gallery)* Hear them in there? *(X back to R. gallery door.)*

GOOPER: *(stands above BIG MAMA. Leaning over her)* Big Mama, what you said just now was not at all true, an' you know it. I've always loved Big Daddy in my own quiet way. I never made a show of it. I know that Big Daddy has always been fond of me in a quiet way, too. *(MARGARET drifts U.R. on gallery. MAE returns, X to GOOPER'S L. with briefcase.)*

MAE: Here's your briefcase, Gooper, honey. *(Hands it to him.)*

GOOPER: *(hands briefcase back to MAE)* Thank you. Of cou'se, my relationship with Big Daddy is different from Brick's.

MAE: You're eight years older'n Brick an' always had t'carry a bigger load of th' responsibilities than Brick ever had t'carry; he never carried a thing in his life but a football or a highball.

GOOPER: Mae, will y'let me talk, please?

MAE: Yes, honey.

GOOPER: Now, a twenty-eight thousand acre plantation's a mighty big thing t'run.

MAE: Almost single-handed!

BIG MAMA: You never had t'run this place, Brother Man, what're you talkin' about, as if Big Daddy was dead an' in his grave, you had to run it? Why, you just had t'help him out with a few business details an' had your law practice at the same time in Memphis.

MAE: Oh, Mommy, Mommy, Mommy! Let's be fair! Why, Gooper has given himself body an' soul t'keepin' this place up fo' the past five years since Big Daddy's health started failin'. Gooper won't say it, Gooper never thought of it as a duty, he just did it. An' what did Brick do? Brick kep' livin' in his past glory at college! *(GOOPER places a restraining hand on MAE's leg; MARGARET drifts D.S. in gallery.)*

GOOPER: Still a football player at twenty-seven!

MARGARET: *(bursts into U.R. door)* Who are you talkin' about now? Brick? A football player? He isn't a football player an' you know it! Brick is a sports announcer on TV an' one of the best-known ones in the country!

MAE: *(breaks U.C.)* I'm talkin' about what he was!

MARGARET: *(X to above lower gallery door)* Well, I wish you would just stop talkin' about my husband!

GOOPER: *(X to above MARGARET)* Listen, Margaret, I've got a right to discuss my own brother with other members of my own fam'ly, which don't include *you*! *(Pokes finger at her; she slaps his finger away.)*

Now, why don't you go on out there an' drink with Brick?

MARGARET: I've never seen such malice toward a brother.

GOOPER: How about his for me? Why he can't stand to be in the same room with me!

BRICK: *(on lower gallery)* That's the truth!

MARGARET: This is a deliberate campaign of vilification for the most disgusting and sordid reason on earth, and I know what it is! *It's avarice, avarice, greed, greed!*

BIG MAMA: Oh, I'll scream, I will scream in a moment unless this stops! Margaret, child, come here, sit next to Big Mama.

MARGARET: *(X to* BIG MAMA, *sits above her)* Precious Mommy.

(GOOPER X to bar.)

MAE: How beautiful, how touchin' this display of devotion! Do you know why she's childless? She's childless because that big, beautiful athlete husband of hers won't go to bed with her, that's why!

(X to L. of bed, looks at GOOPER.)

GOOPER: You jest won't let me do this the nice way, will yuh? Aw right—

(X to above wicker seat.)

I don't give a goddam if Big Daddy likes me or don't like me or did or never did or will or will never! I'm just appealin' to a sense of common decency an' fair play! I'm tellin' you th' truth—

(X D.S. through lower door to BRICK *on* D.R. *gallery.)*

I've resented Big Daddy's partiality to Brick ever since th' goddam day you were born, son, an' th' way I've been treated, like I was just barely good enough to spit on, an' sometimes not even good enough for that.

(X back through room to above wicker seat.)

Big Daddy is dyin' of cancer an' it's spread all through him an' it's attacked all his vital organs includin' the kidneys an' right now he is sinkin' into uremia, an' you all know what uremia is, it's poisonin' of the whole system due to th' failure of th' body to eliminate its poisons.

MARGARET: Poisons, poisons, venomous thoughts and words! In hearts and minds! That's poisons!

GOOPER: I'm askin' for a square deal an' by God I expect to get one. But if I don't get one, if there's any peculiar shenanigans goin' on around here behind my back, well I'm not a corporation lawyer for nothin'!

(X D.S. toward lower gallery door, on apex.)

I know how to protect my own interests.

(Rumble of distant thunder.)

BRICK: *(entering the room through* D.S. *door)* Storm comin' up.

GOOPER: Oh, a late arrival!

MAE: *(X through* C. *to below bar,* L.C.O.*)* Behold, the conquerin' hero comes!

GOOPER: *(X through* C. *to bar, following* BRICK, *imitating his limp)* The fabulous Brick Pollitt! Remember him? Who could forget him?

MAE: He looks like he's been injured in a game!

GOOPER: Yep, I'm afraid you'll have to warm th' bench at the Sugar Bowl this year, Brick! Or was it the Rose Bowl that he made his famous run in.

(Another rumble of thunder, sound of wind rising.)

MAE: *(X to* L. *of* BRICK, *who has reached the bar)* The punch bowl, honey, it was the punch bowl, the cut-glass punch bowl!

GOOPER: That's right! I'm always gettin' the boy's *bowls* mixed up!

(Pats BRICK *on the butt.)*

MARGARET: *(rushes at* GOOPER, *striking him)* Stop that! You stop that!

(Thunder.)

(MAE X toward MARGARET *from* L. *of* GOOPER, *flails at* MARGARET; GOOPER *keeps the women apart.* LACEY *runs through the* U.S. *lawn area in a raincoat.)*

DAISY and SOOKEY: *(off* U.L.*)* Storm! Storm comin'! Storm! Storm!

LACEY: *(running out* U.R.*)* Brightie, close them shutters!

GOOPER: *(X onto* R. *gallery, calls after* LACEY*)* Lacey, put the top up on my Cadillac, will yuh?

LACEY: *(off* R.*)* Yes, suh, Mistah Pollitt!

GOOPER: *(X to above* BIG MAMA*)* Big Mama, you know it's goin' to be necessary for me t'go back to Memphis in th' mornin' t'represent the Parker estate in a lawsuit.

*(*MAE *sits on* L. *side bed, arranges papers she removes from briefcase.)*

BIG MAMA: Is it, Gooper?

MAE: Yaiss.

GOOPER: That's why I'm forced to—to bring up a problem that—

MAE: Somethin' that's too important t' be put off!

GOOPER: If Brick was sober, he ought to be in on this. I think he ought to be present when I present this plan.

MARGARET: *(*U.C.*)* Brick is present, we're present!

GOOPER: Well, good. I will now give you this outline my partner, Tom Bullitt, an' me have drawn up—a sort of dummy—trusteeship!

MARGARET: Oh, that's it! You'll be in charge an' dole out remittances, will you?

GOOPER: This we did as soon as we got the report on Big Daddy from th' Ochsner Laboratories. We did this thing, I mean we drew up this dummy outline with the advice and assistance of the Chairman of the Boa'd of Directors of th' Southern Plantuhs Bank and Trust Company in Memphis, C. C. Bellowes, a man who handles estates for all th' prominent fam'lies in West Tennessee and th' Delta!

BIG MAMA: Gooper?

GOOPER: *(X behind seat to below* BIG MAMA*)* Now this is not—not final, or anything like it, this is just a preliminary outline. But it does provide a—basis—a design—a—possible, feasible—*plan!*

(He waves papers MAE *has thrust into his hand,* U.S.*)*

MARGARET: *(X* D.L.*)* Yes, I'll bet it's a plan!

(Thunder rolls. Interior lighting dims.)

MAE: It's a plan to protect the biggest estate in the Delta from irresponsibility an'—

BIG MAMA: Now you listen to me, all of you, you listen here! They's not goin' to be no more catty talk in my house! And Gooper, you put that away

before I grab it out of your hand and tear it right up! I don't know what the hell's in it, and I don't want to know what the hell's in it. I'm talkin' in Big Daddy's language now, I'm his *wife*, not his *widow*, I'm still his *wife!* And I'm talkin' to you in his language an'—

GOOPER: Big Mama, what I have here is—

MAE: Gooper explained that it's just a plan . . .

BIG MAMA: I don't care what you got there, just put it back where it come from an' don't let me see it again, not even the outside of the envelope of it! Is that understood? Basis! Plan! Preliminary! Design!—I say—what is it that Big Daddy always says when he's disgusted?

(Storm clouds race across sky.)

BRICK: *(from bar)* Big Daddy says "crap" when he is disgusted.

BIG MAMA: *(rising)* That's right—*CRAPPPP!* I say *CRAP* too, like Big Daddy!

(Thunder rolls.)

MAE: Coarse language don't seem called for in this—

GOOPER: Somethin' in me is *deeply outraged* by this.

BIG MAMA: *Nobody's goin' to do nothin'!* till Big Daddy lets go of it, and maybe just possibly not—not even then! No, not even then!

(Thunder clap. Glass crash, off L.*)*

(Off U.R., *children commence crying. Many storm sounds,* L. *and* R. *barnyard animals in terror, papers crackling, shutters rattling.* SOOKEY *and* DAISY *hurry from* L. *to* R. *in lawn area. Inexplicably,* DAISY *hits together two leather pillows. They cry, "Storm! Storm!"* SOOKEY *waves a piece of wrapping paper to cover lawn furniture.* MAE *exits to hall and upper gallery. Strange man runs across lawn,* R. *to* L.*)*

(Thunder rolls repeatedly.)

MAE: Sookey, hurry up an' git that po'ch fu'niture covahed; want th' paint to come off?

(Starts D.R. *on gallery.)*

*(*GOOPER *runs through hall to* R. *gallery.)*

GOOPER: *(yells to* LACEY, *who appears from* R.*)* Lacey, put mah car away!

LACEY: Cain't, Mistah Pollitt, you got the keys!
(Exit U.S.*)*
GOOPER: Naw, you got 'em, man.
(Exit D.R. *Reappears* U.R. *calls to* MAE*)* Where th' keys to th' car, honey?
(Runs C.*)*
MAE: *(*D.R. *on gallery)* You got 'em in your pocket!
(Exit D.R.*)*
*(*GOOPER *exits* U.R. DOG *howls.* DAISY *and* SOOKEY *sing off* U.R. *to comfort children.* MAE *is heard placating the children.)*
(Storm fades away.)
(During the storm, MARGARET *X and sits on couch,* D.R. BIG MAMA *X* D.C.*)*
BIG MAMA: BRICK! Come here, Brick, I need you.
(Thunder distantly.)
*(*CHILDREN *whimper, off* L. MAE *consoles them.* BRICK *X to* R. *of* BIG MAMA.*)*
BIG MAMA: Tonight Brick looks like he used to look when he was a little boy just like he did when he played wild games in the orchard back of the house and used to come home when I hollered myself hoarse for him! all—sweaty— and pink-cheeked—an' sleepy with his curls shinin'—
(Thunder distantly.)
*(*CHILDREN *whimper, off* L. MAE *consoles them.* DOG *howls, off.)*
Time goes by so fast. Nothin' can outrun it. Death commences too early—almost before you're half-acquainted with life—you meet with the other. Oh, you know we just got to love each other, an' stay together all of us just as close as we can, specially now that such a *black* thing has come and moved into this place without invitation.
*(*DOG *howls, off.)*
Oh, Brick, son of Big Daddy, Big Daddy does so love you. Y'know what would be his fondest dream come true? If before he passed on, if Big Daddy has to pass on . . .
*(*DOG *howls, off.)*
You give him a child of yours, a grandson as much like his son as his son is like Big Daddy. . . .

MARGARET: I know that's Big Daddy's dream.
BIG MAMA: That's his dream.
BIG DADDY: *(off* D.R. *on gallery)* Looks like the wind was takin' liberties with this place.
*(*LACEY *appears* U.L., *X to* U.C. *in lawn area;* BRIGHTIE *and* SMALL *appear* U.R. *on lawn.* BIG DADDY *X onto the* U.R. *gallery.)*
LACEY: Evenin', Mr Pollitt.
BRIGHTIE *and* SMALL: Evenin', Cap'n. Hello, Cap'n.
MARGARET: *(X to* R. *door)* Big Daddy's on the gall'ry.
BIG DADDY: Stawm crossed th' river, Lacey?
LACEY: Gone to Arkansas, Cap'n.
*(*BIG MAMA *has turned toward the hall door at the sound of* BIG DADDY'S *voice on the gallery. Now she X's* D.S.R. *and out the* D.S. *door onto the gallery.)*
BIG MAMA: I can't stay here. He'll see somethin' in my eyes.
BIG DADDY: *(on upper gallery, to the boys)* Stawm done any damage around here?
BRIGHTIE: Took the po'ch off ole Aunt Crawley's house.
BIG DADDY: Ole Aunt Crawley should of been settin' on it. It's time fo' th' wind to blow that ole girl away!
(Field-hands laugh, exit, U.R. BIG DADDY *enters room,* U.C., *hall door.)*
Can I come in?
(Puts his cigar in ash tray on bar.)
*(*MAE *and* GOOPER *hurry along the upper gallery and stand behind* BIG DADDY *in hall door.)*
MARGARET: Did the storm wake you up, Big Daddy?
BIG DADDY: Which stawm are you talkin' about— th' one outside or th' hullabaloo in here?
*(*GOOPER *squeezes past* BIG DADDY.*)*
GOOPER: *(X toward bed, where legal papers are strewn)* 'Scuse me, sir . . .
*(*MAE *tries to squeeze past* BIG DADDY *to join* GOOPER, *but* BIG DADDY *puts his arm firmly around her.)*
BIG DADDY: I heard some mighty loud talk. Sounded like somethin' important was bein' discussed. What was the powwow about?

MAE: *(flustered)* Why—nothin', Big Daddy . . .

BIG DADDY: *(X D.L.C., taking* MAE *with him)* What is that pregnant-lookin' envelope you're puttin' back in your briefcase, Gooper?

GOOPER: *(at foot of bed, caught, as he stuffs papers into envelope)* That? Nothin', suh—nothin' much of anythin' at all . . .

BIG DADDY: Nothin'? It looks like a whole lot of nothing!
(Turns U.S. *to group:)*
You all know th' story about th' young married couple—

GOOPER: Yes, sir!

BIG DADDY: Hello, Brick—

BRICK: Hello, Big Daddy.
(The group is arranged in a semi-circle above BIG DADDY, MARGARET *at the extreme* R., *then* MAE *and* GOOPER, *then* BIG MAMA, *with* BRICK *at* L.*)*

BIG DADDY: Young married couple took Junior out to th' zoo one Sunday, inspected all of God's creatures in their cages, with satisfaction.

GOOPER: Satisfaction.

BIG DADDY: *(X* U.S.C., *face front)* This afternoon was a warm afternoon in spring an' that ole elephant had somethin' else on his mind which was bigger'n peanuts. You know this story, Brick?
*(*GOOPER *nods.)*

BRICK: No, sir, I don't know it.

BIG DADDY: Y'see, in th' cage adjoinin' they was a young female elephant in heat!

BIG MAMA: *(at* BIG DADDY'S *shoulder)* Oh, Big Daddy!

BIG DADDY: What's the matter, preacher's gone, ain't he? All right. That female elephant in the next cage was permeatin' the atmosphere about her with a powerful and excitin' odor of female fertility! Huh! Ain't that a nice way to put it, Brick?

BRICK: Yes, sir, nothin' wrong with it.

BIG DADDY: Brick says the's nothin' wrong with it!

BIG MAMA: Oh, Big Daddy!

BIG DADDY: *(X* D.S.C.*)* So this ole bull elephant still had a couple of fornications left in him. He reared back his trunk an' got a whiff of that elephant lady next door!—began to paw at the dirt in his cage an' butt his head against the separatin' partition and, first thing y'know, there was a conspicuous change in his *profile*—very *conspicuous!* Ain't I tellin' this story in decent language, Brick?

BRICK: Yes, sir, too ruttin' decent!

BIG DADDY: So, the little boy pointed at it and said, "What's that?" His Mam said, "Oh, that's—nothin'!"—His Papa said, "She's spoiled!"
(Field-hands sing off R., *featuring* SOOKEY: "I Just Can't Stay Here by Myself," *through following scene.)*
*(*BIG DADDY *X to* BRICK *at* L.*)*

BIG DADDY: You didn't laugh at that story, Brick.
*(*BIG MAMA *X* D.R.C. *crying.* MARGARET *goes to her.* MAE *and* GOOPER *hold* U.R.C.*)*

BRICK: No, sir, I didn't laugh at that story.
(On the lower gallery, BIG MAMA *sobs.* BIG DADDY *looks toward her.)*

BIG DADDY: What's wrong with that long, thin woman over there, loaded with diamonds? Hey, what's-your-name, what's the matter with you?

MARGARET: *(X toward* BIG DADDY*)* She had a slight dizzy spell, Big Daddy.

BIG DADDY: *(*U.L.C.*)* You better watch that, Big Mama. A stroke is a bad way to go.

MARGARET: *(X to* BIG DADDY *at* C.*)* Oh, Brick, Big Daddy has on your birthday present to him, Brick, he has on your cashmere robe, the softest material I have ever felt.

BIG DADDY: Yeah, this is my soft birthday, Maggie. . . .
Not my gold or my silver birthday, but my soft birthday, everything's got to be soft for Big Daddy on this soft birthday.
*(*MAGGIE *kneels before* BIG DADDY C. *As* GOOPER *and* MAE *speak,* BIG MAMA *X* U.S.R.C. *in front of them, hushing them with a gesture.)*

GOOPER: Maggie, I hate to make such a crude observation, but there is somethin' a little indecent about your—

MAE: Like a slow-motion football tackle—

MARGARET: Big Daddy's got on his Chinese slippers that I gave him, Brick. Big Daddy, I haven't given you my big present yet, but now I will, now's the time for me to present it to you! I have an announcement to make!

MAE: What? What kind of announcement?

GOOPER: A sports announcement, Maggie?

MARGARET: Announcement of life beginning! A child is coming, sired by Brick, and out of Maggie the Cat! I have Brick's child in my body, an' that's my birthday present to Big Daddy on this birthday!

(BIG DADDY looks at BRICK who X behind BIG DADDY to D.S. portal, L.)

BIG DADDY: Get up, girl, get up off your knees, girl.

(BIG DADDY helps MARGARET rise. He X above her, to her R., bites off the end of a fresh cigar, taken from his bathrobe pocket, as he studies MARGARET.)

Uh-huh, this girl has life in her body, that's no lie!

BIG MAMA: BIG DADDY'S DREAM COME TRUE!

BRICK: JESUS!

BIG DADDY: *(X R. below wicker seat)* Gooper, I want my lawyer in the mornin'.

BRICK: Where are you goin', Big Daddy?

BIG DADDY: Son, I'm goin' up on the roof to the belvedere on th' roof to look over my kingdom before I give up my kingdom—twenty-eight thousand acres of th' richest land this side of the valley Nile!

(Exit through R. doors, and D.R. on gallery.)

BIG MAMA: *(following)* Sweetheart, sweetheart, sweetheart—can I come with you?

(Exits D.R.)

(MARGARET is D.S.C. in mirror area.)

GOOPER: *(X to bar)* Brick, could you possibly spare me one small shot of that liquor?

BRICK: *(D.L.C.)* Why, help yourself, Gooper boy.

GOOPER: I will.

MAE: *(X forward)* Of course we know that this is a lie!

GOOPER: *(drinks)* Be still, Mae!

MAE: *(X to GOOPER at bar)* I won't be still! I know she's made this up!

GOOPER: God damn it, I said to shut up!

MAE: That woman isn't pregnant!

GOOPER: Who said she was?

MAE: She did.

GOOPER: The doctor didn't. Doc Baugh didn't.

MARGARET: *(X R. to above couch)* I haven't gone to Doc Baugh.

GOOPER: *(X through to L. of MARGARET)* Then who'd you go to, Maggie?

(Offstage song finishes.)

MARGARET: One of the best gynecologists in the South.

GOOPER: Uh-huh, I see—

(Foot on end of couch, trapping MARGARET:)

May we have his name please?

MARGARET: No, you may not, Mister—Prosecutin' Attorney!

MAE: *(X to R. of MARGARET, above)* He doesn't have any name, he doesn't exist!

MARGARET: He does so exist, and so does my baby, Brick's baby!

MAE: You can't conceive a child by a man that won't sleep with you unless you think you're— *(Forces MARGARET onto couch, turns away C.)*

(BRICK starts C. for MAE.)

He drinks all the time to be able to tolerate you! Sleeps on the sofa to keep out of contact with you!

GOOPER: *(X above MARGARET, who lies face down on couch)* Don't try to kid us, Margaret—

MAE: *(X to bed, L. side, rumpling pillows)* How can you conceive a child by a man that won't sleep with you? How can you conceive? How can you? How can you!

GOOPER: *(sharply):* MAE!

BRICK: *(X below MAE to her R., takes hold of her)* Mae, Sister Woman, how d'you know that I don't sleep with Maggie?

MAE: We occupy the next room an' th' wall between isn't soundproof.

BRICK: Oh . . .

MAE: We hear the nightly pleadin' and the nightly refusal. So don't imagine you're goin' t'put a trick over on us, to fool a dyin' man with—a—

BRICK: Mae, Sister Woman, not everybody makes much noise about love. Oh, I know some people are huffers an' puffers, but others are silent lovers.

GOOPER: (behind seat, R.) This talk is pointless, completely.

BRICK: How d'y'know that we're not silent lovers? Even if y'got a peep-hole drilled in the wall, how can y'tell if sometime when Gooper's got business in Memphis an' you're playin' Scrabble at the country club with other ex-queens of cotton, Maggie and I don't come to some temporary agreement? How do you know that—?
(He X above wicker seat to above R. and couch.)

MAE: Brick, I never thought that you would stoop to her level, I just never dreamed that you would stoop to her level.

GOOPER: I don't think Brick will stoop to her level.

BRICK: (sits R. of MARGARET on couch) What is your level? Tell me your level so I can sink or rise to it.
(Rises.)
You heard what Big Daddy said. This girl has life in her body.

MAE: That is a lie!

BRICK: No, truth is something desperate, an' she's got it. Believe me, it's somethin' desperate, an' she's got it.
(X below seat to below bar.)
An' now if you will stop actin' as if Brick Pollitt was dead an' buried, invisible, not heard, an' go on back to your peep-hole in the wall—I'm drunk, and sleepy—not as alive as Maggie, but still alive. . . .
(Pours drink, drinks.)

GOOPER: (picks up briefcase from R. foot of bed) Come on, Mae. We'll leave these love birds together in their nest.

MAE: Yeah, nest of lice! Liars!

GOOPER: Mae—Mae, you jes' go on back to our room—

MAE: Liars!
(Exits through hall.)

GOOPER: (D.R. above MARGARET) We're just goin' to wait an' see. Time will tell.
(X to R. of bar.)
Yes, sir, little brother, we're just goin' to wait an' see!
(Exit, hall.)
(The clock strikes twelve.)
(MAGGIE and BRICK exchange a look. He drinks deeply, puts his glass on the bar. Gradually, his expression changes. He utters a sharp exhalation.)
(The exhalation is echoed by the singers, off U.R., who commence vocalizing with "Gimme a Cool Drink of Water Fo' I Die," and continue till end of act.)

MARGARET: (as she hears BRICK's exhalation) The click?
(BRICK looks toward the singers, happily, almost gratefully. He X R. to bed, picks up his pillow, and starts toward head of couch, D.R., Xing above wicker seat. MARGARET seizes the pillow from his grasp, rises, stands facing C., holding the pillow close. BRICK watches her with growing admiration. She moves quickly U.S.C., throwing pillow onto bed. She X to bar. BRICK counters below wicker seat, watching her. MARGARET grabs all the bottles from the bar. She goes into hall, pitches the bottles, one after the other, off the platform into the U.L. lawn area. Bottles break, off L. MARGARET re-enters the room, stands U.C., facing BRICK.)
Echo Spring has gone dry, and no one but me could drive you to town for more.

BRICK: Lacey will get me—

MARGARET: Lacey's been told not to!

BRICK: I could drive—

MARGARET: And you lost your driver's license! I'd phone ahead and have you stopped on the highway before you got halfway to Ruby Lightfoot's gin mill. I told a lie to Big Daddy, but we can make that lie come true. And then I'll bring you liquor, and we'll get drunk together, here, tonight, in this place that death has come into! What do you say? What do you say, Baby?

BRICK: *(X to* L. *side bed)* I admire you, Maggie. *(*BRICK *sits on edge of bed. He looks up at the overhead light, then at* MARGARET. *She reaches for the light, turns it out; then she kneels quickly beside* BRICK *at foot of bed.)*

MARGARET: Oh, you weak, beautiful people who give up with such grace. What you need is someone to take hold of you—gently, with love, and hand your life back to you, like something gold you let go of—and I can! I'm determined to do it—and nothing's more determined than a cat on a tin roof—is there? Is there, Baby?

(She touches his cheek, gently.)

CURTAIN

CONTEMPORARY

✦

EDWARD ALBEE, *The Zoo Story* (1959)

AMIRI BARAKA (LEROI JONES), *Dutchman* (1964)

SAM SHEPARD, *The Tooth of Crime* (1972)

DAVID RABE, *Streamers* (1976)

ADRIENNE KENNEDY, *A Movie Star Has to Star in Black and White* (1976)

MARSHA NORMAN, *Getting Out* (1977)

NTOZAKE SHANGE, *spell #7* (1979)

AUGUST WILSON, *Ma Rainey's Black Bottom* (1984)

LUIS VALDEZ, *I Don't Have to Show You No Stinking Badges!* (1986)

DAVID HENRY HWANG, *M. Butterfly* (1988)

KAREN FINLEY, *We Keep Our Victims Ready* (1989/1991)

LARRY KRAMER, *The Destiny of Me* (1992)

DAVID MAMET, *Oleanna* (1992)

CHERRÍE MORAGA, *Giving Up the Ghost* (1994)

Photo by Jay Thompson

DUTCHMAN

THE ZOO
STORY

©1993 William Gibson/Martha Swope Associate

THE DESTINY OF ME

©George E. Joseph

A MOVIE STAR HAS TO STAR IN BLACK AND WHITE

OLEANNA

©1992 Gerry Goodstein

Photo Credit: Alan McEwen

I DON'T HAVE TO SHOW YOU NO STINKING BADGES!

Virtually every single important period term still in (awkward) use has been declared to be inadequate, misleading, arbitrary, hopelessly abstract or distressingly banal.

MATEI CALINESCU IS RIGHT, BOTH IN THIS OBSERVATION ABOUT HISTORICAL periodization and in his later remark that, regardless of the difficulties in conceptualizing history as constituted of distinct periods, "those who explicitly or implicitly reject the idea of periodization . . . [often] end up unreflectively adopting periodizing schemes whose rigidity and lack of sophistication are in ironic contrast with the sophistication they may display in other respects." Like most delineations of a literary or theatrical history—attempts both to mark a course of intellectual or generic development and to identify detours or obstructions along the way—that informing *American Drama: Colonial to Contemporary* is necessarily imperfect. This imperfection originates, at least in part, in the inherently problematic activity of establishing the parameters of historical periods. In the specific instance of organizing a volume of American plays, one might quite justifiably ask when modern drama ends and gives way to the contemporary—or question if such a demonstrable shift has even occurred. If it has, what forces enabled or caused it, and how are they inscribed upon a "contemporary" American drama? How do such recognitions affect our reading of individual texts and influence our understanding of the evolution of theatre in America? And what about **postmodernism**? Labeling something as "contemporary" is largely a periodizing gesture, while asserting a text's postmodernity is to situate it not only within an inventory of certain aesthetic practices—fragmented narratives as opposed to "unified plots," pastiches of features appropriated from mass culture, and so on—but also within a larger context of social, intellectual, and economic conditions. Entitling this last section "contemporary," in short, implies a conception of theatre history that requires examination, something we provide below, albeit in necessarily brief fashion.

We are certainly not the first editors to frame such questions, the answers to which are, not surprisingly, as varied as the scholars who have reflected upon them. Thus, although most theatre historians agree that the 1960s and 1970s brought radical changes in American drama—its narrative forms and structures, politics, and thematic preoccupations—and in the larger enterprise of the professional theatre, there is considerable disagreement about how such changes relate to earlier moments in the evolution of this theatre. C. W. E. Bigsby, for example, emphasizes the centrifugal movement of American drama in the 1950s and 1960s away from Broadway theatres and toward alternative, in some instances more experimental, sites **Off-Broadway**, **Off-Off Broadway**, and at newly created regional theatres across the country. Yet the very title of his *Modern American Drama, 1945–1990* (1992) conveys a sense of an underlying continuity in the history of American drama, a continuity furthered by the later work of Eugene O'Neill, whom Bigsby regards as the "bridge between the pre-war and post-war world of the American theatre." While connections might certainly be forged between O'Neill's *Hughie* (1941) and his later work *The Iceman Cometh*, reprinted earlier in this book, and many of the plays in this section on contemporary drama, we believe on the contrary that readers of *American Drama: Colonial to Contemporary* will find more intriguing differences, especially where issues of realism, the representation of reality, and language are concerned. The disturbing, sudden, and some believe excessively violent realism of David Rabe's *Streamers* (1976) and David Mamet's controversial *Oleanna* (1992), both of which are reprinted here, come immediately to mind in this regard. The 1960s and 1970s saw a transformation of dramatic form, not only an overturning of conventional **realism** and the long-enduring **well-made play**, but also a surpassing of the **expressionistic** or "gauzy realism" made famous by Tennessee Williams and Arthur Miller.

Martin Esslin offers a different historical thesis near the end of his widely influential *The Theatre of the Absurd* (1961), delineating the ways in which several young American playwrights—Jack Gelber, Arthur Kopit, and, most notably, Edward Albee—follow in the footsteps of Samuel Beckett, Eugene Ionesco, and other "absurdists." For Esslin, Beckett's *Waiting for Godot* (1953) led the way for such works as Albee's *The Zoo Story* (1959) and *The American Dream* (1960), Gelber's *The Connection* (1959), and Kopit's *Oh Dad, Poor Dad, Mamma's Hung You in the Closet and I'm Feelin' So Sad* (1962). Still, Esslin argues, because **absurdism** "springs from a deep disillusionment, the draining away of the sense of meaning and purpose in life, which has been characteristic of countries like France and Britain in the years after the Second World War," the so-called **Theatre of the Absurd** never really took root in postwar America. Perhaps, although much of Albee's work, such as *The Zoo Story* included here, shares the disillusionment and ironic humor of Beckett's plays without making their more universal and **existential** gestures. More important than adducing similarities between Beckett and the generation of American writers that came of age in the 1960s—Albee, Sam Shepard, Amiri Baraka, Adrienne Kennedy, Megan Terry—is the recognition that Off-Broadway productions of absurdist drama clearly influenced American theatre in the 1960s and 1970s. In their movement away from the conventions of dramatic realism, and in their analogous "disillusionment" with the orthodoxies of American society in the 1960s, many of the plays in this section of *American Drama: Colonial to Contemporary* borrow from European absurdism, if not necessarily from the existential leanings of Beckett in *Waiting for Godot* and *Endgame* (1957).

That is to say, if Beckettian absurdism, per se, never flourished in America, other innovative dramatic forms certainly did, as Richard Schechner, an influential director and critic, underscores in his characterization of the "burst of experimental energy" in American theatre from the early 1960s until the middle 1970s as "another wave" of the "historical avant-garde." Implicitly agreeing with Esslin about the importance of experimental dramatic writing in the late 1950s and 1960s, Schechner also reminds students of the American theatre that this revolution manifested itself in a myriad of ways that goes far beyond experiments in dramatic form. Innovative directors, conceptual and visual artists, producers, actors, theatre managers—the 1960s brought with them remarkable changes on nearly every front connected with American drama and theatre. Of course, American society itself was undergoing significant restructuring and ideological revaluation as the civil rights movement, protests over American involvement in Vietnam, the feminist movement, and the expansion of popular culture through mass media were all exerting profound effects on everyday life in the United States. Through its 13 plays and script of a performance piece by Karen Finley, this final unit on the contemporary drama attempts to recapture the enormous vitality of American theatre in the 1960s and 1970s—and that of more recent years as well. Particular care has been taken in selecting these works to emphasize both evolving dramatic forms—the absurdist characteristics of Albee's *The Zoo Story* or postmodernist elements of Shepard's *The Tooth of Crime* (1972) and Kennedy's *A Movie Star Has to Star in Black and White* (1976), for example—and the social and political commitments of the contemporary American theatre: Luis Valdez's ironic look at ethnic stereotyping in *I Don't Have to Show You No Stinking Badges!* (1986), for instance; Larry Kramer's treatment of the AIDS epidemic in *The Destiny of Me* (1992); and Cherríe Moraga's expanded 1994 version of her earlier work, *Giving Up the Ghost* (first read in performance in 1984), which concerns, among other things, a central character's internal negotiations with her Chicana and lesbian identities.

It is to this "burst of experimental energy" in the 1960s and 1970s—and the historical conditions to which this experimentation responded—that we now turn.

OFF-BROADWAY AND BEYOND: THE 1960S AND 1970S

The falsehood of ideals. Death from Broadway. Ideal clothing, ideal speech. Death from compromise, certain death from luxury and lack of it. Aspects of the stage that are not the world but vanity. This is the vanity stage against which we have pitted our being.

In this statement from 1962, Julian Beck summarizes not only the project of the **Living Theatre** he cofounded in 1948 with his wife, Judith Malina, but also that of many artists involved in what became known as the Off-Off Broadway movement in New York. An earlier movement Off Broadway in the 1950s was marked by the singular achievements of such theatres as The Circle in the Square, cofounded by director José Quintero; the New York Shakespeare Festival, founded by Joseph Papp; the Chelsea Theatre Center, founded by Robert Kalfin; and others. Off-Broadway productions of works by Williams and O'Neill in particular, but also by such dramatists as Jean Genet, Peter Handke, Edward Bond, Albee, Beckett, and numerous others in the 1950s and 1960s both invigorated the contemporary theatre and helped launch the careers of some of America's finest actors: Jason Robards, Jr., George C. Scott, Colleen Dewhurst, Dustin Hoffman, Ruby Dee, Al Pacino, Morgan Freeman, and many more. But by 1962, the year of Beck's self-described "meditation" quoted above, Off-Broadway theatres, so vital in the 1950s, seemed to many indistinguishable from the commercial houses against which they had initially reacted and defined themselves. At the same time, sweeping changes were taking place in American society that inevitably affected the course of drama and were, in turn, supplemented by that drama. The civil rights movement and protests against an American military intervention in Vietnam serve as two of the most important instances from the early and mid-1960s of the strong relationship between an at-times volatile political climate and the contemporary theatre.

The 1960s brought both advances in civil rights for African Americans and seething frustrations ready to boil over, particularly in major northern cities to which large numbers of blacks moved after World War I. In 1910, over 90 percent of all African Americans lived in the South; by 1960, according to sociologist Thomas Mayer, this figure was reduced to approximately 55 percent, as a flood of "in-migrants" headed toward cities in the

North and West. Some 70 percent of these migrants relocated in California, Illinois, Michigan, New York, Ohio, and Pennsylvania, creating in many instances deplorable living conditions and widespread unemployment. (In 1967, for example, the unemployment rate of blacks in America was twice that of whites.) For African Americans who remained in the South, the early 1960s were marked by prominent, albeit typically hard-fought, social gains. In a case that garnered national attention, James Meredith was admitted to the University of Mississippi in 1962, three years after Little Rock, Arkansas' Central High School was successfully desegregated. Inspired by the vision of Martin Luther King, Jr., peaceful demonstrations and marches took place in many cities throughout the country as the 1960s began; in 1963, for instance, some 125,000 blacks and whites marched in the Detroit Walk to Freedom. But by the mid-1960s unrest in large cities and on college campuses began to simmer toward the explosive rioting of 1967; and widespread student protests against America's escalating involvement in Southeast Asia in 1968, 1969, and 1970—this last year that of the shooting of students by the Ohio National Guard at Kent State University—led to the closings of colleges and universities across America in the spring of 1970. In a 1964 speech, "The Ballot or the Bullet," Malcolm X observed, "There's more racial animosity, more racial hatred, more racial violence today in 1964, than there was in 1954. Where is the progress?" And, in a prediction of things to come, he concluded his speech with an ominous warning: "Just as guerrilla warfare is prevailing in Asia and in parts of Africa and in parts of Latin America, you've got to be mighty naive, or you've got to play the black man cheap, if you don't think some day he's going to wake up and find that it's got to be the ballot or the bullet."

Although clear "progress" was made in 1964 when the Civil Rights Act prohibiting discrimination in employment came before the Congress, three years later during the summer of 1967 the bullet reigned supreme, as violence ripped through American cities. During one week in July in Detroit, four years earlier the scene of the peaceful Walk to Freedom, 43 people were killed, thousands injured, 7,200 arrested, and nearly 700 buildings burned at a cost approaching 100 million dollars. This scene was played out in many major American cities in 1967, with the worst violence in Detroit and Newark, New Jersey; over 80 percent of 83 deaths and more than half of the thousands of injuries reported in urban rioting nationwide occurred in these two locales. A National Advisory Commission on Civil Disorders was appointed to study the causes of the 1967 riots, and determined that a number of factors were responsible. In addition to the obvious material issues of inadequate housing for, and the grinding poverty of, blacks "in which white society is deeply implicated"—that is to say, the creation of a racial ghetto that "white society condones"—one of these factors was the agitation of "militant organizations" and black nationalists. And in the 1960s so-called protest dramas and self-styled **guerrilla theatre** played a significant part in the raising of playgoers' consciousnesses about life in America's inner cities and brought issues of social justice directly to their audiences.

The postwar theatre witnessed the success of a number of plays by African-American playwrights on Broadway and off: Alice Childress's *Trouble in Mind* (1955), Loften Mitchell's *A Land Beyond the River* (1957), Lorraine Hansberry's *A Raisin in the Sun* (1959), and Ossie Davis's *Purlie Victorious* (1961). Some, like Mitchell's play, dealt directly with issues of civil rights for African Americans, and Childress's **Obie** Award–winning play concerns the problems of black actors working for a white director. Through such plays as

Dutchman (1964, reprinted here) and *The Slave* (1964), however, both of which were produced Off-Broadway, Amiri Baraka (LeRoi Jones) introduced a level of intense theatrical discourse on race in America unlike any seen before. Baraka was joined by such dramatists as Ed Bullins and Ron Milner in bringing issues of racial identity and frustration over the pace of social reform to the foreground of American drama in the 1960s. Baraka in particular was a leading force in the **Black Arts Movement**, helping found, with Charles and William Patterson, Clarence Reed, and others, the Black Arts Repertory Theatre and School in Harlem in 1964, and in the later 1960s organizing a number of groups dedicated to fostering a black nationalist culture. The Black Arts Movement, as Larry Neal describes it, advocated the destruction of the "white thing," of "white ideas," and of "white ways of looking at the world," and the creation of a separate "symbolism, mythology, critique, and iconology"—or, as Baraka's poem "Black Art" expresses it, the creation of a "black poem," which is in reality a "Black World." In its strong will "toward self-determination and nationhood" for African Americans, Baraka's work—*Experimental Death Unit #1* (1965), *A Black Mass* (1966), and *The Slave Ship* (1967)—epitomizes what critics frequently characterized as the "militancy" of black protest drama in the 1960s and 1970s. And, while the decade of the 1960s ended with Charles Gordone winning a Pulitzer Prize for *No Place to Be Somebody* (1969), the first time an African-American dramatist had been so honored, Baraka was moving from Off-Broadway to Harlem and Newark—Off-Broadway and beyond.

At the same time in California, Luis Valdez was directing short dramatic sketches to aid labor leader César Chávez and the United Farmworkers in the organization of migrant farmworkers. Valdez drew on his experience working with the San Francisco Mime Troupe, a theatre collective known for its mime performances, **happenings**, and political commitment, for these sketches or *actos*, drawing elements from **agitprop** drama of the 1930s and from the tradition of the Italian ***commedia dell'arte***. In 1965, Valdez organized workers into a performance group, inaugurating, with the help of other less-heralded members of this theatre collective, what is today known as **El Teatro Campesino** and transforming the *acto* into a more authentic Chicano theatre. Much like the writers associated with the Black Arts Movement—and like such dramatists as Hanay Geiogamah of the Native American Theatre Ensemble (NATE), founded in 1972—Valdez's several principles for establishing a Chicano theatre include the recognition of an authentic culture and mythology, the project of remaining closely attuned to the dilemmas of the Mexican-American community, and the commitment to a drama of social action. Valdez discusses this political agenda in his preface to *Actos* (1971), an anthology of work by El Teatro Campesino: "Inspire the audience to social action. Illuminate specific points about social problems. . . . Show or hint at [a] solution. Express what people are feeling." More recently, after his success as a screenwriter and director of the film *La Bamba* (1987), Valdez has announced a similar pledge to increase opportunities for Mexican Americans in the film industry.

American drama of the 1960s and early 1970s was thus, in one sense, returning to the sociopolitical ambitions of agitprop drama and the **Living Newspapers** of the 1930s; formally, however, much American drama was moving in directions scarcely seen before. In 1972, Albert Poland and Bruce Mailman edited what was, at the time, the most exciting anthology of contemporary American drama ever published. *The Off, Off Broadway Book: The Plays, People, Theatre* collects some 37 plays produced between 1961 and 1972 at 13 theatres in New York and such notable regional venues as the Guthrie Theatre in Minneapolis. It includes plays by Terrence McNally, Jean-Claude van Itallie, John Guare, Lanford Wilson, Ed Bullins, Julie Bovasso, Megan Terry, Amiri Baraka, Maria Irene Fornes, William M. Hoffman, Adrienne Kennedy, Sam Shepard, David Rabe, and Charles Ludlam—and brief accounts of the theatres that produced them. Schechner is surely right in underscoring the importance not only of these writers, but also of the teacher-visionaries who, when they were not writing themselves, helped lead an avant-garde American drama in new directions: Ellen Stewart of Café La MaMa, Ralph Cook of Theatre Genesis, Joseph Chaikin of the Open Theatre, Charles Ludlam of the Ridiculous Theatrical Company, Richard Foreman of the Ontological-Hysterical Theatre, and Schechner himself of the Performance Group (later the Wooster Group, founded in 1975 under the direction of Elizabeth LeCompte). Julian Beck perhaps expressed the ambitions of the Off-Off Broadway movement best in his opposition to what Peter Brook would later call in *The Empty Space* (1978) the "Deadly Theatre" that was Broadway in the 1960s: "There is something wrong when I go to the theatre whose province is the world and instead of being brought closer to the world I am cut off from it."

The methods by which American drama of the 1960s and 1970s brought its audience "closer to the world" are various indeed. Paramount among these was, first, a repudiation of the expensive spectacle Broadway had become. Like Brook and Beck, Poland and Mailman lament a Broadway theatre that by the 1950s had reached "an appalling economic state": fewer and more expensive plays produced, and the casting of recognizable stars to assure a better box office, hence the creation of a smaller, more affluent audience to support the theatre. Brook muses in *The Empty Space* that, if carried to its illogical and self-destructive extreme, Broadway would reach an ultimate theatre audience consisting of "one last millionaire" paying a fortune for a private performance. Off-Broadway theatres that, in Poland and Mailman's view, had once supported the theatrical experiments of Beckett, Ionesco, Pinter, and Genet, found themselves rapidly approaching an economic crisis similar to that which paralyzed Broadway: namely, the continued staging of revivals of classic and avant-garde drama, but the inability to gamble with unproven new playwrights just beginning to refine a radically different theatrical language in their plays. Nearly a century ago, Bernard Shaw in London complained about an analogous state of theatrical affairs, for the economics of late-Victorian theatre management dictated that star-managers like Sir Henry Irving stage spectacular revivals of long-established plays or mount dreary runs of thoroughly predictable melodramas. In what Shaw lambasted as a theatrical "fool's paradise of popular romance" and "insipid taste," plays with either "brains or heart" had little chance of ever finding professional production or even a modest audience. What to do?

For Shaw and Great Britain, one answer resided in the founding of a state-subsidized National Theatre where classical plays could be revived and the newer, at times commercially unviable, works of younger playwrights nurtured. For a new generation of American dramatists in the 1960s, a similar answer resided in Off-Off Broadway in coffeehouses, lofts, and church halls; another emerged in the growth of important *regional theatres* like the Guthrie Theatre (founded by Tyrone Guthrie in 1963), the Actors Theatre of Louisville (1964), the Trinity Repertory Company in Providence, Rhode Island (1964), the Long Wharf Theatre in New Haven (1965), the American Conservatory

Theatre in San Francisco (1965), and the Mark Taper Forum in Los Angeles (1967), and the professional revival of Chicago's Goodman Theatre in 1969. To a considerable extent, in the 1970s and today regional theatres, through such series as the Humana Festival of New American Plays inaugurated in 1977 at the Actors Theatre of Louisville, provide the forums for younger playwrights that Shaw had envisioned as one mission of a national theatre. This same theatre's fall series "Classics in Context," begun in 1986—which includes a lecture series, concerts, and various exhibitions—also enriches the community with historical and cultural education commercial Broadway theatres cannot afford to offer. The Goodman Theatre, the American Conservatory Theatre, and numerous other regional venues continue today with similar projects.

While there is not sufficient space here to delineate the numerous formal shapes American drama assumed in the 1960s and 1970s—and the innovations in performance that accompanied them—we might sketch just a few before moving briefly to the 1980s and 1990s, and weighing the progress of performance art, a protean theatrical entertainment that grew in prominence in the 1980s. Such concepts as the "transformation," for example, developed by Joseph Chaikin at the Open Theatre in the 1960s in relation to works by Megan Terry and Jean-Claude van Itallie, anticipate more recent developments both in contemporary drama and performance art. The Open Theatre, founded in 1963 as a theatre where actors could collaborate with writers in the composition of a script, appropriated techniques from a variety of sources, among them improvisational exercises from Chicago's Second City comedy troupe. In the introduction to Terry's *Viet Rock and Other Plays* (1967), Open Theatre director Peter Feldman describes the transformation as

> an improvisation in which the established realities or "given circumstances" (the Method phrase) of the scene changes several different times during the course of the action. . . . Whatever realities are established at the beginning are destroyed after a few minutes and replaced by others. Then these are in turn destroyed and replaced. These changes occur swiftly and *almost without transition*, until the audience's dependence upon any fixed reality is called into question.

Plays based on such a technique, therefore, are hardly naturalistic, and in such a collaborative environment scripts begin more as "notions" than finished texts handed to the actor to reproduce as faithfully as possible. Further, both acting in and responding to such transformations place different demands on performer and audience than realistic drama and *representational* staging require. In a sense, such techniques—narrative and scenic— place the audience on uncertain and constantly shifting epistemological ground; as soon as consoling certainties are produced by the text, they are erased and an entirely new set of narrative factors introduced.

Playwrights of the Off-Off Broadway movement also reclaimed the stage for actors and directors by insisting upon simple, often nonrepresentational sets for their plays. Moreover, many writers and directors attempted to break down the imaginary "fourth wall" dividing audience from performer, drawing the spectator more centrally into the theatrical experience. One method of accomplishing this, as Beckett had shown, was to make numerous self-conscious or **metatheatrical** references in the dramatic text to the event of the production itself. Thus, the Living Theatre's much-discussed production of Gelber's *The Connection* in 1959 begins with a character playing the show's producer addressing the audience: "Hello there! I'm Jim Dunn and I'm producing *The Connection.* . . . With the help of [name of director] we have selected a few addicts to improvise on Jaybird's [the author's] themes." Here, Gelber attempts to blur distinctions between staged performance and reality outside the theatre: perhaps these are addicts, the audience is invited to ask, not actors? In the Living Theatre's production of Gelber's *The Apple* (1962), the audience is made not only to recognize the fictionality of the action, but to feel threatened by what might transpire: "You're going to witness and may be part of some destructive scenes. . . . This is no joking matter. We are going to eat up the set, the audience." As critic Lionel Abel complained, this "gimmick" of effacing the line between textual fiction and the reality of performance is "not exactly new," but the extent to which directors like Schechner at the Performance Group attempted to forge an **environmental theatre** is. So, for its 1973 production of Shepard's *The Tooth of Crime,* Schechner surrounded a circular playing space with used auto parts and musical instruments, creating an arena in which audience and performer were surrounded by the "set." The language of the play, emerging from Shepard's "fantastic ear for all the subcultural vernaculars of American life and the polyglottism of regional speech"—in this case, language taken from rock music, the drug subculture, and the car culture of Southern California—thus merges with Schechner's design to create a more wholistic "environment" than conventional staging would permit.

Nowhere has the questioning of representational staging, linear dramatic narrative, and *"mimetic"* or "mirror-like" representation received more scrutiny and revision than from feminist playwrights and critics. Ntozake Shange, whose *Spell #7* (1979) is reprinted in this section of *American Drama: Colonial to Contemporary,* begins her essay "foreword/unrecovered losses/black theatre traditions" by making this very point: "for too long now afroamericans in theatre have been duped by the same artificial aesthetics that plague our white counterparts/'the perfect play,' as we know it to be/a truly european framework for european psychology/cannot function efficiently for those of us from this hemisphere." Feminist critic Lynda Hart agrees, insisting that the reigning dramatic aesthetic since the time of Aristotle of "holding the mirror up to nature" is a "particularly pernicious concept for the feminist critic of the theatre." For Hart, this "aesthetic of mimesis has maintained the hegemony of realism in the drama which effectively masks the *recreational* power of mimesis," and the "assumption of objectivity which informs mimetic theory presupposes a division of experience, encoding differences as Difference grounded in gender polarity." It is perhaps because of the enduring strength of this aesthetic—or because America in the 1960s was somewhat slower to focus on and endorse issues of women's equality given the considerable demands of the civil rights movement and the Vietnam War—that even the most gifted or politically motivated of playwrights from this period seem surprisingly orthodox or retrograde in their representation of women. Herbert Blau therefore seems justified in asserting that "it remains to be seen. . . . whether [Shepard] can portray the female body as something other than the old stuff," and Yolanda Broyles Gonzalez, among others, complains of Valdez' depiction of Chicanas. In addition, serious questions have been raised concerning the representation of women within the conventional emplotment and *mise-en-scène* of realism. In some instances these questions have been asked of the work of some of America's most celebrated women playwrights of the later 1970s and 1980s: Pulitzer Prize-winners Beth Henley, Marsha Norman (whose 1977 play *Getting Out* is included here), and Wendy Wasserstein.

The later 1960s and 1970s brought significant advances—and some bitter disappointments—for the women's movement: The National Organization for Women (NOW) was founded in 1966; Congress passed the Equal Rights Amendment in March, 1972, although by 1979 it remained unratified by the requisite number of states; *Roe v. Wade* in 1973 changed the law of the land on abortion. And a number of important companies dedicated to the production of feminist plays and/or gay and lesbian drama began their operations. Megan Terry became literary manager of the Omaha Magic Theatre in 1974 to provide a fecund environment for feminist drama, and in 1978 Julia Miles initiated the Women's Project at the American Place Theatre, which has staged rehearsed readings and studio productions of plays by such writers as Lavonne Mueller, Joan Shenkar, Kathleen Collins, and Dorothy Silver. In 1987, the Women's Project and Productions became an independent organization, and as of 1993 boasts some 290 members including Constance Congdon, Emily Mann, Maria Irene Fornés, and Paula Vogel. The Split Britches Company, composed of Peggy Shaw, Lois Weaver, and Deborah Margolin, has been producing feminist and lesbian plays since 1981; and Shaw and Weaver cofounded the WOW Café the following year to provide a performance space for feminist and lesbian work. What Julian Beck denigrated as the "vanity stage" of Broadway has been countered by a veritable explosion of theatres and playing spaces across the country, one able to address a greater, more diverse audience. More so than at any other moment in the history of the American stage, in the 1970s women began to transform the American theatre. They continue to do so today.

FROM THE 1980s TO THE PRESENT: POLITICS, PERFORMANCE ART, AND A NOTE ON THE STATE OF THE THEATRE

In his introduction to *Anti-Naturalism* (1989), an anthology of six contemporary plays by Craig Lucas, Richard Nelson, Eric Overmyer, and others, Christopher Gould observes that whatever few exceptions exist, the "American naturalistic/realistic play is stuck in a dreary dead-end." Hence, in Gould's view the forms of such "anti-realistic" plays as Nelson's *Bal* (1980) and Lucas's *Reckless* (1983) represent a new drama of "poetry" and "overwhelming imagination," a drama countering a tradition of realistic drama grown moldy and "piled high in kitchen sinks and trailer parks." These observations about dramatic realism and those of Lynda Hart concerning the sexual politics of mimetic or putatively objective representation suggest the extent of the contemporary theatre's attack on dramatic tradition, on the conventions of dramatic realism or the so-called well-made play of an earlier modern period, and even on the sacrosanct nature of the written text. This is not to say, of course, that realistic plays are not still written and performed in the 1990s, or that the texts of influential playwrights are not still granted primacy in their theatrical production—or that the residues of what were once dominant dramatic forms no longer exist. But some of the American theatre's most interesting work continues to subvert realistic conventions and refine earlier expressionist ones, to question the relationship of written text to theatrical performance, and to redefine the basic dynamics of the theatre event.

Nowhere has this been more evident in the recent past than in the emergence of **performance art** and the controversy it has sparked. And because of its very nature—

privileging the event over the text—it is difficult to include much recent work in performance in a book such as this one. What happens, one might ask, to a presentational form such as performance art when it can only be represented by a scrivened text? We hope to compensate somewhat for the necessarily limited selection of performance art in this book by the extended discussion that follows, all the while suggesting that performance art might be seen as a symptom of changes in the American drama brought into being in the 1960s and developed in the last two decades of this century.

The positioning of this discussion might seem to imply that the diverse artistic practices describable as performance art are only recent cultural phenomena, devised in the 1980s and refined in the present decade. Not so. As *was* the case in the Off-Off Broadway movement and *is* the case in numerous contemporary cultural forms, performance art emerged from such various sources of the 1960s and early 1970s as the women's movement, theatrical happenings and experimental dance, video and the visual arts, male **body art**, gay rights activism, and many others. Perhaps more significant than any other point of origin, performance art emerged in the late 1960s as **conceptual art** rose to challenge the preeminence of the art object and so-called "museum culture." Disdain for the art object, regarded by many artists as merely the currency exchanged between powerful institutions and profiteers, led to the rise of the "concept"—and the performance—as the immaterial counter to a corrupt orthodoxy. Through such techniques as the "transformation" and the metatheatrical emphasis on self-conscious performance, drama in the 1960s was moving in similar directions. Body artists Vito Acconci and Dennis Oppenheim in the late 1960s and early 70s experimented with placing themselves in larger designs, some of which involved their self-exposure or foregrounded their sexuality. Performance art thus played the same role in the 1970s that performance more broadly construed has done throughout the twentieth century, as RoseLee Goldberg reminds us: "Whenever a certain school, be it Cubism, Minimalism, or conceptual art, seemed to have reached an impasse, artists have turned to performance as a way of breaking down categories and indicating new directions." In the later 1960s, in the words of Lenora Champagne, interest in performance coincided neatly with various political agendas, that of the free speech and women's movements in particular: "The performance-art form has subversive origins and tendencies. . . . [Its] roots are not in the theatre, but in the art world and in dissent." Paramount among its aims are to "challenge established standards and definitions of art" and "to shake up social conventions with shocking, outrageous behavior in public appearances."

In recent years, this is precisely what has happened, as performance art is vilified in some ideological quarters as immoral or irreligious, and defended in others as important sociopolitical critique especially vulnerable to governmental censorship. In the spring of 1990, a much-publicized controversy erupted over the National Endowment for the Art's (NEA) funding of artists whom such groups as the American Family Association and politicians like North Carolina Senator Jesse Helms regarded as obscene. Precipitated by the earlier objections to NEA support of the work of photographers Robert Mapplethorpe and Andres Serrano—and volatized by such syndicated newspaper columnists as Rowland Evans and Robert Novak—this debate eventually brought performance artists Karen Finley, John Fleck, Holly Hughes, and Tim Miller into its ideological ambit. Labeled by many as the "NEA 4," these performers were unanimously recommended for grants by the NEA's peer review panel—endorsements eventually overturned by the National Council of the Arts, the appointed advisory board of the NEA, and embattled NEA chairman, John Frohnmayer. For many observers, the NEA decision amounted to an attack on gay rights, as three of the four affected writer-performers openly treat issues of gay and lesbian sexuality in their work. For Karen Finley, whose monologues frequently concern the victimization of women and whose performances foreground her own body as a site of patriarchal control, the decision represented several interrelated political realities: a desperate effort by Frohnmayer to save an NEA that some politicians and ideologues sought to dismantle; and, as she phrases it, a last-ditch attempt by some politicians "to maintain the power structure of the straight white male" by silencing those artists who challenge it.

Just as it is difficult to separate performance art from recent debates over governmental funding of the arts and the larger issue of censorship, it is equally difficult to isolate a single variety of this inherently hybridized form and eclectic mixture of conventions from various entertainments. In *World Without End* (1988), lesbian artist Holly Hughes appears in a red silk dress and addresses her audience directly, achieving "shocks" through the stories she tells and their often sexually explicit references. In some performance art, sexually explicit language is accompanied by nudity, or shock value is achieved by exploiting one or another bodily function. In his monologue *Blessed Are All the Little Fishes* (1989), for example, gay California artist John Fleck appears dressed as a mermaid on top of a toilet, from which he extracts a bottle of tequila and a goldfish and into which he later urinates. In "Hate Yellow" from *The Constant State of Desire,* Karen Finley takes off her clothes and uses stuffed animals to anoint herself with smashed eggs, glitter, and confetti. All performance art, of course, is not calculated to shock—Spalding Gray's *Monster in a Box* (1990), for instance. But while significant thematic and formal differences obtain between performance texts, several conventions inform most performance monologues: their often autobiographical nature, their fragmented narratives or tendency to weave together several stories as opposed to sustaining a single narrative, their appropriations of techniques from such other genres as stand-up comedy or dance, and their improvisational or site-specific quality. Still, however descriptive, this brief catalog cannot adequately capture the wide variety of practices generally described as performance art, for the most celebrated performers bring a unique combination of talents and life experiences to their art.

Since the 1970s, for example, Laurie Anderson has combined storytelling with elaborate visual and musical effects, forming a kind of multimedia autobiography. The high-tech form of her *Stories from the Nerve Bible* (1993), to mention one such instance, is about as far from Spalding Gray's minimalist mode—a man sitting behind a table telling his story, or Holly Hughes's recitation style in *World Without End*—as one can imagine. For the premiere of Anderson's *Stories* in Philadelphia's Annenberg Center, 15 television monitors were set into the stage's apron; four rectangular large screens were moved on and off the upstage areas; and enormous spherical and cube-shaped screens were occasionally lowered from the ceiling. A series of images and collages—in one segment, of the spectacularly lit night sky over Baghdad during the Persian Gulf conflict of 1991, in another of hang gliders floating over Rio de Janeiro—flashed across these screens as Anderson conveyed her stories, a narration modulated by sound effects created by voice filters on her several microphones. All the while, she provided musical accompaniment on a variety of synthesizers and an electric violin, supported by a bassist, accordion player, and percussionist. Aided by striking statistics and quotations flashing on the screens and a cyclone machine far upstage with elaborate laser lighting into which she moved at the end of her performance, Anderson dazzled many of her viewers. As the audience exited, a long list of credits appeared on the screens, replicating the style so common in film crediting and attesting to the fact that her elaborate, technically complicated aural and visual effects were anything but "minimalist."

Another way of describing performance art is to contextualize it within the larger contemporary reaction against traditional conceptions of drama. As Patrice Pavis discusses in *Theatre at the Crossroads of Culture* (1992), performance art, much like other varieties of "new dramatic writing," has "banished conversational dialogue from the stage as a relic of a dramaturgy based on conflict and exchange." Today, Pavis asserts, "nobody believes in the specificity of the dramatic text, or in the existence of rules and regulations governing dialogue, character, dramatic structure, etc." Because we all know people who in fact *do* "believe in the specificity of the dramatic text" and in a certain rulefulness, however loosely defined, to even the most improvisational or spontaneous of theatrical events, Pavis' point seems either overstated or naive. Nevertheless, performance art would seem particularly resistant to rules and regulations of any kind, to the establishment of any conventions governing matters of form or content (if the two can be legitimately divided from one another). Indeed, the specificity of the dramatic text, its priority and privileged position in the theatre event, is precisely what performance art challenges. In an interview with Richard Schechner in 1988, Finley makes this very point, distinguishing between a "performance procedure"—changeable and "site-specific"—and a more stabilized piece of "experimental theatre." Once monologues like *We Keep Our Victims Ready,* reprinted here, become repeatable night after night, concretized by publication and familiarity, they begin to take on a different shape than the "performance procedures" improvised in the small spaces of clubs and inflected by interactions with the intimate audiences that patronize them. In some respects, then, the development of performance art follows or, rather, parallels changing perceptions in the contemporary theatre of the relationship between dramatic text and production, the relationship between character and identity, and the place of the theatre and the theatre event in what many have called an increasingly postmodern culture.

How performance art evolves in the 1990s and what varieties of entertainment will eventually be identifiable as performance art are in some ways difficult to predict. But given the increased popularity in our culture of both the monologue and the so-called "talk" format in the media—talk radio, talk shows on television, stand-up comedy, and the like—and the ever-accelerating costs of full-blown productions in the contemporary theatre, performance art would seem to be a form custom-made for the economic and electronic times. And given the prospect of even more vitriolic debate between the political left and right in America over such issues as gays in the military, funding for AIDS research, government funding for the arts, and violence and sexuality in mass culture, the transgressive aesthetics and subversive politics of much performance art would seem likely to attract even larger—and perhaps more politically energized—audiences.

Two additional things would appear to be certain as well: American drama will continue to address matters of social and political import, and the contemporary American drama will continue to evolve formally, even on Broadway, as David Henry Hwang's *M. Butterfly* (1988), reprinted here, indicates. A new generation of African-American dramatists like George C. Wolfe, Suzan-Lori Parks, Robbie McCauley, Anna Deavere Smith, and two-time Pulitzer Prize-winner August Wilson, whose first major play *Ma Rainey's Black Bottom* (1984) is included in this section, has experienced continued, in the case of Wilson's *Fences* (1987) unprecedented, success in bringing issues of significance to the black community to a broader national audience. And, as M. Elizabeth Osborn's anthology *The Way We Live Now: American Plays & the AIDS Crisis* (1990) demonstrates, American drama, perhaps more so than any other artistic medium, has responded quickly and passionately to what has become an international tragedy of horrific proportions. Yet drama reacts not only to political or social turmoil, but also thrives on formal innovation. Borrowing terms from Raymond Williams, we might speculate that the American theatre will continue to be defined by the dynamic interplay of *residual* forms from the modern and classical theatre, more recent forms that have assumed a *dominant* stature in the theatre, and more radical *emergent* forms yet to be imagined. We hope in this final section of *American Drama: Colonial to Contemporary* on contemporary drama to have captured all three.

WORKS CONSULTED

Abel, Lionel. *Metatheatre: A New View of Dramatic Form.* New York: Hill & Wang, 1963.

Beck, Julian. *The Life of the Theatre.* New York: Limelight Editions, 1986.

Bigsby, C.W.E. *Modern American Drama, 1945–1990.* Cambridge: Cambridge University Press, 1992.

———. "O'Neill's *Endgame.*" *Eugene O'Neill and the Emergence of American Drama.* Ed. Marc Maufort. Amsterdam/Atlanta: Rodopi, 1989. 159–168.

Blau, Herbert. *The Eye of Prey: Subversions of the Postmodern.* Bloomington: Indiana University Press, 1987.

Branch, William B., ed. *Black Thunder: An Anthology of Contemporary African American Drama.* New York: Mentor Books, 1992.

Brook, Peter. *The Empty Space.* New York: Atheneum, 1978.

Calinescu, Matei. "Postmodernism and Some Paradoxes of Periodization." *Approaching Postmodernism.* Eds. Douwe Fokkema and Hans Bertens. Amsterdam/Philadelphia: John Benjamins, 1986. 239–254.

Champagne, Lenora, ed. *Out from Under: Texts by Women Performance Artists.* New York: Theatre Communications Group, 1990.

Dubin, Steven C. *Arresting Images: Impolitic Art and Uncivil Actions.* New York: Routledge, 1992.

Esslin, Martin. *The Theatre of the Absurd.* New York: Anchor Books, 1961.

Goldberg, RoseLee. *Performance Art: From Futurism to the Present,* revised edition. New York: Abrams, 1988.

Gonzalez, Yolanda Broyles. "Toward a Re-Vision of Chicano Theatre History: The Women of El Teatro Campesino." *Making a Spectacle: Feminist Essays on Contemporary Women's Theatre.* Ann Arbor: University of Michigan Press, 1989. 209–238.

Gould, Christopher, ed. *Anti-Naturalism: Six Full-Length Contemporary Plays.* New York: Broadway Play Publishing, 1989.

Hart, Lynda, ed. *Making a Spectacle: Feminist Essays on Contemporary Women's Theatre.* Ann Arbor: University of Michigan Press, 1989.

Hart, Lynda, and Peggy Phelan, eds. *Acting Out: Feminist Performances.* Ann Arbor: University of Michigan Press, 1993.

Huntsman, Jeffrey F. "Native American Theatre." *Ethnic Theatre in the United States.* Ed. Maxine Schwartz Seller. Westport, CT: Greenwood Press, 1983. 355–385.

Mahone, Sydné, ed. *Moon Marked and Touched by Sun: Plays by African-American Women.* New York: Theatre Communications Group, 1994.

Malcolm X. "The Ballot or the Bullet." *Malcolm X Speaks: Selected Speeches and Statements.* New York: Merit Publishers, 1965. 23–38.

Mayer, Thomas F. "The Position and Progress of Black America: Some Pertinent Statistics." *The Uptight Society: A Book of Readings.* Eds. Howard Gadlin and Bertram E. Garskof. Belmont, CA: Brooks/Cole, 1970. 102–116.

Mills, Julia, ed. *The Women's Project: Seven New Plays by Women.* New York: Performing Arts Journal Publications and the American Place Theatre, 1980.

Neal, Larry. "The Black Arts Movement." *The Black Aesthetic.* Ed. Addison Gayle, Jr. New York: Doubleday, 1972. 257–274.

Osborn, M. Elizabeth, ed. *The Way We Live Now: American Plays & the AIDS Crisis.* New York: Theatre Communications Group, 1990.

Pavis, Patrice. *Theatre at the Crossroads of Culture,* trans. Loren Kruger. New York: Routledge, 1992.

Poland, Albert, and Bruce Mailman, eds. *The Off, Off Broadway Book: The Plays, People, Theatre.* Indianapolis: Bobbs-Merrill, 1972.

Roth, Moira, ed. *The Amazing Decade: Women and Performance Art in America 1970–1980.* Los Angeles: Astro Artz, 1983.

Schechner, Richard. *The End of Humanism: Writings on Performance.* New York: Performing Arts Journal Publications, 1982.

Shange, Ntozake. *Three Pieces.* New York: St. Martin's, 1981.

Terry, Megan. *Viet Rock and Other Plays.* New York: Touchstone Books, 1967.

Valdez, Luis, and El Teatro Campesino. *Actos.* San Juan Bautista, CA: Cucaracha, 1971.

Williams, Raymond. *Marxism and Literature.* Oxford: Oxford University Press, 1977.

Wilmeth, Don B., and Tice Miller, eds. *The Cambridge Guide to American Theatre.* Cambridge: Cambridge University Press, 1993.

THE ZOO STORY (1959)

What . . . could be more absurd than a theatre in which the esthetic criterion is something like this: A "good" play is one which makes money; a "bad" play (in the sense of "Naughty! Naughty!" I guess) is one which does not; a theatre in which playwrights are encouraged (what a funny word!) to think of themselves as cogs in a great big wheel; a theatre in which imitation has given way to imitation of imitation; a theatre in which London "hits" are, willy nilly, in a kind of reverse chauvinism, greeted in a manner not unlike a colony's obeisance to the Crown; a theatre in which real estate owners and theatre party managements predetermine the success of unknown quantities; a theatre in which everybody scratches and bites for billing as though it meant access to the last bomb shelter on earth; a theatre in which, in a given season, there was not a single performance of a play by Beckett, Brecht, Chekhov, Genet, Ibsen, O'Casey, Pirandello, Shaw, Strindberg—or Shakespeare? What . . . could be more absurd than that?

With slight revision—removing the reference to "bomb shelter" and adding one to "revivals of American musicals," for instance—this broadside directed at Broadway theatre might have been delivered last year as opposed to 1962 when Edward Albee wrote it for the *New York Times Magazine.* Albee's indictments of the Broadway establishment reflect not only a particular young playwright's anger at being denied the broader audience available through the larger Broadway houses, but also the abiding twentieth-century tension between commercial and noncommercial theatres. Since the beginning of the century—first in New York City and then in regional theatres—experimental drama and unknown dramatists have persistently sought to find venues for a theatre not driven primarily by profit. Albee's remarks also bespeak the intense frustration of a younger generation of playwrights at the perceived moribund state of American theatre in the late 1950s and early 1960s. The icons of the classical repertoire were being ignored; the plays of the best contemporary foreign writers were being passed over; and the previous generation of American giants were dead (O'Neill), in the midst of a prolonged period of seeming nonproductivity (Miller), or already beginning to show signs of decline (Williams). Thus, Albee merely straightforwardly expressed an opinion that would have been echoed by such playwrighting contemporaries as Jack Richardson, Arthur Kopit, Jack Gelber, and Amiri Baraka. But in his confrontational style, in his resistance to the naive deployment of critical language, in his disdain for the commercial ethic, and in the irony that he was the American playwright who was to reap enormous financial and critical rewards by bridging the gap between Off-Broadway and Broadway, these comments are classic Albee.

Edward Franklin Albee III was born on 12 March 1928 and adopted by Reed and Frances Albee two weeks later. His paternal grandfather had made a fortune as the co-owner of the Keith-Albee theatre chain which, at one point, was composed of over 200 **vaudeville** houses, and his namesake's early life was a privileged one of winters in Miami and Palm Beach and summers sailing Long Island Sound. Albee's adopted father was a short, unassuming man who retired from his father's business to raise horses. Despite his father's constant presence at home, Albee's youth was dominated by his mother, a distant and formidable woman, whose spectral presence many critics have discovered in the shrewish, domineering women who regularly appear in his early plays. Moving quite often with his parents, Albee did poorly in his early schooling. Eventually sent away to boarding schools, Albee continued to perform unsatisfactorily, being kicked out of two preparatory schools before graduating from Choate in 1946. Albee's temporarily improved academic performance can probably be accounted for by the encouragement some of his instructors gave him to direct his energies toward writing. He attended Trinity College but was dismissed after three semesters. Thereafter, he remained at home writing material for radio programs until he moved to Greenwich Village in New York City in 1950, intent upon becoming a writer. Combining the income from a trust fund that his grandmother had established for him in 1949 with wages from a series of odd jobs—office boy for an advertising agency, salesclerk for record and book shops, counterman in a luncheonette, and, finally, delivery person for Western Union—Albee secured sufficient income to devote himself to writing, honing his craft in a series of unpublished plays.

Albee asserts that he wrote his first produced play, *The Zoo Story*, in three weeks in 1958, typing away at the kitchen table in his apartment. Through a circuitous route of friends and acquaintances of friends, *The Zoo Story* found its way to Europe where, in a German translation, it premiered at the Schiller Theatre *Werkstatt* in Berlin, 28 September 1959 on a program that included Samuel Beckett's *Krapp's Last Tape.* After that mounting captured the Berlin Festival Award, *The Zoo Story* had its American premiere at New York's Provincetown Playhouse on 14 January 1960. In quick succession Albee added to his own fame with *The Sandbox, The Death of Bessie Smith,* and *Fam and Yam* (all 1960) while at the same time giving new artistic credibility to the Off-Broadway movement. Albee added to his luster in 1961 with *The American Dream* and capped his early successes (and silenced Broadway skeptics who continued to wonder about the commercial potential of Off-Broadway writers) with his best-known

work to date, *Who's Afraid of Virginia Woolf?* (1962). Winner of the Drama Critics Award and numerous other prizes, *Who's Afraid of Virginia Woolf?* firmly established Albee as the major new voice in American drama. Perhaps more important to Albee, the play's royalties together with the proceeds from the sale of the motion-picture rights established him as that rare creature in the American theatre, a financially independent dramatist. His later works in the decade—*Tiny Alice* (1964), *A Delicate Balance* (1966), and *Box* and *Quotations from Chairman Mao Tse-Tung* (both 1968)—solidified Albee's reputation and gave him his first Pulitzer Prize for *A Delicate Balance.* During this decade he also penned several adaptations, but with the exception of his reworking of Carson McCullers' novella *The Ballad of the Sad Cafe* (1963), none was successful. Though Albee has remained a major figure on the American drama and theatrical scene, the intervening decades have been something of a critical roller coaster.

The 1970s brought Albee his second Pulitzer Prize for *Seascape* (1975), but increasingly his plays were castigated by the New York critics as obscure and inaccessible. The 1980s and early 1990s have been an equally tumultuous period for him. For most of the 1980s his work continued to be slighted in New York, even in Off-Broadway productions, and Albee increasingly turned to what he has sardonically called "Off-Off Broadway" venues. Three of Albee's latest plays have benefited from the generally more hospitable receptions in these locales—*The Man Who Had Three Arms* (1982) premiered in Chicago while *Marriage Play* (1987) and *Three Tall Women* (1991) were first produced in Vienna, Austria. Given the abiding antipathy of his New York reviewers, Albee has not seemed eager to bring his plays back to New York. In fact, Albee did not produce *Marriage Play* in New York until the fall of 1993, at which time the *New York Times* reviewer's suggestion that "at its core, the play is little more than turgid male menopausal ruminations" seemed to vindicate Albee's diffidence toward Broadway. The critical tide turned, however, with *Three Tall Women,* which premiered in New York in February 1994 and has brought him a third Pulitzer Prize.

Unlike its immediate predecessors, *Three Tall Women* received generally good reviews, with Ben Brantley of the *New York Times* noting that despite its flaws the play possesses "an undeniably affecting emotional core and a shimmeringly black sense of humor." Jack Kroll of *Newsweek* was more enthusiastic: "Albee is back with a powerful and moving work, his most emotionally affecting play since 'Who's Afraid of Virginia Woolf?' exploded in 1962." As these varied responses to his latest plays suggest, the ultimate assessment of Albee remains to be written. At 67, he remains very much a working playwright.

The Zoo Story has been read as, among other things, a failed or limited experiment with **absurdism**, an attack on the corrupt values of American materialist society, a contemporary morality play on the themes of isolation and salvation through sacrifice, and even a Greek-style tragedy. Given the play's compression and the disparate thematic threads that it weaves into its arresting tapestry, such critical diversity is understandable. Despite the variety of readings it has inspired, *The Zoo Story* is both structurally and thematically typical of many of Albee's subsequent pieces.

Like many of Albee's later one-act plays, *The Zoo Story* is deceptively straightforward. Two characters meet in Central Park and talk. One character dies. The other character runs away crying ambiguously "OH MY GOD!" But as Jerry comments twice, "sometimes a person has to go a very long distance out of his way to come back a short distance correctly." In the process of coming to the "point," of arriving at the resolution to the play's conflict, Albee is able to delve into many of the corners of what he asserts is modern humanity's too often sterile lives. The central issues around which the play is structured are the alternative responses to the isolation of modern life and the potential of language as a means of overcoming isolation and facilitating authentic communication.

Concealed behind a façade of material and social success, Peter contentedly refuses to face the emptiness of his life. But his snug Sundays in Central Park are destroyed forever by his encounter with Jerry, a "permanent transient," whose desire to reach beyond himself pulls an unwilling Peter steadily out of his insular world into a new existence. Insinuating himself into Peter's presence and alternatively attacking and retreating from him, Jerry teaches Peter the nature of an ambivalent existence which seems to partake of love and aggression in equal amounts. Escalating from verbal to physical attack, Jerry precipitates his own death and, in a carefully modulated echo of Peter's anguished "OH MY GOD!" wryly evokes the bleak prospects of a humanity facing mortality without the traditional reassurance of a faith in the divine.

The play's language is a masterful example of Albee's facility with dialogue, a talent that has led Ruby Cohn to comment that Albee arrived on the dramatic scene already in "perfect command of contemporary colloquial stylized dialogue." In this play that adroitness is seen in the distinctive language that serves to characterize Jerry and Peter and in the suggestive images through which Albee develops many of the play's ideas. Peter's studied multisyllabic reserve nicely contrasts with Jerry's increasingly frenetic diatribes. Albee's images are equally rich. For example, Jerry at first deems Peter a "vegetable" but allows that Peter has evolved into an "animal" over the course of the play. Jerry's desire for a relationship with God presents God as "a colored queen who wears a kimono and plucks his eyebrows." Clearly, Albee has reframed his images to the new psychological realities of his era.

While examining many of the same ontological questions that have been associated with the "theatre of the absurd," Albee's vision is ultimately shaped by American life rather than European philosophy and aesthetics. Albee is, finally, American to the core. Though radically recontextualized, his is fundamentally the idealistic vision often associated with American letters. With the materialist illusion shattered and the search for transcendent meaning transferred from one person to the next, there is a chance that individuals and, ultimately, society as a whole may be revitalized. That Jerry must die for Peter to have an opportunity for such a quest is part of Albee's point. If, as some have argued, Jerry is the founder of a new spiritual quest, the sacrifice necessary to transform Peter into a "disciple" remains enormous.

WORKS CONSULTED

Albee, Edward. "Which Theatre is the Absurd One?" *New York Times Magazine.* 25 February 1962: 30–31, 64, 66.

Amacher, Richard E. *Edward Albee.* Rev. ed. Boston: Twayne, 1982.

Baxandall, Lee. "The Theatre of Edward Albee." *Tulane Drama Review* 9 (1965): 19–40.

Bigsby, C. W. E. *A Critical Introduction to Twentieth-Century American Drama.* Volume Two: *Tennessee Williams, Arthur*

Miller, Edward Albee. Cambridge: Cambridge University Press, 1984.

Brantley, Ben. Rev. of *Marriage Play* by Edward Albee. *The New York Times.* Feb. 14, 1994: B 1, 3.

Cohn, Ruby. *Dialogue in American Drama.* Bloomington: Indiana University Press, 1971.

Esslin, Martin. *The Theatre of the Absurd.* Rev. ed. Garden City, NY: Anchor, 1969.

Kroll, Jack. "Trinity of Women." *Newsweek.* Feb. 21, 1994: 62.

Way, Brian. "Albee and the Absurd: *The American Dream* and *The Zoo Story.*" *American Theatre.* Stratford-upon-Avon Studies 10. New York: St. Martin's Press, 1967. 189–207.

Zimbardo, Rose A. "Symbolism and Naturalism in Edward Albee's *The Zoo Story.*" *Twentieth Century Literature* 8 (1962): 10–17.

CHARACTERS

PETER . . . . A man in his early forties, neither fat nor gaunt, neither handsome nor homely. He wears tweeds, smokes a pipe, carries horn-rimmed glasses. Although he is moving into middle age, his dress and his manner would suggest a man younger.

JERRY . . . . A man in his late thirties, not poorly dressed, but carelessly. What was once a trim and lightly muscled body has begun to go to fat; and while he is no longer handsome, it is evident that he once was. His fall from physical grace should not suggest debauchery; he has, to come closest to it, a great weariness.

THE SCENE: *It is Central Park; a Sunday afternoon in summer; the present. There are two park benches, one toward either side of the stage; they both face the audience. Behind them: foliage, trees, sky. At the beginning,* PETER *is seated on one of the benches.*

STAGE DIRECTIONS: *As the curtain rises,* PETER *is seated on the bench stage-right. He is reading a book. He stops reading, cleans his glasses, goes back to reading.* JERRY *enters.*

JERRY: I've been to the zoo. (PETER *doesn't notice*) I said, I've been to the zoo. MISTER, I'VE BEEN TO THE ZOO!

PETER: Hm? . . . What? . . . I'm sorry, were you talking to me?

JERRY: I went to the zoo, and then I walked until I came here. Have I been walking north?

PETER: (*puzzled*) North? Why . . . I . . . I think so. Let me see.

JERRY: (*pointing past the audience*) Is that Fifth Avenue?

PETER: Why yes; yes, it is.

JERRY: And what is that cross street there; that one, to the right?

PETER: That? Oh, that's Seventy-fourth Street.

JERRY: And the zoo is around Sixty-fifth Street; so, I've been walking north.

PETER: *(anxious to get back to his reading)* Yes; it would seem so.

JERRY: Good old north.

PETER: *(lightly, by reflex)* Ha, ha.

JERRY: *(after a slight pause)* But not due north.

PETER: I . . . well, no, not due north; but, we . . . call it north. It's northerly.

JERRY: *(watches as* PETER, *anxious to dismiss him, prepares his pipe)* Well, boy; you're not going to get lung cancer, are you?

PETER: *(looks up, a little annoyed, then smiles)* No, sir. Not from this.

JERRY: No, sir. What you'll probably get is cancer of the mouth, and then you'll have to wear one of those things Freud wore after they took one whole side of his jaw away. What do they call those things?

PETER: *(uncomfortable)* A prosthesis?

JERRY: The very thing! A prosthesis. You're an educated man, aren't you? Are you a doctor?

PETER: Oh, no; no. I read about it somewhere; *Time* magazine, I think. *(He turns to his book)*

JERRY: Well, *Time* magazine isn't for blockheads.

PETER: No, I suppose not.

JERRY: *(after a pause)* Boy, I'm glad that's Fifth Avenue there.

PETER: *(vaguely)* Yes.

JERRY: I don't like the west side of the park much.

PETER: Oh? *(then, slightly wary, but interested)* Why?

JERRY: *(offhand)* I don't know.

PETER: Oh. *(He returns to his book)*

JERRY: *(he stands for a few seconds, looking at* PETER, *who finally looks up again, puzzled)* Do you mind if we talk?

PETER: *(obviously minding)* Why . . . no, no.

JERRY: Yes you do; you do.

PETER: *(puts his book down, his pipe out and away, smiling)* No, really; I don't mind.

JERRY: Yes you do.

PETER: *(finally decided)* No; I don't mind at all, really.

JERRY: It's . . . it's a nice day.

PETER: *(stares unnecessarily at the sky)* Yes. Yes, it is; lovely.

JERRY: I've been to the zoo.

PETER: Yes, I think you said so . . . didn't you?

JERRY: You'll read about it in the papers tomorrow, if you don't see it on your TV tonight. You have TV, haven't you?

PETER: Why yes, we have two; one for the children.

JERRY: You're married!

PETER: *(with pleased emphasis)* Why, certainly.

JERRY: It isn't a law, for God's sake.

PETER: No . . . no, of course not.

JERRY: And you have a wife.

PETER: *(bewildered by the seeming lack of communication)* Yes!

JERRY: And you have children.

PETER: Yes; two.

JERRY: Boys?

PETER: No, girls . . . both girls.

JERRY: But you wanted boys.

PETER: Well . . . naturally, every man wants a son, but . . .

JERRY: *(lightly mocking)* But that's the way the cookie crumbles?

PETER: *(annoyed)* I wasn't going to say that.

JERRY: And you're not going to have any more kids, are you?

PETER: *(a bit distantly)* No. No more. *(Then back, and irksome)* Why did you say that? How would you know about that?

JERRY: The way you cross your legs, perhaps; something in the voice. Or maybe I'm just guessing. Is it your wife?

PETER: *(furious)* That's none of your business! *(A silence)* Do you understand? *(*JERRY *nods.* PETER *is quiet now)* Well, you're right. We'll have no more children.

JERRY: *(softly)* That *is* the way the cookie crumbles.

PETER: *(forgiving)* Yes . . . I guess so.

JERRY: Well, now; what else?

PETER: What were you saying about the zoo . . . that I'd read about it, or see . . . ?

JERRY: I'll tell you about it, soon. Do you mind if I ask you questions?

PETER: Oh, not really.

JERRY: I'll tell you why I do it; I don't talk to many people—except to say like: give me a beer, or where's the john, or what time does the feature go on, or keep your hands to yourself, buddy. You know—things like that.

PETER: I must say I don't . . .

JERRY: But every once in a while I like to talk to somebody, really *talk;* like to get to know somebody, know all about him.

PETER: *(lightly laughing, still a little uncomfortable)* And am I the guinea pig for today?

JERRY: On a sun-drenched Sunday afternoon like this? Who better than a nice married man with two daughters and . . . uh . . . a dog? *(PETER shakes his head)* No? Two dogs. *(PETER shakes his head again)* Hm. No dogs? *(PETER shakes his head, sadly)* Oh, that's a shame. But you look like an animal man. CATS? *(PETER nods his head, ruefully)* Cats! But, that can't be your idea. No, sir. Your wife and daughters? *(PETER nods his head)* Is there anything else I should know?

PETER: *(he has to clear his throat)* There are . . . there are two parakeets. One . . . uh . . . one for each of my daughters.

JERRY: Birds.

PETER: My daughters keep them in a cage in their bedroom.

JERRY: Do they carry disease? The birds.

PETER: I don't believe so.

JERRY: That's too bad. If they did you could set them loose in the house and the cats could eat them and die, maybe. *(PETER looks blank for a moment, then laughs)* And what else? What do you do to support your enormous household?

PETER: I . . . uh . . . I have an executive position with a . . . a small publishing house. We . . . uh . . . we publish textbooks.

JERRY: That sounds nice; very nice. What do you make?

PETER: *(still cheerful)* Now look here!

JERRY: Oh, come on.

PETER: Well, I make around eighteen thousand a year, but I don't carry more than forty dollars at any one time . . . in case you're a . . . a holdup man . . . ha, ha, ha.

JERRY: *(ignoring the above)* Where do you live? *(PETER is reluctant)* Oh, look; I'm not going to rob you, and I'm not going to kidnap your parakeets, your cats, or your daughters.

PETER: *(too loud)* I live between Lexington and Third Avenue, on Seventy-fourth Street.

JERRY: That wasn't so hard, was it?

PETER: I didn't mean to seem . . . ah . . . it's that you don't really carry on a conversation; you just ask questions. and I'm . . . I'm normally . . . uh . . . reticent. Why do you just stand there?

JERRY: I'll start walking around in a little while, and eventually I'll sit down. *(Recalling)* Wait until you see the expression on his face.

PETER: What? Whose face? Look here; is this something about the zoo?

JERRY: *(distantly)* The what?

PETER: The zoo; the zoo. Something about the zoo.

JERRY: The zoo?

PETER: You've mentioned it several times.

JERRY: *(still distant, but returning abruptly)* The zoo? Oh, yes; the zoo. I was there before I came here. I told you that. Say, what's the dividing line between upper-middle-middle-class and lower-upper-middle-class?

PETER: My dear fellow, I . . .

JERRY: Don't my dear fellow me.

PETER: *(unhappily)* Was I patronizing? I believe I was; I'm sorry. But, you see, your question about the classes bewildered me.

JERRY: And when you're bewildered you become patronizing?

PETER: I . . . I don't express myself too well, sometimes. *(He attempts a joke on himself)* I'm in publishing, not writing.

JERRY: *(amused, but not at the humor)* So be it. The truth *is:* I was being patronizing.

PETER: Oh, now; you needn't say that.

(It is at this point that JERRY *may begin to move about the stage with slowly increasing determination and authority, but pacing himself, so that the long speech about the dog comes at the high point of the arc)*

JERRY: All right. Who are your favorite writers? Baudelaire and J. P. Marquand?

PETER: *(wary)* Well, I like a great many writers; I have a considerable . . . catholicity of taste, if

I may say so. Those two men are fine, each in his way. *(Warming up)* Baudelaire, of course . . . uh . . . is by far the finer of the two, but Marquand has a place . . . in our . . . uh . . . national . . .

JERRY: Skip it.

PETER: I . . . sorry.

JERRY: Do you know what I did before I went to the zoo today? I walked all the way up Fifth Avenue from Washington Square; all the way.

PETER: Oh; you live in the Village! *(This seems to enlighten* PETER)

JERRY: No, I don't. I took the subway down to the Village so I could walk all the way up Fifth Avenue to the zoo. It's one of those things a person has to do; sometimes a person has to go a very long distance out of his way to come back a short distance correctly.

PETER: *(almost pouting)* Oh, I thought you lived in the Village.

JERRY: What were you trying to do? Make sense out of things? Bring order? The old pigeonhole bit? Well, that's easy; I'll tell you. I live in a four-story brownstone roominghouse on the upper West Side between Columbus Avenue and Central Park West. I live on the top floor; rear; west. It's a laughably small room, and one of my walls is made of beaverboard; this beaverboard separates my room from another laughably small room, so I assume that the two rooms were once one room, a small room, but not necessarily laughable. The room beyond my beaverboard wall is occupied by a colored queen who always keeps his door open; well, not always, but *always* when he's plucking his eyebrows, which he does with Buddhist concentration. This colored queen has rotten teeth, which is rare, and he has a Japanese kimono, which is also pretty rare; and he wears this kimono to and from the john in the hall, which is pretty frequent. I mean, he goes to the john a lot. He never bothers me, and he never brings anyone up to his room. All he does is pluck his eyebrows, wear his kimono and go to the john. Now, the two front rooms on my floor are a little larger, I guess; but they're pretty small, too. There's a Puerto Rican family in one of them, a husband, a wife, and some kids; I don't know how many. These people entertain a lot. And in the other front room, there's somebody living there, but I don't know who it is. I've never seen who it is. Never. Never ever.

PETER: *(embarrassed)* Why . . . why do you live there?

JERRY: *(from a distance again)* I don't know.

PETER: It doesn't sound like a very nice place . . . where you live.

JERRY: Well, no; it isn't an apartment in the East Seventies. But, then again, I don't have one wife, two daughters, two cats and two parakeets. What I do have, I have toilet articles, a few clothes, a hot plate that I'm not supposed to have, a can opener, one that works with a key, you know; a knife, two forks, and two spoons, one small, one large; three plates, a cup, a saucer, a drinking glass, two picture frames, both empty, eight or nine books, a pack of pornographic playing cards, regular deck, an old Western Union typewriter that prints nothing but capital letters, and a small strongbox without a lock which has in it . . . what? Rocks! Some rocks . . . sea-rounded rocks I picked up on the beach when I was a kid. Under which . . . weighed down . . . are some letters . . . please letters . . . please why don't you do this, and please when will you do that letters. And when letters, too. When will you write? When will you come? When? These letters are from more recent years.

PETER: *(stares glumly at his shoes, then)* About those two empty picture frames . . . ?

JERRY: I don't see why they need any explanation at all. Isn't it clear? I don't have pictures of anyone to put in them.

PETER: Your parents . . . perhaps . . . a girl friend . . .

JERRY: You're a very sweet man, and you're possessed of a truly enviable innocence. But good old Mom and good old Pop are dead . . . you know? . . . I'm broken up about it, too . . .

I mean really. BUT. That particular vaudeville act is playing the cloud circuit now, so I don't see how I can look at them, all neat and framed. Besides, or, rather, to be pointed about it, good old Mom walked out on good old Pop when I was ten and a half years old; she embarked on an adulterous turn of our southern states . . . a journey of a year's duration . . . and her most constant companion . . . among others, among many others . . . was a Mr. Barleycorn. At least, that's what good old Pop told me after he went down . . . came back . . . brought her body north. We'd received the news between Christmas and New Year's, you see, that good old Mom had parted with the ghost in some dump in Alabama. And, without the ghost . . . she was less welcome. I mean, what was she? A stiff . . . a northern stiff. At any rate, good old Pop celebrated the New Year for an even two weeks and then slapped into the front of a somewhat moving city omnibus, which sort of cleaned things out family-wise. Well no; then there was Mom's sister, who was given neither to sin nor the consolations of the bottle. I moved in on her, and my memory of her is slight excepting I remember still that she did all things dourly: sleeping, eating, working, praying. She dropped dead on the stairs to her apartment, my apartment then, too, on the afternoon of my high school graduation. A terribly middle-European joke, if you ask me.

PETER: Oh, my; oh, my.

JERRY: Oh, your what? But that was a long time ago, and I have no feeling about any of it that I care to admit to myself. Perhaps you can see, though, why good old Mom and good old Pop are frameless. What's your name? Your first name?

PETER: I'm Peter.

JERRY: I'd forgotten to ask you. I'm Jerry.

PETER: (with a slight, nervous laugh) Hello, Jerry.

JERRY: (nods his hello) And let's see now; what's the point of having a girl's picture, especially in two frames? I have two picture frames, you

remember. I never see the pretty little ladies more than once, and most of them wouldn't be caught in the same room with a camera. It's odd, and I wonder if it's sad.

PETER: The girls?

JERRY: No. I wonder if it's sad that I never see the little ladies more than once. I've never been able to have sex with, or, how is it put? . . . make love to anybody more than once. Once; that's it. . . . Oh, wait; for a week and a half, when I was fifteen . . . and I hang my head in shame that puberty was late . . . I was a h-o-m-o-s-e-x-u-a-l. I mean, I was queer . . . (Very fast) . . . queer, queer, queer . . . with bells ringing, banners snapping in the wind. And for those eleven days, I met at least twice a day with the park superintendent's son . . . a Greek boy, whose birthday was the same as mine, except he was a year older. I think I was very much in love . . . maybe just with sex. But that was the jazz of a very special hotel, wasn't it? And now; oh, do I love the little ladies; really, I love them. For about an hour.

PETER: Well, it seems perfectly simple to me. . . .

JERRY: (angry) Look! Are you going to tell me to get married and have parakeets?

PETER: (angry himself) Forget the parakeets! And stay single if you want to. It's no business of mine. I didn't start this conversation in the . . .

JERRY: All right, all right. I'm sorry. All right? You're not angry?

PETER: (laughing) No, I'm not angry.

JERRY: (relieved) Good. (Now back to his previous tone) Interesting that you asked me about the picture frames. I would have thought that you would have asked me about the pornographic playing cards.

PETER: (with a knowing smile) Oh, I've seen those cards.

JERRY: That's not the point. (Laughs) I suppose when you were a kid you and your pals passed them around, or you had a pack of your own.

PETER: Well, I guess a lot of us did.

JERRY: And you threw them away just before you got married.

PETER: Oh, now; look here. I didn't *need* anything like that when I got older.

JERRY: No?

PETER: *(embarrassed)* I'd rather not talk about these things.

JERRY: So? Don't. Besides, I wasn't trying to plumb your post-adolescent sexual life and hard times; what I wanted to get at is the value difference between pornographic playing cards when you're a kid, and pornographic playing cards when you're older. It's that when you're a kid you use the cards as a substitute for a real experience, and when you're older you use real experience as a substitute for the fantasy. But I imagine you'd rather hear about what happened at the zoo.

PETER: *(enthusiastic)* Oh, yes; the zoo. *(Then, awkward)* That is . . . if you. . . .

JERRY: Let me tell you about why I went . . . well, let me tell you some things. I've told you about the fourth floor of the roominghouse where I live. I think the rooms are better as you go down, floor by floor. I guess they are; I don't know. I don't know any of the people on the third and second floors. Oh, wait! I do know that there's a lady living on the third floor, in the front. I know because she cries all the time. Whenever I go out or come back in, whenever I pass her door, I always hear her crying, muffled, but . . . very determined. Very determined indeed. But the one I'm getting to, and all about the dog, is the landlady. I don't like to use words that are too harsh in describing people. I don't like to. But the landlady is a fat, ugly, mean, stupid, unwashed, misanthropic, cheap, drunken bag of garbage. And you may have noticed that I very seldom use profanity, so I can't describe her as well as I might.

PETER: You describe her . . . vividly.

JERRY: Well, thanks. Anyway, she has a dog, and I will tell you about the dog, and she and her dog are the gatekeepers of my dwelling. The woman is bad enough; she leans around in the entrance hall, spying to see that I don't bring in things or people, and when she's had her mid-afternoon pint of lemon-flavored gin she always stops me in the hall, and grabs ahold of my coat or my arm, and she presses her disgusting body up against me to keep me in a corner so she can talk to me. The smell of her body and her breath . . . you can't imagine it . . . and somewhere, somewhere in the back of that pea-sized brain of hers, an organ developed just enough to let her eat, drink, and emit, she has some foul parody of sexual desire. And I, Peter, I am the object of her sweaty lust.

PETER: That's disgusting. That's . . . horrible.

JERRY: But I have found a way to keep her off. When she talks to me, when she presses herself to my body and mumbles about her room and how I should come there, I merely say: but, Love; wasn't yesterday enough for you, and the day before? Then she puzzles, she makes slits of her tiny eyes, she sways a little, and then, Peter . . . and it is at this moment that I think I might be doing some good in that tormented house . . . a simple-minded smile begins to form on her unthinkable face, and she giggles and groans as she thinks about yesterday and the day before; as she believes and relives what never happened. Then, she motions to that black monster of a dog she has, and she goes back to her room. And I am safe until our next meeting.

PETER: It's so . . . unthinkable. I find it hard to believe that people such as that really *are*.

JERRY: *(lightly mocking)* It's for reading about, isn't it?

PETER: *(seriously)* Yes.

JERRY: And fact is better left to fiction. You're right, Peter. Well, what I have been meaning to tell you about is the dog; I shall, now.

PETER: *(nervously)* Oh, yes; the dog.

JERRY: Don't go. You're not thinking of going, are you?

PETER: Well . . . no, I don't think so.

JERRY: *(as if to a child)* Because after I tell you about the dog, do you know what then?

Then . . . then I'll tell you about what happened at the zoo.

PETER: *(laughing faintly)* You're . . . you're full of stories, aren't you?

JERRY: You don't *have* to listen. Nobody is holding you here; remember that. Keep that in your mind.

PETER: *(irritably)* I know that.

JERRY: You do? Good.

(The following long speech, it seems to me, should be done with a great deal of action, to achieve a hypnotic effect on PETER, *and on the audience, too. Some specific actions have been suggested, but the director and the actor playing* JERRY *might best work it out for themselves)* ALL RIGHT. *(As if reading from a huge billboard)* THE STORY OF JERRY AND THE DOG! *(Natural again)* What I am going to tell you has something to do with how sometimes it's necessary to go a long distance out of the way in order to come back a short distance correctly; or, maybe I only think that it has something to do with that. But, it's why I went to the zoo today, and why I walked north . . . northerly, rather . . . until I came here. All right. The dog, I think I told you, is a black monster of a beast: an oversized head, tiny, tiny ears, and eyes . . . bloodshot, infected, maybe; and a body you can see the ribs through the skin. The dog is black, all black; all black except for the bloodshot eyes, and . . . yes . . . and an open sore on its . . . *right* forepaw; that is red, too. And, oh yes; the poor monster, and I do believe it's an old dog . . . it's certainly a misused one . . . almost always has an erection . . . of sorts. That's red, too. And . . . what else? . . . oh, yes; there's a gray-yellow-white color, too, when he bares his fangs. Like this: Grrrrrr! Which is what he did when he saw me for the first time . . . the day I moved in. I worried about that animal the very first minute I met him. Now, animals don't take to me like Saint Francis had birds hanging off him all the time. What I mean is: animals are indifferent to me . . . like people *(He smiles slightly)* . . . most of the time. But this dog wasn't indifferent. From the very beginning he'd snarl and then go for me, to get one of my legs. Not like he was rabid, you know; he was sort of a stumbly dog, but he wasn't half-assed, either. It was a good, stumbly run; but I always got away. He got a piece of my trouser leg, look, you can see right here, where it's mended; he got that the second day I lived there; but, I kicked free and got upstairs fast, so that was that. *(Puzzles)* I still don't know to this day how the other roomers manage it, but you know what I *think:* I think it had to do only with me. Cozy. So. Anyway, this went on for over a week, whenever I came in; but never when I went out. That's funny. Or, it *was* funny. I could pack up and live in the street for all the dog cared. Well, I thought about it up in my room one day, one of the times after I'd bolted upstairs, and I made up my mind. I decided: First, I'll kill the dog with kindness, and if that doesn't work . . . I'll just kill him. *(PETER winces)* Don't react, Peter; just listen. So, the next day I went out and bought a bag of hamburgers, medium rare, no catsup, no onion; and on the way home I threw away all the rolls and kept just the meat.

(Action for the following, perhaps)

When I got back to the roominghouse the dog was waiting for me. I half opened the door that led into the entrance hall, and there he was; waiting for me. It figured. I went in, very cautiously, and I had the hamburgers, you remember; I opened the bag, and I set the meat down about twelve feet from where the dog was snarling at me. Like so! He snarled; stopped snarling; sniffed; moved slowly; then faster; then faster toward the meat. Well, when he got to it he stopped, and he looked at me. I smiled; but tentatively, you understand. He turned his face back to the hamburgers, smelled, sniffed some more, and then . . . RRRAAAAGGGGGHHHH, like that . . . he tore into them. It was as if he had never eaten anything in his life before, except like garbage. Which might very well have been the truth. I don't think the landlady ever eats anything but garbage. But. He ate all the hamburgers, almost all at once, making sounds in his throat like a woman. *Then,* when he'd finished the meat, the hamburger, and tried to eat the paper, too, he sat down and smiled. I think he smiled; I know cats do. It was a very gratifying few moments. Then, BAM, he snarled and made for me again. He didn't get me this time, either. So, I got upstairs, and I lay down on my bed and started to think about the dog again. To be truthful, I was offended, and I was damn mad, too. It was six perfectly good hamburgers with not enough pork in them to make it disgusting. I was offended. But, after a while, I decided to try it for a few more days. If you think about it, this dog had what amounted to an antipathy toward me; really. And, I wondered if I mightn't overcome this antipathy. So, I tried it for five more days, but it was always the same: snarl, sniff; move; faster; stare; gobble; RAAGGGHHH; smile; snarl; BAM. Well, now; by this time Columbus Avenue was strewn with hamburger rolls and I was less offended than disgusted. So, I decided to kill the dog.

(PETER *raises a hand in protest*)

Oh, don't be so alarmed, Peter; I didn't succeed. The day I tried to kill the dog I bought only one hamburger and what I thought was a murderous portion of rat poison. When I bought the hamburger I asked the man not to bother with the roll, all I wanted was the meat. I expected some reaction from him, like: we don't sell no hamburgers without rolls; or, wha' d'ya wanna do, eat it out'a ya han's? But no; he smiled benignly, wrapped up the hamburger in waxed paper, and said: A bite for ya pussy-cat? I wanted to say: No, not really; it's part of a plan to poison a dog I know. But, you can't say "a dog I know" without sounding funny; so I said, a little too loud, I'm afraid, and too formally: YES, A BITE FOR MY PUSSY-CAT.

People looked up. It always happens when I try to simplify things; people look up. But that's neither hither nor thither. So. On my way back to the roominghouse, I kneaded the hamburger and the rat poison together between my hands, at that point feeling as much sadness as disgust. I opened the door to the entrance hall, and there the monster was, waiting to take the offering and then jump me. Poor bastard; he never learned that the moment he took to smile before he went for me gave me time enough to get out of range. BUT, there he was; malevolence with an erection, waiting. I put the poison patty down, moved toward the stairs and watched. The poor animal gobbled the food down as usual, smiled, which made me almost sick, and then, BAM. But, I sprinted up the stairs, as usual, and the dog didn't get me, as usual. AND IT CAME TO PASS THAT THE BEAST WAS DEATHLY ILL. I knew this because he no longer attended me, and because the landlady sobered up. She stopped me in the hall the same evening of the attempted murder and confided the information that God had struck her puppy-dog a surely fatal blow. She had forgotten her bewildered lust, and her eyes were wide open for the first time. They looked like the dog's eyes. She sniveled and implored me to pray for the animal. I wanted to say to her: Madam, I have myself to pray for, the colored queen, the Puerto Rican family, the person in the front room whom I've never seen, the woman who cries deliberately behind her closed door, and the rest of the people in all roominghouses, everywhere; besides, Madam, I don't understand how to pray. But . . . to simplify things . . . I told her I would pray. She looked up. She said that I was a liar, and that I probably wanted the dog to die. I told her, and there was so much truth here, that I didn't want the dog to die. I didn't, and not just because I'd poisoned him. I'm afraid that I must tell you I wanted the dog to live so that I could see what our new relationship might come to.

(PETER indicates his increasing displeasure and slowly growing antagonism)
Please understand, Peter; that sort of thing is important. You must believe me; it *is* important. We have to know the effect of our actions. *(Another deep sigh)* Well, anyway; the dog recovered. I have no idea why, unless he was a descendant of the puppy that guarded the gates of hell or some such resort. I'm not up on my mythology. *(He pronounces the word myth-o-* logy) Are you?
(PETER sets to thinking, but JERRY goes on)
At any rate, and you've missed the eight-thousand-dollar question, Peter; at any rate, the dog recovered his health and the landlady recovered her thirst, in no way altered by the bow-wow's deliverance. When I came home from a movie that was playing on Forty-second Street, a movie I'd seen, or one that was very much like one or several I'd seen, after the landlady told me puppykins was better, I was so hoping for the dog to be waiting for me. I was . . . well, how would you put it . . . enticed? . . . fascinated? . . . no, I don't think so . . . heart-shatteringly anxious, that's it; I was heart-shatteringly anxious to confront my friend again.
(PETER reacts scoffingly)
Yes, Peter; friend. That's the only word for it. I was heart-shatteringly et cetera to confront my doggy friend again. I came in the door and advanced, unafraid, to the center of the entrance hall. The beast was there . . . looking at me. And, you know, he looked better for his scrape with the nevermind. I stopped; I looked at him; he looked at me. I think . . . I think we stayed a long time that way . . . still, stone-statue . . . just looking at one another. I looked more into his face than he looked into mine. I mean, I can concentrate longer at looking into a dog's face than a dog can concentrate at looking into mine, or into anybody else's face, for that matter. But during that twenty seconds or two hours that we looked into each other's face, we made contact. Now, here is

what I had wanted to happen: I loved the dog now, and I wanted him to love me. I had tried to love, and I had tried to kill, and both had been unsuccessful by themselves. I hoped . . . and I don't really know why I expected the dog to understand anything, much less my motivations . . . I hoped that the dog would understand.
(PETER seems to be hypnotized)
It's just . . . it's just that . . . *(JERRY is abnormally tense, now)* . . . it's just that if you can't deal with people, you have to make a start somewhere. WITH ANIMALS! *(Much faster now, and like a conspirator)* Don't you see? A person has to have some way of dealing with SOMETHING. If not with people . . . if not with people . . . SOMETHING. With a bed, with a cockroach, with a mirror . . . no, that's too hard, that's one of the last steps. With a cockroach, with a . . . with a . . . with a carpet, a roll of toilet paper . . . no, not that, either . . . that's a mirror, too; always check bleeding. You see how hard it is to find things? With a street corner, and too many lights, all colors reflecting on the oily-wet streets . . . with a wisp of smoke, a wisp . . . of smoke . . . with . . . with pornographic playing cards, with a strongbox . . . WITHOUT A LOCK . . . with love, with vomiting, with crying, with fury because the pretty little ladies aren't pretty little ladies, with making money with your body which is an act of love and I could prove it, with howling because you're alive; with God. How about that? WITH GOD WHO IS A COLORED QUEEN WHO WEARS A KIMONO AND PLUCKS HIS EYEBROWS, WHO IS A WOMAN WHO CRIES WITH DETERMINATION BEHIND HER CLOSED DOOR . . . with God who, I'm told, turned his back on the whole thing some time ago . . . with . . . some day, with people. *(JERRY sighs the next word heavily)* People. With an idea; a concept. And where better, where ever better in this humiliating excuse for a jail, where better to communicate one single, simple-minded idea than

in an entrance hall? Where? It would be A START! Where better to make a beginning . . . to understand and just possibly be understood . . . a beginning of an understanding, than with . . .

(Here JERRY *seems to fall into almost grotesque fatigue)*

. . . than with A DOG. Just that; a dog.

(Here there is a silence that might be prolonged for a moment or so; then JERRY *wearily finishes his story)*

A dog. It seemed like a perfectly sensible idea. Man is a dog's best friend, remember. So: the dog and I looked at each other. I longer than the dog. And what I saw then has been the same ever since. Whenever the dog and I see each other we both stop where we are. We regard each other with a mixture of sadness and suspicion, and then we feign indifference. We walk past each other safely; we have an understanding. It's very sad, but you'll have to admit that it is an understanding. We had made many attempts at contact, and we had failed. The dog has returned to garbage, and I to solitary but free passage. I have not returned. I mean to say, I have *gained* solitary free passage, if that much further loss can be said to be gain. I have learned that neither kindness nor cruelty by themselves, independent of each other, creates any effect beyond themselves; and I have learned that the two combined, together, at the same time, are the teaching emotion. And what is gained is loss. And what has been the result: the dog and I have attained a compromise; more of a bargain, really. We neither love nor hurt because we do not try to reach each other. And, *was* trying to feed the dog an act of love? And, perhaps, was the dog's attempt to bite me *not* an act of love? If we can so misunderstand, well then, why have we invented the word love in the first place?

(There is silence. JERRY *moves to* PETER'S *bench and sits down beside him. This is the first time* JERRY *has sat down during the play)*

The Story of Jerry and the Dog: the end.

*(*PETER *is silent)*

Well, Peter? *(*JERRY *is suddenly cheerful)* Well, Peter? Do you think I could sell that story to the *Reader's Digest* and make a couple of hundred bucks for *The Most Unforgettable Character I've Ever Met?* Huh?

*(*JERRY *is animated, but* PETER *is disturbed)*

Oh, come on now, Peter; tell me what you think.

PETER: *(numb)* I . . . I don't understand what . . . I don't think I . . . *(Now, almost tearfully)* Why did you tell me all of this?

JERRY: Why not?

PETER: I DON'T UNDERSTAND!

JERRY: *(furious, but whispering)* That's a lie.

PETER: No. No, it's not.

JERRY: *(quietly)* I tried to explain it to you as I went along. I went slowly; it all has to do with . . .

PETER: I DON'T WANT TO HEAR ANY MORE. I don't understand you, or your landlady, or her dog. . . .

JERRY: *Her* dog! I thought it was my . . . No. No, you're right. It *is* her dog. *(Looks at* PETER *intently, shaking his head)* I don't know what I was thinking about; of course you don't understand. *(In a monotone, wearily)* I don't live in your block; I'm not married to two parakeets, or whatever your setup is. I am a *permanent transient,* and my home is the sickening roominghouses on the West Side of New York City, which is the greatest city in the world. Amen.

PETER: I'm . . . I'm sorry; I didn't mean to . . .

JERRY: Forget it. I suppose you don't quite know what to make of me, eh?

PETER: *(a joke)* We get all kinds in publishing. *(Chuckles)*

JERRY: You're a funny man. *(He forces a laugh)* You know that? You're a very . . . a richly comic person.

PETER: *(modestly, but amused)* Oh, now, not really. *(Still chuckling)*

JERRY: Peter, do I annoy you, or confuse you?

PETER: *(lightly)* Well, I must confess that this wasn't the kind of afternoon I'd anticipated.

JERRY: You mean, I'm not the gentleman you were expecting.

PETER: I wasn't expecting anybody.

JERRY: No, I don't imagine you were. But I'm here, and I'm not leaving.

PETER: *(consulting his watch)* Well, you may not be, but I must be getting home soon.

JERRY: Oh, come on; stay a while longer.

PETER: I really should get home; you see . . .

JERRY: *(tickles* PETER'S *ribs with his fingers)* Oh, come on.

PETER: *(He is very ticklish; as* JERRY *continues to tickle him his voice becomes falsetto)*
No, I . . . OHHHHH! Don't do that. Stop, Stop. Ohhh, no, no.

JERRY: Oh, come on.

PETER: *(as* JERRY *tickles)* Oh, hee, hee, hee. I must go. I . . . hee, hee, hee. After all, stop, stop, hee, hee, hee, after all, the parakeets will be getting dinner ready soon. Hee, hee. And the cats are setting the table. Stop, stop, and, and . . . *(*PETER *is beside himself now)* . . . and we're having . . . hee, hee . . . uh . . . ho, ho, ho.
*(*JERRY *stops tickling* PETER, *but the combination of the tickling and his own mad whimsy has* PETER *laughing almost hysterically. As his laughter continues, then subsides,* JERRY *watches him, with a curious fixed smile)*

JERRY: Peter?

PETER: Oh, ha, ha, ha, ha, ha. What? What?

JERRY: Listen, now.

PETER: Oh, ho, ho. What . . . what is it, Jerry? Oh, my.

JERRY: *(mysteriously)* Peter, do you want to know what happened at the zoo?

PETER: Ah, ha, ha. The what? Oh, yes; the zoo. Oh, ho, ho. Well, I had my own zoo there for a moment with . . . hee, hee, the parakeets getting dinner ready, and the . . . ha, ha, whatever it was, the . . .

JERRY: *(calmly)* Yes, that was very funny, Peter. I wouldn't have expected it. But do you want to hear about what happened at the zoo, or not?

PETER: Yes. Yes, by all means; tell me what happened at the zoo. Oh, my. I don't know what happened to me.

JERRY: Now I'll let you in on what happened at the zoo; but first, I should tell you why I went to the zoo. I went to the zoo to find out more about the way people exist with animals, and the way animals exist with each other, and with people too. It probably wasn't a fair test, what with everyone separated by bars from everyone else, the animals for the most part from each other, and always the people from the animals. But, if it's a zoo, that's the way it is. *(He pokes* PETER *on the arm)* Move over.

PETER: *(friendly)* I'm sorry, haven't you enough room? *(He shifts a little)*

JERRY: *(smiling slightly)* Well, all the animals are there, and all the people are there, and it's Sunday and all the children are there. *(He pokes* PETER *again)* Move over.

PETER: *(patiently, still friendly)* All right.
(He moves some more, and JERRY *has all the room he might need)*

JERRY: And it's a hot day, so all the stench is there, too, and all the balloon sellers, and all the ice cream sellers, and all the seals are barking, and all the birds are screaming. *(Pokes* PETER *harder)* Move over!

PETER: *(beginning to be annoyed)* Look here, you have more than enough room! *(But he moves more, and is now fairly cramped at one end of the bench)*

JERRY: And I am there, and it's feeding time at the lions' house, and the lion keeper comes into the lion cage, one of the lion cages, to feed one of the lions. *(Punches* PETER *on the arm, hard)* MOVE OVER!

PETER: *(very annoyed)* I can't move over any more, and stop hitting me. What's the matter with you?

JERRY: Do you want to hear the story? *(Punches* PETER'S *arm again)*

PETER: *(flabbergasted)* I'm not so sure! I certainly don't want to be punched in the arm.

JERRY: *(punches* PETER'S *arm again)* Like that?

PETER: Stop it! What's the matter with you?

JERRY: I'm crazy, you bastard.

PETER: That isn't funny.

JERRY: Listen to me, Peter. I want this bench. You go sit on the bench over there, and if you're good I'll tell you the rest of the story.

PETER: *(flustered)* But . . . whatever for? What *is* the matter with you? Besides, I see no reason why I should give up this bench. I sit on this bench almost every Sunday afternoon, in good weather. It's secluded here; there's never anyone sitting here, so I have it all to myself.

JERRY: *(softly)* Get off this bench, Peter; I want it.

PETER: *(almost whining)* No.

JERRY: I said I want this bench, and I'm going to have it. Now get over there.

PETER: People can't have everything they want. You should know that; it's a rule; people can have some of the things they want, but they can't have everything.

JERRY: *(laughs)* Imbecile! You're slow-witted!

PETER: Stop that!

JERRY: You're a vegetable! Go lie down on the ground.

PETER: *(intense)* Now *you* listen to me. I've put up with you all afternoon.

JERRY: Not really.

PETER: LONG ENOUGH. I've put up with you long enough. I've listened to you because you seemed . . . well, because I thought you wanted to talk to somebody.

JERRY: You put things well; economically, and, yet . . . oh, what is the word I want to put justice to your . . . JESUS, you make me sick . . . get off here and give me my bench.

PETER: MY BENCH!

JERRY: *(pushes* PETER *almost, but not quite, off the bench)* Get out of my sight.

PETER: *(regaining his position)* God da . . . mn you. That's enough! I've had enough of you. I will not give up this bench; you can't have it, and that's that. Now, go away.

*(*JERRY *snorts but does not move)*

Go away, I said.

*(*JERRY *does not move)*

Get away from here. If you don't move on . . . you're a bum . . . that's what you are. . . . If you don't move on, I'll get a policeman here and make you go.

*(*JERRY *laughs, stays)*

I warn you, I'll call a policeman.

JERRY: *(softly)* You won't find a policeman around here; they're all over on the west side of the park chasing fairies down from trees or out of the bushes. That's all they do. That's their function. So scream your head off; it won't do you any good.

PETER: POLICE! I warn you, I'll have you arrested. POLICE! *(Pause)* I said POLICE! *(Pause)* I feel ridiculous.

JERRY: You look ridiculous: a grown man screaming for the police on a bright Sunday afternoon in the park with nobody harming you. If a policeman *did* fill his quota and come sludging over this way he'd probably take you in as a nut.

PETER: *(with disgust and impotence)* Great God, I just came here to read, and now you want me to give up the bench. You're mad.

JERRY: Hey, I got news for you, as they say. I'm on your precious bench, and you're never going to have it for yourself again.

PETER: *(furious)* Look, you; get off my bench. I don't care if it makes any sense or not. I want this bench to myself; I want you OFF IT!

JERRY: *(mocking)* Aw . . . look who's mad.

PETER: GET OUT!

JERRY: No.

PETER: I WARN YOU!

JERRY: Do you know how ridiculous you look *now?*

PETER: *(his fury and self-consciousness have possessed him)* It doesn't matter. *(He is almost crying)* GET AWAY FROM MY BENCH!

JERRY: Why? You have everything in the world you want; you've told me about your home, and your family, and *your own* little zoo. You have everything, and now you want this bench. Are these the things men fight for? Tell me, Peter, is this bench, this iron and this wood, is this your honor? Is this the thing in the world you'd fight for? Can you think of anything more absurd?

PETER: Absurd? Look, I'm not going to talk to you about honor, or even try to explain it to you. Besides, it isn't a question of honor; but even if it were, you wouldn't understand.

JERRY: (contemptuously) You don't even know what you're saying, do you? This is probably the first time in your life you've had anything more trying to face than changing your cats' toilet box. Stupid! Don't you have any idea, not even the slightest, what other people *need?*

PETER: Oh, boy, listen to you; well, you don't need this bench. That's for sure.

JERRY: Yes; yes, I do.

PETER: (quivering) I've come here for years; I have hours of great pleasure, great satisfaction, right here. And that's important to a man. I'm a responsible person, and I'm a GROWNUP. This is my bench, and you have no right to take it away from me.

JERRY: Fight for it, then. Defend yourself; defend your bench.

PETER: You've *pushed* me to it. Get up and fight.

JERRY: Like a man?

PETER: (still angry) Yes, like a man, if you insist on mocking me even further.

JERRY: I'll have to give you credit for one thing: you *are* a vegetable, and a slightly nearsighted one, I think . . .

PETER: THAT'S ENOUGH. . . .

JERRY: . . . but, you know, as they say on TV all the time—you know—and I mean this, Peter, you have a certain dignity; it surprises me. . . .

PETER: STOP!

JERRY: (rises lazily) Very well, Peter, we'll battle for the bench, but we're not evenly matched. (He takes out and clicks open an ugly-looking knife)

PETER: (suddenly awakening to the reality of the situation) You *are* mad! You're stark raving mad! YOU'RE GOING TO KILL ME! (But before PETER has time to think what to do, JERRY tosses the knife at PETER's feet)

JERRY: There you go. Pick it up. You have the knife and we'll be more evenly matched.

PETER: (horrified) No!

JERRY: (rushes over to PETER, grabs him by the collar; PETER rises; their faces almost touch) Now you pick up that knife and you fight with me. You fight for your self-respect; you fight for that goddamned bench.

PETER: (struggling) No! Let . . . let go of me! He . . . Help!

JERRY: (slaps PETER on each "fight") You fight, you miserable bastard; fight for that bench; fight for your parakeets; fight for your cats, fight for your two daughters; fight for your wife; fight for your manhood, you pathetic little vegetable. (Spits in PETER's face) You couldn't even get your wife with a male child.

PETER: (breaks away, enraged) It's a matter of genetics, not manhood, you . . . you monster. (He darts down, picks up the knife and backs off a little; he is breathing heavily) I'll give you one last chance; get out of here and leave me alone! (He holds the knife with a firm arm, but far in front of him, not to attack, but to defend)

JERRY: (sighs heavily) So be it! (With a rush he charges PETER and impales himself on the knife. Tableau: For just a moment, complete silence, JERRY impaled on the knife at the end of PETER's still firm arm. Then PETER screams, pulls away, leaving the knife in JERRY. JERRY is motionless, on point. Then he, too, screams, and it must be the sound of an infuriated and fatally wounded animal. With the knife in him, he stumbles back to the bench that PETER had vacated. He crumbles there, sitting, facing PETER, his eyes wide in agony, his mouth open)

PETER: (whispering) Oh my God, oh my God, oh my God. . . . (He repeats these words many times, very rapidly)

JERRY: (JERRY is dying; but now his expression seems to change. His features relax, and while his voice varies, sometimes wrenched with pain, for the most part he seems removed from his dying. He smiles)

Thank you, Peter. I mean that, now; thank you very much.

(PETER'S *mouth drops open. He cannot move; he is transfixed*)

Oh, Peter, I was so afraid I'd drive you away. (*He laughs as best he can*) You don't know how afraid I was you'd go away and leave me. And now I'll tell you what happened at the zoo. I think . . . I think this is what happened at the zoo . . . I think. I think that while I was at the zoo I decided that I would walk north . . . northerly, rather . . . until I found you . . . or somebody . . . and I decided that I would talk to you . . . I would tell you things . . . and things that I would tell you would . . . Well, here we are. You see? Here we *are*. But . . . I don't know . . . could I have planned all this? No . . . no, I couldn't have. But I think I did. And now I've told you what you wanted to know, haven't I? And now you know all about what happened at the zoo. And now you know what you'll see in your TV, and the face I told you about . . . you remember . . . the face I told you about . . . my face, the face you see right now. Peter . . . Peter? . . . Peter . . . thank you. I came unto you (*He laughs, so faintly*) and you have comforted me. Dear Peter.

PETER: (*almost fainting*) Oh my God!

JERRY: You'd better go now. Somebody might come by, and you don't want to be here when anyone comes.

PETER: (*does not move, but begins to weep*) Oh my God, oh my God.

JERRY: (*Most faintly, now; he is very near death*) You won't be coming back here any more, Peter; you've been dispossessed. You've lost your bench, but you've defended your honor. And Peter, I'll tell you something now; you're not really a vegetable; it's all right, you're an animal. You're an animal, too. But you'd better hurry now, Peter. Hurry, you'd better go . . . see?

(JERRY *takes a handkerchief and with great effort and pain wipes the knife handle clean of fingerprints*)

Hurry away, Peter.

(PETER *begins to stagger away*)

Wait . . . wait, Peter. Take your book . . . book. Right here . . . beside me . . . on your bench . . . my bench, rather. Come . . . take your book.

(PETER *starts for the book, but retreats*)

Hurry . . . Peter.

(PETER *rushes to the bench, grabs the book, retreats*)

Very good, Peter . . . very good. Now . . . hurry away.

(PETER *hesitates for a moment, then flees, stage-left*)

Hurry away. . . . (*His eyes are closed now*) Hurry away, your parakeets are making the dinner . . . the cats . . . are setting the table . . .

PETER: (*off stage*)(*A pitiful howl*) OH MY GOD!

JERRY: (*His eyes still closed, he shakes his head and speaks; a combination of scornful mimicry and supplication*)

Oh . . . my . . . God.

(*He is dead*)

CURTAIN

DUTCHMAN (1964)

There seemed to me a kind of overwhelming sense from [the reviews of Dutchman*] that something explosive had gone down. I had a strange sensation, standing there like that. I could tell from the reviews that now my life would change again. I wasn't sure how, but I could perceive that and it sent a chill through me. I walked back home slowly, looking at my name in the newspapers, and I felt very weird indeed.*

Amiri Baraka's memories of his reaction to the reviews of *Dutchman*'s initial commercial production recapture in miniature the sense of explosive transformation that would be a hallmark of the tumultuous social changes of the later 1960s and early 1970s. In some ways emblematic of those changes, *Dutchman* sits at the confluence of a host of theatrical, dramatic, and, most important, social forces which burst forth upon the American dramatic and theatrical scene in LeRoi Jones' first widely received play. (Baraka retains his former name in referring to material produced before he changed his name in 1968.) As ideological statement and as artistic production within the framework of the **Black Arts Movement**, *Dutchman* announced to the world that a much different type of African-American drama had arrived on the American scene.

Amiri Baraka entered the world as Everett LeRoi Jones on 7 October 1934. Born in Newark, New Jersey, to Coyette LeRoy Jones, a postal worker, and Anna Lois Russ Jones, a social worker, Jones attended public schools in Newark, graduating from high school in 1951. He attended the Newark campus of Rutgers University for a year, afterwards transferring to Howard University in Washington, DC. For two years as an English major

and philosophy minor, Jones immersed himself in the intellectual life of the campus. Toward the end of his tenure at Howard, Jones, evidencing an inclination that would later become more pronounced and systematic, became increasingly disaffected with his more conservative colleagues' responses to emerging black nationalism. He left Howard and entered the U.S. Air Force for a three-year stint. He returned to New York City in 1957, quickly becoming part of the bohemian community. In 1958 he met and married Hetti Roberta Cohen, a Jewish-American woman with whom he had two daughters. For the next few years Jones worked primarily as a poet under the influence of such antibourgeois Black Mountain and Beat poets as Robert Creeley, Charles Olson, and Allen Ginsberg. In addition, he wrote essays, music, and play reviews for such avant-garde journals as *Evergreen Review* and *Kulcher*. In 1959 he began Totem Press, his own publishing company, which published his first book of verse, *Preface to a Twenty Volume Suicide Note . . . .* (1961). And in 1960, in an episode of far-ranging political and artistic import, he travelled to Cuba where he encountered Third World artists who fundamentally challenged his stance as an apolitical poet.

About 1963, Jones entered what William Harris has called (with Baraka's approval) a transitional period which marked his movement from bohemian counterculture to black revolution. Jones' influential ruminations on black music in America, *Blues People: Negro Music in White America* (1963), and his novel *The System of Dante's Hell* (1965) date from this period, as do the plays which were to bring him to wider public attention: *Dutchman, The Toilet,* and *The Slave* (all produced in 1964).

This brief transitional period was followed by a decade in which Jones devoted his energies to black nationalism, an era in which he marked his own metamorphosis by changing his name to Imamu (later dropped) Amiri Baraka. In his autobiography, Baraka points to the moment—the assassination of Malcolm X in February 1965—that galvanized him to make the final break with the bohemian culture of Greenwich Village and depart for the blackness of Harlem. The riots in the Watts section of Los Angeles the following summer confirmed his new dedication to black nationalism. After a year in Harlem (during which time he formed the short-lived but influential Black Arts Repertory Theatre and School), Baraka returned to his native Newark. There, in 1966, he married Sylvia Robinson (who subsequently changed her name to Amina Baraka) and alternatively engaged in transforming local politics, in developing aesthetic pronouncements of what would become known as the Black Arts Movement, and in putting into practice a new, highly ideological art designed to speak directly from and to the African-American experience. In such poetry as *Black Magic* (1969) and such **agitprop** plays as *Great Goodness of Life (A Coon Show)* (1967), *Madheart* (1967), and *Police* (1968), Baraka increasingly rejected the aesthetics of traditional Western representational drama in favor of a more ritualistic drama designed to generate a collective emotional response and spur action within the African-American community.

Since the middle 1970s, Baraka's writings have been grounded in a Third-World Marxist-Leninist ideology. Explaining his ideological shift, Baraka has stated:

> I think fundamentally my intentions are similar to those I had when I was a Nationalist. That might seem contradictory, but they were similar in the sense I see art as a weapon, and a weapon of revolution. It's just now . . . I define revolution in Marxist terms. . . . I came to my Marxist view as a result of having struggled as a Nationalist and found certain dead ends theoretically and ideologically, as far as

Nationalism was concerned, and had to reach out for a communist ideology.

Such collections of poetry as *Hard Facts* (1975) and *Poetry for the Advanced* (1979) and plays such as *What Was the Relationship of the Lone Ranger to the Means of Production?* (1979) and *Boy and Tarzan Appear in a Clearing* (1981) reveal Baraka's insistence upon turning his talents to what many critics have argued is a more systematic but less emotionally immediate art.

Though written before Baraka had entered his active black nationalist phase or espoused the tenets which would become the hallmarks of the black aesthetic, *Dutchman* is nevertheless best understood in terms of those two intimately related phenomena. The intricacies—both political and aesthetic—of the Black Arts Movement as presented in Addison Gayle's seminal collection *The Black Aesthetic* are obviously beyond the scope of this introduction. However, a few general observations might prove useful. First, the Black Arts Movement saw itself as the aesthetic wing of a revolution against oppressive white Western civilization, a culture which had failed to acknowledge the black experience as worthy of artistic consideration. Thus, according to black nationalists, the primary duty of black art was to facilitate the emergence of a black nation. As Ron Karenga succinctly put it, "Black art must expose the enemy, praise the people, and support the revolution." Second, black art was to embody a new, black aesthetic, one which emphasized the artist's relationship not to an abstract world of universals but to the community which collectively should provide the artist's subject matter. Ultimately, the Black Arts Movement added a third criterion for black art. Having earlier motivated the audience to seek change, it must, again in Karenga's words, "be committing"—a means of reaffirming the artist's and audience's pledge to bring about change. The implications for drama are perhaps put best by Baraka himself in "The Revolutionary Theatre" (1964):

> what we show must cause the blood to rush, so that prerevolutionary temperaments will

be bathed in this blood, and it will cause their deepest souls to move, and they will find themselves tensed and clenched, even ready to die, at what the soul has been taught. We will scream and cry, murder, run through the streets in agony, if it means some soul will be moved.

Despite its performance date and the fact that the play was first commercially mounted at Edward Albee's Cherry Lane Theatre and opened, thus, to an integrated audience, *Dutchman* has many of the features that would come to be associated with plays of the Black Arts Movement. First, its subject matter is deliberately focused on a black issue. *Dutchman* is clearly meant to express Baraka's vision of the irredeemable social oppression and death that is the black fate in white America. And the unbridgeable gulf between African-American and white experience dramatized in the play's action speaks most resonantly to African Americans and implicitly argues for a political response for black nationalism.

Second, in its dramatic style the play evidences the beginnings of the process that would eventually lead Baraka to repudiate traditional mimetic representation in favor of a more accessible, communal, and participatory drama. The play's title—suggesting at once the legend of the Flying Dutchman and the Dutch traders who brought slaves to the New World—hints at the mythic quality of the action. Written as a one-act parable in two scenes, *Dutchman* anatomizes the destruction of Clay, a middle-class African American, at the hands of Lula, a white, demonic seductress. While Robert Hooks and Jennifer West (the Clay and Lula of the Cherry Lane production) were both praised for their portrayals, neither character is individualized, for this is not a play designed for character exploration. As Baraka has noted, his interest in drama during this period stemmed from his desire for an "action literature, where one has to put characters upon a stage and make them living metaphors." Like Albee's Peter and Jerry, Clay and Lula are designed as poles in a philosophical

discussion. Unlike Albee's pair, however, both Clay and Lula are representative of historically determined racial groups, not metaphysical alternatives to a common experience.

Finally, in its use of language *Dutchman* foreshadows Baraka's later plays. Clay's carefully crafted *petit bourgeois* discourse gives way in his final outburst to a violent reappropriation of elements of black idiom that Lula has attempted to co-opt. In its deliberate vulgarity, in its explosive emotionality, and in its reliance upon dialect (ironically brought into the play by Lula), *Dutchman* points the way toward the black audience pieces of the black nationalist period in which these elements would be transformed from devices utilized for their shock value into artistic means of solidifying linguistic links between the play and its audiences. The words and phrases of the community would, in these later plays, become the language of art.

Though Baraka has written many more pieces in the last 30 years, *Dutchman* remains his most widely known play with general theatre audiences. While its reliance upon Western aesthetic assumptions distinguishes it from his later, more thoroughly black nationalistic pieces, *Dutchman* established Baraka as a major force within American drama and paved the way for black nationalist theatre. Perhaps its continuing power arises from its mythic frame which links it to the ghostly ships that haunt our imaginations. More likely, the racial conflict at the play's core seems sadly still part of our national subterranean life. Hurtling through history we have not yet found a way of putting racism off the train.

WORKS CONSULTED

Baraka, Amiri. *The autobiography of Leroi Jones/Amiri Baraka.* New York: Freundlich Books, 1984.

Benston, Kimberly, ed. *Imamu Amiri Baraka (LeRoi Jones): A Collection of Critical Essays.* Englewood Cliffs, NJ: Prentice-Hall, 1978.

———. *Baraka: The Renegade and the Mask.* New Haven: Yale University Press, 1976.

Brown, Lloyd W. *Amiri Baraka.* Boston: Twayne, 1980.

Fox, Robert Elliot. *Conscientious Sorcerers: The Black Postmodernist Fiction of LeRoi Jones/Amiri Baraka, Ishmael Reed, and Samuel R. Delany.* New York: Greenwood Press, 1987.

Gayle, Addison, Jr., ed. *The Black Aesthetic.* New York: Doubleday, 1971.

Gwynne, James B., ed. *Amiri Baraka: The Kaleidoscopic Torch.* New York: Steppingstones Press, 1985.

Harris, William J., ed. *The LeRoi Jones/Amiri Baraka Reader.* New York: Thunder's Mouth Press, 1991.

Hay, Samuel A. *African American Theatre: A Historical and Critical Analysis.* Cambridge, MA: Cambridge University Press, 1994.

Hudson, Theodore. *From LeRoi Jones to Amiri Baraka: The Literary Works.* Durham, NC: Duke University Press, 1973.

Sollors, Werner. *Amiri Baraka/LeRoi Jones: The Quest for a "Populist Modernism."* New York: Columbia University Press, 1978.

C H A R A C T E R S

CLAY .... twenty-year-old Negro

LULA .... thirty-year-old white woman

RIDERS OF COACH .... white and black

YOUNG NEGRO

CONDUCTOR

In the flying underbelly of the city. Steaming hot, and summer on top, outside. Underground. The subway heaped in modern myth.

Opening scene is a man sitting in a subway seat, holding a magazine but looking vacantly just above its wilting pages. Occasionally he looks blankly toward the window on his right. Dim lights and darkness whistling by against the glass. (Or paste the lights, as admitted props, right on the subway windows. Have them move, even dim and flicker. But give the sense of speed. Also stations, whether the train is stopped or the glitter and activity of these stations merely flashes by the windows.)

The man is sitting alone. That is, only his seat is visible, though the rest of the car is outfitted as a complete subway car. But only his seat is shown. There might be, for a time, as the play begins, a loud scream of the actual train. And it can recur throughout the play, or continue on a lower key once the dialogue starts.

The train slows after a time, pulling to a brief stop at one of the stations. The man looks idly up, until he sees a woman's face staring at him through the window; when it realizes that the man has noticed the face, it begins very premeditatedly to smile. The man smiles too, for a moment, without a trace of self-consciousness. Almost an instinctive though undesirable response. Then a kind of awkwardness or embarrassment sets in, and the man makes to look away, is further embarrassed, so he brings back his eyes to where the face was, but by now the train is moving again, and the face would seem to be left behind by the way the man turns his head to look back through the other windows at the slowly fading platform. He smiles then; more comfortably confident, hoping perhaps that his memory of this brief encounter will be pleasant. And then he is idle again.

Scene I

Train roars. Lights flash outside the windows. LULA enters from the rear of the car in bright, skimpy summer clothes and sandals. She carries a net bag full of paper books, fruit, and other anonymous articles. She *is wearing sunglasses, which she pushes up on her forehead from time to time.* LULA *is a tall, slender, beautiful woman with long red hair hanging straight down her back, wearing only loud lipstick in somebody's good taste. She is eating an apple, very daintily. Coming down the car toward* CLAY.

She stops beside CLAY'S *seat and hangs languidly from the strap, still managing to eat the apple. It is apparent that she is going to sit in the seat next to* CLAY, *and that she is only waiting for him to notice her before she sits.*

CLAY *sits as before, looking just beyond his magazine, now and again pulling the magazine slowly back and forth in front of his face in a hopeless effort to fan himself. Then he sees the woman hanging there beside him and he looks up into her face, smiling quizzically.*

LULA: Hello.
CLAY: Uh, hi're you?
LULA: I'm going to sit down. . . . O.K.?
CLAY: Sure.
LULA: (*Swings down onto the seat, pushing her legs straight out as if she is very weary*) Ooooof! Too much weight.
CLAY: Ha, doesn't look like much to me.
        (*Leaning back against the window, a little surprised and maybe stiff*)
LULA: It's so anyway.
        (*And she moves her toes in the sandals, then pulls her right leg up on the left knee, better to inspect the bottoms of the sandals and the back of her heel. She appears for a second not to notice that* CLAY *is sitting next to her or that she has spoken to him just a second before.* CLAY *looks at the magazine, then out the black window. As he does this, she turns very quickly toward him*)
        Weren't you staring at me through the window?
CLAY: (*wheeling around and very much stiffened*) What?
LULA: Weren't you staring at me through the window? At the last stop?
CLAY: Staring at you? What do you mean?
LULA: Don't you know what staring means?

CLAY: I saw you through the window . . . if that's what it means. I don't know if I was staring. Seems to me you were staring through the window at me.
LULA: I was. But only after I'd turned around and saw you staring through that window down in the vicinity of my ass and legs.
CLAY: Really?
LULA: Really. I guess you were just taking those idle potshots. Nothing else to do. Run your mind over people's flesh.
CLAY: Oh boy. Wow, now I admit I was looking in your direction. But the rest of that weight is yours.
LULA: I suppose.
CLAY: Staring through train windows is weird business. Much weirder than staring very sedately at abstract asses.
LULA: That's why I came looking through the window . . . so you'd have more than that to go on. I even smiled at you.
CLAY: That's right.
LULA: I even got into this train, going some other way than mine. Walked down the aisle . . . searching you out.
CLAY: Really? That's pretty funny.
LULA: That's pretty funny. . . . God, you're dull.
CLAY: Well, I'm sorry, lady, but I really wasn't prepared for party talk.
LULA: No, you're not. What are you prepared for? (*Wrapping the apple core in a Kleenex and dropping it on the floor*)
CLAY: (*takes her conversation as pure sex talk. He turns to confront her squarely with this idea*) I'm prepared for anything. How about you?
LULA: (*laughing loudly and cutting it off abruptly*) What do you think you're doing?
CLAY: What?
LULA: You think I want to pick you up, get you to take me somewhere and screw me, huh?
CLAY: Is that the way I look?
LULA: You look like you been trying to grow a beard. That's exactly what you look like. You look like you live in New Jersey with your parents and are trying to grow a beard. That's what.

You look like you've been reading Chinese po-
etry and drinking lukewarm sugarless tea.
(Laughs, uncrossing and recrossing her legs)
You look like death eating a soda cracker.

CLAY: *(cocking his head from one side to the other,
embarrassed and trying to make some comeback,
but also intrigued by what the woman is saying
. . . even the sharp city coarseness of her voice,
which is still a kind of gentle sidewalk throb)*
Really? I look like all that?

LULA: Not all of it.
*(She feigns a seriousness to cover an actual
somber tone)*
I lie a lot.
(Smiling)
It helps me control the world.

CLAY: *(relieved and laughing louder than the humor)* Yeah, I bet.

LULA: But it's true, most of it, right? Jersey? Your
bumpy neck?

CLAY: How'd you know all that? Huh? Really, I
mean about Jersey . . . and even the beard. I
met you before? You know Warren Enright?

LULA: You tried to make it with your sister when
you were ten.
*(CLAY leans back hard against the back of the
seat, his eyes opening now, still trying to look
amused)*
But I succeeded a few weeks ago.
(She starts to laugh again)

CLAY: What're you talking about? Warren tell you
that? You're a friend of Georgia's?

LULA: I told you I lie. I don't know your sister. I
don't know Warren Enright.

CLAY: You mean you're just picking these things
out of the air?

LULA: Is Warren Enright a tall skinny black black
boy with a phony English accent?

CLAY: I figured you knew him.

LULA: But I don't. I just figured you would know
somebody like that.
(Laughs)

CLAY: Yeah, yeah.

LULA: You're probably on your way to his house
now.

CLAY: That's right.

LULA: *(putting her hand on CLAY's closer knee,
drawing it from the knee up to the thigh's hinge,
then removing it, watching his face very closely,
and continuing to laugh, perhaps more gently
than before)* Dull, dull, dull. I bet you think I'm
exciting.

CLAY: You're O.K.

LULA: Am I exciting you now?

CLAY: Right. That's not what's supposed to happen?

LULA: How do I know?
*(She returns her hand, without moving it, then
takes it away and plunges it in her bag to draw
out an apple)*
You want this?

CLAY: Sure.

LULA: *(she gets one out of the bag for herself)* Eating apples together is always the first step. Or
walking up uninhabited Seventh Avenue in the
twenties on weekends.
*(Bites and giggles, glancing at CLAY and speak-
ing in loose singsong)*
Can get you involved . . . boy! Get us involved. Um-huh.
(Mock seriousness)
Would you like to get involved with me, Mister
Man?

CLAY: *(trying to be as flippant as LULA, whack-
ing happily at the apple)* Sure. Why not? A
beautiful woman like you. Huh, I'd be a fool
not to.

LULA: And I bet you're sure you know what you're
talking about.
*(Taking him a little roughly by the wrist, so he
cannot eat the apple, then shaking the wrist)*
I bet you're sure of almost everything anybody
ever asked you about . . . right?
(Shakes his wrist harder)
Right?

CLAY: Yeah, right. . . . Wow, you're pretty strong,
you know? Whatta you, a lady wrestler or something?

LULA: What's wrong with lady wrestlers? And
don't answer because you never knew any. Huh.
(Cynically)

That's for sure. They don't have any lady wrestlers in that part of Jersey. That's for sure.

CLAY: Hey, you still haven't tole me how you know so much about me.

LULA: I told you I didn't know anything about *you* . . . you're a well-known type.

CLAY: Really?

LULA: Or at least I know the type very well. And your skinny English friend too.

CLAY: Anonymously?

LULA: (*settles back in seat, single-mindedly finishing her apple and humming snatches of rhythm and blues song*) What?

CLAY: Without knowing us specifically?

LULA: Oh boy.
(*Looking quickly at* CLAY)
What a face. You know, you could be a handsome man.

CLAY: I can't argue with you.

LULA: (*vague, off-center response*) What?

CLAY: (*raising his voice, thinking the train noise has drowned part of his sentence*) I can't argue with you.

LULA: My hair is turning gray. A gray hair for each year and type I've come through.

CLAY: Why do you want to sound so old?

LULA: But it's always gentle when it starts.
(*Attention drifting*)
Hugged against tenements, day or night.

CLAY: What?

LULA: (*refocusing*) Hey, why don't you take me to that party you're going to?

CLAY: You must be a friend of Warren's to know about the party.

LULA: Wouldn't you like to take me to the party?
(*Imitates clinging vine*)
Oh, come on, ask me to your party.

CLAY: Of course I'll ask you to come with me to the party. And I'll bet you're a friend of Warren's.

LULA: Why not be a friend of Warren's? Why not?
(*Taking his arm*)
Have you asked me yet?

CLAY: How can I ask you when I don't know your name?

LULA: Are you talking to my name?

CLAY: What is it, a secret?

LULA: I'm Lena the Hyena.

CLAY: The famous woman poet?

LULA: Poetess! The same!

CLAY: Well, you know so much about me . . . what's my name?

LULA: Morris the Hyena.

CLAY: The famous woman poet?

LULA: The same.
(*Laughing and going into her bag*)
You want another apple?

CLAY: Can't make it, lady. I only have to keep one doctor away a day.

LULA: I bet your name is . . . something like . . . uh, Gerald or Walter. Huh?

CLAY: God, no.

LULA: Lloyd, Norman? One of those hopeless colored names creeping out of New Jersey. Leonard? Gag. . . .

CLAY: Like Warren?

LULA: Definitely. Just exactly like Warren. Or Everett.

CLAY: Gag. . . .

LULA: Well, for sure, it's not Willie.

CLAY: It's Clay.

LULA: Clay? Really? Clay what?

CLAY: Take your pick. Jackson, Johnson, or Williams.

LULA: Oh really? Good for you. But it's got to be Williams. You're too pretentious to be a Jackson or Johnson.

CLAY: Thass right.

LULA: But Clay's O.K.

CLAY: So's Lena.

LULA: It's Lula.

CLAY: Oh?

LULA: Lula the Hyena.

CLAY: Very good.

LULA: (*starts laughing again*) Now you say to me, "Lula, Lula, why don't you go to this party with me tonight?" It's your turn, and let those be your lines.

CLAY: Lula, why don't you go to this party with me tonight, Huh?

LULA: Say my name twice before you ask, and no huh's.

CLAY: Lula, Lula, why don't you go to this party with me tonight?

LULA: I'd like to go, Clay, but how can you ask me to go when you barely know me?

CLAY: That is strange, isn't it?

LULA: What kind of reaction is that? You're supposed to say, "Aw, come on, we'll get to know each other better at the party."

CLAY: That's pretty corny.

LULA: What are you into anyway?
(Looking at him half sullenly but still amused)
What thing are you playing at, Mister? Mister Clay Williams?
(Grabs his thigh, up near the crotch)
What are *you* thinking about?

CLAY: Watch it now, you're gonna excite me for real.

LULA: *(taking her hand away and throwing her apple core through the window)* I bet.
(She slumps in the seat and is heavily silent)

CLAY: I thought you knew everything about me? What happened?
(LULA looks at him, then looks slowly away, then over where the other aisle would be. Noise of the train. She reaches in her bag and pulls out one of the paper books. She puts it on her leg and thumbs the pages listlessly. CLAY cocks his head to see the title of the book. Noise of the train. LULA flips pages and her eyes drift. Both remain silent)
Are you going to the party with me, Lula?

LULA: *(bored and not even looking)* I don't even know you.

CLAY: You said you know my type.
(Strangely irritated)
Don't get smart with me, Buster. I know you like the palm of my hand.

CLAY: The one you eat the apples with?

LULA: Yeh. And the one I open doors late Saturday evening with. That's my door. Up at the top of the stairs. Five flights. Above a lot of Italians and lying Americans. And scrape carrots with. Also . . .
(looks at him)

the same hand I unbutton my dress with, or let my skirt fall down. Same hand. Lover.

CLAY: Are you angry about anything? Did I say something wrong?

LULA: Everything you say is wrong.
(Mock smile)
That's what makes you so attractive. Ha. In that funnybook jacket with all the buttons.
(More animate, taking hold of his jacket)
What've you got the jacket and tie on in all this heat for? And why're you wearing a jacket and tie like that? Did your people ever burn witches or start revolutions over the price of tea? Boy, those narrow-shoulder clothes come from a tradition you ought to feel oppressed by. A three-button suit. What right do you have to be wearing a three-button suit and striped tie? Your grandfather was a slave, he didn't go to Harvard.

CLAY: My grandfather was a night watchman.

LULA: And you went to a colored college where everybody thought they were Averell Harriman.

CLAY: All except me.

LULA: And who did you think you were? Who do you think you are now?

CLAY: *(laughs as if to make light of the whole trend of the conversation)* Well, in college I thought I was Baudelaire. But I've slowed down since.

LULA: I bet you never once thought you were a black nigger.
(Mock serious, then she howls with laughter. CLAY is stunned but after initial reaction, he quickly tries to appreciate the humor. LULA almost shrieks)
A black Baudelaire.

CLAY: That's right.

LULA: Boy, are you corny. I take back what I said before. Everything you say is not wrong. It's perfect. You should be on television.

CLAY: You act like you're on television already.

LULA: That's because I'm an actress.

CLAY: I thought so.

LULA: Well, you're wrong. I'm no actress. I told you I always lie. I'm nothing, honey, and don't you ever forget it.
(Lighter)

Although my mother was a Communist. The only person in my family ever to amount to anything.

CLAY: My mother was a Republican.

LULA: And your father voted for the man rather than the party.

CLAY: Right!

LULA: Yea for him. Yea, yea for him.

CLAY: Yea!

LULA: And yea for America where he is free to vote for the mediocrity of his choice! Yea!

CLAY: Yea!

LULA: And yea for both your parents who even though they differ about so crucial a matter as the body politic still forged a union of love and sacrifice that was destined to flower at the birth of the noble Clay . . . what's your middle name?

CLAY: Clay.

LULA: A union of love and sacrifice that was destined to flower at the birth of the noble Clay Clay Williams. Yea! And most of all yea yea for you, Clay Clay. The Black Baudelaire! Yes!
(And with knifelike cynicism)
My Christ. My Christ.

CLAY: Thank you, ma'am.

LULA: May the people accept you as a ghost of the future. And love you, that you might not kill them when you can.

CLAY: What?

LULA: You're a murderer, Clay, and you know it.
(Her voice darkening with significance)
You know goddamn well what I mean.

CLAY: I do?

LULA: So we'll pretend the air is light and full of perfume.

CLAY: *(sniffing at her blouse)* It is.

LULA: And we'll pretend the people cannot see you. That is, the citizens. And that you are free of your own history. And I am free of my history. We'll pretend that we are both anonymous beauties smashing along through the city's entrails.
(She yells as loud as she can)
GROOVE!

B L A C K

Scene II

Scene is the same as before, though now there are other seats visible in the car. And throughout the scene other people get on the subway. There are maybe one or two seated in the car as the scene opens, though neither CLAY *nor* LULA *notices them.* CLAY'S *tie is open.* LULA *is hugging his arm.*

CLAY: The party!

LULA: I know it'll be something good. You can come in with me, looking casual and significant. I'll be strange, haughty, and silent, and walk with long slow strides.

CLAY: Right.

LULA: When you get drunk, pat me once, very lovingly on the flanks, and I'll look at you cryptically, licking my lips.

CLAY: It sounds like something we can do.

LULA: You'll go around talking to young men about your mind, and to old men about your plans. If you meet a very close friend who is also with someone like me, we can stand together, sipping our drinks and exchanging codes of lust. The atmosphere will be slithering in love and half-love and very open moral decision.

CLAY: Great. Great.

LULA: And everyone will pretend they don't know your name, and then . . .
(She pauses heavily)
later, when they have to, they'll claim a friendship that denies your sterling character.

CLAY: *(kissing her neck and fingers)* And then what?

LULA: Then? Well, then we'll go down the street, late night, eating apples and winding very deliberately toward my house.

CLAY: Deliberately?

LULA: I mean, we'll look in all the shopwindows, and make fun of the queers. Maybe we'll meet a Jewish Buddhist and flatten his conceits over some pretentious coffee.

CLAY: In honor of whose God?

LULA: Mine.

CLAY: Who is . . . ?

LULA: Me . . . and you?

CLAY: A corporate Godhead.

LULA: Exactly. Exactly.

(Notices one of the other people entering)

CLAY: Go on with the chronicle. Then what happens to us?

LULA: (a mild depression, but she still makes her description triumphant and increasingly direct) To my house, of course.

CLAY: Of course.

LULA: And up the narrow steps of the tenement.

CLAY: You live in a tenement?

LULA: Wouldn't live anywhere else. Reminds me specifically of my novel form of insanity.

CLAY: Up the tenement stairs.

LULA: And with my apple-eating hand I push open the door and lead you, my tender big-eyed prey, into my . . . God, what can I call it . . . into my hovel.

CLAY: Then what happens?

LULA: After the dancing and games, after the long drinks and long walks, the real fun begins.

CLAY: Ah, the real fun.

(Embarrassed, in spite of himself)

Which is . . . ?

LULA: (laughs at him) Real fun in the dark house. Hah! Real fun in the dark house, high up above the street and the ignorant cowboys. I lead you in, holding your wet hand gently in my hand . . .

CLAY: Which is not wet?

LULA: Which is dry as ashes.

CLAY: And cold?

LULA: Don't think you'll get out of your responsibility that way. It's not cold at all. You Fascist! Into my dark living room. Where we'll sit and talk endlessly, endlessly.

CLAY: About what?

LULA: About what? About your manhood, what do you think? What do you think we've been talking about all this time?

CLAY: Well, I didn't know it was that. That's for sure. Every other thing in the world but that. (Notices another person entering, looks quickly, almost involuntarily, up and down the car, seeing the other people in the car)

Hey, I didn't even notice when those people got on.

LULA: Yeah, I know.

CLAY: Man, this subway is slow.

LULA: Yeah, I know.

CLAY: Well, go on. We were talking about my manhood.

LULA: We still are. All the time.

CLAY: We were in your living room.

LULA: My dark living room. Talking endlessly.

CLAY: About my manhood.

LULA: I'll make you a map of it. Just as soon as we get to my house.

CLAY: Well, that's great.

LULA: One of the things we do while we talk. And screw.

CLAY: (trying to make his smile broader and less shaky) We finally got there.

LULA: And you'll call my rooms black as a grave. You'll say, "This place is like Juliet's tomb."

CLAY: (laughs) I might.

LULA: I know. You've probably said it before.

CLAY: And is that all? The whole grand tour?

LULA: Not all. You'll say to me very close to my face, many, many times, you'll say, even whisper, that you love me.

CLAY: Maybe I will.

LULA: And you'll be lying.

CLAY: I wouldn't lie about something like that.

LULA: Hah. It's the only kind of thing you will lie about. Especially if you think it'll keep me alive.

CLAY: Keep you alive? I don't understand.

LULA: (bursting out laughing, but too shrilly) Don't understand? Well, don't look at me. It's the path I take, that's all. Where both feet take me when I set them down. One in front of the other.

CLAY: Morbid. Morbid. You sure you're not an actress? All that self-aggrandizement.

LULA: Well, I told you I wasn't an actress . . . but I also told you I lie all the time. Draw your own conclusions.

CLAY: And is that all of our lives together you've described? There's no more?

LULA: I've told you all I know. Or almost all.

CLAY: There's no funny parts?

LULA: I thought it was all funny.

CLAY: But you mean peculiar, not ha-ha.

LULA: You don't know what I mean.

CLAY: Well, tell me the almost part then. You said almost all. What else? I want the whole story.

LULA: (*searching aimlessly through her bag. She begins to talk breathlessly, with a light and silly tone*) All stories are whole stories. All of 'em. Our whole story . . . nothing but change. How could things go on like that forever? Huh?
(*Slaps him on the shoulder, begins finding things in her bag, taking them out and throwing them over her shoulder into the aisle*)
Except I do go on as I do. Apples and long walks with deathless intelligent lovers. But you mix it up. Look out the window, all the time. Turning pages. Change change change. Till, shit, I don't know you. Wouldn't, for that matter. You're too serious. I bet you're even too serious to be psychoanalyzed. Like all those Jewish poets from Yonkers, who leave their mothers looking for other mothers, or others' mothers, on whose baggy tits they lay their fumbling heads. Their poems are always funny, and all about sex.

CLAY: They sound great. Like movies.

LULA: But you change.
(*Blankly*)
And things work on you till you hate them.
(*More people come into the train. They come closer to the couple, some of them not sitting, but swinging drearily on the straps, staring at the two with uncertain interest*)

CLAY: Wow. All these people, so suddenly. They must all come from the same place.

LULA: Right. That they do.

CLAY: Oh? You know about them too?

LULA: Oh yeah. About them more than I know about you. Do they frighten you?

CLAY: Frighten me? Why should they frighten me?

LULA: 'Cause you're an escaped nigger.

CLAY: Yeah?

LULA: 'Cause you crawled through the wire and made tracks to my side.

CLAY: Wire?

LULA: Don't they have wire around plantations?

CLAY: You must be Jewish. All you can think about is wire. Plantations didn't have any wire. Plantations were big open whitewashed places like heaven, and everybody on 'em was grooved to be there. Just strummin' and hummin' all day.

LULA: Yes, yes.

CLAY: And that's how the blues was born.

LULA: Yes, yes. And that's how the blues was born. (*Begins to make up a song that becomes quickly hysterical. As she sings she rises from her seat, still throwing things out of her bag into the aisle, beginning a rhythmical shudder and twistlike wiggle, which she continues up and down the aisle, bumping into many of the standing people and tripping over the feet of those sitting. Each time she runs into a person she lets out a very vicious piece of profanity, wiggling and stepping all the time*)
And that's how the blues was born. Yes. Yes. Son of a bitch, get out of the way. Yes. Quack. Yes. Yes. And that's how the blues was born. Ten little niggers sitting on a limb, but none of them ever looked like him.
(*Points to* CLAY, *returns toward the seat, with her hands extended for him to rise and dance with her*)
And that's how blues was born. Yes. Come on, Clay. Let's do the nasty. Rub bellies. Rub bellies.

CLAY: (*waves his hands to refuse. He is embarrassed, but determined to get a kick out of the proceedings*) Hey, what was in those apples? Mirror, mirror on the wall, who's the fairest one of all? Snow White, baby, and don't you forget it.

LULA: (*grabbing for his hands, which he draws away*) Come on, Clay. Let's rub bellies on the train. The nasty. The nasty. Do the gritty grind, like your ol' rag-head mammy. Grind till you lose your mind. Shake it, shake it, shake it, shake it! OOOOweeee! Come on, Clay. Let's do the choo-choo train shuffle, the navel scratcher.

CLAY: Hey, you coming on like the lady who smoked up her grass skirt.

LULA: (*becoming annoyed that he will not dance, and becoming more animated as if to embarrass him still further*) Come on, Clay . . . let's do the thing. Uhh! Uhh! Clay! Clay! You middle-class black bastard. Forget your social-working mother for a few seconds and let's knock stomachs. Clay, you liver-lipped white man. You would-be Christian. You ain't no nigger, you're just a dirty white man. Get up, Clay. Dance with me, Clay.

CLAY: Lula! Sit down, now. Be cool.

LULA: *(mocking him, in wild dance)* Be cool. Be cool. That's all you know . . . shaking that wildroot cream-oil on your knotty head, jackets buttoning up to your chin, so full of white man's words. Christ! God! Get up and scream at these people. Like scream meaningless shit in these hopeless faces.

(She screams at people in train, still dancing)

Red trains cough Jewish underwear for keeps! Expanding smells of silence. Gravy snot whistling like sea birds. Clay. Clay, you got to break out. Don't sit there dying the way they want you to die. Get up.

CLAY: Oh, sit the fuck down.

(He moves to restrain her)

Sit down, goddamn it.

LULA: *(twisting out of his reach)* Screw yourself, Uncle Tom. Thomas Woolly-Head.

(Begins to dance a kind of jig, mocking CLAY with loud forced humor)

There is Uncle Tom . . . I mean, Uncle Thomas Woolly-Head. With old white matted mane. He hobbles on his wooden cane. Old Tom. Old Tom. Let the white man hump his ol' mama, and he jes' shuffle off in the woods and hide his gentle gray head. Ol' Thomas Woolly-Head.

(Some of the other riders are laughing now. A drunk gets up and joins LULA in her dance, singing, as best he can, her "song." CLAY gets up out of his seat and visibly scans the faces of the other riders)

CLAY: Lula! Lula!

(She is dancing and turning, still shouting as loud as she can. The drunk too is shouting, and waving his hands wildly)

Lula . . . you dumb bitch. Why don't you stop it?

(He rushes half stumbling from his seat, and grabs one of her flailing arms)

LULA: Let me go! You black son of a bitch.

(She struggles against him)

Let me go! Help!

(CLAY is dragging her towards her seat, and the drunk seeks to interfere. He grabs CLAY around the shoulders and begins wrestling with him. CLAY clubs the drunk to the floor without releasing LULA, who is still screaming. CLAY finally gets her to the seat and throws her into it)

CLAY: Now you shut the hell up.

(Grabbing her shoulders)

Just shut up. You don't know what you're talking about. You don't know anything. So just keep your stupid mouth closed.

LULA: You're afraid of white people. And your father was. Uncle Tom Big Lip!

CLAY: *(slaps her as hard as he can, across the mouth. LULA's head bangs against the back of the seat. When she raises it again, CLAY slaps her again)* Now shut up and let me talk.

(He turns toward the other riders, some of whom are sitting on the edge of their seats. The drunk is on one knee, rubbing his head, and singing softly the same song. He shuts up too when he sees CLAY watching him. The others go back to newspapers or stare out the windows)

Shit, you don't have any sense, Lula, nor feelings either. I could murder you now. Such a tiny ugly throat. I could squeeze it flat, and watch you turn blue, on a humble. For dull kicks. And all these weak-faced ofays squatting around here, staring over their papers at me. Murder them too. Even if they expected it. That man there . . .

(Points to well-dressed man)

I could rip that *Times* right out of his hand, as skinny and middle-classed as I am, I could rip that paper out of his hand and just as easily rip out his throat. It takes no great effort. For what? To kill you soft idiots? You don't understand anything but luxury.

LULA: You fool!

CLAY: *(pushing her against the seat)* I'm not telling you again, Tallulah Bankhead! Luxury. In your face and your fingers. You telling me what I ought to do.

(Sudden scream frightening the whole coach)

Well, don't! Don't you tell me anything! If I'm a middle-class fake white man . . . let me be. And let me be in the way I want.

(Through his teeth)

I'll rip your lousy breasts off! Let me be who I feel like being. Uncle Tom. Thomas. Whoever. It's none of your business. You don't know anything except what's there for you to see. An act. Lies. Device. Not the pure heart, the pumping black heart. You don't ever know that. And I sit here, in this buttoned-up suit, to keep myself from cutting all your throats. I mean wantonly. You great liberated whore! You fuck some black man, and right away you're an expert on black people. What a lotta shit that is. The only thing you know is that you come if he bangs you hard enough. And that's all. The belly rub? You wanted to do the belly rub? Shit, you don't even know how. You don't know how. That ol' dipty-dip shit you do, rolling your ass like an elephant. That's not my kind of belly rub. Belly rub is not Queens. Belly rub is dark places, with big hats and overcoats held up with one arm. Belly rub hates you. Old bald-headed four-eyed ofays popping their fingers . . . and don't know yet what they're doing. They say, "I love Bessie Smith." And don't even understand that Bessie Smith is saying, "Kiss my ass, kiss my black unruly ass." Before love, suffering, desire, anything you can explain, she's saying, and very plainly, "Kiss my black ass." And if you don't know that, it's you that's doing the kissing.

Charlie Parker? Charlie Parker. All the hip white boys scream for Bird. And Bird saying, "Up your ass, feebleminded ofay! Up your ass." And they sit there talking about the tortured genius of Charlie Parker. Bird would've played not a note of music if he just walked up to East Sixty-seventh Street and killed the first ten white people he saw. Not a note! And I'm the great would-be poet. Yes. That's right! Poet. Some kind of bastard literature . . . all it needs is a simple knife thrust. Just let me bleed you, you loud whore, and one poem vanished. A whole people of neurotics, struggling to keep from being sane. And the only thing that would cure the neurosis would be your murder. Simple as that. I mean if I murdered you, then other white people would begin to understand me. You understand? No. I guess not. If Bessie Smith had killed some white people she wouldn't have needed that music. She could have talked very straight and plain about the world. No metaphors. No grunts. No wiggles in the dark of her soul. Just straight two and two are four. Money. Power. Luxury. Like that. All of them. Crazy niggers turning their backs on sanity. When all it needs is that simple act. Murder. Just murder! Would make us all sane.

(Suddenly weary)

Ahhh. Shit. But who needs it? I'd rather be a fool. Insane. Safe with my words, and no deaths, and clean, hard thoughts, urging me to new conquests. My people's madness. Hah! That's a laugh. My people. They don't need me to claim them. They got legs and arms of their own. Personal insanities. Mirrors. They don't need all those words. They don't need any defense. But listen, though, one more thing. And you tell this to your father, who's probably the kind of man who needs to know at once. So he can plan ahead. Tell him not to preach so much rationalism and cold logic to these niggers. Let them alone. Let them sing curses at you in code and see your filth as simple lack of style. Don't make the mistake, through some irresponsible surge of Christian charity, of talking too much about the advantages of Western rationalism, or the great intellectual legacy of the white man, or maybe they'll begin to listen. And then, maybe one day, you'll find they actually do understand exactly what you are talking about, all these fantasy people. All these blues people. And on that day, as sure as shit, when you really believe you can "accept" them into your fold, as half-white trusties late of the subject peoples. With no more blues, except the very old ones, and not a watermelon in sight, the great missionary heart will have triumphed, and all of those ex-coons will be stand-up Western men, with eyes for clean hard useful lives, sober, pious and sane, and they'll murder you. They'll murder you, and have very rational explanations. Very much like your own. They'll cut your throats, and drag you out to the edge of your cities so the flesh can fall away from your bones, in sanitary isolation.

LULA: *(her voice takes on a different, more businesslike quality)* I've heard enough.

CLAY: *(reaching for his books)* I bet you have. I guess I better collect my stuff and get off this train. Looks like we won't be acting out that little pageant you outlined before.

LULA: No. We won't. You're right about that, at least.
(She turns to look quickly around the rest of the car)
All right!
(The others respond)

CLAY: *(bending across the girl to retrieve his belongings)* Sorry, baby, I don't think we could make it.
(As he is bending over her, the girl brings up a small knife and plunges it into CLAY's chest. Twice. He slumps across her knees, his mouth working stupidly)

LULA: Sorry is right.
(Turning to the others in the car who have already gotten up from their seats)

Sorry is the rightest thing you've said. Get this man off me! Hurry, now!
(The others come and drag CLAY's body down the aisle)
Open the door and throw his body out.
(They throw him off)
And all of you get off at the next stop.
(LULA busies herself straightening her things. Getting everything in order. She takes out a notebook and makes a quick scribbling note. Drops it in her bag. The train apparently stops and all the others get off, leaving her alone in the coach.

Very soon a young Negro of about twenty comes into the coach, with a couple of books under his arm. He sits a few seats in back of LULA. When he is seated she turns and gives him a long slow look. He looks up from his book and drops the book on his lap. Then an old Negro conductor comes into the car, doing a sort of restrained soft shoe, and half mumbling the words of some song. He looks at the young man, briefly, with a quick greeting)

CONDUCTOR: Hey, brother!

YOUNG MAN: Hey.
(The conductor continues down the aisle with his little dance and the mumbled song. LULA turns to stare at him and follows his movements down the aisle. The conductor tips his hat when he reaches her seat, and continues out the car)

CURTAIN

T H E   T O O T H   O F   C R I M E   (1 9 7 2)

Obviously one thinks of Sam Shepard as a writer for whom the discourse of popular culture assumes a richness and density. . . . But Shepard might be considered our poet of the postmodern condition for reasons other than his use of pop discourse and pop myth. For beyond their preoccupation with popular culture Shepard's plays exhibit postmodern characteristics and address postmodern concerns.

Leonard Wilcox's view of Sam Shepard is shared by many critics both of the contemporary theatre and of a larger cultural condition describable as "postmodern." Since the early 1970s or so, **postmodernism** has been the object of intense and, at times, highly contentious debate, and an introduction to Shepard's *The Tooth of Crime* is not the place to revisit this large body of cultural criticism. Yet the terms of Wilcox's characterization of Shepard are central to charting one trajectory American drama of the 1970s and after has taken; they form, moreover, a suggestive context against which to assess Shepard's enormous contribution to American theatre. Wilcox's emphasis on Shepard's appropriations from popular culture is particularly relevant to a reading of *The Tooth of Crime.*

Wilcox takes this emphasis from, among others, the influential theoretical work of Fredric Jameson and the premise that one project of "high modernism" earlier in the century—the literary experimentation of James Joyce, T. S. Eliot, and Virginia Woolf, for example—was to separate itself from popular cultural forms. For Marxist scholar Terry Eagleton, **modernism** is "among other things a strategy whereby the work of art resists commodification"; hence, the "modernist work brackets off the referent or real historical world,

thickens its textures and deranges its forms to forestall instant consumability." Thus, to borrow a phrase from Andreas Huyssen, there exists a "great divide" between modernist *art* and the popular *commodities* mass audiences consume: films, comic books, dime novels, and television programs. Writers like Shepard, however, celebrate popular culture, indeed depend upon it for the very construction and reception of their texts. *The Tooth of Crime* is an exemplary instance of the postmodernist effacement of distinctions between high and low art—if the plays of a dramatist who has won nearly a dozen **Obies** and a Pulitzer Prize count as "high" art—drawing as they do from science fiction, rock music, and movie Westerns for their emplotment and characterization, and from the 1960s drug and Southern California car subcultures for much of their language. Explanations of postmodernism, though, involve a good deal more than the assessment of contemporary art's borrowings from the growing mass culture of the electronic "global village," as Wilcox's references to Shepard's "postmodern characteristics" and "postmodern concerns" imply. What are these, and how do they manifest themselves in *The Tooth of Crime*? In sum, what is entailed in being a "poet of the postmodern condition," and how does this relate to the perhaps more commonly received notion that Shepard is *par excellence* an exemplar of the **Off-Off Broadway** movement of the 1960s?

Samuel Shepard Rogers II (1943–   ) was born in Fort Sheridan, Illinois, and as a child lived on numerous army bases, including one on the island of Guam. After retiring from the military, his father moved his family to South Pasadena and then to Duarte, California, where the younger Shepard settled in more permanently and, apparently, quite happily on an avocado ranch complete with horses and domestic animals. Shepard's father, remembered by his son as "very strict" in an interview given shortly after *The Tooth of Crime* opened in London in 1972, loved music and played the drums in a local band. Shepard followed in his father's footsteps by playing drums himself, most famously in the rock and roll band The Holy Modal Rounders, and while attending high school in Duarte first became interested in drama and theatre. While in high school, Shepard recalls he read works of the "beat generation"— Jack Kerouac and Lawrence Ferlinghetti—and was introduced to Samuel Beckett's *Waiting for Godot.* He also attended junior college for a year and joined a touring repertory company as an actor. The experiences of his teen years—the combination of rock music, cars, films, and the rugged Western landscape—inform much of Shepard's work, his plays as well as two collections of his poetry and short prose sketches, *Hawk Moon* (1973, published in 1981) and *Motel Chronicles* (1982). "Dream Band" from *Hawk Moon* provides one example of this thematic mixture: "Jeeps in four wheel drive. Sand and beach. Endless. . . . The Beach Boys. Duarte High. . . . The Sierra Madre Mountains. The Arizona border. Dylan in shades. The ship. The missile. Rattle." And perhaps the most consistent influence from his earlier years is his father, who, foregrounded in several prose fragments in *Motel Chronicles,* resembles the fathers or absent fathers in several of Shepard's most successful plays: *Curse of the Starving Class* (1977), the Pulitzer Prize–winning *Buried Child* (1978), *True West* (1980), and *Fool for Love* (1983). In *Motel Chronicles,* Shepard visits his father's small house in the New Mexico desert, a structure filled with dusty record albums, "wall-to-wall magazine clippings" taped everywhere, and a refrigerator filled with bottles of Bourbon: "My Dad lives alone on the desert. He says he doesn't fit with people." Fragments of popular culture sustaining a lonely identity, popular music, alcohol abuse, and eccentricity in a ruptured family—this combination of elements surfaces in many of Shepard's plays.

Shepard arrived in New York in 1963 and found work as a busboy at The Village Gate, a popular jazz club. There he met Ralph Cook, founder of Theatre

Genesis, an Off-Off Broadway company, which opened in 1964 at St. Mark's Episcopal Church-in-the-Bowery. As Albert Poland and Bruce Mailman describe it, Theatre Genesis in the 1960s was "closely tied" with a subculture in which "politics and drugs" played important parts. There were "no frills" in Genesis productions, according to Poland and Mailman. "Everything is stripped away and we get right down to basics: *how to survive* in a world of political, social and ecological chaos." Shepard became one of the best-known playwrights in this subculture with such plays as *Cowboys* (1964), *The Rock Garden* (1964), *Chicago* (1965), and *Mad Dog Blues* (1965), all produced at Theatre Genesis; *Dog* (1965), *The Unseen Hand* (1969), and *Shaved Splits* (1970) at Café La MaMa (later La MaMa ETC); *Icarus's Mother* (1965) at Caffe Cino; and *La Turista* (1967) at the American Place Theatre. Shepard went on in the 1970s and early 1980s to serve as playwright-in-residence at San Francisco's Magic Theatre where *Angel City* (1976) and *Fool for Love* premiered; to write such plays as *A Lie of the Mind* (1985) and *States of Shock* (1991), and screenplays for *Paris, Texas* (1984, winner of the Palm D'Or at the 1985 Cannes Film Festival) and *Far North* (1988); and to act in such films as *Raggedy Man* (1981), *Frances* (1982, with his longtime companion Jessica Lange), *The Right Stuff* (1983, for which he was nominated for an Academy Award), *Crimes of the Heart* (1986, based on Beth Henley's play), and *The Pelican Brief* (1993). He was elected to the American Academy of Arts and Letters in 1986.

But shortly after his play *Operation Sidewinder* opened at the repertory theatre of Lincoln Center in 1970, Shepard grew increasingly unhappy with both New York and the "theatre scene." Things "got more and more insane," he told British director Kenneth Chubb. "And also I was into a lot of drugs then—it became very difficult you know, everything seemed to be sort of shattering. . . . So I had this fantasy that I'd come [to London] and somehow fall into a rock 'n' roll band." Shepard, his former wife O-Lan Johnson, and his son moved to London, where his "fantasy" of being a rock star was not realized, but where he wrote several plays, including *The Tooth of Crime.* The play received its first production at the Open Space in July 1972, and the next year was staged in New York by the Performance Group under the direction of Richard Schechner. The marriage of Shepard's play and Schechner's artistic agenda, one influenced by Polish theoretician Jerzy Grotowski and dedicated to the creation of an **environmental theatre**, was not initially a blissful one. Schechner strove to create a ritualistic theatre in which the audience actively participated, and this necessarily meant, as he informed Shepard, that a play was merely *"part of an artwork yet to be completed* [Schechner's emphasis]." The Performance Group, for example, had no musicians with experience in rock music, so he wrote Shepard that "we will not use electric music done electrically. We will have to find out how to do electric music with our bodies." Shepard's response was clear and emphatic: "It's gotta be electric! No other way for it to work." Schechner worked on creating what he termed a "modular environment" for the production, littering the entire theatre (not just a playing space) with automobile parts and musical instruments. Staging *The Tooth of Crime* in a circle of about 30 feet in diameter, Schechner and his designer created spaces ("windows") in the environment that resembled the frames on a strip of film to create a cinematic experience for the audience. Shepard, who had learned so much from the experimental theatre in which he participated in the 1960s, was to learn a great deal more, not only from this experience with the Performance Group but also from his later collaboration with Joseph Chaikin at the Open Theatre.

An environment composed of junked car parts and musical instruments seems appropriate to the language and form of *The Tooth of Crime*, which begins with Hoss singing "The Way Things Are," the last line of which immediately transports the audience into the realm of the fantastic: "So here's another fantasy/About the way things seem to be to me." This suggestion of the play's monodramatic or dreamlike nature—of its fantastical, nonrealistic world of Markers and Gypsies, hit records and mob "hits," drugs and cars—is realized by the action that follows, all of which leads to an inevitable showdown between Hoss and his young rival, Crow. A combination of a heavyweight prizefight and the conventional gunfight in Westerns, the confrontation between Hoss and Crow is fought with music and competing styles. Hoss, who early in the play tells Becky that she would be "O. K." if she had a "self"—"Something to fall back on in a moment of doubt or terror or even surprise"—seems to discover before his suicide that his "self" is linked to rules and codes that Crow ignores. Before putting a gun in his mouth, Hoss claims to be a "true killer" in whom "Everything's whole and unshakeable. . . . Knows where he stands. Lives by a code. His own code." Crow has shaken all of this, has "pulled and pushed" Hoss around "from one image to another. Nothin' takes a solid form. Nothin' sure and final." Crow, conversely, forms himself from a congeries of images, as he boasts in his song: "But I believe in my mask—The man I made up is me/ And I believe in my dance—And my destiny." In Round Three of their showdown, Crow warns Hoss to "get the image in line. Get the image in line boy," but Hoss fails to do so, and Crow scores the "T.K.O." over his badly beaten opponent. "The Way Things Are" for Hoss is defeat, not only personal defeat but also the destruction of the entire system in which he found self-definition.

Analogous, then, to "postmodern concerns" about the preeminence of the image in contemporary culture and its effect on human subjectivity, the image in *The Tooth of Crime*, or the aggregation of surface images that Crow represents, reigns supreme over Hoss who, despite his seeming lack of a self to "fall back on," clearly is "centered" by the rules by which a "true killer" lives. At the same time, there exists some slippage between Shepard's Crow and the postmodern subject, for such a subject is typically regarded as lacking the ability or "agency" to manipulate images in the manner that Crow does. Nevertheless, as Gay Gibson Cima argues, it is self-evident that characters in such plays as *The Tooth of Crime* are not coherent "psychological entities in the tradition of Ibsen [or Arthur Miller] with clearly demarcated, if contradictory, motivations." Shepard's plays, like a number of postmodern works in other media, combine realistic and nonrealistic elements; playfully and ironically point to the elements of their own fabrication from popular cultural forms; offer dramatic meditation on the subject formed within and, to a great extent, determined by contemporary culture; and exhibit other "postmodern characteristics" as well. Or, as Shepard put it in a poem in *Motel Chronicles*, "Men turning themselves into advertisements of Men/. . . Women turning themselves into advertisements of Women"—at the boundary between authenticity and cultural construction, who can discern the real from the unreal? Does such a boundary exist at all? *Is* there an authentic self apart from and immune to the incursions of culture? *The Tooth of Crime* probes these issues and, in the process, illuminates important differences between much contemporary American drama and that which preceded it on the modern stage.

WORKS CONSULTED

Chubb, Kenneth, and the editors of *Theatre Quarterly*. "Metaphors, Mad Dogs and Old Time Cowboys: An Interview with Sam Shepard." *Theatre Quarterly*, (1974); Rpt. Marranca, 187–209.

Cima, Gay Gibson. "Shifting Perspectives: Combining Shepard and Rauschenberg." *Theatre Journal* 38 (1986): 67–81.

Eagleton, Terry. *Against the Grain: Selected Essays*. London: Verso, 1986.

Huyssen, Andreas. *After the Great Divide: Modernism, Mass Culture, Postmodernism*. Bloomington: Indiana University Press, 1986.

Jameson, Fredric. *Postmodernism, or, The Cultural Logic of Late Capitalism*. Durham, NC: Duke University Press, 1991.

Marranca, Bonnie, ed. *American Dreams: The Imagination of Sam Shepard*. New York: PAJ Publications, 1981.

Poland, Albert, and Bruce Mailman, eds. *The Off, Off Broadway Book*. Indianapolis/New York: Bobbs-Merrill, 1972.

Schechner, Richard. "The Writer and the Performance Group: Rehearsing *The Tooth of Crime*." *Performance* 5 (1973); Rpt. Marranca, 162–168.

Shepard, Sam. *Hawk Moon*. New York: PAJ Publications, 1981.

———. *Motel Chronicles*. San Francisco: City Lights Books, 1982.

———. *Seven Plays*. New York: Bantam, 1984.

Wilcox, Leonard. "Modernism vs. Postmodernism: Shepard's *The Tooth of Crime* and the Discourses of Popular Culture." *Modern Drama* 30 (1987): 560–573.

CHARACTERS

HOSS	REFEREE
BECKY LOU	CHEYENNE
STAR-MAN	DOC
GALACTIC JACK	CROW

ACT ONE

SCENE: *A bare stage except for an evil-looking black chair with silver studs and a very high back, something like an Egyptian pharaoh's throne but simple, centre stage. In the dark, heavy lurking rock and roll starts low and builds as the lights come up. The band should be hidden. The sound should be like "Heroin" by the Velvet Underground. When the lights are up full,* HOSS *enters in black rocker gear with silver studs and black kid gloves. He holds a microphone. He should look like a mean Rip Torn but a little younger. He takes the stage and sings "The Way Things Are." The words of the song should be understood, so the band has to back off on volume when he starts singing.*

"The Way Things Are"
You may think every picture you see is a true history
  of the way things used to be or the way things are

While you're ridin' in your radio or walkin' through
    the late late show ain't it a drag to know you just
    don't know
you just don't know
So here's another illusion to add to your confusion
Of the way things are
Everybody's doin' time for everybody else's crime
    and
I can't swim for the waves in the ocean
All the heroes is dyin' like flies they say it's a sign
    a' the times
And everybody's walkin' asleep eyes open—eyes
    open

So here's another sleep-walkin' dream
A livin' talkin' show of the way things seem
I used to believe in rhythm and blues
Always wore my blue suede shoes
Now everything I do goes down in doubt
But sometimes in the blackest night I can see a lit-
    tle light
That's the only thing that keeps me rockin'—keeps
    me rockin'

So here's another fantasy
About the way things seem to be to me.
    *(He finishes the song and throws down the mi-
    crophone and yells off stage.)*
    Becky Lou!
    *(BECKY comes on in black rock and roll gear.
    She's very tall and blonde. She holds two black
    satchels, one in each hand. They should look
    like old country-doctor bags.)*
BECKY: Ready just about.
HOSS: Let's have a look at the gear.
    *(BECKY sets the bags down on the floor and
    opens them. She pulls out a black velvet piece of
    cloth and lays it carefully on the floor, then be-
    gins to take out pearl-handled revolvers, pis-
    tols, derringers and rifles with scopes, shotguns
    broken down. All the weapons should look re-
    ally beautiful and clean. She sets them care-
    fully on the velvet cloth. HOSS picks up the
    rifles and handles them like a pro, cocking
    them and looking down the barrel through the
    scope, checking out the chambers on the pistols*

*and running his hands over them as though
they were alive.)*
    How's the Maserati?
BECKY: Clean. Greased like a bullet. Cheyenne
    took it up to 180 on the Ventura Freeway then
    backed her right down. Said she didn't bark
    once.
HOSS: Good. About time he stopped them quarter-
    mile orgasms. They were rippin' her up. Gotta
    let the gas flow in a machine like that. She's
    Italian. Likes a full-tilt feel.
BECKY: Cheyenne's hungry for long distance now.
    Couldn't hold him back with nails. Got lead in
    his gas foot.
HOSS: These look nice and blue. Did the Jeweler
    check 'em out?
BECKY: Yeah, Hoss. Everything's taken care of.
HOSS: Good. Now we can boogie.
BECKY: What's the moon chart say?
HOSS: Don't ask me! I hired a fucking star-man. A
    gazer. What the fuck's he been doin' up there.
BECKY: I don't know. Last I knew it was the next
    first quarter moon. That's when he said things'd
    be right.
HOSS: Get that fucker down here! I wanna see
    him. I gave him thirteen grand to get this chart
    in line. Tell him to get his ass down here!
BECKY: O.K., O.K.
    (She exits, HOSS caresses the guns.)
HOSS: That fuckin' Scorpion's gonna crawl if this
    gets turned around now. Now is right. I can feel
    it's right. I need the points! Can't they see that!
    I'm winning in three fucking States! I'm con-
    trolling more borders than any a' them punk
    Markers. The El Camino Boys. Bunch a' fuckin'
    punks. GET THAT FUCKER DOWN HERE!!!
    *(STAR-MAN enters with BECKY. He's dressed in
    silver but shouldn't look like Star Trek, more con-
    temporary silver.)*
    O.K., slick face, what's the scoop. Can we move
    now?
STAR-MAN: Pretty risky, Hoss.
HOSS: I knew it! I knew it! You fuckin' creep! Ev-
    ery time we get hot to trot you throw on the ice
    water. Whatsa matter now.

STAR-MAN: Venus is entering Scorpio.

HOSS: I don't give a shit if it's entering Brigitte Bardot. I'm ready for a kill!

STAR-MAN: You'll blow it.

HOSS: I'll blow it. What do you know. I've always moved on a sixth sense. I don't need you, meatball.

BECKY: Hoss, you never went against the charts before.

HOSS: Fuck before. This time I feel it. I can smell blood. It's right. The time is right! I'm fallin' behind. Maybe you don't understand that.

STAR-MAN: Not true, Hoss. The El Caminos are about six points off the pace. Mojo Root Force is the only one close enough to even worry about.

HOSS: Mojo? That fruit? What'd he knock over?

STAR-MAN: Vegas, Hoss. He rolled the big one.

HOSS: Vegas! He can't take Vegas, that's my mark! That's against the code!

STAR-MAN: He took it.

HOSS: I don't believe it.

BECKY: We picked it up on the bleeper.

HOSS: When? How come I'm the last to find out?

STAR-MAN: We thought it'd rattle you too much.

HOSS: When did it happen!

STAR-MAN: This morning from what the TeleprompTers read.

HOSS: I'm gonna get that chump. I'm gonna have him. He can't do that. He knew Vegas was on my ticket. He's trying to shake me. He thinks I'll just jump borders and try suburban shots. Well he's fuckin' crazy. I'm gonna roll him good.

BECKY: You can't go against the code, Hoss. Once a Marker strikes and sets up colors, that's his turf. You can't strike claimed turf. They'll throw you out of the game.

HOSS: *He* did it! He took my mark. It was on my ticket, goddamnit!

STAR-MAN: He can just claim his wave system blew and he didn't find out till too late.

HOSS: Well he's gonna find out now. I'll get a fleet together and wipe him out.

BECKY: But, Hoss, you'll be forced to change class. You won't have solo rights no more. You'll be a gang man. A punk.

HOSS: I don't care. I want that fuckin' gold record and nobody's gonna stop me. Nobody!

STAR-MAN: You gotta hold steady, Hoss. This is a tender time. The wrong move'll throw you back a year or more. You can't afford that now. The charts are moving too fast. Every week there's a new star. You don't wanna be a fly-by-night mug in the crowd. You want something durable, something lasting. How're you gonna cop an immortal shot if you give up soloing and go into a gang war. They'll rip you up in a night. Sure you'll have a few moments of global glow, maybe even an interplanetary flash. But it won't last, Hoss, it won't last.

BECKY: He's right, Hoss.

HOSS: O.K., O.K. I'm just gettin' hungry that's all. I need a kill. I haven't had a kill for months now. You know what that's like. I gotta kill. It's my whole life. If I don't kill I get crazy. I start eating away at myself. It's not good. I was born to kill.

STAR-MAN: Nobody knows that better than us, Hoss. But you gotta listen to management. That's what we're here for. To advise and direct. Without us you'd be just like a mad dog again. Can't you remember what that was like.

HOSS: Yeah, yeah! Go away now. Go on! I wanna be alone with Becky.

STAR-MAN: O.K. Just try and take it easy. I know you were wired for a big kill but your time is coming. Don't forget that.

HOSS: Yeah, all right. Beat it!

(STAR-MAN *exits leaving* HOSS *alone with* BECKY. *He looks around the stage dejected. He kicks at the guns and pulls off his gloves.*)

I'm too old fashioned. That's it. Gotta kick out the scruples. Go against the code. That's what they used to do. The big ones. Dylan, Jagger, Townsend. All them cats broke codes. Time can't change that.

BECKY: But they were playin' pussy, Hoss. They weren't killers . . . You're a killer, man. You're in the big time.

HOSS: So were they. My Pa told me what it was like. They were killers in their day too. Cold killers.

BECKY: Come on. You're talkin' treason against the game. You could get the slammer for less than that.

HOSS: Fuck 'em. I know my power. I can go on Gypsy Kill and still gain status. There's a whole underground movement going on. There's a lot of Gypsy Markers comin' up.

BECKY: Why do you wanna throw everything away. You were always suicidal like that. Right from the start.

HOSS: It's part of my nature.

BECKY: That's what we saved you from, your nature. Maybe you forgot that. When we first landed you, you were a complete beast of nature. A sideways killer. Then we molded and shaped you and sharpened you down to perfection because we saw in you a true genius killer. A killer to end them all. A killer's killer.

HOSS: Aw fuck off. I don't believe that shit no more. That stuff is for schoolies. Sure I'm good. I might even be great but I ain't no genius. Genius is something outside the game. The game can't contain a true genius. It's too small. The next genius is gonna be a Gypsy Killer. I can feel it. I know it's goin' down right now. We don't have the whole picture. We're too successful . . . We're insulated from what's really happening by our own fame.

BECKY: You're really trying to self-destruct aren't you? Whatsa matter, you can't take fame no more? You can't hold down the pressure circuits? Maybe you need a good lay or two.

HOSS: Your ass. I can handle the image like a fuckin' jockey. It's just that I don't trust the race no more. I dropped the blinkers.

BECKY: You're not gettin' buck fever are ya'?

HOSS: Get outa' here!

BECKY: Come on. Put it in fourth for a while, Hoss. Cruise it. You can afford to take it easy.

HOSS: GET THE FUCK OUTA' HERE!!!

BECKY: O.K., O.K. I'm your friend. Remember?

HOSS: Yeah, sure.

BECKY: I am. You're in a tough racket. The toughest. But now ain't the time to crack. You're knockin' at the door, Hoss. You gotta hold on. Once you get the gold then you can back off. But not now.

HOSS: I'm not backin' off. I'm just havin' a doubt dose.

BECKY: Maybe I should call a D.J. One a' the big ones. Then you could sit down with him and he could lay the charts out right in front of you. Show you exactly where you stand.

HOSS: That's a good idea. Good. Go get one. Get Galactic Jack and his Railroad Track. Tell him to bring his latest charts. Go on!

BECKY: O.K. I'll be back.

(She exits. HOSS *stalks around the stage building up his confidence.)*

HOSS: She's right! She's right goddamnit! I'm so fucking close. Knockin' at the door. I can't chicken out of it now. This is my last chance. I'm gettin' old. I can't do a Lee Marvin in the late sixties. I can't pull that number off. I've stomped too many heads. I'm past shitkicker class now. Past the rumble. I'm in the big time. Really big. It's now or never. Come on, Hoss, be a killer, man. Be a killer!

(Music starts. He sings "Cold Killer.")

"Cold Killer"

I'm a cold killer Mama—I got blood on my jeans
I got a Scorpion star hangin' over me
I got snakes in my pockets and a razor in my boot
You better watch it don't get you—It's faster'n you can shoot
I got the fastest action in East L.A.
I got the fastest action in San Berdoo
And if you don't believe it lemme shoot it to you

Now watch me slide into power glide—supercharged down the line
There ain't no way for you to hide from the killer's eye

My silver studs, my black kid gloves make you
    cry inside
But there ain't no way for you to hide from the
    killer's eye

I'm a cold killer Mama—and I've earned my
    tattoo
I got a Pachooko cross hangin' over you
I got whiplash magic and a rattlesnake tongue
My John the Conqueroot says I'm the cold gun

Now watch me slide into power glide super-
    charged down the line
There ain't no way for you to hide from the
    killer's eye
My silver studs, my black kid gloves make you
    cry inside
But there ain't no way for you to hide from the
    killer's eye.

*(The song ends. BECKY enters with GALACTIC
JACK the disc jockey. He's white and dressed like
a 42nd Street pimp, pink shirt, black tie, black
patent leather shoes, white panama straw hat
and a flash suit. He talks like Wolfman Jack
and carries a bundle of huge charts.)*

Ah! The man. Galactic Jack and his Railroad
Track.

GALACTIC JACK: That's me, Jim. Heavy duty and
on the whim. Back flappin', side trackin', finger poppin', reelin' rockin' with the tips on the
picks in the great killer race. All tricks, no
sale, no avail. It's in the can and on the lam.
Grease it, daddyo!

*(He holds out his hand palm up for HOSS to give
him five. HOSS holds back.)*

HOSS: Back down, Jack. Just give it to me straight.
Am I risin' or fallin'.

GALACTIC JACK: A shootin' star, baby. High flyin'
and no jivin'. You is off to number nine.

HOSS: Show me what you got. Just lay it out on the
floor.

BECKY: Shall I get ya'll some drinks?

HOSS: Yeah. Tequila Gold. What do you take,
Jack?

GALACTIC JACK: Not me, baby. I'm runnin' reds all
down the spine. Feelin' fine and mixin's a crime.

BECKY: Right.

*(She exits. JACK lays his chart on the floor.
HOSS and JACK crouch down to get a close inspection.)*

GALACTIC JACK: O.K. Here's the stand on the national band. The game's clean now. Solo is the
word. Gang war is takin' a back seat. The Low
Riders are outa' the picture and you is in, Jim.
In like a stone winner.

HOSS: Don't type it up, Jack. Just show me how it's
movin'. I was ready to take Nevada clean and
that meathead Mojo Root Force rolled Vegas.

GALACTIC JACK: Yeah I heard that. Supposed to
be on your ticket too. Bad news.

HOSS: He can't get away with that can he?

GALACTIC JACK: I can't dope them sheets, Hoss.
You'll have to consult a Ref for the rules or go
straight to the Keepers.

HOSS: I can't go to the game Keepers. They'll ask
for an itinerary and question past kills. I can't
afford a penalty now. I need every point.

GALACTIC JACK: Well lookee here. There's movement all around but no numero uno. That's
what they're backin' their chips on you for, boy.
The bookies got you two to one.

HOSS: That close?

GALACTIC JACK: All of 'em runnin' it down to you.
There's Little Willard from the East in his formula Lotus. Fast machine. Doin' O.K. with a
stainless steel Baretta.

HOSS: Willard's solo now?

GALACTIC JACK: Yeah but no threat. Just a front
runner. Lots a' early speed but can't go the
distance. Here's one outa Tupalo called
Studie Willcock. Drivin' a hot Merc, dual
cams, Chrysler through and through. Fast but
not deadly. He's offered four in a week and almost had Arkansas wrapped up but he's fadin'
fast. You're it, Jim. You is the coldest on the
circuit.

HOSS: What about this mark? *(pointing at the
charts)*

GALACTIC JACK: Oh yeah, that's Grease Jam. Got a
supercharged Mini Cooper. Takes the corners.
Tried a hit on St. Paul and almost had Minnesota

to its knees when he blew a head gasket. Some say he's even been offed by the El Caminos.

HOSS: Those guys are pressin' it pretty hard. They're gonna get blown off sooner or later.

GALACTIC JACK: No doubt. No need to pout. The course is clear. Maybe a few Gypsy Killers comin' into the picture but nothin' to fret your set.

HOSS: Gypsies? Where? I knew it. I got a feeling.

GALACTIC JACK: Just some side bets. They go anonymous 'cause a' the code. One slip and they is pissed. You can dig it. They's playin' with the king fire.

HOSS: But they got a following right? They're growing in the poles?

GALACTIC JACK: Hard to suss it yet, man. Some poles don't even mention their kills for fear of the Keepers comin' down on 'em. I could maybe sound some flies for ya'. See if I could whiff some sniff on that action.

HOSS: Yeah, do.

GALACTIC JACK: What's the keen to the Gypsy scene. These boys are losin' to the cruisin' baby.

HOSS: They've got time on their side. Can't you see that. The youth's goin' to 'em. The kids are flocking to Gypsy Kills. It's a market opening up, Jack. I got a feeling. I know they're on their way in and we're going out. We're gettin' old, Jack.

GALACTIC JACK: You just got the buggered blues, man. You been talkin' to the wrong visions. You gotta get a head set. Put yer ears on straight. Zoot yerself down, boy. These Gypsies is committin' suicide. We got the power. We got the game. If the Keepers whimsy it all they do is scratch 'em out. Simple. They're losers, man. The bookies don't even look past their left shoulder at a Gypsy Mark. They won't last, man. Believe me.

HOSS: I don't know. There's power there. Full blown.

GALACTIC JACK: They don't know the ropes, man. Rules is out. They're into slaughter straight off. Not a clean kill in the bunch.

HOSS: But they got balls. They're on their own.

GALACTIC JACK: So are you. Solo's the payolo.

HOSS: But I'm inside and they're out. They could unseat us all.

GALACTIC JACK: Not a King. The crown sticks where it fits and right now it looks about your size.

HOSS: What if they turned the game against us. What if they started marking us!

GALACTIC JACK: That's revolution, man.

HOSS: You hit it.

GALACTIC JACK: Old time shuffle. Don't stand a chance at this dance.

HOSS: But that's how we started ain't it. We went up against the Dudes. Wiped 'em out.

GALACTIC JACK: The Dudes weren't pros, man. You gotta see where you stand. I do believe you is tastin' fear. Runnin' scared. These Gypsies is just muckrakers. Second hand, one night stand. They ain't worth shit on Shinola in your league. Dig yourself on the flip side. You're number one with a bullet and you ain't even got the needle in the groove.

HOSS: We'll see. Somethin's goin' down big out there. The shit's gonna hit the fan before we can get to the bank.

GALACTIC JACK: Take a deep knee bend, Hoss. It's just the pre-victory shakes. Tomorrow you'll have the gold in your hand. The bigee. Don't be shy, I tell no lie. Catch ya' on the re-bop. Say bye and keep the slide greased down.

HOSS: Yeah. Thanks.

(JACK *collects his charts and exits.* HOSS *paces and talks to himself.*)

(*to himself*) Come on, come on. Confidence, man. Confidence. Don't go on the skids now. Keep it together. Tighten down. Talk it out. Quit jumpin' at shadows. They got you goose bumped and they ain't even present. Put yourself in their place. They got nothin'. You got it all. All the chips. Come on dice! Come on dice! That's it. Roll 'em sweet. The sweet machine. Candy in the gas tank. Floor it. Now you got the wheel. Take it. Take it!

(BECKY *enters with the drink.* HOSS *catches himself.*)

BECKY: What happened to Jack?

HOSS: We ran the session.

BECKY: Here's your drink.

HOSS: Thanks. Listen, Becky, is Cheyenne ready to roll?

BECKY: Yeah. He's hot. Why?

HOSS: Maybe we could just do a cruise. No action. Just some scouting. I'm really feelin' cooped up in here. This place is drivin' me nuts.

BECKY: Too dangerous, Hoss. We just got word that Eyes sussed somebody's marked you.

HOSS: What! Marked *me?* Who?

BECKY: One a' the Gypsies.

HOSS: It's all comin' down like I said. I must be top gun then.

BECKY: That's it.

HOSS: They gotta be fools, man. A Gypsy's marked *me?*

BECKY: That's the word from Eyes.

HOSS: Where is he?

BECKY: Vegas.

HOSS: Vegas? Oh now I get it. Mojo. He's hired a Gypsy to off me clean. That's it. That fuckin' chicken shit. I'm gonna blast him good. Doesn't have the balls to come down to me. Gotta hire a Gypsy.

BECKY: Might be just a renegade solo, Hoss. They're all lookin' to put you under. You're the main trigger. The word's out.

HOSS: Don't you get it? The Root Force is slipstreamin' my time. Takin' my marks and hirin' amateurs to rub me out. It's a gang shot. They're workin' doubles. I gotta team up now. It's down to that. I gotta get ahold a' Little Willard. Get him on the line.

BECKY: Hoss, don't fly off, man. You're safe here.

HOSS: Safe! Safe and amputated from the neck down! I'm a Marker man, not a desk clerk. Get fucking Willard to the phone! And tell Cheyenne to come in here!

(*BECKY exits*)

O.K. Now the picture brightens. I can play for high stakes now. I can draw to the straight, outside or in. I'm ready to take on any a' these flash heads. Vegas is mine, man. It belongs in my pocket. The West is mine. I could even take on

the Keepers. That's it. I'll live outside the fucking law altogether. Outside the whole shot. That's it. Why didn't I think a' that before! (*CHEYENNE enters in green velvet with silver boots and racing gloves.*)

CHEYENNE: You want me, Hoss?

HOSS: Yeah! Yeah I want you! You're my main man. (*He gives* CHEYENNE *a bear hug.*) Listen, Cheyenne, we done a lotta' marks in our time. Right?

CHEYENNE: Yeah.

HOSS: Good clean kills. Honest kills. But now the times are changin'. The race is deadly. Mojo Root Force is movin' in on turf marks and tryin' to put me out with a Gypsy.

CHEYENNE: A Gypsy?

HOSS: Yeah.

CHEYENNE: They can't do that. It's against the code.

HOSS: Fuck the code. Nobody's playin' by the rules no more. We been suckers to the code for too long now. Now we move outside. You remember Little Willard?

CHEYENNE: East Coast. Drove a Galaxie. Into Remington over and unders.

HOSS: Yeah. He's changed his style now. Got himself a Lotus Formula 2 and a Baretta.

CHEYENNE: Sounds mean.

HOSS: He is, man. And I trust him. He was right with me when we took off the Dudes. Becky's on the phone to him now. He's our man. Just him and us.

CHEYENNE: But Root Force has probably got Vegas locked up, Hoss. It's gonna be hard penetration.

HOSS: We rolled Phoenix didn't we?

CHEYENNE: Yeah.

HOSS: Tucson?

CHEYENNE: Yeah.

HOSS: San Berdoo?

CHEYENNE: Yeah.

HOSS: So Vegas ain't no Fort Knox.

CHEYENNE: So it's back to the rumble?

HOSS: Temporary. Just temporary. We can't sit back and let the good times roll when the game's breakin' down.

CHEYENNE: I don't know. I love the game, Hoss. I ain't hot to go back to gang war.

HOSS: We got to now! Otherwise we're down the tubes.

CHEYENNE: What about the Keepers?

HOSS: Fuck them too. We'll take 'em all on.

CHEYENNE: The critics won't like it.

HOSS: The critics! They're outside, man. They don't know what's goin' on.

CHEYENNE: What about our reputation. We worked hard to get where we are. I'm not ready to throw that away. I want a taste a' that gold.

HOSS: I'm surrounded by assholes! Can't you see what's happened to us. We ain't Markers no more. We ain't even Rockers. We're punk chumps cowering under the Keepers and the Refs and the critics and the public eye. We ain't free no more! Goddamnit! We ain't flyin' in the eye of contempt. We've become respectable and safe. Soft, mushy chewable ass lickers. What's happened to our killer heart. What's happened to our blind fucking courage! Cheyenne, we ain't got much time, man. We were warriors once.

CHEYENNE: That was a long time ago.

HOSS: Then you're backing down?

CHEYENNE: No. I'm just playin' the game.

(CHEYENNE *exits.*)

HOSS: God! Goddamnit! This is gettin' weird now. Solo ain't the word for it. It's gettin' lonely as an ocean in here. My driver's gone against me and my time's runnin' thin. Little Willard's my last chance. Him and me. He's runnin' without a driver, so can I. The two of us. Just the two of us. That's enough against the Root Force. He's East Coast though. Maybe he don't know the Western Ropes. He could learn it. We'll cruise the action. He'll pick up the streets. Cheyenne knows the West though. Born and raised like me. Backyard schoolin'. Goddamn! Why's he have to go soft now! Why now!

(BECKY *enters.*)

You get Willard?

BECKY: No.

HOSS: How come! I need him bad. Keep tryin'!!

BECKY: He's dead, Hoss. Shot himself in the mouth.

HOSS: Who told you?

BECKY: His Rep. They just found him in New Haven slumped over an intersection. They say his car was still runnin'.

HOSS: Why'd he go and do that? He was in the top ten and risin'.

BECKY: Couldn't take it I guess. Too vulnerable. They found a pound of Meth in the back seat.

HOSS: Becky, I'm marked. What the fuck am I gonna do? I can't just sit here and wait for him to come.

BECKY: Least you'll know he's comin'. If you go out cruisin' he's liable to strike anywhere, any time. A Gypsy's got the jump on you that way.

HOSS: What if I busted into Vegas myself? Just me. They'd never expect somethin' like that. I could take off Mojo and split before they knew what happened.

BECKY: You're dealin' with a pack now, man. It ain't one against one no more.

HOSS: Well what am I gonna do!

BECKY: Wait him out. Meet him on a singles match and bounce him hard. Challenge him.

HOSS: What if he snipes me?

BECKY: We got the watch out. We'll give him the usher routine. Say that you've been expecting him. That'll challenge his pride. Then fight him with shivs.

HOSS: Shivs! I ain't used a blade for over ten years. I'm out of practice.

BECKY: Practice up. I'll get you a set and a dummy.

HOSS: O.K. And call in the Doc. I need a good shot.

BECKY: Good.

(She exits. HOSS *stalks the stage.*)

HOSS: Backed into a fucking box. I can't believe it. Things have changed that much. They don't even apprentice no more. Just mark for the big one. No respect no more. When I was that age I'd sell my leathers to get a crack at a good teacher. I would. And I had some a' the best.

There's no sense of tradition in the game no more. There's no game. It's just back to how it was. Rolling night clubs, strip joints. Bustin' up poker games. Zip guns in the junk yard. Rock fights, dirt clods, bustin' windows. Vandals, juvies, *West Side Story*. Can't they see where they're goin'! Without a code its just crime. No art involved. No technique, finesse. No sense of mastery. The touch is gone.

(BECKY *enters with* DOC *who is dressed in red.* BECKY *has two knives and a dummy which she sets up centre stage right.* HOSS *sits in his chair.* DOC *has a syringe and a vial of dope and a rubber surgical hose.* HOSS *rolls his sleeve up and* DOC *goes about shooting him up.*)

Oh, Doc, it's good to see ya'. I'm in need. I'm under the gun, Doc.

DOC: Yeah. Things are tough now. This'll cool you out.

HOSS: Good. Doc, what do you think about Gypsy Kills. Do you think it's ethical?

DOC: Haven't thought too much about it actually. I suppose it was bound to happen. Once I remember this early Gypsy. I guess you'd call him a Gypsy now but at the time he was just a hard luck fella name a' Doc Carter. Little got to be known of the man on account a' the fact that he was ridin' a certain William F. Cody's shirt-tail all through the West, and, for that matter, half around the planet. Anyhow, ole Doc came to be known as the "Spirit Gun of the West" and a well-deserved title it was, too. That boy could shoot the hump off a buffalo on the back-side of a nickel at a hundred paces. To this very day his saddle is settin' in some musty ole Wyoming museum decorated with a hundred silver coins. Each one shot through and through with his Colt .45. And all surroundin' this saddle is pictures tall as a man of this William F. Cody fella pallin' it up with the Indians. Ole Doc never got out from behind the shadow a' that Cody. But I suppose nowadays he'd just take over the whole show. Don't rightly know what made me think a' that. Just popped into my mind.

HOSS: Yeah. It's just funny finding myself on the other side.

BECKY: It ain't revolution, man. This Gypsy's a hired trigger from Mojo. He ain't a martyr.

HOSS: But he works outside the code.

BECKY: Fuck it. All you gotta worry about is gettin' him before he gets you.

HOSS: You were one of the ones who taught me the code. Now you can throw it away like that.

BECKY: It's back down to survival, Hoss. Temporary suspension. That's all.

HOSS: I don't think so. I think the whole system's gettin' shot to shit. I think the code's going down the tubes. These are gonna be the last days of honor. I can see it comin'.

DOC: There. That oughta' do you for a while.

HOSS: Thanks, Doc.

DOC: If you need any crystal later just call me down.

HOSS: Thanks, man.

(DOC *exits.*)

BECKY: You wanna try these out?

(*She offers the knives to* HOSS. *He goes limp and relaxed in the chair.*)

HOSS: Not now. Just come and sit with me for a while.

(BECKY *sits at his feet. He strokes her hair.*)

Becky?

BECKY: Yeah?

HOSS: You remember the El Monte Legion Stadium?

BECKY: Yeah?

HOSS: Ripple Wine?

BECKY: Yeah.

HOSS: The Coasters?

BECKY: (*she sings a snatch*) "Take out the papers and the trash or you don't get no spendin' cash."

HOSS: (*sings*) "Just tell your hoodlum friend outside. You ain't got time to take a ride."

BECKY: "Yackety yack."

HOSS: "Don't talk back."

(*They laugh.* HOSS *stops himself.*)

Don't let me go too soft.

BECKY: Why not. You've earned it.

HOSS: Earned it? I ain't earned nothin'. Everything just happened. Just fell like cards. I never made a choice.

BECKY: But you're here now. A hero. All those losers out there barkin' at the moon.

HOSS: But where am I goin'? The future's just like the past.

BECKY: You gotta believe, Hoss.

HOSS: In what?

BECKY: Power. That's all there is. The power of the machine. The killer Machine. That's what you live and die for. That's what you wake up for. Every breath you take you breathe the power. You live the power. You are the power.

HOSS: Then why do I feel so weak!

BECKY: The knife's gotta be pulled out before you can stab again. The gun's gotta be cocked. The energy's gotta be stored. You're just gettin' a trickle charge now. The ignition's gotta turn yet.

HOSS: Yeah. It's just hard to wait.

BECKY: It's harder for movers. You're a mover, Hoss. Some people, all they do is wait.

HOSS: Maybe I should take a ramble.

BECKY: Where to?

HOSS: Anywhere. Just to get out for a while.

BECKY: You carry your gun wherever you go.

HOSS: Listen, maybe I should go on the lam.

BECKY: Are you crazy?

HOSS: No, I'm serious. I'm gettin' too old for this. I need some peace.

BECKY: Do you know what it's like out there, outside the game? You wouldn't recognize it.

HOSS: What about New York? Second Avenue.

BECKY: What Second Avenue? There ain't no Second Avenue. They're all zoned out. You wouldn't stand a snowball's chance in hell of makin' it outside the game. You're too professional. It'd be like keepin' a wild animal as a pet then turnin' him back loose again. You couldn't cope, Hoss.

HOSS: I did it once. I was good on the streets. I was a true hustler.

BECKY: The streets are controlled by the packs. They got it locked up. The packs are controlled by the gangs. The gangs and the Low Riders. They're controlled by cross syndicates. The next step is the Keepers.

HOSS: What about the country. Ain't there any farmers left, ranchers, cowboys, open space? Nobody just livin' their life.

BECKY: You ain't playin' with a full deck, Hoss. All that's gone. That's old time boogie. The only way to be an individual is in the game. You're it. You're on top. You're free.

HOSS: What free! How free! I'm tearin' myself inside out from this fuckin' sport. That's free? That's being alive? Fuck it. I just wanna have some fun. I wanna be a fuck-off again. I don't wanna compete no more.

BECKY: And what about the kill? You don't need that?

HOSS: I don't know, maybe not. Maybe I could live without it.

BECKY: You're talkin' loser now, baby.

HOSS: Maybe so. Maybe I am a loser. Maybe we're all fuckin' losers. I don't care no more.

BECKY: What about the gold record. You don't need that?

HOSS: I don't know! I just wanna back off for a while. I can't think straight. I need a change. A vacation or something.

BECKY: Maybe so. I heard about a place, an island where they don't play the game. Everybody's on downers all day.

HOSS: That sounds good. What about that. Maybe you could find out for me. All I need is a week or two. Just to rest and think things out.

BECKY: I'll see what I can do.

HOSS: Jesus. How'd I get like this?

BECKY: It'll pass.

HOSS: Sing me a song or somethin', would ya? Somethin' to cool me off.

BECKY: O.K.
(She sings.)
"Becky's Song"
Lemme take you for a ride down the road
Lean back in the tuck and roll
The radio's broken and I got no beer
But I can ease your load

Listen to the song that the V-8 sings
Watch the rhythm of the line
Isn't it some magic that the night-time
    brings
Ain't the highway fine

Tell me where ya' wanna go just take yer
    pick
All I'm really doin' is cruisin'
Take ya' down to Baton Rouge—New
    Orleans
Pick us up a Louisiana trick

Listen to the song that the V-8 sings
Watch the rhythm of the line
Isn't it some magic that the night-time
    brings
Ain't the highway fine

You could tell me stories of your yesterdays
I could break out a few a' mine
Roll down the window and kiss the wind
Anyway ya' want to ease the time

    Listen to the song that the V-8 sings
    Watch the rhythm of the line
    Isn't it some magic that the night-time
        brings
    Ain't the highway fine

(The song ends and CHEYENNE *enters.)*

CHEYENNE: Say, Hoss. We just got tapped that the Gypsy's made it through zone five. He's headed this way.

HOSS: Already? What's he drivin'?

CHEYENNE: You won't believe this. A '58 black Impala, fuel injected, bored and stroked, full blown Vet underneath.

HOSS: I'm gonna like this dude. O.K. let him through.

CHEYENNE: All the way?

HOSS: Yeah. Stop him at the mote and sound him on a shiv duel.

CHEYENNE: Shivs? You ain't in shape for blades, Hoss.

HOSS: I can handle it. Walk on.

CHEYENNE: O.K. *(He exits.)*

BECKY: Good. He's finally comin'. This'll get ya' back on your feet, Hoss. Your waitin' time is over.

HOSS: Go tell the Doc I want some snow.

BECKY: You want the fit or snort?

HOSS: Snort. Hurry up.

BECKY: Right.

*(*BECKY *exits.* HOSS *picks up the knives and stalks the dummy. He circles it and talks to the dummy and himself. As he talks he stabs the dummy with sudden violent lunges, then backs away again. Blood pours from the dummy onto the floor.)*

HOSS: O.K. Gypsy King, where's your true heart. Let's get down now. Let's get down. You talk a good story. You got the true flash but where's yer heart. That's the whole secret. The heart of a Gypsy must be there!

(He stabs at the heart of the dummy, then backs off.)

Maybe not. Maybe yer colder than that. Maybe in the neck. Maybe it pumps from the neck down. Maybe there!

(He stabs at the neck, then backs off. Blood gushes out.)

All right. All right. A secret's a secret. I can give you that much. But it comes from this end too. I'm your mystery. Figure me. Run me down to your experience. Go ahead. Make a move. Put me in a place. An inch is fatal. Just an inch. The wrong move'll leave you murdered. Come on. Lemme see it. Where's the action? That's not good enough for the back lot even. Here's one!

(He makes a quick move and stabs the dummy in the stomach.)

Now I get it. There ain't no heart to a Gypsy. Just bone. Just blind raging courage. Well that won't do you, boy. That won't take you the full length. Yer up against a pro, kid. A true champion Marker. Yer outclassed before the bell rings. Now you've stepped across the line, boy. No goin' back. Dead on yer feet. *(to himself)* What am I gettin' so wired about? This kid is a punk. It ain't even a contest. He's still ridin' in the fifties. Beach Boys behind the eyeballs. A blonde boy. A fair head. Gang bangs, cheap wine and bonfires. I could take him in my sleep. I could. I could—

(BECKY *enters with* DOC. DOC *has a large sheet of foil with mounds of cocaine on it. He sets it down on the chair.*)

BECKY: How's it goin'?

HOSS: Something's lacking. I can't seem to get it up like the other kills. My heart's not in it.

DOC: Have some a' this.

(*He holds out a rolled-up hundred dollar bill.* HOSS *takes it and goes to the coke.*)

HOSS: Yeah. Maybe that'll help.

(*He takes the bill and snorts the coke as he talks.*)

You know, I been thinkin'. What if the neutral field state failed. One time. Just once.

BECKY: Like this time for instance?

HOSS: Yeah. Like this time.

BECKY: Then you're a goner.

DOC: It shouldn't fail, Hoss. You've been trained.

HOSS: I know, but what if an emotional field came through stronger.

BECKY: Like love or hate?

HOSS: Not that gross, not that simple. Something subtle like the sound of his voice or a gesture or his timing. Something like that could throw me off.

BECKY: You're really worried about this Gypsy.

HOSS: Not worried. Intrigued. His style is copping my patterns. I can feel it already and he's not even here yet. He's got a presence. Maybe even star quality. His movements have an aura. Even his short. I mean nobody rides a '58 Impala to do battle with a star Marker.

BECKY: He's just a fool.

DOC: You gotta stay disengaged, Hoss. The other way is fatal.

HOSS: Maybe not. Maybe there's an opening. A ground wire.

BECKY: For what. He's come to knock you over, man.

HOSS: O.K. but I can play in his key. Find his tuning. Jam a little before the big kill. I don't have to off him soon's he walks in the door.

DOC: You'd be better off. He's probably got eyes to work that on you.

HOSS: I don't think so. He's got more class than that. I can feel him coming. We might even be in the same stream. He's got respect.

BECKY: Respect! He's a killer, man.

HOSS: So am I. There's another code in focus here. An outside code. Once I knew this cat in High School who was a Creole. His name was Moose. He was real light skinned and big, curly blond hair, blue eyes. He could pass easy as a jock. Good musician. Tough in football but kinda dumb. Dumb in that way—that people put you down for in High School. Dumb in class. He passed as white until his sister started hangin' around with the black chicks. Then the white kids figured it out. He was black to them even though he looked white. He was a nigger, a coon, a jungle bunny. A Rock Town boy from that day on. We ran together, Moose and me and another cat from Canada who dressed and wore his hair like Elvis. They put him down too because he was too smart. His name was Cruise and he got straight A's without readin' none a' the books. Slept in a garage with his aunt. Built himself a cot right over an old Studebaker. His mother was killed by his father who drove skidders for a lumber company up near Vancouver. Got drunk and busted her in the head with a tire iron. The three of us had a brotherhood, a trust. Something unspoken. Then one day it came to the test. I was sorta' ridin' between 'em. I'd shift my personality from one to the other but they dug me 'cause I'd go crazy drunk all the time. We all went out to Bob's Big Boy in Pasadena to cruise the chicks and this time we got spotted by some jocks from our High School. Our own High School. There were eight of 'em, all crew cut and hot for blood. This was the old days ya' know. So they started in on Cruise 'cause he was the skinniest. Smackin' him around and pushin' him into the car. We was right in the parking lot there. Moose told 'em to ease off but they kept it up. They were really out to choose Moose. He was their mark. They wanted him bad. Girls and dates started gathering around until we was right in the center of a huge crowd a' kids. Then I saw it. This was a class war. These were rich white kids from Arcadia who got T-birds and deuce coupes for Xmas from Mommy and Daddy. All them cardigan sweaters and chicks with ponytails and pedal pushers and bubble hairdos. Soon as I saw that I flipped out. I found my strength. I started kickin' shit, man. Hard and fast. Three of 'em went down screamin' and holdin' their balls. Moose and Cruise went right into action. It was like John Wayne, Robert Mitchum and Kirk Douglas all in one movie. Those chumps must a' swung on us three times and that was all she wrote. We had all eight of 'em bleedin' and cryin' for Ma right there in the parking lot at Bob's Big Boy. I'll never forget that. The courage we had. The look in all them rich kids' faces. The way they stepped aside just like they did for "Big John." The three of us had a silent pride. We just walked strong, straight into that fuckin' burger palace and ordered three cherry Cokes with lemon and a order a' fries.

DOC: Those were the old days.

HOSS: Yeah. Look at me now. Impotent. Can't strike a kill unless the charts are right. Stuck in my image. Stuck in a mansion. Waiting. Waiting for a kid who's probably just like me. Just like I was then. A young blood. And I gotta off him. I gotta roll him or he'll roll me. We're fightin' ourselves. Just like turnin' the blade on ourselves. Suicide, man. Maybe Little Willard was right. Blow your fuckin' brains out. The whole thing's a joke. Stick a gun in your fuckin' mouth and pull the trigger. That's what it's all about. That's what we're doin'. He's my brother and I gotta kill him. He's gotta kill me. Jimmy Dean was right. Drive the fuckin' Spider till it stings ya' to death. Crack up your soul! Jackson Pollock! Duane Allman! Break it open! Pull the trigger! Trigger me! Trigger you! Drive it off the cliff! It's all an open highway. Long and clean and deadly beautiful. Deadly and lonesome as a jukebox.

DOC: Come on, Becky, let's leave him alone.

HOSS: Yeah. Right. Alone. That's me. Alone. That's us. All fucking alone. All of us. So don't go off in your private rooms with pity in mind. Your day is comin'. The mark'll come down to you one way or the other.

BECKY: You better rest, Hoss.

HOSS: Ya' know, you'd be O.K., Becky, if you had a self. So would I. Something to fall back on in a moment of doubt or terror or even surprise. Nothin' surprises me no more. I'm ready to take it all on. The whole shot. The big one. Look at the Doc. A slave. An educated slave. Look at me. A trained slave. We're all so pathetic it's downright pathetic. And confidence is just a hype to keep away the open-ended shakes. Ain't that the truth, Doc?

DOC: I don't know.

HOSS: Right. Right. "I don't know" is exactly right. Now beat it, both of ya' before I rip your fuckin' teeth out a' yer heads!! GO ON BEAT IT!!!

(BECKY and DOC exit. HOSS sits in his chair and stares out in front of him. He talks to himself, sometimes shifting voices from his own into an older man's.)

(old) All right, Hoss, this is me talkin'. Yer old Dad. Yer old fishin' buddy. We used to catch eels side by side down by the dump. The full moon lit up the stream and the junk. The rusty chrome flashin' across the marsh. The fireflies dancin' like a faraway city. They'd swallow the hook all the way down. You remember that? (himself) Yeah. Sure. (old) O.K. You're not so bad off. It's good to change. Good to feel your blood pump. (himself) But where to? Where am I going? (old) It don't matter. The road's what counts. Just look at the road. Don't worry about where it's goin'. (himself) I feel so trapped. So fucking unsure. Everything's a mystery. I had it all in the palm of my hand. The gold, the silver. I knew. I was sure. How could it slip away like that? (old) It'll come back. (himself) But I'm not a true Marker no more. Not really. They're all countin' on me. The bookies, the agents, the Keepers. I'm a fucking industry. I even affect the stocks and bonds. (old) You're just a man,

Hoss. Just a man. *(himself)* Yeah, maybe you're right. I'm just a man.
(CHEYENNE enters.)
CHEYENNE: Hoss. He's here.
(HOSS stays seated, relaxed. He has an air of complete acceptance.)
HOSS: Good. He's here. That's good. What's his name?
CHEYENNE: He calls himself Crow.
HOSS: Crow. That's a good name. Did you sound him on the duel?
CHEYENNE: Yeah. He's game. He looks tougher than I thought, Hoss.
HOSS: Tough. Tough? *(he laughs)* Good. A tough Crow.
CHEYENNE: What'll I tell him?
HOSS: Tell him I like his style. Tell him I'm very tired right now and I'm gonna cop some z's. He can take a swim, have a sauna and a massage, some drinks, watch a movie, have a girl, dope, whatever he wants. Tell him to relax. I'll see him when I come to.
CHEYENNE: O.K. You all right, Hoss?
HOSS: Yeah. Just tired. Just a little tired.
CHEYENNE: O.K.
HOSS: Thanks, man.
CHEYENNE: Sure.
(CHEYENNE exits. HOSS stays seated looking out.)
HOSS: Maybe the night'll roll in. A New Mexico night. All gold and red and blue. That would be nice. A long slow New Mexico night. Put that in your dream, Hoss, and sleep tight. Tomorrow you live or die.

ACT TWO

SCENE: *The stage is the same. The lights come up on* CROW. *He looks just like Keith Richard. He wears high-heeled green rock and roll boots, tight greasy blue jeans, a tight yellow T-shirt, a green velvet coat, a shark tooth earring, a silver swastika hanging from his neck and a black eye-patch covering the left eye. He holds a short piece of silver chain in his hand and* twirls *it constantly, tossing it from hand to hand. He chews a stick of gum with violent chomps. He exudes violent arrogance and cruises the stage with true contempt. Sometimes he stops to examine the guns on the floor, or check out the knives and the dummy. Finally he winds up sitting in* HOSS' *chair. A pause as he chews gum at the audience.* HOSS *enters dressed the same as in Act One.* CROW *doesn't move or behave any different than when he was alone. They just stare at each other for a while.*

HOSS: My sleuth tells me you're drivin' a '58 Impala with a Vet underneath.
CROW: Razor, Leathers. Very razor.
HOSS: Did you rest up?
CROW: Got the molar chomps. Eyes stitched. You can vision what's sittin'. Very razor to cop z's sussin' me to be on the far end of the spectrum.
HOSS: It wasn't strategy man. I was really tired. You steal a lotta' energy from a distance.
CROW: No shrewd from this end either. We both bow to bigger fields.
HOSS: You wanna drink or somethin'?
CROW: *(he laughs with a cackle)* Lush in sun time gotta smell of lettuce or turn of the century. Sure Leathers, squeeze on the grape vine one time.
HOSS: White or red?
CROW: Blood.
HOSS: Be right back.
CROW: No slaves in this crib?
HOSS: They're all in the pool watchin' a movie.
CROW: Very Greek.
HOSS: Yeah. Just relax, I'll be right back.
(HOSS exits. CROW gets up and walks around thinking out loud.)
CROW: Very razor. Polished. A gleam to the movements. Weighs out in the eighties from first to third. Keen on the left side even though he's born on the right. Maybe forced his hand to change. Butched some instincts down. Work them through his high range. Cut at the gait. Heel-toe action rhythms of New Orleans. Can't suss that particular. That's well covered. Meshing patterns. Easy mistakes here. Suss the bounce.

(CROW *tries to copy* HOSS' *walk. He goes back and forth across the stage practicing different styles until he gets the exact one. It's important that he gets inside the feeling of* HOSS' *walk and not just the outer form.*)

Too heavy on the toe. Maybe work the shoulders down. Here's a mode. Three-four cut time copped from Keith Moon. Early. Very early. Now. Where's that pattern. Gotta be in the "Happy Jack" album. Right around there. Triplets. Six-eight. Here it comes. Battery. Double bass talk. Fresh Cream influence. Where's that? Which track. Yeah. The old Skip James tunes. Question there. Right there. *(sings it)* "I'm so glad, I'm so glad, I'm glad, I'm glad, I'm glad." Yeah. Ancient. Inborn. Has to be a surgery. Grind down.

(*He hears* HOSS *coming and darts back to the chair and sits as though he'd never moved.* HOSS *enters with a bottle of red wine and two glasses. He hands one to* CROW *and then he pours himself one and sets the bottle down.*)

HOSS: Ya know I had a feeling you were comin' this way. A sense. I was onto a Gypsy pattern early yesterday. Even conjured going that way myself.

CROW: Cold, Leathers. Very icy. Back seat nights. Tuck and roll pillow time. You got fur on the skin in this trunk.

HOSS: Yeah, yeah. I'm just gettin' bored I guess. I want out.

CROW: I pattern a conflict to that line. The animal says no. The blood won't go the route. Re-do me right or wrong?

HOSS: Right I guess. Can't you back the language up, man. I'm too old to follow the flash.

CROW: Choose an argot Leathers. Singles or LPs. 45, 78, 33⅓.

HOSS: I musta' misfed my data somehow. I thought you were raw, unschooled. Ya' know? I mean, maybe the training's changed since my time. Look, I wanna just sound you for a while before we get down to the cut. O.K.? You don't know how lonely it's been. I can talk to Cheyenne but we mostly reminisce on old kills. Ya' know. I don't get new information. I'm starving for new

food. Ya' know? That don't mean I won't be game to mark you when the time comes. I don't sleep standin' up. Ya' know what I mean? It's just that I wanna find out what's going on. None of us knows. I'm surrounded by boobs who're still playin' in the sixties. That's where I figured you were. Earlier. I figured you for Beach Boys in fact.

CROW: That sand stayed on the beach with me. You can suss me in detail Leathers. What's your key?

HOSS: This is really weird, me learnin' from you. I mean I can't believe myself admitting it. Ya' know? I thought I could teach you somethin'. I thought you were playin' to the inside. Choosin' me off just to get in the door. I mean I know you must be Mojo's trigger, right?

CROW: De-rail Leathers. You're smokin' the track.

HOSS: Eyes traced a Nevada route. It don't matter. If you ain't from the Root Force you're on the Killin' floor Jack. Anyway you cut it you're a corpse. So let's lay that one on the rack for now. Let's just suspend and stretch it out.

CROW: We can breathe thin or thick. The air is your genius.

HOSS: Good. Now, first I wanna find out how the Gypsy Killers feature the stars. Like me. How do I come off. Are we playin' to a packed house like the Keepers all say?

CROW: *(he cackles)* Image shots are blown, man. No fuse to match the hole. Only power forces weigh the points in our match.

HOSS: You mean we're just ignored? Nobody's payin' attention?

CROW: We catch debris beams from your set. We scope it to our action then send it back to garbage game.

HOSS: Listen chump, a lotta' cats take this game serious. There's a lotta' good Markers in this league.

CROW: You chose ears against tongue Leathers. Not me, I can switch to suit. You wanna patter on my screen for a while?

HOSS: Sorry. It's just hard to take. If it's true. I don't believe we could be that cut off. How did it happen? We're playing in a vacuum?

All these years. All the kills and no one's watching?

CROW: Watching takes a side seat. Outside. The Game hammered the outside.

HOSS: And now you hammer us with fucking indifference! This is incredible. It's just like I thought. The Outside is the Inside now.

CROW: *(he cackles)* Harrison, Beatle did that ancient. It cuts a thinner slice with us. Roles fall to birth blood. We're star marked and playing inter-galactic modes. Some travel past earthbound and score on Venus, Neptune, Mars.

HOSS: How do you get to fucking Neptune in a '58 Impala!

CROW: How did you get to earth in a Maserati?

HOSS: There! Why'd you slip just then? Why'd you suddenly talk like a person? You're into a wider scope than I thought. You're playin' my time Gypsy but it ain't gonna work. And get the fuck outa' my chair!!

(CROW slides out of the chair and starts walking around, twirling his chain and chomping his gum. HOSS sits down. He sips his wine. Slowly through the dialogue CROW starts to get into HOSS' walk until he's doing it perfect.)

CROW: Your tappets are knockin' rock-man. I sense an internal smokin' at the seams.

HOSS: Yeah, so this is how you play the game. A style match. I'm beginning to suss the mode. Very deadly but no show. Time is still down to the mark, kid. How's your feel for shivs anyway?

CROW: Breakdown lane. Side a' the road days.

HOSS: Yeah, well that's the way it's gonna be. I ain't used a blade myself for over ten years. I reckon it's even longer for you. Maybe never.

(HOSS begins to switch into a kind of Cowboy-Western image.)

I reckon you ain't never even seen a knife. A pup like you. Up in Utah we'd use yer kind fer skunk bait and throw away the skunk.

CROW: Throwin' to snake-eyes now Leathers.

HOSS: So you gambled your measly grub stake for a showdown with the champ. Ain't that pathetic. I said that before and I'll say it again. Pathetic.

(CROW is getting nervous. He feels he's losing the match. He tries to force himself into the walk. He chews more desperately and twirls the chain faster.)

You young guns comin' up outa' prairie stock and readin' dime novels over breakfast. Drippin' hot chocolate down yer zipper. Pathetic.

CROW: Time warps don't shift the purpose, just the style. You're clickin' door handles now. There'll be more paint on your side than mine.

HOSS: We'd drag you through the street fer a nickel. Naw. Wouldn't even waste the horse. Just break yer legs and leave ya' fer dog meat.

CROW: That's about all you'll get outa' second. Better shift it now Leathers.

(HOSS shifts to 1920s gangster style.)

HOSS: You mugs expect to horn in on our district and not have to pay da' price? Da' bosses don't sell out dat cheap to small-time racketeers. You gotta tow da' line punk or you'll wind up just like Mugsy.

(CROW begins to feel more confident now that he's got HOSS to switch.)

CROW: Good undertow. A riptide invisible moon shot. Very nice slide Leathers.

(HOSS goes back to his own style.)

HOSS: Don't give me that. I had you hurtin'. You were down on one knee Crow Bait. I saw you shakin'.

CROW: Fuel injected. Sometimes the skin deceives. Shows a power ripple. Misconstrucd Leathers.

(CROW is into HOSS' walk now and does it perfect.)

HOSS: You were fishtailin' all over the track meathead! I had you tagged!

CROW: Posi-traction rear end. No pit stops the whole route. Maybe you got a warp in your mirror.

HOSS: There's no fuckin' warp. You were down!

CROW: Sounds like a bad condenser. Points and plugs.

HOSS: Suck ass! I had you clean! And stop walkin' like that! That's not the way you walk! That's the way I walk!

(CROW stops still. They stare at each other for a second. HOSS rises slow.)

All right. I can handle this action but we need a Ref. I ain't playin' unless we score.

CROW: It's your turf.

HOSS: Yeah, and it's stayin' that way. I'm gonna beat you Gypsy. I'm gonna whip you so bad you'll wish we *had* done the shivs. And then I'm gonna send you back with a mark on your forehead. Just a mark that won't never heal.

CROW: You're crossin' wires now Leathers. My send is to lay you cold. I'll play flat out to the myth but the blood runs when the times comes.

HOSS: We'll see. You're well padded Crow Bait but the layers'll peel like a skinned buck. I'm goin' to get a Ref now. You best use the time to work out. You ain't got your chops down. You're gonna need some sharpening up. When I get back it's head to head till one's dead.

(HOSS *exits. The band starts the music to* CROW'S *song. He sings.*)

"Crow's Song"

CROW: What he doesn't know—the four winds blow
Just the same for him as me
We're clutchin' at the straw and no one knows the law
That keeps us lost at sea

But I believe in my mask—The man I made up is me
And I believe in my dance—And my destiny

I coulda' gone the route—of beggin' for my life
Crawlin' on my hands and knees
But there ain't no Gods or saviors who'll give you flesh and blood
It's time to squeeze the trigger
But I believe in my mask—The man I made up is me
And I believe in my dance—And my destiny
The killer time—will leave us on the line
Before the cards are dealt
It's a blindman's bluff—without the stuff
To reason or to tell

But I believe in my mask—The man I made up is me
And I believe in my dance—And my destiny

(The song ends. HOSS *enters with the* REFEREE.

He's dressed just like an N.B.A. ref with black pants, striped shirt, sneakers, a whistle, baseball cap and a huge scoreboard which he sets up down right. He draws a big "H" on the top left side of the board and a big "C" on the other. He separates the letters with a line down the middle. As he goes about his business HOSS *talks to* CROW.)

HOSS: I suppose you wouldn't know what's happened to my people? Becky. Cheyenne, Doc, Star-Man—they're all gone. So's my short.

CROW: Lotsa' force concentration in this spot Leathers. Could be they got bumped out to another sphere. They'll be back when the furnace cools.

HOSS: I don't fancy tap dancers Crow Bait. I like both feet on the ground. Nailed. Joe Frazier mode.

CROW: I vision you brought the rule, man.

HOSS: Yeah. He's gonna see that things stay clean. Points scored and lost on deviation from the neutral field state.

CROW: I'd say you already broke the mercury in round one.

HOSS: That don't count! We start when he's ready.

CROW: I can't cipher why you wanna play this course, Leathers. It's a long way from shivs.

HOSS: Just to prove I ain't outside.

CROW: To me or you?

(HOSS *considers for a second but shakes it off.*)

HOSS: I don't know how it is with you but for me it's like looking down a long pipe. All the time figurin' that to be the total picture. You take your eye away for a second and see you been gyped.

CROW: "Gyped"—coming from "Gypsy."

(Through all this the REF *puts himself through several yoga positions and regulated breathing exercises, cracks his knuckles, shakes his legs out like a track star and runs in place.*)

HOSS: I'm gonna have fun skinnin' you.

CROW: If narrow in the eyeball is your handicap then runnin' a gestalt match figures suicidal. Look, Leathers, may be best to run the blades and forget it.

HOSS: No! You ain't no better than me.

CROW: You smell loser, Leathers. This ain't your stompin' turf.

HOSS: We'll see.

CROW: It took me five seconds to suss your gait. I ran it down to Skip James via Ginger Baker. How long's it gonna take you to cop mine?

HOSS: I ain't a Warlock, I'm a Marker.

CROW: So stick to steel. Pistols. How 'bout the ancient chicken? Maserati against the Chevy. That's fair.

HOSS: I see you turnin' me in. I ain't stupid. I'm stickin' with this route Gypsy and that's what you want so can the horseshit. There's no Marker on the planet can out-kill me with no kinda' weapon or machine. You'd die with the flag still in the air. That's straight on. But too easy. I'm tired of easy marks. I'm drawin' to the flush. I'm gonna leave you paralyzed alive. Amputated from the neck down.

CROW: Just like you.

HOSS: We'll see.

(REF *wipes himself off with a towel and tests his whistle.*)

REF: All right. Let's get the show on the road. We all know the rules. When the bell rings, come out swingin'. When it rings again go to your corners. No bear hugs, rabbit punches, body pins or holdin' on. If a man goes down we give him five and that's it. After that you can kick the shit out of him. Ready? Let's have it!

(*An off-stage bell rings. The band starts slow, low-keyed lead guitar and bass music, it should be a lurking evil sound like the "Sister Morphine" cut on "Sticky Fingers." HOSS and CROW begin to move to the music, not really dancing but feeling the power in their movements through the music. They each pick up microphones. They begin their assaults just talking the words in rhythmic patterns, sometimes going with the music, sometimes counterpointing it. As the round progresses the music builds with drums and piano coming in, maybe a rhythm guitar too. Their voices build so that sometimes they sing the words or shout. The words remain as intelligible as possible like a sort of talking opera.*)

Round 1

CROW: Pants down. The moon show. Ass out the window. Belt lash. Whip lash. Side slash to the kid with a lisp. The dumb kid. The loser. The runt. The mutt. The shame kid. Kid on his belly. Belly to the blacktop. Slide on the rooftop. Slide through the parkin' lot. Slide kid. Shame kid. Slide. Slide.

HOSS: Never catch me with beer in my hand. Never caught me with my pecker out. Never get caught. Never once. Never, never. Fast on the hoof. Fast on the roof. Fast through the still night. Faster than the headlight. Fast to the move.

CROW: Catch ya' outa' breath by the railroad track.

HOSS: Never got caught!

CROW: Catch ya' with yer pants down. Whip ya' with a belt. Whup ya' up one side and down to the other. Whup ya' all night long. Whup ya' to the train time. Leave ya' bleedin' and cryin'. Leave ya' cryin' for Ma. All through the night. All through the night long. Shame on the kid. Little dumb kid with a lisp in his mouth. Bleedin' up one side and down to the other.

HOSS: No! Moved to a hard town. Moved in the midnight.

CROW: Comin' in a wet dream. Pissin' on the pillow. Naked on a pillow. Naked in a bedroom. Naked in a bathroom. Beatin' meat to the face in a mirror. Beatin' it raw. Beatin' till the blood come. Pissin' blood on the floor. Hidin' dirty pictures. Hide 'em from his Ma. Hide 'em from his Pa. Hide 'em from the teacher.

HOSS: Never did happen! You got a high heel. Step to the lisp. Counter you, never me. Back steppin' Crow Bait. History don't cut it. History's in the pocket.

CROW: The marks show clean through. Look to the guard. That's where it hides. Lurkin' like a wet hawk. Scuffle mark. Belt mark. Tune to the rumble. The first to run. The shame kid. The first on his heel. Shame on the shame kid. Never live it down. Never show his true face. Last in line. Never face a showdown. Never meet a face-off.

Never make a clean break. Long line a' losers. *(All the other characters from Act One come on dressed in purple cheerleader outfits. Each has a pom-pom in one hand and a big card with the word "Victory" printed on it. They do a silent routine, mouthing the word "Victory" over and over and shaking their pom-poms. They move around the stage doing a shuffle step and stupid routines just like at the football games.* CROW *and* HOSS *keep up the battle concentrating on each other. The* REF *bobs in and out between them, watching their moves closely like a fight ref.)*

HOSS: Missed the whole era. Never touched the back seat.

CROW: Coughin' in the corner. Dyin' from pneumonia. Can't play after dinner. Lonely in a bedroom. Dyin' for attention. Starts to hit the small time. Knockin' over pay phones. Rollin' over Beethoven. Rockin' pneumonia. Beboppin' to the Fat Man. Driving' to the small talk. Gotta make his big mark. Take a crack at the teacher. Find him in the can can. There he's doin' time time. Losin' like a wino. Got losin' on his mind. Got losin' all the time.

HOSS: You can't do that!

(At some point the cheerleaders all come downstage in a line, turn their backs on the audience, take their pants down and bend over bare assed. When the bell rings marking the end of the round, they all turn around and show the reverse side of their cards which has the word "Fight" in big letters. Then they all hobble off with their pants around their ankles giggling like school kids.)

CROW: In the slammer he's a useless. But he does his schoolin'. Tries to keep a blind face. Storin' up his hate cells. Thinks he's got it comin'. Bangin' out the street signs. Tryin' to do his time time. Turns into a candy-cock just to get a reprieve. Lost in the long sleeve. Couldn't get a back up. So he takes his lock up. Calls it bitter medicine. Makes a sour face. Gotta pay his dues back. Fakin' like a guru. Finally gets his big chance and sucks the warden's dinger. Gotta be a good boy. Put away the stinger. Put away the

gun boy. I'll take away your time. Just gimme some head boy. Just get down on your knees. Gimme some blow boy. I'll give ya' back the key. I'll give ya' back the key boy! Just get down on my thing boy! Just get down! Get on down! Get on down! Get down! Get down! Get down! Come on!

(The bell rings. The music stops. The cheerleaders flash their cards and exit. REF *goes to the scoreboard and without hesitation chalks up a big mark for* CROW. CROW *lies flat on his back and relaxes completely. He looks like he's dead.* HOSS *paces around nervous.)*

HOSS: What the fuck! What the fuck was that! *(to the* REF) You call that fair? You're chalkin' that round up to him! On what fucking grounds!

CROW: Good clean body punches. Nice left jab. Straight from the shoulder. Had you rocked on your heels two or three times. No doubt about it.

HOSS: Are you kiddin' me! If flash and intensity is what you want I can give you plenty a' that. I thought we were shootin' honest pool. This kid's a fuckin' fish man. Nothin' but flash. No heart. Look at him. Wasted on his back and I'm still smokin'.

CROW: *(looking at his watch)* Better get some rest. You got thirty seconds left.

HOSS: I don't need rest. I'm ready to rock. It's him that's stroked out on the fuckin' floor, not me. Look at him. How can you give him the round when he's in that kinda' shape.

REF: Good clean attack.

HOSS: Clean! You call that clean? He was pickin' at a past that ain't even there. Fantasy marks. Like a dog scratchin' on ice. I can play that way if I was a liar. The reason I brought you into this match was to keep everything above the table. How can you give points to a liar.

REF: I don't. I give 'em to the winner.

(The bell rings. CROW *jumps to his feet. The band strikes a note.* HOSS *steps in. He speaks to the band.)*

HOSS: All right look. Can the music. This ain't Broadway. Let's get this down to the skinny.

REF: What's going on! Play the round!

HOSS: What'sa matter, Crow Bait? Afraid to do it naked? Drop the echo stick and square me off.

CROW: You should be past roots on this scale, Leathers. Very retrograde.

HOSS: Don't gimme that. I wanna strip this down to what's necessary.

CROW: *(laughing)* Necessity?

REF: This is against the code. Either play this round or it's no match.

CROW: We'll walk this dance so long as sounds can push Round 3. Certain muscles have gone green on me, Leathers. You can cipher.
(The bell rings again. HOSS *and* CROW *put down their mikes slowly and deliberately as though they both had knives and agreed instead to wrestle.* REF *moves around them. The band remains quiet.)*

Round 2

HOSS: *(talking like an ancient delta blues singer)* Chicago. Yeah, well I hear about all that kinda 'lectric machine gun music. All that kinda 'lectric shuffle, you dig? I hear you boys hook up in the toilet and play to da mirror all tru the night.

CROW: *(nervously)* Yeah. Well, you know, twelve bars goes a long way.

HOSS: *(growing physically older)* It come down a long way. It come down by every damn black back street you can move sideways through. 'Fore that even it was snakin' thru rubber plants. It had Cheetahs movin' to its rhythm. You dig?

CROW: Yeah. Sure. It's a matter a' course.
*(*CROW *moves to get away from him as* HOSS *becomes a menacing ancient spirit. Like a voodoo man.)*

HOSS: Yo' "yeah" is tryin' to shake a lie, boy. The radio's lost the jungle. You can't hear that space 'tween the radio and the jungle.

CROW: It's in my blood. I got genius.

HOSS: Fast fingers don't mean they hold magic. That's lost to you, dude. That's somethin' sunk on another continent and I don't mean Atlantis. You can dig where the true rhymes hold down. Yo' blood know that if nothin' else.

CROW: Blood. Well listen, I need some spray on my callouses now and then, but it's not about endurance.

HOSS: Ha! Yo' lost dewclaw. Extra weight. You ain't come inside the South. You ain't even opened the door. The brass band contain yo' world a million times over.

CROW: Electricity brought it home. Without juice you'd be long forgot.

HOSS: Who's doin' the rememberin'? The fields opened up red in Georgia, South Carolina. A moan lasted years back then. The grey and blue went down like a harvest and what was left?

CROW: That scale hung itself short.

HOSS: What was left was the clarinet, the bass drum, the trumpet. The fixin's for a salad. All hung gold and black in the pawnshop window. All them niggers with their hollers hangin' echoes from the fields. All the secret messages sent through a day a' blazin' work.

CROW: I can't do nothing about that. I'm in a different time.

HOSS: And what brought their heads up off the cement? Not no Abraham Lincoln. Not no Emancipation. Not no John Brown. It was the gold and black behind them windows. The music of somethin' inside that no boss man could touch.

CROW: I touch down here, Leathers. Bring it to now.

HOSS: You'd like a free ride on a black man's back.

CROW: I got no guilt to conjure! Fence me with the present.

HOSS: But you miss the origins, milk face. Little Brother Montegomery with the keyboard on his back. The turpentine circuit. Piano ringin' through the woods. Back then you get hung you couldn't play the blues. Back when the boogie wasn't named and every cathouse had a professor. Hookers movin' to the ivory tinkle. Diplomats and sailors gettin' laid side by side to the blues. Gettin' laid so bad the U.S. Navy have to close down Storyville. That's how the move began. King Oliver got Chicago talkin' New

Orleans, Ma Rainey, Blind Lemon Jefferson. They all come and got the gangsters hoppin'.

CROW: I'm a Rocker, not a hick!

HOSS: You could use a little cow flop on yer shoes, boy. Yo' music's in yo' head. You a blind minstrel with a phony shuffle. You got a wound gapin' 'tween the chords and the pickin'. Chuck Berry can't even mend you up. You doin' a pantomime in the eye of a hurricane. Ain't even got the sense to signal for help. You lost the barrelhouse, you lost the honky-tonk. You lost your feelings in a suburban country club the first time they ask you to play "Risin' River Blues" for the debutante ball. You ripped your own self off and now all you got is yo' poison to call yo' gift. You a punk chump with a sequin nose and you'll need more'n a Les Paul Gibson to bring you home.

(REF blows his whistle.)

REF: Hold it, hold it, hold it!

(HOSS snaps back to himself.)

HOSS: What's wrong?

REF: I don't know. Somethin's funny. Somethin's outa' whack here. We'll call this one a draw.

HOSS: A draw!

REF: I can't make heads or tails outa' this.

HOSS: I had him cut over both eyes!

REF: We leave it. Let's get on with Round 3.

HOSS: Look at him! He's unconscious standin' up.

REF: Play the round!

(The bell rings. CROW jumps into action, dancing like Muhammad Ali. HOSS moves flatfooted trying to avoid him. CROW is now on the offensive. The music starts again.)

Round 3.

CROW: So ya' wanna be a rocker. Study the moves. Jerry Lee Lewis. Buy some blue suede shoes. Move yer head like Rod Stewart. Put yer ass in a grind. Talkin' sock it to it, get the image in line. Get the image in line boy. The fantasy rhyme. It's all over the streets and you can't buy the time. You can't buy the bebop. You can't buy the slide. Got the fantasy blues and no place to hide.

HOSS: O.K., this time I stay solid. You ain't suckin' me into jive rhythms. I got my own. I got my patterns. Original. I'm my own man. Original. I stand solid. It's just a matter of time. I'll wear you to the bone.

CROW: Collectin' the South. Collectin' the blues. Flat busted in Chicago and payin' yer dues.

HOSS: Kick it out fish face! This time you bleed!

(REF blows his whistle. The music stops.)

REF: *(to HOSS)* No clinches. This ain't a wrestlin' match.

HOSS: I was counterin'.

REF: Just keep daylight between ya'. Let's go.

(The music starts again. HOSS goes back to the offense.)

HOSS: *(to REF)* I was counterin', man!

CROW: Ain't got his chops yet but listens to Hendrix. Ears in the stereo lappin' it up. Likes snortin' his horses too chicken to fix. Still gets a hard on but can't get it up.

HOSS: Backward tactics! I call a foul!

(REF blows his whistle again.)

REF: No stalls. Keep it movin'. Keep it movin'.

HOSS: I call a foul. He can't shift in midstream.

REF: Let's go, let's go.

HOSS: He can't do that!

(REF blows his whistle again. The music comes up.)

CROW: Can't get it sideways walkin' the dog. Tries trainin' his voice to sound like a frog. Sound like a Dylan, sound like a Jagger, sound like an earthquake all over the Fender. Wearin' a shag now, looks like a fag now. Can't get it together with chicks in the mag. Can't get it together for all of his tryin'. Can't get it together for fear that he's dyin'. Fear that he's crackin' busted in two. Busted in three parts. Busted in four. Busted and dyin' and cryin' for more. Busted and bleedin' all over the floor. All bleedin' and wasted and tryin' to score.

(REF blows his whistle.)

HOSS: What the fuck's wrong now?

REF: I'm gonna have to call that a T.K.O.

HOSS: Are you fuckin' crazy?

REF: That's the way I see it. The match is over.

HOSS: I ain't even started to make my move yet!

REF: Sorry.

(HOSS *lets loose a blood-curdling animal scream and runs to one of the pistols on the floor, picks it up and fires, emptying the gun into the* REF. REF *falls dead.* HOSS *should be out of control, then snap himself back. He just stands there paralyzed and shaking.*)

CROW: Now the Keepers'll be knockin' down your hickory, Leathers.

HOSS: Fuck 'em. Let 'em come. I'm a Gypsy now. Just like you.

CROW: Just like me?

HOSS: Yeah. Outside the game.

CROW: And into a bigger one. You think you can cope?

HOSS: With the Gypsies? Why not. You could teach me. I could pick it up fast.

CROW: You wanna be like me now?

HOSS: Not exactly. Just help me into the style. I'll develop my own image. I'm an original man. A one and only. I just need some help.

CROW: But I beat you cold. I don't owe you nothin'.

HOSS: All right. Look. I'll set you up with a new short and some threads in exchange for some lessons.

CROW: No throw Leathers.

HOSS: I'll give ya' all my weapons and throw in some dope. How's that?

CROW: Can't hack it.

HOSS: All right, what do you want? Anything. It's all yours.

(CROW *pauses*)

CROW: O.K. This is what I want. All your turf from Phoenix to San Berdoo clear up to Napa Valley and back. The whole shot. That's what I want.

(HOSS *pauses for a while, stunned. Then a smile of recognition comes over him.*)

HOSS: Now I get it. I should cut you in half right now. I shoulda' slit yer throat soon's you came through the door. You must be outa' yer fuckin' cake man! All my turf?! You know how long it's taken me to collect that ground. You know how many kills it's taken! I'm a fuckin' champion man. Not an amateur. All my turf! That's all I got.

CROW: Yer throwin' away yer reputation, so why not give me yer turf. You got nothin' to lose. It won't do you no good once the Keepers suss this murder.

HOSS: I still got power. The turf is my power. Without that I'm nothin'. I can survive without the image, but a Marker without no turf is just out to lunch.

CROW: I thought you wanted to cop Gypsy style.

HOSS: I do but I need my turf!

CROW: The Gypsies float their ground, man. Nobody sets up colors.

HOSS: *You* want it bad enough. What's a' matter with you. You movin' outa' Gypsy ranks?

CROW: Razor Leathers.

HOSS: Wait a minute. You tricked me. You wanna trade places with me? You had this planned right from the start.

CROW: Very razor. An even trade. I give you my style and I take your turf.

HOSS: That's easy for you and hard for me.

CROW: You got no choice.

HOSS: I could just move out like I am and keep everything. I could make it like that.

CROW: Try it.

HOSS: You got it all worked out don't ya, fish face? You run me through a few tricks, take everything I got and send me out to die like a chump. Well I ain't fallin' for it.

CROW: Then what're you gonna do?

HOSS: I'll think a' somethin'. What if we teamed up? Yeah! That's it! You, me and Cheyenne. We start a Gypsy pack.

CROW: I'm a solo man. So are you. We'd do each other in. Who'd be the leader?

HOSS: We don't need a leader. Cheyenne could be the leader.

CROW: Not on my time. Rip that one up, Leathers.

HOSS: How did this happen? This ain't the way it's supposed to happen. Why do you wanna be like me anyway. Look at me. Everything was going so good. I had everything at my fingertips. Now I'm outa' control. I'm pulled and pushed around from one image to another. Nothin' takes a solid form. Nothin' sure and final. Where do I stand! Where the fuck do I stand!

CROW: Alone, Leathers.

HOSS: Yeah, well I guess I don't got your smarts. That's for sure. You played me just right. Sucked me right into it. There's nothin' to do but call ya'. All right. The turf's yours. The whole shot. Now show me how to be a man.

CROW: A man's too hard, Leathers. Too many doors to that room. A Gypsy's easy. Here, chew on some sap.

(*He hands* HOSS *a stick of gum.* HOSS *chews it in a defeated way.*)

Bite down. Chew beyond yourself. That's what ya' wanna shoot for. Beyond. Walk like ya' got knives on yer heels. Talk like a fire. The eyes are important. First you gotta learn yer eyes. Now look here. Look in my eyes. Straight out.

(HOSS *stands close to* CROW'S *face and looks in his eyes.* CROW *stares back.*)

No! Yer lookin' in. Back at yourself. You gotta look out. Straight into me and out the back a' my head. Like my eyes were tunnels goin' straight through to daylight. That's better. More. Cut me in half. Get mean. There's too much pity, man. Too much empathy. That's not the target. Use yer eyes like a weapon. Not defensive. Offensive. Always on the offense. You gotta get this down. You can paralyze a mark with a good set of eyes.

HOSS: How's that?

CROW: Better. Get down to it. Too much searchin'. I got no answers. Go beyond confidence. Beyond loathing. Just kill with the eyes. That's it. That's better. Now. How do you feel?

HOSS: Paralyzed.

CROW: That'll change. The power'll shift to the other side. Feel it?

HOSS: No.

CROW: It'll come. Just hang in there. Feel it now?

HOSS: No. Can I blink now?

CROW: Yeah. Give 'em a rest.

(HOSS *blinks his eyes and moves away.*)

It'll come. You gotta practice like a musician. You don't learn all yer licks in one session. Now try out yer walk. Start movin' to a different

drummer man. Ginger Baker's burned down. Get into Danny Richmond, Sonny Murray, Tony Williams. One a' them cats. More Jazz licks. Check out Mongo Santamaria, he might get yer heels burnin'.

(HOSS *starts moving awkwardly around the stage.*)

HOSS: I never heard a' them guys.

CROW: O.K. pick one. Any one. Pick one ya' like.

HOSS: Capaldi.

CROW: Too clean man. Try out Ainsley Dunbar. Nice hot licks. Anyone that gets the knife goin'. You gotta slice blacktop man. Melt asphalt.

HOSS: Keith Moon.

CROW: Too much flash. Get off the cymbals. Stop flyin' around the kit. Get down to it. Get down.

HOSS: Buddy Miles.

CROW: Just loud, man. Blind strength but no touch.

HOSS: Let's go on to somethin' else.

CROW: O.K. Body moves. Do a few chick moves. Fluff up yer feathers. Side a' the head shots. Hand on the hip. Let the weight slide to one side. Straight leg and the opposite bent. Pull on yer basket.

(HOSS *tries to follow.* CROW *acts out all the gestures with a slick cool.*)

Spit out yer teeth. Ear pulls. Nose pulls. Pull out a booger. Slow scratches from shoulder to belly. Hitch up yer shirt. Sex man. Tighten your ass. Tighten one cheek and loosen the other. Play off yer thighs to yer calves. Get it all talkin' a language.

HOSS: Slow down! I ain't a fuckin' machine.

CROW: Yer gettin' it. Yer doin' O.K. It's comin'. Talk to yer blood. Get it together. Get it runnin' hot on the left side and cold on the right. Now split it. Now put it in halves. Get the top half churnin', the bottom relaxed. Control, Leathers. Ya' gotta learn control. Pull it together.

HOSS: I'm not prepared. I can't just plunge into this. I gotta have some preliminaries.

CROW: O.K. You're right. Tell ya' what. Sit down in the chair and relax. Just take it easy. Come on.

HOSS: Maybe I'm too old.

CROW: Come on, just sit yerself down.

(HOSS *sits in the chair.* CROW *paces around him.*) We gotta break yer patterns down, Leathers. Too many bad habits. Re-program the tapes. Now just relax. Start breathin' deep and slow. Empty your head. Shift your attention to immediate sounds. The floor. The space around you. The sound of your heart. Keep away from fantasy. Shake off the image. No pictures just pure focus. How does it feel?

HOSS: I don't know. Different I guess.

CROW: Just ease down. Let everything go.

(BECKY *comes on down left facing the audience. She wears a black wig and is dressed like Anna Karina in "Alphaville." She caresses herself as though her hands were a man's, feeling her tits, her thighs, her waist. Sometimes when one hand seems to take too much advantage she seizes it with the other hand and pushes it away.* HOSS *seems to turn into a little boy.*)

HOSS: You won't let nobody hurt me will ya'?

CROW: Nobody's gonna hurt ya'.

HOSS: Where have I been. All this time. No memory. I was never there.

(BECKY *talks straight out to the audience. But directs it at* HOSS.)

BECKY: I never knew you were that kind of a guy. I thought you were nice. A nice guy. I never thought you'd be like the others. Why do you do that? You know I'm not that kind of a girl. Come on. I just wanna talk. I wanna have a conversation. Tell me about yourself. Come on. Don't do that. Can't we just talk or something. All right, I wanna go then. Take me home. Come on. Let's go get a Coke. Come on. I mean it. Don't do that! Don't!

(*Her hands pull off her sweater. The wig comes off with it. She's wearing a stiff white bra underneath. She struggles against her hands, then lets them go, then struggles again.*)

Can't we go back? I'm going to be late. Can't we just kiss? No! Don't! Come on. I don't wanna do this. I'm not that kind of a girl. Look, just keep your hands off! I mean it. I don't like it. I just wanna talk. Tell me something nice.

(*Her hands rip off her bra and feel her tits.*)

Just talk to me. Tell me about your car. What kind of an engine has it got? Come on. Don't! Do you go racing a lot? Don't you take it down to the strip. No! Don't do that! Has it got overhead lifters. I really like those fat tires. They're really boss. Cut it out! No! Stop it! Don't!

(*Her hands unzip her skirt and tear it off. One hand tries to get inside her panties while the other hand fights it off.*)

I don't go all the way. I can't. I've never ever gone this far before. I don't wanna go all the way. I'm not that kind of a girl. I'll get pregnant. Stop it! All right, just get away from me! Get away! I'm getting out. Let me outa' the car! Let me out! Don't! Let go of me! Let go! (*she starts screaming*) Let me out! Let me out! Let me out! Let me out!

(*She picks up her clothes and runs off.*)

CROW: How is it now?

HOSS: I don't know. Trapped. Defeated. Shot down.

CROW: Just a wave. Time to scoop a Gypsy shot. Start with a clean screen. Are you blank now?

HOSS: I guess.

CROW: Good. Now vision him comin'. Walking towards you from a distance. Can't make out the face yet. Just feel his form. Get down his animal. Like a cat. Lethal and silent. Comin' from far off. Takin' his time. Pull him to ya'. Can you feel him?

HOSS: I think so. It's me. He's just like me only younger. More dangerous. Takes bigger chances. No doubt. No fear.

CROW: Keep him comin'. Pull him into ya'. Put on his gestures. Wear him like a suit a' clothes.

HOSS: Yeah. It *is* me. Just like I always wanted to be.

(*The band starts playing the first two chords to "Slips Away." CHEYENNE, STAR-MAN, DOC and GALACTIC JACK come on dressed in white tuxedos with pink carnations in their lapels. They stand in a tight group and sing harmony notes to the music. They move in perfect choreographed movements like the old a capella bands. The music should build slowly with HOSS' voice until he stops talking and the* SINGERS *go right into the song.)*

Mean and tough and cool. Untouchable. A true killer. Don't take no shit from nobody. True to his heart. True to his voice. Everything's whole and unshakeable. His eyes cut through the jive. He knows his own fate. Beyond doubt. True courage in every move. Trusts every action to be what it is. Knows where he stands. Lives by a code. His own code. Knows something timeless. Unending trust in himself. No hesitation. Beyond pride or modesty. Speaks the truth without trying. Can't do anything false. Lived out his fantasies. Plunged into fear and come out the other side. Died a million deaths. Tortured and pampered. Holds no grudge. No blame. No guilt. Laughs with his whole being. Passed beyond tears. Beyond ache for the world. Pitiless. Indifferent and riding a state of grace. It ain't me! IT AIN'T ME! IT AIN'T ME! IT AIN'T ME!!

(He collapses in a ball and holds himself tight. The FOUR GUYS *sing.)*

"Slips Away"

FOUR GUYS:

I saw my face in yours—I took you for
    myself
I took you by mistake—for me
I learned your walk and talk—I learned
    your mouth
I learned the secrets in your eye

    But now I find the feelin' slips away
    What's with me night and day is gone

Where you left off and I begin
It took me time to break the line
And on your own is tough enough
Without the thread that we got broken

    But now I find the feelin' slips away
    What's with me night and day is gone

If we could signify from far away
Just close enough to get the touch
You'd find your face in mine
And all my faces tryin' to bring you back
    to me

But now I find the feelin' slips away
What's with me night and day is gone
(repeat chorus)
(The song ends. The FOUR GUYS *exit.)*

CROW: Hey, Leathers. Come on man it's time to cope. Get ready to bop. The world's waitin'.
*(*HOSS *doesn't move.)*
Leathers, you gotta move out to it now. I taught ya' all I know. Now it's up to you. You got the power.
*(*HOSS *rises holding the gun in his hand.)*

HOSS: In the palm a' my hand. I got the last say.

CROW: That's it. Get ready to roll. You're gonna knock 'em dead.

HOSS: Knock 'em dead.

CROW: Yeah. What about it.

HOSS: You know somethin' Crow? I really like you. I really have respect for you. You know who you are and you don't give a shit.

CROW: Thanks, Leathers.

HOSS: I just hope you never see yourself from the outside. Just a flash of what you're really like. A pitiful flash.

CROW: Like you?

HOSS: Like me.

CROW: No chance, Leathers. The image is my survival kit.

HOSS: Survival. Yeah. You'll last a long time Crow. A real long time. You're a master adapter. A visionary adapter.

CROW: Switch to suit, Leathers, and mark to kill.

HOSS: Tough as a blind man.

CROW: Tough enough to beat the champ.

HOSS: Yeah. You win all right. All this. Body and soul. All this invisible gold. All this collection of torture. It's all yours. You're the winner and I'm the loser. That's the way it stands. But I'm losin' big, Crow Bait. I'm losin' to the big power. All the way. I couldn't take my life in my hands while I was alive but now I can take it in death. I'm a born Marker Crow Bait. That's more than you'll ever be. Now stand back and watch some true style. The mark of a lifetime. A true gesture that won't never cheat on itself 'cause it's the last of its kind. It can't be taught or copied or stolen or sold. It's mine. An original. It's my life and my death in one clean shot. (HOSS *turns his back to the audience. And puts the gun in his mouth. He raises one hand high in the air and pulls the trigger with the other. He falls in a heap. This gesture should not be in slow motion or use any jive theatrical gimmicks other than the actor's own courage on stage. To save the actor's face from powder burns an off-stage gun should be fired at the right moment.* CROW *stands silent for a while.*)

CROW: Perfect, Leathers. Perfect. A genius mark. I gotta hand it to ya'. It took ya' long enough but you slid right home. (*he calls off stage*) All right! Let's go!

(BECKY *and* CHEYENNE *enter, dressed like they were in Act One.*)

Becky, get some biceps to drag out these stiffs. Get the place lookin' a little decent. We're gonna have us a celebration.

BECKY: I had a feeling you'd take him. Was it hard?

CROW: Yeah. He was pretty tough. Went out in the old style. Clung right up to the drop.

BECKY: He was a good Marker man. One a' the great ones.

CROW: Not great enough.

BECKY: I guess not.

(*She exits.* CROW *talks to* CHEYENNE *who eyes him.*)

CROW: You eye me bitter wheel-boy. What's the skinny?

CHEYENNE: I guess you want me to drive for you now.

CROW: Maybe I hear you're the top handler in the gold circuit.

CHEYENNE: You hear good.

CROW: I cipher you turnin' sour through. Suicidal like the master. I don't fashion goin' down to a kamikaze collision just after I knock the top.

CHEYENNE: You're cuttin' me loose?

CROW: That's it.

CHEYENNE: You got big shoes to fill Gypsy. They'll be comin' for you next.

CROW: Naw. That's fer lames. I'm throwin' the shoes away. I'm runnin' flat out to a new course.

CHEYENNE: (*looking at* HOSS' *body*) He was knockin' at the door. He was right up there. He came the long route. Not like you. He earned his style. He was a Marker. A true Marker.

CROW: He was backed up by his own suction, man. Didn't answer to no name but loser. All that power goin' backwards. It's good he shut the oven. If he hadn't he'd be blowin' poison in non-directions. I did him a favor. Now the power shifts and sits till a bigger wind blows. Not in my life run but one to come. And all the ones after that. Changin' hands like a snake dance to heaven. This is my time Cowboy and I'm runnin' it up the middle. You best grab your ticket and leave the Maserati with the keys.

CHEYENNE: Sure.

(*He reaches in his pocket and pulls out the keys to the car.*)

Good luck.

(*He throws the keys at* CROW'S *feet and exits.* CROW *smiles, bends down slowly and picks up the keys. He tosses them in his hand. The band starts the music.* CROW *sings "Rollin' Down."*)

"Rollin' Down"

CROW:

Keep me rollin' down
Keep me rollin' down
Keep me in my state a' grace
Just keep me rollin' down

I've fooled the Devil's hand
I've fooled the Ace of Spades
I've called the bluff in God's own face
Now keep me from my fate

If I'm a fool then keep me blind
I'd rather feel my way
If I'm a tool for a bigger game
You better get down—you better get down
    and pray

Just keep me rollin' down
Keep me rollin' down
Keep me in my state a' grace
Just keep me rollin' down.

(*The song ends. The lights go to black.*)

DAVID RABE

STREAMERS (1976)

At this point [when Carlyle stabs Rooney in Streamers] the atmosphere in the auditorium changed radically, boiled over. A rather substantial portion of the audience got to its feet noisily, not hesitating to call out to companions to join them in leaving.

In a review of the opening of David Rabe's *Streamers* at the Long Wharf Theatre in New Haven, Connecticut, Walter Kerr describes the exodus of audience members exasperated with the play's considerable gore. Kerr wonders aloud if these spectators were "unable to assimilate the sudden violence that author Rabe and director Mike Nichols had made incontestably real? Or was the violence not incontestably real. . . ? Was there too much blood, had it come too suddenly upon them?" He quickly decides that neither was the case, indicting instead the play's narrative construction: "What the audience asks for is a pattern, a design, a shape that will embrace what they are now looking at and place it in significant relationship to what has gone before and may come after." Rabe fails to provide this, Kerr concludes, seemingly basing his verdict on Aristotle's notion of the **unity of action**: the desideratum that all the events of a tragic plot be linked by "probability and necessity." Unable to discern such a "unity," Rabe's New Haven audience stalked out in protest. This explanation, however, begs at least one question Rabe frequently raises when discussing his work: namely, how "realistic" is such a conception of "realism"? Must dramatic representation of the "real" always be rational? Is reality itself rational? Since its brief run in Connecticut from late January through February 1976, *Streamers* has found more receptive audiences. It opened in April 1976 at the Mitzi Newhouse Theatre at Lincoln Center, running for some 478 performances and winning the New York Drama Critics

Circle Award as best play of the year. Thereafter, it quickly found a place in the repertories of such important regional theatres as the Goodman Theatre in Chicago and the Arena Stage in Washington, and was made into a film in 1983 by Robert Altman. *Streamers* remains both a frequently revived play in the contemporary repertory and, along with such films as Oliver Stone's *Platoon* (1986), Stanley Kubrick's *Full Metal Jacket* (1987), and Brian DePalma's *Casualties of War* (1989), for which Rabe wrote the screenplay, a provocative commentary on America during the Vietnam War era.

Like Clive Barnes of *The New York Times*, many critics regard *Streamers* as completing a "Vietnam Trilogy" that began with *The Basic Training of Pavlo Hummel* (1971) and *Sticks and Bones* (1972; an earlier version was staged at Villanova University in 1969). Rabe himself, in discussing *Pavlo Hummel* and *Sticks and Bones*, both of which are more formally experimental than *Streamers*, resists their categorization as antiwar texts or mere "political tracts." Yet if his interest in Vietnam is undeniable, so too is his concern about the effects of mass culture on present-day consumers. In a 1990 interview with Toby Silverman Zinman, Rabe conflates both interests, bemoaning the "high-tech sheen" that television in particular has applied liberally to the reality of Vietnam—among other aspects of American life—transforming it into something "glossed over" with false images and, therefore, "quite unreal." Especially in the **surreal** *Sticks and Bones*, Rabe seems committed to a project both of exploring the realities of xenophobia and misogyny underlying the idealized image of American family life perpetrated by mass culture, and, as he does in *Streamers*, of representing through a linguistic and physical violence that some deem excessive the irrational forces raging beneath the surface of everyday life.

From its opening stage directions through to its climactic sacrifice of the returning son-soldier, *Sticks and Bones* conveys Rabe's critiques both of mass culture's re-writing of the Vietnam War and its inflection of its consumers' subjectivities. That is, Rabe's stage directions emphasize that while there should exist an aura of "naturalness" to the living room in which much of the action is located, there should also be a "sense" that parts of the room belong more properly to "the gloss of an advertisement." When David, a blinded young soldier, returns to his situation comedy household (that of the popular 1950s and 1960s TV series *The Adventures of Ozzie and Harriet*), the reality of Vietnam collides with and finally subverts the mass cultural "reality" projected by his family. Rabe's non-Vietnam plays present a similar collision, as deeper psychological truths frequently compete with the lures of mass culture in the formation of a character's desire and sense of identity. *In the Boom Boom Room* (1974), for example, shows Chrissy, an unhappy go-go dancer who forms most of her notions of marriage and love from Top Forty records; and the protagonist of *Hurlyburly* (1984) theorizes that watching "about a million hours of TV a week" has rendered an acquaintance's brain "a fog of TV thoughts" in a "hurlyburly" that is a "spin-off of what was once prime-time life." According to Rabe, such realities, like the tensions inside the barracks of *Streamers,* cannot be represented adequately by the so-called **realistic** dramas of

> Ibsen, Lillian Hellman, Inge, Odets. It's the idea of the well-made play. I've never done that, and maybe that's part of why people seeing my work get confused sometimes. Sam Shepard, for example, makes it clear where he's not operating in a conventionally realistic mode, so people know how to take him, whereas I've placed plays like *Streamers* and so on in realistic sites and situations . . . for a while, and then this other thing comes out of them.

This "other thing" originates in, among other sources, Rabe's experiences in Vietnam.

Born in Dubuque, Iowa, and graduated in 1962 from Loras College, a Catholic liberal-arts institution there, Rabe (1940–) then enrolled as a graduate student in theatre at Villanova. Before completing his master's degree, he was drafted into the U.S. Army, serving from early 1965 to January 1967, and spending some 11 months in a support unit for hospitals in Vietnam. After returning from southeast Asia, Rabe completed his degree at Villanova in 1968, and worked from May 1969 to August 1970 as a staff writer for the *New Haven Register.* Among other critics, Philip C. Kolin cites the importance of Rabe's tenure as a journalist during which time the stories he published "reflect his approach to a host of contemporary topics that repeatedly surface in his plays": the war and American dissent over it, drug use, the arts, and so on. Rabe returned briefly to Villanova to teach, and in the spring of 1971 Joseph Papp produced *The Basic Training of Pavlo Hummel* at the New York Shakespeare Festival Public Theatre. Rabe won an **Obie** Award for Distinguished Playwriting for *Pavlo Hummel,* and in 1972 *Sticks and Bones* won a **Tony** for the best play on Broadway. This latter drama also sparked a large-scale controversy the following year, particularly over the issue of censorship, when CBS postponed a scheduled showing of it on national television. *The Orphan* (1973) and *In the Boom Boom Room* were, by comparison, commercial and critical failures, but *Streamers* brought Rabe back into prominence in 1976. Since then, he has written, among others, such plays as *Goose and Tomtom* (1982), *Hurlyburly* (1984), and *Those the River Keeps* (1991); the films *I'm Dancing as Fast as I Can* (1982, starring his wife, Jill Clayburgh) and *Casualties of War;* and a novel, *Recital of the Dog* (1993).

Streamers depicts the lives of several young soldiers after they have completed basic training and await their next assignment, most likely to Vietnam, and the drunken reunion of two older sergeants, veterans of Korea, Vietnam, and bars too numerous to mention. The barracks in which the play is set serve as home for three younger soldiers from vastly different backgrounds: Richie, a gay soldier from an affluent family who reads film books and openly discusses his homosexuality; Billy, a middle-class soldier from Wisconsin with whom Richie is infatuated; and Roger, a black from the inner city who later attempts to moderate conflicts between his friend Billy and another soldier, Carlyle. Richie, Billy, and Roger together have a "sweet deal," a kind of home, as Carlyle, a newcomer displaced from his former company and angry at an army run by white men, terms it. In a sense, the barracks *are* their home, one in which racial and class differences are effaced, in part by the use of a common language of ungrammatical sentences and profane phrases. Early in the play Richie advises Billy to say "shit," "ain't," and "motherfucker," which he increasingly does, so that educational differences between them and other soldiers may be erased. And, for a time, these and the differences of Richie's sexuality are subdued. Yet when Carlyle intrudes upon the scene early in the play and recognizes that he may not be warmly received by the others, the "happy home" of the barracks is placed in jeopardy. He ominously declares as he leaves in Act I, "You gonna hear from me." And later they do, with violent ramifications.

In Act II of *Streamers*, Richie's flirtations with Carlyle accelerate into the possibility of sexual relations in the barracks, a possibility that Billy cannot allow in his "house." Conflict is inevitable, and frighteningly sudden. In the flash of a second, Carlyle wields a switchblade and cuts Billy, who finds a straight razor and racial slurs of which he thought he was incapable. Carlyle stabs him and later kills an inebriated Sergeant Rooney, who staggers into the room looking for his drinking buddy, Sergeant Cokes, and decides to confront Carlyle himself with the shard of a broken bottle. This explosion of violence, this profusion of blood, leads to two deaths and the arrest of a frightened, irrational Carlyle, who declares that the barracks are his "house," his place. The play concludes with Cokes, drunken and sentimental, looking for pal Rooney, the **miles gloriosus** (braggart soldier) character from classical comedy, and unable to find him. Cokes ends the play with two long speeches, one of which foregrounds his memory

of killing a helpless enemy during the Korean War that liquor can never wash away, and an elegaic version of "Beautiful Streamer," sung earlier about the paratrooper who discovers in mid-jump that his parachute will not open. A streamer, as Cokes describes it earlier in the play, is a parachute hopelessly "twisted" and hanging upright like a tulip—or a "big icicle sticking straight up"—above the jumper. Streamers don't open, and the parachutists below them plummet helplessly to earth and stick into the ground "like a knife."

The reality of the streamer, then, is a sudden one for which there is no preparation and from which there is no escape. And it is an apt metaphor for the violence in much of Rabe's work: the concealed booby traps of punji sticks working their instantaneous and horrible perfection in the Vietnamese jungles of *Casualties of War*, and the fragmentation-type grenade thrown "by a hand that merely flashes" into view at the beginning of *Pavlo Hummel*. *Streamers* in performance delivers this reality to its audience and, as Walter Kerr discovered at the play's premiere, not every audience member is eager to experience it.

WORKS CONSULTED

Barnes, Clive. "Rabe Brings Vietnam Trilogy to a Close." *New York Times*, April 22, 1976: 38.

Kerr, Walter. "Stage View: When Does Gore Get Gratuitous?" *New York Times*, February 22, 1976, sec. 2: 1, 7.

Kolin, Philip C. *David Rabe: A Stage History and A Primary and Secondary Bibliography*. New York: Garland, 1988.

Rabe, David. "Introduction." *The Basic Training of Pavlo Hummel and Sticks and Bones*. New York: Viking, 1973. ix–xxv.

Watt, Stephen. "In Mass Culture's Image: The Subject of (in) Rabe's Boom Boom Rooms." *David Rabe: A Casebook*, ed. Toby Silverman Zinman. New York: Garland, 1991. 49–67.

Zinman, Toby Silverman, ed. *David Rabe: A Casebook*. New York: Garland, 1991.

MASTER SSU, MASTER YÜ, MASTER LI AND MASTER LAI

All at once Master Yü fell ill, and Master Ssu went to ask how he was. "Amazing!" exclaimed Master Yü. "Look, the Creator is making me all crookedy! My back sticks up like a hunchback's so that my vital organs are on top of me. My chin is hidden down around my navel, my shoulders are up above my head, and my pigtail points at the sky. It must be due to some dislocation of the forces of the yin and the yang. . . ."

"Do you resent it?" asked Master Ssu.

"Why, no," replied Master Yü. "What is there to resent . . .?"

Then suddenly Master Lai also fell ill. Gasping for breath, he lay at the point of death. His wife and children gathered round in a circle and wept. Master Li, who had come to find out how he was, said to them, "Shooooo! Get back! Don't disturb the process of change."

And he leaned against the doorway and chatted with Master Lai. "How marvelous the Creator is!" he exclaimed. "What is he going to make out of you next? Where is he going to send you? Will he make

you into a rat's liver? Will he make you into a bug's arm?"

"A child obeys his father and mother and goes wherever he is told, east or west, south or north," said Master Lai. "And the yin and the yang—how much more are they to a man than father or mother! Now that they have brought me to the verge of death, how perverse it would be of me to refuse to obey them. . . . So now I think of heaven and earth as a great furnace and the Creator as a skilled smith. What place could he send me that would not be all right? I will go off peacefully to sleep, and then with a start I will wake up."

—CHUANG-TZU

They so mean around here, they steal your sweat.

—SONNY LISTON

CHARACTERS

MARTIN	ROONEY
RICHIE	M.P. LIEUTENANT
CARLYLE	PFC HINSON (M.P.)
BILLY	PFC CLARK (M.P.)
ROGER	FOURTH M.P.
COKES	

ACT I

The set is a large cadre room thrusting angularly toward the audience. The floor is wooden and brown. Brightly waxed in places, it is worn and dull in other sections. The back wall is brown and angled. There are two lights at the center of the ceiling. They hang covered by green metal shades. Against the back wall and to the stage right side are three wall lockers, side by side. Stage center in the back wall is the door, the only entrance to the room. It opens onto a hallway that runs off to the latrines, showers, other cadre rooms and larger barracks

rooms. There are three bunks. BILLY'S bunk is parallel to ROGER'S bunk. They are upstage and on either side of the room, and face downstage. RICHIE'S bunk is downstage and at a right angle to BILLY'S bunk. At the foot of each bunk is a green wooden footlocker. There is a floor outlet near ROGER'S bunk. He uses it for his radio. A reading lamp is clamped on to the metal piping at the head of RICHIE'S bunk. A wooden chair stands beside the wall lockers. Two mops hang in the stage left corner near a trash can.

It is dusk as the lights rise on the room. RICHIE is seated and bowed forward wearily on his bunk. He

*wears his long-sleeved khaki summer dress uniform.
Upstage behind him is* MARTIN, *a thin, dark young
man, pacing, worried. A white towel stained red with
blood is wrapped around his wrist. He paces several
steps and falters, stops. He stands there.*

RICHIE: Honest to God, Martin, I don't know what
    to say anymore. I don't know what to tell you.
MARTIN: *(beginning to pace again)* I mean it. I just
    can't stand it. Look at me.
RICHIE: I know.
MARTIN: I hate it.
RICHIE: We've got to make up a story. They'll ask
    you a hundred questions.
MARTIN: Do you know how I hate it?
RICHIE: Everybody does. Don't you think I hate it,
    too?
MARTIN: I enlisted, though. I enlisted and I hate it.
RICHIE: I enlisted, too.
MARTIN: I vomit every morning. I get the dry
    heaves. In the middle of every night.
    (He flops down on the corner of BILLY'S *bed and
    sits there, slumped forward, shaking his head.)*
RICHIE: You can stop that. You can.
MARTIN: No.
RICHIE: You're just scared. It's just fear.
MARTIN: They're all so mean; they're all so awful.
    I've got two years to go. Just thinking about it
    is going to make me sick. I thought it would be
    different from the way it is.
RICHIE: But you could have died, for God's sake.
    (RICHIE has turned now; he is facing MARTIN.)
MARTIN: I just wanted out.
RICHIE: I might not have found you, though. I
    might not have come up here.
MARTIN: I don't care. I'd be out.
    *(The door opens and a black man in filthy fa-
    tigues—they are grease-stained and dark with
    sweat—stands there. He is* CARLYLE, *looking
    about.* RICHIE, *seeing him, rises and moves to-
    ward him.)*
RICHIE: No. Roger isn't here right now.
CARLYLE: Who isn't?
RICHIE: He isn't here.
CARLYLE: They tole me a black boy livin' in here.
    I don't see him.

(He looks suspiciously about the room.)

RICHIE: That's what I'm saying. He isn't here.
    He'll be back later. You can come back later.
    His name is Roger.
MARTIN: I slit my wrist.
    *(Thrusting out the bloody, towel-wrapped wrist
    toward* CARLYLE.)
RICHIE: Martin! Jesus!
MARTIN: I did.
RICHIE: He's kidding. He's kidding.
CARLYLE: What was his name? Martin?
    *(CARLYLE is confused and the confusion has
    made him angry. He moves toward* MARTIN.)
    You Martin?
MARTIN: Yes.
    (As BILLY, *a white in his mid-twenties, blond and
    trim, appears in the door, whistling, carrying a
    slice of pie on a paper napkin. Sensing some-
    thing, he falters, looks at* CARLYLE, *then* RICHIE.)
BILLY: Hey, what's goin' on?
CARLYLE: *(turning, leaving)* Nothin', man. Not a
    thing.
    (BILLY looks questioningly at RICHIE. *Then, af-
    ter placing the piece of pie on the chair beside
    the door, he crosses to his footlocker.)*
RICHIE: He came in looking for Roger, but he
    didn't even know his name.
BILLY: *(sitting on his footlocker, he starts taking off
    his shoes)* How come you weren't at dinner,
    Rich? I brought you a piece of pie. Hey, Martin.
    (MARTIN thrusts out his towel-wrapped wrist.)
MARTIN: I cut my wrist, Billy.
RICHIE: Oh, for God's sake, Martin!
    (He whirls away.)
BILLY: Huh?
MARTIN: I did.
RICHIE: You are disgusting, Martin.
MARTIN: No. It's the truth. I did. I am not dis-
    gusting.
RICHIE: Well, maybe it isn't disgusting, but it cer-
    tainly is disappointing.
BILLY: What are you guys talking about?
    *(Sitting there, he really doesn't know what is
    going on.)*
MARTIN: I cut my wrists, I slashed them, and
    Richie is pretending I didn't.

RICHIE: I am not. And you only cut one wrist and you didn't slash it.

MARTIN: I can't stand the army anymore, Billy.
(He is moving now to petition BILLY, *and* RICHIE *steps between them.)*

RICHIE: Billy, listen to me. This is between Martin and me.

MARTIN: It's between me and the army, Richie.

RICHIE: *(taking* MARTIN *by the shoulders as* BILLY *is now trying to get near* MARTIN*)* Let's just go outside and talk, Martin. You don't know what you're saying.

BILLY: Can I see? I mean, did he really do it?

RICHIE: No!

MARTIN: I did.

BILLY: That's awful. Jesus. Maybe you should go to the infirmary.

RICHIE: I washed it with peroxide. It's not deep. Just let us be. Please. He just needs to straighten out his thinking a little, that's all.

BILLY: Well, maybe I could help him?

MARTIN: Maybe he could.

RICHIE: *(suddenly pushing at* MARTIN, RICHIE *is angry and exasperated. He wants* MARTIN *out of the room.)* Get out of here, Martin. Billy, you do some push-ups or something.
(Having been pushed toward the door, MARTIN *wanders out.)*

BILLY: No.

RICHIE: I know what Martin needs.
*(*RICHIE *whirls and rushes into the hall after* MARTIN, *leaving* BILLY *scrambling to get his shoes on.)*

BILLY: You're no doctor, are you? I just want to make sure he doesn't have to go to the infirmary, then I'll leave you alone.
(One shoe on, he grabs up the second and runs out the door into the hall after them.)
Martin! Martin, wait up!
(Silence. The door has been left open. Fifteen or twenty seconds pass. Then someone is heard coming down the hall. He is singing "Get a Job" and trying to do the voices and harmonies of a vocal group. ROGER, *a tall, well-built black in long-sleeved khakis, comes in the door. He has a laundry bag over his shoulder, a pair of clean civilian*

trousers and a shirt on a hanger in his other hand. After dropping the bag on his bed, he goes to his wall locker, where he carefully hangs up the civilian clothes. Returning to the bed, he picks up the laundry and then, as if struck, he throws the bag down on the bed, tears off his tie and sits down angrily on the bed. For a moment, with his head in his hands, he sits there. Then, resolutely, he rises, takes up the position of attention, and simply topples forward, his hands leaping out to break his fall at the last instant and put him into the push-up position. Counting in a hissing, whispering voice, he does ten push-ups before giving up and flopping onto his belly. He simply doesn't have the will to do any more. Lying there, he counts rapidly on.)

ROGER: Fourteen, fifteen. Twenty. Twenty-five.
*(*BILLY, *shuffling dejectedly back in, sees* ROGER *lying there.* ROGER *springs to his feet, heads toward his footlocker, out of which he takes an ashtray and a pack of cigarettes.)*
You come in this area, you come in here marchin', boy: standin' tall.
*(*BILLY, *having gone to his wall locker, is tossing a* Playboy *magazine onto his bunk. He will also remove a towel, a Dopp kit and a can of foot powder.)*

BILLY: I was marchin'.

ROGER: You call that marchin'?

BILLY: I was as tall as I am; I was marchin'—what do you want?

ROGER: Outa here, man; outa this goddamn typin'-terrors outfit and into some kinda real army. Or else out and free.

BILLY: So go; who's stoppin' you; get out. Go on.

ROGER: Ain't you a bitch.

BILLY: You and me more regular army than the goddamn sergeants around this place, you know that?

ROGER: I was you, Billy boy, I wouldn't be talkin' so sacrilegious so loud, or they be doin' you like they did the ole sarge.

BILLY: He'll get off.

ROGER: Sheee-it, he'll get off.
(Sitting down on the side of his bed and facing BILLY, ROGER *lights up a cigarette.* BILLY *has*

arranged the towel, Dopp kit and foot powder on his own bed.)

Don't you think L.B.J. want to have some sergeants in that Vietnam, man? In Disneyland, baby? Lord have mercy on the ole sarge. He goin' over there to be Mickey Mouse.

BILLY: Do him a lot of good. Make a man outa him.

ROGER: That's right, that's right. He said the same damn thing about himself and you, too, I do believe. You know what's the ole boy's MOS? His Military Occupation Specialty? Demolitions, baby. Expert is his name.

BILLY: *(taking off his shoes and beginning to work on a sore toe,* BILLY *hardly looks up.)* You're kiddin' me.

ROGER: Do I jive?

BILLY: You mean that poor ole bastard who cannot light his own cigar for shakin' is supposed to go over there blowin' up bridges and shit? Do they wanna win this war or not, man?

ROGER: Ole sarge was over in Europe in the big one, Billy. Did all kinds a bad things.

BILLY: *(swinging his feet up onto the bed,* BILLY *sits, cutting the cuticles on his toes, powdering his feet)* Was he drinkin' since he got the word?

ROGER: Was he breathin', Billy? Was he breathin'?

BILLY: Well, at least he ain't cuttin' his fuckin' wrists.

(Silence. ROGER *looks at* BILLY, *who keeps on working.)*

Man, that's the real damn army over there, ain't it? That ain't shinin' your belt buckle and standin' tall. And we might end up in it, man. *(Silence.* ROGER, *rising, begins to sort his laundry.)*

Roger . . . you ever ask yourself if you'd rather fight in a war where it was freezin' cold or one where there was awful snakes? You ever ask that question?

ROGER: Can't say I ever did.

BILLY: We used to ask it all the time. All the time. I mean, us kids sittin' out on the back porch tellin' ghost stories at night. 'Cause it was Korea time and the newspapers were fulla pictures of soldiers in snow with white frozen beards; they

got these rags tied around their feet. And snakes. We hated snakes. Hated 'em. I mean, it's bad enough to be in the jungle duckin' bullets, but then you crawl right into a goddamn snake. That's awful. That's awful.

ROGER: It don't sound none too good.

BILLY: I got my draft notice, goddamn Vietnam didn't even exist. I mean, it existed, but not as in a war we might be in. I started crawlin' around the floor a this house where I was stayin' 'cause I'd dropped outa school, and I was goin' "Bang, bang," pretendin'. Jesus.

ROGER: *(continuing with his laundry, he tries to joke)* My first goddamn formation in basic, Billy, this NCO's up there jammin' away about how some a us are goin' to be dyin' in the war. I'm sayin', "What war? What that crazy man talkin' about?"

BILLY: Us, too. I couldn't believe it. I couldn't believe it. And now we got three people goin' from here.

ROGER: Five.

(They look at each other, and then turn away, each returning to his task.)

BILLY: It don't seem possible. I mean, people shootin' at you. Shootin' at you to kill you.
(Slight pause.)
It's somethin'.

ROGER: What did you decide you preferred?

BILLY: Huh?

ROGER: Did you decide you would prefer the snakes or would you prefer the snow? 'Cause it look like it is going to be the snakes.

BILLY: I think I had pretty much made my mind up on the snow.

ROGER: Well, you just let 'em know that, Billy. Maybe they get one goin' special just for you up in Alaska. You can go to the Klondike. Fightin' some snowmen.

*(*RICHIE *bounds into the room and shuts the door as if to keep out something dreadful. He looks at* ROGER *and* BILLY *and crosses to his wall locker, pulling off his tie as he moves. Tossing the tie into the locker, he begins unbuttoning the cuffs of his shirt.)*

RICHIE: Hi, hi, hi, everybody. Billy, hello.

BILLY: Hey.

ROGER: What's happenin', Rich?

(Moving to the chair beside the door, RICHIE *picks up the pie* BILLY *left there. He will place the pie atop the locker, and then, sitting, he will remove his shoes and socks.)*

RICHIE: I simply did this rather wonderful thing for a friend of mine, helped him see himself in a clearer, more hopeful light—little room in his life for hope? And I feel very good. Didn't Billy tell you?

ROGER: About what?

RICHIE: About Martin.

ROGER: No.

BILLY: *(looking up and speaking pointedly)* No.

*(*RICHIE *looks at* BILLY *and then at* ROGER. RICHIE *is truly confused.)*

RICHIE: No? No?

BILLY: What do I wanna gossip about Martin for?

RICHIE: *(he really can't figure out what is going on with* BILLY. *Shoes and socks in hand, he heads for his wall locker)* Who was planning to gossip? I mean, it did happen. We could talk about it. I mean, I wasn't hearing his goddamn confession. Oh, my sister told me Catholics were boring.

BILLY: Good thing I ain't one anymore.

RICHIE: *(taking off his shirt, he moves toward* ROGER*)* It really wasn't anything, Roger, except Martin made this rather desperate, pathetic gesture for attention that seems to have brought to the surface Billy's more humane and protective side.

(Reaching out, he tousles BILLY'S *hair.)*

BILLY: Man, I am gonna have to obliterate you.

RICHIE: *(tossing his shirt into his locker)* I don't know what you're so embarrassed about.

BILLY: I just think Martin's got enough trouble without me yappin' to everybody.

*(*RICHIE *has moved nearer* BILLY, *his manner playful and teasing.)*

RICHIE: "Obliterate"? "Obliterate," did you say? Oh, Billy, you better say "shit," "ain't" and "motherfucker" real quick now or we'll

all know just how far beyond the fourth grade you went.

ROGER: *(having moved to his locker, into which he is placing his folded clothes)* You hear about the ole sarge, Richard?

BILLY: *(grinning)* You ain't . . . shit . . . motherfucker.

ROGER: *(laughing)* All right.

RICHIE: *(moving center and beginning to remove his trousers)* Billy, no, no. Wit is my domain. You're in charge of sweat and running around the block.

ROGER: You hear about the ole sarge?

RICHIE: What about the ole sarge? Oh, who cares? Let's go to a movie. Billy, wanna? Let's go. C'mon.

(Trousers off, he hurries to his locker.)

BILLY: Sure. What's playin'?

RICHIE: I don't know. Can't remember. Something good, though.

(With a Playboy *magazine he has taken from his locker,* ROGER *is settling down on his bunk, his back toward both* BILLY *and* RICHIE.*)*

BILLY: You wanna go, Rog?

RICHIE: *(in mock irritation)* Don't ask Roger! How are we going to kiss and hug and stuff if he's there?

BILLY: That ain't funny, man.

(He is stretched out on his bunk, and RICHIE *comes bounding over to flop down and lie beside him.)*

RICHIE: And what time will you pick me up?

BILLY: *(he pushes at* RICHIE, *knocking him off the bed and onto the floor)* Well, you just fall down and wait, all right?

RICHIE: Can I help it if I love you?

(Leaping to his feet, he will head to his locker, remove his shorts, put on a robe.)

ROGER: You gonna take a shower, Richard?

RICHIE: Cleanliness is nakedness, Roger.

ROGER: Is that right? I didn't know that. Not too many people know that. You may be the only person in the world who know that.

RICHIE: And godliness is in there somewhere, of course.

(Putting a towel around his neck, he is gathering toiletries to carry to the shower.)

ROGER: You got your own way a lookin' at things, man. You cute.

RICHIE: That's right.

ROGER: You g'wan, have a good time in that shower.

RICHIE: Oh, I will.

BILLY: *(without looking up from his feet, which he is powdering)* And don't drop your soap.

RICHIE: I will if I want to.

(Already out the door, he slams it shut with a flourish.)

BILLY: Can you imagine bein' in combat with Richie—people blastin' away at you—he'd probably want to hold your hand.

ROGER: Ain't he somethin'?

BILLY: Who's zat?

ROGER: He's all right.

BILLY: *(rising, he heads toward his wall locker, where he will put the powder and Dopp kit)* Sure he is, except he's livin' under water.

(Looking at BILLY, ROGER senses something unnerving; it makes ROGER rise, and return his magazine to his footlocker.)

ROGER: I think we oughta do this area, man. I think we oughta do our area. Mop and buff this floor.

BILLY: You really don't think he means that shit he talks, do you?

ROGER: Huh? Awwww, man . . . Billy, no.

BILLY: I'd put money on it, Roger, and I ain't got much money.

(BILLY is trying to face ROGER with this, but ROGER, seated on his bed, has turned away. He is unbuttoning his shirt.)

ROGER: Man, no, no. I'm tellin' you, lad, you listen to the ole Rog. You seen that picture a that little dolly he's got in his locker? He ain't swish, man, believe me—he's cool.

BILLY: It's just that ever since we been in this room, he's been different somehow. Somethin'.

ROGER: No, he ain't.

(BILLY turns to his bed, where he carefully starts folding the towel. Then he looks at ROGER.)

BILLY: You ever talk to any a these guys—queers, I mean? You ever sit down, just rap with one of 'em?

ROGER: Hell, no; what I wanna do that for? Shit, no.

BILLY: *(crossing to the trash can in the corner, where he will shake the towel empty)* I mean, some of 'em are okay guys, just way up this bad alley, and you say to 'em, "I'm straight, be cool," they go their own way. But then there's these other ones, these bitches, man, and they're so crazy they think anybody can be had. Because they been had themselves. So you tell 'em you're straight and they just nod and smile. You ain't real to 'em. They can't see nothin' but themselves and these goddamn games they're always playin'.

(Having returned to his bunk, he is putting on his shoes.)

I mean, you can be decent about anything, Roger, you see what I'm sayin'? We're all just people, man, and some of us are hardly that. That's all I'm sayin'.

(There is a slight pause as he sits there thinking. Then he gets to his feet.)

I'll go get some buckets and stuff so we can clean up, okay? This area's a mess. This area ain't standin' tall.

ROGER: That's good talk, lad; this area a midget you put it next to an area standin' tall.

BILLY: Got to be good fuckin' troopers.

ROGER: That's right, that's right. I know the meanin' of the words.

BILLY: I mean, I just think we all got to be honest with each other—you understand me?

ROGER: No, I don't understand you; one stupid fuckin' nigger like me—how's that gonna be?

BILLY: That's right; mock me, man. That's what I need. I'll go get the wax.

(Out he goes, talking to himself and leaving the door open. For a moment ROGER sits, thinking, and then he looks at RICHIE's locker and gets to his feet and walks to the locker, which he opens and looks at the pinup hanging on the inside of the door. He takes a step backward, looking.)

ROGER: Sheee-it.

(Through the open door comes CARLYLE. ROGER *doesn't see him. And* CARLYLE *stands there looking at* ROGER *and the picture in the locker.)*

CARLYLE: Boy . . . whose locker you lookin' into?

ROGER: *(he is startled, but recovers)* Hey, baby, what's happenin'?

CARLYLE: That ain't your locker, is what I'm askin', nigger. I mean, you ain't got no white goddamn woman hangin' on your wall.

ROGER: Oh, no—no, no.

CARLYLE: You don't wanna be lyin' to me, 'cause I got to turn you in you lyin' and you do got the body a some white goddamn woman hangin' there for you to peek at nobody around but you—you can be thinkin' about that sweet wet pussy an' maybe it hot an' maybe it cool.

ROGER: I could be thinkin' all that, except I know the penalty for lyin'.

CARLYLE: Thank God for that.

(Extending his hand, palm up.)

ROGER: That's right. This here the locker of a faggot.

(And ROGER *slaps* CARLYLE'S *hand, palm to palm.)*

CARLYLE: Course it is; I see that; any damn body know that.

*(*ROGER *crosses toward his bunk and* CARLYLE *swaggers about, pulling a pint of whiskey from his hip pocket.)*

You want a shot? Have you a little taste, my man.

ROGER: Naw.

CARLYLE: C'mon. C'mon. I think you a Tom you don't drink outa my bottle.

(He thrusts the bottle toward ROGER *and wipes a sweat- and grease-stained sleeve across his mouth.)*

ROGER: *(taking the bottle)* Shit.

CARLYLE: That right. How do I know? I just got in. New boy in town. Somewhere over there; I dunno. They dump me in amongst a whole bunch a pale, boring motherfuckers.

*(*CARLYLE *is exploring the room. Finding* BILLY'S Playboy, *he edges onto* BILLY'S *bed and leafs nervously through the pages.)*

I just come in from P Company, man, and I been all over this place, don't see too damn many of us. This outfit look like it a little short on soul. I been walkin' all around, I tell you, and the number is small. Like one hand you can tabulate the lot of 'em. We got few brothers I been able to see, is what I'm sayin'. You and me and two cats down in the small bay. That's all I found.

(As ROGER *is about to hand the bottle back,* CARLYLE, *almost angrily, waves him off.)*

No, no, you take another; take you a real taste.

ROGER: It ain't so bad here. We do all right.

CARLYLE: *(he moves, shutting the door. Suspiciously, he approaches* ROGER*)* How about the white guys? They give you any sweat? What's the situation? No jive. I like to know what is goin' on within the situation before that situation get a chance to be closin' in on me.

ROGER: *(putting the bottle on the footlocker, he sits down)* Man, I'm tellin' you, it ain't bad. They're just pale, most of 'em, you know. They can't help it; how they gonna help it? Some of 'em got little bit a soul, couple real good boys around this way. Get 'em little bit of Coppertone, they be straight, man.

CARLYLE: How about the NCOs? We got any brother NCO watchin' out for us or they all white, like I goddamn well KNOW all the officers are? Fuckin' officers always white, man; fuckin' snow cones and bars everywhere you look.

*(*CARLYLE *cannot stay still. He moves to his right, his left; he sits, he stands.)*

ROGER: First sergeant's a black man.

CARLYLE: All right; good news. Hey, hey, you wanna go over the club with me, or maybe downtown? I got wheels. Let's be free.

(Now he rushes at ROGER.)*

Let's be free.

ROGER: Naw . . .

CARLYLE: Ohhh, baby . . . !

(He is wildly pulling at ROGER *to get him to the door.)*

ROGER: Some other time. I gotta get the area straight. Me and the guy sleeps in here too are gonna shape the place up a little.

(ROGER has pulled free, and CARLYLE cannot understand. It hurts him, depresses him.)

CARLYLE: You got a sweet deal here an' you wanna keep it, that right?

(He paces about the room, opens a footlocker, looks inside.)

How you rate you get a room like this for yourself—you and a couple guys?

ROGER: Spec 4. The three of us in here Spec 4.

CARLYLE: You get a room then, huh?

(And suddenly, without warning or transition, he is angry.)

Oh, man, I hate this goddamn army. I hate this bastard army. I mean, I just got outa basic—off leave—you know? Back on the block for two weeks—and now here. They don't pull any a that petty shit, now, do they—that goddamn petty basic training bullshit? They do and I'm gonna be bustin' some head—my hand is gonna be upside all kinds a heads, 'cause I ain't gonna be able to endure it, man, not that kinda crap—understand?

(And again, he is rushing at ROGER.)

Hey, hey, oh, c'mon, let's get my wheels and make it, man, do me the favor.

ROGER: How'm I gonna? I got my obligations.

(And CARLYLE spins away in anger.)

CARLYLE: Jesus, baby, can't you remember the outside? How long it been since you been on leave? It is so sweet out there, nigger; you got it all forgot. I had such a sweet, sweet time. They doin' dances, baby, make you wanna cry. I hate this damn army.

(The anger overwhelms him.)

All these mother-actin' jacks givin' you jive about what you gotta do and what you can't do. I had a bad scene in basic—up the hill and down the hill; it ain't somethin' I enjoyed even a little. So they do me wrong here, Jim, they gonna be sorry. Some-damn-body! And this whole Vietnam THING—I do not dig it.

(He falls on his knees before ROGER. It is a gesture that begins as a joke, a mockery. And then a real fear pulses through him to nearly fill the pose he has taken.)

Lord, Lord, don't let 'em touch me. Christ, what will I do, they DO! Whooooooooooooooo! And they pullin' guys outa here, too, ain't they? Pullin' 'em like weeds, man; throwin' 'em into the fire. It's shit, man.

ROGER: They got this ole sarge sleeps down the hall—just today they got him.

CARLYLE: Which ole sarge?

ROGER: He sleeps just down the hall. Little guy.

CARLYLE: Wino, right?

ROGER: Booze hound.

CARLYLE: Yeh; I seen him. They got him, huh?

ROGER: He's goin'; gotta be packin' his bags. And three other guys two days ago. And two guys last week.

CARLYLE: *(leaping up from BILLY'S bed)* Ohhh, them bastards. And everybody just takes it. It ain't our war, brother. I'm tellin' you. That's what gets me, nigger. It ain't our war nohow because it ain't our country, and that's what burns my ass—that and everybody just sittin' and takin' it. They gonna be bustin' balls, man— kickin' and stompin'. Everybody here maybe one week from shippin' out to get blown clean away and, man, whata they doin'? They doin' what they told. That what they doin'. Like you? Shit! You gonna straighten up your goddamn area! Well, that ain't for me; I'm gettin' hat, and makin' it out where it's sweet and the people's livin'. I can't cut this jive here, man. I'm tellin' you. I can't cut it.

He has moved toward ROGER, and behind him now RICHIE enters, running, his hair wet, traces of shaving cream on his face. Toweling his hair, he falters, seeing CARLYLE. Then he crosses to his locker. CARLYLE grins at ROGER, looks at RICHIE, steps toward him and gives a little bow.)

My name is Carlyle; what is yours?

RICHIE: Richie.

CARLYLE: *(he turns toward ROGER to share his joke)* Hello. Where is Martin? That cute little Martin.

(And RICHIE has just taken off his robe as CARLYLE turns back.)

You cute, too, Richie.

RICHIE: Martin doesn't live here.

(*Hurriedly putting on underpants to cover his nakedness.*)

CARLYLE: (*watching* RICHIE, *he slowly turns toward* ROGER) You ain't gonna make it with me, man?

ROGER: Naw . . . like I tole you. I'll catch you later.

CARLYLE: That's sad, man; make me cry in my heart.

ROGER: You g'wan get your head smokin'. Stop on back.

CARLYLE: Okay, okay. Got to be one man one more time.

(*On the move for the door, his hand extended palm up behind him, demanding the appropriate response.*)

Baby! Gimme! Gimme!

(*Lunging,* ROGER *slaps the hand.*)

ROGER: G'wan home! G'wan home.

CARLYLE: You gonna hear from me.

(*And he is gone out the door and down the hallway.*)

ROGER: I can . . . and do . . . believe . . . that.

(RICHIE, *putting on his T-shirt, watches* ROGER, *who stubs out his cigarette, then crosses to the trash can to empty the ashtray.*)

RICHIE: Who was that?

ROGER: Man's new, Rich. Dunno his name more than that "Carlyle" he said. He's new—just outa basic.

RICHIE: (*powdering his thighs and under his arms*) Oh, my God . . .

(*As* BILLY *enters, pushing a mop bucket with a wringer attached and carrying a container of wax.*)

ROGER: Me and Billy's gonna straighten up the area. You wanna help?

RICHIE: Sure, sure; help, help.

BILLY: (*talking to* ROGER, *but turning to look at* RICHIE, *who is still putting powder under his arms*) I hadda steal the wax from Third Platoon.

ROGER: Good man.

BILLY: (*moving to* RICHIE, *joking, yet really irritated in some strange way*) What? Whata you

doin', singin'? Look at that, Rog. He's got enough jazz there for an entire beauty parlor. (*grabbing the can from* RICHIE'S *hand*) What is this? Baby powder! BABY POWDER!

RICHIE: I get rashes.

BILLY: Okay, okay, you get rashes, so what? They got powder for rashes that isn't baby powder.

RICHIE: It doesn't work as good; I've tried it. Have you tried it?

(*Grabbing* BILLY'S *waist,* RICHIE *pulls him close.* BILLY *knocks* RICHIE'S *hands away.*)

BILLY: Man, I wish you could get yourself straight. I'll mop, too, Roger—okay? Then I'll put down the wax and you can spread it?

(*He has walked away from* RICHIE.)

RICHIE: What about buffing?

ROGER: In the morning.

(*He is already busy mopping up near the door.*)

RICHIE: What do you want me to do?

BILLY: (*grabbing up a mop, he heads downstage to work*) Get inside your locker and shut the door and don't holler for help. Nobody'll know you're there; you'll stay there.

RICHIE: But I'm so pretty.

BILLY: NOW!

(*Pointing to* ROGER. *He wants to get this clear*) Tell that man you mean what you're sayin', Richie.

RICHIE: Mean what?

BILLY: That you really think you're pretty.

RICHIE: Of course I do; I am. Don't you think I am? Don't you think I am, Roger?

ROGER: I tole you—you fulla shit and you cute, man. Carlyle just tole you you cute, too.

RICHIE: Don't you think it's true, Billy?

BILLY: It's like I tole you, Rog.

RICHIE: What did you tell him?

BILLY: That you go down; that you go up and down like a yo-yo and you go blowin' all the trees like the wind.

(RICHIE *is stunned. He looks at* ROGER, *and then he turns and stares into his own locker. The others keep mopping.* RICHIE *takes out a towel, and putting it around his neck, he walks to where*

BILLY *is working. He stands there, hurt, looking at* BILLY.)

RICHIE: What the hell made you tell him I been down, Billy?

BILLY: *(still mopping)* It's in your eyes; I seen it.

RICHIE: What?

BILLY: You.

RICHIE: What is it, Billy, you think you're trying to say? You and all your wit and intelligence— your *humanity.*

BILLY: I said it, Rich; I said what I was tryin' to say.

RICHIE: *Did* you?

BILLY: I think I did.

RICHIE: *Do* you?

BILLY: Loud and clear, baby.
(Still mopping.)

ROGER: They got to put me in with the weirdos. Why is that, huh? How come the army *hate* me, do this shit to me—*know* what to do.
(Whimsical and then suddenly loud, angered, violent.)
Now you guys put socks in your mouths, right now—get shut up—or I am gonna beat you to death with each other. Roger got work to do. To be doin' it!

RICHIE: *(turning to his bed, he kneels upon it)* Roger, I think you're so innocent sometimes. Honestly, it's not such a terrible thing. Is it, Billy?

BILLY: How would I know?
(He slams his mop into the bucket.)
Oh, go fuck yourself.

RICHIE: Well, I can give it a try, if that's what you want. Can I think of you as I do?

BILLY: *(throwing down his mop)* GODDAMMIT! That's it! IT!
(He exits, rushing into the hall and slamming the door behind him. ROGER *looks at* RICHIE. *Neither quite knows what is going on. Suddenly the door bursts open and* BILLY *storms straight over to* RICHIE, *who still kneels on the bed.)*
Now I am gonna level with you. Are you gonna listen? You gonna hear what I say, Rich, and not what you think I'm sayin'?

*(*RICHIE *turns away as if to rise, his manner flippant, disdainful.)*
No! Don't get cute; don't turn away cute. I wanna say somethin' straight out to you and I want you to hear it!

RICHIE: I'm all ears, goddammit! For what, however, I do not know, except some boring evasion.

BILLY: At least wait the hell till you hear me!

RICHIE: *(in irritation)* Okay, okay! What?

BILLY: Now this is level, Rich; this is straight talk.
(He is quiet, intense. This is difficult for him. He seeks the exactly appropriate words of explanation.)
No b.s. No tricks. What you do on the side, that's your business and I don't care about it. But if you don't cut the cute shit with me, I'm gonna turn you off. Completely. You ain't gonna get a good mornin' outa me, you understand, because it's gettin' bad around here. I mean, I know how you think—how you keep lookin' out and seein' yourself, and that's what I'm tryin' to tell you because that's all that's happenin', Rich. That's all there is to it when you look out at me and think there's some kind of approval or whatever you see in my eyes—you're just seein' yourself. And I'm talkin' the simple quiet truth to you, Rich. I swear I am.
*(*BILLY *looks away from* RICHIE *now and tries to go back to the mopping. It is embarrassing for them all.* ROGER *has watched, has tried to keep working.* RICHIE *has flopped back on his bunk. There is a silence.)*

RICHIE: How . . . do . . . you want me to be? I don't know how else to be.

BILLY: Ohhh, man, that ain't any part of it.
(The mop is clenched in his hands.)

RICHIE: Well, I don't come from the same kind of world as you do.

BILLY: Damn, Richie, you think Roger and I come off the same street?

ROGER: Shit . . .

RICHIE: All right. Okay. But I've just done what I wanted all of my life. If I wanted to do something, I just did it. Honestly. I've never had to work or anything like that and I've always had nice clothing and money for cab fare. Money for whatever I wanted. Always. I'm not like you are.

ROGER: You ain't sayin' you really done that stuff, though, Rich.

RICHIE: What?

ROGER: That fag stuff.

RICHIE: *(he continues looking at* ROGER *and then he looks away)* Yes.

ROGER: Do you even know what you're sayin', Richie? Do you even know what it means to be a fag?

RICHIE: Roger, of course I know what it is. I just told you I've done it. I thought you black people were supposed to understand all about suffering and human strangeness. I thought you had depth and vision from all your suffering. Has someone been misleading me? I just told you I did it. I know all about it. Everything. All the various positions.

ROGER: Yeh, so maybe you think you've tried it, but that don't make you it. I mean, we used to . . . in the old neighborhood, man, we had a couple dudes swung that way. But they was weird, man. There was this one little fella, he was a screamin' goddamn faggot . . . uh . . .

(He considers RICHIE, *wondering if perhaps he has offended him.)*

Ohhh, ohhh, you ain't no screamin' goddamn faggot, Richie, no matter what you say. And the baddest man on the block was my boy Jerry Lemon. So one day Jerry's got the faggot in one a them ole deserted stairways and he's bouncin' him off the walls. I'm just a little fella, see, and I'm watchin' the baddest man on the block do his thing. So he come bouncin' back into me instead of Jerry, and just when he hit, he gave his ass this little twitch, man, like he thought he was gonna turn me on. I'd never a thought that was possible, man, for a man to be twitchin' his ass on me, just like he thought he was a broad. Scared me to death. I took off runnin'. Oh, oh, that ole neighborhood put me into all kinds a crap. I did some sufferin', just

like Richie says. Like this once, I'm swingin' on up the street after school, and outa this phone booth comes this man with a goddamned knife stickin' outa his gut. So he sees me and starts tryin' to pull his motherfuckin' coat out over the handle, like he's worried about how he looks, man. "I didn't know this was gonna happen," he says. And then he falls over. He was just all of a sudden dead, man; just all of a sudden dead. You ever seen anything like that, Billy? Any crap like that?

*(*BILLY, *sitting on* ROGER'S *bunk, is staring at* ROGER.*)*

BILLY: You really seen that?

ROGER: Richie's a big-city boy.

RICHIE: Oh, no; never anything like that.

ROGER: "Momma, help me," I am screamin'. "Jesus, Momma, help me." Little fella, he don't know how to act, he sees somethin' like that.

(For a moment they are still, each thinking.)

BILLY: How long you think we got?

ROGER: What do you mean?

*(*ROGER *is hanging up the mops;* BILLY *is now kneeling on* ROGER'S *bunk.)*

BILLY: Till they pack us up, man, ship us out.

ROGER: To the war, you mean? To Disneyland? Man, I dunno; that up to them IBM's. Them machines is figurin' that. Maybe tomorrow, maybe next week, maybe never.

(The war—the threat of it—is the one thing they share.)

RICHIE: I was reading they're planning to build it all up to more than five hundred thousand men over there. Americans. And they're going to keep it that way until they win.

BILLY: Be a great place to come back from, man, you know? I keep thinkin' about that. To have gone there, to have been there, to have seen it and lived.

ROGER: *(settling onto* BILLY'S *bunk, he lights a cigarette)* Well, what we got right here is a fool, gonna probably be one a them five hundred thousand, too. Do you know I cry at the goddamn anthem yet sometimes? The flag is flyin' at a ball game, the ole Roger gets all wet in the eye. After all the shit been done to his black ass. But I don't know what I think about this war. I do not know.

BILLY: I'm tellin' you, Rog—I've been doin' a lot a readin' and I think it's right we go. I mean, it's just like when North Korea invaded South Korea or when Hitler invaded Poland and all those other countries. He just kept testin' everybody and when nobody said no to him, he got so committed he couldn't back out even if he wanted. And that's what this Ho Chi Minh is doin'. And all these other Communists. If we let 'em know somebody is gonna stand up against 'em, they'll back off, just like Hitler would have.

ROGER: There is folks, you know, who are sayin' L.B.J. is the Hitler, and not ole Ho Chi Minh at all.

RICHIE: (talking as if this is the best news he's heard in years) Well, I don't know anything at all about all that, but I am certain I don't want to go—whatever is going on. I mean, those Vietcong don't just shoot you and blow you up, you know. My God, they've got these other awful things they do: putting elephant shit on these stakes in the ground and then you step on 'em and you got elephant shit in a wound in your foot. The infection is horrendous. And then there's these caves they hide in and when you go in after 'em, they've got these snakes that they've tied by their tails to the ceiling. So it's dark and the snake is furious from having been hung by its tail and you crawl right into them—your face. My God.

BILLY: They do not.

(BILLY knows he has been caught; they all know it.)

RICHIE: I read it, Billy. They do.

BILLY: (completely facetious, yet the fear is real) That's bullshit, Richie.

ROGER: That's right, Richie. They maybe do that stuff with the elephant shit, but nobody's gonna tie a snake by its tail, let ole Billy walk into it.

BILLY: That's disgusting, man.

ROGER: Guess you better get ready for the Klondike, my man.

BILLY: That is probably the most disgusting thing I ever heard of. I DO NOT WANT TO GO! NOT TO NOWHERE WHERE THAT KINDA SHIT IS GOIN' ON! L.B.J. is Hitler; suddenly I see it all very clearly.

ROGER: Billy got him a hatred for snakes.

RICHIE: I hate them, too. They're hideous.

BILLY: (and now, as a kind of apology to RICHIE, BILLY continues his self-ridicule far into the extreme) I mean, that is one of the most awful things I ever heard of any person doing. I mean, any person who would hang a snake by its tail in the dark of a cave in the hope that some other person might crawl into it and get bitten to death, that first person is somebody who oughta be shot. And I hope the five hundred thousand other guys that get sent over there kill 'em all—all them gooks—get 'em all driven back into Germany, where they belong. And in the meantime, I'll be holding the northern border against the snowmen.

ROGER: (rising from BILLY's bed) And in the meantime before that, we better be gettin' at the ole area here. Got to be strike troopers.

BILLY: Right.

RICHIE: Can I help?

ROGER: Sure. Be good.

(And ROGER crosses to his footlocker and takes out a radio.)

Think maybe I put on a little music, though it's gettin' late. We got time. Billy, you think?

BILLY: Sure.

(Getting nervously to his feet.)

ROGER: Sure. All right. We can be doin' it to the music.

(He plugs the radio into the floor outlet as BILLY bolts for the door.)

BILLY: I gotta go pee.

ROGER: You watch out for the snakes.

BILLY: It's the snowmen, man; the snowmen.

(BILLY is gone and "Ruby," sung by Ray Charles, comes from the radio. For a moment, as the music plays, ROGER watches RICHIE wander about the room, pouring little splashes of wax onto the floor. Then RICHIE moves to his bed *and lies down, and* ROGER, *shaking his head, starts leisurely to spread the wax, with* RICHIE *watching.*)

RICHIE: How come you and Billy take all this so seriously—you know.

ROGER: What?

RICHIE: This army nonsense. You're always shining your brass and keeping your footlocker neat and your locker so neat. There's no point to any of it.

ROGER: We here, ain't we, Richie? We in the army.

(Still working the wax.)

RICHIE: There's no point to any of it. And doing those push-ups, the two of you.

ROGER: We just see a lot of things the same way is all. Army ought to be a serious business, even if sometimes it ain't.

RICHIE: You're lucky, you know, the two of you. Having each other for friends the way you do. I never had that kind of friend ever. Not even when I was little.

ROGER: *(after a pause during which* ROGER, *working, sort of peeks at* RICHIE *every now and then)* You ain't really inta that stuff, are you, Richie?

(It is a question that is a statement.)

RICHIE: *(coyly he looks at* ROGER*)* What stuff is that, Roger?

ROGER: That fag stuff, man. You know. You ain't really into it, are you? You maybe messed in it a little is all—am I right?

RICHIE: I'm very weak, Roger. And by that I simply mean that if I have an impulse to do something, I don't know how to deny myself. If I feel like doing something, I just do it. I . . . will . . . admit to sometimes wishin' I . . . was a little more like you . . . and Billy, even, but not to any severe extent.

ROGER: But that's such a bad scene, Rich. You don't want that. Nobody wants that. Nobody wants to be a punk. Not nobody. You wanna know what I think it is? You just got in with the wrong bunch. Am I right? You just got in with a bad bunch. That can happen. And that's what I

think happened to you. I bet you never had a chance to really run with the boys before. I mean, regular normal guys like Billy and me. How'd you come in the army, huh, Richie? You get drafted?

RICHIE: No.

ROGER: That's my point, see.

(He has stopped working. He stands, leaning on the mop, looking at RICHIE.*)*

RICHIE: About four years ago, I went to this party. I was very young, and I went to this party with a friend who was older and . . . this "fag stuff," as you call it, was going on . . . so I did it.

ROGER: And then you come in the army to get away from it, right? Huh?

RICHIE: I don't know.

ROGER: Sure.

RICHIE: I don't know, Roger.

ROGER: Sure; sure. And now you're gettin' a chance to run with the boys for a little, you'll get yourself straightened around. I know it for a fact; I know that thing.

(From off there is the sudden loud bellowing sound of Sergeant ROONEY.*)*

ROONEY: THERE AIN'T BEEN NO SOLDIERS IN THIS CAMP BUT ME. I BEEN THE ONLY ONE—I BEEN THE ONLY ME!

(And BILLY *comes dashing into the room.)*

BILLY: Oh, boy.

ROGER: Guess who?

ROONEY: FOR SO LONG I BEEN THE ONLY GODDAMN ONE!

BILLY: *(leaping onto his bed and covering his face with a* Playboy *magazine as* RICHIE *is trying to disappear under his sheets and blankets and* ROGER *is trying to get the wax put away so he can get into his own bunk)* Hut who hee whor— he's got some yo-yo with him, Rog!

ROGER: Huh?

(As COKES *and* ROONEY *enter. Both are in fatigues and drunk and big-bellied. They are in their fifties, their hair whitish and cut short. Both men carry whiskey bottles, beer bottles.* COKES *is a little neater than* ROONEY, *his fatigue*

jacket tucked in and not so rumpled, and he wears canvas-sided jungle boots. ROONEY, *very disheveled, chomps on the stub of a big cigar. They swagger in, looking for fun, and stand there side by side.*)

ROONEY: What kinda platoon I got here? You buncha shit sacks. Everybody look sharp.

(*The three boys lie there, unmoving.*)

Off and on!

COKES: OFF AND ON!

(*He seems barely conscious, wavering as he stands.*)

ROGER: What's happenin', Sergeant?

ROONEY: (*shoving his bottle of whiskey at* ROGER, *who is sitting up*) Shut up, Moore! You want a belt?

(*Splashing whiskey on* ROGER'S *chest.*)

ROGER: How can I say no?

COKES: My name is Cokes!

BILLY: (*rising to sit on the side of his bed*) How about me, too?

COKES: You wait your turn.

ROONEY: (*he looks at the three of them as if they are fools. Indicates* COKES *with a gesture*) Don't you see what I got here?

BILLY: Who do I follow for my turn?

ROONEY: (*suddenly, crazily petulant*) Don't you see what I got here? Everybody on their feet and at attention!

(BILLY *and* ROGER *climb from their bunks and stand at attention. They don't know what* ROONEY *is mad at.*)

I mean it!

(RICHIE *bounds to the position of attention.*)

This here is my friend, who in addition just come back from the war! The goddamn war! He been to it and he come back.

(ROONEY *is patting* COKES *gently, proudly.*)

The man's a fuckin' hero!

(ROONEY *hugs* COKES, *almost kissing him on the cheek.*)

He's always been a fuckin' hero.

(COKES, *embarrassed in his stupor, kind of wobbles a little from side to side.*)

COKES: No-o-o-o-o-o . . .

(And ROONEY *grabs him, starts pushing him toward* BILLY'S *footlocker.*)

ROONEY: Show 'em your boots, Cokes. Show 'em your jungle boots.

(*With a long, clumsy step,* COKES *climbs onto the footlocker,* ROONEY *supporting him from behind and then bending to lift one of* COKES' *booted feet and display it for the boys.*)

Lookee that boot. That ain't no everyday goddamn army boot. That is a goddamn jungle boot! That green canvas is a jungle boot 'cause a the heat, and them little holes in the bottom are so the water can run out when you been walkin' in a lotta water like in a jungle swamp.

(*He is extremely proud of all this; he looks at them.*)

The army ain't no goddamn fool. You see a man wearin' boots like that, you might as well see he's got a chestful a medals, 'cause he been to the war. He don't have no boots like that unless he been to the war! Which is where I'm goin' and all you slaphappy motherfuckers, too. Got to go kill some gooks.

(*He is nodding at them, smiling.*)

That's right.

COKES: (*bursting loudly from his stupor*) Gonna piss on 'em. Old booze. 'At's what I did. Piss in the rivers. Goddamn GI's secret weapon is old booze and he's pissin' it in all their runnin' water. Makes 'em yellow. Ahhhha ha, ha, ha!

(*He laughs and laughs, and* ROONEY *laughs, too, hugging* COKES.)

ROONEY: Me and Cokesy been in so much shit together we oughta be brown.

(And then he catches himself, looks at ROGER.)

Don't take no offense at that, Moore. We been swimmin' in it. One Hundred and First Airborne, together. One-oh-one. Screamin' goddamn Eagles!

(*Looking at each other, face to face, eyes glinting, they make sudden loud screaming-eagle sounds.*)

This ain't the army; you punks ain't in the army. You ain't ever seen the army. The army is Airborne! Airborne!

COKES: *(beginning to stomp his feet)* Airborne, Airborne! ALL THE WAY!

(As RICHIE, *amused and hoping for a drink, too, reaches out toward* ROONEY.)

RICHIE: Sergeant, Sergeant, I can have a little drink, too.

*(*ROONEY *looks at him and clutches the bottle.)*

ROONEY: Are you kiddin' me? You gotta be kiddin' me.

(He looks to ROGER.)

He's kiddin' me, ain't he, Moore?

(And then to BILLY *and then to* COKES.)

Ain't he, Cokesy?

*(*COKES *steps forward and down with a thump, taking charge for his bewildered friend.)*

COKES: Don't you know you are tryin' to take the booze from the hand a the future goddamn Congressional Honor winner . . . Medal . . . ?

(And he looks lovingly at ROONEY. *He beams.)*

Ole Rooney, Ole Rooney.

(He hugs ROONEY'S *head.)*

He almost done it already.

(And ROONEY, *overwhelmed, starts screaming "Aggggggghhhhhhhhhh," a screaming-eagle sound, and making clawing-eagle gestures at the air. He jumps up and down, stomping his feet.* COKES *instantly joins in, stomping and jumping and yelling.)*

ROONEY: Let's show these shit sacks how men are men jumpin' outa planes. Aggggggghhhhhhhhhh.

(Stomping and yelling, they move in a circle, ROONEY *followed by* COKES.)

A plane fulla yellin' stompin' men!

COKES: All yellin' stompin' men!

(They yell and stomp, making eagle sounds, and then ROONEY *leaps up on* BILLY'S *bed and runs the length of it until he is on the footlocker,* COKES *still on the floor, stomping.* ROONEY *makes a gesture of hooking his rip cord to the line inside the plane. They yell louder and louder and* ROONEY *leaps high into the air, yelling,* "GERONIMO-O-O-O!" *They stand side by side, their arms held up in the air as if grasping the shroud lines of open chutes. They seem to float there in silence.)*

What a feelin' . . .

ROONEY: Beautiful feelin' . . .

(For a moment more they float there, adrift in the room, the sky, their memory. COKES *smiles at* ROONEY.)

COKES: Remember that one guy, O'Flannigan . . . ?

ROONEY: *(nodding, smiling, remembering)* O'Flannigan . . .

COKES: He was this one guy . . . O'Flannigan . . .

(He moves now toward the boys, BILLY, ROGER *and* RICHIE, *who have gathered on* ROGER'S *bed and footlocker.* ROONEY *follows several steps, then drifts backward onto* BILLY'S *bed, where he sits and then lies back, listening to* COKES.)

We was testing chutes where you could just pull a lever by your ribs here when you hit the ground—see—and the chute would come off you, because it was just after a whole bunch a guys had been dragged to death in an unexpected and terrible wind at Fort Bragg. So they wanted you to be able to release the chute when you hit if there was a bad wind when you hit. So O'Flannigan was this kinda joker who had the goddamn sense a humor of a clown and nerves, I tell you, of steel, and he says he's gonna release the lever midair, then reach up, grab the lines and float on down, hanging.

(His hand paws at the air, seeking a rope that isn't there.)

So I seen him pull the lever at five hundred feet and he reaches up to two fistfuls a air, the chute's twenty feet above him, and he went into the ground like a knife.

(The bottle, held high over his head, falls through the air to the bed, all watching it.)

BILLY: Geezus.

ROONEY: *(nodding gently)* Didn't get to sing the song, I bet.

COKES: *(standing, staring at the fallen bottle)* No way.

RICHIE: What song?

ROONEY: *(he rises up, mysteriously angry)* Shit sack! Shit sack!

RICHIE: What song, Sergeant Rooney?

ROONEY: "Beautiful Streamer," shit sack.

(COKES, *gone into another reverie, is staring skyward.*)

COKES: I saw this one guy—never forget it. Never.

BILLY: That's Richie, Sergeant Rooney. He's a beautiful screamer.

RICHIE: He said "streamer," not "screamer," asshole.

(COKES *is still in his reverie.*)

COKES: This guy with his chute goin' straight up above him in a streamer, like a tulip, only white, you know. All twisted and never gonna open. Like a big icicle sticking straight up above him. He went right by me. We met eyes, sort of. He was lookin' real puzzled. He looks right at me. Then he looks up in the air at the chute, then down at the ground.

ROONEY: Did *he* sing it?

COKES: He didn't sing it. He started going like this.

(COKES *reaches desperately upward with both hands and begins to claw at the sky while his legs pump up and down.*)

Like he was gonna climb right up the air.

RICHIE: Ohhhhh, Geezus.

BILLY: God.

(ROONEY *has collapsed backward on* BILLY'S *bed and he lies there and then he rises.*)

ROONEY: Cokes got the Silver Star for rollin' a barrel a oil down a hill in Korea into forty-seven chinky Chinese gooks who were climbin' up the hill and when he shot into it with his machine gun, it blew them all to grape jelly.

(COKES, *rocking a little on his feet, begins to hum and then sing "Beautiful Streamer," to the tune of Stephen Foster's "Beautiful Dreamer."*)

COKES: "Beautiful streamer, open for me . . . The sky is above me . . . "

(*And then the singing stops.*)

But the one I remember is this little guy in his spider hole, which is a hole in the ground with a lid over it.

(*And he is using* RICHIE'S *footlocker before him as the spider hole. He has fixed on it, is moving toward it.*)

And he shot me in the ass as I was runnin' by, but the bullet hit me so hard—

(*His body kind of jerks and he runs several steps.*)

—it knocked me into this ditch where he couldn't see me. I got behind him.

(*Now at the head of* RICHIE'S *bed, he begins to creep along the side of the bed as if sneaking up on the footlocker.*)

Crawlin'. And I dropped a grenade into his hole.

(*He jams a whiskey bottle into the footlocker, then slams down the lid.*)

Then sat on the lid, him bouncin' and yellin' under me. Bouncin' and yellin' under the lid. I could hear him. Feel him. I just sat there.

(*Silence.* ROONEY *waits, thinking, then leans forward.*)

ROONEY: He was probably singin' it.

COKES: (*sitting there*) I think so.

ROONEY: You think we should let 'em hear it?

BILLY: We're good boys. We're good ole boys.

COKES: (*jerking himself to his feet, he staggers sideways to join* ROONEY *on* BILLY'S *bed.*) I don't care who hears it, I just wanna be singin' it.

(ROONEY *rises; he goes to the boys on* ROGER'S *bed and speaks to them carefully, as if lecturing people on something of great importance.*)

ROONEY: You listen up; you just be listenin' up, 'cause if you hear it right you can maybe stop bein' shit sacks. This is what a man sings, he's goin' down through the air, his chute don't open.

(*Flopping back down on the bunk beside* COKES, ROONEY *looks at* COKES *and then at the boys. The two older men put their arms around each other and they begin to sing.*)

ROONEY AND COKES: (*singing*)

Beautiful streamer,
Open for me,
The sky is above me,
But no canopy.

BILLY: (*murmuring*) I don't believe it.

ROONEY AND COKES:
> Counted ten thousand,
> Pulled on the cord.
> My chute didn't open,
> I shouted, "Dear Lord."
>
> Beautiful streamer,
> This looks like the end,
> The earth is below me,
> My body won't end.
>
> Just like a mother
> Watching o'er me,
> Beautiful streamer,
> Ohhhhh, open for me.

ROGER: Un-fuckin'-believable.

ROONEY: *(beaming with pride)* Ain't that a beauty.
(And then COKES *topples forward onto his face and flops limply to his side. The three boys leap to their feet.* ROONEY *lunges toward* COKES.*)*

RICHIE: Sergeant!

ROONEY: Cokie! Cokie!

BILLY: Jesus.

ROGER: Hey!

COKES: Huh? Huh?
*(*COKES *sits up.* ROONEY *is kneeling beside him.)*

ROONEY: Jesus, Cokie.

COKES: I been doin' that; I been doin' that. It don't mean nothin'.

ROONEY: No, no.

COKES: *(pushing at* ROONEY, *who is trying to help him get back to the bed.* ROONEY *agrees with everything* COKES *is now saying and the noises he makes are little animal noises)* I told 'em when they wanted to send me back I ain't got no leukemia; they wanna check it. They think I got it. I don't think I got it. Rooney? Whata you think?

ROONEY: No.

COKES: My mother had it. She had it. Just 'cause she did and I been fallin' down.

ROONEY: It don't mean nothin'.

COKES: *(he lunges back and up onto the bed)* I tole 'em I fall down 'cause I'm drunk. I'm drunk all the time.

ROONEY: You'll be goin' back over there with me, is what I know, Cokie.
(He is patting COKES, *nodding, dusting him off.)*
That's what I know.
(As BILLY *comes up to them, almost seeming to want to be a part of the intimacy they are sharing.)*

BILLY: That was somethin', Sergeant Cokes. Jesus.
*(*ROONEY *whirls on him, ferocious, pushing him.)*

ROONEY: Get the fuck away, Wilson! Whata you know? Get the fuck away. You don't know shit. Get away! You don't know shit.
(And he turns to COKES, *who is standing up from the bed.)*
Me and Cokes are goin' to the war zone like we oughta. Gonna blow it to shit.
(He is grabbing at COKES, *who is laughing. They are both laughing.* ROONEY *whirls on the boys.)*
Ohhh, I'm gonna be so happy to be away from you assholes; you pussies. Not one regular army people among you possible. I swear it to my mother who is holy. You just be watchin' the papers for doin' darin' brave deeds. 'Cause we're old hands at it. Makin' shit disappear. Goddamn whooosh!

COKES: Whooosh!

ROONEY: Demnalitions. Me and . . .
(And then he knows he hasn't said it right.)
Me and Cokie . . . Demnal . . . Demnali . . .

RICHIE: *(still sitting on* ROGER'S *bed)* You can do it, Sergeant.

BILLY: Get it.
(He stands by the lockers and ROONEY *glares at him.)*

ROGER: 'Cause you're cool with dynamite, is what you're tryin' to say.

ROONEY: *(charging at* ROGER, *bellowing)* Shut the fuck up, that's what you can do; and go to goddamn sleep. You buncha shit . . . sacks. Buncha mothers—know-it-all motherin' shit sacks—that's what you are.

COKES: *(shoulders back, he is taking charge)* Just goin' to sleep is what you can do, 'cause Rooney and me fought it through two wars already and we can make it through this one more and leukemia that comes or doesn't come—who gives a shit? Not guys like us. We're goin' just pretty as pie. And it's lights-out time, ain't it, Rooney?

ROONEY: Past it. goddammit. So the lights are goin' out.

(There is fear in the room, and the three boys rush to their wall lockers, where they start to strip to their underwear, preparing for bed. ROONEY *paces the room, watching them, glaring.)*

Somebody's gotta teach you soldierin'. You hear me? Or you wanna go outside and march around awhile, huh? We can do that if you wanna. Huh? You tell me? Marchin' or sleepin'? What's it gonna be?

RICHIE: *(rushing to get into bed)* Flick out the ole lights, Sergeant; that's what we say.

BILLY: *(climbing into bed)* Put out the ole lights.

ROGER: *(in bed and pulling up the covers)* Do it.

COKES: Shut up.

(He rocks forward and back, trying to stand at attention. He is saying good night.)

And that's an order. Just shut up. I got grenades down the hall. I got a pistol. I know where to get nitro. You don't shut up, I'll blow . . . you . . . to . . . fuck.

(Making a military left face, he stalks to the wall switch and turns the lights out. ROONEY *is watching proudly, as* COKES *faces the boys again. He looks at them.)*

That's right.

(In the dark, there is only a spill of light from the hall coming in the open door. COKES *and* ROONEY *put their arms around each other and go out the door, leaving it partly open.* RICHIE, ROGER *and* BILLY *lie in their bunks, staring. They do not move. They lie there. The sergeants seem to have vanished soundlessly once they went out the door. Light touches each of the boys as they lie there.)*

ROGER: *(he does not move)* Lord have mercy, if that ain't a pair. If that ain't one pair of beauties.

BILLY: Oh, yeh.

(He does not move.)

ROGER: Too much, man—too, too much.

RICHIE: They made me sad; but I loved them, sort of. Better than movies.

ROGER: Too much. Too, too much.

(Silence.)

BILLY: What time is it?

ROGER: Sleep time, men. Sleep time.

(Silence.)

BILLY: Right.

ROGER: They were somethin'. Too much.

BILLY: Too much.

RICHIE: Night.

ROGER: Night.

(Silence.)

Night, Billy.

BILLY: Night.

*(*RICHIE *stirs in his bed.* ROGER *turns onto his side.* BILLY *is motionless.)*

BILLY: I . . . had a buddy, Rog—and this is the whole thing, this is the whole point—a kid I grew up with, played ball with in high school, and he was tough little cat, a real bad man sometimes. Used to have gangster pictures up in his room. Anyway, we got into this deal where we'd drive on down to the big city, man, you know, hit the bad spots, let some queer pick us up . . . sort of . . . long enough to buy us some good stuff. It was kinda the thing to do for a while, and we all did it, the whole gang of us. So we'd let these cats pick us up, most of 'em old guys, and they were hurtin' and happy as hell to have us, and we'd get a lot of free booze, maybe a meal, and we'd turn 'em on. Then pretty soon they'd ask us did we want to go over to their place. Sure, we'd say, and order one more drink, and then when we hit the street, we'd tell 'em to kiss off. We'd call 'em fag and queer and jazz like that and tell 'em to kiss off. And Frankie, the kid I'm tellin' you about, he had a mean streak in him and if they gave us a bad time at all, he'd put 'em down. That's the way he was. So that kinda jazz went on and on for sort of a long time and it was a good deal if we were low on cash or needed a laugh and it went on for a while. And then Frankie—one day he come up to me—and he says he was goin' home with the guy he was with. He said, what the hell, what did it matter? And he's sayin'—Frankie's sayin'—why don't I tag along? What the hell, he's sayin', what does it matter who does it to you, some broad or some old guy, you close your eyes, a mouth's a mouth, it don't matter—that's what he's sayin'. I tried to talk him out of it, but he wasn't hearin' anything I was sayin'. So the next day, see, he calls me up to tell me about it. Okay, okay, he says, it was a cool scene, he says; they played poker, a buck minimum, and he made a fortune. Frankie was eatin' it up, man. It was a pretty way to live, he says. So he stayed at it, and he had this nice little girl he was goin' with at the time. You know the way a real bad cat can sometimes do that—have a good little girl who's crazy about him and he is for her, too, and he's a different cat when he's with her?

ROGER: Uh-huh.

(The hall light slants across BILLY'S *face.)*

BILLY: Well, that was him and Linda, and then one day he dropped her, he cut her loose. He was hooked, man. He was into it, with no way he knew out—you understand what I'm sayin'? He had got his ass hooked. He had never thought he would and then one day he woke up and he was on it. He just hadn't been told, that's the way I figure it; somebody didn't tell him somethin' he shoulda been told and he come to me wailin' one day, man, all broke up and wailin', my boy Frankie, my main man, and he was a fag. He was a faggot, black Roger, and I'm not lyin'. I am not lyin' to you.

ROGER: Damn.

BILLY: So that's the whole thing, man; that's the whole thing.

(Silence. They lie there.)

ROGER: Holy . . . Christ. Richie . . . you hear him? You hear what he said?

RICHIE: He's a storyteller.

ROGER: What you mean?

RICHIE: I mean, he's a storyteller, all right; he tells stories, all right.

ROGER: What are we into now? You wanna end up like that friend a his, or you don't believe what he said? Which are you sayin'?

(The door bursts open. The sounds of machine guns and cannon are being made by someone, and CARLYLE, *drunk and playing, comes crawling in.* ROGER, RICHIE *and* BILLY *all pop up, startled, to look at him.)*

Hey, hey, what's happenin'?

BILLY: Who's happenin'?

ROGER: You attackin' or you retreatin', man?

CARLYLE: *(looking up; big grin)* Hey, baby . . . ?

(Continues shooting, crawling. The three boys look at each other.)

ROGER: What's happenin', man? Whatcha doin'?

CARLYLE: I dunno, soul; I dunno. Practicin' my duties, my new abilities.

(Half sitting, he flops onto his side, starts to crawl.)

The low crawl, man; like I was taught in basic, that's what I'm doin'. You gotta know your shit, man, else you get your ass blown so far away you don't ever see it again. Oh, sure, you guys don't care. I know it. You got it made. You got it made. I don't got it made. You got a little home here, got friends, people to talk to. I got nothin'. You got jobs they probably ain't ever gonna ship you out, you got so important jobs. I got no job. They don't even wanna give me a job. I know it. They are gonna kill me. They are gonna send me over there to get me killed, goddammit. WHAT'S A MATTER WITH ALL YOU PEOPLE?

(The anger explodes out of the grieving and ROGER *rushes to kneel beside* CARLYLE. *He speaks gently, firmly.)*

ROGER: Hey, man, get cool, get some cool; purchase some cool, man.

CARLYLE: Awwwww . . .

(Clumsily, he turns away.)

ROGER: Just hang in there.

CARLYLE: I don't wanna be no DEAD man. I don't wanna be the one they all thinkin' is so stupid he's the only one'll go, they tell him; they don't even have to give him a job. I got thoughts, man, in my head; alla time, burnin', burnin' thoughts a understandin'.

ROGER: Don't you think we know that, man? It ain't the way you're sayin' it.

CARLYLE: It is.

ROGER: No. I mean, we all probably gonna go. We all probably gonna have to go.

CARLYLE: No-o-o-o-o.

ROGER: I mean it.

CARLYLE: *(suddenly he nearly topples over)* I am very drunk.
(And he looks up at ROGER.*)*
You think so?

ROGER: I'm sayin' so. And I am sayin', "No sweat." No point.
*(*CARLYLE *angrily pushes at* ROGER, *knocking him backward.)*

CARLYLE: Awwwww, dammit, dammit, mother . . . shit . . . it . . . ohhhhhhh.
(Sliding to the floor, the rage and anguish softening into only breathing.)
I mean it. I mean it.
(Silence. He lies there.)

ROGER: What . . . a you doin' . . . ?

CARLYLE: Huh?

ROGER: I don't know what you're up to on our freshly mopped floor.

CARLYLE: Gonna go sleep—okay? No sweat . . .
(Suddenly very polite, he is looking up.)
Can I, soul? Izzit all right?

ROGER: Sure, man, sure, if you wanna, but why don't you go where you got a bed? Don't you like beds?

CARLYLE: Dunno where's zat. My bed. I can' fin' it. I can' fin' my own bed. I looked all over, but I can' fin' it anywhere. GONE!
(Slipping back down now, he squirms to make a nest. He hugs his bottle.)

ROGER: *(moving to his bunk, where he grabs a blanket)* Okay, okay, man. But get on top a this, man.
(He is spreading the blanket on the floor, trying to help CARLYLE *get on it.)*

Make it softer. C'mon, c'mon . . . get on this.
*(*BILLY *has risen with his own blanket, and is moving now to hand it to* ROGER.*)*

BILLY: Cat's hurtin', Rog.

ROGER: Ohhhhh, yeh.

CARLYLE: Ohhhhh . . . it was so sweet at home . . . it was so sweet, baby; so-o-o good. They doin' dances make you wanna cry. . . .
(Hugging the blankets now, he drifts in a kind of dream.)

ROGER: I know, man.

CARLYLE: So sweet . . . !
*(*BILLY *is moving back to his own bed, where, quietly, he sits.)*

ROGER: I know, man.

CARLYLE: So sweet . . . !

ROGER: Yeh.

CARLYLE: How come I gotta be here?
(On his way to the door to close it, ROGER *falters, looks at* CARLYLE, *then moves on toward the door.)*

ROGER: I dunno, Jim.
*(*BILLY *is sitting and watching as* ROGER *goes on to the door, gently closes it and returns to his bed.)*

BILLY: I know why he's gotta be here, Roger. You wanna know? Why don't you ask me?

ROGER: Okay. How come he gotta be here?

BILLY: *(smiling)* Freedom's frontier, man. That's why.

ROGER: *(settled on the edge of his bed and about to lie back)* Oh . . . yeh . . .
(As a distant bugle begins to play taps and RICHIE, *carrying a blanket, is approaching* CARLYLE. ROGER *settles back;* BILLY *is staring at* RICHIE; CARLYLE *does not stir; the bugle plays.)*
Bet that ole sarge don't live a year, Billy. Fuckin' blow his own ass sky high.
*(*RICHIE *has covered* CARLYLE. *He pats* CARLYLE'S *arm, and then straightens in order to return to his bed.)*

BILLY: Richie . . . !
*(*BILLY'S *hissing voice freezes* RICHIE. *He stands, and then he starts again to move, and* BILLY'S *voice comes again and* RICHIE *cannot move.)*

Richie . . . how come you gotta keep doin' that stuff?

(ROGER *looks at* BILLY, *staring at* RICHIE, *who stands still as a stone over the sleeping* CARLYLE.) How come?

ROGER: He dunno, man. Do you? You dunno, do you, Rich?

RICHIE: No.

CARLYLE: *(from deep in his sleep and grieving)* It . . . was . . . so . . . pretty . . . !

RICHIE: No.

(*The lights are fading with the last soft notes of taps.*)

ACT II

SCENE 1: *Lights come up on the cadre room. It is late afternoon and* BILLY *is lying on his stomach, his head at the foot of the bed, his chin resting on his hands. He wears gym shorts and sweat socks; his T-shirt lies on the bed and his sneakers are on the floor.* ROGER *is at his footlocker, taking out a pair of sweat socks. His sneakers and his basketball are on his bed. He is wearing his khakis.*

A silence passes, and then ROGER *closes his footlocker and sits on his bed, where he starts lacing his sneakers, holding them on his lap.*

BILLY: Rog . . . you think I'm a busybody? In any way?

(*Silence.* ROGER *laces his sneakers.*)

Roger?

ROGER: Huh? Uh-uh.

BILLY: Some people do. I mean, back home.

(*He rolls slightly to look at* ROGER.)

Or that I didn't know how to behave. Sort of.

ROGER: It's time we maybe get changed, don't you think?

(ROGER *rises and goes to his locker. He takes off his trousers, shoes and socks.*)

BILLY: Yeh. I guess. I don't feel like it, though. I don't feel good, don't know why.

ROGER: Be good for you, man; be good for you.

(*Pulling on his gym shorts,* ROGER *returns to his bed, carrying his shoes and socks.*)

BILLY: Yeh.

(BILLY *sits up on the edge of his bed.* ROGER, *sitting, is bowed over, putting on his socks.*)

I mean, a lot a people thought like I didn't know how to behave in a simple way. You know? That I overcomplicated everything. I didn't think so. Don't think so. I just thought I was seein' complications that were there but nobody else saw.

(*He is struggling now to put on his T-shirt. He seems weary, almost weak.*)

I mean, Wisconsin's a funny place. All those clear-eyed people sayin' "Hello" and lookin' you straight in the eye. Everybody's good, you think, and happy and honest. And then there's all of a sudden a neighbor who goes mad as a hatter. I had a neighbor who came out of his house one morning with axes in both hands. He started then attackin' the cars that were driving up and down in front of his house. An' we all knew why he did it, sorta.

(*He pauses; he thinks.*)

It made me wanna be a priest. I wanted to be a priest then. I was sixteen. Priests could help people. Could take away what hurt 'em. I wanted that, I thought. Somethin', huh?

ROGER: *(he has the basketball in his hands)* Yeh. But everybody's got feelin's like that sometimes.

BILLY: I don't know.

ROGER: You know, you oughta work on a little jump shot, my man. Get you some kinda fall-away jumper to go with that beauty of a hook. Make you tough out there.

BILLY: Can't fuckin' do it. Not my game. I mean, like that bar we go to. You think I could get a job there bartendin', maybe? I could learn the ropes.

(*He is watching* ROGER, *who has risen to walk to his locker.*)

You think I could get a job there off-duty hours?

ROGER: *(pulling his locker open to display the pinup on the inside of the door)* You don't want no job. It's that little black-haired waitress you wantin' to know.

BILLY: No, man. Not really.

ROGER: It's okay. She tough, man.

(He begins to remove his uniform shirt. He will put on an O.D. T-shirt to go to the gym.)

BILLY: I mean, not the way you're sayin' it, is all. Sure, there's somethin' about her. I don't know what. I ain't even spoke to her yet. But somethin'. I mean, what's she doin' there? When she's dancin', it's like she knows somethin'. She's degradin' herself, I sometimes feel. You think she is?

ROGER: Man, you don't even know the girl. She's workin'.

BILLY: I'd like to talk to her. Tell her stuff. Find out about her. Sometimes I'm thinkin' about her and it and I got a job there, I get to know her and she and I get to be real tight, man—close, you know. Maybe we screw, maybe we don't. It's nice . . . whatever.

ROGER: Sure. She a real fine-lookin' chippy, Billy. Got nice cakes. Nice little titties.

BILLY: I think she's smart, too.

(ROGER starts laughing so hard he almost falls into his locker.)

Oh, all I do is talk. "Yabba-yabba." I mean, my mom and dad are really terrific people. How'd they ever end up with somebody so weird as me?

(ROGER moves to him, jostles him.)

ROGER: I'm tellin' you, the gym and a little ball is what you need. Little exercise. Little bumpin' into people. The soul is tellin' you.

(BILLY rises and goes to his locker, where he starts putting on his sweat clothes.)

BILLY: I mean, Roger, you remember how we met in P Company? Both of us brand-new. You started talkin' to me. You just started talkin' to me and you didn't stop.

ROGER: *(hardly looking up)* Yeh.

BILLY: Did you see somethin' in me made you pick me?

ROGER: I was talkin' to everybody, man. For that whole day. Two whole days. You was just the first one to talk back friendly. Though you didn't say much, as I recall.

BILLY: The first white person, you mean.

(Wearing his sweat pants, BILLY is now at his bed, putting on his sneakers.)

ROGER: Yeh. I was tryin' to come outa myself a little. Do like the fuckin' head shrinker been tellin' me to stop them fuckin' headaches I was havin', you know. Now let us do fifteen or twenty push-ups and get over to that gymnasium, like I been sayin'. Then we can take our civvies with us—we can shower and change at the gym.

(ROGER crosses to BILLY, who flops down on his belly on the bed.)

BILLY: I don't know . . . I don't know what it is I'm feelin'. Sick like.

(ROGER forces BILLY up onto his feet and shoves him playfully downstage, where they both fall forward into the push-up position, side by side.)

ROGER: Do 'em, trooper. Do 'em. Get it.

(ROGER starts. BILLY joins in. After five, ROGER realizes that BILLY has his knees on the floor. They start again. This time, BILLY counts in double time. They start again. At about "seven," RICHIE enters. Neither BILLY nor ROGER sees him. They keep going.)

ROGER and BILLY: . . . seven, eight, nine, ten . . .

RICHIE: No, no; no, no; no, no, no. That's not it; that's not it.

(They keep going, yelling the numbers louder and louder.)

ROGER and BILLY: . . . eleven, twelve, thirteen . . .

(RICHIE crosses to his locker and gets his bottle of cologne, and then returning to the center of the room to stare at them, he stands there dabbing cologne on his face.)

ROGER and BILLY: . . . fourteen, fifteen.

RICHIE: You'll never get it like that. You're so far apart and you're both humping at the same time. And all that counting. It's so unromantic.

ROGER: *(rising and moving to his bed to pick up the basketball)* We was exercisin', Richard. You heard a that?

RICHIE: Call it what you will, Roger.

(With a flick of his wrist, ROGER tosses the basketball to BILLY.)

Everybody has their own cute little pet names for it.

BILLY: Hey!

(And he tosses the ball at RICHIE, hitting him in the chest, sending the cologne bottle flying. RICHIE yelps, as BILLY retrieves the ball and, grabbing up his sweat jacket from the bed, heads for the door. ROGER, at his own locker, has taken out his suit bag of civilian clothes.) You missed.

RICHIE: Billy, Billy, Billy, please, please, the ruffian approach will not work with me. It impresses me not even one tiny little bit. All you've done is spill my cologne.

(He bends to pick up the cologne from the floor.)

BILLY: That was my aim.

ROGER: See you.

(BILLY is passing RICHIE. Suddenly RICHIE sprays BILLY with cologne, some of it getting on ROGER, as ROGER and BILLY, groaning and cursing at RICHIE, rush out the door.)

RICHIE: Try the more delicate approach next time, Bill.

(Having crossed to the door, he stands a moment, leaning against the frame. Then he bounces to BILLY'S bed, sings "He's just my Bill," and squirts cologne on the pillow. At his locker, he deposits the cologne, takes off his shirt, shoes and socks. Removing a hard-cover copy of Pauline Kael's I Lost It at the Movies *from the top shelf of the locker, he bounds to the center of the room and tosses the book the rest of the way to the bed. Quite pleased with himself, he fidgets, pats his stomach, then lowers himself into the push-up position, goes to his knees and stands up.)*

Am I out of my fucking mind? Those two are crazy. I'm not crazy.

(RICHIE pivots and strides to his locker. With an ashtray, a pack of matches and a pack of cigarettes, he hurries to his bed and makes himself comfortable to read, his head propped up on a pillow. Settling himself, he opens the book, finds his place, thinks a little, starts to read. For a moment he lies there. And then CARLYLE steps into the room. He comes through the doorway looking to his left and right. He comes several steps into the room and looks at RICHIE. RICHIE sees him. They look at each other.)

CARLYLE: Ain't nobody here, man?

RICHIE: Hello, Carlyle. How are you today?

CARLYLE: Ain't nobody here?

(He is nervous and angrily disappointed.)

RICHIE: Who do you want?

CARLYLE: Where's the black boy?

RICHIE: Roger? My God, why do you keep calling him that? Don't you know his name yet? Roger. Roger.

(He thickens his voice at this, imitating someone very stupid. CARLYLE stares at him.)

CARLYLE: Yeh. Where is he?

RICHIE: I am not his keeper, you know. I am not his private secretary, you know.

CARLYLE: I do not know. I do not know. That is why I am asking. I come to see him. You are here. I ask you. I don't know. I mean, Carlyle made a fool outa himself comin' in here the other night, talkin' on and on like how he did. Lay on the floor. He remember. You remember? It all one hype, man; that all one hype. You know what I mean. That ain't the real Carlyle was in here. This one here and now the real Carlyle. Who the real Richie?

RICHIE: Well . . . the real Richie . . . has gone home. To Manhattan. I, however, am about to read this book.

(Which he again starts to try to do.)

CARLYLE: Oh. Shit. Jus' you the only one here, then, huh?

RICHIE: So it would seem.

(He looks at the air and then under the bed as if to find someone.)

So it would seem. Did you hear about Martin?

CARLYLE: What happened to Martin? I ain't seen him.

RICHIE: They are shipping him home. Someone told about what he did to himself. I don't know who.

CARLYLE: Wasn't me. Not me. I keep that secret.

RICHIE: I'm sure you did.

(Rising, walking toward CARLYLE *and the door, cigarette pack in hand.)*

You want a cigarette? Or don't you smoke? Or do you have to go right away?

(Closing the door.)

There's a chill sometimes coming down the hall, I don't know from where.

(Crossing back to his bed and climbing in.)

And I think I've got the start of a little cold. Did you want the cigarette?

*(*CARLYLE *is staring at him. Then he examines the door and looks again at* RICHIE. *He stares at* RICHIE, *thinking, and then he walks toward him.)*

CARLYLE: You know what I bet? I been lookin' at you real close. It just a way I got about me. And I bet if I was to hang my boy out in front of you, my big boy, man, you'd start wantin' to touch him. Be beggin' and talkin' sweet to ole Carlyle. Am I right or wrong?

(He leans over RICHIE.)

What do you say?

RICHIE: Pardon?

CARLYLE: You heard me. Ohhh. I am so restless, I don't even understand it. My big black boy is what I was talkin' about. My thing, man; my rope, Jim. HEY, RICHIE!

(And he lunges, then moves his fingers through RICHIE'S *hair.)*

How long you been a punk? Can you hear me? Am I clear? Do I talk funny?

(He is leaning close.)

Can you smell the gin on my mouth?

RICHIE: I mean, if you really came looking for Roger, he and Billy are gone to the gymnasium. They were—

CARLYLE: No.

(He slides down on the bed, his arm placed over RICHIE'S *legs.)*

I got no athletic abilities. I got none. No moves. I don't know. HEY, RICHIE!

(Leaning close again.)

I just got this question I asked. I got no answer.

RICHIE: I don't know . . . what . . . you mean.

CARLYLE: I heard me. I understood me. "How long you been a punk?" is the question I asked. Have you got a reply?

RICHIE: *(confused, irritated, but fascinated)* Not to that question.

CARLYLE: Who do if you don't? I don't. How'm I gonna?

(Suddenly there is whistling in the hall, as if someone might enter, footsteps approaching, and RICHIE *leaps to his feet and scurries away toward the door, tucking in his undershirt as he goes.)*

Man, don't you wanna talk to me? Don't you wanna talk to ole Carlyle?

RICHIE: Not at the moment.

CARLYLE: *(he is rising, starting after* RICHIE, *who stands nervously near* ROGER'S *bed)* I want to talk to you, man; why don't you want to talk to me? We can be friends. Talkin' back and forth, sharin' thoughts and bein' happy.

RICHIE: I don't think that's what you want.

CARLYLE: *(he is very near to* RICHIE) What do I want?

RICHIE: I mean, to talk to me.

*(*RICHIE, *as if repulsed, crosses away. But it is hard to tell if the move is genuine or coy.)*

CARLYLE: What am I doin'? I am talkin'. DON'T YOU TELL ME I AIN'T TALKIN' WHEN I AM TALKIN'! COURSE I AM. Bendin' over backwards.

(And pressing his hands against himself in his anger, he has touched the grease on his shirt, the filth of his clothing, and this ignites the anger.)

Do you know they still got me in that goddamn P Company? That goddamn transient company. It like they think I ain't got no notion what a home is. No nose for no home—like I ain't never had no home. I had a home. IT LIKE THEY THINK THERE AIN'T NO PLACE FOR ME IN THIS MOTHER ARMY BUT K.P. ALL SUDSY AND WRINKLED AND SWEATIN'. EVERY DAY SINCE I GOT TO THIS SHIT HOUSE, MISTER! HOW MANY TIMES YOU BEEN ON K.P.? WHEN'S THE LAST TIME YOU PULLED K.P.?

(He has roared down to where RICHIE *has moved, the rage possessing him.)*

RICHIE: I'm E.D.

CARLYLE: You E.D.? You E.D.? You Edie, are you? I didn't ask you what you friends call you, I asked you when's the last time you had K.P.?

RICHIE: *(edging toward his bed. He will go there, get and light a cigarette)* E.D. is "Exempt from Duty."

CARLYLE: *(moving after* RICHIE*)* You ain't got no duties? What shit you talkin' about? Everybody in this fuckin' army got duties. That what the fuckin' army all about. You ain't got no duties, who got 'em?

RICHIE: Because of my job, Carlyle. I have a very special job. And my friends don't call me Edie. *(Big smile.)* They call me Irene.

CARLYLE: That mean what you sayin' is you kiss ass for somebody, don't it? Good for you. *(Seemingly relaxed and gentle, he settles down on* RICHIE'S *bed. He seems playful and charming.)* You know the other night I was sleepin' there. You know.

RICHIE: Yes.

CARLYLE: *(gleefully, enormously pleased)* You remember that? How come you remember that? You sweet.

RICHIE: We don't have people sleeping on our floor that often, Carlyle.

CARLYLE: But the way you crawl over in the night, gimme a big kiss on my joint. That nice.

RICHIE: *(shocked, he blinks)* What?

CARLYLE: Or did I dream that?

RICHIE: *(laughing in spite of himself)* My God, you're outrageous!

CARLYLE: Maybe you dreamed it.

RICHIE: What . . . ? No. I don't know.

CARLYLE: Maybe you did it, then; you didn't dream it.

RICHIE: How come you talk so much?

CARLYLE: I don't talk, man, who's gonna talk? YOU? *(He is laughing and amused, but there is an anger near the surface now, an ugliness.)* That bore me to death. I don't like nobody's voice but my own. I am so pretty. Don't like nobody else face. *(And then viciously, he spits out at* RICHIE.*)* You goddamn face ugly fuckin' queer punk! *(And* RICHIE *jumps in confusion.)*

RICHIE: What's the matter with you?

CARLYLE: You goddamn ugly punk face. YOU UGLY!

RICHIE: Nice mouth.

CARLYLE: That's right. That's right. And you got a weird mouth. Like to suck joints. *(As* RICHIE *storms to his locker, throwing the book inside. He pivots, grabbing a towel, marching toward the door.)* Hey, you gonna jus' walk out on me? Where you goin'? You c'mon back. Hear?

RICHIE: That's my bed, for chrissake. *(He lunges into the hall.)*

CARLYLE: You'd best. *(Lying there, he makes himself comfortable. He takes a pint bottle from his back pocket.)* You come back, Richie, I tell you a good joke. Make you laugh, make you cry. *(He takes a big drink.)* That's right. Ole Frank and Jesse, they got the stagecoach stopped, all the peoples lined up— Frank say, "All right, peoples, we gonna rape all the men and rob all the women." Jesse say, "Frank, no no—that ain't it—we gonna—" And this one little man yell real loud, "You shut up, Jesse; Frank knows what he's doin'." *(Loudly, he laughs and laughs.* BILLY *enters. Startled at the sight of* CARLYLE *there in*

RICHIE'S *bed,* BILLY *falters, as* CARLYLE *gestures toward him.)*

Hey, man ; . . . ! Hey, you know, they send me over to that Vietnam, I be cool, 'cause I been dodgin' bullets and shit since I been old enough to get on pussy make it happy to know me. I can get on, I can do my job.

*(*BILLY *looks weary and depressed. Languidly he crosses to his bed. He still wears his sweat clothes.* CARLYLE *studies him, then stares at the ceiling.)*

Yeh. I was just layin' here thinkin' that and you come in and out it come, words to say my feelin'. That my problem. That the black man's problem altogether. You ever considered that? Too much feelin'. He too close to everthing. He is, man; too close to his blood, to his body. It ain't that he don't have no good mind, but he BELIEVE in his body. Is . . . that Richie the only punk in this room, or is there more?

BILLY: What?

CARLYLE: The punk; is he the only punk?
(Carefully he takes one of RICHIE'S *cigarettes and lights it.)*

BILLY: He's all right.

CARLYLE: I ain't askin' about the quality of his talent, but is he the only one, is my question?

BILLY: *(he does not want to deal with this. He sits there)* You get your orders yet?

CARLYLE: Orders for what?

BILLY: To tell you where you work.

CARLYLE: I'm P Company, man. I work in P Company. I do K.P. That all. Don't deserve no more. Do you know I been in this army three months and ten days and everbody still doin' the same shit and sayin' the same shit and wearin' the same green shitty clothes? I ain't been happy one day, and that a lotta goddamn misery back to back in this ole boy. Is that Richie a good punk? Huh? Is he? He takes care of you and Roger—that how come you in this room, the three of you?

BILLY: What?

CARLYLE: *(emphatically)* You and Roger are hittin' on Richie, right?

BILLY: He's not queer, if that's what you're sayin'. A little effeminate, but that's all, no more; if that's what you're sayin'.

CARLYLE: I'd like to get some of him myself if he a good punk, is what I'm sayin'. That's what I'm sayin'! You don't got no understandin' how a man can maybe be a little diplomatic about what he's sayin' sorta sideways, do you? Jesus.

BILLY: He don't do that stuff.

CARLYLE: *(lying there)* What stuff?

BILLY: Listen, man. I don't feel too good, you don't mind.

CARLYLE: What stuff?

BILLY: What you're thinkin'.

CARLYLE: What . . . am I thinkin'?

BILLY: You . . . know.

CARLYLE: Yes, I do. It in my head, that how come I know. But how do you know? I can see your heart, Billy boy, but you cannot see mine. I am unknown. You . . . are known.

BILLY: *(as if he is about to vomit, and fighting it)* You just . . . talk fast and keep movin', don't you? Don't ever stay still.

CARLYLE: Words to say my feelin', Billy boy.
*(*RICHIE *steps into the room. He sees* BILLY *and* CARLYLE, *and freezes.)*
There he is. There he be.
*(*RICHIE *moves to his locker to put away the towel.)*

RICHIE: He's one of them who hasn't come down far out of the trees yet, Billy; believe me.

CARLYLE: You got rudeness in your voice, Richie—you got meanness I can hear about ole Carlyle. You tellin' me I oughta leave—is that what you think you're doin'? You don't want me here?

RICHIE: You come to see Roger, who isn't here, right? Man like you must have important matters to take care of all over the quad; I can't imagine a man like you not having extremely important things to do all over the world, as a matter of fact, Carlyle.

CARLYLE: *(he rises. He begins to smooth the sheets and straighten the pillow. He will put the pint bottle in his back pocket and cross near to*

RICHIE) Ohhhh, listen—don't mind all the shit I say. I just talk bad, is all I do; I don't do bad. I got to have friends just like anybody else. I'm just bored and restless, that all; takin' it out on you two. I mean, I know Richie here ain't really no punk, not really. I was just talkin', just jivin' and entertainin' my own self. Don't take me serious, not ever. I get on out and see you all later.

(He moves for the door, RICHIE *right behind him, almost ushering him.)*

You be cool, hear? Man don't do the jivin', he the one gettin' jived. That what my little brother Henry tell me and tell me.

(Moving leisurely, he backs out the door and is gone. RICHIE *shuts the door. There is a silence as* RICHIE *stands by the door.* BILLY *looks at him and then looks away.)*

BILLY: I am gonna have to move myself outa here, Roger decides to adopt that sonofabitch.

RICHIE: He's an animal.

BILLY: Yeh, and on top a that, he's a rotten person.

RICHIE: *(he laughs nervously, crossing nearer to* BILLY*)* I think you're probably right.

(Still laughing a little, he pats BILLY'S *shoulder and* BILLY *freezes at the touch. Awkwardly* RICHIE *removes his hand and crosses to his bed. When he has lain down,* BILLY *bends to take off his sneakers, then lies back on his pillow staring, thinking, and there is a silence.* RICHIE *does not move. He lies there, struggling to prepare himself for something.)*

Hey . . . Billy?

(Very slight pause.)

Billy?

BILLY: Yeh.

RICHIE: You know that story you told the other night?

BILLY: Yeh . . . ?

RICHIE: You know . . .

BILLY: What . . . about it?

RICHIE: Well, was it . . . about you?

(Pause.)

I mean, was it . . . ABOUT you? Were you Frankie?

(This is difficult for him.)

Are . . . you Frankie? Billy?

(BILLY is slowly sitting up.)

BILLY: You sonofabitch . . . !

RICHIE: Or was it really about somebody you knew . . . ?

BILLY: *(sitting, outraged and glaring)* You didn't hear me at all!

RICHIE: I'm just asking a simple question, Billy, that's all I'm doing.

BILLY: You are really sick. You know that? Your brain is really, truly rancid! Do you know there's a theory now it's genetic? That it's all a matter of genes and shit like that?

RICHIE: Everything is not so ungodly cryptic, Billy.

BILLY: You. You, man, and the rot it's makin' outa your feeble fuckin' brain.

(ROGER, dressed in civilian clothes, bursts in and BILLY *leaps to his feet.)*

ROGER: Hey, hey, anyone got a couple bucks he can loan me?

BILLY: Rog, where you been?

ROGER: *(throwing the basketball and his sweat clothes into his locker)* I need five. C'mon.

BILLY: Where you been? That asshole friend a yours was here.

ROGER: I know, I know. Can you gimme five?

RICHIE: *(he jumps to the floor and heads for his locker)* You want five. I got it. You want ten or more, even?

(BILLY, watching RICHIE, *turns, and nervously paces down right, where he moves about, worried.)*

BILLY: I mean, we gotta talk about him, man; we gotta talk about him.

ROGER: *(as* RICHIE *is handing him two fives)* 'Cause we goin' to town together. I jus' run into him out on the quad, man, and he was feelin' real bad 'bout the way he acted, how you guys done him, he was fallin' down apologizin' all over the place.

BILLY: *(as* RICHIE *marches back to his bed and sits down)* I mean, he's got a lotta weird ideas about us; I'm tellin' you.

ROGER: He's just a little fucked up in his head is all, but he ain't trouble.

(He takes a pair of sunglasses from the locker and puts them on.)

BILLY: Who needs him? I mean, we don't need him.

ROGER: You gettin' too nervous, man. Nobody said anything about anybody needin' anybody. I been on the street all my life; he brings back home. I played me a little ball, Billy; took me a shower. I'm feelin' good!

(He has moved down to BILLY.*)*

BILLY: I'm tellin' you there's something wrong with him, though.

ROGER: *(face to face with* BILLY, ROGER *is a little irritated)* Every black man in the world ain't like me, man; you get used to that idea. You get to know him, and you gonna like him. I'm tellin' you. You get to be laughin' just like me to hear him talk his shit. But you gotta relax.

RICHIE: I agree with Billy, Roger.

ROGER: Well, you guys got it all worked out and that's good, but I am goin' to town with him. Man's got wheels. Got a good head. You got any sense, you'll come with us.

BILLY: What are you talkin' about—come with you? I just tole you he's crazy.

ROGER: And I tole you you're wrong.

RICHIE: We weren't invited.

ROGER: I'm invitin' you.

RICHIE: No, I don't wanna.

ROGER: *(he moves to* RICHIE; *it seems he really wants* RICHIE *to go)* You sure, Richie? C'mon.

RICHIE: No.

ROGER: Billy? He got wheels, we goin' in drinkin', see if gettin' our heads real bad don't just make us feel real good. You know what I mean. I got him right; you got him wrong.

BILLY: But what if I'm right?

ROGER: Billy, Billy, the man is waitin' on me. You know you wanna. Jesus. Bad cat like that gotta know the way. He been to D.C. before. Got cousins here. Got wheels for the weekend. You always talkin' how you don't do nothin'—

you just talk it. Let's do it tonight—stop talkin'. Be cruisin' up and down the strip, leanin' out the window, bad as we wanna be. True cool is a car. We can flip a cigarette out the window— we can watch it bounce. Get us some chippies. You know we can. And if we don't, he knows a cathouse, it fulla cats.

BILLY: You serious?

RICHIE: You mean you're going to a whorehouse? That's disgusting.

BILLY: Listen who's talkin'. What do you want me to do? Stay here with you?

RICHIE: We could go to a movie or something.

ROGER: I am done with this talkin'. You goin', you stayin'?

(He crosses to his locker, pulls into view a wide-brimmed black and shiny hat, and puts it on, cocking it at a sharp angle.)

BILLY: I don't know.

ROGER: *(stepping for the door)* I am goin'.

BILLY: *(turning,* BILLY *sees the hat)* I'm going. Okay! I'm going! Going, going, going!

(And he runs to his locker.)

RICHIE: Oh, Billy, you'll be scared to death in a cathouse and you know it.

BILLY: BULLSHIT!

(He is removing his sweat pants and putting on a pair of gray corduroy trousers.)

ROGER: Billy got him a lion-tamer 'tween his legs!

(The door bangs open and CARLYLE *is there, still clad in his filthy fatigues, but wearing a going-to-town black knit cap on his head and carrying a bottle.)*

CARLYLE: Man, what's goin' on? I been waitin' like throughout my fuckin' life.

ROGER: Billy's goin', too. He's gotta change.

CARLYLE: He goin', too! Hey! Beautiful! That beautiful!

(His grin is large, his laugh is loud.)

ROGER: Didn't I tell you, Billy?

CARLYLE: That beautiful, man; we all goin' to be friends!

RICHIE: *(sitting on his bed)* What about me, Carlyle?

(CARLYLE *looks at* RICHIE, *and then at* ROGER *and then he and* ROGER *begin to laugh.* CAR-LYLE *pokes* ROGER *and they laugh as they are leaving.* BILLY, *grabbing up his sneakers to fol-low, stops at the door, looking only briefly at* RICHIE. *Then* BILLY *goes and shuts the door. The lights are fading to black.*)

SCENE 2: *In the dark, taps begins to play. And then slowly the lights rise, but the room remains dim. Only the lamp attached to* RICHIE'S *bed burns and there is the glow and spill of the hallway coming through the transom.* BILLY, CARLYLE, ROGER *and* RICHIE *are sprawled about the room.* BILLY, *lying on his stomach, has his head at the foot of his bed, a half-empty bottle of beer dangling in his hand. He wears a blue oxford-cloth shirt and his sneakers lie beside his bed.* ROGER, *collapsed in his own bed, lies upon his back, his head also at the foot, a Playboy magazine covering his face and a half-empty bottle of beer in his hands, folded on his belly. Having re-moved his civilian shirt, he wears a white T-shirt.* CARLYLE *is lying on his belly on* RICHIE'S *bed, his head at the foot, and he is facing out.* RICHIE *is sit-ting on the floor, resting against* ROGER'S *footlocker. He is wrapped in a blanket. Beside him is an un-opened bottle of beer and a bottle opener.*

They are all dreamy in the dimness as taps plays sadly on and then fades into silence. No one moves.

RICHIE: I don't know where it was, but it wasn't here. And we were all in it—it felt like—but we all had different faces. After you guys left, I only dozed for a few minutes, so it couldn't have been long. Roger laughed a lot and Billy was taller. I don't remember all the details ex-actly, and even though we were the ones in it, I know it was about my father. He was a big man. I was six. He was a very big man when I was six and he went away, but I remember him. He started drinking and staying home making model airplanes and boats and paintings by the numbers. We had money from mom's family, so

he was just home all the time. And then one day I was coming home from kindergarten, and as I was starting up the front walk he came out the door and he had these suitcases in his hands. He was leaving, see, sneaking out, and I'd caught him. We looked at each other and I just knew and I started crying. He yelled at me, "Don't you cry; don't you start crying." I tried to grab him and he pushed me down in the grass. And then he was gone. G-O-N-E.

BILLY: And that was it? That was it?

RICHIE: I remember hiding my eyes. I lay in the grass and hid my eyes and waited.

BILLY: He never came back?

RICHIE: No.

CARLYLE: Ain't that some shit. Now, I'm a jive-time street nigger. I knew where my daddy was all the while. He workin' in this butcher shop two blocks up the street. Ole Mom used to point him out. "There he go. That him—that your daddy." We'd see him on the street, "There he go."

ROGER: Man couldn't see his way to livin' with you—that what you're sayin'?

CARLYLE: Never saw the day.

ROGER: And still couldn't get his ass outa the neighborhood?

(RICHIE *begins trying to open his bottle of beer.*)

CARLYLE: Ain't that a bitch. Poor ole bastard just duck his head—Mom pointin' at him—he git this real goddamn hangdog look like he don't know who we talkin' about and he walk a little faster. Why the hell he never move away I don't know, unless he was crazy. But I don't think so. He come up to me once—I was playin'. "Boy," he says, "I ain't your daddy. I ain't. Your momma's crazy." "Don't you be callin' my momma crazy, Daddy," I tole him. Poor ole thing didn't know what to do.

RICHIE: (*giving up; he can't get the beer open*) Somebody open this for me? I can't get this open.

(BILLY *seems about to move to help, but* CAR-LYLE *is quicker, rising a little on the bunk and reaching.*)

CARLYLE: Ole Carlyle get it.

(RICHIE *slides along the floor until he can place the bottle in* CARLYLE'S *outstretched hand.*)

RICHIE: Then there was this once—there was this TV documentary about these bums in San Francisco, this TV guy interviewing all these bums, and just for maybe ten seconds while he was talkin' . . .

(*Smiling,* CARLYLE *hands* RICHIE *the opened bottle.*)

. . . to this one bum, there was this other one in the background jumpin' around like he thought he was dancin' and wavin' his hat, and even though there wasn't anything about him like my father and I didn't really ever see his face at all, I just kept thinkin': That's him. My dad. He thinks he's dancin'.

(*They lie there in silence and suddenly, softly,* BILLY *giggles, and then he giggles a little more and louder.*)

BILLY: Jesus!

RICHIE: What?

BILLY: That's ridiculous, Richie; sayin' that, thinkin' that. If it didn't look like him, it wasn't him, but you gotta be makin' up a story.

CARLYLE: (*shifting now for a more comfortable position, he moves his head to the pillow at the top of the bed*) Richie first saw me, he didn't like me much nohow, but he thought it over now, he changed his way a thinkin'. I can see that clear. We gonna be one big happy family.

RICHIE: Carlyle likes me, Billy; he thinks I'm pretty.

CARLYLE: (*sitting up a little to make his point clear*) No, I don't think you pretty. A broad is pretty. Punks ain't pretty. Punk—if he good-lookin'—is cute. You cute.

RICHIE: He's gonna steal me right away, little Billy. You're so slow, Bill. I prefer a man who's decisive.

(*He is lying down now on the floor at the foot of his bed.*)

BILLY: You just keep at it, you're gonna have us all believin' you are just what you say you are.

RICHIE: Which is more than we can say for you.

(*Now* ROGER *rises on his elbow to light a cigarette.*)

BILLY: Jive, jive.

RICHIE: You're arrogant, Billy. So arrogant.

BILLY: What are you—on the rag?

RICHIE: Wouldn't it just bang your little balls if I were!

ROGER: (*to* RICHIE) Hey, man. What's with you?

RICHIE: Stupidity offends me; lies and ignorance offend me.

BILLY: You know where we was? The three of us? All three of us, earlier on? To the wrong side of the tracks, Richard. One good black upside-down whorehouse where you get what you buy, no jive along with it—so if it's a lay you want and need, you go! Or don't they have faggot whorehouses?

ROGER: IF YOU GUYS DON'T CUT THIS SHIT OUT I'M GONNA BUST SOMEBODY'S HEAD!

(*Angrily he flops back on his bed. There is a silence as they all lie there.*)

RICHIE: "Where we *was*," he says. Listen to him. "Where we *was*." And he's got more school, Carlyle, than you have fingers and . . .

(*He has lifted his foot onto the bed; it touches, presses,* CARLYLE'S *foot.*)

. . . toes. It's this pseudo-earthy quality he feigns—but inside he's all cashmere.

BILLY: That's a lie.

(*Giggling, he is staring at the floor.*)

I'm polyester, worsted and mohair.

RICHIE: You have a lot of school, Billy; don't say you don't.

BILLY: You said "fingers and toes"; you didn't say "a lot."

CARLYLE: I think people get dumber the more they put their butts into some schoolhouse door.

BILLY: It depends on what the hell you're talkin' about.

(*Now he looks at* CARLYLE, *and sees the feet touching.*)

CARLYLE: I seen cats back on the block, they knew what was shakin'—then they got into all this school jive and, man, every year they went, they come back they didn't know nothin'.

(BILLY *is staring at* RICHIE'S *foot pressed and rubbing* CARLYLE'S *foot.* RICHIE *sees* BILLY *looking.* BILLY *cannot believe what he is seeing. It fills him with fear. The silence goes on and on.*)

RICHIE: Billy, why don't you and Roger go for a walk?

BILLY: What?

(*He bolts to his knees. He is frozen on his knees on the bed.*)

RICHIE: Roger asked you to go downtown, you went, you had fun.

ROGER: (*having turned, he knows almost instantly what is going on*) I asked you, too.

RICHIE: You asked me; you *begged* Billy. I said no. Billy said no. You took my ten dollars. You begged Billy. I'm asking you a favor now—go for a walk. Let Carlyle and me have some time. (*Silence.*)

CARLYLE: (*he sits up, uneasy and wary*) That how you work it?

ROGER: Work what?

CARLYLE: Whosever turn it be.

BILLY: No, no, that ain't the way we work it, because we don't work it.

CARLYLE: See? See? There it is—that goddamn education showin' through. All them years in school. Man, didn't we have a good time tonight? You rode in my car. I showed you a good cathouse, all that sweet black pussy. Ain't we friends? Richie likes me. How come you don't like me?

BILLY: 'Cause if you really are doin' what I think you're doin', you're a fuckin' animal!

(CARLYLE *leaps to his feet, hand snaking to his pocket to draw a weapon.*)

ROGER: Billy, no.

BILLY: NO, WHAT?!

ROGER: Relax, man; no need.

(*He turns to* CARLYLE; *patiently, wearily, he speaks.*)

Man, I tole you it ain't goin' on here. We both tole you it ain't goin' on here.

CARLYLE: Don't you jive me, nigger. You goin' for a walk like I'm askin', or not? I wanna get this clear.

ROGER: Man, we live here.

RICHIE: It's my house, too, Roger; I live here, too.

(RICHIE *bounds to his feet, flinging the blanket that has been covering him so it flies and lands on the floor near* ROGER'S *footlocker.*)

ROGER: Don't I know that? Did I say somethin' to make you think I didn't know that?

(*Standing,* RICHIE *is removing his trousers and throwing them down on his footlocker.*)

RICHIE: Carlyle is my guest.

(*Sitting down on the side of his bed and facing out, he puts his arms around* CARLYLE'S *thigh.* ROGER *jumps to his feet and grabs the blanket from the foot of his bed. Shaking it open, he drops onto the bed, his head at the foot of the bed and facing off as he covers himself.*)

ROGER: Fine. He your friend. This you home. So that mean he can stay. It don't mean I gotta leave. I'll catch you all in the mornin'.

BILLY: Roger, what the hell are you doin'?

ROGER: What you better do, Billy. It's gettin' late. I'm goin' to sleep.

BILLY: What?

ROGER: Go to fucking bed, Billy. Get up in the rack, turn your back and look at the wall.

BILLY: You gotta be kiddin'.

ROGER: DO IT!

BILLY: Man . . . !

ROGER: Yeah . . . !

BILLY: You mean just . . .

ROGER: It been goin' on a long damn time, man. You ain't gonna put no stop to it.

CARLYLE: You . . . ain't . . . serious.

RICHIE: (*both he and* CARLYLE *are staring at* ROGER *and then* BILLY, *who is staring at* ROGER) Well, I don't believe it. Of all the childish . . . infantile . . .

CARLYLE: Hey!

(*Silence.*)

HEY! Even I got to say this is a little weird, but if this the way you do it . . .

(*And he turns toward* RICHIE *below him.*)

. . . it the way I do it. I don't know.

RICHIE: With them right there? Are you kidding? My God, Carlyle, that'd be obscene.

(Pulling slightly away from CARLYLE.*)*

CARLYLE: Ohhh, man . . . they backs turned.

RICHIE: No.

CARLYLE: What I'm gonna do?

(Silence. He looks at them, all three of them.)
Don't you got no feelin' for how a man feel? I don't understand you two boys. Unless'n you a pair of motherfuckers. That what you are, you a pair of motherfuckers? You slits, man. DON'T YOU HEAR ME!? I DON'T UNDERSTAND THIS SITUATION HERE. I THOUGHT WE MADE A DEAL!

(RICHIE rises, starts to pull on his trousers. CARLYLE grabs him.)
YOU GET ON YOUR KNEES, YOU PUNK, I MEAN NOW, AND YOU GONNA BE ON MY JOINT FAST OR YOU GONNA BE ONE BUSTED PUNK. AM I UNDERSTOOD?

(He hurls RICHIE *down to the floor.)*

BILLY: I ain't gonna have this going on here; Roger, I can't.

ROGER: I been turnin' my back on one thing or another all my life.

RICHIE: Jealous, Billy?

BILLY: *(getting to his feet)* Just go out that door, the two of you. Go. Go on out in the bushes or out in some field. See if I follow you. See if I care. I'll be right here and I'll be sleepin', but it ain't gonna be done in my house. I don't have much in this goddamn army, but *here* is mine.

(He stands beside his bed.)

CARLYLE: I WANT MY FUCKIN' NUT! HOW COME YOU SO UPTIGHT? HE WANTS ME! THIS BOY HERE WANTS ME! WHO YOU TO STOP IT?

ROGER: *(spinning to face* CARLYLE *and* RICHIE*)* *That's right,* Billy. Richie one a those people want to get fucked by niggers, man. It what he know was gonna happen all his life—can be his dream come true. Ain't that right, Richie!

(Jumping to his feet, RICHIE *starts putting on his trousers.)*
Want to make it real in the world, how a nigger is an animal. Give 'em an inch, gonna take a mile. Ain't you some kinda fool, Richie? Hear me, Carlyle.

CARLYLE: Man, don't make me no nevermind what he think he's provin' an' shit, long as I get my nut. I KNOW I ain't no animal, don't have to prove it.

RICHIE: *(pulling at* CARLYLE'S *arm, wanting to move him toward the door)* Let's go. Let's go outside. The hell with it.

(But CARLYLE *tears himself free; he squats furiously down on the bunk, his hands seizing it, his back to all of them.)*

CARLYLE: Bull shit. Bullshit! I ain't goin' no-fuckin'-where—this jive ass ain't runnin' me. Is this you house or not?

(He doesn't know what is going on; he can hardly look at any of them.)

ROGER: *(bounding out of bed, hurling his pillow across the room)* I'm goin' to the fuckin' john, Billy. Hang it up, man; let 'em be.

BILLY: No.

ROGER: I'm smarter than you—do like I'm sayin'.

BILLY: It ain't right.

ROGER: Who gives a big rat's ass!

CARLYLE: Right on, bro! That boy know; he do.

(He circles the bed toward them.)
Hear him. Look into his eyes.

BILLY: This fuckin' army takin' everything else away from me, they ain't takin' more than they got. I see what I see—I don't run, don't hide.

ROGER: *(turning away from* BILLY, *he stomps out the door, slamming it)* You fuckin' well better learn.

CARLYLE: That right. Time for more schoolin'. Lesson number one.

(Stealthily he steps and snaps out the only light, the lamp clamped to RICHIE'S *bed.)*
You don't see what you see so well in the dark. It dark in the night. Black man got a black body—he disappear.

(The darkness is so total they are all no more than shadows.)

RICHIE: Not to the hands; not to the fingers.

(Moving from across the room toward CARLYLE.*)*

CARLYLE: You do like you talk, boy, you gonna make me happy.

(As BILLY, *nervously clutching his sneaker, is moving backward.)*

BILLY: Who says the lights go out? Nobody goddamn asked me if the lights go out.

(BILLY, *lunging to the wall switch, throws it.
The overhead lights flash on, flooding the
room with light.* CARLYLE *is seated on the
edge of* RICHIE'S *bed,* RICHIE *kneeling before
him.*)

CARLYLE: I DO, MOTHERFUCKER, I SAY!

(*And the switchblade seems to leap from his
pocket to his hand.*)

I SAY! CAN'T YOU LET PEOPLE BE?

(BILLY *hurls his sneaker at the floor at* CAR-
LYLE'S *feet. Instantly* CARLYLE *is across the
room, blocking* BILLY'S *escape out the door.*)

Goddamn you, boy! I'm gonna cut your ass, just
to show you how it feel—and cuttin' can happen. This knife true.

RICHIE: Carlyle, now c'mon.

CARLYLE: Shut up, pussy.

RICHIE: Don't hurt him, for chrissake.

CARLYLE: Goddamn man throw a shoe at me, he
don't walk around clean in the world thinkin'
he can throw another. He get some shit come
back at him.

(BILLY *doesn't know which way to go, and then*
CARLYLE, *jabbing the knife at the air before*
BILLY'S *chest, has* BILLY *running backward, his
eyes fixed on the moving blade. He stumbles,
having run into* RICHIE'S *bed. He sprawls backward and* CARLYLE *is over him.*)

No, no; no, no. Put you hand out there. Put it
out.

(*Slight pause;* BILLY *is terrified.*)

DO THE THING I'M TELLIN'!

(BILLY *lets his hand rise in the air and* CARLYLE
grabs it, holds it.)

That's it. That's good. See? See?

(*The knife flashes across* BILLY'S *palm; the blood
flows.* BILLY *winces, recoils, but* CARLYLE'S *hand
still clenches and holds.*)

BILLY: Motherfucker.

(*Again the knife darts, cutting, and* BILLY
yelps. RICHIE, *on his knees beside them, turns
away.*)

RICHIE: Oh, my God, what are you—

CARLYLE: (*in his own sudden distress,* CARLYLE
flings the hand away) That you blood. The
blood inside you, you don't ever see it there.
Take a look how easy it come out—and
enough of it come out, you in the middle of the
worst goddamn trouble you ever gonna see.
And know I'm the man can deal that kinda
trouble, easy as I smile. And I smile . . .
easy. Yeah.

(BILLY *is curled in upon himself, holding the
hand to his stomach as* RICHIE *now reaches tentatively and shyly out as if to console* BILLY,
who repulses the gesture. CARLYLE *is angry and
strangely depressed. Forlornly he slumps onto*
BILLY'S *footlocker as* BILLY *staggers up to his
wall locker and takes out a towel.*)

Bastard ruin my mood, Richie. He ruin my
mood. Fightin' and lovin' real different in the
feelin's I got. I see blood come outa somebody
like that, it don't make me feel good—hurt
me—hurt on somebody I thought was my friend.
But I ain't supposed to see. One dumb nigger.
No mind, he thinks, no heart, no feelings a gentleness. You see how that ain't true, Richie.
Goddamn man threw a shoe at me. A lotta people woulda cut his heart out. I gotta make him
know he throw shit, he get shit. But I don't hurt
him bad, you see what I mean?

(BILLY'S *back is to them, as he stands hunched
at his locker, and suddenly his voice, hissing,
erupts.*)

BILLY: Jesus . . . H. . . . Christ . . . ! Do
you know what I'm doin'? Do you know what
I'm standin' here doin'?

(*He whirls now; he holds a straight razor in his
hand. A bloody towel is wrapped around the hurt
hand.* CARLYLE *tenses, rises, seeing the razor.*)

I'm a twenty-four-year-old goddamn college
graduate—intellectual goddamn scholar type—
and I got a razor in my hand. I'm thinkin' about
comin' up behind one black human being
and I'm thinkin' nigger this and nigger that—I
wanna cut his throat. THAT IS RIDICULOUS. I
NEVER FACED ANYBODY IN MY LIFE WITH ANY-
THING TO KILL THEM. YOU UNDERSTAND ME? I

DON'T HAVE A GODDAMN THING ON THE LINE
HERE!

(The door opens and ROGER *rushes in, having heard the yelling.* BILLY *flings the razor into his locker.)*

Look at me, Roger, look at me. I got a cut palm—I don't know what happened. Jesus Christ, I got sweat all over me when I think a what I was near to doin'. I swear it. I mean, do I think I need a reputation as a killer, a bad man with a knife?

(He is wild with the energy of feeling free and with the anger at what these others almost made him do. CARLYLE *slumps down on the footlocker; he sits there.)*

Bullshit! I need shit! I got sweat all over me. I got the mile record in my hometown. I did four forty-two in high school and that's the goddamn record in Windsor County. I don't need approval from either one of the pair of you.

(And he rushes at RICHIE.)

You wanna be a goddamn swish—a goddamn faggot-queer—GO! Suckin' cocks and takin' it in the ass, the thing of which you dream—GO! AND YOU—

(Whirling on CARLYLE.)

You wanna be a bad-assed animal, man, get it on—go—but I wash my hands. I am not human as you are. I put you down, I put you down—

(He almost hurls himself at RICHIE.)

—you gay little piece a shit cake—SHIT CAKE. AND YOU—

(Hurt, confused, RICHIE *turns away, nearly pressing his face into the bed beside which he kneels, as* BILLY *has spun back to tower over the pulsing, weary* CARLYLE.)

—you are your own goddamn fault, SAMBO! SAMBO!

(And the knife flashes up in CARLYLE'S *hand into* BILLY'S *stomach, and* BILLY *yelps.)*

Ahhhhhhhhh.

(And pushes at the hand. RICHIE *is still turned away.)*

RICHIE: Well, fuck you, Billy.

BILLY: *(he backs off the knife)* Get away, get away.

RICHIE: *(as* ROGER, *who could not see because* BILLY'S *back is to him, is approaching* CARLYLE *and* BILLY *goes walking up toward the lockers as if he knows where he is going, as if he is going to go out the door and to a movie, his hands holding his belly)* You're so-o messed up.

ROGER: *(to* CARLYLE*)* Man, what's the matter with you?

CARLYLE: Don't nobody talk that weird shit to me, you understand?

ROGER: You jive, man. That's all you do—jive!

*(*BILLY, *striding swiftly, walks flat into the wall lockers; he bounces, turns. They are all looking at him.)*

RICHIE: Billy! Oh, Billy!

*(*ROGER *looks at* RICHIE.)

BILLY: Ahhhhhhh. Ahhhhhhh.

*(*ROGER *looks at* CARLYLE *as if he is about to scream, and beyond him,* BILLY *turns from the lockers, starts to walk again, now staggering and moving toward them.)*

RICHIE: I think . . . he stabbed him. I think Carlyle stabbed Billy. Roger!

*(*ROGER *whirls to go to* BILLY, *who is staggering downstage and angled away, hands clenched over his belly.)*

BILLY: Shut up! It's just a cut, it's just a cut. He cut my hand, he cut gut.

(He collapses onto his knees just beyond ROGER'S *footlocker.)*

It took the wind out of me, scared me, that's all.

(Fiercely he tries to hide the wound and remain calm.)

ROGER: Man, are you all right?

(He moves to BILLY, *who turns to hide the wound. Till now no one is sure what happened.* RICHIE *only "thinks"* BILLY *has been stabbed.* BILLY *is pretending he isn't hurt. As* BILLY *turns from* ROGER, *he turns toward* RICHIE *and* RICHIE *sees the blood.* RICHIE *yelps and they all begin talking and yelling simultaneously.)*

CARLYLE: You know what I was learnin', he was learnin' to talk all that weird shit,	ROGER: You all right? Or what? He slit you? BILLY: Just took the wind outa me, scared me.

cuttin', baby, cuttin',
the ways and means
a shit, man, razors.

RICHIE: Carlyle, you stabbed him; you stabbed him.

CARLYLE: Ohhhh, pussy, pussy, pussy, Carlyle know what he do.

ROGER: *(trying to lift* BILLY*)* Get up, okay? Get up on the bed.

BILLY: *(irritated, pulling free)* I am on the bed.

ROGER: What?

RICHIE: No, Billy, no, you're not.

BILLY: Shut up!

RICHIE: You're on the floor.

BILLY: I'm on the bed. I'm on the bed.
(Emphatically. And then he looks at the floor.)
What?

ROGER: Let me see what he did.
*(*BILLY'S *hands are clenched on the wound.)*
Billy, let me see where he got you.

BILLY: *(recoiling)* NO-O-O-O-O-O, you nigger!

ROGER: *(he leaps at* CARLYLE*)* What did you do?

CARLYLE: *(hunching his shoulders, ducking his head)* Shut up.

ROGER: What did you do, nigger—you slit him or stick him?
(And then he tries to get back to BILLY*.)*
Billy, let me see.

BILLY: *(doubling over till his head hits the floor)* NO-O-O-O-O-O! Shit, shit, shit.

RICHIE: *(suddenly sobbing and yelling)* Oh, my God, my God, ohhhh, ohhhh, ohhhh.
(Bouncing on his knees on the bed.)

CARLYLE: FUCK IT, FUCK IT, I STUCK HIM. I TURNED IT. This mother army break my heart. I can't be out there where it pretty, don't wanna live! Wash me clean, shit face!

RICHIE: Ohhhh, ohhhhh, ohhhhhhhhhhh. Carlyle stabbed Billy, oh, ohhhh, I never saw such a thing in my life. Ohhhhhh.
(As ROGER *is trying gently, fearfully, to straighten* BILLY *up.)*
Don't die, Billy; don't die.

ROGER: Shut up and go find somebody to help. Richie, go!

RICHIE: Who? I'll go, I'll go.
(Scrambling off the bed.)

ROGER: I don't know. JESUS CHRIST! DO IT!

RICHIE: Okay. Okay. Billy, don't die. Don't die.
(Backing for the door, he turns and runs.)

ROGER: The sarge, or C.Q.

BILLY: *(suddenly doubling over, vomiting blood.* RICHIE *is gone)* Ohhhhhhhhhh. Blood. Blood.

ROGER: Be still, be still.

BILLY: *(pulling at a blanket on the floor beside him)* I want to stand up. I'm——vomiting——
(Making no move to stand, only to cover himself.)
—blood. What does that mean?

ROGER: *(slowly standing)* I don't know.

BILLY: Yes, yes, I want to stand up. Give me blanket, blanket. *(He rolls back and forth, fighting to get the blanket over him.)*

ROGER: RIICCHHHIIIEEEE!
(As BILLY *is furiously grappling with the blanket.)*
No, no.
(He looks at CARLYLE, *who is slumped over, muttering to himself.* ROGER *runs for the door.)*
Wait on, be tight, be cool.

BILLY: Cover me. Cover me.
(At last he gets the blanket over his face. The dark makes him grow still. He lies there beneath his blanket. Silence. No one moves. And then CARLYLE *senses the quiet; he turns, looks. Slowly, wearily, he rises and walks to where* BILLY *lies. He stands over him, the knife hanging loosely from his left hand as he reaches with his right to gently take the blanket and lift it slowly from* BILLY'S *face. They look at each other.* BILLY *reaches up and pats* CARLYLE'S *hand holding the blanket.)*
I don't want to talk to you right now, Carlyle. All right? Where's Roger? Do you know where he is?
(Slight pause.)
Don't stab me anymore, Carlyle, okay? I was dead wrong doin' what I did. I know that now. Carlyle, promise me you won't stab me anymore. I couldn't take it. Okay? I'm cold . . . my blood . . . is . . .

(From off comes a voice.)

ROONEY: Cokesy? Cokesy wokesy?

(And ROONEY *staggers into the doorway, very drunk, a beer bottle in his hand.)*

Ollie-ollie oxen-freeee.

(He looks at them. CARLYLE *quickly, secretly, slips the knife into his pocket.)*

How you all doin'? Everybody drunk, huh? I los' my friend.

(He is staggering sideways toward BILLY'S *bunk, where he finally drops down, sitting.)*

Who are you, soldier?

*(*CARLYLE *has straightened, his head ducked down as he is edging for the door.)*

Who are you, soldier?

(And RICHIE, *running, comes roaring into the room. He looks at* ROONEY *and cannot understand what is going on.* CARLYLE *is standing.* ROONEY *is just sitting there. What is going on?* RICHIE *moves along the lockers, trying to get behind* ROONEY, *his eyes never off* CARLYLE.*)*

RICHIE: Ohhhhh, Sergeant Rooney, I've been looking for you everywhere—where have you been? Carlyle stabbed Billy, he stabbed him.

ROONEY: *(sitting there)* What?

RICHIE: Carlyle stabbed Billy.

ROONEY: Who's Carlyle?

RICHIE: He's Carlyle.

(As CARLYLE *seems about to advance, the knife again showing in his hand.)*

Carlyle, don't hurt anybody more!

ROONEY: *(on his feet, he is staggering toward the door)* You got a knife there? What's with the knife? What's goin' on here?

*(*CARLYLE *steps as if to bolt for the door, but* ROONEY *is in the way, having inserted himself between* CARLYLE *and* RICHIE, *who has backed into the doorway.)*

Wait! Now wait!

RICHIE: *(as* CARLYLE *raises the knife)* Carlyle, don't!

*(*RICHIE *runs from the room.)*

ROONEY: You watch your step, you understand. You see what I got here?

(He lifts the beer bottle, waves it threateningly.)

You watch your step, motherfucker. Relax. I mean, we can straighten all this out. We—

*(*CARLYLE *lunges at* ROONEY, *who tenses.)*

I'm just askin' what's goin' on, that's all I'm doin'. No need to get all—

(And CARLYLE *swipes at the air again;* ROONEY *recoils.)*

Motherfucker. Motherfucker.

(He seems to be tensing, his body gathering itself for some mighty effort. And he throws his head back and gives the eagle yell.)

Eeeeeeeeeeeaaaaaaaaaaaaaaaaaahhhhhh! Eeeeaaaaaaaaaaaaaahhhhhhhhhhhhh!

*(*CARLYLE *jumps; he looks left and right.)*

Goddammit, I'll cut you good.

(He lunges to break the bottle on the edge of the wall lockers. The bottle shatters and he yelps, dropping everything.)

Ohhhhhhhh! Ohhhhhhhhhhhhhh!

*(*CARLYLE *bolts, running from the room.)*

I hurt myself, I cut myself. I hurt my hand.

(Holding the wounded hand, he scurries to BILLY'S *bed, where he sits on the edge, trying to wipe the blood away so he can see the wound.)*

I cut—

(Hearing a noise, he whirls, looks; CARLYLE *is plummeting in the door and toward him.* ROONEY *stands.)*

I hurt my hand, goddammit!

(The knife goes into ROONEY'S *belly. He flails at* CARLYLE.*)*

I HURT MY HAND! WHAT ARE YOU DOING? WHAT ARE YOU DOING? WAIT! WAIT!

(He turns away, falling to his knees, and the knife goes into him again and again.)

No fair. No fair!

*(*ROGER, *running, skids into the room, headed for* BILLY, *and then he sees* CARLYLE *on* ROONEY, *the leaping knife.* ROGER *lunges, grabbing* CARLYLE, *pulling him to get him off* ROONEY. CARLYLE *leaps free of* ROGER, *sending* ROGER *flying backward. And then* CARLYLE *begins to circle* ROGER'S *bed. He is whimpering, wiping at the blood on his shirt as if to wipe it away.* ROGER *backs away as* CARLYLE *keeps waving the knife*

at him. ROONEY *is crawling along the floor under* BILLY'S *bed and then he stops crawling, lies there.*)

CARLYLE: You don't tell nobody on me you saw me do this, I let you go, okay? Ohhhhhhhhh. *(Rubbing, rubbing at the shirt.)* Ohhhhhh, how'm I gonna get back to the world now, I got all this mess to—

ROGER: What happened? That you—I don't understand that you did this! That you did—

CARLYLE: YOU SHUT UP! Don't be talkin' all that weird shit to me—don't you go talkin' all that weird shit!

ROGER: Nooooooooooooo!

CARLYLE: I'm Carlyle, man. You know me. You know me. *(He turns, he flees out the door.* ROGER, *alone, looks about the room.* BILLY *is there.* ROGER *moves toward* BILLY, *who is shifting, undulating on his back.)*

BILLY: Carlyle, no; oh, Christ, don't stab me anymore. I'll die. I will—I'll die. Don't make me die. I'll get my dog after you. I'LL GET MY DOG AFTER YOU! *(*ROGER *is saying, "Oh, Billy, man, Billy." He is trying to hold* BILLY. *Now he lifts* BILLY *into his arms.)*

ROGER: Oh, Billy; oh, man. GODDAMMIT, BILLY! *(As a* MILITARY POLICE LIEUTENANT *comes running in the door, his .45 automatic drawn, and he levels it at* ROGER.)*

LIEUTENANT: Freeze, soldier! Not a quick move out of you. Just real slow, straighten your ass up. *(*ROGER *has gone rigid; the* LIEUTENANT *is advancing on him. Tentatively* ROGER *turns, looks.)*

ROGER: Huh? No.

LIEUTENANT: Get your ass against the lockers.

ROGER: Sir, no. I—

LIEUTENANT: *(hurling* ROGER *away toward the wall lockers)* MOVE! *(As another M.P., Pfc* HINSON, *comes in, followed by* RICHIE, *flushed and breathless.)* Hinson, cover this bastard.

HINSON: *(drawing his .45 automatic, moving on* ROGER*)* Yes, sir.

(The LIEUTENANT *frisks* ROGER, *who is spread-eagled at the lockers.)*

RICHIE: What? Oh, sir, no, no. Roger, what's going on?

LIEUTENANT: I'll straighten this shit out.

ROGER: Tell 'em to get the gun off me, Richie.

LIEUTENANT: SHUT UP!

RICHIE: But, sir, sir, he didn't do it. Not him.

LIEUTENANT: *(fiercely he shoves* RICHIE *out of the way)* I told you, all of you, to shut up. *(He moves to* ROONEY'S *body.)* Jesus, God, this Sfc is cut to shit. He's cut to shit. *(He hurries to* BILLY'S *body.)* This man is cut to shit. *(As* CARLYLE *appears in the doorway, his hands cuffed behind him, a third M.P., Pfc* CLARK, *shoving him forward.* CARLYLE *seems shocked and cunning, his mind whirring.)*

CLARK: Sir, I got this guy on the street, runnin' like a streak a shit. *(He hurls the struggling* CARLYLE *forward and* CARLYLE *stumbles toward the head of* RICHIE'S *bed as* RICHIE, *seeing him coming, hurries away along* BILLY'S *bed and toward the wall lockers.)*

RICHIE: He did it! Him, him!

CARLYLE: What is going on here? I don't know what is going on here!

CLARK: *(club at the ready, he stations himself beside* CARLYLE*)* He's got blood all over him, sir. All over him.

LIEUTENANT: What about the knife?

CLARK: No, sir, he must have thrown it away. *(As a fourth M.P. has entered to stand in the doorway, and* HINSON, *leaving* ROGER, *bends to examine* ROONEY. *He will also kneel and look for life in* BILLY.)*

LIEUTENANT: You throw it away, soldier?

CARLYLE: Oh, you thinkin' about how my sister got happened, too. Oh, you ain't so smart as you think you are! No way!

ROGER: Jesus God almighty.

LIEUTENANT: What happened here? I want to know what happened here.

HINSON: *(Rising from* BILLY'S *body)* They're both dead, sir. Both of them.

LIEUTENANT: *(confidential, almost whispering)* I know they're both dead. That's what I'm talkin' about.

CARLYLE: Chicken blood, sir. Chicken blood and chicken hearts is what all over me. I was goin' on my way, these people jump out the bushes be pourin' it all over me. Chicken blood and chicken hearts.

(Thrusting his hands out at CLARK.)

You goin' take these cuffs off me, boy?

LIEUTENANT: Sit him down, Clark. Sit him down and shut him up.

CARLYLE: This my house, sir. This my goddamn house.

(CLARK grabs him, begins to move him.)

LIEUTENANT: I said to shut him up.

CLARK: Move it; move!

(Struggling to get CARLYLE over to ROGER's footlocker as HINSON and the other M.P. exit.)

CARLYLE: I want these cuffs taken off my hands.

CLARK: You better do like you been told. You better sit and shut up!

CARLYLE: I'm gonna be thinkin' over here. I'm gonna be thinkin' it all over. I got plannin' to do. I'm gonna be thinkin' in my quietness; don't you be makin' no mistake.

(He slumps over, muttering to himself. HINSON and the other M.P. return, carrying a stretcher. They cross to BILLY, chatting with each other about how to go about the lift. They will lift him; they will carry him out.)

LIEUTENANT: *(to RICHIE)* You're Wilson?

RICHIE: No, sir.

(Indicating BILLY.)

That's Wilson. I'm Douglas.

ROGER: *(to ROGER)* And you're Moore. And you sleep here.

ROGER: Yes, sir.

RICHIE: Yes, sir. And Billy slept here and Sergeant Rooney was our platoon sergeant and Carlyle was a transient, sir. He was a transient from P Company.

LIEUTENANT: *(scrutinizing ROGER)* And you had nothing to do with his?

(To RICHIE.)

He had nothing to do with this?

ROGER: No, sir, I didn't.

RICHIE: No, sir, he didn't. I didn't either. Carlyle went crazy and he got into a fight and it was awful. I didn't even know what it was about exactly.

LIEUTENANT: How'd the Sfc get involved?

RICHIE: Well, he came in, sir.

ROGER: I had to run off to call you, sir. I wasn't here.

RICHIE: Sergeant Rooney just came in—I don't know why—he heard all the yelling, I guess— and Carlyle went after him. Billy was already stabbed.

CARLYLE: *(rising, his manner that of a man who is taking charge)* All right now, you gotta be gettin' the fuck outa here. All of you. I have decided enough of the shit has been goin' on around here and I am tellin' you to be gettin' these mother-fuckin' cuffs off me and you be gettin' me a bus ticket home. I am quittin' this jive-time army.

LIEUTENANT: You are doin' what?

CARLYLE: No, I ain't gonna be quiet. No way. I am quittin' this goddamn—

LIEUTENANT: You shut the hell up, soldier. I am ordering you.

CARLYLE: I don't understand you people! Don't you people understand when a man be talkin' Eng-lish at you to say his mind? I have quit the army!

(As HINSON returns.)

LIEUTENANT: Get him outa here!

RICHIE: What's the matter with him?

LIEUTENANT: Hinson! Clark!

(They move, grabbing CARLYLE, and drag him, struggling, toward the door.)

CARLYLE: Oh, no. Oh, no. You ain't gonna be doin' me no more. I been tellin' you. To get away from me. I am stayin' here. This my place, not your place. You take these cuffs off me like I been tellin' you! My poor little sister Lin Sue under-stood what was goin' on here! She tole me! She knew!

(He is howling in the hallway now.)

You better be gettin' these cuffs off me!

(Silence. ROGER, RICHIE *and the* LIEUTENANT *are all staring at the door. The* LIEUTENANT *turns, crosses to the foot of* ROGER'S *bed.)*

LIEUTENANT: All right now. I will be getting to the bottom of this. You know I will be getting to the bottom of this.

(He is taking two forms from his clipboard.)

RICHIE: Yes, sir.

*(*HINSON *and the fourth M.P. return with another stretcher. They walk to* ROONEY, *talking to one another about how to lift him. They drag him from under the bed. They will roll him onto the stretcher, lift him and walk out.* ROGER *moves, watching them, down along the edge of* BILLY'S *bed.)*

LIEUTENANT: Fill out these forms. I want your serial number, rank, your MOS, the NCOIC of your work. Any leave coming up will be canceled. Tomorrow at 0800 you will report to my office at the provost marshal's headquarters. You know where that is?

ROGER: *(as the two M.P.'s are leaving with the stretcher and* ROONEY'S *body)* Yes, sir.

RICHIE: Yes, sir.

LIEUTENANT: *(crossing to* ROGER, *he hands him two cards.)* Be prepared to do some talking. Two perfectly trained and primed strong pieces of U.S. Army property got cut to shit up here. We are going to find out how and why. Is that clear?

RICHIE: Yes, sir.

ROGER: Yes, sir.

(The LIEUTENANT *looks at each of them. He surveys the room. He marches out.)*

RICHIE: Oh, my God. Oh. Oh.

(He runs to his bed and collapses, sitting hunched down at the foot. He holds himself and rocks as if very cold. ROGER, *quietly, is weeping. He stands and then walks to his bed. He puts down the two cards. He moves purposefully up to the mops hanging on the wall in the corner. He takes one down. He moves with the mop and the bucket to* BILLY'S *bed, where* ROONEY'S *blood stains the floor. He mops.* RICHIE, *in horror, is watching.)*

RICHIE: What . . . are you doing?

ROGER: This area a mess, man.

(Dragging the bucket, carrying the mop, he moves to the spot where BILLY *had lain. He begins to mop.)*

RICHIE: That's Billy's blood, Roger. His blood.

ROGER: Is it?

RICHIE: I feel awful.

ROGER: *(he keeps mopping)* How come you made me waste all that time talkin' shit to you, Richie? All my time talkin' shit, and all the time you was a faggot, man; you really was. You shoulda jus' tole ole Roger. He don't care. All you gotta do is tell me.

RICHIE: I've been telling you. I did.

ROGER: Jive, man, jive!

RICHIE: No!

ROGER: You did bullshit all over us! ALL OVER US!

RICHIE: I just wanted to hold his hand, Billy's hand, to talk to him, go to the movies hand in hand like he would with a girl or I would with someone back home.

ROGER: But he didn't wanna; *he* didn't wanna.

(Finished now, ROGER *drags the mop and bucket back toward the corner.* RICHIE *is sobbing; he is at the edge of hysteria.)*

RICHIE: He did.

ROGER: No, man.

RICHIE: He did. He did. It's not my fault.

*(*ROGER *slams the bucket into the corner and rams the mop into the bucket. Furious, he marches down to* RICHIE. *Behind him* SERGEANT COKES, *grinning and lifting a wine bottle, appears in the doorway.)*

COKES: Hey!

*(*RICHIE, *in despair, rolls onto his belly.* COKES *is very, very happy.)*

Hey! What a day, gen'l'men. How you all doin'?

ROGER: *(crossing up near the head of his own bed)* Hello, Sergeant Cokes.

COKES: *(affectionate and casual, he moves near to* ROGER) How you all doin'? Where's ole Rooney? I lost him.

ROGER: What?

COKES: We had a hell of a day, ole Rooney and me, lemme tell you. We been playin' hide-and-go-seek, and I was hidin', and now I think maybe he started hidin' without tellin' me he was gonna and I can't find him and I thought maybe he was hidin' up here.

RICHIE: Sergeant, he—

ROGER: No. No, we ain't seen him.

COKES: I gotta find him. He knows how to react in a tough situation. He didn't come up here looking for me?

(ROGER *moves around to the far side of his bed, turning his back to* COKES. *Sitting,* ROGER *takes out a cigarette, but he does not light it.*)

ROGER: We was goin' to sleep, Sarge. Got to get up early. You know the way this mother army is.

COKES: (*nodding, drifting backward, he sits down on* BILLY'S *bed*) You don't mind I sit here a little. Wait on him. Got a little wine. You can have some. (*Tilting his head way back, he takes a big drink and then, looking straight ahead, corks the bottle with a whack of his hand.*) We got back into the area—we had been downtown—he wanted to play hide-and-go-seek. I tole him okay, I was ready for that. He hid his eyes. So I run and hid in the bushes and then under this Jeep. 'Cause I thought it was better. I hid and I hid and I hid. He never did come. So finally, I got tired—I figured I'd give up, come lookin' for him. I was way over by the movie theater. I don't know how I got there. Anyway, I got back here and I figured maybe he come up here lookin' for me, figurin' I was hidin' up with you guys. You ain't seen him, huh?

ROGER: No, we ain't seen him. I tole you that, Sarge.

COKES: Oh.

RICHIE: Roger!

ROGER: He's drunk, Richie! He's blasted drunk. Got a brain turned to mush!

COKES: (*in deep agreement*) That ain't no lie.

ROGER: Let it be for the night, Richie. Let him be for the night.

COKES: I still know what's goin' on, though. Never no worry about that. I always know what's goin' on. I always know. Don't matter what I drink or how much I drink. I always still know what's goin' on. But . . . I'll be goin' maybe and look for Rooney.

(*But rising, he wanders down center.*)

But . . . I mean, we could be doin' that forever. Him and me. Me under the Jeep. He wants to find me, he goes to the Jeep. I'm over here. He comes here. I'm gone. You know, maybe I'll just wait a little while more I'm here. He'll find me then if he comes here. You guys want another drink.

(*Turning, he goes to* BILLY'S *footlocker, where he sits and takes another enormous guzzle of wine.*)

Jesus, what a goddamn day we had. Me and Rooney started drivin' and we was comin' to this intersection and out comes this goddamn Chevy. I try to get around her, but no dice. BINGO! I hit her in the left rear. She was furious. I didn't care. I gave her my name and number. My car had a headlight out, the fender bashed in. Rooney wouldn't stop laughin'. I didn't know what to do. So we went to D.C. to this private club I know. Had ten or more snorts and decided to get back here after playin' some snooker. That was fun. On the way, we picked up this kid from the engineering unit, hitchhiking. I'm starting to feel real clear-headed now. So I'm comin' around this corner and all of a sudden there's this car stopped dead in front of me. He's not blinkin' to turn or anything. I slam on the brakes, but it's like puddin' the way I slide into him. There's a big noise and we yell. Rooney starts laughin' like crazy and the kid jumps outa the back and says he's gonna take a fuckin' bus. The guy from the other car is swearin' at me. My car's still workin' fine, so I move it off to the side and tell him to do the same, while we wait for the cops. He says he wants his car right where it is and he had the right of way 'cause he was makin' a legal turn. So we're waitin' for the cops. Some cars go by. The guy's car is this big fuckin' Buick. Around the corner comes this little red Triumph. The driver's this blond kid got this blond girl next to him. You can see what's gonna happen. There's this fuckin' car sittin' there, nobody in it. So the Triumph goes crashin' into the back of the Buick with nobody in it. BIFF-BANG-BOOM. And everything stops.

We're staring. It's all still. And then that fuckin' Buick kinda shudders and starts to move. With nobody in it. It starts to roll from the impact. And it rolls just far enough to get where the road starts a downgrade. It's driftin' to the right. It's driftin' to the shoulder and over it and onto this hill, where it's pickin' up speed 'cause the hill is steep and then it disappears over the side, and into the dark, just rollin' real quiet. Rooney falls over, he's laughin' so hard. I don't know what to do. In a minute the cops come and in another minute some guy comes runnin' up over the hill to tell us some other guy had got run over by this car with nobody in it. We didn't know what to think. This was fuckin' unbelievable to us. But we found out later from the cops that this wasn't true and some guy had got hit over the head with a bottle in a bar and when he staggered out the door it was just at the instant that the fuckin' Buick with nobody in it went by. Seein' this, the guy stops cold and turns around and just goes back into the bar. Rooney is screamin' at me how we been in four goddamn accidents and fights and how we have got out clean. So then we got everything all straightened out and we come back here to play hide-and-seek 'cause that's what ole Rooney wanted.

(He is taking another drink, but finding the bottle empty.)

Only now I can't find him.

(Near RICHIE'S *footlocker stands a beer bottle and* COKES *begins to move toward it. Slowly he bends and grasps the bottle; he straightens, looking at it. He drinks. And settles down on* RICHIE'S *footlocker.)*

I'll just sit a little.

*(*RICHIE, *lying on his belly, shudders. The sobs burst out of him. He is shaking.* COKES, *blinking, turns to study* RICHIE.)*

What's up? Hey, what're you cryin' about, soldier? Hey?

*(*RICHIE *cannot help himself.)*

What's he cryin' about?

ROGER: *(disgustedly, he sits there)* He's cryin' 'cause he's a queer.

COKES: Oh. You a queer, boy?

RICHIE: Yes, Sergeant.

COKES: Oh.

(Pause.)

How long you been a queer?

ROGER: All his fuckin' life.

RICHIE: I don't know.

COKES: *(turning to scold* ROGER*)* Don't be yellin' mean at him. Boy, I tell you it's a real strange thing the way havin' leukemia gives you a lotta funny thoughts about things. Two months ago— or maybe even yesterday—I'da called a boy who was a queer a lotta awful names. But now I just wanna be figurin' things out. I mean, you ain't kiddin' me out about ole Rooney, are you, boys, 'cause of how I'm a sergeant and you're enlisted men, so you got some idea a vengeance on me? You ain't doin' that, are you, boys?

ROGER: No.

RICHIE: Ohhhh. Jesus. Ohhhh! I don't know what's hurtin' in me.

COKES: No, no, boy. You listen to me. You gonna be okay. There's a lotta worse things in this world than bein' a queer. I seen a lot of 'em, too. I mean, you could have leukemia. That's worse. That can kill you. I mean, it's okay. You listen to the ole sarge. I mean, maybe I was a queer, I wouldn't have leukemia. Who's to say? Lived a whole different life. Who's to say? I keep thinkin' there was maybe somethin' I coulda done different. Maybe not drunk so much. Or if I'd killed more gooks, or more Krauts or more dinks. I was kind-hearted sometimes. Or if I'd had a wife and I had some kids. Never had any. But my mother did and she died of it anyway. Gives you a whole funny different way a lookin' at things, I'll tell you. Ohhhhh, Rooney, Rooney.

(Slight pause.)

Or if I'd let that little gook outa that spider hole he was in, I was sittin' on it. I'd let him out now, he was in there.

(He rattles the footlocker lid under him.)

Oh, how'm I ever gonna forget it? That funny little guy. I'm runnin' along, he pops up outa that hole. I'm never gonna forget him—how'm

I ever gonna forget him? I see him and dive, goddamn bullet hits me in the side, I'm midair, everything's turnin' around. I go over the edge of this ditch and I'm crawlin' real fast. I lost my rifle. Can't find it. Then I come up behind him. He's half out of the hole. I bang him on top of his head, stuff him back into the hole with a grenade for company. Then I'm sittin' on the lid and it's made outa steel. I can feel him in there, though, bangin' and yellin' under me, and his yelling I can hear is begging for me to let him out. It was like a goddamn Charlie Chaplin movie, everybody fallin' down and clumsy, and him in there yellin' and bangin' away, and I'm just sittin' there lookin' around. And he was Charlie Chaplin. I don't know who I was. And then he blew up.

(Pause.)

Maybe I'll just get a little shut-eye right sittin' here while I'm waitin' for ole Rooney. We figure it out. All of it. You don't mind I just doze a little here, you boys?

ROGER: No.

RICHIE: No.

(ROGER rises and walks to the door. He switches off the light and gently closes the door. The transom glows. COKES sits in a flower of light. ROGER crosses back to his bunk and settles in, sitting.)

COKES: Night, boys.

RICHIE: Night, Sergeant.

(COKES sits there, fingers entwined, trying to sleep.)

COKES: I mean, he was like Charlie Chaplin. And then he blew up.

ROGER: *(suddenly feeling very sad for this old man)* Sergeant . . . maybe you was Charlie Chaplin, too.

COKES: No. No.

(Pause.)

No. I don't know who I was. Night.

ROGER: You think he was singin' it?

COKES: What?

ROGER: You think he was singin' it?

COKES: Oh, yeah. Oh, yeah; he was singin' it.

(Slight pause. COKES, sitting on the footlocker, begins to sing a makeshift language imitating Korean, to the tune of "Beautiful Streamer." He begins with an angry, mocking energy that slowly becomes a dream, a lullaby, a farewell, a lament.)

Yo no som lo no
Ung toe lo knee
Ra so me la lo
La see see oh doe.
Doe no tee ta ta
Too low see see
Ra mae me lo lo
Ah boo boo boo eee.
Boo boo eee booo eeee
La so lee lem
Lem lo lee da ung
Uhhh so ba booooo ohhhh.
Boo booo eee ung ba
Eee eee la looo
Lem lo lala la
Eeee oohhh ohhh ohhh ohhhhh.

(In the silence, he makes the soft, whispering sound of a child imitating an explosion, and his entwined fingers come apart. The dark figures of RICHIE and ROGER are near. The lingering light fades.)

THE END

A MOVIE STAR HAS TO STAR IN BLACK AND WHITE (1976)

Adrienne Kennedy's plays are not easily placed into any of the traditional categories of contemporary American drama. For example, although she is concerned with unmasking the racism that she has experienced, her plays are not so immediately cited as those of Ntozake Shange or Amiri Baraka as examples of a quintessentially African-American theatre. Likewise, although her plays also seek to expose those social constructs that determine women's constricted roles, the highly personal nature of Kennedy's quest makes her plays more opaque and does not immediately mark her as a consciously feminist playwright. Her plays are **expressionist**, even fragmented in their creation of characters with multiple personas. The **surreal** nature of the landscapes Kennedy draws and the self-introspection that frequently occurs in them have led to largely psychological and biographical readings of her work; recent criticism, however, particularly that of *A Movie Star Has to Star in Black and White* (1976), has sought to complicate these readings by seeking out the social agenda that coexists in her plays with the personal quest for identity.

Adrienne Kennedy (1931–) grew up in solidly middle-class surroundings in Cleveland, Ohio. Her parents, Cornell Wallace Hawkins and Etta Haugabook Hawkins, were both professionals who graduated from predominantly black colleges. A community leader and a teacher, respectively, her father and mother encouraged young Adrienne likewise to realize her potential to its fullest. Growing up in an ethnically diverse neighborhood with access to books and the arts, she began her writing at an early age.

Unfortunately, Kennedy found herself caught up in a much more complicated milieu when she enrolled at Ohio State University. This was the first of a series of life experiences that impressed upon her a consciousness of the societal barriers existing for her in the world outside her neighborhood. Her marriage to Joseph Kennedy after her graduation in 1953 (they would later divorce amicably) led eventually to a keen sense of the limitations placed upon her as a woman. She was left on her own, expecting their first child, when her husband left to fight in Korea; upon his return, they moved to New York City so he could study at Columbia University. In both Cleveland and New York City, Kennedy turned to writing as a means of combatting loneliness and engaging in self-discovery. She eventually pursued studies in creative writing alternately at Columbia and the American Theatre Wing.

A trip to Africa in 1961 served as the impetus for the creation of what was to become her first professionally produced play, *Funnyhouse of a Negro* (1962), for on this trip Kennedy had time both to encounter new experiences and to reflect upon those from her past. In writing about the inner self in search of a voice, she replicated a project central to the work of two of her favorite playwrights, Tennessee Williams and Federico García Lorca, but *Funnyhouse of a Negro* marked the creation of a unique dramatic style that would continue in its various forms down through *A Movie Star Has to Star in Black and White*. This style combined images and experiences from Kennedy's own life, adapting both personal and public figures that had exerted considerable influence on her. Thus it is that in a play such as *Funnyhouse of a Negro*, while a young African-American woman is ostensibly the center of the action, our sense of a linear narrative and fixed, conventional characters is upset. Though the racist world within which the heroine, Sarah, must operate is certainly a type of nightmarish funnyhouse, the real setting is the place of confusion that is Sarah's mind, where public personas such as Queen Victoria, Patrice Lumumba, and Jesus Christ manifest the multiple facets of her and others' selves. Kennedy sent the manuscript to Edward Albee, with whom she later studied in his Circle-in-the-Square playwriting workshop. Albee, who greatly admired Kennedy's work, optioned the play, and it opened **Off-Broadway** in 1964. It proved a critical and commercial success, garnering Kennedy an **Obie**, and also marked the start of a productive era in her career. Seven of her plays were professionally produced between 1963 and 1969: *The Owl Answers* (1963), *A Rat's Mass* (1966), *The Lennon Play: In His Own Write* (1967), *A Lesson in a Dead Language* (1968), *Sun: A Poem for Malcolm X Inspired by His Murder* (1968), *A Beast Story* (1969), and *Boats* (1969).

The Owl Answers, her next play after *Funnyhouse of a Negro*, continued to extend several of the themes and theatrical devices later used in *A Movie Star Has to Star in Black and White*. It introduced Clara Passmore, also the Clara of the latter play (and, many critics argue, an older version of *Funnyhouse*'s Sarah), and continued the process of identity-seeking with which Kennedy's plays are so concerned. This Clara, illegitimate daughter of a black mother and a white father, looks for herself in England, confronting such figures as Chaucer and Shakespeare during her search. Besides encountering many different figures from her heritage, Clara's own character is given multiple representations to suggest the complexity of her personality; she is identified by Kennedy as "SHE who is CLARA PASSMORE who is the VIRGIN MARY who is the BASTARD who is the OWL."

A Movie Star Has to Star in Black and White came a few years after this prolific period in Kennedy's writing, and continued to extend Kennedy's use of both public and personal sources arranged in a surrealistic form. The heroine's difficult negotiations with both racism and racial identities in *Funnyhouse of a Negro* and *The Owl Answers* not only grow out of Kennedy's own personal reflections, but also, according to Susan Meigs, "address the cultural and political fragmentation of black Americans that occurs when a dominant (white) social structure interrupts efforts to construct a black community." This is no less true of *A Movie Star Has to Star in Black and White*. At its most basic level, *Movie Star* charts the struggle for self-actualization of its heroine, Clara, who watches episodes from her life performed by actors within recreated scenes from the Hollywood movies *Now, Voyager* (1942), *Viva Zapata* (1952), and *A Place in the Sun* (1951). And while Kennedy was not the first playwright to use film techniques, her agenda was quite unique. Clara, as Meigs suggests, is one more of Kennedy's "black women who fail to unite the fragmented elements of their identities into harmonic, dynamic wholes." Called to the bedside of her comatose brother, Wally, who has been in a car crash, Clara is reunited in his hospital room with her estranged parents; the room proves a point of departure from which she can explore the different aspects of her persona that have not been allowed to reconcile themselves into a cohesive whole. This inner exploration takes the form of a type of highlights film of her life, one rendered by actors chosen specifically to resemble those who starred in the original Hollywood versions of the scenes evoked here.

Several intersecting forces seem to have rendered Clara unable to reconcile her disparate roles of wife, mother, daughter, and artist. Chief among them is her place in a society that devalues the role of women, for Clara has had to struggle beyond the patriarchal constructs of a family unsupportive of her efforts to write, constructs that made her own mother feel herself a failure because she could not pass on to her daughter the capacity to be happy in a male-dominated world. Clara's efforts to realize her own vision are juxtaposed in an ironic fashion against Hollywood's view of the "correct" roles for women. These include being a trustworthy sidekick who will help further a man's success without making physical or emotional demands upon him, as do the self-effacing heroines played by Bette Davis in *Now, Voyager* and Jean Peters in *Viva Zapata*, or as a sexual plaything readily cast aside in favor of a purer woman, as Shelley Winters is in *A Place in the Sun*. Amidst these appropriations from Hollywood film are echoes of Kennedy's frustration with those years at Columbia when her husband's research interests were given primacy over her own. These, in his eyes, could not compare with her "real" first duty: to their child. Even Clara's relation to her female physicality needs to be reconstructed. As Linda Kintz has pointed out, Kennedy's obsession with the bleeding of Clara's first miscarriage, as well as Clara's insistence that her first play will be one whose "main image is a girl in a white organdy dress covered with menstrual blood," is a foregrounding of the female body that has been previously hidden. For the society in which Clara lives, anything less than cleanliness, than purity, is unacceptable. By contrast, the process of birth is messy and fraught with anxiety, rendering it analogous to the creative process.

That the stars from "well-made" Hollywood productions are used to act out Clara's recollections of her life is telling on more than one level. The social constructs represented by the movies not only reinforce the secondary place of women, but also allow no recognition of African Americans. As Elin Diamond suggests, Kennedy's audience becomes acutely aware of the irony of watching actors specifically chosen to represent white movie icons of the 1950s perform the life episodes of an aspiring African-American playwright. Granted, Clara, and thus Kennedy, has found these movie stars alluring; but in this play, identifying with them becomes "an occasion for dreaming as well as for critique." African Americans in general, let alone African-American women, held little place outside a roster of familiar stereotypes in the cultural imagination of

1950 Hollywood or the society for which it tried to set the standards. As reinforcement of this reality, Clara's mother speaks more directly and bitterly of racism she has encountered. The black-and-white choices enshrined in black-and-white film are clear: in this society, it is white over black.

Kennedy continues to write such dramatic works as *The Alexander Plays* (1992), as well as teach at such institutions as Stanford and Rutgers universities. She also has authored *People Who Led to My Plays* (1987), a book extremely important in the study of the personal and public sources from which she has drawn her work. The intensely personal nature of Kennedy's drama may explain why it does not enjoy so wide an audience as other plays by African-American artists. Still, Kennedy's plays are especially significant in their rich representations of the personal and cultural milieus in which the individual is, or is not, encouraged to fulfill her potential.

WORKS CONSULTED

Bryant-Jackson, Paul K., and Lois More Overbeck, eds. *Intersecting Boundaries: The Theatre of Adrienne Kennedy*. Minneapolis: University of Minnesota Press, 1992.

Diamond, Elin. "Rethinking Identification: Kennedy, Freud, Brecht." *The Kenyon Review* 15 (1993): 86–99.

Hay, Samuel A. *African-American Theatre: A Historical and Critical Analysis*. Cambridge: Cambridge University Press, 1994.

Kintz, Linda. "The Sanitized Spectacle: What's Birth Got to Do with It? Adrienne Kennedy's *A Movie Star Has to Star in Black and White*." *Theatre Journal* 44 (1992): 67–86.

Meigs, Susan. "No Place But the Funnyhouse: The Struggle for Identity in Three Adrienne Kennedy Plays." *Modern American Drama: The Female Canon*. Ed. June Schleuter. London and Toronto: Associated University Presses, 1990. 172–183.

NOTES: *The movie music throughout is romantic.*

The ship, the deck, the railings and the dark boat can all be done with lights and silhouettes.

All the colors are shades of black and white.

These movie stars are romantic and moving, never camp or farcical, and the attitudes of the supporting players to the movie stars is deadly serious.

The movie music sometimes plays at intervals when Clara's thought is still.

Characters

Clara

"Leading Roles" are played by actors who look exactly like:
Bette Davis
Paul Henreid
Jean Peters
Marlon Brando
Montgomery Clift
Shelley Winters

(They all look exactly like their movie roles.)

Supporting roles by
the mother
the father
the husband

(They all look like photographs Clara keeps of them except when they're in the hospital.)

S C E N E S :
I Hospital lobby and *Now, Voyager*
II Brother's room and *Viva Zapata*
III Clara's old room and *A Place in the Sun*

Dark stage. From darkness center appears the COLUMBIA PICTURES LADY *in a bright light.*

COLUMBIA PICTURES LADY: Summer, New York, 1955. Summer, Ohio, 1963. The scenes are *Now, Voyager, Viva Zapata,* and *A Place in the Sun.*

The leading roles are played by Bette Davis, Paul Henreid, Jean Peters, Marlon Brando, Montgomery Clift and Shelley Winters. Supporting roles are played by the mother, the father, the husband. A bit role is played by Clara.

Now, Voyager takes place in the hospital lobby. *Viva Zapata* takes place in the brother's room. *A Place in the Sun* takes place in Clara's old room.
June 1963.

My producer is Joel Steinberg. He looks different from what I once thought, not at all like that picture in *Vogue.* He was in *Vogue* with a group of people who were going to do a musical about Socrates. In the photograph Joel's hair looked dark and his skin smooth. In real life his skin is blotched. Everyone says he drinks a lot.

Lately I think often of killing myself. Eddie Jr. plays outside in the playground. I'm very lonely . . . Met Lee Strasberg: the members of the playwrights unit were invited to watch his scene. Geraldine Page, Rip Torn and Norman Mailer were there. . . . I wonder why I lie so much to my mother about how I feel. . . . My father once said his life has been nothing but a life of hypocrisy and that's why his photograph smiled. While Eddie Jr. plays outside I read Edith Wharton, a book on Egypt and Chinua Achebe. LeRoi Jones, Ted Joans and Allen Ginsburg are reading in the Village. Eddie comes every evening right before dark. He wants to know if I'll go back to him for the sake of our son.

(She fades. At the back of the stage as in a distance a dim light goes on a large doorway in the hospital. Visible is the foot of the white hospital bed and a figure lying upon it. Movie music. CLARA *stands at the doorway of the room. She is a Negro woman of thirty-three wearing a maternity dress. She does not enter the room but turns away and stands very still. Movie music.)*

CLARA: *(Reflective; very still facing away from the room.)* My brother is the same . . . my father is coming . . . very depressed.

Before I left New York I got my typewriter from the pawnshop. I'm terribly tired, trying to do a page a day, yet my play is coming together.

Each day I wonder with what or with whom can I co-exist in a true union?

(She turns and stares into her brother's room. Scene fades out; then bright lights that convey an ocean liner in motion.)

[SCENE I]: *Movie music. On the deck of the ocean liner from* Now, Voyager *are* BETTE DAVIS *and* PAUL HENREID. *They sit at a table slightly off stage center.* BETTE DAVIS *has on a large white summer hat and* PAUL HENREID *a dark summer suit. The light is romantic and glamorous. Beyond backstage left are deck chairs. It is bright sunlight on the deck.*

BETTE DAVIS: *(To* PAUL.*)* June 1955.

When I have the baby I wonder will I turn into a river of blood and die? My mother almost died when I was born. I've always felt sad that I couldn't have been an angel of mercy to my father and mother and saved them from their torment.

I used to hope when I was a little girl that one day I would rise above them, an angel with glowing wings and cover them with peace. But I failed. When I came among them it seems to me I did not bring them peace . . . but made them more disconsolate. The crosses they bore always made we sad.

The one reality I wanted never came true . . . to be their angel of mercy to unite them. I keep remembering the time my mother threatened to kill my father with the shotgun. I keep remembering my father's going away to marry a girl who talked to willow trees.

(Onto the deck wander the MOTHER, *the* FATHER, *and the* HUSBAND. *They are Negroes. The parents are as they were when young in 1929 in Atlanta, Georgia. The* MOTHER *is small, pale and very beautiful. She has on a white summer dress and white shoes. The* FATHER *is small and dark skinned. He has on a Morehouse sweater, knickers and a cap. They both are emotional and nervous. In presence both are romanticized. The* HUSBAND

is twenty-eight and handsome. He is dressed as in the summer of 1955 wearing a seersucker suit from Kleins that cost thirteen dollars.)

BETTE DAVIS: In the scrapbook that my father left is a picture of my mother in Savannah, Georgia, in 1929.

MOTHER: *(Sitting down in a deck chair, takes a cigarette out of a beaded purse and smokes nervously. She speaks bitterly in a voice with a strong Georgia accent.)* In our Georgia town the white people lived on one side. It had pavement on the streets and sidewalks and mail was delivered. The Negroes lived on the other side and the roads were dirt and had no sidewalk and you had to go to the post office to pick up your mail. In the center of Main Street was a fountain and white people drank on one side and Negroes drank on the other.

When a Negro bought something in a store he couldn't try it on. A Negro couldn't sit down at the soda fountain in the drugstore but had to take his drink out. In the movies at Montefore you had to go in the side and up the stairs and sit in the last four rows.

When you arrived on the train from Cincinnati the first thing you saw was the WHITE AND COLORED signs at the depot. White people had one waiting room and we Negroes had another. We sat in only two cars and white people had the rest of the train.

(She is facing PAUL HENREID *and* BETTE DAVIS. *The* FATHER *and the* HUSBAND *sit in deck chairs that face the other side of the sea. The* FATHER *also smokes. He sits hunched over with his head down thinking. The* HUSBAND *takes an old textbook out of a battered briefcase and starts to study. He looks exhausted and has dark circles under his eyes. His suit is worn.)*

BETTE DAVIS: My father used to say John Hope Franklin, Du Bois and Benjamin Mays were fine men.

(Bright sunlight on FATHER *sitting on other side of deck.* FATHER *gets up and comes toward them . . . to* BETTE DAVIS.*)*

FATHER: Cleveland is a place for opportunity, leadership, a progressive city, a place for education, a chance to come out of the back woods of Georgia. We Negro leaders dream of leading our people out of the wilderness.

(He passes her and goes along the deck whistling. Movie music. BETTE DAVIS *stands up looking after the* FATHER . . . *then distractedly to* PAUL HENREID.)

BETTE DAVIS: *(Very passionate.)* I'd give anything in the world if I could just once talk to Jesus.

Sometimes he walks through my room but he doesn't stop long enough for us to talk . . . he has an aureole. *(Then to the* FATHER *who is almost out of sight on the deck whistling.)* Why did you marry the girl who talked to willow trees? *(To* PAUL HENREID.) He left us to marry a girl who talked to willow trees.

*(*FATHER *is whistling,* MOTHER *is smoking, then the* FATHER *vanishes into a door on deck.* BETTE DAVIS *walks down to railing.* PAUL HENREID *follows her.)*

BETTE DAVIS: June 1955.

My mother said when she was a girl in the summers she didn't like to go out. She'd sit in the house and help her grandmother iron or shell peas and sometimes she'd sit on the steps.

My father used to come and sit on the steps. He asked her for her first "date." They went for a walk up the road and had an ice cream at Miss Ida's Icecream Parlor and walked back down the road. She was fifteen.

My mother says that my father was one of the most well thought of boys in the town, Negro or white. And he was so friendly. He always had a friendly word for everybody.

He used to tell my mother his dreams how he was going to go up north. There was opportunity for Negroes up north and when he was finished at Morehouse he was going to get a job in some place like New York.

And she said when she walked down the road with my father people were so friendly.

He organized a colored baseball team in Montefore and he was the Captain. And she used to go and watch him play baseball and everybody called him "Cap."

Seven more months and the baby.

Eddie and I don't talk too much these days.

Very often I try to be in bed by the time he comes home.

Most nights I'm wide awake until at least four. I wake up about eight and then I have a headache.

When I'm wide awake I see Jesus a lot.

My mother is giving us the money for the doctor bill. Eddie told her he will pay it back.

Also got a letter from her; it said I hope things work out for you both. And pray, pray sometimes. Love Mother.

We also got a letter from Eddie's mother. Eddie's brother had told her that Eddie and I were having some problems. In her letter which was enclosed in a card she said when Eddie's sister had visited us she noticed that Eddie and I don't go to church. She said we mustn't forget the Lord, because God takes care of everything . . . God gives us peace and no matter what problems Eddie and I were having if we trusted in Him God would help us. It was the only letter from Eddie's mother that I ever saved.

Even though the card was Hallmark.

July 1955.

Eddie doesn't seem like the same person since he came back from Korea. And now I'm pregnant again. When I lost the baby he was thousands of miles away. All that bleeding. I'll never forgive him. The Red Cross let him send me a telegram to say he was sorry. I can't believe we used to be so in love on the campus and park the car and kiss and kiss. Yet I was a virgin when we married. A virgin who was to bleed and bleed . . . when I was in the hospital all I had was a photograph of Eddie in GI clothes standing in a woods in Korea. *(Pause.)* Eddie and I went to the Thalia on 95th and Broadway. There's a film festival this summer. We saw *Double Indemnity, The Red Shoes* and *A Place in the Sun.* Next week *Viva Zapata* is coming. Afterwards we went to Reinzis on Macdougal Street and had Viennese coffee. We forced an enthusiasm we didn't feel. We took the subway back up to 116th Street and walked to Bencroft Hall. In the middle of the night I woke up and wrote in my diary.

(A bright light at hospital doorway. CLARA *younger, fragile, anxious. Movie music. She leaves hospital doorway and comes onto the deck from the door her father entered. She wears maternity dress, white wedgies, her hair is straightened as in the fifties. She has a passive beauty and is totally preoccupied. She pays no attention to anyone, only writing in a notebook. Her movie stars speak for her.* CLARA *lets her movie stars star in her life.* BETTE DAVIS *and* PAUL HENREID *are at the railing. The* MOTHER *is smoking. The* HUSBAND *gets up and comes across the deck carrying his battered briefcase. He speaks to* CLARA *who looks away.* PAUL HENREID *goes on staring at the sea.)*

HUSBAND: Clara, please tell me everything the doctor said about the delivery and how many days you'll be in the hospital.

(Instead of CLARA, BETTE DAVIS *replies.* PAUL HENREID *is oblivious of him.)*

BETTE DAVIS: *(Very remote.)* I get very jealous of you Eddie. You're doing something with your life.

(He tries to kiss CLARA. *She moves away and walks along the deck and writes in notebook.)*

BETTE DAVIS: *(To* EDDIE.*)* Eddie, do you think I have floating anxiety? You said everyone in Korea had floating anxiety. I think I might have it. *(Pause.)* Do you think I'm catatonic?

EDDIE: *(Staring at* CLARA.*)* I'm late to class now. We'll talk when I come home. *(He leaves.)* When I get paid I'm going to take you to Birdland. Dizzy's coming back.

(Movie music.)

CLARA: July.

I can't sleep. My head always full of thoughts night and day. I feel so nervous. Sometimes I hardly hear what people are saying. I'm writing a lot of my play, I don't want to show it to anyone though. Suppose it's no good. *(Reads her play.)*

They are dragging his body across the green his white hair hanging down. They are taking off his shoes and he is stiff. I must get into the chapel to see him. I must. He is my blood father. God, let me in to his burial. *(He grabs her down center. She, kneeling.)* I call God and the Owl answers. *(Softer.)* It haunts my Tower calling, its feathers are blowing against the cell wall, speckled in the garden on the fig tree, it comes, feathered, great hollow-eyed with yellow skin and yellow eyes, the flying bastard. From my Tower I keep calling and the only answer is the Owl, God. *(Pause. Stands.)* I am only yearning for our kingdom, God.

(Movie music.)

BETTE DAVIS: *(At railing.)* My father tried to commit suicide once when I was in high school. It was the afternoon he was presented an award by the Mayor of Cleveland at a banquet celebrating the completion of the New Settlement building. It had taken my father seven years to raise money for the New Settlement which was the center of Negro life in our community. He was given credit for being the one without whom it couldn't have been done. It was his biggest achievement.

I went upstairs and found him whistling in his room. I asked him what was wrong. I want to see my dead mama and papa he said, that's all I really live for is to see my mama and papa. I stared at him. As I was about to leave the room he said I've been waiting to jump off the roof of the Settlement for a long time. I just had to wait until it was completed . . . and he went on whistling.

He had tried to jump off the roof but had fallen on a scaffold.

(Movie music. The deck has grown dark except for the light on BETTE DAVIS *and* PAUL HENREID *and* CLARA.*)*

CLARA: I loved the wedding night scene from *Viva Zapata* and the scene where the peasants met Zapata on the road and forced the soldiers to take the rope from his neck . . . when they shot Zapata at the end I cried.

(Deck darker. She walks along the deck and into door, leaving PAUL HENREID *and* BETTE DAVIS *at railing. She arrives at the hospital doorway, then enters her brother's room, standing at the foot of his bed. Her brother is in a coma.)*

CLARA: *(To her brother.)* Once I asked you romantically when you came back to the United States on a short leave, how do you like Europe Wally? You were silent. Finally you said, I get into a lot of fights with the Germans. You stared at me. And got up and went into the dining room to the dark sideboard and got a drink. *(Darkness. Movie music.)*

[SCENE II]: *Hospital room and* Viva Zapata. *The hospital bed is now totally visible. In it lies Wally in a white gown. The light of the room is twilight on a summer evening.* CLARA'S *brother is handsome and in his late twenties. Beyond the bed is steel hospital apparatus.* CLARA *stands by her brother's bedside. There is no real separation from the hospital room and* Viva Zapata *and the ship lights as there should have been none in* Now, Voyager. *Simultaneously brighter lights come up stage center. Wedding night scene in* Viva Zapata. *Yet it is still the stateroom within the ship. Movie music.* MARLON BRANDO *and* JEAN PETERS *are sitting on the bed. They are both dressed as in* Viva Zapata.

JEAN PETERS: *(To* BRANDO.*)* July 11.

I saw my father today. He's come from Georgia to see my brother. He lives in Savannah with his second wife. He seemed smaller and hunched over. When I was young he seemed energetic, speaking before civic groups and rallying people to give money to the Negro Settlement.

In the last years he seems introspective, petty and angry. Today he was wearing a white nylon sports shirt that looked slightly too big . . . his dark arms thin. He had on a little straw sport hat cocked slightly to the side.

We stood together in my brother's room. My father touched my brother's bare foot with his hand. My brother is in a coma. *(Silent.)*

Eddie and I were married downstairs in this house. My brother was best man. We went to Colorado, but soon after Eddie was sent to Korea. My mother has always said that she felt if she and my father hadn't been fighting so much maybe I wouldn't have lost the baby. After I lost the baby I stopped writing to Eddie and decided I wanted to get a divorce when he came back from Korea. He hadn't been at Columbia long before I got pregnant again with Eddie Jr.

*(*MARLON BRANDO *listens. They kiss tenderly. She stands up. She is bleeding. She falls back on her bed.* BRANDO *pulls a sheet out from under her. The sheets are black. Movie music.)*

JEAN PETERS: The doctor says I have to stay in bed when I'm not at the hospital.

(From now until the end MARLON BRANDO *continuously helps* JEAN PETERS *change sheets. He puts the black sheets on the floor around them.)*

CLARA: *(To her brother, at the same time.)* Wally, you just have to get well. I know you will, even though you do not move or speak.

(Sits down by his bedside watching him. Her MOTHER *enters. She is wearing a rose-colored summer dress and small hat. The mother is in her fifties now. She sits down by her son's bedside and holds his hand. Silence in the room. The light of the room is constant twilight. They are in the constant dim twilight while* BRANDO *and* PETERS *star in a dazzling wedding night light. Mexican peasant wedding music,* Zapata *remains throughout compassionate, heroic, tender. While* CLARA *and her* MOTHER *talk* BRANDO *and* PETERS *sit on the bed, then enact the* Zapata *teach-me-to-read scene in which* BRANDO *asks* PETERS *to get him a book and teach him to read.)*

MOTHER: What did I do? What did I do?

CLARA: What do you mean?

MOTHER: I don't know what I did to make my children so unhappy.

*(*JEAN PETERS *gets book for* BRANDO.*)*

CLARA: I'm not unhappy mother.

MOTHER: Yes you are.

CLARA: I'm not unhappy. I'm very happy. I just want to be a writer. Please don't think I'm unhappy.

MOTHER: Your family's not together and you don't seem happy. *(They sit and read.)*

CLARA: I'm very happy mother. Very. I've just won an award and I'm going to have a play produced. I'm very happy.
(Silence. The mother straightens the sheet on her son's bed.)

MOTHER: When you grow up in boarding school like I did, the thing you dream of most is to see your children together with their families.

CLARA: Mother you mustn't think I'm unhappy because I am, I really am, very happy.

MOTHER: I just pray you'll soon get yourself together and make some decisions about your life. I pray for you every night. Shouldn't you go back to Eddie especially since you're pregnant?
(There are shadows of the ship's lights as if Now, Voyager *is still in motion.)*

CLARA: Mother, Eddie doesn't understand me.
(Silence. Twilight dimmer, MOTHER *holds Wally's hand. Movie light bright on* JEAN PETERS *and* MARLON BRANDO.)

JEAN PETERS: My brother Wally's still alive.

CLARA: *(To her diary.)* Wally was in an accident. A telegram from my mother. Your brother was in an automobile accident . . . has been unconscious since last night in St. Luke's hospital. Love, Mother.

JEAN PETERS: Depressed.

CLARA: Came to Cleveland. Eddie came to La Guardia to bring me money for my plane ticket and to say he was sorry about Wally who was best man at our wedding. Eddie looks at me with such sadness. It fills me with hatred for him and myself.
*(*BRANDO *is at the window looking down on the peasants. Mexican wedding music.)*

JEAN PETERS: Very depressed, and afraid at night since Eddie and I separated. I try to write a page a day on another play. It's going to be called a Lesson In Dead Language. The main image is a girl in a white organdy dress covered with menstrual blood.

*(*CLARA *is writing to her diary. Her* MOTHER *sits holding Wally's hand,* BRANDO *stares out the window,* JEAN PETERS *sits on the bed. Now,* Voyager *ship, shadows and light.)*

CLARA: It is twilight outside and very warm. The window faces a lawn, very green, with a fountain beyond. Wally does not speak or move. He is in a coma. *(Twilight dims.)*
    It bothers me that Eddie had to give me money for the ticket to come home. I don't have any money of my own: the option from my play is gone and I don't know how I will be able to work and take care of Eddie Jr. Maybe Eddie and I should go back together.

*(*FATHER *enters the room, stands at the foot of his son's bed. He is in his fifties now and wears a white nylon sports shirt a little too big, his dark arms thin, baggy pants and a little straw sports hat cocked to the side. He has been drinking. The moment he enters the room the mother takes out a cigarette and starts to nervously smoke. They do not look at each other. He speaks to* CLARA, *then glances in the direction of the* MOTHER. *He then touches his son's bare feet. Wally is lying on his back, his hands to his sides.* CLARA *gets up and goes to the window.* BRANDO *comes back and sits on the bed next to* JEAN PETERS. *They all remain for a long while silent. Suddenly the* MOTHER *goes and throws herself into her daughter's arms and cries.)*

MOTHER: The doctor said he doesn't see how Wally has much of a chance of surviving: his brain is damaged.
(She clings to her daughter and cries. Simultaneously.)

JEAN PETERS: *(To* BRANDO.) I'm writing on my play. It's about a girl who turns into an Owl. Ow. *(Recites from her writings.)* He came to me in the outhouse, in the fig tree. He told me, You are an owl, I am your beginning. I call God and the Owl answers. It haunts my tower, calling.
(Silence. FATHER *slightly drunk goes toward his former wife and his daughter. The* MOTHER *runs out of the room into the lobby.)*

MOTHER: I did everything to make you happy and still you left me for another woman.

(CLARA *stares out of the window.* FATHER *follows the* MOTHER *into the lobby and stares at her.* JEAN PETERS *stands up. She is bleeding. She falls back on the bed.* MARLON BRANDO *pulls a sheet out from under her. The sheets are black. Movie music.*)

JEAN PETERS: The doctor says I have to stay in bed when I'm not at the hospital.

(From now until the end MARLON BRANDO *continuously helps* JEAN PETERS *change sheets. He puts the black sheets on the floor around them.)*

JEAN PETERS: This reminds me of when Eddie was in Korea and I had the miscarriage. For days there was blood on the sheets. Eddie's letters from Korea were about a green hill. He sent me photographs of himself. The Red Cross, the letter said, says I cannot call you and I cannot come.

For a soldier to come home there has to be a death in the family.

MOTHER: *(In the hallway she breaks down further.)* I have never wanted to go back to the south to live. I hate it. I suffered nothing but humiliation and why should I have gone back there?

FATHER: You ought to have gone back with me. It's what I wanted to do.

MOTHER: I never wanted to go back.

FATHER: You yellow bastard. You're a yellow bastard. That's why you didn't want to go back.

MOTHER: You black nigger.

JEAN PETERS: *(Reciting her play.)* I call God and the Owl answers, it haunts my tower, calling, its feathers are blowing against the cell wall, it comes feathered, great hollow-eyes . . . with yellow skin and yellow eyes, the flying bastard. From my tower I keep calling and the only answer is the Owl.

July 8 I got a telegram from my mother. It said your brother has been in an accident and has been unconscious since last night in St. Luke's hospital. Love, Mother. I came home.

My brother is in a white gown on white sheets.

(The MOTHER *and the* FATHER *walk away from one another. A sudden bright light on the*

Hospital Lobby and on Wally's room. CLARA *has come to the doorway and watches her parents.)*

MOTHER: *(To both her former husband and her daughter.)* I was asleep and the police called and told me Wally didn't feel well and would I please come down to the police station and pick him up. When I arrived at the police station they told me they had just taken him to the hospital because he felt worse and they would drive to the hospital. When I arrived here the doctor told me the truth: Wally's car had crashed into another car at an intersection and Wally had been thrown from the car, his body hitting a mail box and he was close to death.

(Darkness.)

[SCENE III]: JEAN PETERS *and* BRANDO *are still sitting in* Viva Zapata *but now there are photographs above the bed of* CLARA'S *parents when they were young, as they were in* Now, Voyager. *Wally's room is dark. Lights of the ship from* Now, Voyager.

JEAN PETERS: Wally is not expected to live. *(She tries to stand.)* He does not move. He is in a coma. *(Pause.)* There are so many memories in this house. The rooms besiege me.

My brother has been living here in his old room with my mother. He is separated from his wife and every night has been driving his car crazily around the street where she now lives. On one of these nights was when he had the accident.

*(*JEAN PETERS *and* BRANDO *stare at each other. A small dark boat from side opposite Wally's room. In it are* SHELLEY WINTERS *and* MONTGOMERY CLIFT. CLARA *sits behind* SHELLEY WINTERS *writing in her notebook.* MONTGOMERY CLIFT *is rowing. It is* A Place in the Sun. *Movie music.* BRANDO *and* JEAN PETERS *continue to change sheets.)*

CLARA: I am bleeding. When I'm not at the hospital I have to stay in bed. I am writing my poems. Eddie's come from New York to see my brother. My brother does not speak or move.

*(*MONTGOMERY CLIFT *silently rows dark boat*

across. CLARA *has on a nightgown and looks as if she has been very sick, and heartbroken by her brother's accident.* MONTGOMERY CLIFT, *as was* HENREID *and* BRANDO, *is mute. If they did speak they would speak lines from their actual movies. As the boat comes across* BRANDO *and* PETERS *are still. Movie music.* EDDIE *comes in room with* JEAN PETERS *and* BRANDO. *He still has his textbook and briefcase.* SHELLEY WINTERS *sits opposite* MONTGOMERY CLIFT *as in* A Place in the Sun. CLARA *is writing in her notebook.*)

EDDIE: (*To* JEAN PETERS; *simultaneously* CLARA *is writing in her diary.*) Are you sure you want to go on with this?

JEAN PETERS: This?

EDDIE: You know what I mean, this obsession of yours?

JEAN PETERS: Obsession?

EDDIE: Yes, this obsession to be a writer?

JEAN PETERS: Of course I'm sure.

(BRANDO *is reading.* CLARA *from the boat.*)

CLARA: I think the Steinbergs have lost interest in my play. I got a letter from them that said they have to go to Italy and would be in touch when they came back.

EDDIE: I have enough money for us to live well with my teaching. We could all be so happy.

CLARA: (*From boat.*) Ever since I was twelve I have secretly dreamed of being a writer. Everyone says it's unrealistic for a Negro to want to write.

Eddie says I've become shy and secretive and I can't accept the passage of time, and that my diaries consume me and that my diaries make me a spectator watching my life like watching a black and white movie.

He thinks sometimes . . . to me my life is one of my black and white movies that I love so . . . with me playing a bit part.

EDDIE: (*To* JEAN PETERS *looking up at the photographs.*) I wonder about your obsession to write about your parents when they were young. You didn't know them. Your mother's not young, your father's not young and we are not that young couple who came to New York in 1955, yet all you ever say to me is Eddie you don't seem the same since you came back from Korea.

(EDDIE *leaves.* MONTGOMERY CLIFT *rows as* SHELLEY WINTERS *speaks to him. Lights on* BRANDO *and* PETERS *start slowly to dim.*)

SHELLEY WINTERS: (*To* MONTGOMERY CLIFT.) A Sunday Rain . . . our next door neighbor drove me through the empty Sunday streets to see my brother. He's the same. My father came by the house last night for the first time since he left Cleveland and he and my mother got into a fight and my mother started laughing. She just kept saying see I can laugh ha ha nothing can hurt me anymore. Nothing you can ever do, Wallace, will ever hurt me again, no one can hurt me since my baby is lying out there in that hospital and nobody knows whether he's going to live or die. And very loudly again she said ha ha and started walking in circles in her white shoes. My father said how goddamn crazy she was and they started pushing each other. I begged them to stop. My father looked about crazily.

I hate this house. But it was my money that helped make a down payment on it and I can come here anytime I want. I can come here and see my daughter and you can't stop me, he said.

CLARA: (*To diary.*) The last week in March I called up my mother and I told her that Eddie and I were getting a divorce and I wanted to come to Cleveland right away.

She said I'm coming up there.

When, I said. When?

It was four o'clock in the afternoon.

When can you come I said.

I'll take the train tonight. I'll call you from the station.

Should I come and meet you?

No, I'll call you from the station.

She called at 10:35 that morning. She said she would take a taxi. I went down to the courtyard and waited. When she got out of the taxi I will never forget the expression on her face. Her face had a hundred lines in it. I'd never seen her look so sad.

CLARA: (*Reciting her play.*) They said: I had lost my mind, read so much, buried myself in my books. They said I should stay and teach summer school. But I went. All the way to London. Out there in the black taxi my cold hands were colder than ever. No sooner than I left the taxi and passed down a gray walk through a dark gate and into a garden where there were black ravens on the grass, when I broke down. Oow . . . oww.

SHELLEY WINTERS: This morning my father came by again. He said Clara I want to talk to you. I want you to know my side. Now, your mother has always thought she was better than me. You know Mr. Harrison raised her like a white girl, and your mother, mark my word, thinks she's better than me. (It was then I could smell the whiskey on his breath . . . he had already taken a drink from the bottle in his suitcase.) *(She looks anxiously at* MONTGOMERY CLIFT *trying to get him to listen.)*

CLARA: *(Reading from her notebook.)* He came to me in the outhouse, in the garden, in the fig tree. He told me you are an owl, ow, oww, I am your beginning, ow. You belong here with us owls in the fig tree, not to somebody that cooks for your Goddamn Father, oww, and I ran to the outhouse in the night crying oww. Bastard they say, the people in the town all say Bastard, but I—I belong to God and the owls, ow, and I sat in the fig tree. My Goddamn Father is the Richest White Man in the Town, but I belong to the owls. *(Putting down her notebook. Lights shift back to* PETERS *and* BRANDO *on the bed.)*

JEAN PETERS: When my brother was in the army in Germany, he was involved in a crime and was court-martialled. He won't talk about it. I went to visit him in the stockade.

It was in a Quonset hut in New Jersey.

His head was shaven and he didn't have on any shoes. He has a vein that runs down his forehead and large brown eyes. When he was in high school he was in All City track in the two-twenty dash. We all thought he was going to be a great athlete. His dream was the Olympics. After high school he went to several colleges and left them; Morehouse (where my father went), Ohio State (where I went), and Western Reserve. I'm a failure he said. I can't make it in those schools. I'm tired. He suddenly joined the army.

After Wally left the army he worked nights as an orderly in hospitals; he liked the mental wards. For a few years every fall he started to school but dropped out after a few months. He and his wife married right before he was sent to Germany. He met her at Western Reserve and she graduated cum laude while he was a prisoner in the stockade. *(Movie music. Dark boat with* MONTGOMERY CLIFT *and* SHELLEY WINTERS *reappears from opposite side.* MONTGOMERY CLIFT *rows.* CLARA *is crying.)*

SHELLEY WINTERS and CLARA: Eddie's come from New York because my brother might die. He did not speak again today and did not move. We don't really know his condition. All we know is that his brain is possibly badly damaged. He doesn't speak or move.

JEAN PETERS: I am bleeding. *(Lights suddenly dim on* MARLON BRANDO *and* JEAN PETERS. *Quite suddenly* SHELLEY WINTERS *stands up and falls "into the water." She is in the water, only her head is visible, calling silently.* MONTGOMERY CLIFT *stares at her. She continues to call silently as for help, but* MONTGOMERY CLIFT *only stares at her. Movie music.* CLARA *starts to speak as* SHELLEY WINTERS *continues to cry silently for help.)*

CLARA: The doctor said today that my brother will live; he will be brain damaged and paralyzed.

After he told us, my mother cried in my arms outside the hospital. We were standing on the steps, and she shook so that I thought both of us were going to fall headlong down the steps. *(*SHELLEY WINTERS *drowns. Light goes down on* MONTGOMERY CLIFT *as he stares at* SHELLEY WINTERS *drowning. Lights on* CLARA. *Movie music. Darkness. Brief dazzling image of* CO-LUMBIA PICTURES LADY.*)*

END

G E T T I N G   O U T   (1 9 7 7)

With the plays of Marsha Norman (1947–   ) comes the reminder that the most ordinary people and the least world-shattering events can provide materials for deep dramatic introspection. As Norman herself has put it, she writes about "those folks you wouldn't even notice in life," everyday people who somehow manage to scrape together the will to go on, even in the most daunting of circumstances. Norman set this tone for her work with her first play, *Getting Out* (1977), a drama that gradually yet relentlessly exposes the social and personal forces preventing a recently released prison inmate, Arlene Holsclaw, from finding the means by which to fully liberate herself. Arlene's ultimate hope is to make choices for herself in a way that she has never been able to; such a quest for self-determination is a pervasive theme in Norman's writing. In *Getting Out*, Arlene must wrest her rehabilitation from a society that really does not want to see her freed from the limits that others place upon her.

Marsha Norman's own biography reveals her familiarity with dilemmas like those Arlene faces. Born Marsha Williams in Louisville, Kentucky, she was the daughter of strict fundamentalists. There was little in her childhood to suggest that she would later burst onto the American playwriting scene; at one point, she was kept isolated from neighborhood children for fear she would be exposed to questionable ideas, and conversation in her own house was strictly limited. Norman recalled a "very serious code about what you could and could not say" in her home: "You particularly could not say anything that was in the least angry or had any conflict in it at all." She, did, however, find solace in the arts at an early age, and became a successful student at Durrett High School, where she was active on the newspaper and yearbook staffs. It was there that she won an award for an essay prophetically entitled "Why Good Men Suffer," a question that reemerges in many of her plays. During her time at Agnes Scott College as a philosophy major, she confronted it head-on by working as a volunteer in the pediatric burn unit of Grady Memorial Hospital in Atlanta.

Upon graduation and return to Louisville in 1969, she married her former teacher, Michael Norman (they would divorce in 1974). She simultaneously worked on a master's degree from the University of Louisville and taught disturbed children at Central State Hospital, where she met the young woman who would become the model for Arlene's younger version, Arlie. According to Norman, this patient was "absolutely terrifying," so "violent and vicious that people would get bruises when she walked in a room." Continuing to mix her work and writing, Norman taught at the Brown School for gifted children, while submitting occasional pieces to newspapers for publication. Eventually, the latter evolved into a full-time occupation, and as early as 1976 Norman was regularly writing for a local newspaper; she even created a children's supplement called "The Jelly Bean Journal."

It was through Norman's interest in young people (she had already written a children's musical) and a young people's program she was developing that she first came into contact with Jon Jory, artistic director of the Actors Theatre of Louisville. He, in turn, commissioned her to write a play for its annual festival of new plays, the Humana Festival of New American Plays. *Getting Out* resulted, and Norman became an overnight sensation. The play won both local and national prizes, including an Outer Critics' Award for best new playwright, and was eventually produced at the Mark Taper Forum in Los Angeles and the Theatre de Lys in New York. Norman's life changed profoundly from her early days in Louisville; she married Dann Nyck, Jr., first president of the Actors Theatre, and served as the theatre's playwright-in-residence. She subsequently authored plays such as *Third and Oak* (1978), *Circus Valentine* (1979), and *The Holdup* (1983). Later she was named playwright-in-residence at the Mark Taper Forum, and wrote successful works such as the Pulitzer Prize–winning *'night Mother* (1983), the musical *The Secret Garden* (1992), and numerous teleplays and screenplays.

Getting Out is a play about transformation. At the beginning of the play, it is apparent that although Arlene's life has been turned around, it has not been resolved. After her release from Pine Ridge Correctional Institute in Alabama, she returns to her native Louisville to begin her new life, but is still constrained by forces from within and without. This is quite literally staged in front of the audience, since the set representing Arlene's dingy, one-room efficiency (the former home of her prostitute sister) is framed by the catwalk of her old prison, with her former cell off to one side. In a fashion similar to the collision of dual selves at the center of Cherríe Moraga's *Giving Up the Ghost,* Arlene's former self and counterpart in the play, Arlie, prowls the walks, remaining on the edge of Arlene's consciousness constantly, and appearing before the audience in a series of flashbacks.

Arlene/Arlie has been first and foremost a victim of a man's world that still seeks to control her, a world represented by such characters as the prison guard Bennie, who drives Arlene to Louisville in the hopes of settling down with her. Although he has not treated her so cruelly as other prison guards have, he views women as objects whose affections can be bought with his bribes of taboo items. Indeed, his possessiveness of Arlene nearly reaches the point of rape before she frees herself of him. Her former pimp, Carl, also claims ownership of Arlene, and tries to convince her to turn tricks for him once again. He mocks her resolve to make a go of her life, ridiculing her determination to work to the point of exhaustion so that she can provide a home for the son she had to give up while in prison. The most chilling male influence, however, comes from Arlene's father, who is never onstage but is resurrected

in Arlene's conversation with her mother. Arlie's intermittent appearances reveal to us that Arlene was the victim of ongoing sexual abuse by a father who abused the entire family.

But while the **split character** is used by Norman to suggest the forces that have made Arlene who she is, the device also signifies the psychical reconciliation she needs before she can move on with her life. And, although Arlie represents Arlene's victimization by a male-dominated society with which her mother has complied, she is also a persona whom the born-again Arlene must allow herself to remember fondly. Arlene does this by the end of the play, accepting the idea that a multiplicity of selves exists in everyone. She learns to do this through the help of another former convict, Ruby, who shares the same apartment building. Critics have varied in their response to this ending. Patricia Schroeder, for example, sees it as empowerment through the establishment of a community of women; Timothy Murray, conversely, eschews it as a too-romantic interpretation, one easily adopted by an audience not willing to be implicated for its part in producing the social conditions that have put Arlie/Arlene where she is. According to Murray, such an ending should be read as a frame for the joking that ends the play, a more subtle way of undercutting social norms. No matter how Arlene relates to other women, however, a key reason for her success is her increasing sense of self-reliance—a sense of self-determination as to how she will earn her money and with whom she will share her future.

In many ways, *Getting Out* was a fitting start for Norman's playwriting career, as it embraced signature themes and devices that would repeat themselves in her later work. Although Norman has rejected categorizing her work as "women's theatre," and some commentators have questioned the play's feminism on the basis of its realistic structure (a traditional, male-created and male-influenced theatrical method that cannot adequately represent women), many of her plays center around women coming to terms with their lives. Very often, as in plays such as *Getting Out* and *'night Mother*, the central focus is on a mother (or mother surrogate) and child. Those works which most strongly typify her playwriting, *Getting Out, Third and Oak,* and *'night Mother,* all have several thematic and performative features in common. Each operates within confined, realistic, and quite modest settings: Arlene's "new" apartment, a Laundromat, a poolroom, or a country home. The **realism** of the plays is further extended by the everyday speech of the characters, matching their profanities, dialect, and clipped conversational speech. Ultimately, the protagonists of the plays must make choices that those around them may not agree with, but ones that are necessary for their own sense of self-direction. Thus it is that Arlene can throw away the matchbook with Carl's number on it, and Jessie in *'night Mother* can choose to end her life. There is a leave-taking of the past and its paralyzing influence in these plays; and while they do not always offer satisfactory conclusions, they warn us of the potential sources of oppression for the individual spirit.

Norman's playwriting continues to have a significant impact on the development of modern American drama. Her attention to reading everyday life should not be underestimated, for it is in the spaces where day-to-day lives are lived that many significant dramas are played out. Norman is aware of this, and in drawing our attention to it, makes us examine our own conditions and surroundings all the more carefully.

WORKS CONSULTED

Hart, Lynda. "Doing Time: Hunger for Power in Marsha Norman's Plays." *The Southern Quarterly* 25 (1987): 67–79.

Kane, Leslie. "The Way Out, the Way In: Paths to Self in the Plays of Marsha Norman." *Feminine Focus: The New Women Playwrights.* Ed. Enoch Brater. Oxford: Oxford UP, 1989. 255–274.

Murray, Timothy. "Patriarchal Panopticism, or The Seduction of a Bad Joke: *Getting Out* in Theory." *Theatre Journal* 35 (1983): 376–388.

Norman, Marsha. *Four Plays.* New York: Theatre Communications Group, 1988.

Schroeder, Patricia R. "Locked Behind the Proscenium: Feminist Strategies in *Getting Out* and *My Sister in This House.*" *Modern Drama* 32 (1989): 104–114.

CHARACTERS

ARLENE	a thin, drawn woman in her late twenties who has just served an eight-year prison term for murder
ARLIE	Arlene at various times earlier in her life
BENNIE	an Alabama prison guard in his fifties
GUARD (EVANS)	
GUARD (CALDWELL)	
DOCTOR	a psychiatrist in a juvenile institution
MOTHER	Arlene's mother
SCHOOL PRINCIPAL	female
RONNIE	a teenager in a juvenile institution
CARL	Arlene's former pimp and partner in various crimes, in his late twenties
WARDEN	superintendent of Pine Ridge Correctional Institute for Women
RUBY	Arlene's upstairs neighbor, a cook in a diner, also an ex-con, in her late thirties

Prologue

Beginning five minutes before the houselights come down, the following announcements are broadcast over the loudspeaker. A woman's voice is preferred, a droning tone is essential.

LOUDSPEAKER VOICE: Kitchen workers, all kitchen workers report immediately to the kitchen. Kitchen workers to the kitchen. The library will not be open today. Those scheduled for book checkout should remain in morning work assignments. Kitchen workers to the kitchen. No library hours today. Library hours resume tomorrow as usual. All kitchen workers to the kitchen.

Frances Mills, you have a visitor at the front gate. All residents and staff, all residents and staff . . . Do not, repeat, do not, walk on the front lawn today or use the picnic tables on the front lawn during your break after lunch or dinner.

Your attention please. The exercise class for Dorm A residents has been cancelled. Mrs. Fischer should be back at work in another month. She thanks you for your cards and wants all her girls to know she had an eight-pound baby girl.

Doris Creech, see Mrs. Adams at the library before lunch. Frances Mills, you have a visitor at the front gate. The Women's Associates' picnic for the beauty school class has been postponed until Friday. As picnic lunches have already been prepared, any beauty school member who so wishes, may pick up a picnic lunch and eat it at her assigned lunch table during the regular lunch period.

Frances Mills, you have a visitor at the front gate. Doris Creech to see Mrs. Adams at the library before lunch. I'm sorry, that's Frankie Hill, you have a visitor at the front gate. Repeat, Frankie Hill, not Frances Mills, you have a visitor at the front gate.

The play is set in a dingy one-room apartment in a rundown section of downtown Louisville, Kentucky. There is a twin bed and one chair. There is a sink, an apartment-size combination stove and refrigerator, and a counter with cabinets above. Dirty curtains conceal the bars on the outside of the single window. There is one closet and a door to the bathroom. The door to the apartment opens into a hall.

A catwalk stretches above the apartment and a prison cell, stage right, connects to it by stairways. An area downstage and another stage left complete the enclosure of the apartment by playing areas for the past. The apartment must seem imprisoned.

Following the prologue, lights fade to black and the WARDEN'S VOICE *is heard on tape.*

WARDEN'S VOICE: The Alabama State Parole Board hereby grants parole to Holsclaw, Arlene, subject having served eight years at Pine Ridge Correctional Institute for the second-degree murder of a cab driver in conjunction with a filling station robbery involving attempted kidnapping of attendant. Crime occurred during escape from Lakewood State Prison where subject Holsclaw was serving three years for forgery and prostitution. Extensive juvenile records from the state of Kentucky appended hereto.

(As the warden continues, light comes up on ARLENE, *walking around the cell, waiting to be picked up for the ride home.* ARLIE *is visible, but just barely, down center.)*

WARDEN'S VOICE: Subject now considered completely rehabilitated is returned to Kentucky under interstate parole agreement in consideration of family residence and appropriate support personnel in the area. Subject will remain under the supervision of Kentucky parole officers for a period of five years. Prospects for successful integration into community rated good. Psychological evaluation, institutional history and health records attached in Appendix C, this document.

BENNIE'S VOICE: Arlie!

(ARLENE *leaves the cell as light comes up on* AR-LIE, *seated down center. She tells this story rather simply. She enjoys it, but its horror is not lost on her. She may be doing some semiabsorbing activity such as painting her toenails.*)

ARLIE: So, there was this little kid, see, this creepy little fucker next door. Had glasses an somethin' wrong with his foot. I don't know, seven, maybe. Anyhow, ever time his daddy went fishin', he'd bring this kid back some frogs. They built this little fence around 'em in the backyard like they was pets or somethin'. An we'd try to go over an see 'em but he'd start screamin' to his mother to come out an git rid of us. Real snotty like. So we got sick of him bein' such a goody-goody an one night me an June snuck over there an put all his dumb ol' frogs in this sack. You never heared such a fuss. *(makes croaking sounds)* Slimy bastards, frogs. We was plannin' to let 'em go all over the place, but when they started jumpin' an all, we just figured they was askin' for it. So, we taken 'em out front to the porch an we throwed 'em, one at a time, into the street. *(laughs)* Some of 'em hit cars goin' by but most of 'em jus' got squashed, you know, runned over? It was great, seein' how far we could throw 'em, over back of our backs an under our legs an God, it was really fun watchin' 'em fly through the air then *splat (claps hands)* all over somebody's car window or somethin'. Then the next day, we was waitin' and this little kid comes out in his backyard lookin' for his stupid frogs and he don't see any an he gets so crazy, cryin' and everthing. So me an June goes over an tells him we seen this big mess out in the street, an he goes out an sees all them frogs' legs and bodies an shit all over the everwhere, an, man, it was so funny. We 'bout killed ourselves laughin'. Then his mother come out and she wouldn't let him go out an pick up all the pieces, so he jus' had to stand there watchin' all the cars go by

smush his little babies right into the street. I's gonna run out an git him a frog's head, but June yellin' at me "Arlie, git over here fore some car slips on them frog guts an crashes into you." *(pause)* I never had so much fun in one day in my whole life.

(ARLIE *remains seated as* ARLENE *enters the apartment. It is late evening. Two sets of footsteps are heard coming up the stairs.* ARLENE *opens the door and walks into the room. She stands still, surveying the littered apartment.* BENNIE *is heard dragging a heavy trunk up the stairs.* BENNIE *is wearing his guard uniform. He is a heavy man, but obviously used to physical work.*)

BENNIE: *(from outside)* Arlie?

ARLENE: Arlene.

BENNIE: Arlene? *(Bringing the trunk just inside the door.)*

ARLENE: Leave it. I'll git it later.

BENNIE: Oh, now, let me bring it in for you. You ain't as strong as you was.

ARLENE: I ain't as mean as I was. I'm strong as ever. You go on now. *(Beginning to walk around the room.)*

ARLIE: *(irritated, as though someone is calling her)* Lay off! *(Gets up and walks past* BENNIE.)*

BENNIE: *(scoots the trunk into the room a little further)* Go on where, Arlie?

ARLENE: I don't know where. How'd I know where you'd be goin'?

BENNIE: I can't go till I know you're gonna do all right.

ARLENE: Look, I'm gonna do all right. I done all right before Pine Ridge, an I done all right at Pine Ridge. An I'm gonna do all right here.

BENNIE: But you don't know nobody. I mean, nobody nice.

ARLENE: Lay off.

BENNIE: Nobody to take care of you.

ARLENE: *(picking up old newspapers and other trash from the floor)* I kin take care of myself. I been doin' it long enough.

BENNIE: Sure you have, an you landed yourself in prison doin' it, Arlie girl.

ARLENE: *(wheels around)* Arlie girl landed herself in prison. Arlene is out, okay?

BENNIE: Hey, now, I know we said we wasn't gonna say nuthin' about that, but I been lookin' after you for a long time. I been watchin' you eat your dinner for eight years now. I got used to it, you know?

ARLENE: Well, you kin jus' git unused to it.

BENNIE: Then why'd you ask me to drive you all the way up here?

ARLENE: I didn't, now. That was all your big ideal.

BENNIE: And what were you gonna do? Ride the bus, pick up some soldier, git yourself in another mess of trouble?

(ARLIE struts back into the apartment, speaking as if to a soldier in a bar.)

ARLIE: Okay, who's gonna buy me a beer?

ARLENE: You oughta go by Fort Knox on your way home.

ARLIE: Fuckin' soldiers, don't care where they get theirself drunk.

ARLENE: You'd like it.

ARLIE: Well, Arlie girl, take your pick.

ARLENE: They got tanks right out on the grass to look at.

ARLIE: *(now appears to lean on a bar rail)* You git that haircut today, honey?

BENNIE: I just didn't want you givin' your twenty dollars the warden gave you to the first pusher you come across.

(ARLIE laughs.)

ARLENE: That's what you think I been waitin' for? *(A GUARD appears and motions for ARLIE to follow him.)*

ARLIE: Yeah! I heard ya.

(The GUARD takes ARLIE to the cell and slams the door.)

BENNIE: But God almighty, I hate to think what you'd done to the first ol' bugger tried to make you in that bus station. You got grit, Arlie girl. I gotta credit you for that.

ARLIE: *(from the cell, as she dumps a plate of food on the floor)* Officer!

BENNIE: The screamin' you'd do. Wake the dead.

ARLENE: Uh-huh.

BENNIE: *(proudly)* An there ain't nobody can beat you for throwin' plates.

ARLIE: Are you gonna clean up this shit or do I have to sit here and look at it till I vomit? *(A guard comes in to clean it up.)*

BENNIE: Listen, ever prison in Alabama's usin' plastic forks now on account of what you done.

ARLENE: You can quit talkin' just anytime now.

ARLIE: Some life you got, fatso. Bringin' me my dinner then wipin' it off the walls. *(Laughs.)*

BENNIE: Some of them officers was pretty leery of you. Even the chaplain.

ARLENE: No he wasn't either.

BENNIE: Not me, though. You was just wild, that's all.

ARLENE: Animals is wild, not people. That's what he said.

ARLIE: *(mocking)* Good behavior, good behavior. Shit.

BENNIE: Now what could that four-eyes chaplain know about wild? *(ARLENE looks up sharply)* Okay. Not wild, then . . .

ARLIE: I kin git outta here anytime I want. *(Leaves the cell.)*

BENNIE: But you got grit, Arlie.

ARLENE: I have said for you to call me Arlene.

BENNIE: Okay okay.

ARLENE: Huh?

BENNIE: Don't git riled. You want me to call you Arlene, then Arlene it is. Yes ma'am. Now, *(slapping the trunk)* where do you want this? *(no response)* Arlene, I said, where do you want this trunk?

ARLENE: I don't care. *(BENNIE starts to put it at the foot of the bed)* No! *(then calmer)* I seen it there too long. *(BENNIE is irritated)* Maybe over here. *(points to a spot near the window)* I could put a cloth on it and sit an look out the . . . *(she pulls the curtains apart, sees the bars on the window)* What's these bars doin' here?

BENNIE: *(stops moving the trunk)* I think they're to keep out burglars, you know. *(Sits on the trunk.)*

ARLENE: Yeah, I know.

(ARLIE appears on the catwalk, as if stopped during a break-in.)

ARLIE: We ain't breakin' in, cop, we're just admirin' this beautiful window.

ARLENE: I don't want them there. Pull them out.

BENNIE: You can't go tearin' up the place, Arlene. Landlord wouldn't like it.

ARLIE: *(to the unseen policeman)* Maybe I got a brick in my hand and maybe I don't.

BENNIE: Not one bit.

ARLIE: An I'm standin' on this garbage can because I like to, all right?

ARLENE: *(walking back toward* BENNIE*)* I ain't gonna let no landlord tell me what to do.

BENNIE: The landlord owns the building. You gotta do what he says or he'll throw you out right on your pretty little *be*hind. *(Gives her a familiar pat.)*

ARLIE: *(slaps his hand away)* You watch your mouth. I won't have no dirty talk.

ARLIE: Just shut the fuck up, cop! Go bust a wino or somethin'. *(Returns to the cell.)*

ARLENE: *(points down right)* Here, put the trunk over here.

BENNIE: *(carrying the trunk over to the spot she has picked)* What you got in here, anyhow? Rocks? Rocks from the rock pile?

ARLENE: That ain't funny.

BENNIE: Oh sweetie, I didn't mean nuthin' by that.

ARLENE: And I ain't your sweetie.

BENNIE: We really did have us a rock pile, you know, at the old men's prison, yes we did. And those boys, time they did nine or ten years carryin' rocks around, they was pret-ty mean, I'm here to tell you. And strong? God.

ARLENE: Well, what did you expect? *(Beginning to unpack the trunk.)*

BENNIE: You're tellin' me. It was dumb, I kept tellin' the warden that. They coulda killed us all, easy, anytime, that outfit. Except, we did have the guns.

ARLENE: Uh-huh.

BENNIE: One old bastard sailed a throwin' rock at me one day, woulda took my eye out if I hadn't turned around just then. Still got the scar, see? *(Reaches up to the back of his head.)*

ARLENE: You shoot him?

BENNIE: Nope. Somebody else did. I forget who. Hey! *(walking over to the window)* These bars won't be so bad. Maybe you could get you some plants so's you don't even see them. Yeah, plants'd do it up just fine. Just fine.

ARLENE: *(pulls a cheaply framed picture of Jesus out of the trunk)* Chaplain give me this.

BENNIE: He got it for free, I bet.

ARLENE: Now, look here. That chaplain was good to me, so you can shut up about him.

BENNIE: *(backing down)* Fine. Fine.

ARLENE: Here. *(handing him the picture)* You might as well be useful fore you go.

BENNIE: Where you want it?

ARLENE: Don't matter.

BENNIE: Course it matters. Wouldn't want me puttin' it inside the closet, would you? You gotta make decisions now, Arlene. Gotta decide things.

ARLENE: I don't care.

BENNIE: *(insisting)* Arlene.

ARLENE: *(pointing to a prominent position on the apartment wall, center)* There.

BENNIE: Yeah. Good place. See it first thing when you get up.
*(*ARLENE *lights a cigarette, as* ARLIE *retrieves a hidden lighter from the toilet in the cell.)*

ARLIE: There's ways . . . gettin' outta bars . . .
(Lights a fire in the cell, catching her blouse on fire too.)

BENNIE: *(as* ARLIE *is lighting the fire)* This ol' nail's pretty loose. I'll find something better to hang it with . . . somewhere or other . . .
*(*ARLIE *screams and the doctor runs toward her, getting the attention of a guard who has been goofing off on the catwalk.)*

ARLIE: Let me outta here! There's a fuckin' fire in here!
(The DOCTOR *arrives at the cell, pats his pockets as if looking for the keys.)*

ARLIE: Officer!

DOCTOR: Guard!
*(*GUARD *begins his run to the cell.)*

ARLIE: It's burnin' me!

DOCTOR: Hurry!

GUARD (EVANS): I'm comin'! I'm comin'!

DOCTOR: What the hell were you—

GUARD (EVANS): *(fumbling for the right key)* Come on, come on.

DOCTOR: *(urgent)* For Chrissake!

(The GUARD gets the door open, they rush in. The DOCTOR, wrestling ARLIE to the ground, opens his bag.)

DOCTOR: Lay still, dammit.

(ARLIE collapses. The DOCTOR gives an injection.)

DOCTOR: *(grabbing his hand)* Ow!

GUARD (EVANS): *(lifting ARLIE up to the bed)* Get bit, Doc?

DOCTOR: You going to let her burn this place down before you start payin' attention up there?

GUARD (EVANS): *(walks to the toilet, feels under the rim)* Uh-huh.

BENNIE: There, that what you had in mind?

ARLENE: Yeah, thanks.

GUARD (EVANS): She musta had them matches hid right here.

BENNIE: *(staring at the picture he's hung)* How you think he kept his beard trimmed all nice?

ARLENE: *(preoccupied with unloading the trunk)* Who?

BENNIE: *(pointing to the picture)* Jesus.

DOCTOR: I'll have to report you for this, Evans.

ARLENE: I don't know.

DOCTOR: That injection should hold her. I'll check back later. *(Leaves.)*

GUARD (EVANS): *(walking over to the bed)* Report me, my ass. We got cells don't have potties, Holsclaw. *(begins to search her and the bed, handling her very roughly)* So where is it now? Got it up your pookie, I bet. Oh, that'd be good. Doc comin' back an me with my fingers up your . . . roll over . . . don't weigh hardly nuthin', do you, dollie?

BENNIE: Never seen him without a moustache either.

ARLENE: Huh?

BENNIE: The picture.

GUARD (EVANS): Aw now . . . *(finding the lighter under the mattress)* That wasn't hard at all. Don't you know 'bout hide an seek, Arlie, girl? Gonna hide somethin', hide it where it's fun to find it. *(standing up, going to the door)* Crazy fuckin' someday-we-ain't-gonna-come-save-you bitch!

(GUARD slams cell door and leaves.)

BENNIE: Well, Arlie girl, that ol' trunk's 'bout as empty as my belly.

ARLENE: You have been talkin' 'bout your belly ever since we left this mornin'.

BENNIE: You hungry? Them hotdogs we had give out around Nashville.

ARLENE: No. Not really.

BENNIE: You gotta eat, Arlene.

ARLENE: Says who?

BENNIE: *(laughs)* How 'bout I pick us up some chicken, give you time to clean yourself up. We'll have a nice little dinner, just the two of us.

ARLENE: I git sick if I eat this late. Besides, I'm tired.

BENNIE: You'll feel better soon's you git somethin' on your stomach. Like I always said, "Can't plow less'n you feed the mule."

ARLENE: I ain't never heard you say that.

BENNIE: There's lots you don't know about me, Arlene. You been seein' me ever day, but you ain't been payin' attention. You'll get to like me now we're out.

ARLENE: You . . . was always out.

BENNIE: Yes sir, I'm gonna like bein' retired. I kin tell already. An I can take care of you, like I been, only now—

ARLENE: You tol' me you was jus' takin' a vacation.

BENNIE: I was gonna tell you.

ARLENE: You had some time off an nothin' to do . . .

BENNIE: Figured you knew already.

ARLENE: You said you ain't never seen Kentucky like you always wanted to. Now you tell me you done quit at the prison?

BENNIE: They wouldn't let me drive you up here if I was still on the payroll, you know. Rules, against the rules. Coulda got me in big trouble doin' that.

ARLENE: You ain't goin' back to Pine Ridge?

BENNIE: Nope.

ARLENE: An you drove me all the way up here plannin' to stay here?

BENNIE: I was thinkin' on it.

ARLENE: Well what are you gonna do?

BENNIE: *(not positive, just a possibility)* Hardware.

ARLENE: Sell guns?

BENNIE: *(laughs)* Nails. Always wanted to. Some little store with bins and barrels full of nails and screws. Count 'em out. Put 'em in little sacks.

ARLENE: I don't need nobody hangin' around remindin' me where I been.

BENNIE: We had us a good time drivin' up here, didn't we? You throwin' that tomato outta the car . . . hit that no litterin' sign square in the middle. *(grabs her arm as if to feel the muscle)* Good arm you got.

ARLENE: *(pulling away sharply)* Don't you go grabbin' me.

BENNIE: Listen, you take off them clothes and have yourself a nice hot bath. *(heading for the bathroom)* See, I'll start the water. And me, I'll go get us some chicken. *(coming out of the bathroom)* You like slaw or potato salad?

ARLENE: Don't matter.

BENNIE: *(asking her to decide)* Arlene . . .

ARLENE: Slaw.

BENNIE: One big bucket of slaw comin' right up. An extra rolls. You have a nice bath, now, you hear? I'll take my time so's you don't have to hurry fixin' yourself up.

ARLENE: I ain't gonna do no fixin'.

BENNIE: *(a knowing smile)* I know how you gals are when you get in the tub. You got any bubbles?

ARLENE: What?

BENNIE: Bubbles. You know, stuff to make bubbles with. Bubble bath.

ARLENE: I thought you was goin'.

BENNIE: Right. Right. Goin' right now.

(BENNIE leaves, locking the door behind him. He has left his hat on the bed. ARLENE checks the stove and refrigerator.)

GUARD (CALDWELL):   *(opening the cell door, carrying a plastic dinner carton)* Got your grub, girlie.

ARLIE: Get out!

GUARD (CALDWELL):   Can't. Doc says you gotta take the sun today.

ARLIE: You take it! I ain't hungry.

(The GUARD and ARLIE begin to walk to the downstage table area.)

GUARD (CALDWELL):   You gotta eat, Arlie.

ARLIE: Says who?

GUARD (CALDWELL):   Says me. Says the warden. Says the Department of Corrections. Brung you two rolls.

ARLIE: And you know what you can do with your—

GUARD (CALDWELL):   Stuff 'em in your bra, why don't you?

ARLIE: Ain't you got somebody to go beat up somewhere?

GUARD (CALDWELL):   Gotta see you get fattened up.

ARLIE: What do you care?

(ARLENE goes into the bathroom.)

GUARD (CALDWELL):   Oh, we care all right. *(setting the food down on the table)* Got us a two-way mirror in the shower room. *(she looks up, hostile)* And you don't know which one it is, do you? *(he forces her onto the seat)* Yes ma'am. Eat. *(pointing to the food)* We sure do care if you go gittin' too skinny. *(walks away but continues to watch her)* Yes ma'am. We care a hog-lickin' lot.

ARLIE: *(throws the whole carton at him)* Sons-a-bitches!

(MOTHER's knock is heard on the apartment door.)

MOTHER'S VOICE: Arlie? Arlie girl you in there?

(ARLENE walks out of the bathroom. She stands still, looking at the door. ARLIE hears the knock at the same time and slips into the apartment and over to the bed, putting the pillow between her legs and holding the yellow teddy bear ARLENE has unpacked. The knocking gets louder.)

MOTHER'S VOICE: Arlie?

ARLIE: *(pulling herself up weakly on one elbow, speaking with the voice of a very young child)* Mama? Mama?

(ARLENE walks slowly toward the door.)

MOTHER'S VOICE: *(now pulling the doorknob from the outside, angry that the door is locked)* Arlie? I know you're in there.

ARLIE: I can't git up, Mama. *(hands between her legs)* My legs is hurt.

MOTHER'S VOICE: What's takin' you so long?

ARLENE: *(smoothing out her dress)* Yeah, I'm comin'. *(puts* BENNIE'S *hat out of sight under the bed)* Hold on.

MOTHER'S VOICE: I brung you some stuff but I ain't gonna stand here all night.

*(*ARLENE *opens the door and stands back.* MOTHER *looks strong but badly worn. She is wearing her cab driver's uniform and is carrying a plastic laundry basket stuffed with cleaning fluids, towels, bug spray, etc.)*

ARLENE: I didn't know if you'd come.

MOTHER: Ain't I always?

ARLENE: How are you?

*(*ARLENE *moves as if to hug her.* MOTHER *stands still,* ARLENE *backs off.)*

MOTHER: 'Bout the same. *(Walking into the room.)*

ARLENE: I'm glad to see you.

MOTHER: *(not looking at* ARLENE*)* You look tired.

ARLENE: It was a long drive.

MOTHER: *(putting the laundry basket on the trunk)* Didn't fatten you up none, I see. *(walks around the room, looking the place over)* You always was too skinny. *(*ARLENE *straightens her clothes again)* Shoulda beat you like your daddy said. Make you eat.

ARLIE: Nobody done this to me, Mama. *(protesting, in pain)* No! No!

MOTHER: He weren't a mean man, though, your daddy.

ARLIE: Was . . . *(quickly)* my bike. My bike hurt me. The seat bumped me.

MOTHER: You remember that black chewing gum he got you when you was sick?

ARLENE: I remember he beat up on you.

MOTHER: Yeah, *(proudly)* and he was real sorry a coupla times. *(looking in the closet)* Filthy dirty. Hey! *(slamming the closet door.* ARLENE *jumps at the noise)* I brung you all kinda stuff. Just like Candy not leavin' you nuthin'. *(walking back to the basket)* Some kids I got.

ARLIE: *(curling up into a ball)* No, Mama, don't touch it. It'll git well. It git well before.

ARLENE: Where is Candy?

MOTHER: You got her place so what do you care? I got her outta my house so whatta I care? This'll be a good place for you.

ARLENE: *(going to the window)* Wish there was a yard, here.

MOTHER: *(beginning to empty the basket)* Nice things, see? Bet you ain't had no colored towels where you been.

ARLENE: No.

MOTHER: *(putting some things away in cabinets)* No place like home. Got that up on the kitchen wall now.

ARLIE: I don't want no tea, Mama.

ARLENE: Yeah?

MOTHER: *(repeating* ARLENE'S *answers)* No . . . yeah? . . . You forgit how to talk? I ain't gonna be here all that long. Least you can talk to me while I'm here.

ARLENE: You ever git that swing you wanted?

MOTHER: Dish towels, an see here? June sent along this teapot. You drink tea, Arlie?

ARLENE: No.

MOTHER: June's havin' another baby. Don't know when to quit, that girl. Course, I ain't one to talk. *(Starting to pick up trash on the floor.)*

ARLENE: Have you seen Joey?

ARLIE: I'm tellin' you the truth.

MOTHER: An Ray . . .

ARLIE: *(pleading)* Daddy didn't do nuthin' to me.

MOTHER: Ray ain't had a day of luck in his life.

ARLIE: Ask him. He saw me fall on my bike.

MOTHER: Least bein' locked up now, he'll keep off June till the baby gits here.

ARLENE: Have you seen Joey?

MOTHER: Your daddy ain't doin' too good right now. Man's been dyin' for ten years, to hear him tell it. You'd think he'd git tired of it an jus' go ahead . . . pass on.

ARLENE: *(wanting an answer)* Mother . . .

MOTHER: Yeah, I seen 'im. 'Bout two years ago. Got your stringy hair.

ARLENE: You got a picture?

MOTHER: You was right to give him up. Foster homes is good for some kids.

ARLIE: Where's my Joey-bear? Yellow Joey-bear? Mama?

ARLENE: How'd you see him?

MOTHER: I was down at Detention Center pickin' up Pete. *(Beginning her serious cleaning now.)*

ARLENE: *(less than interested)* How is he?

MOTHER: I could be workin' at the Detention Center I been there so much. All I gotta do's have somethin' big goin' on an I git a call to come after one of you. Can't jus' have kids, no, gotta be pickin' 'em up all over town.

ARLENE: You was just tellin' me—

MOTHER: Pete is taller, that's all.

ARLENE: You was just tellin' me how you saw Joey.

MOTHER: I'm comin' back in the cab an I seen him waitin' for the bus.

ARLENE: What'd he say?

MOTHER: Oh, I didn't stop. *(ARLENE looks up quickly, hurt and angry)* If the kid don't even know you, Arlie, he sure ain't gonna know who I am.

ARLENE: How come he couldn't stay at Shirley's?

MOTHER: 'Cause Shirley never was crazy about washin' more diapers. She's the only smart kid I got. Anyway, social worker only put him there till she could find him a foster home.

ARLENE: But I coulda seen him.

MOTHER: Thatta been trouble, him bein' in the family. Kid wouldn't have known who to listen to, Shirley or you.

ARLENE: But I'm his mother.

MOTHER: See, now you don't have to be worryin' about him. No kids, no worryin'.

ARLENE: He just had his birthday, you know.

ARLIE: Don't let Daddy come in here, Mama. Just you an me. Mama?

ARLENE: When I git workin', I'll git a nice rug for this place. He could come live here with me.

MOTHER: Fat chance.

ARLENE: I done my time.

MOTHER: You never really got attached to him anyway.

ARLENE: How do you know that?

MOTHER: Now don't you go gettin' het up. I'm telling you . . .

ARLENE: But . . .

MOTHER: Kids need rules to go by an he'll git 'em over there.

ARLIE: *(screaming)* No Daddy! I didn't tell her nuthin'. I didn't! I didn't! *(Gets up from the bed, terrified.)*

MOTHER: Here, help me with these sheets. *(hands ARLENE the sheets from the laundry basket)* Even got you a spread. Kinda goes with them curtains. *(ARLENE is silent)* You ain't thanked me, Arlie girl.

ARLENE: *(going to the other side of the bed)* They don't call me Arlie no more. It's Arlene now.
   (ARLENE and MOTHER make up the bed. ARLIE jumps up, looks around and goes over to MOTHER'S purse. She looks through it hurriedly and pulls out the wallet. She takes some money and runs down left, where she is caught by a school principal.)

PRINCIPAL: Arlie? You're in an awfully big hurry for such a little girl. *(brushes at ARLIE'S hair)* That is you under all that hair, isn't it? *(ARLIE resists this gesture)* Now, you can watch where you're going.

ARLIE: Gotta git home.

PRINCIPAL: But school isn't over for another three hours. And there's peanut butter and chili today.

ARLIE: Ain't hungry. *(Struggling free.)*
   (The PRINCIPAL now sees ARLIE'S hands clenched behind her back.)

PRINCIPAL: What do we have in our hands, Arlie?

ARLIE: Nuthin'.

PRINCIPAL: Let me see your hands, Arlie. Open up your hands.
   (ARLIE brings her hands around in front, opening them, showing crumpled dollars.)

ARLIE: It's my money. I earned it.

PRINCIPAL: *(taking the money)* And how did we earn this money?

ARLIE: Doin' things.

PRINCIPAL: What kind of things?

ARLIE: For my daddy.

PRINCIPAL: Well, we'll see about that. You'll have to come with me.

(ARLIE *resists as the principal pulls her.*)

ARLIE: No.

PRINCIPAL: Your mother was right after all. She said put you in a special school. *(quickly)* No, what she said was put you away somewhere and I said, no, she's too young, well I was wrong. I have four hundred other children to take care of here and what have I been doing? Breaking up your fights, talking to your truant officer and washing your writing off the bathroom wall. Well, I've had enough. You've made your choice. You *want* out of regular school and you're going to *get* out of regular school.

ARLIE: *(becoming more violent)* You can't make me go nowhere, bitch!

PRINCIPAL: *(backing off in cold anger)* I'm not making you go. You've earned it. You've worked hard for this, well, they're used to your type over there. They'll know exactly what to do with you.

(*She stalks off, leaving* ARLIE *alone.*)

MOTHER: *(smoothing out the spread)* Spread ain't new, but it don't look so bad. Think we got it right after we got you. No, I remember now. I was pregnant with you an been real sick the whole time.

(ARLIE *lights a cigarette,* MOTHER *takes one,* ARLENE *retrieves the pack quickly.*)

MOTHER: Your daddy brung me home this big bowl of chili an some jelly doughnuts. Some fare from the airport give him a big tip. Anyway, I'd been eatin' peanut brittle all day, only thing that tasted any good. Then in he come with this chili an no sooner'n I got in bed I thrown up all over everwhere. Lucky I didn't throw you up, Arlie girl. Anyhow, that's how come us to get a new spread. This one here. *(Sits on the bed.)*

ARLENE: You drivin' the cab any?

MOTHER: Any? Your daddy ain't drove it at all a long time now. Six years, seven maybe.

ARLENE: You meet anybody nice?

MOTHER: Not anymore. Mostly drivin' old ladies to get their shoes. Guess it got around the nursin' homes I was reliable. *(sounds funny to her)* You remember that time I took you drivin' with me that night after you been in a fight an that soldier bought us a beer? Shitty place, hole in the wall?

ARLENE: You made me wait in the car.

MOTHER: *(standing up)* Think I'd take a child of mine into a dump like that?

ARLENE: You went in.

MOTHER: Weren't no harm in it. *(walking over for the bug spray)* I didn't always look so bad, you know.

ARLENE: You was pretty.

MOTHER: *(beginning to spray the floor)* You could look better'n you do. Do somethin' with your hair. I always thought if you'd looked better you wouldn't have got in so much trouble.

ARLENE: *(pleased and curious)* Joey got my hair?

MOTHER: And skinny.

ARLENE: I took some beauty school at Pine Ridge.

MOTHER: Yeah, a beautician?

ARLENE: I don't guess so.

MOTHER: Said you was gonna work.

ARLENE: They got a law here. Ex-cons can't get no license.

MOTHER: Shoulda stayed in Alabama, then. Worked there.

ARLENE: They got a law there, too.

MOTHER: Then why'd they give you the trainin'?

ARLENE: I don't know.

MOTHER: Maybe they thought it'd straighten you out.

ARLENE: Yeah.

MOTHER: But you are gonna work, right?

ARLENE: Yeah. Cookin' maybe. Somethin' that pays good.

MOTHER: You? Cook? *(Laughs.)*

ARLENE: I could learn it.

MOTHER: Your daddy ain't never forgive you for that bologna sandwich. (ARLENE *laughs a little, finally enjoying a memory*) Oh, I wish I'd seen you spreadin' that Colgate on that bread. He'd have smelled that toothpaste if he hadn't been so sloshed. Little snotty-nosed kid tryin' to kill her daddy with a bologna sandwich. An him bein' so pleased when you brung it to him . . . *(Laughing.)*

ARLENE: He beat me good.

MOTHER: Well, now, Arlie, you gotta admit you had it comin' to you. *(Wiping tears from laughing.)*

ARLENE: I guess.

MOTHER: You got a broom?

ARLENE: No.

MOTHER: Well, I got one in the cab I brung just in case. I can't leave it here, but I'll sweep up fore I go. *(walking toward the door)* You jus' rest till I git back. Won't find no work lookin' the way you do.

(MOTHER leaves. ARLENE finds some lipstick and a mirror in her purse, makes an attempt to look better while MOTHER is gone.)

ARLIE: *(jumps up, as if talking to another kid)* She is not skinny!

ARLENE: *(looking at herself in the mirror)* I guess I could . . .

ARLIE: And she don't have to git them stinky permanents. Her hair just comes outta her head curly.

ARLENE: Some lipstick.

ARLIE: *(serious)* She drives the cab to buy us stuff, 'cause we don't take no charity from nobody, 'cause we got money 'cause she earned it.

ARLENE: *(closing the mirror, dejected, afraid MOTHER might be right)* But you're too skinny and you got stringy hair. *(Sitting on the floor.)*

ARLIE: *(more angry)* She drives at night 'cause people needs rides at night. People goin' to see their friends that are sick, or people's cars broken down an they gotta get to work at the . . . nobody calls my mama a whore!

MOTHER: *(coming back in with the broom)* If I'd known you were gonna sweep up with your butt, I wouldn't have got this broom. Get up! *(Sweeps at ARLENE to get her to move.)*

ARLIE: You're gonna take that back or I'm gonna rip out all your ugly hair and stuff it down your ugly throat.

ARLENE: *(tugging at her own hair)* You still cut hair?

MOTHER: *(noticing some spot on the floor)* Gonna take a razor blade to get out this paint.

ARLENE: Nail polish.

ARLIE: Wanna know what I know about your mama? She's dyin'. Somethin's eatin' up her insides piece by piece, only she don't want you to know it.

MOTHER: *(continuing to sweep)* So, you're callin' yourself Arlene, now?

ARLENE: Yes.

MOTHER: Don't want your girlie name no more?

ARLENE: Somethin' like that.

MOTHER: They call you Arlene in prison?

ARLENE: Not at first when I was bein' hateful. Just my number then.

MOTHER: You always been hateful.

ARLENE: There was this chaplain, he called me Arlene from the first day he come to talk to me. Here, let me help you. *(She reaches for the broom.)*

MOTHER: I'll do it.

ARLENE: You kin rest.

MOTHER: Since when? *(ARLENE backs off)* I ain't hateful, how come I got so many hateful kids? *(sweeping harder now)* Poor dumb-as-hell Pat, stealin' them wigs, Candy screwin' since day one, Pete cuttin' up ol' Mac down at the grocery, June sellin' dope like it was Girl Scout cookies, and you . . . thank God I can't remember it all.

ARLENE: *(a very serious request)* Maybe I could come out on Sunday for . . . you still make that pot roast?

MOTHER: *(now sweeping over by the picture of Jesus)* That your picture?

ARLENE: That chaplain give it to me.

MOTHER: The one give you your "new name."

ARLENE: Yes.

MOTHER: It's crooked. *(Doesn't straighten it.)*

ARLENE: I liked those potatoes with no skins. An that ketchup squirter we had, jus' like in a real restaurant.

MOTHER: People that run them institutions now, they jus' don't know how to teach kids right. Let 'em run around an get in more trouble. They should get you up at the crack of dawn and set you to scrubbin' the floor. That's what kids need. Trainin'. Hard work.

ARLENE: *(a clear request)* I'll probably git my Sundays off.

MOTHER: Sunday . . . is my day to clean house now.

(ARLENE gets the message, finally walks over to straighten the picture. MOTHER now feels a little bad about this rejection, stops sweeping for a moment.)

MOTHER: I woulda wrote you but I didn't have nuthin' to say. An no money to send, so what's the use?

ARLENE: I made out.

MOTHER: They pay you for workin'?

ARLENE: 'Bout three dollars a month.

MOTHER: How'd you make it on three dollars a month? *(answers her own question)* You do some favors?

ARLENE: *(sitting down in the chair under the picture, a somewhat smug look)* You jus' can't make it by yourself.

MOTHER: *(pauses, suspicious, then contemptuous)* You play, Arlie?

ARLENE: You don't know nuthin' about that.

MOTHER: I hear things. Girls callin' each other "mommy" an bringin' things back from the canteen for their "husbands." Makes me sick. You got family, Arlie, what you want with that playin'? Don't want nobody like that in my house.

ARLENE: You don't know what you're talkin' about.

MOTHER: I still got two kids at home. Don't want no bad example. *(Not finishing the sweeping. Has all the dirt in one place, but doesn't get it up off the floor yet.)*

ARLENE: I could tell them some things.

MOTHER: *(vicious)* Like about that cab driver.

ARLENE: Look, that was a long time ago. I wanna work, now, make somethin' of myself. I learned to knit. People'll buy nice sweaters. Make some extra money.

MOTHER: We sure could use it.

ARLENE: An then if I have money, maybe they'd let me take Joey to the fair, buy him hotdogs an talk to him. Make sure he ain't foolin' around.

MOTHER: What makes you think he'd listen to you? Alice, across the street? Her sister took care her kids while she was at Lexington. You think they pay any attention to her now? Ashamed, that's what. One of 'em told me his mother done died. Gone to see a friend and died there.

ARLENE: Be different with me and Joey.

MOTHER: He don't even know who you are, Arlie.

ARLENE: *(wearily)* Arlene.

MOTHER: You forgot already what you was like as a kid. At Waverly, tellin' them lies about that campin' trip we took, sayin' your daddy made you watch while he an me . . . you know. I'd have killed you then if them social workers hadn't been watchin'.

ARLENE: Yeah.

MOTHER: Didn't want them thinkin' I weren't fit. Well, what do they know? Each time you'd get out of one of them places, you'd be actin' worse than ever. Go right back to that junkie, pimp, Carl, sellin' the stuff he steals, savin' his ass from the police. He follow you home this time, too?

ARLENE: He's got four more years at Bricktown.

MOTHER: Glad to hear it. Here . . . *(handing her a bucket)* Water.

(ARLENE fills up the bucket and MOTHER washes several dirty spots on the walls, floor and furniture. ARLENE knows better than to try to help. The DOCTOR walks downstage to find ARLIE for their counseling session.)

DOCTOR: So you refuse to go to camp?

ARLIE: Now why'd I want to go to your fuckin' camp? Camp's for babies. You can go shit in the woods if you want to, but I ain't goin'.

DOCTOR: Oh, you're goin'.

ARLIE: Wanna bet?

MOTHER: Arlie, I'm waitin'. *(For the water.)*

ARLIE: 'Sides, I'm waitin'.

DOCTOR: Waiting for what?

ARLIE: For Carl to come git me.

DOCTOR: And who is Carl?

ARLIE: Jus' some guy. We're goin' to Alabama.

DOCTOR: You don't go till we say you can go.

ARLIE: Carl's got a car.

DOCTOR: Does he have a driver's license to go with it?

ARLIE: *(enraged, impatient)* I'm goin' now.
(ARLIE *stalks away, then backs up toward the* DOCTOR *again. He has information she wants.)*

DOCTOR: Hey!

ARLENE: June picked out a name for the baby?

MOTHER: Clara . . . or Clarence. Got it from this fancy shampoo she bought.

ARLIE: I don't feel good. I'm pregnant, you know.

DOCTOR: The test was negative.

ARLIE: Well, I should know, shouldn't I?

DOCTOR: No. You want to be pregnant, is that it?

ARLIE: I wouldn't mind. Kids need somebody to bring 'em up right.

DOCTOR: Raising children is a big responsibility, you know.

ARLIE: Yeah, I know it. I ain't dumb. Everybody always thinks I'm so dumb.

DOCTOR: You could learn if you wanted to. That's what the teachers are here for.

ARLIE: Shit.

DOCTOR: Or so they say.

ARLIE: All they teach us is about geography. Why'd I need to know about Africa. Jungles and shit.

DOCTOR: They want you to know about other parts of the world.

ARLIE: Well, I ain't goin' there so whatta I care?

DOCTOR: What's this about Cindy?

ARLIE: *(hostile)* She told Mr. Dawson some lies about me.

DOCTOR: I bet.

ARLIE: She said I fuck my daddy for money.

DOCTOR: And what did you do when she said that?

ARLIE: What do you think I did? I beat the shit out of her.

DOCTOR: And that's a good way to work out your problem?

ARLIE: *(proudly)* She ain't done it since.

DOCTOR: She's been in traction, since.

ARLIE: So, whatta I care? She say it again, I'll do it again. Bitch!

ARLENE: *(looking down at the dirt* MOTHER *is gathering on the floor)* I ain't got a can. Just leave it.

MOTHER: And have you sweep it under the bed after I go? *(Wraps the dirt in a piece of newspaper and puts it in her laundry basket.)*

DOCTOR: *(looking at his clipboard)* You're on unit cleanup this week.

ARLIE: I done it last week!

DOCTOR: Then you should remember what to do. The session is over. *(getting up, walking away)* And stand up straight! And take off that hat!
(DOCTOR *and* ARLIE *go offstage as* MOTHER *finds* BENNIE's *hat.)*

MOTHER: This your hat?

ARLENE: No.

MOTHER: Guess Candy left it here.

ARLENE: Candy didn't leave nuthin'.

MOTHER: Then whose is it? *(ARLENE doesn't answer)* Do you know whose hat this is? *(ARLENE knows she made a mistake)* I'm askin' you a question and I want an answer. *(ARLENE turns her back)* Whose hat is this? You tell me right now, whose hat is this?

ARLENE: It's Bennie's.

MOTHER: And who's Bennie?

ARLENE: Guy drove me home from Pine Ridge. A guard.

MOTHER: *(upset)* I knew it. You been screwin' a goddamn guard. *(Throws the hat on the bed.)*

ARLENE: He jus' drove me up here, that's all.

MOTHER: Sure.

ARLENE: I git sick on the bus.

MOTHER: You expect me to believe that?

ARLENE: I'm tellin' you, he jus'—

MOTHER: No man alive gonna drive a girl five hundred miles for nuthin'.

ARLENE: He ain't never seen Kentucky.

MOTHER: It ain't Kentucky he wants to see.

ARLENE: He ain't gettin' nuthin' from me.

MOTHER: That's what you think.

ARLENE: He done some nice things for me at Pine Ridge. Gum, funny stories.

MOTHER: He'd be tellin' stories all right, tellin' his buddies where to find you.

ARLENE: He's gettin' us some dinner right now.

MOTHER: And how're you gonna pay him? Huh? Tell me that.

ARLENE: I ain't like that no more.

MOTHER: Oh you ain't. I'm your mother. I know what you'll do.

ARLENE: I tell you I ain't.

MOTHER: I knew it. Well, when you got another bastard in you, don't come cryin' to me, 'cause I done told you.

ARLENE: Don't worry.

MOTHER: An I'm gettin' myself outta here fore your boyfriend comes back.

ARLENE: (increasing anger) He ain't my boyfriend.

MOTHER: I been a lotta things, but I ain't dumb, Arlene. ("Arlene" is mocking.)

ARLENE: I didn't say you was. (Beginning to know how this is going to turn out.)

MOTHER: Oh no? You lied to me!

ARLENE: How?

MOTHER: You took my spread without even sayin' thank you. You're hintin' at comin' to my house for pot roast just like nuthin' ever happened, an all the time you're hidin' a goddamn guard under your bed. (furious) Uh-huh.

ARLENE: (quietly) Mama?

MOTHER: (cold, fierce) What?

ARLENE: What kind of meat makes a pot roast?

MOTHER: A roast makes a pot roast. Buy a roast. Shoulder, chuck . . .

ARLENE: Are you comin' back?

MOTHER: You ain't got no need for me.

ARLENE: I gotta ask you to come see me?

MOTHER: I come tonight, didn't I, an nobody asked me?

ARLENE: Just forget it.

MOTHER: (getting her things together) An if I hadn't told them about this apartment, you wouldn't be out at all, how 'bout that!

ARLENE: Forget it!

MOTHER: Don't you go talkin' to me that way. You remember who I am. I'm the one took you back after all you done all them years. I brung you that teapot. I scrubbed your place. You remember that when you talk to me.

ARLENE: Sure.

MOTHER: Uh-huh. (now goes to the bed, rips off the spread and stuffs it in her basket) I knowed

I shouldn't have come. You ain't changed a bit.

ARLENE: Same hateful brat, right?

MOTHER: (arms full, heading for the door) Same hateful brat. Right.

ARLENE: (rushing toward her) Mama . . .

MOTHER: Don't you touch me.
(MOTHER leaves. ARLENE stares out the door, stunned and hurt. Finally, she slams the door and turns back into the room.)

ARLENE: No! Don't you touch Mama, Arlie.
(RONNIE, a fellow juvenile offender, runs across the catwalk, waving a necklace and being chased by ARLIE.)

RONNIE: Arlie got a boyfriend, Arlie got a boyfriend. (throws the necklace downstage) Whoo!

ARLIE: (chasing him) Ronnie, you ugly mother, I'll smash your fuckin'—

ARLENE: (getting more angry) You might steal all—

RONNIE: (running down the stairs) Arlie got a boyfriend . . .

ARLIE: Gimme that necklace or I'll—

ARLENE: —or eat all Mama's precious pot roast.

RONNIE: (as they wrestle downstage) You'll tell the doctor on me? And get your private room back? (Laughing.)

ARLENE: (cold and hostile) No, don't touch Mama, Arlie. 'Cause you might slit Mama's throat. (Goes into the bathroom.)

ARLIE: You wanna swallow all them dirty teeth?

RONNIE: Tell me who give it to you.

ARLIE: No, you tell me where it's at.
(RONNIE breaks away, pushing ARLIE in the opposite direction, and runs for the necklace.)

RONNIE: It's right here. (drops it down his pants) Come an git it.

ARLIE: Oh now, that was really ignorant, you stupid pig.

RONNIE: (backing away, daring her) Jus' reach right in. First come, first served.

ARLIE: Now, how you gonna pee after I throw your weenie over the fence?

RONNIE: You ain't gonna do that, girl. You gonna fall in love.

(ARLIE turns vicious, pins RONNIE down, attacking. This is no longer play. He screams. The DOCTOR appears on the catwalk.)

DOCTOR: Arlie! *(Heads down the stairs to stop this.)*

CARL'S VOICE: *(from outside the apartment door)* Arlie!

DOCTOR: Arlie!

ARLIE: Stupid, ugly—

RONNIE: Help!

(ARLIE runs away and hides down left.)

DOCTOR: That's three more weeks of isolation, Arlie. *(bending down to RONNIE)* You all right? Can you walk?

RONNIE: *(looking back to ARLIE as he gets up in great pain)* She was tryin' to kill me.

DOCTOR: Yeah. Easy now. You should've known, Ronnie.

ARLIE: *(yelling at RONNIE)* You'll get yours, crybaby.

CARL'S VOICE: Arlie . . .

ARLIE: Yeah, I'm comin'!

CARL'S VOICE: Bad-lookin' dude says move your ass an open up this here door, girl.

(ARLENE does not come out of the bathroom. CARL twists the door knob violently, then kicks in the door and walks in. CARL is thin and cheaply dressed. CARL'S walk and manner are imitative of black pimps, but he can't quite carry it off.)

CARL: Where you at, mama?

ARLENE: Carl?

CARL: Who else? You 'spectin' Leroy Brown?

ARLENE: I'm takin' a bath!

CARL: *(walking toward the bathroom)* I like my ladies clean. Matter of professional pride.

ARLENE: Don't come in here.

CARL: *(mocking her tone)* Don't come in here. I seen it all before, girl.

ARLENE: I'm gittin' out. Sit down or somethin'.

CARL: *(talking loud enough for her to hear him through the door)* Ain't got the time. *(opens her purse, then searches the trunk)* Jus' come by to tell you it's tomorrow. We be takin' our feet to the New York street. *(as though she will be pleased)* No more fuckin' around with these jiveass southern turkeys. We're goin' to the big

city, baby. Get you some red shades and some red shorts an' the johns be linin' up fore we hit town. Four tricks a night. How's that sound? No use wearin' out that cute ass you got. Way I hear it, only way to git busted up there's be stupid, an I ain't lived this long bein' stupid.

ARLENE: *(coming out of the bathroom wearing a towel)* That's exactly how you lived your whole life—bein' stupid.

CARL: Arlie . . . *(moving in on her)* be sweet, sugar.

ARLENE: Still got your curls.

CARL: *(trying to hug her)* You're looking okay yourself.

ARLENE: Oh, Carl. *(Noticing the damage to the door, breaking away from any closeness he might try to force.)*

CARL: *(amused)* Bent up your door, some.

ARLENE: How come you're out?

CARL: Sweetheart, you done broke out once, been nabbed and sent to Pine Ridge and got yourself paroled since I been in. I got a right to a little free time too, ain't that right?

ARLENE: You escape?

CARL: Am I standin' here or am I standin' here? They been fuckin' with you, I can tell.

ARLENE: They gonna catch you.

CARL: *(going to the window)* Not where we're going. Not a chance.

ARLENE: Where you goin' they won't git you?

CARL: Remember that green hat you picked out for me down in Birmingham? Well, I ain't ever wore it yet, but I kin wear it in New York 'cause New York's where you wear whatever you feel like. One guy tol' me he saw this dude wearin' a whole ring of feathers roun' his leg, right here *(grabs his leg above the knee)* an he weren't in no circus nor no Indian neither.

ARLENE: I ain't seen you since Birmingham. How come you think I wanna see you now?

(ARLIE appears suddenly, confronts CARL.)

ARLIE: *(pointing as if there is a trick waiting)* Carl, I ain't goin' with that dude, he's weird.

CARL: 'Cause we gotta go collect the johns' money, that's "how come."

ARLIE: I don't need you pimpin' for me.

ARLENE: *(very strong)* I'm gonna work.

CARL: Work?

ARLENE: Yeah.

CARL: What's this "work"?

ARLIE: You always sendin' me to them ol' droolers . . .

CARL: You kin do two things, girl—

ARLIE: They slobberin' all over me . . .

CARL: Breakin' out an hookin'.

ARLIE: They tyin' me to the bed!

ARLENE: I mean real work.

ARLIE: *(now screaming, gets further away from him)* I could git killed working for you. Some sicko, some crazy drunk . . .
(ARLIE goes offstage. A GUARD puts her in the cell sometime before BENNIE's entrance.)

CARL: You forget, we seen it all on TV in the day room, you bustin' outta Lakewood like that. Fakin' that palsy fit, then beatin' that guard half to death with his own key ring. Whoo-ee! Then that spree you went on . . . stoppin' at that fillin' station for some cash, then kidnappin' the old dude pumpin' the gas.

ARLENE: Yeah.

CARL: Then that cab driver comes outta the bathroom an tries to mess with you and you shoots him with his own piece. *(fires an imaginary pistol)* That there's nice work, mama. *(Going over to her, putting his arms around her.)*

ARLENE: That gun . . . it went off, Carl.

CARL: *(getting more determined with his affection)* That's what guns do, doll. They go off.

BENNIE'S VOICE: *(from outside)* Arlene? Arlene?

CARL: Arlene? *(jumping up)* Well, la-de-da.
(BENNIE opens the door, carrying the chicken dinners. He is confused, seeing ARLENE wearing a towel and talking to CARL.)

ARLENE: Bennie, this here's Carl.

CARL: You're interruptin', Jack. Me an Arlie got business.

BENNIE: She's callin' herself Arlene.

CARL: I call my ladies what I feel like, chicken man, an you call yourself "gone."

BENNIE: I don't take orders from you.

CARL: Well, you been takin' orders from somebody, or did you git that outfit at the army surplus store?

ARLENE: Bennie brung me home from Pine Ridge.

CARL: *(walking toward him)* Oh, it's a guard now, is it? That chicken break out or what? *(Grabs the chicken.)*

BENNIE: I don't know what you're doin' here, but—

CARL: What you gonna do about it, huh? Lock me up in the toilet? You an who else, Batman?

BENNIE: *(taking the chicken back, walking calmly to the counter)* Watch your mouth, punk.

CARL: *(kicks a chair toward BENNIE)* Punk!

ARLENE: *(trying to stop this)* I'm hungry.

BENNIE: You heard her, she's hungry.

CARL: *(vicious)* Shut up! *(mocking)* Ossifer.

BENNIE: Arlene, tell this guy if he knows what's good for him . . .

CARL: *(walking to the counter where BENNIE has left the chicken)* Why don't you write me a parkin' ticket? *(shoves the chicken on the floor)* Don't fuck with me, dad. It ain't healthy.
(BENNIE pauses. A real standoff. Finally BENNIE bends down and picks up the chicken.)

BENNIE: You ain't worth dirtyin' my hands.
(CARL walks by him, laughing.)

CARL: Hey, Arlie. I got some dude to see. *(for BENNIE's benefit as he struts to the door)* What I need with another beat-up guard? All that blood, jus' ugly up my threads. *(very sarcastic)* Bye y'all.

ARLENE: Bye, Carl.
(CARL turns back quickly at the door, stopping BENNIE, who was following him.)

CARL: You really oughta shine them shoes, man. *(Vindictive laugh, slams the door in BENNIE's face.)*

BENNIE: *(relieved, trying to change the atmosphere)* Well, how 'bout if we eat? You'll catch your death dressed like that.

ARLENE: Turn around then.
(ARLENE gets a shabby housecoat from the closet. She puts it on over her towel, buttons it up, then pulls the towel out from under it. This has the look of a prison ritual.)

BENNIE: *(as she is dressing)* Your parole officer's gonna tell you to keep away from guys like that . . . for your own good, you know. Those types, just like the suckers on my tomatoes back home. Take everything right outta you. Gotta pull 'em off, Arlie, uh, Arlene.

ARLENE: Now, I'm decent now.

BENNIE: You hear what I said?

ARLENE: *(going to the bathroom for her hairbrush)* I told him that. That's exactly what I did tell him.

BENNIE: Who was that anyhow? *(Sits down on the bed, opens up the chicken.)*

ARLENE: *(from the bathroom)* Long time ago, me and Carl took a trip together.

BENNIE: When you was a kid, you mean?

ARLENE: I was at this place for kids.

BENNIE: And Carl was there?

ARLENE: No, he picked me up an we went to Alabama. There was this wreck an all. I ended up at Lakewood for forgery. It was him that done it. Got me pregnant too.

BENNIE: That was Joey's father?

ARLENE: Yeah, but he don't know that. *(Sits down.)*

BENNIE: Just as well. Guy like that, don't know what they'd do.

ARLENE: Mother was here while ago. Says she's seen Joey. *(Taking a napkin from* BENNIE.*)*

BENNIE: Wish I had a kid. Life ain't, well, complete, without no kids to play ball with an take fishin'. Dorrie, though, she had them backaches an that neuralgia, day I married her to the day she died. Good woman though. No drinkin', no card playin', real sweet voice . . . what was that song she used to sing? . . . Oh, yeah . . .

ARLENE: She says Joey's a real good-lookin' kid.

BENNIE: Well, his mom ain't bad.

ARLENE: At Lakewood, they tried to git me to have an abortion.

BENNIE: They was just thinkin' of you, Arlene.

ARLENE: *(matter-of-fact, no self-pity)* I told 'em I'd kill myself if they done that. I would have too.

BENNIE: But they took him away after he was born.

ARLENE: Yeah. *(BENNIE *waits, knowing she is about to say more)* An I guess I went crazy after that. Thought if I could jus' git out an find him . . .

BENNIE: I don't remember any of that on the TV.

ARLENE: No.

BENNIE: Just remember you smilin' at the cameras, yellin' how you tol' that cab driver not to touch you.

ARLENE: I never seen his cab. *(Forces herself to eat.)*

ARLIE: *(in the cell, holding a pillow and singing)* Rock-a-bye baby, in the tree top, when the wind blows, the cradle will . . . *(not remembering)* cradle will . . . *(now talking)* What you gonna be when you grow up, pretty boy baby? You gonna be a doctor? You gonna give people medicine an take out they . . . no, don't be no doctor . . . be . . . be a preacher . . . sayin' Our Father who is in heaven . . . heaven, that's where people go when they dies, when doctors can't save 'em or somebody kills 'em fore they even git a chance to . . . no, don't be no preacher neither . . . be . . . go to school an learn good *(tone begins to change)* so you kin . . . make everbody else feel so stupid all the time. Best thing you to be is stay a baby 'cause nobody beats up on babies or puts them . . . *(much more quiet)* that ain't true, baby. People is mean to babies, so you stay right here with me so nobody kin git you an make you cry and they lay one finger on you *(hostile)* an I'll beat the screamin' shit right out of 'em. They even blow on you an I'll kill 'em.

*(BENNIE *and* ARLENE *have finished their dinner.* BENNIE *puts one carton of slaw in the refrigerator, then picks up all the paper, making a garbage bag out of one of the sacks.)*

BENNIE: Ain't got a can, I guess. Jus' use this ol' sack for now.

ARLENE: I ain't never emptyin' another garbage can.

BENNIE: Yeah, I reckon you know how by now. *(yawns)* You 'bout ready for bed?

ARLENE: *(stands up)* I s'pose.

BENNIE: *(stretches)* Little tired myself.

ARLENE: *(dusting the crumbs off the bed)* Thanks for the chicken.

BENNIE: You're right welcome. You look beat. How 'bout I rub your back. *(Grabs her shoulders.)*

ARLENE: *(pulling away)* No. *(walking to the sink)* You go on now.

BENNIE: Oh come on. *(wiping his hands on his pants)* I ain't all that tired.

ARLENE: *I'm* tired.

BENNIE: Well, see then, a back rub is just what the doctor ordered.

ARLENE: No. I don't . . . *(pulling away)*
(BENNIE grabs her shoulders and turns her around, sits her down hard on the trunk, starts rubbing her back and neck.)

BENNIE: Muscles git real tightlike, right in here.

ARLENE: You hurtin' me.

BENNIE: Has to hurt a little or it won't do no good.

ARLENE: *(jumps, he has hurt her)* Oh, stop it! *(She slips away from him and out into the room. She is frightened.)*

BENNIE: *(smiling, coming after her, toward the bed)* Be lot nicer if you was layin' down. Wouldn't hurt as much.

ARLENE: Now, I ain't gonna start yellin'. I'm jus' tellin' you to go.

BENNIE: *(straightens up as though he's going to cooperate)* Okay then. I'll jus' git my hat.
(He reaches for the hat, then turns quickly, grabs her and throws her down on the bed. He starts rubbing again.)

BENNIE: Now, you just relax. Don't you go bein' scared of me.

ARLENE: You ain't gettin' nuthin' from me.

BENNIE: I don't want nuthin', honey. Jus' tryin' to help you sleep.

ARLENE: *(struggling)* Don't you call me honey.
(BENNIE stops rubbing, but keeps one hand on her back. He rubs her hair with his free hand.)

BENNIE: See? Don't that feel better?

ARLENE: Let me up.

BENNIE: Why, I ain't holdin' you down.

ARLENE: Then let me up.

BENNIE: *(takes hands off)* Okay. Git up.
(ARLENE turns over slowly, begins to lift herself up on her elbows. BENNIE puts one hand on her leg.)

ARLENE: Move your hand. *(She gets up, moves across the room.)*

BENNIE: I'd be happy to stay here with you tonight. Make sure you'll be all right. You ain't spent a night by yourself for a long time.

ARLENE: I remember how.

BENNIE: Well how you gonna git up? You got a alarm?

ARLENE: It ain't all that hard.

BENNIE: *(puts one hand in his pocket, leers a little)* Oh yeah it is. *(walks toward her again)* Gimme a kiss. Then I'll go.

ARLENE: *(edging along the counter, seeing she's trapped)* You stay away from me.
(BENNIE reaches for her, clamping her hands behind her, pressing up against her.)

BENNIE: Now what's it going to hurt you to give me a little ol' kiss?

ARLENE: *(struggling)* Git out! I said git out!

BENNIE: You don't want me to go. You're jus' beginning to git interested. Your ol' girlie temper's flarin' up. I like that in a woman.

ARLENE: Yeah, you'd love it if I'd swat you one. *(Getting away from him.)*

BENNIE: I been hit by you before. I kin take anything you got.

ARLENE: I could mess you up good.

BENNIE: Now, Arlie. You ain't had a man in a long time. And the ones you had been no-count.

ARLENE: Git out!
(She slaps him. He returns the slap.)

BENNIE: *(moving in)* Ain't natural goin' without it too long. Young thing like you. Git all shriveled up.

ARLENE: All right, you sunuvabitch, you asked for it!
(She goes into a violent rage, hitting and kicking him. BENNIE overpowers her capably, prison-guard style.)

BENNIE: *(amused)* Little outta practice, ain't you?

ARLENE: *(screaming)* I'll kill you, you creep!
(The struggle continues, BENNIE pinning her arms under his legs as he kneels over her on the bed. ARLENE is terrified and in pain.)

BENNIE: You will? You'll kill ol' Bennie . . . kill ol' Bennie like you done that cab driver?

(A cruel reminder he employs to stun and mock her. ARLENE *looks as though she has been hit.* BENNIE, *still fired up, unzips his pants.)*

ARLENE: *(passive, cold and bitter)* This how you got your Dorrie, rapin'?

BENNIE: *(unbuttoning his shirt)* That what you think this is, rape?

ARLENE: I oughta know.

BENNIE: Uh-huh.

ARLENE: First they unzip their pants.

*(*BENNIE *pulls his shirttail out.)*

ARLENE: Sometimes they take off their shirt.

BENNIE: They do huh?

ARLENE: But mostly, they just pull it out and stick it in.

*(*BENNIE *stops, finally hearing what she has been saying. He straightens up, obviously shocked. He puts his arms back in his shirt.)*

BENNIE: Don't you call me no rapist. *(pause, then insistent)* No, I ain't no rapist, Arlie. *(Gets up, begins to tuck his shirt back in and zip up his pants.)*

ARLENE: And I ain't Arlie.

*(*ARLENE *remains on the bed as he continues dressing.)*

BENNIE: No I guess you ain't.

ARLENE: *(quietly and painfully)* Arlie coulda killed you.

E N D   O F   A C T   O N E

Prologue

These announcements are heard during the last five minutes of the intermission.

LOUDSPEAKER VOICE: Garden workers will, repeat, will, report for work this afternoon. Bring a hat and raincoat and wear boots. All raincoats will be checked at the front gate at the end of work period and returned to you after supper.

Your attention please. A checkerboard was not returned to the recreation area after dinner last night. Anyone with information regarding the black and red checkerboard missing from the recreation area will please contact Mrs. Duvall after lunch. No checkerboards or checkers will be distributed until this board is returned.

Betty Rickey and Mary Alice Wolf report to the laundry. Doris Creech and Arlie Holsclaw report immediately to the superintendent's office. The movie this evening will be *Dirty Harry* starring Clint Eastwood. Doris Creech and Arlie Holsclaw report to the superintendent's office immediately.

The bus from St. Mary's this Sunday will arrive at 1:00 P.M. as usual. Those residents expecting visitors on that bus will gather on the front steps promptly at 1:20 and proceed with the duty officer to the visiting area after it has been confirmed that you have a visitor on the bus.

Attention all residents. Attention all residents. *(pause)* Mrs. Helen Carson has taught needlework classes here at Pine Ridge for thirty years. She will be retiring at the end of this month and moving to Florida where her husband has bought a trailer park. The resident council and the superintendent's staff has decided on a suitable retirement present. We want every resident to participate in this project— which is—a quilt, made from scraps of material collected from the residents and sewn together by residents and staff alike. The procedure will be as follows. A quilting room has been set up in an empty storage area just off the infirmary. Scraps of fabric will be collected as officers do evening count. Those residents who would enjoy cutting up old uniforms and bedding no longer in use should sign up for this detail with your dorm officer. If you would like to sign your name and send Mrs. Carson some special message on your square of fabric, the officers will have tubes of embroidery paint for that purpose. The backing for the quilt has been donated by the Women's Associates as well as the refreshments for the retirement party to be held after lunch on the thirtieth. Thank you very much for your attention and participation in this worthwhile tribute to someone we are all very fond of here. You may resume work at this time. Doris Creech and Arlie Holsclaw report to the superintendent's office immediately.

ACT TWO

Lights fade. When they come up, it is the next morning. ARLENE *is asleep on the bed.* ARLIE *is locked in a maximum-security cell. We do not see the officer to whom she speaks.*

ARLIE: No, I don't have to shut up, neither. You already got me in seg-re-ga-tion, what else you gonna do? I got all day to sleep, while everybody else is out bustin' ass in the laundry. *(laughs)* Hey! I know . . . you ain't gotta go do no dorm count, I'll just tell you an you jus' sit. Huh? You 'preciate that? Ease them corns you been moanin' about . . . yeah . . . okay. Write this down. *(pride, mixed with alternating contempt and amusement)* Startin' down by the john on the back side, we got Mary Alice. Sleeps with her pillow stuffed in her mouth. Says her mom says it'd keep her from grindin' down her teeth or somethin'. She be suckin' that pillow like she gettin' paid for it. *(laughs)* Next, it's Betty the Frog. Got her legs all opened out like some fuckin' . . . *(makes croaking noises)* Then it's Doris eatin' pork rinds. Thinks somebody gonna grab 'em outta her mouth if she eats 'em during the day. Doris ain't dumb. She fat, but she ain't dumb. Hey! You notice how many girls is fat here? Then it be Rhonda, snorin', Marvene, wheezin', and Suzanne, coughin'. Then Clara an Ellie be still whisperin'. Family shit, who's gettin' outta line, which girls is gittin' a new work 'signment, an who kin git extra desserts an for how much. Them's the two really run this place. My bed right next to Ellie, for sure it's got some of her shit hid in it by now. Crackers or some

crap gonna leak out all over my sheets. Last time I found a fuckin' grilled cheese in my pillow. Even had two of them little warty pickles. Christ! Okay. Linda and Lucille. They be real quiet, but they ain't sleepin'. Prayin', that's them. Linda be sayin' them Hell Marys till you kin just about scream. An Lucille, she tol' me once she didn't believe in no God, jus' some stupid spirits whooshin' aroun' everwhere makin' people do stuff. Weird. Now, I'm goin' back down the other side, there's . . . *(screams)* I'd like to see you try it! I been listenin' at you for the last three hours. Your husband's gettin' laid off an your lettuce is gettin' eat by rabbits. Crap City. *You* shut up! Whadda I care if I wake everybody up? I want the nurse . . . I'm gittin' sick in here . . . an there's bugs in here!

(The light comes up in the apartment. Faint morning traffic sounds are heard. ARLENE *does not wake up. The* WARDEN *walks across the catwalk. A* GUARD *catches up with him near* ARLIE'S *cell.* BENNIE *is stationed at the far end of the walk.)*

LOUDSPEAKER VOICE: Dorm A may now eat lunch.

GUARD (EVANS): Warden, I thought 456 . . . *(nodding in* ARLIE'S *direction)* was leavin' here.

WARDEN: Is there some problem?

GUARD (EVANS): Oh, we can take care of her all right. We're just tired of takin' her shit, if you'll pardon the expression.

ARLIE: You ain't seen nuthin' yet, you mother.

WARDEN: Washington will decide on her transfer. Till then, you do your job.

GUARD (EVANS): She don't belong here. Rest of—

LOUDSPEAKER VOICE: Betty Rickey and Mary Alice Wolf report to the laundry.

GUARD (EVANS): Most of these girls are mostly nice people, go along with things. She needs a cage.

ARLIE: *(vicious)* I need a knife.

WARDEN: *(very curt)* Had it occurred to you that we could send the rest of them home and just keep her? *(Walks away.)*

LOUDSPEAKER VOICE: Dorm A may now eat lunch. A Dorm to lunch.

GUARD (EVANS):   *(turning around, muttering to himself)* Oh, that's a swell idea. Let everybody out except bitches like Holsclaw. *(she makes an obscene gesture at him, he turns back toward the catwalk)* Smartass warden, thinks he's runnin' a hotel.

BENNIE: Give you some trouble, did she?

GUARD (EVANS):   I can wait.

BENNIE: For what?

GUARD (EVANS):   For the day she tries gettin' out an I'm here by myself. I'll show that screechin' slut a thing or two.

BENNIE: That ain't the way, Evans.

GUARD (EVANS):   The hell it ain't. Beat the livin'—

BENNIE: Outta a little thing like her? Gotta do her like all the rest. You got your shorts washed by givin' Betty Rickey Milky Ways. You git your chairs fixed givin' Frankie Hill extra time in the shower with Lucille Smith. An you git ol' Arlie girl to behave herself with a stick of gum. Gotta have her brand, though.

GUARD (EVANS):   You screwin' that wildcat?

BENNIE: *(starts walk to* ARLIE's *cell)* Watch. *(*ARLIE *is silent as he approaches, but is watching intently)* Now, *(to nobody in particular)* where was that piece of Juicy Fruit I had in this pocket. Gotta be here somewhere. *(takes a piece of gum out of his pocket and drops it within* ARLIE's *reach)* Well, *(feigning disappointment)* I guess I already chewed it. *(*ARLIE *reaches for the gum and gets it)* Oh, *(looking down at her now)* how's it goin', kid?

ARLIE: Okay.

*(*ARLIE *says nothing more, but unwraps the gum and chews it.* BENNIE *leaves the cell area, motioning to the other guard as if to say, "See, that's how it's done." A loud siren goes by in the street below the apartment.* ARLENE *bolts up out of bed, then turns back to it quickly, making it up in a frenzied, ritual manner. As she tucks the spread up under the pillow, the siren stops and so does she. For the first time, now, she realizes where she is and the inappropriateness of the*

habit she has just played out. A jackhammer noise gets louder. She walks over to the window and looks out. There is a wolf whistle from a worker below. She shuts the window in a fury. She looks around the room as if trying to remember what she is doing there. She looks at her watch, now aware that it is late and that she has slept in her clothes.)

ARLENE: People don't sleep in their clothes, Arlene. An people git up fore noon.

*(*ARLENE *makes a still-disoriented attempt to pull herself together—changing shoes, combing her hair, washing her face—as prison life continues on the catwalk. The* WARDEN *walks toward* ARLIE, *stopping some distance from her but talking directly to her, as he checks files or papers.)*

WARDEN: Good afternoon, Arlie.

ARLIE: Fuck you. *(*WARDEN *walks away)* Wait! I wanna talk to you.

WARDEN: I'm listening.

ARLIE: When am I gittin' outta here?

WARDEN: That's up to you.

ARLIE: The hell it is.

WARDEN: When you can show that you can be with the other girls, you can get out.

ARLIE: How'm I supposed to prove that bein' in here?

WARDEN: And then you can have mail again and visitors.

ARLIE: You're just fuckin' with me. You ain't ever gonna let me out. I been in this ad-just-ment room four months, I think.

WARDEN: Arlie, you see the other girls in the dorm walking around, free to do whatever they want? If we felt the way you seem to think we do, everyone would be in lockup. When you get out of segregation, you can go to the records office and have your time explained to you.

ARLIE: It won't make no sense.

WARDEN: They'll go through it all very slowly . . . when you're eligible for parole, how many days of good time you have, how many industrial days you've earned, what constitutes meritorious good time . . . and how many days you're set back for your write-ups and all your time in segregation.

ARLIE: I don't even remember what I done to git this lockup.

WARDEN: Well, I do. And if you ever do it again, or anything like it again, you'll be right back in lockup where you will stay until you forget *how* to do it.

ARLIE: What was it?

WARDEN: You just remember what I said.

ARLENE: Now then . . . *(Sounds as if she has something in mind to do. Looks as though she doesn't.)*

ARLIE: What was it?

WARDEN: Oh, and Arlie, the prison chaplain will be coming by to visit you today.

ARLIE: I don't want to see no chaplain!

WARDEN: Did I ask you if you wanted to see the chaplain? No, I did not. I said, the chaplain will be coming by to visit you today. *(to an unseen guard)* Mrs. Roberts, why hasn't this light bulb been replaced?

ARLIE: *(screaming)* Get out of my hall!

(The WARDEN *walks away.* ARLENE *walks to the refrigerator and opens it. She picks out the carton of slaw* BENNIE *put there last night. She walks away from the door, then turns around, remembering to close it. She looks at the slaw, as a* GUARD *comes up to* ARLIE's *cell with a plate.)*

ARLENE: I ain't never eatin' no more scrambled eggs.

GUARD (CALDWELL): Chow time, cutie pie.

ARLIE: These eggs ain't scrambled, they's throwed up! And I want a fork!

*(*ARLENE *realizes she has no fork, then fishes one out of the garbage sack from last night. She returns to the bed, takes a bite of slaw and gets her wallet out of her purse. She lays the bills out on the bed one at a time.)*

ARLENE: That's for coffee . . . and that's for milk and bread . . . an that's cookies . . . an cheese and crackers . . . and shampoo an soap . . . and bacon an livercheese. No, pickle loaf . . . an ketchup and some onions . . . an peanut butter an jelly . . . and shoe polish.

Well, ain't no need gettin' everything all at once. Coffee, milk, ketchup, cookies, cheese, onions, jelly. Coffee, milk . . . oh, shampoo . . . *(There is a banging on the door.)*

RUBY'S VOICE: *(yelling)* Candy, I gotta have my five dollars back.

ARLENE: *(quickly stuffing her money back in her wallet)* Candy ain't here!

RUBY'S VOICE: It's Ruby, upstairs. She's got five dollars I loaned her . . . Arlie? That Arlie? Candy told me her sister be . . . *(*ARLENE *opens the door hesitantly.)*

RUBY: It is Arlie, right?

ARLENE: It's Arlene. *(Does not extend her hand.)*

RUBY: See, I got these shoes in layaway . . . *(puts her hand back in her pocket)* she said you been . . . you just got . . . you seen my money?

ARLENE: No.

RUBY: I don't get 'em out today they go back on the shelf.

ARLENE: *(doesn't understand)* They sell your shoes?

RUBY: Yeah. Welcome back.

ARLENE: Thank you.

RUBY: She coulda put it in my mailbox. *(*RUBY *starts to leave.* ARLENE *is closing the door when* RUBY *turns around.)*

RUBY: Uh . . . listen . . . if you need a phone, I got one most of the time.

ARLENE: I do have to make this call.

RUBY: Ain't got a book though . . . well, I got one but it's holdin' up my bed. *(Laughs.)*

ARLENE: I got the number.

RUBY: Well, then . . .

ARLENE: Would you . . . wanna come in?

RUBY: You sure I'm not interruptin' anything?

ARLENE: I'm s'posed to call my parole officer.

RUBY: Good girl. Most of them can't talk but you call 'em anyway. *(*ARLENE *does not laugh)* Candy go back to that creep?

ARLENE: I guess.

RUBY: I's afraid of that. *(looking around)* Maybe an envelope with my name on it? Really cleaned out the place, didn't she?

ARLENE: Yeah. Took everything.
(They laugh a little.)

RUBY: Didn't have much. Didn't do nuthin' here 'cept . . . sleep.

ARLENE: Least the rent's paid till the end of the month. I'll be workin' by then.

RUBY: You ain't seen Candy in a while.

ARLENE: No. Think she was in the seventh grade when—

RUBY: She's growed up now, you know.

ARLENE: Yeah. I was thinkin' she might come by.

RUBY: Honey, she won't be comin' by. He keeps all his . . . *(starting over)* his place is pretty far from here. But . . . *(Stops, trying to decide what to say.)*

ARLENE: But what?

RUBY: But she had a lot of friends, you know. *They* might be comin' by.

ARLENE: Men, you mean.

RUBY: Yeah. *(Quietly, waiting for* ARLENE'S *reaction.)*

ARLENE: *(realizing the truth)* Mother said he was her boyfriend.

RUBY: I shouldn't have said nuthin'. I jus' didn't want you to be surprised if some john showed up, his tongue hangin' out an all. *(Sits down on the bed.)*

ARLENE: It's okay. I shoulda known anyway. *(now suddenly angry)* No, it ain't okay. Guys got their dirty fingernails all over her. Some pimp's out buyin' green pants while she . . . Goddamn her.

RUBY: Hey now, that ain't your problem. *(Moves toward her,* ARLENE *backs away.)*

ARLIE: *(pointing)* You stick your hand in here again Doris an I'll bite it off.

RUBY: She'll figure it out soon enough.

ARLIE: *(pointing to another person)* An you, you ain't my mama, so you can cut the mama crap.

ARLENE: I wasn't gonna cuss no more.

RUBY: Nuthin' in the parole rules says you can't get pissed. My first day outta Gilbertsville I done the damn craziest . . . *(*ARLENE *looks around, surprised to hear she has done time)* Oh yeah, a long time ago, but . . . hell, I

heaved a whole gallon of milk right out the window my first day.

ARLENE: *(somewhat cheered)* It hit anybody?

RUBY: It bounced! Made me feel a helluva lot better. I said, "Ruby, if a gallon of milk can bounce back, so kin you."

ARLENE: That's really what you thought?

RUBY: Well, not exactly. I had to keep sayin' it for 'bout a year fore I finally believed it. I's moppin' this lady's floor once an she come in an heard me saying "gallon a milk, gallon a milk," fired me. She did. Thought I was too crazy to mop her floors.
*(*RUBY *laughs, but is still bitter.* ARLENE *wasn't listening.* RUBY *wants to change the subject now.)*

RUBY: Hey! You have a good trip? Candy said you was in Arkansas.

ARLENE: Alabama. It was okay. This guard, well he used to be a guard, he just quit. He ain't never seen Kentucky, so he drove me. *(Watching for* RUBY'S *response.)*

RUBY: Pine Ridge?

ARLENE: Yeah.

RUBY: It's coed now, ain't it?

ARLENE: Yeah. That's dumb, you know. They put you with men so's they can git you if you're seen with 'em.

RUBY: S'posed to be more natural, I guess.

ARLENE: I guess.

RUBY: Well, I say it sucks. Still a prison. No matter how many pictures they stick up on the walls or how many dirty movies they show, you still gotta be counted five times a day. *(now beginning to worry about* ARLENE'S *silence)* You don't seem like Candy said.

ARLENE: She tell you I was a killer?

RUBY: More like the meanest bitch that ever walked. I seen lots worse than you.

ARLENE: I been lots worse.

RUBY: Got to you, didn't it?
*(*ARLENE *doesn't respond, but* RUBY *knows she's right.)*

RUBY: Well, you jus' gotta git over it. Bein' out, you gotta—

ARLENE: Don't you start in on me.

RUBY: *(realizing her tone)* Right, sorry.

ARLENE: It's okay.

RUBY: Ex-cons is the worst. I'm sorry.

ARLENE: It's okay.

RUBY: Done that about a year ago. New waitress we had. Gave my little goin'-straight speech, "No booze, no men, no buyin' on credit," shit like that, she quit that very night. Stole my fuckin' raincoat on her way out. Some speech, huh? *(Laughs, no longer resenting this theft.)*

ARLENE: You a waitress?

RUBY: I am the Queen of Grease. Make the finest french fries you ever did see.

ARLENE: You make a lot of money?

RUBY: I sure know how to. But I ain't about to go back inside for doin' it. Cookin' out's better'n eatin' in, I say.

ARLENE: You think up all these things you say?

RUBY: Know what I hate? Makin' salads—cuttin' up all that stuff 'n floppin' it in a bowl. Some day . . . some day . . . I'm gonna hear "tossed salad" an I'm gonna do jus' that. Toss out a tomato, toss out a head a lettuce, toss out a big ol' carrot. *(Miming the throwing and enjoying herself immensely.)*

ARLENE: *(laughing)* Be funny seein' all that stuff flyin' outta the kitchen.

RUBY: Hey Arlene! *(gives her a friendly pat)* You had your lunch yet?

ARLENE: *(pulling away immediately)* I ain't hungry.

RUBY: *(carefully)* I got raisin toast.

ARLENE: No. *(Goes over to the sink, twists knobs as if to stop a leak.)*

ARLIE: Whaddaya mean, what did she do to me? You got eyes or is they broke? You only seein' what you feel like seein'. I git ready to protect myself from a bunch of weirdos an then you look.

ARLENE: Sink's stopped up. *(Begins to work on it.)*

ARLIE: You ain't seein' when they's leavin' packs of cigarettes on my bed an then thinking I owe 'em or somethin'.

RUBY: Stopped up, huh? *(Squashing a bug on the floor.)*

ARLIE: You ain't lookin' when them kitchen workers lets up their mommies in line nights they know they only baked half enough brownies.

RUBY: Let me try.

ARLIE: You ain't seein' all the letters comin' in an goin' out with visitors. I'll tell you somethin'. One of them workmen buries dope for Betty Rickey in little plastic bottles under them sticker bushes at the water tower. You see that? No, you only seein' me. Well, you don't see shit.

RUBY: *(a quiet attempt)* Gotta git you some Drano if you're gonna stay here.

ARLIE: I'll tell you what she done. Doris brung me some rollers from the beauty-school class. Three fuckin' pink rollers. Them plastic ones with the little holes. I didn't ask her. She jus' done it.

RUBY: Let me give her a try.

ARLENE: I can fix my own sink.

ARLIE: I's stupid. I's thinkin' maybe she were different from all them others. Then that night everbody disappears from the john and she's wantin' to brush my hair. Sure, brush my hair. How'd I know she was gonna crack her head open on the sink. I jus' barely even touched her.

RUBY: *(walking to the bed now, digging through her purse)* Want a Chiclet?

ARLIE: You ain't asked what she was gonna do to me. Huh? When you gonna ask that? You don't give a shit about that 'cause Doris such a good girl.

ARLENE: *(giving up)* Don't work.

RUBY: We got a dishwasher quittin' this week if you're interested.

ARLENE: I need somethin' that pays good.

RUBY: You type?

ARLENE: No.

RUBY: Do any clerk work?

ARLENE: No.

RUBY: Any keypunch?

ARLENE: No.

RUBY: Well, then I hate to tell you, but all us old-timers already got all the good cookin' and cleanin' jobs. *(smashes another bug, goes to the cabinet to look for the bug spray)* She even took the can of Raid! Just as well, empty anyway. (ARLENE *doesn't respond*) She hit the bugs with it. (*still no response*) Now, there's that phone call you was talkin' about.

ARLENE: Yeah.

RUBY: (*walking toward the door*) An I'll git you that number for the dishwashin' job, just in case. (ARLENE *backs off*) How 'bout cards? You play any cards? Course you do. I get sick of beatin' myself all the time at solitaire. Damn borin' bein' so good at it.

ARLENE: (*goes for her purse*) Maybe I'll jus' walk to the corner an make my call from there.

RUBY: It's always broke.

ARLENE: What?

RUBY: The phone . . . at the corner. Only it ain't at the corner. It's inside the A & P.

ARLENE: Maybe it'll be fixed.

RUBY: Look, I ain't gonna force you to play cards with me. It's time for my programs anyway.

ARLENE: I gotta git some pickle loaf an . . . things.

RUBY: Suit yourself. I'll be there if you change your mind.

ARLENE: I have some things I gotta do here first.

RUBY: (*trying to leave on a friendly basis*) Look, I'll charge you a dime if it'll make you feel better.

ARLENE: (*takes her seriously*) Okay.

RUBY: (*laughs, then realizes* ARLENE *is serious*) Mine's the one with the little picture of Johnny Cash on the door.

(RUBY *leaves. Singing to the tune of "I'll Toe the Line,"* BENNIE *walks across the catwalk carrying a tray with cups and a pitcher of water.* ARLENE *walks toward the closet. She is delaying going to the store, but is determined to go. She checks little things in the room, remembers to get a scarf, changes shoes, checks her wallet. Finally, as she is walking out, she stops and looks at the picture of Jesus, then moves closer, having noticed a dirty spot. She goes back into the bathroom for a tissue, wets it in her mouth, then dabs at the offending spot. She puts the tissue in her purse, then leaves the room when noted.*)

BENNIE: I keep my pants up with a piece of twine. I keep my eyes wide open all the time. Da da da

da-da da da da da da. If you'll be mine, please pull the twine.

ARLIE: You can't sing for shit.

BENNIE: (*starts down the stairs toward* ARLIE'S *cell*) You know what elephants got between their toes?

ARLIE: I don't care.

BENNIE: Slow natives. (*Laughs.*)

ARLIE: That ain't funny.

GUARD (EVANS): (*as* BENNIE *opens* ARLIE'S *door*) Hey, Davis.

BENNIE: Conversation is rehabilitatin', Evans. Want some water?

ARLIE: Okay.

BENNIE: How about some Kool-Aid to go in it? (*Gives her a glass of water.*)

ARLIE: When does the chaplain come?

BENNIE: Want some gum?

ARLIE: Is it today?

BENNIE: Kool-Aid's gone up, you know. Fifteen cents and tax. You get out, you'll learn all about that.

ARLIE: Does the chaplain come today?

BENNIE: (*going back up the catwalk*) Income tax, sales tax, property tax, gas and electric, water, rent—

ARLIE: Hey!

BENNIE: Yeah, he's comin', so don't mess up.

ARLIE: I ain't.

BENNIE: What's he tell you anyway, get you so starry-eyed?

ARLIE: He jus' talks to me.

BENNIE: I talk to you.

ARLIE: Where's Frankie Hill?

BENNIE: Gone.

ARLIE: Out?

BENNIE: Pretty soon.

ARLIE: When.

BENNIE: Miss her don't you? Ain't got nobody to bullshit with. Stories you gals tell . . . whoo-ee!

ARLIE: Get to cut that grass now, Frankie, honey.

BENNIE: Huh?

ARLIE: Stupidest thing she said. (*gently*) Said first thing she was gonna do when she got out— (ARLENE *leaves the apartment.*)

BENNIE: Get laid.

ARLIE: Shut up. First thing was gonna be going to the garage. Said it always smelled like car grease an turpur . . . somethin'.

BENNIE: Turpentine.

ARLIE: Yeah, an gasoline, wet. An she'll bend down an squirt oil in the lawnmower, red can with a long pointy spout. Then cut the grass in the backyard, up an back, up an back. They got this grass catcher on it. Says she likes scoopin' up that cut grass and spreadin' it out under the trees. Says it makes her real hungry for some lunch. *(A quiet curiosity about all this.)*

BENNIE: I got a power mower, myself.

ARLIE: They done somethin' to her. Took out her nerves or somethin'. She . . .

BENNIE: She jus' got better, that's all.

ARLIE: Hah. Know what else? They give her a fork to eat with last week. A fork. A fuckin' fork. Now how long's it been since I had a fork to eat with?

BENNIE: *(getting ready to leave the cell)* Wish I could help you with that, honey.

ARLIE: *(loud)* Don't call me honey.

BENNIE: *(locks the door behind him)* That's my girl.

ARLIE: I ain't your girl.

BENNIE: *(on his way back up the stairs)* Screechin' wildcat.

ARLIE: *(very quiet)* What time is it?

(ARLENE walks back into the apartment. She is out of breath and has some trouble getting the door open. She is carrying a big sack of groceries. As she sets the bag on the counter, it breaks open, spilling cans and packages all over the floor. She just stands and looks at the mess. She takes off her scarf and sets down her purse, still looking at the spilled groceries. Finally, she bends down and picks up the package of pickle loaf. She starts to put it on the counter, then turns suddenly and throws it at the door. She stares at it as it falls.)

ARLENE: Bounce? *(in disgust)* Shit.

(ARLENE sinks to the floor. She tears open the package of pickle loaf and eats a piece of it. She is still angry, but is completely unable to do anything about her anger.)

ARLIE: Who's out there? Is anybody out there? *(reading)* Depart from evil and do good. *(yelling)* Now, you pay attention out there 'cause this is right out of the Lord's mouth. *(reading)* And dwell, that means live, dwell for-ever-more. *(speaking)* That's like for longer than I've been in here or longer than . . . this Bible the chaplain give me's got my name right in the front of it. Hey! Somebody's s'posed to be out there watchin' me. Wanna hear some more? *(reading)* For the Lord for . . . *(the word is "forsaketh")* I can't read in here, you turn on my light, you hear me? Or let me out and I'll go read it in the TV room. Please let me out. I won't scream or nuthin'? I'll just go right to sleep, okay? Somebody! I'll go right to sleep. Okay? You won't even know I'm there. Hey! Goddammit, somebody let me out of here, I can't stand it in here anymore. Somebody! *(Her spirit finally broken.)*

ARLENE: *(she draws her knees up, wraps her arms around them and rests her head on her arms)* Jus' gotta git a job an make some money an everything will be all right. You hear me, Arlene? You git yourself up an go find a job. *(continues to sit)* An you kin start by cleanin' up this mess you made 'cause food don't belong on the floor.

(ARLENE still doesn't get up. CARL appears in the doorway of the apartment. When he sees ARLENE on the floor, he goes into a fit of vicious, sadistic laughter.)

CARL: What's happenin', mama? You havin' lunch with the bugs?

ARLENE: *(quietly)* Fuck off.

CARL: *(threatening)* What'd you say?

ARLENE: *(reconsidering)* Go away.

CARL: You watch your mouth or I'll close it up for you.

(ARLENE stands up now. CARL goes to the window and looks out, as if checking for someone.)

ARLENE: They after you, ain't they?

(CARL sniffs, scratches at his arm. He finds a plastic bag near the bed, stuffed with brightly colored knitted things. He pulls out baby sweaters, booties and caps.)

CARL: What the fuck is this?

ARLENE: You leave them be.

CARL: You got a baby hid here somewhere? I found its little shoes. (*Laughs, dangling them in front of him.*)

ARLENE: (*chasing him*) Them's mine.

CARL: Aw, sugar, I ain't botherin' nuthin'. Just lookin'. (*Pulls more out of the sack, dropping one or two booties on the floor, kicking them away.*)

ARLENE: (*picking up what he's dropped*) I ain't tellin' you again. Give me them.

CARL: (*turns around quickly, walking away with a few of the sweaters*) How much these go for?

ARLENE: I don't know yet.

CARL: I'll jus' take care of 'em for you—a few coin for the trip. You *are* gonna have to pay your share, you know.

ARLENE: You give me them. I ain't goin' with you. (*She walks toward him.*)

CARL: You ain't?

(*Mocking,* ARLENE *walks up close to him now, taking the bag in her hands. He knocks her away and onto the bed.*)

CARL: Straighten up, girlie. (*now kneels over her*) You done forgot how to behave yourself. (*Moves as if to threaten her, but kisses her on the forehead, then moves out into the room.*)

ARLENE: (*sitting up*) I worked hard on them things. They's nice, too, for babies and little kids.

CARL: I bet you fooled them officers good, doin' this shit. (*Throws the bag in the sink.*)

ARLENE: I weren't—

CARL: I kin see that scene. They sayin' . . . (*puts on a high southern voice*) "I'd jus' love one a them nice yella sweaters."

ARLENE: They liked them.

CARL: Those turkeys, sure they did. Where else you gonna git your free sweaters an free washin' an free step-right-up-git-your-convict-special-shoe-shine. No, don't give me no money, officer. I's jus' doin' this 'cause I likes you.

ARLENE: They give 'em for Christmas presents.

CARL: (*checks the window again, then peers into the grocery sack*) What you got sweet, mama? (*Pulls out a box of cookies and begins to eat them.*)

ARLIE: I'm sweepin', Doris, 'cause it's like a pigpen in here. So you might like it, but I don't, so if you got some mops, I'll take one of them too.

ARLENE: You caught another habit, didn't you?

CARL: You turned into a narc or what?

ARLENE: You scratchin' an sniffin' like crazy.

CARL: I see a man eatin' cookies an that's what you see too.

ARLENE: An you was laughin' at me sittin' on the floor! You got cops lookin' for you an you ain't scored yet this morning. You better get yourself back to prison where you can git all you need.

CARL: Since when Carl couldn't find it if he really wanted it?

ARLENE: An I bought them cookies for me.

CARL: An I wouldn't come no closer if I's you.

ARLENE: (*stops, then walks to the door*) Then take the cookies an git out.

CARL: (*imitating* BENNIE) Oh, please, Miss Arlene, come go with Carl to the big city. We'll jus' have us the best time.

ARLENE: I'm gonna stay here an git a job an save up money so's I kin git Joey. (*opening the door*) Now, I ain't s'posed to see no ex-cons.

CARL: (*big laugh*) You don't know nobody else. Huh, Arlie? Who you know ain't a con-vict?

ARLENE: I'll meet 'em.

CARL: And what if they don't wanna meet you? You ain't exactly a nice girl, you know. An you gotta be jivin' about that job shit. (*Throws the sack of cookies on the floor.*)

ARLENE: (*retrieving the cookies*) I kin work.

CARL: Doin' what?

ARLENE: I don't know. Cookin', cleanin', somethin' that pays good.

CARL: You got your choice, honey. You can do cookin' an cleanin' *or* you can do somethin' that pays good. You ain't gonna git rich working on your knees. You come with me an you'll have money. You stay here, you won't have shit.

ARLENE: Ruby works an she does okay.

CARL: You got any Kool-Aid? (*looking in the cabinets, moving Arlene out of his way*) Ruby who?

ARLENE: Upstairs. She cooks. Works nights an has all day to do jus' what she wants.

CARL: And what, exactly, do she do? See flicks take rides in cabs to pick up see-through shoes?

ARLENE: She watches TV, plays cards, you know.

CARL: Yeah, I know. Sounds just like the day room in the fuckin' joint.

ARLENE: She likes it.

CARL: *(exasperated)* All right. Say you stay here an *finally* find yourself some job. *(grabs the picture of Jesus off the wall)* This your boyfriend?

ARLENE: The chaplain give it to me.

CARL: Say it's dishwashin', okay? *(ARLENE doesn't answer)* Okay?

ARLENE: Okay. *(Takes the picture, hangs it back up.)*

CARL: An you git maybe seventy-five a week. Seventy-five for standin' over a sink full of greasy gray water, fishin' out blobs of bread an lettuce. People puttin' pieces of chewed-up meat in their napkins and you gotta pick it out. Eight hours a day, six days a week, to make seventy-five lousy pictures of Big Daddy George. Now, how long it'll take you to make seventy-five workin' for me?

ARLENE: A night.

(She sits on the bed, CARL pacing in front of her.)

CARL: Less than a night. Two hours maybe. Now, it's the same fuckin' seventy-five bills. You can either work all week for it or make it in two hours. You work two hours a night for me an how much you got in a week? *(ARLENE looks puzzled by the multiplication required. He sits down beside her, even more disgusted)* Two seventy-five's is a hundred and fifty. Three hundred-and-fifties is four hundred and fifty. You stay here you git seventy-five a week. You come with me an you git four hundred and fifty a week. Now, four hundred and fifty, Arlie, is *more* than seventy-five. You stay here you gotta work eight hours a day and your hands git wrinkled and your feet swell up. *(suddenly distracted)* There was this guy at Bricktown had webby toes like a duck. *(back now)* You come home with me you work two hours a night an you kin sleep all mornin' an spend the day buyin' eyelashes and tryin' out perfume. Come home, have some guy openin' the door for you sayin', "Good evenin', Miss Holsclaw, nice night now ain't it?" *(Puts his arm around her.)*

ARLENE: It's Joey I'm thinkin' about.

CARL: If you was a kid, would you want your mom to git so dragged out washin' dishes she don't have no time for you an no money to spend on you? You come with me, you kin send him big orange bears an Sting-Ray bikes with his name wrote on the fenders. He'll like that. Holsclaw. *(amused)* Kinda sounds like coleslaw, don't it? Joey be tellin' all his friends 'bout his mom livin' up in New York City an bein' so rich an sendin' him stuff all the time.

ARLENE: I want to be with him.

CARL: *(now stretches out on the bed, his head in her lap)* So, fly him up to see you. Take him on that boat they got goes roun' the island. Take him up to the Empire State Building, let him play King Kong. *(rubs her hair, unstudied tenderness)* He be talkin' 'bout that trip his whole life.

ARLENE: *(smoothing his hair)* I don't want to go back to prison, Carl.

CARL: *(jumps up, moves toward the refrigerator)* There any chocolate milk? *(distracted again)* You know they got this motel down in Mexico named after me? Carlsbad Cabins. *(proudly)* Who said anything about goin' back to prison? *(slams the refrigerator door, really hostile)* What do you think I'm gonna be doin'? Keepin' you out, that's what!

ARLENE: *(stands up)* Like last time? Like you gettin' drunk? Like you lookin' for kid junkies to beat up?

CARL: God, ain't it hot in this dump. You gonna come or not? You wanna wash dishes, I could give a shit. *(yelling)* But you comin' with me, you say it right now, lady! *(grabs her by the arm)* Huh?

(There is a knock on the door.)

RUBY'S VOICE: Arlene?

CARL: *(yelling)* She ain't here!

RUBY'S VOICE: (alarmed) Arlene! You all right?

ARLENE: That's Ruby I was tellin' you about.

CARL: (catches ARLENE'S arms again, very rough) We ain't through!

RUBY: (opening the door) Hey! (seeing the rough treatment) Goin' to the store. (very firm) Thought maybe you forgot somethin'.

CARL: (turns ARLENE loose) You this cook I been hearin' about?

RUBY: I cook. So what?

CARL: Buys you nice shoes, don't it, cookin'? Why don't you hock your watch an have somethin' done to your hair? If you got a watch.

RUBY: Why don't you drop by the coffee shop. I'll spit in your eggs.

CARL: They let you bring home the half-eat chili dogs?

RUBY: You . . . you got half-eat chili dogs for brains. (to ARLENE) I'll stop by later. (Contemptuous look for CARL.)

ARLENE: No. Stay.

(CARL gets the message. He goes over to the sink to get a drink of water out of the faucet, then looks down at his watch.)

CARL: Piece a shit. (thumps it with his finger) Shoulda took the dude's hat, Jack. Guy preachin' about the end of the world ain't gonna own a watch that works.

ARLENE: (walks over to the sink, bends over CARL) You don't need me. I'm gittin' too old for it, anyway.

CARL: I don't discuss my business with strangers in the room. (Heads for the door.)

ARLENE: When you leavin'?

CARL: Six. You wanna come, meet me at this bar. (gives her a brightly colored matchbook) I'm havin' my wheels delivered.

ARLENE: You stealin' a car?

CARL: Take a cab. (gives her a dollar) You don't come . . . well, I already laid it out for you. I ain't never lied to you, have I girl?

ARLENE: No.

CARL: Then you be there. That's all the words I got. (makes an unconscious move toward her) I don't beg nobody. (backs off) Be there.

(He turns abruptly and leaves. ARLENE watches him go, folding up the money in the matchbook. The door remains open.)

ARLIE: (reading, or trying to, from a small Testament) For the Lord forsaketh not his saints, but the seed of the wicked shall be cut off.

(RUBY walks over to the counter, starts to pick up some of the groceries lying on the floor, then stops.)

RUBY: I 'magine you'll want to be puttin' these up yourself. (ARLENE continues to stare out the door) He do this?

ARLENE: No.

RUBY: Can't trust these sacks. I seen bag boys punchin' holes in 'em at the store.

ARLENE: Can't trust anybody. (Finally turning around.)

RUBY: Well, you don't want to trust him, that's for sure.

ARLENE: We spent a lot of time together, me an Carl.

RUBY: He live here?

ARLENE: No, he jus' broke outta Bricktown near where I was. I got word there sayin' he'd meet me. I didn't believe it then, but he don't lie, Carl don't.

RUBY: You thinkin' of goin' with him?

ARLENE: They'll catch him. I told him but he don't listen.

RUBY: Funny ain't it, the number a men come without ears.

ARLENE: How much that dishwashin' job pay?

RUBY: I don't know. Maybe seventy-five.

ARLENE: That's what he said.

RUBY: He tell you you was gonna wear out your hands and knees grubbin' for nuthin', git old an be broke an never have a nice dress to wear? (Sitting down.)

ARLENE: Yeah.

RUBY: He tell you nobody's gonna wanna be with you 'cause you done time?

ARLENE: Yeah.

RUBY: He tell you your kid gonna be ashamed of you an nobody's gonna believe you if you tell 'em you changed?

ARLENE: Yeah.

RUBY: Then he was right. *(pauses)* But when you make your two nickels, you can keep both of 'em.

ARLENE: *(shattered by these words)* Well, I can't do that.

RUBY: Can't do what?

ARLENE: Live like that. Be like bein' dead.

RUBY: You kin always call in sick . . . stay home, send out for pizza an watch your Johnny Carson on TV . . . or git a bus way out Preston Street an go bowlin'.

ARLENE: *(anger building)* What am I gonna do? I can't git no work that will pay good 'cause I can't do nuthin'. It'll be years fore I have a nice rug for this place. I'll never even have some ol' Ford to drive around, I'll never take Joey to no fair. I won't be invited home for pot roast and I'll have to wear this fuckin' dress for the rest of my life. What kind of life is that?

RUBY: It's outside.

ARLENE: Outside? Honey I'll either be *inside* this apartment or *inside* some kitchen sweatin' over the sink. Outside's where you get to do what you want, not where you gotta do some shit job jus' so's you can eat worse than you did in prison. That ain't why I quit bein' so hateful, so I could come back and rot in some slum.

RUBY: *(word "slum" hits hard)* Well, you can wash dishes to pay the rent on your "slum," or you can spread your legs for any shit that's got the ten dollars.

ARLENE: *(not hostile)* I don't need you agitatin' me.

RUBY: An I don't live in no slum.

ARLENE: *(sensing RUBY'S hurt)* Well, I'm sorry . . . it's just . . . I thought . . . *(Increasingly upset.)*

RUBY: *(finishing her sentence)* . . . it was gonna be different. Well, it ain't. And the sooner you believe it, the better off you'll be. *(A GUARD enters ARLIE'S cell.)*

ARLIE: Where's the chaplain? I got somethin' to tell him.

ARLENE: They said I's . . .

GUARD (CALDWELL): He ain't comin'.

ARLENE: . . . he tol' me if . . . I thought once Arlie . . .

ARLIE: It's Tuesday. He comes to see me on Tuesday.

GUARD (CALDWELL): Chaplain's been transferred, dollie. Gone. Bye-bye. You know.

ARLENE: He said the meek, meek, them that's quiet and good . . . the meek . . . as soon as Arlie . . .

RUBY: What, Arlene? Who said what?

ARLIE: He's not comin' back?

ARLENE: At Pine Ridge there was . . .

ARLIE: He woulda told me if he couldn't come back.

ARLENE: I was . . .

GUARD (CALDWELL): He left this for you.

ARLENE: I was . . .

GUARD (CALDWELL): Picture of Jesus, looks like.

ARLENE: . . . this chaplain . . .

RUBY: *(trying to call her back from this hysteria)* Arlene . . .

ARLIE: *(hysterical)* I need to talk to him.

ARLENE: This chaplain . . .

ARLIE: You tell him to come back and see me.

ARLENE: I was in lockup . . .

ARLIE: *(a final, anguished plea)* I want the chaplain!

ARLENE: I don't know . . . years . . .

RUBY: And . . .

ARLENE: This chaplain said I had . . . said Arlie was my hateful self and she was hurtin' me and God would find some way to take her away . . . and it was God's will so I could be the meek . . . the meek, them that's quiet and good an git whatever they want . . . I forgit that word . . . they git the earth.

RUBY: Inherit.

ARLENE: Yeah. And that's why I done it.

RUBY: Done what?

ARLENE: What I done. 'Cause the chaplain he said . . . I'd sit up nights waitin' for him to come talk to me.

RUBY: Arlene, what did you do? What are you talkin' about?

ARLENE: They tol' me . . . after I's out an it was all over . . . they said after the chaplain got transferred . . . I didn't know why he didn't come no more till after . . . they said it was three whole nights at first, me screamin' to God to come git Arlie an kill her. They give me this medicine an thought I's better . . . then that night it happened, the officer was in the dorm doin' count . . . an they didn't hear nuthin' but they come back out where I was an I'm standin' there tellin' 'em to come see, real quiet I'm tellin' 'em, but there's all this blood all over my shirt an I got this fork I'm holdin' real tight in my hand . . . *(clenches one hand now, the other hand fumbling with the front of her dress as if she's going to show* RUBY*)* this fork, they said Doris stole it from the kitchen an give it to me so I'd kill myself and shut up botherin' her . . . an there's all these holes all over me where I been stabbin' myself an I'm sayin' Arlie is dead for what she done to me, Arlie is dead an it's God's will . . . I didn't scream it, I was jus' sayin' it over and over . . . Arlie is dead, Arlie is dead . . . they couldn't git that fork outta my hand till . . . I woke up in the infirmary an they said I almost died. They said they's glad I didn't. *(smiling)* They said did I feel better now an they was real nice, bringing me chocolate puddin' . . .

RUBY: I'm sorry, Arlene.

*(*RUBY *reaches out for her, but* ARLENE *pulls away sharply.)*

ARLENE: I'd be eatin' or jus' lookin' at the ceiling an git a tear in my eye, but it'd jus' dry up, you know, it didn't run out or nuthin'. An then pretty soon, I's well, an officers was sayin' they's seein' such a change in me an givin' me yarn to knit sweaters an how'd I like to have a new skirt to wear an sometimes lettin' me chew gum. They said things ain't never been as clean as when I's doin' the housekeepin' at the dorm. *(so proud)* An then I got in the honor cottage an nobody was foolin' with me no more or nuthin'. An I didn't git mad like before or nuthin'. I jus' done my work an

knit . . . an I don't think about it, what happened, 'cept . . . *(now losing control)* people here keep callin' me Arlie an . . . *(has trouble saying "Arlie")* I didn't mean to do it, what I done . . .

RUBY: Oh, honey . . .

ARLENE: I did . . . *(this is very difficult)* I mean, Arlie was a pretty mean kid, but I did . . . *(very quickly)* I didn't know what I . . .

*(*ARLENE *breaks down completely, screaming, crying, falling over into* RUBY'S *lap.)*

ARLENE: *(grieving for this lost self)* Arlie!

*(*RUBY *rubs her back, her hair, waiting for the calm she knows will come.)*

RUBY: *(finally, but very quietly)* You can still . . . *(stops to think of how to say it)* . . . you can still love people that's gone.

*(*RUBY *continues to hold her tenderly, rocking as with a baby. A terrible crash is heard on the steps outside the apartment.)*

BENNIE'S VOICE: Well, chicken-pluckin', hog-kickin' shit!

RUBY: Don't you move now, it's just somebody out in the hall.

ARLENE: That's—

RUBY: It's okay Arlene. Everything's gonna be just fine. Nice and quiet now.

ARLENE: That's Bennie that guard I told you about.

RUBY: I'll get it. You stay still now. *(she walks to the door and looks out into the hall, hands on hips)* Why you dumpin' them flowers on the stairs like that? Won't git no sun at all! *(turns back to* ARLENE*)* Arlene, there's a man plantin' a garden out in the hall. You think we should call the police or get him a waterin' can?

*(*BENNIE *appears in the doorway, carrying a box of dead-looking plants.)*

BENNIE: I didn't try to fall, you know.

RUBY: *(blocking the door)* Well, when you git ready to *try,* I wanna watch!

ARLENE: I thought you's gone.

RUBY: *(to* BENNIE*)* You got a visitin' pass?

BENNIE: *(coming into the room)* Arlie . . .

(quickly) Arlene. I brung you some plants. You know, plants for your window. Like we talked about, so's you don't see them bars.

RUBY: *(picking up one of the plants)* They sure is scraggly-lookin' things. Next time, git plastic.

BENNIE: I'm sorry I dropped 'em, Arlene. We kin get 'em back together an they'll do real good. *(setting them down on the trunk)* These ones don't take the sun. I asked just to make sure. Arlene?

RUBY: You up for seein' this petunia killer?

ARLENE: It's okay. Bennie, this is Ruby, upstairs.

BENNIE: *(bringing one flower over to show ARLENE, stuffing it back into its pot)* See? It ain't dead.

RUBY: Poor little plant. It comes from a broken home.

BENNIE: *(walks over to the window, getting the box and holding it up)* That's gonna look real pretty. Cheerful-like.

RUBY: Arlene ain't gettin' the picture yet. *(walking to the window and holding her plant up too, posing)* Now.

(ARLENE looks, but is not amused.)

BENNIE: *(putting the plants back down)* I jus' thought, after what I done last night . . . I jus' wanted to do somethin' nice.

ARLENE: *(calmer now)* They is nice. Thanks.

RUBY: Arlene says you're a guard.

BENNIE: I was. I quit. Retired.

ARLENE: Bennie's goin' back to Alabama.

BENNIE: Well, I ain't leavin' right away. There's this guy at the motel says the bass is hittin' pretty good right now. Thought I might fish some first.

ARLENE: Then he's goin' back.

BENNIE: *(to RUBY as he washes his hands)* I'm real fond of this little girl. I ain't goin' till I'm sure she's gonna do okay. Thought I might help some.

RUBY: Arlene's had about all the help she can stand.

BENNIE: I got a car, Arlene. An money. An . . . *(reaching into his pocket)* I brung you some gum.

ARLENE: That's real nice, too. An I 'preciate what you done, bringin' me here an all, but . . .

BENNIE: Well, look. Least you can take my number at the motel an give me a ring if you need somethin'. *(holds out a piece of paper)* Here, I wrote it down for you. *(ARLENE takes the paper)* Oh, an somethin' else, these towel things . . . *(reaching into his pocket, pulling out a package of towelettes)* they was in the chicken last night. I thought I might be needin' 'em, but they give us new towels every day at that motel.

ARLENE: Okay then. I got your number.

BENNIE: *(backing up toward the door)* Right. Right. Any ol' thing, now. Jus' any ol' thing. You even run outta gum an you call.

RUBY: Careful goin' down.

ARLENE: Bye Bennie.

BENNIE: Right. The number now. Don't lose it. You know, in case you need somethin'.

ARLENE: No.

(BENNIE leaves, ARLENE gets up and picks up the matchbook CARL gave her and holds it with BENNIE'S piece of paper. RUBY watches a moment, sees ARLENE trying to make this decision, knows that what she says now is very important.)

RUBY: We had this waitress put her phone number in matchbooks, give 'em to guys left her nice tips. Anyway, one night this little ol' guy calls her and comes over and says he works at this museum an he don't have any money but he's got this hat belonged to Queen Victoria. An she felt real sorry for him so she screwed him for this little ol' lacy hat. Then she takes the hat back the next day to the museum thinkin' she'll git a reward or somethin' an you know what they done? *(pause)* Give her a free membership. Tellin' her thanks so much an we're so grateful an wouldn't she like to see this mummy they got downstairs . . . an all the time jus' stallin' . . . waiting 'cause they called the police.

ARLENE: You do any time for that?

RUBY: *(admitting the story was about her)* County jail.

ARLENE: *(quietly, looking at the matchbook)* County jail. *(she tears up the matchbook and drops it in the sack of trash)* You got any Old Maids?

RUBY: Huh?

ARLENE: You know.

RUBY: *(surprised and pleased)* Cards?

ARLENE: *(laughs a little)* It's the only one I know.

RUBY: Old Maid, huh? *(Not her favorite game.)*

ARLENE: I gotta put my food up first.

RUBY: 'Bout an hour?

ARLENE: I'll come up.

RUBY: Great. *(stops by the plants on her way to the door, smiles)* These plants is real ugly.
(RUBY exits. ARLENE watches her, then turns back to the groceries still on the floor. Slowly, but with great determination, she picks up the items one at a time and puts them away in the cabinet above the counter. ARLIE appears on the catwalk. There is one light on each of them.)

ARLIE: Hey! You 'member that time we was playin' policeman an June locked me up in Mama's closet an then took off swimmin'? An I stood around with them dresses itchin' my ears an crashin' into that door tryin' to git outta there? It was dark in there. So, finally, *(very proud)* I went around an peed in all Mama's shoes. But then she come home an tried to git in the closet only June taken the key so she said, "Who's in there?" an I said, "It's me!" and she said, "What you doin' in there?" an I started gigglin' an she started pullin' on the door an yellin', "Arlie, what you doin' in there?" *(big laugh)*
(ARLENE has begun to smile during the story. Now they speak together, both standing as Mama did, one hand on her hip.)

ARLIE and ARLENE: Arlie, what you doin' in there?

ARLENE: *(still smiling and remembering, stage dark except for one light on her face)* Aw shoot.
(Light dims on ARLENE's fond smile as ARLIE laughs once more.)

E N D   O F   P L A Y

SPELL #7: GEECHEE JIBARA QUIK MAGIC TRANCE MANUAL FOR TECHNOLOGICALLY STRESSED THIRD WORLD PEOPLE (1979)

Ntozake Shange's work, particularly her play *spell #7; geechee jibara quik magic trance manual for technologically stressed third world people*, represents the intersection of two artistic goals: first, to articulate an African-American theatre tradition: and second, to make it one in which woman's voice is not silenced. Because, as Hortense Spillers has observed, racial discrimination only compounds the effects of gender discrimination in the experience of African-American women, writers like Shange have felt themselves doubly silenced. Aware of this double bind in her own life, Shange employs *spell #7* and her other works to assault contemporary theatrical styles she finds "overwhelmingly shallow/stilted & imitative," in short, paralyzing in their Europeanness. In doing so, she fulfills both aforementioned goals, presenting alternatives to dominant dramatic forms and refusing the societal domination over black women they represent. As José David Saldivar argues, she "reproduces a version of the black female experience designed to encourage women of color 'to tell their stories'" in order to combat the combined effects of racism and sexism.

Born Paulette Williams to Paul T. Williams, a surgeon, and Eloise Williams, a psychiatric social worker and educator, Shange (1948–) lived her early life in Trenton, New Jersey, moving with her family to St. Louis when she was eight. As a child she enjoyed works from the traditional literary canon, and was also exposed to figures important to the African-American cultural community of the time, including W. E. B. DuBois and Josephine Baker, among others. Despite her middle-class upbringing, Shange experienced racism early in her life in the reaction to her forced busing to a German-

American school, an experience she speaks of in *spell #7* in a bitter litany describing the obstacles African-American children face. This experience was compounded by her increasing awareness in high school of her relative "unimportance" as an African-American woman. Nevertheless, she began college at Barnard and earned a bachelor's degree in 1970, although her intellectual development was not without inner turmoils; she made the first of several suicide attempts a year after starting college, shortly after separating from her law student husband. She later renamed herself as a recognition of her struggle to re-create her life: *Ntozake* means "she who comes with her own things"; *Shange,* "she who walks like a lion." Shange earned a master's degree in American Studies in 1973 from UCLA, and until 1975 taught Afro-American Studies, Women's Studies, and humanities at several colleges in California.

The production of her **choreopoem** *for colored girls who have considered suicide/when the rainbow is enuf* (1975) sparked Shange's move to New York City. Shange had been writing poetry and dancing with several companies, including her own, For Colored Girls Who Have Considered Suicide, and the choreopoem form was an outgrowth of such combined experiences with different artistic media. This first play marked the start of Shange's literary career, and introduced several tropes characteristic of Shange as poet/performer. For example, the figures in Shange's drama cannot be easily described as "characters." In *for colored girls* seven women appear on stage, identified only by the color of their respective costumes. The figures in a choreopoem, whether it be *for colored girls,* *boogie woogie landscapes* (1978), or *spell #7*, even when they have more concrete identities as named figures, slip between identities, becoming other characters and figures whose tales they tell. This transformational technique carries several implications: It undercuts the tradition of the rounded character in the **well-made play**; it allows the characters to shift before the eyes of the audience, assuming the identity of each of the different personae to whom they give voice; finally, this technique allows for a range of individuals far beyond what the worlds of most plays allow. The characters in a Shange play, while themselves unique, by no means exhaust the range of experiences, cultural backgrounds, and concerns extant in the wider African-American community. This outcome is essential to Shange's playwriting, supporting her sense that in order to become part of an African-American aesthetic, cultural texts must eschew any notion that there is a single African-American or female identity, speaking rather to experiences that overlap.

Shange rejects the title "playwright" as representative of a tradition she feels little in common with as an African-American woman. Her poetry constantly recounts a process of becoming; likewise, her plays are performed with intermittent music, dance, and movement, interrupting and therefore subverting any sense of a linear narrative. Readers of Shange's plays also experience this subversion of convention, largely because in writing her choreopoems, she abolishes capital letters, breaks the flow of lines by use of virgules (/), and shortens words to abbreviated forms. There is also a joyful quality to this, for Shange has pointed out that she likes the idea that "letters dance, not just that words dance; of course the words also dance." A reader of Shange's plays is forced to slow down and reevaluate the nature of her undermining of convention.

Shange's *spell #7*, originally produced in 1979 by Joseph Papp's New York Shakespeare Festival, contains all these performative and editorial innovations. In one sense, the play is a continuation of the subject matter that so concerned her in *for colored girls;* here, too, African-American women struggle with the pain of everyday life, mustering the will to survive and confronting the difficulty of creating a self and simply enjoying life. As John Timpane points out, however, Shange is not concerned just with criticizing those who have subjugated African Americans, but rather with celebrating the development of an African-American consciousness. Indeed, as he suggests, "none of these epiphanies . . . 'solve' the future, but they are communal starting points for a large number of possible futures."

Shange's consciousness-raising takes place on two levels. That the play opens upon the figure of an enormous minstrel mask and introduces several players outfitted in minstrel garb implicates white America in constructing blackness in its own terms. Shange is sympathetic and cautionary in her use of the minstrel motif: "I had the minstrel dance because that's what happens to black people in the arts no matter how famous we become. . . . Black Theatre is not moving forward the way people like to think it is. We're not free of our paint yet!" One of the few male characters in the play is the magician, lou, who convinces us that he is going to "make us colored and love it" to reverse the negative implications of theatrical blackness. His character gives way to a collection of African-American actors who have retreated to a bar to discuss their frustration at being unable to find work except in stereotypical roles. They have been unable to perform both on the professional stage and in the greater society, a situation that Shange seeks to rectify as she has them, in turn, present different stories of those in the African-American community.

The actors' frustration with a profession that will allow them to play only bit parts stands for a larger frustration with a society which values too little of the black community. And, while Shange pokes fun at stereotypical white pursuits, she also challenges her audience to revalue African-American experience through the collage of portraits she presents. It is here that a second level of consciousness-raising on Shange's part becomes apparent. That is, many of these stories celebrate the different types of African-American womanhood; Shange's articulating these experiences, Saldivar suggests, allows "black women to insert themselves into the cultural conversations of U.S. history." We hear of fay, so full of the joy of living that white onlookers think her stoned; of sue-jean, a woman who 'always wanted to have a baby/ a lil boy / named myself'; of the different experiences of the actresses at the bar. In this way, as Timpane suggests, "Shange's most characteristic gesture is . . . toward possibility rather than closure; her works evoke the complexity of human relations rather than the completion of given actions or characters." As in other Shange plays, sympathetic female characters outnumber the male characters; however, in *spell #7*, even the latter are given the chance to reveal their frustrations or to enact male stereotypes in order to deflate them. Although there is always a pervasive sense that we are experiencing a collage, Timpane suggests that the political purposes in the midst of the play keep it from being a series of unconnected speech acts.

spell #7 was published in 1981 as part of a collection of plays entitled *Three Pieces,* which also includes the plays *a photograph: lovers-in-motion* (1977) and *boogie woogie landscapes.* Shange has continued her commitment to articulating the cause of the African-American woman through further writing; in recent years, she has produced poems, plays, and the novels *Betsey Brown* (1985), adapted for the stage by Shange and Emily Mann in 1991, and recently *I Live in Music: Poem* (1994). Interestingly enough, some critics of Shange continue to evaluate her in terms of traditional playwriting, critiquing her, for example, for failing to develop her characters. Yet, as lou points out in *spell #7*, "aint no colored magician in his right mind / gonna make you white / cuz this is blk magic you lookin at"; likewise, Shange continues to exercise her own particular powers outside mainstream theatrical conventions—not to exclude parts of her audience, but to make it recognize the value of conventions and peoples who have been ignored for too long.

WORKS CONSULTED

Cronacher, Karen. "Unmasking the Minstrel Mask's Black Magic in Ntozake Shange's *spell #7.*" *Theatre Journal* 11 (1992): 177–193.

Geis, Deborah. *Postmodern Theatric(k)s: Monologue in Contemporary American Drama.* Ann Arbor: University of Michigan Press, 1993.

Hay, Samuel A., *African-American Theatre: A Historical and Critical Analysis.* Cambridge: Cambridge University Press, 1994.

Mahone, Sydné, ed. *Moon Marked & Touched by Sun: Plays by African-American Women.* New York: Theatre Communications Group, 1994.

Pinkney, Mikell. "Theatrical Expressionism in the Structure and Language of Ntozake Shange's *spell # 7.*" *Theatre Studies* 37 (1992): 5–15.

Saldivar, José David. *The Dialectics of Our America: Genealogy, Cultural Critique, and Literary History.* Durham, NC: Duke University Press, 1991.

Spillers, Hortense. "Mama's Baby, Papa's Maybe: An American Grammar Book." *Diacritics* 17 (1987): 65–81.

Timpane, John. "'The Poetry of a Moment': Politics and the Open Form in the Drama of Ntozake Shange." *Modern American Drama: The Female Canon.* Ed. June Schleuter. London and Toronto: Associated University Presses, 1990. 198–206.

CHARACTERS

lou . . . . a practicing magician

alec . . . . a frustrated, angry actor's actor

dahlia . . . . young gypsy (singer/dancer)

eli . . . . a bartender who is also a poet

bettina . . . . dahlia's co-worker in a chorus

lily . . . . an unemployed actress working as a barmaid

natalie . . . . a not-too-successful performer
ross . . . . guitarist-singer with natalie
maxine . . . . an experienced actress

ACT I

(there is a huge black-face mask hanging from the ceiling of the theatre as the audience enters. in a way the show has already begun, for the members of the audience must integrate this grotesque, larger than life misrepresentation of life into their pre-show chatter. slowly the house lights fade, but the mask looms even larger in the darkness.

once the mask is all that can be seen, LOU, *the magician, enters. he is dressed in the traditional costume of Mr. Interlocutor: tuxedo, bow-tie, top hat festooned with all kinds of whatnots that are obviously meant for good luck. he does a few catchy "soft-shoe" steps & begins singing a traditional version of a black play song)*

LOU: *(singing)*
10 lil picaninnies all in bed
one fell out and the other nine said:
i sees yr hiney
all black & shiny
i see yr hiney
all black & shiny/shiny
(as a greeting)
yes/yes/yes   isnt life wonderful
(confidentially)
my father is a retired magician
which accounts for my irregular behavior
everything comes outta magic hats
or bottles wit no bottoms & parakeets
are as easy to get as a couple a rabbits
or 3 fifty-cent pieces/1958
my daddy retired from magic & took
up another trade cuz this friend a mine
from the 3rd grade/asked to be made white
on the spot

what cd any self-respectin colored american
    magician
do wit such an outlandish request/cept
put all them razzamatazz hocus pocus zippity-
    doo-dah
thingamajigs away   cuz
colored chirren believin in magic
waz becomin politically dangerous for the race
& waznt nobody gonna be made white
on the spot just
from a clap of my daddy's hands
& the reason i'm so peculiar's
cuz i been studyin up on my daddy's technique
& everything i do is magic these days
& it's very colored/very now you see it/now you
dont mess wit me
(boastfully)
                         i come from a family of retired
sorcerers/active houngans & pennyante for-
    tune tellers
wit 41 million spirits/critturs & celestial bodies
on our side
        i'll listen to yr problems
        help wit yr career/yr lover/yr wanderin
        spouse
        make yr grandma's stay in heaven more
        gratifyin
        ease yr mother thru menopause & show yr
        son
        how to clean his room
(while LOU *has been easing the audience into acceptance of his appearance & the mask (his father, the ancestors, our magic), the rest of the company enters in tattered fieldhand garb, blackface, and the countenance of stepan fetchit when he waz frightened. their presence belies the magician's promise that "you'll be colored n love it," just as the minstrel shows were lies, but* LOU *continues)*

YES YES YES 3 wishes is all you get
   scarlet ribbons for yr hair
   a farm in mississippi
   someone to love you madly
all things are possible
but aint no colored magician in his right mind
gonna make you   white
i mean
    this is blk magic
you lookin at
& i'm fixin you up good/fixin you up good &
   colored
& you gonna be colored all yr life
& you gonna love it/bein colored/all yr life/
   colored & love it
love it/bein colored. SPELL #7!
*(LOU claps his hands, & the company which
had been absolutely still til this moment jumps
up. with a rhythm set on a washboard carried
by one of them/they begin a series of steps that
identify every period of afro-american entertainment: from acrobats, comedians, tap-
dancers, calindy dancers, cotton club choruses,
apollo theatre du-wop groups, til they reach a
frenzy in the midst of "hambone, hambone
where ya been"/& then take a bow à la bert
williams/the lights bump up abruptly.*
*the magician, LOU, walks thru the black-faced
figures in their kneeling poses, arms outstretched
as if they were going to sing "mammy." he
speaks now (as a companion of the mask) to the
same audience who fell so easily into his hands
& who were so aroused by the way the black-
faced figures "sang n danced")*

LOU: why dont you go on & integrate a german-
american school in st. louis mo./1955/better
yet why dont ya go on & be a red niggah in a
blk school in 1954/i got it/try & make one
friend at camp in the ozarks in 1957/crawl thru
one a jesse james' caves wit a class of white
kids waitin outside to see the whites of yr eyes/
why dontcha invade a clique of working class
italians trying to be protestant in a jewish com-
munity/& come up a spade/be a lil too dark/
lips a lil too full/hair entirely too nappy/to be

beautiful/be a smart child trying to be dumb/
you go meet somebody who wants/always/a lil
less/be cool when yr body says hot/& more/be
a mistake in racial integrity/an error in white
folks' most absurd fantasies/be a blk kid in
1954/who's not blk enuf to lovingly ignore/not
beautiful enuf to leave alone/not smart enuf to
move outta the way/not bitter enuf to die at an
early age/why dontchu c'mon & live my life for
me/since the dreams aint enuf/go on & live my
life for me/i didnt want certain moments at all/
i'd give em to anybody . . . awright. alec.
*(the black-faced ALEC gives his minstrel mask to
LOU when he hears his name/ALEC rises. the rest
of the company is intimidated by this figure daring to talk without the protection of black-face.
they move away from him/or move in place as if
in mourning)*

ALEC: st. louis/such a colored town/a whiskey
black space of history & neighborhood/forever
ours to lawrenceville/where the only road open
to me waz cleared by colonial slaves/whose
children never moved/never seems like mended
the torments of the Depression or the stains of
demented spittle/dropped from the lips of crystal women/still makin independence flags/

   st. louis/on a halloween's eve to the veiled
prophet/usurpin the mystery of mardi gras/i
made it mine tho the queen waz always fair/
that parade of pagan floats & tambourines/
commemorates me/unlike the lonely walks wit
liberal trick or treaters/back to my front door/
bag half empty/

   my face enuf to scare anyone i passed/gee/
a colored kid/whatta gas. here/a tree/wanderin
the horizon/dipped in blues/untended bones/
usedta hugs drawls rhythm & decency here a
tree/waitin to be hanged

   sumner high school/squat & pale on the
corner/like our vision waz to be vague/our memory of the war/that made us free/to be forgotten/
becomin paler/linear movement from sous'
carolina to missouri/freedmen/landin in jackie
wilson's yelp/daughters of the manumitted swimmin in tina turner's grinds/this is chuck berry's

town disavowin miscega-nation/in any situa-
tion/& they let us be/electric blues & bo didley/
the rockin pneumonia & boogie-woogie flu/the
slop & short fried heads/runnin always to the
river chambersburg/lil italy/i passed everyday
at the sweet shoppe/& waz afraid/the cops
raided truants/regularly/& after dark i wd not
be seen wit any other colored/sane & lovin
my life

*(shouts n cries that are those of a white mob are
heard, very loud . . . the still black-faced figures try to move away from the menacing voices
& memories)*

VOICES: hey niggah/over here

ALEC: behind the truck lay five hands claspin
    chains

VOICES: hey niggah/over here

ALEC: round the trees/4 more sucklin steel

VOICES: hey niggah/over here

ALEC: this is the borderline

VOICES: hey niggah/over here

ALEC: a territorial dispute

VOICES: hey niggah/over here

ALEC: *(crouched on floor)*
    cars loaded with families/fellas from the factory/
    one or two practical nurses/become our
        trenches/
    some dig into cement wit elbows/under engines/
    do not be seen in yr hometown
    after sunset/we suck up our shadows
    *(finally moved to tear off their "shadows," all
    but two of the company leave with their true
    faces bared to the audience. DAHLIA has, as
    if by some magical cause, shed not only her
    mask, but also her hideous overalls & picaninny-
    buckwheat wig, to reveal a finely laced unitard/
    the body of a modern dancer. she throws her
    mask to ALEC, who tosses it away. DAHLIA be-
    gins a lyrical but pained solo as ALEC speaks
    for them)*

ALEC: we will stand here
    our shoulders embrace an enormous spirit
    my dreams waddle in my lap
    run round to miz bertha's
    where lil richard gets his process

run backward to the rosebushes
& a drunk man lyin
down the block to the nuns
in pink habits/prayin in a pink chapel
my dreams run to meet aunt marie
my dreams haunt me like the little geechee
    river
our dreams draw blood from old sores
this is our space
we are not movin

*(DAHLIA finishes her movement/ALEC is seen
reaching for her/lights out. in the blackout they
exit as LOU enters. lights come up on LOU who
repeats bitterly his challenge to the audience)*

LOU: why dontchu go on & live my life for me
    i didnt want certain moments at all
    i'd give them to anybody

*(LOU waves his hand commanding the minstrel
mask to disappear, which it does. he signals to
his left & again by magic, the lights come up
higher revealing the interior of a lower manhattan bar & its bartender, ELI, setting up for the
night. ELI greets LOU as he continues to set up tables, chairs, candles, etc., for the night's activities. LOU goes over to the jukebox, & plays "we
are family" by sister sledge. LOU starts to tell us
exactly where we are, but ELI takes over as characters are liable to do. throughout ELI's poem,
the other members of the company enter the bar
in their street clothes, & doing steps reminiscent
of their solos during the minstrel sequence. as
each enters, the audience is made aware that
these ordinary people are the minstrels. the company continues to dance individually as ELI
speaks)*

this is . . .

ELI:

    MY kingdom.
    there shall be no trespassers/no marauders
    no tourists in my land
    you nurture these gardens   or   be shot on
        sight
    carelessness & other priorities
    are not permitted within these walls
    i am mantling an array of strength & beauty

no one shall interfere with this
the construction of myself
my city   my theater
my bar   come to my poems
but understand we speak english carefully
& perfect antillean french
our toilets are disinfected
the plants here sing to me each morning
come to my kitchen my parlor even my bed
i sleep on satin   surrounded by hand made
infants who bring me good luck & warmth
come even to my door
the burglar alarm/armed guards vault from the
    east side
if i am in danger   a siren shouts
you are welcome
to my kingdom   my city   my self
but yr presence must not disturb these inhabi-
    tants
leave nothing out of place/push no dust under
    my rugs
leave not a crack in my wine glasses
no finger prints
clean up after yrself in the bathroom
there are no maids here   no days off
for healing   no insurance policies
for dislocation of the psyche
aliens/foreigners/are granted resident status
we give them a little green card
as they prove themselves non-injurious
to the joy of my nation
i sustain no intrusions/no double-entendre ro-
    mance
no soliciting of sadness   in my life
are those who love me well
the rest are denied their visas . . .
is everyone ready to boogie
(finally, when ELI *calls for a boogie, the com-*
pany does a dance that indicates these people
have worked & played together a long time. as
dance ends, the company sits & chats at the ta-
bles & at the bar. this is now a safe haven for
these "minstrels" off from work. here they are
free to be themselves, to reveal secrets, fantasies,
nightmares, or hope. it is safe because it is seg-
regated & magic reigns.

LILY, *the waitress, is continually moving abt the*
bar, taking orders for drinks & generally stay-
ing on top of things)
ALEC: gimme a triple bourbon/& a glass of angel
    dust
        these thursday nite audiences are abt to
kill me
(ELI *goes behind bar to get drinks)*
DAHLIA: why do i drink so much?
BETTINA, LILY, NATALIE: *(in unison)* who cares?
DAHLIA: but i'm an actress. i have to ask myself
    these questions
LILY: that's a good reason to drink
DAHLIA: no/i mean the character/alec, you're a
    director/give me some motivation
ALEC: motivation/if you didn't drink you wd re-
    member that you're not workin
LILY: i wish i cd get just one decent part
LOU: say as lady macbeth or mother courage
ELI: how the hell is she gonna play lady macbeth
    and macbeth's a white dude?
LILY: ross & natalie/why are you countin pennies
    like that?
NATALIE: we had to wait on our money again
ROSS: and then we didn't get it
BETTINA: maybe they think we still accept beads
    & ribbons
NATALIE: i had to go around wit my tambourine
    just to get subway fare
ELI: dont worry abt it/have one on me
NATALIE: thank you eli
BETTINA: *(falling out of her chair)* oh . . .
ALEC: cut her off eli/dont give her no more
LILY: what's the matter bettina/is yr show closin?
BETTINA: *(gets up, resets chair)* no/my show is not
    closin/but if that director asks me to play it any
    blacker/i'm gonna have to do it in a mammy
    dress
LOU: you know/countin pennies/lookin for parts/
    breakin tambourines/we must be outta our
    minds for doin this
BETTINA: no we're not outta our minds/we're just
    sorta outta our minds
LILY: no/we're not outta our minds/we've been do-
    ing this shit a long time . . . ross/captain
    theophilis conneau/in a *slaver's logbook*/says

that "youths of both sexes wear rings in the nose and lower lip and stick porcupine quills thru the cartilage of the ear." ross/when ringlin' bros. comes to madison square garden/dontcha know the white people just go

ROSS: in their cb radios

DAHLIA: in their mcdonald's hats

ELI: with their save america t-shirts & those chirren who score higher on IQ tests for the white chirren who speak english

ALEC: when the hockey games absorb all america's attention in winter/they go with their fists clenched & their tongues battering their women who dont know a puck from a 3-yr-old harness racer

BETTINA: they go & sweat in fierce anger

ROSS: these factories

NATALIE: these middle management positions

ROSS: make madison square garden

BETTINA: the temple of the primal scream
        (LILY gets money from cash register & heads toward jukebox)

LILY: oh how they love blood

NATALIE: & how they dont even dress for the occasion/all inconspicuous & pink

ELI: now if willie colon come there

BETTINA: if/we say/the fania all stars gonna be there
        in that nasty fantasy of the city council

ROSS: where the hot dogs are not even hebrew national

LILY: and the bread is stale

ROSS: even in such a place where dance is an obscure notion

BETTINA: where one's joy is good cause for a boring chat with the pinkerton guard

DAHLIA: where the halls lead nowhere

ELI: & "back to yr seat/folks"

LILY: when all one's budget for cruisin

LOU: one's budget for that special dinner with you know who

LILY: the one you wd like to love you

BETTINA: when yr whole reasonable allowance for leisure activity/
        buys you a seat where what's goin on dont matter

DAHLIA: cuz you so high up/you might be in seattle

LILY: even in such a tawdry space

ELI: where vorster & his pals wd spit & expect black folks to lick it up

ROSS: *(stands on chair)* in such a place i've seen miracles

ALL: oh yeah/aw/ross

ROSS: the miracles
        ("music for the love of it," by butch morris, comes up on the jukebox/this is a catchy uptempo rhythm & blues post WW II. as they speak the company does a dance that highlights their ease with one another & their familiarity with "all the new dance steps")

LILY: the commodores

DAHLIA: muhammad ali

NATALIE: bob marley

ALEC: & these folks who upset alla 7th avenue with their glow/
        how the gold in their braids is new in this world of hard hats & men with the grace of wounded buffalo/how these folks in silk & satin/in bodies reekin of good love comin/these pretty muthafuckahs

DAHLIA: make this barn

LILY: this insult to good taste

BETTINA: a foray into paradise

DAHLIA, LILY, ALEC, NATALIE, and ROSS: *(in unison)* we dress up

BETTINA, ELI, and LOU: *(in unison)* we dress up

DAHLIA: cuz we got good manners

ROSS: cd you really ask dr. funkenstein to come all that way & greet him in the clothes you sweep yr kitchen in?

ALL: NO!

BETTINA: cd you say to muhammad ali/well/i just didnt have a chance to change/you see i have a job/& then i went jogging & well, you know its just madison square garden

LOU: my dear/you know that wont do

NATALIE: we honor our guests/if it costs us all we got

DAHLIA: when stevie wonder sings/he don't want us lookin like we ain't got no common sense/he wants us to be as lovely as we really are/so we strut & reggae

ELI: i seen some doing the jump up/i myself just got happy/but i'm tellin you one thing for sure

LILY: we fill up where we at

BETTINA: no police

NATALIE: no cheap beer

DAHLIA: no nasty smellin bano

ROSS: no hallways fulla derelicts & hustlers

NATALIE: gonna interfere wit alla this beauty

ALEC: if it wasnt for us/in our latino chic/our rasta-fare our outer space funk suits & all the rest i have never seen

BETTINA: tho my daddy cd tell you bout them fox furs & stacked heels/the diamonds & marie antoinette wigs

ELI: it's not cuz we got money

NATALIE: it's not cuz if we had money we wd spend it on luxury

LILY: it's just when you gotta audience with the pope/you look yr best

BETTINA: when you gonna see the queen of england/you polish yr nails

NATALIE: when you gonna see one of them/& you know who i mean

ALEC: they gotta really know

BETTINA: we gotta make em feel

ELI: we dont do this for any old body

LOU: we're doin this for you

NATALIE: we dress up

ALEC: is our way of sayin/you gettin the very best

DAHLIA: we cant do less/we love too much to be stingy

ROSS: they give us too much to be loved ordinary

LILY: we simply have good manners

ROSS: & an addiction to joy

FEMALE CAST MEMBERS: *(in unison)* WHEE . . .

DAHLIA: we dress up

MALE CAST MEMBERS: *(in unison)* HEY . . .

BETTINA: we gotta show the world/we gotta corner on the color

ROSS: happiness just jumped right outta us/& we are lookin good
    (everyone in the bar is having so much fun/that MAXINE *takes on an exaggerated character as she enters/in order to bring them to attention,*

the company freezes, half in respect/half in parody)

MAXINE: cognac!
(the company relaxes, goes to tables or the bar. in the meantime, ROSS *has remained in the spell of the character that* MAXINE *had introduced when she came in. he goes over to* MAXINE *who is having a drink/& begins an improvisation)*

ROSS: she left the front gate open/not quite knowing she wanted someone to walk on thru the wrought iron fence/scrambled in whiskey bottles broken round old bike spokes/some nice brown man to wind up in her bed/she really didnt know/the sombrero that enveloped her face was a lil too much for an april nite on the bowery/& the silver halter dug out from summer cookouts near riis beach/didnt sparkle with the intensity of her promise to have one good time/before the children came back from carolina. brooklyn cd be such a drag. every street cept flatbush & nostrand/reminiscent of europe during the plague/seems like nobody but sickness waz out walkin/drivels & hypes/a few youngsters lookin for more than they cd handle/& then there waz fay/
(MAXINE *rises, begins acting the story out)*
        waitin for a cab. anyone of the cars inchin along the boulevard cd see fay waznt no whore/ just a good clean woman out for the nite/& tho her left titty jumped out from under her silver halter/she didnt notice cuz she waz lookin for a cab. the dank air fondled her long saggin bosom like a possible companion/she felt good. she stuck her tin-ringed hand on her waist & watched her own ankles dance in the nite. she waz gonna have a good time tonight/she waz awright/a whole lotta woman/wit that special brooklyn bottom strut. knowin she waznt comin in til dawn/fay covered herself/sorta/wit a light kacky jacket that just kept her titties from rompin in the wind/& she pulled it closer to her/the winds waz comin/from nowhere jabbin/& there waznt no cabs/the winds waz beatin her behind/whisperin/gigglin/you aint

goin noplace/you an ol bitch/shd be at home wit ur kids. fay beat off the voices/& an EBONY-TRUE-TO-YOU cab climbed the curb to get her. *(as cabdriver)*

hope you aint plannin on stayin in brook-lyn/after 8:00 you dead in brooklyn. *(as narrator)*

she let her titty shake like she thot her mouth oughtta bubble like/wd she take off her panties/i'd take her anywhere.

MAXINE: *(as if in cab)* i'm into havin a good time/ yr arms/veins burstin/like you usedta lift to-bacco onto trucks or cut cane/i want you to be happy/long as we dont haveta stay in brooklyn

ROSS: & she made like she waz gypsy rose lee/or the hotsy totsy girls in the carnival round from waycross/when it waz segregated

MAXINE: what's yr name?

ROSS: my name is raphael

MAXINE: oh that's nice

ROSS: & fay moved where i cd see her out the rear view mirror/waz tellin me all bout her children & big eddie who waz away/while we crossed the manhattan bridge/i kept smilin. *(as cab-driver)* where exactly you goin?

MAXINE: i dont really know. i just want to have a good time. take me where i can see famous peo-ple/& act bizarre like sinatra at the kennedys/ maybe even go round & beat up folks like jim brown/throw somebody offa balcony/you know/ for a good time

ROSS: the only place i knew/i took her/after i kisst the spaces she'd been layin open to me. fay had alla her $17 cuz i hadnt charged her nothin/ turned the meter off/said it waz wonderful to pick up a lady like her on atlantic avenue/i saw nobody but those goddamn whores/& fay

(MAXINE moves in to ROSS & gives him a very long kiss)

now fay waz a gd clean woman/& she waz burstin with pride & enthusiasm when she walked into the place where I swore/all the ac-tresses & actors hung out

(the company joins in ROSS' story; responding to MAXINE as tho she waz entering their bar)

oh yes/there were actresses in braids & lipstick/wigs & winged tip pumps/fay as-sumed the posture of someone she'd always admired/etta james/the waitress asked her to leave cuz she waz high/& fay knew better than that

MAXINE: *(responding to LILY'S indication of throw-ing her out)* i aint high/i'm enthusiastic/and i'm gonna have me a goooooooood/ol time

ROSS: she waz all dressed up/she came all the way from brooklyn/she must look high cuz i/the taxi-man/well i got her a lil excited/that waz all/ but she waz gonna cool out/cuz she waz gonna meet her friends/at this place/yes. she knew that/& she pushed a bunch of rhododendrum/ outta her way so she cd get over to that table/& stood over the man with the biggest niggah eyes & warmest smellin mouth

MAXINE: please/let me join you/i come all the way from brooklyn/to have a good time/you dont think i'm high do ya/cd i please join ya/i just wanna have a good ol time

ROSS: *(as BETTINA turns away)* the woman sipped chablis & looked out the window hopin to see one of the bowery drunks fall down somewhere/ fay's voice hoverin/flirtin wit hope

LOU: *(turning to face MAXINE)* why dont you go downstairs & put yr titty in yr shirt/you cant have no good time lookin like that/now go on down & then come up & join us

(BETTINA & LOU rise & move to another table)

ROSS: fay tried to shove her flesh anywhere/ she took off her hat/bummed a kool/swal-lowed somebody's cognac/& sat down/waitin/ for a gd time

MAXINE: *(rises & hugs ROSS)* aw ross/when am i gonna get a chance to feel somethin like that/i got into this business cuz i wanted to feel things all the time/& all they want me to do is put my leg in my face/smile/&

LILY: you better knock on some wood/maxine/at least yr workin

BETTINA: & at least yr not playin a whore/if some other woman comes in here & tells me she's playin a whore/i think i might kill her

ELI: you'd kill her so you cd say/oh dahlia died &
i know all her lines

BETTINA: aw hush up eli/dnt you know what i
mean?

ELI: no miss/i dont/are you in the theater?

BETTINA: mr. bartender/poet sir/i am theater

DAHLIA: well miss theater/that's a surprise/espe-
cially since you fell all over the damn stage in
the middle of my solo

LILY: she did

ELI: miss theater herself fell down?

DAHLIA: yeah/she cant figure out how to get attention without makin somebody else look
bad

MAXINE: now dahlia/it waznt that bad/i hardly
noticed her

DAHLIA: it waz my solo/you werent sposed to notice her at all!

BETTINA: you know dahlia/i didnt do it on pur-
pose/i cda hurt myself

DAHLIA: that wd be unfortunate

BETTINA: well miss thing with those big ass hips
you got/i dont know why you think you can do
the ballet anyway
(the company breaks; they're expecting a fight)

DAHLIA: (crossing to BETTINA) i got this
(demonstrates her leg extension)
& alla this
(DAHLIA turns her back to BETTINA/& slaps her
own backside. BETTINA grabs DAHLIA, turns her
around & they begin a series of finger snaps
that are a paraphrase of ailey choreography for
very dangerous fights. ELI comes to break up the
impending altercation)

ELI: ladies ladies ladies
(ELI separates the two)

ELI:
people keep tellin me to put my feet on the
ground
i get mad & scream/there is no ground
only shit pieces from dogs horses & men who
dont live
anywhere/they tell me think straight & make
myself

somethin/i shout & sigh/i am a poet/i write poems
i make words cartwheel & somersault down
pages
outta my mouth come visions distilled like
bootleg
whiskey/i am like a radio but i am a channel of
my own
i keep sayin i write poems/& people keep
askin me
what do i do/what in the hell is going on?
people keep tellin me these are hard times/
what are
you gonna be doin ten years from now/
what in the hell do you think/i am gonna be
writin poems
i will have poems inchin up the walls of the lincoln tunnel/
i am gonna feed my children poems on rye
bread with horseradish/
i am gonna send my mailman off with a poem
for his wagon/
give my doctor a poem for his heart/i am a
poet/
i am not a part-time poet/i am not a amateur
poet/
i dont even know what that person cd be/who-
ever that is
authorizing poetry as an avocation/is a fraud/
put yr own feet on the ground

BETTINA: i'm sorry eli/i just dont want to be a
gypsy all my life
(the bar returns to normal humming & sipping.
the lights change to focus on LILY/who begins to
say what's really been on her mind. the rest of the
company is not aware of LILY'S private thoughts.
only BETTINA responds to LILY, but as a partner
in fantasy, not as a voyeur)

LILY: (illustrating her words with movement) i'm
gonna simply brush my hair. rapunzel pull yr
tresses back into the tower. & lady godiva give
up horseback riding. i'm gonna alter my social
& professional life dramatically. i will brush
100 strokes in the morning/100 strokes midday

& 100 strokes before retiring. i will have a very busy schedule. between the local trains & the express/i'm gonna brush. i brush between telephone calls. at the disco i'm gonna brush on the slow songs/i dont slow dance with strangers. i'ma brush my hair before making love & after. i'll brush my hair in taxis. while windowshopping. when i have visitors over the kitchen table/i'ma brush. i brush my hair while thinking abt anything. mostly i think abt how it will be when i get my full heada hair. like lifting my head in the morning will become a chore. i'll try to turn my cheek & my hair will weigh me down (LILY *falls to the floor.* BETTINA *helps lift her to her knees, then begins to dance & mime as* LILY *speaks)*

i dream of chaka khan/chocolate from graham central station with all seven wigs/& medusa. i brush & brush. i use olive oil hair food/& posner's vitamin E. but mostly i brush & brush. i may lose contact with most of my friends. i cd lose my job/but i'm on unemployment & brush while waiting on line for my check. i'm sure i get good recommendations from my social worker: such a fastidious woman/that lily/always brushing her hair. nothing in my dreams suggests that hair brushing/per se/has anything to do with my particular heada hair. a therapist might say that the head fulla hair has to do with something else/like: a symbol of lily's unconscious desires. but i have no therapist *(she takes imaginary pen from* BETTINA, *who was pretending to be a therapist/& sits down at table across from her)*

& my dreams mean things to me/like if you dreamed abt tobias/then something has happened to tobias/or he is gonna show up. if you dream abt yr grandma who's dead/then you must be doing something she doesnt like/or she wdnta gone to all the trouble to leave heaven like that. if you dream something red/you shd stop. if you dream something green/you shd keep doing it. if a blue person appears in yr dreams/then that person is yr true friend

& that's how i see my dreams. & this head fulla hair i have in my dreams is lavender & nappy as a 3-yr-old's in a apple tree. i can fry an egg & see the white of the egg spreadin in the grease like my hair is gonna spread in the air/but i'm not egg-yolk yellow/i am brown & the egg white isnt white at all/it is my actual hair/& it wd go on & on forever/irregular like a rasta-man's hair. irregular/gargantuan & lavender. nestled on blue satin pillows/pillows like the sky. & so i fry my eggs. i buy daisies dyed lavender & laced lavender tablemats & lavender nail polish. though i never admit it/i really do believe in magic/& can do strange things when something comes over me. soon everything around me will be lavender/fluffy & consuming. i will know not a moment of bitterness/through all the wrist aching & tennis elbow from brushing/i'll smile. no regrets/"je ne regrette rien" i'll sing like edith piaf. when my friends want me to go see tina turner or pacheco/i'll croon "sorry/i have to brush my hair."

i'll find ambrosia. my hair'll grow pomegranates & soil/rich as round the aswan/i wake in my bed to bananas/avocados/collard greens/the tramps' latest disco hit/fresh croissant/pouilly fuissé/ishmael reed's essays/charlotte carter's stories/all stream from my hair.

& with the bricks that plop from where a 9-year-old's top braid wd be/i will brush myself a house with running water & a bidet. i'll have a closet full of clean bed linen & the lil girl from the castro convertible commercial will come & open the bed repeatedly & stay on as a helper to brush my hair. lily is the only person i know whose every word leaves a purple haze on the tip of yr tongue. when this happens i says clouds are forming/& i has to close the windows. violet rain is hard to remove from blue satin pillows *(LOU, the magician, gets up. he points to* LILY *sitting very still. he reminds us that it is only thru him that we are able to know these people without the "masks"/the lies/& he cautions that all their thoughts are not benign. they are not safe from what they remember or imagine)*

LOU: you have t come with me/to this place where magic is/

to hear my song/some times i forget & leave my tune

in the corner of the closet under all the dirty clothes/

in this place/magic asks me where i've been/how i've

been singin/lately i leave my self in all the wrong hands/

in this place where magic is involved in

undoin our masks/i am able to smile & answer that.

in this place where magic always asks for me

i discovered a lot of other people who talk without mouths

who listen to what you say/by watchin yr jewelry dance

& in this place where magic stays

you can let yrself in or out

but when you leave yrself at home/burglars & daylight thieves

pounce on you & sell yr skin/at cut-rates on tenth avenue

(ROSS has been playing the acoustic guitar softly as LOU spoke. ALEC picks up on the train of LOU's thoughts & tells a story that in turn captures NATALIE's attention. slowly, NATALIE becomes the woman ALEC describes)

ALEC: she had always wanted a baby/never a family /never a man/

she had always wanted a baby/who wd suckle & sleep

a baby boy who wd wet/& cry/& smile suckle & sleep

when she sat in bars/on the stool/near the door/& cross from the juke box/with her legs straddled & revealin red lace pants/& lil hair smashed under the stockings/she wd think how she wanted this baby & how she wd call the baby/"myself" & as she thot/bout this brown lil thing/she ordered another bourbon/double

& tilted her head as if to cuddle some infant/not present/the men in the bar never imagined her as someone's mother/she rarely tended her own self carefully/

(NATALIE rises slowly, sits astride on the floor) just enough to exude a languid sexuality that teased the men off work/& the bartender/ray who waz her only friend/women didnt take to her/so she spent her afternoons with ray/in the bar round the corner from her lil house/that shook winsomely in a hard wind/surrounded by three weepin willows

NATALIE: my name is sue-jean & i grew here/a ordinary colored girl with no claims to any thing/ or anyone/i drink now/bourbon/in harder times/beer/but i always wanted to have a baby/ a lil boy/named myself

ALEC: one time/she made it with ray

NATALIE: & there waz nothin special there/only a hot rough bangin/a brusque barrelin throwin of torso/legs & sweat/ray wanted to kiss me/ but i screamed/cuz i didnt like kissin/only fuckin/& we rolled round/i waz a peculiar sorta woman/wantin no kisses/no caresses/ just power/heat & no eaziness of thrust/ray pulled himself outa me/with no particular exclamation/he smacked me on my behind/i waz grinnin/& he took that as a indication of his skill/he believed he waz a good lover/& a woman like me/didnt never want nothin but a hard dick/& everyone believed that/tho no one in town really knew

ALEC: so ray/went on behind the bar cuz he had got his

NATALIE: & i lay in the corner laughin/with my drawers/twisted round my ankles & my hair standin every which way/i waz laughin/knowin i wd have this child/myself/& no one wd ever claim him/cept me cuz i waz a low-down thing/ layin in sawdust & whiskey stains/i laughed & had a good time masturbatin in the shadows.

ALEC: sue-jean ate starch for good luck

NATALIE: like mama kareena/tol me

ALEC: & she planted five okras/five collards/& five tomatoes

NATALIE: for good luck too/i waz gonna have this baby/i even went over to the hospital to learn prenatal care/& i kept myself clean

ALEC: sue-jean's lanky body got ta spreadin & her stomach waz taut & round high in her chest/a high pregnancy is sure to be a boy/& she smiled

NATALIE: i stopped goin to the bar

ALEC: started cannin food

NATALIE: knittin lil booties

ALEC: even goin to church wit the late nite radio evangelist

NATALIE: i gotta prayer cloth for the boy/myself waz gonna be safe from all that his mama/waz prey to

ALEC: sure/sue-jean waz a scandal/but that waz to be expected/cuz she waz always a po criterish chile

NATALIE: & wont no man bout step my way/ever/ just cuz i hadda bad omen on me/from the very womb/i waz bewitched is what the ol women usedta say

ALEC: sue-jean waz born on a full moon/the year of the flood/the night the river raised her skirts & sat over alla the towns & settlements for 30 miles in each direction/the nite the river waz in labor/gruntin & groanin/splittin trees & families/spillin cupboards over the ground/ waz the nite sue-jean waz born

NATALIE: & my mother died/drownin/holdin me up over the mud crawlin in her mouth

ALEC: somebody took her & she lived to be the town's no one/now with the boy achin & dancin in her belly/sue-jean waz a gay & gracious woman/she made pies/she baked cakes & left them on the stoop of the church she had never entered just cuz she wanted/& she grew plants & swept her floors/she waz someone she had never known/she waz herself with child/& she waz a wonderful bulbous thing

NATALIE: the nite/myself waz born/ol mama kareena from the hills came down to see bout me/ i hollered & breathed/i did exactly like mama kareena said/& i pushed & pushed & there waz a earthquake up in my womb/i wanted to sit up & pull the tons of logs trapped in my

crotch out/so i cd sleep/but it wdnt go way/i pushed & thot i saw 19 horses runnin in my pussy/i waz sure there waz a locomotive stalled up in there burnin coal & steamin & pushin gainst a mountain

ALEC: finally the child's head waz within reach & mama kareena/brought the boy into this world

NATALIE: & he waz awright/with alla his toes & fingers/his lil dick & eyes/elbows that bent/& legs/ straight/i wanted a big glassa bourbon/& mama kareena brought it/right away/we sat drinkin the bourbon/& lookin at the child whose name waz myself/like i had wanted/& the two of us ate placenta stew . . . i waznt really sure . . .

ALEC: sue-jean you werent really sure you wanted myself to wake up/you always wanted him to sleep/or at most to nurse/the nites yr dreams were disturbed by his cryin

NATALIE: i had no one to help me

ALEC: so you were always with him/& you didnt mind/you knew this waz yr baby/myself/& you cuddled him/carried him all over the house with you all day/no matter/what

NATALIE: everythin waz going awright til/myself wanted to crawl

ALEC: (*moving closer to* NATALIE) & discover a world of his own/then you became despondent/ & yr tits began to dry & you lost the fullness of yr womb/where myself/had lived

NATALIE: i wanted that back

ALEC: you wanted back the milk

NATALIE: & the tight gourd of a stomach i had when myself waz bein in me

ALEC: so you slit his wrists

NATALIE: he waz sleepin

ALEC: sucked the blood back into yrself/& waited/ myself shriveled up in his crib

NATALIE: a dank lil blk thing/i never touched him again

ALEC: you were always holdin yr womb/feelin him kick & sing to you bout love/& you wd hold yr tit in yr hand

NATALIE: like i always did when i fed him

ALEC: & you waited & waited/for a new myself. tho there were labor pains

NATALIE: & i screamed in my bed

ALEC: yr legs pinnin to the air

NATALIE: spinnin sometimes like a ferris wheel/i cd get no child to fall from me

ALEC: & she forgot abt the child bein born/& waz heavy & full all her life/with "myself"

NATALIE: who'll be out/any day now

(ELI moves from behind the bar to help NATALIE/ or to clean tables. he doesnt really know. he stops suddenly)

ELI: aint that a goddamn shame/aint that a way to come into the world

sometimes i really cant write

sometimes i cant even talk

(the minstrel mask comes down very slowly. blackout, except for lights on the big minstrel mask which remains visible throughout inter- mission)

ACT II

(all players onstage are frozen, except LOU, who makes a motion for the big minstrel mask to dis- appear again. as the mask flies up, LOU begins)

LOU: in this place where magic stays

you can let yrself in or out

(he makes a magic motion. a samba is heard from the jukebox & activity is begun in the bar again. DAHLIA, NATALIE & LILY enter, appar- ently from the ladies room)

NATALIE: i swear we went to that audition in good faith/& that man asked us where we learned to speak english so well/i swear this foreigner/ asked us/from the city of new york/where we learned to speak english.

LILY: all i did was say "bom dia/como vai"/and the englishman got red in the face

LOU: *(as the englishman)* yr from the states/aren't you?

LILY: "sim"/i said/in good portuguese

LOU: but you speak portuguese

LILY: "sim" i said/in good portuguese

LOU: how did you pick that up?

LILY: i hadda answer so simple/i cdnt say i learned it/cuz niggahs cant learn & that wda been too hard on the man/so i said/in good english: i held my ear to the ground & listened to the samba from bêlim

DAHLIA: you should have said: i make a lotta phone calls to casçais, portugao

BETTINA: i gotta bahiano boyfriend

NATALIE: how abt: i waz an angolan freedom fighter

MAXINE: no/lily/tell him: i'm a great admirer of zeza motto & leci brandao

LILY: when the japanese red army invaded san juan/they poisoned the papaya with portuguese. i eat a lotta papaya. last week/i developed a strange schizophrenic condition/with 4 mani- fest personalities: one spoke english & under- stood nothing/one spoke french & had access to the world/one spoke spanish & voted against statehood for puerto rico/one spoke portuguese. "eu naõ falo ingles entaõ y voce"/i dont speak english anymore/& you?

(all the women in the company have been doing samba steps as the others spoke/now they all dance around a table in their own ritual/which stirs ALEC & LOU to interrupt this female segre- gation. the women scatter to different tables, leaving the two interlopers alone. so, ALEC & LOU begin their conversation)

ALEC: not only waz she without a tan, but she held her purse close to her hip like a new yorker. someone who rode the paris métro or listened to mariachis in plaza santa cecilia. she waz not from here

(he sits at table)

LOU: *(following suit)* but from there

ALEC: some there where coloureds/mulattoes/ negroes/blacks cd make a living big enough to leave there to come here/where no one went there much any more for all sorts of reasons

LOU: the big reasons being immigration restric- tions & unemployment. nowadays, immigra- tion restrictions of every kind apply to any

noneuropean persons who want to go there
from here

ALEC: some who want to go there from here risk
fetching trouble with the customs authority
there

LOU: or later with the police, who can tell who's
not from there cuz the shoes are pointed &
laced strange

ALEC: the pants be for august & yet it's january

LOU: the accent is patterned for pétionville, but
working in crown heights

ALEC: what makes a person comfortably ordinary
here cd make him dangerously conspicuous
there

LOU: so some go to london or amsterdam or paris/
where they are so abounding no one tries to tell
who is from where

ALEC: still the far right wing of every there prints
lil pamphlets that say everyone from there shd
leave & go back where they came from

LOU: this is manifest legally thru immigration restrictions & personally thru unemployment

ALEC: anyway the yng woman waz from there/&
she waz alone. that waz good. cuz if a person
had no big brother in gronigen/no aunt in rouen

LOU: no sponsor in chicago

ALEC: this brown woman from there might be a
good idea. everybody in the world/european &
non-european alike/everybody knows that rich
white girls are hard to find. some of them joined
the weather underground/some the baader-
meinhof gang

LOU: a whole bunch of them gave up men entirely

ALEC: so the exotic lover in the sun routine
becomes more difficult to swing/if she wants
to talk abt plastic explosives & the resistance
of the black masses to socialism/instead of
giving head as the tide slips in or lending
money

LOU: just for the next few days

ALEC: is hard to find a rich white girl who is so
dumb/too

LOU: anyway. the whole world knows/european &
non-european alike/the whole world knows
that nobody loves the black woman like they

love farrah fawcett-majors. the whole world
dont turn out for a dead black woman like they
did for marilyn monroe

ALEC: actually/the demise of josephine baker waz
an international event

LOU: but she was a war hero
the worldwide un-beloved black woman is a
good idea/if she is from there & one is a young
man with gd looks/piercing eyes/& knowledge
of several romantic languages
(*throughout this conversation, ALEC & LOU
will make attempts to seduce, cajole, & woo the
women of the bar as their narrative indicates.
the women play the roles as described, being so
moved by romance*)

ALEC: the best dancing spots/the hill where one
can see the entire bay at twilight

LOU: the beach where the seals & pelicans run
free/the hidden "local" restaurants

ALEC: "aw babee/you so pretty" begins often in
the lobby of hotels where the bright handsome
yng men wd be loiterers

LOU: were they not needed to tend the needs of
the black women from there

ALEC: tourists are usually white people or asians
who didnt come all this way to meet a black
woman who isnt even foreign

LOU: so hotel managers wink an eye at the yng men
in the lobby or by the bar who wd be loitering/
but are gonna help her have a gd time

ALEC: maybe help themselves too

LOU: everybody in the world/european & non-
european alike/everybody knows the black
woman from there is not treated as a princess/as
a jewel/a cherished lover

ALEC: that's not how sapphire got her reputation/
nor how mrs. jefferson perceives the world

LOU: you know/babee/you dont act like them. aw
babee/you so pretty

ALEC: the yng man in the hotel watches the yng
blk woman sit & sit & sit/while the european
tourists dance with each other/& the dapper local fellas mambo frenetically with secretaries
from arizona/in search of the missing rich white
girl. our girl sits &

FEMALE CAST MEMBERS: *(in unison)* sits & sits & sits

ALEC: *(to* DAHLIA *&* NATALIE, *who move to the music)* maybe she is courageous & taps her foot. maybe she is bold & enjoys the music/ smiling/shaking shoulders. let her sit & let her know she is unwanted

LOU: she is not white & she is not from here

ALEC: let her know she is not pretty enuf to dance the next merengue. then appear/mysteriously/ in the corner of the bar. stare at her. just stare. when stevie wonder's song/"isnt she lovely"/ blares thru the red-tinted light/ask her to dance & hold her as tyrone power wda. hold her & stare

*(*ROSS *&* ELI *sing the chorus to stevie wonder's "isn't she lovely")*

LOU: dance yr ass off. she has been discovered by the non-european fred astaire

ALEC: let her know she is a surprise/an event. by the look on yr face you've never seen anyone like this black woman from there. you say: "aw/you not from here?"/totally astonished. she murmurs that she is from there. as if to apologize for her unfortunate place of birth

LOU: you say

ALEC: aw babee/you so pretty, & it's all over

LOU: a night in a pension near the sorbonne. pick her up from the mattress. throw her gainst the wall in a show of exotic temper & passion: "maintenant/tu es ma femme. nous nous sommes mariés." unions of this sort are common wherever the yng black women travel alone. a woman traveling alone is an affront to the non-european man who is known the world over/to european & non-european alike/for his way with women

ALEC: his sense of romance/how he can say:

LOU: aw babee/you so pretty . . . and even a beautiful woman will believe no one else ever recognized her loveliness

ELI: or else/he comes to a cafe in willemstad in the height of the sunset. an able-bodied/sinewy yng man who wants to buy one beer for the yng woman. after the first round/he discovers he

has run out of money/so she must buy the next round/when he discovers/what beautiful legs you have/how yr mouth is like the breath of tiger lilies. we shall make love in the/how you call it/ yes in the earth/in the dirt/i will have you in my/ how you say/where things grow/aw/yes/i will have you in the soil. probably under the stars & smelling of wine/an unforgettable international affair can be consummated

(the company sings "tara's theme" as ELI *ends his speech.* ELI *&* BETTINA *take a tango walk to the bar, while* MAXINE *mimics a 1930's photographer, shooting them as they sail off into the sunset)*

MAXINE: at 11:30 one evening i waz at the port authority/new york/united states/myself. now i waz there & i spoke english & waz holding approximately $7 american currency/when a yng man from there came up to me from the front of the line of people waiting for the princeton new jersey united states local bus. i mean to say/he gave up his chance for a good seat to come say to me:

ROSS: i never saw a black woman reading nietzsche

MAXINE: i waz demure enough/i said i have to for a philosophy class. but as the night went on i noticed this yng man waz so much like the other yng men from here/who use their bodies as bait & their smiles as passport alternatives. anyway the night did go on. we were snuggled together in the rear of the bus going down the jersey turnpike. he told me in english/that he had spoken all his life in st. louis/where he waz raised:

ROSS: i've wanted all my life to meet someone like you. i want you to meet my family/who haven't seen me in a long time/since i left missouri looking for opportunity . . .

(he is lost for words)

LOU: *(stage whisper)* opportunity to sculpt

ROSS: thank you/opportunity to sculpt

MAXINE: he had been everyplace/he said

ROSS: you arent like any black woman i've ever met anywhere

MAXINE: here or there

ROSS: i had to come back to new york cuz of immigration restrictions & high unemployment among black american sculptors abroad

MAXINE: just as we got to princeton/he picked my face up from his shoulder & said:

ROSS: aw babee/you so pretty

MAXINE: aw babee/you so pretty. i believe that night i must have looked beautiful for a black woman from there/though i cd be asked at any moment to tour the universe/to climb a 6-story walkup with a brilliant & starving painter/to share kadushi/to meet mama/to getta kiss each time the swing falls toward the willow branch/to imagine where he say he from/& more. i cd/i cd have all of it/but i cd not be taken/long as i don't let a stranger be the first to say:

LOU: aw babee/you so pretty

MAXINE: after all/immigration restrictions & unemployment cd drive a man to drink or to lie
  (she breaks away from ROSS*)*
     so if you know yr beautiful & bright & cherishable awready/when he say/in whatever language:

ALEC: *(to* NATALIE*)* aw babee/you so pretty

MAXINE: you cd say:

NATALIE: i know. thank you

MAXINE: then he'll smile/& you'll smile. he'll say:

ELI: *(stroking* BETTINA'S *thigh)* what nice legs you have

MAXINE: you can say:

BETTINA: *(removing his hand)* yes. they run in the family

MAXINE: oh! whatta universe of beautiful & well traveled women!

MALE CAST MEMBERS: *(in unison)* aw babee/i've never met anyone like you

FEMALE CAST MEMBERS: *(in unison, pulling away from men to stage edges)* that's strange/there are millions of us!
  (men all cluster after unsuccessful attempts to persuade their women to talk. ALEC *gets the idea to serenade the women;* ROSS *takes the first verse, with men singing back-up. song is "ooh baby," by smokey robinson)*

ROSS: *(singing)* i did you wrong/my heart went out to play/but in the game
     i lost you/what a price to pay/i'm cryin . . .

MALE PLAYERS: *(singing)* oo oo oo/baby baby . . . oo oo oo/baby baby
  (this brings no response from the women; the men elect ELI *to lead the second verse)*

ELI: mistakes i know i've made a few/but i'm only human
     you've made mistakes too/i'm cryin . . .
       oo oo oo/baby baby . . . oo oo oo/baby baby
  (the women slowly forsake their staunch indignation/returning to the arms of their partners. all that is except LILY, *who walks abt the room of couples awkwardly)*

MALE CAST MEMBERS & LILY: *(singing)* i'm just about at the end of my rope
     but i can't stop trying/i cant give up hope
     cause i/i believe one day/i'll hold you near
     whisper i love you/until that day is here
     i'm cryin . . . oo oo oo/baby baby
  *(*LILY *begins as the company continues to sing)*

LILY: unfortunately
     the most beautiful man in the world
     is unavailable
     that's what he told me
     i saw him wandering abt/said well this is one of
       a kind
     & i might be able to help him out
     so alone & pretty in all this ganja & bodies
       melting
     he danced with me & i cd become that
     a certain way to be held that's considered in advance
     a way a thoughtful man wd kiss a woman who
     cd be offended easily/but waznt cuz
     of course the most beautiful man in the world
     knows exactly what to do
     with someone who knows that's who he is/
     these dreads fallin thru my dress
     so my nipples just stood up
     these hands playin the guitar on my back
     the lips somewhere between my neck
     & my forehead

talking bout ocho rios & how i really must go
marcus garvey cda come in the door & we/
we wd still be dancin that dance
the motion that has more to do with kinetic
   energy
than shootin stars/more to do with the impossibility
of all this/& how it waz awready bein too much
our reason failed
we tried to go away & be just together
aside from the silence that weeped
with greed/we didnt need/anything/but one another
for tonite
but he is the most beautiful man in the world
   says he's unavailable/
& this man whose eyes made me
half-naked & still & brazen/was singin with
   me
since we cd not talk/we sang
(male players end their chorus with a flourish)
LILY: we sang with bob marley
   this man/surely the most beautiful man in the
      world/& i
   sang/"i wanna love you & treat you right/
   *(the couples begin different kinds of reggae
   dances)*
   I wanna love you every day & every nite"
THE COMPANY: *(dancing & singing)* we'll be together with the roof right over our heads
   we'll share the shelter of my single bed
   we'll share the same room/jah provide the
      bread
DAHLIA: *(stops dancing during conversation)* i tell
   you it's not just the part that makes me love you
   so much
LOU: what is it/wait/i know/you like my legs
DAHLIA: yes/uh huh/yr legs & yr arms/& . . .
LOU: but that's just my body/you started off saying
   you loved me & now i see it's just my body
DAHLIA: oh/i didnt mean that/it's just i dont know
   you/except as the character i'm sposed to love/
   & well i know rehearsal is over/but i'm still in
   love with you

*(they go to the bar to get drinks, then sit at a
table)*
ROSS: but baby/you have to go on the road. we
   need the money
NATALIE: i'm not going on the road so you can
   fuck all these aspiring actresses
ROSS: aw/just some of them/baby
NATALIE: that's why i'm not going
ROSS: if you dont go on the road i'll still be fuckin
   em/but you & me/we'll be in trouble/you under-
   stand?
NATALIE: *(stops dancing)* no i dont understand
ROSS: well let me break it down to you
NATALIE: please/break it down to me
BETTINA: *(stops dancing)* hey/natalie/why dont
   you make him go on the road/they always want
   us to be so goddamned conscientious
ALEC: *(stops dancing)* dont you think you shd
   mind yr own bizness?
NATALIE: yeah bettina/mind yr own bizness
   (she pulls ROSS *to a table with her)*
BETTINA: *(to* ALEC*)* no/i'm tired of having to take
   any & every old job to support us/& you get to
   have artistic integrity & refuse parts that are
   beneath you
ALEC: thats right/i'm not playing the fool or the
   black buck pimp circus/i'm an actor not
   a stereotype/i've been trained. you know i'm a
   classically trained actor
BETTINA: & just what do you think we are?
MAXINE: well/i got offered another whore part
   downtown
ELI: you gonna take it?
MAXINE: yeah
LILY: if you dont/i know someone who will
ALEC: *(to* BETTINA*)* i told you/we arent gonna get
   anyplace/by doin every bit part for a niggah
   that someone waves in fronta my face
BETTINA: & we arent gonna live long on nothin/
   either/cuz i'm quittin my job
ALEC: be in the real world for once & try to un-
   derstand me
BETTINA: you mean/i shd understand that you are
   the great artist & i'm the trouper.

ALEC: i'm not sayin that we cant be gigglin & laughin all the time dancin around/but i cant stay in these "hate whitey" shows/cuz they arent true

BETTINA: a failure of imagination on yr part/i take it

ALEC: no/an insult to my person

BETTINA: oh i see/you wanna give the people some more make-believe

ALEC: i cd always black up again & do minstrel work/wd that make you happy?

BETTINA: there is nothin niggardly abt a decent job. work is honorable/work!

ALEC: well/i got a problem. i got lots of problems/ but i got one i want you to fix & if you can fix it/i'll do anything you say. last spring this niggah from the midwest asked for president carter to say he waz sorry for that forgettable phenomenon/slavery/which brought us all together. i never did get it/none of us ever got no apology from no white folks abt not bein considered human beings/that makes me mad & tired. someone told me "roots" waz the way white folks worked out their guilt/the success of "roots" is the way white folks assuaged their consciences/i dont know this/this is what i waz told. I dont get any pleasure from nobody watchin me trying to be a slave i once waz/who got away/when we all know they had an emancipation proclamation/ that the civil war waz not fought over us. we all know that we/actually dont exist unless we play football or basketball or baseball or soccer/pélé/ see they still import a strong niggah to earn money. art here/isnt like in the old country/ where we had some spare time & did what we liked to do/i dont know this either/this is also something i've been told. i just want to find out why no one has even been able to sound a gong & all the reporters recite that the gong is ringin/ while we watch all the white people/immigrants & invaders/conquistadors & relatives of london debtors from georgia/kneel & apologize to us/ just for three or four minutes. now/this is not impossible/& someone shd make a day where a few

minutes of the pain of our lives is acknowledged. i have never been very interested in what white people did/cuz i waz able/like most of us/to have very lil to do with them/but if i become a success that means i have to talk to white folks more than in high school/they are everywhere/ you know how they talk abt a neighborhood changin/we suddenly become all over the place/ they are now all over my life/& i dont like it. i am not talkin abt poets & painters/not abt women & lovers of beauty/i am talkin abt that proverbial white person who is usually a man who just/ turns yr body around/looks at yr teeth & yr ass/ who feels yr calves & back/& agrees on a price. we are/you see/now able to sell ourselves/& i am still a person who is tired/a person who is not into his demise/just three minutes for our lives/ just three minutes of silence & a gong in st. louis/oakland/in los angeles . . .

(the entire company looks at him as if he's crazy/he tries to leave the bar/but BETTINA stops him)

BETTINA: you're still outta yr mind. ain't no apologies keeping us alive.

LOU: what are you gonna do with white folks kneeling all over the country anyway/man
(LOU signals everyone to kneel)

LILY: they say i'm too light to work/but when i asked him what he meant/he said i didnt actually look black. but i said/my mama knows i'm black & my daddy/damn sure knows i'm black/ & he is the only one who has a problem thinkin i'm black/i said so let me play a white girl/i'm a classically trained actress & i need the work & i can do it/he said that wdnt be very ethical of him. can you imagine that shit/not ethical

NATALIE: as a red-blooded white woman/i cant allow you all to go on like that
(NATALIE starts jocularly)

cuz today i'm gonna be a white girl/i'll retroactively wake myself up/ah low & behold/ a white girl in my bed/but first i'll haveta call a white girl i know to have some more accurate information/what's the first thing white girls think in the morning/do they get up being glad they aint niggahs/do they remember mama/or worry abt gettin to work/do they work?/do they play isadora & wrap themselves in sheets & go tip toeing to the kitchen to make maxwell house coffee/oh i know/the first thing a white girl does in the morning is fling her hair/

so now i'm done with that/i'm gonna water my plants/but am i a po white trash white girl with a old jellyjar/or am i a sophisticated & protestant suburbanite with 2 valiums slugged awready & a porcelain water carrier leading me up the stairs strewn with heads of dolls & nasty smellin white husband person's underwear/if i was really protected from the niggahs/i might go to early morning mass & pick up a tomato pie on the way home/so i cd eat it during the young & the restless. in williams arizona as a white girl/i cd push the navaho women outta my way in the supermarket & push my nose in the air so i wdnt haveta smell them. coming from bay ridge on the train i cd smile at all the black & puerto rican people/& hope they cant tell i want them to go back where they came from/or at least be invisible

i'm still in my kitchen/so i guess i'll just have to fling my hair again & sit down. i shd pinch my cheeks to bring the color back/i wonder why the colored lady hasnt arrived to clean my house yet/so i cd go to the beauty parlor & sit under a sunlamp to get some more color back/it's terrible how god gave those colored women such clear complexions/it take em years to develop wrinkles/but beauty can be bought & flattered into the world.

as a white girl on the street/i can assume since i am a white girl on the streets/that everyone notices how beautiful i am/especially lil black & caribbean boys/they love to look at me/ i'm exotic/no one in their families looks like me/poor things. if i waz one of those white girls who loves one of those grown black fellas/i cd say with my eyes wide open/totally sincere/oh i didnt know that/i cd say i didnt know/i cant/i

dont know how/cuz i'ma white girl & i dont have to do much of anything.

all of this is the fault of the white man's sexism/oh how i loathe tight-assed thin-lipped pink white men/even the football players lack a certain relaxed virility. that's why my heroes are either just like my father/who while he still cdnt speak english knew enough to tell me how the niggers shd go back where they came from/or my heroes are psychotic faggots who are white/ or else they are/oh/you know/colored men.

being a white girl by dint of my will/is much more complicated than i thought it wd be/but i wanted to try it cuz so many men like white girls/white men/black men/latin men/ jewish men/asians/everybody. so i thought if i waz a white girl for a day i might understand this better/after all gertrude stein wanted to know abt the black women/alice adams wrote *thinking abt billie*/joyce carol oates has three different black characters all with the same name/i guess cuz we are underdeveloped individuals or cuz we are all the same/at any rate i'm gonna call this thinkin abt white girls/cuz helmut newton's awready gotta book called *white women*/see what i mean/that's a best seller/one store i passed/hadda sign said/

> ## WHITE WOMEN
> ## SOLD OUT

it's this kinda pressure that forces us white girls to be so absolutely pathological abt the other women in the world/who now that they're not all servants or peasants want to be considered beautiful too. we simply krinkle our hair/ learn to dance the woogie dances/slant our eyes with make-up or surgery/learn spanish & claim argentinian background/or as a real trump card/show up looking like a real white girl. you know all western civilization depends on us/

i still havent left my house. i think i'll fling my hair once more/but this time with a pout/cuz i think i havent been fair to the sisterhood/ women's movement faction of white girls/although/they always ask what do you people really want. as if the colored woman of the world were a strange sort of neutered workhorse/which isnt too far from reality/since i'm still waiting for my cleaning lady & the lady who takes care of my children & the lady who caters my parties & the lady who accepts quarters at the bathroom in sardi's. those poor creatures shd be sterilized/no one shd have to live such a life. cd you hand me a towel/thank-you caroline. i've left all of maxime's last winter clothes in a pile for you by the back door. they have to be cleaned but i hope yr girls can make gd use of them.

oh/i'm still not being fair/all the white women in the world dont wake up being glad they aint niggahs/only some of them/the ones who dont/wake up thinking how can i survive another day of this culturally condoned incompetence. i know i'll play a tenor horn & tell all the colored artists i meet/that now i'm just like them/i'm colored i'll say cuz i have a struggle too. or i cd punish this white beleaguered body of mine with the advances of a thousand ebony bodies/all built like franco harris or peter tosh/ a thousand of them may take me & do what they want/cuz i'm so sorry/yes i'm so sorry they were born niggahs. but then if i cant punish myself to death for being white/i certainly cant in good conscience keep waiting for the cleaning lady/& everytime i attempt even the smallest venture into the world someone comes to help me/like if i do anything/anything at all i'm extending myself as a white girl/cuz part of being a white girl is being absent/like those women who are just with a man but whose names the black people never remember/they just say oh yeah his white girl waz with him/or a white girl got beat & killed today/why someone will say/cuz some niggah told her to give him her money & she said no/cuz she thought he realized that she waz a white girl/& he did know but he didnt care/so he killed her & took the money/but the cops knew she waz a white girl & cdnt be killed by a niggah especially/when she had awreddy said no. the niggah was sposed to hop round the corner backwards/you dig/so the cops/found the culprit within 24 hours/cuz just like emmett till/niggahs do not kill white girls.

i'm still in my house/having flung my hair-do for the last time/what with having to take 20 valium a day/to consider the ERA/& all the men in the world/& my ignorance of the world/ it is overwhelming. i'm so glad i'm colored. boy i cd wake up in the morning & think abt anything. i can remember emmett till & not haveta smile at anybody.

MAXINE: *(compelled to speak by* NATALIE'S *pain)* whenever these things happened to me/& i waz young/i wd eat a lot/or buy new fancy underwear with rhinestones & lace/or go to the movies/ maybe call a friend/talk to made-up boyfriends til dawn. this waz when i waz under my parents' roof/& trees that grew into my room had to be cut back once a year/this waz when the birds sometimes flew thru the halls of the house as if the ceilings were sky & i/simply another winged creature. yet no one around me noticed me especially. no one around saw anything but a precocious brown girl with peculiar ideas. like during the polio epidemic/i wanted to have a celebration/which nobody cd understand since iron lungs & not going swimming waznt nothing to celebrate. but i explained that i waz celebrating the bounty of the lord/which more people didnt understand/til i went on to say that/it waz obvious that god had protected the colored folks from polio/nobody understood that. i did/if god had made colored people susceptible to polio/ then we wd be on the pictures & the television with the white children. i knew only white folks cd get that particular disease/& i celebrated. that's how come i always commemorated anything that affected me or the colored people. according to my history of the colored race/not enough attention was paid to small victories or small personal defeats of the colored. i celebrated the colored trolley driver/the colored basketball team/the colored blues singer/&

the colored light heavy weight champion of the world. then too/i had a baptist child's version of high mass for the slaves in new orleans whom i had read abt/& i tried to grow watermelons & rice for the dead slaves from the east. as a child i took on the burden of easing the ghost-colored-folks' souls & trying hard to keep up with the affairs of my own colored world.

when i became a woman, my world got smaller. my grandma closed up the windows/so the birds wdnt fly in the house any more. waz bad luck for a girl so yng & in my condition to have the shadows of flying creatures over my head. i didnt celebrate the trolley driver any-more/cuz he might know i waz in this condition. i didnt celebrate the basketball team anymore/cuz they were yng & handsome & yng & hand-some cd mean trouble. but trouble waz when white kids called you names or beat you up cuz you had no older brother/trouble waz when someone died/or the tornado hit yr house/now trouble meant something abt yng & handsome/& white or colored. if he waz yng & handsome that meant trouble. seemed like every one who didnt have this condition/so birds cdnt fly over yr head/waz trouble. as i understood it/my mama & my grandma were sending me out to be with trouble/but not to get into trouble. the yng & handsome cd dance with me & call for sunday supper/the yng & handsome cd write my name on their notebooks/cd carry my ribbons on the field for gd luck/the uncles cd hug me & chat for hours abt my growing up/so i counted all 492 times this condition wd make me victim to this trouble/before i wd be immune to it/the way colored folks were immune to polio.

i had discovered innumerable manifestations of trouble: jealousy/fear/indignation & recurring fits of vulnerability that lead me right back to the contradiction i had never understood/even as a child/how half the world's population cd be bad news/be yng & handsome/& later/eligible & interested/& trouble.

plus/according to my own version of the history of the colored people/only white people hurt little colored girls or grown colored women/ my mama told me only white people had social disease & molested children/and my grandma told me only white people committed unnatural acts. that's how come i knew only white folks got polio/muscular dystrophy/sclerosis/& mental illness/this waz all verified by the television. but i found out that the colored folks knew abt the same vicious & disease-ridden passions that the white folks knew.

the pain i succumbed to each time a colored person did something that i believed only white people did waz staggering. my entire life seems to be worthless/if my own folks arent better than white folks/then surely the sagas of slavery & the jim crow hadnt convinced anyone that we were better than them. i commenced to buying pieces of gold/14 carat/24 carat/18 carat gold/ every time some black person did something that waz beneath him as a black person & more like a white person. i bought gold cuz it came from the earth/& more than likely it came from south africa/where the black people are humili-ated & oppressed like in slavery. i wear all these things at once/to remind the black people that it cost a lot for us to be here/our value/can be known instinctively/but since so many black people are having a hard time not being like white folks/i wear these gold pieces to protest their ignorance/their disconnect from history. i buy gold with a vengeance/each time someone appropriates my space or my time without per-mission/each time someone is discourteous or actually cruel to me/if my mind is not respected/ my body toyed with/i buy gold/& weep. i weep as i fix the chains round my neck/my wrists/my an-kles. i weep cuz all my childhood ceremonies for the ghost-slaves have been in vain. colored peo-ple can get polio & mental illness. slavery is not unfamiliar to me. no one on this planet knows/ what i know abt gold/abt anything hard to get & beautiful/anything lasting/wrought from pain. no one understands that surviving the impossi-ble is sposed to accentuate the positive aspects of a people.

(ALEC *is the only member of the company able to come immediately to* MAXINE. *when he reaches her,* LOU, *in his full magician's regalia, freezes the whole company*)

LOU: yes yes yes   3 wishes is all you get
        scarlet ribbons for yr hair
        a farm in mississippi
        someone to love you madly
all things are possible
but aint no colored magician in his right mind
gonna make you white
cuz this is blk magic you lookin at
& i'm fixin you up good/fixin you up good & col-
    ored
& you gonna be colored all yr life

& you gonna love it/bein colored/all yr life
colored & love it/love it/bein colored
(LOU *beckons the others to join him in the chant,* "colored & love it." *it becomes a serious celebration, like church/like home/but then* LOU *freezes them suddenly*)

LOU: crackers are born with the right to be
alive/i'm making ours up right here
in yr face/& we gonna be
colored & love it
(*the huge minstrel mask comes down as company continues to sing* "colored & love it/love it being colored." *blackout/but the minstrel mask remains visible. the company is singing* "colored & love it being colored" *as audience exits*)

MA RAINEY'S BLACK BOTTOM (1984)

The blues impulse transferred . . . containing a race, and its expression. . . . Through its many changes, it remained the exact replication of The Black Man In The West.

As Amiri Baraka's comments in *Black Music* indicate, blacks have long recognized and acknowledged the centrality of the blues to African-American culture. And in its various transmutations and derivatives—ragtime, jazz, rhythm and blues, rock, hip-hop, and rap—blues has become a vital part of both American and world culture. In 1965, in a Pittsburgh rooming house the energy of blues and its significance for African Americans were driven home to the young August Wilson when he discovered a Bessie Smith recording which for the first time in his life, Wilson asserts, alerted him to "a world that contained my image, a world at once rich and varied, marked and marking, brutal and beautiful, and at crucial odds with the larger world that contained it and pressed it from every conceivable angle." Twenty years later Wilson was to give dramatic form to the blues in his first commercial success, *Ma Rainey's Black Bottom.* In Wilson's hands, the blues, as part of the history of African Americans in this century, becomes a means of recovering not only the events of black life in America but also the textures of that life. As Wilson notes in his Preface to *Three Plays:*

> I saw blues as a cultural response of a non-literate people whose history and culture were rooted in the oral tradition. . . . [T]he blues was a flag bearer of self-definition, and within the scope of the larger world which lay beyond its doorstep, it carved out a life, set down rules, and urged a manner of being that corresponded to the temperament and sensibilities of its creators. It was a spiritual conduit that gave spontaneous expression to the spirit that was locked in combat and devising new strategies for engaging life and enlarging itself. It was a true and articulate literature that was in the forefront of the development of both character and consciousness.

At once a paean to the spirit of those who live the blues and a lamentation for the circumstances which have engendered this response, *Ma Rainey's Black Bottom* seeks to reconfigure American history, to present the 1920s from the perspective of those heretofore silenced except for their music.

August Wilson was born in Pittsburgh, Pennsylvania, in 1945 and grew up there in a black slum community called the Hill. His father was a white baker named August Wilson who other than fathering August and his five siblings had little to do with the family. His mother, Daisy Wilson, who had moved from North Carolina to Pittsburgh, supported her family's life in a cold-water apartment on welfare checks and wages from cleaning jobs. Still, Daisy Wilson found time to instill in her son a desire to read, a skill he mastered by age four. Despite his precocity, Wilson eventually left high school without graduating. As he told Bill Moyers, alienated by the persistent racism he encountered and, finally by a teacher's refusal to believe that he had written a term paper on Napoleon, Wilson turned his back on formal education and embraced the alternative of the local library. There, he began reading the works of Paul Laurence Dunbar, Ralph Ellison, Langston Hughes, and Richard Wright, among others, and supplemented his reading with jobs as a short-order cook and stock clerk, which allowed him to observe and listen to members of his contemporary community.

By 1965 he had decided that he would be a writer and began publishing in the emerging little magazines. Embracing the Black Power movement and under the influence of such Black Nationalist dramatists as Amiri Baraka, Wilson and playwright-teacher Rob Penny formed the Black Horizons Theatre in Pittsburgh in 1968. In an interview with David Savran, Wilson acknowledged that during this period he knew nothing about the theatre and that by 1971 he had initially given up on writing drama and had returned to poetry and fiction.

In 1976, however, Charles Purdy convinced Wilson to write a play about Black Bart, a recurrent character in Wilson's poetry, and a musical satire, *Black Bart and the Sacred Hills,* was born. When Purdy began working with the Penumbra Theatre in St. Paul, Minnesota, he invited Wilson to visit and rewrite the play. Wilson's 1977 revision subsequently received a staged reading by the Inner City Theatre of Los Angeles in 1978. Wilson eventually moved to St. Paul, began working at the Science Museum of Minnesota, writing dramatic sketches to accompany the exhibitions, and became affiliated with the Playwrights' Center in Minneapolis. With Purdy's encouragement, Wilson wrote *Jitney,* a play set in 1971 Pittsburgh at a gypsy cabstand that was eventually produced by the Allegheny Repertory Theatre in Pittsburgh in 1982. This was followed by *Fullerton Street*, which received a staged reading at the Playwrights' Center.

The turning point in Wilson's playwrighting career came in 1982 when *Ma Rainey's Black Bottom* was accepted at the O'Neill National Playwright's Workshop. After a series of rewritings, *Ma Rainey's Black Bottom* premiered at the Yale Repertory Theatre on 6 April 1984 directed by Wilson's mentor and friend, Lloyd Richards. Moving to Broadway in October of the same year, *Ma Rainey* ran for 267 performances, garnered overwhelmingly favorable reviews, and received the New York Drama Critics Circle Award for Best Play. Wilson's next play, *Fences* (1983), has proved his most popular play to date. An exploration of the central character Troy Maxon's failed dreams and relationships set against the changing roles of African Americans in the

1950s, *Fences* again employed the route to Broadway that *Ma Rainey* had pioneered. Establishing a pattern that all but his most recent play have followed, *Fences* opened at the Yale Repertory Theatre again under the direction of Lloyd Richards and saw additional performances in regional theatres—in this case Chicago and San Francisco—before opening on Broadway. An immediate hit, *Fences* swept the major drama prizes in 1987, winning the Drama Critics Circle Award, the Antoinette Perry (or **Tony**) Award and Pulitzer Prize for best play. Perhaps more importantly, by grossing $11 million in its first year (a record for nonmusicals on Broadway), *Fences* guaranteed Wilson's future artistic freedom. In *Joe Turner's Come and Gone* (1986; Broadway 1988), Wilson turns his attention to 1911 and examines the legacy of slavery in the rural South and the dislocations attendant to the Great Migration to the North by southern blacks in the early years of this century. *The Piano Lesson* (1988; Broadway 1990) won Wilson the 1990 Pulitzer Prize. Set in 1930s Pittsburgh, *The Piano Lesson* dramatizes the alternative uses of familial history in a brother and sister's conflict over the fate of a piano that can either become the means of securing land their father had worked as a slave, or remain as a reminder of the family's sometimes violent path from slavery to freedom. In *Two Trains Running* (1990; Broadway 1992), Wilson examines the hopes and dreams of a small Pittsburgh diner's patrons in the waning days of the civil rights movement. *Seven Guitars* (1995) reprises Wilson's musical interest, exploring the lives of 1940s blues musicians. Collectively, these plays represent Wilson's rewriting of the history of the African-American experience in the twentieth century, a project which, he has said, will generate one play for each decade.

Talking to Bill Moyers, Wilson asserted that one of the things that his plays try to accomplish is to illuminate the choices that blacks in America have made. In *Ma Rainey's Black Bottom*, Wilson examines the choice of blacks to transform the blues from a soul-sustaining music within the African-American community into entertainment for white America. Just as he would later in *Fences* with sports, Wilson takes a central element of American popular culture—music—and dismantles the myth that music can ultimately provide a means of escaping the grinding poverty and soul-numbing effects of racism. He reveals how the economic system of the period rather than liberating musically talented African Americans inexorably commodifies and exploits them and their skills, thereby replicating the social and economic order against which the subversive power of the blues has been deployed. The anger and sense of powerlessness at their circumstances manifest themselves along a continuum from Ma Rainey's aggressive hijacking of the process of production to carve out transitory moments of self-assertion and identity to the stoic acceptance of Cutler, a man who lives his life as he plays his music—absorbed totally by immediate reality. But it is in the trumpet player, Levee, that Wilson provides his most telling commentary on the cruel paradoxes of this particular choice.

Wilson carefully weaves together the historical figure of Gertrude "Ma" Rainey (1886–1939), the "Mother of the Blues," with a group of fictional characters including her "sidemen," or backup musicians, who come together in a 1927 Chicago studio to record some of Ma's most popular tunes including "Ma Rainey's Black Bottom," from which the play takes its title. Wilson's division of the acting area allows him to establish spatially the racial dynamics of the world. The recording area effectively represents the point of shared economic interest for both the whites—record producer, Sturdyvant, and Ma's manager, Irvin—and the blacks—Ma, her band, and her retinue. Literally over this area sits the aptly named "control booth" into which the whites quickly retreat and from which they manipulate the process that turns talent into wax and wax into profit. The other part of the stage is reserved for the band's rehearsal area. While many critics have acknowledged the pervasive thematic importance of the blues to *Ma Rainey's Black Bottom,* most have argued, as Frank Rich does, that the structural influence of the blues is most evident in the moments in the band's rehearsal room when each of the men steps forward—like blues musicians taking turns

as soloists—to tell a story that grounds his blues. But Wilson's division of the action allows him not only to provide an arena in which the blacks can speak revelatorily without the presence of whites, but also to counterpoint the action of one venue with the reality of the other. Thus, for example, Levee's assertions of Sturdyvant's primacy in the studio is radically modified by the forceful presence of Ma and her refusal to record Levee's version of "Ma Rainey's Black Bottom." Sturdyvant will accede to Ma's momentary requests only until he possesses her songs. As she wryly comments, "They ain't got what they wanted yet. As soon as they get my voice down on them recording machines, then it's just like I'd be some whore and they roll over and put their pants on."

But Ma Rainey's ability to live expansively within the confines established by pervasive white racism is ultimately an individual triumph that cannot be shared with her fellow sufferers. The acid of racism takes a much heavier toll in the band room. There, as Wilson related to Kim Powers, Levee confronts the question, "How can I live this life in a society that refuses to recognize my worth, that refuses to allow me to contribute to its welfare—how can I live this life and remain a whole and complete person?" Finally incapable of manipulating the white economic system into providing him the means to success that the general society insists is the determinant of personal worth, Levee seems to become the stereotypical black male who resorts to violence. Unable to attack the white man, he transfers his anger to Toledo, the voice of black nationalism who has earlier warned Levee that "We done sold Africa for the price of tomatoes. We done sold ourselves to the white men in order to be like him." With Toledo's death the black nationalist intellectual is symbolically torn from the African-American community (just as Marcus Garvey was deported in 1927 by President Calvin Coolidge) and the vitality of Levee is doomed to prison. While critics such as Edwin Wilson have seen Toledo's death as melodramatic, Sandra G. Shannon argues convincingly that Wilson carefully lays the psychic groundwork for Levee's action.

Ma Rainey's Black Bottom is finally as ineffable as the blues itself. Ma's description of the blues is as apt to Wilson's art as her own: "White folks don't understand about the blues. They hear it come out, but they don't know how it got there. They don't understand that's life's way of talking. You don't sing to feel better. You sing 'cause that's a way of understanding life."

WORKS CONSULTED

Baraka, Amiri. *Black Music.* New York: William Morrow, 1968.

Bigsby, C. W. E. *Modern American Drama, 1945–1990.* Cambridge: Cambridge University Press, 1992.

Hay, Samuel A. *African-American Theatre: A Historical and Critical Analysis.* Cambridge: Cambridge University Press, 1994.

Lieb, Sandra R. *Mother of the Blues: A Study of Ma Rainey.* Amherst: University of Massachusetts Press, 1981.

Moyers, Bill. *A World of Ideas.* New York: Doubleday, 1989.

Powers, Kim. "An Interview with August Wilson." *Theatre* 16 (5): 50–55.

Rich, Frank. "Wilson's 'Ma Rainey's' Opens." *New York Times.* Oct. 12, 1984: C1, C3.

Savran, David. "August Wilson." *In Their Own Words: Contemporary American Playwrights.* New York: Theatre Communications Group, 1988. 288–305.

Shannon, Sandra G. "The Long Wait: August Wilson's *Ma Rainey's Black Bottom.*" *Black American Literature Forum* 25:1 (1991): 135–146.

Wilmeth, Don B., and Tice L. Miller. *Cambridge Guide to American Theatre.* New York: Cambridge University Press, 1993.

Wilson, August. *Three Plays.* Pittsburgh: University of Pittsburgh Press, 1991.

Wilson, Edwin. "Ma Rainey." *Wall Street Journal.* Oct. 16, 1984: 26.

They tore the railroad down
so the Sunshine Special can't run
I'm going away baby
build me a railroad of my own

—Blind Lemon Jefferson

CHARACTERS

STURDYVANT	LEVEE
IRVIN	MA RAINEY
CUTLER	POLICEMAN
TOLEDO	DUSSIE MAE
SLOW DRAG	SYLVESTER

The Setting

There are two playing areas: what is called the "band room," and the recording studio. The band room is at stage left and is in the basement of the building. It is entered through a door up left. There are benches and chairs scattered about, a piano, a row of lockers, and miscellaneous paraphernalia stacked in a corner and long since forgotten. A mirror hangs on a wall with various posters.

The studio is upstairs at stage right, and resembles a recording studio of the late 1920s. The entrance is from a hall on the right wall. A small control booth is at the rear and its access is gained by means of a spiral staircase. Against one wall there is a line of chairs, and a horn through which the control room communicates with the performers. A door in the rear wall allows access to the band room.

The Play

It is early March in Chicago, 1927. There is a bit of a chill in the air. Winter has broken but the wind coming off the lake does not carry the promise of spring. The people of the city are bundled and brisk in their defense against such misfortunes as the weather, and the business of the city proceeds largely undisturbed.

Chicago in 1927 is a rough city, a bruising city, a city of millionaires and derelicts, gangsters and roughhouse dandies, whores and Irish grandmothers who move through its streets fingering long black rosaries. Somewhere a man is wrestling with the taste of a woman in his cheek. Somewhere a dog is barking. Somewhere the moon has fallen through a window and broken into thirty pieces of silver.

It is one o'clock in the afternoon. Secretaries are returning from their lunch, the noon Mass at St. Anthony's is over, and the priest is mumbling over his vestments while the altar boys practice their Latin. The procession of cattle cars through the stockyards continues unabated. The busboys in Mac's Place are cleaning away the last of the corned beef and cabbage, and on the city's Southside, sleepy-eyed negroes move lazily toward their small cold-water flats and rented rooms to await the onslaught of night, which will find them crowded in the bars and juke joints both dazed and dazzling in their rapport with life. It is with these negroes that our concern lies most heavily: their values, their attitudes, and particularly their music.

It is hard to define this music. Suffice it to say that it is music that breathes and touches. That connects. That is in itself a way of being, separate and distinct from any other. This music is called blues. Whether this music came from Alabama or Mississippi or other parts of the South doesn't matter anymore. The men and women who make this music have learned it from the narrow crooked streets of East St. Louis, or the streets of the city's Southside, and the Alabama or Mississippi roots have been strangled by the northern manners and customs of free men of definite and sincere worth, men for whom this music often lies at the forefront of their conscience and concerns. Thus they are laid open to be consumed by it; its warmth and redress, its braggadocio and roughly poignant comments, its vision and prayer, which would instruct and allow them to

reconnect, to reassemble and gird up for the next battle in which they would be both victim and the ten thousand slain.

ACT ONE

The lights come up in the studio. IRVIN *enters, carrying a microphone. He is a tall, fleshy man who prides himself on his knowledge of blacks and his ability to deal with them. He hooks up the microphone, blows into it, taps it, etc. He crosses over to the piano, opens it, and fingers a few keys.* STURDYVANT *is visible in the control booth. Preoccupied with money, he is insensitive to black performers and prefers to deal with them at arm's length. He puts on a pair of earphones.*

STURDYVANT: *(over speaker)* Irv . . . let's crack that mike, huh? Let's do a check on it.

IRVIN: *(crosses to mike, speaks into it)* Testing . . . one . . . two . . . three . . .
(There is a loud feedback. STURDYVANT *fiddles with the dials.)*
Testing . . . one . . . two . . . three . . . testing. How's that, Mel?
*(*STURDYVANT *doesn't respond.)*
Testing . . . one . . . two . . .

STURDYVANT: *(taking off earphones)* Okay . . . that checks. We got a good reading.
(Pause.)
You got that list, Irv?

IRVIN: Yeah . . . yeah, I got it. Don't worry about nothing.

STURDYVANT: Listen, Irv . . . you keep her in line, okay? I'm holding you responsible for her . . . If she starts any of her . . .

IRVIN: Mel, what's with the goddamn horn? You wanna talk to me . . . okay! I can't talk to you over the goddamn horn . . . Christ!

STURDYVANT: I'm not putting up with any shenanigans. You hear, Irv?
*(*IRVIN *crosses over to the piano and mindlessly runs his fingers over the keys.)*
I'm just not gonna stand for it. I want you to keep her in line. Irv?

(STURDYVANT *enters from the control booth.*)
Listen, Irv . . . you're her manager . . . she's your responsibility . . .

IRVIN: Okay, okay, Mel . . . let me handle it.

STURDYVANT: She's your responsibility. I'm not putting up with any Royal Highness . . . Queen of the Blues bullshit!

IRVIN: Mother of the Blues, Mel. Mother of the Blues.

STURDYVANT: I don't care what she calls herself. I'm not putting up with it. I just want to get her in here . . . record those songs on that list . . . and get her out. Just like clockwork, huh?

IRVIN: Like clockwork, Mel. You just stay out of the way and let me handle it.

STURDYVANT: Yeah . . . yeah . . . you handled it last time. Remember? She marches in here like she owns the damn place . . . doesn't like the songs we picked out . . . says her throat is sore . . . doesn't want to do more than one take . . .

IRVIN: Okay . . . okay . . . I was here! I know all about it.

STURDYVANT: Complains about the building being cold . . . and then . . . trips over the mike wire and threatens to sue me. That's taking care of it?

IRVIN: I've got it all worked out this time. I talked with her last night. Her throat is fine . . . We went over the songs together . . . I got everything straight, Mel.

STURDYVANT: Irv, that horn player . . . the one who gave me those songs . . . is he gonna be here today? Good. I want to hear more of that sound. Times are changing. This is a tricky business now. We've got to jazz it up . . . put in something different. You know, something wild . . . with a lot of rhythm.
(*Pause.*)
You know what we put out last time, Irv? We put out garbage last time. It was garbage. I don't even know why I bother with this anymore.

IRVIN: You did all right last time, Mel. Not as good as you did before, but you did all right.

STURDYVANT: You know how many records we sold in New York? You wanna see the sheet? And you know what's in New York, Irv? Harlem. Harlem's in New York, Irv.

IRVIN: Okay, so they didn't sell in New York. But look at Memphis . . . Birmingham . . . Atlanta. Christ, you made a bundle.

STURDYVANT: It's not the money, Irv. You know I couldn't sleep last night? This business is bad for my nerves. My wife is after me to slow down and take a vacation. Two more years and I'm gonna get out . . . get into something respectable. Textiles. That's a respectable business. You know what you could do with a shipload of textiles from Ireland?
(*A buzzer is heard offstage.*)

IRVIN: Why don't you go upstairs and let me handle it, Mel?

STURDYVANT: Remember . . . you're responsible for her.
(STURDYVANT *exits to the control booth.* IRVIN *crosses to get the door.* CUTLER, SLOW DRAG, *and* TOLEDO *enter.* CUTLER *is in his mid-fifties, as are most of the others. He plays guitar and trombone and is the leader of the group, possibly because he is the most sensible. His playing is solid and almost totally unembellished. His understanding of his music is limited to the chord he is playing at the time he is playing it. He has all the qualities of a loner except the introspection.* SLOW DRAG, *the bass player, is perhaps the one most bored by life. He resembles* CUTLER, *but lacks* CUTLER'S *energy. He is deceptively intelligent, though, as his name implies, he appears to be slow. He is a rather large man with a wicked smile. Innate African rhythms underlie everything he plays, and he plays with an ease that is at times startling.* TOLEDO *is the piano player. In control of his instrument, he understands and recognizes that its limitations are an extension of himself. He is the only one in the group who can read. He is self-taught but misunderstands and misapplies his knowledge, though he is quick to penetrate to the core of a situation and his insights are thought-provoking. All of the men are dressed in*

a style of clothing befitting the members of a successful band of the era.)

IRVIN: How you boys doing, Cutler? Come on in. *(Pause.)* Where's Ma? Is she with you?

CUTLER: I don't know, Mr. Irvin. She told us to be here at one o'clock. That's all I know.

IRVIN: Where's . . . huh . . . the horn player? Is he coming with Ma?

CUTLER: Levee's supposed to be here same as we is. I reckon he'll be here in a minute. I can't rightly say.

IRVIN: Well, come on . . . I'll show you to the band room, let you get set up and rehearsed. You boys hungry? I'll call over to the deli and get some sandwiches. Get you fed and ready to make some music. Cutler . . . here's the list of songs we're gonna record.

STURDYVANT: *(over speaker)* Irvin, what's happening? Where's Ma?

IRVIN: Everything under control, Mel. I got it under control.

STURDYVANT: Where's Ma? How come she isn't with the band?

IRVIN: She'll be here in a minute, Mel. Let me get these fellows down to the band room, huh? *(They exit the studio. The lights go down in the studio and up in the band room. IRVIN opens the door and allows them to pass as they enter.)* You boys go ahead and rehearse. I'll let you know when Ma comes.

(IRVIN exits. CUTLER hands TOLEDO the list of songs.)

CUTLER: What we got here, Toledo?

TOLEDO: *(reading)* We got . . . "Prove It on Me" . . . "Hear Me Talking to You" . . . "Ma Rainey's Black Bottom" . . . and "Moonshine Blues."

CUTLER: Where Mr. Irvin go? Them ain't the songs Ma told me.

SLOW DRAG: I wouldn't worry about it if I were you, Cutler. They'll get it straightened out. Ma will get it straightened out.

CUTLER: I just don't want no trouble about these songs, that's all. Ma ain't told me them songs. She told me something else.

SLOW DRAG: What she tell you?

CUTLER: This "Moonshine Blues" wasn't in it. That's one of Bessie's songs.

TOLEDO: Slow Drag's right . . . I wouldn't worry about it. Let them straighten it up.

CUTLER: Levee know what time he supposed to be here?

SLOW DRAG: Levee gone out to spend your four dollars. He left the hotel this morning talking about he was gonna go buy some shoes. Say it's the first time he ever beat you shooting craps.

CUTLER: Do he know what time he supposed to be here? That's what I wanna know. I ain't thinking about no four dollars.

SLOW DRAG: Levee sure was thinking about it. That four dollars liked to burn a hole in his pocket.

CUTLER: Well, he's supposed to be here at one o'clock. That's what time Ma said. That nigger get out in the streets with that four dollars and ain't no telling when he's liable to show. You ought to have seen him at the club last night, Toledo. Trying to talk to some gal Ma had with her.

TOLEDO: You ain't got to tell me. I know how Levee do.

(Buzzer is heard offstage.)

SLOW DRAG: Levee tried to talk to that gal and got his feelings hurt. She didn't want no part of him. She told Levee he'd have to turn his money green before he could talk with her.

CUTLER: She out for what she can get. Anybody could see that.

SLOW DRAG: That's why Levee run out to buy some shoes. He's looking to make an impression on that gal.

CUTLER: What the hell she gonna do with his shoes? She can't do nothing with the nigger's shoes.

(SLOW DRAG takes out a pint bottle and drinks.)

TOLEDO: Let me hit that, Slow Drag.

SLOW DRAG: *(handing him the bottle)* This some of that good Chicago bourbon!

(The door opens and LEVEE enters, carrying a shoe box. In his early thirties, LEVEE is

younger than the other men. His flamboyance is sometimes subtle and sneaks up on you. His temper is rakish and bright. He lacks fuel for himself and is somewhat of a buffoon. But it is an intelligent buffoonery, clearly calculated to shift control of the situation to where he can grasp it. He plays trumpet. His voice is strident and totally dependent on his manipulation of breath. He plays wrong notes frequently. He often gets his skill and talent confused with each other.)

CUTLER: Levee . . . where Mr. Irvin go?

LEVEE: Hell, I don't know. I ain't none of his keeper.

SLOW DRAG: What you got there, Levee?

LEVEE: Look here, Cutler . . . I got me some shoes!

CUTLER: Nigger, I ain't studying you.

(LEVEE takes the shoes out of the box and starts to put them on.)

TOLEDO: How much you pay for something like that, Levee?

LEVEE: Eleven dollars. Four dollars of it belong to Cutler.

SLOW DRAG: Levee say if it wasn't for Cutler . . . he wouldn't have no new shoes.

CUTLER: I ain't thinking about Levee or his shoes. Come on . . . let's get ready to rehearse.

SLOW DRAG: I'm with you on that score, Cutler. I wanna get out of here. I don't want to be around here all night. When it comes time to go up there and record them songs . . . I just wanna go up there and do it. Last time it took us all day and half the night.

TOLEDO: Ain't but four songs on the list. Last time we recorded six songs.

SLOW DRAG: It felt like it was sixteen!

LEVEE: *(finishes with his shoes)* Yeah! Now I'm ready! I can play some good music now!

(He goes to put up his old shoes and looks around the room.)

Damn! They done changed things around. Don't never leave well enough alone.

TOLEDO: Everything changing all the time. Even the air you breathing change. You got, monoxide, hydrogen . . . changing all the time. Skin changing . . . different molecules and everything.

LEVEE: Nigger, what is you talking about? I'm talking about the room. I ain't talking about no skin and air. I'm talking about something I can see! Last time the band room was upstairs. This time it's downstairs. Next time it be over there. I'm talking about what I can see. I ain't talking about no molecules or nothing.

TOLEDO: Hell, I know what you talking about. I just said everything changin'. I know what you talking about, but you don't know what I'm talking about.

LEVEE: That door! Nigger, you see that door? That's what I'm talking about. That door wasn't there before.

CUTLER: Levee, you wouldn't know your right from your left. This is where they used to keep the recording horns and things . . . and damn if that door wasn't there. How in hell else you gonna get in here? Now, if you talking about they done switched rooms, you right. But don't go telling me that damn door wasn't there!

SLOW DRAG: Damn the door and let's get set up. I wanna get out of here.

LEVEE: Toledo started all that about the door. I'm just saying that things change.

TOLEDO: What the hell you think I was saying? Things change. The air and everything. Now you gonna say you was saying it. You gonna fit two propositions on the same track . . . run them into each other, and because they crash, you gonna say it's the same train.

LEVEE: Now this nigger talking about trains! We done went from the air to the skin to the door . . . and now trains. Toledo, I'd just like to be inside your head for five minutes. Just to see how you think. You done got more shit piled up and mixed up in there than the devil got sinners. You been reading too many goddamn books.

TOLEDO: What you care about how much I read? I'm gonna ignore you 'cause you ignorant.

(LEVEE takes off his coat and hangs it in the locker.)

SLOW DRAG: Come on, let's rehearse the music.

LEVEE: You ain't gotta rehearse that . . . ain't nothing but old jug-band music. They need one of them jug bands for this.

SLOW DRAG: Don't make me no difference. Long as we get paid.

LEVEE: That ain't what I'm talking about, nigger. I'm talking about art!

SLOW DRAG: What's drawing got to do with it?

LEVEE: Where you get this nigger from, Cutler? He sound like one of them Alabama niggers.

CUTLER: Slow Drag's all right. It's you talking all that weird shit about art. Just play the piece, nigger. You wanna be one of them . . . what you call . . . virtuoso or something, you in the wrong place. You ain't no Buddy Bolden or King Oliver . . . you just an old trumpet player come a dime a dozen. Talking about art.

LEVEE: What is you? I don't see your name in lights.

CUTLER: I just play the piece. Whatever they want. I don't go talking about art and criticizing other people's music.

LEVEE: I ain't like you, Cutler. I got talent! Me and this horn . . . we's tight. If my daddy knowed I was gonna turn out like this, he would've named me Gabriel. I'm gonna get me a band and make me some records. I gone give Mr. Sturdyvant some of my songs I wrote and he say he's gonna let me record them when I get my band together.

(Takes some papers out of his pocket.)

I just gotta finish the last part of this song. And Mr. Sturdyvant want me to write another part to this song.

SLOW DRAG: How you learn to write music, Levee?

LEVEE: I just picked it up . . . like you pick up anything. Miss Eula used to play the piano . . . she learned me a lot. I knows how to play *real* music . . . not this old jug-band shit. I got style!

TOLEDO: Everybody got style. Style ain't nothing but keeping the same idea from beginning to end. Everybody got it.

LEVEE: But everybody can't play like I do. Everybody can't have their own band.

CUTLER: Well, until you get your own band where you can play what you want, you just play the piece and stop complaining. I told you when you came on here, this ain't none of them hot bands. This is an accompaniment band. You play Ma's music when you here.

LEVEE: I got sense enough to know that. Hell, I can look at you all and see what kind of band it is. I can look at Toledo and see what kind of band it is.

TOLEDO: Toledo ain't said nothing to you now. Don't let Toledo get started. You can't even spell music, much less play it.

LEVEE: What you talking about? I can spell music. I got a dollar say I can spell it! Put your dollar up. Where your dollar?

(TOLEDO waves him away.)

Now come on. Put your dollar up. Talking about I can't spell music.

(LEVEE peels a dollar off his roll and slams it down on the bench beside TOLEDO.)

TOLEDO: All right, I'm gonna show you. Cutler. Slow Drag. You hear this? The nigger betting me a dollar he can spell music. I don't want no shit now!

(TOLEDO lays a dollar down beside LEVEE's.)

All right. Go ahead. Spell it.

LEVEE: It's a bet then. Talking about I can't spell music.

TOLEDO: Go ahead, then. Spell it. Music. Spell it.

LEVEE: I can spell it, nigger! M-U-S-I-K. There!

(He reaches for the money.)

TOLEDO: Naw! Naw! Leave that money alone! You ain't spelled it.

LEVEE: What you mean I ain't spelled it? I said M-U-S-I-K!

TOLEDO: That ain't how you spell it! That ain't how you spell it! It's M-U-S-I-*C!* C, nigger. Not K! C! M-U-S-I-C!

LEVEE: What you mean, C? Who say it's C?

TOLEDO: Cutler. Slow Drag. Tell this fool.

(They look at each other and then away.)

Well, I'll be a monkey's uncle!

(TOLEDO *picks up the money and hands* LEVEE *his dollar back.*)

Here's your dollar back, Levee. I done won it, you understand. I done won the dollar. But if don't nobody know but me, how am I gonna prove it to you?

LEVEE: You just mad 'cause I spelled it.

TOLEDO: Spelled what! M-U-S-I-K don't spell nothing. I just wish there was some way I could show you the right and wrong of it. How you gonna know something if the other fellow don't know if you're right or not? Now I can't even be sure that I'm spelling it right.

LEVEE: That's what I'm talking about. You don't know it. Talking about C. You ought to give me that dollar I won from you.

TOLEDO: All right. All right. I'm gonna show you how ridiculous you sound. You know the Lord's Prayer?

LEVEE: Why? You wanna bet a dollar on that?

TOLEDO: Just answer the question. Do you know the Lord's Prayer or don't you?

LEVEE: Yeah, I know it. What of it?

TOLEDO: Cutler?

CUTLER: What you Cutlering me for? I ain't got nothing to do with it.

TOLEDO: I just want to show the man how ridiculous he is.

CUTLER: Both of you all sound like damn fools. Arguing about something silly. Yeah, I know the Lord's Prayer. My daddy was a deacon in the church. Come asking me if I know the Lord's Prayer. Yeah, I know it.

TOLEDO: Slow Drag?

SLOW DRAG: Yeah.

TOLEDO: All right. Now I'm gonna tell you a story to show just how ridiculous he sound. There was these two fellows, see. So, the one of them go up to this church and commence to taking up the church learning. The other fellow see him out on the road and he say, "I done heard you taking up the church learning," say, "Is you learning anything up there?" The other one say, "Yeah, I done take up the church learning and I's learning all

kinds of things about the Bible and what it say and all. Why you be asking?" The other one say, "Well, do you know the Lord's Prayer?" And he say, "Why, sure I know the Lord's Prayer, I'm taking up learning at the church ain't I? I know the Lord's Prayer backwards and forwards." And the other fellow says, "I bet you five dollars you don't know the Lord's Prayer, 'cause I don't think you knows it. I think you be going up to the church 'cause the Widow Jenkins be going up there and you just wanna be sitting in the same room with her when she cross them big, fine, pretty legs she got." And the other one say, "Well, I'm gonna prove you wrong and I'm gonna bet you that five dollars." So he say, "Well, go on and say it then." So he commenced to saying the Lord's Prayer. He say, "Now I lay me down to sleep, I pray the Lord my soul to keep." The other one say, "Here's your five dollars. I didn't think you knew it."

(*They all laugh.*)

Now, that's just how ridiculous Levee sound. Only 'cause I knowed how to spell music, I still got my dollar.

LEVEE: That don't prove nothing. What's that supposed to prove?

(TOLEDO *takes a newspaper out of his back pocket and begins to read.*)

TOLEDO: I'm through with it.

SLOW DRAG: Is you all gonna rehearse this music or ain't you?

(CUTLER *takes out some papers and starts to roll a reefer.*)

LEVEE: How many times you done played them songs? What you gotta rehearse for?

SLOW DRAG: This a recording session. I wanna get it right the first time and get on out of here.

CUTLER: Slow Drag's right. Let's go on and rehearse and get it over with.

LEVEE: You all go and rehearse, then. I got to finish this song for Mr. Sturdyvant.

CUTLER: Come on, Levee . . . I don't want no shit now. You rehearse like everybody else.

You in the band like everybody else. Mr. Sturdyvant just gonna have to wait. You go to do that on your own time. This is the band's time.

LEVEE: Well, what is you doing? You sitting there rolling a reefer talking about let's rehearse. Toledo reading a newspaper. Hell, I'm ready if you wanna rehearse. I just say there ain't no point in it. Ma ain't here. What's the point in it?

CUTLER: Nigger, why you gotta complain all the time?

TOLEDO: Levee would complain if a gal ain't laid across his bed just right.

CUTLER: That's what I know. That's why I try to tell him just play the music and forget about it. It ain't no big thing.

TOLEDO: Levee ain't got an eye for that. He wants to tie on to some abstract component and sit down on the elemental.

LEVEE: This is get-on-Levee time, huh? Levee ain't said nothing except this some old jug-band music.

TOLEDO: Under the right circumstances you'd play anything. If you know music, then you play it. Straight on or off to the side. Ain't nothing abstract about it.

LEVEE: Toledo, you sound like you got a mouth full of marbles. You the only cracker-talking nigger I know.

TOLEDO: You ought to have learned yourself to read . . . then you'd understand the basic understanding of everything.

SLOW DRAG: Both of you all gonna drive me crazy with that philosophy bullshit. Cutler, give me a reefer.

CUTLER: Ain't you got some reefer? Where's your reefer? Why you all the time asking me?

SLOW DRAG: Cutler, how long I done known you? How long we been together? Twenty-two years. We been doing this together for twenty-two years. All up and down the back roads, the side roads, the front roads . . . We done played the juke joints, the whorehouses, the barn dances, and city sit-downs . . . I

done lied for you and lied with you . . . We done laughed together, fought together, slept in the same bed together, done sucked on the same titty . . . and now you don't wanna give me no reefer.

CUTLER: You see this nigger trying to talk me out of my reefer, Toledo? Running all that about how long he done knowed me and how we done sucked on the same titty. Nigger, you *still* ain't getting none of my reefer!

TOLEDO: That's African.

SLOW DRAG: What? What you talking about? What's African?

LEVEE: I know he ain't talking about me. You don't see me running around in no jungle with no bone between my nose.

TOLEDO: Levee, you worse than ignorant. You ignorant without a premise.

(Pauses.)

Now, what I was saying is what Slow Drag was doing is African. That's what you call an African conceptualization. That's when you name the gods or call on the ancestors to achieve whatever your desires are.

SLOW DRAG: Nigger, I ain't no African! I ain't doing no African nothing!

TOLEDO: Naming all those things you and Cutler done together is like trying to solicit some reefer based on a bond of kinship. That's African. An ancestral retention. Only you forgot the name of the gods.

SLOW DRAG: I ain't forgot nothing. I was telling the nigger how cheap he is. Don't come talking that African nonsense to me.

TOLEDO: You just like Levee. No eye for taking an abstract and fixing it to a specific. There's so much that goes on around you and you can't even see it.

CUTLER: Wait a minute . . . wait a minute. Toledo, now when this nigger . . . when an African do all them things you say and name all the gods and whatnot . . . then what happens?

TOLEDO: Depends on if the gods is sympathetic with his cause for which he is calling them with the right names. Then his success comes with the right proportion of his naming. That's the way that go.

CUTLER: *(taking out a reefer)* Here, Slow Drag. Here's a reefer. You done talked yourself up on that one.

SLOW DRAG: Thank you. You ought to have done that in the first place and saved me all the aggravation.

CUTLER: What I wants to know is . . . what's the same titty we done sucked on. That's what I want to know.

SLOW DRAG: Oh, I just threw that in there to make it sound good.

(They all laugh.)

CUTLER: Nigger, you ain't right.

SLOW DRAG: I knows it.

CUTLER: Well, come on . . . let's get it rehearsed. Time's wasting.

(The musicians pick up their instruments.)

Let's do it. "Ma Rainey's Black Bottom." One . . . two . . . You know what to do.

(They begin to play. LEVEE is playing something different. He stops.)

LEVEE: Naw! Naw! We ain't doing it that way.

(TOLEDO stops playing, then SLOW DRAG.)

We doing my version. It say so right there on that piece of paper you got. Ask Toledo. That's what Mr. Irvin told me . . . say it's on the list he gave you.

CUTLER: Let me worry about what's on the list and what ain't on the list. How you gonna tell me what's on the list?

LEVEE: 'Cause I know what Mr. Irvin told me! Ask Toledo!

CUTLER: Let me worry about what's on the list. You just play the song I say.

LEVEE: What kind of sense it make to rehearse the wrong version of the song? That's what I wanna know. Why you wanna rehearse that version?

SLOW DRAG: You supposed to rehearse what you gonna play. That's the way they taught me. Now, *whatever* version we gonna play . . . let's go on and rehearse it.

LEVEE: That's what I'm trying to tell the man.

CUTLER: You trying to tell me what we is and ain't gonna play. And that ain't none of your business. Your business is to play what I say.

LEVEE: Oh, I see now. You done got jealous 'cause Mr. Irvin using my version. You done got jealous 'cause I proved I know something about music.

CUTLER: What the hell . . . nigger, you talk like a fool! What the hell I got to be jealous of you about? The day I get jealous of you I may as well lay down and die.

TOLEDO: Levee started all that 'cause he too lazy to rehearse.

(To LEVEE.)

You ought to just go on and play the song . . . What difference does it make?

LEVEE: Where's the paper? Look at the paper! Get the paper and look at it! See what it say. Gonna tell me I'm too lazy to rehearse.

CUTLER: We ain't talking about the paper. We talking about you understanding where you fit in when you around here. You just play what I say.

LEVEE: Look . . . I don't care what you play! All right? It don't matter to me. Mr. Irvin gonna straighten it up! I don't care what you play.

CUTLER: Thank you.

(Pauses.)

Let's play this "Hear Me Talking to You" till we find out what's happening with the "Black Bottom." Slow Drag, you sing Ma's part.

(Pauses.)

"Hear Me Talking to You." Let's do it. One . . . Two . . . You know what to do.

(They play.)

SLOW DRAG: *(singing)*

Rambling man makes no change in me
I'm gonna ramble back to my used-to-be
Ah, you hear me talking to you
I don't bite my tongue
You wants to be my man
You got to fetch it with you when you come.

Eve and Adam in the garden taking a chance
Adam didn't take time to get his pants
Ah, you hear me talking to you

I don't bite my tongue
You wants to be my man
You got to fetch it with you when you come.

Our old cat swallowed a ball of yarn
When the kittens were born they had sweaters on
Ah, you hear me talking to you
I don't bite my tongue
You wants to be my man
You got to fetch it with you when you come.
(IRVIN *enters. The musicians stop playing.*)

IRVIN: Any of you boys know what's keeping Ma?

CUTLER: Can't say, Mr. Irvin. She'll be along directly, I reckon. I talked to her this morning, she say she'll be here in time to rehearse.

IRVIN: Well, you boys go ahead.
(He starts to exit.)

CUTLER: Mr. Irvin, about these songs . . . Levee say . . .

IRVIN: Whatever's on the list, Cutler. You got that list I gave you?

CUTLER: Yessir, I got it right here.

IRVIN: Whatever's on there. Whatever that says.

CUTLER: I'm asking about this "Black Bottom" piece . . . Levee say . . .

IRVIN: Oh, it's on the list. "Ma Rainey's Black Bottom" on the list.

CUTLER: I know it's on the list. I wanna know what version. We got two versions of that song.

IRVIN: Oh. Levee's arrangement. We're using Levee's arrangement.

CUTLER: Ok. I got that straight. Now, this "Moonshine Blues" . . .

IRVIN: We'll work it out with Ma, Cutler. Just rehearse whatever's on the list and use Levee's arrangement on that "Black Bottom" piece.
(He exits.)

LEVEE: See, I told you! It don't mean nothing when I say it. You got to wait for Mr. Irvin to say it. Well, I told you the way it is.

CUTLER: Levee, the sooner you understand it ain't what you say, or what Mr. Irvin say . . . it's what Ma say that counts.

SLOW DRAG: Don't nobody say when it come to Ma. She's gonna do what she wants to do. Ma says what happens with her.

LEVEE: Hell, the man's the one putting out the record! He's gonna put out what he wanna put out!

SLOW DRAG: He's gonna put out what Ma want him to put out.

LEVEE: You heard what the man told you . . . "Ma Rainey's Black Bottom," Levee's arrangement. There you go! That's what he told you.

SLOW DRAG: What you gonna do, Cutler?

CUTLER: Ma ain't told me what version. Let's go on and play it Levee's way.

TOLEDO: See, now . . . I'll tell you something. As long as the colored man look to white folks to put the crown on what he say . . . as long as he looks to white folks for approval . . . then he ain't never gonna find out who he is and what he's about. He's just gonna be about what white folks want him to be about. That's one sure thing.

LEVEE: I'm just trying to show Cutler where he's wrong.

CUTLER: Cutler don't need you to show him nothing.

SLOW DRAG: *(irritated)* Come on, let's get this shit rehearsed! You all can bicker afterward!

CUTLER: Levee's confused about who the boss is. He don't know Ma's the boss.

LEVEE: Ma's the boss on the road! We at a recording session. Mr. Sturdyvant and Mr. Irvin say what's gonna be here! We's in Chicago, we ain't in Memphis! I don't know why you all wanna pick me about it, shit! I'm with Slow Drag . . . Let's go on and get it rehearsed.

CUTLER: All right. All right. I know how to solve this. "Ma Rainey's Black Bottom." Levee's version. Let's do it. Come on.

TOLEDO: How that first part go again, Levee?

LEVEE: It go like this.
(He plays.)
That's to get the people's attention to the song. That's when you and Slow Drag come in with the rhythm part. Me and Cutler play on the breaks.

(Becoming animated.)

Now we gonna dance it . . . but we ain't gonna countrify it. This ain't no barn dance. We gonna play it like . . .

CUTLER: The man ask you how the first part go. He don't wanna hear all that. Just tell him how the piece go.

TOLEDO: I got it. I got it. Let's go. I know how to do it.

CUTLER: "Ma Rainey's Black Bottom." One . . . two . . . You know what to do.

(They begin to play. LEVEE *stops.)*

LEVEE: You all got to keep up now. You playing in the wrong time. Ma come in over the top. She got to find her own way in.

CUTLER: Nigger, will you let us play this song? When you get your own band . . . then you tell them that nonsense. We know how to play the piece. I was playing music before you was born. Gonna tell me how to play . . . All right. Let's try it again.

SLOW DRAG: Cutler, wait till I fix this. This string started to unravel.

(Playfully.)

And you know I want to play Levee's music right.

LEVEE: If you was any kind of musician, you'd take care of your instrument. Keep it in tip-top order. If you was any kind of musician, I'd let you be in my band.

SLOW DRAG: Shhheeeeet!

(He crosses to get his string and steps on LEVEE'S *shoes.)*

LEVEE: Damn, Slow Drag! Watch them big-ass shoes you got.

SLOW DRAG: Boy, ain't nobody done nothing to you.

LEVEE: You done stepped on my shoes.

SLOW DRAG: Move them the hell out the way, then. You was in my way . . . I wasn't in your way.

*(CUTLER *lights up another reefer.* SLOW DRAG *rummages around in his belongings for a string.* LEVEE *takes out a rag and begins to shine his shoes.)*

You can shine these when you get done, Levee.

CUTLER: If I had them shoes Levee got, I could buy me a whole suit of clothes.

LEVEE: What kind of difference it make what kind of shoes I got? Ain't nothing wrong with having nice shoes. I ain't said nothing about your shoes. Why you wanna talk about me and my Florsheims?

CUTLER: Any man who takes a whole week's pay and puts it on some shoes—you understand what I mean, what you walk around on the ground with—is a fool! And I don't mind telling you.

LEVEE: *(irritated)* What difference it make to you, Cutler?

SLOW DRAG: The man ain't said nothing about your shoes. Ain't nothing wrong with having nice shoes. Look at Toledo.

TOLEDO: What about Toledo?

SLOW DRAG: I said ain't nothing wrong with having nice shoes.

LEVEE: Nigger got them clodhoppers! Old brogans! He ain't nothing but a sharecropper.

TOLEDO: You can make all the fun you want. It don't mean nothing. I'm satisfied with them and that's what counts.

LEVEE: Nigger, why don't you get some decent shoes? Got nerve to put on a suit and tie with them farming boots.

CUTLER: What you just tell me? It don't make no difference about the man's shoes. That's what you told me.

LEVEE: Aw, hell, I don't care what the nigger wear. I'll be honest with you. I don't care if he went barefoot.

*(SLOW DRAG *has put his string on the bass and is tuning it.)*

Play something for me, Slow Drag.

*(SLOW DRAG *plays.)*

A man got to have some shoes to dance like this! You can't dance like this with them clodhoppers Toledo got.

*(LEVEE *sings.)*

Hello Central give me Doctor Jazz
He's got just what I need I'll say he has
When the world goes wrong and I have got the blues

He's the man who makes me get on my dancing shoes.

TOLEDO: That's the trouble with colored folks . . . always wanna have a good time. Good times done got more niggers killed than God got ways to count. What the hell having a good time mean? That's what I wanna know.

LEVEE: Hell, nigger . . . it don't need explaining. Ain't you never had no good time before?

TOLEDO: The more niggers get killed having a good time, the more good times niggers wanna have.

(SLOW DRAG *stops playing.*)

There's more to life than having a good time. If there ain't, then this is a piss-poor life we're having . . . if that's all there is to be got out of it.

SLOW DRAG: Toledo, just 'cause you like to read them books and study and whatnot . . . that's your good time. People get other things they likes to do to have a good time. Ain't no need you picking them about it.

CUTLER: Niggers been having a good time before you was born, and they gonna keep having a good time after you gone.

TOLEDO: Yeah, but what else they gonna do? Ain't nobody talking about making the lot of the colored man better for him here in America.

LEVEE: Now you gonna be Booker T. Washington.

TOLEDO: Everybody worried about having a good time. Ain't nobody thinking about what kind of world they gonna leave their youngens. "Just give me the good time, that's all I want." It just makes me sick.

SLOW DRAG: Well, the colored man's gonna be all right. He got through slavery, and he'll get through whatever else the white man put on him. I ain't worried about that. Good times is what makes life worth living. Now, you take the white man . . . The white man don't know how to have a good time. That's why he's troubled all the time. He don't know how to have a good time. He don't know how to laugh at life.

LEVEE: That's what the problem is with Toledo . . . reading all them books and things. He done got to the point where he forgot how to laugh and have a good time. Just like the white man.

TOLEDO: I know how to have a good time as well as the next man. I said, there's got to be more to life than having a good time. I said the colored man ought to be doing more than just trying to have a good time all the time.

LEVEE: Well, what is you doing, nigger? Talking all them highfalutin ideas about making a better world for the colored man. What is you doing to make it better? You playing the music and looking for your next piece of pussy same as we is. What is you doing? That's what I wanna know. Tell him, Cutler.

CUTLER: You all leave Cutler out of this. Cutler ain't got nothing to do with it.

TOLEDO: Levee, you just about the most ignorant nigger I know. Sometimes I wonder why I ever bother to try and talk with you.

LEVEE: Well, what is you doing? Talking that shit to me about I'm ignorant! What is you doing? You just a whole lot of mouth. A great big windbag. Thinking you smarter than everybody else. What is you doing, huh?

TOLEDO: It ain't just me, fool! It's everybody! What you think . . . I'm gonna solve the colored man's problems by myself? I said, we. You understand that? We. That's every living colored man in the world got to do his share. Got to do his part. I ain't talking about what I'm gonna do . . . or what you or Cutler or Slow Drag or anybody else. I'm talking about all of us together. What all of us is gonna do. That's what I'm talking about, nigger!

LEVEE: Well, why didn't you say that, then?

CUTLER: Toledo, I don't know why you waste your time on this fool.

TOLEDO: That's what I'm trying to figure out.

LEVEE: Now there go Cutler with his shit. Calling me a fool. You wasn't even in the conversation. Now you gonna take sides and call me a fool.

CUTLER: Hell, I was listening to the man. I got sense enough to know what he was saying. I could tell it straight back to you.

LEVEE: Well, you go on with it. But I'll tell you this . . . I ain't gonna be too many more of your fools. I'll tell you that. Now you put that in your pipe and smoke it.

CUTLER: Boy, ain't nobody studying you. Telling me what to put in my pipe. Who's you to tell me what to do?

LEVEE: All right, I ain't nobody. Don't pay me no mind. I ain't nobody.

TOLEDO: Levee, you ain't nothing but the devil.

LEVEE: There you go! That's who I am. I'm the devil. I ain't nothing but the devil.

CUTLER: I can see that. That's something you know about. You know all about the devil.

LEVEE: I ain't saying what I know. I know plenty. What you know about the devil? Telling me what I know. What you know?

SLOW DRAG: I know a man sold his soul to the devil.

LEVEE: There you go! That's the only thing I ask about the devil . . . to see him coming so I can sell him this one I got. 'Cause if there's a god up there, he done went to sleep.

SLOW DRAG: Sold his soul to the devil himself. Name of Eliza Cotter. Lived in Tuscaloosa County, Alabama. The devil came by and he done upped and sold him his soul.

CUTLER: How you know the man done sold his soul to the devil, nigger? You talking that old-woman foolishness.

SLOW DRAG: Everybody know. It wasn't no secret. He went around working for the devil and everybody knowed it. Carried him a bag . . . one of them carpetbags. Folks say he carried the devil's papers and whatnot where he put your fingerprint on the paper with blood.

LEVEE: Where he at now? That's what I want to know. He can put my whole handprint if he want to!

CUTLER: That's the damnedest thing I ever heard! Folks kill me with that talk.

TOLEDO: Oh, that's real enough, all right. Some folks go arm in arm with the devil, shoulder to shoulder, and talk to him all the time. That's real, ain't nothing wrong in believing that.

SLOW DRAG: That's what I'm saying. Eliza Cotter is one of them. All right. The man living up in an old shack on Ben Foster's place, shoeing mules and horses, making them charms and things in secret. He done hooked up with the devil, showed up one day all fancied out with just the finest clothes you ever seen on a colored man . . . dressed just like one of them crackers . . . and carrying this bag with them papers and things. All right. Had a pocketful of money, just living the life of a rich man. Ain't done no more work or nothing. Just had him a string of women he run around with and throw his money away on. Bought him a big fine house . . . Well, it wasn't all that big, but it did have one of them white picket fences around it. Used to hire a man once a week just to paint that fence. Messed around there and one of the fellows of them gals he was messing with got fixed on him wrong and Eliza killed him. And he laughed about it. Sheriff come and arrest him, and then let him go. And he went around in that town laughing about killing this fellow. Trial come up, and the judge cut him loose. He must have been in converse with the devil too . . . 'cause he cut him loose and give him a bottle of whiskey! Folks ask what done happened to make him change, and he'd tell them straight out he done sold his soul to the devil and ask them if they wanted to sell theirs 'cause he could arrange it for them. Preacher see him coming, used to cross on the other side of the road. He'd just stand there and laugh at the preacher and call him a fool to his face.

CUTLER: Well, whatever happened to this fellow? What come of him? A man who, as you say, done sold his soul to the devil is bound to come to a bad end.

TOLEDO: I don't know about that. The devil's strong. The devil ain't no pushover.

SLOW DRAG: Oh, the devil had him under his wing, all right. Took good care of him. He ain't wanted for nothing.

CUTLER: What happened to him? That's what I want to know.

SLOW DRAG: Last I heard, he headed north with that bag of his, handing out hundred-dollar bills on the spot to whoever wanted to sign on with the devil. That's what I hear tell of him.

CUTLER: That's a bunch of fool talk. I don't know how you fix your mouth to tell that story. I don't believe that.

SLOW DRAG: I ain't asking you to believe it. I'm just telling you the facts of it.

LEVEE: I sure wish I knew where he went. He wouldn't have to convince me long. Hell, I'd even help him sign people up.

CUTLER: Nigger, God's gonna strike you down with that blasphemy you talking.

LEVEE: Oh, shit! God don't mean nothing to me. Let him strike me! Here I am, standing right here. What you talking about he's gonna strike me? Here I am! Let him strike me! I ain't scared of him. Talking that stuff to me.

CUTLER: All right. You gonna be sorry. You gonna fix yourself to have bad luck. Ain't nothing gonna work for you.

(Buzzer sounds offstage.)

LEVEE: Bad luck? What I care about some bad luck? You talking simple. I ain't knowed nothing but bad luck all my life. Couldn't get no worse. What the hell I care about some bad luck? Hell, I eat it every day for breakfast! You dumber than I thought you was . . . talking about bad luck.

CUTLER: All right, nigger, you'll see! Can't tell a fool nothing. You'll see!

IRVIN: (IRVIN enters the studio, checks his watch, and calls down the stairs) Cutler . . . you boys' sandwiches are up here . . . Cutler?

CUTLER: Yessir, Mr. Irvin . . . be right there.

TOLEDO: I'll walk up there and get them.

(TOLEDO exits. The lights go down in the band room and up in the studio. IRVIN paces back and forth in an agitated manner. STURDYVANT enters.)

STURDYVANT: Irv, what's happening? Is she here yet? Was that her?

IRVIN: It's the sandwiches, Mel. I told you . . . I'll let you know when she comes, huh?

STURDYVANT: What's keeping her? Do you know what time it is? Have you looked at the clock? You told me she'd be here. You told me you'd take care of it.

IRVIN: Mel, for Chrissakes! What do you want from me? What do you want me to do?

STURDYVANT: Look what time it is, Irv. You told me she'd be here.

IRVIN: She'll be here, okay? I don't know what's keeping her. You know they're always late, Mel.

STURDYVANT: You should have went by the hotel and made sure she was on time. You should have taken care of this. That's what you told me, huh? "I'll take care of it."

IRVIN: Okay! Okay! I didn't go by the hotel! What do you want me to do? She'll be here, okay? The band's here . . . she'll be here.

STURDYVANT: Okay, Irv. I'll take your word. But if she doesn't come . . . if she doesn't come . . .

(STURDYVANT exits to the control booth as TOLEDO enters.)

TOLEDO: Mr. Irvin . . . I come up to get the sandwiches.

IRVIN: Say . . . uh . . . look . . . one o'clock, right? She said one o'clock.

TOLEDO: That's what time she told us. Say be here at one o'clock.

IRVIN: Do you know what's keeping her? Do you know why she ain't here?

TOLEDO: I can't say, Mr. Irvin. Told us one o'clock.

(The buzzer sounds. IRVIN goes to the door. There is a flurry of commotion as MA RAINEY enters, followed closely by the POLICEMAN, DUSSIE MAE, and SYLVESTER. MA RAINEY is a short, heavy woman. She is dressed in a full-length fur coat with matching hat, an emerald-green dress, and several strands of pearls of varying lengths. Her hair is secured by a headband that matches her dress. Her manner is simple and direct, and she carries herself in a royal fashion. DUSSIE MAE is a young, dark-skinned woman whose greatest asset is the *sensual energy which seems to flow from her. She is dressed in a fur jacket and a tight-fitting canary-yellow dress.* SYLVESTER *is an Arkansas country boy, the size of a fullback. He wears a new suit and coat, in which he is obviously uncomfortable. Most of the time, he stutters when he speaks.)*

MA RAINEY: Irvin . . . you better tell this man who I am! You better get him straight!

IRVIN: Ma, do you know what time it is? Do you have any idea? We've been waiting . . .

DUSSIE MAE: *(to* SYLVESTER*)* If you was watching where you was going . . .

SYLVESTER: I was watching . . . What you mean?

IRVIN: *(notices* POLICEMAN*)* What's going on here? Officer, what's the matter?

MA RAINEY: Tell the man who he's messing with!

POLICEMAN: Do you know this lady?

MA RAINEY: Just tell the man who I am! That's all you gotta do.

POLICEMAN: Lady, will you let me talk, huh?

MA RAINEY: Tell the man who I am!

IRVIN: Wait a minute . . . wait a minute! Let me handle it. Ma, will you let me handle it?

MA RAINEY: Tell him who he's messing with!

IRVIN: Okay! Okay! Give me a chance! Officer, this is one of our recording artists . . . Ma Rainey.

MA RAINEY: Madame Rainey! Get it straight! Madame Rainey! Talking about taking me to jail!

IRVIN: Look, Ma . . . give me a chance, okay? Here . . . sit down. I'll take care of it. Officer, what's the problem?

DUSSIE MAE: *(to* SYLVESTER*)* It's all your fault.

SYLVESTER: I ain't done nothing . . . Ask Ma.

POLICEMAN: Well . . . when I walked up on the incident . . .

DUSSIE MAE: Sylvester wrecked Ma's car.

SYLVESTER: I d-d-did not! The m-m-man ran into me!

POLICEMAN: *(to* IRVIN*)* Look, buddy . . . if you want it in a nutshell, we got her charged with assault and battery.

MA RAINEY: Assault and what for what!

DUSSIE MAE: See . . . we was trying to get a cab . . . and so Ma . . .

MA RAINEY: Wait a minute! I'll tell you if you wanna know what happened. *(She points to* SYLVESTER*.)*
Now, that's Sylvester. That's my nephew. He was driving my car . . .

POLICEMAN: Lady, we don't know whose car he was driving.

MA RAINEY: That's my car!

DUSSIE MAE and SYLVESTER: That's Ma's car!

MA RAINEY: What you mean you don't know whose car it is? I bought and paid for that car.

POLICEMAN: That's what you say, lady . . . We still gotta check.
(To IRVIN*.)*
They hit a car on Market Street. The guy said the kid ran a stoplight.

SYLVESTER: What you mean? The man c-c-come around the corner and hit m-m-me!

POLICEMAN: While I was calling a paddy wagon to haul them to the station, they try to hop into a parked cab. The cabbie said he was waiting on a fare . . .

MA RAINEY: The man was just sitting there. Wasn't waiting for nobody. I don't know why he wanna tell that lie.

POLICEMAN: Look, lady . . . will you let me tell the story?

MA RAINEY: Go ahead and tell it then. But tell it right!

POLICEMAN: Like I say . . . she tries to get in this cab. The cabbie's waiting on a fare. She starts creating a disturbance. The cabbie gets out to try and explain the situation to her . . . and she knocks him down.

DUSSIE MAE: She ain't hit him! He just fell!

SYLVESTER: He just s-s-s-slipped!

POLICEMAN: He claims she knocked him down. We got her charged with assault and battery.

MA RAINEY: If that don't beat all to hell. I ain't touched the man! The man was trying to reach around me to keep his car door closed. I opened the door and it hit him and he fell down. I ain't touched the man!

IRVIN: Okay. Okay . . . I got it straight now, Ma. You didn't touch him. All right? Officer, can I see you for a minute?

DUSSIE MAE: Ma was just trying to open the door.

SYLVESTER: He j-j-just got in t-t-the way!

MA RAINEY: Said he wasn't gonna haul no colored folks . . . if you want to know the truth of it.

IRVIN: Okay, Ma . . . I got it straight now. Officer?

(IRVIN *pulls the* POLICEMAN *off to the side.*)

MA RAINEY: (*noticing* TOLEDO) Toledo, Cutler and everybody here?

TOLEDO: Yeah, they down in the band room. What happened to your car?

STURDYVANT: (*entering*) Irv, what's the problem? What's going on? Officer . . .

IRVIN: Mel, let me take care of it. I can handle it.

STURDYVANT: What's happening? What the hell's going on?

IRVIN: Let me handle it, Mel, huh?

(STURDYVANT *crosses over to* MA RAINEY.)

STURDYVANT: What's going on, Ma. What'd you do?

MA RAINEY: Sturdyvant, get on away from me! That's the last thing I need . . . to go through some of your shit!

IRVIN: Mel, I'll take care of it. I'll explain it all to you. Let me handle it, huh?

(STURDYVANT *reluctantly returns to the control booth.*)

POLICEMAN: Look, buddy, like I say . . . we got her charged with assault and battery . . . and the kid with threatening the cabbie.

SYLVESTER: I ain't done n-n-nothing!

MA RAINEY: You leave the boy out of it. He ain't done nothing. What's he supposed to have done?

POLICEMAN: He threatened the cabbie, lady! You just can't go around threatening people.

SYLVESTER: I ain't done nothing to him! He's the one talking about he g-g-gonna get a b-b-baseball bat on me! I just told him what I'd do with it. But I ain't done nothing 'cause he didn't get the b-b-bat!

IRVIN: (*pulling the* POLICEMAN *aside*) Officer . . . look here . . .

POLICEMAN: We was on our way down to the precinct . . . but I figured I'd do you a favor and bring her by here. I mean, if she's as important as she says she is . . .

IRVIN: (*slides a bill from his pocket*) Look, Officer . . . I'm Madame Rainey's manager . . . It's good to meet you.

(*He shakes the* POLICEMAN'S *hand and passes him the bill.*)

As soon as we're finished with the recording session, I'll personally stop by the precinct house and straighten up this misunderstanding.

POLICEMAN: Well . . . I guess that's all right. As long as someone is responsible for them.

(*He pockets the bill and winks at* IRVIN.)

No need to come down . . . I'll take care of it myself. Of course, we wouldn't want nothing like this to happen again.

IRVIN: Don't worry, Officer . . . I'll take care of everything. Thanks for your help.

(IRVIN *escorts the* POLICEMAN *to the door and returns. He crosses over to* MA RAINEY.)

Here, Ma . . . let me take your coat.

(*To* SYLVESTER.)

I don't believe I know you.

MA RAINEY: That's my nephew, Sylvester.

IRVIN: I'm very pleased to meet you. Here . . . you can give me your coat.

MA RAINEY: That there is Dussie Mae.

IRVIN: Hello . . .

(DUSSIE MAE *hands* IRVIN *her coat.*)

Listen, Ma, just sit there and relax. The boys are in the band room rehearsing. You just sit and relax a minute.

MA RAINEY: I ain't for no sitting. I ain't never heard of such. Talking about taking me to jail. Irvin, call down there and see about my car.

IRVIN: Okay, Ma . . . I'll take care of it. You just relax.

(IRVIN *exits with the coats.*)

MA RAINEY: Why you all keep it so cold in here? Sturdyvant try and pinch every penny he can. You all wanna make some records, you better put some heat on in here or give me back my coat.

IRVIN: *(entering)* We got the heat turned up, Ma. It's warming up. It'll be warm in a minute.

DUSSIE MAE: *(whispering to* MA RAINEY*)* Where's the bathroom?

MA RAINEY: It's in the back. Down the hall next to Sturdyvant's office. Come on, I'll show you where it is. Irvin, call down there and see about my car. I want my car fixed today.

IRVIN: I'll take care of everything, Ma.
(He notices TOLEDO.*)*
Say . . . uh . . . uh . . .

TOLEDO: Toledo.

IRVIN: Yeah . . . Toledo. I got the sandwiches, you can take down to the rest of the boys. We'll be ready to go in a minute. Give you boys a chance to eat and then we'll be ready to go.
*(*IRVIN *and* TOLEDO *exit. The lights go down in the studio and come up in the band room.)*

LEVEE: Slow Drag, you ever been to New Orleans?

SLOW DRAG: What's in New Orleans that I want?

LEVEE: How you call yourself a musician and ain't never been to New Orleans.

SLOW DRAG: You ever been to Fat Back, Arkansas?
(Pauses.)
All right, then. Ain't never been nothing in New Orleans that I couldn't get in Fat Back.

LEVEE: That's why you backwards. You just an old country boy talking about Fat Back, Arkansas, and New Orleans in the same breath.

CUTLER: I been to New Orleans. What about it?

LEVEE: You ever been to Lula White's?

CUTLER: Lula White's? I ain't never heard of it.

LEVEE: Man, they got some gals in there just won't wait! I seen a man get killed in there once. Got drunk and grabbed one of the gals wrong . . . I don't know what the matter of it was. But he grabbed her and she stuck a knife in him all the way up to the hilt. He ain't even fell. He just stood there and choked on his own blood. I was just asking Slow Drag 'cause I was gonna take him to Lula White's when we get down to New Orleans and show him a good time. Introduce him to one of them gals I know down there.

CUTLER: Slow Drag don't need you to find him no pussy. He can take care of his own self. Fact is . . . you better watch your gal when Slow Drag's around. They don't call him Slow Drag for nothing.
(He laughs.)
Tell him how you got your name Slow Drag.

SLOW DRAG: I ain't thinking about Levee.

CUTLER: Slow Drag break a woman's back when he dance. They had this contest one time in this little town called Bolingbroke about a hundred miles outside of Macon. We was playing for this dance and they was giving twenty dollars to the best slow draggers. Slow Drag looked over the competition, got down off the bandstand, grabbed hold of one of them gals, and stuck to her like a fly to jelly. Like wood to glue. Man had that gal whooping and hollering so . . . everybody stopped to watch. This fellow come in . . . this gal's fellow . . . and pulled a knife a foot long on Slow Drag. 'Member that, Slow Drag?

SLOW DRAG: Boy that mama was hot! The front of her dress was wet as a dishrag!

LEVEE: So what happened? What the man do?

CUTLER: Slow Drag ain't missed a stroke. The gal, she just look at her man with that sweet dizzy look in her eye. She ain't about to stop! Folks was clearing out, ducking and hiding under tables, figuring there's gonna be a fight. Slow Drag just looked over the gal's shoulder at the man and said, "Mister, if you'd quit hollering and wait a minute . . . you'll see I'm doing you a favor. I'm helping this gal win ten dollars so she can buy you a gold watch." The man just stood there and looked at him, all the while stroking that knife. Told Slow Drag, say, "All right, then, nigger. You just better make damn sure you win." That's when folks started calling him Slow Drag. The women got to hanging around him so bad after that, them fellows in that town ran us out of there.
*(*TOLEDO *enters, carrying a small cardboard box with the sandwiches.)*

LEVEE: Yeah . . . well, them gals in Lula White's will put a harness on his ass.

TOLEDO: Ma's up there. Some kind of commotion with the police.

CUTLER: Police? What the police up there for?

TOLEDO: I couldn't get it straight. Something about her car. They gone now . . . she's all right. Mr. Irvin sent some sandwiches.

(LEVEE springs across the floor.)

LEVEE: Yeah, all right. What we got here?

(He takes two sandwiches out of the box.)

TOLEDO: What you doing grabbing two? There ain't but five in there . . . How you figure you get two?

LEVEE: 'Cause I grabbed them first. There's enough for everybody . . . What you talking about? It ain't like I'm taking food out of nobody's mouth.

CUTLER: That's all right. He can have mine too. I don't want none.

(LEVEE starts toward the box to get another sandwich.)

TOLEDO: Nigger, you better get out of here. Slow Drag, you want this?

SLOW DRAG: Naw, you can have it.

TOLEDO: With Levee around, you don't have to worry about no leftovers. I can see that.

LEVEE: What's the matter with you? Ain't you eating two sandwiches? Then why you wanna talk about me? Talking about there won't be no leftovers with Levee around. Look at your own self before you look at me.

TOLEDO: That's what you is. That's what we all is. A leftover from history. You see now, I'll show you.

LEVEE: Aw, shit . . . I done got the nigger started now.

TOLEDO: Now, I'm gonna show you how this goes . . . where you just a leftover from history. Everybody come from different places in Africa, right? Come from different tribes and things. Soonawhile they began to make one big stew. You had the carrots, the peas, and potatoes and whatnot over here. And over there you had the meat, the nuts, the okra, corn . . . and then you mix it up and let it cook right through to get the flavors flowing together . . . then you got one thing. You got a stew.

Now you take and eat the stew. You take and make your history with that stew. All right. Now it's over. Your history's over and you done ate the stew. But you look around and you see some carrots over here, some potatoes over there. That stew's still there. You done made your history and it's still there. You can't eat it all. So what you got? You got some leftovers. That's what it is. You got leftovers and you can't do nothing with it. You already making you another history . . . cooking you another meal, and you don't need them leftovers no more. What to do?

See, we's the leftovers. The colored man is the leftovers. Now, what's the colored man gonna do with himself? That's what we waiting to find out. But first we gotta know we the leftovers. Now, who knows that? You find me a nigger that knows that and I'll turn any whichaway you want me to. I'll bend over for you. You ain't gonna find that. And that's what the problem is. The problem ain't with the white man. The white man knows you just a leftover. 'Cause he the one who done the eating and he know what he done ate. But we don't know that we been took and made history out of. Done went and filled the white man's belly and now he's full and tired and wants you to get out the way and let him be by himself. Now, I know what I'm talking about. And if you wanna find out, you just ask Mr. Irvin what he had for supper yesterday. And if he's an honest white man . . . which is asking for a whole heap of a lot . . . he'll tell you he done ate your black ass and if you please I'm full up with you . . . so go on and get off the plate and let me eat something else.

SLOW DRAG: What that mean? What's eating got to do with how the white man treat you? He don't treat you no different according to what he ate.

TOLEDO: I ain't said it had nothing to do with how he treat you.

CUTLER: The man's trying to tell you something, fool!

SLOW DRAG: What he trying to tell me? Ain't you here. Why you say he was trying to tell *me* something? Wasn't he trying to tell you too?

LEVEE: He was trying all right. He was trying a whole heap. I'll say that for him. But trying ain't worth a damn. I got lost right there trying to figure out who puts nuts in their stew.

SLOW DRAG: I knowed that before. My grandpappy used to put nuts in his stew. He and my grandmama both. That ain't nothing new.

TOLEDO: They put nuts in their stew all over Africa. But the stew they eat, and the stew your grandpappy made, and all the stew that you and me eat, and the stew Mr. Irvin eats . . . ain't in no way the same stew. That's the way that go. I'm through with it. That's the last you know me to ever try and explain something to you.

CUTLER: *(after a pause)* Well, time's getting along . . . Come on, let's finish rehearsing.

LEVEE: *(stretching out on a bench)* I don't feel like rehearsing. I ain't nothing but a leftover. You go and rehearse with Toledo . . . He's gonna teach you how to make a stew.

SLOW DRAG: Cutler, what you gonna do? I don't want to be around here all day.

LEVEE: I know my part. You all go on and rehearse your part. You all need some rehearsal.

CUTLER: Come on, Levee, get up off your ass and rehearse the songs.

LEVEE: I already know them songs . . . What I wanna rehearse them for?

SLOW DRAG: You in the band, ain't you? You supposed to rehearse when the band rehearse.

TOLEDO: Levee think he the king of the barnyard. He thinks he's the only rooster know how to crow.

LEVEE: All right! All right! Come on, I'm gonna show you I know them songs. Come on, let's rehearse. I bet you the first one mess be Toledo. Come on . . . I wanna see if he know how to crow.

CUTLER: "Ma Rainey's Black Bottom," Levee's version. Let's do it.

(They begin to rehearse. The lights go down in the band room and up in the studio. MA RAINEY *sits and takes off her shoes, rubs her feet.* DUSSIE MAE *wanders about looking at the studio.* SYLVESTER *is over by the piano.)*

MA RAINEY: *(singing to herself)*
Oh, Lord, these dogs of mine
They sure do worry me all the time
The reason why I don't know
Lord, I beg to be excused
I can't wear me no sharp-toed shoes.
I went for a walk
I stopped to talk
Oh, how my corns did bark.

DUSSIE MAE: It feels kinda spooky in here. I ain't never been in no recording studio before. Where's the band at?

MA RAINEY: They off somewhere rehearsing. I don't know where Irvin went to. All this hurry up and he goes off back there with Sturdyvant. I know he better come on 'cause Ma ain't gonna be waiting. Come here . . . let me see that dress. *(*DUSSIE MAE *crosses over.* MA RAINEY *tugs at the dress around the waist, appraising the fit.)* That dress looks nice. I'm gonna take you tomorrow and get you some more things before I take you down to Memphis. They got clothes up here you can't get in Memphis. I want you to look nice for me. If you gonna travel with the show you got to look nice.

DUSSIE MAE: I need me some more shoes. These hurt my feet.

MA RAINEY: You get you some shoes that fit your feet. Don't you be messing around with no shoes that pinch your feet. Ma know something about bad feet. Hand me my slippers out my bag over yonder.

*(*DUSSIE MAE *brings the slippers.)*

DUSSIE MAE: I just want to get a pair of them yellow ones. About a half-size bigger.

MA RAINEY: We'll get you whatever you need. Sylvester, too . . . I'm gonna get him some more clothes. Sylvester, tuck your clothes in. Straighten them up and look nice. Look like a gentleman.

DUSSIE MAE: Look at Sylvester with that hat on.

MA RAINEY: Sylvester, take your hat off inside. Act like your mama taught you something. I know she taught you better than that.

(SYLVESTER *bangs on the piano.*)

Come on over here and leave that piano alone.

SYLVESTER: I ain't d-d-doing nothing to the p-p-piano. I'm just l-l-looking at it.

MA RAINEY: Well. Come on over here and sit down. As soon as Mr. Irvin comes back, I'll have him take you down and introduce you to the band.

(SYLVESTER *comes over.*)

He's gonna take you down there and introduce you in a minute . . . have Cutler show you how your part go. And when you get your money, you gonna send some of it home to your mama. Let her know you doing all right. Make her feel good to know you doing all right in the world.

(DUSSIE MAE *wanders about the studio and opens the door leading to the band room. The strains of* LEVEE'S *version of "Ma Rainey's Black Bottom" can be heard.* IRVIN *enters.*)

IRVIN: Ma, I called down to the garage and checked on your car. It's just a scratch. They'll have it ready for you this afternoon. They're gonna send it over with one of their fellows.

MA RAINEY: They better have my car fixed right too. I ain't going for that. Brand-new car . . . they better fix it like new.

IRVIN: It was just a scratch on the fender, Ma . . . They'll take care of it . . . don't worry . . . they'll have it like new.

MA RAINEY: Irvin, what is that I hear? What is that the band's rehearsing? I know they ain't rehearsing Levee's "Black Bottom." I know I ain't hearing that?

IRVIN: Ma, listen . . . that's what I wanted to talk to you about. Levee's version of that song . . . it's got a nice arrangement . . . a nice horn in-tro . . . It really picks it up . . .

MA RAINEY: I ain't studying Levee nothing. I know what he done to that song and I don't like to sing it that way. I'm doing it the old way. That's why I brought my nephew to do the voice intro.

IRVIN: Ma, that's what the people want now. They want something they can dance to. Times are changing. Levee's arrangement gives the people what they want. It gets them excited . . . makes them forget about their troubles.

MA RAINEY: I don't care what you say, Irvin. Levee ain't messing up my song. If he got what the people want, let him take it somewhere else. I'm singing Ma Rainey's song. I ain't singing Levee's song. Now that's all there is to it. Carry my nephew on down there and introduce him to the band. I promised my sister I'd look out for him and he's gonna do the voice in-tro on the song my way.

IRVIN: Ma, we just figured that . . .

MA RAINEY: Who's this "we"? What you mean "we"? I ain't studying Levee nothing. Come talking this "we" stuff. Who's "we"?

IRVIN: Me and Sturdyvant. We decided that it would . . .

MA RAINEY: You decided, huh? I'm just a bump on the log. I'm gonna go which ever way the river drift. Is that it? You and Sturdyvant decided.

IRVIN: Ma, it was just that we thought it would be better.

MA RAINEY: I ain't got good sense. I don't know nothing about music. I don't know what's a good song and what ain't. You know more about my fans than I do.

IRVIN: It's not that, Ma. It would just be easier to do. It's more what the people want.

MA RAINEY: I'm gonna tell you something, Irvin . . . and you go on up there and tell Sturdyvant. What you all say don't count with me. You understand? Ma listens to her heart. Ma listens to the voice inside her. That's what counts with Ma. Now, you carry my nephew on down there . . . tell Cutler he's gonna do the voice intro on that "Black Bottom" song and that Levee ain't messing up my song with none of his music shit. Now, if that don't set right with you and Sturdyvant . . . then I can carry my black bottom on back down South to my tour, 'cause I don't like it up here no ways.

IRVIN: Okay, Ma . . . I don't care. I just thought . . .

MA RAINEY: Damn what you thought! What you look like telling me how to sing my song? This Levee and Sturdyvant nonsense . . . I ain't going for it! Sylvester, go on down there and introduce yourself. I'm through playing with Irvin.

SYLVESTER: Which way you go? Where they at?

MA RAINEY: Here . . . I'll carry you down there myself.

DUSSIE MAE: Can I go? I wanna see the band.

MA RAINEY: You stay your behind up here. Ain't no cause in you being down there. Come on, Sylvester.

IRVIN: Okay, Ma. Have it your way. We'll be ready to go in fifteen minutes.

MA RAINEY: We'll be ready to go when Madame says we're ready. That's the way it goes around here.

(MA RAINEY *and* SYLVESTER *exit. The lights go down in the studio and up in the band room.* MA RAINEY *enters with* SYLVESTER.)

Cutler, this here is my nephew Sylvester. He's gonna do that voice intro on the "Black Bottom" song using the old version.

LEVEE: What you talking about? Mr. Irvin say he's using my version. What you talking about?

MA RAINEY: Levee, I ain't studying you or Mr. Irvin. Cutler, get him straightened out on how to do his part. I ain't thinking about Levee. These folks done messed with the wrong person this day. Sylvester, Cutler gonna teach you your part. You go ahead and get it straight. Don't worry about what nobody else say.

(MA RAINEY *exits.*)

CUTLER: Well, come on in, boy. I'm Cutler. You got Slow Drag . . . Levee . . . and that's Toledo over there. Sylvester, huh?

SYLVESTER: Sylvester Brown.

LEVEE: I done wrote a version of that song what picks it up and sets it down in the people's lap! Now she come talking this! You don't need that old circus bullshit! I know what I'm talking about. You gonna mess up the song Cutler and you know it.

CUTLER: I ain't gonna mess up nothing. Ma say . . .

LEVEE: I don't care what Ma say! I'm talking about what the intro gonna do to the song. The peoples in the North ain't gonna buy all that tent-show nonsense. They wanna hear some music!

CUTLER: Nigger, I done told you time and again . . . you just in the band. You plays the piece . . . whatever they want! Ma says what to play! Not you! You ain't here to be doing no creating, Your job is to play whatever Ma says!

LEVEE: I might not play nothing! I might quit!

CUTLER: Nigger, don't nobody care if you quit. Whose heart you gonna break?

TOLEDO: Levee ain't gonna quit. He got to make some money to keep him in shoe polish.

LEVEE: I done told you all . . . you all don't know me. You don't know what I'll do.

CUTLER: I don't think nobody too much give a damn! Sylvester, here's the way your part go. The band plays the intro . . . I'll tell you where to come in. The band plays the intro and then you say, "All right, boys, you done seen the rest . . . Now I'm gonna show you the best. Ma Rainey's gonna show you her black bottom." You got that?

(SYLVESTER *nods.*)

Let me hear you say it one time.

SYLVESTER: "All right, boys, you done s-s-seen the rest n-n-now I'm gonna show you the best. M-m-m-m-m-m-ma Rainey's gonna s-s-show you her black b-b-bottom."

LEVEE: What kind of . . . All right, Cutler! Let me see you fix that! You straighten that out! You hear that shit, Slow Drag? How in the hell the boy gonna do the part and he can't even talk!

SYLVESTER: W-w-w-who's you to tell me what to do, nigger! This ain't your band! Ma tell me to d-d-d-do it and I'm gonna do it. You can go to hell, n-n-n-nigger!

LEVEE: B-b-b-boy, ain't nobody studying you. You go on and fix that one, Cutler. You fix that one and I'll . . . I'll shine your shoes for you. You go on and fix that one!

TOLEDO: You say you Ma's nephew, huh?

SYLVESTER: Yeah. So w-w-what that mean?

TOLEDO: Oh, I ain't meant nothing . . . I was just asking.

SLOW DRAG: Well, come on and let's rehearse so the boy can get it right.

LEVEE: I ain't rehearsing nothing! You just wait till I get my band. I'm gonna record that song and show you how it supposed to go!

CUTLER: We can do it without Levee. Let him sit on over there. Sylvester, you remember your part?

SYLVESTER: I remember it pretty g-g-g-good.

CUTLER: Well, come on, let's do it, then.

(*The band begins to play.* LEVEE *sits and pouts.* STURDYVANT *enters the band room.*)

STURDYVANT: Good . . . you boys are rehearsing, I see.

LEVEE: (*jumping up*) Yessir! We rehearsing. We know them songs real good.

STURDYVANT: Good! Say, Levee, did you finish that song?

LEVEE: Yessir, Mr. Sturdyvant. I got it right here. I wrote that other part just like you say. It go like:
You can shake it, you can break it
You can dance at any hall
You can slide across the floor
You'll never have to stall
My jelly, my roll,
Sweet Mama, don't you let it fall.
Then I put that part in there for the people to dance, like you say, for them to forget about their troubles.

STURDYVANT: Good! Good! I'll just take this. I wanna see you about your songs as soon as I get the chance.

LEVEE: Yessir! As soon as you get the chance, Mr. Sturdyvant.

(STURDYVANT *exits.*)

CUTLER: You hear, Levee? You hear this nigger? "Yessuh, we's rehearsing, boss."

SLOW DRAG: I heard him. Seen him too. Shuffling them feet.

TOLEDO: Aw, Levee can't help it none. He's like all of us. Spooked up with the white men.

LEVEE: I'm spooked up with him, all right. You let one of them crackers fix on me wrong. I'll show you how spooked up I am with him.

TOLEDO: That's the trouble of it. You wouldn't know if he was fixed on you wrong or not. You so spooked up by him you ain't had the time to study him.

LEVEE: I studies the white man. I got him studied good. The first time one fixes on me wrong, I'm gonna let him know just how much I studied. Come telling me I'm spooked up with the white man. You let one of them mess with me, I'll show you how spooked up I am.

CUTLER: You talking out your hat. The man come in here, call you a boy, tell you to get up off your ass and rehearse, and you ain't had nothing to say to him, except "Yessir!"

LEVEE: I can say "yessir" to whoever I please. What you got to do with it? I know how to handle white folks. I been handling them for thirty-two years, and now you gonna tell me how to do it. Just 'cause I say "yessir" don't mean I'm spooked up with him. I know what I'm doing. Let me handle him my way.

CUTLER: Well, go on and handle it, then.

LEVEE: Toledo, you always messing with somebody! Always agitating somebody with that old philosophy bullshit you be talking. You stay out of my way about what I do and say. I'm my own person. Just let me alone.

TOLEDO: You right, Levee. I apologize. It ain't none of my business that you spooked up by the white man.

LEVEE: All right! See! That's the shit I'm talking about. You all back up and leave Levee alone.

SLOW DRAG: Aw, Levee, we was all just having fun. Toledo ain't said nothing about you he ain't said about me. You just taking it all wrong.

TOLEDO: I ain't meant nothing by it Levee.

(*Pauses.*)
Cutler, you ready to rehearse?

LEVEE: Levee got to be Levee! And he don't need nobody messing with him about the white man— 'cause you don't know nothing about me. You don't know Levee. You don't know nothing about what kind of blood I got! What kind of heart I got beating here!

(*He pounds his chest.*)

I was eight years old when I watched a gang of white mens come into my daddy's house and have to do with my mama any way they wanted. *(Pauses.)*

We was living in Jefferson County, about eighty miles outside of Natchez. My daddy's name was Memphis . . . Memphis Lee Green . . . had him near fifty acres of good farming land. I'm talking about good land! Grow anything you want! He done gone off of shares and bought this land from Mr. Hallie's widow woman after he done passed on. Folks called him an uppity nigger 'cause he done saved and borrowed to where he could buy this land and be independent. *(Pauses.)*

It was coming on planting time and my daddy went into Natchez to get him some seed and fertilizer. Called me, say, "Levee you the man of the house now. Take care of your mama while I'm gone." I wasn't but a little boy, eight years old. *(Pauses.)*

My mama was frying up some chicken when them mens come in that house. Must have been eight or nine of them. She standing there frying that chicken and them mens come and took hold of her just like you take hold of a mule and make him do what you want. *(Pauses.)*

There was my mama with a gang of white mens. She tried to fight them off, but I could see where it wasn't gonna do her any good, I didn't know what they were doing to her . . . but I figured whatever it was they may as well do to me too. My daddy had a knife that he kept around there for hunting and working and whatnot. I knew where he kept it and I went and got it.

I'm gonna show you how spooked up I was by the white man. I tried my damndest to cut one of them's throat! I hit him on the shoulder with it. He reached back and grabbed hold of that knife and whacked me across the chest with it.

(LEVEE raises his shirt to show a long ugly scar.)

That's what made them stop. They was scared I was gonna bleed to death. My mama wrapped a sheet around me and carried me two miles down to the Furlow place and they drove me up to Doc Albans. He was waiting on a calf to be born, and say he ain't had time to see me. They carried me up to Miss Etta, the midwife, and she fixed me up.

My daddy came back and acted like he done accepted the facts of what happened. But he got the names of them mens from mama. He found out who they was and then we announced we was moving out of that county. Said good-bye to everybody . . . all the neighbors. My daddy went and smiled in the face of one of them crackers who had been with my mama. Smiled in his face and sold him our land. We moved over with relations in Caldwell. He got us settled in and then he took off one day. I ain't never seen him since. He sneaked back, hiding up in the woods, laying to get them eight or nine men. *(Pauses.)*

He got four of them before they got him. They tracked him down in the woods. Caught up with him and hung him and set him afire. *(Pauses.)*

My daddy wasn't spooked up by the white man. Nosir! And that taught me how to handle them. I seen my daddy go up and grin in this cracker's face . . . smile in his face and sell him his land. All the while he's planning how he's gonna get him and what he's gonna do to him. That taught me how to handle them. So you all just back up and leave Levee alone about the white man. I can smile and say "yessir" to whoever I please. I got time coming to me. You all just leave Levee alone about the white man.

(There is a long pause. SLOW DRAG begins playing on the bass and sings.)

SLOW DRAG: *(singing)*
If I had my way
If I had my way
If I had my way
I would tear this old building down.

ACT TWO

(The lights come up in the studio. The musicians are setting up their instruments. MA RAINEY *walks about shoeless, singing softly to herself.* LEVEE *stands near* DUSSIE MAE, *who hikes up her dress and crosses her leg.* CUTLER *speaks to* IRVIN *off to the side.)*

CUTLER: Mr. Irvin, I don't know what you gonna do. I ain't got nothing to do with it, but the boy can't do the part. He stutters. He can't get it right. He stutters right through it every time.

IRVIN: Christ! Okay. We'll . . . Shit! We'll just do it like we planned. We'll do Levee's version. I'll handle it, Cutler. Come on, let's go. I'll think of something.
(He exits to the control booth.)

MA RAINEY: *(calling* CUTLER *over)* Levee's got his eyes in the wrong place. You better school him, Cutler.

CUTLER: Come on, Levee . . . let's get ready to play! Get your mind on your work!

IRVIN: *(over speaker)* Okay, boys, we're gonna do "Moonshine Blues" first. "Moonshine Blues," Ma.

MA RAINEY: I ain't doing no "Moonshine" nothing. I'm doing the "Black Bottom" first. Come on, Sylvester.
(To IRVIN.*)*
Where's Sylvester's mike? You need a mike for Sylvester. Irvin . . . get him a mike.

IRVIN: Uh . . . Ma, the boys say he can't do it. We'll have to do Levee's version.

MA RAINEY: What you mean he can't do it? Who say he can't do it? What boys say he can't do it?

IRVIN: The band, Ma . . . the boys in the band.

MA RAINEY: What band? The band work for me! I say what goes! Cutler, what's he talking about? Levee, this some of your shit?

IRVIN: He stutters, Ma. They say he stutters.

MA RAINEY: I don't care if he do. I promised the boy he could do the part . . . and he's gonna do it! That's all there is to it. He don't stutter all the time. Get a microphone down here for him.

IRVIN: Ma, we don't have time. We can't . . .

MA RAINEY: If you wanna make a record, you gonna find time. I ain't playing with you, Irvin. I can walk out of here and go back to my tour. I got plenty fans. I don't need to go through all of this. Just go and get the boy a microphone.
*(IRVIN *and* STURDYVANT *consult in the booth,* IRVIN *exits.)*

STURDYVANT: All right, Ma . . . we'll get him a microphone. But if he messes up . . . He's only getting one chance . . . The cost . . .

MA RAINEY: Damn the cost. You always talking about the cost. I make more money for this outfit than anybody else you got put together. If he messes up he'll just do it till he gets it right. Levee, I know you had something to do with this. You better watch yourself.

LEVEE: It was Cutler!

SYLVESTER: It was you! You the only one m-m-mad about it.

LEVEE: The boy stutter. He can't do the part. Everybody see that. I don't know why you want the boy to do the part no ways.

MA RAINEY: Well, can or can't . . . he's gonna do it! You ain't got nothing to do with it!

LEVEE: I don't care what you do! He can sing the whole goddamned song for all I care!

MA RAINEY: Well, all right. Thank you.
*(IRVIN *enters with a microphone and hooks it up. He exits to the control booth.)*

MA RAINEY: Come on, Sylvester. You just stand here and hold your hands like I told you. Just remember the words and say them . . . That's all there is to it. Don't worry about messing up. If you mess up, we'll do it again. Now, let me hear you say it. Play for him, Cutler.

CUTLER: One . . . two . . . you know what to do.
(The band begins to play and SYLVESTER *curls his fingers and clasps his hands together in front of his chest, pulling in opposite directions as he says his lines.)*

SYLVESTER: "All right, boys, you d-d-done s-s-s-seen the best . . .
*(LEVEE *stops playing.)*

Now I'm g-g-g-gonna show you the rest
. . . Ma R-r-rainey's gonna show you her
b-b-b-black b-b-b-bottom."
(The rest of the band stops playing.)

MA RAINEY: That's all right. That's real good. You
take your time, you'll get it right.

STURDYVANT: *(over speaker)* Listen, Ma . . . now,
when you come in, don't wait so long to come in.
Don't take so long on the intro, huh?

MA RAINEY: Sturdyvant, don't you go trying to tell
me how to sing. You just take care of that up
there and let me take care of this down here.
Where's my Coke?

IRVIN: Okay, Ma. We're all set up to go up here.
"Ma Rainey's Black Bottom," boys.

MA RAINEY: Where's my Coke? I need a Coke.
You ain't got no Coke down here? Where's my
Coke?

IRVIN: What's the matter, Ma? What's . . .

MA RAINEY: Where's my Coke? I need a Coca-Cola.

IRVIN: Uh . . . Ma, look, I forgot the Coke, huh?
Let's do it without it, huh? Just this one song.
What say, boys?

MA RAINEY: Damn what the band say! You know I
don't sing nothing without my Coca-Cola!

STURDYVANT: We don't have any, Ma. There's no
Coca-Cola here. We're all set up and we'll just
go ahead and . . .

MA RAINEY: You supposed to have Coca-Cola.
Irvin knew that. I ain't singing nothing without
my Coca-Cola!
*(She walks away from the mike, singing to her-
self.* STURDYVANT *enters from the control
booth.)*

STURDYVANT: Now, just a minute here, Ma. You
come in an hour late . . . we're way behind
schedule as it is . . . the band is set up and
ready to go . . . I'm burning my lights . . .
I've turned up the heat . . . We're ready to
make a record and what? You decide you want a
Coca-Cola?

MA RAINEY: Sturdyvant, get out of my face.
*(IRVIN *enters.)*
Irvin . . . I told you keep him away from me.

IRVIN: Mel, I'll handle it.

STURDYVANT: I'm tired of her nonsense, Irv. I'm
not gonna put up with this!

IRVIN: Let me handle it, Mel. I know how to handle
her.
*(IRVIN *to* MA RAINEY.)*
Look, Ma . . . I'll call down to the deli and
get you a Coke. But let's get started, huh?
Sylvester's standing there ready to go . . .
the band's set up . . . let's do this one song,
huh?

MA RAINEY: If you too cheap to buy me a Coke,
I'll buy my own. Slow Drag! Sylvester, go with
Slow Drag and get me a Coca-Cola.
*(SLOW DRAG *comes over.)*
Slow Drag, walk down to that store on the cor-
ner and get me three bottles of Coca-Cola. Get
out my face, Irvin. You all just wait until I get
my Coke. It ain't gonna kill you.

IRVIN: Okay, Ma. Get your Coke, for Chrissakes!
Get your Coke!
*(IRVIN *and* STURDYVANT *exit into the hall-
way followed by* SLOW DRAG *and* SYLVESTER.
TOLEDO, CUTLER *and* LEVEE *head for the
band room.)*

MA RAINEY: Cutler, come here a minute. I want to
talk to you.
*(CUTLER *crosses over somewhat reluctantly.)*
What's all this about "the boys in the band
say"? I tells you what to do. I says what the
matter is with the band. I say who can and can't
do what.

CUTLER: We just say 'cause the boy stutter . . .

MA RAINEY: I know he stutters. Don't you think I
know he stutters. This is what's gonna help
him.

CUTLER: Well, how can he do the part if he stutters? You want him to stutter through it? We
just thought it be easier to go on and let Levee
do it like we planned.

MA RAINEY: I don't care if he stutters or not! He's
doing the part and I don't wanna hear any more
of this shit about what the band says. And I
want you to find somebody to replace Levee
when we get to Memphis. Levee ain't nothing
but trouble.

CUTLER: Levee's all right. He plays good music when he puts his mind to it. He knows how to write music too.

MA RAINEY: I don't care what he know. He ain't nothing but bad news. Find somebody else. I know it was his idea about who to say who can do what.

(DUSSIE MAE *wanders over to where they are sitting.*)

Dussie Mae, go sit your behind down somewhere and quit flaunting yourself around.

DUSSIE MAE: I ain't doing nothing.

MA RAINEY: Well, just go on somewhere and stay out of the way.

CUTLER: I been meaning to ask you, Ma . . . about these songs. This "Moonshine Blues" . . . that's one of them songs Bessie Smith sang, I believes.

MA RAINEY: Bessie what? Ain't nobody thinking about Bessie. I taught Bessie. She ain't doing nothing but imitating me. What I care about Bessie? I don't care if she sell a million records. She got her people and I got mine. I don't care what nobody else do. Ma was the *first* and don't you forget it!

CUTLER: Ain't nobody said nothing about that. I just said that's the same song she sang.

MA RAINEY: I been doing this a long time. Ever since I was a little girl. I don't care what nobody else do. That's what gets me so mad with Irvin. White folks try to be put out with you all the time. Too cheap to buy me a Coca-Cola. I lets them know it, though. Ma don't stand for no shit. Wanna take my voice and trap it in them fancy boxes with all them buttons and dials . . . and then too cheap to buy me a Coca-Cola. And it don't cost but a nickel a bottle.

CUTLER: I knows what you mean about that.

MA RAINEY: They don't care nothing about me. All they want is my voice. Well, I done learned that, and they gonna treat me like I want to be treated no matter how much it hurt them. They back there now calling me all kinds of names . . . calling me everything but a child of god.

But they can't do nothing else. They ain't got what they wanted yet. As soon as they get my voice down on them recording machines, then it's just like if I'd be some whore and they roll over and put their pants on. Ain't got no use for me then. I know what I'm talking about. You watch. Irvin right there with the rest of them. He don't care nothing about me either. He's been my manager for six years, always talking about sticking together, and the only time he had me in his house was to sing for some of his friends.

CUTLER: I know how they do.

MA RAINEY: If you colored and can make them some money, then you all right with them. Otherwise, you just a dog in the alley. I done made this company more money from my records than all the other recording artists they got together. And they wanna balk about how much this session is costing them.

CUTLER: I don't see where it's costing them all what they say.

MA RAINEY: It ain't! I don't pay that kind of talk no mind.

(*The lights go down on the studio and come up on the band room.* TOLEDO *sits reading a newspaper.* LEVEE *sings and hums his song.*)

LEVEE: (*singing*)
You can shake it, you can break it
You can dance at any hall
You can slide across the floor
You'll never have to stall
My jelly, my roll,
Sweet Mama, don't you let it fall.

Wait till Sturdyvant hear me play that! I'm talking about some real music, Toledo! I'm talking about *real* music!

(*The door opens and* DUSSIE MAE *enters.*)

Hey, mama! Come on in.

DUSSIE MAE: Oh, hi! I just wanted to see what it looks like down here.

LEVEE: Well, come on in . . . I don't bite.

DUSSIE MAE: I didn't know you could really write music. I thought you was just jiving me at the club last night.

LEVEE: Naw, baby . . . I knows how to write music. I done give Mr. Sturdyvant some of my songs and he says he's gonna let me record them. Ask Toledo. I'm gonna have my own band! Toledo, ain't I give Mr. Sturdyvant some of my songs I wrote?

TOLEDO: Don't get Toledo mixed up in nothing.
  (He exits.)

DUSSIE MAE: You gonna get your own band sure enough?

LEVEE: That's right! Levee Green and his Footstompers.

DUSSIE MAE: That's real nice.

LEVEE: That's what I was trying to tell you last night. A man what's gonna get his own band need to have a woman like you.

DUSSIE MAE: A woman like me wants somebody to bring it and put it in my hand. I don't need nobody wanna get something for nothing and leave me standing in my door.

LEVEE: That ain't Levee's style, sugar. I got more style than that. I knows how to treat a woman. Buy her presents and things . . . treat her like she wants to be treated.

DUSSIE MAE: That's what they all say . . . till it come time to be buying the presents.

LEVEE: When we get down to Memphis, I'm gonna show you what I'm talking about. I'm gonna take you out and show you a good time. Show you Levee knows how to treat a woman.

DUSSIE MAE: When you getting your own band?

LEVEE: *(moves closer to slip his arm around her)* Soon as Mr. Sturdyvant say. I done got my fellows already picked out. Getting me some good fellows know how to play real sweet music.

DUSSIE MAE: *(moves away)* Go on now, I don't go for all that pawing and stuff. When you get your own band, maybe we can see about this stuff you talking.

LEVEE: *(moving toward her)* I just wanna show you I know what the women like. They don't call me Sweet Lemonade for nothing.
  (LEVEE takes her in his arms and attempts to kiss her.)

DUSSIE MAE: Stop it now. Somebody's gonna come in here.

LEVEE: Naw they ain't. Look here, sugar . . . what I wanna know is . . . can I introduce my red rooster to your brown hen?

DUSSIE MAE: You get your band, then we'll see if that rooster know how to crow.
  (He grinds up against her and feels her buttocks.)

LEVEE: Now I know why my grandpappy sat on the back porch with his straight razor when grandma hung out the wash.

DUSSIE MAE: Nigger, you crazy!

LEVEE: I bet you sound like the midnight train from Alabama when it crosses the Mason-Dixon line.

DUSSIE MAE: How's you get so crazy?

LEVEE: It's women like you . . . drives me that way.
  (He moves to kiss her as the lights go down in the band room and up in the studio. MA RAINEY *sits with* CUTLER *and* TOLEDO.*)*

MA RAINEY: It sure done got quiet in here. I never could stand no silence. I always got to have some music going on in my head somewhere. It keeps things balanced. Music will do that. It fills things up. The more music you got in the world, the fuller it is.

CUTLER: I can agree with that. I got to have my music too.

MA RAINEY: White folks don't understand about the blues. They hear it come out, but they don't know how it got there. They don't understand that's life's way of talking. You don't sing to feel better. You sing 'cause that's a way of understanding life.

CUTLER: That's right. You get that understanding and you done got a grip on life to where you can hold your head up and go on to see what else life got to offer.

MA RAINEY: The blues help you get out of bed in the morning. You get up knowing you ain't alone. There's something else in the world. Something's been added by that song. This be an empty world without the blues. I take that emptiness and try to fill it up with something.

TOLEDO: You fill it up with something the people can't be without, Ma. That's why they call you the Mother of the Blues. You fill up that emptiness in a way ain't nobody ever thought of doing before. And now they can't be without it.

MA RAINEY: I ain't started the blues way of singing. The blues always been here.

CUTLER: In the church sometimes you find that way of singing. They got blues in the church.

MA RAINEY: They say I started it . . . but I didn't. I just helped it out. Filled up that empty space a little bit. That's all. But if they wanna call me the Mother of the Blues, that's all right with me. It don't hurt none.
(SLOW DRAG *and* SYLVESTER *enter with the Cokes.*)
It sure took you long enough. That store ain't but on the corner.

SLOW DRAG: That one was closed. We had to find another one.

MA RAINEY: Sylvester, go and find Mr. Irvin and tell him we ready to go.
(SYLVESTER *exits. The lights in the band room come up while the lights in the studio stay on.* LEVEE *and* DUSSIE MAE *are kissing.* SLOW DRAG *enters. They break their embrace.* DUSSIE MAE *straightens up her clothes.*)

SLOW DRAG: Cold out. I just wanted to warm up with a little sip.
(*He goes to his locker, takes out his bottle and drinks.*)
Ma got her Coke, Levee. We about ready to start.
(SLOW DRAG *exits.* LEVEE *attempts to kiss* DUSSIE MAE *again.*)

DUSSIE MAE: No . . . Come on! I got to go. You gonna get me in trouble.
(*She pulls away and exits up the stairs.* LEVEE *watches after her.*)

LEVEE: Good God! Happy birthday to the lady with the cakes!
(*The lights go down in the band room and come up in the studio.* MA RAINEY *drinks her Coke.* LEVEE *enters from the band room. The musicians take their places.* SYLVESTER *stands by his mike.*

IRVIN *and* STURDYVANT *look on from the control booth.*)

IRVIN: We're all set up here, Ma. We're all set to go. You ready down there?

MA RAINEY: Sylvester you just remember your part and say it. That's all there is to it.
(*To* IRVIN.)
Yeah, we ready.

IRVIN: Okay, boys. "Ma Rainey's Black Bottom." Take one.

CUTLER: One . . . two . . . You know what to do.
(*The band plays.*)

SYLVESTER: All right boys, you d-d-done s-s-seen the rest . . .

IRVIN: Hold it!
(*The band stops.* STURDYVANT *changes the recording disk and nods to* IRVIN.)
Okay. Take two.

CUTLER: One . . . two . . . You know what to do.
(*The band plays.*)

SYLVESTER: All right, boys, you done seen the rest . . . now I'm gonna show you the best. Ma Rainey's g-g-gonna s-s-show you her b-b-black bottom.

IRVIN: Hold it! Hold it!
(*The band stops.* STURDYVANT *changes the recording disk.*)
Okay. Take three. Ma, let's do it without the intro, huh? No voice intro . . . you just come in singing.

MA RAINEY: Irvin, I done told you . . . the boy's gonna do the part. He don't stutter all the time. Just give him a chance. Sylvester, hold your hands like I told you and just relax. Just relax and concentrate.

IRVIN: All right. Take three.

CUTLER: One . . . two . . . You know what to do.
(*The band plays.*)

SYLVESTER: All right, boys, you done seen the rest . . . now, I'm gonna show you the best. Ma Rainey's gonna show you her black bottom.

MA RAINEY: *(singing)*
    Way down south in Alabamy
    I got a friend they call dancing Sammy
    Who's crazy about all the latest dances
    Black Bottom stomping, two babies prancing

    The other night at a swell affair
    As soon as the boys found out that I was there
    They said, come on, Ma, let's go to the cabaret.
    When I got there, you ought to hear them say,

    I want to see the dance you call the black bottom
    I want to learn that dance
    I want to see the dance you call your big black
        bottom
    It'll put you in a trance.

    All the boys in the neighborhood
    They say your black bottom is really good
    Come on and show me your black bottom
    I want to learn that dance

    I want to see the dance you call the black bottom
    I want to learn that dance
    Come on and show the dance you call your big
        black bottom
    It puts you in a trance.

    Early last morning about the break of day
    Grandpa told my grandma, I heard him say,
    Get up and show your old man your black bottom
    I want to learn that dance
    (Instrumental break.)
    I done showed you all my black bottom
    You ought to learn that dance.

IRVIN: Okay, that's good, Ma. That sounded great!
    Good job, boys!

MA RAINEY: *(to* SYLVESTER*)* See! I told you. I
    knew you could do it. You just have to put your
    mind to it. Didn't he do good, Cutler? Sound
    real good. I told him he could do it.

CUTLER: He sure did. He did better than I
    thought he was gonna do.

IRVIN: *(entering to remove* SYLVESTER'S *mike)*
    Okay, boys . . . Ma . . . let's do "Moonshine
    Blues" next, huh? "Moonshine Blues," boys.

STURDYVANT: *(over speaker)* Irv! Something's
    wrong down there. We don't have it right.

IRVIN: What? What's the matter Mel . . .

STURDYVANT: We don't have it right. Something
    happened. We don't have the goddamn song
    recorded!

IRVIN: What's the matter? Mel, what happened?
    You sure you don't have nothing?

STURDYVANT: Check that mike, huh, Irv. It's the
    kid's mike. Something's wrong with the mike.
    We've got everything all screwed up here.

IRVIN: Christ almighty! Ma, we got to do it again.
    We don't have it. We didn't record the song.

MA RAINEY: What you mean you didn't record it?
    What was you and Sturdyvant doing up there?

IRVIN: *(following the mike wire)* Here . . . Levee
    must have kicked the plug out.

LEVEE: I ain't done nothing: I ain't kicked nothing!

SLOW DRAG: If Levee had his mind on what he's
    doing . . .

MA RAINEY: Levee, if it ain't one thing, it's an-
    other. You better straighten yourself up!

LEVEE: Hell . . . it ain't my fault. I ain't done
    nothing!

STURDYVANT: What's the matter with that mike,
    Irv? What's the problem?

IRVIN: It's the cord, Mel. The cord's all chewed
    up. We need another cord.

MA RAINEY: This is the most disorganized . . .
    Irvin, I'm going home! Come on. Come on,
    Dussie.
    *(*MA RAINEY *walks past* STURDYVANT *as he en-
    ters from the control booth. She exits offstage to
    get her coat.)*

STURDYVANT: *(to* IRVIN*)* Where's she going?

IRVIN: She said she's going home.

STURDYVANT: Irvin, you get her! If she walks out
    of here . . .
    *(*MA RAINEY *enters carrying her and* DUSSIE
    MAE'S *coat.)*

MA RAINEY: Come on, Sylvester.

IRVIN: *(helping her with her coat)* Ma . . . Ma
    . . . listen. Fifteen minutes! All I ask is fifteen
    minutes!

MA RAINEY: Come on, Sylvester, get your coat.

STURDYVANT: Ma, if you walk out of this studio . . .

IRVIN: Fifteen minutes, Ma!

STURDYVANT: You'll be through . . . washed up! If you walk out on me . . .

IRVIN: Mel, for Chrissakes, shut up and let me handle it!

(He goes after MA RAINEY, *who has started for the door.)*

Ma, listen. These records are gonna be hits! They're gonna sell like crazy! Hell, even Sylvester will be a star. Fifteen minutes. That's all I'm asking! Fifteen minutes.

MA RAINEY: *(crosses to a chair and sits with her coat on)* Fifteen minutes! You hear me, Irvin? Fifteen minutes . . . and then I'm gonna take my black bottom on back down to Georgia. Fifteen minutes. Then Madame Rainey is leaving!

IRVIN: *(kisses her)* All right, Ma . . . fifteen minutes. I promise.

(To the band.)

You boys go ahead and take a break. Fifteen minutes and we'll be ready to go.

CUTLER: Slow Drag, you got any of that bourbon left?

SLOW DRAG: Yeah, there's some down there.

CUTLER: I could use a little nip.

*(*CUTLER *and* SLOW DRAG *exit to the band room, followed by* LEVEE *and* TOLEDO. *The lights go down in the studio and up in the band room.)*

SLOW DRAG: Don't make me no difference if she leave or not. I was kinda hoping she would leave.

CUTLER: I'm like Mr. Irvin . . . After all this time we done put in here, it's best to go ahead and get something out of it.

TOLEDO: Ma gonna do what she wanna do, that's for sure. If I was Mr. Irvin, I'd best go on and get them cords and things hooked up right. And I wouldn't take no longer than fifteen minutes doing it.

CUTLER: If Levee had his mind on his work, we wouldn't be in this fix. We'd be up there finishing up. Now we got to go back and see if that boy

get that part right. Ain't no telling if he ever get that right again in his life.

LEVEE: Hey, Levee ain't done nothing!

SLOW DRAG: Levee up there got one eye on the gal and the other on his trumpet.

CUTLER: Nigger, don't you know that's Ma's gal?

LEVEE: I don't care whose gal it is. I ain't done nothing to her. I just talk to her like I talk to anybody else.

CUTLER: Well, that being Ma's gal, and that being that boy's gal, is one and two different things. The boy is liable to kill you . . . but you' ass gonna be out there scraping the concrete looking for a job if you messing with Ma's gal.

LEVEE: How am I messing with her? I ain't done nothing to the gal. I just asked her her name. Now, if you telling me I can't do that, then Ma will just have to go to hell.

CUTLER: All I can do is warn you.

SLOW DRAG: Let him hang himself, Cutler. Let him string his neck out.

LEVEE: I ain't done nothing to the gal! You all talk like I done went and done something to her. Leave me go with my business.

CUTLER: I'm through with it. Try and talk to a fool . . .

TOLEDO: Some mens got it worse than others . . . this foolishness I'm talking about. Some mens is excited to be fools. That excitement is something else. I know about it. I done experienced it. It makes you feel good to be a fool. But it don't last long. It's over in a minute. Then you got to tend with the consequences. You got to tend with what comes after. That's when you wish you had learned something about it.

LEVEE: That's the best sense you made all day. Talking about being a fool. That's the only sensible thing you said today. Admitting you was a fool.

TOLEDO: I admits it, all right. Ain't nothing wrong with it. I done been a little bit of everything.

LEVEE: Now you're talking. You's as big a fool as they make.

TOLEDO: Gonna be a bit more things before I'm finished with it. Gonna be foolish again. But I ain't never been the same fool twice. I might be a different kind of fool, but I ain't gonna be the same fool twice. That's where we parts ways.

SLOW DRAG: Toledo, you done been a fool about a woman?

TOLEDO: Sure. Sure I have. Same as everybody.

SLOW DRAG: Hell, I ain't never seen you mess with no woman. I thought them books was your woman.

TOLEDO: Sure I messed with them. Done messed with a whole heap of them. And gonna mess with some more. But I ain't gonna be no fool about them. What you think? I done come in the world full-grown, with my head in a book? I done been young. Married. Got kids. I done been around and I done loved women to where you shake in your shoes just at the sight of them. Feel it all up and down your spine.

SLOW DRAG: I didn't know you was married.

TOLEDO: Sure. Legally. I been married legally. Got the papers and all. I done been through life. Made my marks. Followed some signs on the road. Ignored some others. I done been all through it. I touched and been touched by it. But I ain't never been the same fool twice. That's what I can say.

LEVEE: But you been a fool. That's what counts. Talking about I'm a fool for asking the gal her name and here you is one yourself.

TOLEDO: Now, I married a woman. A good woman. To this day I can't say she wasn't a good woman. I can't say nothing bad about her. I married that woman with all the good graces and intentions of being hooked up and bound to her for the rest of my life. I was looking for her to put me in my grave. But, you see . . . it ain't all the time what you' intentions and wishes are. She went out and joined the church. All right. There ain't nothing wrong with that. A good Christian woman going to church and wanna do right by her god. There ain't nothing wrong with that. But she got up there, got to seeing them good Christian mens and wondering why I ain't like that. Soon she figure she got a heathen on her hands. She figured she couldn't live like that. The church was more important than I was. So she left. Packed up one day and moved out. To this day I ain't never said another word to her. Come home one day and my house was empty! And I sat down and figured out that I was a fool not to see that she needed something that I wasn't giving her. Else she wouldn't have been up there at the church in the first place. I ain't blaming her. I just said it wasn't gonna happen to me again. So, yeah, Toledo been a fool about a woman. That's part of making life.

CUTLER: Well, yeah, I been a fool too. Everybody done been a fool once or twice. But, you see, Toledo, what you call a fool and what I call a fool is two different things. I can't see where you was being a fool for that. You ain't done nothing foolish. You can't help what happened, and I wouldn't call you a fool for it. A fool is responsible for what happens to him. A fool cause it to happen. Like Levee . . . if he keeps messing with Ma's gal and his feet be out there scraping the ground. That's a fool.

LEVEE: Ain't nothing gonna happen to Levee. Levee ain't gonna let nothing happen to him. Now, I'm gonna say it again. I asked the gal her name. That's all I done. And if that's being a fool, then you looking at the biggest fool in the world . . . 'cause I sure as hell asked her.

SLOW DRAG: You just better not let Ma see you ask her. That's what the man's trying to tell you.

LEVEE: I don't need nobody to tell me nothing.

CUTLER: Well, Toledo, all I gots to say is that from the looks of it . . . from your story . . . I don't think life did you fair.

TOLEDO: Oh, life is fair. It's just in the taking what it gives you.

LEVEE: Life ain't shit. You can put it in a paper bag and carry it around with you. It ain't got no balls. Now, death . . . death got some style! Death will kick your ass and make you wish you never been born! That's how bad death is! But you can rule over life. Life ain't nothing.

TOLEDO: Cutler, how's your brother doing?

CUTLER: Who, Nevada? Oh, he's doing all right. Staying in St. Louis. Got a bunch of kids, last I heard.

TOLEDO: Me and him was all right with each other. Done a lot of farming together down in Plattsville.

CUTLER: Yeah, I know you all was tight. He in St. Louis now. Running an elevator, last I hear about it.

SLOW DRAG: That's better than stepping in mule-shit.

TOLEDO: Oh, I don't know now. I like farming. Get out there in the sun . . . smell that dirt. Be out there by yourself . . . nice and peaceful. Yeah, farming was all right by me. Sometimes I think I'd like to get me a little old place . . . but I done got too old to be following behind one of them balky mules now.

LEVEE: Nigger talking about life is fair. And ain't got a pot to piss in.

TOLEDO: See, now, I'm gonna tell you something. A nigger gonna be dissatisfied no matter what. Give a nigger some bread and butter . . . and he'll cry 'cause he ain't got no jelly. Give him some jelly, and he'll cry 'cause he ain't got no knife to put it on with. If there's one thing I done learned in this life, it's that you can't satisfy a nigger no matter what you do. A nigger's gonna make his own dissatisfaction.

LEVEE: Niggers got a right to be dissatisfied. Is you gonna be satisfied with a bone somebody done throwed you when you see them eating the whole hog?

TOLEDO: You lucky they let you be an entertainer. They ain't got to accept your way of entertaining. You lucky and don't even know it. You's entertaining and the rest of the people is hauling wood. That's the only kind of job for the colored man.

SLOW DRAG: Ain't nothing wrong with hauling wood. I done hauled plenty wood. My daddy used to haul wood. Ain't nothing wrong with that. That's honest work.

LEVEE: That ain't what I'm talking about. I ain't talking about hauling no wood. I'm talking about being satisfied with a bone somebody done throwed you. That's what's the matter with you all. You satisfied sitting in one place. You got to move on down the road from where you sitting . . . and all the time you got to keep an eye out for that devil who's looking to buy up souls. And hope you get lucky and find him!

CUTLER: I done told you about that blasphemy. Talking about selling your soul to the devil.

TOLEDO: We done the same thing, Cutler. There ain't no difference. We done sold Africa for the price of tomatoes. We done sold ourselves to the white man in order to be like him. Look at the way you dressed . . . That ain't African. That's the white man. We trying to be just like him. We done sold who we are in order to become someone else. We's imitation white men.

CUTLER: What else we gonna be, living over here?

LEVEE: I'm Levee. Just me. I ain't no imitation nothing!

SLOW DRAG: You can't change who you are by how you dress. That's what I got to say.

TOLEDO: It ain't all how you dress. It's how you act, how you see the world. It's how you follow life.

LEVEE: It don't matter what you talking about. I ain't no imitation white man. And I don't want to be no white man. As soon as I get my band together and make them records like Mr. Sturdyvant done told me I can make, I'm gonna be like Ma and tell the white man just what he can do. Ma tell Mr. Irvin she gonna leave . . . and Mr. Irvin get down on his knees and beg her to stay! That's the way I'm gonna be! Make the white man respect me!

CUTLER: The white man don't care nothing about Ma. The colored folks made Ma a star. White folks don't care nothing about who she is . . . what kind of music she make.

SLOW DRAG: That's the truth about that. You let her go down to one of them white-folks hotels and see how big she is.

CUTLER: Hell, she ain't got to do that. She can't even get a cab up here in the North. I'm gonna tell you something. Reverend Gates . . . you know Reverend Gates? . . . Slow Drag know who I'm talking about. Reverend Gates . . . now I'm gonna show you how this go where the white man don't care a thing about who you is. Reverend Gates was coming from Tallahassee to Atlanta, going to see his sister, who was sick at that time with the consumption. The train come up through Thomasville, then past Moultrie, and stopped in this little town called Sigsbee . . .

LEVEE: You can stop telling that right there! That train don't stop in Sigsbee. I know what train you talking about. That train got four stops before it reach Macon to go on to Atlanta. One in Thomasville, one in Moultrie, one in Cordele . . . and it stop in Centerville.

CUTLER: Nigger, I know what I'm talking about. You gonna tell me where the train stop?

LEVEE: Hell, yeah, if you talking about it stop in Sigsbee. I'm gonna tell you the truth.

CUTLER: I'm talking about *this* train! I don't know what train you been riding. I'm talking about *this* train!

LEVEE: Ain't but one train. Ain't but one train come out of Tallahassee heading north to Atlanta, and it don't stop at Sigsbee. Tell him, Toledo . . . that train don't stop at Sigsbee. The only train that stops at Sigsbee is the Yazoo Delta, and you have to transfer at Moultrie to get it!

CUTLER: Well, hell, maybe that what he done! I don't know. I'm just telling you the man got off the train at Sigsbee . . .

LEVEE: All right . . . you telling it. Tell it your way. Just make up anything.

SLOW DRAG: Levee, leave the man alone and let him finish.

CUTLER: I ain't paying Levee no never mind.

LEVEE: Go one and tell it your way.

CUTLER: Anyway . . . Reverend Gates got off this train in Sigsbee. The train done stopped there and he figured he'd get off and check the schedule to be sure he arrive in time for somebody to pick him up. All right. While he's there checking the schedule, it come upon him that he had to go to the bathroom. Now, they ain't had no colored rest rooms at the station. The only colored rest room is an outhouse they got sitting way back two hundred yards or so from the station. All right. He in the outhouse and the train go off and leave him there. He don't know nothing about this town. Ain't never been there before—in fact, ain't never even heard of it before.

LEVEE: I heard of it! I know just where it's at . . . and he ain't got off no train coming out of Tallahassee in Sigsbee!

CUTLER: The man standing there, trying to figure out what he's gonna do . . . where this train done left him in this strange town. It started getting dark. He see where the sun's getting low in the sky and he's trying to figure out what he's gonna do, when he noticed a couple of white fellows standing across the street from this station. Just standing there, watching him. And then two or three more come up and joined the other ones. He look around, ain't seen no colored folks nowhere. He didn't know what was getting in these here fellows' minds, so he commence to walking. He ain't knowed where he was going. He just walking down the railroad tracks when he hear them call him. "Hey, nigger!" See, just like that. "Hey, nigger!" He kept on walking. They called him some more and he just keep walking. Just going down the tracks. And then he heard a gunshot where somebody done fired a gun in the air. He stopped then, you know.

TOLEDO: You don't even have to tell me no more. I know the facts of it. I done heard the same story a hundred times. It happened to me too. Same thing.

CUTLER: Naw, I'm gonna show you how the white folks don't care nothing about who or what you is. They crowded around him. These gang of mens made a circle around him. Now, he's standing there, you understand . . . got his cross around his neck like them preachers wear. Had his little Bible with him what he carry all the time. So they crowd on around him and one of them ask who he is. He told them he was Reverend Gates and that he was going to see his sister who was sick and the train left without him. And they said, "Yeah, nigger . . . but can you dance?" He looked at them and commenced to dancing. One of them reached up and tore his cross off his neck. Said he was committing a heresy by dancing with a cross and Bible. Took his Bible and tore it up and had him dancing till they got tired of watching him.

SLOW DRAG: White folks ain't never had no respect for the colored minister.

CUTLER: That's the only way he got out of there alive . . . was to dance. Ain't even had no respect for a man of God! Wanna make him into a clown. Reverend Gates sat right in my house and told me that story from his own mouth. So . . . the white folks don't care nothing about Ma Rainey. She's just another nigger who they can use to make some money.

LEVEE: What I wants to know is . . . if he's a man of God, then where the hell was God when all of this was going on? Why wasn't God looking out for him. Why didn't God strike down them crackers with some of this lightning you talk about to me?

CUTLER: Levee, you gonna burn in hell.

LEVEE: What I care about burning in hell? You talk like a fool . . . burning in hell. Why didn't God strike some of them crackers down? Tell me that! That's the question! Don't come telling me this burning-in-hell shit! He a man of God . . . why didn't God strike some of them crackers down? I'll tell you why! I'll tell you the truth! It's sitting out there as plain as day! 'Cause he a white man's God. That's why! God ain't never listened to no nigger's prayers. God take a nigger's prayers and throw them in the garbage. God don't pay niggers no mind. In fact . . . God hate niggers! Hate them with all the fury in his heart. Jesus don't love you, nigger! Jesus hate your black ass! Come talking that shit to me. Talking about burning in hell! God can kiss my ass.

(CUTLER *can stand no more. He jumps up and punches* LEVEE *in the mouth. The force of the blow knocks* LEVEE *down and* CUTLER *jumps on him.*)

CUTLER: You worthless . . . That's my God! That's my God! That's my God! You wanna blaspheme my God!

(TOLEDO *and* SLOW DRAG *grab* CUTLER *and try to pull him off* LEVEE.)

SLOW DRAG: Come on, Cutler . . . let it go! It don't mean nothing!

(CUTLER *has* LEVEE *down on the floor and pounds on him with a fury.*)

CUTLER: Wanna blaspheme my God! You worthless . . . talking about my God!

(TOLEDO *and* SLOW DRAG *succeed in pulling* CUTLER *off* LEVEE, *who is bleeding at the nose and mouth.*)

LEVEE: Naw, let him go! Let him go!
(*He pulls out a knife.*)
That's your God, huh? That's your God, huh? Is that right? Your God, huh? All right. I'm gonna give your God a chance. I'm gonna give your God a chance. I'm gonna give him a chance to save your black ass.

(LEVEE *circles* CUTLER *with the knife.* CUTLER *picks up a chair to protect himself.*)

TOLEDO: Come on, Levee . . . put the knife up!

LEVEE: Stay out of this, Toledo!

TOLEDO: That ain't no way to solve nothing.

(LEVEE *alternately swipes at* CUTLER *during the following.*)

LEVEE: I'm calling Cutler's God! I'm talking to Cutler's God! You hear me? Cutler's God! I'm calling Cutler's God. Come on and save this nigger! Strike me down before I cut his throat!

SLOW DRAG: Watch him, Cutler! Put that knife up, Levee!

LEVEE: *(to* CUTLER*)* I'm calling your God! I'm gonna give him a chance to save you! I'm calling your God! We gonna find out whose God he is!

CUTLER: You gonna burn in hell, nigger!

LEVEE: Cutler's God! Come on and save this nigger! Come on and save him like you did my mama! Save him like you did my mama! I heard her when she called you! I heard her when she said, "Lord, have mercy! Jesus, help me! Please, God, have mercy on me, Lord Jesus, help me!" And did you turn your back? Did you turn your back, motherfucker? Did you turn your back?

*(*LEVEE *becomes so caught up in his dialogue with God that he forgets about* CUTLER *and begins to stab upward in the air, trying to reach God.)*

Come on! Come on and turn your back on me! Turn your back on me! Come on! Where is you? Come on and turn your back on me! Turn your back on me, motherfucker! I'll cut your heart out! Come on, turn your back on me! Come on! What's the matter? Where is you? Come on and turn your back on me! Come on, what you scared of? Turn your back on me! Come on! Coward, motherfucker!

*(*LEVEE *folds his knife and stands triumphantly.)*

Your God ain't shit, Cutler.

(The lights fade to black.)

MA RAINEY: *(singing)*

Ah, you hear me talking to you
I don't bite my tongue
You wants to be my man
You got to fetch it with you when you come.

(Lights come up in the studio. The last bars of the last song of the session are dying out.)

IRVIN: *(over speaker)* Good! Wonderful! We have that, boys. Good session. That's great, Ma. We've got ourselves some winners.

TOLEDO: Well, I'm glad that's over.

MA RAINEY: Slow Drag, where you learn to play the bass at? You had it singing! I heard you! Had that bass jumping all over the place.

SLOW DRAG: I was following Toledo. Nigger got them long fingers striding all over the piano. I was trying to keep up with him.

TOLEDO: That's what you supposed to do, ain't it? Play the music. Ain't nothing abstract about it.

MA RAINEY: Cutler, you hear Slow Drag on that bass? He make it do what he want it to do! Spank it just like you spank a baby.

CUTLER: Don't be telling him that. Nigger's head get so big his hat won't fit him.

SLOW DRAG: If Cutler tune that guitar up, we would really have something!

CUTLER: You wouldn't know what a tuned-up guitar sounded like if you heard one.

TOLEDO: Cutler was talking. I heard him moaning. He was all up in it.

MA RAINEY: Levee . . . what is that you doing? Why you playing all them notes? You play ten notes for every one you supposed to play. It don't call for that.

LEVEE: You supposed to improvise on the theme. That's what I was doing.

MA RAINEY: You supposed to play the song the way I sing it. The way everybody else play it. You ain't supposed to go off by yourself and play what you want.

LEVEE: I was playing the song. I was playing it the way I felt it.

MA RAINEY: I couldn't keep up with what was going on. I'm trying to sing the song and you up there messing up my ear. That's what you was doing. Call yourself playing music.

LEVEE: Hey . . . I know what I'm doing. I know what I'm doing, all right. I know how to play music. You all back up and leave me alone about my music.

CUTLER: I done told you . . . it ain't about *your* music. It's about *Ma's* music.

MA RAINEY: That's all right, Cutler. I done told you what to do.

LEVEE: I don't care what you do. You supposed to improvise on the theme. Not play note for note the same thing over and over again.

MA RAINEY: You just better watch yourself. You hear me?

LEVEE: What I care what you or Cutler do? Come telling me to watch myself. What's that supposed to mean?

MA RAINEY: All right . . . you gonna find out what it means.

LEVEE: Go ahead and fire me. I don't care. I'm gonna get my own band anyway.

MA RAINEY: You keep messing with me.

LEVEE: Ain't nobody studying you. You ain't gonna do nothing to me. Ain't nobody gonna do nothing to Levee.

MA RAINEY: All right, nigger . . . you fired!

LEVEE: You think I care about being fired? I don't care nothing about that. You doing me a favor.

MA RAINEY: Cutler, Levee's out! He don't play in my band no more.

LEVEE: I'm fired . . . Good! Best thing that ever happened to me. I don't need this shit!
(LEVEE exits to the band room. IRVIN enters from the control booth.)

MA RAINEY: Cutler, I'll see you back at the hotel.

IRVIN: Okay, boys . . . you can pack up. I'll get your money for you.

CUTLER: That's cash money, Mr. Irvin. I don't want no check.

IRVIN: I'll see what I can do. I can't promise you nothing.

CUTLER: As long as it ain't no check. I ain't got no use for a check.

IRVIN: I'll see what I can do, Cutler.
(CUTLER, TOLEDO, and SLOW DRAG exit to the band room.)
Oh, Ma, listen . . . I talked to Sturdyvant, and he said . . . Now, I tried to talk him out of it . . . He said the best he can do is to take your twenty-five dollars of your money and give it to Sylvester.

MA RAINEY: Take what and do what? If I wanted the boy to have twenty-five dollars of my money, I'd give it to him. He supposed to get his own money. He supposed to get paid like everybody else.

IRVIN: Ma, I talked to him . . . He said . . .

MA RAINEY: Go talk to him again! Tell him if he don't pay that boy, he'll never make another record of mine again. Tell him that. You supposed to be my manager. All this talk about sticking together. Start sticking! Go on up there and get that boy his money!

IRVIN: Okay, Ma . . . I'll talk to him again. I'll see what I can do.

MA RAINEY: Ain't no see about it! You bring that boy's money back here!
(IRVIN exits. The lights stay on in the studio and come up in the band room. The men have their instruments packed and sit waiting for IRVIN to come and pay them. SLOW DRAG has a pack of cards.)

SLOW DRAG: Come on, Levee, let me show you a card trick.

LEVEE: I don't want to see no card trick. What you wanna show me for? Why you wanna bother me with that?

SLOW DRAG: I was just trying to be nice.

LEVEE: I don't need you to be nice to me. What I need you to be nice to me for? I ain't gonna be nice to you. I ain't even gonna let you be in my band no more.

SLOW DRAG: Toledo, let me show you a card trick.

CUTLER: I just hope Mr. Irvin don't bring no check down here. What the hell I'm gonna do with a check?

SLOW DRAG: All right now . . . pick a card. Any card . . . go on . . . take any of them. I'm gonna show you something.

TOLEDO: I agrees with you, Cutler. I don't want no check either.

CUTLER: It don't make no sense to give a nigger a check.

SLOW DRAG: Okay, now. Remember your card. Remember which one you got. Now . . . put it back in the deck. Anywhere you want. I'm gonna show you something.
(TOLEDO puts the card in the deck.)
You remember your card? All right. Now I'm gonna shuffle the deck. Now . . . I'm gonna show you what card you picked. Don't say

nothing now. I'm gonna tell you what card you picked.

CUTLER: Slow Drag, that trick is as old as my mama.

SLOW DRAG: Naw, naw . . . wait a minute! I'm gonna show him his card . . . There it go! The six of diamonds. Ain't that your card? Ain't that it?

TOLEDO: Yeah, that's it . . . the six of diamonds.

SLOW DRAG: Told you! Told you I'd show him what it was!

(The lights fade in the band room and come up full on the studio. STURDYVANT enters with IRVIN.)

STURDYVANT: Ma, is there something wrong? Is there a problem?

MA RAINEY: Sturdyvant, I want you to pay that boy his money.

STURDYVANT: Sure, Ma. I got it right here. Two hundred for you and twenty-five for the kid, right?

(STURDYVANT hands the money to IRVIN, who hands it to MA RAINEY and SYLVESTER.)

Irvin misunderstood me. It was all a mistake. Irv made a mistake.

MA RAINEY: A mistake, huh?

IRVIN: Sure, Ma. I made a mistake. He's paid, right? I straightened it out.

MA RAINEY: The only mistake was when you found out I hadn't signed the release forms. That was the mistake. Come on, Sylvester.

(She starts to exit.)

STURDYVANT: Hey, Ma . . . come on, sign the forms, huh?

IRVIN: Ma . . . come on now.

MA RAINEY: Get your coat, Sylvester. Irvin, where's my car?

IRVIN: It's right out front, Ma. Here . . . I got the keys right here. Come on, sign the forms, huh?

MA RAINEY: Irvin, give me my car keys!

IRVIN: Sure, Ma . . . just sign the forms, huh?

(He gives her the keys, expecting a trade-off.)

MA RAINEY: Send them to my address and I'll get around to them.

IRVIN: Come on, Ma . . . I took care of everything, right? I straightened everything out.

MA RAINEY: Give me the pen, Irvin.

(She signs the forms.)

You tell Sturdyvant . . . one more mistake like that and I can make my records someplace else.

(She turns to exit.)

Sylvester, straighten up your clothes. Come on, Dussie Mae.

(She exits, followed by DUSSIE MAE and SYLVESTER. The lights go down in the studio and come up on the band room.)

CUTLER: I know what's keeping him so long. He up there writing out checks. You watch. I ain't gonna stand for it. He ain't gonna bring me no check down here. If he do, he's gonna take it right back upstairs and get some cash.

TOLEDO: Don't get yourself all worked up about it. Wait and see. Think positive.

CUTLER: I am thinking positive. He positively gonna give me some cash. Man give me a check last time . . . you remember . . . we went all over Chicago trying to get it cashed. See a nigger with a check, the first thing they think is he done stole it someplace.

LEVEE: I ain't had no trouble cashing mine.

CUTLER: I don't visit no whorehouses.

LEVEE: You don't know about my business. So don't start nothing. I'm tired of you as it is. I ain't but two seconds off your ass no way.

TOLEDO: Don't you all start nothing now.

CUTLER: What the hell I care what you tired of. I wasn't even talking to you. I was talking to this man right here.

(IRVIN and STURDYVANT enter.)

IRVIN: Okay boys. Mr. Sturdyvant has your pay.

CUTLER: As long as it's cash money, Mr. Sturdyvant. 'Cause I have too much trouble trying to cash a check.

STURDYVANT: Oh, yes . . . I'm aware of that. Mr. Irvin told me you boys prefer cash, and that's what I have for you.

(He starts handing out the money.)

That was a good session you boys put in . . . That's twenty-five for you. Yessir, you boys really know your business and we are going to . . . Twenty-five for you . . . We are going to get you back in here real soon . . . twenty-five . . . and have another session so you can make some more money . . . and twenty-five for you. Okay, thank you, boys. You can get your things together and Mr. Irvin will make sure you find your way out.

IRVIN: I'll be out front when you get your things together, Cutler.

(IRVIN *exits.* STURDYVANT *starts to follow.*)

LEVEE: Mr. Sturdyvant, sir. About them songs I give you? . . .

STURDYVANT: Oh,   yes, . . . uh . . . Levee. About them songs you gave me. I've thought about it and I just don't think the people will buy them. They're not the type of songs we're looking for.

LEVEE: Mr. Sturdyvant, sir . . . I done got my band picked out and they's real good fellows. They knows how to play real good. I know if the peoples hear the music, they'll buy it.

STURDYVANT: Well, Levee, I'll be fair with you . . . but they're just not the right songs.

LEVEE: Mr. Sturdyvant, you got to understand about that music. That music is what the people is looking for. They's tired of jug-band music. They wants something that excites them. Something with some fire to it.

STURDYVANT: Okay, Levee. I'll tell you what I'll do. I'll give you five dollars apiece for them. Now that's the best I can do.

LEVEE: I don't want no five dollars, Mr. Sturdyvant. I wants to record them songs, like you say.

STURDYVANT: Well, Levee, like I say . . . they just aren't the kind of songs we're looking for.

LEVEE: Mr. Sturdyvant, you asked me to write them songs. Now, why didn't you tell me that before when I first give them to you? You told me you was gonna let me record them. What's the difference between then and now?

STURDYVANT: Well, look . . . I'll pay you for your trouble . . .

LEVEE: What's the difference, Mr. Sturdyvant? That's what I wanna know.

STURDYVANT: I had my fellows play your songs, and when I heard them, they just didn't sound like the kind of songs I'm looking for right now.

LEVEE: You got to hear *me* play them, Mr. Sturdyvant! You ain't heard *me* play them. That's what's gonna make them sound right.

STURDYVANT: Well, Levee, I don't doubt that really. It's just that . . . well, I don't think they'd sell like Ma's records. But I'll take them off your hands for you.

LEVEE: The people's tired of jug-band music, Mr. Sturdyvant. They wants something that's gonna excite them! They wants something with some fire! I don't know what fellows you had playing them songs . . . but if I could play them! I'd set them down in the people's lap! Now you told me I could record them songs!

STURDYVANT: Well, there's nothing I can do about that. Like I say, it's five dollars apiece. That's what I'll give you. I'm doing you a favor. Now, if you write any more, I'll help you out and take them off your hands. The price is five dollars apiece. Just like now.

(He attempts to hand LEVEE the money, finally shoves it in LEVEE'S coat pocket and is gone in a flash. LEVEE follows him to the door and it slams in his face. He takes the money from his pocket, balls it up and throws it on the floor. The other musicians silently gather up their belongings. TOLEDO walks past LEVEE and steps on his shoe.)

LEVEE: Hey! Watch it . . . Shit Toledo! You stepped on my shoe!

TOLEDO: Excuse me there, Levee.

LEVEE: Look at that! Look at that! Nigger, you stepped on my shoe. What you do that for?

TOLEDO: I said I'm sorry.

LEVEE: Nigger gonna step on my goddamn shoe! You done fucked up my shoe! Look at that! Look at what you done to my shoe, nigger! I ain't stepped on your shoe! What you wanna step on my shoe for?

CUTLER: The man said he's sorry.

LEVEE: Sorry! How the hell he gonna be sorry after he gone ruint my shoe? Come talking about sorry!
(Turns his attention back to TOLEDO.*)*
Nigger, you stepped on my shoe! You know that!
*(*LEVEE *snatches his shoe off his foot and holds it up for* TOLEDO *to see.)*
See what you done done?

TOLEDO: What you want me to do about it? It's done now. I said excuse me.

LEVEE: Wanna go and fuck up my shoe like that. I ain't done nothing to your shoe. Look at this!
*(*TOLEDO *turns and continues to gather up his things.* LEVEE *spins him around by his shoulder.)*

LEVEE: Naw . . . naw . . . look what you done!
(He shoves the shoe in TOLEDO'S *face.)*
Look at that! That's my shoe! Look at that! You did it! You did it! You fucked up my shoe! You stepped on my shoe with them raggedy-ass clodhoppers!

TOLEDO: Nigger, ain't nobody studying you and your shoe! I said excuse me. If you can't accept that, then the hell with it. What you want me to do?
*(*LEVEE *is in a near rage, breathing hard. He is trying to get a grip on himself, as even he senses, or perhaps only he senses, he is about to lose control. He looks around, uncertain of what to do.* TOLEDO *has gone back to packing, as have* CUTLER *and* SLOW DRAG. *They purposefully avoid looking at* LEVEE *in hopes he'll calm down if he doesn't have an audience. All the weight in the world suddenly falls on* LEVEE *and he rushes at* TOLEDO *with his knife in his hand.)*

LEVEE: Nigger, you stepped on my shoe!
(He plunges the knife into TOLEDO'S *back up to the hilt.* TOLEDO *lets out a sound of surprise and agony.* CUTLER *and* SLOW DRAG *freeze.* TOLEDO *falls backward with* LEVEE, *his hand still on the knife, holding him up.* LEVEE *is suddenly faced with the realization of what he has done. He shoves* TOLEDO *forward and takes a step back.* TOLEDO *slumps to the floor.)*
He . . . he stepped on my shoe. He did. Honest, Cutler, he stepped on my shoe. What he do that for? Toledo, what you do that for? Cutler, help me. He stepped on my shoe, Cutler.
(He turns his attention to TOLEDO.*)*
Toledo! Toledo, get up.
(He crosses to TOLEDO *and tries to pick him up.)*
It's okay, Toledo. Come on . . . I'll help you. Come on, stand up now. Levee'll help you.
*(*TOLEDO *is limp and heavy and awkward. He slumps back to the floor.* LEVEE *gets mad at him.)*
Don't look at me like that! Toledo! Nigger, don't look at me like that! I'm warning you, nigger! Close your eyes! Don't you look at me like that!
(He turns to CUTLER.*)*
Tell him to close his eyes. Cutler. Tell him don't look at me like that.

CUTLER: Slow Drag, get Mr. Irvin down here.
(The sound of a trumpet is heard, LEVEE'S *trumpet, a muted trumpet struggling for the highest of possibilities and blowing pain and warning.)*
(Black out.)

THE END

I DON'T HAVE TO SHOW YOU NO STINKING BADGES! (1986)

No other individual has made as important an impact on Chicano theatre as Luis Valdez.

–Jorge Huerta

The world is not black and white. It is a multitude of colors. I only wait for the day when it will be possible to speak truthfully about the true racial makeup of the only true race on the planet earth, the Human race, La Raza Humana.

–Luis Valdez

In his introduction to Luis Valdez's *Zoot Suit and Other Plays* (1992), Jorge Huerta reprises his earlier praise of Valdez in *Necessary Theatre: Six Plays about the Chicano Experience* (1989), emphasizing the undeniable importance of Valdez's work to Chicano theatre in America. Since the early 1960s, Valdez has been a tireless force in the Mexican-American community, an important writer and director, and in 1965 a founding member of **El Teatro Campesino** (The Farmworkers' Theatre) in San Juan Bautista, California. And although few would question Huerta's assessment of Valdez as "the leading Chicano playwright and director" in America whose work "inspired a national movement of theatre troupes dedicated to the exposure of sociopolitical problems within the Chicano communities of the United States," Valdez is not without his critics. Nor is Huerta. For Yolanda Broyles González, Huerta's historical view of El Teatro Campesino distorts its collaborative origins, subsuming them under the name of a single "great man": Valdez. González's critique of Huerta's "heroic and monolithic vision" of El Teatro Campesino and Valdez includes a sharp indictment of the theatre's repertory of plays, one that

regardless of its "strong progressive strides in the treatment of labor issues, of Chicano culture, [and] of historical issues" consistently demonstrates "stagnation" in its treatment of women. In 1992, Valdez sparked further criticism by casting an Anglo actress (Laura San Giacomo) to play Frida Kahlo, Mexican artist and wife of muralist Diego Rivera, in his film *Frida and Diego*. Valdez responded with a strong "Statement on Artistic Freedom," which concludes with the epigraph quoted above and the complaint that, as a "Chicano filmmaker in Hollywood," he is "damned if I do, and damned if I don't make this movie the way others see it." Although in the same statement he announced the suspension of this film project, he insisted that by casting San Giacomo he had "not turned his back on a lifelong effort to gain equal opportunities for Latinos in the entertainment industry"—and that he would not be "intimidated" into making his "vision of America coincide with whatever is politically correct at the moment."

I Don't Have to Show You No Stinking Badges! concerns many of these same issues, suggesting not only the considerable irony of the controversy surrounding *Frida and Diego*, but also indicating the broader ambit of Valdez's career in the 1980s and 90s. Luis Miguel Valdez (1940–) was born into a family of migrant farmworkers in Delano, California, the second of ten children. While still in high school, he appeared regularly on local television programs, and later majored in English at San Jose State College. There, his interest in theatre grew, and his first play, *The Shrunken Head of Pancho Villa*, was produced by the drama department in 1963. After graduating in 1964, he joined the San Francisco Mime Troupe, acting in agitprop dramas that protested, among other things, American involvement in the

Vietnam War. In 1965, he returned to Delano to help César Chávez and the United Farm Workers organize agricultural workers by staging *actos*, short dramatic pieces (some of them performed on the backs of flatbed trucks) structured so as to provide narrative space both for comic improvisation, satire, and more direct political commentary. In his preface to El Teatro Campesino's *Actos* (1971), Valdez explains their purpose: "Inspire the audience to social action. Illuminate specific points about social problems. Satirize the opposition." And in his "Notes on Chicano Theatre," published in *Luis Valdez—Early Works* (1990), Valdez expands this agenda in directions analogous to those taken by the **Black Arts Movement** of the 1960s: This theatre must foster the idea of a cultural nationalism emerging from Chicanos' Amerindian past which importantly includes the development of a unique mythology, and it must remain focused on *la Raza*—Mexican Americans and their everyday lives. Valdez's work from the 1960s and 1970s concerns such issues as the unionization of exploited agricultural workers and the improvement of their labor conditions, the drafting of Chicanos to fight in Vietnam, and the dilemmas of Spanish-speaking children enrolled in U.S. schools. Important plays from this early period include *Las dos caras del patroncito* (*The Two Faces of the Little Boss*, 1965), *Los vendidos* (*The Sell-Outs*, 1967), *No saco nada de la escuela* (*I Don't Get Anything Out of School*, 1969), *Soldado Razo* (*Buck Private*, 1970), and *Bernabé* (1970).

In 1967, Valdez left the United Farm Workers to develop his own career as a dramatist—writing *mitos* (myths) and, later in the 1970s, *corridos* (traditional ballads)—and to help establish an independent El Teatro Campesino. In several plays of the early 1970s, Valdez returns to the dramatic forms of more traditional entertainments, adapting conventions from *carpas* (Mexican tent shows) in *La gran carpa de la Familia Rascuachi* (*The Great Tent of the Rascuachi Family*, 1971), and reviving religious drama in *Las cuatro apariciones de la Virgen de Guadalupe* (*The Four Apparitions of Our Lady of Guadalupe*, 1971). He also began to reach a larger audience in the 1970s and 1980s with such plays as *Zoot Suit*

(1978), a musical docudrama of the Sleepy Lagoon murder trial in Los Angeles in 1942, which opened at the Mark Taper Forum and eventually went to Broadway; *Bandido!* (1981), described by Valdez as an "anti-melodrama" about a nineteenth-century California bandit; *Corridos* (1982), a pageant of Mexican and Mexican-American ballads adapted in 1987 by Valdez for the Corporation for Public Broadcasting and, subsequently, winner of a Peabody Award; and *I Don't Have to Show You No Stinking Badges!* In addition, in 1987 he wrote and directed the film *La Bamba*, based on the life of 1950s rock star Ritchie Valens, marking in Huerta's historical schema a new phase in Valdez's career: from the union days, to those of the independent teatro, to the creative directorship of a more professionalized and more national theatre around 1980, and, in the later 1980s and 90s, to new projects as a filmmaker as well as continuing his involvement with El Teatro Campesino.

I Don't Have to Show You No Stinking Badges! takes its title from a line in the John Huston film, *The Treasure of the Sierra Madre* (1948), a film in which Valdez's Buddy Villa, the bit-actor, restaurant-owner, and patriarch in *Badges!*, claims to have appeared. With good humor but an inevitable bitterness, Buddy and his wife Connie attempt throughout much of the play to find more substantial parts in television and movies than the predictable, stereotypical roles from which they have made a decent living: for Buddy, bandido, gardener, pimp; for Connie, devoted mother, housekeeper, or whore. Parents of an extremely successful daughter and a son (Sonny) studying a prelaw curriculum at Harvard, Buddy and Connie return home to find Sonny, home from school and, to their great disappointment, planning to drop out and become an actor. Sonny's ambition, however, goes beyond landing the "marginal" roles his parents have performed and, as a consequence, beyond attaining what he deprecates as their virtually "invisible" status in the "larger scheme of Hollywood." Yet Sonny is also aware of the limited roles that would be made available to him, most of which would subscribe to a well-known stereotypical pattern: "the indispensable cholo gang member–heroin addict–born-to-lose-image . . . hostile, dumb, and potentially violent. Preferably with rape on the mind." He has other ideas.

In the second scene of Act Two, Sonny enters the house moments before the police surround it, telling Anita, his new girlfriend, that he has just robbed a fast-food restaurant. He was just acting out the robbery, he tells her, but in the "cheap imitation of Anglo life he has lived," the line between reality and simulation is often indistinct. This issue, the effacement of boundaries between staged or filmed image and everyday reality, is not only a constant theme in contemporary literature—in Adrienne Kennedy's *A Movie Star Has to Star in Black and White*, for example—but also one Valdez frequently explores. So, in *Zoot Suit* when Henry, a Chicano gang member, prepares to draw his knife on a rival, El Pachuco stops him with "That's exactly what the play needs right now. Two more Mexicans killing each other," later adding while looking at the audience, "That's exactly what they paid to see. Think about it." This **metatheatrical** moment deliberately challenges the audience's suspension of disbelief, causing it to reconsider its participation in the theatrical event and creating a momentary distance between them and the action of the play. Further, as Valdez explains in the opening stage directions to his first play, *The Shrunken Head of Pancho Villa*, the "psychological reality of the barrio" cannot be adequately represented by conventionally **realistic** drama; thus, the play combines "realistic and surrealistic elements working together to achieve a transcendental expression of the social condition of La Raza in los Estados Unidos." Somewhat similarly, *Badges!* combines realistic dialogue and action with the simulations of a televised drama, for at the crucial moment of confrontation between Sonny and the Los Angeles police who surround the house, the lights lower and after a brief pause a director's voice reminds the audience of what it might have forgotten: that it has been watching a television program. The set for the play, which includes television monitors and video cameras, conspicuous scenery flats and "assorted equipment," supplements the play's development of a metatheatrical self-consciousness and its distance from conventional realism.

One further rationale for framing the action of *Badges!* around the mechanisms of television production—in some ways similar to Kennedy's motivation for borrowing scenes from well-known movies in *Movie Star*—would seem to be Valdez's hypothesis that mass cultural images not only promote stereotypes to be resisted, but also create strong senses of identification *and* identity in young viewers like Sonny. At one moment in Act One, he reminds his parents that while part of his interest in the law originated in Charles Laughton's performance as a barrister in the film *Witness for the Prosecution*, this interest was little different from—and finally no more intense than—his desire to buy a white suit after seeing *Saturday Night Fever* or to search for gold in Mexico after watching *Raiders of the Lost Ark*. Thus, one "psychological reality of the barrio," as Valdez terms it in *The Shrunken Head of Pancho Villa*, and of the suburban neighborhood in which Sonny's family lives, involves the subject's negotiations of traditional Mexican influences, mass cultural texts, and the myriad of images and roles these provide. *Badges!*, with its scores of references to classic films of the 1940s and more recent movies, to popular television series of the 1950s, and to music from the 1960s, blends the influences (and reductions) of popular culture with a variety of elements from the Chicano community to create an intricate network of cultural references within which identity (and this importantly includes gender) is formed. This play, then, both recalls the satirical and political edge of Valdez's earlier protest dramas as it also anticipates some of the very issues in which he has been embroiled in the making of *Frida and Diego*. And if, as he suggests in his "Statement on Artistic Freedom," he has "helped define the Latino identity in America" through his plays and films, then *Badges!* confirms the complexity of this identity and the substantial role popular culture plays in its formation for Latino consumers.

WORKS CONSULTED

González, Yolanda Broyles. "Toward a Re-Vision of Chicano Theatre History: The Women of El Teatro Campesino." *Making a Spectacle: Feminist Essays on Contemporary Theatre.* Ed. Lynda Hart. Ann Arbor: University of Michigan Press, 1989. 209–238.

Huerta, Jorge, ed. *Necessary Theatre: Six Plays about the Chicano Experience.* Houston: Arte Publico Press, 1989.

Morales, Ed. "Shadowing Valdez." *American Theatre.* November 1992: 14–19.

Valdez, Luis. *Luis Valdez—Early Works: Actos, Barnabé, and Pensamiento serpentino.* Houston: Arte Publico, 1990.

———. "A Statement on Artistic Freedom." *American Theatre* 9 (November 1992): 18.

———. *Zoot Suit and Other Plays.* Houston: Arte Publico Press, 1992.

Valdez, Luis, and El Teatro Campesino. *Actos.* San Juan Bautista: Cucaracha, 1971.

CHARACTERS

BUDDY VILLA

CONNIE . . . . his wife

SONNY . . . . their son

ANITA . . . . Sonny's friend

Scene

The den of a comfortable, middle-class, suburban tract home in Southern California. Built some twenty years ago, the large den has all the features one might expect: black leather couches, bookshelves, trophies (bowling, golf, football, baseball, basketball), family photographs, liquor cabinet, fireplace, 25" console TV, stereo, VCR, etc. Upstage left, overlooking the sunken den, is the breakfast bar with stools, plus all the standard appliances beyond. A long hallway juts off diagonally, upstage right, toward the front of the house. Downstage right, through a large portico, is the formal dining and living room, rarely used and largely unseen. Another door, down left of the breakfast bar, opens onto a two-car garage. Extreme doors open onto a worn wooden deck, supposedly overlooking a huge, neglected, imaginary swimming pool.

The entire scene has a comfortable, lived-in quality, particularly the den which is certainly the most lived-in room in the house. It is the family cockpit.

Perhaps the only sign of the family's ancestral heritage is the familiar, round Aztec calendar stone, cast in plaster and painted gold, hanging above the fireplace. An old framed poster of Humphrey Bogart's 1948 classic "The Treasure of the Sierra Madre" hangs on another wall, and one of those electrical plastic signs hawking Asahi beer stands in the corner.

Time

The Reagan years, early in 1985.

Place

Monterey Park—a suburb of greater Los Angeles, on the distant fringe of Hollywood, USA.

Note

The entire set sits within the confines of a TV studio. The scenery flats and their supports are entirely visible, as they might be to a live studio audience at a taping. Huge TV lamps hang above the set, and assorted equipment looms here and there above and beyond the limits of the set. A studio boom is poised above one of the flats, as if waiting to come on. Two studio monitors sit at extreme upstage right and upstage left, unobtrusive but activated from time to time with shots of the play picked up by two live video cameras in the house, and with shots on video tape.

The video-taped inserts must be pre-recorded, showing the family pool, cars coming and going, the front door, etc. The presence and participation of television equipment in this play must remain in the background until the final scene, but it is an integral part of the theatrical reality at hand in our story.

The use of music in this play approximates the sort of underscoring found in television and on film. Buddy must definitely have a "theme," but it is also appropriate for each of the four characters to have their own leitmotif.

Prologue

Darkness. A single clear note from a clarinet pierces the dark and plays the opening to Gershwin's "Rhapsody in Blue" slowly and hauntingly.

DIRECTOR: *(voice over. On the studio speakers)* Lights . . .
(In the den: A lamp slowly comes on, revealing BUDDY VILLA, *54, sitting asleep late at night in front of the TV [unseen and invisible] at extreme downstage right.)*

DIRECTOR: *(voice over)* Video . . . Action!
(Behind BUDDY VILLA, *the VCR on, a rack comes on, playing a scene from "The Treasure of Sierra*

Madre." On the studio monitors: A wily Mexican bandit is confronting a scruffy Humphrey Bogart with toothy disdain, somewhere in the wilds of Mexico.)

BANDIDO: *(affronted)* Badges? We don't have no badges. I don't have to show you any stinkin' badges!
(Gunfire. Action. In a mist, SONNY *appears in the patio, dressed as a Hollywood director. The French doors open automatically, and* SONNY *enters in slow motion, as in a dream, riding in on a dolly behind a phosphorescent camera.* BUDDY *stirs from his sleep and walks over to him, also in slow motion, moving his lips silently as if to say "Sonny what are you doing here?"* SONNY *commands him to sit down and sleep, and* BUDDY *does as he is told.* SONNY *then turns off the TV, affectionately kisses his father on the forehead, and exits out the French doors which close automatically behind him.*

Slow fade to black.)

ACT ONE

SCENE ONE: *Early morning.*
At rise: Coffee is perking in the kitchen. We hear the upbeat sounds of a '50s rock 'n' roll classic. In the den, CONNIE VILLA, *an attractive 48-year-old Chicana, is dancing. Dressed in a fluffy pink nightgown, she ambles over to the phone and makes a call, while the music on the stereo tape deck plays. Sitting on a wooden stool at the breakfast bar,* CONNIE *dials carefully, dangling a fluffy pink bedroom slipper from her foot. As the music ends, she is talking into the phone with a laid-back, brassy tone and worldly air.*

CONNIE: *(on phone)* Hello, Betty? This is Constance D'Ville—Connie Villa! How ya doin' today? . . . Great. Listen, any word on that Jack Nicholson picture? . . . Well, when was I supposed to go back for that interview? I know we talked about it yesterday, but . . . well, I was wondering . . . Did you get a chance to ask the casting director about Buddy? . . . Nothing? Nothing at all? Please, Betty. Without him I'm sunk! Central America's out of the question . . . Yeah . . . yeah. I'll hold, sure. *(the back door, down the hall, opens and closes. The sound of heavy breathing and footsteps)* Buddy? . . . Is that you, *viejo?*

BUDDY: *(enters, jogging in place)* Viejo my ass. Look at me—I'm an animal! *(BUDDY is a hefty, well-preserved Chicano, hungover but dressed in a jogging suit and running shoes, with the balding hair and body weight of an aging prizefighter. He jogs up to CONNIE, tosses her the morning paper and then picks her up and spins her around while she is still talking to her agent)*

CONNIE: Wait a minute, Betty. There's an animal in the house! No, it's only Buddy. *(BUDDY drops to the floor and does ten, grunting and counting vociferously)* What? . . . Oh. What about Buddy? . . . Nothing, huh? A part in what? . . . "The Hairy Ape"?

BUDDY: *(puffing)* All right! ¿No que no?

CONNIE: No, Betty. I don't think so. We don't do waiver theatre. Screw the exposure. We don't work for free.

BUDDY: Twenty minutes flat, old lady! *(CONNIE makes a face and stands, still on the phone. She wipes his sweat off the floor. BUDDY hops on the exercise bike)*

CONNIE: He's right here, dripping sweat all over my floor . . . Yeah, he was out jogging. Or as we say in Spanish—"hogging." *(BUDDY playfully grunts like a hog, heading for the kitchen)* Which reminds me: the residuals for the AT&T commercial, when do they start? . . . Well okay, keep me posted. See you at the banquet tonight. *Ciao (hangs up).* Betty says there might be something in a couple of days. *(BUDDY opens the refrigerator door, we hear a beer pop open)* Beer, hombre? It's still morning.

BUDDY: Gotta replace my body fluids. Would you believe I just ran five miles?

CONNIE: No.

BUDDY: Okay. Would you believe three miles?

CONNIE: I believe you ran around the house, slowly.

BUDDY: Honest. *Hice jog hasta la* freeway and back. Ran like an Apache . . . *(CONNIE reaches up to the cabinet for vitamins; BUDDY eyes her over)* What's for breakfast?

CONNIE: What would you like?

BUDDY: How about a little *chorizo con huevos* . . . in bed?

CONNIE: Don't start, *señor.*

BUDDY: *(sidling up to her)* Jogging always makes me horny.

CONNIE: Breathing makes you horny.

BUDDY: At my age I hate to let a good erection go to waste.

CONNIE: Down, boy. *(flicks at his feigned erection)* How about some butterless toast?

BUDDY: I'll stay on my liquid diet. *(he takes a long swig on his beer, and straddles one of the breakfast stools, noticing a letter on the counter. He picks it up as CONNIE pours orange juice and sets out the vitamins for BUDDY)* What's this?

CONNIE: *(exchanges BUDDY'S beer for a glass of juice)* It's from Lucy. She says Bob and her are doing just fine. Bob just got tenure in the Economics Department at Arizona State, and she's about to open her own practice in pediatrics in downtown Phoenix, which is why they've decided to wait to have a baby of their own. Go ahead, read it.

BUDDY: What the hell for? You just told me all that's in it.

CONNIE: Pick up your beer cans. *(he tosses the letter back on the counter; then he crosses down into the den, taking his beer, and starts picking up other empty beer cans)* At least your daughter writes. Sonny, on the other hand, forget it. Not one written word since he got back East. We're lucky if he even calls once a month to ask for money. Do you think he's okay?

BUDDY: Sixteen years old and studying pre-law at Harvard? What could go wrong? A bad case of zits? The kid's a prodigy. He'll own his own law firm by the time he's twenty-five.

CONNIE: God knows, the last thing I want to be is one of those clinging *madrecitas* that won't let their kids grow up or they lose their purpose in life. *Chale,* man, not me, boy. I hung up my uterus a long time ago. I like my freedom, and I'm ready to go places. (BUDDY *crosses up into the kitchen, carrying several empty beer cans*) How late did you stay up last night?

BUDDY: Late. I was listening to a little Gershwin and I fell asleep watching my favorite picture. (*he deposits the cans into a garbage bag under the sink*)

CONNIE: (*archly*) What's that, a whole twelve pack? I thought you looked a little hung over this morning!

BUDDY: I always look hung over in the morning.

CONNIE: After twenty-five years, you think I don't . . . ?

BUDDY: (*laughs defensively*) It was just a few beers, *chingao.* Can't I have a few lousy beers—alone, by myself, in my own *pinche* den, in my own *pinche* house?

CONNIE: Not when you had a *pinche* drinking problem, just a few *pinche* years ago . . .

BUDDY: (*drops cans into a trash bag*) That's ancient history.

CONNIE: Especially if you drink alone.

BUDDY: Actually, I had a weird dream Sonny was here in the house, right here in the den. I was there in my chair, there was someone outside and he came in, setting up shots, like he was directing a new "Twilight Zone" or something, can you beat that?

CONNIE: Mm, hmm, Harvard School of Law, Class of '92.

BUDDY: Anyway, this morning I woke up with a new movie idea.

CONNIE: Finish taking out the garbage.

BUDDY: This one's real hot. You wanna hear it? It'll only take a second. (BUDDY *crosses to the stereo, and turns on the "Star Wars" theme, on cassette*)

CONNIE: (*patiently tolerating him*) Go on.

BUDDY: Well, the first shot shows him speeding across the giant screen in his space ship, blasting all rockets. Right? And his little ship sorta resembles a chopped down '56 Chevy, with fuzzy dice hanging over the dashboard, while the hero sits in the cockpit, down low, see? His head barely visible. *Órale, mamacita.*

CONNIE: (*dully*) Like a lowrider.

BUDDY: You got it. Well, suddenly there's these laser beams shooting at his tail, see? And the screen fills up with this giant space battle cruiser in hot pursuit.

CONNIE: Sounds familiar.

BUDDY: Except that the giant battle cruiser looks like a huge sombrero! A sombrero flying saucer! (*laughs, enthused*) And it's chasing the Chicano spaceman, 'cause they're the Interplanetary Border Patrol, the Space Migra, and he's trying to escape across the border to Earth! You get it?

CONNIE: (*crosses to the stereo and turns it off*) Take out the garbage.

BUDDY: It's a satire.

CONNIE: It won't sell, Buddy.

BUDDY: (*angered*) How the hell do you know? You're trying to tell me I don't know the *pinche* business? Shit, I was personal friends with Humphrey Bogart when you were still in grammar school, lady. Bogey and me were like that! (BUDDY *takes the garbage to service patio*) Won't sell, my ass. I could pick up that *pinche* phone right now and peddle this *pinche* idea to a dozen *pinche* big-time directors. (*offstage. Exits to garage*) Spielberg, Redford, Brian de Palma—they all know me! (*we hear the trash can lid slammed on. Pause.* BUDDY *re-enters*)

CONNIE: (*concerned*) What's with all the *pinches*? What's eating you?

BUDDY: The Garcías' German shepherd chased me down the *pinche* block this morning.

CONNIE: (*crosses to hall closet for cleaning equipment*) Again, *hombre*?

BUDDY: Fifth time. And he's not the only one. The new Oriental families on the other block have pit bulls. *¡Pinches perros!* Why is it all the rich *gabachos* over in Beverly Hills have all these lousy little Chihuahuas, and all the Mexicans and Chinks on this side of town have these big Nazi killers?

CONNIE: *(carpet sweeping)* We could use a guard dog ourselves, for when we go out of town. It's been years since we went to Mexico. Wouldn't it be nice to travel now that the kids are out of the house?

BUDDY: *(looks out toward the backyard, with a darkening mood)* Dogtown . . . Here we are in Monterey Park, and all these people still live in Dogtown. Know what I mean? In their minds, they never left.

CONNIE: And you did?

BUDDY: Lock, stock and *perros.* I was drafted.

CONNIE: Well, personally, I like "this side of town." I'm glad we left the barrio, but I wouldn't live in Beverly Hills if they paid me. Too many Latina maids at the bus stops.

BUDDY: In Korea I even ate some *perro* once.

CONNIE: East is east, and west is west, especially in L.A. Of course, there is always north and south, south of the border—way south? Honduras would be nice. Or Belize. Or Costa Rica.

BUDDY: *(puts his arms around her)* We never use the goddamn pool anymore . . . Remember when we first put it in? Sonny and Lucy went crazy out there. We had some great times together.

CONNIE: *(squirts armpits, getting away)* That was ten, fifteen years ago, *señor.* That pool hasn't been cleaned in so long, there's something slimy growing at the bottom.

BUDDY: *(tongue in cheek)* I'm growing some class "A" Colombian seaweed.

CONNIE: Be serious. *(he turns and faces her tensely, in a showdown of sorts)*

BUDDY: Okay. Then let's talk about the Nicholson movie.

CONNIE: So that's what's eating you!

BUDDY: I know damn well you really want to do it.

CONNIE: *(cautiously)* Betty says I still have a good chance at the part of the madam.

BUDDY: *(scoffing, spreads legs into the air)* Another Mexican whore?

CONNIE: *(trying to joke, sliding up to him)* Of course not, she's Costa Rican! Come on, at least I own the house! Buddy, it's a great part. A speaking part. I'd only be on location for three weeks. A month's shoot at the most.

BUDDY: *(tightening)* I got news for you. They're already shooting down there.

CONNIE: Where?

BUDDY: Everywhere! Nicaragua, El Salvador, Miami.

CONNIE: The location's in Costa Rica.

BUDDY: *(blowing up)* People are KILLING each other down there! Don't you understand? You'd be all alone. You wanna get killed, or even worse, raped to death?

CONNIE: *(cleaning trophies)* Then come with me.

BUDDY: I've got a business to run.

CONNIE: Betty can talk to them. Get you some kind of small role.

BUDDY: Small role? I read for those people, same as you. If they don't want me, I ain't gonna beg them. Fuck 'em. Who needs their two-bit TV movies, anyway? Cecil B. De Mille once ate at my restaurant.

CONNIE: *(pleading)* It's a feature, Buddy . . .

BUDDY: *(goes to fridge for beer)* Outta town we work as a team or no dice! Remember? Nobody goes anywhere alone. (CONNIE'S *face takes on an undaunted look)*

CONNIE: What about the Stallone picture last year in Mexico? You went alone.

BUDDY: On restaurant business. I brought back Pedro Wong, didn't I? Where else was I to find a Chinese-Mexican cook?

CONNIE: But you acted.

BUDDY: *(goes to the phone and dials)* For Pedro's sake, I saved our business! Fried rice and re-fried beans, our chile relleno runneth over now. In this case, Wong was right. (CONNIE *groans, returns stuff to hall closet.* BUDDY'S *call connects with his restaurant; he talks to his cook. On the phone)* Pedro, joe san! . . . *Frijoles* ju ho mee-ah? *Menudo* ju ho mee-ah? *Tortillas* gow mee-ah? Ngaw dee you jew-ng mole? Gup gaee chicken chow yuk? Ngaw, chee dee lai gwaw. *¡Hay te watcho! (Hangs up)* Besides, Sly cut my scene out of the picture, so it didn't count, sweetheart.

CONNIE: Well, maybe Jack will cut my scene out of the picture and it won't count either, sweetheart.

BUDDY: *¿Sabes qué?* Before you start getting on a first-name basis with stars, you better make damn sure you've even got a job.

CONNIE: Oh, that's cruel, Buddy. That's really cruel.

BUDDY: It's a cruel business.

CONNIE: I'm only asking for a little support and encouragement. Is that such a big deal?

BUDDY: I knew it was a mistake to let you start acting.

CONNIE: All I want is a little harmless fun in my life! Who knows, maybe I've got a talent or two I never had a chance to develop before. Is that so bad?

BUDDY: *(like Jackie Gleason)* Put 'em in a couple of pictures, way in the background, and suddenly everybody wants to be a star!

CONNIE: Why do you have to be such a fat ass *cabezudo?*

BUDDY: *(pause)* Okay . . . now you're hitting below the belt, see? Enough's enough. Get this whole crazy scheme outta your head. Get dressed and get on the phone and work on your little real estate sideline. *¡Ya estuvo!* No more show business today. I'm gonna drain the pool. *(BUDDY heads for the backyard. CONNIE follows him)*

CONNIE: If it weren't for my little real estate sideline, we wouldn't even have the goddamn pool! *(the phone rings. CONNIE and BUDDY look at each other, then race to the phone. CONNIE answers)*

CONNIE: Hello? Oh, hi, Betty . . . Yeah? *(brightening)* Really?

BUDDY: *(hanging on her shoulder)* I'm serious, Connie. Don't take it.

CONNIE: *(on phone)* I'll take it! . . . When? That soon? . . . Right . . . MGM, soundstage eighteen. Great! Got it . . . Thanks, Betty. *Ciao. (hangs up)*

BUDDY: *(frustrated)* What? What?

CONNIE: "DALLAS" over at MGM. They want both of us.

BUDDY: *(impressed)* Both of us? *(BUDDY turns to tuck shirt into pants)*

CONNIE: *(with a caustic edge)* Work for a whole two days, *mi amor.* Both of us—right here in town, just the way you like it. A maid and a gardener. Are you happy now?

BUDDY: *(with gardener accent)* Well, you could have consulted me before you agreed to do it.

CONNIE: *(blowing up, furious, hits BUDDY in the stomach)* Look, Buddy, if you don't want the goddamn job, you call Betty! I'm taking it. Interview's on the lot in fifty minutes. *(CONNIE starts to storm out; BUDDY chases her, looking like the cat who ate the canary)*

BUDDY: *(holding CONNIE)* Heh, heh, wait a minute. How much is the Nicholson picture worth? You know the score. We haven't gotten this far by fooling ourselves, right? I'm the Silent Bit King and you're my Queen! No more, no less. Right?

CONNIE: *(deadly serious, pushes BUDDY away)* Buddy, I'm tired of being silent. *(CONNIE walks out without another word. BUDDY holds back for a beat, then glances at the Bogart poster)*

BUDDY: So, who am I, Charlie Chaplin? *(BUDDY exits, walking like "The Little Tramp")*
(Fade to black.)

SCENE TWO: *Early evening. Mozart's "Rondo in C" plays sprightly, as the lights come up to half, simulating dusk.* SONNY *enters the house, coming down the hallway, carrying a suitcase. He is a tall, slim seventeen-year-old law student, looking quite Anglo in his casual winter wear, despite his classic handsome Latin features. He enters tentatively, apprehensively calling out "Mom" and then "Dad?" as he checks the garage. Confident no one is home, he tosses his suitcase on the couch, and looks about the den with an ironic haughty demeanor. He then steps out onto the wooden deck and looks out towards the pool. Shuddering suddenly, he spins around and heads for his suitcase. Opening it up, he extracts a portable cassette recorder, and presses PLAY and draws an anxious breath, before he speaks.*

SONNY: Greater East Los Angeles. February 20th. 6:30 P.M. Home away from home away from home. Concept for possible "Twilight Zone." i.e.—"Sonny, the Harvard Homeboy Comes Home." So what's on your mind, homes? *(pause)* Sonny's mind is on my mind, homes. Little Son, *mamacita's* little *m'ijo*, daddy's little chicken. Chicken Little. The sky is falling! *(paces, growing agitated)* Fuck. The whole inside of your refried skull is falling, Sonny boy! Raining cats and dogs. A veritable *chubasco* of cranial slime, drowning your brain in your own biological soup, the primordial chicken broth of your own egg, your *huevo*, one egg instead of two. With two *huevos* you might have been born a human. Add a Polish sausage and you might have been born a man. A Lech Walesa in solidarity with your Polish balls! *(As SONNY pours out his anxieties, ANITA SAKAI, gorgeous but frazzled twenty-eight-year-old Asian-American brunette, enters from the rear and pauses, crossing her arms and leaning against the corner of the hallway, pops a Valium.)* What are you doing here, Sonny? Your *mamá* and *papá* have great expectations. Are you real or are you Memorex? Reach out, reach out and touch someone, asshole!

ANITA: Sonny?

SONNY: *(startled)* What?

ANITA: Remember me? *(SONNY stares at her with embarrassment, suddenly tongue-tied. ANITA comes down and examines her surroundings, toting her baggy purse)*

ANITA: *(on edge but playful)* Hello, hello? Is this the Villa household? Does Sonny Villa live here?

SONNY: Sorry. I'm still in rapid transit between realities.

ANITA: Your folks are out, huh?

SONNY: *(SONNY and ANITA kiss and hug)* Uh . . . yeah. Right. The place is all ours, baby. *(SONNY regains his composure, superficially putting on the sophisticated airs of a "Harvard Man." He nuzzles into her neck and kisses her)*

ANITA: Nice place. At least one of us is home.

SONNY: Just your standard Southern California suburban tract home. Nothing special. *(ANITA notices the Aztec calendar clock above the fireplace)*

ANITA: What's that?

SONNY: An Aztec Timex, I think. Same category as Tijuana tincan sculptures and paintings on black felt. My parent's taste—not mine.

ANITA: Listen to you. Where did the Ivy League snob come from?

SONNY: Harvard, where else? *(ANITA looks out into the backyard, affecting a snobbish accent)*

ANITA: Oh. We have a pool!

SONNY: *(playing back)* Doesn't everybody? That's where I first learned all about sex.

ANITA: *(knowingly)* Skinny-dipping with the girls?

SONNY: Playing squirrel with the boys.

ANITA: Squirrel?

SONNY: Grab nuts and run. *(ANITA laughs playfully, sits on the rug and begins to stretch)*

ANITA: I keep forgetting you still remember puberty. *(SONNY'S sophistication melts in a sudden flush of adolescent chagrin)*

SONNY: *(looking at a picture of LUCY)* Actually, it was fat dipping my big sister, who tried to drown me more than once. She knew all the medical terms by the time she was eleven. I was an embryo. I was born believing *genitalia* was the name of an opera star. *(ANITA groans as SONNY holds her from behind)* Tired? *(as he rubs her inner thighs and midriff)*

ANITA: *(stretching)* Wired, actually. I'm just quietly going out of my fucking mind. The Peugeot finally wheezed and crapped out on me. It won't even turn over. It's just sitting out there, sagging on its last tires, waiting for the final bullet.

SONNY: Maybe it just needs another rest? I mean, it worked in Las Vegas. Didn't it? Overnight?

ANITA: *(jumping out of SONNY'S arms)* Never mind last night. Everything I own is sitting out there in that car. Poor baby. We've been through a lot together. I can't believe this is the end of the road, but then, the way my life has been going lately, I feel Peugeot'd out myself.

SONNY: *(solicitously, pulls her to him)* How about some Coke? Pepsi, milk or anything? Tea! How about some hot tea?

ANITA: Okay. Red Zinger, *(grabs his butt)* if you have it.

SONNY: *(pausing)* Red Zinger? I can't promise that. This is more of a Lipton Tea house.

ANITA: *(bending over, looking in bag)* Mind if I use your phone? It's a local call. Pacific Palisades.

SONNY: Who do you know in Palisades? *(SONNY comes up behind ANITA and holds her by the waist and presses himself up to her butt)*

ANITA: My brother. I was going to call him last night, when we got to Vegas, except, well, you know. Somebody distracted me. I thought all you Latino dudes knew about sex and cars. I was half right. *(SONNY looks for the tea in the kitchen cabinet; ANITA crosses to her purse on the couch, extracting her phone book)*

SONNY: *(looking for tea)* Sorry. I'm a mechanical idiot. Auto shop just wasn't my thing in high school. Fact is, I was never a Latino dude, per se. My Mom insisted on my taking college prep. My Dad's a Chicano tho'. He fixes cars. Maybe he can fix yours. *(ANITA pauses before the "Treasure of Sierra Madre" poster)*

ANITA: I can't ask him to do that, especially since he was in "Treasure of Sierra Madre," and I've never even seen it. My old boyfriend and I never owned a TV. *(pops a Valium)*

SONNY: *(serves himself wine)* I'll be damned. They do have Red Zinger! What was that?

ANITA: *(crossing up)* The Bogart movie . . . in the poster. Didn't you say your folks were in it?

SONNY: My Dad.

ANITA: He was the head bandit, right?

SONNY: More like the tail. My Dad's brought up the rear in a lot of movies. I told you he's only an extra. Like my Mom. They've made a career of playing nothing but bit parts.

ANITA: Hey, I'd still put Humphrey Bogart on my resume.

SONNY: Wouldn't work. He's dead. Old Bogey cashed in his chips before we were born. *(ANITA dials the phone, sitting on one of the breakfast bar stools. SONNY fills a cup with water and puts it in the microwave to heat)*

ANITA: Your folks have worked Hollywood a long time, huh? I'm beginning to understand you better. *(SONNY smirks bitterly. ANITA'S call connects on the other end)* Hello? This is Anita Sakai, Doctor Sakai's sister. May I speak to my brother, please? You're his answering service? . . . But . . . when do you expect him back? . . . What! Did he leave me a key or anything? I'm supposed to stay with him . . . I see . . . No, no, there's no message . . . Wait! Yes, there is . . . Tell him: Thanks a lot for leaving me stranded, Kuso Tare! K-U-S-O T-A-R-E. That's right. Sign it: Anita. Bye.

SONNY: *(perking up)* KUSO TARE—that's your brother's name?

ANITA: *(devastated)* It means "shithead." He's out of town. Left L.A. about the same time we left Cambridge and won't be back for ten days. Gone to a conference in Hawaii, of all places . . . to push some of his grass.

SONNY: Your brother pushes pot?

ANITA: *(laughing and crying)* He sells lawn seed. He's a turf doctor, retained by several professional football stadiums around the country, including the Rose Bowl. I told him I was coming, but he's always got fertilizer on the mind. Anita, girl, you're on your own.

SONNY: So, what are you going to do?

ANITA: *(clicking glass to cup)* I don't know. Call up one of my gypsy friends, I guess. It's as if my life just came to a sudden halt, and it's sitting out there in that pooped-out Peugeot, waiting to get towed someplace else.

SONNY: *(serious pause)* Wherever that is, I'll come with you.

ANITA: You're home, Sonny.

SONNY: Stay here then with me. At least for tonight.

ANITA: Sleep with you in your parent's house? Sorry. That would be like making love in church.

SONNY: *(holding ANITA'S hand)* You'd have your privacy. My sister's room hasn't been used since she moved out. It's really huge—like my sister. How about it? I promise to only indulge in the passions of the mind. *(kisses* ANITA *up the arm to forehead)*

ANITA: That's no fun.

SONNY: *(hugging* ANITA *from behind)* In essence, my life didn't make sense until I met you. You're my only reality now. And my fantasy. Did we really make love last night at the Bluebird Motel, or was I dreaming? The last few days have been the most exhilarating period in my life! Is it my fault I love you? *(*SONNY *approaches her tenderly)*

ANITA: *(not unkindly)* I knew I shouldn't have jumped your bones.

SONNY: Symbolically, you're the distillation of everything beautiful in my life.

ANITA: *(tongue in cheek)* Symbolically?

SONNY: The woman of my dreams.

ANITA: That's what scares me. How old are you really? Eighteen? Nineteen? I'm at least ten years older than you are.

SONNY: So? I've always preferred older women.

ANITA: Thanks. But I can't make love to you again, Sonny. Honestly now. I shouldn't have ever let you come on this trip . . . it sure knocked the hell out of your studies. Your parents are going to love me for that.

SONNY: *(angrily, forcefully)* My parents don't have a damn thing to say about this! Okay? This is my life. Come on, stay one night and one night, only. Please?

ANITA: *(sighing)* I know I'll regret this, but what the hell, I'm too tired to think about it. Okay! I'm yours! *(*ANITA *hugs and kisses him passionately, rolling onto the floor with* SONNY. *The phone rings and the answering machine picks up.* ANITA *perks up when she hears* CONNIE'S *voice. She stops the ensuing actions by gathering her things together)*

ANITA: But first! I'd like a long hot shower. Think your folks would mind?

SONNY: First door on the right, upstairs . . . I Love You!

ANITA: Passions of the mind, remember? *(*ANITA *smiles and exits, swinging her bag.* SONNY *picks up his suitcase and takes it to the couch. He*

opens *and pulls out a tiny cassette recorder. Then he reaches over, turns on a lamp in the darkening room, clicks on the recorder and settles back. He pauses breathing deeply)*

SONNY: So what's on your mind now, Sonny? Sex is on my mind, Sonny. Time to take the cosmic plunge into the orgasmic sea of your own creation, just to see what's there . . . With all the sharks and crabs and little fishes. Are you a man or a sea urchin? Like the night in Harvard you thought you caught a glimpse of a white whale in there, deep down? Scared the piss out of you, didn't it? The friggin' whale was bigger than you! Is that possible? Do you suppose there might be an ocean inside of you, Sonny? A Moby Dick. Are you here to save the white whale? *(he laughs suddenly, self-mockingly talking "Chicano.")* ¡ÓRALE! Is that why you came back, es-saaay? To save Moby's WHITE DICK? *(we hear the sound of a car pulling into the driveway.* SONNY *snaps off the recorder and freezes. The garage door opens, and the car pulls in and parks.* SONNY *is galvanized into action at the sound of* CONNIE'S *voice)*

CONNIE: *(offstage)* Viejo, don't forget to get the groceries outa the back. *(car doors slam. Almost panicking,* SONNY *gathers his coat, cassette recorder and suitcase. Spinning around to see if he's forgotten anything, he bounds out of the den and down the hallway.* CONNIE *enters from the side door, followed by* BUDDY *carrying the groceries. They are completely transformed in appearance, wearing old shabby clothes.* BUDDY'S *slouch hat, worn flannel shirt, faded jeans and boots complete his "gardener look."* CONNIE, *dressed as a Mexican maid in a print dress and sweater, looks a generation older than she is)* Am I glad to be home or what? I hope you're not starving. I'm gonna soak in the tub for a while. *(*BUDDY *enters singing "Born in East L.A." He crosses up into the kitchen where he unpacks groceries.* CONNIE *flops on the couch)*

BUDDY: *(putting stuff in fridge)* Where's my beer? Store-bought *tortillas,* woman? What kind of 7-Eleven *groserías* did you buy? Some kinda Mexican maid you are.

CONNIE: Made in the U.S.A., *cabrón.* Can you believe we still have the L.A. Latino Actors banquet tonight?

BUDDY: *(pulling out a fryer)* LALA? Forget it. Let's stay home and I'll fix dinner. Suchi Shicken. You like raw *gallina,* Mama San? *(laughs)* Beats the rubber chicken at the Hilton.

CONNIE: You're in an awfully good mood.

BUDDY: Hey, is it my fault they used me in a shot and not you? Speaking part *y todo!* How did you like the way I said: *Sí Señor . . . No, Señor . . . Pronto,* J.R.!

CONNIE: *(peeved)* Up yours, Buddy. The whole day was a complete waste of time.

BUDDY: Speak for yourself. Today between takes on the soundstage—I got another movie idea. This one's really hot!

CONNIE: No, Buddy, please, no more hot ideas! I need a hot bath. *(BUDDY snaps on a tape on his portable cassette recorder. The sound of the music holds CONNIE in the room. She falls back onto the couch and listens. BUDDY starts the tape with James Bond "Goldfinger" theme)*

BUDDY: There's a Chicano James Bond type, see? It's one of those international spy thrillers—set in Guadalajara, where an American narcotics agent has been kidnapped, maybe snuffed. So who do they call?

CONNIE: *(already bored)* Ghostbusters.

BUDDY: *(fanfare)* Ta-raan! NIGEL LÓPEZ—Agent Double-O Eleven—the brilliant, suave, sophisticated Chicano spy and international Latin lover! *(CONNIE turns to sneak away, and suddenly notices that the lamp in the den is on. She pauses, staring at it quizzically, as BUDDY rattles on, self-absorbed)*

CONNIE: Buddy? What's this lamp doing on?

BUDDY: Lighting up the room. Who cares? Son of an English mother and a Mexican father, Nigel López is a black belt in karate. In fact, he's mastered judo, tae kwan do, jujitsu—all the *Chino* stuff.

CONNIE: Did you turn it on this morning?

BUDDY: *(distracted)* What?

CONNIE: The lamp.

BUDDY: *(peeved)* How should I know? Maybe. I dunno. I don't think so. Aren't you listening? *(CONNIE crosses down into the den, spotting something)*

CONNIE: There's a glass of wine here! You weren't drinking wine this morning.

BUDDY: *(puzzled, turning off the tape player)* Correct. You're the *wina* in this family. *(CONNIE sniffs the glass, then surveys the room, growing apprehensive. BUDDY starts paying attention)*

CONNIE: Somebody's been here.

BUDDY: *(tongue in cheek)* Maybe there's a little blonde asleep on our bed upstairs? Little Goldifingers?

CONNIE: This is no joke, *hombre!* No home in L.A. is safe anymore.

BUDDY: *(checking around)* The stereo's still here, the TV, VCR. If it was burglars, why should they just go after our fine Gallo wines? *(the same thought strikes them simultaneously)*

CONNIE: Unless . . . ? *(there is a sound upstairs)*

TOGETHER: They're—still—here? *(BUDDY puts a finger to his lips and signals CONNIE to back up. He grabs a big trophy and sneaks to the hallway, then shouts)*

BUDDY: OKAY, *CABRONES!* I HAVE A THIRTY-EIGHT HERE, IF YOU'RE STILL IN THE HOUSE . . . *(he looks to CONNIE for inspiration)*

CONNIE: . . . Get the fuck out . . .

BUDDY: GET THE FUCK OUT!

SONNY: *(SONNY calls back from within)* You don't have a thirty-eight! It's a twenty-two, and it's upstairs. *(BUDDY and CONNIE exchange surprised glances)*

CONNIE: Sonny?

SONNY: *(SONNY comes out reading* Shogun*)* Hi, Mom.

BUDDY: *(shocked)* Well, I'll be! It is him!

SONNY: Hi, Dad.

CONNIE: SONNY! *(CONNIE comes running up to SONNY and showers him with motherly hugs and kisses, as he stiffens and tries to shy away)*

CONNIE: *M'ijo,* what a surprise! What's the idea of playing games? Why didn't you call and let us know you were coming?

BUDDY: *(puts away the trophy and comes up to* SONNY, *as well, giving him fatherly backslaps. The questions come fast)* Good to see you, *m'ijo!* Are you all right? This sure is one hellava surprise!

CONNIE: When did you arrive?

SONNY: Just a little while ago.

BUDDY: But how? When? Did you fly?

SONNY: Drove. (BUDDY *and* CONNIE *exchange a puzzled look)*

CONNIE: You drove?

BUDDY: I thought I noticed? . . . Who's overstuffed Peugeot is that parked outside?

SONNY: Anita's. We drove out together. How's the 'Vette?

BUDDY: Who's Anita? Some French babe?

CONNIE: You drove all the way from the East Coast? (SONNY *nods mysteriously, giving them a nervous smile. He strolls into the den, trying to sound casual, but sounding cocky)*

SONNY: We ran into a couple of snowstorms in the Midwest, but aside from that, it was a breeze. I-80 to Salt Lake City, then down to San Berdoo. Made it in four and a half days with, uh, a brief pitstop in Vegas. The rites of passages, folks. No sweat.

BUDDY: *(flabbergasted)* No sweat? They're having blizzards back there! It was on the 11 o'clock news just last night. Worst winter on record.

SONNY: *(superciliously)* Really? Well, I haven't watched any TV since I left home. We made it okay.

CONNIE: *(sighs)* Thank God. Maybe it's good you didn't tell me you were coming, after all. I would've died from worrying.

SONNY: You sound like a Jewish mother.

CONNIE: *(suddenly peeved)* Qué Jewish mother *ni que madres, ¡cabrón!* First you don't call in months, and then you come breezing in here, driving through blizzards? Who do you think you are, Sergeant Preston of the Yukon?

SONNY: Sergeant Who?

BUDDY: Why aren't you in law school? Aren't you in the middle of the semester or something?

SONNY: *(evasively)* Spring break's coming up. What's this? "The Grapes of Wrath"—in Spanish? *(he indicates* BUDDY *and* CONNIE'S *clothes)*

CONNIE: We had an audition today.

SONNY: Get the job?

CONNIE: Don't we always?

BUDDY: Who's Anita?

SONNY: *(shaking his head)* You must be awfully tired of playing Mexican maids.

CONNIE: *(archly)* As Hattie McDaniel used to say: "I'd rather play a maid than be one."

SONNY: What's the difference? (CONNIE *is a little stunned by* SONNY'S *flippant, slightly supercilious manner. She glances at* BUDDY)

BUDDY: Don't look at me. I'm just the wetback gardener. Who's Anita?

SONNY: A friend.

CONNIE: Girl friend?

SONNY: *(annoyed)* A woman friend. A lovely human being, if you must know. She was coming out to the West Coast, so we shared the driving and gas expenses. She's from New York.

CONNIE: A Chicana from New York? *Oy vey.*

SONNY: No, Mom.

CONNIE: *(smiling wisely)* Ah. A *Puertorriqueña,* then.

SONNY: *(exasperated)* What difference does it make? There's other people in the world besides Latins, you know!

BUDDY: *(responds, insulted and angered)* Oye, oye, watch the attitude, eh? *¡Pos, mira!* We're your parents, remember? The ones putting you through Harvard Law School? We don't deserve this!

SONNY: *(pause.* SONNY *calms down and takes a deep breath)* I'm sorry.

BUDDY: *(perturbed)* You still haven't told us what you're doing back here. (SONNY *looks at* BUDDY, *then at* CONNIE, *holding back his surging emotions. He begins to pace nervously)*

CONNIE: *(concerned)* What's the matter, Sonny? Did something happen to you at Harvard?

BUDDY: *(pause)* You didn't . . . flunk out . . . did you, *m'ijo?* (SONNY *looks at* BUDDY, *with a strangely sad smile, and slowly shakes his head.* BUDDY *seems relieved*)

CONNIE: Of course, he didn't flunk out, *Señor!* How could he? He's always been an honor student.

BUDDY: *(paternally)* ¿*Sabes qué?* We'd better sit down. Come on. (SONNY *reluctantly sits between* BUDDY *and* CONNIE *on the couch*)

SONNY: I'm not a kid, you know.

BUDDY: Now, you just tell your ol' *jefe* straight out. What's the problem? It can't be money. *(suddenly worried)* Can it?

SONNY: No.

BUDDY: *(cautiously)* Drugs?

SONNY: Sure. I'm snorting $100 worth of flaked Peruvian coke a day. Do you want a toot?

BUDDY: Toot, my ass! I'll rip your nose off.

SONNY: Why? You smoke majoon.

BUDDY: I smoke what?

SONNY: Hemp, bhang, ganja, cannabis, weed, boo, mota, maui waui. In a word, *Shit*, Daddy-O.

BUDDY: *(guiltily)* Since when?

SONNY: *(coolly cynical)* Since we lived in Boyle Heights. Lucy and I used to smell it in the house all the time. At least cocaine is more sophisticated—the drug of choice of the upwardly mobile.

CONNIE: *(mocking* SONNY*)* The drug of choice of the upwardly mobile!

BUDDY: Bullshit! You oughta see some of your "sophisticates" in the studios. A Mack truck could park in one of their nostrils.

SONNY: It's not drugs, okay? My problem's a bit more personal than that. (SONNY *unleases his ponytail, to reveal a shock of long black hair*)

CONNIE: It's a girl, isn't it, *m'ijo?* Are you having troubles with your love life?

SONNY: *(wincing)* Come on, Mom.

BUDDY: (BUDDY *grimaces with uneasiness*) When did you let your hair grow out like that? You look like a fugitive from a Cochise picture.

CONNIE: *(playing with* SONNY'S *hair)* He's a handsome *Indio,* ¿*qué quieres?* Pero, ay m'ijo, shouldn't you cut off your split ends at least?

SONNY: (SONNY *stands up impatiently*) Look, both of you, give me a break, will you? Part of my problem is that you've always assumed certain things about me.

CONNIE: *(pause)* What do you mean?

SONNY: *(deadly serious)* My entire life has been an act. I've decided to come out of the closet.

BUDDY: *(suddenly suspicious)* Oye, cabrón, you didn't come back here to tell us you've gone, ¿*tú sabes?*

SONNY: Gay?

BUDDY: You said it, I didn't.

CONNIE: *(objecting)* Buddy!

BUDDY: But it isn't true, right? (SONNY *smiles noncommitally*) Right?

SONNY: *(superior air)* What if it is? What's wrong with being gay?

BUDDY: *(reacting)* WHAT? YOU WANNA GIVE ME A HEART ATTACK?! *(he lunges after* SONNY, *who backs up defensively;* CONNIE *goes after* BUDDY, *grabbing his arm*)

CONNIE: *Viejo,* don't! Stop it!

BUDDY: *(swiping at* SONNY*)* Is that your big news, *baboso?* THAT YOU'RE A PALOBLANCO? (SONNY *blows a kiss at* BUDDY. BUDDY *chases* SONNY *through the kitchen and out into the backyard and ends up being held outside the French doors by* CONNIE, *as* SONNY *runs back into the den*)

SONNY: *(shouting)* NO! DAD, WAIT! I'm not GAY, all right?

CONNIE: Then you knocked somebody up.

SONNY: And I didn't get anybody PREGNANT! And I'm not fleeing from the LAW! May we dispense with the family melodrama, PLEASE? What's Anita going to think?

BUDDY: (CONNIE *lets him inside*) Anita again? What the hell does Anita have to do with this?

SONNY: Just sit down.

BUDDY: Who's Anita?

SONNY: Be rational, please. I'll explain everything.

CONNIE: *(anxious)* Yes, Buddy. Let's all sit down and be calm about this. *Ándale, hombre. Siéntate, por favor.* (BUDDY *and* CONNIE *sit down.*

There is a tense pause. SONNY *takes a deep breath)*

SONNY: *(nervously)* Thank you. Now the reason I've returned is . . . *(pause)* Well, the simple fact of the matter is . . . *(pause)* I quit.

CONNIE: Quit?

SONNY: *(simply)* Quit.

BUDDY: *(swallowing hard)* You quit Harvard?

SONNY: Dropped out. As of last week, I am no longer enrolled as a pre-law student at Harvard University. *(BUDDY and CONNIE sag on the couch, as SONNY begins to pace—a lawyer before his jury)* I know this must come as bit of a shock. However, judge me harshly, if you wish. Find me guilty of irresponsibility, if you will. I won't dispute you. I simply enter a plea of *nolo contendere*. No contest. For I am finally, completely, joyfully, and irrevocably through with academic life. In short, I am a free man! The defense rests.

BUDDY: *(BUDDY and CONNIE in hysterics)* He quit Harvard. After two years and twenty thousand dollars down the drain, he quit Harvard.

BUDDY and CONNIE: YOU QUIT HARVARD?!

SONNY: *(less assured)* To follow my own destiny, Dad.

CONNIE: *(deeply disappointed)* Sonny, how could you? Your father and me were hoping . . .

SONNY: *(correcting her)* Your father and I.

CONNIE: Your father and I were . . . *(stops)* Don't correct me, *cabrón*! Don't you realize what you've done? All our dreams, our hopes, our aspirations—you've thrown them out the window!

BUDDY: Not to speak of the money.

CONNIE: *(emotionally)* All these years—what have me and your Dad worked for? The money? . . . the money's not important. For you, *m'ijo!*, for your future, the future of both our children, our children's children's future . . . How can you just come back here and tell us you've quit? Just like that—no sign, no warning, nothing . . . and from Harvard! Do you know how many Chicanos get the chance to go to Harvard?

SONNY: *(aloof)* I was there, Mom.

CONNIE: *(impassioned)* You're one in a million, *m'ijito*! Millions! You're a jewel, a rare jewel, our crown jewel. Look at you—young, handsome . . .

BUDDY: Stupid.

CONNIE: The valedictorian of your class in high school and the university. Our pride! That's what you're throwing out the window. Our very pride! *(CONNIE goes to the fridge, opens a beer, chugs it down in a theatrical display. BUDDY is sagging on the couch. SONNY maintains a superior attitude. Short silence)*

BUDDY: *(baffled)* Why? That's what I don't understand. Why did you do it?

SONNY: *(shrugging)* I was bored. Tired of being a . . . *Ha'va'd* man. Just . . . burned out.

BUDDY: Bullshit! What about all the Koreans around here—and all the boat people. You don't see their kids burning out. Hell no. They're going like Zippo lighters.

SONNY: I'm not admitting defeat.

BUDDY: That's what you said when you went from anthropology to sociology to Englishology to who knows what cacaology!

SONNY: Thirteen years, Dad. That's how long I've been in school. That's almost my entire lifetime.

CONNIE: *(quietly intense)* Your sister went through all that, too. High school, university, medical school. She never quit. *Summa cum laude, summa summa cum laude, maxima summa cum laude!*

SONNY: *(stung)* Lucy thrived on the pressure! She was born competitive. You never saw what she used to do to frogs in our backyard, did you? She'd dissect them just for the fun of it. Once when I was eating a peanut butter sandwich, she even made me throw up. "Sonny?" she says in that obnoxious, smart-alecky voice she used to have. "You wanna see the fastest dissection in the world?" Then she stuck a straw up a frog's ass and blew it apart! *(BUDDY inadvertently cracks up laughing. CONNIE cools him with a look)*

BUDDY: Yep. That's Lucy all right.

SONNY: *(painfully)* She was always making me cry.

BUDDY: (hitching his pants) Yeah, well, that was a long time ago. You're a man now, and I didn't raise you up to be a *chillón*. You're a winner. (proudly) Look at all your trophies—basketball, baseball, football. Shit. You could've been an All-American quarterback. Another Jim Plunkett . . . except you were only twelve and 4'11" in high school.

SONNY: (SONNY *looks at his trophies without emotion*) Most of these are for debate.

CONNIE: Precisely! The mark of a true lawyer, if there ever was one.

SONNY: (solemnly) I never wanted to be a lawyer, Mom. (BUDDY *stares at* SONNY, *then laughs in disbelief*)

BUDDY: That's a lotta baloney. Remember how much you loved "Witness for the Prosecution"? We saw that video dozens of times. Why? Because your mom kept renting it? *Chale.* It was because you loved Charles Laughton. And wanted to be a great barrister, just like him.

SONNY: Well, I looked like Charles Laughton then. After I saw "Saturday Night Fever," I wanted to be like John Travolta. Mom even bought me a little white disco suit, when I lost all that weight. Remember? Then came Indiana Jones in "Raiders of the Lost Ark," and we went to Mexico, to the Yucatan. You never realized who talked you into that trip, did you? A stumpy, brown Harrison Ford seeking lost Mayan gold.

CONNIE: (slightly alarmed) Sonny, this is crazy, *m'ijo*. What are you trying to tell us?

SONNY: I'm saying the time has come for me to be honest with myself . . . and with you. Even on the debate team, what I really wanted was to compete in dramatic interpretation, but I didn't think you'd approve.

BUDDY: Why wouldn't we approve?

SONNY: Too close to home, maybe? I wanted to save you the embarrassment.

CONNIE: (genuinely puzzled) What are you talking about?

SONNY: (emotionally) The truth! I knew you and Dad didn't want me to be an actor. You wanted me to be somebody. Lucy was a doctor, so I had to be a lawyer. Acting just wasn't respectable enough. Or even masculine.

BUDDY: (recoiling) Oh, *sí*! And what does that make me? A *pinche vieja*? I'm an actor and I'm proud of it.

CONNIE: So am I. And I'm just as proud to be a *vieja. ¡Pinche viejo!* (BUDDY *and* CONNIE *begin to act like they will start a fist fight.* SONNY *breaks them up, laughs cynically and starts to pace again, cruelly expressing his true feelings*)

SONNY: Come on, Mom, Dad. You know what you are. Let's be honest. You're nothing but glorified Hollywood extras. Bit players who have managed to eke out a comfortable existence for yourselves—for me and Lucy. But, let's face it, in the larger scheme of Hollywood, you're only marginal. Atmosphere at best. Invisible, for all intents and purposes. (BUDDY *and* CONNIE *are astonished*)

BUDDY: Invisible?

CONNIE: Marginal?

SONNY: (pompous but sincere) I just want to add, with all due respect, I appreciate all you've done for me, Mom. However, I am now prepared to take my own chances in the school of hard knocks.

BUDDY: (bristling angrily) Hard knocks, eh? I'll give this idiot some hard knocks!

CONNIE: Be my guest. (BUDDY *once again chases* SONNY *around the room. They rush* CONNIE, *both of them spinning her crazily*)

BUDDY: (incensed) You're going back to law school, *cabrón*! And you're going back to-DAY! I'm taking you to the airport! (SONNY *keeps backing off, hiding behind the couches, staying out of* BUDDY'S *reach*)

SONNY: (throwing words at him) It won't work anymore, Dad. I've grown INURED to your VITUPERATIVE displays and threats of physical PERSUASION! I know it's only bad ACTING!

BUDDY: (BUDDY *throws a cushion at him*) INURED, MANURED! (ANITA *enters quietly down the hallway, dressed in a floppy robe, still wet from her shower.* SONNY *spots her immediately;*

his face drops) Some Chicano progress! *(steaming)* My son, the Harvard dropout! Maybe you should've been born into a family of BOAT PEOPLE!

CONNIE: *(seeing* ANITA*)* Buddy?

BUDDY: At least all those CHINOS know how to apply themselves. They never QUIT, that's for damn sure! I may have fought in Korea, but I'll be the first to admit it, the GOOKS are taking over Monterey Park, because . . .

CONNIE: *(pinching him)* Enough, *señor!* (CONNIE *gives* BUDDY *a small, hard pinch and he recoils, rubbing the spot)*

BUDDY: *¡Ay, jodido!* What was that for?

CONNIE: We have company. (BUDDY *turns and finally sees* ANITA. *He fumbles and mumbles and goes speechless.)*

SONNY: *(red-faced)* This is Anita—Anita Sakai from Brooklyn, New York.

BUDDY: That's Anita. (BUDDY *and* CONNIE *nod together, unconsciously bending slightly at the waist, Japanese style.* ANITA *smiles, blissfully stoned on tranquilizers)*

ANITA: *(speaking Japanese) Do itashimashite.*

SONNY: Welcome to the "Teahouse of the August Moon"! (BUDDY *and* CONNIE *self-consciously snap right up.* SONNY *reassumes his haughty, superior air.* ANITA *just smiles)*

ANITA: You must be Buddy and Connie. Hi ya!

SONNY: Sorry you had to walk into this little domestic scene, Anita. My parents and I seem to be embroiled in a typical middle-class squabble. My Dad was only trying to drag my ass to the airport and ship me back East. Right, Pop?

CONNIE: *(chagrined) Ay,* Sonny . . .

BUDDY: . . . That's a hellava thing to say.

ANITA: *(cheerily)* Hey, don't mind me. I'm just passing through. *Hasta la vista.* I'll leave you alone to talk.

SONNY: *(calling urgently)* We're only acting! You know how it is. A show business family? *(turning to his parents)* Anita's a dancer and an actor as well. She's even danced on Broadway . . . and now she's here to make it in Hollywood. Right, Anita?

ANITA: I don't belong in this conversation, Sonny.

SONNY: *(sotto voce)* On the contrary, I need you to save my *gluteus maximus.* *(Putting* ANITA'S *hands on his butt)* Come on, everybody, make friends! (BUDDY, CONNIE *and* ANITA *look at each other, puzzled and feeling awkward. Short pause)*

SONNY: *(wryly)* Well, come on—we're all Americans! (CONNIE *steps forward trying to be civil at least)*

CONNIE: Won't you sit down, Anita? I'm sorry we didn't hear you come in.

ANITA: Didn't Sonny tell you?

SONNY: *(quickly)* She was upstairs taking a shower.

CONNIE: There's a lot Sonny doesn't tell us.

ANITA: *(feeling no pain)* I had to borrow this robe. I hope you don't mind? Our last stop was, uh, breakfast in Vegas, and we drove straight through. Actually, I was just going to drop Sonny off, and head for Pacific Palisades, where my brother lives, when he's not in Hawaii or some such place, but my Peugeot crapped out on me and left me stranded, and I really felt stressed out and just needed to relax with a hot shower, you know what I mean? Great shower, by the way. Big Thanks for the hospitality. Am I talking too much? Why don't I just go back up and come down again? *(she climbs stairs and re-enters)* Hi ya! You must be Buddy and Connie. Boy am I tired. (BUDDY *looks at* CONNIE, *subtly raising an eyebrow.* SONNY *catches it)*

CONNIE: *Pobrecita* . . . you must be exhausted! Please, make yourself at home. Are you two hungry? (BUDDY *comes forward, somewhat intrigued by* ANITA'S *presence)*

BUDDY: How about some wine, Anita? Beer?

ANITA: I'll have some wine now. (BUDDY *gets the wine.* CONNIE *is starting to fix dinner, masking her emotions.* SONNY *is watching her, waiting to seize the moment)*

CONNIE: Have you two eaten? Buddy and I have to go to a banquet tonight, but I can easily pop a chicken into the microwave, make a salad. Why don't I do that?

SONNY: Actually, Mom, I've invited Anita to spend the night in Lucy's room. Okay? (CONNIE *pauses, suddenly overtaken by maternal jealousy*)

CONNIE: Sure . . . fine! Whatever you wish, *m'ijo.* What do you say, Buddy? Shall we all stay home?

SONNY: Hey, don't change your plans on my account.

CONNIE: No problem.

SONNY: Really?

CONNIE: Your father didn't want to go, anyway.

BUDDY: *Whoa.* Don't blame it on me. *Douzo, douzo.* (BUDDY *brings* ANITA *her glass of wine, bowing graciously: the genial host*)

ANITA: *Dōmo arigatō gozaimasu.*

BUDDY: Don't touch your mustache, too. (ANITA *laughs.* SONNY *takes a beer from* BUDDY'S *hand, a little jealous*)

SONNY: Thanks, Dad.

ANITA: Sonny's been telling me about all your experiences in "the industry," Buddy. You've done a lot. When did you start making movies?

BUDDY: 1948—thereabouts.

ANITA: How about you, Connie?

CONNIE: *(pointedly)* Only since 1980 when Sonny finished elementary school.

SONNY: Don't let the false modesty fool you, Anita. Together they've been in hundreds of films. How many would you say you've made, Dad?

BUDDY: With or without TV shows?

SONNY: Movies. Let's start with the big stuff.

BUDDY: Maybe two, two hundred and fifty pictures. To tell the truth, I lost count after "Jaws."

ANITA: *(with admiration)* You were in that?

SONNY: *(tongue in cheek)* Was he ever! He was one of the first guys to get eaten!

ANITA: *(to* CONNIE*)* May I help you with anything?

CONNIE: No, thank you. Just sit.

SONNY: Tell her what else you've done, Dad.

BUDDY: "Close Encounters of the Third Kind," "Raiders of the Lost Ark," "E.T." . . . I've been in most of Spielberg's biggest blockbusters.

ANITA: Wow! Great!

SONNY: *(subtly sarcastic)* Can you beat that? And nobody knows it.

CONNIE: *(sharply)* Somebody knows it. He keeps on working.

BUDDY: Damn right. Bought me my restaurant.

ANITA: You have a restaurant, too?

BUDDY: BUDDY'S HOLLYWOOD VILLA over on Garfield. Chinese-Mexican cuisine. Nothing fancy, but it pays the bills, between pictures, know what I mean?

SONNY: I'll have to take you there sometime, Anita. You oughta see the walls. Dad's covered it with blowups of himself, posing with all the stars he's ever worked with. Bogart, Cagney, Raft, next to Bandit, Wino, Wetback. What is it you call yourself, Dad? The silent something or other?

BUDDY: *(pause)* The Silent Bit King.

SONNY: Right. The Silent Bit *King* and *Queen* of Hollywood . . . So! These are my folks, Anita. My roots and heritage. They're the reason I went to Harvard, and they're the reason I've returned—to vindicate their silence. *(there is an uncomfortable, funny silence)*

CONNIE: *(coming back)* What silence? They're offering us speaking roles now. Your Dad and I left the Extras and joined the Screen Actors Guild. You know what SAG is, don't you, Anita? You're a dancer?

ANITA: Choreographer. A little classical Japanese dance, as well as modern, jazz, ballet . . . actually, my plans are to concentrate on acting. TV, movies, HBO, whatever. *(pause)* I hear there's lots of work during pilot season, which is now, right?

BUDDY: *(playfully sarcastic)* Sure, sure, there's work if you're not choosy. As an extra, I used to work all the time, nighttime, daytime, overtime. Now she's got us killing time by the phone waiting for speaking roles. SAG, is right.

CONNIE: *(with an edge)* Some of us are getting offers? Don't listen to him, Anita. I can show you the ropes. The important thing is not to pigeon-hole yourself. Go for it! The sky's the limit.

ANITA: *(stoned)* I like your energy. (ANITA *hugs* CONNIE, *high on life)*

CONNIE: *(disarmed)* Are you into energy? Positive energy, that's my motto! Our daughter's an M.D. . . . in Phoenix. "Out on a Limb"?

ANITA: Shirley Maclaine. "Gradual Awakening"?!

CONNIE: Steven Levine!

CONNIE and ANITA: Passages!

SONNY: *(laughing)* Sky's the limit! *(another pause. They all stare at* SONNY, *who smiles back)*

CONNIE: What are your plans, *m'ijo*?

SONNY: I was, uh, coming to it. Especially with all this positive show biz energy. Anita already knows, so it's cool, know what I mean? The stage is a world, the world is a stage . . . of entertainment.

BUDDY: *(with carrot)* So, what's up, Doc?

SONNY: *(dramatically)* What's up is . . . I've finally discovered my real purpose in life, Dad.

BUDDY: And that is?

SONNY: To follow in your footsteps.

BUDDY: What . . . do you mean . . . my footsteps?

CONNIE: You quit Harvard to become an *extra*?

SONNY: *(superior)* On the contrary, I'm not that foolish. No, Mom, the only way I can ever justify my leaving Harvard is by . . . *(matter-of-factly)* becoming the newest superstar in Hollywood.

CONNIE: (BUDDY *and* CONNIE'S *mouths drop open)* Sonny, you can't be serious.

SONNY: Deadly serious. You always told me I could be anything I ever wanted in life, and this is what I want. I'm going to act, write, direct, produce and generally turn this town on its tinsel ear. In short, you're looking at the next Woody Allen. I didn't realize it until I met Anita, but I've been an auteur all my life . . . Right, baby? I'm going to make stars out of all of us, All-American All-Stars!

BUDDY: Sonny, you can't mean it.

CONNIE: Of course, he doesn't mean it.

ANITA: He means it.

BUDDY and CONNIE: *(simultaneously)* ¡¡¡Me lleva la chingada!!!

ANITA: *(rising)* I'll drink to that. L'chaim! I think I'll go bring in the rest of my bags. *(she drains her glass)*

SONNY: I'll help you.

ANITA: No, no thank you. I can handle it. (ANITA *exits with* SONNY *right behind her)*

CONNIE: I'm gonna nuke a chicken.

BUDDY: *(sagging on the couch)* I feel like Marlon Brando in "The Godfather." When his youngest son decides to go into the mob? "I didn't want this for you, Michael. I wanted more—Senator Corleone, Governor Corleone—but there just wasn't enough time . . . "

SONNY: *(overhearing on his way back in)* I'll be all right, Dad.

BUDDY: That's what Al Pacino said. Look where he ended up.

SONNY: It made him a star.

BUDDY: He's Italian, *baboso*! The wops have been in since all those crime pictures in the '30s. They're still doing the mob, except now they get to play bigshots. We don't have any bigshots!

SONNY: Don't worry about it, Daddy-O! The Wild One is here. *(outside we hear the sound of a car starting up. Turning)* Hold it! What the hell . . . ? That's Anita's car. *(panicking)* ANITA! (SONNY *bounds out of the den and down the hallway.* BUDDY *and* CONNIE *look at each other totally frustrated)*

BUDDY: What the hell's going on?

CONNIE: *(puzzled)* I don't know! Maybe he's head over heels in love? Like father, like son.

BUDDY: What's that supposed to mean?

CONNIE: Figure it out.

BUDDY: *(disturbed)* I hope you're not talking about Korea? That was a long time ago—before I even met you!

CONNIE: Forget it, Buddy. It was just a bad joke. Maybe Sonny's right. Maybe all he needs is a couple of months to come back to his senses, to experience Hollywood for himself, to get it out of his system. But . . . that older woman? (I just can't see her in the sack with my baby!) (SONNY *comes rushing back in again, looking disoriented)*

CONNIE: Where's Anita?

SONNY: (embarrassed) Coming in. My mistake . . . I ran halfway down the block before I realized it was the neighbor's car . . . I, uh, better help her upstairs with her luggage.

CONNIE: (concerned) M'ijo, are you all right? (ANITA enters with her bags and goes directly upstairs)

SONNY: (smiling poignantly) Don't worry about it. I'll keep this situation comedy from turning into a soap opera. In fact, let's make it a prime time series . . . before a live studio audience . . . (he finds this strangely hilarious and exits clucking like a chicken)

CONNIE: (confused) Live studio audience? I don't know whether to laugh or cry.

BUDDY: (shaking his head) He's the fruit of my loins, but something's gone rotten . . . Where's the chingas?

CONNIE: The what?

BUDDY: The remote. I gotta turn on the tube for sanity's sake. (BUDDY finds the remote control and aims it toward the invisible TV console at extreme downstage right. The faint sound of the set comes on, as BUDDY sits in his easy chair. CONNIE sits beside him deep in thought)

CONNIE: Situation comedy? Buddy, that's not funny.

BUDDY: (muttering) Hah! I wish our life was a situation comedy. At least we'd be working steady! (he turns up the volume on the TV. Music comes up full; on the background monitors, closing credits are rolling on an old rerun of "I Love Lucy." The show's theme swells to a climactic flourish and fades out. Fade to black)

ACT TWO

SCENE ONE: Two hours later. Early evening. In the dark, we hear SONNY's voice bark out commands with an imperious, directorial air.

SONNY: QUIET ON THE SET . . . ! ROLLING . . . SPEED . . . SLATE! HOMEBOY

HOME MOVIE, SCENE FOUR, TAKE TWO. ACTION!

(Music: We hear a song opening in stereo, as the lights come up full on CONNIE and BUDDY in Mexican regalia, posing for SONNY's video camera in the den. They go through a musical comedy routine, as SONNY "shoots" and ANITA watches, drinking wine and laughing with amusement. BUDDY and CONNIE mime a holdup, with outrageous stereotypical accents. SONNY's outrageous shots appear live on the studio monitors)

SONNY: Dance! (CONNIE and BUDDY dance. They finish with a final glint of the eye and a flash of the teeth in a musical comedy flourish)

SONNY: CUT! Reloading . . . That's a print, folks. (SONNY reloads his camera, all business with the technical stuff. CONNIE and BUDDY laugh, relaxing their final pose. ANITA applauds)

ANITA: Ole! Bravo, mucho bueno!

BUDDY: ¿No que no? I told you we'd still remember it!

CONNIE: I can't believe Sonny actually talked us into doing this! Look at us! A couple of stereotypes! We're such suckers for the camera.

ANITA: Aren't we all?

CONNIE: We did this number three years ago, Anita, at the LALA banquet? What a disaster, it totally misfired!

BUDDY: Did Mel Brooks misfire with "Blazing Saddles"? This routine could have been the start of something big!

CONNIE: Yeah, like another refried bean commercial. It took us till this year to have the courage to go back to another banquet, and here we are instead, doing "Blazing Frijoles."

BUDDY: (mugging) As my compadre Mel Brooks would say . . . (lifts leg and blows a Bronx cheer) More wine, ladies?

CONNIE: Sure, why not? I've lost all shame. How about you, Anita?

ANITA: I'm not driving tonight, that's for sure. (BUDDY goes to the breakfast bar, and opens another bottle of wine)

CONNIE: The things we do for our kids . . .

ANITA: That's what my mother used to say all the time.

CONNIE: Oh? Was she a dancer, too?

ANITA: Traditional odori. When she was young.

CONNIE: Back in Japan?

ANITA: No, actually it was here, in L.A.

CONNIE: I thought you were from Brooklyn.

ANITA: It's a long story. (BUDDY *comes back with the wine bottle, singing operatically to the tune of "O Solo Mio"*)

BUDDY: (*singing*) There's no tortillas, there's only bread. There's no tortillas, that's why I'm so sad. My grief I cannot hide. There's no tortillas. For my refried. (*speaking with Italian accent*) *Su vino, señorina.* A delicate Tokay from Tokyo. Just kidding. It's a white Zin from the Sa-napa Noma country. Enjoy!

ANITA: *Molto grazie.*

BUDDY: And you, *bella mia*?

CONNIE: (*Italian accent*) Just a half a glass, Luciano. I still have to wash the dishes. You oughta watch it too.

BUDDY: I'm watching it, I'm watching it. It isn't every day a son fulfills his *jefe's* dreams. I feel like Pancho Villa when he raided Columbus, New Mexico. The only other way a Mexican can shoot gringos and get away with it is by becoming a Hollywood director. Right, Sonny?

SONNY: Whatever you say, *jefe.*

BUDDY: What are you calling our movie, anyway?

SONNY: "TYPES IN STEREO."

BUDDY: (*pause*) ¡Cantinero! ¡Otro tequila para el General! (BUDDY *heads back to the breakfast bar, doing a Mexican general. He pops open a bottle of tequila*)

CONNIE: Weren't you only going to have one shot of that stuff?

BUDDY: ¡Viva Villa, chingao! (BUDDY *downs the whole shot glass, and* CONNIE *is not happy.* SONNY *hoists the camera on his shoulder, obsessed, as he turns toward* ANITA)

SONNY: Okay, folks, here we go again. Mom, playback. Rolling . . . speed . . . Your turn, Anita. Slate! SCENE FIVE, TAKE ONE! ACTION, sweetheart.

ANITA: (*doing Ingrid Bergman*) I love you Rick . . . and I will always love you, but you must stay here in Casablanca, and I must fly off to a new life or there's no end to this movie . . .

SONNY: (*shooting*) Great, Ingrid. Now how about a little Anita Sakai? A little classical Japanese dance? Jazz, modern? Better yet, just tell us about yourself. Cinema verité! How did you end up in Brooklyn?

ANITA: (*laughing*) I was born there.

SONNY: When? (SONNY *waits with bated camera, still rolling, on* ANITA, *close-up*)

ANITA: Hate to spoil the shoot, Sonny, but I'm not really into this. My life is enough of a soap opera.

SONNY: Tell us about your radish legs.

BUDDY: Her what? Did he say "radish legs"?

ANITA: (*a little hurt*) Sonny, that's a really personal story.

SONNY: (*seriously*) That's why I want it. Trust me, baby. I'm still rolling. (ANITA *pauses a beat, taking a breath, looking at* SONNY)

ANITA: All right. As a kid, they used to call me "radish legs." *Daikonashi.* Like the Japanese radish? That's because I had these big thick ankles and calves I couldn't stand. So I became a dancer. I fell in love with ballet. I was classically trained from the age of seven . . . By the time I was thirteen, I was dancing on point, graceful as a swan.

SONNY: So how did you learn Japanese dance?

ANITA: Before I could study ballet, Mama always insisted that I first learn classical Japanese dance. I resented her for it. It had nothing to do with anything I saw around me in Brooklyn. I didn't realize until I was much older that my mother was trying to help me become a woman, a woman able to draw from the wellsprings of her own life. Okay? (BUDDY *and* CONNIE *have been listening with rapt attention*)

CONNIE: Okay! I mean, it's true. It's a very personal story.

SONNY: How about that dance?

ANITA: Sorry. My music's packed away. In the Peugeot.

BUDDY: *(feeling good)* So, unpack it! Come on, be a sport.

CONNIE: *(dryly)* Anybody for some more chicken salad? If not, this scullery maid is going to clean up the kitchen.

ANITA: I'll help you wash the dishes.

SONNY: *(with bullhorn)* And CUT! *(ANITA helps CONNIE pick up plates, heading up to the kitchen. SONNY lowers his camera, looking angry, intense and preoccupied)* Listen, PEOPLE. We're seriously SHOOTING A MOVIE here. Would you MIND giving me your undivided attention and a little GODDAMN COOPERATION? Is that TOO MUCH to ASK?! . . . Sorry, I didn't mean to shout. *(BUDDY, CONNIE and ANITA are momentarily aghast)* Never mind. I'll get the friggin' music myself! It's in that little red suitcase behind the green trunk, right? Take a break, and rest your honkers. I'll be right back. *(he storms out the back, toward the garage)*

BUDDY: He's good at bossing people around, isn't he?

CONNIE: This is getting out of hand, Buddy. He's never talked to us with such disrespect before. Who does he think he is? Otto Preminger?

BUDDY: *(angered)* Look, whose idea was it to let him pull out all the video equipment? Now let's get it straight. Do you want to humor the idiot genius or do you want me to talk to him? Let me slap some sense into him man to man.

CONNIE: Don't hurt him.

BUDDY: When I was his age, I still had to kiss my father's hand. I'll show that *mocoso* who his *padre* is! *(BUDDY puts on his sombrero, grabs CONNIE and kisses her theatrically, then walks off with comic macho bravado, his prop gun in hand. CONNIE and ANITA are left alone in the kitchen for the first time. There is a pause)*

CONNIE: So.

ANITA: So?

CONNIE: So how long have you known Sonny? If you don't mind my asking?

ANITA: *(pauses, she smiles)* About a week. He answered my ad in *The Village Voice* for a driving companion, and he seemed like a safe bet.

CONNIE: I'll bet he did.

ANITA: He's a sweet kid. I've grown very fond of him in seven days.

CONNIE: Anything happen on the trip I should know about?

ANITA: Why? Did he say something?

CONNIE: He's just acting strange . . . stranger than when he left for Harvard, I mean. It's hard to tell with Sonny. He was always a little eccentric. Brilliant but absurd, as one of his teachers said. But he was always shy, especially with girls. Something must have happened to him. He's acting awfully cocky for sixteen.

ANITA: Sixteen?

CONNIE: Technically. His 17th birthday isn't until next month. Not that it matters. He's not a virgin anymore. Is he? I saw it in his eyes right away. They aren't innocent anymore. They glistened with that horny look men get. My baby!

ANITA: *(feeling bad)* Gee, I'm sorry. *(CONNIE stares at her without malice)*

CONNIE: I knew it had to happen sooner or later . . . Anyway, I'm glad I heard you say what you said about your mother? It's a nice thing for a daughter to recognize her mom.

ANITA: It was a while ago. When she still talked to me. *(CONNIE registers interest in following the topic, but she doesn't want to be obvious about it. She pours more wine for both of them)*

CONNIE: You say your mom grew up in L.A.?

ANITA: *(sadly)* Born in Japan, and brought here as a four-year-old. My Dad was born in East Los Angeles, though, in a place called Dogtown. Can there be such a place?

CONNIE: *(amazed)* Wait till I tell Buddy. He'll hound you to death about the place.

ANITA: Of course, that was before World War II.

CONNIE: Of course. The '50s were more my time, but I saw all the John Wayne movies. "Wake Island," "Sands of Iwo Jima," "Guadalcanal Diary" . . . Which camp was your family concentrated into?

ANITA: None. *(ANITA suddenly chokes with emotion. It's been welling up inside her all evening and now the dam is about to break)*

CONNIE: Excuse me?

ANITA: They escaped!

CONNIE: I'm sorry. I mean, that's okay. I understand. You don't have to talk about it. (ANITA *lets some tears go, but she takes control of herself, blowing her nose and shaking her head*)

ANITA: No, I'm fine. It's better that I talk about it. It's no big deal. It's just my fucking anonymous life . . .

CONNIE: Your "effing" what?

ANITA: Anonymous life. Yeah, it'd make a great movie on PBS. Instead of waiting for the Army to pack them up, my old man packed up his wife and son and musical instruments and headed east in his 1936 Chevy. It was called voluntary self-evacuation in those days.

CONNIE: Voluntary self-evacuation?

ANITA: Permissible by law, but my family's trek made headlines clear across the country. It was even on nationwide radio. Daily reports of their whereabouts as they crossed city, county and state lines.

CONNIE: At least they were famous.

ANITA: Oh yeah. "The Japs are coming, hide the kids!" When they finally arrived in New York City, my dad got my mother and brother and settled in Brooklyn, hoping just to live in quiet anonymity . . . I wasn't born until 1960, but I grew up in that anonymity. (*she fondles the Valium container*)

CONNIE: (*moved*) I know what you mean. Have you ever been married? What about your Mom?

ANITA: She grew old at home. My Dad eventually got a job playing the cello with the New York Philharmonic. My brother ended up chasing football fields around the country . . . I figured it was time for me to come back to L.A.

CONNIE: (*blunt but not kind*) Why? Now, I mean.

ANITA: (*straight in the eye*) I just broke up with my boyfriend. We lived together for five years. He was a black choreographer. (*looks at the Valium*) I don't need this shit!

CONNIE: You've got a lot of guts, girl. (SONNY *calls from the hallway and comes running in, carrying* ANITA'S *red suitcase of audiotapes*)

SONNY: (*enters on a skateboard*) HO! Here we go-o! Thumbs up on the *música!* We'll just lay these puppies down right here. (*he lays the tapes down and picks up his camera, adjusting the lights and slapping a cassette into the stereo*)

CONNIE: Where's your dad?

SONNY: You'll find out. Pick up the camera, change the mood, add a little soundtrack . . . and this movie outfit is back in action! Mom, you're in the shot. Mom, you're still in the shot! I want this whole area clear! Anita, be my dolly grip.

ANITA: Your what?

SONNY: Push the skateboard. Mom, playback . . . ROLLING . . . SPEED . . . GO FOR IT, DAD! SCENE SIX, TAKE ONE, ACTION!! (*we hear music from the soundtrack of "Treasure of Sierra Madre."* BUDDY *enters, his bandit costume all disheveled, his face dirty. He pulls out his .22 pistol*)

CONNIE: Buddy, what is this? What are you doing with that pistol?

SONNY: QUIET ON THE SET, MOM. PLEASE? It's a PROP, okay? Come ahead, Dad. We're still rolling. ACTION! (BUDDY *shrugs at* CONNIE *and keeps going toward* SONNY'S *camera*)

CONNIE: Did you check to see if it was loaded?

BUDDY: (*stopping*) Sorry, Boss, I lost it.

SONNY: CUT! SHIT!

CONNIE: Watch your language, young man! Who the hell do you think you're talking to? Rodney Dangerfield? What happened to the "man to man" talk, Boss?

BUDDY: (*pause*) We had it, *verdad, m'ijo?* We got to talking about the old days, when he was just a squirt, and we used to do that scene from my favorite movie. Anita, did I ever tell you the story of my favorite picture?

CONNIE: Here it comes. I knew we'd get to it sooner or later. (BUDDY *crosses to the poster*)

BUDDY: "The Treasure of the Sierra Madre," starring Humphrey Bogart . . . It was my first job. I was only eighteen then and still living in Dogtown.

CONNIE: So was Anita's father.

BUDDY: *(oblivious)* In downtown L.A. there were still signs saying "No Dogs or Mexicans Allowed," so the thought of working with Bogart made my head spin . . . But the main guy for me turned out to be Alfonso Bedoya. He was the leader of the *bandidos*, see? With that toothy smile and greasy look he built his career on, and the rest of us Mexicans, well, we were his men . . . Right, Sonny? Start your cameras rolling, *m'ijo* . . . Remember how we used to do it? Anita, he used to do Bogey. *(SONNY, who has been studying the gun, lifts the camera and starts to roll)*

SONNY: *(doing Bogart)* ¡ALTO! Sweetheart.

BUDDY: *(doing Bedoya)* ¡Ay jijo! Mira la palomita que me encontré en su nido.

SONNY: Don't come any closer!

BUDDY: *Oiga señor,* we don't try to do you any harm, why don't you try to be a little more polite? Give us your gun and we'll leave you in peace.

SONNY: I need my gun myself!

BUDDY: Ah. Throw that old iron over here. We'll pick it up and go on our way. We're not federales.

SONNY: If you're the police, where are your badges?

BUDDY: Badges? We ain't got no badges. We don't need no badges. I don't have to show you any stinking . . . *(the phone rings)*

SONNY: GODDAMIT! CUT!!

BUDDY: *(to ANITA)* Your father used to live in Dogtown? *(SONNY storms out into the patio. ANITA goes out to talk to him. CONNIE answers the phone)*

CONNIE: Hello? Oh . . . hello, Betty. Yes, we're still here. *(cupping the speaker)* She sounds pissed . . . Oh no, no, just relaxing. We had some unexpected company, and decided not to go . . . Sonny, our Harvard dropout? What? Yes, yes I know, Betty, but really, it's so late, and . . . who's there? *(cupping the speaker)* The casting director from the Nicholson picture! He's looking for Hispanic faces at the banquet. What? He wanted to see Buddy? For a speaking role? The part of a Costa Rican general? Buddy!

BUDDY: A general?

CONNIE: Betty, it's already past nine o'clock. We'll never make it on time.

BUDDY: The hell we won't. In my red hot 'Vette? Monterey Park to Beverly Hills? Gimme forty-five minutes and a lead foot. A job's a job.

CONNIE: Can you hold him for an hour? We're on our way! *(CONNIE hangs up)* My God. How are we going to do it? We're not even dressed!

BUDDY: We'll dress at the hotel! I know the waiters. *(CONNIE and BUDDY head for the hallway)*

SONNY: MOM! DAD! Aren't you forgetting something?

CONNIE: *(stopping, calm for a second)* Of course. Our clothes! We forgot to pick up our clothes, Buddy.

SONNY: NO!

CONNIE: No? Oh! Anita, how rude of me, please excuse us. We're just going to drop in on the LALA banquet for a moment. It's a movie, you see. Gotta see a man about a horse.

BUDDY: *(happy)* A general's horse!

ANITA: Go for it.

CONNIE: Now behave yourselves, you two. We'll be back by midnight. *Viejo,* shouldn't we take my LTD instead? *(BUDDY and CONNIE exit to the bedroom. SONNY looks at ANITA, like a spoiled child)*

SONNY: Do you see? Do you see what's going on here? They forgot completely about my movie.

ANITA: Those are the breaks. Parents grow up, just like everybody else.

SONNY: I don't see you spending quality time with your parents. They won't even talk to you, because of your black boyfriend.

ANITA: Are you deliberately being nasty, or is that just more juvenile angst? *(SONNY picks up his camera)*

SONNY: What if it is? Half the successful directors in Hollywood are juvenile assholes, why should I be any different?

ANITA: Because you are different. Or at least I thought you were. *(SONNY follows her with the camera)*

SONNY: Remember Little America, that truck stop in Wyoming? The one with all the redneck cowboys? It was like a scene out of a movie, wouldn't you say?

ANITA: I suppose.

SONNY: Which movie?

ANITA: I don't know . . . "Easy Rider"?

SONNY: The sixties flick? With Jack "The Border" Nicholson? How about "The Geisha and the Greaser," crossing the Western Divide in a snow-covered Peugeot? (ANITA *looks at* SONNY *with impatience*)

ANITA: Are you kidding me?

SONNY: Too unreal or just uncommercial?

ANITA: Too weird.

SONNY: Precisely. Rednecks won't pay to see us making love. Unless it's a porno.

ANITA: (*pause*) I'm not buying any of this bullshit, Sonny.

SONNY: (*sarcastically*) The real question is will anybody in the movies buy you? Or will you just settle for the local anchor spot on the "Eleven O'Clock News"? (ANITA *looks at* SONNY, *furious and hurt. He continues to shoot*)

ANITA: Stop this, will you?

SONNY: Am I getting to you?

ANITA: You're messing with me.

SONNY: Well, I'm a Messican.

ANITA: Fuck you! This is Nancy Nissan, signing off! (ANITA *hits aside* SONNY'S *camera, and storms upstairs.* SONNY *holds for a moment, trying to laugh*)

SONNY: (*lowering his camera*) CUT! . . . bad cut. (CONNIE *and* BUDDY *come out of the bedroom, carrying their clothes, shoes and make-up kits, heading toward the garage*)

CONNIE: Okay, *m'ijo*, this is it! We're on our way.

BUDDY: Wish us luck, eh? The part of a Mexican general, *fijate!* Opposite my buddy, Jack Nicholson.

CONNIE: The general is Costa Rican. Not Mexican.

BUDDY: Did you ever meet a casting director who could tell the difference? (BUDDY *and* CONNIE *exit down the hall, and they are heard getting into their car and driving away.* SONNY *studies his camera, and then turns around to face himself. He records his close-up*)

SONNY: (*changing shirts*) Greater East Los Angeles. February 20th. 9:30 P.M. Continuing script and production notes RE: HARVARD HOMEBOY MOVIE . . . (*putting his wool cap on*) You're fucking up, homeboy! You're not fooling anybody, *ese.* You didn't fool nobody in Harvard, and you ain't fooling jack shit here, *bato!* (SONNY *starts talking to himself, as if he is a group of cholos, raking him over the coals*) We're the echo from the barrio streets of your mind, loco! We know you're middle class; pussy, aye. Harvard and all that shit. Well, you're nothing, dude. A little Mexican-American fart, still sucking Momma's tit. Or is it Moby's Dick? What about that fine woman upstairs? You oughta be up there right now banging the bitch sideways, and you're down here, thinking about how you hurt her feelings . . . ? Pussssyyy . . . (*disgusted with himself*) Get out into the streets, and find something real to do, motherfucker. Don't just sit there, going out of your fucking mind. OUT INTO REALITY! (SONNY *turns off the camera and picks up the gun. He pauses for a beat, then pocketing the gun, picks up the skateboard and exits, strutting with street-wise cool. Fade to black*)

SCENE TWO: *In the dark, we hear a soundtrack of police calls and siren, overlaid with rap music. It holds for a few moments, then fades out. The music of tiko drums, giving way to melody: "Odori" played by Hiroshima. The lights come up to reveal* ANITA *dancing a graceful odori in the den. It is midnight, and she is alone. Presently,* SONNY *appears in the shadows from the hallway, still dressed as a cholo and carrying a fast food hamburger bag. He watches her, until* ANITA *senses his presence.*

ANITA: (*stopping*) Sonny? Is that you?

SONNY: Simón. Go on. (ANITA *throws the fan at him and changes into modern dance. In the midst of the dance she stops, hugs* SONNY, *and turns off the stereo*)

SONNY: That was fuckin' beautiful. What'd you stop for?

ANITA: I've been waiting for you. What time is it? Jesus, it's past midnight. My ride oughta be here in a few minutes.

SONNY: Ride?

ANITA: My brother called me back again. The service has been trying to reach me. Turns out my *kuso tare* brother was still home, waiting for me. He's bringing a tow truck.

SONNY: How did your brother get this number? (ANITA *pauses, realizing* SONNY *is not buying it*)

ANITA: I left it with them, didn't I? All right . . . So it's a gypsy friend from Santa Monica. What's the difference? May I leave some presents with you? (ANITA *goes to the coffee table, where she has laid out gifts*) This is a gift for your mom. And this is for Buddy. It's a *daruma* doll. Tell him to make a wish and paint in the right eye, and when it comes true, paint in the left eye. And I want you to have one of my fans.

SONNY: What's with the gifts?

ANITA: It's *omiage*. Thank-you gifts for all their hospitality. I'll be going now.

SONNY: Just like that?

ANITA: No, not just like that. I'm going to miss you. But it's obvious you need some time alone with your parents. I should have known you were only sixteen. Anyway, I'm proud and happy to have been your first lay. (SONNY'S *face hardens into a cholo mask*)

SONNY: You mean like . . . ? "I'm glad to be in AMERICA, so fine to be een AMEERICAA! Aiee, Aiee!" (*his face hardens into a cholo mask*) What's that again, aye?

ANITA: You heard me, aye.

SONNY: *¿Sabes qué?* Pity the existential condition of the dude, eh? *Sayonara.* (ANITA *studies him a little regretfully*)

ANITA: I was hoping we could part friends.

SONNY: (*sarcastically*) Maybe I could buy you dinner sometime. Over at the local Crap-in-the-Box? See, I've always suspected they put something in this garbage to give you . . . a feeling . . . of emptiness. (SONNY *empties the hamburger bag. Styrofoam containers, empty soft drink cups, and assorted wrappings fall out. He kicks them around. Exploding*) And want! And CONFUSION! AND ANOMIE!!

ANITA: (*shocked*) Sonny, what? What are you doing! (*she starts to pick up an empty container.* SONNY *drops into his cholo stance*)

SONNY: No! Don't touch it—leave it!

ANITA: But what will your Mom say when . . .

SONNY: (*fiercely*) I SAID LEAVE IT, *ESA!* (ANITA *freezes.* SONNY *advances, sauntering and lapsing into his cholo accent*) Did I scare you? Sorry. It's just that this is all . . . creative garbage . . . and evidence. We're all on trial here, see? In a decidedly precarious pseudo-psycho-juridical conundrum. Can you dig it?

ANITA: Is this some kind of joke?

SONNY: Fuckin'ey. A case in point. What's the difference between a chicken and a Chicano? A chicken is born out of one egg, the Chicano out of two . . . (*grabs his balls*) . . . and that's schizoo . . . (*we hear the sudden siren of police cars as they roll down the street outside, shining a spotlight, on the house.* SONNY *dives for the switch, and kills the kitchen lights*) Shit! Get down, be quiet, it's the cops.

ANITA: (*wilting*) Cops? Sonny, I can't handle this.

SONNY: Fuck! Somebody must have seen me running into the house. Assholes! Just because I wear a Pendleton, I'm some kind of burglar! Don't they know I live here?

ANITA: Why don't you just go out and tell them?

SONNY: (*pause*) I robbed the local Crap-in-the-Box.

ANITA: (*after a beat*) Come again?

SONNY: (*surprisingly clear*) I pulled a heist. It was over before I knew what happened. I just walked in there, with my Dad's little .22 and held up the joint. Two Fat Jacks and a Big Bopper. Is that weird? Do I seem dangerous to you? Criminally dangerous or merely Hispanic?

ANITA: Let me get this straight, you robbed a burger joint? (SONNY *laughs with a brooding undertone*)

SONNY: *(pulls off cap and glasses)* I was ACTING! I'm acting—see? No more threatening East L.A. cholo. Check it out. Here's my straight-on, neutral shot with an innocuous shit-eating smile all casting directors require? See?

ANITA: What's the matter with you? What are you doing robbing Crap-in-the-Boxes, for Christ's sake! Do you want to go to prison? *(SONNY puts on his blue beanie again)*

SONNY: What's the difference? Here's the main event: the indispensable illiterate cholo gang member-heroin-addict-born-to-lose image, which I suppose could account for 99 percent of my future employment in TV land. Just look hostile, dumb, and potentially violent. Preferably with rape on the mind, know what I mean? *(he gives ANITA a lascivious leer—overacting—wiping his mouth with his hand)*

ANITA: Sonny, stop it. What are you up to?

SONNY: *(grabbing ANITA)* ACTING! Am I being CONVINCING?

ANITA: Let me GO! Are you OUT OF YOUR MIND?

SONNY: *(struggling with her)* Are you—AFRAID—I'LL RAPE YOU? Is that it? Do you—EXPECT ME—to act the type?

ANITA: LET ME GO!!! *(ANITA grabs SONNY's arm and flips him completely over)*

SONNY: What . . . was that . . . martial arts?

ANITA: Modern dance. Seriously, Sonny. What's going on?

SONNY: Have I been screwing up, fortune cookie?

ANITA: No, just screwed up, bean dip!

SONNY: *(pause)* I'm having a spiritual hernia. A cathartic outburst below the belt. I'm a scholastic disgrace. Thanks to you.

ANITA: No you don't. Don't start pretending you left Harvard because of me. I told you back in New York this was a mistake. Whatever your problem is, it's gotten worse since we arrived in L.A. Come back to reality, Sonny.

SONNY: Which reality? Your particular suspension of disbelief? Look around you. Does any of this look real to you? I knew what I was getting myself into—coming here. I grew up in this low-rated situation comedy! *(looks out at audience)* You can almost imagine a studio audience out there . . . sitting, watching, waiting to laugh at this cheap imitation of Anglo life. Superficial innocuous bullshit that has to conceal its humorless emptiness with canned laughter! *(we hear more police cars coming up, sirens blowing. Street sounds, traffic, then the voices of men. Then canned laughter)* ¿Órale? Did you hear that? *(ANITA sneaks to the kitchen window and looks out)*

ANITA: My God! The place is surrounded by cops. They're standing across the street, looking this way! *(spotlights trace the side of the house. ANITA ducks. More canned laughter)*

SONNY: There it is again. Canned laughter.

ANITA: Cut the act, will you? Get a hold of yourself. Honestly, you sound like you're going off the deep end. What are we going to do?

SONNY: You wanna make love. *(ANITA looks at him lovingly, in spite of the circumstances)*

ANITA: You're hopeless. I really have a talent for finding the basket cases.

SONNY: *(gently)* My Dad fell in love with an Asian girl, when he was in Korea. Wanted to marry her, but the Army discouraged him . . . So he came back to the States, promising to send for her. He never did. The family pressure was so against it, he ended up marrying my Mom instead. Rumor has it he might even have left a son behind . . . I guess he'd be older than me now—poor bastard. A Korean Chicano . . . *(the front door bell chimes, followed by a solid pounding)*

ANITA: They're knocking at the front door! *(SONNY snaps to life again, wielding his pistol)*

SONNY: Stay put. Don't move! Nobody here but us chickens . . . *(more knocking. A police bullhorn blares outside. SONNY carefully opens the side door)*

BULLHORN: *(offstage. Sounding like Bogart)* THIS IS LIEUTENANT SMILEY, L.A.P.D. WE KNOW YOU'RE IN THERE, KID. DO US ALL A BIG FAVOR: THROW OUT YOUR WEAPON AND COME OUT WITH YOUR HANDS OVER YOUR HEAD. REPEAT. YOUR HANDS

OVER YOUR HEAD! WE HAVE YOU SUR-
ROUNDED.

SONNY: *(yelling outside)* SCREW YOU, COPPERS!
REPEAT, SCREW YOU!! YOU'LL NEVER
TAKE ME ALIVE! (SONNY *fires off the .22—
pop! pop! pop!—then slams the door)* HIT THE
DECK! (ANITA *hits the floor beside* SONNY, *just
as a barrage of gunfire smokes the outside of the
house. We hear the sound of shattering glass.
Pause)*

ANITA: Sonny . . . ? (ANITA *starts punching him
with a vengeance)*

ANITA: *(fuming)* What's the matter with you,
man? Just what the fuck is your problem?

SONNY: I'm trying to break through this ridiculous
situation comedy into some contact with reality,
goddammit! Real life! You know what I'm talking about. Come on, let it out.

ANITA: Let what out?

SONNY: Your emotions. Your guts. Your chaos!
Don't you ever take off that Kabuki mask?
Don't you ever explode?

ANITA: *(tears)* NEVER! A good Japanese girl learns
to control her feelings. A good Japanese girl
learns to control her guilt. You *gaman,* you endure! (ANITA *stares into* SONNY'S *burning eyes,
then out of care or compassion or both, she leans
into his arms and they kiss—passionately—
slowly sinking to the floor. Short pause, then the
sound of the bullhorn blows again)*

CONNIE: *(offstage. On the bullhorn)* SONNY?
THIS IS YOUR MOTHER, *M'IJO,* OUT HERE
WITH THE POLICE. YOUR FATHER AND I
JUST DROVE UP A FEW MINUTES AGO.
MY GOD! THEY SAY YOU JUST ROBBED A
FAST-FOOD PLACE! *POR DIOS, M'IJO!*
WHAT HAVE YOU DONE? *¿QUÉ CHIN-
GADOS HAS HECHO?*

SONNY: *¡Yo no speako Españole!*

BUDDY: *(taking the bullhorn)* SONNY, THIS IS
YOUR FATHER, BUDDY VILLA.

SONNY: Why is he telling me his name? I know
who he is . . . unless . . . ?

BUDDY: TURN ON THE TV IN THE DEN, *M'IJO.*
YOUR MOM AND I ARE ON "LIVE"—COAST

TO COAST—ON CNM. (SONNY *turns on the
imaginary TV set. The monitors go on.* BUDDY *is
drunk but trying to control it, performing for the
camera)*

REPORTER: *(live footage camera crew, outside
Villa home)* . . . That's right, Blair, I'm
right here at the scene, as this drama unfolds
directly behind me. The details as we know
them at this moment are sketchy, but we have
been able to piece together this scenario. Earlier this evening, the suspect, now barricaded
in this house and, as you can see, completely
surrounded by police, was identified as local
sixteen-year-old SONNY VILLA, "the skateboard bandit" who terrorized employees and
patrons at a local fast-food restaurant. His
parents, BUDDY and CONNIE VILLA, alleged "show-biz" folks, were alerted by the
police and called away from the gala LALA
banquet in Hollywood, and are now pleading
with their son to give himself up. Ah . . .
here's Mr. and Mrs. Villa now . . . Mr. Villa,
do you know what this is all about?

BUDDY: I DON'T KNOW WHAT'S GOING ON
HERE, SON, BUT I JUST WANT AMERICA
TO KNOW THAT I FOUGHT IN KOREA,
AND THAT WE'RE PROUD TO BE MED-
SICAN AMERICANS. OUR SON IS AN
HONOR STUDENT AT HARVARD UNIVER-
SITY, AND LIKE RICHARD NIXON, HIM IS
NOT A CROOK!

CONNIE: GOD BLESS YOU, *M'IJO.* WE'RE
COMING IN!

BUDDY: THE POLICE ARE GIVING US A
CHANCE TO TALK TO YOU, SONNY.

CONNIE: DON'T SHOOT. (CONNIE *and* BUDDY
walk away from the CNM cameras. SONNY *is
incredulous)*

REPORTER: And there you have it, Blair. A tense
and highly volatile situation, probably gang-
related, here in Monterey Park in East Los Angeles. Reporting live, this is Chico Chingón for
CNM, The Chicano Media News Network.

SONNY: Can you believe this? I can't break out of
this INANE situation comedy! MOTHER-

FUCKERS!!!! (SONNY *gets out another couple of pops! A barrage of gunfire slams into the house again.* SONNY *and* ANITA *eat dust. Pause. The phone rings.* SONNY *answers it with a heavy street-wise accent*) Simón? What can I do for you, man? I mean, ma'am . . . uh, *esa* . . . no *chale, La* Connie's not here. She and Buddy went out tonight. Who's this? Lucy? Lucy, my *carnala?* . . . *¡Órale!* This is Sonny! (*he gives the phone the finger*) All right, all right, Lucy . . . Hold it a second. Before you jump . . . wait, give me a chance . . . WAIT, GOD-DAMMIT! I DON'T CARE IF IT'S ON CNM! I don't care if you're disgusted. GO ON, GO ON, call me a failure! I don't give a damn! I'VE GOT CONTROL OVER MY OWN LIFE, LUCY! YOU STAY OUT OF IT—IT'S MY PRISON TERM! FUCKIN' EY!—Stick that up a FROG'S ASS AND BLOW IT, SISTER—I LOVE YOU TOO! GOODBYE! (*he hangs up*)

CONNIE: (*offstage. Cheerily*) Yoo-hoo? It's me, kids. Are you decent?

ANITA: (*hiding his gun*) Shit. Don't say anything about this—be cool. (SONNY *collapses onto the kitchen floor, spread-eagled and faking mortal injury.* CONNIE *enters, dressed to the nines and looking like a million bucks in a formal evening gown, high heels, jewelry, imitation mink and sweeping glamorous hairstyle. She screams, but proceeds past* SONNY *to the mess in the den*)

CONNIE: *¡Santo Niño de Atocha!* What hit this place? Punk rockers?

SONNY: (*the cholo again*) I had to set the scene, Mom! (CONNIE *comes down into den, dismayed, shaking her head*)

CONNIE: *Mira nomás* . . . It looks like you've been feeding dogs in here!

ANITA: We can clean it up in a second. It's all empty garbage.

SONNY: I said leave it, *esa!*

CONNIE: *¿Esa?* What do you think this is? "Hill Street Blues"? TV cholos are a dime a dozen.

SONNY: (*cryptically*) I'm a Korean Chicano . . . part of the Chinatown suicide prevention squad. Right, Anita? (CONNIE *signals* ANITA *to let her carry the ball*)

CONNIE: Forget it. I've got a real job for you. On the Big Screen! Are you ready for this, *m'ijo?* I just landed you a role in your first movie!

SONNY: (*stunned*) Me? How?

CONNIE: (*picking up trash*) At the LALA banquet. We sat with Betty, our agent, and Jack Nicholson's casting director. You should have seen the main room of the Beverly Hilton. It was packed! And the stars—everywhere! Ricardo Montalbán, Mario Moreno "Cantinflas," Katy Jurado, Raquel Welch, Martin Sheen (aka Ramón Estevez), Linda Ronstadt, the Lennon Sisters . . . Did you know their grandmother was Mexican? (CONNIE *looks at the garbage in her hands, stuffed into a hamburger bag*) What am I doing? This is your job, Sonny. Slowly but surely all these Hollywood stars with brown roots are coming out of the closet. If the gays can do it, why can't we? Right, Anita?

ANITA: Right on.

CONNIE: At least once a year we can get together to hand out awards and put on the dog. How do you like my stole?

ANITA: (*distracted, watching* SONNY) Um? Oh . . . I love it. Mink?

CONNIE: Dog. Just kidding. It's imitation mink. I wouldn't kill a rat for its fur.

ANITA: (*looking*) Where is Buddy? Wasn't he with you?

CONNIE: He stopped to throw up. (SONNY *kneels in the kitchen and ritualistically stabs the burger bag hari-kari fashion. Trash spills out. There is a pause*)

ANITA: So what's the movie about, Connie? I mean, does Sonny have a good role?

CONNIE: It's not bad.

SONNY: Is it any good, Mom?

CONNIE: (*philosophically*) It's a movie—what do you want? And on international location—in Panama! A lot of guys would give an arm and a leg for chance like that. Starring with Jack Nicholson? You'd better believe it!

ANITA: *(impressed)* Jack Nicholson? Sonny, that's great.

CONNIE: Or maybe Sylvester Stallone. They haven't nailed down the main lead yet.

SONNY: *(suspiciously)* What part do I play?

CONNIE: *(cautiously)* Sort of a soldier . . . A *guerrilla*. The story takes place in Central America, see? And there's this American Marine who's down there advising the *contras*. Well, you're one of the boys he's training.

SONNY: *(sharply)* To overthrow what, Nicaragua?

CONNIE: Who said anything about Nicaragua?

SONNY: Who's financing this thing, the Sandinistas or the CIA? Why doesn't it have Arnie Schwarzenegger?

CONNIE: *(perplexed)* No, you don't understand . . .

SONNY: *(angry)* I'm not participating in any reactionary fascist film.

CONNIE: *(on the defensive)* M'ijo, you've got it all wrong. It's a comedy, sort of a funny love story set in El Salvador.

SONNY: *(SONNY glances at ANITA. Pauses)* So what's your role, *Consuelo?*

CONNIE: *(peeved)* Sort of a hostess, and don't call me Consuelo.

SONNY: *(snide)* What kind of hostess?

CONNIE: *(evasively)* A hostess with the mostess. I run the canteen in the mountains.

SONNY: *(bitterly)* Canteen or *cantina?*

CONNIE: *(shrugs)* I sell the gringos a few drinks. So what?

SONNY: What else do you sell them—"gorls"?

CONNIE: It's only a movie, for Pete's sake.

SONNY: It's a whorehouse isn't it?

CONNIE: It's a job!

SONNY: *(seething)* And what am I suppose to be— one of the customers, too, or just a pimp? I probably don't even speak English, do I?

CONNIE: *(affronted)* You don't even get to speak at all.

SONNY: So I'm an EXTRA, is that it? An extra in a goddamn CIA WHOREHOUSE? That's sick, Mom. SICK! How much is a FUCKING MOVIE worth?

CONNIE: WHAT?

SONNY: I don't want your fucking job, and I don't need your fucking agent!

CONNIE: *(slaps SONNY)* Don't you use that language with me, *cabrón! ¡Soy tu madre! Pos mira . . .* What's the matter with you? I didn't want to do that, especially in front of Anita, but it's time you showed some respect and appreciation for what I've tried to do for you, eh? Being your mom doesn't mean I'm your dishrag! I've got hopes and dreams for myself, just like you, and I need my space to do it. You hear what I'm saying? Grow up! *(SONNY turns and pathetically exits up the hall. There is a pause. CONNIE is distraught)* He's getting worse, isn't he?

ANITA: *(anxiously)* That's putting it mildly. He's got Buddy's gun, Connie. He could hurt himself.

CONNIE: *(guilty)* But how-why? Buddy and I have done everything for that kid and his sister. He's had a great life, a middle-class life. Is it our fault he doesn't know what to do with it!

BUDDY: *(enters, tipsily rocking to and fro, with a gloriously drunken smile on his lips, impeccably attired in a tuxedo. With his tie straight and every hair on his balding head in place, he nevertheless looks quite dapper. Slurring)* Cheerio! Good evening.

CONNIE: *(incensed)* Señor, are you still drunk? *(BUDDY smiles and suddenly straightens out, dropping his drunken routine, but in high spirits)*

BUDDY: *(almost British)* No, actually. I'm quite in control of my faculties, after a bit of an upchuck. López is the name, Nigel López. *(lisping) Señorita princesa, ¿cómo está usted? (He nods to ANITA)*

CONNIE: *(disgusted)* You're ridiculous.

BUDDY: Would you prefer a little Noel Coward? Where's Sonny?

CONNIE: For your information, Mr. Coward, your son is upstairs with a gun about to blow his brains out, for all we know, with your gun!

BUDDY: *(relieved)* That old thing? It hasn't been fired in twenty years. *(a gunshot goes off.*

Silence. BUDDY, CONNIE *and* ANITA *look at each other horrified)*

CONNIE: *(screaming)* SONNY!!! (BUDDY *leaps out of the den and runs up the hallway, followed by* CONNIE *and* ANITA. *Long pause. The den remains empty.* BUDDY, CONNIE *and* ANITA *return slowly, backing down the hallway, with their arms slightly raised in caution.* SONNY *has the gun aimed at them. Smiling insanely, he is wearing shades and a green beret)*

SONNY: *(sings)*
"Put silver wings on my hairy chest
make me one of America's best . . ."

BUDDY: *(bewildered)* What's going on, Sonny? Is this some kind of game?

SONNY: *(sick smile)* The only game in town, a little game of life and death.

CONNIE: *(emotionally)* Are you CRAZY?!

BUDDY: *(turns to her anxiously)* ¡Cállate, mujer! He isn't being serious. Right, Sonny? You're acting, aren't you, *m'ijo?*

SONNY: *(spaced out)* Do you really think so?

BUDDY: *(humoring him)* That outfit you're wearing, isn't that part of my costume for "The Green Berets"?

SONNY: *(shakes his head vigorously. Wild-eyed)* Screw John Wayne! I'm going to Central America to make my own movie! YO!

BUDDY: *(glares at* CONNIE*)* Central América?

SONNY: *(laughing crazily)* It's a comedy, Dad. A laff riot set in El Salvador. We're going down there to kick some brown ass and have a ball, huh Mom?

BUDDY: What have you been . . . ? Did you offer him a job in the Nicholson picture?

CONNIE: *(helpless)* I was only humoring him, *hombre.*

SONNY: *(fiercely intense)* It appears both of you are having trouble taking me seriously. Would it help if we played a little game of Russian roulette a la Robert DeNiro in "The Deer Hunter"?! Motherfucker, huh? Motherfucker! *(he spins the chamber on the gun and holds it up.* BUDDY *stands tall before his son shielding* CONNIE *and* ANITA*)*

BUDDY: Come on, *m'ijo*! Enough's enough. Settle down and give me the gun.

CONNIE: *(fearfully)* M'ijo, por el amor de Dios, what are you going to do?

SONNY: *(stepping on hearth with an insane smile)* One of us may not get out of here alive. The only question is which one? The maid, the gardener, the ballerina or me?

ANITA: You're ill, Sonny seriously ill.

SONNY: *(holding up the gun to his own throat)* SHUT UP!! Or the beaner gets it. Now SIT DOWN!

BUDDY: *(standing steadily)* If you're going to shoot me, you may as well do it now, Sonny, I don't take orders in my own house.

SONNY: *(bitterly)* Right, the Silent Bit King in his castle! What about all those cops outside, King? Are you going to close up the moat and keep them out? Or did you come to talk me into surrendering? What chance do I have of going back to Harvard now, huh, Pop? Your prince and heir? They're going to throw my ass in prison, Daddy-O! I'm going to do EXTRA time!

BUDDY: *(angered)* So who told you to leave Harvard? Sonny, you had it made!

SONNY: *(desolate)* You still don't get it, do you? What it's like being a Chicano at Harvard? The sense of isolation and guilt.

CONNIE: *(emotionally)* No more, *m'ijo,* please.

SONNY: *(shaking his head morosely in desperation. Anguished)* Do you know how many times I've denied you? Lucy used to do it all the time. Do you think she gave a damn? I'm talking about SHAME! HUMILIATION!—all those scum-sucking roles you've played in the movies all these years! DRUNKS and WHORES and ASS-LICKING GREASERS! And for what? So Lucy and I could make something of ourselves? Well, we have, Dad! We've become SOMEBODY ELSE! Anybody else but your CHILDREN!— ACTORS faking our roles to fit into the GREAT AMERICAN SUCCESS STORY: go away, move away, change your name and deny your origins, change your SEX if need be, but become NEUTER, like everybody else! You see, in order to

ACT TRULY AMERICAN, you have to kill your parents: no fatherland, no motherland, no MEXICAN, Japanese, African, Jewish, Puertorican, Filipino, Armenian, Latvian, Chinese, Indian, Arabian, Norwegian, old-country SHIT! Well, I damn near succeeded . . . Thanks to good old Anglo-Saxon Protestant, MONROE JAMES! *(music: We hear Mozart's "Rondo in C" in underscore)*

BUDDY: Monroe who?

SONNY: *(obsessively)* My roommate at Harvard . . . He was everything I ever wanted to be. Tall, rich, blonde, but he wasn't much company, so I preferred to do my homework in the library. One night I was working on a paper— writing with all my conscious skill to make the syntax of my English sentences as perfect as they could be. I couldn't tolerate the thought of being anything less than brilliant, you see. If you're not white, you have to be brilliant, just to be considered acceptable. Well, I got stuck . . . on one paragraph . . . First, I restructured the sentences, hoping to eliminate a certain kind of circular logic in the paragraph. I hate being REDUNDANT . . . Then the linear order of the words began to bother me. MY ENGLISH WAS BREAKING DOWN! Then I couldn't tolerate the space between the words. Finally, I got stuck on a hyphen, a lousy hyphen, so I scratched it out. And the HOLE between the two words became an unbridgeable GAP, and I FELL! . . . into a sea of nothingness. So I ran, I ran like my life depended on it all the way back to the dorm. Then . . . when I opened the door to our room, I spotted Monroe, holding a gun to his head. Neither of us said anything. He just smiled, and pulled the trigger. My fucking role model! He blew his brains out! *(he collapses in silent tears. There is a pause.* CONNIE *crosses to* SONNY, *and sits beside him, overwhelmed with maternal concern, also in tears)*

CONNIE: Whatever we've done, *m'ijo*, it's been for you. We wanted to be proud of you, but more than anything we wanted you to be at peace with yourself. I just don't honestly know what's gone wrong. You had everything going for you!

ANITA: It's time to grow up, Sonny. Accept your parents for what they are and maybe you'll accept yourself. We're all only human.

BUDDY: You know, Sonny. After a while, making movies can be just like any other job, but it's never been scum-sucking work. You don't like the roles we've played? That's tough. You see, *m'ijo* . . . Bedoya was right. Inside yourself you know your own worth. And I should know. I'm your father and I don't have to show you any stinking badges. NOW, GIVE ME THE GUN! *(*BUDDY *holds his hand out for the gun.* SONNY *is about to hand it to him when the L.A.P.D. interrupts and brings* SONNY *back to his craziness. The L.A.P.D. bullhorn blares out again in front of the house)*

BULLHORN: THIS IS THE L.A.P.D. TIME'S UP! YOU'VE GOT TWO MINUTES TO COME OUT WITH YOUR HANDS UP, OR WE'RE COMING IN!

SONNY: Nice try, Dad, but it won't work! Your speeches were a bit too predictable.

CONNIE: Sonny, please!

BUDDY: Let's have it, *cabrón.* *(*BUDDY *reaches for the gun.* SONNY *backs off, raising the pistol to his head)*

SONNY: DON'T, DAD! OR I'LL SHOOT!! *(*BUDDY *stops.* ANITA *comforts* CONNIE*)*

ANITA: Sonny, why are you torturing your parents like this?

SONNY: *(laughs insanely, his face a tragicomic mask. With suicidal irony)* Torture? . . . You mean I'm finally being convincing? . . . I don't know if I'm acting or not anymore . . . Am I being melodramatic? I don't know . . . and I don't care . . . I only know that I'm not going to prison and that the white whale must die. Would you believe I'm going after white whale—inside my head? I now understand why, so if the gun is still loaded, this is GOODBYE! *(he places the barrel of the gun between his eyes, shutting his eyes tight)*

CONNIE: *(pleading)*
M'ijo . . . please . . . don't.
(Blackout.)

SCENE THREE: *In the dark, immediately following, we hear a recording of Los Lobos singing "Will the Wolf Survive?" Half lights come up. A* STAGEHAND *walks onstage, takes the gun from* SONNY *and begins to clear props.*

SONNY: *(opening his eyes)* Hey, wait. Stop it, I said. CUT!!!
(Lights black out, except for a single spot on SONNY. BUDDY, CONNIE *and* ANITA *sit in the background. There is a pause. We suddenly hear the* DIRECTOR'S *voice—Speaking to* SONNY *from the booth, his face on the studio monitors, looking and sounding exactly like* SONNY!*)*

DIRECTOR: WHAT'S THE MATTER, SWEET-HEART?

SONNY: *(talking to the booth)* It's not working out, man. You're messing with the tragic implications of my entire story here. What happened to the final shot?

DIRECTOR: *(offstage)* WE GOTTA KEEP IT LIGHT. ENTERTAINING, ESE.

SONNY: *(intensely)* Don't *ese* me! It's idiotic! This isn't reality!

DIRECTOR: WHO SAID ANYTHING ABOUT RE-ALITY? THIS IS TELEVISION. FRANKLY, REALITY'S A BIG BORING PAIN IN THE ASS. WE'RE IN THE ENTERTAINMENT BUSINESS. LAUGHS, SONNY, THAT'S MORE IMPORTANT THAN REALITY. LOTS OF LAUGHS.

SONNY: *(pained)* You promised to respect my script.

DIRECTOR: *(offstage)* AND I MOST CERTAINLY DO. I JUST CAN'T USE IT. NOT IN THIS PI-LOT SHOW. LATER PERHAPS? ONCE WE'VE EARNED SOME DECENT RATINGS.

SONNY: What if I disappear for a while. I go away for six months back to Yucatan, to the sacred pyramids of the Mayan jungle. I go through my own psychic death and rebirth in Mexico. I plummet to the schizophrenic depths of my own cosmic root and emerge from the dark side of my own soul cleansed and enlightened. Would that be amusing?

DIRECTOR: IN A SITUATION COMEDY? 'FRAID NOT, SONNY. PERHAPS YOU CAN FASH-ION AN ART FILM OUT OF THOSE EXPE-RIENCES.

SONNY: And the politics? I go on to Guatemala and Nicaragua. What about all the stuff on Ameri-can foreign policy in Latin America?

DIRECTOR: DITTO. WRITE AN EDITORIAL. THE ONLY LATINS OUR AUDIENCES CARE ABOUT ARE THOSE WHO DANCE AND SING AND STAMP THEIR FEET . . . AND SAY FUNNY THINGS, CROSSOVER VALUE, SONNY! IF IT CAN'T COME ACROSS IN BUFFALO, YOU CAN FORGET IT. THE COS-MIC TRUTHS ARE FINE, BUT DOWN HERE ON EARTH, PROGRESS MOVES LIKE A SNAIL. GIVE IT A CHANCE. NOW, SHALL WE WRAP THIS MOTHER UP? FOR THE SAKE OF PROGRESS?

SONNY: *(cagily)* Can you get rid of the cops? And the burglary rap at the Crap-in-the-Box?

DIRECTOR: *(pause)* WHY SHOULD I?

SONNY: *(passionately)* Because you can change the ending if you want to . . . It's our story. Right? We can't leave all these high school dropouts with this downer, man! Give the peo-ple some hope. Save the Harvard Homeboy. Be honest with yourself, Sonny. Am I talking to myself?

DIRECTOR: *(offstage)* TO THE BONE, SONNY BOY. TO THE BONE.

SONNY: *(confidently)* All right, then I wanna make this ending my own. A spectacular ending!

DIRECTOR: *(offstage)* OKAY! OKAY, FINE. IT'S ALL YOURS, JUST DON'T SCREW IT UP. MAKE IT EMOTIONALLY SATISFYING, HOMEBOY.

SONNY: BELIEVE. *(he turns and slowly starts to exit down the hall, then stops and turns)* ACTION!!! *(he hurries out as the lights fade to black)*

Epilogue

BUDDY *and* CONNIE'S *dream.*

In the dark: The DIRECTOR'S *voice comes over the audio system.*

DIRECTOR: *(offstage)* LADIES AND GENTLE-MEN, WE WOULD LIKE TO TAKE THIS OPPORTUNITY TO THANK YOU FOR PARTICIPATING AS A LIVE STUDIO AUDIENCE IN THE TAPING OF THIS SHOW. WE HOPE THAT YOU WILL FIND OUR ENDING POSITIVELY HILARIOUS.
(Music: Lights come up on the den to reveal BUDDY *and* CONNIE *asleep, still wearing their evening clothes.* BUDDY *is in his chair, and* CONNIE *is on the couch, covered with her imitation mink. They stir to the sound of the driving music of hypnotic flutes, shamisens and drums. Out in the patio, through the night mist, a body of great flashing lights descends from the heavens, indicating the arrival of an extraterrestrial object.* BUDDY *rises and goes to the patio doors, and looks out with utter amazement.)*

BUDDY: GOD BLESS AMERICA *¡y que viva México, chingao!*

CONNIE: *(getting up)* What is it?

BUDDY: Come and look at this beautiful sight, *viejita!*

CONNIE: *(looks out, with equal amazement)* My God. It's a flying saucer!

BUDDY: *(laughing like a child)* A GIANT, SOMBRERO FLYING SAUCER! Didn't I tell you? There it is! It wasn't just a crazy movie idea, it's real! Isn't it?

CONNIE: Are we dreaming?

BUDDY: How can we both be having the same dream? *(*SONNY *and* ANITA *come down the stairs, dressed and ready to travel, carrying suitcases. Their New Age American look is stunning, the stuff of the 21st century)*

SONNY: Mommy-O and Daddy-O? It's my dream. We're on our way.

CONNIE: You're leaving? Where are you going?

BUDDY: What are you doing, Sonny?

SONNY: *(seriously)* Trying to give this situation a fantastic solution. To do that I've got to convince you that my recent misadventures were only aberrations of my stressed-out overactive brain. You see, we're only as real as we believe ourselves to be. In show-biz terms, I'm asking you to suspend your disbelief in me and to believe me when I tell you I'm mentally, physically and spiritually okay. *Mens sana in corpore sano.* I have found my own mind again. Are you ready for this? I'm going back to Harvard, to finish what I started.

CONNIE: *(delighted)* ¡M'ijo!

ANITA: Sonny, that's wonderful!

BUDDY: I knew you'd come through, *m'ijo!* (BUDDY *puts his arm around him)*

SONNY: *(thoughtful)* I've been thinking a lot about this, Dad. To be honest, I still don't know what the hell I'm going to be, but I'm going to make you proud of me, whatever I become. Lawyer, filmmaker or cosmic lowrider.

BUDDY: Cosmic lowrider?

SONNY: I'm only sorry I put you all through this melodramatic violence. I just had to come back to the Twilight Zone to find out who I was.

BUDDY: *(head up)* And so . . . who are you?

SONNY: *(with maturity)* Your spaced-out son, for one. *(there is a quiet moment.* BUDDY *embraces* SONNY, *then* CONNIE *joins them, then* ANITA)

BUDDY: *(ironically)* Well, at least we've managed to save our *pinche* dignity, *chingao!*

CONNIE: I'm beginning to see a happy ending to all of this! *(a whirring sound is heard offstage, the great light starts to glow out in the patio.* SONNY *puts his arm around* ANITA)

SONNY: Anita's coming back to the East Coast with me, for a while anyway.

ANITA: *(excited)* I'm going back to see my folks. It wasn't right of me to leave without saying good-bye, so I'm going back to say hello and mend some broken fences. The Peugeot is going with us, by the way. Thanks for the fantastic ride Sonny conjured up.

SONNY: Actually, it was my Dad's idea. He deserves all the credit.

BUDDY: *(proudly)* The Flying Saucer Sombrero . . . how does it fly, Sonny?

SONNY: Heliotropic waves. Aztechnology. Mayan Solar Lord stuff. The stuff of dreams and science fiction. Everybody's got a right to star in their own movie, right? This one's mine. From now on, we're going nowhere but UP. Straight up, into the brightest stars of our wildest dreams. Ready to go, baby?

ANITA: Hey, after the crazy cholo, I'm ready for anything.

SONNY: Then let's go, Mom, Dad? *(BUDDY and CONNIE both embrace their son. ANITA holds back)*

CONNIE: *(tears)* Go on, now. Your father and I have our own dreams and world to conquer. We're perfectly happy staying in our own home. Right, *viejo?*

BUDDY: Sure.

SONNY: Sure sure?

BUDDY: Don't sweat it. Get going!

SONNY: *(laughs and kisses CONNIE on the cheek)* Thanks, Mom, Dad. It's great to be home for a while. I just want you to know you're both a fine pair of human beings. And that I LOVE YOU!

ANITA: *(joining the embrace)* That goes for me, too.

BUDDY: *Sayonara.*

ANITA: *¡ADIÓS!*

SONNY: *¡Ay los watcho! (Offstage) Ese,* Scotty, beam me up, homes! *(SONNY and ANITA step out into the patio, glowing with light. The flying saucer sombrero takes off, in a spectacular ascent, making a great whoosh as it flies away. There is a pause. BUDDY is standing in the den. They look at each other. BUDDY heads to the fireplace mantle and picks up the daruma doll)*

CONNIE: What are you doing?

BUDDY: Filling in the left eye. *¿No que no?* Our wish came true! Sonny went back to Harvard. Well, *vieja,* shall we call it a day or work up a little more sweat? We gotta be in shape, you know, if we're gonna make that anti-war Nicholson movie together.

CONNIE: Forget it, Buddy. I'm hitting the showers.

BUDDY: I'll join you.

CONNIE: We won't fit.

BUDDY: I'll make us fit . . . Come on.

CONNIE: *(tempted)* Let's go for a real Hollywood ending, like in all those movies in the '40s.

BUDDY: Let George do it.

CONNIE: *(loving it) Cómo eres señor*—look at you. The middle-aged father of an established doctor and an up-and-coming cosmic lowrider. Well, Nigel, what do you have to say for yourself?

BUDDY: *(with monocle, British accent)* What else? I don't have to show you no stinking badges! *(he turns on the tape deck, which plays "Rhapsody in Blue." BUDDY and CONNIE cross slowly and romantically towards each other, meeting center stage. BUDDY holds CONNIE in his arms and they do an old-fashioned kiss as the lights fade to black)*

CURTAIN

M. BUTTERFLY (1988)

Thus the Orient acquired representatives, so to speak, and representations, each one more concrete, more internally congruent with some Western exigency, than the ones that preceded it. It is as if, having once settled on the Orient as a locale suitable for incarnating the infinite in a finite shape, Europe could not stop the practice.

Edward Said's insightful suggestion of the process by which Europeans, for a host of purposes, constructed the "Orient" and "Orientals," provides a useful point of departure for a discussion of David Henry Hwang's *M. Butterfly*. For at the heart of this finely crafted play is an examination of the impulse to create such categories and the tragically destructive results that adherence to them can cause. Hwang's inspiration came from an actual set of events. In 1986 a French diplomat, who off and on for 20 years had supplied his Chinese lover with classified documents, was convicted of spying for the Republic of China and sentenced to six years in prison. At his trial, the diplomat firmly maintained that he had never known that his "mistress" was, in actuality, a man. In Hwang's reworking, the prurient question of how, in an intimate relationship, one might mistake a man for a woman is quickly dismissed. Instead, through the relationship between the French diplomat, Gallimard, and his Chinese lover, Song Liling, Hwang explores the ways in which Eastern and Western versions of racism and sexism have provided psychic underpinnings for both Euro-American imperialism in Asia and Eastern attempts to manipulate the stereotypes to political and economic advantage.

David Henry Hwang was born in 1957 to Henry Yuan and Dorothy Huang Hwang in Los Angeles. While his parents emigrated to the United States, their professional status (his father as a banker and his mother a professor of piano) meant that David Hwang's childhood in San Gabriel, California, was securely middle-class. He attended Stanford University, graduating in 1979 with a degree in English. Though his quick movement from student to professionally produced playwright may suggest a long-standing interest in theatre, Hwang has said that it was not until late in his college career that he began writing plays. As he told David Savran, in the summer of 1978 he studied with Sam Shepard and Maria Irene Fornés at the first Padua Hills Playwrights' Festival. Under their tutelage he began what would become his first play, *F.O.B.*, produced in his Stanford dormitory during his senior year, accepted for production at the National Playwright's Conference at the O'Neill Theater Center in 1979, and finally produced **Off-Broadway** by Joseph Papp, where it won an **Obie** for best new play of the 1980 season. His affiliation with Papp continued with Off-Broadway productions of a series of plays exploring Asian and Asian-American issues: *The Dance and the Railroad* (1981), *Family Devotions* (1981), and "Sound and Beauty" (1983), a mounting of two of Hwang's one-acts, *The House of Sleeping Beauties* and *The Sound of a Voice*. After a two-year absence from the New York theatres, Hwang returned to Off Broadway with *Rich Relations*, a play in which he dramatized his own family's experiences in the guise of a Euro-American family. Though Hwang remains proud of it, the play is generally regarded as a critical failure. His best-known play to date, *M. Butterfly*, premiered in Washington, DC, in 1988 and moved quickly to Broadway where it won the **Tony Award** for best play and was nominated for the Pulitzer Prize. Calling upon his musical training as well as his skills as a dramatist, he has since worked with Philip Glass and Jerome Sirlin on a musical fantasy entitled *1000 Airplanes on the Roof*, which premiered in an airplane hangar in Vienna, Austria, in 1988. His recent play, *Face Value* (1993), pushes the ideas of *M. Butterfly* even further, arguing, in effect, that race doesn't exist.

But in a very real sense, issues of race and ethnicity have been and continue to be a part of David Henry Hwang's career and the professional lives of other Asian-American playwrights. Until relatively recently, representations of Asian Americans were little seen in mainstream culture except, as James Moy has persuasively argued, as a series of negatively inscribed stereotypes. Living primarily in ethnically homogeneous neighborhoods, Asian Americans themselves were often removed from the view of the general population. While they had written plays earlier in the century, only in the 1960s did Asian Americans begin to explore seriously and persistently the possibilities of Western-style theatre. It was not until 1965 that the first Asian-American theatre group was founded with the formation of the **East West Players** in Los Angeles. That was followed by the establishment of Kumu Kahua at the University of Hawaii in 1970 and the San Francisco Asian American Theatre Workshop in 1973.

Asian-American playwrighting received its first big boost when the East West Players sponsored a playwrighting contest that encouraged Momoko Iko to rework her novel about the internment of Japanese Americans during World War II into a play entitled *Gold Watch*, which was performed at the Inner City Cultural Center in Los Angeles in 1972. The next year, the Asian American Theatre Workshop's Frank Chin wrote *Chickencoop Chinaman*, generally regarded as the first major play by an Asian American. In 1977 Chin's *The Year of the Dragon* became the first Asian-American drama ever produced in a mainstream New York house when it was mounted by the American Place Theatre. These events and the formation of Asian-American companies such as New York's Pan Asian Repertory, Seattle's Northwest Asian American Theatre Company (originally the Asian Exclusion Act), and the Toronto-based Canadian Artists Group, as well as more recent companies in San Diego, San Francisco, and Chicago, have provided an increasingly broad forum for Asian-American drama, and a host of dramatists have arisen to provide representations authentic to the varied experiences of the Asian-American community. In addition to Hwang, Asian-American playwrights such as Ping Chong, Philip Kan Gotanda, Jessica Hagedorn, Velina Hasu Houston, Genny Lim, Wakako Yamauchi, and Laurence Yep have all made significant contributions to the increasingly multiethnic reality of American drama.

As an instance of this body of ethnic drama, *M. Butterfly* reveals a double perspective, a current that Misha Berson has noted is part of much—but not all—Asian-American stage literature. This point of view leaves Asian-American authors constantly aware of their emotional and familial existence between the countries from which they or their families departed and the nation of which they are now a part either by choice or birth. Perhaps reflecting this double perspective, *M. Butterfly* (in a fashion typical of most of Hwang's earlier pieces) deploys a host of Eastern and Western, elite and popular, representational styles. Kabuki theatre, Chinese opera, Western opera, and television sitcoms all provide elements; and thus it distinguishes itself from stylistically traditional Eastern or Western theatres while simultaneously declaring the play's affinity with **postmodern** experimentations within Western theatre and pushing those techniques in new directions.

The backbone of the drama is what Hwang himself in his "Afterword" to the play has called a "deconstructivist *Madame Butterfly*." Puccini's 1904 opera tells the story of a nineteenth-century American naval officer, Benjamin Franklin Pinkerton, who while stationed in Nagasaki, Japan, conducts a sham marriage with Cio-Cio-San, also known as Butterfly, the fifteen-year-old geisha embodiment of the male-constructed feminine ideal. Pinkerton is posted home and Cio-Cio-San, having borne him a child, waits three years patiently for his return. When he finally comes back he brings with him Kate, his American wife, who goes to Cio-Cio-San's house to secure Pinkerton's son. Butterfly agrees to give up the child and, having placed a doll and an American flag in her child's arms, blindfolds her son and stabs herself, to the horror of Kate and the belatedly remorseful Pinkerton, who enters as Butterfly lies dying on the floor. Hwang uses this story to establish an emotional trajectory against which his own play's action can be understood. At the same time, the constant counterpointing of the Cio-Cio-San and Pinkerton story with a much more complicated reworking played out in Beijing and Paris during the twentieth century allows Hwang to explore the abiding gender and racial stereotypes that have perpetuated East-West misperceptions and the seemingly willful misunderstandings metaphorically rendered in the affair between Gallimard and Song.

Gallimard's construction of Song as a latter-day Butterfly precipitates a series of events that parodies the typical narrative pattern of Western patriarchy's family romance—courtship, marriage, family, and, of more recent vintage, divorce. In Gallimard's mind, the virile Westerner has once again found true love in the arms of a passively submissive Eastern beauty. In effect, he plays out in the Beijing boudoir what the United States is trying to do at the same time in Vietnam, a distant background to the action of the play. But, as later events make clear, Gallimard has fallen in love not with Song but with the ideal she represents. In fact that ideal has little to do with women at all, for as Song remarks, "only a man knows how a woman is supposed to act." Gallimard's decision at the play's end to reassert and embrace illusion even at the cost of his life is reminiscent of Pirandello and links Hwang's play to an antirealist tradition of drama which has sought to question the foundations of identity. In the process of examining the relationship between Gallimard and Song, *M. Butterfly* goes further than even such works as Jean Genet's *The Maids*, arguing that foundational assumptions about gender, as opposed to the biological realities of sex, are much more problematic and culturally relative than we might choose to believe.

This strategy is both daring and dangerous, for it proposes to use stereotypes against themselves. For some critics—notably Robert Brustein, John

Simon, and Gabrielle Cody—the device is ultimately a failure because the play tends to substitute a new set of stereotypes for those of an earlier age (Brustein), because the power relationship between the characters is too fluid to make the stereotypes seem accurately ascribable to one person or another (Simon), or because the action of the play merely reinscribes the sexist stereotypes it is ostensibly engaging (Cody). For most critics, however, Hwang's ploy is applauded as a masterstroke. Even given its status as a Broadway "hit," Robert Skloot argues, no matter how one chooses to answer the racial and gender questions the play raises, audiences are forced to confront them. Similarly, Karen Shimakawa suggests that Hwang's play has the benefit of forcing a dominant culture audience to recognize the extent to which its expectations "construct" individuals, coercing them into roles rather than allowing them to form their own identities.

Like many of the plays in the contemporary American theatrical scene, David Henry Hwang's *M. Butterfly* reminds us of the varied ways American drama and theatre are confronting with imagination and spirit some of the more vexed political and social issues of our day. Racism, sexism, and imperialism remain part of the subject matter of our theatre, despite general assertions of a pervasive political quietism in the nation's drama. More important, perhaps, *M. Butterfly* also emphasizes for us that, as in previous ages, American drama continues to find new voices to speak to the peoples of the nation.

WORKS CONSULTED

Berson, Misha, ed. *Between Worlds: Contemporary Asian-American Plays.* New York: Theatre Communications Group, 1990.
Brustein, Robert. "Transcultural Blends." *Reimagining American Theatre.* New York: Hill and Wang, 1991. 57–62.
Cody, Gabrielle. "David Hwang's *M. Butterfly*: Perpetuating the Misogynist Myth." *Theater* 20 (1989): 24–27.
DiGaetani, John Louis. "*M. Butterfly*: An Interview with David Henry Hwang." *TDR* 33 (1989): 141–153.
Houston, Velina Hasu, ed. *The Politics of Life: Four Plays by Asian American Women.* Philadelphia: Temple University Press, 1993.

Hwang, David Henry. *M. Butterfly*. New York: Plume, 1989.

Moy, James S. *Marginal Sights: Staging the Chinese in America.* Iowa City: University of Iowa Press, 1993.

Said, Edward. *Orientalism.* New York: Random House, 1978.

Savran, David. "David Hwang." *In Their Own Words: Contemporary American Playwrights.* New York: Theatre Communications Group, 1988. 117–131.

Shimakawa, Karen. "'Who's to Say?' Or, Making Space for Gender and Ethnicity in *M. Butterfly*." *Theatre Journal* 45 (1993): 349–361.

Simon, John. "Finding Your Song." *New York Magazine,* 11 April, 1988: 117–119.

Skloot, Robert. "Breaking the Butterfly: The Politics of David Henry Hwang." *Modern Drama* 33 (1990): 59–66.

C H A R A C T E R S

KUROGO	GIRL IN MAGAZINE
RENE GALLIMARD	COMRADE CHIN
SONG LILING	SUZUKI
MARC	SHU FANG
MAN #2	HELGA
CONSUL SHARPLESS	M. TOULON
RENEE	MAN #1
WOMAN AT PARTY	JUDGE

The action of the play takes place in a Paris prison in the present, and in recall, during the decade 1960 to 1970 in Beijing, and from 1966 to the present in Paris.

A C T   O N E

SCENE I:　M. GALLIMARD'S *prison cell. Paris. Present. Lights fade up to reveal* RENE GALLIMARD, *65, in a prison cell. He wears a comfortable bathrobe, and looks old and tired. The sparsely furnished cell contains a wooden crate upon which sits a hot plate with a kettle, and a portable tape recorder.* GALLIMARD *sits on the crate staring at the recorder, a sad smile on his face.*

Upstage SONG, *who appears as a beautiful woman in traditional Chinese garb, dances a traditional piece from the Peking Opera, surrounded by the percussive clatter of Chinese music.*

Then, slowly, lights and sound cross-fade; the Chinese opera music dissolves into a Western opera, the "Love Duet" from Puccini's Madame Butterfly. SONG *continues dancing, now to the Western accompaniment. Though her movements are the same, the difference in music now gives them a balletic quality.*

GALLIMARD *rises, and turns upstage towards the figure of* SONG, *who dances without acknowledging him.*

GALLIMARD:　Butterfly, Butterfly . . .
　　(He forces himself to turn away, as the image of SONG *fades out, and talks to us.)*

GALLIMARD:　The limits of my cell are as such: four-and-a-half meters by five. There's one window against the far wall; a door, very strong, to protect me from autograph hounds. I'm responsible for the tape recorder, the hot plate, and this charming coffee table.
　　　When I want to eat, I'm marched off to the dining room—hot, steaming slop appears on my plate. When I want to sleep, the light bulb

turns itself off—the work of fairies. It's an enchanted space I occupy. The French—we know how to run a prison.

But, to be honest, I'm not treated like an ordinary prisoner. Why? Because I'm a celebrity. You see, I make people laugh.

I never dreamed this day would arrive. I've never been considered witty or clever. In fact, as a young boy, in an informal poll among my grammar school classmates, I was voted "least likely to be invited to a party." It's a title I managed to hold onto for many years. Despite some stiff competition.

But now, how the tables turn! Look at me: the life of every social function in Paris. Paris? Why be modest? My fame has spread to Amsterdam, London, New York. Listen to them! In the world's smartest parlors. I'm the one who lifts their spirits!

(*With a flourish,* GALLIMARD *directs our attention to another part of the stage.*)

SCENE II: *A party. Present.*

Lights go up on a chic-looking parlor, where a well-dressed trio, two men and one woman, make conversation. GALLIMARD *also remains lit; he observes them from his cell.*

WOMAN: And what of Gallimard?
MAN 1: Gallimard?
MAN 2: Gallimard!
GALLIMARD: (*to us*) You see? They're all determined to say my name, as if it were some new dance.
WOMAN: He still claims not to believe the truth.
MAN 1: What? Still? Even since the trial?
WOMAN: Yes. Isn't it mad?
MAN 2: (*laughing*) He says . . . it was dark . . . and she was very modest!
(*The trio break into laughter.*)
MAN 1: So—what? He never touched her with his hands?
MAN 2: Perhaps he did, and simply misidentified the equipment. A compelling case for sex education in the schools.

WOMAN: To protect the National Security—the Church can't argue with that.
MAN 1: That's impossible! How could he not know?
MAN 2: Simple ignorance.
MAN 1: For twenty years?
MAN 2: Time flies when you're being stupid.
WOMAN: Well, I thought the French were ladies' men.
MAN 2: It seems Monsieur Gallimard was overly anxious to live up to his national reputation.
WOMAN: Well, he's not very good-looking.
MAN 1: No, he's not.
MAN 2: Certainly not.
WOMAN: Actually, I feel sorry for him.
MAN 2: A toast! To Monsieur Gallimard!
WOMAN: Yes! To Gallimard!
MAN 1: To Gallimard!
MAN 2: Vive la différence!
(*They toast, laughing. Lights down on them.*)

SCENE III: M. GALLIMARD'S *cell.*

GALLIMARD: (*smiling*) You see? They toast me. I've become patron saint of the socially inept. Can they really be so foolish? Men like that—they should be scratching at my door, begging to learn my secrets! For I, Rene Gallimard, you see, I have known, and been loved by . . . the Perfect Woman.

Alone in this cell, I sit night after night, watching our story play through my head, always searching for a new ending, one which redeems my honor, where she returns at last to my arms. And I imagine you—my ideal audience—who come to understand and even, perhaps just a little, to envy me.
(*He turns on his tape recorder. Over the house speakers, we hear the opening phrases of* Madame Butterfly.)
GALLIMARD: In order for you to understand what I did and why, I must introduce you to my favorite opera: *Madame Butterfly*. By Giacomo Puccini. First produced at La Scala, Milan, in 1904, it is now beloved throughout the Western world.

(As GALLIMARD *describes the opera, the tape sequences in and out to sections he may be describing.)*

GALLIMARD: And why not? Its heroine, Cio-Cio-San, also known as Butterfly, is a feminine ideal, beautiful and brave. And its hero, the man for whom she gives up everything, is—*(he pulls out a naval officer's cap from under his crate, pops it on his head, and struts about)*—not very good-looking, not too bright, and pretty much a wimp: Benjamin Franklin Pinkerton of the U.S. Navy. As the curtain rises, he's just closed on two great bargains: one on a house, the other on a woman—call it a package deal.

Pinkerton purchased the rights to Butterfly for one hundred yen—in modern currency, equivalent to about . . . sixty-six cents. So, he's feeling pretty pleased with himself as Sharpless, the American consul, arrives to witness the marriage.

*(*MARC, *wearing an official cap to designate* SHARPLESS, *enters and plays the character.)*

SHARPLESS/MARC: Pinkerton!

PINKERTON/GALLIMARD: Sharpless! How's it hangin'? It's a great day, just great. Between my house, my wife, and the rickshaw ride in from town, I've saved nineteen cents just this morning.

SHARPLESS: Wonderful. I can see the inscription on your tombstone already: "I saved a dollar, here I lie." *(he looks around)* Nice house.

PINKERTON: It's artistic. Artistic, don't you think? Like the way the shoji screens slide open to reveal the wet bar and disco mirror ball? Classy, huh? Great for impressing the chicks.

SHARPLESS: "Chicks"? Pinkerton, you're going to be a married man!

PINKERTON: Well, sort of.

SHARPLESS: What do you mean?

PINKERTON: This country—Sharpless, it is okay. You got all these geisha girls running around—

SHARPLESS: I know! I live here!

PINKERTON: Then, you know the marriage laws, right? I split for one month, it's annulled!

SHARPLESS: Leave it to you to read the fine print. Who's the lucky girl?

PINKERTON: Cio-Cio-San. Her friends call her Butterfly. Sharpless, she eats out of my hand!

SHARPLESS: She's probably very hungry.

PINKERTON: Not like American girls. It's true what they say about Oriental girls. They want to be treated bad!

SHARPLESS: Oh, please!

PINKERTON: It's true!

SHARPLESS: Are you serious about this girl?

PINKERTON: I'm marrying her, aren't I?

SHARPLESS: Yes—with generous trade-in terms.

PINKERTON: When I leave, she'll know what it's like to have loved a real man. And I'll even buy her a few nylons.

SHARPLESS: You aren't planning to take her with you?

PINKERTON: Huh? Where?

SHARPLESS: Home!

PINKERTON: You mean, America? Are you crazy? Can you see her trying to buy rice in St. Louis?

SHARPLESS: So, you're not serious.

(Pause.)

PINKERTON/GALLIMARD: *(as* PINKERTON*)* Consul, I am a sailor in port. *(as* GALLIMARD*)* They then proceed to sing the famous duet, "The Whole World Over."

(The duet plays on the speakers. GALLIMARD, *as* PINKERTON, *lip-syncs his lines from the opera.)*

GALLIMARD: To give a rough translation: "The whole world over, the Yankee travels, casting his anchor wherever he wants. Life's not worth living unless he can win the hearts of the fairest maidens, then hotfoot it off the premises ASAP." *(he turns towards* MARC*)* In the preceding scene, I played Pinkerton, the womanizing cad, and my friend Marc from school . . . *(*MARC *bows grandly for our benefit)* played Sharpless, the sensitive soul of reason. In life, however, our positions were usually—no, always—reversed.

SCENE IV: *École Nationale. Aix-en-Provence. 1947.*

GALLIMARD: No, Marc, I think I'd rather stay home.

MARC: Are you crazy?! We are going to Dad's condo in Marseille! You know what happened last time?

GALLIMARD: Of course I do.

MARC: Of course you don't! You never know . . . They stripped, Rene!

GALLIMARD: Who stripped?

MARC: The girls!

GALLIMARD: Girls? Who said anything about girls?

MARC: Rene, we're a buncha university guys goin' up to the woods. What are we gonna do— talk philosophy?

GALLIMARD: What girls? Where do you get them?

MARC: Who cares? The point is, they come. On trucks. Packed in like sardines. The back flips open, babes hop out, we're ready to roll.

GALLIMARD: You mean, they just—?

MARC: Before you know it, every last one of them—they're stripped and splashing around my pool. There's no moon out, they can't see what's going on, their boobs are flapping, right? You close your eyes, reach out—it's grab bag, get it? Doesn't matter whose ass is between whose legs, whose teeth are sinking into who. You're just in there, going at it, eyes closed, on and on for as long as you can stand. *(pause)* Some fun, huh?

GALLIMARD: What happens in the morning?

MARC: In the morning, you're ready to talk some philosophy. *(beat)* So how 'bout it?

GALLIMARD: Marc, I can't . . . I'm afraid they'll say no—the girls. So I never ask.

MARC: You don't have to ask! That's the beauty— don't you see? They don't have to say yes. It's perfect for a guy like you, really.

GALLIMARD: You go ahead . . . I may come later.

MARC: Hey, Rene—it doesn't matter that you're clumsy and got zits—they're not looking!

GALLIMARD: Thank you very much.

MARC: Wimp.

(MARC walks over to the other side of the stage, and starts waving and smiling at women in the audience.)

GALLIMARD: *(to us)* We now return to my version of *Madame Butterfly* and the events leading to my recent conviction for treason.

(GALLIMARD notices MARC making lewd gestures.)

Marc, what are you doing?

MARC: Huh? *(sotto voce)* Rene, there're a lotta great babes out there. They're probably lookin' at me and thinking, "What a dangerous guy."

GALLIMARD: Yes—how could they help but be impressed by your cool sophistication?

(GALLIMARD pops the SHARPLESS cap on MARC's head, and points him offstage. MARC exits, leering.)

SCENE V: M. GALLIMARD'S *cell.*

GALLIMARD: Next, Butterfly makes her entrance. We learn her age—fifteen . . . but very mature for her years.

(Lights come up on the area where we saw SONG dancing at the top of the play. She appears there again, now dressed as MADAME BUTTERFLY, moving to the "Love Duet." GALLIMARD turns upstage slightly to watch, transfixed.)

GALLIMARD: But as she glides past him, beautiful, laughing softly behind her fan, don't we who are men sigh with hope? We, who are not handsome, nor brave, nor powerful, yet somehow believe, like Pinkerton, that we deserve a Butterfly. She arrives with all her possessions in the folds of her sleeves, lays them all out, for her man to do with as he pleases. Even her life itself—she bows her head as she whispers that she's not even worth the hundred yen he paid for her. He's already given too much, when we know he's really had to give nothing at all.

(Music and lights on SONG out. GALLIMARD sits at his crate.)

GALLIMARD: In real life, women who put their total worth at less than sixty-six cents are quite hard to find. The closest we come is in the pages of these magazines. *(he reaches into his crate, pulls out a stack of girlie magazines, and begins flipping through them)* Quite a necessity in prison. For three or four dollars, you get seven or eight women.

I first discovered these magazines at my uncle's house. One day, as a boy of twelve. The first time I saw them in his closet . . . all lined up—my body shook. Not with lust—no, with power. Here were women—a shelfful—who would do exactly as I wanted.

(The "Love Duet" creeps in over the speakers. Special comes up, revealing, not Song *this time, but a pinup girl in a sexy negligee, her back to us.* GALLIMARD *turns upstage and looks at her.)*

GIRL: I know you're watching me.

GALLIMARD: My throat . . . it's dry.

GIRL: I leave my blinds open every night before I go to bed.

GALLIMARD: I can't move.

GIRL: I leave my blinds open and the lights on.

GALLIMARD: I'm shaking. My skin is hot, but my penis is soft. Why?

GIRL: I stand in front of the window.

GALLIMARD: What is she going to do?

GIRL: I toss my hair, and I let my lips part . . . barely.

GALLIMARD: I shouldn't be seeing this. It's so dirty. I'm so bad.

GIRL: Then, slowly, I lift off my nightdress.

GALLIMARD: Oh, god. I can't believe it. I can't—

GIRL: I toss it to the ground.

GALLIMARD: Now, she's going to walk away. She's going to—

GIRL: I stand there, in the light, displaying myself.

GALLIMARD: No. She's—why is she naked?

GIRL: To you.

GALLIMARD: In front of a window? This is wrong. No—

GIRL: Without shame.

GALLIMARD: No, she must . . . like it.

GIRL: I like it.

GALLIMARD: She . . . she wants me to see.

GIRL: I want you to see.

GALLIMARD: I can't believe it! She's getting excited!

GIRL: I can't see you. You can do whatever you want.

GALLIMARD: I can't do a thing. Why?

GIRL: What would you like me to do . . . next?

(Lights go down on her. Music off. Silence, as GALLIMARD *puts away his magazines. Then he resumes talking to us.)*

GALLIMARD: Act Two begins with Butterfly staring at the ocean. Pinkerton's been called back to the U.S., and he's given his wife a detailed schedule of his plans. In the column marked "return date," he's written "when the robins nest." This failed to ignite her suspicions. Now, three years have passed without a peep from him. Which brings a response from her faithful servant, Suzuki.

*(*COMRADE CHIN *enters, playing* SUZUKI.*)*

SUZUKI: Girl, he's a loser. What'd he ever give you? Nineteen cents and those ugly Day-Glo stockings? Look, it's finished! Kaput! Done! And you should be glad! I mean, the guy was a woofer! He tried before, you know—before he met you, he went down to geisha central and plunked down his spare change in front of the usual candidates—everyone else gagged! These are hungry prostitutes, and they were not interested, get the picture? Now, stop slathering when an American ship sails in, and let's make some bucks—I mean, yen! We are broke!

Now, what about Yamadori? Hey, hey—don't look away—the man is a prince—figuratively, and, what's even better, literally. He's rich, he's handsome, he says he'll die if you don't marry him—and he's even willing to overlook the little fact that you've been deflowered all over the place by a foreign devil. What do you mean, "But he's Japanese"? You're Japanese! You think you've been touched by the whitey god? He was a sailor with dirty hands!

*(*SUZUKI *stalks offstage.)*

GALLIMARD: She's also visited by Consul Sharpless, sent by Pinkerton on a minor errand.

*(*MARC *enters, as* SHARPLESS.*)*

SHARPLESS: I hate this job.

GALLIMARD: This Pinkerton—he doesn't show up personally to tell his wife he's abandoning her.

No, he sends a government diplomat . . . at taxpayers' expense.

SHARPLESS: Butterfly? Butterfly? I have some bad—I'm going to be ill. Butterfly, I came to tell you—

GALLIMARD: Butterfly says she knows he'll return and if he doesn't she'll kill herself rather than go back to her own people. *(beat)* This causes a lull in the conversation.

SHARPLESS: Let's put it this way . . .

GALLIMARD: Butterfly runs into the next room, and returns holding—
(Sound cue: a baby crying. SHARPLESS, "seeing" this, backs away.)

SHARPLESS: Well, good. Happy to see things going so well. I suppose I'll be going now. Ta ta. Ciao. *(he turns away. Sound cue out)* I hate this job. *(he exits)*

GALLIMARD: At that moment, Butterfly spots in the harbor an American ship—the *Abramo Lincoln!* *(Music cue: "The Flower Duet." SONG, still dressed as BUTTERFLY, changes into a wedding kimono, moving to the music.)*

GALLIMARD: This is the moment that redeems her years of waiting. With Suzuki's help, they cover the room with flowers—
(CHIN, as SUZUKI, trudges onstage and drops a lone flower without much enthusiasm.)

GALLIMARD: —and she changes into her wedding dress to prepare for Pinkerton's arrival.
(SUZUKI helps BUTTERFLY change. HELGA enters, and helps GALLIMARD change into a tuxedo.)

GALLIMARD: I married a woman older than myself—Helga.

HELGA: My father was ambassador to Australia. I grew up among criminals and kangaroos.

GALLIMARD: Hearing that brought me to the altar—
(HELGA exits.)

GALLIMARD: —where I took a vow renouncing love. No fantasy woman would ever want me, so, yes, I would settle for a quick leap up the career ladder. Passion, I banish, and in its place—practicality!

But my vows had long since lost their charm by the time we arrived in China. The sad truth is that all men want a beautiful woman, and the uglier the man, the greater the want.
(SUZUKI makes final adjustments of BUTTERFLY's costume, as does GALLIMARD of his tuxedo.)

GALLIMARD: I married late, at age thirty-one. I was faithful to my marriage for eight years. Until the day when, as a junior-level diplomat in puritanical Peking, in a parlor at the German ambassador's house, during the "Reign of a Hundred Flowers," I first saw her . . . singing the death scene from *Madame Butterfly*.
(SUZUKI runs offstage.)

SCENE VI: *German ambassador's house. Beijing. 1960.*

The upstage special area now becomes a stage. Several chairs face upstage, representing seating for some twenty guests in the parlor. A few "diplomats"— RENEE, MARC, TOULON—in formal dress enter and take seats.

GALLIMARD *also sits down, but turns towards us and continues to talk. Orchestral accompaniment on the tape is now replaced by a simple piano.* SONG *picks up the death scene from the point where* BUTTERFLY *uncovers the hara-kiri knife.*

GALLIMARD: The ending is pitiful. Pinkerton, in an act of great courage, stays home and sends his American wife to pick up Butterfly's child. The truth, long deferred, has come up to her door.
(SONG, playing BUTTERFLY, sings the lines from the opera in her own voice—which, though not classical, should be decent.)

SONG: "Con onor muore/chi non puo serbar/vita con onore."

GALLIMARD: *(simultaneously)* "Death with honor/ Is better than life/Life with dishonor."
(The stage is illuminated; we are now completely within an elegant diplomat's residence. SONG proceeds to play out an abbreviated death scene. Everyone in the room applauds.

SONG, *shyly, takes her bows. Others in the room rush to congratulate her.* GALLIMARD *remains with us.)*

GALLIMARD: They say in opera the voice is everything. That's probably why I'd never before enjoyed opera. Here . . . here was a Butterfly with little or no voice—but she had the grace, the delicacy . . . I believed this girl. I believed her suffering. I wanted to take her in my arms—so delicate, even I could protect her, take her home, pamper her until she smiled. *(Over the course of the preceding speech,* SONG *has broken from the upstage crowd and moved directly upstage of* GALLIMARD.)

SONG: Excuse me, Monsieur . . . ?

*(*GALLIMARD *turns upstage, shocked.)*

GALLIMARD: Oh! Gallimard. Mademoiselle . . . ? A beautiful . . .

SONG: Song Liling.

GALLIMARD: A beautiful performance.

SONG: Oh, please.

GALLIMARD: I usually—

SONG: You make me blush. I'm no opera singer at all.

GALLIMARD: I usually don't like *Butterfly.*

SONG: I can't blame you in the least.

GALLIMARD: I mean, the story—

SONG: Ridiculous.

GALLIMARD: I like the story, but . . . what?

SONG: Oh, you like it?

GALLIMARD: I . . . what I mean is, I've always seen it played by huge women in so much bad makeup.

SONG: Bad makeup is not unique to the West.

GALLIMARD: But, who can believe them?

SONG: And you believe me?

GALLIMARD: Absolutely. You were utterly convincing. It's the first time—

SONG: Convincing? As a Japanese woman? The Japanese used hundreds of our people for medical experiments during the war, you know. But I gather such an irony is lost on you.

GALLIMARD: No! I was about to say, it's the first time I've seen the beauty of the story.

SONG: Really?

GALLIMARD: Of her death. It's a . . . a pure sacrifice. He's unworthy, but what can she do? She loves him . . . so much. It's a very beautiful story.

SONG: Well, yes, to a Westerner.

GALLIMARD: Excuse me?

SONG: It's one of your favorite fantasies, isn't it? The submissive Oriental woman and the cruel white man.

GALLIMARD: Well, I didn't quite mean . . .

SONG: Consider it this way: what would you say if a blonde homecoming queen fell in love with a short Japanese businessman? He treats her cruelly, then goes home for three years, during which time she prays to his picture and turns down marriage from a young Kennedy. Then, when she learns he has remarried, she kills herself. Now, I believe you would consider this girl to be a deranged idiot, correct? But because it's an Oriental who kills herself for a Westerner— ah!—you find it beautiful.

(Silence.)

GALLIMARD: Yes . . . well . . . I see your point . . .

SONG: I will never do Butterfly again, Monsieur Gallimard. If you wish to see some real theatre, come to the Peking Opera sometime. Expand your mind.

*(*SONG *walks offstage.)*

GALLIMARD: *(to us)* So much for protecting her in my big Western arms.

SCENE VII: M. GALLIMARD'S *apartment. Beijing. 1960.*

GALLIMARD *changes from his tux into a casual suit.* HELGA *enters.*

GALLIMARD: The Chinese are an incredibly arrogant people.

HELGA: They warned us about that in Paris, remember?

GALLIMARD: Even Parisians consider them arrogant. That's a switch.

HELGA: What is it that Madame Su says? "We are a very old civilization." I never know if she's talking about her country or herself.

GALLIMARD: I walk around here, all I hear every day, everywhere is how *old* this culture is. The fact that "old" may be synonymous with "senile" doesn't occur to them.

HELGA: You're not going to change them. "East is east, west is west, and . . ." whatever that guy said.

GALLIMARD: It's just that—silly. I met . . . at Ambassador Koening's tonight—you should've been there.

HELGA: Koening? Oh god, no. Did he enchant you all again with the history of Bavaria?

GALLIMARD: No. I met, I suppose, the Chinese equivalent of a diva. She's a singer in the Chinese opera.

HELGA: They have an opera, too? Do they sing in Chinese? Or maybe—in Italian?

GALLIMARD: Tonight, she did sing in Italian.

HELGA: How'd she manage that?

GALLIMARD: She must've been educated in the West before the Revolution. Her French is very good also. Anyway, she sang the death scene from *Madame Butterfly.*

HELGA: *Madame Butterfly!* Then I should have come. *(she begins humming, floating around the room as if dragging long kimono sleeves)* Did she have a nice costume? I think it's a classic piece of music.

GALLIMARD: That's what *I* thought, too. Don't let her hear you say that.

HELGA: What's wrong?

GALLIMARD: Evidently the Chinese hate it.

HELGA: She hated it, but she performed it anyway? Is she perverse?

GALLIMARD: They hate it because the white man gets the girl. Sour grapes if you ask me.

HELGA: Politics again? Why can't they just hear it as a piece of beautiful music? So, what's in their opera?

GALLIMARD: I don't know. But, whatever it is, I'm sure it must be *old.*
(HELGA exits.)

SCENE VIII: *Chinese opera house and the streets of Beijing. 1960.*

The sound of gongs clanging fills the stage.

GALLIMARD: My wife's innocent question kept ringing in my ears. I asked around, but no one knew anything about the Chinese opera. It took four weeks, but my curiosity overcame my cowardice. This Chinese diva—this unwilling Butterfly—what did she do to make her so proud?

The room was hot, and full of smoke. Wrinkled faces, old women, teeth missing—a man with a growth on his neck, like a human toad. All smiling, pipes falling from their mouths, cracking nuts between their teeth, a live chicken pecking at my foot—all looking, screaming, gawking . . . at her.
(The upstage area is suddenly hit with a harsh white light. It has become the stage for the Chinese opera performance. Two dancers enter, along with SONG. GALLIMARD *stands apart, watching.* SONG *glides gracefully amidst the two dancers. Drums suddenly slam to a halt.* SONG *strikes a pose, looking straight at* GALLIMARD. *Dancers exit. Light change. Pause, then* SONG *walks right off the stage and straight up to* GALLIMARD.)

SONG: Yes. You. White man. I'm looking straight at you.

GALLIMARD: Me?

SONG: You see any other white men? It was too easy to spot you. How often does a man in my audience come in a tie?
(SONG starts to remove her costume. Underneath, she wears simple baggy clothes. They are now backstage. The show is over.)

SONG: So, you are an adventurous imperialist?

GALLIMARD: I . . . thought it would further my education.

SONG: It took you four weeks. Why?

GALLIMARD: I've been busy.

SONG: Well, education has always been undervalued in the West, hasn't it?

GALLIMARD: *(laughing)* I don't think it's true.

SONG: No, you wouldn't. You're a Westerner. How can you objectively judge your own values?

GALLIMARD: I think it's possible to achieve some distance.

SONG: Do you? *(pause)* It stinks in here. Let's go.

GALLIMARD: These are the smells of your loyal fans.

SONG: I love them for being my fans, I hate the smell they leave behind. I too can distance myself from my people. *(she looks around, then whispers in his ear)* "Art for the masses" is a shitty excuse to keep artists poor. *(she pops a cigarette in her mouth)* Be a gentleman, will you? And light my cigarette.

(GALLIMARD fumbles for a match.)

GALLIMARD: I don't . . . smoke.

SONG: *(lighting her own)* Your loss. Had you lit my cigarette, I might have blown a puff of smoke right between your eyes. Come.

(They start to walk about the stage. It is a summer night on the Beijing streets. Sounds of the city play on the house speakers.)

SONG: How I wish there were even a tiny cafe to sit in. With cappuccinos, and men in tuxedos and bad expatriate jazz.

GALLIMARD: If my history serves me correctly, you weren't even allowed into the clubs in Shanghai before the Revolution.

SONG: Your history serves you poorly, Monsieur Gallimard. True, there were signs reading "No dogs and Chinamen." But a woman, especially a delicate Oriental woman—we always go where we please. Could you imagine it otherwise? Clubs in China filled with pasty, big-thighed white women, while thousands of slender lotus blossoms wait just outside the door? Never. The clubs would be empty. *(beat)* We have always held a certain fascination for you Caucasian men, have we not?

GALLIMARD: But . . . that fascination is imperialist, or so you tell me.

SONG: Do you believe everything I tell you? Yes. It is always imperialist. But sometimes . . . sometimes, it is also mutual. Oh—this is my flat.

GALLIMARD: I didn't even—

SONG: Thank you. Come another time and we will further expand your mind.

(SONG exits. GALLIMARD continues roaming the streets as he speaks to us.)

GALLIMARD: What was that? What did she mean, "Sometimes . . . it is mutual"? Women do not flirt with me. And I normally can't talk to them. But tonight, I held up my end of the conversation.

SCENE IX: GALLIMARD'S *bedroom. Beijing. 1960.*

HELGA *enters.*

HELGA: You didn't tell me you'd be home late.

GALLIMARD: I didn't intend to. Something came up.

HELGA: Oh! Like what?

GALLIMARD: I went to the . . . to the Dutch ambassador's home.

HELGA: Again?

GALLIMARD: There was a reception for a visiting scholar. He's writing a six-volume treatise on the Chinese revolution. We all gathered that meant he'd have to live here long enough to actually write six volumes, and we all expressed our deepest sympathies.

HELGA: Well, I had a good night too. I went with the ladies to a martial arts demonstration. Some of those men—when they break those thick boards—*(she mimes fanning herself)* whoo-whoo!

(HELGA exits. Lights dim.)

GALLIMARD: I lied to my wife. Why? I've never had any reason to lie before. But what reason did I have tonight? I didn't do anything wrong. That night, I had a dream. Other people, I've been told, have dreams where angels appear. Or dragons, or Sophia Loren in a towel. In my dream, Marc from school appeared.

(MARC enters, in a nightshirt and cap.)

MARC: Rene! You met a girl!

(GALLIMARD and MARC stumble down the Beijing streets. Night sounds over the speakers.)

GALLIMARD: It's not that amazing, thank you.

MARC: No! It's so monumental, I heard about it halfway around the world in my sleep!

GALLIMARD: I've met girls before, you know.

MARC: Name one. I've come across time and space to congratulate you. *(he hands* GALLIMARD *a bottle of wine)*

GALLIMARD: Marc, this is expensive.

MARC: On those rare occasions when you become a formless spirit, why not steal the best? *(*MARC *pops open the bottle, begins to share it with* GALLIMARD.*)*

GALLIMARD: You embarrass me. She . . . there's no reason to think she likes me.

MARC: "Sometimes, it is mutual"?

GALLIMARD: Oh.

MARC: "Mutual"? "Mutual"? What does that mean?

GALLIMARD: You heard!

MARC: It means the money is in the bank, you only have to write the check!

GALLIMARD: I am a married man!

MARC: And an excellent one too. I cheated after . . . six months. Then again and again, until now—three hundred girls in twelve years.

GALLIMARD: I don't think we should hold that up as a model.

MARC: Of course not! My life—it is disgusting! Phooey! Phooey! But, you—you are the model husband.

GALLIMARD: Anyway, it's impossible. I'm a foreigner.

MARC: Ah, yes. She cannot love you, it is taboo, but something deep inside her heart . . . she cannot help herself . . . she must surrender to you. It is her destiny.

GALLIMARD: How do you imagine all this?

MARC: The same way you do. It's an old story. It's in our blood. They fear us, Rene. Their women fear us. And their men—their men hate us. And, you know something? They are all correct. *(They spot a light in a window.)*

MARC: There! There, Rene!

GALLIMARD: It's her window.

MARC: Late at night—it burns. The light—it burns for you.

GALLIMARD: I won't look. It's not respectful.

MARC: We don't have to be respectful. We're foreign devils. *(Enter* SONG, *in a sheer robe. The "One Fine Day" aria creeps in over the speakers. With her back to us,* SONG *mimes attending to her toilette. Her robe comes loose, revealing her white shoulders.)*

MARC: All your life you've waited for a beautiful girl who would lay down for you. All your life you've smiled like a saint when it's happened to every other man you know. And you see them in magazines and you see them in movies. And you wonder, what's wrong with me? Will anyone beautiful ever want me? As the years pass, your hair thins and you struggle to hold onto even your hopes. Stop struggling, Rene. The wait is over. *(he exits.)*

GALLIMARD: Marc? Marc? *(At that moment,* SONG, *her back still towards us, drops her robe. A second of her naked back, then a sound cue: a phone ringing, very loud. Blackout, followed in the next beat by a special up on the bedroom area, where a phone now sits.* GALLIMARD *stumbles across the stage and picks up the phone. Sound cue out. Over the course of his conversation, area lights fill in the vicinity of his bed. It is the following morning.)*

GALLIMARD: Yes? Hello?

SONG: *(offstage)* Is it very early?

GALLIMARD: Why, yes.

SONG: *(offstage)* How early?

GALLIMARD: It's . . . it's 5:30. Why are you—?

SONG: *(offstage)* But it's light outside. Already.

GALLIMARD: It is. The sun must be in confusion today. *(Over the course of* SONG'S *next speech, her upstage special comes up again. She sits in a chair, legs crossed, in a robe, telephone to her ear.)*

SONG: I waited until I saw the sun. That was as much discipline as I could manage for one night. Do you forgive me?

GALLIMARD: Of course . . . for what?

SONG: Then I'll ask you quickly. Are you really interested in the opera?

GALLIMARD: Why, yes. Yes I am.

SONG: Then come again next Thursday. I am playing *The Drunken Beauty.* May I count on you?

GALLIMARD: Yes. You may.

SONG: Perfect. Well, I must be getting to bed. I'm exhausted. It's been a very long night for me.
(SONG *hangs up; special on her goes off.* GALLIMARD *begins to dress for work.*)

SCENE X: SONG LILING'S *apartment. Beijing. 1960.*

GALLIMARD: I returned to the opera that next week, and the week after that . . . she keeps our meetings so short—perhaps fifteen, twenty minutes at most. So I am left each week with a thirst which is intensified. In this way, fifteen weeks have gone by. I am starting to doubt the words of my friend Marc. But no, not really. In my heart, I know she has . . . an interest in me. I suspect this is her way. She is outwardly bold and outspoken, yet her heart is shy and afraid. It is the Oriental in her at war with her Western education.

SONG: *(offstage)* I will be out in an instant. Ask the servant for anything you want.

GALLIMARD: Tonight, I have finally been invited to enter her apartment. Though the idea is almost beyond belief, I believe she is afraid of me.
(GALLIMARD *looks around the room. He picks up a picture in a frame, studies it. Without his noticing,* SONG *enters, dressed elegantly in a black gown from the twenties. She stands in the doorway looking like Anna May Wong.*)

SONG: That is my father.

GALLIMARD: *(surprised)* Mademoiselle Song . . .
(She *glides up to him, snatches away the picture.*)

SONG: It is very good that he did not live to see the Revolution. They would, no doubt, have made him kneel on broken glass. Not that he didn't deserve such a punishment. But he is my father. I would've hated to see it happen.

GALLIMARD: I'm very honored that you've allowed me to visit your home.
(SONG *curtsys.*)

SONG: Thank you. Oh! Haven't you been poured any tea?

GALLIMARD: I'm really not—

SONG: *(to her offstage servant)* Shu-Fang! Cha! Kwai-lah! *(to* GALLIMARD) I'm sorry. You want everything to be perfect—

GALLIMARD: Please.

SONG: —and before the evening even begins—

GALLIMARD: I'm really not thirsty.

SONG: —it's ruined.

GALLIMARD: *(sharply)* Mademoiselle Song!
(SONG *sits down.*)

SONG: I'm sorry.

GALLIMARD: What are you apologizing for now?
(*Pause;* SONG *starts to giggle.*)

SONG: I don't know!
(GALLIMARD *laughs.*)

GALLIMARD: Exactly my point.

SONG: Oh, I am silly. Lightheaded. I promise not to apologize for anything else tonight, do you hear me?

GALLIMARD: That's a good girl!
(SHU-FANG, *a servant girl, comes out with a tea tray and starts to pour.*)

SONG: *(to* SHU-FANG) No! I'll pour myself for the gentleman!
(SHU-FANG, *staring at* GALLIMARD, *exits.*)

SONG: No, I . . . I don't even know why I invited you up.

GALLIMARD: Well, I'm glad you did.
(SONG *looks around the room.*)

SONG: There is an element of danger to your presence.

GALLIMARD: Oh?

SONG: You must know.

GALLIMARD: It doesn't concern me. We both know why I'm here.

SONG: It doesn't concern me either. No . . . well perhaps . . .

GALLIMARD: What?

SONG: Perhaps I am slightly afraid of scandal.

GALLIMARD: What are we doing?

SONG: I'm entertaining you. In my parlor.

GALLIMARD: In France, that would hardly—

SONG: France. France is a country living in the modern era. Perhaps even ahead of it. China is a nation whose soul is firmly rooted two thousand years in the past. What I do, even pouring the tea for you now . . . it has . . . implications. The walls and windows say so. Even my own heart, strapped inside this Western dress . . . even it says things—things I don't care to hear. *(SONG hands GALLIMARD a cup of tea. GALLI-MARD puts his hand over both the teacup and SONG'S hand.)*

GALLIMARD: This is a beautiful dress.

SONG: Don't.

GALLIMARD: What?

SONG: I don't even know if it looks right on me.

GALLIMARD: Believe me—

SONG: You are from France. You see so many beautiful women.

GALLIMARD: France? Since when are the European women—?

SONG: Oh! What am I trying to do, anyway?! *(SONG runs to the door, composes herself, then turns towards GALLIMARD.)*

SONG: Monsieur Gallimard, perhaps you should go.

GALLIMARD: But . . . why?

SONG: There's something wrong about this.

GALLIMARD: I don't see what.

SONG: I feel . . . I am not myself.

GALLIMARD: No. You're nervous.

SONG: Please. Hard as I try to be modern, to speak like a man, to hold a Western woman's strong face up to my own . . . in the end, I fail. A small, frightened heart beats too quickly and gives me away. Monsieur Gallimard, I'm a Chinese girl. I've never . . . never invited a man up to my flat before. The forwardness of my actions makes my skin burn.

GALLIMARD: What are you afraid of? Certainly not me, I hope.

SONG: I'm a modest girl.

GALLIMARD: I know. And very beautiful. *(he touches her hair)*

SONG: Please—go now. The next time you see me, I shall again be myself.

GALLIMARD: I like you the way you are right now.

SONG: You are a cad.

GALLIMARD: What do you expect? I'm a foreign devil. *(GALLIMARD walks downstage. SONG exits.)*

GALLIMARD: *(to us)* Did you hear the way she talked about Western women? Much differently than the first night. She does—she feels inferior to them—and to me.

SCENE XI: *The French embassy. Beijing. 1960.*

GALLIMARD *moves towards a desk.*

GALLIMARD: I determined to try an experiment. In *Madame Butterfly*, Cio-Cio-San fears that the Western man who catches a butterfly will pierce its heart with a needle, then leave it to perish. I began to wonder: had I, too, caught a butterfly who would writhe on a needle? *(MARC enters, dressed as a bureaucrat, holding a stack of papers. As GALLIMARD speaks, MARC hands papers to him. He peruses, then signs, stamps or rejects them.)*

GALLIMARD: Over the next five weeks, I worked like a dynamo. I stopped going to the opera, I didn't phone or write her. I knew this little flower was waiting for me to call, and, as I wickedly refused to do so, I felt for the first time that rush of power—the absolute power of a man. *(MARC continues acting as the bureaucrat, but he now speaks as himself.)*

MARC: Rene! It's me!

GALLIMARD: Marc—I hear your voice everywhere now. Even in the midst of work.

MARC: That's because I'm watching you—all the time.

GALLIMARD: You were always the most popular guy in school.

MARC: Well, there's no guarantee of failure in life like happiness in high school. Somehow I knew I'd end up in the suburbs working for Renault and you'd be in the Orient picking exotic women off the trees. And they say there's no justice.

GALLIMARD: That's why you were my friend?

MARC: I gave you a little of my life, so that now you can give me some of yours. *(pause)* Remember Isabelle?

GALLIMARD: Of course I remember! She was my first experience.

MARC: We all wanted to ball her. But she only wanted me.

GALLIMARD: I had her.

MARC: Right. You balled her.

GALLIMARD: You were the only one who ever believed me.

MARC: Well, there's a good reason for that. *(beat)* C'mon. You must've guessed.

GALLIMARD: You told me to wait in the bushes by the cafeteria that night. The next thing I knew, she was on me. Dress up in the air.

MARC: She never wore underwear.

GALLIMARD: My arms were pinned to the dirt.

MARC: She loved the superior position. A girl ahead of her time.

GALLIMARD: I looked up, and there was this woman . . . bouncing up and down on my loins.

MARC: Screaming, right?

GALLIMARD: Screaming, and breaking off the branches all around me, and pounding my butt up and down into the dirt.

MARC: Huffing and puffing like a locomotive.

GALLIMARD: And in the middle of all this, the leaves were getting into my mouth, my legs were losing circulation, I thought, "God. So this is *it?*"

MARC: You thought that?

GALLIMARD: Well, I was worried about my legs falling off.

MARC: You didn't have a good time?

GALLIMARD: No, that's not what I—I had a great time!

MARC: You're sure?

GALLIMARD: Yeah. Really.

MARC: 'Cuz I wanted you to have a good time.

GALLIMARD: I did.

(Pause.)

MARC: Shit. *(pause)* When all is said and done, she was kind of a lousy lay, wasn't she? I mean, there was a lot of energy there, but you never knew what she was doing with it. Like when she yelled "I'm coming!"—hell, it was so loud, you wanted to go "Look, it's not that big a deal."

GALLIMARD: I got scared. I thought she meant someone was actually coming. *(pause)* But, Marc?

MARC: What?

GALLIMARD: Thanks.

MARC: Oh, don't mention it.

GALLIMARD: It was my first experience.

MARC: Yeah. You got her.

GALLIMARD: I got her.

MARC: Wait! Look at that letter again!

(GALLIMARD picks up one of the papers he's been stamping, and rereads it.)

GALLIMARD: *(to us)* After six weeks, they began to arrive. The letters.

(Upstage special on SONG, as MADAME BUTTERFLY. The scene is underscored by the "Love Duet.")

SONG: Did we fight? I do not know. Is the opera no longer of interest to you? Please come—my audiences miss the white devil in their midst.

(GALLIMARD looks up from the letter, towards us.)

GALLIMARD: *(to us)* A concession, but much too dignified. *(beat; he discards the letter)* I skipped the opera again that week to complete a position paper on trade.

(The bureaucrat hands him another letter.)

SONG: Six weeks have passed since last we met. Is this your practice—to leave friends in the lurch? Sometimes I hate you, sometimes I hate myself, but always I miss you.

GALLIMARD: *(to us)* Better, but I don't like the way she calls me "friend." When a woman calls a man her "friend," she's calling him a eunuch or a homosexual. *(beat; he discards the letter)* I was absent from the opera for the seventh week, feeling a sudden urge to clean out my files.

(Bureaucrat hands him another letter.)

SONG: Your rudeness is beyond belief. I don't deserve this cruelty. Don't bother to call. I'll have you turned away at the door.

GALLIMARD: *(to us)* I didn't. *(he discards the letter; bureaucrat hands him another)* And then finally, the letter that concluded my experiment.

SONG: I am out of words. I can hide behind dignity no longer. What do you want? I have already given you my shame.

(GALLIMARD gives the letter back to MARC, slowly. Special on SONG fades out.)

GALLIMARD: *(to us)* Reading it, I became suddenly ashamed. Yes, my experiment had been a success. She was turning on my needle. But the victory seemed hollow.

MARC: Hollow? Are you crazy?

GALLIMARD: Nothing, Marc. Please go away.

MARC: *(exiting, with papers)* Haven't I taught you anything?

GALLIMARD: "I have already given you my shame." I had to attend a reception that evening. On the way, I felt sick. If there is a God, surely he would punish me now. I had finally gained power over a beautiful woman, only to abuse it cruelly. There must be justice in the world. I had the strange feeling that the ax would fall this very evening.

SCENE XII: AMBASSADOR TOULON'S *residence. Beijing. 1960.*

Sound cue: party noises. Light change. We are now in a spacious residence. TOULON, *the French ambassador, enters and taps* GALLIMARD *on the shoulder.*

TOULON: Gallimard? Can I have a word? Over here.

GALLIMARD: *(to us)* Manuel Toulon. French ambassador to China. He likes to think of us all as his children. Rather like God.

TOULON: Look, Gallimard, there's not much to say. I've liked you. From the day you walked in. You were no leader, but you were tidy and efficient.

GALLIMARD: Thank you, sir.

TOULON: Don't jump the gun. Okay, our needs in China are changing. It's embarrassing that we lost Indochina. Someone just wasn't on the ball there. I don't mean you personally, of course.

GALLIMARD: Thank you, sir.

TOULON: We're going to be doing a lot more information-gathering in the future. The nature of our work here is changing. Some people are just going to have to go. It's nothing personal.

GALLIMARD: Oh.

TOULON: Want to know a secret? Vice-Consul LeBon is being transferred.

GALLIMARD: *(to us)* My immediate superior!

TOULON: And most of his department.

GALLIMARD: *(to us)* Just as I feared! God has seen my evil heart—

TOULON: But not you.

GALLIMARD: *(to us)*—and he's taking her away just as . . . *(to* TOULON*)* Excuse me, sir?

TOULON: Scare you? I think I did. Cheer up, Gallimard. I want you to replace LeBon as vice-consul.

GALLIMARD: You—? Yes, well, thank you, sir.

TOULON: Anytime.

GALLIMARD: I . . . accept with great humility.

TOULON: Humility won't be part of the job. You're going to coordinate the revamped intelligence division. Want to know a secret? A year ago, you would've been out. But the past few months, I don't know how it happened, you've become this new aggressive confident . . . thing. And they also tell me you get along with the Chinese. So I think you're a lucky man, Gallimard. Congratulations.

(They shake hands. TOULON *exits. Party noises out.* GALLIMARD *stumbles across a darkened stage.)*

GALLIMARD: Vice-consul? Impossible! As I stumbled out of the party, I saw it written across the sky: There is no God. Or, no—say that there is a God. But that God . . . understands. Of course! God who creates Eve to serve Adam, who blesses Solomon with his harem but ties Jezebel to a burning bed—that God is a man. And he understands! At age thirty-nine, I was suddenly initiated into the way of the world.

SCENE XIII: SONG LILING'S *apartment. Beijing. 1960.*

SONG *enters, in a sheer dressing gown.*

SONG: Are you crazy?

GALLIMARD: Mademoiselle Song—

SONG: To come here—at this hour? After . . . after eight weeks?

GALLIMARD: It's the most amazing—

SONG: You bang on my door? Scare my servants, scandalize the neighbors?

GALLIMARD: I've been promoted. To vice-consul. (*Pause.*)

SONG: And what is that supposed to mean to me?

GALLIMARD: Are you my Butterfly?

SONG: What are you saying?

GALLIMARD: I've come tonight for an answer: are you my Butterfly?

SONG: Don't you know already?

GALLIMARD: I want you to say it.

SONG: I don't want to say it.

GALLIMARD: So, that is your answer?

SONG: You know how I feel about—

GALLIMARD: I do remember one thing.

SONG: What?

GALLIMARD: In the letter I received today.

SONG: Don't.

GALLIMARD: "I have already given you my shame."

SONG: It's enough that I even wrote it.

GALLIMARD: Well, then—

SONG: I shouldn't have it splashed across my face.

GALLIMARD: —if that's all true—

SONG: Stop!

GALLIMARD: Then what is one more short answer?

SONG: I don't want to!

GALLIMARD: Are you my Butterfly? (*silence; he crosses the room and begins to touch her hair*) I want from you honesty. There should be nothing false between us. No false pride. (*Pause.*)

SONG: Yes, I am. I am your Butterfly.

GALLIMARD: Then let me be honest with you. It is because of you that I was promoted tonight. You have changed my life forever. My little Butterfly, there should be no more secrets: I love you.
(*He starts to kiss her roughly. She resists slightly.*)

SONG: No . . . no . . . gently . . . please, I've never . . .

GALLIMARD: No?

SONG: I've tried to appear experienced, but . . . the truth is . . . no.

GALLIMARD: Are you cold?

SONG: Yes. Cold.

GALLIMARD: Then we will go very, very slowly. (*He starts to caress her; her gown begins to open.*)

SONG: No . . . let me . . . keep my clothes . . .

GALLIMARD: But . . .

SONG: Please . . . it all frightens me. I'm a modest Chinese girl.

GALLIMARD: My poor little treasure.

SONG: I am your treasure. Though inexperienced, I am not . . . ignorant. They teach us things, our mothers, about pleasing a man.

GALLIMARD: Yes?

SONG: I'll do my best to make you happy. Turn off the lights.
(*GALLIMARD gets up and heads for a lamp. SONG, propped up on one elbow, tosses her hair back and smiles.*)

SONG: Monsieur Gallimard?

GALLIMARD: Yes, Butterfly?

SONG: "Vieni, vieni!"

GALLIMARD: "Come, darling."

SONG: "Ah! Dolce notte!"

GALLIMARD: "Beautiful night."

SONG: "Tutto estatico d'amor ride il ciel!"

GALLIMARD: "All ecstatic with love, the heavens are filled with laughter."
(*He turns off the lamp. Blackout.*)

ACT TWO

SCENE I: M. GALLIMARD'S *cell. Paris. Present.*

Lights up on GALLIMARD. *He sits in his cell, reading from a leaflet.*

GALLIMARD: This, from a contemporary critic's commentary on *Madame Butterfly:* "Pinkerton suffers from . . . being an obnoxious bounder whom every man in the audience itches to kick." Bully for us men in the audience! Then, in the same note: "Butterfly is the most irresistibly appealing of Puccini's 'Little Women.' Watching the succession of her humiliations is like watching a child under torture." *(he tosses the pamphlet over his shoulder)* I suggest that, while we men may all want to kick Pinkerton, very few of us would pass up the opportunity to *be* Pinkerton.

(GALLIMARD moves out of his cell.)

SCENE II: GALLIMARD *and* BUTTERFLY'S *flat. Beijing. 1960.*

We are in a simple but well-decorated parlor. GALLIMARD *moves to sit on a sofa, while* SONG, *dressed in a chong sam, enters and curls up at his feet.*

GALLIMARD: *(to us)* We secured a flat on the outskirts of Peking. Butterfly, as I was calling her now, decorated our "home" with Western furniture and Chinese antiques. And there, on a few stolen afternoons or evenings each week, Butterfly commenced her education.

SONG: The Chinese men—they keep us down.

GALLIMARD: Even in the "New Society"?

SONG: In the "New Society," we are all kept ignorant equally. That's one of the exciting things about loving a Western man. I know you are not threatened by a woman's education.

GALLIMARD: I'm no saint, Butterfly.

SONG: But you come from a progressive society.

GALLIMARD: We're not always reminding each other how "old" we are, if that's what you mean.

SONG: Exactly. We Chinese—once, I suppose, it is true, we ruled the world. But so what? How much more exciting to be part of the society ruling the world today. Tell me—what's happening in Vietnam?

GALLIMARD: Oh, Butterfly—you want me to bring my work home?

SONG: I want to know what you know. To be impressed by my man. It's not the particulars so much as the fact that you're making decisions which change the shape of the world.

GALLIMARD: Not the world. At best, a small corner.
(TOULON enters, and sits at a desk upstage.)

SCENE III: *French embassy. Beijing. 1961.*

GALLIMARD *moves downstage, to* TOULON'S *desk.* SONG *remains upstage, watching.*

TOULON: And a more troublesome corner is hard to imagine.

GALLIMARD: So, the Americans plan to begin bombing?

TOULON: This is very secret, Gallimard: yes. The Americans don't have an embassy here. They're asking us to be their eyes and ears. Say Jack Kennedy signed an order to bomb North Vietnam, Laos. How would the Chinese react?

GALLIMARD: I think the Chinese will squawk—

TOULON: Uh-huh.

GALLIMARD: —but, in their hearts, they don't even like Ho Chi Minh.
(Pause.)

TOULON: What a bunch of jerks. Vietnam was *our* colony. Not only didn't the Americans help us fight to keep them, but now, seven years later, they've come back to grab the territory for themselves. It's very irritating.

GALLIMARD: With all due respect, sir, why should the Americans have won our war for us back in '54 if we didn't have the will to win it ourselves?

TOULON: You're kidding, aren't you?
(Pause.)

GALLIMARD: The Orientals simply want to be associated with whoever shows the most strength and power. You live with the Chinese, sir. Do you think they like Communism?

TOULON: I live in China. Not with the Chinese.

GALLIMARD: Well, I—

TOULON: *You* live with the Chinese.

GALLIMARD: Excuse me?

TOULON: I can't keep a secret.

GALLIMARD: What are you saying?

TOULON: Only that I'm not immune to gossip. So, you're keeping a native mistress. Don't answer. It's none of my business. *(pause)* I'm sure she must be gorgeous.

GALLIMARD: Well . . .

TOULON: I'm impressed. You have the stamina to go out into the streets and hunt one down. Some of us have to be content with the wives of the expatriate community.

GALLIMARD: I do feel . . . fortunate.

TOULON: So, Gallimard, you've got the inside knowledge—what *do* the Chinese think?

GALLIMARD: Deep down, they miss the old days. You know, cappuccinos, men in tuxedos—

TOULON: So what do we tell the Americans about Vietnam?

GALLIMARD: Tell them there's a natural affinity between the West and the Orient.

TOULON: And that you speak from experience?

GALLIMARD: The Orientals are people too. They want the good things we can give them. If the Americans demonstrate the will to win, the Vietnamese will welcome them into a mutually beneficial union.

TOULON: I don't see how the Vietnamese can stand up to American firepower.

GALLIMARD: Orientals will always submit to a greater force.

TOULON: I'll note your opinions in my report. The Americans always love to hear how "welcome" they'll be. *(he starts to exit)*

GALLIMARD: Sir?

TOULON: Mmmm?

GALLIMARD: This . . . rumor you've heard.

TOULON: Uh-huh?

GALLIMARD: How . . . widespread do you think it is?

TOULON: It's only widespread within this embassy. Where nobody talks because everybody is guilty. We were worried about you, Gallimard. We thought you were the only one here without a secret. Now you go and find a lotus blossom . . . and top us all. *(he exits)*

GALLIMARD: *(to us)* Toulon knows! And he approves! I was learning the benefits of being a man. We form our own clubs, sit behind thick doors, smoke—and celebrate the fact that we're still boys. *(he starts to move downstage, towards* SONG*)* So, over the—

(Suddenly COMRADE CHIN *enters.* GALLIMARD *backs away.)*

GALLIMARD: *(to* SONG*)* No! Why does she have to come in?

SONG: Rene, be sensible. How can they understand the story without her? Now, don't embarrass yourself.

*(*GALLIMARD *moves down center.)*

GALLIMARD: *(to us)* Now, you will see why my story is so amusing to so many people. Why they snicker at parties in disbelief. Please—try to understand it from my point of view. We are all prisoners of our time and place. *(he exits)*

SCENE IV: GALLIMARD *and* BUTTERFLY'S *flat. Beijing. 1961.*

SONG: *(to us)* 1961. The flat Monsieur Gallimard rented for us. An evening after he has gone.

CHIN: Okay, see if you find out when the Americans plan to start bombing Vietnam. If you can find out what cities, even better.

SONG: I'll do my best, but I don't want to arouse his suspicions.

CHIN: Yeah, sure, of course. So, what else?

SONG: The Americans will increase troops in Vietnam to 170,000 soldiers with 120,000 militia and 11,000 American advisors.

CHIN: *(writing)* Wait, wait. 120,000 militia and—

SONG: —11,000 American—

CHIN: —American advisors. *(beat)* How do you remember so much?

SONG: I'm an actor.

CHIN: Yeah. *(beat)* Is that how come you dress like that?

SONG: Like what, Miss Chin?

CHIN: Like that dress! You're wearing a dress. And every time I come here, you're wearing a dress. Is that because you're an actor? Or what?

SONG: It's a . . . disguise, Miss Chin.

CHIN: Actors, I think they're all weirdos. My mother tells me actors are like gamblers or prostitutes or—

SONG: It helps me in my assignment.

(Pause.)

CHIN: You're not gathering information in any way that violates Communist Party principles, are you?

SONG: Why would I do that?

CHIN: Just checking. Remember: when working for the Great Proletarian State, you represent our Chairman Mao in every position you take.

SONG: I'll try to imagine the Chairman taking my positions.

CHIN: We all think of him this way. Good-bye, comrade. *(she starts to exit)* Comrade?

SONG: Yes?

CHIN: Don't forget: there is no homosexuality in China!

SONG: Yes, I've heard.

CHIN: Just checking. *(she exits)*

SONG: *(to us)* What passes for a woman in modern China.

(GALLIMARD sticks his head out from the wings.)

GALLIMARD: Is she gone?

SONG: Yes, Rene. Please continue in your own fashion.

SCENE V: *Beijing. 1961–63.*

GALLIMARD *moves to the couch where* SONG *still sits. He lies down in her lap, and she strokes his forehead.*

GALLIMARD: *(to us)* And so, over the years 1961, '62, '63, we settled into our routine, Butterfly and I. She would always have prepared a light snack and then, ever so delicately, and only if I agreed, she would start to pleasure me. With her hands, her mouth . . . too many ways to explain, and too sad, given my present situation. But mostly we would talk. About my life. Perhaps there is nothing more rare than to find a woman who passionately listens.

(SONG remains upstage, listening, as HELGA enters and plays a scene downstage with GALLIMARD.)

HELGA: Rene, I visited Dr. Bolleart this morning.

GALLIMARD: Why? Are you ill?

HELGA: No, no. You see, I wanted to ask him . . . that question we've been discussing.

GALLIMARD: And I told you, it's only a matter of time. Why did you bring a doctor into this? We just have to keep trying—like a crapshoot, actually.

HELGA: I went, I'm sorry. But listen: he says there's nothing wrong with me.

GALLIMARD: You see? Now, will you stop—?

HELGA: Rene, he says he'd like you to go in and take some tests.

GALLIMARD: Why? So he can find there's nothing wrong with both of us?

HELGA: Rene, I don't ask for much. One trip! One visit! And then, whatever you want to do about it—you decide.

GALLIMARD: You're assuming he'll find something defective!

HELGA: No! Of course not! Whatever he finds—if he finds nothing, we decide what to do about nothing! But go!

GALLIMARD: If he finds nothing, we keep trying. Just like we do now.

HELGA: But at least we'll know! *(pause)* I'm sorry. *(she starts to exit)*

GALLIMARD: Do you really want me to see Dr. Bolleart?

HELGA: Only if you want a child, Rene. We have to face the fact that time is running out. Only if you want a child. *(she exits)*

GALLIMARD: *(to SONG)* I'm a modern man, Butterfly. And yet, I don't want to go. It's the same old voodoo. I feel like God himself is laughing at me if I can't produce a child.

SONG: You men of the West—you're obsessed by your odd desire for equality. Your wife can't give you a child, and *you're* going to the doctor?

GALLIMARD: Well, you see, she's already gone.

SONG: And because this incompetent can't find the defect, you now have to subject yourself to him? It's unnatural.

GALLIMARD: Well, what is the "natural" solution?

SONG: In Imperial China, when a man found that one wife was inadequate, he turned to another—to give him his son.

GALLIMARD: What do you—? I can't . . . marry you, yet.

SONG: Please. I'm not asking you to be my husband. But I am already your wife.

GALLIMARD: Do you want to . . . have my child?

SONG: I thought you'd never ask.

GALLIMARD: But, your career . . . your—

SONG: Phooey on my career! That's your Western
mind, twisting itself into strange shapes again.
Of course I love my career. But what would I
love most of all? To feel something inside me—
day and night—something I know is yours.
(pause) Promise me . . . you won't go to this
doctor. Who is this Western quack to set himself as judge over the man I love? I know who is
a man, and who is not. *(she exits)*

GALLIMARD: *(to us)* Dr. Bolleart? Of course I
didn't go. What man would?

SCENE VI: *Beijing. 1963.*

Party noises over the house speakers. RENEE *enters,
wearing a revealing gown.*

GALLIMARD: 1963. A party at the Austrian embassy. None of us could remember the Austrian
ambassador's name, which seemed somehow
appropriate. *(to* RENEE*)* So, I tell the Americans, Diem must go. The U.S. wants to be respected by the Vietnamese, and yet they're
propping up this nobody seminarian as her
president. A man whose claim to fame is his
sister-in-law imposing fanatic "moral order"
campaigns? Oriental women—when they're
good, they're very good, but when they're bad,
they're Christians.

RENEE: Yeah.

GALLIMARD: And what do you do?

RENEE: I'm a student. My father exports a lot of
useless stuff to the Third World.

GALLIMARD: How useless?

RENEE: You know. Squirt guns, confectioner's
sugar, Hoola Hoops . . .

GALLIMARD: I'm sure they appreciate the sugar.

RENEE: I'm here for two years to study Chinese.

GALLIMARD: Two years?

RENEE: That's what everybody says.

GALLIMARD: When did you arrive?

RENEE: Three weeks ago.

GALLIMARD: And?

RENEE: I like it. It's primitive, but . . . well,
this is the place to learn Chinese, so here I am.

GALLIMARD: Why Chinese?

RENEE: I think it'll be important someday.

GALLIMARD: You do?

RENEE: Don't ask me when, but . . . that's what
I think.

GALLIMARD: Well, I agree with you. One hundred
percent. That's very farsighted.

RENEE: Yeah. Well of course, my father thinks
I'm a complete weirdo.

GALLIMARD: He'll thank you someday.

RENEE: Like when the Chinese start buying
Hoola Hoops?

GALLIMARD: There're a billion bellies out there.

RENEE: And if they end up taking over the world—
well, then I'll be lucky to know Chinese too,
right?
(Pause.)

GALLIMARD: At this point, I don't see how the
Chinese can possibly take—

RENEE: You know what I *don't* like about China?

GALLIMARD: Excuse me? No—what?

RENEE: Nothing to do at night.

GALLIMARD: You come to parties at embassies
like everyone else.

RENEE: Yeah, but they get out at ten. And then
what?

GALLIMARD: I'm afraid the Chinese idea of a dance
hall is a dirt floor and a man with a flute.

RENEE: Are you married?

GALLIMARD: Yes. Why?

RENEE: You wanna . . . fool around?
(Pause.)

GALLIMARD: Sure.

RENEE: I'll wait for you outside. What's your name?

GALLIMARD: Gallimard. Rene.

RENEE: Weird. I'm Renee too. *(she exits)*

GALLIMARD: *(to us)* And so, I embarked on my first
extra-extra-marital affair. Renee was picture
perfect. With a body like those girls in the
magazines. If I put a tissue paper over my eyes, I

wouldn't have been able to tell the difference. And it was exciting to be with someone who wasn't afraid to be seen completely naked. But is it possible for a woman to be *too* uninhibited, *too* willing, so as to seem almost too . . . masculine?

(CHUCK BERRY *blares from the house speakers, then comes down in volume as* RENEE *enters, toweling her hair.*)

RENEE: You have a nice weenie.

GALLIMARD: What?

RENEE: You have a nice penis.

GALLIMARD: Oh. Well, thank you. That's very . . .

RENEE: What—can't take a compliment?

GALLIMARD: No, it's very . . . reassuring.

RENEE: But most girls don't come out and say it, huh?

GALLIMARD: And also . . . what did you call it?

RENEE: Oh. Most girls don't call it a "weenie," huh?

GALLIMARD: It sounds very—

RENEE: Small, I know.

GALLIMARD: I was going to say, "young."

RENEE: Yeah. Young, small, same thing. Most guys are pretty, uh, sensitive about that. Like, you know, I had a boyfriend back home in Denmark. I got mad at him once and called him a little weeniehead. He got so mad! He said at least I should call him a great big weeniehead.

GALLIMARD: I suppose I just say "penis."

RENEE: Yeah. That's pretty clinical. There's "cock," but that sounds like a chicken. And "prick" is painful, and "dick" is like you're talking about someone who's not in the room.

GALLIMARD: Yes. It's a . . . bigger problem than I imagined.

RENEE: I—I think maybe it's because I really don't know what to do with them—that's why I call them "weenies."

GALLIMARD: Well, you did quite well with . . . mine.

RENEE: Thanks, but I mean, really *do* with them. Like, okay, have you ever looked at one? I mean, really?

GALLIMARD: No, I suppose when it's part of you, you sort of take it for granted.

RENEE: I guess. But, like, it just hangs there. This little . . . flap of flesh. And there's so much fuss that we make about it. Like, I think the reason we fight wars is because we wear clothes. Because no one knows—between the men, I mean—who has the bigger . . . weenie. So, if I'm a guy with a small one, I'm going to build a really big building or take over a really big piece of land or write a really long book so the other men don't know, right? But, see, it never really works, that's the problem. I mean, you conquer the country, or whatever, but you're still wearing clothes, so there's no way to prove absolutely whose is bigger or smaller. And that's what we call a civilized society. The whole world run by a bunch of men with pricks the size of pins. (*she exits*)

GALLIMARD: (*to us*) This was simply not acceptable.

(*A high-pitched chime rings through the air.* SONG, *dressed as* BUTTERFLY, *appears in the up-stage special. She is obviously distressed. Her body swoons as she attempts to clip the stems of flowers she's arranging in a vase.*)

GALLIMARD: But I kept up our affair, wildly, for several months. Why? I believe because of Butterfly. She knew the secret I was trying to hide. But, unlike a Western woman, she didn't confront me, threaten, even pout. I remembered the words of Puccini's *Butterfly:*

SONG: "Noi siamo gente avvezza/alle piccole cose/umili e silenziose."

GALLIMARD: "I come from a people/Who are accustomed to little/Humble and silent." I saw Pinkerton and Butterfly, and what she would say if he were unfaithful . . . nothing. She would cry, alone, into those wildly soft sleeves, once full of possessions, now empty to collect her tears. It was her tears and her silence that excited me, every time I visited Renee.

TOULON: (*offstage*) Gallimard!

(TOULON *enters.* GALLIMARD *turns towards him. During the next section,* SONG, *up center, begins to dance with the flowers. It is a drunken dance, where she breaks small pieces off the stems.)*

TOULON: They're killing him.

GALLIMARD: Who? I'm sorry? What?

TOULON: Bother you to come over at this late hour?

GALLIMARD: No . . . of course not.

TOULON: Not after you hear my secret. Champagne?

GALLIMARD: Um . . . thank you.

TOULON: You're surprised. There's something that you've wanted, Gallimard. No, not a promotion. Next time. Something in the world. You're not aware of this, but there's an informal gossip circle among intelligence agents. And some of ours heard from some of the Americans—

GALLIMARD: Yes?

TOULON: That the U.S. will allow the Vietnamese generals to stage a coup . . . and assassinate President Diem.

(The chime rings again. TOULON freezes. GALLIMARD turns upstage and looks at BUTTERFLY, who slowly and deliberately clips a flower off its stem. GALLIMARD turns back towards TOULON.)

GALLIMARD: I think . . . that's a very wise move!

(TOULON unfreezes.)

TOULON: It's what you've been advocating. A toast?

GALLIMARD: Sure. I consider this a vindication.

TOULON: Not exactly. "To the test. Let's hope you pass."

(They drink. The chime rings again. TOULON freezes. GALLIMARD turns upstage, and SONG clips another flower.)

GALLIMARD: *(to TOULON)* The test?

TOULON: *(unfreezing)* It's a test of everything you've been saying. I personally think the generals probably will stop the Communists. And you'll be a hero. But if anything goes wrong, then your opinions won't be worth a pig's ear. I'm sure that won't happen. But sometimes it's easier when they don't listen to you.

GALLIMARD: They're your opinions too, aren't they?

TOULON: Personally, yes.

GALLIMARD: So we agree.

TOULON: But my opinions aren't on that report. Yours are. Cheers.

(TOULON turns away from GALLIMARD and raises his glass. At that instant SONG picks up the vase and hurls it to the ground. It shatters. SONG sinks down amidst the shards of the vase, in a calm, childlike trance. She sings softly, as if reciting a child's nursery rhyme.)

SONG: *(repeat as necessary)* "The whole world over, the white man travels, setting anchor, wherever he likes. Life's not worth living, unless he finds, the finest maidens, of every land . . ."

(GALLIMARD turns downstage towards us. SONG continues singing.)

GALLIMARD: I shook as I left his house. That coward! That worm! To put the burden for his decisions on my shoulders!

  I started for Renee's. But no, that was all I needed. A schoolgirl who would question the role of the penis in modern society. What I wanted was revenge. A vessel to contain my humiliation. Though I hadn't seen her in several weeks, I headed for Butterfly's.

(GALLIMARD enters SONG's apartment.)

SONG: Oh! Rene . . . I was dreaming!

GALLIMARD: You've been drinking?

SONG: If I can't sleep, then yes, I drink. But then, it gives me these dreams which—Rene, it's been almost three weeks since you visited me last.

GALLIMARD: I know. There's been a lot going on in the world.

SONG: Fortunately I am drunk. So I can speak freely. It's not the world, it's you and me. And an old problem. Even the softest skin becomes like leather to a man who's touched it too often. I confess I don't know how to stop it. I don't know how to become another woman.

GALLIMARD: I have a request.

SONG: Is this a solution? Or are you ready to give up the flat?

GALLIMARD: It may be a solution. But I'm sure you won't like it.

SONG: Oh well, that's very important. "Like it"? Do you think I "like" lying here alone, waiting, always waiting for your return? Please—don't worry about what I may not "like."

GALLIMARD: I want to see you . . . naked.

(Silence.)

SONG: I thought you understood my modesty. So you want me to—what—strip? Like a big cowboy girl? Shiny pasties on my breasts? Shall I fling my kimono over my head and yell "ya-hoo" in the process? I thought you respected my shame!

GALLIMARD: I believe you gave me your shame many years ago.

SONG: Yes—and it is just like a white devil to use it against me. I can't believe it. I thought myself so repulsed by the passive Oriental and the cruel white man. Now I see—we are always most revolted by the things hidden within us.

GALLIMARD: I just mean—

SONG: Yes?

GALLIMARD: —that it will remove the only barrier left between us.

SONG: No, Rene. Don't couch your request in sweet words. Be yourself—a cad—and know that my love is enough, that I submit—submit to the worst you can give me. (pause) Well, come. Strip me. Whatever happens, know that you have willed it. Our love, in your hands. I'm helpless before my man.

(GALLIMARD starts to cross the room.)

GALLIMARD: Did I not undress her because I knew, somewhere deep down, what I would find? Perhaps. Happiness is so rare that our mind can turn somersaults to protect it.

   At the time, I only knew that I was seeing Pinkerton stalking towards his Butterfly, ready to reward her love with his lecherous hands. The image sickened me, pulled me to my knees, so I was crawling towards her like a worm. By the time I reached her, Pinkerton . . . had vanished from my heart. To be replaced by something new, something unnatural, that flew in the face of all I'd learned in the world—something very close to love.

(He grabs her around the waist; she strokes his hair.)

GALLIMARD: Butterfly, forgive me.

SONG: Rene . . .

GALLIMARD: For everything. From the start.

SONG: I'm . . .

GALLIMARD: I want to—

SONG: I'm pregnant. (beat) I'm pregnant. (beat) I'm pregnant.

(Beat.)

GALLIMARD: I want to marry you!

SCENE VII: GALLIMARD and BUTTERFLY'S flat. Beijing. 1963.

Downstage, SONG paces as COMRADE CHIN reads from her notepad. Upstage, GALLIMARD is still kneeling. He remains on his knees throughout the scene, watching it.

SONG: I need a baby.

CHIN: (from pad) He's been spotted going to a dorm.

SONG: I need a baby.

CHIN: At the Foreign Language Institute.

SONG: I need a baby.

CHIN: The room of a Danish girl . . . What do you mean, you need a baby?!

SONG: Tell Comrade Kang—last night, the entire mission, it could've ended.

CHIN: What do you mean?

SONG: Tell Kang—he told me to strip.

CHIN: Strip?!

SONG: Write!

CHIN: I tell you, I don't understand nothing about this case anymore. Nothing.

SONG: He told me to strip, and I took a chance. Oh, we Chinese, we know how to gamble.

CHIN: (writing) ". . . told him to strip."

SONG: My palms were wet, I had to make a split-second decision.

CHIN: Hey! Can you slow down?!

(Pause.)

SONG: You write faster, I'm the artist here. Suddenly, it hit me—"All he wants is for her to submit. Once a woman submits, a man is always ready to become 'generous.'"

CHIN: You're just gonna end up with rough notes.

SONG: And it worked! He gave in! Now, if I can just present him with a baby. A Chinese baby with blond hair—he'll be mine for life!

CHIN: Kang will never agree! The trading of babies has to be a counterrevolutionary act.

SONG: Sometimes, a counterrevolutionary act is necessary to counter a counterrevolutionary act. *(Pause.)*

CHIN: Wait.

SONG: I need one . . . in seven months. Make sure it's a boy.

CHIN: This doesn't sound like something the Chairman would do. Maybe you'd better talk to Comrade Kang yourself.

SONG: Good. I will.

(CHIN gets up to leave.)

SONG: Miss Chin? Why, in the Peking Opera, are women's roles played by men?

CHIN: I don't know. Maybe, a reactionary remnant of male—

SONG: No. *(beat)* Because only a man knows how a woman is supposed to act.

(CHIN exits. SONG turns upstage, towards GALLIMARD.)

GALLIMARD: *(calling after CHIN)* Good riddance! *(to SONG)* I could forget all that betrayal in an instant, you know. If you'd just come back and become Butterfly again.

SONG: Fat chance. You're here in prison, rotting in a cell. And I'm on a plane, winging my way back to China. Your President pardoned me of our treason, you know.

GALLIMARD: Yes, I read about that.

SONG: Must make you feel . . . lower than shit.

GALLIMARD: But don't you, even a little bit, wish you were here with me?

SONG: I'm an artist, Rene. You were my greatest . . . acting challenge. *(she laughs)* It doesn't matter how rotten I answer, does it? You still adore me. That's why I love you, Rene. *(she points to us)* So—you were telling your audience about the night I announced I was pregnant.

(GALLIMARD puts his arms around SONG's waist. He and SONG are in the positions they were in at the end of Scene VI.)

SCENE VIII: *Same.*

GALLIMARD: I'll divorce my wife. We'll live together here, and then later in France.

SONG: I feel so . . . ashamed.

GALLIMARD: Why?

SONG: I had begun to lose faith. And now, you shame me with your generosity.

GALLIMARD: Generosity? No, I'm proposing for very selfish reasons.

SONG: Your apologies only make me feel more ashamed. My outburst a moment ago!

GALLIMARD: Your outburst? What about my request?!

SONG: You've been very patient dealing with my . . . eccentricities. A Western man, used to women freer with their bodies—

GALLIMARD: It was sick! Don't make excuses for me.

SONG: I have to. You don't seem willing to make them for yourself. *(Pause.)*

GALLIMARD: You're crazy.

SONG: I'm happy. Which often looks like crazy.

GALLIMARD: Then make me crazy. Marry me. *(Pause.)*

SONG: No.

GALLIMARD: What?

SONG: Do I sound silly, a slave, if I say I'm not worthy?

GALLIMARD: Yes. In fact you do. No one has loved me like you.

SONG: Thank you. And no one ever will. I'll see to that.

GALLIMARD: So what is the problem?

SONG: Rene, we Chinese are realists. We understand rice, gold, and guns. You are a diplomat. Your career is skyrocketing. Now, what would happen if you divorced your wife to marry a Communist Chinese actress?

GALLIMARD: That's not being realistic. That's defeating yourself before you begin.

SONG: We must conserve our strength for the battles we can win.

GALLIMARD: That sounds like a fortune cookie!

SONG: Where do you think fortune cookies come from?

GALLIMARD: I don't care.

SONG: You do. So do I. And we should. That is why I say I'm not worthy. I'm worthy to love and even to be loved by you. But I am not worthy to end the career of one of the West's most promising diplomats.

GALLIMARD: It's not that great a career! I made it sound like more than it is!

SONG: Modesty will get you nowhere. Flatter yourself, and you flatter me. I'm flattered to decline your offer. *(she exits)*

GALLIMARD: *(to us)* Butterfly and I argued all night. And, in the end, I left, knowing I would never be her husband. She went away for several months—to the countryside, like a small animal. Until the night I received her call.

(A baby's cry from offstage. SONG *enters, carrying a child.)*

SONG: He looks like you.

GALLIMARD: Oh! *(beat; he approaches the baby)* Well, babies are never very attractive at birth.

SONG: Stop!

GALLIMARD: I'm sure he'll grow more beautiful with age. More like his mother.

SONG: "Chi vide mai/a bimbo del Giappon . . ."

GALLIMARD: "What baby, I wonder, was ever born in Japan"—or China, for that matter—

SONG: ". . . occhi azzurrini?"

GALLIMARD: "With azure eyes?"—they're actually sort of brown, wouldn't you say?

SONG: "E il labbro."

GALLIMARD: "And such lips!" *(he kisses* SONG*)* And such lips.

SONG: "E i ricciolini d'oro schietto?"

GALLIMARD: "And such a head of golden"—if slightly patchy—"curls?"

SONG: I'm going to call him "Peepee."

GALLIMARD: Darling, could you repeat that because I'm sure a rickshaw just flew by overhead.

SONG: You heard me.

GALLIMARD: "Song Peepee"? May I suggest Michael, or Stephan, or Adolph?

SONG: You may, but I won't listen.

GALLIMARD: You can't be serious. Can you imagine the time this child will have in school?

SONG: In the West, yes.

GALLIMARD: It's worse than naming him Ping Pong or Long Dong or—

SONG: But he's never going to live in the West, is he?

(Pause.)

GALLIMARD: That wasn't my choice.

SONG: It is mine. And this is my promise to you: I will raise him, he will be our child, but he will never burden you outside of China.

GALLIMARD: Why do you make these promises? I want to be burdened! I want a scandal to cover the papers!

SONG: *(to us)* Prophetic.

GALLIMARD: I'm serious.

SONG: So am I. His name is as I registered it. And he will never live in the West.

*(*SONG *exits with the child.)*

GALLIMARD: *(to us)* It is possible that her stubbornness only made me want her more. That drawing back at the moment of my capitulation was the most brilliant strategy she could have chosen. It is possible. But it is also possible that by this point she could have said, could have done . . . anything, and I would have adored her still.

SCENE IX: *Beijing. 1966.*

A driving rhythm of Chinese percussion fills the stage.

GALLIMARD: And then, China began to change. Mao became very old, and his cult became very strong. And, like many old men, he entered his second childhood. So he handed over the reins of state to those with minds like his own. And children ruled the Middle Kingdom with complete caprice. The doctrine of the Cultural Revolution implied continuous anarchy. Contact between Chinese and foreigners became impossible. Our flat was confiscated. Her fame and my money now counted against us.

(Two dancers in Mao suits and red-starred caps enter, and begin crudely mimicking revolutionary violence, in an agitprop fashion.)

GALLIMARD: And somehow the American war went wrong too. Four hundred thousand dollars were being spent for every Viet Cong killed; so General Westmoreland's remark that the Oriental does not value life the way Americans do was oddly accurate. Why weren't the Vietnamese people giving in? Why were they content instead to die and die and die again?

(TOULON enters.)

TOULON: Congratulations, Gallimard.

GALLIMARD: Excuse me, sir?

TOULON: Not a promotion. That was last time. You're going home.

GALLIMARD: What?

TOULON: Don't say I didn't warn you.

GALLIMARD: I'm being transferred . . . because I was wrong about the American war?

TOULON: Of course not. We don't care about the Americans. We care about your mind. The quality of your analysis. In general, everything you've predicted here in the Orient . . . just hasn't happened.

GALLIMARD: I think that's premature.

TOULON: Don't force me to be blunt. Okay, you said China was ready to open to Western trade. The only thing they're trading out there are Western heads. And, yes, you said the Americans would succeed in Indochina. You were kidding, right?

GALLIMARD: I think the end is in sight.

TOULON: Don't be pathetic. And don't take this personally. You were wrong. It's not your fault.

GALLIMARD: But I'm going home.

TOULON: Right. Could I have the number of your mistress? *(beat)* Joke! Joke! Eat a croissant for me.

(TOULON exits. SONG, wearing a Mao suit, is dragged in from the wings as part of the upstage dance. They "beat" her, then lampoon the acrobatics of the Chinese opera, as she is made to kneel onstage.)

GALLIMARD: *(simultaneously)* I don't care to recall how Butterfly and I said our hurried farewell. Perhaps it was better to end our affair before it killed her.

(GALLIMARD exits. COMRADE CHIN walks across the stage with a banner reading: "The Actor Renounces His Decadent Profession!" She reaches the kneeling SONG. Percussion stops with a thud. Dancers strike poses.)

CHIN: Actor-oppressor, for years you have lived above the common people and looked down on their labor. While the farmer ate millet—

SONG: I ate pastries from France and sweetmeats from silver trays.

CHIN: And how did you come to live in such an exalted position?

SONG: I was a plaything for the imperialists!

CHIN: What did you do?

SONG: I shamed China by allowing myself to be corrupted by a foreigner . . .

CHIN: What does this mean? The People demand a full confession!

SONG: I engaged in the lowest perversions with China's enemies!

CHIN: What perversions? Be more clear!

SONG: I let him put it up my ass!

(Dancers look over, disgusted.)

CHIN: Aaaa-ya! How can you use such sickening language?!

SONG: My language . . . is only as foul as the crimes I committed . . .

CHIN: Yeah. That's better. So—what do you want to do now?

SONG: I want to serve the people.

(Percussion starts up, with Chinese strings.)

CHIN: What?

SONG: I want to serve the people!

(Dancers regain their revolutionary smiles, and begin a dance of victory.)

CHIN: What?!

SONG: I want to serve the people!!

(Dancers unveil a banner: "The Actor Is Rehabilitated!" SONG remains kneeling before CHIN, as the dancers bounce around them, then exit. Music out.)

SCENE X: *A commune. Hunan Province. 1970.*

CHIN: How you planning to do that?

SONG: I've already worked four years in the fields of Hunan, Comrade Chin.

CHIN: So? Farmers work all their lives. Let me see your hands.

(SONG holds them out for her inspection.)

CHIN: Goddamn! Still so smooth! How long does it take to turn you actors into good anythings? Hunh. You've just spent too many years in luxury to be any good to the Revolution.

SONG: I served the Revolution.

CHIN: Serve the Resolution? Bullshit! You wore dresses! Don't tell me—I was there. I saw you! You and your white vice-consul! Stuck up there in your flat, living off the People's Treasury! Yeah, I knew what was going on! You two . . . homos! Homos! Homos! *(pause; she composes herself)* Ah! Well . . . you will serve the people, all right. But not with the Revolution's money. This time, you use your own money.

SONG: I have no money.

CHIN: Shut up! And you won't stink up China anymore with your pervert stuff. You'll pollute the place where pollution begins—the West.

SONG: What do you mean?

CHIN: Shut up! You're going to France. Without a cent in your pocket. You find your consul's house, you make him pay your expenses—

SONG: No.

CHIN: And you give us weekly reports! Useful information!

SONG: That's crazy. It's been four years.

CHIN: Either that, or back to rehabilitation center!

SONG: Comrade Chin, he's not going to support me! Not in France! He's a white man! I was just his plaything—

CHIN: Oh yuck! Again with the sickening language. Where's my stick?

SONG: You don't understand the mind of a man.

(Pause.)

CHIN: Oh no? No I don't? Then how come I'm married, huh? How come I got a man? Five, six years ago, you always tell me those kinds of

things, I felt very bad. But not now! Because what does the Chairman say? He tells us *I'm now the smart one, you're now the nincompoop! You're* the blackhead, the harebrain, the nitwit! You think you're so smart? You understand "The Mind of a Man"? Good! Then *you* go to France and be a pervert for Chairman Mao!

(CHIN and SONG exit in opposite directions)

SCENE XI: *Paris. 1968–70.*

GALLIMARD *enters.*

GALLIMARD: And what was waiting for me back in Paris? Well, better Chinese food than I'd eaten in China. Friends and relatives. A little accounting, regular schedule, keeping track of traffic violations in the suburbs. . . . And the indignity of students shouting the slogans of Chairman Mao at me—in French.

HELGA: Rene? Rene? *(she enters, soaking wet)* I've had a . . . a problem. *(she sneezes)*

GALLIMARD: You're wet.

HELGA: Yes, I . . . coming back from the grocer's. A group of students, waving red flags, they—

(GALLIMARD fetches a towel.)

HELGA: —they ran by, I was caught up along with them. Before I knew what was happening—

(GALLIMARD gives her the towel.)

HELGA: Thank you. The police started firing water cannons at us. I tried to shout, to tell them I was the wife of a diplomat, but—you know how it is . . . *(pause)* Needless to say, I lost the groceries. Rene, what's happening to France?

GALLIMARD: What's—? Well, nothing, really.

HELGA: Nothing? The storefronts are in flames, there's glass in the streets, buildings are toppling—and I'm wet!

GALLIMARD: Nothing! . . . that I care to think about.

HELGA: And is that why you stay in this room?

GALLIMARD: Yes, in fact.

HELGA: With the incense burning? You know something? I hate incense. It smells so sickly sweet.

GALLIMARD: Well, I hate the French. Who just smell—period!

HELGA: And the Chinese were better?

GALLIMARD: Please—don't start.

HELGA: When we left, this exact same thing, the riots—

GALLIMARD: No, no . . .

HELGA: Students screaming slogans, smashing down doors—

GALLIMARD: Helga—

HELGA: It was all going on in China, too. Don't you remember?!

GALLIMARD: Helga! Please! *(pause)* You have never understood China, have you? You walk in here with these ridiculous ideas, that the West is falling apart, that China was spitting in our faces. You come in, dripping of the streets, and you leave water all over my floor. *(he grabs* HELGA's *towel, begins mopping up the floor)*

HELGA: But it's the truth!

GALLIMARD: Helga, I want a divorce.

   (Pause; GALLIMARD *continues, mopping the floor.)*

HELGA: I take it back. China is . . . beautiful. Incense, I like incense.

GALLIMARD: I've had a mistress.

HELGA: So?

GALLIMARD: For eight years.

HELGA: I knew you would. I knew you would the day I married you. And now what? You want to marry her?

GALLIMARD: I can't. She's in China.

HELGA: I see. You want to leave. For someone who's not here, is that right?

GALLIMARD: That's right.

HELGA: You can't live with her, but still you don't want to live with me.

GALLIMARD: That's right.

   (Pause.)

HELGA: Shit. How terrible that I can figure that out. *(pause)* I never thought I'd say it. But, in China, I was happy. I knew, in my own way, I knew that you were not everything you pretended to be. But the pretense—going on your arm to the embassy ball, visiting your office

and the guards saying, "Good morning, good morning, Madame Gallimard"—the pretense . . . was very good indeed. *(pause)* I hope everyone is mean to you for the rest of your life. *(she exits)*

GALLIMARD: *(to us)* Prophetic.

   *(*MARC *enters with two drinks.)*

GALLIMARD: *(to* MARC*)* In China, I was different from all other men.

MARC: Sure. You were white. Here's your drink.

GALLIMARD: I felt . . . touched.

MARC: In the head? Rene, I don't want to hear about the Oriental love goddess. Okay? One night—can we just drink and throw up without a lot of conversation?

GALLIMARD: You still don't believe me, do you?

MARC: Sure I do. She was the most beautiful, et cetera, et cetera, blasé blasé.

   (Pause.)

GALLIMARD: My life in the West has been such a disappointment.

MARC: Life in the West is like that. You'll get used to it. Look, you're driving me away. I'm leaving. Happy, now? *(he exits, then returns)* Look, I have a date tomorrow night. You wanna come? I can fix you up with—

GALLIMARD: Of course. I would love to come.

   (Pause.)

MARC: Uh—on second thought, no. You'd better get ahold of yourself first.

   (He exits; GALLIMARD *nurses his drink.)*

GALLIMARD: *(to us)* This is the ultimate cruelty, isn't it? That I can talk and talk and to anyone listening, it's only air—too rich a diet to be swallowed by a mundane world. Why can't anyone understand? That in China, I once loved, and was loved by, very simply, the Perfect Woman.

   *(*SONG *enters, dressed as* BUTTERFLY *in wedding dress.)*

GALLIMARD: *(to* SONG*)* Not again. My imagination is hell. Am I asleep this time? Or did I drink too much?

SONG: Rene?

GALLIMARD: God, it's too painful! That you speak?

SONG: What are you talking about? Rene—touch me.

GALLIMARD: Why?

SONG: I'm real. Take my hand.

GALLIMARD: Why? So you can disappear again and leave me clutching at the air? For the entertainment of my neighbors who—?

(SONG touches GALLIMARD.)

SONG: Rene?

(GALLIMARD takes SONG'S hand. Silence.)

GALLIMARD: Butterfly? I never doubted you'd return.

SONG: You hadn't . . . forgotten—?

GALLIMARD: Yes, actually, I've forgotten everything. My mind, you see—there wasn't enough room in this hard head—not for the world *and* for you. No, there was only room for one. *(beat)* Come, look. See? Your bed has been waiting, with the Klimt poster you like, and—see? The xiang lu [incense burner] you gave me?

SONG: I . . . I don't know what to say.

GALLIMARD: There's nothing to say. Not at the end of a long trip. Can I make you some tea?

SONG: But where's your wife?

GALLIMARD: She's by my side. She's by my side at last.

(GALLIMARD reaches to embrace SONG. SONG sidesteps, dodging him.)

GALLIMARD: Why?

SONG: *(to us)* So I did return to Rene in Paris. Where I found—

GALLIMARD: Why do you run away? Can't we show them how we embraced that evening?

SONG: Please. I'm talking.

GALLIMARD: You have to do what I say! I'm conjuring you up in *my* mind!

SONG: Rene, I've never done what you've said. Why should it be any different in your mind? Now split—the story moves on, and I must change.

GALLIMARD: I welcomed you into my home! I didn't have to, you know! I could've left you penniless on the streets of Paris! But I took you in!

SONG: Thank you.

GALLIMARD: So . . . please . . . don't change.

SONG: You know I have to. You know I will. And anyway, what difference does it make? No matter what your eyes tell you, you can't ignore the truth. You already know too much.

(GALLIMARD exits. SONG turns to us.)

SONG: The change I'm going to make requires about five minutes. So I thought you might want to take this opportunity to stretch your legs, enjoy a drink, or listen to the musicians. I'll be here, when you return, right where you left me.

(SONG goes to a mirror in front of which is a wash basin of water. She starts to remove her makeup as stagelights go to half and houselights come up.)

ACT THREE

SCENE I: *A courthouse in Paris. 1986.*

As he promised, SONG *has completed the bulk of his transformation onstage by the time the houselights go down and the stagelights come up full. He removes his wig and kimono, leaving them on the floor. Underneath, he wears a well-cut suit.*

SONG: So I'd done my job better than I had a right to expect. Well, give him some credit, too. He's right—I was in a fix when I arrived in Paris. I walked from the airport into town, then I located, by blind groping, the Chinatown district. Let me make one thing clear: whatever else may be said about the Chinese, they are stingy! I slept in doorways three days until I could find a tailor who would make me this kimono on credit. As it turns out, maybe I didn't even need it. Maybe he would've been happy to see me in a simple shift and mascara. But . . . better safe than sorry.

That was 1970, when I arrived in Paris. For the next fifteen years, yes, I lived in a very comfy life. Some relief, believe me, after four years on a fucking commune in Nowheresville, China. Rene supported the boy and me, and I did some demonstrations around the country as part of my "cultural exchange" cover. And then there was the spying.

*(*SONG *moves upstage, to a chair.* TOULON *enters as a judge, wearing the appropriate wig and robes. He sits near* SONG*. It's 1986, and* SONG *is testifying in a courtroom.)*

SONG: Not much at first. Rene had lost all his high-level contacts. Comrade Chin wasn't very interested in parking-ticket statistics. But finally, at my urging, Rene got a job as a courier, handling sensitive documents. He'd photograph them for me, and I'd pass them on to the Chinese embassy.

JUDGE: Did he understand the extent of his activity?

SONG: He didn't ask. He knew that I needed those documents, and that was enough.

JUDGE: But he must've known he was passing classified information.

SONG: I can't say.

JUDGE: He never asked what you were going to do with them?

SONG: Nope.
          (Pause.)

JUDGE: There is one thing that the court—indeed, that all of France—would like to know.

SONG: Fire away.

JUDGE: Did Monsieur Gallimard know you were a man?

SONG: Well, he never saw me completely naked. Ever.

JUDGE: But surely, he must've . . . how can I put this?

SONG: Put it however you like. I'm not shy. He must've felt around?

JUDGE: Mmmmm.

SONG: Not really. I did all the work. He just laid back. Of course we did enjoy more . . . complete union, and I suppose he *might* have wondered why I was always on my stomach, but . . . But what you're thinking is, "Of course a wrist must've brushed . . . a hand hit . . . over twenty years!" Yeah. Well, Your Honor, it was my job to make him think I was a woman. And chew on this: it wasn't all that hard. See, my mother was a prostitute along the Bundt before the Revolution. And, uh, I think it's fair to say she learned a few things about Western men. So I borrowed her knowledge. In service to my country.

JUDGE: Would you care to enlighten the court with this secret knowledge? I'm sure we're all very curious.

SONG: I'm sure you are. *(pause)* Okay, Rule One is: Men always believe what they want to hear. So a girl can tell the most obnoxious lies and the guys will believe them every time—"This is my first time"—"That's the biggest I've ever seen"—or *both*, which, if you really think about it, is not possible in a single lifetime. You've maybe heard those phrases a few times in your own life, yes, Your Honor?

JUDGE: It's not my life, Monsieur Song, which is on trial today.

SONG: Okay, okay, just trying to lighten up the proceedings. Tough room.

JUDGE: Go on.

SONG: Rule Two: As soon as a Western man comes into contact with the East—he's already confused. The West has sort of an international rape mentality towards the East. Do you know rape mentality?

JUDGE: Give us your definition, please.

SONG: Basically, "Her mouth says no, but her eyes say yes." The West thinks of itself as masculine—big guns, big industry, big money—so the East is feminine—weak, delicate, poor . . . but good at art, and full of inscrutable wisdom—the feminine mystique.

       Her mouth says no, but her eyes say yes. The West believes the East, deep down, *wants* to be dominated—because a woman can't think for herself.

JUDGE: What does this have to do with my question?

SONG: You expect Oriental countries to submit to your guns, and you expect Oriental women to be submissive to your men. That's why you say they make the best wives.

JUDGE: But why would that make it possible for you to fool Monsieur Gallimard? Please—get to the point.

SONG: One, because when he finally met his fantasy woman, he wanted more than anything to

believe that she was, in fact, a woman. And second, I am an Oriental. And being an Oriental, I could never be completely a man.
(Pause.)

JUDGE: Your armchair political theory is tenuous, Monsieur Song.

SONG: You think so? That's why you'll lose in all your dealings with the East.

JUDGE: Just answer my question: did he know you were a man?
(Pause.)

SONG: You know, Your Honor, I never asked.

SCENE II: *Same.*

Music from the "Death Scene" from Butterfly *blares over the house speakers. It is the loudest thing we've heard in this play.*

GALLIMARD *enters, crawling towards* SONG'S *wig and kimono.*

GALLIMARD: Butterfly? Butterfly?
*(*SONG *remains a man, in the witness box, delivering a testimony we do not hear.)*

GALLIMARD: *(to us)* In my moment of greatest shame, here, in this courtroom—with that . . . person up there, telling the world. . . . What strikes me especially is how swallow he is, how glib and obsequious . . . completely . . . without substance! The type that prowls around discos with a gold medallion stinking of garlic. So little like my Butterfly.

Yet even in this moment my mind remains agile, flip-flopping like a man on a trampoline. Even now, my picture dissolves, and I see that . . . witness . . . talking to me.
*(*SONG *suddenly stands straight up in his witness box, and looks at* GALLIMARD.*)*

SONG: Yes. You. White man.
*(*SONG *steps out of the witness box, and moves downstage towards* GALLIMARD. *Light change.)*

GALLIMARD: *(to* SONG*)* Who? Me?

SONG: Do you see any other white men?

GALLIMARD: Yes. There're white men all around. This is a French courtroom.

SONG: So you are an adventurous imperialist. Tell me, why did it take you so long? To come back to this place?

GALLIMARD: What place?

SONG: This theatre in China. Where we met many years ago.

GALLIMARD: *(to us)* And once again, against my will, I am transported.
(Chinese opera music comes up on the speakers. SONG *begins to do opera moves, as he did the night they met.)*

SONG: Do you remember? The night you gave your heart?

GALLIMARD: It was a long time ago.

SONG: Not long enough. A night that turned your world upside down.

GALLIMARD: Perhaps.

SONG: Oh, be honest with me. What's another bit of flattery when you've already given me twenty years' worth? It's a wonder my head hasn't swollen to the size of China.

GALLIMARD: Who's to say it hasn't?

SONG: Who's to say? And what's the shame? In pride? You think I could've pulled this off if I wasn't already full of pride when we met? No, not just pride. Arrogance. It takes arrogance, really—to believe you can will, with your eyes and your lips, the destiny of another. *(he dances)* C'mon. Admit it. You still want me. Even in slacks and a button-down collar.

GALLIMARD: I don't see what the point of—

SONG: You don't? Well, maybe, Rene, just maybe—I want you.

GALLIMARD: You do?

SONG: Then again, maybe I'm just playing with you. How can you tell? *(reprising his feminine character, he sidles up to* GALLIMARD*)* "How I wish there were even a small cafe to sit in. With men in tuxedos, and cappuccinos, and bad expatriate jazz." Now you want to kiss me, don't you?

GALLIMARD: *(pulling away)* What makes you—?

SONG: —so sure? See? I take the words from your mouth. Then I wait for you to come and retrieve them. *(he reclines on the floor)*

GALLIMARD: Why? Why do you treat me so cruelly?

SONG: Perhaps I *was* treating you cruelly. But now—I'm being nice. Come here, my little one.

GALLIMARD: I'm not your little one!

SONG: My mistake. It's I who am *your* little one, right?

GALLIMARD: Yes, I—

SONG: So come get your little one. If you like. I may even let you strip me.

GALLIMARD: I mean, you were! Before . . . but not like this!

SONG: I was? Then perhaps I still am. If you look hard enough. *(he starts to remove his clothes)*

GALLIMARD: What—what are you doing?

SONG: Helping you to see through my act.

GALLIMARD: Stop that! I don't want to! I don't—

SONG: Oh, but you asked me to strip, remember?

GALLIMARD: What? That was years ago! And I took it back!

SONG: No. You postponed it. Postponed the inevitable. Today, the inevitable has come calling.

(From the speakers, cacophony: BUTTERFLY mixed in with Chinese gongs.)

GALLIMARD: No! Stop! I don't want to see!

SONG: Then look away.

GALLIMARD: You're only in my mind! All this is in my mind! I order you! To stop!

SONG: To what? To strip? That's just what I'm—

GALLIMARD: No! Stop! I want you—!

SONG: You want me?

GALLIMARD: To stop!

SONG: You know something, Rene? Your mouth says no, but your eyes say yes. Turn them away. I dare you.

GALLIMARD: I don't have to! Every night, you say you're going to strip, but then I beg you and you stop!

SONG: I guess tonight is different.

GALLIMARD: Why? Why should that be?

SONG: Maybe I've become frustrated. Maybe I'm saying "Look at me, you fool!" Or maybe I'm just feeling . . . sexy. *(he is down to his briefs)*

GALLIMARD: Please. This is unnecessary. I know what you are.

SONG: Do you? What am I?

GALLIMARD: A—a man.

SONG: You don't really believe that.

GALLIMARD: Yes I do! I knew all the time somewhere that my happiness was temporary, my love a deception. But my mind kept the knowledge at bay. To make the wait bearable.

SONG: Monsieur Gallimard—the wait is over.

(SONG drops his briefs. He is naked. Sound cue out. Slowly, we and SONG come to the realization that what we had thought to be GALLIMARD'S sobbing is actually his laughter.)

GALLIMARD: Oh god! What an idiot! Of course!

SONG: Rene—what?

GALLIMARD: Look at you! You're a man! *(he bursts into laughter again)*

SONG: I fail to see what's so funny!

GALLIMARD: "You fail to see—!" I mean, you never did have much of a sense of humor, did you? I just think it's ridiculously funny that I've wasted so much time on just a man!

SONG: Wait. I'm not "just a man."

GALLIMARD: No? Isn't that what you've been trying to convince me of?

SONG: Yes, but what I mean—

GALLIMARD: And now, I finally believe you, and you tell me it's not true? I think you must have some kind of identity problem.

SONG: Will you listen to me?

GALLIMARD: Why?! I've been listening to you for twenty years. Don't I deserve a vacation?

SONG: I'm not just any man!

GALLIMARD: Then, what exactly are you?

SONG: Rene, how can you ask—? Okay, what about this?

(He picks up BUTTERFLY'S robes, starts to dance around. No music.)

GALLIMARD: Yes, that's very nice. I have to admit.

(SONG holds out his arm to GALLIMARD.)

SONG: It's the same skin you've worshiped for years. Touch it.

GALLIMARD: Yes, it does feel the same.

SONG: Now—close your eyes.

(SONG covers GALLIMARD'S eyes with one hand. With the other, SONG draws GALLIMARD'S hand

up to his face. GALLIMARD, *like a blind man, lets his hands run over* SONG'S *face.)*

GALLIMARD: This skin, I remember. The curve of her face, the softness of her cheek, her hair against the back of my hand . . .

SONG: I'm your Butterfly. Under the robes, beneath everything, it was always me. Now, open your eyes and admit it—you adore me. *(he removes his hand from* GALLIMARD'S *eyes)*

GALLIMARD: You, who knew every inch of my desires—how could you, of all people, have made such a mistake?

SONG: What?

GALLIMARD: You showed me your true self. When all I loved was the lie. A perfect lie, which you let fall to the ground—and now, it's old and soiled.

SONG: So—you never really loved me? Only when I was playing a part?

GALLIMARD: I'm a man who loved a woman created by a man. Everything else—simply falls short.
(Pause.)

SONG: What am I supposed to do now?

GALLIMARD: You were a fine spy, Monsieur Song, with an even finer accomplice. But now I believe you should go. Get out of my life!

SONG: Go where? Rene, you can't live without me. Not after twenty years.

GALLIMARD: I certainly can't live with you—not after twenty years of betrayal.

SONG: Don't be so stubborn! Where will you go?

GALLIMARD: I have a date . . . with my Butterfly.

SONG: So, throw away your pride. And come . . .

GALLIMARD: Get away from me! Tonight, I've finally learned to tell fantasy from reality. And, knowing the difference, I choose fantasy.

SONG: *I'm* your fantasy!

GALLIMARD: You? You're as real as hamburger. Now get out! I have a date with my Butterfly and I don't want your body polluting the room! *(he tosses* SONG'S *suit at him)* Look at these— you dress like a pimp.

SONG: Hey! These are Armani slacks and—! *(he puts on his briefs and slacks)* Let's just say . . .

I'm disappointed in you, Rene. In the crush of your adoration, I thought you'd become something more. More like . . . a woman.

But no. Men. You're like the rest of them. It's all in the way we dress, and make up our faces, and bat our eyelashes. You really have so little imagination!

GALLIMARD: You, Monsieur Song? Accuse me of too little imagination? You, if anyone, should know—I am pure imagination. And in imagination I will remain. Now get out!
*(*GALLIMARD *bodily removes* SONG *from the stage, taking his kimono.)*

SONG: Rene! I'll never put on those robes again! You'll be sorry!

GALLIMARD: *(to* SONG) I'm already sorry! *(looking at the kimono in his hands)* Exactly as sorry . . . as a Butterfly.

SCENE III: M. GALLIMARD'S *prison cell. Paris. Present.*

GALLIMARD: I've played out the events of my life night after night, always searching for a new ending to my story, one where I leave this cell and return forever to my Butterfly's arms.

Tonight I realize my search is over. That I've looked all along in the wrong place. And now, to you, I will prove that my love was not in vain—by returning to the world of fantasy where I first met her.
(He picks up the kimono; dancers enter.)

GALLIMARD: There is a vision of the Orient that I have. Of slender women in chong sams and kimonos who die for the love of unworthy foreign devils. Who are born and raised to be the perfect women. Who take whatever punishment we give them, and bounce back, strengthened by love, unconditionally. It is a vision that has become my life.
(Dancers bring the wash basin to him and help him make up his face.)

GALLIMARD: In public, I have continued to deny that Song Liling is a man. This brings me headlines, and is a source of great embarrassment to my French colleagues, who can now be sent into a coughing fit by the mere mention of Chinese food. But alone, in my cell, I have long since faced the truth.

And the truth demands a sacrifice. For mistakes made over the course of a lifetime. My mistakes were simple and absolute—the man I loved was a cad, a bounder. He deserved nothing but a kick in the behind, and instead I gave him . . . all my love.

Yes—love. Why not admit it all? That was my undoing, wasn't it? Love warped my judgment, blinded my eyes, rearranged the very lines on my face . . . until I could look in the mirror and see nothing but . . . a woman.

(Dancers help him put on the BUTTERFLY *wig.)*

GALLIMARD: I have a vision. Of the Orient. That, deep within its almond eyes, there are still women. Women willing to sacrifice themselves for the love of a man. Even a man whose love is completely without worth.

(Dancers assist GALLIMARD *in donning the kimono. They hand him a knife.)*

GALLIMARD: Death with honor is better than life . . . life with dishonor. *(he sets himself center stage, in a seppuku position)* The love of a Butterfly can withstand many things—unfaithfulness, loss, even abandonment. But how can it face the one sin that implies all others? The devastating knowledge that, underneath it all, the object of her love was nothing more, nothing less than . . . a man. *(he sets the tip of the knife against his body)* It is 19—. And I have found her at last. In a prison on the outskirts of Paris. My name is Rene Gallimard— also known as Madame Butterfly.

*(*GALLIMARD *turns upstage and plunges his knife into his body, as music from the "Love Duet" blares over the speakers. He collapses into the arms of the dancers, who lay him reverently on the floor. The image holds for several beats. Then a tight special up on* SONG, *who stands as a man, staring at the dead* GALLIMARD. *He smokes a cigarette; the smoke filters up through the lights. Two words leave his lips.)*

SONG: Butterfly? Butterfly?

(Smoke rises as lights fade slowly to black.)

THE END

WE KEEP OUR VICTIMS READY (1989/1991)

"Deconstructive" of "systems of oppression," "subversive" of a dominant patriarchal culture, a "manifestation of postmodernist feminist theory"—these characterizations resonate throughout scholarly accounts of Karen Finley's **performance art.** For other commentators, particularly those unsympathetic to her politics, writing, or style of performance, Finley is disturbing, bizarre, even obscene; her monologues are strident in their polemics and profanity, and her frequent use of her own body as text borders on the pornographic. Her art, as unique as it is, thus represents both those aspects of performance art that its admirers laud and those conventions intended to outrage bourgeois morality that its opponents revile.

Raised in Evanston, Illinois, a suburb of Chicago, Finley (1956–   ) is the oldest of six children and the daughter of a jazz drummer who, when she was 21 and home on Christmas break from school, went into the family garage and shot himself. By her own account, his suicide affected her greatly, reminding her that "reality is stronger than art." Returning to school at the San Francisco Art Institute, Finley supported herself for a brief time as a stripper and began her career as a performance artist. In San Francisco she met and later married Brian Routh, her graduate advisor at the Art Institute and a member of the controversial performance tandem the Kipper Kids, with whom she performed in Europe in 1981. Since then (and after the breakup of her marriage to Routh), Finley has played in clubs, performance venues, and college campuses, writing her own material and gaining particular notoriety in the spring of 1990 when controversy erupted over the National Endowment for the Arts' funding of photographers, playwrights, and performance artists whom some politicians and fundamentalist religious groups found offensive. Finley and three other performers

(the so-called "NEA 4" or "Defunded Four") became a kind of eye in a political storm instigated by, among others, Senator Jesse Helms of North Carolina, the Reverend Donald Wildmon of the American Family Association, and newspaper columnists Rowland Evans and Robert Novak (all of whom are named and castigated in *We Keep Our Victims Ready*). Finley, unanimously endorsed by a peer review panel to receive an NEA grant, was along with the others denied funding in the summer of 1990, although in January 1991 the grant was finally made available to her. Not long after the grant's original revocation, Finley hypothesized that the political imbroglio over the NEA represented some ideologues' efforts to suppress works that dealt with "social issues they don't want to hear about," and constituted a desperate "last chance at trying to maintain the power structure of the straight white male."

Finley's body of work includes numerous performance pieces, several of which are collected in the volume *Shock Treatment* (1990); the plays *The Theory of Total Blame* (1989) and *Lamb of God Hotel* (1991); and several compact discs such as *Jump in the River; Never Get Old* (1988, with Sinéad O'Connor) and *The Truth Is Hard to Swallow* (1989). Much of this work deals directly, often in sexually explicit terms, with such issues as violence against women (rape and incest in particular), psychoanalytic pseudo-explanations of human behavior, the AIDS crisis, and the effects of mass culture on its consumers. Most important, Finley's work continually interrogates society's devaluation and persistent victimization of women. In *The Theory of Total Blame*, for example, Finley plays Irene, an abusive, drunken matriarch and victim of incest who, in turn, verbally batters her four grown children. Her dysfunctional family includes Jan, Irene's daughter who was raped at eleven and whose child Irene "took away"; Jan's upper-class husband who longs for the kind of ideal family promoted by television situation comedies; and Irene's three sons. One is comatose and lies on the couch; one has just returned from ten years of spiritual "soul-searching"; and the other is fixated with being in the army, although he has never served in the military, and visiting the garage in which his father committed suicide. As the play evolves—and as Irene's depictions of past sexual violence become more intense—it becomes clear that not only Irene's reliance on her late husband for her own self-definition but also her family's dysfunctional behavior originate in the few roles afforded women in a male-dominated society. She tells Jan, "The sooner you realize that women are second-class citizens, the better off you'll be"; and drunkenly proclaims, "I had five kids, three miscarriages, and one abortion. I've been a mother, a whore, and a slave. I've been needed, rejected, and desired but never valued by any of you." Like Finley, Irene regards society as inherently cruel to women, as allowing women only biological opportunities to reproduce and reviling those who aspire to anything greater. Yet, sadly, Irene longs to keep the memory of her dead husband alive, a longing that may constitute her greatest victimization, for without her husband and the roles of mother and wife, she has no identity of her own.

Finley's most provocative monologues, *The Constant State of Desire* and *We Keep Our Victims Ready*, concern similar issues, yet in a much different, more controversial presentational form. *The Constant State of Desire* is composed of five smaller narrative units that, as several commentators have noted, allow Finley to move between several "subject positions." A victim of incest in "Strangling Baby Birds," she is a male rapist and sodomist in "The Father in All of Us"; in "Enter Entrepreneur," she takes revenge against an affluent "yuppie" class that exploits its victims economically; and in "Common Sense" she constructs a dialogue critical of Freudian psychoanalysis and the concept of "penis envy" (society seems more centered around "womb envy," Finley declares in an interview). Finley's monologues move from one story line to another, with little

attempt on her part at realistic acting or impersonation. Instead, her performance style, as described by Richard Schechner in an interview with her, resembles a "kind of surrealistic, automatic talking" and a "sing-song delivery of lines." Agreeing with this description, Finley adds that what she does is *not* acting; instead, she considers herself a "vehicle" or "medium" for real emotions. Hence, at her performances the audience is not always viewing a fictional character, but often Finley herself, as the fictionality of her stories blends into the realities of her life. Her audiences are also compelled to contemplate their own voyeurism, their complicity in her victimization or that of her characters, particularly at those moments in her monologues when she appears in the nude. Interested in exposing what she calls the "sexuality of violence" and the "violence of sexuality" in contemporary society, Finley frequently applies various substances to her body, offering viewers what Maria T. Pramaggiore terms a "grotesque" female body: a counter to idealized representations of the feminine and a "reminder that no body conforms to the specifications of the female nude," thereby thwarting any attempt "to objectify her as that image." Violence, thus, not only means rape and the acts of feminine revenge she delineates in "Enter Entrepreneur" (violations and degradations of yuppies, castrations of Wall Street brokers), but also entails the matter of representation—the ways in which our culture, by representing women's physical appearances in certain privileged ways, legislates their career choices and lives.

We Keep Our Victims Ready continues with these themes and performance strategies, and for *American Drama: Colonial to Contemporary*, Finley has generously provided a revised version of her earlier monologue, complete with stage directions. The version printed here differs from that published in *Shock Treatment* in several respects, the most important of which concern the indications of Finley's movements on stage and the transposition of the Prologue "It's Only Art" into this performance. Of course, performance art, reborn in the 1960s from a movement in **conceptual art** designed to replace or circumvent an art object grown into commodity, retains an irreducibly improvisational quality: A performance piece thus lacks the fixed or finished status of a play. *We Keep Our Victims Ready* is no exception, as former parts of the monologue are modified and combined with a prologue whose politics take on an added resonance after the NEA controversy (and, in the opening reference to T-shirts with "Karen Finley—World Tour 1991" emblazoned upon them, look forward to later performances). The censorship and cultural fascism alluded to in the Prologue anticipate Finley's later analogies between Hitler's Nazis and contemporary politicians on the ideological right, making it a fascinating and appropriate preface to the three acts that follow.

Finley's art, much like **agitprop** drama both of the 1930s and the 1960s as practiced by **El Teatro Campesino**, art so carefully calculated to overturn expectations and shake bourgeois morality, is designed to shock its audience into a new awareness of social injustice. Whether or not she is always successful in achieving this goal—whether her cultural critique is appreciated only by a coterie of academics and is largely misunderstood by more general audiences—is another matter. Yet one thing seems to be certain: In the 1980s and early 1990s, Finley's art has become one of the most visible and often discussed examples of experimentation in the American theatre. Her work has come to epitomize the subversive edge of performance art and will continue to attract attention from both the media and the academy.

WORKS CONSULTED

Carr, C., "'Telling the Awfullest Truth': An Interview with Karen Finley." 1991. Rpt. in *Acting Out: Feminist Performances*, eds. Lynda Hart and Peggy Phelan. Ann Arbor: University of Michigan Press, 1993. 153–160.

———. "Unspeakable Practices, Unnatural Acts: The Taboo Art of Karen Finley." 1986. Rpt. in *Acting Out: Feminist Performances*. 141–151.

Finley, Karen. *Shock Treatment*. San Francisco: City Lights, 1990.

———. *The Theory of Total Blame. Grove New American Theatre.* Ed. Michael Feingold. New York: Grove Press, 1993. 217–257.

Forte, Jeanie. "Women's Performance Art: Feminism and Postmodernism." *Theatre Journal* 40 (1988): 217–235.

Pramaggiore, Maria T. "Resisting/Performing/Femininity: Words, Flesh, and Feminism in Karen Finley's *The Constant State of Desire.*" *Theatre Journal* 44 (1992): 269–290.

Schechner, Richard. "Karen Finley: A Constant State of Becoming." *TDR* 32 (1988): 152–158.

Schuler, Catherine. "Spectator Response and Comprehension: The Problem of Karen Finley's *Constant State of Desire.*" *TDR: The Drama Review* 33 (1990): 131–145.

Span, Paula, and Carla Hall. "At Home with the NEA 4." *American Theatre.* September 1990: 14–19.

SETTING: *Purple satin curtains in background. A wooden rocking chair is positioned stage left, a kitchen table and bar stool are center stage and a single bed with bedside chair is stage right. A mirror lying flat on a gallery block is positioned upstage between the rocker and the table.*

PROPS: *On the table are four baskets containing bean sprouts, Red Hots, wrapped candy, and Christmas tinsel. Also on the table are a Valentine's Day chocolate box, two store-bought containers of pre-made Jell-O, a chocolate cake with little American flags stuck in it like candles, five T-shirts that have their logo crossed out and have "Karen Finley—World Tour 1991" written on them. On the mirror is a clear glass bowl and pitcher. The pitcher is filled with water. On the bed is a white sheet.*

COSTUME: *Costume consists of purple and black cocktail dress over a black corset with a pair of red bikini briefs, a red scarf tied on head like a turban, red socks with red rubber galoshes. Hair should be up in a bun under the turban. No make-up.*

Prologue

(Enter—sit in rocker. Talk to audience with jokes and chatter before beginning with the prologue.)

It's Only Art

I went into a museum, but they had taken down all the art—all that was left was empty frames. Pieces of masking tape were up with the names of the paintings and the artists and why they were removed. The guards had nothing to guard. The white walls yellowed. Toilets were locked up in museums because people might think someone peeing is art. Someone might think that pee flushing down that toilet is art. Someone might think that the act of peeing is a work of art. And the government pays for that pee flushing down that toilet. There were many bladder infections amongst those who inspected the museum to make sure that there was no offensive art. They might lose their jobs. A good life is one that no one thinks that you ever piss or shit.

In the empty frames were the reasons why art was confiscated.

Jasper Johns—for desecrating the flag.

Michelangelo—for being a homosexual.

Mary Cassatt—for painting nude children.

Van Gogh—for contributing to psychedelia.

Georgia O'Keeffe—for painting cow skulls (the dairy industry complained).

Picasso—for apparently urinating on his sculptures with the help of his children to achieve the desired patina effect.

Edward Hopper—Repressed lust.

Jeff Koons—for offending Michael Jackson.

All ceramicists were gone, for working with clay was too much like playing with your own shit.

All glassblowers became extinct for it was too much like a blow job.

All art from cultures that didn't believe in one male god was banned for being blasphemous.

We looked for the show of Early American quilts, but it had been taken down. One guard said that a period stain was found on one, besides you can imagine what happened under those quilts at night!

Since the Confiscation of Art occurred an Art Propaganda Army was started by the government. Last month the national assignment for the army artists was to make Dan Quayle look smart. For the army writers the assignment was to make the Stealth bomber as important as a microwave oven.

Musicians were asked to write a tune that the S&L scandal was no big deal, like taking sugar packets from a cafe. Dancers were to choreograph a dance showing that the Iran-Contra affair was as harmless as your dog going into your neighbor's yard. And filmmakers were asked to make films about homelessness, poverty, and AIDS saying that God has a plan for us all.

But no art came out.

No art was made.

Newspapers became thin and stopped because there was no criticism. There was nothing to gossip about. Schools closed, for learning got in the way of patriotism. You couldn't experiment, for that was the way of the devil.

There was no theory. No academia. No debate teams. No Jeopardy.

Everyone became old overnight. There was no more reason for anything.

Everything became old and gray. Everyone had blue-gray skin like the color of bones, unfriendly seas and navy bean soup.

And then The Punishers, The Executioners, The Judges of creativity grew weary, for there was no creativity left to condemn. So they snorted and they squawked but they held in their boredom.

All that was printed in newspapers, journals, and magazines was the phrase I DON'T KNOW.

All actresses and actors were gone from TV except for Charlton Heston. Charlton did TV shows 24 hours a day.

One day, Jesse Helms was having some guests arrive from Europe. A dignitary, a land developer or a king. Mrs. Helms asked them where they'd like to go in America. The king said, "Disneyland."

Mr. Helms said, "Oh, that's been closed down for we saw Disney's film *Fantasia.*"

So the guests said, "Nathan's Hotdogs in Coney Island."

Mr. Helms answered, "Sorry, but hotdogs are too phallic—Nathan's is history."

"Well," the guests said, "we'd like to go to the Museum of Modern Art—and if we can't go there then why come to America?"

Mr. Helms was stuck. He wanted everyone to think he was cool having Europeans visit him. But he had an idea—he'd make art to put back into the empty museums. He'd get George Bush, Dana Rohrbacher, George Will, Tipper Gore, and William Buckley and some other conservative allies to come over and make some art on the White House lawn. So he called all of his cronies to come on down and make some Art. And everyone came 'cause it was better than watching Charlton Heston on TV.

Mr. and Mrs. Helms looked all over for art supplies—they came up with old wallpaper, scissors, and house paint and laid it all out for their friends to express themselves.

When the friends arrived they were scared to make art, for they never had before. Never even used a crayon. But then a child picked up a crayon and drew a picture of her cat having babies. Then she drew a picture of her father hitting her. Then a picture of her alone and bruised. The mother looked at the picture and cried and told the daughter she didn't know that happened to her. The child screamed out, "DRAW YOUR DREAMS! DRAW YOUR NIGHTMARES! DRAW YOUR FEARS! DRAW YOUR REALITIES!"

Everyone started making pictures of houses on fire, monsters, trees became penises, pictures of making love with someone of the same sex, of being naked on street corners, of pain and dirty words, and things you never admitted in real life.

For 13 days and nights everyone drew and drew nonstop. Some started telling stories, writing poems, neighbors saw the artmaking and joined in. Somehow pretend was back in. Somehow expression sprang up from nowhere.

But then the Confiscation Police arrived and they took everyone away. (The father of the child who drew the father hitting the child complained.) Everyone was arrested. They even arrested Jesse Helms, for he was painting his soul out, which was HATE AND ENVY AND CRIME AND DARKNESS AND PAIN. And they threw him into the slammer. He was tried for treason and lost. On his day of execution his last words were: "It was only art."

ACT 1
LIFE OF LIES

I woke up smelling the flowered, flanneled sheets of my dog's urine. The smell was not distinct but distant, for Bill had turned over the futon the night before after we discovered our pet's piss on our bed.

Last night, I cried till dawn. We had invited some of Bill's friends over to the house for smoked butt. Yes, we are suburban, but that isn't what depressed me. It's how I want a daughter but instead I have had three sons. I have never been out of the county, nor have I ever been to New York City, even though my husband goes to work there every day. I am a committed waitress and mother. And I look forward to purchasing a new thousand-dollar sofa set. Isn't that what working is for?

One of my children limps, the other crawls—and the other stutters—but still I want a daughter—because, maybe if I have a daughter I can give her chances I didn't have. Something that perhaps only women would understand—like up to this very day girls, daughters are killed for being just that—girls, daughters. Females. No wonder that the entire psyche of women is universally coached to be as desirable as possible, as cute as possible, as boring as possible. It's survival of the female species.

Maybe my daughter could have the chances I didn't have. I'd encourage my daughter, and maybe my daughter would have other opportunities besides biological opportunities. Maybe she could get another kind of job instead of one that involved serving, nurturing for a pay scale that most men would never work for. Of course, our society does not put much value on traditional female vocations such as nurses or teachers or child-care workers.

I've never talked about the fact that as a waitress there is no pregnancy leave. In fact, there is rarely maternity leave of any realistic length for any vocation. The ability to bear children often means the end of a career. The fact that there is a severe shortage of good affordable child care supported by our government proves that the government wants to make it as hard as possible for women to have a fair share along with men. Waitressing, which is shift-work and never nine to five, does not correspond with day-care facilities. Sitters can be expensive and can cost more than half of a woman's salary. There is rarely insurance protection for the service employee who is not in a union. No sick leave. No paid vacations. In fact, in many states restaurants can pay below minimum wage. In fact, in many up-scale hotels and restaurants, women are discriminated against from not working the dinner shift for their option of hiring men. Equality? It has just been recent history that the waitresses in the sky could be fired for being 35, pregnant, above a certain weight or married. This decision was considered fair by Supreme Court Judge Kennedy.

I keep this all to myself because I WAS NOT EXPECTED TO BE TALENTED. You see, I WAS NOT EXPECTED TO BE TALENTED. That is why I wanted a daughter—whom I could encourage, to lead, to eventually leave the domestic cycle. But I've been told by the doctors that I could not have any more children. I worked too hard and long into my pregnancy, even though most waitresses stop working when "they show" since most customers find a pregnant woman serving food unappetizing.

Yeah, you just tell me I'm supposed to stop thinkin' about everyone else's problem and start thinking about my own. Well, as soon as I start doing that, everyone else's life collapses and I'm left to pick up the pieces. Then you say, "One day at a time." Well, it's a slow death! Then I'm told to remember those who are less fortunate than myself. Remember the homeless, the poor, the suffering. WELL, I'M SUFFERING INSIDE! Anytime I see someone caring or sharing, I burn up inside with envy. You know why I feel comfortable only around the collapsed, the broken, the inebriated, the helpless and poor—'CAUSE IT LOOKS LIKE WHAT I FEEL INSIDE! It looks, it looks, it looks like what I feel inside!

And when I see you
after you beat me
after you degraded me
and you stand on top of me
in some God-awful museum
where I see the posters of the white man,
	cigar-chompin',
drinking-with-the-collector artist
My gender is the exception
and you say to me,
"There are no great women artists"
I hate museums and galleries that show mostly
	white, male artists

And instead of going to church
I walk past the sites in Central Park
where women have been raped and murdered—
and think about the men who just walked away
after they performed their deed
and then I think of this country's heroes
and how they treated their women—
Like the Kennedys—
how they treated their women—
treated Marilyn Monroe LIKE SHIT
They killed her—left her for dead
Mary Jo Kopechne—
Abandoned her like shit—
But we're used to it—
and all the single women
with children

with no health care, no child care, no child
    support—
We're used to it.
We can only fuck to get access to the power
and if we don't we're raped anyway

And I barf whenever I see William Hurt
He thought he was so cool when he played a queen
In *Kiss of the Spider Woman*
When he made love to a deaf woman—Marlee
    Matlin
For the world to see
It's a life of Lies—
It's a life of Selling Out—

And the last time I saw my mother she had a
    skillet above my head.

Why should I pretend to stop drinking? For
the children? Shit, they're the reason I drink! My
so-called daughter hasn't called me in years for
my so-called intoxicated life-style—who cares if
my decisions are intoxicated, liquor-motivated, no
one cares, no one listens. No one cares about me.
Why should I care about me? Let's see how low
they'll let me fall before they'll let me up—
besides, I can stop whenever I want to. And you
know children, as soon as they're in trouble it's always the Mother they call on to bail them out.

I know everything, that's my problem. I'm too
smart for this world. My analysis can be so deliberate
that I'm known for my psychic pain. Clever, smart,
driven pain. I'm always right.

I feel your shiver when you suspect me drinking,
but you'll never find my vodka behind the Kitty Litter
box! 'Cause I'm the only one who works around here.
No matter how much I drink I always make it to work
on time!

You don't know. You don't know the pain of
raising a family alone. I don't get any widow benefits. People and family members are scared of me.
They don't know what to do with a widow. Everyone
blames his death on me.

Everyone blames his life on me. Even though
he pointed the trigger. The only consoling words I

ever get are, "You're so lucky he didn't kill
you and the children, too" or "You're so lucky he
blew his brains out in the garage and not in the
living room." I hate people who like to rationalize
suffering.

People like to know a reason to blame on everything. They just can't accept that bad things
happen to good people. Because if they did they'd
be out of control. They'd be like me—out of control. Yeah, I admit it, I'm out of control.

Soon my words will slur—my muscles and fa-
cial expressions will drop and change. My head
will bob and my sentences will run on and on and
on 'til you want me to stop but I won't. I'm a living
Hell and I intend to keep my devil out.

'Cause
I live in a state of never getting better—
I live in a world of caving in
I live in a life where
pleasure means death
I HATE REHAB
I HATE DENIAL
I HATE POST-MODERN, NON-FEELING ART
I HATE BANK ART—
I HATE ART THAT LOOKS GOOD
    on white walls

Why is it I hate independence
Independence Day?
I want Dependence Day.
I want to be dependent on drugs, alcohol, and sex
    again
I want dependency
But this country takes all my independency away
They are trying to take abortion away
and freedom of speech
Because this country spends more time on this
    burning flag
When our own citizens' stomachs are burning
    with hunger
When AIDS babies and victims are burning with
    fever
Let me tell you God has failed
And God is bureaucracy—

God is statistics
God is what you make and not what you feel
  We've been oppressed
  We've tolerated
and they say we're lucky 'cause we don't live in
    China
I want more than a biological opportunity—
Listen to me

I grew up to the stories of my Aunt Mandy—in
        public it was cancer of the uterus—in private
        Aunt Mandy died because she was
        butchered—
She died from an abortion
a hatchet job—
She lay dying in the basement—they found rats
        eating her insides out—
in fact, all of her blood drained out of her—
All of the women bowed their heads at the story of
        Aunt Mandy
'Cause they knew it could have been them—
It could have been them
It was talk amongst women, mothers
mothers
a chance you took to be a mother—
to be a woman
Whatever the reason—the decision
a woman would make the decision knowing she
        could die—
Because in this world a woman isn't worth
        much—
Sometimes it's a hanger—
Sharp, rusty, bleeding
Sometimes it's a knife—
to cut out our soul—
Sometimes it's fire, falling from buildings
stairs, drowning, or suicide
Like I said, a woman isn't worth much
A woman's life isn't worth much

and as a child I would sit with the women
whose lives were mothers
only valued as mothers
grandmothers who remembered when women
        couldn't vote,

mothers who remembered not having credit
couldn't buy their own car, house, or dream
A woman can't be president
But the mother never abandoned her children
Children are her life
She'd die for her children
War, famine, plague, and drought
A woman must always be a mother
Children were their lives
They never questioned when a mother couldn't be
        a mother,
for no matter what else a woman accomplishes,
A WOMAN MUST ALWAYS BE A MOTHER
A WOMAN MUST ALWAYS BE A MOTHER
A WOMAN MUST ALWAYS BE A MOTHER
'Cause a woman isn't nothing if she isn't a mother
A woman must always be love but never treated
        like it's her own body—
There is mother earth who creates famine and
        plenty
                                      calm and storm

it's my body
it's not Pepsi's body
it's not Nancy Reagan's body
it's not Congress's body
it's not the Supreme Court's body
it's not *Cosmopolitan's* pink twat body
it's not George Bush's ugly-conscience,
        never-be-responsible, let-the-world-rot body
It's not Cardinal O'Connor's Catholic
        Church-homophobic-hate women-hate
queers-oppressive-DEVIL-SATAN-no children
        body
IT'S NOT YOUR BODY

You know nothing about God—
God is dead.
God is death—if he cared about life
He wouldn't kill with AIDS, he wouldn't allow
Chinese students to die and be executed and
be forgotten about a year later
He wouldn't allow Jennifer Levin to die
Yeah, God is death
    God is dead

I want my body—
But it's never been mine—
It's only for creating babies—
with a man's name on it—
'cause my name is never good enough—
My name is not good enough—
'Cause if I use my name it's real name is
BASTARD BASTARD BASTARD
I ain't got health insurance
'cause I refuse to take the HIV test
and, baby, I can't afford it
My body is the government's, let them pay me
MY BODY IS PAID FOR IN FULL BY ME.
MY body is mine.

It's funny but in this country if you test positive
    you ain't gonna be covered.
It's the sick that need the insurance.
WE have no-fault car insurance.
So why not no-fault health insurance?
'Cause we care more about cars than we do people.

One day I hope to God BUSH, the Pope,
Cardinal O'Connor, and the Right to Lifers
return back to life as an unwanted
pregnant 13-year-old girl working at
McDonald's at minimum wage—
and she's on the floor of some rat-scum alley—
screaming with a rag in her throat
with no anesthesia
nothing clean
and the doctor is not a real doctor—
Who cares—She's dead—
Who cares—She's dead anyway—
Who cares—She's already dead
Who cares—She's a goner—
Who cares—She's poor trash anyway.
To be slaves to their biology
so we aren't successful
so we make the beds and vacuum the carpet—

But the abortions will never stop—
Aunt Mandy watches us from above

There will always be Aunt Mandys
Who are
BUTCHERED LIKE A PIG
BUTCHERED LIKE A PIG

and forget God and religion
for all they do is represent fantasies of men
that perpetuate hatred to women and gays—
I want a FEMALE GODDESS
I want a lesbian goddess
I want a homosexual god
I want a black goddess
I want a brown god
I want a red goddess
I want a yellow god
I want a god in the image of the real humans here
    now—
Remember we have the right to feel
But all I'm hearing is
Are my tits big enough?
    (*Walk to centerstage next to table—Take off
    dress, revealing black corset and red under-
    pants. Put containers of Jell-O in bra, one for
    each breast. Wiggle so that Jell-O bounces.
    Light flags on the cake as if they were candles.
    Give out T-shirts and wrapped candy to audi-
    ence. Return to stool area.*)

ACT 2
WHY CAN'T THIS VEAL
CALF WALK?

I was afraid of being loved
    so I loved being hated—
I was afraid of being wanted—
    so I wanted to be abused.
I was afraid of being alone—
    so I alone became afraid.
I was afraid of being successful—
    so I successfully became nothing.
I was afraid of not being in control—
    so I lost control of my own life.

I was afraid that I was worth nothing—
  so I wasted my body to nothing.
I was afraid of eating—
  so I eat to my heart's content
  so I drink to my heart's content
    I party to my heart's content
    I fuck to my heart's content
    I spend to my heart's content
    I eat to my heart's content
and then I puke it all up
    then I take laxatives
      and shit and shit and shit and shit
I'm afraid I shit a long time
for I'm nothing but shit—
  (Peel off corset, open chocolate box, revealing
  chocolate frosting, and smear frosting on body.)
I've had my share of love letters.
I'm writing to tell you that I love you but I don't ever
  want to see you again,
I never want to talk to you again, hear your voice,
  smell you, touch you,
hold you, I want you out of my life—I love you but I
  want you out of my life!
But remember—I will never love anyone as much
  as I love you!

I'm beating you with this belt, this whip, this stick
  because I love you.
You talked back to me and your mother. Your
  bloody back, your scars, are
evidence of my love, I beat you as a child because I
  loved you.

The only emotion I ever saw from my parents was
  anger.

I'm sleeping with your best friend because I want to
  make you jealous
and make you realize that you love me. I make you
  jealous because I love
you. I sleep with your best friend because I love
  you.
I am hurting you because I love you.

I ignore you because I don't want you to know that I
  love you till you show
me that you love me. I ignore you because I love
  you.

I tied your hands together as a child because you
  were touching your penis
too much. I tied up your penis because I love you.

I put you down as a child—for I didn't want you to
  expect much out of life—
I ridiculed you—I belittled you because I loved
  you.

I abuse my children sexually—because I didn't
  want someone else to who
didn't love them. I didn't hate them—I love them. I
  show them love.

I shot myself because I love you—
if I loved myself I'd be shooting you.

I drink myself to death for I never loved myself. I
  love you. But I love
my liquor more.
Yes, I know love. That is the reason I hate the peo-
  ple I love
My whole life is untangling what was hate and what
  was love.
My whole life is falling in love with those that hate
  me while loving me.
I always fall in love with the cruel, the sadistic—
For it's better to feel abuse than to feel nothing at
  all.
It's better to feel abuse than to feel nothing at all.
  (Take basket of Red Hots and sprinkle on body.)

IN COMMEMORATION of St. Valentine's Day Mas-
  sacre that killed violently 62 years ago
America commemorates this event by killing thou-
  sands of its citizens.
The first plan of death will be called THE YEAR
  OF THE CHILD—

All policemen will use infants and toddlers as bul-
letproof vests—
All 6-year-old children will be issued a gun upon
entering school—
All 10-year-old children will be required to sell
crack to sponsor after-school programs because of limited government funding.
Other forms of death are the following:
freezing, starvation, homelessness, AIDS, lead poisoning, poor health care,
no drug rehab programs, no free needles, AIDS, no
prenatal care, child abuse,
rat bites, polluted lakes, river, seas, oceans, and
air, toxic waste, and AIDS.

Grab your dick
grab your maleness
Girls grab it.
Girls grab your energy
fucking pussy
tie bandages to their pussies
I like to cut off the ears of males—he said.
I like to cut off male naughty bits
string foreskin as necklaces.
Sure, I've eaten a doggie out
Cuz I'm a man. Nothing better.
I'll eat dog pussy. 'Cause I'm a pet lover.
I'll eat chicken hearts
bite snake heads
I'm a military kind of guy.
I saw a guy shoot himself
happened to be my dad—
I saw a man go berserk
happened to be myself
I saw a child cut himself with razors
never knew his name
I saw a guy tear up his stereo
just for the hell of it.

'Cause I'm a man—a man don't have friends like a
woman—
We don't tell our feelings. We don't show our feelings.
The only feelings we show are NO No feelings at
all.

Ain't got a friend, but I got a drinking partner—
Ain't got a confidant, but I got a hunting buddy—
Ain't got a shoulder to cry on but I got a shoulder to
carry my gun.
'Cause the only feelings I show are no feelings at
all.
The only feelings I show are no feelings at all.
*(Take basket with bean sprouts and sprinkle
bean sprouts over body.)*

Hitler likes to have Eva Braun shit on him.
That's what Eva likes, too. Adolph wants Eva to
take a Big, Brown, hot steamy shit on him. Shit in
my mouth. I want a blond Aryan shit in the Fuhrer's
mouth now.
    The Fuhrer has a fear of pubic hair. It looks
like sperm. I don't like pubes—that's why I like to
fuck big, hairy ears.
    Don't be alarmed, I have a small penis and Eva
has very large ears and the Fuhrer never comes.
    The Fuhrer's first dream was of attacking his
mother's womb and destroying his brothers and sisters. He blamed his disturbing dreams on being delivered by ice tongs.

At 8 she was molested by her brother—
At 10 she was fingered by her daddy—
At 12 she was beaten by her mother—
At 14 her white baby was kidnapped by the Nazis.

It isn't your penis that gives me pleasure, it's
my clitoris—she'd say as she masturbated and
sucked her arm and pretended she was sucking her
own breast.

You said that you don't lift your son for the potty at
night. When he wets the bed, what do you do?
—I BEAT THE SHIT OUT OF HIM!
When you son cries?
—I BEAT THE SHIT OUT OF HIM!

Berlin 1938—the campaign toward the elimi-
nation of Jews and the handicapped intensified.
November 10, 1938—Night of Broken Glass—

Jewish shops were demolished, synagogues set on fire. Germany, 1938—Jews were not allowed to own property, have businesses, and live in certain areas. Civil rights were taken away—this was the beginning toward the setting up of death camps, ovens for the Jewish people.

America NOW—it is in many minds that the junkies and victims of AIDS deserve to die. That women who are dependent on the state should be forced to be sterilized. Because they are unproductive citizens, say the zealots—
In spirit we are not very different.
We keep our victims ready.
Who are our form of 1938 Nazism? Who are our zealots with evil ways?
Our Christian holymen preach as if all homosexuals will burn in hell.
Our politicians allow the homeless to rot on the pavement.
Many believe HIV carriers should be identified like branded cattle.
Many believe that by giving IV drug users clean needles we are giving them
the wrong message.
WE JUST KILL BY NOT DOING ANYTHING AND ALLOW DEATH FOR NO APPARENT REASON.
Our own SS—The 700 Club with charter member David Duke
We have our own Himmler, our own Goebbels—
William Buckley, Evans & Novak, Patrick Buchanan,
our conservative political columnists who maliciously condemn "the other"
Donald Wildmon, Jesse Helms, and Pat Robertson,
our religious fanatics who try to destroy and distort the artist and the gay and lesbian voice
Now they can't kill the commie so they're out to kill the soul of America—ME AND YOU
IT'S JUST THAT OUR OVENS ARE AT A SLOWER SPEED
IT'S JUST THAT OUR OVENS ARE AT A SLOWER SPEED

WE KEEP OUR VICTIMS READY—

Those religious fanatics only want a voice that is their voice and not a voice
of diversity, a voice of difference, a voice of choice, a voice of strength of togetherness.
You see the wall is beginning to crumble for the white-male power. They are going to have to share the power, share the planet, and they don't want to.
But I cry at nights for I know that someone is dying.
Remember:
You can still die because of the color of your skin.
You can still die because of your sexual preference.
We have our fascist state, our Auschwitz, our racist attacks,
Howard Beach, Bensonhurst, Tawana Brawley, and never forget Michael
Stewart, although they want us to

WE KEEP OUR VICTIMS READY—

We don't have time for statistics
We don't have time for studies
We don't have time for presidential inquiries
People are dying
People with AIDS in hospital wards in urine-soaked sheets with no AZT,
there's no money for follow-up care
Homeless, ill and unfed bodies walked over in Grand Central Station
And the rich would rather build the world's tallest building rather than
provide the world's largest low-income housing project.

Some folks who call themselves Christians would like to see all homosexuals
and people with AIDS in concentration camps
It's not surprising, America had concentration camps for Japanese Americans
in WWII where innocents died or went insane

WE KEEP OUR VICTIMS READY—

And in the coming years—after 1938 in Germany
Music would be made of
murdered children's bones.

Exhaled airs burnt with martyrs' cries.
Lampshades from human skins.
IT ONLY TOOK A ZEALOT AND A FOLLOWER

I'll never forgive Adolph Hitler and the Nazis.
There are some things that I'll never forgive—
I'll never forgive Robert Chambers for committing
    murder
I'll never forgive Cardinal O'Connor
I'll never forgive the Pope for saying that it is better
    to get AIDS than to use a condom
I'll never forgive the whites in power in South
    Africa—
I'll never forgive our Constitution for including
    slavery—
I'll never forgive us for stealing this land from the
    Indians—
There are just some things I won't forgive.

WE are the oven.
Our homeless the victims
and our narrowed American minds
wish to exterminate the victims of AIDS
instead of exterminating the disease,
wish to exterminate the poor, the suffering, the de-
    pendent—
We'll happily pay for their death and never their
    life.
No, we aren't decadent
we are violent, cruel, and deliberately unjust.

What's at the end of the tunnel?
Oh, I come here tonight and try and have a good
    time.
'Cause outside it's only a bad time.
What's at the end of the tunnel?
Where the sick and suffering are comforted.
Where the homeless are housed.
Where humanity is more valuable than money.
Where the soul, the heart, and mind meet.
What's at the end of the tunnel?
Where every empty hand is held.
    *(Take basket with tinsel and drape silver tinsel
    over body.)*

You sold my soul before I could speak.
Raped by an uncle at eight
Known addiction all my lives
let me dance for you
my daddy was a preacher
preach the bible
        beat my mama—
        I sell my babies.
        I sell my bodies.

To keep 'em from stealing the women had to strip
    and had to work naked—
It looks bad but to me it looks normal.

Why can't this veal calf walk?
'cause she's kept in a wooden box that she can't
    turn around in.
She's fed some antibiotic-laced formula—and she
    sleeps in her own diarrhea—
chained in a darkened building—immobilized and
    sick
and then we kill her and eat her.

Him hurting me is not my fault.
Your hurting me is not my fault.
After I was raped by my doctor—
I didn't want to be close to anyone.
I cut off my hair—
I cut off my breasts
I cut off my hips
I cut off my buttocks.
nothing revealing, nothing tight
neutered.
You say I got what I deserved.
I let the doctor examine my crotch.
My legs were in the stirrups pinned down.
And you gave me a shot—
I couldn't see you but I could feel you. I couldn't do
    nothing.
Everyone always told me I couldn't do nothing my
    whole life.
Just seeing the veal calf now.

Everyone says I deserved it—
I'm a hussy. I'm a tramp.
I'm a whore—
'cause I wear lipstick?
work at nights?
and drink bourbon straight?
I'm a preacher girl.
Daddy, teach me right.

When I said NO
you didn't listen to me.
When I said NO
You fucked me anyway.
When I said NO
I meant NO
When I said NO
I wasn't playing hard to get.
And I never meant yes.
You raped me.
I took a shower, a hot one.
but I couldn't get clean
    his sweat his semen
    his skin smells near
another bath another shower
my whole body was covered with hickey—
I just cried—I just cried.
When I reported it
Policeman said, "Hey, Slut, you led him on."
The doctor cleaned me up, stuffed me with gauze—
bled three days with the morning-after pill.
And when they returned my empty wallet
Mr. Policeman said, "If you don't suck me I'll blow
    your brains out."

Get me used to it! Get me used to it!
But I can't. I want something better for my sisters,
    my daughters.
And every day I hear them laughing at me from
    street corners. Sizing me up.
They don't say it, though, when I walk down the
    street with a man
'cause then I'm "his" property.
And the menfolk say as I pass:
"I prefer small women."

"I like to dominate women."
"I enjoy the conquest of sex."
"Some women are asking for it."
"I get excited when a woman struggles."
"I'd like to make it with her."
"I hope I score tonight."

And when the last man said his violence—
I knew I couldn't do anything to them so I'd so
    something to me—
I went and took a knife and I cut out my hole
but it just became a bigger hole—
and all the men just laughed and said "she's too big
    now." And I felt relief
but instead they said "we can all fuck her at the
    same time"—
But I was bleeding so they left me alone—
men don't touch women so much when they bleed—
it's unclean—unless, of course, they cause the
    bleeding.
And then I hoped I would die but, of course, I
    didn't
I heard a sound, a whimper
and I realized I was in the same room as the veal
    calf—
And veal calf walked over to me.
Veal calf limps. Veal calf stinks.
And I look into veal calf's eyes—and I knew veal
    calf's story.
And said I was sorry for her.
And she said I got to keep trying—
And she asked why I was there, too.
And I spoke my story:

And when the big man like a big daddy like a big
    uncle, big uncle who I
loved—when the cop, the teacher, the country doc-
    tor, the date, the neighbor,
the authority man whom I trusted and respected—
    visited me in my own
bed, broke into my own house, lived with me, in my
    own street in my own
car, looked at me, grabbed me, mangled and hurt
    me, slapped me and

pushed me, touched my privacy, destroyed my fem-
    inine instinct, entered
and took and hurt and screams and bruises—new
    colors on my skin.
When I see a rainbow in the sky I only see an angel
    being raped.

When I said NO I meant No
But you did it anyway
When you were gone your body—your stink
    stayed.
Tried to wash you wash you off of me my body my
    skin
    in me in me in me.
    wash it off of me still not gone—scrub it off—
    burn you off of me—
    try to kill me—I don't like me—'cause I smell
    like you.

I'm hurt abused. I slice me.
I burn me. I hit me. I want this body to die. I want
    to be old and
undesired—
I want my body back.
I want my personhood back.
Society, Culture, and History
Media, Entertainment, and Art.
I'm more than a hole.
But you hate us for we can have babies and you
    can't.
I'm more than a hole.
But you envy us for we can have children who love
    us unquestionably.
I'm more than a set of tits.
And if I don't have the right size for you I'm never
    enough for you.
So, we make implants and surgery just for you.
We create a woman that never existed.
It's survival of the species.
And I'm more than a pair of legs—
but if they don't do more than walk
I'm a dog.
If I nurse my babies and my tits sag
I'm told you won't desire me.
You can't be a mother and a whore—

No one loves a smart woman.
I'm more than a piece of ass, a good fuck, and lay.
For the woman—our society relates and values you
    only for your desirability.
The Woman as Private Property.
    (*Walk over to mirror, pour water from pitcher
    into bowl and wash face. Cross stage to chair by
    the bed.*)
    (*Pick up white sheet and wrap it around body.
    Sit in chair facing the empty bed.*)

ACT 3
DEPARTURE

Tell me what to say when I visit the sick
And your sick friend says—
    When am I going to get better?
and all you can say is
    If we could make you better we would—
and your lover says
    I want you to find someone after I die
and you say
Don't talk like that—
Let's not think about it—
I'll never forget you—
and just hold your lover's hand
and keep holding it—
but it's too weak—
and that hand is inside you now

Your friend says
    I'm going to die but I'm not ready
and you say
    Well, even though you're young you've led a full
    life—
or there is a time for everything
or it's not easy for you now—
or just hold their hand
    look into their eyes
    and think to yourself
    GOD IS DEATH
and the friend tries to make you feel better and says
    I'm going to get better, aren't I?
    and hold your friend's hand

harder
HARDER
and in time your friend says
   I'm going to die now—

And after they've died. There's something in me
   that dies—something is
always lost and I have something more in common
   with the other side than
with this side. And you think about ending it all but
   you don't for someone
needs you.
And you do different things—the widower, the
   widow—different rituals
the friend that is left behind, the lover who is left
   behind.
With some, the passing to the other side means
We burn, we burn, we burn their clothes
'Cause we are cold inside without you
Sometimes we destroy their memories for our lives
   now mean nothing
We give everything away that was theirs
'Cause we have been giving and giving and giving
   and we want to continue
that lost continuation, that thread, that same feeling
That if we become as good, as good, as good
maybe we could make you better
and maybe if we keep on giving
we'll get you back one day.
When you were holding the departed you were
   whispering in their breath
You smelled that last breath
You tasted that last breath
you feel you failed and you became their mother,
   their father
You became their connection with the outside world
And when you were holding the body—
We know we still have to bid the soul farewell
And sometimes the spirit stays for days. Scared and
   tired from bodies that
wouldn't give up. Lives that had to make it—be the
   best
some souls deny their death while the living deny
   their life
At first you're gentle

Release child, release into clear blue, into the soft
   world of fragrances,
of musk
Become the first words of a child—become the first
   feelings of love
become the reasons for me to go on living or I'll go
   on dying
And you know it's not over
for you still must scatter ashes
at a place that as you pass in the future will make
   you relive the loss.
You laugh, too.
He planned it that way.
Sometimes you place them in a coffin with gifts and
   charms and talismans.
Beds of silk and brocades—and smells of Oriental
   Jasmine
But once the coffin door is closed
you don't sleep with doors closed ever again
Your sides, where his arms held you
like two spoons as you slept, ache.
When you hear sand and earth shoveled you relive
   the saddest time again
and then you are empty.
And so you run home and open his closet
and wrap your arms around his clothes, you take all
   the sleeves and wrap them
around your neck—and you breathe your lover's
   smell
and cry and cry.
All the lights flicker in the house, butterflies follow
   you and sit on your
shoulder,
mirrors break,
pictures fall out of their frames,
birds fly into windows,
His initials appear on license plates on cars in
   front of you.
He was always so good at leaving messages.

After a funeral someone said to me—
You know I only see you at funerals
it's been three since June—
been five since June for me—
He said I've made a vow—

I only go to death parties if I know someone before
      they were sick—
Why?
'cause—'cause—'cause I feel I feel so
sad 'cause I never knew their life—
and now I only know their death
And because we are members of the
Black Sheep family—

We are sheep with no shepherd—
We are sheep with no straight and narrow
We are sheep with no meadow
We are sheep who take the dangerous
pathway through the mountain range
to get to the other side of our soul.
We are the black sheep of the family
called Black Sheep folk.
We always speak our mind.
   appreciate differences in culture
   believe in sexual preferences
   believe in no racism
            no sexism
            no religionism
and we'll fight for what we believe
but usually we're pagans,
There's always one in every family
Even when we're surrounded by bodies
we're always alone—
You're born alone
and you die alone
written by a black sheep.
You can't take it with you—
written by a former black sheep.

Black Sheep folk look different from their family—
The way they look at the world
We're a quirk of nature—
We're a quirk of fate—
Usually our family, our city, our country
never understand us—
We knew this from when we were very young
that we weren't meant to be understood.
That's right. That's our job.
Usually we're not appreciated
until the next generation.

That's our life. That's our story.
Usually we're outcasts, outsiders
in our own family.
Don't worry—get used to it.
My sister says I don't understand you!
But I have hundreds of sisters with me tonight.
My brother says I don't want you!
But I have hundreds of brothers with me here
      tonight!
My mother says I don't know how to love someone
      like you!
You're so different from the rest!
But I have hundreds of mamas with me here tonight!
My father says I don't know how to hold you!
But I have hundreds of daddies with me here tonight!

We're related to people we love who can't say—
I love you, Black Sheep daughter
I love you, Black Sheep son—
I love you, outcast, I love you, outsider
But tonight we love each other—
That's why we're here—
to be around others like ourselves—
So it doesn't hurt quite so much—
In our world our temple of difference—
I am at my loneliest when I have
something to celebrate and try
to share it with those I love but
who don't love me back.
There's always silence at the end
of the phone—
There's always silence at the end
of the phone—

Sister—congratulate me!
NO, I CAN'T, YOU'RE TOO LOUD—
GRANDMA, LOVE ME
NO, I DON'T KNOW HOW TO LOVE
SOMEONE LIKE YOU
Sometimes the Black Sheep is a soothsayer,
a psychic, a magician of sorts—
Black Sheep see the invisible
We know each other's thoughts
We feel fear and hatred

Sometimes, some sheep are chosen to be sick
to finally have average, flat, boring
people say I love you.
Sometimes, Black Sheep are chosen to be sick
so families can finally come together
and say I love you.
Sometimes, some Black Sheep are chosen to die
so loved ones and families can finally say
Your life was worth living
Your life meant something to me!
Black Sheeps' destinies are not in
necessarily having families,
having prescribed existences—
like the American Dream.
Black Sheeps' Destinies are to give
meaning in life—to be angels,
to be conscience, to be nightmares,
to be actors in dreams.

Black Sheep can be family to strangers
We can love each other like MOTHER
FATHER SISTER BROTHER CHILD
We understand universal love

We understand unconditional love.
We feel a unique responsibility
a human responsibility for feelings for others
We can be all things to all people—
We are there at 3:30 AM when you call
We are here tonight 'cause I just can't
go to sleep. I have nowhere else to go—
I'm a creature of the night—
I travel in your dreams
I feel your nightmares—
We are your holding hand—
We are your pillow, your receiver,
your cuddly toy.
I feel your pain.
I wish I could relieve you of your suffering.
I wish I could relieve you of your pain.
I wish I could relieve you of your death.
Silence at the end of the phone.
Silence at the end of the phone.
Silence at the end of the phone.

THE END

T H E   D E S T I N Y   O F   M E   (1 9 9 2)

The only way [AIDS] ceases to be a news story is this—you, or someone you care for, gets it. Then it is transformed, immediately, from a bizarre, depressing media topic into a fact that is indescribably cruel.

AIDS. For us, it terrifies like "PLAGUE" did for our medieval ancestors. But it was not always so. For too long, as Andrew Holleran intimates above, AIDS was merely another one of those depressing stories that flowed from the lips of smartly dressed news commentators or quietly stared back at us from newspaper stories filled with mystery and grim statistics. But then the deaths began to come closer. Our acquaintances. Our friends. Our lovers. Our brothers and sisters and mothers and fathers. And then it was no longer their disease, the disease of faceless numbers. It was ours. And like our medieval forebears quaking before the inexplicable horror of the Black Death, we—the ill and the as-yet well—came to look to our dramatic art to understand the physical, emotional, political, economic, and spiritual elements of this relentless and devastating fact. No playwright in America has done more to put and keep this topic before the public both in the nation's theatres and in its streets than Larry Kramer, cofounder of the Gay Men's Health Crisis, ACT UP (AIDS Coalition to Unleash Power), and author of *The Normal Heart* (1985) and his 1993 **Obie** Award–winning *The Destiny of Me.*

In some senses, Larry Kramer (1935–) is an unlikely activist. Born into a middle-class family in Bridgeport, Connecticut, Kramer grew up in Washington, D.C., where he apparently spent a troubled childhood in a family fictionalized in *The Normal Heart* and *The Destiny of Me* as rife with more than the usual share of generational and sexual tensions. Escaping this environment, Kramer studied at Yale,

graduating in 1957. He quickly settled upon a career in the movies, becoming initially an assistant story editor based in New York City in 1960 for Columbia Pictures. He later moved to London, England, and became a production executive for Columbia Pictures from 1961–1965. Kramer transferred his talents to United Artists, serving briefly in 1965 as assistant to the president of that company. He then became more fully involved with the production of motion pictures, serving as associate producer of *Here We Go Round the Mulberry Bush* (1967) and ultimately as producer, as well as screenwriter, for the 1969 film of D. H. Lawrence's novel *Women in Love.* Kramer was nominated for the 1970 Academy Award for that screenplay by the American Academy of Motion Picture Arts and Sciences, an honor that was replicated by the British Film Academy. He turned his attention to fiction in 1978 with the novel *Faggots,* the author's uncompromising vision of what Martin Duberman disparagingly called "that fatuous segment of the gay male population which defines existence wholly in terms of gyms, discos, orgies and Fire Island phantasmagoria." Though widely deprecated when it appeared, *Faggots* remained in print as something of a cult classic, becoming over a decade a best-seller. When it was republished in 1987, the novel was acclaimed for its unflinchingly honest examination of a segment of gay life in the 1970s.

Though both *Women in Love* and *Faggots* explore, to a lesser or greater degree, male homosexuality, Kramer's generalized speculations gave way to very particular concerns with the advent of the AIDS epidemic. To the extent that both *The Normal Heart* and *The Destiny of Me* have sought to counter the oppressive discourses which have traditionally fashioned the general culture's perceptions of gays and lesbians and to the extent that his plays have presented his gay characters as human beings whose sexual orientation, while important—even crucial to their senses of self—is ultimately only part of their beings, Kramer has aided the general cause of a more open gay and lesbian theatre. But the greater part of *The Normal Heart*—as well as a significant portion of *The Destiny of Me*—is designed as polemic. Especially for the Kramer of *The Normal Heart,* all narrower concerns are secondary before the specter of AIDS.

Nineteen hundred eighty-five was the watershed year in American drama, for in that year AIDS became commercially acceptable, and AIDS moved from the narrow confines of gay and lesbian community centers to mainstream theatres. In March, William M. Hoffman's *As Is* opened at New York's Circle Repertory Company, and the next month Joseph Papp produced Kramer's *The Normal Heart* at New York's Public Theatre. Hoffman's play is generally acknowledged as the more tempered artistic statement, utilizing as it does conventional realistic techniques to arouse sympathy for its AIDS-stricken protagonist who, faced with rejection by both his lover and family, finally finds acceptance "as is" with a former lover. But acceptance cannot stay the course of the disease. The play's closing lines, delivered by a hospice worker, leave little doubt about the future—death will soon claim another victim. While Marshall W. Mason's staging sought to distance the audience emotionally by using Brechtian techniques such as **demonstration** (in which actors remain on stage as themselves rather than the characters they play), Hoffman's decision to focus on the fate of an AIDS patient inevitably operated to draw the audience within the emotionally intense ambit of tragedy. In some respects, Hoffman's play is another instance of the homosexual-martyr play that John M. Clum has described.

Kramer's thinly disguised autobiographical *The Normal Heart* carefully elicits the audience's distanced identification with the hard-to-love Ned Weeks, the activist who enters the play enraged, gets progressively angrier, and ends the play livid, though very painfully alive in the wake of his lover's death from AIDS. Though Weeks's fury is warranted (and a fully accurate reflection of Kramer's public

persona of the early 1980s), it drives a wedge between him and the audience as well as his fellow activists. As Ned prophetically tells his brother in the play, "Everyone's afraid of me anyway. I frighten them away." Kramer clearly recognizes both Weeks's potential and his limitations, for he carefully augments Weeks's off-putting outrage with a host of Brechtian devices designed to transform the anger that Weeks has helped to generate into political action. By painting the walls of the theatre and the sets with the data of AIDS' progression, by pointing up the neglect of major media organs and governmental agencies to the epidemic, by analogizing the early reactions of gay community leaders and governmental officials to AIDS to the response of American Jewish leaders and governmental bureaucrats to the Holocaust, by taking to task actual public figures such as New York Mayor Edward Koch, and by fictionalizing himself as the not easily embraced Ned Weeks, Kramer seeks to achieve not so much sympathy for his central character as audience outrage at the state of affairs. Thus, in the tradition of **agit-prop** dramas of the 1930s, *The Normal Heart* seeks to galvanize its audience to demand immediate political transformation. While he tempers this approach somewhat in *The Destiny of Me,* Kramer's trademark anger remains one of his distinctive contributions to the drama of AIDS.

Since *As Is* and *The Normal Heart* premiered, theatrical representations of AIDS have become increasingly varied, and the pictures of gays—and others—facing this disease and its aftermath have become more elaborate. While some plays—such as Lanford Wilson's one-act *A Poster of the Cosmos* (1988)—have continued to feature central characters who are martyrs to a traditional homophobic bigotry made more rabid by homosexuality's abiding association with AIDS, other plays have employed quite different strategies: Paula Vogel's *The Baltimore Waltz* (1990) renders the heartbreaking legacy of AIDS through an intriguing role reversal in which a sister tries to cope with the loss of her brother to AIDS by changing places with him in her fantasy of a trip to Europe. Tony Kushner's two-part epic *Angels in America: A Gay Fantasia on National Themes*

(Part One, *Millennium Approaches* [1991] and Part Two, *Perestroika* [1992]) utilizes the epidemic and the general state of gay life in 1980s America to examine some of America's most cherished myths as well as the moral climate of the nation itself. Harvey Fierstein's *Safe Sex* (1987) and Paul Rudnick's *Jeffrey* (1993) suggest that comedy, rather than being inappropriate, may actually be a necessity in the era of AIDS. Even the formally improbable musical has found various ways of accommodating the disease. As David Román observes, in an ironic turn, several members of ACT UP/Los Angeles redirected the theatrical impulses for which ACT UP has been so noted to their source of origin by serving in the cast of the campy *AIDS! The Musical!* (1991), wryly promoted with the slogan "You've had the disease, you've been to the demonstration, now see the musical!"

The years since the premiere of *The Normal Heart* have seen many changes in Larry Kramer's life. He has helped to found ACT UP and he has broken with it. He has written a powerfully personal account of the first decade of the AIDS epidemic, *Reports from the Holocaust: The Making of an AIDS Activist* (1989). Far from the least significant event of the intervening years was his diagnosis as HIV positive in 1988. That circumstance prompted him to complete the play that was to become *The Destiny of Me*. As he remarked in an article for the *New York Times*, having been working for years on "one of those 'family' slash 'memory' plays I suspect most playwrights feel compelled at some point to try their hand at in a feeble attempt, before it's too late, to find out what their lives have been all about," he sought to arrange for its production. But Kramer escaped death and the play was initially rejected by several companies. By the time it premiered in October of 1992, *The Destiny of Me* had become more a mechanism for delineating what Kramer himself has called "a journey to acceptance of one's homosexuality" than a snapshot of the current frontlines of the war on AIDS.

Kramer signals his dual focus in the first act when the play opens with Ned Weeks entering what he calls the "National Institutes of Quacks" to undergo an experimental treatment while the nameless AIDS activist group which Weeks has helped to found is protesting outside. As in *The Normal Heart*, much of the scene is peppered with Weeks's sarcasm and outrage though, as David Richards notes, they seem almost reflex reactions. In fact, Ned himself ruefully notes, "It's funny how everyone's afraid of me. And my mouth. And my temper. They should only know I can't get angry now to save my soul." Kramer quickly balances the present soul-weary and seriously ill patient with Alexander Weeks—Ned's ungainly younger self— an adolescent just beginning to come to grips with the fact that his feelings of alienation transcend the usual adolescent angst. As the hospital room is transformed into the home of Weeks's parents in the sardonically named Eden Heights, a dialogue begins between youth and age which moves *The Destiny of Me* beyond the memory-play models of Arthur Miller and Tennessee Williams. Unlike *Death of a Salesman* or *A Streetcar Named Desire*, which foreground their characters' reliving of the past or conversing with the long dead, Ned and Alexander occupy an emotional time frame in which youth and age coexist, linked but autonomous, capable of providing each other insight and, eventually, support.

The byplay of Alexander and Ned over *The Destiny of Me*'s three acts serves to do for Ned's relationship with his family what his earlier confrontations with the political and medical establishments have done to his sense of those who have controlled the public policy of AIDS: "When we were on the outside, fighting to get in, it was easier to call everyone names. But they were smart. They invited us inside. And we saw they looked human. And that makes hate harder." As Ned watches his younger self, he comes to realize that his mother and father's sad lives in large measure explain—without justifying— their debilitating attitudes toward him. When he confronts again through his younger self the family rejection that greeted his announcement of his homosexuality, and when he comes to recognize the partial truth of Alexander's plaintive cry, "I gave you great stuff to work with. How did you fuck it up? Excuse me for saying so, but I think you're a mess," Ned can finally begin the process of accepting himself.

As the play ends, an exhausted Ned sits on a hospital floor covered with blood from transfusion bags that he has destroyed in a paroxysm of anger over the news that the procedure has failed. His destiny remains unchanged. He is doomed. But his humor, anguished though it may be, remains:

> ALEXANDER: What's going to happen to me?
> NED: You're going to go to eleven shrinks. You won't fall in love for forty years. And when a nice man finally comes along and tries to teach you to love him and love yourself, he dies from a plague. Which is waiting to kill you, too.
> ALEXANDER: I'm sorry I asked.

In a touching scene of rebirth, Ned gives Alexander the embrace he has craved throughout the play as they sing a duet of "It's Only Make Believe" ending with the lines: "Might as well make believe I love you . . . For to tell the truth . . . I do." The destiny of Larry Kramer is to face himself and finally find, as Frank Rich said, that he has been "blessed and cursed by a far larger than normal heart." So has *The Destiny of Me.*

WORKS CONSULTED

Bergman, David. "Larry Kramer and the Rhetoric of AIDS." *AIDS: The Literary Response.* Ed. Emmanuel S. Nelson. New York: Twayne, 1992. 175–186.

Clum, John M. "A Culture That Isn't Just Sexual: Dramatizing Gay Male History." *Theatre Journal* 41 (1989): 169–189.

———. *Acting Gay: Male Homosexuality in Modern Drama.* New York: Columbia University Press, 1992.

Curtin, Kaier. *"We Can Always Call Them Bulgarians": The Emergence of Lesbians and Gay Men on the American Stage.* Boston: Alyson Publications, 1987.

De Jongh, Nicholas. *Not in Front of the Audience: Homosexuality on Stage.* London: Routledge, 1992.

Duberman, Martin. Rev. of *Faggots,* by Larry Kramer. *The New Republic,* 6 January 1979: 30–32.

Gross, Gregory. "Coming Up for Air: Three AIDS Plays." *Journal of American Culture* 15 (1992): 63–67.

Holleran, Andrew. "Introduction." *The Normal Heart,* by Larry Kramer. New York: Plume, 1985.

Kramer, Larry. "A Man's Life, and the Path to Acceptance." *New York Times,* 4 October 1992, sec. 2: 1+.

———. *The Destiny of Me.* New York: Plume, 1993.

———. *The Normal Heart.* New York: Plume, 1985.

Osborn, M. Elizabeth, ed. *The Way We Live Now: American Plays & The AIDS Crisis.* New York: Theatre Communications Group, 1990.

Rich, Frank. "Larry Kramer Tells His Own Anguished Story." *New York Times,* 21 October 1992: C15+.

Richards, David. "An Author in Search of 2 Characters: Himself." *New York Times,* 25 October 1992, sec. 2, 5+.

Román, David. "'It's My Party and I'll Die If I Want to!': Gay Men, AIDS, and the Circulation of Camp in U.S. Theatre." *Theatre Journal* 44 (1992): 305–327.

CHARACTERS

NED WEEKS
NURSE HANNIMAN
DR ANTHONY DELLA VIDA
ALEXANDER WEEKS

RICHARD WEEKS
RENA WEEKS
BENJAMIN WEEKS

About the Production

As with all plays, I hope there are many ways to design *The Destiny of Me*.

The original New York production turned out to be much more elaborate than I'd conceived it in my head as I wrote it. As I worked with the director, Marshall Mason, I began to fear I'd written an undesignable play (not that there should ever be such a thing!).

On *The Normal Heart* I'd had the talent of the enormously gifted Eugene Lee, ever adept at solving problems of this nature in miraculously ingenious ways, and ways that were not expensive. I suspect that Eugene's design for *The Normal Heart*—the way he solved not dissimilar problems—has been utilized unknowingly all over the world, just from the participants in one production seeing photographs of another.

This time, and it was also a great gift, I had the opportunity to work with John Lee Beatty, who'd designed many of Marshall's other productions. John Lee is another kind of theatrical genius, as obsessed with minute details as Eugene is off-the-cuff. Our set was a realistic, technical marvel, with the scenes from the past zipping in and out on clever winches. We even had a sink on stage, with running water, so that the doctors and nurses and orderlies who were constantly coming into the hospital environment could wash their hands, as they would in a real hospital.

The elaborate apparatus for the medical treatment Ned is undergoing, as well as everything having to do with blood, was also worked out meticulously. I have not, in this published version, completely detailed all this medical minutiae, or the comings and goings of the nonspeaking hospital staff that the availability of a group of young Circle Rep interns allowed us to utilize in peopling our stage. Nor have I gone into too much detail about how the blood machinery looked and worked, beyond cursory descriptions.

I guess what I'm saying, and hoping, is that a lot of inventive ways will be found to deal with any problems designing and producing my play might raise—that there is no *right* way, and that, as in all theater, imagination is also one of the actors, and there are many ways to play the part.

Introduction

I began arranging for the production of *The Destiny of Me* when I thought I was shortly going to die. It's a play I've been working on for years—one of those "family" slash "memory" plays I suspect most playwrights feel compelled at some point to try their hand at in a feeble attempt, before it's too late, to find out what their lives have been all about. I figured it would be the last words of this opinionated author.

Not only did I think my play would be done while I was on my deathbed or after, I decided I would definitely leave word that it would not be done while my mother, who is now approaching ninety-three, was still alive. I certainly didn't want to be around to discover how she would react to the portrayal, by her fifty-seven-year-old homosexual son, of some fifty years of *her* life.

As destiny would have it, I appear to have received a respite from my expected imminent demise, at least one sufficient enough to ask myself: what have I gone and done?

I call *The Destiny of Me* a companion play to the one I wrote in 1985, *The Normal Heart*, about the early years of AIDS. It's about the same leading character, Ned Weeks, and the events of the earlier play have transpired before the curtain rises on the new one; it is not necessary, as they say, to have seen one to see the other. (The deathbed play remains to be written; now I have the chance to write a trilogy.)

Oh, I've had to make a few little changes. Instead of facing death so closely, Ned Weeks now only fears it mightily. And the hospital where he'd gone to die is now the hospital where he goes to try to live a little longer.

He still tries to figure out what his life's been all about.

This play now seems very naked to me. I'm overwhelmed with questions that didn't bother me before. Why was it necessary for me to write it? Why do I want people to see it? What earthly use is served by washing so much of "the Weeks family" linen in public?

When I wrote *The Normal Heart*, I had no such qualms. I knew exactly what I wanted to achieve and there was no amount of *anything* that could repress my hell-or-high-water determination to see that play produced, to hear my words screamed out in a theater, and to hope I'd change the world.

In what possible way could *The Destiny of Me* ever change the world?

About a dozen years ago I found myself talking to a little boy. I realized the little boy was me. And he was talking back. I was not only talking to myself but this myself was a completely different individual, with his own thoughts, defenses, and character, and a personality often most at odds with his grown-up self. These conversations frightened me. It's taken me years of psychoanalysis to rid myself of just such schizophrenic tendencies.

I found myself talking to this kid more and more. I found myself writing little scenes between the two of us. I was in trouble. I was falling in love with this kid. I, who face a mirror—and the world—each day with difficulty, had found something, inside myself, to love. I found myself writing this kid's journey—one that could only complete itself in death.

I should point out that I have always hated *anything* that borders on the nonrealistic. I hate science fiction and horror movies. I do not want to see a play, be it by Herb Gardner or Neil Simon or Luigi Pirandello, in which one actor (the author) talks to himself as embodied in another actor. My life has always been too bound up in harsh realities to believe in such fantastic possibilities, theatrical or otherwise. Nor have I ever been one to write comfortably in styles not realistic, not filled with facts and figures and *truth*. (Some readers tell me my novel, *Faggots*, is about as surreal a portrayal of

the gay world as could be, but it was all the real McCoy to me.)

As I wrote on, in addition to worrying about my mother's reaction, I began to taunt myself with other fears. There is only one *Long Day's Journey into Night*. There is only one *Death of a Salesman*. And a million feeble attempts to duplicate their truth and to provoke their tears. And each playwright has only one family story to tell. And only one chance to tell it. Most, if they're lucky, throw their feeble attempts in the waste basket or file them with the stuff they plan to bequeath to their alma mater or unload on the University of Texas.

I further complicated my task by determining to write a personal history: a journey to acceptance of one's own homosexuality. My generation has had special, if not unique, problems along this way. We were the generation psychoanalysts tried to change. This journey, from discovery through guilt to momentary joy and toward AIDS, has been my longest, most important journey, as important—no, more important—than my life with my parents, than my life as a writer, than my life as an activist. Indeed, my homosexuality, as unsatisfying as much of it was for so long, has been the single most important defining characteristic of my life.

As I wrote of these journeys, and as we entered rehearsals, I found myself, over and over again, learning new things no amount of analysis had taught me. The father I'd hated became someone sad to me; and the mother I'd adored became a little less adorable, and no less sad. And although I'd set out, at the least, to have my day in court, actors, those magicians, grabbed hold of my words, and what had been my characters asserted themselves, and my harsh judgments were turned around in my face! My mother and father were showing me who they were, and not the other way around.

Oh, why had I written this damn play anyway!

I'd started out wanting to write a tragedy. I'd read all sorts of books that tried to define precisely what one is, including not a few that told me I couldn't write one anymore. I think the lives that many gay men have been forced to lead, with AIDS awaiting them after the decades-long journey from self-hate, is the stuff of tragedy. And I'd thought that the marriage my parents had was tragic, too; they could have had much better lives without each other.

But, once again, I discovered some surprising things. My younger self was very funny and spunky, and it's the me of today who, despite one hundred years of therapy, has lost resilience. As for my parents' lives, well, there is a difference between tragedy and sadness. I cannot bring myself to see my father as Willy Loman. Nor my mother as Medea or Clytemnestra or Antigone or Phèdre. Or Mary Tyrone. Or Joan of Arc. The stakes (pun intended) just weren't the same.

So was my determination to see this play produced a desire for vengeance? For blame? For catharsis? Was it only hubris? (Anita Brookner enunciated many writers' main motivation in the very title of one of her own books, *Look at Me.*)

I discovered long ago that writing doesn't bring catharsis. Writing *The Normal Heart* did not release my anger or make me hate Ed Koch and Ronald Reagan less or alter the present sorry state of the AIDS plague for the better. Writing *Faggots* did not find me true love or make me any more lovable or, so far as I can see, start any mass migration by the gay community to monogamous relationships. No, getting things off your chest doesn't get them off for very long.

Carole Rothman, the artistic director at Second Stage in New York, herself a parent, said she was uncomfortable about doing a play that "blamed" parents. (Joe Papp said he wouldn't put on any play where a father hit a son. I always thought this said more about Joe than my play.) "Blame" began to be a word that haunted me. Did I blame my parents? Is this what my play was saying? Over and over I reread my words. I wasn't blaming them. I was trying to understand what in their own lives made them the way they were and how this affected the lives of their children. I didn't see this as blame or vengeance.

In fact, I came to see their behavior as destined as my own. I even decided to change the play's title, which had been *The Furniture of Home* (taken from the same W. H. Auden poem as *The Normal Heart*). I don't know what sent me to Walt Whitman (beyond the desire to find my title in the words of another gay poet; I wonder now if it was as simple as one aging and physically deteriorating gay writer seeking inspiration from another), but I found myself reading and rereading his collected works. Sure enough, in "Out of the Cradle Endlessly Rocking," that haunting ode to life without love, I found what I was looking for—"the destiny of me."

Now I had a play and I had a title and I had a director—Marshall Mason. Then my leading actors, Colleen Dewhurst and Brad Davis, died. I lost my next leading man, Ron Rifkin, because of an unfortunate disagreement I had with the playwright Jon Robin Baitz. Ron, for whom Robbie wrote his greatest role, in *The Substance of Fire*, bowed out. It would be some time before Tanya Berezin of the Circle Repertory Company would read my play in March 1991 and immediately accept it. Like me by the men in my life, my play had first to have its own history of rejections: by the Public Theater (both Joe Papp and JoAnne Akalaitis), Manhattan Theater Club, Lincoln Center, Playwrights Horizons (both André Bishop and Don Scardino), American Place Theater, Second Stage, Long Wharf in New Haven, Hartford Stage, Yale Rep (both Lloyd Richards and Stan Wojewodski, Jr.), South Coast Rep in California, the Goodman and Steppenwolf in Chicago, and Circle in the Square on Broadway.

I list these not to either tempt fate (oh, the nightmare possibility of those reviews that begin, "The numerous theaters that turned down Larry Kramer's new play were wise indeed . . .") or flaunt my rejections (*The Normal Heart, Faggots,* and my screenplay for *Women in Love* were originally turned down by even larger numbers), but to offer this thought to other writers, and to the little child inside that one talks to: almost more than talent you need tenacity, and an infinite capacity for rejection if you are to succeed. I still don't know where you get these even after writing this play to try to find the answer.

I guess that's what my play's about. I guess that's what my life's been about.

Not much of a message, huh? Well, maybe it's about a little more. I'll have to wait and see. Each day my family surprises me more and more. And that little boy inside me.

I'll bet you didn't expect Larry Kramer to talk like this.

I set out to make sense of my life. And I found out that one's life, particularly *after* one has written about it, doesn't make sense. *Life* doesn't make sense.

But change does. And there is no change without tenacity. And change is usually very hard. With precious few gratifications along the way to encourage you to carry on. And some change is good. And necessary. And some change must not be allowed.

This sounds more like Larry Kramer.

Yes, I can make sense out of *this*.

You may not agree, and you may not change your opinion, but you will have heard me make my case. And maybe, just maybe, you will think twice before slugging your kid tonight because he or she is gay, or you will not vote for any candidate who would allow AIDS to become a plague.

Yes, I know the possibilities are slim.

So what?

The little boy in me still believes everything is possible.

Mom, you taught me this.

And you lied.

But so does art and so does hope.

O you singer solitary, singing by yourself, projecting me,
O solitary me listening, never more shall I cease perpetuating you,
Never more shall I escape, never more the reverberations,
Never more the cries of unsatisfied love be absent from me,
Never again leave me to be the peaceful child I was before what there in the night,
By the sea under the yellow and sagging moon,
The messenger there arous'd, the fire, the sweet hell within,
The unknown want, the destiny of me.

From "Out of the Cradle Endlessly Rocking"
WALT WHITMAN

ACT ONE

(NED WEEKS, *middle-aged, enters a hospital room with his suitcase.*)

NED: I grew up not far from here. The trees were just being chopped down. To make room for Eden Heights. That's where we lived. That's what they named places then.
(HANNIMAN, *a nurse, pushes in a cart with medical stuff on it, including* NED'S *records. She is black.*)

HANNIMAN: The eleventh floor is our floor—Infectious Diseases. We ask that you don't leave this floor, or the hospital, or the Institute's grounds, or indeed go to any other floor, where other illnesses are housed. Dr Della Vida says it's better to have you on our side. I tell him you're never going to be on our side. You're not here to cause some sort of political ruckus? Are you?

NED: (*unpacking some books*) What better time and place to read *The Magic Mountain?*

HANNIMAN: Are you?

NED: I'm here for you to save my life. Is that too political?
(DR ANTHONY DELLA VIDA *enters. He is short, dynamic, handsome, and very smooth, a consummate bureaucrat. He beams hugely and warmly embraces* NED.)

TONY: Hello, you monster!

NED: I never understand why you talk to me . . .

TONY: I'm very fond of you.

NED: . . . after all I say about you.

HANNIMAN: "Dr Della Vida runs the biggest waste of taxpayers' money after the Defense Department." In the Washington *Post.*

TONY: No, in the Washington *Post* he compared me to Hitler.

HANNIMAN: No, that was in the *Village Voice.* And it was "you fucking son-of-a-bitch of a Hitler."

TONY: Where was it he accused me of pulling off the biggest case of scientific fraud since laetrile?

NED: *Vanity Fair.*

TONY: *(studying* NED'S *file)* All your numbers are going down pretty consistently. You didn't listen to me when you should have.

NED: Ah, Tony, nobody wants to take that shit.

TONY: They're wrong.

NED: It doesn't work.

TONY: Nothing works for everybody.

NED: Nobody believes you.

TONY: Then why are you here?

NED: I'm more desperate. And you sold me a bill of goods.

TONY: You begged me you were ready to try anything.

NED: I asked you when you were going to strike gold with *something.* You've spent two billion dollars.

TONY: No, sir! You asked me if I had anything I would take if I were you.

NED: No, sir! You said to me, "I've got it." And I said, "The cure!" And you said, "If you quote me I'll deny it." You slippery bastard.

TONY: You're the slippery bastard!

HANNIMAN: Yep, he sure is on our side.

NED: *(reading from a newspaper clipping)* "Dr Della Vida has discovered a method to suppress the growth of the virus in mice by 80–90% . . ." The *New York Times.*

TONY: For over a decade you have mercilessly condemned that newspaper's coverage of this illness. Suddenly they're your experts?

NED: *(another clipping)* ". . . reconstituted genes will be introduced in transfusions of the patient's own blood . . . cells given new genetic instructions, to self-destruct if they are infected." *The Lancet. (a third clipping)* "Conclusion: The success of this theory in *in vitro* experiments, followed by the successful inoculation of three West African sooty mangabey monkeys, leads one to hope that human experimentation can commence without further delay." The *New England Journal of Monkeys.* I'll be your monkey.

HANNIMAN: Don't say that. We have to guarantee each chimp a thirty-thousand-dollar retirement endowment. Their activists are better than your activists.

TONY: How have you been feeling? *(starts examining* NED.)

NED: Okay physically. Emotionally shitty. We've lost.

TONY: You *are* depressed. That's too bad. You've been very useful.

HANNIMAN: Useful?

TONY: All your anger has kept us on our toes.

HANNIMAN: They have yelled at, screamed at, threatened, insulted, castigated, crucified every person on our staff. In every publication. On every network. From every street corner. Useful?

NED: Who is she? I've been infected for so long, and I still don't get sick. What's that all about? Everyone thinks I *am* sick. Everyone around me *is* sick. I keep waiting *to* get sick. I don't know why I'm *not* sick. All my friends are dead. I think I'm guilty I'm still alive.

TONY: Not everybody dies in any disease. You know that. Your numbers could even go back up on their own. Why is my hospital surrounded by your army of activists? Am I going to be burned at the stake if I can't restore your immune system?

NED: I'm not so active these days.

TONY: You?

NED: *(softly)* They don't know I'm here.

HANNIMAN: Why don't I believe that?

NED: What have we achieved? I'm here begging. *(*NED *suddenly reaches out and touches* TONY'S *face.* HANNIMAN'S *back is turned.)* This new treatment—you can't even stick it into me legally. Can you?

TONY: Ned—I do think I'm on to something. You've really got to keep your mouth shut. You've got to promise me. And then you've got to keep that promise.

NED: The world can't be saved with our mouths shut.

TONY: Give me lessons later.

NED: How long can you keep me alive? I've got work to finish. Two years. Can you do that?

TONY: You know there aren't any promises. Two years, the way you look now, doesn't seem impossible.

NED: How about three? It's a very long novel. Why are you willing to do this for me?

HANNIMAN: Because if it works, you'll scream bloody murder if anyone stands in his way. Because if it doesn't work, you'll scream bloody murder for him to find something else. That's *his* reasoning. Now *I* would just as soon you weren't here. Period.

TONY: *(to* HANNIMAN.*)* Give him the double d.d.b.m. *(leaves)*

NED: What's a double d.d.b.m.?

(From the cart, HANNIMAN *wields an enormous needle.* ALEXANDER, *a young boy, is seen dimly on the side. He's wet from a shower, and wrapped in towels. He comes closer to see what's going on.)*

HANNIMAN: Mice and chimps were easy. You're our first one who can talk back. Drop your drawers and bend over.

ALEXANDER: What's she doing?

NED: I want my Mommy.

ALEXANDER: Mommy's not home yet.

HANNIMAN: You even wrote in *The Advocate* you'd heard I was a lesbian.

NED: You're Mrs. Dr Della Vida?

(She rams the hypodermic into his ass.)

(Screams) We consider that a compliment!

ALEXANDER: Why are you here? *(no answer)* Please tell me what's happening!

HANNIMAN: *(still injecting him)* I think it takes great courage for you to set foot anywhere near here. My husband works twenty hours a day and usually sleeps the other four in one of these rooms. I'm pregnant and I don't know how. Or why. With the number of patients we're seeing, I'm bearing an orphan. *(extracts the hypodermic and takes a larger one)*

NED: That wasn't it?

(She laughs. She administers the second needle even deeper. He screams again, louder.)

ALEXANDER: Tell me what's going on!

NED: I'm starring in this wonderful play about euthanasia.

(HANNIMAN finishes and leaves.)

ALEXANDER: Where's Benjamin? Where's *anyone?* Don't you have any friends? At a time like this? Something awful's happening. Isn't it? *(no answer)* Will you give me a hug?

NED: Get lost, Lemon.

ALEXANDER: Just remember—*I* was here. *(leaves)*

NED: *(changing from his street clothes)* What do you do when you're dying from a disease you need not be dying from? What do you do when the only system set up to save you is a pile of shit run by idiots and quacks? What do you do when your own people won't unite and fight together to save their own lives? What do you do when you've tried every tactic you can think of to fight back and none of them has worked and you are now not only completely destitute of new ideas but suddenly more frightened than you've been before that your days are finally and at last more numbered and finite and that an obit in the *New York Times* is shortly to be yours? Why, you talk yourself into believing the quack is a genius *(massages his sore ass)* and his latest vat of voodoo is a major scientific breakthrough. And you check yourself in. So, here I am. At the National Institutes of Quacks.

They still don't know how this virus works inside our bodies. They still don't know how this disease progresses and what really triggers this progression. They still don't know if the virus could be hiding someplace else—its major home might not even be in the blood at all. Finally, in total desperation, my kids out there prepared a whole long list of what they still don't know; we even identified the best scientists anywhere in the world to find the answers.

When we were on the outside, fighting to get in, it was easier to call everyone names. But they were smart. They invited us inside. And we saw they looked human. And that makes hate harder.

It's funny how everyone's afraid of me. And my mouth. And my temper. They should only know I can't get angry now to save my soul. Eight years of screaming at one idiot to wake up and four more years of trying to get another idiot to even say the word can do that. They knew we couldn't keep up the fight and that eventually they'd be able to kill off all the faggots and spics and niggers. When I started yelling, there were forty-one cases of a mysterious disease. Now a doctor at Harvard is predicting a billion by the new century. And it's still mysterious. And the mystery isn't why they don't know anything, it's why they don't *want* to know anything.

So what does all this say about the usefulness of . . . anything?

Yes, the war is lost.

And I'd give anything to get angry again.

ALEXANDER: *(reappearing, still wrapped in towel)* You are not going to die!

NED: Go away.

ALEXANDER: If you die I die!

NED: Please go away.

ALEXANDER: I kept you alive for quite some time, thank you very much!

NED: Lemon—get the fuck out of here.

ALEXANDER: I was here first! Are you rich and successful and famous? Two of them? One? Did you fall in love? *(no answers)* Every single second of my entire life I've wanted there to be somebody! I gave you great stuff to work with. How did you fuck it up? Excuse me for saying so, but I think you're a mess.

(He goes to his Eden Heights bedroom. The walls are plastered with theatrical posters from hit shows—South Pacific, Mister Roberts, A Streetcar Named Desire, The Glass Menagerie.)

(To NED *and the audience)* Alexander the Great ruled the entire known world, from east to west and north to south! He conquered it, with his faithful companions. He was very handsome. He was very fearless. Everybody knew who he was and everybody loved him and worshiped him and cherished him. He was king of everything! *(singing)* "Give me some men who are stouthearted men who will fight for the right they adore!" Good evening, Mr Murrow. Thank you for coming into my home. This is where I wrote my Pulitzer Prize play and this, of course,

is where I practiced my Academy Award–winning performance. An Alexander can be anything he wants to be! Dressed up for battle in shining armor and a helmet and plumes, or a gorgeous purple royal cloak. *(singing)* "Who cares if my boat goes upstream, Or if the gale bids me go with the river's flow? I drift along with my fancy, Sometimes I thank my lucky stars my heart is free—And other times I wonder where's the mate for me?" *(speaking dialogue)* "Hello."

NED: "How do you do? Are you an actress?"

ALEXANDER: "Oh, no. But I'd give anything if I could be."

NED: "Why?"

ALEXANDER: "Because you can make believe so many wonderful things that never happen in real life." *(singing)* "The game of just supposing is the sweetest game I know, Our dreams are more romantic, Than the world we see."

NED: *(singing)* "And if the things we dream about, Don't happen to be so . . ."

ALEXANDER: "That just an unimportant technicality." *Show Boat* was the first show I saw on Broadway. *(singing)* "Only make believe I love you . . ."

NED: "Only make believe that you love me . . ." Oh, get dressed. Before Pop catches you.

ALEXANDER: I can be Henry Fonda in *Mister Roberts* or Cornelia Otis Skinner in *Lady Windermere's Fan.* The second balcony of the National Theater is only ninety cents and I go every other week when they change the show. I can be Ezio Pinza or Mary Martin in *South Pacific.* "One dream in my heart. One love to be living for . . ." And I am performing on the biggest stage and everyone is applauding me like crazy. *(bowing)* Thank you. Thank you very much. Oh, Ned! Nobody I know is interested in what I'm interested in. And I'm not interested in what they're interested in.

NED: And you're never going to be able to accept or understand that.

ALEXANDER: Do you get in trouble when you try to find out things?

NED: Only if you're nosey.

ALEXANDER: I'm nosey.

NED: The best people are nosey.

ALEXANDER: Thank you. I ran away once. To New York. I used all my baby-sitting money. I'd see a Broadway show every day for the rest of my life. Mom traced me to Aunt Fran's just as I was leaving to see Judith Anderson in *Medea.* Ma said under no circumstances was I allowed to see a play about a mother who murders both her children.

NED: I said, Why not?

ALEXANDER and NED: Pop wants to murder me all the time.

ALEXANDER: *(making a turban from a towel and singing)* "I'm gonna wash that man right out-a my hair, And send him on his way."
(Sounds of RICHARD WEEKS *coming home.)*
My God, Pop's home! *(furiously getting dressed,* NED *helping him)* I always say Hope for the Best and Expect the Worst. Ned, Alexander means Helper and Defender of All Mankind. Why'd you change my name?

NED: Alexander the Great died very young.
*(*RICHARD WEEKS *enters. He is almost the same age* NED *is now, but he looks much older. He is impeccably dressed. He puts down his newspaper and takes off his jacket and tie and cufflinks and rolls up his shirtsleeves. He keeps on his vest with its gold chain that holds his Phi Beta Kappa and Yale Law Journal keys. He comes across some of* ALEXANDER'S *comic books.)*

RICHARD: Come here, you!

ALEXANDER: *(from his room)* I'm not home from school yet!

RICHARD: I warned you if I caught you buying comic books one more time I'd take away your allowance. You'll never get into Yale.

ALEXANDER: I'm going to go to Harvard.

RICHARD: You are not going to go to Harvard.

ALEXANDER: *(to* NED*)* What am I supposed to say? Poppa, this strange man who lives down the block *gives* me the comic books. If I let him stick his finger up my tushie and suck my penis. He says he's in medical school and I'm helping him learn. Isn't it all right to have comic books if I don't spend my own money on them?

NED: Mordecai Rushmore.

ALEXANDER: Why do I have to lie? *(entering, dressed)* Hi, Pop. What's a penis? *(grabbing the offending comic books)*

RICHARD: *(leaving to wash up)* Look it up in the dictionary.

ALEXANDER: It isn't in the dictionary.

RICHARD: Then ask your mother. *(exits)*

HANNIMAN: *(enters with a large bottle of pills)* Take two of these every two hours. You have a watch. I won't have to remind you.

NED: *(as* ALEXANDER *stuffs the comics behind a book on a shelf)* What are you doing?

ALEXANDER: I always hide them here.

NED: *(reading the book's spine)* Psychopathia Sexualis *by Dr Richard von Krafft-Ebing.*

HANNIMAN: There seem to be more and more unusually dressed people gathering outside. What are they going to do?

NED: Look, can we please try and be friends?

ALEXANDER: Hey! I think if you're going to be with me, you really should be with me.

NED: I'm sorry if I upset you.

HANNIMAN: You're not sorry. You're scared shitless. *(leaves)*

RENA'S VOICE: Somebody please help me!
*(*RENA WEEKS *manages to open the front door, carrying large bags of groceries. She is in her forties. She wears a Red Cross uniform—skirt, jacket, and hat.)*

ALEXANDER: *(helping her)* Hi, Mom. Dad says to ask you what's a penis?

RENA: I told you.

ALEXANDER: Tell me again.

RENA: When you grow up, you'll insert it into the woman's sexual organ, which is called the vagina. The penis goes into the vagina and deposits semen into my uterus, and, if it's the right time of the month, pregnancy occurs, resulting, nine months later, in a child.

ALEXANDER: That's all?

RENA: What else would you like?

(RICHARD *returns, drying his hands on a towel, which he then puts around his neck. The telephone starts to ring.*)

RICHARD: Why are you so late?

RENA: You want to eat, don't you? Can't anyone else ever answer the phone?

RICHARD: Who calls me? (*takes out some new money, peels a bill off*)

RENA: (*answering the phone*) Hello.

RICHARD: I'm raising your allowance from fifty cents to one dollar.

ALEXANDER: (*surprised*) Thanks, Pop.

RENA: Oh, Mrs Noble! This is Rena Weeks, Home Service Director, Suburban Maryland Chapter American Red Cross.

RICHARD: (*trying to give the rest of the money to* RENA) Count it. I got a raise!

RENA: (*taking the money and putting it down*) Could you possibly send some of your wonderful Gray Ladies to help us out driving our paraplegic vets to the ball game this Saturday while our regular volunteers work the monthly Bloodmobile?

RICHARD: I hate it that you work.

RENA: Yes, it is hard finding volunteers now the war is almost over.

(ALEXANDER *accidentally drops some canned goods.*)

RICHARD: That table cost two hundred dollars!

ALEXANDER: One hundred and seventy-five.

RENA: Yes, some other time. (*hangs up*)

RICHARD: They fired fifty more. Abe Lesser and his wife moved out of their apartment in the middle of the night. Nobody heard them leave. How could anybody not hear them leave?

(ALEXANDER *sits down and reads part of* RICHARD'S *newspaper, unconsciously jiggling his leg up and down with increasing speed.* RENA *puts out a cold meal; in a hurry, she'll rush through the serving, eating, and clearing.*)

RENA: It's been a terrible day for tragedy.

RICHARD: Abe Lesser is no more a Communist than Joe DiMaggio.

RENA: We had a dreadful fire in Hyattsville.

RICHARD: I went to Yale with Abie.

RENA: Six entire families were burned out of everything they owned.

RICHARD: I don't want to hear about it.

RENA: I found shelter for all of them. Six entire families, Richard.

RICHARD: That's enough! I asked you not to talk about it.

ALEXANDER: Louella Parsons is very angry at Rita Hayworth.

RENA: (*telling* ALEXANDER) And I had to call a lovely young bride and break the news that her husband—he was just drafted, they didn't even have time for a honeymoon—he was killed on his very first training flight.

ALEXANDER: Louella says playing bold hussies only gets Rita into trouble.

RENA: His plane just fell from the sky.

RICHARD: Didn't you hear me!

RENA: She hadn't even started receiving his paychecks and he's dead!

ALEXANDER: Louella says she should start playing nice girls like Loretta Young.

RENA: Somebody has to take care of them!

RICHARD: And I never get a hot meal!

RENA: Oh, you do too get hot meals!

RICHARD: I like my tuna salad with egg and you know it!

RENA: I didn't have time to boil eggs!

ALEXANDER: But Rita says the bold and the brazen are the only parts they offer her.

(RICHARD *suddenly and furiously swats* ALEXANDER'S *leg with his part of the newspaper.*) What'd I do now!

RICHARD: You're boring a hole in the rug!

ALEXANDER: Four hundred dollars.

RENA: Alexander, eat.

RICHARD: Five hundred dollars!

ALEXANDER: Four hundred and forty-nine ninety-five.

RICHARD: Isn't Ben coming home again?

RENA: I don't know.

RICHARD: Four hundred and ninety-nine ninety-five! Tax, delivery, and installation. He's Alexander again?

ALEXANDER: At least seven full weeks ago I changed my name to Alexander. Alex, which I thought suited me, was only the whim of a foolish child, a mere moment in time. And Benjamin has always, *always*, preferred Benjamin. You're the only one who insists on shortening him to Ben. And no, Benjamin is not coming home. He had football practice this afternoon, tonight he puts the school paper to bed, and then he's sleeping over at one of his chums. And, *and*, he has told me confidentially that he hates eating at home. With us. Everyone fights too much. *(salts his food vigorously)*

RENA: He didn't say any such thing.

RICHARD: *(slapping* ALEXANDER'S *hand)* You cannot put so much salt on everything! Do you want your stomach to fall apart when you grow up?

ALEXANDER and NED: I'll let you know when I grow up.

NED: It did.

RICHARD: *(to* NED*)* What did I tell you? *(to* ALEXANDER*)* Ben your bosom buddy? He doesn't even know you're alive.

ALEXANDER: He does so! *(salts his food vigorously)*

RICHARD: Do you see what he's doing?

RENA: Richard, please don't say things like that to the boy.

RICHARD: Am I talking to the wall?

RENA: They love each other very much. Benjamin was dying for a brother. He ran all the way to the hospital.

ALEXANDER: And when he saw me he said, "God, he's ugly. What a lemon!" Why do you always have to tell that story? *(salts vigorously again)*

RICHARD: I wash my hands of him. He's your son.

RENA: He's your son, too. I forgot to put any salt in, I was in such a hurry.

RICHARD: You always take his side.

RENA: There aren't any sides. We're all on the same side. We're a family.

RICHARD: Where's my Gelusil? My ulcer's acting up.

NED: Take Alka-Seltzer. It's the only thing that works for me. *(gives* RICHARD *one)*

ALEXANDER: Here it comes, Alexander's ulcer.

NED: Did they have Alka-Seltzer then?

RICHARD: *(preparing it in one of* NED'S *hospital cups)* I get these pains in my gut and the doctor says there's no cure and I said, of course not, how can you be cured of your own son.

NED: Of course they had Alka-Seltzer then. Adam, Noah, Abraham, Moses—all the Jews took Alka-Seltzer.

RICHARD: You haven't shut up since the day you were born.

NED: The Jews *invented* Alka-Seltzer.

ALEXANDER: And I won't shut up until the day I die!

NED: Jesus took Alka-Seltzer.

RENA: Both of you stop it! Where did this fight come from?

ALEXANDER: *(to* RICHARD*)* Why don't fights with Benjamin cause your ulcer? Why is it always Alexander's ulcer?

RENA: You fought with Benjamin?

ALEXANDER: When he won his appointment it didn't look like the war would ever be over.

RICHARD: I won't let him throw away a West Point education!

ALEXANDER: But now there's no point to West Point.

RICHARD: A war isn't over just because you say it's over.

NED: World War II ended in '45 and McCarthy was the early fifties. I'm not remembering this properly.

ALEXANDER: Yes, you are, you are! You're remembering it just fine.

NED: *(starting to take some of the pills* HANNIMAN *left)* I don't remember what I'm remembering.

ALEXANDER: Isn't that the point? I'll tell you when you're wrong.

NED: I'm sure you will. *(noticing the container)* He knows I won't take this poison! *(pumps the nurse's bell)*

RENA: Richard, you're going to have to work the Bloodmobile on Saturday.

RICHARD: I'll be goddamned if I'll work the Bloodmobile on Saturday or any other day.

RENA: Then you can drive the paraplegics to the ball game. Take your pick. And watch your language.

RICHARD: The Bloodmobile on Saturday, Sunday you teach at Temple, and I never get a hot meal.

RENA: Now I'm not supposed to teach at Temple? How else could we pay for Alexander to learn about the history of our people?

ALEXANDER: Don't blame that one on me.

RENA: It's bad enough living in a place where we're the only Jews. It was bad enough his not being bar mitzvahed. My mother would die if she knew.

ALEXANDER: How will she know? You made me write her how sad we all were she couldn't come all the way from L.A. to see me become a man and thank you for your generous check.

NED: *(to RENA)* Do you know I think that was my first conscious lie?

RENA: *(to NED)* I was only trying not to break my mother's heart.

(Goes into her bedroom.)

ALEXANDER: Mordecai Rushmore was my first lie.

NED: He was kind of humpy.

ALEXANDER: I don't have to tell you there are a lot of comic books hidden behind Dr Krafft-Ebing.

NED: So you like it?

ALEXANDER: It feels good. Except when it's over. Then it feels bad.

RICHARD: *(taking the money RENA has left by the phone)* I got a raise.

ALEXANDER: How could I be bar mitzvahed when I don't believe in God?

RICHARD: Why do you say things like that?

ALEXANDER: What's wrong with saying what you believe?

RICHARD: You're just an obnoxious show-off!

ALEXANDER: And you're my father!

(RICHARD raises his hand to hit him. ALEXANDER moves adeptly out of the way.)

Do you believe in God?

RICHARD: Of course I believe in God!

ALEXANDER: I don't know why. He hasn't been very good to you.

NED: *(impressed)* Did we learn how to fight from them?

RICHARD: Then go live in Hyattsville with those goddamned six dozen burned-out families on their goddamned training flights.

ALEXANDER: I didn't learn one thing from them! Not one goddamned thing!

NED: Then where did we come from?

ALEXANDER: We made it on our own! With lots of help from me!

HANNIMAN: *(rushing in)* What's wrong?

NED: *(to ALEXANDER)* So we sprang full-grown from the head of Zeus?

HANNIMAN: Are you having some sort of drug reaction?

ALEXANDER: Yes!

NED: Yes! *(to HANNIMAN)* I started an organization of activists. Slowly we have lessened from ten to two the years required for a drug to meander through your maze from that first spark in a scientist's eye to your much-sought-after Good Housekeeping Seal. So what do you give us as our first reward? You have studied this rat shit in one hundred and fifty cities, on four continents, in a quarter-million suffering, desperate, docile bodies. You have tested it alone, in numerous combinations, in high dose and low dose, in early intervention and late. You have spent over $300 million attempting to disguise the truth we told you seven years ago, based on our own experience using bootleg supplies we smuggled out of the factories of its manufacturer in the dead of night, that rat shit is rat shit. But do you listen to us? Of course not. We are not scientists. Our results are not based on "good science," "controlled" studies that cost $300 million. How dare you still dispense this . . . this . . . this rat shit?!

HANNIMAN: When will you tell me how you really feel? *(angry)* Why do you and yours always and automatically believe the worst about everything we do? This "rat shit" has become the standard of care against which we must test anything new. That's the only way we can find out if *anything* is better. And you know as well as I do that so far there's *nothing else* to use as a control! To measure new "rat shit" against! *(looking out the window)* Oh, why are you here! We're all doing the best we can. Do you want vengeance or do you want a cure!

NED: I'm here to try the top-secret experimental miracle your husband has up his high-tech ass to redeem his wretched reputation *(brandishing the bottle again)* before all of the billion presently predicted cases die. It's called a last-ditch stand.

HANNIMAN: You've already been given the first part of the top-secret experimental miracle. What do you think it was I rammed up your low-tech ass? And you have to take this with it. *(getting a glass of water and practically ramming some pills down his throat)* Because the protocol we've submitted to the seventeen committees Congress mandates must repeat must vote approval every time Tony pisses requires that you cannot take one without the other. You want to be saved? Shut your fucking mouth and let us save you our way. Swallow! *(leaves when she sees he does)*

(RENA returns wearing a different uniform.)

RICHARD: Now he doesn't believe in God.

RENA: Come with me tonight for a change.

ALEXANDER: All God is is just a little black book in the sky where it's written down exactly when we're going to die.

RENA: That's very original. Alexander, the dishes.

RICHARD: You're going out again?

ALEXANDER: That's all God is. A little black book.

RENA: You know tonight is my night for being a hostess to the servicemen at the Stage Door Canteen. Come with me. We could dance.

ALEXANDER: Saying when we're going to die.

RICHARD: I don't want to dance.

ALEXANDER: It sure would save a lot of time if I could read it right now.

RENA: We used to go everywhere. Mrs Roosevelt might be there. And those Andrews Sisters.

ALEXANDER: Ma, I know all their songs!

RICHARD: I'm tired. Sometimes I feel real old, Rene.

ALEXANDER: Take *me!*

RENA: Don't say that. You'll talk yourself into it.

RICHARD: And like I'm not going to make it.

NED: *(directed toward RICHARD)* You're the same age I am now.

ALEXANDER: Don't you dare feel sorry for him!

RENA: You're fine and your health is fine and you finally have a full-time job. We're all fine.

NED: You have . . . thirty years before you die . . .

RENA: I feel I'm really doing something useful. I love my job.

RICHARD: Which one? You have so many.

RENA: I like helping people. Why does that bother you so? What's wrong with my feeling good? *(starts clearing the table)*

RICHARD: I don't feel good. I've never felt at home here. I can't wait to go back home.

NED: You can't retire for twenty years.

RICHARD: Nineteen.

NED: Almost twenty.

RICHARD: Nineteen and a half.

ALEXANDER: Nineteen and three-quarters.

RENA: *(to ALEXANDER)* Didn't you forget something?

ALEXANDER: *(giving her a ritual kiss)* A kiss for the cook.

RICHARD: A kiss for the cook? What did she cook?

RENA: Washington is such a transient city. Everyone's always talking about going back to someplace else. Funny how nobody ever thinks this place is home.

ALEXANDER: We don't live *in* Washington. We live on the wrong side of the District Line. We are *of* the Capital of the United States but we are not *in* it.

RICHARD: We never should have left Connecticut. We're going back.

ALEXANDER: We are outsiders.

RENA: I like it here. People do all sorts of interesting, important things. I got a new assignment.

I'm going to help avert the many accidents suffered by returning servicemen just out of military hospitals and with prosthetic limbs.

ALEXANDER: What's prosthetic limbs?

NED: (*starts singing softly, then a little dance*) "Blue skies, smiling at me . . ."

RENA: Artificial arms and legs and hands. Made of wood and metal. When these wounded men go into stores, the sales personnel recoil in fear and horror. I'm going to be trained at the Pentagon! And then I'll be sent to department stores like Garfinkel's and specialty stores, like Rich's Shoes. And I'll bring these arms and hands and legs with me so the staff can see and feel them and then they won't be so frightened of them and they can come right up to these men and say, "May I help you, sir?"

ALEXANDER: Mom, that's very depressing. I know all the Andrews Sisters' songs!

RICHARD: That's very depressing.

ALEXANDER: Please!

(*RENA goes back into her bedroom, ALEXANDER begins to sing a medley of Andrews Sisters' songs.*)

"Oh give me land lots of land under starry skies above . . ." "Drinking rum and Coca-Cola . . ." "Don't sit under the apple tree with anyone else but me . . ." "There's going to be a hallelujah day, When the boys have all come home to stay . . ."

RICHARD: Stop that.

ALEXANDER: (*dancing, kicking high*) "And a million bands begin to play . . ."

RICHARD: I said stop it!

ALEXANDER: "We'll be dancing the Victory Polka!"

NED: "Never saw the sun shining so bright . . ."

ALEXANDER: You like the way Fred Astaire dances.

RICHARD: You don't dance like Fred Astaire.

NED: "Noticing the days hurrying by . . ."

ALEXANDER: How do you know I won't develop? Even Fred started somewhere. "When you're in love, my how time flies . . ."

(*RICHARD pounces on him suddenly, trying to restrain the dance movements. But the kid refuses to stop and RICHARD finds himself becoming more violent than he intended.*)

Poppa!

(*RICHARD lets go, shaking his head at what has come over him; he sits down and stares into space, before taking up his paper again.*)

Why can't I do what I want to?

NED: (*helping him up from the floor*) That is probably the least satisfactorily answered question in the history of man.

ALEXANDER: (*defiantly*) Oh, I am going to do with my life every single thing I want to do I don't care what and you better, too!

(*RENA comes out wearing an outfit for hostessing at the Stage Door Canteen. She carries a wooden leg and an arm with a metal hook. She takes NED's hand and makes him touch the limbs.*)

RENA: I want my son to become a leader in the fight against discrimination and prejudice. Don't stay up too late. (*unloads the limbs on NED and kisses him good night. Starting out, passing RICHARD*) Last chance. It will cheer you up. (*leaves*)

RICHARD: Yes, I have a good job. Yes, the government is a good employer that'll never fire me if I keep my mouth shut.

(*NED gives the limbs to ALEXANDER.*)

(*laying out utensils, bowl, and cereal for his breakfast*) I supervise the documentation of all the ocean-going vessels that come anywhere near or leave our shores. I verify their seaworthiness. I study their manifests and any supporting documents. Then I make a decision. Yes or No. There's not much evidence of crime on the high seas anymore, so usually there isn't any reason to say No. Each day is like the one before. Each week and month and year are the same. For this I went to Yale and Yale Law School. For this I get up every day at dawn while everyone's asleep. So I can go through life stamping papers Yes. I got a raise.

ALEXANDER: So did I. Thank you, Poppa. (*tries to hug him, still holding the limbs*) Poppa, would you like me to get up early and have breakfast with you?

RICHARD: *(taking the limbs from him and moving away)* That's okay. You finish your homework, boy?

ALEXANDER: Yes, Poppa.

RICHARD: That's good. You've got to get into Yale. Good night, boy.

ALEXANDER: Good night, Poppa. Poppa . . . *(ALEXANDER wants to kiss him and be kissed. But RICHARD goes into his bedroom, taking the limbs.)* Does the fighting stop someday?

NED: No.

ALEXANDER: Does any dream come true? *(no answer)* Should I stop wishing?

NED: *(pause)* A few dreams do.

ALEXANDER: You had me worried.

NED: Not many.

ALEXANDER: Are you afraid if you tell me the truth I'll slit my wrists?

NED: I wish you could know now everything that happened so you could avoid the things that hurt.

ALEXANDER: Would I do anything differently?

NED: I don't know if we can.

ALEXANDER: Then don't tell me. I guess it wouldn't be much fun anyway if I knew everything in advance. It *will* become fun . . . ? Oh, Ned, I want a friend so bad . . . ly!

NED: I know.

ALEXANDER: *(taking out Dr Krafft-Ebing and reading from it)* "X, a young student in North Germany, began his sexual life in his thirteenth year when he became acquainted with another boy. From that point, he frequently indulged in *immissio penis in os,* although his ambition was always *penem viri in anum.* My advice was to strenuously combat these impulses, perform marital duties, eschew masturbation, and undergo treatment." You sort of get the feeling that, whatever it is, Dr Krafft-Ebing doesn't want you to do it. Ned, who am I? Who can tell me?

NED: There isn't anyone.

ALEXANDER: I'll talk to Benjamin! Why haven't I done it before?

NED: *(trying to hold him back)* Alexander . . .

ALEXANDER: Let go!

NED: Don't tell Ben!

ALEXANDER: Benjamin is the most important person in my life.

NED: Not yet. You're not good friends yet.

ALEXANDER: We are too! Don't you say that too! *(The lights change to nighttime. There is moonlight. BENJAMIN, in a West Point uniform and carrying a small duffel bag, comes home. BENJAMIN rarely raises his voice; his anger is inside of him and his quiet and serious determination is pervasive.)*

NED: Ben, you were so handsome. *(HANNIMAN enters and turns on the light, breaking the mood. She carries a tray on which are four plastic cups, each with a different-colored liquid.)*

HANNIMAN: Before we extract your blood and process it to insert the necessary genetic material, we must determine if you are capable of being transfected—that is, hospitable to receiving our retroviruses containing new genetic instructions without becoming infected or infectious. Each colored liquid contains a different radioactive antibody tracer which will be able to locate that part of your declining immune system that will be the best host for our new virus. L'chaim. *(handing him each glass and seeing that he empties each one completely)* I thought you should know, since of course you don't, that those picketers outside, who, of course, aren't in any way connected with your being here, are growing in number. They have sleeping bags and seem to be camping out. Is something going to happen in the morning that's awful? Last year a bunch sneaked in and chained themselves to Tony's lab tables. The police had to saw off the metal legs before they could take them to jail. OMB charged our budget $300,000 for new tables so we have $300,000 less to save your life. *(as NED finishes by taking his pills)* What a good boy. Now we'll be able to see if a straight path can be cleared. *(turns out the light and leaves)*

(BENJAMIN *crosses in the dark and turns on a light in the bedroom.* ALEXANDER *wakes up and throws himself into his arms.*)

ALEXANDER: Benjamin! I must talk to you! When you're not here, I talk to you from my bed to yours. Do you talk to me? *(no answer)* I pretend Mom and Pop are both dead in a car crash and you and I live together happily ever after.

BENJAMIN: Hey, cheer me up, Lemon.

ALEXANDER: Guess what I got voted in class? *(no answer)* Most talkative. *(no answer)* Oh, Benjamin, I have so much to say. It's imperative I talk to you.

(RICHARD, *in pajamas and slippers, enters, pulling on a robe.* RENA, *in nightgown and slippers only, follows, bearing a plate of brownies.*)

BENJAMIN: I'd hoped you, not Uncle Leon, would be there for my pretrial deposition. Not as my lawyer. As my father.

RICHARD: I almost died!

BENJAMIN: My trial was scheduled long before your operation. Your operation wasn't an emergency. I was court-martialed.

RICHARD: I had to go when the doctor was free.

RENA: He's very famous.

BENJAMIN: Uncle Leon showed up three days late. They put me in detention until he came. The first thing he said to me was: "Your Daddy has more money to pay for a lawyer than you think." You went to Uncle Leon, after not talking to him all these years, so you wouldn't have to pay for a lawyer?

RICHARD: I don't know anything about the kind of law that governs the trouble you're in!

BENJAMIN: What else is there to know when your own son says he's innocent?

ALEXANDER: Benjamin, I must talk to you.

NED: He really does have something important in his own life right now. Try and understand.

RICHARD: How did you plead?

BENJAMIN: Not guilty.

RICHARD: I didn't expect you to listen to me. *(pause)* I almost died. Did you know that?

BENJAMIN: That's why I'm here. They don't just let you out of beast barracks. How do you feel?

RICHARD: They cut out my insides. I had a hemorrhage. I almost bled to death.

RENA: Then the nurse left a window open and he got pneumonia. There was a sudden summer storm. By the time we finally got back here this room was flooded. Alexander and I got down on our hands and knees and sopped up water all night.

BENJAMIN: If either of you has any notions of my staying at West Point, please disabuse yourselves of them immediately. Ma, please put on a robe.

RENA: That's very thoughtful of you, darling. *(to* ALEXANDER*)* Get me my robe.

(ALEXANDER *rushes in and out so he won't miss anything.*)

RICHARD: Why are you deliberately choosing to fight the system!

BENJAMIN: Where do you find choice? I'm accused of turning my head all of two inches during a dress parade because the man next to me tripped. For this a lieutenant colonel, a major, a captain, eight cadets have spent two months haggling over whether it was really four inches instead of two inches. But in reality I lose a year of my life not because I turned my head at all but because my drill inspector, Lieutenant Futrell, hates Jews.

RICHARD: That's right. They don't like Jew boys. Why do you want to make so much trouble?

BENJAMIN: Why do you take their side?

RICHARD: It's your word against theirs.

BENJAMIN: He lied.

RICHARD: Yes, he called you a liar.

BENJAMIN: He called me a kike. At four-thirty in the morning, I was pulled out of my bed, and hauled naked out into the snow by a bunch of upperclassmen, and forced to stand up against a brick wall, which was covered with ice . . .

ALEXANDER: Poor Benjamin.

RENA: Such a good education going to waste.

BENJAMIN: Please stop saying things like that.

RICHARD: Can't you see how impossible it is to be the only one on your side?

BENJAMIN: Can't you see I don't mind being the only one on my side?

ALEXANDER: Neither do I! *(as* RICHARD *is about to turn on him)* Why can't you believe my brother!

BENJAMIN: Thanks, boy. I guess it was too much to expect I'd have the support of my parents.

RENA: Don't say that.

BENJAMIN: Why not? You're asking me to say I'm guilty, when I'm not, and to allow such black marks to enter my permanent record, and to carry on as if nothing has happened. The only thing that keeps me going is some inexplicable sense of my own worth and an intense desire not to develop the habit of quitting.

NED: Where did we come from, Ben?

ALEXANDER: He's magnificent!

RICHARD: Go to bed!

ALEXANDER: Never!

BENJAMIN: I am going to *force* them into declaring me guilty or innocent. They will be compelled to disprove the validity of my word.

ALEXANDER: It's the only way.

BENJAMIN: And unless you are willing to back up my judgment, we shall be coming to a parting of the ways.

ALEXANDER: *(to* NED*)* How can he not help me?

RICHARD: I thought you came home to see me because I almost bled to death. *(starts to leave, then turns)* My own brother! We were going to be partners for life. He threw me out at the height of the Depression. Your mother says I quit because he made my life so miserable that I had no choice but to resign. Her and her peculiar version of the truth. My own brother fired me! I loved him and looked up to him like he was God and that's what he did. Your Mom and I couldn't afford the rent so we had to default on our lease and move to some place cheaper and Leon, for some reason I could never understand, buys up the remainder of that apartment's lease and twenty years later when Mom dies and leaves her few bucks to me, Leon, my brother, sues me for the $3,000 back rent we didn't have in our pocket to pay plus interest for the twenty years. What kind of brother is that? We were going to be partners for life. Yes, I sent for him to help save you in your troubles. He has connections in high places that I'll never have. He's the best

lawyer I know, the best lawyer I ever knew and ever will. Even if I don't talk to him. *(leaves)*

RENA: *(kissing* BENJAMIN *good night)* Everything will be fine. *(kissing* ALEXANDER *good night)* I love you both very much. *(picking up plate and offering brownies)* I made your favorites. I warned him Grandma Sybil should have left her money equally to both her sons. The funny thing is, after Leon was paid back, all it bought me was a new winter coat. You would have thought she'd left us the Hope Diamond. There's nothing in the world my sons can't do. *(leaves)*

*(*BENJAMIN *strips down to his undershorts.* ALEXANDER *tries not to look at him, but peeks anyway.)*

ALEXANDER: Do you have a favorite song? *(no answer)* "One dream in my heart, One love to be living for . . ." You're not coming home, are you?

BENJAMIN: *(looking out the window)* There's not much safety around. As best we can, Alexander, we've got to tough it out. I left home a long time ago.

ALEXANDER: How do I get out? *(no answer)* "One love to be dreaming of . . ." Honestly, sometimes I think I live here all alone.

NED: You do.

ALEXANDER: Oh, shut up. Benjamin, I need help.

NED: Boy, you have some mouth on you.

BENJAMIN: I'm going to go to Yale. It's the surest way I know to get rich.

ALEXANDER: It didn't help Pop.

BENJAMIN: Yes, it did. He found his job down here through some classmate. He'd still be unemployed.

ALEXANDER: What am I going to do?

BENJAMIN: You'll be at Yale soon enough.

ALEXANDER: I can't wait *that* long!

BENJAMIN: You'd be better off at some small liberal-artsy place where they don't mind you being different.

ALEXANDER: *(pause)* You can see I'm different?

BENJAMIN: A blind man can see you're different.

ALEXANDER: *(pause)* How am I different? *(no answer)* Please tell me.

BENJAMIN: Lemon, I'm in trouble. Let's get some shut-eye. *(turns out light)*

ALEXANDER: "Close to my heart he came, Only to fly away, Only to fly as day flies from moonlight . . ."

(HANNIMAN enters and yanks open the blinds, letting in the light. She has equipment for drawing blood.)

HANNIMAN: Not a morning person? Now we take some tests. I thought you would be out there directing your troops. There are twice as many. Thousands. Speeches. Firecrackers. Bullhorns. Rockets. Red glares. Colored smoke. It actually was very pretty. Lots of men dressed up like nurses. There don't seem to be any TV cameras.

NED: That's too bad.

HANNIMAN: Isn't it. Over fifty arrests so far. Mounted police and tear gas. One of the horses crushed somebody's foot. Why don't you like my husband? Is it some sort of sin to work for the government? Do you have any idea how much work all this involves? Tony's been up all night, culturing healthy cells to mix with your unhealthy ones. Then they'll be centrifuged together so they can be put into your blood. Then, from this, additional cells will be drawn off, which then are also genetically altered, so that the infecting part is rendered harmless before it's put back into you. That's for the anti-sense part. To sort of fake out the infected cells and lead them over the cliff to their doom. If it works . . . Well, it's worked with a little girl with another disease. If it works on you . . . I don't let myself think how proud I'll be. Why don't they know out there that you're in here? *(no answer)* Would they think you'd crossed over to the enemy? *(no answer)* They hate us that much?

NED: Too many of us have been allowed to die.

HANNIMAN: Allowed?

NED: There's not one person out there who doesn't believe that intentional genocide is going on.

HANNIMAN: So. Their saint is now a sinner.

NED: A sinner. My late lover's ex-wife, Darlene, whom Felix hadn't seen for over fifteen years, and who had remarried immediately after their divorce an exceptionally rich man, turned up at the memorial service. She brought her own preacher from Oklahoma. Uninvited, he got up and delivered a sermon. To a church filled with hundreds of gay men and lesbians, he yelled out: "Oh, God, take this sinner, Felix Turner, for he knew not what he did." There was utter silence. Then I stood up and walked over and stood right under his nose and screamed as loud as I think I've ever screamed: "Felix Turner was not a sinner! Felix Turner was a good man! The best I ever knew."

ALEXANDER: *(rushing in)* Who's Felix Turner!

NED: In due course.

(ALEXANDER withdraws.)

Darlene drew herself up and marched right over to me and shouted even louder: "I now know that I have been placed on this earth to make you and all like you miserable for your sins." And we've been in court ever since, fighting over his will, which left everything to me. I was in love for five minutes with someone who was dying. I guess that's all I get.

HANNIMAN: *(finishes taking blood)* "The desires of the heart are as crooked as corkscrews."

NED: "Not to be born is the best for man." W. H. Auden.

HANNIMAN: I know.

NED: He was a gay poet.

HANNIMAN: Well, I agree with him anyway.

NED: How do you know that poem?

HANNIMAN: If I were one of your activists, I would respond to that insulting question: Go fuck yourself. But I am only a beleaguered nurse, with a B.A., an M.S., and a Ph.D., who is breaking her butt on the front lines of an endless battle, so I reply: Go fuck yourself. "This long disease, my life."

NED: Alexander Pope.

HANNIMAN: Not a gay poet.

NED: *(taking more pills)* These are making me sick to my stomach.

HANNIMAN: Take an Alka-Seltzer. *(leaves)*

ALEXANDER: *(rushing back in)* Did I hear you correctly? You were only in love for five minutes?

That's terrible! What did you mean, That's all you get? Mommy! What's wrong with me?
*(*ALEXANDER *runs into her bedroom.* RENA *wears only a half-slip and is having trouble hooking her bra up in the back. He automatically hooks her up.)*

RENA: I need new brassieres. It's time to visit Aunt Leona. What's wrong?

ALEXANDER: I'm *different!* Even Benjamin says so.

RENA: Her company won't give her one extra penny from all the millions they make from her designs. They're hers! You see how impossible it is for a woman to be independent? "Different" doesn't tell me enough.

NED: Ma, why don't you put on a dress?

RENA: If you're going to become a writer, you must learn to be more precise with words.

NED: Do not sit half-naked with your adolescent son. Is that precise enough?

ALEXANDER: *(to* NED*)* Why does it bother you guys so much? She does it all the time. I don't even look. *(to* RENA*)* I don't want to be a writer anymore. *The Glass Menagerie* didn't win the Pulitzer Prize. Ma, how could they not know it was such a great play? They gave it to a play about a man who talks to an invisible rabbit. I'm going to be an actor.

NED: What do you mean, you don't look?

ALEXANDER: I look at Ponzo Lombardo. In gym. He's growing these huge tufts of pub-ic hair. Around his penis. Around his huge penis. Which she doesn't know how to tell me about and he tells me to look up in the dictionary.

NED: Pubic hair.

ALEXANDER: Pubic hair.

RENA: I was going to be an actress.

ALEXANDER: Around his huge penis.

NED: That you pronounced correctly.

RENA: I had an audition for a radio program. On NBC. Coast to coast.

ALEXANDER: You never told me that. What happened?

RENA: I was summoned to the station. Oh, I was so excited.

ALEXANDER: Then what happened?

RENA: I walked round and around the block.

ALEXANDER: Then what happened?

RENA: I walked around again.

ALEXANDER: You never went inside?

RENA: Benjamin was just a baby. I couldn't leave him.

NED: You were going to tell her how you feel so different.

ALEXANDER: But she could have become a star of the airwaves!

NED: She didn't become a star of the airwaves.

ALEXANDER: Mommy—isn't it a good thing . . . being different?

RENA: We're all different in many ways and alike in many ways and special in some sort of way. What are you trying to tell me?

ALEXANDER: Is it okay for me to . . . marry a . . . for instance . . . colored girl?

NED: Oh, for goodness' sake.

RENA: You know how important it is for Jewish people to marry Jewish people. There are many famous Jews—Jascha Heifetz and Dinah Shore and Albert Einstein and that baseball player your father's so crazy about, Hank Whatshisname. But we can't name them out loud.

ALEXANDER: Why not?

RENA: If they know who we are, they come after us. That's what Hitler taught us, and Senator McCarthy is teaching us all over again.

ALEXANDER: What if I find a colored girl who's Jewish?
(She puts her hand to his forehead to see if he has a fever.)
(breaking away) All I know is I feel different! From as long ago as I remember! You always taught me to be tolerant of *everyone.* You did mean it, didn't you? I *can* trust you?

RENA: Give me an example of what makes you think you're different.

ALEXANDER: I don't ever want to get married.

RENA: Of course you do. Everyone gets married. That's what you do in life. You get married. You fall in love with someone wonderful and you get married.

ALEXANDER: Are you really happy with Daddy?

RENA: Than with whom?

ALEXANDER: Cary Grant.

RENA: I never met Mr. Grant.

ALEXANDER: He's gorgeous.

RENA: Alexander, gorgeous is . . . well, it's a word that's better for me than for you.

ALEXANDER: Why can't I say gorgeous?

RENA: It's too . . . effusive for a man, too generous.

ALEXANDER: What's wrong with being generous? You would have been happier with Cary Grant, too. We could all have lived happily ever after in Hollywood—you and me and Benjamin and Cary. Why'd you settle for Richard Weeks?

RENA: Don't you think I love your father?

ALEXANDER: *I* don't.

NED: I actually said it out loud.

ALEXANDER: No, *I* said it out loud.

NED: Once again, I remind you, this is not what you set out to talk about.

ALEXANDER: But doesn't it fit in nicely?

RENA: I had lots of beaux. One was very handsome. But your father took me in his arms on our very first date and looked deep into my eyes and said, You're the girl I'm going to marry.

ALEXANDER: (cuddling seductively close to her) Tell me about the handsome one.

RENA: (running her hand along his leg) You're growing up so.

NED: Please, Ma.

RENA: You never tell me how much you love me anymore. You used to tell me all the time, Mommy, I love you more than anyone and anything in the whole wide world.

ALEXANDER: (touched and guilty) Oh, Mommy, I'm grown up now and I'm not supposed to say things like that.

RENA: Oh, silly billy, who says?

ALEXANDER: Please tell me what to do!

RENA: About what!

ALEXANDER: I've got to get ready for my Halloween Pageant.
(He breaks away and runs into the living room, where he opens an old trunk.)

HANNIMAN: (entering with medical cart) Now we take some blood.
(She will take blood and put some in each of four containers.)

NED: The straight path has been cleared?
(HANNIMAN nods.)
I am transfectious and not infectious?

HANNIMAN: Transfected. Now I didn't say that. That's our goal. And by all Tony's measurements and calculations, you appear to be—so far—a good candidate.

RENA: (pulling on a housedress and joining ALEXANDER) That's all that's left from when we were in Russia and they came after all the Jews and we had to run if we wanted to stay alive. You'd think they'd give us a rest. Why does someone always want someone else dead?

ALEXANDER: I'll bet the handsome one wasn't Jewish.

RENA: No, he wasn't.

ALEXANDER: What was his name?

RENA: Drew.

ALEXANDER: Drew.

RENA: Drew Keenlymore.

ALEXANDER: Drew Keenlymore! Oh! What did he do?

RENA: He was my professor.

ALEXANDER: A poor gentile.

RENA: No, he wasn't. He was from one of the oldest families in Canada and his brother was Prime Minister.

ALEXANDER: Oh, Mom! Did he take you in his arms and kiss you all over and say he wanted to marry you?

RENA: They didn't do things like that in those days.

ALEXANDER: You just said Pop did.
(He is putting on Russian clothing from the trunk—a peasant blouse, skirt, sash, babushka, from RENA's youth.)

RENA: Your Aunt Emma married a gentile. Momma wouldn't talk to her for twenty years. (helps him)

ALEXANDER: Did you love Drew?

RENA: I had long auburn hair. Everyone said I was very pretty. I had many chances.
(HANNIMAN exits)

ALEXANDER: What happened to him?

RENA: I met your father.

NED: Who comes home and finds you in a dress.

RENA: No, I knew him already.

ALEXANDER: And you never saw Drew Keenly-more again. *(stuffs Kleenex from* NED'S *bedside table into the blouse to make breasts. To* NED*)* Mickey Rooney did this in *Babes on Broadway.*

NED: You hate Mickey Rooney.

ALEXANDER: I'm not so crazy about Pop either.

NED: That is a motivation that had not occurred to me.

ALEXANDER: That's what we're here for, kid. *(tosses him back the Kleenex box)*

RENA: No. I saw him again.

ALEXANDER: You did?

RENA: He wrote me he was coming to New York. This was before you were born and Richard was still with Leon and it wasn't working out, Leon bullied Richard mercilessly, the one thing I always pray is you and Benjamin will never fight and always love each other—will you promise me?

ALEXANDER: Don't worry about that—what happened!

RENA: He took me to Delmonico's. I didn't have a nice dress. But I dressed up as best I could. I felt like a child, going back to my teacher, with a marriage that was in trouble, I shouldn't be telling you all of this, I wish you could like him more . . . There was no money! In the bank, in the country. Everyone was poor, except your Uncle Leon, he and Aunt Judith living so high off the hog, you should have seen their apartment, in the El Dorado, with two full-time maids. *(gets some makeup from her vanity and puts some lipstick and rouge on him)*

ALEXANDER: Go back to Delmonico's.

RENA: After lunch, Drew asked me to come back to his hotel. The Savoy Plaza.

ALEXANDER: And?

RENA: I didn't go.

ALEXANDER: Not again! Alexander Keenlymore, farewell!

RENA: I had a baby to feed.

ALEXANDER: Benjamin could have had two full-time maids! Momma, don't you want to be different?
  *(*RICHARD *suddenly appears, home from work, exhausted. He is furious at what he sees.)*

RICHARD: What are you doing to him?

RENA: Don't use that tone of voice to me.

RICHARD: Look at him! He's a sissy! Your son is a sissy!

RENA: He's your son, too!

RICHARD: If he were my son, he wouldn't be wearing a dress. If he were my son, he'd come with me to ball games instead of going to your la-de-da theater. Your son is a sissy! *(hits him)*

RENA: Richard!
  *(*RICHARD *hits him again.* ALEXANDER *is strangely passive.* RICHARD *corners him and can't stop swatting him.)*
  Stop it!

RICHARD: Sissy! Sissy! Sissy!

NED: Why aren't you fighting back?

ALEXANDER: When he hit me last week I vowed I'd never talk to him again. *(singing to himself)* "Waste no time, make a switch, drop him in the nearest ditch . . ."

RENA: This time I won't come back when you turn up begging.

NED: Never run from a fight.

ALEXANDER: "Don't try to patch it up, Tear it up, Tear it up . . ."

RICHARD: That was a million years ago in another lifetime.

ALEXANDER: "You can't put back a petal when it falls from a flower . . ."

RENA: I can do it again!

ALEXANDER: "Or sweeten up a fella when he starts turning sour. Oh, no! . . ."

RENA: It's never too late to correct our mistakes.

ALEXANDER: "Oh, nooooo!"

NED: *(to* RICHARD*)* Daddy, why did you hit me?

RICHARD: You have an awful life ahead of you if you're a sissy.

NED: How do you know?

RICHARD: Everybody knows. *(to* RENA*)* You want to see something? You who always defends her darling son. You want to see what he does to himself?

ALEXANDER: "If you laugh at diff'rent comics, If you root for diff'rent teams . . ."
*(*RICHARD *rips the skirt and underpants off him.)*

RENA: Stop tearing my dress! It's all that's left!

ALEXANDER: "Waste no time, Weep no more . . ."

RICHARD: I come home from the ball game, I smell this awful smell, like something died. I caught him. Rena, I really let him have it.
*(*RICHARD *is trying to get ahold of* ALEXANDER'S *penis. It becomes a tussle of him almost getting it and* ALEXANDER *evading his grasp just in time.)*

RENA: You hit him?

RICHARD: Of course I hit him!

ALEXANDER: "Show him what the door is for . . ."

RICHARD: He had his privates all covered up with depilatory cream!

ALEXANDER: "Rub him out-a the roll call and drum him out-a your dreams!" LET GO!

RICHARD: *(to* RENA*)* Don't you even care?

RENA: I do care!

ALEXANDER: I'm the only boy in my entire class except Ponzo Lombardo who has any puberty hair and everybody laughs at him!

RICHARD: *(starts ripping down the theater posters from the walls)* Thank God at least I've got one son who's a man.

ALEXANDER: Don't! They're the most precious thing I have!

RICHARD: So this is what it takes to get you to talk to me.

RENA: Don't do that to the boy!

RICHARD: This is what we do to sissies.
*(*ALEXANDER *crawls around trying to smooth out his beloved posters and piece them back together.)*

ALEXANDER: It's Halloween! I wrote a play. Mr. Mills divided my scout troop, half into boys and half into girls. I didn't have any choice!

RICHARD: You wrote a play?

RENA: Tonight's his opening night. He invited us.

ALEXANDER: *(screaming with all his might)* I hate you!

RENA: Don't say that!

ALEXANDER: You taught me to always tell the truth!

NED: Go for it! *(feels dizzy. Swallows more pills)*

ALEXANDER: *(to* NED, *furious)* Get me out of this!

RENA: Apologize to your father immediately!

ALEXANDER: *(to* RENA *and* RICHARD*)* I hate both of you!

RICHARD: *(really hitting him)* Do what your mother says!

ALEXANDER: *(grabbing the Russian shawl, stepping into women's shoes, and standing up to both of them)* Go to hell! *(running off, as best he can, yelling)* Trick or treat! Trick or treat!
*(*HANNIMAN *rushes into the room. Her white coat is heavily bloodied.)*

HANNIMAN: Are you happy now? Look what your people did to me!

 E N D   O F   A C T   O N E

A C T   T W O

NED *enters in a wheelchair, singing an Andrews Sisters' song.* HANNIMAN, *in a clean white coat, wheels in a cart with a small insulated chest.* DR DELLA VIDA *follows.* NED *carries a huge poster that reads* TONY AND GEORGE, YOU ARE MURDERING US *over big blow-ups of* DELLA VIDA *and George Bush. He holds it in front of the window, which provokes cheers from outside.*

TONY: Why do they hate me?

HANNIMAN: These are all over the hospital. Plastered on the corridor walls, in the johns, in the cafeteria, in the Director's office. On the X-ray machines!

NED: *(putting up the poster on a wall)* I had my CAT scan lying under a picture of you. It was very sexy.

TONY: You wish. Get into bed.

(NED *does so.* HANNIMAN *pulls back a curtain along the wall, revealing elaborate equipment—a high-tech orgy of gleaming cylinders, dials, tubes, bells, and lights, all connected to a computer.*)

NED: This is it? Wouldn't it be easier if I just checked into a monastery and took sleeping pills?

TONY: You drown my wife in fake blood. You chop the legs off my lab tables. You've got some crazy gay newspaper up in New York that claims I'm not even studying the right virus. They call me Public Enemy Number One. Why aren't you guys proud of me? If I'm not in my lab, I'm testifying, lobbying, pressuring, I'm on TV ten times a week, I fly to conferences all over the world, I churn out papers for the journals, I supervise hundreds of scientists, I dole out research grants like I'm Santa Claus— what more do you want?

(HANNIMAN *carefully takes a sack of blood from the container and gives it to* TONY. *He inserts it into part of the machine. They repeat the procedure for two more sacks.*)

NED: A cure.

TONY: I'm not a magician.

NED: Now's not the time to tell me. There's no end in sight. That's why they hate you. You tell every reporter you have enough money. That's why they hate you. You tell Congress you have everything you need. That's why they hate you. You say more has been learned about this disease than any disease in the history of disease. That's why they hate you. You say the President cares. That's why they hate you.

(TONY *and* HANNIMAN *attach* NED *to the machine.*)

TONY: He does care! He tells me all the time how much he cares!

NED: You asked me, I told you. You're the one in charge and you're an apologist for your boss. That's why they . . .

TONY: If I weren't, do you think I'd get *any-thing!* You don't understand the realities of this town.

NED: The reality of this town is that nobody can say the word "penis" without blushing.

(RENA, ALEXANDER, *and* RICHARD *enter. It's evening, shadowy, at a seaside boardinghouse in Connecticut, on Long Island Sound.*)

HANNIMAN: The President named him a hero.

NED: No comment. On the grounds he might murder *me.* Wait!

TONY: (*pulling a lever to release the blood into* NED) This construct is the first transfect of anti-sense. Competing protein mechanisms will effect a cross-reactive anti-self.

RENA: (*talking into a pay phone on a wall. Dropping in coins with each call*) Jane, we've finally made it!

NED: That's what we want?

TONY: That's what we want.

RENA: Get your datebook out. You're first!

TONY: If we're—, it will screw up your reproductive process.

NED: I'd assumed that already was screwed up.

TONY: Of your *viral* load.

RENA: It's been the longest year.

NED: Tell me again there isn't any down side.

TONY: I never told you there wasn't any down side.

NED: You did too!

TONY: It's too late now.

ALEXANDER: (*to* NED) Come with me.

TONY: (*taking* NED'S *hand*) Relax.

NED: (*grabbing* TONY) Tony, I'm afraid.

TONY: We're going to be just fine.

RENA: Friday night at seven! Perfect! We can hardly wait! (*hangs up, enters the engagement in her datebook*)

ALEXANDER: Ned, come back. Only two more weeks to Yale! No more Eden Heights. My new life! We don't have much time left before I grow into you and you kick me out. (*pulls* NED *with him*) Come on!

(TONY *and* HANNIMAN *leave.* ALEXANDER *helps* NED, *still connected by tubes to the machinery, get out of bed and walk to sit beside* RICHARD *on a porch swing.*)

NED: *(applying salt liberally to some food)* Hi, Poppa.

RENA: *(to RICHARD, as she dials another number)* Jane and Barney are taking us to their new country club that costs a thousand dollars a year per family just to join. *(into phone)* Grace, darling, this is Rena! Just this minute! Tell me when you're free!

ALEXANDER: *(to the audience)* Every summer we come back to Connecticut for two weeks at Mrs Pennington's Seaside Boarding House, and every year everyone Mom and Pop grew up with has become richer and richer.

(RICHARD grabs the salt away from NED)

(to NED) Did I say that well?

NED: First-rate. And every summer you feel more and more different.

ALEXANDER: *(to the audience)* And every summer I feel more and more frightened. Of what I don't know.

RENA: A swim in your new pool and lobsters for luncheon! Saturday at noon. We can hardly wait! *(she hangs up, enters the engagement, checks her address book, and dials another number)*

(NED grabs the salt back from RICHARD.)

Grace and Percy bought that big estate in Westport.

(RICHARD grabs the salt back from NED.)

Cole Porter wrote some famous song there.

(NED grabs the salt back from RICHARD.)

NED: I want to eat it the way I want to eat it.

RENA: Percy sold his business for a million dollars and retired.

RICHARD: Who's going to pay the bills when you get sick?

NED and ALEXANDER: I'll let you know when I get sick.

ALEXANDER: Tradition means a great deal in our family.

RENA: Dolores, darling, this is Rena! Quiet, both of you! Oh, my God! *(to RICHARD)* Dolores and Nathan are going around the world for an entire year.

RICHARD: I can't take it anymore. *(to NED)* Why are you always so ungrateful?

RENA: I've always dreamed of a trip like that.

NED: Everything you always blame me for demands I defend myself.

ALEXANDER: You're playing me really well.

RICHARD: Blame? What are you talking about? *(grabs the salt back)* Blame!

RENA: An informal candlelight dinner for fifty on your outdoor terrace under the stars! Saturday at nine. You'll send a car and driver! We can hardly wait! *(slamming down the phone)* I've heard this fight for the last time! This is supposed to be a wonderful vacation! I've been on the phone calling people I haven't seen or spoken to or heard from in a year. Why don't you ever call them? They're your old childhood chums, too. I feel like such a suppliant. Inviting people to take us out and feed us. *(having dialed another number)* Tessie, it's Rena!

RICHARD: What I need's a vacation from him.

RENA: Are you free on Sunday?

ALEXANDER: Just two more weeks you won't ever have to see me again.

RENA: Don't say that!

RICHARD: Maybe then I'll feel better. Where's Ben?

RENA: You think he confides in me? *(into phone)* A cruise on your *yacht?* Cocktails at five to watch the sunset. We can hardly wait. *(hangs up)* Tessie and Isadore have a yacht.

(NED suddenly feels a little woozy. He stands up uncertainly. A bell rings softly. A yellow light goes on. He indicates to a concerned ALEXANDER that he should carry on. He makes his way back to bed.)

ALEXANDER: Benjamin is driving from New Haven in the new secondhand Ford he bought with his own money. He has jobs and he has scholarships and he's paying his own way and he's free, he's a free man, ever since he beat West Point and they said he wasn't a liar. So what do you know what's right for him or me or anybody?

He won! My brother, whom you said wouldn't win, won!

(RICHARD *is standing directly in front of him.* ALEXANDER *holds his ground.* RICHARD *turns and leaves*)

RENA: Who.

ALEXANDER: Who. *(trying to kiss* RENA*)* A kiss for the cook. *(as she pointedly ignores him)* Now, Alexander, you know I don't like it when you talk back to your father like that. Yes, Momma, I know. I know you didn't mean it, dear. But I did mean it, Momma. Oh, boy, did I mean it. And I don't think I did anything wrong. Well, you can do your Mom a great big favor. Even if you don't mean it. Just do it for me. For the Mommy you love. I will not apologize! Ever!

(The yellow light goes off)

RENA: You used to say, Mommy, I'll do anything you ask me.

ALEXANDER: Ma, every kid says that.

RENA: Oh, do they? What else do they say?

NED: Mommy, I am going to become so famous someday, just so I can get away from here!

RENA: My last case before we left was a family without a father. They lived in a shack. The lovely young mother. With two adorable children. Who threw up all over the house. And bled all over the sheets. From some strange illness.

NED: And I must never forget that those two diseased babies might have been me and Benjamin.

RENA: The point is we're all healthy and together and he loves you very much.

NED: The point is in my entire life I never believed for one single minute that my father ever loved me. The point is I can't even figure out if I've ever been loved at all.

*(*ALEXANDER *is troubled by this.)*

RENA: The point is I love him and I love you and he loves me and he loves you and we all love each other very very much!

*(*ALEXANDER *goes to sit on the swing.)*

I was so proud, being asked to be an official hostess. But you didn't dance with your own mother at your own graduation prom, not once.

ALEXANDER: Nobody danced with their *mother!*

RENA: Bernie Krukoff did. Neil Nelson did. Skipper with the red hair did. Do you know how much I wanted you? Do you? Mr Know-It-All. You think you know it all. Some things you don't know.

ALEXANDER: You told me about Drew Keenlymore.

RENA: I did not.

NED: You did, too.

ALEXANDER: Before I found his letters.

RENA: I don't even know where they are.

NED: Hidden in a navy crocheted purse inside an old Macy's hatbox at the back of the top of your bedroom closet, over on the far right.

ALEXANDER: The purse is cable stitch.

RENA: Your great-grandmother crocheted that purse. She was married three times and she divorced each one of them. She traveled all over the world. And then she came home and my Poppa took care of her until the day she died. She was ninety-nine. She was one gutsy lady.

NED: She was one scary lady. Always reading her Bible out loud, day and night, and barking orders in Hebrew.

ALEXANDER: Grandma Sybil was the scary one!

RENA: *(sitting between them)* After we got married, your Grandmother Sybil made Daddy promise he'd never leave her, that one of her sons would always look out for her. Richard kept his promise, which is why she left him the money. He worshiped her. Her great sinful secret was her husband's infidelity. What was his name? I can't even remember his name. She would never let his name be said out loud. She threw him out for sleeping with another woman. Kicked him out. Just like that. Judith divorced Leon, too. He kissed his mistress in his and Judith's very bedroom. I caught them accidentally. He laughed at me! "Why don't you go out and have some pleasure in life? Why are you always so faithful to that loser?" Imagine saying that about your own brother? I'd been to a doctor. The doctor examined me and told me I wasn't pregnant. Richard—where was Richard? Well, he wasn't there and I'd gone to spend the night with Mother Sybil. She terrified me, too. She was a mean, unloving, self-centered . . . bitch. Grandma Sybil only had one bed. I had to sleep with her. Oh, her smells! Her old-lady unguents and liniments. Don't open the window. I feel a draft. I feel a draft. She started talking to me in the dark. Telling me how much she'd loved him. Her husband. When they first came to America they scrubbed floors together. They'd meet in the middle and kiss. I don't know why but I thought that was very romantic. Then one day someone told her he was cavorting with a woman in Atlantic City. She didn't even let him pack. Her heart was still broken, she said, and she fell asleep crying. I kept waking up. I had to go to the toilet. I tiptoed in the dark. I didn't even flush. I was terrified I'd disturb her. The third or fourth time I smelled a bad smell. Like something spoiled or rotten. The fifth time I turned on the light. The toilet bowl was filled with blood. And lumps of stringy fibers. Like liver. Pieces of raw liver. From the butcher. I was so sleepy. The doctor had given me something to sleep. Why was liver coming out of me? And this awful smell? I went back to her bed. I had to go to the toilet again. And again. By morning I must have been close to death. She demanded her tea in bed. I pulled myself to the kitchen. I fell on the floor in a heap. What must have saved me was the kettle whistling. I couldn't reach up to turn it off. Where's my tea? What's wrong with you, girl? You can't even make my tea. I woke up in a hospital. I'd had a miscarriage. So you see how much I wanted you. Can't you? Can't you see how much I want you? *(clutching* ALEXANDER *physically)*

ALEXANDER: Momma, don't. I'm beginning to feel really unhappy.

RENA: Can't you see?

ALEXANDER: *(breaking away from her)* It comes out of nowhere.

NED: I get scared.

RENA: Can't you see?

*(*ALEXANDER *runs away from her.* RENA *has no arms to go to but* NED'S; *he accepts her reluctantly.)*

NED: Don't cry, Momma. *(in* ALEXANDER'S *direction)* Come back!

RENA: *(clutching* NED*)* You're leaving me. What am I supposed to do?
*(*BENJAMIN *enters; he doesn't like what he sees.* RENA *quickly relinquishes* NED.*)*

BENJAMIN: Hi, Mom.

RENA: I made your favorites. Remember when you were captain of the football team and drank three quarts of milk every meal?

BENJAMIN: I'm not on any team anymore. *(to* ALEXANDER*)* Lemon, come help me.
*(*BENJAMIN *and* ALEXANDER *go off.* NED *returns to bed; he's not feeling well. Several yellow lights go on. The soft bell rings. He presses his buzzer.)*

RENA: *(alone)* Aren't you glad to see me?
*(*RENA *sits on the swing. After a moment,* RICHARD *enters.)*

RENA: Your other son has arrived.

RICHARD: I hate using everyone's toilet.

RENA: Year after year, you're the one who insists on coming back here to Mrs Pennington's. We could go to that place in New Hampshire Manny and Teresa rave about. You even told me to send for a brochure. I've never been to Europe.

RICHARD: I've been to Europe. Leon and I tried to find where Pop was born. We couldn't find it. I like it here. Except for the toilet. *(angry)* We can't afford Europe, for Christ's sake!

RENA: I can dream! Let's have a nice time.

RICHARD: I didn't come here not to have a nice time. Why couldn't he have turned out like Ben?

RENA: You want another Ben? A son who never comes home. Who never writes except when he wants something. This is the first time the family has been together in years. I should've bought flowers. I wonder why he's come.

RICHARD: Come here.

RENA: What do you want?

RICHARD: *(as she sits beside him)* You're a good egg. It hasn't been easy for you.

RENA: Why are you talking like this all of a sudden?

RICHARD: I'm just trying to be nice.

RENA: I don't even recognize it anymore.

RICHARD: You wanted more.

RENA: Everybody wants more.

RICHARD: I've always been crazy about you.

RENA: What's wrong with wanting more?
    (NED *presses the buzzer more urgently.*)

RICHARD: Things will be better soon. Four more years and we'll have nothing to spend money on but ourselves.

RENA: Just the two of us again.

RICHARD: It will be better. We'll move back here for good.

RENA: You've never stopped loving me for one minute, have you?

RICHARD: No, Mommy, I haven't. And I never shall.

RENA: Richard, they're both gone now. I want to go out on my own now, too.

RICHARD: Don't start those dumb, stupid, asinine threats one more time!
    (BENJAMIN *and* ALEXANDER *enter, carrying a tennis racket, books, a suitcase.*)

BENJAMIN: You could show a little more enthusiasm.

ALEXANDER: (*offering his hand*) Congratulations, Benjamin. I hope you'll be very happy.
    (*But* BENJAMIN'S *hands are full.*)

RICHARD: Hey, son!

BENJAMIN: Who won?

RICHARD: We slaughtered you. Yankees ten, Red Sox two.

BENJAMIN: We're still ahead in the series.
    (HANNIMAN *runs in.*)

NED: I'm boiling! I feel like I'm going to explode!
    (*She feels him, then quickly checks the monitoring devices.*)

RENA: (*trying to kiss* BENJAMIN *hello*) Tell me all about Yale. I want to know everything so I can be proud. What's your thesis on?

BENJAMIN: Ma, I've told you a dozen times.

RENA: Tell me again.

ALEXANDER: Twentieth Century Negro Poets.
    (HANNIMAN *leaves quickly.*)

RENA: Isn't that fascinating.

RICHARD: Studying all that literature stuff is crap!

RENA: Don't be such a philistine!

BENJAMIN: It's my money and my education and my life.
    (HANNIMAN *returns with* DR DELLA VIDA. NED *begins to convulse slightly.*)

TONY: (*checking the computer, then* NED) He's going into shock! (*turns off the machinery*)
    (HANNIMAN *hands him a huge syringe, which he injects into* NED'S *groin or neck.*)

ALEXANDER: Benjamin doesn't want to go to law school. He wants to be a teacher or a writer. He wants to help people. Ned, what are they doing to you?

BENJAMIN: I'll be all right, Lemon. Law is helping people, too.

ALEXANDER: That's not what you told me! Ned, what's wrong? Why aren't you answering?

RICHARD: (*to* BENJAMIN) Listen, mister smart ass big guy, don't make it sound like such a holy sacrifice! I got you this far. I got both of you this far. I got all of us this far.

RENA: Stop it, stop it, stop it!

ALEXANDER: *NED!*

RICHARD: You and your ungrateful prick of a brother!

RENA: We are not going to fight!

ALEXANDER: Why do you bring us back to this stupid place every year anyway? Just so we can feel poor? Benjamin is going to marry a rich girl he doesn't even love!

RENA: You're getting married?

RICHARD: Hey, I always say it's just as easy to marry a rich one.

BENJAMIN: You promised me you'd keep your mouth shut. Let's go for a swim. (*throws* ALEXANDER *his suit*)

RENA: Don't go. It's getting dark.

BENJAMIN: (*gets his own suit*) Fast!

RENA: It's too dark. Wait until tomorrow. I'll go with you.

RICHARD: *(grabbing* ALEXANDER *as he starts out)*
Every time I look at you, every single time I
see you, I wish to Christ your mother'd had that
abortion!

RENA: *(a wail)* NOOOOOO!

RICHARD: She wouldn't have another one. And
I've been paying for it ever since.

RENA: I beg you!

ALEXANDER: Ned, help me! Where are you?
*(*NED *tries to get up, but is restrained by* DR
DELLA VIDA.*)*
*(*BENJAMIN *physically lifts* ALEXANDER *away
from* RICHARD *and they start out.* RICHARD *grabs*
RENA, *who is also leaving.)*
I'm going to be sick. *(runs to sink)*

TONY: It's okay, Ned. We're going to get through
this.

RICHARD: Where do you think you're going? We
can't afford another child, Rene. He'll just take
all our pleasure away. All our money and all our
hope.

RENA: Let go of me, Richard.

RICHARD: Listen to me, Rene. It's the Depression.

RENA: This time I mean it. This time I'm going for
good.
*(*RICHARD *restrains her from leaving.)*
I only came back because you begged me!
What else could I do? A woman can't get a decent job to use her brain. I had to sell lace and
pins at Macy's for twelve dollars a week. I lost
my chance with Drew Keenlymore.

RICHARD: We're back to him again? Miss Flirt!
Miss Goddamn Flirt!

BENJAMIN: *(helping* ALEXANDER *at the sink)*
Lemon, are you all right?

ALEXANDER: Please don't call me Lemon anymore.

RICHARD: What does anyone know about not taking it anymore? Spending each day of my life
at a job I hate, with people who don't know how
smart I am.

BENJAMIN: Come on.

ALEXANDER: I can't throw up.

RICHARD: Not seeing my sons turn into anything I
want as my sons—the one I love never at home,
the other one always at home, to remind me of
what a sissy's come out of my loving you. Don't
leave me, Rene!

RENA: I am, I am. Let me go!
*(*RICHARD *is trying to hold a woman who doesn't
want to be held. He hits her. She screams.)*

RICHARD: I don't want to live without you!

RENA: I'm supposed to stay here? For the rest of
my life?
*(*RENA *breaks loose and runs off.* BENJAMIN
runs after her. RICHARD *yanks* ALEXANDER
*away from the sink and hurls him to the floor,
falling on top of him, pinioning him beneath
him and letting out all his venom and fury on
his younger son.)*

RICHARD: You were a mistake! I didn't want you! I
never wanted you! I should have shot my load
in the toilet!

ALEXANDER: Mommy!

NED: *(screaming out)* Ben!
*(*BENJAMIN *runs back in. He somehow sepa-
rates his father from his brother. He carries
ALEXANDER *off in his arms.)*

BENJAMIN: It's too late. There's nothing we can do.
I shouldn't have come.
*(*RICHARD *pulls himself up off the floor. He
doesn't know which way to go. He stumbles first
in one direction, then in another, finally going
off.)*

NED: It's too late. There's nothing we can do. I
shouldn't have come.

HANNIMAN: Why, we're just starting.

TONY: You just had a little imbalance. It's a good
sign. It means we're knocking out more of your
infected cells than we expected. I think we just
may be seeing some progress.

NED: That was awful. You sure it's not just poison?
Would you tell me it's working, even when it's
killing me? Did anyone anywhere in the entire
history of the world have a happy childhood?

TONY: I'm sure George Bush was a very happy
child.

HANNIMAN and NED: He still is.
(They all smile. TONY *turns the switch to the
equipment on again and leaves.* HANNIMAN *wipes*
NED'S *damp brow.)*

NED: In eighteenth-century Holland—a country and culture that had never acted this way—there was a hysterical uprising against gays that resulted in the most awful witch hunts. Young boys were condemned, persecuted, throttled, executed . . . a fourteen-year-old boy was found guilty and drowned with a two hundred pound weight. Who was that kid? What was his name? What could he possibly ever have done to deserve such punishment, and in a Christian land?

Centuries later, historians, searching for a reason, discovered that, when all that happened, the sea walls along the Dutch coast were collapsing because of massive, unrelenting pressure from floods, accompanied by a plague of very hungry pile worms consuming the foundations.

The people, in that perverse cause-and-effect way that never seems to stop, had blamed the destruction of their coastline and its fortifications on the gay kids. God would inundate their Republic until it was punished and penance was paid to relieve the wrath of the Almighty.

When I was a little boy I thought colored girls were much sexier than white girls.

HANNIMAN: What happened?

NED: Boys. Any color. How did you meet Tony?

HANNIMAN: I was head nurse of this division when he was appointed director.

NED: Was it love at first sight?

HANNIMAN: None of your business.

NED: You don't seem very happy. Is it because he's such a . . . Republican?

HANNIMAN: You think anyone black has anything to be happy about?

NED: It seems more personal.

HANNIMAN: Everyone in this entire hospital in every room on every floor is dying from something. They all come here to be saved. This is the new Lourdes. Congress gives us nine billion dollars a year to perform miracles. And God's a bit slow these days in the miracle department. You don't think that's enough to get you down?

NED: Still not personal enough.

HANNIMAN: You always say just what you want to?

NED: Pretty much. No matter what you say, x number of people are going to approve and x number aren't. You might as well say what you want to.

HANNIMAN: You obviously don't work for the government.

NED: So marrying a white man didn't solve any of your problems?

HANNIMAN: Did not marrying a colored girl solve any of yours? *(starts to leave)*

NED: Hey! I thought we were seeing some progress!

HANNIMAN: We are. *(leaves)*

ALEXANDER: *(entering his Yale room, dressed most collegiately)* The first thing upon entering a new life is to change one's name.

BEN: *(entering with brownies and milk, wearing a Y athletic sweater)* Ned?

ALEXANDER: Ben?

BEN: But Ben is logically the nickname for Benjamin.

ALEXANDER: I read this play called *Holiday* where there's a Ned. It could be a nickname for Alexander. It sounds very fresh and spiffy, don't you think? Ned. She still makes a good brownie.

BEN: *(noticing some papers)* What kind of dreadful way is this to start out? What happened?

ALEXANDER: What happened? I'm flunking psychology. And astronomy. And geology. And German. So far. What do I do?

BEN: Study.

ALEXANDER: That's very helpful. What did you win that letter for?

BEN: This one? Boxing, I think.

ALEXANDER: Boxing. Football. Squash. Tennis. Dean's List. Phi Bete. A after A after A. Prom committees, elected offices, scholarships, friends, girls . . . You have done your parents and your alma mater and your country proud. You're even marrying a rich girl.

BEN: It's time to get married.

ALEXANDER: Do you love her yet?

BEN: She's as good as anyone.

ALEXANDER: What kind of dreadful way is this to start out? I don't want to be a lawyer.

BEN: Nobody's asked you to be a lawyer.

ALEXANDER: I always dreamed we'd be partners in something.

BEN: Why aren't you going to Europe with Theo?

ALEXANDER: Boy, is *Moby Dick* a bitch to get excited about. Are you sorry Pop made you go to law school?

BEN: I don't believe anybody makes you do anything you don't really want to.

ALEXANDER: That's good to know.

BEN: Why aren't you going to Europe this summer with Theo all expenses paid? It sounded like a wonderful offer.

(NED *has left his bed and moved closer to* ALEXANDER.)

NED: This is one of those moments in life we talked about. Would life be otherwise if you did or didn't do something differently? You're about to tell your brother . . . something both painful and precious, something you don't understand, something you need help with. You want him to understand. Oh, how you want him to understand! He's not going to understand.

ALEXANDER: Will it be better if I don't tell him?

NED: I've always thought it would have been. I don't know. Why do you have to tell him at all?

ALEXANDER: Why not? Is it something so awful?

NED: *(helplessly)* But Ben is going to . . .

ALEXANDER: Going to what?

NED: *(feebly)* Make you . . .

ALEXANDER: Make me what?

NED: Make you do something I'd rather not have done. Just yet. They didn't know enough then!

ALEXANDER: How much do they know now! In my limited experience, so far as I can see, you don't have a very good record on just about anything concerning me. Or yourself. Why are you even here? Why are you letting them do all this to you? Do you trust that doctor? I don't. He's much too gorgeous. *(to* BEN) We were lovers.

BEN: We were what!

ALEXANDER: Me and Theo!

NED: And so the journey begins. Do you feel any better?

BEN: Did he ask you?

ALEXANDER: *(to* BEN) Yes. *(to* NED) Yes!

BEN: He shouldn't have done that.

ALEXANDER: Oh, I wanted to do it.

BEN: How can you be so certain of that?

ALEXANDER: I don't believe anybody makes you do anything you don't really want to.

BEN: This is about you, not me. Sometimes we do things we don't want to.

ALEXANDER: Like become a lawyer and get married to someone you don't love?

BEN: Look, Sara and I are just getting started, and, listen, get off my case. What happened with Theo?

ALEXANDER: We made love. Right here. I went to Theo and asked him: I'm flunking out of your German class, could I do something for extra credit, and we went out and drank beer, and we came back here, and he asked me: would you like to make love, and I walked to this door, and opened it, and said: I think you'd better go, and I closed the door, and ran right back into his arms. And I passed.

BEN: I believe this is something they now think they can change.

ALEXANDER: It felt wonderful!

BEN: It's unhealthy, it's caused by something unhealthy, it'll do nothing but make you unhappy.

NED: How are all the men in my family such experts in these matters?

BEN: Everybody knows.

NED: Everybody does not know! Everybody is told!

BEN: What's the difference?

ALEXANDER: Unhealthy? *(*BEN *nods)* Caused by something?

BEN: A possessive mother. An absent father.

NED: That's what they thought then.

ALEXANDER: Absent? Richard was always there. That was the problem. Possessive doesn't sound precise enough for Rena. *(to* NED) Where do I get more up-to-date information?

BEN: You see a psychiatrist.

ALEXANDER: See him do what?

BEN: You talk to him.

ALEXANDER: Talk to *him?*

BEN: About this.

ALEXANDER: I'm talking to you.

BEN: What do you expect me to say?

ALEXANDER: "I don't care if you've got purple spots, I love you." Theo said there are lots of us. We can tell each other like Jewish people can.

BEN: Horseshit!

ALEXANDER: *We* mustn't fight, Benjamin.

NED: Why not? If you don't agree, fight, Alexander. Fight back! Never run away from a fight.

ALEXANDER: Which one of you am I supposed to fight? It's like Richard and Rena—each one is pulling so hard in opposite directions I'm being torn in two. *(to NED)* Please call me Ned. *(to BEN)* So you do think I'm sick? *(no answer)* You do. I told Theo that going to Europe as his assistant on his Guggenheim was a terrific opportunity but that after walking round and around the block all night long I decided not to go.

BEN: Good man.

ALEXANDER: I told him no because I don't love him.

BEN: You told him no because you know it's wrong.

NED: *(to BEN)* I told him no because . . . because I knew you wanted me to tell him no.

BEN: *(to NED)* You told him no because you knew it was considered wrong and unhealthy and sick.

ALEXANDER: Don't I just not love Theo because I just don't love Theo?

BEN: There's something called psychoanalysis. It's the latest thing. You lie down on a couch every day and say whatever comes into your head.

NED: *(as ALEXANDER look at him, suddenly worried)* Why listen to me? I can only predict epidemics and plagues.

ALEXANDER: What have I done?

NED: You're letting Ben push you on to a treadmill of revolving doctors, not one of whom will know a fucking thing about what makes *your* heart tick.

ALEXANDER: What will they do to me?

NED: They will turn you into a productive human being.

ALEXANDER: What's wrong with that? I'm flunking every course.

NED: While they teach you to love yourself they will also teach you to hate your heart. It's their one great trick. All these old Jewish doctors—the sons of Sigmund—exiled from their homelands, running from Hitler's death camps, for some queer reason celebrated their freedom on our shores by deciding to eliminate homosexuals. That's what you are. It's going to be a long time before you can say the word out loud. Over and over and over again they will pound into your consciousness through constant repetition: you're sick, you're sick, you're sick. So your heart is going to lie alone. So you see, you should have gone to Europe with Theo.

ALEXANDER: Ben—I'm scared.

BEN: You're making all the right decisions. I'll always fight for you and defend you and protect you. All I ask is that you try. The talking cure, it's called. *(puts his arm around ALEXANDER's shoulder)*

ALEXANDER: Talking? I should be cured real fast. *(leaving with BEN)* Theo gave me crabs. Do you know what crabs are? *(BEN nods)* I didn't but I do now.

(They exit. HANNIMAN enters with her cart. Sounds of chanting outside can be dimly heard.)

HANNIMAN: We need more blood.

NED: What are you opening, a store? Do you know how many blood tests I've had in the past twelve years? It's definitely a growth industry. The tyranny of the blood test. Ladies and gentlemen, step right up and watch the truth drawn right before your very eyes. We are being tested for the presence of a virus that may or may not be the killer. We are being tested to discover if this and/or that miraculous new discovery that may or may not kill the virus which may or may not be the killer is working. We live in constant terror that the number of healthy cells, which may or may not be an accurate indicator of anything at all and which the virus that may or may not be the killer may or may not be destroying, will decline and fall. What does any of this *mean*? Before each blood test, no one sleeps. *(singing)* "Nessun dorma." Awaiting each result, the same. The final moments are agony. On a piece of paper crowded with computerized chitchat that, depending on whom you ask, is open to at least two and often more contradictory interpretations, and which your doctor is holding in his hand, is printed the latest clairvoyance of your life expectancy. May I have the winning envelope, please?

HANNIMAN: Boy, you are one piece of cake. What happened between you and your people out there?

NED: You ran out of miracles.

HANNIMAN: Not personal enough.

NED: They look to me for leadership and I don't know how to guide them. I'm going to die and they're going to die, only they're nineteen and twenty-four and somehow born into this world and I feel so fucking guilty that I've failed them. I wanted to be Moses but I only could be Cassandra.

HANNIMAN: And you lay all that on yourself?

NED: Why not?

HANNIMAN: If people don't want to be led, they don't want to be led. You're not as grand and important as you think you are.

NED: In a few more years more Africans will be dying from this plague than are being born. If this stuff works, only rich white men will get it. I call that genocide. What do you call it? How do you go to sleep at night lying beside your husband knowing all that? What are you doing for *your* people out there?

HANNIMAN: I don't have to take this shit. *(walks out)*

NED: *(Calling after her)* You're as grand and important as you want to be!
(Loud banging is heard, then BEN'S *voice.)*

BEN: Ned! Your landlady says you're in there! Open up. Open up the goddamned door! Alexander!

*(*BEN *is banging on the door of a sparsely furnished New York studio apartment.* ALEXANDER *sits staring into space.* BEN *finally breaks the door down. He carries a bottle of champagne.)*
You haven't been to work in a week. Your office said you were home sick. Why don't you answer the phone? Does Dr . . . I can't remember the new one's name . . . know you're like this? Ned, come on, talk to me. You always talk to me. Ned, goddamn it, please answer me! You know, you're not a very good uncle. You never come and see my kids. Alexandra would like to see her namesake. Timmy wants to know all about the movie business. Betsy—sometimes I think my feelings for my firstborn are unnatural. Have you been staring into space for a week? Come on—congratulations! You're going to London! Your career is progressing nicely. Are you going to talk to me?
*(*BEN *uncorks the champagne.* NED *gives him a cup.* BEN *pours some and offers it to* ALEXANDER, *who refuses.)*

ALEXANDER: Be careful you don't ever give me one of your secrets.

NED: I told you not to tell him.

ALEXANDER: Fuck you! *(mimicking)* "I told you this!" "I told you that!" I've had enough of your . . . lack of cooperation.

NED: Well, tough shit and fuck you yourself, you little parasite.

ALEXANDER: Parasite?

NED: Bloodsucker. Leech. Hanger-on. Freeloader. You're like the very virus itself and I can't get rid of you.

ALEXANDER: I didn't know that's what you wanted to do.

NED: There's never been a virus that's been successfully eradicated.

ALEXANDER: *(repeating)* I didn't know that's what you wanted to do.

BEN: Who is it this time?
*(*BEN *offers him the cup of champagne again. This time* ALEXANDER *takes it.* BEN *drinks out of the bottle.)*

ALEXANDER: Six shrinks later I'm still the most talkative one in class. When do I graduate?

You always take care of me. Why? *(no answer)* Why?

BEN: Tell me about him.

ALEXANDER: Which one?

BEN: Any one.

ALEXANDER: Dr Schwartz kept calling me a pervert. Dr Grossman said I was violating God's laws by not fathering children. Dr Nussbaum was also very uncomplimentary. I ran into him getting fucked in the Provincetown dunes. Dr . . . I go to all the doctors you send me to. One doesn't do the trick, you find me another.

BEN: What's wrong!

ALEXANDER: I didn't know life could be so lonely.

BEN: I'm sorry. You'll meet someone.

ALEXANDER: Oh, that. I already tried that. Hundreds of times. At first I wanted love back. But now I'm willing to give that up if someone would just stay put and let me love him. That's really a person who likes himself a lot, huh?

BEN: Don't give up. Your self-pity will . . . diminish.

ALEXANDER: I did meet someone. He loved every book I loved. Every symphony and pop song and junk food. I couldn't believe this man was interested in me. He was so . . . beautiful. Beauty rarely looks at me. I couldn't stop feeling his skin, touching his face. *(pointing to mattress)* Right there. There! All night long, two days through, we couldn't let go of each other.

   And then came the brainwashing session. What did that mind-bender say to turn me into such a monster? I walked home very slowly. I came in here. Peter had made breakfast. Nobody ever made me breakfast. He smiled and said, "I've missed you." He missed me. "We have one more day before I have to go back." He was finishing his doctorate at Harvard. The perfect man for *anyone* to take home to the folks. And I said . . . I actually said . . . I don't know where the words came from or how I could say them . . . but I said: "You have to leave now." God damn you!

BEN: Me?

ALEXANDER: They're your witch doctors! *(to* NED*)* All this psychoanalysis shit and you're what I've got to show for it?

NED: I did not send you into psychoanalysis.

ALEXANDER: Stop trying to keep your hands so fucking clean! *You're* the bloodsucker!

BEN: Ned . . . ?

ALEXANDER: Why do I go to them? One after another. One doesn't do the trick: step right up, your turn at bat. Why do I listen to them? Why do I listen to you? How do we still love each other, when all we do is . . . this? Peter could be here *(holding out his empty arms)* right now. Why are you so insistent? Why do I obey you? You don't put a gun to my head. Why don't I say: get out of my life, I'll make my own rules? I could be loved! But you do put a gun to my head. You won't love me unless I change. Well, it's too powerful a force to change! It's got to be a part of me! It doesn't want to die. And fights tenaciously to stay alive, against all odds. And no matter what anyone does to try and kill it. Why don't you just leave me alone? We don't have to see each other. Are you afraid to let go of me, too? Why? Why am I—why are we both—such collaborators? And how can I love you when part of me thinks you're murdering me?

BEN: You're very strange. You just lay it all right out there. You always have.

NED: *(to* BEN*)* Answer him!

BEN: What do you want me to say! *(pause)* Change is hard.

ALEXANDER: How about grief? And sadness. And mourning for lost life and love and what might have been.

BEN: Try not to be so melodramatic.

ALEXANDER: Melodramatic? Who are you? Do I know you? Sometimes you can be a very mysterious person.

BEN: I've heard excellent things about another doctor. In London.

ALEXANDER: Why'd you stay away from home so much? *(no answer)* Why'd you stay away from home? *(no answer)* Why did you run away?

BEN: I didn't run away.

ALEXANDER: You were never there.

NED: Answer him!

BEN: *(after a long pause)* I didn't have a mother.

ALEXANDER: You never had a *mother?*

BEN: You asked me why I never came home. That's why I never came home.

ALEXANDER: You thought Rena didn't love you?

BEN: She doesn't.

ALEXANDER: Mommy doesn't love you? *(to* NED*)* Did you know this?

NED: That's what he believes.

BEN: She was never there! She had so many jobs. She was always out taking care of everyone in the entire world except me. So I went out and did a thousand projects at a time because I thought that was how I'd get my mother's love. If I got *another* A or headed up *another* organization, she'd notice me and pay attention to me and I'd win some approval from her. I needed her and she wasn't there and I resent it bitterly. *(long pause)* And I'll never forgive her for that.

ALEXANDER: *(shaken, feeling he must defend her)* She had to work! Pop didn't make enough! She was doing her best.

BEN: That's all she cares about. *Her* best. She *made* Daddy quit working for Uncle Leon. It was a good job. All through the Depression, Leon was rich. Pop had been making big bucks. Suddenly he's no longer the breadwinner, with no self-respect. He was out of work for something like seven, eight years before the war finally came and there was work in Washington for everybody. So we moved to Washington where he made ten times less than he'd made with Leon.

ALEXANDER: You can't blame that on her!

BEN: Why not! She had to be the star. She never stopped. She had a million jobs. She had a few spare hours she ran over to take dictation from a couple of bozos who repaired wrecked trucks. Leon found Pop a job as American counsel in the Virgin Islands. A big house, servants, tax-free salary. A fortune in those days. They turned it down.

ALEXANDER: She said there wasn't any milk for babies. You were just born.

BEN: You boil milk. You use powdered. What did all the tens of thousands of babies born there drink? Have you heard about any mass demise of Virgin Island babies? She didn't want to go! She felt so "useful." And so he stayed home, unemployed, playing pinochle with the boys.

ALEXANDER: Why didn't he hustle his ass like she did?

BEN: You're not listening to me. She took his balls away! Why are you defending her so? She almost smothered you to death.

ALEXANDER: She was the only one interested in me!

BEN: Interested in you? What did she ever do to help you develop one single ability or interest or gift you ever had? You wanted to act, sing, dance, write, create . . . whatever. That's what parents are supposed to do! Richard crucified every single one of those desires and she stood by and let him. All she does is talk endlessly and forever about herself!

ALEXANDER: It wasn't her. It wasn't! It was him. It was all him. It was Richard. Why aren't you mad at him for being so weak instead of her for trying to be strong?

BEN: She called all the shots and she called them from her own selfish point of view.

ALEXANDER: You don't like her as much as I don't like him. What happens when a kid is chosen for the wrong team? It's as if we each took one parent for our very own. And each of them chose one of us. The whole procedure had nothing to do with love. Can you say I love you? Out loud? To anyone? And mean it? *(no answer. To* NED*)* Can you? *(no answer)*

BEN: There's just an anger inside me that never goes away. I've got to get out of here. I'm late. Walk me back to the office.

ALEXANDER: How'd you figure all this out? *(no answer)* You have just told me I shouldn't love my mother. How did you figure this all out!

BEN: *(another long pause)* I'm being psychoanalyzed.

ALEXANDER: *(pause)* I don't know why but that scares the shit out of me.

BEN: It should make you feel better you're not the only one.

ALEXANDER: It's all the decisions I let you make for me because you were the only one. What happened? God, wouldn't it be wonderful if it were another man.

BEN: You know how Richard always yelled at you, no matter what you did, you couldn't do anything right? That's how Sara treats Timmy. She says I . . . I withhold. I don't show how I feel toward anyone and that makes her overreact and overreach and vent her anger on young Timmy. My son . . . he . . . she . . . she's so hard on him, she takes everything out on him that's meant for me. I called her . . . a controlling bitch. She says she can't stop herself from doing it. Alexander, it's a mess. The poor kid's got some kind of stomach ulceration now. He'll suddenly start bleeding, he can never be out of range of a toilet, and he's only a kid, he'll have this all his life. He's such a good kid. He came into my room and started crying. I want him to be smart in school and the kid just isn't. And he knows it disappoints the shit out of me. Ned, why doesn't he do better? He's smart. I just know it! He was crying. He started screaming I didn't love him. And I'd never loved him. Why are you looking at me that way? We're working on it! Sara's in therapy, too. She's learning. I'm learning. Richard and Rena couldn't learn. We can learn. We mustn't stop trying to learn.

NED: "And the sins of the fathers shall visit unto the third and fourth generations."

BEN: No! I don't believe that! We *can* change it!

NED: And all those years you told me it was worse for me and I believed you!

BEN: It was. It was worse for you.

NED: No, it wasn't. Why was it so important for you to hold on to that? Why was it so important to you to make me the sick one? Were you so angry at Rena that you had to make my homosexuality so awful just to blame her? It wasn't so hot for either of us! It made you stay away from home. And it didn't make me gay. It made

both of us have a great deal of difficulty saying "I love you."

BEN: Ned—go and call Peter back.

ALEXANDER: Thank you, Ben. I called Peter back. I asked him to meet me. Which he did. At the Savoy Plaza. I took this grand suite and ordered filet mignon and champagne and flowers, tons of flowers. I apologized over and over again for what I had done. He said he recalled our time together as very pleasant. I practically pounced on him and threw him on the bed and held him in my arms and kissed him all over. He told me he was very happily in love with someone else and he thought it best that he leave. Which he did.

BEN: I'm sorry. I have to get back to the office. I really am sorry. I have a meeting. Good luck in London. Maybe you'll meet someone.

ALEXANDER: Are you saying loving a man is now okay?

BEN: Keep fighting. Keep on fighting. Don't give up. The answers will present themselves. They really will. For both of us!
(They go off.)

NED: I haven't been honest with you. I left out the hardest part for me to talk about. It was done by another Ned, someone inside of me who took possession of me and did something I've been terrified, every day of my life ever since, he might come back and do again. And, this time, succeed. After my father beat me and Mom up and told me he'd never wanted me and after I told my brother I was gay and after my brother got married and before my first year's final exams that I knew I'd flunk, I pulled a bottle of some kind of pills which belonged to my roommate who's father was a doctor out of his bureau drawer and swallowed them all. I had wanted to take a knife and slice a foot or arm off. I had wanted to see blood, gushing everywhere, making a huge mess, and floating me away on its sea. But there were only pills. I'm only going to take two for a headache and two more to help me sleep. I have finals on Monday and there's no way I can pass. Where else can I go? Back to

Eden Heights? I'd rather be dead. So where? Every social structure I'm supposed to be a part of—my family, my religion, my school, my friends, my neighborhood, my work, my city, my state, my country, my government, my newspaper, my television . . . —tells me over and over what I feel and see and think and do is sick. The only safe place left is the dark. I want to go to sleep. It's Friday. I want to sleep till Tuesday. *(swallowing* HANNIMAN'S *pills with* BEN'S *champagne)* This couple of pills will take me till tomorrow and these until Sunday and . . . Monday . . . now I can sleep till Tuesday. Might as well take a few more. Just in case. Pop's right, of course. I'm a failure. *(looking at himself in the mirror over the sink)* You even look like Richard. You'll look like him for the rest of your life. I am more my father's child than ever I wanted to be. I've fought so hard not to look like you. I've fought so hard not to inherit your failure. Poor newly-named Ned. Trying so hard to fight failure. Now increasing at an awful rate. I woke up in the hospital and Ben was there beside me.

ALEXANDER'S VOICE: Help! I'm drowning! Don't let me drown!

NED: That night at Mrs Pennington's when Benjamin stopped Poppa from beating me up, he put me on his shoulders and carried me down to the shore. We swam and played and ducked under each other's arms and legs. We lay on the big raft, way out on the Sound, side by side, not saying a word, looking at the stars. I held his hand. He said, Come dive with me. I dived in after he did and I got caught under the raft and I couldn't get out from under. I thrashed desperately this way and that and I had no more breath.

ALEXANDER'S VOICE: Help! I'm drowning! Don't let me drown!

NED: When I thought I would surely die, he rescued me and saved me, Benjamin did.

*(*BENJAMIN *carries in a limp* ALEXANDER *and lays him on the ground. Both are wet from the ocean.)*

He got me to the shore and he laid me out on the sand and he pressed my stomach so the poison came out and he kissed me on the lips so I might breathe again.

TONY: *(entering)* Ned, I've run the tests. The new genes are adhering. We're halfway there. We can go on with the final part. Say Thank You. Say Congratulations. You begged for a few more years. I may have bought you life. *(leaves)*

NED: Okay, Ned—be happy. Be exuberant! You're halfway there. *(singing)* "Hold my hand and we're halfway there, Hold my hand and I'll take you there. Someday. Somewhere. Somehow . . ."

END OF ACT TWO

ACT THREE

HANNIMAN *removes three more sacks of blood from the small insulated chest on her cart and inserts them into the wall machine.* DR DELLA VIDA, *wearing the white dress uniform of a Public Health Service officer, checks that everything is in readiness.* NED, *wearing a navy blue robe with a red ribbon on the lapel, looks out the window.*

NED: Three hundred and seventy arrests and not one lousy reporter or camera so no one sees it but a couple hundred of your scientists with nothing better to do than look out their windows because their microscopes are constipated.

TONY: I thought your soapbox was in retirement.

NED: You bought me life.

TONY: Nice robe.

NED: Navy blue and red. The smart colors, Felix always called them.

*(*TONY *wheels in from the outside hallway a new machine—the Ex-Cell-Aerator, another elaborate invention, replete with its own dials and switches and tubings and lights.)*

What's that?

TONY: *(proudly)* I call it the Ex-Cell-Aerator. Your reassembled blood will be pumped through it so it can be exposed to particles of—

NED: That's it? I thought it was the other one.

TONY: It's both of them.

NED: It takes two? Did you dream all this up?

TONY: I try to be as creative as the law allows.

NED: *(re: the sacks of blood)* The little buggers went and multiplied.

TONY: Enriched. They got enriched. Hey, don't touch those.

NED: Do genes get loose and act uncontrollably, like viruses?

TONY: You bet. It's scary trying to modify nature.

NED: Despite everything I know and said and stood for, I have fucked with the enemy and he has given me hope.

TONY: I'm not your enemy.

NED: Why are you all dressed up?

TONY: The President wants to know all about this. *(indicates that NED should get in bed)*

NED: Any of my blood you want to slip him, hey . . . You're going to the White House!

TONY: Yes, I am. I go quite often.

NED: *(as TONY and HANNIMAN reconnect him to the wall tubing)* Tell me . . . you're a doctor, but you're also an officer in the service of your country. You're compelled to obey orders. How can research be legislated? You're an artist. How can you be free enough to create? It's like asking writers to write not using any vowels.

TONY: *(connecting the Ex-Cell-Aerator to the wall apparatus)* I run the premier research facility in the entire world. The American people are very lucky to have a place like this. And you got him all wrong. He's a good guy. He's got a heart. He really wants this disease to go away.

NED: He's brain dead and you're brainwashed.

TONY: Lay off my wife, will you? Any fights you got with me, pick them with me. *(hits a computer key to start everything going)*

NED: Tony, all your top assistants are gay. What's that all about? When I bring down all my young men for meetings, you look at them so . . . *(can't find the word)*

TONY: So what?

NED: You can't take your eyes off them.

TONY: It's very sad . . . what's happening.

NED: Yes, it is. What kind of life do you want to be leading that you're not? Why is everyone down here afraid to call a plague a plague? Are you punishing us or yourself? *(calling after him as he leaves)* You get away with murder because you're real cute and everybody wants to go to bed with you! Nobody wanted to go to bed with Ed Koch. Him we could get rid of. *(talking to the Ex-Cell-Aerator)* You're the cure? I hope you come in a portable version, like a laptop. Can you find me a boy friend while you're at it? Way to win the charm contest, Ned. You'll never get them in your arms that way. Mom, you said there wasn't anything in the world your son couldn't do.

(HANNIMAN comes in and pulls a curtain around the bed.

RENA, *now about seventy, sits in a hospital waiting area trying unsuccessfully to read some old magazines. Occasionally she gets up to look inside a room through an open door.*

After a moment, NED, wearing an overcoat and carrying a suitcase, enters. They are strangely distant with each other. Sounds of baseball game on the TV.)

RENA: *(to the unseen RICHARD)* I'm closing this so I don't have to hear that ball game. *(does so)* When he sees you here he'll put two and two together and realize we sent for you.

NED: Doesn't he know?

RENA: Some things you don't want to know, even if you know. How's London? You never write to me.

NED: It's great. Very productive. Where's Ben?

RENA: They took a break. Sara's been wonderful. She hasn't left my side. So.

NED: You always wanted to travel.

RENA: He isn't dead yet.

NED: I'm just saying you've got something to look forward to.

RENA: How about giving me a chance to mourn first? Why are we talking like this to each other? I haven't seen you in six, seven years. Are you still going to a psychiatrist?

NED: I can go every day for seventy-five dollars a week.

RENA: That used to be three months' rent. How in God's name do you find enough to talk about every day?

NED: I fall asleep a lot.

RENA: You pay someone to fall asleep? You kids, you and your psychiatrists think you know it all. Then why aren't we perfect after all these years?

NED: Did you and Richard have a good sex life?

RENA: That's none of your business.

NED: I just thought I'd ask.

RENA: Well, don't.

NED: Did he want sex more than you, or did you want it and he wouldn't?

RENA: Stop it!

NED: You used to tell me everything.

RENA: Well, here's something I'm not going to. Our lives weren't about sex. Is sex what controls your life?

NED: I don't know. Why don't you try and look up Drew Keenlymore?

RENA: Why don't you try and stop being so fresh?

NED: Didn't you love him?

RENA: Why are you so obsessed with Drew Keenlymore?

NED: One should be able to have the man one loves.

RENA: Life should be a lot of things.

NED: Did he ever ask you to marry him? Did he?

RENA: I was invited to the Keenlymore private island estate in Western Canada for the entire summer. What does that tell you?

NED: But you didn't go.

RENA: He was ready to marry me. There! Does that make you happy?

NED: If you'd listened to your heart, and not been so afraid, that would have made me happy.

RENA: Listen to my heart. You've seen too many movies. Have you listened to your heart? I don't hear about any secret long-lost love you're keeping in a purse on the top shelf of your closet.

NED: I don't fall in love. People don't fall in love with me.

RENA: That's too bad.

NED: I want to love them. I want them to love me back.

RENA: Everyone should have someone.

NED: Kids are some sort of sum total of both their parents. We pick up a lot of traits from whatever kind of emotional subtext is going on.

RENA: I'm supposed to understand that mouthful of jargon?

NED: We've got both of you in us.

RENA: Are we getting blamed for all of this?

NED: I've just finally got the courage to say what I want to say.

RENA: I don't recall your ever being delinquent in that department. Well, I always tried to instill courage in you. But you can't always just say what you think.

NED: You saw how much Pop hated me. You must have had some sense that if you'd only left him, I wouldn't have had to go through all that shit.

RENA: Don't use that language. I tried to make up for it by loving you more.

NED: It doesn't work that way.

RENA: It would appear it doesn't.

NED: Why didn't you leave him for good?

RENA: You don't run away when things don't work out.

NED: You ran away from Drew.

RENA: Some courage I had and some courage I didn't have. I don't cry over spilt milk.

NED: Are you admitting you didn't love your husband?

RENA: I am not! You don't have so many choices as you seem to think!

NED: I'm homosexual. I would like you to accept that but I don't care if you don't, because I have.

RENA: You don't care? So I was a lousy mother.

NED: Don't do that.

RENA: Why not? You just said I was. Not very good value for all my years, is it? Some psychiatrist, some stranger, turns your son against you and declares me a bad mother.

NED: The preference now is to stay away from judgmental words like "good" or "bad."

RENA: Of course it's judgmental! Is this some kind of joke? You think any mother likes her son to be a . . . I'm not even going to say the word, that's how judgmental I think it is. I never criticized my parents. I worshiped the ground my mother walked on. I respected my father, even if he wasn't the most affectionate man in the world.

NED: Your father never smiled a day in his life.

RENA: Life was hard! They ran a tiny grocery store in a hostile neighborhood where neither of them spoke English and all the customers were Irish Catholics who hated us and never paid their bills. My parents didn't marry for love. They married to stay alive! Most kids grow up and leave home. You left home and found new parents called psychiatrists. I'm sorry the old ones were so disappointing. Sum total? Of both of us? You can also be so much more than that. I always told your father he should show his feelings more. He couldn't do it. He never would talk about his dreams. I don't even know what his dreams were. I guess they were taken away from him before I even knew him. He really did love you! I knew someday we'd reap the whirlwind. Why didn't Ben become one, too? He was there, too.

NED: I'm beginning to think it isn't caused by anything. I was born this way.

RENA: I don't believe that.

NED: I like being gay. It's taken me a very, very, very long time. I don't want to waste any more, tolerating your being ashamed of me, or anyone I care about being ashamed of me. If you can't accept that, you won't see your younger son again.

RENA: He has to die for you even to come home as it is. It makes you happy? Anything that makes you happy makes me happy. Miss Pollyanna, that's me. Go say hello to your father. Please don't tell him your wonderful news that makes you so happy.

(She takes his suitcase from him and goes off. NED *pulls the curtain around the bed, revealing* RICHARD *it in, half asleep, with the ball game still on.* NED *comes in and turns the TV off.* RICHARD *wakes up.)*

RICHARD: Who won?

NED: Hi, Pop.

RICHARD: This is it, boy. I'm not going to make it.

NED: Sure you are.

RICHARD: I'm ready to go.

NED: Hey, I want you to see my first movie. I wrote it and produced it. It's good!

RICHARD: My goddamned Yankees can't break their losing streak. Ben's goddamned Red Sox may win the pennant.

NED: It cost two million dollars. I was paid a quarter of a million dollars.

RICHARD: Movies. The thee-ay-ter. When are you going to grow up?

NED: I've discovered how to make a living from it.

RICHARD: At least Ben listened to me. He's raking it in. He's senior partner over two hundred lawyers. Two million dollars. That's a hot one. I'm glad it's over. What's your name now?

NED: I've been Ned since I was eighteen.

RICHARD: Eighteen. That's when your mother started signing over her paychecks to your psychiatrist. I wouldn't have anything to do with it. She could have bought lots of nice clothes. She could have looked real pretty. I never felt good. I've felt sick all my life. In and out of doctors' offices and still the pain in my bloody gut. Nothing ever took it away. I never had a father either. So long, boy. *(he rolls over, with his back to* NED*)*

NED: What do you mean, you never had a father either? *(no answer)* Pop? Poppa? *(*RICHARD *doesn't answer.* NED *starts out . . .)*

RICHARD: My father was a mohel. You know what that is?

NED: The man who does the circumcision.

RICHARD: It was supposed to be a holy honor. God was supposed to bless him and his issue forever. One day he cut too much foreskin and this rich baby was mutilated for life. My Mom and Pop ran away and changed our name. Then Pop ran away. Forever.

NED: Mom said Grandma Sybil threw him out for sleeping with another woman in Atlantic City.

RICHARD: That's what she told people. He ran away when the kid he mutilated grew up and tracked him down. He couldn't have an erection without great pain and he was out for Pop's blood. I never told anyone. Not even your mother. I was afraid if I told her she wouldn't marry me. Maybe I should have told her. I wanted her more than she wanted me. I thought I could convince her and I never could. I helped my father. I was his assistant. All the time, the blood. Bawling babies terrified out of their wits. Tiny little cocks with pieces peeled off them. I had to dispose of the pieces. I buried them. He made me memorize all the Orthodox laws. If I made a mistake, he beat me. "You are forbidden to touch your membrum in self-gratification. You are forbidden to bring on an erection. It is forbidden to discharge semen in vain. Two bachelors must not sleep together. Two bachelors must not gaze upon each other. Two bachelors who lie down together and know each other and touch each other, it is equal to killing a person and saying blood is all over my hands. It is forbidden . . . It is forbidden . . ." He made me learn all that and then he ran away. I never stopped hating him. It's hard living with your gut filled with hate. Good luck to you, boy. Anything you want to say to me?

(RICHARD *rolls over and turns his back on him.* NED *stands there, trying to work up his courage to say what he has to say. Finally, finally, he does so.*)

NED: I'm sorry your life was a disappointment, Poppa. Poppa, you were cruel to me, Poppa.

(*There is no answer. He pulls the curtain closed again.*)

Poppa died. I didn't cry. My movie was a success. I made another. I realized how little pleasure achievement gave me. Slowly I became a writer. It suited me. I'd finally found a way to make myself heard. And "useful"—that word

Rena so reveled in trumpeting. I would address the problems of my new world. Every gay man I knew was fucking himself to death. I wrote about that. Every gay man I knew wanted a lover. I wrote about that. I said that having so much sex made finding love impossible. I made my new world very angry. As when I was a child, such defiance made me flourish. My writing and my notoriety prospered.

I stopped going to psychoanalysts. I'd analyzed, observed, regurgitated, parsed, declined, X-rayed, and stared down every action, memory, dream, recollection, thought, instinct, and deed, from every angle I'd been able to come up with.

(NED *pulls back the curtain and gets into bed. He reconnects himself to the tubing.*)

I spent many years looking for love—in the very manner I'd criticized. How needy man is. And with good reason. When I finally met someone, I was middle-aged. His name was Felix Turner. Eleven months later he was sick and nineteen months later he was dead. I had spent so many years looking for and preparing for and waiting for Felix. Just as he came into my arms and just as I was about to say "I love you, Felix," the plague came along and killed him. And the further away I've got from the love I had, the more I question I ever had it in the first place.

Ben invested my money wisely and I am rich. When I get angry with him for not joining me in fighting this plague, he points out that he has made me financially independent so I could afford to be an activist. Ben has made all the Weeks family, including Rena and his children, rich. That's what he wanted to do—indeed I believe that's been his mission in life—to give all of us what he and I never had as children—and he's accomplished it.

(BEN *stands in the Eden Heights apartment, smoking a cigar. Scattered cartons and packing crates.*)

NED: Did you ever think you'd spend one more night in Eden Heights?

BEN: I consider it one of the greatest achievements of my life that I got out of here alive.

NED: Don't you ever stop and think how far we've come?

BEN: No. Never.

(RENA *is on the phone. She is now almost ninety.* BEN *sits in a chair and reads a business magazine.*)

RENA: *(loudly)* I'm coming home! I'll be there tomorrow! Back with all you dear chums I've loved since childhood! I can hardly wait! *(hangs up)* The woman's deaf. Paula's deaf and Nettie's moved to an old people's kibbutz in Israel and Belle is blind and Lydia's dead. Belle's husband brought you both into this world. Lydia introduced me to Richard. She didn't want him. *(starts rummaging in a carton)* All our past—in one battered carton from the Safeway. Aah, I'm going to throw it all away.

NED: No, I want it. It's our history.

RENA: Some history. So you can dredge up more unhappy memories to tell a psychiatrist how much you hated your father.

NED: *(to BEN)* Don't you want to take anything for a memento?

BEN: You're the family historian. I leave the past to you.

NED: Your West Point letters, your yearbooks . . .

BEN: I've burned the mortgage. You're the one with the passion for remembering.

NED: Is that the way we handle it? I remember and you don't?

BEN: Maybe so. Maybe you've hit the nail on the head, young brother.

RENA: *(comes across* RICHARD's *watch chain)* He was Phi Beta Kappa and Law Journal. He majored in Greek and Latin. They didn't let many Jews into Yale in those days. You would have thought he'd have done better.

NED: Both brothers such failures. Uncle Leon wound up broke, hanging around the Yale Club trying to bum loans off old Yalies. I could never understand why you paid for his funeral.

BEN: He wasn't such a bad guy.

RENA: Aunt Judith threw him out when she discovered all his bimbos.

BEN: Some old judge I met told me, "If only Leon had been castrated instead of circumcised, he'd have wound up on the Supreme Court."

RENA: I've lived in this room for over fifty years. We moved down here on a three-month temporary job. Some man had almost burned to death and they needed a new one fast. The poor chap died and the job was Richard's. *(comes across the navy blue crocheted purse and pulls out the letters and tries to read them)*

NED: Ah, the famous letters. *(knows them by heart)* "I find my schedule will perhaps bring me into the vicinity of New York on 4th May; might you be available for luncheon?"

RENA: That was at Delmonico's.

NED: "I find I must reschedule; will you be available instead on the 10th inst.?" "It now appears the 10th must be replaced by the 20th and even this is not firm." Why did I think they were so romantic?

RENA: They were romantic. They are romantic.

NED: Maybe you'll meet another man at the home.

RENA: It's called an adult residence. I don't want to meet another man. One was enough. I always thought Richard was inadequate. I just never had the guts to really leave him. It's no great crime to choose security over passion. My grand passion was the two of you. *(to BEN)* You have the wonderful wife and the wonderful marriage and have given me my wonderful grandchildren. *(to NED)* You have the artistic talent, which you inherited from me. Hurry up and write whatever it is you're going to write about me so I can get through all the pain it'll no doubt cause me.

NED: Why do you automatically assume it will be painful?

RENA: Knowing you it will be. I want to show you something. *(goes into her bedroom)*

BEN: We can't die. We're indestructible. We have her genes inside us. Sara called. Timmy has to have an operation. But then it should be fine. His bleeding will stop. Finally. All these years we blamed ourselves. It wasn't bad parenting. It wasn't psychosomatic. It was genetic. Ulcerated nerve ends not dissimilar to what Richard must have had.

NED: I'm glad. Genetic. That's what they say now about homosexuality. In a few more minutes the Religious Right is going to turn violently Pro-Choice.

BEN: Now if Betsy wouldn't keep falling for all these wretched young men who treat her so terribly.

NED: Yes, that's a tough one.

BEN: But I've found her the best therapist I could find.

NED: Her very own first therapist.

BEN: We learned how to attack problems and not be defeated by them. We found the tools to do this, probably by luck and the accident of history. Rena and Richard didn't. For them it was more about missed opportunities. It was the wrong time for them and it hasn't been for us.

NED: For you.

BEN: Ned, you're not going to die. Tell Rena I'll be here with the car in the morning at nine sharp.

(RENA *comes back dressed in the Russian peasant clothing.*)

NED: How *did* we get out of here alive?

BEN: A lot of expensive therapy. *(sneaks out)*

RENA: I wore this when I got off the boat from Russia.

NED: You were two years old when you got off the boat from Russia. *(pause)* I wore it, too.

RENA: You never wore this.

NED: Daddy beat me up for it.

RENA: Oh, he did not. He never laid a finger on you. How can you say such an awful thing? How about giving us one tiny little bit of credit while I'm still alive.

NED: Mom . . . aren't you afraid of dying?

(HANNIMAN *comes in to take a sample of* NED's *blood.*)

RENA: Of course I'm frightened. Who isn't? What time is it? My friends are throwing me a farewell party. I see your brother left without saying goodbye. It's as if he's punishing me. He thinks I never notice. You think I don't know how you both treat me with such disdain? So many of my friends have kids who never see them at all. So I guess I must consider myself fortunate. You'll never guess what happened. I called Drew Keenlymore! He's listed in Vancouver. His very first words to me were, "My dear, I called every Weeks in the New York directory trying to find you." He tried to find me. He tried to find me. *(re:* HANNIMAN*)* What is she doing?

NED: A blood test.

RENA: Is my son going to be all right?

NED: My mother, Mrs Weeks. Nurse Hanniman.

HANNIMAN: What a kind, pleasant, thoughtful, considerate son you have. I'm so enjoying taking care of him.

NED: Nurse Hanniman and I enjoy a rare bonding. (HANNIMAN *leaves.*)

Momma . . . you may outlive me.

RENA: Don't say that. My momma was ninety-five years old when she died. She was withered beyond recognition. She was in a crib, mewling, wetting her pants, not knowing anyone, and me trying not to vomit from the putrid smell of urine and her runny stools. She simply would not let go. This old people's home had taken her every last cent for this tiny crib, for no nurse to come and wipe her. I wiped her. I came every day. I sat beside her. She didn't know who I was. My own mother. I'll bet you won't do all that for me. People stick articles under my door. "Your son's sick with that queer disease." "I saw your pervert son on TV saying homosexuals are the same as everyone else." Then, in our current events class we had a report on all the progress that's been made and how much your activists had to do with it and all the women came over and congratulated me. I don't know why, after ninety years, I'm surprised by anything.

NED: There hasn't been any progress.

RENA: Of course there has. Alexander . . .

NED: Yes, Momma?

RENA: He's dead. Drew Keenlymore is dead. I planned a trip to British Columbia, to Banff and

Lake Louise, and I called to let him know I was going to be in the vicinity and he's gone and died. I guess we couldn't expect him to wait around for me forever, could we?

NED: No, Momma. I'm sorry.

RENA: Goodbye, darling. It's a long trip back. And I'm having trouble with my tooth. Every time I say goodbye I'm never sure I'm going to see you again. Give me a kiss.

(They kiss. NED *hugs her as best he can with his arms connected to the tubing.)*

NED: *(as she begins to leave)* I wouldn't be a writer if you guys hadn't done what you did.

RENA: Is that something else I'm meant to feel guilty for?

NED: I love being a writer.

RENA: At last.

*(*RENA *walks off, slowly, holding on to things. She is almost blind.*

HANNIMAN *enters, with* DR DELLA VIDA, *no longer in official uniform, and takes another blood test.)*

NED: Another one? Why am I having another one so quickly? What happened at the White House? What did *he* say?

TONY: They're cutting our budget.

NED: Your buddy. Is it too pushy of me to inquire as to my and/or your progress?

TONY: We have a fifty-fifty chance.

NED: That's your idea of progress?

TONY: You're not only pushy, you're . . . how do your people say it—a *kvetch?* Just imagine this is the cure and you're the first person getting it.

NED: Can I also imagine the Republicans never being re-elected?

HANNIMAN: He'd never work again.

TONY: Oh, I'll find a way. *(leaves)*

NED: Did the mouth of Weeks cause a little friction in the house of Della Vida?

HANNIMAN: Congratulations. You're my last patient.

NED: Where are you going?

HANNIMAN: To raise my baby. And be a pushy *kvetch* wife.

NED: How come?

HANNIMAN: It's somebody else's turn now. I think you can identify with that.

NED: Good luck.

HANNIMAN: You, too. Sweet dreams.

(She turns out the lights and leaves.

Darkness. NED *is tossing and turning.)*

NED: *(screaming out)* Ben!

BEN: *(lying on a cot next to him)* I'm here, Ned.

NED: Ben?

BEN: Yes, Ned.

NED: I'm scared.

BEN: It's all right. Go to sleep.

NED: Ben, I love you.

BEN: I love you, too.

NED: I can't say it enough. It's funny, but life is very precious now.

BEN: Why's it funny? I understand, and it is for me, too. A colleague of mine with terminal cancer went into his bathroom last week and blew his brains out with a shotgun.

(Dawn is breaking outside. BEN *gets up. He throws some cold water on his face at the sink.)*

NED: Hey, cheer me up, Lemon.

BEN: They haven't struck us out yet.

NED: What if this doesn't work?

BEN: It's going to work. *(sits beside him on bed)*

NED: Even if it does, it will only work for a while.

BEN: Then we'll worry about it in a while.

NED: You've certainly spent a great deal of your life trying to keep me alive, and I've been so much trouble, always trying to kill myself, asking your advice on every breath I take, putting you to the test endlessly.

BEN: I beat you up once.

NED: You beat me up? When?

BEN: We were kids. I was trying to teach you how to tackle in football. You were fast, quick. I thought you could be a quarterback. And you wouldn't do it right. You didn't want to learn. It was just perversity on your part. So I decided to teach you a lesson. I blocked you and blocked you, as hard as I could, much harder than I had to. And then I tackled you, and you'd get up and I'd tackle you again, harder. You just kept getting up for more. I beat you up real bad.

NED: I don't remember any of that. Now why did you go and do all that?

BEN: A thousand reasons and who knows?

NED: I don't want to be cremated. I want to be buried, with a tombstone, so people can come and find me and visit. Do you want to be buried or cremated?

BEN: Neither.

NED: What will they do with you?

BEN: I don't care.

NED: How can you not care?

BEN: I won't be here.

NED: You don't want people to remember you?

BEN: I've never thought about it.

NED: It seems like I've spent my whole life thinking about it. How can you never have thought about it?

BEN: I never thought about it.

NED: Well, think about it.

BEN: I don't want to think about it.

NED: I just thought we could be buried side by side.

BEN: Please, Ned. You're not go—

NED: I've picked out the cemetery. It's a pretty place. George Balanchine is buried there. I danced around his grave. When no one could see me.

BEN: Are we finished with the morbid part of this conversation?

NED: No. I want my name on something. A building. At Yale, for gay students, or in New York. Will you look after that for me?

BEN: You'll have many years to arrange all that yourself.

NED: But you're my lawyer!

BEN: Everything will be taken care of.

NED: Then, the rest of my money, you give to the kids and Sara, please give something special to Sara. You married her and you didn't even love her. And you grew to love her. I'm sorry I never really had that. For very long.

BEN: I want you to know . . . I want you to know . . . I'm proud you've stood up for what you've believed in. I've even been a little jealous of all the attention you've received. I think

to myself that if I'd gone off on my own instead of built the firm, I could have taken up some cause and done it better than you. But I didn't do that and you have and I admire you for that.

NED: I guess you could have lived without me. I never could have lived without you. Go back to your hotel.

BEN: I'll see you tomorrow.

(Lights up. DR DELLA VIDA *enters, carrying a long computer printout. He turns off the computer and then the Ex-Cell-Aerator.)*

NED: The results are in. May I have the winning envelope, please?

TONY: I don't know how much more we can take. Your hoodlums infiltrated my hospital. They destroyed my entire laboratory. *(throwing him the printout)*

NED: I guess they want you to admit you don't know what the fuck's going on and go back to the drawing board. I'm worse? I'm worse!

TONY: Yes.

NED: What are you going to do?

TONY: There's nothing I can do.

NED: What do you mean there's nothing you can do? You gave me the fucking stuff! You must have considered such a possibility! You must have some emergency measures!

TONY: Oh, shut up! I am sick to death of you, your mouth, your offspring! You think changing Presidents will change anything? Will make any difference? The system will always be here. The system doesn't change. No matter who's President. It doesn't make any difference who's President! You're scared of dying? Let me tell you the facts of life: it isn't easy to die: you don't die until you have tubes in every single, possible, opening and orifice and vent and passage and outlet and hole and slit in your ungrateful body. Why, it can take years and years to die. It's much worse than you can even imagine. You haven't suffered nearly enough. *(leaves)*

NED: *(pulls the tubes from his arms. Blood spurts out. Gets out of bed)* What do you do when you're dying from a disease you need not be dying from? What do you do when the only system set up to save you is a pile of shit run by idiots and quacks? *(yanks the tubes violently out of the wall apparatus, causing blood to gush out. Then pulls out the six bags of blood, smashing them, one by one, against the walls and floor, to punctuate the next speech)*

My straight friends ask me over and over and over again: Why is it so hard for you to find love? Ah, that is the question, answered, I hope, for you tonight. Why do I never stop believing this fucking plague can be cured!

ALEXANDER: *(appearing in the bath towels he was first seen in)* What's going to happen to me?

NED: You're going to go to eleven shrinks. You won't fall in love for forty years. And when a nice man finally comes along and tries to teach you to love him and love yourself, he dies from a plague. Which is waiting to kill you, too.

ALEXANDER: I'm sorry I asked. Do I learn anything?

NED: Does it make any sense, a life? *(singing)* "Only make believe I love you . . ."

ALEXANDER: *(singing)* "Only make believe that you love me . . ."

NED: When Felix was offered the morphine drip for the first time in the hospital, I asked him, "Do you want it now or later?" Felix somehow found the strength to answer back, "I want to stay a little longer."

NED and ALEXANDER: "Might as well make believe I love you . . ."

NED: "For to tell the truth . . ."

NED and ALEXANDER: "I do."

NED: I want to stay a little longer.

THE END

O L E A N N A   (1 9 9 2)

When *Oleanna* was originally mounted by The Back Bay Theatre Company in association with the American Repertory Theatre in Cambridge, Massachusetts, in May 1992, David Mamet walked headlong into a morass of gender issues that has become an often vexatious part of the landscape of American college and university campuses. More specifically, Mamet used his case of actual or imagined sexual harassment on a nameless college campus to explore wider concerns about gender that had received unprecedented national attention in the wake of the October 1991 confirmation hearings for Clarence Thomas, President George Bush's nominee to become a justice on the Supreme Court of the United States. During those hearings Anita Hill, a professor of law at the University of Oklahoma and former subordinate of Thomas's at the Equal Employment Opportunity Commission and the Department of Education, alleged that Thomas had sexually harassed her by talking about pornographic materials and describing his own sexual prowess. Thomas categorically denied the allegations. The all-male Senate Judiciary Committee questioned both Hill and Thomas at length, adducing evidence to support each party's positions. But the questioning, motivated to some degree by partisan politics with Republicans trying to "save" a nominee made by a president of their party and Democrats trying to shore up their party's reputation for pursuing social justice, was seen by many feminists as another example of the insensitivity of men to the plight of women who, having been harassed, must then appeal to other men, who might be equally or more insensitive, to redress the situation. In this view, the tactics of certain Judiciary Committee members went beyond party politics and validated the general assessment that men "just don't get it"—that sexual harassment is a serious and degrading daily reality for many women in the country.

Although Mamet maintained that he had started *Oleanna* months before the Hill–Thomas matter and that the hearings merely provided an impetus to finish the play, he has clearly relished his role as agent provocateur. Arthur Holmberg quotes Mamet as responding to a student who challenged what she saw as the play's refusal to take a position:

> As a playwright I have no political responsibility. I'm an artist. I write plays, not political propaganda. If you want easy solutions, turn on the boob tube. Social and political issues on TV are cartoons; the good guy wears a white hat; the bad guy a black hat. Cartoons don't interest me. We are living through a time of deep transition, so everyone is unsettled. I'm as angry, scared and confused as the rest of you. I don't have answers.

Such assertions of independence from the politics of the moment have been a prominent theme in Mamet's occasional writings and essays about the theatre. But Mamet has been personally outspoken on a number of contemporary political issues and as a cursory examination of some of his major plays indicates, his representations of an American civilization in decline have inevitably forced him to speak, indirectly at least, on a number of important social and political questions.

David Mamet is a Chicagoan, born 30 November 1947 to Leonore Silver Mamet, a teacher, and Bernard Mamet, an attorney. He grew up in a Jewish section on Chicago's South Side until his parents divorced and he moved with his mother to Olympia Fields, a Chicago suburb. During high school he attended private school in Chicago, bussed tables at the improvisational comedy cabaret Second City, and worked backstage at Chicago's Hull House

Theatre. Mamet matriculated at Goddard College, where he received a B.A. in 1969. While at Goddard, he took a year (1968–1969) to study acting under Sanford Meisner at New York City's Neighborhood Playhouse School of the Theatre. Under Meisner's influence, Mamet was exposed to the **Stanislavsky-**inspired acting **method,** a system Mamet has maintained did much to teach him about writing and the way language shapes behavior. After graduation, Mamet took a job at Marlboro College in Vermont where he wrote *Lakeboat,* a one-act play that his students staged in 1970. After his single year at Marlboro, Mamet returned to Chicago, where he worked a series of jobs including cab driver and telephone salesman. In 1971 he took an appointment at Goddard to teach and write drama, but after a year, he returned to Chicago. He began submitting plays to experimental Chicago theatre groups and several were produced, including *Duck Variations* (1972) and *Sexual Perversity in Chicago* (1974), which won the Joseph Jefferson Award as Chicago's best new play. In 1974 he also was a founding member of the Saint Nicholas Players, a group with which he was closely associated until 1976. (Among Mamet's cofounders was William H. Macy, who played John in the Cambridge and New York productions of *Oleanna.*) His New York premiere came with a 1975 double bill of *Duck Variations* and *Sexual Perversity in Chicago,* first at the **Off-Off Broadway** Saint Clements Theatre and then at the Cherry Lane Theatre (**Off-Broadway**).

American Buffalo, Mamet's first major work and winner of a New York Drama Critics Circle Award, premiered at the Goodman Theatre in Chicago in 1975 and was revised for a 1977 presentation at Broadway's Ethel Barrymore Theatre. Set in a rundown junk shop in Chicago, the play delineates the symbiotic relationships of three young men who plan a robbery of a valuable buffalo nickel only to have the plot fall apart. Although a relatively early work, *American Buffalo* evidences many of the characteristics that have since become Mamet's trademarks: a reliance upon contemporary American urban vernacular and social environment, a meticulous use of his characters' fractured utterances and pauses to chart their inner conflicts and psychological shifts, an examination of the influence of American popular culture's myths upon the nation's citizens, a nearly exclusionary focus on the relationships among men, and a recurring concern with the world of American business in both its respectable and illegal incarnations.

Mamet returned to the theme of American business in 1982 in his most acclaimed work to date, *Glengarry Glen Ross,* winner of both the **Pulitzer Prize** for drama and the New York Drama Critics Circle Award. A scathing look at the relationships among a group of unethical real estate salesmen, *Glengarry Glen Ross* posits the ways in which the clients' needs to believe in something or someone are exploited by salesmen whose abilities as improvisational storytellers earn the grudging respect (perhaps even sympathy, as Bigsby has suggested) of both playwright and audience. In *Speed-the-Plow* (1988) Mamet makes use of his increasing knowledge of Hollywood to provide an updated, insider's look at the city emblematic of both success and corruption to generations of American actors and dramatists. Unlike some other dramatists who have critiqued Hollywood, Mamet can speak with authority. In the last decade or so Mamet has served as screenwriter for such motion pictures as *The Postman Always Rings Twice* (1981), *The Verdict* (1982), and *The Untouchables* (1987), and has written and directed *House of Games* (1987), *Things Change* (1988), and *Homicide* (1991). Thus, *Speed-the-Plow*'s portrait of the "buddy-movie" formula that has been unconsciously internalized by motion-picture executives Bobby Gould and Charlie Fox rings with the wry humor of one who has observed the pattern at close range. The competition between Gould and Fox to see who can more successfully manipulate the other is complicated by the addition of a woman, Gould's temporary secretary. For the play's men, she becomes a means of reinforcing the male hierarchy when Gould manages to seduce the young and willing Karen, a woman with her own ambitions. As David Richards notes, Karen, though ultimately unsuccessful in manipulating Gould, may become a formidable adversary when she has gained the experience of Gould and Fox, a fact that the Broadway production tried to emphasize by casting the ultimate "material girl," rock diva Madonna, as Karen. Certainly Karen is hardly the female cipher of many of Mamet's earlier plays. While Bobby, Charlie, and Karen can occasionally indulge a self-aggrandizing thought or gesture, the dance of exploitation here is deftly handled, and unlike in either *American Buffalo* or *Glengarry Glen Ross,* Mamet keeps the stakes low—money, not survival, is at issue. As Robert Brustein has argued, despite its ironizing of the "buddy" formula, the play seems ultimately to argue for the values of personal loyalty and male friendship in a world whose emotional note is cynical hypocrisy.

When Mamet shifted focus from Hollywood to the academy in *Oleanna,* he ostensibly turned his back on the cutthroat economic world of Hollywood executives and real estate salesmen. The conflict in *Oleanna* certainly seems to deal much more with social roles than economic competition. But playing upon the myth of the university as an institution free of the economic forces that drive his protagonists in *American Buffalo, Glengarry Glen Ross,* and *Speed-the-Plow,* Mamet explores the personal and public implications of two emblematic individuals caught up in the profound and interrelated social and economic transformations overtaking American higher education and America more generally.

Always part of the nation's economic system, American colleges and universities have become one of the primary institutions responsible for producing the affluent consumers who have driven the American economic dream in the post–World War II era. Constantly called upon by the general economy to "credential" prospective members of the work force, American higher education is cast and casts itself more and more as a "service industry," the intellectual handmaiden to American business. Complicating this economic realignment are the more general social modifications in the gender roles of men and women that find expression in colleges and universities. As Deborah Tannen remarks in *You Just Don't Understand,* women have not traditionally placed

their primary focus on achieving status or avoiding failure, inevitably part of American higher education as well as the workplace; but that reality has been steadily changing in the last thirty years. As older social formations have eroded, more women have entered American campuses with an eye to establishing their own independent intellectual, social, and economic identities. And it is in this last domain—the economic—that women have come most squarely into conflict with an entrenched male hierarchy. As American males consistently tend to define their masculinity by their economic earning power, their perceived sense of increased competition from women, as Susan Faludi notes in *Backlash,* generates anxiety, especially when men see heightened competition and potential displacement accompanied by a changing social environment which compromises many of the devices of control that men have wielded over women. These underlying frictions inform the play's overt conflict over sexual harassment.

For Mamet, the altercation between John and Carol is fraught with ironic, contradictory, and unacknowledged misapprehensions on both characters' parts which ultimately result in a grotesque reenactment of stereotypical roles of men and women. The inarticulate Carol of the first act is the ironic beneficiary of the hard-fought battles by feminists for more extensive access to higher education for women. But the potentials for personal liberation and individual growth—two of the widely espoused ideals of feminism—have been co-opted by society's pervasive materialism. A woman of her era, Carol seeks knowledge not from some thirst for enlightenment or as part of a search for individual betterment, but to qualify for credentials so that, as she says, she might "get on in the world." For Carol this nameless university is where she has come "to be *helped*" (her passive voice, in typical Mamet fashion, reflecting her giving of herself over to institutional authority). She has done everything that those in control have told her to do. Yet she is failing. For Carol, following the rules and failing are incompatible; somewhere the system must be breaking down. For her, a system that takes her money in tuition but cannot "guarantee" an education, the traditional *passe porteau* to economic security, must be being mismanaged by those who control it. She locates an instance of the problem in John.

An ostensible liberal who scrutinizes the academy from a self-styled "outsider's" perspective, John stands on the threshold of the very economic security for which Carol longs. In Mamet's indictment of what he perceives as liberal educational theorists' naive abrogation of their authority, John focuses primarily on ameliorating Carol's emotional pain rather than her ignorance. Pedantic and self-satisfied, John smugly assures Carol that she can have her "A" for the term, if she will meet with him so that he can answer her questions and raise her interest in the subject. When pressed by Carol as to why he would be willing to break the rules, John assures her that he "likes" her. When he ambiguously adds "There's no one here but you and me," Carol, for once, thinks she grasps what John is saying: "All right. I did not understand." But John's complaisance in removing what he terms the "artificial stricture" between student and teacher disguises from him his reluctance to accept equality beyond that which he prescribes. He will give her an "A," but this antiauthoritarian gesture still proceeds under the teacher's prerogative, for he still controls her grade. When Carol, ironically feeling that she has been the victim of a harassment grounded in the disparate power relationship between student and teacher, seeks to treat him as a true equal, the problematic nature of John's position slowly becomes apparent to him. By shifting the essential issue from the intellectual to social arena, Carol can call upon institutional authority—ironically "disciplining" John while at the same time serving her now more fully recognized and articulated economic and ideological ends.

In the second and third acts, Mamet clearly stacks the play's emotional deck, making Carol something of an automaton of "political correctness," a variety of witch, as Deborah Tannen suggests in the *New York Times* forum on the play, *"He Said . . . She Said . . . Who Did What?"* Stripped of potential tenure, suspended from his

job, and perhaps to be charged with attempted rape, John becomes a Kafkaesque victim ground down by an implacable foe and by a venal institution which just seems to want the whole issue to go away. Meantime, Carol, reworking one of the play's reiterated phrases in a gruesome evocation of Tannen's book's title, insists "I don't want 'revenge.' I WANT UNDERSTANDING." But Mamet compromises the audience's sympathy for John in the spasm of violence that ends the play. Goaded beyond his endurance, John becomes the very sexist brute that Carol has accused him of being. Carol, at the same time, becomes the cowering victim of the very male oppression that she has ostensibly resisted. Even more troubling is her ambiguous response to the attack—"That's right." The frozen action of John standing over Carol ready to bash her with a chair grotesquely suggests that the ideals employed by these two characters have done little, if anything, to move women and men to closer understanding. Indeed, a return to the caves of prehistory seems in the offing.

Whether one agrees with Mamet's vision of gender relationships or sees *Oleanna* as a cynical exploitation of a legitimate social concern, the play does raise a host of compelling questions: What constitutes sexual harassment? Whose interpretation of a word or an action is to be privileged when interpretation itself is no longer grounded (if it ever was) in a linguistic and ethical communality? Can—or how can—language remain a viable means of human interaction in a period of enormous social and economic flux? Can power be given away yet retained? Does the exercise of power inevitably lead to abuses no matter who controls the levers of authority? Are men and women doomed to remain adversaries forever, constantly battling for supremacy? While Mamet does not answer these questions, he certainly forces us to confront them. After grossing an estimated five million dollars in its New York run, and with productions from Brazil to Japan to Iceland in 1994, *Oleanna* continues to spark controversy. And, for Mamet at least, thoughtful questioning, not the formulation answers, is the function of dramatic art.

WORKS CONSULTED

Bigsby, C. W. E. *David Mamet.* London: Methuen, 1985.

———. *Modern American Drama: 1945–1990.* Cambridge: Cambridge University Press, 1992.

Brustein, Robert. "The Last Refuge of Scoundrels." *Reimagining American Theatre.* New York: Hill and Wang, 1991. 62–65.

Carroll, Dennis. *David Mamet.* New York: St. Martin's, 1987.

Dean, Anne. *David Mamet: Language as Dramatic Action.* Rutherford, NJ: Fairleigh Dickinson University Press, 1990.

Faludi, Susan. *Backlash: The Undeclared War Against American Women.* New York: Anchor Books, 1991.

Greene, Alexis. "Theatre Review." *TheatreWeek,* 30 Nov. 1992: 30+.

"He Said . . . She Said . . . Who Did What?" New York Times, 15 Nov. 1992, sec. 2: 6+.

Holmberg, Arthur. "The Language of Misunderstanding." *American Theatre* October 1992: 94–95.

Kane, Leslie. *David Mamet: A Casebook.* New York: Garland, 1992.

Lahr, John. "Dogma Days." *The New Yorker,* 16 Nov. 1992: 121–125.

Mamet, David. *Oleanna.* New York: Pantheon, 1992.

McDonough, Carla. "Every Fear Hides a Wish: Unstable Masculinity in Mamet's Drama." *Theatre Journal* 44 (1992): 195–205.

Mufson, Daniel. "Sexual Perversity in Viragos." *Theatre* 24 (1993): 111–113.

Resnikova, Eva. "Fool's Paradise." *The National Review,* 18 Jan. 1993: 54–56.

Richards, David. "The Jackhammer Voice of Mamet's 'Oleanna.'" *New York Times,* 8 Nov. 1992, sec. 2: 1+.

———. "Mamet's Women." *New York Times,* 3 Jan. 1993, sec. 2: 1+.

Savran, David. "David Mamet." *In Their Own Words.* New York: Theatre Communications Group, 1988. 132–144.

———. "New Realism: Mamet, Mann, and Nelson." *Contemporary American Theatre.* Ed. Bruce King. New York: St. Martin's, 1991. 63–69.

Showalter, Elaine. "Acts of Violence: David Mamet and the Language of Men." *Times Literary Supplement,* 6 Nov. 1992: 16+.

Silverthorne, Jeanne. "PC Playhouse." *ArtForum* (March 1993): 10.

Tannen, Deborah. *You Just Don't Understand: Women and Men in Conversation.* New York: Ballantine Books, 1990.

Weales, Gerald. "Gender Wars." *Commonweal.* 4 Dec. 1992 15+.

Weber, Bruce. "On Stage and Off." *New York Times,* 14 Jan. 1994: C2.

The want of fresh air does not seem much to affect the happiness of children in a London alley: the greater part of them sing and play as though they were on a moor in Scotland. So the absence of a genial mental atmosphere is not commonly recognized by children who have never known it. Young people have a marvelous faculty of either dying or adapting themselves to circumstances. Even if they are unhappy—very unhappy—it is astonishing how easily they can be prevented from finding it out, or at any rate from attributing it to any other cause than their own sinfulness.

The Way of All Flesh
Samuel Butler

Oh, to be in *Oleanna,*
That's where I would rather be.
Than be bound in Norway
And drag the chains of slavery.

—folk song

CHARACTERS

CAROL . . . . A woman of twenty

JOHN . . . . A man in his forties

The play takes place in John's office.

ACT ONE

JOHN *is talking on the phone.* CAROL *is seated across the desk from him.*

JOHN: *(on phone)* And what about the land. *(pause)* The land. And what about the land? *(pause)* What about it? *(pause)* No. I don't understand. Well, yes, I'm I'm . . . no, I'm *sure* it's signif . . . I'm sure it's significant. *(pause)* Because it's significant to mmmmmm . . . did you call Jerry? *(pause)* Because . . . no, no, no, no, no. What did they say . . . ? Did you speak to the *real* estate . . . where *is* she . . . ? Well, well, all right. Where are her notes? Where are the notes we took with her. *(pause)* I thought you were? No. No, I'm sorry, I didn't mean that, I just thought that I saw you, when we were there . . . what . . . ? I thought I saw you with a *pencil.* WHY NOW? is what I'm say . . . well, that's why I say "call Jerry." Well, I can't right now, be . . . no, I *didn't* schedule any . . . Grace: I *didn't* . . . I'm well aware . . . Look: Look. Did you call Jerry? Will you call Jerry . . . ? Because I can't now. I'll be there, I'm sure I'll be there in fifteen, in twenty. I intend to. No, we aren't *going* to lose the, we aren't *going* to lose the house. Look: Look, I'm not minimizing it. The "easement." Did she say "easement"? *(pause)* What did she *say; is* it a "term of art," are we *bound* by it . . . I'm sorry . . . *(pause)* are: we: yes. *Bound* by . . . Look: *(he checks his watch)* before the other side *goes home,* all right? "a term of art." Because: that's right *(pause)* The yard for the boy. Well, that's the whole . . . Look: I'm going to meet you there . . . *(he checks his watch)* Is the Realtor there? All right, tell her to show you the basement again. Look at the *this* because . . .

Bec . . . I'm leaving in, I'm leaving in ten or fifteen . . . Yes. No, no, I'll meet you at the new . . . That's a good. If he thinks it's nec . . . you tell Jerry to meet . . . All right? We *aren't* going to lose the deposit. All right? I'm sure it's going to be . . . *(pause)* I hope so. *(pause)* I love you, too. *(pause)* I love you, too. As soon as . . . I will.

(He hangs up) (he bends over the desk and makes a note) (he looks up) (to CAROL*)* I'm sorry . . .

CAROL: *(pause)* What is a "term of art"?

JOHN: *(pause)* I'm sorry . . . ?

CAROL: *(pause)* What is a "term of art"?

JOHN: Is that what you want to talk about?

CAROL: . . . to talk about . . . ?

JOHN: Let's take the mysticism out of it, shall we? Carol? *(pause)* Don't you think? I'll tell you: when you have some "thing." Which must be broached. *(pause)* Don't you think . . . ? *(pause)*

CAROL: . . . don't I think . . . ?

JOHN: Mmm?

CAROL: . . . did I . . . ?

JOHN: . . . what?

CAROL: Did . . . did I . . . did I say something wr . . .

JOHN: *(pause)* No. I'm sorry. No. You're right. I'm very sorry. I'm somewhat rushed. As you see. I'm sorry. You're right. *(pause)* What is a "term of art"? It seems to mean a *term,* which has come, through its use, to mean something *more specific* than the words would, to someone *not acquainted* with them . . . indicate. That, I believe, is what a "term of art," would mean. *(pause)*

CAROL: You don't know what it means . . . ?

JOHN: I'm not sure that I know what it means. It's one of those things, perhaps you've had them, that, you look them up, or have someone explain them to you, and you say "aha," and, you immediately *forget* what . . .

CAROL: You don't do that.

JOHN: . . . I . . . ?

CAROL: You don't do . . .

JOHN: . . . I don't, what . . . ?

CAROL: . . . for . . .

JOHN: . . . I don't for . . .

CAROL: . . . no . . .

JOHN: . . . forget things? Everybody does that.

CAROL: No, they don't.

JOHN: They don't . . .

CAROL: No.

JOHN: *(pause)* No. Everybody does that.

CAROL: Why would they do that . . . ?

JOHN: Because. I don't know. Because it doesn't interest them.

CAROL: No.

JOHN: I think so, though. *(pause)* I'm sorry that I was distracted.

CAROL: You don't have to say that to me.

JOHN: You paid me the compliment, or the "obeisance"—all right—of coming in here . . . All right. *Carol.* I find that I am at a *standstill.* I find that I . . .

CAROL: . . . what . . .

JOHN: . . . one moment. In regard to your . . . to your . . .

CAROL: Oh, oh. You're buying a new house!

JOHN: No, let's get on with it.

CAROL: "get on"? *(pause)*

JOHN: I know how . . . *believe* me. I know how . . . potentially *humiliating* these . . . I have no desire to . . . I have no desire other than to help you. But: *(he picks up some papers on his desk)* I won't even say "but." I'll say that as I go back over the . . .

CAROL: I'm just, I'm just trying to . . .

JOHN: . . . no, it will not do.

CAROL: . . . what? What will . . . ?

JOHN: No. I see, I see what you, it . . . *(he gestures to the papers)* but your work . . .

CAROL: I'm just: I sit in class I . . . *(she holds up her notebook)* I take notes . . .

JOHN: *(simultaneously with* "notes"*)* Yes. I understand. What I am trying to *tell* you is that some, some basic . . .

CAROL: . . . I . . .

JOHN: . . . one moment: some basic missed communi . . .

CAROL: I'm doing what I'm told. I bought your book, I read your . . .

JOHN: No, I'm sure you . . .

CAROL: No, no, no. I'm doing what I'm told. It's *difficult* for me. It's *difficult* . . .

JOHN: . . . but . . .

CAROL: I don't . . . lots of the *language* . . .

JOHN: . . . please . . .

CAROL: The *language*, the "things" that you say . . .

JOHN: I'm sorry. No. I don't think that that's true.

CAROL: It *is* true. I . . .

JOHN: I think . . .

CAROL: It *is* true.

JOHN: . . . I . . .

CAROL: Why would I . . . ?

JOHN: I'll tell you why: you're an incredibly bright girl.

CAROL: . . . I . . .

JOHN: You're an incredibly . . . you have no problem with the . . . Who's kidding who?

CAROL: . . . I . . .

JOHN: No. No. I'll tell you why. I'll tell . . . I think you're *angry*, I . . .

CAROL: . . . why would I . . .

JOHN: . . . wait one moment. I . . .

CAROL: It *is* true. I have *problems* . . .

JOHN: . . . every . . .

CAROL: . . . I come from a different *social* . . .

JOHN: . . . ev . . .

CAROL: a different economic . . .

JOHN: . . . Look:

CAROL: No. I: when I *came* to this school:

JOHN: Yes. Quite . . . *(pause)*

CAROL: . . . does that mean nothing . . . ?

JOHN: . . . but look: look . . .

CAROL: . . . I . . .

JOHN: *(picks up paper)* Here: Please: Sit down. *(pause)* Sit down. *(reads from her paper)* "I think that the ideas contained in this work express the author's feelings in a way that he intended, based on his results." What can that mean? Do you see? What . . .

CAROL: I, the best that I . . .

JOHN: I'm saying, that perhaps this course . . .

CAROL: No, no, no, you can't, you can't . . . I have to . . .

JOHN: . . . how . . .

CAROL: . . . I have to pass it . . .

JOHN: Carol, I:

CAROL: I *have* to pass this course, I . . .

JOHN: Well.

CAROL: . . . don't you . . .

JOHN: Either the . . .

CAROL: . . . I . . .

JOHN: . . . either the, I . . . either the *criteria* for judging progress in the class are . . .

CAROL: No, no, no, no, I have to pass it.

JOHN: Now, look: I'm a human being, I . . .

CAROL: I did what you told me. I did, I did everything that, I read your *book,* you told me to buy your book and read it. Everything you *say* I . . . *(she gestures to her notebook) (the phone rings)* I do . . . Ev . . .

JOHN: . . . look:

CAROL: . . . everything I'm told . . .

JOHN: Look. Look. I'm not your *father. (pause)*

CAROL: What?

JOHN: I'm.

CAROL: Did I say you were my father?

JOHN: . . . no . . .

CAROL: Why did you say that . . . ?

JOHN: I . . .

CAROL: . . . why . . . ?

JOHN: . . . in class I . . . *(he picks up the phone) (into phone)* Hello. I can't talk now. Jerry? Yes? I underst . . . I can't talk now. I know . . . I know . . . Jerry. I can't *talk* now. Yes, I. Call me back in . . . Thank you. *(he hangs up) (to* CAROL*)* What do you want me to do? We are two people, all right? Both of whom have subscribed to . . .

CAROL: No, no . . .

JOHN: . . . certain arbitrary . . .

CAROL: No. You have to help me.

JOHN: Certain institutional . . . you tell me what you want me to do . . . You tell me what you want me to . . .

CAROL: How can I go back and tell them the *grades* that I . . .

JOHN: . . . what can I do . . . ?

CAROL: *Teach* me. *Teach* me.

JOHN: . . . I'm trying to teach you.

CAROL: I read your book. I read it. I don't under . . .

JOHN: . . . you don't understand it.

CAROL: No.

JOHN: Well, perhaps it's not well *written* . . .

CAROL: *(simultaneously with* "written"*)* No. No. No. I want to *understand* it.

JOHN: What don't you understand? *(pause)*

CAROL: *Any* of it. What you're trying to say. When you talk about . . .

JOHN: . . . yes . . . ? *(she consults her notes)*

CAROL: "Virtual warehousing of the young" . . .

JOHN: "Virtual warehousing of the young." If we artificially prolong adolescence . . .

CAROL: . . . and about "The Curse of Modern Education."

JOHN: . . . well . . .

CAROL: I don't . . .

JOHN: Look. It's just a *course,* it's just a *book,* it's just a . . .

CAROL: No. No. There are *people* out there. People who came *here.* To know something they didn't *know.* Who *came* here. To be *helped.* To be *helped.* So someone would *help* them. To *do* something. To *know* something. To get, what do they say? "To get on in the world." How can I do that if I don't, if I fail? But I don't *understand.* I don't *understand.* I don't understand what anything means . . . and I walk around. From morning 'til night: with this one thought in my head. I'm *stupid.*

JOHN: No one thinks you're stupid.

CAROL: No? What am I . . . ?

JOHN: I . . .

CAROL: . . . what am I, then?

JOHN: I think you're angry. Many people are. I have a *telephone* call that I have to make. And an *appointment,* which is rather *pressing;* though I sympathize with your concerns, and though I wish I had the time, this was not a previously scheduled meeting and I . . .

CAROL: . . . you think I'm nothing . . .

JOHN: . . . have an appointment with a *Realtor*, and with my wife and . . .

CAROL: You think that I'm stupid.

JOHN: No. I certainly don't.

CAROL: You said it.

JOHN: No. I did not.

CAROL: You did.

JOHN: When?

CAROL: . . . you . . .

JOHN: No. I never did, or never would say that to a student, and . . .

CAROL: You said, "What can that mean?" *(pause)* "What can that mean?" . . . *(pause)*

JOHN: . . . and what did that mean to you . . . ?

CAROL: That meant I'm stupid. And I'll never learn. That's what that meant. And you're right.

JOHN: . . . I . . .

CAROL: But then. But then, what am I doing here . . . ?

JOHN: . . . if you thought that I . . .

CAROL: . . . when nobody wants me, and . . .

JOHN: . . . if you interpreted . . .

CAROL: Nobody *tells* me anything. And I *sit* there . . . in the *corner*. In the *back*. And everybody's talking about "this" all the time. And "concepts," and "precepts" and, and, and, and, and, WHAT IN THE WORLD ARE YOU *TALKING* ABOUT? And I read your book. And they said, "Fine, go in that class." Because you talked about responsibility to the young. I DON'T KNOW WHAT IT MEANS AND I'M *FAILING* . . .

JOHN: May . . .

CAROL: No, you're right. "Oh, hell." I failed. Flunk me out of it. It's garbage. Everything I do. "The ideas contained in this work express the author's feelings." That's right. That's right. I know I'm stupid. I know what I am. *(pause)* I know what I am, Professor. You don't have to tell me. *(pause)* It's pathetic. Isn't it?

JOHN: . . . Aha . . . *(pause)* Sit down. Sit down. Please. *(pause)* Please sit down.

CAROL: Why?

JOHN: I want to talk to you.

CAROL: Why?

JOHN: Just sit down. *(pause)* Please. Sit down. Will you, please . . . ? *(pause. She does so)* Thank you.

CAROL: What?

JOHN: I want to tell you something.

CAROL: *(pause)* What?

JOHN: Well, I know what you're talking about.

CAROL: No. You don't.

JOHN: I think I do. *(pause)*

CAROL: How can you?

JOHN: I'll tell you a story about myself. *(pause)* Do you mind? *(pause)* I was raised to think myself stupid. That's what I want to tell you. *(pause)*

CAROL: What do you mean?

JOHN: Just what I said. I was brought up, and my earliest, and most persistent memories are of being told that I was stupid. "You have such *intelligence*. Why must you behave so *stupidly?*" Or, "Can't you *understand?* Can't you *understand?*" And I could *not* understand. I could *not* understand.

CAROL: What?

JOHN: The simplest problem. Was beyond me. It was a mystery.

CAROL: What was a mystery?

JOHN: How people learn. How *I* could learn. Which is what I've been speaking of in class. And of *course* you can't hear it. Carol. Of *course* you can't. *(pause)* I used to speak of "real people," and wonder what the *real* people did. The *real* people. Who were they? *They* were the people other than myself. The *good* people. The *capable* people. The people who could do the things, *I* could not do: learn, study, retain . . . all that *garbage*—which is what I have been talking of in class, and that *exactly* what I have been talking of—If you are told . . . Listen to this. If the young child is told he cannot understand. Then he takes it as a *description* of himself. What am I? I am *that which can not understand*. And I saw you out there, when we were speaking of the concepts of . . .

CAROL: I can't understand any of them.

JOHN: Well, then, that's *my* fault. That's not your fault. And that is not verbiage. That's what I firmly hold to be the truth. And I am sorry, and I owe you an apology.

CAROL: Why?

JOHN: And I suppose that I have had some *things* on my mind . . . We're buying a *house,* and . . .

CAROL: People said that you were stupid . . . ?

JOHN: Yes.

CAROL: When?

JOHN: I'll tell you when. Through my life. In my childhood; and, perhaps, they stopped. But I heard them continue.

CAROL: And what did they say?

JOHN: They said I was incompetent. Do you see? And when I'm tested the, the, the *feelings* of my youth about the *very subject of learning* come up. And I . . . I become, I feel "unworthy," and "unprepared." . . .

CAROL: . . . yes.

JOHN: . . . eh?

CAROL: . . . yes.

JOHN: And I feel that I must fail. *(pause)*

CAROL: . . . but then you *do* fail. *(pause)* You have to. *(pause)* Don't you?

JOHN: A *pilot.* Flying a plane. The pilot is flying the plane. He thinks: Oh, my *God,* my mind's been drifting! Oh, my God! What kind of a cursed imbecile am I, that I, with this so precious cargo of *Life* in my charge, would allow my attention to wander. Why was I born? How deluded are those who put their trust in me, . . . et cetera, so on, and he crashes the plane.

CAROL: *(pause)* He could just . . .

JOHN: That's right.

CAROL: He could say:

JOHN: My attention *wandered* for a moment . . .

CAROL: . . . uh huh . . .

JOHN: I had a *thought* I did not like . . . but now:

CAROL: . . . but now it's . . .

JOHN: That's what I'm telling you. It's time to put my attention . . . see: it is not: this is what I learned. It is Not Magic. Yes. Yes. *You.* You are

going to be frightened. When faced with what may or may not be but which you are going to perceive as a test. You will become frightened. And you will say: "I am incapable of . . ." and everything *in* you will think these two things. "I must. But I can't." And you will think: Why was I born to be the laughingstock of a world in which everyone is better than I? In which I am entitled to nothing. Where I can not learn. *(pause)*

CAROL: Is that . . . *(pause)* Is that what I have . . . ?

JOHN: Well. I don't know if I'd put it that way. Listen: I'm talking to you as I'd talk to my son. Because that's what I'd like him to have that I never had. I'm talking to you the way I wish that someone had talked to me. I don't know how to do it, other than to be *personal,* . . . but . . .

CAROL: Why would you want to be personal with me?

JOHN: Well, you see? That's what I'm saying. We can only interpret the behavior of others through the screen we . . . *(the phone rings)* Through . . . *(to phone)* Hello . . . ? *(to CAROL)* Through the screen we create. *(to phone)* Hello. *(to CAROL)* Excuse me a moment. *(to phone)* Hello? No, I can't talk nnn . . . I know I did. In a few . . . I'm . . . is he coming to the . . . yes. I talked to him. We'll meet you at the No, because I'm with a *student.* It's going to be fff . . . This is important, too. I'm with a *student,* Jerry's going to . . . Listen: the sooner I get off, the sooner I'll be down, all right. I love you. Listen, listen, I said "I love you," it's going to work *out* with the, because I feel that it is, I'll be right down. All right? Well, then it's going to take as long as it takes. *(he hangs up) (to CAROL)* I'm sorry.

CAROL: What was that?

JOHN: There are some problems, as there usually are, about the final agreements for the new house.

CAROL: You're buying a new house.

JOHN: That's right.

CAROL: Because of your promotion.

JOHN: Well, I suppose that that's right.

CAROL: Why did you stay here with me?

JOHN: Stay here.

CAROL: Yes. When you should have gone.

JOHN: Because I like you.

CAROL: You like me.

JOHN: Yes.

CAROL: Why?

JOHN: Why? Well? Perhaps we're similar. *(pause)* Yes. *(pause)*

CAROL: You said "everyone has problems."

JOHN: Everyone has problems.

CAROL: Do they?

JOHN: Certainly.

CAROL: You do?

JOHN: Yes.

CAROL: What are they?

JOHN: Well. *(pause)* Well, you're perfectly right. *(pause)* If we're going to take off the Artificial *Stricture,* of "Teacher," and "Student," why should *my* problems be any more a mystery than your own? Of *course* I have problems. As you saw.

CAROL: . . . with what?

JOHN: With my *wife* . . . with *work* . . .

CAROL: With work?

JOHN: Yes. And, and, perhaps my problems are, do you see? *Similar* to yours.

CAROL: Would you tell me?

JOHN: All right. *(pause)* I came *late* to teaching. And I found it Artificial. The notion of "I know and you do not"; and I saw an *exploitation* in the education process. I told you. I hated school, I hated teachers. I hated everyone who was in the position of a "boss" because I *knew*—I didn't *think,* mind you, I *knew* I was going to fail. Because I was a fuckup. I was just no goddamned good. When I . . . late in life . . . *(pause)* When I *got out from under* . . . when I worked my way out of the need to fail. When I . . .

CAROL: How do you do that? *(pause)*

JOHN: You have to look at what you are, and what you feel, and how you act. And, finally, you have to look at how you act. And say: If that's what I *did,* that must be how I think of myself.

CAROL: I don't understand.

JOHN: If I fail all the time, it must be that I think of myself as a failure. If I do not want to think of myself as a failure, perhaps I should begin by *succeeding* now and again. Look. The tests, you see, which you encounter, in school, in college, in life, were designed, in the most part, for idiots. *By* idiots. There is no need to fail at them. They are not a test of your worth. They are a test of your ability to retain and spout back misinformation. Of *course* you fail them. They're *nonsense.* And I . . .

CAROL: . . . no . . .

JOHN: Yes. They're *garbage.* They're a *joke.* Look at me. Look at me. The Tenure Committee. The Tenure Committee. Come to judge me. The Bad Tenure Committee.

The "Test." Do you see? They put me to the test. Why, they had people voting on me I wouldn't employ to wax my car. And yet, I go before the Great Tenure Committee, and I have an urge, to *vomit,* to, to, to puke my *badness* on the table, to show them: "I'm no good. Why would you pick *me?*"

CAROL: They granted you tenure.

JOHN: Oh no, they announced it, but they haven't *signed.* Do you see? "At any moment . . ."

CAROL: . . . mmm . . .

JOHN: "They might not *sign*" . . . I might not . . . the *house* might not go through . . . Eh? Eh? They'll find out my "dark secret." *(pause)*

CAROL: . . . what is it . . . ?

JOHN: There *isn't* one. But *they* will find an index of my badness . . .

CAROL: Index?

JOHN: A ". . . pointer." A "Pointer." You see? Do you see? I *understand* you. I. Know. That. Feeling. Am I entitled to my job, and my nice *home,* and my *wife,* and my *family,* and so on. This is what I'm saying: That theory of education which, that *theory:*

CAROL: I . . . I . . . *(pause)*

JOHN: What?

CAROL: I . . .

JOHN: What?

CAROL: I want to know about my grade *(long pause)*

JOHN: Of course you do.

CAROL: Is that bad?

JOHN: No.

CAROL: Is it bad that I asked you that?

JOHN: No.

CAROL: Did I upset you?

JOHN: No. And I apologize. Of *course* you want to know about your grade. And, of course, you can't concentrate on anyth . . . *(the telephone starts to ring)* Wait a moment.

CAROL: I should go.

JOHN: I'll make you a deal.

CAROL: No, you have to . . .

JOHN: Let it ring. I'll make you a deal. You stay here. We'll start the whole course over. I'm going to say it was not you, it was I who was not paying attention. We'll start the whole course over. Your grade is an "A." Your final grade is an "A." *(the phone stops ringing)*

CAROL: But the class is only half over . . .

JOHN: *(simultaneously with* "over"*)* Your grade for the whole term is an "A." If you will come back and meet with me. A few more times. Your grade's an "A." Forget about the paper. You didn't like it, you didn't like writing it. It's not important. What's important is that I awake your interest, if I can, and that I answer your questions. Let's start over. *(pause)*

CAROL: Over. With what?

JOHN: Say this is the beginning.

CAROL: The beginning.

JOHN: Yes.

CAROL: Of what?

JOHN: Of the class.

CAROL: But we can't start over.

JOHN: I say we can. *(pause)* I say we can.

CAROL: But I don't believe it.

JOHN: Yes, I know that. But it's true. What is The Class but you and me? *(pause)*

CAROL: There are rules.

JOHN: Well. We'll break them.

CAROL: How can we?

JOHN: We won't tell anybody.

CAROL: Is that all right?

JOHN: I say that it's fine.

CAROL: Why would you do this for me?

JOHN: I like you. Is that so difficult for you to . . .

CAROL: Um . . .

JOHN: There's no one here but you and me. *(pause)*

CAROL: All right. I did not understand. When you referred . . .

JOHN: All right, yes?

CAROL: When you referred to hazing.

JOHN: Hazing.

CAROL: You wrote, in your book. About the comparative . . . the comparative . . . *(she checks her notes)*

JOHN: Are you checking your notes . . . ?

CAROL: Yes.

JOHN: Tell me in your own . . .

CAROL: I want to make sure that I have it right.

JOHN: No. Of course. You want to be exact.

CAROL: I want to know everything that went on.

JOHN: . . . that's good.

CAROL: . . . so I . . .

JOHN: That's very good. But I was suggesting, many times, that that which we wish to retain is retained oftentimes, I think, *better* with less expenditure of effort.

CAROL: *(of notes)* Here it is: you wrote of *hazing.*

JOHN: . . . that's correct. Now: I said "hazing." It means ritualized annoyance. We shove this book at you, we say read it. Now, you say you've read it? I think that you're *lying.* I'll *grill* you, and when I find you've lied, you'll be disgraced, and your life will be ruined. It's a sick game. Why do we do it? Does it educate? In no sense. Well, then, what is higher education? It is something-other-than-useful.

CAROL: What is "something-other-than-useful"?

JOHN: It has become a ritual, it has become an article of faith. That all must be subjected to, or to put it differently, that all are entitled to Higher Education. And my point . . .

CAROL: You disagree with that?

JOHN: Well, let's address that. What do you think?

CAROL: I don't know.

JOHN: What do you think, though? *(pause)*

CAROL: I don't know.

JOHN: I spoke of it in class. Do you remember my example?

CAROL: Justice.

JOHN: Yes. Can you repeat it to me? *(she looks down at her notebook)* Without your notes? I ask you as a favor to me, so that I can see if my idea was interesting.

CAROL: You said "justice" . . .

JOHN: Yes?

CAROL: . . . that all are entitled . . . *(pause)* I . . . I . . . I . . .

JOHN: Yes. To a speedy trial. To a fair trial. But they needn't be given a trial *at all* unless they stand accused. Eh? Justice is their right, should they choose to avail themselves of it, they should have a fair trial. It does not follow, of necessity, a person's life is incomplete without a trial in it. Do you see?

My point is a confusion between equity and *utility* arose. So we confound the *usefulness* of higher education with our, granted, right to equal access to the same. We, in effect, create a *prejudice* toward it, completely independent of . . .

CAROL: . . . that it is prejudice that we should go to school?

JOHN: Exactly. *(pause)*

CAROL: How can you say that? How . . .

JOHN: Good. Good. *Good.* That's right! Speak up! What is a prejudice? An unreasoned belief. We are all subject to it. None of us is not. When it is threatened, or opposed, we feel anger, and feel, do we not? As you do now. Do you not? Good.

CAROL: . . . but how can you . . .

JOHN: . . . let us examine. Good.

CAROL: How . . .

JOHN: Good. Good. When . . .

CAROL: I'M SPEAKING . . . *(pause)*

JOHN: I'm sorry.

CAROL: How can you . . .

JOHN: . . . I beg your pardon.

CAROL: That's all right.

JOHN: I beg your pardon.

CAROL: That's all right.

JOHN: I'm sorry I interrupted you.

CAROL: That's all right.

JOHN: You were saying?

CAROL: I was saying . . . I was saying . . . *(she checks her notes)* How can you say in a class. Say in a college class, that college education is prejudice?

JOHN: I said that our predilection for it . . .

CAROL: Predilection . . .

JOHN: . . . you know what that means.

CAROL: Does it mean "liking"?

JOHN: Yes.

CAROL: But how can you say that? That College . . .

JOHN: . . . that's my *job*, don't you know.

CAROL: What is?

JOHN: To provoke you.

CAROL: No.

JOHN: Oh. Yes, though.

CAROL: To provoke me?

JOHN: That's right.

CAROL: To make me mad?

JOHN: That's right. To force you . . .

CAROL: . . . to make me mad is your job?

JOHN: To force you to . . . listen: *(pause)* Ah. *(pause)* When I was young somebody told me, are you ready, the rich copulate less often than the poor. But when they do, they take more of their clothes off. Years. Years, mind you, I would compare experiences of my own to this dictum, saying, aha, this fits the norm, or ah, this is a variation from it. What did it mean? Nothing. It was some jerk thing, some school kid told me that took up room inside my head. *(pause)*

Somebody told *you,* and you hold it as an article of faith, that higher education is an unassailable good. This notion is so dear to you that when I question it you become angry. Good. Good, I say. Are not those the very things which we should question? I say college education, since the war, has become so a matter of course, and such a fashionable necessity, for those either of or aspiring *to* to the new vast middle class, that we *espouse* it, as a matter of right, and have ceased to ask, "What is it good for?" *(pause)*

What might be some reasons for pursuit of higher education?

One: A love of learning.

Two: The wish for mastery of a skill.

Three: For economic betterment.

(stops. Makes a note)

CAROL: I'm keeping you.

JOHN: One moment. I have to make a note . . .

CAROL: It's something that I said?

JOHN: No, we're buying a house.

CAROL: You're buying the new house.

JOHN: To go with the tenure. That's right. Nice *house,* close to the *private school . . . (he continues making his note) . . .* We were talking of economic *betterment* (CAROL *writes in her notebook) . . .* I was thinking of the School Tax. *(he continues writing) (to himself) . . . where is it written* that I have to send my child to public school. . . . Is it a law that I have to improve the City Schools at the expense of my own interest? And, is this not simply *The White Man's Burden?* Good. And *(looks up to* CAROL*) . . .* does this interest you?

CAROL: No. I'm taking notes . . .

JOHN: You don't have to take notes, you know, you can just listen.

CAROL: I want to make sure I remember it. *(pause)*

JOHN: I'm not lecturing you, I'm just trying to tell you some things I think.

CAROL: What do you think?

JOHN: Should all kids go to college? *Why . . .*

CAROL: *(pause)* To learn.

JOHN: But if he does not learn.

CAROL: If the child does not learn?

JOHN: Then why is he in college? Because he was told it was his "right"?

CAROL: Some might find college instructive.

JOHN: I would hope so.

CAROL: But how do they feel? Being told they are wasting their time?

JOHN: I don't think I'm telling them that.

CAROL: You said that education was "prolonged and systematic hazing."

JOHN: Yes. It can be so.

CAROL: . . . if education is so *bad,* why do you do it?

JOHN: I do it because I love it. *(pause)* Let's . . . I suggest you look at the demographics, wage-earning capacity, college- and non-college-educated men and women, 1855 to 1980, and let's see if we can wring some worth from the statistics. Eh? And . . .

CAROL: No.

JOHN: What?

CAROL: I can't understand them.

JOHN: . . . you . . . ?

CAROL: . . . the "charts." The *Concepts,* the . . .

JOHN: "Charts" are simply . . .

CAROL: When I leave here . . .

JOHN: Charts, do you see . . .

CAROL: No, I can't . . .

JOHN: You can, though.

CAROL: NO, NO—I DON'T UNDERSTAND. DO YOU SEE??? I DON'T *UNDERSTAND* . . .

JOHN: What?

CAROL: *Any* of it. *Any* of it. I'm *smiling* in class, I'm *smiling,* the whole time. What are you *talking* about? What is everyone *talking* about? I don't *understand.* I don't know what it *means.* I don't know what it means to *be* here . . . you tell me I'm intelligent, and then you tell me I should not be *here,* what do you *want* with me? What does it *mean?* Who should I *listen* to . . . I . . .

(He goes over to her and puts his arm around her shoulder.)

NO! *(she walks away from him)*

JOHN: Sshhhh.

CAROL: No, I don't under . . .

JOHN: Sshhhhh.

CAROL: I don't know what you're *saying* . . .

JOHN: Sshhhhh. It's all right.

CAROL: . . . I have no . . .

JOHN: Sshhhhh. Sshhhhh. Let it go a moment. *(pause)* Sshhhhh . . . let it go. *(pause)* Just let it go. *(pause)* Just let it go. It's all right. *(pause)*

Sshhhhh. *(pause)* I understand . . . *(pause)* What do you feel?

CAROL: I feel bad.

JOHN: I know. It's all right.

CAROL: I . . . *(pause)*

JOHN: What?

CAROL: I . . .

JOHN: What? Tell me.

CAROL: I don't understand you.

JOHN: I know. It's all right.

CAROL: I . . .

JOHN: What? *(pause)* What? *Tell* me.

CAROL: I can't tell you.

JOHN: No, you must.

CAROL: I can't.

JOHN: No. Tell me. *(pause)*

CAROL: I'm bad. *(pause)* Oh, God. *(pause)*

JOHN: It's all right.

CAROL: I'm . . .

JOHN: It's all right.

CAROL: I can't talk about this.

JOHN: It's all right. Tell me.

CAROL: Why do you want to know this?

JOHN: I don't want to know. I want to know whatever you . . .

CAROL: I always . . .

JOHN: . . . good . . .

CAROL: I always . . . all my life . . . I have never told anyone this . . .

JOHN: Yes. Go on. *(pause)* Go on.

CAROL: All of my life . . . *(the phone rings)* *(pause.* JOHN *goes to the phone and picks it up)*

JOHN: *(into phone)* I can't talk now. *(pause)* What? *(pause)* Hmm. *(pause)* All right, I . . . I. Can't. Talk. Now. No, no, no, I *Know* I did, but . . . What? Hello. What? She *what?* She *can't,* she said the agreement is void? How, how is the agreement *void? That's Our House.*

I have the *paper;* when we come down, next week, with the payment, and the paper, that house is . . . wait, wait, wait, wait, wait, wait, wait: Did Jerry . . . is Jerry there? *(pause)* Is *she* there . . . ? Does she have a *lawyer* . . . ? How the *hell,* how the *Hell.* That

is . . . it's a question, you said, of the *easement.* I don't underst . . . it's not the *whole agreement.* It's just the *easement,* why would she? Put, put, put, *Jerry* on. *(pause)* Jer, *Jerry:* What the *Hell* . . . that's my *house.* That's . . . Well, I'm, no, no, no, I'm *not* coming ddd . . . List, *Listen, screw* her. You *tell* her. You, listen: I want you to take *Grace,* you take Grace, and get out of that house. You *leave* her there. Her and her lawyer, and you *tell* them, we'll see them in court next . . . no. No. Leave her there, leave her to *stew* in it: You tell her, we're *getting* that house, and we are going to . . . No. I'm *not* coming down. I'll be damned if I'll sit in the same rrr . . . the next, you tell her the next time I *see* her is in court . . . I . . . *(pause)* What? *(pause)* What? I don't understand. *(pause)* Well, what about the house? *(pause)* There isn't any problem with the hhh . . . *(pause)* No, no, no, that's all right. All ri . . . All right . . . *(pause)* Of course. Tha . . . Thank you. No, I will. Right away. *(he hangs up)* *(pause)*

CAROL: What is it? *(pause)*

JOHN: It's a surprise party.

CAROL: It is.

JOHN: Yes.

CAROL: A party for you.

JOHN: Yes.

CAROL: Is it your birthday?

JOHN: No.

CAROL: What is it?

JOHN: The tenure announcement.

CAROL: The tenure announcement.

JOHN: They're throwing a party for us in our new house.

CAROL: Your new house.

JOHN: The house that we're buying.

CAROL: You have to go.

JOHN: It seems that I do.

CAROL: *(pause)* They're proud of you.

JOHN: Well, there are those who would say it's a form of aggression.

CAROL: What is?

JOHN: A surprise.

ACT TWO

JOHN *and* CAROL *seated across the desk from each other.*

JOHN: You see *(pause)*, I love to teach. And flatter myself I am *skilled* at it. And I love the, the aspect of *performance.* I think I must confess that.

When I found I loved to teach I swore that I would not become that cold, rigid automaton of an instructor which I had encountered as a child.

Now, I was not unconscious that it was given me to err upon the other side. And, so, I asked and *ask* myself if I engaged in heterodoxy, I will not say "gratuitously" for I do not care to posit orthodoxy as a given good—but, "to the detriment of, of my students." *(pause)*

As I said. When the possibility of tenure opened, and, of course, I'd long pursued it, I was, of course *happy,* and *covetous* of it.

I asked myself if I was wrong to covet it. And thought about it long, and, I hope, truthfully, and saw in myself several things in, I think, no particular order. *(pause)*

That I *would* pursue it. That I *desired* it, that I was not pure of longing for security, and that that, perhaps, was not reprehensible in me. That I had duties *beyond* the school, and that my duty to my home, for instance, was, or should be, if it were not, of an equal weight. That tenure, and security, and yes, and *comfort,* were not, of themselves, to be scorned; and were even worthy of honorable pursuit. And that it was given me. Here, in this place, which I enjoy, and in which I find comfort, to assure myself of—as far as it rests in The Material—a continuation of that joy and comfort. In exchange for what? Teaching. Which I love.

What was the price of this security? To obtain *tenure.* Which tenure the committee is in the process of granting me. And on the basis of which I contracted to purchase a house. Now, as you don't have your own family, at this point, you may not know what that means. But to me it is important. A home. A Good Home. To raise my family. Now: The Tenure Committee will meet. This is the process, and a *good* process. Under which the school has functioned for quite a long time. They will meet, and hear your complaint— which you have the right to make; and they will dismiss it. They will *dismiss* your complaint; and, in the intervening period, I will lose my house. I will not be able to close on my house. I will lose my *deposit,* and the home I'd picked out for my wife and son will go by the boards. Now: I see I have angered you. I understand your anger at teachers. I was angry with mine. I felt hurt and humiliated by them. Which is one of the reasons that I went into education.

CAROL: What do you want of me?

JOHN: *(pause)* I was hurt. When I received the report. Of the tenure committee. I was shocked. And I was hurt. No, I don't mean to subject you to my weak sensibilities. All right. Finally, I didn't understand. Then I thought: is it not always at those points at which we reckon ourselves unassailable that we are most vulnerable and . . . *(pause)* Yes. All right. You find me pedantic. Yes. I am. By nature, by *birth,* by profession, I don't know . . . I'm always looking for a *paradigm* for . . .

CAROL: I don't know what a paradigm is.

JOHN: It's a model.

CAROL: Then why can't you use that word? *(pause)*

JOHN: If it is important to you. Yes, all right. I was looking for a model. To continue: I feel that one point . . .

CAROL: I . . .

JOHN: One second . . . upon which I am unassailable is my unflinching concern for my students' dignity. I asked you here to . . . in the spirit of *investigation,* to ask you . . . to ask . . . *(pause)* What have I done to you? *(pause)*

And, and, I suppose, how I can make amends. Can we not settle this now? It's pointless, really, and I want to know.

CAROL: What you can do to force me to retract?

JOHN: That is not what I meant at all.

CAROL: To bribe me, to convince me . . .

JOHN: . . . No.

CAROL: To retract . . .

JOHN: That is not what I meant at all. I think that you know it is not.

CAROL: That is not what I know. I *wish* I . . .

JOHN: I do not want to . . . you wish what?

CAROL: No, you said what amends can you make. To force me to retract.

JOHN: That is not what I said.

CAROL: I have my notes.

JOHN: Look. Look. The Stoics say . . .

CAROL: The Stoics?

JOHN: The Stoical Philosophers say if you remove the phrase "I have been injured," you have removed the injury. Now: Think: I know that you're upset. Just tell me. Literally. Literally: what wrong have I done you?

CAROL: Whatever you have done to me—to the extent that you've done it to *me*, do you know, rather than to me as a *student*, and, so, to the student body, is contained in my report. To the tenure committee.

JOHN: Well, all right. *(pause)* Let's see. *(he reads)* I find that I am sexist. That I am *elitist*. I'm not sure I know what that means, other than it's a derogatory word, meaning "bad." That I . . . That I insist on wasting time, in nonprescribed, in self-aggrandizing and theatrical *diversions* from the prescribed *text* . . . that these have taken both sexist and pornographic forms . . . here we find listed . . . *(pause)* Here we find listed . . . instances ". . . closeted with a student" . . . "Told a rambling, sexually explicit story, in which the frequency and attitudes of fornication of the poor and rich are, it would seem, the central point . . . moved to *embrace* said student and . . . all part of a pattern . . ." *(pause)*

(He reads) That I used the phrase "The White Man's Burden" . . . that I told you how I'd asked you to my room because I quote like you. *(pause)*

(He reads) "He said he 'liked' me. That he 'liked being with me.' He'd let me write my examination paper over, if I could come back oftener to see him in his office." *(pause)* *(to* CAROL*)* It's *ludicrous.* Don't you know that? It's not *necessary.* It's going to *humiliate* you, and it's going to cost me my *house,* and . . .

CAROL: It's "*ludicrous* . . ."?

*(*JOHN *picks up the report and reads again.)*

JOHN: "He told me he had problems with his wife; and that he wanted to take off the artificial stricture of Teacher and Student. He put his arm around me . . ."

CAROL: Do you deny it? Can you deny it . . . ? Do you see? *(pause)* Don't you see? You don't see, do you?

JOHN: I don't see . . .

CAROL: You think, you think you can deny that these things happened; or, if they *did*, if they *did*, that they meant what you *said* they meant. Don't you see? You drag me in here, you drag us, to listen to you "go on"; and "go on" about this, or that, or we don't "express" ourselves very well. We don't say what we mean. Don't we? Don't we? We *do* say what we mean. And you say that "I don't understand you . . .": Then *you* . . . *(points)*

JOHN: "Consult the Report"?

CAROL: . . . that's right.

JOHN: You see. You see. Can't you . . . You see what I'm saying? Can't you tell me in your own words?

CAROL: Those are my own words. *(pause)*

JOHN: *(he reads)* "He told me that if I would stay alone with him in his office, he would change my grade to an A." *(to* CAROL*)* What have I done to you? Oh. My God, are you so hurt?

CAROL: What I "feel" is irrelevant. *(pause)*

JOHN: Do you know that I tried to help you?

CAROL: What I know I have reported.

JOHN: I would like to help you now. I would. Before this escalates.

CAROL: (*simultaneously with* "escalates") You see. I don't think that I need your help. I don't think I need anything you have.

JOHN: I feel . . .

CAROL: I don't *care* what you feel. Do you see? DO YOU SEE? You can't *do* that anymore. You. Do. Not. Have. The. Power. Did you misuse it? *Someone* did. Are you part of that group? *Yes.* Yes. You Are. You've *done* these things. And to say, and to say, "Oh. Let me help you with your problem . . ."

JOHN: Yes. I understand. I understand. You're *hurt.* You're *angry.* Yes. I think your *anger* is *betraying* you. Down a path which helps no one.

CAROL: I don't *care* what you think.

JOHN: You don't? (*pause*) But you talk of *rights.* Don't you see? *I* have rights too. Do you see? I have a *house* . . . part of the *real* world; and The Tenure Committee, Good Men and True . . .

CAROL: . . . Professor . . .

JOHN: . . . Please: *Also* part of that world: you understand? This is my *life.* I'm not a *bogeyman.* I don't "stand" for something, I . . .

CAROL: . . . Professor . . .

JOHN: . . . I . . .

CAROL: Professor. I came here as a *favor.* At your personal request. Perhaps I should not have done so. But I did. On my behalf, and on behalf of my group. And you speak of the tenure committee, one of whose members is a woman, as you know. And though you might call it Good Fun, or An Historical Phrase, or An Oversight, or, All of the Above, to refer to the committee as Good Men and True, it is a demeaning remark. It is a sexist remark, and to overlook it is to countenance continuation of that method of thought. It's a remark . . .

JOHN: OH COME ON. Come on . . . Sufficient to deprive a family of . . .

CAROL: Sufficient? Sufficient? Sufficient? Yes. It is a *fact* . . . and that story, which I quote, is

vile and *classist,* and *manipulative* and *pornographic.* It . . .

JOHN: . . . it's pornographic . . . ?

CAROL: What gives you the *right.* Yes. To speak to a *woman* in your private . . . Yes. Yes. I'm sorry. I'm sorry. You feel yourself empowered . . . you say so yourself. To *strut.* To *posture.* To "perform." To "Call me in here . . ." Eh? You say that higher education is a joke. And treat it as such, you *treat* it as such. And *confess* to a taste to play the *Patriarch* in your class. To grant *this.* To deny *that.* To embrace your students.

JOHN: How can you assert. How can you stand there and . . .

CAROL: How can you *deny* it. You did it to me. *Here.* You *did* . . . . You *confess.* You love the Power. To *deviate.* To *invent,* to transgress . . . to *transgress* whatever norms have been established for us. And you think it's charming to "question" in yourself this taste to mock and destroy. But you should question it. Professor. And you pick those things which you feel *advance* you: publication, *tenure,* and the steps to get them you call "harmless rituals." And you perform those steps. Although you say it is hypocrisy. But to the aspirations of your students. Of *hardworking students,* who come here, who *slave* to come here—you have no idea what it cost me to come to this school—you *mock* us. You call education "hazing," and from your so-protected, so-elitist seat you hold our confusion as a *joke,* and our hopes and efforts with it. Then you sit there and say "what have I done?" And ask me to understand that *you* have aspirations too. But I tell you. I tell you. That you are vile. And that you are exploitative. And if you possess one ounce of that inner honesty you describe in your book, you can look in yourself and see those things that I see. And you can find revulsion equal to my own. Good day. (*she prepares to leave the room*)

JOHN: Wait a second, will you, just one moment. (*pause*) Nice day today.

CAROL: What?

JOHN: You said "Good day." I think that it is a nice day today.

CAROL: *Is* it?

JOHN: Yes, I think it is.

CAROL: And why is that important?

JOHN: Because it is the essence of all human communication. I say something conventional, you respond, and the information we exchange is not about the "weather," but that we both agree to converse. In effect, we agree that we are both human. *(pause)*

I'm not a . . . "exploiter," and you're not a . . . "deranged," what? *Revolutionary* . . . that we may, that we may have . . . positions, and that we may have . . . desires, which are in *conflict*, but that we're just human. *(pause)* That means that sometimes we're *imperfect*. *(pause)* Often we're in conflict . . . *(pause)* *Much* of what we do, you're right, in the name of "principles" is *self-serving* . . . much of what we do is *conventional*. *(pause)* You're right. *(pause)* You said you came in the class because you wanted to learn about *education*. I don't know that I can teach you about education. But I know that I can tell you what I *think* about education, and then *you* decide. And you don't have to fight with me. *I'm* not the subject. *(pause)* And where I'm *wrong* . . . perhaps it's not your job to "fix" me. I don't want to fix *you*. I would like to tell you what I *think*, because that *is* my job, conventional as it is, and flawed as I may be. And then, if you can show me some better *form*, then we can proceed from there. But, just like "nice day, isn't it . . . ?" I don't think we can proceed until we accept that each of us is human. *(pause)* And we still can have difficulties. We *will* have them . . . that's all right too. *(pause)* Now:

CAROL: . . . wait . . .

JOHN: Yes. I want to hear it.

CAROL: . . . the . . .

JOHN: Yes. Tell me frankly.

CAROL: . . . my position . . .

JOHN: I want to hear it. In your own words. What you want. And what you feel.

CAROL: . . . I . . .

JOHN: . . . yes . . .

CAROL: My Group.

JOHN: Your "Group" . . . ? *(pause)*

CAROL: The people I've been talking to . . .

JOHN: There's no shame in that. Everybody needs advisers. Everyone needs to expose themselves. To various points of view. It's not wrong. It's essential. Good. Good. Now: You and I . . . *(the phone rings)*

You and I . . .

(he hesitates for a moment, and then picks it up) (into phone) Hello. *(pause)* Um . . . no, I know they do. *(pause)* I know she does. Tell her that I . . . can I call you back? . . . Then tell her that I think it's going to be fine. *(pause)* Tell her just, just hold on, I'll . . . can I get back to you? . . . Well . . . no, no, no, we're *tak-ing* the house . . . we're . . . no, no, nn . . . no, she will nnn, it's not a *question* of refunding the dep . . . no . . . it's not a *question* of the deposit . . . will you call Jerry? Babe, baby, will you just call Jerry? Tell him, nnn . . . tell him they, well, they're to keep the deposit, because the deal, be . . . because the deal is going to go *through* . . . because I know . . . be . . . will you please? Just *trust* me. Be . . . well, I'm dealing with the complaint. Yes. Right *Now*. Which is why I . . . yes, no, no, it's really, I can't *talk* about it now. Call Jerry, and I can't talk now. Ff . . . fine. Gg . . . good-bye. *(hangs up) (pause)* I'm sorry we were interrupted.

CAROL: No . . .

JOHN: I . . . I was saying:

CAROL: You said that we should agree to talk about my complaint.

JOHN: That's correct.

CAROL: But we *are* talking about it.

JOHN: Well, that's correct too. You see? This is the *gist* of education.

CAROL: No, no. I mean, we're talking about it at the Tenure Committee Hearing. *(pause)*

JOHN: Yes, but I'm saying: we can talk about it *now*, as easily as . . .

CAROL: No. I think that we should stick to the process . . .

JOHN: . . . wait a . . .

CAROL: . . . the "conventional" process. As you said. *(she gets up)* And you're right, I'm sorry if I was, um, if I was "discourteous" to you. You're right.

JOHN: Wait, wait a . . .

CAROL: I really should go.

JOHN: Now, look, granted. I have an interest. In the status quo. All right? Everyone does. But what I'm saying is that the *committee* . . .

CAROL: Professor, you're right. Just don't impinge on me. We'll take our differences, and . . .

JOHN: You're going to make a . . . look, look, look, you're going to . . .

CAROL: I shouldn't have come here. They told me . . .

JOHN: One moment. No. No. There are *norms,* here, and there's no reason. Look: I'm trying to *save* you . . .

CAROL: No one *asked* you to . . . you're trying to save *me?* Do me the courtesy to . . .

JOHN: I *am* doing you the courtesy. I'm talking *straight* to you. We can settle this *now.* And I want you to sit *down* and . . .

CAROL: You must excuse me . . . *(she starts to leave the room)*

JOHN: Sit down, it seems we each have a . . . Wait one moment. Wait one moment . . . just do me the courtesy to . . .
(he restrains her from leaving)

CAROL: LET ME GO.

JOHN: I have no desire to *hold* you, I just want to *talk* to you . . .

CAROL: LET ME GO. LET ME GO. WOULD SOMEBODY *HELP* ME? WOULD SOME-BODY *HELP* ME PLEASE . . . ?

ACT THREE

(At rise, CAROL *and* JOHN *are seated.)*

JOHN: I have asked you here. *(pause)* I have asked you here against, against my . . .

CAROL: I was most surprised you asked me.

JOHN: . . . against   my   better   *judgment,* against . . .

CAROL: I was most surprised . . .

JOHN: . . . against the . . . yes. I'm sure.

CAROL: . . . If you would like me to leave, I'll leave. I'll go right now . . . *(she rises)*

JOHN: Let us begin *correctly,* may we? I feel . . .

CAROL: That is what I wished to do. That's why I came here, but now . . .

JOHN: . . . I feel . . .

CAROL: But now perhaps you'd like me to leave . . .

JOHN: I don't want you to leave. I asked you to come . . .

CAROL: I didn't have to come here.

JOHN: No. *(pause)* Thank you.

CAROL: All right. *(pause) (she sits down)*

JOHN: Although I feel that it *profits,* it would *profit* you something, to . . .

CAROL: . . . what I . . .

JOHN: If you would hear me out, if you would hear me out.

CAROL: I came here to, the court officers told me not to come.

JOHN: . . . the "court" officers . . . ?

CAROL: I was shocked that you asked.

JOHN: . . . wait . . .

CAROL: Yes. But I did *not* come here to hear what it "profits" me.

JOHN: The "court" officers . . .

CAROL: . . . no, no, perhaps I should leave . . . *(she gets up)*

JOHN: Wait.

CAROL: No. I shouldn't have . . .

JOHN: . . . wait. Wait. Wait a moment.

CAROL: Yes? What is it you want? *(pause)* What is it you want?

JOHN: I'd like you to stay.

CAROL: You want me to stay.

JOHN: Yes.

CAROL: You do.

JOHN: Yes. *(pause)* Yes. I would like to have you hear me out. If you would. *(pause)* Would you please? If you would do that I would be in your debt. *(pause) (she sits)* Thank You. *(pause)*

CAROL: What is it you wish to tell me?

JOHN: All right. I cannot . . . *(pause)* I cannot help but feel you are owed an apology. *(pause) (of papers in his hands)* I have read. *(pause)* And reread these accusations.

CAROL: What "accusations"?

JOHN: The, the tenure comm . . . what other accusations . . . ?

CAROL: The tenure committee . . . ?

JOHN: Yes.

CAROL: Excuse me, but those are not accusations. They have been *proved*. They are facts.

JOHN: . . . I . . .

CAROL: No. Those are not "accusations."

JOHN: . . . those?

CAROL: . . . the committee *(the phone starts to ring)* the committee has . . .

JOHN: . . . All right . . .

CAROL: . . . those are not accusations. The Tenure Committee.

JOHN: ALL RIGHT. ALL RIGHT. ALL RIGHT. *(he picks up the phone)* Hello. Yes. No. I'm here. Tell Mister . . . No, I can't talk to him now . . . I'm sure he has, but I'm fff . . . I know . . . No, I have no time t . . . tell Mister . . . tell Mist . . . tell Jerry that I'm *fine* and that I'll call him right aw . . . *(pause)* My wife . . . Yes. I'm sure she has. Yes, thank you. Yes, I'll call her too. I cannot talk to you now. *(he hangs up) (pause)* All right. It was good of you to come. Thank you. I have studied. I have spent some time studying the indictment.

CAROL: You will have to explain that word to me.

JOHN: An "indictment" . . .

CAROL: Yes.

JOHN: Is a "bill of particulars." A . . .

CAROL: All right. Yes.

JOHN: In which is alleged . . .

CAROL: No. I cannot allow that. I cannot allow that. Nothing is alleged. Everything is proved . . .

JOHN: Please, wait a sec . . .

CAROL: I cannot *come* to allow . . .

JOHN: If I may . . . If I may, from whatever you feel is "established," by . . .

CAROL: The issue here is not what I "feel." It is not my "feelings," but the feelings of women. And men. Your superiors, who've been "polled," do you see? To whom *evidence* has been presented, who have *ruled*, do you see? Who have weighed the testimony and the evidence, and have *ruled*, do you see? That you are *negligent*. That you are *guilty*, that you are found *wanting*, and in *error*; and are *not*, for the reasons so-told, to be given tenure. That you are to be disciplined. For facts. For *facts*. Not "alleged," what is the word? But *proved*. Do you see? *By your own actions.*

That is what the tenure committee has said. That is what my lawyer said. For what you did in class. For what you did *in this office.*

JOHN: They're going to discharge me.

CAROL: As full well they should. You don't understand? You're angry? What had *led* you to this place? Not your sex. Not your race. Not your class. YOUR OWN ACTIONS. And you're *angry*. You *ask* me here. What *do* you want? You want to "charm" me. You want to "convince" me. You want me to recant. I will *not* recant. Why should I . . . ? What I say is right. You tell me, you are going to tell me that you have a wife and child. You are going to say that you have a career and that you've worked for twenty years for this. Do you know what you've *worked* for? *Power*. For *power*. Do you understand? And you sit there, and you tell me *stories*. About your *house*, about all the private *schools*, and about *privilege*, and how you are entitled. To *buy*, to *spend*, to *mock*, to *summon*. All your stories. All your silly weak *guilt*, it's all about *privilege*; and you won't know it. Don't you see? You worked twenty years for the right to *insult* me. And you feel entitled to be *paid* for it. Your Home. Your Wife . . . Your sweet "deposit" on your house . . .

JOHN: Don't you have feelings?

CAROL: That's my point. You see? Don't you have feelings? Your final argument. What is it that has no feelings. *Animals*. I don't take your side, you question if I'm Human.

JOHN: Don't you have feelings?

CAROL: I have a responsibility. I . . .

JOHN: . . . to . . . ?

CAROL: To? This institution. To the *students*. To my *group*.

JOHN: . . . your "group." . . .

CAROL: Because I speak, yes, not for myself. But for the group; for those who suffer what I suffer. On behalf of whom, even if I, were, inclined, to what, forgive? Forget? What? Overlook your . . .

JOHN: . . . my behavior?

CAROL: . . . it would be wrong.

JOHN: Even if you were inclined to "forgive" me.

CAROL: It would be wrong.

JOHN: And what would transpire.

CAROL: Transpire?

JOHN: Yes.

CAROL: "Happen"?

JOHN: Yes.

CAROL: Then *say* it. For Christ's sake. Who the *hell* do you think that you are? You want a post. You want unlimited power. To do and to say what you want. As it pleases you—Testing, Questioning, Flirting . . .

JOHN: I never . . .

CAROL: Excuse me, one moment, will you?
(she reads from her notes)
The twelfth: "Have a good day, dear."

The fifteenth: "Now, don't *you* look fetching . . ."

April seventeenth: "If you girls would come over here . . ." I saw you. I saw you, Professor. For two semesters sit there, stand there and exploit our, as you thought, "paternal prerogative," and what is that but rape; I swear to God. You asked me in here to explain something to me, as a child, that I did not understand. But I came to explain something to you. You Are Not God. You ask me why I came? I came here to instruct you.
(she produces his book)
And your book? You think you're going to show me some "light"? You *"maverick."* Outside of tradition. No, no, *(she reads from the book's liner notes)* "of* that fine tradition of *inquiry.* Of Polite *skepticism"* . . . and you say you believe in free intellectual discourse. YOU BELIEVE IN NOTHING. YOU BELIEVE IN NOTHING AT ALL.

JOHN: I believe in freedom of thought.

CAROL: Isn't that fine. *Do* you?

JOHN: Yes. I do.

CAROL: Then why do you question, for one moment, the committee's decision refusing your tenure? Why do you question your suspension? You believe in what *you call* freedom of thought. Then, fine. *You* believe in freedom-of-thought *and* a home, and, *and* prerogatives for your kid, *and* tenure. And I'm going to tell you. You believe *not* in "freedom of thought," but in an elitist, in, in a protected hierarchy which rewards you. And for whom you are the clown. And you mock and exploit the system which pays your rent. You're wrong. I'm not wrong. You're wrong. You think that I'm full of hatred. I know what you think I am.

JOHN: Do you?

CAROL: You think I'm a, of course I do. You think I am a frightened, repressed, confused, I don't know, abandoned young thing of some doubtful sexuality, who wants, power and revenge. *(pause)* Don't you? *(pause)*

JOHN: Yes. I do. *(pause)*

CAROL: Isn't that better? And I feel that that is the first moment which you've treated me with respect. For you told me the truth. *(pause)* I did not come here, as you are assured, to gloat. Why would I want to gloat? I've profited nothing from your, your, as you say, your "misfortune." I came here, as you did me the honor to *ask* me here, I came here to *tell* you something.

(Pause) That I think . . . that I think you've been wrong. That I think you've been terribly wrong. Do you hate me now? *(pause)*

JOHN: Yes.

CAROL: Why do you hate me? Because you think me wrong? No. Because I have, you think, *power* over you. Listen to me. Listen to me,

Professor. *(pause)* It is the power that you hate. So deeply that, that any atmosphere of free discussion is impossible. It's not "unlikely." It's *impossible.* Isn't it?

JOHN: Yes.

CAROL: *Isn't* it . . . ?

JOHN: Yes. I suppose.

CAROL: Now. The thing which you find so cruel is the selfsame process of selection I, and my group, go through *every day of our lives.* In admittance to school. In our tests, in our class rankings. . . . Is it unfair? I can't tell you. But, if it is fair. Or even if it is "unfortunate but necessary" for us, then, by God, so must it be for you. *(pause)* You write of your "responsibility to the young." Treat us with respect, and that will *show* you your responsibility. You write that education is just hazing. *(pause)* But we worked to get to this school. *(pause)* And some of us. *(pause)* Overcame prejudices. Economic, sexual, you cannot begin to imagine. And endured humiliations I *pray* that you and those you love never will encounter. *(pause)* To gain admittance here. To pursue that same dream of security *you* pursue. We, who, who are, at any moment, in danger of being deprived of it. By . . .

JOHN: . . . by . . . ?

CAROL: By the administration. By the teachers. By *you.* By, say, one low grade, that keeps us out of graduate school; by one, say, one capricious or inventive answer on our parts, which, perhaps, you don't find amusing. Now you *know,* do you see? What it is to be subject to that power. *(pause)*

JOHN: I don't understand. *(pause)*

CAROL: My charges are not trivial. You see that in the haste, I think, with which they were accepted. A *joke* you have told, with a sexist tinge. The language you use, a verbal or physical caress, yes, yes, I know, you say that it is meaningless. I understand. I differ from you. To lay a hand on someone's shoulder.

JOHN: It was devoid of sexual content.

CAROL: I say it was not. I SAY IT WAS NOT. Don't you begin to *see* . . . ? Don't you begin to understand? IT'S NOT FOR YOU TO SAY.

JOHN: I take your point, and I see there is much good in what you refer to.

CAROL: . . . do you think so . . . ?

JOHN: . . . but, and this is not to say that I cannot change, in those things in which I am deficient . . . But, the . . .

CAROL: Do you hold yourself harmless from the charge of sexual exploitativeness . . . ? *(pause)*

JOHN: Well, I . . . I . . . I . . . You know I, as I said. I . . . think I am not too old to *learn,* and I *can* learn, I . . .

CAROL: Do you hold yourself innocent of the charge of . . .

JOHN: . . . wait, wait, wait . . . All right, let's go back to . . .

CAROL: YOU FOOL. Who do you think I am? To come here and be taken in by a *smile.* You little yapping fool. You think I want "revenge." I don't want revenge. I WANT UNDERSTANDING.

JOHN: . . . *do* you?

CAROL: I do. *(pause)*

JOHN: What's the use. It's over.

CAROL: Is it? What is?

JOHN: My job.

CAROL: Oh. Your job. That's what you want to talk about. *(pause) (she starts to leave the room. She steps and turns back to him)* All right. *(pause)* What if it were possible that my Group withdraws its complaint. *(pause)*

JOHN: What?

CAROL: That's right. *(pause)*

JOHN: Why.

CAROL: Well, let's say as an act of friendship.

JOHN: An act of friendship.

CAROL: Yes. *(pause)*

JOHN: In exchange for what.

CAROL: Yes. But I don't think, "exchange." Not "in exchange." For what do we derive from it? *(pause)*

JOHN: "Derive."

CAROL: Yes.

JOHN: *(pause)* Nothing. *(pause)*

CAROL: That's right. We derive nothing. *(pause)* Do you see that?

JOHN: Yes.

CAROL: That is a little word, Professor. "Yes." "I see that." But you will.

JOHN: And you might speak to the committee . . . ?

CAROL: To the committee?

JOHN: Yes.

CAROL: Well. Of course. That's on your mind. We might.

JOHN: "If" what?

CAROL: "Given" what. Perhaps. I think that that is more friendly.

JOHN: GIVEN WHAT?

CAROL: And, believe me, I understand your rage. It is not that I don't feel it. But I do not see that it is deserved, so I do not resent it . . . All right. I have a list.

JOHN: . . . a list.

CAROL: Here is a list of books, which we . . .

JOHN: . . . a list of books . . . ?

CAROL: That's right. Which we find questionable.

JOHN: What?

CAROL: Is this so bizarre . . . ?

JOHN: I can't believe . . .

CAROL: It's not necessary you believe it.

JOHN: Academic freedom . . .

CAROL: Someone chooses the books. If you can choose them, others can. What are you, "God"?

JOHN: . . . no, no, the "dangerous." . . .

CAROL: You have an agenda, we have an agenda. I am not interested in your feelings or your motivation, but your actions. If you would like me to speak to the Tenure Committee, here is my list. You are a Free Person, you decide. *(pause)*

JOHN: Give me the list. *(she does so. He reads)*

CAROL: I think you'll find . . .

JOHN: I'm capable of reading it. Thank you.

CAROL: We have a number of *texts* we need re . . .

JOHN: I see that.

CAROL: We're amenable to . . .

JOHN: Aha. Well, let me look over the . . . *(he reads)*

CAROL: I think that . . .

JOHN: LOOK. I'm reading your demands. All right?! *(he reads) (pause)* you want to ban my book?

CAROL: We do not . . .

JOHN: *(of list)* It says here . . .

CAROL: . . . We want it removed from inclusion as a representative example of the university.

JOHN: Get out of here.

CAROL: If you put aside the issues of personalities.

JOHN: Get the fuck out of my office.

CAROL: No, I think I would reconsider.

JOHN: . . . you think you can.

CAROL: We can and we *will*. Do you want our support? That is the only quest . . .

JOHN: . . . to ban my *book* . . . ?

CAROL: . . . that is correct . . .

JOHN: . . . this . . . this is a *university* . . . we . . .

CAROL: . . . and we have a statement . . . which we need you to . . . *(she hands him a sheet of paper)*

JOHN: No, no. It's out of the question. I'm sorry. I don't know what I was thinking of. I want to tell you something. I'm a teacher. I am a teacher. Eh? It's my *name* on the door, and *I* teach the class, and that's what I do. I've got a book with my name on it. And my son will *see* that *book* someday. And I have a respon . . . No, I'm sorry I have a *responsibility* . . . to *myself*, to my *son*, to my *profession* . . . I haven't been *home* for two days, do you know that? Thinking this out.

CAROL: . . . you haven't?

JOHN: I've been, no. If it's of interest to you. I've been in a *hotel. Thinking.* *(the phone starts ringing)* Thinking . . .

CAROL: . . . you haven't been home?

JOHN: . . . *thinking,* do you see.

CAROL: Oh.

JOHN: And, and, I owe you a debt, I see that now. *(pause)* You're *dangerous,* you're *wrong* and it's my *job* . . . to say no to you. That's my job. You are absolutely right. You want to ban my book? Go to *hell,* and they can do whatever they want to me.

CAROL: . . . you haven't been home in two days . . .

JOHN: I think I told you that.

CAROL: . . . you'd better get that phone. *(pause)* I think that you should pick up the phone. *(pause)*

(JOHN picks up the phone)

JOHN: *(on phone)* Yes. *(pause)* Yes. Wh . . . I. I. I had to be away. All ri . . . did they wor . . . did they worry ab . . . No. I'm all right, now, Jerry. I'm f . . . I got a little turned *around,* but I'm *sitting* here and . . . I've got it figured out. I'm fine. I'm fine don't worry about me. I got a little bit mixed up. But I am not sure that it's not a blessing. It cost me my job? Fine. Then the job was not worth having. Tell Grace that I'm coming home and everything is fff . . . *(pause)* What? *(pause) What? (pause)* What do you *mean?* WHAT? Jerry . . . Jerry. They . . . Who, who, what can they do . . . ? *(pause)* NO. *(pause)* NO. They can't do th . . . What do you mean? *(pause)* But how . . . *(pause)* She's, she's, she's *here* with me. To . . . Jerry. I don't underst . . . *(pause) (he hangs up) (To* CAROL*)* What does this mean?

CAROL: I thought you knew.

JOHN: What. *(pause)* What does it mean. *(pause)*

CAROL: You tried to rape me. *(pause)* According to the law. *(pause)*

JOHN: . . . what . . . ?

CAROL: You tried to rape me. I was leaving this office, you "pressed" yourself into me. You "pressed" your body into me.

JOHN: . . . I . . .

CAROL: My Group has told your lawyer that we may pursue criminal charges.

JOHN: . . . no . . .

CAROL: . . . under the statute. I am told. It was battery.

JOHN: . . . no . . .

CAROL: Yes. And attempted rape. That's right. *(pause)*

JOHN: I think that you should go.

CAROL: Of course. I thought you knew.

JOHN: I have to talk to my lawyer.

CAROL: Yes. Perhaps you should.

(The phone rings again) (pause)

JOHN: *(picks up phone. Into phone)* Hello? I . . . Hello . . . ? I . . . Yes, he just called. No . . . I. I can't talk to you now, Baby. *(to* CAROL*)* Get out.

CAROL: . . . your wife . . . ?

JOHN: . . . who it is is no concern of yours. Get out. *(to phone)* No, no, it's going to be all right. I. I can't talk now, Baby. *(to* CAROL*)* Get out of here.

CAROL: I'm going.

JOHN: Good.

CAROL: *(exiting)* . . . and don't call your wife "baby."

JOHN: What?

CAROL: Don't call your wife baby. You heard what I said.

*(*CAROL *starts to leave the room.* JOHN *grabs her and begins to beat her.)*

JOHN: You vicious little bitch. You think you can come in here with your political correctness and destroy my life?

(He knocks her to the floor.)

After how I treated you . . . ? You should be . . . *Rape you* . . . ? Are you kidding me . . . ?

(He picks up a chair, raises it above his head, and advances on her.)

I wouldn't touch you with a ten-foot pole. You little *cunt* . . .

(She cowers on the floor below him. Pause. He looks down at her. He lowers the chair. He moves to his desk, and arranges the papers on it. Pause. He looks over at her.)

. . . well . . .

(Pause. She looks at him.)

CAROL: Yes. That's right.

(She looks away from him, and lowers her head. To herself) . . . yes. That's right.

E N D

GIVING UP THE GHOST: A STAGE PLAY IN THREE PORTRAITS (1994)

"Breaking Silence" was one of the first accomplishments of the early movement in establishing a feminist voice [one distinct from "the patriarchal masculine voice"] . . .

In contrast, "breaking silence" for the lesbian feminist voice has been situated primarily within the context of feminism and only secondarily within that of the dominant culture. The compound identification, "lesbian feminist," suggests a more complex referent.

Sue-Ellen Case's observation about the inherent complexity of the term "lesbian feminism"—the plurality of voices and intellectual positions the term contains, the many silences it must break—is exemplified by much of Cherríe Moraga's work. This includes the 1994 revision of *Giving Up the Ghost* reprinted here, a play Moraga originally wrote some ten years earlier. It was first given a staged reading at the Foot of the Mountain Theatre in Minneapolis in the summer of 1984, and was published by West End Press in 1986. It was later produced in 1987 by both the Front Room Theatre in Seattle and the Mission Cultural Center in San Francisco, and in 1989 a significantly revised version was staged at the Theatre Rhinoceros in San Francisco. The play reproduced here, as Moraga has explained, is based on this last production and, while similar to the 1986 published text, represents an expansion and refinement of it, intimated by its revised subtitle: *Giving Up the Ghost: Teatro in Two Acts* from the 1980s has evolved into *Giving Up the Ghost: A Stage Play in Three Portraits* in the 1990s. The poetic and largely monologic form of *Giving Up the Ghost*, unlike that of any other selection in this anthology, also suggests

the manner in which more conventional **realism** is not particularly well-suited for the melding of lesbian, feminist, and Chicana voices that speak in much of Moraga's writing. In short, the implications of the complete title of her autobiographical *Loving in the War Years: (lo que nunca pasó por sus labios)* (1983)—"what never passed her lips"—are in many ways realized by her subsequent writing. Much passes Moraga's lips in such plays as *Giving Up the Ghost*, in the process breaking crucial silences in her life and in the lives of her characters.

Cherríe Moraga (1952–) was born in Whittier, California, to a Chicana mother and an Anglo father, and when she was nine the entire family moved to San Gabriel, near Los Angeles. Completing her undergraduate studies in 1974, she taught English in a high school in Los Angeles for two years and then moved to San Francisco. There, she completed a master's degree in feminist writing at San Francisco State University, submitting her anthology *This Bridge Called My Back: Writings by Radical Women of Color* (1981), co-edited with Gloria Anzaldúa, as her M.A. thesis. In addition to co-editing the volume, Moraga contributed poems and essays, one of which, "La Güera," delineates the privileged subject-position of the light-skinned Chicana within Latino communities. "No one ever quite told me this (that light was right)," Moraga recalls, "but I knew that being light was something valued in my family (who were all Chicano, with the exception of my father). In fact everything about my upbringing . . . attempted to bleach me of what color I did have." So, although her mother was fluent in Spanish, little Spanish was spoken in her home; although her mother came from a poor Latino family, she attempted to suppress memory of it, because "being

Chicana meant being 'less.'" In this essay, Moraga explains that when she "finally lifted the lid" on her lesbianism, a "profound connection" with her mother was "re-awakened." She was newly able to experience a "heartfelt identification with and empathy for" her mother's "oppression—due to being poor, uneducated, and Chicana." This reawakening, in turn, motivated her to study feminist and lesbian writing, to cofound Kitchen Table/Women of Color Press, and to become an important cultural critic who interrogates in her poetry, prose, and dramas the sociocultural forces that subjugate Chicanas. Her work includes the volumes cited above, *The Sexuality of Latinas* (1993), *The Last Generation: Prose and Poetry* (1993), and three plays: *Giving Up the Ghost, The Shadow of a Man* (1990), and *Heroes and Saints* (1992), the latter two of which were produced or coproduced by Brava! For Women in the Arts, a women's theatre and visual arts collective in San Francisco.

In such works as *Shadow of a Man* and the essay "A Long Line of Vendidas" ("A Long Line of Sell-outs") from *Loving in the War Years*, Moraga focuses her attention on those ideological institutions—the Catholic Church and the traditional family structure, for example—that subordinate women and, in several instances, devastate the lives of men as well. In *Shadow of a Man*, Hortensia, an abused wife in her forties, cooks, cleans, presses her husband Manuel's clothes, and helps him dress and undress; her younger daughter Lupe shines his dress shoes and helps her mother fold clothing. But Manuel and Hortensia's loveless marriage is ruined by a deeper and more secret subjugation of Hortensia in the past—Manuel's giving of her to his *compadre*, Conradio. Hortensia, Manuel's gift to Conradio to cement the relationship of the two men, suffers as a consequence, but so too do Manuel and the entire family. The "love" between these two men and the social codes it sanctions finally kill Manuel; drunken and disconsolate, he takes his own life at the end of the play. The "shadow" in the play's title thus takes on several connotations: Conradio's shadow has hung over the family ever since the night of his assignation with Hortensia, reducing Manuel—and his

marriage—to "shadows" of their former selves. The bond between Manuel and his *compadre*, traditionally one of great strength in Chicano households, destroys the entire family. And it is precisely for this reason that Hortensia's older, rebellious daughter Leticia, much to her mother's horror, blithely gives away her virginity, what she describes as "that special secret, that valuable commodity, waiting for some lucky guy to put his name on it." Leticia craves a level of agency her mother can only equate with maleness—"Tha's [sic] what you want, isn't it? To be free like a man?"—and the status of virgin-commodity can only ensure her further subordination to men. In "A Long Line of Vendidas" Moraga makes the point even more succinctly: "Chicanas begin to turn our backs on each other either to gain male approval or to avoid being sexually stigmatized" by men. Sexism and "heterosexism" are thus causes of oppression for most Chicanas.

Because, in Moraga's view, the "control of women begins through the institution of heterosexuality," her lesbianism "challenges the very foundation of *la familia*"—and with it one source of domination over women. Moreover, Moraga's acknowledgement of her lesbianism affects her identification with her mother, her mother's culture, and her language. So, in *Giving Up the Ghost* both Spanish and English are spoken, a combination of languages Moraga heard as a child in her mother's kitchen: "The sounds of my mother and aunts gossiping—half in English, half in Spanish—while drinking cerveza in the kitchen." In "La Güera," Moraga recalls hearing Ntozake Shange give a reading in the late 1970s in "a language that I knew." What Shange sparked in her, Moraga recalls, is "the realization that in my development as a poet, I have, in many ways, denied the voice of my own brown mother—the brown in me." Moraga had, as she speculates in the same essay, internalized an "oppressive imagery" sponsored by Western culture that equates what is "dark and female" with "evil," thereby forming an **Other** against which the oppressor defines himself. Split genetically between brown and white—linguistically, between Spanish and English—Moraga "urgently" feels the need for dialogue, not simply between one or two voices, but between many. Finally, as she asserts in "A Long Line of Vendidas," lesbian feminists must seize *"the right to passion* expressed in our own cultural tongue."

Giving Up the Ghost is about the expression of this passion, as Marisa reveals to the audience both her constant negotiation with Corky, her former self, and her love for Amalia, an older woman. In a manner resembling Arlene's dealings with Arlie, her former self, in Marsha Norman's *Getting Out,* Marisa is often forced to rationalize or modulate Corky's aggressiveness, her tough *cholo* appearance and talk. Corky's fantasies of being "big 'n tough," as Marisa explains, are not so much the product of her longing to be a man, but rather the expression of her desire to be free and have a woman want her. As the audience learns later, Corky was raped by a school janitor when she was 12, a violation Marisa claims she does not regret, because it "only convinced" her of "her own name." This experience, made even more disturbing by the janitor's strong resemblance to Corky/Marisa's father and by its occurring in school, serves to foreground the institutions complicitous in Marisa's oppression. As the play progresses, Marisa and Amalia's sexual intimacy causes Corky—with her toughness and her rage—to disappear. Yet Amalia must finally express her deep reservations about their relationship, her troubled dreams of their "breaking of the taboo," and admit her heterosexuality as the play's penultimate scene concludes: "I never wanted you the way I wanted a man." As the last scene begins, Marisa stands alone on stage, recalling her belief that she could "save" Amalia from the prison of heterosexuality she has so painfully inhabited. She apparently cannot. Nevertheless, Marisa concludes the play with an expression of her determination to make a new "familia from scratch" if necessary, "each time all over again."

In her contextualization of *Giving Up the Ghost* within larger developments in Chicano theatre in the 1980s and 1990s, Yvonne Yarbro-Bejarno emphasizes the manner in which writers like Moraga and groups like **El Teatro de la Esperanza** are helping to "undermine the unifying concept of identity promulgated by the cultural nationalism of the 1960s movements." In *Giving Up the Ghost,* Moraga replaces this sense of shared identity with a poetic meditation on the forces that construct and restrict female identity for Chicanas like Marisa and Amalia. Yarbro-Bejarno lists these forces in terms of oppositions—"masculine/feminine, active/passive, subject/object, penetrator/penetrated defined in Chicano-specific cultural terms"—terms that expose the highly gendered realities and inequities that underlie the concepts of cultural nationalism and common identity. The nonchronological ordering of the play presents no "facile resolution" to these very powerful and determinative cultural forces; Marisa and Amalia may find methods of overcoming them, and they may not. In any event, *Giving Up the Ghost* provides a moving, often quite beautiful articulation—or breaking of silences—of the complexities of being Chicana *and* lesbian in contemporary America.

WORKS CONSULTED

Case, Sue-Ellen. "Judy Grahn's Gynopoetics: *The Queen of Swords.*" *Studies in the Literary Imagination* 21 (1988): 47–67.

Moraga, Cherríe. *Heroes and Saints & Other Plays.* Albuquerque: West End Press, 1994.

———. *Loving in the War Years: lo que nunca pasó por sus labios.* Boston: South End Press, 1983.

———. *Shadow of a Man. Shattering the Myth: Plays by Hispanic Women.* Ed. Linda Feyder. Houston: Arte Publico Press, 1992. 9–49.

———. "La Güera." *This Bridge Called My Back: Writings by Radical Women of Color.* Eds. Cherríe Moraga and Gloria Anzaldúa. New York: Kitchen Table/Women of Color Press, 1981. 27–34.

Saldivar, José David. *The Dialectics of Our America: Genealogy, Cultural Critique, and Literary History.* Durham: Duke University Press, 1991.

Winn, Steven. "Brava Bucks the Status Quo." *American Theatre* May–June 1994: 56–57.

Yarbro-Bejarno, Yvonne. "Cherríe Moraga." *Dictionary of Literary Biography,* Volume 82. Eds. Francisco A. Lomeli and Carl Shirley. Detroit: Gale Research Press, 1989. 165–177.

———. "Cherríe Moraga's 'Shadow of a Man': Touching the Wound in Order to Heal." *Acting Out: Feminist Performances.* Eds. Lynda Hart and Peggy Phelan. Ann Arbor: University of Michigan Press, 1993. 85–104.

———. "The Female Subject in Chicano Theatre: Sexuality, 'Race,' and Class." *Theatre Journal* 38 (1986): 389–407.

CHARACTERS

MARISA .... Chicana in her late 20s
CORKY .... MARISA as a young teenager
AMALIA .... Mexican-born, a generation older than MARISA
THE PEOPLE .... those viewing the performance or reading the play

If I had wings like an angel
over these prison walls
I would fly
  (song my mother would sing me)

Set

The stage set should be simple, with as few props as possible. A crate is used for street scenes downstage. A raised platform, stage left, serves as the bed in a variety of settings, including a hotel room, a mental hospital, and both AMALIA'S and MARISA'S apartments. A simple wooden table and two chairs, stage right, represent AMALIA'S kitchen. Windows, doorways, and furniture appear in the imagination when needed. The suggestion of a Mexican desert landscape is illuminated upstage during scenes evoking indigenous Mexican imagery. Scrims can be used for the dreamlike sequences. Aside from the minimal set pieces mentioned above, lighting and music should be the main features in providing setting. Music should be used to re-create the "streetwise ritmo" of the urban life of these Chicanas, spanning a generation of Motown, soul, Tex-Mex, and Latin rock. It should also reflect the profound influence of traditional Mexican folk music—rancheras, corridos, mariachi, etc.—as well as the more ancient indigenous sounds of the flauta, concha, and tambor. Throughout the long monologues (unless otherwise indicated) when the non-speaking actors remain on stage, the lighting and direction should give the impression that the characters both disappear and remain within hearing range of the speaker. In short, direction should reflect that each character knows, on an intuitive level, the minds of the other characters.

RETRATO I: "LA PACHUCA"

Prologue

This is the urban Southwest, a Chicano barrio within the sprawling Los Angeles basin. Street sounds fill the air: traffic, children's schoolyard voices, street repairs, etc. MARISA sits on a wooden crate, centerstage. She wears a pair of Levi's, tennis shoes and a bright-colored shirt. Her black hair is pulled back, revealing a face of dark intensity and definite Indian features. She holds a large sketch book on her lap. CORKY enters upstage. Their eyes meet. As MARISA'S younger self, CORKY tries to act tough but displays a wide open-heartedness in her face which betrays the toughness. She dresses "Cholo style"—khaki pants with razor-sharp creases, pressed white undershirt. Her hair is cut short and slicked back. She approaches the upstage wall, spray can in hand, feigning the false bravado of her teenage male counterparts. She writes *in large, Chicano graffiti-style letters, as* MARISA *writes in her sketchbook.*

Dedicación

Don't know where this woman
and I will find each other again,
but I am grateful to her   to something
that feels like a blessing

that I am, in fact, not trapped

which brings me to the question of prisons
politics
sex.

(CORKY *tosses the spray can to* MARISA.)

MARISA/CORKY: I'm only telling you this to stay
my hand.

MARISA: But why, cheezus, why me?

Why'd I hafta get into a situation where all my
ghosts come to visit?
I always see that man . . . thick-skinned,
dark, muscular.
He's a boulder between us.
I can't lift him and her, too . . . carrying him.

He's a ghost, always haunting her . . .
lingering.
(*Fade out.*)

SCENE ONE: *A Chicano "oldie" rises. Crossfade to* CORKY *coming downstage, moving "low & slow" to the tune.*

CORKY: the smarter I get the older I get the
meaner I get
tough a tough cookie my mom calls me
sometimes I even pack a blade
no one knows I never use it or nut'ing
but can feel it there there in my pants pocket
run the pad of my thumb over it to remind me I
carry somet'ing
am sharp secretly
always envy those batos who get all cut up at
the weddings
getting their rented tuxes all bloody

that red 'n' clean color
against the white starched collars
I love that shit!

the best part is the chicks all climbing into the
ball of the fight
"Chuy, déjalo! Leave him go, Güero!" tú sabes
you know how the chicks get all excited 'n'
upset 'n' stuff
they always pulling on the carnales 'n' getting
nowhere
'cept messed up themselves 'n' everybody
looks so
like they digging the whole t'ing tú sabes
their dresses ripped here 'n' there . . . like a
movie
it's all like a movie

when I was a real little kid I useta love the
movies
every Saturday you could find me there
my eyeballs glued to the screen
then later my friend Arturo 'n' me
we'd make up our own movies
one was where we'd be out in the desert
'n' we'd capture these chicks 'n' hold 'em up
for ransom
we'd string 'em up 'n' make 'em take their
clothes off
"strip" we'd say to the wall all cool-like
funny . . . now when I think about how little I
was at the time
and a girl but in my mind I was big 'n' tough 'n'
a dude
in my *mind* I had all their freedom
the freedom to see a girl   kina
the way   you see
an animal   you know?

like imagining
they got a difernt set
of blood vessels or somet'ing   like   so
when you mess with 'em
it don' affect 'em the way   it do   you
like like they got a difernt gland system or
somet'ing that

that makes their pain cells
more dense

hell I dunno

but you see
I never could
quite
pull it off

always knew I was a girl
deep down inside
no matter how I tried to pull the other off

I knew
always knew
I was an animal that kicked back . . .

(with MARISA) . . . cuz it hurt!
(CORKY exits)

MARISA: (from the platform, coming downstage) I never wanted to be a man, only wanted a woman to want me that bad. And they have, you know, plenty of them, but there's always that one you can't pin down, who's undecided. (Beat) My mother was a heterosexual, I couldn't save her. My failures follow thereafter.

AMALIA (entering): I am a failure.

AMALIA is visibly "soft" in just the ways that MARISA appears "hard." She chooses her clothes with an artist's eye for color and placement. They appear to be draped over her, rather than worn: a rebozo wrapped around her shoulders, a blouse falling over the waist of an embroidered skirt. Her hair is long and worn down or loosely braided. As a woman nearing fifty, she gives the impression of someone who was once a rare beauty, now trading that for a fierce dignity in bearing.

AMALIA: I see the Americans. Their security. Their houses. Their dogs. Their children are happy. They are not un . . . happy. Sure, they have their struggles, their problemas, but . . . it's a life. I always say this, it's a life. (She sits at the table stacked with art books, puts on a pair of wire-rim glasses, leafs through a book.)

MARISA: My friend Marta bought her mother a house. I admire her. Even after the family talked bad about her like that for leaving home with a gabacha, she went back cash in hand and bought her mother a casita kina on the outskirts of town. Ten grand was all it took, that's nothing here, but it did save her mother from the poverty her dead father left behind. I envy her. For the first time wished my father'd die so I could do my mother that kind of rescue routine.

I wanna talk about betrayal, about a battle I will never win and never stop fighting. The dick beats me every time. I know I'm not supposed to be sayin' this cuz it's like confession, like still cryin' your sins to a priest you long ago stopped believing was god or god's sit-in, but still confessing what you'd hoped had been forgiven in you. . . . (Looking to AMALIA.) That prison . . . that passion to beat men at their own game.

AMALIA: I worry about La Pachuca. That's my nickname for her. I have trouble calling her by her Christian name. (Savoring it.) Marisa. ("Rain sticks" in the background.) I worry about La Pachuca. I worry what will happen to the beautiful corn she is growing if it continues to rain so hard and much.

CORKY (entering): one time Tury 'n' me stripped
for real
there was this minister 'n' his family down the
street
they was presbyterians or methodists or
somet'ing
you know one of those gringo religions
'n' they had a bunch a kids
the oldest was named Lisa or somet'ing
lightweight like that
'n' the littlest was about three or so, named
Chrissy
I mean you couldn't really complain about
Chrissy
cuz she wasn't old enough yet to be a pain in
the cola
but you knew that was coming

Lisa'd be hassling me 'n' my sister Patsy all the
time

telling us how we wernt really christians

cuz cath-lics worshipped the virgin mary or
somet'ing

I dint let this worry me though cuz we was being
tole at school

how being cath-lic was the one true numero
uno church 'n' all

so I jus' let myself be real cool with her

'n' the rest of her little pagan baby brothers 'n'
sisters

that's all they was to me as far as I was
concerned

they dint even have no mass

jus' some paddy preaching up there with a
dark suit on

very weird

not a damn candle for miles

dint seem to me that there was any god
happening in that place at all

so one day Tury comes up with this idea how
we should strip

"for real"

I wasn't that hot on the idea but still go along
with him

checkin' out the neighborhood looking for prey

then we run into Chrissy 'n' Tury 'n' me eye
each other

the trouble is I'm still not completely sold on
the idea

pero ni modo cuz I already hear comin' outta
my mouth

real syrupy-like

"come heeeeere Chrissy, we got somet'ing to
shooooow you"

well, a'course she comes cuz I was a big kid 'n'
all

'n' we take her into this shed

I have her hand 'n' Tury tells her . . .

no *I* told her this

I tell her we think she's got somet'ing wrong
with her

"down there"

I think . . . I think I said she had a cut or
somet'ing

'n' Tury 'n' me had to check it out

so I pull her little shorts down 'n' then her
chones

'n' then jus' as I catch a glimpse of her little
fuchi fachi . . .

it was so tender-looking all pink 'n' real sweet
like a bun

then stupid Tury like a menso goes 'n' sticks
his dirty finger on it

like it was burning hot

'n' jus' at that moment . . . I see this little
Chrissy-kid

look up at me like . . . like I was her mom or
somet'ing

like tú sabes she has this little kid's frown on
her face

the chubby skin on her forehead all rumpled
up

like . . . like she knew somet'ing was wrong
with what we was doing

'n' was looking to me to reassure her

that everyt'ing was cool 'n' regular 'n' all

what a jerk I felt like!

*(She pushes "Tury" away, bends down to
"Chrissy.")*

so, I pull up her shorts 'n' whisper to her

"no no you're fine really there's nut'ing wrong
with you

but don' tell nobody we looked

we don' want nobody to worry about you"

what else was I supposed to say? ¡Tonta!

'n' Tury 'n' me make a beeline into the alley 'n'
outta there!

(She exits.)

SCENE TWO: *Crossfade to* AMALIA *rising from the
bed. It is morning.*

AMALIA: I remember the first time I met her, the
day she first began to bring me her work. It was
early morning, too early really, and there was
someone at the door. At first I think it is my
son, Che. Like him to appear at my doorstep
with the least amount of warning. *(She goes to
the "window," looks down to the front steps.
MARISA appears, carrying a portfolio.)* But it

was Marisa, standing there with a red jacket on, I remember, a beautiful color of red. Maybe if I had not dreamed the color the night before I might not even have bothered to open the door so early, such a hermit I am. *(To* MARISA*)* ¿Sí?

MARISA: Hello. I got these . . . paintings. I . . . heard you could help me.

AMALIA: ¿Quién eres?

MARISA: Marisa. Marisa Moreno.

AMALIA: It's a little early ¿qué no?

MARISA: I'm sorry. Frank Delgado—

AMALIA: Súbete.

AMALIA *"buzzes"* MARISA *in.* AMALIA *puts on a robe, brushes back her hair.* MARISA *enters.*

MARISA: Good morning.

AMALIA: It's too early to tell.

MARISA: I'm sorry.

AMALIA: That's two "sorrys" already and I don't even got my eyes on yet.

MARISA: Sor . . .

MARISA *(smiling):* Pásale. Pásale.

MARISA *(handing her a small paper sack):* Here, this is for you.

AMALIA: Siéntate.

MARISA: It's pandulce.

AMALIA *(looking inside):* Conchas. They're my favorites.

AMALIA *puts the pastry on the table.* MARISA *sits down, holds the portfolio awkwardly in her lap. During the following scene there are brief lapses in the conversation.*

AMALIA: ¿Quieres café?

MARISA: Gracias. No.

AMALIA: Pues, yo . . . sí. *(Goes to prepare the coffee.)* I can't even talk before I have a cup of coffee in me. Help yourself to the pandulce.

MARISA *(indicating the books on the table):* Are all these yours?

AMALIA: The books? Claro.

MARISA: They're wonderful.

AMALIA: Take a look at them if you want.

MARISA *carefully props up her portfolio onto a chair and begins to leaf through one of the books.* AMALIA *reenters, looking for her glasses.*

MARISA: You got a lotta . . . things.

AMALIA: What? Yes. Too much. My son, Che, he calls me a . . . rat pack.

MARISA: A pack rat.

AMALIA: Whatever you call it, I can't even find my glasses.

MARISA *(pointing to the painting on the upstage wall):* And this?

AMALIA: Well, I couldn't afford a room with a view, so . . . bueno, pues I improvised a little. ¿Te gusta? *(She finds her glasses in her robe pocket, puts them on.)*

MARISA: Yeah. Mucho.

AMALIA *(observing her):* You don't seem quite as awesome as Delgado described you.

MARISA: He told you about me?

AMALIA: Ay, all los boys at El Centro were talking about you, telling me how I should see your work . . . this new "Eastlos import."

MARISA: I didn't think they liked me.

AMALIA: Pues, I didn't say they *liked* you.

MARISA: Oh.

AMALIA: I think you scared them a little. Una pintora bien chingona, me dijo Frank.

MARISA: That's what he said?

AMALIA: Más o menos. Bueno. . . . *(Indicating the portfolio.)* Abrélo. Let's see what makes those machos shake in their botas so much.

As MARISA *opens the portfolio, the lights cross-fade to* CORKY *entering.*

CORKY: the weird thing was that after that episode with Chrissy

I was like a maniac all summer

snotty Lisa kept harassing me about the virgin mary 'n' all

'n' jus' in general being a pain in the coolie

things began to break down with her 'n' her minister's family

when me 'n' Patsy stopped going to their church meetings

on wednesday nights

we'd only go cuz they had cookies 'n' treats after all the bible stuff

'n' sometimes had arts 'n' crafts where you got to paint

little clay statues of blond jesus in a robe
'n' the little children coming to him
the drag was that you also had to do these
    prayer sessions
where everybody'd stand in a circle squeezing
    hands
'n' each kid'd say a little prayer
you know like "for the starving people in china"
Patsy 'n' me always passed when we got
    squeezed
jus' shaked our heads no
cuz it was against our religion to pray with
    them
well, one time, this Lisa punk has the nerve to
    pray that Patsy 'n' me
would *(mimicking)* "come to the light of the
    one true Christian faith"
shi-it can you get to that? 'course we never
    went again
AMALIA *puts on an apron, becomes* CORKY'S
"mother."

CORKY: but I remember coming home 'n' telling
my mom . . .
"MOTHER": It's better mi'jitas, I think, if you don'
go no more.
CORKY: 'n' it was so nice to hear her voice so
warm
like she loved us a lot
'n' that night being cath-lic felt like my mom
real warm 'n' dark 'n' kind
Fade out.

SCENE THREE: *At rise,* MARISA *straddles the kitchen
chair, addresses* THE PEOPLE. AMALIA *is upstage by
the bed. During* MARISAS'S *monologue,* AMALIA *ties
her hair back into a tight bun, applies a grey powder
to her face, and draws dark circles under her eyes.*

MARISA: The women I have loved the most have
always loved the man more than me, even in
their hatred of him. I'm queer I am. Sí, soy jota
because I have never been crazy about a man.
(Pause.) My friend Sally the hooker told me the
day she decided to stop tricking was when
once, by accident, a john made her come. That

was strictly forbidden. She'd forgotten to re-
sist, to keep business business. It was very un-
professional . . . and dangerous. No, I've
never been in love with a man and I never understood women who were, although I've certainly been around to pick up the pieces. My
sister was in love with my brother.
CORKY *(entering):* My mother loved her father.
MARISA: My first woman
CORKY: The man who put her away.
MARISA: The crazy house. Camarillo, Califas.
Sixteen years old.
Blue light. Haunting music. AMALIA *becomes
"*NORMA,*"* MARISA'S *"first woman." She sits on
the bed in a kind of psychotic stupor.* CORKY *goes
over to her.* MARISA *observes.*
MARISA: When I come to get my cousin Norma,
she has eyes like saucers, spinning black and
glass. I can see through them, my face, my
name. She says . . .
"NORMA": I am Buddha.
CORKY: How'd you get that black eye? ¿Quién te
pegó?
"NORMA": I am Buddha.
Fade out.

SCENE FOUR: CORKY *is alone on stage. She takes
out a yo-yo, tries a few tricks. She is quite good.*

CORKY: since that prayer meeting night
when Patsy 'n' me wouldn't get squeezed into
    the minister's jesus
Lisa's nose was gettin' higher 'n' higher in the air

one day Patsy 'n' her are playing dolls up
on the second story porch of Mrs. Rodríguez's
    house
it was nice up there cuz Mrs. R would let you
    move the tables
'n' chairs 'n' stuff around to play "pertend"

my sister had jus' gotten this nice doll for her
    birthday
with this great curly hair
Lisa only had this kina stupid doll
with plastic painted-on hair 'n' only one leg

she'd always put long dresses on it to disguise
  the missing leg
but we all knew it was gone

anyway, one day this brat Lisa throws my sister's
  new doll
into this mud puddle right down from Mrs. R's
  porch
(She lets out the yo-yo. It dangles helplessly.)

Patsy comes back into our yard crying like crazy
her doll's all muddy 'n' the hair has turned
  bone straight
I mean like an arrow!
I wanted to kill that punk Lisa!
so me 'n' Patsy go over to Lisa's house
where we find the little creep all pleased with
  herself
I mean not even feeling bad
suddenly I see her bike which is really a trike
but it's huge . . . I mean hu-u-uge!
to this day, I never seen a trike that big
it useta bug me to no end that she wasn't even
  trying
to learn to ride a two-wheeler
so all of a sudden . . . *(Winding up with the
  yo-yo like a pitcher.)*
that trike 'n' Lisa's wimpiness come together
  in my mind
'n' I got that thing 'n' *(throwing the pitch)*
I threw the sucker into the street

I dint even wreck it none
(She stuffs the yo-yo back in her pocket.)
but it was the principle of the thing

a'course she goes 'n' tells her mom on me
'n' this lady who by my mind don' even seem
  like a mom
she dint wear no makeup 'n' was real skinny 'n'
  tall
'n' wore her hair in some kina dumb bun
she has the nerve to call my mom 'n' tell her
  what I done
AMALIA, *as* CORKY'S *"mom," appears upstage
in an apron. She is stirring a pot in her arms.
She observes* CORKY.

CORKY: so a'course my mom calls me on the carpet
  wants to know the story
  'n' I tell her 'bout the doll 'n' Patsy 'n' the
    principle of the thing
  'n' Patsy's telling the same story 'n' I can see in
    my mom's eyes
  she don' believe I did nut'ing so bad but she
    tells me . . .
"MOTHER":   We got to keep some peace in the
  neighborhood, hija.
CORKY: Cuz we was already getting pedo from the
  paddy neighbors 'bout how my mom hollered
  too much at her kids . . . her own kids! I mean
  if you can't yell at your own kids who *can* you
  yell at? but she don' let on that this is the real
  reason I hafta go over to the minister's house
  and apologize. She jus' kina turns back to the
  stove 'n' keeps on with what she was doing.
"MOTHER":   Andale, mija, dinner's almost ready.
  *(*CORKY *hesitates)* Andale. Andale.
CORKY *(coming downstage):*   so, a'course I go . . .
  I go by myself
  with no one to watch me to see if I really do it
  but my mom knows I will cuz she tole me to
  'n' I ring the doorbell 'n' Mrs. Minister answers
  'n' as I begin to talk that little wimp Lisa runs
    up
  'n' peeks out at me from behind her mother's
    skirt
  with the ugliest most snottiest shit-eating grin
  I'd ever seen in a person
  while all the while *I* say *I'm* sorry
  'n' as the door shuts in front of my face
  I vow I'll never make that mistake again . . .

  (with MARISA*)* I'll never show nobody how mad I
    can get!

  Black out.

SCENE FIVE: MARISA *is pacing about* AMALIA'S *room.*
AMALIA *sits on the floor mixing paints. She wears a
paint-splattered apron.*

MARISA *(to* THE PEOPLE*):*   I have a very long
  memory. I try to warn people that when I get

hurt, I don't forget it. I use it against them. I blame women for everything. My mistakes. Missed opportunities. My grief. I usually leave just when I wanna lay a woman flat. When I feel that vengeance rise up in me, I split. I desert.

AMALIA: Desert. Desierto. For some reason, I could always picture mi cholita in the desert, amid the mesquite y nopal. Always when I closed my eyes to search for her, it was in the Mexican desert that I found her. I *had* intended to take her . . . to México. She would never have gone alone, sin gente allá.

MARISA: This *is* México! What are you talking about? It was those gringos that put up those fences between us!

AMALIA *brings* MARISA *to the table, takes out a piece of charcoal from her apron, puts it into* MARISA'S *hand.* MARISA *begins to sketch.*

AMALIA: She was hardly convincing. Her nostalgia for the land she had never seen was everywhere. In her face, her drawings, her love of the hottest sand by the sea.

Coming around behind her, AMALIA *wraps her arms around* MARISA'S *neck. Indigenous flutes and drums can be heard in the background.*

AMALIA: Desierto de Sonora. Tierra de tu memoria. *(Turning* MARISA'S *face to her.)* Same chata face. Yaqui. *(They hesitate, then kiss their first kiss.)*

MARISA: I've just never believed a woman capable of loving a man was capable of loving . . . me. Some part of me remains amazed that I'm not the only lesbian in the world and that I can always manage to find someone to love me. *(Pause.)* But I am never satisfied because there are always those women left alone . . . and unloved.

Lights slowly fade to black. Musical interlude.

RETRATO II: "LA LOCA"

SCENE SIX: *A sunny morning.* AMALIA *is kneeling on a chair, bent over the table, painting in thick*

strokes and occasionally sipping at a cup of coffee. Her hair is combed into a braid and tied up. MARISA lies on the bed, hands behind her head.

AMALIA: I've only been crazy over one man in my life. Alejandro was nothing special. Era pescador, indio. Once we took a drive out of the small town he lived in, and he was terrified, like a baby. I'm driving through the mountains and he's squirming in his seat, "Amalia, ¿pá dónde vamos? Are you sure you know where we're going?" I was so amused to see this big macho break out into a cold sweat just from going no more than twenty miles from his home town. Pero ¡Ay, Dios! How I loved that man! I still ask myself what I saw in him, really. *(Pause.)* He was one of the cleanest people I had ever met. Took two, three baths a day. You have to, you know. That part of la Costa is like steam baths some seasons. I remember how he'd even put powder in his shorts and under his huevos to keep dry. He was that clean. I always loved knowing that when I touched him I would find him like a saint. Pure, somehow . . . that no matter where he had been or who he had been with, he would always have washed himself for me. He always smelled . . . so clean. (She wipes her hands, sits at the foot of the bed.) When I went back home that first time, after my son was already grown, I had never dreamed of falling in love. Too many damn men under the bridge. I can see them all floating down the river like so many sacks of potatoes. "Making love," they call it, was like having sex with children. They rub your chichis a little, then they stick it in you. Nada más. It's all over in a few minutes. ¡Un río de cuerpos muertos!

MARISA: Sometimes I only see the other river on your face. I see it running behind your eyes. Remember the time we woke up together and your eye was a bowl of blood? I thought the river had broken open inside you.

AMALIA: I was crazy about Alejandro. But what I loved was not so much him . . . I loved his children. I loved the way he had made México my home again. *(Pause.)* He was not a strong man really. He was soft. An inside softness, I could feel even as his desire swelled into a rock hardness. Once he said that with me he felt as thought he were "a heart that knew no sex." No man-woman, he meant, only heat and a heart and that even a man could be entered in this way. *(Indigenous music rises in the background.)* I, on the other hand, was *not* clean, forgot sometimes to wash. Not when I was around others, pero con mí misma, I became like the animals. Uncombed. El olor del suelo.

MARISA: I remember the story you told me about the village children, how they had put una muñeca at the door of your casita. How you had found it there . . . there, in your likeness and you thought—

AMALIA: I must be mad.

Suddenly, the beat of tambores. CORKY *enters, wearing a native bruja mask. She dances across the stage with rattles in her hand. As she exits,* MARISA *goes to* AMALIA, *unbraids her hair.*

MARISA: So we take each other in doses. I learn to swallow my desire, work my fear slowly through the strands of your hair.

MARISA *bends to kiss* AMALIA *on the neck.* AMALIA *pulls away, comes downstage.*

AMALIA: Of course, soon after, Alejandro ran to every whore he could find, but not without first calling me that: "puta, bruja." He claimed I was trying to work some kind of mala suerte on him, that I was trying to take from him his manhood, make him something less than a man. *(Pause, to* MARISA*)* I have always felt like an outsider.

MARISA *starts toward her, then changes her mind and exits.*

AMALIA *(to* THE PEOPLE*):*   Ni de aquí, ni de allá. Ask me in one word to describe to you the source of all my loneliness and I will tell you, "México." Not that I would have been any happier staying there. How *could* I have stayed there, been some man's wife . . . after so many years in this country, so many years on my own?

(Pause.) I'll never forget the trip, the day our whole tribe left para el norte.

Sudden spiritedness. A Mexican mariachi instrumental rises. AMALIA *ties a bandana around her head. She is a young girl.*

AMALIA: All of us packed into the old blue Chevy. I was thirteen and la regla had started, the bleeding, and I was ashamed to tell my mother. Tía Fita had been the one to warn me that at my age, any day, I could expect to become sick. "Mala," she said, and that when it happened I should come to her and she would bless me and tell me how to protect myself. It came the morning of our long jornada to California.

AMALIA *sees the "blood" coming down her leg. She takes the bandana from her head, looks around nervously, then stuffs it under her skirt, flattening it back into place.*

AMALIA: Tía Fita was not speaking to my mother so angry was she for all of us leaving. We had asked her to come with us. "What business do I have up there with all those pochos y gringos?" My father said she had no sense. It broke her heart to see us go. So, there was no running to Tía Fita that morning. It seemed too selfish to tell her my troubles when *I* was the one leaving *her.*

Southwestern desert and distant highway sounds can be heard. AMALIA, *trying to hide from the others, pulls the bandana out from under her skirt. Kneeling by the "river," she secretly begins to wash the blood from it. Sound and lights gradually fade out.*

SCENE SEVEN: MARISA *sits at the table in soft light sipping at a beer. She is dressed for the evening in a man's suit jacket. She wears a kind of classic androgynous look.* AMALIA *enters in a slip, crosses to the bed where she begins to dress.*

MARISA: If I were a man, things would've been a lot simpler between us, except . . . she never would've wanted me. I mean, she would've seen me more and all, fit me more conveniently into her life, but she never would've, tú sabes . . . wanted me.

AMALIA: Sometimes I think, with me, that she only wanted to feel herself so much a woman that she would no longer be hungry for one. Pero, siempre tiene hambre. Siempre tiene pena.

MARISA: She'd come to me sometimes I swear like heat on wheels. I'd open the door and find her there, wet from the outta nowhere June rains, and, without her even opening her mouth, I knew what she had come for. I never knew when to expect her this way, just like the rains. Never ever when I wanted it, asked for it, begged for it, only when she decided.

AMALIA: I always had to have a few traguitos and then things would cloud between us a little and I could feel her as if underwater, my hands swimming towards her in the darkness, discovering breasts, not mine . . . not these empty baldes, pero senos firmes, like small stones of heat. Y como un recién nacido, I drink and drink and drink y no me traga la tierra.

Lights suggest memory. Nighttime freeway sounds, car radio music. MARISA and AMALIA hold each other's eyes. Voice over.

MARISA: I'll keep driving if you promise not to stop touching me.

AMALIA: You want me to stop touching you?

MARISA: No, if you promise *not* to stop.

AMALIA crosses in front of MARISA. She prepares herself a drink. MARISA watches her.

MARISA: It's odd being queer. It's not that you don't want a man, you just don't want a man in a man. You want a man in a woman. The woman part goes without saying. That's what you always learn to want first. Maybe the first time you see your dad touch your mom in that way. . . .

CORKY *(entering):* ¡Hiiiijo! I remember the first time I got hip to that! My mom standing at the stove making chile colorado and flippin' tortillas. She asks my dad . . .

AMALIA *(as "MOM," to MARISA):* ¿Quieres otra, viejo?

CORKY: Kina like she's sorta hassled 'n' being poquita fría, tú sabes, but she's really digging my dad to no end. 'N' jus' as she comes over to him, kina tossing the tort onto the plate, he slides his hand, real suave-like, up the inside of her thigh. Cheezus! I coulda died! I musta been only about nine or so, but I got that tingling, tú sabes, that now I know what it means. *As CORKY exits, she throws her chin out to MARISA "bato style." MARISA, amused, returns the gesture. The lights shift. MARISA puts on a tape. A Mexican ballad is played—"Adios Paloma" by Chavela Vargas. AMALIA hums softly along with it.*

MARISA: Hay un hombre en esta mujer. Lo he sentido. La miro, cocinando para nosotras. Pienso . . . ¿cómo puede haber un hombre en una persona, tan feminina? Su pelo, sus movimientos de una serenidad imposible de describir.

AMALIA *(softly singing):*

"Ya se va tu paloma, mi vida
Ileva en sus alas dolor
Ileva en sus ojos tristeza
y es un lamento su voz."

MARISA *(going to her):* Tu voz que me acaricia con cada palabra . . . tan suave . . . tan rica. *(Takes her by the hand.)* Vente.
The music rises. They dance for a few moments, then MARISA takes AMALIA to the bed. The music fades as MARISA slowly removes AMALIA'S blouse.

MARISA: Con ella, me siento como un joven lleno de deseo. I move on top of her. She wants this. The worn denim and metal buttons are cotton and cool ice on my skin. And she is full of slips and lace and stockings . . .

AMALIA: Quítate los pantalones.

MARISA: And yet it is she who's taking me.
A soft jazz rises. MARISA takes off her jacket. They kiss each other, at first tenderly, then passionately. They hold and caress each other. MARISA takes AMALIA'S hand, brings it to her chest. The music softens.

MARISA: I held the moment. Prayed that if I looked long and hard enough at your hand full inside me, if I could keep this pictured forever in my mind . . . how beneath that moon blasting through the window . . . how everything was changing at that moment in both of us.

AMALIA: How everything was changing . . . in both of us.

The jazz rises again. The lights slowly fade as they hold a deep kiss.

RETRATO III:
"LA SALVADORA"

SCENE EIGHT: CORKY *writes graffiti-style on upstage wall.*

I have this rock in my hand
it is my memory
the weight is solid
in my palm   it cannot fly away

because I still remember
that woman
not my savior, but an angel
with wings
that did once lift me
to another
self.

MARISA *and* AMALIA *appear in shadow on opposite ends of the stage.*

AMALIA: You have the rest of your life to forgive me.

MARISA: Forgive you for what?

AMALIA: Por lo que soy.

   (Black out.)

SCENE NINE: AMALIA *enters carrying a small suitcase. She sets it down at the foot of the bed, removes her rebozo and holds it in her lap.*

AMALIA: All I was concerned about was getting my health back together. It was not so much that I had been sick, only I lacked . . . energy. My body felt like a rag, squeezed dry of any feeling. Possibly it was the "change" coming on. But the women in my family did not go through the change so young. I wasn't even fifty. I thought . . . maybe it was the American influence that causes the blood to be sucked dry from you so early. Nothing was wrong with me, really. My bones ached. I needed rest. Nothing México couldn't cure.

She lies down, covers herself with the rebozo.
MARISA *enters, barefoot.*

MARISA: For the whole summer, I watched the people fly in bright-colored sails over the Califas sea, waiting for her. Red- and gold- and blue-striped wings blazing the sky. Lifting off the sandy cliffs, dangling gringo legs. Always imagined myself up there in their place, flying for real. Never ever coming back down to earth, just leaving my body behind. *(Pause.)* One morning I awoke to find a bird dead on the beach. I knew it wasn't a rock because it was light enough to roll with the tide . . . I saw this from a distance. Later that day, they found a woman dead there at the very same spot, I swear. Una viejita. *(A soft grey light washes over* AMALIA.*)* A crowd gathered 'round her as a young man in a blue swimsuit tried to spoon the sand from her throat with his finger. Putting his breath to her was too late. She was so very very grey and wet, como la arena . . . y una mexicana, I could tell by her housedress. How did she drown? Then I remembered what Amalia had told me about bad omens. *(A sudden ominous tambor,* AMALIA *bolts up in bed.)* I stopped going. I stopped waiting.

MARISA *exits.*

AMALIA: When I learned of Alejandro's death, I died too. I just started bleeding and the blood wouldn't stop, not until his ghost had passed through me or was born in me. I don't know which. That Mexican morning I had awakened to find the hotel sheets red with blood. It had come out in torrents and thick clots that looked like a fetus. But I was not pregnant, my tubes

had been tied for years. Yet, lying there in the cool dampness of my own blood, I felt my womanhood leave me. And it was Alejandro being born in me. Does this make sense? I can't say exactly how I knew this, except . . . again . . . for the smell, the unmistakable smell of the man, as if we had just made love. And coming from my mouth was *his* voice . . . "¡Ay mi Marisa! ¡Te deseo! ¡Te deseo!" *(Her eyes search for Marisa.)* Marisa!
Lights rise. Morning in Mexico City. AMALIA *gets up from the bed.*

AMALIA: It is barely dawn and the sun has already entered my hotel window. Afuera los hombres are already at work tearing up the Mexican earth with their steel claws. *(Indigenous music.)* Pero La Tierra is not as passive as they think. "Regresaré," Ella nos recuerda. "Regresaré," nos promete. When they "discovered" El Templo Mayor beneath the walls of this city, they had not realized that is was She who discovered them. Nothing remains buried forever. Not even memory. Especially not memory.
Fade out.

SCENE TEN: *The indigenous music blends into Chicano urban sounds.* MARISA *enters. Her posture is noticeably more guarded than in the previous scene. The music fades. There is a pause as* MARISA *scans the faces of* THE PEOPLE.

MARISA: Got raped once. When I was a kid. Taken me a long time to say that was exactly what happened, but that was exactly what happened. Makes you more aware than ever that you are one hunerd percent female, just in case you had any doubts. One hunerd percent female whether you act it . . . or like it . . . or not. Y'see, I never ever really let myself think about it, the possibility of rape, even after it happened. Not like other girls, I didn't walk down the street like there were men lurking everywhere, every corner, to devour me. Yeah, the street was a war zone, but for different rea-

sons, . . . for muggers, mexicanos sucking their damn lips at you, gringo stupidity, drunks like old garbage sacks thrown around the street, and the rape of other women and the people I loved. They weren't safe and I worried each time they left the house . . . but never, never me. I guess I never wanted to believe I was raped. If someone took me that bad, I wouldn't really want to think I was took, you follow me? But the truth is . . .

CORKY *(entering):* I was took.
MARISA *crosses to the platform.* CORKY *"stakes out the territory."*

CORKY: I was about twelve years old
I was still going to cath-lic school then
'n' we wore those stupid checkered jumpers
they looked purty shitty on the seventh 'n' eighth grade girls
cuz here we was getting chi-chis 'n' all
'n' still trying to shove 'em into the tops of these play suits
I wasn't too big pero the big girls looked terrible!

anyway in the seventh grade I was trying to mend my ways
so would hang after school 'n' try to be helpful 'n' all to the nuns
I guess cuz my cousin Norma got straight A's
'n' was taking me into her bed by then
so I figured . . . that was the way to go
she'd get really pissed when I fucked up in school
threatened to "take it away" tú saves if I dint behave
can you get to that? ¡Qué fría! ¿no?

anyway Norma was the only one I ever tole
about the janitor doing it to me
'n' then she took it away for good
I'd still like to whip her butt for that
her 'n' her goddamn hubby 'n' kids now   shi-it
puros gabachos, little blond-haired blue-eyed things
the oldest is a little joto if you ask me sure
he's barely four years old but you can already tell

the way he goes around primping all over the
place
pleases me to no end
what goes around comes around
"Jason" they call him
no, not "Ha-són" pero "Jay-sun"
puro gringo.

anyway so I was walking by Sister Mary
Dominic's classroom
"the Hawk" we called her cuz she had a nose
'n' attitude like one
when this man a mexicano motions to me to
come on inside
"Ven p'aca," he says
I dint recognize him but the parish was always
hiring
mexicanos to work around the grounds 'n' stuff
I guess cuz they dint need to know English
'n' the priests dint need to pay 'em much
they'd do it "por Dios" tú sabes
so he asks me, "Señorita, ¿hablas español?"
muy polite y todo
'n' I answer, "Sí poquito," which I always say
to strangers
cuz I dunno how much they're gonna expect
outta me
"Ven p'aca," he says otra vez
'n' I do outta respect for my primo Enrique
cuz he looks a lot like him but somet'ing was
funny
his Spanish   I couldn't quite make it out cuz
he mumbled a lot
which made me feel kina bad about myself tú
sabes
that I was Mexican too but couldn't understand
him that good

he's trying to fix this drawer that's loose in the
Hawk's desk
I knew already about the drawer
cuz she was always bitchin' n' moanin'
about it getting stuck cuz the bottom kept
falling out
so he tells me he needs someone to hold the
bottom of the drawer up
so he can screw the sides in

(She goes to the "desk," demonstrates.)
so standing to the side I lean over
and hold the drawer in place así
then he says all frustrated-like, "No, así, así."
it turns out he wants me to stand in front of the
drawer
with my hands holding each side up así
*(She stands with her legs apart, her pelvis
pressed up against the edge of the "desk.")*
'n' believe it or not this cabrón sits behind me
on the floor
'n' reaches his arm up between my legs
that I'm straining to keep closed
even though he keeps saying all business-like,
"Abrete más por favor las piernas. Abretelas
un poco más."
'n' like a pendeja I do
(She grips the edge of the "desk.")
I feel my face getting hotter
'n' I can kina feel him jiggling the drawer
pressed up against me down there
I'm staring straight ahead don' wanna look at
what's happening
then worry how someone would see us like this
this guy's arm up between my legs
'n' then it begins to kina brush past the inside
of my thigh
I can feel the hair   that first
then the heat of his skin
(Almost tenderly.) the skin is so soft I hafta admit
young kina like a girl's like Norma's shoulder
I try to think about Norma 'n' her shoulders
to kina pass the time hoping to hurry things
along
while he keeps saying, "Casi termino. Casi termino."
'n' I keep saying back, "Señor me tengo que ir,
mi mamá me espera"
still all polite como mensa!
until finally I feel the screwdriver by my leg
like ice
then suddenly the tip of it   it feels like to me
is against the cotton of my chones

"Don't move," he tells me. In English. His
accent gone. 'n' I don'

from then on all I see in my mind's eye . . .
were my eyes shut?
is this screwdriver he's got in his sweaty palm
yellow   glass   handle
shiny metal
the kind my father useta use to fix things
    around the house
remembered how I'd help him how he'd take
    me on his jobs with him
'n' I kept getting him confused in mind
this man 'n' his arm with my father
kept imagining he was my father returned
    come back
the arm was so soft but this other thing . . .
hielo   hielo   ice!
I wanted to cry, "¡Papi! ¡Papi!"
'n' then I started crying for real
cuz I knew I musta done somet'ing real wrong
to get myself in this mess

I figure he's gonna shove the damn thing up me
he's trying to get my chones down, "Por favor
    señor please don'."
but I can hear my voice through my own ears
not from the inside out but the other way
    around
'n' I know I'm not fighting this one
I know I don' even sound convinced
"¿Dónde 'stás, Papi? ¿Dónde 'stás?"
'n' finally I hear the man answering, "Aquí
estoy.
    Soy tu papá."
'n' this gives me permission to go 'head to not
    hafta fight

by the time he gets my chones down to my
    knees
I suddenly feel like I'm floating in the air
my thing kina attached to no body
flapping in the wind like a bird a wounded bird
I'm relieved when I hear the metal drop to the
    floor
only worry *who will see me doing this?*
(Gritting her teeth.) get-this-over-with-get-this
    over-with
'n' he does gracias a dios bringin me down to
    earth

linoleum floor   cold
the smell of wax
polish

y ya 'stoy lista for what long ago waited for me
there is no surprise
'n' I open my legs wide wide open
for the angry animal that springs outta the
    opening in his pants
'n' all I wanna do is have it over so I can go
    back to being myself
'n' a kid again

then he hit me with it
into what was supposed to be a hole
(Tenderly.) that I remembered had to be
cuz Norma had found it once wet 'n' forbidden
'n' showed me too how wide 'n' deep like a
    cueva hers got
when she wanted it to only with me she said
MARISA: Only with you, Corky.
CORKY: but with this one there was no hole he
    had to make it
'n' I saw myself down there like a face with no
    opening
a face with no features
no eyes no nose no mouth
only little lines where they shoulda been
so I dint cry
I never cried as he shoved the thing
into what was supposed to be a mouth
with no teeth
with no hate
with no voice
only a hole
a hole!

He made me a hole!
MARISA approaches, wraps a rebozo around
CORKY'S *shoulders, holds her.*
MARISA: I don't regret it. I don't regret nuthin'.
He only convinced me of my own name. From
an early age you learn to live with it, being a
woman. I just got a head start over some. And
then, years later, after I got to be with some
other men, I admired how their things had no
opening . . . only a tiny tiny pinhole dot to
pee from, to come from. I thought . . . how

lucky they were, that they could release all that stuff, all that pent-up shit from the day, through a hole that *nobody* could get into.

SCENE ELEVEN: MARISA *and* CORKY *remain on stage. The lighting slowly shifts. Indigenous music, lively tambores.* AMALIA *enters wearing a rebozo. She covers* MARISA'S *shoulders with one as well. All three, now in rebozos, have become indias. They enter a dream.* CORKY *comes downstage, kneels. She begins making tortillas, slapping her hands together.* MARISA *and* AMALIA *join her on each side, forming a half circle. They, too, clap tortillas to the rhythm of the tambores. They are very happy. The rhythm quickens, accelerates.*

MARISA *and* AMALIA *slowly bend toward each other, their faces crossing in front of* CORKY'S. *They kiss. Suddenly the scene darkens, the drumming becomes sinister, the clapping frantic. Thunder. Lightning. The gods have been angered. The three scatter. The stage is a maze of colliding lights, searching out the women.* CORKY *has disappeared.* AMALIA *cowers beneath her rebozo.* MARISA *appears upstage in shadow. She is out of breath. She is being hunted, her arms spread, her body pressed up against an invisible wall.*

MARISA: Amalia, let me in! ¡Abre la puerta! ¡Vienen a agarrarme!
AMALIA wrestles in bed with her "pesadilla."

MARISA: ¡No me dejes, Amalia! ¡No me dejes sola! Let me in!
AMALIA can't bear to hear her, covers her ears.

MARISA: Amalia! . . . Amalia! . . . Let . . . me . . . in!
The lights fade out and rise again. CORKY *can be seen in shadow standing where* MARISA *had been seconds before. She holds a beer bottle in the air above her head. She comes down with it, like a weapon. The sound of glass breaking. Black out.*

AMALIA *(in the darkness):*   ¿Quién es? ¿Quién es? Who is it? ¿Eres tú, Che?
Lights rise. AMALIA *is sitting up in bed. There is an opened, unpacked suitcase on the floor and a*

photo *of a man with a candle next to it on the table.* MARISA *appears in the doorway. She is very drunk, almost in a stupor.*

AMALIA: Marisa.

MARISA: Where the . . . where have you been? *(*AMALIA *gets out of bed, puts on a robe.)*

AMALIA: What are you doing here?

MARISA *(menacingly):*   I'm asking you a question.

AMALIA: Don't come near me.

MARISA: I said, where have you been?

AMALIA: What do you want?

MARISA: I wanna know . . . *(She stalks* AMALIA.*)* I wanna know where you been.

AMALIA: You're drunk.

MARISA: Good observation, maestra. Now are you gonna answer me?

AMALIA: Stay away from me. Don't touch me.

MARISA: I'm not gonna touch you. No, no. These hands? No, no, Doña Amalia . . . us jotas learn to keep our hands to ourselves.

AMALIA: ¡Adió!

MARISA: Answer me!

AMALIA: You know where I was.

MARISA: I waited for you. I waited three goddamn months! Count them! June, July—

AMALIA: I can count.

MARISA: Well, jus' cuz it aint all hanging out on the outside don' mean I don' feel nuthin'. What did you expect from me anyway?

AMALIA: Well, not this.

MARISA: Well, honey, this is what you got. Aint I a purty picture?

AMALIA: Estás borracha. Estás loca.

MARISA: Bueno, 'stoy loca. Tal vez quieres que te hable en español, eh? A lo mejor you could understand me then. I'm sorry, y'know, us pochas don' speak it as purty as you do.

AMALIA: What are you talking about?

MARISA: I'm talking about going to the goddamn mailbox every day, thinking every llamadita would be you. "Ven, Chatita. Meet me in México." You lied to me.

AMALIA: I didn't lie.

MARISA: No?

AMALIA: No. *(She turns away.)*

MARISA: What then?

There is a pause.

MARISA: Look at you. You don' got nuthin' to say to me. You don' feel a thing.

AMALIA: It's three o'clock in the morning, what am I supposed to feel?

MARISA *(after a beat):* Nuthin'. You're supposed to feel nuthin'.

AMALIA: I'm going to get you some coffee.

MARISA: I don' want no coffee! You went back to him, didn't you?

AMALIA: Ay, Marisa, por favor no empieces.

MARISA *(seeing the photo):* What is this? A little altar we have for the man? *(She picks it up.)*

AMALIA: Don't.

MARISA: ¡Vela y todo! What is he, a saint now?

AMALIA: ¡Déjalo!

MARISA: You're still in love with him, aren't you?

AMALIA: Put it down, te digo.

MARISA *(approaching):* I'm asking you a question.

AMALIA: Stay away from me.

MARISA: Answer me! *(Grabs* AMALIA.*):* Are you in love with him or not?

AMALIA: ¡Déjame

MARISA *(shaking her):* Did you sleep with him?

AMALIA: No! Stop it!

MARISA: Did you? Tell me the truth!

AMALIA: No! ¡Déjame! *(They struggle. The picture falls to the floor.* AMALIA *breaks* MARISA'S *hold.)* I'm not an animal! What gives you the right to come in here like this? Do you think you're the only person in the world who's ever been left waiting?

MARISA: What was I supposed to think . . . that you were dead? That you were dead or you were with him, those were my two choices.

AMALIA *(bitterly):* He's the one who's dead.

MARISA *(after a pause):* What?

AMALIA: He's dead.

AMALIA *slowly walks over to the picture, picks it up, replaces it by the candle. She sits down on the bed, her face impassive.*

AMALIA *(after a pause):* When I got the news, I was in a hotel in Mexico City. I didn't stop to think about it, I took a bus right away to la Costa. Then I hired a boy to give me a lift in a truck. When I got to the river, I knew where to go. The exact spot. The place under the tamarindo where we used to make love. And for hours until dark I sat there by la orilla as I imagined he had that last time.

MARISA: He drowned.

AMALIA: He drowned himself.

MARISA *(going to her):* It's not your fault, Amalia.

AMALIA *(after a pause):* Whose face do you think he saw in the belly of that river moments before it swallowed him?

MARISA: It's not your fault. *(There is a long silence.* MARISA *makes a gesture to touch* AMALIA, *but is unable to.)* I shouldn't have come. I'm sorry.

AMALIA: No, stay. Stay and keep an old woman company.

MARISA: I'll come back tomorrow . . . fix the window. *(She starts to exit.)*

AMALIA: Soñé contigo.

MARISA: You did?

AMALIA: Last night. *(Pause.)* I dreamed we were indias. In our village, some terrible taboo had been broken. There was thunder and lightning. I am crouched down in terror, unable to move when I realize it is *you* who have gone against the code of our people. But I was not afraid of being punished. I did not fear that los dioses would enact their wrath against el pueblo for the breaking of the taboo. It was merely that the taboo *could* be broken. And if this law nearly transcribed in blood could go, then what else? What *was* there to hold to? What immutable truths were left? *(Pause. She turns to* MARISA.*)* I never wanted you the way I wanted a man. With a man, I just would have left him. Punto. *(Pause.)* Like I left Alejandro.

The lights slowly fade to black.

SCENE TWELVE: MARISA *sits on the platform.* AMALIA'S *rebozo has been left there.*

MARISA: I must admit I wanted to save her. That's probably the whole truth of the story. And the problem is . . . sometimes I actually believed I could, and *sometimes* she did too.

She was like no woman I had ever had. I think it was in the quality of her skin. Some people, you know, their skin is like a covering. They're supposed to be showing you something when the clothes fall into a heap around your four ankles, but nothing is lost, y'know what I mean? They jus' don' give up nuthin'. Pero Amalia . . . ¡Híjole!

She picks up AMALIA'S *rebozo, fingers it.*

She was never fully naked in front of me, always had to keep some piece of clothing on, a shirt or something always wrapped up around her throat, her arms all outta it and flying. What she did reveal, though, each item of clothing removed was a gift, I swear, a small offering, a suggestion of all that could be lost and found in our making love together. It was like she was saying to me, "I'll lay down my underslip, ¿Y tú? ¿Qué me vas a dar?" And I'd give her the palm of my hand to warm the spot she had just exposed. Everything was a risk. Everything took time. Was slow and deliberate.

I'll never forget after the first time we made love, I was feeling muy orgullosa y todo, like a good lover, and she says to me.

AMALIA (*voice-over, memory*): You make love to me like worship.

MARISA: And I nearly died, it was so powerful what she was saying. And I wanted to answer, "Sí, la mujer es mi religion." If only sex coulda saved us.

Y'know, sometimes when me and her were in the middle of it, making love, I'd look up at her face, kinda grey from being indoors so much with all those books of hers, and I'd see it change, turn this real deep color of brown and olive, like she was cooking inside. Tan. Kind. Very very very kind to me, to herself, to the pinche planet . . . and I'd watch it move from outside the house where that crazy espíritu of hers had been out makin' tracks. I'd watch it come inside, through the door, watch it travel all through her own private miseries and settle itself, finally, right there in the room with us. This bed. This fucking dreary season. This cement city. With us. With me. No part of her begging to have it over . . . forget. And I could feel all the parts of her move into operation. Waiting. Held. Suspended. Praying for me to put my tongue to her and I knew and she knew we would find her . . . como fuego. And just as I pressed my mouth to her, I'd think . . . *I could save your life.*

(*Coming downstage.*) It's not often you get to see people this way in all their pus and glory and still love them. It makes you feel so good, like your hands are weapons of war. And as they move up into el corazón de esta mujer, you are making her body remember, it didn't have to be that hurt. ¿Me entiendes? It was not natural or right that she got beat down so damn hard, and that all those crimes had nothing to do with the girl she once was two, three, four decades ago.

Pause. Music rises softly in the background.

MARISA: It's like making familia from scratch, each time all over again . . .
with strangers, if I must.
If I must, I will.

I am preparing myself for the worst
so I cling to her in my heart
my daydream with pencil in my mouth

when I put my fingers
to my own forgotten places.
The lights gradually fade out. Music.

THE END

SELECT BIBLIOGRAPHY

EDITORIAL NOTE

The following bibliography is intended as a preliminary resource for students interested in further reading. For each writer listed in the *"Individual Authors"* section—and only those dramatists represented in this book have been included—we have, in most cases, cited a primary edition or two, a biographical or introductory study, and a small number of critical works dedicated either largely or solely to the author's oeuvre.

General

HISTORY AND REFERENCE

Atkinson, Brooks. *Broadway*. New York: Macmillan, 1970.

Bernheim, Alfred. *The Business of the American Theatre: An Economic History of the American Theatre, 1750–1932*. 1932. Rpt. New York: Benjamin Blom, 1964.

Bordman, Gerald. *American Musical Comedy: From Adonis to Dreamgirls*. New York: Oxford University Press, 1982.

———. *American Musical Theatre: A Chronicle*. New York: Oxford University Press, 1978.

———. *The American Theatre: A Chronicle of Comedy and Drama, 1869–1914*. New York: Oxford University Press, 1994.

———. *The Oxford Companion to American Theatre*. New York: Oxford University Press, 1984.

Dorman, James H. *Theatre in the Antebellum South, 1815–1861*. Chapel Hill: University of North Carolina Press, 1967.

Goldberg, RuthLee. *Performance Art: From Futurism to the Present*. Rev. ed. New York: Abrams, 1988.

Hewitt, Barnard. *Theatre U.S.A., 1665 to 1957*. New York: McGraw-Hill, 1959.

Huntsman, Jeffrey F. "Native American Theatre." *Ethnic Theatre in the United States*. Ed. Maxine Schwartz Seller. Westport, CT: Greenwood Press, 1983. 355–385.

Krutch, Joseph Wood. *The American Drama Since 1918: An Informal History*. New York: George Braziller, 1957.

Meserve, Walter J. *An Emerging Entertainment: The Drama of the American People to 1828*. Bloomington: Indiana University Press, 1977.

———. *An Outline History of American Drama*. Totowa, NJ: Littlefield, Adams, 1970.

Miller, Jordan Y., and Winifred L. Frazer. *American Drama Between the Wars: A Critical History*. Boston: G. K. Hall, 1991.

Mordden, Eric. *The American Theatre*. New York: Oxford University Press, 1981.

Moses, Montrose J., and John Mason Brown, eds. *The American Theatre as Seen by Its Critics, 1752–1934*. New York: Norton, 1934.

Quinn, Arthur Hobson. *A History of the American Drama from the Beginning to the Civil War*. New York: Harper & Brothers, 1923.

———. *A History of the American Drama from the Civil War to the Present*. Rev. ed. 2 vols. New York: Appleton-Century-Crofts, 1936.

Richardson, Gary A. *American Drama From the Colonial Period Through World War I: A Critical History*. New York: Twayne, 1993.

Roth, Moira, ed. *The Amazing Decade: Women and Performance Art in America 1970–1980*. Los Angeles: Astro Artz, 1983.

Seller, Maxine Schwartz, ed. *Ethnic Theatre in the United States*. Westport, CT: Greenwood Press, 1983.

Weales, Gerald. *American Drama Since World War II*. New York: Harcourt, Brace & World, 1962.

Wilmeth, Don B., and Tice Miller, eds. *The Cambridge Guide to American Theatre*. Cambridge: Cambridge University Press, 1993.

ANTHOLOGIES

Berson, Misha, ed. *Between Worlds: Contemporary Asian-American Plays*. New York: Theatre Communications Group, 1990.

Branch, William B., ed. *Black Thunder: An Anthology of Contemporary African American Drama*. New York: Mentor Books, 1992.

Champagne, Lenora, ed. *Out from Under: Texts by Women Performance Artists.* New York: Theatre Communications Group, 1990.

Clark, Barrett H., gen. ed. *America's Lost Plays.* 20 vols. Princeton: Princeton University Press, 1940–1942.

Feingold, Michael, ed. *Grove New American Theatre.* New York: Grove Press, 1993.

Feyder, Linda, ed. *Shattering the Myth: Plays by Hispanic Women.* Houston: Arte Publico Press, 1992.

Geiogamah, Hanay. *New Native American Drama: Three Plays.* Norman: University of Oklahoma Press, 1980.

Hatch, James V., ed. *Black Theater, U.S.A.: Forty-Five Plays by Black Americans, 1847–1974.* New York: The Free Press, 1974.

Houston, Velina Hasu, ed. *The Politics of Life: Four Plays by Asian-American Women.* Philadelphia: Temple University Press, 1993.

Huerta, Jorge, ed. *Necessary Theatre: Six Plays About the Chicano Experience.* Houston: Arte Publico Press, 1989.

Gould, Christopher, ed. *Anti-Naturalism: Six Full-Length Contemporary Plays.* New York: Broadway Play Publishing, 1989.

Jacobus, Lee A., ed. *The Longman Anthology of American Drama.* New York: Longman, 1982.

Mahone, Sydné, ed. *Moon Marked & Touched by Sun: Plays by African-American Women.* New York: Theatre Communications Group, 1994.

Mills, Julia, ed. *The Women's Project: Seven New Plays by Women.* New York: Performing Arts Journal Publications and the American Place Theatre, 1980.

Moody, Richard, ed. *Dramas from the American Theatre, 1762–1909.* Cleveland: World Publishing Company, 1966.

Osborn, M. Elizabeth, ed. *The Way We Live Now: American Plays and the AIDS Crisis.* New York: Theatre Communications Group, 1990.

Poland, Albert, and Bruce Mailman, eds. *The Off, Off Broadway Book: The Plays, People, Theatre.* Indianapolis: Bobbs-Merrill, 1972.

Richardson, Willis, ed. *Plays and Pageants from The Life of the Negro.* 1930. Rpt. Jackson: University of Mississippi Press, 1993.

CRITICISM AND COMMENTARY

Abel, Lionel. *Metatheatre: A New View of Dramatic Form.* New York: Hill & Wang, 1963.

Adler, Thomas P. *Mirror on the Stage: The Pulitzer Plays as an Approach to American Drama.* West Lafayette, IN: Purdue University Press, 1987.

Auslander, Philip. *Presence and Resistance: Postmodernism and Cultural Politics in Contemporary American Performance.* Ann Arbor: University of Michigan Press, 1992.

Beck, Julian. *The Life of the Theatre.* San Francisco: City Lights, 1972.

Bigsby, C. W. E. *A Critical Introduction to Twentieth-Century American Drama.* 3 vols. Cambridge: Cambridge University Press, 1984.

———. *Modern American Drama, 1945–1990.* Cambridge: Cambridge University Press, 1992.

Blau, Herbert. *The Eye of Prey: Subversions of the Postmodern.* Bloomington: Indiana University Press, 1987.

Brook, Peter. *The Empty Space.* New York: Atheneum, 1978.

Brown, Janet. *Taking Center Stage: Feminism in Contemporary U.S. Drama.* Metuchen, NJ: Scarecrow Press, 1991.

Brustein, Robert. *Reimagining American Theatre.* New York: Hill & Wang, 1991.

Case, Sue-Ellen. *Feminism and Theatre.* New York: Methuen, 1988.

———. *Performing Feminisms: Feminist Critical Theory and Theatre.* Baltimore: Johns Hopkins University Press, 1990.

Chinoy, Helen Krich, and Linda Walsh Jenkins, eds. *Women in American Theatre.* Rev. ed. New York: Theatre Communications Group, 1987.

Clum, John M. *Acting Gay: Male Homosexuality in Modern American Drama.* New York: Columbia University Press, 1992.

Cohn, Ruby. *Dialogue in American Drama.* Bloomington: Indiana University Press, 1971.

Curtin, Kaier. *"We Can Always Call Them Bulgarians": The Emergence of Lesbians and Gay Men on the American Stage.* Boston: Alyson, 1987.

Debusscher, Gilbert, and Henry I. Schey, eds. *New Essays on American Drama.* Amsterdam/Atlanta: Rodopi, 1989.

de Jongh, Nicholas. *Not in Front of the Audience: Homosexuality on Stage.* London: Routledge, 1992.

Demastes, William W. *Beyond Naturalism: A New Realism in American Theatre.* Westport, CT: Greenwood, 1988.

Dolan, Jill. *The Feminist Spectator as Critic.* Ann Arbor: University of Michigan Press, 1988.

————. *Presence and Desire: Essays on Gender, Sexuality, Performance.* Ann Arbor: University of Michigan Press, 1993.

Downer, Alan S., ed. *American Drama and Its Critics.* Chicago: University of Chicago Press, 1965.

Fisher, Judith L., and Stephen Watt, eds. *When They Weren't Doing Shakespeare: Essays on Nineteenth-Century British and American Theatre.* Athens: University of Georgia Press, 1989.

Geis, Deborah R. *Postmodern Theatric(k)s: Monologue in Contemporary American Drama.* Ann Arbor: University of Michigan Press, 1993.

Grimsted, David. *Melodrama Unveiled: American Theatre and Culture, 1800–1850.* Chicago: University of Chicago Press, 1968.

Hart, Lynda, ed. *Making a Spectacle: Feminist Essays on Contemporary Women's Theatre.* Ann Arbor: University of Michigan Press, 1989.

Hart, Lynda, and Peggy Phelan, eds. *Acting Out: Feminist Performances.* Ann Arbor: University of Michigan Press, 1993.

Hay, Samuel A. *African-American Theatre: A Historical and Critical Analysis.* New York: Cambridge University Press, 1994.

Heilman, Robert Bechtold. *The Iceman, the Arsonist, and the Troubled Agent: Tragedy and Melodrama on the Modern Stage.* Seattle: University of Washington Press, 1973.

Mason, Jeffrey D. *Melodrama and the Myth of America.* Bloomington: Indiana University Press, 1993.

McConachie, Bruce A. *Melodramatic Formations.* Iowa City: University of Iowa Press, 1992.

Moy, James S. *Marginal Sights: Staging the Chinese in America.* Iowa City: University of Iowa Press, 1993.

Murphy, Brenda. *American Realism and American Drama, 1880–1940.* Cambridge: Cambridge University Press, 1987.

Pavis, Patrice. *Theatre at the Crossroads of Culture.* Trans. Loren Kruger. New York: Routledge, 1992.

Rabkin, Gerald. *Drama and Commitment: Politics in the American Theatre of the 30's.* Bloomington: Indiana University Press, 1964.

Reinelt, Janelle G., and Joseph R. Roach, eds. *Critical Theory and Performance.* Ann Arbor: University of Michigan Press, 1992.

Roudané, Matthew C., ed. *Public Issues, Private Tensions: Contemporary American Drama.* New York: AMS Press, 1993.

Savran, David. *In Their Own Words: Contemporary American Playwrights.* New York: Theatre Communications Group, 1988.

Schroeder, Patricia. *The Presence of the Past in Modern American Drama.* Rutherford, NJ: Fairleigh Dickinson University Press, 1989.

Schechner, Richard. *The End of Humanism: Writings on Performance.* New York: Performing Arts Journal Publications, 1982.

Schlueter, June, ed. *Modern American Drama: The Female Canon.* Rutherford, NJ: Fairleigh Dickinson University Press, 1990.

Smiley, Sam. *The Drama of Attack: Didactic Plays of the American Depression.* Columbia: University of Missouri Press, 1972.

Szondi, Peter. *Theory of the Modern Drama,* trans. Michael Hays. Minneapolis: University of Minnesota Press, 1987.

Individual Authors

EDWARD ALBEE

Albee, Edward. *Plays.* 4 vols. New York: Coward, McCann and Geoghegan, 1981–1982.

————. "Which Theatre Is the Absurd One?" *New York Times Magazine,* 25 February 1962: 30+.

Amacher, Richard E. *Edward Albee.* Rev. ed. Boston: Twayne, 1982.

Baxandall, Lee. "The Theatre of Edward Albee." *Tulane Drama Review* 9 (Summer 1965): 19–40.

Bigsby, C. W. E. *A Critical Introduction to Twentieth-Century American Drama.* Volume Two: *Tennessee Williams, Arthur Miller, Edward Albee.* Cambridge: Cambridge University Press, 1984.

Kolin, Philip C., ed. *Conversations with Edward Albee.* Jackson: University of Mississippi Press, 1988.

McCarthy, Gerry. *Edward Albee.* London: Macmillan, 1987.

"On Edward Albee." Special issue of *American Drama.* Volume 2, Spring 1993.

Paolucci, Anne. *From Tension to Tonic: The Plays of Edward Albee.* Carbondale: Southern Illinois Press, 1972.

Rutenberg, Michael E. *Edward Albee: Playwright in Protest.* New York: Discuss/Avon, 1970.

AMIRI BARAKA (LEROI JONES)

Baraka, Amiri. *The Autobiography of LeRoi Jones/Amiri Baraka.* New York: Freundlich Books, 1984.

Bentson, Kimberly W., ed. *Imamu Amiri Baraka (LeRoi Jones): A Collection of Critical Essays.* Englewood Cliffs, NJ: Prentice-Hall, 1978.

———. *Baraka: The Renegade and the Mask.* New Haven: Yale University Press, 1976.

Brown, Lloyd W. *Amiri Baraka.* Boston: Twayne, 1980.

Fox, Robert Elliot. *Conscientious Sorcerers: The Black Post-Modernist Fiction of LeRoi Jones/Amiri Baraka, Ishmael Reed, and Samuel R. Delany.* New York: Greenwood Press, 1987.

Gwynne, James B., ed. *Amiri Baraka: The Kaleidoscopic Torch.* New York: Steppingstones Press, 1985.

Harris, William J., ed. *The LeRoi Jones/Amiri Baraka Reader.* New York: Thunder's Mouth Press, 1991.

Hudson, Theodore. *From LeRoi Jones to Amiri Baraka: The Literary Works.* Durham, NC: Duke University Press, 1973.

Sollors, Werner. *Amiri Baraka/LeRoi Jones: The Quest for a "Populist Modernism."* New York: Columbia University Press, 1978.

PHILIP BARRY

Barry, Philip. *States of Grace: Eight Plays.* New York: Harcourt Brace Jovanovich, 1975.

Carmer, Carl. "Philip Barry." *Theatre Arts Monthly* (November 1929): 819–826.

Krutch, Joseph Wood. *The American Drama Since 1918: An Informal History.* New York: George Braziller, 1957.

Roppolo, Joseph Patrick. *Philip Barry.* New York: Twayne, 1965.

DION BOUCICAULT

Boucicault, Dion. "Theatres, Halls, and Audiences." *The North American Review* 149 (October 1889): 425–436.

Fawkes, Richard. *Dion Boucicault: A Biography.* London: Quartet Books, 1979.

Hogan, Robert. *Dion Boucicault.* New York: Twayne, 1969.

Krause, David. "Introduction." *The Dolmen Boucicault.* Dublin: Dolmen, 1964. 9–47.

Molin, Sven Eric, and Robin Goodefellowe. *Dion Boucicault: The Shaughraun.* Newark, DE: Proscenium, 1979.

Richardson, Gary A. "Boucicault's *The Octoroon* and American Law." *Theatre Journal* 34 (1982): 155–164.

Roach, Joseph R. "Slave Spectacles and Tragic Octoroons: A Cultural Geneaology of Antebellum Performance." *Theatre Survey* 33 (1992): 167–187.

Walsh, Townsend. *The Career of Dion Boucicault.* New York: The Dunlap Society, 1915.

RACHEL CROTHERS

Abramson, Doris. "Rachel Crothers: Broadway Feminist." *Modern American Drama: The Female Canon.* Ed. June Schleuter. London and Toronto: Associated University Presses, 1990. 55–65.

Friedman, Sharon. "Feminism as Theme in Twentieth-Century American Women's Drama." *American Studies* 25 (1984): 69–89.

Gottlieb, Lois C. *Rachel Crothers.* Boston: Twayne, 1979.

Sutherland, Cynthia. "American Women Playwrights as Mediators of the 'Woman Problem.'" *Modern Drama* 21 (1978): 319–336.

AUGUSTIN DALY

Daly, Augustin. *Plays.* Eds. Don B. Wilmeth and Rosemary Cullen. Cambridge: Cambridge University Press, 1984.

Daly, Joseph Francis. *The Life of Augustin Daly.* New York: Macmillan, 1917.

Felheim, Marvin. *The Theatre of Augustin Daly.* Cambridge, MA: Harvard University Press, 1956.

KAREN FINLEY

Carr, C. "Unspeakable Practices, Unnatural Acts: The Taboo Art of Karen Finley." Rpt. in *Acting Out: Feminist Performances.* Eds. Lynda Hart and Peggy

Phelan. Ann Arbor: University of Michigan Press, 1993. 141–151.

Finley, Karen. *Shock Treatment*. San Francisco: City Lights Books, 1990.

———. *The Theory of Total Blame. Grove New American Theatre*. Ed. Michael Feingold. New York: Grove Press, 1993. 217–257.

Forte, Jeanie. "Women's Performance Art: Feminism and Postmodernism." *Theatre Journal* 40 (1988): 217–235.

Pramaggiore, Maria T. "Resisting/Performing/Femininity: Words, Flesh, and Feminism in Karen Finley's *The Constant State of Desire*." *Theatre Journal* 44 (1992): 269–290.

Schechner, Richard. "Karen Finley: A Constant State of Becoming." *TDR: The Drama Review* 33 (1988): 152–158.

SUSAN GLASPELL

Ben-Zvi, Linda. "Susan Glaspell's Contributions to Contemporary Women Playwrights." *Feminine Focus: The New Women Playwrights*. Ed. Enoch Brater. New York: Oxford University Press, 1989. 147–166.

Dymkowsky, Christine. "On the Edge: The Plays of Susan Glaspell." *Modern Drama* 31 (1988): 91–105.

Makowsky, Veronica. *Susan Glaspell's Century of American Women: A Critical Interpretation of Her Work*. New York: Oxford University Press, 1993.

Stein, Karen F. "The Women's World of Glaspell's *Trifles*." *Women in American Theatre*. Eds. Helen Krich Chinoy and Linda Walsh Jenkins. Rev. ed. New York: Theatre Communications Group, 1987, 253–256.

Waterman, Arthur E. *Susan Glaspell*. New York: Twayne, 1966.

LILLIAN HELLMAN

Hellman, Lillian. *The Collected Plays*. Boston: Little, Brown, 1972.

———. *Conversations with Lillian Hellman*. Jackson: University Press of Mississippi, 1986.

———. *Pentimento*. New York: NAL, 1973.

———. *An Unfinished Woman: A Memoir*. Boston: Little, Brown, 1969.

Moody, Richard. *Lillian Hellman, Playwright*. New York: Pegasus, 1972.

Wright, William. *Lillian Hellman: The Image, The Woman*. New York: Simon and Schuster, 1986.

JAMES A. HERNE

Bucks, Dorothy S., and A.H. Nethercot. "Ibsen and Herne's *Margaret Fleming*: A Study of the Early Ibsen Movement in America." *American Literature* 17 (1946): 311–333.

Edwards, Herbert J., and Julie A. Herne. *James A. Herne: The Rise of Realism in the American Drama*. Orono: University of Maine Press, 1964.

Herne, James A. "Art for Truth's Sake in the Drama." *Arena* 17 (1897): 361–370. Rpt. *American Drama and Its Critics*. Ed. Alan S. Downer. Chicago: University of Chicago Press, 1965. 1–9.

Howells, William Dean. "Editor's Study." *Harper's Monthly*, August 1891: 478.

Perry, John. *James A. Herne: The American Ibsen*. Chicago: Nelson-Hall, 1978.

BRONSON HOWARD

Bloomfield, Maxwell. "Mirror for Businessmen: Bronson Howard's Melodramas, 1870–1890." *Mid-Continent American Studies Journal* 5 (1964): 38–49.

Dithmar, Edward A. Rev. of *Shenandoah* by Bronson Howard. *New York Times*, 10 September 1889: 4.

———. Rev. of *Shenandoah* by Bronson Howard. *New York Times* 15 September 1889: 3.

Howard, Bronson. *Autobiography of a Play*. New York: Dramatic Museum of Columbia University, 1914.

———. "The American Drama." *Sunday Magazine* (New York), October 7, 1906. Rpt. *Representative Plays by American Dramatists*. 3 vols. Ed. Montrose J. Moses. New York: Dutton, 1918–1921. III: 365–370.

Howells, William Dean. "Editor's Study." *Harper's Monthly*, June 1890: 155.

LANGSTON HUGHES

Hughes, Langston. *Five Plays by Langston Hughes*. Ed. Webster Smalley. Bloomington: Indiana University Press, 1963.

———. *The Big Sea*. New York: Knopf, 1940.

———. *I Wonder as I Wander*. New York: Rinehart, 1956.

Kent, George. *Blackness and the Adventure of Western Culture.* Chicago: Third World Press, 1972.

Miller, R. Baxter. *Langston Hughes and Gwendolyn Brooks: A Reference Guide.* Boston: G.K. Hall, 1978.

O'Daniel, Therman, ed. *Langston Hughes, Black Genius: A Critical Evaluation.* New York: Morrow, 1971.

Rampersad, Arnold. *The Life of Langston Hughes.* 2 vols. New York: Oxford University Press, 1986.

DAVID HENRY HWANG

Berson, Misha, ed. *Between Worlds: Contemporary Asian-American Plays.* New York: Theatre Communications Group, 1990.

Hwang, David Henry. *FOB and Other Plays.* New York: New American Library, 1990.

Savran, David. "David Hwang." *In Their Own Words: Contemporary American Playwrights.* New York: Theatre Communications Group, 1988. 117-131.

Shimakawa, Karen. "'Who's to Say?' or, Making Space for Gender and Ethnicity in *M. Butterfly.*" *Theatre Journal* 45 (1993): 349–361.

Skloot, Robert. "Breaking the Butterfly: The Politics of David Henry Hwang." *Modern Drama* 33 (1990): 59–66.

ADRIENNE KENNEDY

Blau, Herbert. "The American Dream in American Gothic: The Plays of Sam Shepard and Adrienne Kennedy." *The Eye of Prey: Subversions of the Postmodern.* Bloomington: Indiana University Press, 1987. 42–64.

Bryant-Jackson, Paul K., and Lois More Overbeck, eds. *Intersecting Boundaries: The Theatre of Adrienne Kennedy.* Minneapolis: University of Minnesota Press, 1992.

Diamond, Elin. "Rethinking Identification: Kennedy, Freud, Brecht." *The Kenyon Review* 15 (1993): 86–99.

Kennedy, Adrienne. *Adrienne Kennedy in One Act.* Minneapolis: University of Minnesota Press, 1988.

———. *People Who Led to My Plays.* New York: Theatre Communications Group, 1988.

Kintz, Linda. "The Sanitized Spectacle: What's Birth Got to Do with It? Adrienne Kennedy's *A Movie Star*

Has to Star in Black and White." *Theatre Journal* 44 (1992): 67–86.

LARRY KRAMER

Bergman, David. "Larry Kramer and the Rhetoric of AIDS." *AIDS: The Literary Response.* Ed. Emmanuel S. Nelson. New York: Twayne, 1992. 175–186.

de Jongh, Nicholas. "The Return of the Outcast: 1981–1985." *Not in Front of the Audience: Homosexuality on Stage.* London: Routledge, 1992. 175–190.

Kramer, Larry. *The Normal Heart.* New York: Plume, 1985.

Gross, Gregory. "Coming Up for Air: Three AIDS Plays." *Journal of American Culture* 15 (1992): 63–67.

Román, David. "'It's My Party and I'll Die If I Want to!': Gay Men, AIDS, and the Circulation of Camp in U.S. Theatre." *Theatre Journal* 44 (1992): 305–327.

DAVID MAMET

Bigsby, C. W. E. *David Mamet.* London: Methuen, 1985.

Carroll, Dennis. *David Mamet.* New York: St. Martin's, 1987.

Dean, Anne. *David Mamet: Language as Dramatic Action.* Rutherford, NJ: Fairleigh Dickinson University Press, 1990.

Kane, Leslie, ed. *David Mamet: A Casebook.* New York: Garland, 1992.

ARTHUR MILLER

Centola, Steve. *Arthur Miller in Conversation.* Dallas: Northouse & Northouse, 1993.

Hayman, Ronald. *Arthur Miller.* New York: Ungar, 1972.

Miller, Arthur. *Arthur Miller's Collected Plays,* 2 vols. New York: Viking, 1957–1981.

———. *The Theatre Essays of Arthur Miller,* ed. Robert A. Martin. New York: Viking, 1978.

———. *Timebends: A Life.* New York: Grove Press, 1987.

Roudané, Matthew C., ed. *Conversations with Arthur Miller.* Jackson: University Press of Mississippi, 1987.

Savran, David. *Cowboys, Communists, and Queers: The Politics of Masculinity in the Work of Arthur Miller and Tennessee Williams.* Minneapolis: University of Minnesota Press, 1992.

WILLIAM VAUGHN MOODY

The Plays and Poems of William Vaughn Moody. 2 Vols. Ed. John M. Manly. Boston and New York: Houghton Mifflin, 1912.

Brown, Maurice. *Estranging Dawn: The Life and Works of William Vaughn Moody.* Carbondale: Southern Illinois University Press, 1973.

Corbin, John. Rev. of *The Great Divide.* Rep. in *New York Sun*, 4 October 1906. Rpt. *The American Theatre as Seen by Its Critics, 1752–1934.* Eds. Montrose J. Moses and John Mason Brown. New York: Norton, 1934. 176–178.

Halpern, Martin. *William Vaughn Moody.* New York: Twayne, 1964.

Moody, William Vaughn. *Some Letters of William Vaughn Moody.* Ed. Daniel Gregory Mason. Boston and New York: Houghton Mifflin, 1913.

———. *Letters to Harriet.* Ed. Percy MacKaye. Boston: Houghton Mifflin, 1931.

CHERRÍE MORAGA

Alarcón, Norma. "Interview with Cherríe Moraga. *Third Woman* 3 (1986): 127–134.

de Lauretis, Teresa. *The Practice of Love: Lesbian Sexuality and Perverse Desire.* Bloomington: Indiana University Press, 1994. 203–253.

Moraga, Cherríe. *Heroes and Saints & Other Plays.* Albuquerque: West End Press, 1994.

Moraga, Cherríe. *Loving in the War Years: (lo que nunca pasó por sus labios).* Boston: South End Press, 1983.

Moraga, Cherríe, and Gloria Anzaldúa, eds. *This Bridge Called My Back: Writings by Radical Women of Color.* New York: Kitchen Table: Women of Color Press, 1983.

Umpierre, Luz María. "With Cherríe Moraga." *Americas Review: A Review of Hispanic Literature and Art of the USA* 14 (1986): 54–67.

Yarbro-Bejarno, Yvonne. "Cherríe Moraga's 'Shadow of a Man': Touching the Wound in Order to Heal." *Acting Out: Feminist Performances.* Eds. Lynda Hart and Peggy Phelan. Ann Arbor: University of Michigan Press, 1993. 85–104.

———. "The Female Subject in Chicano Theatre: Sexuality, 'Race,' and Class." *Theatre Journal* 38 (1986): 389–407.

ANNA CORA MOWATT

Barnes, Eric Wollencott. *The Lady of Fashion: The Life and Theatre of Anna Cora Mowatt.* New York: Charles Scribner's Sons, 1954.

Mowatt, Anna Cora. *Autobiography of an Actress; or, Eight Years on the Stage.* Boston: Ticknor, Reed, and Fields, 1854.

Poe, Edgar Allan. "Mrs. Mowatt's Comedy Reconsidered." Rep. in *The American Theatre as Seen by Its Critics, 1752–1934.* Eds. Montrose J. Moses and John Mason Brown. New York: Norton, 1934. 63–66.

MARSHA NORMAN

Hart, Lynda. "Doing Time: Hunger for Power in Marsha Norman's Plays." *The Southern Quarterly* 25 (1987): 67–79.

Kane, Leslie. "The Way Out, the Way In: Paths to Self in the Plays of Marsha Norman." *Feminine Focus: The New Woman Playwrights.* Ed. Enoch Brater. New York: Oxford University Press, 1989. 255–274.

Murray, Timothy. "Patriarchal Panopticism, or the Seduction of a Bad Joke: *Getting Out* in Theory." *Theatre Journal* 35 (1983): 376–388.

Norman, Marsha. *Four Plays.* New York: Theatre Communications Group, 1988.

Schroeder, Patricia R. "Locked Behind the Proscenium: Feminist Strategies in *Getting Out* and *My Sister in This House.*" *Modern Drama* 32 (1989): 104–114.

Spencer, Jenny S. "Marsha Norman's *She-tragedies.*" *Making a Spectacle: Feminist Essays on Contemporary Women's Theatre.* Ed. Lynda Hart. Ann Arbor: University of Michigan Press, 1989. 147–165.

CLIFFORD ODETS

Cantor, Harold. *Clifford Odets: Playwright-Poet.* Metuchen, NJ: Scarecrow Press, 1978.

Cooperman, Robert. *Clifford Odets: An Annotated Bibliography, 1935–1989.* Westport, CT: Meckler, 1990.

Demastes, William W. *Clifford Odets: A Research and Production Sourcebook.* Westport, CT: Greenwood Press, 1991.

Miller, Gabriel, ed. *Critical Essays on Clifford Odets.* Boston: G. K. Hall, 1991.

Shuman, R. Baird. *Clifford Odets.* New York: Twayne, 1962.

EUGENE O'NEILL

Bogard, Travis. *Contour in Time: The Plays of Eugene O'Neill.* Rev. ed. New York: Oxford University Press, 1988.

Gelb, Arthur and Barbara. *O'Neill.* Enlarged ed. New York: Harper & Row, 1973.

O'Neill, Eugene. *Nine Plays.* New York: Modern Library, 1952.

Sanborn, Ralph, and Barrett H. Clark. *A Bibliography of the Works of Eugene O'Neill.* New York: Random House, 1931.

Sheaffer, Louis. *O'Neill: Son and Artist.* Boston: Little, Brown, 1973.

———. *O'Neill: Son and Playwright.* Boston: Little, Brown, 1968.

Stroupe, John H., ed. *Critical Approaches to O'Neill.* New York: AMS, 1987.

DAVID RABE

Christie, N. Bradley. "Still a Vietnam Playwright After All These Years." *David Rabe: A Casebook.* Ed. Toby Silverman Zinman. New York: Garland, 1991.

Kolin, Philip C. *David Rabe: A Stage History and A Primary and Secondary Bibliography.* New York: Garland, 1988.

Watt, Stephen. "In Mass Culture's Image: The Subject of (in) Rabe's Boom Boom Rooms." *David Rabe: A Casebook.* Ed. Toby Silverman Zinman. New York: Garland, 1991. 49–67.

Zinman, Toby Silverman, ed. *David Rabe: A Casebook.* New York: Garland, 1991.

NTOZAKE SHANGE

Cronacher, Karen. "Unmasking the Minstrel Mask's Black Magic in Ntozake Shange's *spell #7.*" *Theatre Journal* 44 (1992): 177–193.

Pinkney, Mikell. "Theatrical Expressionism in the Structure and Language of Ntozake Shange's *spell #7.*" *Theatre Studies* 37 (1992): 5–15.

Saldívar, José David. "The Real and the Marvelous in Charleston, South Carolina: Ntozake Shange's *Sassafrass, Cypress and Indigo.*" *The Dialectics of Our America: Genealogy, Cultural Critique, and Literary History.* Durham, NC: Duke University Press, 1991. 87–104.

Shange, Ntozake. *Three Pieces.* New York: St. Martin's, 1981.

Timpane, John. "'The Poetry of a Moment': Politics and the Open Form in the Drama of Ntozake Shange." *Modern American Drama: The Female Canon.* Ed. June Schlueter. London and Toronto: Associated University Presses, 1990. 198–206.

SAM SHEPARD

Chubb, Kenneth, and the Editors of *Theatre Quarterly.* "Metaphors, Mad Dogs and Old Time Cowboys: An Interview with Sam Shepard." *Theatre Quarterly* 4, 15 (1974); Rpt. in Marranca, 187–209.

Hart, Lynda. *Sam Shepard's Metaphorical Stages.* Westport, CT: Greenwood Press, 1987.

Marranca, Bonnie, ed. *American Dreams: The Imagination of Sam Shepard.* New York: PAJ Publications, 1981.

Mottram, Ron. *Inner Landscapes: The Theatre of Sam Shepard.* Columbia: University of Missouri Press, 1984.

Shepard, Sam. *Hawk Moon.* New York: PAJ Publications, 1981.

———. *Motel Chronicles.* San Francisco: City Lights Books, 1982.

———. *Seven Plays.* New York: Bantam, 1984.

Tucker, Martin. *Sam Shepard.* New York: Continuum, 1992.

JOHN AUGUSTUS STONE

Grose, B. Donald. "Edwin Forrest, *Metamora,* and the Indian Removal Act of 1830." *Theatre Journal* 37 (1985): 181–191.

McConachie, Bruce A. "The Theatre of Edwin Forrest and Jacksonian Hero Worship." *When They Weren't Doing*

Shakespeare: Essays on Nineteenth-Century British and American Theatre. Eds. Judith L. Fisher and Stephen Watt. Athens: University of Georgia Press, 1989. 3–18.

SOPHIE TREADWELL

Heck-Rabi, Louise. "Sophie Treadwell: Agent for Change." *Women in American Theater.* Eds. Helen Crich Chinoy and Linda Walsh Jenkins. New York: Theatre Communications Group, 1987. 157–162.

Parent, Jennifer. "Arthur Hopkins' Production of Sophie Treadwell's *Machinal.*" *The Drama Review* 26 (1982): 87–100.

Strand, Ginger. "Treadwell's Neologism: *Machinal.*" *Theatre Journal* 44 (1992): 163–175.

ROYALL TYLER

Carson, Ada Lou, and Herbert L. Carson. *Royall Tyler.* Boston: Twayne, 1979.

Lauber, John. "*The Contrast:* A Study in the Concept of Innocence." *English Language Notes* 1 (1963): 33–37.

Seibert, Donald T., Jr. "Royall Tyler's 'Bold Example': *The Contrast* and the English Comedy of Manners." *Early American Literature* 13 (1978): 3–11.

Stein, Roger. "Royall Tyler and the Question of Our Speech." *New England Quarterly* 38 (1965): 454–474.

Tanselle, G. Thomas. *Royall Tyler.* Cambridge, MA: Harvard University Press, 1967.

LUIS VALDEZ

Huerta, Jorge, ed. *Necessary Theatre: Six Plays about the Chicano Experience.* Houston: Arte Publico Press, 1989.

Morales, Ed. "Shadowing Valdez." *American Theatre* November 1992: 14–19.

Valdez, Luis. *Luis Valdez—Early Works: Actos, Bernabé, and Pensamiento Serpentino.* Houston: Arte Publico Press, 1990.

———. *Zoot Suit and Other Plays.* Houston: Arte Publico Press, 1992.

Valdez, Luis, and El Teatro Campesino. *Actos.* San Juan Bautista, CA: Cucaracha, 1971.

TENNESSEE WILLIAMS

Devlin, Albert J., ed. *Conversations with Tennessee Williams.* Jackson: University of Mississippi Press, 1986.

Londré, Felicia Hardison. *Tennessee Williams.* New York: Frederick Ungar, 1979.

Murphy, Brenda. *Tennessee Williams and Elia Kazan: A Collaboration in the Theatre.* New York: Cambridge University Press, 1992.

Stanton, Stephen S., ed. *Tennessee Williams: A Collection of Critical Essays.* Englewood Cliffs, NJ: Prentice-Hall, 1977.

Williams, Tennessee. *The Theatre of Tennessee Williams.* 8 vols. New York: New Directions, 1971.

AUGUST WILSON

Hay, Samuel A. *African-American Theatre: A Historical and Critical Analysis.* New York: Cambridge University Press, 1994.

Powers, Kim. "An Interview with August Wilson." *Theatre* 16 (1984): 50–55.

Savran, David. "August Wilson." *In Their Own Words: Contemporary American Playwrights.* New York: Theatre Communications Group, 1988. 288–305.

Shannon, Sandra G. "The Long Wait: August Wilson's *Ma Rainey's Black Bottom.*" *Black American Literature Forum* 25, 1 (1991): 125–146.

Wilson, August. *Three Plays.* Pittsburgh: University of Pittsburgh Press, 1991.

SELECT FILMOGRAPHY

Editorial Note: Below is a brief list of filmed versions of plays written by the dramatists represented in this volume and, in some instances, of films scripted or co-written by these dramatists. In the case of these dramatists' adaptations of prior material, only representative screenplays have been included.

EDWARD ALBEE

Death of Bessie Smith. ITV (London), 1965. (Made for TV.)
A Delicate Balance. Director, Tony Richardson. American Film Theatre, 1973.
Who's Afraid of Virginia Woolf? Director, Mike Nichols. Warner Bros., 1966.

AMIRI BARAKA

Dutchman. Director, Anthony Harvey. Gene Persson 1966.
A Fable. Director, Al Freeman Jr. MFR, 1971. (Also known as *The Slave*.)

PHILIP BARRY

The Animal Kingdom. Director, Edward H. Griffith. RKO, 1932.
Holiday. Director, George Cukor. Columbia, 1938. (An earlier version, starring Mary Astor and directed by Edward H. Griffith, was produced in 1930.)
The Philadelphia Story. Director, George Cukor. Metro-Goldwyn-Mayer (MGM), 1940.

DION BOUCICAULT

Bride of the Lake. American Anglo Corporation, 1934. (Based on *The Colleen Bawn*, 1860.)
Kathleen Mavourneen. (Director unknown.) Tiffany Productions Incorporated, 1929.

RACHEL CROTHERS

As Husbands Go. Director, Hamilton McFadden. Fox Film Corporation, 1934.
The Captain is a Lady. Director, Robert Sinclair. MGM, 1940. (Based on *Old Lady 31.*)
Let Us Be Gay. Director, Robert Z. Leonard. MGM, 1930.
Splendor. Director, Eliott Nugent. UAC (Samuel Goldwyn), 1935.
Susan and God. Director, George Cukor. MGM, 1940.
When Ladies Meet. Director, Harry Beaumont. MGM, 1933. (Produced by MGM again in 1941, directed by Robert Z. Leonard.)

SUSAN GLASPELL

The Right to Love. Director, Richard Wallace. Paramount, 1930. (Based on the 1928 novel *Brook Evans.*)

LILLIAN HELLMAN

Another Part of the Forest. Director, Michael Gordon. Universal, 1948.
The Chase. Director, Arthur Penn. Columbia/Sam Spiegel, 1966. (Based on the novel by Horton Foote.)
The Children's Hour. Director, William Wyler. United Artists (UA), 1961. (Wyler also made a version of this play entitled *These Three* in 1936.)
The Dark Angel. Director, Sidney Franklin. Samuel Goldwyn, 1935. (Screenplay with Mordaunt Shairp.)
Julia. Director, Fred Zinneman. Twentieth-Century Fox Productions (20 Fox), 1977. (Based on story from *Pentimento.*)
The Little Foxes. Director, William Wyler. RKO, 1941.
North Star. Director, Lewis Milestone. Samuel Goldwyn, 1943. (Revised and re-released as *Armored Attack* in 1957.)
The Searching Wind. Director, William Dieterle. Paramount/Hal B. Wallis Productions, 1946.
Toys in the Attic. Director, Arthur Penn. United Artists (UA), 1962.
Watch on the Rhine. Director, Herman Schumlin. Warner Bros., 1943.

LANGSTON HUGHES

Way Down South. Director, Bernard Vorhaus. RKO, 1939.

DAVID HENRY HWANG

M. Butterfly. Director, David Cronenberg. Geffen Pictures, 1993.

DAVID MAMET

Glengarry Glen Ross. Director, James Foley. Rank/Zupnik Enterprises, 1992.
Homicide. Director, David Mamet. First Independent/J&M Entertainment/Cinehaus. Released by Bison Films, 1991.
House of Games. Director, David Mamet. Orion Pictures, 1987.
The Postman Always Rings Twice. Director, Bob Rafelson. Lorimar/Northstar International, 1981. (Based on the novel by John M. Cain.)
Things Change. Director, David Mamet. RCA/Columbia Pictures Home Video, 1988.
The Untouchables. Director, Brian DePalma. Paramount, 1987.
The Verdict. Director, Sidney Lumet. TCF/Zanuck-Brown, 1982. (Based on the novel by Barry Reed.)

ARTHUR MILLER

All My Sons. Director, Irving Reis. Universal, 1948.
All My Sons. Director, Jack O'Brien (for PBS, *American Playhouse*). MCA Home Video, 1987.
Clara. Director, Burt Brinckerhoff. General Motors Playwrights Theatre (Made for TV), 1991.
Death of a Salesman. Director, Laslo Benedek. Columbia: 1952.
Death of a Salesman. Director, Volker Schlondorff. Karl-Lorimar Home Video, 1986.
Enemy of the People. Director, George Schaefer. Warner Bros., 1978.
The Misfits. Director, John Huston. UA, 1961.
View From the Bridge. Director, Sidney Lumet. Continental Film Distribution, 1962.
Witches of Salem. Kingsley-International, 1959. (Based on *The Crucible.*)

WILLIAM VAUGHN MOODY

Woman Hungry. First National Pictures, Incorporated, 1930. (Based on *The Great Divide.*)

MARSHA NORMAN

Getting Out. Director, John Korty. Signpost Hill (with ABC Television), 1993.
'night, Mother. Director, Tom Moore. Universal/Aaron Spelling, 1986.

CLIFFORD ODETS

The Big Knife. Director, Robert Aldrich. UA, 1955.
Clash By Night. Director, Fritz Lang. RKO Radio, 1952.
The Country Girl. Director, George Seaton. Paramount, 1954.
Golden Boy. Director, Rouben Mamoulian. Columbia, 1939.
None but the Lonely Heart. Director, Clifford Odets. RKO, 1944.
Rocket to the Moon. Director, John Jacobs (for PBS, *American Playhouse*). Program Development Company, 1987.
The Story on Page One. Director, Clifford Odets. TCF/Company of Artists, 1959.

EUGENE O'NEILL

Ah, Wilderness! Director, Clarence Brown. MGM, 1935.
Anna Christie. Director, Clarence Brown. MGM, 1930.
Constant Woman. KBS Productions, 1933. (Based on *Recklessness*.)
Desire Under the Elms. Director, Delbert Mann. Paramount, 1958.
The Hairy Ape. Director, Alfred Santell. UA, 1944.
Long Day's Journey Into Night. Director, Sidney Lumet. Ely Landau/Embassy Pictures, 1962. (Also, 1987 version starring Jack Lemmon and directed by Jonathan Miller.)
Long Voyage Home. Director, John Ford. UA, 1940. (Based on one-act play of the same title and other "plays of the sea.")
Mourning Becomes Electra. Director, Dudley Nichols. RKO Radio Pictures, 1947.
Strange Interlude. Director, Robert Z. Leonard. MGM, 1932.
Strange Interlude. Director, Herbert Wise (for PBS, *American Playhouse*). Fries Home Video, 1988. (Also, 1932 film starring Norma Shearer and Clark Gable.)

Summer Holiday. Director, Rouben Mamoulian. MGM, 1948. (Musical based on *Ah, Wilderness!*)

DAVID RABE

Casualties of War. Director, Brian DePalma. Columbia TriStar, 1989. (Based on the story by Daniel Lang.)

The Firm. Director, Sydney Pollack. Paramount, 1993. (Based on the novel by John Grisham.)

I'm Dancing as Fast as I Can. Director, Jack Hofiss. Paramount, 1982.

Streamers. Director, Robert Altman. UA Classics, 1983.

SAM SHEPARD

Far North. Director, Sam Shepard. Alive Films, 1988.

Fool For Love. Director, Robert Altman. Cannon, 1985.

Paris, Texas. Director, Wim Wenders. Road Movies & Greno, 1984.

Silent Tongue. Director, Sam Shepard. Belbo/Alive Films, 1993.

True West. Director, Allan Goldstein. Academy Home Entertainment, 1987.

LUIS VALDEZ

La Bamba. Director, Luis Valdez. Columbia, 1986.

Los Mineros (The Miners). Director, Luis Valdez (for PBS, *The American Experience*). PBS Video, 1991.

La Pastorela (The Shepherd's Tale). Director, Luis Valdez. El Teatro Campesino/Richard Soto Productions, 1991.

Zoot Suit. Director, Luis Valdez. Universal, 1982; MCA Universal Home Video, 1991.

TENNESSEE WILLIAMS

Baby Doll. Director, Elia Kazan. Warner Bros., 1956.

Cat on a Hot Tin Roof. Director, Richard Brooks. MGM, 1958.

The Fugitive Kind. Director, Sidney Lumet. UA, 1960. (Based on *Orpheus Descending.*)

The Glass Menagerie. Director, Irving Rapper. Warner Bros., 1950. (Also, a TV movie, directed by Anthony Harvey, 1973.)

The Glass Menagerie. Director, Paul Newman. Cineplex, 1987.

The Night of the Iguana. Director, John Huston. MGM/Seven Arts, 1964.

Orpheus Descending. Director, Peter Hall, 1990.

The Rose Tattoo. Director, Daniel Mann. Paramount/Hal B. Wallis, 1955.

A Streetcar Named Desire. Director, Elia Kazan. Warner Bros., 1951. (Also 1984 version starring Ann-Margret and Treat Williams.)

Suddenly, Last Summer. Director, Joseph L. Mankiewicz. Columbia/Horizon, 1959.

Summer and Smoke. Director, Peter Glenville. Paramount, 1961.

Sweet Bird of Youth. Director, Richard Brooks. MGM, 1962.

WORKS CONSULTED

Aros, Andrew A. *Title Guide to the Talkies 1964–1974.* Metuchen, NJ: Scarecrow Press, 1977.

———. *Title Guide to the Talkies 1975–1984.* Metuchen, NJ and London: Scarecrow Press, 1986.

Contemporary Theatre, Film, and Television. 11 Vols. Detroit: Gale Research Company, 1984–1994.

Dimmitt, Richard Bertrand. *Title Guide to the Talkies 1927–1963.* New York and London: Scarecrow Press, 1965.

Halliwell, Leslie. *Halliwell's Filmgoer's Companion.* 9th ed. New York: Charles Scribner's Sons, 1988.

Katz, Ephraim. *The Film Encyclopedia.* New York: Thomas Y. Crowell, 1979.

Magill's Survey of Cinema. 1st Series. 4 Vols. Englewood Cliffs, NJ: Salem Press, 1980.

Magill's Survey of Cinema. 2nd Series. 6 Vols. Englewood Cliffs, NJ: Salem Press, 1981.

Museum of Modern Art (New York). *Film Catalog: A List of Holdings in the Museum of Modern Art.* Boston: G.K. Hall and Co., 1985.

New York Times Encyclopedia of Film. 13 Vols. New York: Times Books, 1984.

Walker, John, ed. *Halliwell's Film Guide 1994.* New York: HarperPerennial, 1994.

GLOSSARY

Abbey Theatre   Dublin, Ireland theatre founded by W. B. Yeats, Lady Augusta Gregory, and others. Now home of the National Theatre of Ireland.

Absurdism   see Theatre of the Absurd

actos   Short satirical plays dramatizing the conditions of California farm workers developed by Luis Valdez and El Teatro Campesino in the 1960s.

affective or emotional memory   Stanislavskian acting technique in which an actor recreates an emotion on stage by remembering a parallel experience in his or her life.

agitprop   (Term combined from the words *agitation* and *propaganda*) A form of political theatre originated in the 1920s by German director Erwin Piscator, associated in Depression-era America with workers' rights movements. Agitprop often employs multiple stages and multimedia including film, slides, posters, and music-hall routines to present the dilemmas of an oppressed working class.

anagnorisis   From Aristotle's *Poetics*, the protagonist's recognition or self-discovery.

Augustan Tragedy   Tragedy written in imitation of classical models during the first half of the eighteenth century. Such plays as Joseph Addison's *Cato* (1713) rigidly observed the "unities" of place, time, and action supposedly mandated by classical authorities such as Aristotle.

avant-garde   A general term in the arts referring to those on the cutting edge. In American drama, the term has been particularly used to describe unorthodox and experimental works such as Megan Terry's rock-musical protest play *Viet Rock* (1966) and acting groups such as the Off-Off Broadway La MaMa Troupe.

benefit performance   A staging of a play given to profit either an actor, author or manager. The system emerged in the eighteenth and continued throughout the nineteenth century.

Black Arts Movement   An artistic movement of the 1960s in which African-American writers sought to redefine art within an aesthetic and nationalistic framework grounded in African-American experience.

body art   Art produced using the body itself as the medium of expression or as an artistic object in itself.

Like **conceptual art,** part of the 1960s revolt in artistic circles against the commodification of art.

Broadway   The name of a Manhattan boulevard which gives the New York City theatre district its name.

canon   Strictly, an accepted list of plays by an author. More generally, a group of works widely accepted as manifesting characteristics particular to a specific literary period, artistic movement or form, or some other critical construct, e.g. American drama.

choreopoem   Term coined by Ntozake Shange to describe a staging blending music, dance, and poetry. Used specifically by Shange to refer to *for colored girls who have considered suicide / when the rainbow is enuf* (1975).

comedy   Generally, a play designed to amuse which avoids the disasters of tragedy and ends happily. Unlike farce, comedy has a more substantial plot, relies on more meaningful and subtler dialogue, utilizes lifelike characters, and a less raucous action. Traditionally, the subject matter of comedy has been either the intrigues of love (often called **romantic comedy**) or the follies and foibles of human beings and their institutions (also known as **satiric comedy**). See also **comedy of manners, high comedies, Restoration comedy,** and **romantic comedy.**

comedy of manners   A variety of comedy concerned with the mores and manners of an artificial and highly sophisticated segment of society.

commedia dell'arte   Italian comedy of the sixteenth to eighteenth centuries. Although originally improvisational, this comedy eventually evolved into set pieces called *lazzi*, derived in the main from Roman comedy. The *commedi dell'arte* relied upon a series of masked stock characters—a wily servant, an impudent maid, a clown servant, a businessman, a stupid fellow, and a womanizing tippler or braggart soldier—whose descendants still populate plays today.

conceptual art   A style of art that emerged in the 1960s which claims that art is not in the physical objects created by artists but is rather the ideas or "concepts" which artists attempt to communicate through the vehicles which the viewer sees.

demonstration   Brechtian acting technique in which actors do not fully identify with their characters (cf. **Stanislavsky method**). Such a technique keeps the audience aware of both the character and the actor playing the character and thereby serves to enhance the "alienation" or emotional detachment of the audience.

East West Players   The first contemporary Asian-American theatre company, East West Players founded in 1965 has consistently provided a venue for new Asian-American dramatists.

environmental theatre   Commonly used late 1960s phrase to describe performances which encompass the total theatrical environment making no distinction between the playing area and the audience.

Existentialism   A group of ideas and attitudes that emerged during and after World War II in philosophical, theological, and artistic thought. Existentialism asserts the primacy of existence (as opposed to essence) and suggests that the basic philosophical question is human reason's inadequacy to explain the mystery of the universe. As an ethical framework, it emphasizes individual responsibility in the face of the meaninglessness that surrounds human existence.

existentialist   see **Existentialism**

Expressionism   An artistic movement particularly strong in the theatre of the 1920s which sought to replace the representational use of external objects to create a verisimilar reality with an emotional use in which objects became the depictions of a character's or author's moods, understanding, or subjectivity.

form   A literary work's structure as opposed to its content; often defined as a system of relationships that make up an aesthetic text. In drama, form is usually denoted in terms of acts, scenes, and speeches.

fourth wall   The convention in realistic theatre that the playing area is a room with one wall missing. The audience observes the action through this transparent wall and is never acknowledged or addressed by the actors.

Group Theatre, The   An acting and production company founded in 1931 by Harold Clurman, Lee Strasberg, and Cheryl Crawford. Dedicated to exacting acting training along Stanislavskian lines and to presenting new, socially significant American plays, the Group was largely responsible for popularizing the **method** acting technique and encouraging young playwrights such as Clifford Odets.

guerrilla drama/theatre   Short, compelling dramatic pieces on controversial subjects often staged in public places to draw attention to a specific cause.

happenings   A variety of performance which came to prominence in the late 1950s and continued into the 1960s which made use of both scripted and improvisational materials as well as dance and music.

Harlem Renaissance   The post-World War I African-American artistic movement centered in the Harlem section of New York City. Prominent among the literary participants were Zora Neale Hurston, Nella Larsen, Jean Toomer, Countee Cullen, and the dramatist/poet Langston Hughes.

high comedies   Those comedies which appeal to the intellect and evoke serious laughter by focusing on the contradictions and absurdities of human nature and exhibiting the frivolities of social mores.

House Un-American Activities Committee (HUAC)   A committee of the United States House of Representatives notably active in the 1940s and 1950s which sought to ferret out politically subversive persons in all walks of American life, including the theatre and film industry.

HUAC   see **House Un-American Activities Committee**

Imagistic   see **imagism**

Imagism   A poetic movement associated with F. S. Flint, H.D. (Hilda Doolittle), and Ezra Pound. Specifically, these poets sought to present what Pound termed "an intellectual and emotional complex in an instant of time"—with visual images bearing the intellectual content and auditory images the emotional.

Indian plays   A group of American plays in the first half of the nineteenth century taking as their subject Native-American peoples. Their popularity eventually faded in the face of John Brougham's burlesques of the form at mid-century.

Little Theatre Movement   The name given to the sudden growth of American amateur theatrical groups in the early decades of the twentieth century. By 1940 the number of groups offering non-commerical or socially relevant theatre experiences to small groups (usually subscribers) had grown to over 100. Today there are approximately 5,000 such groups in the country.

Living Newspapers   Originated by the theatre project of the WPA (Works Progress Administration) in the 1930s, Living Newspapers presented a series of brief skits based upon topical social and political issues. They were so named because of their use of documentary materials and the involvement in them of newspaper and theatrical workers.

Living Theatre Founded in 1948 by Julian Beck and his wife Judith Malina and still active, the Living Theatre is credited with beginning the **Off-Off Broadway** movement. Wedding political and artistic radicalism, the Living Theatre has arguably been the one of the most influential **avant-garde** theatre groups in American history.

lost generation Phrase attributed to Gertrude Stein and applied to several American writers born about 1900 who came to prominence in the 1920s. Their work is characterized by a loss of faith in the values of an earlier generation and a sense of alienation from post-World War I American life. Often included in this group are F. Scott Fitzgerald, Ernest Hemingway, Hart Crane, and Malcolm Cowley.

manners comedy see **comedy of manners**

melodrama A term coined in the eighteenth century to describe a play employing music. In the nineteenth century used to describe a play which used music to heighten emotional tension and reinforce the moral judgments portrayed by the action. More recently, the term has been applied to works utilizing stark contrasts between good and evil. See also, **sensation melodrama.**

metatheatrical see **metatheatre**

metatheatre The term used to denote plays which self-consciously comment upon the theatrical process, often commenting thereby on the relationship between the theatre and life. While some plays utilize the play-within-a-play device, it is not necessary. Examples range from *Six Characters in Search of an Author* to *A Chorus Line.*

method or method acting see **Stanislavsky method**

miles gloriosus The title character of the Roman playwright Plautus's *Miles Gloriosus,* he is the stock figure of the braggart soldier in classical Greek and Roman drama.

minstrel show A form of entertainment very popular in late nineteenth-century and early twentieth-century America in which a group of white men with blackened faces assumed the guise of stereotypical African-Americans to present a series of unrelated songs, dances, and comic exchanges.

mise-en-scène French phrase for the "putting on-stage" of a play, it refers to the total environment of a play including the blocking, props, visual effects, setting, scenery, and costumes. Effectively, the "look" of the play.

mitos Lyrical plays dealing with Mexican-American life developed by Luis Valdez and El Teatro Campesino in the 1960s and 1970s.

modernism A term denoting a direction in the arts in the twentieth century characterized by a break with traditional forms and techniques of expression, by greater concern for the individual per se rather than as a social being, by an increased emphasis on the unconscious, and by embracing the concept of an imagination that is self-referential.

Naturalism A late-nineteenth- and early-twentieth century literary movement in France, England, and the United States which sought to apply the principles of scientific determinism to literature. Stylistically dominated by a scrupulous verisimilitude, naturalism sought thematically to emphasize the operation of biological or socioeconomic determinism on human actions.

new stagecraft Non-representational stagecraft emphasizing the interplay of dominate colors, abstract shapes, and lighting effects associated with the work of Gordon Craig, early twentieth-century theatrical artist and son of the Victorian actress Ellen Terry.

Obie(s) Awards established in 1956 by the *Village Voice* to recognize achievement in Off-Broadway theatre.

Off-Broadway A term coined in the 1950s to describe small New York City theatres outside of the commercial (**Broadway**) district and the productions given there. A descendent of the **Little Theatre Movement,** Off-Broadway has been a mecca for experimental plays and staging experiments, but that role has been increasingly assumed by **Off-Off Broadway.**

Off-Off Broadway An expression coined in the 1960s to distinguish between non-commercial theatre presented in traditionally non-theatrical venues such as coffeehouses, churches, and storefronts from the commercial theatres of **Broadway** and **Off-Broadway.**

Otherness A critical term derived from the writings of French psychoanalysts Jacques Lacan, Julia Kristeva and others to describe the alien, the unknown in the unconscious of any given Subject. For Lacan, the **Other** is the repository of the Subject's unconscious desires and as modified by other theorists like Julia Kristeva often refers to the projection of despised or bestial characteristics on to representations of racial and sexual difference.

patent theatre   A theatre given a patent or license from the British crown to give dramatic performances. The granting of patents effectively created a theatrical monopoly in London and precluded others from staging "legitimate" (non-musical) plays. This system inadvertently spurred the development of new dramatic forms such as **melodrama.**

performance art   An art form which emerged in the 1960s and 1970s combining impulses from such currents as the "free-speech" and women's political movements, the radical art world's rejection of "museum culture," and the commodification of the art object, and theatrical experiments designed to escape the perceived tyranny of the dramatic text. Performance art remains popular as the latest incarnation of the **avant-garde.**

peripeteia   From Artistole's *Poetics*, the reversal of fortunes of a play's protagonist.

persona   A mask. The term is widely used to distinguish between a supposed authentic self (such as an author, for example) and a fictive creation designed to serve a particular function within a play or other work of literature (such as present to the author's views without exposing the author to censure). By extension, the identity assumed by a character in a play.

postmodern   see **postmodernism**

postmodernism   A highly contested critical term developed by such theorists as Ihab Hassan, Fredric Jameson, Jean Baudrillard, Jean-François Lyotard and numerous others. For Jameson, postmodernism refers to a stage of late-capitalism emerging in the late 1960s which has come to dominance in the present. Jameson and others refer to postmodernism as a "cultural dominant" of contemporary America that manifests itself in such aesthetic features as emphasis on surface as opposed to depth, on the video and otherwise simulated image, in the use of pastiche in the aesthetic text, and the erosion of the boundaries between high art and mass culture.

Provincetown Players   Originally an amateur company led by George Cram Cook that took its name from Provincetown, Massachusetts where it was organized in 1915. Joined by Eugene O'Neill in 1916, the Provincetown Players relocated to New York City's Greenwich Village, producing many of Susan Glaspell and O'Neill's early works, most notably *Trifles* and *The Emperor Jones*. Like many other experimental companies, it was a fatality of the Depression, disbanding in 1929.

Pulitzer Prize   One of several literary awards established by the will of Joseph Pulitzer. In drama, the prize is given for the best play written by an American preferrably on an American topic showing the power and the educational value of the theatre.

Realism   A nineteenth-century literary movement in France, England, and the United States which arose, at least in part, as a reaction against the perceived excesses of Romanticism. William Dean Howells defined realism as "the truthful treatment of material" by which he seems to have meant a relative truth which could be verified by experience of the commonplace or everyday. In the theatrical practice, realism has been less concerned with superficial verisimilitude and more with psychological motivation and the "inner reality" of characters. Unlike naturalism, realism is not committed to producing art that shows the operation of universal laws.

regional theatre   Also called resident or repertory theatre. Gaining momentum in the 1960s to provide a decentralized theatre alternative to the commercial New York City houses, the regional theatres are professional, non-profit sites dedicated to fostering new American drama, to producing the classical and contemporary repertory, to developing dedicated theatre professionals, and, in many cases, to serving the communities of which they are parts.

repertoire companies   Theatrical troupes that perform several plays in rotation throughout a season.

Restoration [drama]   Drama written in England between the Restoration of the Stuart monarchy in 1660 and the end of the seventeenth century.

Restoration comedy   A particularly witty, skeptical, and acerbic variety of manners comedy written during the Restoration period. Its most notable practitioners were John Dryden, Sir George Etherege, William Wycherley, and William Congreve.

romantic comedy   A type of comedy developed on the English Renaissance stage by Robert Greene and William Shakespeare which takes as its central issue serious love. Commonly, these plays utilize outdoor action, an idealized, cross-dressing heroine, multiple pairs of characters in similar romantic situations, significant obstacles to love's fulfillment, and a happy resolution.

romantic tragedy   Tragedy which employs a wider variety of themes and subjects, places greater emphasis on character, has a looser structure, indulges greater stylistic diversity, and incorporates a wider assortment of material than its classical antecedents. Elizabethan tragedy generally and Shakespearean tragedy particularly are often deemed romantic.

sensation melodrama   A style of mid-Victorian melodrama in which sensational physical action was a dominate feature of the play. Rendered as accurately as possible and designed to tantalize the audience, tenements burned, trains bore down on innocents, and floods coursed across the stage. Both Boucicault's *The Octoroon* and Daly's *Under the Gaslight* evidence the influence of sensation melodrama.

split character   A device of dramatic characterization in which aspects or manifestations of a single personality are divided and given representation on the stage.

Stanislavsky method   An acting technique developed by Konstantin Stanislavsky for the Moscow Art Theatre at the turn of the twentieth century. Dedicated to the idea of a play's inner truth, Stanislavsky repudiated the external dramatic effect of older acting styles and developed a series of exercises which would allow actors to reach the essence of the personalities of the characters they were to portray. Starting with information about the historical situation and moving through improvisation and concentration exercises, Stanislavsky's method sought to allow the actor to "be" rather than "seem to be" the character. Associated in the United States theatre particularly with the teaching efforts of Lee Strasberg in the **Group Theatre** and, afterwards, the Actors Studio.

stock company   A permanent company of actors, usually headed by a manager-actor, presenting plays in repertory rotation either in residence or on tour. The dominant theatrical model for much of the nineteenth century, the stock company cast its members by "line" with actors assuming the same type of role in play after play. Such casting gave rise to "stock" characterizations which were complemented by the company's use of "stock" scenery and props. This system of production was undermined first in the early nineteenth century by the emergence of the "star system" in which leading players temporarily joined a company for a limited engagement and later by the emergence of "combination companies" which toured, usually by rail, complete with star and full cast, as well as props, scenery, and costumes.

surreal   see **Surrealism**

Surrealism   A literary and artistic movement developed in France in the 1920s under the leadership of André Breton and dedicated to presenting the imagination as perceived in dreams with as little conscious control as possible. In drama, surrealism is associated with the works of Antonin Artaud and finds expression in elements of the Theatre of the Absurd.

Symbolist   see **Symbolism**

Symbolism   Generally, using of one object to represent or suggest another; the use of symbols in literature. More narrowly, a literary movement that emerged in France in the 1880s and associated with poets such as Charles Baudelaire, Stéphane Mallarmé, and Paul Valéry. A reaction against realism, symbolism sought to represent the unique emotional responses of the artist to experience through poetry characterized by private, often seemingly disconnected, symbols arranged in an evocative pattern. In drama, symbolism was influential on Yeats, Synge, and O'Neill, among others.

[El] Teatro Campesino   Group founded in 1965 by Luis Valdez and Chicano farm workers originally to assist César Chávez's efforts to unionize farm laborers. Subsequently, the theatre has become one of the major venues for Latino plays, and Valdez has continued to write dramas and has extended his efforts into the writing and production of films based upon Chicano life in America.

[El] Teatro de la Esperanza (Theatre of Hope)   Founded in 1971 in Santa Barbara, California, this Latino theatre group is noted for its docudramas and collaborative efforts among artists of both sexes. It moved to the Mission Cultural Center in San Francisco in the 1980s.

Theatre Guild   The successor to the **Washington Street Players,** the Theatre Guild was founded in 1919 when former members of the Players decided to move "uptown" and begin producing full-length plays on Broadway. Using a subscription system that guaranteed a knowledgeable audience and financial stability, the Guild quickly drew attention by mounting world premiers of several plays by George Bernard Shaw. By the later 1920s, the Guild had become a significant venue for major American dramatists, especially O'Neill. After defections by some of its younger members to begin the **Group Theatre** in 1931 and the establishment of the

Playwrights' Company in 1938 by many of its former writers, the Guild continued to produce, but its experimental impulse was gone. Nevertheless, its influence upon American theatre, especially in the 1920s and 1930 was profound.

Theatre of the Absurd   A critical term coined by Martin Esslin to describe a host of plays which he argues are "striving to express [their] sense of the senselessness of the human condition and the inadequacy of the rational approach by the open abandonment of rational devices and discursive thought." Fundamentally existential in ideology and metaphysical in orientation, the Theatre of the Absurd presents generally confused beings adrift in an incomprehensible universe. Most often associated with the work of Samuel Beckett and Eugène Ionesco, the Theatre of the Absurd has been widely influential on American playwrights such as Edward Albee, Arthur Kopit, and John Guare.

Theatrical Syndicate   A theatrical monopoly which effectively controlled first-class theatrical production between its founding in 1896 and 1916 when its last agreements expired and it was replaced by an even more efficient Shubert Brothers monopoly. The primary members of the Syndicate were Charles Frohman, a producer, and Marc Klaw and Abraham Erlanger, booking agents.

Tony   The popular name for the Antoinette Perry Awards given since 1947 for "Distinguished Achievement in the Theatre." The awards are presented for numerous areas of Broadway performance and production.

tragedy   A variety of drama first defined in Aristotle's *Poetics* which seeks to celebrate human dignity and courage when confronted with destruction. According to Aristotle, through a dignified and serious treatment, tragedy rehearses the fate of a generally superior person whose descent from happiness to misery is charted by a plot whose arranged incidents are such as to arouse fear and pity in the average person. For Aristotle, the ultimate end of tragedy is the catharsis or purgation of these emotions. As a literary form, tragedy has been continuously scrutinized and interrogated since the Greek period with each successive age inevitably redefining various elements for itself. The advent of more democratic social structures has led to a significant discussion of whether protagonists of sufficient stature any longer exist to elevate the protagonist's condition above

those of the average citizen and, thus, provide the play's action the seriousness to qualify as tragedy. One of the most spirited defenses of the possibility of tragedy in a democratic age is Arthur Miller's essay "Tragedy and the Common Man."

trope   A figure of speech which involves a non-literal use of a word. Comparative figures such as metaphors and similes as well as ironic expressions are tropes.

unity of action   A precept of dramatic plot construction taken from Aristotle's *Poetics*. Unity of action dictates that a play have a single action or plot without subplots.

vaudeville   A type of stage entertainment popular in the United States from roughly the mid-nineteenth century to the early 1930s. Fundamentally, a variety show in which audiences could see singers, dancers, animal acts, acrobats, comedians, magicians—or anything else managers thought would be popular—vaudeville fell victim to the Depression as well as to rival entertainment forms such as radio and motion pictures.

Washington Square Players   A theatrical company founded in 1915 and named for the area of New York City in which it was organized. Initially, mounting one-act productions in the 40-seat Bandbox Theatre, they relocated to the larger Comedy Theatre seating 600 in 1916. Although they sought to emphasize American drama and, in fact, produced the Broadway premier of O'Neill's *In the Zone*, the Players are probably best known for productions of George Bernard Shaw, Maurice Maeterlinck, and Anton Chekhov. The company disbanded in 1918, but many of its members reunited the next year to form the **Theatre Guild.**

well-made play   A type of play originated by the nineteenth-century French playwright, Eugène Scribe emphasizing tight and logical play construction. Such plays are usually characterized by a plot based on a withheld secret; by steadily mounting suspense resulting from rising action, mistaken identities, exactly timed entrances and exits, lost documents and letters containing key information, and a battle of wits between hero and villain; a climax in which the secret is revealed and the hero's fortune is happily reversed; and by a logical dénouement. This structure was immensely influential on Ibsen, who directed Scribe in Norway, and through Ibsen's influence on early realist play construction.

CREDITS AND ACKNOWLEDGMENTS

CLIFFORD ODETS

EUGENE O'NEILL

DAVID WILLIAM RABE

NTOZAKE SHANGE

SAM SHEPHARD

Shepard. Used by permission of Bantam Books, a division of Bantam Doubleday Dell Publishing Group, Inc.

JOHN AUGUSTUS STONE "Metamora or The Last of the Wampanoags" by John Augustus Stone from DRAMAS FROM THE AMERICAN THEATRE 1762–1909, edited by Richard Moody, Houghton Mifflin 1969. Reprinted by permission of Richard Moody, Professor Emeritus of Theatre and Drama, Indiana University.

SOPHIE TREADWELL MACHINAL by Sophie Treadwell was produced Off-Broadway by the New York Shakespeare Festival, Joseph Papp, Producer. The rights to this work are owned by the Roman Catholic Church of the Diocese of Tucson: A Corporation Sole, from whom production rights must be obtained. It is reprinted here by permission of the Diocese of Tucson. Proceeds from the printing or production of this play and others written by Sophie Treadwell are used for the aid and benefit of Native American children in Arizona.

LUIS VALDEZ "I Don't Have to Show You No Stinking Badges" by Luis Valdez from ZOOT SUIT AND OTHER PLAYS. Copyright © 1992 Luis Valdez. Reprinted by permission of Luis Valdez and El Teatro Campesino.

TENNESSEE WILLIAMS CAT ON A HOT TIN ROOF. Copyright © 1954, 1955, 1971, 1975 by Tennessee Williams. Reprinted by permission of New Directions Publishing Corp.

CAUTION: Professionals and amateurs are hereby warned that CAT ON A HOT TIN ROOF, being fully protected under the copyright laws of the United States of America, the British Empire, including the Dominion of Canada, and all other countries of the Copyright Union, and other countries of the world, is subject to royalty. All rights, including professional, amateur, motion picture, recitation, lecturing, public reading, radio broadcasting, television and the rights of translation into foreign languages are strictly reserved. Particular emphasis is laid on the question of readings, permission for which must be secured from the author's agent: Mr. Bill Barnes, International Famous Agency, Inc., 1301 Avenue of the Americas, New York, N.Y. 10019.

AUGUST WILSON "Ma Rainey's Black Bottom" from MA RAINEY'S BLACK BOTTOM by August Wilson. Copyright © 1985 by August Wilson. Used by permission of New American Library, a division of Penguin Books USA Inc.

Public-domain versions of the following plays appear in AMERICAN DRAMA:

DION BOUCICAULT THE OCTOROON, originally performed in 1850.

HOWARD BRONSON SHENANDOAH, first published in 1888.

RACHEL CROTHERS HE AND SHE, first published in 1912.

AUGUSTIN DALY UNDER THE GASLIGHT, first published in 1867.

SUSAN GLASPELL TRIFLES, first published in 1916.

JAMES A. HERNE MARGARET FLEMING, first published in 1890.

WILLIAM VAUGHN MOODY THE GREAT DIVIDE, first published in 1903.

ANNA CORA MOWATT FASHION; OR LIFE IN NEW YORK, first published in 1845.

ROYALL TYLER THE CONTRAST, first published in 1787.